A PRINTED LIST FROM THE DATABASE DOC.

The Millers and Mills of Ireland

THE MOST COMPREHENSIVE LIST OF THE OLD AND SOME ANCIENT MILLS OF ALL THE COUNTIES OF IRELAND TAKEN FROM A BROAD ASSORTMENT OF ARCHIVAL AND MODERN DOCUMENTARY SOURCES

Information concerning all aspects of the database are contained in the INTRODUCTION on a following page.

This edition of ***The Millers & The Mills of Ireland,*** in database form, was printed in Dublin, by Betaprint Services, 2011. Cover design by Susan Waine incorporating the Glenoe watercolour picture by Jack Calderwood.

Previous editions :
Revised (second) edition (paperback) ISBN 0-9532246-3-5
(hardback) ISBN 0-9532246-4-3
Original database edition (paperback) ISBN 0-9532246-5 -1

This improved 2011 database edition (paperback) ISBN 978-0-9566964-0-3

Milling was not simply the grain trade and its extensive business but rather the entire industrial scene of previous centuries. From numerous record sources more than seventy different types of mills have been noted, they are :-

ALABASTER BARK BARLEY BEETLING BERE BLADE BLEACH BLUE BOLTING BONE BREWERY

CARDING CHARCOAL CHEMICAL CHINA CHURNING CLOTH COPPER CORN COTTON CUTLING

DAMASK DISTILLERY DYESTUFF FLAX FLAX-SPINNING FLOUR FRIEZE FULLING GIG GLUE

GRIST GORSE GRINDING GUNPOWDER HACKLING HAMMER HORSE INDIGO IRON LEAD

LEATHER LINEN LINGERY LOGWOOD MARBLE MALT MUSTARD NAPPING OAT OATMEAL

OIL PAPER PATCH PRINTING RAPE REAPING-HOOK RIND SALT SAW SCUTCH SPADE

SPINNING STARCH TILE THREAD THRESHING TREAD TUCK WASH WHIN WOOLLEN.

ACKNOWLEDGEMENTS :
The author wishes to express gratitude for the co-operation and approvals granted for use of an abundance of detail collected and used by the publisher, at National Archives, Dublin; Public Record Office of Northern Ireland; Royal Irish Academy, Dublin; Queens University, Belfast; The National Library of Ireland; The Registry of Deeds, Dublin; Dublin City Library, Pearse Street; The Irish Architectural Archive; Moore Institute and NUI Galway. Appreciation also for un-named sources, publications and friends who have supplied items of history concerning a mill, a photograph, or permission to take or use one.

INTRODUCTION

This LIST type publication is a printout of a database document. As it is impossible without basic knowledge to know how many mills existed in a townland the detail located in each archival source has been allocated a separate record (i.e. a single line in the database) rather than amalgamate the several that might refer to the same mill.

INFORMATION CONCERNING THE FIELD HEADINGS USED IN THE DATABASE :

TOWNLAND Though many townland names are no longer spoken of today they were formerly much used. Townlands varied considerably in size, sometimes under 50 acres and also exceeding 2,000 acres. Names have changed over the years and may now be presented in different ways that can make recognition difficult.
Place-names under the TOWNLAND heading that cannot be found in the Index of Townlands of Ireland (NB many of such still remain within old documents and cause interpretation difficulties.) These are denoted by the addition of an * in the column.

MILLER In property records the name was usually that of the proprietor or lessee, may or may not also have been the miller.

TYPE The List covers the range of industrial activity found in Ireland (mining & sea-shore activities are not included.) Descriptions of less known milling operations are located in ***The Millers & The Mills of Ireland of about 1850.***

HOUSE In each case the first set of dimensions given is for the **mill building**; detail for others (if provided) also - kilns, dwelling house, workshop, barns, stores, etc. Significant small details and descriptions of buildings and machinery provided in Valuation Office House Books that are useful have been included.

WHEEL etc. Initial figures provided under this heading are feet and inch measurements of - wheel diameter, breadth of wheel (or bucket) and fall of water. The type of wheel may be noted and detail of mill stones, and other equipment driven by the water wheel of mills of a non-grinding variety. In the database document, column width is inadequate to carry this often extensive detail, accordingly any spill-over is indicated by **':'** (and is available in a database 'Form' document on request) under all headings including : '**HOUSE**' & '**WHEEL etc.**'

(continued next page)

RECORD. The many abbreviations used under this heading may be grouped under one of three categories :-

(1) Records from Valuation Office Documents, viz. primary books of R. Griffith`s Valuation of Tenements :
vmb/ = V.O. Mill Book (dated usually from 1835 to 1840) ; **hob/** = V.O. House Book (*) ;
fdb/ = V.O. Field Book ; **valCB/(no.)** = Cancellation (i.e. updating of valuation) Book.
(*) Reference letters & numbers may vary according to the archival source (ex Dublin or N. Ireland.).
And significantly : **gr/** = Sir Richard Griffith`s Primary Valuations, dated from 1848 to 1858.

(2) Other important sources :
dd/ = Memorials of Deeds at Registry of Deeds, Dublin. References specify book number, folio and deed number. Date is that of the implementation of a legal transaction and the **PROPRIETORS** column lists the names of the parties then involved.
1"os/ = A record from the early series 1" per mile Ordnance Survey maps originating about 1835, later revised and usually printed about 1902.
6"os/ = Site locations noted from 6" per mile Ordnance Survey maps 1835 series, some records are also found in O. S. 25" Series maps.
osm/ = Record from Ordnance Survey Memoirs, i.e. notes taken by secretaries employed by the officers who created the early O. S. maps. For a complete list of the nation's mills carefully marked in historic maps see the separate publication – ***Mills of Ireland, A List Dated About 1850***, published 2008, by this author.
P (etc.) = A photograph is available in a Collection, famous or private (the abbreviations denote :) W. A. Green, R. J. Walsh, W. A. McCutcheon, W. E. Hogg.

3) Reports & survey from :-
iaa/ = The Irish Architectural Archive; **aii/** = record in The Architectural Inventory of Ireland series; **sv/ (xx)** = work, providing author's name ; **mmSv/** = Mills & Millers of Ireland Survey (member's initials); **lic. /no.** = 1963 Oireachtas report of milling licenses, holder /tonnage; **hcJ** = Stills licenses in House of Commons Journals (1779-1782) ; **thom** = Thom's Directory; **turb** = report by electricity authority of about 1947. And from research via the internet :- **a.a.ire.ie**. = Ask about Ireland via Griffith's record at National Archives; **Ld.Est.db** = per database of NUI Galway and the Moore Institute.

SURVEYS : In order to maintain and forward its interest in the preservation of ancient and traditional mills the society Mills and Millers of Ireland has been active through simple survey of mills wherever and whenever possible. The substantial number of such surveys already conducted goes some way to providing an interesting indication of the general condition of several types of old Irish mills. The letter found at the extreme right of each **mmSv** record in the database indicates the current state of mill at that site :- **A** = Active mill, **B** = Building 75% remains substantial, **C** = Converted, **D** = Dilapidated [= probably beyond repair,] **R** = Ruins only, **Z** = Zero mill on site.

A summary of the findings of the MMOI and other parties' survey is provided in the following table. This provides an indication of the state of mills throughout the nation and a suggestion for the considerable number of old mill buildings that might still be worthy of conservation or adaptation for modern purposes.

From a CLASSIFICATION of mills & an **ESTIMATED** total number **(say 5,000)**

CLASS	**DESCRIPTION**	**%**	**Est. TOTAL no.**
A	Active mills	5.5	275
B	Buildings substantially (75%) complete	19.9	995
C	Buildings converted or restored	19.7	985
D	Dilapidated buildings	7.6	380
R	RUINS only remain (or small pieces)	20.4	1020
Z	Zero located or site obliterated	26.9	1345
		(**Estimated** -) TOTAL :	5000

NOTES : This publication is the development of ***The Millers & The Mills of Ireland of about 1850***, first published in 1989. Since the latter date further research and additional sources have been investigated from which milling information and data may be obtained, thus providing a more useful record.

Every source now available to the researcher was prepared for a specific purpose; but each was peculiar and interesting in a different manner. And if some provide information concerning milling (i.e. the working activity of our ancestors) it becomes clear that certain records, specially the legal documents concerning transfer of property, contain a abundant detail concerning the names and status of the parties concerned. Hence such information satisfies the reader's further interest as a genealogist. The data base accordingly contains numerous such references and though they too are hidden in the normal printout of the List, they are available in the database Form type document already mentioned. See ref. to columns with a ':'

OLD IRISH MILL BUILDINGS

On the one hand, so great was the variety of architectural design applied to mill buildings that it is quite difficult to locate two that can be said to be alike. On the other hand it becomes clear to the researcher when listing the measurements and detail of the huge number of structures across the nation that in very many localities, the smaller buildings at least, do seem to be of similar pattern or offshoots of the one design, originating perhaps from in the head of a particular millwright or architect.

One thing is certain that no mill was casually constructed or thrown up where a miller might have wished it to be. Indeed, we cannot know how much thought and care needed to be applied, primarily with view to obtaining adequate supply and power of water source, after which thought could be given to access and convenience of the workers. Continuity of water could of course not be assumed and it is clear that a considerable proportion of Irish mills remained idle for four or five months during summer-time.

The selection of photographs that now follows portrays mills in a variety of size shape and conditions and from a good number of our counties. The database will make clear if conservation measures have been taken should this not be obvious in the picture.

How pleasing to the eye we may find even an old derelict structure on a river bank to be, or however familiar may some old building become as we regularly pass it by - it unfortunate that so many have passed from usefulness and will never again support a workforce ! For Dubliners it is a joy to be able still, while 'darting' along nearby to behold one of our finest survivors; though sad that it still appears to contain empty rooms.

Dublin City, Dock Mill

Co. Offaly, Fancroft Mill

Co. Tyrone, Sion Mills

Co. Kilkenny, Duninga, Malthouse

Co. Down, Ballydugan Flour Mill (photo. N. Killen)
Co. Westmeath, Coola Mills

Co. Dublin, Tallaght Corn Mill
Co. Meath, Higginstown Corn Mill

Co. Meath, Mentrim Mill
Co. Cork, Glanworth Woollen Mill

Co. Carlow, Clonmoney Woollen Mill
Co. Donegal, Rathmelton, Old Brewery

Co. Kilkenny, Kells Corn & Tuck Mills
Co. Dublin, Mill – submerged near Salmon Leap

Co. Carlow, Paupish, Old Mill
Co. Kerry, Ballybrack, Old Mill

Co. Carlow, Dunleckny Corn Mill
Co, Meath, Bective Mill.

Co. Kildare, Crookstown Corn Mill
Co. Donegal, Churchtown Corn Kiln

Co. Wexford, Ballygerry, Windmill Stump
Co. Mayo, Ardkill, Windmill Ruins

Co. Donegal, Tully Mill, Ballyarr, Flax
Co. Kilkenny, Bennetsbridge, Pottery

Co. Dublin, Skerries Mills
Co. Fermanagh, Mullycovet Corn Mill

Co. Cavan, Lackan Flax Mill
Galway City, West Bridge small Mill

Co. Antrim, Tamnabrick, Sprucefield Mill
Co. Roscommon, Castlereagh Flour Mill

Co. Tyrone, Dyan Mill
Co. Louth, Dunleer, White River Mill

Co. Offaly, Cadamstown Corn Mill
Co. Galway, Templetogher Corn Mill

Co. Meath, Tullog Mill (photo. S. Lancaster)
Co. Wexford, Garrylough Mill

Co. Cavan, Wotoraghy, Corn Mill & Kiln
Co. Kerry, Knocknagoshel, Corn & Tuck Mills

Co. Meath, Moynalty, Annesbrook Mill (photo. R. Jacob)
Co. Limerick, Croom, Mill Granary

Co. Antrim, Flax Mill, near Claddy Water
Co. Meath, Macetown Mill

Dublin City, Bolands Flour Mill.
Co. Antrim, Newtownabbey, Mossley Mill
(photos. left: S. Pilgrim & right: S. Bourke)

Co. Waterford, Dungarvan Mills
Co. Wicklow, Tinakilly Upper, Aughrim Mill

Co. Offaly, Bunrevan Flour Mill
Co. Meath, Slane Mill

OLD MILL WHEELS

As it was with the buildings, so also a considerable variety of water wheels were designed to suit both water supply and the mill building. Firstly as to one of four basic types that were named according to how (and at what level) the water struck the wheel, viz. at the bottom of a vertical mill wheel, somewhere about mid-way up, or at the top – on the near side or side opposite from the flow. The work to be done and the power that was accordingly required had everything to do with the size of the wheel – the range of output of Irish wheels varied from just a fraction of a h.p. up to 10 or 12 h.p., when the diameter was in the region of 20 feet. For further information on calculation of horse power and also information found in Valuation Office documents that concerned mill buildings the reader is referred to the 2000 publication of ***The Millers and The Mills of Ireland of about 1850.***

The earlier wheels in many cases were comprised of buckets of strange shape but those seen in the following photographs portray some of the more regular designs and size. The first wheel photograph here displayed does not portray its immense size until one spies and compares that of the person immediately at r.h.s. of this wheel.

WHEELS : Kells, Co. Kilkenny, Newmills, Co. Donegal, R. Barrow, Co. Carlow;
Bruree, Co. Limerick, Old Mill, Co. Down; Martry Mill, Co. Meath.

OLD MILL STONES

The grinding machinery and the technology of the grist mill's interior, though it did steadily improve in design and efficiency, did not change as dramatically as the water wheels that provided power. The majority of old 18th & 19th century mills operated with millstones of 4 feet diameter for shelling and 4ft. 6ins. for grinding purposes.

In the earlier small mills that were driven by a horizontal type water wheel the power provided was just capable of turning a stone of about 3 feet in diameter. Very few of these very old horizontal wheel mills remain intact or on view today though there must have been many hundreds of them across the country at one time. The sites of over one hundred of mills of this type are listed in the database of this volume.

As a result of loss of water supply or lack of its consistency many mills converted to using electricity as power source. Such is the case for the mill stones seen smoothly in motion in the photograph opposite are at Martry Mill, County Meath, it being one of the very few old Irish mills still grinding and active for business in 2011.

Very old stone – date no known.
Old stones displayed near gateway/

Old stones (modern) still grinding at Martry Mill.

WHIN MILL,

COUNTY WICKLOW.

This nicely preserved mill with its adjacent small millhouse is one of many that operated in rural parts of Ireland both north and south.

Driven by horse or mule they were used for chopping roots to feed to animals, or in this case the whins.

MILLS and MILLERS of IRELAND

The Society of Mills and Millers of Ireland was established in 2001 to encourage and assist in the preservation and appreciation of mills as part of our industrial heritage. Membership is well spread throughout the nation and comprises both mill owners and others who either regard themselves as mill-folk or who would wish to support the aims of the organisation.

Copies of this publication are available from the Society; it is recommended to students or anybody engaging in serious research or investigations concerning Irish mills.

MILLS & MILLERS of IRELAND DATA BASE

Containing more than 22,000 references, notes and items of statistics relating to some 4,500 old mills; in many cases the condition in which they are found today is recorded. Twenty differing sources have been researched for the completion of the data base list.

PARISH	TOWNLAND	MILLER	TYPE	HOUSE	Land	£Val	PROPRIETORS	Date	WHEEL etc.	Record	Ref.
Drumaul	Aghaboy	-	mill	-	-	-	-	-	wheel	pWAM	-
Drumaul	Aghaboy	Davidson Adam	corn & flax	-	-	-	-	-	16x5 16x4	osm/	-
Drumaul	Aghaboy	Davidson Adam	corn & kiln	-	-	-	-	-	- 2 pair stones	v1B/	-
Drumaul	Aghaboy	Davidson Adam	flax	-	-	-	-	-	- 4 berths	v1B/	-
Skerry	Aghafatten	-	mill	-	-	-	-	-	wheel	pWAM	-
Aghagallon	Aghagallon	-	mill	-	-	-	-	-	wheel	pWAM	-
Aghalee	Aghalee	Ferris William	flour & bleach	-	-	-	-	-	15x3 13x2	osm/	-
Antrim	Aghislone	McWaters John	corn	-	-	-	McWaters - Richardson :	1819	-	dd/	742 2 505137
Racavan	Aghnadore	unoc./ Martin James	old flax mill	-	-	-	-	-	-	gr/	-
Ahoghill	Ahoghill	Weir Robt	corn	-	-	-	-	-	-	v1B/	-
Armoy	Alcrossagh	-	corn kiln	-	-	-	-	-	-	6"os/	-
Lisburn district	Annahilt	- on Ravernet R.	corn	-	-	-	-	2006	-	mmSv/	jd - Cr
Rasharkin	Anticur	-	corn	-	-	-	-	-	14x2	osm/	-
Rasharkin	Anticur	Heany James	corn & kiln	-	-	-	-	-	-	v1B/	-
Rasharkin	Anticur	Henry Wmilliam	corn & flax	-	-	-	-	-	-	gr/	-
Larne	Antiville	Barclay Archibald	beetling	-	-	-	-	-	-	v1B/	-
Larne	Antiville	Barklie	beetling	-	-	-	-	-	-	gr/	-
Larne	Antivillie	-	mill	-	-	-	-	-	-	pWAM	-
Antrim	Antrim T`parks	-	brewery	-	-	-	-	-	-	6"os/	-
Antrim	Antrim T`parks	-	houses	-	-	-	-	-	-	pWAM	-
Antrim	Antrim T`parks	-	mill	-	-	-	-	-	-	pWAM	-
Antrim	Antrim T`parks	-	mill / several	-	-	-	-	-	-	pWAM	-
Antrim	Antrim T`parks	-	paper	-	-	-	-	-	-	6"os/	-
Antrim	Antrim T`parks	-	paper	-	-	-	-	-	-	6"os/	-
Antrim	Antrim T`parks	Clarke George J	flour & kiln	-	5a.	-	-	-	-	gr/	-
Antrim	Antrim T`parks	Ferguson John F	corn	-	-	-	-	-	-	v1B/	-
Antrim	Antrim T`parks	Ferguson John F	paper	-	-	-	-	-	-	v1B/	-
Antrim	Antrim T`parks	Fowke & Ferguson	brewery	-	-	-	-	-	-	v1B/	-
Antrim	Antrim Town	- at Mill Row	paper	-	-	-	-	-	-	gr/	-
Antrim	Antrim Town	Brooke Basil	mill & weir	-	-	-	Brooke - Macartney Geo	1843	-	dd/	1843 14 198
Antrim	Antrim Town	Brooke Basil	mills	-	-	-	Brooke B - Hamilton Thos	1840	-	dd/	1840 8 5
Antrim	Antrim Town	Brooke Basil	tuck or fulling	-	-	-	Brooke - Macartney Geo	1843	-	dd/	1843 14 198
Antrim	Antrim Town	Celtic Paper Co.	paper	-	-	-	Celtic Paper - Coleman Jas	1888	-	dd/	1888 55 212
Antrim	Antrim Town	Coleman James	tucking & fulling	-	-	-	Coleman Jas - Boal Hugh	1891	-	dd/	1891 32 277
Antrim	Antrim Town	Crawford William	paper	-	-	-	Crawford - Holford Thos	1880	-	dd/	1880 32 80
Antrim	Antrim Town	Crawford William	paper	-	-	-	Crawford W - Holford :	1880	-	dd/	1880 27 173
Antrim	Antrim Town	Grant Lewis Sir	Castle & Mills	-	-	-	Grant - Harvey Sir Robt J	1851	-	dd/	1851 14 282
Antrim	Antrim Town	Holford Thomas	paper	-	-	-	Holford Thos - Barbour Jas	1885	-	dd/	1885 49 53
Antrim	Antrim Town	Judges Lord	paper :	-	-	-	Judges - Ferguson John	1878	-	dd/	1878 27 60
Antrim	Antrim Town	Land. Estate Courts	paper	-	-	-	Ld. Est. Cts. - Birkhead :	1875	-	dd/	18775 54 118
Antrim	Antrim Town	Massereene Visc.	Manor Mills	-	-	-	Mass. Visc. - Leech :	1877	-	dd/	1877 7 60
Antrim	Antrim Town	Massereene Visc.	tucking or fulling	-	-	-	Mass`ne - Ferguson Jno	1851	-	dd/	1851 19 167
Antrim	Antrim Town	Massereene Visc.	tucking or fulling	-	-	-	Massereene - Taggart J	1851	-	dd/	1851 20 67
Antrim	Antrim Town	McConehy James	The Mill	-	-	-	McConehy Jas - Jane	1836	-	dd/	1836 2 210
Antrim	Antrim Town	O`Neill Hon. Edward	Manor mills :	-	-	-	O`Neill Ed - Fitzgerald :	1877	-	dd/	1877 2 192
Antrim	Antrim Town :	Mass. & Ferr. Visc.	mill	-	-	-	Mass. Visc. - Boal John	1896	-	dd/	1896 8 75
Antrim	Antrim Town :	Cinnamond Joseph :	mill	-	-	-	Cinnamond J - McConchy :	1832	-	dd/	889 81 588081
Antrim	Antrim Town :	Casement Charles :	land	- dw., hos, offs.	20a.	-	Casement C - Crozier Wm :	1832	Mort. 3 Feb. 1829	dd/	843 47 585047
Antrim	Antrim Town :	Magill Rev Robert :	land	-	-	-	Magill R - Allen William :	1830	-	dd/	863 250 575250
Antrim	Antrim Town :	Hughes Jane	mill race	-	-	-	-	1849	-	dd/	1849 21 84
Billy	Ardihannon	-	flax	-	-	-	-	-	13x1.8	osm/	-
Billy	Ardihannon	Taylor James	corn & flax, kiln	-	-	-	-	-	flax mill - 2 beetles	v1B/	-

PARISH	TOWNLAND	MILLER	TYPE	HOUSE	Land	£Val	PROPRIETORS	Date	WHEEL etc.	Record	Ref.
Toome	Artogues	Black Joseph	mill	-	-	-	Balck Jos - Heffron John	1891	-	dd/	1891 7 81
Toome	Artogues	Heffron John	mill	-	-	-	Heffron J - Ant Co Ld Inv Co	1891	-	dd/	1891 7 82
Ahoghill	Aughnacleagh	-	flax	-	-	-	-	-	13x2	osm/	-
Killead	Aughnamullan	-	corn	-	-	-	-	-	18x2x18 & 18x2x18	osm/	-
Killead	Aughnamullan	-	flax	-	-	-	-	-	18x2x18	osm/	-
Killead	Aughnamullan	- on Dundesert R.	mill	-	-	-	-	-	-	1"os/	28
Killead	Aughnamullan	Cunningham George	corn & flax	-	-	-	-	-	14x2x8	osm/	-
Killead	Aughnamullan	Cunningham George	corn & kiln	-	-	-	-	-	- 2 pair stones	v1B/	-
Killead	Aughnamullan	Cunningham George	flax	-	-	-	-	-	3 stocks & 1 bruising m/c	v1B/	-
Killead	Aughnamullan	Fleming James	corn & kiln	-	-	-	-	-	-	gr/	-
Killead	Aughnamullen	-	mill	-	-	-	-	-	-	pWAM	-
Ballymoney	Ballaghmore	-	factory	-	-	-	-	-	-	1"os/	13
Ballymoney	Ballaghmore	Anderson & McAnally	corn & kiln	-	-	-	-	-	-	v1B/	-
Ballymoney	Ballaghmore	Dinsmore W G	corn, flax, kilns	-	-	-	-	-	15 ft. dia., fall 10 ft.	v1B/	-
Culfeightrin	Ballindam	McNeill John	corn & kiln	-	-	-	-	-	-	v1B/	-
Ballinderry	Ballinderry	-	mill	-	-	-	-	-	-	pWAM	-
Ballinderry	Ballinderry	Walkington Thomas	corn & kiln	-	-	-	-	-	1 1/2 pr. stones	v1B/	-
Ballinderry	Ballinderry Lr	Walkington Thomas	corn	-	-	-	-	-	15x3 13x2	osm/	-
Ballintoy	Ballinlea	-	mill	-	-	-	-	-	wheel	pWAM	-
Ballintoy	Ballinlea Lr	-	flax	-	-	-	-	-	-	6"os/	-
Ballintoy	Ballinlea Lr	-	mill	-	-	-	-	-	-	6"os/	-
Ballintoy	Ballinlea Lr	-	mill & kiln	-	-	-	-	-	-	6"os/	-
Ballintoy	Ballinlea Lr	Fleming George	flax	-	-	-	-	-	-	gr/	-
Ballintoy	Ballinlea Lr	McCaughen Sam	flax	-	-	-	-	-	-	v1B/	-
Ballintoy	Ballinlea Upr	Moore James S	corn & kiln	-	-	-	-	-	fall 8ft., breast wh.	v1B/	-
Ballintoy	Ballintoy Upr	Moore James S	corn & kilns	-	-	-	-	-	-	gr/	-
Gr. Muckamore	Balloo	-	corn & kiln	-	-	-	-	-	-	6"os/	-
Gr. Muckamore	Ballyarnot	-	mill	-	-	-	-	-	-	1"os/	28
Ahoghill	Ballybeg	Hardy Joseph	mill pond	-	2.2.5	-	-	-	-	gr/	-
Nilteen Grange	Ballybentragh	Cameron James	thrashing	-	-	-	-	-	-	osm/	-
Nilteen Grange	Ballybentragh	Cameron Robert	thrashing	-	-	-	-	-	-	osm/	-
Nilteen Grange	Ballybentragh	Wallace John	thrashing	-	-	-	-	-	-	osm/	-
Dunluce	Ballyboggy	Montgomery John	mills	-	-	-	Montgomery - Lecky Hugh	1893	-	dd/	1893 44 140
Dunluce	Ballybogy	-	flax	-	-	-	-	-	12x2.2	osm/	-
Dunluce	Ballybogy	-	flax	-	-	-	-	-	14x2	osm/	-
Dunluce	Ballybogy	-	mill	-	-	-	-	-	-	pWAM	-
Dunluce	Ballybogy	M`Naughten Catherine	corn, flax, kilns	-	-	-	-	-	-	gr/	-
Dunluce	Ballybogy	Nevin Thomas	flax	-	-	-	-	-	-	v1B/	-
Dunluce	Ballybogy	Taggart John	corn & flax, kiln	-	-	-	-	-	-	v1B/	-
Ballymoney	Ballybolands Lr	-	mill	-	-	-	-	-	-	6"os/	-
Ballymoney	Ballybolands Lr	-	mill	-	-	-	-	-	-	6"os/	-
Ballymoney	Ballybolands Lr	-	mill	-	-	-	-	-	-	6"os/	-
Larne/Ballycor	Ballyboley	-	flax	-	-	-	-	-	-	6"os/	-
Larne/Ballycor	Ballyboley	-	flax	-	-	-	-	-	13x2.6	osm/	-
Larne/Ballycor	Ballyboley	-	flax hole	-	-	-	-	-	-	6"os/	-
Drumaul	Ballybollen	O`Neill Ambrose	corn	-	-	-	-	-	-	dd/	-
Dunluce Upper	Ballyboylands	-	flax	-	-	-	-	-	-	1"os/	13
Dunluce Upper	Ballyboylands	-	mill	-	-	-	-	-	wheel	pWAM	-
Dunluce Upper	Ballyboylands Lr	-	beetling	-	-	-	-	-	17x4.2x12	osm/	-
Dunluce Upper	Ballyboylands Lr	-	corn & flax	-	-	-	-	-	16x3.6x8 & 12x3x11	osm/	-
Dunluce Upper	Ballyboylands Lr	Moore Lawrence	beetling	-	-	-	-	-	-	v1B/	-
Dunluce Upper	Ballyboylands Lr	Moore Lawrence	beetling (2)	-	-	-	-	-	-	gr/	-

PARISH	TOWNLAND	MILLER	TYPE	HOUSE	Land	£Val	PROPRIETORS	Date	WHEEL etc.	Record	Ref.
Dunluce Upper	Ballyboylands Lr	Moore Lawrence	corn & kiln	-	-	-	-	-	-	v1B/	-
Dunluce Upper	Ballyboylands Lr	Moore Lawrence	corn & kilns	-	-	-	-	-	-	gr/	-
Dunluce Upper	Ballyboylands Lr	Moore Lawrence	flax	-	-	-	-	-	-	v1B/	-
Rathlin Island	Ballycarry	McBride Wm Alex	thrashing	-	-	-	-	-	no wheel	osm/	-
Ramoan	Ballycastle Town :	Dunlop John	corn	-	-	-	-	-	-	gr/	-
Ballynure	Ballyclare	-	beetling	-	-	-	-	-	-	pWSH	-
Ballynure	Ballyclare	-	bleach	-	-	-	-	-	-	pWAG	-
Ballynure	Ballyclare	-	bleach	-	-	-	-	-	-	pWSH	-
Ballynure	Ballyclare	-	mill	-	-	-	-	-	-	pWAM	-
Ballynure	Ballyclare	-	mills	-	-	-	-	-	-	6"os/	-
Ballynure	Ballyclare	-	paper	-	-	-	-	-	-	6"os/	-
Ballynure	Ballyclare	- on Doagh R.	flax	-	-	-	-	-	-	1"os/	28
Ballynure	Ballyclare	- at Grahamstown	paper	-	-	-	-	-	-	1"os/	28
Ballynure	Ballyclare	Bell John	bleach	-	-	-	-	-	-	gr/	-
Ballynure	Ballyclare	Bell John & George	bleach	-	-	-	-	-	28x4x20	v1B/	-
Ballynure	Ballyclare	Greenfield Robert	corn & kiln	32x21x16 & :	-	-	-	-	2 pr. st. water for 8 mos.	v1B/	-
Ballynure	Ballyclare	Greenfield Robert	paper	-	-	-	-	-	28x5 18x5 18x2	osm/	-
Ballynure	Ballyclare	Greenfield Robert	paper	62x28x26 & :	-	82.7.0	-	-	14x5x30 & 28x7x30 :	v1B/	-
Ballynure	Ballyclare	Ledie George	corn	-	-	-	-	-	-	gr/	-
Ballynure	Ballyclare	N.I. Paper Mill Co.	mill	-	-	-	NI Paper Mill Co - Thornley :	1894	-	dd/	1894 72 287
Ballynure	Ballyclare	unoc.	old paper mill	-	-	-	-	-	-	gr/	-
Derryaghy	Ballycollin	Roberts John	bleach	-	-	-	-	-	-	v1B/	-
Ballycor	Ballycor	-	corn	-	-	-	-	-	-	6"os/	-
Ballycor	Ballycor	-	corn	-	-	-	-	-	-	6"os/	-
Ballycor	Ballycor	-	corn	-	-	-	-	-	13x1.8 13x1.8	osm/	-
Ballycor	Ballycor	-	mill	-	-	-	-	-	large wheel	pWAM	-
Ballycor	Ballycor	Ferguson J C	beetling	-	-	-	-	-	-	gr/	-
Ballycor	Ballycor	Inc. Estate Commrs.	mill	-	-	-	I.E.C. - Ferguson	1856	-	dd/	1856 25 84
Ballycor	Ballycor	Smith M/s	beetling & wash	-	-	-	-	-	26x5.6 (+ 3 ors)	osm/	-
Ballycor	Ballycor	Smith M/s	bleach green	-	24a.	-	-	-	-	osm/	-
Ballycor	Ballycor	unoc.	old mill (dilap.)	-	-	-	-	-	-	gr/	-
Dunaghy	Ballycregagh	- on Flesk Water	flax	-	-	-	-	-	-	1"os/	13
Dunaghy	Ballycregagh	Hanna Andrew	mill	-	-	-	Hanna Andrew - David	1890	-	dd/	1890 57 163
Dunaghy	Ballycregagh	Hanna David	mill	-	-	-	Hanna David - John	1890	-	dd/	1890 57 165
Dunaghy	Ballycregagh	Henry Wiliam	flax	-	-	-	-	-	-	gr/	-
Loughguile	Ballycregagh Lr	-	beetling	-	-	-	-	-	12x2.6	osm/	-
Loughguile	Ballycregagh Lr	-	flax	-	-	-	-	-	14x1.10	osm/	-
Loughguile	Ballycregagh Lr	-	flax	-	-	-	-	-	13x1.8	osm/	-
Loughguile	Ballycregagh Lr	Henry Mathew	beetling	-	-	-	-	-	-	v1B/	-
Loughguile	Ballycregagh Lr	Henry Mathew	flax	-	-	-	-	-	-	v1B/	-
Ballyclug	Ballycreggy	-	mill	-	-	-	-	-	-	6"os/	-
Ballyclug	Ballycreggy	Johnston Margt & Rob	corn & flax	-	-	-	-	-	-	v1B/	-
Templeparick	Ballycushan	-	corn	-	-	-	-	-	-	1"os/	28
Templeparick	Ballycushan	-	flax	-	-	-	-	-	-	1"os/	28
Templeparick	Ballycushan	Wiley Mr	thrashing	-	-	-	-	-	13x3x6	osm/	-
Rasharkin	Ballydonnelly	-	corn	-	-	-	-	-	13x2	osm/	-
Rasharkin	Ballydonnelly	-	flax	-	-	-	-	-	20x3	osm/	-
Duneane	Ballydonnelly	-	mill	-	-	-	-	-	-	pWAM	-
Rasharkin	Ballydonnelly	McCulloch John	corn & kiln	-	-	-	-	-	-	v1B/	-
Islandmagee	Ballydown	-	ruins	-	-	-	-	-	-	pWAM	-
Ballycor	Ballyeaston	-	mill	-	-	-	-	-	-	1"os/	28
Castlecarn	Ballygalley	-	cotton factory	-	-	-	-	-	-	6"os/	-

PARISH	TOWNLAND	MILLER	TYPE	HOUSE	Land	£Val	PROPRIETORS	Date	WHEEL etc.	Record	Ref.
Castlecarn	Ballygalley	Agnew Jones	corn & kiln	-	-	-	-	-	-	v1B/	-
Castlecarn	Ballygalley	Rennie Hugh	spinning	-	-	-	-	-	-	v1B/	-
Castlecarn	Ballygally	-	mill	-	-	-	-	-	-	pWAM	-
Castlecarn	Ballygally	Aiken Robert	corn	-	-	-	-	-	-	gr/	-
Kirkinriola	Ballygarvey	-	flax	-	-	-	-	-	-	1"os/	20
Kirkinriola	Ballygarvey	-	linen	-	-	-	-	-	-	1"os/	20
Kirkinriola	Ballygarvey	-	linen factory	-	-	-	-	-	-	1"os/	20
Kirkinriola	Ballygarvey	-	mill	-	-	-	-	-	-	pWAM	-
Kirkinriola	Ballygarvey	Craig Daniel	corn & flax	-	-	-	-	-	-	gr/	-
Kirkinriola	Ballygarvey	Currell Andrew	beetling, bleach	-	-	-	-	-	-	gr/	-
Kirkinriola	Ballygarvey	Currie Daniel	beetling	-	-	-	-	-	16x6	osm/	-
Kirkinriola	Ballygarvey	Currie Daniel	beetling & wash	-	-	-	-	-	15x5 15x5	osm/	-
Kirkinriola	Ballygarvey	Currill Daniel	bleach	-	-	-	-	-	-	v1B/	-
Kirkinriola	Ballygarvey	Hunter Harris	corn & kiln	-	-	-	-	-	-	v1B/	-
Killead	Ballyginniff	-	corn	-	-	-	-	-	14x2x8	osm/	-
Killead	Ballyginniff	-	mill	-	-	-	-	-	-	6"os/	-
Killead	Ballyginniff	George Alex	corn & kiln	42x23x8 & :	-	-	-	-	-	v1B/	-
Killead	Ballyginniff	Wiley James	corn & kiln	-	-	-	-	-	-	gr/	-
Carnmoney	Ballygolan	-	mill	-	-	-	-	-	-	pWAM	-
Carnmoney	Ballygolan	- at Glenmount	flax	-	-	-	-	-	-	1"os/	28
Carnmoney	Ballygolan	Grimshaw James	flax spinning	93x28x25 & :	-	-	-	-	-	v1B/	-
Carnmoney	Ballygolan	Grimshaw James & :	spinning-mill	stores, offs., yd.	0.3.20	260	-	1865	-	gr/	a.a.ire.ie
Carnmoney	Ballygolan	Grimshaw Thomas	print works	-	-	-	-	-	-	v1B/	-
Carnmoney	Ballygolan	Walker Robert	dye-works	house, offs. & ld.	18a.	108	-	1865	-	gr/	a.a.ire.ie
Carnmoney	Ballygoland W`ho	Grimshaw Jas & Son	flax spinning	-	-	-	-	-	35x4.6x30	osm/	-
Shankill	Ballygomartin	-	mill houses	-	-	-	-	-	-	pWAM	-
Shankill	Ballygomartin	Ewart William	bleachgreen	-	-	-	-	-	-	gr/	-
Shankill	Ballygomartin	Moore James	bleach	-	-	-	-	-	-	v1B/	-
Camlin	Ballygortgarve	-	corn	-	-	-	-	-	-	6"os/	-
Camlin	Ballygortgarve	-	corn & flax	-	-	-	-	-	16x3x3, 14x3x5	osm/	-
Camlin	Ballygortgarve	-	flax	-	-	-	-	-	-	6"os/	-
Camlin	Ballygortgarve	-	flax mill	-	-	-	-	-	-	6"os/	-
Camlin	Ballygortgarve	-	mill	-	-	-	-	-	-	pWAM	-
Camlin	Ballygortgarve	McCawley Robert	flax	-	-	-	-	-	-	v1B/	-
Camlin	Ballygortgarve	McCawley Robert	flour	-	-	-	-	-	- 3 pr. stones	v1B/	-
Carnmoney	Ballygowan	-	flax	-	-	-	-	-	-	6"os/	-
Carnmoney	Ballygowan	Grimshaw James	spinning	-	-	-	-	-	-	gr/	-
Carnmoney	Ballygowan	Moore Robert	flax	-	-	-	-	-	17x2x20	osm/	-
Carnmoney	Ballygowan	Moore Robert	flax	-	-	-	-	-	16x2x22	v1B/	-
Drumaul	Ballygrooby	-	corn	-	-	-	-	-	-	6"os/	-
Drumaul	Ballygrooby	-	cotton mfy	-	-	-	-	-	-	6"os/	-
Drumaul	Ballygrooby	-	mill	-	-	-	-	-	-	pWAM	-
Drumaul	Ballygrooby	-	old bleach	-	-	-	-	-	-	pWSH	-
Drumaul	Ballygrooby	Black James	bleach	-	-	-	-	-	-	v1B/	-
Drumaul	Ballygrooby	Black James	corn	-	-	-	-	-	14x3 & 12x5	osm/	-
Drumaul	Ballygrooby	Black James	cotton	-	-	-	-	-	14x12x0 (4)	osm/	-
Drumaul	Ballygrooby	Black James	cotton	-	-	-	-	-	-	v1B/	-
Drumaul	Ballygrooby	Connor Foster	corn & kiln	-	-	-	-	-	-	gr/	-
Drumaul	Ballygrooby	Cooper John	corn	-	-	-	-	-	14x3 12x5	osm/	-
Drumaul	Ballygrooby	Cooper John	corn & kiln (2)	-	-	-	-	-	-	v1B/	-
Drumaul	Ballygrooby	Fenton & Sons	beetling, bleach	-	-	-	-	-	-	gr/	-
Drumaul	Ballygrooby	unoc.	flax (dilap.)	-	-	-	-	-	-	gr/	-

PARISH	TOWNLAND	MILLER	TYPE	HOUSE	Land	£Val	PROPRIETORS	Date	WHEEL etc.	Record	Ref.
Drumaul	Ballygrooby	unoc.	old flax spinning	-	-	-	-	-	-	gr/	-
Kilbride	Ballyhamage	Dickey & Raphael	beetling	66x23x16 & :	-	13.12	-	-	-	v1B/	-
Kilbride	Ballyhamage	Rowan John	beetling	-	-	-	-	-	-	gr/	-
Kilwaughter	Ballyhampton	-	cotton factory	-	-	-	-	-	-	6"os/	-
Islandmagee	Ballyharry	-	ruins	-	-	-	-	-	-	pWAM	-
Carnmoney	Ballyhenry	-	cotton works	-	-	-	-	-	-	6"os/	-
Carnmoney	Ballyhenry	-	mill	-	-	-	-	-	-	pWAM	-
Carnmoney	Ballyhenry	-	mill hos.	-	-	-	-	-	-	pWAM	-
Carnmoney	Ballyhenry	Campbell Henry & Co.	flax spinning	Mill expanded :	-	-	Purs. from Edmd Grimshaw	1859	20x2.8x20	IHAI	editor
Carnmoney	Ballyhenry	Council N'townabbey :	industrial museun	- at Mossley Mill	-	-	-	-	-	IHAI	editor
Carnmoney	Ballyhenry	Grimshaw Edmund	flax spinning	-	-	-	-	-	20x2.8x20	osm/	-
Carnmoney	Ballyhenry	Grimshaw Edmund	flax spinning	-	-	-	-	-	35x4.6x35	osm/	-
Carnmoney	Ballyhenry	Grimshaw Mr	spinning	4 spinning hos :	-	-	-	-	-	v1B/	-
Carnmoney	Ballyhenry	Grimshaw Mr	spinning (cont.)	eng. ho 26x23x21	-	67.11	-	-	-	v1B/	-
Carnmoney	Ballyhenry		ruins of houses	-	-	-	-	-	-	pWAM	-
Carnmoney	Ballyhenry W`ho	Thompson Mr	beetling, bleach	-	-	-	-	-	20x2.8x20	osm/	-
Kilroot	Ballyhill	-	mill	-	-	-	-	-	-	pWAM	-
Kilroot	Ballyhill	Hevey Timothy	corn & kiln	-	-	-	-	-	-	gr/	-
Kilroot	Ballyhill	Holmes William	corn & kiln	-	-	-	-	-	16x3x19	v1B/	-
Kilroot	Ballyhill	unoc.	mill	-	-	-	-	-	-	gr/	-
Glynn	Ballyhone	-	cotton mills	-	-	-	-	-	-	6"os/	-
Glynn	Ballyhone	-	mill	-	-	-	-	-	-	pWAM	-
Glynn	Ballyhone	Taylor James	bleach	-	-	-	Taylor Jas - Bell	-	-	dd/	-
Carnmoney	Ballyhowne	Grimshaw & Duffin	logwood	-	-	-	-	-	16x5 16x3	v1B/	-
Carnmoney	Ballyhowne	Grimshaw Robert	logwood	-	-	-	-	-	14x3x12 & 16x4x12	osm/	-
Carnmoney	Ballyhowne	Henderson James	corn	-	-	-	-	-	20x3.6x24	osm/	-
Carnmoney	Ballyhowne	Henderson James	corn	-	-	-	-	-	-	v1B/	-
Carnmoney	Ballyhowne	Henderson James	flax	-	-	-	-	-	-	v1B/	-
Carnmoney	Ballyhowne	McConnell Agnes	corn	-	-	-	-	-	-	gr/	-
Dunluce	Ballyhunsley S.	-	flax	-	-	-	-	-	14x2	osm/	-
Dunluce	Ballyhunsley S.	McElfatrick	flax	-	-	-	-	-	-	v1B/	-
Ballyclug	Ballykeel	Bell Robert	corn & beetling	30x22x12 & :	-	12.8	-	-	16 ft dia. breast wheel :	v1B/	-
Ballyclug	Ballykeel	McPeake William	mills	-	-	-	McPeake Wm - Dunlop	1860	-	dd/	1860 6 107
Antrim	Ballykeel /Ballylig	-	mill	-	-	-	-	-	-	pWAM	-
Armoy	Ballykenver	- Armoy on Flesk W.	flax	-	-	-	-	-	-	1"os/	13
Glynn	Ballylig	-	mill	-	-	-	-	-	-	6"os/	-
Glynn	Ballylig	Miller Alex	corn	43x23x8	-	-	-	-	-	v1B/	-
Glynn	Ballylig	Hogg Quintin	lands	-	-	-	Hogg Quintin - Stuart	1891	-	dd/	1891 55 126
Ballylinny	Ballylinny	-	flax	-	-	-	-	-	-	6"os/	-
Ballylinny	Ballylinully D`ne	Chesney Robert	flax	-	-	-	-	-	14x2x6	v1B/	-
Larne	Ballyloran	-	corn, flax & kiln	-	-	-	-	-	-	6"os/	-
Larne	Ballyloran	-	mill	-	-	-	-	-	-	pWAM	-
Larne	Ballyloran	Coey James	corn	-	-	-	-	-	-	gr/	-
Larne	Ballyloran	Whitla George	flax	-	-	-	-	-	-	v1B/	-
Larne	Ballyloran	Whitla George	flour, corn & kiln	-	-	-	-	-	-	v1B/	-
Ahoghill	Ballyloughan	Morton Robert	mill pond	-	7a.	-	-	-		gr/	-
Ahoghill	Ballyloughan	Strahan George	corn & flax	-	23a.	-	-	-	-	gr/	-
Islandmagee	Ballylumford	-	mill	-	-	-	-	-	-	pWAM	-
Ahoghill	Ballylummin	-	mill	-	-	-	-	-	-	1"os/	19
Glynn	Ballylune	Tucker Edward	cotton	-	-	-	-	-	-	osm/	-
Drumaul	Ballylurgan	-	mill	-	-	-	-	-	-	pWAM	-
Kirkinriola	Ballym`a R.Braid	-	spinning	-	-	-	-	-	-	pWAG	-

PARISH	TOWNLAND	MILLER	TYPE	HOUSE	Land	£Val	PROPRIETORS	Date	WHEEL etc.	Record	Ref.
Aghagallon	Ballymacilrany	Usher Robert	corn	-	-	-	-	-	-	osm/	-
Shankill	Ballymagarry	Coates Maurice L	cotton	-	-	-	-	-	-	gr/	-
Shankill	Ballymagarry	M`Ewan John	thread works	-	-	-	-	-	-	gr/	-
Shankill	Ballymagarry	Stevenson Messrs	bleach	-	-	-	-	-	25x5x20 25x5	v1B/	-
Shankill	Ballymagarry	Stevenson Messrs	cotton spinning	-	-	-	-	-	-	v1B/	-
Ballyclug	Ballymarlagh	-	old mill dam	-	-	-	-	-	-	6"os/	-
Ballyclug	Ballymarlagh	Irwin Thomas	corn & kiln	-	-	-	-	-	-	v1B/	-
Ballyclug	Ballymarlagh	Irwin Thomas	flax	28x26x11	-	0.18.3	-	-	-	v1B/	-
Ballyclug	Ballymarlagh	Wilson James	corn kiln	-	-	-	-	-	-	v1B/	-
Ballymartin	Ballymartin	Finlay William	tuck	-	-	-	-	-	-	osm/	-
Killead	Ballymather	-	cotton print	-	-	-	-	-	-	6"os/	-
Killead	Ballymather	-	mill	-	-	-	-	-	-	pWAM	-
Killead	Ballymather	Hunter & Elgee	printing	-	-	-	-	-	16x4x8	osm/	-
Killead	Ballymather Lr	Algie Thomas	corn, flax, kiln	-	-	-	-	-	-	gr/	-
Killead	Ballymather Lr	Algie Thomas	print & dye	-	-	-	-	-	-	gr/	-
Killead	Ballymather Lr	Hunter M & Algee T	print works	35x25x8 & :	-	-	-	-	-	v1B/	-
Killead	Ballymather Lr	zero name	corn & kiln	-	-	-	-	-	26x6 72 bkts	v1B/	-
Duneane	Ballymatoskerty	-	corn	-	-	-	-	-	16x3.3x9	osm/	-
Duneane	Ballymatoskerty	O`Neill Earl	corn & kiln	-	-	-	-	-	16x2x16	v1B/	-
Duneane	Ballymatuskerty	Dobbin William	corn	-	-	-	-	-	16x2x12	osm/	-
Kirkinriola	Ballymena	-	corn	-	-	-	-	-	16x6 16x6	osm/	-
Kirkinriola	Ballymena	-	corn	-	-	-	-	-	11x5 18x5	osm/	-
Kirkinriola	Ballymena	-	flax spinning	-	-	-	-	-	-	pWSH	-
Kirkinriola	Ballymena	Gihon Andrew	beetling	-	-	-	-	-	10x5 18x5	osm/	-
Kirkinriola	Ballymena	Gihon Andrew	beetling & wash	-	-	-	-	-	16x6 16x6	osm/	-
Kirkinriola	Ballymena	Gihon Andrew	corn	-	-	-	-	-	18x4	osm/	-
Kirkinriola	Ballymena	Gihon Andrew	distillery	-	-	-	-	-	26x3x21	osm/	-
Kirkinriola	Ballymena T`pks	Gihon William Jun	beetling, bleach	-	-	-	-	-	-	gr/	-
Kirkinriola	Ballymena T`pks :	unoc.	beetling	-	-	-	-	-	-	gr/	-
Kirkinriola	Ballymena T`pks :	Morton Robert	flour & corn	-	-	-	-	-	-	gr/	-
Kirkinriola	Ballymena town	-	corn	-	-	-	-	-	16x5.8 (2)	osm/	-
Kirkinriola	Ballymena town	-	corn	-	-	-	-	-	10.8x5 18x5	osm/	-
Kirkinriola	Ballymena Town	-	corn	-	-	-	-	-	18x4	osm/	-
Kirkinriola	Ballymena town	-	distillery	-	-	-	-	-	-	6"os/	-
Kirkinriola	Ballymena Town	-	distillery	-	-	-	-	-	26x3x21	osm/	-
Ahoghill	Ballyminstra	-	flax	-	-	-	-	-	-	6"os/	-
Ahoghill	Ballyminstra	-	mill	-	-	-	-	-	-	6"os/	-
Ahoghill	Ballyminstra	- at Straid Bridge	mill	-	-	-	-	-	-	1"os/	19
Ballymoney	Ballymoney	Moore James	brewery	-	-	-	-	-	-	v1B/	-
Ballymoney	Ballymoney :	Cameron James	waring factory	& yard	-	7	-	1865	-	gr/	a.a.lre.ie
Ballymoney	Ballymoney :	Cameron James	yarn factory	yard & garden	0.0.35	8	- [+ 15 tenants' houses]	1865	-	gr/	a.a.lre.ie
Glenavy	Ballymoneyman	Gregg T	old mill	45x22x16 & :	-	3.12.3	-	-	mill out of repair	v1B/	-
Gr. Nilteen	Ballymorris	-	beetling	v. good	-	-	- Peter Heuston	1997	now residence	pWEH	- Cr
Billy	Ballymoy	-	mill	-	-	-	-	-	-	pWAM	-
Connor	Ballymucvea	-	mill	-	-	-	-	-	-	pWAM	-
Shankill	Ballymurphy	-	bleachgreen	-	-	-	-	-	-	6"os/	-
Shankill	Ballymurphy	-	bleachgreen	-	-	-	-	-	-	6"os/	-
Shankill	Ballymurphy	Arthur William	beetling	-	-	-	-	-	-	v1B/	-
Shankill	Ballymurphy	Ferguson William	bleach	-	-	-	-	-	-	gr/	-
Shankill	Ballymurphy	Girwood Thomas	beetling	-	-	-	-	-	-	gr/	-
Shankill	Ballymurphy	Girwood Thomas	dye wks, pond	-	-	-	-	-	-	gr/	-
Shankill	Ballymurphy	Hamill Thomas	beetling	-	-	-	-	-	-	gr/	-

PARISH	TOWNLAND	MILLER	TYPE	HOUSE	Land	£Val	PROPRIETORS	Date	WHEEL etc.	Record	Ref.
Shankill	Ballymurphy	Orr William	bleach	-	-	-	-	-	-	v1B/	-
Shankill	Ballymurphy	Sinclair John	bleach	-	-	-	-	-	-	v1B/	-
Shankill	Ballymurphy	unoc./ Patterson John	beetling, bleach	-	-	-	-	-	-	gr/	-
Shankill	Ballymurphy	unoc./ Sinclair Thomas	bleach (dilap.)	-	-	-	-	-	-	gr/	-
Racavan	Ballynacaird	-	mill	-	-	-	-	-	-	6"os/	-
Racavan	Ballynacaird	-	mill	-	-	-	-	-	-	6"os/	-
Racavan	Ballynacaird	-	mill	-	-	-	-	-	-	6"os/	-
Racavan	Ballynacaird	-	mill	-	-	-	-	-	-	pWAM	-
Racavan	Ballynacaird	M`Neill Andrew	flax	-	-	-	-	-	-	gr/	-
Racavan	Ballynacaird	McNeill Andrew	flax	30x17x6	-	10.10	-	-	-	v1B/	-
Racavan	Ballynacaird	Montgomery Thomas	corn & kiln	-	-	-	-	-	-	v1B/	-
Racavan	Ballynacaird	O`Neill Chas	flax	-	-	-	-	-	-	v1B/	-
Racavan	Ballynacaird	Shaw James	flax	-	-	-	-	-	-	gr/	-
Racavan	Ballynacaird	Shaw James	flax	23x17x8	-	0.7.11	-	-	-	v1B/	-
Racavan	Ballynacaird	Thompson William	corn & flax	-	-	-	-	-	-	gr/	-
Ballymoney	Ballynacree More	O`Bryan James T	spinning	-	-	-	-	-	21x11x14 & steam	v1B/	-
Ballymoney	Ballynacreeskein	-	mill	-	-	-	-	-	-	pWAM	-
Ballymoney	Ballynacreeskein	Smith Mr	spinning	-	-	-	-	-	18x5.6x20	osm/	-
Ballymoney	Ballynacreeskein	Smith Samuel	corn & kiln	-	-	-	-	-	-	v1B/	-
Ballymoney	Ballynacreeskein	Smith Samuel	spin & bleach	-	-	-	-	-	-	v1B/	-
Ballymoney	Ballynacreeskein	Thompson James	spinning	ho., offs. & land	24a.	151	- [+ 35 tenants' houses]	1865	-	gr/	a.a.Ire.ie
Drumaul	Ballynagraigy	-	corn	-	-	-	-	-	14x2	osm/	-
Killagan	Ballynaloob	- near Killagan Br.	mill	-	-	-	-	-	-	1"os/	13
Kilbvride	Ballynamage	Dickey & Raphael	beetling	66x23x16 & :	-	-	-	-	-	v1B/	-
Rashee	Ballynashee	-	corn & kiln	-	-	-	-	-	-	6"os/	-
Rashee	Ballynashee	Beggs James	mill ruins	-	-	-	-	-	-	gr/	-
Rashee	Ballynashee	Logan John	corn & kiln	55x21x13	-	2.4.0	-	-	- 1 pair stones	v1B/	-
Loughguile	Ballyneely Upr	Montgomery Hugh	corn & kiln	29x22x15 & :	-	-	-	-	- m/cy not good :	v1B/	-
Ballymoney	Ballyness	-	-	-	-	500	-	-	-	osm/	-
Billy	Ballyness	McNaul Robert	flax	-	-	-	-	-	- mc/y bad	v1B/	-
Donegore	Ballynoe	unoc.	old flax mill	-	-	-	-	-	-	gr/	-
Ballynure	Ballynure	- at B`nure Town	mill	-	-	-	-	-	-	1"os/	28
Ballynure	Ballynure Village	Bell Mrs	bleach	-	-	-	-	-	20x4x17	osm/	-
Ballynure	Ballynure Village	Bell Mrs	wash	-	-	-	-	-	8x2 28x5x28	osm/	-
Ballynure	Ballynure Village	Howe Robert	cotton	-	-	-	-	-	-	osm/	-
Ballynure	Ballynure Village	Hunter Harris	corn	-	-	-	-	-	12x4x14	osm/	-
Ballynure	Ballynure Village	Park James	logwood	-	-	-	-	-	16x3x24 16x3	osm/	-
Culfeightrin	Ballypatrick	-	mill	-	-	-	-	-	-	pWAM	-
Culfeightrin	Ballypatrick	M`Aulay James	corn	-	-	-	-	-	-	gr/	-
Culfeightrin	Ballypatrick	McGildowney C & E	corn & kiln	-	-	-	-	-	-	v1B/	-
Loughguile	Ballyportery	-	flax	-	-	-	-	-	-	1"os/	-
Loughguile	Ballyportery	-	flax	-	-	-	-	-	11x2.10	osm/	-
Loughguile	Ballyportery	- on Killagan Water	mill	-	-	-	-	-	-	1"os/	13
Loughguile	Ballyportery N	-	corn	-	-	-	-	-	13x2.4	osm/	-
Loughguile	Ballyportery N	-	mill	-	-	-	-	-	-	pWAM	-
Loughguile	Ballyportery N	Dinsmore William	corn & flax	-	-	-	-	-	-	gr/	-
Loughguile	Ballyportery N	Elder Robert	corn & kiln	-	-	-	-	-	-	v1B/	-
Loughguile	Ballyportery N	Elder Robert	flax	-	-	-	-	-	-	v1B/	-
Loughguile	Ballyportery S	-	beetling	-	-	-	-	-	-	6"os/	-
Loughguile	Ballyportery S	-	beetling	-	-	-	-	-	14x3.6	osm/	-
Loughguile	Ballyportery S	-	mill	-	-	-	-	-	-	pWAM	-
Loughguile	Ballyportery S	Cruit Robert	beetling	-	-	-	-	-	-	gr/	-

PARISH	TOWNLAND	MILLER	TYPE	HOUSE	Land	£Val	PROPRIETORS	Date	WHEEL etc.	Record	Ref.
Loughguile	Ballyportery S	Stevelly Wm & John	beetling	-	-	-	-	-	-	v1B/	-
Killead	Ballyquillan	-	corn	-	-	-	-	-	-	6"os/	-
Killead	Ballyquillan	Armstrong James	corn	-	-	-	-	-	12x12x12	osm/	-
Killead	Ballyquillan	unoc.	corn & kiln	-	-	-	-	-	-	gr/	-
Killead	Ballyquillin	McConnell James	corn & kiln	-	-	-	-	-	-	v1B/	-
Derrykeighan	Ballyratahan	-	mill	-	-	-	-	-	-	pWAM	-
Dunaghy	Ballyreagh	-	corn	-	-	-	-	-	-	1"os/	20
Dunaghy	Ballyreagh	Dowds Patrick	mills & kiln	-	-	-	-	-	-	gr/	-
Dunaghy	Ballyreagh	Strachan John	flax	49x17x8 new mill	-	6.6.0	-	-	3 berths	v1B/	-
Killead	Ballyrobin	-	flax	-	-	-	-	-	-	6"os/	-
Killead	Ballyrobin	-	flax	-	-	-	-	-	15x2x16	osm/	-
Killead	Ballyrobin	-	flax - ruins	-	-	-	-	-	-	6"os/	-
Killead	Ballyrobin	-	mill	-	-	-	-	-	-	6"os/	-
Killead	Ballyrobin	Johnston John	corn & flax	-	-	-	-	-	-	gr/	-
Killead	Ballyrobin	Johnston John	corn & kiln	-	-	-	-	-	- new wheel	v1B/	-
Killead	Ballyrobin	Johnston John	flax	-	-	-	-	-	- 4 stocks	v1B/	-
Killead	Ballyrobin	Munniss John	corn & flax	-	-	-	-	-	18x4x16 & 15x12x8	osm/	-
Carncastle	Ballyruther	Dale Jane	corn & kiln	-	-	-	-	-	-	v1B/	-
Raloo	Ballyryland	-	mill	-	-	-	-	-	-	6"os/	-
Raloo	Ballyryland	-	mill ruins	-	-	-	-	-	-	6"os/	-
Shankill	Ballysillan	Emerson Jno	mill	-	-	-	Emerson J - Richardson	1861	-	dd/	1861 37 207
Shankill	Ballysillan	Emerson John	flax spinning	-	-	-	-	-	-	gr/	-
Shankill	Ballysillan	Ferguson John	bleach	-	-	-	-	-	14x6x11 & 16x6x14	v1B/	-
Shankill	Ballysillan	Mackey Mr	bleach	-	-	-	-	-		v1B/	-
Shankill	Ballysillan	Moore John	bleach	-	-	-	-	-	30x6x26	v1B/	-
Shankill	Ballysillan	Saddler B G & :	flax spinning	-	-	-	-	-	-	gr/	-
Shankill	Ballysillan Lr	-	mill	-	-	-	-	-	-	pWAM	-
Shankill	Ballysillan Lr		houses	-	-	-	-	-	-	pWAM	-
Shankill	Ballysillan Upr	-	mill	-	-	-	-	-	-	pWAM	-
Shankill	Ballysillan Vge.	Ewart William & S	bleach	-	-	-	-	-	-	gr/	-
Lambeg	Ballyskeagh	Charley Wiliam	bleach works	-	45a.	179	-	-	-	gr/	-
Is`mg/C`castle	Ballytober	-	ruins	-	-	-	-	-	-	pWAM	-
Camlin	Ballytromery	-	flax	-	-	-	-	-	12x1	osm/	-
Camlin	Ballytromery	-	ruins	-	-	-	-	-	-	pWAM	-
Tickmacrevan	Ballyvaddy	-	ruins	-	-	-	-	-	-	pWAM	-
Tickmacrevan	Ballyvaddy		old houses	-	-	-	-	-	-	pWAM	-
Loughguile	Ballyveely Lr	-	corn	-	-	-	-	-	14x2	osm/	-
Culfeightrin	Ballyvenagh	-	mill	-	-	-	-	-	wheel	pWAM	-
Culfeightrin	Ballyvenagh	Casement John	corn & kiln	-	-	-	-	-	-	gr/	-
Culfeightrin	Ballyvenagh	McGarry Neal	corn & kiln	-	-	-	-	-	-	v1B/	-
Carnmoney	Ballyvesey	-	bleach & dye	-	-	-	-	-	-	1"os/	28
Carnmoney	Ballyvesey	-	flax	-	-	-	-	-	-	1"os/	28
Camlin	Ballyvorally	-	bleach	-	-	-	-	-	30x4x34	osm/	-
Camlin	Ballyvorally	-	mill	-	-	-	-	-	-	6"os/	-
Camlin	Ballyvorally	-	mill	-	-	-	-	-	-	pWAM	-
Camlin	Ballyvorally	Browne John & Hugh	bleach	-	-	-	-	-	2 engines & 6ft wash	v1B/	-
Camlin	Ballyvorally	Hunter James	flour	-	-	-	-	-	-	gr/	-
Craigs	Ballywatermoy	-	mill	-	-	-	-	-	-	1"os/	19
Craigs	Ballywatermoy	Paul John	corn	-	-	-	-	-	-	gr/	-
Ballyrashane	Ballywatt East	-	flax	-	-	-	-	-	-	6"os/	-
Ballyrashane	Ballywatt East	Lamont Hugh	flax	-	-	-	-	-	-	v1B/	-
Ballyrashane	Ballywatt Leggs	Paton Robert	corn & kiln	48x21x8 & kiln	-	-	-	-	water scarce 6 mos.	v1B/	-

PARISH	TOWNLAND	MILLER	TYPE	HOUSE	Land	£Val	PROPRIETORS	Date	WHEEL etc.	Record	Ref.
Kilbride	Ballywee	-	mill	-	-	-	-	-	-	1"os/	28
Kilbride	Ballywee	-	mill	-	-	-	-	-	-	6"os/	-
Kilbride	Ballywee	-	mill	-	-	-	-	-	wheel	pWAM	-
Kilbride	Ballywee	-	mill pond	-	-	-	-	-	-	6"os/	-
Kilbride	Ballywee	Baird Jackson	corn & kiln	33x19x12 & :	-	3.17	-	-	-	v1B/	-
Kilbride	Ballywee	Baird Jackson	flax	29x18x7	-	18/2	-	-	-	v1B/	-
Kilbride	Ballywee	Baird John	corn & kilns	-	-	-	-	-	-	gr/	-
Kilbride	Ballywee	Baird John (Miller)	flax	& land	-	2a.	- [+ 4 tenants' houses]	1865	-	gr/	a.a.ire.ie
Loughguile	Ballyweeny	-	corn & kiln	-	-	-	-	-	-	6"os/	-
Loughguile	Ballyweeny	-	mill	-	-	-	-	-	-	pWAM	-
Raloo	Ballywillin	-	corn	-	-	-	-	-	15x2x7	osm/	-
Raloo	Ballywillin	-	corn	-	-	-	-	-	15x2	osm/	-
Raloo	Ballywillin	McClaverty Miss	corn	-	-	-	-	-	17x3x24	osm/	-
Raloo	Ballywillin	McClaverty Miss	flax	-	-	-	-	-	16x2x22	osm/	-
Raloo	Ballywillin	McDowell George	corn	67x18x17	-	-	-	-	18x3x24	v1B/	-
Raloo	Ballywillin	McDowell George	flax	28x28x18	-	-	-	-	17x2.5x23	v1B/	-
Raloo	Ballywillin	Shaw Richard	corn	-	-	-	-	-	-	gr/	-
Islandmagee	Baloo	Holmes Wiliam	corn & kiln	27x19x10 kiln :	-	1.19.0	-	-	14x2.6x18 water for 6 mos	v1B/	-
Antrim	Bank Head	- on Kells R.	mill	-	-	-	-	-	-	1"os/	20
Shankill	Belfast	Shaw Jno	mill	-	-	-	Shaw Jno - N Banking	1860	-	dd/	1860 37 90
Shankill	Belfast Divis St	-	grain mill	-	-	-	-	-	-	pWSH	-
Shankill	Belfast York St	-	flax spinning	-	-	-	-	-	-	pWSH	-
Shankill	Belfast York St	-	spinning	-	-	-	-	-	-	pWAG	-
Shankill	Belfast T`parks	-	distillery	-	-	-	-	-	-	6"os/	-
Shankill	Belfast T`parks	-	flour	-	-	-	-	-	-	6"os/	-
Shankill	Belfast T`parks :	Edwards Hugh & Benj	glass factory	-	-	-	-	1808	-	dir/	Smith
Shankill	Belfast T`parks :	Napier William	brewery	-	-	-	-	1807	-	dir/	Smith
Shankill	Belfast T`parks :	Coats Victor	starch factory	-	-	-	-	1807	-	dir/	Smith
Shankill	Belfast T`parks :	Finlay Robert	cotton factory	-	-	-	-	1807	-	dir/	Smith
Shankill	Belfast T`parks :	Ireland Thomas	cotton factory	-	-	-	-	1807	-	dir/	Smith
Shankill	Belfast T`parks :	Edwards Benjamin	glass factory	-	-	-	-	1807	-	dir/	Smith
Shankill	Belfast T`parks :	Greg & Boyd	vitriol works	-	-	-	-	1807	-	dir/	Smith
Shankill	Belfast T`parks :	Maphet William & Co.	salt works	-	-	-	-	1807	-	dir/	Smith
Shankill	Belfast Town	-	cotton factory	-	-	-	-	-	-	6"os/	-
Shankill	Belfast Town	-	flour	-	-	-	-	-	-	6"os/	-
Shankill	Belfast Town	-	linen	-	-	-	-	-	-	6"os/	-
Shankill	Belfast Town	-	linen	-	-	-	-	-	-	6"os/	-
Shankill	Belfast Town	-	linen factory	-	-	-	-	-	-	6"os/	-
Shankill	Belfast Town	-	linen hall	-	-	-	-	-	-	6"os/	-
Shankill	Belfast Town	-	paper	-	-	-	-	-	-	6"os/	-
Shankill	Belfast Town	-	vitriol works	-	-	-	-	-	-	6"os/	-
Shankill	Belfast Town :	- on Forth River	beetling	-	-	-	-	1931	-	15"/	AG60.12
Shankill	Belfast Town :	Radcliffe & Black	cotton factory	-	-	-	-	1807	-	dir/	Smith
Shankill	Belfast Town :	Park James	cotton factory	-	-	-	-	1807	-	dir/	Smith
Shankill	Belfast Town :	McCrum John	cotton & muslin	-	-	-	-	1807	-	dir/	Smith
Shankill	Belfast Town :	Mc+C521Ilroy Archibal	muslin factory	-	-	-	-	1807	-	dir/	Smith
Shankill	Belfast Town :	Rutherford John	muslin factory	-	-	-	-	1807	-	dir/	Smith
Shankill	Belfast Town :	Porter Edward	cutlers	-	-	-	-	1807	-	dir/	Smith
Shankill	Belfast Town :	Reilly & Co.	food factory	-	-	-	-	1807	-	dir/	Smith
Shankill	Belfast Town :	Sloan David & Co.	fustian & calico	-	-	-	-	1807	-	dir/	Smith
Shankill	Belfast Town :	M`Cracken William	cotton factory	-	-	-	-	1807	-	dir/	Smith
Shankill	Belfast Town :	Reid & Calvert	fustian factory	-	-	-	-	1807	-	dir/	Smith

PARISH	TOWNLAND		MILLER	TYPE	HOUSE	Land	£Val	PROPRIETORS	Date	WHEEL etc.	Record	Ref.
Shankill	Belfast Town	:	Rowan Henry & Co.	distillery	-	-	-	-	1807	-	dir/	Smith
Shankill	Belfast Town	:	Snell George & Co.	muslin factory	-	-	-	-	1807	-	dir/	Smith
Shankill	Belfast Town	:	Watt William	cotton factory	-	-	-	-	1807	-	dir/	Smith
Shankill	Belfast Town	:	-	iron & brass	-	-	-	-	1931	-	15"/	AG60.12
Shankill	Belfast Town	:	-	bleach greens (2)	-	-	-	-	1931	-	15"/	AG60.12
Shankill	Belfast Town	:	- Broadway	Damask Works	-	-	-	-	1931	-	15"/	AG60.12
Shankill	Belfast Town	:	Gordon James	cotton factory	-	-	-	-	1808	-	dir/	Smith
Shankill	Belfast Town	:	Tucker William	muslin factory	-	-	-	-	1807	-	dir/	Smith
Shankill	Belfast Town	:	-	flax spinning	-	-	-	-	1931	-	15"/	AG60.12
Shankill	Belfast Town	:	-	flax spinning (2)	-	-	-	-	1931	-	15"/	AG60.12
Shankill	Belfast Town	:	-	print works (dis.)	-	-	-	-	1931	-	15"/	AG60.12
Shankill	Belfast Town	:	- Forth River Mills	flax spinning	-	-	-	-	1931	-	15"/	AG60.12
Shankill	Belfast Town	:	-	print works (dis.)	-	-	-	-	1931	-	15"/	AG60.12
Shankill	Belfast Town	:	-	weaving	-	-	-	-	1931	-	15"/	AG60.12
Shankill	Belfast Town	:	M`Cracken John & Co.	cotton spinning	-	-	-	-	1807	-	dir/	Smith
Shankill	Belfast Town	:	- Docks area	saw	-	-	-	-	1920	-	15"/	AG61.5
Shankill	Belfast Town	:	- York Road Mills	spinning & wv	-	-	-	-	1920	-	15"/	AG61.5
Shankill	Belfast Town	:	- City Saw Mills	saw	-	-	-	-	1920	-	15"/	AG61.5
Shankill	Belfast Town	:	- Docks area	saw	-	-	-	-	1920	-	15"/	AG61.5
Shankill	Belfast Town	:	- Donegall Quay Mill	flour& meal	-	-	-	-	1920	-	15"/	AG61.5
Shankill	Belfast Town	:	-	printing works	-	-	-	-	1931	-	15"/	AG60.12
Shankill	Belfast Town	:	-	weaving	-	-	-	-	1931	-	15"/	AG60.12
Shankill	Belfast Town	:	New Northern S.& W	spinning & wv	-	-	-	-	1931	-	15"/	AG60.12
Shankill	Belfast Town	:	-	StarFactory	-	-	-	-	1931	-	15"/	AG60.12
Shankill	Belfast Town	:	M`Millan Neil	muslin factory	-	-	-	-	1808	-	dir/	Smith
Shankill	Belfast Town	:	-	match factory	-	-	-	-	1931	-	15"/	AG60.12
Shankill	Belfast Town	:	- Springfield	Cotton Factory	-	-	-	-	1931	-	15"/	AG60.12
Shankill	Belfast Town	:	- Springfield	Linen Factory	-	-	-	-	1931	-	15"/	AG60.12
Shankill	Belfast Town	:	- Bath Place Mill	flax spinning	-	-	-	-	1920	-	15"/	AG61.5
Shankill	Belfast Town	:	White John	muslin factory	-	-	-	-	1807	-	dir/	Smith
Shankill	Belfast Town	:	-	flour	-	-	-	-	1920	-	15"/	AG61.5
Shankill	Belfast Town	:	-	weaving	-	-	-	-	1920	-	15"/	AG61.5
Shankill	Belfast Town	:	Ross John	cambric factory	-	-	-	-	1807	-	dir/	Smith
Shankill	Belfast Town	:	Russell & Woods	cotton spinning	-	-	-	-	1807	-	dir/	Smith
Shankill	Belfast Town	:	McConnell William	utensil factory	-	-	-	-	1807	-	dir/	Smith
Shankill	Belfast Town	:	Gemmill Robert	muslin factory	-	-	-	-	1807	-	dir/	Smith
Shankill	Belfast Town	:	Bell John	brewery	-	-	-	-	1807	-	dir/	Smith
Shankill	Belfast Town	:	Blow Ward & Co.	paper	-	-	-	-	1807	-	dir/	Smith
Shankill	Belfast Town	:	Herdman, Gibson &Cc	brewery	-	-	-	-	1807	-	dir/	Smith
Shankill	Belfast Town	:	How, John & Thomas	muslin factory	-	-	-	-	1807	-	dir/	Smith
Shankill	Belfast Town	:	Miller Samuel	starch factory	-	-	-	-	1807	-	dir/	Smith
Shankill	Belfast Town	:	Finlay Alexander	soap factory	-	-	-	-	1807	-	dir/	Smith
Shankill	Belfast Town	:	Bell John	muslin factory	-	-	-	-	1807	-	dir/	Smith
Shankill	Belfast Town	:	Mollyneaux Joseph	starch factory	-	-	-	-	1807	-	dir/	Smith
Shankill	Belfast Town	:	Huddleson Fran & Co.	muslin factory	-	-	-	-	1807	-	dir/	Smith
Shankill	Belfast Town	:	Mountford John	cotton factory	-	-	-	-	1807	-	dir/	Smith
Shankill	Belfast Town	:	McCracken Margaret	muslin factory	-	-	-	-	1807	-	dir/	Smith
Shankill	Belfast Town	:	Alexander John	cotton factory	-	-	-	-	1807	-	dir/	Smith
Shankill	Belfast Town	:	Milford John	cotton factory	-	-	-	-	1807	-	dir/	Smith
Shankill	Belfast Town	:	Crossen James	calico factory	-	-	-	-	1807	-	dir/	Smith
Shankill	Belfast Town	:	Crossen William & Jas	muslin factory	-	-	-	-	1807	-	dir/	Smith
Shankill	Belfast Town	:	Gordon James	muslin factory	-	-	-	-	1807	-	dir/	Smith

PARISH	TOWNLAND	MILLER	TYPE	HOUSE	Land	£Val	PROPRIETORS	Date	WHEEL etc.	Record	Ref.
Shankill	Belfast Town :	Horner Anthony	muslin factory	-	-	-	-	1807	-	dir/	Smith
Shankill	Belfast Town :	Boomer James	cotton factory	-	-	-	-	1807	-	dir/	Smith
Shankill	Belfast Town :	Gibson Samuel	brewery	-	-	-	-	1807	-	dir/	Smith
Shankill	Belfast Town :	Kennedy Daniel	cutler	-	-	-	-	1807	-	dir/	Smith
Shankill	Belfast Town :	Broadley Ben & Co.	cotton factory	-	-	-	-	1807	-	dir/	Smith
Shankill	Belfast Town :	Byers William & Co.	muslin factory	-	-	-	-	1807	-	dir/	Smith
Shankill	Belfast Town :	- Belfast	Porter Brewery	-	-	-	-	1807	-	dir/	Smith
Shankill	Belfast Town :	Dickson William	cotton factory	-	-	-	-	1807	-	dir/	Smith
Shankill	Belfast Town :	BakerJames	muslin factory	-	-	-	-	1807	-	dir/	Smith
Shankill	Belfast Town :	Bentley George	machine maker	-	-	-	-	1807	-	dir/	Smith
Shankill	Belfast Town :	Cunningham John :	brewery	-	-	-	-	1807	-	dir/	Smith
Shankill	Belfast Town :	Joy James & Co.	cotton factory	-	-	-	-	1807	-	dir/	Smith
Shankill	Belfast Town :	Armstrong Robert	cotton factory	-	-	-	-	1807	-	dir/	Smith
Kilroot	Bellahill	Dalway Marriot	corn	-	-	-	-	-	14ft.	osm/	-
Antrim	Bellenan	-	mill	-	-	-	-	-	-	1"os/	8
Raloo	Beltoy	-	flax	-	-	-	-	-	-	6"os/	-
Raloo	Beltoy	-	flax	-	-	-	-	-	17x2	osm/	-
Raloo	Beltoy	Robinson Sam	scutch	-	-	-	-	-	-	gr/	-
Antrim	bo. BELFAST	Barr David	Upper Mill	-	-	-	Barr D - Andrews Jas	1890	-	dd/	1890 20 69
Antrim	bo. BELFAST	McMeekin William	Upper mill	-	-	-	McMeekin - Whitehouse Sp.	1890	-	dd/	1890 27 177
Antrim	bo.GLENARM	Jamieson Daniel	old kiln lot	-	-	-	Jamieson Daniel - John	1891	-	dd/	1891 43 43
Gr. Muckamore	Boghead	Chaine Wm	-	-	-	-	-	-	15x4x19	osm/	-
Antrim	Bogstown	-	flax	-	-	-	-	-	-	1"os/	20
Culfeightrin	Bonamargy	Boyd Hugh	corn & kiln	-	-	-	-	-	-	v1B/	-
Derraghy	Bovolcan	Dickson John	cotton	-	-	-	-	-	-	v1B/	-
Portglenone	Bracknamuckley	-	corn	-	-	-	-	-	-	6"os/	-
Portglenone	Bracknamuckley	-	corn	-	-	-	-	-	14x2	osm/	-
Portglenone	Bracknamuckley	-	mill	-	-	-	-	-	wheel	pWAM	-
Portglenone	Bracknamuckley	Andrews James	corn & kilns	-	-	-	-	-	-	gr/	-
Portglenone	Bracknamuckley	Henderson John	corn & kiln	-	-	-	-	-	-	v1B/	-
Portglenone	Bracknamuckley	M`Caw Thos	flax	-	-	-	-	-	-	gr/	-
Skerry	Breckagh	-	mill	-	-	-	-	-	-	6"os/	-
Skerry	Breckagh	Montgomery John	corn & kiln	-	-	-	-	-	-	v1B/	-
Ahoghill	Brocklamont	-	mill	-	-	-	-	-	-	pWAM	-
Ahoghill	Brocklamont	Dickey John	beetling, bleach		62a	-	-	-	-	gr/	-
Ahoghill	Brocklamont	Dickey Mr	beetling	-	-	-	-	-	-	v1B/	-
Antrim	Brookfield	-	flax	-	-	-	-	-	-	1"os/	28
Antrim	Brookfield	Brown William	mills	-	-	-	Brown Wm - Keoghler	1861	-	dd/	1861 6 67
Antrim	Brookfield	Prentor Nath	mills	-	-	-	Prenter Nath - Fenton	1857	-	dd/	1857 36 72
Culfeightrin	Broughanlea	McDonnell John	corn & kilns	-	-	-	-	-	-	gr/	-
Racavan	Broughshane	-	beetling	-	-	-	-	-	15.6x4	osm/	-
Racavan	Broughshane	-	flax	-	-	-	-	-	15.6x3	osm/	-
Racavan	Broughshane	-	houses	-	-	-	-	-	-	pWAM	-
Racavan	Broughshane	-	mill	-	-	-	-	-	-	1"os/	-
Racavan	Broughshane	-	paper	-	-	-	-	-	16x2	osm/	-
Racavan	Broughshane	-	spinning	-	-	-	-	-	16x11 16x6.6	osm/	-
Racavan	Broughshane	- at Nuns Bridge	flax	-	-	-	-	-	-	1"os/	20
Racavan	Broughshane	Eccles Thos	paper	-	-	-	-	-	-	v1B/	-
Racavan	Broughshane Tn	-	flax	-	-	-	-	-	-	1"os/	-
Racavan	Broughshane Tn :	Black Joseph	beetling & flax	-	-	-	-	-	-	gr/	-
Racavan	Broughshane Upr	-	mill	-	-	-	-	-	-	6"os/	-
Racavan	Broughshane Upr	-	mill	-	-	-	-	-	-	6"os/	-

PARISH	TOWNLAND	MILLER	TYPE	HOUSE	Land	£Val	PROPRIETORS	Date	WHEEL etc.	Record	Ref.
Racavan	Broughshane Upr	-	mill ruins	-	-	-	-	-	-	6"os/	-
Racavan	Broughshane Upr	Currie Daniel	bleach	-	-	-	-	-	-	v1B/	-
Racavan	Broughshane Upr	Davidson Jn & Alex	spinning & wv	-	-	-	-	-	-	gr/	-
Racavan	Broughshane Upr	Montgomery Charles	flax	-	-	-	-	-	-	v1B/	-
Racavan	Broughshane Upr	Moore Archibald	cloth	-	-	-	-	-	-	gr/	-
Ballylinny	Bruslee	-	flax - ruins	-	-	-	-	-	-	osm/	-
Ballylinny	Bruslee	-	mill	-	-	-	-	-	-	pWAM	-
Ballylinny	Bruslee	-	spade	-	-	-	-	-	-	6"os/	-
Ballylinny	Bruslee	Atkinson James	spade	-	-	-	-	-	14x2x6	osm/	-
Ballylinny	Bruslee	Atkinson James	spade & forge	-	-	-	-	-	14x2x14	v1B/	-
Balynure	Bryantang	- at Straid	mill	-	-	-	-	-	-	1"os/	28
Racavan	Buckna	-	mill	-	-	-	-	-	-	1"os/	20
Racavan	Buckna	Dunlop Charles	flax	-	-	-	-	-	-	v1B/	-
Racavan	Buckna	Montgomery Charles	corn & kiln	-	-	-	-	-	-	v1B/	-
Kilbride	Burnside	-	mill	-	-	-	-	-	wheel	pWAM	-
Kilbride	Burnside	Prenter Nath A	spinning	-	-	-	-	-	-	gr/	-
Kilbride	Burnside	Watt R & R	spinning	22x25x14 & :	-	35.4	-	-	-	v1B/	-
Dunluce	Bushmills	-	corn	-	-	-	-	-	12x2 12x2	osm/	-
Dunluce	Bushmills	-	distillery	-	-	-	-	-	wheel	pWAM	-
Dunluce	Bushmills	-	grain mill	-	-	-	-	-	-	pWSH	-
Dunluce	Bushmills	-	mill	-	-	-	-	-	wheel	pWAM	-
Dunluce	Bushmills	-	spade factory	-	-	-	-	-	12x3 12x1.6	osm/	-
Dunluce	Bushmills	Anderson Stewart	distillery	-	-	-	Anderson S - McColgan	1860	-	dd/	1860 28 147
Derryaghy	Buvolcan	Howie Robert	bleach	-	-	-	-	-	-	gr/	-
Antrim	Calisnagh *	Dixon Daniel	mill	-	-	-	Dixon D - McVicker Donald	1890	-	dd/	1890 9 112
Layd	Callisnagh	-	flax	-	-	-	-	-	-	1"os/	-
Layd	Callisnagh	-	flax	-	-	-	-	-	13X2	osm/	-
Layd	Callisnagh	-	mill	-	-	-	-	-	-	pWAM	-
Layd	Callisnagh	Jameson Samuel &	flax	-	-	-	-	-	-	v1B/	-
Antrim	Cappobeg	Neilson James	mills	-	-	-	Neilson Jas - Shaw	1859	-	dd/	1859 5 290
Cary	Carey Mill	-	mill	-	-	-	-	-	-	pWAM	
Cary	Carey Mill	McGildowney Edmond	corn	-	-	-	-	-	-	v1B/	-
Loughguile	Carnagall	-	saw	-	-	-	-	-	-	1"os/	14
Loughguile	Carnagall	- on Killagan Water	mill	-	-	-	-	-	-	1"os/	13
Loughguile	Carnamenagh	-	corn & flax	-	-	-	-	-	12x2.8x1.4 u`s	osm/	-
Loughguile	Carnamenagh	Mullen Felix	corn & kiln	-	-	-	-	-	-	v1B/	-
Loughguile	Carnamenagh	O`Mullan Felix	corn & flax	-	-	-	-	-	-	gr/	-
Ballylinny	Carnanee	-	mill	-	-	-	-	-	-	1"os/	28
Ballylinny	Carnanee	-	paper	-	-	-	-	-	-	1"os/	28
Ballylinny	Carnanee	-	spade	-	-	-	-	-	-	pWAM	-
Ballylinny	Carnanee	McClean	mill	-	-	-	McClean - Sloan	1856	-	dd/	1856 26 26
Ballylinny	Carnanee	Parker James	corn & kiln	32x20x12 & :	-	2.14	-	-	-	v1B/	-
Ballylinny	Carnanee	Parker James	flax	29x20x6 & :	-	1.2.2	-	-	- 5 stocks	v1B/	-
Ballylinny	Carnanee	Sloan Mr	paper	-	-	-	-	-	25x6x25 & : 14x1.	osm/	-
Ballylinny	Carnanee	Sloane Wiliam	paper	-	-	-	-	-	-	gr/	-
Killagan	Carnbeg	-	corn	-	-	-	-	-	-	1"os/	20
Killagan	Carnbeg	- at Carnlea Clogh R.	corn	-	-	-	-	-	-	1"os/	20
Templecorran	Carnbrock	-	corn & kiln	-	-	-	-	-	-	6"os/	-
Templecorran	Carnbrock	Stevelly Edward	thrashing	-	-	-	-	-	no wheel	osm/	-
Carncastle	Carncastle	-	mill	-	-	-	-	-	-	1"os/	-
Derrykeighan	Carncloghey	-	flax	-	-	-	-	-	-	osm/	-
Ahoghill	Carndonaghy	-	corn	-	-	-	-	-	-	6"os/	-

PARISH	TOWNLAND	MILLER	TYPE	HOUSE	Land	£Val	PROPRIETORS	Date	WHEEL etc.	Record	Ref.
Ahoghill	Carndonaghy	-	corn	-	-	-	-	-	14x2	osm/	-
Ahoghill	Carndonaghy	- on R. Main	flax	-	-	-	-	-	-	1"os/	19
Ahoghill	Carndonaghy	Dixon Joseph	flax	-	-	-	-	-	-	v1B/	-
Raloo	Carneal	-	mill	-	-	-	-	-	-	6"os/	-
Raloo	Carneal	-	ruins	-	-	-	-	-	wheel	pWAM	-
Raloo	Carneal	Crawford James	turning	-	-	-	-	-	-	gr/	-
Ballymoney	Carnealty	-	flax	-	-	-	-	-	-	1"os/	8
Ahoghill	Carnearney	-	corn & flax	-	-	-	-	-	13x3 13x2	osm/	-
Ahoghill	Carnearney	Adair Thomas Benj	corn & kiln	-	-	-	-	-	-	v1B/	-
Ahoghill	Carnearney	Hardy Joseph	corn & flax		9a.	-	-	-	-	gr/	-
Ramoan / B`my	Carneatly	-	mill	-	-	-	-	-	-	pWAM	-
Ramoan / B`my	Carneatly	Hill John	flax	31x19x7 & :	-	2.1.0	-	-	-	v1B/	-
Kirkinriola	Carnlea	-	corn	-	-	-	-	-	-	1"os/	20
Kirkinriola	Carnlea	-	mill	-	-	-	-	-	-	pWAM	-
Kirkinriola	Carnlea	Cunning Robert	corn & kiln	-	-	-	-	-	-	v1B/	-
Ardclinis	Carnlough	-	corn	-	-	-	-	-	10x2	osm/	-
Ardclinis	Carnlough	-	mill	-	-	-	-	-	-	1"os/	14
Ardclinis	Carnlough	-	mill	-	-	-	-	-	-	pWAM	-
Ardclinis	Carnlough South	-	whiting	-	-	-	-	-	-	pWSH	-
Ardclinis	Carnlough South	McLaughlin Charles	corn & kiln	48x18x8 & :	-	6.7.6	-	-	-	v1B/	-
Ardclinis	Carnlough Town	-	mill tenement	-	-	-	-	-	-	6"os/	-
Ardclinis	Carnlough Town	M`Loughlin Hon`ia	corn & kilns	-	-	-	-	-	-	gr/	-
Carnmoney	Carnmoney	Kennedy Thos M.	corn	-	-	-	-	-	14x2x14	osm/	-
Carnmoney	Carnmoney	Kennedy Thos M.	flax	-	-	-	-	-	16x2x16	osm/	-
Carnmoney	Carnmoney	McKenny	corn & kiln	-	-	-	-	-	-	v1B/	-
Carnmoney	Carnmoney	McKenny Thomas	corn & kiln	-	-	-	-	-	-	v1B/	-
Carnmoney	Carnmoney	McKinney Thomas	flax	25x19x6 & :	-	-	-	-	- 3 berths	v1B/	-
Islandmagee	Carnspindle	Holmes Wiliam	corn & kiln	-	-	-	-	-	12x2.6x14	v1B/	-
Ballylinny	Carntall	Campbell Henry & :	spinning	engine ho. & yard	2a.	380	- [+ 24 tenants' houses]	1865	-	gr/	a.a.lre.ie
Derrykeighan	Carracloghy	McCloy John	flax	-	-	-	-	-	-	v1B/	-
Carrickfergus	Carrickferfus Tn	Gamble James	Woodburn Mill	-	-	-	Gamble James - William	1853	-	dd/	1853 16 89
Carrickfergus	Carrickferfus Tn	Maxwell William	Woodburn Mill	-	-	-	Maxwell W - Gamble Jas	1851	-	dd/	1851 4 230
Carrickfergus	Carrickferfus Tn	Maxwell William	Woodburn Mill	-	-	-	Maxwell Wm - N. Bank	1851	-	dd/	1851 22 214
Carrickfergus	Carrickferfus Tn	Thomson Charles	Woodburn Mill	-	-	-	Thomson C - Maxwell Wm	1851	-	dd/	1851 5 82
Carrickfergus	Carrickferfus Tn	Vance Jno	Woodburn Mill	-	-	-	Vance J - Musewell Wm	1847	-	dd/	1847 9 17
Carrickfergus	Carrickferfus Tn	Walker William	Scotch Qr. Mill	-	-	-	Walker Wm - Duffin Chas	1853	-	dd/	1853 31 111
Carrickfergus	Carrickfergus	-	flax	-	-	-	-	-	-	1"os/	29
Carrickfergus	Carrickfergus	-	mill	-	-	-	-	-	-	pWAM	-
Carrickfergus	Carrickfergus	Barnett James	distillery	-	-	-	-	-	-	v1B/	-
Carrickfergus	Carrickfergus	Walker & Stevenson	spinning	-	-	-	-	-	-	v1B/	-
Carrickfergus	Carrickfergus	Wilson James	flour & corn	-	-	-	-	-	- 4 pr. st	v1B/	-
Carrickfergus	Carrickfergus :	Cinnamond Joseph :	mill	-	-	-	Cinnamond J - McConchy :	1832	Mort. 24 Oct.	dd/	889 81 588081
Carrickfergus	Carrickfergus :	Beverley Alex	mill	-	-	-	Beverley A - N Bank Co	1895	-	dd/	1895 41 124
Carrickfergus	Carrickfergus :	N. Banking Co.	mill	-	-	-	N. Bk. Co - Williamson Jn	1895	-	dd/	1895 56 110
Carrickfergus	Carrickfergus E	Shaftsbury Lord & :	mills	-	-	-	Shaftsbury - Sullatober :	1895	-	dd/	1895 41 124
Carrickfergus	Carrickfergus Irish	Barnet James	oats	-	-	-	-	-	14x7x17	osm/	-
Carrickfergus	Carrickfergus Irish	Waterson Wiliam	corn & kiln	-	-	-	-	-	14ft., 2 pr. st.	v1B/	-
Carrickfergus	Carrickfergus Irish	Wilson James	corn	-	-	-	-	-	17.6x1.6x17	osm/	-
Carrickfergus	Carrickfergus Irish	Wilson James	flour	-	-	-	-	-	17.6x4.6x17	osm/	-
Carrickfergus	Carrickfergus Irish	Wilson James	flour & corn	-	-	-	-	-	17x4x17 & 17x1x17	v1B/	-
Carrickfergus	Carrickfergus Mid.	-	cotton mfy	-	-	-	-	-	-	6"os/	-
Carrickfergus	Carrickfergus Mid.	-	cotton print	-	-	-	-	-	-	6"os/	-

PARISH	TOWNLAND	MILLER	TYPE	HOUSE	Land	£Val	PROPRIETORS	Date	WHEEL etc.	Record	Ref.
Carrickfergus	Carrickfergus Mid.	Cowan Reps William	linen factory	mill-dam & land	21a	21	- [+ 11 tenants' houses]	1865	-	a.a.Ire.ie	-
Carrickfergus	Carrickfergus Mid.	Gamble & Bruce	linen factory	& land	30a.	31	- [+ 18 tenants' houses]	1865	-	a.a.Ire.ie	-
Carrickfergus	Carrickfergus NE	-	corn	-	-	-	-	-	-	6"os/	-
Carrickfergus	Carrickfergus NE	-	cotton mfy	-	-	-	-	-	-	6"os/	-
Carrickfergus	Carrickfergus NE	-	cotton print	-	-	-	-	-	-	6"os/	-
Carrickfergus	Carrickfergus NE	-	flax	-	-	-	-	-	-	6"os/	-
Carrickfergus	Carrickfergus NE	-	old corn - ruins	-	-	-	-	-	-	6"os/	-
Carrickfergus	Carrickfergus NE	-	old mill	-	-	-	-	-	-	6"os/	-
Carrickfergus	Carrickfergus NE	- on Woodburn R.	linen	-	-	-	-	-	-	1"os/	29
Carrickfergus	Carrickfergus NE	Duncan Dr	old cotton mill	-	-	-	-	-	-	v1B/	-
Carrickfergus	Carrickfergus NE	Johns Alex	old print mill	-	-	-	-	-	-	v1B/	-
Carrickfergus	Carrickfergus NE	Preston John	flax spinning	-	-	-	-	-	-	gr/	-
Carrickfergus	Carrickfergus NE	Taylor James	flax spinning	-	-	-	-	-	-	gr/	-
Carrickfergus	Carrickfergus NE	Taylor James	hackling factory	-	-	-	-	-	-	gr/	-
Carrickfergus	Carrickfergus NE	Woods Hill	spinning	-	-	-	-	-	-	gr/	-
Carrickfergus	Carrickfergus Tn	-	printing	-	-	-	-	-	13x2.4x13	osm/	-
Carrickfergus	Carrickfergus Tn	Belfast Banking Co.	Barn Mills Farm	-	-	-	Belfast B Co - Taylor Jas	1887	-	dd/	1887 24 56
Carrickfergus	Carrickfergus Tn	Berry James	corn	-	-	-	-	-	18.6x3x15	osm/	-
Carrickfergus	Carrickfergus Tn	Cowan James	spinning	-	-	-	-	-	50x4.6x50	osm/	-
Carrickfergus	Carrickfergus Tn	Draper Elizabeth	Western Mills	-	-	-	Draper E - Northern Bk Co	1889	-	dd/	1889 49 153
Carrickfergus	Carrickfergus Tn	Dunne Stewart	flax	-	-	-	-	-	30x4.6x15	osm/	-
Carrickfergus	Carrickfergus Tn	Girwood John	Woodburn Mill	-	-	-	Girwood John - Hamilton G	1886	-	dd/	1886 49 282
Carrickfergus	Carrickfergus Tn	Hamilton William	Woodburn Mills	-	-	-	Hamilton - Wodburn Wv Co	1894	-	dd/	1894 21 169
Carrickfergus	Carrickfergus Tn	Hanna Dr (Belfast)	spinning	-	-	-	-	-	34x5.6x34	osm/	-
Carrickfergus	Carrickfergus Tn	How Thomas	Woodburn Mill	-	-	-	How Thos - Vance John	1836	-	dd/	1836 14 290
Carrickfergus	Carrickfergus Tn	Lindon & Co.	beetling	-	-	-	-	-	13x6x10	osm/	-
Carrickfergus	Carrickfergus Tn	McAuliffe George	Western Mills	-	-	-	McAuliffe G - Dreaper Eliza	1889	-	dd/	1889 37 232
Carrickfergus	Carrickfergus Tn	Preston George	Woodburn Mill :	& farm			Preston - Co D. Weaving Cc	1904		dd/	1904 54 69
Carrickfergus	Carrickfergus Tn	Smith Bryce	Woodburn Mill				Smith B - McKean Wm	1900		dd/	1900 12 244
Carrickfergus	Carrickfergus Tn	Thompson Henry	bl. green (NE)	-	-	-	Thompson H - Sullatober :	1888	-	dd/	1888 47227
Carrickfergus	Carrickfergus Tn	Wallace William	Scotch Qr Mill	-	-	-	Wallace William - Robert	1885	-	dd/	1885 1 199
Carrickfergus	Carrickfergus Tn	Whiteabbey Flax :	Duncrue Mill	-	-	-	Whiteabbey - Beverly Alex	1889	-	dd/	1889 8 270
Carrickfergus	Carrickfergus Tn	Alexander Robert :	Farmhill Mills	-	-	-	Alexander Robt - Dunne :	1828	-	dd/	842 245 564745
Carrickfergus	Carrickfergus Tn :	Reade Robert	use of water	-	-	-	Reade Robt - Cowan Wm	1852	-	dd/	1852 22 246
Carrickfergus	Carrickfergus Tn :	Walker William	mill	-	-	-	Walker Wm- Duffin Chas	1852	-	dd/	1852 1 74
Carrickfergus	Carrickfergus Tn :	Johns Alexander	corn	-	-	-	Johns Alex - Walker Wm	1843	-	dd/	1843 4 208
Carrickfergus	Carrickfergus Tn :	How Robert	mill	-	-	-	How R - Vance Jno	1845	-	dd/	1845 19 127
Carrickfergus	Carrickfergus Tn :	Downshire Marq.	corn	-	-	-	Downshire - Landys Lord	1837	-	dd/	1837 20 68
Carrickfergus	Carrickfergus Tn :	Reilly William E	corn	-	-	-	Reilly W - Downshire Mq.	1837	-	dd/	1837 1 126
Carrickfergus	Carrickfergus Tn :	Johns Thomas D	mill	-	-	-	Johns Thos - Reid James	1880	-	dd/	1880 51 150
Carrickfergus	Carrickfergus Tn :	Reid James J	mill	-	-	-	Reid James - Johns Thos	1883	-	dd/	1883 20 75
Carrickfergus	Carrickfergus Tn :	Reid James J	mill	-	-	-	Reid James - Reid Mary	1883	-	dd/	1883 20 76
Carrickfergus	Carrickfergus Tn :	Reid James J	mill	-	-	-	Reid James - Reid Mary	1883	-	dd/	1883 20 77
Carrickfergus	Carrickfergus Tn :	Reid James J	mill	-	-	-	Reid James - Reid Mary	1883	-	dd/	1883 20 78
Carrickfergus	Carrickfergus Tn :	Cowan James	mill	-	-	-	Cowan J - Ire.Bank Govs	1842	-	dd/	1842 14 255
St Nicholas	Carrickfergus Tn :	Woods James	mill	-	-	-	Woods J - Newton Josh	1841	-	dd/	1841 19 11
Carrickfergus	Carrickfergus Tn :	Bennett Robert	bleach	-	-	-	Bennet - McMurray Robt	1884	-	dd/	1884 5 140
Carrickfergus	Carrickfergus Tn :	McMurray Robert	bleach	-	-	-	McMurray - Bennet Robt	1879	-	dd/	1879 3 119
Carrickfergus	Carrickfergus Tn :	Donegall Most Hon. :	mill	-	-	-	Marq. - MacArtney	1830	Conv. 2 J784 -Feb.1830	dd/	881 268 284268
Carrickfergus	Carrickfergus Tn :	Hamlet Thomas	mill	-	-	-	Hamlet Thos - Linnet John	1834	-	dd/	1834 20 36
Carrickfergus	Carrickfergus Tn :	Donegall Marq.	mills	-	-	-	Donegall - Chaine Wm	1841	-	dd/	1841 11 75
Carrickfergus	Carrickfergus Tn :	Goddard James	mill	-	-	-	Goddard J - Walker Wm	1833	-	dd/	1833 19 136

PARISH	TOWNLAND	MILLER	TYPE	HOUSE	Land	£Val	PROPRIETORS	Date	WHEEL etc.	Record	Ref.
Carrickfergus	Carrickfergus Tn :	Cowan James	mill	-	-	-	Cowan Jas - Walker Wm	1833	-	dd/	1833 18 202
Carrickfergus	Carrickfergus Tn :	Walker William	mill	-	-	-	Walker - Campbell Henry	1843	-	dd/	1843 10 238
Carrickfergus	Carrickfergus Tn :	Walker William	mill & mill dam	-	-	-	Walker Wm - Johns Alex	1839	-	dd/	1839 2 28
Carrickfergus	Carrickfergus Tn :	Niven Richard	mill	-	-	-	Niven R - Brown Robert	1836	-	dd/	1836 21 294
Carrickfergus	Carrickfergus Tn :	Vance Jno	mill	-	-	-	Vance Jno - Samuel	1848	-	dd/	1845 11 163
Carrickfergus	Carrickfergus Tn :	Derbyshire Herbert	mill	-	-	-	Derbyshire - Girdwood Jn	1847	-	dd/	1875 1 230
Carrickfergus	Carrickfergus Tn :	Derbyshire Herbert	mill	-	-	-	Derbyshire - Girdwood Jn	1847	-	dd/	1878 16 115
Carrickfergus	Carrickfergus Tn :	Derbyshire Herbert	mill	-	-	-	Derbyshire - Girdwood Jn	1847	-	dd/	1878 16 257
Carrickfergus	Carrickfergus Tn :	Girdwood John	mill	-	-	-	Girdwood J - Fenton Sam	1847	-	dd/	1878 47 273
Carrickfergus	Carrickfergus Tn :	Derbyshire George	mill	-	-	-	Derbyshire Geo - Herbert	1880	-	dd/	1880 16 174
Carrickfergus	Carrickfergus Tn :	Derbyshire Herbert	mill	-	-	-	Derbyshire - Girdwood Jn	1880	-	dd/	1880 16 175
Carrickfergus	Carrickfergus Tn :	Derbyshire James	mill	-	-	-	Derbyshire - Girdwood Jn	1880	-	dd/	1880 16 176
Carrickfergus	Carrickfergus Tn :	Fenton Samuel	mill	-	-	-	Fenton S - Girdwood Jn	1879	-	dd/	1879 41 11
Carrickfergus	Carrickfergus Tn :	Girdwood John	mill	-	-	-	Girdwood - Girdwood Jn	1880	-	dd/	1880 16 177
Carrickfergus	Carrickfergus Tn :	Girdwooh John	mill	-	-	-	Girdwood - Hamilton Jas	1880	-	dd/	1880 16 178
Carrickfergus	Carrickfergus Tn :	N. Banking Co.	mill	-	-	-	NB Co - Derbyshire Herb	1880	-	dd/	1880 16 173
Carrickfergus	Carrickfergus Tn :	-	mill	-	-	-			-	dd/	
Carrickfergus	Carrickfergus W	-	cotton print	-	-	-	-	-	-	6"os/	-
Carrickfergus	Carrickfergus W	-	cotton print	-	-	-	-	-	-	6"os/	-
Carrickfergus	Carrickfergus W	-	cotton print	-	-	-	-	-	-	6"os/	-
Carrickfergus	Carrickfergus W	-	ruins	-	-	-	-	-	-	6"os/	-
Carrickfergus	Carrickfergus W	-	ruins	-	-	-	-	-	-	6"os/	-
Carrickfergus	Carrickfergus W	-	windmill ruins	-	-	-	-	-	-	6"os/	-
Carrickfergus	Carrickfergus W	Bragg Henry	bleachgreen	-	-	-	-	-	-	gr/	-
Carrickfergus	Carrickfergus W	Brown, Warnock &Co.	linen thread	-	-	-	-	-	-	v1B/	-
Carrickfergus	Carrickfergus W	Richardson Bros.	flax spinning	-	-	-	-	-	-	gr/	-
Portglenone	Castletown	-	flax - ruins	-	-	-	-	-	-	6"os/	-
Carrickfergus	Catruckfergus Tn	Hamilton John	corn & starch	-	-	-	-	-	-	gr/	-
Derrykeighan	Chathamhall	-	corn	-	-	-	-	-	-	6"os/	-
Derrykeighan	Chathamhall	-	corn	-	-	-	-	-	-	osm/	-
Derrykeighan	Chathamhall	-	flax	-	-	-	-	-	-	1"os/	13
Derrykeighan	Chathamhall	-	mill	-	-	-	-	-	-	pWAM	-
Derrykeighan	Chathamhall	Moore James	flax	-	-	-	-	-	-	gr/	-
Derrykeighan	Chathamhall	Moore James	flax	-	-	-	-	-	20x4x18	v1B/	-
Derrykeighan	Chathamhall	Stewart Henry	corn & kiln	-	-	-	-	-	-	v1B/	-
Derrykeighan	Chathamhall	Stewart Henry	old bleach mill	-	-	-	-	-	-	v1B/	-
Tickmacrevan	Claddy	-	beetling	-	-	-	-	-	-	1"os/	28
Tickmacrevan	Clady Lower	Wm Heany`s	corn	blds G, also kiln & stores			Ron Burns	1997	residence	pWEH	C
Tickmacrevan	Clady Upper	-	-	walls ok, no roof	-	-	-	1997	derelict	pWEH	D
Glenwhirry	Clateryknowes	-	mill	-	-	-	-	-	-	pWAM	-
Glenwhirry	Clatteryknowes	-	corn	-	-	-	-	-	14x3	osm/	-
Glenwhirry	Clatteryknowes	-	mill	-	-	-	-	-	-	6"os/	-
Glenwhirry	Clatteryknowes	McConnell Fran	corn & kiln	-	-	-	-	-	17x4x21	v1B/	-
Ballymoney	Claughey	-	flour	-	-	-	-	-	30x12x23	osm/	-
Armoy	Cleggan	McMullan John	flax	-	-	-	-	-	-	v1B/	-
Killagan	Clogh Mills	-	mill	-	-	-	-	-	-	pWAM	-
Killagan	Clogh Mills	Hill Jn & Bros	flax	-	-	-	-	-	-	v1B/	-
Killagan	Clogh Mills	Moore Sampson	corn & kiln	-	-	-	-	-	14 & 12 ft, fall 7ft.	v1B/	-
Killagan	Clogh Mills	Murray Mary	corn, flax & kiln	-	-	-	-	-	-	gr/	-
Templepatrick	Cloghanduff	-	corn	-	-	-	-	-	14x3x6 12x2 6	osm/	-
Templepatrick	Cloghanduff	-	mill	-	-	-	-	-	-	pWAM	-
Templepatrick	Cloghanduff	Bell David	corn & kilns	-	-	-	-	-	-	gr/	-

PARISH	TOWNLAND	MILLER	TYPE	HOUSE	Land	£Val	PROPRIETORS	Date	WHEEL etc.	Record	Ref.
Templepatrick	Cloghanduff	Bell David	flax	ho., offs. & land	26a.	60	- [+ 3 tenants' houses]	1865	-	gr/	a.a.Ire.ie
Ramoan	Cloghanmurry	Land Judges Co.	mills	-	-	-	Ld Jdg. Co - Boyd Andrew	1892	-	dd/	1982 8 154
Ramoan	Cloghanmurry	Land Judges Co.	mills	-	-	-	Ld. Jdg. Co - Douglas Richd	1892	-	dd/	1982 8 155
Ramoan	Cloghanmurry	McCormick & ano	flax	-	-	-	-	-	-	v1B/	-
Ramoan	Cloghanmurry	Mullan Hugh	corn	-	-	-	-	-	-	v1B/	-
Billy	Clogher North	-	mill	-	-	-	-	-	-	pWAM	-
Billy	Clogher North	Gwymae John	mill	-	-	-	-	-	-	v1B/	-
Loughguile	Clonty	-	mill	-	-	-	-	-	-	pWAM	-
Loughguile	Clontyfinnan	- on Bush R.	mills	-	-	-	-	-	-	1"os/	13
Loughguile	Clontyfinnan	Ferguson Hugh	corn	-	-	-	-	-	-	gr/	-
Layd	Clorey	McElherin	bark	-	-	-	-	-	-	v1B/	-
Cart	Clough Murry	-	mill	-	-	-	-	-	-	6"os/	-
Killagan	Cloughmills	-	corn	-	-	-	-	-	24x2.5	osm/	-
Killagan	Cloughmills	-	flax	-	-	-	-	-	-	6"os/	-
Killead	Coggrey	-	mill	-	-	-	-	-	-	pWAM	-
Killead	Coggrey	Moone Wiliam	flax spinning	-	-	-	-	-	-	gr/	-
Ballymoney	Coldagh	-	flax	-	-	-	-	-	13.8x2.6x7	osm/	-
Ballymoney	Coldagh	-	mill	-	-	-	-	-	-	6"os/	-
Ballymoney	Coldagh	Cramsie Alex	flax	-	-	-	-	-	-	gr/	-
Ballymoney	Coldagh	Cramsie Alex	flax	-	-	-	-	-	-	v1B/	-
Derryaghy	Collin Mountain	Roberts John	bleach & wash	-	-	-	-	-	28x5x1 + 2 ors	osm/	-
Carnmoney	Collinward	-	mill	-	-	-	-	-	-	pWAM	-
Connor	Connor	-	houses	-	-	-	-	-	-	pWAM	-
Connor	Connor	-	mill	-	-	-	-	-	-	pWAM	-
Connor	Connor	Bones James	corn & kiln	36x20x9 & :	-	-	-	-	14x3x14, 1 pr.st.	v1B/	-
Connor	Connor	Densmore Mr	beetling & tuck	-	-	-	-	-	-	v1B/	-
Connor	Connor	M`Cormack Fran	corn & kilns	-	-	-	-	-	-	gr/	-
Killagan	Corby Br.	- on Clough R.	beetling	-	-	-	-	-	-	1"os/	20
Killagan	Corby Br.	- on Clough R.	flax	-	-	-	-	-	-	1"os/	20
Killagan	Corby Br. Clogh R.	-	beetling	-	-	-	-	-	-	6"os/	-
Loughguile	Corkey Little S.	Campbell John	corn & flax	-	-	-	-	-	-	gr/	-
Loughguile	Corkey Middle	-	corn & flax	-	-	-	-	-	18x5 18x5	osm/	-
Loughguile	Corkey South	-	ruins	-	-	-	-	-	-	pWAM	-
Loughguile	Corkey South	McCartney George	corn & kiln	-	-	-	-	-	-	v1B/	-
Loughguile	Corkey South	McCartney George	flax	32x20x12 & :	-	-	-	-	- good m/cy	v1B/	-
Skerry	Correen	-	beetling	-	-	-	-	-	24x4 18x4	osm/	-
Skerry	Correen	Young J & R	beetling	-	-	-	-	-	-	v1B/	-
Ballywillin	Craigahulliar	-	mill	-	-	-	-	-	-	pWAM	-
Templepatrick	Craigarogan	-	bleach	-	-	-	-	-	-	gr/	-
Templepatrick	Craigarogan	-	cottages	-	-	-	-	-	-	pWAM	-
Templepatrick	Craigarogan	-	mill	-	-	-	-	-	-	pWAM	-
Templepatrick	Craigarogan	Bragg Henry	bleach	-	-	-	-	-	- 10s. engines	v1B/	-
Templepatrick	Craigarogan	Dickey James	printing	-	-	-	-	-	-	v1B/	-
Templepatrick	Craigarogan	M'Alister Joseph	bleach (unocc.)	offs., ponds, yd.	2a.	120	- [+ 8 mill hos., occupied]	1865	-	a.a.ire.ie	-
Templepatrick	Craigarogan	Pullen Matt	bleach	-	-	-	-	-	-	gr/	-
Templepatrick	Craigarogan	Williamson John	flax	-	-	-	-	-	-	gr/	-
Kilwaughter	Craiginorne	-	cotton	-	-	-	-	-	-	6"os/	-
Kilwaughter	Craiginorne	Raphael Mrs	cotton spinning	-	-	-	-	-	20x4 overshot	v1B/	-
Craigs	Craigs	-	bleach	-	-	-	-	-	18x8	osm/	-
Craigs	Craigs	-	mill	-	-	-	-	-	-	6"os/	-
Craigs	Craigs	-	mill	-	-	-	-	-	-	6"os/	-
Craigs	Craigs	-	mill	-	-	-	-	-	-	6"os/	-

PARISH	TOWNLAND	MILLER	TYPE	HOUSE	Land	£Val	PROPRIETORS	Date	WHEEL etc.	Record	Ref.
Craigs	Craigs	-	mill	-	-	-	-	-	-	pWAM	-
Craigs	Craigs	Beggs William	beetling	-	-	-	-	-	-	v1B/	-
Craigs	Craigs	Carr Henry & :	beetling & flax	house & land	10a.	62	- [+ 2 tenants' houses]	1865	-	gr/	a.a.Ire.ie
Craigs	Craigs	Cunningham William	beetling	-	-	-	-	-	-	v1B/	-
Craigs	Craigs	Cunningham William	beetling	-	-	-	-	-	-	v1B/	-
Craigs	Craigs	Cunningham William	corn & flax	-	-	-	-	-	-	v1B/	-
Craigs	Craigs	Currell Andrew	beetling	-	-	-	-	-	-	gr/	-
Craigs	Craigs	Kilpatrick George S	flax & thrashing	steward's ho, ld.	104a.	122	- [+ 10 tenants' houses]	1865	-	gr/	a.a.Ire.ie
Craigs	Craigs	Wright James	corn & kiln	-	-	-	-	-	-	v1B/	-
Craigs	Craigs	Wright Matthew	corn & kiln	ho., offs. & land	22a.	24.10.	-	1865	-	gr/	a.a.Ire.ie
Craigs	Craigs	Young Robert	beetling	-	-	-	-	-	-	v1B/	-
Craigs	Craigs	Young Robert	beetling & bleach	ho., offs. & land	153a.	355	- [+ 33 tenants' houses]	1865	-	gr/	a.a.Ire.ie
Craigs	Craigs Lower	-	bleach	-	-	-	-	-	14x5	osm/	-
Antrim	Craigtempin	-	mill	-	-	-	-	-	-	1"os/	13
Ballyclug	Crebilly	-	beetling	-	-	-	-	-	25x7 14x8	osm/	-
Ballyclug	Crebilly	-	beetling, flax	-	-	-	-	-	30x6 14x2.6	osm/	-
Ballyclug	Crebilly	-	bleach green	-	-	-	-	-	-	osm/	-
Racavan	Creeramoy	-	beetling, wash	-	-	-	-	-	14x3 14x2.8 : & 13x3	osm/	-
Racavan	Creevamoy	-	beetling	-	-	-	-	-	-	1"os/	20
Racavan	Creevamoy	-	mill	-	-	-	-	-	-	6"os/	-
Racavan	Creevamoy	-	mill	-	-	-	-	-	-	pWAM	-
Racavan	Creevamoy	Mabin Patrick	flax	-	-	-	-	-	-	gr/	-
Antrim	Creggagh	-	flax	-	-	-	-	-	-	1"os/	14
Duneane	Creggan	-	corn	-	-	-	-	-	-	6"os/	-
Duneane	Creggan	-	flax	-	-	-	-	-	-	6"os/	-
Duneane	Creggan	-	flax	-	-	-	-	-	15x2	osm/	-
Duneane	Creggan	Baker & Quinn	flax	-	-	-	-	-	14x2x10	v1B/	-
Racavan	Crevamoy	-	mill	-	-	-	-	-	-	6"os/	-
Connor	Crevilly Valley	-	beetling & dye	-	-	-	-	-	-	1"os/	20
Connor	Crevilly Valley	-	mill	-	-	-	-	-	-	pWAM	-
Connor	Crevillyvalley	-	beetling, wash	-	-	-	-	-	18x3 18x3 & 14x2	osm/	-
Connor	Crevillyvalley	-	bleach green	-	8a.	-	-	-	-	osm/	-
Connor	Crevillyvalley	Miller Jesse	beetling 2 & dye	-	-	-	-	-	-	gr/	-
Connor	Crevilly-valley	-	beetling	-	-	-	-	-	16x5.6	osm/	-
Connor	Crevilly-valley	Giffin William	bleach, beetling	-	-	-	-	-	-	v1B/	-
Connor	Crevilly-valley	Miller David	beetling	38x21x8 & :	-	35.15	-	-	2 whs. 8 rollers	v1B/	-
Connor	Crevilly-valley	Miller Wiliam	beetling	53x27x18 & :	-	16.7	-	-	-	v1B/	-
Carnmoney	Croghfern	-	bleach	-	-	-	-	-	-	1"os/	28
Carnmoney	Croghfern	-	mill	-	-	-	-	-	-	pWAM	-
Carnmoney	Croghfern	- at Monkstown	spinning	-	-	-	-	-	-	1"os/	28
Antrim	Cromack	Cunningham	paper	-	-	-	Cunningham - Jas Blow	1850	-	dd/	1850 12 83/84
Armoy	Cromaghs	-	mill	-	-	-	-	-	-	1"os/	14
Killead	Crookedstone	-	corn	-	-	-	-	-	-	6"os/	-
Killead	Crookedstone	-	corn	-	-	-	-	-	-	6"os/	-
Killead	Crookedstone	-	mill	-	-	-	-	-	-	1"os/	28
Killead	Crookedstone	-	mill	-	-	-	-	-	wheel	pWAM	-
Killead	Crookedstone	Moore George	corn	-	-	-	-	-	14x3x14	osm/	-
Killead	Crookedstone	Moore George	corn & kiln	-	-	-	-	-	- 2 pr. st.	v1B/	-
Killead	Crookedstone	Moore James	corn & kiln	-	-	-	-	-	-	gr/	-
Killead	Crookedstone	Rea John	corn	-	-	-	-	-	18x4x14 & 14x3x12	osm/	-
Killead	Crookedstone	Rea John	corn & kiln	-	-	-	-	-	- 2 pr. st.	v1B/	-
Killead	Crookedstone	Wilson John	corn	-	-	-	-	-	-	gr/	-

PARISH	TOWNLAND	MILLER	TYPE	HOUSE	Land	£Val	PROPRIETORS	Date	WHEEL etc.	Record	Ref.
Connor	Cross	-	bleach green	-	5a.	-	-	-	-	osm/	-
Connor	Cross	Hamilton	flax	-	-	-	-	-	-	v1B/	-
Connor	Cross	Kirks David	bleach	-	-	-	-	-	-	v1B/	-
Killead	Crosshill	-	mill	-	-	-	-	-	-	pWAM	-
Killead	Crosshill	Hunter James	flour	-	-	-	-	-	-	gr/	-
Killead	Crosshill	McCauley Robert	corn	-	-	-	-	-	14x4x7	osm/	-
Killead	Crosshill	McCauley Robert	corn & kiln	-	-	-	-	-	-	v1B/	-
Killead	Crosshill	McCauley Robert	flour	-	-	-	-	-	14x5x18 (3)	osm/	-
Killead	Crosshill	McCauley Robert	flour & windmill	-	-	-	-	-	-	v1B/	-
Killead	Crosshill	McCauley Robert	windmill	-	-	-	-	-	77 feet wings	osm/	-
Killead	Crosshill	unoc.	corn & kiln	-	-	-	-	-	-	gr/	-
Carnmoney	Croughfern	Bragg Henry	bleach	-	-	-	-	-	-	gr/	-
Camlin	Crumlin	Greer James	corn & flax	-	-	-	-	-	12x1x3 16x1x3	osm/	-
Camlin	Crumlin	McCauley Robert	flax	-	-	-	-	-	14x2x5	osm/	-
Loughguile	Culbane	-	corn	-	-	-	-	-	12x3	osm/	-
Loughguile	Culbane	Ferguson James	corn & kiln	-	-	-	-	-	-	v1B/	-
Loughguile	Culbane	Kilpatrick James	corn & kilns	-	-	-	-	-	-	gr/	-
Loughguile	Culbane	McDonnell Bernard	mills	-	-	-	McDonnell - Ant Co LB Inv. (	1892	-	dd/	1892 63 233
Loughguile	Culbane	McMichael Anne	mills	-	-	-	McMichael - McNaughton :	1892	-	dd/	1892 53 63
Antrim	Culcron	-	corn	-	-	-	-	-	-	6"os/	-
Craigs	Culllybackey	Casement Thomas	beetling, bleach	-	-	-	-	-	-	gr/	-
Craigs	Cullybackey	-	bleach	-	-	-	-	-	16x4.6 (+ 3)	osm/	-
Craigs	Cullybackey	-	bleach	-	-	-	-	-	-	pWSH	-
Craigs	Cullybackey	-	corn	-	-	-	-	-	14x3	osm/	-
Craigs	Cullybackey	-	mill	-	-	-	-	-	-	pWAM	-
Craigs	Cullybackey	Casement Thomas	corn & kilns	-	-	-	-	-	-	gr/	-
Craigs	Cullybackey	Dickey A	bleach	-	-	-	-	-	-	v1B/	-
Craigs	Cullybackey	Leslie Rev Peter	corn	-	-	-	Leslie - Colville	1745	-	dd/	120 86 81930
Craigs	Cullybackey	Leslie Rev Peter	tuck	-	-	-	Leslie - Colville	1745	-	dd/	120 86 81930
Craigs	Cullybackey	Nichol Joseph	bleach	-	-	-	-	-	-	v1B/	-
Craigs	Cullybackey	Nichol Joseph	corn & kiln	-	-	-	-	-	-	v1B/	-
Craigs	Cullybackey	river below Town	flax	blds. on Island only remain			ref. to as Free State	2001	-	pWEH	B
Craigs	Cullybackey	Woods James	thrashing	-	-	-	-	-	-	gr/	-
Ballintoy	Currysheskin	-	ruins	-	-	-	-	-	-	pWAM	-
Ballintoy	Currysheskin	McAlister John	corn & kilns	-	-	-	-	-	-	gr/	-
Ballintoy	Currysheskin	McKenkie N ano	corn & kiln	-	-	-	-	-	-	v1B/	-
Layd	Cushendall	-	corn	-	-	-	-	-	-	6"os/	-
Layd	Cushendall	-	corn	-	-	-	-	-	16x4 o`shot + ano.	osm/	-
Layd	Cushendall	-	old corn mill	-	-	-	-	-	13x2	osm/	-
Layd	Cushendall	Mc Donald R ano	corn & kiln	-	-	-	-	-	-	v1B/	-
Layd	Cushendall	Turnley Fran	corn & kiln	-	-	-	-	-	-	v1B/	-
Layd	Cushendall Dem.	-	mill	-	-	-	-	-	-	pWAM	-
Layd	Cushendall Town	-	corn	-	-	-	-	-	-	6"os/	-
Antrim	Dairyland	-	flax	-	-	-	-	-	-	1"os/	28
Tickmacrevin	Deerpark Farms	Morrow David	corn & kiln	-	-	-	-	-	-	gr/	-
Derryaghy	Derriaghy	Dunlap Samuel	flax	-	-	-	-	-	12x3x4	osm/	-
Derryaghy	Derriaghy	Johnston Mr	corn	-	-	-	-	-	15x3x8	osm/	-
Derryaghy	Derriaghy	Lewson Mr	flax	-	-	-	-	-	22x5	osm/	-
Derryaghy	Derriaghy	Thompson Ross	corn	-	-	-	-	-	14x3x1	osm/	-
Derryaghy	Derryaghy	- (Milltown)	no mill	-	-	-	-	-	-	6"os/	-
Derryaghy	Derryaghy	Dunlop Samuel	flax	-	-	-	-	-	-	v1B/	-
Derryaghy	Derryaghy	Hertford Marq.	corn & kiln	-	-	-	-	-	-	v1B/	-

PARISH	TOWNLAND	MILLER	TYPE	HOUSE	Land	£Val	PROPRIETORS	Date	WHEEL etc.	Record	Ref.
Derryaghy	Derryaghy	Hertford Marq.	spade mfy	-	-	-	-	-	-	v1B/	-
Derryaghy	Derryaghy	Hutchinson James	spade & shovel	-	-	-	-	-	-	v1B/	-
Derryaghy	Derryaghy	Markey Thomas	corn	-	-	-	-	-	-	gr/	-
Derryaghy	Derryaghy	Newell Wiliam	corn	-	-	-	-	-	-	gr/	-
Derryaghy	Derryaghy	Rogers Robert	bleach	-	-	-	-	-	-	v1B/	-
Duneane	Derryhollagh	-	corn	-	-	-	-	-	-	6"os/	-
Duneane	Derryhollagh	Black Joseph	corn & kilns	-	-	-	-	-	-	gr/	-
Duneane	Derryhollagh	Black Joseph	flax	-	-	-	-	-	-	gr/	-
Duneane	Derryhollagh	O`Neill Earl	corn	-	-	-	-	-	14x2.6x20	v1B/	-
Duneane	Derryslough	-	corn	-	-	-	-	-	14x3	osm/	-
Derrykeighan	Dervock	-	ruins	-	-	-	-	-	-	pWAM	-
Derrykeighan	Dervock	- on Stranocum R.	flax	-	-	-	-	-	-	1"os/	13
Derrykeighan	Dervock	Douglas Charles	corn & beetling	-	-	-	-	-	-	v1B/	-
Derrykeighan	Dervock	Laghlin Andr	bark	-	-	-	-	-	-	v1B/	-
Derrykeighan	Dervock	Palmer Hamilton	mills	-	-	-	Palmer H - Black Wm	1891	-	dd/	1891 8 220
Derrykeighan	Dervock town	-	corn	-	-	-	-	-	-	osm/	-
Derrykeighan	Dervock town	Mackay Hugh B	corn & kiln	-	-	-	-	-	-	gr/	-
Derrykeighan	Dervog	Macartney Catharnack	The Mills	-	-	-	MaCartney C - Butler Walter	1890	-	dd/	1890 40 285
Gr. Doagh	Doagh	-	mill	-	-	-	-	-	-	pWAM	-
Gr. Doagh	Doagh	- on Doagh R.	flax	-	-	-	-	-	-	1"os/	28
Gr. Doagh	Doagh	Dickey & Raphael	beetling	-	-	-	-	-	-	v1B/	-
Gr. Doagh	Doagh	Hollybank Sp. Co.	flax spinning	-	-	-	-	-	-	gr/	-
Gr. Doagh	Doagh	Rowan James	beetling	-	-	-	-	-	-	gr/	-
Gr. Doagh	Doagh	Swan & Gilliland	beetling	-	-	-	-	-	-	v1B/	-
Gr. Doagh	Doagh	Swan & Gilliland	corn	-	-	-	-	-	-	v1B/	-
Gr. Doagh	Doagh	Swan & Gilliland	flax	-	-	-	-	-	-	v1B/	-
Gr. Doagh	Doagh	unoc.	beetling	-	-	-	-	-	-	gr/	-
Gr. Doagh	Doagh	unoc.	beetling (dilap.)	-	-	-	-	-	-	gr/	-
Gr. Nilteen	Donegore	-	mill	-	-	-	-	-	-	6"os/	-
Gr. Nilteen	Donegore	-	mill	-	-	-	-	-	-	pWAM	-
Gr. Nilteen	Donegore	Black James & Son	beetling	-	-	-	-	-	-	v1B/	-
Gr. Nilteen	Donegore	Black Mr	beetling	-	-	-	-	-	17x5	osm/	-
Gr. Nilteen	Donegore	Lawther C	corn & flax	-	-	-	-	-	16x4, 13x3, 13x4	osm/	-
Gr. Nilteen	Donegore	Lawther Charles	corn & kiln	-	-	-	-	-	-	v1B/	-
Gr. Nilteen	Donegore	Lawther Charles	flax	-	-	-	-	-	-	v1B/	-
Gr. Nilteen	Donegore	Lawther Henry	beetling mill	-	-	-	-	-	-	gr/	-
Gr. Nilteen	Donegore	Lawther Henry	bleach works	ho., offs. & land	52a.	137	- [+ 14 tenants' hos. unoc.]	1865	-	gr/	a.a.Ire.ie
Gr. Nilteen	Donegore	McDonell	mills	-	-	-	-	-	-	dd/	-
Gr. Nilteen	Donegore	McDonell Thomas	mills	-	-	-	McDonell Thos - Tucker	-	-	dd/	-
Killead	Dongon	-	corn	-	-	-	-	-	14x2x16	osm/	-
Armoy	Doonans	-	corn	-	-	-	-	-	-	6"os/	-
Armoy	Doonans	-	mill	-	-	-	-	-	wheel	pWAM	-
Armoy	Doonans	Gillan Alex	corn	-	-	-	-	-	-	gr/	-
Armoy	Doonans	Gillin Alex	corn & kiln	-	-	-	-	-	13x-x7 1pr. st.	v1B/	-
Dunaghy	Doonbough	-	flax	-	-	-	-	-	13x2	osm/	-
Dunaghy	Doonbought	-	flax	-	-	-	-	-	-	6"os/	-
Dunaghy	Doonbought	-	mill	-	-	-	-	-	-	pWAM	-
Dunaghy	Doonbought	Cupples Henry	flax	-	-	-	-	-	-	v1B/	-
Gr. Killyglen	Drains	-	mill	-	-	-	-	-	wheel c 20 ft.	pWAM	-
Ahoghill	Dreen	-	flax	-	-	-	-	-	-	6"os/	-
Rasharkin	Dreen	-	flax	-	-	-	-	-	14x2	osm/	-
Ahoghill	Dreen	McGuigan Arthur	flax	-	-	-	-	-	- 3 berths	v1B/	-

PARISH	TOWNLAND	MILLER	TYPE	HOUSE	Land	£Val	PROPRIETORS	Date	WHEEL etc.	Record	Ref.
Kilraghts	Drumabeest	-	flax	-	-	-	-	-	14x1.10	osm/	-
Loughguile	Drumadallagh	-	corn	-	-	-	-	-	15x3	osm/	-
Loughguile	Drumadallagh	-	mill	-	-	-	-	-	-	6"os/	-
Loughguile	Drumadallagh	-	mill	-	-	-	-	-	-	6"os/	-
Loughguile	Drumadallagh	Warren George	bleach	-	-	-	-	-	-	v1B/	-
Loughguile	Drumadallagh	Warren George	corn & kiln	-	-	-	-	-	-	v1B/	-
Loughguile	Drumadallagh	Warren Mr	beetling & wash	-	-	-	-	-	14x4 12x3.2	osm/	-
Loughguile	Drumadallagh	Warren Mr	bleach green	-	-	-	-	-	8 acres	osm/	-
Ballymoney	Drumaheglis	-	distillery	-	-	-	-	-	-	6"os/	-
Ballymoney	Drumaheglis	-	distillery	-	-	-	-	-	-	osm/	-
Ballymoney	Drumaheglis	-	mill	-	-	-	-	-	-	pWAM	-
Ballymoney	Drumaheglis	Moore Fran	distillery	-	-	-	-	-	-	v1B/	-
Ballymoney	Drumaheglis	Moore William	corn	-	-	-	-	-	-	gr/	-
Ballymoney	Drumaheglis	unoc./ Moore William	old distillery	& offices	-	15	- [+ 2 tenants' hos. unoc.]	1865	-	gr/	a.a.Ire.ie
Antrim	Drumahore	-	cotton factory	-	-	-	-	-	-	6"os/	-
Antrim	Drumasod	- on Carey R.	mill	-	-	-	-	-	-	1"os/	8
Ramoan	Drumawillin	-	mill	-	-	-	-	-	-	6"os/	-
Ramoan	Drumawillin	Fullerton Dug	flax	-	-	-	-	-	-	v1B/	-
Kilraghts	Drumbest	Young Mrs	flax	-	-	-	-	-	-	v1B/	-
Loughguile	Drumdallagh	-	flax	-	-	-	-	-	13x1.8	osm/	-
Loughguile	Drumdallagh	-	ruins	-	-	-	-	-	-	pWAM	-
Loughguile	Drumdallagh	- on Flesk Water	flax	-	-	-	-	-	-	1"os/	13
Loughguile	Drumdallagh	- on Flesk Water	mills	-	-	-	-	-	-	1"os/	13
Loughguile	Drumdallagh	Ferguson James	flax	-	-	-	-	-	-	v1B/	-
Loughguile	Drumdallagh	Thompson Daniel	flax	-	-	-	-	-	-	gr/	-
Carnmoney	Drumnadrough	-	houses	-	-	-	-	-	-	pWAM	-
Carnmoney	Drumnadrough	-	mill	-	-	-	-	-	-	pWAM	-
Carnmoney	Drumnadrough	Bell R & J & ors	spinning	-	-	-	-	-	-	gr/	-
Carnmoney	Drumnadrough	Bells & Calvert	flax spinning	-	-	-	-	-	30x8x27.6	osm/	-
Carnmoney	Drumnadrough	Grimshaw James & :	mill-pond	& embankment	4a.	26	-	1865	-	gr/	a.a.Ire.ie
Carnmoney	Drumnadrough	Grimshaw James & :	spinning mill, weaving f'cty & pond		24a.	260	- [+ 6 tenants' hos. unoc.]	1865	-	gr/	a.a.Ire.ie
Carnmoney	Drumnadrough	Grimshaw M/s	gas works	-	-	-	-	-	-	v1B/	-
Carnmoney	Drumnadrough	Grimshaw Thomas	bleach & dye	-	-	-	-	-	-	v1B/	-
Loughguile	Drumnafivey	-	flax	-	-	-	-	-	12x1.10	osm/	-
Kilwaughter	Drumnahone	-	houses	-	-	-	-	-	-	pWAM	-
Kilwaughter	Drumnahone	-	mill	-	-	-	-	-	-	pWAM	-
Kilwaughter	Drumnahone	unoc.	spinning	-	-	-	-	-	-	gr/	-
Culfeightrin	Drumnakeel	Jolly Charles	flax	-	-	-	-	-	-	gr/	-
Culfeightrin	Drumnakeel	Jolly Charles	flax	-	-	-	-	-	-	v1B/	-
Antrim	Drumnamoe	Bell & Co	cotton spinning	-	-	-	-	-	36x5 34x5 o`shot	v1B/	-
Craigs	Drumrankin	-	corn	-	-	-	-	-	13x2	osm/	-
Craigs	Drumrankin	-	mill	-	-	-	-	-	-	pWAM	-
Craigs	Drumrankin	Cowan Alexander	corn & kiln	-	-	-	-	-	-	v1B/	-
Craigs	Drumrankin	Cowan Alexander	mill	-	-	-	Cowan A - Clarke Henry	1892	-	dd/	1892 13 261
Craigs	Drumrankin	Cowan William	corn & flax	-	-	-	-	-	-	gr/	-
Craigs	Drumrankin	White James	mill	-	-	-	White J - Cowan Margt	1892	-	dd/	1892 13 260
Ramoan	Drumwillin	Fulerton Marcella	thrashing	-	-	-	-	-	-	gr/	-
Ramoan	Drumwillin	Fulerton Marcella	tuck	-	-	-	-	-	-	gr/	-
Ramoan	Drumwillin	Fullerton	tuck	-	-	-	-	-	-	v1B/	-
Gr. Nilteen	Dunadry	-	bleach	-	-	-	-	-	-	1"os/	28
Gr. Nilteen	Dunadry	-	mill	-	-	-	-	-	-	6"os/	-
Gr. Nilteen	Dunadry	-	mill	-	-	-	-	-	wheel	pWAM	-

PARISH	TOWNLAND	MILLER	TYPE	HOUSE	Land	£Val	PROPRIETORS	Date	WHEEL etc.	Record	Ref.
Gr. Nilteen	Dunadry	-	paper	-	-	-	-	-	-	6"os/	-
Gr. Nilteen	Dunadry	Belfast Banking Co.	mills	-	-	-	Bft Bk Co - Fremantle Arth	1891	-	dd/	1891 11 183
Gr. Nilteen	Dunadry	Blow	mill	-	-	-	-	-	-	dd/	-
Gr. Nilteen	Dunadry	Blow Edwin	paper	-	-	-	-	-	18x7x9 9x3x9	osm/	-
Gr. Nilteen	Dunadry	Blow Edwin	paper	-	-	-	-	-	-	v1B/	-
Gr. Nilteen	Dunadry	Boyd	mill	-	-	-	-	-	-	dd/	-
Gr. Nilteen	Dunadry	Dill Robert	beetling	-	-	-	-	-	-	gr/	-
Gr. Nilteen	Dunadry	Marshall William	flax	-	-	-	-	-	-	v1B/	-
Gr. Nilteen	Dunadry	Orr	mill	-	-	-	-	-	-	dd/	-
Gr. Nilteen	Dunadry	The Old Mill	beetling - ruins	being demolished		-	-	1999	for residences	pWEH	C
Racavan	Dunaird	-	flax	-	-	-	-	-	16.6x1.10	osm/	-
Racavan	Dunaird	Black John	flax	-	-	-	-	-	-	gr/	-
Racavan	Dunaird	Montgomery Hugh	flax	-	-	-	-	-	-	v1B/	-
Rashee	Dunamoy	Langtry Charles	corn & kiln	-	34a.	ú69	-	-	-	gr/	-
Carnmoney	Dunanney	Green & Moffet	corn	-	-	-	-	-	13x3x15	v1B/	-
Carnmoney	Dunanney	Holmes David	corn	-	-	-	-	-	-	gr/	-
Killead	Dundesert	-	mill	-	-	-	-	-	-	6"os/	-
Tullyrusk	Dundrod	-	corn	-	-	-	-	-	-	6"os/	-
Tullyrusk	Dundrod	-	flax - ruins	-	-	-	-	-	-	6"os/	-
Tullyrusk	Dundrod	Willis John	corn & kiln	-	-	-	-	-	- 2 pr. st	v1B/	-
Tullyrusk	Dundrod Bridge	-	corn & flax	-	-	-	-	-	-	osm/	-
Duneane	Duneane	Courtney James	corn	-	-	-	-	-	-	osm/	-
Carnmoney	Duneaney	Patterson William	corn	-	-	-	-	-	14x3.6x14	osm/	-
Killead	Dungonnell	-	corn	-	-	-	-	-	13x3x8	osm/	-
Killead	Dungonnell	M`Ilwrath Deb	corn & kiln	-	-	-	-	-	-	gr/	-
Killead	Dungonnell	McIlrath William	corn	-	-	-	-	-	- 1 pr. st.	v1B/	-
Kilraghts	Dungorberry	-	corn	-	-	-	-	-	13x1.5	osm/	-
Kilraghts	Dungorberry	Chesnut John	flax	-	-	-	-	-	-	v1B/	-
Kilraghts	Dungorbery	-	flax	-	-	-	-	-	-	6"os/	-
Ardclinis	Dunmall	-	mill	-	-	-	-	-	wheel	pWAM	-
Rasharkin	Dunminning	-	beetling	-	-	-	-	-	-	1"os/	19
Rasharkin	Dunminning	-	mill	-	-	-	-	-	-	pWAM	-
Rasharkin	Dunminning	-	ruins	-	-	-	-	-	-	pWAM	-
Rasharkin	Dunminning	Cunningham John	beetling	-	-	-	-	-	20x4 20x4	osm/	-
Rasharkin	Dunminning	Cunningham John	beetling & wash	-	-	-	-	-	40x7	osm/	-
Rasharkin	Dunminning	Cunningham John	bleach	-	-	-	-	-	-	v1B/	-
Rasharkin	Dunminning	Cunningham John	engine ho	-	-	-	-	-	-	v1B/	-
Rasharkin	Dunminning	McBirnie Thomas	beetling	-	-	-	-	-	-	v1B/	-
Rasharkin	Dunminning	McBirnie Thomas (?)	bleach	-	-	-	-	-	-	v1B/	-
Rasharkin	Dunminning	Patrick John	beetling & dye	-	-	-	-	-	-	gr/	-
Rasharkin	Dunminning	unoc./ Ulster Bank	beetling & dye	-	-	-	-	-	-	gr/	-
Drumbeg	Dunmurry	-	flax	-	-	-	-	-	-	6"os/	-
Drumbeg	Dunmurry	-	flax spinning	-	-	-	-	-	-	pWSH	-
Drumbeg	Dunmurry	-	ruins	-	-	-	-	-	-	pWAM	-
Drumbeg	Dunmurry	Barbour Wm & Son	thread works	-	-	-	-	-	-	pWAG	-
Drumbeg	Dunmurry	Curtis Mr	beetling	-	-	-	-	-	-	v1B/	-
Drumbeg	Dunmurry	Hunter Alex	bleach	-	-	-	-	-	2 wheels	v1B/	-
Drumbeg	Dunmurry	Hunter Alex	bleach	-	-	-	-	-	20x4x20 22x5 & 18x6	v1B/	-
Drumbeg	Dunmurry	Hunter William	corn	-	-	-	-	-	20x5x0	osm/	-
Drumbeg	Dunmurry	Hunter William	corn, flour, kiln	-	-	-	-	-	-	v1B/	-
Drumbeg	Dunmurry	Hunter William	flour	-	-	-	-	-	24x6x0	osm/	-
Drumbeg	Dunmurry	Hunter William	mills	-	-	-	Hunter Wm - Hunter	1812	-	dd/	652 393 488399

PARISH	TOWNLAND	MILLER	TYPE	HOUSE	Land	£Val	PROPRIETORS	Date	WHEEL etc.	Record	Ref.
Drumbeg	Dunmurry	McCance John W S	beetling mills	ho., offs. & land	57a.	282	- [+ 9 tenants' hos. unoc.]	1865	-	gr/	a.a.lre.ie
Drumbeg	Dunmurry	McGuigan Jn	beetling	-	-	-	-	-	-	gr/	-
Drumbeg	Dunmurry	Weir A	spinning	-	-	-	-	-	-	gr/	-
Drumbeg	Dunmurry (pt.of)	-	mill	-	-	-	-	-	-	6"os/	-
Racavan	Dunnaird	-	flax	-	-	-	-	-	14x2.4	osm/	-
Layd	Dunouragan	-	flax	-	-	-	-	-	-	6"os/	-
Ballynure	Dunturkey	-	corn	-	-	-	-	-	-	6"os/	-
Ballynure	Dunturkey	Howe Robert	corn	-	-	-	-	-	12x4	osm/	-
Ballynure	Dunturkey	McKinstry Thomas+C1	corn	-	-	-	-	-	-	gr/	-
Ballynure	Dunturkey	Majury Robert	corn & kiln	-	-	-	-	-	-	gr/	-
Ballynure	Dunturkey	McMurtry William	corn & kiln	-	-	-	-	-	12x4x8 2 pr st.	v1B/	-
Eagry	Eagry	-	distillery	-	-	-	-	-	-	6"os/	-
Billy	Eagry	-	distillery	-	-	-	-	-	-	osm/	-
Billy	Eagry	-	flax	-	-	-	-	-	12x1.10	osm/	-
Billy	Eagry	-	mill	-	-	-	-	-	-	pWAM	-
Billy	Eagry	Anderson Stewart	distillery	-	-	-	-	-	-	v1B/	-
Billy	Eagry	McKibbon James	distillery	-	-	-	-	-	-	v1B/	-
Shankill	Ed`derry Falls Rd	Alexander Lor & Jas	flour	-	-	-	-	-	-	gr/	-
Shankill	Ed`derry Falls Rd	Campbell James & Co	flax spinning	-	-	-	-	-	-	gr/	-
Shankill	Ed`derry Falls Rd	Charters John & ors	flax spinning	-	-	-	-	-	-	gr/	-
Shankill	Ed`derry Falls Rd	Craig John ano	flax spinning	-	-	-	-	-	-	gr/	-
Shankill	Ed`derry Falls Rd	Gordon Robert ano	flax spinning	-	-	-	-	-	-	gr/	-
Shankill	Ed`derry Falls Rd	unoc./ trustees	flax spinning	-	-	-	-	-	-	gr/	-
Shankill	Edenderry	-	boiler room	-	-	-	-	1999	-	pWEH	B
Shankill	Edenderry	-	Estate Entrance	-	-	-	St. Ellen Industrial Est.	1999	-	pWEH	-
Shankill	Edenderry	-	logwood	-	-	-	-	-	-	6"os/	-
Shankill	Edenderry	-	mill houses	-	-	-	-	1999	-	pWEH	-
Shankill	Edenderry	-	old mill complex	-	-	-	St. Ellen Industrial Est.	1999	-	pWEH	B
Shankill	Edenderry	Alexander John	flour	-	-	-	-	-	-	v1B/	-
Shankill	Edenderry	Andrews Mr	damask, bleach	-	-	-	-	-	-	v1B/	-
Shankill	Edenderry	Boomer James	old mill, stores	-	-	-	-	-	-	v1B/	-
Shankill	Edenderry	Coates, Gamble &	flax spinning	-	-	-	-	-	- steam	v1B/	-
Shankill	Edenderry	Craig A W	weaving	-	-	-	-	-	-	v1B/	-
Shankill	Edenderry	Howe Robt & Co.	bleach & dye	-	-	-	-	-	-	v1B/	-
Shankill	Edenderry	M`Kavanagh John	saw	-	-	-	-	-	-	gr/	-
Shankill	Edenderry	Tripp & Co	corn	-	-	-	-	-	-	v1B/	-
Glenavy	Edenturcher	-	old buildings	-	-	-	-	-	-	pWAM	-
Glenavy	Edenturcher	Larmour Andrew	beetling	-	-	-	-	-	-	gr/	-
Glenavy	Edenturcher	Larmour Andrew	flax	-	-	-	-	-	-	gr/	-
Glenavy	Edenturcher	Larmour Andrew	flour	-	-	-	-	-	-	gr/	-
Shankill	Englisgtown	Hodgkinson Alfred	bleach green	-	-	-	-	-	-	gr/	-
Shankill	Englishtown	-	mill	-	-	-	-	-	-	pWAM	-
Shankill	Englishtown	Hodgkinson Alfred	beetling, bleach	-	-	-	-	-	-	gr/	-
Shankill	Englishtown	McCance & Co.	bleach	-	-	-	-	-	24x5x22 & 17x6x15	v1B/	-
Shankill	Englishtown	McCance & Co.	bleach	-	-	-	-	-	23x5x23 & 16x6x16	v1B/	-
Skerry	Evishnablay	-	ruins	-	-	-	-	-	-	pWAM	-
Ahoghill	Fanaghy	-	bleach	-	-	-	-	-	16x5 11x4 & 10x2	osm/	-
Ahoghill	Fenaghy	-	mill	-	-	-	-	-	-	pWAM	-
Ahoghill	Fenaghy	Cunningham John	beetling	-	-	-	-	-	-	v1B/	-
Ahoghill	Fenaghy	Young William	beetling & dye	-	38a	-	-	-	-	gr/	-
Donegore	Ferguson`s Land	-	flax	-	-	-	-	-	-	6"os/	-
Donegore	Ferguson`s Land	-	mill	-	-	-	-	-	-	pWAM	-

PARISH	TOWNLAND	MILLER	TYPE	HOUSE	Land	£Val	PROPRIETORS	Date	WHEEL etc.	Record	Ref.
Donegore	Ferguson`s Land	Ferguson James	corn & flax	-	-	-	-	-	-	gr/	-
Donegore	Ferguson`s Land	Ferguson Margaret	corn, flax & kiln	-	-	-	-	-	-	v1B/	-
Donegore	Ferguson`s Land		-	-	-	-	-	-	primitive mcy	pWAM	-
Armoy	Five Acres	Smith Daniel	flax	-	-	-	-	-	12x - x5	v1B/	-
Antrim	Freaghduff	-	mills	-	-	-	-	-	-	1"os/	13
Donegore	Freemanstown	Finton Samuel G	flax spinning	-	-	-	-	-	-	gr/	-
Tickmacrevan	Galdanagh	-	flax	-	-	-	-	-	-	6"os/	-
Galgorm	Galgorm	-	mill	-	-	-	-	-	-	pWAM	-
Galgorm	Galgorm Parks	Gillen George	flax	-	-	-	-	-	-	v1B/	-
Galgorm	Galgorn T`parks	-	whiting	-	-	-	-	-	-	pWSH	-
Ardclinis	Gallanagh	-	tuck	-	-	-	-	-	-	6"os/	-
Ardclinis	Gallanagh	-	tuck	-	-	-	-	-	13x2 o`shot	osm/	-
Tickmacrevan	Glenarm Dem.	McDonnell Edward	mill & kiln	-	-	-	-	-	-	v1B/	-
Glenavy	Glenavy	-	cotton	-	-	-	-	-	-	6"os/	-
Glenavy	Glenavy	-	mill	-	-	-	-	-	wheel	pWAM	-
Glenavy	Glenavy	Esther Wallace	old mill	-	-	-	-	-	-	gr/	-
Glenavy	Glenavy	Howe John	cotton mfy	-	-	-	-	-	52 carding engs.	v1B/	-
Glenavy	Glenavy	Howe John	flax (2)	-	-	-	-	-	-	v1B/	-
Glenavy	Glenavy	Larmour Andrew	corn & kiln	-	-	-	-	-	- 2 pr.st	v1B/	-
Glenavy	Glenavy	Lorimer John	corn & kilns	-	-	-	-	-	-	gr/	-
Glenavy	Glenavy Town	-	corn	-	-	-	-	-	14x2	osm/	-
Glenavy	Glenavy Town	Howe Thos	cotton	-	-	-	-	-	26x5x24	osm/	-
Drumbeg	Glenburn	Hunter William Jun.	bleach	-	-	-	-	-	16x7x0 (2)	osm/	-
Drumbeg	Glenburn	Hunter William Jun.	bleach & wash	-	-	-	-	-	14x6x7 24x5x0	osm/	-
Carnmoney	Glengormley	Browne Allen	thrashing	-	-	-	-	-	16x4x16	osm/	-
Carnmoney	Glengormly	Brown Allen G	thrashing	-	-	-	-	-	-	v1B/	-
Carnmoney	Glengormly	Wallace Hugh	thrashing	-	-	-	-	-	-	gr/	-
Antrim	Glenmount	-	-	old, small ruins	-	-	-	1997	-	pWEH	R
Larne	Glenoe	-	mill	-	-	-	-	-	-	1"os/	21
Larne	Glenoe	-	mill race	-	-	-	-	1997	-	pWEH	-
Larne	Glenoe	-	old mill/ kiln	-	-	-	-	1997	-	pWEH	R
Ballintoy	Glenstall	-	mill	-	-	-	-	-	-	6"os/	-
Ballintoy	Glenstall	Blair James	corn & kiln	-	-	-	-	-	-	v1B/	-
Ballintoy	Glenstall	Blair James	flax	-	-	-	-	-	-	v1B/	-
Ballintoy	Glenstall	Moore Wm	flour	-	-	-	-	-	32x12	v1B/	-
Glenwhirry	Glenville	- on Glenwhirry R.	mill	-	-	-	-	-	-	1"os/	-
Glenwhirry	Glenwhirry	McCullagh John	corn	-	-	-	-	-	- 1 pr.st.	v1B/	-
Glenwhirry	Glenwhirry River	-	bleach green	-	-	-	-	-	-	osm/	-
Ahoghill	Gloonan	-	corn	-	-	-	-	-	-	6"os/	-
Ahoghill	Gloonan	-	flax	-	-	-	-	-	-	1"os/	19
Ahoghill	Gloonan	-	flax	-	-	-	-	-	-	6"os/	-
Ahoghill	Gloonan	-	mill	-	-	-	-	-	-	1"os/	19
Ahoghill	Gloonan	-	mill	-	-	-	-	-	wheel	pWAM	-
Ahoghill	Gloonan	McKelvey James	corn & kiln	-	-	-	-	-	-	v1B/	-
Ahoghill	Gloonan	McKelvey James	flax	-	-	-	-	-	-	v1B/	-
Ahoghill	Gloonan	Weir John	corn & flax	-	28a.	-	-	-	-	gr/	-
Glynn	Glynn	-	mill	-	-	-	-	-	-	1"os/	21
Glynn	Glynn	-	mill	-	-	-	-	-	-	6"os/	-
Glynn	Glynn	-	mill	-	-	-	-	-	-	6"os/	-
Glynn	Glynn	-	mill	-	-	-	-	-	-	pWAM	-
Glynn	Glynn	Baines George	corn	-	-	-	-	-	-	gr/	-
Glynn	Glynn	Conliffe John	cotton spinning	-	-	-	-	-	fall 10 ft	v1B/	-

PARISH	TOWNLAND	MILLER	TYPE	HOUSE	Land	£Val	PROPRIETORS	Date	WHEEL etc.	Record	Ref.
Glynn	Glynn	Conliffe Mr	spinning	-	-	-	-	-	16x2.6x10	v1B/	-
Glynn	Glynn	Johnston R W	corn & kiln	-	-	-	-	-	18x4x16	v1B/	-
Glynn	Glynn	Wilson Wiliam	whiting	-	-	-	-	-	-	gr/	-
Glynn	Glynn Village	-	spinning	-	-	-	-	-	13ft. 6ins. dia.	osm/	-
Glynn	Glynn Village	Cunliffe William	flax	-	-	-	-	-	16x2x10	osm/	-
Glynn	Glynn Village	Johnston Mrs	corn	-	-	-	-	-	14x5x12	osm/	-
Antrim	Goldanagh	-	mill	-	-	-	-	-	-	pWAM	-
Antrim	Gormalsland	- on Copeland Water	corn	-	-	-	-	-	-	1"os/	29
Portglenone	Gortaherran	-	corn	-	-	-	-	-	-	6"os/	-
Portglenone	Gortaherran	Law John	corn	-	-	-	-	-	-	gr/	-
Portglenone	Gortaherran	Law William	corn & kiln	-	-	-	-	-	- old m/cy	v1B/	-
Rasharkin	Gortereghy	-	flax	-	-	-	-	-	14x2	osm/	-
Rasharkin	Gortereghy	-	mill	-	-	-	-	-	-	pWAM	-
Rasharkin	Gortereigh	Elder Robert	flax	-	-	-	-	-	-	gr/	-
Rasharkin	Gortereigh	Elder Robert	flax	-	-	-	-	-	- old m/cy	v1B/	-
Ahoghill	Gortgole	-	corn & flax	-	-	-	-	-	14x2 13x2	osm/	-
Ahoghill	Gortgole	-	flax	-	-	-	-	-	-	6"os/	-
Ahoghill	Gortgole	Duffin John	flax	-	-	-	-	-		v1B/	-
Magheramesk	Gortnacor	Bennet John	corn	-	-	-	-	-	13x2x5	osm/	-
Magheramesk	Gortnacor Upr	-	corn	-	-	-	-	-	16x2x9	osm/	-
Magheramesk	Gortnacor Upr	-	corn	-	-	-	-	-	-	6"os/	-
Magheramesk	Gortnacor Upr	Bennett John	corn & kiln	-	-	-	-	-	- 1 pr.st.	v1B/	-
Ahoghill	Gracehill	-	flax	-	-	-	-	-	-	6"os/	-
Gr. Ballyscullion	Grange Park	Carmichael Hugh	corn	-	-	-	-	-	14x3	osm/	-
Gr. Ballyscullion	Grange Park	Carmichael Hugh	corn & kiln	-	-	-	-	-	-	v1B/	-
Gr. Ballyscullion	Grange Park	Goodwin Wilkin	corn & kiln	-	-	-	-	-	-	gr/	-
Gr. Ballyscullion	Grange Park	Goodwin Wilkin	starch	-	-	-	-	-	-	gr/	-
Gr. Ballyscullion	Grangepark	-	mill	-	-	-	-	-	-	pWAM	-
Shankill	Green Castle	unoc./ Gray George	bleach	-	-	-	-	-	-	gr/	-
Shankill	Greencastle	Gray William	bleach	-	-	-	-	-	25 h.p. steam.	v1B/	-
Gr. Muckamore	Greenmount	-	beetling	-	-	-	-	-	-	1"os/	28
Gr. Muckamore	Greenmount	-	linen	-	-	-	-	-	-	1"os/	28
Gr. Muckamore	Greenmount	-	mill	-	-	-	-	-	-	1"os/	28
Gr. Muckamore	Greenmount	-	ruins	-	-	-	-	-	-	pWEH	R
Gr. Muckamore	Greenmount	Chaine William	bleach	-	-	-	-	-	16x4x19 & 12x3x19	osm/	-
Ballymoney	Greenshields	Thompson George	flax	-	-	-	-	-	-	v1B/	-
Ballymoney	Greenshields Up	-	flax	-	-	-	-	-	12.4x2.1x5	osm/	-
Ballymoney	Greenshields Up	Nevin John	flax	-	-	-	-	-	-	gr/	-
Ahoghill	Gruba	-	bleach	-	-	-	-	-	44/0 x 3/6	osm/	-
Antrim	Hardhill	-	ruins	-	-	-	-	-	-	pWAM	-
Tickmacrevin	Harphall	-	grain mill	-	-	-	-	-	-	pWSH	-
Tickmacrevin	Harphall	-	mill	-	-	-	-	-	-	6"os/	-
Tickmacrevin	Harphall	Banford	mill & kiln	-	-	-	-	-	-	v1B/	-
Tickmacrevin	Harphall	Wilson Arthur	corn & kiln	-	-	-	-	-	-	gr/	-
Ahoghill	Hill Mount Green	-	bleach	-	-	-	-	-	18x5 14x6 & 12x4	osm/	-
Antrim	Hyde Park	-	bleach	-	-	-	-	-	-	1"os/	28
Magheramesk	Inishloughlin	Crooks George	corn	-	-	-	-	-	-	osm/	-
Inver	Inver	-	mill	-	-	-	-	-	-	6"os/	-
Inver	Inver	-	mill	-	-	-	-	-	-	6"os/	-
Inver	Inver	-	mill	-	-	-	-	-	-	pWAM	-
Inver	Inver	-	ruins	-	-	-	-	-	-	pWAM	-
Inver	Inver	Barclay Archibald	bleach	-	-	-	-	-	-	v1B/	-

PARISH	TOWNLAND	MILLER	TYPE	HOUSE	Land	£Val	PROPRIETORS	Date	WHEEL etc.	Record	Ref.
Inver	Inver	Barklie Archibald	wash	-	-	-	-	-	12 ft. dia. (2)	osm/	-
Inver	Inver	Casement Mr	thrashing	-	-	-	-	-	14x3x28	osm/	-
Inver	Inver	Ross James	tuck	-	-	-	-	-	10.6x2.6	osm/	-
Inver	Inver	Whitla H	flour	-	-	-	-	-	35x7x35	v1B/	-
Gr. Muckamore	Islandbane	Back James	beetling	-	-	-	-	-	3 whs., 4 engines.	v1B/	-
Gr. Muckamore	Islandbane	Beck William	beetling	-	-	-	-	-	16x3x14	osm/	-
Gr. Muckamore	Islandbane	Beck William	beetling & wash	-	-	-	-	-	15x3x14 & 16x3x14	osm/	-
Gr. Muckamore	Islandbane	Chaine Wiliam	beetling	-	-	-	-	-	-	gr/	-
Gr. Muckamore	Islandbane	Chaine Wiliam	bleach	-	-	-	-	-	-	gr/	-
Gr. Nilteen	Islandreagh	Benson Robert S	beetling, bleach	-	-	-	-	-	-	gr/	-
Gr. Nilteen	Islandreagh	Ferguson John	bleach	-	-	-	-	-	-	v1B/	-
Gr. Nilteen	Islandreagh	Ferguson Mr	beetling, bleach	-	-	-	Wallace J - Blenerhasset	-	14x4, 13x4, 13x4	osm/	-
Gr. Nilteen	Islandreagh	McClure Samuel	beetling	-	-	-	-	1998	turbine & tailrace	pWEH	B
Gr. Nilteen	Islandreagh	Park John	mill	-	-	-	Jno Park - Hunter	1851	-	dd/	1851 4 98
Skerry	Islandstown	-	beetling	-	-	-	-	-	-	1"os/	
Skerry	Islandstown	-	flax	-	-	-	-	-	-	1"os/	-
Carrickfergus	Joymount	-	bleach	-	-	-	-	-	-	pWSH	-
Connor	Kells	-	beetling	-	-	-	-	-	16x4 18x5	osm/	-
Connor	Kells	-	beetling	-	-	-	-	-	14x3.4 14.8x4	osm/	-
Connor	Kells	-	beetling, wash	-	-	-	-	-	16x4 16x4	osm/	-
Connor	Kells	-	bleach green	-	-	-	-	-	-	osm/	-
Connor	Kells	-	corn	-	-	-	-	-	-	6"os/	-
Connor	Kells	-	corn	-	-	-	-	-	15x6.6	osm/	-
Connor	Kells	-	mill	-	-	-	-	-	-	pWAM	-
Connor	Kells	-	tuck	-	-	-	-	-	13x1.6	osm/	-
Connor	Kells	Browne Robert	beetling & dye	-	-	-	-	-	-	gr/	-
Connor	Kells	Johnston W C	beetling	-	-	-	-	-	-	v1B/	-
Connor	Kells	Johnston W C	corn & kiln	-	-	-	-	-	-	v1B/	-
Connor	Kells	Miller Jesse Jun	beetling	-	-	-	-	-	-	gr/	-
Connor	Kells	Miller Wiliam	beetling	-	-	-	-	-	2 wh., 6 rollers	v1B/	-
Connor	Kells Town	-	beetling & dye	-	-	-	-	-	-	1"os/	20
Antrim	Kilbegs	-	mill	-	-	-	-	-	-	pWAM	-
Antrim	Kilbegs	Kerr James	corn & kiln	offices & land	20a.	57.10	- [+ 7 tenants' houses]	1856	-	gr/	a.a.Ire.ie
Kilbride	Kilbride	-	flax	-	-	-	-	-	-	1"os/	28
Kilbride	Kilbride	-	mill	-	-	-	-	-	-	1"os/	28
Kilbride	Kilbride	- near B`hamage Ho	beetling	-	-	-	-	-	-	1"os/	28
Kilbride	Kilbride	Arthur Alex	corn	-	-	-	-	-	2 pr. st. 5ft. dia.	v1B/	-
Portglenone	Kilcurry	Hogg Edward	corn	-	-	-	Hogg Edw - Casement	1804	-	dd/	561 540 378531
Portglenone	Kilcurry	Hogg Edward	mill	-	-	-	Hogg Edw - Casement	1807	-	dd/	599 266 399623
Connor	Kildrum	-	beetling	-	-	-	-	-	18x3 15x2.6	osm/	-
Connor	Kildrum	-	beetling	-	-	-	-	-	17x2.6	osm/	-
Connor	Kildrum	-	beetling, wash	-	-	-	-	-	18x3.6 15x4	osm/	-
Connor	Kildrum	-	bleach green	-	-	-	-	-	2 acres	osm/	-
Connor	Kildrum	-	flax	-	-	-	-	-	-	1"os/	20
Connor	Kildrum	-	flax	-	-	-	-	-	-	6"os/	-
Connor	Kildrum	-	flax	-	-	-	-	-	12x2.2	osm/	-
Connor	Kildrum	-	mill	-	-	-	-	-	-	pWAM	-
Connor	Kildrum	Barker Robert	flax	-	-	-	-	-	-	v1B/	-
Connor	Kildrum	Hanna John	beetling	-	-	-	-	-	-	gr/	-
Connor	Kildrum	Miller Jesse Jun.	beetling & dye	-	-	-	-	-	-	gr/	-
Connor	Kildrum	Miller William	beetling, bleach	-	-	-	-	-	-	v1B/	-
Connor	Kildrum	Miller William	beetling, bleach	-	-	-	-	-	17x5 17x5	v1B/	-

PARISH	TOWNLAND	MILLER	TYPE	HOUSE	Land	£Val	PROPRIETORS	Date	WHEEL etc.	Record	Ref.
Connor	Kildrum	Parker Robt	flax	-	-	-	-	-	-	gr/	-
Connor	Kilgad	-	beetling	-	-	-	-	-	20x3.6 18x3.6	osm/	-
Connor	Kilgad	-	beetling etc.	-	-	-	-	-	14x3.6	osm/	-
Connor	Kilgad	-	wash & rubbing	-	-	-	-	-	16x2.4 14x2.6	osm/	-
Connor	Kilgad	Miller Wiliam	beetling	-	-	-	-	-	2 wh. 8 rollers	v1B/	-
Connor	Kilgad	Miller Wiliam	beetling	-	-	-	-	-	14x3.6x11 & 18x3.6	v1B/	-
Connor	Kilgad	Smith William & ano	beetling, bleach	-	-	-	-	-	-	gr/	-
Templepatrick	Kilgreel	-	corn	-	-	-	-	-	14x2x20	osm/	-
Templepatrick	Kilgreel	-	ruins	-	-	-	-	-	-	pWAM	-
Templepatrick	Kilgreel	Byrne Patrick	corn & kiln	-	-	-	-	-	-	v1B/	-
Templepatrick	Kilgreel	Byrne Patrick	printing	29x26x12 & :	-	-	-	-	3 singe beetling engs. :	v1B/	-
Templepatrick	Kilgreel	Sloane William	corn & kiln	-	15a.	-	-	-	-	gr/	-
Templepatrick	Kilgreel	Sloane William	paper	& offices	-	12	-	1856	-	gr/	a.a.Ire.ie
Templepatrick	Kilgreel	Wiley Jane	corn	kiln & land	21a.	38	- [+ 3 tenants' houses]	1856	-	gr/	a.a.Ire.ie
Ballycastle	Killoughag	-	corn	-	-	-	-	-	-	6"os/	-
Ballycastle	Killoughag	-	corn	-	-	-	-	-	12x1.8	osm/	-
Skerry	Killycarn	-	mill & mill pond	-	-	-	-	-	-	6"os/	-
Ahoghill	Killycoogan	-	flax	-	-	-	-	-	-	6"os/	-
Ahoghill	Killycoogan	McCaw Thomas	flax	-	-	-	-	-	-	v1B/	-
Rasharkin	Killycreen	-	corn	-	-	-	-	-	-	6"os/	-
Rasharkin	Killycreen	-	corn	-	-	-	-	-	12x2	osm/	-
Rasharkin	Killycreen	-	mill	-	-	-	-	-	-	1"os/	19
Rasharkin	Killycreen	Gaston David	corn & kiln	-	-	-	-	-	-	gr/	-
Rasharkin	Killycreen	Gaston David	corn & kiln	-	-	-	-	-	-	v1B/	-
Rasharkin	Killydonnelly	-	beetling & flax	-	-	-	-	-	-	1"os/	19
Rasharkin	Killydonnelly	Robinson Hugh	beetling	-	-	-	-	-	-	v1B/	-
Rasharkin	Killydonnelly	Walsh James	beetling & flax	-	-	-	-	-	-	gr/	-
Drumaul	Killyfad	-	corn	-	-	-	-	-	-	6"os/	-
Drumaul	Killyfad	-	corn	-	-	-	-	-	14x1	osm/	-
Drumaul	Killyfad	-	flax	-	-	-	-	-	15x2x17	osm/	-
Drumaul	Killyfad	Boyle Neal	mill & kilns	-	-	-	-	-	-	gr/	-
Drumaul	Killyfad	Moor James	corn & kiln	-	-	-	-	-	-	v1B/	-
Kirkinriola	Killyflugh	-	flax	-	-	-	-	-	-	1"os/	20
Portglenone	Killygarn	-	- brick field	-	-	-	-	-	-	osm/	-
Portglenone	Killygarn	-	flax	-	-	-	-	-	-	1"os/	19
Portglenone	Killygarn	-	mill	-	-	-	-	-	-	6"os/	-
Portglenone	Killygarn	-	mill	-	-	-	-	-	-	pWAM	-
Portglenone	Killygarn	Chesney James	flax	-	-	-	-	-	-	gr/	-
Portglenone	Killygarn	Chesney John	corn	-	-	-	-	-	-	gr/	-
Portglenone	Killygarn	Chesney John	corn	-	-	-	-	-	-	v1B/	-
Skerry	Killygore	-	mill	-	-	-	-	-	-	6"os/	-
Skerry	Killygore	-	ruins	-	-	-	-	-	-	pWAM	-
Skerry	Killygore	Curry John	flax	-	-	-	-	-	3x12	v1B/	-
Ballymoney	Killyramer	-	corn	-	-	-	-	-	13.8x2.2x30	osm/	-
Ballymoney	Killyramer	-	mill	-	-	-	-	-	-	6"os/	-
Ballymoney	Killyramer	-	mill	-	-	-	-	-	-	pWAM	-
Ballymoney	Killyramer	Percy James	corn & kiln	-	-	-	-	-	-	v1B/	-
Dunaghy	Killyree	-	mill	-	-	-	-	-	-	pWAM	-
Antrim	Killyrogan	-	mill	-	-	-	-	-	-	pWAM	-
Ballintoy	Kilmahamogue	-	corn	-	-	-	-	-	-	1"os/	7
Derryaghy	Kilmakee	-	bleach	-	-	-	-	-	-	v1B/	-
Derryaghy	Kilmakee	-	house	-	-	-	-	-	-	pWAM	-

PARISH	TOWNLAND	MILLER	TYPE	HOUSE	Land	£Val	PROPRIETORS	Date	WHEEL etc.	Record	Ref.
Derryaghy	Kilmakee	Charley Jno & Wm	bleach	-	-	-	-	-	-	gr/	-
Layd	Kilmore	-	flax	-	-	-	-	-	-	1"os/	13
Layd	Kilnadore	-	flax	-	-	-	-	-	13x2.5	osm/	-
Layd	Kilnadore	McIntyre James	flax	-	-	-	-	-	-	v1B/	-
Kilraghts	Kilraghts	-	corn	-	-	-	-	-	14x2	osm/	-
Kilraghts	Kilraghts	-	mill	-	-	-	-	-	-	6"os/	-
Kilraghts	Kilraghts	Dawson James	flax	-	-	-	-	-	-	gr/	-
Kilraghts	Kilraghts	Wallace Thomas	corn & kiln	-	-	-	-	-	-	v1B/	-
Kilroot	Kilroot	-	bleach	-	-	-	-	-	-	6"os/	-
Kilroot	Kilroot	-	bleach	-	-	-	-	-	-	6"os/	-
Kilroot	Kilroot	-	corn & kiln	-	-	-	-	-	-	6"os/	-
Kilroot	Kilroot	Andrews Mlichael	bleach & engine	-	-	-	-	-	-	gr/	-
Kilroot	Kilroot	Andrews Mr	beetling	-	-	-	-	-	26x4x23	v1B/	-
Kilroot	Kilroot	Andrews Mr	beetling	-	-	-	-	-	26x4x23	v1B/	-
Kilroot	Kilroot	Stevenson James	corn & kiln	-	-	-	-	-	-	gr/	-
Kilroot	Kilroot	Stevenson Samuel	corn & kiln	-	-	-	-	-	14x3x14	v1B/	-
Kilwaughter	Kilwaughter	-	corn	-	-	-	-	-	-	1"os/	20
Kilwaughter	Kilwaughter	McCleverty William	mill	-	-	-	McCleverty - McNeale Henry	1892	-	dd/	1892 17 216
Skerry	Kinbally	-	flax	-	-	-	-	-	-	6"os/	-
Skerry	Kinbally	Walsh John	flax	-	-	-	-	-	-	v1B/	-
Loughguile	Kingariff	-	flax	-	-	-	-	-	12.6x2	osm/	-
Loughguile	Kingariff	McElhatten Armour	corn & kiln	-	-	-	-	-	-	v1B/	-
Loughguile	Kingarriff	- at Flesk Br.	flax	-	-	-	-	-	-	1"os/	13
Rathlin Island	Kinkeel	Gage Robert	corn & kiln	-	-	-	-	-	-	gr/	-
Rathlin Island	Kinkeel	Gage Robert	corn & kiln	-	-	-	-	-	-	v1B/	-
Kirkinriola	Kirkinriola T`parks	Bell Robert	bleach	-	-	-	-	-	-	v1B/	-
Kirkinriola	Kirkinriola T`parks	Clotworthy W`shaw	corn & kiln	-	-	-	-	-	-	v1B/	-
Kirkinriola	Kirkinriola T`parks	Clotworthy W`shaw	distillery	-	-	-	-	-	-	v1B/	-
Kirkinriola	Kirkinriola T`parks	Gehon Andrew	bleach	-	-	-	-	-	-	v1B/	-
Derrykeighan	Knockanboy	-	flax	-	-	-	-	-	-	6"os/	-
Derrykeighan	Knockanboy	-	flax	-	-	-	-	-	-	osm/	-
Derrykeighan	Knockanboy	Lyle Thomas	flax	-	-	-	-	-	-	v1B/	-
Derrykeighan	Knockanboy	Sloan Mary	flax	-	-	-	-	-	-	gr/	-
Skerry	Knockanully	-	mill	-	-	-	-	-	-	1"os/	20
Skerry	Knockanully	Blair John	corn & kiln	-	-	-	-	-	18x3x6	v1B/	-
Antrim	Knockbane	-	flax	-	-	-	-	-	-	1"os/	14
Antrim	Knockbane	-	mill	-	-	-	-	-	-	1"os/	14
Skerry	Knockboy	-	beetling	-	-	-	-	-	18x4.4	osm/	-
Skerry	Knockboy	-	beetling, bleach	-	-	-	-	-	-	6"os/	-
Skerry	Knockboy	-	bleach	-	-	-	-	-	-	6"os/	-
Skerry	Knockboy	-	bleach	-	-	-	-	-	-	6"os/	-
Skerry	Knockboy	-	corn	-	-	-	-	-	13x2.8	osm/	-
Skerry	Knockboy	-	corn & kiln	-	-	-	-	-	-	6"os/	-
Skerry	Knockboy	-	flax	-	-	-	-	-	47x4	osm/	-
Skerry	Knockboy	-	mill	-	-	-	-	-	-	1"os/	-
Skerry	Knockboy	-	mill	-	-	-	-	-	-	pWAM	-
Skerry	Knockboy	-	spinning	-	-	-	-	-	-	6"os/	-
Skerry	Knockboy	-	spinning fcty	-	-	-	-	-	-	6"os/	-
Skerry	Knockboy	Davison Alex	hackling	-	-	-	-	-	-	v1B/	-
Skerry	Knockboy	Logan James	beetling	-	-	-	-	-	-	v1B/	-
Skerry	Knockboy	Logan James	corn & kiln	-	-	-	-	-	-	v1B/	-
Lambeg	Lambeg	Richardson James	bleach	-	-	-	-	-	16x5x0 14x5x0	osm/	-

PARISH	TOWNLAND	MILLER	TYPE	HOUSE	Land	£Val	PROPRIETORS	Date	WHEEL etc.	Record	Ref.
Lambeg	Lambeg	Wolfenden James	tuck	-	-	-	-	-	13x1x8	osm/	-
Lambeg	Lambeg North	-	house	-	-	-	-	-	-	pWAM	-
Lambeg	Lambeg North	-	houses	-	-	-	-	-	-	pWAM	-
Lambeg	Lambeg North	-	mill	-	-	-	-	-	-	pWAM	-
Lambeg	Lambeg North	-	tuck	-	-	-	-	-	-	6"os/	-
Lambeg	Lambeg North	Lucen Samuel	fullers	-	-	-	-	-	-	v1B/	-
Lambeg	Lambeg South	Barber William	thread	-	-	-	-	-	-	v1B/	-
Lambeg	Lambeg South	Richardson James	bleach	-	-	-	-	-	-	v1B/	-
Antrim	Largymore	-	mill	-	-	-	-	-	-	pWAM	-
Inver	Larne Town	Hamilton John	corn & kiln	-	-	-	-	-	-	gr/	-
Inver	Larne Town	Macaulay Robert	flour	-	-	-	-	-	-	gr/	-
Inver	Larne Town	Ross James	tuck	-	-	-	-	-	-	gr/	-
Larne	Larne Town :	-	bleach	-	-	-	-	-	-	pWSH	-
Larne	Larne Townsparks	-	mill	-	-	-	-	-	-	6"os/	-
Larne	Larne Townsparks	-	mill	-	-	-	-	-	-	pWAM	-
Larne	Larne Townsparks	Simpson Wiliam	corn & kiln	-	-	-	-	-	-	v1B/	-
Larne	Larne Townsparks	Smith Alex	tanning	-	-	-	-	-	-	v1B/	-
Kilwaughter	Lealies	Jones Miss	corn & kiln	-	-	-	-	-	15x4.6x13	v1B/	-
Kilwaughter	Learies	-	corn	-	-	-	-	-	-	6"os/	-
Kilwaughter	Learies	-	mill	-	-	-	-	-	-	6"os/	-
Shankill	Legoneil	-	bleachgreen	-	-	-	-	-	-	6"os/	-
Shankill	Legoneil	-	houses	-	-	-	-	-	-	pWAM	-
Shankill	Legoneil	-	mill	-	-	-	-	-	-	pWAM	-
Shankill	Legoneil	Duncan William :	flax spinning	-	-	-	-	-	-	gr/	-
Shankill	Legoneil	Stewart Alex	beetling	-	-	-	-	-	20x4x18 & 18x3x20	v1B/	-
Shankill	Legoneil	Stewart Alex	bleach	-	-	-	-	-	22x3x20 & 24x6x20	v1B/	-
Shankill	Legoneil	Stewart Alex	linen factory	-	-	-	-	-	-	v1B/	-
Shankill	Legoneil	Thompson Mr	flax spinning	-	-	-	-	-	40x8x34	v1B/	-
Shankill	Legoneil WolfHill	M`Clure Thomas	spinning	-	-	-	-	-	-	gr/	-
Ahoghill	Leighmore	-	bleach	-	-	-	-	-	15x3x6 14x2x6	osm/	-
Ahoghill	Leymore	-	old chimney	-	-	-	-	-	-	pWAM	-
Ahoghill	Leymore	Lougheridge J & W	corn & flax	-	39a.	-	-	-	-	gr/	-
Ahoghill	Leymore	Lougheridge J & W	machine ho.	-	-	-	-	-	-	gr/	-
Dunaghy	Limavallaghan	-	corn & flax	-	-	-	-	-	16x4 13x2	osm/	-
Dunaghy	Limavallaghan	-	mill	-	-	-	-	-	-	6"os/	-
Dunaghy	Limavallaghan	-	mill	-	-	-	-	-	-	pWAM	-
Dunaghy	Limavallaghan	Russell Thomas H	flax	-	-	-	-	-	-	v1B/	-
Dunaghy	Limavallaghan	Shaw Robert	corn & kiln	-	-	-	-	-	-	v1B/	-
Carncastle	Linfield	Grimshaw William H	mill & prems	-	-	-	Grimshaw Wm - Nich	1894	-	dd/	1894 4 103
Blaris	Lisburn	Hogg Edward :	corn	-	-	-	Hogg Edw - Hogg William :	1789	-	dd/	404 18 266475
Blaris	Lisburn	Kennedy Mr	wheat & corn	-	-	-	-	-	13x7x0 13x7x0	osm/	-
Blaris	Lisburn	Millar John	corn	-	-	-	-	-	14x3x0	osm/	-
Blaris	Lisburn Millbrook	-	flax spinning	-	-	-	-	-	-	pWSH	-
Blaris	Lisburn Millbrook	Richardson James	beetling	-	-	-	-	-	14x6x0 15x6x0	osm/	-
Blaris	Lisburn Island	-	flax spinning	-	-	-	-	-	-	pWSH	-
Blaris	Lisburn Island	-	spinning	-	-	-	-	-	-	pWAG	-
Blaris	Lisburn Tn`parks	McNally Willaim	mills	-	-	-	McNally W - Harvey Wm	1895	-	dd/	1895 48 133
Blaris	Lisburn Tn`parks :	Harvey William	mill	-	-	-	Harvey Wm - Hope Jos	1898	-	dd/	1898 28 21
Blaris	Lisburn Town	Richardson James	mill	-	-	-	Richardson J - Josh	1847	-	dd/	1847 3 62
Blaris	Lisburn Town	Richardson James N	mill	-	-	-	Richardson Jas - Joshua	1874	-	dd/	1847 3 62
Blaris	Lisburn Town :	Vaughan William	land	-	-	-	Vaughan - O`Connor Jn	1879	-	dd/	1879 13 51
Blaris	Lisburn Town :	Pelan George	land	-	-	-	Pelan G - Ulster Land & :	1875	-	dd/	1875 26 12

PARISH	TOWNLAND	MILLER	TYPE	HOUSE	Land	£Val	PROPRIETORS	Date	WHEEL etc.	Record	Ref.
Blaris	Lisburn Town :	Charley Frederick	mills	-	-	-	Charley Fred - Phineas	1880	-	dd/	1880 53 38
Blaris	Lisburn Town :	Barbour James	mills	-	-	-	Barbour James - William	1883	-	dd/	1883 41 23
Blaris	Lisburn Town :	Richardson James	corn	-	-	-	Richardson J - R.J.S.& O	1876	-	dd/	1876 27254
Blaris	Lisburn Town :	Richardson Jno	Lisburn Mill	-	-	-	Richardson Jno - James	1839	-	dd/	1839 18 240
Blaris	Lisburn Town :	Casement Hugh	land	-	-	-	Casement Hu - Thos	1849	-	dd/	1849 21 137
Blaris	Lisburn Town :	-	saw	-	-	-	-	1902	-	15"/	AG68.02
Blaris	Lisburn Town :	-	damask m/fty.	-	-	-	-	1902	-	15"/	AG68.02
Blaris	Lisburn Town :	- on R. Lagan	corn	-	-	-	-	1902	-	15"/	AG68.02
Blaris	Lisburn Town :	- on R. Lagan	corn (disused)	-	-	-	-	1902	-	15"/	AG68.02
Blaris	Lisburn Town :	- Largymore Factory	weaving	-	-	-	-	1902	-	15"/	AG68.02
Blaris	Lisburn Town :	-	handkerchief wks	-	-	-	-	1902	-	15"/	AG68.02
Blaris	Lisburn Town :	-	damask m/fts.	-	-	-	-	1902	-	15"/	AG68.02
Blaris	Lisburn Town :	Hartford Marquess	mill	-	-	-	Hartford - Richardson J N	1848	-	dd/	1848 15 82
Blaris	Lisburn Town :	Carleton	land	-	-	-	Carleton - Carleton	1845	-	dd/	1845 16 211
Blaris	Lisburn Town :	- on R. Lagan	betling	-	-	-	-	1902	-	15"/	AG68.02
Blaris	Lisburn Town :	-	bl. green, ponds	-	-	-	-	1902	-	15"/	AG68.02
Blaris	Lisburn Town :	-	flax spinning	-	-	-	-	1902	-	15"/	AG68.02
Blaris	Lisburn Town :	-	saw	-	-	-	-	1902	-	15"/	AG68.02
Blaris	Lisburn Town :	- on R. Lagan	flax spinning	-	-	-	-	1902	-	15"/	AG68.02
Blaris	Lisburn Town :	- Lagan Factory	weaving	-	-	-	-	1902	-	15"/	AG68.02
Derrykeighan	Lisconnan	-	corn	-	-	-	-	-	-	6"os/	-
Derrykeighan	Lisconnan	-	corn	-	-	-	-	-	-	osm/	-
Derrykeighan	Lisconnan	-	tannery	-	-	-	-	-	-	6"os/	
Derrykeighan	Lisconnan	Allen Saml	corn & kiln	-	-	-	-	-	14 or 15 ft.	v1B/	-
Derrykeighan	Lisconnan	Taggart John	corn, flax & kiln	-	-	-	-	-	-	gr/	
Duneane	Lismacloskey	-	corn	-	-	-	-	-	-	6"os/	-
Duneane	Lismacloskey	Meath Ld. Bishop	corn & kiln	30x19x10 & :	-	-	-	-	wheel broken mill out :	v1B/	-
Dunaghy	Lismavallaghan	Caruth Robert	corn & beetling	-	-	-	-	-	-	gr/	-
Ahoghill	Lisnafillan	-	mill	-	-	-	-	-	-	pWAM	-
Ahoghill	Lisnafillon	-	bleach	-	-	-	-	-	18x6 (2) & 15x6x12	osm/	-
Ahoghill	Lisnafillon	-	bleach	-	-	-	-	-	18x6x12 (3)	osm/	-
Ahoghill	Lisnafillon	Gehan John	beetling	-	-	-	-	-	-	v1B/	-
Ahoghill	Lisnafillon	Gihon William Jun	beetling, bleach	& land	54a.	443	- [+ 6 tenants' houses]	1856	-	gr/	a.a.Ire.ie
Blaris	Lisnagarvey	-	bleach	-	-	-	-	-	-	6"os/	-
Blaris	Lisnagarvey	-	mill	-	-	-	-	-	-	6"os/	-
Blaris	Lisnagarvey	-	mill	-	-	-	-	-	-	6"os/	-
Blaris	Lisnagarvey	-	vitriol works	-	-	-	-	-	-	6"os/	-
Blaris	Lisnagarvey	Hartford Marq.	mill	-	-	-	Hertford - Richardson	1840	-	dd/	1840 15 82
Blaris	Lisnagarvey	Kennedy Samuel	mills	-	-	-	Kennedy S - Boyd Jane	1860	-	dd/	1860 8 209
Blaris	Lisnagarvey	Kennedy Samuell	flour	-	-	-	-	-	-	v1B/	-
Blaris	Lisnagarvey	Richardson Jas N	bleach	-	-	-	-	-	41 pairs engs.	v1B/	-
Blaris	Lisnagarvey	Richardson Jas N	corn & kiln	-	-	-	-	-	-	v1B/	-
Racavan	Lisnamurrikin	-	flax	-	-	-	-	-	17x2.2	osm/	-
Racavan	Lisnamurrikin	-	ruins	-	-	-	-	-	-	pWAM	-
Racavan	Lisnamurrikin	- at Lisnamurkin Br.	mill	-	-	-	-	-	-	1"os/	20
Racavan	Lisnamurrikin	Esler Robeert	corn	-	-	-	-	-	-	gr/	-
Racavan	Lisnamurrikin	Ester Robert	flax	-	-	-	-	-	-	v1B/	-
Racavan	Lisnamurrikin	Montford John	flax	-	-	-	-	-	-	gr/	-
Connor	Lisnawhiggel	-	beetling, wash	-	-	-	-	-	12.6x3 17x4	osm/	-
Connor	Lisnawhiggel	-	mill	-	-	-	-	-	wheel	pWAM	-
Connor	Lisnawhiggel	Dinsmore Fran	beetling	-	-	-	-	-	-	gr/	-
Connor	Lisnawhiggel	Johnston William	beetling	72x24x24 & :	-	-	-	-	14x4x11 : & 1	v1B/	-

PARISH	TOWNLAND	MILLER	TYPE	HOUSE	Land	£Val	PROPRIETORS	Date	WHEEL etc.	Record	Ref.
Ballyrashane	Lisnisk	-	flax	-	-	-	-	-	-	6"os/	-
Ballyrashane	Lisnisk	-	mill	-	-	-	-	-	-	pWAM	-
Ballyrashane	Lisnisk	Nevin Robert A	flax & eng. ho.	-	-	-	-	-	-	gr/	-
Ballyrashane	Lisnisk	Nivan Thomas	bleach & flax	-	-	-	-	-	-	v1B/	-
Antrim	Loaning	McCreery William	paper	-	-	-	McCreery Wm - Stevenson	1859	-	dd/	1859 39 294
Killaghan	Loughill	-	flax	-	-	-	-	-	12x2	osm/	-
Ahoghill	Low Park	-	bleach	-	-	-	-	-	16x5 16x3	osm/	-
Kilwaughter	Lowtown	-	mill	-	-	-	-	-	-	1"os/	28
Layd	Lubitavish	-	flax	-	-	-	-	-	13x2	osm/	-
Layd	Lubitavish	-	ruins	-	-	-	-	-	wheel	pWAM	-
Layd	Lubitavish	Alex J & M`Allister	flax	-	-	-	-	-	-	gr/	-
Layd	Lubitavish	McAllister Alex	flax	-	-	-	-	-	-	v1B/	-
Rasharkin	Magheraboy	-	corn	-	-	-	-	-	14x2	osm/	-
Rasharkin	Magheraboy	-	flax	-	-	-	-	-	-	1"os/	19
Rasharkin	Magheraboy	-	mill	-	-	-	-	-	wheel	pWAM	-
Rasharkin	Magheraboy	Dunlop Hugh	flax	-	-	-	-	-	-	v1B/	-
Rasharkin	Magheraboy	Dunlop John	flax	-	-	-	-	-	-	gr/	-
Rasharkin	Magheraboy	Kinley Mary	flax	-	-	-	-	-	-	gr/	-
Magheragall	Magheragall	-	mill	-	-	-	-	-	wheel	pWAM	-
Magheragall	Magheragall	Crossin James	corn & kilns	-	-	-	-	-	-	gr/	-
Magheragall	Magheragall	Larmor John	corn	-	-	-	-	-	26x5x24	osm/	-
Magheragall	Magheragall	Larmour John	corn & kiln	-	-	-	-	-	-	v1B/	-
Loughguile	Magherahoney	-	corn	-	-	-	-	-	13x2	osm/	-
Loughguile	Magherahoney	-	mill	-	-	-	-	-	-	1"os/	14
Loughguile	Magherahoney	Adams Alex	corn & kiln	-	-	-	-	-	-	v1B/	-
Loughguile	Magherahoney	Kyle James	corn	-	-	-	-	-	-	gr/	-
Drumaul	Magheralane	- (no name)	mill	-	-	-	-	-	15 & 14ft. Breast wheels	osm/	-
Drumaul	Magheralane	-	bleach	-	-	-	-	-	-	6"os/	-
Drumaul	Magheralane	-	cottage	-	-	-	-	-	-	pWAM	-
Drumaul	Magheralane	-	mill	-	-	-	-	-	-	pWAM	-
Drumaul	Magheralane	-	mills	-	-	-	-	-	-	1"os/	28
Drumaul	Magheralane	Dickey Adam	beetling	-	-	-	-	-	3 wheels, 2 engines	v1B/	-
Derryaghy	Magheralave	Crone John	corn (ancient)	-	-	-	-	-	-	osm/	-
Derryaghy	Magheralave	Richardson J N R	bleach	-	-	-	-	-	-	gr/	-
Derryaghy	Magheralin	Richardson James	bleach	67x24x18 & :	-	48.8	-	-	-	v1B/	-
Antrim	Magherintemple	- on Carey R.	mill	-	-	-	-	-	-	1"os/	8
Antrim	Magherintemple	- 1 m from B`castle	mill	-	-	-	-	-	-	1"os/	8
Shankill	Malone Lower	Blow Wm & Edward	paper	-	-	-	-	-	-	v1B/	-
Shankill	Malone Lower	Pelan James	brewery	-	-	-	-	-	-	v1B/	-
Shankill	Malone Lower	Tucker Edward	glue works	-	-	-	-	-	-	v1B/	-
Shankill	Malone Lower :	Murphy William & :	flax	-	-	-	-	-	-	v1B/	-
Lambeg	Malone Upper	Ferguson Jas & Sons	bleach	-	-	-	-	-	-	gr/	-
Lambeg	Malone Upper	Ferguson Wm & Jas	bleach	-	-	-	-	-	12x3x5 15x4x5	v1B/	-
Carrickfergus	Marshalstown	Melville William	mills	-	-	-	Melville - McMurtry Jo`na	1898	-	dd/	1898 33 256
Skerry	Martinstown	-	corn	-	-	-	-	-	-	6"os/	-
Skerry	Martinstown	-	mill	-	-	-	-	-	-	1"os/	20
Connor	Maxwell`s Walls	-	flax	-	-	-	-	-	-	6"os/	-
Connor	Maxwell`s Walls	-	flax	-	-	-	-	-	14x2	osm/	-
Connor	Maxwell`s Walls	Egleson Samuel	flax	-	-	-	-	-	-	v1B/	-
Carrickfergus	Middle Division	-	mill	-	-	-	-	-	-	pWAM	-
Carrickfergus	Middle Division	-	ruins	-	-	-	-	-	-	pWAM	-
Layd	Middle Park	-	mill	-	-	-	-	-	-	pWAM	-

PARISH	TOWNLAND	MILLER	TYPE	HOUSE	Land	£Val	PROPRIETORS	Date	WHEEL etc.	Record	Ref.
Layd	Middle Park	-	mill	-	-	-	-	-	looms	pWAM	-
Armoy	Mill Five Acre	-	mill	-	-	-	-	-	old wheel	pWAM	-
Armoy	Mill Five Acre	-	mill	-	-	-	-	-	wheel	pWAM	-
Armoy	Mill Five Acre	Fulton Hugh	flax	-	-	-	-	-	-	gr/	-
Antrim	Mill Quarter	-	mill	-	-	-	-	-	-	pWAM	-
Toome	Mill Quarter	Harris Charlotte	mill	-	-	-	Harris C - Armstrong John	1891	-	dd/	1891 15 289
Antrim	Millfield	Forsyth	mill	-	-	-	-	-	-	dd/	-
Antrim	Milllands	Cranston	mills & dams	-	-	-	-	-	-	dd/	-
Antrim	Milllands	Marquis/Alexander	mill	-	-	-	-	-	-	dd/	
Gr Ballyscullion	Millq`r Manybrook	Shuldam & McManus	mill	-	-	-	-	-	-	dd/	-
Toome	Millquarter	-	corn	-	-	-	-	-	15x3x8	osm/	-
Gr Ballyscullion	Millquarter	-	flax	-	-	-	-	-	-	6"os/	-
Ballymoney	Millquarter	-	flour	-	-	-	-	-	-	osm/	-
Ballymoney	Millquarter	-	mill	-	-	-	-	-	-	6"os/	-
Ballymoney	Millquarter	Cameron James	flour, corn, kilns	-	-	-	-	-	-	gr/	-
Gr. Ballyscullion	Millquarter	Harris Joseph	corn & kiln	32x19x10 & :	-	14.5	-	-	-	v1B/	-
Gr. Ballyscullion	Millquarter	Quin	mill	-	-	-	-	-	-	dd/	-
Ballymoney	Millquarter	Ross John	flour, corn & kiln	-	-	-	-	-	-	v1B/	-
Ballycarry	Milltown	-	mill	-	-	-	-	-	-	1"os/	29
Ballycastle	Milltown	-	mill	-	-	-	-	-	-	pWAM	-
Ballymoney	Milltown	-	mill	-	-	-	-	-	-	pWAM	-
Ballymoney	Milltown	-	mill	-	-	-	-	-	sluice-gate	pWAM	-
Layd	Milltown	-	no mill	-	-	-	-	-	-	1"os/	14
Island Magee	Milltown	-	no mill	-	-	-	-	-	-	1"os/	21
Antrim	Milltown	-	no mill	-	-	-	-	-	-	1"os/	28
Ballycastle	Milltown	-	ruins	-	-	-	-	-	-	pWAM	-
Antrim	Milltown	- near Damstown	mills	-	-	-	-	-	-	1"os/	13
Kilroot	Milltown	- on Copeland Wate	no mill	-	-	-	-	-	-	1"os/	29
Killead	Milltown D`gonnell		no mill	-	-	-	-	-	-	1"os/	-
Finvoy	Milltown Eden	-	mill	-	-	-	-	-	-	1"os/	29
Layd	Milltown Red Bay	-	no mill	-	-	-	-	-	-	1"os/	14
Gllenwhirry	Mistyburn	-	corn	-	-	-	-	-	15x2.6	osm/	-
Templepatrick	Molusk	-	cottage	-	-	-	-	-	-	pWAM	-
Templepatrick	Molusk	-	mill	-	-	-	-	-	-	pWAM	-
Templepatrick	Molusk	-	old house	-	-	-	-	-	-	pWAM	-
Templepatrick	Molusk	-	ruins	-	-	-	-	-	-	pWAM	-
Templepatrick	Molusk	Bath William & Co.	54x20x9 & :	-	-	-	-	-	-	v1B/	-
Templepatrick	Molusk	Bath William & Co.	printing	mills 41x42x16 &	-	-	-	-	-	v1B/	-
Templepatrick	Molusk	Bath William & Co.	printing (cont.)	148x33x40 print	-	-	-	-	-	v1B/	-
Templepatrick	Molusk	Byrne Patrick	mill	-	-	-	-	-	-	dd/	-
Templepatrick	Molusk	Cameron Jas	mill	-	-	-	-	-	-	dd/	-
Templepatrick	Molusk	Hyde John	printing	-	-	-	-	-	18x5x64 8x5x64	osm/	-
Templepatrick	Molusk	Hyde John	wash	-	-	-	-	-	17x3x64	osm/	-
Magheragall	Moneybroom	-	corn	-	-	-	-	-	14x2x14	osm/	-
Magheragall	Moneybroom	-	corn	-	-	-	-	-	13x2x14	osm/	-
Finvoy	Moneycannon	-	mill	-	-	-	-	-	-	1"os/	13
Rasharkin	Moneyleck	- nr Curragh Ctge.	flax	-	-	-	-	-	-	1"os/	19
Duneane	Moneynick	-	old cottages	-	-	-	-	-	-	pWAM	-
Carnmoney	Monkstown	-	logwood	-	-	-	-	-	-	6"os/	-
Carnmoney	Monkstown	-	mill	-	-	-	-	-	-	pWAM	-
Carnmoney	Monkstown	-	mill hos	-	-	-	-	-	-	pWAM	-
Carnmoney	Monkstown	-	print works	-	-	-	-	-	-	6"os/	-

PARISH	TOWNLAND	MILLER	TYPE	HOUSE	Land	£Val	PROPRIETORS	Date	WHEEL etc.	Record	Ref.
Carnmoney	Monkstown	-	ruins	-	-	-	-	-	-	pWAM	-
Carnmoney	Monkstown	Cooper Jn & Wm	print works	-	-	-	-	-	40x4 breast	v1B/	-
Carnmoney	Monkstown	Cooper John & Wm	printing calico	-	-	-	-	-	40x5x36	osm/	-
Carnmoney	Monkstown :	Carter John T	spinning	ho., offs. stores,	36a.	370	-	1865	-	gr/	a.a.Ire.ie
Antrim	Montalto	-	flax	-	-	-	-	-	-	1"os/	14
Antrim	Moorfields	- on Kells R	beetling & dye	-	-	-	-	-	-	1"os/	20
Antrim	Moorfields	Antrim Land B. Inv. Cc	mill	-	-	-	Ant. LBI Co. - Kennedy Wm	1894	-	dd/	1894 38 95
Antrim	Moorfields	Joy Robert	Cromac Paper Mi	-	-	-	Joy Robert - Joy Robert	1892	-	dd/	1892 51 146
Blaris	Mosside	-	corn	-	-	-	-	-	14x2	osm/	-
Blaris	Mosside	-	flax	-	-	-	-	-	-	6"os/	-
Blaris	Mosside	-	flax	-	-	-	-	-	13x1.9	osm/	-
Blaris	Mosside	-	mill	-	-	-	-	-	-	pWAM	-
Blaris	Mosside	Mackay Hugh	corn & kiln	-	-	-	-	-	-	v1B/	-
Blaris	Mosside	Mackay Hugh	flax	-	-	-	-	-	-	v1B/	-
Ramoan	Moyarget Lr	-	mill	-	-	-	-	-	-	6"os/	-
Ramoan	Moyarget Lr	Kean Bernard	flax	-	-	-	-	-	-	v1B/	-
Billy	Moycraig Ham`	Thompson George	flax	-	-	-	-	-	-	v1B/	-
Billy	Moycraig Upr	Hamil Dan & William	corn & kiln	-	-	-	-	-	-	v1B/	-
Billy	Moycraig Upr	Hamill William	corn & 2 kilns	-	-	-	-	-	-	gr/	-
Craigs	Moylarg	-	finishing	-	-	-	-	-	-	pWSH	-
Craigs	Moylarg	-	mill	-	-	-	-	-	-	6"os/	-
Craigs	Moylarg	-	ruins	-	-	-	-	-	-	pWAM	-
Craigs	Moylarg	Cunningham William	beetling	-	-	-	-	-	-	v1B/	-
Craigs	Moylarg	M`Vicker John	beetling, bleach	-	-	-	-	-	-	gr/	-
Antrim	Moylinny	-	mill	-	-	-	-	-	wheel	pWAM	-
Antrim	Moylinny	-	paper	-	-	-	-	-	-	6"os/	-
Antrim	Moylinny	-	ruins	-	-	-	-	-	-	pWAM	-
Antrim	Moylinny	Chaine William	beetling	-	127a.	-	-	-	-	gr/	-
Antrim	Moylinny	Chaine William	beetling	-	-	-	-	-	- 6 engines	v1B/	-
Gr. Muckamore	Muckamore	-	beetling	-	-	-	-	-	-	1"os/	28
Gr. Muckamore	Muckamore	-	beetling	-	-	-	-	-	-	6"os/	-
Gr. Muckamore	Muckamore	-	beetling	v. well preserved	-	-	Samuel M`Clure	1997	power source	pWEH	A
Gr. Muckamore	Muckamore	-	bleach	-	-	-	-	-	-	pWSH	-
Gr. Muckamore	Muckamore	-	chimney	-	-	-	-	-	-	pWAM	-
Gr. Muckamore	Muckamore	-	mill	-	-	-	-	-	-	1"os/	28
Gr. Muckamore	Muckamore	-	mill	-	-	-	-	-	-	6"os/	-
Gr. Muckamore	Muckamore	-	mill	-	-	-	-	-	-	pWAM	-
Gr. Muckamore	Muckamore	-	mill house	-	-	-	-	-	-	pWAM	-
Gr. Muckamore	Muckamore	-	miller`s house	in poor condition	-	-	-	1997	-	pWEH	R
Gr. Muckamore	Muckamore	-	miller's house	small building :	-	-	-	1997	-	pWEH	D
Gr. Muckamore	Muckamore	-	village	-	-	-	-	-	-	pWAM	-
Gr. Muckamore	Muckamore	Chain William	bleach	-	-	-	-	-	- double eng.	v1B/	-
Gr. Muckamore	Muckamore	Chaine Mr & Son	beetling & wash	-	-	-	-	-	15x6x19 (3)	osm/	-
Gr. Muckamore	Muckamore	Chaine William	bleach	-	-	-	-	-	-	gr/	-
Gr. Muckamore	Muckamore	Clotworthy	mill	-	-	-	-	-	-	dd/	-
Gr. Muckamore	Muckamore	Groves	mill	-	-	-	-	-	-	dd/	-
Gr. Muckamore	Muckamore	McCourt Joseph	flax	-	-	-	-	-	-	v1B/	-
Gr. Muckamore	Muckamore	near Antrim Town	beetling	large, cond. bad	-	-	-	1997	-	pWEH	D
Gr. Muckamore	Muckamore	White James	flour & corn	-	-	-	-	-	-	gr/	-
Gr. Muckamore	Muckamore	Whittle Fran	corn, flour & kiln	-	-	-	-	-	-	v1B/	-
Magheragall	Mullaghcartin	-	flax	-	-	-	-	-	15x3x0	osm/	-
Magheragall	Mullaghcartin	Larmour John	flax	-	-	-	-	-	-	v1B/	-

PARISH	TOWNLAND	MILLER	TYPE	HOUSE	Land	£Val	PROPRIETORS	Date	WHEEL etc.	Record	Ref.
Derrykeighan	Mullaghduff	-	flax	-	-	-	-	-	-	6"os/	-
Derrykeighan	Mullaghduff	-	flax	-	-	-	-	-	-	osm/	-
Derrykeighan	Mullaghduff	-	mill	-	-	-	-	-	-	pWAM	-
Derrykeighan	Mullaghduff	Hoy Michael	flax	-	-	-	-	-	-	v1B/	-
Derrykeighan	Mullaghduff	Hoy Michael	paper	-	-	-	-	-	-	v1B/	-
Derrykeighan	Mullaghduff	Moore John	flax	-	-	-	-	-	-	gr/	-
Derryaghy	Mullaglass	Roberts John	bleach	-	-	-	-	-	-	gr/	-
Ahoghill	Mullinsallagh	Alexander	mills	-	-	-	Alexander - Godfrey	-	?	dd/	761 596 517131
Carrickfergus	N.E. Division	-	mill	-	-	-	-	-	-	pWAM	-
Carrickfergus	N.E. Division	-	ruins	-	-	-	-	-	-	pWAM	-
Antrim	New Mill	-	salt works	-	-	-	-	-	-	1"os/	29
Antrim	Newmill	-	spinning	-	-	-	-	-	-	1"os/	29
N`t`ncrommelin	Newt`ncrommelin	Crommelin Mr	corn	-	-	-	-	-	24.6x5	osm/	-
Drumbeg	Old Forge	-	mill	-	-	-	-	-	-	6"os/	-
Drumbeg	Old Forge	-	mill	-	-	-	-	-	-	6"os/	-
Drumbeg	Old Forge	-	mill	-	-	-	-	-	-	pWAM	-
Drumbeg	Old Forge	Bank Liverpool B`ro	bleach	-	-	-	-	-	-	gr/	-
Drumbeg	Old Forge	Curtis Mr	bleaching	97x26x16 & :	-	22.17	-	-	- water all yr.	v1B/	-
Antrim	Old Mill	-	mill	-	-	-	-	-	-	1"os/	21
Shankill	Old Park	-	beetling	-	-	-	-	-	-	1"os/	28
Shankill	Old Park	-	print works	-	-	-	-	-	-	1"os/	28
Shankill	Old Park	-	print works	-	-	-	-	-	-	6"os/	-
Shankill	Old Park	-	ruins	-	-	-	-	-	-	pWAM	-
Shankill	Old Park	Girwood William	beetling	-	-	-	-	-	-	gr/	-
Shankill	Old Park	Lyons Henry	printing	19x25x6, vat ho.:	-	-	-	-	11ft. - m/cy all rotten : r	v1B/	-
Shankill	Old Park	McPherson Dug	printing	-	-	-	-	-	- steam engine	v1B/	-
Blaris	Old Warren	-	mill	-	-	-	-	-	-	pWAM	-
Blaris	Old Warren	-	ruins	-	-	-	-	-	-	pWAM	-
Blaris	Old Warren	Coulson Messrs	wv fcty Lisburn	-	-	-	-	-	-	v1B/	-
Blaris	Old Warren	Coulson William	weaving factory	-	-	-	-	-	-	v1B/	-
N`t`ncrommelin	Omerbane	-	flax	-	-	-	-	-	-	1"os/	14
Armoy	Park	-	mill	-	-	-	-	-	-	pWAM	-
Armoy	Park	Knox Thos & ors	corn	-	-	-	-	-	-	gr/	-
Armoy	Park	Peacock John	corn & kiln	-	-	-	-	-	-	v1B/	-
Armoy	Park	Peacock John	flax	-	-	-	-	-	-	v1B/	-
Derryaghy	Poleglass	-	corn	-	-	-	-	-	-	6"os/	-
Derryaghy	Poleglass	-	mill	-	-	-	-	-	-	pWAM	-
Derryaghy	Poleglass	Lewson Mr	corn	-	-	-	-	-	16x3x2	osm/	-
Derryaghy	Poleglass	Lewson William	corn & kiln	-	-	-	-	-	-	v1B/	-
Aghalee	Poobles	-	Old Mill Bridge	-	-	-	-	-	-	6"os/	-
Ballywillin	Port Rush	Kerr Lord Mark	fish house	-	-	-	-	-	-	v1B/	-
Ahoghill	Portglenone	Hogg William :	corn	-	-	-	Hogg William - Hogg James	1820	Rel. 22 Aug.	dd/	754 584 512919
Island Magee	Portmuck	-	ruins	-	-	-	-	-	-	pWAM	-
Drumaul	Randalstown	-	beetling	-	-	-	-	-	16x4 16x4	osm/	-
Drumaul	Randalstown	-	corn	-	-	-	-	-	14x3x3	osm/	-
Drumaul	Randalstown	-	cotton	-	-	-	-	-	14/0 x 9/9	osm/	-
Drumaul	Randalstown	-	cotton	-	-	-	-	-	14/0 x 9/9 x 3/6	osm/	-
Drumaul	Randalstown	Davidson Mr	corn	-	-	-	-	-	17/0 x 4/6 x 1/6	osm/	-
Drumaul	Randalstown		corn	-	-	-	-	-	-	osm/	-
Drumaul	Randalstown Br.	-	corn	-	-	-	-	-	14x3x3	osm/	-
Rashee	Rashee	Moon William	flax	-	-	-	-	-	-	gr/	-
Templecorran	Redhall	-	corn	-	-	-	-	-	-	6"os/	-

PARISH	TOWNLAND	MILLER	TYPE	HOUSE	Land	£Val	PROPRIETORS	Date	WHEEL etc.	Record	Ref.
Templecorran	Redhall	-	corn & kiln	-	-	-	-	-	-	6"os/	-
Templecorran	Redhall	-	flax	-	-	-	-	-	-	6"os/	-
Templecorran	Redhall	-	mill	-	-	-	-	-	-	pWAM	-
Templecorran	Redhall	-	ruins	-	-	-	-	-	-	pWAM	-
Templecorran	Redhall	-	thrashing	-	-	-	-	-	16x3.10x20	osm/	-
Templecorran	Redhall	Ker David	flax	-	-	-	-	-	16x4x11	osm/	-
Templecorran	Redhall	Kerr David	corn & kiln	-	-	-	-	-	-	v1B/	-
Templecorran	Redhall	Kerr David	flax	-	-	-	-	-	-	v1B/	-
Templecorran	Redhall	Orr Wm	corn & kilns	-	-	-	-	-	-	gr/	-
Templecorran	Redhall	Wright Mr	corn	-	-	-	-	-	20x4x2	osm/	-
Duncuce	Revallagh	-	flax	-	-	-	-	-	-	6"os/	-
Duncuce	Revallagh N	McDonald Andrew	flax	-	-	-	-	-	- machinery bad	v1B/	-
Templepatrick	Rickamore	-	flax	-	-	-	-	-	-	6"os/	-
Templepatrick	Rickamore	-	flax	-	-	-	-	-	15x2x8	osm/	-
Templepatrick	Rickamore	vacant	flax	-	-	-	-	-	-	gr/	-
Rasharkin	River Main	Birnie, Cunningham	beetling & wash	-	-	-	-	-	18x5 (3) 13x12	osm/	-
Rasharkin	River Main	Birnie, Cunningham	bleach greens	-	-	-	-	-	-	osm/	-
Antrim	Rockstown	-	flax	-	-	-	-	-	-	1"os/	13
Kilwaughter	Rory`s Glen	-	flax	-	-	-	-	-	-	6"os/	-
Kilwaughter	Rory`s Glen	-	flax	-	-	-	-	-	-	v1B/	-
Kilwaughter	Rory`s Glen	-	mill	-	-	-	-	-	-	pWAM	-
Kilwaughter	Rory`s Glen	-	ruins	-	-	-	-	-	-	pWAM	-
Kilwaughter	Rory`s Glen	Agnew William	corn & kiln	-	-	-	-	-	-	gr/	-
Kilwaughter	Rory`s Glen	Agnew William	flax	-	-	-	-	-	-	gr/	-
Finvoy	Rosnashane	unoc./ W Anderson	flax	-	-	-	-	-	-	gr/	-
Carncastle	Saint Cunning	-	flax	-	-	-	-	-	-	6"os/	-
Dunluce	Seneirl	McKeon William	flax	-	-	-	-	-	-	v1B/	-
Dunluce	Seneirl	Paton Robert	corn & kiln	-	-	-	-	-	-	v1B/	-
Derryaghy	Seymour Hill	Charley William	bleach	-	-	-	-	-	20x5x1 10x5x1	osm/	-
Gr. Muckamore	Shaneoguestown	-	beetling	-	-	-	-	-	-	6"os/	-
Gr. Muckamore	Shaneoguestown	-	beetling		64a.	-	-	-	-	gr/	-
Gr. Muckamore	Shaneoguestown	-	cottages	-	-	-	-	-	-	pWAM	-
Gr. Muckamore	Shaneoguestown	-	dye works	-	-	-	-	-	-	1"os/	28
Gr. Muckamore	Shaneoguestown	-	mill	-	-	-	-	-	-	6"os/	-
Gr. Muckamore	Shaneoguestown	-	mill	-	-	-	-	-	-	pWAM	-
Gr. Muckamore	Shaneoguestown	-	ruins	-	-	-	-	-	-	pWAM	-
Gr. Muckamore	Shaneoguestown	-	ruins / beetling	-	-	-	-	1999	-	pWEH	- R
Gr. Muckamore	Shaneoguestown	-	ruins miller`s ho	-	-	-	-	1999	-	pWEH	- R
Gr. Muckamore	Shaneoguestown	Cantwell	mill	-	-	-	-	-	-	dd/	-
Gr. Muckamore	Shaneoguestown	Chain William	beetling	-	-	-	-	-	- 2 engines	v1B/	-
Gr. Muckamore	Shaneoguestown	Chaine Mr & Son	beetling & wash	-	-	-	-	-	20x6x19 & 20x5x19	osm/	-
Gr. Muckamore	Shaneoguestown	Chaine William	beetling	-	-	-	-	-	-	gr/	-
Gr. Muckamore	Shaneoguestown	Swan	mill	-	-	-	-	-	-	dd/	-
Gr. Muckamore	Shaneoguestown	Swan	mill	-	-	-	-	-	-	dd/	-
Gr. Muckamore	Shaneoguestown	White	mill	-	-	-	-	-	-	dd/	-
Gr. Muckamore	Shaneoguestown	White	mill	-	-	-	-	-	-	dd/	-
Gr. Muckamore	Shaneoguestown	Whittle Lattimer	flour & corn	-	-	-	-	-	17x5x11 & 15x5x11	osm/	-
Antrim	Shank Bridge	-	beetling	-	-	-	-	-	-	1"os/	20
Shankill	Shankill T`parks	Duffin Charles & Co.	spinning	-	-	-	-	-	-	gr/	-
Shankill	Shankill T`parks	Emerson Jn & ors	flax spinning	-	-	-	-	-	-	gr/	-
Shankill	Shankill T`parks	Hodgkinson Alfred	beetling	-	-	-	-	-	-	gr/	-
Shankill	Shankill T`parks	Hodgkinson Alfred	bleach	-	-	-	-	-	-	gr/	-

PARISH	TOWNLAND	MILLER	TYPE	HOUSE	Land	£Val	PROPRIETORS	Date	WHEEL etc.	Record	Ref.
Shankill	Shankill T`parks	Johnston William	spinning	-	-	-	-	-	-	gr/	-
Shankill	Shankill T`parks	Murphy Wm & ors	flax spinning	-	-	-	-	-	-	gr/	-
Shankill	Shankill T`parks	unoc./ Ulster Bank	spining & corn	-	-	-	-	-	-	gr/	-
Shankill	Shankill T`parks :	Hind John, Jas & Jos	spinning mill & :	-	-	-	-	-	-	gr/	-
Shankill	Shankill T`parks :	Mitchell William S	flax spinning	-	-	-	-	-	-	gr/	-
Shankill	Shankill T`parks :	Charters John	flax spinning	-	-	-	-	-	-	gr/	-
Shankill	Shankill T`parks :	Kennedy James & :	flax spinning	-	-	-	-	-	-	gr/	-
Shankill	Shankill T`parks :	Valentine Thomas &	flax spinning & :	-	-	-	-	-	-	gr/	-
Shankill	Shankill T`parks :	Ewart William	flax spinning	-	-	-	-	-	-	gr/	-
Shankill	Shankill T`parks :	Ferguson John	beetling	-	-	-	-	-	-	gr/	-
Shankill	Shankill T`parks :	Ferguson John	bleachgreen pt.	-	-	-	-	-	-	gr/	-
Shankill	Shankill T`parks :	Johnston Philip & :	flax spinning	-	-	-	-	-	-	gr/	-
Shankill	Shankill T`parks :	Boyd John & John K	spinning & wv	-	-	-	-	-	-	gr/	-
Shankill	Shankill T`parks :	unoc./ Ewart Wm	old corn mill	-	-	-	-	-	-	gr/	-
Shankill	Shankill T`parks :	M`Cullough William &	flour	-	-	-	-	-	-	gr/	-
Shankill	Shankill T`parks :	M`Cammon Thomas	flour & tannery	-	-	-	-	-	-	gr/	-
Shankill	Shankill T`parks :	Lepper Robt C. & :	cotton spinning	-	-	-	-	-	-	gr/	-
Shankill	Shankill T`parks :	Ronan John, Wm & R	spinning	-	-	-	-	-	-	gr/	-
Shankill	Shankill T`parks :	Campbell John &	flax spinning	-	-	-	-	-	-	gr/	-
Shankill	Shankill T`parks :	Little Jn & Brown A	corn & starch	-	-	-	-	-	-	gr/	-
Shankill	Shankill T`parks :	Ross William & :	flax spinning	-	-	-	-	-	-	gr/	-
Shankill	Shankill T`parks :	Stevenson Peter	flour	-	-	-	-	-	-	gr/	-
Shankill	Shankill T`parks :	Mulholland John & :	spinning & wv	-	-	-	-	-	-	gr/	-
Skerry	Skerry East	-	ruins	-	-	-	-	-	-	pWAM	-
Skerry	Skerry East	Russel Thomas H	corn & kiln	-	-	-	-	-	-	v1B/	-
Skerry	Skerry West	-	corn	-	-	-	-	-	-	6"os/	-
Ballynure	Skilganaban	-	mill	-	-	-	-	-	-	1"os/	28
Ahoghill	Slievenagh	-	corn	-	-	-	-	-	-	6"os/	-
Ahoghill	Slievenagh	-	corn & flax	-	-	-	-	-	12x2 13x2	osm/	-
Ahoghill	Slievenagh	-	flax	-	-	-	-	-	-	6"os/	-
Finvoy	Slievenaghy	-	corn	-	-	-	-	-	-	1"os/	13
Finvoy	Slievenaghy	Chesnutt Andrew	corn & kiln	-	-	-	-	-	-	v1B/	-
Antrim	Springfield	Coates Victor	mill	-	-	-	Coates V - Weir William	1892	-	dd/	1892 22 54
Antrim	Springfield	Weir William	mill	-	-	-	Weir Wim - N. Banking Co	1892	-	dd/	1892 22 192
Gr. Dundermot	Springmount	-	corn	-	-	-	-	-	16x3	osm/	-
Gr. Dundermot	Springmount	-	mill	-	-	-	-	-	-	6"os/	-
Gr. Dundermot	Springmount	-	ruins	-	-	-	-	-	-	pWAM	-
Gr. Dundermot	Springmount	Higginson Jno O`N	corn & kiln	-	-	-	-	-	-	gr/	-
Gr. Dundermot	Springmount	McQuade William	corn & kiln	-	-	-	-	-	-	v1B/	-
Antrim	St Catherine`s	-	bleach & print	-	-	-	-	-	-	1"os/	29
Derryaghy	Stoneyford	Dickson John	spinning	-	-	-	-	-	32x5	osm/	-
Templepatrick	Stradbally	Steen James	corn & kiln	-	-	-	-	-	-	gr/	-
Templepatrick	Stradbally	unoc.	beetling	-	-	-	-	-	-	gr/	-
Templepatrick	Stradballymorris	-	mill	-	-	-	-	-	-	6"os/	-
Templepatrick	Stradballymorris	-	mill /several	-	-	-	-	-	-	pWAM	-
Templepatrick	Stradballymorris	- on Clady Water	bleach & dye	-	-	-	-	-	-	1"os/	28
Templepatrick	Stradballymorris	Steen A	flax	-	-	-	-	-	-	v1B/	-
Templepatrick	Stradballymorris	Steen Alex	beetling	-	-	-	-	-	-	v1B/	-
Templepatrick	Stradballymorris	Steen Alex	corn	-	-	-	-	-	-	v1B/	-
Templepatrick	Stradballymorris	Steen Mr	corn	-	-	-	-	-	18x5x16	osm/	-
Templepatrick	Stradballymorris	Steen Mr	corn	-	-	-	-	-	13x3x8	osm/	-
Templepatrick	Stradballymorris	Steen Mr	thrashing	-	-	-	-	-	14x2x10	osm/	-

PARISH	TOWNLAND	MILLER	TYPE	HOUSE	Land	£Val	PROPRIETORS	Date	WHEEL etc.	Record	Ref.
Templepatrick	Stradballymorris	Swan Mr	bleach	-	-	-	-	-	-	v1B/	-
Templepatrick	Stradballymorris	Swan Mr	flax	-	-	-	-	-	-	v1B/	-
Templepatrick	Stradballymorris	Swann Hugh	beetling	-	-	-	-	-	12x1.6x12	osm/	-
Templepatrick	Stradballymorris	Swann Hugh	beetling & wash	-	-	-	-	-	32x6x20 & 4x2x14	osm/	-
Templepatrick	Stradballymorris	Wallace Thomas	beetling mills	-	-	-	-	-	-	gr/	-
Templepatrick	Stradballymorris	Wallace Thomas	linen dye works	-	-	-	-	-	-	gr/	-
Ahoghill	Straid	-	corn	-	-	-	-	-	13x2	osm/	-
Ahoghill	Straid	-	flax	-	-	-	-	-	-	6"os/	-
Ahoghill	Straid	-	flax	-	-	-	-	-	13x2	osm/	-
Ahoghill	Straid	-	flax	-	-	-	-	-	13x2	osm/	-
Ballynure	Straid	-	mill	-	-	-	-	-	-	6"os/	-
Ballynure	Straid	-	mill	-	-	-	-	-	-	pWAM	-
Ahoghill	Straid	Weir Alex	corn & kilns	-	44a.	-	-	-	-	gr/	-
Ahoghill	Straid	Weir Robert	flax	-	-	-	-	-	-	v1B/	-
Ballynure	Straid	Wilson John	corn & kiln	-	-	-	-	-	-	gr/	-
Billy	Straidbilly	Cowan William	spinning & pond	-	-	-	-	-	-	gr/	-
Killead	Straidhaven	-	new mill	-	-	-	-	-	-	6"os/	-
Killead	Straidhaven	Montgomery Alex	corn	-	-	-	-	-	15x4x12 16x4	osm/	-
Killead	Straidhaven	Montgomery Alex	corn & kiln	-	-	-	-	-	-	v1B/	-
Killead	Straidhaven	unoc.	corn & kiln	-	-	-	-	-	-	gr/	-
Ballynure	Straidland	Hutcheson Margaret	flax	-	-	-	-	-	14x2x20	v1B/	-
Ballynure	Straidland	Hutchinson Mrs	flax	-	-	-	-	-	19x3x19	osm/	-
Ballynure	Straidland	Wilson John	corn	-	-	-	-	-	17x3x12	osm/	-
Ballymoney	Stranocum	-	corn	-	-	-	-	-	12x2x6	osm/	-
Ballymoney	Stranocum	-	corn & kiln	-	-	-	-	-	-	v1B/	-
Ballymoney	Stranocum	-	flax	-	-	-	-	-	12x2x6	osm/	-
Ballymoney	Stranocum	-	flax	-	-	-	-	-	11.8x1.8x20	osm/	-
Ballymoney	Stranocum	-	flax	-	-	-	-	-	-	v1B/	-
Ballymoney	Stranocum	-	mill	-	-	-	-	-	-	6"os/	-
Ballymoney	Stranocum	-	mill / several	-	-	-	-	-	-	pWAM	-
Ballymoney	Stranocum	- on Bush R.	mills	-	-	-	-	-	-	1"os/	13
Ballymoney	Stranocum	Adams Dav	corn & kiln	-	-	-	-	-	-	v1B/	-
Ballymoney	Stranocum	Hutch William F	corn & flax	-	-	-	-	-	-	gr/	-
Ballymoney	Stranocum	Hutch William F	saw	-	-	-	-	-	-	gr/	-
Ballymoney	Stranocum	McKane Neill	flax	-	-	-	-	-	-	v1B/	-
Ballymoney	Stranocum	McLean James	flax	-	-	-	-	-	-	v1B/	-
Layd	Tavnaghdrissagh	Cuppage Edmond F	corn, flax, kilns	-	-	-	-	-	-	gr/	-
Connor	Tawnybrack	-	beetling	-	-	-	-	-	18x7	osm/	-
Connor	Tawnybrack	-	beetling	-	-	-	-	-	18x3.6 18x3.8	osm/	-
Connor	Tawnybrack	-	beetling	-	-	-	-	-	16x4 16x4	osm/	-
Connor	Tawnybrack	-	bleach green	-	-	-	-	-	51a. 1r. 13 p.	osm/	-
Connor	Tawnybrack	-	long mill-race	-	-	-	-	-	-	6"os/	-
Connor	Tawnybrack	-	mill	-	-	-	-	-	-	pWAM	-
Connor	Tawnybrack	Kirk Daniel	beetling	-	-	-	-	-	-	gr/	-
Connor	Tawnybrack	Kirk Daniel	beetling	-	-	-	-	-	18x6x13	v1B/	-
Connor	Tawnybrack	McCord & Smith	beetling	-	-	-	-	-	-	gr/	-
Connor	Tawnybrack	Miller William	beetling	107x28x18 & :	-	27.16	-	-	8 sets engines	v1B/	-
Connor	Tawnybrack	Miller William	beetling	53x27x18 & :	-	16.7.0	-	-	20x4x15 2 wh.	v1B/	-
Ahoghill	Teeshan	-	corn	-	-	-	-	-	-	1"os/	20
Ahoghill	Teeshan	-	flax	-	-	-	-	-	-	1"os/	20
Ahoghill	Teeshan	-	flax	-	-	-	-	-	-	1"os/	20
Templepatrick	Templepatrick	Barron Joseph	mill	-	-	-	-	-	-	dd/	-

PARISH	TOWNLAND	MILLER	TYPE	HOUSE	Land	£Val	PROPRIETORS	Date	WHEEL etc.	Record	Ref.
Antrim	The Trench	- at Mollusk	linen	-	-	-	-	-	-	1"os/	28
Antrim	Thorntown	-	corn	-	-	-	-	-	-	1"os/	20
Antrim	Thorntown	-	flax	-	-	-	-	-	-	1"os/	20
Skerry	Tickloy	Craigs James	flax	-	-	-	-	-	11x3	v1B/	-
Rashee	Tildarg	-	mill / several	-	-	-	-	-	-	pWAM	-
Rashee	Tildarg	Allen John	bleach	-	-	-	-	-	-	v1B/	-
Rashee	Tildarg	Ewart William & Son	beetling	-	-	-	-	-	-	gr/	-
Gr. Muckamore	Tiregracy	Chaine Mr & Son	beetling & wash	-	-	-	-	-	15x4x19	osm/	-
Gr. Muckamore	Tirgracey	-	beetling	-	-	-	-	-	-	6"os/	-
Gr. Muckamore	Tirgracey	-	paper	-	-	-	-	-	-	6"os/	-
Gr. Muckamore	Tirgracey	Chain William	beetling (2)	-	-	-	-	-	-	gr/	-
Gr. Muckamore	Tirgracey	Chain William	bleach	-	-	-	-	-	-	gr/	-
Gr. Muckamore	Tirgracey	Chain William	bleach	-	-	-	-	-	3 engines	v1B/	-
Gr. Muckamore	Tirgracey	Chain William	paper	-	-	-	-	-	-	v1B/	-
Gr. Muckamore	Tirgracey	Chaine Mr & Son	beetling	-	-	-	-	-	16x4x9 12x3x9	osm/	-
Gr. Muckamore	Tirgracey		houses	-	-	-	-	-	-	pWAM	-
Ballynure	Toberdowney	-	cotton	-	-	-	-	-	-	6"os/	-
Ballynure	Toberdowney	-	logwood	-	-	-	-	-	-	6"os/	-
Ballynure	Toberdowney	How Robt	cotton	-	-	-	-	-	28x5	v1B/	-
Ballynure	Toberdowney	Park James	logwood	-	-	-	-	-	16x3 16x3	osm/	-
Ballynure	Toberdowney	Park James	logwood	-	-	-	-	-	16x3x18 & 14x3x18	v1B/	-
Ballynure	Toberdowney	Rowan Jn & Sons	beetling	-	-	-	-	-	-	gr/	-
Ballynure	Toberdowney		houses	-	-	-	-	-	-	pWAM	-
Ballynure	Toberdowney		v. old ruin	-	-	-	-	-	-	pWAM	-
Blaris	Tonagh		houses	-	-	-	-	-	-	pWAM	-
Blaris	Tonagh		large mill	-	-	-	-	-	-	pWAM	-
Blaris	Tonagh		thread factory	-	-	-	-	-	-	pWAM	-
Toome	Toome	-	flax	-	-	-	-	-	-	pWSH	-
Toome	Toome	-	flax	-	-	-	-	-	-	pWSH	-
Toome	Toome	-	flax	-	-	-	-	-	-	pWSH	-
Toome	Toome	-	grain mill	-	-	-	-	-	-	pWSH	-
Toome	Toome	-	grain mill	-	-	-	-	-	-	pWSH	-
Duneane	Toome	-	scutch	-	-	-	-	-	-	pWAG	-
Ballymoney	Topp	- above Breekagh Br.	mill	-	-	-	-	-	-	1"os/	13
Ballymoney	Topp	- on Breekagh Burn	mill	-	-	-	-	-	-	1"os/	13
Ballymoney	Topp		mill	-	-	-	-	-	-	pWAM	-
Ballymoney	Topp Lower	-	flax	-	-	-	-	-	12x1.6x10	osm/	-
Ballymoney	Topp Lower	-	flax	-	-	-	-	-	11.4x1.6x8	osm/	-
Ballymoney	Topp Lower	Cathcart Matthew	flax	-	-	-	-	-	-	gr/	-
Ballymoney	Topp Lower	Henderson William	flax & rolling	-	-	-	-	-	-	v1B/	-
Antrim	Townland Co. Ant	-	saddle quern	-	-	-	-	-	-	pWAG	-
Ramoan	Townsparks R`mn	Dunlop Mrs.	corn & kiln	-	-	-	-	-	-	v1B/	-
Antrim	Townsparks sdry	-	mills / several	-	-	-	-	-	-	pWAM	-
Dunaghy	Tullaghbane	-	flax	-	-	-	-	-	-	1"os/	14
Dunaghy	Tullaghbane	-	mill	-	-	-	-	-	-	1"os/	14
Dunaghy	Tullaghbane	Hood Adam	corn & kiln	-	-	-	-	-	- machinery old	v1B/	-
Dunaghy	Tullaghbane	Hood John	corn	-	-	-	-	-	-	gr/	-
Dunaghy	Tullaghbane	Hood John	flax	-	-	-	-	-	-	gr/	-
Dunaghy	Tullaghbane	Stewart Alex	flax	-	-	-	-	-	-	v1B/	-
Dunaghy	Tullaghbane	Stewart Hugh	corn, flax & kiln	-	-	-	-	-	-	gr/	-
Dunaghy	Tullaghbane	Stewart Hugh	mill	-	-	-	Stewart Hugh - Jane	1891	-	dd/	1891 43 119
Dunaghy	Tulloughbane	-	corn & flax	-	-	-	-	-	16x4 12x2	osm/	-

PARISH	TOWNLAND	MILLER	TYPE	HOUSE	Land	£Val	PROPRIETORS	Date	WHEEL etc.	Record	Ref.
Antrim	Tullycreenaght	Frew William	flax	-	-	-	-	-	-	v1B/	-
Antrim	Tullycreenaght	Read James	flax	-	-	-	-	-	-	v1B/	-
Antrim	Tullycreenaght	unoc. / Frew John	old mill	-	-	-	-	-	-	gr/	-
Antrim	Tullycreenaghy	-	flax	-	-	-	-	-	-	6"os/	-
Skery	Tullymore	-	beetling	-	-	-	-	-	24x4	osm/	-
Skerry	Tullymore	-	corn	-	-	-	-	-	-	6"os/	-
Skery	Tullymore	-	corn	-	-	-	-	-	14x4	osm/	-
Skerry	Tullymore	Fulton Adam	beetling	-	-	-	-	-	-	v1B/	-
Skerry	Tullymore	Fulton Adam	corn & kiln	-	-	-	-	-	-	v1B/	-
Skerry	Tullymore		mill	-	-	-	-	-	-	pWAM	-
Lambeg	Tullynacross	Richardson J.N & Son:	mill pond, ld & :	-	96a.	ú167	-	-	-	gr/	-
Lambeg	Tullynacross	Richardson Jonathan	bleach works	-	97a.	ú430	-	-	-	gr/	-
Connor	Tullynamullan	McFarlane Andrew	thrashing	-	-	-	-	-	12x4.6	gr/	-
Dunaghy	Tullynewy	-	flax	-	-	-	-	-	-	6"os/	-
Dunaghy	Tullynewy	-	flax	-	-	-	-	-	14x2	osm/	-
Armoy / Raloo	Tureagh	-	flax	-	-	-	-	-	-	6"os/	-
Armoy / Raloo	Tureagh	Robinson William	flax	-	-	-	-	-	14x2.6x18	v1B/	-
Armoy	Turnarobert	-	mill	-	-	-	-	-	-	6"os/	-
Raloo	Turreagh	-	flax	-	-	-	-	-	12 x -	osm/	-
Raloo	Turreagh	Robinson William	flax	-	-	-	-	-	13x2x14	osm/	-
Finvoy	Vow	-	corn & flax	-	-	-	-	-	13x1.10 12x2.4	osm/	-
Finvoy	Vow	-	mill	-	-	-	-	-	-	6"os/	-
Finvoy	Vow	-	mills	-	-	-	-	-	-	1"os/	13
Finvoy	Vow	Harte Solomon	corn, flax & kiln	-	-	-	-	-	-	gr/	-
Finvoy	Vow	McAuley Alex	corn & kiln	-	-	-	-	-	-	v1B/	-
Finvoy	Vow	McAuley Alex	flax	-	-	-	-	-	-	v1B/	-
Kilbride	Walk Mill	Prenter Nathaniel &Co	mill pond & land	-	17a.	-	-	-	-	pWAM	-
Dunluce	Walk Mill	Warde Dav Fran	paper	-	-	-	-	-	-	v1B/	-
Kilbride	Walk Mill	Watt James	spinning factory	-	-	-	-	-	-	v1B/	-
Kilbride	Walk Mill		mill	-	-	-	-	-	-	pWAM	-
Kilbride	Walkmill	-	factory	-	-	-	-	-	-	6"os/	-
Billy	Walkmill	-	mill	-	-	-	-	-	-	6"os/	-
Ballymoney	Walkmill	-	paper	-	-	-	-	-	18x4	osm/	-
Kilbride	Walkmill	-	spinning	-	-	-	-	-	-	1"os/	28
Kilbride	Walkmill	Prenter Nathaniel A	mill pond	-	-	-	-	-	-	gr/	-
Antrim	Waterheadstown	-	beetling	-	-	-	-	-	-	1"os/	28
Carrickfergus	West Division	-	houses	-	-	-	-	-	-	pWAM	-
Carrickfergus	West Division	-	mills	-	-	-	-	-	-	pWAM	-
Templecorran	White Head	Dunan John	thrashing	-	-	-	-	-	no wheel	osm/	-
Carnmoney	White House	-	mill	-	-	-	-	-	-	pWAM	-
Carnmoney	Whiteabbey	-	cotton works	-	-	-	-	-	-	6"os/	-
Carnmoney	Whiteabbey	-	houses	-	-	-	-	-	-	pWAM	-
Carnmoney	Whiteabbey	-	mill	-	-	-	-	-	-	pWAM	-
Carnmoney	Whiteabbey	Cowan & Co.	flax spinning	-	-	-	-	-	43x5x40	v1B/	-
Carnmoney	Whiteabbey	Cowan & Reid	flax spinning	-	-	-	-	-	46x6x62	osm/	-
Carnmoney	Whiteabbey	Cowan Reps William	spinning & wv	-	-	-	-	-	-	gr/	-
Carnmoney	Whiteabbey	William Wallace	beetling, bleach	-	-	-	-	-	28x8x23	osm/	-
Culfeightrin	Whitehouse	-	scutch mill	-	-	-	-	-	-	pWAM	-
Carnmoney	Whitehouse Upr	Bells & Calvert	cotton	-	-	-	-	-	-	osm/	-
Carnmoney	Whitehouse Upr	Grimshaw Nicholas	cotton	-	-	-	-	-	-	osm/	-
Antrim	Woodburn	-	linen	-	-	-	-	-	-	1"os/	29

PARISH	TOWNLAND	MILLER	TYPE	HOUSE	Land	£Val	PROPRIETORS	Date	WHEEL etc.	Record	Ref.
Ballymore	Acton Manor	Stewart	mills	-	-	-	Stewart - Stewart	-	-	dd/	103 600 73001
Killevey	Aghayalloge	Hughes James	corn	-	-	-	-	-	-	vmb/	28
Killevy	Aghayalloge	Hughes James	corn & kiln	25x22x9 & 32x19x6 :	-	5.8	-	1836	1 pr. stones used 2 yrs.:	v1B/	244b
Kilmore	Aghory	-	flax	mill o`grown (in-access.) -						mmiS/	PW - R
Kilmore	Aghory	-	flax	-	-	-	-	2004	Jas McFadden	mmiS/	PW - Z
Kilmore	Aghory	-	corn	-	-	-	-	2004	-	mmiS/	PW - Z
Kilmore	Aghory	-	flax	-	-	-	-	-	-	6"os/	13
Kilmore	Aghory	-	flax	-	-	-	-	2004	-	mmiS/	PW - (I)
Kilmore	Aghory	-	flax	-	-	-	-	2004	-	mmiS/	PW - Z
Kilmore	Aghory	Atkinson	mills	-	-	-	Atkinson - Atkinson	-	? (not listed)	dd/	339 489 229610
Kilmore	Aghory	Atkinson John	mills	-	-	-	Atkinson Jn - Donely Robt	1786	? (not listed)	dd/	482 272 308872
Kilmore	Aghory	Atkinson John :	mills	-	-	-	Atkinson J - Glendenning :	1796	Rent Cge. 15 Oct.	dd/	517 475 339400
Kilmore	Aghory	Atkinson John :	mills	-	-	-	Atkinson J - Atkinson Wm	1809	Lse. 4 May	dd/	614 23 417346
Kilmore	Aghory	McFadden James	flax	-	-	-	-	-	16x3x15	vmb/	28
Kilmore	Aghory	McFadden James	flax	-	-	-	-	-	21x3x18 8 stocks	vmb/	28
Kilmore	Aghory	McFaden James	flax	44x29x13 & 63x28x20 :	-	12.11	-	1837	new wheel and works :	v1B/	229b
Kilmore	Aghory	McFaden James	flax mills	44x25x20, 21x25x14 :	-	12.11	-	1837	wheel & works old :	v1B/	229b
Kilmore	Aghory	Richardson	mill	-	-	-	Richardson - Coleman	-	? (not listed)	dd/	567 521 382061
Kilmore	Aghory	Williamson Robert	flax	-	-	-	-	-	20x4x12 8 stocks	vmb/	28
Kilmore	Aghory	Williamson Robert	flax	-	-	-	-	-	14x4x14 10 stocks	vmb/	28
Kilmore	Aghory	Williamson Robert	flax (f'mly corn)	50x29x17, 16x17x15 :	-	11.6	-	1837	metal wheel drives :	v1B/	229`
Kilmore	Aghory :	-	corn	-	-	-	-	-	-	6"os/	13
Kilmore	Aghory :	-	flax & dam	-	-	-	-	-	-	6"os/	13
Grange	Allistragh	-	beetling	-	-	-	-	-	-	1"os/	47
Grange	Allistragh	- on Callan R. :	beetling	-	-	-	-	-	-	6"os/	12
Grange	Allistragh	Donaldson	mills	-	-	-	Donaldson - Jones	-	?	dd/	102 415 71542
Grange	Allistragh	Donaldson	mills	-	-	-	Donaldson - Donaldson	-	?	dd/	181 13 119240
Grange	Allistragh	Farnham	mills	-	-	-	Farnham Lord - Scott	-	? (not listed)	dd/	384 89 254255
Grange	Allistragh	Hutchinson William :	mill	-	-	-	Hutchinson - Oliver Jos. :	1813	-	dd/	661 290 455110
Grange	Allistragh	McBride Robert	beetling	118x21x18, 17x30x8 :	-	7.11	-	1836	2 water wheels, fall 7ft.	v1B/	25
Grange	Allistragh	McBride Robert	bleach	-	-	-	-	-	14x4x5	vmb/	28
Grange	Allistragh	McBride Robert	corn	-	-	-	-	-	14x2x5	vmb/	28
Grange	Allistragh	McBride Robert	corn & kiln	31x25x15, 11x17x10 :	-	7.8	-	1836	supply during summer	v1B/	25
Grange	Allistragh	McBride Robert :	mill	-	-	-	McBride R - Cauldwell Eliz	1801	M. Arts. 4 Apl.	dd/	537 474 353955
Grange	Allistragh	Scott	mills	-	-	-	Scott - Smith	-	-	dd/	268 576 171503
Grange	Allistragh	Scott	mills	-	-	-	Scott - Smith	-	-	dd/	283 625 187686
Grange	Allistragh	Stringer Francis	mills	-	-	-	Stringer Fran - Greer Thos	1796	-	dd/	493 416 323621
Loughgilly	Alogly	Markey Michael	flax	-	-	-	-	-	13x4x1	vmb/	28
Armagh	Anagh	Burnside James	distillery	-	-	-	-	1782	1 still - 200g.	hcJ	lic.
Armagh	Anaghgary	Jones	mill	-	-	-	Jones - Tipping	-	-	dd/	214 732 140922
Armagh	Anaghgary	Jones Eliz Widow :	-	-	-	-	Jones E - Jones Richard :	1796	Agmt. 24 Dec.	dd/	505 612 331216
Armagh	Anaghgary	Tipping Francis :	mill	-	-	-	Tipping F - Wilde Rebecca	1798	Smt. 15 Apl.	dd/	513 291 337314
Creggan	Annaghmare	McGeough	corn & kiln	34x18x7, kiln 31x18x7	-	4.13	-	1837	- 1 pair stones :	v1B/	229a
Creggan	Annaghmore	McGeogh William	corn	-	-	-	-	-	13x2x8	vmb/	28
Kilmore	Annareagh	Greer Nathaniel	flax	-	-	-	-	-	16x3x9 6 stocks	vmb/	28
Kilmore	Annareagh	Grier Nathaniel	flax	53x22x8	-	4.9	-	1837	- 1 set rollers :	v1B/	229a
Armagh	Annavale	Kirk William	mills	-	-	-	Kirk Wm - Gardiner Wm	1880	-	dd/	1880 41 13
Armagh	Annsborough	Aicken Graves	mills	-	-	-	Aicken Graves - Chamney	1793	-	dd/	468 104 299353
Armagh	Annsborough	Ellis William	mils	-	-	-	Ellis William - Turtle James	1815	-	dd/	701 144 480668
Armagh	Annsborough	Mercer Ann	mills	-	-	-	Mercer Ann - Dixon	1795	-	dd/	490 460 315630
Armagh	Annsborough	Owens	mills	-	-	-	Owens - Ellis	-	-	dd/	582 292 393654
Loughgall	Ardressel	Alexander Jno	mill	-	-	-	Alexander J - Bell David :	1788	Conv. 17 Nov.	dd/	403 122 265571

PARISH	TOWNLAND	MILLER	TYPE	HOUSE	Land	£Val	PROPRIETORS	Date	WHEEL etc.	Record	Ref.
Loughgall	Ardressel	Walker	mill	-	-	-	Walker - Ensor	-	-	dd/	330 360 223418
Armagh	Armagh	McCully Robert	distillery	-	-	-	-	1782	1 still - 238g.	hcJ	lic.
Armagh	Armagh	McWilliams James	distillery	-	-	-	-	1782	1 still - 243g.	hcJ	lic.
Armagh	Armagh	Stringer Thomas	distillery	-	-	-	-	1782	1 still - 268g.	hcJ	lic.
Armagh	Armagh :	Jackson John	wind mill & kiln	dia. 25ft., height 52ft. :	-	11.0	-	1835	-	v1B/	21a/b
Armagh	Armagh :	Henchey Pat	coach factory	15x44x16 & 17x9x13	-	6.0	-	1835	-	v1B/	21a/b
Armagh	Armagh :	Lyle Andrew & Alex	brewery & kiln	95x26x17, 11x13x14 :	-	41.4	-	1835	in good working conditic	v1B/	21a/b
Armagh	Armagh :	Vogan Dr.	flour	47x28x52, 77x23x16 :	-	40.0	-	1835	-	v1B/	21a/b
Armagh	Armagh Town	-	mill	-	-	-	-	-	-	1"os/	47
Armagh	Armagh Town	-	Umgola Mills	-	-	-	-	-	-	1"os/	47
Armagh	Armagh Town	Ulster Bank Co.	old brewery	-	-	-	-	1895	-	dd/	1895 32 162
Armagh	Armagh Town :	Moore William	flour	-	-	-	Moore William - Andrew	1836	-	dd/	1836 6 217
Armagh	Armagh Town :	Campbell Henry	old brewery	-	-	-	Campbell Henry - U B Co	1895	-	dd/	1895 32 162
Drumcree	Artabrackagh	Robinson James	corn & kiln	23x19x14, kiln 46x21x9	-	2.2	-	1836	1 pr. sts., 1 new, 1 worn	v1B/	226a
Drumcree	Artabracken	Robinson James	corn	-	-	-	-	-	12x3x5	vmb/	28
Armagh	Aughariel	Atkinson John :	mill	-	-	-	Atkinson J - Peebles Benj :	1814	-	dd/	713 547 488282
Clogher	Augher	Ley George	distillery	-	-	-	-	1782	1 still - 230g.	hcJ	lic.
Clogher	Augher	Richarson William	distillery	-	-	-	-	1782	1 still - 215g.	hcJ	lic.
Clogher	Augher	Scott William	distillery	-	-	-	-	1782	1 still - 218g.	hcJ	lic.
Clogher	Augher Town	Brockman Edward	mill & grist	-	-	-	Brockman - Ankettell F`m	1879	-	dd/	1879 47 272
Clogher	Augher Town	Bunbery Emily R	mill, grist & toll	-	-	-	Bunbury - Ankettell F`mne	1877	-	dd/	1877 49 204
Clogher	Augher Town	Bunbury Diana R	Mill of Augher	-	-	-	Bunbury - Ankettell F`mne	1878	-	dd/	1878 24 262
Armagh	Augher Town	Bunbury James	Mill of Augher	-	-	-	Bunbury Sir James - John	1835	-	dd/	1835 15 71
Clogher	Augher Town	Bunbury John A	miller`s ho & gdn	-	-	-	Bunbury - Ankettell F`mne	1876	-	dd/	1876 35 246
Clogher	Augher Town	Moutray John	mill, grist & toll	-	-	-	Moutray - Ankettell F`mne	1878	-	dd/	1878 12 74
Clogher	Augher Town	Moutray Whitney	Shillin Mill & :	-	-	-	Moutray - Ankettell F`mne	1878	-	dd/	1878 12 75
Clogher	Augher Town	Murray Abraham	mill	-	-	-	Murray - Bunbury Mervyn	1876	-	dd/	1876 37 187
Clogher	Augher Town	Tenner John K Jun	mill	-	-	-	Tenner Jn - Hurst Francis	1878	-	dd/	1878 45 297
Grange	Aughnacloy	Cochran John	distillery	-	-	-	-	1782	1 still - 220g.	hcJ	lic.
Grange	Aughnacloy	Jackson Robert Jun. :	mill	-	-	-	Jackson R - Pringle Mcl :	1819	-	dd/	741 268 504803
Grange	Aughnacloy	Montgomery Thomas	distillery	-	-	-	-	1782	1 still - 238g.	hcJ	lic.
Grange	Aughnacloy	Reilly James	distillery	-	-	-	-	1782	1 still - 208g.	hcJ	lic.
Keady	Aughnagurgan	-	flax	-	-	-	-	-	-	1"os/	59
Keady	Aughnagurgan	Kidd Samuel	beetling	-	-	-	-	-	19x5x16	vmb/	28
Keady	Aughnagurgan	Kidd Samuel	beetling	-	-	-	-	-	16x4x14	vmb/	28
Keady	Aughnagurgan	Kidd Samuel	bleach	-	-	-	-	-	18x4x16 drives 2 beams	vmb/	28
Keady	Aughnagurgan	Kidd Samuel A	beetling	79x28x28, 67x22x18 & :	-	21.2	-	1836	19x5x14 7 16x4x14 :	v1B/	26c/d
Keady	Aughnagurgan	Kidd Samuel A	bleach & beelting	35x22x14, 51x28x18 & :	-	11.18	-	1836	18x4x16 4 sets beetles	v1B/	26c/d
Keady	Aughnagurgan	Morrison James :	bleach	- & offices	-	130	-	-	-	gr	-
Armagh	Aughover	Peebles Benjamin :	mills	-	-	-	Peebles B - Pebles Harris :	1819	Mort. 28 Aug.	dd/	744 157 586492
Eglish	Ballaghy	-	corn	-	-	-	-	-	-	6"os/	12
Eglish	Ballaghy	-	corn	-	-	-	-	-	-	6"os/	12
Eglish	Ballaghy	-	flax	-	-	-	-	-	-	6"os/	12
Eglish	Ballaghy	Armstrong George	flour	-	-	-	-	-	16x4x14	vmb/	28
Eglish	Ballaghy	Armstrong George	flour	56x23x31	-	6.19	-	1836	18x23x26 overshot :	v1B/	24
Eglish	Ballaghy	Carson Thomas	flax	-	-	-	-	-	14x5x8 6 berths	vmb/	28
Eglish	Ballaghy	Carson Thomas	flax	45x20x14	-	3.12	-	1836	17x3x4 new wheel	v1B/	24
Eglish	Ballaghy	Carson Thomas	flax	ho., offices & land	22a.	32	-	1856	-	gr/	a.a.Ire.ie
Eglish	Ballaghy	Hagan Pat	corn	45x22x22 & 33x18x15	-	5.12	-	1836	16x3x4 2 pair stones :	v1B/	24
Eglish	Ballaghy	Hagan Patrick	corn	-	-	-	-	-	16x3x10	vmb/	28
Eglish	Ballaghy	Knipe Thomas	corn	(mill unfinished) & land	0-2-0	15	-	1856	-	gr/	a.a.Ire.ie
Eglish	Ballaghy	Land Judges	mill	-	-	-	Land Judges - Edgar Jas	1881	-	dd/	1881 9 169

PARISH	TOWNLAND	MILLER	TYPE	HOUSE	Land	£Val	PROPRIETORS	Date	WHEEL etc.	Record	Ref.
Lisnadill	Balleer	-	flax	-	-	-	-	-	-	6"os/	16
Lisnadill	Balleer	Boyd James	bleaching	-	-	-	-	-	15x4x9	vmb/	28
Lisnadill	Balleer	Ferguson Thomas	mills	-	-	-	Ferguson Thos - Stitt Alex	1886	-	dd/	1886 8 231
Lisnadill	Balleer	McMahon John	flax	34x24x17 & 9x9x6	-	6.12	-	1837	22x4x16 drives 6 stocks	v1B/	2411
Lisnadill	Balleer	McMahon Johnston	flax	-	-	-	-	-	22x4x16 6 stocks	vmb/	28
Lisnadill	Balleer	McMahon Johnston	flax	-	-	-	-	2002	5 blade fmly beetling	mmSv/	- Z
Lisnadill	Balleer	Rusk William	beetling	-	-	-	-	-	13x4x3	vmb/	28
Lisnadill	Balleer	Rusk William	beetling	44x22x17, 18x22x8 & :	-	4.6	-	1837	14x3x8 depth bucket 1ft	v1B/	211
Armagh	Ballinaclosh	Eastwood Francis :	mills	-	-	-	Eastwood F - Page John :	1785	M.Smt./ Rel. 15 Jan.	dd/	360 577 245198
Armagh	Ballinaclosh	Eastwood John :	mills	-	-	-	Eastwood - Johnston Jn :	1779	Lse. 22 Nov.	dd/	363 464 245199
Armagh	Ballinaclosh	Eastwood Samuel	mills	-	-	-	Eastwood, Sam - James	-	-	dd/	472 381 301685
Armagh	Ballinaclosh	Majoriebanks	mills	-	-	-	Majoriebanks - Buxton	-	??	dd/	505 455 324511
Newry	Ballinlare :	Boyd Samuel	brewery	95x18x18, 13x26x15 & :	-	77	-	1836	-	v1B/	246a
Newry	Ballinlare :	Guy George	Corn Market	33x63x12 & 19x30x12	-	24.0	-	1836	-	v1B/	246a
Newry	Ballinlare :	Davis Thomas	ofices	67x22x15, 38x29x18 & :	-	23.0	-	1836	-	v1B/	246a
Newry	Ballinlare :	Henry William	brewery	29x23x34, 38x22x14 & :	-	-	-	1836	-	v1B/	246b
Newry	Ballinlare :	Henry William	brewery	malt ho. 100x21x16 & :	-	57.1	-	1836	-	v1B/	246b
Newry	Ballinlare :	Russell Arthur	brewery	brew ho. 72x42x20 & :	-	52.16	-	1836	-	v1B/	246b
Killevey	Ballinliss	Cromey Thomas	corn	-	-	-	-	-	-	vmb/	28
Killevy	Ballinliss	Cromie James	corn & kiln	27x21x11 & kiln :	-	8.5.0	-	1836	- 1 pair stones :	v1B/	244b
Lisnadill	Ballyards	Ballyards Bleach Wks	mill	-	-	-	-	-	-	6"os/	16
Lisnadill	Ballyards	Barnes & Simpson	flour	-	-	-	-	-	16x5x8 18x4x8	vmb/	28
Lisnadill	Ballyards	Barnes George	flour & kiln	42x27x40, 27x18x18 :	-	44.18	-	1836	16x4x8 & 16x4x8 :	v1B/	27
Lisnadill	Ballyards	James McQuay	beetling	-	-	-	-	-	15x3x8 drives :	vmb/	28
Lisnadill	Ballyards	James McQuay	bleach	-	-	-	-	-	17x5x8 drives :	vmb/	28
Lisnadill	Ballyards	James McQuay	bleach	-	-	-	-	-	16x3x8 drives :	vmb/	28
Lisnadill	Ballyards	Kirk William	bleach	81x21x19, 23x22x11 :	-	34.2	-	1836	-	v1B/	27
Lisnadill	Ballyards	Macquay James	bleach	56x17x17, 30x17x8 & :	-	45	-	1836	-	v1B/	27
Lisnadill	Ballyards	Maxwell Margaret	mill	-	-	-	Maxwell Margt - Simpson	-	-	dd/	126 837 87542
Lisnadill	Ballyards	Maxwell Margaret	mill	-	-	-	Maxwell Margt - Simpson	-	-	dd/	128 454 87546?
Lisnadill	Ballyards	Parker Samuel :	bleach & m/cy	-	-	-	Parker S - Carroll Edward :	1811	-	dd/	455 257 451345
Lisnadill	Ballyards	Simpson	mill	-	-	-	Simpson - Simpson	-	-	dd/	706 229 490185
Lisnadill	Ballyards	Simpson Thomas :	mill	-	-	-	Simpson T - Simpson Jn :	1816	Mort. 7 Sep.	dd/	706 288 483763
Lisnadill	Ballyards	Stephenson	mill	-	-	-	Strphenson - Stephenson	-	-	dd/	135 295 90564
Lisnadill	Ballyards district	Kirk William	Bleach Green	-	-	-	Kirk Wm - Gardiner Wm	1881	-	dd/	1881 41 19
Kilmore	Ballybreagh	-	flax	-	-	-	-	2004	-	mmiS/	PW - Z
Kilmore	Ballybreagh	-	flax & pond	-	-	-	-	-	-	6"os/	13
Kilmore	Ballybreagh	Neill Mrs	flax	old mill 27x20x5 & :	-	1.4.4	-	1837	- 6 metal stocks :	v1B/	229b
Kilmore	Ballybreagh	Neill Widow	flax	-	-	-	-	-	16x4x9 6 stocks	vmb/	28
Lisnadill	Ballybrolly	Henry George	flax	-	-	-	-	-	22x4x - 10 stocks	vmb/	28
Lisnadill	Ballybrolly	Henry John	flax	55x24x18 & 19x29x10	-	11.13	-	1837	22x4 drives10 stocks :	v1B/	211
Lisnadill	Ballybrolly	Wilson Samuel	mill reservoir	- land waste -	1.1.20		-	1856	-	gr/	a.a.Ire.ie
Armagh	Ballycargan	Mandeville Viscount	mills	-	-	-	Mandeville Visc - Harison :	1885	-	dd/	1885 16 135
Armagh	Ballycrummy	Gainford George	distillery	80x21x20, 14x16x14 :	-	25.9	-	1835	-	v1B/	21a
Armagh	Ballycrummy :	Kidd Messrs	distillery	-	-	-	-	-	16x3x6	vmb/	28
Armagh	Ballycrummy :	-	distillery	-	-	-	-	-	-	6"os/	12
Loughgilly	Ballydogherty	-	corn	-	-	-	-	-	-	6"os/	22
Loughgilly	Ballydogherty	-	flax	-	-	-	-	-	-	6"os/	22
Loughgilly	Ballydogherty	Caldwell Robert	flax	-	-	-	-	-	12x4x4	vmb/	28
Loughgilly	Ballydogherty	Gracy Robert	corn	-	-	-	-	-	13x3x13	vmb/	28
Loughgilly	Ballydogherty	Gracy Robert	flax	-	-	-	-	-	14x3x14	vmb/	28
Loughgilly	Ballydogherty	Hanna Hugh	corn	-	-	-	-	-	16x2x20	vmb/	28

PARISH	TOWNLAND	MILLER	TYPE	HOUSE	Land	£Val	PROPRIETORS	Date	WHEEL etc.	Record	Ref.
Loughgilly	Ballydogherty	Hanna John	corn & kiln & flax	44x23x19 & 18x24x6 :	-	6.7.0	-	1836	wooden 2 pair stones :	v1B/	219
Seagoe	Ballydonaghy	Joyce Thomas	flax	64x19x14	-	4.14	-	1836	no water, mill not used	v1B/	222
Loughgall	Ballygasey	Jackson Wiliam	corn & kiln	46x28x19 & kiln :	-	17.4	-	1837	18x4x6 3 pair stones :	v1B/	230
Loughgall	Ballygasey	Jackson William	corn	-	-	-	-	-	18x4x18	vmb/	28
Loughgall	Ballygasey	Jackson William	corn & kiln	17x20x14, 16x20x15 :	-	15.2	-	1837	18x4x16 3 pr. stones :	v1B/	230
Forkhill	Ballykeel	Delaney William	corn	-	-	-	-	-	-	vmb/	28
Forkhill	Ballykeel	Delany William	corn & kiln	37x19x11 & kiln :	-	4.0.0	-	1836	- 1 pair stones :	v1B/	247
Forkhill	Ballykeel Bridge	-	flax	-	-	-	-	-	-	1"os/	59
Grange	Ballyknick	- nr Bonds Bridge	mill	-	-	-	-	-	-	1"os/	47
Kilclooney	Ballylane	Black Samuel	mill	-	-	-	Black S - Wiliamson Jas	1886	-	dd/	1886 44 12
Kilclooney	Ballylane	Harcourt	mill	-	-	-	Harcourt - Harcourt	-	-	dd/	488 475 311872
Kilcloney	Ballylane	Leeper William	flax	-	-	-	-	-	14x4x8 6 berths	vmb/	28
Kilclooney	Ballylane	Leeper William	flax	24x19x6 & 31x18x6	-	3.15	-	1837	14x4x8 drives 6 stocks	v1B/	210a
Kilcloney	Ballylane	Martin S & I	flax	-	-	-	-	-	15x3x8	vmb/	28
Kilclooney	Ballylane	Martin Samuel & Jn	flax	23x19x8, 24x18x8 & :	-	3.7.0	-	1837	15x3x8 drives 4 stocks	v1B/	210a
Kilclooney	Ballylane	Richardson William	mill	-	-	-	Richardson - Langtry Jno :	1806	Lse. 1 Nov.	dd/	596 426 408375
Kilclooney	Ballylane	Woodhouse	mill	-	-	-	Woodhouse - Walker	-	-	dd/	447 178 286524
Kilmore	Ballyloughan	Andrews Robert :	mill	-	-	-	Andrews R - Patten Dav :	1787	Rel. 8 Jan.	dd/	413 143 231135
Kilmore	Ballyloughan	Andrews	mill	-	-	-	Andrews - Patton	-	?	dd/	415 126 273031
Kilmore	Ballyloughan	Andrews	mill	-	-	-	Andrews - Andrews	-	-	dd/	427 402 279257
Kilmore	Ballyloughan	Andrews Joseph	mill	-	-	-	Andrews J - Greer James :	1810	Lse. 19 Apl.	dd/	623 294 428268
Kilmore	Ballyloughan	Ballantine Adam	flax	20x27x5	-	4.2.0	-	1836	- 4 stocks & :	v1B/	229b
Kilmore	Ballyloughan	Hoey James	flax	-	-	-	-	-	14x3x5 6 stocks	vmb/	28
Kilmore	Ballyloughan	McQuillan Ephraim	mill	-	35a.	-	McQuillan - Thompson Jn	1794	-	dd/	480 485 305763
Kilmore	Ballyloughan	Thompson Jno :	mill	-	-	-	Thompson J - Orr James :	1798	Asgt. 1 Nov.	dd/	521 891 339926
Kilmore	Ballyloughan	Thompson William	flax	24x19x6	-	-	-	1837	- 6 stocks :	v1B/	229b
Armagh	Ballymacranagan	Sparrow Milicent :	mill	-	-	-	Sparrow M - Blacker Sam :	1819	-	dd/	752 152 511287
Armagh	Ballymahon More	Dobbin Leo	corn	-	-	-	-	-	20x4x18	vmb/	28
Armagh	Ballymahon More	Matthews Joseph	flour	-	-	-	-	-	14x4x12	vmb/	28
Lisnadill	Ballymoran	-	mill	-	-	-	-	-	-	1"os/	47
Lisnadill	Ballymoran	McKinstry James	corn	-	-	-	-	-	17x4x13	vmb/	28
Lisnadill	Ballymoran	McKinstry James	corn & kiln	41x20x12, 13x12x8 & :	-	12.10	-	1837	16x3x13 2 pr. stones :	v1B/	211
Lisnadill	Ballymoran :	-	corn	-	-	-	-	-	-	6"os/	16
Ballymore	Ballymore :	Mairs Jeremiah	corn kiln & store	19x19x18, store :	-	35.11	-	1836	-	v1B/	15
Creggan	Ballynaclosha	Crilly Thomas	corn & kiln	39x22x21 & kiln :	-	5.4.3	-	1837	- 3 pair stones :	v1B/	240a
Creggan	Ballynaclosha	Crilly Thomas	corn	-	-	-	-	-	15x2x15 3 pair stones	vmb/	28
Creggan	Ballynaclosha	Eastwood Samuel	mills	-	-	-	Eastwood Sam - James :	1793	-	dd/	472 381 301685
Lisnadill	Ballynagalliagh	-	beetling	-	-	-	-	-	-	1"os/	47
Seagoe	Ballynaghy	Blacker William :	mill	-	-	-	Blacker W - Hunter Dav :	1744	Lse. 25 Jul.	dd/	147 39 98651
Seagoe	Ballynaghy	Blacker	mill	-	-	-	Blacker - Mathers	-	-	dd/	199 250 132116
Seagoe	Ballynaghy	Joyce Thomas	corn	-	-	-	-	-	14x2x17 3 pr st	vmb/	28
Seagoe	Ballynaghy	Joyce Thomas	corn & kiln	29x19x11, 17x20x12 :	-	4.0.8	-	1836	- new stones old m/cy	v1B/	222
Seagoe	Ballynaghy	Joyce Thomas	flax	-	-	-	-	-	16x3x16 6 stocks	vmb/	28
Seagoe	Ballynaghy	Joyce Thomas	flax	49x19x14	-	5.13	-	1836	- 3 pairs stocks :	v1B/	222
Seagoe	Ballynaghy	Mathers	mill	-	-	-	Mathers - Tade	-	-	dd/	214 345 141438
Seagoe	Ballynaghy	Wakefield	mill	-	-	-	Wakefield - Phelps	-	-	dd/	445 460 285891
Lisnadill	Ballynahone	Bell	mill	-	-	-	Bell - Glenny	-	-	dd/	192 346 127908
Lisnadill	Ballynahone	Hall	mill	-	-	-	Hall & wife - Jackson	-	-	dd/	281 349 186831
Lisnadill	Ballynahone	Hill	mill	-	-	-	Hill - Mee	-	-	dd/	526 352 344727
Lisnadill	Ballynahone	Scott	mill	-	-	-	Scott - Kidd	-	-	dd/	611 510 419394
Lisnadill	Ballynahone	Tullamore Charles W	mill	-	-	-	Tullamore - Atkinson Ed :	1799	15 Feb.	dd/	519 147 338492
Lisnadill	Ballynahone Beg	Jackson Robert :	bl. green & mill	-	-	-	Jackson, Oliver & Seaver :	1782	27 Sep.	dd/	360 236 242429

PARISH	TOWNLAND	MILLER	TYPE	HOUSE	Land	£Val	PROPRIETORS	Date	WHEEL etc.	Record	Ref.
Lisnadill	Ballynahone Beg	Jackson Robert :	bleach green	-	-	-	Jackson R - Waugh John	-	-	dd/	724 472 494807
Lisnadill	Ballynahone Beg	Kid Thomas Osborne	distillery	22x26x12, 62x21x40 :	-	48.11	-	1836	- good supply water:	v1B/	27
Lisnadill	Ballynahone Beg	Kidd T O	malt & distillery	-	-	-	-	-	20x5x7	vmb/	28
Lisnadill	Ballynahone Beg	Mazur Barth	bl. green & mill	-	-	-	Mazur Barth - Prentice	-	-	dd/	461 392 296013
Lisnadill	Ballynahone Beg	M'Williams George	thrashing	house, offs., & land	148a.	225	-	1856	-	gr/	a.a.lre.ie
Lisnadill	Ballynahone Beg	Oliver	bl. green & mill	-	-	-	Oliver - Jaskson	-	-	dd/	404 2 264884
Lisnadill	Ballynahone Beg	Oliver John	bl. green & mill	-	-	-	Oliver John - Scott John :	1796	Lse. 1 Apl.	dd/	510 33 328019
Lisnadill	Ballynahone Beg	Oliver Jn, Mary, Eliz.	bl. green & mill	-	-	-	Oliver John - Scott John :	1797	17 Jan.	dd/	506 95 328017
Lisnadill	Ballynahone Beg	Oliver Mary & Eliz :	bl. green & mill	-	-	-	Oliver M & E - Scott John :	1796	Lse. 1 Apl.	dd/	510 33 328019
Armagh	Ballynahone Beg	Pepper	mill	-	-	-	Pepper - Scott	-	-	dd/	642 461 457890
Armagh	Ballynahone Beg	Pepper	mill	-	-	-	Pepper - Scott	-	-	dd/	642 461 457890?
Lisnadill	Ballynahone Beg	Price	bl. green & mill	-	-	-	Price - Jackson	-	-	dd/	384 123 254319
Lisnadill	Ballynahone Beg	Seaver Sarah :	bl. green & mill	-	-	-	Seaver S - Bradford Jas ;	1884	Mort. 10 Feb.	dd/	360 85 241557
Lisnadill	Ballynahone Beg	Seaver Sarah	bl. green & mill	-	-	-	Seaver Sarah - Jackson	1793	-	dd/	464 414 296474
Armagh	Ballynahone More	- near B`nahone Ho.	corn	-	-	-	-	-	-	6"os/	12
Armagh	Ballynahone More	Dobbin Leonard	corn	45x57x32, 37x38x21 :	-	30.14	-	1836	21x4x15 water supply	v1B/	21a
Armagh	Ballynahone More	Levingston Robert :	mill	-	-	-	Levingston - Williams Wm	1813	Conv. 23 Oct.	dd/	665 260 458990
Armagh	Ballynahone More	Mathews Joseph	flour	14x18x15, 17x18x25 :	-	27.1	-	1837	14x5x15 water supply	v1B/	242b
Armagh	Ballynahone More	Whittington	mill	-	-	-	Whittington - Prentice	-	-	dd/	664 570 459237
Armagh	Ballynahone More		flour	-	-	-	-	-	-	6"os/	12
Newt`nhamilton	Ballynarea	Garmoney Hugh	corn	-	-	-	-	-	4x2x8	vmb/	28
Newt`nhamilton	Ballynarea	Garmoney Hugh	corn & kiln	40x20x9 & kiln :	-	4.0.0	-	1836	- 1 pair stones :	v1B/	242 a/b
Mullabrack	Ballynewry	-	corn	-	-	-	-	-	-	6"os/	13
Mullaghbrack	Ballynewry	Atkinson Benjamin	flax	-	-	-	-	-	14x3x5	vmb/	28
Mullabrack	Ballynewry	Atkinson Benjamin	flax	53x19x6	-	1..7.3	-	1837	16x4x5 4 stocks & :	v1B/	213
Mullaghbrack	Ballynewry	Quin Arthur	corn	-	-	-	-	-	16x4x10	vmb/	28
Mullabrack	Ballynewry	Quin Arthur	corn & kiln	26x21x20 & 11x10x6 :	-	4.13	-	1837	16x4x10 2 pairs stones	v1B/	213
Ballymore	Ballysheil Beg	- NE/ Clare Bridge	old bleach mill	-	-	-	-	1845	-	6"os/	13
Ballymore	Ballysheil Beg	Harden Robert	old bleach mill	42x22x18x& 23x22x9	-	3.17	-	1836	-	v1B/	214
Ballymore	Ballyshiel Beg	Langtree James	flax	49x21x6	-	5.9.0	-	1836	- 6 berths :	v1B/	214
Ballymore	Ballyshiel Beg	Langtree John	flax	-	-	-	-	-	16x3x13 6 berths	vmb/	28
Ballymore	Ballyshiel More	Hamilton George	flax	-	-	-	-	-	21x3x13 6 berths	vmb/	28
Ballymore	Ballyshiel More	Hamilton George	flax	33x19x8	-	3.11	-	1836	- 6 berths :	v1B/	214
Lisnadill	Baltarnan	-	mill	-	-	-	-	-	-	1"os/	47
Lisnadill	Baltarran	Hughes James	corn	-	-	-	-	-	14x3x6	vmb/	28
Lisnadill	Baltarran	Hughes James	corn	41x23x12	-	5.11	-	1836	14x3x7 supply "scanty"	v1B/	29b
Lisnadill	Baltarran	Hughes Patrick	mills	-	-	-	Hughes Partick - William	1881	-	dd/	1882 16 140
Lisnadill	Baltarran :	stream to Callan R.	corn	-	-	-	-	-	-	6"os/	12
Tynan	Balteagh	Armstrong Thos Knox	corn	25x20x16, 20x19x25 :	-	23.14	-	1836	15x4x12 good supply	v1B/	29b
Tynan	Balteagh	Knox & Armstrong	corn	-	-	-	-	-	15x4x11	vmb/	28
Tynan	Balteagh	Robertson John	corn & flax	house, offs. & land	101a.	250	-	1856	-	gr/	a.a.lre.ie
Armagh	Bessbrook	-	weaving	-	-	-	-	-	-	1"os/	59
Clonfeacle	Blackwatertown	Harrington John :	mill	-	-	-	Harrington - Read James :	1815	? ?	dd/	698 266 478981
Ballymore	Brannock	Bennett John	corn	-	-	-	-	-	15x2x15	vmb/	28
Ballymore	Brannock	Carrothers Alex	corn	26x24x13	-	2.0.0	-	1836	- 1 pair stones :	v1B/	214
Ballymore	Brannock	Crothers Thomas :	mills	-	-	-	Crothers - Stewart Alex :	1789	Asgt. 2 Dec.	dd/	411 462 272200
Ballymore	Brannock	Sheals Neal & Michae	mills	-	-	-	Sheals N - Doran Peter :	1800	Asgt. Mort. 24 Mar	dd/	528 476 347425
Armagh	Brook	McKenna James	distillery	-	-	-	-	1782	1 still - 241g.	hcJ	lic.
Armagh	Brook	M'Guire Thomas	distillery	-	-	-	-	1782	1 still - 321g.	hcJ	lic.
Derrynoose	Broughan	-	flax	-	-	-	-	-	-	6"os/	16
Derrynoose	Broughan	- nar Cowser`s Br.	paper	-	-	-	-	-	-	6"os/	16
Derrynoose	Broughan	Girvan Mary	beetling	-	-	-	-	-	15x3x6	vmb/	28

PARISH	TOWNLAND	MILLER	TYPE	HOUSE	Land	£Val	PROPRIETORS	Date	WHEEL etc.	Record	Ref.
Derrynoose	Broughan	McCullough Joseph	paper	-	-	-	-	-	14x2x7	vmb/	28
Mullabrack	Bryandrum	Gray John	flax	36x15x6, 11x12x5 & :	-	1.1.0	-	1837	15x4x6 6 new stocks :	v1B/	242a/b
Mullaghbrack	Bryandrum	Grey John	flax	-	-	-	-	-	15x4x5	vmb/	28
Armagh	Calan River	Thompson Livingston	use of water	-	-	-	Thompson L - King Mcl	1880	-	dd/	1880 44 12
Newt`nhamilton	Camly Ball	Walsh Thomas	corn	-	-	-	-	-	14x2x14	vmb/	28
Newt`nhamilton	Camlyball	Mulligan Qwen	corn & kiln	17x18x12 & kiln :	-	2.13	-	1836	-	v1B/	242b
Newt`nhamilton	Camlyball	Walsh Thomas	corn & kiln	34x18x12	-	4.15	-	1837	- 1 pair stones :	v1B/	242a/b
Armagh	Carnally	McCullough John	mills	-	-	-	McCullough - MacGeough	1886	-	dd/	1886 51 30
Loughgilly	Carrickananny	Patten Wm & Sarah	flax	32x22x7	-	19/1	-	1837	15x3 4 berths :	v1B/	245a
Loughgilly	Carrickananny	Patterson Sarah	flax	-	-	-	-	-	15x3x12	vmb/	28
Eglish	Carrickaness	Cross Richard	corn	-	-	-	-	-	14x2x6	vmb/	28
Eglish	Carrickaness	Cross Richard	corn & kiln	29x25x22, 17x17x27 :	-	8.11	-	1837	shelling wheel 14x2x6	v1B/	236
Eglish	Carrickaness	Cross Richard	flax	-	-	-	-	-	13x3x5 6 berths	vmb/	28
Eglish	Carrickaness	Cross Richard	flax	-	-	-	-	-	13x4x4 4 berths	vmb/	28
Eglish	Carrickaness	Cross Richard	flax	46x24x7	-	2.4.7	-	1838	13x3x5 6 stocks & :	v1B/	236
Eglish	Carrickaness	Cross Richard	flax	41x20x7	-	1.5	-	1838	13x4x3 4 stocks & :	v1B/	236
Keady	Carrickduff	Allen Joseph	corn	-	-	-	-	-	16x4x13	vmb/	28
Keady	Carrickduff	Allen Joseph	corn & kiln	31x23x15 & kiln :	-	10.4	-	1837	16x4x13 2 pr. stones	v1B/	237
Keady	Carrickduff	Irwin William A	mill	-	-	-	Irwin W - Walker Richd E	1880	-	dd/	1880 22 18
Loughgilly	Carrickgallogly	Markey Michael	flax	28x19x7	-	18/2	-	1837	good wheel dia. 14ft. :	v1B/	45a
Forkhill	Carrigans	Smith Bernard	corn	-	-	-	-	-	-	vmb/	28
Loughgilly	Carrinane	Toner Loughlin	flax	-	-	-	-	-	14x3x14 8 stocks	vmb/	28
Forkill	Carrive	-	mill	-	-	-	-	-	-	1"os/	70
Derrynoose	Carryhugh	Hall Willaim	flax	-	-	-	-	-	-	vmb/	28
Derrynoose	Carryhugh	Hall William	flax	23x20x20, 27x20x10 :	-	4.5.0	-	1836	- 4 stocks :	v1B/	23
Forkhill	Cashel	Donnelly Michael	corn & kiln	35x19x11 & kiln :	-	4.15	-	1836	- 1 pair stones :	v1B/	247
Forkhill	Cashel	McDonnell Michael	corn	-	-	-	-	-	-	vmb/	28
Kilclooney	Claddymore	Gass William	flax	27x17x6 & 20x13x8	-	1.2.1	-	1837	15x3 o'shot 4 stocks	v1B/	210a
Kilclooney	Claddymore	Gass William Jnr.	corn & kiln	42x22x15, 18x14x7 & :	-	9.12	-	1837	14x2 drives 1 pr. stones	v1B/	210a
Kilclooney	Claddymore	McMurdry Thomas	bleach	40x21x13 & 32x20x8	-	1.18	-	1837	mill no longer in use :	v1B/	210a
Kilcloney	Cladymore	Gass William	flax	-	-	-	-	-	16x3x16	vmb/	28
Kilcloney	Cladymore	Gass Wm & Son	corn	-	-	-	-	-	14x2x -	vmb/	28
Mullaghbrack	Clarbane	Donaghy Terence	corn	-	-	-	-	-	14x2x3	vmb/	28
Creggan	Clarbane	Donaghy terence	corn & kiln	31xs18x7, kiln 23x14x6	-	3.13	-	1837	- 1 pair stones :	v1B/	240
Ballymore	Clare	-	mill	-	-	-	-	-	-	1"os/	47
Ballymore	Clare	McCleland William	corn & kiln	33x24x23 & 24x10x7 :	-	6.16	-	1836	wooden wheel, 1 pr. sts	v1B/	214
Ballymore	Clare	McCleland William	flax	33x25x18, 29x6x5 & :	-	10.15	-	1836	- 8 berths :	v1B/	214
Ballymore	Clare	McClelland William	corn	-	-	-	-	-	16x4x5	vmb/	28
Ballymore	Clare	McClelland William	flax	-	-	-	-	-	14x3x6 12 stocks :	vmb/	28
Ballymore	Clare	McClelland William	mills, water, grist	-	-	-	McClelland Wm - Robert	1881	-	dd/	1881 37 294
Ballymore	Clare	McClelland William	mills, water, grist	-	-	-	McClelland Wm - Margt	1881	-	dd/	1881 37 296
Ballymore	Clare	McClelland William	mills, water, grist	-	-	-	McClelland Wm - Agnes	1881	-	dd/	1881 37 298
Ballymore	Clare	McConnell Joseph	:mill	-	-	-	McConnell J - Atkinson Wn	1816	-	dd/	701 122 480647
Ballymore	Clare	Pepper Jonathan :	mills	-	-	-	Pepper J - Patton George :	1819	-	dd/	746 334 507869
Ballymore	Clare	Trotter Robert	mills, water & gris	-	-	-	Trotter R - McClelland Wm	1881	-	dd/	1881 37 293
Ballymore	Clare Town	-	bleach & corn :	-	-	-	-	2004	-	mmiS/	PW - D
Ballymore	Clare Town :	-	old bleach mill	-	-	-	-	-	-	6"os/	13
Killevey	Clogharavan	Carter & Knox	old spade mill	-	-	-	-	-	16x6x12	vmb/	28
Killevey	Clogharavan	Carter & Knox	spinning	-	-	-	-	-	20x6x18 drives :	vmb/	28
Killevey	Clogharavan	Nicholson Joseph	spinning	-	-	-	-	-	40x18x38 drives :	vmb/	28
Killevy	Clogharevan	Carter & Knox M/s	spinning factory	76x19x7, 114x26x18 :	-	37.0	-	1836	-	v1B/	244b
Killevy	Clogharevan	Jennings Andrew	spade	50x26x8	-	1.15	-	1836	mill no longer in use :	v1B/	244b

PARISH	TOWNLAND	MILLER	TYPE	HOUSE	Land	£Val	PROPRIETORS	Date	WHEEL etc.	Record	Ref.
Killevy	Clogharevan	Nicholson Joseph	spinning factory	46x23x19, 56x20x16 :	-	37.0	-	1836	-	v1B/	244b
Killevey	Cloghreagh	Bell John	flax	-	-	-	-	-	20x5x20 16 stocks	vmb/	28
Killevy	Cloghreagh	Bell John	log wood mill	-	-	-	-	1836	-	v1B/	244b
Killevey	Cloghreagh	Bell John	logwood/ starch	-	-	-	-	-	18x4x18	vmb/	28
Killevy	Cloghreagh	Bell John	starch m'factory	-	-	3.15	-	1836	-	v1B/	244b
Loughgall	Clonmain	Atkinson C	flax	48x21x13	-	3.16	-	1837	- 6 stocks, supply :	v1B/	230
Loughgall	Clonmain	Atkinson Charles	beetling	-	-	-	-	-	2 beams x 7ft 6ins	vmb/	28
Loughgall	Clonmain	Atkinson Charles	beetling & bleach	91x28x16 & 21x16x8	-	9.18	-	1836	16x3x3 1 double eng.:	v1B/	230
Loughgall	Clonmain	Atkinson Charles	flax	-	-	-	-	-	13x3x - undershot	vmb/	28
Loughgall	Clonmain	McCoan Sarah	windmill & kiln	34x11x22 & kiln :	-	4.7.5	-	1837	- 2 pair stones	v1B/	230
Mullaghbrack	Coolmillish	McKee Joseph	corn	-	-	-	-	-	-	vmb/	28
Mullaghbrack	Coolmillish	McKee Joseph	corn & kiln	15x19x5, 42x19x21 & :	-	8.17	-	1836	- 2 pairs stones :	v1B/	213
Mullaghbrack	Coolmillish :	-	mill pond	-	-	-	-	-	-	6"os/	17
Forkill	Copes Mill	Maturin William :	mill	-	-	-	Maturin Wm - Hall Letitia :	1816	Asgt. Mort. 13 May	dd/	702 614 481698
Forkill	Copes Mill	McNaghton Francis :	mill	-	-	-	McNaghton F - Hall Letitia	1818	Mort 10 Aug.	dd/	706 202 483738
Drumcree	Corcullentragh	Wolsey J	corn	-	-	-	-	-	15x5x12	vmb/	28
Drumcree	Corcullentragh	Wolsey J	flax	-	-	-	-	-	15x4x12 6 berths	vmb/	28
Drumcree	Corcullentragh	Woolsey John	corn	56x29x18 & 19x8x6	-	6.4.4	-	1836	old wheel 15x4 supply :	v1B/	226b
Drumcree	Corcullentragh	Woolsey John	flax	51x22x8, 18x14x6 & :	-	2.19	-	1836	supply water for 8 mos.	v1B/	226b
Kilcloney	Cordrummond	Marshall John	flax	-	-	-	-	-	15x3x15 6 berths	vmb/	28
Kilclooney	Cordrummond	Marshall John	flax	48x19x6	-	4.8.0	-	1836	15x6 drives 6 stocks :	v1B/	210a/b
Kilcloney	Cordrummond :	-	flax	-	-	-	-	-	-	6"os/	17
Keady	Corkley	Doran George	flax	-	-	-	-	-	13x3x11	vmb/	28
Keady	Corkley	Hazlip Thomas	flax	30x22x12	-	3.18	-	1836	15x3x10 mill not :	v1B/	26c/d
Keady	Corkley	Hogg William	land	-	-	-	Hogg Wm - McClelland J	1881	-	dd/	1881 22 179
Keady	Corkley	Kirk Wiliam	beetling	19x19x8, 16x9x16 & :	-	27.13	-	1836	-	v1B/	26c
Keady	Corkley	Kirk Wiliam & :	beetling	- offices & land	15a.	71.10.	-	-	-	gr	-
Keady	Corkley	McKee William	beetling	-	-	-	-	-	30x5x23 drives beams:	vmb/	28
Keady	Corkley	Warnock Thomas	flax & land	- ho., offices & land	58a.	-	-	-	-	gr	-
Loughgilly	Cornagrally	-	corn	-	-	-	-	-	-	1"os/	59
Loughgilly	Cornagrally	-	flax	-	-	-	-	-	-	1"os/	59
Armagh	Corporation	Murphy Joseph	mill	-	-	-	Murphy J - Belfast Banking	1884	-	dd/	1884 30 99
Loughgilly	Corrinure	Toner Loughlin	flax	51x19x8, 51x8x6 & :	-	4.17	-	1836	- metal wheel drives :	v1B/	219
Newt`nhamilton	Cortamlat	-	flax	-	-	-	-	-	-	1"os/	59
Newt`nhamilton	Cortamlat	-	mill	-	-	-	-	-	-	1"os/	59
Newt`nhamilton	Cortamlat	Clarke Andrew	flax	-	-	-	-	-	16x3x16	vmb/	28
Newt`nhamilton	Cortamlat	Clarke Andrew	flax	23x20x11, 15x10x5 & :	-	7.16	-	1837	- 8 pair handles :	v1B/	242a
Newt`nhamilton	Cortamlat	Garmany Hugh	corn & kiln	37x20x16 & 17x20x5 :	-	10.3	-	1837	- 2 pair stones :	v1B/	242a/b
Newt`nhamilton	Cortamlat	Garmoney Hugh	corn	-	-	-	-	-	18x4x14	vmb/	28
Armagh	Couller`s Bridge	- on Claddy Water	flax	-	-	-	-	-	-	1"os/	59
Armagh	Craggan Upper	Scott Thomas	corn	-	-	-	-	-	14x3x14	vmb/	28
Armagh	Craggan Upper	Scott Thomas	flax	-	-	-	-	-	16x3x16 8 stocks	vmb/	28
Loughgilly	Crankey	-	corn & flax	-	-	-	-	-	-	1"os/	59
Loughgilly	Crankey	McBride Robert	corn	-	-	-	-	-	15x3x20	vmb/	28
Loughgilly	Crankey	McBride Robert	corn & kiln	20x21x16, 24x20x18 :	-	3.8.0	-	1836	- 1 pair stones :	v1B/	219
Loughgilly	Crankey	McBride Robert	flax	-	-	-	-	-	16x3x16	vmb/	28
Loughgilly	Crankey :	- nr Gamble`s Br.	corn	-	-	-	-	-	-	6"os/	22
Loughgilly	Creggan Upper	Scott Alexander	corn & kiln	32x19x6 & 16x15x6 :	-	7.10	-	1837	15x2x13 old wheel :	v1B/	219
Loughgilly	Creggan Upper	Scott Alexander	flax	43x20x7 & 19x18x8	-	6.10	-	1837	16x3x13 metal 8 berths	v1B/	219
Loughgilly	Creggan Upper	Scott Thomas	corn & kiln	34x19x6, kiln 36x18x7	-	1.8.2	-	1838	14x3x12 drives :	v1B/	245a
Loughgilly	Creggan Upper	Scott Thomas	flax	43x20x7, 12x19x7 & :	-	3.0.7	-	1838	15x4 o'shot 8 stocks	v1B/	245a
Killevey	Cross	Kelly Messrs	corn	-	-	-	-	-	18x5x1	vmb/	28

PARISH	TOWNLAND	MILLER	TYPE	HOUSE	Land	£Val	PROPRIETORS	Date	WHEEL etc.	Record	Ref.
Killevey	Cross	Kelly Messrs	flax	-	-	-	-	-	13x4x13 13x4x12	vmb/	28
Killevy	Cross	Kelly Robert	corn & kiln	49x21x19 & 14x18x12 :	-	9.14	-	1836	- 3 pairs stones :	v1B/	244b
Killevy	Cross	Kelly Robert	flax	old mill 28x16x6, new :	-	2.10	-	1836	4 stocks in new mill :	v1B/	244b
Keady	Crossdened	Kidd Benjamin Sen.	mill	-	-	-	Kidd Benj - Benjamin :	1818	Asgt. 10 Mar.	dd/	737 409 502544
Keady	Crossdened	Kidd Councillor	corn	-	-	-	-	-	16x3x16	vmb/	28
Keady	Crossdened	Kidd Councillor	wheat	-	-	-	-	-	15x2x13 3 pr st.	vmb/	28
Keady	Crossdened	Kidd Count	corn	47x17x15, 47x15x24 &:	-	21.11	-	1836	16x3 & 15x3x20 o'shot	v1B/	26a
Keady	Crossdened	Kidd James	flax	-	-	-	-	-	16x3x13 6 berths	vmb/	28
Keady	Crossdened	Kidd Jo.	flax	41x24x19 & 16x24x8	-	5.1.9	-	1836	16x3x13 formerly :	v1B/	26a
Keady	Crossdened	Matthews & Barnes	corn	-	-	-	-	-	20x5x15 3 pair st.	vmb/	28
Keady	Crossdened	McKane James	flax	-	-	-	-	-	32x4x28	vmb/	28
Keady	Crossdened	McKane James	spinning	-	-	-	-	-	20x4x17 spindles :	vmb/	28
Keady	Crossdened	McKane James	spinning factory	35x23x12, 35x7x9 & :	-	47.2	-	1836	20x4 & 32x4x14 :	v1B/	26a
Keady	Crossdened	Richey John	corn	60x12x10, 65x20x30 :	-	34.4	-	1836	20x5x15 good supply :	v1B/	26a
Creggan	Crossmaglen	Cary Tristan	mill	-	-	-	Cary Tristan - Watt David	1883	-	dd/	1883 43 70
Creggan	Crossmaglen	McDonnell John	mill	-	-	-	McDonnell John - Newry :	1885	-	dd/	1885 1 156
Keady	Crossmore :	M'Kean James	flax spinning	- & yard	-	100	-	1856	-	gr	-
Keady	Crossnamotie	Wilson John	corn	-	-	-	-	-	13x2x10	vmb/	28
Keady	Crossnamotie	Wilson John	corn	-	-	-	-	-	16x2x13	vmb/	28
Keady	Crossnamoyle	-	corn	-	-	-	-	-	-	1"os/	59
Keady	Crossnamoyle	Wilson John	corn & kiln	44x22x16 & kiln :	-	4.16	-	1837	13x2 for shelling & :	v1B/	237
Keady	Darkley	Kidd S A	beetling	-	-	-	-	-	30x5x24 drives 9 beams	vmb/	28
Keady	Darkley	Kidd Samuel :	mills	-	-	-	Kidd Sam - Barklie James	1814	-	dd/	693 507 476223
Keady	Darkley	Kidd Samuel A	beetling & bleach	32x16x6, 22x14x4 & :	-	51.7	-	1836	25x5x20 & 24x5x17 :	v1B/	26c
Keady	Darkley	Kirk William	flax	-	-	-	-	-	15x3x10	vmb/	28
Keady	Darkley	Kirk William & :	spinning & wv.	stores, offs. & yard	2a.	500	-	1856	-	gr/	a.a.Ire.ie
Keady	Darkley	McKane Henry	spinning	-	-	-	-	-	30x5x25 spindles 1232	vmb/	28
Keady	Darkley	McKean Henry	spinning factory	74x37x33, 15x10x26 :	-	35.18	-	1836	32x4x26 & 36x6x26	v1B/	26c/d
Keady	Darkley	Morrison James :	beetling	Manager's ho. & Land	1a.	121.1(	-	1856	-	gr	-
Keady	Darkley	Morrison James :	bleach	- offices & Land	37a.	87	-	1856	-	gr	-
Keady	Darkley :	-	beetling	-	-	-	-	-	-	6"os/	20
Keady	Darkley :	-	beetling	-	-	-	-	-	-	6"os/	20
Keady	Darkley :	-	beetling	-	-	-	-	-	-	6"os/	20
Keady	Darkley :	-	ruins of blech mill	-	-	-	-	-	-	6"os/	20
Keady	Darkley :	-	long mill race	-	-	-	-	-	-	6"os/	20
Keady	Darkley :	-	ruins of bt. mill	-	-	-	-	-	-	6"os/	20
Keady	Darkley :	-	spinning	-	-	-	-	-	-	6"os/	20
Shankill	Demense	Greer & Son	corn	-	-	-	-	-	22x4x17	vmb/	28
Ballymore	Demoan	Boyd Isaac	corn	-	-	-	-	-	13x2x16	vmb/	28
Ballymore	Demoan	Boyd Isaac	corn & kiln	27x19x14 & kiln :	-	5.5.0	-	1836	- 1 pair stones :	v1B/	214
Ballymore	Demoan	Boyd Isaac	flax	-	-	-	-	-	14x3x6	vmb/	28
Loughgilly	Derlet :	-	corn & kiln	-	-	-	-	-	-	6"os/	17
Loughgilly	Derlet :	-	flax	-	-	-	-	-	-	6"os/	17
Shankill	Derry	Greer & Boyd	distillery	81x24x24, 25x28x26 :	-	80.0	-	1836	-	v1B/	2223a
Montiagh	Derryadd	-	old windmill	-	-	-	-	-	-	1"os/	35
Montiaghs	Derryadd	Ford James	corn & kiln	35x24x20, 22x9x7 & :	-	7.16	-	1836	- mill useles no water	v1B/	221
Montiaghs	Derryadd	Ford James	windmill	circum. 62ft., ht. 24ft.	-	1.3.3	-	1836	-	v1B/	221
Montiagh	Derryadd	Forde Francis	-	-	-	-	-	-	-	vmb/	28
Ballymore	Derryallan :	- on Cusher R.	flour & corn	-	-	-	-	-	-	6"os/	14
Ballymore	Derryallen	-	flour & corn	-	-	-	-	2004	-	mmiS/	PW - Rs
Ballymore	Derryallen	Beehan James	boiling house	34x20x12 & 53x23x20	-	6.9.0	-	1836	-	v1B/	214
Tartaraghan	Derryaugh	Smyth Robert	distillery	34x31x13, boiling ho :	-	35.0	-	1837	16x14x10 new metal :	v1B/	233b

PARISH	TOWNLAND	MILLER	TYPE	HOUSE	Land	£Val	PROPRIETORS	Date	WHEEL etc.	Record	Ref.
Tartagallan	Derryaugh	Smyth Robert	malt	-	-	-	-	-	14x6x - undershot	vmb/	28
Kilclooney	Derryaughan	Orr William	corn & kiln	37x18x9 kiln 34x20x6	-	2/.1.4	-	1836	1 pr. sts. wooden m/cy.	v1B/	216
Kilclooney	Derryaughan	Orr William	flax	54x25x10 & 17x25x8	-	4.8.8	-	1836	- 10 berths :	v1B/	233b
Drumcree	Derrybrughas	Robb Mrs	pottery	19x18x9, 6x5x10 & :	-	16.16	-	1837	-	v1B/	226a
Kilcloney	Derrycughan	-	flax	-	-	-	-	-	-	6"os/	17
Kilcloney	Derrycughan	-	mill & kiln	-	-	-	-	-	-	6"os/	17
Kilcloney	Derrycughan	McMurray James :	corn & kiln	-	-	-	McMurray J - McGowan :	1812	Conv. 30 Oct. :	dd/	656 10 449785
Kilcloney	Derrycughan	Orr William	corn	-	-	-	-	-	15x3x17	vmb/	28
Kilcloney	Derrycughan	Orr William	flax	-	-	-	-	-	18x3x18	vmb/	28
Kilcloney	Derrycughan	Trew Andrew	flax	-	-	-	-	-	14x4x1	vmb/	28
Kilcloney	Derrycughan	Trew Andrew	flax	34x21x7 & 53x24x17	-	5.7.9	-	1836	4 berths 1 set rollers	v1B/	216
Kilcloney	Derrycushan	Russell Robert	flax	-	-	-	-	-	14x4x10 6 stocks	vmb/	28
Tynan	Derryhaw	Jiohnston James	flax	49x21x7	-	5.1.0	-	1836	-	v1B/	29b
Tynan	Derryhaw	Johnston James	flax	-	-	-	-	-	14x2x12 6 stocks	vmb/	28
Tynan	Derryhaw	Johnston Robert	flax	-	-	-	-	-	16x3x8 8 stocks	vmb/	28
Tynan	Derryhaw	Johnston Robert	flax	65x20x7 & 16x5x5	-	6.17	-	1836	16x3x8 new wheel	v1B/	29b
Tynan	Derryhaw	Oliver Joseph	flax	-	-	-	-	-	16x4x8 6 stocks	vmb/	28
Tynan	Derryhaw	Oliver Joseph	flax	37x19x14	-	2.14	-	1836	16x3x8	v1B/	29b
Tynan	Derryhaw :	-	flax	-	-	-	-	-	-	6"os/	15
Tartaraghan	Derrylee	Verner Colonel	corn & kiln	30x22x12, 20x9x6 & :	-	5.3.4	-	1837	13ft dia 1 pr st dia. 5ft.	v1B/	233b
Tartagallan	Derrylee	Verner William	corn	-	-	-	-	-	14x3x4	vmb/	28
Newry	Derrymore	Smith Isaac	corn & flour	-	-	-	-	-	24x8x17	vmb/	28
Newry	Derrymore	Smith Isaac	corn & kiln	70x34x43 & kiln :	-	52.0	-	1836	- 4 pairs mill stones	v1B/	246a
Drumcree	Diving	Love David	flax	-	-	-	-	-	13x2x- breast, drives :	vmb/	28
Drumcree	Diviny	Hyde Robert John & :	flax	48x19x13	-	2.1.9	-	1837	14x2 nwe 4 stocks :	v1B/	226b
Newry	Donnybeg	Cochran William :	bl green & mills	-	-	-	Cochran W - Bell Jn Sen. :	1813	-	dd/	664? 174 456937
Tynan	Doogarry	Daley Thomas	corn & kiln	41x21x6, 9x17x11 & :	-	3.16	-	1837	13x2x9 1 pair stones	v1B/	238
Tynan	Doogarry	Johnston Messrs	corn	-	-	-	-	-	13x2x10	vmb/	28
Mullaghbrack	Dorsy	-	mill	-	-	-	-	-	-	1"os/	70
Mullaghbrack	Dorsy	Jerrfes Richard	corn	-	-	-	-	-	14x2x8	vmb/	28
Shankill	Doucher	Greer & Son	corn	-	-	-	-	-	28x3x25 2 wheels	vmb/	28
Armagh	Dounes	Pepper John :	mills	-	-	-	Pepper John - Scott John :	1813	DD R'cvy cons. £1950	dd/	662 461 457090
Armagh	Dounes	Pepper John :	mills	-	-	-	Pepper John - Scott John :	1813	Mort. 20 Jul.	dd/	662 462 457091
Armagh	Drominikelly	Kelly Arthur	mills	-	-	-	Kelly Arthur - Hall Letitia :	1817	-	dd/	717 50 490185
Derrynoose	Drumacanver	Hagan Frances	corn & kiln	37x20x8 & 36x21x9 & :	-	2.6.5	-	1836	12x14x4 2 pair stones	v1B/	23
Derrynoose	Drumacanver	Humphreys D	flax	57x19x14	-	4.6.4	-	1837	18x4x12 6 stocks :	v1B/	23
Mullaghbrack	Drumachee	-	flax & pond	-	-	-	-	-	-	6"os/	17
Mullaghbrack	Drumachee	Allen John	corn & kiln	36x18x15 & 14x15x10 :	-	5.3.5	-	1837	14x3x10 " pair stones	v1B/	213
Mullaghbrack	Drumachee	Allen John	flax	48x19x10 & 22x17x9	-	3.12	-	1837	10x15x3 6 stocks :	v1B/	213
Mullaghbrack	Drumachee	Allen Joseph	corn	-	-	-	-	-	14x3x10	vmb/	28
Mullaghbrack	Drumachee	Allen Joseph	flax	-	-	-	-	-	15x3x10 11x3x4	vmb/	28
Loughgilly	Drumahunshin	Patterson Henry	flax	-	-	-	-	-	14x4x6 wooden rollers	vmb/	28
Armagh	Drumarg	Pepper John	mills	-	-	-	Pepper J - Scott John	1813	-	dd/	662 461 457090
Armagh	Drumarg	Scott John :	mills	-	-	-	Scott John - Kidd Benj :	1809	Lse. 16 Apl.	dd/	665 487 460872
Armagh	Drumarg	Scott John :	mills	- and lands	11a.	-	Scott John - Dobbin John :	1816	-	dd/	706 232 483787
Loughgall	Drumart	Slevin Edward	bleach	18x15x8, 18x19x12 :	-	2.8.3	-	1837	driven by one horse :	v1B/	230
Armagh	Drumcananver	-	corn	-	-	-	-	-	-	6"os/	15
Grange	Drumcarn	- on Callan R.	linen	-	-	-	-	-	-	1"os/	47
Grange	Drumcarn	- near T`elmer Ho.	linen	-	-	-	-	-	-	1"os/	47
Grange	Drumcarn	Belfact Bank Co.	mill	-	-	-	Belfast Bank - Wilson Abr	1884	-	dd/	1884 40 193
Grange	Drumcarn	Murphy Joseph	mill	-	-	-	Murphy J - Belfast Bank	1884	-	dd/	1884 40 192
Lisnadill	Drumconwell	-	mills	-	-	-	-	-	-	1"os/	47

PARISH	TOWNLAND	MILLER	TYPE	HOUSE	Land	£Val	PROPRIETORS	Date	WHEEL etc.	Record Ref.
Loughgily	Drumcrow	-	mill	-	-	-	-	-	-	1"os/ 59
Eglish	Drumduff	-	mill	-	-	-	-	-	-	1"os/ 47
Eglish	Drumduff	Eyres Thomas	beetling	60x27x17 & 23x27x13	-	5.9.0	-	1838	mill no longer in use	v1B/ 236
Eglish	Drumduff	Eyres Thomas	old beetling mill	-	-	-	-	-	machinery removed	vmb/ 28
Loughgilly	Drumgane	Armstrong Archibald	corn & kiln	46x19x7 & kiln :	-	1.7.3	-	1837	13x3x14 2 pir. stones	v1B/ 212
Loughgilly	Drumgane	Armstrong Archibald	flax	52x22x7	-	15.0	-	1837	- 6 berths & roller :	v1B/ 212
Loughgilly	Drumgane	Armstrong Mr	corn	-	-	-	-	-	13x3x9	vmb/ 28
Loughgilly	Drumgane	Armstrong Mr	flax	-	-	-	-	-	16x3x16 6 stocks	vmb/ 28
Loughgilly	Drumgane	Byers John	flax	-	-	-	-	-	16x3x10 8 stocks	vmb/ 28
Loughgilly	Drumgane	Byers John	flax	30x25x9, 20x18x7 & :	-	2.2.1	-	1837	- 8 berths & roller :	v1B/ 212
Armagh	Drumharrif	-	Kings Mill	-	-	-	-	-	-	1"os/ 59
Loughgilly	Drumharrif	Boyle Dennis	corn & flax	19x19x13 & 18x17x8 :	-	1.17	-	1836	- corn mill not used :	v1B/ 214
Loughgilly	Drumharrif	Boyle Dennis	flax	22x21x7, 20x21x7 & :	-	2.5.6	-	1836	- 6 stocks good m/cy	v1B/ 245a
Ballymore	Druminure	-	corn	-	-	-	-	2004	wheel still complete	mmiS/ PW - D
Ballymore	Druminure	Harden Robert	corn	-	-	-	-	-	14x4x6	vmb/ 28
Ballymore	Druminure	Harden Robert	corn & kiln	40x28x20, 42x21x154 :	-	10.0	-	1836	- 2 pairs stones :	v1B/ 214
Ballymore	Druminure :	-	corn	-	-	-	-	-	-	6"os/ 13
Mullaghbrack	Drumman	- on Fall R	mill	-	-	-	-	-	-	1"os/ 47
Tynan	Drummond	-	flax	-	-	-	-	-	-	1"os/ 59
Tynan	Drummond	McCrum James	flax	-	-	-	-	-	13x3x10 6 stocks	vmb/ 28
Tynan	Drummond	McCrum James	flax	32x19x7 & 16x18x7	-	7.0.0	-	1836	13x3x10 o'shot, drives	v1B/ 29b
Derrynoose	Drumnacanner	Hagan Frances	corn	-	-	-	-	-	14x3x11	vmb/ 28
Derrynoose	Drumnacanner	Humphries David	flax	-	-	-	-	-	18x4x15 8 berths	vmb/ 28
Loughgilly	Drumnahunshin	Patterson Henry	flax	25x19x7	-	14/1	-	1837	13x3..6x7 drives :	v1B/ 224a
Drumcree	Drumnakelly	Cummings John	flax	23x16x5, kiln 41x18x9	-	7/8	-	1836	wheel nearly new :	v1B/ 226a
Drumcree	Drumnakelly	Cummins John	corn	-	-	-	-	-	12x2x8	vmb/ 28
Drumcree	Drumnakelly	Cummins John	flax	-	-	-	-	-	12x2x8 5 berths	vmb/ 28
Drumcree	Drumnakelly	Greer James	mill	-	-	-	Greer Jas - Greer Samuel	1812	-	dd/ 645 452 449059
Loughgilly	Drumnarriff	Boyle Denis	flax	-	-	-	-	-	- 6 stocks	vmb/ 28
Keady	Dundrum	Kidd S A	beetling	-	-	-	-	-	14x3x5	vmb/ 28
Keady	Dundrum	McCleane J	corn	-	-	-	-	-	-	vmb/ 28
Keady	Dundrum	McCleane John	corn & kiln	82x22x18 & kiln :	-	10.5	-	1836	14x4x12 2 pair stones	v1B/ 26b
Keady	Dundrum	Morrison James :	beetling	- offices & land	3a.	18	-	1856	-	gr -
Keady	Dundrum	nr Old Dundrum Ho.	beetling	-	-	-	-	-	-	mmSv/ pw - Z
Mullabrack	Dunesmullan	-	falx	-	-	-	-	-	-	6"os/ 17
Mullabrack	Dunesmullan	-	saw	-	-	-	-	-	-	1"os/ 47
Jonesborough	Edenappa	Hughes Francis	corn & kiln	29x19x12 & kiln :	-	10.0	-	1836	2 pair sts. m/cy new :	v1B/ 243
Jonesborough	Edenappa	Hughes Messrs	corn	-	-	-	-	-	14x3x10	vmb/ 28
Kilcloney	Edenkennedy	McDonnell R	flax	-	-	-	-	-	15x3x6	vmb/ 28
Kilclooney	Edenkennedy	McDonnell Robert	flax	20x20x6 * 27x16x7	-	4.7.0	-	1837	-	v1B/ 210b
Eglish	Eglish	-	flax	-	-	-	-	-	-	1"os/ 47
Eglish	Eglish	-	flax	-	-	-	-	-	-	1"os/ 47
Lisnadill	Enagh	-	mills	-	-	-	-	-	-	1"os/ 47
Lisnadill	Ennislare	-	corn	-	-	-	-	-	-	1"os/ 47
Lisnadill	Ennislare	Prentice Henry L	corn	-	-	-	-	-	-	6"os/ 16
Lisnadill	Ennislare	Prentice Henry L	corn & kiln	40x21x24, 21x9x7 & :	-	19.14	-	-	15x4x10	vmb/ 28
Armagh	Finiskin	- on Camlin L.	mill	-	-	-	-	1837	15x4x10 drives 2 pr. st	v1B/ 211
Drumcree	Garvaghy	Hutcheson William	distillery	63x53x21, 24x15x14 :	-	100.0	-	-	-	1"os/ 59
Drumcree	Garvaghy	Hutcheson William	distillery	38x21x29, 40x15x22 :	-	6.15	-	1836	-	v1B/ 226b
Drumcree	Garvaghy :	Shillington Thomas	corn kiln	17x24x20 & :	-	24	-	1836	-	v1B/ 226b
Tynan	Glaslough	Stewart Robert	distillery	-	-	-	-	1836	-	v1B/ 226b
Ballymore	Glassdrumman	Cochran	mills	-	-	-	Cochran - Bell & ors	1782	1 still - 220g.	hcJ lic.
								-	-	dd/ 664 174 456937

PARISH	TOWNLAND	MILLER	TYPE	HOUSE	Land	£Val	PROPRIETORS	Date	WHEEL etc.	Record	Ref.
Ballymore	Glassdrumman	Little	mill	-	-	-	Little - Donaldson	-	-	dd/	692 198 475328
Killevey	Glassdrummond	Atkinson William	beetling	-	-	-	-	-	23x5x21	vmb/	28
Killevy	Glassdrummond	Atkinson William	beetling	92x26x16, 24x24x16 &:	-	22.0	-	1836	constant supply water	v1B/	244b
Killevey	Glassdrummond	Atkinson William	wash	-	-	-	-	-	18x4x8	vmb/	28
Killevey	Glassdrummond	Carville Fran	beetling	-	-	-	-	-	18x4x18	vmb/	28
Killevey	Glassdrummond	Carville Fran	flax	-	-	-	-	-	20x4x20	vmb/	28
Killevey	Glassdrummond	Carville Fran	shovel	-	-	-	-	-	16x4x16	vmb/	28
Killevey	Glassdrummond	Carville Fran	spade	-	-	-	-	-	16x4x16	vmb/	28
Killevey	Glassdrummond	Carville Fran	wash	-	-	-	-	-	14x4x14	vmb/	28
Killevey	Glassdrummond	Carville Francis	beetling	76x24x14	-	4.18	-	1836	mill no longer in use	v1B/	244b
Killevey	Glassdrummond	Carville Francis	flax	29x31x17, 20x8x8 & :	-	15.18	-	1836	- superior mill :	v1B/	244b
Killevey	Glassdrummond	Carville Francis	spade	47x28x10	-	3.12	-	1836	-	v1B/	244b
Armagh	Glen Eyre	-	linen	-	-	-	-	-	-	1"os/	47
Keady	Glencarn	-	mill	-	-	-	-	-	-	1"os/	59
Killevy	Goragh	Pollock & Lochart	spade	29x21x9 & 22x18x8	-	3.10	-	1836	-	v1B/	244b
Killevey	Goragh	Pollock B	spade	-	-	-	-	-	13x2x13	vmb/	28
Keady	Granemore	Burrowes James	grist	-	-	-	Burrowes Jas - Greg : (	1814	Mort. 1 Feb.	dd/	672 387 464382
Armagh	Green	Kirk William	the water course	-	-	-	Kirk Wm - Gardiner Wm	1881	-	dd/	1881 41 15
Grange	Greenan	Mollan	mill	-	-	-	Mollan - Orr	-	-	dd/	685 104 471044
Armagh	Grenhall	Cowdy Anthony	mills	-	-	-	Cowdy Anthony - Belfast:	1885	-	dd/	1885 38 216
Armagh	Hanecrackabee *	-	corn	-	-	-	-	-	-	6"os/	17
Armagh	Hanecrackabee *	-	flax	-	-	-	-	-	-	6"os/	17
Armagh	Hanecrackabee * :	-	flax	-	-	-	-	-	-	6"os/	17
Keady	Iskymeadow :	-	beetling mills	-	-	-	-	-	-	6"os/	16
Keady	Keady	-	corn	-	-	-	-	2004	-	mmSv/	pw - Z
Keady	Keady	- 1m S. of Town	flour & corn	-	-	-	-	2004	-	mmSv/	pw - Cc
Keady	Keady	- at Town Bridge	flour	now Old Mill Restaurant			Kidd	2004	-	mmSv/	pw - Cc
Keady	Keady	Brownlee Richard	distillery	-	-	-	-	1782	1 still - 210g.	hcJ	lic.
Keady	Keady	Kidd	mill	-	-	-	Kidd - Kidd	-	-	dd/	737 409 502544
Keady	Keady	McKean James	mill & fall in	-	-	-	McKean J - Ire Bank Govs	1885	-	dd/	1885 49 256
Keady	Keady	M'Kinstry Thomas	distillery	-	-	-	-	1782	1 still - 250g.	hcJ	lic.
Loughgilly	Keady More	Gracy Robert	flax	-	-	-	-	-	13x3x4	vmb/	28
Loughgilly	Keadybeg	Caldwell Robert	flax	43x17x6, 15x15x5 & :	-	7.17	-	1836	metal wheel :	v1B/	219
Loughgilly	Keadybeg	Gracey Robert	corn & kiln	31x20x16 & kiln :	-	4.12	-	1836	- 1 pair stones :	v1B/	219
Loughgilly	Keadybeg	Gracey Robert	flax	46x15x6, 38x19x6 & :	-	4.14	-	1836	- 4 berths supply :	v1B/	219
Loughgilly	Keadybegg	McGowan	mill	-	-	-	McGowan - McGowan	-	-	dd/	643 208 442611
Loughgilly	Keadymore	- on Blackwater	flax mills	-	-	-	-	-	-	1"os/	59
Loughgilly	Keadymore	Gracey Robert	flax	24x21x6 (Val. 12/6)	-	4.8.0	-	1836	- metal wheel inside :	v1B/	219
Lisnadill	Kennedies	-	flax	-	-	-	-	-	-	1"os/	46
Lisnadill	Kennedies	-	flax	-	-	-	-	-	-	6"os/	12
Lisnadill	Kennedies	- Ballynahone Beg	Distillery	-	-	-	-	-	-	6"os/	12
Lisnadill	Kennedies	- Millford Mills	flour	-	-	-	-	-	-	6"os/	12
Lisnadill	Kennedies	- Millford Mills	rope walk	-	-	-	-	-	-	6"os/	12
Lisnadill	Kennedies	- Millford Mills	spinning	-	-	-	-	-	-	6"os/	12
Lisnadill	Kennedies	- Lishane Mills	mill ruins	-	-	-	-	-	-	6"os/	12
Lisnadill	Kennedies	Henry Anne :	mill	-	-	-	Henry A - McCrum Wm :	1817	-	dd/	739 501 503836
Lisnadill	Kennedies	McCrum Wiliam	flax	-	-	-	-	2004	-	mmSv/	pw - Z
Lisnadill	Kennedies	McCrum Wiliam	flax & corn	68x21x17, 84x21x17 & :	-	16.12	-	1836	-	v1B/	27
Lisnadill	Kennedies	McCrum Wiliam	scutch & spinninç	75x21x15, 15x20x9 & :	-	13.17	-	1836	-	v1B/	27
Lisnadill	Kennedies	McCrum William	corn & flour	-	-	-	-	-	-	vmb/	28
Lisnadill	Kennedies	McCrum William	flax	-	-	-	-	-	14x2x4 14x5x7	vmb/	28
Lisnadill	Kennedies	McCrum William	flax	house, offices & land	46a.	111	-	1856	-	gr/	a.a.Ire.ie

PARISH	TOWNLAND	MILLER	TYPE	HOUSE	Land	£Val	PROPRIETORS	Date	WHEEL etc.	Record Ref.
Lisnadill	Kennedies	Millford Mills	spinning	-	-	-	-	2004	-	mmSv/ pw - Z
Lisnadill	Kennedies	Stanley James	flour	-	-	-	-	-	14x4x7	vmb/ 28
Lisnadill	Kennedies	Stanley James	flour	25x8x20, 48x23x25 & :	-	22.0	-	1836	13x4x8 supply water :	v1B/ 27
Lisnadill	Kennedies	Stanley James	flour	-	-	-	-	2004	-	mmSv/ pw - Z
Kilclooney	Kilbracks	-	flax	-	-	-	-	-	-	1"os/ 59
Kilclooney	Kilbracks	-	flax	-	-	-	-	-	-	1"os/ 59
Kilclooney	Killrockan	Donaldson	mill	-	-	-	Donaldson - Wallace	-	-	dd/ 716 309 489844
Loughgilly	Killybora	- nr Gamble`s Br.	corn	-	-	-	-	-	-	6"os/ 22
Loughgilly	Killycarn	- on Usher R	mill	-	-	-	-	-	-	1"os/ 47
Loughgilly	Killycarn Upper	Douglas David	flax	-	-	-	-	-	14x5x2 10 stocks	vmb/ 28
Loughgilly	Killycarn Upper	Douglass David	flax	67x20x7, 15x9x5 & :	-	3.8.9	-	1836	- 10 berths & :	v1B/ 219
Kilcloney	Kilmachugh	- Claddy Milltown	flax	-	-	-	-	-	-	1"os/ 59
Kilcloney	Kilmachugh	Mitchell Robert	flax	-	-	-	-	-	16x4x9 6 stocks	vmb/ 28
Kilclooney	Kilmachugh	Mitchell Robert	flax	32x18x8 & 19x18x7	-	1.13	-	1837	16x4x9 drives 6 stocks	v1B/ 210a
Tynan	Knockbane	Matthews	mills	-	-	-	Matthews - Boyde	-	-	dd/ 670 499 462293
Armagh	Knockbeg	McGarvan Samuel :	mills	-	-	-	McGarvan - McGowan :	1818	-	dd/ 726 571 496106
Armagh	Knockbeg	McGarvan Samuel :	mills	-	-	-	McGowan - Ferguson : R	1817	-	dd/ 728 225 496960
Armagh	Knockbeg	McKinstry Robert :	mills	-	-	-	McKinstry R - Caulfield :	1818	-	dd/ 727 55 496190
Lisnadill	Latmacollum	McCrum William	corn	-	-	-	-	-	14x3x10	vmb/ 28
Lisnadill	Latmacollum	McCrum William	corn & kiln	38x22x8 & 22x10x6 &:	-	2.15	-	1837	15x3x10 drives :	v1B/ 211
Lisnadill	Latmacollum :	-	corn	-	-	-	-	-	-	6"os/ 16
Lisnadill	Latmacollum	- on Butlerwater	flax	-	-	-	-	-	-	1"os/ 47
Killevey	Latt	Ferris Robert	flax	-	-	-	-	-	14x2x12	vmb/ 28
Killevy	Latt	Ferris Robert	flax	27x18x6	-	7/3	-	1836	- 3 handles :	v1B/ 244b
Kilmore	Legacorry	-	corn	-	-	-	-	2004	-	mmiS/ PW - B
Kilmore	Legacurry	Redmond David	mills	-	-	-	Rednond Dav - Small Alex	1882	-	dd/ 1882 36 17
Armagh	Legarhill :	- on Callan R.	flour & dam	-	-	-	-	-	-	6"os/ 12
Eglish	Lisadian	Anderson & Gillen	corn	-	-	-	-	-	14x2x12	vmb/ 28
Eglish	Lisadian	Anderson William	corn & kiln	miller's ho., offs., land	38a.	7.12	-	1836	-	gr/ a.a.Ire.ie
Eglish	Lisadian	Anderson William	mill reservoir	-	4a.	-	-	1856	-	gr/ a.a.Ire.ie
Eglish	Lisadian	Anderson William &	:corn & kiln	33x27x24, 32x27x17 :	-	7.12	-	1836	15x2x3 2 pr. stones :	v1B/ 24
Eglish	Lisadian :	nr B`martrim Water	corn	-	-	-	-	-	-	6"os/ 12
Kilmore	Lisavague	- converted :	corn	-	-	-	-	2004	-	mmiS/
Kilmore	Lisavague	McCaffrey Thomas :	mill lands	-	-	-	McCaffrey T - Pepper Jn :	1819	13 Jan.	dd/ 741 131 504666
Kilmore	Lisavague	McConnell	mill	-	-	-	McConnell - Mollan & ano	-	-	dd/ 716 90 489625
Kilmore	Lisavague	Mollan James :	mill lands	-	-	-	Mollan - McCaffrey Thos :	1819	Conv. 11 Jan.	dd/ 741 130 504665
Kilmore	Lisavague	Quin Silvester :	mill lands	-	-	-	Quin S - McKinstry Thos :	1819	Mort. 27 Mar.	dd/ 740 179 504114
Kilmore	Lisavague :	-	corn	-	-	-	-	-	-	6"os/ 13
Kilmore	Lisavague :	-	mill	-	-	-	-	-	-	1"os/ 47
Kilmore	Lisavague :	-	weaving fcty.	-	-	-	-	-	-	1"os/ 47
Kilmore	Lisaveague	Grier Moses	corn & kiln	35x15x12 & 35x23x19:	-	6.1.8	-	1836	- 1 pair stones :	v1B/ 218
Ballymore	Lisbane	Achison James	yarn m'factory.	drying ho. 60x21x8 :	-	4.1.9	-	1836	-	v1B/ 214
Lisnadill	Lisbanoe	-	beetling	-	-	-	-	-	-	1"os/ 47
Lisnadill	Lisbanoe	Lisbane Mills	mill ruins	-	-	-	-	2004	-	mmSv/ pw - Z
Lisnadill	Lisbanoe	McCrum	mills	-	-	-	McCrum - Henry	-	-	dd/ 692 605 475725
Grange	Lisdonwilly	-	mills	-	-	-	-	-	-	1"os/ 47
Loughgilly	Lisdrumchor Lr	Atkinson William	cotton spinning	-	-	-	-	-	1224 throstle spindles :	vmb/ 28
Loughgilly	Lisdrumchor Lr	Atkinson William	flax	-	-	-	-	-	17x4x17 6 stocks	vmb/ 28
Loughgilly	Lisdrumchor Lr	Atkinson William	flax	-	-	-	-	-	16x4x13 6 stocks	vmb/ 28
Loughgilly	Lisdrumchor Lr.	Atkinson William	spinning/weaving	16x28x46, 77x29x46 :	-	-	-	1836	24x4x18 drives :	v1B/ 212
Loughgilly	Lisdrumchor Lr.	Atkinson William	spinning factory	83x32x36 & 28x15x13 :	-	28.10	-	1836	29x4x30 m/cy good :	v1B/ 212
Loughgilly	Lisdrumchor Lr.	Mathers Joseph or :	flax	55x24x15, 54x23x9 :	-	13.16	-	1836	-	v1B/ 212

PARISH	TOWNLAND	MILLER	TYPE	HOUSE	Land	£Val	PROPRIETORS	Date	WHEEL etc.	Record	Ref.
Loughgilly	Lisdrumchor Upr.	Atkinson William	cotton factory	39x36x7, 49x19x12 :	-	8.8.2	-	1837	- 1200 spindles :	v1B/	212
Loughgilly	Lisdrumchor Upr.	William Atkinson	cotton weaving	-	-	-	-	-	169 looms :	vmb/	28
Newry	Lisdrumgullion :	McNaghten Rowan	salt works	38x20x21, 46x19x14 :	-	11.3	-	1836	-	v1B/	246a/c/e
Newry	Lisdrumgullion :	Bennie John	metal foundry & :	45x38x11, 45x21x11 :	-	18.2	-	1836	-	v1B/	246a
Newry	Lisdrumgullion :	Boyd & Glenny	stores & kiln	33x14x18, 70x19x26 :	-	20.6	-	1836	-	v1B/	246 a/c/e
Newry	Lisdrumgullion :	Hancock William	store	39x31x26 & 48x16x19	-	11.5	-	1836	-	v1B/	246 a/c/e
Newry	Lisdrumgullion :	Kirkwood & McClure	glass works	31x31x30, 60x49x10 :	-	15.13	-	1836	-	v1B/	246 a/c/e
Newry	Lisdrumgullion :	White, Weir & Hill	metal foundry	77x13x8, 62x10x7 :	-	12.0	-	1836	-	v1B/	246 a/c/e
Newry	Lisdrumgullion :	Corry, Little & Swanzy	flour & corn	63x22x21 & 60x22x18	-	49.8	-	1836	2 pair stones ea. mill :	v1B/	246a
Newry	Lisdrumgullion :	Ogle & Godfrey	stores	33x27x28, 72x11x8 :	-	9.18	-	1836	-	v1B/	246a
Newry	Lisdrumgullion :	Boyd Hugh	store	49x17x9, 24x12x7 :	-	5.8.6	-	1836	-	v1B/	246
Newry	Lisdrumliska :	Maguire Dennis	brewery	malt loft 123x26x18 :	-	171	-	1836	-	v1B/	246a
Newry	Lisdrumliska :	Maguire Dennis	brewery (part)	still house 51x82x27 :	-	-	-	1836	-	v1B/	246a
Newry	Lisdrumliska :	McGuire Dennis &Co.	distillery	brew ho. 126x33x29 :	-	104.0	-	1836	- (no longer in use)	v1B/	246a
Newry	Lisdrumliska :	McGuire Dennis &Co.	distillery (part)	corn kiln 34x34x22 :	-	-	-	1836	- (no longer in use)	v1B/	246a
Newry	Lisdrumullion	Reilly John	corn & flour	-	-	-	-	-	17x8x12	vmb/	28
Armagh	Lisinacartie	McKinstry	mill	-	-	-	McKinstry - Caulfield	-	? ?	dd/	727 55 496190
Tynan	Lislanly	-	corn	-	-	-	-	-	-	6"os/	15
Tynan	Lislanly	Russell Thomas	corn	-	-	-	-	-	15x3x12	vmb/	28
Tynan	Lislanly	Russell Thomas	corn & kiln	25x21x14, 13x13x6 :	-	3.12	-	1837	15x3x12 drives 1 pr. sts	v1B/	213
Loughgall	Lislasly	- nr Green Hall	mill	-	-	-	-	-	-	1"os/	47
Killevey	Lislea	Doran Terence	corn	-	-	-	-	-	13x2x13	vmb/	28
Killevy	Lislea	Doran Terence	corn & kiln	38x18x6, kiln 45x17x6	-	6.0.0	-	1836	inferior mill, 1 pr. sts. :	v1B/	244b
Killevey	Lislea	Doran Terence	flax	-	-	-	-	-	13x2x10 6 stocks	vmb/	28
Kennedies	Lislea	Wynne Mrs	beetling	-	-	-	-	-	12x3x6, 15x4x8 drive :	vmb/	28
Kennedies	Lislea	Wynne Mrs	bleach	5 bay complex	-	-	-	2004	-	mmSv/	pw - B
Kennedies	Lislea	Wynne Mrs	bleaching	-	-	-	-	-	12x2x6 drives 2 beams	vmb/	28
Lisnadill	Lislea	Wynne Thomas	beetling	house, offs. land	79a.	175	-	1856	-	gr/	a.a.lre.ie
Lisnadill	Lislea	Wynne Thomas	bleach	57x24x15, 30x20x13 :	-	22.8	-	1836	-	v1B/	27
Loughgilly	Lisnaee	Boyde Michael	flax	-	-	-	-	-	15x3x15	vmb/	28
Ballymore	Lisnagree	-	flax	-	-	-	-	-	-	1"os/	-
Ballymore	Lisnagree	- at Windy Gap	flax	-	-	-	-	-	-	1"os/	59
Loughgilly	Lisnalee	Boyle Michael	flax	43x17x10 & 19x17x6	-	4.7.0	-	1836	4 berths, m/cy good :	v1B/	219
Kilmore	Lisnaveague	Greer Moses	corn	-	-	-	-	-	13x2x13	vmb/	28
Ballymore	Lisraw	Moody John	corn kiln	39x21x7 & 12x8x5 & :	-	5.8.0	-	1836	-	v1B/	214
Mullaghbrack	Lurgaboy	Watson John	flax	65x18x6	-	3.8.4	-	1836	16x4x10 drives :	v1B/	213
Mullabrack	Lurgaboy :	-	corn	-	-	-	-	-	-	6"os/	17
Shankill	Lurgan	Johnston John	brewery	cellar 43x34x9, addn. :	-	96.0	-	1836	-	v1B/	223a
Ballymyre	Lurgana	Reid Capt.	corn	-	-	-	-	-	20x4x15	vmb/	28
Ballymyre	Lurgana	Reid William	corn & kiln	34x28x23, 19x9x7 & :	-	39.19	-	1837	- 2 pairs stones :	v1B/	239
Mullaghbrack	Lurganboy	Watson John	flax	-	-	-	-	-	16x4x10	vmb/	28
Armagh	Lurgy Valley	Bell Matthew	corn & flour	22x34x22, 27x35x22 :	-	45.17	-	1835	18x8x17 supply water :	v1B/	21a
Armagh	Lurgyvallon	Bell Matthew	corn	-	-	-	-	-	17x6x1.6	vmb/	28
Armagh	Lurgyvallon	Bell Matthew	flour	-	-	-	-	-	18x6x1.6	vmb/	28
Armagh	Lurgyvallon	Irving William :	mill	-	-	-	Irving Wm & ors ag'ment :	1811	-	dd/	714 50 487562
Armagh	Lurgyvallon	McCan	mills	-	-	-	McCan - McCan	-	-	dd/	700 387 480254
Armagh	Lurgyvallon	McDonnell Randall :	mill	-	-	-	McDonnell & ors - King :	1819	L&R. 10/11 Aug.	dd/	744 117 506452
Derrynoose	Maddan	-	flax	-	-	-	-	-	-	1"os/	59
Derrynoose	Maddan	-	patch	-	-	-	-	-	-	1"os/	59
Derrynoose	Maddan		flax	-	-	-	-	-	-	1"os/	59
Armagh	Markethill, Mohan	Gosford Earl of	mills	-	-	-	Gosford - Reynolds Geo	1885	-	dd/	1885 23 201
Mullaghbrack	Marlacoo Beg	-	flax	-	-	-	-	-	-	6"os/	13

PARISH	TOWNLAND	MILLER	TYPE	HOUSE	Land	£Val	PROPRIETORS	Date	WHEEL etc.	Record	Ref.
Mullaghbrack	Marlacoo Beg	Boyd Robert	flax	-	-	-	-	-	16x3x13 6 stocks	vmb/	28
Mullaghbrack	Marlacoo Beg	Boyd Robert	flax	-	-	-	-	-	14x3x15 4 stocks	vmb/	28
Mullaghbrack	Marlacoo More	Johnston James	corn	-	-	-	-	-	-	vmb/	28
Mullaghbrack	Marlacoo More	Johnston James	flax	-	-	-	-	-	13x2x13	vmb/	28
Mullaghbrack	Marlacoo More :	-	flax	-	-	-	-	-	-	6"os/	13
Mullaghbrack	Marlacoomore	Boyd Robert	flax	36x28x26 & 12x11x6 :	-	9.18	-	1837	1st mill 6 stocks & :	v1B/	232
Mullaghbrack	Marlacoomore	Johnston James	corn & kiln	33x21x6, 10x10x6 & :	-	2.16	-	1837	12x2x15 drives 1 pr. st.	v1B/	231
Mullaghbrack	Marlacoomore	Johnston James	flax	17x15x16	-	1.3.8	-	1837	4 stocks water supply :	v1B/	231
Armagh	Marlacoo	Rowntree James :	mill & bog	-	-	-	Rowntree J - Rowntree :	1812	Rel. 2 Apl.	dd/	750 487 510422
Armagh	Marytone *	Gray Joseph H	mills	-	-	-	Gray Jos - Tyndall Wm	1889	-	dd/	1889 21 125
Eglish	Maydown	Dobbin Leonard :	mill	-	-	-	Dobbin L - Eyres Edwd :	1819	23 Apl.	dd/	740 103 504038
Eglish	Maydown	Eyres Thomas	flax	-	-	-	-	-	16x5x7 8 berths	vmb/	28
Eglish	Maydown	Eyres Thomas	flax	58x29x17, 50x23x15 &	-	12.18	-	1838	16x5x7 drives 4 stocks :	v1B/	236
Tynan	Middleton	-	mill	-	-	-	-	-	-	1"os/	46
Tynan	Middleton Town	Johnston Matthew	corn	-	-	-	-	-	18x4x16	vmb/	28
Tynan	Middletown	Connor Anne	distillery	-	-	-	-	1782	1 still - 220g.	hcJ	lic.
Tynan	Middletown	Hughes James	distillery	-	-	-	-	1782	1 still - 200g.	hcJ	lic.
Tynan	Middletown	Hughes Thomas	distillery	-	-	-	-	1782	1 still - 220g.	hcJ	lic.
Tynan	Middletown	Irwin Mountross	distillery	-	-	-	-	1782	1 still - 229g.	hcJ	lic.
Tynan	Middletown	King Robert	distillery	-	-	-	-	1782	1 still - 204g.	hcJ	lic.
Tynan	Middletown	Love Henry	distillery	-	-	-	-	1782	1 still - 219g.	hcJ	lic.
Tynan	Middletown	Patterson & Harkness	distillery	-	-	-	-	1782	1 still - 204g.	hcJ	lic.
Tynan	Middletown Manor	Bond	mills	-	-	-	Bond - Harris	-	-	dd/	738 436 503171
Armagh	Millford	-	linen	-	-	-	-	-	-	1"os/	47
Aghory	Milltown	-	mill	-	-	-	-	-	-	1"os/	47
Armagh	Milltown Claddy	-	mill	-	-	-	-	-	-	1"os/	59
Eglish	Milltown Tamlaght	-	flax	-	-	-	-	-	-	1"os/	47
Armagh	Miltown Inishmore	-	no mill	-	-	-	-	-	-	1"os/	35
Loughgilly	Mohan	-	flax	-	-	-	-	-	-	1"os/	59
Loughgilly	Mohan	-	mill	-	-	-	-	-	-	1"os/	59
Loughgilly	Mohan	Gosford Earl of	mills	-	-	-	Gosford E - Lewis Samuel	1881	-	dd/	1881 23 261
Loughgilly	Mohan	Gosford Earl of	mills	-	-	-	Gosford Earl - Harrison :	1881	-	dd/	1881 32 289
Loughgilly	Mohan	Gosford Earl of	mills	-	-	-	Gosford E - Wann James	1887	-	dd/	1887 47 125
Loughgilly	Mohan	Wynne Margaret	mills	-	-	-	Wynne Margt - Brown Jn	1881	-	dd/	1881 45 126
Lisnadill	Moneyquin	Carroll Edward :	bleach green	-	-	-	Carrol Ed - McQuaide Jn :	1819	Mort. 9 Apl.	dd/	740 107 504042
Ballymore	Moodoge	-	corn & flax :	-	-	-	J. Mains	2004	used as poultry unit	mmiS/	PW - Cc
Ballymore	Moodoge	-	mill	-	-	-	-	-	-	1"os/	47
Ballymore	Moodoge	- on Cusher R.	corn & flax	-	-	-	-	-	-	6"os/	15
Ballymore	Moodoge	Maines Jerry & Hardy	corn & kiln	27x27x16 & 7x26x6 & :	-	14.14	-	1836	2 pr. sts. metal m/cy :	v1B/	219
Ballymore	Moodoge	Maines Jerry & Hardy	flax	60x21x15, rolling mill :	-	5.19	-	1836	20 berths, mill kept in :	v1B/	214
Ballymore	Moodoge	Mains J & Co.	corn	-	-	-	-	-	13x3x4	vmb/	28
Loughgilly	Mountmorris	Byers William	flax	-	-	-	-	-	14x3x14 6 stocks	vmb/	28
Loughgilly	Mountnorris	McCullough John	mills	-	-	-	McCullough Jn - Turretin :	1883	-	dd/	1883 11 87
Loughgilly	Mount-Norris	Byrnes William	flax	61x26x6 & stores :	-	13.6	-	1836	12 berths, 2 sets rollers	v1B/	219
Mullaghbrack	Mullaghbrack	-	flax	-	-	-	-	-	-	1"os/	47
Loughgilly	Mullaghmore	Douglas William	corn	-	-	-	-	-	18x4x17	vmb/	28
Loughgilly	Mullaghmore	Douglas William	flax	-	-	-	-	-	14x3x14 6 stocks	vmb/	28
Loughgilly	Mullaghmore	Douglass William	flax	33x18x6 & 26x17x6	-	4.4.0	-	1836	wooden wheel drives :	v1B/	219
Armagh	Mullaghycasey	Atkinson	mill	-	-	-	Atkinson & Bailies m/arts.	-	-	dd/	721 320 492855
Killevey	Mullaglass	Atkinson William	beetling	-	-	-	-	-	20x4x20	vmb/	28
Killevey	Mullaglass	Atkinson William	beetling	11x26x15, 17x16x16 :	-	17.45	-	1836	-	v1B/	244b
Killevey	Mullaglass	Gray Doctor	spade	-	-	-	-	-	13x3x14	vmb/	28

PARISH	TOWNLAND	MILLER	TYPE	HOUSE	Land	£Val	PROPRIETORS	Date	WHEEL etc.	Record	Ref.
Killevey	Mullaglass	Masterson Alex	spade	32x19x7, 16x4x7 & :	-	4.4.0	-	1836	mill idle & m/cy moved	v1B/	244b
Killevey	Mullaglass	McAlister Alex	corn	-	-	-	-	-	13x3x6	vmb/	28
Killevey	Mullaglass	McAlister Alex	flax	-	-	-	-	-	14x4x7	vmb/	28
Killevey	Mullaglass	McAllister Alex	corn & kiln	40x21x9 & kiln :	-	13.4	-	1836	- 1 pair stones	v1B/	244b
Killevey	Mullaglass	McAllister Alex	flax	34x21x12 & 22x19x6	-	13.4	-	1836	good supply, 5 handles	v1B/	244b
Tynan	Mullanary	-	flax	-	-	-	-	-	-	1"os/	58
Ballymore	Mullantur	Allen William	spade	25x19x6 & smithy :	-	6.7.0	-	1836		v1B/	214
Ballymore	Mullanture	- on Cusher R.	spade	-	-	-	-	-	-	6"os/	14
Ballymore	Mullanture	Allen William	spade	-	-	-	-	-	13x3x2 hammer 4cwts.	vmb/	28
Newt`nhamilton	Newt`nhamilton	-	mill	-	-	-	-	-	-	1"os/	59
Newt`nhamilton	Newt`nhamilton	-	mill	-	-	-	-	-	-	1"os/	59
Newt`nhamilton	Newt`nhamilton	Oliver Andrew	distillery	-	-	-	-	1782	1 still - 234g.	hcJ	lic.
Newt`nhamilton	Newt`nhamilton	Ruxton Henry	distillery	-	-	-	-	1782	1 still - 250g.	hcJ	lic.
Tynan	Portnelligan :	-	corn	-	-	-	-	-	-	6"os/	15
Keady	Racarbery	- at Millmount	flour	-	-	-	-	2004	-	mmSv/	pw - Z
Keady	Racarbery	nr. old Annaville Ho.	beetling	-	-	-	-	2004	-	mmSv/	pw - Z
Keady	Racarbery	nr. old Annaville Ho.	flour	-	-	-	-	2004	-	mmSv/	pw - Z
Keady	Racarbery	Watson Mervyn	beetling	-	-	-	-	2004	-	mmSv/	pw - Z
Keady	Racarby	Kidd	mill	-	-	-	Kidd - Kidd	-	-	dd/	737 409 502544
Keady	Racarby	Kirk William	mills	-	-	-	Kirk Wm - Gardiner Wm	1881	-	dd/	1881 41 15
Keady	Racarby	Kirk Wm, Henry & Jn	beetling	ho., gate ho., offs,. ld.	49a.	162	-	1881	-	dd/	1881 41 15
Keady	Racarby :	-	beetling	-	-	-	-	-	-	6"os/	20
Keady	Racarby :	-	flour	-	-	-	-	-	-	6"os/	20
Keady	Racarby :	Kidd Osborne	flour	44x24x31 & 13x24x31	-	24.7	-	1836	18x4x14	v1B/	26b
Keady	Racarby :	Kirk William	beetling	85x29x18, 21x12x7 :	-	15.0	-	1836	22x7x16 7 sets beetles	v1B/	26a
Keady	Racarby :	Kirk William	beetling	75x25x18 & 10x12x6	-	7.6.9	-	1836	20x4x18 4 sets beetles	v1B/	26b
Keady	Racarby :	Martin Jacob	flour	50x29x33, 15x16x17 :	-	32.6	-	1836	13x3x15 good supply :	v1B/	26b
Mullabrack	Ratarnet	-	flax	-	-	-	-	-	-	1"os/	47
Tynan	Rathtrillick	Johnson Matthew	corn	-	-	-	-	-	15x5x7	vmb/	28
Tynan	Rathtrillick	Johnston Matthew	corn & kiln	71x22x20	-	13.18	-	1837	15x5x7 2 pr. stones :	v1B/	238
Kilmore	Rich Hill	Laughy Charlotte	corn & kiln	72x19x16, 42x26x15 :	-	12.17	-	1837	wheels worn out, m/cy	v1B/	229b
Kilmore	Richhill	- on Tall R. :	corn	-	-	-	-	-	-	6"os/	13
Kilmore	Richhill	Langtree Mrs	corn	-	-	-	-	-	13x2x13 13x2x13	vmb/	28
Kilmore	Richhill	Thompson William	flax	-	-	-	-	-	13x4x6 6 stocks	vmb/	28
Kilmore	Rockmacreeny	-	flax & corn	-	-	-	-	2004	-	mmiS/	PW - B
Kilmore	Rockmacreeny	Sinton William	flax	old mill 50x23x8 & :	-	6.17	-	1837	- 6 stocks in ea. mill :	v1B/	229a
Kilmore	Rockmacreeny	Tinton William	flax	-	-	-	-	-	13x4x13 6 stocks	vmb/	28
Kilmore	Rockmacreeny	Tinton William	flax	-	-	-	-	-	13x4x13 4 stocks	vmb/	28
Kilmore	Rockmacreeny :	- on Tall R. :	flax & pond	-	-	-	-	-	-	6"os/	13
Donaghenry	Roughan	- at Cowser's Br.	paper	-	-	-	-	2004	-	mmSv/	pw - Z
Donaghenry	Roughan	- on Callan R.	flax (ruins)	-	-	-	-	2004	-	mmSv/	pw - Z
Derrynoose	Roughan	Girvan Mary	beetling	45x20x15 old bldg. :	-	2.13	-	1836	15x3x4 2 sets beetles	v1B/	23
Derrynoose	Roughan	McCullagh Joseph	beetling	84x22x16, 23x10x5 :	-	10.4	-	1836	- m/cy in good repair	v1B/	23
Kilclooney	Seasboughan	Hutchinson John	flax	19x19x6 7 23x16x6	-	1.3.4	-	1836	16x3 drives 4 stocks :	v1B/	210a&b
Mullabrack	Shancrackan Beg	Leigh Thomas :	mills	-	-	-	Leigh T - Bacon Mary :	1816	Mort. 11 Oct.	dd/	708 279 485014
Mullabrack	Shancrackan Beg	Morrison John :	mill	-	-	-	Morrison - Cherry Robert, [	1815	Asgt. 16 Sep.	dd/	734 291 500626
Mullabrack	Shancrackan Beg	Patterson John	corn & kiln	21x26x10 & kiln :	-	2.13	-	1837	- 1 pr. stones dia 5ft. :	v1B/	231
Mullabrack	Shancrackan Beg	Patterson John	flax	56x26x18, 19x26x11 :	-	9.17	-	1837	- 4 stocks, water :	supply	231
Mullabrack	Shancrackan Beg	Small Hugh	beetling	50x24x17	-	4.2.6	- 4 sets of beetles :	1837	- 4 sets of beetles :	v1B/	231
Mullabrack	Shancrackan Beg	Small Hugh	corn & kiln	17x24x13 & 10x9x5 :	-	1.8.4	-	1837	- mill idle for 2 yrs. :	v1B/	231
Mullabrack	Shancrackan Beg	Small Hugh	flax	20x37x6	-	17/2d	-	1837	- 10 stocks, water :	v1B/	231
Mullabrack	Shanecrackan	- on Usher R.	mill	-	-	-	-	-	-	1"os/	47

PARISH	TOWNLAND	MILLER	TYPE	HOUSE	Land	£Val	PROPRIETORS	Date	WHEEL etc.	Record	Ref.
Shankill	Shankill	Greer & Boyd Messrs	corn	49x28x27	-	11.8	-	1836	water 2 months/ yr.	v1B/	223a
Forkhill	Shean	Bellew John	corn & kiln	37x21x14 & kiln :	-	9.0.0	-	1836	- 2 pairs stones :	v1B/	247
Forkhill	Shean	Smyth Thomas	corn & kiln	40x22x6 & kiln :	-	15.0	-	1836	- 3 pairs stones :	v1B/	247
Armagh	Sheernageragh	Roberts John	distillery	-	-	-	-	1782	1 still - 200g.	hcJ	lic.
Eglish	Tamlaght	M'Carraher John	corn & kiln	house, offices & land	15a.	24.10.	-	1856	-	gr/	a.a.Ire.ie
Eglish	Tamlaght	McCarragher John	corn	-	-	-	-	-	16x3x10	vmb/	28
Eglish	Tamlaght	McCarrogher John	corn & kiln	18x19x20, 14x18x20 :	-	5.11	-	1836	16x3 water 4 mos.	v1B/	24
Eglish	Tamlaght	nr B`martrim Water	corn & pond	-	-	-	-	-	-	6"os/	12
Lisnadill	Tanderagee	-	spinning	-	-	-	-	-	-	1"os/	47
Lisnadill	Tanderagee	Nugent Peter	corn	-	-	-	-	-	13x2x -	vmb/	28
Lisnadill	Tanderagee Tn :	-	flour & corn	-	-	-	-	-	-	6"os/	14
Lisnadill	Tanderagee Tn :	-	flour & corn :	-	-	-	-	2004	-	mmiS/	PW - Ab
Lisnadill	Tandragee	Nugent Peter	corn & kiln	35x18x6, 13x10x5 :	-	2.15	-	1837		v1B/	211
Shankill	Tannagh	Boyd & Watt Messrs	brewery	32x21x17 & 33x16x16 :	-	26.0	-	1836		v1B/	223a
Shankill	Tannagh	Johnston John	brewery	12x18x15, 29x29x22 : 8	-	40.0	-	1836		v1B/	223a
Shankill	Tannagh More S.	Boyd & Watt Messrs	malt house & kiln	121x22x9 & 72x24x19, r	-	7.0.0	-	1836		v1B/	223a
Keady	Tassagh	-	bleach	-	-	-	-	-	-	6"os/	16
Keady	Tassagh	-	corn & beetling	-	-	-	-	-	-	6"os/	16
Keady	Tassagh	-	corn kiln	-	-	-	-	-	-	6"os/	16
Keady	Tassagh	Boud James	beetling	-	-	-	-	-	16x3x8	vmb/	28
Keady	Tassagh	Boyd James	beetling	565x28x17 & 15x11x5	-	4.13	-	1836	16x4.6x7.6	v1B/	26b
Keady	Tassagh	Boyd James B	beetling	- workman's ho., offs.	-	50	-	-	-	gr	-
Keady	Tassagh	Boyd James B	beetling	-	-	22	-	-	-	gr	-
Keady	Tassagh	Bradley George J	use of water	-	-	-	Bradley Geo - Keating Ada	1881	-	dd/	1881 21 243
Armagh	Tassagh	Greenmount Mills	beetling	-	-	-	-	2004	-	mmSv/	pw - Z
Armagh	Tassagh	k/a paper mill	beetling	-	-	-	-	2004	-	mmSv/	pw - B
Keady	Tassagh	Kidd Samuel	beetling	-	-	-	-	-	14x6x8 drives 3 beams	vmb/	28
Kkeady	Tassagh	Kidd Samuel	beetling	36x17x18 & 9x9x5	-	4.1.3	-	1836		v1B/	26b
Keady	Tassagh	Kirk William	beetling	-	-	-	-	-	15x8x9 drives 5 beams	vmb/	28
Keady	Tassagh	Kirk William	beetling	63x34x30 & 10x9x5	-	16.1	-	1836	15x8x8 drives :	v1B/	7
Armagh	Tassagh	Kirk William	beetling	-	-	-	-	2004	-	mmSv/	pw - Z
Keady	Tassagh	Kirk William	mill	-	-	-	Kirk Wm - Gardiner Wm	1881	-	dd/	1881 41 18
Keady	Tassagh	Kirk Wm., Jn. & Henry	beetling	- offices & land	2a.	51.10.	-	-	-	gr	-
Keady	Tassagh	Lambert Thomas	use of water				Lambert Thos - Boyd Eliz	1881		dd/	1881 43 224
Keady	Tassagh	McKee I	corn	-	-	-	-	-	10x3x6	vmb/	28
Kkeady	Tassagh	McKee J	betling & bleach	50x22x18, 25x22x18 :	-	6.2	-	1836	-	v1B/	23
Kkeady	Tassagh	McKee J	betling & bleach	37x21x14 & 29x6x7	-	3.11	-	1836	14x6x8	v1B/	3
Kkeady	Tassagh	McKee J	corn	49x21x8	-	1.12	-	1836	10x3x6 almost idle :	v1B/	26b
Keady	Tassagh	McKee Joseph	beetling	-	-	-	-	-	14x6x8 drives 3 beams	vmb/	28
Keady	Tassagh	McKee Joseph	beetling	-	-	-	-	-	13x3x7	vmb/	28
Keady	Tassagh	McKee Joseph	beetling	-	-	-	-	-	15x6x8	vmb/	28
Armagh	Tassagh	McKee Joseph	beetling	-	-	-	-	2004	-	mmSv/	pw - Z
Keady	Tassagh	McKee Joseph	betling & bleach	64x28x26 & 20x13x6	-	11.15	-	1836	-	v1B/	3
Armagh	Tassagh	Milk Marketing Board	beetling	-	-	-	-	2004	-	mmSv/	pw - B
Keady	Tassagh	Morrison James :	beetling	-	-	25	-	-	-	gr	-
Keady	Tassagh	Sadler, Ferdon, Kidd	linen weaving	52x22x17 & 52x17x6	-	3.16	-	1836	-	v1B/	13
Keady	Tassagh	Seward Luke M	mills				Seward L M - Boyd Eliz	1882		dd/	1882 7 169
Kkeady	Tassagh	Stringer Fr.	flax	33x25x20	-	4.7.3	-	1836	14x4x8 good supply :	v1B/	11
Keady	Tassagh	Stringer Francis	flax	-	-	-	-	-	14x4x7 6 berths	vmb/	28
Keady	Tassagh	Wynne Thomas	beetling	- & offices	-	38	-	-	-	gr	-
Keady	Tassagh	Wynne Thomas	beetling	-	-	14	-	-	-	gr	-
Drumcree	Tavanagh, High St.	Stanley Henry	stores	37x15x19	-	6.10	-	1837	-	v1B/	5

PARISH	TOWNLAND	MILLER	TYPE	HOUSE	Land	£Val	PROPRIETORS	Date	WHEEL etc.	Record	Ref.
Kilcloney	Teaboughan	Hutchinson John	flax	-	-	-	-	-	17x3x17	vmb/	28
Mullaghbrack	Thanecracken Beg	Patterson John	corn	-	-	-	-	-	13x3x4	vmb/	28
Mullaghbrack	Thanecracken Beg	Patterson John	flax	-	-	-	-	-	13x4x4 8 stocks	vmb/	28
Mullaghbrack	Thanecracken Beg	Small Hugh	corn	-	-	-	-	-	- mill not in use	vmb/	28
Mullaghbrack	Thanecracken Beg	Small Hugh	flax	-	-	-	-	-	- mill not in use	vmb/	28
Armagh	The Fews	-	mill	-	-	-	-	-	-	1"os/	59
Forkhill	Thean	Bellew John	corn	-	-	-	-	-	-	vmb/	28
Forkhill	Thean	Smyth Thomas	corn	-	-	-	-	-	-	vmb/	28
Armagh	Toagh	Kidd	mulcture	-	-	-	Kidd - Kidd	-	-	dd/	737 409 502544
Armagh	Townland ?	Maturin William :	Cope's Mill	-	-	-	Maturin Wm - Hall Letitia :	1816	Mort. 13 May (assgt. of)	dd/	702 614 481698
Loughgilly	Tullyallan	Atkinson William	beetling	-	-	-	-	-	30x4x30 drives 3 beams	vmb/	28
Loughgilly	Tullyallan	Atkinson William	beetling & wash	-	-	-	-	-	27x5x27 drives 2 beams	vmb/	28
Loughgilly	Tullyallan	Gibson Messrs	flax	-	-	-	-	-	14x3x14	vmb/	28
Loughgilly	Tullyallen	-	beetling	-	-	-	-	-	-	1"os/	59
Loughgilly	Tullyallen	Atkinsin William	beetling	50x27x28 & 27x12x11	-	24.7	-	1836	- wooden wheel :	v1B/	219
Loughgilly	Tullyallen	Atkinson mr	linen m'factory	beetling mill 40x34x22 :	-	31.5	-	1836	- wooden wheel :	v1B/	219
Loughgilly	Tullyallen	Gibson Robert Wm	flax	39x20x6 & 34x20x7	-	4.0.0	-	1836	- wooden machinery	v1B/	219 & 106
Loughgilly	Tullyallen	Gray George	mills	-	-	-	Gray Geo - Gray Jos H.	1889	-	dd/	1889 21 126
Tynan	Tullybrick	-	mill pond	-	-	-	-	-	-	6"os/	15
Tynan	Tullybrick Hamilton	Johnston Matthew	corn & kiln	37x24x34, 18x13x18 :	-	10.18	-	1837	18x4x16 2 pr. stones :	v1B/	238
Tynan	Tullybrick Hamilton	Johnston Matthew	distillery	37x24x34, 33x23x16 :	-	10.18	-	1837	-	v1B/	238
Armagh	Tullycondraught	Shirges	mill	-	-	-	Shirges - Mulligan	-	-	dd/	627 448 464653
Armagh	Tullycondraught	Shirges Anna Isbla :	mill	-	-	-	Shirges A - Crawford : (	1814	-	dd/	672 450 464655
Ballymore	Tullycross	Creevy John	corn	-	-	-	-	-	25x5x21 3 pr st.	vmb/	28
Armagh	Tullyelmer	Burges	mills	-	-	-	Burges - Cardwell	-	-	dd/	697 233 478356
Armagh	Tullyelmer	Cardwell Wm & John	corn	-	-	-	-	-	15x3x4.6	vmb/	28
Armagh	Tullyelmer	Cardwell Wm & John	corn & kiln	34x13x7, 80x21x15 :	-	9.15	-	1835	16x2x6	v1B/	1
Armagh	Tullyelmer :	- on Callan R.	corn	-	-	-	-	-	-	6"os/	12
Shankill	Tullygally	-	linen	-	-	-	-	-	-	1"os/	35
Keady	Tullyglush	Finton S & Kidd	bleach	-	-	-	-	-	18x5x12	vmb/	28
Keady	Tullyglush	Finton S & Kidd	bleach	-	-	-	-	-	18x6x12	vmb/	28
Keady	Tullyglush	Higgins Jno :	bleach	-	-	-	Higgins J - Gowin Jno :	1811	Lse. 15 Jne.	dd/	637 337 438657
Keady	Tullyglush	Higgins	bleach	-	-	-	Higgins - Feir	-	-	dd/	641 251 444938
Keady	Tullyglush	Huggins John :	mills	-	-	-	Huggins & ors - Huggins :	1819	Asgt. 16 Dec.	dd/	749 40 509325
Keady	Tullyglush	Huggins John	mills	-	-	-	Huggins John - Huggins :	1819	-	dd/	749 41 509376
Keady	Tullyglush	Kane John	flax	-	-	-	-	-	16x3x12 6 rollers	vmb/	28
Keady	Tullyglush	Kane John	flax	58x19x13, 19x9x7 :	-	17.0	-	1837	16x3x12 6 stocks :	vmb/	238
Keady	Tullyglush	Kidd J A	beetling & bleach	36x21x16, 18x7x8 :	-	13.5	-	1836	17x6x12 & 18x4x12	v1B/	26c & d
Keady	Tullyglush	Kidd J A	beetling & bleach	24x64x16, 15x7x16 :	-	18.11	-	1836	30x5x27 5 pairs rollers	v1B/	26c&d
Keady	Tullyglush	Kidd J A	wash	49x22x13, 27x14x6 :	-	10.4	-	1836	21x2x30	v1B/	26c&d
Keady	Tullyglush	Kidd James	mills	-	-	-	Kidd james - Kidd George	1881	-	dd/	1881 41 207
Keady	Tullyglush	Kidd James A	beetling	-	-	-	-	-	30x5x27 drives 7 beams	vmb/	28
Keady	Tullyglush	Kidd James A	beetling	-	-	-	-	-	16x6x11 drives 3 beams	vmb/	28
Keady	Tullyglush	Kidd James A	beetling	-	-	-	-	-	19x4x11 drives 4 beams	vmb/	28
Keady	Tullyglush	Kidd James A	wash	-	-	-	-	-	20x2x7 drives :	vmb/	28
Keady	Tullyglush	Morrison James & :	bleach	wareho., offs. & land	8.1.2:	122	-	-	-	gr/	a.a.ire.ie
Keady	Tullyglush	nr old Greenmount Ho	beetling	-	-	-	-	2004	-	mmSv/	pw - Z
Keady	Tullyglush	Quinn John	beetling	part remains	-	-	-	2004	-	mmSv/	pw - B
Keady	Tullyglush	Quinn John	beetling & pond	-	-	-	-	2004	-	mmSv/	pw - B
Keady	Tullyglush	Sarlier, Fenton & Kidd	flax	58x19x13, 19x9x7 & :	-	47.18	-	1837	19x5x14 2 double engs	v1B/	238
Ballymore	Tullyhugh	Creery John	flour & corn	62x33x48, 68x29x48 :	-	80.9	-	1836	corn mill 3 pairs stones	v1B/	214
Ballymore	Tullyhugh	Creery John	old starch mfty	45x19x21, 16x26x10 &	-	4.15	-	1836	-	v1B/	214

PARISH	TOWNLAND	MILLER	TYPE	HOUSE	Land	£Val	PROPRIETORS	Date	WHEEL etc.	Record	Ref.
Ballymore	Tullyhugh	Creevy John	flour	-	-	-	-	-	25x8x21 5 pairs stones	vmb/	28
Eglish	Tullymore	Whiteside James :	mill	-	-	-	Whiteside J - McMurren :	1817	-	dd/	718 267 491002
Eglish	Tullymore Etrce	-	spade	-	-	-	-	-	14x3x3	vmb/	28
Eglish	Tullymore Etrce	McNorden M/s	corn	-	-	-	-	-	16x3x4	vmb/	28
Eglish	Tullymore Etrce	McNorden widow	spade	-	-	-	-	-	11x3x5	vmb/	28
Eglish	Tullymoreetra	McMorran Jas & Edw	corn & kiln	38x20x18, 32x22x10 :	-	10.5	-	1838	16x4x7 drives 2 pr. st. :	v1B/	236
Eglish	Tullymoreetra	McMorran Jas & Edw	spade	43x28x10 & 61x17x13	-	6.1.4	-	1838	12x4x5 mill going to ruir	v1B/	236
Eglish	Tullymoreetra	McMorran Widow I	flax	34x21x7 & 36x21x12	-	3.3.4	-	1838	10x4x6 8 stocks & :	v1B/	236
Eglish	Tullymoreetra	McMorran Widow I	spade	27x23x9 & 41x20x9	-	3.7.5	-	1838	12x3x5 machinery bad	v1B/	236
Armagh	Tullynacreeve	-	mill	-	-	-	-	-	-	1"os/	59
Ballymore	Tullynacross	Carrothers Alex	corn & kiln	40x24x16 & kiln :	-	10.15	-	1836	- 1 pair stones :	v1B/	34
Ballymore	Tullynacross	Carrothers William	flax	26x19x12, 18x7x6 7 :	-	6.19	-	1836	- 6 stocks or berths :	v1B/	214
Keady	Tullynamollogue	Kirk William	bleach	-	-	-	-	-	30x2x25 drives 4 beams	vmb/	28
Keady	Tullynamollogue	Kirk William	bleach	105x43x28 & :	-	86.8	-	1836	30x6 7 24x4 overshot :	v1B/	26a & b
Keady	Tullynamollogue	Morrison James :	beetling	- ho., offices & land	28a.	62.10	-	-	-	gr	-
Keady	Tullynamollogue	Simpson Mrs	flax	-	-	-	-	-	16x4x8 6 berths	vmb/	28
Keady	Tullynamollogue	Simpson Mrs	flax	39x24x16 & 25x9x6	-	9.0.3	-	1836	-	v1B/	26a & b
Newt`nhamilton	Tullyvallon	Johnston Robert	corn	-	-	-	-	-	16x4x8	vmb/	28
Newt`nhamilton	Tullyvallon	Johnston Robert	corn	42x24x11, 18x19x17 :	-	3.18	-	1837	14x4x7 2 pairs sts. :	v1B/	238
Newt`nhamilton	Tullyvallon	Johnston Robert	corn & kiln	26x23x14, 29x23x14 :	-	9.4.0	-	1837	- 3 pairs stones :	v1B/	242a/b
Newt`nhamilton	Tullyvallon	Lymes James	flax	46x19x9	-	4.15	-	1837	- 4 stocks :	v1B/	242a/b
Newt`nhamilton	Tullyvallon	Maguire John	corn	-	-	-	-	-	14x2x8	vmb/	28
Newt`nhamilton	Tullyvallon	Maguire John	corn & kiln	33x19x7 & 13z12x5 :	-	3.2.1	-	1837	- 1 pair stones :	v1B/	242a/b
Newt`nhamilton	Tullyvallon	McCosh Mary	corn	-	-	4.8.0	-	1837	- 6 stocks, 1 pr. rollers	v1B/	242b
Newt`nhamilton	Tullyvallon	McShane Neal :	mill	-	-	-	McShane N - McShane :	1816	Conv. 3 Aug.	dd/	707 43 484179
Newt`nhamilton	Tullyvallon	Simpson Mary	flax	47x19x9	-	4.6.0	-	1837	- 4 stocks, 1 pr. rollers	v1B/	242b
Newt`nhamilton	Tullyvallon	Sinton Thomas	spade	25x20x6 & 16x20x7	-	5..6.0	-	1837	-	v1B/	242a/b
Newt`nhamilton	Tullyvallon	Tinton Thomas	spade	-	-	-	-	-	16x4x8 hammer :	vmb/	28
Newt`nhamilton	Tullyvallon	Tymes James	flax	-	-	-	-	-	13x3x13	vmb/	28
Tynan	Tynan	Ferguson John	corn	-	-	-	-	-	14x4x7	vmb/	28
Tynan	Tynan	Ferguson John	flax	-	-	-	-	-	14x4x6	vmb/	28
Tynan	Tynan	Ferguson John	flax	35x20x14	-	2 13	-	1837	14x4x6 4 stocks :	v1B/	238
Tynan	Tynan	Strong James Sir	corn	-	-	-	Mrs G. McDermott	2004	-	mmiS/	wh - B
Armagh	Umgola	-	flour	-	-	-	-	-	-	6"os/	12
Armagh	Umgola	- Umgola Mills	mills & mill race	-	-	-	-	-	-	6"os/	12
Armagh	Umgola	Kidd Thomas	beetling	-	-	-	-	2004	-	mmSv/	pw - B
Armagh	Umgola	Kidd Thomas	beetling	-	-	-	-	2004	-	mmSv/	pw - Z
Armagh	Umgola	Kidd Thomas	corn	-	-	-	-	-	14x5x4.6	vmb/	28
Armagh	Umgola	Kidd Thomas	corn & flour	39x55x27, bldg. bad :	-	39.2	-	1835	corn undershot 14x6x5 :	v1B/	21a
Armagh	Umgola	Kidd Thomas	flour	-	-	-	-	-	15x8x4.6 3 pr stones	vmb/	28
Tynan	Unshog	Hughes James	mills	-	-	-	Hughes James - James	1886	-	dd/	1886 45 115
Tynan	Unshog	Irwin George	starch	42x22x14 & shed :	-	9.5.0	-	1837	14x2x10, machinery :	v1B/	
Tynan	Unshog	Irwin William G	srarch	-	-	-	-	-	14x2x10	vmb/	28
Tynan	Unshog	Matthews	mills	-	-	-	Matthews - Boyde	-	-	dd/	670 499 462293
Tynan	Unshog :	38	corn	-	-	-	-	-	-	6"os/	15
Armagh	Windy Gap	- near Lisnagree	flax	-	-	-	-	-	-	1"os/	-
Armagh	Woodvale	-	Ball`s Mill	-	-	-	-	-	-	1"os/	70

PARISH	TOWNLAND	MILLER	TYPE	HOUSE	Land	£Val	PROPRIETORS	Date	WHEEL etc.	Record	Ref.
Aghade	Aghade	at Ahade Bridge	-	old, in poor condition	-	-	-	1998	-	pWEH	R
Aghade	Aghade	Echlin Alice	-	-	-	-	Echlin A - Lynnan John	1787	-	dd/	394 104 259535
Aghade	Aghade	Lennon Bernard	mill	-	-	-	Lennon B - Keppel Robt	1873	-	dd/	1873 45 36
Aghade	Aghade	Lennon Michael	-	-	-	-	Lennon Bernard - Maria	1871	-	dd/	1871 37 186
Aghade	Aghade	Lennon Michael	-	-	-	-	Lennon B - Keppel Robt	1873	-	dd/	1873 45 35
Aghade	Aghade	Lennon Michael	mill	-	-	-	Lennon Michael - Bernard	1871	-	dd/	1871 37 184
Ardristan	Ardristan	Leggett William	corn	-	54a.	-	-	-	-	gr/	-
Ardristan	Ardristan	Ligate Wiliam	corn	-	-	22	-	1851	2 wheels, 4 pr st :	hob/	5.0019
Ardristan	Ardristan	Ligate William	corn	(1A) 36.6x20x21 kiln :	-	9.0.0	-	1843	13x4.9x6 breast :	hob/	5.0019
Carlow	Badger	Knott Abigail :	mill	-	-	-	Knott Abigail - Sarah	1819	Mort. 28 Aug.	dd/	745 306 507241
Dunleckny	Bagenalstown	Colvill Hester	mill	-	-	-	Colvill Hester - Hugh	1871	-	dd/	1871 29 163
Dunleckny	Bagenalstown	Colvill Hugh	mill	-	-	-	Colvill Hugh - Martha	1875	-	dd/	1875 47 152
Dunleckny	Bagenalstown	Colvill Martha	mill	-	-	-	Colvill Martha - Weld Matt	1876	-	dd/	1876 55 205
Dunleckny	Bagenalstown	Connolly Elizabeth	mill	-	-	-	Connolly E - Hughes Mtn.	1878	-	dd/	1878 23 211
Dunleckny	Bagenalstown	Forbes Matthew	mill	-	-	-	Forbes M - Weld Edmond	1878	-	dd/	1878 25 281
Dunleckny	Bagenalstown	on R. Slaney	seed	v. well preserved	-	-	Minch-Norton Ltd.	1998	maltings	pWEH	A
Dunleckney	Bagenalstown Tn	Crosthwaite Samuel	corn & kiln	- on strip of land :	-	35	-	1851	4 pair stones :	hob/	5.2358
Dunleckney	Bagenalstown Tn	Crosthwaite Samuel	flour	-	-	300	-	1851	2 wheels, small - :	hob/	5.2358
Dunleckney	Bagenalstown Tn	John Casey	malt house	- at The Quay :	-	-	-	1851	-	hob/	5.2358
Dunleckny	Bagnelstown	Bagenal	-	-	-	-	Bagenal - Brennan	-	[not 516]	dd/	516 524 361220
Dunleckny	Bagnelstown	Boulger William	-	-	-	-	Boulger W - Stewart Henry :	1788	-	dd/	391 387 261669
Dunleckny	Bagnelstown	Carter Robert :	-	-	-	-	Carter R - Colville William :	1795	Mort. 13 may	dd/	483 310 314160
Dunleckny	Bagnelstown	Colvill William :	mill	-	-	-	Colvill Wm - Weld Matthew	1781	-	dd/	366 187 244672
Dunleckny	Bagnelstown	Geoghan John	Lodge Mills	-	-	-	-	-	Twin 100-125 :	turb/	c1947
Dunleckny	Bagnelstown	Mercer Richard :	mill	-	-	-	Mercer R - Weld Matthew :	1784	-	dd/	361 358 244692
Dunleckny	Bagnelstown	Vigors Edward Rev.	mill	-	-	-	Vigors E - Merce Mounclierr	1773	-	dd/	395 126 261613
Sliguff	Ballinure	Newton Henry	charcoal	also drying ho	-	-	-	1851	20x3 breast :	hob/	5.0009
Sliguff	Ballinure	Newton Henry	saw &	(1A) 32.6x21x22 :	-	34	-	1851	21x3 full breast :	hob/	5.0007
Sliguff	Ballinure	Newton Henry	thrashing	(1A) 30.6x21x22 :	-	(part)	-	1851	-	hob/	5.0007
Killerrig	Ballybannon	-	malt	-	-	-	-	-	-	1"os/	137
Moyacomb	Ballyedmond	Kavanagh Thomas	old corn mill	- buildings very bad	-	-	-	1851	11ft.x2.6 o'shot :	hob/	5.0036A/note
Ballyellen	Ballyellen	Alexander	mill	-	-	-	Alexander - Stewart	-	-	dd/	828 377 557112
Ballyellin	Ballyellin	Cullen Edmond & Jas	flour	86.6 x 23.6 x 39.6 :	-	-	-	1843	-	hob/	5.0002
Ballyellin	Ballyellin	Cullen Edmond & Jas	flour	miller`s ho 42x18x11 :	-	78	-	-	1st - 15.6x6.6x4 :	hob/	5.0002
Ballyellin	Ballyellin	Cullen James	flour	-	49a.	-	-	-	-	gr/	-
Ballyellin	Ballyellin	Murphy Patrick :	mill & malt ho	-	-	-	Murphy Pat - Murphy Matt :	1820	-	dd/	748 174 508909
Ballyellin	Ballyellin Upper	- near B. Barrow	mill site ?	now has lime quarry :	-	-	-	2002	-	mmSv/	wh - Z
Cloydagh	Ballygowan	- on small canal :	mill complex	- walls only remain :	-	-	-	2002	- phos taken	mmSv/	wh - Z
Cloydagh	Ballygowan	- at Millford Dems.	flour	-	-	-	-	1840	-	6"os/	12
Cloydagh	Ballygowan	Alexander	-	-	-	-	Alexander - Izard & ano	-	?	dd/	338 172 360132
Cloydagh	Ballygowan	Alexander John	flour	(1B) 125x46.6x56 :	-	336	-	1843	16x20x6 dp bkts :	hob/	5.0010
Cloydagh	Ballygowan	Alexander John	malt house	(1B) 50x23x20 kiln :	-	(part)	-	1843	-	hob/	5.0010
Cloydagh	Ballygowan	Alexander John	mill	-	-	-	Alexander - Stewart Wm	1827	-	dd/	828 377 557112
Cloydagh	Ballygowan	Blakeney Walter	-	-	-	-	Blakeney W - Phelan Thos	1785	-	dd/	392 199 250608
Cloydagh	Ballygowan	Connolly James & Wm	mill	-	-	-	Connolly J - Connolly Richd :	1816	Mg. Smt.	dd/	701 522 481025
Cloydagh	Ballygowan	Connolly James :	mill	-	-	-	Connolly J - Connolly John :	1825	-	dd/	809 528 545863
Cloydagh	Ballygowan	Connolly Andrew	mills	-	-	-	Connolly A - Dolan Fran	1871	-	dd/	1871 22 64
Cloydagh	Ballygowan	Connolly James	mill	-	-	-	Connolly J - Alexander Jn	1827	-	dd/	828 316 557052
Cloydagh	Ballygowan	Connolly Richard	mills	-	-	-	Connolly R - Norton Patk	1870	-	dd/	1870 34 130
Cloydagh	Ballygowan	Landed Estate Court	mills	-	-	-	Ld Est Ct - Connolly Richd	1870	-	dd/	1870 13 7
Cloydagh	Ballygowan	Latouche John :	mill	-	-	-	Latouche - Alexander Jn :	1796	-	dd/	495 336 322771
Cloydagh	Ballygowan	Nugenr John	mills	-	-	-	Nugent John - Nat B. I. Co.	1874	-	dd/	1874 29 232

PARISH	TOWNLAND	MILLER	TYPE	HOUSE	Land	£Val	PROPRIETORS	Date	WHEEL etc.	Record	Ref.
Cloydagh	Ballygowan	Nugent James	mills	-	-	-	Nugent James - Kathleen	1874	-	dd/	1874 8 208
Cloydagh	Ballygowan	Nugent James	mills	-	-	-	Nugent Jas - Evans Allen	1874	-	dd/	1874 9 256
Cloydagh	Ballygowan	Nugent John	mills	-	-	-	Nugent Jn - Meldon John	1876	-	dd/	1876 10 283
Cloydagh	Ballygowan	Nugent John	mills	-	-	-	Nugent Jn - Nugent John	1876	-	dd/	1876 23 82
Cloydagh	Ballygowan	Nugent John	mills	-	-	-	Nugent Jn - Baylor Arthur	1876	-	dd/	1876 23 91
Cloydagh	Ballygowan	Nugent John	mills	-	-	-	Nugent Jn - Lewis Sam	1876	-	dd/	1876 47 45
Cloydagh	Ballygowan	Nugent John	mills	-	-	-	Nugent John - Clarke Jos	1876	-	dd/	1876 47 46
Cloydagh	Ballygowan	Nugent Kathleen	mills	-	-	-	Nugent Kathleen - John	1876	-	dd/	1876 10 254
Cloydagh	Ballygowan	Phelan Thomas	mill	-	-	-	Phelan T - Connolly James	1787	-	dd/	387 147 259734
Cloydagh	Ballygowan	Phelan Thomas :	mill & 19 acres.	-	-	-	Phelan T - Connolly James	1790	-	dd/	427 228 278646
Ullard	Ballykeenan	- Cournellan	Corn Mill	-	-	-	-	1840	-	6"os/	22
Ullard	Ballykeenan	- Clashgamma	Flour Mill	-	-	-	-	1840	-	6"os/	22
Ullard	Ballykeenan	McTeir James	flour (new)	(1A) 40x20x38 :	6a.	27.9	-	1843	15ft, dia. o`shot :	hob/	5.0035
Ullard	Ballykeenan	Weir James	flour	-	6.0.3	-	-	-	-	gr/	-
Hacketstown	Ballykilane	-	corn	-	-	-	-	1840	-	6"os/	4
Haroldstown	Ballykilduff Upper	-	dam & mill race	-	-	-	-	1840	-	6"os/	9
Haroldstown	Ballykilduff Upper	-	Milltown Vge.	-	-	-	-	1840	-	6"os/	9
Haroldstown	Ballykilduff Upper :	-	mill	-	-	-	-	1840	-	6"os/	9
Hacketstown	Ballykillane	Hore Patrick	carding	-	-	-	-	-	-	gr/	-
St Mullins	Ballyknock	- nr Paulmont Br.	corn	-	-	-	-	1840	-	6"os/	26
St Mullins	Ballyknock	Kavanagh Dudley	corn	-	78a	-	-	-	-	gr/	-
St Mullins	Ballyknock	Kavanagh Dudley	corn	(3B) 26x21.6x10 :	-	6.15	-	1851	12x2.9x13 o`shot	hob/	5.0034
St Mullins	Ballyknock	Kavanagh Dudley	tuck	-	-	-	-	-	-	gr/	-
St Mullins	Ballyknock	Kavanagh Dudley	tuck, carding	-	-	-	-	1851	wheel overshot	hob/	5.0034
Wells	Ballyknockan	- at Leighlinbridge	brewery	-	-	-	-	-	-	hob/	5.0017
W`lls/F`nagh	Ballyknockan	Dillon Edward :	-	-	-	-	Dillon E - Vigors Edw Rev.	1784	-	dd/	364 210 244 277
Wells	Ballyknockan	Doolan Edward	kiln	-	-	-	-	-	-	hob/	5.0017
W`lls/F`nagh	Ballyknockan	Dowling John	-	-	-	-	Dowling J - Meighan Patrick	1785	-	dd/	373 428 248911
W`lls/F`nagh	Ballyknockan	Maher Michael	corn	-	26a.	-	-	-	-	gr/	-
W`lls/F`nagh	Ballyknockan	Maher Michael	corn	- buildings low, bad	-	-	-	1851	10.6x3 overshot :	hob/	5.0014
Wells	Ballyknockan	Mulroony John	bakery, tea rm	-	-	-	-	-	-	hob/	5.0017
W`lls/F`nagh	Ballyknockan	Ryan David	mill	-	-	-	Ryan D - Parker Joshua	1784	-	dd/	363 29 242578
W`lls/F`nagh	Ballyknockan	Swift	mill	-	-	-	Swift - Cliffe	-	?	dd/	377 479 255270
W`lls/F`nagh	Ballyknockan	Swift Robert :	mills	-	-	-	Swift ano - Parker Josh	1784	-	dd/	362 90 242579
Wells	Ballyknockan	Wynne Edward	kiln, flour & :	-	-	-	-	-	-	hob/	5.0017
St Mullins	Ballyling	- near Turra Bridge	thrashing	- recorded in OS	-	-	- Jonny O'Neill	2002	-	mmSv/	wh - Z
Clonygoose	Ballymartin	-	corn	-	-	-	-	1843	-	6"os/	19
Clonygoose	Ballymartin	Phelan Patrick	corn	House, corn mill & :	-	-	-	1851	-	hob/	5.0003
Clonygoose	Ballymartin	Phelan Patrick	corn	39x20x21.6 & kiln :	-	7.18	-	1843	12ft. buckets :	hob/	5.0003
Clonygoose	Ballymartin	Phelim Patrick	corn	-	.0.20	-	-	-	-	gr/	-
Tullowphelim	Ballymurphy	- on R. Slaney	corn	-	-	-	-	1840	-	6"os/	8
Tullowphelin	Ballymurphy	Fitzgerald Anne	corn	-	-	-	-	-	-	gr/	-
Tullowphelin	Ballymurphy	Fitzgerald Anne	corn (new mill)	(1A) 23.6x17.6x18 :	-	8	-	1851	9x4.10 impulse :	hob/	5.0032
Tullowphelin	Ballymurphy	Fitzgerald Anne	old mill	(2A) 22.6x17x8.6 :	-	-	-	1851	-	hob/	5.0032
St Mullins	Ballymurphy	Joyce Edward	corn	(1A) 37x16.6x13.6 :	-	11	-	1851	12x2.9x13 o`shot	hob/	5.0034
St Mullins	Ballynebranagh	Cahill Thomas :	-	-	-	-	Cahill T - Hartley Humphry :	1802	-	dd/	544 170 361826
St Mullins	Ballynebranagh	Chamney	-	-	-	-	Chamney - Chamney	-	?	dd/	591 520 404850
St Mullins	Ballynebranagh	Hartley Humphry :	-	-	-	-	Hartley H - Lacy Mary :	1802	-	dd/	559 234 374240
St Mullins	Ballynebranagh	Mercer Richard :	mill	-	-	-	Mercer R - Webb Stawell & :	1789	-	dd/	410 516 270283
St Mullins	Ballynebranagh	Webb Stawell :	mill	-	-	-	Webb S - Mercer Richard	1799	-	dd/	518 222 341 337
St Mullins	Ballynkockcrumpin	- on Pollymonty R.	mill	-	-	-	-	-	-	1"os/	157
St Mullins	Ballynkockcrumpin	- on Pollymonty R.	woollen	- (part of complex)	-	-	- Patrick Hickey	2002	-	mmSv/	wh - B

PARISH	TOWNLAND	MILLER	TYPE	HOUSE	Land	£Val	PROPRIETORS	Date	WHEEL etc.	Record	Ref.
St Mullins	Ballynkockcrumpin	- on Pollymonty R. :	dye house	- (part of complex)	-	-	- Patrick Hickey	2002	-	mmSv/	wh - B
Gilbertstown	Ballynunnery	-	mills	-	-	-	-	-	-	iaa/	AI787 os13NPL
Barragh	Ballypierce	Hatchell Rt Hon John	old carding mill	-	-	-	-	-	-	gr/	-
Barragh	Ballypierce	Hatchell Rt Hon John	old corn mill	-	3.2	-	-	-	-	gr/	-
Barragh	Ballypierce	Price	mill	-	-	-	Price - Warren	-	-	dd/	779 310 527654
Hacketstown	Ballysallagh Upper	-	corn	-	-	-	-	1840	-	6"os/	5
Barragh	Barragh	Fletcher John	corn, carding	one house & mill :	-	-	-	1851	-	hob/	5.0036a
Barragh	Barragh	Fletcher John	corn, spinning	(1A)43.6x24.6x15.6 :	-	4.9.7	-	1843	corn o`shot 12x3 :	hob/	5.0036a
Carlow	Barrow River	Hamil	mill	-	-	-	Hamil - Murphy	-	[not 654]	dd/	654 231 454824
Carlow	Bathbrumill *	Malone	-	-	-	-	Malone - Faulkner	-	?	dd/	363 117 243258
Carlow	Bathbrumill *	Malone James	-	-	-	-	Malone Jas - will	-	?	dd/	339 417 229307
Carlow	Bathbrumill *	Warren William :	mill	-	-	-	Warren W - Watson John :	1742	-	dd/	119 500 83372
Carlow	Bathbrumill *	Warren William :	mill	-	-	-	Warren - Corrogon Timothy :	1742	-	dd/	119 507 83421
Ballyellin	Bendinstown	Boileau	mills	-	-	-	Boileau - Phipps	-	-	dd/	739 270 503605
Ballyellin	Bendinstown	Eustace Edward	-	-	-	-	Eustace E - Waddy Richard	1788	-	dd/	396 495 262328
Ballyellin	Bendinstown	Eustace Edward	mill	-	-	-	Eustace Edward - Robt	1746	-	dd/	127 437 87367
Ballyellin	Bendinstown	Eustace Edward	mill	-	-	-	Eustace Ed - Stewart Andr	1765	-	dd/	262 22 166212
Ballyellin	Bendinstown	Eustace Edward	mill	-	-	-	Eustace Ed - Stewart Andr :	1765	-	dd/	263 44 166185
Ballyellin	Bendinstown	Eustace Edward :	-	-	-	-	Eustace E - Elshaw John :	1788	-	dd/	395 501 262581
Ballyellin	Bendinstown	Eustace James :	-	-	-	-	Eustace Jas - Disrael Bergin	1809	-	dd/	617 245 423310
Ballyellin	Bendinstown	Eustace James :	mills	-	-	-	Eustace J - Wolesworth :	1811	-	dd/	645 385 488778
Ballyellin	Bendinstown	Eustace Joseph :	mill	-	-	-	Eustace J - Lyster Edmund :	1760	-	dd/	205 252 135906
Ballyellin	Bendinstown :	Exshaw John :	mills	-	-	-	Exshaw J - Eustace James :	1815	Rent ú137.2.6 pa.	dd/	729 180 497515
Ballyellin	Bendinstown	George John :	mills	-	-	-	George J - Boileau Wilson :	1817	-	dd/	722 81 493216
Ballyellin	Bendinstown	Stewart Andrew :	mill	-	-	-	Stewart A - Butler Thos. :	1767	-	dd/	291 613 193140
Ballyellin	Bendinstown :	Digby John Rev. :	mill	-	-	-	Digby J - Eustace James :	1818	-	dd/	759 372 515708
Ballyellin	Bendinstown :	Eustace Alicia :	mill	-	-	-	Eustace A - Eustace James :	1821	-	dd/	760 418 516354
Ballyellin	Bendinstown :	McPherson William :	mill	-	-	-	McPherson - Eustace Jas :	1819	-	dd/	760 401 516336
Hacketstown	Borough	-	corn	-	-	-	-	1840	-	6"os/	5
Hacketstown	Borough	- N. side Dereen R.	corn	-	-	-	-	1840	-	6"os/	5
Hacketstown	Borough	- N. side Dereen R.	mill ford	-	-	-	-	1840	-	6"os/	5
Hacketstown	Borough	- N. side Dereen R.	mill moat	-	-	-	-	1840	-	6"os/	5
Hacketstown	Borough	- N. side Dereen R.	mill park	-	-	-	-	1840	-	6"os/	5
Hacketstown	Borough	- N. side Dereen R.	Mill spout	-	-	-	-	1840	-	6"os/	5
Hacketstown	Borough	Darcy Thomas	corn	-	0.1.12		-	-	-	gr/	-
Clonygoose	Borris	Brown Robin	Fish Farm	-	-	-	-	-	Gikes / 20kw	turb/	c1947
Clonygoose	Borris	Gliborn Ed	Nores Mill	-	-	-	Gliborn E - Simmons Thos :	1806	-	dd/	619 109 423812
Clonygoose	Borris	Morris John	mill	-	-	-	Morris John - Simmons Thos	1806	-	dd/	619 108 423811
Clonygoose	Borris	Thorpe	mill	-	-	-	Thorpe - Little	-	[not 584]	dd/	548 211 401378
Clonygoose	Borris Town	-	corn	- part dilapidated	-	-	- J. & B. O'Leary	2002	-	mmSv/	wh - B
Clonygoose	Borris Town	- in yard Town centre	old mill ?	- used for storage	-	-	-	2002	-	mmSv/	wh - B
Clonygoose	Borris Town	Whitney George	corn	(1C) 25x20x13.6 :	-	26.6	-	1842	10x3.6x4.6 :	hob/	5.2360
Clonygoose	Borris Town	Whitney Thomas	corn, malt ho	-	1.1.0	-	-	-	-	gr/	-
Wells	Burgage	-	corn	- used for storage	-	-	-	2002	-	mmSv/	wh - B
Wells	Burgage	Maher Michael	corn	(2B) 24x19.6x12.6 :	-	5.3.0	-	1851	10.6x3 overshot :	hob/	5.0016
Wells	Burgage	Maher Michael	corn	(2B) 24x19.6x12.6 :	-	5.3.0	-	1851	10.6x3 overshot :	hob/	5.0016
Rathvilly	Butlersgrange	Fox Thomas	corn	- [no dimensions]	-	7	-	1843	[no dims.] :	hob/	5.0032
Carlow	Carlow	- S. of Town	corn		-	-	-	2002	-	mmSv/	wh - Z
Ballincarig	Carlow	Brown Jane	corn & kiln	-	32a.	-	-	-	-	gr/	-
Carlow	Carlow :	Brennan Jno :	mill	-	-	-	Brennan J - Hughes Wm :	1808	-	dd/	596 283 406645
Carlow	Carlow :	Fitzgerald	mill	-	-	-	Fitzgerald M - Fitzgerald Wm	1802	-	dd/	551 403 364241
Carlow	Carlow :	Fitzgerald	mill	-	-	-	Fitzgerald - Sikes	-	[not 555]	dd/	555 251 372943

PARISH	TOWNLAND	MILLER	TYPE	HOUSE	Land	£Val	PROPRIETORS	Date	WHEEL etc.	Record	Ref.
Carlow	Carlow :	Fitzgerald Martin :	mill	-	-	-	Fitzgerald M - Fitzgerald Wm	1802	-	dd/	549 368 364240
Carlow	Carlow :	Sykes George Sen :	mill & bl green	-	-	-	Sykes G - Goodison O'Neill :	1822	Conv. 10 Sep.	dd/	790 406 534341
Carlow	Carlow Town	-	mill (3 sites)	-	-	-	-	1307	-	iaa/	AI790 os-
Carlow	Carlow Town	- at Canal Lock	flour	-	-	-	-	1840	-	6"os/	7
Carlow	Carlow Town	- nr Evergreen Lo.	brewery	-	-	-	-	1840	-	6"os/	7
Carlow	Carlow Town	- nr Springfield Ho.	mill	-	-	-	-	-	-	1"os/	137
Carlow	Carlow Town	- W. side Barrow	corn	-	-	-	-	1840	-	6"os/	7
Carlow	Carlow Town	- W. side Barrow	corn kiln	-	-	-	-	1840	-	6"os/	7
Carlow	Carlow Town	- W. side Barrow	distillery	-	-	-	-	1840	-	6"os/	7
Carlow	Carlow Town	Bernard Philip	brewery	-	-	-	Bernard P - Proctor Thos	1786	-	dd/	384 299 255006
Carlow	Carlow Town	Boyle John :	corn store, kiln	(1A) 37.7x11x13.6 :	-	10	-	1851	-	hob/	5.2367
Carlow	Carlow Town	Brewster Anthony :	Bridewell Mills	-	-	-	Brewster A - Clarke	1814	-	dd/	673 336 465194/5
Carlow	Carlow Town	Browne John :	brewery	-	-	-	Browne J - Nicholson Jas	1798	-	dd/	516 65 336220
Carlow	Carlow Town	Burgess William :	bleach yard	-	-	-	Burgess Wm - Orpin Thos :	1815	-	dd/	693 149 475892
Carlow	Carlow Town	Burren Street	flour	demolished replaced :	-	-	-	2002	-	mmSv/	wh - Z
Carlow	Carlow Town	Byrne Jno	bolting mill	-	-	-	Byrne J - Hughes John	1794	-	dd/	489 171 307870
Carlow	Carlow Town	Callaghan Thomas :	bolting mill	-	-	-	Callaghan T - Clarke Jno :	1808	Mort, 25 May	dd/	600 336 409791
Carlow	Carlow Town	Carpenter	malt ho & store	-	-	-	Carpenter - Emerson	-	[not 513]	dd/	513 142 338866
Carlow	Carlow Town	Centaur Street	brewery	- demolished :	-	-	-	2002	-	mmSv/	wh - Cc
Carlow	Carlow Town	Church Thomas	brewery	-	-	-	Church Thos - Saul Thomas	1851	-	dd/	1851 3 267
Carlow	Carlow Town	Clarke John :	bolting mill	-	-	-	Clarke J - Callaghan Thos :	1805	Mort. 6 Jan.	dd/	570 271 381347
Carlow	Carlow Town	Clarke	Bridewell Mills	-	-	-	Clarke - Doyle	-	[not 675]	dd/	675 421 465528
Carlow	Carlow Town	Clarke Simon :	Bridewell Mills	-	-	-	Clarke S - Wilson John :	1817	-	dd/	717 288 490423
Carlow	Carlow Town	Collier Peter	Burren Mill	-	-	-	Collier P - Sweeny Marion	1891	-	dd/	1891 44 1
Carlow	Carlow Town	Connor (as Master)	Bridewell Mill	-	-	-	Connor - Fishbourne	-	-	dd/	892 422 568422
Carlow	Carlow Town	Cornwall John F :	Castle Mill	-	-	-	Cornwall J - Hanlon Patrick :	1815	-	dd/	696 590 478087
Carlow	Carlow Town	Cornwall Quay	mill	- well preserved :	-	-	- Dicey Reilly	2002	-	mmSv/	wh - Ce
Carlow	Carlow Town	Cotter	malt house	-	-	-	Cotter - Leech	-	-	dd/	556 232 369634
Carlow	Carlow Town	Dunne Michael	Burren Mill	-	-	-	Dunne M - Sweeny Marion	1891	-	dd/	1891 1 14
Carlow	Carlow Town	English Jno	Bridewell Mills	-	-	-	English Jno - Deed	1851	-	dd/	1851 23 176
Carlow	Carlow Town	English William	Bridewell Mills	-	-	-	English W - Small Thos G	1853	-	dd/	1853 11 178
Carlow	Carlow Town	Faircloth George	brewery	[no meas. ref. note :]	-	29.10	-	1842	-	hob/	5.2377
Carlow	Carlow Town	Finn Susanna :	Castle Mill	-	-	-	Finn Susanna & Michael	1817	-	dd/	712 493 487628
Carlow	Carlow Town	Fishborne William :	Bridewell Mill	-	-	-	Fishbourne Wm - William :	1829	-	dd/	849 422 568423
Carlow	Carlow Town	Fishbourne Gordon	Hanover Mills	-	-	-	Fishbourne Gordon - Wm	1889	-	dd/	1889 36 180
Carlow	Carlow Town	Fishbourne William	Bridewell Mill	-	-	-	Fishbourne - Moore Garrett	1889	-	dd/	1889 36 159
Carlow	Carlow Town	Fishbourne William :	Bridewell Mill	-	-	-	Fishbourne W - Fishbourne :	1832	-	dd/	889 136 588136/7
Carlow	Carlow Town	Furney	Bridewell Mills	-	-	-	Furney - Clarke	-	[not 699]	dd/	699 129 479435
Carlow	Carlow Town	Furney Benjamin	Bridewell Mills	-	-	-	Furney Benj - Clarke John	1797	-	dd/	512 211 333461
Carlow	Carlow Town	Geale Daniel :	bolting mill	-	-	-	Geale D - Carter Robert	1795	-	dd/	487 505 314319
Carlow	Carlow Town	Graigue	distilery	converted, site of :	-	-	-	2002	-	mmSv/	wh - Ca
Carlow	Carlow Town	Graigue	malt house	converted for res.	-	-	-	2002	-	mmSv/	wh - Ca
Carlow	Carlow Town	Graigue	thrashing	- recorded in OS :	-	-	-	2002	-	mmSv/	wh - Z
Carlow	Carlow Town	Graigue, Barrow Mills	flour	- demolished now :	-	-	-	2002	-	mmSv/	wh - Ca
Carlow	Carlow Town	Hamilton Benedict :	Bridewell Mill	-	-	-	Hamilton B - Clarke Simon :	1813	-	dd/	663 451 456897
Carlow	Carlow Town	Hamilton Benedict :	Bridewell Mills	-	-	-	Hamilton B - Heron Edward :	1817	Mort. 4 April	dd/	716 162 489697
Carlow	Carlow Town	Hamilton Benedict :	Burren Mill	-	-	-	Hamilton B - Clarke Simon :	1813	-	dd/	663 451 456897
Carlow	Carlow Town	Hamilton Bernard	bolting mill	-	-	-	Hamilton B - Carter Robert	1787	-	dd/	393 217 260255
Carlow	Carlow Town	Hamilton James	Castle, Estate	-	-	-	Hamilton J - Stewart Chas	1724	-	dd/	39 463 28438
Carlow	Carlow Town	Hamilton Jno	malt house	-	-	-	Hamilton J - Farrell Myles	1787	-	dd/	392 420 259392
Carlow	Carlow Town	Henn (as Master) :	Burren Mill	-	-	-	Henn W - Brewster Edward :	1814	-	dd/	673 153 463254
Carlow	Carlow Town	Henn Wm as Master :	Bridewell Mill	-	-	-	Henn W - Brewster Edward :	1814	-	dd/	673 153 463254

PARISH	TOWNLAND	MILLER	TYPE	HOUSE	Land	£Val	PROPRIETORS	Date	WHEEL etc.	Record	Ref.
Carlow	Carlow Town	Hughes John :	bolting mill	-	-	-	Hughes J - Sykes : George :	1798	-	dd/	512 452 335401?
Carlow	Carlow Town	Hughes John	bolting mill	-	-	-	Hughes John - Crosbie Thos	1795	-	dd/	499 68 314967
Carlow	Carlow Town	Humphrey Michael	malt house	-	-	-	Humphrey - Butler Henry	1839	-	dd/	1839 11 48
Carlow	Carlow Town	John Street	corn	- building still intact	-	-	-	2002	-	mmSv/	wh - B
Carlow	Carlow Town	Kelly Laurence :	corn & kiln	-	-		-	-	steam engine	gr/	-
Carlow	Carlow Town	Kelly Laurence :	corn & kiln	(1B) 48.6x26x38 :	-	38	-	-	steam engine	hob/	5.2367 & 2374
Carlow	Carlow Town	Keogh Elizabeth :	malt ho., store	-	-	-	Keogh Eliz - Emerson John :	1809	-	dd/	619 190 423532
Carlow	Carlow Town	Mangan Partick	The Castle Mill	-	-	-	Mangan P - Haughton Wm	1900		dd/	1900 46 60
Carlow	Carlow Town	McDonnell William :	brewery	-	-	-	McDonnell - Greene Jno :	1798	-	dd/	514 125 335835
Carlow	Carlow Town	McSweeny Marion	bolting mill	-	-	-	McSweeny M - P Wks Com	1894	-	dd/	1894 62 188
Carlow	Carlow Town	Mill Lane	flour	near the Castle (95% :	-	-	-	2002	-	mmSv/	wh - Ca
Carlow	Carlow Town	Mill Lane	house	The Castle Millhouse :	-	-	-	2002	-	pWEH	wh - B
Carlow	Carlow Town	Mill Lane	kilns	nr Castle demolished	-	-	-	2002	-	mmSv/	wh - Z
Carlow	Carlow Town	Moffett William	Castle Mill	-	-	-	Moffett William - William	1850	-	dd/	1850 2 2
Carlow	Carlow Town	Montgomery Street	flour	part of ind. complex	-	-	Minch Norton & Co.	2002	-	mmSv/	wh - B
Carlow	Carlow Town	Newton John :	brewery	-	-	-	Newton J - Box Edward :	1801	-	dd/	541 176 356480
Carlow	Carlow Town	Newton Jno	brewery	-	-	-	Newton J - Morgan Edward :	1799	-	dd/	519 172 338669
Carlow	Carlow Town	Nicholson	brewery	-	-	-	Nicholson - Hamilton	-	-	dd/	493 585 340196
Carlow	Carlow Town	Nicholson James :	brewery	-	-	-	Nicholson J - Browne John :	1797	-	dd/	508 101 328187
Carlow	Carlow Town	O`Reilly Michael M	malthouse	-	-	-	O`Reilly M - Duggan Wm	1882	-	gr/	1882 24 239
Carlow	Carlow Town	One Track Way	entrance to mill	- on riverside to :	-	-	-	2002	-	pWEH	
Carlow	Carlow Town	Proctor Nathaniel	brewery	-	-	-	Proctor N - Alexander John	1810	-	dd/	622 516 430451
Carlow	Carlow Town	Ryan	bolting mill	-	-	-	Ryan - Redmond	-	-	dd/	569 302 383073
Carlow	Carlow Town	Shackleton Theobald	The Barrow Mill:	-	-	-	Shackleton Theo - Theo	1901		dd/	1901 88 77
Carlow	Carlow Town	Walsh Frances R	bleach dround	-	0.2.12		-	-	-	gr/	-
Carlow	Carlow Town	Water Lane	mill	- tall roofless ruin :	-	-	-	2002	-	mmSv/	wh - Ca
Carlow	Carlow Town	Weld Georgina	The Castle Mill	-	-	-	Weld G - Weld Edmond	1900		dd/	1900 1 192
Carlow	Carlow Town	Wright John :	Bridewell Mill	-	-	-	Wright John - Clarke Simon :	1819	-	dd/	747 38 508173
Carlow	Carlow Town :	Paul Richard & Son	brewery :	-	0.2.20		-	-	-	gr/	-
Carlow	Carlow Town :	Alexander John	brewery	(1C) 13x18.6x26 & :	-	32	-	-	-	hob/	5.2364
Carlow	Carlow Town :	Anderson Geo W	corn store, kiln	-	-	-	-	-	-	gr/	-
Carlow	Carlow Town :	Ball Jno	Castle Mill	-	-	-	Ball Jno - Moffett Wm	1849	-	dd/	1849 23 38
Carlow	Carlow Town :	Byrne John	mill	-	-	-	Byrne John - Byrne Jos	1834	-	dd/	1834 20 122
Carlow	Carlow Town :	Malcolmson Henry	bolting mill	-	-	-	Malcolmson H - Dunn Isbl	1834	-	dd/	1834 7 208
Carlow	Carlow Town :	Calwell Nathaniel	mills	-	-	-	Calwemll N - Disclaimer	1851	-	dd/	1851 22 202
Carlow	Carlow Town :	Drum Richard	bolton	-	-	-	Drum Richd - Curran Jno	1845	-	dd/	1845 4 208
Carlow	Carlow Town :	CarterJno	bolting	-	-	-	Carter Jno - Samuel R	1846	-	dd/	1846 18 102
Carlow	Carlow Town :	Mortimer Michael	bolting	-	-	-	Mortimer M - Carton Saml	1851	-	dd/	1851 2 173
Carlow	Carlow Town :	Ball Jno	Castle Mill	-	-	-	Ball Jno - Moffett William	1849	-	dd/	1849 23 38
Carlow	Carlow Town :	Brough	brewery	-	-	-	Brough - Brough	-	-	dd/	519 299 334191
Carlow	Carlow Town :	Dunn Richard	bolting mill	-	-	-	Dunn Richd - Currin Jno	1845	-	dd/	1845 4 208
Carlow	Carlow Town :	Carter Jno	bolting mill	-	-	-	Carter Jno - Carter Saml	1846	-	dd/	1846 18 102
Carlow	Carlow Town :	Dunne Richard	mill	-	-	-	Dume Richard - Deed	1851	-	dd/	1851 26 152
Carlow	Carlow Town :	Clarke Simon	Bridewell Mills	-	-	-	Clarke S - English Wm	1841	-	dd/	1841 1 152
Carlow	Carlow Town :	English William	Bridewell Mills	-	-	-	English W - Clarke Simon	1841	-	dd/	1841 18 46
Carlow	Carlow Town :	English Jno	Bridewell Mill	-	-	-	English Jno - Wilson Josh	1848	-	dd/	1848 16 102
Carlow	Carlow Town :	Sikes John	bleach gn, hos	-	-	-	Sikes Jn - Devereux Laur	1833	-	dd/	1833 5 218
Carlow	Carlow Town :	Sikes John	flour	-	-	-	Sikes Jn - Devereux Laur	1833	-	dd/	1833 5 218
Carlow	Carlow Town :	Michell Juliana Hon.	Malthouse conc	-	-	-	Michell J - Michell George	1885	-	dd/	1885 21 291
Carlow	Carlow Town :	Whitty David	forge	-	-	-	Whitty Dav - Whitty John	1835	-	dd/	1835 8 228
Carlow	Carlow Town :	Hanlon Thomas :	mill	-	-	-	Hanlon T - Murphy John :	1821	Mort. 23 Oct.	dd/	772 199 523334
Carlow	Carlow Town :	Cross	mill	-	-	-	Cross - Mercer	-	?	dd/	390 334 256804

PARISH	TOWNLAND	MILLER	TYPE	HOUSE	Land	£Val	PROPRIETORS	Date	WHEEL etc.	Record	Ref.
Carlow	Carlow Town :	Clarke Smon	Bridewell Mill	-	-	-	Clarke Simon - Ire Bank	1850	-	dd/	1850 19 242
Carlow	Carlow Town :	English Jno	Bridewell Mill	-	-	-	English Jno - Wilson Josh	1848	-	dd/	1848 16 102
Carlow	Carlow Town :	Ryan	land	-	-	-	Ryan - Hamilton	-	-	dd/	804 172 542507
Carlow	Carlow Town :	Hamilton	brewery	-	-	-	Hamilton - Brough	-	-	dd/	465 280 297311
Carlow	Carlow Town :	Hamilton James :	brewery	-	-	-	Hamilton J - Redmond Matt :	1799	-	dd/	524 57 342274
Carlow	Carlow Town :	Scraggs	premises	-	-	-	Scraggs - Minchin	-	-	dd/	775 274 525209
Carlow	Carlow Town :	Juliana Michael	bolting mill	-	-	-	Juliana Mcl - Revocation	1895	-	dd/	1895 32 270
Carlow	Carlow Town :	Brophy	mill	-	-	-	Brophy - Price	-	-	dd/	820 244 552179
Carlow	Carlow Town :	Clarke Simeon	flour	(1B) 47.6x26x38.6 :	-	-	-	-	-	hob/	5.2364
Carlow	Carlow Town :	Clarke Simeon	flour (cont.)	old mill 4.6x20x20.6 :	-	-	-	-	-	hob/	5.2364
Carlow	Carlow Town :	Clarke Simeon & Co.	flour & corn	- [see also note :]	-	-	-	-	steam engine :	gr/	-
Carlow	Carlow Town :	Croghan Edward	mill	-	-	-	Croghan Edwd - Richard	1878	-	dd/	1878 53 162
Carlow	Carlow Town :	Finn	no mill	-	-	-	Finn - Darcy	-	-	dd/	724 575 494910
Carlow	Carlow Town :	King Simon :	malthouse	-	-	-	King S - Mitchell Humphry :	1786	-	dd/	392 96 257954
Carlow	Carlow Town :	Lawless Richard	mill	-	-	-	Lawless R - Croghan Ed	1877	-	dd/	1877 55 300
Carlow	Carlow Town :	Lawless Richard	mill	-	-	-	Lawless R- Gerrard Thos	1878	-	dd/	1878 53 163
Carlow	Carlow Town :	Proctor	brewery	-	-	-	Proctor - Proctor	-	-	dd/	540 553 356849
Carlow	Carlow Town :	Proctor Bridget :	brewery	-	-	-	Proctor B - Proctor Thomas :	1815	-	dd/	694 180 476489
Carlow	Carlow Town :	Proctor Nathaniel	brewery	-	-	-	Proctor N - Alexander John :	1810	-	dd/	622 516 430451
Carlow	Carlow Town :	Fitsimmons Thomas	mill	-	-	-	Fitsimmons Thos - William	1830	-	dd/	863 414 575414
Carlow	Carlow Town :	Brewster Edward :	Bridewell Mill	-	-	-	Brewster Ed - Ryan Henry :	1824	-	dd/	794 253 536588
Carlow	Carlow Town :	Carter Samuel Richd :	mill	-	-	-	Carter S - Clarke Simon :	1814	Rent Cge. 9 Oct.	dd/	680 311 468275
Carlow	Carlow Town :	Carter Robert	bolting mill	-	-	-	Carter R - Geale Daniel	1788	-	dd/	393 218 260256
Carlow	Carlow Town :	Carter Robert	bolting mill	-	-	-	Carter Robt - Ryan James	1795	-	dd/	526 435 345292
Carlow	Carlow Town :	Clarke John :	bolting mill	-	-	-	Clarke J - Callaghan Thos :	1805	Mort. 6 Jan.	dd/	570 271 381347
Carlow	Carlow Town :	Clarke Simeon	corn & kilns	(1B) 58x21x28 :	-	35	-	-	2 u`shot wheels :	hob/	5.2364 & 5.2374
Carlow	Carlow Town :	Clarke Simon :	mill	-	-	-	Clarke S - English William :	1828	-	dd/	836 504 562040
Carlow	Carlow Town :	Connor Roderick :	bolting mill	-	-	-	Connor R - Dunne Richard :	1829	-	dd/	853 61 570061
Carlow	Carlow Town :	Gallagher Thos, Elder	bolting mill	-	-	-	Gallagher Thos - Clarke Jno	1808	Mort. 25 May	dd/	600 336 409791
Carlow	Carlow Town :	Goggin Richard :	brewhouse :	-	-	-	Goggin R - Constantine Thos	1757	-	dd/	183 412 123320
Carlow	Carlow Town :	Goggin Stephen :	brewhouse	-	-	-	Goggin S - Goggin William :	1755	-	dd/	181 30 119325
Carlow	Carlow Town :	Grace	bolting mill	-	-	-	Grace - Carter	-	-	dd/	487 505 314319
Carlow	Carlow Town :	Haughton Sam & S	corn store, kiln	-	-	-	-	-	-	gr/	-
Carlow	Carlow Town :	King	malthouse	-	-	-	King - Dowling	-	?	dd/	237 65 151607
Carlow	Carlow Town :	Redmond	bolting mill	-	-	-	Redmond - Hanlen	-	-	dd/	638 100 44189?2
Carlow	Carlow Town :	Ryan James :	bolting mill	-	-	-	Ryan James - Clarke John	1800	-	dd/	526 536 345293
Carlow	Carlow Town :	Scragg	bolting mill	-	-	-	Scragg - Carter	-	-	dd/	868 231 577731
Carlow	Carlow Town :	Windis Samuel	malthouse	-	-	-	Windis - Costigan John :	1772	-	dd/	294 684 196738
Carlow	Carlow Town :	Byrne John	mill	-	-	-	Byrne John - Joseph	1834	-	dd/	1834 20 122
Carlow	Carlow Town :	Clarke Simeon	corn & flour	- old establishment :	-	-	-	-	-	hob/	5.2377
Carlow	Carlow Town :	Kelly Michael	mill	-	-	-	Kelly M - O`Connor Mary	1878	-	dd/	1878 29 82
Carlow	Carlow Town :	Malcolmson Henry	mill	-	-	-	Malcolmson - Dunne Isbla	1834	-	dd/	1834 7 208
Carlow	Carlow Town :	Clarke Simon	bolting mill	-	-	-	Clarke S - English Wm	1841	-	dd/	1841 1 152
Carlow	Carlow Town :	Dunne James	bolting mill	-	-	-	Dunne J - Comerford Mcl	1876	-	dd/	1876 37 205
Carlow	Carlow Town :	Dunne Kate	bolting mill	-	-	-	Dunne Kate - Dunne Jas	1877	-	dd/	1877 17/19 197
Carlow	Carlow Town :	English William	bolting mill	-	-	-	English W - Clarke Simon	1841	-	dd/	1841 18 46
Carlow	Carlow Town :	Carter	bolting mill	-	-	-	Carter - Ardagh	-	-	dd/	868 294 577794
Carlow	Carlow Town :	McDonnell	brewery mill	-	-	-	McDonnell - Green	-	-	dd/	514 125 335835
Carlow	Carlow Town :	Prossor James	brewery	Dwelling house :	-	-	Prossor J - McDaniel Wm	1786	-	dd/	382 139 253848
Carlow	Carlow Town :	Ferrall Robt & John	brewery	(1C) 18.6x23.6x13 :	-	29.6	-	1851	[no information]	hob/	5.2369
Carlow	Carlow Town :	Mangan Martin	corn	-	-	50	-	-	steam engine	gr/	-
Carlow	Carlow Town :	Mangan Martin	corn	[no measurements] :	-	10	-	1851	steam engine	hob/	5.2367

PARISH	TOWNLAND	MILLER	TYPE	HOUSE	Land	£Val	PROPRIETORS	Date	WHEEL etc.	Record	Ref.
Carlow	Carlow Town :	Mangan Martin	corn stores	(1A) 10.9x25.6x26 :	-	32.15.	-	1851	-	hob/	5.2367
Carlow	Carlow Town :	Mangan Martin	corn stores :	-	-	-	-	-	-	gr/	-
Carlow	Carlow Town :	Keogh John & Eliz	brewery	Dwelling house :	-	-	Keogh J - Prossor James	1785	-	dd/	372 331 248971
Carlow	Carlow Town :	Browne William	bleach yard	-	-	-	Browne W - Byrne Wm :	1746	-	dd/	144 430 98153
Carlow	Carlow Town :	Silkes John	flour	-	-	-	Silkes J - Devereaux Laur	1833	-	dd/	1833 5 218
Carlow	Carlow Town :	Delany Thomas	mill	-	-	-	Delany T - Fishbourne W	1789	-	dd/	408 199 269834
Carlow	Carlow Town :	Fishbourne William	mill	-	-	-	Fishbourne - Browne Rbt	1787	Mort. 26 Jan.	dd/	407 123 269836
Carlow	Carlow Town :	Farrell Edward :	mill	-	-	-	Farrell E - Fitsimmons Thos :	1827	-	dd/	823 127 553862
Carlow	Carlow Town :	Cooper George :	land plot :	-	-	-	Cooper Geo - Meyler John :	1827	Lse. 17 July	dd/	826 254 555789
Carlow	Carlow Town :	Gurley	premises	-	-	-	Gurley - Thompson	-	-	dd/	762 572 517707
Carlow	Carlow Town :	Newton	mill	-	-	-	Newton - Newton	-	-	dd/	829 183 557518?
Carlow	Carlow Town :	Borroughs George	corn	-	-	-	-	-	steam engine	gr/	-
Carlow	Carlow Town :	Borroughs George	corn	[no measurements] :	-	20	-	-	steam engine	hob/	5.2376
Carlow	Carlow Town :	Clarke Simeon	mill & kiln	(1B) 63x24.6x34 & :	-	23	-	1851	2 u`shot wheels :	hob/	5.2364 & 2374
Carlow	Carlow Town :	Lynch Joseph :	mill	-	-	-	Lynch Jos - Bewley James :	1826	-	dd/	825 373 555308
Carlow	Carlow Town :	Malcolmson Frances	malt store	(1B) 96x24x21.6 :	-	15	-	1851	-	hob/	5.2364
Carlow	Carlow Town :	Montgomery Francis :	mill	-	-	-	Montgomery F - Meyler Jn :	1826	-	dd/	814 47 548382
Carlow	Carlow Town :	Montgomery Francis :	land	-	-	-	Montgomery F - Bewly Jas :	1825	Rel. 13 Jul.	dd/	804 590 542933
Carlow	Carlow Town :	Dobbyn	Castle Mill	-	-	-	Dobbyn - O`Brien	-	-	dd/	787 580 527315
Carlow	Carlow Town :	Lynch John :	mill	-	-	-	Lynch John - Bewly James :	1827	-	dd/	827 481 556616
Carlow	Carlow Town :	Thomond Lord :	Castle & Estate	-	-	-	Thomond Ld - Hamilton Jas	1721	-	dd/	33 504 21058
Carlow	Carlow Town :	Grumly John	malt house	-	-	-	Grumly Jn - Good Wm	1716	-	dd/	42 36 25554
Carlow	Carlow Town :	Carpenter	malt ho. & kiln	-	-	-	Carpenter - Emerson	-	- [not 513]	dd/	513 142 338866
Carlow	Carlow Town :	Emerson	malt ho & store	-	-	-	Emersom - Keogh	-	?	dd/	566 28 377576
Carlow	Carlow Town :	Farrell Myles :	brewery	-	-	-	Farrell M - Fitzsimons Thos :	1815	-	dd/	694 301 476586
Carlow	Carlow Town :	Hamilton Jno Carlow	malthouse	-	-	-	Hamilton J - Farrell Myles	1787	-	dd/	392 420 259392
Carlow	Carlow Town :	Hamilton John :	malthouse	-	-	-	Hamilton J - Dargan Andr :	1787	-	dd/	394 32 259393
Carlow	Carlow Town :	Keogh	malt ho. & kiln	-	-	-	Keogh - Emerson	-	-	dd/	619 190 423532
Carlow	Carlow Town :	Ryan John	malt house	-	-	-	Ryan John - Ager John	1724	-	dd/	45 242 29093
Carlow	Carlow Town :	Whelan Thomas	brewhouse	-	-	-	Whelan T - James Wm	1725	-	dd/	45 274 30086
Carlow	Carlow Town :	Humphrey Alex :	premises	-	-	-	Humphrey A - Humphrey	1800	-	dd/	776 46 524381
Carlow	CarlowTown :	Barrow Milling Co.	flour	-	-	-	-	1965	-	lic/2	wheat
Aghade	Carrickslaney	Lennon Michael	flour	-	17a.	-	-	-	-	gr/	-
Myshall	Clashganny	Bull	mill	-	-	-	Bull - Page	-	- (error)	dd/	349 107 233154
Myshall	Clashganny	Doyle	mill	-	-	-	Doyle - Hickey	-	-	dd/	575 326 306415
Myshall	Clashganny	Esmonde Hellen :	mill	-	-	-	Esmonre H - Frizell Richd :	1781	-	dd/	342 133 228864
Myshall	Clashganny	Fraser	mills	-	-	-	Frizell - Lee	-	-	dd/	736 282 501817
Myshall	Clashganny	Fraser William B	mill	-	-	-	Fraser Wm - Armstrong M	1828	-	dd/	832 69 559204
Myshall	Clashganny	Haughton	mill	-	-	-	Haughton - Haughton	-	-	dd/	818 270 551005
Myshall	Clashganny	Haughton	mill	-	-	-	Haughton - Haughton	-	-	dd/	821 170 552705
Myshall	Clashganny	Kelly	mill	-	-	-	Kelly - Roe	-	-	dd/	632 195 433614
Myshall	Clashganny	North	mills	-	-	-	North - Kelly	-	-	dd/	550 409 448956
Cloydagh	Cloghristic	Dowling's mill	corn	demolished	-	-	- (confirmed local hist.)	2002	-	mmSv/	wh - Z
Cloydagh	Cloghristic ?	- on farm :	threshing	-	-	-	-	1840	-	6"os/	12
Cloydagh	Cloghristick	Alexander Harrietta	mill	-	-	-	Alexander Harrieta - John	1875	-	dd/	1875 30 211
Cloydagh	Cloghristick	Alexander John	corn	-	8a.	-	-	-	-	gr/	-
Cloydagh	Cloghristick	Alexander John	mill	-	-	-	Alexander Jn - Harrietta	1875	-	dd/	1875 30 210
Cloydagh	Cloghristick	Baillie	mill	-	-	-	Baillie - Roe	-	-	dd/	625 373 146615
Cloydagh	Cloghristick	Brereton George :	mill	-	-	-	Brereton G - Roe James :	1779	Mort. 13 Sep.	dd/	325 363 220995
Cloydagh	Cloghristick	Butler Antoine	mills	-	-	-	Butler Antoine - R. C. B.	1874	-	dd/	1874 6 130
Cloydagh	Cloghristick	Butler Richard Bt. :	mill	-	-	-	Butler - Warren Wm Paul :	1756	-	dd/	184 53 121999
Cloydagh	Cloghristick	Butler Thomas :	mill	-	-	-	Butler T - Lockington Chris	1756	-	dd/	186 31 122015

PARISH	TOWNLAND	MILLER	TYPE	HOUSE	Land	£Val	PROPRIETORS	Date	WHEEL etc.	Record	Ref.
Cloydagh	Cloghristick	Connolly	mill	-	-	-	Connolly - Nugent	-	-	dd/	701 522 481025
Cloydagh	Cloghristick	Connolly	mill	-	-		Connolly - Connolly	-	-	dd/	809 528 545863
Cloydagh	Cloghristick	Davis Richard	mill	-	-	-	Davis R - Butler Gerald :	1778	-	dd/	316 554 214511
Cloydagh	Cloghristick	Disney	mill	-	-	-	Disney - Wellwood	-	?	dd/	364 490 248257
Cloydagh	Cloghristick	Rochfort Horace	mills	-	-	-	Rochfort Horace - R. C. B.	1874	-	dd/	1874 3 279
Moyacomb	Clonegall	Bell Edmond :	mill	-	-	-	Bell Ed - Bonham Robert :	1813	-	dd/	661 450 455692
Moyacomb	Clonegall	Chamney Graves	mill	-	-	-	Chamney G - Ransford Ml	1749	-	dd/	134 463 91764
Moyacomb	Clonegall	Esmond Sir Jno	mill	-	-	-	Esmond J - Butler Edwd	1753	-	dd/	166 62 110296
Moyacomb	Clonegall	Esmond Sir John	mill	-	-	-	Esmond J - Jackson Geo	1753	-	dd/	164 68 108899
Moyacomb	Clonegall	Putland John	mill	-	-	-	Putland J - Fowkke Sydn.	1753	-	dd/	159 461 107759
Moyacomb	Clongarran	- on Derry R	corn	-	-	-	-	-	-	1"os/	148
Templepeter	Clonmacshane	-	corn & mill dam	-	16a.	-	-	1840	-	6"os/	12
Templepeter	Clonmacshane	Corcoran Patrick	corn & kiln	-	16a.	-	-	-	-	gr/	-
Carlow	Clonmisk *	Beresford John G	mills	-	-	-	Beresford J - Rep. Ch. B.	1874	-	dd/	1874 4 152
Lorum	Corries	Thorpe Samuel	corn	-	24a.	-	-	-	-	gr/	-
Lorum	Corries	Thorpe Samuel	corn & kiln	(1B) 64.6x21x16.6 :	-	9.18	-	1843	13x3x8 breast :	hob/	5.0007
Ullard	Courmellan	Clashganny Mill	corn	large building & roof :	-	-	Hughes	2002	-	mmSv/	wh - B
Ullard	Courmellan	Doyle John	corn, kiln	(1A) 28x18x10.6 :	-	8.8.7	-	1843	12x3 dp. bkt. 1ft :	hob/	5.0035
Ullard	Courmellan	Hennessy's	corn	demolished for res . :	-	-	-	2002	-	mmSv/	wh - Z
Ahade	Craan	- at Whitemill Br	white mill	-	-	-	-	-	-	1"os/	148
Ahade	Craan	- on R Slaney	cloth	-	-	-	-	-	-	1"os/	148
Ardoyne	Craans	- on R. Slaney	beetling	very attractive site :	-	-	- Michael Hogg Watt	2002	wheel operates	mmSv/	wh - R
Ardoyne	Craans	- on R. Slaney	millhouse	on attractive site	-	-	Michael H. Watt	1998	residence	pWEH	B
Ardoyne	Craans	Kelly James	woollen fcty	-	14a.	-	-	-	-	gr/	-
Rathvilly	Derren River :	O'Brien Edward :	mill	-	-	-	O'Brien Ed - Lalor Edward :	1822	-	dd/	770 115 522050
Rathvilly	Derren River :	Kinglsey Daniel :	mill	-	-	-	Kingsley D - O`Brien Edwd :	1821	-	dd/	763 421 518156
Carlow	Dunganstown	-	corn	-	-	-	-	1840	-	6"os/	2
Dunleckny	Dunleckney	-	corn	converted for res.	-	-	-	2002	-	mmSv/	wh - Ca
Dunleckny	Dunleckney	- on R. Slaney	brewery	restored as maltings	-	-	Minch Norton & Co.	2002	-	mmSv/	wh - A
Dunleckny	Dunleckny	Casey John	corn	-	14a.	-	-	-	-	gr/	-
Dunleckny	Dunleckny	Casey John	corn	(1B) 44.6x21.6x18 :	-	-	-	1843	-	hob/	5.0004
Dunleckny	Dunleckny	Casey John	corn (cont.)	malt ho 54x18x17 :	-	57.10	-	1843	-	hob/	5.0004
Dunleckny	Dunleckny	Norton John	thrashing	88x21.6x12 & dw. :	-	70.7	-	1843	17x3 depth bkt :	hob/	5.0004
Gilbertstown	Gilbertstown	Noonan Anne	corn	-	3a.	-	-	-	-	gr/	-
Grangesilva :	Goresbridge	near br. on R. Barrow	corn	- in fine order	-	-	-	2002	-	mmSv/	wh - B
Carlow	Graigue	-	mill	-	-	-	-	-	-	1"os/	137
Grangesilva	Grange Lower	- Red Mill	flour	lge. bldg. long millrace	-	-	-	-	-	6"os/	21
Grangesilva	Grange Lower	- S. road to Gowran	corn	-	-	-	-	1841	-	6"os/	21
Grangesilva	Grange Lower	1m. NW / Goresbridge	flour	old building incorp. in :	-	-	-	-	- pho. taken	mmSv/	wh - A
Killerrig	Grangewat	- W. side R. Slaney	tuck	-	-	-	-	1840	-	6"os/	8
Killerrig	Grangewat	Battley	mill	-	-	-	Battley - Grange	-	- (error)	dd/	351 11 361993
Killerrig	Grangewat	Croker Jno	mills	-	-	-	Croker J - Cudmore Henry	1746	-	dd/	124 335 84912
Killerrig	Grangewat	Flynn John	hook	-	30a.	-	-	-	-	gr/	-
Killerrig	Grangewat	Herbert Edward :	mill	-	-	-	Herbert Ed - Jones George :	1721	-	dd/	283 558 187253
Killerrig	Grangewat	Nowlan Gerard	mill	-	-	-	Nowlan G - Griffin Patrick :	1809	-	dd/	607 197 415576
Killerrig	Grangewat	Scott	mill	-	-	-	Scott - Butler	-	-	dd/	698 379 473720
Dunleckny	Kilcarrig	- at Bagnelstown	flax	converted to res.	-	-	- Anne McKinney	2002	-	mmSv/	wh - Ca
Dunleckny	Kilcarrig	- E. of Kilcarrig Br.	corn	-	-	-	-	1888	-	25"os/	16.10
Dunleckny	Kilcarrig	Ward Thomas	corn	-	-	-	-	-	-	gr/	-
Dunleckny	Kilcarrig	Ward Thomas	corn	66.6x23.6x23.6 & :	-	14.18	-	1852	17.6 dia. breast :	hob/	5.0004
Moyacomb	Kilcarry	Anderson John	corn & sicle	(meas. in orig book)	-	-	-	1851	-	hob/	5.0036a
Moyacomb	Kilcarry	Anderson John	cutling	(2B) 29x16.6x8 & :	-	3.16	-	1843	15x2x2.6 breast :	hob/	5.0036a

PARISH	TOWNLAND	MILLER	TYPE	HOUSE	Land	£Val	PROPRIETORS	Date	WHEEL etc.	Record	Ref.
Moyacomb	Kilcarry	Anderson John	hook	-	-	-	-	-	-	gr/	-
Moyacomb	Kilcarry	Anderson John	old corn mill	-	15a.	-	-	-	-	gr/	-
Moyacomb	Kilcarry	Anderson John	sicle & corn	- buildings bad	-	-	-	1846	Mill to date was :	hob/	5.0036A/note
Moyacomb	Kilcarry *	- close to R Slaney	spade	- [no mill located]	-	-	-	1998	-	no ph	Z?
Clonygoose	Kilcloney	Kealy James	woollen	-	18a.	-	-	-	-	gr/	-
Clonygoose	Kilcloney	Kealy James	woollen fty	28.6x20x12.6 addn.:	-	4.19	-	1850	13x2.9 o`shot :	hob/	5.0003
Carlow	Kiltillahan *	-	mill	-	-	-	-	-	-	1"os/	-
Clonygoose	Knockagundarragh	Murphy James	corn	-	13a.	-	-	-	-	gr/	-
Clonygoose	Knockagundarragh	Murphy James	corn	kiln (new in 1852) :	-	40	-	1852	14x7x11.6 metal	hob/	5.0003
Clonygoose	Knockagundarragh	Murphy Timothy	corn	(1A) 46x20x24.6 :	-	19.10	-	1843	12ft. o`shot bkts. :	hob/	5.0003
Barragh	Knockbarragh	Rourke Hugh	corn & kiln	-	-	-	-	-	-	gr/	-
Rathvilly	Knockloe	Fox Thomas	mill	-	-	-	Fox Thos - National Bank	1873	-	dd/	1873 38 113
Carlow	Knockmill *	Colvill Martha	lodge & mill	-	-	-	Colvill Martha - Weld Matt	1876	-	dd/	1876 55 205/6
Wells	Leighlandbridge	Dillon	mill	-	-	-	Dillon & W - Stewart	-	-	dd/	405 153 265586
Wells	Leighlandbridge	Mercer	mill	-	-	-	Mercer - Phelan	-	-	dd/	471 382 299628
Wells	Leighlandbridge	Swift	mill	-	-	-	Swift - Cliffe	-	?	dd/	319 479 255270
Wells	Leighlinbridge	-	granary	- known as The Mill	-	-	-	2002	-	mmSv/	wh - B
Wells	Leighlinbridge	at Town Park	culm crusher	-	-	-	-	2002	-	pWEH	-
Wells	Leighlinbridge	Church Street	corn	bldg. good new roof	-	-	now Murphy & Co. Engineers	2002	-	mmSv/	wh - Cc
Wells	Leighlinbridge	Church Street	granary	5 sty., recently burnt	-	-	-	2002	-	mmSv/	wh - B
Wells	Leighlinbridge	Kavanagh John :	kiln	22.6x23x12.6 & :	-	17.16.	-	-	-	hob/	5.0017
Wells	Leighlinbridge	on site Lord B. Inn	brewery	- x	-	-	-	2002	-	mmSv/	wh - Z
Wells	Leighlinbridge	on site Lord B. Inn	kiln	demolished large & :	-	-	-	2002	-	mmSv/	wh - Z
Wells	Leighlinbridge	on site Lord B. Inn	malt houses	(2) demolished	-	-	-	2002	-	mmSv/	wh - Z
Rathvilly	Lisnevagh	Bunbury (?)	corn	(1A) 32.6x25.6x18.8 :	-	-	-	-	steam eng. 8 HP :	hob/	5.0030
Rathvilly	Lisnevagh	Bunbury William C	corn	-	796a	-	-	-	-	gr/	-
Cloydagh	Milford	- at Millford Bridge	flour	ruin, in fine state	-	-	-	2002	-	mmSv/	wh - R
Cloydagh	Milford	Alexander George	mills	-	-	-	Alexander George - John	1871	-	dd/	1871 11 65
Cloydagh	Milford	Connolly Andrew	mills	-	-	-	Connolly A - Dolan Fran	1871	-	dd/	1871 22? 64
Cloydagh	Milford	Norton Patrick	mills	-	-	-	Norton P - Alexander Jas	1870	-	dd/	1870 34 131
Cloydagh	Milford	Nugent John	mills	-	-	-	Nugent john - Roche John	1877	-	dd/	1877 14 171
Cloydagh	Milford	Nugent Kathleen	mills	-	-	-	Nugent Kathleen - John	1876	-	dd/	1876 10 254
Cloydagh	Milford	Nugent Kathleen	mills	-	-	-	Nugent Kathleen - John	1876	-	dd/	1876 23 82
Cloydagh	Milford	Nugent Kathleen	mills	-	-	-	Nugent Kathleen - John	1876	-	dd/	1876 23 91
Cloydagh	Milford	Strongstream Ltd	mills	-	-	-	John Alexander	1946	Kaplan, Francis :	turb/	A
Carlow	Mill Land	Clarke Simeon & Co	corn	-	0.0 37	-	-	-	-	gr/	-
Cloydagh	Millford	Connolly	mill	-	-	-	Connolly - Alexander	-	?	dd/	186 6 309729
Carlow	Millpark	- at Castlegrace	New Mills corn	-	-	-	-	-	-	1"os/	148
Carlow	Milltown	Coghlan	mill	-	-	-	Coghlan - Harding	-	-	dd/	470 562 308343
Carlow	Milltown	Duncannon	mill	-	-	-	Duncannon - Cavendish	-	-	dd/	94 548 67233
Feenagh	Milltown	Fitzgerald Thomas	hook & forge	no dimensions	6a.	19/4d	-	1851	10ft dia., buckets :	hob/	5.0004
Clonygoose	Milltown Borris	-	no mill	-	-	-	-	-	-	1"os/	147
Dunleckny	Monebeg	Forbes Edward	mill	-	-	-	Forbes Ed - Weld Edmond	1878	-	dd/	1878 25 281
Dunleckny	Moneybeg	- Bagenalstown :	corn	-	-	-	-	1840	-	6"os/	16
Dunleckny	Moneybeg	Bagnelstown	flour	ceased op. recently	-	-	-	2002	-	mmSv/	wh - B
Dunleckny	Moneybeg	Crosthwaite Samuel	corn & flour	-	-	-	-	-	-	gr/	
Dunleckny	Moneybeg	Crosthwaite Samuel	flour	(1B) 85x69x45.6 :	-	-	-	1843	-	hob/	5.0004
Dunleckny	Moneybeg	Crosthwaite Samuel	flour	kilns 50.6x25x25 :	-	-	-	1851	new wheel & :	hob/	5.0004
Dunleckny	Moneybeg	Crosthwaite Samuel	flour (cont.)	kilns 50.6x25x25 E423	-	-	-	1843	1st - 16x2x9 bkts	hob/	5.0004
Dunleckny	Moneybeg	Ducie Carl	mill	-	-	-	Ducie C - Moreton Algern.	1878	-	dd/	1878 17 263
Dunleckny	Moneybeg	Rudkin's Mill	corn & brewery	large ruin (? soon for :	-	-	-	2002	-	mmSv/	wh - R
Carlow	Mortarstown	- at Millford Br.	corn	-	-	-	-	1840	-	6"os/	12

PARISH	TOWNLAND	MILLER	TYPE	HOUSE	Land	£Val	PROPRIETORS	Date	WHEEL etc.	Record	Ref.
Drumlummin	Mullaghoran	McCormick Michael (?)	corn	(2B) 40x20x8 : k	-	-	-	1838	1 pair stones :	hob/	5.0055
Painstown	Newacre	-	corn	-	-	-	-	1840	-	6"os/	2
Painstown	Newacre	Condell's (1st on R.B.)	corn	-	-	-	- Patrick Mealy	2002	-	mmSv/	wh - R
Painstown	Newacre	Dillon	mill	-	-	-	Dillon - Browne	-	-	dd/	735 145 501080
Painstown	Newacre	Dillon	mill	-	-	-	Dillon - Dyer	-	-	dd/	736 561 502096
Painstown	Newacre	Duigan John	corn	-	25a.	-	-	-	-	gr/	-
Ardoyne	Newstown	- at Newstown Ho.	thrashing	-	-	-	-	1841	-	6"os/	14
Agha	Newtown	Latouche Robt Lt Col. :	mill	-	-	-	LatoucheR - Kelly Edmond :	1828	-	dd/	832 306 559441
Nurney	Nurney	-	corn	-	-	-	-	1840	-	6"os/	12
Nurney	Nurney	McGrath William	old mill	-	144a.	-	-	-	-	gr/	-
Wells	Old Leighlin :	Gordon John	mill	-	-	-	Gordon J - Nixon James	1876	-	dd/	1876 3891
Carlow	Old Park *	Bruen Henry	mill	-	-	-	Bruen H - Pollock Henry	1875	-	dd/	1875 3 174
Carlow	Old Park *	Bruen Henry	mill	-	-	-	Bruen H - Pollock Henry	1875	-	dd/	1875 55 3
Carlow	Old Park *	Bruen Henry	mill	-	-	-	Bruen H - Pollock Henry	1875	-	dd/	1875 56 191
Clonmore	Oldtown :	-	Clonmore Castl	-	-	-	-	-	-	6"os/	9
Clonmore	Oldtown :	-	stone cross :	-	-	-	-	-	-	6"os/	9
Clonmore	Oldtown :	- nr. St. Mogul's Well	mill in ruins	-	-	-	-	-	-	6"os/	9
Carlow	Oldtown (3)	Bagenal	mill	-	-	-	Bagenal - Bruen	-	-	dd/	400 533 264315
Urney	Orchard	- recorded in OS.	corn	demolished, probable:	-	-	-	2002	-	mmSv/	wh - Z
Nurney	Orchard	- at Orchard Bridge	mill	-	-	-	-	-	-	1"os/	-
Nurney	Orchard	- at Orchard Bridge :	corn	-	-	-	-	-	-	6"os/	12
Nurney	Orchard	Goold Mary :	mills	-	-	-	Goold M - O`Connell Maurice	1823	-	dd/	782 232 529367
Nurney	Orchard	Hamilton	mill	-	-	-	Hamilton - Bruen	-	-	dd/	974 126 536461
Tullowphelin	Ouragh	-	corn (in ruins)	-	-	-	-	1843	-	6"os/	13
Tullowphelin	Ouragh	Hickey Michael	corn	-	28a.	-	-	-	-	gr/	-
Tullowphelin	Ouragh	Hickey Michael	corn	house not in proper :	-	-	-	1851	- 3 pair stones :	hob/	5.0032
Carlow	Papish	Brennan Jno :	mill & bl green	-	-	-	Brennan J - Hughes Wm :	1808			
Rathvily	Patrickswell	- on R. Slaney	old corn mill	-	-	-	-	-	-	6"os/	4
Rathvilly	Patrickswell	David Whitty (note) :	corn	-	-	-	-	-	-	hob/	5.0030
Rathvilly	Patrickswell	Faulkner Thomas	corn	-	17a.	-	-	-	-	gr/	-
Rathvilly	Patrickswell	Faulkner Thomas S. :	corn	(1B) 30x22.6x15.6 :	-	-	-	1851	15.6x6x1.6 float :	hob/	5.0030
Carlow	Paupish	- on R. Burren	corn	small bldg. fine order	-	-	- James Murphy Sen.	2002	-	mmSv/	wh - B
Carlow	Paupish	- on R. Burren	corn	v. old building	-	-	- (was) Kathleen Lennon's	2002	- pho. taken	mmSv/	wh - B
Carlow	Poorestown *	Butler	mills	-	-	-	Butler - Bayley	-	?	dd/	199 361 132469
Carlow	Poorestown *	Cooper William :	mills	-	-	-	Cooper W - Stewart Wm	1752	-	dd/	153 394 103284
Carlow	Poorestown *	Meredith	mills	-	-	-	Meredith - Stronde	-	-	dd/	253 *?* **?**
Kilteegan	Portrushen	- on Dereen R.	tuck :	-	-	-	-	1840	-	6"os/	4
Rathvilly	Portrushen Lr	Murphy John	corn	-	82a	-	-	-	-	gr/	-
Tullowmag`a	Rathcrogue	-	corn & mill race	-	-	-	-	1843	-	6"os/	7
Tullowmag`a	Rathcrogue	M`Donnell John	corn	-	23a.	-	-	-	-	gr/	-
Ardoyne	Ratheeragh	-	old corn mill	-	-	-	-	1843	-	6"os/	13
Ardoyne	Ratheeran :	-	saw	-	-	-	-	-	-	1"os/	-
Ardoyne	Ratheeran :	Fairbrother Sarah :	mill	-	-	-	Fairbrother S - Kinsley Dan :	1821	-	dd/	760 139 516074
Rathmore	Rathmore	- on R. Slaney	corn	-	-	-	-	1840	-	6"os/	3
Rathmore	Rathmore	Malone Joseph	corn	-	24a.	-	-	-	-	gr/	-
Rathmore	Rathmore	Walnutt Joseph	corn	(1A) 22.6x37x25.6 :	-	33	-	1843	13.6x5.9x2.6 :	hob/	5.0029
Carlow	Rathnapish	near Carlow Town	starch (remains	at hospital near asylum, strange ancient building				2002	-	mmSv/	wh - R?Z
Carlow	Rathnapish	Walsh Frances R :	bleach ground	-	1a.	-	-	-	-	gr/	-
Carlow	Rathnapish & :	Nolan James	malt house	(1B) 61.6x23x17.6 :	-	11.14	-	-	-	hob/	5.2376
Rathvilly	Rathvilly	-	corn	fine small building E4	-	-	-	2002	- Enrico Tonini	mmSv/	wh - Cc
Rathvilly	Rathvilly	-	mill	-	-	-	Enrico Tononi	1998	restaurant	pWEH	C
Rathvilly	Rathvilly	Butler	mill	-	-	-	Butler - Prim	-	-	dd/	584 525? 398851

PARISH	TOWNLAND	MILLER	TYPE	HOUSE	Land	£Val	PROPRIETORS	Date	WHEEL etc.	Record	Ref.
Rathvilly	Rathvilly	Dobie	mill	-	-	-	Dobie - Butler	-	-	dd/	580 389 398852
Rathvilly	Rathvilly	Dobie	mill	-	-	-	Dobie - Cooke	-	-	dd/	580 389 398853
Rathvilly	Rathvilly	Dobie	mill	-	-	-	Dobie - Cooke	-	-	dd/	588 83 398855
Rathvilly	Rathvilly	in Tullow Town	mill	old, dangerous cond.	-	-	-	1998	-	pWEH	R
Rathvilly	Rathvilly	Minas Robert :	mills	-	-	-	Minas R - Nowlan Thomas :	1814	-	dd/	672 34 461049
Rathvilly	Rathvilly	Nowlan Thomas :	mill	-	-	-	Nowlan T - Fishbourne Jos.:	1813	-	dd/	671 258 461172
Rathvilly	Rathvilly	Tullow Town	mill	old very dilapidated :	-	-	-	2002	- pho. taken	mmSv/	wh - R
Carlow	Red Mills *	near Goresbridge	flour	old building incorp. :	-	-	-	2002	- Connolly's	mmSv/	wh - A
Kiltinnell	Rosdellig	-	cutlery & tuck m	-	-	-	-	1843	-	6"os/	22
Kiltinnell	Rosdellig	-	old corn mill	-	-	-	-	1843	-	6"os/	22
Kiltinnell	Rosdellig	Bagenal Walter	mill	-	-	-	Bagenal W - B`champ R	1740	-	dd/	101 62 69877
Kiltinnell	Rosdellig	BagenalBeauchamp :	mill	-	-	-	Bagenal B - Barnes Bart :	1757	-	dd/	186 486 125569
Kiltinnell	Rosdellig	Clean John	corn	25.6x17.6x9 and : (	-	5.12	-	1843	12x2 overshot :	hob/	5.0006
Kiltinnell	Rosdellig	Clean John	tuck	-	-	-	-	1843	11.6x2 mc/y bad	hob/	5.0006
Kiltinnell	Rosdellig	Evans Nathaniel	mill	-	-	-	Evans - Bagenal B`champ	1756	-	dd/	181 192 120288
Kiltinnell	Rosdellig	Fitzhenry	mill	-	-	-	Fitzhenry - Doyle	-	?	dd/	286 591 171527
Kiltinnell	Rosdellig	James John :	mills	-	-	-	James J - Burgess Eliz. :	1813	-	dd/	667 69 458610
Kiltinnell	Rosdellig	Leech George	corn & kiln	25.6x15.6x8 & kiln : :	-	4.3.8	-	1851	no dimensions :	hob/	5.0006
Kiltinnell	Rosdellig	Martin William	mill	-	-	-	Martin W - Bowycar Fran	1737	-	dd/	99 202 68632
Kiltinnell	Rosdellig	Martin William	mill	-	-	-	Martin - Woollaston Israel	1737	-	dd/	99 205 68633
Clonygoose	Scartreene	Foyle Joseph :	mill	-	-	-	Foyle Joseph - Goff Tadd :	1840	-	dd/	533 497 355142
Clonygoose	Scorteen or :	- Borris	Corn & Flour	-	-	-	-	1840	-	6"os/	22
Clonygoose	Scortreen	Evans John	carding	-	-	-	-	-	-	gr/	-
Clonygoose	Scortreen	Fayle	mill	-	-	-	Fayle - Goffe	-	-	dd/	533 497 355142
Clonygoose	Scortreen	Jordan	mill	-	-	-	Jordan - Jordan	-	-	dd/	537 42 353932
Clonygoose	Scortreen	Moran	mill	-	-	-	Moran - Strphens	-	?	dd/	- - 309051
Clonygoose	Scortreen	Warren John	mill	-	-	-	Warren J - Warren Jacob	1750	-	dd/	141 358 95794
Carlow	Shagten *	Courtown Jas Earl	mills	-	-	-	Courtown - Stoppford Ld	1828	-	dd/	832 589 559724
Carlow	Shagten *	Courtown Earl Hon. :	mills	-	-	-	Courtown Jas - Montague :	1828	Mort. 11 Feb.	dd/	832 590 559725
Grangeford	Slaney Quarter	- W. side R. Slaney	mill in ruins	-	-	-	-	1840	-	6"os/	8
Sliguff	Sliguff	- Ballyellen	Flax Mill	-	-	-	-	1840	-	6"os/	19
St Mullins	St Mullins	-	mill	-	-	-	-	-	-	iaa/	Al800 os26.6.3
St Mullins	St Mullins	- E. side at M. Br.	corn	-	-	-	-	1840	-	6"os/	26
St Mullins	St Mullins	- E. side below Ch.	corn	-	-	-	-	1840	-	6"os/	26
St Mullins	St Mullins	- above village	store house &	-	-	-	-	2002	-	mmSv/	
St Mullins	St Mullins	- Cushion's Mill	woollen	sturdy rect. building	-	-	-	2002	- Mrs Flusky	mmSv/	wh - B
St Mullins	St Mullins	- on Barrow bank	corn	small mill	-	-	-	1998	-	mmSv/	wh - B
St Mullins	St Mullins	- on Barrow bank	flour	large buildings	-	-	-	1998	- pho. taken	mmSv/	wh - B
St Mullins	St Mullins	- stream to R Barrow	mill	-	-	-	-	-	-	1"os/	157
St Mullins	St Mullins	Altham	land	-	-	-	Altham - Paul	-	-	dd/	22 114 11551
St Mullins	St Mullins	Birch	land	-	-	-	Birch - Cooke	-	-	dd/	820 316 552251
St Mullins	St Mullins	Connolly	land	-	-	-	Connolly - Nugent	-	-	dd/	701 522 481025
St Mullins	St Mullins	Coyle	land	-	-	-	Coyle - Wrightby	-	?	dd/	10 60 3063
St Mullins	St Mullins	Kavanagh	land	-	-	-	Kavanagh - Byrne	-	?	dd/	? ? 331986
St Mullins	St Mullins	Kavanagh	land	-	-	-	Kavanagh - Veitch	-	?	dd/	311 130 207730
St Mullins	St Mullins	Kavanagh	land	-	-	-	Kavanagh - Wallace	-	-	dd/	498? 127 316592
St Mullins	St Mullins	Kavanagh	land	-	-	-	Kavanagh - Kavanagh	-	-	dd/	514 19 332767
St Mullins	St Mullins	Knapton Lord	land	-	-	-	Knapton - Clanbrassill E	-	?	dd/	289 48 189163
St Mullins	St Mullins	Kough	land	-	-	-	Kouch - Fowler	-	-	dd/	700 319 480199
St Mullins	St Mullins	Markham	land	-	-	-	Markham - ?	-	?	dd/	34 199 21191
St Mullins	St Mullins	McGrath	land	-	-	-	Mcgrath - Hanly	-	-	dd/	772 170 523305
St Mullins	St Mullins	Phillips	land	-	-	-	Phillips - Harrison	-	-	dd/	7 45 1578

PARISH	TOWNLAND	MILLER	TYPE	HOUSE	Land	£Val	PROPRIETORS	Date	WHEEL etc.	Record	Ref.
St Mullins	St Mullins	Vesey	land	-	-	-	Vesey - Loftus	-	-	dd/	55 308 37068
St Mullins	St Mullins	Vesey	land	-	-	-	Vesey - Marlay	-	-	dd/	81 367 57923
St Mullins	St Mullins	Wilson	land	-	-	-	Wilson - Annesley	-	-	dd/	47 541 31800
Ballinacarrig	Staples Mill	Bagenal Beauchamp :	mill	-	-	-	Bagenal B - Latouche Dav :	1773	-	dd/	293 162 194614
Ballinacarrig	Staples Mill	Barnes Bartholomew :	mill	-	-	-	Barnes B - Baker Walter :	1765	-	dd/	241 193 15800-?
Ballinacarrig	Staples Mill	Butler Walter & Son	mill	-	-	-	Butler W - Grose Edward :	1765	-	dd/	241 191 158000
Ballinacarrig	Staples Mill	Galbraith Samuel :	mill	-	-	-	Galbraith - Gorman Ferdin'd :	1766	-	dd/	287 509 188614
Ballinacarrig	Staplestown	Bagenal Beauchamp	mill	-	-	-	Bagenal B - Bruen Henry	1788	-	dd/	400 533 264315
Ballinacarrig	Staplestown	Bruen Henry	mill	-	-	-	Bruen H - Pollock Henry	1875	-	dd/	1875 55 3
Ballinacarrig	Staplestown	Bruen Henry :	mill	-	-	-	Bruen H - Gorman Patk :	1791	-	dd/	436 222 282250
Ballinacarrig	Staplestown	Gorman Patrick :	mill	-	-	-	Gorman P - Bruen Henry	1789	-	dd/	405 468 266924
Ballinacarrig	Staplestown	stream from Burren R.	flour & mill pond		-	-	-	1843	-	6"os/	7
Ballinacarrig	Staplestown	Thompson	mills	-	-	-	Thompson - Hamilton	-	-	dd/	722 248 523387
Ballinacarrig	Staplestown	Thompson William Rev	mills	-	-	-	Thompson - Hamilton Robt :	1822	Mort. 1 Apl.	dd/	772 248 523383
Straboe	Straboe	- N. side R. Slaney	cutlery	-	-	-	-	1840	-	6"os/	3
Straboe	Straboe	Fitzgerald Patrick	cutlers	(2A) 25x17.6x7 :	-	3.10	-	1843	12x3.8x8.6 breast	hob/	5.0031
Painstown	Strawhall	Morgan Edward :	land	-	-	-	Morgan Ed - Kelly David :	1820	-	dd/	761 43 516578
Cloydagh	Strongstream	Alexander	mill	-	-	-	Alexander - Connolly	-	-	dd/	421 498 428356
Cloydagh	Strongstream	Alexander	mill	-	-	-	Alexander - Connolly	-	-	dd/	621 492 428358
Cloydagh	Strongstream	Alexander Henry	mill holding	-	-	-	Alexander Henry - John	1871	-	dd/	1871 11 64
Cloydagh	Strongstream	Alexander John :	mill	-	-	-	Alexander J - Connolly Jas :	1809	-	dd/	621 498 428356
Cloydagh	Strongstream	Butler Sir Richard Bt. :	mill	-	-	-	Butler R & T - Alexander Jas	1807	-	dd/	621 285 426554
Cloydagh	Strongstream	Connolly	mill	-	-	-	Connolly - Connolly	-	-	dd/	809 528 454863
Cloydagh	Strongstream	Connolly	mill	-	-	-	Connolly - Alexander	-	-	dd/	828 317 557052
Rathvilly	Tobinstown	- W. side Dereen R.	corn	-	-	-	-	1840	-	6"os/	9
Rathvilly	Tobinstown	Bagot	mill	-	-	-	Bagot - Cadell	-	-	dd/	419 199 273667
Rathvilly	Tobinstown	Bagot James John :	mill	-	-	-	Bagot J - O`Callaghan Ellen :	1821	-	dd/	774 437 524772
Rathvilly	Tobinstown	Bagot Burren St	mill	-	-	-	Bagot - Leigh	-	-	dd/	624 448 429490
Rathvilly	Tobinstown	Bagot Eleanor Wid	mill	-	-	-	Bagot E - Ruxton Clarges :	1828	Asgt. 1 Mar.	dd/	833 77 559812
Rathvilly	Tobinstown	Norris Margaret	mill	-	-	-	Norris M - O`Ferral Richd	1872	-	dd/	1872 34 120
Rathvilly	Tobinstown	O`Ferrall Richard	mill	-	-	-	O`Ferrall Rich - Ambrose	1873	-	dd/	1873 38 49
Rathvilly	Tobinstown :	-	Acaun Monastry		-	-	-	1840	-	6"os/	2
Carlow	Townland ?	- near Aghcoig Br.	corn & dam	-	-	-	-	1840	-	6"os/	24
Carlow	Townland ?	Knott	Badger Mill	-	-	-	Knott - Knott	-	-	dd/	745 306 507241
Rathvilly	Tullow	- at Knockloe Br.	mill	-	-	-	-	-	-	1"os/	-
Rathvilly	Tullow	Doyne Robert :	bolting mill	below Tullow Bridge :	-	-	Doyne R - Pim Joseph	1824	-	dd/	806 357 543892
Rathvilly	Tullow	Moore John :	mills	-	-	-	Moore J - Dwyer Garrett :	1815	-	dd/	688 9 472744/5
Rathvilly	Tullow	Moore Edward :	mills	-	-	-	Moore Ed - Burgess Wm :	1815	-	dd/	694 226 476527
Rathvilly	Tullow	Nowlan John :	mills	-	-	-	Nowlan J - Synott Patk Rev. :	1820	-	dd/	752 422 501347
Feenagh / :	Tullow Castleqtr.	Fury William	mill	-	-	-	Fury W - Clibborn Robert	1746	-	dd/	119 440 83158
Feenagh / :	Tullow Town	-	mills (2)	-	-	-	-	1845	-	iaa/	AI802 os8.15.3
Feenagh / :	Tullow Town	Doyle James	corn & kiln	-	-	-	-	-	-	gr/	-
Feenagh / :	Tullow Town	Fox Thomas	corn store, kiln	-	-	-	-	-	-	gr/	-
Feenagh / :	Tullow Town	Keppel John	flour	-	-	-	-	-	-	gr/	-
Tullowphelim	Tullow Town	vac.	brewery	(1B) 34x25x18 & : f	-	11	-	-	[no information]	hob/	5.2383
Tullowphelim	Tullow Town :	- on R. Slaney	corn	-	-	-	-	1840	-	6"os/	8
Tullowphelim	Tullow Town :	Doyle James	corn	(1C) 85x20x24.6 & : k	-	55	-	-	12x6x6 24 bkts :	hob/	5.2383
Fennagh	Tullowbeg	Donoghue Daniel	corn	-	12a.	-	-	-	-	gr/	-
Fennagh	Tullowbeg	Donohoe Daniel	corn	- (see orig. hob.)	-	2.10	-	1850	- 3 pair stones :	hob/	5.0023
Feenagh	Tullowbeg :	- on R. Slaney :	corn	-	-	-	-	1840	-	6"os/	8
Tullowphelim	Tullowphelim	Doyne Charles	mills	-	-	-	Doyne C - Unlacke Cath	1870	-	dd/	1870 24 5
Tullowphelim	Tullowphelim	Fox Thomas	corn	-	9.1.9	-	-	-	-	gr/	-

PARISH	TOWNLAND	MILLER	TYPE	HOUSE	Land	£Val	PROPRIETORS	Date	WHEEL etc.	Record	Ref.
Tullowphelin	Tullowphelim	Fox Thomas	corn	(2B) 24.6x18.6x8 & :	-	5.8.0	-	1843	13x2.6x2 breast :	hob/	5.0032
Tullowphelim	Tullowphelim :	- on Dereen R.	corn	-	-	-	-	1840	-	6"os/	8
Tullowphelim	Tullowphelim :	-	corn	-	-	-	-	1840	-	6"os/	8
Wells	Wells	-	mill	-	-	-	-	-	-	iaa/	AI804 os-
Wells	Wells	- W. side R. Slaney	corn	-	-	-	-	1843	-	6"os/	16
Wells	Wells	Brennan Edmond :	land [no mill]	-	-	-	Brennan E - Rice William :	1817	-	dd/	725 354 495289
Wells	Wells	Brennan Pierce	corn	-	66a.	-	-	-	-	gr/	-
Wells	Wells	Brosnan Pierce	corn	(2A) 20x17.6x12.6 :	-	14.3	-	1843	14ft overshot :	hob/	5.0016
Wells	Wells	Pierce Drea	corn	old small building	-	-	-	2002	-	mmSv/	wh - B

PARISH	TOWNLAND	MILLER	TYPE	HOUSE	Land	£Val	PROPRIETORS	Date	WHEEL etc.	Record	Ref.
Annagh	Aghadreenagh	-	corn & dam	-	-	-	-	-	-	6"os/	16
Annagh	Aghadreenagh	Fitzpatrick Daniel	corn	(2C) 39.6x22.6x9 :	-	-	-	-	13.6 dia. 2 pr st. :	hob/	5.0069
Annagh	Aghadreenagh	Hewston Chas & Co.	corn	-	-	-	formerly Fitzpatrick Dan	-	13x - x10	vmb/	2
Annagh	Aghadreenagh	Prunty John	corn & kiln	-	-	5.15	-	1856	-	gr/	a.a.Ire.ie
Ballintemple	Ardleny	-	malt kiln	-	-	-	-	-	-	6"os/	37
Kildallon	Ardlougher	-	corn & kiln	-	-	-	-	-	-	6"os/	14
Kildallon	Ardlougher	Brady John & Andr	corn	-	-	-	-	-	14x3x4	vmb/	2
Drumlane	Ardue	-	corn	-	-	-	-	-	-	6"os/	10
Drumlane	Ardue	- nr Killywilly Ho.	bleach	-	-	-	-	-	-	6"os/	10
Bailieborough	Bailieborough	-	flax	-	-	-	-	1899	-	1"os/	80
Bailieborough	Bailieborough	- at Spearvale	mill	-	-	-	-	1899	-	1"os/	80
Lurgan	Ballaghanea	-	corn & tuck	-	-	-	-	-	-	6"os/	39
Lurgan	Ballaghanea	Tormry Walter	corn & tuck	ho., offs. & land	36a.	31	-	-	-	gr	-
Lurgan	Ballaghanea	Tormry Walter	corn & tuck	(2C) 33x19x8 & :	-	6.6	-	1837	12x4 drives 1 pr st. :	hob/	5.3768
Lurgan	Ballaghanna	- near L. Ramor	mill	-	-	-	-	1899	-	1"os/	80
Lurgan	Ballaghanna	Tormey Walter	corn	(2C) 32.0x18.6x7 :	-	-	- (valued also Apl. 1837)	1838	11.6 x2.0x14 - corn :	hob/	5.0042
Lurgan	Ballaghanna	Tormey Walter	corn	-	-	-	-	-	11x2x14	vmb/	2
Lurgan	Ballaghanna	Tormey Walter	tuck	-	-	-	-	-	-	vmb/	2
Enniskeen	Balloughly	Moore Patrick	corn	-	-	-	-	-	-	vmb/	2
Ballintemple	Ballyheelan	- nr Cross Roads	corn & kiln	-	-	-	-	-	-	6"os/	37
Ballintemple	Ballyheelan	Parr John Geo	corn	(2B) 34x22x11 :	-	-	-	1839	14.6x2.10x5 2 pr st.	hob/	5.0048
Castlerahan	Ballyjamesduff	- at Laragh Ho.	flax	-	-	-	-	1899	-	1"os/	80
Castlerahan	Ballyjamesduff	- at Laragh Lo.	mill	-	-	-	-	1899	-	1"os/	80
Castlerahan	Ballyjamesduff	- at Rockville	mill	-	-	-	-	1899	-	1"os/	80
Enniskeen	Ballyloughly	Moore Patrick	corn	house, offs. & land	32a.	21.15.	-	1856	-	gr/	a.a.Ire.ie
Templeport	Ballymagauran	-	distillery ruins	-	-	-	-	-	-	6"os/	13
Drung	Ballynacargy	-	corn	-	-	-	-	-	12ft. dia. undershot	osm/	-
Cavan	Ballyness	Taggart	corn	-	-	-	-	1974	-	sv/ff	GBowie
Templeport	Bawnboy	-	corn & tuck	-	-	-	-	-	-	6"os/	9
Templeport	Bawnboy	Burke Mrs	corn	(2C) 35.6x20x10.6 :	-	7-11	-	-	15x2.7x4.6 u`shot	hob/	5.0084
Templeport	Bawnboy	Burke Mrs	corn	-	-	-	-	-	15x2x5	vmb/	2
Templeport	Bawnboy	Burke Mrs	tuck	- (att. to corn mill)	-	-	-	-	-	hob/	5.0084
Templeport	Bawnboy	Coffey James	corn	35.6x20x11 & addn :	-	8-10	-	-	15.5x2.4x5 2 pr st.	hob/	5.0083
Templeport	Bawnboy	Gilroy Owen	tuck	(2B) 33.6x19x7	-	1-19	-	-	12x1.10x3 breast :	hob/	5.0083
Templeport	Bawnboy	Gilroy Owen	tuck	-	-	-	-	-	12x2x8	vmb/	2
Templeport	Bawnboy	King	mill	-	-	-	King - King	-	?	dd/	180 140 528075
Kilmore	Bellananagh	-	corn & pond	-	-	-	-	-	-	6"os/	25
Kilmore	Bellananagh	Bennett	mill	-	-	-	-	1974	-	sv/ff	GBowie
Kilmore	Bellananagh	Bennett`s	corn	-	-	-	-	1998	-	pWEH	- B
Annagh	Belturbet Town	- nr Holburn Hill	brewery	-	-	-	-	-	-	6"os/	11
Kinawley	Binkeeragh	-	corn kiln	-	-	-	-	-	-	6"os/	7
Drumgoon	Boagh	-	beetling	-	-	-	-	-	16ft. dia. undershot	osm/	-
Drumgoon	Boagh	-	bleach field	-	-	-	-	-	-	osm/	-
Drumgoon	Boagh	-	watch ho. (2) :	-	-	-	-	-	18x4x2 3 pr st	vmb/	2
Drumgoon	Boagh	-	watch house	-	-	-	-	1837	-	6"os/	23
Drumgoon	Boagh	Barry Thomas	bleach	-	-	-	-	-	14x3x4	vmb/	2
Drumgoon	Boagh	Hinds Robert	corn	-	-	-	-	-	18x4x2 3 pr st	vmb/	2
Templeport	Boffealan	-	-	-	-	-	-	-	-	vmb/	2
Templeport	Boffealan	- on Crooked R.	corn & kiln	-	-	-	-	-	-	6"os/	10
Templeport	Boffealan	Tegart William	corn	(2C) 40.6x23x7 :	-	7-11	-	-	16x2.5x14 1 pr st.	hob/	5.0083
Drung	Bunnoe	Foy	corn	-	-	-	-	1974	12.6 dia	sv/ff	GBowie
Enniskeen	Cabra	-	saw	-	-	-	-	-	-	6"os/	35

PARISH	TOWNLAND	MILLER	TYPE	HOUSE	Land	£Val	PROPRIETORS	Date	WHEEL etc.	Record	Ref.
Enniskeen	Cabra	Peatt Col.	sawmill	-	-	-	-	-	-	vmb/	2
Drumgoon	Cabragh	-	flax	-	-	-	-	-	-	6"os/	17
Drumgoon	Cabragh	Boyd & Langtry	flax	-	-	-	-	-	16x4x3	vmb/	2
Drumgoon	Cabragh	M'Minn David	house	- (ex Chas Hurphy)	-	1	-	1856	-	gr/	a.a.Ire.ie
Drumgoon	Cabragh	Murphy Charles	flax	stores & land	49a.	35	-	1856	-	gr/	a.a.Ire.ie
Cavan	Canningstown	-	mill	-	-	-	-	1899	-	1"os/	69
Drung	Carravogy	-	corn	-	-	-	-	-	12ft. dia. undershot	osm/	-
Munterconnaght	Carrick	near L. Sheelin	-	low bld. still stands	-	-	-	1998	-	pWEH	- B
Denn	Carrickatobber	McCabe James	corn	(1A) 35x21.6x18 :	-	10-14	-	1837	12x30ins. mc/y old	hob/	5.3789
Denn	Carrickatobber	McCabe John	corn	-	-	-	-	-	12x2x -	vmb/	2
Denn	Carrickatober	- at Tn Crosskeys	corn & kiln	-	-	-	-	-	-	6"os/	32
Denn	Carrickatober	M'Cabe James	corn	House, offs. & land	13a.	30	-	1856	-	gr/	a.a.Ire.ie
Killinkere	Carrickeeshill	- nr Billis Br.	mill (2)	-	-	-	-	1899	-	1"os/	80
Cavan	Carricklevan	- on R. Erne	corne	-	-	-	-	-	-	6"os/	30
Killinagh	Cashel	-	corn kiln	-	-	-	-	-	-	6"os/	5
Urney	Cavan	-		-	-	-	-	-	-	6"os/	7
Urney	Cavan Town	Farnham Ld Baron	bleach	-	-	-	Farnham - Methodist Sc	1880	-	dd/	1880 54 289
Urney	Cavan Town	Lifeforce Mill	corn	v. well preserved	-	-	M. McCluskey	1998	-	pWEH	- A
Urney	Cavan Town :	Hague William	corn	(unfinished)	-	10/-	-	1856	-	gr/	a.a.Ire.ie
Lurgan	Cinnaghmore	-	-	-	-	-	-	-	-	vmb/	2
Castlerahan	Claddagh	-	corn	-	-	-	-	-	-	6"os/	38
Castlerahan	Claddagh	Hunter James	corn	(2C) 45.6x18.0x6 :	-	-	- (valued also Apl. 1837)	1838	13x2x12.6 pr st old :	hob/	5.0037
Castlerahan	Claddagh	Hunter James	corn	-	-	-	-	-	13x2x12	vmb/	2
Kilmore	Clarebane	-	corn & pond	-	-	-	-	-	-	6"os/	25
Kilmore	Clarebane	Carrigan Peter	corn	-	-	-	-	1839	-	hob/	5.0065
Kilmore	Clarebane	Heaslop Samuel	corn & kiln	Herd's house & ld.	1a.	5	-	1856	-	gr/	a.a.Ire.ie
Kilmore	Clarebane	McKeon Frans	corn	- note by Valuator :	-	-	-	1839	-	hob/	5.0065
Crosserlough	Clareboy	-	corn & kiln	-	-	-	-	-	-	6"os/	31
Crosserlough	Clareboy	Cronin John	house	- (ex Patk Innis)	-	5/-	-	1856	-	gr/	a.a.Ire.ie
Crosserlough	Clareboy	Ennis Ann	corn	-	-	-	-	-	11x1x12	vmb/	2
Crosserlough	Clareboy	Ennis Ann Widow	corn	(3B) 32x19x11 :	-	3-5-0	-	1840	- machinery :	hob/	5.0064
Crosserlough	Clareboy	Innis Patrick	corn	house, offs. & land	34a.	27.10.	-	1856	-	gr/	a.a.Ire.ie
Killinkere	Cleffin	-	flax	-	-	-	-	1899	-	1"os/	80
Killinkere	Cleffin	- nr Beagh Glebe	tuck	-	-	-	-	-	-	6"os/	33
Killinkere	Cleffin	Hunter John	corn	(2C) 30.0x17.0x6 :	-	-	-	-	11.6x2x14 1 pr st :	hob/	5.0040
Killinkere	Cleffin	Hunter John	corn	-	-	-	-	-	11x2x14	vmb/	2
Killinkere	Cleffin	Hunter John	tuck	-	-	-	-	-	11x2x14	vmb/	2
Lurgan	Cleggan	McCabe James	corn	(2C) 31X18.6X7 :	-	-	-	1838	12x1.9x10 1 pr. st. :	hob/	5.0042
Larah	Clifferna	-	mill	-	-	-	-	1899	-	1"os/	69
Larah	Clifferna	-	mill kiln	-	-	-	-	-	-	6"os/	27
Laragh	Clifferna	MacChop John	corn	(2C) 21.6x30x8 :	-	4-9-8	-	-	11x6 - 1 pair st.	hob/	5.0077
Larah	Clifferna	Wanhop John	corn	-	-	-	-	-	11x - x6	vmb/	2
Cavan	Clodrum	Goodfellow James :	mill	-	-	-	Goodfellow - Masterson :	1825	Asgt. 3 Dec.	dd/	809 146 545481
Killeshandra	Cloggy	- W side R. Erne	bleaching	-	-	-	-	1843	-	6"os/	25
Killeshandra	Cloggy	- W side R. Erne	bt. engine & :	-	-	-	-	-	-	6"os/	25
Killeshandra	Cloggy	- W side R. Erne	flax (only)	-	-	-	-	1897	-	6"os/	25
Killeshandra	Cloggy	Farris William	bleach	-	-	-	-	-	-	vmb/	2
Killeshandra	Cloggy	Farris William	corn	-	-	-	-	-	12x3x3	vmb/	2
Mullagh	Cloghbally Upr	-	hz mill	-	-	-	-	-	-	iaa/	AI1896 os44.6.1
Castlerahan	Clonkeiffy	-	corn	-	-	-	-	1841	-	6"os/	42
Castlerahan	Clonkeiffy	Love Wiliam Mr.	corn	(2B) 33.6x20.6x15 :	-	5.19	-	1837	old wheel dia. 14ft. :	hob/	5.3764
Castlerahan	Clonkeiffy	Love William & John	corn	34x22x14 & :	-	-	-	-	13x6x2.10x10.6 :	hob/	5.0037

PARISH	TOWNLAND	MILLER	TYPE	HOUSE	Land	£Val	PROPRIETORS	Date	WHEEL etc.	Record	Ref.
Castlerahan	Clonkeiffy	Love Wm & Jno	corn	-	-	-	-	-	13x2x16	vmb/	2
Cavan	Coldrum	Farrell James :	mill	-	-	-	Farrell J - Earl of Farnham	1823	Mort. 29 Mar.	dd/	780 42 527977
Kildrumsherdan	Coppanagh	-	corn & flax	-	-	-	-	-	12x2.6x - u`shot	osm/	-
Kildrumsherdan	Coppanagh	-	corn & flour	-	-	-	-	-	-	6"os/	16
Killdrumsherdan	Coppanagh	Hall David	corn	(1A) 27.6x27x20 :	-	-	-	-	14x5 - 2 pair st.	hob/	5.0075
Kildrumsherdan	Coppanagh	Hall David	corn	-	-	-	-	-	14x5x5	vmb/	2
Kildrumsherdan	Coppanagh	Hall David	corn & flax	(1B) 27x20x26 :	-	8-14	-	-	15x5.6x8 2 pr st. :	hob/	5.0074
Cavan	Coraneary	- nr Shercock	corn	-	-	-	-	1899	-	1"os/	69
Kildrumsherdan	Corbeagh	-	corn	-	-	-	-	-	12ft. dia. undershot	osm/	-
Kildrumsherdan	Corbeagh	- on Dromore R.	kiln	-	-	-	-	-	-	6"os/	16
Kildrumsherdan	Corbeagh	Ellis Henry :	mills	-	-	-	Ellis H - Crofton Morgan :	1824	-	dd/	797 160 538295
Kildrumsherdan	Corbeagh	Maxwell Henry Rev :	mills	-	-	-	Maxwell H - Power Mgt :	1825	-	dd/	806 226 543761
Kildrumsherdan	Corbeagh	Maxwell Henry Rev.:	mills	-	-	-	Maxwell - Orchard Fras :	1821	-	dd/	770 270 522205
Kildrumsherdan	Corbeagh	Maxwell Henry Rev.:	mills	Clerk	-	-	Maxwell - Powell Margt :	1825	-	dd/	805 533 543468
Killdrumsherdan	Corbeagh	Whitley Charles	corn	(2C) 31x19.6x6 :	-	4-14	-	-	12.6x3.6x - 1 pr st.	hob/	5.0075
Kildrumsherdan	Corbeagh	Whitley Charles	corn	-	-	-	-	-	12x2x3	vmb/	2
Drumgoon	Corcloghan	- at Knappagh Ho	clothiers	-	-	-	-	-	-	6"os/	23
Drumgoon	Corcloghan	Caden William	tuck	-	-	-	-	-	11x2x5	vmb/	2
Laragh	Cormeen	Dougherty Matt :	corn	(2C) 30x19.6x6.6 :	-	-	-	-	12ft.dia.	hob/	5.0077
Larah	Cormeen	Plunkett John	corn	-	-	-	-	-	12x4x8	vmb/	2
Drumgoon	Cornacarrow	- W./ Clements Br.	corn & kiln	-	-	-	-	-	-	6"os/	16
Drumgoon	Cornacarrow	Leadbeater Garret	corn	-	-	-	formerly - Drumgool Jn	-	17x5x3 3 pr st	vmb/	2
Enniskeen	Cornagee	- nr Tn Kingscourt	corn & kiln	-	-	-	-	-	-	6"os/	35
Enniskeen	Cornagee	Howel & Donnelly	corn	-	-	-	-	-	13x - x - & 14x3x1	vmb/	2
Enniskeen	Cornagee	Howel John	corn & kiln & ld	-	6a.	9.15.	-	1856	-	gr/	a.a.lre.ie
Enniskeen	Cornagee	Howel John	tuck	-	-	-	-	1856	-	gr/	a.a.lre.ie
Scrabby	Cornagran	-	bleach	-	-	-	-	-	-	6"os/	36
Knockbride	Corraceeran	Hall Thomas	corn	-	-	-	-	-	11x2x5	vmb/	2
Kinawley	Corraclassy	- nr Owensalla` Br.	corn	-	-	-	-	-	-	6"os/	9
Killeshandra	Corradarren	-	corn	-	-	-	-	1841	-	6"os/	24
Killeshandra	Corradarren	Glendinning Misses	corn	-	-	-	-	-	12x2x4	vmb/	2
Shercock	Corrakeeran	- race Skeagh L	corn	-	-	-	-	-	-	6"os/	28
Shercock	Corrakeeran	- race Skeagh L	tuck	-	-	-	-	-	-	6"os/	28
Killinkere	Corratinner	- race Corratinner:	corn	-	-	-	-	-	-	6"os/	34
Killinkere	Corratinner	Smith Brian	corn	-	-	-	-	-	11x1x6	vmb/	2
Killinkere	Corratinner	Smith Brien	corn	(3C) 31.0x18.6x6.6 :	-	-	-	1838	11.3x1.6x6 1 pr st :	hob/	5.0040
Killinkere	Corratinner	Smith Patrick & Geo	corn	offices & land	2a.	5	-	1856	-	gr/	a.a.lre.ie
Shercock	Corravilla	-	-	-	-	-	-	-	-	vmb/	2
Shercock	Corravilla	- N. of Milltown L.	mill & dam	-	-	-	-	-	-	6"os/	28
Shercock	Corravilla	Hall Isaac	corn	(3C) 34x18x8 :	-	-	-	-	11.6x2.9x7.6 1 pr st	hob/	5.0045
Shercock	Corravilla	Hall Thomas	mill	house, offs. & land	33a.	22	-	1856	-	gr/	a.a.lre.ie
Drung	Corravohy	-	corn	-	-	-	-	1974	12.9x3.6x- overshot	sv/ff	GBowie
Drung	Corravohy	Hagerty Patrick	corn	-	-	-	-	-	13x2x13	vmb/	2
Drung	Corravohy	Hegarty Patrick	corn	(2C) 44x23x8 :	-	2-12	-	-	12x2x5 1 pr st. 5ft.	hob/	5.0072
Lavey	Corrawillin	-	corn	-	-	-	-	1974	12x4.6 x- overshot	sv/ff	GBowie
Lavey	Corrawillin	Cussack Patrick	corn & kiln	house, offs. & land	33a.	32.15.	-	1856	-	gr/	a.a.lre.ie
Lurgan	Correagh Glebe	-	-	-	-	-	-	-	-	vmb/	2
Lurgan	Correagh Glebe	- W.side rd. Virginia	corn	-	-	-	-	1841	-	6"os/	39
Lurgan	Correagh Glebe	Brady Bernard & Ed.	corn	miller & kilnsman's hos.		6	-	-	-	gr	-
Cavan	Correagh Glebe	Brady Edward	corn	34.0x20.6x7 :	-	-	- (valued also Apl. 1837)	1838	11.10x2.6x4 new :	hob/	5.0042
Bailirborough	Crocknahattan	Simpson Sam & Son	corn & kilns	house, offs. & land	30a.	50.10.	-	1856	-	gr/	a.a.lre.ie
Bailirborough	Crocknahattan	Simpson Samuel	corn	-	-	-	-	-	15x6x8	vmb/	2

PARISH	TOWNLAND	MILLER	TYPE	HOUSE	Land	£Val	PROPRIETORS	Date	WHEEL etc.	Record	Ref.
Bailieborough	Crocknahattin	-	corn	-	-	-	-	-	-	6"os/	28
Shercock	Crossmakeelan	-	corn kiln	-	-	-	-	-	-	6"os/	28
Ballymachugh	Crover	- near lake	corn	-	-	-	-	-	-	6"os/	38
Ballymachugh	Crover	Telford Henry	corn	(2B) 36.6x20x8 :	-	-	-	-	10.6x2.10x9.6 & :	hob/	5.0048
Denn	Crumlin	-	corn	-	-	-	-	1837	-	6"os/	26
Denn	Crumlin	Cottingham John	corn	-	-	-	-	-	13x2x -	vmb/	2
Denn	Crumlin	Gaffney Bernard	corn	house, offs. & land	23a.	24.10.	-	1856	-	gr/	a.a.Ire.ie
Denn	Crumlin	Gaffney Bernard	corn	(2B) 40x19.6x13.6 :	-	4-17	-	1837	16ft. dia. 24 buckets	hob/	5.3789
Mullagh	Cuilcagh	- race Quilcagh L	mill	-	-	-	-	-	-	6"os/	40
Cavan	Culliagh	-	corn & kiln	-	-	-	-	-	-	6"os/	9
Lurgan	Curraghmore	- nr Lurgan Ch.	corn & kiln	-	-	-	-	-	-	6"os/	39
Lurgan	Curraghmore	Jennings john	corn	-	62a	53	-	-	-	gr	-
Lurgan	Curraghmore	MacKlern Robert	corn	(2C) 42x23x10 :	-	-	-	1838	13.4x2.7x15 2 pr st. :	hob/	5.0042
Shercock	Darkley	-	corn	-	-	-	-	1899	-	1"os/	69
Shercock	Darkley	- race ex Shinan L	corn & kiln	-	-	-	-	-	-	6"os/	23
Shercock	Darkley	Reilly Anne	corn & flax	house, offs. & land	12a.	14	-	1856	-	gr/	a.a.Ire.ie
Shercock	Darkley	Reilly Mrs	corn	30x22x8 11x9x5 :	-	-	-	-	12x1.10x7 1 pair st. :	hob/	5.0045
Shercock	Darkley	Reilly Mrs	flax	-	-	-	-	-	13.6x3x7 4 berths	vmb	2
Shercock	Darkley	Reilly Widow	corn	-	-	-	-	-	12x2x7	vmb/	2
Shercock	Darkley	Reilly Widow	flax	-	-	-	-	-	13x3x7	vmb/	2
Killnagh	Darna	Nixon Mrs	corn	-	-	-	-	-	12x1x4	vmb/	2
Shercock	Derry	-	corn & kiln	-	-	-	-	-	-	6"os/	28
Killinkere	Derryhum	-	corn & race	-	-	-	-	-	-	6"os/	33
Killinkere	Derryhum	Flood Bridget	corn	-	-	-	-	-	10x2x5	vmb/	2
Killinkere	Derryhum	Flood Edward	corn & kiln	house, offs. & land	8a.	6.5.0	-	1856	-	gr/	a.a.Ire.ie
Crosserlough	Derrylea	Clinton John	corn	ho., offs. & land	3a.	10	-	-	-	gr	-
Templeport	Derrynatruan	- river to Lattone L.	corn & kiln	-	-	-	-	-	-	6"os/	3
Templeport	Derrynatruan	Dolan Charles	corn	(2C) 31x17x7.6 :	-	2-0-0	-	-	12.9x1.8x5 u`shot	hob/	5.0084
Cavan	Doagh	-	beetling mills	-	-	-	-	-	-	6"os/	18
Cavan	Doagh	-	corn & flour	-	-	-	-	-	-	6"os/	18
Tomregan	Doon	- on Woodford R.	flour	-	-	-	-	1837	-	6"os/	10
Tomregan	Doon	at Ballyconnell Town	mill & mill race	-	-	-	-	1837	-	6"os/	10
Tomregan	Doon	Benison Capt.	beetling wash	-	-	-	-	-	13x2x3	vmb/	2
Tomregan	Doon	Bennison Capt.	bleach	(2C) 67x26.6x8 :	-	22-6	-	-	13.6x2.10x1.6 :	hob/	5.0084
Tomregan	Doon	Cobaine John	corn	-	-	-	-	-	16x6x4	vmb/	2
Tomregan	Doon	Cobaine John	flour	-	-	-	-	-	16x6x4	vmb/	2
Tomregan	Doon	Cobean John	flour	(1A) 44.6x28x30.6 :	-	32-10	-	-	15.6x6.6x3 2 pr st. :	hob/	5.0085
Killinagh	Dowra	-	corn kiln	-	-	-	-	-	-	6"os/	5
Killinagh	Dowra	- on Owenmore R.	corn & kiln	-	-	-	-	-	-	6"os/	5
Killinagh	Dowra	Belford William	corn	(2C) 30.6x20x6.6 :	-	-	-	-	11.6x2x2.10 u`shot :	hob/	5.0080
Annagh	Drumakeenan	- W./ Tn Redhill	corn & pond	-	-	-	-	-	-	6"os/	16
Annagh	Drumakeenan	Fay Bernard	corn	(1C) 36.6x21.6x10 :	-	5-3-0	-	-	14ft. dia, fall 12ft. :	hob/	5.0069
Annagh	Drumakeenan	Fay Luke	corn	house, offs. & land	21a.	25.12.	-	-	-	gr/	a.a.Ire.ie
Castleterragh	Drumaraw	-	corn & flour	-	-	-	-	1841	-	6"os/	16
Castleterra	Drumaraw	- nr Fort	corn	-	-	-	-	-	-	6"os/	16
Castleterra	Drumaraw	Adams Francis	corn & flour	ofices, hos. & land	47a.	-	-	1856	-	gr/	a.a.Ire.ie
Castleterragh	Drumaraw	Adams Willaim	flour	-	-	-	-	-	4 pr stones	vmb/	2
Castleterragh	Drumaraw	Adams William	corn	-	-	-	-	-	- 4 pr stones	vmb/	2
Urney	Drumavanagh	Clemenger John	coach factory	offices & yard		20		1856	-	gr/	a.a.ire.ie
Drumlumman	Drumbannow	-	corn	-	-	-	-	-	16x2.4x -	osm/	-
Drumlumman	Drumbannow	-	corn & race	-	-	-	-	1841	16x2.4x -	6"os/	31
Denn	Drumbarry	Ellis Henry :	mills	-	-	-	Ellis H - Crofton Morgan :	1824	-	dd/	797 160 538295

PARISH	TOWNLAND	MILLER	TYPE	HOUSE	Land	£Val	PROPRIETORS	Date	WHEEL etc.	Record	Ref.
Denn	Drumbarry	Maxwell Henry :	mills	-	-	-	Maxwell H - Power Mgt	1825	-	dd/	806 226 543761
Denn	Drumbarry	Maxwell Henry Rev.:	mills	-	-	-	Maxwell - Orchard Fras :	1821	-	dd/	770 270 522205
Denn	Drumbarry	Maxwell Henry Rev.:	mills	Clerk	-	-	Maxwell - Powell Margt :	1825	-	dd/	805 553 543468
Annagh	Drumcalpin	Donachs Mrs	corn	-	-	-	-	-	13x2x4	vmb/	2
Annagh	Drumcalpin	Donoghue Mary	corn	(2C) 43x20.6x11.6 :	-	-	-	-	13x2.3x4.6 new	hob/	5.0060
Kinawley	Drumcannon	- at Drumcar	corn	-	-	-	-	1899	-	1"os/	56
Kinawley	Drumcannon	- R. Owensallagh	corn & kiln	-	-	-	-	-	-	6"os/	7
Kinawley	Drumcannon	Howden James	corn	(1B) 41.6x24.6x21 :	-	8-9-4	-	-	20x4.3x17.6 :	hob/	5.0082
Crosserlough	Drumcassidy	-	mill race	-	-	-	-	-	-	6"os/	32
Crosserlough	Drumcassidy	Reilly Peter	corn	(2B) 29x19.0x12.6 :	-	-	(valued also Aug. 1837)	1838	13x2.7x3.6 2 pr st. :	hob/	5.0038
Crosserlough	Drumcassidy	Reilly Peter	corn	-	-	-	-	-	13x3x3	vmb/	2
Urney	Drumconnick	-	-	-	-	-	-	-	-	vmb/	2
Urney	Drumconnick	- 2m. WxS Cavan	corn & pond	-	-	-	-	1841	-	6"os/	20
Kinawley	Drumcor	Hassard Minor :	corn	(1B) 68.6x24.6x32 :	-	10-15	-	-	24x4.11x19	hob/	5.0081
Killinkere	Drumdallagh	Smith Brian	corn	(2C) 45x18.6x7 :	-	-	-	1838	(2) -11.6 & 10 feet	hob/	5.004
Kilawley	Drumersee	-	corn kiln	-	-	-	-	-	-	6"os/	7
Drumgoon	Drumgreen	Buxton John :	mills	-	-	-	Buxton John - Caffray :	1821	Mort. 1 Nov.	dd/	766 293 519828
Knockbride	Drumhillagh	Adams Chas Jas	corn	-	-	-	-	-	16x4x -	vmb/	2
Ballintemple	Drumhillagh	Reilly Michael	corn	(2B) 32x20.6x7	-	-	-	1839	12x2.6x3.6 :	hob/	5.0047
Knockbride	Drumhillagh N.	Henry John	corn	house & land	3a.	21.10.	-	1856	-	gr/	a.a.Ire.ie
Knockbride	Drumhillagh N.	Henry John	flax	& offices	-	10	-	1856	-	gr/	a.a.Ire.ie
Knockbride	Drumhillagh N.	King Peter (Miller)	house	(ex John Henry)	-	10/-	-	1856	-	gr/	a.a.Ire.ie
Knockbride	Drumhillagh North	- Drumhilliagh Mills	mills	-	-	-	-	-	-	6"os/	23
Knockbride	Drumhillagh North	Wallace Thomas	mill	74x50x25 :	-	-	-	1839	16x1.6x16 48 bkts :	hob/	5.3813
Bailirborough	Drumkeery	Simpson Hugh	flax	-	1a.	12.10.	-	1856	-	gr/	a.a.ire.ie
Bailirborough	Drumkeery	Simpson Samuel	flax	-	-	-	-	-	18x4x10	vmb/	2
Crosserloogh	Drumkilly	-	corn	-	-	-	-	-	-	6"os/	31
Crosserloogh	Drumkilly	-	corn	-	-	-	-	1974	11x4.4x -	sv/ff	GBowie
Annagelliff	Drumlark	-	corn (in ruins)	-	-	-	-	-	-	6"os/	20
Bailieborough	Drumlon	Brady Patrick	mill	-	-	-	Brady - Hamilton Stewart :	1821	-	dd/	763 76 517811
Bailieborough	Drumlon	Brady Patrick :	mill	-	-	-	Brady P - Jackson John :	1821	-	dd/	763 40 517775
Drumgoon	Drumlumman	-	corn kiln	-	-	-	-	-	-	6"os/	23
Killinkere	Drummallaght	- nr L. Nadreegeel :	corn	-	-		-	1841	-	6"os/	33
Killinkere	Drummallaght	Lynch Bryan	corn	-	-	-	-	-	11x3x7	vmb/	2
Killinkere	Drummallaght	Lynch Bryan	shelling	-	-	-	-	-	10x2x7	vmb/	2
Killinkere	Drummallaght	Smith Brien	corn	(2C) 45.0x18.6x7 :	-	-	-	-	11.6x2.10x7.6 :	hob/	5.0040
Castleterra	Drummany	- S/ Butler's Br. :	corn	-	-	-	-	1837	-	6"os/	15
Castleterra	Drummany	- SW/ Butler's Br.	corn	-	-	-	-	1841	-	6"os/	15
Killeshandra	Drummany	McDowell Charles	corn	-	-	-	-	-	13x1x6	vmb/	2
Castleterra	Drummany	Reilly John	corn	- & offices	-	5	-	1856	-	gr/	a.a.Ire.ie
Castleterra	Drummany	Reilly John	corn	(2B) 26x17.68.6 :	-	-	-	-	- machinery :	hob/	5.0063
Castleterragh	Drummany	Reilly John	corn	-	-	-	-	-	-	vmb/	2
Castleterra	Drummany	Reilly John :	corn	(2C) 26x18x10 :	-	3-3-6	-	1839	-	hob/	5.0062
Lavey	Drumnabeg	Mulligan James	corn	-	-	-	-	-	no information	vmb/	2
Cavan	Drumnagran	- on Annagh R.	corn & race	-	-	-	-	-	-	6"os/	17
Killdrumsherdan	Drumnagran	- on mill race from :	corn	-	-	-	-	1841	-	6"os/	17
Killdrumsherdan	Drumnagran	Marsden John	corn & kiln	(1A) 28x54x46 :	-	-	-	-	16x10x 4 32 floatboa[r]	hob/	5.0074
Kildrumsherdan	Drumnagran	Townley John	corn	-	-	-	-	-	10x10x4 4 pr st	vmb/	2
Killdrumsherdan	Drumnagran	Townly John	corn & kiln	(1A) 54.6x59x44.6 :	-	37-18	-	-	10.6x10x4 4 pr st. :	hob/	5.0075
Annagh	Drumnakenan	Foy Bernard	corn	-	-	-	-	-	13x - x11	vmb/	2
Cavan	Drumnaquean	Boyle Mr	flour & corn	-	-	-	-	-	16x10.2x -	osm/	-
Lavey	Drumnaveagh	-	corn & kiln	-	-	-	-	-	-	6"os/	33

PARISH	TOWNLAND	MILLER	TYPE	HOUSE	Land	£Val	PROPRIETORS	Date	WHEEL etc.	Record	Ref.
Killashandra	Drumnawall	-	corn & kiln	-	-	-	-	-	-	6"os/	30
Killashandra	Drumnawall	- nr Arvagh Town	bleach mill	-	-	-	-	-	-	6"os/	30
Killeshandra	Drumrae	McGuire Con	corn	-	-	-	-	-	12x2x5	vmb/	2
Cavan	Drumristin	-	mill	-	-	-	-	1899	-	1"os/	56
Killeshandra	Drumrockady	-	corn & pond	-	-	-	-	-	-	6"os/	24
Killeshandra	Drumrockady	-	corn & race	-	-	-	-	1841	-	6"os/	24
Killeshandra	Drumrockady	Cartwright William	corn	-	-	-	-	-	12x1x12	vmb/	2
Killeshandra	Drumroe	-	corn & kiln	-	-	-	-	-	-	6"os/	24
Killeshandra	Drumroosk	-	corn & kiln	-	-	-	-	-	-	6"os/	19
Killeshandra	Drumroosk	-	distillery	-	-	-	-	-	-	6"os/	19
Killeshandra	Drumroosk	Graham John	corn	-	-	-	-	-	13x - x4	vmb/	2
Drumlane	Drumrush	-	corn & kiln	-	-	-	-	1841	-	6"os/	10
Cavan	Drumrush	Patterson John :	mill	-	-	-	Patterson j - Rocers Wm	1822	-	dd/	770 127 522062
Drumlane	Drumrush	Reilly Terence	corn	-	-	-	-	-	13x3x2	vmb/	2
Drumlane	Drumrush	Reilly Thomas (Miler)	corn & kiln	house, offs. & land	31a.	27.5.	-	1856	-	gr/	a.a.ire.ie
Killdrumsherdan	Drumsheil	-	corn	-	-	-	-	1841	-	6"os/	17
Killdrumsherdan	Drumsheil	Carleton Edward	threshing	(2B) dia. 30 x 6ft. :	-	-	-	-	- in bad order	hob/	5.0075
Killdrumsherdan	Drumsheil	Foy Charles	corn	(3C) 30.6x21x7 :	-	-	-	-	- metal undershot :	hob/	5.0075
Kildrumsherdan	Drumsillagh	-	corn	-	-	-	-	-	-	6"os/	22
Kildrumsherdan	Drumsillagh	-	corn	-	-	-	-	-	12x2.6x - overshot	osm/	-
Kildrumsherdan	Drumsillagh	Boyle James Moore :	mill	-	-	-	Boyle J - Prichit Mary :	1817	-	dd/	782 203 529338
Killdrumsherdan	Drumsillagh	Boyle Maxwell J	corn	(2B) 48x22.6x15.6 :	-	-	-	-	11x3x9 2 pr st.	hob/	5.0075
Kildrumsherdan	Drumsillagh	Boyle Maxwell J	corn	-	-	-	-	-	11x3x9	vmb/	2
Kildrumsherdan	Drumsillagh	Boyle Maxwell J :	mill	-	-	-	Boyle M - Montgomery :	1823	-	dd/	782 311 529446
Killdrumsherdan	Drumsillagh	Masterson John	corn	(2C) 22x22x13 :	-	9-18	-	-	- 2 pair stones	hob/	5.0076
Kildrumsherdan	Drumsillagh	Prichard Alicia Boyle:	mill	-	-	-	Prichard Aliocia - Boyle :	1823	Lse. 30 May.	dd/	782 310 529445
Cavan	Drumus	- nr Kinroad L.	corn & kiln	-	-	-	-	-	-	6"os/	10
Urney	Drunconnick	Ellis William	corn	39x23x14 & :	-	-	-	-	14x2x10 2 pr st. :	hob/	5.0068
Lurgan	Fintawan	-	-	-	-	-	-	-	-	vmb/	2
Lurgan	Fintawan	-	corn & race	-	-	-	-	-	-	6"os/	34
Lurgan	Fintawan	Brady Matthew	corn	-	40a.	26	-	-	-	gr	-
Lurgan	Fintawan	Brady Matthew	corn	(2C) 34.0x18.6x5.6 :	-	-	-	-	10.8x2.7x7.6 1 pr. :	hob/	5.0042
Kinawley	Furnaceland	SE/ Swanlinbar R.	iron foundry	-	-	-	-	1837	-	6"os/	7
Bailieborough	Galbolie	-	bleach	-	-	-	-	-	-	6"os/	34
Bailieborough	Galbolie	-	corn & kiln	-	-	-	-	-	-	6"os/	28
Bailieborough	Galbolie	- race ex Parker L.	engine house	-	-	-	-	-	-	6"os/	34
Bailieborough	Galbolie	Spear William	bleach	-	-	-	-	-	13x8x4	vmb/	2
Bailieborough	Galbolie	Young John Sir Bt.	flax & bleaching	- offices & land	10a.	21.10.	-	1856	-	gr/	a.a.Ire.ie
Ballintemple	Garrymore	-	corn	-	-	-	-	1841	- out of repair	6"os/	25
Ballintemple	Garrymore	-	corn	-	-	-	-	1837	-	6"os/	25
Ballintemple	Garrymore	Finnegan John	corn	(2C) 39x20x7 :	-	-	-	-	- out of repair	hob/	5.0047
Killeshandra	Gartylough	-	flax	-	-	-	-	-	-	6"os/	24
Killeshandra	Gartylough	Armstrong James	flax	-	-	-	-	-	-	vmb/	2
Shercock	Glasleck	-	-	-	-	-	-	-	-	vmb/	2
Shercock	Glasleck	-	corn & dam	-	-	-	-	-	-	6"os/	28
Shercock	Glasleck	McCullough Joseph	corn	(3B) 32.0x19.6x8.0 :	-	-	(valued also Dec. 1839)	1838	11x2x6.6 1 pair st.:	hob/	5.0045
Annagh ?	Glassdruman	- on stream to :	corn & kiln	-	-	-	-	1837	-	6"os/	7
Kilmore	Glencorran	-	corn & kiln	-	-	-	-	-	-	6"os/	26
Kinawley	Gorteenaglogh	-	corn kiln	-	-	-	-	1837	-	6"os/	7
Crosserlough	Graddum	-	mill pond	-	-	-	-	-	-	6"os/	32
Crosserlough	Graddum	Mullins Owen	corn	(2B) 29.0x21.0x9.0 :	-	-	-	1838	12.10x3x9 new :	hob/	5.0038
Crosserlough	Graddum	Murphy Owen	corn	-	-	-	-	-	13x3x9	vmb/	2

PARISH	TOWNLAND	MILLER	TYPE	HOUSE	Land	£Val	PROPRIETORS	Date	WHEEL etc.	Record	Ref.
Crosserlough	Graddum	Spinks William :	corn	(2B) 30.0x21.0x9.0 :	-	-	-	1837	dia about 13ft. :	hob/	5.3765
Cavan	Greagduff	-	old mill race	-	-	-	-	-	-	6"os/	33
Mullagh	Greaghnadarragh	- on R. Owenroe	corn	-	-	-	-	-	-	6"os/	40
Mullagh	Greaghnadarragh	Reilly Felix	old mill	(2/3C) 33x21x7 :	28a.	-	-	1838	-	hob/	5.0043
Kinawley	Hawkswood	Gracen George	corn	34.6x28.6x21 & :	-	-	-	-	18X3.3X17 2 pr st.	hob/	5.3808
Kinawley	Hawkswood :	- nr R. Claddagh	corn & kiln	-	-	-	-	-	-	6"os/	7
Urney	Keadew :	Murphy Peter	mills & prems.	-	-	-	-	1846	-	dd/	1841 14 229
Bailieborough	Killan	-	corn & kiln	-	-	-	-	-	-	6"os/	28
Bailieborough	Killan	Adams Robert	corn	house, offs. & land	21a.	25.10.	-	1856	-	gr/	a.a.Ire.ie
Bailieborough	Killan	Adams Robert	corn	-	-	-	-	-	12x2x12	vmb/	2
Killeshandra	Killeshandra	-	-	small ruins, walls	-	-	-	1998	-	pWEH	- R
Killeshandra	Killeshandra	Southwell Robert :	mills	- & mill holding	-	-	Southwell R - Woolsey :	1825	Mort. 5 Jan.	dd/	798 574 539304
Killinagh	Killycarney	-	corn & kiln	-	-	-	-	-	-	6"os/	1
Killinagh	Killycarney	Govern Bernard	corn	(2B) 34x20x8 :	-	3-12	-	-	11.6x1.8x5.9	hob/	5.0080
Killnagh	Killycarney	Magamon Bernard	corn	-	-	-	-	-	12x2x5	vmb/	2
Lavey	Killyconnan	Gilcreest John (Andy)	corn & kiln	House, office & ld.	14a.	15.10.	-	1856	-	gr/a.a.Ire.ie	
Kildrumsherdan	Killycreeny	-	corn & flax	-	-	-	-	-	13x2.6x - breast	osm/	-
Cavan	Killycreeny	- Dromore R. nr Br.	corn & kiln	-	-	-	-	-	-	6"os/	16
Kildrumsherdan	Killycreeny	Brady George	flax	(1B) 33.6x22.6x14.6 :	-	-	-	-	15x4x7 6 berths :	vmb/	2
Killdrumsherdan	Killycreeny	Foy Charles	corn	(3C) 31x21x6.6 :	-	4-12	-	-	1 pair stones :	hob/	5.0076
Kildrumsherdan	Killycreeny	Foy Charles	corn	-	-	-	-	-	12x2x6	vmb/	2
Killdrumsherdan	Killycreeny	Whitley Joseph	flax	(1B) 33x22.6x15 :	-	7-11	-	-	16ft dia. nearly new :	hob/	5.0076
Drung	Killymullin	- on R Annalee	mill	-	-	-	-	1899	-	1"os/	69
Denn	Killyteane	-	corn	-	-	-	-	1841	-	6"os/	26
Denn	Killyteane	Heslop Henry	corn	(2B) 35x19x8 :	-	1-18	-	1837	12x30ins., old	hob/	5.3789
Denn	Killyteane	Heslop John	corn	-	-	-	-	-	12x2x -	vmb/	2
Drumlane	Killywilly	Berry James	bleach	-	-	-	-	-	14x4x3 2 beams	vmb/	2
Drumlane	Killywilly	Berry James	corn	-	-	-	-	-	14x3x2	vmb/	2
Drumlane	Killywilly (NB :)	- nr Killywilly Ho.	corn	-	-	-	-	1897	-	6"os/	10
Crosserlough	Kilnaleck	- nr Kilnaleck Tn	corn & pond	-	-	-	-	-	-	6"os/	37
Crosserlough	Kilnaleck	Brady	-	- burnt c1944	-	-	-	1974	12ft dia	sv/ff	GBowie
Crosserlough	Kilnaleck	Tormey Widow	corn	(3C) 34.6x18.6x6 :	20a.	-	-	-	12x2x6.6 1 pair st :	hob/	5.0038
Crosserlough	Kilnaleck	Tormey widow	corn	-	-	-	-	-	12x2x6	vmb/	2
Drumlumman	Kilsaran	-	corn kiln	-	-	-	-	-	-	6"os/	36
Killinagh	Kiltomulty	- nr. L. Macnean	corn & kiln	-	-	-	-	-	-	6"os/	1
Killinagh	Kiltomulty	Nixon Mrs	corn	(2C) 25x17.6x6.6 :	-	17/1	-	-	13x1.10x12 1 pr st.	hob/	5.0080
Killnagh	Kiltumulty	Nixon Mrs	corn	-	-	-	-	-	13x2x13	vmb/	2
Scrabby	Knockaghy :	Sloan (Millbrook)	mill	-	-	-	-	1974	-	sv/ff	GBowie
Laragh	Knockataggart	-	corn	-	-	-	-	-	-	6"os/	27
Larah	Knockataggart	-	corn	-	-	-	-	-	14x2.6x -	osm/	-
Laragh	Knockataggart	-	tuck	-	-	-	-	-	-	6"os/	27
Larah	Knockataggart	-	tuck	-	-	-	-	-	12x2.6x - overshot	osm/	-
Laragh	Knockataggart	McCabe Edward :	corn	(2B) 29.6x20x10.6 :	-	4-5-2	-	-	12ft. dia., fall 8ft.	hob/	5.0077
Larah	Knockataggart	McCabe John	corn	-	-	-	-	-	12x - x8	vmb/	2
Larah	Knockatudor	-	corn	-	-	-	-	-	12x2.4x - overshot	osm/	-
Larah	Knockatudor	- to NW of Fort	corn	-	-	-	-	-	-	6"os/	21
Laragh	Knockatudor	Smith James	corn	(2B) 38.6x20x8.6 :	-	5-15	-	-	12ft 6ins dia.	hob/	5.0077
Larah	Knockatudor	Smith James	corn	-	-	-	-	-	12x - x10	vmb/	2
Knockbride	Knocknalosset	-	corn	-	-	-	-	-	-	6"os/	23
Knockbride	Knocknalosset	-	tuck	-	-	-	-	-	-	6"os/	23
Knockbride	Knocknalosset	Anderson James	corn & kiln	55x18.6x8 & :	-	-	-	1839	12x2.4x - 30 bkts :	hob/	5.3813
Knockbride	Knocknalosset	Anderson James	tuck	-	-	-	-	1839	11.6x2x6.6 36 bkts :	hob/	5.3813

PARISH	TOWNLAND	MILLER	TYPE	HOUSE	Land	£Val	PROPRIETORS	Date	WHEEL etc.	Record	Ref.
Knockbride	Knocknalosset	Anderson Robert	corn	-	-	-	-	-	12x2x12	vmb/	2
Knockbride	Knocknalosset	Anderson Robert	tuck	-	-	-	-	-	11x2x6	vmb/	2
Ballintemple	Lackan	-	corn & flax	mills fair & :	-	-	Eamonn O`Donoghue	1998	-	pWEH	- B
Ballintemple	Lackan	Brady	corn	-	-	-	-	1974	-	sv/ff	GBowie
Ballintemple	Lackan	Brady	flax	-	-	-	-	1974	13.4 dia	sv/ff	GBowie
Ballintemple	Lackan	Reilly John	bleach	-	-	-	-	-	16x5x1	vmb/	2
Ballintemple	Lackan Lower	- on R. Erne	bleach	-	-	-	-	-	-	6"os/	31
Ballintemple	Lackan Lower	O`Reilly John	bleach	(1A) 53x26x19.6 :	-	-	-	-	16x5.2x1.6 engines :	hob/	5.0047
Annagelliff	Latt	Brady	mill	-	-	-	Brady - Jackson	-	?	dd/	763 40 517775
Annagelliff	Latt	Brady Patrick	mill	-	-	-	Brady Patk - Hamilton :	1821	-	dd/	763 76 517811
Lavey	Lattagloghan	-	corn & kiln	-	-	-	-	-	-	6"os/	32
Lavey	Lattagloghan	Lee Peter	corn	-	-	-	-	-	no information	vmb/	2
Lavey	Lattaloghan	Lee Peter :	corn	(3B) 39x18x8.6 :	-	2-9-7	-	-	- 1 pr st. worn	hob/	5.0067
Templeport	Legatraghta	-	corn kiln	-	-	-	-	-	-	6"os/	6
Templeport	Legnagrow	-	-	-	-	-	-	-	-	vmb/	2
Templeport	Legnagrow	- nr L`nagrow Lo..	corn & kiln	-	-	-	-	-	-	6"os/	6
Templeport	Legnagrow	- nr L`nagrow Lo..	New Mill	-	-	-	-	-	-	6"os/	6
Templeport	Legnagrow	Magaurans Mrs	mill	(3C) 32x17x7.6 :	-	5-5-6	-	-	11.9x1.8x4.6 sts. 5ft.	hob/	5.0083
Drumlumman	Legwee	-	corn	-	-	-	-	-	-	osm/	-
Drumlummon	Legwee	Rogers Thomas	corn	(2B) 32x17x7.6 :	-	1-4-3	-	1837	11x1.9x10 (old) :	hob/	5.0054
Kildrumsherdan	Leighan	-	corn	-	-	-	-	-	11ft.dia. overshot	osm/	-
Kildrumsherdan	Leighan	Fitzpatrick Patrick	corn	(3C) 36x19x9 :	-	1-18-	-	1838	13x2.6 o'shot :	hob/	5.0057
Killdrumsherdan	Leighan	McQuaid James	corn	(2C) 33x18.6x6.6 :	-	4-4-2	-	-	13x2x13 1 pr st. :	hob/	5.0075
Kildrumsherdan	Leighan	McQuaid James	corn	-	-	-	-	-	13x2x13	vmb/	2
Lavey	Leiter	Magloan Robert	corn	(2B) 39x19x8 :	-	4-0-6	-	-	-	hob/	5.0067
Lavey	Leiter	McGlure Robert	corn	-	-	-	-	-	no information	vmb/	2
Lavey	Leiter :	-	corn & pond	-	-	-	-	1841	-	6"os/	26
Lavey	Leiter :	Marley Leila Cath	flour	Miller's & herd's hos. :	34	67	-	1856	-	gr/	a.a.lre.ie
Lavey	Leiter :	Marley Mrs	mill	(1A) 40x22x30 :	-	24-15	-	1855	m/cy no information	hob/	5.3975
Drung	Lisboduff	-	corn	-	-	-	-	-	13x2.6x - breast	osm/	-
Drung	Lisboduff	-	corn & race	-	-	-	-	-	-	6"os/	16
Drung	Lisboduff	Brady Patk Richard :	mill	-	-	-	Brady P - Blackwood :	1823	-	dd/	794 410 536745
Drung	Lisboduff	Brady Patrick	mill	-	-	-	Brady Patk - Hamilton :	1821	-	dd/	763 76 517811
Drung	Lisboduff	Brady Patrick :	mill	-	-	-	Brady P - Jackson John :	1821	-	dd/	763 40 517775
Drung	Lisboduff	Foy Owen	corn	(3C) 21x19.6x6 :	-	4-17	-	-	12x2x5 sts. dia 5ft.	hob/	5.0072
Drung	Lisboduff	Foy Owen	corn	-	77a.	-	-	-	12x2x5	vmb/	2
Drung	Lisboduff & Latt	Blackwood James :	mills	-	-	-	Blackwood Jas - Clarke :	1823	-	dd/	781 252 528787
Knockbride	Lisdonan	-	corn	-	-	-	-	1841	-	6"os/	23
Knockbride	Lisdonan	Mahood Geo & Jas	corn	-	-	-	-	-	11x2x6	vmb/	2
Knockbride	Lisdonan	Mahood James	old corn mill	Ho., offs., kiln & ld.	34a.	27.10.	-	1856	-	gr/	a.a.lre.ie
Drumgoon	Lisnaclea	-	clothier`s	-	-	-	-	-	-	osm/	-
Drumgoon	Lisnaclea	Caden Owen	corn	-	-	-	-	-	12x2x6	vmb/	2
Drumgoon	Lisnageer	-	corn	-	-	-	-	-	-	osm/	-
Drumgoon	Lisnageer	-	corn	-	-	-	-	-	-	osm/	-
Drumgoon	Lisnageer	-	corn & flour	-	-	-	-	-	-	6"os/	17
Drumgoon	Lisnageer	Boyd & Langtry	corn	-	-	-	-	-	18x9x2 3 pr st	vmb/	2
Drumgoon	Lisnageer	Boyd & Langtry	flour	-	-	-	-	-	only 1 wh 3 pr st	vmb/	2
Drumgoon	Lisnageer	Murphy Mr	flour & corn	-	-	-	-	-	18x9x - undershot	osm/	-
Drumgoon	Lisnagoon	-	bleach field	-	-	-	-	-	-	osm/	-
Drumgoon	Lisnagoon	-	bleach in ruins :	-	-	-	-	1841	-	6"os/	23
Drumgoon	Lisnagoon	Worthy William	corn	house, offs. & land	33a.	71	-	1856	-	gr/	a.a.lre.ie
Drumgoon	Lisnagoon	Worthy William	corn	-	-	-	-	-	21x6x16 3 pr st.	vmb/	2

PARISH	TOWNLAND	MILLER	TYPE	HOUSE	Land	£Val	PROPRIETORS	Date	WHEEL etc.	Record	Ref.
Cavan	Logher	- nr Shercock	corn	-	-	-	-	1899	-	1"os/	69
Lurgan	Lurgan	Anderson	mill	-	-	-	Anderson - Reilly	-	- [not 761]	dd/	761 582 520117
Drumgoon	Lurganboy	-	flax	-	-	-	-	-	-	osm/	-
Drumgoon	Lurganboy	Reilly	-	-	-	-	-	1974	14x4.6x -	sv/ff	GBowie
Drumgoon	Lurganboy	Reilly Patrick	corn	-	-	-	-	-	13x3x7	vmb/	2
Drumgoon	Lurganboy	S. side Annagh R.	mill & mill race	-	-	-	-	1841	-	6"os/	23
Urney	Lurganboy :	-	corn	-	-	-	-	1888	-	25"os/	20
Drumlumman	Magheraboy Lr	-	corn	-	-	-	-	-	16x2.4x -	osm/	-
Drumlummon	Magheraboy Upr	-	corn & race	-	-	-	-	-	-	6"os/	41
Drumlummon	Magheraboy Upr	Plunkett Henry	corn	(2B) 35.6x20x8 :	-	2-5-9	-	1837	12x2.3x - 2 p st. :	hob/	5.0054
Urney	Manor Mill	Thompson David :	mill	-	-	-	Thompson D - Waller :	1824	-	dd/	791 46 534581
Shercock	Milltown	-	flax	-	-	-	-	1899	-	1"os/	69
Shercock	Milltown	-	mill	-	-	-	-	1899	-	1"os/	69
Cavan	Milltown	Crawford	-	-	-	-	Crawford - Orr	-	-	dd/	808 576 545311
Lurgan	Minmod	-	-	-	-	-	-	-	-	vmb/	2
Killinagh	Moneen	- S.Tobermore Vge	corn & kiln	-	-	-	-	-	-	6"os/	3
Killinagh	Moneen	Gallagher John	corn	(2C) 30x20x8 :	-	-	-	-	13x1.10x6.4	hob/	5.0080
Killnagh	Moneen	Gilroy Owen	tuck	-	-	-	-	-	12x2x8	vmb/	2
Killinkere	Mullagh Cuilcagh	Burns Denis	corn	-	-	-	-	-	12x1x12	vmb/	2
Killinagh	Mullaghboy	- W/ Garvagh L.	tuck	-	-	-	-	-	-	6"os/	4
Annagh	Mullaghcroghery	-	corn & dam	-	-	-	-	1841	-	6"os/	16
Annagh	Mullaghcroghery	Brady Thomas	corn	house, offs. & land	9a.	11	-	1856	-	gr/	a.a.Ire.ie
Annagh	Mullaghcroghery	Brady Thomas	corn	-	-	-	-	-	12x - x3	vmb/	2
Crosserlough	Mullaghkeel	-	corn & pond	-	-	-	-	-	-	6"os/	31
Ctosserlough	Mullaghkeel	Smith Philip	corn	(2C) 43x20x8 :	-	-	-	1839	12x2.6x5 1 pr st.	hob/	5.0050
Drumlumman	Mullaghoran	-	corn & race	-	-	-	-	-	-	6"os/	37
Drumlumman	Mulloghoran	-	corn	-	-	-	-	-	16x2.4x -	osm/	-
Drumlummon	Mulloghoran	McDermott Thomas	corn	(2B) 40x20x8 :	-	-	-	1837	11x2.9x15 wooden :	hob/	5.0054
Cavan	Mully	-	mill	-	-	-	-	1899	-	1"os/	56
Cavan	Mully Maher	Enery William :	mills	-	-	-	Enery William - Arabin :	1824	Annty. 31 Jul.	dd/	794 326 536661
Lurgan	Murmod	- on R. Ramor	corn & race	-	-	-	-	-	-	6"os/	39
Lurgan	Murmod	Bride James	corn	(2C) 31.0x18.6x7 :	36a.	-	-	-	12x1.9x10 2 pr st :	hob/	5.0042
Kilbride	Pollareagh	Caffrey Charles	corn	(2C) 32.6x21x7 :	-	5-4-4	-	1839	11x1.11x - u`shot	hob/	5.0056
Kilbride	Pollareagh :	-	corn	-	-	-	-	1841	-	6"os/	38
Killeshandra	Portaliff	- at K`shandra Vge.	brewery	-	-	-	-	-	-	6"os/	19
Larah	Raheelagh	-	corn	-	-	-	-	1841	12ft. dia.metal :	6"os/	17
Larah	Raheelagh	Burrows Robert	corn	(1B) 20x30.6x22 :	-	-	-	1840	- machinery :	hob/	5.0066
Larah	Raheelagh	Burrows Robert	corn	(1A) 31x20x20 :	-	10-12	-	1855	12ft. dia.metal :	hob/	5.3794
Larah	Raheelagh	Burrows Robert	corn & kiln	Miller's ho. & land	4a.	17	-	1856	-	gr/	a.a.Ire.ie
Kildrumsherdan	Rakane	-	corn kiln	-	-	-	-	-	-	6"os/	17
Larah	Rakeelagh	Barrows Robert	corn	-	-	-	-	-	12x - x -	vmb/	2
Castlerahan	Ramonan	- nr B`jasduff Vge	corn & flax	-	-	-	-	-	-	6"os/	38
Castlerahan	Ramonan	Morrow Robert	corn	offices & land	15a.	24	-	-	-	gr	-
Castlerahan	Ramonan	Morrow Robert	corn	(1A) 56x24.6x25.6 :	-	-	-	1838	20x4x13 2 pairs st :	hob/	5.0037
Castlerahan	Ramonan	Morrow Robert	corn	-	-	-	-	-	20x4x13	vmb/	2
Castlerahan	Ramonan	Morrow Robert	flax (now idle)	28.6x13.6x8.6	-	-	-	1838	12x3x4 4 stands :	hob/	5.0037
Crosserlough	Rassan	-	corn & tuck	-	-	-	-	1841	-	6"os/	38
Crosserlough	Rassan	Veech Patt	corn	(2C) 27.0x19.6x8 :	-	-	-	-	12x2.9x12 1 pr st :	hob/	5.0038
Crosserlough	Rassan	Veech Patt	corn	-	-	-	-	-	12x3x12	vmb/	2
Castlerahan	Rassudan	-	mill stream	-	-	-	-	-	-	6"os/	38
Castlerahan	Rassudan	Brady Jas (Chas.) :	& corn	-	2a.	2.5.0	-	-	-	gr	-
Castlerahan	Rassudan	McMahon & Brady	corn	-	-	-	-	-	12x2x13	vmb/	2

PARISH	TOWNLAND	MILLER	TYPE	HOUSE	Land	£Val	PROPRIETORS	Date	WHEEL etc.	Record	Ref.
Castlerahan	Rassudan	McMahon Patrick & :	corn	(2C) 29.6x21.6x10 :	-	-	-	1838	11.9x2x13 1 pr st. :	hob/	5.0037
Munterconnaght	Ryefield	-	-	-	-	-	-	-	-	vmb/	2
Munterconnaght	Ryefield	- on Crosswater	mill	-	-	-	-	1899	-	1"os/	80
Munterconnaght	Ryefield	Porter John	corn & kiln	(3C) 39.6x17x6.6 :	-	-	-	1838	10x1.6x11 1 pr. st. :	hob/	5.0044
Munterconnaght	Ryefield	Ryefield Cross Mills	corn & kiln	-	-	-	-	-	-	6"os/	43
Munterconnaght	Ryefield Cross	- Ryefield Cross	Mill	-	-	-	-	1841	-	6"os/	43
Munterconnaght	Ryefield Cross	Brady	oats	-	-	-	-	1974	-	sv/ff	GBowie
Scrabby	Sallaghan	- N/ Sallaghan Br. :	mill in ruins	-	-	-	-	-	-	6"os/	30
Mullagh	Seeharan	-	corn kiln	-	-	-	-	-	-	6"os/	40
Balymachugh	Shankill	Brady Patrick :	mill	-	-	-	Brady P - Jackson John :	1821	-	dd/	763 40 517775
Balymachugh	Shankill	Brady Patrick :	mill	-	-	-	Brady - Blackwood Dorcas	1823	-	dd/	794 410 536745
Annagelliff	Shankill Lower	-	corn & stream :	-	-	-	-	-	-	6"os/	21
Annagelliff	Shankill Lower	McClernon Bernard :	corn	(2B) 20x38.6x7 :	-	-	-	1839	- outside wheel :	hob/	5.0061
Annagelliff	Shankill Lower	McLennon Bernard	corn	-	-	-	-	-	-	vmb/	2
Kilmore	Shantully	-	old corn mill	-	-	-	-	-	-	6"os/	25
Jerpointchurch	Smithstown	Howlin John	mill	(3C) 45x20x9 :	-	-	-	-	- no information	hob/	5.3989
Annagh	Sraheglin	Thompson Jn Dixon	distillery	house., offs., ld.	102a.	303	-	-	-	gr/	a.a.Ire.ie
Larah	Stradone	-	corn	-	-	-	-	-	12x4.2x - breast	osm/	-
Larah	Stradone	-	mill	-	-	-	-	1899	-	1"os/	69
Annagh	Straheglin	- on R. Erne	distillery	-	-	-	-	-	-	6"os/	15
Kinawley	Swanlinbar	Waldron	mills	-	-	-	Waldron - Waldron	-	-	dd/	778 507 527242
Kinawley	Swanlinbar Tn.: -	Gresson	mills	-	-	-	Gresson - Holmes	-	-	dd/	778 85 526820
Killinagh	Termon	-	corn	-	-	-	-	1899	-	1"os/	56
Killinagh	Thornhill	-	corn	-	-	-	-	1899	-	1"os/	56
Kildrumsherdan	Tonyin	-	corn & kiln	-	-	-	-	-	-	6"os/	22
Kildrumsherdan	Tonyin	McEnteer Terence	corn	-	-	-	-	-	12x2x10	vmb/	2
Kildrumsherdan	Tonyin	McIntee Terence	corn	(2B) 22x22x10 :	-	7-11	-	-	14x3 metal o`shot :	hob/	5.0072
Cav	Townland ?	-	corn	-	-	-	-	-	-	6"os/	31
Drumgoon	Townland ?	- on R. Knappagh	cloth	-	-	-	-	-	-	6"os/	23
Drumgoon	Townland ?	- on R. Knappagh	corn	-	-	-	-	-	-	6"os/	23
Castleterra	Townland ?	Adame Francis	flour mills	(1B) 74.6x25x29.6 :	-	-	-	1839	16ft. dia. medium :	hob/	5.0062
Cavan	Townland ?	Porter John Sen.	corn	(3C) 30.6x17.0x6.6 :	-	-	-	-	10x1.6x11 1 pr st.	hob/	5.0044
Knockbride	Tullylorcan	-	corn & kiln	-	-	-	-	-	-	6"os/	27
Knockbride	Tullylorcan	Mahood Edward	corn	-	-	-	-	-	14x3x14	vmb/	2
Killinagh	Tullynamoyle	-	corn kiln	-	-	-	-	-	-	6"os/	3
Templeport	Tullyveela	-	corn kiln	-	-	-	-	-	-	6"os/	8
Cavan	Ummallaght	- N. of Billis Br.	corn & race	-	-	-	-	-	-	6"os/	33
Lurgan	Virginia	-	mill	-	-	-	-	1899	-	1"os/	80
Lurgan	Virginia Town	- NW / Town Br.	brewery	-	-	-	-	-	-	6"os/	39
Lurgan	Virginia Town :	White Robert :	brewery	(1B) 20.6x22x21 :	-	20.1.8	-	1837	13x8 wood :	hob/	5.3768
Ballintemple	Wotoraghy	Brady	corn	-	-	-	-	1974	-	sv/ff	GBowie
Ballintemple	Wotoraghy	Cahill Widow	corn	(2&3C) 29x18x6.6 :	-	-	-	-	12.8x2.4x3.6 1pr st.	hob/	5.0047
Ballintemple	Wotoraghy	on R. Erne	corn	mill, kiln dilapidated	-	-	Ned Brady	1998	-	pWEH	- B

PARISH	TOWNLAND	MILLER	TYPE	HOUSE	Land	£Val	PROPRIETORS	Date	WHEEL etc.	Record	Ref.
Kilmancheen	Ardnacullia N.	Fallon John	corn	-	-	-	-	-	11x3x3	vmb/	3
Kilmancheen	Ardnacullia N.	Fallon John	tuck	-	-	-	-	-	11x2x3	vmb/	3
Kilmanaheen	Ardnacullia North	- S. side Inagh R.	tuck	-	-	-	-	-	-	6"os/	15
Kilmanaheen	Ardnacullia North	- S/ R. Cullenagh	tuck	-	-	-	-	1841	-	6"os/	15
Kilmanaheen	Ardnacullia North	- SW/ Ennistimon	woollen	-	-	-	-	-	-	1"os/	123
(bo.Corcumroe)	Ardrahine *	Inchiquin Baron	Ardrahine Mill	-	-	-	Inchiquin - O`Brien Robt.	1892	-	dd/	1892 50 250
Clare	Ardrahine *	O'Brien Edward :	mill	-	-	-	O'Brien Ed - O'Brien Michael :	1728	-	dd/	60 16 39682
(bo.Corcumroe)	Ardrahine *	Reynolds Francis	Ardrahine Mill	-	-	-	-	1892	-	dd/	1892 50 292
Doora	Ardsolus	- on Ardsolus R.	tuck (in ruins)	-	-	-	-	-	-	6"os/	42
Doora	Ardsolus	- W/ Ardsolus R.	corn mill	-	-	-	-	-	-	6"os/	42
Clare	Ballincurrig *	-	corn kiln	-	-	-	-	-	-	6"os/	28
Clare	Ballincurrig *	on Annamulaghaun R.	corn & tuck	-	-	-	-	-	-	6"os/	28
Inchicronan	Ballinruan		corn kiln	-	-	-	-	-	-	6"os/	18
Kilfintinan	Ballintnea N.	- N/ Ballintlea Lo.	oil mill (ruins)	-	-	-	-	-	-	6"os/	52
Kilfintinan	Ballintnea.	Pease als Clifford	grist & tuck mill	-	-	-	Pease - Pease	-	-	dd/	48 416 32091
	Ballintnea.	Pease als Clifford	grist & tuck mill	-	-	-	Pease - Pease	-	-	dd/	48 418 32092
Bo. Bunraty	Ballycline River	Macghee John	mill or forge	-	-	-	Macghee Jn - Roche Jno	1747	-	dd/	128 366 87236
Killaloe	Ballycorney	- nr Mill Brook Ho.	flour	-	-	-	-	-	-	6"os/	45
Killaloe	Ballycorney	- SE /B'corney Br.	tuck	-	-	-	-	-	-	6"os/	45
Killaloe	Ballycorney	Deniston James	flour	-	-	-	-	-	16x4x17	vmb/	3
Killaloe	Ballycorney :	Jefferys Augustus?	mills	-	-	-	Jefferys A - Reilly	-	-	dd/	622 579 430952
Killaloe	Ballycorney :	Martin William	mills	-	-	-	Martin wM - McNamara Danl	1750	-	dd/	175 92 116322
Killaloe	Ballycorney :	Newton Edward	mills	-	-	-	Newton Ed - Flanagan John	1792	-	dd/	462 499 296489
Quin	Ballykilty	Exre	mills	-	-	-	Exre - McNamara	-	-	dd/	322 249 215767
Quin	Ballykilty	Mahon	mills	-	-	-	Mahon - Brown	-	-	dd/	346 16 230020
Quin	Ballykilty	Mahon Thomas	mills	-	-	-	Mahon Thos - Hewett Henry	1777	-	dd/	319 270 213848
Quin	Ballykilty	Monsello William	mills	-	-	-	Monsello W - Strettle Ambrose	1776	-	dd/	319 11 209230
Bo. Tulla	Ballylinbeg	Butler Theobald	mill	-	-	-	Butler Theo - Butler James	1734	-	dd/	93 358 65829
Clare	Ballylyne *	S/ Balyline Br.	tuck & dam	-	-	-	-	-	-	6"os/	27
Killuran	Ballymacdonnell	O'Callaghan John :	houses & land	- (leased by)	637a.	150	-	1855	-	gr/	-
Kilmaley	Ballymacooda	- E/ Kilclogher Br.	tuck & mill race	-	-	-	-	-	-	6"os/	41
Kilmaley	Ballymacooda	Quealy John	tuck & land	-	54a.	30.10	-	1855	-	gr/	-
Tomgraney	Ballymalone	-	malt kiln	-	-	-	-	-	-	6"os/	29
Tomgraney	Ballyminoge	-	Scarriff Mills	-	-	-	-	-	-	6"os/	28
Tomgraney	Ballyminoge	Wallnutt	mills	-	-	-	-	1855	-	gr/	-
Kilfinaghty	Ballymulcashel	- near Bridge	mill	-	-	-	-	-	-	mmSv/	ms - Z
Kilfinaghty	Ballymulcashel	- S. bridge in field	mill & millhouse	attached, v dilap.	-	-	-	-	-	mmSv/	ms - D
Kilfinaghty	Ballymulcashel	- S/ B'mulcahhel Br.	tuck mill	-	-	-	-	-	-	6"os/	43
Kilfinaghty	Ballymulcashel	Gleeson D & J	tuck	-	-	-	-	-	10x2x5	vmb/	3
Kilfinaghty	Ballymulcashel	McInerney Patrick	Castle Mills	-	-	-	McInerney P - P. W. Com.	1890	-	dd/	1890 59 285
Kilfinaghta	Ballysheenmore	- N/ Annagore Br.	mill (ruins)	-	-	-	-	-	-	6"os/	52
Kilfinaghta	Ballysheenmore	- SE/ Annagore Br.	mill (in ruins)	-	-	-	-	-	-	6"os/	52
Tulla	Ballyslattery	- N/ Newgrove Br	corn (ruins)	-	-	-	-	-	-	6"os/	35
Inchicronan	Ballyvanna	E/side Scarriff R.	corn kiln	-	-	-	-	-	-	6"os/	18
St Patricks	Blackwater	-	Blackwater Mills	-	-	-	-	-	-	6"os/	53
Killquane	Blackwater	Bull	mills	-	-	-	Bull - Mahon	-	-	dd/	31 368 19470
Killquane	Blackwater	Bull	mills	-	-	-	Bull - Bull	-	-	dd/	32 55 18942
St Patrick`s	Blackwater	Caswell Samuel	corn	-	-	-	-	-	18x6x13	vmb/	3
St Patrick`s	Blackwater	Caswell Samuel	flour	-	-	-	-	-	18x8x13	vmb/	3
St Patrick`s	Blackwater	Caswell Samuel	flour, corn :	land & miller's house	2a.	80.5	-	1855	-	gr/	-
Clare	Bow River Bridge	- on Bow R.	mill	-	-	-	-	-	-	1"os/	125
Kilaspuglonan	Caheraddery		cloth	-	-	-	-	-	-	6"os/	15

PARISH	TOWNLAND	MILLER	TYPE	HOUSE	Land	£Val	PROPRIETORS	Date	WHEEL etc.	Record	Ref.
Kilaspuglonan	Caheraderry	Lysaght Henry	corn	-	-	-	-	-	10x1x11	vmb/	3
Killasbuglonane	Caheraderry	Lysaght Henry	corn & tuck	-	-	5	-	1855	-	gr/	-
Kilaspuglonan	Caheraderry	Lysaght Henry	tuck	-	-	-	-	-	9x1x11	vmb/	3
Kilnoe	Caherhurley	Hogan John	corn	-	-	-	-	-	13x2x13	vmb/	3
Kilshanny	Caherlooskaun	Cooleen R. below Br.	tuck	-	-	-	-	-	-	6"os/	15
Clare	Callaghans	Molony	mills	-	-	-	Molony - Knox	-	-	dd/	788 124 532884
Clare *	Cappagh Lower	Pease	ye grist mill	-	-	-	Pease - Roche	-	-	dd/	94 264 66157
Clare *	Cappagh Lower	Pease Hester :	mills	-	-	-	Pease Hester - Pease Geo :	1726	-	dd/	48 416 32091
Kilfinaghta	Cappagh South	on Owenogarney R.	Old Mill Bridge	-	-	-	-	-	-	6"os/	52
Dysert	Carhoo	Synge Francis H	mill, kiln & land	-	28a.	39.10	-	1855	-	gr/	-
Clooney	Carrownaclough	N/ Aroadaroon R.	mill in ruins	-	-	-	-	-	-	6"os/	26
Bo. Inchiquin	Cartron	Browne Emill	mill	-	-	-	Browne E - Browne Thos	1892	-	dd/	1892 46 266
Kilkeedy	Castlequarter	on Windmill Hill	windmill ruins	-	-	-	-	-	-	6"os/	18
Clare	Clare County	Smith Mrs Mai	grain	small stone millhouse	-	-	known as O`Callaghan`s	-	wheel derelict :	iaa/	RPD20.10
Rath	Clifden	Valentine Jas B & Son	flour	-	-	50	-	1855	-	gr/	-
Rath	Clifden	W. side R. Fergus	flour	-	-	-	-	-	-	6"os/	17
Clare *	Clonassy	O'Callaghan	mills	-	-	-	O'Callaghan - O'Callaghan	-	-	dd/	482 401 304583
Clare *	Clonassy	Stackpoole	mills	-	-	-	Stackpoole - Roche	-	-	dd/	403 466 296015
Clare *	Clonassy	Stackpoole	mills	-	-	-	Stackpoole - Roche	-	-	dd/	409 496 269019
Clare *	Clonassy	Stackpoole	mills	-	-	-	Stackpoole - Steele	-	-	dd/	427 27228794
Drumcliff	Clonroad Beg	- Ennis Town	flour	-	-	-	-	-	-	6"os/	33
Drumcliff	Clonroad Beg	- Ennis Town	mill	-	-	-	-	-	-	6"os/	33
Drumcliff	Clonroad Beg	- in Ennis Town	brewery	-	-	-	-	-	-	6"os/	33
Kilmurry	Cloonadrum	-	tuck mills	-	-	-	-	-	-	6"os/	38
Kilmurry	Cloonadrum	- N/ Lissyneilan Br.	Annageeragh Mill	-	-	-	-	-	-	6"os/	38
Tulla	Cloonaleary	Little Michael	corn kiln	21x18x8	-	-	-	-		hob/	5.0088
Kiluran	Clooncool	- on Mill River :	corn & tuck	-	-	-	-	1841	-	6"os/	35
Killuran	Clooncool	Boland John	corn & tuck	-	-	-	-	1883	-	valCB/	9
Killuran	Clooncool	Boland Matthew	corn & land :	-	-	-	-	1860	-	valCB/	9
Killuran	Clooncool	Callaghan	land	-	-	-	Callaghan - Crowe	-	-	dd/	309 607 207787
Killuran	Clooncool	Callaghan	land	-	-	-	Callaghan - Hennessy	-	-	dd/	497 57 317 690
Killuran	Clooncool	Callaghan	land	-	-	-	Callaghan - Hennessy	-	-	dd/	499 562 319689
Killuran	Clooncool	Gleeson Batt	corn & tuck	-	-	-	-	1910	-	valCB/	9
Killuran	Clooncool	Harrison	land	-	-	-	Harrison - Hartney	-	-	dd/	159 33 105911
Killuran	Clooncool	Smith John	corn & yard	-	-	-	-	1932	-	valCB/	9
Killuran	Clooncool	Smyth Nora	corn & yard	-	-	-	-	1941	-	valCB/	9
Killuran	Clooncool, Vge. of :	Boland Matthew	corn & land	-	1a.	15.15	-	1855	-	gr/	-
Kilmurry	Cloonlaheen	Muggevin Patrick	mill, land & :	-	11a.	11.10	-	1855	-	gr/	-
Kilfenora	Cloonomera	Mooney Thomas	tuck	-	-	-	-	-	10x1x6	vmb/	3
Kilfenora	Cloonomra	1/8m W/ Lickeen Lo.	corn & tuck	-	-	-	-	-	-	6"os/	16
Kilfenora	Cloonomra	Mooney Thomas	corn & land	-	18a.	8.10	-	1855	-	gr/	-
Drumcliff	Cloughleagh	- Mill Rd., Ennis	mill	-	-	-	-	1841	-	vmb/	3
Drumcliff	Cloughleagh :	Bannantyne Jas & S.	store, kiln & yard	-	-	55	-	1856	-	gr/	a.a.Ire.ie
Drumcliff	Cloughleagh :	Bannantyne Jas & S.	mills & kiln	house, offices & land	2.0.5	190	-	1856	-	gr/	a.a.Ire.ie
Bo. Unchicronar	Cloun	Butler Theobald	mills	-	-	-	Butler Theo - Butler Paul	1734	-	dd/	77 409 54195
Bo. Unchicronar	Cloun	Butler Theobald	mills	-	-	-	Butler Theo - Butler James	1720	-	dd/	81 532 58648
Bo. Unchicronar	Cloun	Butler Thomas	mills	-	-	-	Butler Thomas - Butler Paul	1734	-	dd/	76 313 54648
Clare *	Coogy West	O'Grady	land	-	-	-	O'Grady - O'Callaghan	-	-	dd/	281 19 179886
Kilfidanne	Coolmeen	- N/ New Bridge	mill	-	-	-	-	-	-	6"os/	59
Kilfiddane	Coolmeen	Conway Edmond	corn	-	41a.	14.10	-	1855	-	gr/	-
Killimor	Corraige	Downes Thomas	corn	-	15a.	16.10	-	1855	-	gr/	-
Clare *	Coshery island	Brady	land	-	-	-	Brady - O'Callaghan	-	-	dd/	503 115 321632

PARISH	TOWNLAND	MILLER	TYPE	HOUSE	Land	£Val	PROPRIETORS	Date	WHEEL etc.	Record	Ref.
Clare *	Craggbryen	Aylmer James	mills	-	-	-	Aylmer J - Stakpoole John	1736	-	dd/	85 467 61009
Drumcliff	Cragleagh	Law Thomas P	mill	-	-	-	Law Thos - Roberts Arthur	1892	-	dd/	1892 13 236
Drumcliff	Cragleagh	Stokes George B	mill	-	-	-	Stokes Geo - Roberts Arth	1892	-	dd/	1892 13 235
Feakle	Curragh	3/4m N/ Ayle Br.	Poulawillin Mill	(in ruins)	-	-	-	-	-	6"os/	27
Doora	Deerpark	Armstrong William	corn & land	-	42a.	21.5	-	1855	-	gr/	-
Kilscily	Derry	-	Derry Mills	-	-	-	-	1842	-	6"os/	44
Kilscily	Derry	-	mill race	-	-	-	-	-	-	6"os/	44
Kilscily	Derry	- nr Broadford	mill	-	-	-	-	-	-	mmSv/	ms - R
Kilscily	Derry	- E/ town bridge	corn	-	-	-	-	-	-	6"os/	44
Kilscily	Derry	- NNE/ Crean Br.	tuck	-	-	-	-	-	-	6"os/	44
Kilscily	Derry	McDonald George	corn	-	-	-	-	-	14x4x7	vmb/	3
Kilscily	Derry	McDonald George	tuck	-	-	-	-	-	10x2x12 2 wheels	vmb/	3
Kilsealy	Derry	McDonnell George	mills & land	-	33a.	35.15	-	1855	-	gr/	-
Clooney	Derrycaliff		corn kiln	-	-	-	-	-	-	6"os/	27
Clooney	Derrycallif Lr		corn & tuck	-	-	-	-	-	-	6"os/	27
Inchieronan	Derrygarrif	imed E/ Lughid Br.	mill	-	-	-	-	-	-	6"os/	18
Kilkeedy	Derrylumman		corn kiln	-	-	-	-	-	-	6"os/	11
Kilmurry	Doonogan	-	mill race	-	-	-	-	-	-	6"os/	39
Kilmurry	Doonogan	- N/ Moyglass Br.	tuck	-	-	-	-	-	-	6"os/	39
Kilfarbog	Dough	McMahon Martin	grist	-	-	-	-	-	12x - x13	vmb/	3
Kilfarbog	Dough	McMahon Martin	tuck	-	-	-	-	-	12x - x13	vmb/	3
Kilfarbog	Dough	M'Mahon Mary	corn & tuck	-	18a.	-	-	1855	-	gr/	-
	Dromin	Egan Michael	land				Egan Mcl - O'Callaghan :	1821		dd/	815 545 584989
Inagh	Drumcarna		Mauricemills (tn.)	-	-	-	-	-	-	6"os/	24
Drumcliff	Ennis	Gore Hon. Brig. Fran	corn & tuck	-	-	-	Gore Fran - Sexton Thomas	1723	-	dd/	38 523 5239
Drumcliff	Ennis Town	- on R. Fergus	stone	-	-	-	-	-	20x6 metal :	iaa/	RPD20.10
Drumcliff	Ennis Town	Bannantyne James	Lifford Mill	-	-	-	Bannantyne Jas - Alex	1898	-	dd/	1898 57 68
Drumcliff	Ennis Town	Caulfield James E :	Mills of Ennis	-	-	-	Caulfield Jas - Charlemount	1832	-	dd/	889 285 588028
Drumcliff	Ennis Town	E. side of Mill Road	mill	conv. to appartments	-	-	-	-	-	mmSv/	ms - Ca
Drumcliff	Ennis Town	Gore Francis	Mills of Ennis	-	-	-	Gore Fras - McBeath Jn	1833	-	dd/	1833 15 158
Drumcliff	Ennis Town	Gore Francis	Mills of Ennis	-	-	-	Gore F - Radcliffe Jos	1838	-	dd/	1838 15 103
Drumcliff	Ennis Town	Gore Francis :	mills	-	-	-	Gore Fras & Peacock Chris :	1797	-	dd/	799 195 539530
Drumcliff	Ennis Town	Mill Road close to R.	mill	2 bay, 6 appartment :	-	-	-	-	-	mmSv/	ms - Ca
Drumcliff	Ennis Town	O`Brien Michael	Mills of Ennis	-	-	-	O`Brien M - Moran Bryan	1834	-	dd/	1834 19 176
Drumcliff	Ennis Town	O`Kelly Jno	Mills of Ennis	-	-	-	O`Kelly - Barmatyne Alx	1848	-	dd/	1848 20 202
Drumcliff	Ennis Town	O`Meara Phillipa	Millsof Ennis	-	-	-	O`Meara P - Gore Ed A	1851	-	dd/	1851 21 6
Drumcliff	Ennis Town	on Isl. W. of mill Br.	mill (small)	- demolished c2002	-	-	-	-	-	mmSv/	ms - Z
Drumcliff	Ennis Town	on Isl. W. of mill Br.	mill (large)	- demolished c1980	-	-	-	-	-	mmSv/	ms - Z
Drumcliff	Ennis Town	Studdert Richard	Ennis Mills	-	-	-	Studdert - O`Meara Eyre	1851	-	dd/	1851 16 93
Drumcliff	Ennis Town :	Gore Edward	mills, kiln & land	-	2a.	190	-	1855	-	gr/	-
Drumcliff	Ennis Town :	O`Kelly	mill	-	-	-	O`Kelly - Bannantyne Alex	1848	-	dd/	1848 20 202
Drumcliff	Ennis Town :	Bannantyne Jas & Son	mill	-	-	30	-	1855	-	gr/	-
Ennis	EnnisTown	Inman Charles	Mills of Ennis		-	-	Inman C - L`pool A. Bank	1841	-	dd/	1841 16 112
Ennis	EnnisTown	Trouton Charles	Mills of Ennis		-	-	Trouton - Bannantyne Ax	1841	-	dd/	1841 22 471
Ennis	EnnisTown	Wright William	Mills of Ennis	-	-	-	Wright Wm - L`pool Bank	1840	-	dd/	1840 6 197
Feakle	Feakle	1/4m due S/ Feakle	tuck	-	-	-	-	-	-	6"os/	28
Feakle	Feakle	1/8m SE/ Feakle Vge	tuck	-	-	-	-	-	-	6"os/	28
Feakle	Feakle	Flynn Hugh	corn & tuck :	-	8a.	8.5	-	1855	-	gr/	-
Kilmacduane	Fenaclough	Breen James	corn & land	-	18a.	10.5	-	1855	-	gr/	-
Kilmurry	Finnor Beg	- 1m E/ Lissy Br.	tuck mills	-	-	-	-	-	-	6"os/	38
Kilnurry	Finnor Beg	Malone David	grist	-	-	-	-	-	12x - x13	vmb/	3
Kilnurry	Finnor Beg	Malone David	tuck	-	-	-	-	-	12x - x13	vmb/	3

PARISH	TOWNLAND	MILLER	TYPE	HOUSE	Land	£Val	PROPRIETORS	Date	WHEEL etc.	Record	Ref.
Kilnurry	Finnor Beg	Malone Laurence	tuck	-	-	-	-	-	-	vmb/	3
Kilmurry	Finor Bog	Malone Daniel	corn, tuck & land	-	3a.	6.10	-	1855	-	gr/	-
Kilmurry	Finor Bog	Malone John	house, offices :	-	3a.	3.5	-	1855	-	gr/	-
Kilmurry	Finor Bog	Malone Laur & David	kiln & land	-	-	-	-	1855	-	gr/	-
Kilmurry	Finor Bog	Malone Laurence	corn, tuck & land	-	3a.	6.15	-	1855	-	gr/	-
Kilmurry	Finor Bog	Muggevin Patrick	mill & forge	-	-	-	-	1855	-	gr/	-
Killuran	Foxandgeese	O'Callaghansmills Tn	- [no mill in Tld.]	-	-	-	-	-	-	6"os/	35
Doora	Gaurus	N. Ennis at G. Br.	flour	33x21 + kiln extn.	-	-	-	-	-	mmSv/	ms - B
Killadysert	Glenconaun More	Conway John	mill	-	9a.	3.5	-	1855	-	gr/	-
Clare *	Gortafeane	Butler	mills	-	-	-	Butler - Butler	-	-	dd/	81 533 58648
Clare *	Gortafeane	Butler Theobald	mills	-	-	-	Butler Theo - Butler James	1734	-	dd/	77 410 54197
Clare *	Gortafeane	Butler Theobald	mills	-	-	-	Butler T - Fran McNamara	-	-	dd/	81 349 57844
Killuran	Gortatrassa	O'Callaghan Reps. H :	houses & land	- (leased by)	484a.	60.13	-	1855	-	gr/	-
Gowlan	Gowlaun		mill	-	-	-	-	-	-	6"os/	8
Kilfinaghta	Ieverstown	Ievers William	mills	-	-	-	Ievers Wm - Millar James	1793	-	dd/	481 149 305957
Kilfinaghta	Ieverstown	Ievers William	mills	-	-	-	Ievers Wm - Clune John	1797	-	dd/	513 317 334893
Kilfinaghta	Ieverstown	Perry Thomas	mills	-	-	-	Perry Thos - Mahon Thos	1800	-	dd/	529 35 346234
Kilfinaghta	Ieverstown	ullin Thomas :	paper	- and offices	-	-	-	1856	-	gr/	a.a.Ire.ie
Clare *	Inchiquin Manor	Bryan John :	mill	-	-	-	Bryan J - Southby Henry	1782	-	dd/	349 176 233474
Clare *	Inchiquin Manor	Foster	mill	-	-	-	Foster - Wheeler	-	-	dd/	365 138 243640
Clare *	Inchiquin Manor	Kildare Hon. Jas Marq.	mill	-	-	-	Kildare Marq. - Freake Jno	1761	-	dd/	218 82 14721
Clare *	Inchiquin Manor	Wheeler	mill	-	-	-	Wheeler - Mooney	-	-	dd/	384 385? 254520
Clare *	Inchiquion	O'Brien Catherine	mills	-	-	-	O'Brien C - Fleming Helen	1725	-	dd/	48 347 31909
Kilfinaghty	Inverstown	Cullen & Donaldson	grist	-	-	-	-	-	14x4x2	vmb/	3
Killuran	Iragh	Callaghan John	house	-	-	10/-	-	1855	-	gr/	-
Killuran	Iragh	O'Callaghansmillls Old	- [no mill at Vge	-	-	-	-	-	-	6"os/	35
Killokennedy	Kilbane	- at Lisroe Vge.	mill	-	-	-	-	-	-	6"os/	44
Killokennedy	Kilbane	O`Connor	mill	-	-	-	O`Connor - McCormick	-	-	dd/	774 438 524773
Kilfarboy	Kildeema South	Windam Col. Geo	corn	-	-	10	-	1855	-	gr/	-
Killadysert	Killadysert Town	O`Grady Daniel	corn	-	-	-	-	-	16x3x17	vmb/	3
Killaloe	Killaloe town	- on Shannon bank	mill	ESB Station :	-	-	-	-	-	mmSv/	ms - B
Killaloe	Killaloe town	Burke Michael	old corn kiln	18x17x17 35x17x17	-	-	-	1853	-	hob/	5.0087
Kilmacduane	Kilmacduane West	Breen Patrick, Mcl. &	corn & kiln	-	3.5a.	13.10	-	1855	-	gr/	-
Kilmaley	Kilmaley	- E/ Kilmaley Br.	tuck mill	-	-	-	-	-	-	6"os/	40
Kilmaley	Kilmaley	Nellan Patrick	tuck	-	-	-	-	-	12x1x7	vmb/	3
Kilrush	Kilrush Town :	Kelly John	store & kiln	-	-	42	-	1855	-	gr/	-
Kilrush	Kilrush Town :	-	woollen	-	-	-	-	1897	-	6"os/	67
Kilrush	Kilrush Town :	-	corn & saw	-	-	-	-	1897	-	6"os/	67
Kilrush	Kilrush Town :	Glynn M & Son	flour	-	-	-	-	1963	-	lic./10	flour
Kilrush	Kilrush Town :	-	lace factory	-	-	-	-	1841	-	6"os/	67
Kilscily	Kiltenanlea	Bindon Samuel	beetling	-	-	-	-	-	12x3x3 14x4x -	vmb/	3
Kilscily	Kiltenanlea	Bindon Samuel	corn	-	-	-	-	-	14x4x3	vmb/	3
Inchicronan	Kilvoyran	Connor Martin	corn	-	-	1.10	-	1855	-	gr/	-
Clondagan	Knockalehia	Bannantine James	flour	-	-	13	-	1855	-	gr/	-
Clonagad	Knockalehid	- on Owenslieve R.	mill	-	-	-	-	-	-	6"os/	50
Feakle	Knockalisheen	-	tuck	-	-	-	-	-	-	6"os/	28
Kilmihil	Lack West	- N/ D'crossaun Br.	tuck	-	-	-	-	-	-	6"os/	58
Killimor	Lack West	Lorihgan Thos & Jane	tuck & grist	-	-	4	-	1855	-	gr/	-
Kilrush	Leadmore West	Paterson J W	distillery idle 3 yr.	-	-	-	-	-	-	vmb/	3
Kilfarboy	Leaghard	-	Milltown House	(no mill)	-	-	-	-	-	6"os/	30
Kilfinaghten	Lenercappagh *	Pease	mills	-	-	-	Pease - Pease	-	-	dd/	92 264 64601
Kilfinaghten	Lenercappagh *	Pease als. Clifford H	mills	-	-	-	Pease Hester - George	1726	-	dd/	48 416 32091

PARISH	TOWNLAND	MILLER	TYPE	HOUSE	Land	£Val	PROPRIETORS	Date	WHEEL etc.	Record	Ref.
Kilfinaghten	Lenercappagh *	Pease George	mills	-	-	-	Pease Geo - Pease Hester	1726	-	dd/	48 418 32092
Drumcliff	Lifford	- mid-R., NW/ Ennis	flour	-	-	-	-	1841	-	vmb/	3
Drumcliff	Lifford	Banantine Cloghlea	corn	-	-	-	-	-	17x8x3	vmb/	3
Drumcliff	Lifford	Banantine Cloghlea	flour	-	-	-	-	-	17x10x4	vmb/	3
Drumcliff	Lifford	Banantine Sam & S	corn	-	-	-	-	-	14x4x4	6"os/	33
Drumcliff	Lifford	Banantine Sam & S	flour	-	-	-	-	-	18x10x4	6"os/	33
Drumcliff	Lifford :	Bannantyne Jas &Son	mill (part of)	-	-	30	-	-	-	gr/	a.a.Ire.ie
Drumcliff	Lifford :	Bannantyne Jas &Son	store & yard	-	-	27	-	-	-	gr/	a.a.Ire.ie
Tulla	Milltown	-	mill (1 mile)	-	-	-	-	-	-	1"os/	131
(bo. Iberkane)	Milltown	National Bank Ltd.	Milltown	-	-	-	Nat. Bank - O`Brien Thos	1890	-	dd/	1890 19 61
Kilkeedy	Monreagh	Keane Denis	mill, kiln & land	-	136a.	52.10	-	1855	-	gr/	-
Killaloe	Moys	- S/ Town	marble mills	-	-	-	-	-	-	6"os/	45
Killaloe	Moys	Deniston James	marble	-	-	-	-	-	16x8x5	vmb/	3
Killaloe	Moys	Sheehan Joseph	marble mill :	-	1a.	50	-	1855	-	gr/	-
Templemaley	New Park	Moylan Mary	flour, kilns & ld.	-	10a.	6.5	-	1855	-	gr/	-
Templemaly	New Park	Moylen Michael	flour	-	-	-	-	-	14x2x3	vmb/	3
Tomfinlough	Newmarket	- imed. S/ Town	mill	-	-	-	-	-	-	6"os/	51
Tomfinlough	Newmarket	Reidy John	flour	-	-	-	-	-	15x3x6	vmb/	3
Tomfinlough	Newmarket :	Gleeson William	flour & kiln	-	-	30	-	1855	-	gr/	-
Killuran	O`Callaghans	Wall	mills	-	-	-	Wall - Browne	-	-	dd/	767 530 520665
Obriensbridge	O'Briensbridge	-	flour	-	-	-	-	-	-	6"os/	54
O'Briensbridge	O'Briensbridge	Davis	mills	-	-	-	Davis - LLoyd	-	-	dd/	537 275 352780
O'Briensbridge	O'Briensbridge	Davis	mills	-	-	-	Davis - O'Callaghan	-	-	dd/	548 518 359357
Obriensbridge	O'Briensbridge	Deniston James	flour	-	-	-	-	-	16x7x16	vmb/	3
Obriensbridge	O'Briensbridge	Deniston James & Co.	Mill-pond	-	3.0.21	1	-	1856	-	gr/	a.a.Ire.ie
O'Briensbridge	O'Briensbridge	Norris	mills	-	-	-	Norris - Ryan	-	-	dd/	499 438 317055
O'Briensbridge	O'Briensbridge	Tomkin	mills	-	-	-	Tomkin - Widenham	-	-	dd/	505 585? 333804
O'Briensbridge	O'Briensbridge Tn	Denniston James	flour & corn :	-	-	130	-	1855	-	gr/	-
Killuran	O'Callaghansmills	Cole John	land	-	-	-	Cole John - Cole Richard	1724	-	dd/	41 382 26416
Killuran	O'Callaghansmills	Gerran	land	-	-	-	Geeran - O'Callaghan	-	-	dd/	585 6 393387
Killuran	O'Callaghansmills	Harrison	land	-	-	-	Harrison - Hartney	-	-	dd/	159 33 105911
Killuran	O'Callaghansmills	O'Callaghan	land	-	-	-	O'Callaghan - Crowe	-	-	dd/	309 607 207787
Killuran	O'Callaghansmills	O'Callaghan Cornelius	land	-	-	-	O'Callaghan C - Bayley Jn	1790	-	dd/	515 557 335993
Killuran	O'Callaghansmills	O'Callaghan Cornelius :	land	-	-	-	O'Callaghan - Henessy Ptk	1792	-	dd/	499 562 316689
Killuran	O'Callaghansmills	O'Callaghan Donal :	land	-	-	-	O'Callaghan - Watson Thos	1795	-	dd/	497 57 317686
Killuran	O'Callaghansmills	O'Callaghan Donalus	land	-	-	-	O'Callaghan D - Campbell W	1802	-	dd/	541 448 375966
Killuran	O'Callaghansmills	Perry	land	-	-	-	Perry - Perry	-	-	dd/	529 238 347019
Killuran	O'Callaghansmills	Ranelagh Hon. Arthur :	land	-	-	-	Ranelagh Lord - Scott Jno	1734	-	dd/	82 145 57308
Killuran	O'Callaghansmills	Wall George Morris :	land	-	-	-	Wall Geo - Bourne Lucinda :	1821	Asgt. of Mort.	dd/	767 530 520665
Killuran	O'Callaghansmills	Wilkinson	land	-	-	-	Wilkinson - Sampson	-	-	dd/	213 252 140990
Clare ?	Portroe	at gate of bungalow	mill	small ruins	-	-	pursd by husband 1938	-	-	mmSv/	ms - R
Tomgraney	Raheen	-	flour	(inf. per local)	-	-	-	-	-	mmSv/	ms - Z
Tomgraney	Raheen	-	mill race & pond	-	-	-	-	-	-	6"os/	29
Tomgraney	Raheen	- W/ Raheen Br.	corn & tuck	-	-	-	-	-	-	6"os/	29
Tomgraney	Raheen	- W/ Raheen Br.	Raheen Mills	-	-	-	-	-	-	6"os/	29
Tomgraney	Raheen	Flynn Patrick	mill & land	-	24a.	13.10	-	1855	-	gr/	-
Torngraney	Raheen Town	Flynn Patrick	corn	-	-	-	-	-	13x3x10ins	vmb/	3
Torngraney	Raheen Town	Flynn Patrick	tuck	-	-	-	-	-	10x2x10ins	vmb/	3
St Patricks	Rath Clifden	Barton Edward W	flour (idle 5 yrs)	-	-	-	-	-	12x3x3	vmb/	3
Killone	Rathmeehan	Toughey Andrew	tuck	-	-	-	-	-	12x2x8	vmb/	3
Killone	Rathmeehan	Toughey Daniel	tuck	-	-	-	-	-	11x1x11	vmb/	3
Kilkeedy	Rockvale		mill	-	-	-	-	-	-	6"os/	11

PARISH	TOWNLAND	MILLER	TYPE	HOUSE	Land	£Val	PROPRIETORS	Date	WHEEL etc.	Record	Ref.
O'Briensbridge	Roo East	Hickey James	corn	house, offs. & land	14a.	7.0.0	-	1856	-	gr/	a.a.Ire.ie
St Patricks	Rossmadda	-	Rossmadda Mills	-	-	-	-	-	-	6"os/	53
St Patricks	Rossmadda	known as The Field	tilery	-	-	-	-	-	-	mmSv/	ms - Z
St Patricks	Rossmadda	Maunsell Dorothea :	mills	-	-	-	Maunsell D - McAdam Thos :	1824	Mort. 10 Dec.	dd/	801 588 541103
St Patricks	Rossmadda	Watson Andrew :	mills	-	-	-	Watson A - Watson Thos :	1824	Recov. 10 Dec.	dd/	801 569 541100
St Patricks	Rossmadda W.	Caswell Samuel	flour	-	-	-	-	-	18x11x13	vmb/	3
St Patricks	Rossmadda W.	Caswell Samuel	flour & land :	-	139a.	100	-	1855	-	gr/	-
Tomgraney	Scarriff Town	Wallnutt Charles	corn	-	-	-	-	-	18x - x -	vmb/	3
Tomgraney	Scarriff Town	Wallnutt Charles	oil	-	-	-	-	-	14x - x -	vmb/	3
Killaloe	Shantrand	Flynn Edmond	flour	-	-	-	-	-	12x2x12	vmb/	3
Killaloe	Shantrand	Flynn Philip Jnr.	corn	21x18x11 2 offs. :	-	-	-	1853	-	hob/	5.0087
Killaloe	Shantrand	Flynn Philip Jnr.	tuck	33.6x15x8	-	-	-	1853	-	hob/	5.0087
Killaloe	Shantraud	-	Manor Mills	-	-	-	-	-	-	6"os/	45
Killaloe	Shantraud	- Killaloe town	brewery	-	-	-	-	-	-	6"os/	45
Killaloe	Shantraud	Flynn Philip Jun.	tuck & corn :	-	20a.	11	-	1855	-	gr/	-
Kilfinaghta	Sixmilebridge	- S/ Town Br.	bleach (in ruins)	-	-	-	-	-	-	6"os/	52
Kilfinaghta	Sixmilebridge Tn :	Donaldson Alexander	paper	-	-	25	-	1855	-	gr/	-
Kilfinaghta	Sooreeny	-	mill in ruins (was paper mill)		-	-	-	-	-	6"os/	52
Kilfinaghty	Sooreeny	- SE/ Annagore Br.	mill in ruins	-	-	-	-	1841	-	6"os/	52
Kilfinaghty	Sooreeny	Annagore Mills	woollen	-	-	-	-	1897	-	6"os/	52
Kilfinaghty	Sooreeny	Kennier Dennis	paper	-	-	-	-	-	16x4x3	vmb/	3
Inchiervevan	Sranagalloon	Butler Austin	corn & land	-	10a.	7	-	1855	-	gr/	-
Inchieronan	Sranagalloon	W/ Lughid Br.	tuck	-	-	-	-	-	-	6"os/	18
Inchieronan	Sranagalloon		corn kilns (2)	-	-	-	-	-	-	6"os/	18
Clare	Stackpoole`s Br.	- on Kildeema R	mill	-	-	-	-	-	-	1"os/	131
Feakle	Stonepark	1/8m NNW/ Ayle Br.	tuck	-	-	-	-	-	-	6"os/	27
Feakle	Stonepark	k/a Tucker's Mill	mill	across fields :	-	-	-	-	-	mmSv/	ms - R
Kiltenanlea	Summerhill	- S/ Waterpark Ho.	Doonan's Bl. Mill	-	-	-	-	-	-	6"os/	54
Kiltenanlea	Summerhill	Quinn John	corn mill & :	- [also 8 houses]	126a.	118	-	1856	-	gr/	a.a.Ire.ie
Killimer	Tarmon	Hickman	tuck	-	-	-	Hickman - Lyllis	-	-	dd/	73 471 52035
Killimer	Tarmon	O`Brian John :	mill	-	-	-	O`Brian J - Meany James :	1820	-	dd/	786 226 536561
Tomgraney	Tomgraney	Wallnutt Charles	mills & land	-	3a.	61	-	1855	-	gr/	-
(bo. Moyarta)	Townland ?	Vandeleur Hector S	old distillery	-	-	-	Vandeleur - McAuliffe :	1892	-	dd/	1892 3142
Kilrush	Tullycrine	O`Donnell Dick	grain	-	-	-	-	-	- exterior :	iaa/	RPD20.10
Clare	Waterpark	Massey John :	'bl. green & mills	-	-	-	Massey J - Bindon Samuel :	-	-	dd/	799 203 539538

PARISH	TOWNLAND	MILLER	TYPE	HOUSE	Land	£Val+	PROPRIETORS	Date	WHEEL etc.	Record	Ref.
Ballinaboy	Adamstown	-	Fivem'br. Mill House		-	-	-	-	-	6"os	86
Ballinaboy	Adamstown	-	mill pond	-	-	-	-	-	-	6"os	86
Ballinaboy	Adamstown	W/ Fivemilebridge	flour	-	-	-	-	-	-	6"os	86
Aghacross	Aghacross	N/ Glenavuddig Br.	flour	-	-	-	-	-	-	6"os	18
Cork	Aghakeiny *	Gubbins Joseph	mill	-	-	-	Gubbins J - Low Francis	1888	-	dd/	1888 26 20
Templebreedy	Aghamarta	W/ Aghamarta Castle	thrashing mill	-	-	-	-	-	-	6"os	99
Kilgarriff	Aghamilla	-	corn & tuck	- roadside complex :	-	-	-	-	-	iaa/	AI3475 os135.2.4
Inishcarra	Agharinagh	-	mill pond	-	-	-	-	-	-	6"os	72
Inishcarra	Agharinagh	Greel Alfred	paper	-	35a.	-	-	-	-	gr/	-
Inishcarra	Agharinagh	- S/ Dripsey Lo.	paper	-	-	-	-	-	-	6"os	72
Aghern	Aghern West	-	corn	2 storey against slope	-	-	-	-	- 2 sandstone st.	iaa/	AI6261
Abbeymahon	Aghmanister	-	corn (in ruins)	- 5 sty roofless mill at	-	-	-	-	-	iaa/	AI3485 os136.2.5
Abbeymahon	Aghmanister	1/4m. long ex pond :	mill pond & race	-	-	-	-	-	-	6"os	136
Abbeymahon	Aghmanister	S/ Spittal Br.	Spittal Corn Mill	-	-	-	-	-	-	6"os	136
Fanlobus	Ahakeera	Neil Cornelius	corn	(1A) 23.6x18.6x11 :	-	-	-	1850	12x3.6x8.6 1 pair st.	hob/	5.0201
Kilgarrif	Ahgamilla	- Aghamilla Mills	corn	-	-	-	-	1841	-	6"os	135
Kilgarrif	Ahgamilla	Bandon Earl of	corn	-	-	-	Bandon E. - Parker Saville	1891	-	dd/	1891 21 190
Kilgarrif	Ahgamilla	Bandon Earl of	mill	-	-	-	Bandon E. - Guiness Henry	1885	-	dd/	1885 20 19
Kilgarrif	Ahgamilla	Bandon Earl of	mills	-	-	-	Bandon E. - Donoghue Jn	1885	-	dd/	1885 20 19
Kilgarrif	Ahgamilla	Bandon Earl of	mills	-	-	-	Bandon E. - Doherty Richd	1885	-	dd/	1885 51 96
Kilgarrif	Ahgamilla	Bernard Percy B	corn	-	-	-	Bernard P - Bandon Earl	1893	-	dd/	1893 23 71
Kilgarrif	Ahgamilla	Gillman Henry	mills	-	-	-	Gillman H - W. E. Life A Co	1886	-	dd/	1886 52 137
Kilgarrif	Ahgamilla	Gillman Henry	mills	-	-	-	Gillman H - WE Fire L As.C(	1886	-	dd/	1886 52 137
Kilgarrif	Ahgamilla	Pratt Robert	mills	-	-	-	Pratt R - W. E. Life A Co	1887	-	dd/	1887 54 271
Inishkenny	Ardarostig	Hallinan Timothy	mill & kiln	(1B) 64x28x39 :	-	30-8	-	1848	no information	hob/	5.0382
Inishteury	Ardarostig	Hanlon Timothy	flour & corn	-	-	-	-	-	42x5x37 5 pr st.	vmb/	4
Inishteury	Ardarostig	Logan William & John	mill	-	-	-	Logan W - Blackall Robt. :	1811	-	dd/	648 127 442562
Cork	Ardclare *	Wall	mill land	-	-	-	Wall & Sullivan	-	-	dd/	675 48 463746
Kilcatherine	Ardgroom	-	carding	- 3 bay single storey :	-	-	-	-	- wheel pit 1.65 m :	iaa/	AI3506 os102.6.2
Desertserges	Ardkitt	Bandon Earl of	mill	-	-	-	Bandon E. - Parker Saville	1891	-	dd/	1891 21 190
Desertserges	Ardkitt	Bandon Earl of	mill & land	-	-	-	Bandon E. - Guiness Henry	1885	-	dd/	1885 20 19
Desertserges	Ardkitt	Bernard Hon. Kath J	mill & land	-	-	-	Bernard K - Gaussen Wm	1885	-	dd/	85 26 114
Desertserges	Ardkitt	Bernard Kath F Hon.	mill & mill land	-	-	-	Bernard K - Gaussen Wm	1885	-	dd/	1885 26 114
Desertserges	Ardkitt	Bernard Percy B	mill	-	-	-	Bernard P - Bandon Earl of	1893	-	dd/	1893 23 71
Desertserges	Ardkitt	Pratt Robert	mill & mill land	-	-	-	Pratt Robert -Pratt Robert	1887	-	dd/	1887 54 271
Templeomalus	Arundelmills	-	hz wheeled	-	-	-	-	-	runner stone 0.82m :	iaa/	AI2725 os135.8.4
Templeomalus	Arundelmills	- N/ Ring Bridge	flour	-	-	-	-	-	-	6"os	135
Cork	Bailer	- on Owenboy R.	corn	in ruins - 1933	-	-	-	-	-	iaa/	AI6262
Tullylease	Ballagh	-	mill	-	-	-	-	-	-	1"os/	164
Liscleary	Ballea	-	corn	-	-	-	-	-	-	6"os	86
Liscleary	Ballea	Hewitt Thomas :	corn	-	-	20	-	1865	-	gr/-	Ld.Est.db
Kilnamanagh	Ballinacarriga	Vincent Arthur E.	mill & mill lands	-	-	-	Vincent A - Rucklet John	1889	-	dd/	1889 44 230
Clontead	Ballinacurra	- on Brinny R.	mill	-	-	-	-	-	-	1"os/	194
Ballinadee	Ballinadee	O`Brien John	flour	-	-	-	-	-	26x6x20	vmb/	4
Ballinadee	Ballinadee	O'Brine John	flour	(1C) 53x32x20 & :	-	-	-	-	26x6.6x20 50 bkts :	hob/	5.0182
Carrigrohane	Ballincollig	- S. side of R. Lee	Royal Gun Powder Mills		-	-	-	-	-	6"os	73
Carrigrohane	Ballincollig	Gunpowder Mills	powder	timber buildings rebuilt	-	22	Heritage Group	-	Visitor Centre & Exh.	pWEH	C
Carrigrohane	Ballincollig	Leslie Charles	powder	-	-	13	Tobin, Liverpool	-	2 incoprorating mills :	iaa/	AI9753 os73.11.1
Carrigrohane	Ballincollig	Tobin Thomas	gunpowder :	charge house & :	-	-	-	-	23x4x7 (9 of metal)	hob/	5.0693
Carrigrohane	Ballincollig	Tobin Thomas	gunpowder :	boiler ho : 11x13.6x6.6	-	-	-	-	-	hob/	5.0693
Carrigrohane	Ballincollig	Tobin Thomas	gunpowder :	office 24.0x21x18.6 & :	-	-	-	-	-	hob/	5.0693
Carrigrohane	Ballincollig	Tobin Thomas	gunpowder :	store, offices & :	-	-	-	-	-	hob/	5.0693

PARISH	TOWNLAND	MILLER	TYPE	HOUSE	Land	£Val+	PROPRIETORS	Date	WHEEL etc.	Record	Ref.
Carrigrohane	Ballincollig	Tobin Thomas	gunpowder :	sifting ho : 18x23.6x7 :	-	-	-	-	-	hob/	5.0693
Carrigrohane	Ballincollig	Tobin Thomas	gunpowder :	black mills : 73x23.6x18	-	-	-	-	-	hob/	5.0693
Carrigrohane	Ballincollig	Tobin Thomas	gunpowder :	offices, house & :	-	-	-	-	-	hob/	5.0693
Carrigrohane	Ballincollig	Tobin Thomas	gunpowder :	powder mills :	-	-	-	-	wheels metal of dia :	hob/	5.0693
Carrigrohane	Ballincollig	Tobin Thomas	gunpowder :	charge house :	-	-	-	-	-	hob/	5.0693
Carrigrohane	Ballincollig	Tobin Thomas	gunpowder :	office, magazine shed :	-	-	-	-	-	hob/	5.0693
Carrigrohane	Ballincollig	Tobin Thomas	match house	-	49a.	-	-	-	-	gr/	-
Carrigrohane	Ballincollig	Tobin Thomas		-	49a.	-	-	-	-	gr/	-
Carrigrohane	Ballincollig W.	-	milling complex	-	-	-	-	-	-	iaa/	AI6278
St. Annes Sh'n	Ballincrockig	- S. / Kilcully	iron mills	-	-	-	-	-	-	6"os	63
Rathcooney	Ballincroney	Daly James & Co.	barley	-	-	-	-	-	20x12x8	vmb/	4
Rathcooney	Ballincrossig	- at Springmount	flour	-	-	-	-	-	-	6"os	63
Rathcooney	Ballincrossig	Murray Maurice	corn	miller's house & land	6a.	67	-	1856	-	gr/	a.a.lre.ie
Ballydeloughy	Ballindangan	-	mill	-	-	-	-	-	-	1"os/	165
Kinalea bo.	Ballindeasig	-	mill (hz)	-	-	-		-	-	iaa/	AI 5155 os113.0.0
Ballymartke	Ballindresrough	Canty Johanna :	mill	-	-	-	Canty Jo - Keeffe Thos :	1813	-	dd/	669 185 462732
Ballymartke	Ballindresrough	Driscoll	mill	-	-	-	Driscoll - Canty	-	-	dd/	661 434 455671?
Ballymartke	Ballindresrough	Keller Daniel	flour	-	-	-	-	-	18x8x16	vmb/	4
Ballymartke	Ballindresrough	Meade Richard Rev.	mill	-	-	-	Meade R - Dricsoll James :	1811	-	dd/	630 347 435225
Ballymartke	Ballindresrough	- S/ Waterford Br.	flour	-	-	-	-	-	-	6"os	98
Caherlag	Ballinglanna	- on Glashboy R.	distillery	remains 3 & 4 sty blds.	-	-	-	-	-	iaa/	AI-6255
Kilcrumper	Ballinglanna	at Riverstown	distillery	-	-	-	-	-	-	6"os	75
Kilcrumper	Ballinglanna	Hoare Edward :	mills	-	-	-	Hoare Ed - Whiting John :	1711	-	dd/	10 363 3838
Kilcrumper	Ballinglanna	Moore	mills	-	-	-	Moore - Moore	-	-	dd/	31 454 19926?
Kilcrumper	Ballinglanna	Moore	mills	-	-	-	Moore - Coughlan	-	-	dd/	38 530 6369
Kilcrumper	Ballinglanna	Pomeroy	mills	-	-	-	Pomeroy - Pomeroy	-	-	dd/	55 231 36705
Kilcrumper	Ballinglanna	Newenham	mills	-	-	-	Newenham - Wallace	-	-	dd/	657 44? 45326?
Kilcrumper	Ballinglanna	S/ Glanmire Br.	flour	-	-	-	-	-	-	6"os	75
Kilcrumper	Ballinglanna N.	John Nunnan	tuck	-	-	-	-	-	10x2x13	vmb/	4
Kilcrumper	Ballinglen North	-	tuck	-	-	-	-	1841	-	6"os/	27
Kilcrumper	Ballinglen North	Noonan John	tuck mills	(3C) 23x21x5.6 :	-	3-13	-	1848	(2) 9.6x2.2 30 bkts. :	hob/	5.0341
Ballinaboy	Ballinhassig	Donigan James :	mill & tolls	-	-	-	Donigan J - Morgan Isaac :	1813	-	dd/	664 511 459029
Ballinaboy	Ballinhassig	Morgan	mill	-	-	-	Morgan - Sullivan	-	-	dd/	691 545 474932
Ballyfeard Pk	Ballinluig W.	-	milling complex	-	-	-		-	millstones still in situ	iaa/	AI6278
Ballyfeard Pk	Ballinluig W.	-	milling complex	-	-	-	-	-	-	pOPW/	(AI6278)
Ballyfeard Pk	Ballinluig W.	- at B'feard Vge.	flour	-	-	-	-	1841	-	6"os/	98
Ballyfeard Pk	Ballinluig W.	- at B'feard Vge.	tuck & carding	-	-	-	-	1841	-	6"os/	112
Ballyfeard Pk	Ballinluig W.	McDonnell Owen	corn	-	-	-	-	-	13x3x13	vmb/	4
Ballyfeard Pk	Ballinluig W.	McDonnell Owen	tuck	-	-	-	-	-	9x2x9	vmb/	4
Ballyfeard Pk	Ballinluig W.	McDonnell Owen	tuck	-	-	-	-	-	11x2x11	vmb/	4
Ballyfeard Pk	Ballinluig W.	McDonnell Owen	tuck & carding	-	-	-	-	-	9x2x9	vmb/	4
Rathcooney	Ballinrossig	Clancy Patrick :	barley	(1C) 99.6x25x35 :	-	-	-	1851	20x12x8.6 40 bkts.	hob/	5.0389
Kilnagross	Ballinrougher	-	Castleview Mill	-	-	-	-	-	-	1"os/	201
Kilnagross	Ballinrougher	-	corn	- 5 bay 5 storey mill	-	-	-	-	- originally housed :	iaa/	AI3486 os122.16.3
Kilnagross	Ballinrougher	Hayes James	flour	-	-	-	-	-	19x5x7	vmb/	4
Kilnagross	Ballinrougher	Hayes James	flour	-	-	-	-	-	16x6x7	vmb/	4
Kilnagross	Ballinrougher	Hayes Jayes	part of	17.6x24.6x24.0 & :	-	-	-	-	no dimensions	hob/	5.0256
Kilnagross	Ballinrougher	on Arggideen R.	Castleview Flour	-	-	-	-	-	-	6"os	122
Ringrone	Ballinspittle		corn	-	-	-	-	-	-	6"os	124
St Finbar`s	Ballintemple	-	flour	-	-	-	-	-	-	1"os/	187
Ardagh	Ballinteosig	NNW/ Inch Vge.	tuck	-	-	-	-	-	-	6"os	55
Inishkenny	Ballinveiltig		corn	-	-	-	-	-	-	6"os	85

PARISH	TOWNLAND	MILLER	TYPE	HOUSE	Land	£Val+	PROPRIETORS	Date	WHEEL etc.	Record	Ref.
Inishkenny	Ballinveiltig		tuck	-	-	-	-	-	-	6"os	85
Castletownroche	Ballinvoher	-	mile race	-	-	-	-	-	-	6"os	26
Castletownroche	Ballinvoher	-	mill (hz)	- (remains)	-	-	-	-	-	iia/	IA5151 os88.0.0
Castletownroche	Ballinvoher	- S/ Anne's Grove	old mill ruins	-	-	-	-	-	-	6"os	26
Castletownroche	Ballyadeen	1/10m S/ Tn Bridge	flour	-	-	-	-	-	-	6"os	26
Castletownroche	Ballyadeen	Webb Robert	flour	(1B) 90.6x24x42.6 :	-	85	-	1849	impulse 10x10x - :	hob	5.2466
Carrigaline	Ballybrack	Lane James Rev.	mill	-	-	-	Lane Jas - Keane Daniel	1888	-	dd/	1888 49 170
Carrigaline	Ballybrack	Whity Mr	flour	-	-	-	-	-	22x7x19 erecting :	vmb/	4
Carrigaline	Ballybrack		flour	-	-	-	-	-	-	6"os	74
Ballyclogh	Ballyclogh	-	corn mill	-	-	-	-	-	-	6"os	24
Ballyclogh	Ballyclogh	-	flour	-	-	-	-	-	-	6"os	24
Ballyclogh	Ballyclogh	-	thrashing mill	-	-	-	-	-	-	6"os	27
Cloyne	Ballycroneen	-	mill	-	-	-	-	-	-	6"os/	1xx
Cloyne	Ballycroneen	Dillon Henry	mill	-	-	-	Dillon Henry - Boyd Chas	1886	-	dd/	1886 10 91
Cloyne	Ballycroneen	Longfield Mountford :	mill	-	-	-	Longfield M - his Heir :	1811	Deed Poll	dd/	639 65 438396
Cloyne	Ballycroneen	Longfield Robert Rev.:	mill	-	-	-	Longfield R - Hugo Cherry :	1813	-	dd/	638 299 441576
Cloyne	Ballycroneen	Regan Edward :	mill	-	-	-	Regan ED - Longfield :	1811	-	dd/	637 324 438640
Cloyne	Ballycroneen	Rochfort Boyd Chas	mill	-	-	-	Rochfort B C - Dillon Henry	1889	-	dd/	1889 18 36
Donaghmore	Ballycunningham	Mill ford	(no mill)	-	-	-	-	-	-	6"os	61
Carrigtohill	Ballycureen	White Edmond	corn	house, offices & land	1.0.1(	7.10.	-	1856	-	gr/	a.a.lol.ie
Carrigtohill	Ballycureen		Glenmore Paper Mill		-	-	-	-	-	6"os	64
St Finbars	Ballycurreen	Kiereen	mill	-	-	-	Kiereen- Joiners & Carps.	-	-	dd/	48 434 26668
Kilcrumper	Ballyderown	Elizabeth Higgins	factory	-	-	-	-	-	16x6x4	vmb/	4
Kilcrumper	Ballyderown	Higgins Elizabeth	wv factory	(2B) 63x18x16 :	-	23-16	-	1848	wooden 18x6 :	hob/	5.0341
Kilcrumper	Ballyderown	N/ Araglin Br	woollen factory	-	-	-	-	-	-	6"os	28
Monanimy	Ballyduff	-	carding & tuck	-	-	-	-	1841	-	6"os/	34
Monanimy	Ballyduff	- stream to B'water	cloth	-	-	-	-	-	10x2.10x - 46 bkts.	hob/	5.0462
Monanimy	Ballyduff	Connor Cornelius	carding, tuck & :	-	-	-	-	-	10x2.10x - 46 bkts.	hob/	5.0462
Cork	Ballydulogher *	Hardman	mill	-	-	-	Hardman - Piersy	-	-	dd/	49 530 332???
Cloyne	Ballyfeard	Irwin	mills	-	-	-	-	1841	-	6"os/	34
Carrigaline	Ballygarvan	Gillman James :	mills	-	-	-	Gillman J - Dennett Elenor :	1814	-	dd/	668 343 464758
Carrigaline	Ballygarvan	Hains Charles :	mills	-	-	-	Haynes C- Ballard John :	1810	-	dd/	638 26 463338
Carrigaline	Ballygarvan	Harris William :	mills	-	-	-	Harris W - Reynolds Benj :	1810	-	dd/	637 102 434299
Carrigaline	Ballygarvan	Montgomery John :	mills	-	-	-	Montgomery J - Sinnick Jn :	1813	-	dd/	662 589 458057
Carrigaline	Ballygarvan	Shimmick John, Miller	bolting & corn	-	-	-	Shimmick - Montg'mry Jn :	1812	-	dd/	645 135 442194
Carrigaline	Ballygarvan	Shimmick Yahine	mills	- mill stream & land	7a.	-	Shimmick Y - Casey Thos :	1812	Mort.15 Jan.	dd/	644 221 442212
Carrigaline	Ballygarvan	Sinnich	mills	-	-	-	Sinnich - Lane	-	?	dd/	664 91 459006
Carrigaline	Ballygarvan	Sinnich Jno :	mills	-	-	-	Sinnich Jn - Carroll John :	1813	Mort. - Sept	dd/	665 95 458062
Carrigaline	Ballygarvan	Sinnich John :	mills	-	-	-	Sinnick J - Casey Thos :	1810	Mort. 8 Feb.	dd/	618 252 424560
Carrigaline	Ballygarvan	Sinnick John :	mills	-	-	-	Sinnick J - Lane Maurice :	1813	Mort. 1 Oct.	dd/	662 589 458056
Cork	Ballygeoganeigy	Gould	mill	-	-	-	Gould - Gould	-	-	dd/	76 401 55048
Castlet`nroche	Ballygrillihan	- at Glenmore	mill	-	-	-	-	-	-	1"os/	176
Fanlobus	Brook Park :	Cox	mill	-	-	-	Cox - Evans	-	-	dd/	59 350 40849
Knockavilly	Ballyhandle	Holland William	corn	-	-	-	-	-	9x2x9 overshot	vmb/	4
Ballymodan	Ballylangley	3/4m E/ Bridge	Alllman's distillery	-	-	-	-	-	-	6"os	110
Monanimy	Ballymacmoy	-	mill pond	-	-	-	-	-	-	6"os	34
Monanimy	Ballymacmoy	E/ Town Bridge	corn mill	-	-	-	-	-	-	6"os	34
Monanimy	Ballymacmoy	Foote B.	flour	(1C) 53.6x29x43.6 :	-	-	-	-	22x6x22 bkts. 56 :	hob/	5.0462
Killathy	Ballymacphilip	-	mill	-	-	-	-	-	-	1"os/	176
Cork	Ballymahane	- on Sall R.	mill	-	-	-	-	-	-	1"os/	194
Caherduggan	Ballymee	-	tuck	-	-	-	-	-	-	6"os	17
Caherduggan	Ballymee	Carney John	corn	(1C) 36x22.6x15	-	5.0.0	-	1850	13x4x - 36 floats :	hob/	5.0438

PARISH	TOWNLAND	MILLER	TYPE	HOUSE	Land	£Val+	PROPRIETORS	Date	WHEEL etc.	Record	Ref.
Caherduggan	Ballymee	S./ R. Awbeg	tuck	-	-	-	-	-	-	6"os	17
Kilnamanagh	Ballynacarrigga	Gillman Edward :	mill	-	-	-	Gillman E - Heazle John :	1814	-	dd/	669 164 461828
Kilnamanagh	Ballynacarrigga	Holmes Francis :	mill	-	-	-	Holmes F - Joye Windpear :	1812	Mort. 29 Jan.	dd/	638 561 444362
Aghada	Ballynafarsid	- on mud Farsid Vge.	flour	-	-	-	-	-	-	6"os	88
St Nathlash	Ballynahalisk	S/ Funshion R.	Rockmills	-	-	-	-	-	-	6"os	18
St Nathlash	Ballynahallisk	Lyster Philip	flour	Old pt. (1C) 55x27.6x43	-	-	-	-	22x16.6x6.6 floats :	hob/	5.0467
Dungourney	Ballynona South		flour mill ruins	-	-	-	-	-	-	6"os	66
Rathcoony	Ballyphilip	- near Sallybrook	woollen	-	-	-	-	-	-	1"os/	187
Killeenemer	Ballyquane	Kelliher Denis	flour	(1B) 24x19x17 & :	-	-	-	-	11.9x5.6x - impeller :	hob/	5.0449
Killeenemer	Ballyquane	S/ Glanworth Br.	flour	-	-	-	-	-	-	6"os	27
Ballintemple	Ballyrobin	Dillon Henry	mill	-	-	-	Dillon Henry - Boyd Chas	1886	-	dd/	1886 10 91
Kilbrin	Ballyrusheen	Lane	paper	-	-	-	Lane - Browne	-	-	dd/	674 59 463736
Kilbrin	Ballyrusheen	Lane Richard :	paper	-	-	-	Lane R - Browne Frances:	1813	-	dd/	674 59 463736
Kilbrin	Ballyrusheen :	Lavitt	mill	-	-	-	Lavitt - Bond	-	-	dd/	40 356 27273
Kilbrin	Ballyrusheen :	-	mill	-	-	-	Bond - Delahoide	-	-	dd/	64 407 444411
Cloyne	Ballyrussell	Irwin	mill	-	-	-	Irwin - Irwin	-	-	dd/	37 167 21701
Cloyne	Ballyrussell	Irwin	mill	-	-	-	Irwin - St Ledger	-	-	dd/	39 290 25327
Cloyne	Ballyrussell	Irwin John :	mill	-	-	-	Irwin Jn - Knox William :	1722	-	dd/	35 204 21985
Farahy	Ballyshonuck	1/4m. NW/ Farahay Br	corn	-	-	-	-	-	-	6"os	18
Ballydeloher	Ballyvisteale Dem.		paper	-	-	-	-	-	-	6"os	64
Ballydeloher	Ballyvisteale Dem.		paper	-	-	-	-	-	-	6"os	64
St Anne`s	Ballyvolane	Callaghan David	corn	-	-	-	-	-	27x6x23	vmb/	4
St Anne`s	Ballyvolane	Callaghan David	malt	-	-	-	-	-	14x5x15	vmb/	4
St Anne`s	Ballyvolane	E/ Dublin St.	Glen distillery	-	-	-	-	-	-	6"os	74
St Anne`s	Ballyvolane	Lambert William	corn	-	-	-	-	-	16x5x16	vmb/	4
St Annes :	Ballyvolane	Lambert William	flour & corn	(1A) 33x20.6x20.6	-	17-4	-	-	10x3.6x12 30 bkts.	hob/	5.0393
St Anne`s	Ballyvolane	Lambert William	iron	-	-	-	-	-	10x3x12	vmb/	4
St Anne`s	Ballyvolane	Murphy Denis	corn	-	-	-	-	-	22x5x19	vmb/	4
St Anne`s	Ballyvolane	Murphy Denis	corn	-	-	-	-	-	16x5x16	vmb/	4
St Annes :	Ballyvolane	Perrot John Esq.	mill & kiln	(1B) 64x33x44 :	-	25-17	-	1850	west mill 3 pr.st. :	hob/	5.0392
St Annes :	Ballyvolane	Perrot John Esq.	mill & kiln	(1B) 64x33x44 :	-	25-17	-	1850	west mill 3 pr.st. :	hob/	5.0392
St Annes :	Ballyvolane	Power John	mills	(1B) 24x21.6x17 :	-	-	-	-	-	hob/	5.0392
St Annes :	Ballyvolane	Power John	mills	(1B) 24x21.6x17 :	-	-	-	-	-	hob/	5.0392
St Annes :	Ballyvolane	Power John	mills etc.	kiln (1B) 21.6x28x39 :	-	-	-	-	-	hob/	5.0392
St Annes :	Ballyvolane	Power John	mills etc.	kiln (1B) 21.6x28x39 :	-	-	-	-	-	hob/	5.0392
St Annes :	Ballyvolane	Shaw Joseph	mills	dw. (1B) 46.6x32x21:	-	-	-	-	-	hob/	5.0392
St Annes :	Ballyvolane	Shaw Joseph	mills	dw. (1B) 46.6x32x21:	-	-	-	-	-	hob/	5.0392
St Anne`s	Ballyvolane		iron works	-	-	-	-	-	-	6"os	74
St Anne`s	Ballyvolane		malt & kiln	-	-	-	-	-	-	6"os	74
St Anne`s	Ballyvolane		malt & pond	-	-	-	-	-	-	6"os	74
St Anne`s	Ballyvolane		mill pond	-	-	-	-	-	-	6"os	74
Tullagh	Baltimore	on coast	corn store	-	-	-	-	-	-	6"os	150
Kinalmeaky	Bandon	Allman Richd Lord	distillery	-	-	-	Allman R Ld - Ire. Bk Govs.	1887	-	dd/	1887 34 61
Ballymodan	Bandon	Biggs Chris :	Bandon R. Mills	-	-	-	Biggs C - Biggs William :	1814	Conv. 8 May	dd/	678 87 466834
Ballymodan	Bandon	Payne Thomas W	Bandon Mills	-	-	-	Payne Thos - Warren Mary	1889	-	dd/	1889 2 90
Ballymodan	Bandon	Shaw William	mills & land	-	-	-	Shaw Wm - Allman Richd	1885	-	dd/	1885 33 59
Kinalmeaky	Bandon Town	Allman Richard	Watergate Bewery	-	-	-	Allman R - Ireland Bk Govs	1887	-	dd/	1887 34 61
Kinalmeaky	Bandon Town	Clerke Mary J	Watergate Bewery	-	-	-	Clerke M - Bird Kate R	1886	-	dd/	1886 31 74
Kinalmeaky	Bandon Town	Clerke Mary J	Watergate Bewery	-	-	-	Clerke M - Payne Somers H	1887	-	dd/	1887 44 147
Kinalmeaky	Bandon Town	Lee Samuel G	Bandon Steam :	-	-	-	Lee Samuel - Shaw Wm	1885	-	dd/	1885 39 271`
Kinalmeaky	Bandon Town :	Crowley Timothy J.	wheatmeal :	-	-	-	-	1963	-	lic/6	wheat
Ballymodan	Bandon Town :	Moore Mary	corn-store	-	-	12	-	-	-	gr/	a.a.Ire.ie

PARISH	TOWNLAND	MILLER	TYPE	HOUSE	Land	£Val+	PROPRIETORS	Date	WHEEL etc.	Record	Ref.
Kinalmeaky	Bandon Town :	Stanley Joseph	soap factory	(1B) 15x12x12.6 :	-	17	-	-	-	hob/	5.2454
Kinalmeaky	Bandon Town :	Stanley Joseph	soap factory	(1B) 15x12x12.6 :	-	17	-	-	-	hob/	5.2454
Kinalmeaky	Bandon Town :	Hurley John	brewery	(1B) 18.6x51x9.6 :	-	39	-	-	-	hob/	5.2454
Kinalmeaky	Bandon Town :	Scott Robert	steam	(1B) 59.6x22.6x26.6 :	-	18	-	-	-	hob/	5.2454
Kinalmeaky	Bandon Town :	Hurley Johanna	brewery	(1B) 76x26.6x20 :	-	47	-	-		hob/	5.2455
Kinalmeaky	Bandon Town :	Sweeny Fran Bern	flour	(1B) 52x20x40.6 :	-	47	-	-	13x5.4 & 35x5x36 :	hob/	5.2455
Kinalmeaky	Bandon Town :	McDonnell William	brewery	(1A) 32x19.6x21 :	-	24	-	-	-	hob/	5.2455
Ballymodan	Bandon Town :	Biggs Jacob	mills (new, old)	(1B) 69x24x42 :	-	58	-	-	18x12x6 & 12.6x7.6 :	hob/	5.2456
Ballymodan	Bandon Town :	Hamilton James	kiln & stores	offices & timber yard	-	30	-	1856	-	gr/	a.a.Ire.ie
Ballymodan	Bandon Town :	Heazle Henry	indigo	(1B) 22x24x14 :	-	26	-	-	9.6x3.6x3.6	hob/	5.2454
Kilmocomoge	Bantry	Glenlough :	-	-	-	-	-	-	Pelton avg. 2.5kw	turb/	c1947
Kilmocomoge	Bantry	Owenbeg Nat. Pr. Co.	printing	-	-	-	-	-	Twin Pelton avg. :	turb/	c1947
Kilmocomoge	Bantry T`plots	-	hz wheeled mill	-	-	-	-	-	hz wheel - descr. :	iaa/	AI2724 os110.0.0
Kilmocomoge	Bantry Town :	Biggs & Co Ltd.	flour	-	-	-	-	1963	- <1,000 barrels	lic/3	wh.meal
Kilmocomoge	Bantry Town Lots		flour	-	-	-	-	-	-	6"os	118
Rathclarin	Barleyfield	-	corn	- 4 bay 3 storey mill :	-	-	-	-	-	iaa/	AI3847 os123.4.4
Rathclarin	Barleyfield	- NNW B'field Br.	flour & pond	-	-	-	-	1841	-	6"os/	123
Rathclarin	Barleyfield	Sealy Elizabeth	flour	-	-	-	-	-	15x8x15	vmb/	4
Kilmaloda	Barrane	Leary Patrick	grist	-	-	-	-	-	15x3x15	vmb/	4
Caheragh	Bauravilla	-	tuck	-	-	-	-	-	-	1"os/	200
Kilbrittain	Baurleigh	Moore Walter B	corn	house, offs. & land	132a.	57.5.	-	1856	-	gr/	a.a.Ire.ie
Dromdaleague	Baurnahulla	Robbinson George	flax	39.0x24.6x17.6 - burnt	-	-	-	-	16x4x11 1 breaker	hob/	5.0291
Dromdaleague	Baurnahulla	Robinson George	corn	29.0x20.0x21	-	-	-	-	18.6x4x10 2 pr st.	hob/	5.0291
Cork	Bawneskertane	Mountcashell Lord	manor mills	-	-	-	Mountcashell Ld - Heir :	1813	-	dd/	664 255 457453
Macroom	Bealick	-	corn	14m x 20m 4 storey		-		-	-	pOPW	(AI9743)
Macroom	Bealick	-	tuck	- not surviving	-	-	-	-	- on same mill-race	iaa/	AI9743 0s71.5.5
Macroom	Bealick	- N side R. Laney	Bealick Mills	-	-	-	-	1841	-	6"os	71
Macroom	Bealick	- N side R. Laney	tuck	-	-	-	-	-	-	iaa/	AI9743 0s71.5.5
Macroom	Bealick	Bandon Earl of	mills	-	-	-	Bandon E. - Doherty Richd	1885	-	dd/	85 51 96
Macroom	Bealick	Hardings of Firville	corn	14m x 20m 4 storey :	-	-	-	1841	-	6"os	71
Kilnagross	Beanhill S.	-	corn	- Shannon Vale Mill :	-	-	-	-	- breast shot wheel	iaa/	AI3488 os122.15.5
Rathcormack	Behernagh Lower	-	mill race 1/2 mile	-	-	-	-	-	-	6"os	44
Rathcormack	Behernagh Lower	1/4m S/ Bridge	tuck	-	-	-	-	-	-	6"os	44
Rathcormack	Behernagh Lower	S/ Glanragh Br.	carding	-	-	-	-	-	-	6"os	44
Moviddy	Bellmount Lower	-	corn	Bellmount Mills original	-	-	-	-	26ft x 7ft & 2 pr st. :	iaa/	AI9744 os83.12.2
Moviddy	Bellmount Lower	SW/ Crookstown Vg.	Bellmount Mills	-	-	-	-	-	-	6"os	83
St Finbar`s	Bishop's-mill-lands	Jennings Thomas	chemical works	offices & land	19a.	104	-	1856	-	gr/	a.a.Ire.ie
St Finbar`s	Bishop's-mill-lands	Mahoney Daniel	corn & flour	-	-	-	-	-	16x5x15	vmb/	4
St Finbar`s	Bishop's-mill-lands	- NW/ Glasheen Br.	Brookfield Chemical Works		-	-	-	-	-	6"os	74
St Finbar`s	Bishop's-mill-lands	- S/ Wellington Br.	-		-	-	-	-	-	6"os	74
St Finbar`s	Bishop's-mill-lands	Mahoney Daniel	woollen	-	-	-	-	-	-	vmb/	4
Garrycloyne	Blarney	Collins Jeremiah :	mills	-	-	-	Collins J - Austen Samuel :	1810	-	dd/	620 409 425749
Garrycloyne	Blarney	Lynch -	mills	-	-	-	Lynch - Davies	-	?	dd/	607 250 423320
Garrycloyne	Blarney	Mahony Thomas M	corn	(1A) 26x40x33 & :	-	8.8	-	1851	2 wheels dr. all mills :	hob/	5.2443
Garrycloyne	Blarney	Mahony Thomas M	cotton	(1A) 50x26x33 & :	-	-	-	1851	-	hob/	5.2443
Garrycloyne	Blarney	Mahony Thomas M	woollen factory	(1B) 85x28x36 & :	-	-	-	1851	3 scribblers & :	hob/	5.2443
Garrycloyne	Blarney	Mahony Thomas M	worsted factory	-	-	-	-	1851	4 coming machines :	hob/	5.2443
Garrycloyne	Blarney	Sullivan Jas Bart :	mills	-	-	-	Sullivan J - Towgood Matt :	1809	-	dd/	617 334 423398
Garrycloyne	Blarney	Willison Samuel :	mills	-	-	-	Willison S - Buckley Daniel	1809	-	dd/	617 256 423319
Kilbritain ?	bo./ Ballymore	Lawe /Alexander W	Upper Mill	-	-	-	Lawe A - Arnott John Sir	1890	-	dd/	1890 28 124
Kilbritain ?	bo./ Barrymore	Hudson Henry	old mills	-	-	-	Hudson H - Kindham Edwd	1886	-	dd/	1886 42 177
Kilbritain ?	bo./ Barrymore	Newenham Edward	Upper Mills	-	-	-	Newenham E - Mayne Sara	1887	-	dd/	1887 48 198

PARISH	TOWNLAND	MILLER	TYPE	HOUSE	Land	£Val+	PROPRIETORS	Date	WHEEL etc.	Record	Ref.
Kilbritain ?	bo./ Carberry EW	Lupton Mary	East Mill	-	-	-	Lupton M - Hennessy Danl	1885	-	dd/	1885 46 209
Kilbritain ?	Bonnybrook	Ireland Bank Govs.	mill	-	-	-	I B Gvs. - Morrogh Bros Co	1889	-	dd/	1889 56 120
Cork	Boulapatrick *	O`Sullivan Bart :	mills	-	-	-	O`Sullivan - Towgood Matt :	1810	-	dd/	617 325 423399
Cork	Boulapatrick *	Towgood Matthew :	mills	-	-	-	Towgood - Williams Robt :	1817	Mort. 15 May	dd/	721 254 492789
Kilmocomoge	Breeny More	-	hz wheeled mill	-	-	-	-	-	hz wheel - found :	iaa/	AI2717 os106.0.0
Castlelions	Bridebridge Tn	Dowling Patrick	flour	(1B) 81x23x27 & :	-	-	-	1852	u`shot 18x6x - :	hob	5.2460
Ardnageehy	Bridestown	SSE / Glanragh br.	old paper mill	-	-	-	-	-	-	6"os	44
Brigtown	Brigown	Mitchellstown :	old brewery & :	-	-	-	-	1841	-	6"os	19
Brigown	Brigown	Mitchellstown :	corn (didused)	-	-	-	-	1888	-	25"os	19.04
Brinny	Brinny	-	corn	4 storey L shaped	-	-	-	-	-	iaa/	AI6264
Brinny	Brinny	- on Brinny R.	mill	-	-	-	-	-	-	1"os/	194
Ballydeloher	Brookhill		spade factory	-	-	-	-	-	-	6"os	64
Ballydeloher	Brooklodge Up	SE/ Brook Lodge Vge.	paper	-	-	-	-	-	-	6"os	64
Middleton	Broomfield	Carden John	woollen	(1A) 50x30x29	-	15	-	-	18x7.4x11.6 :	hob/	5.0546
Middleton	Broomfield	Hackett Bart. James	flour	ho, offs, mill & store	-	-	-	-	-	hob/	5.0546
Middleton	Broomfield West	E/ Owenacurra R.	large distillery	-	-	-	-	-	-	6"os	76
Middleton	Broomfield West	O`Donohoe Mrs	distillery (idle:) :	(1C) 83x37x38 & :	-	-	-	-	new 18x7x12.6	hob/	5.0550
Ringcurran	Brownsmills	Kearney T (Reps.)	mills	-	-	14.10.		-	-	gr/-	Ld.Est.db
Ringcurran	Brownsmills	-	mill complex	-	-	-	part conv. into apartments	2011	-	Sv/-	Ld.Est.db
Ringcurran	Brownsmills	Donnan	mills	-	-	-	Donnan - Regan	-	?	dd/	625 *** 434818
Ringcurran	Brownsmills		Brown's Mills	-	-	-	-	-	-	6"os	112
Caheragh	Bunalunn	-	mill	Hollybrook Mill :	-	-	-	-	- wheelpit 1.7 m.	iaa/	AI3517 os141.4.1
Caheragh	Bunalunn	-	old mill	-	-	-	-	1841	-	6"os/	132
Ross	Burgatia	-	mill	-	-	-	-	-	-	1"os/	200
Ross	Burgatia	Morrogue Henry	flour	30x26x35 40x26.6x35 :	-	-	-	-	24x6x20 4 pr st. :	hob/	5.0248
Ross	Burgatia		mill pond	-	-	-	-	-	-	6"os	143
Ross	Burgatia		Millfield House	-	-	-	-	-	-	6"os	143
Ross	Burgatia		Ross Mill	-	-	-	-	-	-	6"os	143
Kilmaloda	Burrane	Earl Barrymore	mill	-	-	-	Barrymore - Barry	-	-	dd/	91 165 63821
Kilmaloda	Burrane	Earl Barrymore	mill	-	-	-	Barrymore - Gleadon	-	-	dd/	94 120 65583
Cork	Burranness	Moore Emanuel :	mill				Moore E - Phillips William	1810	-	dd/	610 451 427911
Ballydeloher	Butlerstown Gt.	E/ Butlerstown Br.	paper	-	-	-	-	-	-	6"os	64
Ballydeloher	Butlerstown Gt.	W/ Butlerstown Br.	spade factory	-	-	-	-	-	-	6"os	64
St Anne's :	Cahergal	- NW of City	old sailcloth factory		-	-	-	-	-	6"os	74
St Anne's :	Cahergal	Shaw Joseph	flour	(1C) 61x29x21.6 :	-	12-18	-	1850	-	hob/	5.0393
St Anne's :	Cahergal	Shea Joseph	flour & corn	-	1.1.2‹	31	-	1856	-	gr/	a.a.lre.ie
Kilnamanagh	Caminches	N/ Ballydonegan R.	stamp mill	-	-	-	-	-	-	6"os	114
Kilnamanagh	Caminches	N/ Ballydonegan R.	stamp mill	-	-	-	-	-	-	6"os	114
Kilnamanagh	Caminches	N/ Ballydonegan R.	stamp mill	-	-	-	-	-	-	6"os	114
Kilmoe	Cannawe	nr Blowing sands	inlet & river	-	-	-	-	-	╡ x╝m,tidal, chanel :	6"os	147
Skull	Cappaghglass	Capppagh	Copper Mine	-	-	-	-	-	-	6"os	140
Skull	Cappaghglass		engine shaft	-	-	-	-	-	-	6"os	140
Clondulane	Careysville	Carey Edward	corn	Ho., offs., gate-lo., land	270a.	407	-	1856	-	gr/	a.a.lre.ie
Clondulane	Careysville	Carey Edward	corn	-	-	-		-	20x3x20	vmb/	4
Cork	Carignamuck (2)	-	woollen	- large mill complex	-	-	O`Shaughnessy	1903	- electrified 1950s	iaa/	AI9751 os72.3.1
Doneraile	Carker	Barry rps Redmond	flour	(1C) 48x21x24 & ret. :	-	12.4	-	-	13.7x3x8 48 bkts :	hob/	5.0448
Doneraile	Carkerk North	N. / Ogeen River	old mill	-	-	-	-	-	-	6"os	17
Templequinlan	Carrig	- on Ardigeen R.	saw	-	-	-	-	-	-	1"os/	210
Templequinlan	Carrig	E/ Lisselane Br	Carrig Mills	-	-	-	-	-	-	6"os	122
Templequinlan	Carrig	Leary John	corn	25.0x17.0x11 & :	-	-	-	-	12x2.6 overshot	hob/	5.0255
Templequinlan	Carrig	Leary John	corn & tuck mills	house, offs. & land	17a.	16	- (+ tenant's house)	1856	-	gr/	a.a.lre.ie
Templequinlan	Carrig	Leary John	grist	-	-	-	-	-	12x2x12	vmb/	4

PARISH	TOWNLAND	MILLER	TYPE	HOUSE	Land	£Val+	PROPRIETORS	Date	WHEEL etc.	Record	Ref.
Templequinlan	Carrig	Leary John	tuck	18.6x16.6x6.6	-	-	-	-	12x2.2	hob/	5.0255
Templequinlan	Carrig	Leary John	tuck	-	-	-	-	-	12x2x12	vmb/	4
Templequinlan	Carrig	NE/ Carrigboy Br.	mill	-	-	-	-	-	-	6"os	131
Macroom	Carrigagulla	Creed John	mill	-	-	-	Creed John - Sullivan Mary	1889	-	dd/	1889 38 46
Macroom	Carrigagulla	Horgan Timothy O`C	corn	-	-	-	-	-	16x6x20	vmb/	4
Carrigaline	Carrigaline West	Roberts Michael	mill	- Carrigaline Mill	-	100	-	-	-	gr/-	Ld.Est.db
Carrigaline	Carrigaline West	-	mill	-	-	-	-	1910	- demolished	Sv/-	Ld.Est.db
Carrigaline	Carrigaline Middle	NxE/ Carrigaline Br.	flour	-	-	-	-	-	-	6"os	87
Carrigaline	Carrigaline West	NW/ Carrigaline Br.	flour mills	-	-	-	-	-	-	6"os	87
Carrigaline	Carrigaline West	on Owenboy R.	sluice gate & weir		-	-	-	-	-	6"os	87
Aghinagh	Carriganish	E/ Glashagarrif R.	site of mill	-	-	-	-	-	-	6"os	60
Kilmacabea	Carrigbaun	on Saivnose R.	tuck	-	-	-	-	-	-	6"os	133
Kilmacabea	Carrigbaun	Regan John	corn	49.0x16.0x8.6 & :	-	-	-	-	13x2.6x7	hob/	5.0285
Kilmacabea	Carrigbaun	Regan John	tuck	-	-	-	-	-	10x2.3x7	hob/	5.0285
Kilmocomoge	Carrigboy	-	corn	10m x 6.75m roofless :	-	-	-	-	- wheel pit on east :	iaa/	AI3889 os131.5.1
Kilmocomoge	Carrigboy	in Durus on W. bank	corn	rect. building roofless	-	-	-	1902	-	iaa/	Ck/3513
Kilmocomoge	Carrigboy	Sullivan John	corn	38.0x18.6x10	-	-	-	-	11x3.2 overshot	hob/	5.0292
Kilmocomoge	Carrigboy	Sullivan John	tuck	-	-	-	-	-	11x2.9 overshot	hob/	5.0292
Clonfert	Carrigcastle	opp. Castle	cloth	-	-	-	-	-	-	6"os	14
St. Mary's Sh'n	Carrignaveagh	Wise's Quay	distillery	-	-	-	-	-	-	6"os	74
St. Mary's Sh'n	Carrignaveagh	Wise's Quay	malt	-	-	-	-	-	-	6"os	74
Carrigrohan	Carrigrohan	McSweeny Aug.	flour	-	-	-	-	-	20x10x4 7 pr st.	vmb/	4
Carrigrohan	Carrigrohan	W/ Carrigrohan Castle	Water Gate Flour Mills		-	-	-	-	-	6"os	73
Castlehaven	Carrigtishane	-	corn	- Rineen Corn Mill :	-	-	-	-	-	iaa/	AI3490 os142.10.6
Castlehaven	Carrigtishane	at Rinneen estuary	Rinneen Mills	-	-	-	-	1841	-	6"os	142
Castlehaven	Carrigtishane	McNamarra Goold & :	flour	55.6x28x46 & :	-	-	-	-	41x5.6x34 4 pr st.	hob/	5.0247
Island	Cashelisky	-	mill	-	-	-	-	-	-	1"os/	201
Cork	Castledodde *	Fitzgerald	mill	-	-	-	Fitzgerald - Lord Mountjoy	-	-	dd/	85 41 58956
Cork	Castledodde *	Stephens	mill	-	-	-	Stephens - Coghill	-	-	dd/	85 71 59091
Cork	Castlefreeke	-	hz wheeled mill	-	-	-	-	-	hz wheel - found :	iaa/	AI2718
Buttevant	Castleland	LLoyd George	mills	-	-	-	Lloyd Geo - Oliver Richard	1885	-	dd/	1885 31 14
Buttevant	Castle-land	Browning David R	corn	-	-	-	-	-	16x - x10	vmb/	4
Buttevant	Castle-land	Browning David R	flour	-	-	-	-	-	20x - x9	vmb/	4
Buttevant	Castle-land	S./ R. Awbeg	corn	-	-	-	-	-	-	6"os	17
Buttevant	Castleland :	-	corn	-	-	-	-	1841	-	6"os	17
Kinneigh	Castlelands	due N/ bridge	paper	-	-	-	-	-	-	6"os	109
Kinneigh	Castlelands	N side Bandon R.	corn	-	-	-	-	-	-	6"os	109
Templemartin	Castlenalact	N/ Keye's Br.	corn	-	-	-	-	-	-	6"os	96
Templemartin	Castlenalact		tuck	-	-	-	-	-	-	6"os	96
Templemartin	Castlenalact		tuck	-	-	-	-	-	-	6"os	96
Templemartin	Castlenalact (2)	-	corn & tuck	- mill complex roadside	-	-	-	-	- wheelpit 3m wide	iaa/	AI3476 os96.11.1
Castlehaven	Castletownsend	on coast	corn store	-	-	-	-	-	-	6"os	142
Carrigaline	Castletrasna	Besuard Mr	rope walk	-	-	-	-	-	20x4x18	vmb/	4
Castletownroche	Castlewidenham	-	flour	-	-	-	-	-	-	6"os	26
Castletownroche	Castlewidenham	Smith John	flour	(1B) 46.6x28.6x46.9 :	-	-	-	-	impeller 10.4x6.11 :	hob	5.2466
Athnowen	Clashanure	-	corn (disused)	12m x 8.54m 3 bay :	-	-	-	-	-	iaa/	AI9745 os72.8.4
Athnowen	Clashanure	-	mill	7.93m x 5.15m 2 storey	-	-	-	-	-	iaa/	AI9742 os72.8.4
Athnowen	Clashanure	Allen Kyree & Co.	corn	40.6x20.0x30.0 & kiln	-	-	-	-	30x2.6x -	hob/	5.0699
Inchinabacky	Clashduff		Ballynona Flour Mill		-	-	-	-	-	6"os	76
Rathrogan	Clashganniv	Ball Valentine	Castledod Mill	-	-	-	Ball Valentine - Rel.	1887	-	dd/	1887 36 136
Rathrogan	Clashganniv	Harrison Christina	Castledod Mill	-	-	-	Harrison - O`Sh`nessy Wm	1886	-	dd/	1886 21 234
Rathrogan	Clashganniv	Harrison George	Castledod Mill	-	-	-	Harrison George - Rel.	1887	-	dd/	1887 37 58

PARISH	TOWNLAND	MILLER	TYPE	HOUSE	Land	£Val+	PROPRIETORS	Date	WHEEL etc.	Record	Ref.
Rathrogan	Clashganniv	Harrison Standish	Castledod Mill	-	-	-	Harrison S - Barry John	1885	-	dd/	1885 18 74
Rathrogan	Clashganniv	Harrison Standish	Castledod Mill	-	-	-	Harrison S - Ryan John	1886	-	dd/	1886 36 144
Rathrogan	Clashganniv	O`Shaughnessy Wm	Castledod Mill	-	-	-	O`Shaughnessy Wm - Rel.	1887	-	dd/	1887 27 220
Rathrogan	Clashganniv	Warren Graves	Castledod Mill	-	-	-	Warren G - Harrison Stdsh	1887	-	dd/	1887 38 74
Rathrogan	Clashganniv	Wynne Margaret	Castledod Mill	-	-	-	Wynne Mgt - Harrison Geo	1887	-	dd/	1887 12 115
Tullagh	Clodagh	Kingston Jane	corn	26.6x18x13.6 :	-	-	-	-	14x2x7	hob/	5.0288
Ballinadee	Cloghane	Falvey Thomas	grist	(1A) 45x25x21 :	-	-	-	-	18X5X17 40 bkts. :	hob/	5.0182
Ballinadee	Cloghane	Talvey Thomas	grist	(1A) 45x25x24	-	-	-	1850	18x5.6x17 40 bkts.:	hob/	5.1081
Ballinadee	Cloghane	Talvey Thomas	grist	-	-	-	-	-	18x5x17	vmb/	4
Ballymoodan	Clogheenavodig	Allman Robert	corn	house, offs. & land	5a.	22.10.	-	1856	-	gr/	a.a.Ire.ie
Ballymoodan	Clogheenavodig	Allman Robert	grist	(1B) 34x22x27 :	-	-	-	1850	16x5x9.6 48 bkts. :	hob/	5.0184
Ballymodan	Clogheenavodig		flour mill	-	-	-	-	-	-	6"os	110
(? par)	Cloghina *	Neville Henry Rev.	mill	-	-	-	Neville - O`Callaghan Thos	1889	-	dd/	1889 10 195
Matehy	Cloghroe	ExS/ Aghnamuck Br.	flour	-	-	-	-	-	-	6"os	73
Ballymoodan	Cloheenavodig	Allman Robert	grist	-	-	-	-	-	16x5x10	vmb/	4
Kilmoremoy	Clonakilty Town :	Hill Thomas & Co.	wheatmeal :	-	-	-	-	1963	-	lic/14	wheat
Kilmoremoy	Clonakilty Town :	Hurley John J	wheatmeal :	-	-	-	-	1963	-	lic/16	wheat
Kilmoremoy	Clonakilty Town :	Bennett & Co. Ltd.	flour	-	-	-	-	1963	-	lic/3	wheat
Clondulane	Clondulane	- at Glandalane Ho.	mill	-	-	-	-	-	-	1"os/	176
Clondulane	Clondulane	Briscoe Robert	mill	N. end (1B) 40x26x58.6	-	25-15	-	1848	iron 20x12x8 :	hob/	5.0325
Clondulane	Clondulane North	-	flour	-	-	-	-	-	-	6"os	35
Clondulane	Clondulane North	Briscoe Robert	flour	-	-	95	-	1856	-	gr/	a.a.Ire.ie
Clondulane	Clondulane North	Smith Henry	flour	-	-	-	-	-	20x12x8 6 pr. st.	vmb/	4
Kilmichael	Clonmoyle	- on Dripsey R.	mill	-	-	-	-	-	-	1"os/	186
Kilmichael	Clonmoyle E.	-	corn	11.9m x 5.4m 4 storey	-	-	-	-	- wheel-pit 1.7 m.	iaa/	AI9746 os61.14.5
Fanlobus	Cloontiquirk	Gillman Herbert	corn & furze	(1B) 25.6x18x13.6 :	-	-	-	1850	16x3x- under repair	hob/	5.0201
Cork	Clough *	-	mill	-	-	-	-	-	-	1"os/	175
Ballymoodan	Cloughmacsimon	Fitzgerald \Maurice	distillery	[no dimensions]	-	-	-	1850	18x5x8 3 pr. sts. :	hob/	5.0184
Ballymoodan	Cloughmacsimon	Fitzgerald Maurice	distillery	-	-	-	-	-	18x5x18	vmb/	4
Ballymoodan	Cloughmacsimon	Fitzgerald Maurice	distillery & mill	ho., offs. & yard	-	-	-	1856	-	gr/	a.a.Ire.ie
Ballymoodan	Cloughmacsimon	Fitzgerald Maurice	houses	land, yard & street	3a.	-	-	1856	-	gr/	a.a.Ire.ie
Cork	Connonagh *	- at Glenville	mill	-	-	-	-	-	-	1"os/	200
Clonfert	Coolacoosane	-	tuck mills	-	-	-	-	-	-	6"os	23
Clonfert	Coolacoosane	N/ Brogen Bridge	flour (ruins)	-	-	-	-	-	-	6"os	23
Clondrohid	Coolaniddane :	Walton Richard	corn	-	-	-	-	-	10x2x12	vmb/	4
Tullylease	Coolbane	E./ Allow Br.	grist	-	-	-	-	-	-	6"os	6
Kilmichael	Cooldaniel	-	carding disused	5.5m x 4.4m remains	-	-	-	-	- wheel-pit 1.29 m.	iaa/	AI9750 os82.7.2
Rathcoony	Coole	Mullins Hannah	mills	-	-	-	Mullins Hannah - James	1885	-	dd/	1885 25 167
Rathcoony	Coole	Mullins Henry	mills	-	-	-	Mullins Henry - Hannah	1887	-	dd/	1887 41 267
Rathcoony	Coole East	Craig William	bleach	(1A) 28.6x21.6x26 :	-	20-18	-	-	11x4.6x11.6 :	hob/	5.0389
Rathcooney	Coole East	Craig William	corn	-	-	-	-	-	11x4x11	vmb/	4
Rathcooney	Coole East	Craig William	corn	-	-	-	-	-	11x4x11	vmb/	4
Kilbrogan	Coolfadda	Davis	mill	-	-	-	davis - Jones	-	-	dd/	54 443 36361
Kilbrogan	Coolfadda	Dowden William C	mills	-	-	-	Dowden Wm - Allman R Ld	1885	-	dd/	1885 33 59
Kilbrogan	Coolfadda	Payne Thomas W	mills	-	-	-	Payne Thos - Warren Mary	1889	-	dd/	1889 2 90
Kilbrogan	Coolfadda	W/ Bandon Br.	Bandon Mills	-	-	-	-	-	-	6"os	110
Tullylease	Coolhane	Shaughnessy Andr	corn	-	-	-	-	-	12x3x12	vmb/	4
Tullylease	Coolhane	Shaughnessy Andr	tuck	-	-	-	-	-	10x1x10	vmb/	4
Cooliney	Cooliney	NE/ Cooliney Br.	Cooliney Mill	-	-	-	-	-	-	6"os	7
Fanlobus	Coolkellure	- at Hill Farm	threshing :	-	-	-	-	1841	-	hob/	5.0199
Fanlobus	Coolkellure	Sholdam General	flour & corn	(1A) 37x24.6x12 & :	-	-	-	1850	16x4x20.3 12 revs. :	hob/	5.0199
Castleventry	Coolnagay	-	corn & tuck	- mill complex remains	-	-	-	-	- wheel-pit widths :	iaa/	AI3477 os134.8.1

PARISH	TOWNLAND	MILLER	TYPE	HOUSE	Land	£Val+	PROPRIETORS	Date	WHEEL etc.	Record	Ref.
Castleventry	Coolnagay	-	Inchamullen Mills	-	-	-	-	-	-	1"os/	200
Castleventry	Coolnagay	- Inchamullen Mills	tuck	-	-	-	-	1841	-	6"os/	134
Castleventry	Coolnagay	Hurley Patrick	corn & tuck	(3C) 24x17x7.6 :	-	-	-	-	12x2x12 propels :	hob/	5.0189
Litter	Coolroe	-	flour	-	-	-	-	-	-	6"os	35
Litter	Coolroe	Hyde John	flour	& offices	-	40	- (+ tenant's houses)	1856	-	gr/	a.a.Ire.ie
Litter	Coolroe	Smith Henry	flour	(1B) 71x23.6x36.6 :	-	25-19	-	1848	breast 22x7.6x1.6 :	hob/	5.0358
Litter	Coolroe	Smith Henry, Fermoy	flour	(1B) 71x23.6x36.6 :	-	25-19	-	1848	breast 22x7.6x1.6 :	hob/	5.0358
Carrigrohanbeg	Coolyduff	Tobin Thomas	corning	28.6x20.6x9.6 & :	-	-	-	-	20x2.11x3 metal	hob/	5.0699
Carrigrohanbeg	Coolyduff	Tobin Thomas	corning	49.0x22.0x8.0 :	-	-	-	-	20x2.11x3 metal	hob/	5.0699
Carrigrohanbeg	Coolyduff	W/ Royal G. Mills	stoving house	-	-	-	-	-	-	6"os	73
Skull	Cooradarragan	-	corn & carding	- small mill roadside :	-	-	-	-	4.36m dia. x 1.2m &	iaa/	AI3478 os139.16.6
Skull	Cooradarragan	- W. side sm. river:	corn & carding	-	-	-	-	-	-	6"os	138
Skull	Coosheen	-	mill complex	2x1storey structures :	-	-	-	-	9 millstones on site	iaa/	AI3515 os139.16.6
Skull	Coosheen	- at Skull Harbour :	stamp, magazine	-	-	-	-	1841	-	6"os/	I39
Skull	Coosheen	Barytes & Umber	mills & quay :	-	-	-	-	1897	-	6"os/	I39
Clondulane	Coreysville	Carey Edward K	mill & granary	(1A) 43.6x24x21.6 :	-	86-12	-	1848	churning machine :	hob/	5.0325
Cork	Cork City	- Dock Mill	flour	- small remains only	-	-	-	2000	- pho taken	mmSv/	R
Cork	Cork City	Anglesea Road	lime & salt wks	-	-	-	-	-	-	6"os	74
Cork	Cork City	Anglesea Road	lime works	-	-	-	-	-	-	6"os	74
Cork	Cork City	Brockelsby St.	corn & kiln	-	-	-	- millstream from weir to N.	-	-	6"os	74
Cork	Cork City	Brockelsby St.	tannery	-	-	-	-	-	-	6"os	74
Cork	Cork City	Hayes Atwell	Lee Mills	-	-	-	-	1787	- (rebuilt 1825/31)	AB'bg	2003
Cork	Cork City	Ponrose's Quay	foundry	-	-	-	-	-	-	6"os	74
Cork	Cork City	St Patrick's Quay	foundry	-	-	-	-	-	-	6"os	74
Cork	Cork City	Watercourse road	distillery	-	-	-	-	-	-	6"os	74
Cork	Cork City	Wise's Quay	distillery	-	-	-	-	-	-	6"os	74
Cork	Cork City	Wise's Quay	malt	-	-	-	-	-	-	6"os	74
Cork	Cork City	York Street	distillery	-	-	-	-	-	-	6"os	74
Cork	Cork City :	Phipps	mill	-	-	-	Phipps - Spread	-	-	dd/	84 234 59793
Cork	Cork City :	Pigott Thomas :	mill	-	-	-	Pigott T - Gillman Jon Jun :	1708	-	dd/	4 309 978
Cork	Cork City :	Masters William :	mill	-	-	-	Masters W - Davies Rev. :	1722	Lse. 6 Feb.	dd/	35 323 22680
Cork	Cork City :	Daly John :	Arthorans Mill	-	-	-	Daly J - Quinlan Edmond :	1721	Asgt. 1 July	dd/	36 18 20968
Cork	Cork City :	Hedges Richard :	Arthorans Mill	-	-	-	Hedges R - Mitchell John :	1721	Lse. 7 Jan.	dd/	34 154 20998
Cork	Cork City :	Roth John	malt ho. & kiln	-	-	-	Roth J - Chattor Thomas :	1715	-	dd/	14 293 6252
Cork	Cork City :	Roth Philip :	Archdeacons Mill	-	-	-	Roth P - Moore John :	1716	-	dd/	18 182 8802
Cork	Cork City :	Roth Philip :	Archdeacons Mill	-	-	-	Roth P - Porter Samuel :	1719	-	dd/	23 393 13805
Cork	Cork City :	Roth Philip :	Arthorans Mill	-	-	-	Roth Phil - Dawly John :	1709	Lse. 12 Jul.	dd/	4 263 939
Cork	Cork City :	Slattery Darby :	Archdeacons Mill	-	-	-	Slattery - Bonbounous Jn :	1718	-	dd/	29 307 17749
Cork	Cork City :	Harrington Robert	chemical works	Incumb Est consisting :	-	-	(1935) Burke's Chemicals	1851	-	mlyIE	p10
Cork	Cork City :	Beamish & Crawford	Lee Mills	-	-	-	- from -	1872	-	mlyIE	p137
Cork	Cork City :	Beamish Richd P. :	Lee Mills	-	-	-	- from -	1855	-	mlyIE	p137
Cork	Cork City :	Lane William	Lee Mills	Incumb Est consisting :	-	-	-	1855	2 wheels - 20x14 :	mlyIE	p137
Cork	Cork City :	National Flour Mills	flour	-	-	-	-	1963	-	lic/15	wheat
Cork	Cork City :	Jn Furlong & Sons	flour	-	-	-	-	1963	-	lic/9	wheat
Cork	Cork City :	Suttons Ltd.	wheatmeal :	-	-	-	-	1963	-	lic/12	flour
St Anne	Cork City :	Kelleher Daniel	cooperage	house, offs. & yard	-	9	-	1856	-	gr/	a.a.Ire.ie
St Anne	Cork City :	Murray Maurice	distillery	offices & yard	-	85	-	1856	-	gr/	a.a.Ire.ie
St Anne	Cork City :	Murray Maurice	malt stores, kiln	& yard	-	32	-	1856	-	gr/	a.a.Ire.ie
St Anne	Cork City :	Murray Maurice	spirit stores & yd	-	-	23	-	1856	-	gr/	a.a.Ire.ie
St Anne	Cork City :	Deeble Benjamin	bone	house, stable & yard	-	24	-	1856	-	gr/	a.a.Ire.ie
St Anne	Cork City :	Mahony John	steam mill & yard	-	-	13	-	1856	-	gr/	a.a.Ire.ie
St Anne	Cork City :	Murray Maurice	corn store, kiln	& yard	-	65	-	1856	-	gr/	a.a.Ire.ie

PARISH	TOWNLAND	MILLER	TYPE	HOUSE	Land	£Val+	PROPRIETORS	Date	WHEEL etc.	Record	Ref.
St Anne	Cork City :	Killeher Cornelius	flour & corn	& kiln	-	47	-	1856	-	gr/	a.a.lre.ie
St Anne	Cork City :	Killeher Cornelius	glue yard	house, offices & garden	2a.	30	-	1856	-	gr/	a.a.lre.ie
St Anne	Cork City :	Thompson George	soap m'factory	& tan yard	-	48	-	1856	-	gr/	a.a.lre.ie
Cork	Cork City N. Libs	Gaggin Francis :	mills	-	-	-	Gaggin F - Engain Danl :	1721	Mort. 1 May	dd/	23 393 13805
Cork	Cork City N. Libs	King Benjamin :	mills	-	-	-	King B - Gaggin Francis :	1714	Lse. 23 Mar.	dd/	23 261 13315
Cork	Cornaveagh		flour	-	-	-	-	-	-	6"os	67
Cork	Cornaveigh	- on Tourig R.	corn	-	-	-	-	-	-	iaa/	AI6266
Cork	Cornmarket Ward	Fitton St.	tannery	-	-	-	-	-	-	6"os	74
Dunderrow	Corran	E/ Owenboy R.	flour	-	-	-	-	-	-	6"os	86
Kilmacabea	Corran South	-	flax & creamery	24.45m x 6.65m :	-	-	-	-	6m x 1.07 overshot :	iaa/	AI3511 os133.8.4
Cork	Corrydorregan *	Coosheen district	tuck	conv. to small appmts.	-	-	-	2008	- o'shot wheel	mmSv/	Ca
Skull	Croagh Bay	nr.Vge.Seafort	inlet (tidal)	-	-	-	-	-	R.tidal, chnl25ch.wide	6"os	148
Cork	Crookstown	Howard Bros Ltd.	Bellmont Mills :	-	-	-	-	1963	- >1,000 barrels	lic/3	wh.meal
Cullen	Cullen	Harrington & Bowen :	flour	-	-	-	-	-	18x6x30 12x - x -	vmb/	4
Kilmichael	Curradrinagh	-	windmill	remains 4m dia x 0.6m	-	-	-	-	-	iaa/	AI3516 os94.6.4
Clonfert	Curragh	Barry Gerard	flour	-	-	-	-	-	15x8x8 4 pr st.	vmb/	4
Clonfert	Curragh	E / Town Bridge	tuck	-	-	-	-	-	-	6"os	23
Clonfert	Curragh	N. side Dalua R.	large flour	-	-	-	-	-	-	6"os	23
Clonfert	Curragh	on R. Allow	mill	-	-	-	-	-	-	6"os	23
Drinagh	Curraghalicky	Nihan John	corn	22.0x16.6x7 & dw. ho :	-	-	-	-	12x2.6x12	hob/	5.0285
Drinagh	Curraghalicky	Nihan John	tuck	-	-	-	-	-	12x1.8x10	hob/	5.0285
Drinagh	Curraghalicky	W/ Curraghalicky Br.	tuck & corn	-	-	-	-	-	-	6"os	120
Athnowen	Curraghbeg	NNE/ Ovens Br.	Ovens Mill	-	-	-	-	-	-	6"os	73
Kilshannig	Curraghbower	Bolster George	grist	S. ho. (1A) 40x21x29 :	-	10-17	-	-	o`shot 20x4x17.6 :	hob/	5.0425
Kilshannig	Curraghbower	Bolster George	grist	-	-	-	-	-	20x4x17	vmb/	4
Desert	Curraghgrane Beg	Arundel Mills		-	-	-	-	-	-	6"os	135
Templemartin	Currravordy	E/ Tanyard Br.	mill pond	-	-	-	-	-	-	6"os	95
Cork	Danesfort *	-	thrashing	-	-	-	-	-	-	6"os	41
Templeroan	Dannanstown	E / Awbeg R.	flour mill	-	-	-	-	-	-	6"os	26
Fanlobus	Darkwood	-	bleach & bl. green		-	-	-	1841	-	6"os/	107
Fanlobus	Darkwood	-	bleach disused	- remains bl. complex	-	-	-	-	- wheelpit 1.4x1.6m.	iaa/	AI3509 os107.8.5
Fanlobus	Darkwood	Wright James	corn	(1A) 19x19x13 & :	-	-	-	1849	16x4x9.5 40 bkts.	hob/	5.0199
Castlelyons	Deerpark	-	mill pond	-	-	-	-	-	-	6"os	45
Castlelyons	Deerpark	E/ Bride Bridge	flour	-	-	-	-	-	-	6"os	45
Cork	Deerpark *	-	woollen factory	-	-	-	-	-	-	6"os	54
Cork	Deerpark *	7/8 mile	mill race	-	-	-	-	-	-	6"os	54
Magourney	Deeshart	N. Dripsey Br.	carding	-	-	-	-	-	-	6"os	72
Kilmeen	Derrygalun	-	corn & tuck	-	-	-	-	1841	-	6"os/	22
Kilmeen	Derrygalun	Connor James	grist	(1B) 31x18x10.6 :	-	3-8-3	-	-	14x3.4x14.6 :	hob/	5.0425
Desert	Desert	on stream E. Desert	mill (hz)	-	-	-	-	-	-	iaa/	IA5152 os54.1.3
Desert	Desert	Stannard James E	mills	-	-	-	Stannard J - Bird Robert G	1885	-	dd/	1885 14 198
Desert	Desert	Stannard James E	mills	-	-	-	Stannard - Huggard Martin	1886	-	dd/	1886 38 45
Cork	Diviny *	S/Vge. Scotchstreet	corn	-	-	-	-	-	-	6"os	63
Kildorrery	Doonawanly	-	corn kiln	-	-	-	-	-	-	6"os	26
Kildorrery	Doonawanly	Roche John	corn	(3C) 20x19x10.6	-	-	-	-	8.6x4x2.6 bkts. 16 :	hob/	5.0458
Kildorrery	Doonawanly	S/ Awbeg R.	old corn mill	-	-	-	-	-	-	6"os	26
Carrigaline	Douglas	- on Tramore R.	-	-	-	-	-	-	-	1"os/	187
Carrigaline	Douglas	Lane Mr	corn	-	-	-	-	-	16x5x13	vmb/	4
Carrigaline	Douglas	Blesinton Lord	mill	-	-	-	Blesinton - Bustead	-	-	dd/	50 252 32841
Carrigaline	Douglas	Longford Earl of	mills	-	-	-	Longford E. - Stewart Jas	1887	-	dd/	1887 27 252
Drinagh	Driminidy South	Donovan Con	corn	23x16.6x6 20x15x5	-	-	-	-	12x1.8x12	hob/	5.0285
Drinagh	Drinagh East	-	flour	-	-	-	-	1841	-	6"os/	121

PARISH	TOWNLAND	MILLER	TYPE	HOUSE	Land	£Val+	PROPRIETORS	Date	WHEEL etc.	Record	Ref.
Drinagh	Drinagh East	-	flour	-	-	-	-	1841	-	6"os/	121
Drinagh	Drinagh East	-	flour (1842)	- roadside corn mill nr	-	-	-	-	-	iaa/	AI3491 os121.5.5
Drinagh	Drinagh East	Scott William	flour	(1B) 66x23.6x26 & :	-	-	-	-	23.6x6.6x4 metal :	hob/	5.0197
Inishcarra	Dripsey	- on Dripsey R. :	woollen	-	-	-	-	-	-	1"os/	186
Kilfaughnabeg	Drom	-	corn (disused)	- 4 bay 2 storey mill :	-	-	-	-	-	iaa/	AI3492 os142.3.3
Kilfaughnabeg	Drom	-	corn store	-	-	-	-	1841	-	6"os/	142
Cork	Dromaskill *	Toogood	mill	-	-	-	Toogood - Doneraile	-	-	dd/	65 93 44527
Cork	Dromaskill *	Toogood	mill	-	-	-	Toogood - Wraxon	-	-	dd/	67 300 50853
Caheragh	Dromcorragh	on R. Glanaphuca	tuck	-	-	-	-	-	-	6"os	132
Caheragh	Dromcorragh	Blecher	mill	-	-	-	Blecher - Roberts	-	-	dd/	56 123 37246
Kilmaloda	Dromgarrif	-	corn (disused)	on roadside north of :	-	-	-	-	- wheelpit 2.6 m.	iaa/	AI3493 os122.7.6
Kilmaloda	Dromgarrif	W/ Owenkeagh R.	flour	-	-	-	-	-	-	6"os	122
Kilmaloda	Dromgarrif (NB :)	Connell Charles	flour (part of)	28.0x21.6x18.6 & also :	-	-	-	-	no dimensions	hob/	5.0221
Cork	Dromihill *	Morris	mill	-	-	-	Morris - Ash	-	-	dd/	74 524 52390
Cork	Dromihill *	Morris	mill	-	-	-	Morris - Morris	-	-	dd/	86 162 59778
Cork	Dromore	-	mill	- 5 bay 2 storey mill	-	-	-	-	7.3m x 1.9m o`shot :	iaa/	AI3519 os119.9.6
Cork	Dromore	Barry John	corn & tuck	55x23x30 & :	-	-	-	-	11x2.6 overshot	hob/	5.0268
Cork	Dromore	Foster Alfred	mill	-	-	-	Foster Alf - Beasley Chas	1891	-	dd/	1891 34 48
Cork	Drumbrand (?)	- (s. of Cork City)	woollen	-	-	-	-	-	-	1"os/	187
Dunbulloge	Dunbulloge	E/ Dunbologe Br.	tuck	-	-	-	-	-	-	6"os	63
Dunbulloge	Dunbulloge	N. / Dunbuloge Br.	tuck	-	-	-	-	-	-	6"os	63
Cork	Duncanon Br	-	Shinnagh Mills	-	-	-	-	-	-	1"os/	174
Dungourney	Dungourney			-	-	-	-	-	-	6"os	66
caherlag	Dunkettle		mills	-	-	-	Hall - Hoare	-	-	dd/	82 523 58591
Drinagh	Dunmanway	Cox	mills	-	-	-	Cox - Cox	-	-	dd/	54 300 35839
Drinagh	Dunmanway South	-	corn	- rect. 6 bay 6 storey :	-	-	-	-	- wheelpit 2.5 m.	iaa/	AI3494 os107.12.5
Drinagh	Dunmanway South	E/ Green Br.	flour	-	-	-	-	-	-	6"os	107
Drinagh	Dunmanway South	Goulde Wid./ Edmnd	flour	(1B) 20x18x31.6 & :	-	-	-	-	26x8.2x22 bkts. 60	hob/	5.0199
Drinagh	Dunmanway South	SW/ Green Br.	flour mill, mill pond		-	-	-	-	-	6"os	107
Drinagh	Dunmanway South		Brewery Br.	-	-	-	-	-	-	6"os	107
Drinagh	Dunmanway South		mill race	-	-	-	-	-	-	6"os	107
Cork	Dunmark Ho	- on Melagh R.	mill	-	-	-	-	-	-	1"os/	192
Kilmocomoge	Dunnamark	-	corn & tuck	remains (ruins) 3 mills	-	-	-	-	-	iaa/	AI3479 os118.3.2
Kilmocomoge	Dunnamark Mill-lot	on Mealagh R.	tuck & corn	-		-	-	-	-	6"os	118
Kilmocomoge	Dunnamark	Murphy Michael	mill	-	35	-	-	1852	-	gr/	Ld.Est.db
Fermoy	Duntahane	Johnston Francis G	corn	(1A) 25.6x17x21.6 :	-	23-16		1850	wooden 23x4x0.3 :	hob/	5.0333
Ballymodan	East Gully	M & L Bank Ltd.	mills	-	-	-	M & L Bank - Uncles A W	1886	-	dd/	1886 36 176
Ballymodan	East Gully	Unkles Abraham W	mills	-	-	-	Unkles Ab W - Hall Robt	1887	-	dd/	188714 144
Ballymoney	Edencurra	E/ Clubhouse Br.	Clubhouse Mill	-	-	-	-	-	-	6"os	121
Ballymoney	Edencurra	Reilly James	corn	house & sm. garden	-	3.5.0	-	1856	-	gr/	a.a.Ire.ie
Ballymoney	Edencurra	Reilly James	grist	(1C) 46.6x22x20 :	-	9-9	-	1848	17x6x6.6 40 bkts. :	hob/	5.0186
Ballymoney	Edencurra	Reilly James	grist	(1B) 34x24x29 & ret. :	-	18.3	-	-	17x6x6.6 30 bkts. :	hob/	5.0186/7
Ballymoney	Edencurra	Reilly James	grist	-	-	-	-	-	17x6x6	vmb/	4
Kilcatherine	Eyeries	-	corn & tuck	-	-	-	-	1841	-	6"os/	114
Kilcatherine	Eyeries	-	tuck	remains only :	-	-	-	-	- wheelpit 1.35 m.	iaa/	AI3502 os114.4.6
Desertserges	Fananashesherry	Norwood William	flour	128.6x30.0x48.0 & :	-	-	-	-	23x14x4.6 6 pr st.:	hob/	5.0194
Desertserges	Fananashesherry	Norwood William	flour	-	-	-	-	-	23x14x5 8 pr st.	vmb/	4
Desertserges	Fananashesherry	Norwood William	flour & land	- [+ hos. for tenents ?]	23a.	168	-	1856	-	gr/	a.a.Ire.ie
Desertserges	Fananashesherry	SW of Murragh Br. :	flour	-	-	-	-	1841	-	6"os/	109
Farahy	Farahy	1/4m. E/ Farahay Vge.	corn	-	-	-	-	-	-	6"os	18
Farahy	Farahy	Carroll Anthony	corn	(1B) 36x27x27.6 & kiln	-	5.11	-	-	12x3.6x13 24 bkts. :	hob/	5.4050
St Annes S'don	Farrancleary	- off York St.	tannery	-	-	-	-	-	-	6"os	74

PARISH	TOWNLAND	MILLER	TYPE	HOUSE	Land	£Val+	PROPRIETORS	Date	WHEEL etc.	Record	Ref.
St Annes S'don	Farrancleary	- C546on Glen R.	malt & pond	-	-		-	-	-	6"os	74
Kilmocomoge	Farranferris	Cork, Brocklesby St.	tannery	-	-	-	-	-	-	6"os	74
Kilmocomoge	Farranferris	Lane nr York St.	corn	-	-	-	-	-	-	6"os	74
Kilmocomoge	Farranferris	Lane nr York St.	corn kiln	-	-	-	-	-	-	6"os	74
Kinneagh	Farranmareen	-	hz wheeled mill	-	-	-	-	-	-	iaa/	AI2719 os95.0.0
Ballyfeard Pk	Farsha	Potter Leonard	carding & corn	-	-	-	-	-	16x3x16	vmb/	4
Cork	Fenagh *	Hughes Martin	mill & mill land	-	-	-	Hurges Martin - John	1891	-	dd/	1891 49 26
Fermoy	Fermoy	-	short mill	-	-	-	-	-	-	6"os	35
Fermoy	Fermoy	1/4m. E/ bridge	flour	-	-	-	-	-	-	6"os	35
Fermoy	Fermoy	Carroll William	flour	-	-	-	-	-	19x10x7 14x3x7	vmb/	4
Fermoy	Fermoy	opposite Millview	paper	-	-	-	-	-	-	6"os	35
Fermoy	Fermoy (barony)	Hewson George	The Mill Quarter	-	-	-	Hewson - Honywood Wm	1886	-	dd/	1886 5 177
Fermoy	Fermoy Town	Carroll William	flour	(1B) 123x20x34 :	-	88	- (NB- horse driven wheel)	1850	19x10x7, dia.5.6 : I	hob/	5.0335
bo. Kinalea	Finagh	Barrymore Earl of	mills	-	-	-	Barrymore E - Baeey	-	-	dd/	91 165 63821
Mallow	Firville E	- on R Laney	mill	-	-	-	-	-	-	1"os/	186
Killaconenagh	Foildarrig	-	tuck (disused)	rectangular remains :	-	-	-	-	-	iaa/	AI3503 os115.10.4
Killaconenagh	Foildarrig		salt manufactory	-	-	-	-	-	-	6"os	115
Dromtarriff	Garanes South	Sullivan Michael	corn	25.0x17.6x7 & :	-	-	-	-	12x2.4x7	hob/	5.0288
Brigown	Garrane	Artkinson Susanna	bleach	-	-	-	-	-	11x3x14	vmb/	4
Brigown	Garrane	Artkinson Susanna :	carding & tuck	-	-	-	-	1856	-	gr/	a.a.Ire.ie
Brigown	Garrane	Artkinson Susanna :	corn	-	-	-	-	1856	-	gr/	a.a.Ire.ie
Brigown	Garrane	E./ R Funshin	bleach mill	-	-	-	-	-	-	6"os	10
Brigown	Garrane	E./ R Funshin	woollen factory	-	-	-	-	-	-	6"os	10
Clondrohid	Garranenagappul	Danaghy & Riordan :	corn	-	-	-	-	-	12x3x15	vmb/	4
Clondrohid	Garranenagappul	SE/ Garranagappul Br.	mill (in ruins)	-	-	-	-	-	-	6"os	59
Drishane	Garransduff	Niern Richard	corn	-	-	-	-	-	12x4x5	vmb/	4
Mogeely	Garryaughterragh	Carty Patrick	carding & corn	(1C) 40x18.6x14 :	-	-	-	-	12x3x13 2 pr st.	hob/	5.0551
Mogeely	Garryoughtra North	on Womanagh R. :	Mogeely Carding	-	-	-	-	-	-	6"os	66
Cork	Gearagh	N/ Argideen Br	Gearagh Corn & Tuck Mills		-	-	-	-	-	6"os	121
Cork	Gearagh (5)	-	corn & tuck	- mill complex SE :	-	-	-	-	- wheelpit 1.6m.	iaa/	AI3490 os121.12.5
Cork	Gearagh (5)	- Fermoy Town	mill	-	-	-	-	-	-	1"os/	176
Cork	Gearagh (5)	- on Ardigeen R.	mill	-	-	-	-	-	-	1"os/	200
Cork	Glananoudig *	Kingston Lord	mills	-	-	-	Kingston Lord - Condon	-	-	dd/	62 84 41994
Cork	Glananoudig *	Kingston Lord	mills	-	-	-	Kingston Lord - Brien	-	-	dd/	63 12 42418
Youghal	Glanaradotia	SW/ Youghal Town	windmill	-	-	-	-	-	-	6"os	67
Ross	Glanbrack	-	tuck	-	-	-	-	-	-	1"os/	200
Rathclarin	Glanduff	Quinlan Timothy	flour	-	-	-	-	-	12x3x12	vmb/	4
Rathclarin	Glanduff	Quinlan Timothy	tuck	-	-	-	-	-	11x3x11 9x3x9	vmb/	4
Rathclarin	Glanduff	W/ K'brittain Br.	Grace Mill	-	-	-	-	-	-	6"os	123
Rathclarin	Glanduff		tuck	-	-	-	-	-	-	6"os	123
Kilworth1	Glansheskin	S/ Glansheskin Br.	flax	-	-	-	-	-	-	6"os	28
Rathcoony	Glanmire	Hail	mill	-	-	-	Hail - Hoare	-	-	dd/	81 523 58591
Glanworth	Glanworth	Gibbons John	flour	(1B) 44x44x33 & kiln :	-	-	-	-	12.4x5 - 32 floats :	hob/	5.0451
Glanworth	Glanworth	Glanworth Mill	corn	expertly converted	-	-	Lynne Glasscoe	2000	hotel	pWEH	C
Glanworth	Glanworth	W/ R. Funshion	flour	-	-	-	-	-	-	6"os	27
Kilworth	Glensesken	Pierse John	corn	(1A) 54x20x29 :	-	8-6	-	1848	15x3.8x11 2 pr. st.	hob/	5.0349
Kilworth	Glensesken	Pierse John	corn	-	-	-	-	-	15x4x11	vmb/	4
Ardnageehy	Glenville	1/6m S/ Keam Br.	paper	-	-	-	-	-	-	6"os	43
Ardnagehy	Glenville Demse	-	corn	3 storey	-	-	-	-	saw mill in 1950	iaa/	AI6267
Ballinaboy	Gogganshill	-	ponds (2)	-	-	-	-	-	-	6"os	85/97
Kilquane	Gogganstown		Carrigeen Paper Mill		-	-	-	-	-	6"os	64
Cork	Gort - ?	-	mill	-	-	-	-	-	-	1"os/	187

PARISH	TOWNLAND	MILLER	TYPE	HOUSE	Land	£Val+	PROPRIETORS	Date	WHEEL etc.	Record	Ref.
Cork	Gortabullig ?tld	on Kealincha R.	corn & tuck	-	-	-	-	-	-	6"os	114
Ballyspillane	Gortacrue	NxE/ Carrigogna Br.	flour	-	-	-	-	-	-	6"os	65
Mallow	Gortmolire	-	tuck & grist	-	-	-	-	-	-	6"os	32
Creagh	Gortnaclohy	W. side North St.	brewery	-	-	-	-	-	-	6"os	141
Creagh	Gortnaclohy		corn	-	-	-	-	-	-	6"os	141
Ballyhoory	Gortroche	Aldworth John	corn	(1B) 76.6x22x21 :	-	-	-	-	o`shot 17.6x4.6x19 :	hob/	5.0436
Ballyhooly	Gortroche	flour		-	-	-	-	-	-	6"os	35
Kilshannig	Gortroe	-	1/8m E/ Gortroe XRds		-	-	-	-	-	6"os	32
Kilshannig	Gortroe	-	corn	- 3 sty part collapsed	-	-	-	-	- wheelpit 1.3 m.	iaa/	AI3495 os134.13.1
Kilshannig	Gortroe	Smith Richard	grist	-	-	-	-	-	12x2x12	vmb/	4
Kilshannig	Gortroe	Smith Richard	grist & tuck	(3B) 21.6x14x6 :	-	9/4d	-	-	-	hob/	5.0428
Kilshannig	Gortroe	Smith Richard	tuck	-	-	-	-	-	10x2x10	vmb/	4
Kilshannig	Gortroe	SW/ Connonagh Br.	Connonagh Tuck	-	-	-	-	-	-	6"os	134
Kilshannig	Gortroe		mill race	-	-	-	-	-	-	6"os	134
Tracton	Granig	NW/Tracton Bridge	tuck & corn	-	-	-	-	-	-	6"os	99
Carigrohane	Great Island	no name	corning	-	-	-	-	1894	20x - x4.6 metal	hob/	5.0698
Grenagh	Grenagh North	-	woollen factory	-	-	-	-	1841	-	6"os	51
Grenagh	Grenagh North	Power John	tucking	(1C) 24.6x21.6x12.6	-	1.6	-	-	no.1/ 8.9x2.1x0.6 :	hob/	5.3808
Kilnagross	Grillagh	Allen James & Thos	flour	house, offs. & land	23a.	259	- (+ 20 tenant's hos.)	1856	-	gr/	a.a.Ire.ie
Kilnagross	Grillagh	Allen James & Thos :	flour	-	-	-	-	-	24x12x10 10 pr st.	vmb/	4
Kilnagross	Grillagh	Bennett (family)	mill	-	-	-	- later a Rank property	2011	ceased 1963	Sv/-	Ld.Est.db
Kilnagross	Grillagh		long mill race	-	-	-	-	-	-	6"os	122
Kilnagross	Grillagh		Shannonvale Flour Mills		-	-	-	-	-	6"os	122
Kilnagross	Grillagh		tail race	-	-	-	-	-	-	6"os	122
Ballymodan	Gully	- Mill Street	brewery	-	-	-	-	1841	-	6"os	110
Ballymodan	Gully	- W. side Bandon	brewery	- remains located of	-	-	-	-	-	iaa/	AI3471 os135.8.4
Ballymodan	Gully East	Savage	tuck mill		-	-	Savage - Mills	-	-	dd/	82 43 56960
Ballymodan	Gully East	Gookin	tuck mill		-	-	Gookin - Rice	-	-	dd/	34 152 20988
Skull	Gunpoint	on Currin Creek	corn store	-	-	-	-	-	-	6"os	148
Ballymodan	Gurteen	Crowley John :	mill	Gurteen Old Mill	-	10	-	-	-	gr/-	Ld.Est.db
Ballymodan	Gurteen	-	mill	-	-	-	building demolished	2011	-	Sv/-	Ld.Est.db
Dromtarriff	Gurteen	Leared William	flour	-	-	-	-	-	-	vmb/	4
Dromtarriff	Gurteen	W/ B'maquirk Br.	flour, race	-	-	-	-	-	-	6"os	31
Ballymartke	Hill Land	Barry William	corn	-	-	-	-	-	14x2x14	vmb/	4
Templebreedy	Hoddersfield		thrashing mill	-	-	-	-	-	-	6"os	99
Cork	Hollybrook *	Morgan Anthony	mill lot	-	-	-	Moregan A - Lindsay Saml	1887	-	dd/	1887 44147
Cork	Hollybrook *	Sadlier John G	mill lot	-	-	-	Sadlier Jn - Seymour Chas	1887	-	dd/	1887 51 259
Gortroe	Hollyhill	- on Flesk R.	tuck mill ruins	-	-	-	-	-	-	6"os	44
Skull	Horse Island	- N. end of island :	copper mines	-	-	-	-	-	2 shafts	6"os	149
Doneraile	Horseclose	Stawel George	flour	(1B) 90x32x50 & addns:	-	59	-	-	2 ea. 14x7x6 floats :	hob/	5.0448
Doneraile	Horseclose	W. / Town Br.	large flour mill	-	-	-	-	-	-	6"os	17
Ballymoney	Inchafune	- Rock Castle	Mill	-	-	-	-	1841	-	6"os	108
Ballymoney	Inchafune	Heazel John	flour	house, offs. & land	1a.	61.5.	- (+ tenents)	1856	-	gr/	a.a.Ire.ie
Ballymoney	Inchafune	Heazel John	flour	(1B) 46x25x31 :	-	14-15	-	1848	15x8.3x16.6 :	hob/	5.0186
Ballymoney	Inchafune	Heazel John	flour	-	-	-	-	-	15x8x15 5 pr st.	vmb/	4
Abbeystrowry	Inchinagotagh	NE/ Derreeny Bridge	tuck	-	-	-	-	-	-	6"os	132
Castleventry	Inchinattin	Bateman Thomas	corn	18.6x16x8 & kiln :	-	1-19	-	1848	12x3x12 36 bkts. :	hob/	5.0189
Castleventry	Inchinattin	Hurley Patrick	corn & tuck	26x17x7.6 & tuck mill	-	-	-	-	-	hob/	5.0189
Castleventry	Inchinattin	W/ Inchinattin Bridge	tuck	-	-	-	-	-	-	6"os	121
Castleventry	Inchinattin		mill race	-	-	-	-	-	-	6"os	121
Abbeystrowry	Inchingotagh	-	corn & tuck	- 3 storey complex :	-	-	-	-	- wheelpit 1.5 m.	iaa/	AI3481 os132.12.2
Abbeystrowry	Inchingotagh	-	corn & tuck	- 3 storey complex :	-	-	-	-	-	pOPW/	(AI3481)
Abbeystrowry	Inchingotagh	-	tuck	-	-	-	-	1841	-	6"os	132

PARISH	TOWNLAND	MILLER	TYPE	HOUSE	Land	£Val+	PROPRIETORS	Date	WHEEL etc.	Record	Ref.
Island	Inchydoney Isle.	-	hz wheeled mill	-	-	-	-	-	hz wheel - examined	iaa/	AI2720 os135.0.0
Inishannon	Inishannon	between road & R.	mill	- stream but no bldg.	-	-	-	2008	-	mmSv/	Z
Middleton	Innygraga		corn & flax	-	-	-	-	-	-	6"os	76
Middleton	Innygraga		mill dam	-	-	-	-	-	-	6"os	76
Cork	Iverstown	-	bleach & cloth	-	-	-	-	-	-	6"os	63
Cork	Iverstown	-	mill pond	-	-	-	-	-	-	6"os	63
Cork	Iverstown	-	paper	-	-	-	-	-	-	6"os	63
Kilmocomoge	Kealkill	-	carding	- 3 bay 2 storey ruin :	-	-	-	-	- wheelpit 2 m.	iaa/	AI3507 os106.2.1
Kilmacabea	Keamore	Beamish Robert	corn	25.0x17.0x11 & kiln :	-	-	-	-	16x2 overshot	hob/	5.0296
Fanlobus	Keelaraheen	-	hz wheeled mill	-	-	-	-	-	hz wheel - found :	iaa/	AI2721 os93.16.5
St Anne`s	Kilbarry	- on Glenamought R.	corn	3 blds remain - 1935	-	-	-	-	high breast shot	iaa/	6268
Fanlobus	Kilbarry	Brine John	corn	40x22x13	-	-	-	-	-	hob/	5.0199
St Anne`s	Kilbarry	E/ Glenanought Br.	corn	-	-	-	-	-	-	6"os	63
Fanlobus	Kilbarry	Jago John	corn	(1A) 35.6x25x24.6 new	-	-	-	1849	25x8x25 81 bkts. :	hob/	5.0199
St Annes :	Kilbarry	Murphy Denis	old mill	(1B) 49x24x17 :	-	17-3	-	-	20x1.2 50 bkts. :	hob/	5.0392
Fanlobus	Kilbarry		corn & flour	-	-	-	-	-	-	6"os	74
Desertserges	Kilbeloge	-	corn & tuck	mill complex on street :	-	-	-	-	- wheelpits 4.4 m. :	iaa/	AI3482 os121.4.5
Desertserges	Kilbeloge	1/2m N/ Kilmeen Br.	corn	-	-	-	-	-	-	6"os	121
Desertserges	Kilbeloge		tuck	-	-	-	-	-	-	6"os	121
Desertserges	Kilbelogue	Tobin John	corn	- house & garden	0.1.29	£7	-	1856	-	gr/	a.a.Ire.ie
Desertserges	Kilbelogue	Tobin John	grist	-	-	-	-	-	12x3x12	vmb/	4
Desertserges	Kilbelogue	Tobin John	grist	-	-	-	-	-	11x3x11	vmb/	4
Kilbolane	Kilbolane	Barry E R C	flour & corn	-	-	-	-	1856	16x5x10	vmb/	4
Kilbolane	Kilbolane	Caulfield Edmd. R :	flour & kiln	(1A) 22x25x33 & :	-	-	-	1846	gravity 16x5x10 :	hob/	5.0783
Kilbolane	Kilbrittain		Klbrittain Flour Mi	-	-	-	-	-	-	6"os	123
Kilbrittan	Kilbrittan	Crehan Michael	flour	-	-	-	-	-	20x9x13	vmb/	4
Kilbrittan	Kilbrittan	Quinlan Timothy	tuck	18.6x16.6x6.6	-	-	-	-	11x3x11	hob/	5.0245
Desertserges	Kilcolmanpark	-	mill	- 2 storey farm bldg.	-	-	-	-	2.1m x 1.3m	iaa/	AI3520 os109.7.5
Caherlag	Kilcoolishal	Factory Hill	(no mill)	-	-	-	-	-	-	6"os	75
Whitechurch	Kilcronan	McMahon Michael	corn	-	-	-	-	-	8x2x8	vmb/	4
Kilcully	Kilcully	-	corn	-	-	-	-	-	-	6"os	63
Kilcully	Kilcully	-	corn	4 bay 3 storey brick	-	-	-	-	-	iaa/	AI6269
Kilcully	Kilcully	-	mill pond	-	-	-	-	-	-	6"os	63
Kilcully	Kilcully	-	old	-	-	-	-	-	-	6"os	63
Kilcully	Kilcully	-	old mill	- [no dims.]	-	-	-	-	no information :	hob/	5.0384
Kilcully	Kilcully	- 3/8m S / Aname Br.	corn	-	-	-	-	-	-	6"os	63
Kilcully	Kilcully	Harris William	carding (dilap.)	-	-	-	-	1856	-	gr/	a.a.Ire.ie
Kilcully	Kilcully	Hayes Mr	flour	- [no dims.]	-	-	-	-	wood (in repair) :	hob/	5.0384
Kilcully	Kilcully	Hayes William	mill	(1C) 32x32.6x25.6 :	-	13-5	-	-	no information	hob/	5.0384
Kilcully	Kilcully	Haynes William	flour	-	-	-	-	-	19x5x20	vmb/	4
Kilcully	Kilcully	Hays William	mill	- [no dims.]	-	-	-	-	19.6x5.3x- 60 bkts.:	hob/	5.0384
Kilcully	Kilcully	Meenan Cornelius	carding	-	-	-	-	-	15x6x9	vmb/	4
Kilgarriff	Kilgarriff	-	tuck	-	-	-	-	-	-	6"os	135
Timoligue	Killavarrig	Barkley Reps John :	flour	20x20x20 & :	-	-	-	-	13x12x12 5 pr st. :	hob/	5.0259
Timoligue	Killavarrig	Bleazby John	flour	house, offs. & land	30a	110	- (& tenant's hos.)	1856	-	gr/	a.a.Ire.ie
Timoligue	Killavarrig	Brodhead Collins	flour	-	-	-	-	-	20x12x13 7 pr st.	vmb/	4
Timoleague	Killavarrig	W/ Inchy Br.	flour	-	-	-	-	-	-	6"os	123
Timoleague	Killavarrig		Inchy Mill	-	-	-	-	-	-	6"os	123
Timoleague	Killavarrig		long mill race	-	-	-	-	-	-	6"os	123
Cork	Killeagh (5)	-	corn	6 bay 5 storey	-	-	-	1842	- flour and maize	iaa/	AI6260
Imshannon	Killeen	Porter William	corn	-	-	-	-	-	12x2x12	vmb/	4
Imshannon	Killeen		N/ Cross Barry Br.		-	-	-	-	-	6"os	97

PARISH	TOWNLAND	MILLER	TYPE	HOUSE	Land	£Val+	PROPRIETORS	Date	WHEEL etc.	Record	Ref.
Cork	Killowen (5)	-	corn	3 sty - roofless 1935 :	-	-	-	-	-	iaa/	6270
-	Killingly	Newenham	grist	-	-	-	Newenham - Busteed	-	-	dd/	34 193 21166
Kilaspugmullane	Killrussane	N/ Ballingonig Br.	paper	-	-	-	-	-	-	6"os	64
Kilmaloda	Kilmaloda	-	thrashing	5.5m x 5.58 2 storey	-	-	-	-	- wheelpit rock cut :	iaa/	AI3521 os123.9.5
Kilmaloda	Kilmaloda	Beamish Thomas	threshing	16.6x20.6x18 & dw. ho :	-	-	-	-	no dimensions	hob/	5.0221
Kilmaloda	Kilmaloda	Leary Daniel	tuck	-	-	-	-	-	10x4x10	vmb/	4
Kilmaloda	Kilmaloda	Leary Patrick	grist	-	-	-	-	-	11x4x11	vmb/	4
Kilmaloda	Kilmaloda	W/ Kilmaloda Br.	thrashing	-	-	-	-	-	-	6"os	123
Brinny	Kilmore	-	corn	on roadside 3km to N.	-	-	-	-	-	iaa/	AI3496 OS96.8.4
Brinny	Kilmore	-	mill	on farm Ball`curra Ho.	-	-	-	-	- breast shot c.iron	iaa/	AI3522 os96.8.4
Brinny	Kilmore	NW/ Brinny Br	flour	-	-	-	-	-	-	6"os	96
Brinny	Kilmore	W/ Ballinacurra Br.	tuck	-	-	-	-	-	-	6"os	96
Templetrine	Kilmore		flour	-	-	-	-	-	-	6"os	124
Brinny	Kilmore		from Brinny R.	-	-	-	-	-	-	6"os	96
Templetrine	Kilmore		tuck	-	-	-	-	-	-	6"os	124
Templetrine	Kilmore	Jago Richard :	mills		-	16	- (later Garrettstown Mill)	1865	-	gr/-	Ld.Est.db
Carrigaline	Kilnaglery		starch & pond	-	-	-	-	-	-	6"os	99
Killanully	Kilnahone	-	corn	-	-	-	-	1841	-	6"os	86
Killanully	Kilnahone	Hewitt Thomas :	corn	-	-	-	-	1841	-		
St Anne`s	Kilnap	-	corn	-	-	-	-	-	-	iaa/	AI6271
St Anne`s	Kilnap	-	flour	-	-	-	-	-	-	6"os	74
St Anne`s	Kilnap	-	Glen Mills	-	-	-	-	-	-	6"os	74
St Anne`s	Kilnap	-	mill pond	-	-	-	-	-	-	6"os	74
St Anne`s	Kilnap	Dawson Thomas	corn	-	-	-	-	-	18x9x18	vmb/	4
St Anne`s	Kilnap	Dawson Thomas	flour	-	-	-	-	-	20x10x16	vmb/	4
St Anne`s	Kilnap	Dawson Thomas	flour & corn	house, offs., kiln & land	5a.	170	-	1856	-	gr/	a.a.Ire.ie
St Annes :	Kilnap	Dawson Thomas	mills	(1B) 9.6x28.6x32 :	-	109-1	-	1850	20x10.3x- 48 bkts.	hob/	5.0393
St Anne`s	Kilnap	Power John	flour	house, offices & land	9a.	130	-	1856	-	gr/	a.a.Ire.ie
St Annes :	Kilnap	Power John	flour	(1C) 54.6x25.6x46.6 :	-	75-12	-	1850	33x6x29 breast :	hob/	5.0393
St Anne`s	Kilnap	Power John	flour	-	-	-	-	-	33x6x12 4 pr st.	vmb/	4
St Annes :	Kilnap	Shaw William	flour	(1B) 44x21.6x25 :	-	43-2	-	-	28x6x- 72 bkts. :	hob/	5.0392
St Anne`s	Kilnap	Shaw William J	corn	-	-	-	-	-	17x5x17	vmb/	4
St Anne`s	Kilnap	Shaw William J	flour	house, offices & land	8a.	113	-	1856	-	gr/	a.a.Ire.ie
St Anne`s	Kilnap	Shaw William J	flour	-	-	-	-	-	28x6x13	vmb/	4
St Anne`s	Kilnap	Shea Joseph	flour	-	-	-	-	-	15x6x11 a steam :	vmb/	4
Youghal	Kilnatoora	Fitzgerald James	corn & tuck	(1A) 26x19.6x12.6 :	-	-	-	-	13.10x5.9x7 :	hob/	5.5065
Youghal	Kilnatoora	N of K'toora Castle	tuck	-	-	-	-	1841	-	6"os	67
Ballynoe	Kilphillibeen	-	mill (hz)	-	-	-	-	827	-	iaa/	IA5153 os88.5.4
Fanlobus	Kilroney East	Brine Bartholomew	corn	(1A) 35x25x24 & :	-	-	-	1850	28x5.3x28.6 81 bkts.	hob/	5.0201
Kinsale	Kinsale	- on Oyster Haven	corn	4 storey with attic :	-	-	-	-	-	iaa/	AI6265
Kinsale	Kinsale Town	Brickford Robert	Browns Mill	-	-	-	Brickford - McLeod R	1836	-	dd/	1836 12 129
Kinsale	Kinsale Town	Builen William	Browns Mill	-	-	-	Builen - Brickford Rb	1836	-	dd/	3 197
St Multose	Kinsale Town	Hawkes Isaac	Cuckoo Mills	-	-	-	Hawkes - Murphy Ed	1834	-	dd/	1834 2 269
St Multose	Kinsale Town	Moeran Caroline A	Cuckoo Mills	-	-	-	Moeran - Edisburry Emma	1884	-	dd/	1884 46 138
Kinsale	Kinsale Town	Sullivan William C	corn	-	-	-	-	-	18x3x18	vmb/	4
Clonteas	Kinsale Town :	Heard Edward	mills	-	-	-	Heard E- Jn & Isaac	1833	-	dd/	1833 2125
St Multose	Kinsale Town :	Hawkes Isaac	mills	-	-	-	Hawkes - Murphy Ed	1834	-	dd/	1834 2 269
St Multose	Kinsale Town :	Dunn Josias	Cuckoo Mill	-	-	-	Dunn J- Garton Patk	1876	-	dd/	1876 44 238
Kinsale	Kinsale Town :	Sullivan Jno	Browns Mill	-	-	-	Sullivan - Logan Wm	1839	-	dd/	1839 20 57
Kinsale	Kinsale Town :	Ahearne John	mills	-	-	-	Ahearne John - Thomas	1835	-	dd/	1835 6 70
Kinsale	KinsaleTown	Coghlan Joseph	Cookoe Mills	-	-	-	Coghlan - Busteed Susanna	1844	-	dd/	1844 20 175
Kinsale	KinsaleTown	Reynolds Jno	Cookoe Mills	-	-	-	Reynolds - Mahout Denis	1842	-	dd/	1842 19 260

PARISH	TOWNLAND	MILLER	TYPE	HOUSE	Land	£Val+	PROPRIETORS	Date	WHEEL etc.	Record	Ref.
Grenagh	Knockabehy	Crofts James	woollen factory	(1C) 45x30x24.3 :	-	14-11	-	-	17.9x5x -	hob/	5.3808
Kilmeen	Knockaclarig	- on Feale R.	tuck	-	-	-	-	-	-	6"os	4
Cork	Knockaneirk *	- on R. Bride	mill	-	-	-	-	-	-	1"os/	194
Cork	Knockanmore	NW/ Drohidnaglaragh	Bride Flour Mill	-	-	-	-	-	-	6"os	85
Cork	Knockanmore *	Mortens John & Jas	new	24.6x35.0x12	-	-	-	-	no dimensions	hob/	5.0699
Cork	Knockanroe	-	tuck (ruins)	13m x 5m single storey	-	-	-	-	- wheelpit 1.3 m.	iaa/	AI3504 os115.9.6
Kilbrogan	Knockbrogan	- nr bank Bandon R.	brewery	large complex east :	-	-	-	-	-	iaa/	AI3472 os110.3.5
Kilbrogan	Knockbrogan :	Clear Thomas	bark	(1B) 24x21.6x21.6 :	-	27-9	-	-	-	hob/	5.2457
Kilbrogan	Knockbrogan :	Cornwall Henry	brewery	(1B) 36.6x44x22 :	-	109	-	-	-	hob/	5.2457
Kilbrogan	Knockbrogan :	Cornwall Henry	brewery (part)	(1B) 50.6x27.6x21.6 :	-	-	-	-	-	hob/	5.2457
Kilbrogan	Knockbrogan :	- Cornwall's	Brewery	-	-	-	-	1841	-	6"os	110
Kilbrogan	Knockbrogan :	Sullivan William	bark	(1B) 25.6x23.6x13 :	-	8.18	-	-	-	hob/	5.2457
Ihgtermurragh	Knockglass	- at Lady's Br.	mill & pond	-	-	-	-	-	-	6"os	77
St Mary's S'don	Knocknabohilly	- at Cattle Market	glue yard	-	-	-	-	-	-	6"os	74
St Mary's S'don	Knocknabohilly	- at Cattle Market	tannery	-	-	-	-	-	-	6"os	74
Ballymodan	Knocknagarrane	Allman George	cotton disused	14 bay 5 storey :	-	-	-	-	- wheelpit 1.93 m.	iaa/	AI3513 os110.10.3
Ballymodan	Knocknagarrane	SSW/ Old Chapel Br.	Overton Cotton Mill		-	-	-	-	-	6"os	110
Ballymodan	Knocknagarrane	- W/ Old Chapel Br.	old flour mill	-	-	-	-	-	-	6"os	110
Ross	Knocknageehy	-	corn & carding	mill complex roadside :	-	-	-	-	- wheel replaced :	iaa/	AI3483 os143.4.1
Ross	Knocknageehy	-	corn & tuck	-	-	-	-	1841	-	6"os	143
Ross	Knocknageehy	-	mill (? hz)	-	-	-	-	-	millstone found on :	iaa/	AI2716 os140.1.6
Rathcooney	Knocknahoigane	Lyons Thomas	bleach	-	-	-	-	-	22x8x13 14 beams	vmb/	4
Rathcooney	Knocknahorgan	- on Glassboy R.	cloth	-	-	-	-	-	-	iaa/	AI6279
Rathcooney	Knocknahorgan	on Glashaboy R.	bleach & cloth	-	-	-	-	-	-	6"os	63
Rathcooney	Knocknahorgan	Symons Mr	drying loft	(1B) 132x23.6x20 :	-	62-15	-	1851	(cont.) no rub bds. :	hob/	5.0389
Rathcooney	Knocknahorgan	Symons Mr	lingery	(1B) 17x23.6x7.6 :	-	-	-	1851	22x8 & 28x15	hob/	5.0389
Rathcooney	Knocknahorgan	Symons Mr	lingery	(1B) 17x23.6x7.6 :	-	-	-	1851	22x8 & 28x15	hob/	5.0389
Cloyne	Knocknamadderee		old corn mill	-	-	-	-	-	-	6"os	76
Kilmurry	Knocknaneirk	- Hornhill Mill	corn	15.2m x 8m (disused) :	-	-	-	-	- wheelpit 3m x 2m	iaa/	AI9747 os83.14.16
Kilmurry	Knocknaneirk	-	tuck (in ruins)	15.2m x 8m Hornhill Mi	-	-	-	-	-	iaa/	AI9747 os83.14.16
Kilmurry	Knocknaneirk	E/ Knockaneirk Br.	tuck mill ruins	-	-	-	-	-	-	6"os	83
Kilmurry	Knocknaneirk	E/ Knockaneirk Br.		-	-	-	-	-	-	6"os	83
Kilmurry	Knocknaneirk		corn mill ruins	-	-	-	-	-	-	6"os	83
St Nicholas	Knockrea	off Blackrock Road	lime & salt works	-	-	-	-	-	-	6"os	74
St Nicholas	Knockrea	off Blackrock Road	lime works	-	-	-	-	-	-	6"os	74
Cork	Knockroe (4)	-	mill	-	-	-	-	-	-	1"os/	199
Ross	Koocknageehy	1/4m ExN Vge.	tuck	-	-	-	-	-	-	6"os	143
Ross	Koocknageehy		corn	-	-	-	-	-	-	6"os	143
Ross	Koocknageehy		Newmills Village	-	-	-	-	-	-	6"os	143
Aghabulloge	Knockglass	Irwin	mill	-	-	-	Irwin - Knox	-	-	dd/	35 204 21981
Aghabulloge	Knockglass	Irwin	mill	-	-	-	Irwin - Irwin	-	-	dd/	37 167 21701
Kilshannig	Lackendarragh	-	mill	-	-	-	-	-	-	1"os/	175
Caherduggan	Lag	Morrissey John	corn	(1A) 24.6x17x14.6 :	-	3.3.	-	-	9x4x2 24 floats :	hob/	5.0438
Caherduggan	Lag	Morrissey John	tuck	-	-	-	-	-	-	hob/	5.0438
Caherduggan	Lag	on R. Awbeg	tuck	-	-	-	-	-	-	6"os	17
Drinagh	Lahanaght	Connelly Cornelius	corn	29.0x18.0x6.6	-	-	formerly Jago Saml	-	14.6x3.2x9.6	hob/	5.0285
Inishannon	Laherfineen	E side Bandon R.	old bleach green	-	-	-	-	-	-	6"os	97
Inishannon	Laherfineen	E/ bridge.	old bleach mill	-	-	-	-	-	-	6"os	97
Inishannon	Laherfineen	from weir 5/8m W.	mill stream	-	-	-	-	-	-	6"os	97
Ringrone	Lanavaud		salt works	-	-	-	-	-	-	6"os	124
Chuurchtown	Leap	200x W. of Village	corn	- smart neat prems.	-	-	-	2008	-	mmSv/	B
Chuurchtown	Leap	at Vge. in gorge :	tuck	- demolished	-	-	-	2008	-	mmSv/	Z

PARISH	TOWNLAND	MILLER	TYPE	HOUSE	Land	£Val+	PROPRIETORS	Date	WHEEL etc.	Record	Ref.
Chuurchtown	Leap	NW/ Leap Vge.	tuck	-	-	-	-	-	-	6"os	142
Chuurchtown	Leap	SE / Leap Bridge	manganese works		-	-	-	-	-	6"os	142
Chuurchtown	Leap	W/ Leap Vge.	mill	-	-	-	-	-	-	6"os	142
Chuurchtown	Leap		corn store		-	-	-	-	-	6"os	142
Kilmoe	Leehane	Mahony Jeremiah	corn	27.6x17.0x8.0	-	-	-	-	11x2 doing no work	hob/	5.0288
St Finbar's	Lehenagh More	- S/R. at Lee Bank	flour, pond	-	-	-	-	-	-	6"os	74
St Finbar's	Leighcloon	on Roaringwater R.	tuck	-	-	-	-	-	-	6"os	140
Drishane	Liscahane	-	mill	-	-	-	-	-	-	6"os	39
Drishane	Liscahane	O`Donnell Herbert	corn	-	-	-	-	-	20x4x21	vmb/	4
Drishane	Liscahane	Wallis Henry	mill	-	-	-	Wallis H - Logan William C	1887	-	dd/	1887 23 181
Desertserges	Lisnacunna	-	mill	-	-	-	-	-	-	1"os/	194
Templemartin	Lisnagat	- ENE/ Lisnagat Br.	L'nagat Cotton Mill		-	-	-	-	-	6"os	96
Templemartin	Lisnagat	Wheeler John	cotton	-	-	-	-	1856	-	gr/	Ld.Est.db
Castlehaven	Lissarankin	-	mill	-	-	-	-	-	-	1"os/	200
Kilnagross	Lisselane	- C792NE/ Lisselane	mill	-	-	-	-	-	-	6"os	122
Kilshannig	Lombardstown	Bolster Thomas	grist	(2B) 18x17.6x12 & :	-	4	-	-	14x5.6x - 48 bkts. :	hob/	5.0428
Kilshannig	Lombardstown	Bolster Thomas	grist	-	-	-	-	-	14x6x5	vmb/	4
Kilshannig	Lombardstown	SSE Lombardstown Br	grist	-	-	-	-	-	-	6"os	32
Abbeystrowry	Lurriga	Clerke Mary	corn	-	-	-	Clerke M - Payne Somers	1887	-	dd/	1887 44 147
Abbeystrowry	Lurriga	Wright Charlotte	mill	-	-	-	Wright C - Carroll Theodore	1885	-	dd/	1885 14 109
Abbeystrowry	Lurriga	Swanton James H :	mill	-	-	88	-	1865	-	gr/-	Ld.Est.db
Abbeystrowry	Lurriga	Downing Timothy M :	mill	-	-	-	-	1906	-	Sv/-	Ld.Est.db
Dromdaleague	Loughcrot	- Shronacarton X	tuck	-	-	-	-	-	-	1"os/	200
Cork	Loyriga *	- on R. Ilen	Lurriga Flour Mills	-	-	-	-	-	-	6"os	140
Kilminoge	Lybe	- NE/ Belgooly Br.	starch	-	-	-	-	-	-	6"os	112
Kilminoge	Lybe		flour	-	-	-	-	-	-	6"os	112
Kilminoge	Lyhe	-	corn	-	-	-	-	-	-	iaa/	AI6272
Kilminoge	Lyhe	-	starch	blds destroyed c1934	-	-	-	-	-	iaa/	AI6272
Kilminoge	Lyhe	Hayes William H	corn	-	-	-	-	-	28x8x25 3 pr st.	vmb/	4
Kilminoge	Lyhe	Hayes William H	old starch mill	-	-	-	-	-	12x4x12	vmb/	4
Macroney	Macroney Lower	NNE of Araglin Br.	oat mill	-	-	-	-	-	-	6"os	28
Macroney	Macroney Lower	Riordan James	corn	-	-	-	-	-	19x4x19	vmb/	4
Macroney	Macroney Lower	Riordan James	flour	(1C) 47x29x24 :	-	5-0-2	-	1848	19x4.3x19 :	hob/	5.0362
Macroom	Macroom Town	- on Sollane R.	mill	-	-	-	-	-	-	1"os/	186
Kilmaloda	Madame	Connell Charles	flour	-	-	-	-	-	20x7x15	vmb/	4
Kilmaloda	Madame (NB :)	Connell Chas & Co.	flour	62.6x29x28.6 & :	-	-	-	-	20x7x15	hob/	5.0221
Macroom	Maghereen	on R.Sullanee	flour	-	-	-	-	-	-	6"os	71
Macroom	Maghereen	Walton	corn	24m x 6m 2 storey :	-	-	-	-	-	pOPW/	(AI9748)
Macroom	Maghereen	Walton (family)	corn	19.1x12.2m roadside :	-	-	-	-	- wheelpit 1.7 m.	iaa/	AI9749 os71.5.1
Macroom	Maghereen	Walton (family)	corn abandoned	24m x 6m 2 storey :	-	-	-	-	- wheelpit 1.7 m.	iaa/	AI9748 os71.5.1
Macroom	Maghereen		corn mill	-	-	-	-	-	-	6"os	71
Mallow	Mallow	- 1/2m W of Town	salt works	-	-	-	-	-	-	6"os	33
Mallow	Mallow	- 1/4m N / Bridge	salt works	-	-	-	-	-	-	6"os	33
Mallow	Mallow	- Main St	brewery	-	-	-	-	-	-	6"os	33
Mallow	Mallow Town :	- on R Blackwater	mill	-	-	-	-	-	-	1"os/	175
Mallow	Mallow Town :	McMullen Josh	mills	-	-	-	McMullen J - Brady K	1849	-	dd/	1849 16 239
Mallow	Mallow Town :	Jones Thomas	Manor Mill	-	-	-	Jones - Carmichael J	1841	-	dd/	18841 7 33
Mallow	Mallow Town :	McMullen Joshua	mill	-	-	-	McMullen J - Brady :	1849	-	dd/	1849 16 239
Fanlobus	Manch West	McCue Daniel	paper	(1B) 20x20x16 & :	-	-	-	1850	13x4.6x13.6 & mc/y :	hob/	5.0201
Fanlobus	Manch West	- W/ Bandon R.	corn	-	-	-	-	-	-	6"os	108
Fanlobus	Manch West	- W/ Bandon R.	paper	-	-	-	-	-	-	6"os	108
Fanlobus	Manch West		Manch Mills	-	-	-	-	-	-	6"os	108
Fanlobus	Mansion Ho Ward	Dyke Parade	flour	-	-	-	-	-	-	6"os	74

PARISH	TOWNLAND	MILLER	TYPE	HOUSE	Land	£Val+	PROPRIETORS	Date	WHEEL etc.	Record	Ref.
Kilworth	Maryville	Corban Laurence	flour	offices & stores	-	160	-	1856	-	gr/	a.a.Ire.ie
Kilworth	Maryville	Corban Laurence	flour	-	-	-	-	-	20x10x9 6 pr st.	vmb/	4
Kilworth	Maryville	Corban Lucas Arthur	mills	-	-	-	Corbal L - Prov Bank of Ire.	1886	-	dd/	1886 37 250
Kilworth	Maryville	W/ Downing Br.	flour	-	-	-	-	-	-	6"os	27
Ross	Maul	- on Roury R.	mill	-	-	-	-	-	-	1"os/	200
Ross	Maulatanvalley	-	flax & pond	roadside remains :	-	-	-	-	-	iaa/	AI3512 os134.2.2
Abbeystrowry	Maulbrack	-	saw	- in Hollybrook farm	-	-	-	-	- diesel powered	iaa/	AI3514 os141.4.2
Desertserges	Maulbrack	Sarlier John G	mill & mill lot	-	-	-	Sadlier Jn - Seymour Chas	1887	-	dd/	1887 51 259
Desertserges	Maulnarouga	Carty Daniel	grist	-	-	-	-	-	14x3x14	vmb/	4
Desertserges	Maulnarouga	M'Carty Daniel	corn	house, offs. & land	42a.	28.5.	- (+ tenants)	1856	-	gr/	a.a.Ire.ie
Ballintemple	Maytown	Boyd Charles	mill lands	-	-	-	Boyd Chas - Dillon Henry	1889	-	dd/	1889 18 36
Farhy	Meadstown	-	tuck	-	-	-	-	-	-	6"os	18
Mogesha	Middleton T`pks	-	distillery (1825)	complex of buildings :	-	-	builder Marcus Lynch	-	22x15.3 cast iron :	iaa/	AI-6250
Mogesha	Middleton T`pks	-	flour	-	-	-	-	-	-	iaa/	AI6265/6
Mogesha	Middleton Town	-	mill	-	-	-	-	-	-	1"os/	187
Mogesha	Middleton Town	- nr Middleton	mill	-	-	-	-	-	-	1"os/	187
Middleton	Middleton Town :	Dwyer Mrs	brewery	(1B) 56x22.6x18.6 & :	-	23	-	-	-	hob/	5.0569
Middleton	Middleton Town :	Murphy Jas. & Co.	distillery	(1B) 51x74x20 still ho :	-	-	-	-	22x10x12.6 all iron :	hob/	5.0549
Middleton	Middleton Town :	Allen Mr	flour	(1B) 72x58x44 & :	-	-	-	-	iron 24.6x16x10.6 :	hob/	5.0550
Middleton	Middleton T'parks	beside distillery	distillery Cottage	-	-	-	-	-	-	6"os	76
Middleton	Middleton T'parks	N/ Cork Br.	flour	-	-	-	-	-	-	6"os	76
Middleton	Middleton T'parks	N/ Lewis Br.	old brewery	-	-	-	-	-	-	6"os	76
Middleton	Middleton T'parks	NExE. / Lewis Br.	distillery	-	-	-	-	-	-	6"os	76
Middleton	Middleton T'parks :	Hackett Bart Jas. :	distillery	Incumb Est consisting :	-	-	-	1850	-	mlyIE	p2
Fanlobus	Milleenanannig	-	bleach	13.15m x 6.4m & green	-	-	-	-	-	iaa/	AI3510 os108.13.1
Fanlobus	Milleenannig	McGovern Henry	bleach in ruins	-	-	-	-	1850	11x2.6x- 31 floats :	hob/	5.0201
Ballymartle	Mill-land	NW/ Ballymartle Br.	tuck	-	-	-	-	-	-	6"os	98
Drishane	Millstreet :	O`Regan Andrew	wheatmeal :	-	-	-	-	1963	-	lic/22	wheat
Cooliney	Milltown	Milltown Castle	no mill	-	-	-	-	-	-	6"os	7
Cork	Milltown b/ Imokilly	Prov Bank of Ireland	mill	-	-	-	Prov Bank - Roche James	1889	-	dd/	1889 11 218
Kanturk	Millview	- at Boogheen Br.	mill	-	-	-	-	-	-	1"os/	175
Drinagh	Minanes	-	corn & tuck	-	-	-	-	1841	-	6"os	120
Drinagh	Minanes	McCarthy James	corn	40.0x16.6x17.6	-	-	-	-	11.6x2.6x10	hob/	5.0285
Ballymodan	Moanarone	Allman's	Distillery	-	-	-	-	1841	-	6"os	110
Ballymodan	Moanarone	Allman George	distillery	- large complex built :	-	-	-	-	-	iaa/	AI3474 os110.3.6
Ballymoodan	Moanarone	Allman Richard	distillery	(1B) 63x38x21 stillho. :	-	-	-	1850	30x7x30 3 rpm :	hob/	5.0184
Ballymoodan	Moanarone	Allman Richard L	grist	-	-	-	-	-	30x7x30 4 pr st.	vmb/	4
Ballymoodan	Moanarone	Alman Richard	distillery	(1B) 74x36x20 :	-	-	-	1857	- pumps etc.	hob/	5.2458
Ballymoodan	Moanarone	Alman Richard	mill	(1A) 31.6x59x45 :	-	-	-	1857	28x6x7.3x30 :	hob/	5.2458
Ballymoodan	Moanarone	Alman Richard L	distillery	59.0x33.0x44 & still ho :	-	-	-	1850	30x7x30 3 pr st. :	hob/	5.0184/5
Garrycloyne	Monacnapa	-	woollen	large 5 bay 3 storey :	-	-	-	-	-	iaa/	AI9752 os621.16.4
Garrycloyne	Monacnapa	-	woollen	- Blarney Woollen Mills	-	-	-	-	-	pOPW/	(AI9752)
Garrycloyne	Monacnapa	- on R. Martin	woollen factory	-	-	-	-	-	-	6"os	62
Kilworth	Monadrishane	Mountcashel E.	Manor Mills	-	-	-	Mountcashel - Smyth Chas	1888	-	dd/	1888 39 294
Kilworth	Monadrishane	Smyth Chas W	Manor Mill	-	-	-	Smyth Ch. - Nat. Bank Govs	1887	-	dd/	1887 27 51
Whitechurch	Monard	-	Dyewood Mills	-	-	-	-	-	-	6"os	63
Whitechurch	Monard	-	iron mills	-	-	-	-	-	-	6"os	63
Whitechurch	Monard	-	Iron Mills	-	-	-	-	-	-	6"os	63
Whitechurch	Monard	-	Monaroad Iron Works		-	-	-	-	-	6"os	63
Whitechurch	Monard	Beales Abraham	1st iron	-	-	-	-	-	12x4x14	vmb/	4
Whitechurch	Monard	Beales Abraham	2nd iron	-	-	-	-	-	14x5x17	vmb/	4
Whitechurch	Monard	Beales Abraham	bellows	-	-	-	-	-	10x2x13	vmb/	4

PARISH	TOWNLAND	MILLER	TYPE	HOUSE	Land	£Val+	PROPRIETORS	Date	WHEEL etc.	Record	Ref.
Whitechurch	Monard	Beales Abraham	hammer	-	-	-	-	-	12x4x16	vmb/	4
Whitechurch	Monard	Beales Abraham	logwood	-	-	-	-	-	14x5x16	vmb/	4
Whitechurch	Monard	Beales Abraham	not working	-	-	-	-	-	-	vmb/	4
Desertsarges	Moneens	-	hz wheeled mill	-	-	-	-	-	hz wheel - visited :	iaa/	AI2722 os110.0.0
Carrigaline	Monfieldstown	S/ Poulgheric Br.	flour, & pond	-	-	-	-	-	-	6"os	75
Cork	Moor Park	Petre Albert Rt Hon.	Manor Mills	-	-	-	Petre Hon. - Smyth Chas	1888	-	dd/	1888 39 295
Cork	Moore Park	Moore-Smyth Chas :	Manor Mills	-	-	-	Moore-Smyth - Boileau Fras	1887	-	dd/	1887 28 77
Carrigaline	Morefieldstown	Power Mr	flour & corn	-	-	-	-	-	44x5x39 4 pr st.	vmb/	4
Clonfert	Mount Keeffe	James O`Keeffe	corn	-	-	-	-	-	20x5x21	vmb/	4
Mountleader	Mountleader	1m. S/ Millstreet	Mountleader Mills	-	-	-	-	-	-	6"os	39
Drishane	Mountleader	Charles Ford	corn	-	-	-	-	-	12x3x13	vmb/	4
Drishane	Mountleader	Charles Ford	tuck	-	-	-	-	-	9x2x12	vmb/	4
Kilmichael	Mountmusic	Morgan Anthony	mill	-	-	-	Morgan Ant - Lindsay Sam	1889	-	dd/	1889 42 52
Aghabulloge	Mountrivers	on Delehina R. :	site of Mulenroh Mill		-	-	-	-	-	6"os	61
Clontead	Mullendunny	- at M`dunny Br.	mill	-	-	-	-	-	-	1"os/	195
Clontead	Mullendunny	Jago Robt J	flour	-	-	-	-	-	12x - x -	vmb/	4
Clontead	Mullendunny	N/ Mullendunny Br.	flour	-	-	-	-	-	-	6"os	112
Murragh	Murragh	-	corn	- Palace Anne Mills :	-	-	-	-	6m dia. x 2.4 m pit.	iaa/	AI3497 os109.3.4
Murragh	Murragh	- str. to Bandon R.	mill	-	-	-	-	-	-	1"os/	194
Murragh	Murragh	- on road to Bandon	mill	lge. Appartments Res. :	-	-	-	2008	-	mmSv/	Ca
Murragh	Murragh	Norwood William	corn & flour	48x47x41	-	-	-	-	29x7x30	hob/	5.0238
Murragh	Murragh	Norwood William	flour	-	-	34	-	1851	-	gr/	Ld.Est.db
Murragh	Murragh	-	flour	-	-	-	Conv. for appartments	c2000	-	Sv/	Ld.Est.db
Murragh	Murragh	- N. Murragh Lake	corn	-	-	-	-	-	-	6"os	109
Murragh	Murragh	-	mill pond	-	-	-	-	-	-	6"os	109
Cork	New Mills	-	mill	-	-	-	-	-	-	1"os/	200
Kilshannig	Newberry	-	Newberry Corn M	-	-	-	-	-	-	6"os	32
Kilshannig	Newberry	- R. Blackwater :	mills	-	-	-	-	-	-	1"os/	175
Kilshannig	Newberry	Benn Walter	grist	-	-	-	-	-	11x5x7	vmb/	4
Kilshannig	Newberry	- near R. Blackwater	Newberry House	-	-	-	-	-	-	6"os	32
Kilshannig	Newberry :	Benn Walter	grist	(3C) 43x18x11.6 :	-	18/2	-	-	11x5x7.6 48 bkts. :	hob/	5.0428
Clonfert	Newmarket Tn :	Ronaldson Eben'zer	corn	-	-	-	-	-	17x4x16	vmb/	4
Clonfert	Newmarket Tn :	Ronaldson Eben'zer	mill & dw. ho.	(2B) 30x19x7 :	-	12	-	1849	17x4x16.6 48 bkts. :	hob/	5.0431
Cork	Newmill	Donoghoe Michael	mill	-	-	-	Donohoe M - Travers Robt	1885	-	dd/	1885 18 6
Kildoneny	Oldcastletown	- W/ R. Funshion	flour & mill pond	-	-	-	-	8141	-	6"os	18
Kildoneny	Oldcastletown	Catherine Carroll	corn	(1B) 45.6x20x31 :	-	7-5	-	1848	o`shot 13.6x4x13.6 :	hob/	5.3041
Kildoneny	Oldcastletown	Catherine Carroll	flour	-	-	-	-	-	13x4x13	vmb/	4
Doneraile	Park South	-	mill race	-	-	-	-	-	-	6"os	18
Doneraile	Park South	1/4m. S / Park House	Park Mill	-	-	-	-	-	-	6"os	18
Doneraile	Park South	Carroll Michael	flour	(1C) 65x20x32 & :	-	65	-	-	14x5.8x4 30 floats :	hob/	5.0448
Castlelyons	Pellick	- E/ Ballynella Br.	tuck	-	-	-	-	-	-	6"os	45
Cork	Peter's Ward	- C920Gt. George's S	Lee Boot Manufacturing Co.		-	-	-	-	-	6"os	74
Cork	Peter's Ward	Hanover Street	Hive Iron Works	-	-	-	-	-	-	6"os	74
Cork	Peter's Ward	Cremer's Sq	Beamish & Crawford Brewery		-	-	-	-	-	6"os	74
Rathcooney	Poulacurry South	Hurley William	bleach	eng. ho (1B) 60x25x21 :	-	-	-	1851	breast 18.6x6x9 :	hob/	5.0389
Rathcooney	Poulacurry South	N/ Glanmire Br.	cloth	-	-	-	-	-	-	6"os	75
Rathcooney	Poulacurrys	Thorley William	bleach	-	-	-	-	-	18x6x9 & 18x7x9 :	vmb/	4
Kilbolane	Prohust	- at Prohust House	thrashing m/c	-	-	-	-	-	-	6"os	6
Mourneabbey	Quartertown	Brady Kingsmile	carding & tuck	-	-	-	-	-	13.6x4.9x - 46 bkts.	hob/	5.0464
Mourneabbey	Quartertown	Brady M/s Wm & K	flour	(1C) 49x24x45 store :	-	-	-	-	Gravity, 13.9x13x15 :	hob/	5.0464
Mourneabbey	Quartertown	McMullins Joseph	flour	(1B) 69x22.6x39 kiln :	-	-	-	-	Gravity, 15.6x7x9 :	hob/	5.0484
Mourneabbey	Quartertown Lr	- 1/4m SW / River	flour	-	-	-	-	-	-	6"os	33

PARISH	TOWNLAND	MILLER	TYPE	HOUSE	Land	£Val+	PROPRIETORS	Date	WHEEL etc.	Record	Ref.
Mourneabbey	Quartertown Lr	- 1/5m W/ River	Mallow Flour Mills	-	-	-	-	-	-	6"os	33
Mourneabbey	Raffeen / Shanbally			-	-	-	-	-	-	6"os	87
Rathcormack	Rathcormack	- on Shannowen R.	corn	6 bay 4 storey	-	-	-	-	-	iaa/	AI6274
Whitechurch	Rathdeacon	Dublo Benjamin	bone	-	-	-	-	-	13x6x16	vmb/	4
Rathgoggan	Rathgoggan Mid. :	Haines Edward	mill	(1C) 26x23x9 (no loft) :	-	-	-	1849	-	hob/	5.0783
Rathgoggan	Rathgoggan Middle	Ryan Kennedy	flour	-	-	-	-	-	16x5x14 14x5x13	vmb/	4
Rathgoggan	Rathgoggan Middle		Barrack Flour Mill	-	-	-	-	-	-	6"os	2
Rathgoggan	Rathgoggan Middle		corn	-	-	-	-	-	-	6"os	2
Rathgoggan	Rathgoggan Middle		flour -	-	-	-	-	-	-	6"os	2
Rathgoggan	Rathgoggan Middle		tannery (2) -	-	-	-	-	-	-	6"os	2
Rathgoggan	Rathgoggan North	-	Ballincolly Mill-	-	-	-	-	-	-	6"os	3
Rathgoggan	Rathgoggan North	Spillane John	flour & corn	-	-	-	-	-	14x4x12	vmb/	4
Ballyhay	Rathmorgan	Carroll John	flour & corn	-	-	-	-	-	16x6x11	vmb/	4
Ballyhay	Rathmorgan	- N./ Awbeg R.	Ballyhay Mill	-	-	-	-	-	-	6"os	8
Whitechurch	Rathpeacon		corn	-	-	-	-	-	-	6"os	74
Whitechurch	Rathpeacon		mill pond	-	-	-	-	-	-	6"os	74
Skull	Rathruane More	-	tuck	6.8m x 3.6 m west of :	-	-	-	-	-	iaa/	AI3505 os140.5.3
Ross	Reanascreena		flax	-	-	-	-	-	-	1"os/	200
Ross	Reanascreena	Mennis Michael :	woollen :	-	-	-	-	1861	water wheel later :	sv/	ATrim
Ross	Reanascreena N.	Cokely John	corn &kiln	(1B) 24x18x14 :	-	-	-	1848	10x2.6x10 2 pr.st.	hob/	5.025
Ross	Reanascreena N.	Cokely John	tuck (vacant)	(1B) 30x20x12 no loft	-	-	-	-	-	hob/	5.025
Ross	Reanascreena N.	Reanascreena Vge.	woollen	-	-	-	-	1888	mill race & pond	25"os/	134-06
Ross	Reanascreena S. :	-	woollen	remains late 19th C. :	-	-	-	-	-	iaa/	AI3501 os134.6.2
Youghal	Rearour	-	flour	-	-	-	-	-	-	6"os	98
Youghal	Rearour		corn	-	-	-	-	-	-	6"os	96
Youghal	Rearour		tuck	-	-	-	-	-	-	6"os	96
Youghal	Rearour :	Carney John & Son	flour	(1C) 40x22x36.6 :	-	-	-	-	25x5x20 3pr.sts. :	hob/	5.0570
Youghal	Rearour :	Carney John & Son	shelling	(1C) 40x23x36.6 :	-	-	-	-	16.6x4.2x12 :	hob/	5.0570
Cork	Reen (2)	M & L Bank	Ascreena Mill	-	-	-	M & L Bank - Mennis McI	1891	-	dd/	1891 2 168
Kilmaloda	Reengarrigeen	Leary Patrick	linen factory	20.6x15.6x9 addition :	-	-	-	-	11x4x11 dilapidated	hob/	5.0221
Kilmaloda	Reengarrigeen	Leary Patrick	tuck	-	-	-	-	-	10x4x10	hob/	5.0221
Tracton	Ringabella		old lead mines	-	-	-	-	-	-	6"os	99
Ballyfoyle	Ringroe	Shea L I	corn	-	-	-	-	-	16x3x11 (O.S. note) :	vmb/	4
Templeusque	Riverstown	-		-	-	-	-	-	-	6"os	75
Templeusque	Riverstown	Lane Thomas B.	flour	(1B) 75.6x22.6x28.6 :	-	22-17	-	1851	20x12x7.10 40 bkts.	hob/	5.0172
Templeusque	Riverstown	Lane Thomas Biggs	mill	(1B) 137x23x28 :	-	22-17	-	1847	worked by steam :	hob/	5.0172
Templeusque	Riverstown	Logan Ellen	cloth factory & :	(1B) 109x27x32.6 :	-	27-13	-	-	18x6x9 breast shot :	hob/	5.0172
Templeusque	Riverstown	Logan Ellen	tuck	-	-	-	-	-	10x5.2x10 30 bkts.	hob/	5.0172
Templeusque	Riverstown	Thorley William & :	bleach factory	(1B) 79.6x26x24 & :	-	37-6	-	1851	16x5x9 32 bkts. :	hob/	5.0172
Templeusque	Riverstown	Thorley William & :	flour	(1B) 25.6x26x24	-	-	-	1851	- 4 pairs stones :	hob/	5.0172
Templeusque	Riverstown Town	-	woollen	-	-	-	-	-	-	1"os/	187
Brinny	Rockfort	- E/ Brinny R.	corn	-	-	-	-	-	-	6"os	96
Brinny	Rockfort	Hornebrell John I	grist	-	-	-	-	-	20x5x20	vmb/	4
Brinny	Rockfort	Hurly Johanna	grist	(1C) 22x24x33 & :	-	-	-	1849	20x5.2x20 32 bkts.	hob/	5.0188
Ros	Ross Carbery		salt works	-	-	-	-	-	-	6"os	143
Rostellan	Rostellan	-	corn	-	-	-	-	-	-	iaa/	AI6273
Rostellan	Rostellan	- in Demesne	corn & pond	-	-	-	-	-	-	6"os	88
Kilbrogan	Roughgrove East	-	carding & spin	- 5 bay 2 sty gabled :	-	-	-	-	-	iaa/	AI3508 os96.14.1
Kilbrogan	Roughgrove East	- S/ Aghnagire Br.	carding & spinning		-	-	-	-	-	6"os	96
Ballymodan	Roundhill	-	corn	- Roundhill Mills :	-	-	-	-	-	iaa/	AI3499 os110.6.6
Ballymodan	Roundhill	-	flour & tuck	-	-	-	-	-	-	6"os	110
Ballymodan	Roundhill	Crowley Timothy	mills	-	-	-	Crowley Timothy - William	1886	-	dd/	1886 36 267

PARISH	TOWNLAND	MILLER	TYPE	HOUSE	Land	£Val+	PROPRIETORS	Date	WHEEL etc.	Record	Ref.
Ballymodan	Roundhill	Jeremiah Crowley	corn	- 3 bay 3 sty mill also :	-	-	-	-	- wheel undershot :	iaa/	AI2498 os110.6.6
Ballymodan	Roundhill	- NE/ Old Chapel Br.	oat	-	-	-	-	-	-	6"os	110
Ballymodan	Roundhill	- SE/ Old Chapel Br.	tuck	-	-	-	-	-	-	6"os	110
Ross	Rouryglen	-	corn	- complex in valley :	-	-	-	-	- wheel used for :	iaa/	AI3484 os143.1.3
Ross	Rouryglen	Anderson John	corn	(3C) 25x17.6x8	-	-	-	1849	12x2.6x12.6 36 bkts.	hob/	5.0248
Ross	Rouryglen	Anderson John	tuck	(3C) 20x18x16.6	-	-	-	1849	9x1.4x9.6	hob/	5.0248
Ross	Rouryglen	- N/ Roury Br.	Roury Tuck Mill	-	-	-	-	-	-	6"os	143
Ross	Rouryglen		Roury Corn Mill	-	-	-	-	-	-	6"os	142
Clonfert	Rowls Langford N.	- N. / R. Allow	tuck	-	-	-	-	-	-	6"os	4
Cork	Ruineen	Tighe St Laurence	mill	-	-	-	Tighe St. L - Paul Alfred	1889	-	dd/	1889 7 298
Corncomohide	Rusheen	Carroll Patrick	corn	(1B) 53x22x33 & :	-	-	-	1849	breast 15x4.6x8.6 :	hob/	5.0774
Corncomohide	Rusheen	Carroll Patrick	flour & corn	-	-	-	-	1856	15x4x8	vmb/	4
Corcomohide	Rusheen	- on Maigue R.	Ross Corn Mill	-	-	-	-	-	-	6"os	2
Abbeystrowry	Russagh	-	corn	- 3 storey & addition :	-	-	-	-	- wheelpit 1.67 m.	iaa/	AI3500 os141.16.3
Abbeystrowry	Russagh	- SE/ Scibbereen	mill	-	-	-	-	-	-	6"os	141
Abbeystrowry	Russagh	- SE/ Scibbereen	mill	now Adventure Centre	-	-	Michael Murphy	2008	-	mmSv?	Cp
Cork	Saint - Annes *	-	woollen	-	-	-	-	-	-	6"os	45
Rathcooney	Sallybrook	Finn James	mill	-	-	-	Finn James - Mullins Henry	1893	-	dd/	1893 75 274
Rathcooney	Sallybrook	Garde Mary	corn	-	-	-	Garde Mary - Mullins Henry	1893	-	dd/	1893 11 155
Rathcoony	Sallybrook Town	-	mill	-	-	-	-	-	-	1"os/	187
Templeusque	Sarsfieldcourt	- E/ Glanmire Bridge	spade factory	-	-	-	-	-	-	6"os	63
Templeusque	Sarsfieldcourt	Tuomy John	flour	(1B) 27.6x20x30 & :	-	-	-	1851	10x4.8x10.6 32 bkts.	hob/	5.0172
Templeusque	Sarsfieldcourt	Tuomy John	spade factory	(1B) 31.6x9.6x7.6 & :	-	-	-	1851	-	6"os	63
Kildorrery	Scart	-	mill pond	conn. to Funshion R.	-	-	-	-	-	6"os	18
Kilgarrif	Scartagh	- S. side Millstreet	oat	-	-	-	-	-	-	6"os	86
Kilgarriff	Scartagh	Allen Thomas & Jas :	kiln	offices & garden	0.0.3(	27.10.	-	1856	-	gr/	a.a.Ire.ie
Kilgarriff	Scartagh	Fitzpatrick John	corn & kiln	- and yard	-	-	-	1856	-	gr/	a.a.Ire.ie
Kilgarriff	Scartagh	Fitzpatrick John	grist	-	-	-	-	-	10x3x6	vmb/	4
Clonfert	Scarteen Lower	- Newmarket Town	mill in ruins	-	-	-	-	1841	-	6"os/	22
Ballymoney	Shanaway E.	Hurley John	corn	-	-	4.5.	-	1856	-	gr/	a.a.Ire.ie
Ballymoney	Shanaway E.	Hurley John	grist	-	-	-	-	-	11x2x12	vmb/	4
Carrigaline	Shanbally	-	Rathanallig Flour Mill		-	-	-	-	-	6"os	87
Cork	Shancashel *	-	hz wheeled mill	-	-	-	-	-	hz wheel - examined:	iaa/	AI2713 os94.0.0
Abbeystrowry	Skibbereen :	Good Robert & Sons	wheatmeal :	-	-	-	-	1963	-	lic/12	wheat
Abbeystrowry	Skibbereen Town	- W. of Bridge	The Steam mill	- conserved for use :	-	-	-	2008	-	mmSv/	Cc
Abbeystrowry	Skibbereen Town :	Hosford R J	wheatmeal :	-	-	-	-	1963	-	lic/15	wheat
Abbeystrowry	Skibbereen Town :	- Drinagh Co-op	mill	- small 3 sty. building	-	-	now Winterwonderland	2008	-	mmSv/	Cp
Ballyvourney	Slievereagh	-	mill race	-	-	-	-	-	-	6"os	58
Ballyvourney	Slievereagh	- on Sullane R.	flour	-	-	-	-	-	-	6"os	58
Ballyvourney	Slievereagh	- W/ B'vourney Vg. :	tuck	-	-	-	-	-	-	6"os	58
Ballyvoracy	Slievreagh	Colthurst George	corn	-	-	-	-	-	16x4x17	vmb/	4
Ballyvoracy	Slievreagh	Colthurst George	tuck	-	-	-	-	-	12x3x13	vmb/	4
Inishkenny	Sraleigh	-	tuck & pond	-	-	-	-	-	-	6"os	85
Inishkenny	Sraleigh	Hurley Daniel	grist	17.6x22.0x16 & dw. ho :	-	-	-	-	12x2.8x12	hob/	5.0699
Cork City	St Patrick's Ward	- Black Miller's Lane	glue yard	-	-	-	-	-	-	6"os	74
Cork City	St Patrick's Ward	- Broad Lane	tannery	-	-	-	-	-	-	6"os	74
Cork City	St Patrick's Ward	- Leitrim St.	windmill	-	-	-	-	-	-	6"os	74
Cork City	St Patrick's Ward	- off Clarence St.	tannery	-	-	-	-	-	-	6"os	74
Cork City	St Patrick's Ward	- Penrose's Quay		-	-	-	-	-	-	6"os	74
Cork City	St Patrick's Ward	- St Patrick`s Quay	foundry	-	-	-	-	-	-	6"os	74
Cork City	St Patrick's Ward	- Water Lane	tannery	-	-	-	-	-	-	6"os	74
Cork City	St Patrick's Ward	- Watercourse Rd.	tanneries	-	-	-	-	-	-	6"os	74

PARISH	TOWNLAND	MILLER	TYPE	HOUSE	Land	£Val+	PROPRIETORS	Date	WHEEL etc.		Record	Ref.
Cork City	St Patrick's Ward	- York St.	distillery	-	-	-	-	-	-		6"os	74
Cork City	St Patrick's Ward	- York St.	tannery	-	-	-	-	-	-		6"os	74
Cork City	St. Nicholas' Ward	- Poulduff Rd.	bleach green	-	-	-	-	-	-		6"os	74
Clondulane	Straw Hall	Denehy Daniel	thrashing	-	-	-	-	-	18x3x18		vmb/	4
Clondulane	Straw Hall	Roche Nicholas Wm	threshing	-	-	-	-	1856	-		gr/	a.a.lre.ie
Kilgarriff	Tawnies Lower	-	oat	-	-	-	-	-	-		6"os	135
Kilgarriff	Tawnies Lower	-	oat	-	-	-	-	-	-		6"os	135
Kilgarriff	Tawnies Lower	- N. of Tobin's Br.	tuck	-	-	-	-	-	-		6"os	135
Kilgarriff	Tawnies Lower	Allen Thomas	grist	-	-	-	-	-	18x5x18		vmb/	4
Kilgarriff	Tawnies Lower	Allen Thomas & Jas	corn	house, offs. & land	7a.	61	- (+ tenant's ho.)	1856	-		gr/	a.a.lre.ie
Kilgarriff	Tawnies Lower	E/ Tobin's Bridge	brewery	-	-	-	-	-	-		6"os	135
Kilgarriff	Tawnies Lower	- N/ Tobin's Bridge	flour	-	-	-	-	-	-		6"os	135
Kilgarriff	Tawnies Lower	- on Oliver Lane	Linen Hall	-	-	-	-	-	-		6"os	135
Templeusque	Templeusque	-	woollen	-	-	-	-	-	-		1"os/	187
Rathcormack	Terramount	NE/ Rathcormack Vge.	flour	-	-	-	-	-	-		6"os	44
Timoleague	Timoleague	-	corn	-	-	-	-	-	-		6"os	123
Timoleague	Timoleague	-	tuck	-	-	-	-	-	-		6"os	123
Caheragh	Tooreen	- ENE / Derreeny Br.	corn mill ruins	-	-	-	-	-	-		6"os	133
Caheragh	Tooreen	- on Saivnose R.	tuck	-	-	-	-	-	-		6"os	132
bo./ Carbery	Townland ?`	Bennett Thomas	the flax mill	-	-	-	Bennett Thos - Hill Thomas	1893	-		dd/	1893 22 64
bo./ Kinsale	Townland ?`	Delacour James	Browns Mills	-	-	-	Delacour James - Robert	1886	-		dd/	1886 14 294
bo./ Kinsale	Townland ?`	McCausland William	Browns Mills	-	-	-	McCausland W - Franks Th	1885	-		dd/	1885 10 272
bo./ Carbery	Townland ?`	Norwood William	Moragh Mill	-	-	-	Norwood Wm - Daly John	1893	-		dd/	1893 55 238
bo./ Carbery	Townland ?`	Norwood William	Palace Anne Mill	-	-	-	Norwood Wm - Daly John	1893	-		dd/	1893 55 238
bo./ Carbery	Townland ?`	Shorten Joseph	Ross Mill	-	-	-	Shorten Joseph - Thomas	1890	-		dd/	1890 24 63
bo./ Kinsale	Townland ?`	Sibthorpe Thomas	Browns Mills	-	-	-	Sibthorpe Th - Molloy Sarah	1886	-		dd/	1886 6 217
bo./ Carbery	Townland ?`	Swanton James	The Mills	-	-	-	Swanton - Sweetman Wm	1894	-		dd/	94 15 216
bo./ Iban	Townland ?`	Tobin Mark	Tobins Mills	-	-	-	Tobin Mark - Good James	1889	-		dd/	1889 20 118
Tracton Park	Tracton	-	woollen	-	-	-	-	-	-		1"os/	195
Killasbugmullane	Trantstown	-	paper mill	-	-	-	-	-	-		6"os	64
Killasbugmullane	Trantstown	S/ St Valentine's Well	paper	-	-	-	-	-	-		6"os	64
Tracton Park	Tubrid	- S/ Tubrid Town :	woollen	-	-	-	-	-	-		25"os/	99-13
Tracton Park	Tubrid	Covenny Denis	corn	-	-	-	-	-	15x4x10		vmb/	4
Tracton Park	Tubridtown	Sullivan John	corn	-	-	-	-	-	11x2x11		vmb/	4
Tracton Park	Tubridtown	Sullivan John	tuck	-	-	-	-	-	9x2x8		vmb/	4
Balimaboy	Tullig More	NNW / B'nahassig Br.	flour mills, pond	-	-	-	-	-	-		6"os	98
Cork	Upton :	O`Mahony Barth.	flour	-	-	-	-	-	-	<1,000 barrels	lic/21	wh.meal
Little Island	Wallingstown	- N. side Lo. Mahon	mill (hz)	-	-	-	-	-	-		iaa/	IA5154 os75.5.5
Little Island	Wallingstown	-	Flaxfort	ho.N/ L. Mahon	-	-	-	-	-		6"os	75
Mallow	Wilton Mallow	-	mills	-	-	-	-	-	-		1"os/	175
Skull	Woodlands	- at Barytes Vge.	mill (2)	-	-	-	-	-	-		1"os/	199
Mogeely	Woodview	- near Kilmeen Br.	tuck	-	-	-	-	-	-		1"os/	193
Youghal	Youghal Town	-	brewery	-	-	-	-	1841	-		6"os/	67
Youghal	Youghal Town	-	brewery	remains of yard and :	-	-	-	-	-		iaa/	AI3473 os 135.6.3
Youghal	Youghal Town	Durdin Alexander	Windmill Lane	-	-	-	Durdin A - Robertson Thos	1886	-		dd/	1886 39 173
Youghal	Youghal Town	Ld Estate Court	Windmill Lane	-	-	-	Ld Est Ct - Lynch Jas	1876	-		dd/	1876 5 234
Youghal	Youghal Town	O`Keeffe David	clay (part of)	(1B) 24x25.6x10.6 :	-	-	-	-	-		hob/	5.0564
Youghal	Youghal Town	O`Keeffe David	clay (part of)	tile kiln (1B) 30x29x20 :	-	31.17	-	-	-		hob/	5.0564
Youghal	Youghal Town	Pim Joseph Wm	flour & corn	Indian corn & flour mill	-	-	-	-	-		hob/	5.0564
Youghal	Youghal Town	Pratt Robert	mill tenement	-	-	-	Pratt Robert - James	1854	-		dd/	1854 5 17
Youghal	Youghal Town :	Ld Estate Court	windmill	- erected on pillars	-	-	-	1633	-		sv/	old map
Youghal	Youghal Town :	Sweeny Patrick	mills	-	-	-	Sweeny Pat - Thos	1844	-		dd/	1844 13 63

PARISH	TOWNLAND	MILLER	TYPE	HOUSE	Land	£Val+	PROPRIETORS	Date	WHEEL etc.	Record	Ref.
Youghal	Youghal Town :	Pim Joseph W	flax	steam flax mill & store	-	-	-	-	steam engine	hob/	5.2667
Youghal	Youghal Town :	Pim Joseph W	old brewery & :	-	-	-	-	-	-	hob/	5.2667
Youghal	Youghal Town :	Pim Joseph W	starch m`fcty	-	-	-	-	-	-	hob/	5.2667
Youghal	Youghal Town :	Ronayne Thomas	corn	(1A) 15.3x18.6x32 :	-	-	-	-	steam engine 6 h.p.	hob/	5.2662
Youghal	Youghal Town :	O`Sullivan Michael	salt manufactory	(1B) 17.6x21xx19 :	-	19.10.	-	1853	-	hob/	5.2662
Youghal	Youghal Town :	Tallon	saltworks	-	-	-	-	-	-	hob/	5.2662
Youghal	Youghal-Lands	E/ Youghal main st.	pottery	-	-	-	-	-	-	6"os	67
Youghal	Youghal-Lands	- S/ Cork Lane	brewery	-	-	-	-	-	-	6"os	67
Kilgarrif	Youghals	- E/ Tobin's Br.	brewery	-	-	-	-	1841	-	6"os	86
Kilgarrif	Youghals	Deasy Jane	brewery	offices & garden	0.1.18	85	-	1856	-	gr/	a.a.Ire.ie

PARISH	TOWNLAND	MILLER	TYPE	HOUSE	Land	£Val	PROPRIETORS	Date	WHEEL etc.	Record	Ref.
Kilbarron	Abbey Island	NE/ Portnamuck Vg.	flax	-	-	-	-	-	-	6"os/	107
Tirhugh bo	Abbey Mill	Connolly Thomas	corn	-	-	-	Connolly T - Harris Lewis	1870	-	dd/	1870 28 238
Tirhugh bo	Abbey Mill	Connolly Thomas	mill	-	-	-	Connolly T - Harris Lewis	1870	-	dd/	1870 10 100
Tirhugh bo	Abbey Mill	Connolly Thomas	mill	-	-	-	Connolly - Hodges Harry	1870	-	dd/	1870 34 89
Tirhugh bo	Abbey Mill	Connolly Thomas	mill	-	-	-	Connolly T - Reoper Geo	1871	-	dd/	1871 12 262
Tirhugh bo	Abbey Mill	Connolly Thomas	mill tenement	-	-	-	Connolly T - Sant Jas	1871	-	dd/	1871 34 291
Tirhugh bo	Abbey Mill	Connolly Thomas	mill tenement	-	-	-	Connolly T - MCCaul Jas	1874	-	dd/	1874 8 19
Kilbarron	Abbeylands	- W/ Portnamuck Br.	corn	-	-	-	-	-	-	6"os/	107
Kilbarron	Abbeylands	Connolly Hamilton	corn & kiln	- & miller`s ho.	2a.	12	-	-	-	gr/	-
Kilbarron	Abbeylands	Keo John	flax & land	-	16a.	14.5	-	-	-	gr/	-
Muff	Adrmore	Kilpatrick Isaac	kiln	(3B) 39x18x5.3 :	-	-	-	-	-	hob/	5.0818
Aghanunshin	Aghalenty	-	corn kiln	-	-	-	-	-	-	6"os/	53
Culdaff	Aghatubbrid	-	corn	-	-	-	-	2010	-	mmOS/	wh - B
Culdaff	Aghatubbrid	- at Carrowee Br.	corn	-	-	-	-	-	-	6"os/	12
Culdaff	Aghatubbrid	McCawley Hugh	mill	-	-	-	-	1856	12x2.6 overshot :	hob/	5.0813
Allsaints	Aghlehard	-	flax	-	-	-	-	1841	-	6"os/	53
Allsaints	Aghlehard	Davis John	flax	-	106a.	-	-	-	-	gr/	-
Killaghter	Aighan	-	brewery	-	-	-	-	1841	-	6"os/	98
Killaghter	Aighan	Stephens Mrs	brewery	(1B) 56x15.6x12 :	-	25-7	-	1838	18x4.3 buckets 56 :	hob/	5.0807
Killaghter	Aighan	Walker James	corn	(1B) 27.6x20.6x8 :	-	-	-	-	- 1 pair stones	hob/	5.0807
Killaghter	Aighan	Walker James	corn & kiln	(1A) 37.6x22.6x30 :	-	-	-	-	18x4.3 buckets 56 :	hob/	5.0807
Conwal	Altadush	-	corn kiln	-	-	-	-	-	-	6"os/	60
Killlea	Altaghaderry	Maxwell Alex :	corn	(2B) 27x23x7.6 :	-	-	-	-	- works 5 mos. :	hob/	5.0836
Killlea	Altaghaderry	on Co. bdry.	mill & mill pond	-	-	-	-	-	-	6"os/	55
Killlea	Altaghaderry Lr.B71	-	mill ponds (2)	(no mill)	-	-	-	-	-	6"os/	55
Glencolumbkille	Altclogh	-	corn kiln	-	-	-	-	-	-	6"os/	81
Killybegs Lower	Altnagapple	-	corn kiln	-	-	-	-	-	-	6"os/	83
Templecrone	Aphort	- near Village	corn kiln	-	-	-	-	-	-	6"os/	48
Taughboyne	Ardagh	Rolestone Andrew	flax	(1B) 33.6x18.6x10 :	-	-	-	-	2 stocks :	hob/	5.0841
Taughboyne	Ardagh	Rolestone Andrew	flax (new mill)	-	-	-	-	1855	date uncertain	hob/	5.0841
Fahan Lower	Ardaravan	-	corn mills	-	-	-	-	-	-	6"os/	29
Fahan Lower	Ardaravan	- at Millfield Ho.	mill fields	-	-	-	-	-	-	6"os/	29
Mevagh	Ardbane	-	corn	-	-	-	-	2010	-	mmOS/	wh - Z
Mevagh	Ardbane	-	corn & pond	-	-	-	-	1843	-	6"os/	16
Inishmacsaint	Ardfarn	Kilmartin Jas & :	corn & kiln	- & miller`s ho.	14a.	10	-	-	-	gr/	-
Mevagh	Ardhane	-	corn	-	-	-	-	-	-	osm/	-
Mevagh	Ardhane	M`Gettigan	corn	-	-	-	-	-	-	gr/	-
Donaghmore	Ardnagannagh	-	flax & pond	-	-	-	-	-	-	6"os/	78
Donaghmore	Ardnagannagh	Thompson Thomas	flax mill	- + ho. offs & ld. :	24a.	39	-	-	-	gr/	-
Templecarn	Ardnaglass	- on Termon R	mill	-	-	-	-	-	-	1"os/	32
Templecarn	Ardnaglass	- N/ Pettigoe Town	corn	-	-	-	-	1841	-	6"os/	105
Templecarn	Ardnaglass	Leslie John	corn	-	10a.	-	-	-	-	gr/	-
Templecarn	Ardnaglass	Leslie John	flax	-	-	-	-	-	-	gr/	-
Templecarn	Ardnaglass :	Scott Mrs	corn & kiln	-	-	5.18	-	-	-	hob/	5.2671
Tullaghobegly	Ards Beg	-	corn kiln	-	-	-	-	-	-	6"os/	24
Tullaghobegly	Ards Beg	Harkin Jas. (John)	corn	(2B) 27.6x23.6x7.6 :	-	-	-	1855	11x2.2x6 36 bkts. :	hob/	5.0827
Tullaghobegly	Ards Beg	Harkin John	corn	(2B) 27.6x23.6x7.6	-	-	-	1839	- 1 pair stones :	hob/	5.0829
Tullaghobegly	Ards Little	- at Crooked Br.	flax & pond	-	-	-	-	-	-	6"os/	45
Convoy	Aughagault	- at A`gault L.Vg.	flax & mill pond	-	-	-	-	-	-	6"os/	69
Convoy	Aughagault	- 1/3 m SE of Vg.	flax & mill pond	-	-	-	-	-	-	6"os/	69
Convoy	Aughagault	- 1/3 m. E. of Vg.	flax	-	-	-	-	-	-	6"os/	69
Convoy	Aughagault	Black John	flax & land	-	27a.	16	-	-	-	gr/	-

PARISH	TOWNLAND	MILLER	TYPE	HOUSE	Land	£Val	PROPRIETORS	Date	WHEEL etc.	Record	Ref.
Convoy	Aughagault	Black John	flax & land	-	-	-	-	-	-	gr/	-
Convoy	Aughagault	Gallagher Mary	flax	-	43a.	25	-	-	-	gr/	-
Mevagh	Aughalatty	-	corn	-	-	-	-	-	-	osm/	-
Mevagh	Aughalatty	Wilson	corn	-	-	-	-	-	-	gr/	-
Donegal	Aughboy *	- nr Aghboy Vge.	silver mines		-	-	-	-	-	6"os/	20
Aughnish	Aughnish	-	flax	-	-	-	-	1841	-	6"os/	46
Aughnish	Aughnish	-	flax	-	-	-	-	-	-	osm/	-
Aughnish	Aughnish	McCorkel William	flax	(2C) 23.6x17x6 :	-	-	-	1838	- 3 stocks	hob/	5.0819
Tullaghobegly	Aughullies	-	corn kiln	-	-	-	-	-	-	6"os/	49
Donaghmore	Avaltygort	-	corn & 2 kilns	-	-	-	-	-	-	6"os/	78
Donaghmore	Avaltygort	-	corn kiln	-	-	-	-	-	-	6"os/	78
Donaghmore	Avaltygort	-	large pond	-	-	-	-	-	-	6"os/	78
Templecarn	Balatt South	-	corn	-	-	-	-	-	8x -	osm/	-
Conwal	Ballaghderg	Boyce Anthony	corn & kiln	-	1.0.2[illegible]	2.10	-	-	-	gr/	-
Raymoghy	Balleeghan	-	corn	- v. attractive res.	-	-	Denis Mclaughlan	2004	-	pWEH	Cr
Raymoghy	Balleeghan	-	flax	(3C) 20.6x21.6x5.6 :	-	-	-	-	- 3 stocks :	hob/	5.0839
Raymoghy	Balleeghan	Alexander Nath	flax& corn	(2B) 24x19.6x5.6 :	-	-	-	-	1 pr st. & 3 stocks :	hob/	5.0839
Raymoghy	Balleeghan	Cassidy Mark	flax	(1B) 30x17.6x6.6 :	-	-	-	-	- 3 stocks :	hob/	5.0839
Raymoghy	Balleeghan	Park Andrew	flax	(3C) 20.6x21.6x5.6 :	-	-	-	-	- 3 stocks :	hob/	5.0839
Raymoghy	Balleelaghan	-	corn	near Malin Town	-	-	-	-	-	6"os/	4
Raymoghy	Balleelaghan	-	flax & ponds (2)	-	-	-	-	-	-	6"os/	54
Raymoghy	Balleelaghan	- at Meenboy	corn kiln	-	-	-	-	-	-	6"os/	4
Raymoghy	Balleelaghan	- imed. N/ Abbey	corn & kiln	-	-	-	-	-	-	6"os/	54
Raymoghy	Balleelaghan	- near Abbey :	flax	-	-	-	-	-	-	6"os/	54
Raymoghy	Balleelaghan	- on coast	corn & kiln	-	-	-	-	-	-	6"os/	54
Culdaff	Balleelaghan Upr	-	corn	at Culceeny Village	-	-	-	-	-	6"os/	4
Culdaff	Balleelaghan Upr	- at Culceeny Vg.	corn	-	-	-	-	-	-	6"os/	4
Donegal	Ballinacarry *	-	old bleach mill	-	-	-	-	-	-	6"os/	29
Clondavaddog	Ballincrick	- at Polinska	corn	-	-	-	-	-	-	6"os/	8
Clondavaddog	Ballincrick	- coast / Polinsea	corn		-	-	-	-	-	6"os/	8
Clondavaddog	Ballincrick	- on Glassog Burn	mill pond	-	-	-	-	-	-	6"os/	8
Clondavaddog	Ballincrick	Clinton John	corm	-	-	-	-	-	-	hob/	5.0822
Clondavaddog	Ballincrick	- ex Glassog Burn	mill pond		-	-	-	-	-	6"os/	8
Mintiaghs	Ballinlough	- nr Mintiaghs Vg	still house	-	-	-	-	-	-	6"os/	19
Drumhome	Ballintra	- nr Ballintra	corn kiln	-	-	-	-	-	-	6"os/	48
Drumhome	Ballintra Town	-	mill	-	-	-	-	-	-	1"os/	32
Tullaghobegly	Ballyness	- nr Castle Bawne	corn	-	-	-	-	-	-	6"os/	24
Tullyfern	Ballyarr	-	corn	-	-	-	-	-	-	osm/	-
Tullyfern	Ballyarr	-	flax, scutch	finely converted	-	-	-	2001	holiday home	pWEH	C
Tullyfern	Ballyarr	- at Ballyarr Ho.	corn & kiln	-	-	-	-	-	-	6"os/	45
Tullyfern	Ballyarr	Hill George A Lord	corn & kilns	(1A) 38x27x24 & :	-	-	-	1838	18x8x4 breast :	hob/	5.0830
Tullyfern	Ballyarr	Russell`s Mill	flax	usefully converted	-	-	Telson`s Fish Farm	2001	fish farm	pWEH	C
Donaghmore	Ballyarrell	- nr Cromin Vge.	flax & mill race	-	-	-	-	-	-	6"os/	78
Donaghmore	Ballyarrell	- N. / Cromin Vge.	mill	-	-	-	-	-	-	6"os/	78
Allsaints	Ballybegly	-	flax	-	-	-	-	2004	-	mmSv/	wh - Z
Allsaints	Ballybegly	-	mill	- not known local	-	-	-	2004	-	mmSv/	wh - Z
Allsaints	Ballybegly	- N./ B`begly Vge	flax	-	-	-	-	-	-	6"os/	46
Allsaints	Ballybegly	- nr. B`begly Vge	brewery	-	-	-	-	-	-	6"os/	46
Allsaints	Ballybegly Little	Ellison John	flax	-	73a.	-	-	-	-	gr/	-
Convoy	Ballyboe	-	corn kiln	-	-	-	-	-	-	6"os/	25
Convoy	Ballyboe	-	ruin of flax mill	-	-	-	-	-	-	6"os/	69
Convoy	Ballyboe	- near Gortlee	mill ponds (2)	-	-	-	-	-	-	6"os/	53

PARISH	TOWNLAND	MILLER	TYPE	HOUSE	Land	£Val	PROPRIETORS	Date	WHEEL etc.	Record	Ref.
Raymoghy	Ballyboe	- Dromoghill Vge.	flax	- lost in trees	-	-	-	2004	-	pWEH	R
Allsaints	Ballyboe	- S. of Town	tannery	-	-	-	-	-	-	6"os/	78
Convoy	Ballyboe	Elliott Sarah	flax	-	65a.	48	-	-	-	gr/	-
Raymoghy	Ballyboe	Patterson Samuel	flax	-	-	-	-	2004	-	mmSv/	BFK - R
Donegal	Ballyboe (9)	Wray William	mill	-	-	-	Wray W - Morrison Margt	1871	-	dd/	1871 24 102
Donegal	Ballyboe (9)	Wray William	mill	-	-	-	Wray W - Ellis Rev Robt	1871	-	dd/	1871 27 164
Donegal	Ballyboe (9)	Wray William	mill	-	-	-	Wray W - Thorp Margaret	1871	-	dd/	1871 27 267
Donegal	Ballyboe (9)	Wray William	mill	-	-	-	Wray Wm - Scott James	1872	-	dd/	1872 40 36
Donegal	Ballyboe (9)	Wray William	mill	-	-	-	Wray Wm - Malseed Jas	1874	-	dd/	1874 27 276
Stranorlar	Ballybofey	-	mill	-	-	-	-	-	-	1"os/	24
Stranorlar	Ballybofey	- N. Burn Daurnet	corn	-	-	-	-	-	-	6"os/	78
Clonleagh ?	Ballybogan	-	corn	-	-	-	-	1841	-	6"os/	79
Conwal	Ballybolauder	-	corn kiln	-	-	-	-	-	-	6"os/	52
Moville Lower	Ballybrack	-	corn kilns	-	-	-	-	-	-	6"os/	22
Clondavaddog	Ballycallan	-	corn	-	-	-	-	-	10x2	osm/	-
Clondavaddog	Ballycallan	- nr Burnside Vg.	corn & pond	-	-	-	-	-	-	6"os/	18
Clondavaddog	Ballycallan	- nr Burnside Vg.	corn kiln	-	-	-	-	-	-	6"os/	18
Clondavaddog	Ballycallan	Dogherty Hugh	corn	-	-	-	-	-	-	hob/	5.0822
Clondavaddog	Ballycallan	Doherty	corn	-	-	-	-	-	-	gr/	-
Raymunterdoney	Ballyconnell	-	malt kiln	-	-	-	-	-	-	6"os/	25
Allsaints	Ballyconnelly	-	flax	-	-	-	-	-	-	6"os/	61
Allsaints	Ballyconnelly	-	pond & mill race	-	-	-	-	-	-	6"os/	61
Allsaints	Ballyconnelly	M`Aulay John	flax	-	65a.	-	-	-	-	gr/	-
Taughboyne	Ballycushion	-	flax & pond	-	-	-	-	-	-	6"os/	55
Taughboyne	Ballycushion	- at Village	flax & pond	-	-	-	-	-	-	6"os/	55
Taughboyne	Ballycushion	Marshall Samuel	flax	(1B) 23.6x19x6 :	-	-	-	1836	4 stocks 6 rollers :	hob/	5.0841
Taughboyne	Ballycushion	Moore John	flax	(1B) 22x20x7.3 :	-	-	-	1836	3 stocks, m/cy B :	hob/	5.0841
Donegal	Ballyduff *	-	mill	-	-	-	-	-	-	1"os/	16
Donegal	Ballyduff *	-	flax	-	-	-	-	-	-	1"os/	16
Burt	Ballyederowen	-	flax	-	-	-	-	-	-	1"os/	16
Burt	Ballyederowen	- S/ Burnfoot R.	flax & corn	-	-	-	-	1841	-	6"os/	38
Burt	Ballyederowen	Ramsy Henry	corn	(2B) 16.6x19.6x7.6:	-	-	-	-	12x2.4x-	hob/	5.0816
Donegal	Ballyeeghan *	- near L. Swilly	friary	-	-	-	-	2004	-	mmSV/	-
Donegal	Ballyeeghan *	- near L. Swilly	mill	v. attractive conv.	-	-	-	2004	Donal Mclaughlan	mmSV/	wh - Ca
Tullyauglish	Ballygay	-	corn	-	-	-	-	-	-	osm/	-
Tullyfern	Ballygay	-	corn & kiln	-	-	-	-	-	-	mm/OS	wh - Z
Tullyauglish	Ballygay	-	flax	-	-	-	-	-	-	osm/	-
Tullyfern	Ballygay	- NE/ Rathmullan	corn & kiln	-	-	-	-	-	-	6"os/	36
Tullyfern	Ballygay	Reid Jas & Alex	flax	(3C) 37x21x9 :	-	-	-	-	- 4 stocks	hob/	5.0830
Donaghmore	Ballygonigan	1 mile E./ Wilsonstn.	flax & pond	-	-	-	-	-	-	6"os/	79
Donegal	Ballyhayes *	-	mill	-	-	-	-	-	-	1"os/	16
Clondavaddog	Ballyheerin	-	corn	-	-	-	-	-	10x2	osm/	-
Clondavaddog	Ballyheerin	-	corn & pond	-	-	-	-	-	-	6"os/	17
Clondavaddog	Ballyheerin	M`Glinchy	corn	-	-	-	-	-	-	gr/	-
Clondavaddog	Ballyheerin	McGlinchy John	corn	-	-	-	-	-	-	hob/	5.0822
Raphoe	Ballyholy Near	-	flax & mill pond	-	-	-	-	-	-	6"os/	62
Raphoe	Ballyholy Near	Blair Thomas	flax	(3B) 25.6x19x6 :	-	6.8	-	-	- [no information]	hob/	5.0837
Kilmacrenan	Ballykeeran	-	corn kiln (2)	-	-	-	-	-	-	6"os/	76
Kilmacrenan	Ballykeeran	-	tuck	-	-	-	-	-	-	6"os/	45
Kilmacrenan	Ballykeeran	- NE. Milltown Br.	corn	-	-	-	-	-	-	6"os/	45
Clonleigh	Ballylast	Ponsonby Frances	mill	-	-	-	Ponsonby - Babington R'd	1893	-	dd/	1893 23 61
Moville Upper	Ballylawn	-	old salt pans	-	-	-	-	-	-	6"os/	21

PARISH	TOWNLAND	MILLER	TYPE	HOUSE	Land	£Val	PROPRIETORS	Date	WHEEL etc.	Record	Ref.
Raymoghy	Ballylevin	-	flax	-	-	-	-	-	-	6"os/	34
Raymoghy	Ballylevin	Stevenson Robt :	flax	(3B) 2 5.6x21.6x5.6	-	-	-	-	diameter 11ft. :	hob/	5.0839
Donagh	Ballylosky	- at Ard	corn kiln	-	-	-	-	-	-	6"os/	11
Donagh	Ballylosky	- at Village	corn kilns (2)	-	-	-	-	-	-	6"os/	11
Donagh	Ballylosky	- on Donagh R.	flax	-	-	-	-	-	-	6"os/	11
Killaghyee	Ballyloughan	-	corn kiln	-	-	-	-	-	-	6"os/	98
Killaghyee	Ballyloughan	- W. side Oily R.	tuck	-	-	-	-	-	-	6"os/	98
Fahan Lower	Ballymacarry Lr.	- S. side Mill R. :	old bleach mill	-	-	-	-	1841	-	6"os/	29
Conwal	Ballymacool	-	mill	-	-	-	-	-	-	1"os/	16
Clondavaddog	Ballymagahy S.	-	corn & pond	-	-	-	-	-	-	6"os/	17
Clondavaddog	Ballymagahy S.	-	corn kiln	-	-	-	-	-	-	6"os/	17
Culdaff	Ballymagaraghy	- nr Tremone Vg.	mill	-	-	-	-	-	-	6"os/	12
Clondavaddog	Ballymaghy	Doaks Samuel :	mill	(3C) 29.10x19.6x6	-	-	-	-	- 1 pr. st. new	hob/	5.0822
Clondavaddog	Ballymaghy S	-	corn	-	-	-	-	-	-	osm/	-
Killaghtee	Ballymagowan	-	mill pond	-	-	-	-	-	-	6"os/	98
Killaghtee	Ballymagowan	- 1/4m. N. river	corn & kiln	-	-	-	-	-	-	6"os/	98
Killaghtee	Ballymagowan	Gunn Ezekiel	corn	(1B) 30x19x12 :	-	-	-	-	- 1pr. st. class C	hob/	5.0807
Killaghtee	Ballymagowan	Gunn Ezekiel	flax	(1B) 16x10x9	-	-	-	-	- 2 stocks	hob/	5.0807
Killaghtee	Ballymagowan	Major Sophia	corn & kiln	-	7a.	2.15	-	-	-	gr/	-
Aghanunshin	Ballymaleel	-	flax & pond	-	-	-	-	-	-	6"os/	53
Clonleigh	Ballymonaster	- 1 m. N. / Br.	corn & pond	-	-	-	-	-	-	6"os/	70
Clondahorky	Ballymore Lower	-	corn kilns (2)	-	-	-	-	-	-	6"os/	26
Drumhome	Ballynacarrick	- W. rd. at Carry	corn	-	-	-	-	-	-	6"os/	103
Drumhome	Ballynacarrick	- 3/8m.SE Ballintra	corn	-	-	-	-	-	-	6"os/	103
Drumhome	Ballynacarrick	- 1/3m.W. Ballintra	corn	-	-	-	-	-	-	6"os/	103
Moville Lower	Ballynally	-	mill race	-	-	-	-	-	-	6"os/	21
Tullaghobegly	Ballyness	-	corn	-	-	-	-	2010	-	mmOS/	wh - Z
Tullaghobegly	Ballyness	- close to Castle	corn & mill race	-	-	-	-	1843	-	6"os/	24
Tullaghobegly	Ballyness	Mcelroy Edward	corn	(1C) 29x22x16 :	-	-	-	1855	13x1.10x6.6 :	hob/	5.0827
Tullaghobegly	Ballyness	Olphert Wibrants	flax	(1A) 22.6x18x11.6 :	-	-	-	1855	13ft dia. 48 bkts. :	hob/	5.0827
Tullaghobegly	Ballyness	Olphert Wibrants	flax	(1A) 23.6x21x12	-	-	-	1855	10x2.9x7 70 bkts. :	hob/	5.0827
Drumhome	Ballyruddelly	- (no name)	scutch	-	-	-	-	-	machinery defective	osm/	-
Drunhome	Ballyruddelly	Graham Thomas	flax	-	36a.	39	-	-	-	gr/	-
Kilbarron	Ballyshannon	-	mill	-	-	-	-	-	-	1"os/	-
Kilbarron	Ballyshannon :	Kelly Peter	brewery	-	-	40	-	-	-	gr/	-
Kilbarron	Ballyshannon Tn	Benison John	corn	-	-	-	Benison John - Myles John	1891	-	dd/	1891 39 244
Kilbarron	Ballyshannon Tn	Benison John	distillery	-	-	-	Benison John - Myles John	1891	-	dd/	1891 39 244
Kilbarron	Ballyshannon Tn	Benison Joseph	Mill of B`shnn	-	-	-	Benison - Hamilton Andr	1835	-	dd/	1835 1 200
Kilbarron	Ballyshannon Tn	Cope James	Erne Mills	-	-	-	Cope James - Neely Wm	1890	-	dd/	1890 38 90
Kilbarron	Ballyshannon Tn :	Benison Thomas	corn	-	-	-	Benison Thos - Joseph	1835	-	dd/	1835 1 209
Kilbarron	Ballyshannon Tn :	Johnston David	mill	-	-	-	Johnston - Green Finlay	1834	-	dd/	1834 1 278
Kilbarron	Ballyshannon Tn :	Thompson Thomas	bakery	-	-	-	-	1856	-	gr/	-
Kilbarron	Ballyshannon Tn :	Crawford Samuel	land	-	-	-	Crawford - O`neill Chas	1845	-	dd/	1845 7 118
Kilmacrennan	Barrack	-	flax	-	-	-	-	-	-	6"os/	45
Kilmacrennan	Barrack	-	flax	-	-	-	-	2004	-	mmSv/	bfk - Z
Kilmacrennan	Barrack	-	flax	-	-	-	-	2004	-	mmSv/	Z
Kilmacrennan	Barrack	- at Crooket Br.	old mill	-	-	-	-	2004	-	mmSv/	wh - Z
Fahan Lower	Bauville	-	corn kiln	-	-	-	-	-	-	6"os/	29
Killaghtee	Beaughreen Glebe	- E. rd at Spamount	brewery	-	-	-	-	-	-	6"os/	98
Glencolumbkille	Beeefan		corn kiln	-	-	-	-	-	-	6"os/	80
Templecarn	Belalt South		spade	-	-	-	-	-	-	6"os/	105
Raphoe	Beltany	- on farm	corn & flax	- demolished	-	-	-	2007	-	mmSv/	wh - Z

PARISH	TOWNLAND	MILLER	TYPE	HOUSE	Land	£Val	PROPRIETORS	Date	WHEEL etc.	Record	Ref.
Raphoe	Beltany	-	flax	- & millhouse	-	-	- Jn & Jas McDaid	2007	was stream driven	mmSv/	wh - Z
Raphoe	Beltany	- in small R. valley	flax	- site in trees :	-	-	-	2007	-	mmSv/	wh - Z
Conwal	Bohirril Park	Boyce Daniel	corn & kiln	-	24a.	1.5.0	-	-	-	gr/	-
Burt	Bohullian Lower	-	distillery	-	-	-	-	2004	-	mmSv/	bfk - R
Burt	Bohullian Lower	-	threshing	-	-	-	-	2004	-	mmSv/	bfk - Z
Burt	Bohullian Lower	Leathan Samuel	mill	(1B) 24x24x22 :	-	-	-	-	-	hob/	5.0816
Burt	Bohullian Lower	Leathan Samuel	threshing	(1A) 18x24x15 :	-	-	-	-	-	hob/	5.0816
Burt	Bohullian Upper	- N .side road	flax	-	-	-	-	-	-	6"os/	47
Burt	Bohullian Upper	- imed. E/ x-roads.	flax	-	-	-	-	1843	-	6"os/	37
Burt	Bohullian Upper	Scott James	flax	(3B) 24x21x6 :	-	-	-	-	drives 6 stocks :	hob/	5.0816
Burt	Bohullion Lower	- N. side Vge.	distillery	-	-	-	-	-	-	6"os/	47
Burt	Bohullion Lower	- N. side Vge.	distillery	-	-	-	-	2004	-	pWEH	D
Burt	Bohullion Lower	- E. of Boh'n Vge.	flax & pond	-	-	-	-	1843	-	6"os/	37
Burt	Bohullion Lower	- E. of Boh'n Vge.	flax & pond	-	-	-	-	2010	-	mmOS/	wh - Z
Conwal	Bomany	- nr Ardahee Vge.	ruins of corn mill	-	-	-	-	-	-	6"os/	61
Donegal	Brackless *	-	flax	-	-	-	-	-	-	1"os/	16
Inishkeel	Bracky	-	corn kiln	-	-	-	-	-	-	6"os/	82
Inishkeel	Bracky	-	mill (note) :	-	-	-	-	1837	-	hob/	5.0803
Inishkeel	Bracky	-	mill (note) :	-	-	-	-	1837	dia. 12 ft. fall 14ft.	hob/	5.0803
Taughboyne	Bready	-	mill	-	-	-	-	-	-	1"os/	17
Tullyfern	Breaghy	Herron David	flax mills	(3B) 27x20.6x6.6 :	-	-	-	1839	- 4 stocks	hob/	5.0831
Moville Lower	Bredaghglen	- S./ Claggan Vge	tuck	-	-	-	-	-	-	6"os/	21
Killea & T`bne	Brickfield	Levins Mr	linen	-	-	-	-	-	-	osm/	-
Tulyfern	Bridge End	-	mill	-	-	-	-	-	-	1"os/	16
Tulyfern	Bridge End	- at Wooden Br.	bleach	-	-	-	-	-	-	6"os/	45
Tulyfern	Bridge End	- W. R`melton Br.	flour	-	-	-	-	-	-	6"os/	45
Tullyfern	Bridge End	Watt James	bleach (& bt.)	(1B) 55x31x17.6 :	-	12	-	1838	14x5x- buckets 1ft.	hob/	5.0831
Tulyfern	Bridge End	Watt James	corn	no.1 (B) 38x20x33 :	-	-	-	-	17x6x- breast :	hob/	5.0830
Tullyfern	Bridge End	Watt James	corn & kiln	-	-	-	-	1838	-	hob/	5.0831
Tullyfern	Bridge End	Watt James	old beetling	51.6x31x17.6 :	-	-	-	-	16x7.2x- buckets :	hob/	5.0831
Tulyfern	Bridge End	Watt Mr	flour	-	-	-	-	-	-	osm/	-
Tullaghobegly	Brinlack	-	corn kilns (3)	-	-	-	-	-	-	6"os/	23
Killaghtee	Bruckless	-	tannery	-	-	-	-	-	-	6"os/	98
Tullaghobegly	Bunbeg	-	mill	-	-	-	-	-	-	1"os/	9
Tullaghobegly	Bunbeg	- N. side Claddy R.	mill	-	-	-	-	1841	-	6"os/	32
Tullaghobegly	Bunbeg	Hill Geo Agustus	corn	(1A) 32.6x24x31 :	-	15	-	1855	16x4x5 40 bkts. :	hob/	5.0827
Fahan lower	Buncrana	-	mill farm	-	-	-	-	-	-	1"os/	16
Inishkeel	Buncroobeg	-	corn kiln	-	-	-	-	-	-	6"os/	75
Burt	Bunnamayne	-	flax & pond	-	-	-	-	-	-	6"os/	47
Inver	Burnside	Russell Alex & Jas	flax	(3B) 20.6x21x5 :	-	-	-	1838		hob/	5.0805A
Raphoe	Burnside	Russell James	flax mills	(3c) 14x18x5.6 :	-	-	-	-	- 4 stocks :	hob/	5.0837
Templecrone	Burtonport	-	corn kiln	-	-	-	-	-	-	6"os/	48
Convoy	Callan	- ESE/ Callan Vg.	flax & pond	-	-	-	-	-	-	6"os/	69
Convoy	Callan Lower	-	mill	-	-	-	-	-	-	1"os/	-
Convoy	Callan Lrower	-	flax	-	-	-	-	-	-	1"os/	-
Convoy	Callancor	-	flax	-	-	-	-	-	-	6"os/	69
Convoy	Callancor	- N. side R. Deel	corn & mill race	-	-	-	-	-	-	6"os/	69
Donaghmore	Calmhame	-	flax	-	-	-	-	-	-	6"os/	78
Inver	Carickbrack	McConnagher Matt	corn	(3B) 32.6x20.6x6.3	-	-	-	1838	12x2x8.6 :	hob/	5.0805A
Inver	Carickbrack	McConnagher Matt	flax	(3B) 28x18x5 :	-	-	-	1838	-	hob/	5.0805A
Convoy	Cark	-	corn kilns (5)	-	-	-	-	-	-	6"os/	60
Tullyfern	Carn High	- N/ Thorne Lo.	corn kiln	-	-	-	-	1841	-	6"os/	37

PARISH	TOWNLAND	MILLER	TYPE	HOUSE	Land	£Val	PROPRIETORS	Date	WHEEL etc.	Record	Ref.
Tullyfern	Carn High	- on stream to :	mill ruin	-	-	-	-	1841	-	6"os/	37
Tullyfern	Carn Low	- on stream to :	mill ruin	-	-	-	-	1841	-	6"os/	37
Tullyfern	Carn Low	Fullerton John	flax	no.1 [no dims.] no.2 :	-	-	-	-	- 3 & 4 stocks	hob/	5.0830
Donaghmore	Carn Lower	Colins ? Colhoon :	flax mills	(3B) 33x20.6x6.6 E	-	-	-	1838	12x1.3x16 :	hob/	5.0835
Conwal	Carnamogagh Lr	-	flax & pond	-	-	-	-	-	-	6"os/	53
Conwal	Carnamogagh Lr	-	mill pond	-	-	-	-	-	-	6"os/	53
Muff	Carnamoyle	-	flax ruins	-	-	-	-	1841	-	6"os/	93
Conwal	Carnatreantragh	Teas John	flax	-	62a.	12	-	-	-	gr/	-
Donaghmore	Carnowen	- S./ Brockstn.	flax & ponds	-	-	-	-	-	-	6"os/	69
Donaghmore	Carnowen	- SE of Village	flax & pond	-	-	-	-	-	-	6"os/	69
Donaghmore	Carnowen	- at Powderly Mid.	corn kiln	-	-	-	-	-	-	6"os/	69
Donaghmore	Carnowen	- on R. Deel Embt.	mill & pond	-	-	-	-	-	-	6"os/	69
Templecarn	Carntressy	- at Ragarson Vg.	corn kiln	-	-	-	-	-	-	6"os/	105
Donegal	Carraghglebe *	-	corn kiln	-	-	-	-	-	-	6"os/	52
Donaghmore	Carranadore	at Milltown Village	corn & pond	-	-	-	-	-	-	6"os/	79
Kilbarron	Carrangartin	-	old bl. green	-	-	-	-	-	-	osm/	-
Killynard	Carrangartin	- (no name)	bleach	-	-	-	-	-	-	osm/	-
Conwal	Carrick	- N. of river	corn kiln	-	-	-	-	-	-	6"os/	79
Conwal	Carrick	- 1m. S/ C`cashell	spade foundry	-	-	-	-	-	-	6"os/	79
Conwal	Carrick	-	corn kiln	-	-	-	-	-	-	6"os/	79
Conwal	Carrick	Chestly Robert	corn & kiln	-	-	-	-	-	-	gr/	-
Conwal	Carrick	Chestly Robert	flax	-	-	-	-	-	-	gr/	-
Conwal	Carrick	- E. of river	mill pond	-	-	-	-	-	-	6"os/	79
Conwal	Carrick	M`Grenra Patrick	flax (2)	-	-	18	-	-	-	gr/	-
Clondahorky	Carrick Lough	-	corn kiln	-	-	-	-	-	-	6"os/	26
Clondahorky	Carrick Lough	- near Duntally Br.	corn & pond	-	-	-	-	-	-	6"os/	26
Glencolumbkille	Carrick Lower	- E. / small river	corn & race	-	-	-	-	-	-	6"os/	90
Drumhome	Carrick West	-	corn kiln	-	-	-	-	-	-	6"os/	99
Donagh	Carrickafoden	-	mill	-	-	-	-	-	-	1"os/	5
Raymoghy	Carrickballydooey	-	flax	-	-	-	-	-	-	6"os/	54
Raymoghy	Carrickballydooey	-	flax	(2B) 2	-	-	-	-	3 stocks :	hob/	5.0839
Raymoghy	Carrickballydooey	Colquhoun Robt	flax	-	41a.	-	-	-	-	gr/	-
Raymoghy	Carrickballydooey	Colquohoon Robt	flax	(3C) 23x21x5.6 :	-	-	-	-	3 stocks :	hob/	5.0839
Raymoghy	Carrickballydooey	Lecky Robert	flax	-	27a.	-	-	-	-	gr/	-
Inishmacsaint	Carrickboy	-	tan yard	-	-	-	-	-	-	6"os/	107
Inishmacsaint	Carrickboy	- W./ B`shannon :	distillery	-	-	-	-	-	-	6"os/	107
Inishmacsaint	Carrickboy	Saunders M/s	distillery & mill	-	-	85	-	-	-	gr/	-
Raphoe	Carrickbrack	-	corn & flax	-	-	-	-	-	-	6"os/	70
Raphoe	Carrickbrack	-	corn kiln	-	-	-	-	-	-	6"os/	69
Raphoe	Carrickbrack	-	corn kiln	-	-	-	-	-	-	6"os/	70
Raphoe	Carrickbrack	-	mill	-	-	-	-	-	-	1"os/	17
Raphoe	Carrickbrack	-	mill ponds	-	-	-	-	-	-	6"os/	69
Raphoe	Carrickbrack	- S. side R. Deel	corn & flax	-	-	-	-	-	-	6"os/	69
Donaghmore	Carrickmagrath	-	corn kiln	-	-	-	-	-	-	6"os/	77
Donaghmore	Carrickmagrath	- SW./ Ballybofey	corn & kiln	-	-	-	-	-	-	6"os/	78
Raymoghy	Carricknamat	Clarke Dougal	flax	(2B) 24x18x6 :	-	-	-	-	3 stocks :	hob/	5.0839
Donaghmore	Carricknashane	- E. side road :	flax & mill pond	-	-	-	-	-	-	6"os/	79
Donaghmore	Carricknashane	Gallagher James	flax	-	22a.	23	-	-	-	gr/	-
Donaghmore	Carricknashane	near Berwick Hall	corn & kiln	-	-	-	-	-	-	6"os/	79
Donaghmore	Carricknashane		flax	-	-	-	-	-	-	6"os/	79
Donaghmore	Carricknashane		flax mill & pond	-	-	-	-	-	-	6"os/	79
Conwal	Carrickyskanlan	-	corn kiln	-	-	-	-	-	-	6"os/	52

PARISH	TOWNLAND	MILLER	TYPE	HOUSE	Land	£Val	PROPRIETORS	Date	WHEEL etc.	Record	Ref.
Killea & T`bne	Carrigans	-	corn & flax	-	-	-	-	-	-	6"os/	55
Killea & T`bne	Carrigans	-	flour	-	-	-	-	-	-	6"os/	55
Killea & T`bne	Carrigans	Gallagher Mr	linen	-	-	-	-	-	-	osm/	-
Killea & T`bne	Carrigans	McRea James	corn	(1B) 51.6x32.6x30 :	-	-	-	-	- 3 pr. of stones :	hob/	5.0836
Mevagh	Carrigart	-	corn	-	-	-	-	-	-	osm/	-
Mintiaghs	Carroghill	- on Owenbeg R.	still house	-	-	-	-	-	-	6"os/	19
Donegal	Carrowan *	Edwards Robert	kiln	(1B) 72.6x20.8x8	-	-	-	-	-	hob/	5.0816
Donegal	Carrowan *	Leslie William	kinn	(2B) 51x21x6.6	-	-	-	-	-	hob/	5.0816
Moville Lower	Carrowbeg	-	corn kiln	-	-	-	-	-	-	6"os/	12
Tullyfern	Carrowkeeel	Dougherty Elenor	flax	(2B) 23x21x5.6 :	-	5.10	-	1838	- 4 stocks	hob/	5.0831
Tullyfern	Carrowkeel	-	corn	-	-	-	-	-	-	osm/	-
Tullyfern	Carrowkeel	-	mill	-	-	-	-	-	-	1"os/	16
Tullyfern	Carrowkeel	- near coast	corn & pond	-	-	-	-	-	-	6"os/	27
Tullyfern	Carrowkeel	- near Quigley`s Pt	corn & pond	-	-	-	-	-	-	6"os/	30
Tullyfern	Carrowkeel	Brown Susan	mills	-	-	-	Brown S - Stevenson Rb	1870	-	dd/	1870 14 14
Moville Upper	Carrowkeel	Burn James	mill house	(1B) 57x20x14	-	-	-	-	16ft. dia. overshot :	hob/	5.0815
Tullyfern	Carrowkeel	Watson Robert	flax	(2B) 24x20.6x6 :	-	-	-	-	-	hob/	5.0830
Moville Lower	Carrowmenagh	-	corn kiln	-	-	-	-	-	-	6"os/	12
Clonca/Culdaff	Carrowmore	Harvey George M	mill	-	-	-	Harvey Geo - Harvey Ed	1870	-	dd/	1870 7 159
Clonca/Culdaff	Carrowmore	Hawkshaw Cath E	mill	-	-	-	Hawkshaw C - Harvey G	1873	-	dd/	1873 31 186
Burt	Carrowreagh	-	flax	-	-	-	-	-	-	1"os/	16
Burt	Carrowreagh	-	flax	-	-	-	-	-	-	6"os/	47
Burt	Carrowreagh	- at Bridgetown	corn & pond	-	-	-	-	-	-	6"os/	47
Burt	Carrowreagh	- NW. Mannerstn	flax & pond	-	-	-	-	-	-	6"os/	47
Burt	Carrowreagh	- WSW. of Town	flax	-	-	-	-	-	-	6"os/	47
Burt	Carrowreagh	Fleming William	flax & kiln	(3B) 19x20.6x6 :	-	-	-	-	11.4x2x- circ. axle :	hob/	5.0816
Donegal	Carrowtrasna *	-	corn	-	-	-	-	1841	-	6"os/	44
Allsaints	Carrygally	-	flax	-	-	-	-	-	-	6"os/	61
Allsaints	Carrygally	-	Mill Row	-	-	-	-	-	-	6"os/	61
Allsaints	Carrygally	Laird John	flax	-	68a.	-	-	-	-	gr/	-
Allsaints	Carrygally	Wiley Allan	flax	-	73a.	-	-	-	-	gr/	-
Tirhugh bo	Casellard *	Connolly Thomas	corn	-	-	-	Conolly T - Royal Bnk of I.	1871	-	dd/	1871 3 296
Tullyauglish	Cashel	-	corn	-	-	-	-	-	-	osm/	-
Tullaghobegly	Cashel	- at Maam	corn kiln	-	-	-	-	-	-	6"os/	24
Kilcar	Cashelcarn	- E. side river	cloth	-	-	-	-	-	-	6"os/	96
Templecarn	Cashelenny	- near coast	corn kiln	-	-	-	-	-	-	6"os/	102
Tullyauglish	Cashelshanaghan	-	corn	-	-	-	-	-	12x2 -	osm/	-
Tullyauglish	Cashelshanaghan	-	corn (ruins)	-	-	-	-	-	-	6"os/	45
Tullyauglish	Cashelshanaghan	-	corn (ruins)	-	-	-	-	2004	-	mmSv/	BFK - Z
Tullyauglish	Cashelshanaghan	-	flax	-	-	-	-	2004	-	mmSv/	BFK - Z
Tullyauglish	Cashelshanaghan	- E. of P.O.	corn & dams	-	-	-	-	-	-	6"os/	45
Tullyauglish	Cashelshanaghan	Stewart Alex	corn	(1B) 31x22.6x8.6 :	-	-	-	-	- 1 pair stones	hob/	5.0819
Tullyauglish	Cashelshanaghan	Stewart Alex	flax	(1B) 30.6x21x7	-	-	-	-	- 5 stocks	hob/	5.0819
Tullyauglish	Cashelshanaghan	Stewart Alex	flax & corn	[as meas. 1838]	-	-	-	1856	- mill not working	hob/	5.0820
Clondahorky	Castlebane	-	corn	-	-	-	-	-	-	6"os/	15
Clondahorky	Castlebane	- Corcreggan Mill	corn	large building	-	-	Brendan Rohan	2004	-	mmSv/	wh - B
Clondahorky	Castlebane	- Corcreggan Mill	millhouse	conv. to hostel	-	-	Brendan Rohan	2004	-	mmSv/	wh - Cr
Burt	Castlecooly	-	flax	-	-	-	-	-	-	6"os/	47
Burt	Castlecooly	-	flax	-	-	-	-	2004	-	mmSv/	BFK - Z
Donaghmore	Castlefinn	Taylor Samuel	mills	-	-	-	Taylor Sam - Taylor John	1872	-	dd/	1872 36 179
Donaghmore	Castlefinn	Taylor Samuel	mills	-	-	-	Taylor J - McKinley Robt	1872	-	dd/	1872 36 211
Donaghmore	Castlefinn		corn	-	-	-	-	-	-	6"os/	79

PARISH	TOWNLAND	MILLER	TYPE	HOUSE	Land	£Val	PROPRIETORS	Date	WHEEL etc.	Record	Ref.
Taughboune	Castlethird :	William Brogan	corn	-	-	-	-	2004	-	mmSv/	BFK - B
Taughboyne	Castletown	- SSW./ K`lly Vge.	flax mill ruins	-	-	-	-	-	-	6"os/	64
Taughboyne	Castletown	Cunningham ? :	flax	(1B) 32x22x6.9 :	-	-	-	-	5 stocks, m/cy B :	hob/	5.0841
Killea & T`bne	Castletown	Cunningham Rev.	linen	-	-	-	-	-	-	osm/	-
Aghanunshin	Castlewray	Wray William	mill	-	-	-	Wray Wm - Scott James	1872	-	dd/	1872 40 36
Aghanunshin	Castlewray	Wray William	mill	-	-	-	Wray Wm - Kemmis Thos	1874	-	dd/	1874 24 6
Allsaints	Castruse	- at N. of Tld.	old still house	-	-	-	-	1841	-	6"os/	47
Allsaints	Castruse	- SE/ Leitrim Vge.	flax	-	-	-	-	1841	-	6"os/	55
Clonleigh	Cavan	Stewart Alex	mill	-	-	-	Stewart A - Std Life Asc	1871	-	dd/	1871 12 212
Clonleigh	Cavan	Thomson William	mill	-	-	-	Thomson W - Stewart A	1874	-	dd/	1874 10 52
Donaghmore	Cavan Lower	- near Milltown	flax & pond	-	-	-	-	-	-	6"os/	78
Donaghmore	Cavan Lower	Hill Henry	Cavan Mills	-	-	-	Hill Henry - Wilson Robert	1894	-	dd/	1894 60 271
Donaghmore	Cavan Lower	Smith James	flax & pond	-	8.2.5	9.5.0	-	-	-	gr/	-
Donaghmore	Cavan Upper	Wilson John	corn, kiln unfin.	- caretaker`s ho.	56a.	29	-	-	-	gr/	-
Donaghmore	Cavan Upper	Wilson John	flax & land	-	146a.	66	-	-	-	gr/	-
Donegal	Churchland *	-	corn kiln	-	-	-	-	-	-	6"os/	11
Gartan	Churchtown	-	corn & kiln	-	-	-	-	2004	large - c40ft dia x 5	pWEH	B
Gartan	Churchtown	-	old corn kiln	-	-	-	-	1841	-	6"os/	44
Donegal	Clar Lough	-	corn	-	-	-	-	-	-	osm/	-
Donegal	Clar Lough	-	old bl. green	-	-	-	-	-	-	osm/	-
Tullyfern	Claragh	- SE. of Tully Br.	corn	-	-	-	-	-	-	6"os/	45
Taughboyne	Clashgowan	- at Milltown Vge.	corn & mill pond	-	-	-	-	1841	-	6"os/	55
Taughboyne	Clashgowan	McClean Matthew	flax & corn	(3B) 40x21.6x5.9 :	-	-	-	1836	6 stocks, m/cy C :	hob/	5.0841
Taughboyne	Clashgowan	S/Clashygowan Vge.	flax	-	-	-	-	1841	-	6"os/	55
Clonmany	Cleagh	-	corn	-	-	-	-	-	12x2x -	osm/	-
Fahan Lower	Cleenagh	- nr Keelogs Vge.	corn	-	-	-	-	-	-	6"os/	10
Templecrone	Cleenderry	-	corn kiln	-	-	-	-	-	-	6"os/	56
Templecrone	Cleenderry	-	corn kiln	-	-	-	-	-	-	6"os/	56
Templecrone	Cleenderry	-	corn kiln	-	-	-	-	-	-	6"os/	56
Templecrone	Cleenderry		corn kiln	-	-	-	-	-	-	6"os/	56
Inishkeel	Cleengort	-	corn kiln (2)	-	-	-	-	-	-	6"os/	65
Inishkeel	Cleengort	-	old corn kiln	-	-	-	-	-	-	6"os/	65
Donegal	Cleggan *	-	mill	-	-	-	-	-	-	1"os/	-
Glencolumbkille	Cloghan	-	flax (2)	-	-	-	-	-	-	6"os/	55
Glencolumbkille	Cloghan	-	corn kiln	-	-	-	-	-	-	6"os/	55
Glencolumbkille	Cloghan	-	flax & pond	-	-	-	-	-	-	6"os/	55
Donaghmore	Cloghard		mill pond	-	-	-	-	-	-	6"os/	79
Donegal	Cloghbane *	-	flax	-	-	-	-	-	-	1"os/	10
Inishkeel	Clogher East	-	corn kiln (2)	-	-	-	-	-	-	6"os/	76
Templecrone	Clogherdillure	-	corn kiln	-	-	-	-	-	-	6"os/	48
Taughboyne	Cloghfin	-	corn kiln	-	-	-	-	-	-	6"os/	55
Taughboyne	Cloghfin	Alexander David	flax	(2B) 25.6x22.6x6.3 :	-	-	-	-	3 stocks m/cy B :	hob/	5.0841
Taughboyne	Cloghfin	N&S Cloghfin Vge.	flax mills	-	-	-	-	-	-	6"os/	55
Kilbarron	Cloghore	Donaldson Geo	corn	-	2.3.0	23	-	-	-	gr/	-
Donegal	Clonea *	-	mill	-	-	-	-	-	-	1"os/	-
Donaghmore	Clonyreel	-	corn kiln	-	-	-	-	-	-	6"os/	78 (41 sites)
Killea & T`bne	Cloon	MacFarland Mr	linen	-	-	-	-	-	-	osm/	-
Allsaints	Cloon	McFarland William	corn & flax	(3B) 20x10x5.6 :	-	-	-	-	13ft. dia. 1 pr. st. :	hob/	5.0832
Killea & T`bne	Cloon		mill pond	-	-	-	-	-	-	6"os/	55
Killea & T`bne	Cloon	- W. Kildrum Vge.	corn & flax	-	-	-	-	-	-	6"os/	55
Leck	Coaghmill	- SE/ L'kenny	flax	-	-	-	-	1841	-	6"os/	56
Leck	Coaghmill	- at Creanagh Vge.	corn & kiln	-	-	-	-	1841	-	6"os/	56

PARISH	TOWNLAND	MILLER	TYPE	HOUSE	Land	£Val	PROPRIETORS	Date	WHEEL etc.	Record	Ref.
Allsaints	Colehill	- imed. N. Town :	mill & pond	-	-	-	-	-	-	6"os/	46
Inishkeel	Common	-	flax mill in ruins	-	-	-	-	-	-	6"os/	62
Convoy	Convoy	-	woollen	huge complex :	-	-	Enterprise Centre Tr.	2001	commercial	pWEH	Cc
Convoy	Convoy	- Woollen Mills	woollen	-	-	-	-	2001	-	pWEH	Cc
Convoy	Convoy	Gregg John	mill	-	-	-	Gregg Jn - Allen Robt	1871	-	dd/	1871 75 204
Convoy	Convoy	Gregg John	mill	-	-	-	Gregg Jn - Shaw Jas A	1874	-	dd/	1874 38 174
Convoy	Convoy	Montgomery Robert	Convoy Mills	-	-	-	Montgomery - Wilson Robt	1892	-	dd/	1892 5 271
Convoy	Convoy	Wilson Robert	Convoy Mills	-	-	-	Wilson - Convoy Woollen	1894	-	dd/	1894 26 25
Convoy	Convoy Town	Montgomery Robt	corn	-	-	-	-	-	- about 20 h.p.	osm/	-
Convoy	Convoy Town	Norman Mr	flax	-	-	-	-	-	-	osm/	-
Stranorlar	Cooladawson	-	flax	-	-	-	-	-	-	1"os/	24
Stranorlar	Cooladawson	- N. of Village	flax	-	-	-	-	-	-	6"os/	78
Raphoe	Cooladdery	- on Swilly Burn	flax & pond	-	-	-	-	-	-	6"os/	69
Clondahorky	Corcreggan	-	corn	-	-	-	Brendan Rohan	2004	-	pWEH	B
Clondahorky	Corcreggan	-	corn kilns (2)	-	-	-	-	-	-	6"os/	15
Clondahorky	Corcreggan	-	Millhouse	restored as Hostel	-	-	Brendan Rohan	2004	-	pWEH	B
Clondahorky	Corcreggan	McCandlish John	mill	well preserved	-	-	McCandlish J - Stewart A	1874	-	dd/	1874 10 53
Clondahorky	Corcreggan	Stewart Alex	corn	-	-	-	Stewart A - Std Life Asc	1871	-	dd/	1871 19 212
Clondahorky	Corcreggan	Stewart Alex	mill	-	-	-	Stewart A J - Lyle Robt	1873	-	dd/	1873 28 143
Clondahorky	Corcreggan	Stewart Alex	mills	-	-	-	Stewart A - Grove Jas G	1874	-	dd/	1874 10 163
Donaghmore	Corgary	-	old malt kiln	-	-	-	-	-	-	6"os/	78
Killaghtee	Corkermore	-	corn kiln	-	-	-	-	-	-	6"os/	83
Raymoghy	Corkey	-	flax (several) :	-	-	-	-	-	-	osm/	-
Raymoghy	Corkey	- near Milltown	corn & pond	-	-	-	-	-	-	6"os/	61
Raymoghy	Corkey	- N. / Hungry Hill	flax	-	-	-	-	-	-	6"os/	62
Raymoghy	Corkey	- on rd. to Roosky	mill	-	-	-	-	-	-	mmSv/	wh - Z
Raymoghy	Corkey	Biers John	corn	(1A) 40x11x5 :	-	-	-	-	1 pair stones :	hob/	5.0839
Raymoghy	Corkey	Leslie Revd John	corn	-	-	-	-	-	-	osm/	-
Kilbarron	Corlea	- E. side R.Erne :	factory	-	-	-	-	-	-	6"os/	108
Urney	Cormakilly	-	mill	-	-	-	-	-	-	1"os/	25
Kilteevoge	Corraine	- S. side R. Finn	corn & pond	-	-	-	-	-	-	6"os/	77
Kilteevoge	Corraine	Laird James	flax	-	64a.	23	-	-	-	gr/	-
Kilteevoge	Corraine	M`Brerety Patrick	scutch	-	4a.	10	-	-	-	gr/	-
Drumhome	Coxtown	-	flax	-	-	-	-	-	-	1"os/	32
Drumhome	Coxtown	-	mill	-	-	-	-	-	-	1"os/	32
Drumhome	Coxtown	- (no name)	scutch :	-	-	-	-	-	machinery defective	osm/	-
Drumhome	Coxtown BridgeTn	-	mill	-	-	-	-	-	-	1"os/	32
Clondahorky	Craig	Hart George	mill	-	-	-	Hart Geo - Hayden Jas	1872	-	dd/	1872 34 72
Clondahorky	Craig	McGilivay Wid. Sid.	corn & kiln	(1B) 40x21x9 & :	-	-	-	-	12ft dia. float bds :	hob/	5.0818
Clondahorky	Craig	McNickle Robert	new flax mill	-	-	-	-	-	- 2 stocks	hob/	5.0818
Clondahorky	Craig	Watt William	new flax mill	-	-	-	-	-	- 2 stocks	hob/	5.0818
Tullyfern	Cratlagh	-	flax	-	-	-	-	2010	-	mm/OS	wh - Z
Tullyfern	Cratlagh	-	flax	-	-	-	-	-	-	osm/	-
Tullyfern	Cratlagh	- NW Bunlin Br.	flax	-	-	-	-	1841	-	6"os/	36
Tullyfern	Cratlagh	Algeo William	new flax mill	(1A) 30x20x18	-	-	-	-	- 6 stocks :	hob/	5.0830
Tullyfern	Cratlagh	Algeo William	tuck	[no dimensions] :	-	-	-	-	-	hob/	5.0830
Tullyfern	Cratlagh	Gilmore Patrick	corn store, kiln	-	-	-	-	-	-	hob/	5.0830
Tullyfern	Cratlagh	Hay Charles	corn & kiln	mill [no dims.] :	-	-	-	-	steam corn mill 12hp	hob/	5.0830
Donegal	Creaneagh *	-	corn & kiln	-	-	-	-	-	-	6"os/	53
Donegal	Creaneagh *	-	flax	-	-	-	-	-	-	6"os/	53
Donegal	Creaneagh *	- at Bunnagee Vge.	corn kiln	-	-	-	-	-	-	6"os/	53
Clondahorky	Creenasmear	-	corn kiln	-	-	-	-	-	-	6"os/	26

PARISH	TOWNLAND	MILLER	TYPE	HOUSE	Land	£Val	PROPRIETORS	Date	WHEEL etc.	Record	Ref.
Allsaints	Creeve	-	corn kiln	-	-	-	-	-	-	6"os/	54
Raphoe	Creggan Lr. Vge.	-	old corn mill	-	-	-	-	-	-	6"os/	19
Killybegs Upr.	Croaghan	Condy & E.? Cahil	corn	(2B) 29x20x8 :	-	-	-	-	1 pr.st. class B m/cy	hob/	5.0810
Donegal	Croaghcullion *	-	corn kiln	-	-	-	-	-	-	6"os/	81
Killybegs Upr.	Croaghlin		corn & mill race	-	-	-	-	-	-	6"os/	91
Killybegs Upr.	Croaghlin		corn kiln	-	-	-	-	-	-	6"os/	91
Templecrone	Crohy	-	corn kilns (2)	-	-	-	-	-	-	6"os/	56
Templecrone	Crohy	-	corn kilns (2)	-	-	-	-	-	-	6"os/	56
Kilteevoge	Crolack	-	corn kiln	-	-	-	-	-	-	6"os/	76
Donaghmore	Cronalaghy	-	corn kiln	-	-	-	-	-	-	6"os/	87
Killea & T`bne	Cross	Laid Mr	linen	-	-	-	-	-	-	osm/	-
Killea & T`bne	Cross :	-	linen	-	-	-	-	2004	-	mmSv/	BFK - Z
Killea & T`bne	Cross :	-	linen	-	-	-	-	2004	-	pWEH	R
Inishkeel	Croveenananta	-	corn kiln	-	-	-	-	-	-	6"os/	76
Templecrone	Crovehy	-	corn kiln	-	-	-	-	-	-	6"os/	49
Kilcar	Crowanrudda	- on W. side road :	corn	-	-	-	-	-	-	6"os/	91
Kilcar	Croweighter	-	corn kiln (2)	-	-	-	-	-	-	6"os/	82
Templecrone	Cruickamore	-	corn kiln (4)	-	-	-	-	-	-	6"os/	49
Inver	Crumlin	-	corn kiln	-	-	-	-	-	-	6"os/	82
Culdaff	Culdaff	-	corn		-	-	-	-	-	6"os/	5
Culdaff	Culdaff	- nr Culdaff Vge.	corn & pond	-	-	-	-	-	-	6"os/	5
Culdaff	Culdaff	Crudden Owen	tuck	(1B) 34x20.6x8	-	-	-	-	12x1.8x6 drives :	hob/	5.0812
Leck	Cullion	-	flax	-	-	-	-	-	-	1"os/	16
Donegal	Cullion (4)	Scottish Equitable A.	Coagh Mill	-	-	-	Scots Eq. - Newton Andrew	1893	-	dd/	1893 5 243
Donegal	Curraghfeaghan *		corn kiln	-	-	-	-	-	-	6"os/	92
Stranorlar	Curraghomongan	-	corn kiln	-	-	-	-	-	-	6"os/	77
Stranorlar	Curraghomongan	-	flax & mill dam	-	-	-	-	-	-	6"os/	77
Kilteevoge	Dergroagh	-	corn kiln	-	-	-	-	-	-	6"os/	76
Killybegs Lower	Derries	-	corn	-	-	-	-	-	-	6"os/	74
Mevagh	Derrycassan	- near coast	corn	-	-	-	-	-	-	6"os/	16
Templecrone	Derrydruel Lower	-	corn kiln	-	-	-	-	-	-	6"os/	57
Templecrone	Derrydruel Upper	-	corn kiln	-	-	-	-	-	-	6"os/	57
Inishkeel	Derryness	-	old corn kiln	-	-	-	-	-	-	6"os/	73
Raymunterdoney	Derryreel	-	corn kiln	-	-	-	-	-	-	6"os/	25
Mevagh	Devlinmore	- > 1/2 mile NNW :	old mill	-	-	-	-	-	-	6"os/	27
Inver	Disert	-	corn kilns (3)	-	-	-	-	-	-	6"os/	84
Raphoe	Disslin	Shildon Alex :	flax	(2B) 29.6x20.6x7 :	-	2.9	-	-	- 4 stocks :	hob/	5.0837
Donegal	Donegal	-	linen	-	-	-	-	-	-	osm/	-
Donegal	Donegal	-	linen (2)	-	-	-	-	-	-	1"os/	-
Donegal	Donegal	M`Loone Anthony	spade	-	5a.	12	-	-	-	gr/	-
Donegal	Donegal Town	at Milltown Vge.	spade foundry	-	-	-	-	-	-	6"os/	93
Leck	Dooballagh	-	corn kiln	-	-	-	-	-	-	6"os/	61
Leck	Dooballagh	- nr Dooba` Vge.	flax mill pond	-	-	-	-	-	-	6"os/	61
Clondahorky	Doocashel Glebe	-	corn kiln	-	-	-	-	-	-	6"os/	26
Raymoghy	Dooish	-	corn kiln	-	-	-	-	-	-	6"os/	54
Raymoghy	Dooish	-	corn kiln	-	-	-	-	-	-	6"os/	77
Raymoghy	Dooish	Glenn John	corn	(1B) 36.6x19.6x8 :	-	-	-	-	diameter 12 ft.	hob/	5.0839
Kilmacrenan	Doon	- at Newmill Br.	corn	-	-	-	-	-	-	6"os/	60
Kilmacrenan	Doon	- SW Doon Glebe	large mill	-	-	-	-	-	-	6"os/	60
Donaghmore	Dreenan	Johnston James	mill	-	-	-	Johnston J - Keys Letitia	1870	-	dd/	1870 1 284
Donaghmore	Dreenan	Johnston John	corn & flax	-	46a.	93	-	-	-	gr/	-
Donaghmore	Dreenan	Johnston John	rub & wash	(3B) 39x21.6x7 :	-	-	-	1838	13.6x3.8x6 :	hob/	5.0835

COUNTY DONEGAL

PARISH	TOWNLAND	MILLER	TYPE	HOUSE	Land	£Val	PROPRIETORS	Date	WHEEL etc.	Record	Ref.
Donaghmore	Dreenan	M`Cormack Saml	flax	-	5a.	10	-	-	-	gr/	-
Donaghmore	Drennan	-	beetling	-	-	-	-	-	-	6"os/	78
Donaghmore	Drennan	-	corn & pond	-	-	-	-	-	-	6"os/	78
Donaghmore	Drennan	-	mill pond	-	-	-	-	-	-	6"os/	78
Donaghmore	Drennan	- S. of R. Finn	mill pond	-	-	-	-	-	-	6"os/	78
Donaghmore	Drennan	- S. of R. Finn	wash house	-	-	-	-	-	-	6"os/	78
Taughboyne	Drimennan	Bullockshed Jas :	flax	(1B) 25.6x19.6x13 :	-	-	-	-	4 stocks, m/cy B :	hob/	5.0841
Donegal	Drimlecks	-	corn	-	-	-	-	-	-	osm/	-
Culdaff	Dristernan	-	old corn kiln	-	-	-	-	-	-	6"os/	12
Culdaff	Dristernan :	-	corn & pond	-	-	-	-	-	-	6"os/	12
Culdaff	Dristernan :	-	corn kiln	-	-	-	-	-	-	6"os/	12
Allsaints	Dromoghill	Clyde Thomas	flax	-	39a.	-	-	-	-	gr/	-
Conwal	Dromore	-	corn kiln	-	-	-	-	-	-	6"os/	53
Conwal	Dromore	- on R. Finn	corn & kiln	-	-	-	-	-	-	6"os/	78
Conwal	Dromore	- on R. Finn	flour	-	-	-	-	-	-	6"os/	78
Conwal	Dromore	- on R. Finn	tuck	-	-	-	-	-	-	6"os/	78
Conwal	Dromore	- at Dromore Vge.	corn kiln	-	-	-	-	-	-	6"os/	53
Taughboyne	Dromore Big	-	mill pond	-	-	-	-	-	-	6"os/	62
Taughboyne	Dromore Big	-	mill ponds (2)	-	-	-	-	-	-	6"os/	62
Taughboyne	Dromore Big	- at Dromore Vge.	flax	-	-	-	-	-	-	6"os/	62
Taughboyne	Dromore Big	- E./ Dromore Vge.	flax	-	-	-	-	-	-	6"os/	62
Taughboyne	Dromore Little	- nr Dromore Vge.	corn & flax	-	-	-	-	-	-	6"os/	62
Donegal	Druimcruach	-	corn	-	-	-	-	-	-	osm/	-
Donegal	Drumacanoo *	-	corn & kiln	-	-	-	-	-	-	6"os/	52
Inishkeel	Drumalough	-	corn kiln	-	-	-	-	-	-	6"os/	73
Tirhugh bo	Drumaneel	Armstrong William	mills	-	-	-	Armstrong - Baxter Siddle	1870	-	dd/	1870 20 122
Clondavaddog	Drumavoghy	-	corn kilns (2)		-	-	-	-	-	6"os/	4
Clondavaddog	Drumavohy	-	corn kilns (2)	-	-	-	-	-	-	6"os/	4
Moville Lower	Drumaweer	-	corn & pond	-	-	-	-	-	-	6"os/	22
Taughboyne	Drumbeg	-	flax & pond	-	-	-	-	-	-	6"os/	62
Stranorlar	Drumboe	-	large mill dam	-	-	-	-	-	-	6"os/	78
Stranorlar	Drumboe	- near Stranorlar	corn & mill dam	-	-	-	-	-	-	6"os/	77
Inishkeel	Drumboghill	- near coast	corn	-	-	-	-	-	-	6"os/	64
Conwal	Drumbologe	-	corn kiln	-	-	-	-	-	-	6"os/	52
Conwal	Drumbologe	- Drumbologe	Mill & pond	-	-	-	-	-	-	6"os/	52
Clonca	Drumcarbit	-	corn kilns	-	-	-	-	-	-	6"os/	4
Clonca	Drumcarbit	-	corn kilns		-	-	-	-	-	6"os/	4
Raymoghy	Drumcarn	- (no mill)	mill pond	-	-	-	-	-	-	6"os/	62
Conwal	Drumcavan	Russell John	flax	-	55a.	10	-	-	-	gr/	-
Conwal	Drumcavanny	-	flax	-	-	-	-	-	-	6"os/	52
Conwal	Drumcavanny	-	tuck	-	-	-	-	-	-	6"os/	52
Conwal	Drumcavany	-	flax	-	-	-	-	-	-	1"os/	10
Taughboyne	Drumchrow	Lowry Henry :	flax & store	(3B) 66x22.6x6 :	-	-	-	-	4 stocks, m/cy B :	hob/	5.0841
Inver	Drumcoe	-	corn kiln	-	-	-	-	-	-	6"os/	99
Inver	Drumconor	-	corn	-	-	-	-	-	-	1"os/	23
Inver	Drumconor	-	corn kiln	-	-	-	-	-	-	6"os/	98
Taughboyne	Drumcrow	- no mill 3/4 mile	mill pond	-	-	-	-	-	-	6"os/	62
Kilteevoge	Drumderrydonan	-	corn kiln	-	-	-	-	-	-	6"os/	76
Donegal	Drumdroit *	-	flax	-	-	-	-	-	-	1"os/	25
Donegal	Drumdroit *		flax	-	-	-	-	-	-	6"os/	79
Inver	Drumduff	(no mill)	mill race & pond	-	-	-	-	-	-	6"os/	92
Inver	Drumduff	Scott George	corn	(2B) 30.6x22x14 :	-	-	-	-	- machinery C :	hob/	5.0805

PARISH	TOWNLAND	MILLER	TYPE	HOUSE	Land	£Val	PROPRIETORS	Date	WHEEL etc.	Record	Ref.
Inver	Drumduff	Sinclair William	corn & kiln	-	21a.	-	-	-	-	gr/	-
Inver	Drumduff	Sinclair William	mill	(2C) 38x22x12 :	-	-	-	-	- undergoing reps.	hob/	5.0806
Clondahorky	Drumdutton	-	corn kiln	-	-	-	-	-	-	6"os/	26
Taughboyne	Drumenan	N/ Drumenan Lr. Vg.	flax	-	-	-	-	1841	-	6"os/	63
Clondavaddog	Drumfad	Marley Patrick	corn & kiln	-	-	-	-	-	-	hob/	5.0822
Convoy	Drumgumberland	- at Milltown	corn & pond	-	-	-	-	-	-	6"os/	69
Convoy	Drumgumberland	- unoc.	flax & corn	(2B) 22x17.6x5.6 :	-	-	-	-	1 pair st., 4 stocks	hob/	5.0834
Convoy	Drumgumberland	- N. side R. Deel	flax & tuck	-	-	-	-	-	-	6"os/	69
Convoy	Drumgumberland	Black James Rev	corn & kiln	-	26a.	23	-	-	-	gr/	-
Burt	Drumhaggart	-	mills (2) pond :	-	-	-	-	1841	-	6"os/	38
Burt	Drumhaggart	Belfast & Pr. Bank	mill	-	-	-	Belfast Bank - Witherow	1874	-	dd/	1874 23 297
Burt	Drumhaggart	Witherow Thomas	mill	-	-	-	Witherow T - Miller Jos E	1874	-	dd/	1874 8 32
Killygarvan	Drumhallagh	- S. New Br. :	corn & kiln	-	-	-	-	-	-	6"os/	28
Aughnish	Drumherrive	-	corn	-	-	-	-	-	14x1.8x -	osm/	-
Aughnish	Drumherrive	-	flax	-	-	-	-	-	12x2.2x -	osm/	-
Aughnish	Drumherrive	-	flax & pond	-	-	-	-	-	-	6"os/	37
Aughnish	Drumherrive	- W/ Walker's Br.	corn & kiln	-	-	-	-	-	-	6"os/	37
Aughnish	Drumherrive	Donnelly Thomas	corn & flax	[as meas. 1838]	-	-	-	1856	- ea. 6 stocks	hob/	5.0820
Aughnish	Drumherrive	Donnelly Thomas	corn & kilns	(1B) 42x20x11 :	-	-	-	1838	- 1 pair stones	hob/	5.0819
Aughnish	Drumherrive	Donnelly Thomas	flax	(1B) 32x16.6x6 :	5a.	-	-	-	- ea. 6 stocks	hob/	5.0819
Raphoe	Drumineney	-	corn kiln	-	-	-	-	-	-	6"os/	69
Raphoe	Drumineney	-	windmill	-	-	-	-	-	-	1"os/	17
Inishkeel	Drumirrin	-	corn kilns (2)	-	-	-	-	-	-	6"os/	73
Mevagh	Drumlackagh	- at Mullans	corn kiln	-	-	-	-	-	-	6"os/	26
Templecrone	Drumlaghdrid	-	corn kiln	-	-	-	-	-	-	6"os/	57
Donegal	Drumlaght	N. side R Eask	corn	-	-	-	-	-	-	6"os/	94
Clonleigh	Drumleene	- 1/4 mile N. Vge.	flax & pond	-	-	-	-	-	-	6"os/	70
Donegal	Drumlonagher	M`Logue Anthony	corn	-	17a.	64	-	-	-	gr/	-
Killea & T`bne	Drummanon	Alexander Mr	linen	-	-	-	-	-	-	osm/	-
Tullyfern	Drummonaghan	- Kelly's Mills	corn / flour	large complex :	-	-	-	2--1	- phos. taken	mmSv/	wh - D
inver	Drumnacarry	W/ R. Eask & 1/3m. :	mill	-	-	-	-	-	-	6"os/	94
Donegal	Drumnadrought *	-	mill	-	-	-	-	-	-	1"os/	16
Kilcar	Drumnafinagle	-	corn kiln	-	-	-	-	-	-	6"os/	96
Kilcar	Drumnafinagle	- N. of river :	corn	-	-	-	-	-	-	6"os/	96
Clonleigh	Drumnaha	-	old wind mill	-	-	-	-	-	-	1"os/	17
Clonleigh	Drumnaha	-	old windmill	-	-	-	-	-	-	6"os/	70
Clonleigh	Drumnaha	- nr Lifford Rd	windmill	-	-	-	-	-	-	1"os/	17
Clonleigh	Drumnaha	- SW./ M`sessiagh	old wind mill	-	-	-	-	-	-	6"os/	70
Raymoghy	Drumoghill	-	flax	-	-	-	-	-	-	6"os/	54
Raymoghy	Drumoghill	-	flax	-	-	-	-	2004	-	mmSv/	bfk - Z
Raymoghy	Drumonaghan *	Kelly`s Mills	-	large complex, dilap.	-	-	-	2001	-	pWEH	D
Conwal	Drumpologe	James Elizabeth	corn & kiln	-	28a.	20	-	-	-	gr/	-
Donegal	Drumrat	Spence Jacob	corn & kiln	-	63a.	77	-	-	-	gr/	-
Donegal	Drumrat	Spence Jacob	flax	-	-	-	-	-	-	gr/	-
Killymard	Drumroosk	-	mill	-	-	-	-	-	-	1"os/	24
Muff	Drumskellan	- S. side of road	flax (2) & pond	-	-	-	-	1843	-	6"os/	39
Muff	Drumskellan	- S. side of road	tuck	-	-	-	-	2010	-	mmOS/	wh - Z
Muff	Drumskellan	- S. side of road	tuck & mill race	-	-	-	-	1843	-	6"os/	39
Muff	Drumskellan	Lynch Henry	flax	(1B) 25.6x18x12 :	-	-	-	-	- 1 pr st. & 4 stocks	hob/	5.0818
Muff	Drumskellan	Mulhern Thomas	kiln	(3C) 48.6x11x5.9 :	-	-	-	-	-	hob/	5.0818
Muff	Drumskellan	Platt Matthew	kiln	-	-	-	-	-	-	hob/	5.0818
Clondahorky	Dunfanaghy	- near Town	corn kiln	-	-	-	-	-	-	6"os/	15

PARISH	TOWNLAND	MILLER	TYPE	HOUSE	Land	£Val	PROPRIETORS	Date	WHEEL etc.	Record	Ref.
Templecrone	Dunglow	- (on rocky inlet)	mill	-	-	-	-	-	-	1"os/	15
Raymunterdoney	Dunmore	-	corn kiln	-	-	-	-	-	-	6"os/	25
Clondahorky	Dunmore	-	corn kiln	-	-	-	-	-	-	6"os/	26
Inishkeel	Eden	-	corn kiln	-	-	-	-	-	-	6"os/	64
Donegal	Edencarnan *	-	corn kiln	-	-	-	-	-	-	6"os/	45
Aghanunshin	Eighteross	- near Castle Wray	corn & pond	-	-	-	-	-	-	6"os/	53
Aghanunshin	Eighterross	Brooks Mrs	gig house	(2B) 24x12.6x6	-	-	-	-	-	hob/	5.0818
Aghanunshin	Eighterross	McIlhenny Alex	corn & kiln	(1B) 39x20x11.6 :	-	-	-	-	- 1 pair stones	hob/	5.0818
Aghanunshin	Eighterross	McIlhenny Alex	flax	(3B) 24.6x22x5.6	-	-	-	-	- 4 stocks	hob/	5.0818
Moville Lower	Eleven Ballyboes	-	corn kiln	-	-	-	-	-	-	6"os/	22
Moville Lower	Eleven Ballybolus	Morrison Samuel	mill	(1A) 24.6x32.6x41 :	-	-	-	1855	34x4 overshot :	hob/	5.0815
Donegal	Eskymeen ? :	Bell Joseph	kiln	(3C) 39x18x5.3	-	-	-	-	-	hob/	5.0818
(bo Ennishowen)	Fahan *	Hamilton Catherine	corn kiln	-	-	-	-	1892	-	6"os/	4
(bo Ennishowen)	Fahan *	Hamilton David	Fahan Mill	-	-	-	Hamilton Dav - Catherine	1892	-	dd/	1892 40 18
Fahan lower	Fahan Lower	-	corn kiln		-	-	-	-	-	6"os/	4
Tullaghobegly	Falcarragh	-	corn kiln	-	-	-	-	-	-	6"os/	25
Tullaghobegly	Falcarragh :	- SW Tullabegly :	corn	-	-	-	-	-	-	6"os/	25
Conwal	Fallard & Calhame	-	mill pond	-	-	-	-	-	-	6"os/	53
Donegal	Farmhill *	- on Drumeny R	mill	-	-	-	-	-	-	1"os/	24
Templecarn	Fincashel	-	corn kiln	-	-	-	-	-	-	6"os/	105
Urney	Flushtown	-	flax	-	-	-	-	-	-	1"os/	16
Aughnish	Fortstewart	Stewart James Sir	flax	(1B) 60x21x10 & :	-	-	-	-	- 4 pair rollers :	hob/	5.0820
Urney	Foyfin	corn kiln		-	-	-	-	-	-	6"os/	79
Raymoghy	Galdonagh	Gregg Robert	flax	(2B) 25x20x5.6 :	-	-	-	-	3 stocks :	hob/	5.0839
Raymoghy	Galdonagh	near Galdonagh Pt.	flax	-	-	-	-	-	-	6"os/	54
Raymoghy	Galdonagh	Patterson William	flax	(2B) 24x19.6x6 :	-	-	-	-	3 stocks :	hob/	5.0839
Kilteevoge	Galwolie	-	corn kiln	-	-	-	-	-	-	6"os/	68
Kilmacrennan	Garrowcarry	-	corn & kiln	-	-	-	-	-	-	6"os/	53
Kilmacrennan	Garrowcarry	-	corn & ponds	-	-	-	-	-	-	6"os/	53
Kilteevoge	Garvan	-	corn kiln	-	-	-	-	-	-	6"os/	67
Clondahorky	Garvary	-	mill	-	-	-	-	-	-	1"os/	16
Clondahorky	Garvary	Donegal Marq	mill	-	-	-	Donegal - Maxwell Robt	1873	-	dd/	1873 24 25
Clondahorky	Garvary	Hardyman or :	mill	-	-	-	Hardyman or Maxwell - :	1871	-	dd/	1871 16 204
Glencolumbkille	Garveross		corn kiln	-	-	-	-	-	-	6"os/	80
Killea & T`bne	Ginsurry	Roger Mr.	linen	-	-	-	-	-	-	osm/	-
Templecrone	Glashbeggan	-	corn kiln (3)	-	-	-	-	-	-	6"os/	48
Templecarn	Glaskeeragh	-	corn kiln	-	-	-	-	-	-	6"os/	104
Tullaghobegly	Glebe	- on coast	corn kiln	-	-	-	-	-	-	6"os/	24
Donagh	Glenaganon :	- on Donagh R.	tuck	-	-	-	-	-	-	6"os/	11
Donagh	Glenaganon :	- nr Carndonagh	corn & pond	-	-	-	-	-	-	6"os/	11
Aughnish	Glenalla	Harte Thos B	flax	(1B) 63.6x24x20	-	-	-	-	- 6 pairs of new :	hob/	5.0820
Moville Upper	Glencrow	- near Village	corn & kiln	-	-	-	-	-	-	6"os/	21
Glencolumbkille	Glenlough	-	corn kiln	-	-	-	-	-	-	6"os/	72
Clondavaddog	Glenmanagh	McGilligan Patrick	corn mill :	-	-	-	-	1838	-	hob/	5.0826
Clondavaddog	Glenmenagh	-	corn & pond	-	-	-	-	-	-	6"os/	26
Mevagh	Glenoory	- on Rossa Bay	salt pans	-	-	-	-	-	-	6"os/	7
Mevagh	Glenoory	- on Rosses Bay	salt pans		-	-	-	-	-	6"os/	7
Raymoghy	Glensmill	Abercorn Marq. of	corn	-	-	-	-	-	-	osm/	-
Tullyfern	Glentidaly	-	flax	-	-	-	-	-	-	1"os/	16
Convoy	Gobnacastle	McClure David	mill	-	-	-	McClure D - Crawford Margt	1891	-	dd/	1891 6 209
Donaghmore	Goland	-	corn kiln	-	-	-	-	-	-	6"os/	77
Donaghmore	Goland	- S./ Burn Durnett	corn & ponds	-	-	-	-	-	-	6"os/	77

PARISH	TOWNLAND	MILLER	TYPE	HOUSE	Land	£Val	PROPRIETORS	Date	WHEEL etc.	Record	Ref.
Donaghmore	Gortafad	-	mill pond	-	-	-	-	-	-	6"os/	79
Donaghmore	Gortafad	-	ruins of malt kiln	-	-	-	-	-	-	6"os/	79
Tullaghobegly	Gortahork	-	corn kilns (2)	-	-	-	-	-	-	6"os/	24
Tullaghobegly	Gortahork	-	old malt house	-	-	-	-	-	-	6"os/	87
Kilmacrenan	Gortalaban	-	flax	-	-	-	-	-	-	6"os/	53
Donergal	Gortamuck *	at Gortamuck Upper	corn kiln	-	-	-	-	-	-	6"os/	79
Clonleigh	Gortin South	1/3m. W/ Vge.	flax & pond	-	-	-	-	-	-	6"os/	79
Conwal	Gortlee	- nr Letterkenny	corn	-	-	-	-	-	-	6"os/	53
Conwal	Gortlee	- at Lytle`s Grove	corn							6"os/	53
Inishkeel	Gortnasillagh	-	corn kiln (2)	-	-	-	-	-	-	6"os/	65
Kilmacrenan	Gortnaskeagh	-	flax	-	-	-	-	-	-	1"os/	10
Allsaints	Gortree	-	corn	-	-	-	-	-	-	6"os/	54
Allsaints	Gortree	- Glensmill Vge.	flax, corn, pond	-	-	-	-	-	-	6"os/	54
Allsaints	Gortree	- near Milltown	flax	-	-	-	-	-	-	6"os/	54
Fahan Lower	Gransha	- on Mill R.	mills	-	-	-	-	-	-	1"os/	16
Moville Lower	Gulladoo	-	corn kiln	-	-	-	-	-	-	mmSv/	wh - Z
Moville Lower	Gulladoo	- at Village	corn kiln	-	-	-	-	-	-	6"os/	21
Moville Lower	Gulladoo	Anderson Richard	mill	(1B) 39x11x12 :	-	-	-	-	20x5x - no. bkts 50 :	hob/	5.0814
Moville Lower	Gulladoo	Anderson Richard	thrashing m/c	(1B) 31x14x8.6 :	-	-	-	-	-	hob/	5.0814
Killymard	Haugh	Cromer John	corn & flax	(3B) 34.6x19x7.6 :	-	-	-	-	10ft.dia. class B :	hob/	5.0811
Kilymard	Haugh	Crommer John	corn & kiln	-	-	4.10/-	-	-	-	gr/	-
Kilymard	Haugh	Crommer John	flax	-	-	-	-	-	-	gr/	-
Taughboyne	Haw	-	corn & pond	-	-	-	-	-	-	6"os/	55
Taughboyne	Haw	-	corn kiln	-	-	-	-	-	-	6"os/	55
Taughboyne	Haw	Rankin William	corn & flax	(1B) 41x22x8.9 :	-	-	-	-	15ft. dia. metal :	hob/	5.0841
Templecrone	Illion	-	corn kiln (2)	-	-	-	-	-	-	6"os/	48
Killlea	Imlick		mill pond	-	-	-	-	-	-	6"os/	55
Killlea	Imlick		spade m/fty	-	-	-	-	-	-	6"os/	55
Tullaghobegly	Inishbofin (Island)	- E. side at Vge.	still house	-	-	-	-	-	-	6"os/	14
Tullaghobegly	Inishdooey (Island)	-	corn kiln	-	-	-	-	-	-	6"os/	14
Tullaghobegly	Inishdooey (Island)	-	still houses (2)	-	-	-	-	-	-	6"os/	14
Templecrone	Inishfree Upper	-	corn kiln (2)	-	-	-	-	-	-	6"os/	48
Tullaghobegly	Inishirrer Island	-	corn kiln	-	-	-	-	-	-	6"os/	23
Tullaghobegly	Innishirrir	-	corn kiln	-	-	-	-	-	-	6"os/	32
Donegal	Iron Mills *	-	iron works	neat, condition good	-	-	on market Oct. 2001	2001	(accomodation)	pWEH	C
Mevagh	Island Roy	-	corn kiln	-	-	-	-	-	-	6"os/	17
Mevagh	Island Roy	- at Carrickart Vg.	corn & pond	-	-	-	-	-	-	6"os/	17
Killea & T`bne	K`ea /Taughboyne	-	linen (20) :	-	-	-	-	-	-	osm/	-
Conwal	Keeloges	Buchanan Fran	flax	-	-	-	-	-	-	gr/	-
Conwal	Keeloges	Buchanan Robert	flax	-	-	10	-	-	-	gr/	-
Clonca	Keenagh	-	corn & pond		-	-	-	-	-	6"os/	2
Clonca	Keenagh	-	corn, stream :	& pond	-	-	-	-	-	6"os/	2
Banagh	Kilaghtee	-	corn	-	-	-	-	-	-	hob/	5.08
Banagh	Kilaghtee	- near old church	brewery	-	-	-	-	-	-	6"os/	98
Donaghmore	Kilcaddan	-	flax	-	-	-	-	-	-	6"os/	78
Donaghmore	Kilcaddan	- W. side of Vge.	corn & kiln	-	-	-	-	-	-	6"os/	78
Donaghmore	Kilcaddan	Walker William	corn & flax	- & 7 mill hos.	-	190	-	-	-	gr/	-
Kilcar	Kilcar	-	corn kiln	-	-	-	-	-	-	6"os/	96
Kilcar	Kilcar	1/4m./ SW of Town	mill	-	-	-	-	-	-	6"os/	96
Killea & T`bne	Kildrum	Coldwell Mr	linen	-	-	-	-	-	-	osm/	-
Killea & T`bne	Kildrum	Culbert Mr	linen	-	-	-	-	-	-	osm/	-
Clondavaddog	Kildrum	Doherty	corn	-	-	-	-	-	-	gr/	-

PARISH	TOWNLAND	MILLER	TYPE	HOUSE	Land	£Val	PROPRIETORS	Date	WHEEL etc.	Record	Ref.
Clondavaddog	Kildrum	Johnston	corn	-	-	-	-	-	-	gr/	-
Killea & T`bne	Kildrum	McPherson Mr	linen	-	-	-	-	-	-	osm/	-
Killea & T`bne	Kildrum	Mills Mr.	linen	-	-	-	-	-	-	osm/	-
Donegal	Kildrum (2)	Barton Baptist	mill	-	-	-	Barton B - Wilson Robert	1893	-	dd/	1893 23 237
Allsaints	Kildrum Lower	Kilpatrick James	spade	(1B) 30x18.6x7.6 :	-	-	-	-	14x4.4 for hammer :	hob/	5.0832
Drumhome	Kilgole	-	flax	-	-	-	-	-	-	6"os/	99
Glencolumbkille	Kilgoly	-	corn & mill pond	-	-	-	-	-	-	6"os/	81
Donaghmore	Killowen	Patterson William	flax	(2B) 16x20.6x6 :	-	3.9	-	1838	10x1.3x11 :	hob/	5.0835
Tullaghobegly	Killult	-	corn & tuck mills	-	-	-	-	2010	-	mmOS/	wh - Z
Tullaghobegly	Killult	- E. side of road :	tuck	-	-	-	-	-	-	6"os/	24
Tullaghobegly	Killult	- W. side of road :	corn	-	-	-	-	-	-	6"os/	24
Tullaghobegly	Killult	Robinson Thomas	corn	(1C) 26.6x20x8 :	-	-	-	1855	12x1.4x6.6 :	hob/	5.0827
Tullaghobegly	Killult	Wilkilson William	tuck	- in open air & ho.	-	-	-	1855	10.9x1.3x6 :	hob/	5.0827
Killybegs Upr.	Killybegs Town	Blane Thomas	corn stores	(1A) 39x24.6x33 :	-	-	-	-		hob/	5.0810
Killygarvan	Killygarvan	- at Mill Bay	no mill	-	-	-	-	-	-	6"os/	28
Donaghmore	Killygorden	-	flax	-	-	-	-	-	-	6"os/	78
Donaghmore	Killygorden	-	tan yard	-	-	-	-	-	-	6"os/	78
Donaghmore	Killygordon	Mansfield Edmund	mill	-	-	-	Mansfield E - Tagert Robt	1894	-	dd/	1894 35 185
Donaghmore	Killygordon	Mansfield Edmund	mill	-	-	-	Mansfield Ed - Knox Robt	1894	-	dd/	1894 70 284
Conwal	Killymasny	-	malt kiln	-	-	-	-	-	-	6"os/	60
Raymoghy	Killyverry	-	flax & pond	-	-	-	-	1841	-	6"os/	54
Raymoghy	Killyverry	- N/ Killyverry Vge.	flax	-	-	-	-	1841	-	6"os/	54
Raymoghy	Killyverry	Rogers George :	flax	(3B) 28.6x22x5.9 :	-	-	-	-	diameter 13 ft.	hob/	5.0839
Raymoghy	Killyverry	Rogers Jas & Geo	flax	(1A) 27x21.6x6.6 :	-	-	-	-	diameter 12 ft. :	hob/	5.0839
Raymoghy	Killyverry Middle	-	flax mills	-	-	-	-	-	-	1"os/	16
Clondahorky	Kilmackilloo	McCandlish John	mill	-	-	-	McCandlish J - Stewart A	1874	-	dd/	1874 10 53
Clondahorky	Kilmackiloo	-	corn kiln	-	-	-	-	-	-	6"os/	26
Clondahorky	Kilmackiloo	- near shore	tuck	-	-	-	-	-	-	6"os/	26
Kilmacrenan	Kilmacrenan	- ear Bridge	flax	-	-	-	-	2004	-	mmSv/	wh - Z
Kilmacrenan	Kilmacrenan	- SW. of K`nan Br.	flax	-	-	-	-	-	-	6"os/	45
Kilmacrenan	Kilmacrenan	- !/4 m above Br.	tuck	- old small remains	-	-	- Thomas Dillon	2004	-	pWEH	B
Kilmacrenan	Kilmacrenan	Skipton Elizabeth	tuck	-	-	-	Skipton Eliz - Skipton Geo	1874	-	dd/	1874 7 105
Kilmacrenan	Kilmacrenan	Stewart Alex	tuck	-	-	-	Stewart A - Std Life Assc.	1871	-	dd/	1871 19 212`
Donegal	Kiln Hills *	Ramsay Robert	mill	-	-	-	Ramsay Robt - Reid Robt	1873	-	dd/	1873 1 277
Conwal	Kilpheak	- on R. Swilly	corn & pond	-	-	-	-	-	-	6"os/	52
Kilteevoge	Kilrean	-	corn kiln	-	-	-	-	-	-	6"os/	67
Kilteevoge	Kilrean	-	malt kiln	-	-	-	-	-	-	6"os/	67
Kilteevoge	Kilrean	-	mill	-	-	-	-	-	-	1"os/	23
Killybegs Lower	Kilrean lower	Mining Company	engine house	(1A) 12x20.6x35 :	-	-	-	1854	-	hob/	5.0809
Raphoe	Kiltole	- 1m N./ Kiltole Lr.	flax & pond	-	-	-	-	-	-	6"os/	69
Raphoe	Kiltole	Gregg John	mills	-	-	-	Gregg Jn - Allen Robert	1871	-	dd/	1871 25 204
Donaghmore	Kiltown	- N. side R. Finn	flax	-	-	-	-	1841	-	6"os/	78
Donaghmore	Kiltown	Patterson William	flax	-	46a.	41	-	-	-	gr/	-
Aghanunshin	Kiltoy	Boyd William Rev.	gig house	(1B) 21.6x12x6	-	-	-	-	-	hob/	5.0818
Glencolumbkille	Kiltyfanned	-	corn kiln	-	-	-	-	-	-	6"os/	81
Kilteevoge	Kinaderry	-	flax & pond	-	-	-	-	-	-	6"os/	77
Kilteevoge	Kinaderry	Michael Martin	corn	-	-	-	-	-	12x2.6x9 16 h.p :	osm/	-
Kilteevoge	Kinaderry	Michael Martin	flax	-	41a.	-	-	-	10x1.8x6 10 h.p.	osm/	-
Raymoghy	Kincraigy	- N. side of road	flax & pond							6"os/	62
Raymoghy	Kincraigy	- S. side od road	flax							6"os/	62
Inishkeel	Kincrum	-	corn kiln	-	-	-	-	-	-	6"os/	65
Clondavaddog	Kindrum	-	corn	-	-	-	-	-	10x2	osm/	-

PARISH	TOWNLAND	MILLER	TYPE	HOUSE	Land	£Val	PROPRIETORS	Date	WHEEL etc.	Record	Ref.
Clondavaddog	Kindrum	-	corn	-	-	-	-	-	10x2	osm/	-
Clondavaddog	Kindrum	-	corn & tuck		-	-	-	-	-	6"os/	8
Clondavaddog	Kindrum	-	tuck	-	-	-	-	-	-	osm/	-
Clondavaddog	Kindrum	- nr Kindrum Lo.	tuck	-	-	-	-	-	-	6"os/	8
Clondavaddog	Kindrum	- S. / Kindrum Lo.	corn	-	-	-	-	-	-	6"os/	8
Taughboyne	Kinnacally	- at Old Kinacally	corn kiln	-	-	-	-	-	-	6"os/	63
Taughboyne	Kinnacally	- E./ St. Johnstn	flax & mill dam	-	-	-	-	-	-	6"os/	63
Taughboyne	Kinnacally	- nr Old K`lly Vg.	flax & corn	-	-	-	-	-	-	6"os/	63
Taughboyne	Kinnacally	Hamilton Henry	flax	(2C) 50x21x7.6 :	-	-	-	1836	3 stocks, m/cy B :	hob/	5.0841
Taughboyne	Kinnacally	Moody John :	flax	(3C) 34x22x5.6 :	-	-	-	-	4 stocks, m/cy B :	hob/	5.0841
Killea & T`bne	Kinnacally	Shaw Mr	linen	-	-	-	-	-	-	osm/	-
Taughboyne	Kinnacally	Shaw Widow	flax	(3B) 20x18.6x6.6 :	-	-	-	-	4 stocks :	hob/	5.0841
Kilteevoge	Kinnaderry	-	corn kiln	-	-	-	-	-	-	6"os/	68
Kilteevoge	Kinnaderry	- at Milltown	corn	-	-	-	-	-	-	6"os/	68
Kilteevoge	Kinnaderry	- nr Kiladerry Vge.	mill & ponds	-	-	-	-	-	-	6"os/	68
Kilteevoge	Kinnaderry	Martin Michael	corn	-	42a.	28	-	-	-	gr/	-
Kilteevoge	Kinnaderry	Martin Michael	flax	-	-	-	-	-	-	gr/	-
Glencolumbkille	Kinnakillew	-	corn kiln	-	-	-	-	-	-	6"os/	81
Conwal	Kirkneedy	-	malt kilns (2)	-	-	-	-	-	-	6"os/	60
Kilbarron	Knader	Connolly Thomas	spinning & flax :	-	-	-	-	-	-	gr/	-
Donaghmore	Knock	- E. of Fort	flax & lge pond	-	-	-	-	-	-	6"os/	78
Donaghmore	Knock	Gallagher Corns	flax & kiln	-	5a.	-	-	-	-	gr/	-
Donaghmore	Knock	Gallagher Corns	flax, pond, kiln	-	5a.	-	-	-	-	gr/	-
Leck	Knockbrack	- near S.L.Railway	flax	-	-	-	-	-	-	1"os/	17
Leck	Knockbrack	M`Kenny Henry	corn	-	-	-	-	-	-	gr/	-
Leck	Knockbrack	M`Kenny Henry	corn & kiln	-	108a.	-	-	-	-	gr/	-
Leck	Knockbrack	M`Kenny Henry	flax	-	-	-	-	-	-	gr/	-
Tullyfern	Knockdoagh	Glackin James	corn	(1B) 27x21x8.6 :	-	-	-	-	- 1 pair stones :	hob/	5.0831
Tullaghobegly	Knockfola	-	corn kiln	-	-	-	-	-	-	6"os/	23
Clonca	Knockglass	-	still house	-	-	-	-	-	-	mmOS/	wh - Z
Clonca	Knockglass	- at Village	still house		-	-	-	1843	-	6"os/	4
Clondahorky	Knocknafaugher	-	corn kiln	-	-	-	-	-	-	6"os/	26
Donaghmore	Knockrawer	- 1/4m. ExN/ :	flax & mill pond	-	-	-	-	1841	-	6"os/	79
Donaghmore	Knockrawer	Taylor Samuel	mills	-	-	-	Taylor Sam - Taylor John	1872	-	dd/	1872 36 179
Donaghmore	Knockrawer	Taylor Samuel :	corn & flax	(1C) 21.4x17.914 :	-	-	-	1838	12x2.2x15 1 pr. st. :	hob/	5.0835
Donaghmore	Knockrawer	Taylor William :	corn & flax	(1C) 21.4x17.9x14 :	-	-	-	1838	12x2.2x15 :	hob/	5.0835
Raymoghy	Labbadish	-	flax	- some wall only	-	-	-	2004	-	PWEH	R
Raymoghy	Labbadish	Ewing Alex	flax	(3B) 30.6x19x6 :	-	-	-	-	6 stocks :	hob/	5.0839
Raymoghy	Labbadish	Galbraith Mr	flax	-	-	-	-	2004	-	mmSv/	BFK - R
Glencolumbkille	Laghil	corn kiln		-	-	-	-	-	-	6"os/	81
Drumhome	Laghy	- at Laghy Vge	corn kiln	-	-	-	-	-	-	6"os/	100
Killygarvan	Laherdan	-	corn	-	-	-	-	-	- undershot	osm/	-
Killygarvan	Laherdan	-	corn	-	-	-	-	-	- undershot	osm/	-
Killygarvan	Laherdan	-	kiln & pond	-	-	-	-	-	-	6"os/	28
Killygarvan	Laherdan	Donnelly	corn	-	-	-	-	-	-	gr/	-
Inishkeel	Largybrack	-	corn kiln	-	-	-	-	-	-	6"os/	82
Templecrone	Leabgarow	- nr Village	corn kiln	-	-	-	-	-	-	6"os/	48
Donaghmore	Leaght	-	mill pond	-	-	-	-	-	-	6"os/	78
Templecrone	Lefinn	-	corn kiln	-	-	-	-	-	-	6"os/	49
Killlea	Legaduff	S. of Village	corn & pond	-	-	-	-	-	-	6"os/	55
Killlea	Legaduff		corn kilns	-	-	-	-	-	-	6"os/	55
Donegal	Legnachiny Lr *	Robinson John Rev	mill	-	-	-	Robinson J - Wheler Margt	1894	-	dd/	1894 16 214

PARISH	TOWNLAND	MILLER	TYPE	HOUSE	Land	£Val	PROPRIETORS	Date	WHEEL etc.	Record	Ref.
Allsaints	Leitrim	- S./ Leitrim Vge.	flax	-	-	-	-	1841	-	6"os/	55
Donegal	Leitter *	- (on Glendragh R.)	mill	-	-	-	-	-	-	1"os/	31
Donegal	Leitter *	Mackinnon Wm	mill	-	-	-	Mackinnon W - Knox Wm	1870	-	dd/	1870 18 54
Kilteevoge	Letterbrick	-	corn kiln	-	-	-	-	-	-	6"os/	67
Templecrone	Lettercau	-	corn kiln	-	-	-	-	-	-	6"os/	49
Conwal	Letterkenny	-	mill pond :	-	-	-	-	-	-	6"os/	53
Conwal	Letterkenny Town :	Boyd John R	corn	(1A) 42x26x21 :	-	-	-	-	18x4x19 2 pr st. :	hob	5.3811
Conwal	Letterkenny Town :	Boyd John R	saw	(1A) 33x10.6x21	-	-	-	-	-	hob	5.3811
Stranorlar	Lettermakenny	-	flax	-	-	-	-	-	-	6"os/	69
Kilteevoge	Lettershanbo	-	corn kiln	-	-	-	-	-	-	6"os/	60
Killea & T`bne	Lignathraw	Stephenson Mr.	linen	-	-	-	-	-	-	osm/	-
Desertegney	Linsfort	-	corn	-	-	-	-	-	12x2x -	osm/	-
Desertegney	Linsfort	-	corn & pond	-	-	-	-	-	-	6"os/	18
Donaghmore	Liscooly	- N. of R. Finn	corn & kiln	-	-	-	-	1841	-	6"os/	79
Donaghmore	Liscooly	Gallagher Hugh	flax	(3B) 41x21x7 :	-	3.2	-	1838	11.6x1.6x17 :	hob/	5.0835
Killea & T`bne	Lishill	Mackin Mr	linen	-	-	-	-	-	-	osm/	-
Raymoghy	Lismoghy	Mahon John	flax	(3C) 25x21.6x6 :	-	-	-	-	3 stocks :	hob/	5.0839
Donaghmore	Lismullyduff	-	old still house	-	-	-	-	-	-	6"os/	87
Donaghmore	Lismullyduff	at Gallagherstown	corn kiln	-	-	-	-	-	-	6"os/	87
Taughboyne	Listical Lower	-	mill ponds (3)	-	-	-	-	-	-	6"os/	54
Taughboyne	Listical Lower	- near Village	flax & corn kiln	-	-	-	-	-	-	6"os/	54
Taughboyne	Little Dromore	Steen Joseph	flax	(3B) 26.6x18.6x6 :	-	-	-	-	2 stocks, m/cy B :	hob/	5.0841
Taughboyne	Little Dromore	Steen Matthew	flax	(2B) 26.6x16x6 :	-	-	-	-	2 stocks, m/cy B :	hob/	5.0841
Killymara	Lougheask	- 1/4m. W/ L. Eask	corn & mill pond	-	-	-	-	-	-	6"os/	94
Killymara	Lougheask Dem.	-	corn kiln	-	-	-	-	-	-	6"os/	94
Killymara	Lougheask Dem.	- 1/4m. W/ L. Eask	corn & mill pond	-	-	-	-	-	-	6"os/	94
Killymara	Lougheask Dem.	Brooke Thomas	thrashing	(1A) 35x24x14 :	-	-	-	-	-	hob/	5.0811
Donegal	Loughkeel *	-	flax	-	-	-	-	-	-	1"os/	-
Knockbrack	Lurgy	-	corn & kiln	-	-	-	-	-	-	6"os/	61
Knockbrack	Lurgy	-	mill ponds (2)	-	-	-	-	-	-	6"os/	61
Knockbrack	Lurgy	- nr Lurgy cross	flax & corn	-	-	-	-	-	-	6"os/	61
Knockbrack	Lurgy	- E./ Lurgy Mid.Vge.	flax	-	-	-	-	-	-	6"os/	61
Knockbrack	Lurgy	M`Clintock Sam	corn	-	98a.	-	-	-	-	gr/	-
Knockbrack	Lurgy	M`Clintock Sam	flax (2)	-	-	-	-	-	-	gr/	-
Knockbrack	Lurgy	Moore David	flax	-	30a.	-	-	-	-	gr/	-
Taughboyne	Lustical Lower	Rankin Samuel	flax mills	(3B) 42.6x19x6.3 :	-	-	-	-	12ft x 3ft. drives :	hob/	5.0841
Donegal	Maanasillagh *	-	corn kiln (2)	-	-	-	-	-	-	6"os/	81
Inishkeel	Maas	- near Maas Br.	corn	-	-	-	-	-	-	6"os/	65
Inishkeel	Maas	- near Maas Up.	old corn kiln	-	-	-	-	-	-	6"os/	65
Convoy	Macmeenstown	- 1/4 m. W./ Vge.	flax & mill pond	-	-	-	-	-	-	6"os/	69
Lettermasward	Madavagh	-	corn kiln (2)	-	-	-	-	-	-	6"os/	65
Inishmacsaint	Magharacar	- S. side R. Deel	flax & mill pond	-	-	-	-	-	-	6"os/	69
Raphoe	Magheestown	- at Milltown Vge.	corn kiln	-	-	-	-	-	-	6"os/	62
Mevagh	Magherabeg	at Magherabeg Vge.	flax	-	-	-	-	-	-	6"os/	54
Clondahorky	Magherablad	-	corn kiln	-	-	-	-	1841	-	6"os/	26
Donaghmore	Magheraboy	1/8m S. Collons Tn	flax & mill pond	-	-	-	-	-	-	6"os/	79
Raphoe	Magherahaan	-	corn kiln	-	-	-	-	-	-	6"os/	70
Raphoe	Magherahaan	-	malt kiln	-	-	-	-	-	-	6"os/	70
Raphoe	Magherahaan	- 1/4 mile E./ Tn	flax & pond	-	-	-	-	-	-	6"os/	70
Inver	Magherahaana	McCleary James	flax	(3C) 31x20x5.6	-	-	-	1838	11x2x8 4 stocks	hob/	5.0805A
Raphoe	Magherahan	McCleery James	flax	(3B) 21x20x5.6 :	-	7-6-6	-	-	- 4 stocks m/c. C	hob/	5.0837
Mevagh	Magheramorgan	-	corn	-	-	-	-	-	-	osm/	-

PARISH	TOWNLAND	MILLER	TYPE	HOUSE	Land	£Val	PROPRIETORS	Date	WHEEL etc.	Record	Ref.
Mevagh	Magheramorgan	- close to shore	corn	-	-	-	-	-	-	6"os/	26
Convoy	Magheranappan	-	corn	-	-	-	-	-	-	1"os/	16
Convoy	Magheranappan	-	flax (3)	-	-	-	-	-	-	1"os/	16
Convoy	Magheranappan	Dogherty Charles	flax	(1B) 33x20x6	-	-	-	-	- 4 stocks m/cy: B	hob/	5.0834
Clondahorky	Magheraroarty	-	corn kiln	-	-	-	-	-	-	6"os/	26
Clondahorky	Magheraroarty	- NxW. L. Moore	corn & pond	-	-	-	-	-	-	6"os/	26
Donashmore	Magherashanvally	-		-	-	-	-	-	-	6"os/	70
Donashmore	Magherashanvally	- str. to R. Deele	flax	-	-	-	-	-	-	1"os/	17
Raphoe	Magherasolus	-	flax & pond	-	-	-	-	-	-	6"os/	62
Convoy	Magheravall	-	corn kiln	-	-	-	-	-	-	6"os/	68
Clondavaddog	Magherawardan	- at Village	corn kiln	-	-	-	-	-	-	6"os/	18
Donegal	Maghery *	Mackinnon Wm	mill	-	-	-	Mackinnon W - Knox Wm	1870	-	dd/	1870 18 54
Donrgal	Maghery *	MGarvey John	mill	-	-	-	MGarvey J - Kelly Hugh	1872	-	dd/	1872 43 60
Urney	Magherycallaghan	- S. of M'c. Vge.	corn	-	-	-	-	-	-	6"os/	79
Urney	Magherycallaghan		flax	-	-	-	-	-	-	6"os/	79
Donegal	Maghryrenan *	Wray William	mill	-	-	-	Wray W - Morrison Margt	1871	-	dd/	1871 24 102
Clonca	Malin Beg	-	corn kiln	-	-	-	-	-	-	6"os/	89
Clonca	Malin More	-	corn & pond	-	-	-	-	-	-	6"os/	89
Clonca	Malin More	-	corn kiln	-	-	-	-	-	-	6"os/	89
Clonca	Malin Town :	Hervey John	corn	(1A) 46x25x21 :	-	-	-	-	- 2 pr st. 5ft. dia.	hob	5.3812
Clondahorky	Masine	- near shore	corn	-	-	-	-	-	-	6"os/	26
Cnonleigh	Mass More	Stewart Alex	tuck	-	-	-	Stewart A - Grove Jas G	1874	-	dd/	1874 10 163
Templecrone	Meenabollagan	-	corn kilns (2)	-	-	-	-	-	-	6"os/	57
Templecrone	Meenabollagan	-	corn kilns (2)	-	-	-	-	-	-	6"os/	57
Killybegs Lower	Meenachallow	-	tuck & mill race	-	-	-	-	-	-	6"os/	74
Killybegs Lower	Meenachallow	- W. of R.Owena	corn	-	-	-	-	-	-	6"os/	74
Killybegs Lower	Meenachallow	Cunningham Lord	corn & kiln	(1A) 84x24x29.6 : s	-	-	-	-	2 pr. st. good m/cy :	hob/	5.0808
Glencolumbkille	Meenacharvy	-	corn kiln (2)	-	-	-	-	-	-	6"os/	81
Inishkeel	Meenacurrin	E/ Lough Namanfin	corn kiln	-	-	-	-	-	-	6"os/	92
Glencolumbkille	Meenadiff	-	corn kiln	-	-	-	-	-	-	6"os/	81
Mintiaghs	Meenadiff	- S. side small R.	still house							6"os/	19
Inver	Meenagran	-	corn kiln	-	-	-	-	-	-	6"os/	84
Donaghmore	Meenahiniss	-	old malt house	-	-	-	-	-	-	6"os/	87
Inishkeel	Meenakillew	-	corn kiln	-	-	-	-	-	-	6"os/	82
Conwal	Meenatoal ?	Stewart James	new mill	-	-	-	Stewart Jas - Martin Wm	1870	-	dd/	1870 19 147
Conwal	Meenatoal ?	Stewart Sir Jas	new mill	-	-	-	Stewart J - Martin Wm	1870	-	dd/	1870 19 147
Conwal	Meenatoal ?	Stewart Sir Jas	new mill	-	-	-	Stewart J - Hanson Geo	1879	-	dd/	1879 12 287
Glencolumbkille	Meencross	-	corn kiln	-	-	-	-	-	-	6"os/	81
Templecrone	Meenderryherk	-	corn kiln	-	-	-	-	-	-	6"os/	49
Clonmany	Meendoran	-	corn kiln	-	-	-	-	-	-	6"os/	10
Clonmany	Meendoran	-	tuck	-	-	-	-	-	-	6"os/	10
Tullaghobegly	Meenlaragh	-	corn kiln	-	-	-	-	-	-	6"os/	24
Donaghmore	Meenlougher	- NNW / Wilsonstn	flax & kiln	-	-	-	-	-	-	6"os/	79
Templecrone	Meenmore	-	corn & race	-	-	-	-	-	-	6"os/	49
Templecrone	Meenmore	-	corn kiln	-	-	-	-	-	-	6"os/	49
Inishkeel	Meentashesk	-	corn kiln	-	-	-	-	-	-	6"os/	82
Killaghtee	Meentullynagarn		corn kiln	-	-	-	-	-	-	6"os/	92
Inishkeel	Middletown	-	woollen	-	-	-	-	-	-	1"os/	6
Tullyauglish	Milford	-	corn	-	-	-	-	-	-	osm/	-
Tullyauglish	Milford :	Millford Flour Mills	flour	-	-	-	-	-	-	lic/13	flour
Taughboyne	Mill Bay L.Swilly	-	no mill	-	-	-	-	-	-	1"os/	-
Urney	Mill Farm	-	mill pond (only) :	-	-	-	-	1841	-	6"os/	79

PARISH	TOWNLAND	MILLER	TYPE	HOUSE	Land	£Val	PROPRIETORS	Date	WHEEL etc.	Record	Ref.
Urney	Mill Farm	Drummon Wm	mill	-	-	-	Drummon W - Kelly Hugh	1874	-	dd/	1874 36 207
Raymoghy	Mill Town	- near R Swilly	no mill	-	-	-	-	-	-	1"os/	17
Donegal	Millers Holding	Lighton Andrew	mill	-	-	-	Lighton Andr - Hayes Henry	1891	-	dd/	1891 26 157
Urney	Millfarm		corn kiln	-	-	-	-	-	-	6"os/	79
Tullyfern	Millford	Mulroy Bay	flour	mill rebuilt 1932 :	-	-	- (In use till 1980)	2001	-	pWEH	D
Clonleigh	Millsesalagh	MacBith Andrew	corn & kiln	(1B) 46x25x14.9 :	-	-	-	-	15x5x4 2 pr. st.	hob/	5.0833
Clonleigh	Millsesalagh	MacBith Andrew	flax :	(1B) 46x25x14.9 :	-	-	-	-	12x2x4.6 & new :	hob/	5.0832
Clonleigh	Millsessiagh	- in Village	flax & pond	-	-	-	-	-	-	6"os/	70
Clonleigh	Millsessiagh	- in Vge. nr river	corn	-	-	-	-	-	-	6"os/	70
Raymoghy	Milltown	-	(no mill)	-	-	-	-	-	-	6"os/	54
Donegal	Milltown	-	corn kiln	-	-	-	-	-	-	6"os/	69
Cleggan	Milltown	-	mill	-	-	-	-	-	-	1"os/	5
Kilmacrenan	Milltown	-	no mill	-	-	-	-	-	-	1"os/	10
Roosky	Milltown	-	no mill	-	-	-	-	-	-	1"os/	16
Raphoe	Milltown	- on Deele R :	no mill	-	-	-	-	-	-	1"os/	17
Donegal	Milltown	- on Gleenely R	no mill	-	-	-	-	-	-	1"os/	-
Convoy	Milltown	- at Milltown Vge.	corn	-	-	-	-	-	-	6"os/	69
Convoy	Milltown	Allen Robert	corn & flax	-	10a.	28	-	-	-	gr/	-
Convoy	Milltown	Allen Robert :	flax & corn	(1B) 24.6x18x8 :	-	-	-	-	-	hob/	5.0834
(bo. Raphoe)	Milltown	Gallagher Patrick	mills	-	-	-	Gallagher P - Noble John	1891	-	dd/	1891 26 157
(bo. Raphoe)	Milltown	Gardiner Catherine	-	-	-	-	Gardiner C - Coyle Michael	1892	-	dd/	1892 55 74
Killymard	Milltown	Graham William	corn & kilns	(1B) 22.6x20.6x18 :	-	-	-	1838	14x5x7 2 pr. st. :	hob/	5.0810
Killynard	Milltown	Graham William	mills	-	47a.	70	-	-	-	gr/	-
Killymard	Milltown	Graham William	spade	(1B) 36.6x22x8 :	-	-	-	-	12x5x8 & bellows :	hob/	5.0811
Raymoghy	Milltown	Marshall James :	flax	(3C) 47x20x6.6 :	-	-	-	-	diameter 12ft. :	hob/	5.0839
(bo. Raphoe)	Milltown	Moore Margaret	mill	-	-	-	Moore Margt - Wilson Wm	1890	-	dd/	1890 1 128
Raphoe	Milltown	Shaw William	mill	-	-	-	Shaw Wm - Wilson Chas	1873	-	dd/	1873 14 38
Inver	Milltown	Thompson William	corn	(2C) 32x22.6x7 :	-	-	-	-	12x1.9x8 :	hob/	5.0805A
Raphoe	Milltown	Thompson Wm Jn	corn	(3B) 17x22x8 :	-	6.5	-	-	[no information]	hob/	5.0837
Raphoe	Milltown	Walrond Theodore	mill	-	-	-	Walrond T - Rec. O`ship	1870	-	dd/	1870 17 222
Maylin	Milltown	Wicklow E. of	mill	-	-	-	Wicklow E - Scot. Prov.	1870	-	dd/	1870 31 280
Raymoghy	Milltown	Wicklow Earl Of	corn	-	-	-	-	-	-	osm/	-
Convoy	Milltown	Wilson Robert	-	-	-	-	Wilson R - Convoy Woollen	1894	-	dd/	1894 26 25
Convoy	Milltown	Wilson Robert	-	-	-	-	Wilson R - Convoy Woollen	1894	-	dd/	1894 26 25
Ballybofey	Milltown	-	corn	-	-	-	-	-	-	1"os/	16
Ballybofey	Milltown	-	flax	-	-	-	-	-	-	1"os/	16
Donegal	Milltown *	- E. side Oily R	corn & kiln	-	-	-	-	-	-	6"os/	98
Taughboyne	Milltown L.Swilly	-	no mill	-	-	-	-	-	-	1"os/	-
Donegal	Milton	-	corn	-	-	-	-	-	-	osm/	-
Clonmany	Mindoran	-	tuck	-	-	-	-	-	10x2x -	osm/	-
(bo Ennishowen)	Moleng	Anderson James	The Mill Pond	-	-	-	Anderson J - Russell Wm	1890	-	dd/	1890 11 14
Raymoghy	Monclick	Clyde John	flax	(3B) 27x18x6 :	-	-	-	-	-	hob/	5.0839
Raymoghy	Monclick	Gardner James	flax	- (no dims.) :	-	-	-	-	3 stocks :	hob/	5.0839
Raymoghy	Monclick	nr Vge Errity	flax	-	-	-	-	-	-	6"os/	54
Donaghmore	Monellan	-	corn & kiln :	-	-	-	-	1841	-	6"os/	78
Donaghmore	Monellan	Guy James	corn & pond	-	44a.	33	-	-	-	gr/	-
Raymoghy	Moneymore	- S. of Milltown	flax mills	-	-	-	-	-	-	6"os/	54
Raymoghy	Moneymore	Glenn James	flax	(2B) 2	-	-	-	-	3 stocks :	hob/	5.0839
Allsaints	Monfad	-	flax	-	-	-	-	-	-	6"os/	54
Allsaints	Monfad	Allison Richard	flax	(3C) 22x19x5.6 :	-	-	-	-	- 3 stocks m/cy B	hob/	5.0832
Allsaints	Monfad	Craig John	corn & kiln	(3C) 46.6x19.6x7 :	-	exmt.	-	-	-	hob/	5.0832
Allsaints	Monglass	- at Milltown Vge.	flax	-	-	-	-	-	-	6"os/	54

COUNTY DONEGAL

PARISH	TOWNLAND	MILLER	TYPE	HOUSE	Land	£Val	PROPRIETORS	Date	WHEEL etc.	Record	Ref.
Allsaints	Monglass	- at Monglass Vge.	corn kiln	-	-	-	-	-	-	6"os/	54
Inver	Mountcharles	-	cloth	-	-	-	-	-	-	6"os/	93
Inver	Mountcharles	-	corn	-	-	-	-	-	-	6"os/	93
Inver	Mountcharles	-	corn kiln	-	-	-	-	-	-	6"os/	93
Inver	Mountcharles	-	mill & race	-	-	-	-	-	-	6"os/	93
Inver	Mountcharles	Meehan Hugh	house, off., ld	-	5a.	4.15/-	-	-	-	gr/	-
Inver	Mountcharles	Mulbreary Hugh	old corn mill	ruins (no meas.) :	-	15-5	-	1838	-	hob/	5.0802
Inver	Mountcharles	Mulbreary Hugh	tuck (open)	-	-	-	-	1838	-	hob/	5.0802
Inver	Mountcharles	Mulrany Hugh	corn & kiln	-	12a.	28	-	-	-	gr/	-
Inver	Mountcharles	Mulrany Hugh	iron foundry	-	-	-	-	-	-	gr/	-
Inver	Mountcharles	Mulreany Hugh	corn	(1A) 36x23x15 :	-	-	-	1838	18x4x21	hob/	5.0802
Inver	Mountcharles	Mulreany Hugh	corn & kiln	(1B) 83.6x30x25 :	-	-	-	-	18x4x21 breast :	hob/	5.0806
Moville Upper	Moville Town	-	corn	-	-	-	-	-	-	osm/	-
Moville Upper	Moville Town	-	mill	-	-	-	-	-	-	1"os/	6
Tullyauglish	Moyle	-	corn	-	-	-	-	-	-	osm/	-
Tullyauglish	Moyle	-	flax	-	-	-	-	-	-	osm/	-
Tullyauglish	Moyle	- str. ex / L. Nakey	corn & flax :	-	-	-	-	-	-	6"os/	36
Tullyauglish	Moyle	Hay Robert	new mill	-	-	-	Hay Robt - Swiney John	1870	-	dd/	1870 12 86
Tullyfern	Moyle	Malseed James	corn, flax, kiln	(1B) 44x21x11.6 :	-	7	-	1838	- 6 stocks	hob/	5.0831
Tullyfern	Moyle	Sweeney Samuel	corn & flax	(1B) 44x21x11.6 :	-	-	-	-	- 1 pair stones :	hob/	5.0830
Tullyauglish	Moyle	Swiney John	mill	-	-	-	Swiney J - White Henry	1871	-	dd/	1871 30 74
Drumhome	Moyne	Erne Earl of	tuck	-	-	-	Erne Earl - Cole Visc	1871	-	dd/	1871 5 129
Donegal	Muckross	Hamilton John	corn & kiln	-	82a.	140	-	-	-	gr/	-
Donaghmore	Mullaboy	-	corn kiln	-	-	-	-	-	-	6"os/	74
Donaghmore	Mullaboy	-	mill race	-	-	-	-	-	-	6"os/	92
Donaghmore	Mullaboy	-	scutch mill	-	-	-	-	-	-	6"os/	92
Donaghmore	Mullaboy	Master of the Rolls	mills	-	-	-	Master of Rolls - Weir John	1892	-	dd/	1892 23 207
Donaghmore	Mullaboy	W/ rd at Mullanboy	corn & pond	-	-	-	-	-	-	6"os/	79
Donaghmore ?	Mullenigar Millacre	Stewart Alex	land	-	-	-	Stewart A - Lyle Robt	1873	-	dd/	1873 23 143
Burt	Mulleny	- on L. shore	flax (ruins)	-	-	-	-	-	-	6"os/	47
Raphoe	Mullinbuoy Farm	Baird William	flax & corn	-	-	-	Baird W - McIlwaine Jas	1873	-	dd/	1873 29 237
Inishkel	Mully	- N. of Owena R.	tuck	-	-	-	-	-	-	6"os/	75
Inishkeel	Mulmosog	-	corn kilns (3)	-	-	-	-	-	-	6"os/	83
Inishkeel	Mulnamin More	- at Greenany Vge.	corn kiln	-	-	-	-	-	-	6"os/	65
Raphoe	Muntertinny	-	malt house	-	-	-	-	-	-	6"os/	62
Kilmacrenan	Nahoory	-	corn kiln	-	-	-	-	-	-	6"os/	45
Donaghmore	Naveeny	Johnston James	boiling house	(1C) 89.6x23.6x17 :	-	-	-	1838	15x4.6x15.6 :	hob/	5.0835
Donaghmore	Navenny	-	boiling house	-	-	-	-	-	-	6"os/	78
Donaghmore	Navenny	-	flax & pond	-	-	-	-	-	-	6"os/	78
Donaghmore	Navenny	-	millpond	-	-	-	-	-	-	6"os/	78
Donaghmore	Navenny	-	old mill & pond	-	-	-	-	-	-	6"os/	78
Donaghmore	Navenny	- S./ Summerhill	drying house	-	-	-	-	-	-	6"os/	78
Donaghmore	Navenny	- S./ Summerhill	flax	-	-	-	-	-	-	6"os/	78
Donaghmore	Navenny	Johnston John	corn	-	-	82	-	-	-	gr/	-
Donaghmore	Navenny	Johnston John	flax, engine ho. :	-	1.5.0	-	-	-	-	gr/	-
Donaghmore	Navenny	Johnston Joseph	bleach green	-	-	-	Johnston J - Walker Eliz	1874	-	dd/	1874 34 242
Tullyauglish	New Mill	Cavendish Emma :	mill	-	-	-	Cavendish E - Lasalles Hen	1892	-	dd/	1892 7 272
Tullyauglish	Newmill	- 1/2 S. Ramelton	corn	-	-	-	-	-	-	6"os/	46
Tullyauglish	Newmills	-	corn	-	-	-	-	-	18x4x -	osm/	-
Tullyfern	Newmills	Letterkeny	corn, flax	perfectly restored	-	-	Heritage Centre	2001	exhibition	pWEH	C
Tullyauglish	Newmills	Stewart William	flax & store	(3B) 40.6x19x6.6 :	-	-	-	-	- 4 stocks	hob/	5.0819
Allsaints	Newtowncunninghai	- SW. of Town	distillery	-	-	-	-	-	-	6"os/	46

PARISH	TOWNLAND	MILLER	TYPE	HOUSE	Land	£Val	PROPRIETORS	Date	WHEEL etc.	Record	Ref.
Allsaints	Newtowncunninghai	Thompson James :	r mill & store :	(1B) 19.6x23x14 :	-	-	-	-	-	hob/	5.0832
Donegal	Oiley *	Mackinnon Wm	mill	-	-	-	Mackinnon W - Knox Wm	1870	-	dd/	1870 18 54
Killlea	Omlick	Hazlett William	flax	(1A) 32x20.6x7.6 :	-	-	-	-	- 4cwts. flax :	hob/	5.0836
Templecrone	Oughtmeen	-	corn kiln (2)	-	-	-	-	-	-	6"os/	49
Inishkeel	Owenteskiny	-	corn kiln	-	-	-	-	-	-	6"os/	82
Leck	Pluck	-	flax & pond	-	-	-	-	-	-	mmSv/	BFK - Z
Leck	Pluck	-	mill	-	-	-	-	-	-	1"os/	17
Leck	Pluck	- in Village	corn	-	-	-	-	-	-	pWEH	D
Leck	Pluck	- S. of Village	flax	-	-	-	-	-	-	pWEH	Z
Leck	Pluck	- W. Pluck Vge.	corn	-	-	-	-	-	-	6"os/	54
Leck	Pluck	- SW./ Vge.	flax	-	-	-	-	-	-	6"os/	54
Leck	Pluck	Hayes Edmund	corn	-	-	-	-	-	-	osm/	-
Leck	Pluck	Hayes Edmund	scutch	-	-	-	-	-	-	osm/	-
Leck	Pluck	Lecky Samuel Alex	corn	-	-	-	-	-	-	mmSv/	BFK - D
Leck	Pluck	Marshall Jas B	corn	-	63a.	-	-	-	-	gr/	-
Leck	Pluck	Marshall Jas B	flax	-	-	-	-	-	-	gr/	-
Conwal	Pollans	-	corn kiln	-	-	-	-	-	-	6"os/	52
Conwal	Pollans	-	old still house	-	-	-	-	-	-	6"os/	52
Clondahorky	Port	-	corn kilns (2)	-	-	-	-	-	-	6"os/	25
Clondahorky	Port	-	old salt works	-	-	-	-	-	-	6"os/	98
Clondahorky	Port	corn kiln		-	-	-	-	-	-	6"os/	81
Killea & T`bne	Port Lough	Gallagher	linen	-	-	-	-	-	-	osm/	-
Killea & T`bne	Port Lough	Pinkerton	linen	-	-	-	-	-	-	osm/	-
Inishmacsaint	Portnason	- near R. Erne :	corn	-	-	-	-	-	-	6"os/	107
Inishmacsaint	Portnason	- on S. point :	saltworks	-	-	-	-	-	-	6"os/	107
Drumhome	Rafoarty	-	cloth	-	-	-	-	-	-	6"os/	99
Drumhome	Rafoarty	Kerr Robert	corn & kiln	-	17a.	16	-	-	-	gr/	-
Clondavaddog	Rahagorry	-	corn	-	-	-	-	-	10x2	osm/	-
Leck	Rann	- nr Bogtown Vge.	ruins of corn mill	-	-	-	-	-	-	6"os/	61
Lettermacward	Ranny	-	corn kiln	-	-	-	-	-	-	6"os/	65
Drumhome	Rath	-	flax	-	-	-	-	1841	-	6"os/	105
Drumhome	Rath	-	mill	-	-	-	-	-	-	1"os/	32
Drumhome	Rath	- (no name)	scutch	-	-	-	-	-	machinery defective	osm/	-
Drumhome	Rath	Kilpatrick Jas & J	corn	-	37a.	36	-	-	-	gr/	-
Drumhome	Rath	Kilpatrick Jas & J	flax	-	-	-	-	-	-	gr/	-
Drumhome	Rath	Kilpatrick Jos Sen	house, offs, ld	-	24a.	15	-	-	-	gr/	-
Drumhome	Rath	M`Gee William	flax	-	12a.	10	-	-	-	gr/	-
Tirhugh bo.	Rathbalskinney *	Connolly Thomas	mill	-	-	-	Connolly - McBirney Dav	1871	-	dd/	1871 7 8
Aughnish	Rathmelton	-	brewery	-	-	-	-	1841	-	6"os/	46
Aughnish	Rathmelton	-	brewery	-	-	-	-	-	-	osm/	-
Aughnish	Rathmelton	-	brewery	finely preserved	-	-	-	2001	now a residence	pWEH	C
Aughnish	Rathmelton	-	creamery	well preserved	-	-	-	2001	bottling	pWEH	A
Aughnish	Rathmelton	- beside river	spinning	finely restored	-	-	-	2001	holiday flats	pWEH	C
Aughnish	Rathmelton	- on quayside	warehouse	finely preserved	-	-	-	2001	-	pWEH	B
Aughnish	Rathmelton	near bleach green	watch houses	well preserved	-	-	-	2001	-	pWEH	B
Aughnish	Rathmelton	Stewart William	corn	(1B) 38x20x14	-	-	-	-	- 1 pr. stones B :	hob/	5.0820
Aughnish	Rathmelton Town	- S./ Town centre	brewery	-	-	-	-	-	-	6"os/	46
Aughnish	Rathmillor ? :	Stewart Samuel	corn	(1A) 54x23x31	-	-	-	-	- 2 pairs stones	hob/	5.0819
Aughnish	Rathmillor ? :	Stewart Samuel	flax	(1A) 38x20x14.6	-	-	-	-	- 4 stocks	hob/	5.0819
Clondavaddog	Rathmullan	-	corn	-	-	-	-	-	14x2	osm/	-
Clondavaddog	Rathmullan	-	corn mill :	-	-	-	-	-	-	6"os/	37
Clondavaddog	Rathmullan	-	distillery	-	-	-	-	1764	-	osm/	-

PARISH	TOWNLAND	MILLER	TYPE	HOUSE	Land	£Val	PROPRIETORS	Date	WHEEL etc.	Record	Ref.
Clondavaddog	Rathmullan	-	mill	-	-	-	-	-	-	1"os/	16
Clondavaddog	Rathmullan	- at March Burn	saw	-	-	-	-	1764	-	osm/	-
Clondavaddog	Rathmullan	Batt Thomas	corn	-	-	-	Batt Thos - Cairns Baron	1872	-	dd/	1872 15 85
Clondavaddog	Rathmullan	Batt Thomas	corn mill, ferry	-	-	-	Batt Thos - Reid Robt	1872	-	dd/	1872 20 144
Clondavaddog	Rathmullan	Batt Thomas	mill	-	-	-	Batt Thos - Skipton Pitt	1874	-	dd/	1874 12 183
Clondavaddog	Rathmullan	Otway James L	mill & ferry	-	-	-	Otway J - Hoffman Fran	1870	-	dd/	1870 29 278
Clondavaddog	Rathmullan	Starratt	corn	-	-	-	-	-	-	gr/	-
Clondavaddog	Ray	- close to shore	saw mill	-	-	-	-	1841	-	6"os/	37
Aughnish	Ray (note) :	Nixon Alex Rev.	mill	-	-	-	-	1856	-	hob/	5.0826
Raymoghy	Raymoghy	Montgomery Wm	flax	(2B) 30.6x18.6x6 :	-	-	-	-	4 stocks :	hob/	5.0839
Donegal	Red Castle Dems.	- E./ Vge Quigley	tuck	-	-	-	-	-	-	6"os/	31
Inishkeel	Roechrow	-	corn kiln	-	-	-	-	-	-	6"os/	82
Raymoghy	Rooskey	-	Mill Row (house)	-	-	-	-	1841	-	6"os/	62
Raymoghy	Rooskey	- C1151 E. side of r	flax	-	-	-	-	1841	-	6"os/	62
Raymoghy	Rooskey	Colquohoon John	flax	(3B) 27.6x19.6x5.6 :	-	-	-	-	3 stocks :	hob/	5.0839
Allsaints	Rooskey	Gallagher John	corn & kiln	(1B) 60.6x22x8 :	-	-	-	-	12.6dia. 1 pr. st. :	hob/	5.0832
Allsaints	Roosky	- S. Milltown Vge.	corn & mill pond	-	-	-	-	1841	-	6"os/	55
Allsaints	Roosky	below Roosky Br.	corn	-	-	-	-	-	-	6"os/	55
Allsaints	Roosky	S. Roosky Mid. Vge.	mill & mill pond	-	-	-	-	1841	-	6"os/	55
Clondahorky	Roshin	-	corn kiln	-	-	-	-	-	-	6"os/	25
Templecrone	Roshin Acres	-	corn kiln	-	-	-	-	-	-	6"os/	48
Tullyfern	Rossgarrow	-	mill	-	-	-	-	-	-	1"os/	10
Tullyauglish	Rubleshinny	-	corn	-	-	-	-	-	-	osm/	-
Raymoghy	Rylands Upper	-	corn kiln	-	-	-	-	-	-	6"os/	54
Taughboyne	Saintjohnstrown	Fleming Rpbert	mill	-	-	-	Fleming Robert - Allen Jas	1894	-	dd/	1894 x x
Conwal	Sallaghagrane	-	corn & kiln	-	-	-	-	-	-	6"os/	53
Inver	Sallows	-	corn kilns (2)	-	-	-	-	-	-	6"os/	84
Raymoghy	Sallybrook	Marshall James	flax store	(2B) 14x16x5.6	-	0-4-8	-	-	-	hob/	5.0839
Donegal	Salt Pans	Cavendish Emma :	mill	-	-	-	Cavendish E - Lasalles Hen	1892	-	dd/	1892 7 272
Killygarvan	Saltpans	-	old salt pans	-	-	-	-	-	-	6"os/	28
Clondahorky	Sandyhill	-	flax	-	-	-	-	-	-	1"os/	24
Clondahorky	Sandyhill	-	mill	-	-	-	-	-	-	1"os/	24
Tirhugh bo	Scotch *	Connolly Thomas	tuck	-	-	-	Connolly T - McGlvin Jas	1873	-	dd/	1873 3 68
Conwal	Seacor	-	corn kiln	-	-	-	-	-	-	6"os/	52
Donaghmore	Sessiagh	-	flax & pond	-	-	-	-	-	-	6"os/	78
Donaghmore	Sessiagh	- at Sessiagh Lr.	flax & pond	-	-	-	-	-	-	6"os/	78
Donaghmore	Sessiagh O`Neill	Martin Dan	flax	-	44a.	4.8	-	-	-	gr/	-
Templecrone	Sheskin	-	corn kiln	-	-	-	-	-	-	6"os/	49
Urney	Sion Mill	Abercorn Marq.	flour now flax :	-	-	-	-	-	-	osm/	-
Fahan Lower	Sladran	-	corn kiln	-	-	-	-	-	-	6"os/	19
Raphoe	Slievebuck	- nr Sl`buck Vge.	flax	-	-	-	-	-	-	6"os/	62
Raphoe	Slievebuck	LHS rd. to L'kenny	flax	-	-	4.15	-	2007	water still flows nr	mmSv/	wh - Z
Raphoe	Slievebuck	Tinny James	flax	(1B) 40x17.6x14	-	4.15	-	-	3 stocks :	hob/	5.0837
Clondavaddog	Springfield	-	corn kilns (2)	-	-	-	-	-	-	6"os/	17
Clondavaddog	Springfield	-	flax	-	-	-	-	-	-	osm/	-
Clondavaddog	Springfield	- at Spingfield Vg.	flax	-	-	-	-	1841	-	6"os/	17
Clonleigh ?	Springhill	-	flax	-	-	-	-	1841	-	6"os/	70
Killea	St Johnston	Pinkerton Miss	bleach green	-	-	-	-	-	-	osm/	-
Killea	St Johnstown	- 7/8 m. S. Town	flax	-	-	-	-	-	-	6"os/	63
Killea	St Johnstown	Fleming Robert	mill	-	-	-	Fleming R - Allen James	1894	-	dd/	1894 16 85
(bo. Raphoe)	St Johnstown	Lighton Andrew	tuck	-	-	-	-	1891	-	dd/	1891 24 98
Killea	St Johnstown	McClean Mr	linen	-	-	-	-	-	-	osm/	-

PARISH	TOWNLAND	MILLER	TYPE	HOUSE	Land	£Val	PROPRIETORS	Date	WHEEL etc.	Record	Ref.
Convoy	Starritdtown	-	corn kiln, pond	-	-	-	-	-	-	6"os/	61
Convoy	Starritstown	McGowan Wm	corn	-	-	-	-	-	11.6x - x22	osm/	-
Glencolumbkille	Straboy	-	corn kilns (2)	-	-	-	-	-	-	6"os/	81
Clonmany	Straid	-	corn	-	-	-	-	-	12x2x -	osm/	-
Clonmany	Straid	-	corn kiln	-	-	-	-	-	-	6"os/	10
Kilcar	Straleel	-	corn kiln	-	-	-	-	-	-	6"os/	90
Tullaghobegly	Stramackilmartin	- N./ Corveen R.	corn & kiln	-	-	-	-	1841	-	6"os/	32
Tullaghobegly	Stramackilmartin	Harkin Charles	corn & kiln	(3B) 27x21x8 :	-	-	-	1855	13x2x7 42 bkts. :	hob/	5.0827
Tullaghobegly	Stranacorcragh	-	corn & kiln	-	-	-	-	-	-	1"os/	9
Tullaghobegly	Stranacorcragh	E/OwencronahullaR.	corn kiln	-	-	-	-	1841	-	6"os/	32
Stranorlar	Stranorlar	-	flax	-	-	-	-	-	-	6"os/	78
Stranorlar	Stranorlar	- S. Town centre	corn	-	-	-	-	-	-	6"os/	78
Clonmany	Strass	-	corn	-	-	-	-	-	12x2x -	osm/	-
Clonmany	Straths	- NE / Strath Vge.	flax	-	-	-	-	-	-	6"os/	11
Inishkeel	Stravally	-	corn kiln	-	-	-	-	-	-	6"os/	82
Donegal	Struhanreagh *	-	corn kiln	-	-	-	-	-	-	6"os/	24
Inishkeel	Summy	-	corn kilns (2)	-	-	-	-	-	-	6"os/	64
Kilmacrenan	Tawny Lower	-	corn kiln	-	-	-	-	-	-	6"os/	45
Stranorlar	Teangue	-	flax	-	-	-	-	-	-	6"os/	69
Taughboyne	Terioddy ?	Gillilan John	flax	(2B) 26x21x6	-	13/7	-	-	wooden, 3 stocks :	hob/	5.0841
Donegal	The Abbey *	-	mill	-	-	-	-	-	-	1"os/	31
Muff	Threetrees	- near shore :	mill	-	-	-	-	-	-	6"os/	39
Killea	Tibber	Marshall Mr	linen	-	-	-	-	-	-	osm/	-
Raymoghy	Tinklersford	-	flax, mill pond	-	-	-	-	-	-	6"os/	54
Raymoghy	Tinklerstown	Huston Moses	flax	(2B) 28x23.6x6 :	-	-	-	-	-	hob/	5.0839
Raymoghy	Tinklerstown	Huston Moses Jun	flax	(2B) 22x24.6x6 :	-	-	-	-	dia. 11ft. 6ins. :	hob/	5.0839
Raymoghy	Tirharon	-	flax & ponds (2)	-	-	-	-	1841	-	6"os/	54
Raymoghy	Tirharon	Barnhill John	flax	(3C) 22.6x23.6x5.6 :	-	-	-	-	3 stocks :	hob/	5.0839
Clondavaddog	Tirlaydan	-	corn	-	-	-	-	-	10x2	osm/	-
Clondavaddog	Tirlaydan	-	corn & pond	-	-	-	-	-	-	6"os/	28
Clondavaddog	Tirlaydan	-	corn kiln	-	-	-	-	-	-	6"os/	28
Donaghmore	Tirnagushoge		corn kiln	-	-	-	-	-	-	6"os/	79
Taughboyne	Tirroddy	-	flax & pond	-	-	-	-	-	-	6"os/	55
Inishkeel	Tl./S/ Kilcloonybeg	-	tuck	-	-	-	-	-	-	6"os/	64
Killea	Toberslane	nr Magheroy Glebe	old flax mill	-	-	-	-	-	-	6"os/	55
Desertegney	Tonduff	-	corn	-	-	-	-	-	14x2x -	osm/	-
Desertegney	Tonduff	- on Owenersk R.	corn & pond	-	-	-	-	-	-	6"os/	18
Kilmacrenan	Toome	- at ToomeVge.	corn kiln	-	-	-	-	-	-	6"os/	8
Kilmacrenan	Toome	- at Toome Vge.	corn kiln		-	-	-	-	-	6"os/	8
Tullaghobegly	Tor	-	corn kiln	-	-	-	-	-	-	6"os/	50
Burt	Toulett	- Bridgetown Mill	flax	-	-	-	-	2004	-	mmSv/	BFK - Z
par	Townland ?	-	corn kiln	-	-	-	-	-	-	6"os/	97
(W./ Kilclooney)	Townland ?	-	corn kilns (2)	-	-	-	-	-	-	6"os/	73
Taughboyne	Townland ?	-	flax	-	-	-	-	-	4 stocks, m/cy B :	hob/	5.0841
Taughboyne	Townland ?	-	flax	-	-	-	-	-	4 stocks, m/cy B :	hob/	5.0841
Taughboyne	Townland ?	-	flax	-	-	-	-	-	4 stocks, m/cy B :	hob/	5.0841
Taughboyne :	Townland ?	-	flax	-	-	-	-	-	4 stocks, m/cy B :	hob/	5.0841
Kilbarron :	Townland ?	- (no name)	flax	-	-	-	-	-	-	osm/	-
Inniskeel	Townland ?	- (no name)	tuck	-	-	-	-	-	-	osm/	-
par	Townland ?	- (= S/ Stravally)	corn kiln	-	-	-	-	-	-	6"os/	82
Donegal	Townland ?	- at Leannan Br.	corn	-	-	-	-	-	-	6"os/	52
Donegal	Townland ?	- at Leannan Br.	flax	-	-	-	-	-	-	6"os/	52

PARISH	TOWNLAND	MILLER	TYPE	HOUSE	Land	£Val	PROPRIETORS	Date	WHEEL etc.	Record	Ref.
Fahan Lower	Townland ?	- E. Drumriacam	corn & kiln	-	-	-	-	-	-	6"os/	29
Killybegs Upr.	Townland ?	- nr Fintragh Tn	corn	-	-	-	-	-	-	6"os/	97
Donegal	Townland ?	- W./ Gartan Lo.	corn kiln	-	-	-	-	-	-	6"os/	52
(bo Ennishowen)	Townland ?	Hart George	Craig Mill	-	-	-	Hart George - William	1891	-	dd/	1891 42 189
(bo.Tyrhugh)	Townland ?	Lighton Andrew	tuck	-	-	-	Lighton Andr - Hayes Henry	1891	-	dd/	1891 24 89
(bo. Raphoe)	Townland ?	Lighton Andrew	Wilson`s Mill :	-	-	-	-	1891	-	dd/	1891 24 98
Donaghmore	Townland ?	Mansfield Francis	corn & flour	-	0.2.2(	4.15	-	-	-	gr/	-
Clondavaddog	Townland ?	Nixon Alex Rev.	mill	-	-	-	-	-	-	hob/	5.0825
Burt	Townland ?	Porter James	corn	(1C) 36.6x22.6x50 :	-	-	-	-	11.6x2ft. circ. axle :	hob/	5.0816
Donaghmore	Townland ?	Scott James	tuck	-	20a.	27	-	-	-	gr/	-
Burt	Townland ?	Witherow James	corn & flax	corn mill down :	-	-	-	-	12x2.8x- axle circ.:	hob/	5.0816
par	Townland ?		corn kiln	-	-	-	-	-	-	6"os/	90
Killybegs Upr.	Townland ?	Hamilton Mrs	corn	(1B) 20x31x10 :	-	-	-	1838	1 pr. st class B m/cy	hob/	5.0810
Conwal	Treankeel	-	corn kiln	-	-	-	-	-	-	6"os/	60
Conwal	Treankeel	-	old kiln	-	-	-	-	-	-	6"os/	60
Conwal	Treankeel	- at Village.	corn	-	-	-	-	-	-	6"os/	60
Taughboyne	Treantagh	-	flax	-	-	-	-	-	-	1"os/	10
Leck	Trimragh	-	flax & pond	-	-	-	-	-	-	6"os/	53
Donegal	Troopers Hill *	- on R. Finn	mill	-	-	-	-	-	-	1"os/	-
Dromhome	Truman	-	corn kiln	-	-	-	-	-	-	6"os/	99
Killea	Tubberslane ??	Osborne Walter :	(flax	(2B) 26x23x5.3 :	-	8-2-7		-	- 3 stocks :	hob/	5.0836
Tirhugh bo	Tuckmill & Island	Connolly Thomas	tuck	-	-	-	Connolly T - Porter Thos	1871	-	dd/	1871 10 221
Tirhugh bo	Tuckmill & Island	Connolly Thomas	tuck	-	-	-	Connolly - Goodwin Lizie	1873	-	dd/	1873 82 123
Tullaghobegly	Tullaghobegly	- Tullaghobegly R.	mill	-	-	-	-	-	-	1"os/	10
Tullaghobegly	Tullaghobegly Irish	- at N. tip Tld.	corn	-	-	-	-	1841	-	6"os/	25
Tullaghobegly	Tullaghobegly Irish	E/Strahanreagh Vg.	corn kiln	-	-	-	-	1841	-	6"os/	24
Tullaghobegly	Tullaghobegly Irish	Nixon Alex Revd.	corn & kiln	(1B) 30x21.6x11.6 :	-	1.5	-	1855	12x2.4x7.6 :	hob/	5.0827
Donagh	Tullanree	- nr Bridgetown :	mill	-	-	-	-	-	-	6"os/	11
Donegal	Tullarville *	Richardson A. M.	mills	-	-	-	Richardson A - Alex	1893	-	dd/	1893 39 294
Clondavaddog	Tully	-	Old Mill Bridge	- (no mill)	-	-	-	-	-	6"os/	17
Donegal	Tully (4)	Hay Robert	mills	-	-	-	Hay Robt - Swiney John	1870	-	dd/	1870 12 86
Donegal	Tully (4)	Swiney John	mills	-	-	-	Swiney Jn - Swiney Jn	1870	-	dd/	1870 28 222
Fahan Lower	Tullyarvan	-	mill & kiln	-	-	-	-	-	-	6"os/	29
Fahan Lower	Tullyarvan	- C1275 near Tandra	old bl. green	-	-	-	-	-	-	6"os/	29
Tullyfern	Tullybeg	-	kiln	-	-	-	-	1841	-	6"os/	36
Tullyfern	Tullybeg	Malseed James	kiln	(1A) 16x21x8 :	-	-	-	1838	-	hob/	5.0831
Raymoghy	Tullybogly	-	flax	-	-	-	-	2004	-	mmSv/	BFK - Z
Raphoe	Tullydonnell Lower	-		-	-	-	-	-	-	6"os/	69
Raphoe	Tullydonnell Lower	Thompson Galbr.	flax	(1B) 28.6x22x7 :	-	5.11	-	-	- 4 stocks :	hob/	5.0837
Raphoe	Tullydonnell Lower	Verkoyle John	mill & kiln	(1A) 58.6x20.6x14.6 :	-	-	-	-	- 2 pair stones :	hob/	5.0837
Raphoe	Tullydonnell Upper	-		-	-	-	-	-	-	6"os/	69
Drumhome	Tullyear (-l ?)	-	corn	-	-	-	-	-	-	1"os/	32
Drumhome	Tullygallan	-	flax	-	-	-	-	-	-	1"os/	32
Drumhome	Tullygallan	- (no name)	scutch	-	-	-	-	-	machinery defective	osm/	-
Tullyfern	Tullyhall	-	corn	-	-	-	-	-	10x2x -	osm/	-
Tullyfern	Tullyhall	-	flax	-	-	-	?	-	-	osm/	-
Tullyfern	Tullyhall	-	mill	-	-	-	-	-	-	1"os/	10
Tullyfern	Tullyhall	Moor Henry :	r flax & corn	(1B) 44x22x8.6 :	-	-	-	1838	- 8 stocks & :	hob/	5.0831
Tullyfern	Tullyhall	Watt James	old corn mill	(1B) 30x15x13.6	-	-	-	-	-	hob/	5.0830
Tullyfern	Tullyhall	Watt James :	c flax	(1B) 28.6x22x13.6 :	-	-	-	-	- 6 pr. iron rollers :	hob/	5.0830
Tullyfern	Tullyhall	Watt James Esq.	flax & store	(1B) 28.6x22x12.6 :	-	-	-	-	-	hob/	5.0830
Taughboyne	Tullyleague	Johnston Charles	flax	(2A) 18.6x31x16	-	1-1-4	-	1856	breast, 11x2.8x6 :	hob/	5.0841

PARISH	TOWNLAND	MILLER	TYPE	HOUSE	Land	£Val	PROPRIETORS	Date	WHEEL etc.	Record	Ref.
Donegal	Tullyloskan	-	flax & corn	-	-	-	-	-	-	6"os/	100
Donegal	Tullyloskan	Graham John	corn & kiln	-	2a.	7	-	-	-	gr/	-
Donegal	Tullylusgain	-	flax	-	-	-	-	-	-	osm/	-
Kilbarron	Tullymore	- SE. Drumman Br.	churn	-	-	-	-	-	-	6"os/	45
Inishkeel	Tullynagallagan	-	corn kiln	-	-	-	-	-	-	6"os/	83
Moville Upper	Tullynavin	- S/ Mill Mount Vge.	corn & pond	-	-	-	-	1841	-	6"os/	21
Moville Upper	Tullynavin	Douglas John	flax	(1B) 24x15x12 :	-	-	-	1857	12x2.6x- overshot :	hob/	5.0815
Moville Lower	Tullynavinn	-	corn & pond	-	-	-	-	-	-	6"os/	21
Taughboyne	Tullyowen	- (no name)	flax	-	-	-	-	-	-	osm/	-
Taughboyne	Tullyowen	- str. to R Foyle	flax	-	-	-	-	-	-	1"os/	17
Taughboyne	Tullyrap	-	mill	still used as store	-	-	-	2007	-	mmSv/	wh - A
Taughboyne	Tullyrap	- S./ river nr Vge.	corn	-	-	-	-	-	-	6"os/	70
Taughboyne	Tullyrap	- S./ river nr Vge.	flax & pond	-	-	-	-	-	-	6"os/	70
Inver	Tullyvinney	Laird Robert	corn	(1A) 66x22x11 :	-	-	-	1838	12x2x8 1 pair st.	hob/	5.0805A
Inver	Tullyvinney	Laird Robert	flax	(3B) 28x18x5 :	-	-	-	1838	14.6x4x10.6	hob/	5.0805A
Raphoe	Tullyvinny	- at Milltown	flax & ponds (2)	-	-	-	-	-	-	6"os/	69
Raphoe	Tullyvinny	Laird Robert	corn & flax	-	-	-	-	-	14 4.2x - 9 stocks	hob/	5.0837
Drumhome	Tullywee	-	flax	-	-	-	-	-	-	6"os/	100
Drumhome	Tullywee	- (no name)	scutch	-	-	-	-	-	machinery defective	osm/	-
Drumhome	Tullywee	M`Clay James	flax	-	3a.	-	-	-	-	gr/	-
Taughboyne	Tullywee	McClay Andrew :	flax	(2C) 30x16x7	-	5-10	-	1856	11x2 revs./ min. :	hob/	5.0841
Muff	Ture	-	mill	-	-	-	-	-	-	1"os/	16
Muff	Ture	McGinagle Widow	corn & kiln	(1B) 14.6x22x9.9 :	-	-	-	-	- 1 pair stones	hob/	5.0818
Clondahorky	Umerafad	-	corn kiln	-	-	-	-	-	-	6"os/	26
Clondavaddog	Umrycam	-	corn kiln	-	-	-	-	-	-	6"os/	17
Kilcar	Umuskan		corn kiln	-	-	-	-	-	-	6"os/	90
Drumhome	Urbalshinny	-	flour	-	-	-	-	-	-	6"os/	99
Drumhome	Urbalshinny	Armstrong William	corn	-	3.2.0	38	-	-	-	gr/	-
Drumhome	Urbalshinny	Armstrong William	flour	-	4a.	98	-	-	-	gr/	-
Clonmany	Urrismenagh	-	old salt pans	-	-	-	-	-	-	6"os/	9
Donegal	Watdoon *	-	flax	-	-	-	-	-	-	1"os/	16
Kilteevoge	Welchtown	-	corn kiln	-	-	-	-	-	-	6"os/	68
Kilteevoge	Welchtown	-	old mine	-	-	-	-	-	-	6"os/	68
Donegal	Whitehill (5)	-	mill	-	-	-	-	-	-	1"os/	-
bo. Raphoe	Wilson`s Mill	Montgomery Robt	Wilson`s Mill	-	-	-	M`gomery - Boyton Mary	1874	-	dd/	1874 42 38
Raphoe	Winnyhaw	-	malt kiln	-	-	-	-	-	-	6"os/	62
Killymard	Winterhill	1/4m. NxE Chapel	corn	-	-	-	-	-	-	6"os/	93

PARISH	TOWNLAND	MILLER	TYPE	HOUSE	Land	£Val+	PROPRIETORS	Date	WHEEL etc.	Record	Ref.
Annahilt	Aghnaleck	-	windmill	-	-	-	-	-	-	6"os/	15
Down	Aghyohill	Hamieon Hans :	mill	-	-	-	Hamieon H - Hamieon Jas :	1733	-	dd/	71 472 52223
Down	Aghyohill	Shannon Samuel :	mill	-	-	-	Shannon S - Shannon Wm :	1803	Rel. 30 Jne.	dd/	556 267 369692
Down	Aghyohill	Shannon Samuel :	mill	-	-	-	Shannon Sam - William :	1800	Conv. 1 Jan. :	dd/	524 462 343795
Down	Annaclone *	Potts	flax	-	-	-	-	2009	-	mmSv/	nk - Z
Inch	Annacloy	- nr Downpatrick	mill	-	-	-	-	-	-	1"os/	49
Loughlinisland	Annadorn	-	flour	-	-	-	-	-	-	6"os/	37
Loughlinisland	Annadorn	Dickson	mill	-	-	-	Dickson - Miller	-	-	dd/	-
Loughlinisland	Annadorn	Dickson Coslett	mill	-	-	-	Coslette - Smith	-	-	dd/	525 10 343982
Loughlinisland	Annadorn	Dickson Coslett :	mill	-	-	-	Dickson C - Miller George :	1823	-	dd/	780 222 528157
Loughlinisland	Annadorn	Forde Col.	flour	-	-	-	-	-	16x6x18 3 pr st. :	vmb/	5
Loughlinisland	Annadorn	Houghton Joseph :	mill	-	-	-	Houghton J - Coslett Chas :	1823	-	dd/	779 148 527483
Loughlinisland	Annadorn	Latouche	mill	-	-	-	Latouche - Peree	-	-	dd/	441 158 284060
Loughlinisland	Annadorn	Latouche	mill	-	-	-	Latouche - Caslette	-	-	dd/	530 323 348276
Loughlinisland	Annadorn	M`Cammon Andrew	corn & kiln	-	163a.	-	-	-	-	gr/	-
Loughlinisland	Annadorn	M`Cammon Andrew	mill pond	-	1.2.0	-	-	-	-	gr/	-
Loughlinisland	Annadorn	McKibben	mill	-	-	-	McKibben - Coslett	-	-	dd/	799 183 539518
Loughlinisland	Annadorn	Thompson William :	mill	-	-	-	Thompson W - Haven :	1824	Mort. 1 Jan.	dd/	787 562 532697
Loughlinisland	Annadorn	Wardlow	mill	-	-	-	Wardlaw - Coslett	-	-	dd/	456 50 360900
Loughlinisland	Annadorn	Wardlow	mill	-	-	-	Wardlaw - Wardlaw	-	-	dd/	547 422 36125?
Kilkeel	Annalong	- on coast	mill	-	-	-	-	-	-	1"os/	61
Kilkeel	Annalong	Bayley Edward :	land	-	-	-	Bayley E - Murray John :	1715	L&R. 4 Feb.	dd/	16 209 7308
Kilkeel	Annalong	Bayley Edward :	(land (? mill)	-	-	-	Bayley Ed - Murray John :	1715	-	dd/	17 2 8029
Kilkeel	Annalong	Hamilton	land (no mill)	-	-	-	Hamilton - Page	-	-	dd/	19 16 9308
Kilkeel	Annalong	Hamilton Archibald :	mill	-	-	-	Hamilton A - Wallace Wm	1716	L&R 19 Sep.	dd/	17 123 8369
Kilkeel	Annalong	near Kilkeel	corn	finely restored	-	-	Newry County Council	2001	exhibition	pWEH	C
Slanes	Annsborough	-	bleach	-	-	-	-	-	-	1"os/	60
Slanes	Annsborough	-	linen	-	-	-	-	-	-	1"os/	60
Kilcoo	Ardaghy	Bann Reservoir Co.	mill-stream	-	-	-	-	-	-	gr/	-
Newry	Ardarragh :	Newham Robert Jun.	grist mill ye	-	-	-	Newham R - Glenny Isaac :	1734	-	dd/	77 427 54247
Annaclone	Ardbrin	Dickson David	old scutch mill	-	-	-	-	1837	-	dd/	?
Annaclone	Ardbrin	Dickson David	old scutch mill	-	-	-	-	1837	-	inv/	green
Annaclone	Ardbrin	Kirk William	flax	-	42a.	6	-	-	-	gr/	-
Ardglass	Ardglass	Kildare Robt Rt Hon. :	mill & miller's holding		-	-	Kildare R - Montgomery Wm	1728	-	dd/	56 308 38082
Ardkeen	Ardkeen	-	corn	-	-	-	-	-	-	6"os/	25
Ardkeen	Ardkeen	- near Deer Park	corn	-	-	-	-	-	-	6"os/	25
Ardkeen	Ardkeen	Keating Neal	corn & kiln	-	-	-	-	-	-	gr/	-
Ardkeen	Ardkeen	Kirk Ethel E	mill	-	-	-	Kirk Ethel - Wallace Bern	1904	-	dd/	1904 80 286
Ardkeen	Ardkeen	Kirk Ethel E	mill	-	-	-	Kirk Ethel - Sheridan An	1904	-	dd/	1904 81 287
Ardkeen	Ardkeen	Sheridan Augustine	mill	-	-	-	Sheridan A - Kirk Ethel	1904	-	dd/	1904 72 248
Ardkeen	Ardkeen	Tennent Robert	mill	-	-	-	Tennent R - Ross Thos C	1903	-	dd/	1903 69 259
Ardkeen	Ardkeen	Wallace Bernard	mill	-	-	-	Wallace B - Garratt Joseph	1904	-	dd/	1904 50 287
Annaclone	Ardkin * :	Savage Lucy :	corn & land :	-	-	-	Savage L - Lucas Francis, D	1724	-	dd/	41 388 26457
Tullynakill	Ardmillan	-	old windmill	-	-	-	-	-	-	1"os/	37
Tullynakill	Ardmillan	Murphy John :	mill	-	-	-	Murphy J - Dickson Stephen	1823	-	dd/	799 575 539910
Ballyculter	Audleys	- at Grenhouse	corn	-	-	-		-	-	6"os/	31
Donaghmore	Aughnacavan	-	flax	-	-	-		-	-	6"os/	40
Annaclone	Aughnacloy	-	flax	-	-	-		-	-	6"os/	34
Annaclone	Aughnacloy also :	Annesley Francis :	grist & molture	-	-	-	Annesley F - Ward Bern. :	1737	-	dd/	87 218 61348
Kilkeel	Aughnahoory	- on Kilkeel R	mill	-	-	-	-	-	-	1"os/	71
Kilkeel	Aughnahoory	Wamsley James	bleach (2)	-	-	-	-	-	14x2x7.6 & :	vmb/	5
Kilkeel	Aughnahoory	Wamsley James	corn & flax	-	110a.	30	-	-	-	gr/	-

PARISH	TOWNLAND	MILLER	TYPE	HOUSE	Land	£Val+(	PROPRIETORS	Date	WHEEL etc.	Record	Ref.
Kilkeel	Aughnahoory	Wamsley James	flax		-	6	-	-	15x3x8 4 berths	vmb/	5
Dromara	Aughnaskeagh	Pattison James	flax	-	30a.	27	-	-	-	gr/	-
Dromara	Aughnaskeagh	Pattison James	flax	-	6a.	-	-	-	-	gr/	-
Dromara	Aughnaskeagh	Pattison James	old corn mill	-	-	-	-	-	-	gr/	-
Drumgooland	Backaderry	M`Cartan James	flax	-	15a.	18	-	-	-	gr/	-
Seapatrick	Balleevy	Crawford George :	beetling	-	-	-	-	1770	-	dd/	?
Seapatrick	Balleevy	Crawford George :	beetling	-	-	-	-	1770	-	inv/	green
Seapatrick	Balleevy	Crawford Gilbert	bleach green	-	-	-	-	1763	-	dd/	?
Seapatrick	Balleevy	Crawford Gilbert	bleachgreen	-	-	-	-	1763	-	inv/	green
Seapatrick	Balleevy	Henry Thos E	flax	-	79a.	-	-	-	-	gr/	-
Seapatrick	Balleevy	Lindsay Jno	mill	-	-	-	Lindsay Jno - Mulligan	1841	-	dd/	1841 12 270
Seapatrick	Balleevy	McCance John :	mill	-	-	-	McCance Jn - Lindsay Jn :	1822	Mort. 14 Feb.	dd/	769 554 521889
Dromore	Balleny	Archbishop of Dublin	corn	-	-	-	A'b Dublin - Beresford Ld	-	-	dd/	175 514 11847
Dromore	Balleny	Dublin Archb. of	corn	-	-	-	Dublin A'b. - Beresford Ld.	-	-	dd/	175 415 114147
Dromore	Balleny	Knox	corn	-	-	-	Knox - Gamble	-	-	dd/	325 267 220254
Dromore	Balleny	Knox	corn	-	-	-	Knox - Wells Lord Baron	-	-	dd/	334 636 226581
Dromore	Balleny	Knox Thomas :	corn	-	-	-	Knox T- Forde Chathew :	1760	Conv. 10 Mar	dd/	246 519 159775
Dromore	Balleny	Wilson	corn	-	-	-	Wilson - Wacker	-	?	dd/	185 541 124206
Dromore	Balleny	Wilson John :	corn	-	-	-	Wilson John - Walker :	1748	-	dd/	184 541 124206
Newry	Ballincraig	Kidd Hugh	flour	-	-	13	-	-	18x4x4 3 pr st.	vmb/	5
Co. Down	Ballinteskin	- on Lough	corn	-	-	-	-	-	-	1"os/	71
Saul	Ballintogher	Murphy Jno	corn (2)	-	-	7	-	-	15x2x15.7 :	vmb/	5
Saul	Ballintogher	Murphy Mary	corn & kiln	-	34a	-	-	-	-	gr/	-
Klilinchy	Balloo	-	corn & flax	-	-	-	-	-	-	6"os/	17
Klilinchy	Balloo	-	corn kiln	-	-	-	-	-	-	6"os/	17
Klilinchy	Balloo	-	corn mills	-	-	-	-	-	-	6"os/	17
Klilinchy	Balloo	-	mill	-	-	-	-	-	-	6"os/	17
Killinchy :	Balloo	Adair James :	mill	-	-	-	Adair J - Hudson James :	1760	-	dd/	209 290 138526
Killinchy :	Balloo	Andrew	mills	-	-	-	Andrew - Andrew	-	-	dd/	301 119 199319
Klilinchy	Balloo	Cooper William :	mill	-	-	-	Cooper W - Denton Alex :	1735	-	dd/	76 501 55604
Klilinchy	Balloo	Coulter John Jun.	corn & flax	-	27a.	-	-	-	-	gr/	-
Killinchy :	Balloo	Hudson James :	mill	-	-	-	Hudson J - Holmes Jno :	1760	-	dd/	209 291 138527
Killinchy	Balloo	Limerick Lord	mill	-	-	-	Limerick Lord - Potter	-	-	dd/	787 459 54341
Klilinchy	Balloo	Limerick Lord Visc.	mill	-	-	-	Limerick Ld - Potter John :	1733	-	dd/	77 459 54341
Killinchy :	Balloo	Moore	mills	-	-	-	Moore - McMath	-	-	dd/	276 153 176605
Killinchy :	Balloo	Murdagh	mills	-	-	-	Murdagh - Morrison	-	-	dd/	288 649 193318
Killinchy :	Balloo	Potter	mills	-	-	-	Potter - McDowell	-	-	dd/	271 228 176150
Killinchy :	Balloo	Potter John	mills	-	-	-	Potter John - Potter John	1747	-	dd/	128 432 87468
Killinchy	Balloo	Potter John (Elder) :	mill	-	-	-	Potter J - Potter Jno Yngr :	1747	Lse. 1 Oct.	dd/	133 387 91665
Killinchy	Balloo	Purdy	mill	-	-	-	Purdy - Purdy	-	-	dd/	128 432 27468
Killinchy	Balloo	Stewart	mill	-	-	-	Stewart - Potter	-	- [not 135]	dd/	135 292 92901/7
Killinchy :	Balloo	Stewart	mills	-	-	-	Stewart - Potter	-	-	dd/	350 394 237111
Killinchy :	Balloo	Stewart Thomas	mills	-	-	-	Stewart Thos - Moore Jn	1739	-	dd/	125 289 85084
Killinchy :	Balloo	Taylor Jno :	mills	-	-	-	Taylor Jno - Trevor Jno :	1746	-	dd/	124 430 85317
Garvaghy	Ballooly	-	corn & flax	-	-	-		-	-	6"os/	35
Garvaghy	Ballooly More	M`Mullen Daniel	flax, corn	-	69a.	-	-	-	-	gr/	-
Garvaghy	Ballooly More	M`Mullen Daniel	mill dam	-	2.0.20	-	-	-	-	gr/	-
Garvaghy	Ballooly More	Russell Samuel	corn & flax	-	15a.	-	-	-	-	gr/	-
Garvaghy	Ballooly More	Russell Samuel	pond	-	0.3.30	-	-	-	-	gr/	-
Drumbeg	Ballyaghlis	-	old flax mill	-	-	-	-	-	-	6"os/	9
Killyleagh	Ballyalgan	-	mill	-	-	-	-	-	-	6"os/	23
Comber	Ballyallolyy	- nr Comber	mills	-	-	-	-	-	-	1"os/	37

PARISH	TOWNLAND	MILLER	TYPE	HOUSE	Land	£Val+	PROPRIETORS	Date	WHEEL etc.	Record	Ref.
Comber	Ballyaltikilligan	M`Kibben Agnes	flax	-	13a.	18	-	-	-	gr/	-
Newtownards	Ballyalton	-	flax (x 2)	-	-	-	-	-	-	6"os/	5
Kilkeel	Ballyardel	-	flax	-	-	-	-	-	-	1"os/	71
Kilkeel	Ballyardel	-	mill	-	-	-	-	-	-	1"os/	71
Clonduff	Ballyaughian	- on R Bann	flax	-	-	-	-	-	-	1"os/	60
Clonduff	Ballyaughian	Lindsay David	old scutch mill	-	-	-	-	1838	-	dd/	?
Clonduff	Ballyaughian	Lindsay David	old scutch mill	-	-	-	-	1838	-	inv/	green
Clonduff	Ballyaughian	Lindsay James	bleachgreen	-	-	-	-	1825	-	dd/	?
Clonduff	Ballyaughian	O`Neill :	bleachgreen	-	-	-	-	1825	-	dd/	?
Clonduff	Ballyaughian	O`Neill :	bleachgreen	-	-	-	Lindsay James	1825	-	inv/	green
Co. Down	Ballybawn	Clarke Mary	mill	-	-	-	Clarke Mary - Clarke Ed	1840	-	dd/	1840 25 176
Co. Down	Ballybawn	Skelton Frans	mill	-	-	-	Skelton Frans - Hill Ld A	1842	-	dd/	1842 20 219
Co. Down	Ballybawne	Barnsley Richard	corn mill, lands	-	-	-	Barnsley R - Reilly Wm E	1842	-	dd/	1842 221 20
Co. Down	Ballybawne	Fairlie William	corn	-	-	-	Fairlie Wm - Reilly John	1739	-	dd/	99 416 69834
Co. Down	Ballybawne	Murphy John :	mill	-	-	-	Murphy J - Dickson Stephen	1823	-	dd/	799 575 539910
Co. Down	Ballybawne	Reilly	mill	-	-	-	Reilly & ors - Southwell	-	-	dd/	289 39 3689
Co. Down	Ballybawne	Reilly	mill	-	-	-	Reilly - Waddell	1816	-	dd/	708 439 485174
Co. Down	Ballybawne	Reilly Willaim	mill, mill lands	-	-	-	Reilly Wm - Hill Ld Geo	1842	-	dd/	1842 20 274
Co. Down	Ballybawne	White John Nevin :	mill	-	-	-	White J - Hutchinson Hugh :	1816	Mort. 1816	dd/	289 39 3689
Greyabbey	Ballybryan	-	corn & kiln	-	-	-	-	-	-	6"os/	12
Greyabbey	Ballybryan	-	old windmill	-	-	-	-	-	-	1"os/	37
Co. Down	Ballycashan	Fitsimons James	mill	-	-	-	Fitsimons J - Gordon Dav	1821	-	dd/	767 116 520521
Killinchy	Ballycloghan	-	mill	-	-	-	-	-	-	1"os/	37
Killinchy	Ballycloghan	Shaw William	flax, mill pond	-	6a.	9	-	-	-	gr/	-
Magheradrool	Ballyclone Big	- on Ballinahinch R	corn, millpond	-	-	-	-	-	-	6"os/	29
Donaghadee	Ballycopeland	- at Millisle Vge.	corn	-	-	-	-	-	-	6"os/	7
Donaghadee	Ballycopeland	- nr large mill pond	corn	-	-	-	-	-	-	6"os/	6
Donaghadee	Ballycopeland	- on R. Burne	corn	-	-	-	-	-	-	6"os/	7
Donaghadee	Ballycopeland	- on R. Burne	mill	-	-	-	-	-	-	6"os/	7
Donaghadee	Ballycopeland	Carmichael D & W	mill pond	-	12a.	-	-	-	-	gr/	-
Donaghadee	Ballycopeland	Gunning James	flax	-	3.3.0	6	-	-	-	gr/	-
Donaghadee	Ballycopeland	M`Gilteen James	corn	-	6.1.0	8	-	-	-	gr/	-
Donaghadee	Ballycopeland	M`Gilteen James	flax	-	-	-	-	-	-	gr/	-
Clonduff	Ballycoshone	- on R. Bann	flax	-	-	-	-	-	-	1"os/	60
Drumbo	Ballycowan	-	corn & flax	large house :	-	-	-	-	-	mmSv/	nk - Z
Drumbo	Ballycowan	- nr Purdysburn	mill	-	-	-	-	-	-	6"os/	8
Drumbo	Ballycowan	Hunter Andrew	corn & kiln	-	7a.	21	-	-	-	gr/	-
Comber	Ballycreely	Parmenter Samuel	mill	-	-	-	Parmenter S - Bruce Wm	1745	-	dd/	120 85 81929
Down	Ballycreevy	Baillie	mill	-	-	-	Baillie - McClure	-	-	dd/	269 86 171622
Down	Ballycreevy	Baillie	mill	-	-	-	Bailie - Hunter	-	-	dd/	299 235 189143
Down	Ballycreevy	Baillie James & Ann :	mill	-	-	-	Baillie J - Gillespie William :	1772	-	dd/	290 506 193954
Down	Ballycreevy :	Baillie James	mill	-	-	-	Baillie Jmes - Gilmer	-	-	dd/	268 402 170914
Bangor	Ballycroghan	-	old windmill	-	-	-	-	-	-	6"os/	52
Ballyculter	Ballyculter	-	corn	-	-	-	-	-	-	1"os/	49
Ballyculter	Ballyculter	-	corn	-	-	-		-	-	6"os/	31
Ballyculter	Ballyculter	Caughey John A	corn & kiln	-	32a	-	-	-	-	gr/	-
Ballyculter	Ballyculter	Caughey John A	flax	-	-	-	-	-	-	gr/	-
Ballyculter	Ballyculter	Keagh Robert	corn	-	-	9	-	-	14x2x11 1 pr st.	vmb/	5
Ballyculter	Ballyculter	Keagh Robert	flax	-	-	-	-	-	13x2x8 3 berths	vmb/	5
Bright	Ballydargan	Colville William :	windmill	-	-	-	Colville W - Hamilton Alex :	1728	-	dd/	58 125 38824
Bright	Ballydargan	Hamilton George :	mill	-	-	-	Hamilton G - Hamilton Alex :	1827	-	dd/	777 329 526464
Bright	Ballydargan	Hamilton George :	mill	-	-	-	Hamilton - Archdall Henry :	1823	Mort. 7 Feb.	dd/	778 397 527132

PARISH	TOWNLAND	MILLER	TYPE	HOUSE	Land	£Val+	PROPRIETORS	Date	WHEEL etc.	Record	Ref.
Bright	Ballydargan	Hamilton George :	windmill	-	-	-	Hamilton G - Hamilton Alex :	1737	L&R. 4 Jan.	dd/	92 104 64033
Bright	Ballydargan	Limerick James :	windmill	-	-	-	Limerick Lord - Colville Wm :	1722	-	dd/	55 369 37334
Bright	Ballydargan	Limerick Ld. James :	windmill	-	-	-	Limerick Ld J - Hereford Bish	1728	L&R 14 Oct.	dd/	62 128 42214
Bright	Ballydargan	Limerick Lord	windmill	-	-	-	Limerick Lord - Tipping	-	-	dd/	56 361 38301
Bright	Ballydargan Hill	-	old windmill	-	-	-	-	-	-	1"os/	49
Holywood	Ballydavey	Killips Hugh	flax	-	71a.	-	-	-	-	gr/	-
Drumbo	Ballydollaghan	-	mill, pond	-	-	-	-	-	-	6"os/	9
Drumbo	Ballydollaghan	-	mill, pond	stream piped :	-	-	-	2009	-	mmSv/	nk - Z
Drumbo	Ballydollaghan	Hamilton Ann Hon. :	mill	-	-	-	Hamilton A - Limerick Hon. :	1725	-	dd/	45 232 29061
Drumbo	Ballydollaghan	Limerick Lord	mill	-	-	-	Limerick Lord - Knox	-	-	dd/	44 105 27818
Drumbo	Ballydollaghan	Limerick Lord Jas : F	mill	-	-	-	Limerick Lord - Knox Thos :	1726	L&R. 16 Jul.	dd/	51 357 33983
Down	Ballydonety	near Ballydugan	-	small building & :	-	-	-	2001	-	pWEH	B
Down	Ballydourne :	Craige & Wife	mill	-	-	-	Craige - Waddell	-	-	dd/	294 549 195709
Down	Ballydourne :	Greer John :	mill	-	-	-	Greer J - Lowry James : S	1761	Conv. 9 Jne.	dd/	213 73 139565
Seapatrick	Ballydown	Adamson	mills	-	-	-	Adamson - Adamson	-	-	dd/	289 415 191932
Seapatrick	Ballydown	Delzel	mills	-	-	-	Delzel - Delzel	-	-	dd/	446 320 289806
Seapatrick	Ballydown	Greer John	bleach	-	-	-	-	1740	-	inv/	green
Seapatrick	Ballydown	Hudson	mill	-	-	-	Hudson - Crawford	-	-	dd/	776 508 526042
Seapatrick	Ballydown	Hudson John	corn	-	-	-	-	1812	-	inv/	green
Seapatrick	Ballydown	Lindsay Geo & John	bleech & bt	-	47a.	-	-	-	-	gr/	-
Seapatrick	Ballydown	Wallace Susanna :	mill	-	-	-	Wallace S - Birch John :	1824	Mort. 23 Jne.	dd/	793 230 535965
Down	Ballydugan	-	flour	-	-	-	-	-	-	pWAM	-
Down	Ballydugan	-	flour (x 2)	-	-	-		-	-	6"os/	37
Down	Ballydugan	-	flour (x 2)	-	-	-		-	-	6"os/	37
Down	Ballydugan	-	mill site	-	-	-	-	1210	-	piperolls	-
Down	Ballydugan	- at Old Town	flax	-	-	-	-	-	-	1"os/	49
Down	Ballydugan	- at Old Town	flax	-	-	-	-	-	-	1"os/	49
Down	Ballydugan	- Tenants (sundry) :	mill houses :	- 5 hos., 1 unoc.	-	-	-	1856	-	gr/	aai.ie
Down	Ballydugan	Annesley Lord :	land	-	-	-	Annesley Ld - Nevin Wm :	1763	Mort. 3 Nov.	dd/	221 474 148672
Down	Ballydugan	Atkinson John	mill	-	-	-	Atkinson J - Hungerford W	1898	-	dd/	1898 38 74
Down	Ballydugan	Atkinson John	mill	-	-	-	Atkinson J - Hungerford W	1898	-	dd/	1898 38 74
Down	Ballydugan	Bromley Chester	mill	-	-	-	Bromley C - Carson	-	-	dd/	325 392 221359
Down	Ballydugan	Carson	mill	-	-	-	Carson - Phelan	-	-	dd/	469 588 302914?
Down	Ballydugan	Echlin Charles : F	mill	-	-	-	Echlin C - Knox Thomas :	1735	Asgt. 28 June :	dd/	82 252 57725
Down	Ballydugan	Haemill	mill	-	-	-	Haemill - Gordon	-	-	dd/	450 167 290427
Down	Ballydugan	Haemill	mill	-	-	-	Haemill - Hutchison	-	-	dd/	453 257 289946
Down	Ballydugan	Haemill	mill	-	-	-	Haemill - McCormick	-	-	dd/	501 41 317521
Down	Ballydugan	Haemill Hans Mark :	mill	-	-	-	Haemill H - Huggins John :	1792	Mort. 13 Dec. :	dd/	461 353 295088
Down	Ballydugan	Hamilton	land	-	-	-	Hamilton - Harrison	-	-	dd/	284 63 183275
Down	Ballydugan	Hamilton	land	-	-	-	Hamilton - Weir	-	-	dd/	300 600 291569
Down	Ballydugan	Hardy Isaac	flour	-	-	-	-	-	19x9x9 3 pr st.	vmb/	5
Down	Ballydugan	Killen Noel	flour	-	-	-	- reopened as Hotel	2000		mmSv/	nk - C
Down	Ballydugan	Wallace Mrs.	flour	-	-	-	- acquired by Noel Killen	1987	(for conservation)	pWEH	-
Down	Ballydugan	Hardy Isaac	old windmill	-	-	-	-	-	-	pWEH	-
Down	Ballydugan	Harrison	land	-	-	-	Harrison - Upton	-	322.165.215299&	dd/	315 456 215300
Down	Ballydugan	Huggins	mill	-	-	-	Huggins - Bateson	-	-	dd/	537 125 352191
Down	Ballydugan	Killeen Noel	flour	-	-	-	-	1999	-	pWEH	-
Down	Ballydugan	Knox Thomas Mr.	mill	-	-	-	Knox Thos His Will	-	- [Mem. lost !]	dd/	55 536 28383
Down	Ballydugan	McAlister Peter	mill	-	-	-	McAlister P - Connor Mary	1897	-	dd/	1897 4 32
Down	Ballydugan	McAlister Peter	mill	-	-	-	McAlister P - Connor Mary	1897	-	dd/	1897 4 32
Down	Ballydugan	Moira Earl	mill	-	-	-	Moira E - Wallace	-	-	dd/	573 59 383839
Down	Ballydugan	Montgomery	land	-	-	-	Montgomery - Stewart	-	-	dd/	307 261 203973

PARISH	TOWNLAND	MILLER	TYPE	HOUSE	Land	£Val+(	PROPRIETORS	Date	WHEEL etc.	Record	Ref.
Down	Ballydugan	Nevin William Rev.	land	-	-	-	Nevin W - Harrison Nich :	1767	Mort. 10 Oct. :	dd/	262 210 168808
Down	Ballydugan	Taylor	mill	-	-	-	Taylor - Dick	-	-	dd/	410 147 269460
Down	Ballydugan	Wallace Wm & ors	old flour mill	kiln & yard	28a.	45	-	1856	-	gr/	-
Down	Ballydugan	Wallace Wm & ors	old flour mill	kiln & yard	-	5-15/-	- mill cottages in field	1856	-	gr/	aai.ie
Down	Ballydugan	West	land	-	-	-	West - Hall	-	-	dd/	271 507 181931
Down	Ballydugan	West	land	-	-	-	West - Clarge	-	-	dd/	292 344 190831
Down	Ballydugan	West	mill	-	-	-	West - Blackwood	-	-	dd/	332 338 224741
Down	Ballydugan	West	mill	-	-	-	West - Auchenleck	-	-	dd/	430 166 279182
Down	Ballydugan	West	mill	-	-	-	West - Auchenleck	-	-	dd/	434 48 231378
Down	Ballydugan	West	mill	-	-	-	West - McCartan	-	-	dd/	624 50 430174
Down	Ballydugan	West & Son	land	-	-	-	West - Prow	-	-	dd/	282 417 184557
Down	Ballydugan	West Batt	land	-	-	-	West B - Harrison Nicholas	1765	40694	dd/	260 253 168207
Down	Ballydugan	West Henry	flour	(old/ renewed)	-	-	-	1770	-	hist/	n.k.
Down	Ballydugan	West Henry :	mill	-	-	-	West H - Clarges Chris	1754	-	dd/	182 377 122229
Down	Ballydugan	West Richard Henry :	mill	-	-	-	West R - Ward Charles :	1810	Mort. 23 Nov.	dd/	628 339 432130
Down	Ballydugan & :	Maguire James :	land	-	-	-	Maguire J - Clarke Darby :	1715	Mort. 23 Dec.	dd/	24 2 12644
Down	Ballydugan & :	Peppard John J	land	-	-	-	Peppard - Wesr Roger :	1708	-	dd/	2 396 529
Down	Ballydugan & :	West Henry :	land - called :	-	-	-	West H - Maguire James :	1713	-	dd/	22 218 11537
Down	Ballydugan & :	West Henry :	land	-	-	-	West H - McCall Helena :	1738	-	dd/	91 362 64471
Down	Ballydugan & :	West Henry :	land	-	-	-	West H - Clerges Chris :	1738	- [Ref. copy DD]	dd/	91 362 64472
Ballyhalbert	Ballyesborough	-	flax	-	-	-	-	-	-	6"os/	18
Greyabbey	Ballyewry	-	C`burn Mill	-	-	-	-	-	-	6"os/	11
Bright	Ballygallum	Rainey William Ash :	mill	-	-	-	Rainey Wm - Hill Samuel :	1753	14 Feb.	dd/	165 34 108145
Bright	Ballygilbert	-	mill ruin, pond	-	-	-	-	-	-	6"os/	57
Maghera	Ballyginny	- at Maghera	mill	-	-	-	-	-	-	1"os/	61
Kilkeel	Ballygowan	-	corn	-	-	-	-	-	-	1"os/	37
Kilkeel	Ballygowan	-	flax	-	-	-	-	-	-	1"os/	37
Kilkeel	Ballygowan	-	mill	-	-	-	-	-	-	1"os/	71
Kilkeel	Ballygowan	-	mills	-	-	-	-	-	-	1"os/	37
Kilkeel	Ballygowan	- at Mill Bay	corn	-	-	-	-	-	-	1"os/	37
Killinchy	Ballygowan	Adair Thomas B	mill	-	-	-	Adair T - McCamon Wm :	1800	-	dd/	581 480 395008
Killinchy	Ballygowan	Allen John	mill	-	-	-	Allen - Watson Hull James	1787	L&R. 30 Mar.	dd/	390 218 256523
Killinchy	Ballygowan	Arbuckle Co. Down :	mill & shilling hill	-	-	-	Arbuckle - Atkinson	-	-	dd/	378? 219 253445
Killinchy	Ballygowan	Blackwood James :	mill	-	-	-	Blackwood J - Reid Jane :	1806	Mort. 9 Jan.	dd/	578 527 390077
Killinchy	Ballygowan	Blackwood James :	mill	-	-	-	Blackwood J - Wilson Thos :	-	-	dd/	578 531 39093
Killinchy	Ballygowan	Gracey Thomas	flax	-	-	3	-	-	-	gr/	-
Killinchy	Ballygowan	Hillsborough Trevor :	land	- (? mill)	-	-	Hillsborough - Denton Alex :	1735	Dem. 28 Mar.	dd/	76 501 55604
Killinchy	Ballygowan	Hillsborough Trevor :	land	- (? mill)	-	-	Belfast City, Gent.	1735	-	dd/	82 282 57848
Kilkeel	Ballygowan	M`Elroy Hugh	corn	-	18a.	9.2	-	-	-	gr/	-
Killinchy	Ballygowan	May Edward Rev. :	mill	-	-	-	May Edw - Corry Trevor ; I	1809	-	dd/	614 179 419033
Killinchy	Ballygowan	McCamon William :	mill	-	-	-	McCamon Wm - Adair Wm :	1808	-	dd/	598 469 412137
Kilkeel	Ballygowan	McElroy Elizabeth	corn	-	-	3	-	-	13x2x8	vmb/	5
Killinchy	Ballygowan	Nedham	mill & shelling mil	-	-	-	Nedham - Mackay	-	-	dd/	33 503 59997
Killinchy	Ballygowan	Nedham Robert :	mill & shelling mil	-	-	-	Nedham R - Atkinson Jas :	1750	Lse. 13 Feb.	dd/	156 112 108287
Comber	Ballygowan	Reid Alex Orr	corn	-	27a.	29	-	-	-	gr/	-
Comber	Ballygowan	Reid Alex Orr	flax	-	-	-	-	-	-	gr/	-
Kilkeel	Ballygowan	Reilly John	mill, mill lands	-	-	-	Reilly Wm - Hill Ld Geo	1842	-	dd/	1842 20 274
Killinchy	Ballygowan	Simpson John	tuck	-	1.1.36	5	-	-	-	gr/	-
Killinchy	Ballygowan	Sinclair	mill	-	-	-	Sinclair Partnership	-	-	dd/	614 170 419632
Killinchy	Ballygowan	Sinclair George :	mill	-	-	-	Sinclair G - McDonnell Alex :	1823	-	dd/	785 87 531022
Killinchy	Ballygowan	Sinclair George :	mill	-	-	-	Sinclair - McDonnell Alex :	1823	-	dd/	780 202 528137
Holywood	Ballyhackmore	Steen James, Wm :	flax spinning	-	3a.	-	-	-	-	gr/	-

PARISH	TOWNLAND	MILLER	TYPE	HOUSE	Land	£Val+(	PROPRIETORS	Date	WHEEL etc.	Record	Ref.
Newtownards	Ballyhaft	Johnston James :	flax	-	81a.	-	-	-	-	gr/	-
Ballyhalbert	Ballyhalbert	-	windmill	-	-	-	-	-	-	1"os/	37
Ballyhalbert	Ballyhalbert	- on coast	corn	-	-	-	-	-	-	6"os/	-
Ballyhalbert	Ballyhalbert	Colvill	mills	-	-	-	Colvill - Hunter	-		dd/	3? 306 65547
Ballyhalbert	Ballyhalbert	Echlin Charles : E	mills	-	-	-	Echlin C - Echlin James :	1735	L&R. 10 Jan.	dd/	81 339 57796
Ballyhalbert	Ballyhalbert	Hamilton Hans	mill land, tmts.	-	-	-	Hamilton H - Tisdall Richd	1708	-	dd/	2 141 339
Ballyhalbert	Ballyhalbert	Maxwell	mills	-	-	-	Maxwell - Echlin	-	-	dd/	88 350 62853
Ballyhalbert	Ballyhalbert	Ross	mills	-	-	-	Ross - Ross	-	-	dd/	87 506 62854
Ballyhalbert	Ballyhalbert	Ross	mills	-	-	-	Ross - Colvill	-	-	dd/	94 107 6546
Comber	Ballyhanwood	-	corn	-	-	-	-	-	-	6"os/	5
Comber	Ballyhanwood	-	flax	-	-	-	-	-	-	6"os/	5
Comber	Ballyhanwood	-	mill	-	-	-	-	-	-	6"os/	5
Down	Ballyharley	Bustard	mill	-	-	-	Bustard - McConnell	-	- [not 254]	dd/	254 485 162672
Down	Ballyharley	Bustard	mill	-	-	-	Bustard - McConnell	-	-	dd/	254 486 162673
Down	Ballyharley	Bustard Andrew : T	mill	-	-	-	Bustard A - Chambers Jas :	1758	Lse. 27 Jan.	dd/	245 487 162674
Down	Ballyharley	Bustard Andrew : T	mill	-	-	-	Bustard A - McIlwaine Thos :	1766	Agmt. 1 Nov.	dd/	252 224 162693
Down	Ballyharley	Bustard Robert :	mill	-	-	-	Bustard R - Bustard John :	1762	10 Aug.	dd/	230 455 152142
Down	Ballyharley	Hamilton Robert :	mill	-	-	-	Hamilton R - Hamilton Robt :	1760	Lse. 15 Nov.	dd/	230 429 152060
Down	Ballyharley	Hamilton Robert :	mill	-	-	-	Hamilton R - Hamilton Robt :	1760	Lse. 2 May	dd/	230 428 152059
Down	Ballyharley	Ross	mill	-	-	-	Ross - Johnson	-	-	dd/	289 150 190074
Down	Ballyharley	Saul	mill	-	-	-	Saul - Napier	-	-	dd/	493 208 320641
Down	Ballyharley	Saul William :	mill	-	-	-	Saul W- Maxwell Thomas :	1810	14 Sep.	dd/	622 445 430238
Down	Ballyharley :	Hall	mill	-	-	-	Hall & Wife - Savage	-	-	dd/	187 32 123182
Newtownards	Ballyharry	-	mill & mill dam	-	-	-	-	-	-	6"os/	6
Donaghadee	Ballyhaskin	-	flax	-	-	-	-	-	-	6"os/	7
Donaghadee	Ballyhaskin	Ewart Jane Sen.	house, offs. ld.		31a.	9	-	-	-	gr/	-
Donaghadee	Ballyhaskin	M`Caw James	flax	-	-	-	-	-	-	gr/	-
Ballyhalbert	Ballyhemlin	- Ballyhalbert Tn	corn & flax	-	-	-	-	-	-	6"os/	18
Ballyhalbert	Ballyhemlin	- on beach	corn	-	-	-	-	-	-	6"os/	18
Ballyhalbert	Ballyhemlin	Cunningham	mills	-	-	-	Cunningham - Ker	-	-	dd/	262 66 166541
Ballyhalbert	Ballyhemlin	Echlin	mills	-	-	-	Echlin - Ross	-	-	dd/	124 14 83?588
Ballyhalbert	Ballyhemlin	Hamilton James Rev :	mill	-	-	-	Hamilton J - Harrison Nich :	1770	-	dd/	284 63 183275
Ballyhalbert	Ballyhemlin	Hamilton James Rev :	mill	-	-	-	Hamilton J - West Henry :	1774	-	dd/	300 600 201569
Ballyhalbert	Ballyhemlin	Harrison Nicholas	mill	-	-	-	Harrison - Upton	-	-	dd/	315 456 215300
Ballyhalbert	Ballyhemlin	Harrison Nicholas	mill	-	-	-	Harrison N - Upton Henry :	1758	-	dd/	322 165 215 299
Ballyhalbert	Ballyhemlin	Leech	mill	-	-	-	Leech - Dunlop	-	-	dd/	180 379 121229
Ballyhalbert	Ballyhemlin	Montgomery Nath :	mill	-	-	-	Montgomery N - Stuart Wm	1725	-	dd/	307 261 203973
Ballyhalbert	Ballyhemlin	Ross James : E	mills	-	-	-	Ross Jas - Echlin Godfrey :	1748	-	dd/	131 403 89626
Ballyhalbert	Ballyhemlin	Walker Charles :	mills	-	-	-	Walker C - Isaac Simon :	1767	-	dd/	259 17 165320
Ballyhalbert	Ballyhemlin	West Henry & Patrick	mill	-	-	-	West Henry & Patk - Prow :	1755	-	dd/	282 417 184557
Ballyhalbert	Ballyhemlin	West Henry Jun : E	mill	-	-	-	West H - Clarges Chris :	1772	Agmt. 1 May	dd/	292 344 190831
Ballyhalbert	Ballyhemlin	West Patrick :	mill	-	-	-	West Patrick - Hall Roger :	1768	-	dd/	271 587 181931
Comber	Ballyhenry	M`Burney Thomas	flax	-	16a.	19	-	-	-	gr/	-
Ardquin	Ballyherly	-	corn	-	-	-	-	-	-	6"os/	25
Ardquin	Ballyherly	- on Ballyherly L	corn	-	-	-	-	-	-	6"os/	25
Ardquin	Ballyherly	Keown James	corn & kiln	-	-	-	-	-	-	gr/	-
Ardquin	Ballyherly	Maxwell Benjamin	petroleum wks	-	-	-	-	-	-	gr/	-
Ardquin	Ballyherly	Maxwell William	corn	-	-	-	-	-	-	gr/	-
Ardquin	Ballyherly	Maxwell William	starch works	-	-	-	-	-	-	gr/	-
Bangor	Ballyholme	-	flax	-	-	-	-	-	-	6"os/	52
Bangor	Ballyholme	-	mill	-	-	-	-	-	-	1"os/	29
Bangor	Ballyholme	-	windmill	-	-	-	-	-	-	1"os/	29

PARISH	TOWNLAND	MILLER	TYPE	HOUSE	Land	£Val+	PROPRIETORS	Date	WHEEL etc.	Record	Ref.
Bangor	Ballyholme	-	windmill	-	-	-	-	-	-	6"os/	52
Bangor	Ballyholme	Banking Co. North.	flour & kilns	-	0.3.25	-	-	-	-	gr/	-
Bangor	Ballyholme	Maxwell Robert	tuck	-	-	-	Maxwell - Blackwood Jas	1738	-	dd/	95 182 66093
Kilkeel	Ballyinran	Anderson James	tuck	-	24a.	13	-	-	-	gr/	-
Kilkeel	Ballyinran	M`Murray Samuel	flax	-	32a.	29	-	-	-	gr/	-
Kilkeel	Ballykeel	- at Ballykeel Ho	flax	-	-	-	-	-	-	1"os/	71
Kilkeel	Ballykeel	Bradshaw rep Herc	mill pond	-	14a.	13	-	-	-	gr/	-
Kilkeel	Ballykeel	Delzel	mill & grist	-	-	-	Delzel - Delzel	-	-	dd/	446 320 289806
Kilkeel	Ballykeel	M`Comiskey Mary	thread factory	-	13a.	-	-	-	-	gr/	-
Magheralin	Ballykeel	Waddell Mary Jane	corn & kiln	-	37a.	-	-	-	-	gr/	-
Magheralin	Ballykeel	Waddle Maj. James	corn	-	-	5.2	-	-	14x2x8.6	vmb/	5
Kilkeel	Ballykeel	Wamsley Jno	bleach	-	-	-	-	-		vmb/	5
Kilkeel	Ballykeel	Wamsley Jno	rolling & flax	-	-	4	-	-	16x3x16 4 berths	vmb/	5
Kilkeel	Ballykeel	White	mill & grist	-	-	-	White - Lowry	-	-	dd/	312 598 312579?
Bangor	Ballykilare	-	ruins of mill	-	-	-	-	-	-	6"os/	1
Bangor	Ballykilare	-	windmill stump	-	-	-	-	-	-	6"os/	1
Bangor	Ballykilare	- nr Crawfordsburn	mill	-	-	-	-	-	-	6"os/	1
Dromara	Ballykine	Earls James	flax	-	-	-	-	-	13x2x7 2 berths	vmb/	5
Ballykinler	Ballykinler Upr	Megaw Bernard	corn	-	48a	-	-	-	-	gr/	-
Ballykinler	Ballykinler Upr	Russell Charles	corn	-	-	-	-	-	13x2x8.6	vmb/	5
Saintfield	Ballyknockan	Bennett John	corn & kiln	-	4.1.0	9	-	-	-	gr/	-
Saintfield	Ballyknockan	Bennett John	flax	-	-	-	-	-	-	gr/	-
Saintfield	Ballyknockan	Hamilton Ann Hon. :	mill	-	-	-	Hamilton A - Limerick Lord :	1725	L&R. 28 Mar.	dd/	45 232 29061
Saintfield	Ballyknockan	Limerick Lord	mill	-	-	-	Limerick Lord - Knox	-	-	dd/	44 105 27818
Saintfield	Ballyknockan	Limerick Lord James :	mill	-	-	-	Limerick Lord - Knox	-	-	dd/	51 357 33983
(Bo. Ards)	Ballylisbane	Savage Lucy :	corn	-	-	-	Savage L - Lucas Francis, [	1724	-	dd/	41 388 26457
Dundonald	Ballylisbredan	-	mill, mill pond	-	-	-	-	-	-	6"os/	5
Dundonald	Ballylisbredan	- nr Mill Mount	mill	-	-	-	-	-	-	6"os/	5
Dundonald	Ballylisbredan	Bayley John :	mill	-	-	-	Bayley Jonn - Cross :	1720	-	dd/	26 479 16425
Dundonald	Ballylisbredan	Campbell Charles	mill, mill lands	-	-	-	Hamilton H - Tisdall Richd	1708	-	dd/	2 141 339
Dundonald	Ballylisbredan	Campbell Charles :	mill	-	-	-	Campbell C - Tyndall Richd :	1708	-	dd/	2 141 339
Dundonald	Ballylisbredan	Galway William	corn	-	133a	8.7	-	-	-	gr/	-
Dundonald	Ballylisbredan	Galway William	flax	-	-	-	-	-	-	gr/	-
Dundonald	Ballylisbredan	Hamilton Hans	mill lands, mill	-	80a	-	Hamilton H - Tisdall Richd	1708	-	dd/	2 102 307
Dundonald	Ballylisbredan	Lord Dungannon	mill	-	-	-	Dungannon - Alexander	-	-	dd/	745 158 518493
Dundonald	Ballylisbredan	Montgomery William :	mill	-	-	-	Montgomery W - Baillie Jn :	1720	-	dd/	28 81 16423
Dundonald	Ballylisbredan	Tyndall Richard :	mill	-	-	-	Tyndall R - Colvill William :	1716	-	dd/	17 279 8816
Dundonald	Ballylisbredan		mill	-	-	-			-	dd/	
Magheradrool	Ballylone Big	McCullagh Wm	flax	-	-	3 0.0	-	-	14x4x6 4 berths	vmb/	5
Kilmegan	Ballylough	Murland James	spinning	-	-	12	-	-	21x6.8x16.6 :	vmb/	5
Kilmegan	Ballylough	Murland Sam & Chas	flax spinning	-	44a	-	-	-	-	gr/	-
Kilmegan	Ballylough	Murland Sam & Chas	mill pond	-	11a.	-	-	-	-	gr/	-
Co. Down	Ballymacachen	- nr Luskey Br.	mill	-	-	-	-	-	-	1"os/	37
Tullylish	Ballymacanallen	-	bleach	-	-	-	-	-	-	6"os/	26
Aghaderg	Ballymacaratty	-	flax	-	-	-		-	-	6"os/	33
Magheradrool	Ballymacarn	Ferren Terence	old bleach wks	-	-	-	-	-	-	gr/	-
Magheradrool	Ballymacarn	Hurst Chas, CJ & W	water to flax	-	51a	-	-	-	-	gr/	-
Magheradrool	Ballymacarn	Lyons James	flax	-	7a.	-	-	-	-	gr/	-
Magheradrool	Ballymacarn	Lyons James	scutcher`s ho	-	-	-	-	-	-	gr/	-
Magheradrool	Ballymacarn S	-	bleach	-	-	-	-	-	-	6"os/	29
Magheradrool	Ballymacarn S	-	flax	-	-	-	-	-	-	6"os/	29
Magheradrool	Ballymacarn S	Brown James	bleach	-	-	-	-	-	16x4x8.6 2 bms	vmb/	5

PARISH	TOWNLAND	MILLER	TYPE	HOUSE	Land	£Val+(	PROPRIETORS	Date	WHEEL etc.	Record	Ref.
Magheradrool	Ballymacarn S	Lyons James	flax	-	-	-	-	-	13x2x9.6 3 bths	vmb/	5
Magheradrool	Ballymacarn S	McColtra Fras	flax	-	-	-	-	-	14x4x6 3 berths	vmb/	5
Knockbreda	Ballymacarret	-	brickfield	-	-	-	-	-	-	6"os/	3
Knockbreda	Ballymacarret	-	glass works	-	-	-	-	-	-	6"os/	3
Knockbreda	Ballymacarret	-	rope walk	-	-	-	-	-	-	6"os/	3
Knockbreda	Ballymacarret	-	spining	(Elm Grove)	-	-	-	-	-	1"os/	36
Knockbreda	Ballymacarret	-	spinning	(Eden Vale)	-	-	-	-	-	1"os/	36
Knockbreda	Ballymacarret	-	spinning	-	-	-	-	-	-	6"os/	3
Knockbreda	Ballymacarret	-	vitriol works	-	-	-	-	-	-	6"os/	3
Knockbreda	Ballymacarret	Barbour John	mill pond on 6a.	-	-	-	-	-	-	gr/	-
Knockbreda	Ballymacarret	Chichester Lord	mill	-	-	-	-	-	-	d/	544
Knockbreda	Ballymacarret	Coates	mill	-	-	-	Coates - Hunter	-	-	d/	538
Knockbreda	Ballymacarret	Cunninghan C	mill	-	-	-	-	-	-	d/	543
Knockbreda	Ballymacarret	Dunbar	mill	-	-	-	-	-	-	d/	544
Knockbreda	Ballymacarret	Faren Joseph	spinning	-	-	-	-	-	-	gr/	-
Knockbreda	Ballymacarret	Fleming Mary :	part of	-	-	-	Fleming Mary - Duff John :	1735	Mort. 20 Apl.	dd/	72 331 50945
Knockbreda	Ballymacarret	Fleming Mary :	part of	-	-	-	Fleming Eliz - Duff John :	1730	Mort. 11 Jan.	dd/	66 75 45191
Knockbreda	Ballymacarret	Hamilton & ors	corn & oil	-	-	-	-	-	-	gr/	-
Knockbreda	Ballymacarret	Jameson	mill	-	-	-	-	-	-	d/	557
Knockbreda	Ballymacarret	Johnston Acheson :	mill	-	-	-	Johnston Ach - Trail :	1760	-	d/	203 277 135216
Knockbreda	Ballymacarret	Moreland	mill	-	-	-	Moreland - Chambers	-	-	d/	432 347 280853
Knockbreda	Ballymacarret	Murdoch	mill	-	-	-	-	-	-	d/	539
Knockbreda	Ballymacarret	Neill	mill	-	-	-	Neill - Innis	-	-	d/	470 235 301596
Knockbreda	Ballymacarret	Pottinger	mill	-	-	-	-	-	-	d/	537
Knockbreda	Ballymacarret	Pottinger	mill	-	-	-	-	-	-	d/	550
Knockbreda	Ballymacarret	Pottinger Joseph :	fields (pt. of 2)	-	-	-	Pottinger J - Fleming John :	1717	Lse. 26 Apl.	dd/	21 487 12223
Knockbreda	Ballymacarret	Ranken	mill	-	-	-	Ranken - Tracy?	-	-	d/	530 194 347160
Knockbreda	Ballymacarret	Richardson J & Bros.	oil & bone	-	-	-	-	-	-	gr/	-
Knockbreda	Ballymacarret	Roche	mill	-	-	-	-	-	-	d/	548
Knockbreda	Ballymacarret	Stevenson S	mill	-	-	-	-	-	-	d/	548
Knockbreda	Ballymacarret	Vincent	mill	-	-	-	-	-	-	d/	538
Killinchy	Ballymacashen	-	windmill stump	-	-	-	-	-	-	6"os/	16
Magheralin	Ballymacateer	-	mill	-	-	-	-	-	-	pWAM	-
Knockbreda	Ballymackamore	-	Beer`s Mill	-	-	-	-	-	-	6"os/	4
Knockbreda	Ballymackamore	-	spinning fcty	-	-	-	-	-	-	6"os/	4
Knockbreda	Ballymackamore	- nr Beer`s Bridge	mill	-	-	-	-	-	-	6"os/	4
Ballytrustan	Ballymacnamee	-	corn	-	-	-	-	-	-	6"os/	25
Ballytrustan	Ballymacnamee	-	flax	-	-	-	-	-	-	6"os/	25
Knockbreda	Ballymaconaghy	-	bleach	-	-	-	-	-	-	6"os/	3
Knockbreda	Ballymaconaghy	Farrell James :	mills	-	-	-	Farrell J - Netterville Patk :	1725	-	dd/	43 327 28404
Knockbreda	Ballymaconaghy	Johnston	mill	-	-	-	Johnston - Langtry	-	-	dd/	766 478 520013
Knockbreda	Ballymaconaghy	Moreland A, Wm & J	flax spinning	-	1.1 30	-	-	-	-	gr/	-
Knockbreda	Ballymaconaghy	Shakelton	mill	-	-	-	Shakelton - Johnston	-	-	dd/	789 521 533856
Knockbreda	Ballymaconaghy	St Laurence	mill	-	-	-	StLaurence - M`j`banks	-	-	dd/	791 483 535018
Knockbreda	Ballymaconaghy	St Laurence	mill	-	-	-	StLaurence - Thompson	-	-	dd/	804 348 543875
Knockbreda	Ballymaconaghy	St Laurence Isabella:	mill	-	-	-	St Laur. - Thompson Wm	1825	-	dd/	806 339 543875
Bangor	Ballymaconnell	-	corn	-	-	-	-	-	-	6"os/	52
Bangor	Ballymaconnell	-	mill	-	-	-	-	-	-	1"os/	29
Bangor	Ballymaconnell	-	windmill	-	-	-	-	-	-	6"os/	52
Bangor	Ballymaconnell	Barr Samuel	flax	-	17a.	-	-	-	-	gr/	-
Bangor	Ballymaconnell	Lowry Elizabeth	corn	-	79a.	20	-	-	-	gr/	-
Bangor	Ballymaconnell	Lowry Elizabeth	flax	-	-	-	-	-	-	gr/	-

PARISH	TOWNLAND	MILLER	TYPE	HOUSE	Land	£Val+	PROPRIETORS	Date	WHEEL etc.	Record	Ref.
Donaghmore	Ballymacratty	-	corn	-	-	-		-	-	6"os/	40
Donaghadee	Ballymacruise	Carmichael D & W	corn & flax	-	16a.	-	-	-	-	gr/	-
Donaghadee	Ballymacruise	Carmichael D & W	flax & land	-	4a.	25	-	-	-	gr/	-
Kilkeel	Ballymagart	-	corn & flax	reqs. restoration	-	-	Victor & Hea. Cirefice	2001	-	pWEH	B
Kilkeel	Ballymagart	Lindsay James	corn & flax	-	37a.	12	-	-	-	gr/	-
Kilkeel	Ballymagart	McConnell Alex	flax	- burnt in 1835	-	-	-	-	24x6x18 8 bths	vmb/	5
Comber	Ballymagaughey	-	mill & pond	-	-	-	-	-	-	6"os/	10
Bangor	Ballymagee	-	flax	-	-	-	-	-	-	6"os/	-
Bangor	Ballymagee	-	flour, corn	-	-	-	-	-	-	6"os/	-
Down	Ballymakilbrick	McClure James :	mill	-	-	-	McClure Jas - Forsyth John :	1736	Trust 2 March	dd/	68 102 47189
Comber	Ballymalady	-	flax	-	-	-	-	-	-	6"os/	20
Comber	Ballymalady	-	windmill stump	-	-	-	-	-	-	6"os/	10
Co. Down	Ballymartin	Caughy Mary & Mgt	corn & kiln	-	67a.	-	-	-	-	gr/	-
Co. Down	Ballymartin	Caughy Mary & Mgt	thrashing	-	-	-	-	-	-	gr/	-
Co. Down	Ballymegenaghie *	Salkeld Joseph :	mill	-	-	-	Salkeld J - Johnston Geo :	1824	-	dd/	
Co. Down	Ballymegenaghie *	St Laurence Isabella :	mill	-	-	-	St Laurence Lady Is'bla - :	1824	-	dd/	
Kilmood	Ballyminstragh	Bell Thomas	flax	-	4.2.11	-	-	-	-	gr/	-
Kilmood	Ballyminstragh	Frew John	corn	-	27a.	23	-	-	-	gr/	-
Kilmood	Ballyminstragh	Frew John	flax	-	-	-	-	-	-	gr/	-
Co Down	Ballymonestown	Johnson Robert	mill	-	-	-	Johnson R - Bradstreet S	1742	-	dd/	107 185 73713
Co Down	Ballymonestown	Savage Lucy	mills	-	-	-	Savage - Johntson Robt	1739	-	dd/	93 627 67169
Kilcoo	Ballymoney	-	bleach	-	-	-	-	-	-	1"os/	-
Kilcoo	Ballymoney	-	flax	-	-	-	-	-	-	6"os/	-
Kilcoo	Ballymoney	Barns John	flax	-	50a.	20	-	-	-	gr/	-
Kilcoo	Ballymoney	Hill Trevor :	mill	-	-	-	Hill Trevor - O'Neill John :	1716	-	dd/	69 112 47541
Kilcoo	Ballymoney	O`Neill Francis	corn & kiln	-	33a.	-	-	-	-	gr/	-
Killinchy	Ballymorran	Stewart Thomas	mills	-	-	-	Stewart Thos - Moore Jn	1739	-	dd/	125 289 85084
Bangor	Ballymullan	Crawford John S	corn & kiln	-	81a	-	-	-	-	gr/	-
Bangor	Ballymullan	Hamilton	mill	-	-	-	Hamilton - Crawford	-	-	dd/	87 42 62443
Ardquin	Ballymurphy	Magowan John	flax	-	26a.	28	-	-	-	gr/	-
Ardquin	Ballymurphy	Wallace & Stewart J	starch works	-	-	-	-	-	-	gr/	-
Tullylish	Ballynagarrick	Park John	corn	-	23a.	17	-	-	-	gr/	-
Tullylish	Ballynagarrick	Park John	flax	-	-	-	-	-	-	gr/	-
Tullylish	Ballynagarrick	Robinson Jno	corn	-	-	3.5.0	-	-	12x2x10	vmb/	5
Tullylish	Ballynagarrick	Stephenson John	mill lds, mills	-	-	-	Stephenson J - Christie T	1756	-	dd/	182 293 120853
Tullylish	Ballynagarrick	Stephenson Robt	mill lds, mills	-	-	-	Stephenson - Dowglass W	1718	-	dd/	95 350 66758
Drumbo	Ballynahatty	- at Purdysburn	mills	-	-	-	-	-	-	6"os/	8
Magheradrol	Ballynahinch	-	windmill	-	-	-	-	-	-	6"os/	22
Magheradrool	Ballynahinch	Barnett	mill	-	-	-	Barnett - Mitchell	-	-	dd/	308 331 205267
Magheradrool	Ballynahinch	Barnett James Robt :	mill	-	-	-	Barnett J R - Barnett Jno :	1768	L&R. 2 Dec.	dd/	260 406 173656
Magheradrool	Ballynahinch	Kerr David	corn	-	-	18	-	-	17x5x10 2 pr st.	vmb/	5
Magheradrool	Ballynahinch	Kerr David	flax	-	-	6	-	-	15x2x10 3 berths	vmb/	5
Magheradrool	Ballynahinch	Martin John	corn & kiln	-	4.1.0	-	-	-	-	gr/	-
Magheradrool	Ballynahinch	Martin John	flax (unfin)	-	-	-	-	-	-	gr/	-
Magheradrool	Ballynahinch	Rawdon Hon. John :	mills	-	-	-	Rawdon J - Ringland John :	1719	-	dd/	28 280 17614
Magheradrool	Ballynahinch	Tallon Frances :	mill	-	-	-	Tallon F - Hamilton Hugh	1767	-	dd/	486 311 308419
Magheradrool	Ballynahinch	Wilkinson Phillips :	corn	-	-	-	Wilkinson P - Black John :	1767	L&R. 20 Jul.	dd/	255 484 166687
Drumb`yroney	Ballynamagna	Cromie Mary Anne	flax	-	55a.	8	-	-	-	gr/	-
Drumb`yroney	Ballynamagna	David Hanna	corn & kiln	-	32a.	-	-	-	-	gr/	-
Drumbeg	Ballynanally	-	old logwood	-	-	-	-	-	-	6"os/	9
Aghaderg	Ballynaskeagh	M`Kee Rev David	flax	-	45a.	-	-	-	-	gr/	-
Drumbo	Ballynavally	Aikin John	corn	-	9a.	28	-	-	-	gr/	-

PARISH	TOWNLAND		MILLER	TYPE	HOUSE	Land	£Val+(	PROPRIETORS	Date	WHEEL etc.	Record	Ref.
Drumbo	Ballynavally		Aikin John	flax	-	-	-	-	-	-	gr/	-
Rathmullan	Ballynewport		Murphy John Sen.	mill	-	-	-	Murphy J - Murphy Thos	1891	-	dd/	1891 62 170
Down	Ballyoolymore	*	McClelland	scutching	-	-	-	-	2009	-	mmSv/	nk - R
Dundonald	Ballyoran		-	flax	-	-	-	-	-	-	6"os/	5
Dundonald	Ballyoran		-	mills	-	-	-	-	-	-	6"os/	5
Dundonald	Ballyrainey		-	windmill	-	-	-	-	-	-	6"os/	-
Ballee ? Inch	Ballyrenan		- at Saltwater Br.	corn	-	-	-	-	-	-	1"os/	49
Holywood	Ballyrobert		Gordon Robert F	flax	-	153a.	-	-	-	-	gr/	-
Newtownards	Ballyrogan		-	flax	-	-	-	-	-	-	6"os/	5
Newtownards	Ballyrogan		-	windmill stump	-	-	-	-	-	-	6"os/	5
Drumb`yroney	Ballyroney		Birch George :	mill	-	-	-	Birch G - McCardle Cath :	1805	Lse. 22 May	dd/	620 46 426237
Drumb`yroney	Ballyroney		Boyd	mill	-	-	-	Boyd - Gilmer	-	-	dd/	3/5?43 479 363944
Drumb`yroney	Ballyroney		Boyd	mill	-	-	-	Boyd - Carr	-	-	dd/	335 616 227323
Drumb`yroney	Ballyroney		Forsyth Ann :	mill	-	-	-	Forsyth Ann - Scott John :	1747	-	dd/	130 75 88012
Drumb`yroney	Ballyroney		Forsyth Ann Widow	mill	-	-	-	Forsyth A - Fairlie William	1742	-	dd/	112 75 77111
Drumb`yroney	Ballyroney		Haltridge John :	mill	-	-	-	Haltridge J - Maclinchy Jn :	1720	-	dd/	42 164 26001
Drumb`yroney	Ballyroney		McClinchey Samuel	corn	-	-	-	McClinchey - Forsyth Ann	1741	-	dd/	101 558 73941
Drumb`yroney	Ballyroney		McClure James	mill	-	-	-	McClure J - Forsyth John	1739	-	dd/	105 63 72511
Comber	Ballyrush		Gowdy John Alex	flax	-	58a.	-	-	-	-	gr/	-
Ballee/D`more	Ballysallagh		-	flax & pond	-	-	-	-	-	-	6"os/	57
Ballee/D`more	Ballysallagh		-	windmill stump	-	-	-	-	-	-	6"os/	57
Shankill	Ballysillan		-	bleach	-	-	-	-	-	-	1"os/	36
Comber	Ballystockart		Colvill Robert	mill	-	-	-	Colvill Robt - Stewart Alex	1744	-	dd/	114 484 79741
Comber	Ballystockart		Colvill Robert	mill	-	-	-	Colvill Robt - Stewart Alex	1744	-	dd/	115 84 79486
Comber	Ballystockart		Earl Londnderry	mill	-	-	-	Earl L`derry - Clelland	-	-	dd/	548 273 362527
Comber	Ballystockart		Leslie Rev Peter	mill	-	-	-	Leslie Peter - M`Neale Dan	1745	-	dd/	117 546 81930
Comber	Ballystockart		Wallace James Yng :	mill	-	-	-	Wallace & ors - Reid Jas :	1757	-	dd/	187 253 124811
Comber	Ballystokart		Orr Blakeley	corn	-	5.0.10	-	-	-	-	gr/	-
Comber	Ballystokart		Orr Blakeley	flax	-	-	-	-	-	-	gr/	-
Saul	Ballysugagh		-	flax	-	-	-		-	-	6"os/	31
Saul	Ballysugagh		-	mill ponds (3)	-	8a	-	-	-	-	gr/	-
Down	Ballytogher	*	Clifford Lord	mill	-	-	-	Clifford Ld - Price	-	-	dd/	333 120 222757
Down	Ballytogher	*	Harris	mill	-	-	-	Harris - Price	-	-	dd/	333 121 222758
Down	Ballytogher	*	Price	mill	-	-	-	Price - Mordant	-	-	dd/	354 49 238282
Down	Ballytogher	*	Savage	mill	-	-	-	Savage - Butler	-	-	dd/	588? 157 392 799
Killyleagh	Ballytrim		-	flax	-	-	-	-	-	-	6"os/	24
Ballytrustan	Ballytrustan		-	windmill stump	-	-	-	-	-	-	6"os/	25
Seapatrick	Ballyvally		Croathers	mill	-	-	-	Croathers - Seawright	-	- [not 222]	dd/	222 321 163455
Seapatrick	Ballyvally		Fennell Robert & Co.	bleech works	-	2.3.0	21	-	-	-	gr/	-
Seapatrick	Ballyvally		Fennell Robert & Co.	bt & stores	-	21a.	20	-	-	-	gr/	-
Seapatrick	Ballyvally		Knox	mill	-	-	-	Knox - Pollock	-	-	dd/	268 72 168042
Seapatrick	Ballyvally		Knox	mill	-	-	-	Knox - Knox	-	-	dd/	292 51 189379
Seapatrick	Ballyvally		Law James	mill	-	-	-	Law J & G - Clibborn Jas :	1775	-	dd/	308 306 205127
Seapatrick	Ballyvally		Law James & Geo	mill	-	-	-	Law Jas - Clibborn Jas	1775	-	dd/	307 481 205126
Seapatrick	Ballyvally		McCance John :	mill	-	-	-	McCance J - Clibborn Ed :	1822	-	dd/	778 493 727228
Seapatrick	Ballyvally		McCance John :	mill	-	-	-	McCance John - McClelland	1822	-	dd/	778 492 727227
Seapatrick	Ballyvally		McCance John :	mill	-	-	-	McCance J - Clibborn Ed :	1822	-	dd/	779 42 527377
Seapatrick	Ballyvally		Templeton	mill	-	-	-	Templeton - Law	-	-	dd/	273 577 180607
Seapatrick	Ballyvally		Trevor Edward :	mill	-	-	-	Trevor E - Clibborne Geo :	1776	-	dd/	310 599 280073
Dromore	Ballyvicnacally		Anderson William	flax	-	4.1.30	-	-	-	-	gr/	-
Bright	Ballyviggis		-	corn	-	-	-	-	-	-	1"os/	49
Bright	Ballyviggis		Carson Joseph	corn	-	136a.	31	-	-	-	gr/	-

PARISH	TOWNLAND	MILLER	TYPE	HOUSE	Land	£Val+	PROPRIETORS	Date	WHEEL etc.	Record	Ref.
Bright	Ballyviggis	Wilson Robert	corn	-	-	6	-	-	13x3x6.6 1 pr st.	vmb/	5
Ardquin	Ballywadden	Gunning Arthur	mill pond	-	5.1.5	-	-	-	-	gr/	-
Ardquin	Ballywallon	-	Bishop`s Mill	-	-	-	-	-	-	6"os/	25
Ardquin	Ballywallon	-	corn	-	-	-	-	-	-	6"os/	25
Ardquin	Ballywallon	-	flax & pond	-	-	-	-	-	-	6"os/	25
Ardquin	Ballywallon	Gunning Arthur	corn & kiln	-	-	-	-	-	-	gr/	-
Ballywalter	Ballywalter	-	corn & kiln	-	-	-	-	-	-	6"os/	12
Ballywalter	Ballywalter	-	mill (? flax)	-	-	-	-	-	-	6"os/	12
Ballywalter	Ballywalter	Bateson William :	mill	-	-	-	Bates W - Litton Edward :	1817	Mort 15 Feb. :	dd/	781 196 528731
Ballywalter	Ballywalter	Gray Isabella :	mill	-	-	-	Gray Is'bla - Carson Agnes	1824	Mort. 20 Apl.	dd/	791 60 534595
Ballywalter	Ballywalter	Haemil	mill	-	-	-	Haemil - Scott	-	-	dd/	399 68 232982
Ballywalter	Ballywalter	Haemil	mill	-	-	-	Haemil - Hutchison	-	-	dd/	453 257 289946
Ballywalter	Ballywalter	Haemill	mill	-	-	-	Haemill - Gordon	-	-	dd/	450 167 290427
Ballywalter	Ballywalter	Haemill	mill	-	-	-	Haemill - Huggins	-	-	dd/	461 353 295088
Ballywalter	Ballywalter	Haemill	mill	-	-	-	Haemill - McCormick	-	-	dd/	501 41 317521
Ballywalter	Ballywalter	Hamel Hans :	mill	-	-	-	Hamel H - Corbitt Michael :	-	-	dd/	179 392 121475
Ballywalter	Ballywalter	Hamill Frances :	mill	-	-	-	Hamill Fran - Moore Wm :	1818	-	dd/	767 417 520552
Ballywalter	Ballywalter	Huggins	mill	-	-	-	Huggins - Bateson	-	-	dd/	537 125 352191
Ballywalter	Ballywalter	Isaac Jno	mills	-	-	-	Isaac Jno - Isaac Robt	1738	Mort. 1 May	dd/	97 129 67628
Ballywalter	Ballywalter	Isaac Simon	windmill & mill	-	-	-	Isaac S - Hamill Hans	1742	-	dd/	118 76 80056
Ballywalter	Ballywalter	Lusk Arthur :	mill	-	-	-	Lusk A - Tomb Rachel :	1775	Mort. 16 Jan.	dd/	309 109 204896
Ballywalter	Ballywalter	Moore William :	mill	-	-	-	Moore Wm - Hamilton Alex :	1819	-	dd/	767 418 520553
Ballywalter	Ballywalter	Taylor	mill	-	-	-	Taylor - Dick	-	-	dd/	410 147 269460
Ballywalter	Ballywalter & ors.	Montgomery Eliza :	mills	-	-	-	Montgomery E - Matthews :	1729	-	dd/	63 142 42983
Drumgooland	Ballyward	-	mill	-	-	-	-	-	-	6"os/	-
Drumgooland	Ballyward	Blackwood	tuck mill ye	-	-	-	Blackwood - Forsyth	-	-	dd/	86 498 61507
Drumgooland	Ballyward	Blackwood Robert	grist	-	-	-	Blackwood - Forsyth	-	-	dd/	93 97 64977
Drumgooland	Ballyward	Corbett John	flax	-	17a.	-	-	-	-	gr/	-
Drumgooland	Ballyward	Stewart William	corn, pond	- miller`s ho	2.2.5	-	-	-	-	gr/	-
Down	Ballywarren	-	corn	-	-	-		-	-	6"os/	38
Donaghadee	Ballywhiskin	-	old flax mill	-	-	-	-	-	-	6"os/	7
D`dee /Comber	Ballywilliam	-	flax & pond	-	-	-	-	-	-	6"os/	10
D`dee /Comber	Ballywilliam	Boyd William	flax, mill pond	-	76a	-	-	-	-	gr/	-
Slanes	Ballywillwill	Kirkpatrick Andrew	corn	-	17a.	-	-	-	-	gr/	-
Lambeg	Balyskeagh	Richardson Jno	beetling	-	6.0.0	22	-	-	-	gr/	-
Lambeg	Balyskeagh	Richardson Jno	land	- tenant`s hos	48a.	29	-	-	-	gr/	-
Seapatrick	Banbridge Town	-	thread m`fty	-	-	-	-	-	-	6"os/	-
Seapatrick	Banbridge Town	-	weaving fcty	-	-	-	-	2009	-	mmSv/	nk - C
Seapatrick	Banbridge Town	M`Clelland Robert	new wv factory	-	-	25	-	-	-	gr/	-
Seapatrick	Banbridge Town	M`Clelland Robert	old wv factory	-	1a.	13	-	-	-	gr/	-
Seapatrick	Banbridge Town	Malcolmson Wiliam	flour, kiln	-	-	-	-	-	-	gr/	-
Seapatrick	Banbridge Town	McClelland Robert	thread m`fty	-	-	-	-	2009	-	mmSv/	nk - C
Seapatrick	Banbridge Town	Scott & Noble M/s	thread & dye	-		-	-	-	-	gr/	-
Bangor	Bangor	Bangor Lord	mills	-	-	-	Bangor Ld - Ward	-	-	dd/	337 564 228343
Bangor	Bangor	Ward	mills	-	-	-	Ward - Partnership	-	-	dd/	338 410 228315
Bangor	Bangor Corp.	-	corn	-	-	-	-	-	-	6"os/	52
Bangor	Bangor Corp.	-	cotton mfty (2)	-	-	-	-	-	-	6"os/	52
Bangor	Bangor Corp.	-	old mill	-	-	-	-	-	-	6"os/	52
Bangor	Bangor Town	M`Murray Samuel	corn & kiln	-	0.3.15	11	-	-	-	gr/	-
Bangor	Bangor Town	Ward Robert E	cotton (dilap.)	-	-	10	-	-	-	gr/	-
Co. Down	Bannvale	- at Hilltown	mill	-	-	-	-	-	-	1"os/	60
Donaghacloney	Banoge	-	Ranoyle Mill	-	-	-	-	-	-	6"os/	20

PARISH	TOWNLAND	MILLER	TYPE	HOUSE	Land	£Val+(	PROPRIETORS	Date	WHEEL etc.	Record	Ref.
Donaghacloney	Banoge	-	Ranoyle Mill	-	-	-	-	2009	-	mmSv/	nk - B
Donaghacloney	Banoge	Clanbrassil Earl of	mill	-	-	-	Clanbrassil - Waddell	-	-	dd/	339 151 226715
Donaghacloney	Banoge	Liddell & Morris	bleaching works	& land [ten'ts hos.]	32a.	38	-	1856	-	gr/	a.a.lre.ie
Donaghacloney	Banoge	Liddell & Morris	bleaching works	& land [ten'ts hos.]	32a.	38	-	1856	-	gr/	a.a.lre.ie
Donaghacloney	Banoge	McDonnell	mill	-	-	-	McDonnell - Waddell	-	-	dd/	402 66 264475
Donaghacloney	Banoge	Nicholson Mr	bleach (2)	-	-	-	-	-	15x12x7 14x3x7 :	vmb/	5
Donaghacloney	Banoge	Nicholson Mr	bleach (2)	-	-	-	-	-	15x12x7 14x3x7 :	vmb/	5
Donaghacloney	Banoge	Waddell	mill	-	-	-	Waddell - Douglas	-	-	dd/	598 146 405958
Killinchy	Barnamaghery	-	corn	-	-	-	-	-	-	6"os/	23
Killinchy	Barnamaghery	Jackson Thomas	flax	-	26a.	-	-	-	-	gr/	-
Kilmore	Barnmaghery	-	corn	-	-	-	-	-	-	6"os/	23
Drumgath	Barnmeen	-	corn	-	-	-	-	-	-	1"os/	-
Clonallan	Bavan	-	flax	-	-	-	-	-	-	1"os/	60
Clonallan	Baven	Clarke Edward	mill	-	-	-	Clarke Ed - Hood Alex	1841	-	dd/	1841 19 190
Clonallan	Baven	McRobert James	mill	-	-	-	McRobert Jas - Reily W	1842	-	dd/	1842 232 279
Down	Belvor *	Adair	mill	-	-	-	Adair - Hudson	-	-	dd/	209 290 138526
Down	Belvor *	Allen Hugh : N	mill	-	-	-	Allen Hugh+H201 - Russell J	1783	Conv. 26 Sep.	dd/	353 200 238075
Down	Belvor *	Dungannon Lord :	mill	-	-	-	Dunganon Ld - Russell Jn :	1789	Lse. 24 Jul.	dd/	414 68 270140
Down	Belvor *	Dungannon Rt. Hon. :	mill	-	-	-	Dungannon - Russell Jn :	1789	Lse. 24 Feb.	dd/	414 67 270139
Down	Belvor *	Ferguson	mill	-	-	-	Ferguson - Russell	-	-	dd/	490 169 315361
Down	Belvor *	Holmes John :	mill	-	-	-	Holmes Jn - Hudson Jas :	-	-	dd/	283 497 185756
Down	Belvor *	Hudson James :	mill	-	-	-	Hudson J - Hudson Chas	1769	-	dd/	258 568 175124
Down	Belvor *	Morehead Jane :	mill	-	-	-	Morehead J - Russell John :	-	-	dd/	309 316 205831
Down	Belvor *	Russell	mill	-	-	-	Russell - Russell	-	-	dd/	576 564 395657
Newry	Benagh	-	mill	-	-	-	-	-	-	1"os/	60
Dunsfort	Bishops Court	Baillie Jno	corn	-	-	-	-	-	12x3x9 1 pr st.	vmb/	5
Co. Down	Black Causway *	-	mills	-	-	-	McMaster - Hill	-	-	dd/	77 271 53426
Co. Down	Black Causway *	Fitzgerald Ld Henry :	mill	-	-	-	Fitzgerald - Hamilton Hugh :	1786	-	dd/	380 35 252595
Co. Down	Black Causway *	Kildare Mary Rt. Hon.	mill	-	-	-	Kildare Lady - Hill Hon. Arth	1747	L&R. 27 Feb.	dd/	131 34 88009
Co. Down	Black Causway *	Kildare Robt Hoh. Ld	mills	-	-	-	Kildare Ld - Hall Anne Wid. :	1714	-	dd/	13 397 6124
Co. Down	Blakans	Fitzgerald Henry Rt. :	mill	-	-	-	Fitzgerald H - Neville Brent:	1822	Mort. 18 Dec.	dd/	777 558 526693
Tullylish	Bleary & B'doogan :	Greer Henry : L	land (? mill)	-	-	-	Greer h - Jenney Henry :	1725	-	dd/	51 297 33087
Tullylish	Bleary & B'doogan :	Jenney Henry : R	land	-	-	-	Jenney H - Meath Bishop :	1729	L&R 20 Nov.	dd/	62 112 42130
Down	Bo. Castlereagh	Middleton Lord	Board Mill	-	-	-	Middleton Ld - Fairly Wm :	1737	Lse. 14 feb.	dd/	93 321 65212?4
Saintfield	Bresagh	-	corn	-	-	-	-	-	-	6"os/	15
Saintfield	Bressagh	Simpson Elizabeth	corn & kiln	-	20a.	16	-	-	-	gr/	-
Saintfield	Bressagh	Simpson Elizabeth	flax & store	-	-	-	-	-	-	gr/	-
Hillsborough	Cabbragh	Frazer John	corn & kiln	-	17a.	26	-	-	-	gr/	-
Hillsborough	Cabragh	Heron Samuel :	mill	-	-	-	Heron S - Heron Samel :	1713	Lse. 15 Dec.	dd/	16 245 7420
Hillsborough	Cabragh	Hill	mill	-	-	-	Hill - Blosinton	-	-	dd/	8 262 2723
Hillsborough	Cabragh	Hill Trevor :	mill	-	-	-	Hill Trevor - Taylor John Sen	1717	Lse. 1 Jul.	dd/	20 376 10962
Hillsborough	Cabragh	Hill Trevor : F	mill	-	-	-	Hill T - Campbell Charles :	1715	-	dd/	14 478 6639
Hillsborough	Cabragh	Hill Trevor :	mill	-	-	-	Hill Trevor - Mercer Richd :	1716	Lse. 29 Aug.	dd/	24 99 13195
Hillsborough	Cabragh	Middleton Alan Hon.:	mill	-	-	-	Middleton Ld - Wilson Jas :	1720	Lse. 10 Jne.	dd/	27 427 17644
Hillsborough	Cabragh	Tuten James	corn	-	-	-	-	-	14x3x10 1 pr st.	vmb/	5
Hillsborough	Cabragh	Tuten James	flax	-	-	-	-	-	13x3x8 3 berths	vmb/	5
Annaclone	Cappagh	Cowan Wm John	flour, corn, kiln	-	-	-	-	-	-	gr/	-
Annaclone	Cappagh	Potts Andrew	flax	-	44a.	-	-	-	-	gr/	-
Co. Down	Carbet	Mulligan Fran M J	mill, mill lands	-	3a.	-	Muligan F - Mulligan G	1842	-	dd/	1842 1 134
Drumbeg	Cargacroy	Martin John	corn & kiln	-	21a.	24	-	-	-	gr/	-
Drumbeg	Cargacroy	Martin John	flax	-	-	-	-	-	-	gr/	-
Annahilt	Cargygray	-	flax	-	-	-	-	-	-	6"os/	22

PARISH	TOWNLAND	MILLER	TYPE	HOUSE	Land	£Val+	PROPRIETORS	Date	WHEEL etc.	Record	Ref.
Annahilt	Cargygray	Hook Campbell	flax	-	23a.	27	-	-	-	gr/	-
Carlingford	Carlingford	Fortescue William	Mill of the Grange	-	-	-	Fortescue Wm - Hone Ele	1875	-	dd/	
Carlingford	Carlingford	Nugent Thomas Jn :	mill dam & lands	-	-	-	Nugent Thos - Aithin Wm :	1831	-	dd/	868 150 577650
Carlingford	Carlingford Town	Anderson James	mill & mill dam	-	-	-	Anderson J - Nugent Thos	1835	-	dd/	1835 10 49
Carlingford	Carlingford Town	Rainsford Joseph	The Malt House	-	-	-	Rainsford J - Appointments	1896	-	dd/	1896 78197
Carlingford	Carlingford Town :	Panton Paul	manor mill	-	-	-	Panton Paul - Lowe Wm	1849	-	dd/	1849 19 96
Newry	Carmeen	Coulter Richard	bleach	-	-	2.3.0	-	-	20x5x20 2 bms :	vmb/	5
Newry	Carmeen	Coulter Richard	bleach	-	-	-	-	-	20x5x20 4 bms :	vmb/	5
Newry	Carmeen	Coulter Richard	bleach	-	-	-	-	-	20x5x20 2 bms :	vmb/	5
Newry	Carmeen	Coulter Richard	wash	-	-	-	-	-	16x4x16	vmb/	5
Newry	Carmeen	Gordon George	flax	-	-	-	-	-	14x4x5 6 bths :	vmb/	5
Newry	Carmeen	Gordon George	flax	-	-	3.3.0	-	-	14x3x5 4 berths	vmb/	5
Newry	Carmeen :	Coulter Richard	flax & bleach	Incumb Estate :	-	-	- sold to I.W. Dickson	1855	-	mlyIE	p53
K`mre / Newry	Carnacally	-	mills	-	-	-		-	-	6"os/	30
Maghera	Carnacavill	- at Tollymore	corn	-	-	-	-	-	-	1"os/	61
Bangor	Carnalea	-	flax	-	-	-	-	-	-	6"os/	52
Bangor	Carnalea	-	ruins of mill	-	-	-	-	-	-	6"os/	52
Drumgath	Carnany	Fairlie	mill	-	-	-	Fairlie & wife - Reilly John	1739	-	dd/	99 416 69834
Kilmore	Carncally	Harris Arthur	corn & flax	-	26a.	-	-	-	-	gr/	-
Donaghadee	Carney Hill	-		-	-	-	-	-	-	6"os/	7
Killaney	Carrickmaddyroe	-	windmill stump	-	-	-	-	-	-	6"os/	15
Killaney	Carrickmaddyroe	Fitzsimmons Richd	Boardmills	-	20a.	30	-	-	-	gr/	-
Killaney	Carrickmaddyroe	Fitzsimmons Richd	flax & stores	-	-	-	-	-	-	gr/	-
Killinchy	Carrickmannan	Duggan Willaim	corn (unfin.)	-	-	-	-	-	-	gr/	-
Co. Down	Carrickruskey	Spratt John :	E mill	-	-	-	Spratt Jn - Johnston Jas :	1823	Mort. 1 Jan.	dd/	778 322 527057
Co. Down	Carrickruskey	Spratt Thomas :	mill	-	-	-	Spratt Thos - Spratt Andr :	1822	-	dd/	775 471 525406
Ballee	Carrownacaw	-	corn	-	-	-		-	-	6"os/	31
Ballee	Carrownacaw	-	windmill	-	-	-		-	-	6"os/	31
Ballee	Carrownacaw	M`Murray John	corn & kiln	-	40a		-	-	-	gr/	-
Dundonald	Carrowreagh	-	bleach & lake	-	-	-	-	-	-	6"os/	5
Dundonald	Carrowreagh	-	flax & pond	-	-	-	-	-	-	6"os/	5
Dundonald	Carrowreagh	-	mill & pond	-	-	-	-	-	-	6"os/	5
Dundonald	Carrowreagh	M`Ilwaine William	flax	-	26a.	21	-	-	-	gr/	-
Dundonald	Carrowreagh	M`Ilwaine William	old flax mill	-	-	9	-	-	-	gr/	-
Saul	Carrowvanny	McGlennon Patkick	corn	-	-	2.2.0	-	-	15x3x10.6	vmb/	5
Saintfield	Carsonstown	M`Burney Alex	flour	-	-	-	-	-	-	gr/	-
Newry	Castle Ennigan	Scott David	bleach	-	-	-	-	-	- out of lease	vmb/	5
Ballyculter	Castle Ward	-	corn, saw	refurbished	-	-	Castleward Estate	2001	exhibition	pWEH	C
Ballyculter	Castleward	Bangor Viscount	corn	-	-	9.3.0	-	-	13x5x4.6 2 pr st.	vmb/	5
Loughlinisland	Claragh	-	flax	-	-	-		-	-	6"os/	36
Loughlinisland	Claragh	Ash Hugh	flax	-	-	-	-	-	18x2x10 3 bths	vmb/	5
Slanes	Clarkill	-	bleach	(Green Vale)	-	-	-	-	-	6"os/	-
Slanes	Clarkill	-	flax & corn	-	-	-	-	-	-	6"os/	-
Slanes	Clarkill	- nr Annsborough	linen factory	-	-	-	-	-	-	6"os/	-
Slanes	Clarkill	Hanna James	corn	-	1a.	-	-	-	-	gr/	-
Slanes	Clarkill	Hanna James	flax	-	-	-	-	-	-	gr/	-
Slanes	Clarkill	Murland Sam & Chas	bleach	-	8a.	-	-	-	-	gr/	-
Slanes	Clarkill	Murland Sam & Chas	flax spinning	-	-	-	-	-	-	gr/	-
Newry	Cloghanramer	-	corn	(Green`s Farm)	-	-	-	-	-	1"os/	60
Kilmegan	Cloghram	M`Cauley	corn & kiln	-	1.3.30	-	-	-	-	gr/	-
Drumgooland	Cloghskelt	M`Auley	corn	-	16a.	-	-	-	-	gr/	-
Drumgooland	Cloghskelt	Rowan William	flax	-	24a	-	-	-	-	gr/	-

PARISH	TOWNLAND	MILLER	TYPE	HOUSE	Land	£Val+(	PROPRIETORS	Date	WHEEL etc.	Record	Ref.
Co. Down	Clonbroney	-	cloth	-	-	-	-	-	-	1"os/	60
Co. Down	Clonknaverty	Johnston James :	mill	-	-	-	Johnston - Patten	-	-	dd/	806 183 543719
Co. Down	Clonknaverty	Reilly John :	mill	-	-	-	Reilly J - Reilly Miles & Franc	1821	-	dd/	793 524 536259
Kilmegan	Cloughran	Kirkpatrick Matthew	corn	-	-	-	-	-	14x2x7.6 breast	vmb/	5
Castleboy	Cloughy	McDonnell Hugh :	mill	-	-	-	McDonnell Hu. - Echlin Jn	1823	-	dd/	780 355 528290
Castleboy	Cloughy	Miller Henry	corn & kiln	-	-	-	-	-	-	gr/	-
Castleboy	Cloughy	Miller Henry	corn & kiln	-	-	-	-	-	-	gr/	-
Castleboy	Cloughy	Wallace Hugh	mill	-	-	-	Wallace Hugh - Houston Jn	1821	-	dd/	763 92 517827
Annahilt	Cluntagh	-	flax	-	-	-	-	-	-	6"os/	-
Annahilt	Cluntagh	-	mill	-	-	-	-	-	-	6"os/	22
Annahilt	Cluntagh	Mineely Thomas	flax	-	-	5.0.0	-	-	-	gr/	-
Co. Down	Clydesford Br.	-	mills	-	-	-	-	-	-	1"os/	37
Co. Down	Colenecran	Hudson William :	mill toll & mulctur	-	-	-	Hudson W - Crawford Geo:	1822	-	dd/	776 508 526043
Co. Down	Comb`s Bridge	- on R Bann	flax	-	-	-	-	-	-	1"os/	-
Comber	Comber	Caldwell Charles :	tuck mill & land	- house & gdn.	28a.	-	Caldwell C - Humphry John :	1738			
Comber	Comber T`parks	Alexander Alex	corn, mill pond	-	3a.	20	-	-	-	gr/	-
Comber	Comber T`parks	Andrews Reps Jas	beetling	-	-	-	-	-	-	gr/	-
Comber	Comber T`parks	Andrews Reps Jas	flour, store, yd	-	5a.	335	-	-	-	gr/	-
Comber	Comber T`parks	Andrews Reps Jas	thrashing	-	-	-	-	-	-	gr/	-
Comber	Comber T`parks	Andrews William	corn & kiln	-	-	2	-	-	-	gr/	-
Comber	Comber T`parks	Miller John	distillery, malt ho.	-	1.1.9	3	-	-	-	gr/	-
Comber	Comber Town	-	bleach	-	-	-	-	-	-	6"os/	10
Comber	Comber Town	-	distillery (new)	-	-	-	-	-	-	6"os/	10
Comber	Comber Town	-	flour	-	-	-	-	-	-	6"os/	10
Comber	Comber Town	-	saw	-	-	-	-	-	-	6"os/	10
Bangor	Conlig	- nr Balloo Ho	flax	-	-	-	-	-	-	1"os/	-
Bangor	Conlig	Appleton Arthur :	mill	-	-	-	Appleton A - Lowry John :	1825	-	dd/	808 183 544918
Dromore	Coolsallagh	Ardery Robert	beetling, store	-	-	-	-	-	-	gr/	-
Dromore	Coolsallagh	Ardery Robert	corn, flax, kiln	-	15a.	-	-	-	-	gr/	-
Tullylish	Coose	-	bleach	-	-	-	-	-	-	6"os/	26
Tullylish	Coose	-	flax spinning	electricity generation		-	-	2009	-	mmSv/	nk - B
Tullylish	Coose	-	flax spinning	now Business Units		-	-	2009	-	mmSv/	nk - C
Tullylish	Coose	Crawford George	lapping	-	-	8.0.0	-	-	-	gr/	-
Tullylish	Coose	Law Samuel	spinning	-	-	28	-	-	14.0x12.0x6.6 :	vmb/	5
Tullylish	Coose	Law Samuel :	flax spinning	& land [+t'ts. hos.]	80a	290	-	1856	-	gr/	a.a.lre.ie
Co. Down	Cornakelly	Harris Robert :	mill	-	-	-	Harris R - Harris Arthur : (	1822	-	dd/	776 200 525735
Killinchy	Craigaruskey	-	flax	-	-	-	-	-	-	6"os/	17
Newtownards	Craigogantlet	Moore James	flax	-	-	2.0.0	-	-	-	gr/	-
Loughlinisland	Creeghduff	Perry Maxwell	flax	-	-	2.2.0	-	-	15x3x15 4 berths	vmb/	5
Kilmore	Creevycarnonan	-	flax	-	-	-	-	-	-	6"os/	23
Knockbreda	Cregagh	Bernard & Koch	flax	-	14a.	-	-	-	-	gr/	-
Newry	Croreagh	- nr Glenny Br	corn	-	-	-	-	-	-	1"os/	60
Kilcoo	Cross	- nr Trassy Br	flax	-	-	-	-	-	-	1"os/	60
Dromara	Crossgar	- on R. Lagan	flax	-	-	-	-	-	-	6"os/	28
Dromara	Crossgar	- at Glasswater Br.	flax	-	-	-	-	-	-	1"os/	49
Dromara	Crossgar	Boyde John B	corn	-	-	45	-	-	-	gr/	-
Dromara	Crossgar	Boyde John B	flax	-	-	-	-	-	-	gr/	-
Blaris	Culcavey	-	distilery	-	-	-	-	-	-	6"os/	14
Blaris	Culcavey	Bradshaw Hercules	distillery	-	-	17	-	-	36x6x35 2 pr st.	vmb/	5
Blaris	Culcavey	Bradshaw rep Herc	corn & kilns	-	6a.	80	-	-	-	gr/	-
Blaris	Culcavey	Bradshaw rep Herc	old distillery	-	-	-	-	-	-	gr/	-
Comber	Cullintraw	-	flour & corn	-	-	-	-	-	-	6"os/	10

PARISH	TOWNLAND	MILLER	TYPE	HOUSE	Land	£Val+	PROPRIETORS	Date	WHEEL etc.	Record	Ref.
Comber	Cullintraw	Shaw Robert	corn & kiln	-	18a.	40	-	-	-	gr/	-
Comber	Cullintraw	Shaw Robert	flax	-	-	-	-	-	-	gr/	-
Comber	Cullintraw :	Hamilton	mill	-	-	-	Hamilton - Johnson	-	-	dd/	8 305 2804
Comber	Cullintraw :	Johnson	mill	-	-	-	Johnson - Lambert	-	-	dd/	63 21 2468
Comber	Cullintraw :	Lambert	mill	-	-	-	Lambert - Rainey	-	-	dd/	72 133 50091
Newtownards	Cunningburn	Cooper Hugh & :	flax & store	-	-	7	-	-	-	gr/	-
Newtownards	Cunningburn	Cooper Hugh & : F	corn & kiln	-	-	45	-	-	-	gr/	-
Newtownards	Cunningburn	Cooper Hugh & : F	flax & store	-	-	5	-	-	-	gr/	-
Newtownards	Cunningburn	Cooper Hugh & : F	flax, mill pond	-	-	-	-	-	-	gr/	-
Newtownards	Cunningburn	Wallace James	flax	-	51a.	61	-	-	-	gr/	-
Newry	Dalmolly	Boyd & Glenny M/s	corn	-	-	34.1	-	-	16x10x6 4 pr st.	vmb/	5
Newry	Dalmolly	Boyd & Glenny M/s	flour	-	-	20	-	-	16x5x6 3 pr st.	vmb/	5
Newry	Derryboy	Chirrey	mill	-	-	-	Chirrey - Martin	-	-	dd/	798 400 539135
Newry	Derrylekagh	Parsons Samuel	corn	-	-	26	-	-	16x5x6 3 pr st.	vmb/	5
Newry	Derrylekagh	Parsons Samuel	flour	-	-	12	-	-	20x4x20 2 pr st.	vmb/	5
Newry	Derrylekagh	Parsons Samuel	flour	-	-	50	-	-	20x4x18 (x2) :	vmb/	5
Annaclone	Derrylough	Todd	mill	-	-	-	Todd - Potts	-	-	dd/	794 269 536604
Drumgooland	Derryneill	M`Avoy Bernard	flax, corn, kiln	-	8a.	15	-	-	-	gr/	-
Newry	Desert	-	mill	-	-	-	-	-	-	1"os/	60
Newry	Desert	Glenny Isaac	corn	-	-	-	-	-	- out of use	vmb/	5
Newry	Desert	Scott Andrew	flax	-	-	-	-	-	14x3x5 4 berths	vmb/	5
Newry	Desert	Weir William	flax	-	-	-	-	-	15x3x6 4 berths	vmb/	5
Donaghadee	Donaghadee	Cromellin Nicholas :	mill	-	-	-	Cromellin N - Orr James :	1821	-	dd/	759 230 515565
Donaghadee	Donaghadee	Cromellin Nicholas : D	mill	-	-	-	Cromellin N - Wallace John :	1875	Mort. 1 Dec.	dd/	809 158 459494
Donaghadee	Donaghadee	Fulton James	mill	-	-	-	Fulton J - Belfast & Co Dn.	1903	-	dd/	1903 19 186
Donaghadee	Donaghadee	Fulton James	mill	-	-	-	Fulton J - Ulster Bank Ltd.	1903	-	dd/	1903 46 69
Donaghadee	Donaghadee T`pk	Carmichael David	old corn & kiln	-	1.0.4	-	-	-	-	gr/	-
Donaghacloney	Donaghcloney	Brown James	bleach	-	-	-	-	2009	-	mmSv/	nk - Z
D`aghacloney	Donaghcloney	Brown James	bleach (3)	-	-	31.4	-	-	13x5x8 9x5x8 & :	vmb/	5
Donaghcloney	Donaghcloney	Liddal Wm & Morris	bleach	-	27a.	-	-	-	-	gr/	-
Slannnes	Dooey	-	windmill stump	-	-	-		-	-	6"os/	32
Down	Down Demense	-	corn store, kiln	-	-	-		-	-	6"os/	38
Down	Down Demense :	Saul Arthur W	brewery	ho., offs., yd., gdn.	0.0.20	60		1856	-	gr/	a.a.Ire.ie
Down	Downpatrick Town :	Boyd Edmond	brewery & yard	-	-	-	Boyd Edm - Keith Andrew	1890	-	dd/	1890 42 4
Down	Downpatrick Town	Johnson Beauchamp	brewery	-	-	-	Johnson B - White John	1881	-	dd/	1881 38 154
Down	Downpatrick Town	Johnston Arthur :	saw	stores, offices & :	-	60	-	1856	-	gr/	a.a.Ire.ie
Down	Downpatrick Town	McGusty William	Down Brewery	-	-	-	McGusty William - William	1889	-	dd/	188923136
Down	Downpatrick Town	Meredith Henry	Dicksons Mills	-	-	-	Meredith - Hozier Jas H C	1887	-	dd/	1887388
Down	Downpatrick Town	Murland James	The Brewery :	-	-	-	Murland Jas - Perry Mary	1886	-	dd/	1886 34 161
Down	Downpatrick Town	Nicholson John	brewery & Mill	-	-	-	Nicholson John - William	1892	-	dd/	1892 38 244
Down	Downpatrick Town	Perry Joseph	brewery	-	-	-	Perry Jos - Hutton John	1883	-	dd/	1881 44 251
Down	Downpatrick Town	Ward Robert	Mill of Down	-	-	-	Ward Robt - Kennedy Robt	1880	-	dd/	1880 59 112
Down	Downpatrick Town	Watson Hugh	brewery & mill	-	-	-	Watson Hugh - Hugh	1885	-	dd/	1885 20 121
Down	Downpatrick Town	Whisker James	starch works	offices, yd. & gdn.	0.0.22	23	-	1856	-	gr/	a.a.Ire.ie
Down	Downpatrick Town :	Meredyth Henry B	mill	-	-	-	Meredyth H - Harrietta A	1884	-	dd/	1884 3 300
Down	Downpatrick Town :	Ire. Bank Governors	mills	-	-	-	Ir.B.Govs. - Meredyth H`ta	1884	-	dd/	1884 7283
Down	Downpatrick Town :	- - -	brewery	-	-	-	-	1879	-	dd/	1879 34 170
Down	Downpatrick Town :	Ward Robert	corn	-	-	-	Ward Rbt - Dunleath Baron	1896	-	dd/	1896 26 67
Down	Downpatrick Town :	Meredyth Harrrietta	mills	-	-	-	Meredyth H - Ir. Bank Govs.	1880	-	dd/	1880 17 106
Down	Downpatrick Town :	Mulholland William	mills	-	-	-	Mulholland - McClintock Alx	1877	-	dd/	1877 32 16
Down	Downpatrick Town :	Hozier James H C	mills	-	-	-	Hozier - Meredyth Sir Hen	1895	-	dd/	1895 37 83
Down	Downpatrick Town :	Boyd Richard	bleach yard	-	-	-	Boyd R - McClurg Margt.	1883	-	dd/	1883 37 53

PARISH	TOWNLAND	MILLER	TYPE	HOUSE	Land	£Val+(	PROPRIETORS	Date	WHEEL etc.	Record	Ref.
Down	Downpatrick Town :	Irvin William	brewery & bl. yd.	-	-	-	Irvin Wm - McRoberts John	1883	-	dd/	1883 38 223
Down	Downpatrick Town :	Giles John :	Mland	-	-	-	Giles J - Cosgrave Thos :	1829	-	dd/	856 15 571515
Down	Downpatrick Town :	Hope James	mills	-	-	-	Hope Jas - Godfrey Lyle	1878	-	dd/	1878 41 220
Down	Downpatrick Town :	Mulholland William	mills	-	-	-	Mulholland - Brunker Thos	1878	-	dd/	1878 13 108
Down	Downpatrick Town :	Meredyth Sir Henry	mills	-	-	-	Meredyth H - Nat. Bank	1876	-	dd/	1876 22 62
Down	Downpatrick Town :	Landed Estate Court	mills	-	-	-	Ld. Est. Ct. - Mullholland Jn	1876	-	dd/	1876 56 149
Down	Downpatrick Town :	Meredyth Sir Henry	mills	-	-	-	Meredyth H - Mullholland Jn	1876	-	dd/	1880 46 266
Down	Downpatrick Town :	Lithgow Robert T	coach factory	-	-	24	-	1856	-	gr/	a.a.lre.ie
Down	Downpatrick Town :	Boyd Keown	malt kiln	-	-	-	Boyd K - Phillmore Walter	1875	-	dd/	1875 35 41
Down	Downpatrick Town :	Meredyth Henry	mills	-	-	-	Meredyth H - Belcher Jos	1875	-	dd/	1875 3 205
Down	Downpatrick Town :	McMechan James	Mill of Down	-	-	-	McMechan Jas - Elizabeth	1896	-	dd/	1896 11 73
Down	DownpatrickTown	Hale Robert H B	Saul Mill	-	-	-	Hale Robt - Ker David	1839	-	dd/	1839 19 292
Down	DownpatrickTown	Ker Margaret	Saul Mill	-	-	-	Ker Margaret - Hale Robt	1840	-	dd/	1840 4 8
Down	DownpatrickTown	Richardson Jno	distillery & :	-	-	-	Richardson J - Murray Robt	1841	-	dd/	1841 22 296
Down	DownpatrickTown	Richardson Jno	Saul Mill & :	-	-	-	Richardson J - Wallace Wm	1841	-	dd/	1841 16 227
Down	DownpatrickTown	Richardson Jno	tuck mill seat	-	-	-	Richardson J - Murray Robt	1841	-	dd/	1841 22 296
Drumbo	Drennan	- on Boyeagh R.	mill & pond	-	-	-	-	-	-	6"os/	-
Drumbo ?	Drennans	Hamilton Hans	mill, mill lands	-	-	-	Hamilton H - Tisdall Richard	1708	-	dd/	2 141 339
Co. Down	Dromaness	Forde	mill	-	-	-	Forde - Davidson	-	-	dd/	807 131 544266
Dromara	Dromara	- on R Lagan	bleach	-	-	-	-	-	-	6"os/	28
Dromara	Dromara Town	Black Christopher	dilap. mills	-	0.2.0	1.10	-	-	-	gr/	-
Dromara	Dromara Town	Black Christopher	mill pond	-	-	5/-	-	-	-	gr/	-
Dromore	Dromore	Whyte John :	I mill	-	-	-	Whyte J - Moore John :	1721	-	dd/	66 338 47005
Dromore	Dromore Town	Corry Samuel	flax, sawing	-	3a.	-	-	-	-	gr/	-
Dromore	Dromore Town	M`Cartney Edward	corn & kiln	-	-	-	-	-	-	gr/	-
Dromore	Dromore Town	M`Cartney Edward	corn & store	-	-	-	-	-	-	gr/	-
Dromore	Dromore Town	M`Murray Thomas	beetling & bl.	-	14a.	116	-	-	-	gr/	-
Kilmore	Drumacanagher	Filcock Jno	corn	-	-	8.12	-	-	17x5x10 3 pr st.	vmb/	5
Kilmore	Drumacanagher	Filcock Jno	flax	-	-	1.2.0	-	-	14x4x4.6 3 bths	vmb/	5
Kilmore	Drumacanagher	Filcock Jno	flax & tuck	-	-	2.4.0	-	-	13x5x5 3 bths. :	vmb/	5
Kilmore	Drumaghlis	-	flax	-	-	-	-	-	-	6"os/	30
Kilmore	Drumaghlis	M`Murry David	flax	-	43a.	-	-	-	-	gr/	-
Kilmore	Drumaglis	Kinkaird Jno	flax	-	-	2.3.0	-	-	14x2x7 3 berths	vmb/	5
Magheradrool	Drumaness	Davidson Jno	bleach	-	-	17.11	-	-	22x4x21 1 beam	vmb/	5
Magheradrool	Drumaness	Davidson Jno	bleach	-	-	13.3	-	-	22x4x21 4 bms	vmb/	5
Magheradrool	Drumaness	Davidson Jno	corn	-	-	15.7	-	-	22x4x21 2 pr st.	vmb/	5
Magheradrool	Drumaness	Davidson John	corn & flax	-	117a	-	-	-	-	gr/	-
Magheradrool	Drumaness	Hurst Chas, CJ & W	flax spinning	-	4a.	-	-	-	-	gr/	-
Magheradrool	Drumaness	Hurst Chas, CJ & W	mill mgr`s ho	-	1a.	-	-	-	-	gr/	-
Magheradrool	Drumaness	Johnston Samuel	flax	-	-	4.12	-	-	14x2x9 3 bths	vmb/	5
Magheradrool	Drumaness	Macoubrie Robert	flax mills	-	68a.	-	-	-	-	gr/	-
Magheradrool	Drumaness	McCoubry Robert	bleach	-	-	-	-	-	13x1x7.6 2 bms :	vmb/	5
Loughlinisland	Drumaroad	-	corn	-	-	-		-	-	6"os/	36
Loughlinisland	Drumaroad	-	flax	-	-	-		-	-	6"os/	36
Loughlinisland	Drumaroad	- at Ballinahinch	flax	-	-	-	-	-	-	1"os/	49
Loughlinisland	Drumaroad	Shaw Hugh	corn	-	-	5.17	-	-	15x4x14 2 pr st.	vmb/	5
Loughlinisland	Drumaroad	Shaw Hugh	corn, flax, kiln	-	50a.	-	-	-	-	gr/	-
Loughlinisland	Drumaroad	Shaw Hugh	flax	-	-	3.7.0	-	-	16x4x13 6 berths	vmb/	5
Drumb`yroney	Drumballyroney	Hanna David	corn & kiln	-	64a.	-	-	-	-	gr/	-
Moira	Drumbane	-	corn	-	-	-	-	-	-	6"os/	13
Moira	Drumbane	McKinley Jno	corn	-	-	4.7.0	-	-	13x2x11	vmb/	5
Moira	Drumbane	Monroe Daniel	corn (dilap.)	-	-	-	-	-	-	gr/	-

PARISH	TOWNLAND	MILLER	TYPE	HOUSE	Land	£Val+	PROPRIETORS	Date	WHEEL etc.	Record	Ref.
Drumbeg	Drumbeg	-	mill	-	-	-	-	-	-	6"os/	8
Drumbeg	Drumbeg	Hunter Alex	corn & kiln	- miller`s ho	3a.	30	-	-	-	gr/	-
Drumbo	Drumbo	Casement Charles :	mill	-	-	-	Casement C - Lyons Wm :	1823	-	dd/	791 89 534624
Drumbo	Drumbo	Lyons William :	mill	-	-	-	Lyons W - Mercer Henry :	1823	Mort. 27 Nov.	dd/	787 30 532165
Drumbo	Drumbo	Rainey William :	mill	-	-	-	Rainey William - Callwell :	1822	-	dd/	778 224 526959
Drumbo	Drumbo	Young William :	mill	-	-	-	Young - Casement Chas :	1823	-	dd/	782 495 529630
Loughlinisland	Drumcaw	Macauley William	flax, corn	-	23a	-	-	-	-	gr/	-
Loughlinisland	Drumcaw	Moore Jno	corn	-	-	4.8	-	-	13x2x12 1 pr st.	vmb/	5
Magheralin	Drumcrow	Waddle Cosleth	bleach	-	-	-	-	-	13x3x8 2 beams :	vmb/	5
Magheralin	Drumcrow	Waddle Cosleth	corn	-	-	7	-	-	14x2x8 1 pr st.	vmb/	5
Magheralin	Drumcrow	Waddle Cosleth	flax	-	-	3.7	-	-	16x6x9 6 beaths	vmb/	5
Magheralin	Drumcrow	Waddle Cosleth	wheat	-	-	1.13	-	-	13x2x7 1 pr st.	vmb/	5
Drumb`yroney	Drumdreenagh	Morrow Margaret	flax	-	20.3	54	-	-	-	gr/	-
Donaghadee	Drumfad	-	windmill stump	-	-	-	-	-	-	6"os/	7
Loughlinisland	Drumgooland	-	-	- refurbished	-	-	Erskine	2001	residence	pWEH	C
Loughlinisland	Drumgooland	-	corn	-	-	-		-	-	6"os/	37
Loughlinisland	Drumgooland	-	flax	-	-	-		-	-	6"os/	37
Loughlinisland	Drumgooland	M`Cammon John	old mill & kiln	-	-	-	-	-	-	gr/	-
Loughlinisland	Drumgooland	M`Cammon John	old mill & kiln	-	-	-	-	-	-	gr/	-
Loughlinisland	Drumgooland	McCammon Wm	corn	-	-	-	-	-	18x4x18 2 pr st.	vmb/	5
Loughlinisland	Drumgooland	McCammon Wm	flax	-	-	-	-	-	14x3x10.6 3 bths	vmb/	5
Down	Drumguillan	Atkinson John	mill	-	-	-	Atkinson J - Hungerford W	1898	-	dd/	1898 38 74
Newtownards	Drumhirk	-	windmill stump	-	-	-	-	-	-	6"os/	6
Dromore	Drummiller	- on R Lagan	bleach	-	-	-	-	-	-	6"os/	21
Magheralin	Drumnabreeze	Waddell Coslett	flax	-	196a.	254	-	-	-	gr/	-
Kilmore	Drumnaconagher	Silcock Christina	corn, flax, kiln	-	54a	-	-	-	-	gr/	-
Seapatrick	Drumnagally	Anne Dunbar	old thread fcty	-	-	-	-	-	-	gr/	-
Aghaderg	Drumnahare	-	mill	-	-	-	-	-	-	6"os/	34
Tullylish	Drumnascamph	- on R. Bann	flax	-	-	-	-	-	-	1"os/	60
Tullylish	Drumnascamph	Lockart David	flax	& gdn. [+t's. hos.]	0.3.0	19	-	1856	-	gr/	a.a.Ire.ie
Tullylish	Drumnascamph	Read Mary	weaving shop	ho., offices & ld.	19a.	26	-	1856	-	gr/	a.a.Ire.ie
Tullylish	Drumnascamph	Reid Joseph	boiling house	-	-	10/-	-	1856	-	gr/	a.a.Ire.ie
Tullylish	Drumnescamp	Lackard David	corn	-	-	10.7	-	-	14x4x3.6 3 pr st.	vmb/	5
Tullylish	Drumnescamp	Lackard David	flax	-	-	5.18	-	-	14x5x3.6 6 berths	vmb/	5
Magheralin	Drumo & D`cro	- on R. Lagan	bleach	-	-	-	-	-	-	6"os/	13
Magheralin	Drumo & D`cro	- on R. Lagan	corn	-	-	-	-	-	-	6"os/	13
Magheralin	Drumo & D`cro	- New Forge Town	corn	-	-	-	-	-	-	6"os/	13
Magheralin	Drumo & D`cro	Waddell Coslett	beetling & flax	-	-	-	-	-	-	gr/	-
Magheralin	Drumo & D`cro	Waddell Coslett	corn & kiln & offs.	-	-	28	-	-	-	gr/	a.a.Ire.ie
Aghaderg	Drumsallagh	Magaw Hugh	flax	-	34a.	46	-	-	-	gr/	-
Dromore	Drumskee	M`Mullen Joseph	corn & kiln	-	-	-	-	-	-	gr/	-
Co. Down	Dundonnell	Dungannon Arthur :	mill	-	-	-	Dungannon A - Alexander :	1821	Mort. 13 May	dd/	764 158 518493
Kilmegan	Dundrum	Robinson Richard	corn	-	-	-	-	-	14x3x9.6 2 pr st.	vmb/	5
Kilmegan	Dundrum	Robinson Richard	flax	-	-	6.12	-	-	14x2x7.6 4bths	vmb/	5
Blaris	Duneight	-	bleach	-	-	-	-	-	-	6"os/	14
Blaris	Duneight	-	corn	-	-	-	-	-	-	1"os/	36
Blaris	Duneight	-	corn	-	-	-	-	-	-	6"os/	14
Blaris	Duneight	Morrow Robert	beetling, wash	-	34a.	94	-	-	-	gr/	-
Co. Down	Dunnaval	- on coast	slate	-	-	-	-	-	-	1"os/	71
Co. Down	Eastwood	-	old windmill	-	-	-	-	-	-	1"os/	71
Magheralin	Eden Ballycoggill	Greer George	bleach (2)	-	-	21.5	-	-	13x4x7 13x4x5.6	vmb/	5
Magheralin	Eden Ballycoggill	Nicholl & Parks	bleach works	ho., offs. & land	34a.	150	-	1856	-	gr/	a.a.Ire.ie

PARISH	TOWNLAND	MILLER	TYPE	HOUSE	Land	£Val+(	PROPRIETORS	Date	WHEEL etc.	Record	Ref.
Dromara	Edendarrif	McCammon David	corn	-	-	5.5	-	-	14x3x14	vmb/	5
Seapatrick	Edenderry	-	bleach	-	-	-	-	-	-	6"os/	27
Seapatrick	Edenderry	-	bleach green	-	-	-	-	-	-	6"os/	27
Seapatrick	Edenderry	Ferguson Thomas	linen	-	-	-	-	2009	-	mmSv/	nk - Z
Seapatrick	Edenderry	Ferguson Thomas	linen w`house	-		-	-	-	-	gr/	-
Seapatrick	Edenderry	Ferguson Thomas	linen yn. store	-	-	-	-	-	-	gr/	-
Seapatrick	Edenderry	Hayes Richard	bleach	new houses	-	-	-	2009	-	mmSv/	nk - D
Seapatrick	Edenderry	Hayes Richard	bleach & bt	- Millmount	51a.	314	-	-	-	gr/	-
Drumbo	Edenderry	Russell Houston	flour	-	-	-	-	2009	-	mmSv/	nk - Z
Drumbo	Edenderry	Russell Houston	flour & stores	-	46a.	247	-	-	-	gr/	-
Dromore	Edenordinary	-	corn	-	-	-	-	-	-	6"os/	27
Dromore	Edenordinary	-	flax, mill pond	-	-	-	-	-	-	6"os/	27
Dromore	Edenordinary	Watts William	corn	-	24a.	67	-	-	-	gr/	-
Dromore	Edenordinary	Watts William	corn	-	-	-	-	2009	-	mmSv/	nk - Z
Comber	Edenslate	Bennett John	corn & kiln	-	107a	125	-	-	-	gr/	-
Comber	Edenslate	Bennett John	flax	-	-	-	-	-	-	gr/	-
Inch	Finnabrogue	-	corn	-	-	-		-	-	6"os/	31
Inch	Finnabrogue	Maxwell Jno W	corn	-	-	2.13	-	-	14x5x3.6 1 pr st.	vmb/	5
Inch	Finnabrogue	Maxwell John W	corn & kiln	-	-	-	-	-	-	gr/	-
Inch	Finnabrogue	Maxwell John W	stewd`s ho, fm	-	505a	-	-	-	-	gr/	-
Newry	Finnard	Scott George	flax	-	-	3.12	-	-	19x9x13 8 berths	vmb/	5
Dromara	Finnis	-	corn	-	-	-		-	-	6"os/	35
Dromara	Finnis	Singers William	corn	miller`s ho	-	10	-	-	-	gr/	-
Donaghadee	Ganaway	Ewart Francis	flax	-	34a.	57	-	-	-	gr/	-
Drumgooland	Gargarry	-	mill	-	-	-	-	-	-	6"os/	-
Drumgooland	Gargarry	Ward John	corn & flax	-	1.1.0	18.10	-	-	-	gr/	-
Drumgooland	Gargarry	Ward John	pond	miller`s ho	-		-	-	-	gr/	-
Garvaghy	Garvaghy	-	mill (x 2)	-	-	-	-	-	-	6"os/	28
Tullylish	Gilford	Shannon	mill	-	-	-	Shannon - Law	-	-	dd/	799 87 539422
Tullylish	Gilford Town	M`Master Jno W & :	flax spinning	-	-	840	-	-	-	gr/	-
Tullylish	Gilford Town	M`Master Jno W & :	gas wks, wv fty	-	-	50	-	-	-	gr/	-
Tullylish	Gilford Town	M`Master Jno W & :	thread m`fty	-	-	50	-	-	-	gr/	-
Tullylish	Gilford Town	Thompson John	corn	-	-	12	-	-	16x4x10 2 pr st.	vmb/	5
Dromore	Gill Hall Dm`se	- on R Lagan	CoolsallaghMill	-	-	-	-	-	-	6"os/	20
Knockbreda	Gilnahirk	Orr John	flax	-	0.5a.	-	-	-	-	gr/	-
Magheradrool	Glasdrumman	Bennett James	corn, mill pond	-	20a.	35	-	-	-	gr/	-
Aghaderg	Glaskermore	Corbett Robt	corn, flax, kiln	-	-	60	-	-	-	gr/	-
M`drl or K`kel	Glassdrumman	Bennett James	corn & kiln	miller`s house :	20a	-	-	-	-	gr/	-
Saintfield	Glassdrumman	McBurnet Alex	corn & kiln	-	27a.	93	-	-	-	gr/	-
Saintfield	Glassdrumman	McBurnet Alex	flax	-	-	-	-	-	-	gr/	-
Saintfield	Glassdrumman	McBurnet Alex	mill pond (part)	-	4a.	-	-	-	-	gr/	-
Saintfield	Glassdrumman	Thompson John	corn	-	8a.	53	-	-	-	gr/	-
Saintfield	Glassdrumman	Thompson John	flax	-	-	-	-	-	-	gr/	-
Saintfield	Glassdrumman	Thompson John	old flour mill	-	-	25	-	-	-	gr/	-
Co. Down	Glennalina	-	bleach	-	-	-	-	-	-	1"os/	36
Knockbreda	Gortgrib	-	mill	-	-	-	-	-	-	6"os/	5
Drumb`yroney	Grallaghgreenan	Cromie John	flax	-	17a.	-	-	-	-	gr/	-
Drumb`yroney	Grallaghgreenan	Swan Robert	flax	-	73a.	89	-	-	-	gr/	-
Bright	Grangewalls	-	corn	-	-	-		-	-	6"os/	38
Bright	Grangewalls	Carson Joseph	corn & kiln	-	7a.	27	-	-	-	gr/	-
Bright	Grangewalls	Megrann William	corn & flax	-	-	18.3	-	-	16x3x10 2 pr st.	vmb/	5
Bright	Grangewalls	O`Neill Ambrose	corn	-	-	-	O`Neill A - Herv O`Hara	1728	-	dd/	46 90 27805

PARISH	TOWNLAND	MILLER	TYPE	HOUSE	Land	£Val+	PROPRIETORS	Date	WHEEL etc.	Record	Ref.
Newry	Gransha	-	flax	-	-	-	-	2001	-	pWEH	B
Newry	Gransha	-	flour, corn	-	-	-	-	-	-	6"os/	10
Newry	Gransha	-	Gransha Mills	-	-	-	-	-	-	6"os/	10
Newry	Gransha	- at Lisleen Vge.	mill	-	-	-	-	-	-	6"os/	10
Comber	Gransha	Lamont John	corn	-	41a.	102	-	-	-	gr/	-
Newry	Gransha	Little David	flax	-	-	1.4.0	-	-	12x2x12 3 berths	vmb/	5
Comber	Gransha	M`Cullagh John	corn & kiln	-	3a.	13	-	-	-	gr/	-
Comber	Gransha	M`Cullagh John	flax, mill pond	-	129a.	166	-	-	-	gr/	-
Newry	Gransha	near La Mon Hotel	scutch	ruins only	-	-	Leslie Huddleson	2001	-	pWEH	R
Co. Down	Gransha	Roberts	mill	-	-	-	Roberts - Spencer	-	-	dd/	807 401 544536
Co. Down	Gransha	Thompson	mill	-	-	-	Thompson - Spencer	-	-	dd/	807 400 544535
Comber	Gransha	Warnock James	flax	-	10a.	17.10	-	-	-	gr/	-
Co. Down	Gransha	Young	mill	-	-	-	Young - Young	-	-	dd/	808 362 545097
Aghaderg	Greenan	Carswell John	boiling ho. & pon(	-	-	-	-	-	-	gr/	-
Aghaderg	Greenan	M`Clelland John	corn & kiln	-	0.3.0	28	-	-	-	gr/	-
Aghaderg	Greenan	M`Clelland John	flax	(Greenan Ho)	26a.	-	-	-	-	gr/	-
Aghaderg	Greenan	Wallace James	flour	-	5a.	24	-	-	-	gr/	-
Kilkeel	Greencastle	Rainey Robert :	mill	-	-	-	Rainey R - Moore John :	1733	-	dd/	77 108 52988
Grey Abbey	Grey Abbey	-	flax	-	-	-	-	-	-	1"os/	37
Grey Abbey	Greyabbey	-	old flax mill	-	-	-	-	-	-	6"os/	11
Grey Abbey	Greyabbey	Montgomery James :	mill	-	-	-	Montgomery J - Cartney :	1712	-	6"os/	11
Co. Down	Hazel Park	Haris	bl. green, mill	-	-	-	Harris - Harris	-	-	dd/	776 200 525735
Lambeg	Hilden	-	thread, corn	-	-	-	-	-	-	1"os/	36
Drumbeg	Hillhall	-	mill	-	-	-	-	-	-	6"os/	9
Drumbeg	Hillhall	-	windmill	-	-	-	-	-	-	6"os/	15
Drumbeg	Hillhall	Hunter James S	corn, mill pond	-	18a.	40	-	-	-	gr/	-
Co. Down	Hillhead	-	corn	(Agnes Vale)	-	-	-	-	-	1"os/	-
Co. Down	Hillhead	- on Ravernet R.	mill	-	-	-	-	-	-	1"os/	36
Hillsborough	Hillsborough	Henderson James	corn (2)	-	-	9.13	-	-	12x2x7 18x3x18 :	vmb/	5
Kilcoo	Hilltown	-	corn	-	-	-	-	-	-	1"os/	60
Kilcoo	Hilltown	-	flax	-	-	-	-	-	-	1"os/	60
Donaghadee	Hogstown	-	flax & pond	-	-	-	-	-	-	6"os/	52
Co. Down	Hollybank	- nr Dundonald	corn (x2)	-	-	-	-	-	-	1"os/	37
Co. Down	Hollybank	- nr Dundonald	mill	-	-	-	-	-	-	1"os/	37
Bangor	Holywood	-	mill	-	-	-	-	-	-	6"os/	57
Bangor	Holywood	-	mill, mill-pond	-	-	-	-	-	-	6"os/	57
Ballytrustan	Kearney	-	flax	-	-	-		-	-	6"os/	32
Ballytrustan	Kearney	- at Kearney Town	flax	-	-	-		-	-	6"os/	32
Ballytrustan	Kearney	Cavan & Hastings	flax & store	-	9.2.5	-	-	-	-	gr/	-
Ballytrustan	Kearney	M`Mullen William	corn & kiln	-	36a	-	-	-	-	gr/	-
Tullylish	Kernan	-	corn	-	-	-	-	-	-	6"os/	26
Tullylish	Kernan	-	flax	-	-	-	-	-	-	6"os/	26
Tullylish	Kernan	Moles Oliver	corn	-	-	3.7.0	-	-	14x2x18	vmb/	5
Tullylish	Kernan	Moles Oliver	flax	-	-	1.10	-	-	14x2x14 4 berths	vmb/	5
Tullylish	Kernan Upr	Lockhart Thomas	corn	-	55a	-	-	-	-	gr/	-
Tullylish	Kernan Upr	Lockhart Thomas	flax	-	-	-	-	-	-	gr/	-
Kilbroney	Kilbroney	-	cloth	-	-	-	-	-	-	1"os/	-
Kilbroney	Kilbroney	Martin David	bleach & bt	-	53a	-	-	-	-	gr/	-
Kilclief	Kilclief	-	corn	-	-	-	-	-	-	6"os/	39
Kilclief	Kilclief	-	flax	-	-	-	-	-	-	6"os/	39
Kilclief	Kilclief	Hanna Patrick	corn & kiln	-	80a.	105	-	-	-	gr/	-
Kilcliess	Kilcliess	Hanna Patrick	corn	-	-	3.9.0	-	-	13x2x9.6 1 pr st.	vmb/	5

PARISH	TOWNLAND	MILLER	TYPE	HOUSE	Land	£Val+(	PROPRIETORS	Date	WHEEL etc.	Record	Ref.
Kilcliess	Kilcliess	Hanna Patrick	flax	-	-	3.10	-	-	13x2x7.6 3 berths	vmb/	5
Kilkeel	Kilkeel	Wamsley Andrew	corn, flax, kiln	-	100a.	-	-	-	-	gr/	-
Kilkeel	Kilkeel	Wamsley James	corn	-	-	5.17	-	-	14x3x9 1 pr st.	vmb/	5
Kilkeel	Kilkeel	Wamsley James	flax	-	-	-	-	-	14x4x9 4 berths	vmb/	5
Newtownards	Killarn	M`Ilwain William	corn & kiln	Mill Bank Ho.	54a.	88	-	-	-	gr/	-
Killinchy	Killinchy	-	corn	-	-	-	-	-	-	1"os/	37
Klilinchy	Killinchy	-	corn	-	-	-	-	-	-	6"os/	23
Killinchy	Killinchy	-	flax	-	-	-	-	-	-	1"os/	37
Klilinchy	Killinchy	M`Gilton Hugh	corn & flax	-	4.0.10	-	-	-	-	gr/	-
Rathmullan	Killough	Leslie Trs./ Chas A	windmill & kiln	-	-	-	-	-	-	gr/	-
Rathmullan	Killough	unoccupied	wind-mill, kiln	-	-	-	-	-	-	gr/	-
Rathmullan	Killough	Wilson John	ho & garden	-	-	10	-	-	-	gr/	-
Killyleagh	Killyleagh Town	Carr John & Joseph	flax spinning	-	9.0.0	-	-	-	-	gr/	-
Co. Down	Kilmole	-	corn	-	-	-	-	-	-	6"os/	13
Co. Down	Kilmole	-	flax & corn	-	-	-	-	-	-	6"os/	13
Kilmood	Kilmood	-	LuskeyCornmill	-	-	-	-	-	-	6"os/	15
Kilmood	Kilmood	Shaw Frew	corn & kiln	-	1a.	24	-	-	-	gr/	-
Shankill	Kilmore	- nr Crossgar	corn	-	-	-	-	-	-	1"os/	49
Shankill	Kilmore	Clarke John	corn	-	23a.	-	-	-	-	gr/	-
Shankill	Kilmore	Clarke John	corn	-	-	5.2	-	-	14x2x8	vmb/	5
Shankill	Kilmore	Clarke John	flax	-	-	3.19	-	-	14x3x9 4 berths	vmb/	5
Shankill	Kilmore	Hungerford Winspeare	mill	-	-	-	Hungerford - I. Bank Govs.	1903	-	dd/	1903 69 102
Shankill	Kilmore	Langtry George	corn	-	-	4.7	-	-	13x2x7.6	vmb/	5
Seapatrick	Kilpike	-	bleach (x3)	-	-	-	-	-	-	6"os/	27
Seapatrick	Kilpike	-	flax	-	-	-	-	-	-	6"os/	27
Seapatrick	Kilpike	-	flour	-	-	-	-	-	-	6"os/	27
Seapatrick	Kilpike	-	windmill	-	-	-	-	-	-	6"os/	27
Seapatrick	Kilpike	Hayes William	spinning	-	29a.	-	-	-	-	gr/	-
Seapatrick	Kilpike	Hayes William	thread factory	-	-	-	-	-	-	gr/	-
Seapatrick	Kilpike	- Tn of Banbridge	thread m`fty	-	-	-	-	-	-	6"os/	27
Dromore	Kinallen	-	corn	-	-	-	-	-	-	6"os/	27
Dromore	Kinallen	Chambres James	-	miller`s & k`m hos.	-	-	-	-	-	gr/	-
Dromore	Kinallen	Chambres James	corn & kiln	-	28a.	48	-	-	-	gr/	-
Dromore	Kinallen Common	Doake Samuel	old corn mill	-	-	6	-	-	-	gr/	-
Inishargy	Kircubbin	-	mill	-	-	-	-	-	-	1"os/	37
Inishargy	Kircubbin	Hamilton Hans	mill, mill lands	-	-	-	Hamilton H - Tisdall Richard	1708	-	dd/	2 141 339
Dundonald	Knock	Martin	mills	-	-	-	Martin - Hunter	-	-	dd/	737 435 524170
Kilbroney	Knockbarragh	-	corn	-	-	-	-	-	-	1"os/	60
D`bo / K`brda	Knockbrackan	-	mill	-	-	-	-	-	-	6"os/	9
Tullylish	Knocknagore	Lockhart David	corn	-	45a	-	-	-	-	gr/	-
Loughlinisland	Knocksticken	- nr Seaforde	mill	-	-	-	-	-	-	1"os/	49
Loughlinisland	Knocksticken	Macauley William	mill pond	-	18a.	-	-	-	-	gr/	-
Drumb`yroney	Lackan	-	flax	-	-	-	-	-	-	1"os/	60
Lambeg	Lambeg	-	bleach	-	-	-	-	-	-	1"os/	36
Dromore	Lappoges	- on R Lagan	flax	-	-	-	-	-	-	6"os/	21
Dromore	Lappoges	Creighton Alex	flax	-	25a.	25	-	-	-	gr/	-
Blaris	Largymore	Coulson Jas Ward	damask factory	-	1a.	18	-	-	-	gr/	-
Blaris	Largymore	Thompson William	weaving factory	- manager`s ho	2a.	60	-	-	-	gr/	-
Co. Down	Ledliestown	- near Newry	bleach	-	-	-	-	-	-	1"os/	-
Drumbo	Legacurry	-	mill (x 2)	-	-	-	-	-	-	6"os/	15
Drumbo	Legacurry	- on Ravernet R.	Legacurry Mill	-	-	-	-	-	-	1"os/	36
Drumbo	Legacurry	Morrow Robert	corn & kiln	-	51a.	-	-	-	-	gr/	-

PARISH	TOWNLAND	MILLER	TYPE	HOUSE	Land	£Val+	PROPRIETORS	Date	WHEEL etc.	Record	Ref.
Drumbo	Legacurry	near Hillsborough	flax	old, dilapidated :	-	-	-	2001	-	pWEH	D
Drumbo	Legacurry	Walkington Francis	mill	-	-	-	Walkington - Brown Saml	1900	-	dd/	1903 53 217
Drumgooland	Legananny	Hanna William	flax	-	8a.	11	-	-	-	gr/	-
Drumgooland	Legananny	Hanna William	flax	-	20a	-	-	-	-	gr/	-
Saintfield	Leggygowan	-	mill, mill dam	-	-	-	-	-	-	6"os/	23
Drumgooland	Leitrim	-	corn	-	-	-		-	-	6"os/	36
Drumgooland	Leitrim	-	corn, mill pond	-	-	-		-	-	6"os/	36
Drumgooland	Leitrim	Maherg William	corn & flax	-	12a.	30	-	-	-	gr/	-
Drumgooland	Leitrim	Quinn James	flax	-	5a.	8	-	-	-	gr/	-
Tullylish	Lenaderg	-	bleach	-	-	-	-	-	-	6"os/	27
Tullylish	Lenaderg	McClelland James	bleach	-	-	-	-	2009	-	mmSv/	nk - Z
Tullylish	Lenaderg	McClelland James	bleach	-	-	12.9	-	-	15x3x3.6 4 bms	vmb/	5
Tullylish	Lenaderg	McClelland James	bleach	-	-	-	-	-	not in use	vmb/	5
Tullylish	Lenaderg	Smyth Jno	bleach	-	-	18	-	-	15x5x6.6 4 bms	vmb/	5
Tullylish	Lenaderg	Smyth Jno	bleach	-	-	13	-	-	15x3x6.6 2 bms	vmb/	5
Tullylish	Lenaderg	Smyth Jno	bleach	-	-	-	-	-	15x3x6.6 1 beam	vmb/	5
Tullylish	Lenaderg	Smyth Jno	bleach	-	-	15	-	-	14x5x4 4 bms	vmb/	5
Tullylish	Lenaderg	Smyth Jno	corn	-	-	7.5.0	-	-	15x2x6.6 2 pr st.	vmb/	5
Tullylish	Lenaderg	Smyth William	bleach & corn	now Orange Hall	-	-	-	2009	-	mmSv/	nk - C
Tullylish	Lenaderg	Smyth William	old drying ho	-	-	-	-	-	-	gr/	-
Tullylish	Lenaderg	Smyth William :	bleach	old drying ho. & ld.	36a.	86	-	1856	-	gr/	a.a.ire.ie
Tullylish	Lenaderg	Smyth William & :	corn, bleach	lapping room & yd.	-	300	- [+ tenant's houses]	1856	-	gr/	a.a.Ire.ie
Tullylish	Lenederg	Smth	mill	-	-	-	Smith - McClelland	-	-	dd/	807 580 544715
Down	Lisbane	-	old windmill	-	-	-	-	-	-	1"os/	37
Blaris	Lisburn Island	Richardson J Joseph	flax spinning	-	2a.	450	-	-	-	gr/	-
Blaris	Lisburn Town	Magee William Jn	damask fcty	-	-	35	-	-	-	gr/	-
Newry	Lisduff	Gordon William	corn	-	-	-	-	-	- out of use	vmb/	5
Newry	Lisduff	Gordon William	old bleach mill	-	-	-	-	-	- out of use	vmb/	5
Comber	Lisleen Village	-	flax	-	-	-	-	-	-	6"os/	10
Aghaderg	Lisnabrague	-	corn	-	-	-	-	-	-	6"os/	33
Aghaderg	Lisnabrague	Saunderson William	corn & kiln	-	178a.	-	-	-	-	gr/	-
Aghaderg	Lisnabrague	Saunderson William	old kilns (unoc)	-	-	-	-	-	-	gr/	-
Seapatrick	Lisnafiffy	-	bleach	-	-	-	-	-	-	6"os/	27
Seapatrick	Lisnafiffy	Law Samuel	spinning	-	38a.	-	-	-	-	gr/	-
Seapatrick	Lisnafiffy	Law Samuel	spinning	-	-	-	-	2009	-	mmSv/	nk - Z
Annaclone	Lisnaliggan	M`Givern John	old mill	-		-	-	-	-	gr/	-
Down	Lisnamaul	Robinson George	corn	-	-	4	-	-	16x2x8.6	vmb/	5
Down	Lisnamaul	Robinson George	flax	-	20a.	21.10	-	1856	-	gr/	-
Kilmore	Lisnamore	-	flax	-	-	-		-	-	6"os/	30
Clonduff	Lisnamulligan	- on R Bann	flax	-	-	-	-	-	-	1"os/	60
Clonduff	Lisnamulligan	Kelly	grist mills	-	-	-	Kelly - Reilly	-	-	dd/	775 584 525519
Seapatrick	Lisnaree	-	bleach	-	-	-	-	-	-	6"os/	27
Seapatrick	Lisnaree	Malcolmson William	flour	-	-	-	-	2009	-	mmSv/	nk - Z
Dromore	Lisnaward	Dickson Robert	corn & kiln	-	32a.	-	-	-	-	gr/	-
Blaris	Lisnoe	Hart Henry	corn & kiln	-	27a.	50	-	-	-	gr/	-
Blaris	Lisnoe	Hart Henry	flax	-	-	-	-	-	-	gr/	-
Kilmore	Lissara	-	corn & flax	-	-	-		-	-	6"os/	30
Kilmore	Lissara	-	flax	-	-	-		-	-	6"os/	30
Kilmore	Lissara	Galbraith Hugh	corn & flax	-	54a.	-	-	-	-	gr/	-
Kilmore	Listooder	- on Ballinahinch R.	mill	-	-	-	-	-	-	1"os/	49
Kilmore	Listooder	Hamilton Hans	mill, mill lands	-	-	-	Hamilton H - Tisdall Richard	1708	-	dd/	2 141 339
Kilmore	Listooder	Lord Dungannon	mill	-	-	-	Dungannon - Alexander	-	-	dd/	564 158 518493

PARISH	TOWNLAND	MILLER	TYPE	HOUSE	Land	£Val+(	PROPRIETORS	Date	WHEEL etc.	Record	Ref.
Kilmore	Listooder	M`Roberts John	corn & flax	-	8.1.15	-	-	-	-	gr/	-
Down	Littleshiplands *	Bristow Edward J	mill	-	-	-	Bristow E - Orr Mary H	1898	-	dd/	1898 53 287
Down	Littleshiplands *	Wallaca Robert	mill	-	-	-	Wallaca R - Bristow Edw	1989	-	dd/	1898 8 125
Comber	Longlands	-	windmill (2)	-	-	-	-	-	-	6"os/	-
Comber	Longlands	M`Teer Alex	flax	-	30a.	23	-	-	-	gr/	-
Comber	Longlands	Woods Hans	flax	-	11a.	16.10	-	-	-	gr/	-
Down	Lough	Coslett Charles :	mills	-	-	-	Coslett C - McKibbon : F	1821	1 Jul.	dd/	764 587 518922
Down	Loughanisland	Coslett	mill	-	-	-	Coslett - Montgomery	-	-	dd/	805 391 543326
Down	Loughanisland	McKibbon	mill	-	-	-	McKibbon - Coslett	-	-	dd/	799 183 539518
Tullylish	Loughans	-	bleach	-	-	-	-	-	-	6"os/	26
Tullylish	Loughans	-	corn	-	-	-	-	-	-	6"os/	26
Tullylish	Loughans	Haughton Benj	bleach	-	-	-	-	2009	-	mmSv/	nk - Z
Tullylish	Loughans	Haughton Benj	corn	-	-	-	-	2009	-	mmSv/	nk - Z
Tullylish	Loughans	Haughton Benjamin	bleach	-	-	-	-	-	out of use 11yrs.	vmb/	5
Tullylish	Loughans	Haughton Benjamin	spinning	-	-	64	-	-	22x20x19 (note) :	vmb/	5
Tullylish	Loughans	M`Master J W & ors :	corn, logwoood	-	-	54	-	-	-	gr/	-
Tullylish	Loughans	M`Master J W & ors :	dye, drying ho	-	-	23	-	-	-	gr/	-
Tullylish	Loughans	Mercier David	corn	-	-	40	-	-	-	gr/	-
Down	Loughmore *	Wallace Robert H	mill	-	-	-	Wallace R - Bristow Edw	1898	-	dd/	1898 8 121
Newry	Loughorne	Martin Mr Jno	corn	-	-	2.14	-	-	14x3x12 1 pr st.	vmb/	5
Annahilt	Magheraconluce	Black Henry	corn	-	-	-	-	-	-	gr/	-
Annahilt	Magheraconluce	Black Henry	flax & flax kiln	-	58a.	115	-	-	-	gr/	-
Magheradrool	Magheradrool	- on Ballinahinch R.	-	-	-	-	-	-	-	6"os/	29
Magheradrool	Magheradrool	Dogherty Patrick	flax	-	-	4.12	-	-	14x4x6 3 berths	vmb/	5
Magheradrool	Magheradrool	Montgomery Arth H	flax	-	47a.	-	-	-	-	gr/	-
Magheradrool	Magheradrool	Montgomery Arth H	scutcher`s ho	-	-	-	-	-	-	gr/	-
Magheradrool	Magheraknock	-	mill, mill dam	-	-	-	-	-	-	6"os/	22
Magheradrool	Magheraknock	Kerr David	corn	-	-	7.17	-	-	18x2x18 1 pr st.	vmb/	5
Down	Magheralagan	-	corn	-	-	-	-	-	-	6"os/	37
Down	Magheralagan	Hozier James H	mill	-	-	-	Hozier J - Meredyth Henry	1895	-	dd/	1895 37 83
Down	Magheralagan	M`Roberts John	corn & kiln	ho., offs. & land	28a.	35	-	-	-	gr/	-
Down	Magheralagan	McRoberts James	corn	-	-	6.10	-	-	16x2x7	vmb/	5
Drumgooland	Magheramayo	Ward Bernard	flax	-	15a.	17	-	-	-	gr/	-
Kilkeel	Magheramurphy	Floyd William	flax thrashing	-	-	30	-	-	-	gr/	-
Donaghcloney	Magherana	Henning John	cambrick m'fcty	- [+ tenant's hos.]	-	18	-	1856	-	gr/	a.a.Ire.ie
Donaghcloney	Magherana	M'Caw Joseph :	offices (old mill)	houses & sm. gdn.	-	-	-	1856	-	gr/	a.a.Ire.ie
Donaghcloney	Magherana	McCaw Reps. Jos	office (old mill)	-	-	6	-	-	-	gr/	-
Magheradrool	Magheratimpany	-	corn	-	-	-	-	-	-	6"os/	29
Drumbo	Mealough	Hunter John	corn & kiln	-	16a.	32.10	-	-	-	gr/	-
Drumbo	Mealough	Hunter John	flax & store	-	-	-	-	-	-	gr/	-
Aghaderg	Meenan	Woods David	flax	-	2a.	22	-	-	-	gr/	-
Newtownards	Milecross	Bradshaw Joseph	flax	-	84a.	80	-	-	-	gr/	-
Newtownards	Milecross	Bradshaw Joseph	thrashing	-	-	-	-	-	-	gr/	-
Donaghadee	Millisle	-	old windmill	-	-	-	-	-	-	pWAG/	-
Donaghadee	Millisle	Bristow James R	mill	-	-	-	Bristow J - Orr Charles	1903	-	dd/	1903 7 157
Donaghadee	Millisle	Fulton James	mill	-	-	-	Fulton J - Ulster Bank Ltd.	1903	-	dd/	1903 41 60
Donaghadee	Millisle	Roddy Robert :	mills	-	-	-	Roddy R - Roddy John :	1820	Conv. Apl.	dd/	762 534 517489
Seapartick	Millmount Kilpike	-	corn	-	-	-	-	-	-	6"os/	27
Co. Down	Millquarter Bay	- nr Kilclief	corn	-	-	-	-	-	-	1"os/	49
Lenaderg	Milltown	-	bleach	replaced :	-	-	-	2009	-	mmSv/	nk - Z
Co. Down	Milltown	- nr Glasker Br.	corn	-	-	-	-	-	-	1"os/	60
Tullylish	Milltown	Hayes William	spinning	-	-	-	-	2009	-	mmSv/	nk - Z

PARISH	TOWNLAND	MILLER	TYPE	HOUSE	Land	£Val+	PROPRIETORS	Date	WHEEL etc.	Record	Ref.
Co. Down	Milltown	Lowthian	mill	-	-	-	Lowthian - Sweetman	-	-	dd/	801 419 540954
Co. Down	Milltown	Rich	mill	-	-	-	Rich - Lowthian	-	-	dd/	795 40 536975
Down	Milltown *	Hamieon	land	-	-	-	Hamieon - Hamieon	-	-	dd/	71 472 52223
Seapatrick	Milltown B`bridge	- stream,. to R Bann	corn	-	-	-	-	-	-	1"os/	48
Newtownards	Milltown C`gburn	-	mill	-	-	-	-	-	-	1"os/	37
Anaderg	Milltown Cluntagh	-	no mill	-	-	-	-	-	-	6"os/	21
Lenaderg	Milltown L`derg	-	bleach	-	-	-	-	-	-	6"os/	27
Drumgath	Milltown R`friel`d	-	corn	-	-	-	-	-	-	1"os/	60
Down	Milltown Ros`vor	-	no mill	-	-	-	-	-	-	1"os/	60
Garvaghy	Milltown Tull`sky	- on R Lagan	mill	-	-	-	-	-	-	6"os/	28
Hillsorough	Millvale	- nr Hillsborough	distillery	-	-	-	-	-	-	1"os/	-
Moira	Moira	-	hand loom	-	-	-	-	-	-	pWAG/	-
Drumgooland	Moneyslane	-	mill (x 2)	-	-	-		-	-	6"os/	35
Drumgooland	Moneyslane	M`Bride James	corn & flax	-	36a.	108	-	-	-	gr/	-
Drumgooland	Moneyslane	Rowan William	flax	-	24a.	78	-	-	-	gr/	-
Down	Monlehegolly	Crawford	mills	-	-	-	Crawford - Barklie	-	-	dd/	765 261 519196
Down	Monlehegolly	Crawford	mills	-	-	-	Crawforn - Manley	-	-	dd/	779 111 527446
Down	Monlehegolly	Crawford	mills	-	-	-	Crawford - Crawford	-	-	dd/	779 13 527348
Down	Monlehegolly	Crawford	mills	-	-	-	Crawford - Crawford	-	-	dd/	781 86 528621
Down	Monlehegolly	Crawford	mills	-	-	-	Crawford - Smith	-	-	dd/	791 325 534860
Comber	Monlough	Bennett John	mill dam	-	7a.	-	-	-	-	gr/	-
Comber	Mountalexander	Andrews Reps Jas	bleach green	-	39a.	-	-	-	-	gr/	-
Down	Mountpanther	Atkinson	mill	-	-	-	Atkinson - Rainey	-	-	dd/	769 127 521462
Down	Mountpanther	Moore	mill	-	-	-	Moore - Rainey	-	-	dd/	769 67 521402
Down	Mountpanther	Saul	mill	-	-	-	Saul - Moore	-	-	dd/	769 337 521672
Kilkeel /Kilcoo	Moyad	-	flax	-	-	-	-	-	-	6"os/	-
Tullylish	Moyallan	-	vitriol works	-	-	-	-	-	-	6"os/	26
Tullylish	Moyallan	Haughton Benjamin	bleach	-	-	-	-	2009	-	mmSv/	nk - Z
Tullylish	Moyallan	Haughton Benjamin	bleach	-	-	-	-	-	15x3x6 5 bms :	vmb/	5
Tullylish	Moyallan	Haughton Benjamin	flour	-	-	-	-	2009	-	mmSv/	nk - Z
Tullylish	Moyallan	Mercier David	flour	-	-	-	-	-	-	gr/	-
Kilkeel	Mullartown	Atkinson Arthur :	mill	-	-	-	Atkinson Arthur - Henry :	1818	Rel. 24 Apl. :	dd/	759 99 515434
Kilkeel	Mullartown	Atkinson Henry	corn	-	-	-	-	-	15x4x11	vmb/	5
Kilkeel	Mullartown	Atkinson Henry	old corn mill	-	-	-	-	-	-	vmb/	5
Kilkeel	Mullartown	M`Cormack Robert	corn & kiln	-	9a.	20	-	-	-	gr/	-
Knockbreda	Multyhogy	- on Crook R	corn	-	-	-	-	-	-	6"os/	3
Newtownards	N`ards Corp.	Dickson Hugh	corn & kiln	-	0.3.5	18	-	-	-	gr	-
Newtownards	N`ards Corp. N	-	Glen Mill	-	-	-	-	-	-	6"os/	5
Newtownards	N`ards Corp. N	-	windmill stump	-	-	-	-	-	-	6"os/	6
Newtownards	N`ards Corp. S	-	bark, pond	-	-	-	-	-	-	6"os/	5
Newtownards	Newgreen	- on Ballinahinch R.	mill	-	-	-	-	-	-	1"os/	49
Newry	Newry Town	Maguire Charlotte	distillery	-	-	-	Maguire Charlotte - Helena	1889	-	dd/	1889 32 45
Newry	Newry Town	McGeorge James	brewery	-	-	-	McGeorge J - Courtney Jn	1882	-	dd/	1882 14 137
Newry	Newry Town	Walker Mary	mill race	-	-	-	Walker Mary - Mary	1890	-	dd/	1890 170 263
Newry	Newry Town	Dempsters Ltd.	mills	-	-	-	Dempsters - Belfast Bank	1899	-	dd/	1899 78 234
Newry	Newry Town	Ld Judges Cp & Co.	Clanrye Mills	-	-	-	Ld Judges - Sands Robt	1895	-	dd/	1895 9 13
Newry	Newry Town :	Dempster Robert	mills	-	-	-	Dempster R - Belfast Bank	1898	-	dd/	1898 33 117
Newry	Newry Town :	Fivey William	mill & ground	-	-	-	Fivey Wm - Peebles Wm	1837	-	dd/	1837 10 219
Newry	Newry Town :	Bank of Ire. Govs.	mill	-	-	-	B of I Govs. - Walker Mary	1890	-	dd/	1890 17 264
Newry	Newry Town :	Walker Mary	mill	-	-	-	Walker Mary - B of I Govs.	1890	-	dd/	1890 17 256
Newry	Newry Town :	Brady Denis	old distillery	-	-	-	Brady Den - Hoey Thomas	1885	-	dd/	1885 25 251
Newry	Newry Town :	Kilmorery C`tess of	mills	-	-	-	Kilmorery - Dempster Robt	1897	-	dd/	1897 48 102

PARISH	TOWNLAND	MILLER	TYPE	HOUSE	Land	£Val+(	PROPRIETORS	Date	WHEEL etc.	Record	Ref.
Newry	Newry Town :	Kilmorery Earl of	mills	-	-	-	Kilmorery E - Unthank Clem	1882	-	dd/	1882 52 295
Newry	Newry Town :	Needham Fran Visc.	Manor Mill	-	-	-	Needham Fran - Cox Edwd	1880	-	dd/	1880 33 209
Newry	Newry Town :	Cunningham Michael	bark	-	-	-	-	-	-	dd/	1848 14 229
Co. Down	Newtown	Black	mill	-	-	-	Black - Savage	-	-	dd/	733 281 524016
Co. Down	Newtown	Carvill Fran & Son	alabaster	-	34a.	107	-	-	-	gr/	-
Co. Down	Newtown	Carvill Fran & Son	spade factory	-	-	-	-	-	-	gr/	-
Co. Down	Newtown	Ross	mills	-	-	-	Ross - Black	-	-	dd/	766 256 519791
Newtownards	Newtownards	-	calico pr. wks	-	-	-	-	-	-	1"os/	37
Newtownards	Newtownards	-	corn	-	-	-	-	-	-	1"os/	37
Newtownards	Newtownards	- nr Whitespots	old windmill	-	-	-	-	-	-	1"os/	37
Newtownards	Newtownards Cp.	Dickenson Hugh	corn & kiln	-	0.3.5	-	-	-	-	gr/	-
Newtownards	Newtownards Tn	Harrison George	flax store, yd	-	-	-	-	-	-	gr/	-
Co. Down	Nutgrove	Coslett	mill	-	-	-	Coslett - Montgomery	-	-	dd/	805 391 543326
Co. Down	Nutgrove	Houghton	mill	-	-	-	Houghton - Coslett	-	-	dd/	799 148 577483
Co. Down	O.C. Mill	Chichester	mill	-	-	-	Ckichester - Clarke	-	-	dd/	785 451 531386
Co. Down	Owenocork (?)	Dungannon Arthur :	mill	-	-	-	Dungannon - Alexander : L	1828	Mort. 13 May	dd/	764 158 518943
Ballyphilip	Portaferrey Town	Nugent Andrew	corn (dilap.)	-	-	-	-	-	-	gr/	-
Ballyphilip	Portaferrey Town	Wallace & Stewart	starch works	-	-	-	-	-	-	gr/	-
Bangor	Portavoe	- on coast	corn	-	-	-	-	-	-	6"os/	52
Bangor	Portavoe	Fargie James	corn & kiln	-	-	12	-	-	-	gr/	-
Ballyhalbert	Portavogie	-	flax	-	-	-	-	-	uses piped water	6"os/	18
Drumbo	Purdysburn	-	corn	-	-	-	-	-	-	1"os/	-
Dromore	Quilly	M`Murray William	beetling	-	4a.	49	-	-	-	gr/	-
Dromore	Quilly	M`Murray William	workmens` ctgs.	-	-	-	-	-	-	gr/	-
Saul	Quilly & Moss	Hamilton	mills	-	-	-	Hamilton - Stott	-	-	dd/	786 196 520931
Saul	Quoile	-	distillery	-	-	-		-	-	6"os/	31
Saul	Quoile	Macoubry	mill	-	-	-	Macoubry - Clelland	-	-	dd/	767 233 520368
Kilmore	Rademan	M`Roberts John	flour	-	48a.	-	-	-	-	gr/	-
Kilmore	Rademan	McRoberts James	flour	-	-	11.12	-	-	16x4x8 2 pr st.	vmb/	5
Ballyculter	Raholp	Hughes Bernard	corn & kiln	-	170a.	-	-	-	-	gr/	-
Ballyculter	Raholp	Spratt Samuel	corn	-	-	6.14	-	-	14x2x14 1 pr st.	vmb/	5
Ballyculter	Rahopl	-	mill	-	-	-	-	-	-	1"os/	49
Kilmore	Raleagh	- on Ballinahinch R	mill	-	-	-	-	-	-	1"os/	-
	Ravara	Curragh William J	mill	-	-	-	Curragh W - Curragh Saml	1900	-	dd/	1900 81 191
Killinchy	Ravara	Gracey Thomas	corn	-	8a.	25	-	-	-	gr/	-
Killinchy	Ravara	Gracey Thomas	flax	-	-	-	-	-	-	gr/	-
Co. Down	Ravensdale	-	mill	-	-	-	-	-	-	1"os/	71
Blaris	Ravernet	Hart Henry	flour	-	56a.	106	-	-	-	gr/	-
Blaris	Ravernet	Henderson Jno	corn	-	-	19.10	-	-	16x4x7 2 pr st.	vmb/	5
Down	Ringboy	-	old windmill	-	-	-	-	-	-	1"os/	37
Killyleagh	Ringdufferin	-	windmill	-	-	-	-	-	-	6"os/	24
Kilmore	Rossconnor	Browne James	corn	-	-	8.7.0	-	-	15x3x8 2 pr st.	vmb/	5
Kilmore	Rossconnor	Browne James	flax	-	-	3.7.0	-	-	14x3x8 4 bths	vmb/	5
Kilmore	Rossconor	-	corn	-	-	-		-	-	6"os/	30
Kilmore	Rossconor	-	flax	-	-	-		-	-	6"os/	30
Kilmore	Rossconor	Brown Arthur	corn & flax	-	108a.	-	-	-	-	gr/	-
Down	Rostrevor	-	bleach	-	-	-	-	-	-	1"os/	60
Down	Rostrevor	Scott Isaac	corn & kiln	-	-	25	-	-	-	gr/	-
Co. Down	Roundhill	- nr Ballinahinch R.	mill	-	-	-	-	-	-	1"os/	49
Co. Down	Rumnagally	Anne Dunbar	workers` hos	-	-	-	-	-	-	gr/	-
Saintfield	Saintfield	-	mills	-	-	-	-	-	-	1"os/	-
Saintfield	Saintfield	- near Boardmills	corn	-	-	-	-	-	-	1"os/	36

PARISH	TOWNLAND	MILLER	TYPE	HOUSE	Land	£Val+	PROPRIETORS	Date	WHEEL etc.	Record	Ref.
Co. Down	Sandymount	- near Lambeg Br.	bleach works	-	-	-	-	-	-	1"os/	36
Saul	Saul	-	-	dangerour ruins	-	-	-	2001	-	pWEH	R
Saul	Saul	- at Millvale Ctge	mills	-	-	-	-	-	-	1"os/	49
Saul	Saul	Atkinson John	mill	-	-	-	Atkinson - Hungerford W	1898	-	dd/	1898 38 74
Saul	Saul	Campbell James	corn & kiln	-	7a.	32	-	-	-	gr/	-
Saul	Saul	Campbell James	flax	-	5a.	10	-	-	-	gr/	-
Saul	Saul	Hyland Thos & Co	starch	-	1a.	20	-	-	-	gr/	-
Saul	Saul	Kennedy Anne C	mill	-	-	-	Kennedy A - Appointment	1899	-	dd/	1899 11 190
Saul	Saul	Richardson Jno	malt	-	-	10.10	-	-	18x4x18	vmb/	5
Saul	Saul	Taggarh Bernard	corn	-	-	9.16	-	-	14x2x4.6	vmb/	5
Newry	Saval More	Glenny Isaac	chemicals	-	-	-	-	-	(same as corn) : ch	vmb/	5
Newry	Saval More	Glenny Isaac	corn	-	-	2.9.0	-	-	14x4x14 also : f	vmb/	5
Newry	Saval More	Glenny Isaac	flax	-	-	2.9.0	-	-	14x3x10 4 bths	vmb/	5
Aghaderg	Scarva	-	corn & kiln	-	-	-	-	-	-	6"os/	33
Aghaderg	Scarva	Chambers Dines	flax	-	45a.	60	-	-	-	gr/	-
Drumb`yroney	Seafin	Cromie John	flax	-	17a.	20.15	-	-	-	gr/	-
Newry	Shanaghan	McCaffrey Daniel	flax	-	-	1.17	-	-	12x2x0.10 3bths	vmb/	5
Newry	Shanaghan	Murphy David & Jas	corn	-	-	-	-	-	14x8x6	vmb/	5
Newry	Shanaghan	Murphy David & Jas	flax	-	-	-	-	-	14x8x6 note : l	vmb/	5
Newry	Shanaghan	Murphy David & Jas	flour	-	-	8.8.0	-	-	14x8x6 also :	vmb/	5
Newry	Shanaghan	Porter Andrew	corn	-	-	4.10	-	-	14x2.9x14 2pr st.	vmb/	5
Newry	Shanaghan	Porter Andrew	flax	-	-	1.9.0	-	-	14x3x11 4 bths	vmb/	5
Newry	Shannaghan	-	corn & flax	-	-	-		-	-	6"os/	35
Newry	Shannaghan	- on R Bann	corn	-	-	-		-	-	6"os/	35
Newry	Shannaghan	- on R Bann	flax	-	-	-		-	-	6"os/	35
Newry	Shannaghan	Copes Thomas	flax	-	17a.	22	-	-	-	gr/	-
Newry	Shannaghan	Lowry Alexander	bleach	-	-	-	-	1797	-	dd/	?
Newry	Shannaghan	Lowry Alexander	bleach	-	-	-	-	1797	-	inv/	green
Newry	Shannaghan	Murphy James	bleach	-	-	-	-	1797	-	dd/	?
Newry	Shannaghan	Murphy James	bleach	-	-	-	-	1797	-	inv/	green
Newry	Shannaghan	Porter Robt & Alex	corn & kiln	-	-	35	-	-	-	gr/	-
Newry	Shannaghan	Porter Robt & Alex	flax	-	-	-	-	-	-	gr/	-
Newry	Shannaghan	Stewart Hugh	corn	-	23a.	62	-	-	-	gr/	-
Newry	Shannaghan	Stewart Hugh	flax	-	-	-	-	-	-	gr/	-
Garvaghy	Shanrod	McMullen Daniel	flax, corn	-	69a.	77	-	-	-	gr/	-
Dunsfort	Sheepland	-	mill	-	-	-	-	-	-	1"os/	49
Dunsfort	Sheepland Beg	-	corn	-	-	-	-	-	-	6"os/	-
Dunsfort	Sheepland Beg	Corran Margaret	corn & kiln	-	7a.	7	-	-	-	gr/	-
Dunsfort	Sheepland Beg	Corran Margaret	corn & land	-	1a.	8	-	-	-	gr/	-
Dunsfort	Sheepland Beg	Currin William	corn	-	-	4.5.0	-	-	14x2x14 1 pr st.	vmb/	5
Dunsfort	Sheepland More	Corran Margaret	mill-pond	-	6.2.8	5/-	-	-	-	gr/	-
Killyleagh	Shrigley	- nr Killyleagh	mills	-	-	-	-	-	-	1"os/	49
Hilsborough	Small Park	- nr Hilsborough	mills	-	-	-	-	-	-	6"os/	14
Co. Down	Solitude	-	flax	-	-	-	-	-	-	1"os/	37
Ballyculter	Strangford	-	mill	-	-	-	-	-	-	1"os/	49
Ballyculter	Strangford	Fitzgerald	manor mill	-	-	-	Fitzgerald - Neville	-	-	dd/	777 558 526639
Ballyculter	Strangford Lr	-	corn	-	-	-		-	-	6"os/	31
Ballyculter	Strangford Lr	Holton William	corn	-	-	-	-	-	14x2x15 1 pr st.	vmb/	5
Blaris	Taghnabrick	Richardson Jno	beetling	caretaker`s ho.	-	26	-	-	-	gr/	-
Blaris	Taghnabrick	Sprucefield House &	Mill	- (demol. 1960)	-	-	-	1845	-	6"os/	14
Killinchy	Templebrook Vly	- near Killinchy	mill	-	-	-	-	-	-	1"os/	37
Co. Down	Ten Towns	Leslie Rev Peter	corn, windmill	-	-	-	Leslie Peter - Colville	1745	-	dd/	120 86 81930

PARISH	TOWNLAND	MILLER	TYPE	HOUSE	Land	£Val+(	PROPRIETORS	Date	WHEEL etc.	Record	Ref.
Co. Down	Ten Towns	Leslie Rev Peter	tuck	-	-	-	Leslie Peter - Colville	1745	-	dd/	120 86 81930
Down	Tobermoney	Quaile Thomas	corn	-	-	5a.	-	-	14x2x14 2 pr st.	vmb/	5
Down	Tobermoney	Rowan Thomas & :	corn & kiln	- [+ tenant's hos.]	-	4.0.0	-	-	-	gr/	a.a.lre.ie
Kilcoo	Tollymore Park	- on Shina R	saw	-	-	-	-	-	-	1"os/	60
Kilcoo	Tollymore Park	- on Shina R	saw	-	-	-	-	-	-	6"os/	49
Kilcoo	Townland ?	- near Hilltown	mill	-	-	-	-	-	-	1"os/	60
Aghaderg	Townland ?	Wallace James	mill pond	-	1a.	-	-	-	-	gr/	-
Comber	Townsparks	-	flour, mills	-	-	-	-	-	-	6"os/	20
Garvaghy	Tullinsky	Graham John	corn & kilns	-	-	32	-	-	-	gr/	-
Garvaghy	Tullinsky	Graham John	flax	-	-	-	-	-	-	gr/	-
Ballyphilip	Tullyboard	-	corn	-	-	-		-	-	6"os/	32
Ballyphilip	Tullyboard	Curran William	corn & kiln	-	3a.	-	-	-	-	gr/	-
Kilcoo	Tullybranigan	-	ruins of mill	-	-	-	-	-	-	6"os/	49
Kilcoo	Tullybranigan	Newsom	bleach green	-	-	-	Newsom - Murphy	-	-	dd/	581 143 528678
Donaghcloney	Tullycarn	Dickson Matilda	flax, boiling ho	-	99a.	243	-	-	-	gr/	-
Donaghcloney	Tullycarn	Waugh Mrs	flax	-	-	2.12	-	1837	15x3x5.6 8 bths : i	vmb/	5
Dundonald	Tullycarney	Morrow John	corn	-	46a.	-	-	-	-	gr/	-
Co. Down	Tullychin	Blackwood	mill	-	-	-	Blackwood - Sheridan	-	-	dd/	805 536 543471
Co. Down	Tullychin	Lord Dufferin	mill	-	-	-	Dufferin - Foster	-	-	dd/	805 36 524971
Seapatrick	Tullyconnaught	- near Milltown	bleach	-	-	-		-	-	6"os/	34
Seapatrick	Tullyconnaught	Mulligan Fran M J	mill, mill lds	-	-	-	Muligan F - Mulligan G	1842	-	dd/	1842 1 134/5
Seapatrick	Tullyconnaught	Mulligan Fras	mill	-	-	-	-	2009	-	mmSv/	nk - Z
Seapatrick	Tullyconnaught	Mulligan George :	beetling (ruins)	-		-	-	-	-	inv/	green
Seapatrick	Tullyconnaught	Mulligan Gilbert	beetling	-	9a.	79	-	-	-	gr/	-
Seapatrick	Tullyconnaught	Mulligan Gilbert	beetling	-	-	-	-	2009	-	mmSv/	nk - Z
Seapatrick	Tullyconnaught	Mulligan Gilbert	corn & kiln	-	-	30	-	-	-	gr/	-
Seapatrick	Tullyconnaught	Mulligan Gilbert	old bl. mill	-		-	-	-	-	gr/	-
Seapatrick	Tullyconnaught	Mulligan John :	beetling (ruins)	-		-	-	-	-	inv/	green
Co. Down	Tullycreely	Blackwood	mill	-	-	-	Blackwood - Sheridan	-	-	dd/	805 536 543471
Co. Down	Tullycreely	Lord Dufferin	mill	-	-	-	Dufferin - Foster	-	-	dd/	805 36 524971
Kilkeel	Tullyframe	-	flax	-	-	-	-	-	-	1"os/	71
Comber	Tullygarvan	Carr John	flax sp. fcty	-	7a.	120	-	-	-	gr/	-
Comber	Tullygarvan	Ewart Thomas	corn & kiln	-	-	30	-	-	-	gr/	-
Comber	Tullygarvan	Waller Samuel	flax	-	112a.	776	-	-	-	gr/	-
Donaghcloney	Tullyheron	Henning John	cambric finishing	-	0.3.0	45	-	-	-	gr/	-
Comber	Tullyhubbert	-	corn & flax	-	-	-	-	-	-	6"os/	20
Comber	Tullyhubbert	Bennett John	flax, mill pond	-	3a.	7.10	-	-	-	gr/	-
Comber	Tullyhulbert	-	mill	-	-	-	-	-	-	6"os/	20
Grey Abbey	Tullykevin	M`Kee William	corn	-	96a.	97	-	-	-	gr/	-
Grey Abbey	Tullykevin	M`Kee William	flax	-	-	-	-	-	-	gr/	-
Tullylish	Tullylish	-	bleach	-	-	-	-	-	-	6"os/	26
Tullylish	Tullylish	-	flour Glen Mill	-	-	-	-	-	-	6"os/	26
Tullylish	Tullylish	- near Mill Park	bleach	-	-	-	-	-	-	6"os/	26
Tullylish	Tullylish	Christie Jno	bleach	-	-	18.2	-	-	14x6x5 also :	vmb/	5
Tullylish	Tullylish	Christie Jno	bleach (2)	-	-	18.14	-	-	14x6x5 9x5x5	vmb/	5
Tullylish	Tullylish	Crawford George	bleach	now Pot Belly Restaurant			-	2009	-	mmSv/	nk - C
Tullylish	Tullylish	Crawford George	lapping	-	-	-	-	2009	-	mmSv/	nk - D
Tullylish	Tullylish	Haughton B & Co.	flour	-	-	39	-	-	14x9x3.6 3 pr st.	vmb/	5
Tullylish	Tullylish	Haughton B & Co.	flour	-	-	25	-	-	14x8x6.6 2 pr st.	vmb/	5
Tullylish	Tullylish	Haughton Benjamin	bleach	-	-	12.16	-	-	14x5x5.6 4 bms	vmb/	5
Tullylish	Tullylish	Haughton Benjamin	bleach	-	-	2.10	-	-	11x5x5.6	vmb/	5
Tullylish	Tullylish	Haughton Benjamin	bleach	-	-	9.16	-	-	12x5x5.6	vmb/	5

PARISH	TOWNLAND	MILLER	TYPE	HOUSE	Land	£Val+	PROPRIETORS	Date	WHEEL etc.	Record	Ref.
Tullylish	Tullylish	Haughton Thos & :	bleach	-	-	100	-	-	-	gr/	a.a.Ire.ie
Tullylish	Tullylish	Haughton Thos & :	bleach	& land	1.1.5	25	-	1856	-	gr/	a.a.Ire.ie
Tullylish	Tullylish	Mullen George &	: bleach	-	-	18	-	-	-	gr/	-
Tullylish	Tullylish	Mullen George &	: bleach	- [& tenant's hos.]	-	18	-	1856	-	gr/	a.a.Ire.ie
Tullylish	Tullylish	Mullen George &	: flour	-	8a.	82	-	-	-	gr/	-
Tullylish	Tullylish	Mullen George &	: flour	offices & land	13a.	205	-	1856	-	gr/	a.a.Ire.ie
Tullylish	Tullylish	Mullen George &	: flour	stores & land :	8a.	82	-	1856	-	gr/	a.a.Ire.ie
Tullylish	Tullylish	Robbins Robert : C	mill , bl green	-	-	-	Robbins R - Kenney Anne :	1820	Mge. Smt.	dd/	759 498 515833
Tullylish	Tullylish	Stoney Issac	bleach	-	-	14.7	-	-	15x3x4.6	vmb/	5
Tullylish	Tullylish	Stoney Issac	bleach	-	-	35	-	-	15x6x4.6 8bms	vmb/	5
Tullylish	Tullylish	Stoney Issac	bleach	-	-	21	-	-	14x4x5 4 bms	vmb/	5
Tullylish	Tullylish	Uprichard M/s James (	bleach	-	-	18	-	-	15x6x11 4 bms	vmb/	5
Tullylish	Tullylish	Uprichard M/s James (	bleach	-	-	6.7	-	-	15x6x11 2 bms	vmb/	5
Tullylish	Tullylish	Uprichard M/s James (	bleach	-	-	-	-	-	13x5x11	vmb/	5
Tullylish	Tullylish	Uprichard William :	bleach works	(Mill Park - dilap.)	4	-	-	-	-	gr/	a.a.Ire.ie
Tullylish	Tullylish	Uprichard William :	bleach works	- [& tenant's hos.]	-	235	-	-	-	gr/	a.a.Ire.ie
Killyleagh	Tullymacnous	Coulter Thomas	corn	miller`s ho.	1a.	-	-	-	-	gr/	-
Lambeg	Tullynacross	Richardson J.N.R. :	land, mill pond	-	95a.	17.10	-	-	-	gr/	-
Lambeg	Tullynacross	Richardson Jno	bleach works	-	97a.	430	-	-	-	gr/	-
Newtownards	Tullynagardy	Dickenson Hugh	corn	engine house	14a.	29	-	-	-	gr/	-
Garvaghy	Tullyorior	-	flax	-	-	-		-	-	6"os/	34
Garvaghy	Tullyorior	-	flax	-	-	-	-	2009	-	mmSv/	nk - R
Kilcoo	Tullyree	-	corn mills	-	-	-	-	-	-	6"os/	49
Kilcoo	Tullyree	-	flax	-	-	-	-	-	-	1"os/	60
Killyleagh	Tullyveery	-	cotton factory	-	-	-	-	-	-	6"os/	24
Killyleagh	Tullyveery	- near Claylake S.	mill	-	-	-	-	-	-	1"os/	49
Killyleagh	Tullyveery	Martin John	flax	-	-	-	-	-	-	gr/	-
Killyleagh	Tullyveery	Martin John	flax spinning	-	11a.	-	-	-	-	gr/	-
Killyleagh	Tullyveery	Martin John	mill pond	-	11a.	-	-	-	-	gr/	-
Seapatrick	Tullyyear	Fennell Robert & Co.	bleech & bt. :	-	72a.	140	-	-	-	gr/	-
Saintfield	Ty`wasnacunagh	-	old windmill	-	-	-	-	-	-	1"os/	49
Dundonald	Unicarval	Allen George	flax & store	-	148a.	183	-	-	-	gr/	-
Saul	Welshtown	Mayra Castle	corn	reqs. attention	-	-	David Good	2001	-	pWEH	B
Saul	Welshtown	Mayra Castle	gas plant	welll preserved	-	-	David Good	2001	-	pWEH	B
Ballywalter	Whitechurch	- at Bandstown	flax	-	-	-	-	-	-	6"os/	12

PARISH	TOWNLAND	MILLER	TYPE	HOUSE	Land	£Val	PROPRIETORS	Date	WHEEL etc.	Record	Ref.
Aderrig	Adamstown	-	flax	-	-	-	-	-	-	6"os/	17
Aderrig	Adamstown	-	mill	-	-	-	-	-	-	6"os/	17
Aderrig	Adamstown	-	mill	-	-	-	-	2002	-	mmSv/	wh - Z
Aderrig	Adamstown	- N W. of Village	Wind Mill	-	-	-	-	-	-	JRoc	1760 map
Dublin	Ashgrove *	-	corn	-	-	-	-	-	-	dir1800	Dublin
Castleknock	Ashtown	-	oil & pond	-	-	-	-	-	-	6"os/	18
Castleknock	Ashtown	McGary Michael	oil	49x38x47 Val. :	-	110	-	1846	21x18x16 all metal :	hob/	5.3814
Clonsilla	Astagob	-	starch works	-	-	-	-	-	-	6"os/	17
Clonsilla	Astagob	-	wire	-	-	-	-	-	-	6"os/	17
Clonsilla	Astagob	- N. side R. Liffey	New Holland	-	-	-	-	1821	-	WDunc/	2
Clonsilla	Astagob	Eustace Clotilda	mills	-	-	-	Eustace Dame - Folliott :	1713	-	dd/	11 55 3973
Clonsilla	Astagob	Henzey Joshua	mills	-	-	-	Henzey J - Charles Elijah	1727	-	dd/	56 452 38589
Clonsilla	Astagob	Kane Nathaniel :	mill	-	-	-	Kane N - Jackson Adam	1727	-	dd/	54 420 36277
Clonsilla	Astagob	Liddy Thomas	paper	60x24x10 = m/c ho. :	-	50	-	1844	16x2.6 & 16x3 no. :	hob/	5.3814
Clonsilla	Astagob	Maguire Thomas	iron works	68.6x30x11.6 & :	-	-	T Maguire - lease c1832	1844	foundry has 3 wh. :	hob/	5.3814
Clonsilla	Astagob	New Holland	wire & starch	-	-	-	-	2002	-	mmSv/	wh - Z
Clonsilla	Astagob	O`Reilly Mr. :	wire	-	-	-	-	-	4 mill wheels	dir1800	Dublin
Clonsilla	Astagob	Pain David	mills	-	-	-	Pain Dav - De Sallie Chas :	1731	Mort. 8 Nov.	dd/	66 107 45317
Clonsilla	Astagob	Pain David	powder mill	-	-	-	Pain Dav - Lennox Wm	1725		dd/	66 107 45317
Clonsilla	Astagob	Pain David	powder mill	-	-	-	Pain Dav - Lennox Wm	1731	Mort. 8 Nov.	dd/	68 43 46920
Clonsilla	Astagob	Price Samuel	mills	-	-	-	Price Saml - Kennan Thos	1725	-	dd/	47 453 31430
Clonsilla	Astagob	Sherigley Abraham	land	-	-	-	Sherigley A - Keenan Th	1729	-	dd/	62 287 42909
Aderrig	Backwestonpark	- at Salmon Leap	flour	remains of old mill :	-	-	-	2001	-	phoWEH	R
Aderrig	Backwestonpark	- near Leixlip Br.	flour	-	-	-	-	-	-	6"os/	17
Aderrig	Backwestonpark	M`Donnell Michael &	paper	-	-	-	-	-	-	gr/	-
Balrothery	Balbriggan	-	cotton (now flour)		-	-	-	-	-	dir1800	Dublin
Balrothery	Balbriggan	-	mill	-	-	-	-	1899	-	1"os/	92
Balrothery	Balbriggan	- in Town	Salt House	-	-	-	-	-	-	JRoc	1760 map
Balrothery	Balbriggan	- S. of Bridge at :	Windmill	-	-	-	-	-	-	JRoc	1760 map
Balrothery	Balbriggan	Alexander George	cotton	77x33x36 & :	-	-	-	1846	20x7.6x18.6 48 bkt.	hob/	5.0845
Balrothery	Balbriggan	Gribbin James :	mills	-	-	-	Gribbin J - King Joseph :	1805	-	dd/	576 87 386131
Balrothery	Balbriggan	Hamilton Alex :	mills	-	-	-	Hamilton A - Ternan Richd :	1805	-	dd/	572 128 387420
Balrothery	Balbriggan	Hamilton Geo Alex	cotton factory	(1B) 77.6x34x40 :	-	34	-	1845	old steam engine :	hob/	5.2672
Balrothery	Balbriggan	Kiernan Robert	corn	-	-	-	Kiernan R - Ward John	1740	-	dd/	104 288 73034
Balrothery	Balbriggan	Kiernan Robert	corn		-	-	Kiernan R - O`Hara Ann	1741	-	dd/	105 220 73142
Balrothery	Balbriggan	Kiernan Robert	corn	-	-	-	Kiernan R (his will) - Sons :	1741	-	dd/	106 453 74664
Balrothery	Balbriggan	Magee Mr	corn	-	-	-	-	-	-	dir1800	Dublin
Balrothery	Balbriggan	McKay David :	mills	-	-	-	Mckay D - Tighe Laurence	1804	-	dd/	568 84 378746
Balrothery	Balbriggan	Mears Mary :	mills	-	-	-	Mears - Vandeleur Frances	1805	-	dd/	573 126 385251
Balrothery	Balbriggan	Pike William	mills	-	-	-	Pike Wm - Pace Matthew	1806	-	dd/	573 415 391403
Balrothery	Balbriggan	Tiernan Mr	cotton	-	-	-	-	-	-	dir1800	Dublin
Balrothery	Balbriggan :	Kiernan Ann Widow	corn	-	-	-	Kiernan A - Kiernan Jas :	1745	-	dd/	117 465 81467
Balrothery	Balbriggan Tn	Magran Christopher	cotton	-	0.2.1	-	-	-	-	gr/	-
Balrothery	Balbriggan Tn :	Magrain Christopher	hand wv. fcty	(3C) 130.9x18x6	-	1-19	-	1845	-	hob/	5.2672
Balrothery	Balbriggan Tn :	Magrain Christopher	cotton (part of)	(1B) 30x17x19 :	-	-	-	1845	steam engine	hob/	5.2672
Balrothery	Balbriggan Tn :	Magrain Christopher	cotton (part of)	(1B) 48x19x23.3 :	-	1-19	-	1845	steam eng. 16 h.p. :	hob/	5.2672
Swords	Balheary	-	old windmill	-	-	-	-	-	-	6"os/	8
Swords	Balheary	-	windmill - corn	-	-	-	-	-	-	dir1800	Dublin
Swords	Balheary	Cassidy Charlotte :	mill	-	-	-	Cassidy - Archbold Eliz :	1791	-	dd/	448 119 286598
Swords	Balheary	Cassidy Elizabeth :	mill	-	-	-	Cassidy E - Cassidy Ptk :	1789	-	dd/	416 27 272316
Swords	Balheary	Crosbie	mill	-	-	-	Crosbie - Keany	-	- (error)	dd/	569 641 379848
Swords	Balheary	McAlister	mill	-	-	-	McAlister - Archbold	-	- (error)	dd/	534 146 357639

PARISH	TOWNLAND	MILLER	TYPE	HOUSE	Land	£Val	PROPRIETORS	Date	WHEEL etc.	Record	Ref.
Swords	Balheary	McAlister Charles :	mill	-	-	-	McAlister - Archbold Eliz :	1802	-	dd/	541 384 357638
Swords	Balheary	Murphy Michael	mill holding	-	-	-	Murphy Mcl - Murphy Ed.	1860	-	dd/	1860 30 178
Tallaght	Ballinascorney	O'Rahilly Niall	domestic	-	-	-	-	-	Ossenberger 6.5kw :	turb/	1947
Lusk	Ballough	-	windmill	-	-	-	-	-	-	6"os/	8
Lusk	Ballough	-	windmill :	-	-	-	-	-	-	mmSv/	sb - Z
Lusk	Ballough	- at Green		-	-	-	-	-	-	JRoc	1760 map
Lusk	Ballough	- nr Windfield Ho.	mill	-	-	-	-	2003	-	mmSv/	sb - Z
Donnybrook	Ballsbridge	- on R. Dodder	distillery	-	-	-	-	-	-	6"os/	18
Donnybrook	Ballsbridge	- on R. Dodder	flour, mill race	-	-	-	-	-	-	TLtts/	1884
Donnybrook	Ballsbridge	Duffy John	bleach works	(1B) 17x24.6x10 :	-	25.5	-	-	-	hob/	5.2685
Donnybrook	Ballsbridge	Duffy John	bleach works	(1C) 100x18x18.6 :	-	25.5	-	1845	10x1.2x8	hob/	5.2685
Donnybrook	Ballsbridge	Duffy, Byrne, Hamill	cotton wash	-	-	-	-	-	-	dir1800	Dublin
Donnybrook	Ballsbridge	Duffy, Byrne, Hamill	cotton wash	-	-	-	-	-	-	dir1800	Dublin
Donnybrook	Ballsbridge	Duffy, Byrne, Hamill	cotton wash	-	-	-	-	-	-	dir1800	Dublin
Whitechurch	Ballyboden	-	cloth & pond	-	-	-	-	-	-	6"os/	22
Whitechurch	Ballyboden	-	paper	-	-	-	-	-	-	6"os/	22
Whitechurch	Ballyboden	- near entrance :	cloth (?)	demolished, millho ok		-	-	2002	-	phoWEH	Z
Whitechurch	Ballyboden	- nr Somerville	cotton	-	-	-	-	-	-	6"os/	22
Whitechurch	Ballyboden	- Taylor`s Lane	paper factory	-	-	-	-	-	-	6"os/	22
Whitechurch	Ballyboden	Beauchamp Jno	Little Mill	-	-	-	Beauchamp J - Crofton M	1863	-	dd/	1863 22 42
Whitechurch	Ballyboden	Frank Thomas :	paper	-	-	-	Frank T - Chamley John :	1803	-	dd/	575 336 386428
Whitechurch	Ballyboden	King	paper	-	-	-	King - Boswell	-	?	dd/	513 234 336873?
Whitechurch	Ballyboden	M`Donagh John	paper	-	-	-	-	-	-	gr/	-
Whitechurch	Ballyboden	McDonagh Jno	paper	-	-	-	McDonogh J - Stubbs Jno	1862	-	dd/	1862 28 286
Whitechurch	Ballyboden	McDonagh John	paper	76x22x20 dr. loft :	-	-	partner - Pim Wm (dead)	1845	no dimensions :	hob/	5.0930
Whitechurch	Ballyboden	Millho. Appartments	mill	fine restored + wh.	-	-	-	2002	-	phoWEH	C
Whitechurch	Ballyboden	Read John	cloth	56.0x39.6x27.6 & :	-	-	-	-	no dimensions	hob/	5.0930
Whitechurch	Ballyboden	Read John	wollen-cloth	-	0.2.13		-	-	-	gr/	-
Whitechurch	Ballyboden	Ryan Michael	paper	21x5x19.6 = front :	-	-	deleted - Manseigh William	1845	no dimensions	hob/	5.0930
Whitechurch	Ballyboden	Ryan Nicholas	paper	-	-	-	-	-	-	gr/	-
Whitechurch	Ballyboden	Stubbs Robert	paper	-	-	-	Stubbs R - Sullivan Jerm.	1793	-	dd/	467 535 302123
Whitechurch	Ballyboden	Sullivan Daniel	paper	-	-	-	Sullivan Dan - Stubbs Robt	1790	-	dd/	468 45 302122
Kinsaley	Ballycartle	-	old brewery	-	-	-	-	-	-	6"os/	15
Rathmichael	Ballycorus	- at Loughlinstown	mill race	-	-	-	-	-	-	6"os/	26
Rathmichael	Ballycorus	- nr B`corus Castle	shot mfty	-	-	-	-	-	-	6"os/	26
Swords	Ballyhara	- E. side of River	Mill	-	-	-	-	-	-	JRoc	1760 map
Ballymadun	Ballymadun	-	corn	-	-	-	-	-	-	dir1800	Dublin
Ballymadun	Ballymadun	-	windmill - corn	-	-	-	-	-	-	dir1800	Dublin
Kilmactalway	Ballymakaily	-	flour	-	-	-	-	-	-	6"os/	17
Kilmactalway	Ballymakaily	- on Grand Canal	mill	-	-	-	-	1899	-	1"os/	111
Kilmactalway	Ballymakaily	- Rathburn`s Mill :	-	preserved ok	-	-	Paddy McMahon	1997	storage	phoWEH	-
Kilmactalway	Ballymakaily	Palmer Sam & Co.	flour, kiln	-	5a.	-	-	-	-	gr/	-
Balrothery	Balrothery	-	windmill - corn	-	-	-	-	-	-	dir1800	Dublin
Balrothery	Balrothery	Kieran Louisa M	mill	-	-	-	-	1860	-	dd/	1860 23 164
Dublin	Bannoges	-	paper	-	-	-	-	-	-	6"os/	17
Castleknock	Barons Mills	Costilloe	corn mill & ho :	-	-	-	Costilloe - Gill	-	?	dd/	67 358 46411
Castleknock	Barons Mills	Sherigley Abraham	Baron`s Mill & :	-	-	-	Sherigley A - Count John :	1734	-	dd/	75 332 53255
Dublin	Barrington *	-	windmill - corn	-	-	-	-	-	-	dir1800	Dublin
Dublin	Bawther *	-	corn	-	-	-	-	-	-	dir1800	Dublin
Portraine	Beaverstown	- Donabate Commo	Wind Mill	-	-	-	-	-	-	JRoc	1760 map
Donnybrook	Beggarsbush	- on R. Dodder	flour	-	-	-	-	-	-	6"os/	18
Donnybrook	Beggarsbush	Cochlans Patrick	flour	(1B) 42x24x32 :	-	30	-	-	-	hob/	5.2682

PARISH	TOWNLAND	MILLER	TYPE	HOUSE	Land	£Val	PROPRIETORS	Date	WHEEL etc.	Record	Ref.
Donnybrook	Beggarsbush	Robinson Mr	cotton wash	-	-	-	-	-	-	dir1800	Dublin
Donnybrook	Beggarsbush	Robinson Mr	cotton wash	-	-	-	-	-	-	dir1800	Dublin
Dublin	Bellaroy (not)	-	woollen	-	-	-	-	-	-	6"os/	18
Clonsilla	Black Mills (not)	Lovely	mills	-	-	-	Lovely - Flood	-	?	dd/	ref. lost
Castleknock	Blanchardstown	- N. side canal	worsted mill	-	-	-	-	1841	-	6"os/	13
Castleknock	Blanchardstown	- S. side Tolka R.	corn & mill dam	-	-	-	-	1841	-	6"os/	13
Castleknock	Blanchardstown	- S./ Tolka R. :	mill	-	-	-	-	1812	-	WDunc/	2
Castleknock	Blanchardstown	Bryson John	corn	32x19.6x19.6 Val. :	-	18	-	-	14x5.4x3 drives :	hob/	5.3814
Castleknock	Blanchardstown	Delaney Emma	mills	-	-	-	Delaney E - Delaney Emma	1903	-	dd/	1903 77 74
Castleknock	Blanchardstown	Delaney Emma	mills	-	-	-	Delaney E - M. & Lei. Bank	1903	-	dd/	1903 77 86
Castleknock	Blanchardstown	L`Estrange John	mill	-	1.0.2(	-	-	-	-	gr/	-
Castleknock	Blanchardstown	Reilly James	worsted factory	70x27x33.6 & :	-	-	-	1846	28x7 no. bkts 72 :	hob/	5.3814
Drimnagh	Bluebell	-	woollen factory	-	-	-	-	-	-	6"os/	18
Drimnagh	Bluebell	Bourke Henry	worsted m`fy	-	13a.	-	-	-	-	gr/	-
Drimnagh	Bluebell	Milner Henry	mill	-	-	-	Milner Henry - Hill Wm	1863	-	dd/	1863 36 282
Drimnagh	Bluebell	Wall Samuel	cloth mfty	-	14a.	95	-	1832	-	VOf/	OL.X078
Drimnagh	Bluebell	Wall Samuel	woollen fcty	-	14a.	-	-	-	-	gr/	-
Dublin	Boddin *	Eustace Martha :	mill	-	-	-	Eustace M - White Mark	1748	-	dd/	132 491 90118
Dublin	Boddin *	White Mark :	mill	-	-	-	White M - Cuthbert John :	1749	-	dd/	135 264 91313
Swords	Brackenstown	-	corn	-	-	-	-	-	-	6"os/	11
Swords	Brackenstown	Manders Richard	flour	-	-	-	-	-	-	gr/	-
Swords	Brackenstown	Manders Richard	miller`s ho. :	-	-	-	-	-	-	gr/	-
Portmarnock	Burrow	- E/ Portmarnock B	corn	-	-	-	-	1841	-	6"os/	15
Portmarnock	Burrow	Molloy John	corn	34.0x23x25 & kiln :	-	-	-	-	14x3.6x2 drives :	hob/	5.0885
Dublin	Butlers Meadow	Norton Brett	mills	-	-	-	Norton B - Falconberg Henr	1790	-	dd/	431 237 279961
Lucan	Caraghcon	- Lucan Iron Works	iron	-	-	-	-	-	-	6"os/	17
Finglas	Cardiffs Mill	Carrick Thomas :	mill	-	-	-	Carrick - Eustace James :	1729	-	dd/	67 247 46075
Finglas	Cardiffs Mill	Eustace	mill	-	-	-	Eustace - Ormsby	-	?	dd/	48 81 30725
Castleknock	Castleknock	-	flour	-	-	-	-	-	-	6"os/	17
Castleknock	Castleknock	-	starch works	-	-	-	-	-	-	6"os/	17
Castleknock	Castleknock	- at weir on R Liffey	flour	now turbine ho.	-	-	Peter Harte	2002	-	phoWEH	A
Castleknock	Castleknock	Foley & Co	cloth	-	-	-	-	-	-	gr/	-
Castleknock	Castleknock	Foley M/s	cloth	34x36x15 :	-	-	-	1846	15x5.6x3 carding :	hob/	5.3814
Castleknock	Castleknock	Glorney Benjamin	flour	86x22x29, office+E1	-	-	-	1846	15x5x3 no bkts. :	hob/	5.3814
Castleknock	Castleknock	Glorney Benjamin	flour & mill ho	-	-	-	-	-	-	gr/	-
Castleknock	Castleknock	Glorney Benjamin	mustard, indigo	blue mill & stores :	-	-	-	1846	15x3x3 no. bkts :	hob/	5.3814
Castleknock	Castleknock	Glorney Benjamin	mustard, starch	-	-	-	-	-	-	gr/	-
Castleknock	Castleknock	Nixon Frederick	cloth	45.6x34x27 also :	-	-	-	1846	no dimensions :	hob/	5.3814
Castleknock	Castleknock	Peate & Hoyle	cloth	-	-	-	-	-	-	gr/	-
Castleknock	Castleknock	Peate & Hoyle	cloth	25.6x22x19 Val :	-	36	-	1846	15x4 no. bkts. 30 :	hob/	5.3814
Castleknock	Castleknock bo.	Dundas Maria & W	mills	The Blade Mills	-	-	Dundas Maria - Dundas L	1861	-	dd/	1861 27 256
Castleknock	Castleknock bo.	Dundas William	blade mill	-	-	-	Dundas Wm - Lorenzo D	1863	-	dd/	1863 3 124
Dublin	Channon Hill	Hall	windmill	-	-	-	Hall - Rowley	-	-	dd/	84 32 60669
Dublin	Channon Hill	Hamilton	windmill	-	-	-	Hamilton - Hall	-	-	dd/	71 448 52013
Dublin	Channon Hill	Thomond Lord	windmill	-	-	-	Thomond Ld - Hamilton	-	-	dd/	37 100 21517
Chapelizod	Chapelizod	-	flax m`fty	-	-	-	-	-	-	6"os/	18
Chapelizod	Chapelizod	- on R. Liffey	flour	- building demol. :	-	-	- sluice & mill race intact	2010	-	mmSv/	wh - R
Chapelizod	Chapelizod	Armstrong	mill	-	-	-	Armstrong - Stephens	-	?	dd/	890 382 599992
Chapelizod	Chapelizod	Bever & W (ors Watt	mill	-	-	-	Bever - Bever	-	-	dd/	890 234 588734
Chapelizod	Chapelizod	Bever & Wife	mill (near)	-	-	-	Bever - Stephens	-	-	dd/	881 198 584198
Chapelizod	Chapelizod	Blake (Chief Rem.)	mill	-	-	-	Blake - Ormsby	-	-	dd/	839 149 56194
Chapelizod	Chapelizod	Conway Mr	wash	-	-	-	-	-	-	dir1800	Dublin

PARISH	TOWNLAND	MILLER	TYPE	HOUSE	Land	£Val	PROPRIETORS	Date	WHEEL etc.	Record	Ref.
Chapelizod	Chapelizod	Crosthwaite & Sons	bleach & bl-gn	-	3a.	-	-	-	-	gr/	-
Chapelizod	Chapelizod	Crosthwaite & Sons	wv.D218 factory	-	-	-	-	-	-	gr/	-
Chapelizod	Chapelizod	Dargan William	mills	-	-	-	Dargan Wm - Hoey Robt	1864	-	dd/	1864 1 156
Chapelizod	Chapelizod	Hyland Mr	flour	-	-	-	-	-	-	dir1800	Dublin
Chapelizod	Chapelizod	Montgomery	mill	-	-	-	Montgomery - Stephens	-	-	dd/	890 381 588881
Chapelizod	Chapelizod	Nowlan Mr	fulling	-	-	-	-	-	-	dir1800	Dublin
Chapelizod	Chapelizod	Nowlan Mr	fulling	-	-	-	-	-	-	dir1800	Dublin
Chapelizod	Chapelizod	Nowlan Mr	woollen	-	-	-	-	-	-	dir1800	Dublin
Clonaghlis	Clonaghlis	- S. side Gd. Canal	corn	-	-	-	-	-	-	6"os/	20
Clondalkin	Clondalkin	-	paper	-	-	-	-	1899	-	1"os/	111
Clondalkin	Clondalkin	Jolly	mill & pond	-	-	-	Jolly - Simpson	-	-	dd/	50 408 33573
Clondalkin	Clondalkin	Seery Thomas	mill	-	12a.	123	-	1832	-	VOf/	OL.X078
Clondalkin	Clondalkin	Seery Thomas	mills	-	-	-	Seery Thos - Ire Bank Govs	1861	-	dd/	1861 11 205
Clondalkin	Clondalkin	Seery Thomas	paper	-	-	-	-	-	-	gr/	-
Clondalkin	Clondalkin Town	-	corn	-	-	-	-	-	-	6"os/	17
Clondalkin	Clondalkin Town	-	paper &, pond	-	-	-	-	-	-	6"os/	17
Clondalkin	Clondalkin U & Lr	Milne James	corn	-	-	-	Milne James - Nat.Bank Ltd	1894	-	dd/	1894 31 144
Clondalkin	Clondalkin U & Lr	Nolan Richard	mills	-	-	-	Nolan Richard - Ross Alex	1890	-	dd/	1890 47 142
Clondalkin	Clondalkin U & Lr	Ross Alexander	corn	-	-	-	Ross Alex - Milne James	1892	-	dd/	1892 33 273
St George`s	Clonliffe East	- nr Riversdale	corn, mill pond	-	-	-	-	-	-	6"os/	18
St George`s	Clonliffe East	- nr Riversdale	vitriol works	-	-	-	-	-	-	6"os/	18
St George`s	Clonliffe East	Ellis Thomas	flour	43.6x20.6x28.0 & :	-	-	-	-	15.4 & 42 floats 4ft.	hob/	5.0891
St George`s	Clonliffe East	Ellis Thomas	flour & corn	flour 43.6x20.6x18 :	-	-	-	1846	15.4x4x5 8 rpm.	hob/	5.0889
Donnybrook	Clonskeagh	- N/ Clonskeagh Br.	snuff factory	-	-	-	-	-	-	6"os/	22
Donnybrook	Clonskeagh	Hibernian Bank	mill weir & race	-	-	-	Hibernian Bank	1894	-	dd/	1894 56 34
Donnybrook	Clonskeagh	Jackson & White	iron-works	-	-	-	-	-	2 wheels	dir1800	Dublin
Donnybrook	Clonskeagh	Jackson & White	iron-works	-	-	-	-	-	2 wheels	dir1800	Dublin
Donnybrook	Clonskeagh	Rochford Henry	mill	-	land	-	Rochford Henry - do	1861	-	dd/	1861 25 123/4
Donnybrook	Clonskeagh	Stokes Mr & Co	iron-works	-	-	-	-	-	3 wheels	dir1800	Dublin
Lucan	Coldblow	- N. side R. Liffey	Mill	-	-	-	-	1821	-	WDunc/	2
Rathcole	Collegeland	-	corn & mill race	-	-	-	-	-	-	6"os/	21
Rathcole	Collegeland	Connor Thomas	corn	-	1.0.1(	-	-	-	-	gr/	-
Dublin	Comberry	Dixon Mr	corn	-	-	-	-	-	-	dir1800	Dublin
Dublin	Conagh	Riall Pineas	-	-	land	-	Riall Pineas - Bewley Sam	1860	-	dd/	1860 16 290
Dublin	Conyborough	Trimelston Ld Baron	mill	-	-	-	Trimelston Lord - Deed	1861	-	dd/	1861 8 17
Dublin	Coolock (bo)	Hely Edward	mill pond & mill	-	-	-	Hely Edward - Deed	1861	-	dd/	1861 39 193
Dublin	Coolock (bo)	Pirie Gordon	mills	Clonliffe Mills	-	-	Pirie Gordon - Healy Edw	1861	-	dd/	1861 11 210
Tallaght	Corbally	-	windmill - corn	-	-	-	-	-	-	dir1800	Dublin
Dublin	Corduff+B137	-	corn	-	-	-	-	-	-	dir1800	Dublin
Clondalkin	Corkagh	-	Corkagh Mills	-	-	-	-	-	-	6"os/	21
Clondalkin	Corkagh	-	gunpowder	well preserved	-	-	Finlay Colley	2002	-	phoWEH	B
Clondalkin	Corkagh	-	mill (x 3)	-	-	-	-	-	-	6"os/	21
Clondalkin	Corkagh	-	mill (store)	well preserved	-	-	Finlay Colley	2002	-	phoWEH	B
Clondalkin	Corkagh	-	millers` houses	well preserved	-	-	-	2002	-	phoWEH	R
Clondalkin	Corkagh	- opp. Demesne	Powder Mill	-	-	-	-	-	-	JRoc	1760 map
Clondalkin	Corkagh	Arabin John Ladavez	threshing	Incumbant Estate :	-	-	- sold to Philip Grierson	1855	(1907 Col. H. Finlay)	mlyIE	p84
Clondalkin	Corkagh	M`Nally Mr	gunpowder	-	-	-	-	-	-	6"os/	21
Clondalkin	Corkagh	M`Nally Mr	old powder mill	-	-	-	-	-	-	6"os/	21
Clondalkin	Corkagh Dems.	Corkagh House	(no mill)	-	-	-	-	-	-	6"os/	21
Cruagh	Cruagh	- at Rockbrook	paper	-	-	-	-	-	-	6"os/	25
Cruagh	Cruagh	- at Rockbrook X	paper	ruinous but solid	-	-	Rockbrook Park School	2002	-	phoWEH	R
Cruagh	Cruagh	- nr Tibradden Ho.	old silk mfy	-	-	-	-	-	-	6"os/	25

PARISH	TOWNLAND	MILLER	TYPE	HOUSE	Land	£Val	PROPRIETORS	Date	WHEEL etc.	Record	Ref.
Crumlin	Crumlin	-	windmill stump	-	-	-	-	-	-	6"os/	18
Crumlin	Crumlin	Dioderick Joseph :	windmill field	-	-	-	Dioderick J - Carmach Jno :	1735	-	dd/	82 309 57936
Crumlin	Crumlin	Purcell	mill & :	-	-	-	Purcell - Smith	-	?	dd/	21 21 10622?
Crumlin	Crumlin	Smith	new mills :	-	-	-	Smith - Davis	-	?	dd/	43 91 34575
Donnybrook	D`brook Town	Nixon John	flour	(1C) 87x25x22.6 & :	-	100	-	1856	-	hob/	5.2682
Castleknock	Diswellstown	Annaly Baron	Devills mills	-	-	-	Annaly - Antrobus Hugh	1890	-	dd/	1890 22 105
Castleknock	Diswellstown	Bourke Henry	Devils Mills	-	-	-	Bourke H - Annaly Baron	1900	-	dd/	1900 14 260
Castleknock	Diswellstown	Child Samuel :	Devils Mills	-	-	-	Child S - Luttrell Lawes :	1772	-	dd/	291 227 191498
Castleknock	Diswellstown	Delany	Devills mills	-	-	-	Delany - Moran	-	-	dd/	889 5 588005
Castleknock	Diswellstown	Diswells (nr Castle)	no mill	-	-	-	-	-	-	JRoc	1760 map
Castleknock	Diswellstown	Eustace Mary :	mill	-	-	-	Eustace M - Eustace Jas :	1726	-	dd/	56 262 37866
Castleknock	Diswellstown	Hope James	Devils Mills	-	-	-	Hope Jas - Annaly Baron	1900	-	dd/	1900 14 220
Castleknock	Diswellstown	Howard Geo Edm	mills	(named : Devils Mill)	-	-	Howard G - Luttrell Simon :	1765	-	dd/	249 60 158902
Castleknock	Diswellstown	Irnham Lord	mills	-	-	-	Lord Irnham - Waltham Rb	1770	-	dd/	266 537 180066
Castleknock	Diswellstown	Irnham Simon :	Devils Mills	-	-	-	Ld Irnham - Child Saml :	1772	-	dd/	291 226 19496
Castleknock	Diswellstown	Irnham Simon Lord :	Devills mills	-	-	-	Irnham S - Child Samuel	1772	-	dd/	291 226 19197
Castleknock	Diswellstown	Keenan Thomas	Devills mills	-	-	-	Keenan Th - Redmond L	1777	-	dd/	324 219 213166
Castleknock	Diswellstown	Keenan Thomas :	Devills mills	-	-	-	Keenan T - Delany Jno :	1775	25 Mar.	dd/	319 409 216821?
Castleknock	Diswellstown	KeenanThomas :	Devills mills	-	-	-	Keenan T - Irnham Rt Hon :	1772	-	dd/	308 338 205326
Castleknock	Diswellstown	Kennan Thomas	mills	-	-	-	Kennan T - Kennan Robt :	1766	-	dd/	253 351 663630
Castleknock	Diswellstown	Luke White	mills	Devils Mills	-	-	White Luke - E & S Law :	1861	-	dd/	1861 30 28
Castleknock	Diswellstown	Luke White	mills	Devils Mills	-	-	White Luke - E & S Law :	1862	-	dd/	1862 13 245
Castleknock	Diswellstown	Luttrell Hon Henry :	Devills mills	-	-	-	Luttrell HL - Hamilton :	1775	-	dd/	315 55 208636
Castleknock	Diswellstown	Luttrell Hon Henry L	Devills mills	-	-	-	Luttrell L - Wegg Samuel :	1772	-	dd/	291 288 191198
Castleknock	Diswellstown	Luttrell Simon	Devils Mills	-	-	-	Luttrell S - Hatchell Henry	1734	-	dd/	76 346 54794
Castleknock	Diswellstown	Luttrell Simon	Devils Mills	-	-	-	Lutrell S - Lawley Robt Bt	1735	-	dd/	91 341 64445
Castleknock	Diswellstown	Luttrell Simon	Devils Mills	-	-	-	Luttrell S - Robbins Jos	1738	-	dd/	90 150 63502
Castleknock	Diswellstown	Luttrell Simon	mill	-	-	-	Luttrell S - Kennan Thos	1734	-	dd/	79 216 55286
Castleknock	Diswellstown	Luttrell Simon :	Devills mills	-	-	-	Luttrell S - Finlay Thomas :	1766	-	dd/	246 496 158932
Castleknock	Diswellstown	O`Connor Arthur	Devills mills	-	-	-	O`Connor Arthur - Charles	1890	-	dd/	1890 49 270
Castleknock	Diswellstown	Price Samuel	land	-	-	-	Price S - Kennan Thos	1725	-	dd/	47 453 31430
Castleknock	Diswellstown	Shute Edith E	mill	-	-	-	Shute E - Martyn Mary	1900	-	dd/	1900 33 171
Castleknock	Diswellstown	White Charles J	Devills mills	-	-	-	White C - O`Connor Arthur	1890	-	dd/	1890 15 245
Castleknock	Diswellstown	White Francis W	Devills mills	-	-	-	White Fran - Wallis John	1894	-	dd/	1894 58 52
Castleknock	Diswellstown	White Robert	Devills mills	-	-	-	White R - Feeny Margaret	1891	-	dd/	1891 37 234
Lucan	Doddsborough	-	corn, mill pond	-	-	-	-	-	-	6"os/	17
Lucan	Doddsborough	Davis Anne	corn	-	110a	-	-	-	-	gr/	-
St James	Dolphins Barn	Abbot Christopher	mills	-	-	-	Abbot C - Wilde Michael	1785	-	dd/	367 533 250387
St James	Dolphins Barn	Bacon Isaac	mill & kiln	-	-	-	Bacon I - Furlong Nicholas	1738	-	dd/	92 5 63672
St James	Dolphins Barn	Bond John	flour	-	0.1.3;	-	-	-	-	gr/	-
St James	Dolphins Barn	Bond John	mill (unfin.)	44.6x22.6x28 :	-	-	-	1845	machinery not in.	hob/	5.2678
St James	Dolphins Barn	Brown Mr	cotton	-	-	-	-	-	-	dir1800	Dublin
St James	Dolphins Barn	Byrne Michael :	mills	-	-	-	Byrne M - Kevill Eamon :	1800	-	dd/	523 581 340703
St James	Dolphins Barn	Chambre Meredyth	mills	-	-	-	Chambre M - Falkener Mgt.	1785	-	dd/	373 22 247772
St James	Dolphins Barn	Chambre Meredyth (	mills	-	-	-	Chambres M - Fottrell Jn :	1789	-	dd/	401 128 267838
St James	Dolphins Barn	Clarke Abrahame :	old foundary	(1C) 38x21x9 & :	-	11-8	-	1845	-	hob/	5.2678
St James	Dolphins Barn	Connor William :	mills	-	-	-	Connor W - Connor Wm :	1796	-	dd/	532 361 349335
St James	Dolphins Barn	Cullen George :	mills	-	-	-	Cullen G - Kennedy Jas :	1796	-	dd/	513 202 336219
St James	Dolphins Barn	Fairbrother Abraham	old mill	-	2.1.1(	13 :	-	1832	-	VOf/	OL.X078
St James	Dolphins Barn	Fairbrother Mr	cotton	-	-	-	-	-	-	dir1800	Dublin
St James	Dolphins Barn	Gilbert Claudius Rev	mill	-	-	-	Gilbert C - Sands William :	1739	-	dd/	88 139 61976
St James	Dolphins Barn	Guy Robert	iron mills, forge	70.0x31.6x19.6 & :	-	-	-	-	15x8x10 56 bkts. :	hob/	5.0939

PARISH	TOWNLAND	MILLER	TYPE	HOUSE	Land	£Val	PROPRIETORS	Date	WHEEL etc.	Record	Ref.
St James	Dolphins Barn	Guy Robert	iron works	-	8.0.1	109 :	-	1832	-	VOf/	OL.X078
St James	Dolphins Barn	Hall John	mills & :	-	-	-	Hall J - Gilbert Claudins	1726	-	dd/	51 258 33601
St James	Dolphins Barn	Hall William	mills & :	-	-	-	Hall Wm - Percy Henry	1709	-	dd/	2 344 496
St James	Dolphins Barn	Hilton John :	mills & :	-	-	-	Hilton J - Pilkington Thos	1713	-	dd/	20 332 10813
St James	Dolphins Barn	Percy Henry	mills & :	-	-	-	Percy H - Hall William	1708	-	dd/	4 142 801
St James	Dolphins Barn	Pilkington Thomas	mills & :	-	-	-	Pilkington T - Carroll Mchl	1718	Mort. 2 Apl.	dd/	20 333 10815
St James	Dolphins Barn	Robinson Thomas	:mills	-	-	-	Robinson T & Eliz & Croker	1785	-	dd/	364 390 246178
St James	Dolphins Barn	Sands Isaac	mill	-	-	-	Sands I - Bradley James	1710	-	dd/	40 355 26271
St James	Dolphins Barn	Sands William	mill	-	-	-	Sands Wm - Hutton John	1737	-	dd/	91 36 63200
St James	Dolphins Barn	Sands William :	mill	-	-	-	Sands W - Hilliard Jno :	1737	Lease 25 Oct.	dd/	89 57 62032
St James	Dolphins Barn	Wilkinson Peter	mills	-	-	-	Wilkinson P - Wilde Nich	1787	-	dd/	386 359 258789
St James	Dolphins Barn	Wilson John :	mill	-	-	-	Wilson J - Percewall Ewd	1750	-	dd/	142 474 96327
Donabate	Donabate	-	corn	-	-	-	-	-	-	dir1800	Dublin
Donabate	Donabate	-	windmill - corn	-	-	-	-	-	-	dir1800	Dublin
Donabate	Donabate	- E. of Killerough Isl	mill	-	-	-	-	-	-	JRoc	1760 map
Donnybrook	Donnybrook	-	saw	-	-	-	-	-	-	6"os/	18
Donnybrook	Donnybrook	Duffy's	Cotton Mill	- on R. Dodder :	-	-	Associated Feltmakers Est.	1813	-	surv/	jh
Donnybrook	Donnybrook	- E. of Town :	Wind Mill	-	-	-	-	-	-	JRoc	1760 map
Donnybrook	Donnybrook	Fitzwiliam Richd Hor	mill	-	-	-	Fitzwiliam - Charlton Andr	1732	-	dd/	73 338 51324
Donnybrook	Donnybrook	Fitzwiliam Richd Ld.	mill	-	-	-	Fitzwiliam R Hon - Richd	1730	-	dd/	72 453 51534
Donnybrook	Donnybrook	Fitzwilliam Richard	mills	-	-	-	Fitzwilliam R - Wm Morice	1739	-	dd/	93 521 66659
Donnybrook	Donnybrook	Manseragh Edward :	mill & park :	-	-	-	Manseragh E - Rutland A	1717	Mort. 12 Feb.	dd/	20 154 10128
Donnybrook	Donnybrook	McDaniel Christphr	mill seat	-	-	-	McDaniel C - Alkin Wm	1738	-	dd/	89 357 63577
Donnybrook	Donnybrook	Moore George :	red mill	-	-	-	Moore G - Thwaite Geo :	1760	-	dd/	203 533 136606
Donnybrook	Donnybrook	Moreton William	red mill	-	-	-	Moreton W - Roberts Robt	1740	-	dd/	99 371 69585
Donnybrook	Donnybrook	Plunket Plunkett :	mill & mill ho.	-	-	-	Plunket Plunkett - LWT	1743	-	dd/	151 456 102523
Donnybrook	Donnybrook	Plunkett Plunkett	mill	-	-	-	Plunkett P - Manseragh Jn	1726	-	dd/	50 380 33430
Donnybrook	Donnybrook	Plunkett Plunkett	mill & mill ho.	-	-	-	Plunket Pl - Barrett Wm	1737	-	dd/	102 388 70854
Donnybrook	Donnybrook	Sterling	red mill	-	-	-	Sterling - Moore George	1751	-	dd/	145 390 98946
Donnybrook	Donnybrook	Usher Henry :	red mill	-	-	-	Usher H - Dawson Richd :	1751	-	dd/	148 150 98952
Donnybrook	Donnybrook	Usher William	mill seat	-	-	-	Usher W - McDaniel Chrs	1738	-	dd/	91 71 63370
Donnybrook	Donnybrook	Usher William	mills & lands	-	-	-	Usher Wm - Leeson Jos	1709	-	dd/	2 321 515
Donnybrook	Donnybrook	Usher William	tuckmill & seat	-	-	-	Usher Wm - Fenner Richd	1705	-	dd/	31 218 862
Donnybrook	Donnybrook	Williams	mills	-	-	-	Williams - Sherwin	-	?	dd/	183 138 70956
Donnybrook	Donnybrook :	Wright Bros.	Beaver Hat Fty.	-							
Donnybrook	Donnybrook East	- W. side R. Dodde	hat factory	-	-	-	-	-	-	6"os/	22
Donnybrook	Donnybrook Lr	Adair Elenor :	corn	-	-	-	Adair E - Ashworth Mgt	1765	-	dd/	288 302 190770
Donnybrook	Donnybrook Lr	Ashwood Margaret	corn	-	-	-	Ashwood - Ashwood S	1794	-	dd/	484 410 308770
Donnybrook	Donnybrook Lr	McMahon John :	corn	-	-	-	McMahon J - Smith Charles	1768	-	dd/	281 342 18695
Donnybrook	Donnybrook Lr	Smith Ann :	corn	-	-	-	Smith Ann - Duffy John :	1795	Lease 8 Jne.	dd/	499 224 345998
Donnybrook	Donnybrook Lr	Smith Charles	corn	-	-	-	Smith Chas - Madden Wm	1781	-	dd/	342 23 227868
Donnybrook	Donnybrook Lr	Walsh	corn	-	-	-	Walsh - Madden	-	?	dd/	392 316 263081
Donnybrook	Donnybrook Tn	Nixon John	flour	(1C) 87x25x22.6 & :	-	101	-	1856	-	hob/	5.2682
Drimnagh	Donore Liberty	Archibold Charles	mills	-	-	-	Archibold C - Healy Wm	1861	-	dd/	1861 25 120
Drimnagh	Donore Mills of	Busby Jno	mills	-	-	-	Busby Jno - Kappock Mcl	1860	-	dd/	1860 16 225
Naul	Doolagh	Flinn Mr	corn	-	-	-	-	-	-	dir1800	Dublin
Drimnagh	Drimnagh	-	paper	-	-	-	-	-	-	6"os/	18
Drimnagh	Drimnagh	- E. side Vilage	Mill	-	-	-	-	-	-	JRoc	1760 map
Drimnagh	Drimnagh	Donagh John	mill-pond	-	1.2.0	-	-	-	-	gr/	-
Drimnagh	Drimnagh	Pim George	mill	-	15a.	-	-	-	-	gr/	-
Drimnagh	Drimnagh	Sulivan Daniel P	paper	-	28a.	-	-	-	-	gr/	-
Drimnagh	Drimnagh	Sullivan Daniel	paper	-	28a.	166 :	-	1832	-	VOf/	OL.X078

PARISH	TOWNLAND	MILLER	TYPE	HOUSE	Land	£Val	PROPRIETORS	Date	WHEEL etc.	Record	Ref.
Drimnagh	Drimnagh	Warren Christopher	printing	-	15a.	79 :	-	1832	-	VOf/	OL.X078
Clonturk	Drishoge	-	woollen m`fty	-	-	-	-	-	-	6"os/	18
Clonturk	Drishoge	- nr Riversdale	flour	-	-	-	-	-	-	6"os/	18
Clonturk	Drishoge	Butterworth James	woollen fcty	44.6x26.0x24.0 & :	-	-	-	-	16.0x4x5 = 20 hp :	hob/	5.0872
Clonturk	Drishoge	Dignam Thomas	flour	25.5x22x26.6 kiln :	-	-	-	1846	14x6x9 breast :	hob/	5.0872
bo./ Coolock	Drishoge (2)	Nihill Laurence :	mill	-	-	-	Nihill L - Sherlock Patrick :	1793	-	dd/	526 381 34479?
bo./ Coolock	Drishoge (2)	Pearson William	mill	-	-	-	Pearson - O`Connell Thos	1809	-	dd/	1890 44130
bo./ Coolock	Drishoge (2)	Richard Ld Bishop	mill	-	-	-	Armagh B of - Sweetman	1793	-	dd/	481 27 300848
bo./ Coolock	Drishoge (2)	Sherlock	mill	-	-	-	Sherlock - Kennedy	c1805	?	dd/	584 268 397283
bo./ Coolock	Drishoge (2)	Ulster Bank Ltd	mill	-	-	-	Ulster Bank - Pearson Wm	1890	-	dd/	1890 43 280
bo./ Coolock	Drishoge (2) :	Atkinson Joseph	mill	-	-	-	Atkinson Jos - Hines Jos	1795	-	dd/	470 167 300270
Dub (? par.)	Droultuin *	Dunn Valentine :	iron mills	-	-	-	Dunn V - Doyle Terence :	1802	Mort. 30 Mar.	dd/	546 180 359226
Dub (? par.)	Droultuin *	Fausett Charles :	iron mills	-	-	-	Fausett C - Yeates James :	1802	-	dd/	545 110 358805
Dub (? par.)	Droultuin *	Norris Joshua & :	iron mills	-	-	-	Norris J - Stokes John & :	1799	-	dd/	525 169 344477
Dub (? par.)	Droultuin *	Sharman Ann :	iron mills	-	-	-	Sharmon - Norman Robt :	1799	-	dd/	517 238 339643
Clonturk	Drumcondra	Halpin Mr	corn	-	-	-	-	-	-	dir1800	Dublin
Clonturk	Drumcondra	Halpin Mr	corn	-	-	-	-	-	-	dir1800	Dublin
Clonturk	Drumcondra	Montgomery Mr	corn	-	-	-	-	-	-	dir1800	Dublin
Clonturk	Drumcondra	Sherlock Mr	corn	-	-	-	-	-	-	dir1800	Dublin
(? par.)	Dub Port & Cem.	Hamilton Charles	Windmill Hill	-	-	-	Hamilton - Naish Redmond	1891	-	dd/	1891 45 215
bo./ U`cross	Dub Port & Cem.	Hutchinson Frederick	The Strand Mill	-	-	-	Hutchinson F - Neill John	1894	-	dd/	1894 16 40
(? par.)	Dub Port & Cem.	Hyland Mary	Tinkers Mill	-	-	-	Hyland M - Drake Mervyn	1892	-	dd/	1892 33 187
bo./ U`cross	Dub Port & Cem.	Nolan Richard	The Mill Meadow		-	-	Nolan Richd - Ross Alex	1890	-	dd/	1890 47 142
bo./ U`cross	Dub Port & Cem.	Plunkett Oliver	Scots Woollen :	-	-	-	Plunkett Oliver - John	1893	-	dd/	1893 13 229
bo./ N`castle	Dub Port & Cem.	Vesey Charles	bleachyard	-	-	-	Vesey C - Mecredy Isabella	1890	-	dd/	1890 3 83
St Luke`s	Dublin	Horan Mr, Mill St.	dye-stuff	-	-	-	-	-	-	dir1800	Dublin
Dub (? par.)	Dublin	Stephens Mr :	corn (steam)	-	-	-	-	-	-	dir1800	Dublin
Dub (? par.)	Dublin	Sweetman Mr :	brewery steam	-	-	-	-	-	-	dir1800	Dublin
St Luke`s	Dublin	Walsh & Co, Mill St.	dye-stuff, oil	-	-	-	-	-	-	dir1800	Dublin
Crumlin	Dublin :	Purcell William :	mill	-	-	-	Purcell W - Richardson Jn :	1775	-	dd/	306 428 204030
Dub (? par.)	Dublin :	Roe Mr, Coome	oatmeal, malt	-	-	-	-	-	-	dir1800	Dublin
Dub (? par.)	Dublin :	Keating Mr	corn (steam)	-	-	-	-	-	-	dir1800	Dublin
St James	Dublin :	Manders Alderman	corn	-	-	-	-	-	-	dir1800	Dublin
Dub (? par.)	Dublin :	Jackson Mr	corn (steam)	-	-	-	-	-	-	dir1800	Dublin
Dub (? par.)	Dublin :	Clarke & Manders	corn	-	-	-	-	-	-	dir1800	Dublin
Dub (? par.)	Dublin City	- (no name) :	steam engine :	-	-	-	-	-	-	dir1800	Dublin
St James	Dublin City	- at Cork Street	chemical wks	-	-	-	-	2002	-	6"os/	18
St James	Dublin City	- at Cork Street	chemical wks	- nil remains	-	-	-	2002	-	phoWEH	Z
St James	Dublin City	- at Islandbridge	calico print	- demolished	-	-	-	2002	-	mmSv/	wh - Z
Dub (? par.)	Dublin City	- at Pim Street	mill	- dilapidated	-	-	-	2002	-	phoWEH	B
St Audoen`s	Dublin City	- Bridgefoot St.	saw	-	-	-	-	-	-	6"os/	18
St Thomas	Dublin City	- Mayor Street	vitriol works	-	-	-	-	-	-	6"os/	18
StJohn`s	Dublin City	- on Cammock R	flour & mill dam	-	-	-	-	-	-	6"os/	18
St James	Dublin City	- on Cork Street	chemical works	-	-	-	-	-	-	6"os/	18
Dub (? par.)	Dublin City	- on Forbes Lane	distillery	-	-	-	-	-	-	6"os/	18
College Ward	Dublin City	- Hanover St. East	flour	-	-	-	-	-	-	6"os/	18
College Ward	Dublin City	- Hanover St. East	flour	- old tall buildings :	-	-	-	-	-	6"os/	18
Dub (? par.)	Dublin City	- S./Gd Canal Doc	distillery	-	-	-	-	2010	-	phoWEH	B
St James	Dublin City	- nr Old Kilmainhar	flour	-	-	-	-	-	-	6"os/	18
Dub (? par.)	Dublin City	Brannigan Thomas	distillery	-	-	-	-	1782	1 still - 533g.	hcJ	lic.
Dub (? par.)	Dublin City	Byrne John	distillery	-	-	-	-	1782	1 still - 265g.	hcJ	lic.
Dub (? par.)	Dublin City	Byrne John	distillery	-	-	-	-	1782	1 still - 247g.	hcJ	lic.

PARISH	TOWNLAND	MILLER	TYPE	HOUSE	Land	£Val	PROPRIETORS	Date	WHEEL etc.	Record	Ref.
Dub (? par.)	Dublin City	Callahan D	distillery	-	-	-	-	1782	2 stills - 475g.	hcJ	lic.
Dub (? par.)	Dublin City	Callahan N	distillery	-	-	-	-	1782	2 stills - 497g.	hcJ	lic.
St John`s	Dublin City	Clarke & Manders	: corn	-	-	-	-	-	-	dir1800	Dublin
St John`s	Dublin City	Clarke & Manders	: corn	-	-	-	-	-	-	dir1800	Dublin
Dub (? par.)	Dublin City	Dodd W	distillery	-	-	-	-	1782	1 still - 263g.	hcJ	lic.
bo./ N`castle	Dublin City	Du Bedat Charles	Harcourt Mills		-	-	Du Bedat chas - Francis E	1890		dd/	1890 49 10
Finglas	Dublin City	Du Bedat Charles	Rialto Mills	-	-	-	Du Bedat Charles - Francis	1890	-	dd/	1890 49 10
Dub (? par.)	Dublin City	Edward J	distillery	-	-	-	-	1782	2 stills - 286 & 1038g	hcJ	lic.
Dub (? par.)	Dublin City	Ford Mr.	distillery	-	-	-	-	1782	2 stills - 543g.	hcJ	lic.
Dub (? par.)	Dublin City	Ford William	distillery	-	-	-	-	1782	2 stills - 486g.	hcJ	lic.
Dub (? par.)	Dublin City	Fraut R	distillery	-	-	-	-	1782	1 still - 250g.	hcJ	lic.
Dub (? par.)	Dublin City	Heavin R	distillery	-	-	-	-	1782	1 still - 242g.	hcJ	lic.
Dub (? par.)	Dublin City	Heavy B	distillery	-	-	-	-	1782	1 still - 526g.	hcJ	lic.
St Luke`s	Dublin City	Horan Mr, Mill St.	dye-stuff	-	-	-	-	-	-	dir1800	Dublin
Dub (? par.)	Dublin City	Huffey	distillery	-	-	-	-	1782	2 stills - 523g.	hcJ	lic.
St Michael`s	Dublin City	Jackson Mr :	corn (steam)	-	-	-	-	-	-	dir1800	Dublin
Dub (? par.)	Dublin City	Keating Mr :	corn (steam)	-	-	-	-	-	-	dir1800	Dublin
Dub (? par.)	Dublin City	Kelly C	distillery	-	-	-	-	1782	2 stills - 226 & 628g.	hcJ	lic.
Dub (? par.)	Dublin City	Kenny	distillery	-	-	-	-	1782	2 stills - 208 & 513g.	hcJ	lic.
Dub (? par.)	Dublin City	Kerny J	distillery	-	-	-	-	1782	1 still - 261g.	hcJ	lic.
Dub (? par.)	Dublin City	Laundy M	distillery	-	-	-	-	1782	1 still - 229g.	hcJ	lic.
Dub (? par.)	Dublin City	Lynch J	distillery	-	-	-	-	1782	2 stills - 212 & 539g.	hcJ	lic.
Dub (? par.)	Dublin City	Lynham M	distillery	-	-	-	-	1782	1 still - 262g.	hcJ	lic.
St James	Dublin City	McCready Edward	mill	-	-	-	-	-	-	gr/	-
Dub (? par.)	Dublin City	Manders Alderman	:corn	-	-	-		-	-	dir1800	Dublin
Finglas	Dublin City	Morris Mary	Rialto Mills	-	-	-	Morris M - Ir. Portland Cem.	1890	-	dd/	1890 49 10
Dub (? par.)	Dublin City	Mortimer G	distillery	-	-	-	-	1782	1 still - 230g.	hcJ	lic.
Dub (? par.)	Dublin City	Pelin J	distillery	-	-	-	-	1782	1 still - 275g.	hcJ	lic.
Dub (? par.)	Dublin City	Reily James	distillery	-	-	-	-	1782	1 still - 242g.	hcJ	lic.
Dub (? par.)	Dublin City	Rivers J	distillery	-	-	-	-	1782	1 still - 285g.	hcJ	lic.
Dub (? par.)	Dublin City	Roe Mr, Coome :	oatmeal, malt	-	-	-	-	-	-	dir1800	Dublin
Dub (? par.)	Dublin City	Roe R	distillery	-	-	-	-	1782	1still - 234g.	hcJ	lic.
Dub (? par.)	Dublin City	Rooney M	distillery	-	-	-	-	1782	1 still - 233g.	hcJ	lic.
Dub (? par.)	Dublin City	Rooney W	distillery	-	-	-	-	1782	1 still - 257g.	hcJ	lic.
Dublin	Dublin City	Sherigley John	Red Mill	-	-	-	Sherigley J - Hodgins Jos	1737	-	dd/	91 125 63639
Dub (? par.)	Dublin City	Stephens Mr :	corn (steam)	-	-	-	-	-	-	dir1800	Dublin
-	Dublin City	Summers John	Hibernian Mills	-	-	-	Summers J - Whelan E Rev	1891	-	dd/	1891 53 178
Dub (? par.)	Dublin City	Swan J	distillery	-	-	-	-	1782	1 still - 219g.	hcJ	lic.
Dub (? par.)	Dublin City	Sweeny B	distillery	-	-	-	-	1782	1 still - 262g.	hcJ	lic.
Dub (? par.)	Dublin City	Sweetman A	distillery	-	-	-	-	1782	1 still - 265g.	hcJ	lic.
Merrion Ward	Dublin City :	Bolands Patrick	flour	-	-	-	-	1870	- works 63 pr. st.	CRynne	Ind.Ire.1750+
St Ths. / Sep.	Dublin City :	Brookes	brewhouse & :	-	-	-	Brookes J - Gerrard Sam	1717	-	dd/	17 461 9440
StJohn`s	Dublin City :	Mecrery Isabella	Manor Mill	-	-	-	Mecredy Isb - Vesey Chas	1890	-	dd/	1890 56 43
Merrion Ward	Dublin City :	Boland's	Flour Mill	20th cen. buildings :	-	-	-	2010	-	phoWEH	B
Merrion Ward	Dublin City :	Bolands Ltd.	flour	-	-	-	-	1965	-	lic/4	wheat
Merrion Ward	Dublin City :	Boland's Flour Mill	flour	-	-	-	-	2010	-	mmSv/	wh - B
St James	Dublin City :	Story Thomas	Millwright	-	-	-	-	-	-	dir/	Thoms
St James	Dublin City :	Spence William	Millwright	-	-	-	-	-	-	dir/	Thoms
St James	Dublin City :	Manders Robt & Co	brewery, mill	-	-	-	-	-	-	gr/	-
St Thomas	Dublin City :	Crawford William :	flour mills	-	-		-	1898	-	dir/	Thoms
St James	Dublin City :	Byrne Matthew	Millwright	-	-	-	-	-	-	dir/	Thoms
St Thomas	Dublin City :	Brown & Gillmer	Seville Steam : (	-	-	-	-	1898	-	dir/	Thoms

PARISH	TOWNLAND	MILLER	TYPE	HOUSE	Land	£Val	PROPRIETORS	Date	WHEEL etc.	Record	Ref.
St James	Dublin City :	Roberts J F	Millwright	-	-	-	-	-	-	dir/	Thoms
Clonturk	Dublin City :	Smith	rind mill	-	-	-	Smith - Neynoe	-	?	dd/	36 231 22110
St Catherine`s	Dublin City :	Ennis Thomas	corn & kiln	-	-	-	-	-	-	gr/	-
St Thomas	Dublin City :	Jameson John	distillery :	chimney to S. 185ft.	-	-	- late. Acquired by J.J. -	1805	-	IHAI	editor
St Ths. / Sep.	Dublin City :	Sporle John :	brew house :	-	-	-	Sporle - Murgitroide Jno :	1712	D/Poll 21 Oct.	dd/	9 247 3592
St Ths./ Sep.	Dublin City :	Higginson John	mill	-	-	-	Higginson J - Commugham	-	?	dd/	5 62 37
St Mark`s	Dublin City :	Wilson Thomas P	corn & kiln	-	-	-	-	-	-	gr/	-
St James	Dublin City :	Dowling Patrick	mill	-	-	-	-	-	-	gr/	-
St Thomas	Dublin City :	McKenna Arthur	mills	Mabbot`s Mills	-	-	McKenna A - Brady John	1860	-	dd/	1860 14 274
St Luke`s	Dublin City :	Walsh & Co.	dye-stuff, oil	-	-	-	-	-	-	dir1800	Dublin
St Luke`s	Dublin City :	Busby John	mill, kiln	-	-	-	-	-	-	gr/	-
St Luke`s	Dublin City :	Leeson	mill (stream) & :	-	-	-	Leeson - Poole	-	?	dd/	5 443 8037
St Thomas	Dublin City :	Patent Saw Corn Mil	corn, saw	-	-	-	-	-	-	gr/	-
Dublin	Dublin City :	Dobson William	bleach yard				Dobson W - Palliser Wm :	1731	-	dd/	66 259 46147
St Thomas	Dublin City :	-	saw	-	-	-	-	-	-	TLtts/	1884
St Ths. / Sep.	Dublin City :	Sporle	brew house :	-	-	-	Sporle - Kane	1717	Mort. 14 Nov.	dd/	9 248 3594
Donnybrook	Dublin City :	Jeminat	saw mill :	-	-	-	Jeminat - Flanigan	-	?	dd/	73 222 53255
St Thomas	Dublin City :	-	Seville Steam :	-	-	-	-	-	-	TLtts/	1884
St Thomas	Dublin City :	-	Glass Works	-	-	-	-	-	-	TLtts/	1884
St Thomas	Dublin City :	-	Vinegar Works	-	-	-	-	-	-	TLtts/	1884
St Thomas	Dublin City :	McNally Thomas :	steam mills	-	-	-	-	-	-	gr/	-
St James	Dublin City :	Fairbrother Samuel	Millwright	-	-	-	-	-	-	dir/	Thoms
St Thomas	Dublin City :	Meath Earl of	Manor & Mill	-	-	-	Meath Earl - do.	1894	-	dd/	1894 60 257
Dub (? par.)	Dublin City :	Nowlan J	snuff m'factory :	-	-	-	-	1831	-	dir/	Wilson
Donnybrook	Dublin City :	The Dock Milling Co	flour	-	-	-	-	1965	-	lic/6	wheat
St Mary`s	Dublin City :	O'Beirne P & Co.	brewery	-	-	-	-	1898	-	dir/	Wilson
St Ths./ Sep.	Dublin City :	Murphy John	brewery	-	-	-	-	1832	-	dir/	Wilson
St Mary`s	Dublin City :	Moore & Son	corn bruising	-	-	-	-	1898	-	dir/	Thom
Donnybrook	Dublin City :	Cullen	mill "ye - :	-	-	-	Cullen - Martin	-	?	dd/	86 485 61442
Donnybrook	Dublin City :	Martin	mill "ye - :	-	-	-	Martin - Villibois	-	?	dd/	88 418 63137
Clonturk	Dublin City :	Eccles	rind mill (?)	-	-	-	Eccles - Smith	-	?	dd/	34 20 20260
Donnybrook	Dublin City :	Clark	brewhouse & :	-	-	-	Clark - Jones	-	?	dd/	51 449 34313
St Ths./ Sep.	Dublin City :	Challoner	brewhouse & :	-	-	-	Challoner - West	-	?	dd/	8 263 60285
St Ths./ Sep.	Dublin City :	Marriott Joseph	brewhouse & :	-	-	-	Marriott Jos - Jacob John	1710	-	dd/	7 338 2615
St Ths./ Sep.	Dublin City :	Archer	brewhouse & :	-	-	-	Archer - Thresher	-	?	dd/	62 470 43723
St Ths./ Sep.	Dublin City :	Carroll Bryan :	brewhouse & :	-	-	-	Carroll - Sheill	1716	Asgt. 24 Dec.	dd/	15 492 8438
St Ths./ Sep.	Dublin City :	Carroll Bryan :	brewhouse & :	-	-	-	Carroll - Shepheard	1716	Mort. 25 Sep.	dd/	15 441 8033
St Ths./ Sep.	Dublin City :	Thresher Daniel :	brewhouse & :	-	-	-	Thresher D - Madden Jn :	1730	-	dd/	64 255 43716
St Ths./ Sep.	Dublin City :	Brooks John	brewhouse & :	-	-	-	Brooks John - Barry Wm	1717	-	dd/	19 257 10102
St Ths./ Sep.	Dublin City :	Brooks John :	brewhouse & :	-	-	-	Brooks Jn - Brooks Jos	1717	-	dd/	21 104 10898
St Ths./ Sep.	Dublin City :	Brooks Joseph	brewhouse & :	-	-	-	Brooks J - Hamilton Jas	1718	-	dd/	24 24 12868
St Ths./ Sep.	Dublin City :	Gerard Samuel	brewhouse & :	-	-	-	Gerard Sam - Gerard Jno	1717	-	dd/	19 417 10476
St Catherines	Dublin City :	-	Harcourt Mill	- demolished	-	-	-	2002	-	mmSv/	wh - Z
St Catherines	Dublin City :	Mount Shamrock Mil	mill	- demolished	-	-	-	2002	-	mmSv/	wh - Z
St Ths./ Sep.	Dublin City :	Higginson	mill	-	-	-	Higginson - Ford	-	?	dd/	6 381 2300
St Ths./ Sep.	Dublin City :	Higginson John	mill	-	-	-	Higginson Jn - Ford Robt	1711	-	dd/	6 380 2302
St Ths./ Sep.	Dublin City :	Higginson John	mill	-	-	-	Higginson Jn - Ford Robt	1714	-	dd/	14 152 5955
Dub (? par.)	Dublin City :	Dawson Richard :	mill	-	-	-	Dawson R - Forbes Wm :	1761	Lease 12 Dec.	dd/	214 534 142209
Dub (? par.)	Dublin City :	Forbes	mill	-	-	-	Forbes - Chapman	-	?	dd/	312 45 209801
Dub (? par.)	Dublin City :	Halpin	mill	-	-	-	Halpin - Partnership	-	?	dd/	-?- -?- 350989
Dub (? par.)	Dublin City :	Halpin Charles :	mill	-	-	-	Halpin C - Disolution of :	1802	-	dd/	542 273 357602
Dub (? par.)	Dublin City :	Monck Laurence :	mill	-	-	-	Monck L - Christie Thmas :	1767	Lease 1 Jan.	dd/	263 223 167421

PARISH	TOWNLAND	MILLER	TYPE	HOUSE	Land	£Val	PROPRIETORS	Date	WHEEL etc.	Record	Ref.
St Ths./ Sep.	Dublin City :	Bignall Thomas	brewhouse & :	-	-	-	Bignall T - Taylor John	1724	-	dd/	44 140 28627
St Ths./ Sep.	Dublin City :	Bignell Edward :	brewhouse & :	-	-	-	Bignoll E - Bignoll Thos	1709	-	dd/	9 191 3495
St Ths./ Sep.	Dublin City :	Rochfort Jno & Deb :	brewhouse & :	-	-	-	Rochfort J&D - Bignell Thos	1737	-	dd/	86 423 61072
St Mary`s	Dublin City :	Haughton	Baron`s Mill & :	-	-	-	Haughton - Haughton	-	?	dd/	16 201 7287?
St Mary`s	Dublin City :	Lovett	Baron`s Mill & :	-	-	-	Lovett - Shirigley	-	?	dd/	13 229 4645
St Mary`s	Dublin City :	Uniack	Baron`s Mill & :	-	-	-	Uniack - Sherigley	-	?	dd/	45 137 28413
St Luke`s	Dublin City :	Hoult Robert	mill & bark ho	-	-	-	Hoult R - Walker William	1723	-	dd/	38 310 24349
St Luke`s	Dublin City :	Hoult Robert :	bark mill & ho :	-	-	-	Hoult R - Boswell Cath	1719	Mort. 17 Jne	dd/	25 81 13586
St Luke`s	Dublin City :	Leeson Joseph	mill & bark ho	-	-	-	Leeson J - Hoult Robt	1711	-	dd/	6 424 2381
St Luke`s	Dublin City :	Brown Daniel :	mill (stream) & :	-	-	-	Brown D - Gibbon Wm	1722	-	dd/	33 435 20814
St Luke`s	Dublin City :	Poole Jacob :	mill (stream) & :	-	-	-	Poole J - Brown Daniel	1716	-	dd/	18 11 8190
St Luke`s	Dublin City :	Poole Jacob :	mill (stream) & :	-	-	-	Poole J - Brown Daniel	1719	Mort.(2nd) 24 Feb	dd/	27 32 15046
StJohn`s	Dublin City :	Lansdowne Marq.	mill holding	-	-	-	Lansdowne Mq. - Release	1891	-	dd/	1891 54 2
St Ths./ Sep.	Dublin City :	Moorecroft Elizabeth	brewhouse & :	-	-	-	Moorecroft E - Hoey Geo	1725	-	dd/	43 517 29118
St Ths./ Sep.	Dublin City :	Paul William :	brewhouse & :	-	-	-	Paul Wm - Paul Gilbert	1730	-	dd/	65 246 45330
St Ths./ Sep.	Dublin City :	Percy Henry	brewhouse & :	-	-	-	Percy H - Moorecroft Jas	1722	-	dd/	37 244 22671
Donnybrook	Dublin City :	The North City Mills	flour	-	-	-	-	1965	-	lic/7	wheat
St Ths./ Sep.	Dublin City :	Gilbert	brewhouse & :	-	-	-	Gilbert - Hopkins	-	?	dd/	49 491 32973
St Ths./ Sep.	Dublin City :	Gilbert	brewhouse & :	-	-	-	Gilbert - Dudgeon	-	?	dd/	50 221 32974
St Ths./ Sep.	Dublin City :	Hoey George	brewhouse & :	-	-	-	Hoey Geo - Gay Letitia	1725	-	dd/	45 268 29189
St Ths./ Sep.	Dublin City :	Hoey George :	brewhouse & :	-	-	-	Hoey G - Fairbrother Sam :	1729	Mort. 5 Mar.	dd/	62 267 42816?
St Ths./ Sep.	Dublin City :	Hoey George :	brewhouse & :	-	-	-	Hoey G - Fairbrother Sam :	1730	Further Mort.	dd/	63 187 43153
St Paul's	Dublin City :	- Phoenix	Iron Works :	-	-	-	-	2010	-	mmSv/	wh - B
St Paul's	Dublin City :	- R. Liffey Phoenix	Iron Works	-	-	-	-	-	(no sign of wheel)	mmSv/	wh - B
St Paul's	Dublin City :	- (R.Liffey) Phoenix	Iron Works	-	-	-	-	1841	-	6"os/	18
St Paul's	Dublin City :	Robinson Richard	Iron Works	- Royal Phoenix	-	-	-	1832	-	dir/	Wilson
St Ths./ Sep.	Dublin City :	Burn John	brew house :	-	-	-	Burne John - Milne Chas	1718	-	dd/	22 22 11179
St Ths./ Sep.	Dublin City :	Burn John :	brew house :	-	-	-	Burn J - Dowdall Edward	1717	Mort. 27 Jul.	dd/	18 459 9533
St Ths./ Sep.	Dublin City :	Forster Richard	brew house :	-	-	-	Forster R - Sporle John	1710	-	dd/	3 452 1232
St Ths./ Sep.	Dublin City :	Murgitroid Jno	brewhouse :	-	-	-	Murgitroid J - Poole Jacob	1716	-	dd/	17 64 8171
St Ths./ Sep.	Dublin City :	Murgitroide Jno	brew house :	-	-	-	Murgitroid J - Burne John	1716	-	dd/	16 415 5852
St Ths./ Sep.	Dublin City :	Poole Jacob :	brew house :	-	-	-	Poole J - Brown Daniel	1716	-	dd/	18 11 8190
St Ths./ Sep.	Dublin City :	Sporle John :	brew house :	-	-	-	Sporle J - Murgitroid Jno	1712	-	dd/	10 248 3593
St Ths./ Sep.	Dublin City :	Sporle John	brew house :	-	-	-	Sporle Jn - Pecard Peter	1710	-	dd/	4 517 1233
St Ths./ Sep.	Dublin City :	Sporle John :	brew house :	-	-	-	Sporle Jn - Murgitroid Jn	1712	-	dd/	10 248 3591
St Ths./ Sep.	Dublin City :	Pim Crot	brew house :	-	-	-	Sporle J - Murgitroide Jno	1712	-	dd/	9 247 3592
St Ths./ Sep.	Dublin City :	Cliffe John :	brewhouse :	-	-	-	Cliffe J - Winterbottom Jn	1714	-	dd/	13 343 5896
St Ths./ Sep.	Dublin City :	Winterbottom John :	brewhouse :	-	-	-	Winterbottom - Brown Matt	1713	-	dd/	11 224 4393
St Ths./ Sep.	Dublin City :	Dudgeon Richard :	malthouse :	-	-	-	Dudgeon R - Dudgeon Ed	1707	-	dd/	7 391 2739
Stgeorge`s	Dublin City :	-	brewery	-	-	-	-	-	-	TLtts/	1884
St Thomas	Dublin City :	Dudgeon Richard	brewhouse & :	-	-	-	Dudgeon R - Dudgeon Ed	1711	-	dd/	8 259 2721
St Thomas	Dublin City :	Archer Richard	mill :	-	-	-	Archer R - Cooper Jane	1724	-	dd/	42 88 25769
St Thomas	Dublin City :	Archer Richard	mill :	-	-	-	Archer R - Mead Patrick	1725	-	dd/	49 107 31088
St Thomas	Dublin City :	Archer Richard :	mill :	-	-	-	Archer R - Cooper John	1716	-	dd/	16 401 7819
St Thomas	Dublin City :	Foreman John	mill :	-	-	-	Foreman J - Archer Richd	1725	-	dd/	46 534 30853
St Ths./ Sep.	Dublin City :	Garrod Joseph :	brewhouse & :	-	-	-	Garrod Jos - Adair Arch	1712	-	dd/	10 26 2969
St Ths./ Sep.	Dublin City :	Wethorall Henry :	brewhouse & :	-	-	-	Wothorall H - Garrod Jos	1712	-	dd/	10 19 2951
St James	Dublin City :	Manders & Power	brewery	-	-	-	-	1832	-	dir/	Wilson
St Thomas	Dublin City :	Dublin Port Milling C	flour	-	-	-	-	1965	-	lic/8	wheat
St James	Dublin City :	- (back of Brewery)	Vitriol Wks.	large red brick building		-	-	-	-	phoWEH	B
St Luke`s	Dublin City :	Watkins Joseph	malt kiln	-	-	-	-	-	-	gr/	-
St Ths. / Sep.	Dublin City :	Emerson	brewhouse & :	-	-	-	Emerson - Dorty	-	?	dd/	12 327 5288

PARISH	TOWNLAND	MILLER	TYPE	HOUSE	Land	£Val	PROPRIETORS	Date	WHEEL etc.	Record	Ref.
bo./ Coolock	Dublin North *	Byrne Francis	Plunkett`s Mill	-	-	-	Byrne - Public Wks Coms.	1891	-	dd/	1891 4 244
bo./ Coolock	Dublin North *	Coslett Olivia	Plunkett`s Mill	-	-	-	Coslett O - N. Dublin Union	1892	-	dd/	1892 27 270
Taney	Dundrum	Dunn	corn	-	-	-	Dunn - Stoker	-	?	dd/	583 101 394760?
Taney	Dundrum	Fitzwilliam Ld Richd	corn	-	-	-	Fitzwilliam - Hutton Henry :	1802	-	dd/	558 445 372829
Taney	Dundrum	Hall Mrs	paper	-	-	-	-	-	-	dir1800	Dublin
Taney	Dundrum	Hutton Henry Rt.Hon	corn	-	-	-	Hutton H - Blood Meridon :	1804	-	dd/	558 558 373451
Taney	Dundrum	Meyler George	mill	-	0.3.3	-	-	-	-	gr/	-
Taney	Dundrum	Norton John :	corn	-	-	-	Norton J - Bloomfield Wm :	1805	Mort. 12 May	dd/	573 300 389332
Taney	Dundrum	Reynolds Patrick	mill	-	-	-	Reynolds P - Rogan Nich	1737	-	dd/	89 482 64173
Taney	Dundrum	Stokes Mr	iron-works (3)	-	-	-	-	-	3 wheels	dir1800	Dublin
Taney	Dundrum	Sykes George	mill	23x15.5x15.6	-	-	-	-	-	hob/	5.0927
Taney	Dundrum	Walsh John	iron-works, mill	-	0.1.1	-	-	-	-	gr/	-
Taney	Dundrum :	- Dundrum	Iron Wks	-	-	-	-	-	-	6"os	23
Taney	Dundrum Manor	Dobson Isaac :	mill	-	-	-	Dobson I - Reynolds Thos :	1754	-	dd/	168 280 113051/2
Taney	Dundrum Manor	Fitzwilliam Richard :	mill	-	-	-	Fitzwilliam - Dobson Isaac :	1746	-	dd/	123 259 84463
Taney	Dundrum Manor	Taylor Samuel :	mill	-	-	-	Taylor S - Thomas Wm :	1753	-	dd/	168 427 114466
Taney	Dundrum Town :	-	mill pond	-	-	-	-	-	-	6"os/	22
Taney	Dundrumtown	- ? -	flour & corn :	(1B) 40x22.6x15.6 :	-	7.3	-	-	-	hob/	5.2688
Dublin	Dunsoghly Mnr	Phipps John :	mill	-	-	-	Phipps Jn - Mercer Wm :	1774	Mort. 31 Dec.	dd/	116 282 80376
Dublin	Dunsoghly Mnr	Piersy James	mill	-	-	-	Piersy J - Gwyn Lewis :	1739	-	dd/	96 89 66526
Whitechurch	Edmondstown	-	cloth	-	-	-	-	1899	-	1"os/	112
Whitechurch	Edmondstown	-	cotton	- (ref. 6"OS/220	-	-	-	2002	-	mmSv/	wh - Z
Whitechurch	Edmondstown	-	mill	-	-	-	-	1899	-	1"os/	112
Whitechurch	Edmondstown	-	mill	-	-	-	-	1899	-	1"os/	112
Whitechurch	Edmondstown	- on B'roan Estate	corn	complex of buildings:	-	-	-	2002	-	mmSv/	wh - Z
Whitechurch	Edmondstown	- on golf course	corn	small remains of :	-	-	-	2002	-	mmSv/	wh - Z
Whitechurch	Edmondstown	- adj. Reckitts fcty	mill	3 storey building :	-	-	-	2002	-	phoWEH	D
Whitechurch	Edmondstown	Ashworth	mill	-	-	-	Ashworth - Rourke	-	?	dd/	396 434 261108
Whitechurch	Edmondstown	Ashworth	mill	-	-	-	Ashworth - Stubbs	-	- [error]	dd/	676 96 380282
Whitechurch	Edmondstown	Bladen Charles	mill	-	-	-	Bladen C - Borr Christian	1717	-	dd/	17 398 9223
Whitechurch	Edmondstown	Bladen Lettice	mill	-	-	-	Bladen L - Borr Christian	1725	-	dd/	46 358 28911
Whitechurch	Edmondstown	Bor Christian :	mill	-	-	-	Bor C - Burke Edmund :	1729	-	dd/	58 502 40292
Whitechurch	Edmondstown	Bor Christian :	mill	-	-	-	Bor C - Nutley Richard	1717	-	dd/	18 412 9406
Whitechurch	Edmondstown	Boyd Patrick	paper	53x27x18.6 finisning:	-	-	Dollard Richard	1845	steam boiler	hob/	5.0930
Whitechurch	Edmondstown	Dollard Margaret	paper	-	8a.	-	-	-	-	gr/	-
Whitechurch	Edmondstown	Keeling Robert	mill	-	-	-	Keeling - Gore	1792	-	dd/	446 280 289409
Whitechurch	Edmondstown	Keeling Robert :	mill	-	-	-	Keeling R - Reilly Hugh :	1794	-	dd/	505 455 328912
Whitechurch	Edmondstown	Lennon Renngivies :	mill	-	-	-	Lennon R - Ryan Richard :	1792	-	dd/	458 299 295305
Whitechurch	Edmondstown	Nunn James	mill	-	-	-	Nunn James & Theresa :	1798	-	dd/	516 71 336253
Whitechurch	Edmondstown	Nunn Richard	mill	-	-	-	Nunn R - Nunn James	1798	-	dd/	514 46 333567
Whitechurch	Edmondstown	Read John	cloth	52.6x18.6x16.6 new	-	-	-	-	20x5x20	hob/	& gr & osi/112
Whitechurch	Edmondstown	Read John	wollen-cloth	-	1.1.1	-	-	-	-	gr/	-
Whitechurch	Edmondstown	Reilly Hugh	mill	-	-	-	Reilly H - Keeling Robert	1796	-	dd/	512 395 334560
Whitechurch	Edmondstown	Rourke Simon :	mill	-	-	-	Rourke S - Mooney Robert	1738	-	dd/	91 304 64326
Whitechurch	Edmondstown	Ryan Thomas :	mill	-	-	-	Ryan T - Keogh Edward :	1800	Mort. 15 Nov.	dd/	532 387 349435
Whitechurch	Edmondstown	Sherlock Robert	boiling house	33x15.6x15 & :	-	-	-	-	-	hob/	5.0930
Whitechurch	Edmondstown	Sherlock Robert	wash	-	-	-	-	-	-	gr/	-
Whitechurch	Edmondstown	Sherlock Robert	wash	60.6x28x20 wadding	-	-	-	-	15x5.4x12 1 pair :	hob/	5.0930
Whitechurch	Edmondstown	Swift Elizabeth	mill	-	-	-	Swift E - Frizell Richard	1786	-	dd/	378 356 253275
Whitechurch	Edmondstown	Swift Elizabeth	mill	-	-	-	Swift E - Ashworth Thos	1787	-	dd/	348 183 254508
Whitechurch	Edmondstown	Swift Elizabeth	mill	-	-	-	Swift Eliz - Keeling Robt	1791	-	dd/	451 132 289276
Esker	Esker	Hilton Mr	cotton	-	-	-	-	-	-	dir1800	Dublin

PARISH	TOWNLAND	MILLER	TYPE	HOUSE	Land	£Val	PROPRIETORS	Date	WHEEL etc.	Record	Ref.
Clondalkin	Fairview	-	corn	-	-	-	-	-	-	6"os/	21
Clondalkin	Fairview	-	old mill & pond	-	-	-	-	-	-	6"os/	21
Clondalkin	Fairview	Henry Joseph Esq	oil	-	-	-	-	-	-	gr/	-
Clondalkin	Fairview	McNally Michael	corn	-	-	58	-	1832	-	VOf/	OL.X078
Taney	Faranboley	Henderson James	flour, saw	-	-	-	-	-	-	gr/	-
Taney	Faranboley	Lee John	sawing	-	-	-	-	-	-	gr/	-
Taney	Faranboley :	-	starch mill	-	-	-	-	-	-	6"os/	22
Taney	Faranboley :	-	starch	-	-	-	-	-	-	6"os	22
Kinsaley	Feltrim	-	windmill - corn	-	-	-	-	-	-	dir1800	Dublin
Kinsaley	Feltrim	- on Feltrim Hill	Wind Mill	-	-	-	-	-	-	JRoc	1760 map
Kinsaley	Feltrim	Ashenhurst Edwd :	mill	-	-	-	Ashenhurst - Simpson Geo	1762	Lease 15 May	dd/	219 63 142658
Kinsaley	Feltrim	Beresford Earl of	land	-	-	-	Beresford - Eagle	-	-	dd/	626 266 433103
Kinsaley	Feltrim	Beresford Earl of	lime kiln	-	-	-	Beresford - Farran	-	-	dd/	734 73 500408
Kinsaley	Feltrim	Beresford John :	land	- (? mill incl.)	-	-	Beresford John - Eagle :	1808	Rel. 29 Feb.	dd/	598 119 406946
Kinsaley	Feltrim	Bever Edmond :	mill	-	-	-	Bever E&J - Traviere Max :	1802	-	dd/	542 511 359250
Kinsaley	Feltrim	Bever Samuel :	mill	-	-	-	Bever S - Sherry Patrick :	1757	Lease 15 Jne.	dd/	194 267 129465
Kinsaley	Feltrim	Bligh Rev Robert :	mill	-	-	-	Bligh R - Jackson Daniel :	1767	-	dd/	260 175 168262
Kinsaley	Feltrim	Darley Henry S	land	-	-	-	Darley H - Shaw John P	1901	-	dd/	19016 72
Kinsaley	Feltrim	Downes Rev David :	mill	-	-	-	Downes D - Garstin John :	1802	Mort.	dd/	547 483 361511
Kinsaley	Feltrim	Doyle Rev Charles :	mill	-	-	-	Doyle C - Simpson Geo :	1753	-	dd/	161 397 109149
Kinsaley	Feltrim	Doyne Philip	mill	-	-	-	Doyne P - Wilmot John	1785	-	dd/	370 125 247050
Kinsaley	Feltrim	Doyne Philip	mill	-	-	-	Doyne P - Gordon Nich	1785	-	dd/	373 407 249062
Kinsaley	Feltrim	Eagle	land	- (? mill incl.)	-	-	Eagle - Beresford	-	-	dd/	598 119 406965
Kinsaley	Feltrim	Eagle Salamon :	land	- (? mill incl.)	-	-	Eagle S - Sayers Richard	1807	L. & R. 22 Jne.	dd/	591 142 401220
Kinsaley	Feltrim	Eagle Salamon :	land	- (? mill incl.)	-	-	Eagle S - Sayers Richard	-	-	dd/	592 203 401678
Kinsaley	Feltrim	Ellis as Master & ors	land	- (? mill incl.)	-	-	Ellis Ma - Cooper	-	-	dd/	722 550 493485
Kinsaley	Feltrim	Enraght	mill	-	-	-	Enraght - Lehunte	?	?	dd/	198 454 132496
Kinsaley	Feltrim	Enraght Rev John :	mill	-	-	-	Enraght & W - Leslie Jas :	1754	-	dd/	173 298 116252
Kinsaley	Feltrim	Gaffney James	windmill	dwelling : 30x22x12	-	-	-	-	2 pairs Irish stones	hob/	5.0882
Kinsaley	Feltrim	Gaffney James	windmill	39.0x12.6x20 office	-	-	-	-	- windmill :	hob/	5.0882
Kinsaley	Feltrim	Gilbert Jeremiah :	mill	-	-	-	Gilbert - Stewart Annesley :	1766	-	dd/	249 126 159561
Kinsaley	Feltrim	Glasscock Rev Jas :	mill	-	-	-	Glasscock - Chaigneau W:	1757	(N)	dd/	186 169 123753
Kinsaley	Feltrim	Goold Elizabeth	mill	-	-	-	Goold E - Doyne Chas	1752	-	dd/	153 371 103186
Kinsaley	Feltrim	Gordon	mill	-	-	-	Gordon - Fierran	c1805	?	dd/	584 1(?) 359581
Kinsaley	Feltrim	Gordon Alex	mill	-	-	-	Gordon A - Gervais Peter	1796	-	dd/	492 268 323418
Kinsaley	Feltrim	Gordon Alex	mill	-	-	-	Gordon A - Singer James	1798	-	dd/	514 105 335565
Kinsaley	Feltrim	Gordon Alex :	mill	-	-	-	Gordon A - Singer James :	1797	Mort. 14 Apl.	dd/	507 523 329600
Kinsaley	Feltrim	Gordon John :	mill	-	-	-	Gordon J - Beresford Jn :	1800	-	dd/	514 105 335565
Kinsaley	Feltrim	Hamilton Sir Fredk. :	mill	-	-	-	Hamilton F - Beresford Jn :	1801	-	dd/	546 254 359820
Kinsaley	Feltrim	Le Hunt Thomas :	mill	-	-	-	Le Hunt T - Bligh Robert :	1760	L&R 16/17 Apl.	dd/	206 97 153311
Kinsaley	Feltrim	Matthews Rev Wm :	mill	-	-	-	Matthews W - Allan Thos :	1757	Lease 15 Jne.	dd/	189 163 125009
Kinsaley	Feltrim	Montgomery Thomas	mill	-	-	-	Montgomery - Burton Jn	1752	-	dd/	155 277 104577
Kinsaley	Feltrim	Norcott William :	land	- (? mill incl.)	-	-	Norcott W - Bever Edw. :	1810	Lse. 23 Feb.	dd/	622 39 425859
Kinsaley	Feltrim	O`Hara Ann :	mill	-	-	-	O`Hara A - Dalton Thos	1773	-	dd/	304 311 199973?
Kinsaley	Feltrim	O`Hara Kane :	mill	-	-	-	O`Hara K - Echlin Richd :	1763	Mort. 29 Jne.	dd/	226 367 147841
Kinsaley	Feltrim	Sayers Richard :	land	- (? mill incl.)	-	-	Sayers R - Cooper Austin :	1810	24 Nov.	dd/	628 403 432196
Kinsaley	Feltrim	Sherigley Bever :	mill	-	-	-	Sherigley B - Jackson Jn :	1757	-	dd/	185 472 123907
Kinsaley	Feltrim	Sherigley Bever & W	mill	-	-	-	Sherigley B - Gilbert J	1755	-	dd/	175 337 117305
Kinsaley	Feltrim	Sherigley Mary :	mill	-	-	-	Sherigley M - Ormsby :	1752	-	dd/	158 39 104622
Kinsaley	Feltrim	Sherigley Sarah Wid	mill	-	-	-	Sherigley - Simpson Geo :	1746	-	dd/	119 431 83127
Kinsaley	Feltrim	Sherry Patrick :	mill	-	-	-	Sherry P - Lester Agnes :	1760	(N)	dd/	205 216 135766
Kinsaley	Feltrim	Simpson George :	mill	-	-	-	Simpson G - West Robt :	1762	Lease 8 Jne. - N.	dd/	219 249 143538

PARISH	TOWNLAND	MILLER	TYPE	HOUSE	Land	£Val	PROPRIETORS	Date	WHEEL etc.	Record	Ref.
Kinsaley	Feltrim	Simpson George :	mill	-	-	-	Simpson G - Clarke Geo :	1766	-	dd/	219 315 143816
Kinsaley	Feltrim	Wilmot John	mill	-	-	-	Wilmot John - Doyne Philip	1785	-	dd/	362 540 246925
Dublin	Fieldstown	Segrave Mr	threshing	-	-	-	-	1800	-	dir/	Dublin
Finglas	Finglas	Bayley John :	mill	-	-	-	Bayley J - Vipon Chas :	1775	-	dd/	309 20 204183
Finglas	Finglas	Bayly John	mill	-	-	-	Bayley J - Crosbie Henry	1783	-	dd/	358 625 246716
Finglas	Finglas	Bayly John	mill	-	-	-	Bayley J - Gerrard Elloner	1785	-	dd/	372 156 248074
Finglas	Finglas	Clarke Mr	corn	-	-	-	-	1800	-	dir/	Dublin
Finglas	Finglas	Crosbie Henry	mill	-	-	-	Crosbie H - Teeling Walter	1784	-	dd/	358 627 248718
Finglas	Finglas	Crosbie Henry	mill	-	-	-	Crosbie H - McKowen :	1789	-	dd/	403 461 268947
Finglas	Finglas	Crosbie Henry :	mill	-	-	-	Crosbie H - Dickenson :	1788	-	dd/	407 1 266044?
Finglas	Finglas	Dickinson Mr	cotton	-	-	-	-	1800	-	dir1800	Dublin
Finglas	Finglas	Henzell Lucy	mill	-	-	-	Henzell L - Abbot Chris	1790	-	dd/	431 375 286774
Finglas	Finglas	O`Farrell Roger	mill	-	-	-	O`Farrell R - Fox Richard :	1786	-	dd/	376 405 251642
Finglas	Finglas	Teeling Walter :	mill	-	-	-	Teeling W - Crosbie Henry :	1788	-	dd/	410 8 265801
Finglas	Finglas L`dship	Bayley Jno	mill	-	-	-	Bayley J - Char. Don & B. :	1862	-	dd/	1862 6 248
Balrothery	Flemingstown	-	threshing	-	-	-	-	-	-	6"os/	1
Donnybrook	Fortyacres	- at Millmount	saw	-	-	-	-	-	-	6"os/	18
Donnybrook	Fortyacres	- nr Donnybrook	bleach	-	-	-	-	-	-	6"os/	18
Donnybrook	Fortyacres	- nr Donnybrook	windmill stump	-	-	-	-	-	-	6"os/	18
Donnybrook	Fortyacres	- on R. Dodder	calico printing	-	-	-	-	-	-	6"os/	18
Dublin	Freestone	Nun James & Teresa	mill	-	-	-	Nun Jas - Waldron Launc.	1798	-	dd/	516 71 336253
Dublin	Freestone	Taylor Clement	mill	-	-	-	Taylor C - Nun Richard	1794	-	dd/	515 147 335603
Dublin	Gallagh	Brownrigg Armsley	mill	-	-	-	Brownrigg A - Smith Jojn	1785	-	dd/	372 272 248623
Dublin	Gallagh	Dillon Redmond :	mill	-	-	-	Dillon R - Butler Thomas :	1802	-	dd/	544 172 361834
Dublin	Gallagh	Flinn Nicholas :	mill	-	-	-	Flinn N - Cochran Mary :	1798	-	dd/	524 290 342969
Dublin	Gallagh	Rowley	mill	-	-	-	Rowley - Powerscourt	-	?	dd/	427 557 303396
Dublin	Gallagh	Rowley Langford	mill	-	-	-	Rowley L - Stewart Hen	1791	-	dd/	442 392 287641
Dublin	Gallagh	Rowley Rt Hon Herc	mill	-	-	-	Rowley Langford - Baker :	1786	-	dd/	386 42 254372
Clondalkin	Gallans	-	glue m`fty	-	-	-	-	-	-	6"os/	17
Clondalkin	Gallans	-	Killeen Paper	-	-	-	-	-	-	6"os/	17
Ballyfermot	Gallanstowm	McDonnell Chris	paper	-	48a.	255 :	-	1832	-	VOf/	OL.X078
Ballyfermot	Gallanstown	McDonnell Chris	paper	35.6x13x19 = eng. :	-	-	-	-	2 overshot wheels :	hob/	5.0931
Garristown	Garristown	-	windmill	-	-	-	-	-	-	6"os/	3
Garristown	Garristown	-	windmill - corn	-	-	-	-	-	-	dir1800	Dublin
Garristown	Garristown	- E. side River :	Bawthers Mill	-	-	-	-	-	-	JRoc	1760 map
Garristown	Garristown	- NW of Town	WindMill	-	-	-	-	-	-	JRoc	1760 map
Glasnevin	Glasnevin	-	broom	-	-	-	-	1899	-	1"os/	112
Glasnevin	Glasnevin	-	woollen mill	-	-	-	-	-	-	6"os/	18
Glasnevin	Glasnevin	Brickell Robert :	mill	-	-	-	Brickell R - Palmer George	1800	-	dd/	523 322 345608
Glasnevin	Glasnevin	Cavanagh Nath :	mill	-	-	-	Cavanagh N - Stephens :	1789	-	dd/	408 387 271013
Glasnevin	Glasnevin	Crofts William	mill	-	-	-	Crofts Wm - Kathrens Sm	1740	Mort. 10 Apl.	dd/	97 309 68465
Glasnevin	Glasnevin	Crofts William	mill	-	-	-	Crofts W - Crofts Alice :	1741	-	dd/	137 466 949682
Glasnevin	Glasnevin	Crofts William	paper	-	-	-	Crofts Wm - Crofts Alice	1722	-	dd/	33 421 20772
Glasnevin	Glasnevin	Crofts William	paper	-	-	-	Crofts W - Barry William	1725	Mort. 22 Jul.	dd/	47 42 29458
Glasnevin	Glasnevin	Crofts William	paper	-	-	-	Crofts - Pepper Henrietta :	1738	Mort. 5 Aug.	dd/	91 295 64287
Glasnevin	Glasnevin	Croker Edward	mill	-	-	-	Croker Ed - Trotter Jno	1789	-	dd/	441 484 285098
Glasnevin	Glasnevin	Croker Edward	mill	-	-	-	Croker E - Derrickson Frd	1791	-	dd/	438 430 283152
Glasnevin	Glasnevin	Dooley Margaret	paper	-	-	-	Dooley M - Nixon Robert	1732	-	dd/	72 169 40264
Glasnevin	Glasnevin	Dooley Thomas :	mill	-	-	-	Dooley T - Jones Thomas :	1752	-	dd/	151 301 101509
Glasnevin	Glasnevin	Egan Cornelius :	mill	-	-	-	Egan C - Humphries John :	1795	-	dd/	505 189 324907
Glasnevin	Glasnevin	Litton	mill	-	-	-	Litton - Cramer	-	?	dd/	505 95 324059
Glasnevin	Glasnevin	M`Ilwrath Mr	paper	-	-	-	-	-	-	dir1800	Dublin

PARISH	TOWNLAND	MILLER	TYPE	HOUSE	Land	£Val	PROPRIETORS	Date	WHEEL etc.	Record	Ref.
Glasnevin	Glasnevin	Meredith Charles	mill	-	-	-	Meredith C - Cooper Richd	1791	-	dd/	428 643 280810
Glasnevin	Glasnevin	Mullholland Charles	mill	-	-	-	Mullholland C - McCally Th	1781	-	dd/	340 609 323732
Glasnevin	Glasnevin	Raymond George	:mill	-	-	-	Raymond G - Kidd George	1794	-	dd/	510 143 329345
Glasnevin	Glasnevin	Rogers John Cooke	mill	-	-	-	Rogers J C - Weir Robert	1796	-	dd/	493 389 323498
Glasnevin	Glasnevin	Supple Edward :	mill	-	-	-	Supple - McDonnell Henry :	1796	Asgt. 12 Apl.	dd/	498 557 321505
Glasnevin	Glasnevin	Tebb David :	mill	-	-	-	Tebb - Sterling Dorothea :	1799	-	dd/	517 364 348100?
Glasnevin	Glasnevin	Trotter Thomas	mill	-	-	-	Trotter Thos - Quin Mary	1782	-	dd/	464 242 295058
Glasnevin	Glasnevin	-	millhouse	-	-	-	-	-	-	6"os/	18
St James	Goldenbridge	Anderson Richard	mill	-	-	-	Anderson R - Kelly R	1784	-	dd/	439 63 842591
St James	Goldenbridge	Dames Ann :	mill	-	-	-	Dames A - Wilson James :	1761	-	dd/	207 577 138493
St James	Goldenbridge	Dowling Patrick	bark	45.0x22.6x29.0 & :	-	-	-	1845	15x4.9 2 pr st. :	hob/	5.0939
St James	Goldenbridge	Dowling Patrick	flour	76.6x23x21.6 & :	-	-	-	1845	12x10 breast 3 pr st.	hob/	5.0939
St James	Goldenbridge	Francis Journaux	flour	49.6x40.0x27.0 & :	-	-	-	1845	16x8 12 hp breast :	hob/	5.0939
St James	Goldenbridge	Francis Journaux	logwood	103.0x28.6x18.6 & :	-	-	-	-	16x8x11 10 rs./min :	hob/	5.0939
St James	Goldenbridge	Grevill John :	mill	-	-	-	Grevill J - Grevill John :	1796	-	dd/	503 223 322973
St James	Goldenbridge	Halpen	mill	-	-	-	Halpen - Fagan	-	?	dd/	249 46 161658
St James	Goldenbridge	Halpen Richard :	mill	-	-	-	Halpen R - Fagan William :	1762	-	dd/	214 575 142343
St James	Goldenbridge	Harrington William	mill	-	-	-	Harrington W - Fagan Wm	1773	-	dd/	295 429 197263
St James	Goldenbridge	Johnston William G	mills	-	-	-	Johnston W - Murphy Anth	1860	-	dd/	1860 23 53
St James	Goldenbridge	Peyton Charles R	mill	-	-	-	Peyton Chas - Nolan Andr	1862	-	dd/	1862 30 229
St James	Goldenbridge	Sullivan Bart	paper	100x26x9.6 & forge	-	-	-	-	25 HP no dims.	hob/	5.0940
St James	Goldenbridge N	Sullivan Bart	paper	-	12a.	201	-	1832	-	VOf/	OL.X078
St James	Goldenbridge N	Sullivan Bart	paper (part of)	(1B) 100x26x9.6 :	-	-	-	-	- (no dims. 25 h.p.)	hob/	5.2693
St James	Goldenbridge N	Sullivan Bart	paper (part of)	(1B) 62x25x36 :	-	-	-	-	-	hob/	5.2693
St James	Goldenbridge N	Sullivan Bart	paper (part of)	(1B) 42x18x6.6 :	-	-	-	-	-	hob/	5.2693
St James	Goldenbridge N	Sullivan Daniel P	paper	-	3a.	-	-	-	-	gr/	-
St James	Goldenbridge S	-	flour	Mt Shannon Mills	-	-	-	2002	-	mmSv/	wh - Z
St James	Goldenbridge S	-	Harcourt Mills	-	-	-	-	-	-	6"os/	18
St James	Goldenbridge S	-	mill	Rutland Mills	-	-	-	2002	-	mmSv/	wh - Z
St James	Goldenbridge S	-	Mountshannon :	-	-	-	-	-	-	6"os/	18
St James	Goldenbridge S	-	Rutland Mills	-	-	-	-	-	-	6"os/	18
St James	Goldenbridge S	- canal (Davit Rd)	flour	Harcourt Mills	-	-	-	2002	-	mmSv/	wh - Z
St James	Goldenbridge S	- on Gd. Canal :	Harcourt Mills	-	-	-	-	-	-	TLtts/	1884
St James	Goldenbridge S	Dowling Patrick	flour & bark	-	-	82	-	1832	-	VOf/	OL.X078
St James	Goldenbridge S	Du Bedat Charles	Harcourt Mills	-	-	-	Du Bedat Charles - Francis	1890	-	dd/	1890 49 10
St James	Goldenbridge S	Journaux Fran	mill	-	12.2.·	-	-	-	-	gr/	-
St James	Goldenbridge S	Journeaux Francis	logwood	-	12a.	139	-	1832	-	VOf/	OL.X078
St James	Goldenbridge S	Margison Anne	Mountshannon Mills		-	-	Margison A - Cooney Mcl	1894	-	dd/	1894 53 32
St James	Goldenbridge S	Vernon Georgina K	Harcourt Mills	-	-	-	Vernon Georgina - Chas	1891	-	dd/	1891 54 57
Clonturk	Goosegreen	Bracken Paul	woad factory	drying loft 27x10x16	-	-	-	-	-	hob/	5.0872
Balscaddan	Gormanstown	- E. side main rd.	Mills	-	-	-	-	-	-	JRoc	1760 map
Balscaddan	Gormanstown	- N. side Delvin R.	Mills	-	-	-	-	-	-	JRoc	1760 map
Balscaddan	Gormanstown	Boylan Mr	corn	-	-	-	-	-	-	dir1800	Dublin
Balscaddan	Gormanstown	Nowlan Mr	corn	-	-	-	-	-	-	dir1800	Dublin
Lusk	Gracedieu	-	corn	-	-	-	-	2003	-	mmSv/	sb - Z
Lusk	Gracedieu	-	corn & dam	-	-	-	-	-	-	6"os/	7
Lusk	Gracedieu	- S. end of Vge.	Mill	-	-	-	-	-	-	JRoc	1760 map
Lusk	Gracedieu	Brown Patrick	corn	41x21.6x13.6 dw :	-	-	-	-	15.6x4.6x10 40 bkt.	hob/	5.0850
Lusk	Gracedieu	Brown Patrick	corn	41.0x21.6x13.6 & :	-	-	-	-	15.6x4.6x10 1pr st:	hob/	5.0851
Lusk	Gracedieu	Browne Patrick	corn, flour	-	-	-	-	-	-	gr/	-
Lusk	Gracedieu	Wybrants Elizabeth	grist	-	-	-	Wybrants E - Betson John	1719	-	dd/	26 214 15248
Dub (? par.)	Grange	- S. side Gd. Canal	mill & pond	-	-	-	-	-	-	6"os/	17

PARISH	TOWNLAND	MILLER	TYPE	HOUSE	Land	£Val	PROPRIETORS	Date	WHEEL etc.	Record	Ref.
Grangeg`man	Grangegorman	-	mill	-	-	-	-	1899	-	1"os/	112
St Catherines	Greenmount	Pim Jonathan	cotton m`fy	-	5a.	-	-	-	-	gr/	-
Rathcoole	Greenoge	-	Greenoge Mill	-	-	-	-	1899	-	1"os/	111
Rathcoole	Greenoge	- at Ragheredan	Mill	-	-	-	-	-	-	JRoc	1760 map
Rathcoole	Greenoge	- Greenoge Mill	corn & dam	-	-	-	-	-	-	6"os/	21
Rathcoole	Greenoge	Morris William	Greenoge Mill	-	-	-	Morris Wm - Carty James	1893	-	dd/	1893 61 81
Dublin	Haerlem *	Hutchinson Frederic	mills	-	-	-	Hutchinson Fred - Neill Johı	1894	-	dd/	1894 16 40
St Peter`s	Haroldscross	- E. side of River	C Mill	-	-	-	-	-	-	JRoc	1760 map
St Peter`s	Haroldscross	- at Mill View (Ho.):	flour	-	-	-	-	-	-	6"os/	18
St Peter`s	Haroldscross	- S/ Kimmage Vge.	windmill	-	-	-	-	-	-	6"os/	18
St Peter`s	Haroldscross	Adams Thomas	Way Mill	-	-	-	Adams T - Bewley Sam	1863	-	dd/	1863 11 288
St Peter`s	Haroldscross	Archer Richard	Wey Mills	-	-	-	Archer R - Cooper Jane	1724	-	dd/	42 88 25796
St Peter`s	Haroldscross	Archer Richard	Wey Mills	-	-	-	ArcherR - Madden John	1725	-	dd/	46 535 30845
St Peter`s	Haroldscross	Archer Richard :	Wey Mills	-	-	-	Archer R - Cooper John	1716	-	dd/	16 401 7819
St Peter`s	Haroldscross	Armstrong Mr	calender	-	-	-	-	-	-	dir1800	Dublin
St Peter`s	Haroldscross	behind Mount Argos	paper & millrace		-	-	-	-	-	6"os/	18
St Peter`s	Haroldscross	Bermingham & :	corn	-	-	-	-	-	-	dir1800	Dublin
St Peter`s	Haroldscross	Bermingham & :	corn	-	-	-	-	-	-	dir1800	Dublin
St Peter`s	Haroldscross	Cuppaidge Mr	paper	-	-	-	-	-	-	dir1800	Dublin
St Peter`s	Haroldscross	Cuppaidge Mr	paper	-	-	-	-	-	-	dir1800	Dublin
St Peter`s	Haroldscross	Cuppaidge Mr	wire	-	-	-	-	-	-	dir1800	Dublin
St Peter`s	Haroldscross	Figgis Samuel	paper	-	-	114	-	1832	-	VOf/	OL.X078
St Peter`s	Haroldscross	Figgis Samuel :	paper	-	-	-	-	-	-	gr/	-
St Peter`s	Haroldscross	Foreman John	Wey Mills	-	-	-	Foreman J - Archer Richd	1725	-	dd/	46 534 30853
St Peter`s	Haroldscross	Herron Robert Sir	Larkfield Mills	-	-	-	Herron R - Connolly H & Co	1891	-	dd/	1891 21 28
St Peter`s	Haroldscross	Herron, Connolly & C	Larkfield Mills	-	-	-	-	1898	-	dir/	Thoms
St Peter`s	Haroldscross	Hicks Richard John	paper	60x21x38 m/c ho &	-	-	-	-	wheel 20 h.p.	hob/	5.0936
St Peter`s	Haroldscross	Jellicoe Anne	mill	-	-	-	Jellicoe A - Mullin Jno	1863	-	dd/	1863 12 93
St Peter`s	Haroldscross	Mr Hyland	corn	-	-	-	-	-	-	dir1800	Dublin
St Peter`s	Haroldscross	Murphy Peter	flour	-	1.3.1:	98 :	-	1832	-	VOf/	OL.X078
St Peter`s	Haroldscross	Murphy Peter	mill	(1B) 49x37x44 :	-	-	-	-	14x8x12 2 pr. st. :	hob/	5.2694
St Peter`s	Haroldscross	Pim Jonathan	cotton fcty (pt.)	(1A) 47x23.6x11 :	-	-	-	-	22.6x11x19 :	hob/	5.2697
St Peter`s	Haroldscross	Pim Jonathan	cotton fcty (pt.)	(1B) 47x73x35 :	-	-	-	-	-	hob/	5.2697
St Peter`s	Haroldscross	Pim Jonathan	cotton fcty (pt.)	(1A) 28x15x13 :	-	-	-	-	-	hob/	5.2697
St Catherine`s	Haroldscross	Pim Jonathan	cotton mfty	-	5a.	293	-	1832	-	VOf/	OL.X078
St Peter`s	Haroldscross	Spence George	mills	-	-	-	Spence Geo brewer LWT	1708	-	dd/	2 139 338
St Peter`s	Haroldscross	Tuite Francis	mill (part of)	-	1.1.2!	-	-	-	-	gr/	-
St Peter`s	Haroldscross	Wall,Cogan, Murphy	skin	-	-	-	-	-	-	dir1800	Dublin
St Peter`s	HaroldsCross	White Joshua	mill	-	-	-	White Josh - Mulhall Lewis	1894	-	dd/	1894 4 234
St Peter`s	Haroldscross :	Danford Willaim	corn & flour	Larkfield Mills	-	-	-	1885	-	dir/	Thoms
Crumlin	Haroldscross W.	Hicks Richard	paper	(1A) 22x18x10 :	-	-	-	1845	- [no information]	hob/	5.0935
Crumlin	Haroldscross W.	Hicks Richard	paper	(1A) 52x23x10 :	-	54.10	-	1845	- [no information]	hob/	5.0935
Rathfarnham	Haroldsgrange :	Latouche David Hon.	threshing	-	-	-	-	-	-	dir1800	Dublin
Uppercross b.	Hibernian Mills	Chambers George	mill	-	-	-	Chambers G - Star L Asc	1864	-	dd/	1864 36 49
Uppercross b.	Hibernian Mills	Cronheim Theo	mill	-	-	-	Cronheim T - McCormick J	1863	-	dd/	1863 22 7
Uppercross b.	Hibernian Mills	Davis Samuel	mill	-	-	-	Davis S - Baird Jasper	1862	-	dd/	1862 36 174
Uppercross b.	Hibernian Mills	Davis Samuel	mill	-	-	-	Davis S - Bonsall Jno	1862	-	dd/	1862 42 55
Uppercross b.	Hibernian Mills	Davis Samuel	mill	-	-	-	Davis S - Bankruptcy Ct	1864	-	dd/	1864 27 208
Dublin	Hollybrook	Robinson John	mill	-	-	-	-	-	-	mssH/	map/16G49(8)
bo./ Coolock	Hollywell *	Ulster Bank Ltd.	mill	-	-	-	Ulster Bank - Pearson Wm	1894	-	dd/	1894 48 280
Balscadden	Holmpatrick	O`Flynn Patrick	flour	30.3x23.3x28.6 & :	-	-	-	1845	16x6x15.3 40 bkts.	hob/	5.0448
Balscadden	HolmpatrickTpk	-	flour	30x23x27 18x20x27	-	-	-	1845	16x6x15 1 pr st.	hob/	5.0848

PARISH	TOWNLAND	MILLER	TYPE	HOUSE	Land	£Val	PROPRIETORS	Date	WHEEL etc.	Record	Ref.
St James	Inchicore	Doyle Patrick Jos :	paper	Kileen Paper Mills	-	-	-	1885	-	dir/	Thoms
St James	Inchicore	Madder Richard & C(	flour	46x40x32 old mill &	-	-	-	-	20x4.8 undershot :	hob/	5.0942
St James	Inchicore	Manders Richard	flour	-	1a.	260	-	1832	-	VOf/	OL.X078
St James	Inchicore	Sanders Richard	flour (old mill)	(1C) 46x40x33 & :	-	62.2	-	-	-	hob/	5.2698
St James	Inchicore	Steering James	calico printing	dw. 32x29x20 & :	-	209	-	-	-	hob/	5.2698
St James	Inchicore	Steering James	printing factory	25x16.6x6 dye shed	-	-	-	-	no dimensions :	hob/	5.0942
St James	Inchicore	Willans Bros & Co.	cotton fcty	-	5a.	259	-	1832	-	VOf/	OL.X078
St James	Inchicore North	-	calico printing :	-	-	-	-	-	-	6"os/	18
St James	Inchicore North	-	flour mill :	-	-	-	-	-	-	6"os/	18
St James	Inchicore North	Manders Richard	flour	-	1.1 1(	-	-	-	-	gr/	-
St James	Inchicore North	Royal Hospital	water engine	-	-	-	-	-	-	gr/	-
St James	Inchicore North	Willans Bros.	cotton factory	-	5a.	-	-	-	-	gr/	-
St James	Inchicore North :	-	mill race	-	-	-	-	-	-	TLtts/	1884
St James	Inchicore North :	-	wheel :	-	-	-	-	-	-	dir1800	Dublin
St James	Inchicore North :	Alderman Mandera	flour	-	-	-	-	-	-	dir1800	Dublin
St James	Inchicore North :	Anderson George &	mills	-	-	-	Anderson - Burton Benj :	1799	-	dd/	519 48 34113?
St James	Inchicore North :	Beasley Mr.	clothier`s mill	-	-	-	-	-	-	dir1800	Dublin
St James	Inchicore North :	Burton Mr.	wash mill :	-	-	-	-	-	-	dir1800	Dublin
St James	Inchicore North :	Cranfield Richard	mills	-	-	-	Cranfield - Anderson Geo	1799	-	dd/	520 420 341139
St James	Inchicore North :	Edmondson Mr.	marble, malt	-	-	-	-	-	-	dir1800	Dublin
St James	Inchicore North :	Farris William	mill & weyer	-	-	-	Farris W - Griffitts Walter	1722	-	dd/	41 519 27206
St James	Inchicore North :	Farris William	mill & weyer	-	-	-	Farris W - Griffitts Walter	1722	-	dd/	41 519 27209
St James	Inchicore North :	Farris William	mill & weyer	-	-	-	Farris W - Farris Walter	1722	-	dd/	42 510 27207
St James	Inchicore North :	Farris William	mill & weyer	-	-	-	Farris W - Griffitts Walter	1722	-	dd/	43 38 27207
St James	Inchicore North :	Griffitts John	mill & weyer	-	-	-	Griffitts J - Griffitts Walter	1724	-	dd/	43 156 27739
St James	Inchicore North :	Griffitts John	mill & weyer	-	-	-	Griffitts J - Griffitts Walter	1724	-	dd/	45 52 27738
St James	Inchicore North :	Griffitts Walter	mill & weyer	-	-	-	Griffitts W - Benkier Andr	1726	-	dd/	49 187 31494
St James	Inchicore North :	Johnston Benj J :	mills	-	-	-	Johnston - Flood Sir Fred :	1802	-	dd/	538 503 359292
St James	Inchicore North :	Lanauze Anna J	mills	-	-	-	Lanauze A - Scott Thos	1862	-	dd/	1862 16 137
St James	Inchicore South	- Railway Co.	steam cge fcty :	-	-	300	-	1845	-	hob/	5.0940
Donnybrook	Irishtown	-	glass works	-	-	-	-	1841	-	6"os/	18
Donnybrook	Irishtown	-	salt works	-	-	-	-	1841	-	6"os/	18
Donnybrook	Irishtown	- close to R. wall	lime & salt wks	-	-	-	-	1841	-	6"os/	18
Donnybrook	Irishtown	Arthur William	saw	-	-	-	Arthur W - Jemmat Saml	1732	-	dd/	72 5 49430
Donnybrook	Irishtown	Eslington Richard :	saw mill & logh	-	-	-	Eslington R - Ward John :	1732	Mort. 28 May	dd/	29 514 18528
Donnybrook	Irishtown	Fitzwilliam Richd Ho	saw	-	-	-	Fitzwilliam Ld - Arthur Wm	1732	-	dd/	73 1 49429
Donnybrook	Irishtown	Henry Percy :	saw mill & logh	-	-	-	Henry P - Eslington R	1721	-	dd/	29 490 18439
Dublin	Island R. Liffey	Carrick Thomas :	new mill	-	-	-	Carrick - Eustace James :	1729	-	dd/	67 247 46075
Dublin	Island R. Liffey	Carrick Thomas :	new mill	-	-	-	Carrick T - Mears Charles :	1731	-	dd/	66 281 46272
Dublin	Island R. Liffey	Eustace Mary :	new mill	-	-	-	Eustace M - Eustace Jas :	1726	-	dd/	56 262 38766
Dublin	Island R. Liffey	Meares Charles	new mill	-	-	-	Meares C - Carrick Thos	1732	-	dd/	73 70 49829
St James	Islandbridge	Stuttart Elis, Miller :	flour	- (mill vacant)	-	-	-	1885		dir/	Thoms
St James	Islandbridge	Worthington William	corn	'The Old Corn Mills'	-	-	Worthington - Powell Mcl :	1809	Mort. 1 Sept.	dd/	850 381 568882
Swords	Jamestown	- at Ballyhara	Wind Mill	-				-	-	JRoc	1760 map
Dub (? par.)	Johnstown (7)	Clinch James :	windmill	-	-	-	Clinch James - Hunt John :	1776	-	dd/	308 686 209006
Clonsilla	Kellystown	- S. of Cnolsilla :	Weavers Row	-	-	-	-	-	-	6"os	13
Donabate	Kilcrea	- Baltrtay Corn Mill	corn	-	-	-	-	-	-	6"os/	12
Kilgobbin	Kilgobbin	Twigge James	slitting mill :	-	-	-	Twigge J - Neville Benj	1721	-	dd/	32 42 18890
Killeek	Killeek	-	corn	-	-	-	-	-	-	6"os/	11
Newcastle	Killeek	Ambrose William	mill	-	-	-	Ambrose - Molesworth R	1709	-	dd/	4 107 765
Killeek	Killeek	Nolan James	corn	-	56a.	-	-	-	-	gr/	-
Ballyfermot	Killeen	-	paper	-	-	-	-	1812	-	WDunc/	2

PARISH	TOWNLAND	MILLER	TYPE	HOUSE	Land	£Val	PROPRIETORS	Date	WHEEL etc.	Record	Ref.
Ballyfermot	Killeen	-	woollen	-	-	-	-	1899	-	1"os/	112
Ballyfermot	Killeen	M`Donnell Chris Esq	paper	-	47a.	-	-	-	-	gr/	-
Coolock	Killerogh-island	-	corn	-	-	-	-	-	-	dir1800	Dublin
Coolock	Killerough	Keating Maurice	mill	-	-	-	Keating M - Tyrell George	1725	-	dd/	49 239 31782
Coolock	Killerough	Keating Maurice :	mill	-	-	-	Keating - Sherlock Richd :	1716	-	dd/	16 411 7842
Coolock	Killerough	Nicholls Robert	mill	-	-	-	Nicholls R - Smith Hugh	1720	Mort. 11 Aug.	dd/	29 174 16726
Balrothery	Killossery	Bolton Edward H.S.	mills (2)	-	-	-	Bolton Ed - French Edmd :	1723	-	dd/	36 53 23973
Balrothery	Killossery	French Edmond	mills (2)	-	-	-	French Ed - Keating Nich	1723	-	dd/	38 190 23920
Killossery	Killossery	Leany Joseph	corn, wheat :	-	7a.	-	-	-	-	gr/	-
Killossery	Killossery :	Delaney	corn	-	-	-	Mr Daly (prev: Delaney)	2003	wheel gone :	mmSv/	sb - B
Killossery	Killossery :	-	corn	-	-	-	-	1841	-	6"os/	11
Kilmactalway	Kilmactalway	- Castlebagot Est	Bond buildings	-	-	-	-	-	-	6"os/	21
St James	Kilmainham	- on Cammock R	woollen	-	-	-	-	-	-	6"os/	18
St James	Kilmainham	- near R. Liffey	flour	complex of buildings:	-	-	-	2002	-	phoWEH	B
St James	Kilmainham	Benkein Andrew :	mills & weirs	-	-	-	Benkein A - Benkein John :	1731	-	dd/	66 199 45801
St James	Kilmainham	Connelly Philip	corn	-	-	-	Connelly P - Smith Corm.	1722	-	dd/	36 198 27013
St James	Kilmainham	Davis Samuel	mill	-	-	-	Davis S - Sullivan Edwd	1862	-	dd/	1862 14 133
St James	Kilmainham	Davis Samuel	mill	-	-	-	Davis S - Bean Henry	1862	-	dd/	1862 14 134
St James	Kilmainham	Davis Samuel	mill	-	-	-	Davis S - Summers Jno	1864	-	dd/	1864 5 257
St James	Kilmainham	Dillon Mr	corn	-	-	-	-	-	-	dir1800	Dublin
St James	Kilmainham	Dillon Mr	corn	-	-	-	-	-	-	dir1800	Dublin
St James	Kilmainham	Fownes William	mill	-	-	-	Fownes W - Southwell W	1705	-	dd/	3 297 985
St James	Kilmainham	Griffitts	mills & weirs	-	-	-	Griffits - Benkein	-	?	dd/	19 187 31494
St James	Kilmainham	Leland Ralph	mill	-	-	-	Leland R - Kingsbury Thos	1738	-	dd/	92 195 64315
St James	Kilmainham	Leland Ralph	mill	-	-	-	Leland Ralph - Walker Th	1738	-	dd/	93 578 66982
St James	Kilmainham	Magennis Mr.	corn	-	-	-	-	-	-	dir1800	Dublin
St James	Kilmainham	Ross Richard Earl	corn	-	-	-	Ross Ld - Weldon Arthur	1722	-	dd/	36 218 22068
St James	Kilmainham	Ross Richard Earl	corn	-	-	-	Ross Ld - Slicer Edwd	1730	-	dd/	64 204 44408
St James	Kilmainham	Ross Richard Earl	mill	-	-	-	Ross R - Butler John	1724	-	dd/	49 541 32818
St James	Kilmainham	Ross Richard Earl	mill	-	-	-	Ross Earl of - Carroll Alex	1740	-	dd/	103 485 72270
St James	Kilmainham	Ross Richard Earl	tuck	-	-	-	Ross Ld - Berkby Nich	1726	-	dd/	64 406 44408
St James	Kilmainham	Ross Richard Earl	tuck	-	-	-	Rosse Ld - Baggs Isham :	1731	-	dd/	72 39 49605
St James	Kilmainham	Rosse Lord Richard	tuck	-	-	-	Rosse Ld - Onge Samuel :	1734	-	dd/	76 91 52974
St James	Kilmainham	Rosse Richard Earl	corn	-	-	-	Rosse E. of - Slicer Edwd	1722	-	dd/	34 365 21930
St James	Kilmainham	Rosse Richard Lord	tuck	-	-	-	Rosse Ld - Berkby Nich	1723	-	dd/	39 18 23920
St James	Kilmainham	Summers John :	flour	Hibernian Mills	-	-	-	1885	-	dir/	Thoms
St James	Kilmainham	Tuite John	mill	-	-	-	-	-	-	gr/	-
St James	Kilmainham	Whelen Ernest Rev.	Hibernian Mills	-	-	-	Whelen Ern - Brophy Wm	1892	-	dd/	1892 29 103
St James	Kilmainham	Willans Obradish	cloth fcty	-	22a.	445	-	1832	-	VOf/	OL.X078
St James	Kilmainham	Willans Thomas	woollen, pond	-	20a.	-	-	-	-	gr/	-
St Peters	Kilmainham	Willins Thomas :	cloth factory	(1A) 24.6x10.6x18 :	-	140	-	-	-	hob/	5.2699
Tully	Kilmashogue	-	old bds (? mill)	- large old ruins	-	-	S Featherstone	2002	-	mmSv/	wh - R
Tully	Kilmashogue	De Burca Jeannie	old high bld.	? silk manufactory	-	-	Jeannie De Burca	2002	-	phoWEH	B
Tully	Kilmashogue	Dolan Mr	corn	-	-	-	-	-	-	dir1800	Dublin
Tully	Kilmashogue	Ramor Samuel	wollen-cloth	-	1.1.3(	-	-	-	-	gr/	-
Killossery	Kilshogan	- W. of village	Wind Mill	-	-	-	-	-	-	JRoc	1760 map
Kiltiernan	Kiltiernan	-	corn	-	-	-	-	-	-	dir1800	Dublin
Kiltiernan	Kiltiernan	-	cotton	well preserved			J & P Stokes	2002	-	phoWEH	Cr
Kiltiernan	Kiltiernan	-	flax	- small part of :	-	-	-	2002	-	phoWEH	B
Kiltiernan	Kiltiernan	- at Kiltiernan Lo.	paper	well preserved			Monica Carroll	2002	-	phoWEH	Cr
Kiltiernan	Kiltiernan	- S. of P.O.	cotton factory	-	-	-	-	1841	-	6"os/	26
Kiltiernan	Kiltiernan	- W. of Church	paper	Wind Mill	-	-	-	1841	-	6"os/	26

PARISH	TOWNLAND	MILLER	TYPE	HOUSE	Land	£Val	PROPRIETORS	Date	WHEEL etc.	Record	Ref.
Kiltiernan	Kiltiernan	- on R. nr Newtn Hill	Mill	-	-	-	-	-	-	JRoc	1760 map
Kiltiernan	Kiltiernan	Browne Michael	paper	-	9a.	-	-	-	-	gr/	-
Kiltiernan	Kiltiernan	Mosse Samuel	cotton factory	-	32a.	-	-	-	-	gr/	-
Tallaght	Kiltipper	- near R. Dodder	parchment	- site of old mill	-	-		2002	-	mmSv/	wh - Z
Tallaght	Kiltipper	- W side R Dodder	parchment site	-	-	-	-	-	-	6"os/	21
Rathfarnham	Kimmage	- E. of Kimmage X	flour	nil remains	-	-	-	2002	-	phoWEH	Z
Rathfarnham	Kimmage	- nr Whitehall Ho.	cutlers	nil remains	-	-	-	2002	-	mmSv/	wh - Z
Rathfarnham	Kimmage	- nr Whitehall Ho.	flour	nil remains	-	-	-	2002	-	mmSv/	wh - Z
Rathfarnham	Kimmage	- W. of Kimmage X	flour	nil remains	-	-	-	2002	-	phoWEH	Z
Crumlin	Kimmage	Flinn John	flour	(1B) 17.6x18x37 :	-	19.4	-	1845	17x6x11.6 56 bkts. :	hob/	5.0935
Crumlin	Kimmage	Flinn John	flour	-	1.3.2	91 :	-	1832	-	VOf/	OL.X078
Rathfarnham	Kimmage	Grange Mr	flour	-	-	-	-	-	-	dir1800	Dublin
Rathfarnham	Kimmage	Kelly Mr	blade	-	-	-	-	-	-	dir1800	Dublin
Rathfarnham	Kimmage	M`Cann Mr	corn	-	-	-	-	-	-	dir1800	Dublin
Rathfarnham	Kimmage	M`Cann Mr	skin	-	-	-	-	-	-	dir1800	Dublin
Crumlin	Kimmage	Regan Patrick	flour	-	2.2.1	72 :	-	1832	-	VOf/	OL.X078
Crumlin	Kimmage	Regan Patrick	mill	(1B) 44x27x33 :	-	10	-	1845	2 - 12x6.6x12 & :	hob/	5.0935
Rathfarnham	Kimmage	Regan Patrick	mill (part of)	-	-	-	-	-	-	gr/	-
Newcastle	Kings Milltown	Moore Capel :	mill	-	-	-	Moore C - Rachel Mass.	1721	-	dd/	31 478 20020
Newcastle	Kings Miltown	O`Brien Daniel	-	-	-	-	O`Brien Dan - O`Brien Robt	1861	-	dd/	1861 24 185
Dublin	Kingsmillstown	Rorke Laurence	mill	-	-	-	Rorke L - Buckley Jno	1862	-	dd/	1862 30 146
Dub (? par.)	Knightsfield	McDonnell Silvester	mill	-	-	-	McDonnell S - Henning Wm	1862	-	dd/	1862 23 174
Dub (? par.)	Knightsgreen	McDonnell Silvester	mill	Knifgtsfield Mill	-	-	McDonnell S - King Jno	1864	-	dd/	1864 35 162
Balrothery	Knock	- W. side of road	Windmill	-	-	-	-	1760	-	JRoc	1760 map
Balrothery	Knock	- S. of reservoir	windmill stump	-	-	-	-	1841	-	6"os/	5
Balrothery	Knock	Hamilton George	mill-pond	-	25a.	-	-	-	-	gr/	-
Balrothery	Knock	M`Cormick Mr.	windmill - corn	-	-	-	-	-	-	dir1800	Dublin
Rathcoole	Knockbrock *	- on Co. Boundary	The Old Mills	-	-	-	-	-	-	JRoc	1760 map
Dub (? par.)	Knockengen :	Moore Mr	bleach	-	-	-	-	-	-	dir1800	Dublin
Crumlin	Larkfield	- nr Kimmage Vge.	flour & pond	-	-	-	-	-	-	6"os/	22
Crumlin	Larkfield	- nr Kimmage Vge.	windmill	-	-	-	-	-	-	6"os/	22
Crumlin	Larkfield	Tuite Francis	flour	(1B) 73x24x26.6 :	-	9.12	-	1845	13.6x6.6x- breast :	hob/	5.0935
Crumlin	Larkfield	Tuite Francis	flour	-	13a.	86 :	-	1832	-	VOf/	OL.X078
Crumlin	Larkfield	Tuite Francis Esq	flour & pond	-	13a.	-	-	-	-	gr/	-
Westpalstown	Leabstown	Georges Hamilton	mill	-	-	-	Georges H - Macarell Jn	1751	-	dd/	154 155 103170
Westpalstown	Leabstown	Torton? Edward	mill	-	-	-	torton - Litton Thomas	1752	-	dd/	154 154 103169
Leixlip	Leixlip	- Mill Office only	-	-	-	-	-	1997	-	phoWEH	Cc
Leixlip	Leixlip	Goodshaw Mr	corn	-	-	-	-	-	-	dir1800	Dublin
Leixlip	Leixlip	Marsden Mr	iron	-	-	-	-	-	-	dir1800	Dublin
Leixlip	Leixlip :	- N. side R Liffey :	Linen Print Ho.	-	-	-	-	-	-	JRoc	1760 map
Dublin	Leybstowm	Bowles John	mill	-	-	-	Bowles J - Plunkett Plkt	1726	-	dd/	49 361 32452
Dublin	Leybstowm	Plunkett Plunkett	: mill	-	-	-	Plunkett P - Whitshed Jas :	1728	-	dd/	57 459 39257
Dublin	Leybstowm	Plunkett Walter	: mill	-	-	-	Plunkett W - Whitshed :	1728	-	dd/	53 116 34601
Dublin	Leybstown	Bowles John	mill	-	-	-	Bowles J - Plunkett Pkt	1726	-	dd/	48 572 32451
Killossery	Lispopple	-	old flour mill	-	-	-	-	-	-	6"os/	11
St Peter`s	Loaders Park	Andersen John :	mill & windmill	-	-	-	Andersen J - Auchmuty C	1720	Mort. 20 May	dd/	27 102 15718
St Peter`s	Loaders Park	Andersen John :	mill & windmill	-	-	-	Anderson J - Will Anthony :	1729	Mort 30 Jul.	dd/	59 439 41263
St Peter`s	Loaders Park	Goodwin Richard	mill & windmill	-	-	-	Goodwin R - Goodwin F	1721	-	dd/	34 35 20354
St Peter`s	Loaders Park	Gore Georgina	mills	-	-	-	Gore G`gina - Vernon Chas	1891	-	dd/	1891 54 57
St Peter`s	Loaders Park	Vernon Georgina	Upper Mill	-	-	-	Vernon Georgina - Charles	1891	-	dd/	1891 54 56
St Peter`s	Loaders Park :	Goodwin Peter	mill & windmill	-	-	-	Goodwin P - Andersen Jn	1709	-	dd/	26 171 15049
Dublin	Lockswood *	Jackson Adam	tuck mills	-	-	-	Jackson A - Delandre Bart	f lease	-	dd/	103 147 70983

PARISH	TOWNLAND	MILLER	TYPE	HOUSE	Land	£Val	PROPRIETORS	Date	WHEEL etc.	Record	Ref.
Dublin	Lockswood *	Kennan Thomas :	tuck	four houses namely :	-	-	Kennan T - Delandre Wm :	1774	-	dd/	118 278 180745?
Killiney	Loughlinstown	-	old corn mill	-	-	-	-	2002	-	mmSv/	wh - Z
Lucan	Lucan	- N. of R. Liffey	Lucan Mills	-	-	-	-	-	-	JRoc	1760 map
Lucan	Lucan	- N. side R. Liffey	Iron Mill	-	-	-	-	1821	-	WDunc/	2
Lucan	Lucan	Barton John :	new corn mill	-	-	-	Barton Jn - Fellows Chas :	1737	Lse. 6 May.	dd/	85 474 61043
Lucan	Lucan	Blair James	tuck	-	-	-	Blair & Ormston - Redford	1790	-	dd/	417 531 273689
Lucan	Lucan	Blair Mr	iron-works (8)	-	-	-	-	-	8 wheels	dir1800	Dublin
Lucan	Lucan	Delvin Hugh	mill	-	-	-	Delvin Hugh & W - Scalian	1862	-	dd/	1862 18 25
Lucan	Lucan	Long William	mill	-	-	-	Long Wm - Archer Geo	1860	-	dd/	1860 18 201
Lucan	Lucan	M`Donnell Mr	paper	-	-	-	-	-	-	dir1800	Dublin
Lucan	Lucan	Shackleton George	Annaliffey Mills	-	-	-	-	1898	-	dir/	Thoms
Lucan	Lucan	Shackleton George	Annaliffey Mills	-	-	-	-	-	Alcott, Jonval & :	turb/	1947
Lucan	Lucan	Sisson Mr	grist (fmly bl.)	-	-	-	-	-	-	dir1800	Dublin
Lucan	Lucan	Vivian S - Coley Ed	mill	-	-	-	Vivian Sam - Coley Edwd	1861	-	dd/	1861 15 19
Lucan	Lucan	Young Mr	corn	-	-	-	-	-	-	dir1800	Dublin
Lucan	Lucan :	Shakleton Geo & Co	flour	-	-	-	-	1965	-	lic/	wheat23
Lucan	Lucan Town	Hill & Sons	Powers Mill	-	-	-	-	-	Francis 90 & 50kw	turb/	1947
Lucan	Lucan Town :	Sisson Family	printing house	-	-	-	-	1760	-	JRoc	1760 map
Lusk	Lusk	-	thrashing	-	-	-	-	-	-	6"os/	8
Castleknock	Luttrellstown	Luttrell Elizabeth :	land	-	-	-	Luttrell E - Luttrell Robert :	1718	-	dd/	23 529 14319
Castleknock	Luttrellstown	Luttrell Henry :	land	-	-	-	Luttrell H - Hawkins Wm :	1718	-	dd/	20 338 10831
Castleknock	Luttrellstown	Sinnott Patrick :	tuck	-	-	-	Sinnott P - Marples Richd	1718	Mort. 2 May	dd/	20 381 10978
Lucan	Luttrels Park	- near R. Liffey :	(stream) no mill	-	-	-	-	-	-	JRoc	1760 map
Castleknock	Luttrelstown	De Notingham Robe	mill	-	-	-	-	1315	-	mssH/	D.604/605
Castleknock	Luttrelstown	White Mr	mills :	-	-	-	-	-	several wheels	dir1800	Dublin
Malahide	Malahide	- S. side of The Mal	ribband factory	-	-	-	- Covered by small park -	1880	-	6"os/	17
Malahide	Mallahide	- N. side River	Mill	-	-	-	-	-	-	JRoc	1760 map
Newcastle bo.	Manor	Vesey Chas	mill	-	-	-	Vesey - Purdon Arabella	1864	-	dd/	1864 14 220
Newcastle bo.	Manor :	Bayly Selina	Manor Mill	-	-	-	Bayly S - Vesey Charles	1901	-	dd/	1901 3 146
Newcastle bo.	Manor :	Vesey Charles E	Manor Mill	-	-	-	Vesey - Harrison Henry J	1900	-	dd/	1900 52 215
Newcastle bo.	Manor :	Vesey Charles E	Manor Mill	-	-	-	Vesey C - Moran Alicia	1900	-	dd/	1900 6 17
Newcastle	Manor N`castle	Colthurst Charles	Manor Mill	-	-	-	Colthurst C - Hamilton Chs	1860	-	dd/	1860 8 123
Dublin	Mardyke	Haskins Mr	tuck :	-	-	-	-	-	-	dir1800	Dublin
St Margarets	Mill Head	Moss Dennis	windmill	dia. 20.6 x height 26	-	-	-	-	drives 1 pair st. :	hob/	5.0892
Newcastle	Mill Hill	Martin William	land	-	-	-	Martin W - Bagenal Walt	1723	-	dd/	44 438 30021
Balruddery	Mill Hill Farm	Keating James :	land	-	-	-	Keating J - Gibbons Mary :	1738	Mort. 22 Nov.	dd/	91 497 64992
Dublin	Millfield	Healy Edward	mill	-	-	-	Healy Edwd - Pirie Gordon	1861	-	dd/	1861 11 211
St Peter`s	Milltown	-	no mill	-	-	-	-	1899	-	1"os/	112
Newcastle	Milltown	-	no mill	-	-	-	-	-	-	6"os/	21
Newcastle	Milltown	-	no mill	-	-	-	-	-	-	JRoc	1760 map
Newcastle	Milltown	- nr Bankside Ctgs	blue	nil remains	-	-	-	2002	-	mmSv/	wh - Z
St Peter`s	Milltown	Alexander Robert Si	woollen fcty	-	3a.	-	-	-	-	gr/	-
St Peter`s	Milltown	Alexander William :	mill	-	-	-	Alexander W - Shaw Wm :	1796	-	dd/	503 263 323569
Dunlavin	Milltown	Bond Francis :	land	-	-	-	Bond Fran - Bond William :	1736	DD/ Marr.	dd/	83 281 5870
Dub (? par.)	Milltown	Burk & Mullen	woollen :	-	-	-	-	-	-	dir1800	Dublin
Dub (? par.)	Milltown	Burke Waller	mill	-	-	-	Burke W - Wallis John	1801	-	dd/	531 576 353600
Dub (? par.)	Milltown	Butler Richard	-	-	-	-	Butler Richd - Ward Wm	1860	-	dd/	1860 36 257
Castleknock	Milltown	Ford Robert Mr :	iron & brass	-	-	-	Ford Robert & Will	1726	-	dd/	53 13 34267
Castleknock	Milltown	French Humphry	iron & brass	-	-	-	French H - Ford William	1724	-	dd/	39 393 24843
Dub (? par.)	Milltown	Harvey James W	mills	-	-	-	Harvey J W - Crosnie W	1860	-	dd/	1860 14 114
Dub (? par.)	Milltown	Hunt Mr	woollen :	-	-	-	-	-	-	dir1800	Dublin
Dub (? par.)	Milltown	Ld. Estate Court	-	-	land	-	Ld. Est. Ct - Beakey Patk	1860	-	dd/	1860 19 15

PARISH	TOWNLAND	MILLER	TYPE	HOUSE	Land	£Val	PROPRIETORS	Date	WHEEL etc.	Record	Ref.
Castleknock	Milltown	Leeson Joseph	iron & brass	-	-	-	Leeson J - French Humph	1724	-	dd/	42 110 25830
Dub (? par.)	Milltown	Maffett William H	-	-	land	-	Maffett WH - Beakey Patk	1861	-	dd/	1861 2 240
Dub (? par.)	Milltown	Milltown Earl	-	-		-	Millown E. - Minett	-	-	dd/	841 310 564310
Dub (? par.)	Milltown	Milltown Earl	-	-		-	Millown E. - Eyre	-	-	dd/	847 442 567442
Dub (? par.)	Milltown	Milltown Earl	-	-	land	-	Millown E. - Leeson Ed	1861	-	dd/	1861 6 260
Dub (? par.)	Milltown	Minnett	-	-		-	Minnett & ors - Millown E.	-	-	dd/	849 243 568243
St Peter`s	Milltown	Moore Samuel	cloth fcty	-	3a.	62	: -	1832	-	VOf/	OL.X078
St Peter`s	Milltown	Moore Samuel	woollen fcty	42x14.6x11 - press :	-	-	-	1845	16x8 6 revs/ min.	hob/	5.0945
Dub (? par.)	Milltown	Rorke Laurence	-	-	-	-	Rorke Laur - Greene W F	1860	-	dd/	1860 11 297
Newcastle bo.	Milltown	Rorke Laurence	mill ?	-	-	-	Rorke L - Mangan Mcl	1862	-	dd/	1862 26 297
Dub (? par.)	Milltown	Rorke Laurence & P	-	-	-	-	Rourke L & P - Teeling Jno	1860	-	dd/	1860 34 87
Clondalkin	Milltown	Ross Richard Hon.	mill	-	-	-	Ross Ld - E. of Abercorn	1715	-	dd/	16 467 7992
Clondalkin	Milltown	Ross Richard Hon.	mill	-	-	-	Ross Ld - Bellew Thos	1716	-	dd/	17 172 8476
Dub (? par.)	Milltown	Walker Richard	-	-	land	-	Walker R - Thompson Dav	1860	-	dd/	1860 24 282
Dub (? par.)	Milltown	Wall Robert	-	-	-	-	Wall Robt - Keates Thos	1860	-	dd/	1861 1 169
Dub (? par.)	Milltown	Wallis John :	mill	-	-	-	Wallis J - Burke Walter :	1801	-	dd/	537 434 353599
St Peter`s	Milltown Village :	-	starch & glue	-	-	-	-	1827	-	Lewis	pars.
St Peter`s	Milltown Village :	Hartnett Maurice	woollen	-	-	-	-	1827	-	Lewis	pars.
Dub (? par.)	Miltown Kings	Thomas James	-	-	-	-	Thomas Jas - Haliday Geo	1860	-	dd/	1860 29 244
Newcastle bo.	Mount Pl Manor	Hamilton Charles	mill	-	-	-	Hamilton Chas - Fredk	1863	-	dd/	1863 37 49
Dublin	Mountdown	Antrobus John	corn	-	-	-	Antrobus J - Harvey John	1723	-	dd/	39 109 24407
Dublin	Mountdown	Jackson Adam :	tuck	-	-	-	Jackson A - Pilkington Thos	1719	-	dd/	26 422 15954
Rathdown	Mounttown	Barton John	mill	-	-	-	Barton J - Robinson Richd	1763	-	dd/	224 521 147220
Rathdown	Mounttown	Barton John	windmill farm :	-	-	-	Barton J - Robinson Richd	1763	-	dd/	224 521 147226
Rathdown	Mounttown	Fisher	windmill farm :	-	-	-	Fisher - Colaman	1750	-	dd/	170 508 11239
Rathdown	Mounttown	Fisher Thomas	mill	-	-	-	Fisher T - Coleman Chas :	1750	-	dd/	170 508 112391
Rathdown	Mounttown	Lord Matthew :	mill	-	-	-	Lord M - Barton Jonn	1763	-	dd/	227 212 466548
Rathdown	Mounttown	Lord Matthew :	windmill farm :	-	-	-	Lord M - Barton Jonn	1763	-	dd/	227 212 146548
Rathdown	Mounttown	Robinson Richard :	mill	-	-	-	Robinson R - Cavendish :	1763	-	dd/	237 41 151447
Rathdown	Mounttown	Robinson Richard :	windmill farm :	-	-	-	Robinson R - Cavendish :	1763	-	dd/	237 41 151447
Naul	Naul	- E. side of Town :	Mill	-	-	-	-	-	-	JRoc	1760 map
Naul	Naul	Teeling Mr	bleach	-	-	-	-	-		dir1800	Dublin
Naul	Naul	Walsh & Co.	flour	-	-	-	-	-	2 wheels	dir1800	Dublin
Whitechurch	Newbrook Mill	McDonagh Jno	paper	-	-	-	McDonogh J - Stubbs Jno	1862	-	dd/	1862 28 286
Lusk	Newhaggard	- middle of Estuary	Turvey Mill								
Cruagh	Newtown	-	cloth (in ruins)	-	-	-	-	-	-	6"os/	22
Dub (? par.)	Newtown	-	corn & flour	-	-	-	-	-	-	6"os/	11
Cruagh	Newtown	- N`t Little Cloth Mill	cloth	-	-	-	-	-	-	6"os/	22
Cruagh	Newtown	Boyd Patk or Nun Ms	paper	-	15a.	87	: -	1832	-	VOf/	OL.X078
Cruagh	Newtown	Brown Paul	paper	-	2a.	67	: -	1832	-	VOf/	OL.X078
Garristown	Newtown	Mangan Simon	windmill	dia. 18ft ht. 21ft 6in :	-	-	-	-	- 1 pr st. 4ft 10in :	hob/	5.0858
Cruagh	Newtown	Millmount Mill	cloth	-	-	-	-	-	-	6"os/	22
Cruagh	Newtown	N`tn Gt Paper Mill	paper	-	-	-	-	-	-	6"os/	22
Dub (? par.)	Newtown (8)	-	corn	-	-	-	-	-	-	dir1800	Dublin
Dub (? par.)	Nutstown	-	windmill - corn	-	-	-	-	-	-	dir1800	Dublin
Tallaght	Oldbawn	-	ruins (/ mill)	-	-	-	-	2002	-	phoWEH	R
Tallaght	Oldbawn	-	The Old Mill	rebuilt (orig. in Tipp.)	-	-	Luis Fitzgerald	2002	-	phoWEH	C
Tallaght	Oldbawn	- nr Haerlem	flour mill	-	-	-	-	-	-	6"os/	22
Tallaght	Oldbawn	- nr Haerlem	woollen cloth	-	-	-	-	-	-	6"os/	22
Tallaght	Oldbawn	- nr Oldbawn Br.	flour	-	-	-	-	-	-	6"os/	22
Tallaght	Oldbawn	- Oldbawn Paper	paper	-	-	-	-	-	-	6"os/	21
Tallaght	Oldbawn	Dobbin Matthew	miller`s house	-	-	-	-	-	-	gr/	-

PARISH	TOWNLAND	MILLER	TYPE	HOUSE	Land	£Val	PROPRIETORS	Date	WHEEL etc.	Record	Ref.
Tallaght	Oldbawn	M`Cracken John	mills	-	42a.	-	-	-	-	gr/	-
Tallaght	Oldbawn	M`Donnell Michael	paper	-	159a.	-	-	-	-	gr/	-
Tallaght	Oldbawn	McCrackan John	flour	(1B) 37.6x14x18 :	-	32.7	-	1845	water wheel works :	hob/	5.0950
Tallaght	Oldbawn	McCrackan John	flour	(1C) 66.6x18.6x16 :	-	44.7	-	1845	14x8x- breast metal :	hob/	5.0950
Tallaght	Oldbawn	McCracken John	mill	-	15a.	165	-	1832	-	VOf/	OL.X078
Tallaght	Oldbawn	McDonnell Michael	paper	-	191a.	479	-	1832	-	VOf/	OL.X078
Tallaght	Oldbawn	Neil Kate	mill	-	45a.	150	-	1832	-	VOf/	OL.X078
Tallaght	Oldbawn	Neil Samuel	flour	-	46a.	-	-	-	-	gr/	-
Tallaght	Oldbawn	Neil Samuel	wv factory	-	-	-	-	-	-	gr/	-
Tallaght	Oldbawn	O'Reilly Thomas	flour	(1B) 55.6x33x27 :	-	13.0.'	-	1845	9x1.6x-	hob/	5.0950
Tallaght	Oldbawn	O'Reilly Thomas	tuck	(1C) 27x22x7.6	-	19/9d	-	1845	13x4x- drives :	hob/	5.0950
Kilmactalway	Oughterard	-	mill	- demolished :	-	-	-	2002	-	mmSv/	wh - Z
Palmerstown	Palmerston	- S. side R. Liffey	Old Mills	-	-	-	-	1821	-	WDunc/	2
Palmerstown	Palmerston Lr.	-	boiling house	ruins (dilapidated)	-	-	-	2002	-	phoWEH	R
Palmerstown	Palmerston Lr.	-	cotton	-	-	-	-	-	-	6"os/	17
Palmerstown	Palmerston Lr.	-	cotton	well preserved	-	-	M/s Coates (Paint/Ink Mfr)	2002	-	phoWEH	C
Palmerstown	Palmerston Lr.	-	iron mill	-	-	-	-	-	-	6"os/	17
Palmerstown	Palmerston Lr.	-	laundry	ruins (burnt 2001)	-	-	-	2002	-	phoWEH	R
Palmerstown	Palmerston Lr.	-	laundry house	now Studios	-	-	-	2002	-	phoWEH	C
Palmerstown	Palmerston Lr.	-	lead & copper	-	-	-	-	-	-	6"os/	17
Palmerstown	Palmerston Lr.	-	logwood	-	-	-	-	-	-	6"os/	17
Palmerstown	Palmerston Lr.	-	oil mill	-	-	-	-	-	-	6"os/	17
Palmerstown	Palmerston Lr.	-	pump houses	restored	-	-	M/s Coates	2002	-	phoWEH	C
Palmerstown	Palmerston Lr.	-	scutch	ruins (dilapidated)	-	-	-	2002	-	phoWEH	R
Palmerstown	Palmerston Lr.	Ashton John	spade forge	34x22x13 25x18x8	-	-	-	-	14x2.9x8 metal :	hob/	5.0937
Palmerstown	Palmerston Lr.	M M`Garry Esq	cotton factory	-	-	-	-	-	-	gr/	-
Palmerstown	Palmerston Lr.	M M`Garry Esq	lead & copper	-	-	-	-	-	-	gr/	-
Palmerstown	Palmerston Lr.	M M`Garry Esq	logwood	-	-	-	-	-	-	gr/	-
Palmerstown	Palmerston Lr.	M M`Garry Esq	mill-race	-	4a.	-	-	-	-	gr/	-
Palmerstown	Palmerston Lr.	M M`Garry Esq	oil	-	0.0.8	-	-	-	-	gr/	-
Palmerstown	Palmerston Lr.	M M`Garry Esq	spade	-	-	-	-	-	-	gr/	-
Palmerstown	Palmerston Lr.	McGarry Michael	cotton factory	93x37x49 store & :	-	-	-	-	no dimensions :	hob/	5.0937
Palmerstown	Palmerston Lr.	McGarry Michael	lead & copper	85x74x34 & lead-	-	-	-	-	21x6x9.6 u`shot :	hob/	5.0937
Palmerstown	Palmerston Lr.	McGarry Michael	logwood	47x43x19 saw mill :	-	-	-	-	16x8 1 pair Irish st.	hob/	5.0937
Palmerstown	Palmerston Lr.	McGarry Michael	oil mill	64x35x54 boiler ho :	-	-	-	-	16.6x10x10 9 rpm.:	hob/	5.0937
Palmerstown	Palmerstown	- at Mill Lane	cottages	well preserved	-	-	-	2002	-	phoWEH	-
Palmerstown	Palmerstown	- W. of Town :	Dunkirk Mills	-	-	-	-	-	-	JRoc	1760 map
Palmerstown	Palmerstown	- N. side of River :	Mardike Mills	-	-	-	-	-	-	JRoc	1760 map
Palmerstown	Palmerstown	Blair Mr	iron-works :	-	-	-	-	-	17 wheels	dir1800	Dublin
Palmerstown	Palmerstown	Brooks Thomas	mill	-	-	-	Brooks T - Lawless John	1785	-	dd/	370 48 246526
Palmerstown	Palmerstown	Byers John :	mill (stocks)	-	-	-	Byers J - Fortick Tristrum	1719	Mort. 5 Sep.	dd/	24 316 13903
Palmerstown	Palmerstown	Byrne John :	leather :	-	-	-	Byrne J - Henzey Joshua :	1728	-	dd/	55 351 37260
Palmerstown	Palmerstown	Charles Elijah :	leather	-	-	-	Charles E - Vipons Luke :	1729	-	dd/	63 23 42479
Palmerstown	Palmerstown	Clarke Mr	printing (6) :	-	-	-	-	-	-	dir1800	Dublin
Palmerstown	Palmerstown	Clarke Mr	wash (3)	-	-	-	-	-	-	dir1800	Dublin
Palmerstown	Palmerstown	Henzey Joshua	corn & tuck	-	-	-	Henzey Joshua - Joshua	1727	-	dd/	52 222 34335
Palmerstown	Palmerstown	Henzey Joshua :	corn	-	-	-	Henzey - CharlesElijah :	1728	-	dd/	56 432 38589
Palmerstown	Palmerstown	Henzey Joshua :	leather	-	-	-	Henzey - CharlesElijah :	1728	-	dd/	56 432 38589
Palmerstown	Palmerstown	Jones Theophilus	:iron	-	-	-	Jones T - Skellern Richd	1712	-	dd/	10 124 3212
Palmerstown	Palmerstown	Lawless Mr	skin & corn	-	-	-	-	-	-	dir1800	Dublin
Palmerstown	Palmerstown	Macken James	mill	-	4a.	113	-	1832	-	VOf/	OL.X078
Palmerstown	Palmerstown	McGarry Bernard	cotton factory	-	-	30	-	1832	-	VOf/	OL.X078

PARISH	TOWNLAND	MILLER	TYPE	HOUSE	Land	£Val	PROPRIETORS	Date	WHEEL etc.	Record	Ref.
Palmerstown	Palmerstown	McGarry Bernard	lead & coper	-	40a.	236	-	1832	-	VOf/	OL.X078
Palmerstown	Palmerstown	McGarry Bernard	logwood	-	-	56	-	1832	-	VOf/	OL.X078
Palmerstown	Palmerstown	McGarry Bernard	oil	-	-	90	-	1832	-	VOf/	OL.X078
Palmerstown	Palmerstown	McGarry Bernard	spade	-	-	39	-	1832	-	VOf/	OL.X078
Palmerstown	Palmerstown	O`Brien Mr	dye-stuff	-	-	-	-	-	-	dir1800	Dublin
Palmerstown	Palmerstown	O`Brien Mr	oil	-	-	-	-	-	-	dir1800	Dublin
Palmerstown	Palmerstown	O`Brien Mr	oil	-	-	-	-	-	-	dir1800	Dublin
Palmerstown	Palmerstown	Palmerstown Henry :	corn	-	-	-	Palmerst`n - Wilson Josh	1726	-	dd/	51 452 34324
Palmerstown	Palmerstown	Segar Halsall	mill	-	-	-	Segar H - Meldon James	1860	-	dd/	1864 21 157
Palmerstown	Palmerstown	Temple Henry :	Norris`s Mills	-	-	-	Temple H - Wilding Richd	1717	-	dd/	17 314 8966
Palmerstown	Palmerstown	Wilding	Norris`s Mills	-	-	-	Wilding - Bryan	-	?	dd/	84? 422 61683
Palmerstown	Palmerstown	Wilding Richard	Norris`s Mills	-	-	-	Wilding R - Wilding Richd	1722	-	dd/	36 103 21726
Palmerstown	Palmerstown	Wilson	corn :	-	-	-	Charles - Vipont ?	-	?	dd/	63 23 42497
Palmerstown	Palmerstown	Wilson	corn & tuck	-	-	-	Wilson J - Henzey Josh	1727	-	dd/	52 226 34333/4
Palmerstown	Palmerstown	Wilson Joshua	corn :	-	-	-	Wilson J - Henzell Josh	1724	-	dd/	40 282 2574
Palmerstown	Palmerstown	Wilson Joshua	corn & tuck	-	-	-	Wilson J - Yarner Wm	1721	-	dd/	36 78 21351
Palmerstown	Palmerstown	Wilson Joshua	corn & tuck	-	-	-	Wilson J - Henzell Josh	1724	-	dd/	50 250 32884
Palmerstown	Palmerstown	Wilson Joshua :	corn	-	-	-	Wilson J - Charles Eyiah	1720	-	dd/	32 169 19314
Castleknock	Pelletstown	-	corn	-	-	-	-	-	-	dir1800	Dublin
Castleknock	Pelletstown	Pratt William	corn	-	-	-	-	-	-	gr/	-
Castleknock	Pelletstown	Pratt William	corn :	30x20.6x13.6 & :	-	-	-	-	10.6x5.4x4 o`shot :	hob/	5.3814
Castleknock	Pelletstown	Tyrell James	iron works	35x23x10 Val. :	-	-	-	-	11x4.6 42 bkts. :	hob/	5.3814
Crumlin	Perrystown	- at Whitehall	cutlers	-	-	-	-	-	-	6"os/	22
Crumlin	Perrystown	- Mount Down	: Flour Mill	-	-	-	-	-	-	6"os/	22
Crumlin	Perrystown	- Mt. Down Mill	flour & mill race	-	-	-	-	-	-	6"os/	22
Crumlin	Perrystown	Milliken Thomas	cutlery	-	5a.	21 :	-	1832	-	VOf/	OL.X078
Crumlin	Perrystown	Milliken Thos R Esq	cutlery	-	5a.	-	-	-	-	gr/	-
Crumlin	Perrystown :	Milliken Thomas R	cutlery	(1B) 31.6x23.6x8 :	-	4.7.6	-	1845	15x4x- u'shot 32bkt. :	hob/	5.0935
Castleknock	Phibblestown	- near Clonee	mill	-	-	-	-	1899	-	1"os/	111
Portmarnock	Portmarnock	-	corn	-	-	-	-	-	-	6"os/	15
Portmarnock	Portmarnock	- W. side Port`k B	mill	-	-	-	-	-	-	JRoc	1760 map
Portmarnock	Portmarnock	Birch Robert :	mill	-	-	-	Birch - Jenny Brabazon :	1721	-	dd/	287 301 187333
Portmarnock	Portmarnock	Cullen John	mill	-	-	-	Cullen J - Beggs Fran	1792	-	dd/	454 337 292522
Portmarnock	Portmarnock	Dickson Mr	corn	-	-	-	-	-	-	dir1800	Dublin
Portmarnock	Portmarnock	Kingsland Lady	mill	-	-	-	Kingsland - Birch Robert :	1775	-	dd/	308 647 208842
Portmarnock	Portmarnock	Potterton Adelaide	mill	-	-	-	Potterton - Coppinger Chas	1893	-	dd/	1893 2290
St Peter`s	Portobello	- nr Portobello Br.	brewery	-	-	-	-	-	-	TLtts/	1884
St Peter`s	Portobello	- nr Portobello Br.	Greenmount :	-	-	-	-	-	-	TLtts/	1884
St Peter`s	Portobello	- nr Portobello Br.	mill ponds (2)	-	-	-	-	-	-	TLtts/	1884
Dub (? par.)	Raghereden	-	corn	-	-	-	-	-	-	dir1800	Dublin
Raheny	Raheny	- in Town	Windmill of :	-	-	-	-	-	-	JRoc	1760 map
Raheny	Raheny	- in Town	Windmill of :	-	-	-	-	-	-	JRoc	1760 map
Raheny	Raheny	- S. of Town	Mill in ruins	-	-	-	-	-	-	JRoc	1760 map
Raheny	Raheny	- W. side of River	Windmill	-	-	-	-	-	-	JRoc	1760 map
Portraine	Rahillion	-	flour	-	-	-	-	-	-	6"os/	8
Portraine	Rahillion	Kerr John	wind-mill	-	11.2.:	-	-	-	-	gr/	-
Rathcole	Rathcreedan	-	corn & pond	-	-	-	-	-	-	6"os/	21
Rathcole	Rathcreedan	M`Donnell Mary A	corn	-	9a.	-	-	-	-	gr/	-
Dub (? par.)	Rathdown (bo)	Shaw Robert	mill	Subbins Mill	-	-	Shaw Robt - Trufil Robt	1861	-	dd/	1861 30 55
Rathfarnham	Rathfarnham	- Ely Cloth Factory	cloth	-	-	-	-	-	-	6"os/	22
Rathfarnham	Rathfarnham	- nr R`farnham Vge	mill	replaced by Appmts.	-	-	-	2002	-	phoWEH	Cr
Rathfarnham	Rathfarnham	- on Owendogher R	old mill	-	-	-	-	-	-	6"os/	22

PARISH	TOWNLAND	MILLER	TYPE	HOUSE	Land	£Val	PROPRIETORS	Date	WHEEL etc.	Record	Ref.
Rathfarnham	Rathfarnham	Choppin Richard	Mill Hill	-	-	-	Choppin R - Hankison Jn	1726	-	dd/	49 281 31984
Rathfarnham	Rathfarnham	Connolly	paper	-	-	-	Connolly - Slater	-	?	dd/	42 210 31391
Rathfarnham	Rathfarnham	Curraghan, Flanagar	flour	-	-	-	-	-	-	dir1800	Dublin
Rathfarnham	Rathfarnham	Drumgold Mr	corn	-	-	-	-	-	-	dir1800	Dublin
Rathfarnham	Rathfarnham	Freeman Mr	paper	-	-	-	-	-	-	dir1800	Dublin
Rathfarnham	Rathfarnham	Hankison John :	Mill Hill	-	-	-	Hankison - Hutchinson :	1727	-	dd/	53 97 34600
Rathfarnham	Rathfarnham	Horan James :	weedmills ? :	-	-	-	Horan J - Keightly Edwd :	1788	-	dd/	407 19 271234
Rathfarnham	Rathfarnham	Horan Thomas :	weedmills :	-	-	-	Horan T - Moody Jno :	1791	Mort. 7 Aug.	dd/	441 219 284212
Rathfarnham	Rathfarnham	Jones Dorothy :	paper	-	-	-	Jones D - Clayton Mary	1719	Mort. 12 May	dd/	26 122 14837
Rathfarnham	Rathfarnham	Keightly Edward :	weedmills :	-	-	-	Keightly E - Connolly :	1792	Mort. 2 Oct.	dd/	464 75 29333
Rathfarnham	Rathfarnham	Keightly Edward :	woodmills :	-	-	-	Keightly - Gd. Canal Co. :	1789	-	dd/	418 106 272265
Rathfarnham	Rathfarnham	Luke	paper	-	-	-	Luke - Fowles	-	?	dd/	27 110 15774
Rathfarnham	Rathfarnham	Murray Thomas	cloth	-	6.1.1	-	-	-	-	gr/	-
Rathfarnham	Rathfarnham	Newman Mr & Co.	flour	-	-	-	-	-	-	dir1800	Dublin
Rathfarnham	Rathfarnham	Teeling Mr	paper	-	-	-	-	-	-	dir1800	Dublin
Rathfarnham	Rathfarnham :	- nr. R. Dodder	flour & pond	-	-	-	-	-	-	6"os/	22
Rathfarnham	Rathfarnham :	- S. of Castle	saw	-	-	-	-	-	-	25"os/	22/07
Rathfarnham	Rathfarnham :	imed. S/ Willbrook	flour mill :	-	-	-	-	1888	-	25"os/	22/06
Rathfarnham	Rathfarnham :	imed. S/ Willbrook	pin factory :	& -	-	-	-	1845	-	6"os/	22
Rathfarnham	Rathgar	-	calico printing	-	-	-	-	-	-	6"os/	22
Rathfarnham	Rathgar	- at Rathgar Ho.	drying green	-	-	-	-	-	-	6"os/	22
Rathfarnham	Rathgar	- N. side R Dodde	Mills	-	-	-	-	-	-	JRoc	1760 map
Rathfarnham	Rathgar	Dartry Dye Works	dye & print	preserved /enlarged		-	-	-	-	phoWEH	A
Rathfarnham	Rathgar	Osbrey Mr	cotton wash	-	-	-	-	-	-	dir1800	Dublin
Rathfarnham	Rathgar	Osbrey Mr	cotton wash	-	-	-	-	-	-	dir1800	Dublin
Rathfarnham	Rathgar	Rathgar Calico Print	printing	preserved also :	-	-	-	-	-	mmSv/	wh - B
St Catherines	Rathland East	-	cotton	-	-	-	-	-	-	6"os/	18
Rathfarnham	Rathmines	Bellwood Mr	woollen	-	-	-	-	-	-	dir1800	Dublin
Rathfarnham	Rathmines	Williams William	woollen fcty	factory 47x30x40 & :	-	-	-	-	20x14x2 6 revs :	hob/	5.0936
St Peter`s	Rathmines S	Jones Richard	cotton fcty	-	7a.	104	-	1832	-	VOf/	OL.X078
Castleknock	Red Mills	Atkinson Mr	woollen	-	-	-	-	-	-	dir1800	Dublin
Castleknock	Red Mills	Camac	mill	-	-	-	Camac - Malone	-	?	dd/	84 514 52345/6
Castleknock	Red Mills	Chaytor Joshua D	mills	-	-	-	Chator - Guiness Hon Arth	1903	-	dd/	1903 67 65
Castleknock	Red Mills	Macken James	mills	-	-	-	Macken Jas - Segar Hals	1861	-	dd/	1861 35 152
Castleknock	Red Mills	Malone	mill	-	-	-	Malone & Will	1735	-	dd/	81 453 58305
Castleknock	Red Mills	Malone Daniel :	mill	-	-	-	Malone D - Count John :	1727	-	dd/	53 192 35039
Castleknock	Red Mills	Malone Elizabeth :	mill	-	-	-	Malone E - Camack John :	1736	-	dd/	82 378 58232
Castleknock	Red Mills	McDaniel Chris :	mills	-	-	-	McDaniel C - Alkin Wm :	1738	Mort. 1 May	dd/	89 357 63577
Castleknock	Red Mills	Murphy Mr.	cotton	-	-	-	-	-	-	dir1800	Dublin
Castleknock	Red Mills	Nixon Mr.	woollen	-	-	-	-	-	-	dir1800	Dublin
Castleknock	Red Mills	Nixon Mr.	woollen	-	-	-	-	-	-	dir1800	Dublin
Castleknock	Red Mills	Sherigley	mill	-	-	-	Sherigley - Malone	-	?	dd/	84 89 58307
Castleknock	Red Mills	Sherigley Abraham	mill	-	-	-	Sherigley A - Count John	1727	-	dd/	52 401 35037
Castleknock	Red Mills	Sherigley Abraham	mill	-	-	-	Sherigley A - Malone Danl	1727	-	dd/	52 401 35038
Castleknock	Red Mills	Sherigley Abraham	mills	-	-	-	Sherigley A - Read Jas	1718	Mort. 18 Sep.	dd/	22 239 11954
Castleknock	Red Mills	Slater Mr.	paper	-	-	-	-	-	-	dir1800	Dublin
Rathcoole	Redgap	-	old windmill	-	-	-	-	1899	-	1"os/	111
Donnybrook	Ringsend :	-	saw, mill race	-	-	-	-	1706	-	sv/map	jacullen
bo./ U`cross	Riversdale	Mounttemple B`ness	tuck	-	-	-	Mounttemple - Kinkaid Johr	1894	-	dd/	1894 54 291
Cruagh	Rockbrook *	Fry Mr.	paper	-	-	-	-	-	-	dir1800	Dublin
Cruagh	Rockbrook *	Manger Mr.	paper	-	-	-	-	-	-	dir1800	Dublin
Cruagh	Rockbrook *	Nun Mr.	paper	-	-	-	-	-	-	dir1800	Dublin

PARISH	TOWNLAND	MILLER	TYPE	HOUSE	Land	£Val	PROPRIETORS	Date	WHEEL etc.	Record	Ref.
Cruagh	Rockbrook *	Nun Mr.	paper	-	-	-	-	-	-	dir1800	Dublin
Cruagh	Rockbrook *	Sullivan Mr	paper	-	-	-	-	-	-	dir1800	Dublin
Cruagh	Rockbrook *	Taylor Mr	paper	-	-	-	-	-	-	dir1800	Dublin
Taney	Roebuck	- near Rawbuck	paper mill	-	-	-	-	-	-	JRoc	1760 map
Taney	Roebuck	- side R. Dodder :	iron-mills	-	6a.	-	-	-	-	gr/	-
Taney	Roebuck	Rochford John	iron-mills	-	6a.	-	-	-	-	gr/	-
Lusk	Rogerstown	-	- (old mill)	-	-	-	-	-	-	6"os/	8
Lusk	Rogerstown	-	- (old mill)	-	-	-	-	-	-	6"os/	8
Swords	Rogerstown	-	corn	-	-	-	-	-	-	dir1800	Dublin
Killossery	Rowelstown *	- at Killossery Vge.	corn	-	-	-	Mr Daly	2003	wheel removed	mmSv/	sb - B
Lusk	Rush	-	flour	-	-	-	-	1899	-	1"os/	102
Lusk	Rush	Farrel Patrick	windmill - corn	-	-	-	-	-	-	dir1800	Dublin
Saggart	Saggart	-	paper	-	-	-	-	1899	-	1"os/	111
Saggart	Saggart	-	paper	-	-	-	-	1899	-	1"os/	111
Saggart	Saggart	- (Swiftbrook)	paper & pond	-	-	-	-	-	-	6"os/	21
Saggart	Saggart	- at Swiftbrook	mill cottages	- very dilapidated	-	-	-	2002	-	mmSv/	wh - D
Saggart	Saggart	- Swiftbrook Mills	paper	recent period fcty :	-	-	-	2002	-	mmSv/	wh - D
Saggart	Saggart	- in Town nr Castle Mills		-	-	-	-	-	-	JRoc	1760 map
Saggart	Saggart	Herron Connolly &Cc	corn	-	-	-	Herron Connolly - Ire Bank	1891	-	dd/	1891 51 206
Saggart	Saggart	Herron Robert Sir	corn	-	-	-	Herron Robt - Connolly	1891	-	dd/	1891 21 28
Saggart	Saggart	M`Donnell John	paper	-	0.1.3	-	-	-	-	gr/	-
Saggart	Saggart	St Patricks Hospital	corn	-	-	-	St Pats Hos - McDonnell Jn	1891	-	dd/	1891 18 12
Palmerstown	Saintlaurence	-	flour	-	-	-	-	-	-	6"os/	18
Palmerstown	Saintlaurence	Macken James	mill	-	4a.	-	-	-	-	gr/	-
Santry	Santry	-	corn	-	-	-	-	-	-	dir1800	Dublin
Dublin	Shallows Mill	McDonnell Silvester	mill	-	-	-	McDonnell - Foster Sir Wm	1864	-	dd/	1864 22 13
Rathmichael	Shanganagh	-	corn	-	-	-	-	-	-	6"os/	26
Rathmichael	Shanganagh	- Mill Lane, Shankil	mill	v. derelict, walls :	-	-	-	2001	-	phoWEH	R
Rathmichael	Shanganagh	Carter Fras B	-	-	land	-	Carter F B - Larney Bern	1860	-	dd/	1860 12 24
Rathmichael	Shanganagh	Carter Mary	-	-	land	-	Carter M - Maddock Robt	1860	-	dd/	1860 12 281
Rathmichael	Shanganagh	Cullen Patrick	mill	-	-	-	-	-	-	gr/	-
Rathmichael	Shanganagh	Cullen Patrick	mills	11.6x19.6x8 :	-	-	-	-	-	hob/	5.0924
Rathmichael	Shanganagh	Murphy Jeremiah	-	-	land	-	Murphy Jer - Reeves Thos	1860	-	dd/	1860 16 210
Rathmichael	Shanganagh	Plunkett Thomas	-	-	land	-	Plunkett T - Hargrave Thos	1860	-	dd/	1860 22 109
Rathmichael	Shanganagh	Quin William	-	-	land	-	Quin Wm - Middleton Alf	1861	-	dd/	1861 19 174
Rathmichael	Shanganagh	Reeves Thomas	-	-	land	-	Reeves Thos - Gray Robt	1861	-	dd/	1861 37 263
Rathmichael	Shanganagh	Rial Pineas	-	-	land	-	Rial Pineas - Wyer James	1861	-	dd/	1861 31 41
Rathmichael	Shanganagh	Tilly Benjamin	-	-	land	-	Tilly Benj - Db. & Wk R.Co	1860	-	dd/	1860 12 39
St Kevin`s	Shipping`s Mill	Exham Richard :	mill	-	-	-	Exham R - Taylor John :	1728	-	dd/	56 344 38244
St Kevin`s	Shipping`s Mill	Smith William :	mill	-	-	-	Smith W - Wills Anthony :	1728	-	dd/	53 349 35801
St Kevin`s	Shipping`s Mill	Taylor Jno :	mill	-	-	-	Taylor Jno & his Will	1732	-	dd/	69 403 48932
St Kevin`s	Shipping`s Mill	Taylor Martha	mill	-	-	-	Taylor M - Falkiner Danl	1732	-	dd/	72 143 50131
St Kevin`s	Shipping`s Mill	Weld Edmond :	mill	-	-	-	Weld E - Delaney Corns :	1731	-	dd/	66 274 46235
Dub (? par.)	Siddolp *	Walsh Mr	flour	-	-	-	-	-	-	dir1800	Dublin
Holmpatrick	Skerries	-	mill	-	-	-	-	1899	-	1"os/	102
Holmpatrick	Skerries	-	windmill	-	-	-	-	1899	-	1"os/	102
Holmpatrick	Skerries	-	Windmill	-	-	-	-	-	-	JRoc	1760 map
Holmpatrick	Skerries	Duff Luke	windmill - corn	-	-	-	-	-	-	dir1800	Dublin
Holmpatrick	Skerries	Flinn Catherine	-	-	land	-	Flinn Cath - Agreement	1860	-	dd/	1860 5 164
Holmpatrick	Skerries	Skerries Mills	corn	perfectly restored	-	-	Fingal C. C.	1999	exhibition, cafe	phoWEH	C
Holmpatrick	Skerries	Skerries Mills	windmill	perfectly restored	-	-	Fingal C. C.	1999	grinding (demo.)	phoWEH	C
Holmpatrick	Skerries :	Ennis William	wheatmeal :	-	-	-	-	1963	-	lic/8	wheat

PARISH	TOWNLAND	MILLER	TYPE	HOUSE	Land	£Val	PROPRIETORS	Date	WHEEL etc.	Record	Ref.
Holmpatrick	Skerries T`pks	-	corn & dam	-	-	-	-	-	-	6"os/	5
Holmpatrick	Skerries T`pks	-	windmill	-	-	-	-	-	-	6"os/	5
Holmpatrick	Skerries T`pks	Flynn Bridget	flour, corn	-	2.0.37	-	-	-	-	gr/	-
Holmpatrick	Skerries T`pks	Flynn Bridget	mill-pond	-	3.2.0	-	-	-	-	gr/	-
Holmpatrick	Skerries T`pks	Flynn Bridget	windmill	-	-	-	-	-	-	gr/	-
Holmpatrick	Skerries Town	Kieran Joseph	brewery	(1A) 58.6x19x13.3	-	-	-	-	-	hob/	5.0855
Swords	Skidoo	-	thrashing	-	-	-	-	-	-	6"os/	7
Glasnevin	Slutsend	-	logwood, wire	-	-	-	-	-	-	6"os/	18
Leixlip	St Cath`s Park	Ryder Thomas	corn	-	127a.	-	-	-	-	gr/	-
Leixlip	St Catherine`s	- nr Leixlip	corn	-	-	-	-	1899	-	1"os/	111
Coolock	St Margarets	Bolton Thomas	Plunkett`s Mills	-	-	-	Bolton T - Flower William	1726	-	dd/	51 105 32953
Coolock	St Margarets	Bolton Thomas :	Plunkett`s Mills	-	-	-	Bolton T - Fowler James :	1727	-	dd/	54 457 36403
Coolock	St Margarets	Fowler James :	Plunkett`s Mills	-	-	-	Fowler J - Fowler William	1727	-	dd/	78 280 55510
St Margarets	St Margarets	Plunkett Olivia	mill	Plunkett`s Mill	-	-	Plunkett O - Semple Mary	1860	-	dd/	1860 16 27
St Margarets	St Margarets	Plunkett Olivia	mill	Plunkett`s Mill	-	-	Plunket O - McKenna Jno	1860	-	dd/	1860 27 215
Dunshaughlin	St Margrets	- at Carrigeen	Wind Mill	-	-	-	-	-	-	JRoc	1760 map
Dub (? par.)	St Sepulchre b.	Davis Samuel	mills	The Hibernian Mills	-	-	Davis S - Chambers Geo	1860	-	dd/	1860 10 97
Dub (? par.)	St Sepulchre b.	Davis Samuel	mills	The Hibernian Mills	-	-	Davis S - Cronheim Theo	1860	-	dd/	1860 21 7
Dub (? par.)	St Sepulchre b.	Harte Jno F	mill	Mabbot`s Mills	-	-	Harte J F - Archer Richd	1860	-	dd/	1860 29 111
Dub (? par.)	St Sepulchre b.	Ld. Estate Court	mill	Mallett`s Mill	-	-	Ld. Est. Ct. - Murtagh Jno	1861	-	dd/	1861 20 265
Dub (? par.)	St Sepulchre b.	McCullock William R	mill	Water Mill	-	-	McCullock - Henshaw Th	1860	-	dd/	1860 24 88
Dub (? par.)	St Sepulchre b.	Regan Patrick	mill	Stubbin`s Mill	-	-	Regan - McCarthy Helena	1861	-	dd/	1861 5 209
Balrothery	Stephenstown	- near Balbriggan	corn			-	-	1899	-	1"os/	92
Balrothery	Stephenstown	- S/ Balbriggan	corn	-	-	-	-	-	-	6"os/	5
Balrothery	Stephenstown	M`Cabe Patrick	corn & kiln	-	0.2.0	-	-	-	-	gr/	-
Balrothery	Stephenstown	Magee Mary	corn	41.0x23x15 & kiln :	-	-	-	-	17x5.4x16 40 bkts.	hob/	5.0844
Balrothery	Stephenstown	Magee Mary Widow	corn	41x23x15 21x20x12	-	-	-	-	17x5x16 40 bkts.	hob/	5.0843
Balrorhery E.	Stephenstown	McCabe Patrick	corn & kiln	(2/3B) 41X23X15.6 :	-	5.7	-	1845	17x5.4x16 drives :	hob/	5.2673
Balrothery	Stephenstown	Walsh James	mill-pond	-	6a.	-	-	-	-	gr/	-
St Kevin`s	Stopping`s Mill	Delaney Cornelius :	mill & land	-	-	-	Delaney C - Taylor John :	1728	-	dd/	56 428 38576
St Kevin`s	Stopping`s Mill	Dollany	mill & land	-	-	-	Dollany - Kane	-	?	dd/	11 328 4636
St Kevin`s	Stopping`s Mill	Exham Richard	mill & land	-	-	-	Exham R - Weld Nath	1709	-	dd/	4 205 874
St Kevin`s	Stopping`s Mill	Exham Richard	mill & land	-	-	-	Exham R - Dellany Corn	1711	-	dd/	7 323 2568
St Kevin`s	Stopping`s Mill	Smith William	mill & land	-	-	-	Smith Wm - Wills Anthony	1711	-	dd/	6 243 2061
St Kevin`s	Stopping`s Mill	Smith William :	mill & land	-	-	-	Smith Wm - Wills Anthony	1718	Mort. 18 Sep.	dd/	22 239 11907?
Newcastle b.	Stubbins Mill	Ireland Bank Govs.	mill	-	-	-	Ire. Bank - Herron Robt Sir	1891	-	dd/	1891 11 71
Newcastle b.	Stubbins Mill	Ld. Estate Court	mill	-	-	-	Ld. Est. Court - Regan Patk	1861	-	dd/	1861 21 16
Newcastle b.	Stubbins Mill	Regan Patrick	mill	-	-	-	Regan P - Hylands Mary	1864	-	dd/	1864 25 127
Newcastle b.	Stubbins Mill	Regan Patrick	mill	-	-	-	Regan Patk - Adams Thos	1860	-	dd/	1860 27 276
Newcastle b.	Stubbins Mill	Shaw Robert Sir	mill	-	-	-	Shaw Robt - Regan Patk	1861	-	dd/	1861 16 267
Swords	Swords	-	mill	-	-	-	-	1899	-	1"os/	102
Swords	Swords	- W. of Town	Windmill	-	-	-	-	-	-	JRoc	1760 map
Swords	Swords	Meras Mr	corn	-	-	-	-	-	-	dir1800	Dublin
Swords	Swords	Meras Mr	windmill	-	-	-	-	-	-	dir1800	Dublin
Swords	Swords	Molesworth Lord	windmill farm :	-	-	-	Molesworth Ld - Swift	-	?	dd/	87 107 60799
Swords	Swords	Staples Thomas	windmill farm	-	-	-	Staples Thos - Greene Wm		-	dd/	1860 2 208
Swords	Swords	Wade Mr	mill	-	-	-	-	-	-	dir1800	Dublin
Swords	Swords T`parks	-	corn	-	-	-	-	-	-	6"os/	11
Swords	Swords T`parks	Branagan James	flour	-	-	-	-	-	-	gr/	-
Swords	Swords T`parks	O`Neill Terence	corn, flour	-	-	-	-	-	-	gr/	-
Swords	Swords Town	-	Mill	-	-	-	-	-	-	JRoc	1760 map
Swords	Swords Town	Green Catherine	troll mill :	-	-	-	Green C - Sharp Edward :	1753	-	dd/	161 159 10799

PARISH	TOWNLAND	MILLER	TYPE	HOUSE	Land	£Val	PROPRIETORS	Date	WHEEL etc.	Record	Ref.
Swords	Swords Town	Green Catherine	troll mill :	-	-	-	Green C - McCausland W	1755	-	dd/	174 447 117126
Swords	Swords Town	Green John	troll mill :	-	-	-	Green John - Harvey Jn	1749	-	dd/	142 333 95729
Swords	Swords Town	McCausland William	troll mill :	-	-	-	McCausland - Phillips Jn	1756	-	dd/	181 210 120454
Swords	Swords Town	Molesworth Coote :	troll mill :	-	-	-	Molesworth Coote - Edw :	1748	-	dd/	130 307 89185
Swords	Swords Town	Molesworth Ed Hon	troll mill :	-	-	-	Molesworth E - Green Jn	1749	-	dd/	141 341 95727
Swords	Swords Town	Molesworth Hon :	troll mill :	-	-	-	Molesworth Coote - Richd	1743	-	dd/	108 511 77182
Swords	Swords Town	Molesworth Richard	troll mill :	-	-	-	Molesworth Ld - M`worth :	1742	-	dd/	109 213 75620
Swords	Swords Town	O`Neill Terence :	brewery	-	-	-	O'Neill T & Connor John :	1805	-	dd/	572 82 386651
Swords	Swords Town	Phillips Christopher	Bridge Mill	-	-	-	Phillips Chris - John	1741	-	dd/	107 340 74402
Swords	Swords Town	Phillips John	Bridge Mill	-	-	-	Phillips Jn - Kelly Brian	1751	-	dd/	168 162 111949
Swords	Swords Town	Phillips Molesworth	Bridge Mill	-	-	-	Phillips M - Talbot Richard	1786	-	dd/	373 562 249491
Swords	Swords Town	Talbot Rev Nolan :	Bridge Mill	-	-	-	Talbot N - Brangan Chros :	1793	-	dd/	467 578 302357
Swords	Swords Town :	O`Neil Laurence	corn & wheat	-	-	-	-	-	-	hob/	5.2724
Tallaght	Tallaght	-	corn	-	-	-	-	-	-	6"os/	22
Tallaght	Tallaght	- Bolbrook Paper	paper	-	-	-	-	-	-	6"os/	22
Tallaght	Tallaght	- nr R. Dodder	paper	Bollbrook Mill (nil)	-	-	-	2002	-	mmSv/	wh - Z
Tallaght	Tallaght	Butler Edmond	mill	-	-	-	Butler E - Power Geo	1862	-	dd/	1862 30 120
Tallaght	Tallaght	Mahon Michael	corn	(2B) 32x18.6x10.6 :	-	1.10	-	1845	12x2.8x - 3 pr. st.	hob/	5.0950
Tallaght	Tallaght	Mahony Michael	corn	32.6x19x9 & barn	-	-	-	1845	11x2.6x11 32 bkts.	hob/	5.0900
Tallaght	Tallaght	Newman Mr	corn	-	-	-	-	-	-	dir1800	Dublin
Tallaght	Tallaght	Old Bawn Mill	corn	and Restaurant :	-	-	Louis Fitzpatrick	2002		phoWEH	Cc
Tallaght	Tallaght	Palmer Sir Wiliam	mill	-	-	-	Palmer Wm - Deed	1863	-	dd/	1863 14 106
Tallaght	Tallaght	Palmer William	mill	-	-	-	Palmer W - Gresson Geo	1863	-	dd/	1863 36 270
Tallaght	Tallaght	Williamson James	mill	(1C) 32.6x17x17 :	-	-	-	1845	12x2 -	hob/	5.0950
Tallaght	Tallaght	Williamson James	mill	-	7a.	63 :	-	1832	-	VOf/	OL.X078
Tallaght	Tallaght	Williamson James	paper	-	7a.	-	-	-	-	gr/	-
Tallaght	Tallaght Town	Mahon Michael	corn	(2C)32.6x19x9 :	-	-	-	1854	-	hob/	5.2726
Tallaght	Templeogue	-	paper	restored as res.	-	-	Marie Therese Tobin	2002	-	phoWEH	Cr
Tallaght	Templeogue	- near T`ogue Br.	flour	-	-	-	-	-	-	6"os/	22
Tallaght	Templeogue	- near T'ogue Ho.	flour	nil remains	-	-	-	2002	-	mmSv/	wh - Z
Tallaght	Templeogue	- on R. Dodder	paper	-	-	-	-	-	-	6"os/	22
Tallaght	Templeogue	- on R. Dodder :	Paper mills	-	-	-	-	-	-	JRoc	1760 map
Tallaght	Templeogue	- on R. Poddle	flour	-	-	-	-	-	-	6"os/	22
Tallaght	Templeogue	- stream to Dodder:	Paper mills	-	-	-	-	-	-	JRoc	1760 map
Tallaght	Templeogue	Archibald Widow	paper	-	-	-	-	-	-	dir1800	Dublin
Tallaght	Templeogue	Burke Francis	mill	-	2.0.0	-	-	-	-	gr/	-
Tallaght	Templeogue	Burrowes Mr	paper	-	-	-	-	-	-	dir1800	Dublin
Tallaght	Templeogue	Domville Charles Sir	mill	-	-	-	Domvile CCW - Toole Chas	1864	-	dd/	1864 9 157
Tallaght	Templeogue	Domville Compton	mill	-	-	-	Domville C - Burke Wm J	1860	-	dd/	1860 21 98
Tallaght	Templeogue	M`Donnell Joseph	paper	-	17a.	-	-	-	-	gr/	-
Tallaght	Templeogue	M`Donnell Mr	paper	-	-	-	-	-	-	dir1800	Dublin
Tallaght	Templeogue	MacDonnel Joseph	paper	(1A) 38x14x10.6 :	-	69.5	-	1845	14x13x- drives :	hob/	5.0950
Tallaght	Templeogue	MacDonnel Joseph	paper (part)	(1A) 60x223.6x15 :	-	-	-	1845	-	hob/	5.0950
Tallaght	Templeogue	Maconchy Charles	Templ`gue Mills	-	-	-	-	1898	-	dir/	Thoms
Tallaght	Templeogue	Murphy Jeremiah	mill	-	-	-	Murphy J - Colvill James	1863	-	dd/	1863 39 152
Tallaght	Templeogue	Murphy Jeremiah J	mill	-	-	-	Murphy J J - Sharpe James	1861	-	dd/	1861 26 116
Tallaght	Templeogue	Newman Mr	flour	-	-	-	-	-	-	dir1800	Dublin
Tallaght	Templeogue	Sharp James	flour	-	39a.	-	-	-	-	gr/	-
Tallaght	Templeogue	Sharp James	mill	-	39a.	140	-	1832	-	VOf/	OL.X078
Tallaght	Templeogue	Sharpe James	flour	(1B) 35x44.6x20 :	-	12.15	-	1845	11.6x7x- 2 pr. st. :	hob/	5.0950
Tallaght	Templeogue	Sharpe James	mill	-	-	-	Sharpe Jas - Colvill James	1860	-	dd/	1860 30 27
Tallaght	Templogue	Domville Compton	tuck	-	-	-	Domvil C - Madden James	1722	-	dd/	37 450 23438

PARISH	TOWNLAND	MILLER	TYPE	HOUSE	Land	£Val	PROPRIETORS	Date	WHEEL etc.	Record	Ref.
Tallaght	Templogue	Leeson Elizabeth :	mill & land	-	-	-	Leeson E - Antrobus John :	1728	-	dd/	65 78 44462
Tallaght	Templogue	Madden James	tuck	-	-	-	Madden J - Mills Bridgett	1723	Mort. 29 Jne	dd/	38 166 23807
Tallaght	Templogue	Madden James :	tuck	-	-	-	Madden J - Phipps John :	1738	Mort. 14 Jul.	dd/	92 136 64160
Tallaght	Templogue	Madden Jas & Juno	tuck	-	-	-	Madden - Knatchbull	1723	-	dd/	86 359 60759
Cruagh	Tibradden	- at residence of :	silk factory	-	-	-	-	2002	-	mmSv/	wh - B
Tully	Ticknick	-	old corn mill	-	-	-	-	-	-	6"os/	25
Newcastle bo.	Tinkers Mill	Pim James	mill	-	-	-	Pim Jas - Regan Patk	1862	-	dd/	1862 19 278
Glasnevin	Tolka	-	paper	-	-	-	-	-	-	6"os/	18
Tallaght	Townland (?) :	O'Neill Thomas	cloth	(1B) 38.6x39.6x15.6	-	-	-	1845	-	hob/	5.0950
Tallaght	Townland (?) :	O'Neill Thomas	cloth (part)	(1C) 35x21x6 & :	-	24.12	-	1845	20x4.6x- drives :	hob/	5.0950
Dub (? par.)	Townland ?	-	mill	-	-	-	-	1832	-	VOf/	OL.X078
bo./ N`castle	Townland ?	Clancy James	bleach yard	-	-	-	-	1893	-	dd/	1893 15 50
bo./ U`cross	Townland ?	Dub Port & Cem. Co	old mill pond	-	-	-	Dub P&C Co - Irish Port Ce	1891	-	dd/	1891 53 36
Uppercross b.	Tubber	Elsington Richard	mill	-	-	-	Essington R - Ward John	1720	-	dd/	29 514 18525
Uppercross b.	Tubber	Percy	mill	-	-	-	Percy - Elsington	-	?	dd/	24 490 18439
Uppercross b.	Tubber	Percy Henry :	mill	-	-	-	Percy H - Powell Charles :	1772	-	dd/	37 287 22745
Dub (? par.)	Tuckmillown	Long William	tuck mill	-	-	-	Long Wm - Vivian Samuel	1861	-	dd/	1861 1 287
Uppercross b.	Turvey	Kingsland Henry Ld.	mill & land	-	-	-	Kingsland - Kerby Thos	1737	-	dd/	94 35 65315
Dub (? par.)	Turvey (2)	-	corn	-	-	-	-	-	-	dir1800	Dublin
Lusk	Walshestown	-	corn	-	-	-	-	-	-	6"os/	3
Lusk	Walshestown	-	corn	-	-	-	-	-	-	dir1800	Dublin
Lusk	Walshestown	-	corn	-	-	-	-	-	-	mmSv/	sb - Z
Lusk	Walshestown	Knox Thomas	corn & kiln	-	-	-	-	-	-	gr/	-
Lusk	Walshestown	Wogan William	corn	39x16.6x9.6 dw ho :	-	3.9.0	-	-	14x1.9x14 32 bkts.	hob/	5.0849
Lusk	Walshestown	Wogan William	windmill	circum. 59ft ht. 23.3	-	-	-	-	14.6x1.9x13.9 :	hob/	5.0851
Lusk	Walshestown	Wogan William	wind-mill	circum 59x23	-	11/3	-	-	supports corn mill	hob/	5.0849
Stillorgan	Walterstown :	- Stillorgan	Brewery	--	-	-	-	1843	-	6"os/	23
Rathdown	Walterstown :	-	brewery	-	-	-	-	-	-	6"os/	23
Rathdown	Walterstown :	Darley Henry	brewery	55x20x19 ho unoc.:	-	-	-	-	-	hob/	5.0925
St Peter`s	Way Mills	Murphy Jeremiah J	mills	(par. St Sepulchre)	-	-	Murphy J J - Jellicoe Jas	1860	-	dd/	1860 18 27
St Peter`s	Way Mills	Thresher Daniel	mills	-	-	-	Thresher D - Madden Jn	1730	-	dd/	64 255 43716
St Peter`s	Way Mills	Vicars Coral :	mills	-	-	-	Vicars Ch - Caldwell Geo :	1814	Lse. 30 Apl.	dd/	679 313 467663
Newcastle bo.	Weldon`s Mill	Wilcocks	mill	-	-	-	Wilcocks - H- Hutchinson	-	?	dd/	271 354 180448
Rathdown	Welshestown	Blessington Chas Ld	windmill farm	-	-	-	Blessington - Malone Richd	1727	-	dd/	52 390 34997
Rathdown	Welshestown	Blessington Lord :	windmill farm	-	-	-	Blessington - Curtis Geo :	1727	-	dd/	53 325 35706
Rathdown	Welshestown	Mountjoy Lord	windmill farm	-	-	-	Mountjoy Ld - Ribton	-	?	dd/	74 187 50663
Naul	Westown	-	flour	-	-	-	-	-	-	6"os/	3
Naul	Westown	Beaulieu Edward :	mill	-	-	-	Beaulieu E - Walsh Cath :	1793	-	dd/	470 310 302 982
Naul	Westown	Ennis James	corn	29x22x29 34x20x29	-	22.1.[illegible]	-	-	17x6.4	hob/	5.0860
Naul	Westown	Ennis James	corn	29.0x22.0x29.6 & :	-	-	-	-	17.6x6.4 overshot :	hob/	5.0861
Palmerstown	Westpalstown	-	corn	-	-	-	-	2003	- millpond gone	mmSv/	sb - Z
Palmerstown	Westpalstown	-	corn & pond	-	-	-	-	-	-	6"os/	7
Palmerstown	Westpalstown	Coroway Thomas	corn	-	36a.	-	-	-	-	gr/	-
St Peter`s	Wey Mills	Cooper John	Wey Mills :	-	-	-	Cooper J - Gwin	1739	-	dd/	93 498 66543
St Peter`s	Wey Mills	Heron Rev Robert :	Wey Mills :	-	-	-	Heron R - Caldwell Chas :	1767	-	dd/	262 52 136451?
St Peter`s	Wey Mills	Mercer William :	Wey Mills :	-	-	-	Mercer W - Wetherall Thos	1750	-	dd/	139 454 94991
St Peter`s	Wey Mills	Phillips John	Wey Mills :	-	-	-	Phillips Jn - Mercer Wm	1744	-	dd/	116 282 80376
St Peter`s	Wey Mills	Piersey James	Wey Mills :	-	-	-	Piersey J - Gwyn Lewis :	1739	-	dd/	96 89 66526
St Peter`s	Wey Mills	Vicar & Ch St Pats.	Wey Mills :	-	-	-	Vicar & ors - Caldwell	-	?	dd/	293 84 194131
St Peter`s	Wey Mills	Vicar & Ch. St Pats.	Way Mills	-	-	-	Vicar & ors - Caldwell	-	-	dd/	679 313 467663
St Peter`s	Wey Mills	Vicar & Ch. St Pats.	Wey Mills :	-	-	-	Vicar & ors - Given Lewis	1750	-	dd/	144 213 97146?
Whitechurch	Whitechurch	-	laundry mill	-	-	-	-	-	-	6"os/	22

PARISH	TOWNLAND	MILLER	TYPE	HOUSE	Land	£Val	PROPRIETORS	Date	WHEEL etc.	Record	Ref.
Whitechurch	Whitechurch	-	silk	-	-	-	-	-	-	6"os/	22
Whitechurch	Whitechurch	-	silk	-	-	-	-	2002	-	phoWEH	Z
Whitechurch	Whitechurch	-	woollen	-	-	-	-	-	-	6"os/	22
Whitechurch	Whitechurch	- Willbrook	Millhouse	old & well preserved,	-	-	Maura Mullarney	2002	-	phoWEH	-
Whitechurch	Whitechurch	- beside Millhouse	old mill	walls only + extn.	-	-	Jas Featherstone	2002	-	phoWEH	D
Whitechurch	Whitechurch	- near COI Church	laundry	-	-	-	-	2002	-	phoWEH	Z
Whitechurch	Whitechurch	- on Golf Course	mill	small remains only	-	-	-	2002	-	phoWEH	R
Whitechurch	Whitechurch	- Rockbrook 1/2ml	cloth	large solid ruin	-	-	Frank Walsh & Son	2002	-	phoWEH	R
Whitechurch	Whitechurch	Bewley Thomas	wash	45.6x26x16 addition	-	-	-	1845	8x3x8 & 10x3x9	hob/	5.0930
Lusk	Whitestown	-	corn	-	-	-	-	-	-	6"os/	8
Lusk	Whitestown	-	mill	-	-	-	-	1899	-	1"os/	102
Lush	Whitestown	- S. / the Common	Windmill	-	-	-	-	-	-	JRoc	1760 map
Lusk	Whitestown	Rickard Walter	corn	-	-	-	-	-	-	gr/	-
Lusk	Whitestown	Rickards Mr	corn	-	-	-	-	-	-	dir1800	Dublin
Lusk	Whitestown	Rickards Walter	corn	16x18x13 15x19x13	-	-	-	-	14x4x13.6 36 bkt :	hob/	5.0849
Lusk	Whitestown :	-	corn	- recently re-roofed	-	-	Frank Flanagan	2003	-	mmSv/	sb - B
Rathfarnham	Whitetown	Andoe William :	mill	-	-	-	Andoe W - Rickard Walt :	1791	-	dd/	449 510 288907
Rathfarnham	Whitetown	Ledgwidge Thomas :	mill	-	-	-	Ledwidge Thos - Wm :	1800	-	dd/	531 210 349094
Rathfarnham	Whitetown	Rickard Walter :	mill	-	-	-	Rickard W - Walsh Cath :	1797	Mort. 1 Mar.	dd/	513 310 332697
Rathfarnham	Whitetown	Sedwidge	mill	-	-	-	Sedwidge - Coogan	-	- (error)	dd/	547 48 360317
Dublin	Wildings Mill	Wilding	mill :	-	-	-	Wilding - Kean	-	?	dd/	10 95 70041
Rathfarnham	Willbrook	- Whitechurch Rd	flour	-	-	-	-	-	-	6"os/	22
Rathfarnham	Willbrook	- Whitechurch Rd	flour	- demolished 1900s	-	-	Maura Mallarney (House)	2002	-	phoWEH	Z
Rathfarnham	Willbrook	- Whitechurch Rd	pin factory	-	-	-	-	-	-	6"os/	22
Rathfarnham	Willbrook	Batley Thomas :	mill	-	-	-	Battley T - Hawkins John :	1807	-	dd/	588 429 400541
Rathfarnham	Willbrook	Battley John :	mill	-	-	-	Battley J - Freeman Richd :	1796	-	dd/	494 268 323579
Rathfarnham	Willbrook	Batttley Thomas C :	paper	-	-	-	Battley T - Shaw Robert :	1804	Mort. 17 Jan.	dd/	559 122 372884
Rathfarnham	Willbrook	Beauchamp Jno :	mill & kiln	-	-	-	Beauchamp - Murphy Jane	1791	Mort. 13 Jne.	dd/	438 462 283240
Rathfarnham	Willbrook	Bertrand Thomas :	paper	-	-	-	Bertrand T - Keeling Robt :	1781	-	dd/	401 37 267412
Rathfarnham	Willbrook	Choppin Richard	mill	-	-	-	Choppin R - Curtis Thos	1723	-	dd/	38 107 23491
Rathfarnham	Willbrook	Cope William :	mill	-	-	-	Cope W - Wilkinson Ab'am	1793	Mort. 1 May	dd/	463 372 289020
Rathfarnham	Willbrook	Evans William	flour	-	3.0.1:	-	-	-	-	gr/	-
Rathfarnham	Willbrook	Farrell	mill & kiln	-	-	-	Farrell - Beecham	-	(error)	dd/	380 11 257067
Rathfarnham	Willbrook	Gibney Robert	flour	-	-	-	-	-	-	gr/	-
Rathfarnham	Willbrook	Hawkins Jno :	mill	& dw. ho., offs. & ld	60a.	-	Hawkins J - Murphy Thos :	1810	-	dd/	620 386 425711
Rathfarnham	Willbrook	Hawkins John :	mill	-	-	-	Hawkins J - Walker Robt :	1807	-	dd/	588 463 400591
Rathfarnham	Willbrook	Hutchinson William	mill & land	-	-	-	Hutchinson W - Smalley C	1722	-	dd/	37 275 22702
Rathfarnham	Willbrook	Jaffray Alex :	paper	-	-	-	Jaffray S - Keeling Robert :	1792	-	dd/	453 13 288702?
Rathfarnham	Willbrook	Keeling Robert :	paper :	-	-	-	Keeling R - McDonnell Matt	1791	-	dd/	501 446 325758
Rathfarnham	Willbrook	Keeling Robert Esq.	paper	-	-	-	Keeling R - Gore Robert :	1791	-	dd/	446 280 289409
Rathfarnham	Willbrook	Kell	mill	-	-	-	Kell - Cunningham	-	-	dd/	74 244 50960
Rathfarnham	Willbrook	Kell Henry :	mill	-	-	-	Kell H - Cunningham Dan :	1733	Mort. 4 Jne.	dd/	74 244 50962
Rathfarnham	Willbrook	Kell Michael	paper	-	-	-	Kell Mcl - Perry Fras :	1792	-	dd/	453 196 289669
Rathfarnham	Willbrook	Kelly Richard :	mill	-	-	-	Kelly Richd - Battley Thos :	1800	-	dd/	532 96 348239
Rathfarnham	Willbrook	McDonnell Matthew	paper	-	-	-	McDonnell M - McD' Thos :	1796	Mort. 4 oct.	dd/	510 93 329128
Rathfarnham	Willbrook	Moore	mill	-	-	-	Moore - Evans	-	?	dd/	(?) (?) 438933
Rathfarnham	Willbrook	Murphy Thomas :	mill	ground adj & pond	-	-	Murphy T - Murphy T	1811	-	dd/	640 50 441203
Rathfarnham	Willbrook	Smalley Caleb	mill	-	-	-	Smalley C - Callaghan Pat	1723	-	dd/	39 137 24611
Rathfarnham	Willbrook	Smalley Caleb :	mill	-	-	-	Smalley C - Delaney Corn :	1725	Mort. 16 Oct.	dd/	47 157 29957/75
Rathfarnham	Willbrook	Smalley Caleb :	mill	-	-	-	Smalley C - Kellett Henry :	1728	Asgt. 15 Aug.	dd/	57 288 38503
Rathfarnham	Willbrook	Smalley Kaleb	mill	-	-	-	Smalley K - Delaney Corn	1723	-	dd/	39 121 24493
Rathfarnham	Willbrook Lr	Gogarty	mill	-	-	-	Gogarty - Colvill	-	?	dd/	775 17 494952

PARISH	TOWNLAND	MILLER	TYPE	HOUSE	Land	£Val	PROPRIETORS	Date	WHEEL etc.	Record	Ref.
Rathfarnham	Willbrook Lr	Walker Robert :	mill	-	-	-	Walker R - Colvill William C	1819	?	dd/	737 521 562657
Newcastle bo.	Windmill Hill	Skerrett John J.L.	land	-	-	-	Skerrett J - Malliard Parn	1863	-	dd/	1863 34 6
bo./ N`cross	Windmill Hill	* Lewis Henry	land	-	-	-	Lewis H - Walsh Alice	1892	-	dd/	1892 41 168
Kinsaley	Windmill House	Sherigley Abraham :	windmill house :	-	-	-	Sheigley A - Jackson John :	1728	-	dd/	116 505 81799
Swords	Windmill Land	-	windmill stump	-	-	-	-	-	-	6"os/	11
Swords	Windmill Land	Molesworth Richard	land	-	-	-	Molesworth Richd - Coote	1743	-	dd/	110 285 7728
Swords	Windmill Land	Molesworth Richd :	land	-	-	-	Molesworth - Leslie Ghas :	1754	-	dd/	174 123 115437
Newcastle	Windmillhill	Foster James F	lands	-	-	-	Foster J - Ford Jmaes	1901	-	dd/	1901 82 178
Raheny	Windmillhill	Grace	land	-	-	-	Grace - Frayne	-	?	dd/	57 102 22941
Newcastle	Windmillhill	Maxwell Richard A	lands	-	-	-	Maxwell R - Ford James	1901	-	dd/	1901 53 35
Newcastle	Windmillhill	Rathpunnell Baron	lands	-	-	-	Rathpunnell Bn - Refues :	1902	-	dd/	1902 19 223
Newcastle	Windmillhill	Rathpunnell Baron	lands	-	-	-	Rathpunnell Bn - Nugent :	1902	-	dd/	1902 23 118
Newcastle	Windmillhill	Rooke John	lands	-	-	-	Rooke J - Doran Carlton	1904	-	dd/	1904 59 5
Newcastle	Windmillhill	Skerrett Jno	-	-	-	-	Skerrett J - Mallard Parnell	1861	-	dd/	1861 28 174
Newcastle	Windmillhill	Staples Sir John M	lands	-	-	-	Staples J - Dunn James	1903	-	dd/	1903 48 107
Taney	Windy Arbour	- at Millmount Tce.	starch	- nil remains	-	-	-	2002	-	mmSv/	wh - Z
Dublin	Wood Mills	Falkiner Frederick :	mill	-	-	-	Falkiner - Holroyd Isaac :	1761	-	dd/	214 44 139845
Dublin	Wood Mills	Fayle Elizabeth	mill	(bo: St Sepulchre)	-	-	Fayle Eliz - Pim Jonathan	1861	-	dd/	1861 27 240
Dublin	Wood Mills	Moody Jno	mill	-	-	-	Moody J - Latouche Wm D	1782	-	dd/	450 477 292017
Clonsilla	Woodlands	-	flour	-	-	-	-	-	-	6"os/	17
Clonsilla	Woodlands	Barrett Robert	New Holland	-	-	-	Barrett R - McDonnell Jas	1890	-	dd/	1890 47 47
Clonsilla	Woodlands	Brown Lorenzo	New Holland	-	-	-	Brown L- Goggins James	1890	-	dd/	1890 55 266
Clonsilla	Woodlands	Gee Thomas	New Holland	-	-	-	GeeThos - Ire. CS Bd Soc.	1892	-	dd/	1892 7 232
Clonsilla	Woodlands	Rainsford Richard	flour, kilns	-	-	-	-	-	-	gr/	
Clonsilla	Woodlands	Ryder Henry D Hon	land	-	-	-	Ryder H - Annaly Baron	1900	-	dd/	1900 16 296
Clonsilla	Woodlands	Shute Edith E	land	-	-	-	Shute E - Martyn Mary	1900	-	dd/	1900 33 171
Clonsilla	Woodlands	White Francis	smoothing iron :	-	-	-	-	1894	-	dd/	1894 58 52
Clonsilla	Woodlands :	Shackleton Abraham	mills & prems.	Annaliffey Mills	-	-	Shackleton Ab. - George :	1904	-	dd/	1904 20 1
Clonsilla	Woodlands :	Brown Elizabeth	land	-	-	-	Brown Eliz - Byrne John	1891	-	dd/	1891 27 167
Clonsilla	Woodlands :	Delaney William	flour	77x28.6x60 & ret. :	-	47	-	1845	16x9x9 breastshot :	hob/	5.0862
Dub (? par.)	Woodlock`s Gr	Eustace Martha	mill	-	-	-	Eustace M - White Mark	1748	-	dd/	132 492 90118
Dub (? par.)	Woodlock`s Gr	White Mark	mill	-	-	-	White M - Whiteside Mary	1750	-	dd/	179 396 121492
Dub (? par.)	Woodlock`s Gr	WhiteMark :	mill	-	-	-	White M - Wade James :	1769	Lease 18 Jan.	dd/	276 170 176956
Dub (? par.)	Woodlock`s Gr	WhiteMark :	mill	-	-	-	White M - Slater Adam :	1763	-	dd/	224 394 146489
Dub (? par.)	Woodlock`s Gr	Whyte Mark Anthony	mill	-	-	-	White M - Benyon Saml	1785	-	dd/	364 315 245461
Dublin	Woodmills	Connell Patrick :	land	-	-	-	Connell P - Madden Jas	1718	-	dd/	22 262 11963
Dub (? par.)	Woodmills	Falkiner Frederick :	land	-	-	-	Falkiner F - Holroyd Isaac :	1761	-	dd/	214 44 139845
Dublin	Woodmills	Madden James :	land	-	-	-	Madden J - Madden John	1718	-	dd/	21 404 11964
Dub (? par.)	Woodmills	Moody Rev Jno :	land	-	-	-	Moody Jno - Latouche ?	1792	-	dd/	450 477 292017
Coolock	Woodmills	Thomas Joseph	land	-	-	-	Thomas J - Spring Mary	1721	-	dd/	33 106 19803
Lusk	Woodpark	-	corn	-	-	-	-	-	-	6"os/	7
Castleknock b.	Woodpark	Elliott	land	-	-	-	Elliott - Elgin	-	?	dd/	52 415 43455
Castleknock b.	Woodpark	Guidon Christopher	land	-	-	-	Guidon C - Elliott Fran	1718	-	dd/	51 275 33681
Lusk	Woodpark	Hartford Patrick	corn	-	-	-	-	-	-	gr/	-
Lusk	Woodpark	Hartford Patrick	corn	52x23x21	-	16.7.5		-	13x5.7x11 30 bkts.	hob/	5.0849
Lusk	Woodpark	Hartford Patrick	corn	52x23x21	-	-	-	-	13.6x5.7x11 2 pr st.	hob/	5.0851
Castleknock b.	Woodpark	Wetherall Robert	land	-	-	-	Wetherall R - Guidon Chr	1718	-	dd/	27 340 17226
Lusk	Woodpark :	- on a good stream	corn	-	38a.	-	-	2002	-	mmSv/	sb - R
Cruagh	Woodtown	-	cloth	-	-	-	-	1899	-	1"os/	112
Malahide	Yellow Walls	- SW/ Barrack Br.	cotton	120x20 & 60x27 ft.	-	-	- Estab. by Richd Talbot :	1783	- (demol. by 1880)	l.surv/	rg
Clondalkin	Yellowmeadows	-	mill pond	-	-	-	-	-	-	6"os/	17

PARISH	TOWNLAND	MILLER	TYPE	HOUSE	Land	£Val	PROPRIETORS	Date	WHEEL etc.	Record	Ref.
Clones	Aghadrumsee	-	corn	-	-	-	-	-	-	6"os/	35
Clones	Aghadrumsee	-	mill	-	-	-	-	-	-	1"os/	57
Boho	Aghaherish	-	corn & kiln	-	-	-	-	-	-	6"os/	21
Boho	Aghaherrish	Britton George	corn	-	32a.	-	-	-	-	gr/	-
Boho	Aghaherrish	Britton William	corn	27x18x12 & corn kiln :	-	-	-	-	12x1.6 bad wheel	v1B/	41
Boho	Aghamore	-	mill	-	-	-	-	-	-	1"os/	57
Aghavea	Ardmoney	-	corn kiln	-	-	-	-	-	-	6"os/	29
Aghavea	Ardunshin	- E/ Colebrook R.	mill & mill race	-	-	-	-	-	-	6"os/	28
Aghavea	Ardunshin	Ellis Henry	bleach	88x24x18 & boiling ho :	-	-	-	-	-	v1B/	429
Aghalurcher	Attyclannabryan	Kidd Anthony	-	miller`s house	31a.	-	-	-	-	gr/	-
Aghalurcher	Attyclannabryan	Porter John G	corn	-	-	-	-	-	-	gr/	-
Aghalurcher	Attyclannabryan	Porter Rev John G	corn & kiln	miller`s house	-	-	-	-	-	gr/	-
Derryvullan	Ballindullagh Out.	-	corn kiln	-	-	-	-	-	-	6"os/	16
Fermanagh	Ballydollagh *	-	mill dam (no mill)	-	-	-	-	-	-	6"os/	22
Derryvullan	Ballylucas	Armstrong John	corn & kiln	-	59a.	-	-	-	-	gr/	-
Enniskillen	Ballylucas	Wilson Thomas	corn	-	-	-	-	-	-	v1B/	435A
Belleek	Ballymagaghran	-	corn & kiln	-	-	-	-	-	-	6"os/	8
Belleek	Ballymagaghran	Bloomfield John C	corn	-	-	-	-	-	-	gr/	-
Belleek	Ballymagaghran	Neville Robert	corn	37x20x9 & corn kiln :	-	-	-	-	-	v1B/	145A+B
Belleek	Ballymaghran	Bloomfield John C	saw	-	-	-	-	-	-	gr/	-
Magheracross	Bellanmallard	Armstrong J & ano :	corn	42x22x7 & corn kiln :	-	-	-	-	- no dimensions	v1B/	436
Magheracross	Bellanmallard	Crozier Robert	corn & kilns	-	11a.	-	-	-	-	gr/	-
Belleek	Belleek	- E. side R. N./Tn Br.	corn	-	-	-	-	-	-	6"os/	8
Belleek	Belleek Town	M`Birney David	china factory	-	-	-	-	-	-	gr/	-
Belleek	Belleek Town	M`Birney David	felspur	-	1.3.0	-	-	-	-	gr/	-
Belleek	Belleek Town	Stephens Felix	corn & kiln	-	-	-	-	-	-	gr/	-
Belleek	Belleek Town	Stephens Felix	saw	-	-	-	-	-	-	gr/	-
Innishmacsaint	Blaney	- near Derrygonnelly	corn	-	-	-	-	-	-	1"os/	44
Aghavea	Boyhill	-	mill pond & race	-	-	-	-	-	-	6"os/	28
Aghavea	Boyhill	- SE/ Maguiresbridge	corn	-	-	-	-	-	-	6"os/	28
Aghavea	Boyhill	Bogues James	corn & kiln	-	7a.	-	-	-	-	gr/	-
Aghavea	Boyhill	Johnston James	corn	-	-	-	-	-	-	v1B/	-
Innishmacsaint	Braade	-	flax kiln	-	-	-	-	-	-	6"os/	14
Innishmacsaint	Braade	Johnston Simon	loom shop	31x17x6 & dw. ho :	-	-	-	-	- no dimensions	v1B/	426A
Cleenish	Brockagh	-	corn kiln	-	-	-	-	-	-	6"os/	17
Templecarn	Brookhill	-	corn	-	-	-	-	-	-	6"os/	4
Templecarn	Brookhill	-	mill race, dam	-	-	-	-	-	-	6"os/	4
Templecarn	Brookhill	-	woollen cloth	-	-	-	-	-	-	6"os/	4
Templecarn	Brookhill	Hazlett William	corn & kiln	-	-	-	-	-	-	gr/	-
Templecarn	Brookhill	Hazlett William	flax	-	1a.	-	-	-	-	gr/	-
Templecarn	Brookhill	Moore James	tuck	-	14a.	-	-	-	-	gr/	-
Templecarn	Brookhill	Moores James	corn	29x19x7 & corn kiln :	-	-	-	-	-	v1B/	-
Trory	Buninubber	-	corn kiln	-	-	-	-	-	-	6"os/	15
Magheraculmoney	Camplany	Marshall William	flax	-	76a.	-	-	-	-	gr/	-
Derryvullan	Cappy	-	corn		-	-	-	-	-	6"os/	27
Derryvullan	Cappy	Armstrong Adam	corn	-	-	-	-	-	-	v1B/	-
Derryvullan	Cappy	Higgins Thomas	corn	-	3a.	-	-	-	-	gr/	-
Derryvullan	Cappy	Innes Edward	corn kiln	-	-	-	-	-	-	gr/	-
Devenish	Carran West	-	corn mill ruin	-	-	-	-	-	-	6"os/	13
Devenish	Carran West	- at Blair`s Bridge	mill	-	-	-	-	-	-	1"os	44
Devenish	Carran West	Blair Edward	corn	28x17x6 & corn kiln :	-	-	-	-	- no dimensions	v1B/	424A
Devenish	Carran West	Blair William	corn	-	24a.	-	-	-	-	gr/	-

PARISH	TOWNLAND	MILLER	TYPE	HOUSE	Land	£Val	PROPRIETORS	Date	WHEEL etc.	Record	Ref.
Devenish	Carran West	Blair William	corn	-	24a.	-	-	-	-	gr/	-
Innishmacsaunt	Carrick	-	corn	-	-	-	-	-	-	1"os/	57
Innishmacsaunt	Carrick	-	old kiln	-	-	-	-	-	-	6"os/	14
Derryvullan	Castle Irvine	Irvine Henry M D	corn & flour	-	1a.	-	-	-	-	gr/	-
Derryvullan	Castle Irvine	Irvine Henry M D	saw	-	-	-	-	-	-	gr/	-
Derryvullan	Castle Irvine Dem.	Darcy William	oat meal	28x21x13	-	-	-	-	- no dimensions	v1B/	419
Derryvullan	Castle Irvine Dem.	Irvine H M D	corn	-	-	-	-	-	-	gr/	-
Derryvullan	Castle Irvine Dem.	Irvine H M D	flour	-	-	-	-	-	-	gr/	-
Derryvullan	Castle Irvine Dem.	Irvine H M D	saw	-	-	-	-	-	-	gr/	-
Cleenish	Cavancarragh	-	corn	-	-	-	-	-	-	6"os/	25
Cleenish	Cavancarragh	-	old tuck mill	-	-	-	-	-	-	6"os/	25
Cleenish	Cavancarragh	M`Court Patrick	corn	-	-	-	-	-	-	gr/	-
Cleenish	Cavancarragh	M`Court Patrick	tuck	-	-	-	-	-	-	gr/	-
Cleenish	Cavancarragh	Macort Patrick	corn	28x18x6 & corn kiln :	-	-	14x1x7	-	- no dimensions	v1B/	42
Fermanagh	Clabry Village *	-	corn kiln	-	-	-	-	-	-	6"os/	18
Innishmacsaunt	Claragh	-	corn kiln	-	-	-	-	-	-	6"os/	15
Galloon	Clevaghy	- Roosky	Flour & Corn Mills	-	-	-	-	-	-	6"os/	34
Galloon	Clevaghy	Clarke James	corn	-	-	-	-	-	-	V1b/	-
Fermanagh	Clohonan *	Cole John :	mill	-	-	-	Cole Jn - Mulala John :	1731	Lse. 25 Oct.	dd/	74 155 50490
Fermanagh	Clohonan *	Cole John :	mill	-	-	-	Cole Jn - Mulala John :	1733	Lse. 8 Apl.	dd/	71 274? 50491
Fermanagh	Clohonan *	Cole John :	mill	-	-	-	Cole John - Nesbitt Alex :	1727	-	dd/	90 122 63340
Fermanagh	Clohonan *	Montgomery	mill	-	-	-	Montgomery - Hume	-	-	dd/	26 382 60874?
Lurg	Clonee	-	corn kiln	-	-	-	-	-	-	6"os/	6
Galloon	Clonmaulin	-	mill	-	-	-	-	-	-	1"os/	57
Magheraculmoney	Cloy	-	mill race, pond	-	-	-	-	-	-	6"os/	6
Magheraculmoney	Cloy	Armstrong David	corn & kilns	-	19.3.2	-	-	-	-	gr/	-
Magheraculmoney	Cloy	McNalty M	oat	-	-	-	-	-	-	v1B/	-
Derryvullan	Coolaness	-	corn kiln	-	-	-	-	-	-	6"os/	11
Aghalurcher	Cooneen	-	corn & kiln	-	-	-	-	-	-	6"os/	24
Aghalurcher	Cooneen	Graham Robert	corn & kiln	-	1.0.0	-	-	-	-	gr/	-
Aghalurcher	Cooneen	Johnston James	corn	-	-	-	-	-	-	v1B/	-
Aghalurcher	Cooneen	Whitley Robert	tuck	-	86a.	-	-	-	-	gr/	-
Fermanagh	Coonfen *	-	mill & corn kiln	-	-	-	-	-	-	6"os/	29
Clones	Corraleek	Whitsitt Benjamin	corn & kiln	-	3a.	-	-	-	-	gr/	-
Aghalurcher	Corralongford	-	corn & kiln	-	-	-	-	-	-	6"os/	24
Aghalurcher	Corralongford	Johnston James	corn	-	-	-	-	-	-	gr/	-
Aghalurcher	Corralongford	Johnston James	corn	-	22a.	-	-	-	-	gr/	-
Aghalurcher	Corralongford	Johnston James	corn	44x25x13 & dw. ho :	-	-	2 wheels	-	-	v1B/	428A
Aghalurcher	Corralongford	Johnston James	flax	-	-	-	-	-	-	gr/	-
Aghalurcher	Corralongford	Johnston James	flax	-	-	-	-	-	-	gr/	-
Clones	Cortrasna	-	corn kiln	-	-	-	-	-	-	6"os/	35
Fermanagh	Corvaghan *	-	corn & mill race	-	-	-	-	-	-	6"os/	39
Magheracross	Craghan	Armstrong J & Crozier	corn	-	-	-	-	-	-	v1B/	-
Magheracross	Craghan	Haliday William A	corn	-	0.1.0	-	-	-	-	gr/	-
Magheracross	Craghan	Haliday William A	new mill	-	-	-	-	-	-	gr/	-
Magheracross	Craghan	Halliday William A	corn	-	-	-	-	-	-	gr/	-
Magheracross	Craghan	Halliday William A	new	-	-	-	-	-	-	gr/	-
Enniskillen	Creevehill	- on rd. S ex Tempo	corn & kiln	-	-	-	-	-	-	6"os/	24
Enniskillen	Creevehill	Cooke Edward	corn	29x20x14 & corn kilns :	-	-	-	-	- no dimensions	v1B/	435A
Magheraculmoney	Crevinish	-	corn kiln	-	-	-	-	-	-	6"os/	5
Magheraculmoney	Crevinish	Bingham	mill & mountain	-	-	-	Bingham - Irwin	-	-	dd/	x 26 1358
Magheraculmoney	Crevinish	Cochran John :	mill & mountain	-	-	-	Cochran J - Archdall Nich	1818	L&R 14 Aug. 1738	dd/	91 325 64325

PARISH	TOWNLAND	MILLER	TYPE	HOUSE	Land	£Val	PROPRIETORS	Date	WHEEL etc.	Record	Ref.
Magheraculmoney	Crevinish	Cochran John :	mill & mountain	-	-	-	Cothran J - Cathcart Jas :	1707	Mort. 7 Aug.	dd/	6 468 2604
Magheraculmoney	Crevinish	Cothran John :	mill & mountain	-	-	-	Cothran J - Lowry Robert	1715	L&R. 3 Sep.	dd/	16 314 7586
Magheraculmoney	Crevinish	Cothran John :	mill & mountain	-	-	-	Cothran John - Irwin :	-	-	dd/	12 305 5197
Magheraculmoney	Crevinish	Derry Bishop George :	mill & mountain	-	-	-	Derry B - Gore Rt Hon. :	1717	Lse. 12 Feb.	dd/	21 1 10618
Magheraculmoney	Crevinish	Irwin Christopher :	mill & mountain	-	-	-	Irwin C - Nesbitt Alex :	1710	L&R. 6 Jul.	dd/	6 136 1587
Magheraculmoney	Crevinish	Irwin Christopher :	mill & mountain	-	-	-	Irwin C - Clogher Gerge H	1720	8 Jul.	dd/	20 274 10599
Magheraculmoney	Crevinish	Irwine Christopher :	mill & mountain	-	-	-	Irwine C - Corry John :	1718	Rel. 29 Jul.	dd/	22 421 12466
Devenish	Crott	-	mill	-	-	-	-	-	-	1"os/	44
Devenish	Cruntully	-	mill	-	-	-	-	-	-	1"os/	32
Drumkeeran	Culleen	-	corn	-	-	-	-	-	-	1"os/	-
Aghalurcher	Curraghfad	- W side Coonfen R.	tuck	-	-	-	-	-	-	6"os/	29
Aghalurcher	Curraghfad	M`Keown Johnston	tuck	-	30a.	-	-	-	-	gr/	-
Aghalurcher	Cushwash	Balfour	corn	-	-	-	Balfour - Colvill	-	-	dd/	32 429 20314
Aghalurcher	Cushwash	Balfour	corn	-	-	-	Balfour - Colvill	-	-	dd/	322 500 20684
Aghalurcher	Cushwash	Balfour William :	corn	-	-	-	Balfour - Deschamps Ch	1726	Lse. 27 Apl.	dd/	51 12 32597
Aghalurcher	Cushwash	Balfour	corn	-	-	-	Balfour - Willoughby	-	-	dd/	32 446 20393
Aghalurcher	Cushwash	Colvill Robert :	corn	-	-	-	Colvill R - Clements Theo	1724	L&R. 25 Nov.	dd/	47 192 30143
Aghalurcher	Cushwash	Johnson Robt. Maj. :	corn	-	-	-	Johnson R - Johnson :	1729	-	dd/	61 240 41252
Aghalurcher	Cushwash	Little Robert	corn & kiln	-	39a.	-	-	-	-	gr/	-
Aghalurcher	Cushwash	Little Robert	flax	-	-	-	-	-	-	gr/	-
Aghalurcher	Cushwash	Little Robert	tuck	-	-	-	-	-	-	gr/	-
Aghalurcher	Cushwash	Swindell Francis	corn	-	-	-	-	-	-	v1B/	-
Aghalurcher	Cushwash	Turner James :	corn	-	-	-	Turner J - Willis Jas :	1722	31 Oct.	dd/	44 83 27660
Fermanagh	Derrihalla * :	Archdall	mill	-	-	-	Archdall - M'tgomery	-	-	dd/	85 382 60847
Fermanagh	Derrihalla * :	Cole John :	mill	-	-	-	Cole J - Hume Alice Rt. :	1736	L&R. 16 Mar.	dd/	85 137 60873
Fermanagh	Derrihalla * :	Cole John :	mill	-	-	-	Cole - Montgomery Thos :	1733	-	dd/	76 75 52893
Fermanagh	Derrihalla * :	Cole John :	mill	-	-	-	Cole - Willoughby Hugh :	1728	-	dd/	58 231 39295
Fermanagh	Derrihalla * :	Cole John :	mill	-	-	-	Cole J - Campbell Hugh :	1730	-	dd/	72 126 50059
Fermanagh	Derrihalla * :	Cole John :	mill	-	-	-	Cole Jn - Nixon George :	1732	-	dd/	72 228 50527
Fermanagh	Derrihalla * :	Cole John :	mill	-	-	-	Cole John - Nesbitt Alex :	1727	-	dd/	90 122 63340
Innishmacsaint	Derrygonnelly	- N .side Sillcon R.	corn	-	-	-	-	-	-	6"os/	15
Innishmacsaint	Derrygonnelly	Ferguson John	corn & kiln	-	74a.	-	-	-	-	gr/	-
Innishmacsaint	Derrygonnelly	Kitson James	corn	-	-	-	-	-	-	v1B/	-
Innishmacsaint	Derrygonnelly	Nixon John	flax	-	-	-	-	-	-	gr/	-
Innishmacsaint	Derrygonnelly Tn	Nixon John Jun.	flax	-	-	-	-	-	-	gr/	-
Enniskillen	Derrykeeghan	-	corn	-	-	-	-	-	-	6"os/	22
Enniskillen	Derrykeeghan	-	tuck & mill dam	-	-	-	-	-	-	6"os/	22
Enniskillen	Derrykeeghan	Williams Christopher	corn & kiln	-	20a.	-	-	-	-	gr/	-
Enniskillen	Derrykeeghan	Wilson James	corn	-	-	-	-	-	-	v1B/	-
Derryvullan	Derrynanny	- near Irvinstown	mill	-	-	-	-	-	-	1"os/	32
Derryvullan	Derryveone	-	mill	-	-	-	-	-	-	6"os/	11
Rossory	Dinnydoon	-	corn & mill pond	-	-	-	-	-	-	6"os/	21
Rossory	Dinnydoon	Ellis John	corn	-	-	-	-	-	-	v1B/	-
Rossory	Dinnydoon	Storey Joseph	corn	-	-	-	-	-	-	gr/	-
Galloon	Donagh	-	mill	-	-	-	-	-	-	1"os/	57
Galloon	Donagh	Morrow William	corn	-	-	-	-	-	-	v1B/	-
Galloon	Donagh	Skelton Francis	corn & kiln	-	0.1.26	-	-	-	-	gr/	-
Rossory	Dooederny	- E side Silless R.	corn	-	-	-	-	-	-	6"os/	26
Rossorry	Dooederny	Archdall	mill	-	-	-	Archdall - Davis	-	`	dd/	45 60 27793
Rossorry	Dooederny	Archdall Edward :	mill	-	-	-	Archdall E - Cole Fenton :	1778	Agmt. 17 Jan.	dd/	74 380 51716
Rossorry	Dooederny	Archdall Nicholas :	mill	-	-	-	Archdall N - M'tgomery :	1731	-	dd/	67 126 45543
Rossorry	Dooederny	Davis	mill	-	-	-	Davis - Archdall	-	-	dd/	43 170 27788

PARISH	TOWNLAND	MILLER	TYPE	HOUSE	Land	£Val	PROPRIETORS	Date	WHEEL etc.	Record	Ref.
Rossorry	Dooederny	Davis	mill	-	-	-	Davis - Archdall	-	-	dd/	47 16 29343
Rossorry	Dooederny	Elliott Oliver	corn	-	-	-	-	-	13x3x5	v1B/	-
Rossorry	Dooederny	Robinson David	corn & kiln	-	21a.	-	-	-	-	gr/	-
Aghalurcher	Doogarry	-	corn kiln	-	-	-	-	-	-	6"os/	24
Enniskillen	Doon	Collum A	corn	-	-	-	-	-	-	v1B/	-
Enniskillen	Doon	Elliott Simon	corn & kiln	-	0.0.30		-	-	-	gr/	-
Magheraculmoney	Drumadraghy	Bell Francis	flax	-	19a.	-	-	-	-	gr/	-
Magheraculmoney	Drumadraghy	M`Cready James	corn & kiln	-	11a.	-	-	-	-	gr/	-
Fermanagh	Drumara *	-	mill	-	-	-	-	-	-	1"os/	32
Fermanagh	Drumaran (2)	-	corn	-	-	-	-	-	-	1"os	44
Derryvullan	Drumarky	-	old dam	-	-	-	-	-	-	6"os/	10
Derryvullan	Drumarky	- 3/8m.SW of Vge.	mill	-	-	-	-	-	-	6"os/	10
Clenish	Drumawillim	Cole	mill	-	-	-	Cole - Hume	-	-	dd/	85 437 60873
Clenish	Drumawillim	Archdall	mill	-	-	-	Archdall - Montgomery	-	-	dd/	86 382 60874
Clenish	Drumawillim	Cole	mill	-	-	-	Cole - Nesbitt	-	-	dd/	90 122 63340
Innishmacsaint	Drumbadmeen	Johnston Edward	corn	-	6a.	-	-	-	-	gr	-
Innishmacsaint	Drumbadmeen	Johnston Edward	corn	-	6a.	-	-	-	-	gr/	-
Innishmacsaint	Drumbadmeen	McBiren William	corn	-	-	-	-	-	-	v1B/	-
Magheraculmoney	Drumbane	Campbell William	corn	-	-	-	-	-	-	v1B/	-
Magheraculmoney	Drumcahy	- on Dernagh R	mill	-	-	-	-	-	-	1"os/	32
Magheraculmoney	Drumcahy	Johnston George	corn	-	-	-	-	-	-	v1B/	-
Fermanagh	Drumcar *	-	corn	-	-	-	-	-	-	1"os/	56
Killesher	Drumcard	- at Glebe Ho.	mill	-	-	-	-	-	-	1"os	44
Derryvullan	Drumcaw	-	corn kiln	-	-	-	-	-	-	6"os/	15
Fermanagh	Drumcoo (3)	Moffatt Galbraith	corn	-	-	-	-	-	-	v1B/	-
Enniskillen	Drumcor	-	corn kiln	-	-	-	-	-	-	6"os	17
Enniskillen	Drumcor	Moffett Andrew	corn & kiln	-	24a.	-	-	-	-	gr/	-
Fermanagh	Drumgiven *	-	corn kiln	-	-	-	-	-	-	6"os/	6
Aghalurcher	Drumgoon	-	corn	-	-	-	-	-	-	1"os/	57
Aghalurcher	Drumgoon	Wiley Robert	corn	-	-	-	-	-	-	v1B/	-
Aghalurcher	Drumgoon	Wiley Robert	corn & kiln	-	24a.	-	-	-	-	gr/	-
Lurg	Drumgowan West	-	corn kiln	-	-	-	-	-	-	6"os/	1
Magheraculmoney	Drumhoney	Humphries Chris	corn & kilns	-	3a.	-	-	-	-	gr/	-
Belleek	Druminillar	-	corn kiln	-	-	-	-	-	-	6"os/	8
Aghavea	Drumlone	-	corn & flax	-	-	-	-	-	-	6"os/	28
Aghavea	Drumlone	Martin John	corn & kiln	-	1.2.10		-	-	-	gr/	-
Aghavea	Drumlone	Martin John	flax	-	-	-	-	-	-	gr/	-
Aghavea	Drumlone	Martin Joseph	corn	-	-	-	-	-	-	v1B/	-
Aghavea	Drumlone	Martin Joseph	flax	-	-	-	-	-	-	v1B/	-
Lurg	Drummacahan	-	mill, mill race	-	-	-	-	-	-	6"os/	5
Magheraculmoney	Drummadraghy	Bell James	scutch	-	-	-	-	-	-	v1B/	-
Magheraculmoney	Drummadraghy	Duffy Isaac	corn	-	-	-	-	-	-	v1B/	-
Magheracross	Drummurry	-	corn	-	-	-	-	-	-	6"os/	10
Drumkeeran	Drumnagalliagh	-	corn	-	-	-	-	-	-	6"os/	1
Drumkeeran	Drumnagalliagh	Barton George	corn & kiln	-	-	-	-	-	-	gr/	-
Drumkeeran	Drumnagalliagh	Flanagan Patrick	corn	-	-	-	-	-	-	v1B/	-
Fermanagh	Drumristan *	-	corn kiln	-	-	-	-	-	-	6"os/	2
Drumkeeran	Drumskinny	-	corn kion	-	-	-	-	-	-	6"os/	1
Fermanagh	Drumury	-	corn	-	-	-	-	-	-	6"os/	16
Ennisk./ Killesher	Edenmore	- near Tempo Vge.	corn	-	-	-	-	-	-	6"os/	23
Ennisk./ Killesher	Edenmore	Elliott William	corn	-	-	-	-	-	-	v1B/	-
Fermanagh	Emmerroo *	Ritchie William	corn	-	-	-	-	-	-	v1B/	-

PARISH	TOWNLAND	MILLER	TYPE	HOUSE	Land	£Val	PROPRIETORS	Date	WHEEL etc.	Record	Ref.
Enniskillen	Enniskillen	Armstrong & Jones	brewery	-	-	-	-	-	-	v1B/	-
Enniskillen	Enniskillen	Armstrong A	distillery	-	-	-	-	-	-	v1B/	-
Enniskillen	Enniskillen	Cole Jno :	mill	-	-	-	Cole Jn - Clegg Francis :	1734	Lse. 9 May	dd/	82 351 58116
Enniskillen	Enniskillen Town	Hales John	saw	-	-	-	-	-	-	gr/	-
Enniskillen	Enniskillen Town :	Elliott Jno	mill	-	-	-	Elliott J - Constabulory	1847	-	dd/	1847 1 58
Enniskillen	Enniskillen Town :	Elliott Jno	land	-	-	-	Elliott - Willis Mary A	1846	-	dd/	1846 20 30
Enniskillen	Enniskillen Town :	- W. side R.	distillery	-	-	-	-	-	-	6"os/	22
Enniskillen	Enniskillen West :	- imed. N/ Bridge	corn	-	-	-	-	-	-	6"os/	22
Aghavea	Eshnadarragh	-	corn kiln	-	-	-	-	-	-	6"os/	29
Lurg	Fartagh	-	corn kiln	-	-	-	-	-	-	6"os/	2
Magheracross	Faughard	Henderson & Edie	woollen	-	-	-	-	-	-	gr/	-
Magheracross	Faughard	Henderson & Edie	woollen fcty	-	2a.	-	-	-	-	gr/	-
Devenish	Frevagh	-	corn kiln	-	-	-	-	-	-	6"os/	19
Kinawley	Glasdrumman	-	corn & kiln	-	-	-	-	-	-	6"os/	38
Kinawley	Glasdrumman	Tegart John	corn	-	-	-	-	-	-	v1B/	-
Kinawley	Glasdrumman	Veitch Alex	corn & kiln	miller`s house	1.3.15		-	-	-	gr/	-
Derryvullan	Glenall	-	corn kiln	-	-	-	-	-	-	6"os/	11
Innishmacsaint	Glennasheevar	-	cornkiln	-	-	-	-	-	-	6"os/	14
Fermanagh	Gortcommon *	-	corn	-	-	-	-	-	-	6"os/	39
Fermanagh	Gortcommon *	-	corn	-	-	-	-	-	-	6"os/	39
Fermanagh	Gortcommon *	-	corn	-	-	-	-	-	-	6"os/	39
Boho	Gortgall	-	mill	-	-	-	-	-	-	1"os	44
Boho	Gortgall	-	mill & mill race	-	-	-	-	-	-	6"os/	21
Boho	Gortgall	Cadden Patrick	corn	28x19x12 & corn kiln :	-	-	12x2	-	12x2 1 pr st - 5ft	v1B/	41
Boho	Gortgall	Maguire Peter	corn	-	6a.	-	-	-	-	gr/	-
Devenish	Gortgor	Bryans Capt.	corn	29x20x8 & corn kiln :	-	-	-	-	- no dimensions	v1B/	424
Clones	Gortindarragh	-	corn	-	-	-	-	-	-	1"os/	58
Aghavea	Greenhill	- on Tempo R.	mill & mill race	-	-	-	-	-	-	6"os/	23
Aghavea	Greenhill	Irvine Arthur H	corn	-	-	-	-	-	-	gr/	-
Aghavea	Greenhill	Irvine Arthur H	corn & kiln	-	12a.	-	-	-	-	gr/	-
Aghavea	Greenhill	Irvine Major H	corn	-	-	-	-	-	-	v1B/	-
Killesher	Gubbacrock	-	corn 7 mill pond	-	-	-	-	-	-	6"os/	32
Killesher	Gubbacrock	Brogue Bernard	corn & kiln	-	-	-	-	-	-	gr/	-
Killesher	Gubbacrock	Stafford Gerrard	corn	-	-	-	-	-	-	v1B/	-
Fermanagh	Island *	Archdall	mill	-	-	-	Archdall - Davis	-	-	dd/	45 60 27793
Fermanagh	Island *	Archdall Nicholas :	mill	-	-	-	Archdall N - M'tgomery :	1731	-	dd/	67 126 45543
Fermanagh	Island *	Davis	mill	-	-	-	Davis - Adchdall	-	-	dd/	43 170 27788
Fermanagh	Island *	Davis	mill	-	-	-	Davis - Archdall	-	-	dd/	47 16 29343
Drumkeeran	Keeran	-	mill	-	-	-	-	-	-	1"os/	57
Galloon	Keeran Beg	-	corn & mill pond	-	-	-	-	-	-	6"os/	35
Galloon	Keeran Beg	Hean Counseller	corn	-	-	-	-	-	-	v1B/	-
Galloon	Keeran Beg	Little Ellen	corn & kiln	-	-	-	-	-	-	gr/	-
Magheraculmoney	Kesh Town	Vaughan (Govs.)	corn & kiln	-	0.2.30		-	-	-	gr/	-
Enniskillen	Killee	Beatty Robert	corn & kiln	-	-	-	-	-	-	gr/	-
Clones	Killyfoyle	Johnston Joseph	corn & kiln	-	29a.	-	-	-	-	gr/	-
Kinawley	Killymackacrean	Donegan James	corn	-	-	-	-	-	-	gr/	-
Drumkeeran	Killynoogan	Barton F & Keys J	corn & kiln	miller`s house	1.2.5	-	-	-	-	gr/	-
Drumkeeran	Killynoogan	Barton F & Keys J	flax	-	-	-	-	-	-	gr/	-
Drumkeeran	Killynoogan	Keys Messrs.	corn	-	-	-	-	-	-	v1B/	-
Cleenish	Killywillin	Nixon Alex	corn	-	-	-	14x2x7	-	-	v1B/	-
Cleenish	Killywillin	Walsh Christopher	corn & kiln	-	27a.	-	-	-	-	gr/	-
Killesher	Knockagehan	-	corn	-	-	-	-	-	-	1"os/	-

PARISH	TOWNLAND	MILLER	TYPE	HOUSE	Land	£Val	PROPRIETORS	Date	WHEEL etc.	Record	Ref.
Killesher	Knockagehan	- at Moneen	corn	-	-	-	-	-	-	1"os	44
Kinawley	Knockarevan	- nr Garrison Tn Br.	corn & race	-	-	-	-	-	-	6"os/	13
Kinawley	Knockarevan	- nr Garrison Tn Br.	corn kiln	-	-	-	-	-	-	6"os/	13
Enniskillen	Knockennis	-	corn kiln	-	-	-	-	-	-	6"os/	17
Derryvullan	Knockroe Archdall	-	corn kiln	-	-	-	-	-	-	6"os	11
Aghalurcher	Knocks	-	corn	-	-	-	-	-	-	6"os/	34
Aghalurcher	Knocks	-	mill	-	-	-	-	-	-	1"os/	57
Aghalurcher	Knocks	Blaney Leslie	corn	-	1.1.0	-	-	-	-	gr/	-
Aghalurcher	Knocks	Leslie Blaney	corn	-	-	-	-	-	-	gr/	-
Aghalurcher	Knocks	McElroy J	corn	-	-	-	-	-	-	v1B/	-
Clones	Lacky	Benson James	spade factory	-	1-3-0	-	-	-	-	gr/	-
Templecarn	Laragh	-	mill rase, weir	-	-	-	-	-	-	6"os/	16
Templecarn	Laragh	-	old mill	-	-	-	-	-	-	6"os/	16
Templecarn	Laragh	- E side Bell`m`ard R.	old mill	-	-	-	-	-	-	6"os/	10
Templecarn	Laragh	Halliday John	corn & flour	-	-	-	-	-	-	v1B/	-
Templecarn	Laragh	Halliday William A	corn & kiln	-	0.0.3C	-	-	-	-	gr/	-
Templecarn	Laragh	Halliday William A	flour	-	-	-	-	-	-	gr/	-
Kinawley	Leggin	Patterson John	corn & kiln	-	63a.	-	-	-	-	gr/	-
Kinawley	Leginn	-	mill	-	-	-	-	-	-	1"os/	57
Kinawley	Leginn	-	mill	-	-	-	-	-	-	6"os/	38
Kinawley	Leginn	Patterson George	corn	-	-	-	-	-	-	v1B/	-
Kinawley	Leginn	Patterson John	corn	-	-	-	-	-	-	gr/	-
Magheracross	Lisbellaw Town	Porter Rev John G	corn	-	1.2.0	-	-	-	-	gr/	-
Clones	Lisnamallard	-	corn mill (in ruins	-	-	-	-	-	-	6"os/	35
Aghavea	Litlemount	Glass Andrew	corn	-	-	-	-	-	-	v1B/	-
Aghavea	Littlemount	Fowler George	corn & kiln	-	0.1.35		-	-	-	gr/	-
Drumkeeran	Lowery	- 1/2m. SxE. Pettigoe	corn & kiln	-	-	-	-	-	-	6"os/	4
Fermanagh	Lydevenish *	-	pond	-	-	-	-	-	-	6"os/	21
Fermanagh	Maghernegeragh *	Caulfield	tuck	-	-	-	Caulfield - Cuthbert	-	-	dd/	44 178 28353
Fermanagh	Maghernegeragh *	Caulfield Anne :	tuck	-	-	-	Caulfield - Cuthbert Sid :	1720	-	dd/	51 105 32957
Fermanagh	Maghernegeragh *	Caulfield Sidney :	tuck	-	-	-	Caulfield S - Cranston :	1722	L&R. 27 Apl.	dd/	34 96 20537
Fermanagh	Maghernegeragh *	Cranston	tuck	-	-	-	Cranston - Crawford	-	-	dd/	66 136 45469
Fermanagh	Maghernegeragh *	Cranston John :	tuck	-	-	-	Cranston - Carleton Geo	1726	L&R. 11 May	dd/	50 339 33270
Fermanagh	Maghernegeragh *	Crawford James :	tuck	-	-	-	Crawford J - Crozier Jn :	1738	L&R. 18 Aug.	dd/	91 493 64996
Fermanagh	Maghernegeragh *	Cuthbert John :	tuck	-	-	-	Cuthbert J - Mitchell :	1726	-	dd/	50 265 32942
Fermanagh	Maghernegeragh *	Mitchell Andrew :	tuck	-	-	-	Mitchell A - Crozier John :	1734	L&R. 10 Dec.	dd/	85 57 59028
Enniskillen	Magonragh	Chapman James	flax	-	2.3.0	-	-	-	-	gr/	-
Cleenish	Meenawargy	-	corn kiln	-	-	-	-	-	-	6"os/	25
Magheraculmoney	Meenmore	-	corn kiln	-	-	-	-	-	-	6"os/	6
Deryvullan	Milltate	-	mill	-	-	-	-	-	-	6"os/	11
Galloon	Milltate	Clarke James	corn & kiln	-	5a.	-	-	-	-	gr/	-
Galloon	Milltate	Clarke James	flour	-	53a.	-	-	-	-	gr/	-
Galloon	Milltate	Clarke James	flour	-	-	-	-	-	-	v1B/	-
Kinawley	Milltown	-	corn & mill dam	-	-	-	-	-	-	6"os/	38
Kesh	Milltown	-	mill - 1.5 miles	-	-	-	-	-	-	1"os/	32
Blaney	Milltown	Feris Thomas	corn	-	-	-	-	-	-	v1B/	-
Innishmacsaint	Milltown	Ferris Thomas	corn & kiln	31x18x6, kiln 24x14x8 :	-	-	-	1836	-	v1B/	426A
Kinawley	Milltown	Surphlis Richard	corn	-	-	-	-	-	-	gr/	-
Kinawley	Milltown	Surphlis Richard	corn	-	-	-	-	-	-	v1B/	-
Kinawley	Milltown	Surphlis Richard	corn & kiln	-	58a.	-	-	-	-	gr/	-
Innishmacsaint	Milltownblaney	Ferris Matthew	corn & kiln	-	40a	-	-	-	-	gr/	-
Devenish	Monaghan	Brown John	corn	-	-	-	-	-	-	v1B/	-

PARISH	TOWNLAND	MILLER	TYPE	HOUSE	Land	£Val	PROPRIETORS	Date	WHEEL etc.	Record	Ref.
Devenish	Monaghan	Browne Mary	corn & kiln	-	15a.	-	-	-	-	gr/	-
Fermanagh	Monaureece *	-	corn kiln	-	-	-	-	-	-	6"os/	6
Devenish	Monea	-	corn	-	-	-	-	-	-	1"os	44
Killesher	Moneen	-	corn & kiln	-	-	-	-	-	-	6"os/	26
Killesher	Moneen	Stutt James	corn	-	-	-	-	-	-	v1B/	-
Killesher	Moneen	Willis George	corn	-	95a.	-	-	-	-	gr/	-
Drumkeeran	Mulakeran	Fraser William	corn & kiln	-	30a.	-	-	-	-	gr/	-
Lurg	Mullaghmore	-	kiln in ruins	-	-	-	-	-	-	6"os/	5
Lurg	Mullanmeen Under	-	mill & mill race	-	-	-	-	-	-	6"os/	1
Drumkeeran	Mullanmeen Under	Frazer Thomas	corn	-	-	-	-	-	-	v1B/	416B
Clones	Mullans	Lynch Peter	corn & kiln	-	15a.	-	-	-	-	gr/	-
Clones	Mullanvaum	-	corn kiln	-	-	-	-	-	-	6"os/	29
Magheracross	Mullybritt	- SE/ Lisbellaw	corn & kiln	-	-	-	-	-	-	6"os/	27
Magheracross	Mullybritt	Copeland James	corn	37x23x15 & corn kilns :	-	-	-	-	- no dimensions	v1B/	432
Magheracross	Mullybritt	Porter John G	corn	-	-	-	-	-	-	gr/	-
Cleenish	Mullycovet	-	corn & mill dam	-	-	-	-	-	-	6"os/	26
Cleenish	Mullycovet	Hamilton James	corn	25x21x13 & corn kiln :	-	-	-	-	13x1x8 1 pair st. :	v1B/	42
Cleenish	Mullycovet	near Belcoo	corn	perfectly restored	-	-	Belcoo Dev. Group	1999	- milling exhibition	pWEH	A
Enniskillen	Mullyknock	Wilson Henry	corn	-	21a.	-	-	-	-	gr/	-
Enniskillen	Mullyknock	Wilson Henry	corn	-	-	-	-	-	-	v1B/	-
Galloon	Mullynavannoge	-	corn	-	-	-	-	-	-	6"os/	39
Galloon	Mullynavannoge	Hamilton John	corn	-	-	-	-	-	-	v1B/	-
Galloon	Mullynavannoge	Hamilton John	corn & kiln	-	97a.	-	-	-	-	gr/	-
Fermanagh	Prospect Hill *	-	corn	-	-	-	-	-	-	1"os/	-
Belleek	Rathmore	M`Birney & Armstrong	china factory	-	1-3-0	-	-	-	-	gr/	-
Belleek	Rathmore	M`Birney & Armstrong	felspur	-	-	-	-	-	-	gr/	-
Belleek	Rathmore	Stephens Felix	corn	-	-	-	-	-	-	gr/	-
Belleek	Rathmore	Stephens Felix	saw	-	-	-	-	-	-	gr/	-
Belleek	Rathmore	Wright Travers	saw	-	-	-	-	-	-	v1B/	-
Innishmacsaint	Roosky	-	corn kiln	-	-	-	-	-	-	6"os/	15
Innishmacsaint	Roosky	-	mill	-	-	-	-	-	-	6"os/	15
Lurg	Rosscolban	-	corn	-	-	-	-	-	-	6"os/	5
Lurg	Rosscolban	Acheson Guy	corn	-	-	-	-	-	-	v1B/	-
Lurg	Rosscolban	Acheson John	scutch	-	-	-	-	-	-	v1B/	-
Lurg	Rosscolban	Vaughan`s Govs.	corn	-	-	-	-	-	-	gr/	-
Clones	Rosslea	-	corn kiln	-	-	-	-	-	-	6"os/	36
Clones	Rosslea	Whitsitt Benjamin	corn	-	-	-	-	-	-	gr/	-
Clones	Rosslea Town	Whitsitt Benjamin	corn & kiln	-	-	-	-	-	-	gr/	-
Lurg	Rossmore	-	malt kiln	-	-	-	-	-	-	6"os/	10
Rossorry	Rossole	Macaulay John	corn & kiln	-	20a.	-	-	-	-	gr/	-
Rossorry	Rossole	McAuley John	corn	-	-	-	-	-	-	v1B/	-
Lurg	Rotten Mountain	-	corn	-	-	-	-	-	-	6"os/	2
Lurg	Rotten Mountain	-	corn kiln	-	-	-	-	-	-	6"os/	2
Fermanagh	Rotten Mountain	Graham John	corn	34x19x30 & corn kiln :	-	-	-	-	- no dimensions	v1B/	416A+B
Magheracross	Salloon	Haliday William A	kiln	-	4a.	-	-	-	-	gr/	-
Lurg	Sessiaghs	-	kiln in ruins	-	-	-	-	-	-	6"os/	11
Derryvullan	Shallany	Johnston Jas & Fran	corn	-	-	-	-	-	-	v1B/	-
Derryvullan	Shallany	Johnston John	corn	-	-	-	-	-	-	gr/	-
Derryvullan	Shallany	Johnston John	corn & kiln	-	8a.	-	-	-	-	gr/	-
Derryvullan	Shallany	- W. of Milltown	corn & kiln	-	-	-	-	-	-	6"os/	10
Derryvullan	Shallany	- W. of Milltown	mill dam	-	-	-	-	-	-	6"os/	11
Clones	Shannock	McClintock Alfred :	corn	-	-	-	McClintock - Black John :	1727	L&R 11 Oct.	dd/	53 499 36633

PARISH	TOWNLAND	MILLER	TYPE	HOUSE	Land	£Val	PROPRIETORS	Date	WHEEL etc.	Record	Ref.
Clones	Shannock	Nesbitt	corn	-	-	-	Nesbitt - McClintock	-	-	dd/	84 74 58104
Enniskillen	Slee	Payne Wiliam A	saw	-	96a	-	-	-	-	gr/	-
Fermanagh	Springtown	- nr Glasdrumman Br	mill	-	-	-	-	-	-	1"os/	57
Magheraculmoney	Stranadarriff	Johnston David	corn & kilns	-	34a.	-	-	-	-	gr/	-
Magheraculmoney	Stranadarriff	Johnston John	corn	-	-	-	-	-	-	v1B/	-
Aghavea	Stranfeley	-	Mill Hill (no mill)	-	-	-	-	-	-	6"os/	28
Clones	Tattinbar	Madden John	flax	-	-	-	-	-	-	gr/	-
Enniskillen	Tattinweir	-	corn kilns (2)	-	-	-	-	-	-	6"os/	17
Derryvullan	Tattygare		mill dam	-	-	-	-	-	-	6"os/	27
Boho	Tievebunnan	-	corn kiln	-	-	-	-	-	-	6"os/	20
Lurg	Tirmacspird	-	corn kiln	-	-	-	-	-	-	6"os/	2
Fermanagh	Tirwinny	-	corn kiln	-	-	-	-	-	-	6"os/	6
Clones	Tonity Bog	-	corn	-	-	-	-	-	-	6"os/	36
Clones	Tonity Bog	M`Mahon John	corn & kiln	-	23a.	-	-	-	-	gr/	-
Clones	Tonity Bog	M`Mahon John	spade	-	-	-	-	-	-	gr/	-
Enniskillen	Tonystick	- 1/2m E/ Ennisk' Br	corn	-	-	-	-	-	-	6"os/	22
Enniskillen	Tonystick :	Casamayor James	Tonystick Mill	-	-	-	Casaymor - Boyd Jno	1852	-	dd/	1852 16 66
Enniskillen	Tonystick :	Frith Richard	corn	-	-	-	-	-	-	v1B/	-
Enniskillen	Tonystick :	M`Neill Joseph	saw	-	-	-	-	-	-	gr/	-
Devenish	Tower More	-	corn kiln	-	-	-	-	-	-	6"os/	13
Fermanagh	Townland ? :	- E/ Manyburns R.	corn	-	-	-	-	-	-	6"os/	23
Aghalurcher	Tully	-	corn & kiln	-	-	-	-	-	-	6"os/	32
Aghalurcher	Tully	-	mill pond	-	-	-	-	-	-	6"os/	32
Aghalurcher	Tully	- W/ Wooden Br.	candlewick mfy	-	-	-	-	-	-	6"os/	32
Aghalurcher	Tully	- E/ Killywillin Glebe	corn mills	-	-	-	-	-	-	6"os/	27
Aghalurcher	Tully	- over 1m from W.	mill stream	-	-	-	-	-	-	6"os/	32
Aghalurcher	Tully	Enniskillen Earl of	corn	-	-	-	-	-	-	v1B/	-
Aghalurcher	Tully	Wamsley George	corn	-	-	-	-	-	-	gr/	-
Aghalurcher	Tully	Wamsley George	corn, mill pond	-	1a.	-	-	-	-	gr	-
Aghalurcher	Tully	Wamsley George	millpond	-	1a.	-	-	-	-	gr/	-
Aghalurcher	Tully North	Wiley Edward	corn & kiln	-	24a.	-	-	-	-	gr/	-
Aghalurcher	Tully North	Wiley Francis	corn	-	-	-	-	-	-	v1B/	-
Cleenish	Tullybellina	-	corn & mill race	-	-	-	-	-	-	6"os/	19
Cleenish	Tullybellina	-	corn kiln	-	-	-	-	-	-	6"os/	19.
Cleenish	Tullybellina	Collum Archibald	corn	-	24a.	-	-	-	-	gr/	-
Lurg	Tullycallrick	-	kiln	-	-	-	-	-	-	6"os/	5
Lurg	Tullycallrick	- Drumbane	Corn Mill	-	-	-	-	-	-	6"os/	5
Devenish	Tullycreevy	-	corn	-	-	-	-	-	-	6"os/	15
Devenish	Tullycreevy	-	pond & race	-	-	-	-	-	-	6"os/	15
Devenish	Tullycreevy	Dreennan widow	corn	-	-	-	-	-	-	v1B/	-
Devenish	Tullycreevy	Hazlett	corn & kiln	-	7a.	-	-	-	-	gr/	-
Devenish	Tullycreevy	Hazlett Jane	corn	-	-	-	-	-	-	gr/	-
Devenish	Tullycreevy	Johnston John :	mill	-	-	-	Johnston J - Fiddis Alex :	1729	Lse. 13 Nov.	dd/	61 434 56989
Lurg	Tullyhommon	-	corn	-	-	-	-	-	-	6"os/	4
Lurg	Tullyhommon	- 1/4m. N./ Pettigoe	corn	-	-	-	-	-	-	6"os/	4
Aghalurcher	Tullykeneye	-	corn kiln	-	-	-	-	-	-	6"os/	24
Enniskillen	Tullyweel	-	mill race & dam	-	-	-	-	-	-	6"os/	24
Fermanagh	Windmill Hill *	Campbell Robert W	distillery	37x16x11 & malt ho :	-	-	-	-	- no dimensions	v1B/	427A
Magheraboy (Bo.)	Windmill Hill * :	Cole Jno :	mill	-	-	-	Cole Jn - Clegg Francis :	1734	Lse. 9 May	dd/	82 351 58116
Magheraboy (Bo.)	Windmill Hill * :	Cole Jno :	windmill hill	-	-	-	Cole Jn - Nesbitt Alex :	-	-	dd/	90 122 63340

PARISH	TOWNLAND	MILLER	TYPE	HOUSE	Land	£Val	PROPRIETORS	Date	WHEEL etc.	Record	Ref.
Monivea	Abbert Demesne	Cavanagh Thomas	corn	-	-	-	-	-	12x2x4 destroyed :	vmb/	19
Monivea	Abbert Demesne	Cavanagh Thomas	corn & tuck	(2B) 37x19x10 & :	-	4.8.3	-	-	14x2x4 1 pr st. :	hob/	5.1047D
Monivea	Abbert Demesne	Cavanagh Thomas	tuck	-	-	-	-	-	12x2x1 1 stock & :	vmb/	19
Moniver	Abbert Demesne	Thomas Kavanagh	corn	-	57a.	21	-	-	-	gr/	-
Abbeyknockmoy	Abbey	- S side Abbert R.	corn	-	-	-	-	-	-	6"os/	58
Abbeyknockmoy	Abbey	Bell William	corn & kiln	-	8a.	30	-	-	-	gr/	-
Dunmore	Addergoolemore	-	corn	-	-	-	-	-	-	6"os/	17
Dunmore	Addergoolemore	Corcoran Augustine	corn	-	14a.	8.15	-	-	-	gr/	-
Dunmore	Addergoolemore	Corcoran Augustine	corn	-	-	-	-	-	12x2x2	vmb/	19
Dunmore	Addergoolemore	Corcoran Augustine	tuck	-	-	-	-	-	-	gr/	-
Killora	Aggard More	Donoghue	corn	- buildings still intact	-	-	-	1983	-	sv/ff	GBowie
Killora	Aggard More	Donoghue James	corn	-	-	-	-	-	13x2x8	vmb/	19
Killora	Aggard More	Donoghue James	tuck	-	-	-	-	-	13x2x8 1 stock :	vmb/	19
Killora	Aggard More	Donohoe James	corn	-	19a.	15	-	-	-	gr/	-
Killora	Aggard More	Donohoe James	corn	(no dimensions)	-	-	-	-	same as corn :	hob/	5.0989
Killora	Aggard More	Donohoe James	tuck	-	-	-	-	-	-	gr/	-
Killora	Aggard More	Donohoe James	tuck	(no dimensions)	-	-	-	-	breast 13x2x7 :	hob/	5.0989
Kilbegnet	Aghalateeve	-	malt kiln	-	-	-	-	-	-	6"os/	19
Ahascragh	Ahascaragh	Bell Samuel	corn	-	-	-	-	-	16x7x6	vmb/	19
Ahascragh	Ahascragh	Bell Samuel	corn	-	-	-	-	-	16x3x6	vmb/	19
Ahascragh	Ahascragh	Farrell	corn	- in good condition	-	-	-	1983	-	sv/ff	GBowie
Ahascragh	Ahascragh Town	Rathbourne & Hunt	corn & kiln	-	-	-	-	-	-	gr/	-
Ahascragh	Ahascragh Town	Rathbourne & Hunt	corn & kiln	68x23.6x27.6 & :	-	-	-	-	-	hob/	5.2728
Ahascragh	Ahascragh Town :	Alexander Samuel :	corn	(1B) 62x23.6x27.6 :	-	-	-	-	15.8x3.6x6 :	hob/	5.2727
Ahascragh	Ahascragh West	- near Ahascragh R.	corn & kilns	-	-	-	-	-	-	6"os/	61
Tuam	Ahglorogh	- at site of Castle	old mill	-	-	-	-	1841	-	6"os/	44
Tuam	Ahglorogh	Tierney J & Farrell P	mill	-	2.2.0	510	-	-	-	gr/	-
Ballynakill	Alleendarra	Maguire Denis	corn & kiln	-	12a.	5.15	-	-	-	gr/	-
Ballymacward	Alloonbaun	- W/ Annagh Br.	cloth	-	-	-	-	-	-	6"os/	73
Ballymacward	Alloonbaun	- W/ Annagh Br.	corn	-	-	-	-	-	-	6"os/	73
Ballynakill	Allygolla	-	corn & pond	-	-	-	-	-	-	6"os/	116
Ballynakill	Allygolla	Kelly Patrick	corn & kiln	-	13a.	5.5.0	-	-	-	gr/	-
Ahascragh	Annaghbeg	- E/ Bunnow R.	corn & kiln	-	-	-	-	-	-	6"os/	74
Ahascragh	Annaghbeg	- on isle. Bunnow R.	tuck	-	-	-	-	-	-	6"os/	74
Ahascragh	Annaghbeg	Burke Martin	corn	-	-	-	-	-	10x2x4	vmb/	19
Ahascragh	Annaghbeg	Cleary James	corm	-	-	-	-	-	-	gr/	-
Moyrus	Ard West :	- at S. end Mill Lough	horizontal	-	-	-	-	-	- worked till 1900	sv/SAq	ATLucas
Killimorbologue	Ardane East	Gaynard Peter	mill	(no dimensions)	-	-	-	1854	(no information)	hob/	5.1046
Moyrus	Ardbear	Creighton Abraham	corn	-	-	-	-	-	13x2x6	vmb/	19
Moyrus	Ardbear	Creighton Abraham	tuck	-	-	-	-	-	13x2x6 & 1 pr :	vmb/	19
Athenry	Athenry	Fleming Margaret M	corn	-	3a.	18	-	-	-	gr/	-
Athenry	Athenry Town	Browne Dominick :	mills	-	-	-	Browne D - Folkes Sir :	1831	-	dd/	887 202 587202
Athenry	Athenry Town	Burke Bartholomew	Castle Mill :	-	-	-	Irvine R - Meldon Jas D	1878	10x3x5	dd/	1878 16 38
Athenry	Athenry Town	Burke Bartholomew	corn	-	-	-	-	-	10x3x5	vmb/	19
Athenry	Athenry Town	Irvine Elizabeth	Castle Mill	-	-	-	Irvine Eliz -Taylor Saml	1898	-	dd/	1898 32 192
Athenry	Athenry Town	Irvine Robert	Castle Mill :	-	-	-	Irvine Robt - N.B.I. Co.	1877	10x3x5	dd/	1877 18 220
Athenry	Athenry Town	Martin Peter J	mill	Mill of Athenry	-	-	Martin P J - Taylor Walt	1842	-	dd/	1842 21 209
Athenry	Athenry Town	Meldon Joseph	Castle Mill	-	-	-	Meldon J - Green Wm	1897	-	dd/	1897 59 224
Athenry	Athenry Town	Nat. Building Inv. Co.	The Corn Mill :	-	-	-	Irvine Robt - N.B.I. Co.	1881	-	dd/	1881 32 284
Athenry	Athenry Town	Nat. Building Inv. Co.	Castle Mill :	-	-	-	N.B.I. Co. - Irvine Robt	1876	-	dd/	1876 12 194
Athenry	Athenry Town	Nat. Building Inv. Co.	Castle Mill :	-	-	-	N.B.I. Co. - Meldon Jas	1883	-	dd/	1883 16 220
Athenry	Athenry Town	Toole Charles	mill holding	-	-	-	Toole Chas - Perry Jas	1854	-	dd/	1854 17 134

PARISH	TOWNLAND	MILLER	TYPE	HOUSE	Land	£Val	PROPRIETORS	Date	WHEEL etc.	Record	Ref.
Athenry	Athenry Town :	Browne Denis Rt. Hon.	mills	-	-	-	Brown - Glendinning Geo:	1825	-	dd/	875 246 /7/8
Athenry	Athenry Town :	Browne Denis Rt. Hon.	mills	-	-	-	Brown D - Livesay Richd :	1825	-	dd/	875 245 581245
Galway	Athernell	Brown Domnick :	mill	-	-	-	Brown D & ord deed	1818	-	dd/	763 593 518328
Clontuskert	Attibrassil Bridge	-	mill	-	-	-	-	-	-	1"os/	107
Dunmore	Attiflynn	Concannon Francis	corn	-	33a.	16	-	-	-	gr/	-
Dunmore	Attiflynn	Concannon Francis	mill	(2B) 28x20x10 & :	-	3.8.0	-	1845	10x1.3x10.6 drives :	hob/	5.0957
Dunmore	Attiflynn	Concannon John	corn	-	-	-	-	-	10x1x10	vmb/	19
Ballymacward	Attiregan	- nr Ahascragh	mill	-	-	-	-	-	-	1"os/	107
Ballymacward	Attiregan	Rafferty Thomas	corn & kiln	-	43a.	-	-	-	-	gr/	-
Ballymacward	Attiregan (?) :	Raftery Thomas	corn & kiln	(2B) 27.6x20x12 :	-	2.12	-	-	12.10x3.3x12 40 bkts	hob/	5. 0999
Dunmore	Attyflynn	-	mill	-	-	-	-	-	-	6"os/	5
Dunmore	Attyflynn	Concannon Fran	mill	(2B) 28x20x10 & :	-	5.8	-	1845	10x1.3x10.6 drives :	hob/	5.9057
Annaghdown	Aughloggeen	-	corn	-	-	-	-	-	-	6"os/	69
Annaghdown	Aughloggeen	- imed. N. of bridge	mill	-	-	-	-	1841	-	6"os/	69
Annaghdown	Aughloggeen	- N/ Bridge, Clegg R.	corn	-	-	-	-	-	-	mmSv/	sp - Z
Annaghdown	Aughloggeen	- on Clegg R.	corn	-	-	-	-	-	- [2nd mill]	mmSv/	sp - Z
Annaghdown	Aughloggeen	Wade Patrick	corn	mill, return, kiln & offs:	-	10.11	-	-	12x4x4 2 pair st. :	hob/	5.0965
Annaghdown	Aughloggeen	Wade Patrick	corn	-	-	-	-	-	14x4x4	vmb/	19
Boyounagh	Ballinastack	McDonagh	corn	- mill bdg. still intact	-	-	-	1983	- all wooden :	sv/ff	GBowie
Kilconnell	Ballinderry	Burke James U	corn & kiln	-	-	-	-	-	-	gr/	-
Kilchrest	Ballingarry	-	corn	-	-	-	-	-	-	6"os/	105
Kilchrest	Ballingarry	Glynn Thomas	corn & kiln	-	19a.	25	-	-	-	gr/	-
Kilchrest	Ballingarry	Killeen Edward	flour	-	-	-	-	-	14x4x5	vmb/	19
Kilkonickny	Ballingarry (East)	-	corn & flour	-	-	-	-	-	-	6"os/	105
Kilkonickny	Ballingarry (East)	-	tuck	-	-	-	-	-	-	6"os/	105
Killeroran	Ballinlass	- S/ Shiven R.	flour	-	-	-	-	-	-	6"os/	47
Killeroran	Ballinlass	Daly Patrick	corn	-	8a.	35.5	-	-	-	gr/	-
Killeroran	Ballinlass	Daly Patrick	corn	-	-	-	-	-	10x3x2	vmb/	19
Killeroran	Ballinlass	Daly Patrick	tuck	-	-	-	-	-	-	gr/	-
Killoran	Ballooly	Prendergast John	corn	-	56a.	-	-	-	-	gr/	-
Killoran	Ballooly Kelly	Prendergast John	corn	-	-	-	-	-	13x2x - u` shot	vmb/	19
Ahascragh	Ballybaun	Clonbrock Lord	corn	(1A) 27.6x20x24.6 :	-	19.13	-	-	11x4.9x4.6 28 bkts.	hob/	5.0966
Ahascragh	Ballybaun	Clonbrock Lord	corn	-	-	6	-	-	14x5x6	vmb/	19
Ahascgagh	Ballybaun	Clonbtock Lord	flour, corn, kiln	- miller`s house	-	59.7	-	-	-	gr	-
Killimorbologue	Ballycahill	M`Dermot Bryan	corn	-	-	-	-	-	12x2x2	vmb/	19
Killimorbologue	Ballycahill	M`Dermot Bryan	tuck	-	-	-	-	-	11x2x2 1pr cmb	vmb/	19
Killimorbologue	Ballycahill	M`Dermot Martin	corn	-	26a.	24	-	-	-	gr/	-
Killimorbologue	Ballycahill	McDermott Brenoll	corn	(1B) 25x22x13.6 :	-	17.13	-	1845	13x3x2.1 u'shot :	hob/	5.1030
Killimorbologue	Ballycahill	McDermott Brenoll	tuck	(2B-) 24x22x13		-	-	1845	12x2x2 u'shot :	hob/	5.1030
Kilkilvery	Ballyfruit	Phew James :	corn	(2B) 30.6x23x10 :	-	3.15	-	-	14x2x3 machinery:	hob/	5.0974
Kilkilvery	Ballyfruit	Phew Patrick	corn	-	-	-	-	-	14x2x4	vmb/	19
Isertkelly	Ballygarraun	N. side/ Owenshree R.	flour & corn & :	-	-	-	-	1841	-	6"os/	52
Isertkelly	Ballygarraun	Rowland John	corn	(2B) 36x22x15 :	-	7.2.0	-	1853		hob/	5.3843
Isertkelly	Ballygarraun	Rowland John	corn	-	-	-	-	-	12x2x3	vmb/	19
Isertkelly	Ballygarraun	Rowland John	tuck	-	-	-	-	-	- not in use	vmb/	19
Isertkelly	Ballygarraun	Rowland Thomas	corn & kiln	-	15a.	14	-	-	-	gr/	-
Loughrea	Ballygasty	-	corn, kiln, pond	-	-	-	-	1841	-	6"os/	104
Loughrea	Ballygasty	- N/ Loughrea Town	corn, kiln & pond	-	-	-	-	1841	-	6"os/	105
Loughrea	Ballygasty	Nevin Michael	corn	-	-	-	-	-	-	vmb/	19
Loughrea	Ballygasty	Nevin Patrick	corn	-	69a.	43	-	-	-	gr/	-
Loughrea	Ballygasty	Nevin Patrick	tuck	-	-	-	-	-	-	gr	-
Kilmoylan	Ballyglooneen	- E/ Abbey Br.	corn	-	-	-	-	1841	-	6"os/	58

PARISH	TOWNLAND	MILLER	TYPE	HOUSE	Land	£Val	PROPRIETORS	Date	WHEEL etc.	Record	Ref.
Kilmoylan	Ballyglooneen	Morriss Patrick	corn & tuck	(2B) 17x22.6x6.6 :	-	2.7	-	-	9x1.8z4 1 pr. st. :	hob/	5.0979
Ballynakill	Ballygowan	- Ballygowan	Mill (corn)	-	-	-	-	1841	-	6"os/	125
Ballynakill	Ballygowan	Finn John	corn & kilns	-	27a.	28	-	-	-	gr/	-
Ballynakill	Ballygowan	Finn John	corn & tuck	(2C) 55.6x20x10 :	-	5.2	-	-	12x1.2 36 bkts. :	hob/	5.3834
Ballynakill	Ballygowan	St George Stephny :	mills	-	-	-	St George S - St George :	1828	-	dd/	835 158 561094
Cargin	Ballygowan	St George Stephny :	mills	-	-	-	St George S - St George :	1828	-	dd/	835 159 561094
Dun	Ballyhinch	- 1m NxW/ Cregg Lo.	tuck (in ruins)	-	-	-	-	-	-	6"os/	134
Kiltartan	Ballylee	-	tuck & corn	-	-	-	-	1841	-	6"os/	123
Kiltartan	Ballylee	Roland John	corn & tuck	-	-	5.10	-	-	-	gr/	-
Kiltartan	Ballylee	Roonan Patrick	corn	-	-	-	-	-	12x2x4	vmb/	19
Kiltartan	Ballylee	Roonan Patrick	tuck	-	-	-	-	-	12x2x4	vmb/	19
Kiltartan	Ballymantan	O`Loughlin John	corn & tuck	-	35a.	25	-	-	-	gr/	-
Kiltartan	Ballymantan	O`Loughton Murty	corn	-	-	-	-	-	12x2x4	vmb/	19
Kiltartan	Ballymantan	O`Loughton Murty	tuck	-	-	-	-	-	12x2x4	vmb/	19
Kilconierin	Ballynahivnia	- N/ Riverville Br.	flour & mill pond	-	-	-	-	-	-	6"os/	97
Kilconierin	Ballynahivnia	Armstrong Grey	flour	-	-	-	-	-	14x3x2	vmb/	19
Kilconierin	Ballynahivnia	Dunsandla Lord	corn & flour	-	161a.	95	-	-	-	gr/	-
Ballynakill	Ballynakill	-	corn & kiln	-	-	-	-	-	-	6"os/	7
Ballynakill	Ballynakill	-	old windmill	-	-	-	-	-	-	1"os/	117
Ballynakill	Ballynakill	Brennan John	corn	-	9a.	8.0.0	-	-	-	gr/	-
Ballynakill	Ballynakill	Brennan John	corn	-	-	-	-	-	11x2x10	vmb/	19
Ballynakill	Ballynakill	Drennan John	mill	-	-	-	-	-	12x1.11x12.6 :	hob/	5.0952
Killian	Ballynalahy	-	flour & pond	-	-	-	-	1841	-	6"os/	46
Killian	Ballynalahy	Wade John	corn & flour	-	-	-	-	-	13x2x10	vmb/	19
Killian	Ballynalahy	Wade John	flour	-	-	-	-	-	13x2x10 2 sets :	vmb/	19
Killian	Ballynalahy	Wade Mrs	corn	-	26a.	25	-	-	-	gr/	-
Lickmolassy	Ballyshrule	De-Swart	grain & saw	- buildings survive	-	-	- (formerly Clarke`s)	1983	- axle tree & :	sv/ff	GBowie
Omey	Barnanoraun	-	marble quarry	-	-	-	-	-	-	6"os/	36
Killannin	Barraderry	- W/ Glashnacally	corn mill ruins	-	-	-	-	-	-	6"os/	90
Athenry	Baunmore	- S/ Athenry Ch.	corn	-	-	-	-	-	-	6"os/	84
Ballynakill	Baunyknav	- S. side Duniry R.	corn & kiln	-	-	-	-	1841	-	6"os/	116
Ballynakill	Baunyknav	M`Donogh Conr.	corn & kiln	-	7a.	6.10	-	-	-	gr/	-
Ballynakill	Baunyknav	M`Donogh Conr.	tuck	-	-	-	-	-	-	gr/	-
Liskeevy	Belmont	-	mill	-	-	-	-	-	-	6"os/	15
Galway	Bleachgreen	Heffernan Mary	mill	-	-	-	Heffernan - Feeny Ptk	1827	-	dd/	831 432 558967
Omey	Boolard	-	copper mine	-	-	-	-	-	-	6"os/	22
Galway	Boyounagh Bridge	- near Gortaganny	mill	-	-	-	-	-	-	1"os/	86
Kilcroan	Bracklagh	-	corn & kiln	-	-	-	-	-	-	6"os/	2
Kilcroan	Bracklagh	- nr Ballaghaugeag Br.	corn & kiln	-	-	-	-	-	-	sv/04	Z
Kilcroan	Bracklagh	Kennedy Bryan	corn	-	12a.	9.10	-	-	-	gr/	-
Dunmore	Breancra :	-	mill	-	-	-	-	-	-	6"os/	17
Rahoon	Brownville	Rooney Alexander	brush m'factory	ho., offs., gate-lo & ld.	143a.	71	-	1856	-	gr/	a.a.lre.ie
Galway	Bullenfoule	Brown Michael Jos	mill	-	-	-	Brown M - McDonnell Fr	1827	Mort. 13 Nov.	dd/	833 114 559849
Annaghdown	Bunatober	- N. side of river	corn	- old bl1ds & ho. ok :	-	-	Simon Fury	2009	-	mmSv/	sp - Cc
Annaghdown	Bunatober	- NE/ Ballynew Vge.	mill & dam	-	-	-	-	-	-	6"os/	56
Annaghdown	Bunatober	Fury Simon	corn	(2B) 17.6x18x8.6 :	-	5.8	-	1845	11x.6x2.6 28 bkts :	hob/	5.0965
Annaghdown	Bunatober	Fury Simon	corn	-	-	-	-	-	13x1x3	vmb/	19
Ballynakill	Burroge	-	mill & kiln	-	-	-	-	-	-	6"os/	125
Killora	Caheradangan	- N. side R.	Stronfort Mill	-	-	-	-	-	-	6"os/	96
Killora	Caheradangan	Rawland William	old mill	-	10a.	8	-	-	-	gr/	-
Killora	Caheradangan	Rowlan William	corn	- (no dimensions)		3.10	-	-	14x2x3 25 floats :	hob'	5.0989
Killora	Caheradangan	Rowlan William	tuck	- (no dimensions)		-	-	-		hob'	5.0989

PARISH	TOWNLAND	MILLER	TYPE	HOUSE	Land	£Val	PROPRIETORS	Date	WHEEL etc.	Record	Ref.
Killora	Caheradangan	Rowland William	corn	-	-	-	-	-	14x2x3	vmb/	19
Kilconickny	Cahertinny	- E. of Killian Bridge :	old mill	-	-	-	-	1841	-	6"os/	97
Kilconickny	Cahertinny	Heary John	corn & tuck	-	-	-	-	-	- not at work	vmb/	19
Kilconickny	Cahertinny	Heary John	tuck	-	-	-	-	-	12x2 1 pr combs	vmb/	19
Kilcummin	Canrawer West	Hicks William	linen factory	-	2a.	10	-	-	-	gr/	-
Kilcummin	Canrawer West	Walsh Michael	corn	-	1.1.0	1.10.0	-	-	-	gr/	-
Dunmore	Cappanntranhan	Hussey Michael	mill	(2B) 34x18x5.6 :	-	4.89	-	1845	12x2.3x12.6 wood :	hob/	5.0957
Dunmore	Cappantruhann	Vesey George	corn & kiln	-	252a.	80.10	-	-	-	gr/	-
Dunmore	Cappantruhaun	-	mill	-	-	-	-	-	-	6"os/	31
Dunmore	Cappantruhaun	Henry Michael & Matt	corn	-	-	-	-	-	12x2x12	vmb/	19
Ballinakill	Carragh	Blake Ethelslane H	flax	(1A) 67x22x18 & :	-	10.3	-	1833	- 4 stocks & :	hob/	5.0961
Galway	Carriglass	Brown Domnick	mill	-	-	-	Brown Dom & Henry	1818	-	dd/	763 593 518328
Kilcummin	Carrowdulla	- E/ Buffy Lough	mill	-	-	-	-	-	-	6"os/	67
Kilcummin	Carrowdulla	Molloy Patrick	corn	-	15a.	4.5.0	-	-	-	gr/	-
Galway	Carrownareeva *	-	corn kiln	-	-	-	-	-	-	6"os/	46
Athenry	Carrowntober E.	-	corn	-	-	-	-	-	-	6"os/	84
Kilcooly	Carrowroe	-	corn	-	-	-	-	1851	-	6"os/	105
Kilcooly	Carrowroe	Broder Michael	corn	-	-	-	-	-	11x2x5	vmb/	19
Kilcooly	Carrowroe	Daly Arthur	mill & kiln	-	93a.	45	-	-	-	gr/	-
Galway	Castlecoote :	- on R. Suck	mill	-	-	-	-	-	-	1"os/	-
Killower	Castlehacket	- N/ Castle	bleach green	-	-	-	-	-	-	6"os/	41
Killererin	Castlemoyle	- E. side Grange R.	mill (in ruins)	-	-	-	-	-	-	6"os/	44
Killererin	Castlemoyle	- E. side Grange R.	mill (in ruins)	-	-	-	-	-	-	6"os/	44
Killererin	Castlemoyle	Raferty	corn	- deteriorating	-	-	-	1983	- still intact	sv/ff	GBowie
Templetogher	Castletogher	-	corn kiln	-	-	-	-	-	-	6"os/	6
Abbeygoormacai	Castletown	-	corn & mill pond	-	-	-	-	-	-	6"os/	106
Abbeygoormacai	Castletown	Coouchan Michael	tuck	(2B) 11x15.6x6.6 & :	-	8/3d	-	1845	undershot wood :	hob/	5.1051
Galway	Clanbruckley	Corry Thomas :	mills	-	-	-	Corry T - Hartland Thos :	1819	Mort. 5 Aug.	dd/	802 474 541609
Kilcummin	Claremount	-	copper mine	-	-	-	-	-	-	6"os/	54
Kilcummin	Claremount	- S/ Owenree R.	corn	-	-	-	-	-	-	6"os/	54
Kilcummin	Claremount	- N side Owenree R.	mill ruin	-	-	-	-	-	-	6"os/	54
Kilcummin	Claremount	Martin Richard	corn	-	16a.	11.10	-	-	-	gr/	-
Abbeyknockmoy	Clashard	-	flour	-	-	-	-	-	-	6"os/	58
Abbeyknockmoy	Clashard	- NE/ Moyne cross	flour	-	-	-	-	-	-	6"os/	58
Omey	Clifden Town	- on R. Owenglin	mill	-	-	-	-	-	-	6"os/	35
Omey	Clifden Town	- S/ Town	brewery ruins	-	-	-	-	-	-	6"os/	35
Omey	Clifden Town	Creighton Abraham	old brewery	(1B) 64x20 10 :	-	-	-	-	-	hob/	5.2743
Omey	Clifden Town	Eyre Thomas	tuck	-	0.1.5	-	-	-	-	gr/	-
Clonkeen	Clogh	Coen Michael	corn	-	29a.	30	-	-	-	gr/	-
Kiltullagh	Clogharevaun	Coghlan Peter	corn	-	21a.	12.15	-	-	-	gr/	-
Kiltullagh	Clogharevaun	W. side Dooeyertha R.	corn & pond	-	-	-	-	1841	-	6"os/	97
Killererin	Clogherboy	Wade Francis	corn	-	-	8/-	-	-	-	gr/	-
Ahascragh	Clonbrock	Clonbrock Lord	brewery	(1A) 61x20x16.6 :	-	300	-	1845	-	hob/	5.1011
Dunmore	Cloneen	Mannion John	corn	-	10a.	8.5.0	-	-	-	gr/	-
Dunmore	Cloneen	Mannion John	tuck	-	-	-	-	-	-	gr/	-
Galway	Clonmore	Matt Donoghoe	corn	-	-	-	-	-	12x6x3	vmb/	19
Kilbeacanty	Cloon	- W. side Annagh R. :	corn & mill race	-	2.0.0	7.5.0	-	-	-	gr/	-
Kilbeacanty	Cloon	Heffernan Michael	corn	-	-	-	-	-	13x3x13	vmb/	19
Kilbeacanty	Cloon	Heffernan Michael	tuck	-	-	-	-	-	13x2x -	vmb/	19
Kilbeacanty	Cloon	Hynes Patrick	corn & tuck	-	2.0.0	7.5.0	-	-	-	gr/	-
Killcoran	Cloonabrica	- on Shiven R	mill	-	-	-	-	-	-	1"os/	97
Killcoran	Cloonabrica	Kelly Dennis H	grist	-	-	-	-	-	11x3x2	vmb/	19

PARISH	TOWNLAND	MILLER	TYPE	HOUSE	Land	£Val	PROPRIETORS	Date	WHEEL etc.	Record	Ref.
Galway	Cloonahaha *	- at Poldiagh Vge.	corn	-	-	-	-	-	-	6"os/	128
Galway	Cloonarragh :	-	mill	-	-	-	-	-	-	1"os/	-
Fohanagh	Cloonatleva	- NW Callow Lough	corn & pond	-	-	-	-	-	-	6"os/	73
Fohanagh	Cloonatleva	Connor Patrick	corn	-	-	-	-	-	12x2x5	vmb/	19
Fohanagh	Cloonatleva	Tyrell James	corn	-	49a.	41	-	-	-	gr/	-
Fohanagh	Cloonatleva Lower	Connor Patrick	mill	(1A) 30x20.6x11.6 :	-	7.16	-	-	10x2x6 drives :	hob/	5.1001
Killian	Cloonavihony	Wade Mrs	corn kiln	-	6a.	3.15	-	-	-	gr/	-
Killmorbologue	Clooncconabeg :	-	corn	-	-	-	-	-	-	6"os/	117
Killererin	Clooncconra	- S. side Gange R.	corn & kiln	-	-	-	-	1841	-	6"os/	39
Killererin	Cloondahampher	- E. of bridge	mill	-	-	-	-	1841	-	6"os/	39
Dunmore	Cloondergan	Patton Owen	corn & kiln	-	9a.	2.15	-	-	-	gr/	-
Dunmore	Clooneen	-	corn	-	-	-	-	-	-	6"os/	17
Dunmore	Clooneen	Mannion John	corn	-	-	-	-	-	14x2x3	vmb/	19
Dunmore	Clooneen	Mannion John	tuck	-	-	-	-	-	12x1x4	vmb/	19
Beagh	Cloonhana	McColgan Susan	flour	-	-	-	-	-	15x3x3	vmb/	19
Kilkeeran	Cloonkeen Eighter	- W/ Cloonkeen Br.	corn & tuck	-	-	-	-	-	-	6"os/	31
Kilkeeran	Cloonkeen Eighter	Kelly Bryan	corn	-	-	-	-	-	13x1x4	vmb/	19
Kilkeeran	Cloonkeen Eighter	Kelly Bryan	tuck	-	-	-	-	-	13x1x4	vmb/	19
Killoran	Cloonlaghan Geo	Burrell Charles W G	corn & kiln	-	55a.	-	-	-	-	gr/	-
Killoran	Cloonlaghan Geo	Horan Michael	corn	-	-	-	-	-	11x1x3 u`shot	vmb/	19
Killoran	Cloonlahan	-	corn kiln & dam	-	-	-	-	-	-	6"os/	99
Killoran	Cloonmain	-	corn & mill race	-	-	-	-	-	-	6"os/	98
Killoran	Cloonmain	Jackson John	corn	-	-	-	-	-	12x2x7 mc/y :	vmb/	19
Tuam	Cloonmore	- SE/ Claretuam Br.	corn	-	-	-	-	-	-	6"os/	43
Killosolan	Cloonpee	- NE/ Clonbrook Br.	corn	-	-	-	-	-	-	6"os/	60
Killosolan	Cloonpee	M`Guire Thomas	corn	-	17a.	19.7	-	-	-	gr/	-
Killosolan	Cloonpee	M`Guire Thomas	tuck	-	-	-	-	-	-	gr/	-
Killosolan	Cloonpee	Maguire Thomas	corn	-	-	-	-	-	13x3x5	vmb/	19
Killosolan	Cloonpee	Maguire Thomas	tuck	-	-	-	-	-	12x2x5 1 stock & :	vmb/	19
Ballynakill	Cloonreleagh E.	-	corn & mill pond	-	-	-	-	-	-	6"os/	46
Ballykakill	Cloonreleagh E.	Donnelan John	corn	-	-	-	-	-	12x2x3	vmb/	19
Galway	Clough House	O`Brien	corn	- used as cow ho.	-	-	-	1983	- all m/cy gone	sv/ff	GBowie
Balykakill	Clougharevaun	Coghlan Peter	corn	-	-	-	-	-	10x1x4	vmb/	19
Balykakill	Clougharevaun	Coghlan Peter	tuck	-	-	-	-	-	10x1x4	vmb/	19
Balykakill	Clougharevaun	W. side Dooeyertha R.	tuck	-	-	-	-	-	10x1x4	vmb/	19
Galway	Clunbrucky	Richardson Wm H :	mills	-	-	-	Richardson & ors deed	1828	-	dd/	835 556 561491
Galway	Clunbrucky	Richardson Wm Henry :	mills	-	-	-	Richardson - Mahon :	1828	Mort (Asgt.) 1 May	dd/	835 557 501492
Galway	Clunbrucky	Weir Christopher :	mills	-	-	-	Weir - Richardson Jas :	1828	-	dd/	835 558 561493
Dunmore	Conagher	-	corn	-	-	-	-	-	-	6"os/	4
Dunmore	Conagher	- on Dalgan R.	mill & kiln	-	-	-	-	-	-	6"os/	4
Dunmore	Conagher	Farrell John	tuck	-	-	-	-	-	12x3x2	vmb/	19
Dunmore	Conagher	Kirwan	mills	-	-	-	Kirwan & ors - Kirwan	1819	-	dd/	772 25 523160
Dunmore	Conagher	Quin Michael	corn	-	-	-	-	-	12x3x2	vmb/	19
Cong	Cong	Fair William :	mill	-	-	-	Fair W - Fair James Jun :	1821	-	dd/	763 142 517877
Cong	Cong	Fair William :	mill	-	-	-	Fair - O`Malley Michael :	1821	(Mort.)	dd/	763 170 517905
Cong	Cong North	- NW corner/ Island	mill	-	-	-	-	1841	-	6"os/	38
Aughrim	Coololla	Stanford Robert	corn	(1B) 48x22.6x16 :	-	11.11	-	-	9x2.4x9.6 38 bkts. :	hob/	5.0998
Aughrim	Coololla	Stanford Robert	corn	-	-	-	-	-	-	vmb/	19
Killererin	Coolrevagh	- W. side Grange R.	corn	-	-	-	-	-	-	6"os/	44
Killererin	Coolrevagh	Farrell James	corn	-	-	-	-	-	12x2x5	vmb/	19
Killererin	Coolrevagh	Farrell James	corn & tuck	(1B) 27x19.6x18 : t	-	-	-	1846	breast 12x1.9x3.6 :	hob/	5.0976
Killererin	Coolrevagh	Farrell James	tuck	-	-	-	-	-	-	vmb/	19

PARISH	TOWNLAND	MILLER	TYPE	HOUSE	Land	£Val	PROPRIETORS	Date	WHEEL etc.	Record	Ref.
Killererin	Coolrevagh	Munroe John :	corn & tuck	(1B) 27x19.6x12 : t	-	-	-	1853	11x2x5.6 24 bkts.:	hob/	5.0976
Ballynakill	Coos	- W side rd. ab. jctn.	new mill	-	-	-	-	-	-	6"os/	131
Ballynakill	Coos North	- W side rd. ab. jctn.	tuck	-	-	-	-	-	-	6"os/	131
Galway	Coranroe	-	corn	- mill in ruins	-	-	-	1983	-	sv/ff	GBowie
Rahoon	Corcullen	Rooney Alexander	sawing	-	-	4.0.0	-	-	-	gr/	-
Monivea	Cormacuagh West	-	corn	-	-	-	-	-	-	6"os/	72
Monivea	Cormacuagh West	Grady John & Maggie	corn & kiln	(2B) 25x20x12 & :	-	-	-	-	12X3X9 30 bkts :	hob/	5.1047D
Monivea	Cormacuagh West	Grady John & Maggie	old tuck mill	- [no dims.]	-	-	-	-	v. little work done	hob/	5.1047D
Galway	Cornabricka	- S/ Shiven R.	corn & tuck	-	-	-	-	-	-	6"os/	46
Killererin	Cornacartan	-	corn & kiln	-	-	-	-	-	-	6"os/	44
Killererin	Cornacartan	Mang Fran & Denis	corn	-	-	-	-	-	13x2x3	vmb/	19
Killererin	Cornacartan	Morgan Francis	corn	-	75a.	10	-	-	-	gr/	-
Loughrea	Cosmona	-	corn & kiln	-	-	-	-	1841	-	6"os/	105
Loughrea	Cosmona	- N. Loughrea Town	white mill	-	-	-	-	1841	-	6"os/	105
Loughrea	Cosmona	Fahy Laurence	corn	-	-	-	-	-	14x3x2	vmb/	19
Loughrea	Cosmona	Plunkett Walter	corn & kiln	-	-	9.0.0	-	-	-	gr/	-
Galway	Cregg	Henn William Esq :	mills	-	-	-	Henn W - Joyce Walter :	1826	-	dd/	814 79 548414
Galway	Cregg	Kirwan Patrick :	mills	-	-	-	Kirwan P - Kirwan	1819	-	dd/	772 25 523160
Galway	Cregg	Wade	flour	- converted recently :	-	-	-	1983	-	sv/ff	GBowie
Galway	Cregg (6)	Barnwall Thomas :	mill & holding	-	-	-	Barnwall - Joyce Walter :	1825	-	dd/	812 471 547606
Cong	Creggaree	- N. side Polltofil L.	mill	-	-	-	-	-	-	6"os/	27
Cong	Creggaree	- S. side Polltofil L.	mill	-	-	-	-	-	-	6"os/	27
Cong	Creggaree	Hayes John	flour	-	-	-	-	-	15x5x3	vmb/	19
Cong	Creggaree	Malia Charles	flour	(1B) 88x25x37.6 :	-	26.11	-	1854	mill enlarged lately :	hob/	5.1046
Cong	Creggaree	Malley Charles	mill, stores	-	1a.	80	-	-	-	gr/	-
Killora	Creggaun	- E/ Craughwell Br.	mill	-	-	-	-	-	-	6"os/	96
Killora	Creggaun	- (no name)	corn	- (no dimensions)	-	-	-	-	u'shot 13x2.6x3 :	hob/	5.0989
Killora	Creggaun	- (no name)	tuck	- (no dimensions)	-	-	-	-	u'shot 12x2.4x3 :	hob/	5.0989
Killora	Creggaun	Dermody Bart	tuck	-	-	-	-	-	12x1x3	vmb/	19
Killora	Creggaun (5)	Dermody Bart	corn	-	-	-	-	-	13x2x1	vmb/	19
Kilbegnet	Creggauns	-	malt kiln	-	-	-	-	-	-	6"os/	20
Ballynakill	Culfin	-	corn kiln	-	-	-	-	-	-	6"os/	10
Kilbegnet	Curraghbog	- at Mill Park, Millford	corn mills	-	-	-	-	-	-	6"os/	19
Kilbegnet	Curraghbog	- imed. N/ Millpark	corn mills	-	-	-	-	1841	-	6"os/	19
Kilbegnet	Curraghbog	Kelly John	corn	-	61a.	35.5	-	-	-	gr/	-
Kilbegnet	Curraghbog	Kelly John	corn	-	-	-	-	-	15x2x10	vmb/	19
Kilbegnet	Curraghbog	Kelly John	mill	mill, kiln & house	-	5.13	-	1853	15.6x2.5x12.6 :	hob/	5.0958
Tuam	Curraghcreen	- 3/4 m. SE of Tuam	old mill	-	-	-	-	1841	-	6"os/	29
Tuam	Curraghcreen	Kelly Patrick	corn & kiln	workmen`s hos.	36a.	27	-	-	-	gr/	-
Addergoole	Dalgin	Quinn	corn & tuck	- mill building good :	-	-	-	1983	12ft.x 4.6 u`shot :	sv/ff	GBowie
Addergoole	Dalgin Bridge	- on Dalgin R.	corn	-	-	-	-	-	-	1"os/	86
Kilclounny	Deerpark	Horsman James E	corn & kiln	-	5a.	-	-	-	-	gr/	-
Kilclounny	Deerpark	Smith John	corn	-	-	-	-	-	10x2x4	vmb/	19
Kiltormer	Derreen	-	corn & kiln	-	-	-	-	1841	-	6"os/	99
Kiltormer	Derreen	Kenny Francis	corn	-	-	-	-	-	11x2x7 breast :	vmb/	19
Kilcummin	Derreennagucfoor	- S. side of Folure R.	mill (in ruins)	-	-	-	-	1841	-	6"os/	39
Meelick	Derry	-	brewery (ruins)	-	-	-	-	1841	-	6"os/	108
Meelick	Derry	-	corn & kiln	-	-	-	-	-	-	6"os/	108
Meelick	Derry	Larkin Patrick	corn	-	-	-	-	-	12x2x7 breast	vmb/	19
Ballynakill	Derrycrag	- S./ Woodford R.	corn kiln	-	-	-	-	-	-	6"os/	132
Ballynakill	Derrygarrif	- Derrygoolin	Bleach Mill (ruins	-	-	-	-	-	-	6"os/	136
Kilkerrin	Derrynabrin	-	mill	-	-	-	-	-	-	1"os/	97

PARISH	TOWNLAND	MILLER	TYPE	HOUSE	Land	£Val	PROPRIETORS	Date	WHEEL etc.	Record	Ref.
Kilkerrin	Derrynabrin	Noone Martin	corn	-	-	3.0.0	-	-	-	gr/	-
Kilkerrin	Derrynabrin	Noone Martin	corn	-	-	-	-	-	-	gr/	-
Kilkerrin	Derrynabrin	Noone Martin	corn	(2A) 30x17x8	-	1.0.0	-	1853	10x1.6x8 2 pr. st. :	hob/	5.1047C
Tynagh	Drimna West :	-	mills	-	-	-	-	-	-	6"os/	126
Tuam	Drumaskin	- SW/ bridge	mill & pond	-	-	-	-	1841	-	6"os/	30.
Tuam	Drumaskin	Hosty John	corn	-	3a.	2.10	-	-	-	gr/	-
Dunmore	Drumbane	Corcoran John	corn	- deteriorating	-	-	-	1983	12ft. x 4ft. wood :	sv/ff	GBowie
Dunmore	Drumbane	Corcoran Michael	mill & kilns	-	7a.	-	-	-	-	gr/	-
Annaghdown	Drumgriffin	- Cregg Mill	flour	- fine preservation	-	-	D. & Z. Driscoll	2009	-	ssSv/	sp - Cr
Annaghdown	Drumgriffin	- S/ Cregg R. bridge	corn	-	-	-	-	-	-	6"os/	69
Annaghdown	Drumgriffin	Blake Frances :	flour	ho., offs., barns, etc.	-	-	Blake F - Brenan Fran :	1820	-	dd/	786 481 532016
Annaghdown	Drumgriffin	Wade Patrick	flour	-	11a.	26.15	-	-	-	gr/	-
Annaghdown	Drumgriffin	Wade Patrick	flour	-	11a.	-	-	-	-	gr/	-
Annaghdown	Drumgriffin	Wade Patrick	flour	(1B) 66x26x37 & :	-	23.19	-	-	2 wheels, 11x2.6x4 :	hob/	5.0065
Annaghdown	Drumgriffin	Wade Patrick	flour	-	-	-	-	-	13x4x4	vmb/	19
Dunmore	Drumleane	Corcoran Michael	corn	-	-	-	-	-	12x1x2	vmb/	19
Galway	Duckanelly	O`Donnell Barn & W.	mills	-	-	-	O`Donnell - Towers Thos :	1728	(Trust)	dd/	835 267 561202
Galway	Duckanelly	O`Donnell Sir Hugh :	mills	-	-	-	O`Donnell ag`ment	1828	-	dd/	835 279 561214
Duniry	Duniry	- W. side small R.	corn & kiln	-	-	-	-	1841	-	6"os/	116
Duniry	Duniry	Derwin Michael	mill	-	26a.	25.10	-	-	-	gr/	-
Dunmore	Dunmore	- on Sinking R	corn	-	-	-	-	-	-	1"os/	86
Drumatemple	Durrow	Thomas N Baggot	corn	-	-	-	-	-	16x2x2	vmb/	19
Drumatemple	Durrow	Thomas N Baggot	flour	-	-	-	-	-	16x5x2 14x3x2 :	vmb/	19
Drumtemple	Durrow	Treans Patrick	mill & additions	mill, wing & offices (4)	-	12.12	-	-	br. floats 4ft. 10ins. :	hob/	5.0954
Drumtemple	Durrow	Treans Patrick	mill & kilns	-	-	25.10	-	-	-	gr/	-
Drumtemple	Durrow :	-	mill & kiln	-	-	-	-	-	-	6"os/	2
Drumtemple	Durrow :	-	corn & kiln	-	-	-	-	-	-	sv/04	Z
Drumtemple	Durrow :	-	flour	-	-	-	-	-	-	6"os/	16
Killogilleen	Eden Hill	-	corn	-	-	-	-	-	-	6"os/	104
Killogilleen	Eden Hill	Darcy James	flour	(1B) 35x14x6x19 & :	-	8.17	-	1853	-	hob/	5.1040
Killogilleen	Eden Hill	M`Tighe John	corn	-	74a.	39	-	-	-	gr/	-
Clonfert	Esker	-	old corn mill	-	-	-	-	-	-	6"os/	109
Clonfert	Esker	- N. of Esker Br.	brick kilns (2)	-	-	-	-	-	-	6"os/	109
Ballyara	Esker Roe	Staunton Peter	corn	-	-	-	-	-	12x2x5	vmb/	19
Ballyara	Esker Roe	Staunton Peter	tuck	-	-	-	-	-	12x2x5	vmb/	19
Killoscobe	Eskerroe	M`Guire Luke	corn	-	24a.	16	-	-	-	gr/	-
Kilchreest	Eskershanore	-	corn & mill race	-	-	-	-	-	-	6"os/	104
Kilchreest	Eskershanore	-	flour	-	-	-	-	-	-	6"os/	104
Lickmolassy	Fairy Hill	- at Portumna :	corn store	-	-	-	-	-	-	6"os/	127
Fahy	Feaghmore	-	mill in ruins	-	-	-	-	-	-	6"os/	108
Kilkerrin	Fiddaun	Shaughnessy John	corn & tuck	-	4a.	12	-	-	-	gr/	-
Kilkerrin	Fiddaun	Shaughnessy John	corn & tuck	-	4a.	-	-	-	-	gr/	-
Kilkerrin	Fiddaun	Shaughnessy William	corn	-	-	-	-	-	12x2x10	vmb/	19
Kilkerrin	Fiddaun	Shaughnessy William	tuck	-	-	-	-	-	12x2x11 1 stock & :	vmb/	19
Ross	Finny	Philliban John	corn	-	-	10/-	-	-	-	gr/	-
Clontuskert	Fristaun	Sellers Simon	corn	-	-	-	-	-	9x1x10	vmb/	19
St Nicholas	Galway Liberties	Costello James :	Eyres Mills	-	-	-	Costello J - Ryan James :	1824	-	dd/	800 56 539991
St Nicholas	Galway Liberties	Eyre Robert Hedges :	Eyres Mills	-	-	-	Eyre R - Bermingham Jn :	1822	Lse. 20 May	dd/	791 153 534688
Rahoon	Galway T`nsparks	Blake James	corn	-	-	-	-	-	14x2x4	vmb/	19
St Nicholas	Galway T`nsparks	Gunning J. & J. & Co.	bark	(1C) 24.6x32x12.6 :	-	5.0.4	-	-	14x3x1.6 1HP :	hob	5.2749
Rahoon	Galway T`nsparks	M`Laughlin Lo`lan	mill	-	-	-	-	-	-	gr/	-
St Nicholas	Galway Town	-	flour	demolished & replaced :	w	-	-	-	-	phWH/	Cr

PARISH	TOWNLAND	MILLER	TYPE	HOUSE	Land	£Val	PROPRIETORS	Date	WHEEL etc.	Record	Ref.
St Nicholas	Galway Town	- at Bowling Gn	tuck	later Gunning Jap Works		-	-	-	-	phWH/	Z
St Nicholas	Galway Town	- at City Centre	distillery	demolished - replaced :		-	-	-	-	phWH/	Cc
St Nicholas	Galway Town	- Mangan`s Mill	corn	at West Br. converted :		-	-	-	-	phWH/	Cr
St Nicholas	Galway Town	- on Eglinton Canal	distillery	outer walls only stand		-	-	-	-	phWH/	R
St Nicholas	Galway Town	- The Bridge Mill	corn	restored as restaurant		-	-	-	-	phWH/	Cc
St Nicholas	Galway Town	- The Little Corn Mill	corn	at West Br., demolished		-	-	-	-	phWH/	Z
St Nicholas	Galway Town	(vac)/ Persse Burton	flour	- (Nun`s Island)	-	120	-	-	-	gr/	-
St Nicholas	Galway Town	(vac.) /Lady C Eyre	provs. fcty	- (Long Walkl)	-	-	-	1855	-	gr/	-
St Nicholas	Galway Town	BlakeThomas	West Br. Mill	-	-	-	Blake T - Smith James	1832	-	dd/	1832 6 231
St Nicholas	Galway Town	Burke Ed. Cussen	corn	- (Newt`nsmith)	-	-	-	1855	-	gr/	-
Oranmore	Galway Town	Burke Edward	distillery	- (Quay St)	-	-	-	-	-	gr/	-
St Marys	Galway Town	Burke Josephine	old tuck mill plot				Burke J - Kearns Patk	1900		dd/	1900 80 219
Rahoon	Galway Town	Campbell & Miller	flour	- (Mill St)	-	-	-	-	-	gr/	-
St Nicholas	Galway Town	Eyre Robert Hedges :	flour	-	-	-	Eyre Robert - Marshall :	1821	-	dd/	777 428 526563
St Nicholas	Galway Town	Eyre Robert Hedges :	flour	-	-	-	Eyre Robert - Marshall :	1821	-	dd/	777 429 526564
St Nicholas	Galway Town	Fitzgerald Gerald	brewery	- (Nun`s Island)	-	52	-	-	-	gr/	-
St Nicholas	Galway Town	Fitzgerald Gerald	malt store	- (Nun`s Island)	-	20	-	-	-	gr/	-
St Nicholas	Galway Town	Flatley Cath	soap factory	- (Abbeygate St)	-	-	-	-	-	gr/	-
St Nicholas	Galway Town	Franklin Walter & Bros.	marble	- (Nun`s Island)	0.1.30	60	-	-	-	gr/	-
Oranmore	Galway Town	Griffin Michael	foundry	- (Cross St)	-	-	-	-	-	gr/	-
St Nicholas	Galway Town	Guiness Benjamin	corn mill & :	-	-	-	Guiness - St Laurence :	1881	-	dd/	1881 38 1
St Nicholas	Galway Town	Gunning John	flour & corn	- (Wood Quay) :	-	-	-	-	-	gr/	-
St Nicholas	Galway Town	Gunning John	tuck	- (Bowling Grn)	-	-	-	-	-	gr/	-
St Nicholas	Galway Town	Gunning John.	flour (unfin.)	- (Bowling Grn)	-	-	-	-	-	gr/	-
Rahoon	Galway Town	Hughes Maria	flour	- (Mill St)	-	-	-	-	-	gr/	-
St Nicholas	Galway Town	Incumbant Est. Coms.	mill	-	-	-	Inc Est. - Guiness Benj	1852	-	dd/	1852 28 175
St Nicholas	Galway Town	Ireland Arthur	brewery	- (Mill St) :	-	-	-	-	-	gr/	-
St Nicholas	Galway Town	Joyes Patrick	old distillery	-	-	-	Joyes Patk - Atwood :	1832	Mort. 10 Nov.	dd/	889 253 588253
Oranmore	Galway Town	Kearney Matthew	corn	- (Martin`s Lane)	-	-	-	-	-	gr/	-
St Nicholas	Galway Town	Landed Estate Court	flour mill & :	-	-	-	L.E. Ct. - P. Wks. Comm.	1877	-	dd/	1877 33 28
St Nicholas	Galway Town	Lynch Mark	Regans Mill	-	-	-	Lynch Mark	1835	-	dd/	1835 16 209
Rahoon	Galway Town	M`Loone Anthony	brewery	- (New Road W.)	-	-	-	-	-	gr/	-
St Nicholas	Galway Town	Mangan Locke S	flour	- (Nun`s Island)	-	96	-	-	-	gr/	-
St Nicholas	Galway Town	Mangan Locke S	flour (2) :	- (Lr Domnick St.)	-	56	-	-	-	gr/	-
St Nicholas	Galway Town	Mangan Locke S	flour & corn	- (Wood Quay) :	-	-	-	-	-	gr/	-
Galway	Galway Town	Marshall Abraham :	flour	-	-	-	Marshall - Costello Jas :	1822	-	dd/	776 286 252821
St Nicholas	Galway Town	Martin Abraham :	Regans Mill	-	-	-	Martin & ors - Joyce Jas :	1822	-	dd/	781 137 528672
St Nicholas	Galway Town	Martyn James	flour	- (Lr Domnick St.)	-	-	-	-	-	gr/	-
St Nicholas	Galway Town	Martyn James	flour	- (Lr Domnick St.)	-	25	-	-	-	gr/	-
St Nicholas	Galway Town	Martyn Jane	Eyres Mills	-	-	-	Martyn J - Guiness Benj	1898	-	dd/	1898 28 190
St Nicholas	Galway Town	McDonnell Mary J	mill site	-	-	-	McDonnell - Guiness Bnj	1897	-	dd/	1897 77 232
St Nicholas	Galway Town	Morris John	soap fcty	- (Shop St.)	-	-	-	1855	-	gr/	-
St Nicholas	Galway Town	Nolan James :	flour mill :	-	-	-	Nolan J - Gunning James :	1825	-	dd/	808 312 545047
St Nicholas	Galway Town	O`Hara John	Eyres Mills	-	-	-	O`Hara J - Costello Wm	1837	-	dd/	1837 20 191
Oranmore	Galway Town	O`Malley Martin	foundry	- (Merchants Rd.)	-	-	-	-	-	gr/	-
St Nicholas	Galway Town	Oliver John	flour	- (Newt`nsmith)	-	-	-	1855	-	gr/	-
St Nicholas	Galway Town	Regan Ann	flour	- (Nun`s Island)	-	100	-	-	-	gr/	-
St Nicholas	Galway Town	Regan Michael	mill	- (Nun`s Island)	-	-	Regan - Cottingham Geo	1846	-	dd/	1846 11 269
St Nicholas	Galway Town	Rogan William	mill & prems	-	-	-	Rogan Wm - Burke Jas	1837	-	dd/	1837 22 159
St Nicholas	Galway Town	Rogan William	mills & prems.	-	-	-	Rogan William	1837	-	dd/	1837 22 159
St Nicholas	Galway Town	Rush Ambrose	corn	- (Nun`s Island)	-	78	-	-	-	gr/	-
St Nicholas	Galway Town	Rush Ambrose & :	corn	- (Nun`s Island)	-	56	-	-	-	gr/	-

PARISH	TOWNLAND		MILLER	TYPE	HOUSE	Land	£Val	PROPRIETORS	Date	WHEEL etc.	Record	Ref.
Oranmore	Galway Town		Rush Ambrose & :	flour	- (Martin`s Lane)	-	-	-	-	-	gr/	-
St Nicholas	Galway Town		Rush Ambrose & :	flour	- (Lr Domnick St)	-	65	-	-	-	gr/	-
Oranmore	Galway Town		Somerville Richd N	chemical wks	- (Long Walkl)	-	-	-	-	-	gr/	-
St Nicholas	Galway Town		Usher Michael	soap factory	- (Bowling Grn)	-	-	-	-	-	gr/	-
St Nicholas	Galway Town		Wade Edward & :	flour	- (Wood Quay)	-	-	-	-	-	gr/	-
St Nicholas	Galway Town	:	Flynn James & Co	corn stores	& yard	-	30	-	1856	-	gr/	a.a.Ire.ie
St Nicholas	Galway Town	:	Higgins Terence	store, kiln & yard	-	-	5	-	1856	-	gr/	a.a.Ire.ie
St Nicholas	Galway Town	:	Overend John	corn store	& yard	-	31	-	1856	-	gr/	a.a.Ire.ie
St Nicholas	Galway Town	:	Beard Samuel	coach factory	house, offices & yard	-	33	-	1856	-	gr/	a.a.Ire.ie
St Nicholas	Galway Town	:	Flatley Catherine	soap factory	office & yard	-	10	-	1856	-	gr/	a.a.Ire.ie
St Nicholas	Galway Town	:	Stokes Michael	coach factory	house, offices & yard	-	14	-	1856	-	gr/	a.a.Ire.ie
St Nicholas	Galway Town	:	Griffin Michael	foundry	house & offs. & yard	-	25	-	1856	-	gr/	a.a.Ire.ie
St Nicholas	Galway Town	:	Persse Burton	corn store	& yard	-	36	-	1856	-	gr/	a.a.Ire.ie
St Nicholas	Galway Town	:	Persse Thomas	corn store	& yard	-	45	-	1856	-	gr/	a.a.Ire.ie
St Nicholas	Galway Town	:	Lynch Michael M	corn stores	& yard	-	50	-	1856	-	gr/	a.a.Ire.ie
St Nicholas	Galway Town	:	Stephens James	foundry	offices & yard	-	32	-	1856	-	gr/	a.a.Ire.ie
St Nicholas	Galway Town	:	Grealy John	corn store	& yard	-	30	-	1856	-	gr/	a.a.Ire.ie
St Nicholas	Galway Town	:	Rush Ambrose & :	corn stores	& yard	-	43	-	1856	-	gr/	a.a.Ire.ie
St Nicholas	Galway Town	:	Rush Ambrose & :	corn store	& yard	-	47	-	1856	-	gr/	a.a.Ire.ie
St Nicholas	Galway Town	:	Morris John	soap factory	& yard (in rere)	-	12	-	1856	-	gr/	a.a.Ire.ie
St Nicholas	Galway Town	:	Eyre Catherine Lady	provisions factory	& yard	-	23	-	1856	-	gr/	a.a.Ire.ie
St Mary's	Galway Town	:	Connolly Bartholomew	mills				Burke J - Kearns Patk	1900		dd/	1902 2 224
St Nicholas	Galway Town	:	Mangan Locke S	flour	-	-	56	-	1856	-	gr/	a.a.Ire.ie
St Nicholas	Galway Town	:	Martyn james	flour			25	-	1856	-	gr/	a.a.Ire.ie
St Nicholas	Galway Town	:	Rush Ambrose	flour	offices & yard	-	120	-	1856	-	gr/	a.a.Ire.ie
St Nicholas	Galway Town	:	Pearse Burton	flour	offices & yard	-	120	-	1856	-	gr/	a.a.Ire.ie
St Nicholas	Galway Town	:	Ashworth Thos & Edm	salmon fishery	fishery, ho., offs. & yd.	-	120	-	1856	-	gr/	a.a.Ire.ie
St Nicholas	Galway Town	:	Franklin Walter & Bros	marble	ho, offs., yard & gdn	0.1.30	60	-	1856	-	gr/	a.a.Ire.ie
St Nicholas	Galway Town	:	Fitzgerald Gerald	malt stores	offices & yard	-	20	-	1856	-	gr/	a.a.Ire.ie
St Nicholas	Galway Town	:	Fitzgerald Gerald	brewery	offices & yard	-	52	-	1856	-	gr/	a.a.Ire.ie
St Nicholas	Galway Town	:	Mangan Locke S	flour	& yard	-	66	-	1856	-	gr/	a.a.Ire.ie
St Nicholas	Galway Town	:	Concanon Matthew	corn store	-	-	24	-	1856	-	gr/	a.a.Ire.ie
St Nicholas	Galway Town	:	Rush Ambrose	corn store	offices & yard	-	120	-	1856	-	gr/	a.a.Ire.ie
St Nicholas	Galway Town	:	Fitzgerald Francis	corn store	& yard	-	15	-	1856	-	gr/	a.a.Ire.ie
St Nicholas	Galway Town	:	Wright John	Regan`s Mill	-	-	-	Wright J - Witham Wm	1838	-	dd/	1838 18 164
St Nicholas	Galway Town	:	- W. side R. Corrib	bleach	-	-	-	-	-	-	6"os/	94
St Nicholas	Galway Town	:	- W. side R. Corrib	bleach green	-	-	-	-	-	-	6"os/	94
St Nicholas	Galway Town	:	Fallon James & :	paper factory	ho., offs., yd. & sm gdn	-	110	-	1856	-	gr/	a.a.Ire.ie
St Nicholas	Galway Town	:	Ireland Arthur	brewery	offices & yard	-	77	-	1856	-	gr/	a.a.Ire.ie
St Nicholas	Galway Town	:	O`Hara John	Eyres Mills	-	-	-	O`Hara J - Costello Wm	1837	-	dd/	1837 20 191
St Nicholas	Galway Town	:	Fletcher Thomas	Small Mill	-	-	-	Fletcher T - Hosking V	1838	-	dd/	1838 20 77
St Nicholas	Galway Town	:	Michell Anne ors :	bleach	-	-	-	Michell A - O`Hara Jn	1836	-	dd/	1836 17 90
St Nicholas	Galway Town	:	Browne Charles	water& dam	-	-	-	Browne Charles	1834	-	dd/	1834 14 214
St Nicholas	Galway Town	:	Killeen Edward	mills	-	-	-	Killeen Ed - Lynch Patk	1837	-	dd/	1837 3 47
St Nicholas	Galway Town	:	Ardilaun Baron	mill	-	-	-	Ardilaun - Skerritt Patrick	1890	-	dd/	1890 41 199
St Nicholas	Galway Town	:	Galway Jute Co	mill	-	-	-	Galway J Co - Irish Gut Co	1890	-	dd/	1890 26 20
St Nicholas	Galway Town	:	Marshall Abraham	flour	-	-	-	Marshall A - Killeen Ed	1835	-	dd/	1835 20 157
St Nicholas	Galway Town	:	Joyes John Richard :	flour	-	-	-	Joyes J R - Morris Patk	1830	Lse. 30 Sep.	dd/	865 54 576074
St Nicholas	Galway Town	:	Joyes James	distillery	-	-	-	Joyes Jas - Kelly Wm	1839	-	dd/	1839 17 98
St Nicholas	Galway Town	:	Gunning Jno	mill	- (Nun`s Isl.)	-	100	Gunning Jno - B.O.I.	1848	-	dd/	1848 18 212
St Nicholas	Galway Town	:	-	distillery	demolished	-	-	-	-	-	phWH/	Z
St Nicholas	Galway Town	:	Mitchell Walter	mill	-	-	-	Mitchell W - Rush Ambr	1838	-	dd/	1838 16 260

PARISH	TOWNLAND	MILLER	TYPE	HOUSE	Land	£Val	PROPRIETORS	Date	WHEEL etc.	Record	Ref.
St Nicholas	Galway Town :	Wright John	Regans Mill E.	-	-	-	Wright Jn - Witham Wm	1838	-	dd/	1838 18 164
St Nicholas	Galway Town :	Regan Mary	mill	-	-	-	Regan - Cloran Marianne	1887	-	dd/	1887 33 151
St Nicholas	Galway Town :	Bermingham Mary	Eyres Mills	-	-	-	Bermingham - Rush A	1839	-	dd/	1839 18 77
St Nicholas	Galway Town :	Lynch Patrick	Eyres Mills	-	-	-	Lynch P - Palmer Thos	1838	-	dd/	1838 22 110
St Nicholas	Galway Town :	Marshall Abraham	Eyres Mills	-	-	-	Marshall A - O`Hara Jn	1836	-	dd/	1836 12 64
St Nicholas	Galway Town :	Mitchell Walter :	Eyres Mills	-	-	-	Mitchell - Mitchell Colier :	1831	-	dd/	873 22 580022
St Nicholas	Galway Town :	-	tread	demolished	-	-	-	-	-	phWH/	Z
St Nicholas	Galway Town :	Semple Joseph	saw	-	-	-	Semple Joseph - Mary A	1887	-	dd/	1887 43 17
St Nicholas	Galway Town :	Mitchell Celia :	flour	-	-	-	Mitchell C - O`Hara Jn :	1832	Mort. 13 Oct.	dd/	890 284 588785
St Nicholas	Galway Town :	Browne Dominick	Mills	-	-	-	Browne - Strickland Jar	1836	-	dd/	1836 4 137
St Nicholas	Galway Town :	Burke Richard	mill holding	-	-	-	Burke - McDonagh Matt	1839	-	dd/	1839 4 248
St Nicholas	Galway Town :	Palmer Thomas	corn store	-	-	16	-	1856	-	gr/	a.a.Ire.ie
St Nicholas	Galway Town :	Patrick Bodkin	corn store	& yard	-	30	-	1856	-	gr/	a.a.Ire.ie
St Nicholas	Galway Town :	Mullens Denis V	corn stores	& yard	-	38	-	1856	-	gr/	a.a.ire.ie
St Nicholas	Galway Town :	Mangan Locke S	flour & corn	offices & yard	-	38	-	1856	-	gr/	a.a.Ire.ie
St Nicholas	Galway Town :	Guning John	flour & corn	stores & yard	-	52	-	1856	-	gr/	a.a.Ire.ie
St Nicholas	Galway Town :	Wade Edward :	flour	stores & yard	-	55	-	1856	-	gr/	a.a.Ire.ie
St Nicholas	Galway Town :	Burke Edward C	corn stores	house, offices & yard	-	26	-	1856	-	gr/	a.a.Ire.ie
St Nicholas	Galway Town :	Burke Edward C	distillery	offices & yard	-	150	-	1856	-	gr/	a.a.Ire.ie
St Nicholas	Galway Town :	Burke Edward C	corn stores	office & yard	-	23	-	1856	-	gr/	a.a.Ire.ie
St Nicholas	Galway Town :	Burke John	malt house	& yard	-	7	-	1856	-	gr/	a.a.Ire.ie
St Nicholas	Galway Town :	Burke Edward C	corn	- [& mill houses]	-	40	-	1856	-	gr/	a.a.Ire.ie
St Nicholas	Galway Town :	5 Martin's Lane.	flour	-	-	52	-	1856	-	gr/	a.a.Ire.ie
St Nicholas	Galway Town :	Regan Anne	corn store	& yard	-	32	-	1856	-	gr/	a.a.Ire.ie
St Nicholas	Galway Town :	Kearney Matthew	corn	& yard	-	35	-	1856	-	gr/	a.a.Ire.ie
St Nicholas	Galway Town :	Birmingham Mary	Eyres Mills	-	-	-	Birmingham - Rush :	1839	-	dd/	1839 18 77
St Nicholas	Galway Town :	Michell Anne :	bl. green & mill	-	-	-	Michell A - O`Hara Jn	1836	-	dd/	1836 17 90
St Nicholas	Galway Town :	Fletcher Thomas	small mill	-	-	-	Fletcher T - Hosking :	1838	-	dd/	1838 20 77
St Nicholas	Galway Town :	P. Works. Commrs.	Gunnings Mill	-	-	-	P.W.C. - Connolly Barth	1883	-	dd/	1883 23 228
St Nicholas	Galway Town :	Ld. Estate Court ano	mill	-	-	-	L.E. Ct. - P. Wks. Comm.	1877	-	dd/	1877 33 28
St Nicholas	Galway Town :	Guiness Benjamin	Eyres Mills	-	-	-	Guiness B - St Laurence :	1893	-	dd/	1893 57 107
St Nicholas	Galway Town :	Guiness Benjamin	mills	-	-	-	Guiness B - St Laurence :	1893	-	dd/	1893 57 107
St Nicholas	Galway Town :	Killeen Edward	mills	-	-	-	Killeen Ed - Lynch Ptk	1837	-	dd/	1837 3 47
St Nicholas	Galway Town :	Lynch Patrick	Eyres Mills	-	-	-	Lynch P - Palmer Thos	1838	-	dd/	1838 22 110
St Nicholas	Galway Town :	Marshall Abraham	Eyres Mills	-	-	-	Marshall - O`Hara Jno	1836	-	dd/	1836 12 64
St Nicholas	Galway Town :	Ellard George B	tuck	-	-	-	Ellard Geo - Somers :	1852	-	dd/	1852 21 116
St Nicholas	Galway Town :	Guiness Benjamin	mill site or :	-	-	-	Guiness B - Ward Thos	1877	-	dd/	1877 25 41
St Nicholas	Galway Town :	Jesson Thomas	brush factory	-	-	-	Jesson Th - Nat. Bank	1875	-	dd/	1875 29 64
St Nicholas	Galway Town :	Petre Albert Rt Hon.	brush factory	-	-	-	Petre A - De Caen Geo	1895	-	dd/	1895 22 7
St Nicholas	Galway Town :	-	tuck	demolished, replaced :	-	-	-	-	-	phWH/	Cr
St Nicholas	Galway Town :	- Valentine`s Mill	corn	converted for use :	-	-	-	-	-	phWH/	Cr
St Nicholas	Galway Town :	Gunning Jno	engine mill	-	-	-	Gunning Jno - B. of Ire	1848	-	dd/	1848 18 212
St Nicholas	Galway Town :	Joyes James	distillery	-	-	-	Joyes J - Kelly Wm	1839	-	dd/	1839 17 89
St Nicholas	Galway Town :	-	corn	-	-	-	-	-	-	dd/	18 88 88
St Nicholas	Galway Town :	-	distillery	demolished, replaced :	-	-	-	-	-	phWH/	Cr
St Nicholas	Galway Town :	-	flour	refurbished for use :	-	-	-	-	-	phWH/	Ce
St Nicholas	Galway Town :	- Abbeygate St.	corn	-	-	-	-	-	-	6"os/	94
St Nicholas	Galway Town :	- E. side R. Corrib	distillery	-	-	-	-	-	-	6"os/	94
St Nicholas	Galway Town :	- E. side R. Corrib	tuck	-	-	-	-	-	-	6"os/	94
St Nicholas	Galway Town :	- imed. S/ West Br.	corn	-	-	-	-	-	-	6"os/	94
St Nicholas	Galway Town :	- S. end Island	flour	-	-	-	-	-	-	6"os/	94
St Nicholas	Galway Town :	- S/ Dominick St.	flour	-	-	-	-	-	-	6"os/	94

PARISH	TOWNLAND	MILLER	TYPE	HOUSE	Land	£Val	PROPRIETORS	Date	WHEEL etc.	Record	Ref.
St Nicholas	Galway Town :	- straddles R. Corib	flour	-	-	-	-	-	-	6"os/	94
St Nicholas	Galway Town :	- E/ Merchants Row	foundry	-	-	-	-	-	-	6"os/	94
St Nicholas	Galway Town :	- on Presentation Rd.	flour	-	-	-	-	-	-	6"os/	94
St Nicholas	Galway Town :	- on River near Gaol	tread mill	-	-	-	-	-	-	6"os/	94
St Nicholas	Galway Town :	Cottingham Charles	mill	-	-	-	Cottingham - Cloran Mcl	1882	-	dd/	1882 23 228
St Nicholas	Galway Town :	Gallway Jute Sp. Co.	mill wt. course	-	-	-	G. Jute - Guiness Arth	1879	-	dd/	1879 4 135
St Nicholas	Galway Town :	Ld. Judges Ct.	tuck & :	-	-	-	Judges - Kendal Clar`ce	1878	-	dd/	1878 27 23
St Nicholas	Galway Town :	Reagan Michael	mill	-	-	-	Reagan - Cottingham Geo	1846	-	dd/	1846 11 269
St Nicholas	Galway Town :	Mitchell Walter	mill	-	-	-	Mitchell - Rush Ambrose	1838	-	dd/	1838 16 260
St Nicholas	Galway Town :	McDonagh Milling & :	flour	-	-	-	-	1963	-	lic/12	flour
St Nicholas	Galway Town :	McDonagh Mathew	tuck	-	-	-	McDonagh M - Martyn :	1854	-	dd/	1854 4 128
St Nicholas	Galway Town :	-	marble	restored as cycle fcty	-	-	-	-	-	phWH/	Cc
St Nicholas	Galway Town :	Bermingham Mary	Eyres Mills	-	-	-	Bermingham - Fynn Jas	1838	-	dd/	1838 8 100
St Nicholas	Galway Town :	-	distillery	large & dilapidated	-	-	-	-	-	phWH/	D
St Nicholas	Galway Town :	-	bleach green		-	-	-	-	-	phWH/	Z
St Nicholas	Galway Town :	-	saw	demolished	-	-	-	-	-	phWH/	Z
St Nicholas	Galway Town :	Stubber Eleanor	mill site	-	-	-	Stubber E - Duncan Alx	1879	-	dd/	1879 24 13
St Nicholas	Galway Town :	Incb Ests Commrs	Burke`s Mill	-	-	-	Inc.Ests. - Burke Edwd	1852	-	dd/	1852 19 40
St Nicholas	Galway Town :	Burke Marcella	mills	-	-	-	Burke - McCormack Fr	1895	-	dd/	1895 51 98
St Nicholas	Galway Town :	Blakeney Arabella	Castle & mills	-	-	-	Blakeney - Murphy Hen	1898	-	dd/	1898 36 280
St Nicholas	Galway Town :	Flynn James & Co.	corn stores	house & yard	-	140	-	1856	-	gr/	a.a.ire.ie
St Nicholas	Galway Town :	Somerville Richard N	corn store	-	-	47	-	1856	-	gr/	a.a.ire.ie
St Nicholas	Galway Town :	Gunning John	tannery	offices & yard	-	30	-	1856	-	gr/	a.a.ire.ie
St Nicholas	Galway Town :	Gunning John	flour (unfinished)	offices & yard	-	50	-	1856	-	gr/	a.a.ire.ie
St Nicholas	Galway Town :	Gunning John	tuck	-	-	-	-	1856	-	gr/	a.a.ire.ie
St Nicholas	Galway Town :	Burke Edward C	malt stores	kiln & yard	-	24	-	1856	-	gr/	a.a.Ire.ie
St Nicholas	Galway Town :	Usher Michael	soap factory	office & yard	-	6	-	1856	-	gr/	a.a.ire.ie
Kilthomas	Garden Blake	-	old corn mill & kil	-	-	-	-	1841	-	6"os/	123
Kilthomas	Garden Blake	Glenane Patrick	old corn mill	-	30a.	212.5	-	-	-	gr/	-
Kilthomas	Garden Blake	O'Connell James	corn	(2&3B) 28x16x6.6 :	-	4.6.8	-	1852	12x2.6x3.6 34 bkts :	hob/	5.1042
Ballymacward	Garrafine	Ward Michael	corn	33x23x12 & kiln :	-	3	-	1845	10x1.2 undershot :	hob/	5.100
Ballymacward	Garrafine	Ward Michael	corn	-	-	-	-	-	13x1x5	vmb/	19
Dunmore	Garrafrauns	-	corn & mill dam	-	-	-	-	1841	-	6"os/	17
Dunmore	Garrafrauns	-	mill	-	-	-	-	-	-	1"os/	86
Dunmore	Garrafrauns	Heffernan David	corn & kiln	-	4a.	3.5.0	-	-	-	gr/	-
Killeran	Garraun	- E. side Grange R.	corn	-	-	-	-	-	-	6"os/	44
Killeran	Garraun	Munroe Simon	corn	-	-	-	-	-	13x2x5	vmb/	19
Killeran	Garraun	Munroe Simon	corn & tuck	- corn mill bad blds :	-	2.0.0	-	1853	- no information :	hob/	5.0976
Killeran	Garraun	Munroe Simon	tuck	- [no dimensions]	-	-	-	1853	breast 13x1.6 :	hob/	5.0976
Killererin	Gerraun	Munroe Simon	corn	(2B) 18x20x6.6 :	-	5.10	-	-	13x1.8x3.6 1 pr. st. :	hob/	5.0976
Killererin	Gerraun	Munroe Simon	corn & tuck	-	-	15	-	-	-	gr/	-
Boyounagh	Glenamaddy	Concannon William	corn	-	11a.	9	-	-	-	gr/	-
Boyounagh	Glenamaddy	Concannon William	corn	-	11a.	-	-	-	-	gr/	-
Boyounagh	Glennamaddy Tn	-	corn & kiln	-	-	-	-	-	-	6"os/	18
Galway	Glentane	Mannion	corn	- now an outhouse	-	-	-	1983	- ceased 1945	sv/ff	GBowie
Kiltartan	Gort Town	Hynes	corn	- deteriorating :	-	-	-	1983	- wooden axle :	sv/ff	GBowie
Boyounagh	Gortaganny	Connell Michael	corn	-	12a.	13	-	-	-	gr/	-
Boyounagh	Gortaganny	Connell Michael	corn	-	12a.	-	-	-	-	gr/	-
Boyounagh	Gortaganny	Connell Michael	corn	-	-	-	-	-	12x3x10	vmb/	19
Boyounagh	Gortaganny	Connell Michael	tuck	-	-	-	-	-	1 wh. does both	vmb/	19
Galway	Gortamulaun *	-	mill	-	-	-	-	-	-	6"os/	118
Kilmalinoge	Gortawullaun	Bohan Michael	corn	-	-	-	-	-	12x2x7 breast	vmb/	19

PARISH	TOWNLAND	MILLER	TYPE	HOUSE	Land	£Val	PROPRIETORS	Date	WHEEL etc.	Record	Ref.
Athenry	Gorteenacra	- E/ Athenry Town	corn		-		-	-	-	6"os/	84
Boyounagh	Gortganny	- ab. Boyounagh Br.	corn & pond	-	-	-	-	-	-	6"os/	6
Killann	Gortmore	-	corn	-	-	-	-	1841	-	6"os/	86
Killann	Gortmore	Griffin Michael	corn	-	4a.	-	-	-	-	gr/	-
Killann	Gortmore	Griffin Widow	corn	-	-	-	-	-	11x2x12	vmb/	19
Donanaghta	Gortnakilla	-	old brewery	-	-	-	-	-	-	6"os/	108
Kilchrest	Gortnamackan	Phayre Thomas	corn & kiln	-	153a.	114	-	-	-	gr/	-
Killererin	Grange	Farrell Michael	corn	-	12a.	11.10	-	-	-	gr/	-
Killosolan	Greenville	-	corn	-	-	-	-	-	-	6"os/	60
Killosolan	Greenville	Tyrell Peter	corn	-	37a.	24	-	-	-	gr/	-
Killura	Headford	-	windmill stump	-	-	-	-	1841	-	6"os/	42
Kilcoona	Inish	-	Kilroe Mill	-	-	-	-	-	-	6"os/	56
Kilcoona	Inish	Gunning John	flour	house, offs & mill :	-	15	-	1846	-	hob/	5.0972
Kilcoona	Inish	Gunning John	flour	(1B) 63x26x34 & :	-	22	-	1845	(2) 14x4x4.6 drive :	hob/	5.0972
Kilcoona	Inish	Hanley James	flour	-	-	2.8.0	-	-	17x4x4 4 pair st. :	vmb/	19
Oranmore	Innplot :	- E. side Main St.	brewery	-	-	-	-	-	-	6"os/	95
Galway	Keloge *	-	corn	-	-	-	-	-	-	6"os/	109
Ross	Kilbeg Upper	Gibbons Jas & Thos	corn & tuck	-	-	5	-	-	-	gr/	-
Ross	Kilbeg Upper	Gibbons Jas & Thos	mill & kilns	- [no dimensions]	-	10/-	-	1853	[no detail m/cy] :	hob/	5.1047
Ross	Kilbeg Upper	Gibbons Thomas	corn	-	-	-	-	-	11x1x11	vmb/	19
Ross	Kilbeg Upper	Gibbons Thomas	tuck	-	-	-	-	-	12x1x12 no :	vmb/	19
Kilchreest	Kilchreest	-	old bleach house	-	-	-	-	1841	-	6"os/	105
Kilconnell	Kilconnell	Cummins George :	mills	-	-	-	Cummins G - Daly Jas :	1827	?	dd/	770 543 522478
Kilconnell	Kilconnell	Daly James :	mills	-	-	-	Daly J - Cummins Geo :	1822	?	dd/	770 545 522480
Monivea	Kilcornan	- 1m. N/ Athenry	tuck	-	-	-	-	-	-	6"os/	84
Kilbennan	Kilcreevanty	- N. side R. Clare	corn	-	-	-	-	-	-	6"os/	29
Kilbennan	Kilcreevanty	- at Fartamore Br.	mill	-	-	-	-	-	-	6"os/	16
Kilbenan	Kilcreevanty	Acton Patrick	corn	-	-	-	-	-	13x2x1	vmb/	19
Kilbenan	Kilcreevanty	McHugh Redmond	corn	-	-	-	-	-	12x2x2	vmb/	19
Kilgerrill	Kilgerrill	Usher William	corn & kiln	-	186a.	-	-	-	-	gr/	-
Ahascragh	Kilglass	- N/ Clonbrock R.	corn & kiln	-	-	-	-	-	-	6"os/	61
Ahascragh	Kilglass	Clonbrock Lord	corn	(1A) 27.6x20x24.6 :	-	-	-	1845	11x4.9x4.6 drives :	hob/	5.0966
Ahascragh	Kilglass	Clonbrock Lord	corn	-	-	-	-	-	11x5x4	vmb/	19
Ahascragh	Kilglass	Clonbrock Lord	saw	-	-	-	-	-	-	vmb/	19
Ahascragh	Kilglass	Clonbrock Lord	saw mill & store	(1A) 52x20x24.6 :	-	19.13	-	-	- [ref. Valor's note]	hob/	5.0966
Moyrus	Kilkieran	Lynch Nicholas	corn & flour	-	-	-	-	-	-	gr/	-
Killaan	Killaan	- NW/ Killaun Br.	corn mill & kiln	-	-	-	-	-	-	6"os/	86
Killaan	Killaan	Cannon Dudley	corn	-	-	-	-	-	12x1x14	vmb/	19
Killaan	Killaan	Cannon Dudley	corn & kiln	-	30a.	-	-	-	-	gr/	-
Killannin	Killaguile	Fahy	corn	- building collapsed	-	-	-	1983	- was horizontal	sv/ff	GBowie
Killannin	Killaguille	- R. from Buffy Lo.	corn	-	-	-	-	-	-	6"os/	67
Kiltullagh	Killarriv	- E/ Dooyertha R.	corn	-	-	-	-	-	-	6"os/	97
Tynagh	Killeen South	Kelly Edward	mill	-	68a.	48	-	-	-	gr/	-
Galway	Killeery Beg *	-	corn	-	-	-	-	-	-	6"os/	103
Killian	Killian	- N/ Killian R.	cloth	-	-	-	-	-	-	6"os/	46
Killian	Killian	- N/ Killian R.	corn	-	-	-	-	-	-	6"os/	46
Killian	Killian	- on Killian R	mill	-	-	-	-	-	-	1"os/	97
Killian	Killian	Daly	corn	-	-	-	-	1983	11.6 x 3ft. u`shot :	sv/ff	GBowie
Killian	Killian	Noone Patrick & Tom	corn & kiln	(1B) 27x18x18	-	4.18	-	-	11x1.1x4 floats :	hob/	5.1016
Killian	Killian	Noone Timothy & Patk	corn & kiln	-	12a.	20.10	-	-	-	gr/	-
Ballymacward	Killooaun	-	corn	-	-	-	-	-	-	6"os/	72
Killoscobe	Killoscobe	-	corn	-	-	-	-	-	-	6"os/	59

PARISH	TOWNLAND	MILLER	TYPE	HOUSE	Land	£Val	PROPRIETORS	Date	WHEEL etc.	Record	Ref.
Killoscobe	Killoscobe	Gilhooly Michael	corn	-	12a.	11	-	-	-	gr/	-
Killoscobe	Killoscobe	Noon Martin	corn	-	-	-	-	-	10x2x8	vmb/	19
Dunmore	Killuney	- N. side river	mill & mill race	-	-	-	-	-	-	6"os/	17
Dunmore	Killuney	- on Sinking R	corn	-	-	-	-	-	-	1"os/	86
Dunmore	Killuney	Haneran Michael	corn	-	-	-	-	-	12x1x3	vmb/	19
Dunmore	Killuney	Haneran Michael	mill	(2B) 30x22x8.6 :	-	2.10	-	1845	12x1.4x3.6 wood :	hob/	5.0957
Dunmore	Killuney	Haneran Michael	old tuck mill	-	-	-	-	-	-	vmb/	19
Melick	Kilmachugh	- at Eyrec`t Castle	mill	-	-	-	-	-	-	1"os/	117
Kilmeen	Kilmeen	-	corn & kiln	-	-	-	-	1841	-	6"os/	106
Kilmeen	Kilmeen	E. Lecarrow Vge.	mill, kiln & millpor	-	-	-	-	1841	-	6"os/	106
Kilmeen	Kilmeen	Kelly Daniel	corn	-	-	-	-	-	11x2x9	vmb/	19
Kilmeen	Kilmeen	Nokely Patrick	corn & kiln	-	36a.	21.10	-	-	-	gr/	-
Clonfert	Kilnaborris	-	brick kiln	-	-	-	-	-	-	6"os/	109
Clonfert	Kilnaborris	-	corn & mill dam	-	-	-	-	-	-	6"os/	109
Clonfert	Kilnaborris	Rourke John	corn	-	-	-	-	-	14x3x5 breast	vmb/	19
Kilcoona	Kilroe	Furey	flax spinning	- mill bdg. still intact	-	-	-	1983	wheel good order	sv/ff	GBowie
Killannin	Kilroe West	Donohoe Thomas	mill	hos (2) office & land	125a.	6.16.	-	1856	-	gr/	a.a.Ire.ie
Kilcroan	Kilsallagh	- nr Blacker`s Br.	tuck	-	-	-	-	-	-	6"os/	6
Kilconla	Kilshanvy	- E/ Kilshanvy Br.	Kilshanvy mill	-	-	-	-	-	-	6"os/	28
Kilconla	Kilshanvy	Farrell	corn	-	-	-	-	1983	16ft. x 4ft.8ins. :	sv/ff	GBowie
Kilconla	Kilshanvy	Leevin James	corn	-	-	-	-	-	16x3x4	vmb/	19
Kilconla	Kilshanvy	Lewin Carrigue :	mill	-	-	-	Lewin C - Lewin Thos :	1825	-	dd/	810 455 546390
Kilconla	Kilshanvy	Lewin Frederick T	mill	-	3.3.3	12	-	-	-	gr/	-
Galway	Kilymon *	- E/ Inner Bay	old mill	-	-	-	-	-	-	6"os/	35
Templetogher	Knockanarra	- narr Clogh Br.	corn & kiln	-	-	-	-	-	-	6"os/	1
Templetogher	Knockanarra	- Clogh Mill near Br.	corn & kiln	-	-	-	-	-	-	pWEH	B
Templetogher	Knockanarra	O`Brien Morgan	corn	-	-	-	-	-	13x2x4	vmb/	19
Templetogher	Knockanarra	O`Brien William	corn & tuck	-	11a.	14	-	-	-	gr/	-
Dunmore	Knockatee East	-	corn kilns	-	-	-	-	-	-	6"os/	17
Dunmore	Knockatee East	Patten Owen	corn	-	-	-	-	-	11x1x2	vmb/	19
Kilclounny	Knockbrack	-	old malt kiln	-	-	-	-	-	-	6"os/	86
Kilclounny	Knockgalss	Masters Charles	corn	-	11a.	-	-	-	-	gr/	-
Kilgerrill	Knockglass	- E/ Kilmallaw Br.	corn	-	-	-	-	-	-	6"os/	87
Kilclounny	Knockglass	Ashe Norman	corn	-	-	-	-	-	9x2x6	vmb/	19
Beagh	Knocktoby	- N/ R. Corheeny	mill (in ruins)	-	-	-	-	-	-	6"os/	133
Addergoole	Lack	- W. side R. Clare	mill	-	-	-	-	-	-	6"os/	16
Addergoole	Lack	Bermingham John	corn & tuck	miller`s house	173a.	122	-	-	-	gr/	
Addergoole	Lack	Farrell John	corn	-	-	-	-	-	14x3x4	vmb/	19
Kilconicking	Lackfinna South	-	corn	-	-	-	-	-	-	6"os/	97
Kilconicking	Lackfinna South	Quin Patrick	tuck	-	-	-	-	-	12x2x5 2 feet or	vmb/	19
Beagh	Lavally	-	tuck	-	-	-	-	1841	-	6"os/	122
Beagh	Lavally	- E. of Gort Town	corn	-	-	-	-	1841	-	6"os/	122
Beagh	Lavally	Dwyer Michael	corn	-	-	-	-	-	13x2x5	vmb/	19
Beagh	Lavally	Dwyer Michael	tuck	-	-	-	-	-	same wheel	vmb/	19
Kiltartan	Lavally	Mangan John	corn, tuck, kiln	-	16a.	19.5	-	-	-	gr/	-
Beagh	Lavally	Mangan John	flour	-	25a.	77.15	-	-	-	gr/	-
Beagh	Lavally	Mangan John	flour	-	-	-	-	-	16x5x7	vmb/	19
Leitrim	Leitrim	Finnerty Vincent	corn	- structures good	-	-	-	1983	13ft. x 3ft. 9ins. :	sv/ff	GBowie
Leitrim	Leitrim More	- E. of Leitrim Vge.	old tuck mill	-	-	-	-	1841	-	6"os/	116
Leitrim	Leitrim More	- NE./ Leitrim Vge.	corn	-	-	-	-	1841	-	6"os/	116
Leitrim	Leitrim More	Feenarty Michael	corn	-	51a.	37.15	-	-	-	gr/	-
Leitrim	Leitrim More	Feenarty Michael	tuck	-	-	-	-	-	-	gr/	-

PARISH	TOWNLAND	MILLER	TYPE	HOUSE	Land	£Val	PROPRIETORS	Date	WHEEL etc.	Record	Ref.
Leitrim	Leitrim More	Fenaghy Michael	-	-	-	-	-	-	-	vmb/	19
Clonbern	Lettera	-	corn	-	-	-	-	-	-	1"os/	86
Clonbern	Lettera	- S. side small river	corn	-	-	-	-	-	-	6"os/	18
Clonbern	Lettera	Gilmore Joseph	corn	- buildings derelict	-	-	-	1983	13.6 x 2.7 intact :	sv/ff	GBowie
Clonbern	Lettera	Gilmore Michael	corn & kiln	-	4a.	5	-	-	-	gr/	-
Clonbern	Lettera	Gilmore Michael	corn & kilns	-	4a.	-	-	-	-	gr/	-
Templetogher	Lettera	Tully Bryan	corn	-	5a.	3.15.0	-	-	-	gr/	-
Duniry	Limehill	-	corn	-	-	-	-	1841	-	6"os/	106
Duniry	Limehill	Egan Patrick	corn	-	110a.	66	-	-	-	gr/	-
Abbeygorman	Liscoyle	Clarke James	corn	-	62a.	-	-	-	-	gr/	-
Abbeygorman	Liscoyle	Pelly Connor	corn	-	-	-	-	-	11x1x11	vmb/	19
Tynagh	Lisduff	-	corn	-	-	-	-	1841	-	6"os/	99
Tynagh	Lisduff	Ellis Thomas	corn (in prog.)	-	4.1.0	-	-	-	-	gr/	-
Tynagh	Lisduff	Glynn James	corn	- structures good :	-	-	-	1983	- still grinding	sv/ff	GBowie
Tynagh	Lisduff	Kirwan Patrick	corn	(2A) 18x24x9 & :	-	2.1.	-	1845	10x4x3 float boards :	hob/	15.1018
Tynagh	Lisduff	Kirwan Patrick	corn	-	-	-		-	12x2x3	vmb/	19
Donanaghta	Lisfinny	Eyre Giles :	mill	-	-	-	Eyre G - Horsman Edw :	1822	-	dd/	778 284 527019
Donanaghta	Lisfinny	Horsman Edward	corn	-	1.1.21	17	-	-	-	gr/	-
Donanaghta	Lisfinny	Horsman Edward	corn	-	-	-	-	-	16x3x7	vmb/	19
Liskeevy	Liskeevy	- W/ Liskeevy Br.	corn	-	-	-	-	-	-	6"os/	16
Galway	Lismafada	Horsman Edward :	mill	-	-	-	Horsman E - Eyre Gyles : I	1827	-	dd/	778 283 527018
Ballynakill	Liss	Egan Francis	corn & kiln	-	105a.	79	-	-	-	gr/	-
Aughrim	Lissavahaun	- SW/ Ballinavoher	corn & kiln							6"os/	87
Aughrim	Lissavahaun	Egan Fran Kelly	flour	-	-	-	-	-	10x1x6 breast	vmb/	19
Aughrim	Lissavahaun	Kegan Francis	corn	-	60a.	-	-	-	-	gr/	-
Moyrus	Lissoughter	- N/ Recesss R.	mill in ruins	-	-	-	-	-	-	6"os/	37
Dunmore	Lissyconor	-	corn & kiln	-	-	-	-	-	-	6"os/	6
Loughrea	Loughrea Town	Dolphin Henry	corn	-	-	1.10	-	-	-	gr/	-
Loughrea	Loughrea Town	Fahy Rep. Laurence	brewery	-	1a.	41.5	-	-	-	gr/	-
Loughrea	Loughrea Town	Fynn John	corn	-	-	14	-	-	-	gr/	-
Loughrea	Loughrea Town	Fynn John	corn kiln	-	-	3	-	-	-	gr/	-
Loughrea	Loughrea Town	Fynn John	white mill	- recently re-roofed	-	-	-	1983	- m/cy all wood	sv/ff	GBowie
Loughrea	Loughrea Town	O`Brien Samuel	corn	-	-	-	-	-	no dimensions	vmb/	19
Loughrea	Loughrea Town :	-	flour	-	-	-	-	-	-	6"os/	105
Loughrea	Loughrea Town :	-	old brewery	-	-	-	-	-	-	6"os/	105
Loughrea	Loughrea Town :	-	brewery	-	-	-	-	-	-	6"os/	105
Killimorbologue	Magheramore	- E. side Kilcrow R.	corn	-	-	-	-	1841	-	6"os/	107
Killimorbologue	Magheramore	Hardy Joseph	corn	-	34a.	35	-	-	-	gr/	-
Killimorbologue	Magheramore	Hardy Joseph	corn	-	34a.	35	-	-	-	gr/	-
Killimorbologue	Magheramore	Hardy Joseph	corn	-	-	-	-	-	14x4x3 `shot	vmb/	19
Clonrush	Meelick	-	iron mill (ruins)	-	-	-	-	-	-	6"os/	135
Inishcaltra	Middleline North	Bulger James	corn	-	48a.	17.10	-	-	-	gr/	-
Inishcaltra	Middleline North	Bulger James	corn	(2B) 29x21x15 :	-	4.14	-	-	12x1.11x12.6 :	hob/	5.3835
Inishcaltra	Middleline North	Bulger James	tuck		-	-	-	-	-	gr/	-
Oranmore	Millplot	- E/ Oranmore Br.	flour	-	-	-	-	-	-	6"os/	95
Oranmore	Millplot	Cummins Thomas	corn	-	4.0.0	12	-	-	-	gr/	-
Oranmore	Millplot	Cummins Thomas	corn	-	4.0.0	-	-	-	-	gr/	-
Oranmore	Millplot	Cummins Thomas	flour	-	-	-	-	-	18x2x4 `shot	vmb/	19
Addergoole	Milltown	-	Milltown Vge	-	-	-	-	-	-	6"os/	16
Kilkerrin	Milltown	-	Milltown Vge.	-	-	-	-	-	-	6"os/	32
Kilkerrin	Milltown	- S/ Village	mill	-	-	-	-	-	-	6"os/	32
Addergoole	Milltown	- on R. Clare E/ Vge.	mill	-	-	-	-	-	-	6"os/	16

PARISH	TOWNLAND	MILLER	TYPE	HOUSE	Land	£Val	PROPRIETORS	Date	WHEEL etc.	Record	Ref.
Addergoole	Milltown	- on Clare R	mill	-	-	-	-	-	-	1"os/	86
Addergoole	Milltown	Grady Patrick	corn	-	-	-	-	-	12x2x2	vmb/	19
Addergoole	Milltown	Grady Patrick	corn & tuck	-	50a.	30.15	-	-	-	gr/	-
Addergoole	Milltown	Grady Patrick	tuck	-	-	-	-	-	-x-x2 1 pr comb	vmb/	19
Galway	Milltown	Kirwan Patrick :	-	-	-	-	Kirwan P - Kirwan	1819	-	dd/	772 25 523160
Galway	Milltown	Mahon	-	-	-	-	Mahon - McDonnell	-	?	dd/	853 393 561328
Kilkerrin	Milltown	Mannion Thomas	corn	(2A) 23.6x16x8 :	3.19	-	-	1853	- [no information]	hob/	5.1047B
Kilkeeran	Milltown	Mannion Thomas	corn	-	-	-	-	-	10x2x10	vmb/	19
Kilkerrin	Milltown	Mannion Thomas	corn & kiln	-	1.3.0	-	-	-	-	gr/	-
Kilkerrin	Milltown	Mannion Thomas	corn & kiln	-	1.3.0	7	-	-	-	gr/	-
Galway	Milltown Bellew	-	mill	-	-	-	-	-	-	1"os/	97
Tuam	Monacow	-	mill	-	-	-	-	1841	-	6"os/	30
Tuam	Monacow	Hosty Edward	mill	-	18a.	30	-	-	-	gr/	-
Galway	Moneen (5)	-	corn	-	-	-	-	-	-	1"os/	86
Moylough	Mount Bellew	-	mill	-	-	-	-	-	-	6"os/	46
Moylough	Mount Bellew	-	mill in ruins	-	-	-	-	-	-	6"os/	46
Moylough	Mount Bellew	-	old mill pond	-	-	-	-	-	-	6"os/	46
Moylough	Mount Bellew	Farrell John	flour	-	-	-	-	-	- 1,000 barrels	lic/19	wh.meal
Killeany	Mountross	-	mill	-	-	-	-	-	-	6"os/	55
Killeany	Mountross	Fahy Margaret	corn	-	-	1.5	-	-	- [Val. note says:]	hob/	5.0975
Killeany	Mountross	Murray Matthew	gig mill	(2C) 12x18x6.6 & :	-	2.5	-	1845	8x7ins.x2ft. GIG :	hob/	5.0975
Abbeyknockmoy	Moyne	-	corn kiln	-	-	-	-	-	-	6"os/	58
Abbeyknockmoy	Moyne	Wade Francis	corn	-	-	-	-	-	-	gr/	-
Abbeyknockmoy	Moyne	Wade Francis	flour	-	54a.	59	-	-	-	gr/	-
Abbeyknockmoy	Moyne	Wade Francis	flour	-	-	-	-	-	12x4x12 2 pair :	vmb/	19
Athenry	Mulpit	- E/ side river	corn	-	-	-	-	-	-	6"os/	84
Athenry	Mulpit	Taylor Walter	corn	-	42a.	29.5	-	-	-	gr/	-
Athenry	Mulpit	Taylor Walter	corn	(2B) 24.6x20.6x10 :	-	10.8	-	1845	11ft., 24 bkts. 11ins.:	hob/	5.3825
Rahoon	Newcastle	- NW/ Galway Br.	N'cle Distillery	-	-	-	-	-	-	6"os/	94
Rahoon	Newcastle	Persse Burton	distillery	-	21.3.1	-	-	-	-	gr/	-
Abbeyknockmoy	Newtown	Kelly James	corn	-	-	-	-	-	27x4x25	vmb/	19
Galway	Newtownsmith	French Nicholas :	mill ? :	-	-	-	French N - French Peter	1826	-	dd/	815 80 549015
Clonfert	Oghillmore	-	corn mill in ruins	-	-	-	-	1841	-	6"os/	100
Clonfert	Oghillmore	Pollock Allan	mill	-	369a.	-	-	-	-	gr/	-
Donaghpatrick	Olter	St George Stephny :	mills	-	-	-	St George S - St George :	1828	-	dd/	835 159 561094
Oranmore	Oran Beg	- S/ Oranmore Tn.	old brewery	-	-	-	-	-	-	6"os/	95
Oranmore	Oranmore Village	Kelly Thomas	brewery	-	-	-	-	-	-	gr/	-
Oranmore	Oranmore Village	Kelly Thomas	brewery	-	-	13	-	-	-	gr/	-
Killursa	Our	Flynn Bernard	corn	-	-	-	-	-	13x2x3	vmb/	19
Killursa	Our	Flynn Bernard	tuck	-	-	-	-	-	13x2x3	vmb/	19
Killursa	Ower	- S/ Black R.	corn mills (2)	-	-	-	-	-	-	6"os/	41
Killursa	Ower	Hennelly James	old corn mill	-	3a.	2.10.0	-	-	-	gr/	-
Kilbennan	Pollacorragune	- SW/ bridge	old mill	-	-	-	-	-	-	6"os/	29
Templetogher	Pollaneyester	Egan Elizabeth	mill	-	9a.	5	-	-	-	gr/	-
Templetogher	Pollaneyster	- Templetogher Mill	corn	-	-	-	-	-	-	6"os/	6
Kilcloony	Pollboy	- W side R. Suck	corn	-	-	-	-	-	-	6"os/	89
Kilcloony	Pollboy	McDonagh Walter	flour	-	-	-	-	-	10x2x7	vmb/	19
Templetogher	Pollremon	-	corn & pond	-	-	-	-	-	-	6"os/	30
Templetogher	Pollremon	-	corn & pond	-	-	-	-	-	-	6"os/	6
Templetogher	Pollremon	-	corn & pond	-	-	-	-	-	-	sv/04	Z
Lickmolassy	Purtumna Town :	-	brewery	-	-	-	-	-	-	6"os/	127
Lickmolassy	Purtumna Town :	Monaghan John	brewery	(1B) 50x23x18.6 :	-	-	-	-	-	hob/	5.2788

PARISH	TOWNLAND	MILLER	TYPE	HOUSE	Land	£Val	PROPRIETORS	Date	WHEEL etc.	Record	Ref.
Kiltullagh	Raford	- NE of Rafford Br.	corn & mill race	-	-	-	-	-	-	6"os/	85
Kiltullagh	Raford	Bourke Edward	corn	-	32a.	22.15	-	-	-	gr/	-
Ballynakill	Reynclamber	-	mill	-	-	-	-	1841	-	6"os/	131
Ballynakill	Reynclamber	- S/ r. E/ Tooreeny Br.	tuck	-	-	-	-	-	-	6"os/	131
Ballynakill	Reynclamber	M`Dermot John	corn mills (2)	(1B) 28x22x20.6 :	-	10.10	-	-	13x2.2 o'shot :	hob/	5.3834
Ballynakill	Reynclamber	M`Dermott John	corn & kiln	-	112a.	22	-	-	-	gr/	-
Kinvarradoorus	Rinneen	O`Dea Daniel	corn & kiln	-	30a.	50	-	-	-	gr/	-
Kinvarradoorus	Rinneen	O`Dea Daniel	flour	-	-	-	-	-	17x4x4	vmb/	19
Killeeneen	Rockfield	-	mill	-	-	-	-	-	-	1"os/	-
Killinan	Roxborough	-	old corn mill	-	-	-	-	-	-	6"os/	104
Kiltullagh	Ruford	Blake John Henry	corn	-	-	-	-	-	12x2x5 idle 5 yr	vmb/	19
Inishcaltra	Sellernaun East	-	corn	-	-	-	-	-	-	6"os/	134
Ballynakill	Shanboolard	-	corn	-	-	-	-	-	-	6"os/	22
Donaghpatrick	Shrule Grove	- on Black R.	flour	-	-	-	-	-	-	6"os/	28
Donaghpatrick	Shrule Grove	Kearns James	flour	-	-	-	-	-	16x4x3 3 pr sts. :	vmb/	19
Donaghpatrick	Shrulegrove	Richard Golding	herd's ho. offs.:	- (note ref. mill :)	-	-	-	1846	- water cut off	hob	5.0971
Killoran	Springfield	-	corn	-	-	-	-	-	-	6"os/	99
Killoran	Springfield	-	kiln & mill dam	-	-	-	-	-	-	6"os/	99
Killoran	Springfield	Pelly Connor	corn	-	-	-	-	-	9x2x11	vmb/	19
Killoran	Springfield	Pelly Patrick (Thos)	corn & kiln	-	4.0.0	-	-	-	-	gr/	-
Stradbally	Stradbally South	-	corn	-	-	-	-	-	-	6"os/	103
Omey	Streamstown	- W/ Streamst'n Br.	tuck	-	-	-	-	-	12x3x10.6 36 bkts. :	6"os/	22
Omey	Streamstown	Austim William Esq.	tuick	- (no dims.) :	-	22.4	-	-	-	hob/	5.3832
Omey	Streamstown	M`Creight James	corn	-	58a.	-	-	-	-	gr/	-
Omey	Streamstown	M`Creight James	tuck	(2C) 30x17x14 & :	-	2.14	-	-	12x3 smashed :	hob/	5.0963
Killora	Strongfort :	Roland William	corn & tuck :	- mill & house intact	-	-	-	1983	13ft. x 2ft. 6ins. :	sv/ff	GBowie
Ross	Teeranea	- S. of Ballydoo Lo.	tuck	-	-	-	-	1841	-	6"os/	26
Ross	Teeranea	- S/ Ballydoo Lough	tuck	-	-	-	-	1841	-	6"os/	26
Ross	Teeranea	Browne Sam & Thad.	tuck	-	72a.	8	-	-	-	gr/	-
Clonkeen	Templebeg	-	corn	-	-	-	-	-	-	1"os/	107
Templetogher	Templetogher	Egan Thomas	corn	at restored building	-	-	Williamstown Trust	2009	wheel active & :	mmSv/	sp -A
Templetogher	Templetogher	Egan Thomas	corn	- building restored	-	-	-	2004	-	phWH/	B
Templetogher	Templetogher	Egan Thomas	corn	- building still intact	-	-	-	1983	- ceased 1964	sv/ff	GBowie
Killimordaly	Tormaun	- S/ Rafford R.	corn & mill race	-	-	-	-	-	-	6"os/	85
Killimordaly	Tormaun	Holland Michael	corn	-	5a.	5	-	-	-	gr/	-
Killimordaly	Tormaun	Holland Michael :	mill	(2B)12x20x6.6 & :	5a.	5	-	1845	9x1.8x9.6 24 bkts. :	hob/	5.1011
Killimordaly	Tormaun	Holland Mick	corn	-	-	-	-	-	11x2x11	vmb/	19
Killimordaly	Tormaun	Mahon	mills	-	-	-	Mahon - Mahon	-	- [error parties]	dd/	774 498 524833
Killimordaly	Tormaun	Mahon George :	mills	-	-	-	Mahon G - Mahon Ross :	1825	Reconv. 4 Jan.	dd/	800 305 540240
Galway	Townland ?	- E/ Killian Br.	Killian Mill	-	-	-	-	-	-	6"os/	97
Galway	Townland ?	- S/ Killian Br.	Killian Mill	-	-	-	-	-	-	6"os/	97
Liskeevy	Townsparks	- NW/ Liskeevy Br.	corn	-	-	-	-	1841	-	6"os/	16
Liskeevy	Townsparks	Corcoran William	corn	-	-	-	-	-	12x1x2	vmb/	19
Kilcloony	Townsparks :	- on R. Suck	brewery	-	-	-	-	-	-	6"os/	88
Kilcloony	Townsparks :	- on R. Suck	mill	-	-	-	-	-	-	6"os/	88
Kilcloony	Townsparks :	- S/ Bridge St.	corn	-	-	-	-	-	-	6"os/	88
Ballynakill	Trean Park	Mehan James	corn	-	24.0.7	16.10	-	-	-	gr/	-
Galway	Tristane * :	Sellors Simon :	mill	- house & land	-	-	Sellors S - Sellors Mcl. :	1824	-	dd/	794 24 536359
Clontuskert	Tristaun	- on Ballinrun R.	corn & kiln	-	-	-	-	-	-	6"os/	87
Tuam	Tuam T`parks :	Blake Alicia Mary	corn	(1B) 40x19x18 :	-	6-11	-	1855	-	hob/	5.2795
Tuam	Tuam Town	Blake Alicia M	corm & kiln	-	-	16	-	-	-	gr/	-
Tuam	Tuam Town	Farrell Patrick	corn	-	1.0.0	61.0	-	-	-	gr/	-

PARISH	TOWNLAND	MILLER	TYPE	HOUSE	Land	£Val	PROPRIETORS	Date	WHEEL etc.	Record	Ref.
Tuam	Tuam Town :	Blake James	corn	(1B) 40x19x18 :	-	4-7-5	-	-	13.9x2.6x -	hob/	5.2792
Tuam	Tuam Townsparks	- N/ Bishop St.	brewery	-	-	-	-	-	-	6"os/	29
Tuam	Tuam Townsparks	- N/ Sun Street	old mill & dam	-	-	-	-	-	-	6"os/	29
Tuam	Tuam Townsparks	- on R. Nanny N/ tn	mill & dam	-	-	-	-	-	-	6"os/	29
Tuam	Tuam Townsparks	- S/ R. Nanny	corn	-	-	-	-	-	-	6"os/	29
Tuam	Tuam Townsparks	- at Newtown Morris	old windmill	-	-	-	-	-	-	6"os/	29
Tuam	Tuam Townsparks	Blake James	corn	-	-	-	-	-	14x2x4	vmb/	19
Tuam	Tuam Townsparks	Bleke James	flour	-	-	-	-	-	16x4x4	vmb/	19
Tuam	Tuam Townsparks	Concannon Edmond	flour	(1B) 30x28.6x37.6 :	-	15-12	-	1855	16.4x4.4x - :	hob/	5.2795
Tuam	Tuam Townsparks	Farrell Patrick	corn	-	-	-	-	-	12x2x6	vmb/	19
Moycullen	Uggol	-	mill	-	-	-	-	-	-	6"os/	81
Moycullen	Uggol	- SE/ Vge. Moycullen	horizomtal	-	-	-	-	1905	altered from HZ	sv/SAq	ATLucas
Moycullen	Uggol	McCork Richard	corn	(no dimensions) :	-	2.0	-	1853	- (no. dims.)	hob/	5.3847
Ballymacward	Whitepark	Morgan Joseph	corn	-	-	-	-	-	13x2x3	vmb/	19
Ballymacward	Whitepark	Morgan Joseph	corn & kiln	-	882a.	-	-	-	-	gr/	-
Ballymacward	Whitepark	Morgan Joseph	corn & kiln	(2B) 43x23x13.6 :	-	5.6.9	-	1845	11.6x2.6x4.6 32bkt:	hob/	5.0999
Kilbegnet	Woodfield	-	mill	-	-	-	-	-	-	1"os/	86
Kilbegnet	Woodfield :	-	corn	-	-	-	-	-	-	6"os/	18
Ballynakill	Woodford	- N/ Bolag Bridge	mill	-	-	-	-	-	-	6"os/	131
Ballynakill	Woodford	- S/ Woodford R. :	mill & Mill Ho.	-	-	-	-	-	-	1"os/	125
Ballynakill	Woodford	Brunskill Henry :	mill & millhouse	-	-	-	Brunskill H - Tempany Jn :	1846	-	dd/	1846 14 64
Ballynakill	Woodford	Fahy Patrick	corn & kilns	miller`s house	6.1.4	21	-	-	-	gr/	-
Ballynakill	Woodford	Fahy Patrick	corn & kilns	- + offices & land	6a.	21	-	-	-	gr/	-
Ballynakill	Woodford Village	Tempany John	corn	(1B) 48x22.6x24 :	-	-	-	1849	breast 13x3.6x6 :	hob/	5.2739
Meelick	Woodlands	Richardson	mills	-	-	-	Richardson & ors deed	1828	-	dd/	835 556 561491
Meelick	Woodlands	Richardson	mills	-	-	-	Richardson - Mahon :	1828	-	dd/	835 557 561492
Meelick	Woodlands	Weir	mills	-	-	-	Weir - Richardson Jas	1828	-	dd/	835 558 561493
Killaan	Woodlawn	Ashton Lord	saw	-	-	-	-	-	20x2x1 for :	vmb/	19

PARISH	TOWNLAND	MILLER	TYPE	HOUSE	Land	£Val	PROPRIETORS	Date	WHEEL etc.	Record	Ref.
Kerry	Ardagh	Galway Lucinda :	mill	-	-	-	Galway L - Betham Sir Wm :	1822	-	dd/	794 226 536561
Kerry	Ardagh	Hickson James	mills	-	-	-	Hickson Jas - Saunders Arth	1765	-	dd/	244 189 156848
Kerry	Ardagh	Kenmare Lord Val :	mills	-	-	-	Ld Kenmare - Bermingham Ed	1800	-	dd/	532 513 350649
Kerry	Ardagh	McSweeny Roger	mills	-	-	-	McSweeeny R - Saunders Wm	1776	-	dd/	314 25 209044
Kerry	Ardagh	O`Leary Cornelius	mill	-	-	-	O`Leary C - Purcell Hannan :	1824	-	dd/	796 539 538074
Kerry	Ardagh (3)	Brown Lord	mills	-	-	-	Ld Kenmare - Herbert Edwd	1752	-	dd/	148 407 101778
Tralee	Ardfert	Boyle Charles Lord	mill	-	-	-	Boyle Ld Chas - Crosbie Wm	1756	-	dd/	184 51 121975
Tralee	Ardfert	Crosbie Sir Maurice	mill	-	-	-	Crosbie Sir M - Mahon Thos	1748	-	dd/	126 413 88084
Tralee	Ardfert	Crosbie Wm & Jno	Abbey Mill	-	-	-	Earl Glandon - Duke Dorset	1777	-	dd/	315 444 215202
Corkaguiny	Ardruane	Chambers Charles	corn & kiln	(1A) 25.6x20.6x13 :	-	-	-	1851	13.6x4x10 1pair st. :	hob/	5.1063
Kerry	Ashgrove *	Chute Charles	mills	-	-	-	Chute Chas - Hurly Robt C	1868	-	dd/	1868 14 117
Kenmare	Ashtown	Sandview Ltd	mill	ho. over mill race	-	-	-	-	2x Diagonal avge. 1.6	turb/	c1947
Killiney	Aughacasla North	Spellane James :	corn	(2C) 11x18x6 :	-	7/3d.	-	1851	10x2.6x8 1 pair st. :	hob/	5.1079
Killiney	Aughacasla South	- SW of A'casla Br.	tuck	-	-	-	-	-	-	6"os/	36
Killiney	Aughacasla South	Donoghue Henry	corn	(3C) 29x15x6 :	-	-	-	1851	10x2.6x12 1pair st. :	hob/	5.1079
Kerry	Aunagarry *	Chute Francis	mill	-	-	-	Chute Franis - Chute Richard	1869	-	dd/	1869 5 114
Kerry	Ballanhourtagh	-	tuck	-	-	-	-	-	-	6"os/	49
Prior	Ballard Upper	-	corn - gig	- minute remains :	-	-	-	2002	-	mmSv/	wh - Z
Prior	Ballard Upper	-	tuck	-	-	-	-	-	-	6"os/	88
Prior	Ballard Upper	Shea Timothy	corn, tuck - hz	12.6x19.6x6 :	-	-	-	1857	4ft.x1ft. gig wheel :	hob/	5.3849
Kerry	Ballincarrig West	Barry John	mill	-	-	-	Barry J - Gallwey Thomas :	1784	-	dd/	357 118 239648
Kerry	Ballincarrig West	McSherry Bryan :	mills	-	-	-	McSherry B - Sheehy Bart :	1802	-	dd/	567 400 581569
Kerry	Ballincarrig West	McSherry Michael :	mills	-	-	-	McSherry M - Galway Thos :	1791	-	dd/	497 7 317092
Ballyduff	Balliniry	-	corn	-	-	-	-	-	-	6"os/	35
Ballyduff	Balliniry	Corkerry Michael	corn	(3C) 38x15.6x6	-	-	-	1850	5x0.8x4 1pair st. :	hob/	-
Ventry	Ballinleague	Kennedy Maurice	corn	(3C) 18.6x13x5 :	-	1.8.7	-	1850	dia. 4ft. fall 5ft. :	hob/	5.3849
Kerry	Ballintourtane	-	mills	-	-	-	-	1868	-	dd/	-
Kerry	Ballintourtane	Ventry Ld Baron	mills	-	-	-	Ventry Baron - De Moleyns D	1868	-	dd/	1868 16 182
Kerry	Ballintourtone	Carrigue Lansby :	mill	-	-	-	Carrigue L - O'Hara Charles :	1760	-	dd/	251 77 160211
Kerry	Ballintourtone	Day	mill	-	-	-	Day & ors - Rowan	-	?	dd/	584 147 396239
Kerry	Ballintourtone	Denny Rev Maynard :	mill	-	-	-	Denny M - Ponsonby Richard :	1798	-	dd/	514 447 338327
Kerry	Ballintourtone	Ponsonby Thomas :	mill	-	-	-	Ponsonby T - Philips Lowry G :	1772	-	dd/	514 447 338327
Kilcrohane	Ballybrack	- near quarry & :	mill	old dilap. walls	-	-	-	2002	-	mmSv/	wh - R
Kilcrohane	Ballybrack	- on Finglas R.	carding		-	-	-	-	-	1"os/	191
Kilcrohane	Ballybrack	Currane Patrick	corn & tuck	-	7a.	-	-	-	-	gr/	-
Ballyseedy	Ballycarty	- Ballyseedy	Mills	-	-	-	-	-	-	6"os/	29
Ballyseedy	Ballycarty	- close to R. Lee	corn	-	-	-	-	2010	-	mmSv/	wh - Z
Ballyseedy	Ballycarty	- near mill site	cottages	old and ruinous	-	-	-	2010	-	mmSv/	wh - R
Ballyseedy	Ballycarty	Bayly	mill	-	-	-	Bayly & ors - Rice	-	?	dd/	693 91 431811
Ballyseedy	Ballycarty	Blenerhasset	mill	-	-	-	Blenerhassett - Fagan	-	?	dd/	540 568 562151
Ballyseedy	Ballycarty	Blenerhasset William	mill	-	-	-	Blenerhasset - Wetherall Jos	1765	-	dd/	232 536 155143
Ballyseedy	Ballycarty	Blenerhasset Wm :	mill	-	-	-	Blenerhasset Wm - Roland :	1793	-	dd/	475 124 299890
Ballyseedy	Ballycarty	Blenerhassett John	mill			-	Blenerhasset J - Crosbie Arth	1714	-	dd/	50 1 31810
Ballyseedy	Ballycarty	Power Pierce	mill	-	-	-	Power Prce - Sealy Samuel	1731	-	dd/	78 86 53518
Killarney	Ballycasheen	-	bleach & cotton	-	-	-	-	-	-	6"os/	66
Killarney	Ballycasheen	Shebee Michael	corn	-	3.2.0	-	-	-	-	gr/	-
Killarney	Ballycasheen	Shebee Michael	mill-pond	-	-	-	-	-	-	gr/	-
Killarney	Ballycasheen or :	-	bleach	-	-	-	- [no trace or knowledge]	2002	-	mmSv/	wh - Z
Killarney	Ballycasheen or :	-	cotton	-	-	-	- flat green near football pitch	2002	-	mmSv/	wh - Z
Kiltallagh	Ballygamboon Up	-	old tuck mill	-	-	-	-	-	-	6"os/	37
Kiltallagh	Ballygamboon Up	- close to mill site	millhouse	- in fine shape	-	-	-	2010	- pho taken	mmSv/	wh - B
Kiltallagh	Ballygamboon Up	on long narrow lane	- old tuck mill	small section :	-	-	-	2010	- pho taken	mmSv/	wh - R

PARISH	TOWNLAND	MILLER	TYPE	HOUSE	Land	£Val	PROPRIETORS	Date	WHEEL etc.	Record	Ref.
Dysert	Ballyhantouragh	Kelliher Patt	mill	-	-	-	Imed. lessor Wm Twess	1848	-	VOt/	6.0281
Dingle	Ballyheabought	-	corn	-	-	-	-	-	-	6"os/	43
Dingle	Ballyheabought	-	tuck	-	-	-	-	-	-	6"os/	43
Dingle	Ballyheabought	Rourk Michael	tuck	-	-	-	-	-	11x2x7 14x3x9	vmb/	-
Dingle	Ballyheabought	Rourk Michael	tuck	(3C) 15.6x13.6x5 :	-	-	-	1851	11x2.2x7 38 bkts.	vmb/	-
Aghavallan	Ballylongford Town	Blair William	corn store	-	-	-	-	-	-	gr/	-
Kilbonane	Ballymalis	-	paper	-	-	-	-	-	-	6"os/	57
Kilbonane	Ballymallis	Galway Chris	flour	-	5a.	-	-	-	-	gr/	-
Kilbonane	Ballymallis	Sealy Edward	corn	-	-	-	-	-	-	gr/	-
Kerry	Ballymullen	-	distillery	-	-	-	-	-	-	6"os/	29
Dingle	Ballynabooley	Griffin Patrick	corn & tuck	(1B) 12.6x19.6x15 :	-	-	-	1851	10x2x11 36 bkts. :	hob/	5.1066
Dingle	Ballynabooley	Griffin Patrick	tuck	-	-	-	-	-	10xx2x11 10x2x11	vmb/	5.1053
Killury	Ballynoe	-	Ballynoe Mills	-	-	-	-	-	-	6"os/	14
Killury	Ballynoe	Cournehan Patrick	corn	(3C) 18x18x9.6 :	-	-	-	1851	12x3x13.6 1 pair st. :	hob/	?
Killury	Ballynoe	Cournehan Patrick	tuck	-	-	-	-	-	12x3x13	vmb/	-
Castleisland	Beheenagh	Bailey William	bolting & grist	& dwelling & 3a. 2r. 7p. land.			-	1851	-	vfb/	4.2587
Castleisland	Beheenagh	Bailey William	corn, flour	-	4a.	-	-	-	-	gr/	-
Castleisland	Beheenagh	Bailey William	grist & bolting	-	3a.	-	Im. lessor Lady A Headley	1851	-	VOt/	6.0281
Castleisland	Beheenagh	Bailey William	tuck	-	-	-	-	-	-	gr/	
Castleisland	Beheenagh	Bailey William	tuck	-	-	-	-	1851	-	vfb/	4.2587
Castleisland	Beheenagh	Bailey William	tuck	-	3a.	-	Im. lessor Lady A Headley	1851	-	VOt/	6.0281
Castleisland	Beheenagh	Bedford Neil	corn & tuck	-	-	-	-	1999	-	pWEH	B
Annagh	Blennerville	-	windmill	& Visitor Centre	-	-	-	2000	-	pWEH	B
Annagh	Blennerville :	-	wind mill	-	-	-	-	-	-	6"os/	29
Annagh	Blennerville Village	Chute Arthur B	windmill ruins	-	-	-	-	-	-	gr/	-
Annagh	Blennerville Village	Chute Arth B`hassett	old windmill	(1C) dia.22x47ft.	-	-	-	1852	- wings & m/cy :	hob/	5.2799
Kerry	Cagriga *	Brennan Maurice	mills	-	-	-	Brennan M - Mahoney Tim J	1768	-	dd/	277 567 179949
Kerry	Cagriga *	Brennan Maurice	mills	-	-	-	Brennan - Carthy & ano	1768	-	dd/	277 568 179950
Kerry	Cagriga *	Dorset Henry Duke :	mills	-	-	-	Duke of Dorset - Franks Matt :	1806	-	dd/	579 369 392612
Kerry	Cagriga *	Herbert Edward	mills	-	-	-	Herbert E & son - Wallis Robt	1755	-	dd/	172 527 117852
Kerry	Cagrigh *	Bateman Francis :	mill	-	-	-	Bateman F - Lloyde George :	1795	-	dd/	487 445 312221
Kerry	Cagrigh *	Bateman George	mills	-	-	-	Bateman G - Musgrave Chris	1743	-	dd/	119 62 81573
Kerry	Cagrigh *	Bateman William M :	mill	-	-	-	Bateman W - Herbert Henry :	1800	-	dd/	534 191 349935
Kerry	Cagrigh *	Herbert	mill	-	-	-	Herbert - Franks	-	?	dd/	576 405 392536
Kerry	Cagrigh *	Musgrave Chris	mills	-	-	-	Musgrave Chris & Hoar Robt	1739	-	dd/	99 174 68487
Kerry	Calanafersy West	-	store & kiln	-	-	-	-	-	-	6"os/	46
Galey	Carhoonaknock	-	long mill race	-	-	-	-	-	-	6"os/	10
Galey	Carounaknock W	Dillane John	corn	-	6a.	-	-	-	-	gr/	-
Kerry	Castleconway	-	mill (in ruins)	-	-	-	-	-	-	6"os/	56
Kilgarrylander	Castledrum	- Castledrum	Mills	-	-	-	-	-	-	6"os/	46
Kilgarrylander	Castledrum	Spring William	corn	-	43a.	20.15	-	-	-	gr/	-
Kilgarrylander	Castledrum	Sullivan Daniel	corn	-	21a	24	-	-	-	gr/	-
Kilgarrylander	Castledrum	Sullivan Daniel	corn	18x16.4x6.3 :	-	-	-	-	o`shot 8x2.1x6ins. :	hob/	5.1187
Castleisland	Castleisland	-	mill race	-	-	-	-	-	-	6"os/	40
Castleisland	Castleisland	Harington John	bark	(1B) 22x18x12 :	-	-	-	1852	-	hob/	5.2802
Castleisland	Castleisland	Porter Edward :	mill	-	-	-	Porter E - Marshall Richard :	1787	-	dd/	386 308 258460
Kerry	Caunguillet	Mason	mills	-	-	-	Mason - Connor & ors	-	?	dd/	589 507 404487
Kerry	Caunguillet	Mason Richard	grist & tucking	-	-	-	Mason R - Hamott William	1807	-	dd/	589 163 401313
Kry (?)	Charleville	Corke & Orrery Earl	tithes & mill	-	-	-	E Orrery - Duke Manchester	1774	-	dd/	302 40 199165
Kry (?)	Charleville	King Edward :	tithes & mill	-	-	-	King Edwd - Taylor William :	1791	-	dd/	430 203 279247
Kry (?)	Charleville	Orrery Earl of	tithes & mill	-	-	-	Earl Orrery & ors - Harper Jn	1751	-	dd/	147 306 100136
Kerry	Clashcommon	Bayley Jno :	mills	-	-	-	Bayley J - Rice Stephen Edwa	1810	-	dd/	633 91 431811

PARISH	TOWNLAND	MILLER	TYPE	HOUSE	Land	£Val	PROPRIETORS	Date	WHEEL etc.	Record	Ref.
Kerry	Clashcommon	Blenerhasset Arthur :	mills	-	-	-	Blenerhasset A - Wilson Wm :	1808	-	dd/	603 575 413467
Kerry	Clashcommon	Denny Arthur	mills	-	-	-	Denny Arth - Collis Thomas	1764	-	dd/	237 286 152922
Kerry	Clashcommon	Franks	mill	-	-	-	Franks - Sealy	-	?	dd/	115 357 80765
Kerry	Clashcommon	Sealy James	mill	-	-	-	Sealy James - Franks Thomas	1744	-	dd/	118 279 80764
Kerry	Clashcommon	Sealy Samuel	mill	-	-	-	Sealy Sam - Blenerhasset Wm	1746	-	dd/	128 281 86887
Kerry	Clogher	-	tuck	-	-	-	-	-	-	6"os/	30
Kerry	Cloghercade	Blennerhasset Dorcas	mills	-	-	-	Blennerhasset D - King Nich :	1822	-	dd/	770 98 522033
Kerry	Cloghercade	Blennerhasset Dorcas	mills	-	-	-	Blennerhasset D - Purcell Edm	1822	-	dd/	773 88 523823
Kerry	Cloghercade	Denny Edward :	mills	-	-	-	Denny Edd - Blennerhasset :	1822	-	dd/	781 489 529024
Kilorglin	Clooncarrig	Power Thomas	corn store kiln	-	-	-	-	-	-	gr/	-
Kry	Cogreig (not)	Musgrave Richard	mills	-	-	-	Musgrave R - Musgrave Chris	1735	-	dd/	83 59 57540
Killarney	Coolclogher	-	Flesk Mills	-	-	-	-	-	-	6"os/	66
Killarney	Coolclogher	- Flesk Mills	mill		-	-	-	2002	-	mmSv/	wh - R
Killarney	Coolclogher	Leahy Charles	mill & mill land	-	-	-	Leahy Chas & ors - Leahy H	1866	-	dd/	1866 30 213
Killarney	Coolclogher	Leahy John	corn, flour	-	12a.	-	-	-	-	gr/	-
Killarney	Coolclogher	Leahy Susanna	mill & mill land	-	-	-	Leahy Su - Leahy Henry	1866	-	dd/	1866 30 213
Killarney	Coolclogher :	Gallwey John	mill & kiln	Incum. Est. consisting of :		-	- sold to Richard Leahy	1855	26x7 overshot iron :	mlyIE	p134
Killarney	Coolclogher :	Galway	mill	-	-	-	Galway - Betham	-	?	dd/	794 226 536561
Knockane	Coolroe	Malcolmson M/s	cotton factory	-	-	-	-	-	34x16x26 26x15x26 :	vmb/	-
Killorglin	Cottoners	Trewell Ltd	-	-	-	-	-	-	Pelton avg. 6.5kw	turb/	c1947
Kerry	Counguilly *	Mason	mill	-	-	-	Mason - Spring	-	?	dd/	377 133 226096
Kerry	Counguilly *	Mason	mill	-	-	-	Mason - Shanahan	-	?	dd/	580 303 381389
Kerry	Counguilly *	Mason John	mill	-	-	-	Mason J - Connor Timothy	1787	-	dd/	392 395 259321
Kerry	Counguilly *	Twiss	mill	-	-	-	Twiss - Raymond		?	dd/	459 260 322322
Kerry	Curra	-	tuck & corn	-	-	-	-	-	-	6"os/	63
Kilgobban	Curraduff	-	Bunow Mill	-	-	-	-	-	-	6"os/	37
Kilgobban	Curraduff	Palmer John Esq.	flour	(1B) 55x46x36 :	-	-	-	1850	14x5x1.3 overshot :	hob/	5.1077
Prior	Curraghnanav	Crimmins Andrew	corn	17 x 15 x 8 :	-	-	-	1857	8.7 x 1ft.10ins. gig :	hob/	5.3849
Prior	Curraghnanav	Crimmins Andrew	tuck - hz.	-	-	-	-	-	8.7 x 1ft 6ins. gig :	hob/	5.3849
Annagh	Curraheen	-	tuck	-	-	-	-	-	-	6"os/	37
Annagh	Curraheen	- Curraheen	Mill	-	-	-	-	-	-	6"os/	37
Annagh	Curraheen	Counihan Michael	grist & tuck	(3C) 15.6x15x6 :	-	1.11	-	-	idle & in ruins :	hob/	5.1185
Annagh	Curraheen	Counihan Patrick	tuck	-	0.1.29	-	-	-	-	gr/	-
Kry	Currens *	Herbert Arthur	mills	-	-	-	Herbert Arth - Crosbie Maurice	1720	-	dd/	64 197 43453
Kry	Cuyrigns *	Cary Tristan	mill	-	-	-	Cary Tristan - Musgrave Richd	1714	-	dd/	14 64 5181
Kry	Cuyrigns *	Hollow Sword Co Gvs	mill	-	-	-	Hollow SwordCo - Bateman Jn	1709	-	dd/	6 174 1702
Kry	Cuyrigns *	Stotten & Co.	mills	-	-	-	Stotten & Co - Tristan Cary	1709	-	dd/	4 522 1244
Kry	Deanogh *	Chaytor William	mill & mill lands	-	-	-	Chaytor Wm - Castleross Ld	1869	-	dd/	1869 15 152
Kerry	Deewnagh *	Galway Lucinda :	mill	-	-	-	Galway L - Betham Sir Wm :	1822	-	dd/	794 226 536561
Kerry	Dereennamuckla	-	duck	-	-	-	-	-	-	6"os/	100
Killarney	Derreen	Deenagh R. W/ Mill Bı	flour mills	-	-	-	-	1841	-	6"os/	66
Killarney	Derreen	Galway Christopher	flour	-	5a.	-	-	-	-	gr/	-
Killarney	Derreen	Galway Christopher	flour & kiln	(1B) 66x70x50 :	-	84	-	-	new 26x6x29.6 :	hob/	5.1166
Kilcrohane	Derreennamucklag	Shea Cornelius	tuck	-	5a.	-	-	-	-	gr/	
Ballinvoher	Derrygorman	-	mill race	-	-	-	-	-	-	6"os/	45
Ballinvoher	Derrygorman	-	tuck	-	-	-	-	-	-	6"os/	43
Ballinvoher	Derrygorman	Counihan john	corn	(3C) 33.6x16x5.6 :	-	-	-	1851	dia. 12ft., fall 13ft. :	hob/	5.1058
Killinane	Derrymore	-	corn	-	-	-	-	-	-	1"os/	?
Killinane	Derrymore	Donovan	mill	-	-	-	Donovan - Murphy	-	?	dd/	787 10 532145
Annagh	Derrymore West	-	corn	-	-	-	-	-	-	6"os/	37
Annagh	Derrymore West	- 6m. W. of Tralee	corn	- still intact	-	-	-	2010	-	mmSv/	dos - B
Annagh	Derrymore West	Donavan Richard Esq	flour	(1B) 43x25x31.6 :	-	8-10	-	1851	26x6x27 3 pair st. :	hob/	5.1055

PARISH	TOWNLAND	MILLER	TYPE	HOUSE	Land	£Val	PROPRIETORS	Date	WHEEL etc.	Record	Ref.
Kilcrohane	Derryquin	-	corn (in ruins)	-	-	-	-	-	-	6"os/	100
Kerry	Dillons (not)	Headley	mill estate	-	-	-	Headley Baron - Ashton	1866	-	dd/	1866 19 258
Dingle	Dingle	-	mill	-	-	-	-	-	-	6"os/	43
Dingle	Dingle	-	mill	-	-	-	-	-	-	6"os/	43
Dingle	Dingle Town	-	corn	-	-	-	-	-	-	1"os/	171
Dingle	Dingle Town	Hickson Robert	corn store, kiln	-	-	-	-	-	-	gr/	-
Dingle	Dingle Town	McKenna James	corn	-	-	-	-	-	-	gr/	-
Kerry	Dirreen *	-	mill	-	-	-	Ld Est Court - Thompson Wm	1865	-	dd/	1865 14 159
Kerry	Dirreen *	-	mill	-	-	-	Ld Est Court - Saunders Mce	1865	-	dd/	1865 17 49
Kilcummin	Dooneen	-	tuck	-	-	-	-	-	-	6"os/	58
Glanbehy	Drom	-	tuck	-	-	-	-	-	-	6"os/	70
Kenmare	Dromaturk	Mayberry George	corn	-	-	-	-	-	-	gr/	-
Kerry	Dromod	-	tuck	-	-	-	-	-	-	6"os/	89
Ratass	Dromthacker	King Elizabeth :	mills	-	-	-	King Eliz - Connell James :	1824	-	dd/	796 167 538302
Ratass	Dromthacker	Morris Samuel	mill	-	-	-	Morris Sam - Tytor John	1724	-	dd/	43 248 28063
Ratass	Dromthacker	Morris Samuel	mill	-	-	-	Morris Samuel - Morris Rachel	1727	-	dd/	52 466 35321
Ratass	Dromthacker	O`Connell James	mills	-	-	-	O`Connell Jas - Chute Fran B	1865	-	dd/	1865 9 120
Ratass	Dromthacker E.	Colles Edward :	mill	-	-	-	Colles Edw - O`Connell James	1825	-	dd/	804 19 542354
Killarney	Dromyrourk	Crimmin Denis	corn	-	0.0.26	-	-	-	-	gr/	-
Killarney	Dromyrourke	- W/ Cloghereen Poc	mill	-	-	-	-	-	-	6"os/	66
Killarney	Drumyrourk	Crimmen Denis	corn	(2B) 22x16x7 :	-	3	-	-	u`shot 11x2.4x4 :	hob/	5.1166
Knockane	Dunloe Upper	-	tuck	-	-	-	-	-	-	6"os/	65
Knockane	Dunloe Upper	Crimmins Catherine	corn & tuck	-	39a.	-	-	-	-	gr/	-
Knockane	Dunloe Upper	Crimmins Denis	corn & tuck	-	-	-	-	-	-	gr/	-
Kerry	Farrantooleen	-	mill (in ruins)	-	-	-	-	-	-	6"os/	35
Kerry	Farrantooleen	-	tuck & knapping	-	-	-	-	-	-	6"os/	35
Kerry	Ferritersquarter	-	corn	-	-	-	-	-	-	6"os/	52
Garfinny	Flemingstown	Counihan John	corn (& tuck)	(1C) 30x20x13.6 :	-	-	-	-	14x3.6x7 1 pr. st. :	hob/	5.1o7o
Killarney	Flesk	-	corn	-	-	-	-	-		1"os/	173
Killarney	Flesk	Leahy Susanna	mills	-	-	-	Leahy Su - Leahy Henry	1866	-	dd/	1866 30 213
Kerry	Galey *	Raymond Samuel	mill lands	-	-	-	Raymond Samuel - Smith Jn	1867	-	dd/	1867 21 125
Molahiffe	Garraun	Fitzgerald Patrick	corn	(1C) 26x18x6 :	-	-	-	-	o`shot dia. 10ft. :	hob/	5.1179
Kerry	Gearhanorly	-	corn	-	-	-	-	-	-	6"os/	94
B`macelligott	Glanageenty	-	mill	-	-	-	-	2010	-	mmSv/	dos - Z
Templenoe	Gortamullin	- W. side Finnahy R	tuck	-	-	-	-	1841	-	6"os/	93
Templenoe	Gortamullin	Kelliher John	corn & tuck	-	6.3.21	-	-	-	-	gr/	-
Kilgarrylander	Gortaneden	- Gortaneden	Mill	-	-	-	-	-	-	6"os/	43
Kilgarrylander	Gortaneden	Shea James	tuck	-	56a.	-	-	-	-	gr/	-
Kilgarrylander	Gortaneden	Shea James	tuck	(3C) 26x14.6x6	-	-	-	-	o`shot 8x1.7x8.6 :	hob/	5.1187
Dingle	Gortonora	-	brewery	-	-	-	-	-	-	6"os/	43
Dingle	Gortonora	-	flour	-	-	-	-	-	-	6"os/	43
Dingle	Gortonora	O`Donoghue Thomas	corn	-	-	-	-	-	-	gr/	-
Dingle	Gortonora	O`Donoghue Thomas	corn	91B) 24.6x21x10	-	-	-	1851	14x3.6x14.6 48 bkts.	hob/	5.1066
Dingle	Gortonora	O`Donoghue Thomas	mill	-	-	-	-	-	14x3x14	vmb/	-
Knockane	Grenagh	- on R. Loe	corn	-	-	-	-	-		1"os/	173
Aghadoe	Headfort	-	tuck	-	-	-	-	-	-	6"os/	67
Aghadoe	Headfort	Crimmin Timothy	corn	-	6.0.3	-	-	-	-	gr/	-
Dromod	Inchiboy	-	corn gig	- [ref. map]	-	-	-	-	- [not locateed]	mmSv/	wh - Z
Dromod	Inchiboy	Sullivan Timothy	tuck	-	114a.	-	-	-	-	gr/	-
Kerry	Islandganniv North	-	tuck	-	-	-	-	-	-	6"os/	10
Ratass	Keelerisky Manor	Denny Sir Barry :	mills	-	-	-	Denny Barry - Scollard Barth :	1787	-	dd/	463 352 297815
Ratass	Keelerisky Manor	Scollard Bartholomew	mills	-	-	-	Scollard Barth - Day Sir Robt	1795	-	dd/	490 261 313833

PARISH	TOWNLAND	MILLER	TYPE	HOUSE	Land	£Val	PROPRIETORS	Date	WHEEL etc.	Record	Ref.
Killiney	Kilcumminbeg	Griffin John	corn & tuck	(2C) 21x16x8 :	-	-	-	1851	12x1.6x13 1pair st. :	hob/	5.1079
Kildrum	Kilfountan	-	corn	-	-	-	-	-	-	6"os/	43
Kildrum	Kilfountan	Ryan James	hz - mill	(2B) 25x17x5.6 :	-	-	-	-	5ft. dia horizontal :	hob/	5.1073
Kildrum	Kilfountan	Ryan James	hz - mill	(2B) 25x17x5.6 :	-	-	-	-	5ft. dia horizontal :	hob/	5.1073
Molahiffe	Killahane	- Molahiffe	Mills	-	-	-	-	-	-	6"os/	48
Molahiffe	Killahane	- close to road :	corn	-	-	-	-	2010	-	pWEH	R
Molahiffe	Killahane	Counihan John	corn	-	-	-	-	-	10.6x1.2x2 30 bkts. :	hob/	5.1180
Killarney	Killarney Glebe	-	brewery	-	-	-	-	-	-	6"os/	66
Killarney	Killarney Town	Killarney Mills	mill	- site & tail race :	-	-	-	2002	-	mmSv/	wh - Z
Killarney	Killarney Town	O`Sullivan Jeremiah	bark	-	-	-	-	-	-	gr/	-
Ratass	Killerisk	Stephen Samuel	mill, kiln	-	-	-	-	-	-	gr/	-
Ratass	Killerisk	Stephens	mill	-	-	-	Stephens S - Kerry Flax Co	1865	-	dd/	1865 19 120
Ratass	Killierisk	-	brewery	-	-	-	-	-	-	6"os/	29
Ratass	Killierisk	- 1m S/ Tralee Town	brewery	-	-	-	- (McCowan's ?)	2010	-	mmSv/	wh - Z
Caher	Killogrone	- near Caherciveen	corn		-	-	- [no site or inf. located]	2002	-	mmSv/	wh - Z
Kilquane	Kilquane	Begley Thomas :	hz - corn	(3C) 21x15x6	-	-	-	1850	4ft. 2ins. horizontal :	hob/	5.1083
Ballinculsane	Knockaboul	-	tuck	-	-	-	-	-	-	6"os/	50
Ballinculsane	Knockaboul	Healy John	tuck	-	2a.	-	-	-	-	gr/	-
Castleisland	Knockanenore	Crosbie William T	mills	-	-	-	Crosbie Wm - Collis Maurice	1866	-	dd/	1866 31 279
Kerry	Knockanrory	-	tan yard	-	-	-	-	-	-	6"os/	79
Kerry	Knocknagappul	-	corn & tuck	-	-	-	-	-	-	6"os/	68
Aghadoe	Knockreer	Mahon Nicholas :	tuck	-	-	-	Mahon N - Goold Fran & Nich :	1788	-	dd/	396 212 260930
Kerry	Knockrie E & W	:'Grady	mill	-	-	-	Grady - Freeman	-	?	dd/	55 61 35871
Kerry	Knockrie E & W	:'Grady	mill	-	-	-	Grady - Barry	-	?	dd/	654 311 35574
Kerry	Knockrie E & W	:'Grady	mill	-	-	-	Grady - Hehir	-	?	dd/	655 63 35876
Kerry	Knockrie E & W	:'May Charles	mill	-	-	-	May Chas - Freeman Wm	1722		dd/	33 514 21093
Kerry	Knockrower East	-	old mill	-	-	-	-	-	-	6"os/	49
Kerry	Knockrower West	-	tuck	-	-	-	-	-	-	6"os/	49
Ardfert	Liscahane	-	corn	-	-	-	-	1841	-	6"os/	28
Ardfert	Liscahane	Denny Hon Edward	mills	-	-	-	Denny Hon Edwd - Day Edwd	1726	-	dd/	56 295 38027
Ardfert	Liscahane	Denny Madam Mary	mills	-	-	-	Denny Mary - Day Edward	1725	-	dd/	45 179 28896
Ardfert	Liscahane	Denny Mary	mills	-	-	-	Denny Mary - Day Edward	1717	-	dd/	17 413 9277
Ardfert	Liscahane	Denny Mary	mills	-	-	-	Denny Mary - Crosbie Maurice	1725	-	dd/	47 508 31677
Killinane	Liss Lower	-	tuck (in ruins)	-	-	-	-	-	-	6"os/	79
Listowel	Listowel Town	-	mill	-	-	-	-	-	-	6"os/	10
Kilbohane	Listry	-	woolen	-	-	-	-	-		1"os/	173
Ballinvoher	Lougher	Beal Patrick	corn	(2C) 21x15x6 :	-	-	-	1850	11.6x2x12.6 1pr. st. :	hob/	5.1058
Killorglin	Maghancoosaun	Hargrave Joshua	mill	-	-	-	Hargrave Josh - Barry Jn B	1869	-	dd/	1869 6 57
Kilgarvan	Mangerton	Castlerosse Visc.	mill & land	-	-	-	Castlerosse Visc - King Sir R	1867	-	dd/	1867 25 207
Kerry	Maulykeevane	Brocklebank Thomas	mill & land	-	-	-	Brocklebank Thos - Neave S	1865	-	dd/	1865 25 221
Kiltallagh	Meanus	-	Meanus Mill	-	-	-	-	-	-	6"os/	47
Knockane	Meanus	-	mill race	-	-	-	-	-	-	6"os/	57
Knockane	Meanus	Harnett Thomas	corn	-	11a.	-	-	-	-	gr/	-
Kry	Mill Lands	Blennerhasset	-	-	-	-	Blennerhasset - Grady	-	?	dd/	759 219 515554
Tralee	Milltown	-	corn	- lge. L shaped	-	-	-	2002	-	mmSv/	wh - B
Ordorney	Milltown	-	mill	-	-	-	-	-	-	6"os/	21
Kerry	Milltown	-	mill	-	-	-	-	-	-	6"os/	43
Colman	Milltown	-	mill	-	-	-	-	-	-	6"os/	47
Kilcolman	Milltown	-	no mill	-	-	-	-	-	-	1"os/	173
Dingle	Milltown	- on Milltown R	mill	-	-	-	-	-	-	1"os/	171
Corkaguiny	Milltown	Brown Edward	Townland	-	-	-	Brown Edwqrd - White John	1721	-	dd/	32 412 20197
Clanmaurice	Milltown	Crosbie William T	Milltown	-	-	-	Crosbie Wm - Bushe Gervais	1865	-	dd/	1865 20 235

COUNTY KERRY

PARISH	TOWNLAND	MILLER	TYPE	HOUSE	Land	£Val	PROPRIETORS	Date	WHEEL etc.	Record	Ref.
Clanmaurice	Milltown	Crosbie William T	Milltown	-	-	-	Crosbie Wm - Collis Maurice	1866	-	dd/	1866 31 279
Kerry	Milltown	Cunningham	-	-	-	-	Cunningham - Cunningham	-	-	dd/	794 63 536398
Trughanacmy	Milltown	Godfrey	-	-	-	-	Godfrey - Franks	-	-	dd/	759 74 515409
Trughanacmy	Milltown	Godfrey	-	-	-	-	Godfrey - Fitzgerald	-	-	dd/	799 44 539379
Trughanacmy	Milltown	Godfrey	Milltown	-	-	-	Godfrey - Palmer	1869	-	dd/	1869 21 29
Kerry	Milltown	Gun	-	-	-	-	Gun or Kinna - ditto.	-	-	dd/	783 7 529742
Dingle	Milltown	Hickson Robert	corn & flour	(1A) 34x25x28 & :	-	-	-	1851	17x5x18.6 56 bkts. :	hob/	5.1066
Dingle	Milltown	Hickson Robert	flour	-	1a.	-	-	-	-	gr/	-
Dingle	Milltown	Hickson Robert	mill	-	-	-	-	-	17x5x18	vmb/	-
Corkaguiny	Milltown	Hussey Edward	Milltown	-	-	-	Hussey Ed - Hussey Saml	1865	-	dd/	1865 12 221
Corkaguiny	Milltown	Hussey Edward	Milltown	-	-	-	Hussey Ed - Latchfield Richd	1867	-	dd/	1867 25 84
Corkaguiny	Milltown	Hussey Edward	Milltown	-	-	-	Hussey Ed - McGillicuddy Dan	1869	-	dd/	186921 187
Dingle	Milltown	O`Sullivan`s	saw	poor condition	-	-	O`Sullivans	1999	sawing, wholesale	pWEH	A
Kerry	Milltown Village	-	tuck	-	-	-	-	-	-	6"os/	43
Kry (not)	Morakiffe	Chute Richard :	manor mills	-	-	-	Chute R - O`Connell Richard :	1821	?	dd/	764 345 518680
Kerry	Mucknagh *	Kerry Thomas Lord	mill	-	-	-	Ld Kerry - Vesey Rev Fa Thos	1716	-	dd/	15 354 7746
Ordorney	Odorny *	Crosbie David	mills	-	-	-	Crosbie D - F`gerald Maurice	1712	-	dd/	28 144 16961
Killorglin	Ownagarry	-	mill	-	-	-	-	-		1"os/	173
Aghadoe	Pallis	-	mill	-	-	-	-	-	-	6"os/	65
Aghadoe	Pallis	Crimmin Patrick	corn	-	0.2.11	-	-	-	-	gr/	-
Ardkill	Rathmore	-	woollen fcty	-	-	-	-	-	-	1"os/	174
Kilgarrylander	Ross	Rae Edward	mill	-	-	-	Rae Ed - Scottish Nat Ins Co	1866	-	dd/	1866 6 229
Kilgarrylander	Shanakeale	Mulchinock Edward	mill lands	-	-	-	Mulchinock Ed - Maconochie	1867	-	dd/	1867 36 297
Kerry	Shannow *	Carney John	mill	-	-	-	Carney John - Crosbie Wm	1867	-	dd/	1867 20 259
Nohavaldaly	Shinnagh	Shinnagh	Mills	-	-	-	-	-	-	6"os/	60
Nohavaldaly	Shinnagh	Coltsman Daniel C.	corn	13x29x22.6 & :	-	6.19	-	-	14.6x4x9 42 bkts. :	hob/	5.1181
Kerry	Stradbally Town	-	-	-	-	-	-	-	-	6"os/	35
Kilnaughtin	Tarbert	-	-	-	-	-	-	-	-	6"os/	3
Kilnaughtin	Tarbert	Leslie John	mill	-	-	-	Leslie John - Fox Samuel	1731	-	dd/	76 307 54543
Dingle	The Wood	Bowler Widow Mary	tuck	(3C) 13x17x5.6 :	-	-	-	1851	10x1.6x10.6 35 bkts.:	hob/	5.1066
Castleisland	Toberananig	Chambers Mr	mill :	-	2a.	-	Imed. lessor R M Lennon	1851	-	VOt/	6.0281
Castleisland	Tobermaing	-	carding	-	-	-	-	-	-	6"os/	40
Castleisland	Tobermaing	-	flour	-	-	-	-	-	-	6"os/	40
B`macelligott	Tonreagh	Busteed John	corn	-	1.3.7	-	-	-	-	gr/	-
B`macelligott	Tonreagh Lower	-	mill dam	-	-	-	-	-	-	6"os/	30
B`macelligott	Tonreagh Lower	- Ashgrove	Mill	-	-	-	-	-	-	6"os/	30
B`macelligott	Tonreagh Lower	Busteed John & :	mill	-	-	25.15.	vacant in period	1856	-	gr/	Ld.Est.db
Kerry	Tonwbee	-	tuck	-	-	-	-	-	-	6"os/	40
Tralee	Tralee	-	brewery	-	-	-	-	-	-	6"os/	29
Tralee	Tralee Town	- at end New Rd.	steam-mill	conversion :	-	-	-	2010	-	mmSv/	dos - Cc
Tralee	Tralee Town	- on N. Circular Rd.	mill	demolished :	-	-	-	2010	-	mmSv/	dos - Cc
Tralee	Tralee Town	Benner Henry	steam mill	-	-	-	-	-	-	gr/	-
Tralee	Tralee Town	Connor Ellen	The Windmill	-	-	-	Connor E - Hilliard Henry	1843	-	dd/	1843 11 33
Tralee	Tralee Town	Donovan John	store, kiln	-	-	-	-	-	-	gr/	-
Tralee	Tralee Town	Donovan Richard	store, kiln	-	-	-	-	-	-	gr/	-
Tralee	Tralee Town	Harrington Maurice	store, kiln	-	-	-	-	-	-	gr/	-
Tralee	Tralee Town	Hayes Patrick	mill	-	-	-	Hayes P - McCowen Robt	1887	-	dd/	1887 1 51
Tralee	Tralee Town	Jeffcott Joseph	store, kiln	-	1a.	-	-	-	-	gr/	-
Tralee	Tralee Town	Johnston William	brewery	-	3a.	-	-	-	-	gr/	-
Tralee	Tralee Town	Kennedy Jas & Co	store, kiln	-	-	-	-	-	-	gr/	-
Tralee	Tralee Town	Leahy Richard	steam-mill	-	-	-	-	-	-	gr/	-
Tralee	Tralee Town	O`Kelly Thomas	store, kiln	-	-	-	-	-	-	gr/	-

PARISH	TOWNLAND		MILLER	TYPE	HOUSE	Land	£Val	PROPRIETORS	Date	WHEEL etc.	Record	Ref.
Tralee	Tralee Town		Palmer John	store, kiln	-	-	-	-	-	-	gr/	-
Tralee	Tralee Town		Sullivan Patrick	store, kiln	-	-	-	-	-	-	gr/	-
Tralee	Tralee Town		Ushborne Thos M	store, kiln	-	-	-	-	-	-	gr/	-
Tralee	Tralee Town	:	Busteed Jno	mills		-	-	Busteed J - Fitzgerald Rev Jas	1851	-	dd/	1851 5 130
Tralee	Tralee Town	:	Blennerhassett Arthur	mills	-	-	-	Blennerhassett - Donovan John	1836	-	dd/	1836 10 250
Tralee	Tralee Town	:	Ld Judges Corp & Co.	mills	-	-	-	Ld Judges - Finnerty Henry	1896	-	dd/	1896 51 88
Tralee	Tralee Town	:	Daly Myles	brewery	-	-	-	Daly Myles - Flynn John	1877	-	dd/	1877 40 110
Tralee	Tralee Town	:	Flynn John	brewery	-	-	-	Flynn John - Hannafin James	1878	-	dd/	1878 20 292
Tralee	Tralee Town	:	Brice James K	grain store	-	-	-	-	1988	-	valCB/	2
Tralee	Tralee Town	:	O'Dowd Marian	grain store	-	-	-	-	2000	-	valCB/	2
Killiney	Tullaree		-	tuck & corn	-	-	-	-	-	-	6"os/	36
Killiney	Tullaree		McKinna Thomas	corn	(2C) 36x20x15	-	-	-	1851	10x2.6x11 1 pr. st. :	hob/	5.1079
Tralee	Tullymullen		-	woollen	-	-	-	-	-	-	1"os/	162

PARISH	TOWNLAND	MILLER	TYPE	HOUSE	Land	£Val	PROPRIETORS	Date	WHEEL etc.	Record	Ref.
Kildare	Abbyowthry *	Cloncurry Lord	mills	-	-	-	Cloncurry Lord - Kyd	-	-	dd/	-
Ballybought	Aliganstown	Connolly Patrick	corn	(1B) 31x20x25 :	-	-	-	1852	13x4x13.6 o`shot :	hob/	5.3867
Ballybought	Alliganstown	-	corn	-	-	-	-	1851	-	6"os/	29
Ballybought	Alliganstown	Connolly Patrick	corn	-	26a.	-	-	-	-	gr/	-
Kildare	Annsborough *	Montgomery William	mill	-	-	-	Montgomery William - Jno	1787	-	dd/	380 669 258329
Ardee	Ardee	Chargneau William :	mill	-	-	-	Chargneau W - Agreement	1820	-	dd/	763 70 517805
Ardee	Ardee	Sherlock Thomas :	mill & weir	-	-	-	Sherlock T - Sherlock :	1821	M.Smt.10 Feb.	dd/	761 565 517101
B`more Eustace	Ardinode	-	mill	-	-	-	-	-	-	1"os	120
B`more Eustace	Ardinode	- nr Ardinode Ho.	Mill	-	-	-	-	-	-	6"os/	29
B`more Eustace	Ardinode	Ardinode Mill :	corn	-	-	-	-	2010	-	mmSv/	wh - Z
B`more Eustace	Ardinode	Brady Philip	corn	-	13a.	-	-	-	-	gr/	-
B`more Eustace	Ardinode	Brady Philip	corn	(1A) 30x20x11 :	-	5-5	-		13.6x4x13.6 o`shot :	hob/	5.3888
B`more Eustace	Ardinode	Homan Henry	corn	-	82a.	-	-	-	-	gr/	-
B`more Eustace	Ardinode	Homan Henry	corn	(1C) 45x23x24 :	-	-	-	-	15x4x4.6 42 bkts. :	hob/	5.3888
Ardree	Ardnaree	Bell	tuck mills	-	-	-	Bell - Atkinson	1785	-	dd/	361 446 245416
Ardree	Ardnaree	Brown Dorcas :	mills	-	-	-	Brown D - Paget James	1789	-	dd/	404 338 268482
Ardee	Ardnaree	Gore Arthur :	mills	-	-	-	Gore Arth - King Vesey :	1809	-	dd/	630 90 431142
Ardee	Ardnaree	Jones Vaughan :	mills	-	-	-	Jones V - Jones Thomas :	1779	-	dd/	330 608 225417
Ardree	Ardree	Atkinson	mills	-	-	-	Atkinson - Atkinson	1765	-	dd/	282 491 185488
Ardee	Ardree	Burroughs Thomas :	mill	-	-	-	Burroughs T - Kelly Thos :	1780	-	dd/	333 214 223520
Ardee	Ardree	Connolly	mill	-	-	-	Connolly - Hill	1790	-	dd/	423 29 273241
Ardee	Ardree	Connolly	mill	-	-	-	Connolly - Ledwick	-	?	dd/	483 183 312901
Ardree	Ardree	Connolly Arthur Rev	mill	-	-	-	Connolly A - Butler	1786	-	dd/	379 417 253494
Ardee	Ardree	Doherty	mill	-	-	-	Doherty - Richards	-	?	dd/	482 446 312591
Ardree	Ardree	Evans Henry :	mill	-	-	-	Evans H - Walsh James :	1765	-	dd/	254 185 153582
Ardree	Ardree	Evans Henry :	mill	-	-	-	Evans H - Bagnell William	1768	-	dd/	262 505 173862
Ardee	Ardree	Evans Henry :	mills	-	-	-	Evans H - Evans Robert :	1764	-	dd/	239 345 158505
Ardee	Ardree	Farange	mill	-	-	-	Farange - Connolly	c1780	?	dd/	459 10 292679`
Ardree	Ardree	Harding Ambrose :	mill	-	-	-	Harding A - Evans Henry	1763	-	dd/	215 620 145927
Ardree	Ardree	Jones	mills	-	-	-	Jones - Browne	1740	-	dd/	203 xx 134797
Ardee	Ardree	Kelly Thomas :	mill	-	-	-	Kelly T - Evans William :	1780	-	dd/	333 254 223929
Ardree	Ardree	Tyranley James Ld.	mills	-	-	-	Tyranley Ld - Jones Thos	1739	-	dd/	97 43 671295
Ardree	Ardree Town	Alfred Haughton	flour	(1B) 104x21x37 :	-	37-11	-	1851	19x15x3.9 40 floats :	hob/	5.3873
Ardree	Ardrigh	Harding	mill	-	-	-	Harding - Evans	-	-	dd/	215 620 145429
Greatconnell	Athgarvan	- on R. Liffey	mill	-	-	-	-	-	-	6"os/	23
Greatconnell	Athgarvan	Dennell	mill	-	-	-	Dennell - Colvill	-	?	dd/	338 596 229342?
Greatconnell	Athgarvan	Dennell	millhouse etc.	-	-	-	Dennell - Colvill	-	-	dd/	327 310 261504
Greatconnell	Athgarvan	Dennell	millhouse etc.	-	-	-	Dennell - Colvill	-	-	dd/	358 40 238516
Greatconnell	Athgarvan	Dennell John :	mill	-	-	-	Dennell J - Colvill William :	1780	Mort. 12 May	dd/	331 588 223607
Greatconnell	Athgarvan	Reeves Joseph R	flour	-	14a.	-	-	-	-	gr/	-
Greatconnell	Athgarvan	Twigg Thomas :	mill	-	-	-	Twigg T - Dennell Jno :	1787	Lse. 3 May	dd/	400 314 263687
Greatconnell	Athgarvan	Walker & ors :	millhouse etc.	-	-	-	Walker - Colville	-	-	dd/	420 475 297508
St John`s	Athy	- on R. Barrow	mill	-	-		-	-	-	1"os/	128
St Michael`s	Athy Town	- E.side. Barrow	corn mill	-	-		-	-	-	6"os/	35
St Michael`s	Athy Town	- W. side River :	brewery	-	-	-	-	-	-	6"os/	35
St John`s	Athy Town	Bibby Thomas	mills & weirs	-	-	-	Bibby T - Hammon Hen	1851	-	dd/	1851 6 231
Athy	Athy Town	Bibby Thomas	Mills of Athy	-	-	-	Bibby Th - Harmon Henry	1851	-	dd/	1851 6 231
St John`s	Athy Town	Hannon Georgina	mills & weirs	-	-	-	Hannon G - N? Ellen	1899	-	dd/	1899 51 110
St John`s	Athy Town	Hannon Henry	corn	-	-	-	-	-	-	gr/	-
St John`s	Athy Town	Henry Hannon :	corn	(1B) 53x31x25.6 :	-	-	-	1841	15x3.8 24 floats :	hob/	5.2836
St Michael`s	Athy Town	Kavanagh Martin	corn	-	-	-	-	-	-	gr/	-
St John`s	Athy Town	King George	mills	-	-	-	King Geo - Meredith	1848	-	dd/	1848 11 293

PARISH	TOWNLAND	MILLER	TYPE	HOUSE	Land	£Val	PROPRIETORS	Date	WHEEL etc.	Record	Ref.
St John`s	Athy Town	King George	mills & weirs	-	-	-	King Geo - Bibby Thomas	1848	-	dd/	1850 5 184
St John`s	Athy Town	King George	mills & weirs	-	-	-	King Geo - Bibby Thomas	1856	-	dd/	1856 5 184
St John`s	Athy Town	King Jno	mills	-	-	-	King Jno - Meredith Jno	1848	-	dd/	1848 11 293
St Michael`s	Athy Town	Melia William :	bakery	(1C) 27x14x12 :	-	-	-	1851	-	hob/	5.2834
St John`s	Athy Town	Timmons Patrick	bleach	-	-	-	Timmons - Ryan Mary	1897	-	dd/	1897 22 161
Athy	Athy Town :	Bibby Thomas	mills	-	-	-	Bibby Th - Harmon Henry	1852	-	dd/	1852 16 26
St John`s	Athy Town :	Hannon John	mills				Hannon J - Lennon Landon	1902		dd/	1902 51 145
St John`s	Athy Town :	Molloy Robert	brewery	-	-	-	Molloy R - Hannon Jn	1899	-	dd/	1899 41 101
B`more Eustace	B`more Eustace	-	woollen	building old / ruinous	-	-	-	2010	- phos. taken	mmSv/	wh - R
B`more Eustace	B`more Eustace	- due S. of Town	woollen	-	-	-	-	-	-	6"os/	29
B`more Eustace	B`more Eustace	Burton	mill & kiln	-	-	-	Burton - Meredith	-		dd/	-
B`more Eustace	B`more Eustace	Copleton John	mills	-	8a.	-	-	-	-	gr/	-
B`more Eustace	B`more Eustace	Copleton John	mills	-	8a.		-	-	-	gr/	-
B`more Eustace	B`more Eustace	Kehoe/ Keogh Martin	mill & kiln	-	-	-	Kehoe M - Quin Terence	1813	-	dd/	674 390 466147
B`more Eustace	B`more Eustace	Miley	mill & kiln	-	-	-	Miley - Lynch	-		dd/	-
B`more Eustace	B`more Eustace	White John Sir :	mill & kiln	-	-	-	White John Sir - Daly :	1814		dd/	873 467 464595
B`more Eustace	B`more Eustace	Wolfe	mill & kiln	-	-	-	Wolfe - Wolfe	-		dd/	-
Kilrainy	Ballinlig	- near Bunglass	mill	-	-	-	-	-	-	1"os	100
Davidstown	Ballintaggart	Palmerston Henry :	mills	-	-	-	Palmerston Ld - Bonham :	1744	-	dd/	115 267 80420
Davidstown	Ballintaggart	Vincent Richard :	manor & mill	-	-	-	Vincent R - Bonham Fran :	1744	-	dd/	115 268 80421
Rathangan	Ballinure	- on Little Barrow	old mill	-	-	-	-	-	-	6"os/	16
Rathangan	Ballinure	Quinn Thomas	corn	(2C) 25.6x18x6 & :	-	-	-	1842	8.4x3x8.4 bkts. 26 :	hob/	5.3915
Timolin	Ballitore	-	mill	-	-	-	-	-	-	1"os	129
Timolin	Ballitore	- at Greese Mt.	flour	-	-	-	-	-	-	6"os/	36
Timolin	Ballitore	Shackleton`s & Ho.	flour ?	mill large, poor cond.	-		-	1998	-	pWEH	-
Timolin	Ballitore	Shackleton's	Flour Mill	& large House	-	-	-	1998		p/WEH	R
Timolin	Ballitore	Shakleton George	flour	-	32a.	-	-	-	-	gr/	-
Timolin	Ballitore Town	Wilson Stephen	bark	(1B) 28x22x12 :	-	-	-	-	-	hob/	5.2838
Timolin	Ballitore Village	-	corn	-	-	-	-	-	-	6"os/	36
Kildare	Ballyaghmoone *	Burrowes Eliz Lady	mill	-	-	-	Burrowes E - Higgins Patk	1739	-	dd/	100 204 70189?4
Kildare	Ballyaghmoone *	Frost Leonard :	mill	-	-	-	Frost L - Rainsford Thos :	1742	-	dd/	111 112 75848
Kildare	Ballyaghmoone *	Hampton James :	mill	-	-	-	Kild. Sher - Thompson Jas	1757	-	dd/	186 566 125878
Ballybought	Ballybought	Rourke Thomas :	mill	-	-	-	Rourke Thomas - Assgt. :	1820	-	dd/	759 457 515792
Cloncurry	Ballycanon	-	corn & pond	-	-	-	-	-	-	6"os/	5
Cloncurry	Ballycanon	Martin John	corn	-	35a.	-	-	-	-	gr/	-
z ?	Ballygegorge	Touchstone	mill	-	-	-	Touchstone - ditto.	-	-	dd/	-
Carbury	Ballyhagen	-	flax	-	-	-	-	-	-	6"os/	8
Lackagh	Ballykelly	Palmerston Henry :	mills	-	-	-	Palmerston Ld - Bonham :	1744	-	dd/	115 267 80420
Lackagh	Ballykelly	Tyrell George :	mills	-	-	-	Tyrell G - Deey Chris	1780	-	dd/	332 642 1270023
Kildare	Ballynabought *	Rourke Thomas :	mill	-	-		Rourke T - Rourke Peter :	1820	-	dd/	759 457 515792
Kildare	Ballynabought *	Tyrell John	mill	-	-		Tyrell John - Barry Robt	-	-	dd/	-
Kildare	Ballyntagart *	Palmerston Henry :	mills	-	-	-	Palmerston Ld - Bonham :	1744	-	dd/	115 267 80420
Kildare	Ballyntagart *	Vincent Richard :	mills	-	-	-	Vincent R - Bonham Fran :	1744	-	dd/	115 268 80421
Ballynadrumny	Ballyonan	- nr rd. to Moyvally	corn	-	-	-	-	-	-	6"os/	1
Ballynadrumny	Ballyonan	Tyrell John :	mills	-	-	-	Tyrell Jn - Rebecca & :	1821	-	dd/	767 313 520448
Kildare	Ballyoneen *	Rourke Thomas :	mills	-	-		Rourke Thos - Rourke	1820	Asgt.	dd/	750 457 515792
Kildare	Ballyoneen *	Tyrell John :	mills	-	-		Tyrell John - Barry Robert	1821	Conv.	dd/	767 313 520448
Ballyshannon	Ballyshannon	- nr Weevil Vge.	corn	-	-	-	-	-	-	6"os/	32
Ballyshannon	Ballyshannon	Morrin Patrick	corn	-	13a.	-	-	-	-	gr/	-
Balraheen	Ballytracey	Walsh Samuel	corn	(no dimensions)	-	-	-	-	12x3.3x - breast :	hob/	5.3866
Nurney	Balrinnet	-	corn	-	-	-	-	-	-	1"os	110
Nurney	Balrinnet	-	corn	-	-	-	-	-	-	1"os/	

PARISH	TOWNLAND	MILLER	TYPE	HOUSE	Land	£Val	PROPRIETORS	Date	WHEEL etc.	Record	Ref.
Balraheen	Baltracey	-	corn & pond	-	-	-	-	-	-	6"os/	10
Haynestown	Baysland	-	flour	-	-	-	-	-	-	6"os/	19
Haynestown	Baysland	Moran Thomas	flour	(1B) 76x24x41 :	-	27.19	-	1850	18x6x18 breast :	hob/	5.3944
Haynestown	Baysland	Nowlan Patrick	flour	-	71a.	-	-	-	-	gr/	-
Kilhea	Beaconstown	-	flour	-	-	-	-	-	-	6"os/	37
Kilhea	Beaconstown	Greene John	corn	-	78a.	-	-	-	-	gr/	-
Belan	Belan	-	corn	-	-	-	-	-	-	6"os/	388
Moone	Belan	Aldborough Earl	mill	-	-	-	Aldborough - Dunne	-	-	dd/	599 194 409265
Moone	Belan	Dunne	mill	-	-	-	Dunne - Robinson	-	-	dd/	520 275 424638
Belan	Belan	Tate John	corn	-	-	-	-	-	-	gr/	-
Kilberry	Bert Demense	-	mill	-	-		-	-	-	1"os/	
Kilteel	Blackchurch	Greene William	Black Mill & :	-	-	-	Greene Wm N - Mary	1821	-	dd/	770 91 522026
Kilteel	Blackchurch	Killarden John Lord :	mill farm	-	-	-	Killarden Ld - Montgomery	1821	-	dd/	771 486 523021
Kilteel	Blackchurch	Ley James Smith :	mill farm	-	-		Ley Jas - French Robert :	1823	-	dd/	779 16 527351
Bodenstown	Blackhall	- at Alex`dra Br :	mill	-	-	-	-	-	-	1"os	111
Bodenstown	Blackhall	- near Clane Vge.	corn	-	-	-	-	-	-	6"os/	14
Bodenstown	Blackhall	Morrisey John	old corn mill	(3C) 25.6x18x6x10.6 :	-	-	-	1850	14x3.6x2 30 floats :	hob/	5.3951
Davidstown	Blackhall	Tyrell George :	mills	-	-	-	Tyrell G - Deey Chris	1780	-	dd/	332 642 1270023
Narraghmore	Blackrath	Walker as Master	mill	-	-	-	Walker - Colville	-	?	dd/	584 58 392901
Greatconnell	Blackrath and :	-	flour	-	14a.		Goodman (for sale)	2001	-	gr/	-
Greatconnell	Blackrath and :	- near R. Liffey	flour	- appear intact	-		-	2010	- phos. taken	mmSv/	wh - B
Harristown	Boghall	-	mill	-	-		-	-	-	1"os/	
Fontstown	Boley Great	- near Mill Bridge	corn & race	-	-	-	-	-	-	6"os/	31
Kildare	Bonglash *	Jones	mill	-	-	-	Jones - French Arthur :	1743	-	dd/	111 375 77044
Kildare	Bonglash *	Jones Theophilus :	mill (?)	-	-	-	Jones Theo - Daly james :	1755	-	dd/	172 200 115840
Kildare	Bonglash *	Jones Walter	mill	-	-	-	Jones W -Tyrell James	1737	-	dd/	96 450 68862
Kildare	Bonglash *	Jones Walter :	mill	-	-	-	Jones W - Tyrell James :	1736	-	dd/	96 450 68862
Kildare	Bonglash *	Tyrell	mill	-	-	-	Tyrell - Baldwin	c1756	-	dd/	182 335126967
Kildare	Bonglass *	Rourke Thomas :	mills	-	-		Rourke Thos - Rourke	1820	Asgt.	dd/	750 457 515792
Kildare	Bonglass *	Tyrell	mill	-	-	-	Tyrell - Baldwin	-	?	dd/	182 335 126967
Kildare	Bonglass *	Tyrell John	mills	-	-		Tyrell John - Barry Robert	-	-	dd/	-
Kilcock	Boycetown	Balhurst	mill	-	-	-	Balhurst - Dease	c1790	-	dd/	495 39 321986
Kilcock	Boycetown	Cleghorn George	mill	-	-	-	Cleghorn G - Cleghorn :	1777	Annuity 27 Aug.	dd/	415 331 273990
Kilcock	Boycetown	Cleghorn	mill	-	-	-	Cleghorn - Clarke	-	?	dd/	502 251 324494
Kilcock	Boycetown	Cleghorn	mill	-	-	-	Cleghorn - Kelly	-	?	dd/	528 177 346134
Kilcock	Boycetown	Cleghorn George	mill	-	-	-	Cleghorn G - Clarke Jos :	1795	-	dd/	497 19 317326
Kilcock	Boycetown	Creighton	mill	-	-	-	Creighton - Dease	-	-	dd/	498 15 315608
Kilcock	Boycetown	Dease	mill	-	-	-	Dease - Clarke	c1805	-	dd/	583 94 394461
Kilcock	Boycetown	Goslin	mill	-	-	-	Goslin - Crawford	-	?	dd/	565 264 377680
Kilcock	Boycetown	O`Brien	mill	-	-	-	O`Brien - Colcough	-	?	dd/	546 116 358966
Kilcock	Boycetown	Phillips	mill	-	-	-	Phillips - Barber	-	-	dd/	461 247 295050
Kilcock	Boycetown	Savage	mill	-	-	-	Savage - Cruise	-	-	dd/	541 386 357644
Gilltown	Brannockstown	Borrowes Robert	mill	mill houses (tenants) :	-	-	-	1853	- [no details]	hob/	5.3892
Gilltown	Brannockstown	Borrowes Robert	mills	(1A) 64x2220 mill :	-	-	-	1853	- [no details]	hob/	5.3892
Graney	Broadstown	-	old mill & pond	-	-	-	-	-	-	6"os/	40
z ?	Bundriskey *	Tuthill	mill	-	-	-	Tuthill - Greens	-	-	dd/	-
	Bushfield	Russell Solomon :	mill	-	-	-	Russell S - Russell Sam :	1781	Rel. 7 Mar.	dd/	340 98 227209
Kildare	Bushfield :	Russell Samuel :	mill	-	-	-	Russell - Greenwood Sam	1747	-	dd/	129 492 82958
Carberry	Carberry & Castle	Pomeroy John :	mill				Pomeroy J - Robinson Jn :	1822	-	dd/	771 501 523026
Carburry	Carburry	Murphy William	corn	(2B) 22x20.6x17 :	-	-	-	-	12x3x10 bkts 36 :	hob/	5.3853
Carbury	Carbury	- at cross road	corn	-	-	-	-	-	-	6"os/	8
Carbury	Carbury	- lane S. of cross	corn	-	-	-	-	-	-	6"os/	8

PARISH	TOWNLAND	MILLER	TYPE	HOUSE	Land	£Val	PROPRIETORS	Date	WHEEL etc.	Record	Ref.
Carburry	Carbury	Murphy William	corn	-	46a.	-	-	-	-	gr/	-
Carbury	Carbury	Pomeroy	mill	-	-		Pomeroy - Robinson m/arts	-	-	dd/	771 501 523026
Carnalway	Carnalway	-	flour	-	-	-	-	2010	-	mmSv/	wh - Z
Carnalway	Carnalway	- nr. Harristown Ho	corn	-	-	-	-	-	-	6"os/	29
Carnalway	Carnalway	Latouch Robert	flour	(1B) 59x25x27 :	-	-	-	1841	17x5x17 56 bkts. :	hob/	5.3890
Clane	Carrigeen	- at Clane Bridge	woollen fcty	-	-	-	-	-	-	6"os/	14
Clane	Carrigeen	McCracken Peter	woollen fcty	(2B) 51x18x16.6 :	4a.	-	-	1842	17.6x7.9x3.6 :	hob/	5.3857
Clane	Carrigen	-	corn	-	-	-	-	2010	-	mmSv/	wh - Z
Clane	Carrigen	M`Cracken Peter	corn	-	-	-	-	-	-	gr/	-
Dunmanoge	Castleroe West	-	corn	-	-	-	-	-	-	6"os/	37
Dunmanoge	Castleroe West	-	reaping hook	-	-	-	-	-	-	6"os/	37
Dunmanoge	Castleroe West	Lawlor Richard	corn	-	28a.	-	-	-	-	gr/	-
Celbridge	Castletown	-	mill	-	-	-	-			1"os/	
Celbridge	Castletown	Daly	mill	-	-	-	Daly - McNally	c1828	-	dd/	619 337 424442
Celbridge	Castletown	Pentland	mills	-	-	-	Pentland - Revell	-	?	dd/	590 281 399541
Celbridge	Castletown	Spoul Arthur :	mills	-	-	-	Spoul A - Thompson Robt :	1825	Trust 3 May	dd/	802 356 541490
Kildrought	Celbridge	Cotter	mills	-	-	-	Cotter & Aylward - O`Brien	-	?	dd/	352 115 253916
Kildrought	Celbridge	Cotter	mills	-	-	-	Cotter - Grogan	c1790	-	dd/	427 341 279017
Kildrought	Celbridge	Dignum Matthew :	mills	-	-	-	Dignum M - Broe James :	1892	Lse. 13 June	dd/	787 67 532202
Kildrought	Celbridge	Grange	mills	-	-	-	Grange - Sperrin	-	?	dd/	532 338 344231
Kildrought	Celbridge	Jagger Joseph :	mills	-	-	-	Jagger - Houghton Jeremia	1821	-	dd/	799 475 539810
Kildrought	Celbridge	Moran	mills	-	-	-	Moran - Thompson	-	-	dd/	5xx --- 384960
Kildrought	Celbridge	Saporito Ltd	mills	-	-	-	-	-	Francis avg. 3.5 GW	turb/	c1947
Kildrought	Celbridge	Watts John & Eliz :	corn & tuck	- tolls, mulcture &	11a.	-	Watts Jn - Thomson Robt :	1825	-	dd/	802 300 541435
Kildrought	Celbridge Town	Shaw & Houghton	flour, flax	-	-	-	-	-	-	gr/	-
Kildrought	Celbridge Town	Shaw & Houghton :	flour, flax & :	-	-	-	-	1850	-	hob/	5.2844
Kildrought	Celbridge Town :	- vacant	tuck	(1B) 50x45x17.6	-	-	-	1852	- [no details]	hob/	5.3927
Kildrought	Celbridge Town :	-	flour	(1B) 61x34x47 :	-	-	-	1852	- [no details]	hob/	5.3927
Kildrought	Celbridge Town :	- nr Comm. Centre	flax	-	-	-	-	2010	-	mmSv/	wh - B
Kildrought	Celbridge Town :	-	flour	-	-	-	-	2010	-	mmSv/	wh - B
Kildrought	Celbridge Town :	-	woollen fcty	- finely preserved :	-	-	-	2010	-	mmSv/	wh - Cl
Kildrought	Celbridge Town :	Houghton & Shaw	woollen fcty :	(1B) 73x21.6x44.6 :	-	235	-	1851	19x20.6x7.6 38 bkts.	hob	5.2843
Harristown	Cherrymills	- Cherry Mills	corn	- demol. c1950	-	-	-	2007	-	mmSv/	wh - Z
Harristown	Cherrymills	- nr Cherrymills Ho	flour	-	-	-	-	-	-	6"os/	27
Harristown	Cherrymills	- nr Cherrymills Ho	mill	-	-	-	-	-	-	1"os	119
Harristown	Cherrymills	Hanlon Patrick	corn	-	20a.	-	-	-	-	gr/	-
Carn	Churchland	Greene William :	Black Mill	-	-	-	Greene W - Greene Mary :	1821	Lse. 21 Dec.	dd/	770 912 522026
Clane	Clane	Burdett George :	Mills	- on R. Anna Liffey	-		Burdett G - Foss Richard :	1825	-	dd/	801 460 540995
Clane	Clane	Carroll Ephram :	mill	-	-	-	Carroll E - Cuppaidge Geo.	1753	-	dd/	155 607 106275
Clane	Clane	Farrin Richard :	mill	-	-	-	Farrin R - White Henry :	1754	-	dd/	169 169 113224
Clane	Clane	Vesey	mill	-	-	-	Vesey - Maughan	-	-	dd/	376 342 251301
Clane	Clane	Vesey Thomas :	mill	-	-	-	Vesey T - Brickenden Wm	1746	-	dd/	125 212 847780
Clonaghlis	Clonaghlis	-	mill	-	-	-	-	-	-	1"os	111
Clonaghlis	Clonaghlis	-	old windmills	-	-	-	-	-	-	1"os	111
Clonaghs	Clonaghlis	- S. side Canal	corn	-	-	-	-	-	-	6"os/	15
Clonaghs	Clonaghlis	nr. canal / Ardclough	mill	- larbe building	-	-	-	2002	-	mmSv/	wh - B
Clonaghlis	Clonaghlis	Palmer Robert	flour	-	0.0.25		-	-	-	gr/	-
Clonaghs	Clonaghlis	Palmer Robert	flour	(1B) 44x39x37 :	-	-	-	1850	16x6x12 40 bkts. :	hob/	5.3942
Kilrainy	Clonard	Darcy Mary Widow :	mills	-	-	-	Darcy M - Browne Henry :	1808	-	dd/	598 360 410262
Kilrainy	Clonard	Mather Henry :	mills				Mather H - Rooke John Jur	1764	Lse. 16 Apl.	dd/	230 507 152451
Kilrainy	Clonard	McCutchen	mills	-	-	-	McCutcheon - Lynch	-	-	dd/	620 295 424663
Kilrainy	Clonard	Ricards	mills				Rickards - Darcy			dd/	529 526 348493

PARISH	TOWNLAND	MILLER	TYPE	HOUSE	Land	£Val	PROPRIETORS	Date	WHEEL etc.	Record	Ref.
Kilrainy	Clonard	Ricards	mills	-	-	-	Ricards - Darcy	-	-	dd/	529 526 348493
Carbury	Clonkeen	- on R. Boyne	corn	-	-	-	-	-	-	6"os/	8
Carburry	Clonkeen	Rourke Francis	corn	(2B) 27x20x12.6 :	45a.	-	-	-	12.6x3.4x4.6 2 pr st.	hob/	5.3853
Davidstown	Colbinstown	-	saw	-	-	-	-	-	-	1"os/	129
Davidstown	Colbinstown	- nr rd Naas / Cork	corn	-	-	-	-	-	-	6"os/	32
Ardkill	Colbinstown	Couse George :	mill	- with ho. & gdns. :	-	-	Couse G - Eager William :	-	-	dd/	776 243 552577
Laraghbryan	Collegeland	- S. of hospital	brewery	-	-	-	-	-	-	6"os/	5
Morristownbiller	Common	Grady John	corn	-	6a.	-	-	-	-	gr/	-
Kilcock	Commons E	- at top of Town	corn & pond	-	-	-	-	-	-	6"os/	5
Greatconnell	Connell	Farrell Thomas	mill	mill store 67.6x20x19 :	-	-	-	-	15.6x6.6x4.6 floats :	hob/	5.3862
Greatconnell	Connell	Reeves Jos Robt	mill	mills with store over :	-	-	-	-	18x17.6x3.6 floats :	hob/	5.3682
Lackagh	Coolsickin	Card Samuel	mill	-	-	-	Card S - Hutchinson John	1740	-	dd/	101 214 70725
Lackagh	Coolsickin	Card Samuel :	mill	-	-	-	Card S - Hutchinson Jn :	1740	-	dd/	100 409 70993
Lackagh	Coolsickin	Cope Henry :	mill				Cope H - Longfield Robt :	1786	-	dd/	399 107 263035
Lackagh	Coolsickin	Frost	mill	-	-	-	Frost L - Rainsford Thos :	1742	-	dd/	111 112 75848
Lackagh	Coolsickin	Longfield	mill	-	-	-	Longfield R - Cope	-	- ?	dd/	293 36 182569
Lackagh	Coolsickin	Longfield Robert :	mill	-	-	-	Longfield R - Gaven Luke :	1788	In Mort. 16 Feb.	dd/	400 79 263086
Kildare	Corbans *	Burgh	Corbans Mill :	-	-	-	Burgh - Burroughs Dixon	-	?	dd/	157 87 104050
Kildare	Corbans *	Burgh	mill	-	-	-	Burgh - Foster	-	-	dd/	532 584 240530
Kildare	Corbans *	Burgh	mill & bl. yard	-	-	-	Burg - Burrows Dixon	-	?	dd/	157 87 104050
Kildare	Corbans *	Burgh	mill & bl. yard	-	-	-	Burgh - Foster	-	-	dd/	352 584 240530
Kildare	Corbans *	Eustace	Corbans Mill	-	-	-	Eustace - Murphy	c1765	-	dd/	264 124 167333
Kildare	Corbans *	Eustace	mill & bl. yard	-	-	-	Eustace - Murphy	-	?	dd/	264 124 167233
Cloncurry	Corcoranstown	-	old windmill	-	-	-	-	-	-	1"os/	111
Narraghmore	Crookstown	Ballitore Mill	-	v. well preserved :	-	-	James Maher	1998	Heritage Centre :	pWEH	-
Narraghmore	Crookstown East	Minch George	house & land	-	40a	-	-	-	-	gr/	-
Narraghmore	Crookstown Lr	Morrin Peter	corn	-	28a.	-	-	-	-	gr/	-
Carburry	Demesne	Wolstenholm Col A	flax	(1B) 61.6x22x9 :	-	-	-	1842	14x5.6x2.6 40 bkts :	hob/	5.3853
Donaghumper	Donaghumper	- at br. Celbridge	woollen fcty	-	-	-	-	-	-	6"os/	11
Downings	Downings South	- S. of Downings :	mill	-	-	-	-	-	-	6"os/	11
Ballynadrumny	Garrisker	Flanagan Matthew	corn	-	23a.	-	-	-	-	gr/	-
Ballynadrumny	Garrisker	Flanagan Matthew	corn & kiln	(2B) 19x23x12 :	-	-	-	-	10ft fall : 7ft, 3 pair :	hob/	5.3851
Ballynafagh	Gilltown	- near Gilltown Lo.	corn	-	-	-	-	-	-	6"os/	28
Ballynafagh	Gilltown	Staplestown	corn & pond	-	-	-	-	-	-	6"os/	9
Gilltown	Gilltown	Flanagan John	corn	(1C) 30x20x12.6 :	-	-	-	1841	13x2.8x11 bkts 40 :	hob/	5.3892
Ballynafagh	Gilltown	Muray Andrew	corn	(3B) 20x22.6x10 :	-	-	-	-	10x2.10 overshot :	hob/	5.3855
Narraghmore	Glassely	- near Glassely Ho.	corn & pond	-	-	-	-	-	-	6"os/	32
Narraghmore	Glassely	Dawson Robert	corn	-	583a.	-	-	-	-	gr/	-
Downings	Goatstown	- near Clane	mill house	-	-	-	-	-	-	6"os/	13
Drumfierth	Gorteen	- in Metcalf Park	flour	-	-	-	-	-	-	6"os/	4
Ballybracken	Gorteen	Bellew Lord	mill	-	-	-	Bellew Lord - Mansfield	-	-	dd/	269 18 168648
Ballybracken	Gorteen	Boyne Lord	mill	-	-	-	Boyne Lord - Cowen	-	-	dd/	276 120 176759
Drumfierth	Gorteen	Dempsey Patrick	corn	-	10a.	-	-	-	-	gr/	-
Drumfierth	Gorteen	Dempsey Patrick	corn	(2B) 33.6x11.6x11 :	-	-	-	-	10x2.6x11 bkts. 24 :	hob/	5.3854
Ballybracken	Gorteen	Mullally Thomas :	mill	-	-	-	Mullally T - Walsh Joseph	1787	-	dd/	388 271 258098
Ballybracken	Gorteen	O`Brien	mill	-	-	-	O`Brien - Gernon	-	-	dd/	368 294 247922
Ballybracken	Gorteen	Warren	mill	-	-	-	Warren - O`Brien	-	-	dd/	350 341 240950
Ballybracken	Gorteen	Warren Jno :	mill	-	-	-	Warren J - Mullally John :	1779	-	dd/	317 491 218521
Graney	Graney West	- at Graney Vge.	flour (in ruins)	-	-	-	-	-	-	6"os/	40
Gilltown	Grange Beg	Burke William	mills	(1B) 40x23x16.6 :	-	-	-	1841	- [no details] :	hob/	5.3892
Gilltown	Grange Beg	Pratt Fitzmaurics	mills	(1B) 40x23x16.6 :	-	-	-	1853	- [no details] :	hob/	5.3892
Greatconnell	Greatconnell	- nr Priory on site :	mill	- large sections : (	-	-	-	2010	- pho/WEH &	mmSv	sb - B

PARISH	TOWNLAND	MILLER	TYPE	HOUSE	Land	£Val	PROPRIETORS	Date	WHEEL etc.	Record	Ref.
Greatconnell	Greatconnell	Daly Denis :	mill	-	-	-	Daly D - Molone Edmond :	1740	-	dd/	97 491 69301
Greatconnell	Greatconnell	Digby Rev. Benj :	mill	-	-	-	Digby B - Gates Robert :	1753	-	dd/	159 317 107112
Greatconnell	Greatconnell	Farrell Thomas	flour	-	1.0.19		-	-	-	gr/	-
Greatconnell	Greatconnell	Gates Thomas :	mill	-	-	-	Gates T - Gaven Robert :	1754	-	dd/	165 554 113086
Greatconnell	Greatconnell	Jervis Augustin	mill	-	-	-	Jervis Augustin - Will	-	-	dd/	275 256176704
Greatconnell	Greatconnell	Jevers Susannagh :	mill	-	-	-	Jevers S - Bloomer Wm :	1774	-	dd/	303 364 201412
Greatconnell	Greatconnell	Jones Henry :	mill	-	-	-	Jones H - Burchell Peter :	1741	-	dd/	124 287 84710
Greatconnell	Greatconnell	Jones Thomas :	mill	-	-	-	Jones T - Lord Primate HG	1715	-	dd/	110 238 78693
Greatconnell	Greatconnell	Kelly	mill	-	-	-	Kelly - Murphy	-	-	dd/	570 454 382374
Greatconnell	Greatconnell	Moreton William :	mill	-	-	-	Moreton W - Harinan Robt	1743	-	dd/	108 464 77036
Greatconnell	Greatconnell	Murphy John :	corn	-	5a.	-	Murphy Jn - Murphy Jas :	1779	-	dd/	335 90 222527
Greatconnell	Greatconnell	Powell	mill	-	-	-	Powell - Wright	-	-	dd/	342 558 231501
Greatconnell	Greatconnell	Rickard	mill	-	-	-	Rickard - Daly	-	-	dd/	476 520 316264?
Kildare	Greenhills	Fitzgerald Lord :	mill & land	-	-	-	Fitzgerald Ld - Hippsley :	1821	-	dd/	765 201 519136
Ballybracken	Gurty *	Varielles James :	mill	-	-	-	Varielles J - Porter Cooke :	1754	-	dd/	169 436 114492
Ballybracken	Gurty (?) :	Boyne Frederick :	mill	-	-	-	Boyne Lord - Mansfield Jn	1760	-	dd/	214 100 140443
Ballybracken	Gurty (?) :	Boyne Lord	mill	-	-	-	Boyne Lord - Tyrell	-	-	dd/	278 138 177243
Harristown	Harristown Lower	Bierne Patrick	corn	-	48a.	-	-	-	-	gr/	-
Harristown	Harristown Lower	Bierne Patrick	flour	-	7a.	-	-	-	-	gr/	-
Harristown	Harristown Lower :	-	corn	-	-	-	-	-	-	6"os/	27
Kill	Hartwell Upper	Doyle Edward	corn	-	4a.	-	-	-	-	gr/	-
Kill	Hartwell Upper	Flanagan Thomas	corn	(1B) 27.6x13x27 :	-	-	-	1850	12x3.8x12.6 :	hob/	5.3945
Haynestown	Haynestown	-	mill	-	-	-	-	-	-	1"os	120
Haynestown	Haynestown	or Newtown	-	small bld. roadside :	-		Mrs Mooney :	2001	-	pWEH	-
Kildare	Hinges	Dixon Henry :	mill	-	-	-	Dixon H - Babington Wm C	1825	-	dd/	802 338 541473
Ballynafagh	Hodgestown	-	old windmill	-	-	-	-	-	-	1"os/	111
Scullogestown	Hortland	Hort Josiah George :	mill	-	-	-	Hortland J - Eyre Thomas	1766	-	dd/	255 94 16808
Scullogestown	Hortland	Hortland	mill	-	-	-	Hortland - Dever	-	-	dd/	353 183 237696
Scullogestown	Hortland	Tuam Josiah late :	mill ? :	r -	-	-	Tuam Archbishop - & Will	1751	-	dd/	151 415 102009
Narraghmore	Inchaquire	Greenham Leonard	cotton factory	-	72a.		-	-	-	gr/	-
Narraghmore	Inchaquire	Jackson Samuel Jun	mills	called Shorts Mills	-		Jackson S - Chambers Jn :	1824	Mort. 8 Apl.	dd/	796 210 537745
Narraghmore	Inchaquire	Keating	mill	-	-	-	Keating - Drought	-	?	dd/	400 436 246 8?28
Narraghmore	Inchaquire	Keating Catherine :	mill	-	-	-	Keating C - Power Robt :	1789	Asgt. 30 May	dd/	409 506 296044
Narraghmore	Inchaquire	Keating Maurice :	mill	-	-	-	Keating M - Farmer John :	1807	Lse. 14 Mar.	dd/	589 371 403405
Narraghmore	Inchaquire	Rawson William	mill	-	-	-	Keating St L - Vesey	-	-	dd/	192 153 321257
Narraghmore	Inchaquire	Rawson William :	mill	-	-	-	Rawson Wm - Richard	1763	-	dd/	304 606 206642
Narraghmore	Inchemcquethyr	: Dyer John	mill	-	-	-	Dyer Jn - Fitzhenry Dav	1389	-	mssH/	d.1319
Moone	Irishtown	- nr Broomfield Ho	mill	-	-	-	-	-	-	1"os	128
Moone	Irishtown	Finnigan Thomas :	mill	-	-	-	Finnigan Thos - Duff John	1762	-	dd/	230 58 149069
Moone	Irishtown	Hamilton William :	mill	-	-	-	Hamilton - Tisdall Hester :	1758	-	dd/	191 576 129644
Moone	Irishtown	Murphy Partick :	mill	-	-	-	Murphy P - Short John :	1764	-	dd/	278 470179782
Moone	Irishtown	Wills	mill	-	-	-	Wills - Cromie	-	?	dd/	205 440 136350
Moone	Irishtown	Wills Godfrey :	mill	-	-	-	Wills G - Finnigan Thomas	1753	-	dd/	159 424 107585
Johnstown	Johnstown	-	mill	-	-		-	-	-	1"os/	137
Johnstown	Johnstown	-	windmill	-	-	-	-	-	-	6"os/	4
Cadamstown	Johnstown	- Johnstown Vge.	corn	-	-	-	-	-	-	6"os/	1
Cadamstown	Johnstown	- west of Village	windmill	-	-	-	-	-	-	6"os/	4
Johnstown	Johnstown	Fitzpatrick John	mill	-	-		Fitzpatrick John :	1821	M. Arts. 20 Nov.	dd/	767175 520301
Johnstown	Johnstown	Garnett Ann :	mill	-	-		Garnett A - Thompson Wm	1823	-	dd/	778 467 527202?
Johnstown	Johnstown	Hamilton Henry :	mill	-	-		Hamilton H - Wingfield Hon	1822	Mort. 13 Dec.	dd/	781 547 529109
Castledermot	Johnstown	Hannan James & :	flour	(1B) 20x22.6x24 :	-	-	-	1851	18x12x10 breast :	hob/	5.3875
Johnstown	Johnstown	Lattin	mill	-	-	-	Lattin - Rose	-	-	dd/	297 498 195944

PARISH	TOWNLAND	MILLER	TYPE	HOUSE	Land	£Val	PROPRIETORS	Date	WHEEL etc.	Record	Ref.
Johnstown	Johnstown	Lodge Jno :	mill	-	-	-	Lodge J - Bryan Robert :	1808		dd/	592 532 405600
Johnstown	Johnstown	Mooney Morgan :	mill	-	-		Mooney & Keane M/Arts.	1823	-	dd/	785 295 531230
Johnstown	Johnstown	Reynolds	mill	-	-	-	Reynolds - Reynolds	-	-	dd/	505 612 331218
Johnstown	Johnstown	Reynolds Thomas :	mill	-	-	-	Reynolds T - Lodge John :	1807	Lse. 15 Feb.	dd/	592 532 405599
Johnstown	Johnstown	Roberts John Crame	mill	-	-		Roberts John - Ryan Wm :	1822	Mort. 14 Jne.	dd/	772 523 523658
Johnstown	Johnstown	Roberts John Rev :	mill	-	-		Roberts Jn - Connor Geo :	1822	-	dd/	774 287 524622
Johnstown	Johnstown	Rose	mill	-	-	-	Rose - Rose	-	-	dd/	458 79 294325
Johnstown	Johnstown	Rose	mill	-	-	-	Rose - Goodshaw	-	-	dd/	500 296 313187
Castledermot	Johnstown South	Bamberry Thomas	corn	(1C) 34x20x25.6 :	-	-	-	1841	15x3.6x5 breast :	hob/	5.3875
Castledermot	Johnstown South	Hannan James	flour	-	7a.	-	-	-	-	gr/	-
Corncomohide	Kilacolla	Caroll Patrick	corn	-	-	-	-		12x3x12	vmb/	
Kildare	Kilbernon *	Downing	mill	-	-	-	Downing - Kelly	-	-	dd/	355 486 241922
Kildare	Kilbernon *	Kelly	mill	-	-	-	Kelly - Kenny	-	?	dd/	339 321 228920
Kilcock	Kilcock	- on Town Square	brewery	-	-	-	-	-	-	6"os/	5
Kilcock	Kilcock	- on Town Square	distillery	-	-	-	-	-	-	6"os/	5
Kilcock	Kilcock	Bathurst	mill	-	-	-	Bathurst - Bathurst	-	-	dd/	559 555 377507?
Kilcock	Kilcock	Beauchamp Richd :	mills	-	-	-	Beauchamp - Harvey Fran	1750	-	dd/	141 442 961127
Kilcock	Kilcock	Browne	mill	-	-	-	Browne - Rourke	-	?	dd/	554 204 366852
Kilcock	Kilcock	Browne	mill	-	-	-	Browne - Quin	-	?	dd/	556 13 367016
Kilcock	Kilcock	Browne	mill	-	-	-	Browne - Kelly	-	?	dd/	573 336 390305
Kilcock	Kilcock	Caulfielld	mills	-	-	-	Caulfield - Wogan Browne	-	-	dd/	431 422 281131
Kilcock	Kilcock	Cope	mill	-	-	-	Cope - Colgan	-	?	dd/	572 195 388208
Kilcock	Kilcock	Dease	mill	-	-	-	Dease - Walker	-	?	dd/	580 261 395206
Kilcock	Kilcock	Selby Charles :	mills	-	-	-	Selby Chas - Tully John :	1751	-	dd/	154 225 103495
Kilcock	Kilcock	Wogan	mills	-	-	-	Wogan - Browne	-	?	dd/	374 249 284909
Kilcock	Kilcock Town	Byrne James	corn	-	0.0.33		-	-	-	gr/	-
Kilcock	Kilcock Town	Colgan Ed & Sam	brewery	-	-	-	-	-	-	gr/	-
Kilcock	Kilcock Town	Colgan Henry	distillery	-	0.0.20		-	-	-	gr/	-
Kilcullen	Kilcullen	Harris Mary :	brewery & : d	-	-	-	Harris Mary - Connell John	1760	M. Arts.	dd/	200 580 134415
Kilcullen	Kilcullen	Harris Mary :	mill	-	-	-	Harris Mary - Connell John	1760	M. Arts.	dd/	200 580 134415
Kilcullen	Kilcullen	Harris Robert 1(	brewery & : d	-	-	-	Harris R - Tighe Robert :	1752	-	dd/	158 153 105296
Kilcullen	Kilcullen	Harris Robert :	brewery & : d	-	-	-	Harris R - Tighe Robert :	1752	-	dd/	158 153 105296
Kilcullen	Kilcullen	McMahon James :	mill	-	-	-	McMahon James - Patrick	1763	-	dd/	216 622145669
Kilcullen	Kilcullen	Otwell Roland :	brewery	-	-	-	Otwell - Harris Robert :	1747	-	dd/	133 226 90530
Kilcullen	Kilcullen	Otwell Roland :	brewery	-	-	-	Otwell - Harris Robert :	1747	-	dd/	133 226 90530
Kilcullen	Kilcullen	Otwell Roland :	brewery	-	-	-	Otwell - Harris Robert :	1747	-	dd/	133 226 90530
Kilcullen	Kilcullen	Smith Jno :	brewery & :	-	-	-	Smith J - Cooper James :	1764	-	dd/	240 27 152995
Kilcullen	Kilcullen	Smith Jno :	mill	-	-	-	Smith J - Cooper James :	1764	-	dd/	240 27 152995
Kilcullen	Kilcullen	Smith John :	mill	-	-	-	Smith J - Cooper James	1762	-	dd/	216 386 143338
Kilcullen	Kilcullen	Tighe Robert :	brewery	-	-	-	Tighe R - Varielles James :	1755	Assgt.	dd/	1996 24 128929
Kilcullen	Kilcullen	Tighe Robert : (	mill	-	-	-	Tighe R - Varielles James :	1755	Assgt.	dd/	196 24 128929
Kilcullen	Kilcullen	Todd	mill	-	-	-	Todd - Otwell	-	-	dd/	208 26 136294
Kilcullen	Kilcullen Town	Brady Michael	corn	-	107a.	-	-	-	-	gr/	-
Kilcullen	Kilcullen Town	Murphy Michael	corn	-	-	-	-	-	-	gr/	-
Kilcullen	Kilcullen Town :	Murphy Michael	corn	- nicely preserved	-	-	-	2001	-	pWEH/	B
Kilcullen	Kilcullenbridge	- near Kilcullen Br.	mill	-	-	-	-	-	-	1"os	120
Kilcullen	Kilcullenbridge	- E. side R. Liffey :	corn	-	-	-	-	1841	-	6"os	48
Kilcullen	Kilcullenbridge	- Kilcullen Town	corn	-	-	-	-	2001	-	pWEH	-
Kilfinane	Kilfinnane	-	mill	-	-	-	-		-	1"os/	
Kilrainy	Kilglass	- near Kilglass Ho.	corn	-	-	-	-	-	-	6"os/	3
Kilcullen	Kilgowan	- on rd Naas/Cork :	corn & dam	-	-	-	-	-	-	6"os/	32
Kilkea	Kilkea	Dickson	mill	-	-	-	Dickson - Lewis	-	?	dd/	305 737 214279

PARISH	TOWNLAND	MILLER	TYPE	HOUSE	Land	£Val	PROPRIETORS	Date	WHEEL etc.	Record	Ref.
Kilkea	Kilkea	Disney	mill	-	-	-	Disney - Pearson	-	(error)	dd/	138 64 92230
Kilkea	Kilkea	Lewis	mill	-	-	-	Lewis - Lewis	-	?	dd/	390 41 256105
Kilkea	Kilkea	Pearson Robert	mill	-	-	-	Pearson R - Doran Denis :	1754	-	dd/	169 568 115334
Kilkea	Kilkea	White Mark :	mill	-	-	-	White M - Disney Moore :	1747	-	dd/	126 310 87244
Killashee	Killashee	- nr Killashee Ho. :	mill in ruins	-	-	-	-	-	-	6"os/	24
Cloncurry	Killikaweeny	-	old windmill	-	-	-	-	-	-	1"os/	111
Kildare	Kilmore	Coates Thomas :	mill	-	-	-	Coates T - Bomford Steph	1750	Marr. Arts.	dd/	156 472 106863
Kildare	Kilmore	Colley Elizabeth :	mill	-	-	-	Colley E - Hamilton Hon.	1752	-	dd/	155 342 104941
Kildare	Kilmore	Pomeroy Arthur :	mills	-	-	-	Pomeroy - Staunton Thos :	1747	-	dd/	161 132 107915
Kilrush	Kilrush	Cheif Remer	mill	-	-	-	Chief Remer - Sweetman	-	-	dd/	517 325 339976
Kilrush	Kilrush	Fitzgerald	mill	-	-	-	Fitzgerald - Maher	-	-	dd/	537 46 348063
Kilrush	Kilrush	Fitzgerald Ed Lord	mill	-	-	-	Fitzgerald - Fitzgerald	-	-	dd/	528 84? 345750
Kilrush	Kilrush	Frizzell & Wife	mill	-	-	-	Frizell & Wife - Ledwith	-	-	dd/	597 3 405823
Kilrush	Kilrush	Lawlor	mill	-	-	-	Lawlor - Donnell	-	-	dd/	442 438288404
Kilrush	Kilrush	Ogilvie	mill	-	-	-	Ogilvie - Kelly	-	?	dd/	323 277 345411
Kilrush	Kilrush	Sweetman	mill	-	-	-	Sweetman - Ogilvie	-	-	dd/	323 478 345463
Knavinstown	Knavinstown	- at Knavinst`n Ho	mill	-	-	-	-	-	-	6"os/	22
Whitechurch	Ladycastle	Alexander John	corn	-	123a.	-	-	-	-	gr/	-
Whitechurch	Ladycastle	Alexander John	corn	-	-	-	-	-	-	gr/	
Whitechurch	Ladycastle	Atkinson Thomas	flour	(1B) 53.6x28x33.6 :	-	11	-	1841	16x5.6x18 26 floats :	hob/	5.3958
Whitechurch	Ladycastle Lower	-	flour	- blds. demolished	-	-	-	2010	- watercourse alive	mmSv/	wh - Z
Whitechurch	Ladycastle Lower	- nr Straffan Br.	flour	-	-	-	-	-	-	6"os/	14
Leixlip	Leixlip	- at Mill Lane	flour	- demolished :	-	-	-	2002	-	mmSv/	wh Z
Leixlip	Leixlip	Mitchell John	flour	-	0.0.35		-	-	-	gr/	-
Leixlip	Leixlip	Mitchell John	flour	-	0.0.35		-	-	-	gr/	
Leixlip	Leixlip	Mitchell John	flour	(1C) 49.6x22x17 :	-	-	-	1850	(2) 15.6x2x2.6 & :	hob/	5.3934
Leixlip	Leixlip Town	Ennis Thomas	corn	-	0.0.20		-	-	-	gr/	-
Leixlip	Leixlip Town	Ennis Thomas :	corn	(2C) 26x24x10.6 :	-	-	-	1850	16.6x2.9x3 old & :	hob/	5.3960
Leixlip	Leixlip Town :	-	corn	-	-	-	-	-	-	6"os/	11
Leixlip	Leixlip Town :	-	iron works	(1C) 22.6x20.6x15 :	-	-	-	1842	(2) 18ft. & (1) 12ft. :	hob/	5.3934
Leixlip	Leixlip Town :	-	Iron Works	-	-	-	-	-	-	6"os/	11
Leixlip	Leixlip Town :	-	Iron Works	- (modernised)	-	-	-	2002	-	pWEH/	Cc
Leixlip	Leixlip Town :	Mitchell John	flour	(1C) 49.6x22x17 :	-	-	-	1842	(2) 16x2.8x8 ea. :	hob/	5.3934
Tankardstown	Levitstown	- on R. Barrow	flour	- roof burnt :	-	-	-	2002	- Paddy Kelly	mmSv/	wh - D
Tankardstown	Levitstown	- on canal	flour	-	-	-	-	-	-	6"os/	37
Tankardstown	Levitstown	Haughton Fred & C.	flour	house & 7 offices	-	-	-	1851	18x13x7 breast :	hob/	5.3886
Tankardstown	Levitstown	Houghton Fredk	flour	-	172a	-	-	-	-	gr/	-
Tankardstown	Levitstown	Jeffries Edward	Millhouse	-	172a	-	-	-	Francis 60kw	turb/	c1947
Dunmanoge	Maganey Upper	- on R. Greese	corn	-	-	-	-	-	-	6"os/	39
Dunmanoge	Maganey Upper	- on R. Greese	reaping hook	-	-	-	-	-	-	6"os/	39
Dunmanoge	Maganey Upper	Lawlor Patrick	corn, flour	-	45a	-	-	-	-	gr/	-
Naas	Maudlins	Fitzpatrick John	flour	(1B) 55x20.6x37.6 :	-	-	-	1850	14.6x4.10x9 32 bkts.	hob/	5.3954
Naas	Maudlins	Fitzpatrick Thos	flour	-	1.3.36		-	-	-	gr/	-
Laraghbryan	Maynooth	- Maynooth Vge.	kiln	-	-		-	-	-	6"os/	5
Laraghbryan	Maynooth	Casey	mill	-	-	-	Casey - Swords	-	-	dd/	603 20 409938
Laraghbryan	Maynooth	Hughes	mill	-	-	-	Hughes - Hamilton	-	-	dd/	610 396 427828
Laraghbryan	Maynooth	Kavanagh Edward	Manor Mills :	-	-	-	-	1963	-	lic/4	wheat
Laraghbryan	Maynooth	Leinster Duke	mill	-	-	-	Leinster Duke - Langan	-	-	dd/	603 135 410626
Laraghbryan	Maynooth	Nowlan	mill	-	-	-	Nowlan - Bourne	-	-	dd/	627 165 430337
Laraghbryan	Maynooth	Swords	mill	-	-	-	Swords - Keogh	-	-	dd/	603 134 410625
Laraghbryan	Maynooth	Swords	mill	-	-	-	Swords - Casey	-	-	dd/	603 21 409939
Laraghbryan	Maynooth	Thompson	mill	-	-	-	Thompson - Hughes	-	-	dd/	625 59 627098

PARISH	TOWNLAND	MILLER	TYPE	HOUSE	Land	£Val	PROPRIETORS	Date	WHEEL etc.	Record	Ref.
Laraghbryary	Maynooth Town	: -	flour	(1B) 31x17.6x16 :	-	20.16	-	1850	-	hob/	5.3961
Lakagh	Mill Farm	Williams Henry	flour	-	4.1.1	-	-	-	-	gr/	-
Naas	Millbrook	-	mill	-	-	-	-	-	-	1"os/	128
Tankardstown	Millbrook	-	mill	-	-	-	-	-	-	1"os/	
Kildare	Millestown ?	Goodshaw	mill	-	-	-	Goodshaw - Kennedy	-	-	dd/	573 243 391431
Kildare	Millestown ?	Kearney	mill	-	-	-	Kearney - Ryan	-	-	dd/	573 549 393254
Kildare	Millestown ?	O`Reilly	mill	-	-	-	O`Reilly - Goodshaw	-	-	dd/	573 243 391423
Kildare	Millestown ?	Ryan	mill	-	-	-	Ryan - Johnson	-	-	dd/	619 359 424473
Lackagh	Millfarm	- :	corn	-	-	-	-	-	-	6"os/	32
Kilrush	Millfarm	- on Grand Canal	flour & pond	-	-	-	-	-	-	6"os/	21
Timolin	Millquarter Timolin	Roycroft	mill	-	-	-	Roycroft - Harrington	-	?	dd/	107 88 73319
Ratheran	Milltown	- Milltown Mill	mill	-	-	-	-	-	-	6"os/	18
bo./ Ikeathy	Milltown	Bell	mills	-	-	-	Bell - Fitzgerald	-	-	dd/	369 242 382285
? Townland	Milltown	Connell	-	-	-	-	Connell - Roche	-	-	dd/	-
bo./ Kilkea & M	Milltown	Connolly	mills	-	-	-	Connolly - Duke of Leinster	-	-	dd/	482 419 312409
bo./ Ikeathy	Milltown	Connolly	mills	-	-	-	Connolly - Megennis	-	-	dd/	534 143 349776
bo./ Ikeathy	Milltown	Daly William :	mills	-	-	-	Daly W - Hyland Bryan :	1779	-	dd/	330 262 222067
bo./ Ikeathy	Milltown	Dealy William :	mills	-	-	-	Dealy W - Clibborn Josh :	1778	Mort. 15 Aug.	dd/	327 240 216975
bo./ Ikeathy	Milltown	Hyland	mills	-	-	-	Hyland - Connolly	-	-	dd/	447 124 288443
bo./ Kilkea & M	Milltown	Hyland	mills	-	-	-	Hyland - Connolly	-	-	dd/	456 350 293083
Feighcullen	Milltown	Kelly Richard	corn	-	47a.	-	-	-	-	gr/	-
bo./ Kilkea & M	Milltown	Leinster Duke	mills	-	-	-	Leinster Duke - Connolly	-	-	dd/	487 363 313541
bo./ Kilkea & M	Milltown	Magennis	mills	-	-	-	Magennis - Powerscourt :	-	-	dd/	450 43 362369
? Townland	Milltown	Rawley	-	-	-	-	Rawley - Rawley	-	-	dd/	-
Churchtown	Milltown	Wolfe Theobold	mills	-	-	-	Wolfe T - Wolfe Arthur :	1783	Rel. 4 Jul.	dd/	353 435 239946
? Townland	Milltown Ballyea	-	no mill	-	-	-	-		-	1"os/	
Morristownbiller	Milltown Hawkf`ld	-	no mill	-	-	-	-	-	-	1"os/	119
Churchtown	Moatstown	Nolan Michael	corn	-	7a.	-	J Ano - W Ano	-	-	gr/	-
Churchtown	Moatstown	Nolan Michael	corn	(2B) 27x24x18 :	-	-	-	1841	15x4x2.6 42 floats :	hob/	5.3867
Monasterevan	Monasterevan	- SE side Main St.	brewery & :	-	-	-	-	-	-	6"os/	26
Monasterevin	Monasterevin Tn	Cassidy Robert	brewery	-	-	-	-	-	-	gr/	-
Monasterevin	Monasterevin Tn	Cassidy Robert	distillery	-	-	-	-	-	-	gr/	-
Monasterevin	Monasterevin Tn	Cassidy Robert	mill	-	-	-	-	-	-	gr/	-
Moone	Moone	-	mill	-	-	-	-	-	-	1"os	129
Moone	Moone	- near C`dermot :	corn	-	-	-	-	-	-	6"os/	36
Moone	Moone	- near C`dermot :	flour	-	-	-	-	-	-	6"os/	36
Moone	Moone	- nr Moone Bridge	flour	-	-	-	-	-	-	6"os/	36
Timolin	Moone	Ashe Mary :	mills	-	-	-	Ashe M - Yeates Samuel :	1748	-	dd/	138 306 93295
Timolin	Moone	Ashe Mary, Moone :	mills	-	-	-	Ashe M - Nowlan Michael	1741	-	dd/	118 160 80364
Timolin	Moone	Bourke	mill	-	-	-	Bourke - Pendred	-	-	dd/	472 18 295223
Timolin	Moone	Fayle	mill	-	-	-	Fayle - Richardson	-	-	dd/	461 523 596501
Moone	Moone	Glynn Joseph	corn	(2B) 22.6x21.6x15 :	-	-	-	1841	16x2.6x7 40 bkts. :	hob/	5.38??
Timolin	Moone	Kearney	mill	-	-	-	Kearney - Latouche	-	?	dd/	303 343 260641
Timolin	Moone	Miley	mills	-	-	-	Miley - Cogan	-	-	dd/	618 479 434152
Moone	Moone	Miley James :	mill	-	-		Miley Jas - Lawler John :	1824	-	dd/	798 109 538844
Timolin	Moone	O`Brien Simon :	mills	-	-	-	O`Brien S - Whelan Wm :	1778	-	dd/	328 453 224677
Timolin	Moone	O'Mara	mill	-	-	-	O'Mara - Fayle	-	-	dd/	444 407 288008
Timolin	Moone	Richardson	mill	-	-	-	Richardson - Colville	-	-	dd/	472 56 269500
Timolin	Moone	Richardson	mills	-	-	-	Richardson - Lawler	-	-	dd/	597 189 408113
Timolin	Moone	Richardson	mills	-	-	-	Richardson - Miley	-	-	dd/	615 255 420886
Moone	Moone	Shackleton Chengou	flour	(1B) 40x24x29 (+2) :	-	-	-	-	20x9x7.6 32 floats :	hob/	5.38??
Moone	Moone	Shackleton E. Esq.	mill	house, offices, mill :	-	54	-	-	20x9x7.6 32 floats	hob/	5.3882

PARISH	TOWNLAND	MILLER	TYPE	HOUSE	Land	£Val	PROPRIETORS	Date	WHEEL etc.	Record	Ref.
Timolin	Moone	St John	mill	-	-	-	St John - Farrell	-	-	dd/	396 421 262076
Timolin	Moone	Taylor Jno :	mills	-	-	-	Taylor J - Whelan Patt :	1807	-	dd/	590 570 403988
Timolin	Moone	Thomas	mill	-	-	-	Thomas - Kearney	-	-	dd/	379 202 251866
Timolin	Moone	Thomas & Dillon	mill	-	-	-	Thomas & Dillon - Kearney	-	-	dd/	356 519 242326
Timolin	Moone	Yeates	mill	-	-	-	Yeates - Cooke	-	?	dd/	425 401 277572
Timolin	Moone	Yeates	mills	-	-	-	Yeates - Taylor	-	-	dd/	597 553 410112
Timolin	Moone	Yeates	mills	-	-	-	Yeates - Taylor	-	-	dd/	602 481 414256
Timolin	Moone	Yeates Samuel :	mills	-	-	-	Yeates S - Yeates Thomas	1752	-	dd/	156 201 104284
Timolin	Moone	Yeates Samuel :	mills	-	-	-	Yeates S - O`Brien Simon :	1770	-	dd/	299 18 197004
Timolin	Moone Manor	Nowlan	mill & kiln	-	-	-	Nowlan - Fayle	-	?	dd/	370 507 252228
Kildare	Mooretown	- at Mooretown Ho.	mill	-	-	-	-	-	-	6"os/	22
Gilltown	Moorhill	Brownrigg Cath	mill	(1B) 25.6x26.6x11.6 :	-	-	-	1841	- [no details] :	hob/	5.3892
Kildare	Mount Blarney	Kildare James Earl :	mill	-	-	-	Kildare E - Letablere Danl :	1754	-	dd/	174 204 115834
Kildare	Mount Blarney *	Bell	mill	-	-	-	Bell - Picknoll	-	?	dd/	176 388 119268
Kildare	Mount Blarney *	Kildare Earl James	mill	-	-	-	Kildare E. - Mountjoy Lord :	1744	-	dd/	117 242 30637
Kildare	Mount Blarney *	Leinster Duke of	mill	-	-	-	Leinster Duke - Bere	-	?	dd/	330 453 224269
Kildare	Mount Blarney *	Nelson Richard :	mill (?)	-	-	-	Nelson R - Nelson Oliver	1754	-	dd/	165 384 11245
Kildare	Mount Blarney *	Rutledge Thomas &	mill	-	-	-	Rutledge - Cooke James :	1754	-	dd/	170 236 113824
Kildare	Mount Blarney *	Vandeleur Francis	mill	-	-	-	Vandeleur F - Sullivan John	1755	-	dd/	178 338 119117
Kildare	Mount Blarney *	Vandelure John :	mill	-	-	-	Vandelure - Bell Marmaduk	1753	-	dd/	166 19 110159
Kildare	Mount Blarney *	Vandelure John :	mill	-	-	-	Vandelure J - Orford Thos :	1749	-	dd/	157 207 104511
Kildare	Mountblairnet	Leinster Duke :	mill	-	-	-	Leinster - Marr. Arts.	1818	-	dd/	766 183 519718
Kildare	Mountblairnet	Keating Maurice :	mill	-	-	-	Keating M - Hamilton Henry	1825	-	dd/	807 223 544358
Lackagh	Mountrice	Bagot Walter :	mill	-	-	-	Bagot W - Bagot Edward :	1807	Smt. 24 Nov.	dd/	597 97 405296
Lackagh	Mountrice	Boughal	mill	-	-	-	Boughal - Fitzgerald	-	-	dd/	557 195 397367
Lakagh	Mountrice	Farrell Christopher	corn	-	44a.	-	-	-	-	gr/	-
Lackagh	Mountrice	Farrell Christopher	mill	(1B) 66x26x26.6	-	-	-	1851	12x4.8 buckets 36 :	hob/	5.3917
Carnalway	Mullaghboy	- on R. Liffey :	corn	-	-	-	-	-	-	6"os/	29
Carnalway	Mullaghboy	Rochestown Corn	Mill	-	-	-	-	2010	-	mmSv/	wh - Z
Carnalway	Mullaghboy	Lawlor James	mill	- no dimensions	-	-	-	1852	15x6 & ladles :	hob/	5.3890
Carnalway	Mullaghboy	Lawlor James	mill	old mill 27.6x21x22 :	-	-	-	1841	16x4x4 32 floats :	hob/	5.3890
Rathangan	Mullantine	Fallon Cherry	corn	-	59a.	-	-	-	-	gr/	-
Rathangan	Mullantine	Farrell James	flour & corn	(1B) 23.6x21x25.6 :	-	-	-	1842	Flour : 14.7x3x6.6 :	hob/	5.3915
Rathangan	Mullantine	Tyrell Walter	corn	-	62a.	-	-	-	-	gr/	-
Rathangan	Mullantine	Tyrell Walter	flour & corn	(1B) 106.6x22.6x24 :	-	-	-	1842	Flour : 17x4x8 :	hob/	5.3915
Mylerstown	Mylerstown	Lattin George & Jane	mill	-	-	-	Lattin G - Wilson Richard	1740	-	dd/	101 104 70071
Naas	Naas East	Fleming Thomas	corn	(2C) 33x23x8 :	-	-	-	1841	9.6x3x10 o`shot :	hob/	5.3954
Naas	Naas Town	- Spring Gardens	mill	-	-	-	-	-	-	1"os	120
Naas	Naas Town	Collins John	corn & kiln	-	0.0.20		-	-	-	gr/	-
Naas	Naas Town	Harrington Mary	corn & kiln	-	-	-	-	-	-	gr/	-
Naas	Naas Town	Wilson Richard :	Fryars Mill :	-	-	-	Wilson R - Magee James	1739	-	dd/	93 378 65953
Naas	Naas Town	- at Millbrook	mill	-	-	-	-	-	-	1"os/	120
Naas	Naas Town :	Harrington Mary	mills	-	-	-	Harrington M - Moylan Den	1853	-	dd/	1853 14 208
Naas	Naas Town (E.) :	-	corn	-	-	-	-	-	-	6"os/	19
Naas	Naas Town (W.) :	-	corn & pond	-		-	-	-	-	6"os/	19
Ladytown	New Hall Ho.	- near Naas	mill	-	-	-	-	-	-	1"os/	120
Brannockstown	Newabbey	- at Milemill	mill	-	-	-	-	-	-	6"os/	28
Brannockstown	Newabbey	S. side R. Liffey :	corn	-	-	-	-	-	-	mmSv/	wh - Z
Brannockstown	Newabbey	Kelly Edward :	mill	-	-	-	Kelly E - Hackett Patrick :	1821	-	dd/	765 373 519307
Brannockstown	Newabbey	Kelly Edward	mil & land	-	-	-	Kelly Ed - Hackett Patrick :	1821	-	dd/	765 373 519307
Greatconnell	Newbridge	-	mill	-	-	-	-	-	-	1"os	120
Greatconnell	Newbridge	- on R. Deel	mill	-	-	-	-		-	1"os/	

PARISH	TOWNLAND	MILLER	TYPE	HOUSE	Land	£Val	PROPRIETORS	Date	WHEEL etc.	Record	Ref.
Greatconnell	Newbridge	- near Abbey	mill	-	-	-	-	-	-	1"os/	
Morristownbiller	Newbridge	- near Friary	mill	-	-	-	-	-	-	1"os/	120
Ladytown	Newhall	-	corn	-	-	-	-	-	-	6"os/	19
Ladytown	Newhall	- at Newhall Ho.	mill	-	-	-	-	-	-	1"os/	
Ladytown	Newhall	Flood Thomas	corn	-	331a.	-	-	-	-	gr/	-
Ladytown	Newhall	Flood Thomas	mill	(1B) 28.6x20.6x16.6 :	-	-	-	1842	13.6x4.6x4 no. bkts :	hob/	5.3864
Ladytown	Newhall	near Naas	-	small tidy bld., pond	-	-	Shane Flood	01/10	-	pWEH	-
Ladytown	Newhall	Sabine	mill	-	-	-	Sabine - Sherdley	-	?	dd/	103 163 78067
Ladytown	Newhall	Sabine	mill	-	-	-	Sabine - Price	-	-	dd/	460 67 293257
Ladytown	Newhall	Sabine	mill	-	-	-	Sabine - Fitzpatrick	-	-	dd/	503 431 321750
Ladytown	Newhall	Sabine Joshua :	mill	-	-	-	Sabine J - Lowther Jno :	1775	-	dd/	315 338 211944
Killashee	Newland	Dunn	mill	-	-	-	Dunn - Grogan	-	-	dd/	617 15 420419
Killashee	Newland	Sabine	mill	-	-	-	Sabine - Jefferys	-	-	dd/	500 246 312801
Killashee	Newland	Sabine	mill	-	-	-	Sabine - Cockburne	-	-	dd/	504 103 325471
Ladytown	Newtown	-	corn & dam	-	-	-	-	-	-	6"os/	38
Donaghcumper	Newtown	-	Temple Mills	- Millhouse intact :	-	-	Dr. Pierce Phelan	2010	- millrace still alive :	mmSv/	wh - R
Ladytown	Newtown	-	woollen fcty	-	-	-	-	-	-	6"os/	38
Leixlip	Newtown	- 1/2m N. Leixlip	distillery	-	-	-	-	1851	-	6"os/	11
Donaghcumper	Newtown	- E. side R. Liffey :	Temple Mills	-	-	-	-	1841	-	6"os/	11
Leixlip	Newtown	Cartan Laurence & :	brewery	(1B) 64.6x51x24 :	-	-	-	1842	14x7.6x10 42 bkts. :	hob/	5.3934
Leixlip	Newtown	Carton L & Burke A	corn, flour	-	11a.	-	-	-	-	gr/	-
Leixlip	Newtown	Carton L & Burke A	flour	-	7a.	-	-	-	-	gr/	-
Leixlip	Newtown	Carton L & Burke A	old distillery	-	-	-	-	-	-	gr/	-
Leixlip	Newtown	Cave	mill	-	-	-	Cave - Harpur	-	-	dd/	362 467 246236
Leixlip	Newtown	Clinton	mill	-	-	-	Clinton - Otway	-	-	dd/	610 148 418292
Donaghcumper	Newtown	Ellis Mr.	Temple Mills	-	-	-	-	-	Unknown 60kw	turb/	c1947
Leixlip	Newtown	Hackett Esther :	mill	-	-	-	Hackett E - Boyle Chris :	1772	-	dd/	292 359 190874
Leixlip	Newtown	Harpur	mill	-	-	-	Harpur - O`Brien	-	-	dd/	365 525 246237
Leixlip	Newtown	Keighly	mill	-	-	-	Keighly - Keighly	-	-	dd/	553 39 36620?
Leixlip	Newtown	O`Brien	mill	-	-	-	O`Brien - Donnellan	-	-	dd/	525 191 344277
Leixlip	Newtown	O`Brien	mill	-	-	-	O`Brien - Donnellan	-	-	dd/	526 246 344276
Donacumper	Newtown	Shaw Joseph	flax	(1B) 86.6x61x40 :	-	-	-	1852	No.1/ 18x10.6x6.6 :	hob/	5.3921
Donaghcumper	Newtown	Shaw Joseph	flax mfty	-	6a.	-	-	-	-	gr/	-
Killelan	Newtown	Walsh Michael	corn	-	138a.	-	-	-	-	gr/	-
Killelan	Newtown	Walsh Michael Esq.	corn	(1B) 60x22x21 & :	-	-	-	1851	- [no information	hob/	5.3380
Newtown	Newtown O`More	Allen Lord Visc.	mill	-	-	-	Allen Ld & Reilly agreemen	1820	Agreement	dd/	761 19 516544
Kilcullen	Nicholastown	- on R. Liffey	Newabbey Corn Mill		-	-	-	-	-	6"os/	28
Kilcullen	Nicholastown	Morrin Patrick	corn	-	32a.	-	-	-	-	gr/	-
Nurney	Nurney	Fitzgerald Jas W	corn	-	193a.	-	-	-	-	gr/	-
Nurney	Nurney Town	-	mill	-	-	-	-	-	-	1"os/	
Robertstown	Old Abbey	McNamara Laur	corn	-	-	-	-		13x4x14	vmb/	
Kilteel	Oldmilltown	- rd. to Rathcoole	old mill & race	-	-	-	-	-	-	6"os/	20
Kildare	Oldtown (5)	Burgh	mill	-	-	-	Burgh - Foster	-	-	dd/	352 584 240538
Kildare	Oldtown (5)	Burgh	mill	-	-	-	Burgh - Montgomery	-	-	dd/	387 186 260235
Kildare	Oldtown (5)	Burgh	mill	-	-	-	Burgh - Digby	-	-	dd/	500 104 312263
Kildare	Oldtown (5)	Goddard	mill	-	-	-	Goddard - Burgh	-	-	dd/	432 113 386229?
Kildare	Oldtown (5)	Pallis John	mill	-	-	-	Pallis John - Marr. Smt.	-	-	dd/	385 536 256008
Naas	Osberstown	-	Leinster Mills	-	-	-	-	-	-	1"os	120
Naas	Osberstown	- Leinster Mills	flour	-	-	-	-	-	-	6"os/	19
Naas	Osberstown	- Leinster Mills	mills	- blds. dilapidated	-	-	-	2010	-	mmSv/	sb - B
Naas	Osberstown	- Leinster Mills	mills	finely refurbished	-	-	Millenium Park Ind. Est.	2001	-	pWEH	-
Naas	Osberstown	Montgomery	Leinster Mills	-	-	-	Montgomery - Aikens	-	-	dd/	573 247 387817

PARISH	TOWNLAND	MILLER	TYPE	HOUSE	Land	£Val	PROPRIETORS	Date	WHEEL etc.	Record	Ref.
Naas	Osberstown	Montgomery	Leinster Mills	-	-	-	Mon tgomery - Aikens	-	-	dd/	609 423 422568
Naas	Osberstown	Montgomery	Leinster Mills	-	-	-	Montgomery - Lucas	-	-	dd/	609 430 422581
Naas	Osberstown	Montgomery	mill	-	-	-	Montgomery - Colville	-	-	dd/	528 92 345776
Naas	Osberstown	Montgomery	mill	-	-	-	Montgomery - Aickin	-	-	dd/	609 423 422568
Naas	Osberstown	Nolan Simon	flour	(1B) 84x29x49.6 :	-	-	-	1841	15X5X13 new :	hob/	5.3954
Naas	Osberstown	Reed Robert	corn	(2C) 18.6x5.6x18 :	-	-	-	1841	14x4x4 breast n :	hob/	5.3954
Johnstown	Palmerstown	- Johnstown Vge.	flour	-	-	-	-	-	-	6"os/	19
Johnstown	Palmerstown	- Mayo Flour Mills	flour	-	-	-	-	-	-	6"os/	19
Donaghcumper	Parsonstown	- Hopkin's Mill	corn	- small piece wall	-	-	Mr. & Roisin O'Riordan	2002	-	mmSv/	wh - R
Ardkill	Parsonstown	Bayley	mill	-	-	-	Bayley - Randell	-	-	dd/	550 108 362866
Ardkill	Parsonstown	Boardman	mill	-	-	-	Boardman - Bowers	-	-	dd/	494 274 323683
Ardkill	Parsonstown	Boardman	mill	-	-	-	Boardman - Boylan	-	-	dd/	535 177 350272
Ardkill	Parsonstown	Boardman	mill	-	-	-	Boardman - Boardman	-	-	dd/	575 461 387375
Ardkill	Parsonstown	Boardman Joseph	mill	-	-	-	Boardman Joseph - Will	-	-	dd/	608 281 417836
Ardkill	Parsonstown	English William :	mills	-	-	-	English W - McMurray Mar	1820	-	dd/	761 523 517058
Ardkill	Parsonstown	Flood	mill	-	-	-	Flood - O`Brien	-	-	dd/	562 424 374788
Ardkill	Parsonstown	Fury	mill	-	-	-	Fury - Sronge	-	-	dd/	540 246 355292
Donaghcumper	Parsonstown	Hopkins William	corn & flour	(1B) 69x27.6x21 :	-	-	-	1841	16x5.6x5 bkts. 32 :	hob/	5.3922
Ardkill	Parsonstown	Hughes	mill	-	-	-	Hughes - Pentland	-	-	dd/	611 462 419344
Ardkill	Parsonstown	Kearney	mill	-	-	-	Kearney - Tutton	-	-	dd/	629 56 430050
Ardkill	Parsonstown	O`Brien	mill	-	-	-	O`Brien - Shuldan	-	-	dd/	561 348 377790
Ardkill	Parsonstown	Queade	mill	-	-	-	Queade - Langrishe	-	-	dd/	523 236 345226
Ardkill	Parsonstown	Randell	mill	-	-	-	Randell - Tuton	-	-	dd/	549? 173 362896
Ardkill	Parsonstown	Tuton	mill	-	-	-	Tuton - Mahon	-	-	dd/	604 25 410726
Ardkill	Parsonstown	Tuton John :	mills	-	-	-	Tuton John - Tuton Ann :	1824	Trust 10 Mar.	dd/	789 531 533866
Donaghcumper	Parsonstown :	- N. side R. Liffey	flour	-	-	-	-	-	-	6"os/	11
Kilmeage	Pluckerstown	Aylmer	mill	-	-	-	Aylmer - Norris	-	-	dd/	194 22 126497
Kilmeage	Pluckerstown	Aylmer Fitzgerald :	mill	-	-	-	Aylmer Sir F - Young Jn :	1763	-	dd/	232 93 150013
Kilmeage	Pluckerstown	Aylmer Lucy :	mill	-	-	-	Aylmer L - Norris John :	1755	-	dd/	173 529 117153
Kilmeage	Pluckerstown	Brereton Edward :	mill	-	-	-	Brereton E - Bunbury Thos	1773	-	dd/	299 278 198357
Kilmeage	Pluckerstown	Bunbury George :	mill	-	-	-	Bunbury - Burton Sir Chas	1778	Mort. 12 Feb.	dd/	321 204 214880
Kilmeage	Pluckerstown	Burton Sir Charles :	mill	-	-	-	Burton C - Meredyth Josh	1779	-	dd/	325 308 220599
Kilmeage	Pluckerstown	Fisher Robert :	mill	-	-	-	Fisher R - Young John :	1755	-	dd/	178 426 110490
Kilmeage	Pluckerstown	Lefroy Thos Hon	mills	-	-	-	Lefroy T - Wilbreham : Eg	1840	-	dd/	1840 5 61
Kilmeage	Pluckerstown	Matthew Isaac :	mill	-	-	-	Matthew I - Bunbury Thos :	1773	-	dd/	299 284 198394
Kilmeage	Pluckerstown	Meredyth Susanna :	mill	-	-	-	Meredyth S - Burton Chas :	1784	-	dd/	354 451 239670
Pollardstown	Pollardstown :	-	old corn mill	-	-	-	-	-	-	6"os/	23
Castledermot	Prumpelstown	-	flour	-	-	-	-	-	-	6"os/	40
Castledermot	Prumpelstown	-	saw	building in good order	-	-	David Cope	2002	-	mmSv/	wh - B
Oughterard	Quinsborough	Garnett	mill	-	-	-	Garnett - Garnett	-	-	dd/	510 85 329067
Oughterard	Quinsborough	Garnett	mill	-	-	-	Garnett - Thompson	1822	- [error/ parties]	dd/	769 295 521630
Oughterard	Quinsborough	Kelly	mill	-	-	-	Kelly - Brennan	-	-	dd/	563 56 380924
Oughterard	Quinsborough	Nugent John :	mill	-	-	-	Nugent J - Thompson Wm	1823	-	dd/	781 147 528682
Oughterard	Quinsborough	Quin	mill	-	-	-	Quin - Read	-	-	dd/	386 374 258921
Oughterard	Quinsborough	Read	mill	-	-	-	Read - Thompson	-	-	dd/	546 91 359496
Oughterard	Quinsborough	Thompson William :	mill	-	-	-	Thompson Wm - Wisdom	1825	-	dd/	807 223 544358
Naraghmore	Rahoonbeak	-	saw	-	-	-	-	-	-	1"os/	
Kildare	Randalstown	nr Whitestown Br	mill	-	-	-	-	-	-	1"os	-
Rathangan	Rathangan	Haynes George	flour	-	62a	-	-	-	-	gr/	-
Rathangan	Rathangan Dems.	-	flour	-	-	-	-	-	-	6"os/	17
Rathangan	Rathangan Manor	Kildare Earl James	mill	-	-	-	Kildare E. - Mountjoy Lord :	1744	-	dd/	117 242 80637
Rathangan	Rathangan Manor	Kildare Earl James :	mills	-	-	-	Kildare E. - Inchiquin E. Wr	1744	-	dd/	115 382 80638

PARISH	TOWNLAND	MILLER	TYPE	HOUSE	Land	£Val	PROPRIETORS	Date	WHEEL etc.	Record	Ref.
Rathangan	Rathangan Town	- W. of Town Br.	flour	-	-	-	-	-	-	6"os/	17
Rathangan	Rathangan Town	- race ex Slate R :	flour	-	-	-	-	-	-	6"os/	17
Balraheen	Rathcoffey N	- (no name)	old mill	(1B) 30x22.6x8 :	-	-	-	1850	(no dimensions)	hob/	5.3866
Bodenstown	Rathmore	- at Alex Br. Clane	mill	-	-	-	-	1899		1"os/	
Rathmore	Rathmore E.	Ebb Thomas	old mill	(1C) 30x20x11 :	-	5	-	1841	-	hob/	5.3955
Rathmore	Rathmore East	- on Hartwell R.	corn	-	-	-	-	-	-	6"os/	20
St Michael`s	Rathstewart	- on R. bank	malt house	-	-	-	-	-	-	6"os/	35
Kildare	Ryevale *	Byrne David :	mill	-	-	-	Byrne D - O'Donnell Chas :	1824	-	dd/	796 482 537417
Kildare	Ryevale *	Donnellan William :	mill	-	-	-	Donnellan W - O'Donnell :	1824	-	dd/	795 397 537332
Kildare	Ryevale *	Donnellan William :	mill	-	-	-	Donnellan W - Byrne Dav	1824	-	dd/	795 399 537334
Kildare	Ryevale *	Donnellan William :	mill	-	-	-	Donnellan W - Hackett :	1824	-	dd/	795 396 537331
Bodenstown	Sallins	Odlum`s Flour Mill	-	-	-	-	Odlum`s	2001	milling	pWEH	-
Straffan	Strafan	Gallagher Patrick	domestic	-	-	-	-	-	Bovinh 60kw	turb/	c1947
Timolin	Timolin	-	cotton factory	-	-	-	-	-	-	6"os/	36
Timolin	Timolin	-	mill	-	-	-	-	-	-	1"os	129
Timolin	Timolin	-	mill	- restored as res. :	-	-	-	2002	-	pWEH/	A
Timolin	Timolin	- E. of Town	mill ruin	-	-	-	-	-	-	6"os/	36
Timolin	Timolin	Nolan James	corn	-	4a.	-	-	-	-	gr/	-
Fontstown	Tippeenn Lower	Doyle James	corn	-	51a.	-	-	-	-	gr/	-
Fontstown	Tippenan Lower	- on rd Naas/Cork	corn & tuck	-	-	-	-	-	-	6"os/	32
Kilberry	Tomard	Lutrell Alex	corn	(2B) 41.6x22x18.6 :	-	-	-	1841	15.6x3.10x3.6 breast	hob/	5.3898
Kilberry	Tomard	Luttrell Andrew	corn	-	3a.	-	-	-	-	gr/	-
Kildare	Townland ?	Dixon Henry :	Hinges Mill	-	-	-	Dixon H - Babington Wm :	1825	-	ddl	802 338 541473
bo. / Carberry	Townland ? :	Chase	Puck Mill	-	-	-	Chase - Colles	-	-	dd/	6623 37 428772
bo. / Carberry	Townland ? :	Deverell	Puck Mill	-	-	-	Deverell - Chase	-	-	dd/	604 158 413775
Kilteel	Townland?	Kinkead Thomas	old mill farm	-	-	-	Kinkead T - Coultis Chris :	1761	-	dd/	275 597 180308
Oughterard	Tuckmilltown	- on Slane R. :	tuck	-	-	-	-	-	-	6"os/	151
Oughterard	Tuckmilltown	Broughall Nicholas	corn	(2C) 36x16.6x9 :	-	3	-	1841	10.6x3x11 32 bkts :	hob/	5.3948
Tully	Tully West	-	corn & race	-	-	-	-	-	-	6"os/	27
Tully	Tully West	Lee Francis	corn & kiln	(1B) 47.6x25x40 :	-	-	(1842 Mr Jas Higgins)	1853	14.6dia. no. bkts. 48	hob/	5.3917
Tully	Tullywest	Lee Francis	corn	-	139a.	-	-	-	-	gr/	-
Whitechurch	Turnings	Atkinson Thomas	corn	(1B) 53x27.6x23 :	-	38.3	-	1841	13.8x5.4 breast :	hob/	5.3958
Whitechurch	Turnings	Atkinson Thomas	threshing	(1B) 30x21x16	-	-	-	1841	-	hob/	5.3958
Whitechurch	Turnings Lower	-	corn	- demol. mid1900 :	-	-	- res. Mrs Bagwell :	2001	- (pho. taken 2010)	mmSv/	wh - R
Whitechurch	Turnings Lower	- Straffan Mill	corn	-	-	-	-	-	-	6"os/	14
Naas	Victoria Bridge	- on R Liffey	mill	-	-	-	-	-	-	1"os	120
Naas	Victoria Bridge	- near Naas	-	finely refurbished	-	-	Eoin O`Toole	2001	research, art centre	pWEH	-
Lusk	Walshestown	Wogan William	corn	(2C) 25x18x9.9 :	-	-	-	-	14.6x1.9x13.9 :	hob/	5.0853
Lusk	Walshestown	Wogan William	windmill	circ. 59ft., ht. 23.3	-	-	-	-	-	hob/	5.0853
Walterstown	Walterstown	Conlon Patrick	corn	-	11a.	-	-	-	-	gr/	-
Walterstown	Walterstown :	- Nurney Mill	mill	-	-	-	-	-	-	6"os/	27
Carbury	Windmill	- near Edenderry	no mill	-	-	-	-	-	-	1"os/	110
Carbury	Windmill	- near Edenderry	no mill	-	-	-	-	-	-	6"os/	8
Kilmore ?	Windmill Land	Pomeroy	land	-	-		Pomeroy & French m/arts.	-	? (error)	dd/	-
Castledermot	Woodlands E	- on Lerr R.	Big Mill & dam	-	-	-	-	-	-	6"os/	40
Castledermot	Woodlands E	Dempsey Edward	hook	-	30a.	-	-	-	-	gr/	-
Castledermot	Woodlands E	Dempsey John	hook	(2C) 21.6x22x8 :	-	-	-	1841	12.6x3x3 breast :	hob/	5.3875
Castledermot	Woodlands East	Dempsey Edward	hook	-	31a.	-	-	-	-	gr/	-
Carragh	Yeomanstown	-	flour	- buildings fine :	-	-	- res. Stephen Langley	2010	-	mmSv/	sb - Cr
Carragh	Yeomanstown	- near Victoria Br.	flour	-	-	-	-	-	-	6"os/	18
Carragh	Yeomanstown	Doyle Henry	flour	-	32a.	-	-	-	-	gr/	-

PARISH	TOWNLAND	MILLER	TYPE	HOUSE	Land	£Val	PROPRIETORS	Date	WHEEL etc.	Record	Ref.
Danesfort	Annamult	- Marino Mill	mill	-	-	-	-	2002	-	pWEH	R
Danesfort	Annamult	- N. side Kings R/	factory	-	-	-	-	1841	-	6"os/	27
Danesfort	Annamult	- N. side Kings R/	flour	-	-	-	-	1841	-	6"os/	27
Danesfort	Annamult	- on island Kings R.	drying ho. :	-	-	-	-	1841	-	6"os/	27
Danesfort	Annamult	Izod Arthur	flour	house, offs. & land	61a.	182	- [+ tenants' houses]	1856	-	gr/	a.a.Ire,ie
Danesfort	Annamult	Izod Arthur	flour	-	-	-	-	-	18x10x19 5 pr st. :	vmb/	9
Archersgrove	Archersgrove	Sullivan Richard	corn	offices & yard	0.2.0	-	-	-	-	gr/	a.a.Ire.ie
Archersgrove	Archersgrove	Sullivan Richard	corn	offices & yard	0.2.0	150	- [+ tenants' houses]	-	no. 4 - 18x4x3	gr/	a.a.Ire.ie
Archersgrove	Archersgrove	Sullivan Richard	flour	-	-	-	-	-	-	vmb/	9
Archersgrove	Archersgrove	Sullivan Richard	flour	-	-	-	-	-	no. 1 - 18x10x3	vmb/	9
Archersgrove	Archersgrove	Sullivan Richard	flour	-	-	-	-	-	no. 2 - 21x2x3	vmb/	9
Archersgrove	Archersgrove	Sullivan Richard	flour	-	-	-	-	-	no. 3 - 18x2x3	vmb/	9
Archersgrove	Archersgrove	Sullivan Richard	flour	-	-	-	-	-	no. 4 - 18x4x3	vmb/	9
Archersgrove	Archersgrove :	-	Flour Mill	-	-	-	-	-	-	6"os/	19
Kilmenan	Atannagh	-	mill ruins	-	-	-	-	2004	-	pWEH	R
Rathkieran	Ballinlough	Aylward William	corn	-	-	-	-	-	14x3x4	vmb/	9
Rathkieran	Ballinlough :	-	corn & pond	-	-	-	-	-	-	6"os/	42
Pollrone	Ballybrassil	- nr Dornane	mill	-	-	-	-	-	-	1"os/	168
Aharney	Ballyconra	- Ballyconra Mill	corn	-	-	-	-	-	-	6"os/	4
Aharney	Ballyconra	Mosse John	flour	house, offs. & land	60a.	270	- [+ tenants' houses]	1856	-	gr/	a.a.Ire.ie
Kilmacow	Ballydaw	- at Dangan Br.	mill	-	-	-	-	-	-	1"os/	168
Graignamanagh	Ballyduff	-	flour		-	-	-	-	-	6"os/	32
Graignamanagh	Ballyduff	-	starch mfty	-	-	-	-	-	-	6"os/	32
Graignamanagh	Ballyduff	Davis Sydnam	corn	-	-	-	-	-	17x4x15	vmb/	9
Graignamanagh	Ballyduff	near Inistioge	-	preserved	-	-	-	1999	woodwork shop	pWEH	A
Aharney	Ballygrove	Mosse John	flour	-	-	-	-	-	18x12x10	vmb/	9
Clonamery	Ballygub Old	-	threshing		-	-	-	-	-	6"os/	33
Kilmacar	Ballyhimmin	- W. side Dinin R.	bleach	-	-	-	-	1841	-	6"os/	10
Kilmacar	Ballyhimmin	Hayes Nathaniel	bleach & :	-	-	-	-	-	13x6x8 1 beam :	vmb/	9
Dunkitt	Ballykeoghan :	-	flour	-	-	-	-	-	-	6"os/	43
Dunkitt	Ballykeoghan :	-	bleach	-	-	-	-	-	-	6"os/	43
Dunkitt	Ballykeoghan :	-	woollen fcty	-	-	-	-	-	-	6"os/	43
Dysartmoon	Ballyknock	-	mill	-	-	-	-	-	-	1"os/	157
Dysartmoon	Ballyknock	- S/ Ballyneale Vge.	corn	-	-	-	-	1841	-	6"os/	37
Dysartmoon	Ballyknock	Walsh James	corn	-	-	-	-	-	12x3x13	vmb/	9
Jerpointchurch	Ballylowra	-	corn & pond	-	-	-	-	1841	-	6"os/	32
Jerpointchurch	Ballylowra	- nr Thomastown	mill	-	-	-	-	-	-	1"os/	157
Jerpointchurch	Ballylowra	Delaney Thomas	corn	-	-	-	-	-	17x4x6	vmb/	9
Dunkitt	Ballymountain	-	Gaul`s Mill	-	-	-	-	-	-	1"os/	168
Kilkenny	Ballynagronny	-	mill	-	-	-	-	-	-	1"os/	156
Kilcolumb	Ballynavoragh	Donovan Patrick	corn	-	-	-	-	-	12x2x12	vmb/	9
Dysartmoon	Ballyneale	-	mill	-	-	-	-	-	-	1"os/	157
Dysartmoon	Ballyneale	- at curve on R. Nore	corn	-	-	-	-	1841	-	6"os/	37
Donaghmore	Ballyragget Tn	- near R. Nore	flour	-	-	-	-	-	-	6"os/	10
Columbkille	Ballyroe	- near Kilfane	flour	-	-	-	-	-	-	6"os/	28
Columbkille	Ballyroe	Davis Sydmon	flour	-	-	-	-	-	23x5x17 no work	vmb/	9
Kilcolumb	Ballyrowragh	-	corn	-	-	-	-	-	-	6"os/	44
Kilcolumb	Ballyrowragh	- Dnovan's Mill	corn	restored for use as :	-	-	Kieran Williams	2003	-	mmSv/	pg - Cc
Fiddown	Banagher	- SE of Pilltown	corn	-	-	-	-	1841	-	6"os/	39
Fiddown	Banagher	Richardson John	corn	-	-	-	-	-	17x3x3	vmb/	9
Tubbrid	Barrabehy	- nr Killnaspick	mill	-	-	-	-	-	-	1"os/	168
Tubbrid	Barrabehy	N. of Killnaspick Vge.	mill	-	-	-	-	1841	-	6"os/	139

COUNTY KILKENNY

PARISH	TOWNLAND	MILLER	TYPE	HOUSE	Land	£Val	PROPRIETORS	Date	WHEEL etc.	Record	Ref.
Kky	Barraghcore	Harriet Alexander	mill & quarter	-	-	-	Alex Harriet - Handy Fleming	1872	-	dd/	1872 21 83/5
Kky	Baunricken	- near Fertagh Br.	old mills	-	-	-					
Treadingstown	Bennetsbridge	- E. side R. Nore :	flour	-	-	-	-	-	-	6"os/	8
Treadingstown	Bennetsbridge	- on R. Nore	mills	-	-	-	-	-	-	6"os/	24
Treadingstown	Bennetsbridge	- W. side R. Nore :	flour	-	-	-	-	-	-	1"os/	147
Treadingstown	Bennetsbridge	Harvey Thomas & Jn	flour	-	-	-	-	-	-	6"os/	24
Treadingstown	Bennetsbridge	Moss Nicholas	Pottery	-	-	-	-	-	18x6x4	vmb/	9
Treadingstown	Bennetsbridge	Mosse Robert	flour	house, offs. & land	17a.	77.5.	- [+ tenant's house]	-	Francis (x2) :	pWEH	A
Danesfort	Bennetsbridge	Mosse Robert	flour	offices & land	14a.	91.10	- [+ tenants' houses]	1856	-	gr/	a.a.Ire.ie
Threadingstown	Bennetsbridge	The Big Mill	corn	well preerved	-	-	Nicholas Mosse	1856	-	gr/	a.a.Ire.ie
Treadingstown	Bennetsbridge	The Small Mill	corn	well preserved, active	-	-	Nicholas Mosse family	2000	pottery	pWEH	C
Tullaghoughy	Birchwood	- E. side Lingaun R.	corn	-	-	-	-	2000	milling	pWEH	A
Tullaghoughy	Birchwood	Dalton William	rape	-	-	-	-	1841	-	6"os/	34
St John`s	Bleach Green	Kinshela Lewis	bleach	-	-	-	-	-	16x3x4 2 pr st. :	vmb/	9
St John`s	Bleach Green	Luby Cornelius	knapping eng	-	-	-	-	-	11x3x4	vmb/	9
St John`s	Bleach Green	Sullivan Richard	corn	-	-	-	-	-	15x3x4	vmb/	9
St John`s	Bleach Green :	-	bleach	-	-	-	-	-	11x5x5	vmb/	9
Dysartmoon	Brownstown	-	corn	-	-	-	-	-	-	6"os/	19
Dysartmoon	Brownstown	Murphy Widow	corn	-	-	-	-	1841	-	6"os/	37
Thomastown	Burrelspark	S.side R. Nore - Island	Flour Mill	-	-	-	-	-	11x2x12	vmb/	9
Thomastown	Burrelspark ? :	Janis Henry	flour	-	-	-	-	-	-	vmb/	9
Kilkenny	Buston Mills	Madden Hugh	mills	-	-	-	-	-	16x4x5 4 pr st.	vmb/	9
Callan	Callan North	-	flour	-	-	-	Hugh Madden - Mary Speer	1872	-	6"os/	28
Callan	Callan South	- E. end Mill Street	pottery	-	-	-	-	1841	-	6"os/	26
Callan	Callan Town	Baker William	dw ho. & mill	-	-	-	-	1841	-	6"os/	26
Callan	Callan Town :	Lynch Michael	corn	(1B) 17.6x20x21 & :	-	-	Baker Wm - Walsh Thomas	1884	-	dd/	1884 52 19
Callan	Callan Town :	Keating Bridget	bark, tannery	(1B) 32x22.6x12 & :	-	-	-	-	15x4.10x2.7 floats :	hob/	5.2875
Callan	Callan Town :	-	mill house	-	-	-	-	-	-	hob/	5.2857
Callan	Callan Town :	Baker George	mill	-	-	-	-	1841	-	6"os/	26
Gaulskill	Cappagh	-	flour	-	-	-	-	1896	-	dd/	1896 26 298
Gaulskill	Cappagh	Jacob William	flour	-	-	-	-	-	-	6"os/	32
Inistioge	Cappagh	Rasstus William	corn	-	-	-	-	-	18x6x16 3 pr st. :	vmb/	9
St Canice	Castle	Ormonde Mills	corn	-	-	-	-	-	18x4x18	vmb/	9
Castlecomer	Castlecomer	Jacob James	corn	buildings v. dilapidated	-	-	Edward Kelly	2000	(in restoration)	pWEH	D
Castlecomer	Castlecomer	Jacob James	flour	-	-	-	-	-	-	vmb/	9
Castlecomer	Castlecomer Tn	Clarke Southwell	horse	-	-	-	-	-	-	vmb/	9
Castlecomer	Castlecomer Tn :	Jacob James	flour & corn	(1B) 21x15.5x6.6 :	119a.	-	-	-	-	hob/	5.2878
Castlecomer	Castlecomer Tn :	-	laundry	(1B) 66x24x25, corn :	-	-	-	1845	- [no information]	hob/	5.4000
Castlecomer	Castlecomer Tn :	-	flour	-	-	-	-	-	-	6"os/	5
Rosconnell	Castlemarket	-	corn	-	-	-	-	-	-	6"os/	5
Rosconnell	Castlemarket	- on small river	corn	-	-	-	-	1841	-	6"os/	1
Rosconnell	Castlemarket	Talien John	corn	-	-	-	-	1841	-	6"os/	1
Whitechurch	Castlemarket Br.	-	corn	-	-	-	-	-	14x3x14	vmb/	9
Whitechurch	Castletown	- S/ Annsboro' Ho.	flour	-	-	-	-	-	-	1"os/	136
Whitechurch	Castletown	Hetherington Mary	corn	-	-	-	-	1841	-	6"os/	34
Whitechurch	Castletown	O`Neill Thomas	corn	-	-	-	-	-	17x4x3	vmb/	9
Kilkenny	Cilcomb	Glascor William B	mill, mill lands	-	-	-	-	-	14x4x7	vmb/	9
Freshford	Clintstown	- on Nueena R.	corn & kiln	-	-	-	Wm Glascot - H`etta Briscoe	1972	-	dd/	1872 39 284
Freshford	Clintstown	Mulhall Patrick	corn	-	-	-	-	-	-	6"os/	13
The Rower	Clogaralt	- near Cullentragh	corn	-	-	-	-	-	10x2x3	vmb/	9
The Rower	Clogaralt	- str. to Barrow	mill	-	-	-	-	-	-	6"os/	33
The River	Clogaralt	James Fennelly	corn	-	-	-	-	-	-	1"os/	157
								-	14x3x14	vmb/	9

PARISH	TOWNLAND	MILLER	TYPE	HOUSE	Land	£Val	PROPRIETORS	Date	WHEEL etc.	Record	Ref.
Poolrone	Clogga	-	corn	-	-	-	-	1841	-	6"os/	42
Poolrone	Clogga	Bowers Edward	corn	-	-	-	-	-	18x3x19	vmb/	9
Clonamery	Clonamery :	- C153 Clor	Flour Mill	-	-	-	-	-	-	6"os/	33
Rathkieran	Clonassy	Gaffney William	corn	-	-	-	-	-	14x3x15	vmb/	9
Rathkieran	Clonassy Deer Pk	- on Blackwater R	mill	-	-	-	-	-	-	1"os/	168
Castlecomer	Cloneen	- near Clogh Br.	brewery	-	-	-	-	-	-	6"os/	6
Clonmantagh	Clonmantagh Lower	- Clonmantagh	Flour Mill	-	-	-	-	-	-	6"os/	13
Clonmantagh	Clonmantagh Lower	Lyster William	flour	-	-	-	-	-	20x10x15 there are	vmb/	9
Kilmocahill	Columbkille	Shea John	corn	-	-	-	-	-	16x4x -	vmb/	9
Kilkenny	Coolaghmane	-	threshing m/c	-	-	-	-	-	-	6"os/	30
Mothel	Coolcullen	-	flour	-	-	-	-	-	-	6"os/	11
Mothel	Coolcullen	-	threshing	-	-	-	-	-	- now ruinous	vmb/	9
Mothel	Coolcullen	Philips Robert	mill	-	-	-	-	-	- has not worked :	vmb/	9
Clonamery	Coolnamuck	- Clodiagh	Flour Mill	-	-	-	-	1841	-	6"os/	33
Clonamery	Coolnamuck	Allen Robert	flour	-	-	-	-	-	20x4x20	vmb/	9
Clonamery	Coolnamuck	Allen Robert	starch	-	-	-	-	-	11x4x8	vmb/	9
Inistioge	Coolroe	- on Aringle R.	mill	-	-	-	-	-	-	1"os/	157
Inistioge	Coolroe	- W.side Arrigle R.	corn & tuck	-	-	-	-	1841	-	6"os/	33
Inistioge	Coolroe	Gafney Thomas	corn	-	-	-	-	-	11x3x14	vmb/	9
Inistioge	Coolroe	Gafney Thomas	tuck	-	-	-	-	-	- works 1 pair	vmb/	9
Mallardstown	Courtnabooly	- on Kings R.	corn	-	-	-	-	-	-	1"os/	156
Kilmacow	Dangan	- on R. Nore ?	mill	-	-	-	-	-	-	1"os/	157
Kilmacow	Dangan	- on Blackwater R	mill	-	-	-	-	-	-	1"os/	168
Kilmacow	Dangan	Chandler John	flour	-	-	-	Owen Cronin, Waterford	1908	20x15x10 5 pr st.	vmb/	9
Columbkille	Dangan	Clarke John	flour	-	-	-	-	-	19x9x5 4 pr st. :	vmb/	9
Kilmacow	Dangan	Davis John	mills	-	-	-	Davis J - Davis Sydenham	1872	-	dd/	1872 4 148
Kilmacow	Dangan	Davis John	mills	-	-	-	Davis J - Davis Sydenham	1873	-	dd/	1873 22 101
Kilmacow	Dangan	Duggan Patrick	corn	-	5a.	-	Built by the Greens.	-	-	gr/	-
Kilmacow	Dangan	Greene John	flour, spinng.	- large 5 storey bld.	-	-	Built for John Greene by :	-	17x8x15 3 pr st. :	s/KL	205
Kilmacow	Dangan	Greene John	linen factory	48x31x 3 storey	-	-	Built by John Greene on :	-	14x6x8 - :	s/KL	200
Columbkille	Dangan	Shea John	corn	-	-	-	Built by Green family.	-	16x4x6	vmb/	9
Columbkille	Dangan :	-	flour	-	-	-	-	-	-	6"os/	43
Rossinan	Deerpark	-	corn, mill race	-	-	-	-	1841	-	6"os/	40
Rossinan	Deerpark	Hayes Patrick	corn	-	-	-	-	-	14x3x3	vmb/	9
Rathpatrick	Drumdowney	- at Giles` Quay	corn	fine building, bad cond.	-	-	James Butler	2000	-	pWEH	B
Rathpatrick	Drumdowney	- near Frazer`s Hall	mill	-	-	-	-	-	-	1"os/	168
Kilkenny	Dukesmeadow :	- Ormonde	Woollen Fcty	-	-	-	-	-	-	6"os/	19
Grangesilva	Duninga	- on R. Barrow	mill	-	-	-	-	-	-	1"os/	147
Grangesilva	Duninga	- W. side R. Barrow	mill large :	weir & wide millrace	-	-	-	1842	-	6"os/	21
Grangesilva	Duninga	Handy John	flour	-	-	-	-	-	18x10x7 4 pr st.	vmb/	9
Grangesilva	Duninga	Handy John	flour	-	-	-	-	-	28x10x25 6 pr st.	vmb/	9
Kilmacow	Dunkit	- on Blackwater R.	mill	-	-	-	-	-	-	1"os/	168
Kilmacow	Dunkit	Campbell Charles	mill, mill race	-	-	-	Campbell C - Webster Robt	1874	-	dd/	1874 25 136
Dunmore Park	Dunmore	- Dunmore	Woollen Fcty	-	-	-	-	-	-	6"os/	14
Dunmore	Dunmore	Kelly James	corn (new)	(1A) 33.6x21.6x22 : (	-	-	-	-	12x2x - wheels :	hob/	5.3965
Dunmore Park	Dunmore Park	Kelly James	tuck	-	-	-	-	-	14x3x4	vmb/	9
Dunmore Park	Dunmore Park	Kelly James	tuck	-	-	-	-	-	12x2x4 west wheel :	vmb/	9
Dunmore Park	Dunmore Park	Kelly James	woollen fcty	-	-	-	-	-	16x6x4 works	vmb/	9
Ennisnag	Ennisnag	- on Kings R.	mills	-	-	-	-	-	-	1"os/	157
Ennisnag	Ennisnag	Daniel	flour	-	-	-	-	-	18x6x3	vmb/	9
Ennisnag	Ennisnag	Pilsworth Robert	corn	ofices & waste	1a.	60	-	1856	-	gr/	a.a.Ire.ie
Ennisnag	Ennisnag	Pilsworth Robert	flour	house, offices & land	18a.	122	- [+ tenant's house]	1856	-	gr/	a.a.Ire.ie

COUNTY KILKENNY

PARISH	TOWNLAND	MILLER	TYPE	HOUSE	Land	£Val	PROPRIETORS	Date	WHEEL etc.	Record	Ref.
Ennisnag	Ennisnag	Pilsworth Robert	flour	-	-	-	-	-	18x8x10	vmb/	9
Gaulskill	Fahy	-	mill	-	-	-	-	-	-	1"os/	168
Gaulskill	Fahy	- Foulkes	Corn Mill	-	-	-	-	1841	-	6"os/	43
Gaulskill	Fahy	Fallon James	cloth	-	-	-	-	-	11x2x11	vmb/	9
Gaulskill	Fahy	Fallon James	corn	-	-	-	-	-	13x2x13	vmb/	9
Kilkenny	Fassadineen	Lyster Charles	mills	-	-	-	Lyster C - Kavanagh Denis	1874	-	dd/	1874 17 180
Erke	Foulks Court	Hely Georges	mill	-	-	-	Hely Geo - King Richard	1872	-	dd/	1872 14 105
Erke	Foulks Court	Hely Georges	mill	-	-	-	Hely Geo - King Richard	1872	-	dd/	1872 8 101
Freshford	Freshford	-	mills	-	-	-	-	-	-	1"os/	136
Freshford	Freshford	- near Urlingford	mill	-	-	-	-	-	-	1"os/	136
Freshford	Freshford Lots	-	flour	-	-	-	-	-	-	6"os/	13
Freshford	Freshford Lots	-	malt house	-	-	-	-	-	-	6"os/	13
Freshford	Freshford Lots	Ruth Martin	corn	-	-	-	-	-	10x6x16 3 pr st.	vmb/	9
Kilkenny	Friarsinch :	-	factory ho.	-	-	-	-	-	-	6"os/	19
St Patricks	Gallowshill	Colles Richard	marble quarry	- & waste	4a.	20	-	-	-	gr/	a.a.Ire.ie
St Patricks	Gallowshill	Colles Richard	marble quarry	- & waste	2a.	20	-	-	-	gr/	a.a.Ire.ie
Kilkenny	Galmoy Bo	Sinclair William	mill	-	-	-	Wm Sinclair - Marq. Ormonc	1870	-	dd/	1870 7 104
Kilkenny	Garden :	-	Black Mill	-	-	-	-	-	-	6"os/	19
Kilkenny	Garden :	-	woollen fcty	-	-	-	-	-	-	6"os/	19
St Johns	Garden :	-	distillery	-	-	-	-	-	-	6"os/	19
St Marys	Garden :	-	brewery	-	-	-	-	-	-	6"os/	19
Kilmocahill	Garryduff	-	corn	-	-	-	-	1841	-	6"os/	35
Kilmacahill	Garryduff	-	mill	-	-	-	-	-	-	1"os/	156
Kilmocahill	Garryduff	Bridget William	corn	-	-	-	-	-	-	vmb/	9
Kells	Garrynamann Lr	- SE of Kells Br.	flour	-	-	-	-	1841	-	6"os/	27
Kells	Garrynamann Lr	- SE of Kells Br.	tuck	-	-	-	-	1841	-	6"os/	27
Kells	Garrynamann Lr	Mulins Bridget	tuck	-	-	-	-	-	14x3x2	vmb/	9
Kells	Garrynamann Lr	Mullins Bridget	corn	-	-	-	-	-	16x3x21	vmb/	9
Owning	Garrynarea	-	flour	-	-	-	-	1841	-	6"os/	38
Owning	Garrynarea	Roade John	flour	-	-	-	-	-	18x4x18 does little	vmb/	9
Owning	Garrynarea	Roade John	flour	-	-	-	-	-	16x4x8	vmb/	9
Dysartmoon	Glenballyvalley	- on R. Nore	saw	-	-	-	-	-	-	1"os/	157
Shanbogh	Glencloghlea	Handrick Laurence	corn & flour	-	-	-	-	-	16x3x16	vmb/	9
Shanbogh	Glencloghlea	stream to R. Barrow	flour & corn	-	-	-	-	1841	-	6"os/	37
Rossinan	Glendonnell	- E/ Mullinavat Vge.	corn, mill race	-	-	-	-	1841	-	6"os/	40
Rossinan	Glendonnell	Hoban Patrick	corn	-	-	-	-	-	12x2x13	vmb/	9
Kells	Goodwinsgarden	-	corn	-	-	-	-	1841	-	6"os/	27
Kells	Goodwinsgarden	-	mill	-	-	-	-	-	-	1"os/	156
Kells	Goodwinsgarden	Delaney James	mill	-	16a.	20	-	-	-	hob/	5.2876
Kells	Goodwinsgarden	Delany James	corn	-	-	-	-	-	12x4x8	vmb/	9
Grangesilva	Goresbridge	- on R Barrow	(mill)	-	-	-	-	-	-	1"os/	147
Grangesilva	Goresbridge	- on R Barrow	mill	-	-	-	-	-	-	pWEH	B
Grangesilva	Goresbridge :	Burris W.K. Rev.	old brewery	(1B) "37x22x21.6 & :	-	-	-	-	-	hob/	5.2881
Rathpatrick	Gorteens	- near R. Suir	-	v. old mill, gable in ruin	-	-	Michael Murphy	2000	-	pWEH	R
Rathpatrick	Gorteens	- on R. Suir	mill	-	-	-	-	-	-	1"os/	168
Rathpatrick	Gorteens	- W. side R. Suir	flour, mill pond	-	-	-	-	1841	-	6"os/	47
Rathpatrick	Gorteens	Murphy Michael	flour	-	-	-	-	-	18x4x11	vmb/	9
Rathpatrick	Gorteens	Murphy Michael	flour	-	-	-	-	-	20x5x10 4 pr st.	vmb/	9
Rathpatrick	Gorteens	Shallow Robert	corn	-	-	-	-	-	12x3x12	vmb/	9
Rathpatrick	Gorteens *	Hendrick`s Mill	-	Donovan`s deserted :	-	-	(bulldozed early 1900)	2000	-	no ph	- Z
Gowran	Gowran	-	mill	-	-	-	-	-	-	1"os/	147
Gowran	Gowran	Dalton`s Mill :	mill	-	-	-	-	2003	-	pWEH	B

PARISH	TOWNLAND	MILLER	TYPE	HOUSE	Land	£Val	PROPRIETORS	Date	WHEEL etc.	Record	Ref.
Gowran	Gowran	Moran William	corn	-	-	-	-	-	14x3x15	vmb/	9
Gowran	Gowran Demse.	Moran William	flour	-	-	-	-	-	16x6x17	vmb/	9
Gowran	Gowran Town	- S/ Town, Gowran	Flour Mills	-	-	-	-	1841	-	6"os/	20
Gowran	Gowran Town :	Moran William	corn	- house, offs. & mill	-	8.9	-	-	-	hob/	5.2883
Kilmakevoge	Graguenakill	- stream to R. Barrow	corn mills & :	-	-	-	-	1841	-	6"os/	41
Kilmakevoge	Graguenakill	Kearney Patrick	corn	-	-	-	-	-	16x3x13	vmb/	9
Kilmakevoge	Graguenakill	Mackesy George	mill	-	-	-	Mackesy - Strangham Sam	1870	-	dd/	1870 4 44
Graignamanagh	Graignamanagh :	- Valley	Mills	-	-	-	-	1841	-	6"os/	29
Graignamanagh	Graignamanagh :	- E. of Main Street	brewery	-	-	-	-	1841	-	6"os/	29
Graignamanagh	Graignamanagh :	- W. of Main Street	corn	-	-	-	-	1841	-	6"os/	29
Graignamanagh	Graignamanagh :	Bailey John	corn	ho : (2B) 31.6x17.6x7 :	-	-	-	-	overshot - 16x2x16	hob/	5.2884
Graignamanagh	Graignamanagh :	Rebecca Mulligan	corn	(1B) 19x23.6x15.5 :	-	4.9	-	-	breast - 11x3.3x - :	hob/	5.2884
Graignamanagh	Graignamanagh :	Shannon Henry	flour	- house & offices	-	38	-	-	-	hob/	5.2883
Graignamanagh	Graignamanagh :	Mulligan Rebecca	corn	- offices & yard	-	6.6.0	-	-	-	hob/	5.2883
Coolaghmore	Graigue	-	mill	-	-	-	-	-	-	1"os/	137
Coolaghmore	Graigue :	- Valley	Flour Mill	-	-	-	-	-	-	6"os/	29
Graignamanagh	Graiguemanagh	-	Valley Mills	-	-	-	-	-	-	1"os/	157
Graignamanagh	Graiguenamanagh	-	mills	-	-	-	-	-	-	1"os/	157
Graignamanagh	Graiguenamanagh	Baily John	corn	-	-	-	-	-	16x2x16	vmb/	9
Graignamanagh	Graiguenamanagh	Muligan Rebecca	corn	-	-	-	-	-	11xx3x8	vmb/	9
Graignamanagh	Graiguenamanagh	Shannon Hugh	flour	-	-	-	-	-	18x5x18	vmb/	9
Grangesilva	Grange Lower	-	corn, mill race	-	-	-	-	1841	-	6"os/	21
Grangesilva	Grange Lower	- near Goresbridge	Red Mill	-	-	-	-	-	-	1"os/	147
Grangesilva	Grange Lower	- NW./ Goresbridge	Red Mill	-	-	-	- marked disused	1890	-	6"os/	21
Grangesilva	Grange Lower	Joyce Thomas	corn	-	-	-	-	-	13x2x7	vmb/	9
Grangesilva	Grange Lower	Joyce Thomas	tuck	-	-	-	-	-	8x3x8	vmb/	9
Grangesilva	Grange Lower	Smithwick Edmond	Red Mills	-	-	-	Smithwick E - Fleming H	1872	-	dd/	1872 21 82
Kilkenny	Grannagh	Le Botiller James	mill	-	-	-	Mabel Gogane (lessee)	-	-	s/KL	203
Kilmacow	Granny	Chandlee John	corn	-	2a.	-	-	-	-	gr/	-
Kilmacow	Granny	Chandler John	corn	-	-	-	formerly : Shearman Mrs	-	21x5x3	vmb/	9
Kilmacow	Granny	Smith Patrick	linen carding	-	-	-	Built by Patk Smith jnr.	-	-	s/KL	203
Kilmacow	Granny :	-	mill	-	-	-	-	-	-	6"os/	43
Dunkitt	Greenville	- Brown's Mill	flour	- well preserved	-	-	Dan & Kay Laffan	2000	overshot wheel :	mmSv/	wh - B
Dunkitt	Greenville	Caddigan Patrick	flour	-	51a	-	Built by John Greene	-	17x7x17	vmb/	9
Dunkitt	Greenville	Cadigan Alice	flour	-	50a	-	-	-	-	gr/	-
Kilmacow	Greenville	Cadogan	flour	- simple 4 storey bld.	51a.	-	Built by Jn Greene leased :	-	17x7x17 :	s/KL	206
Kilmacow	Greenville	Condon John & Jas	flour	-	-	-	Gouch family from 1850 :	-	18x3x5.6 3 pr st. :	s/KL	214
Dunkitt	Greenville	Goough Benjamin	flour	-	20.1.1	-	-	-	-	gr/	-
Dunkitt	Greenville	Gouch Benjamin	flour	-	-	-	-	-	18xx3x4	vmb/	9
Kilmacow	Greenville	Greene John	linen paper	-	-	-	Built by John Greene	-	16ft dia. produced	s/KL	197
Kilmacow	Greenville :	-	flour	-	-	-	-	-	-	6"os/	43
Kilmacow	Greenville Lower	- Gouche's Mill	flour	- mill in good cond. :	-	-	John Laffan	2000	-	mmSv/	wh - B
Thomastown	Grennan	Bull William	flour	house, offs., yd., gdn.	1a.	134	-	1856	-	gr/	a.a.Ire.ie
Thomastown	Grennan	Bull William	flour	-	-	-	-	-	19x7x4 4 pr st.	vmb/	9
Thomastown	Grennan	Innes Henry	flour	house, offices & mill	-	178	-	-	- 6 pair gr. stones	hob/	5.2883
Thomastown	Grennan	Innis Henry	flour	house, offs. & land	21a.	182	-	-	-	gr	-
Thomastown	Grennan	Janis Henry	flour	-	-	-	-	-	16x9x5 6 pr st.	vmb/	9
Thomastown	Grennan :	Island	Flour Mill	-	-	-	-	-	-	6"os/	28
Columbkill	Grennan Town :	Bull William	flour	(1B) mill & yard	-	55	-	-	- wheel & m/cy :	hob/	5.2883
St Martin`s	Highrath	- E. side R. Nore	flour	-	-	-	-	-	-	6"os/	20
St Martin`s	Highrath	- E. side R. Nore	flour	-	-	-	-	-	-	6"os/	20
St Martin`s	Highrath	- E. side R. Nore	marble saw	-	-	-	-	-	-	6"os/	20

PARISH	TOWNLAND	MILLER	TYPE	HOUSE	Land	£Val	PROPRIETORS	Date	WHEEL etc.	Record	Ref.
St Martin`s	Highrath	Collis Richard	marble	-	-	-	-	-	7x4x4	vmb/	9
Killaghy	Inchalarran ? :	Henebry John	corn	(2A) 35x18.6x9	-	2.10	-	-	12x2.9x12.6 o`shot	hob/	5.3901
Inistioge	Inistioge	- NW. of Town	corn	-	-	-	-	-	-	6"os/	32
Inistioge	Inistioge	Cotteral Michael	corn	-	-	-	-	-	12x3x1	vmb/	9
Inistioge	Inistioge Town	Cotteral Michael	corn	offs. (1A) 18x10x8 :	-	7.14	-	-	-	hob/	5.2886
Inistioge	Inistioge Town :	Cotteral Michael	corn	- offices & yard	-	9.17	-	-	-	hob/	5.2883
Kilcoan	Jamestown	-	mill	-	-	-	-	-	-	1"os/	168
Kilmocahill	Jerpoint Abbey	-	corn	-	-	-	-	-	-	6"os/	32
Kilmocahill	Jerpoint Abbey	-	corn & pond	-	-	-	-	-	-	6"os/	32
Kilmocahill	Jerpoint Abbey	Delany Patrick	corn	-	-	-	-	-	16x3x18	vmb/	9
Kilmocahill	Jerpoint Abbey	Whelan Margaret	flour	-	-	-	-	-	15x5x11	vmb/	9
Jerpointchurch	Jerpointchurch	- Goat`s Bridge	Mill :	-	-	-	-	2003	Paddy Kirwan	pWEH	-
Jerpointchurch	Jerpointchurch	Farrell Mrs	corn	-	-	-	-	-	15x4x16	vmb/	9
Kells	Kells Village	Phelan William	mill	-	38a.	192	-	-	-	hob/	5.2876
Kells	Kellsborough	- N side King's R.	flour	-	-	-	-	1841	-	6"os/	27
Kells	Kellsborough	Phelan William H	flour	-	-	-	-	-	18x8x2 19x5x2	vmb/	9
Kells	Kellsgrange	Phelan Daniel	flour	-	-	-	-	-	16x1x3 4 pairs st. :	vmb/	9
Kells	Kellsgrange	Phelan Daniel	flour	-	-	-	-	-	16x4x3	vmb/	9
Kells	Kellsgrange	Phelan Daniel	mill	-	45a.	174	-	-	-	hob/	5.2876
Kilkenny	Kilconrath	- on Blackwater R	mills	-	-	-	-	-	-	1"os/	167
Inistioge	Kilcross	- N. side R. Nore :	corn	-	-	-	-	1841	-	6"os/	9
Inistioge	Kilcross	Delahunt Bridget	corn	-	-	-	-	-	10x2x13	vmb/	9
Kilkenny	Kilkenny City :	-	-	-	-	-	-	1841	-	6"os/	19
Kilkenny	Kilkenny City :	Smithwick Edmond	brewery	(1B) 86x21.6x27.6 :	-	-	-	1847	- wheel	hob/	5.4034
Kilkenny	Kilkenny City :	Smithwick Edmond	corn	(1B) 32.6x22.6x19 :	-	-	-	1847	15x5x6 breast	hob/	5.4034
St Canice	Kilkenny City :	Bradley Thomas	corn	(1B) 54x24.6x20 :	-	14-6	-	1838	16x4.6x4.6 3 pr st.	hob/	5.2890
St Canice	Kilkenny City :	Bradley Thomas	corn	(1B) 45x17.6x26 & :	-	52.14	-	-	breast 19x3x5	hob/	5.2894
St Canice	Kilkenny City :	Sullivan Richard	bark	31x23.6x15.6 :	-	18	-	-	-	hob/	5.2894
St Canice	Kilkenny City :	- Black Mills	flour, mill pond	-	-	-	-	1841	-	6"os/	19
Kilkenny	Kilkenny City :	Sullivan Richard	old brewery	(1B) 23.6x21x20 :	-	26	-	-	-	hob/	5.2889
Kilkenny	Kilkenny City :	Scott Henry	mills	(1B) 43x18.6x30.6 :	-	91	-	-	breast - 15x3.6x3.6	hob/	5.2894
Kilkenny	Kilkenny City :	Scott Henry	tuck	(2B) 45x20x10 & :	-	-	-	-	undershot 17x4x5 :	hob/	5.2894
Kilkenny	Kilkenny City :	Scott Henry	tuck	- (part of above)	-	-	-	-	undershot 16x2.9x3	hob/	5.2894
St Canice	Kilkenny City :	Hampton Thomas	corn	(1B) 54x24.6x20	-	6.13	-	-	breast 16x4.6x4.6 :	hob/	5.2890
Graignamanagh	Kilkenny City :	Hilsham Geo Capt.	old still house	(1B) 43x33.6x21.6 :	-	43	-	-	- formerly distillery	hob/	5.2894
Kilkenny	Kilkenny City :	Scott Henry	corn	(1B) 60x22.6x26 & :	-	14.5	-	-	16x3x5.6 32 floats	hob/	5.2894
St Canice	Kilkenny City :	Hampton Thomas	mill	(1A) 43x22x19 & :	-	7.10	-	-	16x2.3x4 floats 1.6	hob/	5.2890
Kilkenny	Kilkenny City :	Read Inditt	tuck, spinning	(1B) 37x22.6x37	-	-	-	-	u`shot 18x2.3x3.6 :	hob/	5.2894
Kilkenny	Kilkenny City :	-	woollen fcty	-	-	-	-	1841	-	6"os/	19
St. Marys	Kilkenny City :	-	brewery	-	-	-	-	1841	-	6"os/	19
St Canice	Kilkenny City :	(Townland Gardens)	distillery	-	-	-	-	1841	-	6"os/	19
St Canice	Kilkenny City :	(Townland Gardens)	flour	-	-	-	-	1841	-	6"os/	19
St Canice	Kilkenny City :	(Townland Gardens)	mill	-	-	-	-	1841	-	6"os/	19
Kilkenny	Kilkenny City :	- Ormonde Woollen	Factory	-	-	-	-	1841	-	6"os/	19
St. Marys	Kilkenny City :	-	starch mfty	-	-	-	-	1841	-	6"os/	19
St. Marys	Kilkenny City :	-	brewery	-	-	-	-	1841	-	6"os/	19
St Canice	Kilkenny Town	-	woollen fcty	-	-	-	-	1841	-	6"os/	19
St Canice	Kilkenny Town	- on R. Nore	mill	-	-	-	-	-	-	1"os/	147
St Canice	Kilkenny Town	Sion Mills	-	not in good condition	-	-	-	-	-	1"os/	147
Earlstown	Killbrickan	- on Kings R.	corn, kiln & r	-	-	-	-	2000	saw mill	pWEH	A
Earlstown	Killbrickan	- on Kings R.	mill	-	-	-	-	1841	-	6"os/	26
Kells	Killinny	- W. of Wooden Br.	flour	-	-	-	-	-	-	1"os/	156
								1841	-	6"os/	27

PARISH	TOWNLAND	MILLER	TYPE	HOUSE	Land	£Val	PROPRIETORS	Date	WHEEL etc.	Record	Ref.
Kells	Killinny	Shirley Thomas	flour	-	-	-	-	-	20x7x3 2 pairs st. :	vmb/	9
Tullaghoughy	Kilmacoliver	-	corn & :	-	-	-	-	1841	-	6"os/	34
Tullaghoughy	Kilmacoliver	Crowley Michael	corn	-	-	-	-	-	12x1x13	vmb/	9
Kilmacow	Kilmacow	-	corn	- fine old buildings : |	-	-	-	2000	-	mmSv/	wh - R
Kilmacow	Kilmacow	- close to R. B'water	corn & dam	-	-	-	-	1841	-	6"os/	43
Kilmacow	Kilmacow	Kelly Denis	corn	-	12a.	-	-	-	-	gr/	-
Kilmacow	Kilmacow	Kelly Denis	corn, carding	-	3a.	-	-	-	-	gr/	-
Kilmacow	Kilmacow	Kelly Dennis	corn	-	-	-	-	-	15x3x3	vmb/	9
Kilmacow	Kilmacow	Mackey John	corn	-	9a.	-	-	-	-	gr/	-
Kilmacow	Kilmacow	Mackey John	corn	-	-	-	Andrew (son) till 1868 :	-	-	s/KL	215
Kilmacow	Kilmacow	Martin John	corn	-	-	-	-	-	16x3x4	vmb/	9
Kilnagranny	Kilmaganny Town	-	corn	-	-	-	-	-	-	6"os/	31
Kilnagranny	Kilnagranny Town	Delany John	corn	-	-	-	-	-	16x3x17	vmb/	9
Dunkitt	Kilonerry :	-	flour	-	-	-	-	-	-	6"os/	43
Grangekilree	Kilree	-	corn & kiln	-	-	-	-	1841	-	6"os/	23
Grangekilree	Kilree	Croak James	corn	-	-	-	-	-	14x2x1 machinery:	vmb/	9
Clonmantagh	Kilrush	- on Nuenna R.	flour	-	-	-	-	1841	-	6"os/	13
Clonmantagh	Kilrush	Lyster Charles	mills	-	-	-	Lyster C - Kavanagh Den	1874	-	dd/	1874 17 180
Clonmantagh	Kilrush	Ruth Patrick	flour	-	-	-	-	-	20x10x15	vmb/	9
Derrynahinch	Kiltorcan	- on Little Arrigle R.	corn	-	-	-	-	1841	-	6"os/	31
Derrynahinch	Kiltorcan	Raftis Patrick	corn	-	-	-	-	-	17x4x4	vmb/	9
Kilmanagh	Knockenbaun	-	mill	-	-	-	-	-	-	1"os/	146
Knocktopher	Knocktopher	-	corn	-	-	-	-	-	-	6"os/	31
Knocktopher	Knocktopher	- on Little Irrigle R.	mill (x2)	-	-	-	-	-	-	1"os/	157
Knocktopher	Knocktopher Manor	Garvey John	paper	-	-	-	-	-	17x4x17	vmb/	9
Knocktopher	Knocktopher Manor	Garvey Mr	mill	-	18a.	337	-	-	-	hob/	5.2876
Knocktopher	Knocktopher Tn	-	old flour mill	-	-	-	-	-	-	6"os/	31
St John`s	Lackan :	- N. side R. Suir	-	-	-	-	-	1841	-	6"os/	19
St John`s	Lacken	on Suir near Klky. Br.	-	dilapidated	-	-	-	2000	-	pWEH	D
Lismateige	Lismateige	-	corn	-	-	-	-	-	-	6"os/	35
Lismateige	Lismateige	Tobin Peter	corn	-	-	-	-	-	13x2x13	vmb/	9
Listerlin	Listerlin	Gall James	corn	-	-	-	-	-	11x3x12	vmb/	9
Blackrath	Maddockstown	Sullivan Richard	flour	-	-	-	-	-	-	vmb/	9
Blackrath	Maddockstown	Sullivan Richard	flour	-	-	-	-	-	-	vmb/	9
Blackrath	Maddoxtown	Colles Richard	mills	-	-	-	Richd Colles - N Monsarrat	1870	-	dd/	1870 25 9
Mallardstown	Mill Island	- S/ Island, King's R.	flour	-	-	-	-	1841	-	6"os/	26
Mallardstown	Mill Island	Bryan William B	mill	-	-	-	Wm Bryan - Jas Fitzgerald	1874	-	dd/	1874 15 147
Mallardstown	Mill Island	Phelan William H	flour	-	-	-	-	-	18x8x4	vmb/	9
Derrylacky	Milltown	-	no mill	-	-	-	-	-	-	1"os/	157
Cluan	Milltown	- on Clodiagh R	no mill	-	-	-	-	-	-	1"os/	157
Ida	Milltown	Bomford Samuel	mill	-	-	-	Sam Bomford - Sam Law	1870	-	dd/	1870 3 99
Ullard	Milltown	Dowling Thomas	corn	-	-	-	-	-	9x2x12	vmb/	9
Knocktopher	Milltown	Quin John	mill	-	-	-	Jn Quin - Earl Bessborough	1872	-	dd/	1872 29 14
Ida	Milltown	Wilson John	mill	-	-	-	John Wilson - Jas Edwards	1874	-	dd/	1874 34 256
Callan	Minnauns	- E. end Callan Tn.	corn	-	-	-	-	1841	-	6"os/	26
Callan	Minnauns	Baker William	corn	-	-	-	-	-	-	vmb/	9
Knocktopher	Moanroe Comm.	Madigan John	corn	-	-	-	-	-	13x3x2	vmb/	9
Kilkenny	Mount Argula	Davis Syd	mills	-	-	-	Davis Syd - Davis John : &	1872	-	dd/	1872 4 148
Kilkenny	Mount Argula	Davis Syd	mills	-	-	-	Davis Syd - Davis John : &	1873	-	dd/	1873 22 101
Kilbeacon	Mulinavat	- SW. of Town	corn & kiln :	-	-	-	-	1841	-	6"os/	40
Fiddown	Mullen Beg	-	corn, mill pond	-	-	-	-	1841	-	6"os/	35
Fiddown	Mullen Beg	-	corn, mill pond	-	-	-	-	1841	-	6"os/	35

PARISH	TOWNLAND	MILLER	TYPE	HOUSE	Land	£Val	PROPRIETORS	Date	WHEEL etc.	Record	Ref.
Fiddown	Mullen Beg	Shea Jeoffry	corn	-	-	-	formerly : McEnery Thos	-	17x4x18	vmb/	9
Glenmore Town	Mullenahone	Grace Widow	cloth	-	-	-	-	-	11x2x11	vmb/	9
Glenmore Town	Mullenahone	Grace Widow	corn	-	-	-	-	-	11x2x12	vmb/	9
Glenmore Town	Mullenahone :	-	corn, mill pond	-	-	-	-	1841	-	6"os/	41
Dunkitt	Mullinabro	-	mill - hz.	-	-	-	-	-	-	s/KL	203
Odagh	Naglesland	Bambrick James	distillery	-	-	-	-	-	- mc/y moved	vmb/	9
Odagh	Naglestown	- Mountnagle	Distillery	-	-	-	-	-	-	6"os/	14
Kilmacow	Narraghbaun S. :	-	flour & kiln	-	-	-	-	-	-	6"os/	43
Thomastown	Newtown	Loughlin John	corn	-	-	-	-	-	10x3x10	vmb/	9
Dunkitt	Newtown	Roche Patrick	flour	-	10a.	-	-	-	-	gr/	-
Dunkitt	Newtown	Roche Patrick	flour	-	-	-	-	-	16x3x4	vmb/	9
Dunkitt	Newtown :	Gault`s Mill	flour & pond	-	-	-	-	-	-	6"os/	43
Earlstown	Newtown (Baker)	Delany John & Wm	corn	-	-	-	-	-	15x2x3	vmb/	9
Earlstown	Newtown (Baker)	Delany John & Wm	shelling	-	-	-	-	-	12x2x3	vmb/	9
Pollrone	Nicholastown	-	mill	-	-	-	-	-	-	1"os/	168
Clonmore	Nicholastown :	-	corn & pond	-	-	-	-	-	-	6"os/	42
Kilkenny	nr Blackwater R	Shallow`s Mill	-	ruins small mill & store	-	-	Thomas Butler	2000	-	pWEH	R
Fiddown	Owning	- N. of Village	flour & pond	-	-	-	-	1841	-	6"os/	35
Fiddown	Owning & Town	Rafter William	flour	-	-	-	-	1844	19x4x20 this mill	vmb/	9
Aharney	Parksgrove	- W. side R. Nore	flour	-	-	-	-	1841	-	6"os/	10
Aharney	Parksgrove	Mosse John	flour	-	-	-	-	-	-	vmb/	9
Aharney	Parksgrove	Shea James	mill-race	Ho., offs., R. & land	50a.	41	-	1856	-	gr/	a.a.Ire.ie
Poolrone	Portnascully	Walsh & Henebery	corn	-	-	-	-	1843	14x3x3 not working	vmb/	9
Poolrone	Portnascully	Walsh John	corn	-	-	-	-	-	10x4x12	vmb/	9
Poolrone	Portnascully :	-	corn	-	-	-	-	-	-	6"os/	42
St John`s	Purcellsinch	Davis Martin	cloth tuck	-	-	-	-	-	14x5x2	vmb/	9
St John`s	Purcellsinch :	-	woollen fcty	-	-	-	-	-	-	6"os/	19
Rosbercon	Raheen	- nr Rosbercon	mill	-	-	-	-	-	-	1"os/	157
Rosbercon	Raheen	Scott Edward	corn	-	-	-	-	-	30x6x15	vmb/	9
Mallardstown	Rathcubbin	- S. side King's R.	corn	-	-	-	-	1841	-	6"os/	27
Mallardstown	Rathcubbin	Lunnire John (?)	corn	-	-	-	-	-	16x3x4	vmb/	9
Kells	Rathduff (Baylay)	- S. side King's R.	corn	-	-	-	-	1841	-	6"os/	27
Kells	Rathduff (Baylay)	- on Island King's R.:	tuck	-	-	-	-	1841	-	6"os/	27
Kells	Rathduff (Baylay)	Brannock William	corn	-	-	-	-	-	16x1x3	vmb/	9
Rathpatrick	Rathpatrick	Taylor Nathaniel	corn	-	-	-	-	-	15x4x13	vmb/	9
Kilmakevoge	Robinstown	- E. Glenmore Vge.	corn	-	-	-	-	1841	-	6"os/	41
Glenmore Town	Robinstown	Gafney Nicholas	cloth	-	-	-	-	-	11x2x11	vmb/	9
Glenmore Town	Robinstown	Gafney Nicholas	corn	-	-	-	-	-	13x2x14	vmb/	9
Killamery	Roscon	-	corn & pond	-	-	-	-	-	-	6"os/	30
Kilmenan	Russellstown	-	corn	-	-	-	-	-	-	sv/05	Z
Kilmenan	Russellstown	Mullally Widow Mary	tuck & corn	(2B) 26x15x12.6 :	-	-	-	-	12.6x3.3x - o`shot	hob/	5.3971
Kilmenan	Russelstown	- N. side Glashagal R.	mill & mill race	-	-	-	-	-	12x3x12	vmb/	9
Kilmenan	Russelstown	Mulally Mrs	tuck	-	-	-	-	-	12x3x12	vmb/	9
Dungarvan	Scart	Downey Patrick	corn	-	-	-	-	-	10x2x12	vmb/	9
Kilkenny	Scogh	- Annsborough Ho.	mill	-	-	-	-	-	-	1"os/	156
Kilkenny	Sellstown	- on Glashagal R.	mill & race	-	-	-	-	-	-	6"os/	5
Kilfertagh	Sheastown	- W. side R. Nore	flour	-	-	-	-	-	16x7x30	vmb/	9
Kilfertagh	Sheastown	O`Callaghan Owen	flour	-	-	-	-	-	16x7x30	vmb/	9
Dunkitt	Skeard	- E. side Blackwater	bleach	-	-	-	-	1841	-	6"os/	43
Dunkitt	Skeard	- E. side Blackwater	woollen fcty	-	-	-	-	1841	-	6"os/	43
Dunkitt	Skeard	Sharman John	flour	-	-	-	-	-	17x8x15 3 pr st.	vmb/	9
Dunkitt	Skeard	Sharman Joseph	bleach	-	-	-	-	-	14x6x8	vmb/	9

PARISH	TOWNLAND	MILLER	TYPE	HOUSE	Land	£Val	PROPRIETORS	Date	WHEEL etc.	Record	Ref.
Kilbeacon	Smithstown	- N/ Lukeswell Vge.	mill	-	-	-	-	-	-	6"os/	36
Kilbeacon	Smithstown	- on Derrylacky R :	mill	-	-	-	-	-	-	1"os/	157
Kilbeacon	Smithstown	Hoban John	corn	-	-	-	-	-	12x2x13	vmb/	9
Kilbeacon	Smithstown	Hoban John	tuck	-	-	-	-	-	12x2x12	vmb/	9
Dunkitt	Strangsmill	-	mill	-	-	-	-	-	-	6"os/	43
Dunkitt	Strangsmill	Campbell Charles	mill (?)	-	-	-	Campbell C - Webster Robt	1874	-	dd/	1874 25 136
Dunkitt	Strangsmill	Draper Richard	flour	-	5.0.7	-	-	-	-	gr/	-
Dunkitt	Strangsmill	Nevine Thomas F	flour	-	-	-	-	-	16x6x11	vmb/	9
Kilkenny	The Mill Fall	Philips Robert	mill	-	-	-	Phillips Robert - Chas L	1872	-	dd/	1872 34 53
Kilkenny	The Mill Field	Russell John W	mill	-	-	-	Russell J W - White Pat	1872	-	dd/	1872 31 76
Thomastown	Thomastown	- nr Jerpoint Abbey	mill	-	-	-	-	-	-	1"os/	157
Thomastown	Thomastown	Arland`s Inch	corn	finely restored	-	-	-	1999	residence	pWEH	C
Thomastown	Thomastown	Flood Edward	Ths`town Mill	-	-	-	Flood Edwd - Walker Sam	1876	-	dd/	1876 17 143
Thomastown	Thomastown	Landed Est Court	Ths`town Mill	-	-	-	Ld. Est. Ct. - Budds Chas	1876	-	dd/	1876 33 290
Thomastown	Thomastown :	Loughlin John	corn	-	-	-	-	-	-	hob/	5.2883
Thomastown	Thomastown :	Loughlin Michael	corn & pond	house, offices & gdn.	1a.	16	-	1856	-	gr/	a.a.Ire,ie
Thomastown	Thomastown :	Bull William	flour	(1B) 76x22.6x36 :	-	-	-	-	19x7.6x4.6 5 pr st.	hob/	5.2919
Thomastown	Thomastown :	Clarke Jonathan	flour	-	-	-	-	-	-	hob/	5.2883
Thomastown	Thomastown :	Flood Edward	tuck	-	-	-	Edw Flood - Harvey Crosbie	1871	-	dd/	1871 3 279
Thomastown	Thomastown :	Flood Edward	tuck	-	-	-	Edw Flood - John Devereux	1872	-	dd/	1872 7 139
Thomastown	Thomastown :	Flood Edward	tuck	-	-	-	Edw Flood - Harvey Crosbie	1874	-	dd/	1874 14 4
Thomastown	Thomastown :	O`Callaghan Corns	tuck	-	-	-	O`Callaghan - Flood Henry	1871	-	dd/	1871 3 278
Thomastown	Thomastown :	O`Callaghan Corns	tuck	-	-	-	O`Callaghan - Flood Henry	1872	-	dd/	1872 39 201
Tibberaghny	Tibberaghny	- at Millmount Ho.	corn	-	-	-	-	-	-	6"os/	39
Sheffin	Tifeaghna	Bowden John	corn	house & land	19a.	36.15	-	1856	-	gr/	a.a.Ire.ie
Sheffin	Tifeaghna	Bowden John	corn	-	-	-	-	-	11x2x13	vmb/	9
Fiddown	Tinakelly	-	flour	-	-	-	-	1841	-	6"os/	39
Fiddown	Tinakelly	Carew I & E	flour	-	-	-	-	-	16x3x17	vmb/	9
Kilkenny	Tinnacarrig	- on R. Barrow	mill	-	-	-	-	-	-	1"os/	147
Callan	Town of Callan	Lynch Michael	corn	-	-	-	-	-	-	vmb/	9
Kells	Tulla	Madigan John	mill	-	-	6	-	-	-	hob/	5.2876
Inistioge	Uenamanagh	Shannon Henry	flour	-	-	-	-	-	16x5x18	vmb/	9
Ullid	Ullstown	- Rockbrook	corn & wool	-	-	-	-	-	-	6"os/	11
Urlingford	Urlingford	Holohan John	corn	stores, yards, waste	0.1.2	22	-	1865	-	gr/	a.a.Ire.ie
Urlingford	Urlingford	Holohan Thomas	flour	-	-	-	-	-	14x2x3	vmb/	9
Urlingford	Urlingford Town	-	flour	-	-	-	-	-	-	6"os/	12
Rathkieran	Waddingstown	- W. side R. Nore	distillery	-	-	-	-	-	-	6"os/	20
St Patrick`s	Warrington	- E. side R. Nore :	distillery	-	-	-	-	-	-	6"os/	19
St Patrick`s	Warrington	- Kilkenny Town	distillery	-	-	-	-	-	-	1"os/	147
St Patrick`s	Warrington	- Kilkenny Town	woollen	-	-	-	-	-	-	1"os/	147
St Patrick`s	Warrington	Hyland Michael	corn	-	-	-	-	-	16x3x3	vmb/	9
St Patrick`s	Warrington	Hyland Richard	old distillery	offices & land	12a.	15.15	-	1856	-	gr/	a.a.Ire.ie
St Patrick`s	Warrington	Mellea Still	distillery	buildings v. dilapidated	-	-	-	2000	-	pWEH	D
St Patrick`s	Warrington	Murphy Partick & :	corn	house & store	-	52	-	1856	-	gr/	a.a.Ire.ie
Muckalee	Wildfield	Philips George	corn	-	-	-	-	-	16x2x16 1 pr. st.	vmb/	9
Muckalee	Wildfield	Philips George	worsted fcty	-	-	-	-	-	- no. throstles :	vmb/	9
Woolengrange	Woollengrange	Bryan George	mill	-	-	-	Geo Bryan - Patrick Fenlon	1871	-	dd/	1871 37 83

PARISH	TOWNLAND	MILLER	TYPE	HOUSE	Land	£Val	PROPRIETORS	Date	WHEEL etc.	Record	Ref.
Abbeyleix	Abbeleix Dems. :	-	mills	-	-	-	-	-	-	6"os	23
Abbeyleix	Abbeyleix	- nr Abbeyleix Ho.	mills	-	-	-	-	-	-	1"os	136
Abbeyleix	Abbeyleix	Bell	mills	-	-	-	Bell - Murphy	-	-	dd/	592 393 493751
Abbeyleix	Abbeyleix	Bell Mary	mills	-	-	-	Bell M - Stephens Wm	1799	-	dd/	513 562 839384
Abbeyleix	Abbeyleix	Bell William :	mills	-	-	-	Bell W - Donovan James :	1802	-	dd/	542 524 360729
Abbeyleix	Abbeyleix	Ford Matthew :	mills	-	-	-	Ford M - Hamilton Alev Rev.	1804	-	dd/	560 xxx 374107
Abbeyleix	Abbeyleix	Stephens William	mills	-	-	-	Stephens W - Bell Eliz :	1799	-	dd/	522 96 341813
Laois	Acreavock	Dawson	mill	-	-	-	Dawson - Fortescue	-	-	dd/	87 409 62379
Laois	Acreavock	Dawson	mill	-	-	-	Dawson - Lewis	-	-	dd/	65 453 46366
Laois	Acreavock	Lewis	mill	-	-	-	Lewis - Christmas	-	-	dd/	73 141 50283
Laois	Acreavock	Lewis	mill	-	-	-	Lewis - Laban	-	-	dd/	77 353 53952
Aghaboe	Aghaboe T`parks	Walsh Edward	flour	-	-	-	-	-	16x4x16	vmb/	16
Killaban	Aghanure	-	windmill stump	-	-	-	-	1841	-	6"os	26
Killaban	Aghanure :	-	old windmill	-	-	-	-	-	-	6"os	128
Abbeyleix	Aghmacart	-	flour & kiln	-	-	-	-	-	-	6"os	34
Abbeyleix	Aghmacart	-	mill (site)	- no trace 1995 :	-	-	-	-	-	iaa/	AI1044 os34NPL
Abbeyleix	Aghmacart	-	mill (site)	-	-	-	-	1601	-	iai/	1044
Abbeyleix	Aghmacart	Barrett	the black mill	-	-	-	Barrett - Prosson	-	-	dd/	227 177 147426
Abbeyleix	Aghmacart	Barrett John :	the black mill	-	-	-	Barrett J - Prossan John :	1762	-	dd/	116 177 147426
Abbeyleix	Aghmacart	Cooksey	the black mill	-	-	-	Cooksey - Phillips	-	-	dd/	218 507? 142464
Abbeyleix	Aghmacart	Curtis	the black mill	-	-	-	Curtis - Litton	-	-	dd/	199 556 133296
Abbeyleix	Aghmacart	Delany John	corn	-	-	-	-	-	14x3x3	vmb/	16
Abbeyleix	Aghmacart	French	the black mill	-	-	-	French - Phelan	-	-	dd/	192 220 127354
Abbeyleix	Aghmacart	Minchin	the black mill	-	-	-	Minchin - Cooksey	-	-	dd/	197 356 130834
Abbeyleix	Aghmacart	Minchin	the black mill	-	-	-	Minchin - Phillips	-	-	dd/	215 452 142459
Laois	Ardlea ?	-	mill site HZ	-	-	-	-	-	-	iai/	AI1045 os17.11.6
Attanagh	Attanagh Glebe	- W. side R. Nore	mills	-	-	-	-	-	-	6"os	34
Attanagh	Attanagh Glebe	Moran George	corn	-	-	-	-	-	11x3x10	vmb/	16
Attanagh	Attanagh Glebe	Moran George	tuck	-	-	-	-	-	11x3x11 1pr w/ft	vmb/	16
Laois	Aughnahorna	Baldwin James	mill	-	-	-	Baldwin J - Baldwin Robt :	1808		dd/	601 152 407942
Laois	Aughnahorna	Costello	mill	-	-	-	Costello - Neale	-	-	dd/	527 513 353174
Laois	Aughnahorna	Matthews	mill	-	-	-	Matthews - Blunden	-	-	dd/	586 448 397990
Killabban	Ballickmoyler	-	corn & mill dam	-	-	-	-	-	-	6"os	32
Killabban	Ballickmoyler	Furney James	corn	-	-	-	-	-	13x2x13	vmb/	16
Killabban	Ballickmoyler	Furney Robert	corn	house, offices & ld.	12a.	25.10.	-	1856	-	gr/	a.a.ie
Dysartgallon	Ballinakill Town	-	brewery, pond	-	-	-	-	-	-	6"os	30
Erke	Ballinfrase	-	corn & kiln	-	-	-	-	-	-	6"os	34
Erke	Ballinfrase	Barton Andrew	corn	-	-	-	-	-	16x3x5	vmb/	16
Erke	Ballinfrase	Lewis	mills	-	-	-	Lewis - Lowrenson	-	-	dd/	184 271 123918
Erke	Ballinfrase	Lewis Henry	mills	-	-	-	Lewis H - Hutton Geo	-	-	dd/	132 299 89395
Erke	Ballinfrase	Lewis Henry	mills	-	-	-	Lewis H - Williams Edw	-	-	dd/	131 348 89396
Erke	Ballinfrase	Lewis Henry	mills	-	-	-	Lewis Hen - Lewis Dan	-	-	dd/	133 120 89827
Erke	Ballinfrase	Lewis Henry :	mills	-	-	-	Lewis H - Palmer Jos	1748	-	dd/	133 121 29828
Erke	Ballinfrase	Paul Eliz & Josh	mills	-	-	-	Paul E & J - Paul Thos	-	-	dd/	120 387 82494
Laois	Ballinolart	Dempsey John :	mills	-	-	-	Dempsey J - Hopper Margt.	1774	(M. Arts.)	dd/	305 168 201368
Laois	Ballinolart	Dempsey John :	mills	-	-	-	Dempsey J - Dunn Timothy :	1774	-	dd/	300 584 201380
Laois	Ballinolart	Dempsey Margaret :	mills	-	-	-	Dempsey M - Wilkinson :	1784	-	dd/	352 470 239775
Clonenagh	Bally	Coote Sir Charles	saw	-	-	-	-	-	14x4x15	vmb/	16
Lea	Ballybrittas	- near Mount Henry	Lea Windmill	-	-	-	-	-	-	6"os	9
Rathdowney	Ballybuggy	- S. of Rathdowney	pond (no mill)	-	-	-	-	1841	-	6"os/	28
Rathdowney	Ballybuggy	Adamson	mill	-	-	-	Adamson - Armstrong	-	-	dd/	552 308 366367
Rathdowney	Ballybuggy	Atkinson Robert	Mill pond	-	1.1.24	-	-	1856	-	gr/	a.a.Ire.ie

PARISH	TOWNLAND	MILLER	TYPE	HOUSE	Land	£Val	PROPRIETORS	Date	WHEEL etc.	Record	Ref.
Rathdowney	Ballybuggy	Neale	mill	-	-	-	Neale - Adamson	-	-	dd/	534 106 366365
Rathdowney	Ballybuggy	Palmer Joshua :	mill	-	-	-	Palmer J - Flood Fran	1789	-	dd/	462 337 295725
Rathdowney	Ballybuggy	Prior	mill	-	-	-	Prior - Purcell	-	-	dd/	473 368 308257
Rathdowney	Ballybuggy	PriorThomas	mill	-	-	-	Prior T - Purcell Tobias	1794	-	dd/	490 322 314641
Rathdowney	Ballybuggy	Purcell	mill	-	-	-	Purcell - Curleton	-	-	dd/	505 139 332765
Kilcolemanbane	Ballycarnan	-	corn	-	-	-	-	-	-	1"os	127
Kilcolemanbane	Ballycarnan	-	corn & pond	-	-	-	-	-	-	6"os	18
Kilcolemanbane	Ballycarnan	Campion Samuel	corn	-	-	-	-	-	16x5x12	vmb/	16
Kilcolemanbane	Ballycullenbeg	- nr Irishtown Ho.	woollen factory	-	-	-	-	-	-	6"os	8
Kilcolemanbane	Ballycullenbeg	- Mountmellick Tn :	foundry	-	-	-	-	-	-	6"os	8
Kilcolemanbane	Ballycullenbeg	Roberts Thomas	foundry (part)	House, offs. & yard	-	26	-	-	-	gr/	a.a.ie
Kilcolemanbane	Ballycullenbeg	Roberts Thomas	foundry (part)	Yard & garden	0.0.20	2.15.	-	1856	-	gr/	a.a.ie
Kilcolemanbane	Ballycullenbeg :	Penrose George	saltworks	offs., lime kiln, yd.	-	5.10.	-	1856	-	gr/	a.a.ie
Rathdowney	Ballydavin	-	corn & tuck	-	-	-	-	-	-	6"os	34
Rathdowney	Ballydavin	Kirwan & Walsh	corn	-	-	-	-	-	14x3x4	vmb/	16
(bo. Cullenagh)	Ballyegle	Dawson	mills	-	-	-	Dawson - Wills	-	-	dd/	15 229 7324
(bo. Cullenagh)	Ballyegle	Jones	mills	-	-	-	Jones - Phillips	-	-	dd/	37 431 23349
(bo. Cullenagh)	Ballyegle	Wills	mills	-	-	-	Wills - Jones	-	-	dd/	12 348 5325
Cloneenagh	Ballyfin	-	saw	-	-	-	-	-	-	6"os	12
Cloneenagh	Ballyfin	- near Ballyfin Ho.	corn	-	-	-	-	-	-	6"os	12
Laois	Ballyger	Burry Willam	mills	-	-	-	Burry W - Maunsell John	1785	-	dd/	373 470 249090
Laois	Ballyger	Willis Thomas	mills	-	-	-	Willis - Maunsell Jno	1785	-	dd/	373 469 249089
Laois	Ballygor	Cahill	mill	-	-	-	Cahill - Keeffe	-	-	dd/	459 140 293150
Laois	Ballygor	Murray	mill	-	-	-	Murray - Hume	-	-	dd/	382 394 257144
Laois	Ballygor	Murray John	mill	-	-	-	Murray J - Cahill Michael	1785	-	dd/	376 157 250116
Timahoe	Ballygorman	- on Fuer R.	corn mill ruins	-	-	-	-	-	-	6"os	25
Timahoe	Ballygormill South	-	mill site HZ	- no trace 1995 :	-	-	-	-	-	iaa/	AI1046 os18.8.4
Laois	Ballyguille	Gray Edward :	mill	-	-	-	Gray Edward - Parnell Jno :	1760	-	dd/	206 435 136751
Laois	Ballyguille	Moore Lewis	mill	-	-	-	Moore Lewis - Kelly John :	1754	-	dd/	167 440 113 160
Laois	Ballyguille	Moore Lewis :	mill	-	-	-	Moore Lewis - Parnell John	1758	-	dd/	201 285 132800
Lea	Ballymorris	- on Grand Canal	mill	-	-	-	-	-	-	1"os	119
Lea	Ballymorris	- E. side R. Barrow	mill dam (2) :	-	-	-	-	-	-	6"os/	40
Laois	Ballymowland	Lane Ralph	mill	-	-	-	Lane R - Haslins Haniball	-	-	dd/	135 58 90392
Rathdowney	Ballynakill	-	mill & pond	-	-	-	-	-	-	6"os	2
Rathdowney	Ballynakill	- nr Gurragh R.	corn	-	-	-	-	-	-	6"os	2
Rathdowney	Ballynakill	Baynbrick	iron mills	-	-	-	Baynbrick - Cody	-	-	dd/	498 499 321128
Rathdowney	Ballynakill	Dunn	iron mills	-	-	-	Dunn - Costigan	-	-	dd/	430 5 278721
Rathdowney	Ballynakill	Kingsmill	iron mills	-	-	-	Kingsmill - Flood	-	-	dd/	476 455 315726
Rathdowney	Ballynakill	Lawlor	iron mills	-	-	-	Lawlor - Dease	-	-	dd/	431 280 280068
Rathdowney	Ballynakill	Maher	iron mills	-	-	-	Maher - Cahill	-	-	dd/	507 51? 329907
Rathdowney	Ballynakill	Stubdel	iron mills	-	-	-	Stubdel - Devitt	-	-	dd/	503 277 323677
Ballyroan	Ballyroan	-	mill	-	-	-	-	-	-	1"os	127
Ballyroan	Ballyroan	-	mills	remains ivy cover	-	-	-	2006	- wheel inside	mmSv/	D
Ballyroan	Ballyroan	- to W. of Town	corn	-	-	-	-	-	-	6"os	24
Ballyroan	Ballyroan	Beard	mills	-	-	-	Beard - Mitchell	-	-	dd/	83 246 58633
Ballyroan	Ballyroan	Beard Ellen	mill	-	-	-	Beard E - Barrington Jh	1754	-	dd/	166 399 112010
Ballyroan	Ballyroan	Dawson	mill	-	-	-	Dawson - Mills	-	-	dd/	99 36 67823
Ballyroan	Ballyroan	Dawson	mill	-	-	-	Dawson - Mitchell	-	-	dd/	195 518 131334
Ballyroan	Ballyroan	Dawson Wm Henry	mill	-	-	-	Dawson W - Wills G`fry	-	-	dd/	182 353 12144
Ballyroan	Ballyroan	Dunn John :	mills	-	-	-	Dunn Jn - Kehoe Mary :	1797	-	dd/	492 591 329919
Ballyroan	Ballyroan	Harding	mills	-	-	-	Harding - Brennan	-	-	dd/	529 365 347584
Ballyroan	Ballyroan	Hood	mills	-	-	-	Hood - Hood	-	-	dd/	473 386 308257
Ballyroan	Ballyroan	Hood	mills	-	-	-	Hood - Stoker	-	-	dd/	656 87 374211

PARISH	TOWNLAND	MILLER	TYPE	HOUSE	Land	£Val	PROPRIETORS	Date	WHEEL etc.	Record	Ref.
Ballyroan	Ballyroan	Laurenson	mills	-	-	-	Laurenson - Hanay	-	-	dd/	578? 263 339113
Ballyroan	Ballyroan	McMahon Arthur	corn	-	-	-	-	-	14x5x11	vmb/	16
Ballyroan	Ballyroan	Mills	mill	-	-	-	Mills - Morton	-	-	dd/	189 99 124762
Ballyroan	Ballyroan	Miln	mill	-	-	-	Miln - Mitchell	-	-	dd/	201 28 131524
Ballyroan	Ballyroan	Mitchell	mills	-	-	-	Mitchell - Beard	-	-	dd/	49 70 30912
Ballyroan	Ballyroan	Mitchell	mills	-	-	-	Mitvhell - Kelly	-	-	dd/	87 169 58632
Ballyroan	Ballyroan	M'Mahon John	corn	house. offices & ld.	18a.	40.10.	-	1856	-	gr/	a.a.ie
Ballyroan	Ballyroan	Morton	mills	-	-	-	Morton - Stokes	-	-	dd/	544 450 365128
Ballyroan	Ballyroan	Porter	mills	-	-	-	Porter - Harding	-	-	dd/	475 33 395153
Ballyroan	Ballyroan	Shaw	mills	-	-	-	Shaw - Rorke	-	-	dd/	594 308? 483302
Ballyroan	Ballyroan	Shaw	mills	-	-	-	Shaw - Shaw	-	-	dd/	582 311 393682
Ballyroan	Ballyroan	Stoker	mills	-	-	-	Stoker - White	-	-	dd/	501 261 323050
Ballyroan	Ballyroan	Trench	mills	-	-	-	Trench & wife & Agit	-	-	dd/	597 56 405225
Ballyroan	Ballyroan	Walker William :	mills	-	-	-	Walker W - Mitchell Wm :	1806	-	dd/	574 524 391587
Ballyroan	Ballyroan	Woodward	mills	-	-	-	Woodward - Keenan	-	-	dd/	577 282 337115
Laois	Ballyvadame	-	old windmill	-	-	-	-	-	-	1"os	128
Clonenagh	Barkmill	-	woollen	-	-	-	-	-	-	1"os	118
Clonenagh	Barkmill	Beale M	spin worsted	-	-	-	-	-	40x5x30 30 H.P. :	vmb/	16
Offerlane	Baunbeagh	French William S	corn	Stwt's ho., offs. & ld.	1834a.		-	1856	-	gr/	a.a.lre.ie
Curraclone	Bawn Hill	- nr Stradbally	old windmill	-	-	-	-	-	-	1"os	128
Curraclone	Bawn Hill	- nr Stradbally	saw	-	-	-	-	-	-	1"os	128
Lea	Bohernagrisna	Mulloy Thos Mullock :	corn & kiln	(1B) 38x25x25 & :	11.18.	-	-	1851	undershot 15x8x1 :	hob/	5.1189
Clonenagh	Boley	- Fruitlawn	Worsted Fcty	-	-	-	-	-	-	6"os	23
Clonenagh	Boley	- on R. Nore	spiinig	- lge. building	-	-	-	2006	-	mmSv/	wh - Z
Clonenagh	Boley	Leech Alan	worsted factory	house, offs. & ld.	119a.	138	-	1856	-	gr/	a.a.lre.ie
Clonenagh	Boley	Leech Alan & Thos	spin worsted	-	-	-	-	-	15x9x7	vmb/	16
Borris	Borris	-	corn	now garage site :	-	-	-	2008	-	mmSv/	wh - Cc
Borris	Borris	Combie Solomon :	mill	-	-	-	Combie - Coote Rev. Chas :	1776	-	dd/	312 71 207380
Borris	Borris	Coote	mill	-	-	-	Coote - Robinson	-	-	dd/	590 116 40601?
Borris	Borris	Handcock Joseph :	mill	-	-	-	Handcock J - Combie Sol. :	1775	-	dd/	313 77 207379
Borris	Borris	Johnston Edward :	mill	-	-	-	Johnston - Handcock Jas :	1776	-	dd/	310 443 307237
Borris	Borris	Simmons Thomas :	mill	-	-	-	Simmons T - Simmons Isaa(	1810	-	dd/	622 117 428637
Aghaboe	Borris in Ossory :	Walsh Edward	corn	offices &land	1.1.0	22.10.	-	1856	-	gr/	a.a.lre.ie
Aghaboe	Borris in Ossory :	- stream to R.Nore	flour & corn	-	-	-	-	-	-	6"os	22
Rosenallis	Capard	- near Rosenallis :	windmill ruins	-	-	-	-	-	-	6"os	7
Rosenallis	Cappabeg	-	potter`s kiln	-	-	-	-	-	-	6"os	3
Laois	Cappanapp	Gibson	grist	-	-	-	Gibson - Bradish	-	-	dd/	370 482 253199
Laois	Cappanard	Dawson	grist mill	-	-	-	Gibson - Bradish	-	-	dd/	370 482 253199
Rosenallis	Cappaneary	-	potter`s kiln	-	-	-	-	-	-	6"os	3
Rosenallis	Cappaneary	- near R. Barrow :	corn & pond	-	-	-	-	-	-	6"os	3
Rosenallis	Cappaneary	Watson William	corn & kiln	-	-	-	-	-	10x3x6	vmb/	16
Offerlane	Cardtown	- on Killeen R.	old mill	-	-	-	-	-	-	6"os	11
Offerlane	Cardtown	Berry	m ils	-	-	-	Berry - Berry	-		dd/	222 139 147446
Offerlane	Cardtown	Berry	m ils	-	-	-	Berry - White	-		dd/	242 451 157514
Offerlane	Cardtown	Brandon Thomas :	mill	-	-	-	Brandon - Armstrong Robt :	1806	-	dd/	591 106 400756
Offerlane	Cardtown	Brundram	mil	-	-	-	Brundram - Armstrong	-		dd/	591 106 400756
Offerlane	Cardtown	Dawson Hon Ld Wm	mills	-	-	-	Dawson W - Howard Hu. :	1774	-	dd/	302 468 200968
Offerlane	Cardtown	Despard	m ils	-	-	-	Despard - Berry	-		dd/	116 6 79204
Offerlane	Cardtown	Despard	m ils	-	-	-	Despard - Duff	-		dd/	138 450 93860
Offerlane	Cardtown	Humphries	mills	-	-	-	Humphries - Thompson	-	-	dd/	278 642 182448
Offerlane	Cardtown	Lynes	mills	-	-	-	Lynes - Howard	-	-	dd/	318 316 215822
Offerlane	Cardtown	Symes Jeremiah :	mills	-	-	-	Symes J - Howard Robt :	1778	-	dd/	318 316 215822

PARISH	TOWNLAND	MILLER	TYPE	HOUSE	Land	£Val	PROPRIETORS	Date	WHEEL etc.	Record	Ref.
Kilmanan	Castlecuffe	-	corn	-	-	-	-	-	-	6"os	2
Kilmanan	Castlecuffe	- NE. of Village	corn & pond	-	-	-	-	1841	-	6"os/	2
Kilmanan	Castlecuffe	Casey Thomas	corn	-	-	-	-	-	11x3x8	vmb/	16
Killabban	Castletown	-	corn, mill race	-	-	-	-	-	-	6"os	26
Killabban	Castletown	- near C`town Ho.	thrashing	-	-	-	-	-	-	6"os	26
Killabban	Castletown	Bambrick Henry :	mill	-	-	-	Bambrick H - Colclough Jn :	1800	Mort. 23 June	dd/	529 77 346438
Killabban	Castletown	Bambrick John :	mill	-	-	-	Bamberick - Furney Benj. :	1788	-	dd/	414 540 272822
Killabban	Castletown	Furney Benjamin	corn	house, ofices & ld.	48a.	81	-	1856	-	gr/	a.a.ie
Killabban	Castletown	Furney Benjamin	corn	-	-	-	-	-	16x5x12	vmb/	16
Rearymore	Clarahill	Dawson	mills	-	-	-	Lord Dawson - Howard	-	-	dd/	302 468 200968
Rearymore	Clarahill	Dempsey Martin	corn & kiln	-	-	-	-	-	12x3x12	vmb/	16
Rearymore	Clarahill	Heney	mills	-	-	-	Heany Stph - Large Sam	-	-	dd/	180 250 120405
Rearymore	Clarahill	Heney Stephen	mills	-	-	-	Heney - Shaw S`vester	-	-	dd/	182 214 120562
Rearymore	Clarahill	Humphries	mills	-	-	-	Humphries - Thompson	-	-	dd/	278 642 182448
Rearymore	Clarehill	-	corn & kiln	-	-	-	-	-	-	6"os	3
Laois	Cloghrennan	Rochfort	mill	-	-	-	Rochfort - Rawson	-	-	dd/	422 203 275837
Laois	Cloghrennan	Walker	mill	-	-	-	Walker - Burler	-	-	dd/	316 498 214057
Clonenagh	Clonagh	Dawson	mill	-	-	-	Dawson - Archdall	-	-	dd/	342 107 231265
Clonenagh	Clonagh	Dawson	mill	-	-	-	Dawson - Kerniss	-	-	dd/	446 497 290770
Clonenagh	Clonagh	Dawson	mill	-	-	-	Dawson - Kerniss?	-	-	dd/	446 497 290770
Clonenagh	Clonagh	Dawson Joseph :	mill	-	-	-	Dawson - Archdall :	1782	-	dd/	342 507 231265
Clonenagh	Clonagheen	Roberts Thomas	flour	-	-	-	-	-	20x12x6 4 pr st.	vmb/	16
Kilmanan	Clonaslee	Deigan William	corn	-	-	-	formerly Daley widow	-	14x5x16	vmb/	16
Kilmanan	Clonaslee	Deverell	mill	-	-	-	Deverell - Collins	-	-	dd/	458 336 295857
Kilmanan	Clonaslee	Deverell	mill	-	-	-	Deverell - Collins	-	-	dd/	458 336 295857
Kilmanan	Clonaslee	Deverell	mill	-	-	-	Deverell - Russell	-	-	dd/	479 424 303 ***?
Kilmanan	Clonaslee	Deverell	mill	-	-	-	Deverell - Russell	-	-	dd/	479 424 303***
Kilmanan	Clonaslee	Dunn	mill	-	-	-	Dunn - Deverell	-	-	dd/	453 48 292480
Kilmanan	Clonaslee	Dunn	mill	-	-	-	Dunn - Purcell	-	-	dd/	439 556 302007
Kilmanan	Clonaslee	Dunn Samuel :	mill & dw.	-	-	-	Dunn Sam - Moore John :	1795	-	dd/	491 31 317309
Kilmanan	Clonaslee	Dunn Watkins	mill	-	-	-	Dunn W - Purcell Philip	1793	-	dd/	439 556 302007
Kilmanan	Clonaslee	Dunne	mill	-	-	-	Dunne - Moore	-	-	dd/	491 31 317303
Kilmanan	Clonaslee	Dunne	mill	-	-	-	Dunne - Valiance	-	-	dd/	382 148 253893
Kilmanan	Clonaslee	Dunne	mill	-	-	-	Dunne - Valiance	-	-	dd/	382 148 253893
Killabban	Clonbrock	- N. of Mill Bridge	corn & race	-	-	-	-	-	-	6"os	30
Killabban	Clonbrock	- at Millbridge	mill	-	-	-	-	-	-	1"os	137
Killabban	Clonbrock	Edge John Esq.	corn	house, offices & ld.	155a.	132	-	1856	-	gr/	a.a.ie
Killabban	Clonbrock	Edge John Sen	corn	-	-	-	-	-	21x3x17	vmb/	16
Rosenallis	Cloncannon	- nr Mountmellick	New Mill (disd.)	-	-	-	-	-	-	1"os	118
Rearymore	Clonduff	- on R. Barrow	flour	-	-	-	-	-	-	6"os	3
Clonenagh	Clonenagh Dems.	de Vesci Lord	flour & malt	-	-	-	-	-	17x3x17	vmb/	16
Clonenagh	Clonenagh Dems.	de Vesci Lord	saw, threshing	-	-	-	-	-	-	vmb/	16
Kileeshin	Clonmore	Ross	mill	-	-	-	Ross - O`Brien	-	-	dd/	75 492 54079
Rosenallis	Cloonagh	- at Manor Ho.	flour	-	-	-	-	-	-	1"os	118
Cloonaragh	Cloondarrig	-	old corn mill :	-	-	-	-	1841	-	6"os/	12
Cloonaragh	Cloondarrig	Meredith T & S	corn	-	-	-	-	-	-	vmb/	16
Killabban	Coolanowle	McLaughlin Peter	cutlery	-	-	-	-	-	-	vmb/	16
Laois	Cooleroan or :	Keating	mills	-	-	-	Keating - Desdpard	-	-	dd/	71 51 48770
Laois	Cooleroan or :	Keating Richard :	mills	-	-	-	Keating R - Levin Chas :	1720		dd/	56 500 38917
Cloydagh	Coolgrenan	Mangan Martin	corn	-	-	-	-	-	13x5x6	vmb/	16
Killeshin	Coolhenry	Fishbourne William	thrashing	-	-	-	-	-	14x5x1	vmb/	
Coolkerry	Coolkerry	Baldwin Jno :	mills	-	-	-	Baldwin J - Lambert Robert :	1772	-	dd/	306 191 202968

PARISH	TOWNLAND	MILLER	TYPE	HOUSE	Land	£Val	PROPRIETORS	Date	WHEEL etc.	Record	Ref.
Coolkerry	Coolkerry	Baldwin John	mills	-	-	-	Baldwin - Campbell	-	-	dd/	290 239 191007
Coolkerry	Coolkerry	Baldwin Robert	mills	-	-	-	Baldwin R - Meagher Thos	1749	-	dd/	146 245 97467
Coolkerry	Coolkerry	Baldwin Robert :	mills	-	-	-	Baldwin Robt - Casson :	1770	M.Atrs. 10 Nov.	dd/	292 242 119319
Coolkerry	Coolkerry	Baldwin Robert :	mills	-	-	-	Baldwin - Gasson Stephen :	1770	(M. Arts.)	dd/	292 242 199319
Coolkerry	Coolkerry	Harman	mills	-	-	-	Harman - Baldwin	-	-	dd/	96 54 66365
Coolkerry	Coolkerry	Harman Frances	mills	-	-	-	Harman Frances - Rort	-	-	dd/	171 459 116090
Coolkerry	Coolkerry	Harman Robert	mills	-	-	-	Harman R - Baldwin Jn	1729	-	dd/	96 54 66356
Offerlane	Coolrain	-	mill	-	-	-	-	-	-	1"os	127
Offerlane	Coolrain	- nr Coolrain Vge. :	flour	-	-	-	-	-	-	6"os	16
Offerlane	Coolrain	Neal George	corn	-	-	-	-	-	15x5x15	vmb/	16
Offerlane	Coolrain	Neal George	flour	-	-	-	-	-	19x8x16 3 pr st.	vmb/	16
Offerlane	Coolrain	Neill George Esq.	corn & flour	house, offs. & ld.	44a.	250	-	1856	-	gr/	a.a.ie
Offerlane	Coolrain	on Towet R. nr bridge	corn	neat low building	-	-	-	2006	19x8x16 3 pr st.	pWEH	B
Rosenallis	Corbally	- at Rosenallis	mill	-	-	-	-	-	-	1"os	118
Rosenallis	Corbally	- nr Rosenallis :	corn	-	-	-	-	-	-	6"os	3
Rosenallis	Corbally	Degan John	corn	-	-	-	-	-	10x2x12	vmb/	16
Durrow	Course	- N. side Erkina R.	flour	-	-	-	-	-	-	6"os	29
Durrow	Course	Delany William	flour	-	-	-	-	-	17x6x4 17x5x4 &	vmb/	16
Laois	Crannagh	-	mill horizontal	-	-	-	-	-	-	iai/	AI1047 os16.7.6
Laois	Cullenagh (bo.)	Clarke Richard	iron mills	-	-	-	Clarke - Dawson Wm H	-	-	dd/	175 159 116562
Laois	Cullenagh (bo.)	Paul Christmas	iron mills	-	-	-	Paul C - Christmas Thos	-	-	dd/	103 102 70821
Laois	Cullenagh (bo.)	Paul Christmas	iron mills	-	-	-	Paul Chr - Brennan Dan	-	-	dd/	130 556 91651
Laois	Cullenagh (bo.)	Paul Thomas	iron mills	-	-	-	Paul Thos - Gray William	-	-	dd/	133 570 94241
Laois	Cullenagh (bo.)	Pier James	iron mills	-	-	-	Pier James - Paul Mehet.	-	-	dd/	103 497 72309
Laois	Cullenagh (bo.)	Roberts	iron mills	-	-	-	Roberts - White	-	-	dd/	246 29 157192
Laois	Cullenaghbegg	Barrington Jonah :	mills	-	-	-	Barrington J - Lodge Chris	1744	Lse. 14 Feb.	dd/	120 326 82756
Laois	Cullenaghbegg	Fitzgerald William	mills	-	-	-	Fitzgerald W - Prior Robt	-	-	dd/	120 303 82671
Laois	Cullenaghbegg	Heney	mills	-	-	-	Heany S - Large Samuel	-	-	dd/	180 250 120405
Laois	Cullenaghbegg	Saunders	mills	-	-	-	Saunders - Bennett	-	-	dd/	453 187 359045
Laois	Cullenaghbegg	Saunders	mills	-	-	-	Saunders - Bennett	-	-	dd/	543 187 359045
Killeshin	Curragh	Carey John	corn	house, offices & ld.	156a.	162	-	1856	-	gr/	a.a.ie
Laois	Derrycappy	Shangman Joshua	windmill	-	-	-	Shangman J - Finn John	-	-	dd/	104 151 72364
Offerlane	Derryhay	- near Mountrath	mill	- [nil located]	-	-	-	2006	-	mmSv/	wh - Z
Clandonagh	Donaghmore	Dugdale John	flour	-	-	-	-	-	16x6x16 12x5x12	vmb/	16
Clandonagh	Donaghmore	Jacob	mills	-	-	-	Jacob - Conway	-	-	dd/	533 13 348027
Clandonagh	Donaghmore	Jacob John, M' boro'	mills	-	-	-	Jacob Jn - Alley Patrick :	1807	-	dd/	620 74 423762
Clandonagh	Donaghmore	Kingsmill	mills	-	-	-	Kingsmill - Roberts	-	-	dd/	429 471 348745
Clandonagh	Donaghmore	Knaggs	mills	-	-	-	Knaggs - Odlum	-	-	dd/	532 318 349155?
Donaghmore	Donaghmore :	Dugdale John	flour	offices & yard	-	25	-	1856	-	gr/	a.a.Ire.ie
Clandonagh	Donaghmore :	- on Erkina R.	corn	-	-	-	-	-	-	6"os	28
Clonenagh	Doon	- near Doon Br.	corn	-	-	-	-	-	-	1"os	127
Clonenagh	Doon	- SE/ Doon Bridge :	corn & tuck	-	-	-	-	-	-	6"os	17
Clonenagh	Doon	Baldwin	corn & tuck	-	-	-	Baldwin - Phelan	-	-	dd/	536 553 358407
Clonenagh	Doon	Barnes George	corn & tuck	-	-	-	Barnes G - Knaggs Jno	1754	-	dd/	333 260 223969
Clonenagh	Doon	Cullen Edward	old corn mill	-	-	-	-	-	10x3x10	vmb/	16
Clonenagh	Doon	Knaggs George	corn & tuck	-	-	-	Knaggs Geo - Lalor Pet	1783	-	dd/	477 216 301952
Clonenagh	Doon	Knaggs Jno	corn & tuck	-	-	-	Knaggs J - Banting John	1786	-	dd/	378 411 253582
Clonenagh	Doon	White Thomas :	corn & tuck	-	-	-	White T - Hartt Charles :	1783	-	dd/	514 452 338335
Rosenallis	Drinagh	Jackson	mills	-	-	-	Jackson - Handcock	-	-	dd/	59 316 40680
Rosenallis	Drinagh	Jackson	mills	-	-	-	Jackson - Jackson	-	-	dd/	31 306 19177
Rosenallis	Drinagh	Jackson	mills	-	-	-	Jackson - Loftus	-	-	dd/	35 17 20514
Rosenallis	Drinagh	Jackson	mills	-	-	-	Jackson - Russell	-	-	dd/	38 357 4587

PARISH	TOWNLAND	MILLER	TYPE	HOUSE	Land	£Val	PROPRIETORS	Date	WHEEL etc.	Record	Ref.
Rosenallis	Drinagh	Thwaites	mills	-	-	-	Thwaites - Forbes	-	-	dd/	31 300 1915
Dysartenos	Dysart	Piggot Robert	mill & fairs	-	-	-	Piggot R - Wibrow Richard :	1708	-	dd/	1 20 71
Dysartenos	Dysart	Wibrow Richard	mill & fairs	-	-	-	Wibrow - Westenra	-	-	dd/	8 174 2533
Rathsaran	Eglish	-	corn	-	-	-	-	-	-	6"os	27
Rathsaran	Eglish	Bowe Patrick	corn	-	8a.	13	-	-	-	gr/	a.a.ire.ie
Rathsaran	Eglish	Cullen John	corn	-	-	-	-	-	12x3x5	vmb/	16
Rathdowney	Errill	-	mill in ruins	-	-	-	-	-	-	6"os	27
Laois	Eyne	-	corn	-	-	-	-	-	-	1"os	118
Moyanna	Garrymaddock	-	corn	-	-	-	-	-	-	6"os	14
Moyanna	Garrymaddock	Bailey John	mill	-	-	-	Bailey John - Bailey Jn	1863	-	dd/	1863 36 53
Moyanna	Garrymaddock :	-	corn & pond	-	-	-	-	-	-	6"os	14
Moyanna	Garrymaddock :	-	corn & pond	-	-	-	-	-	-	6"os	14
Aghaboe	Gortnaclea	- on R. Gully	corn	-	-	-	-	-	-	6"os	23
Aghaboe	Gortnaclea	Doolan Thomas	corn	-	28a.	-	J Ano - W Ano	-	13x2x6	vmb/	14
Aghaboe	Graigue	- on R. Barrow	flour	-	-	-	-	-	-	6"os	37
Aghaboe	Graigue	- on R.Barrow	distillery	-	-	-	-	-	-	6"os	37
Aghaboe	Graigue	- N. of Church St.	thrashing m/c	-	-	-	-	-	-	6"os	37
Killeshin	Graigue Town :	Haughton Benj & Co.	flour	offices & yard	-	150	-	1856	-	gr/	a.a.ie
Killeshin	Graigue Town :	Haughton Benj & Co.	tannery	offices & yard	-	10	-	1856	-	gr/	a.a.ie
Killeshin	Graigue Town :	Haughton John	flour	-	-	-	-	-	20x12x3 5 pr st.	vmb/	16
Killeshin	Graigue Town :	Brown John	corn	-	-	-	-	1845	18x5x2	vmb/	16
Killeshin	Graigue Town :	Kavanagh Bridget Mrs	corn	offices & kiln	-	70	-	1856	-	gr/	a.a.ie
Monksgrange	Grange	- W. of R. Barrow	flour & kiln	-	-	-	-	-	-	6"os	32
Monksgrange	Grange	Cuffe Maurice	mill	-	-	-	Cuffe M - White Francis	-	-	dd/	126 449 88282
Monksgrange	Grange	Cuffe Maurice	mill	-	-	-	Cuffe Mce - Gale Ant	-	-	dd/	112 324 78274
Monksgrange	Grange	Cuffe Maurice :	mills (& 500a.)	-	-	-	Cuffe - Redmond Morris	1743	-	dd/	113 99 77593
Monksgrange	Grange	Gale	mill	-	-	-	Gale - Harpole	-	-	dd/	192 344 127879
Monksgrange	Grange	Gale Peter	mill	-	-	-	Gale Peter - William	1781	-	dd/	389 583 230156
Monksgrange	Grange	Geale Anthony	mill	-	-	-	Geale A - Bambrick John	-	-	dd/	174 537 117381
Monksgrange	Grange	McWay Murtagh	corn	-	-	-	-	-	16x6x7	vmb/	16
Monksgrange	Grange	O'Cuffe John	corn	offices & land	72a.	100	-	1856	-	gr/	a.a.ie
Laois	Grelagh	Prior	mill	-	-	-	Prior - Prior	-	-	dd/	595 52 104192
Laois	Grelagh	Prior	mill	-	-	-	Prior - Prior	-	-	dd/	595 52 104192
Laois	Heath	Bagnell John :	mills	-	-	-	Bagnell J - Cooney John :	1810	-	dd/	622 471 429017
Laois	Heath	Crofts	mills	-	-	-	Crofts - Nelands	-	-	dd/	598 495 413904
Laois	Heath	Gore	mills	-	-	-	Gore - Dancer	-	-	dd/	624 467 430126?
Laois	Irishtown	Strangman Joshua	windmill	-	-	-	Shangman J - Finn John	-	-	dd/	104 151 72364
Abbeyleix	Iron Mills	Christmas Paul :	mills	-	-	-	Christmas - Brennan Dan	1743	-	dd/	130 556 91651
Abbeyleix	Iron Mills	Paul	mills	-	-	-	Paul - Christmas	-	-	dd/	3 488 1297
Abbeyleix	Iron Mills	Paul	mills	-	-	-	Paul - Westbury	-	-	dd/	2 410 537
Abbeyleix	Ironmills / Kilrush	- on Owenbeg R.	woollen fcty	-	-	-	-	-	-	6"os	30
Abbeyleix	Ironmills / Kilrush	Fannin David :	iron mills	-	-	-	Fannan D - Woodrosse Jas	1809	-	dd/	607 453 417409
Abbeyleix	Ironmills / Kilrush	Hartpole George	iron mills	-	-	-	Hartpole G - White Simon	1795	-	dd/	485 381 312646
Abbeyleix	Ironmills / Kilrush	Jackson John	iron mills	-	-	-	Jackson J - Ebury Baron	1863	-	dd/	1863 35 103
Abbeyleix	Ironmills / Kilrush	Kingsmill Luke :	iron mills	-	-	-	Kingsmill L - Fannan Jas	1788	-	dd/	464 423 296513
Abbeyleix	Ironmills / Kilrush	Moore Patrick	corn	house & land	67a.	79	-	1856	-	gr/	a.a.Ire.ie
Abbeyleix	Ironmills / Kilrush	Moore Patrick	spinning	-	-	-	-	1856	-	gr/	a.a.Ire.ie
Abbeyleix	Ironmills / Kilrush	Noble Benjamin	iron mills	-	-	-	Noble Benj - Lalor Jas	1791	-	dd/	485 7 300674
Abbeyleix	Ironmills / Kilrush	Tenison Thomas :	iron mills	-	-	-	Tenison T - Lyons Myles :	1761	-	dd/	7 300674
Clonenagh	Iry	- on The Strand :	corn	-	-	-	-	-	-	6"os	12
Laois	Kilbrish	Kelly Annette	woollen factory	-	-	-	-	-	12x2x12	vmb/	16
Laois	Kilbrish	Kelly Mrs	woollen factory	-	-	-	-	-	15x3x15	vmb/	16

PARISH	TOWNLAND	MILLER	TYPE	HOUSE	Land	£Val	PROPRIETORS	Date	WHEEL etc.	Record	Ref.
Killabban	Killeen	- at Killeen Ho.	corn	-	-	-	-	-	-	6"os	32
Killabban	Killeen	Thomas Matthew D	thrashing	-	-	-	-	-	10x3x10	vmb/	16
Offerlane	Killinure	- nr Mountrath R :	corn & kiln	-	-	-	-	-	-	6"os	11
Offerlane	Killinure	Shiels Patrick	corn	-	-	-	-	-	12x1x12	vmb/	16
Dysartgallen	Kilnashane :	- nr Owenbeg R.	corn & old race	-	-	-	-	-	-	6"os	30
Dysartgallen	Kilnashane :	- nr Owenbeg R.	old mill race	-	-	-	-	-	-	6"os	30
Abbeyleix	Knapton Bridge	-	mill	lge. ho. no trace of mill		-	-	2006	-	mmSv/	wh - Z
Borris	Knockageragh :	Kelly Michael	corn	-	-	-	-	-	13x3x6	vmb/	16
Clonenagh	Knockanina	- Millbank Mill	mill	-	-	-	-	2006	metal wheel :	mmSv/	wh - R
Clonenagh	Knockanina :	- The Nore	Nore Flour Mills	-	-	-	-	-	-	6"os	16
Offerlane	Knockbrack	-	mill	-	-	-	-	2008			
Borris	Knocknagroagh	-	corn & pond	-	-	-	(local inf.) Pikes of Rushall	2008	-	mmSv/	wh - Cc
Borris	Knocknagroagh	Kelly Michael	corn	house, offices & ld.	36a.	28.10.	-	1856	-	gr/	a.a.ie
Abbeyleix	Knocknamoe :	-	brewery	-	-	-	-	-	-	6"os	23
Kyle	Kyle	Talbot John	corn	house, offices & ld.	30a.	34.5.	-	1856	-	gr/	a.a.ie
Leix	Kyletalesha	-	corn	-	-	-	-	-	-	1"os	118
Offerlane	Lacka	- nr Bennets Br. :	flour mill site	-	-	-	-	-	-	6"os	11
Lea	Lea	- S. side R. Barrow	corn	-	-	-	-	1841	-	6"os/	5
Lea	Lea	Phelan	mill & mill lands	-	-	-	Phelan - Phelan	-	-	dd/	305 614 204036
Lea	Lea	Phelan Bartholomew	mill & mill lands	-	-	-	Phelan - Phelan Geo (Son)	1774	-	dd/	305 614 204036
Lea	Lea	Quin Bridget	corn	(2/3B) 41x22x22.6 :	-	5.2.0	-	-	undershot 10x2.6 :	hob/	5.1189
Lea	Lea	Quin widow	corn & wheat	-	-	-	-	-	11x4x5 machinery	vmb/	16
Laois	Little Mill	Lewis Henry	mill	-	-	-	Lewis H - White Fran	1786	-	dd/	380 603 258115
Borris	Maryborough	-	mill	-	-	-	-	-	-	1"os	127
Borris	Maryborough	Atkinson Thomas	flour	-	-	-	-	-	17x6x13 4 pr st.	vmb/	16
Borris	Maryborough	Clarke James	flour	-	-	-	-	-	16x6x9 3 pr st.	vmb/	16
Borris	Maryborough	Wheelock Henry	mills	- & dw. house	-	-	Wheelock H & Moore Jn	1800	-	dd/	526 454 345033
Borris	Maryborough Bo.	Drogheda Earl	old mill lands	-	-	-	Drogheda - Strangman Sam	1762	-	dd/	225 76 145138
Borris	Maryborough Tn :	-	old factory	-	-	-	-	-	-	6"os	13
Borris	Maryborough Tn :	Carr Richard	Lalor`s Mill	-	-	-	Carr R - O`Brien Nassau	1847	-	dd/	1847 10 102
Borris	Maryborough Tn :	Shelburne Earl	Lalor`s Mill	-	-	-	Shelburne Earl & Deed	1847	-	dd/	1847 13 127
Maryborough	Maryborough Tn :	Atkinson Thomas	mill	-	-	-	Atkinson Th - Kelly Wm	1845	-	dd/	1845 45 19
Borris	Maryborough Tn :	Kelly William, Sen.	flour	ho., offs,. gdn., ld.	1a.	90	-	1856	-	gr/	a.a.ie
Borris	Maryborough Tn :	Budda	corn store	& office	-	9.10.	-	1856	-	gr/	a.a.ie
Borris	Maryborough Tn :	-	flour & pond	-	-	-	-	-	-	6"os	13
Borris	Maryborough Tn :	Carthy John	iron foundry	offices sm gdn.	-	2.5.0	-	1856	-	gr/	a.a.Ire.ie
Borris	Maryborough Tn :	Mullin Geroge	mill	-	-	-	Mullin G - Dowd Robt	1875	-	dd/	1875 48 147
Borris	Maryborough Tn :	Atkinson Thomas	mill	-	-	-	Atkinson Th - Kelly Wm	1845	-	dd/	1845 15 197
Borris	Maryborough Tn :	-	flour	-	-	-	-	-	-	6"os	13
Borris	Maryborough Tn :	Dond Robert	mill	-	-	-	Dond R - Odlum Wm P	1884	-	dd/	1884 51 211
Kilcolemanbane	Meelick	-	flour & pond	-	-	-	-	-	-	6"os	13
Kilcolemanbane	Meelick	-	mill	-	-	-	-	-	-	1"os	127
Kilcolemanbane	Meelick	-	potter`s kiln	-	-	-	-	-	-	6"os	3
Kilcolemanbane	Meelick	Kelly William	flour	house, offices & ld.	50a.	115	-	1856	-	gr/	a.a.ie
Kilcolemanbane	Meelick	Kelly William	flour	-	-	-	-	-	18x7x13 3 pr st.	vmb/	16
Stradbally	Mill Land	-	fulling	no visible traces :	-	-	-	-	-	iaa/	AI1048 os14.15.2
Stradbally	Mill Land	-	fulling (site)	-	-	-	-	-	-	iai/	1048 os15:15:2
Curraclone	Milland	Walsh Sir Edward	bone	-	-	-	-	-	14x4x11	vmb/	16
Curraclone	Milland	Walsh Sir Edward	corn	-	-	-	-	-	16x6x11 3 pr st.	vmb/	16
Curraclone	Mil-land	-	(no mill)	-	-	-	-	-	-	6"os	7
Curraclone	Mil-land	- Newmills	Worsted Fcty							6"os	7
Curraclone	Mill-land (near)	- on Tonet R. :	corn & pond	-	-	-	-	-	-	6"os	14

PARISH	TOWNLAND	MILLER	TYPE	HOUSE	Land	£Val	PROPRIETORS	Date	WHEEL etc.	Record	Ref.
Laois	Milllands :	- Newmills	Worsted Fcty	-	-	-	-	-	-	6"os	7
Laois	Milllands :	- nr Owenass Br.	flour	-	-	-	-	-	-	6"os	7
Curraclone	Milllands (near)	- nr Owenass Br.	flour & pond							6"os	7
Borris	Milltown M`boro	Casson	-	-	-	-	Casson - Knaggs	-	-	dd/	190 545 128128
Borris	Milltown M`boro	Keeffe Luke :	-	-	-	-	Keeffe L - Dunn William :	1802	-	dd/	552 29 364559
Borris	Milltown M`boro	Knaggs James	-	-	-	-	Knaggs James - Robert	1779	-	dd/	339 549 229962
Dysartgallen	Moat	- on Owenbeg R.	corn	-	-	-	-	-	-	6"os	30
Dysartgallen	Moat	Doolan John	corn	house, offices & ld.	14a.	16	-	1856	-	gr/	a.a.ie
Dysartgallen	Moat	Doolan John	corn	-	-	-	-	-	10x2x10	vmb/	16
Laois	Monksgrange	Barrington Jonah :	mill	-	-	-	Barrington J - Grogan Edw :	1806	-	dd/	580 146 393817
Laois	Monksgrange	Colelough Adam ?	mill	-	-	-	Colelough A - Lecky John :	1810	-	dd/	621 592 428958
Laois	Monksgrange	Cuffe Maurice	mill	-	-	-	Cuffe R - Morris Redmd	-	-	dd/	113 99 77595
Laois	Monksgrange	Dillon Thomas	mill	-	-	-	Dillon Thos - Dillon John	-	-	dd/	108 540 77296
Laois	Monksgrange	Gale	mill	-	-	-	Gale - Fitzmaurice	-	-	dd/	543 418 363177
Laois	Monksgrange	Gale	mills	-	-	-	Gale - Hartpole	-	-	dd/	197 344 127879
Laois	Monksgrange	Gale Peter	mill	-	-	-	Gale P - Fitzmaurice Jas	1799	-	dd/	526 129 343797
Laois	Monksgrange	Hartpole	mill	-	-	-	Hartpole - Stratford	-	-	dd/	154 347 233342
Laois	Monksgrange	Hartpole Robert :	mill	-	-	-	Hartpole R - Stratford Benj :	1765	-	dd/	233 342 154347
Laois	Monksgrange	Lindsay John	mill	-	-	-	Lindsay J - Harrington W :	1750	-	dd/	140 500 96246
Laois	Monlisheal	Prior	mill & land	-	-	-	Prior - Prior	-	-	dd/	592 52 404192
Laois	Morett	- nr Portarlington	mill site HZ	- understructure :	-	-	-	-	-	iai/	AI1049 os9.13.4
Clonenagh	Mounteagle	-	corn	strong lge. remains :	-	-	-	2006	-	mmSv/	wh - B
Clonenagh	Mounteagle	-	flour	-	-	-	-	-	-	6"os	24
Clonenagh	Mounteagle	Bell Wellington	corn	-	-	-	-	-	16x6x13	vmb/	16
Clonenagh	Mounteagle	M'Donnell Mary	corn	ho., offs. & land	24a	32	-	1856	-	gr/	a.a.lre.ie
Clonenagh	Mounteagle	Mills	corn & tuck	-	-	-	Mills - B. of Waterford	-	-	dd/	181 182 120355
Clonenagh	Mounteagle	Pigott Jno	corn & tuck	-	-	-	Pigott J - B. of Waterford	-	-	dd/	178 394 119353
Clonenagh	Mounteagle	Pigott John	corn & tuck	-	-	-	Pigott J - Langton John	1739	-	dd/	95 511 67306
Rosenallis	Mountmellick	Crips	manor mills	-	-	-	Crips - Cusitrul?	-	-	dd/	236 465 11524?
Rosenallis	Mountmellick	Crips John	manor mills	-	-	-	Crips John - Crips Geo	-	-	dd/	125 365 85380
Rosenallis	Mountmellick	Dawson	mill lands	-	-	-	Dawson - Archdall	-	-	dd/	342 507 231265
Rosenallis	Mountmellick	Goodbody	old mill & lands	-	-	-	Goodbody - Tarleton	-	-	dd/	551 392 563717?
Rosenallis	Mountmellick	Shannon Joseph	old mill & lands	-	-	-	Shannon J - Thacker Thos.	1780	Mort. 22 Feb.	dd/	338 185 226848
Rosenallis	Mountmellick T`pks	- N. side Main St	brewery	-	-	-	-	-	-	6"os	8
Rosenallis	Mountmellick T`pks	- on Owenass R.	distillery	-	-	-	-	-	-	6"os	8
Rosenallis	Mountmellick T`pks	- S. side Town :	brewery	-	-	-	-	-	-	6"os	8
Rosenallis	Mountmellick T`pks	- S. side Town :	brewery	-	-	-	-	-	-	6"os	8
Rosenallis	Mountmellick T`pks	Conway Edward	malt	-	-	-	-	-	12x4x7 stone :	vmb/	16
Rosenallis	Mountmellick T`pks	Milner John	spinning	-	-	-	-	-	16x8x14	vmb/	16
Rosenallis	Mountmellick T`pks	Milner John	worsted fcty	-	-	-	-	-	13x5x14	vmb/	16
Rosenallis	Mountmellick T`pks	Sheane James	corn	house, offs. & ld.	17a.	53	-	1856	-	gr/	a.a.lre.ie
Rosenallis	Mountmellick T`pks	Sheane James	corn	-	-	-	-	-	10x10x11	vmb/	16
Rosenallis	Mountmellick T`pks	Sheane James	old brewery	offices & yard	-	14	-	1856	-	gr/	a.a.lre.ie
Rosenallis	Mountmellick T`pks	Sheane James	steam flour mill	offices & yard	-	65	-	1856	-	gr/	a.a.lre.ie
Clonenagh	Mountrath	- near Woodbine Ctg	mill	-	-	-	-	-	-	1"os	128
Clonenagh	Mountrath	Despard	Manor Mills	-	-	-	Despard - Hodgins	-	-	dd/	54 146 35204
Clonenagh	Mountrath	Despard Lambert :	iron works	-	-	-	Despard L - Powell Wm :	1759	-	dd/	223 518 149131
Clonenagh	Mountrath	Despard Richard	iron works	-	-	-	Despard Richard - Richd	-	-	dd/	114 451 79617
Clonenagh	Mountrath	Greenham Robert	cotton	-	-	-	-	-	18x5x14	vmb/	16
Clonenagh	Mountrath	Neale Richard	flour	-	-	-	-	-	14x4x5	vmb/	16
Clonenagh	Mountrath	Roe Peter	flour	-	-	-	-	-	13x11x11	vmb/	16
Clonenagh	Mountrath :	-	corn & rape	-	-	-	-	-	-	6"os	17

PARISH	TOWNLAND	MILLER	TYPE	HOUSE	Land	£Val	PROPRIETORS	Date	WHEEL etc.	Record	Ref.
Clonenagh	Mountrath :	-	old distillery	-	-	-	-	2008	-	mmSv/	wh - Z
Clonenagh	Mountrath :	-	mill	-	-	-	-	-	-	6"os	17
Clonenagh	Mountrath :	-	brewery	-	-	-	-	-	-	6"os	17
Clonenagh	Mountrath :	-	cotton factory	-	-	-	- replaced by housing est. :	2008	-	mmSv/	wh - Z
Clonenagh	Mountrath :	-	foundry	shed & store :	-	-	-	2008	-	mmSv/	wh - Cc
Clonenagh	Mountrath :	-	old distillery & : b	-	-	-	-	-	-	6"os	17
Clonenagh	Mountrath :	- on Limerick Road	mill	-	-	-	-	2008	-	mmSv/	wh - Z
Clonenagh	Mountrath :	-	cotton factory	-	-	-	-	-	-	6"os	17
Clonenagh	Mountrath Manor	Calcutt Joseph :	mill	-	-	-	Calcutt Jos & Marr. Smt. :	1804	-	dd/	567 393 381553
Clonenagh	Mountrath Manor	Harris John	old tuck mill	-	-	-	Mr John Harrin & Will	-	-	dd/	119 45 81290
Clonenagh	Mountrath Town	- at Woodbrook	corn & rape	-	-	-	-	-	-	6"os	17
Aghmacart	Newtown	-	Newtown Mills	-	-	-	-	-	-	1"os	136
Aghmacart	Newtown	-	Newtown Mills	pond & mill race	-	-	-	-	-	6"os	29
Aghmacart	Newtown	- near to Collieries	steam engine	-	-	-	-	-	-	6"os	31
Clonenagh	Nore Mills	Roberts Thomas	corn	-	-	-	-	-	17x5x6	vmb/	16
Offerlane	Northgrove	- on R. Delour	rape mill ruins							6"os	11
Offerlane	Northgrove	- W side R. Delour	old mill	-	-	-	-	-	-	6"os	11
Laois	Olar Esker	Coote Charles Rev	old mill	-	-	-	Coote C - Parnell John Sir	1785	-	dd/	372 116 247757
Laois	Olar Esker	Sydney Lord Crosbie	old mill	-	-	-	Sydney Lord - Farnham E. :	1773	-	dd/	298 542 198574
Stradbally	Old Mill	- SW of Town	flour & mill pond	-	-	-	-	1841	-	6"os	19
Laois	Old Mill	Basill	mill	-	-	-	Basill - Gowran	-	-	dd/	27 165 b1630
Desertenos	Old Mill	Comerford John	flour	house, offs., land	25a.	85.15.	-	1856	-	gr/	a.a.ire.ie
Desertenos	Old Mill	Comerford John	mill	-	25a.	3.0.0	-	1856	-	gr/	a.a.ire.ie
Stradbally	Old Mill	Crosby Emily	old mill	-	-	-	Crosby Emily - Robert	1862	-	dd/	1862 7 216
Stradbally	Old Mill	Crosby Robert	old mill	-	-	-	Crosby Robt - deed	1862	-	dd/	1862 6 18
Desertenos	Old Mill	Leadbeater Richard	flour	-	-	-	-	-	18x12x12	vmb/	16
Laois	Old Mill	Ormsby	mill	-	-	-	Ormsby - Walsh	-	-	dd/	15 275 7487
Laois	Old Mill	Walsh	mill	-	-	-	Walsh - Molyneux	-	-	dd/	83 10 57321
Laois	Old Mill	Walsh	mill	-	-	-	Walsh - Walsh	-	-	dd/	71 420 51841
Laois	Old Mill	Warren	mill	-	-	-	Warren - Ashe	-	-	dd/	14 452 6565
Desertenos	Old Mill :	-	corn	-	-	-	-	1856	-	6"os	19
Laois	Old Mill bo:Ossory	Crosby Poly :	old mill	-	-	-	Crosby P - Kelly William :	1757	-	dd/	218 116 142141
Laois	Old Mill bo:Ossory	Gosby	old mill	-	-	-	Gosby - Powerscourt	-	-	dd/	559 394 375848
Stradbally	Old Mills	Cosby Elizabeth :	old mills	-	-	-	Cosby E - Wingfield Thos	1809	-	dd/	609 85 422030
Stradbally	Old Mills	Landers	old mills	-	-	-	Landers - Dease	-	-	dd/	506 540 334251
Kilaban	Oldleagh	-	threshing m/c	-	-	-	-	-	-	6"os	32
Aghmacart	Oldtown	- S. side R. Goul	old mill	-	-	-	-	1841	-	6"os	34
Laois	Orchard	Cosby	old mill	-	-	-	Cosby - Cosby	-	-	dd/	541 218 356726
Laois	Orchard	Cosby	old mill	-	-	-	Cosby - Marq. of Sligo	-	-	dd/	554 241 366921
Laois	Orchard	Dunn Richard	old mill	-	-	-	Dunn R - Dunn Patrick : (	1807	-	dd/	590 94 399831
Laois	Orchard	Murray John	old mill	-	-	-	Murray J - Dunne Richard	1780	-	dd/	374 464 250081
Ballyroan	Pass	- near Pass House	woollen factory	-	-	-	-	-	-	6"os	18
Ballyroan	Pass	Cooney Alex	woollen factory	-	-	-	-	-	15x3x5	vmb/	16
Ballyroan	Pass	Farrar John	corn	house, offs. & ld.	73a.	100	-	1856	-	gr/	a.a.Ire.ie
Ballyroan	Pass	Farrar John	woollen factory	-	-	-	-	1856	-	gr/	a.a.Ire.ie
Abbeyleix	Poormansbridge	- Bleacfield Mills	spinning	v. old & roofless :	-	-	-	2006	-	mmSv/	wh - D
Abbeyleix	Poormansbridge	- nr Gloreen Br. :	woollen factory	-	-	-	-	-	-	6"os	23
Abbeyleix	Poormansbridge	Lee John	spinning worsted	-	-	-	-	-	27x4x25	vmb/	16
Abbeyleix	Poormansbridge	Leigh John	corn	-	-	-	-	1856	-	gr/	a.a.ire.ie
Abbeyleix	Poormansbridge	Leigh John	woollen factory	house, offs. & ld.	36a.	-	-	1856	-	gr/	a.a.ire.ie
Lea	Portarlington	- on R. Barrow :	flour	-	-	-	-	-	-	6"os	4
Lea	Portarlington	Duron Isaac	miller`s holding	-	-	-	-	1832	-	dd/	1832 2 234

PARISH	TOWNLAND	MILLER	TYPE	HOUSE	Land	£Val	PROPRIETORS	Date	WHEEL etc.	Record	Ref.
Lea	Portarlington	Powell Jno Rev	miller`s holding	-	-	-	Powell Jno - Geo	1839	-	dd/	1839 17 72
Coolbanaghter	Portnahinch	Warburton - Dempsey	mill	-	-	-	-	-	-	dd/	53 461 36407
Rathdowney	Raheen	- E. side Erkina R.	corn mill ruins	-	-	-	-	-	-	6"os	28
Laois	Raheenah	Prior Robert	mills	-	-	-	Prior Robt - Owens Wm :	1750	-	dd/	167 223 112082
Kilaban	Rahin	-	windmill ruins	-	-	-	-	-	-	6"os	25
Rathdowney	Rathdowney	- N. of Tn Br.	brewery	-	-	-	-	-	-	6"os	28
Rathdowney	Rathdowney	- to S. of Tn Br.	flour & corn	-	-	-	-	-	-	6"os	28
Rathdowney	Rathdowney	Adams	mill & customs	-	-	-	Adams - Armstrong	-	-	dd/	552 308 366367
Rathdowney	Rathdowney	Atkinson Robert	flour	-	-	-	-	-	16x4x15	vmb/	16
Rathdowney	Rathdowney	Atkinson Robert & :	flour	offices & yard	-	36	-	1856	-	gr/	a.a.Ire.ie
Rathdowney	Rathdowney	Dunphy	mills	-	-	-	Dunphy - Despard	-	-	dd/	631 16 431525
Rathdowney	Rathdowney	Flintoff Albert	mills	-	-	-	Flintoff Albert - Anne	1862	-	dd/	1862 28 59
Rathdowney	Rathdowney	Kennedy Richard	mills	-	-	-	Kennedy R - Ryan Andr	1863	-	dd/	1863 1 5
Rathdowney	Rathdowney	Mason	mill & customs	-	-	-	Mason - Mason	-	-	dd/	348 55 23196
Rathdowney	Rathdowney	Mason Thomas	mill	-	-	-	Mason T - Vickars Geo	-	-	dd/	125 112 84396
Rathdowney	Rathdowney	Nicholson	mills	-	-	-	Nicholson - Neale	-	-	dd/	658 343 402571
Rathdowney	Rathdowney	Perry Robert	corn & brewery	ho., offs., yd. & ld.	1a.	59	-	1865	-	gr/	a.a.Ire.ie
Rathdowney	Rathdowney	Perry Robert brewer	malt	-	-	-	-	-	16x4x15	vmb/	16
Rathdowney	Rathdowney	Prior	mill	-	-	-	Prior - Oldfield	-	-	dd/	182? 160 75071
Rathdowney	Rathdowney	Prior John Murray	mill & customs	-	-	-	Prior J M - Colgan James :	1796	-	dd/	492 260 323381
Rathdowney	Rathdowney	Prior Murray	mill & customs	-	-	-	Prior M - Palmer Jos	1779	-	dd/	340 413 238428?
Rathdowney	Rathdowney	Prior Thomas	mill	-	-	-	Prior T - Palmer Humphry	-	-	dd/	132 436 89893
Rathdowney	Rathdowney	Prior Thomas	mill	-	-	-	Prior Thos - Dixon James :	1748	-	dd/	149 100 99008
Rathdowney	Rathdowney	Prior Thomas :	mills	-	-	-	Prior Thos - Geale Hannah :	1805	-	dd/	576 82 384900
Rathdowney	Rathdowney	Prior Thomas & Eliz.	mills	-	-	-	Prior Thos - Fisher Robert :	1810	-	dd/	620 552 426678
Rathdowney	Rathdowney	Roberts	mills	-	-	-	Roberts - Palmer	-	-	dd/	625 27 427649?
Rathdowney	Rathdowney	White Robert :	mill & customs	-	-	-	White R- Condran Thos :	1799	-	dd/	519 404 340707
Laois	Rathendock	Darcey	mill	-	-	-	Darcey - Darcey	-	-	dd/	693 401 42634?
Laois	Rathendock	Fayle	mill	-	-	-	Fayle - Walsh	-	-	dd/	459 346 294064
Laois	Rathendock	O`Meara	mill	-	-	-	O`Meara - Colgan	-	-	dd/	625 189 432683
Laois	Rathendock	Phelps	mill	-	-	-	Phelps - Middleton	-	-	dd/	596 44 403890
Laois	Rathendock	Walsh	mill	-	-	-	Walsh - Fayle	-	-	dd/	458 57 294063
Rosenallis	Rinn	- NE of Rosenallis :	corn & pond	-	-	-	-	-	-	6"os	3
Rosenallis	Rinn	Hipwell James	corn	house, offs. & ld.	70a.	38.10.	-	-	-	gr/	a.a.Ire.ie
Rosenallis	Rinn	Hipwell James	corn	-	-	-	-	-	11x3x14	vmb/	16
Offerlane	Rushin	Grennan Robert	mill pond	-	10.3.24		-	1856	-	gr/	a.a.ie
Laois	Sampsons Court	Dawson Jos Hon.	Sibthorp`s mills	-	-	-	Dawson - Archdall Mervyn	-	-	dd/	342 507 231261
Laois	Sampsons Court	Gale	Sibthorp`s mills	-	-	-	Gale & Thomas marr smt.	-	-	dd/	595 304 406513
Sleaty	Sleaty	- W. of R. Barrow	corn & kiln	-	-	-	-	-	-	6"os	32
Sleaty	Sleaty	- W. of R. Barrow	mill pond	-	-	-	-	-	-	6"os	32
Sleaty	Sleaty	Byrne Patrick	corn	house, offs. & ld.	2a.	9.0.0	-	1856	-	gr/	a.a.ie
Sleaty	Sleaty	Byrne Patrick	corn	-	-	-	-	-	12x3x8	vmb/	16
Straboe	Straboe	-	corn & mill pond	-	-	-	-	1841	-	6"os	8
Straboe	Straboe	Brady Andrew	corn	house, offs. & ld.	62a.	43	-	1856	-	gr/	a.a.ie
Straboe	Straboe	Brady Andrew	corn	-	-	-	-	-	14x4x11	vmb/	16
Stradbally	Stradbally	Cosby	mills	-	-	-	Cosby - Cassin	-	-	dd/	98 24 67424
Stradbally	Stradbally	Cosby Pole	mills	-	-	-	Cosby P - Brereton Arth	-	-	dd/	106 190 73334
Stradbally	Stradbally	Fitzgerald (H.Sher.)	mills & bl green	-	-	-	Co. Sherrif - Pringle Geo	1785	-	dd/	368 15 245742
Stradbally	Stradbally	Leadbeater Richard	flour & corn	-	-	-	-	-	16x9x12	vmb/	16
Stradbally	Stradbally	Leadbeater Richd S	flour	offices & land	1a.	80	-	1856	-	gr/	a.a.ie
Stradbally	Stradbally	O`Brien	mills & bl green	-	-	-	O`Brien - Falye	-	-	dd/	457 469 302776
Stradbally	Stradbally	O`Brien	mills & bl green	-	-	-	O`Brien - Falye	-	- (? error)	dd/	587? 246 328034?

PARISH	TOWNLAND	MILLER	TYPE	HOUSE	Land	£Val	PROPRIETORS	Date	WHEEL etc.	Record	Ref.
Stradbally	Stradbally	Roan James :	mills & bl green	-	-	-	Roan J - Roberts Arthur	1784	-	dd/	367 130 246?274
Stradbally	Stradbally	Roberts Arthur	mills	-	-	-	Roberts Arth - Toole Jos	1748	-	dd/	152 118 100982
Stradbally	Stradbally	Williams	mills & bl green	-	-	-	Williams - Brien	-	-	dd/	463 192 297907
Stradbally	Stradbally Abbey	Mitchell	mills	-	-	-	Mitchell - Kelly	-	-	dd/	234 637 154879
Stradbally	Stradbally Abbey	Mitchell Capt. Isreal :	mill	-	-	-	Mitchell I - Kelly Michael	1765	-	dd/	234 537 154879
Stradbally	Stradbally Abbey	Mitchell Nathaniel	mills	-	-	-	Mitchell N - Higgins James :	1739	-	dd/	101 323 71404
Stradbally	Stradbally Abbey	Mitchell Nathaniel	mills	-	-	-	Mitchell N - Walker Richard :	1754	-	dd/	167 281 112459
Stradbally	Stradbally Town	- imed. E/ Town Br.	flour & mill pond	-	-	-	-	1841	-	6"os	14
Stradbally	Stradbally Town :	-	flour	-	-	-	-	1841	-	6"os	19
Laois	Strahbaun	-	corn	-	-	-	-	-	-	1"os	136
Laois	Tallaghwood	-	old windmill	-	-	-	-	-	-	1"os	128
Rathdowney	Templequain	- nr Aghmacart Br.	corn & tuck	-	-	-	-	-	-	6"os	33
Rathdowney	Templequain	Carroll Thomas	corn	house, offs. & ld.	3a.	13	-	1856	-	gr/	a.a.Ire.ie
Rathdowney	Templequain	Carroll Thomas	corn	-	-	-	-	-	10x4x10	vmb/	16
Timahoe	Timahoe	-	corn & saw	-	-	-	-	1841	-	6"os/	18
Timahoe	Timahoe	-	corn & saw & :	-	-	-	-	1888	-	25"os/	18.16
Timahoe	Timahoe	-	mills	-	-	-	-	-	-	1"os	128
Timahoe	Timahoe	Cosby	mills	-	-	-	Cosby - Gowran	-	-	dd/	30 46 16302
Timahoe	Timahoe	Edge Joseph	corn	house, offs. & ld	20a	51	-	1856	-	gr/	a.a.Ire.ie
Timahoe	Timahoe	Freeman	mills	-	-	-	Freeman - Bayley	-	-	dd/	26 248 15363
Timahoe	Timahoe	Freeman	mills	-	-	-	Freeman - Ryan	-	-	dd/	47 381 30852
Timahoe	Timahoe	Freeman	mills	-	-	-	Freeman - Stringer	-	-	dd/	26 268
Timahoe	Timahoe	Freeman	mills	-	-	-	Freeman - Wills	-	-	dd/	25 523 15753
Timahoe	Timahoe	Higgins	mills	-	-	-	Higgins - Dodsworth	-	-	dd/	44 262 29076
Timahoe	Timahoe	Stringer	mills	-	-	-	Stringer - Maturin	-	-	dd/	26 486 16464
Timahoe	Timahoe	Wills	mills	-	-	-	Wills - Freeman	-	-	dd/	35 127 21414
Timahoe	Timahoe Manor	Cosby	mills	-	-	-	Cosby - Casson	-	-	dd/	92 4 67424
Timahoe	Timahoe Manor	Hunter John & Thos :	mills	-	-	-	Hunter J - Doran Edmund :	1766	-	dd/	244 284 157768
Timogue	Timogue	- 1/2 m. N/ Vge.	corn mill ruins	-	-	-	-	1841	-	6"os/	19
Timogue	Timogue	- S/ town bridge	corn	-	-	-	-	1841	-	6"os/	19
Timogue	Timogue	- W. of Village	salt ho. (ruins)	-	-	-	-	-	14x5x6	vmb/	16
Timogue	Timogue	Budds Thomas	corn	-	-	-	-	-	14x5x6	vmb/	16
Timogue	Timogue	Budds Thomas	corn	ho., offices & land	315a.	275	- & tenant's houses (3)	-	-	gr/	a.a.Ire.ie
Moyanna	Tonfarna	Bailey John	corn	-	-	-	-	-	18x4x5	vmb/	16
Moyanna	Tonfarna	Bailey John	corn	ho., offices & land	100a.	57	-	-	-	gr/	a.a.Ire.ie
Moyanna	Tonfarna	Lutteral David	corn	-	-	-	-	-	13x4x7 3 pr st.	vmb/	16
Laois	Townland ?	Fitzpatrick - Vicars	miller's house	-	-	-	-	-	-	dd/	26 352 15679
Laois	Townland ?	Jackson - Jackson	corn & tuck	-	-	-	-	-	-	dd/	31 260 18932
Laois	Townland ?	Vicars - Drought	miller's house	-	-	-	-	-	-	dd/	72 517 51799
Laois	Townland ?	Vicars - Drought	miller's house	-	-	-	-	-	-	dd/	82 290 57877
Abbeyleix	Trioge R.	Mosse Thomas	mills	-	-	-	Mosse & wife - Pigott Jn	-	-	dd/	116 38 79339
Abbeyleix	Trioge R.	Mosse Thomas	mills	-	-	-	Mosse Th - Mosse Wm	-	-	dd/	179 465 121870
Laois	Tully	- at Ram Park	mills & pond	-	-	-	-	-	-	6"os	23
Laois	Tully :	- nr Millbrook Ho.	flour & pond	-	-	-	-	-	-	6"os	23
Clonenagh	Tullyroe	- at Bechford Ho.	mill	-	-	-	-	-	-	1"os	-
Clonenagh	Tullyroe	- near Oldtown	mill	-	-	-	woods & bridge - no trace	2006	-	mmSv/	wh - Z
Clonenagh	Tullyroe	- W/ Millbrook Ho.	flour & mill race	-	-	-	-	1841	-	6"os	23
Clonenagh	Tullyroe	Lister John	flour	-	-	-	-	-	26x6x24	vmb/	16

PARISH	TOWNLAND	MILLER	TYPE	HOUSE	Land	£Val	PROPRIETORS	Date	WHEEL etc.	Record	Ref.
Leitrim	nr Thompson`s Is.	- on R Shanon	mill	-	-	-	-	-	-	1"os/	-
Leitrim	Acre Park Five	Richards Georgina	mill	-	-	-	Richards G - McTiernan J	1840	-	dd/	1940 5 233
Feenagh	Aghaboneil	-	corn & kiln	-	-	-	-	-	-	6"os/	28
Feenagh	Aghaboneil	-	pond & race	-	-	-	-	-	-	6"os/	28
Drumreilly	Aghalough	-	corn & kiln	-	-	-	-	-	-	6"os	29
Drumreilly	Aghalough	Kernan James	corn	(2C) 27x20.6x13.6 :	-	-	-	1838	12x2x4.6 1 pr. st. :	hob/	5.4259
Drumreilly	Aghalough	Kernan James	corn	-	-	-	-	-	12x2x4	vmb/	10
Cloone	Aghavas	O`Brien Achison	mill	-	-	-	O`Brien A - Peyton Chas	1842	-	dd/	1842 2 277
Cloone	Aghavas	O`Brien Achison	mill	-	-	-	O`Brien A - Weldon Wm S	1842	-	dd/	8142 18 257
Cloone	Aghavas	on stream to A'vas Lo.	corn & kiln	-	-	-	-	1841	-	6"os/	33
Carrigallen	Aghawilin	-	corn & kiln	-	-	-	-	1841	-	6"os/	34
Oughteragh	Altakeeran	-	corn kiln	-	-	-	-	-	-	6"os/	21
Mohill	Anaghderg Lower	-	corn kiln	-	-	-	-	-	-	6"os/	28
Mohill	Anaghderg Lower	-	corn mills	-	-	-	-	-	-	6"os/	28
Leitrim	Annageary *	-	corn & kiln	-	-	-	-	-	-	6"os/	28
Leitrim	Annageary *	-	tuck	-	-	-	-	-	-	6"os/	28
Drumreilly	Annagh Upper	-	malt kiln	-	-	-	-	-	-	6"os/	18
Kiltoghert	Annagheurly	Gilmartin Owen	corn	-	-	-	-	-	11x1x1	vmb/	10
Kiltoghert	Annagheurly	Gilmartin Owen	tuck	-	-	-	-	-	9x1x9	vmb/	10
Cloone	Annaghoney	-	corn kiln	-	-	-	-	-	-	6"os	36
Drumreilly	Ardunsaghan	-	corn	-	-	-	-	-	-	6"os/	25
Drumreilly	Ardunsaghan	-	mill	-	-	-	-	-	-	1"os/	67
Drumreilly	Ardunsaghan	Graham John	corn	-	-	-	-	-	12x1x5	vmb/	10
Drumreilly	Ardunsaghan	Graham John	corn & kiln	(2B) 26x17.6x12 :	-	2.2.3	-	1838	12x1.6x5 1 pr. st. :	hob/	5.4259
Mohill	Attimanus	-	large mill pond	-	-	-	-	-	-	6"os/	28
Mohill	Attimanus	-	Milltown	-	-	-	-	-	-	6"os/	28
Mohill	Attimanus :	-	corn & kiln	-	-	-	-	-	-	6"os/	28
Inishmagrath	Aughrim	Early Thady	mill & kiln	(3C) 26x18x5.6 :	-	14/-	-	1841	11x1.6x6 o'shot :	hob/	5.4259
Oughteragh	Ballinamore Town	Farrelly Jno	mills	-	-	-	Farrelly Jno - Ross Jas	1839	-	dd/	1839 21 173
Oughteragh	Ballinamore Town	Mahon Thomas	mill	-	-	-	Mahon T - Cowen Richd	1845	-	dd/	1845 3 213
Oughteragh	Ballinamore Town	Mcmanus Jno	mills	-	-	-	McManus J - Lynch Edw	1837	-	dd/	1837 17 244
Oughteragh	Ballinamore Town	Sharpley Charles	mills	-	-	-	Sharpley C - Mahon Thos	1835	-	dd/	1835 5 66
Oughteragh	Ballinamore Town	Sharpley Charles	mills	-	-	-	Sharpley C - Mahon Thos	1837	-	dd/	1837 3 267
Leitrim	Ballyclogh Mills	- on Slievemoher R.	disused	-	-	-	-	-	-	1"os/	-
Leitrim	Ballysheedy	-	mill	-	-	-	-	-	-	1"os/	-
Leitrim	Balscarra	Norris Berry :	mill	-	-	-	Norris Berry - West John :	1825	-	dd/	799 514 539849
Cloone	Balscarra	West Joihn B	mill	-	-	-	West John - White Saml	1835	-	dd/	1835 10 167
Cloone	Beihy	-	corn	-	-	-	-	1837	-	6"os	36
Leitrim	Blackmill Farm	Gillmor Gowan :	farm (? mill)	-	-	-	Gillmor G - Armstrong Jas :	1837	-	dd/	832 139 559274
Drumreilly	Boarmanshill	- at Clare Br.	woollen	-	-	-	-	-	-	1"os/	-
Drumreilly	Boeeshil	-	bleach	-	-	-	-	-	-	6"os/	25
Drumreilly	Boeeshil	-	corn	-	-	-	-	-	-	6"os/	25
Drumreilly	Boeeshil	-	flax	-	-	-	-	-	-	6"os/	25
Drumreilly	Boeeshil	Gerrard Charles	bleach	-	-	-	-	-	14x2x21 2 beams :	vmb/	10
Drumreilly	Boeeshil	Gerrard Charles	corn	-	-	-	-	-	16x2x21	vmb/	10
Drumreilly	Boeeshil	Gerrard Charles	flax	-	-	-	-	-	20x3x21 6 stocks	vmb/	10
Drumreilly	Boeeshil	Gerrard Charles Esq	corn & kiln	(1B) 33x33x17.6 :	-	7.5	-	-	16ft. diameter :	hob/	5.4259
Drumreilly	Boeeshil	Gerrard Charles Esq	flax	(1A) 26x24.8x16 :	-	3.19	-	-	20x3x21 6 stocks :	hob/	5.4259
Drumreilly	Boeeshil	Gerrard Charles Esq.	bleach	(2B) 72.6x28x15	-	7.5.1	-	-	14x2.5x21 drives :	hob/	5.4259
Dromahaire	Brockagh Lower	- 2m. W. of Esky Br.	corn & pond	-	-	-	-	-	-	6"os/	13
Dromahaire	Brocklagh Lower	Clancy B.	corn & kiln	(2B) 28x17x8 :	-	5.2.5	-	1841	12.6x1.5x6 36 bkts.	hob/	5.2952
Rossinver	Bunduff	- E/ Bunduff Br.	corn	-	-	-	-	1837	-	6"os/	1

PARISH	TOWNLAND	MILLER	TYPE	HOUSE	Land	£Val	PROPRIETORS	Date	WHEEL etc.	Record	Ref.
Rossinver	Bunduff	Walker Catherine :	mills	-	-	-	Walker Cath - Barton Hu	1838	-	dd/	1838 8 225
Drumreilly	Bunkilleen	-	corn	-	-	-	-	-	-	6"os	32
Drumreilly	Bunkilleen	-	corn kilns (2)	-	-	-	-	-	-	6"os	32
Leitrim	Carnacannon	Norris Alex :	mills			-	Norris A - Norris Berry :	1821	Mort. 2 Nov.	dd/	769 459 521794
Leitrim	Carrick (2)	-	mill	-	-	-	-	-	-	1"os/	78
Drumlease	Carrickanurroo	-	corn & kiln	-	-	-	-	-	-	6"os/	10
Drumlease	Carrickanurroo	-	mil race	-	-	-	-	-	-	6"os/	10
Drumlease	Carrickanurroo	Cunningham Patrick	corn & kiln	(3B) 27.6x18x7 :	-	17/-	-	1841	14x1.2x15 28 float :	hob/	5.4258
Killoghert	Carrickevy	-	corn & kiln	-	-	-	-	-	-	6"os/	27
Killoghert	Carrickevy	Brock Patrick :	kiln (new)	(1A) 30x19.3x20 :	-	5.14	-	1855	-	hob/	5.4023
Killoghert	Carrickevy	Peyton Charles R	corn	-	-	-	-	-	13x3x6	vmb/	10
Kiltoghert	Carricknabrack	W. side Drumshanbo	corn	-	-	-	-	1841	-	6"os/	25
Carrigallen	Carrigallen Town	-	mill	-	-	-	-	-	-	1"os/	68
Kilanummery	Carrigeen	-	old corn mill	-	-	-	-	-	-	6"os/	14
Kilanummery	Carrigeen	- S/ Bellanagare Br.	old corn mill	-	-	-	-	1837	-	6"os/	14
Drumlease	Carrigeencor	Green Michael	corn & kiln	(2B) 28.6x19x8 :	-	3.10	-	1841	13x2.6x6 36 floats :	hob/	5.4258
Inishmagrath	Cartronbeg	-	corn kiln	-	-	-	-	-	-	6"os/	20
Cloone	Cattan	-	corn kiln	-	-	-	-	-	-	6"os	36
Leitrim	Cavan Park	Malcolm Ellenor	mill	-	-	-	Maccolm E - Garstin Wm	1833	-	dd/	1833 1 80
Leitrim	Cavan Park	Marsh Digby :	mill	-	-	-	Marsh D - Malcom Andr :	1822	Mort. 19 July	dd/	775 75 525010
Leitrim	Cavan Park	Rowley Rev Jno	mill	-	-	-	Rowley John - William	1846	-	dd/	1846 3 1
Carrigallen	Clooncorick	-	corn & kiln	-	-	-	-	-	-	6"os	30
Cloone	Cloone	- near Kinlough	mill	-	-	-	-	-	-	1"os/	43
Leitrim	Cloonlaugher *	-	corn kiln	-	-	-	-	-	-	6"os	38
Drumreilly	Coragh	-	corn	-	-	-	-	-	-	1"os/	67
Mohill	Corduff	-	corn kiln	-	-	-	-	-	-	6"os	32
Mohill	Corgallion	-	corn & kiln	-	-	-	-	-	-	6"os/	28
Cloone	Cornagher	-	corn & kiln	-	-	-	-	-	-	6"os	29
Drumahaire	Cornamarve	-	corn & kiln	-	-	-	-	-	-	6"os/	15
Drumahaire	Cornamarve	-	corn & kiln	(2B) 34x26x10 :	-	5	-	1841	11x1.4x10 32 bkts. :	hob/	5.2925
Drumreilly	Cornamucklagh	-	corn kilns (2)	-	-	-	-	-	-	6"os/	20
Drumreilly	Cornamucklagh	-	mill	-	-	-	-	-	-	1"os/	78
Drumreilly	Cornamucklagh	Bedford William :	corn & kiln	(3B) 23x17x8 :	-	4.6.6	-	1841	11x1.3x12 overshot :	hob/	5.4259
Drumreilly	Corraleehan	-	corn & kiln	-	-	-	-	-	-	6"os/	22
Drumreilly	Corraleehan	McManus Cornelius	corn	(2B) 34.9x20.6x8 :	-	7.14	-	1838	12x2x14 old axle :	hob/	5.4259
Drumreilly	Corraleehan	McManus Cornelius	corn	-	-	-	-	-	12x2x14	vmb/	10
Leitrim	Corryarga	Kernan William :	mill	-	-	-	Kiernan & Maguire M/arts. :	1826	-	dd/	836 201 561736
Leitrim	Creaneleagh	Richards Georgina	mills	-	-	-	Richards G - McTiernan J	1840	-	dd/	1840 5 223
Leitrim	Creaneleagh Abbey	Richards Georgina	mills	-	-	-	Richards G - McTiernan J	1847	-	dd/	1841 25 94
Leitrim	Creaveleagh	Johnson	mills	-	-	-	Johnson - Lane	1828	-	dd/	887 442 587447
Leitrim	Creaveleagh	Johnston Andrew :	F mill	-	-	-	Johnston A - Cooper Ewd :	1826	Mort. 23 May	dd/	814 503 548838
Leitrim	Creaveleagh Abbey	Palmer Thomas :	mill	-	-	-	Palmer T & Palmer William	1827	Conv. 9 Sep.	dd/	826 238 556773
Killanummery	Creevelea	- W. of Dromahair	wash	-	-	-	-	1841	-	6"os/	14
Leitrim	Creeves	- at Millview	mill	-	-	-	-	-	-	1"os/	-
Leitrim	Dergvone	- on Owennayle R.	corn	-	-	-	-	-	-	6"os/	16
Oughteragh	Derrinkeher	-	corn kiln	-	-	-	-	-	-	6"os/	24
Drumahaire	Derrynahinch	- beside L. Allen	corn	-	-	-	-	-	-	6"os/	18
Drumahaire	Derrynahinch	Keenan Hugh	corn & kiln	(2B) 34x20x9 & :	-	4.5.7	-	1840	11.6x1.8x12 30 bkts.	6"os/	18
Drumahaire	Derrynahona	-	corn kiln	-	-	-	-	-	-	6"os/	18
Inishmagrath	Derryvalannagher G	- on Owennayle R.	corn	-	-	-	-	-	-	6"os/	16
Leitrim	Derrywillin	-	malt kiln	-	-	-	-	-	-	6"os/	18
Leitrim	Doogree	Nicholls John :	mills	-	20a	-	Nicholls J - Nicholls Geo :	1824	Lse. 6 May	dd/	809 566 545901

PARISH	TOWNLAND	MILLER	TYPE	HOUSE	Land	£Val	PROPRIETORS	Date	WHEEL etc.	Record	Ref.
Mohill	Doonarah	-	corn	-	-	-	-	-	-	1"os/	67
Annaduff	Doora	-	corn kiln	-	-	-	-	-	-	6"os	35
	Dowra	- imed. W. of Vge.	corn & kiln	-	-	-	-	1841	-	6"os	26
Dromahaire	Dromahaire	- E. side River	corn	-	-	-	-	-	-	6"os/	14
Dromahaire	Dromahaire	- W. side River	wash	-	-	-	-	-	-	6"os/	14
Dromahaire	Dromahaire	Hosey John	corn & kiln	(2B) 28.6x20x16 :	-	5.17	-	1841	16x3x4.6 36 float :	hob/	5.2925
Dromahaire	Dromahaire	Kernaghan Thomas	flour & corn	(1A) 65.6x62.6x32 :	-	40.17	-	1841	30x6x30 o'shot :	hob/	5.2925
Annaduff	Dromod Beg	-	corn & kiln	-	-	-	-	1837	-	6"os	35
Annadyff	Dromod Beg :	-	store house	-	-	-	-	-	-	6"os	35
Kiltubrid	Drumad	Keenan Widow	corn	-	-	-	-	-	12x1x2	vmb/	10
Carrigallen	Drumbreanlis	- C46 on Cullies R.	mill	-	-	-	-	-	-	1"os/	68
Drumreilly	Drumbrick	-	corn kiln	-	-	-	-	-	-	6"os/	22
Carrigallen	Drumcanon	-	corn & race	-	-	-	-	-	-	6"os	30
Annaduff	Drumcree	-	corn	-	-	-	-	-	-	6"os	32
Annaduff	Drumcree	-	mill	-	-	-	-	-	-	1"os/	78
Annaduff	Drumcree	Notley Robert :	mill	-	-	-	Notley R & Riggs Thomas :	1821	-	dd/	765 18 518953
Annaduff	Drumcree	Acheson Alexander :	mill	-	-	-	-	1856	-	gr/	Ld.Est.db
Kiltoghert	Drumcroman	-	corn & kiln	-	-	-	-	-	-	6"os/	23
Kiltoghert	Drumcroman	-	corn kiln	-	-	-	-	-	-	6"os/	22
Killoghert	Drumcroman	Mulvey Jas & Son	corn	-	-	13	-	-	10x1x16	vmb/	10
Cloone	Drumgilra	-	corn kiln	-	-	-	-	-	-	6"os	36
Killoghert	Drumherriff	-	corn	-	-	-	-	-	-	1"os/	67
Kiltoghert	Drumherriff	-	corn & kiln	-	-	-	-	-	-	6"os/	23
Killoghert	Drumherriff	Crawford John	corn	-	-	-	-	-	14x2x3	vmb/	10
Killoghert	Drumherriff	Crawford John	tuck	-	-	-	-	-	12x2x3	vmb/	10
Drumreilly	Druminalass	-	corn kiln	-	-	-	-	-	-	6"os/	18
Cloonclare	Druminshin Glebe	-	mill	-	-	-	-	-	-	1"os/	68
Kiltoghert	Drumkeelan Beg	-	old corn kilns	-	-	-	-	-	-	6"os/	23
Kiltoghert	Drumkeelan Beg	-	old corn mill	-	-	-	-	-	-	6"os/	23
Fenagh	Drumlaheen	-	corn	-	-	-	-	-	-	6"os/	24
Fenagh	Drumlaheen	-	corn kilns	-	-	-	-	-	-	6"os/	24
Oughteragh	Drumrackan	-	corn kiln	-	-	-	-	-	-	6"os/	24
Mohill	Drumraghool North	-	corn kiln	-	-	-	-	-	-	6"os	32
Drumreilly	Drumristin	-	corn kiln	-	-	-	-	-	-	6"os/	18
Kiltoghert	Drumshanbo	-	corn kiln	-	-	-	-	-	-	6"os	36
Annaduff	Drumsna :	-	corn store	-	-	-	-	-	-	6"os	31
Rossinver	Edenvella	-	mill	-	-	-	-	-	-	1"os/	-
Kiltoghert	Farnagh	-	old corn kiln	-	-	-	-	-	-	6"os/	27
Annaduff	Finnalagh	-	corn kiln	-	-	-	-	-	-	6"os	35
Leitrim	Garvagh (3)	- near Addon Stn.	mill	-	-	-	-	-	-	1"os/	67
Cloonclare	Glenboy	-	bleach	-	-	-	-	-	-	6"os/	12
Cloonclare	Glenboy	-	corn	-	-	-	-	-	-	6"os/	12
Cloonclare	Glenboy	-	watch house	-	-	-	-	-	-	6"os/	12
Cloonclare	Glenboy	Algee Louis	bleach	-	-	-	-	-	15x3x15 2 beams :	vmb/	10
Cloonclare	Glenboy	Algeo Lewis	bleach, scutch	(1C) 43.6x22.6x14 :	-	9.2.8	-	1841	beetling engines 2 :	hob/	5.4257
Cloonclare	Glenboy	Algeo Lewis	corn	(2C) 29x19x8 :	-	4.5	-	1841	13.6x2.8x6 36 bkts. :	hob/	5.4257
Dromahaire	Gleneige	-	malt kiln	-	-	-	-	-	-	6"os/	6
Mohill	Gortanure North	-	corn & kiln	-	-	-	-	-	-	6"os/	28
Mohill	Gortanure North	-	mill dam	-	-	-	-	-	-	6"os/	28
Annaduff	Gortinee	-	iron mines	-	-	-	-	-	-	6"os	35
Killarga	Greagh	- SW. / Behavel Lo.	old mill	-	-	-	-	-	-	6"os/	15
Kiltoghert	Greaghnaguillaun	-	corn & kiln	-	-	-	-	-	-	6"os/	20

PARISH	TOWNLAND	MILLER	TYPE	HOUSE	Land	£Val	PROPRIETORS	Date	WHEEL etc.	Record	Ref.
Kiltoghert	Greaghnaguillaun	-	old corn kiln	-	-	-	-	-	-	6"os/	20
Kiltoghert	Greaghnaguillaun	Griffin Philip & Co	corn	-	-	-	-	-	12x1x12	vmb/	10
Leitrim	Grubnageer	- on Ballagh R.	corn & kiln	-	-	-	-	-	-	6"os/	5
Cloone	Gubadorris	-	corn kiln	-	-	-	-	-	-	6"os	38
Kiltoghert	Jamestown	-	flour	-	-	-	-	-	-	6"os	31
Cloone	Keeldra	- NW. Keeldra Lo.	corn	-	-	-	-	-	-	6"os	33
Cloone	Keeldra	- NW. Keeldra Lo.	tuck	-	-	-	-	-	-	6"os	33
Cloone	Keeldra	Norris Berry :	mill & bl green	-	-	-	Norris Berry - West John :	1825	-	dd/	799 514 539849
Kiltubbrid	Kilclare	-	Mill School	-	-	-	-	-	-	1"os/	67
Kiltubbrid	Kilclare More	-	corn & kiln	-	-	-	-	-	-	6"os/	27
Kiltubbrid	Kilclure More	Dougherty Patrick	corn	-	-	-	-	-	10x1x5	vmb/	10
Leitrim	Killacarn *	-	corn kiln	-	-	-	-	-	-	6"os/	27
Killanummery	Killavoggy	-	corn & kiln	-	-	-	-	1841	-	6"os	15
Killanummery	Killavoggy	McTiernan Edward	corn	-	-	-	-	-	12x1x18	vmb/	10
Cloone	Killtvehy	-	corn & kiln	-	-	-	-	1837	-	6"os	36
Cloone	Killyfea	-	corn & kiln	-	-	-	-	-	-	6"os	29
Oughteragh	Killynashinnagh	Knox Alex	beetling eng.	-	-	-	-	-	14x2x16	vmb/	10
Oughteragh	Killynashinnagh	Knox Alex	corn	-	-	-	-	-	14x2x16	vmb/	10
Oughteragh	Killynashinnagh	Knox Alexander	beetling	(2B) 28.6x28.9x16.6	-	2.14.7	-	-	uses corn wheel	vmb/	5.2923
Oughteragh	Killynashinnagh	Knox Alexander	corn	(2B) 36.6x21x14 :	-	2.4.8	-	-	14x2.2x16 2 pr. st. :	hob/	5.2923
Cloone	Killyvehy	-	mill	-	-	-	-	-	-	1"os/	78
Cloone	Kilmakeeny	Rodgers Patrick	corn & kiln	(3B) 33x17.6x7 :	-	3.0.5	-	1855	10x2.3 new :	hob/	5.2924
Cloone	Kilmakeeny (?)	Reilly John :	corn & kiln	(2B) 29x20x10 :	-	4.13	-	1855	12x1.9x12 1 pr. st. :	hob/	5.2924
Inishmagrath	Kilnagany Lower	O'Donnell John	corn & kiln	(3C) 36x19x7 :	-	2.0.1	-	1841	10.6x1.3 36 bkts. :	hob/	5.4250
Inishmagrath	Kilnagarns	-	corn	-	-	-	-	-	-	6"os/	18
Oughtera	Kiltyhugh	-	corn kiln	-	-	-	-	-	-	6"os/	22
Oughtera	Kiltynashinnagh	-	corn & kiln	-	-	-	-	-	-	6"os/	24
Oughtera	Knockacullon	-	corn kilns (2)	-	-	-	-	-	-	6"os/	21
Mohill	Lagheen North :	-	corn & race	-	-	-	-	-	-	6"os	32
Mohill	Lagheen North :	-	corn kiln	-	-	-	-	-	-	6"os	32
Leitrim	Laheen (2) :	-	mill	-	-	-	-	-	-	1"os/	43
Leitrim	Laheen (2) :	Peyton John R	mill	-	-	-	Peyton J - Simpson Pierce	1836	-	dd/	1836 21 72
Leitrim	Laheen (2) :	Peyton John R	mills	-	-	-	Peyton John - Peyton J H	1835	-	dd/	1835 13 100
Rosclogher	Launtaggart	-	corn & pond	-	-	-	-	-	-	6"os/	6
Kiltoghert	Lavaul	-	corn & kiln	-	-	-	-	-	-	6"os/	20
Kiltoghert	Lavaul	-	mill dam	-	-	-	-	-	-	6"os/	20
Kiltoghert	Lavaur	Tiernan William	corn	-	-	-	-	-	11x2x11	vmb/	10
Kiltoghert	Leitrim	-	corn kiln	-	-	-	-	-	-	6"os/	27
Kiltoghert	Leitrim	-	Potter`s kiln	-	-	-	-	-	-	6"os/	27
Leitrim	Limerick Manor	De Clifford Sophia Rt. :	mills	-	-	-	De Clifford Ldy - Meade :	1822	-	dd/	776 41 525576
Leitrim	Limerick Manor	Rowley Josias Sir :	mills	-	-	-	Rowley J - Dunne Josias :	1822	-	dd/	777 37 526172
Inishmagrath	Lisacoghil	- E. of Wooden Br.	corn & kiln	-	-	-	-	-	-	6"os/	16
Inishmagrath	Lisacoghil	Holmes Robert	corn & kiln	(1B) 27x20x11.6 :	-	2.	-	1849	-	hob/	5.4018
Inishmagrath	Lisacoghil	Palmer John	corn & kiln	(2B) 28.6x20x10 :	-	2.9	-	1841	10x13x4.6 30 float :	hob/	5.4260
Kiltoghert	Lisdromarea	-	corn kiln	-	-	-	-	-	-	6"os	32
Cloonaclare	Lismackniff	Peyton John	Laheen Mills	-	-	-	Peyton J - Hone Brindley	1847	-	dd/	1847 7 3
Cloonaclare	Lismackniff	Tottenham Nicholas	mill	-	-	-	Tottenham - Johnston Wm	1838	-	dd/	1838 7 232
Kiltoghert	Lismakegan	-	old corn mill	-	-	-	-	-	-	6"os/	27
Kiltoghert	Mahanagh	-	corn & kiln	-	-	-	-	-	-	6"os/	23
Kiltoghert	Mahanagh	-	mill stream	-	-	-	-	-	-	6"os/	23
Killoghert	Mahanagh	Cain James	corn	-	-	-	-	-	12x3x2	vmb/	10
Cloonclare	Manor Hamilton	Ferguson William	corn & kiln	(2B) 32x20x8 :	-	2.13	-	1841	13.6x1.10x6 u'shot :	hob/	5.4257

PARISH	TOWNLAND	MILLER	TYPE	HOUSE	Land	£Val	PROPRIETORS	Date	WHEEL etc.	Record	Ref.
Clooncl are	Manorhamilton	-	tannery (2)	-	-	-	-	-	-	6"os/	11
Clooncl are	Manorhamilton	- E. Whittaker`s Br.	tuck	-	-	-	-	-	-	6"os/	11
Clooncl are	Manorhamilton	- to R. Owenmore	mill stream	-	-	-	-	-	-	6"os/	11
Clooncl are	Manorhamilton :	-	tuck	-	-	-	-	1844	-	6"os/	11
Mohill	Meelick	-	corn kiln	-	-	-	-	-	-	6"os/	28
Mohill	Meelick	-	tannery	-	-	-	-	-	-	6"os/	28
Drumahaire	Meenagh	-	corn kiln	-	-	-	-	-	-	6"os/	9
Leitrim	Millacre	Tottenham Nicholas	mill	-	-	-	Tottenham - Gallagher Jas	1838	-	dd/	1838 7 231
Killasnet	Milltown	-	corn	-	-	-	-	-	-	6"os/	7
Killasnet	Milltown	-	Milltown Vge.	-	-	-	-	1844	-	6"os/	7
Killasnet	Milltown	Wynne Jno	mill	-	-	-	Wynne Jno - Deed	1849	-	dd/	1849 1 235
Rossinver	Moneen	-	corn & kiln	-	-	-	-	-	-	6"os/	2
Rossinver	Moneen	-	mill pond	-	-	-	-	-	-	6"os/	2
Fenagh	Muckros	-	corn kiln	-	-	-	-	-	-	6"os/	24
Rossinver	Mulanaleck	- NW. /Drownes R.	corn & kiln	-	-	-	-	-	-	6"os/	2
Kiltubbrid	Mullaghboy	-	corn kiln	-	-	-	-	-	-	6"os/	28
Leitrim	Newbridge	- on Deel R.	mill	-	-	-	-	-	-	1"os/	-
Leitrim	Newtown	Cunningham Peter :	mill	-	-	-	Cunningham Pet - Patrick :	1821	-	dd/	769 600 521935
Carrigallae	Newtowngore	-	corn	-	-	-	-	-	-	6"os/	26
Carrigallae	Newtowngore	-	corn & kiln	-	-	-	-	-	-	6"os/	26
Carrigallae	Newtowngore	-	mill race	-	-	-	-	-	-	6"os/	26
Clooncl are	Patrick`s Island	-	still ho.	-	-	-	-	-	-	6"os/	9
Cloonlogher	Pollboy	-	old gold mine	-	-	-	-	1844	-	6"os/	11
Oughterah	Prabagh	-	corn kiln	-	-	-	-	-	-	6"os/	22
Rossinver	Redbrae	- on Drowes R.	mill	-	-	-	-	-	-	1"os/	43
Leitrim	Rhadermott	Sharpley Charles :	mill	-	-	-	Sherpley - Hayes Lyndon :	-	-	dd/	783 228 529963
Rossinver	Rossclogher	Dickson Hyacinth	mills	-	-	-	Dickson - Eccles Jemmina	1843	-	dd/	1843 16 209
Rossinver	Rossclogher	Dickson Jno	mill	-	-	-	Dickson J - Johnston Jas	1846	-	dd/	1846 12 202
Rossinver	Rossclogher	Dickson John	mill	-	-	-	Dickson J - Dickson Wm	1833	-	dd/	1833 21 109
Rossinver	Rossclogher	Dickson John :	mill	-	-	-	Dickson J - Dickson Wm :	1829	Mort. 22 Sep.	dd/	850 389 568889
Rossinver	Rossclogher	Dickson John R	mills	-	-	-	Dickson J - Cullen Henry	1837	-	dd/	1837 14 354
Rossinver	Rossclogher	Reynolds Richard	mills	-	-	-	Reynolds R - White Saml	1838	-	dd/	1838 11 271
Leitrim	Scart	-	corn	-	-	-	-	-	-	1"os/	-
Inishmagrath	Sheena	-	corn kiln	-	-	-	-	-	-	6"os/	18
Inishmagrath	Sheena	- on Owengar R.	mill	-	-	-	-	-	-	6"os/	18
Inishmagrath	Sheena	Comyn William	corn & kiln	(2B) 21x18x8 :	-	1.19	-	1841	- [rebuilding :]	hob/	5.4260
Kiltoghert	Sheskinacurry	-	corn kiln	-	-	-	-	-	-	6"os/	23
Drumreilly	Slievenakilla	-	corn kiln	-	-	-	-	-	-	6"os/	19
Leitrim	Srabagarvanagh *	-	corn kiln	-	-	-	-	-	-	6"os/	19
Kilanummery	Sradoon	-	old corn mill	-	-	-	-	-	-	6"os/	14
Drumreilly	Sradrinagh	- N. side Stony R.	corn kiln	-	-	-	-	-	-	6"os/	20
Clooncl are	Sradrine	- N. side of road :	corn & kiln	-	-	-	-	-	-	6"os/	12
Clooncl are	Sradrine	- S. side of road	corn	-	-	-	-	-	-	6"os/	12
Clooncl are	Sradrine	Clancy Phillip	corn & kiln	(2B) 19x31x8 :	-	1.19	-	1841	1ft. 10ins. broad :	hob/	5.4257
Clooncl are	Sradrine	Trower Hugh	corn & kiln	(2C) 32.6x16x7 :	-	19/-	-	1841	12x2.6x4.6 u'shot :	hob/	5.4257
Rosclogher	Sraduff	S/ Kiltyclogher Vge.	corn & kiln	-	-	-	-	-	-	6"os/	8
Leitrim	Sraud Ferguson	- on Glenaniffa R.	corn & kiln	-	-	-	-	-	-	6"os/	5
Oughteragh	Stradermot	- on Yellow River	corn & kiln	-	-	-	-	-	-	6"os/	25
Oughteragh	Stradermot	Shortley Charles	corn	-	-	-	-	-	18x3x3	vmb/	10
Oughteragh	Stradermot	Shortley Charles	corn & kiln	(1B) 33x24.3x23 :	-	-	-	-	18x3x3 2 pr. stones :	hob/	5.2923
Leitrim	Stragarn *	-	corn kiln	-	-	-	-	-	-	6"os/	28
Killasnet	Tawnamachugh	-	corn	-	-	-	-	-	-	1"os/	43

COUNTY LEITRIM

PARISH	TOWNLAND	MILLER	TYPE	HOUSE	Land	£Val	PROPRIETORS	Date	WHEEL etc.	Record	Ref.
Killasnet	Tawnamachugh	-	corn	-	-	-	-	-	-	6"os/	6
Killarga	Tawnylea	- near Belhavil Lo.	corn	-	-	-	-	1841	-	6"os/	15
Killarga	Tawnylea	Holmes Mathew	corn	(2C) 34x19x7 :	-	16/8d	-	1845	-	hob/	5.4022
Killarga	Tawnylea	Johnson	mills	-	-	-	Johnson - Lane	1828	-	dd/	887 442 587447
Oughteragh	Tomloskan	-	bleach ruin	-	-	-	-	-	-	6"os/	24
Oughteragh	Tomloskan	-	corn	-	-	-	-	-	-	6"os/	24
Oughteragh	Tomloskan	Magowan Michael	corn	(2B) 37x24x16 :	-	-	-	-	16x3.10x3.6 :	hob/	10
Oughteragh	Tomloskan	Magowan Michael	corn	-	-	-	-	-	16x4x3	vmb/	10
Cloone	Toomaline	- near Doon	mill	-	-	-	-	-	-	1"os/	-
Killarga	Tormahoony	Buchanan Patk Mgr.	iron works :	127x27x27 :	-	-	-	1845	-	hob/	5.4022
Clooncare	Tuckmillpark	-	corn	-	-	-	-	1844	-	6"os/	11
Killarga	Tullinwillin	-	mill	-	-	-	-	-	-	1"os/	55
Killarga	Tullinwillin	Holmes Mathew	mill	(2B) 34x18.6x7 :	-	1.19	-	1841	13x1x5 undershot ;	hob/	5.4022
Killarga	Tullinwillin	Holmes Robert	mill	(2B) 35x25.6x17.6 :	-	-	-	1845	-	hob/	5.4022
Killarga	Tullinwillin	McGaughren	corn	(3B) 20x17x6 & :	-	1.17	-	1841	12x1.6x13 o'shot :	hob/	5.4262
Leitrim	Tullyoran (2) :	-	corn & kiln	-	-	-	-	-	-	6"os	33
Drumreilly	Tullyveacan	-	corn kiln	-	-	-	-	-	-	6"os/	18
Killasnet	Twiggs Park	-	silver mines	-	-	-	-	1844	-	6"os/	7
Annaduff	Umera	-	corn kilns (2)	-	-	-	-	-	-	6"os	32
Leitrim	Umeryroe	Keogh Anthony	mill	-	-	-	Keogh A - Shaw William :	1825	-	dd/	803 326 542061
Drumreilly	Urbal	Carrigan Farell	corn & kiln	(2C) 27x17x8 :	-	17/8	-	1841	11x1.7 undershot :	hob/	5.4259
Drumreilly	Urbal Barr	-	corn kiln	-	-	-	-	-	-	6"os/	19
Leitrim	Watercourse	O`Brien Achison	mill	-	-	-	O`Brien A - King Jno	1844	-	dd/	1844 7 10

PARISH	TOWNLAND	MILLER	TYPE	HOUSE	Land	£Val	PROPRIETORS	Date	WHEEL etc.	Record	Ref.
St Peter & Paul	Abbeyfarm	-	Kilmallock Mill	-	-	-	-	1844	-	6"os/	47
St Peter & Paul	Abbeyfarm	Henry Dennis	corn	-	-	148	-	-	13x3x-	vmb/	26
Limerick *	Abbeylowthry	Cloncurry Valentine :	mills	-	-	-	Cloncurry - Hyde Alex :	-	-	dd/	624 423 438560
Abington	Abington	- N side Mulkear R.	mill	-	-	-	-	1844	-	6"os/	14
Abbington	Abington	Keays Benjamin :	Manor Mills	-	-	-	Keays - Hargrave Ab'ram	1818	Mort. 9 Oct. :	dd/	732 451 499586
Askeaton	Aghalacka	Russell Jn Norris & Sons	flour	(1A) 42x25x43	-	45	-	1849	15x5.6x4.8 :	hob/	5.119
Askeaton	Aghalacka	Russell John & son	flour	-	-	-	-	-	15x5x2	vmb/	26
Askeaton	Aghalacka	Russell John & son	flour	-	-	-	-	-	17x7x12	vmb/	26
Askeaton	Aghalacka	Russell John & son	flour	-	-	-	-	-	14x10x9	vmb/	26
Askeaton	Aghalacka	Russell John & sons	flour	(1A) 64x50x44 :	-	156	-	-	14x10.7 :	hob/	5.1190
Askeaton	Aghalacka	Russell John Norris Sons	flour	-	-	45	-	-	-	gr	-
Askeaton	Aghalacka	Russell John Norris Sons	flour, offs, land	-	21a.	164	-	-	-	gr	-
Nantinan	Altavilla	- on Deel R.	corn	-	-	-	-	1844	-	6"os/	20
Nantinan	Altavilla	- on Deel R.	tuck	-	-	-	-	1844	-	6"os/	20
Nantinan	Altavilla	Griffin P G	corn	60x18x14	-	-	-	1848	10.3x3.6 & :	hob/	5.1212
Nantinan	Altavilla	Griffin Peter G	corn	-	-	-	-	-	12x4x4	vmb/	26
Nantinan	Altavilla	Griffin Peter G	corn	-	-	-	-	-	10x3x1	vmb/	26
Nantinan	Altavilla	Griffin Peter G	corn & carding	offices & land	53a.	66	-	1856	-	gr/	a.a.lre.ie
Abington	Ashroe	- near Clare Bridge	mills	-	-	-	-	1844	-	6"os/	17
Abington	Ashroe	Flynn John	corn	-	-	-	-	-	12x3x5	vmb/	26
Abington	Ashroe	Flynn John	mills & land	-	15a.	21.15	-	-	-	gr	-
Abington	Ashroe	Flynn John	spinning	-	-	-	-	-	12x2x9	vmb/	26
Abington	Ashroe	Flynn John	tuck	-	-	-	-	-	10x2x5	vmb/	26
Askeaton	Askeaton	-	Abbey Mills	-	-	-	-	-	-	1"os/	-
Askeaton	Askeaton	- on R. Deel	corn	4 storey	-	-	-	-	18x17.8 :	iaa/	-
Askeaton :	Askeaton	Dundon Philip	tuck	-	-	-	Dundon - Prescottt Robt	1849	-	dd/	1849 3 96
Askeaton	Askeaton	Evans	mill	-	-	-	Evans - Nordblad	-	-	dd/	-
Askeaton	Askeaton	Hunt	mill	-	-	-	Hunt - Leland	-	-	dd/	-
Askeaton	Askeaton	Kelly	mill	-	-	-	Kelly - Maunsell	-	-	dd/	790 335 534270
Askeaton	Askeaton :	Kelly	mill	-	-	-	Kelly - Eason	-	-	dd/	850 498 568998
Askeaton :	Askeaton :	Russell Jno	mill	-	-	-	Russell - Gubbins Geo	1848	-	dd/	1848 20 48
Askeaton	Askeaton Town	Corbett Nicholas	brewery	-	-	-	Corbett N - Quin Michael	1840	-	dd/	1840 23 7
Askeaton	Askeaton Town	Hamilton Jno	mills	-	-	-	Hamilton Jno - Russell Jno	1840	-	dd/	1840 15 181
Askeaton	Askeaton Town	Hewson John	mills				Hewson J - Hewson Wm	1904		dd/	1904 38 145
Askeaton	Askeaton Town	Hewson William	mill holding :	-	-	-	Hewson Wm - Russell Jn	1837	-	dd/	1837 13 289
Askeaton :	Askeaton Town	Kelly Francis	mill	-	-	-	Kelly Fran - Kelly Mcl	1875	-	dd/	1875 - -
Askeaton :	Askeaton Town	Russell Richard	Askeaton Mills	-	-	-	Russell Richd - John	1899	-	dd/	1899 71 269
Askeaton :	Askeaton Town	Russell Richard	mill holding	-	-	-	Russell Richd - Edmond	1899	-	dd/	1899 32 162
Askeaton	Askeaton Town :	Erson Paul	mill	-	-	-	Erson P - Hamilton John	1838	-	dd/	1838 20 70
Askeaton	Askeaton Town :	Erson Paul	The Mills	-	-	-	Erson P - Hamilton John	1841	-	dd/	1841 10 245
Limerick	Ballindra *	King	mills	-	-	-	King & Wife - Lorton Ld	-	-	dd/	-
Limerick	Ballindra *	Kingston Geoge Rt. Hon. :	mills	-	-	-	Kingston G - Hodder Wm :	1827	-	dd/	768 548 532083
Limerick	Ballindra *	King James Wm Hon. :	mills	-	-	-	King - Lorton King Rt. Hon.	1822		dd/	773 95 523830
Newcastle	Ballinena	- on Dooally Stream	Old Mill Bridge	- (no mill)	-	-	-	1844	-	6"os/	28
Ballingarry	Ballingarry	Barker	mill	-	-	-	Barker - Smyth	-	?	dd/	621 345 468913
Ballingarry	Ballingarry	Filaan	mill	-	-	-	Filaan - Cormody	-	-	dd/	688 170 472907
Ballingarry	Ballingarry	Graves	mill	-	-	-	Graves - Croker	-	-	dd/	730 214 481976
Ballingarry	Ballingarry	Graves James William	mill	-	-	-	Graves J - Simpson Edmd. :	1820	-	dd/	751 290 510825
Ballingarry	Ballingarry	Graves James Wm Rev. :	mill	-	-	-	Graves J - Foot Jeffrey :	{ 1818	-	dd/	736 343 501879
Ballingarry	Ballingarry	Graves John Rev	mill	-	-	-	Graves J - Trool Jeffery	1816	-	dd/	718 418 491153
Cahercorney	Ballingoola	- W. of Sixmilebridge	paper	-	-	-	-	1844	-	6"os/	23
Cahercorney	Ballingoola	Garvey Timothy	flour	46x24x26 :	-	-	-	1853	-	hob/	-

PARISH	TOWNLAND	MILLER	TYPE	HOUSE	Land	£Val	PROPRIETORS	Date	WHEEL etc.	Record	Ref.
Cahercorney	Ballingoola	Garvey Timothy	flour & corn	-	-	-	-	-	16x4x4	vmb/	26
Cahercorney	Ballingoola	Garvey Timothy	paper	51x6x20 :	-	-	-	1853	-	hob/	-
Kilfinnane	Ballinlyna Lower	Connors Brian	tuck	(3B) 45x18x4 :	-	1	-	-	-	hob/	5.4031
Kilfinnane	Ballinlyna Lower	Connors Bryan	tuck	-	-	2.5	-	-	-	gr	-
Kilfinnane	Ballinlyna Lower	Connors Bryan	tuck	-	-	-	-	-	8x2x10	vmb/	26
Monaster North	Bally	- N. side Camoge R.	mill (in ruin)	-	-	-	-	1844	-	6"os/	31
St Nicholas	Ballyclogh	-	mill	-	-	-	-	-	-	1"os/	-
Knocknagaul	Ballyclogh	- NW/ Routagh Bridge	Ballyclogh Mills	-	-	-	-	1844	-	6"os/	13
Knocknagaul	Ballyclogh	- NW/ Routagh Bridge	woollen	-	-	-	-	1844	-	6"os/	13
Kilmurry	Ballyclogh	- 3/4m S/ Annacoty Br.	Balluclogh Mills	-	-	-	-	1844	-	6"os/	6
Kilmurry	Ballyclogh	- on Mulkear R.	mill dam	-	-	-	-	1844	-	6"os/	6
Knocknagaul	Ballyclogh		Mill Cottage	-	-	-	-	1844	-	6"os/	13
Kilmurry	Ballyclough	-	mill (disused)	-	-	-	-	-	-	1"os/	-
Knockagaul	Ballyclough	Brownrigg Joseph	woollen	-	-	-	-	-	18x14x13	vmb/	26
Kilmurry	Ballyclough	Cudmore Paul	paper	-	-	-	-	-	16x5x6	vmb/	26
Kilmurry	Ballyclough	Maconchy John	mills	-	-	-	Maconchy J - Bannantyne :	1892	-	dd/	1892 30 109
Kilmurry	Ballyclough	Nash Cornelius	corn	-	-	-	-	-	12x10x8	vmb/	26
Kilmurry	Ballyclough	Nash Cornelius	flour	-	-	-	-	-	12x10x8	vmb/	26
Kilmurry	Ballyclough	Nash Cornelius	flour & corn :	-	7a.	54.10	-	-	-	gr	-
Kilfergus	Ballydonohoe	Connor Elen	corn	14.6x17.6x10.6 :	-	-	-	-	12x2.3	hob/	-
Kilfergus	Ballydonohoe	Connor Elen	tuck	14x16.6x7 :	-	-	-	1850	10x2.2	hob/	-
Kilfergus	Ballydonohue	- S/ Ballyorgan Vge.	corn & tuck	-	-	-	-	1844	-	6"os/	56
Particles	Ballygeagoge	Touchstone	mill ?	-	-	-	Touchstone - Touchstone	-	-	dd/	792 593 535728
Ballylanders	Ballylanders	-	Ballylanders mills	-	-	-	-	1844	-	6"os/	49
Ballylanders	Ballylanders	- (no name)	corn	-	-	-	-	1849	10x2.6 :	hob/	5.1243
Ballylanders	Ballylanders	- (no name)	tuck	-	-	-	-	1849	11x2 :	hob/	5.1243
Ballylanders	Ballylanders	Doherty Patrick	corn	-	-	-	-	-	10x2x10	vmb/	26
Ballylanders	Ballylanders	Doherty Patrick	corn & tuck	house 29x19.6x15 :	-	-	-	1851	10x2.6 :	hob/	5.4026
Ballylanders	Ballylanders	Doherty Patrick	tuck	-	-	-	-	-	11x2x11	vmb/	26
St Michael`s	Ballynacurra Hart	Wheeler Robert	windmill	-	-	-	-	-	-	vmb/	26
Rathkeale	Ballynamuckly	- near Fortwilliam Ho.	saw	-	-	-	-	-	-	1"os/	-
Clonelty	Ballynoe	-	mill	-	-	-	-	-	-	1"os/	-
Clonelty	Ballynoe	-	tuck & mill race	-	-	-	-	1844	-	6"os/	37
Clonelty	Ballynoe	Shine Michael	corn	(2B) 20x18x11 :	-	1-16	-	-	o`shot 12ft. :	hob/	5.1257
Clonelty	Ballynoe	Shine Michael	corn	-	-	-	-	-	12x-	vmb/	-
Clonelty	Ballynoe	Shine Michael	corn & land	-	10a.	2.10	-	-	-	gr	-
Clonelty	Ballynoe	Shine Michael	tuck	(2B) 10x18x6	-	0-4-1	-	-	12ft overshot	hob/	5.1257
Kilfinnane	Ballynoe Lower	Trench Chas F Esq.	brick & tile yard	-	1a.	7.15	-	-	-	gr	-
Askeaton	Ballynort	-	mill (in ruins)	-	-	-	-	1844	-	6"os/	11
Kilmurry	Ballysimon	- at Ballysimon Br.	marble factory	-	-	-	-	1844	-	6"os/	5
Kilmurry	Ballysimon	- due N/ Ballysimon Br.	Ballysimon Mills	-	-	-	-	1844	-	6"os/	5
Kilmurry	Ballysimon	Boyd James	corn & kiln :	-	1.5a.	26	-	-	-	gr	-
Kilmurry	Ballysimon	Butler James	Indian corn	-	-	-	-	-	14x6x17	vmb/	-
Killeenagariff	Ballyvarra	- on Slievemore R.	corn	-	-	-	-	-	-	1"os/	-
Kilbradran	Balyan	- on N side R.Dee :	corn & tuck	-	-	-	- (named Altavalla Mill)	1887	-	6"os/	19/20
Drehidtarsna	Beabus	Spearing Thomas	corn	offices & land	37a.	25	- [+ tenant's house]	1856	-	gr/	a.a.ire.ie
Drehidtarsna	Beabus	Spearing Thomas	corn	-	-	-	-	-	10x3x10	vmb/	26
Kilbeheny	Behanagh	- E. side Behanagh R.	Knockrour Mill	-	-	-	-	1844	-	6"os/	60
Kilbeheny	Behanagh	Broderick Michael	corn	-	-	-	-	-	11x3x11	vmb/	26
Kilbeheny	Behanagh	Broderick Michael	corn, kiln & land	-	-	-	-	-	-	gr	-
Adare	Black Abbey	Smith John	flour	-	-	-	-	-	steam	vmb/	26
Adare	Black Abbey :	Smith John	flour	-	-	-	-	-	-	gr	-

PARISH	TOWNLAND	MILLER	TYPE	HOUSE	Land	£Val	PROPRIETORS	Date	WHEEL etc.	Record	Ref.
Limerick	Brudy *	Foster	mill	-	-	-	Foster - Ryan	-	-	dd/	682 49 469819
Limerick	Brudy *	Higgins	mill	-	-	-	Higgins - Greighton (M.Art)	-	?	dd/	640 447 458714
Limerick	Brudy *	Ryan	mill	-	-	-	Ryan - Higgins	-	-	dd/	682 50 469190
Lim	Bruff	- on Morningstar R.	flour	-	-	-	-	1844	-	6"os/	32
Bruff	Bruff	Carroll John	new mill	-	-	-	-	-	-	vmb/	26
Bruff	Bruff	Graves	mills	-	-	-	Graves - Croker	-	-	dd/	-
Bruff	Bruff	Keane	mills	-	-	-	Keane - Keane	-	-	dd/	47 260 30481
Bruff	Bruff	Limerick Henry Hon. Earl :	mills	-	-	-	E. Limerick - Wilson Thos :	1816	Mort. 1 Dec.	dd/	710 430 486365
Bruff	Bruff :	Carroll John	corn & flour	-	-	20	-	-	-	gr	-
Bruree	Bruree	-	flour	-	-	-	Benedict & Jessie Griffin	2005	-	pWEH	Cr
Bruree	Bruree	- on R. Maigue	mills	4 storey	-	-	Bruree Co-op.	-	20x13 metal :	iaa/	-
Bruree	Bruree	- SW of Town	tuck & carding	-	-	-	-	1844	-	6"os/	39
Bruree	Bruree	Carroll Honora	flour	(1A) 47.0x26.6x28:	-	-	-	-	18x8x12 :	hob/	5.1226
Bruree	Bruree	Carroll Honora	flour	-	-	-	-	-	18x8x12	vmb/	26
Bruree	Bruree	Carroll Honora	flour	-	-	-	-	-	17x6x8	vmb/	26
Bruree	Bruree	Carroll Honora	mill	28x15.6x13.6	-	1-7	-	-	10.6, d/shrd. 1ft.:	hob/	5.1226
Bruree	Bruree	Carroll Honora	tuck	-	-	-	-	-	10x1x -	vmb/	26
Bruree	Bruree	Carroll Honora	tuck	-	-	-	-	-	11x3x6	vmb/	26
Bruree	Bruree	Carroll Honoria	tuck	house & land	6a.	5	-	gr/	-	gr/	a.a.Ire,ie
Bruree	Bruree	Lyons Barry	(dwelling ho)	(3B) 20x18x6.6	-	-	-	-	-	hob/	5.1226
Bruree	Bruree	Ryan Michael	flour	90x25x32 :	-	-	-	-	18x8x10	hob/	-
Bruree	Bruree Town	Ryan Michael	flour	-	-	-	-	-	22x14x11	hob/	-
Bruree	Bruree Town	Ryan Michael	flour	(1B) 90x25x32 & :	-	39-11	-	1850	18x8x10 :	hob/	5.1226
Bruree	Bruree Town	Ryan Michael	flour	-	-	-	-	-	8x8x10	vmb/	26
Bruree	Bruree Town	Ryan Michael	flour	-	-	-	-	-	22x15x7	vmb/	26
Bruree	Bruree Town	Ryan Michael	mill & kiln	-	-	160	-	1856	-	gr/	a.a.Ire.ie
Limerick *	Bundriskehy	Tuthill	mills	-	-	-	Tuthill - Greens	-	?	dd/	651 551 452606
Croom	Caherass	- N. side R. Maigue	flour & mill race	-	-	-	-	1844	-	6"os/	21
Croom	Caherass	Roche David	flour	-	-	-	-	-	28x16x14	vmb/	26
Croom	Caherass	Roche David	old flour mill	-	-	-	-	-	22x12x11	vmb/	26
Croom	Caherass	Roche David Elder :	mill	-	-	-	Roche D - Blood Neptune :	1820	-	dd/	750 391 510326
Croom	Caherass	Roche David Elder :	mill	-	-	-	Roche D - Blood Neptune :	1818	yearly rent ú150	dd/	730 384 489319
Croom	Caherass	Roche Sir David Bart.	flour	offs. land, ten'ts hos	186a.	325	-	1856	-	gr/	a.a.Ire.ie
Abington	Cappanhanagh	- at Clare Bridge	woollen	-	-	-	-	-	-	1"os/	-
Dysert	Carrigeen	W/ Croom Bridge	thrashing	-	-	-	-	1844	-	6"os/	30
Mitchelstown	Carrigeen	- on R Funshin	saw	-	-	-	-	-	-	1"os/	-
Rathkeale	Castlematrix	- S. side R. Deel	Castlematrix Mill	-	-	-	-	1844	-	6"os/	29
Rathkeale	Castlematrix	Brown John S	corn	-	-	-	-	-	21x6x3	vmb/	26
Rathkeale	Castlematrix	Brown John S	flour	-	-	-	-	-	18x9x7	vmb/	26
Rathkeale	Castlematrix	Browne John S	flour	94x49.6x35	-	-	-	-	18x8.10x7	hob/	-
Rathkeale	Castlematrix	Browne John S	flour	(1A) 94x49.6x35	-	118	-	1850	no.1 - 18x8.10x7	hob/	5.1216
Rathkeale	Castlematrix	Browne John S	mills	house, offs. & land	105a.	204	-	1856	-	gr/	a.a.Ire.ie
Rathkeale	Castlematrix	Casey Cornelius :	mills	orchard & gardens :	-	-	Casey C - Casey Patrick	1818	-	dd/	727 303 496439
Rathkeale	Castlematrix	Casey Thomas & Patrick :	mills	-	-	-	Casey T&P - Dartnell Wm :	1813	Mort. 11 June	dd/	661 465 456711
Rathkeale	Castlematrix	Fitzgerald Thomas	mills	-	-	-	Fitzgerald - Southerwell :	1893	-	dd/	1893 30 13
Rathkeale	Castlematrix	Oliver Charles Dean :	mills	-	-	-	Oliver C - Rose Richard :	1819	-	dd/	740 526 504461
Rathkeale	Castlematrix	Southwell John	mill	Incumb Est consisting :		-	(lease 1862 to Tim. Enright)	1850	-	mlyIE	p52
Rathkeale	Castlematrix	Walsh Wiliam	mills	-	-	-	Walsh W - Fitzgerald Thos	1893	-	dd/	1893 25 213
Rathkeale	Castlematrix	Woodlock Bartholemew	mills	-	-	-	Woodlock B - Walsh Wm	1892	-	dd/	1892 16 202
Doondonnell	Cloghanarold	-	corn	-	-	-	-	1844	-	6"os/	29
Doondonnell	Cloghanarold	Frauly Ellen	corn	25.6x21.6x10 :	-	4-19	-	1850	12.6x9x3 :	hob/	5.1203
Doondonnell	Cloghanarold	Frauly Ellen	corn	-	-	-	-	-	12x9x3	vmb/	26

PARISH	TOWNLAND	MILLER	TYPE	HOUSE	Land	£Val	PROPRIETORS	Date	WHEEL etc.	Record	Ref.
Doondonnell	Cloghanarold	Frawley Ellen	corn & land	-	10a.	14	-	-	-	gr	-
Doondonnell	Cloghanarold	Frawley Maurice	corn	(2B) 25.6x21.6x10	-	4-9-4	-	1850	12.6x9x3 :	hob/	5.1196
Clonkeen	Clonkeen	- on Slievemohera R.	corn	-	-	-	-	1844	-	6"os/	14
Clonkeen	Clonkeen	O`Brien Patrick	corn	-	-	-	-	-	11x7x4	vmb/	26
Kilflyn	Clovers	Trench Chas Fred Esq.	kiln & store	-	-	16/-	-	-	-	gr	-
Limerick	Colbans	Heydon	mills	-	-	-	Heydon - Sinnott	-	-	dd/	-
Dromcolliher	Coolaboy	- on Avavarragh Stream	Coolaboy Mill	-	-	-	-	1844	-	6"os/	54
Clonshire	Coolballyshane	-	corn	-	-	-	-	-	-	1"os/	-
Clonshire	Coolballyshane	- E. side Clonshire R	mill race (1 mile)	-	-	-	-	1844	-	6"os/	20
Clonshire	Coolballyshane	- E. side Clonshire R.	corn & mill race	-	-	-	-	1844	-	6"os/	20
Clonshire	Coolballyshane	Enright Timothy	flour	66.6x20x20.6 :	-	10-0	-	1850	13x5.6x9 :	hob/	5.1198
Clonshire	Coolballyshane	Enright Timothy	flour	-	-	-	-	-	13x5x13	vmb/	26
Clonshire	Coolballyshane	Enright Timothy	flour & land :	-	3a.	34.5	-	-	-	gr	-
Ballingarry	Coolrus	- NE/ Coolrus Br.	tuck	-	-	-	-	1844	-	6"os/	38
? Townland	Creeves (2)	-	mill	-	-	-	-	-	-	1"os/	-
Croagh	Croagh	-	mill race	-	-	-	-	1844	-	6"os/	20
Croagh	Croagh	- W. side Clonshire R.	Smithfield Mill	-	-	-	-	1844	-	6"os/	20
Croagh	Croagh	Ferguson Maria	grist	-	-	-	-	-	11x6x7	vmb/	26
Croagh	Croagh	Ferguson Maria Mrs	flour	64.6x25.0x27 :	-	6-7-2	-	-	11x5.9x7 :	hob/	5.1201
Croagh	Croagh	Smith Richard :	mills	-	-	-	Smith - Walcott Thomas L :	-	-	dd/	763 442 518177
Croagh	Croagh	Smyth	mills	-	-	-	Smyth - Volkes	-	-	dd/	754 491 512826
Croom	Croom	- NW/ Croom Bridge	mill	-	-	-	-	1844	-	6"os/	30
Croom	Croom	- on Maigue R.	old mill	-	-	-	-	1844	-	6"os/	30
Croom	Croom	Lyons James D	flour	-	-	-	-	-	18x13x7	vmb/	26
Croom	Croom	Lyons James D Esq.	flour	ho., gate-lo., offs., ld	44a.	123	- [also tenants' houses]	1856	-	gr/	a.a.Ire.ie
Croom	Croom	Maxwell Robert	flour & corn	-	-	-	-	-	13x6x3	vmb/	26
Croom	Croom	Maxwell Robert Esq.	flour, corn & land	-	16a.	30.10.	-	1856	-	gr	-
Croom	Croom Village	Maguire M	corn	-	-	-	-	-	18x12 all metal	iaa/	-
Toughcluggin	Cross	-	Cross Tuck Mills	-	-	-	-	1844	-	6"os/	24
Toughcluggin	Cross	English Michael	corn	-	-	-	-	-	12x2x13	vmb/	26
Toughcluggin	Cross	English Michael	corn & land	-	56a.	41.10	-	-	-	gr	-
Glenquin	Cullenagh	-	bleach field (2)	-	-	-	-	1844	-	6"os/	36
Glenquin	Cullenagh	-	bleach mill	-	-	-	-	1844	-	6"os/	36
Glenquin	Cullenagh	-	sluice & mill race	-	-	-	-	1844	-	6"os/	36
Doon	Cullenagh	Flynn John	corn	-	-	-	-	-	12x2x12	vmb/	26
Doon	Cullenagh	Flynn John	mill & land	-	-	-	-	-	-	gr	-
Monagay	Cullenagh	Griffin Patrick	corn	(1C) 65.0x28.6x22	-	18-6	-	1851	17x4.6 v.old :	hob/	5.1264
Monagay	Cullenagh	Griffin Patrick	corn	-	-	-	-	-	17x4x1	vmb/	26
St Peter & Paul	Deebert	-	Mil View	-	-	-	-	1844	-	6"os/	47
St Peter & Paul	Deebert	- Mullenshane	Corn mill	-	-	-	-	1844	-	6"os/	47
St Peter & Paul	Deebert	Crea James	flour	-	-	-	-	-	18x9x-	vmb/	26
St Peter & Paul	Deebert	Creed Edward :	mill	-	-	-	Creed Edw - Sanders Jn :	1813	-	dd/	661 97 460557
St Peter & Paul	Deebert	Creed James :	mill	-	-	-	Creed Jas - Creed Edm :	1812	-	dd/	661 552 457712
St Peter & Paul	Deebert	Holmes Henry Rev. Sir :	mill	-	-	-	Holmes H - Holmes William :	1807	-	dd/	661 552 457713
Croom	Derryvinane	-	saw	-	-	-	-	-	-	1"os/	-
Mungret	Dooradoyle	-	Mill View (Ho.)	-	-	-	-	1844	-	6"os/	13
Mungret	Dooradoyle	-	Shanwillin Old Mill	-	-	-	-	1844	-	6"os/	13
Corncomohide	Drewscourt East	- E/ Ballybane Bridge	corn	-	-	-	-	1844	-	6"os/	46
Corncomohide	Drewscourt East	- on Maigue R.	corn	-	-	-	-	1844	-	6"os/	46
Corncomohide	Drewscourt East	Connors William	corn	-	-	-	-	-	17x5x9 17x5x8	vmb/	26
Corncomohide	Drewscourt East	O`Connor William	corn	(1C) 62x20x33 :	-	11	-	-	17x5.4x8 :	hob/	5.1226
Corncomohide	Drewscourt East	O`Shaughnessy William	corn	(3B) 23x16x6, kiln :	-	2-1	-	-	10x-x 5 breast :	hob/	5.1226

PARISH	TOWNLAND	MILLER	TYPE	HOUSE	Land	£Val	PROPRIETORS	Date	WHEEL etc.	Record	Ref.
Corncomohide	Drewscourt East	Shaughnessy William	corn	-	-	-	-	-	10x2x5	vmb/	26
Corncomohide	Drewscourt East	Shaughnessy William	corn & land	-	4a.	8.10	-	1856	-	gr	-
Abington	Dromeliagh	Keyes John	corn	-	-	-	-	-	14x3x3	vmb/	26
Abington	Dromellagh	- on Mulkear R.	flax (Millbank)	-	-	-	-	1844	-	6"os/	14
Bruree	Drumacummer E.	Carroll Martin	corn	-	-	-	-	-	7x5x2	vmb/	26
Bruree	Drumacummer E.	Carroll Martin	corn & land	-	69a.	63	-	-	-	gr	-
Rathkeale	Englishtenements	- NW/ R. Deel	brewery	-	-	-	-	1844	-	6"os/	29
Kilmurry	Freelane	Harvey Reuban	corn	-	-	-	-	-	-	vmb/	26
Kilmurry	Freelane	Harvey Reuban	flour	-	-	-	-	-	13x14x10	vmb/	26
Galbally	Galbally	Bishop John	corn & land		20a.	32	-	-	-	gr	-
Monagay	Glenduff	Gwynn John Rev.	mills	-	-	-	Gwynn John - John	1893	-	dd/	1893 9 197
Monagay	Glenduff	Plummer Richard	mills	-	-	-	Plummer R - O`Brien Robt.	1893	-	dd/	1893 52 193
St Peter & Paul	Glenfield	-	mill	-	-	-	-	-	-	1"os/	-
St Peter & Paul	Glenfield	- W/ Kilmallock Br.	Glenfield Mills	-	-	-	-	1844	-	6"os/	47
St Peter & Paul	Glenfield	Ivers James	corn	-	-	-	-	-	15x5x-	vmb/	26
Glenogra	Glenogra	- E/ Camoge R.	old mill & mill race	-	-	-	-	1844	-	6"os/	31
Limerick	Gortanoe *	-	woollen	-	-	-	-	-	-	1"os/	-
Newcastle	Gortboy	-	Newtown Brewery	-	-	-	-	1844	-	6"os/	36
Newcastle	Gortboy	(vacant)	brewery	(1C) 73x19x23.6 :	-	30-3	-	1850	-	hob/	5.1266
Newcastle	Gortboy :	McCarthy Daniel	brewery	-	-	-	-	1850	-	hob/	5.1266
Limerick	Greenmills *	Fitzgerald Lord	garden & kiln	-	-	-	Fitzgerald Ld - Hippesley	-	-	dd/	-
Limerick	Hingesmill *	Dixon	mill	-	-	-	Dixon - Babington	-	-	dd/	-
Hospital	Hospital	Browne Valentine	mill land	-	-	-	Browne Val - Lon. W Bank	1894	-	dd/	1894 54 79
Limerick	Inch *	Langton	mill race	-	-	-	Langton - Fisher	-	-	dd/	-
Kilcornan	Kilbreedy	-	corn	-	-	-	-	1844	-	6"os/	11
Kilcornan	Kilbreedy	Smyth John	corn	-	-	-	-	-	18x8x12	vmb/	26
Loghill	Kilfergus	Browne & Dore	corn	-	-	-	-	-	16x4x17	vmb/	26
Kilfinnane	Kilfinnane	- S. side Main St.	corn	-	-	-	-	1844	-	6"os/	48
Kilfinnane	Kilfinnane	Gascoigne Miss	carding	-	-	-	-	-	-	vmb/	26
Kilfinnane	Kilfinnane	Oliver, Trench, Gascoigne	corn	-	-	-	-	-	15x5x16	vmb/	26
Kilfinnane	Kilfinnane	Oliver, Trench, Gascoigne	corn	-	-	-	-	-	12x4x14	vmb/	26
Kilfinnane	Kilfinnane	Oliver, Trench, Gascoigne	flax	-	-	-	-	-	-	vmb/	26
Kilfinnane	Kilfinnane	Olliver William Esq.	corn & kiln	-	-	20	-	-	-	gr	-
Kilfinnane	Kilfinnane	Trench Fred Chas Esq. :	flax. corn, carding	-	-	17.10	-	-	-	gr	-
Kilfinnane	Kilfinny	- SSE/ Kilfinny Castle	windmill	- at ht. : 222	-	-	-	1844	-	6"os/	30
Kilfinnane	Kilfinny	- SSE/ Kilfinny Castle	windmill	- at ht. : 245	-	-	-	1844	-	6"os/	30
Kilbeheny	Kilglass	M'Carthy Walter	corn & land	-	8a.	12.11	-	-	-	gr	-
Kilbeheny	Kilglass	McCarthy Walter	corn	61x26x41.6 :	-	-	-	-	18x6x16 o`shot :	hob/	5,4030
Corncomohide	Killacolla	Carroll Patrick	corn & land	-	124a.	106	-	-	-	gr	-
Adare	Killeen	- Clarke`s Mill	corn	-	-	-	-	-	-	pWEH	D
Kilmallock	Kilmallock	Jeevers James	Glenfield Mills	-	-	-	-	1846	-	dir/	Slater
Kilmallock	Kilmallock	Mount William	mill	-	-	-	Mount W - Weldon Thos	1848		dd/	1849 3 180
Kilmallock	Kilmallock	Shaughnessy	Glenfield Mills	-	-	-	Shaughnessy - Ivers	-	-		
Kilmallock	Kilmallock	Shinkwin Capt.	mill	-	-	-	-	1846	-	dir/	Slater
Kilmallock	Kilmallock Town	Morris Edith	The Bleach Yd	-	-	-	Morris E - Fitzgerald Jas	1881	-	dd/	1881 39 100
Kilmallock	Kilmallock Town	Oliver Maria E	Streaks Mills & :	-	-	-	Oliver - Townsend Henry	1838	-	dd/	1838 9 99
Kilmallock	Kilmallock Town :	Stewart Spencer	mill	-	-	-	Stewart S - Ryan John	1877	-	dd/	1877 18 149
Kilmallock	Kilmallock Town :	Hallinan John Jun	mills	-	-	-	Hallinan - O`Shaughnessy	1881	-	dd/	1881 20 23
Ballingarry	Kilmore	Holohan Michael	corn	(1B) 28x22x17 :	-	9-5	-	1849	-	hob	5.1223
Ballingarry	Kilmore	Holohan Michael	corn	-	-	-	-	-	13x5x10	vmb/	26
Ballingarry	Kilmore Demesne	-	old corn mill	-	-	-	-	1844	-	6"os/	38
Ballingarry	Kilmore Demesne	-	old mill race & weii	-	-	-	-	1844	-	6"os/	38

PARISH	TOWNLAND	MILLER	TYPE	HOUSE	Land	£Val	PROPRIETORS	Date	WHEEL etc.	Record	Ref.
Abbeyfeale	Knockbrack	McAuliffe John	tuck	-	-	-	-	-	-	vmb/	26
Bruree	Knockfenora	Carroll Honoria Mrs	flour, tuck, carding	& land	8.0.8	38	-	1856	-	gr/	a.a.Ire.ie
Knockainy	Kyle	-	Milltown Lodge	-	-	-	-	1844	-	6"os/	40
St Patricks	Limerick City	- on R Shannon	mill	-	-	-	-	-	-	1"os/	-
St Marys	Limerick City :	Fitt Mathew Esq.	brewery & garden	-	00.26	67.15	-	-	-	gr	-
St Peters	Limerick City :	- Newtown Perry Mill	flour	-	-	-	- (estab. by J. N. Russell)	-	-	hist./	Ranks
St Michaels	Limerick City :	Bannantyne James	flour	- (later k/a City Mills	-	-	(sold to Goodbodys 1893)	1858	-	hist./	Ranks
St Marys	Limerick City :	Byrne David / vacant	corn store & kiln	-	-	19	-	-	-	gr	-
St Peters	Limerick City :	- N side Canal :	Canal Brewery	-	-	-	-	1844	-	6"os/	5
St Patricks	Limerick City :	Russell John N	flour	(1A) 40.6x50x34 :	-	-	-	1848	2 wheels :	hob/	5.4034
St Marys	Limerick City :	- imed. S/ Wellseley Br.	brewery	-	-	-	-	1844	-	6"os/	5
St Marys	Limerick City :	- S/ Wellseley Br. :	mill	-	-	-	-	1844	-	6"os/	5
St Peters	Limerick City :	- N side Canal	Lock Mills	-	-	-	-	1844	-	6"os/	5
St Michaels	Limerick City :	- SW/ Wellseley Br.	Newtown Pery	-	-	-	-	1844	-	6"os/	5
Killeely	Limerick City :	- W side R. Shannon	distillery	-	-	-	-	1844	-	6"os/	5
St Lawrence's	Limerick City :	Shaw & Duffield Messrs	steam mill :	-	2.0.0	-	-	-	-	gr	-
St John's	Limerick City :	Benson John	corn store, kiln, yd	-	15a.	14.10	-	-	-	gr	-
St John's	Limerick City :	Russell Francis P (vacant)	corn store & yard	-	-	18	-	-	-	gr	-
St John's	Limerick City :	- E/ Wellseley Br.	brewery	-	-	-	-	1844	-	6"os/	5
St John's	Limerick City :	O'Brien Patrick	kiln & corn store	-	-	15	-	-	-	gr	-
St John's	Limerick City :	Mossop John	corn store & yard	-	-	20	-	-	-	gr	-
St John's	Limerick City :	O'Connell William	kiln & store	-	-	19	-	-	-	gr	-
St John's	Limerick City :	- 1/2m E/ Wellseley Br.	brewery	-	-	-	-	1844	-	6"os/	5
St John's	Limerick City :	-	cotton factory	-	-	-	-	1844	-	6"os/	5
St Patricks	Limerick City :	Russell John R	mills	(1B) 64.6 28x34.6 :	-	-	-	-	16x22x8.6 :	hob/	5.4034
Loghill	Loghill	- on White R.	old mill	-	-	-	-	1844	-	6"os/	9
Loghill	Loghill	Wallace Michael	flour	-	-	-	-	-	12x2x13	vmb/	26
Loghill	Loghill	Wallace Michael	grist	-	-	-	-	-	12x2x13	vmb/	26
Loghill	Loghill	Wallace Michael	tuck	-	-	-	-	-	12x2x13	vmb/	26
Glenquin	Mahoonagh	Roche R & R	corn	-	-	-	-	-	11x-x5	vmb/	26
Glenquin	Mahoonagh	Roche R & R	tuck	-	-	-	-	-	9x2x4	vmb/	26
Mahoonagh	Mahoonagh More	- W/ Castlemahon Br.	corn & tuck	-	-	-	-	1844	-	6"os/	36
Mahoonagh	Mahoonagh More	Roche Robt & Richard	corn	(2B) 25.6x19x12.0 :	-	2-2	-	1850	10.9x-x5 breast :	hob/	5.1263
Mahoonagh	Mahoonagh More	Roche Robt & Richard	tuck	(2B) 13x12.6x8	-	0-6-4	-	1850	29.6x2x4.6 :	hob/	5.1263
Glenogra	Meanns	Gleeson Michael	corn	-	-	-	-	-	10x3x2	vmb/	-
Glenogra	Meanus	-	tuck	-	-	-	-	1844	-	6"os/	31
Limerick	Milletstown *	Fitzpatrick	mill	-	-	-	Fitzpatrick & Flood :	-	-	dd/	-
Derrygalvin	Milltown	-	mill	-	-	-	-	1844	-	6"os/	6
Uregare	Milltown	-	Milltown George Vge.		-	-	-	1844	-	6"os/	39
Knockainy	Milltown	-	Milltown Lodge	-	-	-	-	1844	-	6"os/	40
Aglishcormick	Milltown	-	no mill	-	-	-	-	1844	-	6"os/	24
Ardpatrick	Milltown	-	no mill	-	-	-	-	1844	-	6"os/	48
Croagh	Milltown	-	no mill	-	-	-	-	1851	-	hob/	-
Aglish	Milltown	-	no mill	- (other buildings :	-	-	-	1850		hob/	5.1237
Croagh	Milltown	- on road from Croom	Milltown Bridge	- (no mill)	-	-	-	1844	-	6"os/	29
Derrygalvin	Milltown	Browne William	corn, kiln & land	-	24a.	48	-	1844	-	gr	-
Limerick	Milltown	Longford Lord	-	-	-	-	Longford Ld & ors (dd)	-	-	dd/	-
Derrygalvin	Milltown	Roche William	corn	-	-	-	-	-	14x6x7	vmb/	26
(bo. Coonagh)	Milltown	Wise Jane	mill	-	-	-	Wise Jane - Cameron Alex	1893	-	dd/	1893 25 161
Ardkill	Milltown :	-	no mill	-	-	-	-	-	-	hob/	-
Knockainy	Milltown 117.2.33	-	no mill	-	-	-	-	1844	-	6"os/	40
Uregare	Milltown 118.2.33	-	no mill	-	-	-	-	1844	-	6"os/	39

PARISH	TOWNLAND	MILLER	TYPE	HOUSE	Land	£Val	PROPRIETORS	Date	WHEEL etc.	Record	Ref.
Lismakeery	Milltown North	-	no milll	- (other buildings:	-	-	-	1850	-	hob/	5.1206
Lismakeery	Milltown South	-	no mill	- (other buildings:	-	-	-	1850	-	hob/	5.1206
(bo. Connello)	Milltown South	O`Leary Henry	mill	-	-	-	O`Leary H - Cregan Thos	1890	-	dd/	1890 49 106
Kilcoran	Moig West	-	Washpool Corn Mill		-	-	-	1844	-	6"os/	11
Rathkeale	Moig West	- near Milltown Ho.	washpool	-	-	-	-	-	-	1"os/	-
Kilcornan	Moig West	Wallace William	corn	-	-	-	-	-	14x2x16	vmb/	26
Limerick	Mountblainey * :	Keatinge	mill	-	-	-	Keatinge - Hamilton	-	-	dd/	-
Limerick	Mountblainey * :	Leinster Duke of	mill & mill-lands	-	-	-	Leinster Duke & Lady :	-	-	dd/	-
Stradbally	Mountshannon :	-	corn mill site	-	-	-	-	-	-	sv/05	Z
Stradbally	Mountshannon :	-	old market ho.	-	-	-	-	-	-	pWEH	-
Kilmoylan	Mullagh	-	Mill View (Ho.)	-	-	-	-	1844	-	6"os/	18
Kilmoylan	Mullagh	- NW/ Creeves Br.	Nutgrove Flour Mill		-	-	-	1844	-	6"os/	18
Kilmoylan	Mullagh	- NW/ Creeves Br.	tuck & mill dam	-	-	-	-	1844	-	6"os/	18
Kilmoylan	Mullagh	Donovan Ellen	flour	-	-	-	-	-	20x5x20	vmb/	26
Limerick	Mullagh	Enraght	mill & lands	-	-	-	Enraght - Enraght	-	-	dd/	-
Dromcolliher	Mundellihy	- W. side R. Deel	Accrour Corn Mill	-	-	-	-	1844	-	6"os/	45
Galbally	Park	- 1/2 m.W/ Galbally Br.	tuck	-	-	-	-	1844	-	6"os/	49
Galbally	Park	- on R. Aherlow	corn	-	-	-	-	1844	-	6"os/	49
Galbally	Park	Bishop John	corn	-	-	-	-	-	14x4x9	vmb/	26
Galbally	Park	Wilkinson Philip	corn	-	-	-	-	-	12x3x7	vmb/	26
Galbally	Park	Wilkinson Philip	corn & land	-	4a.	1.5	-	-	-	gr	-
Kilmurry	Peafield	- at Peafield Ho.	mill	-	-	-	-	1844	-	6"os/	5
Stradbally	Prospect	- on R. Shannon	River Bleach Mill	-	-	-	-	1844	-	6"os/	6
Stradbally	Prospect	Harrison Joseph	mill & spinning fty.	-	-	30	-	-	-	gr	-
Stradbally	Prospect	Harrison Joseph	woollen	-	-	-	-	-	10x5x4	vmb/	26
St Patrick`s	Reboge	Bevan Mrs G	bleach	-	-	-	-	-	11x6x3	vmb/	26
St Patricks	Reboge Meadows	-	mill	-	-	-	-	1844	-	6"os/	5
St Patricks	Reboge Meadows	- close to beetling mill	bleach	-	-	-	-	1844	-	6"os/	5
St Patricks	Reboge Meadows	Cochran Thomas	bleach & land	-	28a.	60.10	-	-	-	gr	-
Kilmurry	Rivers	- imed. S/ Annacoty Br.	mills	-	-	-	-	1844	-	6"os/	6
Kilmurry	Rivers	Grubbs Robert	corn & land	-	6a.	45	-	-	-	gr	-
Kilmurry	Rivers	Grubbs Robert	Indian corn	-	-	-	-	-	12x4x4 9x10	vmb/	26
St Michael`s	Rossbrien	-	paper & mill pond	-	-	-	-	1844	-	6"os/	13
St Michael`s	Rossbrien	Brennan Daniel	corn	-	-	-	-	-	14x3x14	vmb/	26
Limerick	Ryevale *	Donnellan	mill	-	-	-	Donnellan - Hackett	-	-	dd/	-
Limerick	Ryevale *	Donnellan	mill	-	-	-	Donnellan - O`Donnell	-	-	dd/	-
Limerick	Ryevale *	Donnellan	mill	-	-	-	Donnellan - Byrne	-	-	dd/	-
Ballingarry	Rylanes	- NW/ Ballingarry Ch.	old mill	-	-	-	-	1844	-	6"os/	29
Ballingarry	Rylanes	Basey & Brownrick	flour	-	-	-	-	-	13x3x14	vmb/	-
Ballingarry	Rylanes	Pruderman Barry	flour	(1C) 41x23.6x40	-	-	-	-	-	hob/	5.1223
Killonan	Scart	-	Scart Mill & kiln	-	-	-	-	1844	-	6"os/	6
Derrygalvin	Scart	- on Slievemore R.	corn	-	-	-	-	-	-	1"os/	-
Derrygalvin	Scart	Flynn Paul	carding	-	-	-	-	-	15x3x2	vmb/	26
Derrygalvin	Scart	Flynn Paul	corn	-	-	-	-	-	9x4x2	vmb/	26
Derrygalvin	Scart	Flynn Paul	corn & kiln :	-	24a.	22	-	-	-	gr	-
Derrygalvin	Scart	Flynn Paul	old corn mill	-	-	-	-	-	15x3x2	vmb/	26
St Patricks	Singland	-	beetling & bl. greei	-	-	-	-	1844	-	6"os/	5
St Patrick`s	Singland	Beven Mrs G	beetling	-	-	-	-	-	11x2x4	vmb/	26
St Particks	Singland	Cochrane Thomas	beetling & bleach	-	11a.	25.5	-	-	-	gr	-
St Particks	Singland	Cochrane Thomas	mill	-	-	-	Cochrane T - Limk. Manure C	1894	-	dd/	1894 15 86
Croom	Skeagh	Roche Sir David Bart.	mill race & land	-	5a.	2.10	-	-	-	gr	-
Kilmurry	Sreelane	- on R. Shannon	Plassy Mills	-	-	-	-	1844	-	6"os/	5

PARISH	TOWNLAND	MILLER	TYPE	HOUSE	Land	£Val	PROPRIETORS	Date	WHEEL etc.	Record	Ref.
Kilmurry	Sreelane	Harvey Reuben	flour & corn :	-	22a.	134	-	-	-	gr	-
Kilcornan	Stonehall	- N/ Mullamosheen Br.	corn	-	-	-	-	1844	-	6"os/	21
Particles	Sunville	Oliver Richard	corn	-	-	-	- leased from John Lowe	1863	-	mlylE	p48
Particles	Sunville :	Sayers Edward	corn	Incumb Est. consisting :	-	-	- sold to Chas G. Mahon	1853	o'shot dia. 20ft. :	mlylE	p48
Particles	Sunville Lower	- NE/ Ardpatrick	corn	-	-	-	-	1844	-	6"os/	56
Particles	Sunville Lower	Sayers Edward	corn	-	-	-	-	-	18x10x21	vmb/	26
Particles	Sunville Lower	Sayers Edward Esq.	corn & land	-	89a.	109	-	-	-	gr	-
Limerick	The Mill Holding	Wolseley Constance	mill	-	-	-	Wolseley Cons - Fry Wm	1890	-	dd/	1890 28 225
Doon	Toomalene	-	mill	-	-	-	-	-	-	1"os/	-
Doon	Toomalene Upr	Dwyer Thomas	corn	-	-	-	-	-	13x2x14	vmb/	26
Doon	Toomaline	- on Cahernahallia R.	Toomaline Mill	-	-	-	-	1844	-	6"os/	16
(bo. Clanwm.)	Windmill Hill	Deane Matthew	mill	-	-	-	Deane Matt - Thomson Robt	1894	-	dd/	1894 29 241
Ballingarry	Woodstock	Smith John	flour	(1C) 57x26x31 & :	-	8-8-1	-	1849	21x5x12 3pr.st.	hob/	51.112
Ballingarry	Woodstock	Smith John	flour	-	-	-	-	-	21x5x12	vmb/	26

PARISH	TOWNLAND	MILLER	TYPE	HOUSE	Land	£Val	PROPRIETORS	Date	WHEEL etc.	Record	Ref.
Aghadowey	Aghadowey	Hunter, Hempill & :	beetling	-	-	-	-	-	14x4.6x9 breast	osm/	-
Aghadowey	Aghadowey	Hunter, Hempill & :	bleach green	- 2 slated houses	25a	-	-	-	-	osm/	-
Aghadowey	Aghadowey	Hunter, Hempill & :	wash	-	-	-	-	-	12x3x4.6 wheels	osm/	-
Aghadowey	Aghadowey	Smith James & Co.	beetling	-	-	-	-	-	-	gr/	-
Aghadowey	Aghadowey	Smith James & Co.	drying & green	-	36a.	53	-	-	-	gr/	-
Londonderry	Altagasky *	Jackson William Sen :	corn	-	-	-	Jackson W - Mauleverer :	1737	-	dd/	88 77 61667
Londonderry	Altagasky *	Mauleverer Bellingham	mill	-	-	-	Mauleverer - McNeil A :	1750	-	dd/	155 273 104585
Londonderry	Altagasky *	McNeill Archibald :	mill	-	-	-	McNeill A - Duff John	1751	-	dd/	150 152 100606
Londonderry	Altagasky *	Saurin James Rev. :	mill	-	-	-	Saurin - Besnard Peter :	1755	-	dd/	179 82 118957
Desertmartin	Annagh	-	corn	-	-	-	-	-	12x2x -	osm/	-
Desertmartin	Annagh	Bunton John	corn	-	22a.	-	-	-	-	gr/	-
Desertmartin	Annagh	Bunton John	flax	-	-	-	-	-	-	gr/	-
Desertmartin	Annagh	Glenholme Mr	flax	-	-	-	-	-	11x1.4x -	osm/	-
Derryloran	Annahavil	-	flax & dam	-	-	-	-	1839	-	6"os/	48
Derryloran	Annahavil	- on Lissan Water	flax	-	-	-	-	-	-	1"os/	-
Derryloran	Annahavil	Cowan John	flax	-	57a.	-	-	-	-	gr/	-
Drumachose	Ardgarvan	- Largy Br. R. Roe	mill	-	-	-	-	-	-	1"os/	12
Cumber lower	Ardground	-	old mill & stream	-	-	-	-	1839	-	6"os/	22
Dunboe	Ardina	Smith John	flax	-	-	-	-	-	14x2x10 4 rollers & :	osm/	-
Boveagh	Ardinarive	Douglas James	corn	miller`s house	148a.	-	-	-	-	gr/	-
Boveagh	Ardinarrive	-	corn	38x21	-	-	-	-	13x0.11x12.6	osm/	-
Clandermot	Ardkill	- W side R. Faughan	corn kiln, pond	-	-	-	-	1839	-	6"os/	21
Clandermot	Ardkill	- W side R. Faughan	iron spade mfy	-	-	-	-	1839	-	6"os/	21
Clandermot	Ardkill	Blaquire John Rt. Hon.	mill	-	-	-	Blaquoire - Montgomery :	1775	-	dd/	308 534 207238
Clandermot	Ardkill	Dobson Anne Maria	mill	-	-	-	Mrs Dobson / Tomkins :	1751	-	dd/	176 457 119523
Clandermot	Ardkill	Dobson Robert Capt.	mill	-	-	-	Dobson - Bowyer Fran	1754	-	dd/	166 395 111996
Clandermot	Ardkill	Dobson Robert Capt. :	mill	-	-	-	Dobson - Bowyer Fran	1854	-	dd/	166 359 111856
Clandermot	Ardkill	Douglas Joseph	corn	-	4a.	-	-	-	-	gr/	-
Clandermot	Ardkill	Henderson James	flax	-	10a.	-	-	-	-	gr/	-
Clandermot	Ardkill	Tomkins Anna Maria	mill	-	-	-	Tomkin A - Smith Robt	1757	-	dd/	167 412 113028
Clandermot	Ardlogh	Hanly Peter :	mill	-	-	-	Hanly Pet. - Wilson Wm :	1751	-	dd/	182 468 121610
Clondermot	Ardlough	- W. side Faughan R.	mills	-	-	-	-	1839	-	6"os/	14
Clondermot	Ardlough	Ballantine Thomas	flax	-	27a.	-	-	-	-	gr/	-
Clandermot	Ardlough	Moncrief Robert	corn	-	0-1-20		-	-	-	gr/	-
Clandermot	Ardlough	Semple John	flax & store	-	2a.	-	-	-	-	gr/	-
Clandermot	Ardlough	Semple John	flax & store	steward`s house	45a.	-	-	-	-	gr/	-
Clandermot	Ardlough	Semple John	flax rolling	-	-	-	-	-	-	gr/	-
Pelipers	Ardlough	Walker James :	mill	-	-	-	Walker - Batchell Robt :	1801	-	dd/	531 157 348546?
Balteagh	Ardmore	-	flax	-	-	-	-	-	12x1.2x - 3 rollers :	osm/	-
Balteagh	Ardmore	- at Wooden Br.	bleaching	-	-	-	-	1839	-	6"os/	21
Balteagh	Ardmore	- unoccupied	bleach green	-	-	-	-	-	- ceased 1802	osm/	-
Balteagh	Ardmore	Gault Thomas	flax scutching	-	106a.	-	-	-	-	gr/	-
Clondermot	Ardmore	M`Clelland Cary & Co.	bleaching	-	14a.	-	-	-	-	gr/	-
Balteagh	Ardmore	M`Rory Robert	corn	-	43a.	-	-	-	-	gr/	-
Balteagh	Ardmore	McRory Robert	flour	-	-	-	-	-	34x - x -	osm/	-
Balteagh	Ardmore :	-	corn & pond	-	-	-	-	-	-	6"os/	10
Balteagh	Ardmore :	-	corn & pond	-	-	-	-	1839	-	6"os/	17
Clondermot	Ardnabrocky	-	flax hole	-	-	-	-	1839	-	6"os/	20
Clondermot	Ardnabrocky	-	flax holes	-	-	-	-	1839	-	6"os/	20
Faughanvale	Ardnaguniog	- E. of Faughan R.	flax	-	-	-	-	1839	-	6"os/	14
Faughanvale	Ardnaguniog	- E. of Faughan R.	flax kiln, holes	-	-	-	-	1839	-	6"os/	14
Macosquin	Ardvarness	Bennett Mary	thrashing	-	-	-	-	-	-	gr/	-

PARISH	TOWNLAND	MILLER	TYPE	HOUSE	Land	£Val	PROPRIETORS	Date	WHEEL etc.	Record	Ref.
Castledawson	Arlogh	Bernard Anthony	corn	-	-	-	Bernard A - Dumeny Jn	1721	-	dd/	32 312 19838
Castledawson	Arlogh	Bernard Anthony	corn	-	-	-	Bernard A - Wallis Mtha	1713	-	dd/	32 316 18943
Castledawson	Arlogh	Du Petit	mill	-	-	-	Du Petit & W - Legrand	-	?	dd/	142 418 96141
Castledawson	Arlough	Wallis Gilbert	corn	-	-	-	Wallis G - Legrand C J	1725	-	dd/	49 32 30584
Dunboe	Articlave	Clarke James	flax	-	-	-	Cochrane William - 1831	-	16x4x -	osm/	-
Dunboe	Articlave Bridge	-	flax	-	-	-	-	-	-	1"os/	18
Dunboe	Articlave Lower	Kerr Robert	flax	-	13a.	-	-	-	-	gr/	-
Dunboe	Articlave Town	- near Dartress Br.	corn	-	-	-	-	-	-	1"os/	18
Dunboe	Articlave Town	Kerr Robert	flax	-	-	-	-	-	-	gr/	-
Dunboe	Articlave Village	Alexander John	flax	-	-	-	-	-	16x4x - 4 rollers & :	osm/	-
Dunboe	Articlave Village	Alexander John	corn & kiln	-	-	-	Alexander John	-	13x1.2x15 13x1.9x15	osm/	-
Dunboe	Articlave Village	Clarke James	flax	-	-	-	-	-	12x1.8x6	osm/	-
Ballyrashane	Articrunaght	Ferguson John	flax	-	-	-	-	-	13.3x1.6x9	osm/	-
Ballyrashane	Articrunaght N.	-	flax	-	-	-	-	-	-	6"os/	4
Ballyrashane	Articrunaght S.	-	barley	-	-	-	-	-	-	6"os/	8
Ballyrashane	Articrunaght S.	-	corn	-	-	-	-	-	-	6"os/	-
Ballyrashane	Articrunaught :	-	corn & pond	-	-	-	-	-	-	6"os/	8
Lissan	at LittleBr	- on Lissan Water	mill	-	-	-	-	-	-	1"os/	-
Magilligan	Aughil	-	mill & kiln	-	-	-	-	1839	-	6"os/	2
Magilligan	Aughil :	-	kiln & mill	-	-	-	-	-	-	6"os/	1
Artrea	Aughrim	-	spade, mill dam	-	-	-	-	1839	-	6"os/	42
Banagher	Auglish	Witherow James	flax	-	92a.	-	-	-	-	gr/	-
Macosquin	Ballinacanon	Steen James	flax	-	-	-	-	-	12x1.5x4.6	osm/	-
Comber Lower	Ballinamore	Long William	thrashing	-	110a.	-	-	-	-	gr/	-
Aghadowey	Ballincally Beg	- on Aghadowey R.	mill	-	-	-	-	-	-	1"os/	13
Artrea	Ballindrum Town	-	flax	-	-	-	-	-	-	1"os/	-
Aghadowey	Ballinrees	Bartley Alex, Geo &Co.	beetling	-	-	-	-	-	-	gr/	-
Aghadowey	Ballinrees	Wilson Maria	flax & stores	-	1a.	-	-	-	-	gr/	-
Desertoghill	Ballyagan	- E. of Agivey R.	flax mills	-	-	-	-	1839	-	6"os/	18
Desertoghill	Ballyagan	Rankin David	flax	- thatched house :	-	-	-	1837	13x2.10x5.6 breast	osm/	-
Desertoghill	Ballyagan	Rankin David	flax & stores	-	17a.	-	-	-	-	gr/	-
Desertoghill	Ballyagan	Rankin David	small flax	-	-	-	Logan John (decd) :	-	13x2x5.6 breast	osm/	-
Desertoghill	Ballyagan Lower	- on Agivie R.	flax	-	-	-	-	-	-	1"os/	13
Cumber Upper	Ballyartan	- W. side R. Faughan	bleach	-	-	-	-	1839	-	6"os/	22
Cumber Upper	Ballyartan	Irwin John	corn	-	30a.	-	-	-	-	gr/	-
Cumber Upper	Ballyartan	Irwin John	corn	-	-	-	Bishop of Meath	-	-	osm/	-
Cumber Upper	Ballyartan	Irwin John	flax	-	-	-	Bishop of Meath	-	-	osm/	-
Lissan	Ballybriest	- N. of Barony Bridge	bleach & race	-	-	-	-	1839	-	6"os/	45
Lissan	Ballybriest	Miller Rowley	bleach (in ruins)	-	-	-	Morgan Williams ceased	1831	-	osm/	-
Lissan	Ballybriest	Smyth William	corn	miller`s house	43a.	-	-	-	-	gr/	-
Lissan	Ballybriest	Smyth William	flax	-	-	-	-	-	-	gr/	-
Aghadowey	Ballybritain	Hunter, Hempill & :	beetling	-	-	-	-	-	20x4x4 14x4x -	osm/	-
Aghadowey	Ballybritain	Hunter, Hempill & :	bleach green	-	-	-	-	-	-	osm/	-
Aghadowey	Ballybritain	Hunter, Hempill & :	wash	-	-	-	-	-	13.6x2.8x8.6	osm/	-
Magilligan	Ballycarton	- near Roe Bridge :	mill	-	-	-	-	-	-	1"os/	12
Magilligan	Ballycarton	Lane Benjamin	corn	-	-	-	-	-	13.6x12.4x -	osm/	-
Magilligan	Ballycarton	Lane Benjamin	corn & kiln	-	126a.	-	-	-	-	gr/	-
Magilligan	Ballycarton :	-	mill & pond	-	-	-	-	-	-	6"os/	5
Drumachose	Ballydarrog	Connor John	corn & kiln	-	1a.	-	-	-	-	gr/	-
Drumachose	Ballydarrog	Connor John	flax	-	11a.	18	-	-	-	gr/	-
Drumachose	Ballydarrog	Connor John	foundry	-	4a.	3	-	-	-	gr/	-
Tamlaght	Ballydawley Town	- at Tamlaght	mill	-	-	-	-	-	-	1"os/	27

PARISH	TOWNLAND	MILLER	TYPE	HOUSE	Land	£Val	PROPRIETORS	Date	WHEEL etc.	Record	Ref.
Tamlaght-Fin.	Ballyderg	-	corn & dam	-	-	-	-	1839	-	6"os/	16
Tamlaght-Fin.	Ballyderg	- near Fort	flax	-	-	-	-	1839	-	6"os/	16
Tamlaght-Fin.	Ballyderg	Wallace Robert	flax	-	-	-	-	-	12x2.8x9 4 stocks	osm/	-
Tamlaght-Fin.	Ballyderg	Wallace Robert	spade	-	-	-	-	-	12.4x1.8x -	osm/	-
Ballyscullion	Ballydermot	- stream to R. Bann	spade	-	-	-	-	-	-	1"os/	27
Aghadowey	Ballydevit	Adams John & Bennett	bleach & green	-	31a.	-	-	-	-	gr/	-
Aghadowey	Ballydevitt	Bennett Thomas & :	beetling	-	-	-	-	-	18x4.8x10 & :	osm/	-
Aghadowey	Ballydevitt	Bennett Thomas & :	bleach green	-	-	140	-	-	-	osm/	-
Aghadowey	Ballydevitt	Bennett Thomas & :	wash	-	-	-	-	-	12.7x4.7x4 2 wheels	osm/	-
Ballinderry	Ballydonneil	-	flax	-	-	-	-	-	-	1"os/	-
Ballyaghram	Ballygalagh	Cromie John	flax	-	-	-	-	-	12x1.2x5	osm/	-
Arboe	Ballygonny Beg	Nesbitt Hugh	flax	-	27a.	-	-	-	-	gr/	-
Artrea	Ballygurk	-	mill	-	-	-	Given - Adair Bell	-	?	dd/	485 524 315240
Artrea	Ballygurk	- E. side rd./ Coagh	mill race, dam :	-	-	-	-	1839	-	6"os/	47
Artrea	Ballygurk	Boune Andrew	corn & kiln	miller`s house	19a.	-	-	-	-	gr/	-
Artrea	Ballygurk	Boyle James	mill	-	-	-	Boyle Jas - Haslett Wm	1780	-	dd/	334 307 223320
Artrea	Ballygurk	Given James :	mill	-	-	-	Given J - Goold Pierce :	1805	Mort. 1 Sug.	dd/	573 174 386174
Artrea	Ballygurk	Mauleverer Bellingham	mill	Maul`ver - Erskin :	-	-	Mauleveer - Erskin :	1750	-	dd/	155 273 104565
Artrea	Ballygurk	Strean Samuel	mill	-	-	-	Strean S - Given Jas	1780	-	dd/	330 629 225671
Dunboe	Ballyhacket	- at Milltown	flax	-	-	-	-	-	-	1"os/	18
Boveagh	Ballyharigan	Osborne William	corn	-	-	-	-	-	12x2x11	osm/	-
Boveagh	Ballyharigan	Osborne William	flax	miller`s house	1a.	-	-	-	-	gr/	-
Boveagh	Ballyharigan	Osborne William	flax	-	-	-	-	-	11x2.2x8	osm/	-
Ldy	Ballyharrig	- N./ B`harrig Ho.	mill	-	-	-	-	1839	-	6"os/	24
Tamlaght (?)	Ballykellaghan	Annesley William	mill	-	-	-	Annesley - Meade Jane	1750	-	dd/	142 533 97827
Tamlaght (?)	Ballykellaghan	Cary Edward Hon. :	mill	-	-	-	Cary - Blacker Stewart :	1791	-	dd/	430 548 280228
Tamlaght (?)	Ballykellaghan	Cary Henry & Edwd	mill	-	-	-	Cary H - Hamilton Geo	1743	-	dd/	112 331 78323
Tamlaght (?)	Ballykellaghan	O`Gilby Robert :	mill	-	-	-	O`Gilby r - Ash Benj :	1803	-	dd/	558 458 372856
Tamlaght (?)	Ballykellaghan	O`Gilby Robert :	mill	-	-	-	O`Gilby R - Scott Joice :	1804	-	dd/	617 135 421664
Tamlaght (?)	Ballykellaghan	Skinners Company	mill	-	-	-	Skinners Co - Cary Hen	1740	-	dd/	110 177 76448
Tamlaght-Fin.	Ballykelly	Fishmongers W`full :	flax & store	-	2-3-5	-	-	-	-	gr/	-
Tamlaght-Fin.	Ballykelly :	-	factory	-	-	-	-	-	-	6"os/	9
Tamlaght-Fin.	Ballykelly Village	-	mill	- 2 storey	-	-	-	-	-	osm/	-
Killelagh	Ballyknock	Clarke Alex	corn	-	-	-	-	-	16x3.8x1.6 oversho	osm/	-
Killelagh	Ballyknock	Clarke James J	corn	-	-	-	-	-	-	gr/	-
Killelagh	Ballyknock	M`Coy Michael	flax	-	2a.	-	-	-	-	gr/	-
Killelagh	Ballyknock	McKenna Cornelius	flax	-	-	-	-	-	12x1.6x6 bad repair	osm/	-
Balteagh	Ballyleaghry	Irwin James	corn	-	-	-	-	-	13x1.2x10 breast :	osm/	-
Balteagh	Ballyleaghry	Miller Robert	corn	-	4a.	-	-	-	-	gr/	-
Balteagh	Ballyleagry	- nr Lislane	flax	-	-	-	-	-	-	1"os/	
Aghadowey	Ballylintagh	- nr Macosquin R.	flax	-	-	-	-	1839	-	6"os/	11
Aghadowey	Ballylintagh	Hanson George	flax & stores	-	88a.	95	-	-	-	gr/	-
Maghera	Ballymacilcur	Houston David & Wm	flax	-	12a.	-	-	-	-	gr/	-
Maghera	Ballymacilcur	Huston Wiliam	flax	-	-	-	-	-	11x1.6x11	osm/	-
Dunboe	Ballymadigan	Bruce Henry Sir H Bart	flax	-	131a.	-	-	-	-	gr/	-
Templemore	Ballymagrorty	-	corn	-	-	-	-	1839	-	6"os/	13
Templemore	Ballymagrorty	-	flax	-	-	-	-	1839	-	6"os/	13
Templemore	Ballymagrorty	Doak James	corn & kiln	-	33a.	-	-	-	-	gr/	-
Boveagh	Ballymoney	- on Agivey R.	pond (no mill)	-	-	-	-	1839	-	6"os/	24
Boveagh	Ballymoney	Carton James	corn & kiln	-	2a.	-	-	-	-	gr/	-
Boveagh	Ballymoney	Kane William	corn & kiln	-	-	-	Olpher Mr	-	11.6x1x8	osm/	-
Carrick	Ballymore	-	flax	-	-	-	-	1839	-	6"os/	16

PARISH	TOWNLAND	MILLER	TYPE	HOUSE	Land	£Val	PROPRIETORS	Date	WHEEL etc.	Record	Ref.
Carrrick	Ballymore	-	flax12	-	-	-	-	-	-	1"os/	-
Carrick	Ballymore	-	stream & pond	-	-	-	-	1839	-	6"os/	16
Carrrick	Ballymore	M`Clelland James	flax & store	-	17a.	-	-	-	-	gr/	-
Balteagh	Ballymully	-	corn	-	-	-	-	-	16x2.6x -	osm/	-
Balteagh	Ballymully	- near Castle R.	corn	-	-	-	-	-	-	1"os/	12
Balteagh	Ballymully	Grant Thomas	cloth	-	-	-	-	-	11.6x20x10 breast :	osm/	-
Ballinderry	Ballymultrea :	- near Furnace Br.	race & pond :	-	-	-	-	1839	-	6"os/	47
Aghadowey	Ballynacally	Baird Alexander	flax	-	21a.	-	-	-	-	gr/	-
Aghadowey	Ballynacally	Bartley Alex, Geo &Co.	beetling	-	-	-	-	-	-	gr/	-
Aghadowey	Ballynacally Beg	Baird William & Alex	flax	-	-	-	-	-	13x2x10	osm/	-
Aghadowey	Ballynacally Beg	on stream to Agh`dy R.	flax	-	-	-	-	1839	-	6"os/	18
Templemore	Ballynagalliagh	-	-	-	-	-	-	-	-	ct.co./	-
Templemore	Ballynagard	Smith Joseph	flax	-	40a.	-	-	-	-	gr/	-
Drumachose	Ballynaheery	M`Leod James	corn & flax	-	33a.	-	-	-	-	gr/	-
Drumachose	Ballynaheery	M`Leod William	flax	-	27a.	-	-	-	-	gr/	-
Desertoghill	Ballynameen	-	corn	-	-	-	-	-	-	osm/	-
Desertoghill	Ballynameen	- at Tirekeeran Vge.	mill	-	-	-	-	-	-	1"os/	19
Artrea	Ballynenagh	-	mill	-	-	-	-	-	-	1"os/	-
Dungiven	Ballyness	-	mill	-	-	-	-	-	-	1"os/	18
Dungiven	Ballyness	-	mill	-	-	-	Given - Adair Bell	-	?	dd/	485 524 315240
Dungiven	Ballyness	- N. side Gelvin R.	mill	-	-	-	-	1839	-	6"os/	25
Dungiven	Ballyness	- on R. Bann	mill	-	-	-	-	-	-	1"os/	13
Dungiven	Ballyness	Boyle James	mill	-	-	-	Boyle Jas - Haslett Wm	1780	-	dd/	334 307 223320
Dungiven	Ballyness	Connolly Thos Hon.	mill & weir	-	-	-	Connolly T - Fox Henry :	1760	-	dd/	209 572 139585
Dungiven	Ballyness	Donegal Hon. Marq.	mill	-	-	-	Donegal Marq - May Ed :	1809	Lse. 1 Feb.	dd/	607 184 415421
Dungiven	Ballyness	Fox	mill & weir	-	-	-	Fox - Hoare	-	?	dd/	387 63 258854
Dungiven	Ballyness	Given James :	mill	-	-	-	Given J - Goold Pierce :	1805	Mort. 1 Sug.	dd/	573 174 386174
Dungiven	Ballyness	Grocers Company	mill & weir	-	-	-	Grocers Co - Connolly :	1761	-	dd/	209 566 139584
Dungiven	Ballyness	Hamilton H. T. Sir :	mill & weir	-	-	-	Hamilton - Macky Robt :	1775	-	dd/	370 358 252791
Dungiven	Ballyness	Hamilton Henry :	mill & weir	-	-	-	Hamilton - Nedham Robt :	1758	-	dd/	211 299 140138
Macosquin	Ballyness	Heyland Rowley	corn	-	-	-	-	-	14x4.11x4.6	osm/	-
Dungiven	Ballyness	Irwin Robert	corn & kiln	-	49a.	-	-	-	-	gr/	-
Dungiven	Ballyness	Masserene Wm Lynden	mill & weir	-	-	-	Masserene - Ashe Ben	1780	-	dd/	336 119 224085
Dungiven	Ballyness	Mauleverer Bellingham	mill	-	-	-	Mauleveer - Erskin :	1750	-	dd/	155 273 104565
Dungiven	Ballyness	McDougal Joseph	corn	- burned :	-	-	-	-	13.6x2 - undershot	osm/	-
Macosquin	Ballyness	Society The Irish	ruined mill	89.2x42.2 5 sty. :	-	-	-	c1808	-	osm/	-
Macosquin	Ballyness	Spencer John	corn & kiln	-	0-2-5	-	-	-	-	gr/	-
Dungiven	Ballyness	Strean Samuel	mill	-	-	-	Strean Sam - Given Jas	1780	-	dd/	330 629 225671
Tamlaght O`C.	Ballynian	Crilly John	flax	-	-	-	-	-	-	osm/	-
Aghadowey	Ballyoan	-	flax holes	-	-	-	-	1839	-	6"os/	14
Aghadowey	Ballyore	- R. Foyle, S. of City	mill	-	-	-	-	1839	-	6"os/	20
Aghadowey	Ballyquin	Knox John	beetling	-	-	-	-	-	18x4x4	osm/	-
Aghadowey	Ballyquin	Knox John	bleach green	- 2 slated houses	-	-	-	-	-	osm/	-
Aghadowey	Ballyquin	Knox John	wash	-	-	-	-	-	17x4x4	osm/	-
Artera	Ballyrogully	-	flax	-	-	-	-	-	-	1"os/	27
Artera	Ballyrogully	-	mill	-	-	-	-	-	-	1"os/	27
Ballinderry	Ballyronan	-	mill	-	-	-	-	-	-	1"os/	-
Arboe	Ballyronan Beg	- 1/8m. from L. Neagh	distillery	-	-	-	-	1839	-	6"os/	47
Arboe	Ballyronan Beg	Gaussen William	flax	-	-	-	-	-	-	gr/	-
Arboe	Ballyronan Beg	Gaussen William	flour	-	2a.	-	-	-	-	gr/	-
Arboe	Ballyronan More	-	dam & sluice	-	-	-	-	1839	-	6"os/	47
Aghadowey	Ballyshasky	- W side R. Faughan	bleaching	-	-	-	-	1839	-	6"os/	21

PARISH	TOWNLAND	MILLER	TYPE	HOUSE	Land	£Val	PROPRIETORS	Date	WHEEL etc.	Record	Ref.
Clondermot	Ballyshasky	M`Clelland Cary	bleaching	-	37a.	-	-	-	-	gr/	-
Ballyrashane	Ballyvelton Upr :	-	mill	-	-	-	-	-	-	6"os/	7
Macosquin	Ballyvennox	- Macosquin Town	mill	-	-	-	-	-	-	1"os/	13
Ballyrashane	Ballywatt East	-	flax	-	-	-	-	-	12x1.9x -	osm/	-
Ballyrashane	Ballywatt Leggs	-	corn	-	-	-	-	-	-	6"os/	4
Ballyrashane	Ballywatt Leggs	-	corn	-	-	-	-	-	13x1.10x -	osm/	-
Dunboe	Ballywildrick	Blair James	flax	-	-	-	-	-	11.2x1.6x3 breast :	osm/	-
Dunboe	Ballywildrick	Blair John Jun & Matt	flax	-	30a.	-	-	-	-	gr/	-
Aghadowey	Ballywillin	Bennett Thomas	corn	-	-	-	-	-	12x2x6	osm/	-
Aghadowey	Ballywillin	Bennett Thomas	flax	-	-	-	-	-	12.8x2.6x6	osm/	-
Aghadowey	Ballywillin	Thomas James	corn & kiln	-	-	-	-	-	-	gr/	-
Aghadowey	Ballywillin	Thomas James	flax	-	7-1-0		-	-	-	gr/	-
Dunboe	Ballywoodock	Blanchcard	mill	-	-	-	Blanchard - Ford	-	?	dd/	115 141 97313
Dunboe	Ballywoodock	Bruce	mill	-	-	-	Bruce & ors Decl Trust	-	?	dd/	562 561 375592
Dunboe	Ballywoodock	Bruce Henry Sir H. Bt.	mill pond	-	1.0.20		-	-	-	gr/	-
Dunboe	Ballywoodock	Graham Moses	flax	-	49a.	-	-	-	-	gr/	-
Dunboe	Ballywoodock	Graham William	corn & kiln	-	-	-	-	-	13.6x2x23	osm/	-
Dunboe	Ballywoodock	Graham William	flax	-	-	-	-	-	11.8x4.6x8	osm/	-
Dunboe	Ballywoodock :	Ford William :	mill	-	-	-	Ford William - Ford Jas :	1750	-	dd/	153 40 101536
Dunboe	Ballywoolen	Duggan isaac	corn & kiln	-	13a.	-	-	-	-	gr/	-
Coleraine	Balnamore	-	flax	-	-	-	-	-	-	1"os/	-
Coleraine	Balnamore	-	flax	-	-	-	-	-	-	1"os/	-
Coleraine	Balnamore	-	mill	-	-	-	-	-	-	1"os/	-
Macosquin	Balteagh Lower	Bullion John	flax	-	-	-	-	-	12.6x1.8x4.6	osm/	-
Ldy	Beech Hill *	McKenny Patrick :	mill	-	-	-	McKenny P - McKenny :	1759	-	dd/	202 168 133665
Magilligan	Belareena	Gage Connolly	corn & kiln	-	-	-	-	-	15.4x4.6x -	osm/	-
Ballyscullion	Bellaghy	- nr Bellaghy Town	flax	-	-	-	-	-	-	1"os/	27
Ballyscullion	Bellaghy	Connolly	corn & tuck	-	-	-	Connolly - Dougherty :	1734	8 Apl.	dd/	89 76 62140
Ballyscullion	Bellaghy	Boyle James	grist mill	-	-	-	Boyle Jas - Haslett Wm	1780	-	dd/	334 307 223326
Ballyscullion	Bellaghy	Connolly William Hon.	corn & tuck	-	-	-	Connolly - Dougherty Neil	1734	-	dd/	89 76 62140
Ballyscullion	Bellaghy	Given	grist mill	-	-	-	Given - Adair Bell	-	?	dd/	485 524 315240
Ballyscullion	Bellaghy	Given James :	grist mill :	-	-	-	Given J - Goold Pierce :	1805	Mort. 1 Sug.	dd/	573 174 386174
Ballyscullion	Bellaghy	Mauleverer Bellingham	mill	-	-	-	Mauleveer B - Erskin :	1750	-	dd/	155 273 104565
Ballyscullion	Bellaghy	Strean Samuel	grist mill	-	-	-	Strean S - Given James	1780	-	dd/	330 629 225671
Ballyscullion	Bellaghy Town	Cullen Andrew	corn	-	0-1-23		-	-	-	gr/	-
Magilligan	Bellarena	M`Quaid William	mill & kiln	-	-	-	-	-	-	gr/	-
Desertoghill	Boghilboy	Adams John	corn	-	134a.	-	-	-	-	gr/	-
Desertoghill	Boghilboy	Adams John	flax	-	-	-	-	-	-	gr/	-
Drumachose	Bolea	Hamilton Alex	mill	-	-	-	Hamilton A - E. Tyrone	1752	-	dd/	160 361 107867
Drumachose	Bolea :	Ker David	mill	-	-	-	Ker D - Alexander Robt	1780	-	dd/	332 360 224825
Drumachose	Bolea :	Bigham John of Bolea	mill	-	-	-	Bigham J - Erskin Henry	1750	-	dd/	155 488 105538
Drumachose	Bolea :	Erskine Henry :	mill	-	-	-	Erskine - Alexander Wm	1754	-	dd/	167 426 113092
Drumachose	Bolea :	-	pond, mill race	-	-	-	-	-	-	6"os/	10
Ldy	Boughilboy *	Jameson Robert	corn & 2 kilns	-	-	-	-	-	18x1.6x20.4	osm/	-
Ldy	Boughilboy *	Jameson Robert	flax	-	-	-	-	-	13x1.6x20.4 :	osm/	-
Aghadowey	Bovagh	-	corn	-	-	-	-	-	-	6"os/	-
Aghadowey	Bovagh	- at White Hill	mill	-	-	-	-	-	-	1"os/	27
Aghadowey	Bovagh	Leyland Langford :	mill	-	-	-	Heyland - Carleton Corns	1803	-	dd/	553 218 367661
Aghadowey	Bovagh	Milliken Wiliam	corn & kiln	-	32a.	-	-	-	-	gr/	-
Aghadowey	Bovagh	Milliken William	corn	-	-	-	-	-	14x1.10x -	osm/	-
Aghadowey	Bovagh	Tracy Athur :	I mill	-	-	-	Tracy A - Dickson Gus :	1789	-	dd/	416 44 273264
Desertmartin	Boveagh	-	flax	-	-	-	-	-	-	1"os/	27

PARISH	TOWNLAND	MILLER	TYPE	HOUSE	Land	£Val	PROPRIETORS	Date	WHEEL etc.	Record	Ref.
Desertmartin	Boveagh	-	flax	-	-	-	-	-	-	1"os/	27
Desertmartin	Boveagh	Bodkin James	corn & kiln	-	34a.	-	-	-	-	gr/	-
Desertmartin	Boveagh	Douglas James	flax	-	-	-	-	-	12x2.4x - & :	osm/	-
Desertmartin	Boveagh	Douglas James	flax & store	-	26a.	-	-	-	-	gr/	-
Tamlaght O`C	Bovedy	Warwick Robert	corn	-	81a.	50	-	-	-	gr/	-
Londonderry	Bovevagh	- S. side R. Roe	mill & stream	-	-	-	-	1839	-	6"os/	24
Londonderry	Boyagh	- S. side Agivey R.	corn & kiln	-	-	-	-	1839	-	6"os/	19
Lissan	Brackagh	Glendenning Robert	flax	-	21a.	-	-	-	-	gr/	-
Cumber Lr	Brackfield	Lyle Samuel	bleach	-	279a.	-	-	-	-	gr/	-
Termoneeny	Broagh	-	mill pond :	-	-	-	-	1839	-	6"os/	42
Termoneeny	Broagh	Miller Hugh	beetling	-	-	-	-	-	-	gr/	-
Termoneeny	Broagh	Miller Hugh	flax	-	9a.	-	-	-	-	gr/	-
Termoneeny	Broagh	Miller Thomas	beetling	-	-	-	-	-	-	gr/	-
Termoneeny	Broagh	Miller Thomas	flax	-	8a.	-	-	-	-	gr/	-
Londonderry	Brookhill *	-	mill	-	-	-	-	-	-	1"os/	11
Termoneeny	Cabragh	- near Knockadoo	flax	-	-	-	-	-	-	1"os/	27
Londonderry	Calmoney *	-	flax kiln	-	-	-	-	1839	-	6"os/	14
Kilcronaghan	Calmore	Wisner Andrew	corn	-	-	-	-	-	12x1.6x -	osm/	-
Lissan	Caneese	-	flax	-	-	-	-	-	-	1"os/	27
lissan	Caneese	-	flax	-	-	-	-	-	-	1"os/	27
Clondermot	Carn	- at Brackagh Br.	flax	-	-	-	-	-	-	1"os/	27
Ballywillin	Carnalridge	Livingstone Hugh	corn	-	-	-	-	-	- ceased 1828	osm/	-
Ballywillin	Carnalridge	Livingstone Hugh	flax	-	-	-	-	-	14x1.9x10	osm/	-
Banagher	Carnanbane	Stevenson James	flax	miller`s house	37a.	-	-	-	-	gr/	-
Learmount	Carnanreagh	- N. side Glenrandal R.	corn & kiln	-	-	-	-	1839	-	6"os/	29
Learmount	Carnanreagh	- N. side Glenrandal R.	tuck	-	-	-	-	1839	-	6"os/	29
Desertlyn	Carndaisy	Stewart Hannah	flax, mill pond	-	16a.	-	-	-	-	gr/	-
Balteagh	Carnet	- stream to Castle R.	walkmills	-	-	-	-	-	-	1"os/	12
Faughanvale	Carnkilly Upper	Duddy Edward	flax	-	23a.	-	-	-	-	gr/	-
Aghadowey	Carnrallagh	- on Aghadowey R.	bleach	-	-	-	-	-	-	1"os/	13
Artrea	Carraloan	-	corn kiln	-	-	-	-	1839	-	6"os/	47
Balteagh	Carrick East	Rodgers Marcus	bleach green	-	-	-	-	-	- ceased 1812	osm/	-
Faughanvale	Carrickhugh :	-	corn & flour	-	-	-	-	-	-	6"os/	9
Faughanvale	Carrickhugh :	-	flour	-	-	-	-	-	-	6"os/	10
Desertlyn	Carrydarragh	- NW. Moneymore Tn	mill, long race	-	-	-	-	1839	-	6"os/	46
Drumachose	Carrydoo	- at Bolea	flax	-	-	-	-	-	-	1"os/	18
Drumachose	Carrydoo	Cluskey Nathaniel	flax	-	57a.	33	-	-	-	gr/	-
Desertoghill	Carthabalintober	Linton William	flax	-	-	-	-	-	12x2.2x9.5	osm/	-
Macosquinn :	Cashel	-	bleach green	-	-	-	-	-	- on R Roe :	osm/	-
Ballynascreen	Cavanreagh	-	corn kiln, shed	-	-	-	-	1839	-	6"os/	40
Ballynascreen	Cavanreagh	-	mill & pond	-	-	-	-	1839	-	6"os/	40
Ballynascreen	Cavanreagh	McKelvey Neill	corn & 2 kilns	-	-	-	-	-	13.6x2x -	osm/	-
Ballynascreen	Cavanreagh	Patterson Alexander	corn	-	19a.	-	-	-	-	gr/	-
Londonderry	Churchtown *	-	flax	-	-	-	-	-	-	1"os/	27
Cumber Upper	Clady	- N. of R. Faughan	bleach	-	-	-	-	1839	-	6"os/	23
Cumber Upper	Clady	Courtnay James	corn	-	-	-	-	-	12x2.4x -	osm/	-
Cumber Upper	Clady Village	Marjetson Welch	shirt factory	-	-	-	-	-	-	gr/	-
Cumber Upper	Clady Village	Tillis & Henderson	shirt factory	-	-	-	-	-	-	gr/	-
Lissan	Clagan	-	spade or plate	-	-	-	-	-	- demolished	osm/	-
Lissan	Clagan	- at Dunman Bridge	flax	-	-	-	-	-	-	1"os/	-
Lissan	Clagan	- on Co. boundary	corn & dam	-	-	-	-	1839	-	6"os/	45
Lissan	Clagan	Aiken Robert	flax	-	91a.	-	-	-	-	gr/	-

PARISH	TOWNLAND	MILLER	TYPE	HOUSE	Land	£Val	PROPRIETORS	Date	WHEEL etc.	Record	Ref.
Lissan	Clagan	Conlon Mathew	corn	-	-	-	Ransay John	-	13.6x2.2x10	osm/	-
Lissan	Clagan	M`Keever John	beetling	-	24a.	-	-	-	-	gr/	-
Lissan	Clagan	Ramsay William & J	bleach	-	-	-	-	-	- ceased 1806 :	osm/	-
Kilrea	Claragh	- Kilreagh Town	mill	-	-	-	-	-	-	1"os/	19
Cumber Upr	Claudy	-	mills	-	-	-	-	-	-	1"os/	19
Balteagh	Cloghan	- near Castle R.	flax	-	-	-	-	-	-	1"os/	12
Derryloran	Cloghog	Glascow Reps Robert	spinning	-	40a.	-	-	-	-	gr/	-
Faughanvale	Cloghole	- E. side Faughan R.	corn & kiln	-	-	-	-	1839	-	6"os/	14
Clandermot	Clondermot	Douglas Joseph	corn	-	4a.	-	-	-	-	gr/	-
Clandermot	Clondermot	Henderson James	flax	-	10a.	-	-	-	-	gr/	-
Clandermot	Clooney	- Tobermore Town	mills	-	-	-	-	-	-	1"os/	19
Clandermot	Clooney	Meehan John	brewery	-	5a.	-	-	-	-	gr/	-
Ballynascreen	Cloughfin	-	corn kiln	-	-	-	-	1839	-	6"os/	40
Templemore	Cloughglass	Smith William D	thrashing	-	87a.	-	-	-	-	gr/	-
Coleraine	Coleraine	- at Farm Hill		-	-	-	-	-	-	1"os/	13
Coleraine	Coleraine	Glenn William	flax	-	-	-	-	-	12x1.6x -	osm/	-
Coleraine	Coleraine	Rennie John Hill	corn & 5 kilns	- 4 storey	-	-	-	-	24x5x15	osm/	-
Coleraine	Coleraine :	Jackson William :	bleach yard	-	-	-	Jackson W - Todd Isaac	1734	-	dd/	82 207 57560
Coleraine	Coleraine Libs.	Brown William	mill	-	-	-	Brown W - Bacon Robt	1711	-	dd/	10 44 3015
Coleraine	Coleraine Libs.	Browne William :	mill	-	-	-	Brown W - Bacon Robt :	1729	-	dd/	63 346 43857
Coleraine	Coleraine Town	Bellas Hugh & Thos	corn store, kiln	-	-	-	-	-	-	gr/	-
Coleraine	Coleraine Town	Bellas Hugh & Thos	kiln & store	-	-	-	-	-	-	gr/	-
Coleraine	Coleraine Town	Coyle Jas Hamilton	sawing	-	-	-	-	-	-	gr/	-
Coleraine	Coleraine Town	Coyle Mary	old saw mill	-	-	-	Coyle Mary - Church Wm	1892	-	dd/	1892 55 24
Coleraine	Coleraine Town	Crookshank William	Tullans Mill	-	-	-	Crookshank - Keith Andr	1888	-	dd/	1888 39 123
Coleraine	Coleraine Town	Gribben Edward	weaving fcty	-	-	-	-	-	-	gr/	-
Coleraine	Coleraine Town	Gribben John	hand weaving	-	-	-	-	-	-	gr/	-
Coleraine	Coleraine Town	Hamilton James	sawing	-	-	-	-	-	-	gr/	-
Coleraine	Coleraine Town	Irwin John	corn & kilns	-	-	-	-	-	-	gr/	-
Coleraine	Coleraine Town	Kennedy Hugh	iron foundry	-	0-0-23		-	-	-	gr/	-
Coleraine	Coleraine Town	Lawrence Samuel	steam mill, kiln	-	-	-	-	-	-	gr/	-
Coleraine	Coleraine Town	Montgomery Robert	Rashane Mill	-	-	-	Montgomery Robt - Hu.	1852	-	dd/	1852 17 155
Coleraine	Coleraine Town	Moore James	corn & kiln	-	-	-	-	-	-	gr/	-
Coleraine	Coleraine Town	Moore James	distillery	-	-	-	-	-	-	gr/	-
Coleraine	Coleraine Town	Moore James	flax & stores	-	-	-	-	-	-	gr/	-
Coleraine	Coleraine Town	Moore James	malt houses	-	-	-	-	-	-	gr/	-
Coleraine	Coleraine Town	Northern Bank Co.	Coleraine Distillery		-	-	N.B. C. - Taylor Daniel	1888	-	dd/	1888 24 180
Coleraine	Coleraine Town	Taylor Robert	mills	-	-	-	Taylor R - Taylor Daniel	1878	-	dd/	1878 33 158
Coleraine	Coleraine Town :	Patton Samuel	mill	-	-	-	Patton S - McNeill Jno	1852	-	dd/	1852 29 124
Coleraine	Coleraine Town :	Patton Samuel	mill	-	-	-	Patton - Anderson Hen	1853	-	dd/	1853 8 36
Coleraine	Coleraine Town :	Henn William	mill	-	-	-	Henn Wm - Church Wm	1846	-	dd/	1846 12 266
Coleraine	Coleraine Town :	McNaughton Barth.	mill	-	-	-	Mcnaughton - M`gomery	1839	-	dd/	1839 12 97
Coleraine	Coleraine Town :	Taylor John	distillery	-	-	-	Taylor J - Taylor Robt.	1895	-	dd/	1895 6277
Coleraine	Coleraine Town :	Given Andrew	mills	-	-	-	Given A - McCurdy Jno	1843	-	dd/	1843 13 76
Coleraine	Coleraine Town :	Remember 2nd	mills	-	-	-	Rember - Given Andr	1842	-	dd/	1842 7 230
Coleraine	Coleraine Town :	Boyd John	corn & kiln	-	-	-	Boyd John - Rennie Jn	1835	-	dd/	1835 5 253
Coleraine	Coleraine Town :	Hayes Robert	mill	-	-	-	Hughes - McFadden J	1879	-	dd/	1879 40 255
Coleraine	Coleraine Town :	McFadden John	mill	-	-	-	McFadden - Cr`shank R	1879	-	dd/	1879 40 256
Coleraine	Coleraine Town :	Andrews William	mill	-	-	-	Andrews - Boyse Sam	1834	-	dd/	1834 19 65
Coleraine	Coleraine Town :	McNaughten Barth.	mill	-	-	-	Mcnaughten B - DD Poll	1845	-	dd/	1845 19 127
Coleraine	Coleraine Town :	McNeale Jno	distillery	-	-	-	McNeale J - Moore Jas	1848	-	dd/	1848 19 92
Coleraine	Coleraine Town :	Henn William	new mill	-	-	-	Henn Wm - Church Wm	1846	-	dd/	1846 12 266

PARISH	TOWNLAND	MILLER	TYPE	HOUSE	Land	£Val	PROPRIETORS	Date	WHEEL etc.	Record	Ref.
Coleraine	Coleraine Town :	Taylor Paul	corn	-	-	-	Taylor - Leech Hunt W	1878	-	dd/	1878 18 252
Aghadowey	Collins	-	corn	-	-	-	-	1839	-	6"os/	1
Aghadowey	Collins	Wilson John	beetling	-	-	-	-	-	17x5x13	osm/	-
Aghadowey	Collins	Wilson John	bleach green	long 2 storey slated	-	-	-	-	-	osm/	-
Aghadowey	Collins	Wilson John	corn	-	-	-	-	-	13x1.8x6	osm/	-
Aghadowey	Collins	Wilson John	wash	-	-	-	-	-	16.6x4.9x13	osm/	-
Aghadowey	Collins	Wilson Maria	corn & kiln	-	-	-	-	-	-	gr/	-
Aghadowey	Collins	Wilson Maria	flax	-	81a.	-	-	-	-	gr/	-
Aghadowey	Collins Lower	- on Macosquin R.	flax	-	-	-	-	-	-	1"os/	13
Lissan	Coltrim	-	ladle	-	-	-	-	-	- ancient ladle mill	osm/	-
Drumachose	Coolessan	Lane Hugh	distillery	-	-	-	-	-	-	gr/	-
Drumachose	Coolessan	Lane Hugh	mill	-	0-2-5	110.0	-	-	-	gr/	-
Drumachose	Coolessan :	-	distillery	-	-	-	-	-	-	6"os/	9
Errigal	Coolnasillagh	Mullan Patrick	corn	ceased in 1795	-	-	-	-	-	osm/	-
Kilcronaghan	Coolsaragh	Otterson James	flax	-	42a.	-	-	-	-	gr/	-
Templemore	Coshquin	Gibson Charles	corn	-	102a.	-	-	-	-	gr/	-
Templemore	Coshquin	Gibson Charles	flax	-	-	-	-	-	-	gr/	-
Templemore	Coshquin	Young James	flax	-	52a.	-	-	-	-	gr/	-
Dungiven	Crabarkey	- N. side R. Roe	mill	-	-	-	-	1839	-	6"os/	31
Dungiven	Crabarkey	- N. side R. Roe	mill	-	-	-	-	1839	-	6"os/	31
Dungiven	Crabarkey	- on Glen R	flax	-	-	-	-	-	-	1"os/	18
Magilligan	Craig	M`Corstin George	mill & kiln	-	3a.	-	-	-	-	gr/	-
Magilligan	Craig	McCoriston Edward	corn	-	-	-	-	-	14x2.4x -	osm/	-
Maghera	Craigadick	Clarke Alex	corn	-	-	-	-	-	14x2.4x10	osm/	-
Maghera	Craigadick	Craig James J	corn & kilns	-	134a.	-	-	-	-	gr/	-
Maghera	Craigadick :	-	brewery	-	-	-	-	1839	-	6"os/	36
Desertoghill	Craigavole	-	flax	-	-	-	-	1839	-	6"os/	26
Desertoghill	Craigavole	Boyle John	snuff	-	-	-	-	-	-	osm/	-
Desertoghill	Craigavole	Garvin James	flax	-	-	-	-	-	11.6x1.10x9.6	osm/	-
Ballyaughran	Craigtown More	Keith Isaac	flax	-	-	-	-	-	-	gr/	-
Dungiven	Crebarkley	- on R. Roe	flax	-	-	-	-	-	13x2x10 & :	osm/	-
Dungiven	Crebarkley	Ogilby Robert	flax	- burned/rebuilt `32	-	-	-	-	13x2x10	osm/	-
Clondermot	Creeve	- nr Greggan Br.	flax	-	-	-	-	-	-	1"os/	-
Cumber Upper	Cregg	M`Candless Thomas	corn	-	-	-	-	-	-	gr/	-
Cumber Upper	Cregg	M`Candless Thomas	corn	-	19a.	-	-	-	-	gr/	-
Cumber Upper	Cregg	M`Candless Thomas	old flax mill	-	19a.	-	-	-	-	gr/	-
Cumber Upper	Cregg	McCandless Thomas	corn	-	-	-	Browne John, Comber	-	-	osm/	-
Cumber Upper	Cregg	McCandless Thomas	flax	-	-	-	Browne John, Comber	-	-	osm/	-
Maghera	Crew	Kissick William	flax	-	-	-	-	-	12x1.8x14	osm/	-
Maghera	Crew	Kissock William	flax (2)	-	19a.	-	-	-	-	gr/	-
Errigal	Crockindollagh	Wilson Robert	flax	-	-	-	Wallace John & William	1836	12x1.8x7.6	osm/	-
Londonderry	Crossare	- nr Macosquin R.	mill	-	-	-	-	1839	-	6"os/	11
Errigal	Crosshill	- at Crockindollagh	flax	-	-	-	-	-	-	1"os/	13
Desertoghill	Cullyramer	-	flax	-	-	-	-	1839	-	6"os/	19
Maghera	Culnady	-	pond (no mill)	-	-	-	-	1839	-	6"os/	32
Maghera	Culnady	Clarke Alex	corn	-	-	-	-	-	14x2.3x9.6	osm/	-
Maghera	Culnady	Henry John	flax	-	-	-	-	-	12x2x6.4	osm/	-
Maghera	Culnady	Henry John	flax	-	-	-	-	-	12x2x9	osm/	-
Maghera	Culnady	Henry John Jun	flax (2)	-	24a.	-	-	-	-	gr/	-
Maghera	Culnady	Lytle James	corn	-	18-2-C	-	-	-	-	gr/	-
Maghera	Culnady	Lytle James	flax	-	-	-	-	-	-	gr/	-
Killelagh	Culnagrew	Donnelly Patrick	flax	-	7a.	-	-	-	-	gr/	-

PARISH	TOWNLAND	MILLER	TYPE	HOUSE	Land	£Val	PROPRIETORS	Date	WHEEL etc.	Record	Ref.
Maghera	Culnagrew	McReynolds Thomas	flax	-	-	-	-	-	12x2.2x8	osm/	-
Agivey	Culrow	- at Milltown	mill	-	-	-	-	-	-	1"os/	13
Agivey	Culrow	- S. bridge Agivey R.	mill	-	-	-	-	1839	-	6"os/	12
Agivey	Culrow	M`Intyre William	corn & kiln	-	1a.	2	-	-	-	gr/	-
Agivey	Culrow	Wilson John	corn	-	-	-	-	-	13x1.3x6.6	osm/	-
Maghera	Curragh	Dorrety William	flax 1833 corn	-	-	-	-	-	12.4x1.7x8.6	osm/	-
Maghera	Curragh	Houston John	flax	-	7a.	-	-	-	-	gr/	-
Maghera	Curran	Connolly William Hon.	corn & tuck	-	-	-	Connolly - Dougherty Neil	1734	-	dd/	89 76 62140
Maghera	Curran	Rodgers George	corn	-	-	-	-	-	12x4.3x3	osm/	-
Maghera	Curran	Rogers George	mill	-	-	-	-	-	-	gr/	-
Faughvane	Curryfree	Hamilton William J	thrashing	-	143a.	-	-	-	-	gr/	-
Londonderry	Deer Park	- N. side R. Roe	bleach	-	-	-	-	1839	-	6"os/	16
Faughanvale	Derryarkin	Cowan William	flax	-	149a.	-	-	-	-	gr/	-
Banagher	Derrychrier	-	corn & tuck	-	-	-	-	1839	-	6"os/	30
Banagher	Derrychrier	- E. of Owenbeg R.	flax	-	-	-	-	1839	-	6"os/	24
Banagher	Derrychrier	- nr Owenbeg Br.	mill	-	-	-	-	-	-	1"os/	18
Banagher	Derrychrier	- on Owenbeg R.	flax	-	-	-	-	-	-	1"os/	18
Banagher	Derrychrier	Cooke Margaret	corn	-	60a.	-	-	-	-	gr/	-
Banagher	Derrychrier	Wilson George	flax	-	26a.	-	-	-	-	gr/	-
Londonderry	Derrycrin	- SW. Ballinderry Br.	corn & pond	-	-	-	-	1839	-	6"os/	49
Derryloran	Derrycrummy	- near Glebe House	flax	-	-	-	-	-	-	1"os/	-
Derryloran	Derrycrummy	Lyn John	flax	-	52a.	47.15/	-	-	-	gr/	-
Boveagh	Derrylane	-	mill & pond	-	-	-	-	1839	-	6"os/	24
Boveagh	Derrylane	Kane Thomas	corn & kiln	miller`s house	5a.	-	-	-	-	gr/	-
Boveagh	Derrylane	McSparran John Arch	corn	-	-	-	-	-	12x1.9x9	osm/	-
Boveagh	Derrylane	Ritchie John	ancient mill	-	-	-	-	-	-	osm/	-
Dungiven	Derryork	- Derryork	Flax Mill	-	-	-	-	1839	-	6"os/	25
Dungiven	Derryork	McCloskey John	flax	-	-	-	-	-	12x2x - undershot	osm/	-
Dungiven	Derryork	Miller William	flax	-	5a.	12.15/	-	-	-	gr/	-
Faughanvane	Deryarkin Upr	Cowan William	flax	-	159a.	-	-	-	-	gr/	-
Desertmartin	Desertmartin	- on Grangewater	corn	-	-	-	-	-	-	1"os/	27
Desertmartin	Desertmartin Tn	- on Grangewater	mill	-	-	-	-	-	-	1"os/	27
Tamlaght Ard	Dondoan :	-	mill	-	-	-	-	-	-	6"os/	3
Faughanvane	Donnybrewer	Scott Thomas	flax	-	241a.	-	-	-	-	gr/	-
Tamlaght-Fin.	Dromore	-	corn & stream	-	-	-	-	1839	-	6"os/	16
Tamlaght-Fin.	Dromore	Gilfillen J & Forrest D	flax & store	-	-	-	-	-	-	gr/	-
Tamlaght-Fin.	Dromore	Gilfillen John	corn	-	5a.	-	-	-	-	gr/	-
Tamlaght-Fin.	Dromore	Morrison Robert	flax	-	-	-	-	-	12x1.8x4 & :	osm/	-
Tamlaght-Fin.	Drum	Cavin Samuel	flax	-	3a.	-	-	-	-	gr/	-
Tamlaght-Fin.	Drum	Cavin Samuel	mill dam	-	0-0-35	-	-	-	-	gr/	-
Tamlaght O`C.	Drumacannon	Smyth Andrew	corn	-	-	-	-	-	13.6x1.10x -	osm/	-
Balteagh	Drumagoosker	- on Castle R.	flax	-	-	-	-	1839	-	6"os/	17
Balteagh	Drumagoosker	- on Castle R.	flax & kiln	-	-	-	-	1839	-	6"os/	17
Balteagh	Drumagoosker	- on Castle R.	flax pond	-	-	-	-	1839	-	6"os/	17
Balteagh	Drumagoosker	Boyce John	flax	-	-	-	-	-	14x2.6x8 & :	osm/	-
Balteagh	Drumagoosker	Boyle Edward	flax scutching	-	2a.	-	-	-	-	gr/	-
Clandermot	Drumahoe	-	flax holes	-	-	-	-	1839	-	6"os/	21
Clandermot	Drumahoe	- on R. Faughan	mills	-	-	-	-	-	-	1"os/	-
Clandermot	Drumahoe	M`Clelland Wm & Co.	corn	-	-	-	-	-	-	gr/	-
Clandermot	Drumahoe	Smith William D & Co.	flour	-	-	-	-	-	-	gr/	-
Ballyscullion	Drumanee	Bateson Earl Sir Robt	flax & mill dam	-	-	-	-	-	-	gr/	-
Lissan	Drumard	Barfoot Henry	flax	-	34a.	-	-	-	-	gr/	-

PARISH	TOWNLAND	MILLER	TYPE	HOUSE	Land	£Val	PROPRIETORS	Date	WHEEL etc.	Record	Ref.
Faughvane	Drumconan	Bredin Ezekiel & Sam	flax	-	59a.	-	-	-	-	gr/	-
Macosquin	Drumcroon	Wilson John	beetling	-	-	-	-	-	16.10x5x12 & :	osm/	-
Macosquin	Drumcroon	Wilson John	bleach green	-	-	-	-	-	- ceased bl. 1820	osm/	-
Macosquin	Drumcroon	Wilson John	wash	-	-	-	-	-	4.6x3x2x9.6 & :	osm/	-
Balteagh	Drumgavenny	-	flax	-	-	-	-	-	-	1"os/	12
Balteagh	Drumgavenny	-	flax	-	-	-	-	-	13x2.6x12 breast :	osm/	-
Balteagh	Drumgavenny	-	rolling flax	-	-	-	-	-	- breast	osm/	-
Balteagh	Drumgavenny	- above Black Rd.	flax & pond	-	-	-	-	1839	-	6"os/	17
Balteagh	Drumgavenny Lr	Loughry William	flax scutching	-	61a.	-	-	-	-	gr/	-
Tamlaght	Druminard	Hutchinson Thomas	flax	-	17a.	-	-	-	-	gr/	-
Maghera	Drumlamph	Cavin Samuel	flax & mill dam	-	3a.	-	-	-	-	gr/	-
Maghera	Drumlamph	Cunnungham David	flax	-	-	-	-	-	12x4x6 12 berths	osm/	-
Ballynaherry	Drummond	- on Castle R.	corn	-	-	-	-	-	-	1"os/	12
Arboe	Drummullan	Dunbar John	corn & kiln	-	20a.	-	-	-	-	gr/	-
Arboe	Drummullan	Dunbar John	flax	-	-	-	-	-	-	gr/	-
Londonderry	Drumnacanon :	-	dam & mill race	(no mill)	-	-	-	1839	-	6"os/	33
Macosquin	Drumoyagh	- on Macosquin R.	flax	-	-	-	-	-	-	1"os/	13
Tamlaght-Fin.	Drumraghland	Gresham David	turning	-	-	-	-	-	5x1x3	osm/	-
Derryloran	Drumrot	-	corn kiln	-	-	-	-	1839	-	6"os/	48
Ballyaughran	Drumslade	Leslie Henry	mill	-	80a.	-	-	-	-	gr/	-
Aghadowey	Drumsteeple	Barr Higginbotham	flax	-	-	-	-	-	-	gr/	-
Balteagh	Drumsurn	- near Castle R.	flax	-	-	-	-	-	-	1"os/	12
Balteagh	Drumsurn Upr	-	"Giants Mill"	-	-	-	-	-	- large pieces :	osm/	-
Londonderry	Drumulan	- N. of Little Bridge	corn & stream	-	-	-	-	1839	-	6"os/	48
Magheraghfelt	Dunamoney	- nr Magherafelt	flax	-	-	-	-	-	-	1"os/	27
Londonderry	Dunboe	Duggan Isaac Jun	corn & kiln	-	18a.	-	-	-	-	gr/	-
Magilligan	Duncrun	Gage Connolly	flax	- formerly bl green	-	-	-	-	15x2.4	osm/	-
Macosquin	Dunderg	Thompson Robert	bleach	-	12a.	-	-	-	-	gr/	-
Macosquin	Dunderg	Thompson Robert	bleach green	-	14a.	-	-	-	-	osm/	-
Macosquin	Dunderg	Thompson Robert	engine ho	-	-	-	-	-	16x2.11x6, 14x4.9x7	osm/	-
Macosquin	Dunderg	Thompson Robert	wash	-	-	-	-	-	16x4x6	osm/	-
Coleraine	Dundoonan	-	corn	destroyed 1820 :	-	-	-	-	-	osm/	-
Coleraine	Dundoonan	Black William	corn	-	-	-	-	-	13x1.6x8	osm/	-
Coleraine	Dundoonan	Glenn William	flax	-	-	-	-	-	11.6x1.4x10	osm/	-
Balteagh	Dungavanny Lr	- unoccupied	bleach green	-	-	-	-	-	- ceased 1800	osm/	-
Balteagh	Dungavanny Lr	- unoccupied	bleach green	-	-	-	-	-	- ceased 1819	osm/	-
Dungiven	Dungiven	-	bleach green	-	-	-	-	-	- on R Roe	osm/	-
Dungiven	Dungiven	Irwin James	corn & kiln	-	-	228	-	-	-	gr/	-
Dungiven	Dungiven	Irwin Samuel	corn & 2 kilns	-	-	-	-	-	14x3 mill very old &	osm/	-
Cumber Upper	Dungorkin	-	flax	-	-	-	-	-	-	osm/	-
Cumber Upper	Dungorkin	Gibson Thomas	flax	-	70a.	-	-	-	-	gr/	-
Desertmartin	Durnascallon	- at Hollymount	mill	-	-	-	-	-	-	1"os/	27
Desertmartin	Durnascallon	Leeper William	flax	-	67a.	-	-	-	-	gr/	-
Londonderry	Eden	- E. of Eden Br.	tuck, dam, race	-	-	-	-	1839	-	6"os/	30
Templemore	Edenballymore	- 3/4m. NW. L`derry	corn & pond	-	-	-	-	1839	-	6"os/	13
Templemore	Edenballymore	Stewart Abraham H	thrashing	-	30a.	-	-	-	-	gr/	-
Templemore	Edenballymore	Watt David & Samuel	steam	-	-	-	-	-	-	gr/	-
Templemore	Edenballymore :	M`Clelland Matthew	saw	-	-	-	-	-	-	gr/	-
Templemore	Edenballymore :	Carson James & Co.	brewery	-	-	-	-	-	-	gr/	-
Templemore	Edenballymore :	Coppin William	foundry	-	-	-	-	-	-	gr/	-
Templemore	Edenballymore :	Watt David & Samuel	distillery	-	-	-	-	-	-	gr/	-
Templemore	Edenballymore :	Allen Robert	old brewery	-	-	-	-	-	-	gr/	-

PARISH	TOWNLAND	MILLER	TYPE	HOUSE	Land	£Val	PROPRIETORS	Date	WHEEL etc.	Record	Ref.
Clondermot	Edenreaghmore	-	flax hole	-	-	-	-	1839	-	6"os/	14
Clondermot	Edenreaghmore	-	Grocer`s Mill	-	-	-	-	1839	-	6"os/	14
Macosquin	Englishtown	Pollock William	bleach	-	-	10	-	-	-	gr/	-
Macosquin	Englishtown	Smith John A	beetling	-	-	-	-	-	16x6.10x10 & :	osm/	-
Macosquin	Englishtown	Smith John A	bleach green	-	-	-	-	-	-	osm/	-
Macosquin	Englishtown	Smith John A	wash	-	-	-	-	-	14x4x10	osm/	-
Enniskillen	Enniskillen Town	Enniskillen Earl of	Windmill Hill	-	-	-	Enniskillen - Hunter Rd	1878		dd/	1878 29 92
Enniskillen	Enniskillen Town	Nolan Elizabeth	Windmill Hill	-	-	-	Nolan Eliz - Enniskillen E	1879		dd/	1879 29 121
Enniskillen	Enniskillen Town:	Gamble Baptist	brewery	-	-	-	Gamble - Downes Wm	1877		dd/	1877 24255
Kilrea	Fallahogy	Gordon James	flax	stone, thatched ho.	-	-	-	-	13.6x1.6x6	osm/	-
Londonderry	Fallowlea	-	Grocer`s Hall	-	-	-	-	1839	-	6"os/	14
Londonderry	Faltgortreevy	- at Milltown	mill	-	-	-	-	-	-	1"os/	19
Londonderry	Fawney	- at The Cross	mills	-	-	-	-	-	-	1"os/	17
Banagher	Fincarn	Mc+C677Cluskey Denis	flax	-	20a.	-	-	-	-	gr/	-
Kildollagh	Fishloughan	-	flax	-	-	-	-	-	-	6"os/	-
Killdollagh	Fishloughan	Cox Robert	mill	-	34a.	-	-	-	-	gr/	-
Londonderry	Flanders	- nr Kilblought Br	corn	-	-	-	-	-	-	1"os/	18
Londonderry	Gallanny	- N. of Fincarn Br.	corn & old dam	-	-	-	-	1839	-	6"os/	30
Londonderry	Gallanny	- N. side of Water	old flax mill	-	-	-	-	1839	-	6"os/	30
Banagher	Gallany	Stevenson John	flax	-	81a.	-	-	-	-	gr/	-
Banagher	Gallany	Witherow George	flax	-	23a.	-	-	-	-	gr/	-
Ballyaghram	Galvally	Campbell William	corn	-	-	-	Cromie John	-	14x1.6x8	osm/	-
Cumber Upper	Galvally	Cromie John	flax	-	-	-	-	-	12x1.6x7	osm/	-
Errigal	Garvagh Town	- on Agive R.	mill	-	-	-	-	-	-	1"os/	13
Londonderry	Glasgort	- S. siide Agivey R.	pottery	-	-	-	-	1839	-	6"os/	12
Tamlaght-Fin.	Glasvey	Limerick George	flax	-	-	-	-	-	14x3.6x - & :	osm/	-
Errigal	Glenkeen	Kerr Bernard	corn	single storey :	-	-	-	-	13x1.8x8	osm/	-
Ballywillin	Glenmanus	-	corn	-	-	-	-	-	-	6"os/	3
Ballywillin	Glenmanus	Glenn Hugh	corn & kiln	-	-	-	-	-	-	osm/	-
Tamlaght O`C	Glenone	Courtney James	beetling	-	-	-	-	-	-	gr/	-
Tamlaght O`C	Glenone	Courtney James	corn	-	26a.	-	-	-	-	gr/	-
Clandermot	Gobnascale :	M`Kinlay John	saw	-	-	-	-	-	-	gr/	-
Clandermot	Gobnascale :	Newton Robert William	steam	-	-	-	-	-	-	gr/	-
Londonderry	Gortaheerty Upr	-	flax hole	-	-	-	-	1839	-	6"os/	14
Kilcronaghan	Gortahurk	Orr George	corn	-	-	-	-	-	-	osm/	-
Londonderry	Gorteeny	- near Eglinton	flax	-	-	-	-	-	-	1"os/	12
Errigal	Gortfad	Dripps Robert	corn	-	1a.	-	-	-	-	gr/	-
Errigal	Gortfad	M`Cluskey	flax	-	17a.	-	-	-	-	gr/	-
Errigal	Gortfad	McCullagh James	sawing	-	-	-	-	-	12.7x1.9x -	osm/	-
Errigal	Gortfad	Ogilby Robert (formerly	beetling	-	-	-	-	-	13.10x4x machinery	osm/	-
Errigal	Gortfad	Ogilby Robert (formerly	bleach green	-	-	-	-	-	-	osm/	-
Errigal	Gortfad	Ogilby Robert (formerly	wash	-	-	-	-	-	12.3x3.8x -	osm/	-
Errigal	Gortfad	Woodburn William	flax	-	-	-	-	-	12.7x1.9x6	osm/	-
Ldy	Gorticross	-	flax holes	-	-	-	-	1839	-	6"os/	14
Coolhill	Gortin	-	flax	-	-	-	-	-	-	1"os/	13
Mayoghill	Gortin	Clarke William	beetling	-	3.0.20	-	-	-	-	gr/	-
Aghadowey	Gortin	Conn Samuel	beetling	-	-	-	-	-	14.8x5x3 13x4.4x1	osm/	-
Aghadowey	Gortin	Conn Samuel	bleach green	-	-	-	Orr Andrews Keely	-	-	osm/	-
Aghadowey	Gortin	Conn Samuel	wash	-	-	-	-	-	13x3.7x2	osm/	-
Londonderry	Gortnaran	- N. of R. Faughan	corn & mill race	-	-	-	-	1839	-	6"os/	23
Londonderry	Gortnaran	- nr Lettermuck Br.	corn	-	-	-	-	-	-	1"os/	18
Londonderry	Gracefield	- on Burnbunley	flax	-	-	-	-	-	-	1"os/	-

PARISH	TOWNLAND	MILLER	TYPE	HOUSE	Land	£Val	PROPRIETORS	Date	WHEEL etc.	Record	Ref.
Killelagh	Granacohan	MacAnellagh James	flax	-	-	-	Built by Mercers` Co.	-	12x1.10x4.6	osm/	-
Londonderry	Granagh	- S./ Swatragh Town	mill & dam	-	-	-	-	1839	-	6"os/	32
Killelagh	Granaghan	Quinn James	flax	-	17a.	-	-	-	-	gr/	-
Desertmartin	Grange	-	old mill pond :	-	-	-	-	1839	-	6"os/	41
Londonderry	Greenan	-	flax holes	-	-	-	-	1839	-	6"os/	14
Londonderry	Gregardvardan *	Stewart	mills	-	-	-	Stewart - Bacon	-	-	dd/	74 453 52036
Maghera	Grillagh	Cunningham Robert	flax	-	43a.	-	-	-	-	gr/	-
Tamlaght O`C.	Inisrush	Courtnay James	corn	-	-	-	-	-	14x2.8x2	osm/	-
Tamlaght O`C.	Inisrush	Courtnay James	flax	-	-	-	-	-	12.6x2.2x -	osm/	-
Tamlaght O`C.	Inisrush	Courtnay James	shelling	-	-	-	-	-	14x2.8x2	osm/	-
Errigal	Inshaleen	- W side Agivey R.	bleach	-	-	-	-	1839	-	6"os/	18
Errigal	Inshaleen	Rankin David	beetling	-	-	-	-	-	14.8x3.2x -	osm/	-
Errigal	Inshaleen	Rankin David	bleach	-	-	-	-	-	14x3.8x -	osm/	-
Errigal	Inshaleen	Rankin David	bleach green	-	-	-	-	-	-	osm/	-
Londonderry	Inshrush	-	race (no mill)	-	-	-	-	1839	-	6"os/	33
Ballyrashane	Island Effrick	-	paper	-	-	-	-	-	29x3.3x - breast :	osm/	-
Aghadowey	Keely	- on Aghadowey R.	flax	-	-	-	-	-	-	1"os/	13
Aghadowey	Keely & Rusky	Blair John	beetling	-	-	-	Orr Andrew of Keely	-	18x5.4x12	osm/	-
Aghadowey	Keely & Rusky	Blair John	bleach green	-	-	-	Orr Andrew of Keely	-	-	osm/	-
Aghadowey	Keely & Rusky	Blair John	wash	-	-	-	Orr Andrew of Keely	-	20x3x20 13x2x20	osm/	-
Ballyscullion	Kilberry	Orral James	mill dam	-	3-3-0		-	-	-	gr/	-
Desertmartin	Kilboggin	Palmer Jane Widow :	grist mills	-	-	-	Palmer J - Palmer Ann	1734	Conv. 24 May	dd/	76 162 53395
Templemore	Killea	Hagan Patrick	flax	-	35a.	-	-	-	-	gr/	-
Londonderry	Killta	- nr Co. boundary	mill & pond	-	-	-	-	1839	-	6"os/	20
Londonderry	Killtoney	-	flax	-	-	-	-	-	-	1"os/	27
Macosquin	Killure	Lynd John	flax	-	70a.	-	-	-	-	gr/	-
Macosquin	Killure	Lynn John	flax	-	-	-	-	-	15.6x3.5x12.10	osm/	-
Londonderry	Killybasky	- nr The Mullans	flax	-	-	-	-	-	-	1"os/	27
Londonderry	Killybasky	- W. side sm. river	corn kiln	-	-	-	-	1839	-	6"os/	48
Londonderry	Killybasky	- W. side sm. river	old mill	-	-	-	-	1839	-	6"os/	48
Desertmartin	Killyboggin	-	corn	-	-	-	-	-	12x2	osm/	-
Desertmartin	Killyboggin	Pherson Wiliam	corn & kiln	-	2-3-0		-	-	-	gr/	-
Cumber Upper	Killycor	- E. side R. Faughan	mill	-	-	-	-	1839	-	6"os/	23
Cumber Upper	Killycor	- in field, N. of river	old mill	-	-	-	-	1839	-	6"os/	23
Cumber Upper	Killycor	- on R. Faughan	mill	-	-	-	-	-	-	1"os/	8
Cumber Upper	Killycor	Miller John	corn	-	-	-	Fishmongers` Co.	-	-	osm/	-
Cumber Upper	Killycor	Miller John	corn & kiln	-	-	-	-	-	-	gr/	-
Cumber Upper	Killycor	Miller John	flax	miller`s house	20a.	-	-	-	-	gr/	-
Cumber Upper	Killycor	Miller John	flax	-	-	-	Fishmongers` Co.	-	-	osm/	-
Tamlaght O`C	Killygullib Glebe	Anderson Robert	flax	-	20a.	-	-	-	-	gr/	-
Aghadowey	Killykergan	Nolan & Taffe	beetling	-	-	-	-	-	14x4x -	osm/	-
Aghadowey	Killykergan	Nolan & Taffe	bleach green	-	-	-	-	-	-	osm/	-
Aghadowey	Killykergan	Nolan & Taffe	wash	-	-	-	-	-	14x4x -	osm/	-
Desertoghill	Killyvally	- imed. E. Garvagh Tn	corn	-	-	-	-	1839	-	6"os/	18
Desertoghill	Killyvally	Cochran John	corn & kiln	-	-	-	Bishop of Meath	-	-	osm/	-
Desertoghill	Killyvally	M`Alister Alexander	corn	-	5a.	-	-	-	-	gr/	-
Kilrea	Kilrea	Craig Alex	corn & flour	old mill on site :	-	-	-	-	20x4x12 3 pr st.	osm/	-
Kilrea	Kilrea	Craig Andrew	corn & kiln	-	5a.	-	-	-	-	gr/	-
Kilrea	Kilrea	Diamond Thomasina	weaving fcty	-	-	1.5	-	-	-	gr/	-
Macosquin	Kiltinny Lower	Miller John	flax	-	-	-	-	-	11x1.7x3.3	osm/	-
Ballyrashane	Kirkistown	McNaughton Barth.	mills	-	-	-	Mcnaughton - M`gomery	1839	-	dd/	1839 12 97
Ballyrashane	Kirkistown	Workman James	barley	-	-	-	-	-	12x1.7x10	osm/	-

PARISH	TOWNLAND	MILLER	TYPE	HOUSE	Land	£Val	PROPRIETORS	Date	WHEEL etc.	Record	Ref.
Ballyrashane	Kirkistown	Workman James	corn	-	-	-	-	-	12.6x1.6x11.6	osm/	-
Ballyrashane	Kirkistown	Workman Samuel	corn	-	5-2-15	-	-	-	-	gr/	-
Londonderry	Knockan	- W. of R. Owenbeg	beetling & dam	-	-	-	-	1839	-	6"os/	30
Londonderry	Knockanduff	- nr Ballinrees	flax	-	-	-	-	-	-	1"os/	13
Coleraine	Knockantern :	-	flax	-	-	-	-	-	-	6"os/	7
Dungiven	Lackagh	King Michael	bone	-	-	-	-	-	-	gr/	-
Dungiven	Lackagh	King Michael	flax	miller`s house	21a.	54	-	-	-	gr/	-
Dungiven	Lackagh	King Michael	thrashing	-	-	-	-	-	-	gr/	-
Dungiven	Lakagh	Ogilby Les & King :	bleach green	-	-	-	-	-	-	osm/	-
Dungiven	Lakagh	Ogilby Les & King :	wash	-	-	-	-	-	14x2.11 eng : 18x3.3	osm/	-
Londonderry	Larrycormick	-	flax	-	-	-	-	-	-	1"os/	27
Macosquin	Learden	Moore William	flax	-	-	-	-	-	12.2x1.6x3.4	osm/	-
Macosquin	Learden	Moore William	flax & store	-	37a.	-	-	-	-	gr/	-
Dunboe	Leardon :	-	mill	-	-	-	-	-	-	6"os/	7
Londonderry	Learmount	Connor Samuel	corn	-	-	-	-	-	-	gr/	-
Londonderry	Learmount	Connor Samuel	flax	-	-	-	-	-	-	gr/	-
Londonderry	Leck	-	flax	-	-	-	-	1839	-	6"os/	11
Magherafelt	Leckagh	Walsh William	flax	-	11a.	-	-	-	-	gr/	-
Londonderry	Legaghory	- at Oaks Lodge	bleaching	-	-	-	-	1839	-	6"os/	21
Londonderry	Legaghory	Lyle Samuel	bleach	-	-	-	-	-	-	gr/	-
Faughanvane	Legg	Orrr John	flax	-	76a.	-	-	-	-	gr/	-
Termoneeny	Lemnaboy	Dobbin John	-	miller`s house	-	-	-	-	-	gr/	-
Termoneeny	Lemnaboy	Mullholland Henry	corn & kiln	-	30a.	-	-	-	-	gr/	-
Cumber Upper	Lettermuck	-	paper	-	-	-	-	1839	-	6"os/	22
Cumber Upper	Lettermuck	Irwin John	mill	miller`s house	6a.	-	-	-	-	gr/	-
Cumber Upper	Lettermuck	Matthews Robert	paper	-	-	-	-	-	-	osm/	-
Faughanvale	Liggavish	-	flax & pond	-	-	-	-	1839	-	6"os/	14
Clondermot	Lismacarol	-	flax holes	-	-	-	-	1839	-	6"os/	21
Clandermot	Lismacarol	M`Pherson Joseph	corn	-	15a.	-	-	-	-	gr/	-
Lissan	Lismoney	Staunton John	flax	-	41a.	39	-	-	-	gr/	-
Tamlaght O`C.	Lismoyle	Gilmore John	flax	-	-	-	-	-	10x2x -	osm/	-
Tamlaght O`C.	Lisnagroat	Campbell William	flax	-	-	-	-	-	11.4x1.6x -	osm/	-
Tamlaght O`C.	Lisnagroat	Craig Alex	corn	-	-	-	-	-	13.1x2x -	osm/	-
Ballyrashane	Lisnisk	-	beetling	-	-	-	-	-	12x1.9x -	osm/	-
Ballyrashane	Lisnisk	-	flax	-	-	-	-	-	13x1.8x -	osm/	-
Cumber Upper	Listress	-	corn	-	-	-	-	-	12x2x -	osm/	-
Cumber Upper	Listress	-	flax	-	-	-	-	-	12x2x -	osm/	-
Kildorrogh	Loghran	Browne William :	corn	-	-	-	Browne - Moore Jas :	1729	-	dd/	63 247 43409
Ballywillin	Loguestown :	-	flax	-		-	-	-	-	6"os/	3
Templemore	Londonderry :	Allen Jane :	mill	- Termonbaclo		-	Allen J - Marshall Wm :	1746	-	dd/	131 310 89268
Templemore	Londonderry :	M`Intyre, Hogg & Co.	shirt factory	-	-	-	-	-	-	gr/	-
Templemore	Londonderry :	Munn John Jun	flax & spinning	-	-	-	-	-	-	gr/	-
Templemore	Londonderry :	Tillie W & Henderson J	shirt factory	-	-	-	-	-	-	gr/	-
Templemore	Londonderry :	M`Clure James	coach factory	-	-	-	-	-	-	gr/	-
Templemore	Londonderry :	Christy John	steam	-	-	-	-	-	-	gr/	-
Templemore	Londonderry :	Harbour Commrs.	old sping. mill	-	-	-	-	-	-	gr/	-
Templemore	Londonderry :	Leatham John & Wm	steam	-	-	-	-	-	-	gr/	-
Templemore	Londonderry :	Thompson James	soap factory	-	-	-	-	-	-	gr/	-
Templemore	Londonderry Tn	Cunningham Robert	steam	-	-	-	-	-	-	gr/	-
Desertmartin	Longfield	- near Desertmartin	flax	-	-	-	-	-	-	1"os/	27
Desertmartin	Longfield	Bodkin James	flax	-	-	-	-	-	-	gr/	-
Desertmartin	Longfield	Charles William	flax	-	45a.	-	-	-	-	gr/	-

PARISH	TOWNLAND	MILLER	TYPE	HOUSE	Land	£Val	PROPRIETORS	Date	WHEEL etc.	Record	Ref.
Kildollagh	Loughan	- on R. Bann	flax	-	-	-	-	-	-	1"os/	-
Kildollagh	Loughan Mill	- on R. Bann	mill	-	-	-	-	-	-	1"os/	-
Kildollagh	Loughan Water	Adams John	flax	-	-	-	-	-	13x2x8 water 4 mos	osm/	-
Kildollagh	Loughan Water	Rowan William	corn	-	-	-	-	-	13.8x2x6	osm/	-
Kildollagh	Loughan Water	Rowan William	flax	-	-	-	-	-	13x1.10x4	osm/	-
Desertmartin	Luney	Kelly Henry	brewery	-	-	-	-	-	-	gr/	-
Desertmartin	Luney	Kelly Henry	corn	-	15a.	-	-	-	-	gr/	-
Desertmartin	Luney	Kelly Henry	flax	-	-	-	-	-	-	gr/	-
Maghera	Macknagh	Moore Alex	flax	-	-	-	Mercers` Company	-	14x3x8	osm/	-
Maghera	Macknagh	Moore Alexander	flax	-	12a.	-	-	-	-	gr/	-
Macosquin	Macleary	Bennett Stephen	bleach	-	-	-	-	-	-	gr/	-
Macosquin	Macleary	Bennett Stephen	bleach gren	-	20a	-	-	-	-	osm/	-
Macosquin	Macleary	Bennett Stephen	engine ho	-	-	-	-	-	15x3.7x5.6 15x4.6x5.	osm/	-
Macosquin	Macleary	Bennett Stephen	wash	-	-	-	-	-	16x4.3x5.6	osm/	-
Macosquin	Macosquin	Mooney John	corn	-	8-3-0		-	-	-	gr/	-
Macosquin	Macosquin	Mooney John	corn	-	-	-	-	-	16.6x4.1x13.9	osm/	-
Macosquin	Macosquin	Mooney John	flax	-	-	-	-	-	-	gr/	-
Macosquin	Macosquin	Mooney John	flax	-	-	-	-	-	15x2.2x12	osm/	-
Artrea	Maghadone	- nr Moneymore Tn	old flax mill	-	-	-	-	1839	-	6"os/	46
Maghera	Maghera	Deniston James	mill	-	-	-	Deniston - Clark J`son :	1738	-	dd/	92 31 64749
Maghera	Maghera Town	Clarke Alex	brewery	-	-	-	-	-	-	osm/	-
Dungiven	Magheraboy	-	flax	-	-	-	-	-	12x6x -	osm/	-
Dungiven	Magheraboy	Toner Thomas	flax (x 2)	-	11a.	215	-	-	-	gr/	-
Magherafelt	Magherafelt	- 1/2 m. W. of town	brewery	-	-	-	-	1839	-	6"os/	42
Magherafelt	Magherafelt	Clark	grist mills	-	-	-	Clark - Nicholson	-	?	dd/	92 354 64849
Magherafelt	Magherafelt	Palmer Jane Widow :	grist mills	-	-	-	Palmer J - Palmer Ann	1734	-	dd/	76 162 53395
Balteagh	Maine	-	corn	-	-	-	-	-	-	1"os/	12
Balteagh	Maine North	- W. side Castle R.	corn	-	-	-	-	1839	-	6"os/	17
Balteagh	Maine North	Boyle Edward	corn	miller`s house	10a.	-	-	-	-	gr/	-
Balteagh	Maine North	Forsythe Andrew	flax scutching	-	4-2-0	-	-	-	-	gr/	-
Artrea	Mawillian	Carleton William Jun	flax	-	22a.	-	-	-	-	gr/	-
Magherafelt	Megargy	- 2m SE Desertmartin	mill	-	-	-	-	1839	-	6"os/	41
Killdollagh	Mill Loughan	Warwick Thomas	flax mills (2)	-	22a.	-	-	-	-	gr/	-
Magherafelt	Millbrook	- near Magherafelt	mill	-	-	-	-	-	-	1"os/	27
Coleraine	Millloughan :	-	flax	-	-	-	-	-	-	6"os/	7
Kilrea	Monegram	- near R. Bann	race* (no mill) :	-	-	-	-	1839	-	6"os/	27
Kilrea	Monegram	McKiney John	flax	-	-	-	-	-	13.6x4.6x2.6	osm/	-
Ballynascreen	Moneyguiggy	- on Moyola R	corn	-	-	-	-	-	-	1"os/	19
Ballynascreen	Moneyguiggy	Dixon John	flax	-	-	-	-	-	-	osm/	-
Artrea	Moneymore	Boyle James	corn & kiln	-	0-1-35		-	-	-	gr/	-
Artrea	Moneymore Town	-	mill race :	-	-	-	-	1839	-	6"os/	46
Tamlaght O`C.	Moneysallin	Bradley Andrew	flax	-	-	-	-	-	12.2x1.9x -	osm/	-
Kilcronaghan	Moneysharere	Walker Samuel	corn	-	-	-	-	-	-	osm/	-
Killelagh	Moneysharvan	Lyle Archibald	flax	-	20a.	-	-	-	-	gr/	-
Desertmartin	Moneysterling	- nr Desertmartin Tn	mill, race, pond	-	-	-	-	1839	-	6"os/	41
Kilcronaghan	Mormeal	- nr Altagoan Bridge	flax	-	-	-	-	-	-	1"os/	-
Kilcronaghan	Mormeal	Lyle Martha	corn & kiln	-	-	-	-	-	-	gr/	-
Londonderry	Moss Side *	-	flax	-	-	-	-	-	-	1"os/	-
Desertoghill	Movenis	Wallace Henry	flax	-	-	-	Waterford Marq.	-	13.6x2x10	osm/	-
Faughanvale	Moyboy	-	flax	-	-	-	-	1839	-	6"os/	14
Faughanvale	Moyboy	-	flax holes	-	-	-	-	1839	-	6"os/	14
Ballynascreen	Moydamlaght	Morgan Michael	corn	-	16a.	-	-	-	-	gr/	-

PARISH	TOWNLAND	MILLER	TYPE	HOUSE	Land	£Val	PROPRIETORS	Date	WHEEL etc.	Record	Ref.
Ballynascreen	Moydamlaght	Morgan Michael	flax	-	-	-	-	-	-	gr/	-
Ballynascreen	Moyheeland	Hanna Samuel	corn	-	89a.	-	-	-	-	gr/	-
Ballynascreen	Moyheeland	Hanna Samuel	flax	-	-	-	-	-	-	gr/	-
Ballynascreen	Moykeeran	Stewart James	old millstead	-	-	-	-	-	no measurements	osm/	-
Desertoghill	Moyletra	Loughlin Thomas	-	-	-	-	-	-	-	osm/	-
Desertoghill	Moyletrakill	-	flax	-	-	-	-	1839	-	6"os/	26
Desertoghill	Moyletrakill	Leighlin John	flax	-	68a.	-	-	-	-	gr/	-
Londonderry	Moyne North *	-	corn	-	-	-	-	-	14x3.4x8 breast :	osm/	-
Londonderry	Moyne North *	-	flax	-	-	-	-	-	14x1.6x - breast &	osm/	-
Londonderry	Moyne North *	- unoccupied	bleach green	-	-	-	-	-	- ceased 1810	osm/	-
Faughanvane	Muff	Wiggins Henry	flax	-	63a.	-	-	-	-	gr/	-
Boveagh	Muladonagh	M`Fadden Archibald	old corn mill	-	10a.	-	-	-	-	gr/	-
Boveagh	Muladonagh	Pollock Samuel	corn	-	-	-	Hamilton John	-	11x0.11x2	osm/	-
Aghadowey	Mullaghinch	Bartley Alex & Geo &Cc	bleach	-	3-0-0	-	-	-	-	gr/	-
Aghadowey	Mullaghinch	Bartley Alexander	flax	-	91a.	-	-	-	-	gr/	-
Aghadowey	Mullaghmore	-	dyeing	-	-	-	-	-	-	1"os/	13
Aghadowey	Mullaghmore	Barklie Alex & George	beetling	-	-	-	-	-	17.6x5x5 17x4.10x4	osm/	-
Aghadowey	Mullaghmore	Barklie Alex & George	bleach green	-	23a	-	-	-	-	osm/	-
Aghadowey	Mullaghmore	Barklie Alex & George	wash	-	-	-	-	-	15x3.6x4	osm/	-
Aghadowey	Mullan	Hunter, Hempill and :	beetling	-	-	-	-	-	15.6x4x4 16.6x4.8x4	osm/	-
Aghadowey	Mullan	Hunter, Hempill and :	bleach green	- 2 houses	25a	-	-	-	-	osm/	-
Aghadowey	Mullan	Hunter, Hempill and :	wash	-	-	-	-	-	15x4x4	osm/	-
Templemore	Mulleenan	- near R. Foyle	flax & ponds	-	-	-	-	1839	-	6"os/	20
Templemore	Mulleenan	- par/ Tremplemore	Anna`s Mill	-	-	-	-	-	-	ct.co./	-
Drumachose	Newt`nlimavady	Cather George	distillery	-	-	-	-	-	-	gr/	-
Drumachose	Newt`nlimavady	Forsythe Mary Anne	old distillery	-	0-1-20		-	-	-	gr/	-
Londonderry	nr Crosskeys	- stream to L Neagh	mill	-	-	-	-	-	-	1"os/	-
Cumber Upper	nr Cumber Br.	- on R. Faughan	corn	-	-	-	-	-	-	1"os/	-
Cumber Upper	Oaks Lodge	-	bleach green	-	-	-	-	-	-	osm/	-
Cumber Upper	Oaks Lodge	-	rubbing	-	-	-	-	-	14x3.6x -	osm/	-
Cumber Upper	Oaks Lodge	-	wash	-	-	-	-	-	14x3.6x -	osm/	-
Ballyscullion	Old Town :	-	flax	-	-	-	-	-	-	1"os/	-
Ballyscullion	Old Town :	-	mill	-	-	-	-	-	-	1"os/	-
Templemore	Pennyburn	-	flour	-	-	-	-	1839	-	6"os/	13
Templemore	Pennyburn	- Pennyburn	Distillery	-	-	-	-	1839	-	6"os/	13
Templemore	Pennyburn	Ash William :	mills	-	-	-	Ash W - Averell Isabella :	1731	Mort. 18 May	dd/	67 264 46124
Templemore	Pennyburn	Bond Oliver	flour	-	-	-		-	-	gr/	-
Templemore	Pennyburn	Bond Oliver	old distillery	-	-	-	-	-	-	gr/	-
Templemore	Pennyburn	Bond Oliver	windmill, flour	-	-	-	-	-	-	gr/	-
Magherafelt	Polepatrick	Cassidy Francis P	corn & kilns	-	101a.	-	-	-	-	gr/	-
Magherafelt	Polepatrick	Cassidy Francis P	flax	-	-	-	-	-	-	gr/	-
Faughvane	Primity	Anderson James	starch works :	-	2.5a.	27	-	-	-	gr/	-
Cumber Upper	Raspberry Hill	- near Co. Boundary	flax & stream	-	-	-	-	1839	-	6"os/	28
Cumber Upper	Raspberry Hill	Danton Henry	flax	-	71a.	-	-	-	-	gr/	-
Cumber Upper	Raspberry Hill	Danton Henry	flax	-	71a.	-	-	-	-	gr/	-
Drumachose	Rathbrady	Purcell William K	brewery	-	10a.	50	-	-	-	gr/	-
Ballyrashane	Ravallagh N.	-	flax	-	-	-	-	-	12x1.6x -	osm/	-
Ballyrashane	Revallagh N. :	-	flax	-	-	-	-	-	-	6"os/	4
Macosquin	Ringsend Bridge	- on Macosquin R.	flax	-	-	-	-	-	-	1"os/	13
Londonderry	Rosebrook *	-	mill/18	-	-	-	-	-	-	1"os/	-
Desertmartin	Rosgarran	- on Grangewater	corn	-	-	-	-	-	-	1"os/	27
Desertmartin	Rosgarran	- on Grangewater	flax	-	-	-	-	-	-	1"os/	27

PARISH	TOWNLAND	MILLER	TYPE	HOUSE	Land	£Val	PROPRIETORS	Date	WHEEL etc.	Record	Ref.
Faughanvale	Saltworks	Major James	no mill	-	39a.	-	-	-	-	gr/	-
Tamlaght Fin.	Sesnagh	- on Burnfoot R.	flax	-	-	-	-	-	-	1"os/	12
Aghadowey	Shanlonford	- S. rd. to N`town	mill	-	-	-	-	1839	-	6"os/	11
Aghadowey	Shanlongford	Cochran William	corn	-	-	-	-	-	13.3x2x7	osm/	-
Aghadowey	Shanlongford	Cochrane Alexander	corn & kiln	-	11a.	15	-	-	-	gr/	-
Aghadowey	Shanlongford	Millan John	flax	-	18a.	-	-	-	-	gr/	-
Aghadowey	Shanlongford	Miller John	flax	-	-	-	-	-	12x1.7x6	osm/	-
Banagher	Straid	Connor Samuel	corn	-	-	-	-	-	-	gr/	-
Banagher	Straid	Connor Samuel	flax	-	-	-	-	-	-	gr/	-
Londonderry	Straidarran *	- at ford R. Faughan	mills	-	-	-	-	-	-	1"os/	-
Cumber Upper	Stranagalwilly	-	corn	-	-	-	-	-	12x1.4x -	osm/	-
Cumber Upper	Stranagalwilly	-	tuck	-	-	-	-	-	12x1.4x -	osm/	-
Desertmartin	Stranagard	-	corn	-	-	-	-	-	12x1.4x -	osm/	-
Desertmartin	Stranagard	-	flax	-	-	-	-	-	11x1.3x -	osm/	-
Desertmartin	Stranagard	- SW Desertmartin	mill	-	-	-	-	1839	-	6"os/	41
Desertmartin	Stranagard	Leeper James	corn & kiln	-	29a.	-	-	-	-	gr/	-
Desertmartin	Stranagard	Leeper James	flax	-	-	-	-	-	-	gr/	-
Londonderry	Stranawilly	- on Glenrandal R.	corn kiln	-	-	-	-	1839	-	6"os/	28
Ballynascreen	Straw	- near Chapel	tuck	-	-	-	-	1839	-	6"os/	40
Ballynascreen	Straw	- E./ White Water	corn	-	-	-	-	1839	-	6"os/	40
Boveagh	Straw	Crawford Joseph	corn & kiln	-	-	-	-	-	-	gr/	-
Boveagh	Straw	Crawford Joseph	flax	-	41a.	-	-	-	-	gr/	-
Ballynascreen	Straw	Donnelly Bernard	corn & kiln	-	15a.	-	-	-	-	gr/	-
Ballynascreen	Straw	Donnelly Philip	flax	-	25a.	-	-	-	-	gr/	-
Boveagh	Straw	Edwards Mrs	corn	-	-	-	-	-	13.6x3x -	osm/	-
Boveagh	Straw	Edwards Mrs	flax	-	-	-	-	-	-	osm/	-
Ballynascreen	Straw	Kelly Eleanor	corn	-	31a.	-	-	-	-	gr/	-
Ballynascreen	Straw	Kelly Eleanor	tuck	-	-	-	-	-	-	gr/	-
Ballynascreen	Straw	Kelly Peter	flax	-	-	-	-	-	12.6x2x2	osm/	-
Ballynascreen	Straw	Kelly Peter	tuck	-	-	-	-	-	12.6x2x2	osm/	-
Killelagh	Swatragh	Clarke Alex	corn	-	-	-	-	-	14x2.6x14	osm/	-
Killelagh	Swatragh	Clarke William & John	corn & kiln	miller`s house	0-1-30		-	-	-	gr/	-
Tamlaght-Fin.	Tamlaght	Cather David	stone	-	-	-	-	-	4.6x0x11x - :	osm/	-
Tamlaght-Fin.	Tamlaght	Cather William	mill & pond	-	0-3-30		-	-	-	gr/	-
Tamlaght-Fin.	Tamlaght	Cather William	spade foundry	-	40a.	-	-	-	-	gr/	-
Tamlaght	Tamlaght :	-	flax & pond	-	-	-	-	-	-	6"os/	9
Derryloan	Tamlaght More	-	8 wells 0 mills	-	-	-	-	-	-		
Ballyscullion	Tamniaran	- on Mayola R.	cotton mfty	-	-	-	-	1839	-	6"os/	48
Ballyscullion	Tamniaran	M`Hugh Edward	beetling	engine house	-	-	-	1839	-	6"os/	42
Ballyscullion	Tamniaran	Shaw George	beetling	-	-	-	-	-	-	gr/	-
Ballyscullion	Tamniaran	Shaw George	corn	-	7-0-2C	-	-	-	-	gr/	-
Ballyscullion	Tamniarin	- on R. Roe	flax	-	-	-	-	-	-	gr/	-
Ballyscullion	Tamniarin	Crommie James	flax	-	-	-	-	-	12x2x8 & :	osm/	-
Faughanvane	Templemoyle	-	Agric. College	-	48a.	26	-	-	-	gr/	-
Faughanvane	Templemoyle	Cowan	mill	-	-	-	-	1839	-	6"os/	14
Faughanvane	Templemoyle	Gallagher Martha	corn	-	-	-	Cowan - Bolson	-	?	dd/	98 335 17798
Templemore	Termonbacca	-	-	-	4.5a.	-	-	-	-	gr/	-
Templemore	Termonbacca	-	corn	-	-	-	-	-	-	ct.co./	-
Templemore	Termonbacca	-	flax & pond	-	-	-	-	1839	-	6"os/	20
Templemore	Termonbacca	-	mill ponds	-	-	-	-	1839	-	6"os/	20
Templemore	Termonbacca	Allen Jane	mill, mill house	-	-	-	-	1839	-	6"os/	20
Balteagh	Terrydremont	- on R. Roe	flax	-	-	-	Allen Jne - Marshall Wm	1746	-	dd/	131 310 89268
					-	-	-	-	-	1"os/	12

PARISH	TOWNLAND	MILLER	TYPE	HOUSE	Land	£Val	PROPRIETORS	Date	WHEEL etc.	Record	Ref.
Balteagh	Terrydremont N	-	mill pond	-	-	-	-	1839	-	6"os/	16
Balteagh	Terrydremont N.	Boyd John	corn	-	19a.	-	-	-	-	gr/	-
Balteagh	Terrydremont N.	Boyd John	flax scutching	-	-	-	-	-	-	gr/	-
Balteagh	Terrydremont S	- on R. Roe :	mill dam	-	-	-	-	1839	-	6"os/	16
Balteagh	Terrydremont S	- close to R. Roe	flax	-	-	-	-	1839	-	6"os/	16
Balteagh	Terrydremont S.	Given Andrew	flour	miller`s house	8a.	-	-	-	-	gr/	-
Balteagh	Terrydremount	- unoccupied	bleach green	-	-	-	-	-	- ceased c1827	osm/	-
Balteagh	Terrydremount	George William	flax	-	-	-	Rodgers Marcus	-	14.6x3.4x10 & :	osm/	-
Balteagh	Terrydremount	Heaslit Henry	flax	-	-	-	-	-	-	osm/	-
Dungiven	The Castle	- Dungiven Town	mill	-	-	-	-	-	-	1"os/	18
Tamlaght O`C.	Timaconway	Acheson James	ancient mill	-	-	-	-	-	-	osm/	-
Tamlaght O`C.	Timaconway	Green Robert	flax	-	-	-	-	-	11.10x2x -	osm/	-
Tamlaght O`C.	Timaconway Upr	- at Lisgranaghan :	mill	-	-	-	-	-	-	1"os/	19
Killelagh	Timony	Clarke William	bleach green	-	-	-	-	-	-	osm/	-
Lissan	Tintagh	-	flax	-	-	-	-	-	-	1"os/	27
Learmount	Tireighter	- S. of Faughan R.	corn & stream	-	-	-	-	1839	-	6"os/	29
Learmount	Tireighter	- S. of Faughan R.	flax	-	-	-	-	1839	-	6"os/	29
Learmount	Tireighter	Douglas Joseph	corn	-	0-3-0		-	-	-	gr/	-
Desertoghill	Tirekeran	M`Alister Alexander	corn	-	21a.	-	-	-	-	gr/	-
Desertoghill	Tirekeran	M`Alister Alexander	flax	-	-	-	-	-	-	gr/	-
Maghera	Tirgarvil	- on Grillagh R.	flax	-	-	-	-	-	-	1"os/	19
Maghera	Tirgarvil	- at Ampertain	bleach	-	-	-	-	-	-	1"os/	19
Maghera	Tirgarvil	- at Ampertain	mill	-	-	-	-	-	-	1"os/	19
Maghera	Tirgarvil	Clarke Alex	corn	-	-	-	-	-	12x2x6	osm/	-
Maghera	Tirgarvil	Clarke William & John	beetling	-	-	-	-	-	-	gr/	-
Maghera	Tirgarvil	Clarke William & John	corn & kiln	miller`s house	24a.	-	-	-	-	gr/	
Maghera	Tirgarvil	Clarke Wm & John A	beetling	-	-	-	-	-	-	gr/	-
Maghera	Tirgarvil	Clarke Wm & John A	corn & kiln	miller`s house	24a.	-	-	-	-	gr/	-
Banagher	Tirglassan	Eakin Andrew Jun	corn	-	14a.	-	-	-	-	gr/	-
Banagher	Tirglassan	Eakin Andrew Jun	flax	-	-	-	-	-	-	gr/	-
Desertoghill	Tirkeeran	- S. of Garvagh	flax & mill race	-	-	-	-	1839	-	6"os/	18
Desertoghill	Tirkeeran	Cochran Alex	corn	-	-	-	Hill Sir George	-	14x1.8x16	osm/	-
Desertoghill	Tirkeeran	Coningham	mills	-	-	-	Coningham - Macky Pat :	1734	-	dd/	79 145 55042
Desertoghill	Tirkeeran	Lecky Henry :	mills	-	-	-	Lecky H - Macky Patrick :	1734	-	dd/	78 232 55043
Killelagh	Tirnony	Clarke Joseph MD	flax	-	37a.	-	-	-	-	gr/	-
Maghera	Toberhead	- on Grangewater	mill	-	-	-	-	-	-	1"os/	27
Londonderry	Toberlane *	- nr Cookstown	weaving fcty.	-	-	-	-	-	-	1"os/	27
Kilcronaghan	Tobermore	- south of Town	mill & dam	-	-	-	-	1839	-	6"os/	?
Kilcronaghan	Tobermore	Wisiner James	corn & kiln	-	11a.	-	-	-	-	gr/	-
Kilcronaghan	Tobermore	Wisiner James	flax	-	-	-	-	-	-	gr/	-
Learmount	Tonduff	-	corn	-	-	-	-	-	12x1.10 works v. old	osm/	-
Learmount	Toneduff	- W/ R. Faughan	mill & pond	-	-	-	-	1839	-	6"os/	22
Learmount	Toneduff	Carter Arthur	corn	-	5a.	-	-	-	-	gr/	-
Coleraine	Tullans	- New Mills	mill	-	-	-	-	-	-	6"os/	1
Coleraine	Tullans	Boyse Samuel	paper	-	-	-	Church Robert till 1804 :	-	16x3x15	osm/	-
Coleraine	Tullans	Coleraine Corp.	new mill	-	-	-	Coleraine Corp - Church	-	-	dd/	58 286 37959?
Coleraine Libs	Tullans	Coleraine Mayor & :	(mill	-	-	-	C`raine Cp - Church Art	1724	-	dd/	42 438 26964
Coleraine	Tullans	Moore James Jun.	corn & malt ho.	-	39a.	-	-	-	-	gr/	-
Coleraine	Tullans Lower	Coleraine Corporation	mill	-	-	-	Coleraine Corp - Church	1724	-	dd/	42 438 26964
Cumber Upr	Tullintrain	-	mill	-	-	-	-	-	-	1"os/	18
Faughvane	Tully	-	flax kiln	-	-	-	-	1839	-	6"os/	14
Faughvane	Tullyally Lower	- small R. to Foyle	mill & stream	-	-	-	-	1839	-	6"os/	20

PARISH	TOWNLAND	MILLER	TYPE	HOUSE	Land	£Val	PROPRIETORS	Date	WHEEL etc.	Record	Ref.
Faughvane	Tullyally Lower	Stephenson Margaret	thrashing	-	147a.	-	-	-	-	gr/	-
Killelagh	Tullyheran	Dunlop John	flax	-	9a.	-	-	-	-	gr/	-
Killelagh	Tullyheran	Lytle James	flax	-	8a.	-	-	-	-	gr/	-
Magherafelt	Tullylinkisay	- stream to Movolar R.	flax	-	-	-	-	-	-	1"os/	27
Magherafelt	Tullylinkisay	- stream to Movolar R.	flax	-	-	-	-	-	-	1"os/	27
Magherafelt	Tullylinkisay	Hutchinson Andrew	flax	-	30a.	-	-	-	-	gr/	-
Magherafelt	Tullylinkisee	Ash Thomas	iron works	-	-	-	Ash Thos - Ash Wm	1724	-	dd/	43 242 28045
Faughanvane	Tullymain	Cather George	corn & kiln	miller`s house	28a.	-	-	-	-	gr/	-
Faughanvane	Tullymain	Cather George	flour	miller`s house	-	-	-	-	-	gr/	-
Faughanvane	Tullymain	Cather George	mill pond	-	1-0-0	-	-	-	-	gr/	-
Faughanvane	Tullyverry	- W. side Faughan R.	corn & pond	-	-	-	-	1839	-	6"os/	15
Faughanvane	Tullyverry	- W. side Faughan R.	flax & stream	-	-	-	-	1839	-	6"os/	15
Faughanvane	Tullyverry	Connor James	corn & kiln	-	12a.	-	-	-	-	gr/	-
Faughanvane	Tullyverry	Connor James	flax	-	-	-	-	-	-	gr/	-
Faughanvane	Tullyverry	Connor James	pond	-	0-2-0	-	-	-	-	gr/	-
Maghera	Turnaface	-	corn kiln	-	-	-	-	1839	-	6"os/	46
Maghera	Turnaface	- near Keithstown	flax	-	-	-	-	-	-	1"os/	27
Faughanvale	Tygore	-	flax hole	-	-	-	-	1839	-	6"os/	15
Maghera	Upperland	Alex Clarke	beetling	-	-	-	-	-	16x5x - & 19x4.6x -	osm/	-
Maghera	Upperland	Alex Clarke	bleach green	-	-	-	-	-	-	osm/	-
Maghera	Upperland	Alex Clarke	wash	-	-	-	-	-	14x5.4x -	osm/	-
Maghera	Upperlands	Clarke William & John	beetling	-	-	-	-	-	-	gr/	
Maghera	Upperlands	Clarke William & John	bleech	-	109a.	-	-	-	-	gr/	
Maghera	Upperlands	Clarke William & John /	beetling	-	-	-	-	-	-	gr/	-
Maghera	Upperlands	Clarke William & John /	bleach	-	109a.	-	-	-	-	gr/	-
Maghera	Upperlands	Moore Jacob	tuck	-	-	-	Mercers` Co.	-	12x2x4	osm/	-
Londonderry	Vintners Propn.	Connolly William Hon.	corn & tuck	-	-	-	Connolly - Ransterne Wm	1732	-	dd/	72 468 51600
Londonderry	Vintners Propn.	Connolly William Hon.	corn & tuck	-	-	-	Connolly - Mullhollan :	1734	-	dd/	75 374 53464
Londonderry	Vintners Propn.	Connolly William Hon.	corn & tuck	-	-	-	Connolly - Donnington Wr	1734	-	dd/	76 173 53463
Londonderry	Vintners Propn.	Connolly William Hon.	corn & tuck	-	-	-	Connolly W - Mullholland	1734	-	dd/	76 174 53467
Londonderry	Vintners Propn.	Connolly William Hon.	corn & tuck	-	-	-	Connolly - Rooney Thos :	1734	-	dd/	77 228 53465
Londonderry	Vintners Propn.	Connolly William Hon.	corn & tuck	-	-	-	Connolly W - Jennings Jn	1734	-	dd/	78 81 53466
Londonderry	Vintners Propn.	Rankin	corn & tuck	-	-	-	Rankin - Davidson	-	?	dd/	84 527 62414
Londonderry	Vintners Propn.	Vintners Corporation	corn & tuck	-	-	-	Vintners - Connolly Wm :	1729	-	dd/	88 234 62369
Tamlaght-Fin.	Walworth	Fishmongers W`full :	flax (steam)	-	-	-	-	-	-	gr/	-
Tamlaght-Fin.	Walworth	Fishmongers W`full :	saw (steam)	-	-	-	-	-	-	gr/	-
Tamlaght-Fin.	Walworth	M`Cormack William	thrashing	-	98a.	-	-	-	-	gr/	-
Clondermot	Waterside :	Ballintine Thomas	steam	-	-	-	-	-	-	gr/	-
Clondermot	Waterside :	Meehan John	distillery	-	3a.	-	-	-	-	gr/	-
Clondermot	Waterside :	Meehan John	steam	-	-	-	-	-	-	gr/	-
Faughanvale	Whitehill	- on Agivey R.	flax	-	-	-	-	-	-	gr/	-
Templemore	Whitehouse	-	mill ponds	-	-	-	-	-	-	1"os/	13
Templemore	Whitehouse	Allen Robert	corn	-	104a.	-	-	1839	-	6"os/	13
Londonderry	Windmill Perches	Ash William	land	Ferryquarry St. :	-	-	Wm Ash - Wm Hogg	1752	-	dd/	160 151 106798

PARISH	TOWNLAND	MILLER	TYPE	HOUSE	Land	£Val	PROPRIETORS	Date	WHEEL etc.	Record	Ref.
Templemichael	Abbeycartron :	- N. side Camlin R.	corn	-	-	-	-	1837	-	6"os/	13
Shrule	Abbeyshrule	-	corn	-	-	-	-	1837	-	6"os/	23
Shrule	Abbeyshrule	Coates Edward :	mills	-	-	-	Coates Ed - Coates James	1822	-	dd/	772 171 523306
Shrule	Abbeyshrule	Coates James :	mill	-	-	-	Coates J - Holmes Jas :	1822	-	dd/	775 309 525244
Longford	Abbeyshrule Vge.	-	old mill ?	-	-	-	-	2002	-	phWEH	R
Killoe	Aghaboy	-	corn, kiln :	-	-	-	-	1841	-	6"os/	9
Killoe	Aghaboy	Heslin James	corn	-	11a.	-	-	1854	-	gr/	-
Killoe	Aghadowry	-	corn kiln	-	-	-	-	1837	-	6"os/	5
Aghara	Aghara	O`Reilly Richard	corn & kiln	-	396a.	-	-	1854	-	gr/	-
Agharra	Agharra	- W/ B'nacarrow Br.	corn	-	-	-	-	1837	-	6"os/	24
Columbkille	Aghnacliff	-	corn & kiln	-	-	-	-	1837	-	6"os/	6
Columbkille	Aghnacliff	- near L. Gowna	corn kiln :	-	-	-	-	1841	-	6"os/	6
Columbkille	Aghnacliff	Keernam Edward	tuck	-	-	-	-	-	12x2x8 1 stock	vmb/	13
Columbkille	Aghnacliff	Keernan Thomas	corn	-	-	-	-	-	12x2x13	vmb/	13
Columbkille	Aghnacliff	Kiernan Edward	mill	-	45a.	-	-	1854	-	gr/	-
Columbkille	Aghnacliff	McKiernan	mill	-	-	-	McKiernan - McKiernan	-	- [not 774]	dd/	774 457 526592
Clonbroney	Aghnashannagh	- on Camlin R	mill	-	-	-	-	-	-	1"os/	79
Clonbroney	Aghnashannagh	- N/ Ballinalee Br.	corn & kiln	-	-	-	-	1841	-	6"os/	9
Clonbroney	Aghnashannagh	Foster William	corn	27.6x23.0x12 :	-	-	-	1854	14x3.3x6.6 32 bkts.	hob/	5.1293
Clonbroney	Aghnashannagh	Foster William	corn	-	-	-	-	-	12x3x6 & 12x3x6	vmb/	13
Clonbroney	Aghnashannagh	Foster William	mill,	-	80a.	-	-	1854	-	gr/	-
Killoe	Annagh	-	corn kiln	-	-	-	-	1837	-	6"os/	2
Longford	Arboula	Fetherston George :	mill	-	-	-	Fetherston G & Solly :	1821	-	dd/	767 84 520219
Longford	Arboula	Waldron Edward :	mill	-	-	-	Waldron - Fetherston Sir :	1821	-	dd/	768 86 520821
Columbkille	Ballinulty	-	corn kiln	-	-	-	-	1837	-	6"os/	6
Kilglass	Ballycloghan	-	corn & mill pond	-	-	-	-	1837	-	6"os/	19
Kilglass	Ballycloghan	Allen Joseph	corn	-	3a.	-	-	1854	-	gr/	-
Killoe	Ballyduffy	-	corn, kiln :	-	-	-	-	1841	-	6"os/	1
Killoe	Ballyduffy	- stream to Black L.	mill	-	-	-	-	-	-	1"os/	-
Killoe	Ballyduffy	Donaghoe James	corn	-	-	-	-	-	13x2x13	vmb/	13
Killoe	Ballyduffy	Donaghoe James	corn	-	-	-	-	-	13x2x13	vmb/	13
Killoe	Ballyduffy	Kiernan James	mill	-	27a.	-	-	1854	-	gr/	-
Clongesh	Ballykenny	- S. side Camlin R.	corn	-	-	-	-	1841	-	6"os/	8
Clongesh	Ballykenny	Granard Earl	mill	-	-	-	Granard Earlf - Sankey	-	?	dd/	633 441 455952
Clongesh	Ballykenny	Granard Earl	mill	-	-	-	Farrell - Granard Earl	-	- [not 640]	dd/	640 151 454380
Clongesh	Ballykenny	Granard Earl :	mill	-	-	-	Granard E.- Ferrall Edw :	1811	-	dd/	639 474 443466
Clongesh	Ballykenny Upr	Granard Geo. Earl :	mill	-	-	-	Granard E. - Forde Henry	1813	-	dd/	653 441 455952
Clongesh	Ballykenny Upr	Granard Geo. Earl	mill	-	-	-	Granard E. - Forde Henry	1812	-	dd/	642 235 443102
Granard	Ballymacroly	- at Millbrook	mill	-	-	-	-	-	-	1"os/	-
Granard	Ballymacroly	- at Millbrook [Ho.]	brewery, corn :	-	-	-	-	-	-	vmb/	13
Granard	Ballymacroly	- at Millbrook [Ho.]	corn & kiln	-	-	-	-	1841	-	6"os/	10
Granard	Ballymacroly	c1m. SW/ Granard	mill	-	-	-	-	-	-	1"os/	-
Granard	Ballymacroly	Flynn Patrick	corn	-	28a.	-	-	1854	-	gr/	-
Granard	Ballymacroly	Flynn Patrick	corn	31.9x19.0x7.0 :	-	-	-	1853	12x3x6 - formerly :	hob/	5.1292
Granard	Ballymacroly	Flynn Patrick	corn	-	-	-	-	-	11x3x11	vmb/	13
Granard	Ballymacroly	Flynn Patrick	corn	-	-	-	-	-	11x3x11	vmb/	13
Granard	Ballymacroly	Flynn Patrick	old brewery	-	-	-	-	-	-	hob/	5.1292
Granard	Ballymacroly	Flynn Patrick	shelling wheel	-	-	-	-	1841	-	6"os/	10
Shrule	Ballymahon	- E. side R. Inny	corn	-	-	-	-	1837	-	6"os/	27
Shrule	Ballymahon	- near Shrule Br.	corn	-	-	-	-	-	-	1"os/	-
Shrule	Ballymahon	- N. of bridge	mill	-	-	-	-	1841	-	6"os/	27
Shrule	Ballymahon Tn.	Slator Henry B & Co	flour & corn	-	-	-	-	1854	-	gr/	-

PARISH	TOWNLAND	MILLER	TYPE	HOUSE	Land	£Val	PROPRIETORS	Date	WHEEL etc.	Record	Ref.
Shrule	Ballymulvey	-	woollen factory :	-	-	-	-	1854	- & mill race	25"os/	27
Shrule	Ballymulvey	Shuldam John	flax	-	339a.	-	-	1854	-	gr/	-
Kilronan	Ballyrohan	Darby Jane Widow	mill	-	-	-	Darby J - Edgeworth Ed	1716	-	dd/	24 527 14613
Kilronan	Ballyrohan	Edgeworth Robert	mill	-	-	-	Edgeworth R - Langley Th	1711	-	dd/	5 419 2304
Kilronan	Ballyrohan	Edgeworth Robert :	mill	-	-	-	Edgeworth Robert - Jno	1721	-	dd/	53 117 346?84
Kilronan	Ballyrohan	Edgeworth Robert :	mill	-	-	-	Edgeworth R - Domty	1707	-	dd/	8 ? 2569
Granard	Ballywillin	- stream to L. Kinale	corn, mill dam :	-	-	-	-	1841	-	6"os/	11
Kilronan	Ballywillin	Hewison James	mill	-	-	-	Hewison J - Falkiner Thos	1708	-	dd/	11 10 3873
Granard	Ballywillin	M`Cue James	corn	-	21a.	-	-	1854	-	gr/	-
Granard	Ballywillin	M`Cue Mr	tuck	-	-	-	-	-	-	hob/	5.1292
Granard	Ballywillin	M`Cue Mr :	corn	(2B) 36.6x19x7 :	-	-	-	-	11x2x11 2 pr stones :	hob/	5.1292
Granard	Ballywillin	McCue Elizabeth	corn	-	-	-	-	-	11x2x11	vmb/	13
Granard	Ballywillin	McCue Elizabeth	tuck & shelling	-	-	-	-	-	12x2x11	vmb/	13
Rarhcline	Barnacor	- S./ Curraroe Br.	corn	-	-	-	-	1837	-	6"os/	17
Rathcline	Barnacor	Costello John	mill	-	3a.	-	-	1854	-	gr/	-
Shrule	Barnacor	Fox George Lane :	mills	-	-	-	Fox Geo - Fox James :	1819	-	dd/	744 29 506366
Shrule	Barnacor	Fox James :	mills	-	-	-	Fox J & G - Farris Thos :	1814	-	dd/	675 225 465776
Milloe	Barragh More	-	corn kilns (2)	-	-	-	-	1837	-	6"os/	5
Taghshinny	Barry	-	corn & kiln	-	-	-	-	1837	-	6"os/	23
Taghshinny	Barry	Christie Robert	corn	-	0.0.30		-	1854	-	gr/	-
Longford	Bellamock	Graham Charity	mill	-	-	-	Graham Ch - Ford Mathew	1724	-	dd/	45 39 27616
Longford	Bellanchowen	Greville William	mills	-	-	-	Greville W - Combermere :	1821	-	dd/	765 465 519399
Longford	Bellanchowen	McClintock William :	mills	-	-	-	McClintock W - Brown Jn :	1821	Mort. 20 Nov.	dd/	767 329 520464
Longford	Bellanchower	Graham Charity	mill	-	-	-	Graham Ch - Ford Mathew	1724	-	dd/	45 39 27616
Longford	Bellanchower	Graham Charity	mill	-	-	-	Graham Ch - Henry Hugh	1727	-	dd/	52 308 34668
Longford	Bellanchower	Henry	mill	-	-	-	Henry - McCartney	-	?	dd/	53 112 34669
Longford	Bellanchower	McCartney James :	mill	-	-	-	McCartney - Coghill Rt Hon	1737	-	dd/	87 196 61257
Longford	Bellemack	Greville William	mills	-	-	-	Greville W - Combermere :	1821	-	dd/	765 465 519399
Longford	Bellemack	McClintock William :	mills	-	-	-	McClintock W - Brown Jn :	1821	Mort. 20 Nov.	dd/	767 329 520464
Killoe	Birrinagh	stream to L. Naback	corn, kiln :	-	-	-	-	1841	-	6"os/	3
Killoe	Birrinagh	Duffy James	corn	-	-	-	-	-	11x2x12	vmb/	13
Killoe	Birrinagh	Duffy James	corn	-	-	-	-	-	11x2x12	vmb/	13
Longford	Bleach Green	Gauldsbury Cath :	bleach green	-	-	-	Gouldsbury C - Price Richd	1826	?	dd/	820 245 555780
Longford	Bleach Green	Gouldsbury Arthur :	bleach green	-	-	-	Gouldsbury Arth - Richard :	1811	-	dd/	826 245 555780
Clongesh	Breanrisk	-	corn & pond	-	-	-	-	1837	-	6"os/	4
Clongesh	Briskil	-	corn & pond	-	-	-	-	1841	-	6"os/	8
Clongesh	Briskil	Morecroft John :	mill	-	-	-	Morecroft J - Ellis Thomas :	1826	Lse. 19 May	dd/	814 92 548427
Mohill	Bunanass	-	corn kiln	-	-	-	-	1837	-	6"os/	4
Kilglass	Carrickboy										
Clongesh	Cartrons	Granard George Hon.	-	-	-	-	Earl of Granard - Tickell Ed	1825	-	dd/	825 90 555025
Shrule	Castlecore	- NW/ R. Inny	corn & pond	-	-	-	-	1837	-	6"os/	26
Clonbroney	Cavan	-	corn & kiln	-	-	-	-	1841	-	6"os/	9
Clonbroney	Cavan	Wilson William	corn	-	-	-	-	-	16x4x9	vmb/	13
Clonbroney	Cavan	Wilson William	corn	-	-	-	-	-	16x4x9	vmb/	13
Columbkille	Cleenragh	-	iron mines	-	-	-	-	1837	-	6"os/	3
Columbkille	Cleenragh	- stream/ L.Gowna	mill	-	-	-	-	-	-	1"os/	-
Longford	Clonaghill	Bond James :	mills	-	-	-	Bond Jas - Turner John :	1814	Mort. 28 July	dd/	681 158 448709
Longford	Clonaghill	Percival Robert :	mills	-	-	-	Percival R - Turner Sir Chas	1808	-	dd/	641 282 446691
Longford	Clonaghill	Turner John :	mills	-	-	-	Turner J - Bond Winsley :	1814	-	dd/	681 107 468563
Longford	Clonaghlis	Percival Robert :	mills	-	-	-	Percival R - Westby Wm :	1750	-	dd/	146 5 96419
Killashee	Clondora (-dera)	Fox George	Townlands	-	-	-	Fox Geo - Gunning Robt	1741	-	dd/	103 533 72409
Killashee	Clondora (-dera)	Fox George	Townlands	-	-	-	Fox Geo - Gunning Robt	1741	-	dd/	108 117 74856

PARISH	TOWNLAND	MILLER	TYPE	HOUSE	Land	£Val	PROPRIETORS	Date	WHEEL etc.	Record	Ref.
Killashee	Clondora (-dera)	Gunning	Townlands	-	-	-	Gunning R - Keon Ambr	1744	-	dd/	116 225 80350
Killashee	Clondora (-dera)	Gunning Robert	Townlands	-	-	-	Gunning R - O`Connor Mcl	1747	-	dd/	150 462 103110
Killashee	Clondora (-dera)	Gunning Sir Robert	Townlands	-	-	-	Robert Gunning - Fox Geo	1740	-	dd/	103 534 72410
Killashee	Clondora (-dera)	Keon Ambrose :	Townlands	-	-	-	Keon A - Gunning Robt :	1748	-	dd/	133 23 88840
Killashee	Clondora (-dera)	Shelburne E.	Townlands	-	-	-	Shelburne E. of - Fox Geo	1740	-	dd/	101 14 69551
Killashee	Clondra	Fleming	mill	-	-	-	Fleming - & ors	1870		dd/	1870 11 63
Killashee	Clondra	Fleming David :	mill	-	-	-	Fleming D - Fleming Eliz :	1813	-	dd/	662 576 458040
Killashee	Clondra	Fleming William	mill	-	-	-	Fleming W - Gunning Robt	1850	-	dd/	1850 13 177
Killashee	Clondra	Fleming William	mill	-	-	-	Fleming William deed	1850	-	dd/	1850 19 148
Killashee	Clondra	Fleming William	mill	-	-	-	Fleming William - William	1875	-	dd/	1875 4 50
Killashee	Clondra	Fleming William	mill	-	-	-	Fleming Wm - Nat Bank	1886	-	dd/	1886 52 244
Killashee	Clondra	Fleming William	mill	-	-	-	Fleming Wm - P W Comms	1887	-	dd/	1887 19 11
Killashee	Clondra	Fox George	mill	-	-	-	Fox G - Shelburn Ld Henry	1725	-	dd/	49 13 30487
Killashee	Clondra	Gunning George	mill	-	-	-	Gunning Geo - PW Comms	1880	-	dd/	1880 23 1
Killashee	Clondra	Gunning Robert	mill	-	-	-	Gunning R - Fladgate Wm	1861	-	dd/	1861 17 298
Killashee	Clondra	Gunning Robert King	mill	-	-	-	Gunning R K - Fleming Wm	1831	-	dd/	875 443 581443
Killashee	Clondra	Ives John	mill	-	-	-	Ives John - Fleming Wm	1833	-	dd/	1833 18 174
Killashee	Clondra	Paymaster	mill	-	-	-	Paymaster - Marshall Thos	1858	-	dd/	1858 7 109
Longford	Clonloman	Gunning Robert	mill	-	-	-	Gunning R. - Fleming Wm	1843	-	dd/	1843 18 238
Street	Clonmore	- at Moatsvilla Ho.	mill	-	-	-	-	-	-	1"os/	-
Rathreagh	Clontimullan	- near Belderg	corn	- (application)	-	-	Doris Affeldt	2004	-	pWEH	D
Forgney	Clooncallon	Manny William	tuck	-	3.1.2	-	-	1854	-	gr/	-
Shrule	Clooncallow	-	flour	-	-	-	-	1837	-	6"os/	27
Shrule	Clooncallow	- E/ B'mahon Br.	tuck	-	-	-	-	1837	-	6"os/	27
Shrule	Clooncallow	- on R. Inny	woollen	-	-	-	-	-	-	1"os/	-
Mohill	Clooncolligan	-	corn kilns (2)	-	-	-	-	1837	-	6"os/	4
Killashee	Cloondara	- NW/ Richmond Br.	distillery	-	-	-	-	1837	-	6"os/	13
Killashee	Cloondara	Fleming William	corn & kilns	-	216a.	-	-	1854	-	gr/	-
Killashee	Cloondara	Fleming William	mill	-	-	-	Fleming William deed	1856	-	dd/	1856 9 190
Killashee	Cloondara	Gunning Robert	mill	-	-	-	Gunning Robert deed	1850	-	dd/	1850 13 275
Killashee	Cloondara	Marshall Thos Rev.	mill	-	-	-	Marshall Thomas deed	1850	-	dd/	1850 9 234
Killashee	Cloondarra	Civil Service	mill	-	-	-	S. Service - Gunning Robt.	1858	-	dd/	1858 7 109
Columbkille	Clooneen	-	corn kiln	-	-	-	-	1837	-	6"os/	6
Columbkille	Clooneen	- at Clooneen Br.	mill	-	-	-	-	-	-	1"os/	79
Columbkille	Clooneen	- S./ Clooneen Br.	corn	-	-	-	-	1837	-	6"os/	6
Columbkille	Clooneen	- N. of Clooneen Br.	corn & kiln	-	-	-	-	1841	-	6"os/	6
Columbkille	Clooneen	- near Clooneen Br.	mill	-	-	-	-	-	-	1"os/	-
Columbkille	Clooneen	Major Charles	corn	-	-	-	-	-	12x2x2	vmb/	13
Columbkille	Clooneen	Major Charles	corn	-	-	-	-	-	12x2x2	vmb/	13
Columbkille	Clooneen	Major Charles	mill	-	37a.	-	-	1854	-	gr/	-
Columbkille	Clooneen	Winter John Pratt :	- ?	-	-	-	Winter J - Amuty Samuel :	1828	Asgt. Mort. 10 May	dd	836 242 561777
Killoe	Cloonelly	-	corn kiln	-	-	-	-	1837	-	6"os/	2
Ballymacormick	Cloonkeen	Fox Richard :	(no mill)	-	-	-	Fox Richard - Henn Jno :	1822	-	dd/	771 191 522726
Ballymacormick	Cloonkeen	Jessop Fran	mill	-	-	-	Jessop Fran - Robert	1833	-	dd/	1833 16 17
Ballymacormick	Cloonkeen	Shuldham John :	(no mill)	-	-	-	Shuldham - Crosthwaite :	1825	Mort. 12 Feb.	dd/	804 457 542793
Moydow	Cloonker	-	corn	-	-	-	-	1837	-	6"os/	18
Moydow	Cloonker	Donelan Barnabas	corn	-	15a.	-	-	1854	-	gr/	-
Moydow	Cloonker	Ferrall James :	mill	-		-	Ferall J - Willington Charles	1725	-	dd/	48 67 30680
Longford	Cloonker :	-	corn	-	-	-	recently Ned Donovan	2002	-	phWEH	A
Killashee	Cloonmore	-	corn & kiln	-	-	-	-	1837	-	6"os/	13
Moydow	Cloonmucker	-	corn & :	m -	-	-	-	1841	-	6"os/	18
Moydow	Cloonmucker	Coughlan James	corn	-	125a.	-	-	1854	-	gr/	-

COUNTY LONGFORD

PARISH	TOWNLAND	MILLER	TYPE	HOUSE	Land	£Val	PROPRIETORS	Date	WHEEL etc.	Record	Ref.
Ballymacormick	Cloonturk	- N/ Cloonturk Br.	corn & kiln	-	-	-	-	1837	-	6"os/	13
Ballymacormick	Cloonturk	Grenville William	mills	-	-	-	Greville W - Combermere :	1821	-	dd/	765 465 519399
Ballymacormick	Cloonturk	McCord Alex :	mill	-	-	-	McCord A - McCord Chas :	1818	-	dd/	638 523 444130
Ballymacormick	Cloonturk	Shaw James	corn	-	43a.	-	-	1854	-	gr/	-
Ballymacormick	Cloonturk	Shaw`s Mill	corn	-	-	-	-	2002	-	phWEH	R
Longford	Cloraghill	Turner John :	mill	-	-	-	Turner Jn - Bond James :	1821	-	dd/	764 453 518788
Longford	Cooleroy	Fox James :	mills	-	-	-	Fox J & G - Farris Thos H2(	1814	-	dd/	675 225 675776
Longford	Cooleroy	Fox James :	mills	-	-	-	Fox James - White Luke :	1819	Mort. 13 July	dd/	744 18 506353
Killoe	Corboy	-	corn & kiln	-	-	-	-	1837	-	6"os/	14
Ballycormick	Cordivin	-	corn & kiln	-	-	-	-	1837	-	6"os/	19
Ballymacormick	Cordivin	Ganley James	corn	-	48a.	-	-	1854	-	gr/	-
Killoe	Cornacullew	stream to Annagh L.	mill	-	-	-	-	-	-	1"os/	78
Columbkille	Cornadrung	-	corn kiln	-	-	-	-	1837	-	6"os/	3
Forgney	Cornamucklagh	-	corn	-	-	-	-	1837	-	6"os/	27
Forgney	Cornamucklagh	Mann Edward	mills	-	6.2.3	-	-	1854	-	gr/	-
Forgney	Cornamucklagh		corn	-	-	-	-	-	-	1"os/	99
Columbkille	Corrinagh	-	corn kiln	-	-	-	-	1837	-	6"os/	2
Abbeylara	Cranally (?)	Edgewoorth	mill	-		-	Edgeworth - Carty	-	?	dd/	33 396 208612
Longford	Crane Grove	Bagnall Timothy :	-	-	-	-	Bagnall T - Irwin Margaret :	1825	-	dd/	836 285 561820
Kilcommock	Creagh	Granard Geo. Earl :	mill	-	-	-	Granard E. - Forde Henry	1813	-	dd/	653 441 455952
Kilcommock	Creagh	Granard Geo. Earl	mill	-	-	-	Granard E. - Forde Henry	1812	-	dd/	642 235 443107
Kilcommock	Creagh	Hall William	mills	-	-	-	Hall William - Forde Henry	1813	-	dd/	653 303 453777
Killoe	Creelaghta	-	corn mill :	-	-	-	-	1841	-	6"os/	5
Killoe	Creelaghta	Flynn John	mills	-	13a.	-	-	1854	-	gr/	-
Killoe	Creelaghta	Hall William, Miller	mills	-	-	-	Hall W - McLaughlin Peter :	1809	Lse. 25 Oct.	dd/	653 303 453777
Killoe	Creeve, Milltown	-	corn	-	-	-	-	1837	-	6"os/	14
Killoe	Creeve, Milltown	-	corn kilns, pond	-	-	-	-	1837	-	6"os/	14
Killoe	Crowdrumman	-	corn kiln	-	-	-	-	1841	-	6"os/	5
Killoe	Crowdrumman	-	mill	-	-	-	-	-	-	1"os/	78
Mostrim	Cullynore	Armstrong Richard :	mill	-	-	-	Armstrong - Maxwell Henry	1815	-	dd/	697 98 478243
Mostrim	Cullynore	Armstrong Richard :	mill	-	-	-	Armstrong R - Borroughs :	1816	-	dd/	700 671 480500
Mostrim	Cullynore	Beatty Charles	mill	-	-	-	Beatty C - Blake Francis	1732	-	dd/	68 385 48579
Mostrim	Cullynore	Edgewoorth Henry :	mill	-	-	-	Edgeworth - Beatty Chas :	1731	-	dd/	69 212 47980
Mostrim	Cullynore	Edgewoorth Henry : F	mill	-	-	-	Edgeworth - Beatty Chas :	1731	-	dd/	70 330 48576
Mostrim	Cullynore	Reel John	mill	-	-	-	Reel John - O`Farrell Roger	1812	Mort. 23 Nov.	dd/	694 657 476922
Mostrim	Cullynore	Reel John	mill	-	-	-	Reel John - Reel Mary :	1815	Mort. 1 Nov.	dd/	695 41 476960
Longford	Curcunny	Hynes Jno :	mill	-	-	-	Hynes j - Ledwith Edwd :	1738	-	dd/	93 269 654499
Killoe	Derawley	-	corn kilns (3)	-	-	-	-	1837	-	6"os/	5
Killoe	Derawley	- trib. to Black R.	corn	-	-	-	-	-	-	1"os/	78
Cashel	Derrydarragh	-	mill	-	-	-	-	1837	-	6"os/	25
Cashel	Derrydarragh	Coghlan Wm & John	corn	-	-	-	-	1854	-	gr/	-
Columbkille	Dring	stream to L. Gowna	corn & kiln	-	-	-	-	1841	-	6"os/	6
Columbkille	Dring	Jones David	mill & kiln	-	22a.	-	-	1854	-	gr/	-
Columbkille	Dring	Jones Dvaid	corn	-	-	-	-	-	13x3x3	vmb/	13
Columbkille	Dring	Jones Dvaid	shelling wheel	-	-	-	-	-	13x3x3	vmb/	13
Abbeyshrule	Drumanure	- W. side Inny R.	corn	-	-	-	-	1841	-	6"os/	23
Abbeyshrule	Drumanure	- W. side R. Inny	corn	-	-	-	-	1837	-	6"0s/	23
Abbeyshrule	Drumanure	Byrne Charles	bere & rye	54.6x24x30.9 :	-	-	-	1853	14x3.9x3 revs /min 9	hob/	5.1294/5
Abbeyshrule	Drumanure	Byrne Charles	corn	47x21x30	-	-	-	1853	13x4x3 revs /min 11	hob/	5.1294/5
Abbeyshrule	Drumanure	Byrne Charles	corn & flour	-	20a.	-	-	1854	-	gr/	-
Killoe	Drumlish	-	corn & kiln	-	-	-	-	1837	-	6"os/	5
Killoe	Drumlish	Rodgers Thomas	mill &kiln	-	12a.	-	-	1854	-	gr/	-

PARISH	TOWNLAND	MILLER	TYPE	HOUSE	Land	£Val	PROPRIETORS	Date	WHEEL etc.	Record	Ref.
Killoe	Drumlish Vge.	Rodgers Thomas	corn & kiln	-	-	9.0.0	-	1854	-	hob/	5.3171
Columbkille	Dunbeggan	-	old tuck mill	-	-	-	-	1837	-	6"os/	6
Columbkille	Dunbeggan	-	tuck	-	-	-	-	1837	-	6"os/	6
Columbkille	Dunbeggan	- near L. Gowna	old tuck mill :	-	-	-	-	1841	-	6"os/	6
Columbkille	Dunbeggan	- stream /L Gowna	mill	-	-	-	-	-	-	1"os/	79
Forgney	Forgney	Edgeworth	mill	-	-	-	Edgeworth - Herview	-	-	dd/	777 43 524***?
Forgney	Forgney	Edgeworth Frances :	mill	-	-	-	Edgeworth F - Fox John :	1821	-	dd/	771 261 522796
Forgney	Forgney	Edgeworth Lovell :	mill	-	-	-	Edgeworth E - Jerrard Jos ;	1824	Mort. 2 Mar.	dd/	789 418 533753
Forgney	Forgney	Fetherston George :	Fort Mill	-	-	-	Fetherston & Solly m.arts.	1821	-	dd/	767 84 520219
Cashel	Forthill	-	corn & mill dam	-	-	-	-	1837	-	6"os/	22
Cashel	Forthill	Glennon Peter	mill & kiln	-	-	-	-	1854	-	gr/	-
Cashel	Forthill	Glennon Peter	mill dam & land	-	21a.	-	-	1854	-	gr/	-
Street	Freaghmeen	-	corn & kiln :	-	-	-	-	1841	-	6"os/	15
Street	Freaghmeen	Carragig John	mill	-	21a.	-	-	1854	-	gr/	-
Killoe	Gaigue	-	corn, kiln, pond	-	-	-	-	1837	-	6"os/	5
Killoe	Gaigue	Maconchy John :	mill	-	-	-	Machonchy J - Johnston :	1825	Mort. 1 June	dd	803 320 542055
Killoe	Gaigue	Maconchy John :	mill	-	-	-	Maconchy J - Johnston Jas	1825	Mort. 1 June	dd/	803 320 542055
Noughaval	Garrynagh	- on R. Inny	flour	-	-	-	-	1837	-	6"os/	26
Noughval	Garrynagh	stream to Camlin R.	corn	-	-	-	-	1841	-	6"os/	9
Noughval	Garrynagh	McDermott Lucy :	-	-	-	-	Mcdermott L - Conran Patk	1826	-	dd/	812 202 547337
Noughval	Garrynagh	Murtagh Michael	flour & kiln	-	71a	-	-	1854	-	gr/	-
Noughval	Garrynagh	Shuldam	mill	-	-	-	Shuldam - McDermott	-	?	dd/	780 126 528061
Clonbroney	Garvagh	stream to Camlin R.	corn	-	-	-	-	1841	-	6"os/	9
Clonbroney	Garvagh	Harrison Mrs Alex	corn	-	-	-	-	-	12x3x14	vmb/	13
Clonbroney	Garvagh	Rogers Thomas	mill	-	15a.	-	-	1854	-	gr/	-
Killashee	Glebe	- N/ Richmond Hbr.	old bleach mill	-	-	-	-	1837	-	6"os/	13
Ballymacormick	Gorteenboy	Egan James	corn	-	77a.	-	-	1854	-	gr/	-
Clongesh	Gorteenora	Quinn Patrick	mill & kiln	-	-	-	-	1854	-	gr/	-
Killashee	Grillagh	-	corn & kilns	-	-	-	-	1837	-	6"os/	18
Killashee	Grillagh	-	long mill pond	-	-	-	-	1837	-	6"os/	18
Killashee	Grillagh	Trelford Edward	corn	-	66a.	-	-	1854	-	gr/	-
Abbeylara	Kilbride	-	corn & kiln	-	-	-	-	1837	-	6"os/	11
Granard	Killasona	-	corn	-	-	-	-	1841	-	6"os/	16
Granard	Killasona	- nr Abbeylara	mill	-	-	-	-	-	-	1"os/	-
Granard	Killasona	Mitchell Francis	corn	-	11a.	-	-	1854	-	gr/	-
Clongesh	Killeen	- N. side Camlin R.	corn & kiln	-	-	-	-	1841	-	6"os/	8
Clongesh	Killeen	Gouldsbury Robert :	mill	-	-	-	Gouldsbury R - Kiernan :	1823	-	dd/	778 290 527025
Clongesh	Killeen	Gouldsbury Robert :	mill	-	-	-	Gouldsbury R - Kiernan :	1822	-	dd/	786 385 531920
Clongesh	Killeen	Turkington	mill	-	-	-	Turkington - Kiernan	-	- [not 779]	dd/	779 291 527026
Ardagh	Killincastra	-	corn	-	-	-	-	1837	-	6"os/	14
Ardagh	Killincastra	Blackman Patrick	mill	-	26a.	-	-	1854	-	gr/	-
Columbkille	Kilmore	-	corn	-	-	-	-	1837	-	6"os/	6
Columbkille	Kilmore	-	kiln & pond	-	-	-	-	1837	-	6"os/	6
Columbkille	Kilmore	- stream to L Erne	mill	-	-	-	-	-	-	1"os/	-
Longford	Kilnavoge	-	corn & kilns	-	-	-	-	1837	-	6"os/	14
Longford	Kilnplot	Shuldam Jn Brady :	mill	-	-	-	Shuldam - Lewis John :	1825	Mort. 12 Feb.	dd/	804 458 542793
Longford	Kilnplot	Shuldam Jn Brady :	mill	-	-	-	Shuldam - Crosthwaite Jn :	1825	Mort. 12 Feb.	dd/	804 457 542792
Mostrim	Kilshilagh	- nr Edgeworthstn	corn	-	-	-	-	-	-	1"os/	-
Granard	Kilshruly	- beside Camlin R.	mill	-	-	-	-	-	-	1"os/	79
Granard	Kilshruly	- N. side Camlin R	bleach & tuck	-	-	-	-	1841	-	6"os/	10
Granard	Kilshruly	- N. side Camlin R	corn & kiln	-	-	-	-	1841	-	6"os/	9
Clonbroney	Kilshruly	- on co. boundary	corn & kiln :	-	-	-	-	1851	-	vmb/	13

PARISH	TOWNLAND	MILLER	TYPE	HOUSE	Land	£Val	PROPRIETORS	Date	WHEEL etc.	Record	Ref.
Clonbroney	Kilshruly	M`Manus John	bleach	-	-	-	-	1854	-	gr/	-
Clonbroney	Kilshruly	M`Manus John	corn & flour	-	89a.	-	-	1854	-	gr/	-
Clonbroney	Kilshruly	McManus Jno	bleach	-	-	-	-	-	13x3x8 2 beams ea.	vmb/	13
Clonbroney	Kilshruly	McManus Jno	bleach	-	-	-	-	-	10x2x8 4 H.P.	vmb/	13
Clonbroney	Kilshruly	McManus Jno	corn	-	-	-	-	-	15x2x15 & 15x2x15	vmb/	13
Clonbroney	Kilshruly	McManus Jno	shelling	-	-	-	-	-	12x4x -	vmb/	13
Clonbroney	Kilshruly	McManus Jno	tuck	-	-	-	-	-	10x2x8 4 H.P.	vmb/	13
Killashee	Knock	1/4m SE/ L'borough	winmill	- note :	-	-	-	1841	-	6"os/	17
Killashee	Lanesborough	-	mill	-	-	-	-	-	-	1"os/	88
Longford	Lanesborough :	Cline`s Mill	corn	nicely restored	-	-	-	-	-	phWEH	Cr
Kilcommock	Ledwithstown	-	corn & corn kiln	-	-	-	-	1837	-	6"os/	22
Kilcommock	Ledwithstown	Moody William	mill	-	10a.	-	-	1854	-	gr/	-
Longford	Lisduff	-	mill	conv. for res.	-	-	-	2002		phWEH	Cr
Clonbroney	Lislea	-	corn kiln ruins	-	-	-	-	1841	-	6"os/	9
Clonbroney	Lislea	- SW/ Lislea Br.	corn & kiln	-	-	-	-	1841	-	6"os/	9
Clonbroney	Lislea	Tracy Cornelius	corn	-	-	-	-	-	12x2x13 & 12x2x13	vmb/	13
Clonbroney	Lislea	Treacy Cornelius	mill	-	67a.	-	-	1854	-	gr/	-
Mostrim	Lisnagrish	-	corn	-	-	-	-	-	-	1"os/	89
Mostrim	Lissanure	-	corn & mill pond	-	-	-	-	1837	-	6"os/	20
Granard	Lissanure	Cox William	mill	-	23a.	-	-	1854	-	gr/	-
Templemichael	Longford Town	Dublin NC Milling Co.	mill	-	-	-	DNCM Co - Longford E.	1887	-	dd/	1897 31 56
Templemichael	Longford Town	Dublin NC Milling Co.	steam corn	-	-	-	DNCMC - McCarthy Mary E	1880	-	dd/	1880 30 203
Templemichael	Longford Town	Fee Thomas	corn	-	-	-	Fee Thos - Ulster Bank	1887	-	dd/	1887 25 169
Templemichael	Longford Town	Hughes James	corn	-	-	-	-	1854	-	gr/	-
Templemichael	Longford Town	Kennedy Thomas	Manor Mills	-	-	-	Kennedy - O`Connell Mrce	1837	-	dd/	1837 10 49
Templemichael	Longford Town	Kincaird Joseph	mill & water	-	-	-	Kincaird Jos - Thos Revs	1837	-	dd/	1837 22 201
Templemichael	Longford Town	Longford Earl	Manor Mill	-	-	-	Longford Earl - Fee Thos	1884	-	dd/	1884 44 209
Templemichael	Longford Town	Longford Earl+C48	Murtagh`s Mills	-	-	-	Longford E - DC Milling Co.	1880	-	dd/	1880 3 31
Templemichael	Longford Town	Martin Richard Sen	Manor Mill	-	-	-	Martin Richd - Ulster Bank	1896	-	dd/	1896 50 40
Templemichael	Longford Town	Murtagh Micl & Mcl	corn	-	-	-	-	1854	-	gr/	-
Templemichael	Longford Town	Pendleton Richard	Longford Mills	-	-	-	Pendleton - McCarthy Mary	1879	-	dd/	1879 55 273
Templemichael	Longford Town	Rember Chief	mill & water	-	-	-	Re Ch. - McCarthy Amarill	1850	-	dd/	1850 6 275
Templemichael	Longford Town :	Hughes James	corn & store	-	-	32	-	-	new metal 14x3.6x5 :	hob/	5.3069
Templemichael	Longford Town :	Murtagh Michael	new mill	(1A) 50x50x45 :	-	-	-	-	new wheel 16x7.6x5 :	hob/	5.3069
Templemichael	Longford Town :	-	potter's kiln	-	-	-	-	1837	-	6"os/	13
Templemichael	Longford Town :	- N. side Camlin R.	corn	-	-	-	-	1837	-	6"os/	13
Templemichael	Longford Town :	- on Gt Water St.	brewery	-	-	-	-	1837	-	6"os/	13
Templemichael	Longford Town :	- on Gt Water St.	distillery	-	-	-	-	1837	-	6"os/	13
Templemichael	Longford Town :	- S. side River	old corn mill	-	-	-	-	1837	-	6"os/	13
Templemichael	Longford Town :	Costello Charles	distillery & mill	-	-	-	Costello C - Murtagh Jas	1875	-	dd/	1875 41 194
Templemichael	Longford Town :	Murtagh Elizabeth	distillery & mill	-	-	-	Murtagh - Dub. Milling Co.	1876	-	dd/	1876 252
Templemichael	Longford Town :	Murtagh Michael	steam corn	(1B) 86x21x15	-	-	-	1854	steam & new wheel :	hob/	5.3067
Taghsheenod	Loughsheedan	-	corn & kiln	-	-	-	-	1837	-	6"os/	23
Taghsheenod	Loughsheedan	-	mill ponds (2)	-	-	-	-	1837	-	6"os/	23
Taghsheenod	Loughsheedan	M`Donnell Laur	corn	-	42a.	-	-	1854	-	gr/	-
Killoe	Melkagh	-	corn kiln	-	-	-	-	1841	-	6"os/	5
Killoe	Melkagh	Corrigan John	corn	-	37a.	-	-	1854	-	gr/	-
Granard	Millbrook		mill	-	-	-	-	-	-	1"os/	-
Granard	Monadarragh	- SW/ Mullingar Rd.	old corn mill : &	-	-	-	-	1841	-	6"os/	15
Granard	Monadarragh	Duffy John	old corn mill	-	52a.	-	-	1854	-	gr/	-
Ardagh	Moor	Little John :	mill	-	-	-	Little J - Mullaniff James :	1821	-	dd/	765 343 519278
Kilcommock	Mosstown	- S/ Coolnahinch Br.	flour	-	-	-	-	1837	-	6"os/	22

PARISH	TOWNLAND	MILLER	TYPE	HOUSE	Land	£Val	PROPRIETORS	Date	WHEEL etc.	Record phWEH	Ref. R
Longford	Mosstown :	Kellick`s Mill	flour	a large ruins	-	-	-	-	-		
Killashee	Moygh	Bond Richard	tile kiln	-	2.0.6	-	-	1854	-	gr/	-
Shrule	nr Ballmahon	- on Inny R.	woollen fcty	-	-	-	-	-	-	1"os/	-
Columbkille	Rathmore	-	ruin of a mill	-	-	-	-	1837	-	6"os/	6
Columbkille	Rosduff	-	corn kilns (3)	-	-	-	-	1837	-	6"os/	3
Columbkille	Rosduff	Victory Francis	mill	-	10a.	-	-	1854	-	gr/	-
Columbkille	Roseduff	- stream / L Gowna	mill	-	-	-	-	-	-	1"os/	-
Columbkille	Roseduff	McNaboe Francis	corn	-	-	-	-	-	12x2x12	vmb/	13
Columbkille	Rossduff	-	corn	-	-	-	-	1837	-	6"os/	3
Clonbroney	Sheeroe	-	corn & kilns	-	-	-	-	1837	-	6"os/	15
Clonbroney	Sheeroe	-	mill race, pond	-	-	-	-	1837	-	6"os/	15
Clonbroney	Sheeroe	Browne John :	-	-	-	-	Browne Jn - Edgeworth :	1827	-	dd/	822 505 533640
Clonbroney	Sheeroe	Edgeworth Connell :	mill	-	-	-	Edgeworth C - Herview :	1822	-	dd/	774 43 524378
Clonbroney	Sheeroe	Edgeworth Lovell :	mill	-	-	-	Edgeworth - Pemberton Jn	1820	-	dd/	758 397 515038
Clonbroney	Sheeroe	Edgeworth Lovell :	mill	-	-	-	Edgeworth L - Duigan Mcl :	1821	-	dd/	760 538 526475
Clonbroney	Sheeroe	Edgeworth Lovell :	mill	-	-	-	Edgeworth L - Jackson Jn :	1822	-	dd/	769 31 521366
Clonbroney	Sheeroe	Edgeworth Lovell :	mill	-	-	-	Edgeworth - Parker Sidney:	1822	-	dd/	771 506 523041
Clonbroney	Sheeroe	Jackson John :	-	-	-	-	Jackson Jn - Edgeworth :	1827	-	dd/	822 504 533639
Clonbroney	Sheeroe	Slator George W W	corn	-	18a.	-	-	1854	-	gr/	-
Clonbroney	Sheeroe	Sneyd Mary :	-	-	-	-	Sneydyan M - Fox Richard :	1826	-	dd/	810 525 564460
Shrule	Shrule	- W. side R. Inny	corn	-	-	-	-	1837	-	6"os/	26
Shrule	Shrule	Butler Nicholas	corn		43a.	-	-	1854	-	gr/	-
Shrule	Shrule	McDermot Chris. :	mill	-	-	-	McDermott C - McDermott :	-	?	dd/	790 445 534380
Shrule	Shrule	McDermott	-	-	-	-	McDermott - Conran	-	-	dd/	812 202 547337
Shrule	Shrule	McGlynn Philip	corn	-	-	-	-	-	11x2x12 & 11x2x12	vmb/	13
Shrule	Shrule	Shuldam John Brady:	mill	-	-	-	Shuldam J - McDermott Mcl	1822	Conv. 20 Sept.	dd/	780 126 528061
Columbkille	Smear	-	corn & kiln	-	-	-	-	1837	-	6"os/	3
Columbkille	Smear	M`Coy Thomas :	corn & kiln		0.2.0	-	-	1854	-	gr/	-
Columbkille	Smear	McCoy Jno & Richd	corn	-	-	-	-	-	12x2x13	vmb/	13
Columbkille	Smear	Mulligan William	corn kiln		-	-	-	1854	-	gr/	-
Kilglass	Smithfield	-	corn & pond	-	-	-	-	1837	-	6"os/	24
Granard	Springtown	- near Ballywillin	mill	-	-	-	-	-	-	1"os/	-
Killoe	Tawnagh	- nr Crowdrumman	mill	-	-	-	-	-	-	1"os/	-
Taghshinny	Tennalick	- on Inny R. :	cirn	-	-	-	-	1841	-	6"os/	27
Taghshinny	Tennalick	M'Cann John &Sons	corn	house, offs. & ld.	36.2.	174	-	1865	-	gr/	-
Taghshinny	Tennalick	M'Cann John &Sons	corn (part of)	- & land	1.3.	9	-	1865	-	gr/	aai.ie
Taghshinny	Tennalick	M'Cann John &Sons	house	offices & land	74a.	69.10.	-	1865	-	gr/	aai.ie
Taghshinny	Tennalick	M'Cann John &Sons	store	- on canal bank	2a.	30	-	1865	-	gr/	aai.ie
Taghshinny	Tennalick :	Christie Robert	corn	- & garden	0.0.30	16	-	1865	-	gr/	aai.ie
Taghshinny	Tennalick :	McCann Mrs :	house	offices & garden	0.0.30	4	-	1865	-	gr/	aai.ie
Mostrim	Tinnynarr	Sneyd Mary :	-	-	-	-	Sneydyan M - Fox Richard :	1826	-	dd/	810 525 546460
Columbkille	Toome	-	corn & kiln	-	-	-	-	1837	-	6"os/	6
Columbkille	Toome	Sloan James	corn	-	-	-	-	-	11x2x14	vmb/	13
Columbkille	Toome	Sloan James	corn	-	-	-	-	-	11x2x14	vmb/	13
Columbkille	Toome	Sloane Thomas	mill & kiln	-	2.3.7	-	-	1854	-	gr/	-
Longford	Treely (3)	Fox Richard :	mill	-	-	-	Fox Richard - Henn Jno :	1822	Annuity 25 Apl.	dd/	771 191 522726
Granard	Tully, Milltown Vge.	-	old mill	-	-	-	-	1837	-	6"os/	15
Longford	Windmill Hill	Jackson	mill	-	-	-	Jackson - Park	-	?	dd/	778 35 526770
Killashee	Woodlawn	Bond R W	tile kiln	-	71a.	-	-	1854	-	gr/	-

PARISH	TOWNLAND	MILLER	TYPE	HOUSE	Land	£Val	PROPRIETORS	Date	WHEEL etc.	Record	Ref.
B`mascanlan	Aghaboys	Bellew James	corn	-	-	-	-	-	15x3x13	vmb/	-
B`mascanlan	Aghaboys	Martin Mary Anne	corn	(1B) 30x20x18.6 :	-	2-15	-	1853	14.6x3.6x - o`shot	hob/	5.4046
B`mascanlan	Aghaboys	McNeill John	flax	(1A) 78x30.6x18.6 :	-	43-9	-	1853	- steam power	hob/	5.4046
Drumcar	Annagassan	-	mill	-	-	-	-	-	-	1"os/	82
Drumcar	Annagassan	Thompson	mills	-	-	-	Thompson - Iles	-	-	dd/	798 148 538883
Drumcar	Annagassan :	Dougherty Chas & Co	flour	-	-	-	-	1963	-	lic./12	flour
B`mascanlan	Annaloughan	Moore Samuel	threshing	-	-	-	-	-	13x2x13	vmb/	-
B`mascanlan	Annaverna	- nr Ravensdale Br.	corn	-	-	-	-	-	-	6"os/	4
B`mascanlan	Annaverna	Thompson B & Co.	corn	-	-	-	-	-	19x6x17	vmb/	-
Ardee	Ardee	-	Bridge Mills	-	-	-	-	1886	-	dir/	lou.bstt
Ardee	Ardee	Greenville Mill	corn	foundations only & offices remain			- Frank Aiken	1998	-	pWEH	R
Ardee	Ardee	Addy Edward	corn	-	-	-	-	-	14x3x14	vmb/	-
Ardee	Ardee	Breaghy Joseph :	mill	-	-	-	Breaghy J - Ward Patk :	1819	Asgt. 5 Nov.	dd/	746 172 507707
Ardee	Ardee	Davis Fran Louia :	mill	-	-	-	Davis F - McCann Richd :	1818	Smt. 12 May	dd/	728 29 496764
Ardee	Ardee	Fleming Christopher :	mill	-	-	-	Fleming C - Webb Hugh :	1819	Asgt. 21 Jan.	dd/	745 470 507405
Ardee	Ardee	Foster Baron	corn	-	-	-	-	-	18x4x3	vmb/	-
Ardee	Ardee	Foster Baron	flour	-	-	-	-	-	18x4x3	vmb/	-
Ardee	Ardee	Halpenny M & Co.	steam	-	-	-	Builder : Wm Munkittrick	1886	-	dir/	lou.bstt
Ardee	Ardee	Montgomery Robert :	mill	-	-	-	Montgomery R - Pepper :	1816	Renl. Lse. 2 Mar.	dd/	745 467 507402
Ardee	Ardee	Ruxton	mill	-	-	-	Ruxton - Filgate	-	-	dd/	639 366 442357
Ardee	Ardee	Thompson	mill	-	-	-	Thompson - Thompson	-	?	dd/	723 234 493696
Ardee	Ardee	Thompson	mill	-	-	-	Thompson - McClelland	-	-	dd/	742 297 505432
Ardee	Ardee	Thorpe Frank Thos :	mill	-	-	-	Thorpe F - Thorpe Rchd :	1819	Rel. 25 Mar.	dd/	747 34 508169
Ardee	Ardee T`parks	Gray James	corn	-	8a.	-	-	-	-	gr/	-
Ardee	Ardee T`parks	Gray James	corn	-	-	-	-	-	13x3x13	vmb/	-
Ardee	Ardee Town	- on R Dee	mill	-	-	-	-	-	-	1"os/	81
Ardee	Ardee Town	- S. side of Town	corn & kiln	-	-	-	-	-	-	6"os/	17
Ardee	Ardee Town	- S. side of Town	mill race	-	-	-	-	-	-	6"os/	17
Ardee	Ardee Town	- S. side R. Dee :	corn	-	-	-	-	-	-	6"os/	17
Ardee	Ardee Town	- S. side R. Dee :	tan yard	-	-	-	-	-	-	6"os/	17
Ardee	Ardee Town	Ball (as Master) :	mill	-	-	-	Filgate T - Filgate Alex :	1821	Conv. 25 Aug.	dd/	767 458 520593
Ardee	Ardee Town	Ball Thomas :	mill	-	-	-	Ball T - Filgate Townly P	1819	Conv. 19 Oct.	dd/	767 500 520635
Ardee	Ardee Town	Bayley Caroline	mills	-	-	-	-	1895	-	-	-
Ardee	Ardee Town	Bayly Caroline	Addys Mill	-	-	-	Bayly C - Munkittriick Alex	1892	-	dd/	1892 57 54
Ardee	Ardee Town	Bradley Thomas	corn	-	0.0.15		-	-	-	gr/	-
Ardee	Ardee Town	Bradley Thomas	corn	-	-	-	-	-	17x4x2 16x4x4	vmb/	-
Ardee	Ardee Town	Brooks William Jas	Bridge Mills	-	-	-	Brooks WJ - Bradley Patk	1851	-	dd/	1851 9244
Ardee	Ardee Town	Cole Maria Se Le P	Old Bridge Mill	-	-	-	Cole Maria - Blair Edw S	1884	-	dd/	1884 33 44
Ardee	Ardee Town	Douglas William G	Atherdee Mill :	-	9a.	-	Douglas W - Ruxton Wm	1880	-	dd/	1880 28 217
Ardee	Ardee Town	Foster Jno	Bridge Mills	-	-	-	Foster J - North Letitia	1841	-	dd/	1841 9 259
Ardee	Ardee Town	Halpenny Peter	Old Bridge mills	-	-	-	Halpenny Peter - Bernard	1884	-	dd/	1884 34 21
Ardee	Ardee Town	Home Gustavius	Bridge Mills	-	-	-	-	1895	-	-	-
Ardee	Ardee Town	Irwin Crinus	Mill of Ardee	-	-	-	Irwin C - Ruxton Clarges	1840	-	dd/	1840 7 129
Ardee	Ardee Town	Kidd Hugh	Bridge Mills	-	-	-	KiddHugh - Kidd Wm	1836	-	dd/	1836 20 18
Ardee	Ardee Town	Magee or Browne	mill	-	-	-	Magee - Jackson James	1850	-	dd/	1850 19 92
Ardee	Ardee Town	Monkittrick Robert	mills	-	-	-	Monkittrick - Bayley C`line	1895	-	dd/	1895 8 75
Ardee	Ardee Town	Montgomery Alex	mill	-	-	-	Montgomery Alex - Sophia	1846	-	dd/	1846 17 153
Ardee	Ardee Town	Montgomery Alex	Mills of Atherdee	-	-	-	Montgomery - Prescott Rb	1845	-	dd/	1845 2 248
Ardee	Ardee Town	Montgomery Richard	Mill of Atherdee	-	-	-	Montgomery - Barrington :	1891	-	dd/	1891 5 235
Ardee	Ardee Town	Montgomery Richard	mills & fields	-	-	-	Montgomery - Swanzy Th	1884	-	dd/	1884 5 56
Ardee	Ardee Town	Morgan Richard :	Bridge Mills	-	-	-	Morgan - Kinstry Lee	1828	-	dd/	836 287 561822
Ardee	Ardee Town	Munkillrick William	corn	-	-	-	-	-	- steam engine	vmb/	-

PARISH	TOWNLAND	MILLER	TYPE	HOUSE	Land	£Val	PROPRIETORS	Date	WHEEL etc.	Record	Ref.
Ardee	Ardee Town	Ruxton	mill	-	-	-	Ruxton - Lee	-	?	dd/	862 305 574805
Ardee	Ardee Town	Ruxton Arthur	Mill of Atherdee	-	-	-	Ruxton A - Knox Robt J	1841	-	dd/	1841 4 57
Ardee	Ardee Town	Ruxton John	Atherdee Mill	-	-	-	Ruxton John - Mary	1892	-	dd/	1892 31 231
Ardee	Ardee Town	Ruxton William	Atherdee Mill	-	-	-	Ruxton Wm - King Richd	1880	-	dd/	1880 33 108
Ardee	Ardee Town	Ruxton William	Atherdee Mill	-	-	-	Ruxton Wm - Hayes Wm	1881	-	dd/	1881 29 76
Ardee	Ardee Town	Ruxton William	Atherdee Mill :	-	-	-	Ruxton W - Singleton Reg	1884	-	dd/	1884 58 127
Ardee	Ardee Town	Ruxton William	Atherdee Mill :	-	-	-	Ruxton W - Keily Henry	1884	-	dd/	1884 59 126
Ardee	Ardee Town	Ruxton William	Atherdee Mill :	-	-	-	Ruxton W - Meredith Wm	1884	-	dd/	1884 59 171
Ardee	Ardee Town	Ruxton William	Bridge Mills	-	-	-	Ruxton Wm - Home G`vus	1895	-	dd/	1895 62 271
Ardee	Ardee Town :	Addy John	mills	-	-	-	Addy Jn - Addy Edward	1835	-	dd/	1835 21 276
Ardee	Ardee Town :	Addy	mill	-	-	-	Addy - Addy	-	?	dd/	880 367 583867
Ardee	Ardee Town :	Armitage	mill	-	-	-	Armitage - Disney	-	-	dd/	875 301 581301
Ardee	Ardee Town :	Addy Edward	mills	-	-	-	Addy Ed - Duffy Chas	1837	-	dd/	1837 20 2
Ardee	Ardee Town :	Gare Francis	mills	-	-	-	Gare Fras - Smyth Lucas	1839	-	dd/	1839 9 182
Ardee	Ardee Town :	Addy John	mill	-	-	-	Addy John - Addy Edwd	1835	-	dd/	1835 21 276
Ardee	Ardee Town :	Bradley Thomas	(cont.) kiln :	(1B) 48x25.6x18.6 :	-	72-15	-	1852	2 wheels, 4 pr. st. :	hob/	5.3071
Ardee	Ardee Town :	Bradley Thomas	corn & oat	(1B) 23.6x23.6x34 :	-	-	-	1852	-	hob/	5.3072
Ardee	Ardee Town :	Foster Breen :	flour & corn	- not working :	-	-	-	1852	2 mid-shot 18x4x3 :	hob/	5.3072
Ardee	Ardee Town :	Addy Edward	malt store	-	-	-	-	1852	-	hob/	5.3072
Ardee	Ardee Town :	Mankitrick William	new mill	(1B) 23x36x45 :	-	80	-	1852	steam engine 12 hp	hob/	5.3071
Ardee	Ardee Town :	Addy Edward	corn	mill, store, offs & yd	-	51-6	- prems. going to ruin :	1852	14.6x3x14.6 2 pr.st.	hob/	5.3072
Ardee	Ardee Town :	Ruxton William	The Mill	-	-	-	Ruxton Wm - Wilson Thos	1851	-	dd/	1851 9 280
Ardee	Ardee Town :	Ruxton Wiliam	mills	-	-	-	Ruxton William - Jno	1853	-	dd/	1853 26 34
Ardee	Ardee Town :	Ruxton Wiliam	prems & mills	-	-	-	Ruxton W - Bowden Wm	1853	-	dd/	1853 24 99
Ardee	ArdeeTown	Monk Richard Hon.	Old Bridge Mill	-	-	-	Monk Richard - Richard	1886	-	dd/	1886 22 41
Ardee	ArdeeTown	Ruxton William	Atherdee Mill	-	-	-	Ruxton W - Guiness Henry	1881	-	dd/	1881 5 165
Ardee	ArdeeTown	Ruxton William	Atherdee Mill	-	-	-	Ruxton Wm - Rooke W. Bt	1888	-	dd/	1888 42 65
Ardee	ArdeeTown	Ruxton William	mill	-	-	-	Ruxton W - Scottish Prov.	1885	-	dd/	1885 14 180
Ardee	ArdeeTown	Ruxton William	mills	-	-	-	Ruxton Wm - Meredith Wn	1885	-	dd/	1885 13 217
Ardmulchan	Ardmulchan	Boyne Lord	mill & race	-	-	-	Boyne Ld - Smith	-	-	dd/	743 506 506241
Ardmulchan	Ardmulchan	Jones	mill & race	-	-	-	Jones & Jackson	-	-	dd/	743 527 506262
Ardree	Ardnaree	Brown Dorcas Hon. :	mills	-	-	-	Dorcas Hon. - Paget Jame	1787	-	dd/	404 338 268482
Ardree	Ardree	- mid. of River :	flour	-	-	-	-	-	-	6"os/	35
Ardree	Ardree	Chargneau Wm :	mill & weir	-	-	-	Chargneau W & Agmt	1821	-	dd/	763 70 517805
Ardree	Ardree	Colville Wm Charg	mill & weir	-	-	-	Colville & Farange (agmt.)	-	-	dd/	-
Ardree	Ardree	Haughton Alfred	flour	-	2.0.27		-	-	-	gr/	-
Ardree	Ardree	Kelly Rev Thomas	mills	-	-	-	Kelly T - Meyler Jno	1841	-	dd/	1841 22 182
Ardree	Ardree	Sherlock Thomas	mill & weir	-	-	-	Sherlock Thomas & :	1821	-	dd/	761 565 517101
Ardree	Ardree Town	Haughton Alfred	flour	(1B) 86x13x37 :	-	-	-	1851	(no meas m/cy etc.)	hob/	5.3873
Ardree	Ardree Town	Haughton Alfred	flour	104x21x37 :	-	-	-	1851	19x15x3.9 no. floats	hob/	5.3873
Ardree	Ardree Town	Kidd Hugh	Bridge Mills	-	-	-	-	1836	-	dd/	1836 20 18
Ardree	Ardree Town	Kidd William	Bridge Mills	-	-	-	-	1841	-	dd/	1836 20 18
Louth	Ashlittle	Smith Patrick	flax	(3C) 29x20x9.6 :	-	-	-	1838	13.3x1.9 o`shot :	hob/	5.4074
Louth	Ashlittle	Smith Patrick	malt store	(1B) 76x24x17.6 :	-	-	-	1838		hob/	5.4074
Louth	Ashlittle	Smyth Patrick	flax	-	-	-	-	-	13x2x13 3 berths	vmb/	-
Roche	Ballinfriel	Campbell Peter	corn & kiln	(1B) 25x23x18 :	-	6-13	-	1838	14x2.6x - o`shot	hob/	5.4068
Roche	Ballinfull	Campbell Peter	corn	-	-	-	-	-	14x2x14 idle 3 yrs	vmb/	-
Carlingford	Ballinteskin	-	corn	-	-	-	-	-	-	6"os/	4
Carlingford	Ballinteskin	Rice Bernard	corn & tuck	-	-	-	-	-	14x2x10 tuck mill :	vmb/	-
Carlingford	Ballintiskin	Rice Bernard	corn	-	-	-	-	-	13x3x -	osm/	-
Barronstown	Ballinurd	-	threshing	-	-	-	-	-	-	6"os/	6
Barronstown	Ballybinaby	- ab. B`binaby Br.	mill	-	-	-	-	-	-	6"os/	3

PARISH	TOWNLAND	MILLER	TYPE	HOUSE	Land	£Val	PROPRIETORS	Date	WHEEL etc.	Record	Ref.
Roche	Ballybinaby	Murphy Thomas	corn	-	-	-	-	-	13x2x7 1 set fans	vmb/	-
Louth	Ballybony	-	corn	-	-	-	-	-	-	1"os/	-
B`mascanlan	Ballymascanlan	-	corn	-	-	-	-	-	-	6"os/	7
B`mascanlan	Ballymascanlan	Brush	mill	-	-	-	Brush - Fortescue	-	?	dd/	750 403 510336
B`mascanlan	Ballymascanlan	Colter Launcelot	corn	(1B) 66x23.6x31 :	-	21-3	-	1853	16x5x13 40 bkts. :	hob/	5.4046
B`mascanlan	Ballymascanlan	McNeale Wolfe	corn	-	-	-	-	-	16x5x13	vmb/	-
B`mascanlan	Ballymascanlan	McNeale Wolfe	threshing	-	-	-	-	-	15x4x12	vmb/	-
B`mascanlan	Ballymascanlan	Ruxton	mills	-	-	-	Ruxton - Carter	-	-	dd/	771 496 523031
Louth	Ballynamenan	Beatty	mill	-	-	-	Beatty - Fortescue	-	-	dd/	749 213 509548
Louth	Ballynamenan	Brush	mill	-	-	-	Brush - Thompson	-	-	dd/	751 469 511004
Louth	Ballynamenan	Ruxton	mills	-	-	-	Ruxton - Carter	-	-	dd/	771 496 523031
Louth	Ballynamenan	Tallan	mill	-	-	-	Tallan - Tallan	-	-	dd/	749 416 509751
Castletown	Balregan	-	flour	-	-	-	-	-	-	6"os/	7
Castletown	Balregan	-	mill	-	-	-	-	-	-	6"os/	4
Castletown	Balregan	-	mill& weir	-	-	-	-	-	-	6"os/	4
Castletown	Balregan	- Scotch Green Mill	mill	-	-	-	-	-	-	6"os/	7
Castletown	Balregan	Callan	mills	-	-	-	Callan - Bryans	-	-	dd/	807 291 544426
Castletown	Balregan	Coleman John	corn	house & land	11a.	53	- [+ tenants' houses]	1856	-	gr/	a.a.Ire.ie
Castletown	Balregan	Coleman Michael	spade, shovel	-	-	-	-	-	14x3x14 & 13x4x13	vmb/	-
Castletown	Balregan	Colman Michael	spade foundry	(1B) 56x32x30.6 :	-	17-5	-	1838	13.4x4.2x1.3 o`shot	hob/	5.4052
Castletown	Balregan	Kelly Denis & Michael	flour	-	13a.	-	-	-	-	gr/	-
Castletown	Balregan	Kelly Michael	flour	(1C) 93x24x46 :	-	52	-	1848	16x7x8 & 14x5.6x8	hob/	5.4052
Castletown	Balregan	Kelly Michael	flour	-	-	-	-	-	16x7x8 & 14x5x8	vmb/	-
Castletown	Balregan	Sherry	mills	-	-	-	Sherry - Callan	-	?	dd/	801 492 540964
Castletown	Balregan :	Dennis James	mill	-	-	-	-	1886	-	dir/	lou.bstt
Castletown	Balregan :	Sherif Co Louth	mills	-	-	-	Sherif Co Louth - Callan	-	-	dd/	803 208 541943
Faughart	Balriggan	Callon John	corn & flour	-	-	-	-	-	20x6x13 3 pr st.	vmb/	-
Faughart	Balriggan	Kieran John	corn	ofices & land	11a.	73	- [+ tenants' houses]	1856	-	gr/	a.a.ire.ie
Bealieu	Banktown	Wright Alex	corn & flour	-	-	-	-	-	13x4x13 3 pr st	vmb/	-
Beaulieu	Banktown	Wright Joseph	corn & flour	(1B) 28x20x14 :	-	-	-	-	13x4x - 3 pair st.	hob/	5.1300
Bealieu	Banktown	Wright Joseph	mill & kiln	(1B)28x20x14 :	-	-	-	-	o`shot 13x4 32 bkts.	hob/	5.1300
Bealieu	Banktown Up & Lr	Johnston	mills	-	-	-	Johnston - Adams	-	-	dd/	808 341 545076
Duleek	Beamond Mills	McCann John	brewery	150 ft x 5 storey :	2a.	-	Mr Patrick Casey Connolly	1886	no dimensions :	dir/	lou.bstt
Ballyboys	Bellurgan	-	tuck mill ruins	-	-	-	-	-	-	6"os/	7
Ballyboys	Bellurgan	Tipping Richard	threshing	-	-	-	-	-	12x4x12	vmb/	-
Collon	Belpatrick	-	corn	-	-	-	-	-	-	1"os/	81
Collon	Belpatrick	Magennis Thomas	corn	-	23a.	-	-	-	-	gr/	-
Collon	Belpatrick	McGinnis Patrick	flax	-	-	-	-	-	12x2x12 3 berths	vmb/	-
Dundalk	Cambrickville	Duffy Arthur	brewery	-	15a.	-	Built by Mr P Wynne JP	1886	-	dir/	lou.bstt
Dundalk	Cambrickville	McAlister James	brewery	(1B) 27x15.6x8 :	71a.	-	-	1838	-	hob/	5.4057
Ardee	Cappocks	Carnhampton Earl	mill	-	-	-	Carhampton - Cremorne	-	-	dd/	769 83 521418
Ardee	Cappocks	Cooper	mill	-	-	-	Cooper - Mitchell	-	-	dd/	769 81 521416
Ardee	Cappocks	Faviere	mill	-	-	-	Faviere - Faviere	-	-	dd/	789 85 533420
Ardee	Cappocks	Grimwood	mill	-	-	-	Grimwood - Mitchell	-	-	dd/	769 82 521417
Knockbride	Cappocksgreen	- N. side R. Dee :	corn	-	-	-	-	-	-	6"os/	17
Knockbride	Cappocksgreen	- N. side R. Dee :	flax	-	-	-	-	-	-	6"os/	17
Carlingford	Carlingford	McKivitt Mr	corn	-	-	-	-	-	13.10x2x -	osm/	-
Carlingford	Carlingford	Nugent	land & mill dam	-	-	-	-	-	-	dd/	868 150 577650
Carlingford	Carlingford	Rainsford Joseph	malt house				Rainsford J - Appointment	1896		dd/	1896 78 197
Carlingford	Carlingford Tn	Fortescue William	Grange Mill	-	-	-	Fortescue Wm - HoneEif	1875	-	dd/	1875 53 252
Carlingford	Carlingford Town	- 1/4 m. SE of Town	corn & dam	-	-	-	-	-	-	6"os/	5
Carlingford	Carlingford Town	Anderson James	mill & mill dam	-	-	-	Anderson J - Nugent Thos	1835	-	dd/	1835 10 49

PARISH	TOWNLAND	MILLER	TYPE	HOUSE	Land	£Val	PROPRIETORS	Date	WHEEL etc.	Record	Ref.
Carlingford	Carlingford Town :	Moore Hugh	mill	-	-	-	Moore Hugh - Ross	1853	-	dd/	1853 6 121
Dundalk	Carnabregagh	-	windmill stump	-	-	-	-	-	-	6"os/	7
Ballymakenny	Carntown	Norris Nicholas	corn	-	-	-	-	-	14x4x14	vmb/	-
Ballymakenny	Carntown	Norris Nicholas	mill	(2B) 25x19x9 & :	-	64	-	1852	14x4x2x15 o`shot	hob/	5.4035
Termonfeckin	Carstown	McGill William	corn	-	-	-	-	-	13x4x13	vmb/	-
Gernonstown	Castlebellingham	- on Glyde R. :	brewery	-	-	-	-	-	-	6"os/	15
Gernonstown	Castlebellingham	- on Glyde R. :	mill	-	-	-	-	-	-	6"os/	15
Gernonstown	Castlebellingham	Drumgoole Bridget	corn & kiln	-	0.1.0	-	-	-	-	gr/	-
Gernonstown	Castlebellingham	Woolsey John & Co.	brewery	4 storey building :	-	-	Bellingham family	1886	f`mly bleach green	dir/	lou.bstt
Louth	Castlering	- on Fane R.	mills	-	-	-	-	-	-	6"os/	11
Louth	Castlering	Hughes Patrick	corn	-	147a.	-	-	-	-	gr/	-
Louth	Castlering	Hughes Patrick	corn	-	-	-	-	-	13x3x13	vmb/	-
Louth	Castlering	Hughes Patrick	corn & tuck	(1A) 38.6x22.6x11 & :	-	-	-	1838	12.9x2.7 o`shot :	hob/	5.4074
Louth	Castlering	Hughes Patrick	tuck	-	-	-	-	-	12x2x7 1 stock & :	vmb/	-
Castletown	Castletown	-	corn	-	-	-	-	-	-	6"os/	8
Castletown	Castletown	-	flour	-	-	-	-	-	-	6"os/	7
Mullary	Castletown	Byrne Patrick	corn	(3C) 30x25x12 :	-	-	-	1852	-	hob/	5.1299
Mullary	Castletown	Byrnes Patrick	corn	-	-	-	-	-	11x3x11	vmb/	-
Castletown	Castletown	Callan	mill	-	-	-	Callan - Bryans	-	-	dd/	807 290 544425
Castletown	Castletown	Callan Patrick	flour	(1B) 46x23.6x43 :	-	17-3	-	1838	18x6x16 3 pr. st.	hob/	5.4052
Castletown	Castletown	Callon Patrick	flour	-	-	-	-	-	18x6x17 3 pr st.	vmb/	-
Castletown	Castletown	Colman John	corn :	-	-	24	-	1852	20x6x1.6	hob/	5.4052
Castletown	Castletown	M'Cann Richard	corn	house, offs. & land	3a.	46	- [+ tenant's house]	1856	-	gr/	a.a.ire.ie
Carlingford	Castletowncooley	E. side Castletown R.	corn	-	-	-	-	1841	-	6"os/	8
Carlingford	Castletowncooley	Feehan John	corn	-	-	-	-	-	16x3x13	vmb/	-
Carlingford	Castletowncooley	Feehan John	tuck	-	-	-	-	-	- 2 stocks /berths	vmb/	-
Carlingford	Castletowncooley	Murphy John	corn	-	-	-	-	-	14x2x6	vmb/	-
Chanonrock	Chanonrock	- Ch`rock Flour Mill	flour & dam	-	-	-	-	-	-	6"os/	6
Chanonrock	Chanonrock	Fortescue Faithful	flour	(1A) 75.6x29.6x60.6 :	-	-	-	1838	14x4x7	hob/	5.4074
Chanonrock	Chanonrock	Fortescue Faithful	flour	-	-	-	-	-	20x9x6 4 pr st & :	vmb/	-
Chanonrock	Chanonrock	Fortescue Faithful	flour	-	-	-	-	-	14x4x7	vmb/	-
Chanonrock	Chanonrock	Fortescue Faithful	flour (cont.)	(1A) 15x38x30 eng. :	-	-	-	1838	-	hob/	5.4074
Chanonrock	Chanonrock	Kiernan John	flour	-	52a.	-	-	-	-	gr/	-
Collon	Collon	M`Givey Luke	mill	-	34a.	-	-	-	-	gr/	-
Collon	Collon	McGivney L	oatmeal	-	-	-	Formerly Mellifont Abbey.	1886	-	dir/	lou.bstt
Collon	Collon	Qiun Henry	corn	-	-	-	-	-	18x6x18 4 pr st	vmb/	-
Collon	Collon	Sheckleton James	mills	-	75a.	-	-	-	-	gr/	-
Collon	Collon	Sheckleton Margaret	corn	-	140a.	-	-	-	-	gr/	-
Collon	Collon	Shekleton James	beetling	-	-	-	-	-	- steam engine &	vmb/	-
Collon	Collon	Shekleton James	bleach	-	-	-	-	-	14x6x6 2 beams	vmb/	-
Collon	Collon	Shekleton Mrs	corn	-	-	-	-	-	15x4x11 3 pr st	vmb/	-
Collon	Collon	Smith & Co.	corn	-	-	-	-	-	16x3x16 3 pr st	vmb/	-
Collon	Collon	Traynor Mary Ann	mill	-	160a.	-	-	-	-	gr/	-
Collon	Collon Town	-	old windmill	-	-	-	-	-	-	1"os/	81
Collon	Collon Town	McGivney Luke	corn	-	19a.	15-6	-	1852	20x6x- 3 pr.st. :	hob/	5.3075
Collon	Collon Town	Shekleton James	bleach	-	45a.	25 0	-	1852	15x5x12 drives :	hob/	5.3075
Collon	Collon Town	Shekleton James	corn	- (not much used)	-	40-0	-	1852	-	hob/	5.3075
Collon	Collon Town	Shekleton Margaret	corn	-	-	30-0	-	1852	15x4x6 3 pair st. :	hob/	5.3075
Collon	Collon Town	Traynor Mary Anne	mill	house, offices & land	150	100	-	1856	-	gr/	a.a.ire.ie
Collon	Collon Town	Traynor Mrs Mary A	corn	-	-	5-10	-	1852	16x4x16 2pr. st. :	hob/	5.3075
Louth	Comm. Corp. Lds	Johnston	mill	-	-	-	Johnston - Adams	-	-	dd/	808 341 545076
Louth	Corcreaghagh	Smyth	mill	-	-	-	Smyth - Daniel	-	-	dd/	770 515 522450

PARISH	TOWNLAND	MILLER	TYPE	HOUSE	Land	£Val	PROPRIETORS	Date	WHEEL etc.	Record	Ref.
Parsonstown	Cruisetown	-	corn	-	-	-	-	-	-	1"os/	82
Parsonstown	Cruisetown	- 1/2m from shore	corn	-	-	-	-	1841	-	6'os/	19
Parsonstown	Cruisetown	Collier John	corn	-	160a.	-	-	-	-	gr/	-
Parsonstown	Cruisetown	Collier Peter	corn	-	-	-	-	-	12x3x12 3 pr st	vmb/	-
Louth	Cushellstown	McClintock	mill	-	-	-	McClintock - King	-	-	dd/	759 444 515779
Ardee	Dawson`s Dems.	Hale Henry	corn	-	-	-	-	-	13x3x2	vmb/	-
Ardee	Dawson`s Dems.	Hale Henry	flax	-	-	-	-	-	13x3x2	vmb/	-
Ardee	Dawson`s Dems.	Hale Nathaniel	corn	-	18a.	-	-	-	-	gr/	-
Ardee	Dawson`s Dems.	Hale Nathaniel	corn	-	-	-	-	-	12x6x3 mill also :	vmb/	-
Drumcar	Dillonstown	- nr Anagassan Br.	flour	-	-	-	-	-	-	6"os/	15
Drumcar	Dillonstown	- nr Anagassan Br.	windmill	-	-	-	-	-	-	6"os/	15
Drumcar	Dillonstown	Dougherty Charles	mill	-	2.0.0	-	-	-	-	gr/	-
Drumcar	Dillonstown	Thompson Robert	corn	-	-	-	-	-	21x9x4	vmb/	-
Drumcar	Dillonstown	Thompson Robert	flour	-	-	-	-	-	18x8x4	vmb/	-
B`mascanlan	Doolargy	- at Taylor`s Br.	spade m`fcty	-	-	-	-	-	-	6"os/	4
B`mascanlan	Doolargy	- E. Thompson`s Br.	bleach	-	-	-	-	-	-	6"os/	4
B`mascanlan	Doolargy	- E. Thompson`s Br.	bleach	-	-	-	-	-	-	6"os/	4
B`mascanlan	Doolargy	- above Taylor`s Br.	spade m`fcty	-	-	-	-	-	-	6"os/	4
B`mascanlan	Doolargy	- nr Thompson`s Br.	bleach	-	-	-	-	-	-	6"os/	4
B`mascanlon	Doolargy	Benison Mrs Nichola	bleach & flax	(1C) 18x27x14 :	28-14	-	-	1853	-	hob/	5.4046
B`mascanlan	Doolargy	Benison Richard	bleach	-	-	-	-	-	14x3x14 16x6x16 & :	vmb/	-
B`mascanlan	Doolargy	Benison Richard	flax	-	-	-	-	-	16x6x16	vmb/	-
B`mascanlan	Doolargy	Berry John	bleach	-	-	-	-	-	14x4x11 13x3x13	vmb/	-
B`mascanlon	Doolargy	Thompson Benjamin	bleach	(1B) 92x25x17 :	11a.		-	1853	20.6x7x17 bkts. 50	hob/	5.4045
B`mascanlon	Doolargy	Thompson Benjamin	bleach	(1C) 19.6x23x15 :	10-7	-	-	1853	15x6.9x15.6 50 bkts	hob/	5.4046
B`mascanlan	Doolargy O`Hara	O`Hara Pat & Owen	bleach	-	-	-	-	-	12x4x12	vmb/	-
B`mascanlan	Doolargy O`Hara	O`Hara Pat & Owen	spade, shovel :	-	-	-	-	-	11x2x - 12x3x12	vmb/	-
B`mascanlan	Doolargy O`Hara	O`Hara Pat & Owen	spade, shovel :	-	-	-	-	-	11x2x9 14x4x6	vmb/	-
St Peter`s	Drogheda	-	cotton factory	-	-	-	-	-	-	1"os/	92
St Peter`s	Drogheda	-	mill	-	-	-	-	-	-	1"os/	92
St Peter`s	Drogheda Town	Allison Evan	corn	-	-	-	-	-	10x3x10	vmb/	-
St Peter`s	Drogheda Town	Cairns William	brewery	-	0.0.25		-	-	-	gr/	-
St Peters	Drogheda Town	CarpenterThomas	Cottage Mills	-	-	-	-	1886	-	dir/	lou.bstt
St Peter`s	Drogheda Town	Chadwick Jn & Fran	corn	-	-	-	-	-	-	gr/	-
St Peter`s	Drogheda Town	Ennis Thomas	steam corn-mill	-	-	-	-	-	-	gr/	-
St Peter`s	Drogheda Town	Grapwell & Chadwick	flax	-	-	-	-	-	-	gr/	-
St Peter`s	Drogheda Town	Grapwell & Chadwick	flax steam mill	-	-	-	-	-	-	gr/	-
St Peter`s	Drogheda Town	Grapwell & Chadwick	flax store	-	-	-	-	-	-	gr/	-
St Peter`s	Drogheda Town	Gray Robert	cotton factory	-	-	-	-	-	-	gr/	-
St Peter`s	Drogheda Town	Hill R A	flour - (steam)	150ft. front x 100ft	-	-	Mr Nathaniel Hill	1886	-	dir/	lou.bstt
St Peter`s	Drogheda Town	Hill Richard R	steam corn-mill	-	-	-	-	-	-	gr/	-
St Peter`s	Drogheda Town	Jameson, Pim & Co.	corn stores	-	-	-	-	-	-	gr/	-
St Peter`s	Drogheda Town	M`Cann John & Ann	corn store, kiln	-	-	-	-	-	-	gr/	-
St Peter`s	Drogheda Town	M`Carthy George	corn store, kiln	-	-	-	-	-	-	gr/	-
St Peter`s	Drogheda Town	Moore Thomas	corn	-	-	-	-	-	12x4x12	vmb/	-
St Peter`s	Drogheda Town	Morton John & Robt	corn (steam)	-	-	-	-	-	-	gr/	-
St Peter`s	Drogheda Town	Peter Verdon	rope factoty	-	7a.	-	-	-	-	gr/	-
St Peter`s	Drogheda Town	Ridgeway Thomas	corn & kiln	-	-	-	-	-	-	gr/	-
St Peter`s	Drogheda Town	Smith F St George	saw mill	-	-	-	-	1886	-	dir/	lou.bstt
St Peter`s	Drogheda Town	St Mary`s F.S. Co.	flax spinning	-	-	-	-	1886	-	dir/	lou.bstt
St Peter`s	Drogheda Town	Wetherill Thomas B	corn (steam)	-	-	-	-	-	-	gr/	-
St Peter`s	Drogheda Town :	Lyons Peter	wheatmeal :	-	-	-	-	1963	-	lic./39	wheat

PARISH	TOWNLAND	MILLER	TYPE	HOUSE	Land	£Val	PROPRIETORS	Date	WHEEL etc.	Record	Ref.
Tullyallan	Drogheda Town :	Clarke & Ennis	scutch	(1A) 75x40x24 & :	-	23.15	-	1850	-	hob/	5.4037
Tullyallan	Drogheda Town :	Heeny Patrick	bleach grnds	-	-	-	-	1850	-	hob/	5.4037
Tullyallan	Drogheda Town :	Heeny Patrick	flax (steam)	- ho., off, stores.	-	-	-	-	-	hob/	5.4037
Tullyallan	Drogheda Town :	Heeny Patrick	Mell Flax Mill	- ho., offs & yd.	-	-	-	1850	-	hob/	5.4037
St Peters	Drogheda Town :	Hill R.H.	The Steam Mill	-	-	-	-	1886	-	dir/	lou.bstt
St Peters	Drogheda Town :	Derepas John	Sail Cloth Fcty	Incumb Est consisting of :		-	-	1851	-	mlyIE	p22
St Peters	Drogheda Town :	Smith & Son	- (millers)	-	-	-	-	1886	-	dir/	lou.bstt
St Peters	Drogheda Town :	Ternan Patrick	- (miller)	-	-	-	-	1886	-	dir/	lou.bstt
St Peters	Drogheda Town :	Sheils John Joseph	wheatmeal :	-	-	-	-	1963	-	lic./32	wheat
St Peters	Drogheda Town :	Allison Evan	corn & pond	(2C) 30.6x21x14 :	-	3-18	-	1838	10x3.2x - o`shot	hob/	5.4043
St Peters	Drogheda Town :	McCann	Beamond Mills	-	-	-	-	1886	-	dir/	lou.bstt
St Peters	Drogheda Town :	Moore Thomas	corn	(2B) 13x21.6x10.6 :	-	4-9	-	1838	11.8x3.7x - o`shot	hob/	5.4043
Louth	Dromad	Tallan	mill	-	-	-	Tallan - Tallan	-	-	dd/	749 416 509751
Louth	Dromod	Brush	mill	-	-	-	Brush - Thompson	-	-	dd/	751 470 511005
Inishkeen	Drumcamil	-	thrashing	-	-	-	-	-	-	6"os/	11
Drumcar	Drumcar	-	mill	-	-	-	-	-	-	1"os/	81
Drumcar	Drumcar	- on White R.	corn, mill race	-	-	-	-	-	-	6"os/	18
Drumcar	Drumcar	Callan Patrick	corn & flour	-	-	-	-	-	14x3x4	vmb/	-
Drumcar	Drumcar	M`Clintock John	flour & corn	-	369a.	-	-	-	-	gr/	-
Stabannan	Drumgoolestown	Skeckleton James	bleach	-	-	-	-	-	-	gr/	-
Stabannan	Drumgoolestown	Skeckleton James	corn	-	17a.	-	-	-	-	gr/	-
Stabannan	Drumgoolestown	Wynne	mill	-	-	-	Wynne - Brennan	-	-	dd/	788 304 533039
Stabannan	Drumgoolstown	Crawley Robert	bleach	-	-	-	-	-	14x3x5	vmb/	-
Stabannan	Drumgoolstown	Crawley Robert	corn	-	-	-	-	-	13x3x5	vmb/	-
Dunleer	Drumin	Gannon Michael	corn	-	-	-	-	-	11x4x11	vmb/	-
Dunleer	Drumin	Gannon Michael	mill	-	11a.	-	-	-	-	gr/	-
Dunleer	Drummin	- SSE Dunleer Vge.	corn	-	-	-	-	-	-	6"os/	18
Dundalk	Dundalk	Browne Malcolm &Co.	distillery	-	-	-	Built 18th C. by Mr Gilligha	1886	-	dir/	lou.bstt
Dundalk	Dundalk	Browne Thomas	windmill	height 7storeys	-	-	Builder : Mr Martin	-	- sails last set for :	dir/	lou.bstt
Dundalk	Dundalk	Connick John	saw	-	-	-	-	1886	-	dir/	lou.bstt
Dundalk	Dundalk	Kieran Owen	windmill	-	-	-	-	1845	-	dd/	1848 9 257
Dundalk	Dundalk	Magrath Margaret	Ravensdale Mill	-	-	-	-	1849	-	dd/	1849 18 121
Dundalk	Dundalk	Manisty E (millwright)	iron works	-	-	-	-	1886	-	dir/	lou.bstt
St Peters	Dundalk :	McConnon Patrick	wheatmeal :	-	-	-	-	1963	-	lic./18	wheat
Dundalk	Dundalk T`parks	-	wind mill	-	-		-	-	-	6"os/	7
Dundalk	Dundalk T`parks	- at SE edge Town	distillery	-	-		-	-	-	6"os/	7
Dundalk	Dundalk Town	Byrne James	malthouse	-	-	-	Byrne Jas - O`Hagan Patk	1896	-	dd/	1896 45 3
Dundalk	Dundalk Town	Johnston Henry	Wellington Mills	-	-	-	Johnston H - Nat. Bank	1882	-	dd/	1882 37 57
Dunalk	Dundalk Town	McMaster Anna C	Victoria Steam Mills		-	-	McMaster A - Kidd Louisa	1886	-	dd/	1886 35201
St Peters	Dundalk Town	Murray John	brewery	-	-	-	Murray Jn - Straton John	1834	-	dd/	1834 15 113
St Peters	Dundalk Town	Murray John	distillery	-	-	-	Murray Jn - Straton John	1834	-	dd/	1834 15 113
Dunalk	Dundalk Town	Nat. Bank Ltd.	Wellington Mills	-	-	-	Nat. Bk - Dundalk Woollen	1888	-	dd/	1888 55 178
Dundalk	Dundalk Town	Page	distillery	-	-	-	Page - Browne	-	-	dd/	657 192 450938
Dundalk	Dundalk Town	Reid or Brown Margt	Marlfield Dist`y	-	-	-	Reid - Stratton Isabella	1854	-	dd/	1854 11 178
Dundalk	Dundalk Town	Semple	Windmill Road	-	-	-	Semole - Smith	-	-	dd/	754 80 512415
Dundalk	Dundalk Town :	Brown Thomas	salt works	-	-	-	Brown T - Connick Thos	1875	-	dd/	1875 38 66
Dundalk	Dundalk Town :	Magrath Margaret	mill	-	-	-	Magrath Margt - Daniel	1849	-	dd/	1849 18 121
St Peters	Dundalk Town :	Murray John	bleach green :	-	-	-	Murray Jn - Straton John	1834	-	dd/	1834 15 113
Dundalk	Dundalk Town :	Browne Stephen	steam	200 feet x 5 storey :	-	-	-	1886	-	dir/	lou.bstt
Dundalk	Dundalk Town :	Callan John	miller`s holding	-	-	-	Calan John - Townley Jn	1839	-	dd/	1839 5 111
Dundalk	Dundalk Town :	Johnston, Murray &C	flax spinning	-	-	-	Builder G. Kelso, Toronto :	1886	-	dir/	lou.bstt
Dundalk	Dundalk Town :	Murtagh James	factory	-	-	-	Murtagh J - Kennedy J J	1879	-	dd/	1879 48 195

PARISH	TOWNLAND	MILLER	TYPE	HOUSE	Land	£Val	PROPRIETORS	Date	WHEEL etc.	Record	Ref.
Dundalk	Dundalk Town :	Bryans Richard	miller`s holding	-	-	-	Bryans R - Calan John	1838	-	dd/	1838 3 113
Dundalk	Dundalk Town :	O`Neill Elizabeth	factory	-	-	-	O`Neill E - Kennedy Jn J	1878	-	dd/	1878 29 29
Dundalk	Dundalk Town :	Kennedy John J	factory	-	-	-	Kennedy J - Byrne Owen	1879	-	dd/	1879 48 196
St Peters	Dundalk Town :	Magee Robert	The Factory	-	-	-	Magee R - Coleman Neil	1833	-	dd/	1833 13 39
Dundalk	Dundalk Town :	Kidd Hugh	steam mills	-	-	-	Kidd H- Kidd Frederick	1884	-	dd/	1884 55 78
Dundalk	Dundalk Town :	Kidd Louisa S	steam mills	-	-	-	Kidd Louisa - Kidd Eliz.	1884	-	dd/	1884 55 76
Dundalk	Dundalk Town :	Kidd Louisa S	steam mills	-	-	-	Kidd L - McMaster Anna	1884	-	dd/	1884 55 77
Dundalk	Dundalk Town :	Skelton Hamilton	old salt works	-	-	-	Skelton Hamilton - Jno	1854	-	dd/	1854 12 243
Dundalk	Dundalk Town :	Owen Kieron	windmill	-	-	-	Owen K - Robinson Jno	1848	-	dd/	1848 9 257
St Peters	Dundalk Town :	Robinson John	Brewery prems	-	-	-	Robinson J - Belfast Bank	1851	-	dd/	1851 5 159
St Peters	Dundalk Town :	Robinson John	steam mill	(1A) 47.6x45.6x18.6 :	-	-	-	-	- 2 pairs sones	hob/	5.4044
St Peters	Dundalk Town :	Robinson John	wind mill	(1A) dia. 30x80 :	-	13-6	-	-	- 3 pairs stones	hob/	5.4044
St Peters	Dundalk Town :	Morgan P.& Co.	- (millers)	-	-	-	-	1886	-	dir/	lou.bstt
St Peters	Dundalk Town :	Robinson John	Windmill	-	-	-	Robinson J - Belfast Bank	1851	-	dd/	1851 5 159
St Peters	Dundalk Town :	McGinity & Co.	- (millers)	-	-	-	-	1886	-	dir/	lou.bstt
St Peters	Dundalk Town :	Kidd F.W. & Co.	- (millers)	-	-	-	-	1886	-	dir/	lou.bstt
St Peters	Dundalk Town :	Murray John & Co.	distillery & mill	(1B) 60x33.6x18.6 :	-	300	-	-	-	hob/	5.4044
St Peters	Dundalk Town :	Murray John & Co.	mill	(1A) 33x34x40 :	-	-	-	-	-	hob/	5.4044
St Peters	Dundalk Town :	Dennis James	- (miller)	-	-	-	-	1886	-	dir/	lou.bstt
St Peters	Dundalk Town :	Dewhurst Thomas	flour (stem)	(1A) 55x57x43 :	-	51	-	-	-	hob/	5.4044
Dundalk	Dundalk Town :	Brown Paul	corn	buildings & yd. dilap.	-	-	now Byrne & Maguire :	2004	-	mmSv/	wh - B
St Peters	Dundalk Town :	Kelly Michael	- (miller)	-	-	-	-	1886	-	dir/	lou.bstt
St Peters	Dundalk Town :	City Governor	tread mill	(1A) 21.6x17x9 :	-	116	-	-	-	hob/	5.4044
St Peters	Dundalk Town :	Manisty E (millwright)	Iron Works	-	-	-	-	1886	-	dir/	lou.bstt
St Peters	Dundalk Town :	Russell A & W :	-	-	-	-	-	1886	-	dir/	lou.bstt
Dundalk	Dundalk Town :	Brown Paul	salt works	-	-	-	Brown P - Brown Robert	1900	-	dd/	1900 10 178
Dundalk	DundalkTown	McMaster William	Windmill House	-	-	-	McMaster Wiliam - John	1892	-	dd/	1892 13 105
Faughart	Dungooly	Edmondson John	corn	- mill has 2 lofts	-	-	-	-	15x4x13	vmb/	-
Faughart	Dungooly	Edmondson John	tuck	-	-	-	-	-	13x2x10	vmb/	-
Faughart	Dungooly	Murdock William	corn	house, offs. & land	31a.	50	-	1856	-	gr/	a.a.Ire.ie
Faughart	Dungooly	NW. of Dungooly Br.	flax & corn	-	-	-	-	1888	-	25"os/	3.8
Dunleer	Dunleer	- on White R.	corn	restored & grinding	-	-	- Gerard Connor	1999	-	pWEH	A
Louth	Grange	- on Fane R.	corn	-	-	-	-	-	-	6"os/	11
Louth	Grange	M`Cann Neill	corn	-	45a.	-	-	-	-	gr/	-
Louth	Grange	McCann Neill	corn	(3B) 25x21.6x7.6 :	-	19	-	1838	13.3x4.6x5 1 pr.st.	hob/	5.4074
Louth	Grange	McCann Neill	corn	-	-	-	-	-	13x2x4	vmb/	-
Louth	Grange	McCann Neill	corn & wheat	-	-	-	-	-	13x2x5	vmb/	-
Drogheda	Green Hills	Usher Robert & Co.	linen factory	200ft x 30ft x 5 sty :	-	-	1/ Jn Oates 2/ Henry Hull	1886	- f`mly cotton mill.	dir/	bstt
Haggardstown	Haggardstown	- N. of cross road	windmill stump	-	-	-	-	-	-	6"os/	12
B`mascanlan	Jenkinstown	-	bleach	-	-	-	-	-	-	6"os/	8
B`mascanlan	Jenkinstown	McArdle Edward	bleach	(1C) 47.6x20x15 :	-	3-14	-	-	14x3x14.6	hob/	5.4046
B`mascanlan	Jenkinstown	McArdle Edward	bleach	-	-	-	-	-	14x3x13	vmb/	-
Drumshallow	Kercock	Johnston	mill	-	-	-	Johnston - Adams	-	-	dd/	808 341 545076
Drumshallow	Kercock	Rourke Peter	corn	-	-	-	-	-	10x3x10	vmb/	-
Dunbin	Kilcurly	McKeon Messrs	corn	-	-	-	-	-	16x3x14	vmb/	-
Dunbin	Kilcurly	McKeown Miss	corn & kiln	(2B) 53.6x22x12 :	-	12	-	1838	15.9x3.3x14 2 pr.st.	hob/	5.4055
Dunbin	Kilcurry	-	mill	-	-	-	-	-	-	1"os/	70
Dunbin	Kilcurry	- near Kilcurry Ho.	corn & dam	-	-	-	-	-	-	6"os/	6
Killaney	Killaney	-	mill	-	-	-	-	-	-	1"os/	70
Killaney	Killanny	- close to Church	corn	-	-	-	-	-	-	6"os/	10
Killaney	Killanny	Roddy John	corn	-	-	-	-	-	15x3x5	vmb/	-
Killaney	Killanny	Roddy John	mill & kiln	-	4a.	-	-	-	-	gr/	-

PARISH	TOWNLAND	MILLER	TYPE	HOUSE	Land	£Val	PROPRIETORS	Date	WHEEL etc.	Record	Ref.
Louth	Killeen	-	windmill stump	-	-	-	-	-	-	6"os/	11
Killincoole	Killincoole	-	corn & kiln	-	-	-	-	-	-	6"os/	12
Killincoole	Killincoole	Dullahane Patrick	mill & land	-	22a.	-	-	-	-	gr/	-
Killincoole	Killincoole	Fortescue Faithful	corn	(1B) 40.6x23.6x27 :	3-19	-	-	1838	14.3x4x8 3 pr. st.	hob/	5.4073
Killincoole	Killincoole	Fortescue Faithful	corn & wheat	-	-	-	-	-	14x4x8 3 pr st	vmb/	-
Louth	Knock	Clive	mills	-	-	-	Clive - Powis	-	-	dd/	679 112 476444
Louth	Knockalinnin	-	mill	-	-	-	-	-	-	1"os/	81
Louth	Knockbridle	- on Fane R.	mill	-	-	-	-	-	-	1"os/	-
Dromin	Knockdinnin	Drumgoole Peter	corn	-	-	-	-	-	-	vmb/	-
Dromin	Knockdinnin	Drumgoole Peter	corn & flax	-	14a.	-	-	-	-	gr/	-
Dromin	Knockdinnin	Drumgoole Peter	flax	-	-	-	-	-	10x2x10	vmb/	-
Clonkeen ?	Lagan Water	Clements	mill	-	-	-	Clements - Hazelwood	-	-	dd/	641 471 447940
Carlingford	Liberties	McEvitty	corn	-	-	-	-	-	14x2x12	vmb/	-
Mosstown	Listulk	-	corn	-	-	-	-	1843	-	6"os	18
Mosstown	Listulk	Rodgers John	corn	-	-	-	-	-	12x3x14	vmb/	-
Mosstown	Listulk	Rogers John	mill	-	15a.	-	-	-	-	gr/	-
Ballybarrack	Little Mill	-	corn & kiln	-	-	-	-	1843	-	6"os/	7
Ballybarrack	Little Mill	Ball (as Master)	mill	-	-	-	Ball - Filgate	-	-	dd/	767 500 520635
Ballybarrack	Little Mill	Henry	mill	-	-	-	Henry - Richardson	-	-	dd/	766 110 519645
Ballybarrack	Little Mill	Henry Robert	corn	(2B) 32.6x23.6x15 :	-	2-11	-	1838	13x2.6x - 2 prs. st.	hob/	5.4049
Ballybarrack	Little Mill	Henry Robert	corn	-	-	-	-	-	13x2x13	vmb/	-
Ballybarrack	Little Mill	O`Rourke Michael	mill	-	-	6	-	1852	-	hob/	5.4049
Ballybarrack	Little Mill	Rourke Michael	corn	-	2a.	-	-	-	-	gr/	-
Louth	Lowrath	Louth Lord	corn	(2B) 23x23x11.6 :	-	-	-	1838	16.6x3x5 2nd wh. :	hob/	5.4074
Louth	Lowrath North	-	corn, kiln & dam	-	-	-	-	1843	-	6"os/	11
Louth	Lowrath North	Louth Lord	corn	-	-	-	-	-	16x3x5	vmb/	-
Louth	Lowrath North	Louth Lord	wheat	-	-	-	-	-	16x3x5	vmb/	-
Tullyallen	Mellifont	Cowdroy Alfred	flour	-	-	-	-	-	- 3 pr st	vmb/	-
Tullyallen	Mellifont	Cowdroy Alfred	oatmeal & flour	-	-	-	-	-	17x5x15	vmb/	-
Tullyallen	Mellifont	M`Cartin John	mill	-	6a.	-	-	-	-	gr/	-
Tullyallen	Mellifont Park	Tiernan Thomas	corn	-	-	-	-	-	13x3x13	vmb/	-
Carlingford	Mill Grange	not occupied	mills (2)	-	-	-	-	-	-	osm/	-
Barronstown	Milltown	-	corn	-	-		-	-	-	6"os/	6
Barronstown	Milltown	-	old wind mill	-	-		-	-	-	6"os/	6
Killally	Milltown	- near Clogher	mill	-	-	-	-	-	-	1"os/	82
Dysart	Milltown	Butterly Peter	corn	-	25a.	-	-	-	-	gr/	-
Dysart	Milltown	Butterly Peter	flax	-	-	-	-	-	-	gr/	-
Dysart	Milltown	Butterly Thomas	corn	-	-	-	-	-	14x3x14 3 pr st	vmb/	-
Barronstown	Milltown	Morgan Patrick	mill	-	8.1.5	-	-	-	-	gr/	-
Barronstown	Milltown	Morgan Peter & Patk	corn	-	-	-	-	-	12x2x12	vmb/	-
c	Milltown :	-	corn	-	-	-	-	-	-	6"os/	18
c	Milltown :	-	flax	-	-	-	-	-	-	6"os/	18
c	Milltown Old :	-	no mill	-	-	-	-	-	-	6"os/	12
Dysart	Miltown	Butterly Thomas	flax	-	-	-	-	-	13x3x13 4 berths	vmb/	-
Dromiskin	Mooretown	- ab. Lurgangn. Br.	old windmill	-	-	-	-	-	-	6"os/	12
Louth	Newtown Bog	Forster	mill	-	-	-	Forster - Waldron	-	-	dd/	692 585 475789
Louth	Newtown Bog	Graham	mill	-	-	-	Graham - Porter	-	-	dd/	736 314 503649
Louth	Newtown Bog	Kelly	mill	-	-	-	Kelly - Cruise	-	-	dd/	734 334 500669
Louth	Newtown Bog	Mansfield	mill	-	-	-	Mansfield - Waldron	-	-	dd/	644 391 458343
Louth	Newtown Bog	Murphy	mill	-	-	-	Murphy - Greg	-	-	dd/	675 40 463648
Tullyallen	Newtownstalaban	M`Carthy George	mill	-	181a.	-	-	-	-	gr/	-
Tullyallen	Newtownstalaban	Ridley Stephen	corn	-	-	-	-	-	16x3x12 3 pr st	vmb/	-

PARISH	TOWNLAND	MILLER	TYPE	HOUSE	Land	£Val	PROPRIETORS	Date	WHEEL etc.	Record	Ref.
Philipstown	Philipstown	-	flour	-	-		-	-	-	6"os/	6
Philipstown	Philipstown	- on R. Glyde	corn	-	-	-	-	-	-	6"os/	11
Philipstown	Philipstown	- on R. Glyde	Mills of Louth	-	-	-	-	-	-	6"os/	11
Philipstown	Philipstown	Godley	mill	-	-	-	Godley - Henzell	-	-	dd/	646 397 446507
Philipstown	Philipstown	Keeran Messrs	corn	-	-	-	-	-	25x5x23	vmb/	-
Philipstown	Philipstown	Keeran Messrs	flour	-	-	-	-	-	14x10x23	vmb/	-
Philipstown	Philipstown	King	mill	-	-	-	King (as Master) - Kiernan	-	-	dd/	648 59 441742
Philipstown	Philipstown	O`Callaghan	mill	-	-	-	O`Callaghan - Gernon	-	-	dd/	805 240 543175
Philipstown	Philipstown	Ward	mills	-	-	-	Ward - Rogers	-	?	dd/	640 331 493356
B`mascanlan	Piedmont	-	corn	-	-		-	-	-	6"os/	8
B`mascanlan	Piedmont	Drumgoold John	corn	(1B) 30.6x18x10 :	-	5-9	-	1853	13.6x2.8x11.6	hob/	5.4046
B`mascanlan	Piedmont	Drumgoole Peter	corn	-	-	-	-	-	13x2x11	vmb/	-
B`mascanlan	Ram Park	O`Hara Eugene	spade factory	-	-	12-0	-	1853	4 old wheels :	hob/	5.4046
Louth	Rathcassan	-	corn windmill	-	-	-	-	-	-	6"os/	11
Carlingford	Rathcor	-	corn & kiln	-	-		-	-	-	6"os/	8
Carlingford	Rathcor	-	flax	-	-		-	-	-	6"os/	8
Carlingford	Rathcor	Barrett Richard	corn	-	-	2-15	-	-	13.9dia. 32 bkts.	hob/	5.4047
Carlingford	Rathcor	Marks James	corn	-	-	-	-	-	14x2x14	vmb/	-
Carlingford	Rathcor	Marks James	flax	-	-	-	-	-	13x3x12	vmb/	-
Carlingford	Rathcor	Marks Mr	corn	-	-	-	-	-	13x2x -	osm/	-
B`mascanlan	Ravensdale Park	-	bleach in ruins	-	-		-	-	-	6"os/	4
B`mascanlan	Ravensdale Park	Lindsay Francis	beetling	(1B) 50x26x20 :	-	5-15	-	1853	20.6x5.6x18 :	hob/	5.4046
B`mascanlan	Ravensdale Park	Lindsay Francis	corn	(1B) 34x32.6x42 :	-	13	-	1853	19x6.6x16.6 60 bkts	hob/	5.4046
Philipstown	Reaghstown	- S. of cross roads	corn & kiln	-	-	-	-	-	-	6"os/	13
Philipstown	Reaghstown	Reenan Peter	corn	-	2a.	-	-	-	-	gr/	-
Philipstown	Reaghstown	Reenan Peter	corn	house, offs. & land	25a.	-	- [+ tenants' houses]	1856	-	gr/	a.a.ire.ie
Richardstown	Richardstown	-	old flax mill	-	-	-	-	-	-	6"os/	18
Richardstown	Richardstown	-	old mill race	-	-	-	-	-	-	6"os/	18
Richardstown	Richardstown	near Cappoge Br.	boiling house	-	-	-	-	-	-	6"os/	18
Richardstown	Richardstown	- N. side R. Dee	corn	-	-	-	-	-	-	6"os/	18
Richardstown	Richardstown	- N. side R. Dee	white	-	-	-	-	-	-	6"os/	18
Richardstown	Richardstown	- nr Dr`goolstown Br.	black mills	-	-	-	-	-	-	6"os/	18
Richardstown	Richardstown	- nr Dr`goolstown Br.	bleach	-	-	-	-	-	-	6"os/	18
Dunleer	Skibbolmore	Hay Eugene	flax factory	(1B) 131x31.6x20.6 :	-	-	-	1852	-	hob/	5.1297
Dunleer	Skibbolmore	Hay Eugene	flax factory :	-	17a.	-	-	-	-	gr/	-
Dunleer	Skibbolmore	M`Cartin John	flour	-	7a.	-	-	-	-	gr/	-
Dunleer	Skibbolmore	McCartan John	flour	(1C) 54x26.6x30 :	3a.	-	-	1852	-	hob/	5.1297
Ardee	Smarmore	- on county border	corn & dam	-	-	-	-	-	-	6"os/	17
Ardee	Smarmore	- on county border	corn kiln	-	-	-	-	-	-	6"os/	17
Stabannan	Stabannan	- on R Dee	blackmill	-	-	-	-	-	-	1"os/	81
Louth	Stephenstown	Balfour	Slane Mills	-	-	-	Balfour - Moore	-	-	dd/	753 398 512333
Louth	Stephenstown	Balfour	Slane Mills	-	-	-	Balfour - Moore	-	-	dd/	754 170 512505
Louth	Stephenstown	Fortescue Matthew	threshing	-	-	-	-	-	17x3x16	vmb/	
Louth	Stephenstown	French	Slane Mills	-	-	-	French - French	-	-	dd/	772 21 523156
Louth	Stirue	- at Mullary Cross	mill	-	-	-	-	-	-	1"os/	81
Castletown	Stranacarry	Dullaghan Jas & Co.	corn & kiln	(1B) 78.6x23.6x37 :	-	-	-	1838	18.6x8x7.6 2pr. st.	hob/	5.4052
Castletown	Stranacarry	Dullaghan Jas & Co.	old starch mill	(1B) 59x20x11 :	-	-	-	-	-	hob/	5.4052
Castletown	Stranacarry	Dullaghan Messrs	corn	-	-	-	-	-	18x8x7	vmb/	-
Castletown	Stranacarry	O'Hare Terence	corn	miller's ho., offs. & ld.	69a.	126	- [+ tenants' houses]	1856	-	gr/	a.a.ire.ie
Louth	Sundayswell	Thompson	mills	-	-	-	Thompson & Separation	-	-	dd/	782 574 529649
Louth	Sundayswell	Thompson	mills	-	-	-	Thompson - Iles	-	-	dd/	798 148 538883
Roche	Tarnadarra	Murphy Thomas	corn & kiln	(2C) 41.6x17.6x10	-	1-2	-	1838	13x2x7.6 1 pr.st.	hob/	5.4068

PARISH	TOWNLAND	MILLER	TYPE	HOUSE	Land	£Val	PROPRIETORS	Date	WHEEL etc.	Record	Ref.
Carlingford	Templetown	- close to coast	old mill	-	-	-	-	-	-	6"os/	9
Termonfeckin	Termonfeckin	-	corn	-	-	-	-	-	-	1"os/	82
Termonfeckin	Termonfeckin	Maguire James	corn	-	73a.	-	-	-	-	gr/	-
Philipstown	Thomastown	Henry	mill	-	-	-	Henry - Richardson M/As	-	-	dd/	776 110 519645
Philipstown	Thomastown	Irving	mill	-	-	-	Irving - McAlister	-	-	dd/	740 472 504407
Philipstown	Thomastown	Maxwell	mill	-	-	-	Maxwell - Tris(?)ing	-	?	dd/	661 340 455168
Philipstown	Thomastown	Wolden	mill	-	-	-	Wolden - Filgate	-	-	dd/	663 170 454881
Clonmore	Togher	- 1/2 mile E. Vge.	corn & pond	-	-	-	-	-	-	6"os/	19
Clonmore	Togher	Molloy Anne	corn	-	32a.	-	-	-	-	gr/	-
Clonmore	Togher	Molloy James	corn	-	-	-	-	-	10x3x10	vmb/	-
Philipstown	Townland ?	Kirwan James & Co.	corn & kiln	(1A) 105x44.6x70 :	-	-	-	1838	-	hob/	5.4067
Philipstown	Townland ?	Kirwan James & Co.	flour	(1B) 76.6x40x60 :	-	115	-	1838	24x10x23 7 pr.st. :	hob/	5.4067
Tullyallen	Tullyallan	-	flax	- fine restoration :	-	-	Peter & Anne Lyons	1999	-	pWEH	Cr
Louth	Water Lodge	-	mill	-	-	-	-	-	-	1"os/	70
B`mascanlon	White Mill	Porteus Matthew	spade	-	-	-	-	-	14x4x9	vmb/	-
B`mascanlon	White Mill	Sherif Co. Louth	mills	-	-	-	Sherif Co Louth - Rispin	-	-	dd/	732 594 499729
Tullyallen	Woodmill *	- near Mellifont Park	flax	- small remains only	-	-	-	1999	-	mmSv/	wh - R
St Peter`s	Yellowbatter	-	mill	-	-	-	-	-	-	1"os/	92
St Peter`s	Yellowbatter	Moore Isaiah	mill	-	3a.	-	-	-	-	gr/	-
St Peter`s	Yellowbatter	Moore Thomas	mill	-	4a.	-	-	-	-	gr	-

PARISH	TOWNLAND	MILLER	TYPE	HOUSE	Land	£Val	PROPRIETORS	Date	WHEEL etc.	Record	Ref.
Crossmolina	Abbeytown	- on Rosserk R.	mill	-	-	-	-	-	-	1"os/	53
Achill	Achill	- at Cashel Vge.	corn kiln	-	-	-	-	-	-	6"os/	55
Lackan	Aghaleague	Bourke Walter	land	-	-	-	Bourke W - Kirwan Thos	1834	-	dd/	1834 2 241
Templemore	Aghalusky	-	corn kilns (2)	-	-	-	-	1844	-	6"os/	70/71
Aghamore	Aghataharn	-	mill dam & kiln	-	-	-	-	-	-	6"os/	82
Aghamore	Aghatharn	- near L. Urlaur	mill	-	-	-	-	-	-	6"os/	83
Annagh	Agloragh	-	corn & kiln	-	-	-	-	-	-	6"os/	103
Annagh	Agloragh	Judge Owen	corn GIG	-	-	-	-	-	-	vmb/	15
Annagh	Agloragh	Judge Owen	tuck	-	-	-	-	-	12x1x5	vmb/	15
Aghagower	Aille	- on R. Aille	tuck	-	-	-	-	-	-	6"os/	88
Meelick	Ardhoom	- E. side R. Moy	corn kilns (3)	-	-	-	-	-	-	6"os/	61
Kilcommon	Ardkill	-	windmill stump	-	-	-	-	2003	-	pWEH	R
Kilcommon	Ardkill :	- Highwood Mill	mill	-	-	-	-	-	-	6"os/	119
Annagh	Ardnaree	Atkinson Chas	mills	-	-	-	Atkinson - Vaughan Arth :	1804	Lse. 6 Feb.	dd/	563 548 380766?
Annagh	Ardnaree	Atkinson William :	mills	-	-	-	Atkinson William - Geo :	1765	Lse. 20 Mar.	dd/	282 491 185488
Annagh	Ardnaree	Bell	corn & tuck	-	-	-	Bell - Atkinson & ors	c1810	- [? Error]	dd/	631 446 245416
Annagh	Ardnaree	Brown Dorcas Hon.	mills	-	-	-	Brown D - Paget James	1789	-	dd/	404 338 268482
Annagh	Ardnaree	Carshore Thomas :	mills	-	-	-	Carshore T - Burke Oliver :	1769	-	dd/	275 136 175859
Annagh	Ardnaree	Gore Arthur	mills	-	-	-	Gore A Hon. - King Henry :	1809	-	dd/	630 90 431142
Annagh	Ardnaree	Gore Arthur Rt. Hon. :	mills	-	-	-	Gore A - Tyawley Mary :	1751	-	dd/	148 458 101478
Annagh	Ardnaree	Jones Vaughan :	mills	-	-	-	Jones V - Browne Kath :	1758	-	dd/	203 23 134979
Annagh	Ardnaree	Roger Palmer :	mills	-	-	-	Roger P - Palmer Francis :	1769	LWT 31 Aug.	dd/	281 51 180358
Annagh	Ardnaree	Tyrawley Lord	mills	-	-	-	Tyrawley - Gore	c1720	-	dd/	48 455 101478
Annagh	Ardnaree	Tyrawley Lord James	mills	-	-	-	Tyrawley Ld - Jones Thos	1739	-	dd/	97 43 67195
Annagh	Ardnaree :	Knox Annesley	mills	-	-	-	Knox A - Hammon Wm	1835	-	dd/	1835 6 269
Annagh	Ardnaree :	Attwod Mathias	mills	-	-	-	Atwood M - Fair John	1833	-	dd/	1833 2 255
Killedan	Attavally	-	corn & kiln	-	-	-	-	-	-	6"os/	80
Kilcommon	Attavally	- 1m N / Bangor	corn kiln	-	-	-	-	-	-	6"os/	26
Kilcommon	Attavally :	-	corn kilns	-	-	-	-	-	-	6"os/	80
bo. Gallen	Baghtiduffe	Dillon Viscount	mill	-	-	-	Dillon V - Dunsany Ld	1834	-	dd/	1834 6 24
Kilcolman	Ballaghaderreen	-	mills	-	-	-	-	-	-	1"os/	75
Turlough	Ballanierin	-	mill	-	-	-	-	-	hz wheel	sv/	CLawless
Kilmoremoy	Ballina	Gore Hon Richard	mills	-	-	-	Gore R - Cuffe James	1782		dd/	340 446 230839
Kilmoremoy	Ballina	Gore Hon Richard	mills	-	-	-	Gore A - King Henry :	1782	-	dd/	340 504 231348
Kilmoremoy	Ballina	Gore Hon Richard	mills	-	-	-	Gore R - Milltown Earl :	1776	-	dd/	309 689 209403
Kilmoremoy	Ballina	Gore Hon Richard	mills	-	-	-	Gore R - Hume Gustavus :	1776	-	dd/	309 690 209404
Kilmoremoy	Ballina	Hendry John	mill	-	-	-	Hendry Jn - Daky Jas	1833	-	dd/	1833 2 105
Kilmoremoy	Ballina	Jones	mills	-	-	-	Jones & Settlement	c1790	- (?)	dd/	330 608 227417
Kilmoremoy	Ballina	Jones Thomas	mills	-	-	-	Jones T - Waldron Fran	1779	-	dd/	365 157 243810
Kilmoremoy	Ballina	Jones Vaughan	mills	-	-	-	Jones V - Waldron Fran	1779	-	dd/	365 157 243810
Kilmoremoy	Ballina Town	Bourke John JP :	corn kiln	20.6x18.6x20 :	-	16.4	-	1854	-	hob/	5.3114
Kilmoremoy	Ballina Town	Daly James	corn mill	23x16x12 :	-	-	-	-	-	hob/	5.3113
Kilmoremoy	Ballina Town :	Ballina Flour Mills Ltd.	flour	-	-	-	-	1965	-	gLic/	wheat1
Ballina	Ballina Town :	- on R. Moy	brewery	-	-	-	-	-	-	6"os/	30
Ballina	Ballina Town :	- on R. Moy	corn	-	-	-	-	-	-	6"os/	30
Aghamore	Ballinacostello	- nr Tn Fairgreen	mill & mill race	-	-	-	-	-	-	6"os/	81
Aghamore	Ballinacostello	Brehany Patrick	corn	-	-	-	-	-	13x3x4	vmb/	15
Aghamore	Ballinacostello	Brehany Patrick	tuck	-	-	-	-	-	13x1x4	vmb/	15
Kilfian	Ballinagavna	- on Owenmore R.	corn	-	-	-	-	-	-	6"os/	21
Killedan	Ballinamona	Rooney Patrick	gig	-	-	-	-	-	-	hob/	5.4148
Killeden	Ballinamona	Rooney Patrick	tuck	-	-	-	-	-	13x2x6	vmb/	15
Killeden	Ballinamore	- on Geestaun R. :	corn & kiln	-	-	-	-	-	-	6"os/	80

PARISH	TOWNLAND	MILLER	TYPE	HOUSE	Land	£Val	PROPRIETORS	Date	WHEEL etc.	Record	Ref.
Killeden	Ballinamore :	- on Geestown R.	corn & kiln	-	-	-	-	-	-	6"os/	80
Mayo	Ballinaster	-	mill	stone buildings :	-	-	Patricia Nestor (family) :	2003	-	pWEH	R
Mayo	Ballinaster	Costello Patrick	gig	(3B) 33.6x16x5 :	-	1.12	-	-	4ft. 2ins. GIG :	hob/	5.4087
Mayo	Ballinaster :	-	corn	-	-	-	-	-	-	6"os/	90
Mayo	Ballinaster :	-	corn	-	-	-	-	-	-	6"os/	90
Crossboyne	Ballindine N. :	-	brewery	-	-	-	-	-	-	6"os/	112
Turlough	Ballingarden	-	mill & mill dam	-	-	-	-	-	-	6"os/	60
Turlough	Ballingarden	-	mill & mill dam	- (no trace 1984)	-	-	-	-	hz wheel	sv/	CLawless
Ballinrobe	Ballinrobe	Cuffe	mills	-	-	-	Cuffe - Kenny	c1751	-	dd/	492 442 320714
Balinrobe	Ballinrobe Glebe	- on Robe R. :	mill	-	-	-	-	-	-	6"os/	118
Ballinrobe	Ballinrobe Town	Tighe Robert :	brewery	59x22.6x18.6 :	-	-	-	-	16x5.9 u`shot :	hob/	5.3122
Ballinrobe	Ballinrobe Town :	Tighe Robert	brewery	-	-	-	-	-	-	hob/	5.4152
Kilfian	Ballintober	-	corn	-	-	-	-	-	-	1"os/	65
Kilfian	Ballintober	- near Ballintober Br.	mill	-	-	-	-	-	-	6"os/	21
Annagh	Ballybaun	-	corn	-	-	-	-	-	-	1"os/	86
Annagh	Ballybaun	-	corn	-	-	-	-	-	-	6"os/	102
Annagh	Ballybaun	Mulloy James	corn	-	-	-	-	-	11x2x -	vmb/	15
Kilcommon	Ballybeg	- near Bangor Vge.	old corn mill	-	-	-	-	-	-	6"os/	26
Kilcolman	Ballybeg	Heffernan Thomas	tuck	-	-	-	-	-	10x1x6	vmb/	15
Burriscarra	Ballycally Lough	-	Kiln Island	-	-	-	-	-	-	6"os/	100
Drum	Ballycarra	Gibbons Patrick	corn	-	-	-	-	-	14x3x2	vmb/	15
Drum	Ballycarra	Gibbons Patrick	corn & kiln	(1B) 21.6x20.6x9.6 :	1a.	1.17	-	-	14x2.9x2.6 :	hob/	5.4106
Drum	Ballycarra	Gibbons Patrick	tuck	-	-	-	-	-	14x1.4x2 v. old :	hob/	5.4106
Drum	Ballycarra	Joyce Martin	tuck	-	-	-	-	-	14x1x2	vmb/	15
Doonfeeny	Ballycastle	Hart Phelim	corn	-	-	-	-	-	11x1x2	vmb/	15
Doonfeeny	Ballycastle :	Hart Phelim	corn & kiln	-	-	-	-	1842	-	hob/	5.4177
Doonfeeny	Ballycastle :	Madden Daniel	corn & tuck	-	-	-	-	-	-	hob/	5.4178
Attymass	Ballycong	-	corn & kiln	-	-	-	-	-	-	6"os/	40
Attymass	Ballycong	-	tuck	-	-	-	-	-	-	6"os/	40
Addergoole	Ballyduffy	Burke Walter	corn	(1B) 24x24x14 :	-	-	-	-	o`shot 15.6xx4x16 :	hob/	5.4167
Turlough	Ballygarriff	-	mill	-	-	-	-	-	hz wheel	sv/	CLawless
Kilbeagh	Ballyglass	-	corn & pond	-	-	-	-	-	-	6"os/	63
Aghamore	Ballyglass	-	mill & mill race	-	-	-	-	-	-	6"os/	81
Doonfeeny	Ballyglass	-	mill & pond	-	-	-	-	-	-	6"os/	7
Kilbeagh	Ballyglass	Murphy John	corn & kiln	-	-	-	-	-	-	hob/	5.4139
Kilbeagh	Ballyglass :	-	mill & mil race	-	-	-	-	-	-	6"os/	81
Kilbeagh	Ballyglass E.	Murphy John & Phil	corn	-	-	-	-	-	12x2x6	vmb/	15
Kilbeagh	Ballyglass E.	Murphy John & Phil	tuck	-	-	-	-	-	12x1x6 1 stock	vmb/	15
Kilbeagh	Ballyglass West	-	old corn kiln	-	-	-	-	-	-	6"os/	63
Turlough	Ballyguin	-	corn	-	-	-	-	-	-	6"os/	70
Turlough	Ballyguin	-	corn & kilns	T shaped buildings	-	-	-	2003	-	pWEH	R
Turlough	Ballyguin	-	corn & kilns	-	-	-	-	-	hz wheel	sv/	CLawless
Turlough	Ballyguin	- on Clydagh R.	corn	-	-	-	-	-	-	1"os/	75
Turlough	Ballyguin	McAdam James	corn	-	-	-	-	-	-	hob/	5.4126
Turlough	Ballyguinn	-	mill & millrace	-	-	-	-	-	hz wheel	sv/	CLawless
Bekan	Ballyhaunis Tn :	-	mill	-	-	-	-	-	-	6"os/	93
Addergoole	Ballyknock	- nr Cuilmullagh Vge	corn & dam	-	-	-	-	-	-	6"os/	59
Kilfian	Ballymagauna	Swiney Edward	corn	-	-	-	-	-	12x1x8	vmb/	15
Attymass	Ballymore	-	corn & kiln	-	-	-	-	-	-	6"os/	40
Attymass	Ballymore	-	tuck	-	-	-	-	-	-	6"os/	40
Attymass	Ballymore	- on Yellow R.	-	has unusual wheel	-	-	Mary Loftus (n/Brogan)	2003	- (phos. poor)	pWEH	R
Moygawnagh	Ballynagor	- at Vge. Plott	mill	-	-	-	-	-	-	6"os/	21

PARISH	TOWNLAND	MILLER	TYPE	HOUSE	Land	£Val	PROPRIETORS	Date	WHEEL etc.	Record	Ref.
Shrule	Ballynalty :	-	mill	-	-	-	-	-	-	6"os/	123
Aglish	Ballynew	Hughes Patrick	flour & corn	(1C) 55.6x22x22.6 :	-	15.4	-	-	flour 16.3x3.72.6 :	hob/	5.4089/90
Aglish	Ballynew :	- E.side Castlebar	flour	-	-	-	-	-	-	6"os/	78
Annagh	Ballynew (3)	Lucan Hon. Ld. Chas	mills	-	-	-	Lucan Lord - Shuffle Robt :	1787	-	dd/	397 369 264949
Kilfian	Ballyrinlettragh	- on Keerglen R.	mill	-	-	-	-	-	-	6"os/	14
Ballysakeery	Ballysakeery	Cardin John	old mill	(1C) 27x24?x8 :	-	-	-	-	-	hob/	5.4174
Crossmolina	Ballyscanlan	- on Deel R.	corn	-	-	-	-	-	-	6"os/	38
Crossmolina	Ballyscanlan	Gate Hugh	corn	-	-	-	-	-	13x2x4	vmb/	15
Crossmolina	Ballyscanlan	Gate Hugh	tuck	-	-	-	-	-	12x2x4	vmb/	15
Clare	Ballytoohymore	on E. coast Clare Isle	corn & kiln	-	-	-	-	-	-	6"os/	84
Knock	Balyhowly	- SW./ Knock Vge.	corn & kiln	-	-	-	-	1844	-	6"os/	92
Kilcummin	Banagher	Robinson Edward	mill & kiln	(3C) 23x16x6.6 :	-	2.3.4	-	-	breast, broken & :	hob/	5.4180
Kilbeagh	Barnacahoge	- near Vge. Kilkally	mill	-	-	-	-	-	-	6"os/	72
Burrishoole	Barrack Hill	- Owendarra`diva R.	corn & tuck	-	-	-	-	-	-	6"os/	68
Burrishoole	Barrack Hill	Cobden Charles	flax	-	-	-	-	-	-	hob/	5.4080
Burrishoole	Barrack Hill	O`Donnell Sir Richard	corn & flax	-	-	-	-	-	-	hob/	5.4079
Burrishoole	Barrack Hill	Swaine Jonas	corn & kiln	-	-	-	-	-	-	hob/	5.4079
Burrishoole	Barrack Hill	Swaine Jonas	mill (raised)	-	-	-	-	-	-	hob/	5.4080
Burrishoole	Barrack Hill	Swaine Joseph	corn	-	-	-	-	-	14x3x11 42 bkts	vmb/	15
Bekan	Bekan	-	mill	-	-	-	-	-	-	1"os/	86
Bekan	Bekan	O`Brien Patrick	corn	-	-	-	-	-	11x2x -	vmb/	15
Bekan	Bekan :	-	corn & kiln	-	-	-	-	-	-	6"os/	92
Oughaval	Belclare :	-	bleach	-	-	-	-	-	-	6"os/	87
Oughaval	Belclare :	-	cotton factory	-	-	-	-	-	-	6"os/	87
Bekan	Belesker	O'Hara Darby :	corn & tuck	-	-	-	O'Hara D - Atkinson Chas :	1722	Lse. 2 Apl.	dd/	34 391 22556
Bekan	Belesker	Tyrawly Charles :	H corn & tuck	-	-	-	Tyrawly - Atkinson Chas :	1717	Lse. 7 Feb.	dd/	36 241 22147
Bekan	Belesker	Tyrawly Charles :	H corn & tuck :	Mill House and all :	-	-	Tyrawly C - O'Hara Darby :	1718	Lse. 15 Nov.	dd/	21 478 18191
Achill	Belfarsad	-	corn	-	-	-	-	-	-	6"os/	65
Achill	Belfarsad	Heffernan Benjamin	corn GIG	-	-	-	-	-	-	hob/	5.4077
Ballynahaglish	Bellass	- near R. Moy Br.	corn	-	-	-	-	-	-	6"os/	59
Ballynahaglish	Bellass	Brogan Denis	corn & kiln	(2C) 26.6x22x7 :	-	2.10.9	-	-	-	hob/	5.4171
Oughaval	Bellataleen :	- Murrisk Mill	corn	-	-	-	-	-	-	6"os/	86
Kildacommoge	Bellavarry	O`Mally William	corn	-	-	-	-	-	-	hob/	5.4147
Kildacommoge	Bellavary	-	mill	-	-	-	-	-	-	1"os/	75
Kilmoremoy	Belleek	Atkinson	mills	-	-	-	Atkinson - Vaughan	1804	-	dd/	563 548 380766
Kilmoremoy	Belleek	Atkinson Charles	mills	-	-	-	Atkinson C - Moore James	1742	-	dd/	106 527 75105
Kilmoremoy	Belleek	Atkinson George :	mills	-	-	-	Atkinson G - Pilkington Jn :	1766	-	dd/	241 317 159195
Kilmoremoy	Belleek	Atkinson William	mills	-	-	-	Atkinson - Black Thos	1834	-	dd/	1834 12 104
Kilmoremoy	Belleek	Atkinson William :	mills	-	-	-	Atkinson W - Walker Chas :	1766	-	dd/	253 39 161600
Kilmoremoy	Belleek	Knox John	mills	-	-	-	Knox J - Atkinson Geo :	1771	-	dd/	285 98 185490
Kilmoremoy	Belleek	Paget James	mills	-	-	-	Paget J - Atkinson Chas	1791	-	dd/	449 17 287232
Kilmoremoy	Belleek	Tyrawley James Lord	mills	-	-	-	Tyrawley - Atkinson Chas	1742	-	dd/	106 406 74407
Kilmoremoy	Belleek	Vaughan Matthew	mills	-	-	-	Vaughan - Atkinson Chas	1785	-	dd/	365 427 245457?
Aghagower	Bofara	-	mill & kilns	-	-	-	-	-	-	6"os/	87
Aghagower	Bofara	- at top of hill :	mill & kilns	- :	-	-	Mrs Sonia Kelly	2003	-	pWEH	Z
Aghagower	Bofara	1m. above Aghamore	corn	-	-	-	Kilian O`Mauroine	2003	-	pWEH	Z
Aghagower	Bofara :	-	flour	-	-	-	-	-	-	6"os/	87
Aghagower	Bofara :	-	corn	-	-	-	-	-	-	6"os/	87
Addergoole	Bofeenaun	-	corn kiln	-	-	-	-	-	-	6"os/	59
Toomore	Boherhallagh	-	mill & kiln	-	-	-	-	-	-	6"os/	49
Toomore	Boherhallagh	- nr Moortown Ho.	corn	- :	-	-	Wills family	2003	-	pWEH	R
Toomore	Boherhallagh	Sturgeon Hubert	horizontal	-	-	-	-	-	prism of buckets	hob/	5.4191
Turlough	Bovogonnell	-	mill (tradition of)	-	-	-	-	-	hz wheel	sv/	CLawless

PARISH	TOWNLAND	MILLER	TYPE	HOUSE	Land	£Val	PROPRIETORS	Date	WHEEL etc.	Record	Ref.
Addergoole	Brackley	Roland William	corn & frieze	(2C) 25x18x8 :	-	-	-	-	u`shot 12x1.6x4 :	hob/	5.4167
Bekan	Brackloon East	-	mill & mill dam	-	-	-	-	-	-	6"os/	93
Bekan	Brickeens	-	corn	-	-	-	-	-	-	1"os/	86
Bekan	Brickeens	Gilmor James	corn & tuck	-	-	-	-	-	-	hob/	5.4131
Bekan	Brickeens :	-	mill	-	-	-	-	-	-	6"os/	102
Kilcommon	Briska	-	tuck & dam	-	-	-	-	-	-	6"os/	27
Kilmaclasser	Brockagh	Moore Richard	corn	-	-	-	-	-	15x5x -	vmb/	15
Kilmaclasser	Brockagh	Moore Richard	tuck	-	-	-	-	-	13x3x - 1 pr combs	vmb/	15
Kilmaclasser	Brocklagh	- nr Brocklagh Vge.	bleach	-	-	-	-	-	-	6"os/	77
Kilmaclasser	Brocklagh	- nr Brocklagh Vge.	corn & tuck	-	-	-	-	-	-	6"os/	77
Kilmaclasser	Brocklagh	Coffey Martin	corn & tuck	(1B) 43.6x24.6x24	-	-	-	-	15.5x4.11x14	hob/	5
Crossboyne	Brookhill :	Broockhill Flour Mill	flour	-	-	-	-	-	-	6"os/	101
Turlough	Bunduvowen	-	mill & mill race	-	-	-	-	-	hz wheel	sv/	CLawless
Turlough	Bunduvowen	-	mill & race	-	-	-	-	-	-	6"os/	60
Kilcommon	Bunmore West	-	kiln	-	-	-	-	-	-	6"os/	35
Ballincholla	Bunnadober	Burke Peter	corn GIG	-	-	-	-	-	-	hob/	5.4150
Ballina	Bunree	at Rathkib (nr Balina)	flax	no buildings located	-	-	-	2003	-	pWEH	Z
Manulla	Burris	- on R. Manulla :	corn	-	-	-	-	-	-	6"os/	79
Manulla	Burris	Corrigan James	grist	(3C) 21x17.6x8 :	-	1.6	-	-	9.6x1.6x3 floats :	hob/	5.4117
Manulla	Burris	Corrigan James	grist & kiln	-	-	-	-	-	-	hob/	5.4115
Manulla	Burris :	-	corn	-	-	-	-	-	-	6"os/	79
Oughval	Cahemamart	-	mill	-	-	-	-	-	-	6"os/	
Oughval	Cahemamart	Levingston William	corn	-	-	-	-	-	36x6x20	vmb/	15
Oughval	Cahemamart	Levingston William	flour	-	-	-	-	-	20x4x20	vmb/	15
Oughval	Cahemamart	Levingston William	flour	-	-	-	-	-	26x4x20	vmb/	15
Oughval	Cahemamart	Levingston William	malt	-	-	-	-	-	14x4x14 & :	vmb/	15
Kilbefad	Cappanaglogh	- near coast	corn kiln	-	-	-	-	1844	-	6"os/	39
Kilbeagh	Cappulcorragh	-	old mill	-	-	-	-	-	-	6"os/	63
Mayo	Cardroon	Duell Thomas :	-	-	-	-	Duell Thos - Cromie Wm :	1753	-	dd/	164 86 110173
Ballyovey	Carheen :	-	mill	-	-	-	-	-	-	6"os/	109
Crossboyne	Carraghdooey	Hughes Peter	corn	-	-	-	-	-	12 x2x3	vmb/	15
Crossboyne	Carraghdooey	Hughes Peter	tuck	-	-	-	-	-	13xz2x3	vmb/	15
Killedan	Carrick	-	mill dam :	-	-	-	-	-	-	6"os/	80
Mayo	Carrickbelfarsad	-	corn & tuck	-	-	-	-	-	-	6"os/	65
Kilbeagh	Carrountobber	Doyle Thomas	corn	-	-	-	-	-	12x1x -	vmb/	15
Kilbeagh	Carrountobber	Doyle Thomas	tuck	-	-	-	-	-	12x1x -	vmb/	15
Kilconduff	Carrowbaun	-	corn	-	-	-	-	-	-	6"os/	72
Annagh	Carrowbeg	- nr Carrowbeg Ho.	mill ruin	-	-	-	-	-	-	6"os/	82
Annagh	Carrowbeg	Behany Roger	corn GIG	-	-	-	-	-	4x - x3	vmb/	15
Annagh	Carrowbeg :	-	mill ruin	-	-	-	-	-	-	6"os/	82
Kilgarvan	Carrowcrom	-	flax lough	-	-	-	-	-	-	6"os/	39
Turlough	Carrowkeel	McHugh James	horizontal	(2C) 25x15x6 & :	-	5/4	-	-	dia. 4 feet	hob/	5.4124
Turlough	Carrowkeel	McHugh James	horizontal	-	-	-	-	-	-	hob/	5.4126
Crossboyne	Carrowmarley :	-	mill	-	-	-	-	-	-	6"os/	101
Lackan	Carrowmore	- on Cloonalaghan R.	corn & dam	-	-	-	-	-	-	6"os/	14
Killasser	Carrowmoremoy	-	corn & tuck	-	-	-	-	-	-	6"os/	61
Killasser	Carrowmoremoy	-	tuck	-	-	-	-	-	-	1"os/	65
Kilgarvan	Carrownaglogh	- nr Bunnyconnelan	corn (ruins)	-	-	-	-	-	-	6"os/	31
Kilgarvan	Carrownaglogh	- nr Bunnyconnelan	kiln	-	-	-	-	-	-	6"os/	31
Crossboyne	Carrownlough	-	dye	-	-	-	-	-	-	1"os/	86
Kilmainbeg	Carrownoultore	Bingham	mills	-	-	-	Bingham - Gildea	c1751	-	dd/	126 301 87189
Kilbeagh	Carrowntober	-	mill	-	-	-	-	-	-	6"os/	

PARISH	TOWNLAND	MILLER	TYPE	HOUSE	Land	£Val	PROPRIETORS	Date	WHEEL etc.	Record	Ref.
Kilbeagh	Carrowntober	-	mill & kiln	-	-	-	-	-	-	6"os/	63
Kilbeagh	Carrowntober	Mangan Martin	corn & tuck	-	-	-	-	-	-	hob/	5.4139
Bekan	Carrowreagh	- near Togher L.	corn & dam	-	-	-	-	-	-	6"os/	93
Bekan	Carrowreagh	Judge Edward	corn	-	-	-	-	-	14x3x8	vmb/	15
Bekan	Carrowreagh	Judge Edward	corn & tuck	-	-	-	-	-	-	hob/	5.4131
Bekan	Carrowreagh	Judge Edward	tuck	-	-	-	-	-	13x1x8	vmb/	15
Attymass	Cartron	-	corn kiln	-	-	-	-	-	-	6"os/	39
Kilbeagh	Cartron	-	old mill	-	-	-	-	-	-	6"os/	62
Kilcolman	Cartrumnacross	Craghan Peter	corn	-	-	-	-	-	12x2x8	vmb/	15
Burrishoole	Castle Bourke	Morris Michael	land	-	-	-	Morris Mcl - Tighe Robt	1834	-	dd/	1834 11 176
Burrishoole	Castlebar	O`Malley Owen	brewery prems	-	-	-	O`Malley - Galloghly Th	1850	-	dd/	1850 14 227
Killala	Castlereagh	- on Palmerstown R.	corn	-	-	-	-	1897	-	25"os/	14.16
Killala	Castlereagh	Knox Ernest	corn	(1B) 62x24x19 :	-	4.4	-	-	-	hob/	5.4183
Killala	Castlereagh :	Knox John, Arthur E. :	corn	corn mill (struck off):	-	15.0	- sold to Ernest Knox	1856	-	mlyIE	p80
Islandeady	Claggarnagh :	-	corn	-	-	-	-	-	-	6"os/	78
Islandeady	Claggarnagh E.	- near Islandeady L.	corn	-	-	-	-	-	-	6"os/	78
Bekan	Clagnagh	-	corn kiln	-	-	-	-	-	-	6"os/	93
Kilcolman	Clare Town :	-	brewery	-	-	-	-	-	-	6"os/	101
Turlough	Cloghadockan	Becket Nathaniel	corn & tuck	-	-	-	-	-	-	hob/	5.4125
Turlough	Cloghadockan	Bicket Nathaniel	mill	-	-	-	-	-	-	hob/	5.4127
Touaghty	Cloghadockan	Bucket Nathaniel	corn & kiln	(2C) 24x16x7 :	-	14/8	-	-	u`shot 14x1.10x6 :	hob/	5.4124
Touaghty	Cloghadockan	S. side of Clydagh R.	corn & kiln	-	-	-	-	1844	-	6"os/	70
Islandeady	Clogher	-	mill	-	-	-	-	-	-	6"os/	77
Turlough	Clogher	-	tuck & corn	- (no trace 1984)	-	-	-	-	hz wheel	sv/	CLawless
Turlough	Clogher	- near Clogher L.	mill	-	-	-	-	-	-	6"os/	77
Turlough	Clogher	Fitzgerald	mills	-	-	-	Fitzgerald - McDonnell	c1751	-	dd/	131 412 8?9641
Turlough	Clogher	Kirwan	mills	-	-	-	Kirwan - Dillon	c1751	-	dd/	741 208 95057
Turlough	Clogher	Moore James :	mills	-	-	-	Moore J - Kirwan Chris :	1750	-	dd/	139 443 94297
Turlough	Clogher	Westport Water Wks.	corn	small section walls :	-	-	Chris Gibbons	2003	-	pWEH	Z
Myo	Cloghermore	-	mill	-	-	-	-	2003	-	pWEH	Z
Tagheen	Cloghermore	Hughes Patrick	gig & kiln	(3A) 30.6x15x5 :	-	1.7.0	-	-	gig dia. not ascert. :	hob/	5.4088
Tagheen	Cloghermore (?)	Donnelly Thomas	gig	(2B) 21.6x14.6x5.0	-	2.4.7	-	-	4ft. 2ins. GIG :	hob/	5.4088
Tagheen	Cloghernagh	-	-	-	-	-		2003	-	pWEH	Z
Annagh	Clonbullig	Grogan Muchael	corn	-	-	-	-	-	- x - x3	vmb/	15
Templemore	Clonconra	- on Cloonlee R.	mill	-	-	-	-	-	-	6"os/	71
Aghagower	Cloonagh	-	mill	-	-	-	-	2003	-	pWEH	R
Aghagower	Cloonagh	- Cloonagh Mill	corn	conversion for use :	-	-	-	2003	-	pWEH	Cr
Aghagower	Cloonagh	- nr Aghamore Br.	bleach	-	-	-	-	2003	-	pWEH	R
Aghagower	Cloonagh	Bellamount Earl of	mills	-	-	-	Bellamount - McDonnell	c1751	-	dd/	455 496 295824?
Aghagower	Cloonagh	Cloonagh Health Cen.	bleach (?)	recently conv. to res.	-	-	-	2003	-	pWEH	Cr
Aghagower	Cloonagh	McDonnell	mills	-	-	-	McDonnell - Fitzgerald	c1751	-	dd/	612 309 418622
Aghagower	Cloonagh	Whittle Mary	mill	-	-	-	Whittle M - Fielden Jn	1835	-	dd/	1835 15 186
Aghagower	Cloonagh :	- nr Owenwee R.	bleach	-	-	-	-	-	-	6"os/	87
Aghagower	Cloonagh :	- stream to O`wee	mill	-	-	-	-	-	-	6"os/	87
Crossmolina	Cloonawillin	-	flax	farm still operates	-	-	-	2003	-	pWEH	Z
Crossmolina	Cloonawillin	- near Farragh Ho.	flax	- (no trace :)	-	-	-	2003	-	pWEH	Z
Crossmolina	Cloonawillin	- near Farragh Ho.	mill	-	-	-	-	-	-	1"os/	53
Annagh	Cloonbullig :	-	corn & dam	-	-	-	-	-	-	6"os/	103
Touaghty	Clooneencarra	Blake Edward	corn	-	-	-	-	-	14x4x4 6 rev./min.	VOms/	5.4123 (+MS)
Touaghty	Clooneencarra	Blake Edward	corn & kilns	-	-	-	-	-	-	hob/	5.4122
Kilmovee	Cloonfeaghra	-	mill	-	-	-	-	-	-	6"os/	82
Kilmovee	Cloonfeaghra	- on small stream :	mill	-	-	-	-	-	-	6"os/	82

PARISH	TOWNLAND	MILLER	TYPE	HOUSE	Land	£Val	PROPRIETORS	Date	WHEEL etc.	Record	Ref.
Templemore	Cloongee	Annally Lord John :	mills	-	-	-	Annally Ld - Knox Francis :	1778	-	dd/	324 550 217827
Kilconduff	Cloongullaun	- nr br. on R. Moy	corn & sluice	-	-	-	-	-	-	6"os/	61
Kilfian	Cloonkee	Gledstones Thomas :	mills	-	-	-	Gledstanes T - Annally :	1773	-	dd/	295 348 196585
Kilfian	Cloonkee	Westly Edward :	mills	-	-	-	Westby (Ma.) - Knox Fras:	1803	-	dd/	559 75 372310
Turlough	Cloonkesh	-	corn & kiln	-	-	-	-	1844	-	6"os/	70
Turlough	Cloonkesh	-	mill	- (no trace 1984)	-	-	-	-	hz wheel	sv/	CLawless
Turlough	Cloonkesh	stream to Clydagh R.	corn kiln	-	-	-	-	1844	-	6"os/	70
Kilgeever	Cloonlaur	-	gig mill	-	-	-	-	-	-	6"os/	95
Kilgeever	Cloonlaur	- at Clapper Bridge	gig	-	-	-	-	2003	-	pWEH	Z
Kilgeever	Cloonlaur	- at Clapper Bridge	old mill	- (disappeared)	-	-	-	2003	-	pWEH	Z
Kilmovee	Cloonnamana	-	corn & pond	-	-	-	-	-	-	6"os/	73
Kilbefad	Cloontally	-	corn kiln	-	-	-	-	-	-	6"os/	39
Turlough	Clough	- near Turlough :	mill in ruins	-	-	-	-	-	-	6"os/	70
Addergoole	Cloughbrack Far	-	corn & kiln	-	-	-	-	-	-	6"os/	47
Addergoole	Cloughbrack Far	-	corn & kiln	-	-	-	-	-	-	6"os/	47
Islandeady	Cogaula	-	corn	old farm building :	-	-	Patk, Martin, Tony Kelly	2003	-	pWEH	B
Islandeady	Cogaula	-	corn & pond	-	-	-	-	-	-	6"os/	77
Islandeady	Cogaula	-	corn & pond	-	-	-	-	-	-	6"os/	77
Islandeady	Cogaula	-	gig corn	- site recognisable	-	-	-	2003	-	pWEH	Z
Islandeady	Cogaula	-	hz mill	site of old mill :	-	-	Patk, Martin, Tony Kelly	2003	-	pWEH	Z
Islandeady	Cogaula	Filbin Patrick	gig	-	-	-	-	-	-	hob/	5.4081
Kiolbefad	Colladussaun	-	corn kiln	-	-	-	-	-	-	6"os/	48
Cong	Cong North	Edwood Thomas	flour	-	-	-	-	-	20x5x5 3 pr st.	vmb/	15
Cong	Cong North	Edwood Thomas	flour	-	-	-	-	-	16x5x3 4 pr st.	vmb/	15
Cong	Cong North	Moran Patrick	corn	45x26x30 new :	-	15.3.6	-	-	new	hob/	5.3135
Cong	Cong North	Moran Patrick	flour	45x26x30 :	-	12.0.0	-	-	-	hob/	5.3135
Cong	Cong North :	-	mills	-	-	-	-	-	-	6"os/	120
Cong	Cong Town	Elwood Thomas	flour & kiln	-	-	-	-	-	-	hob/	5.4153
Kilbefad	Coolcran	-	corn kiln	-	-	-	-	-	-	6"os/	39
Ballynahaglish	Coolcronaun	-	corn kiln	-	-	-	-	-	-	6"os/	48
Killasser	Coollagagh	-	mill	-	-	-	-	-	-	6"os/	49
Annagh	Coolnafarna	-	corn, mill dam :	-	-	-	-	-	-	6"os/	93
Annagh	Coolnafarna	Moran John	corn	-	-	-	-	-	11x2x -	vmb/	15
Cong	Cordroon	Cromie	mills	-	-	-	Cromie - Blake	c1751	-	dd/	368 140 246369
Cong	Cordroon	Duell Thomas :	mill	-	-	-	Duell T - Cromie William :	1753	-	dd/	164 189 110173
Kilasser	Cornageeha	-	corn	-	-	-	-	-	-	6"os/	62
Kilgeever	Corragaun :	-	mill	-	-	-	-	-	-	6"os/	105
Killeden	Corrahoor	-	gig corn	- [site not located]	-	-	-	2003	-	pWEH	?
Killeden	Corrahoor	- near Kiltimagh	mill	-	-	-	-	-	-	6"os/	80
Killeden	Corrahoor	Pherick Patrick	corn	-	-	-	-	-	12x2x11	vmb/	15
Killedan	Corrahoor	Pherick Patrick	corn & kiln	-	-	-	-	-	-	hob/	5.4148
Killedan	Corrahoor :	-	corn	-	-	-	-	-	-	6"os/	80
Ballynahaglish	Corroy	- near Ballina	corn	now factory site	-	-	-	2003	- pho. old chimney	pWEH	Cc
Ballynahaglish	Corroy	Fcty on Industrial site	mill	part old buildings :	-	-	-	2003	-	pWEH	Cc
Ballynahaglish	Corroy	Brogan Dennis	corn	-	-	-	-	-	11x2x4	vmb/	15
Ballynahaglish	Corroy	Jackson James	corn	(1A) 73x19x23	-	8.9	-	-	12x2.2x6	hob/	5.4171
Ballynahaglish	Corroy	Jackson James	corn	-	-	-	-	-	12x2x6	vmb/	15
Ballynahaglish	Corroy	Jackson James	tuck	-	-	-	-	-	11.4x ?x 4.6 :	hob/	5.4171
Ballinahaglish	Corroy	Jackson James Vau.	mill	-	-	-	-	-	-	hob/	5.4169
Ballynahaglish	Corroy	Vaughan J	corn	(1A) 73x19x22 :	-	7.14	-	-	-	hob/	5.4171
Kilvine	Creeveeshel	- on Dalgan R.	mill	-	-	-	-	-	-	1"os/	86
Toomore	Creggagh	-	tuck	- small building :	-	-	James & Jack McGraoil	2003	-	pWEH	B

PARISH	TOWNLAND	MILLER	TYPE	HOUSE	Land	£Val	PROPRIETORS	Date	WHEEL etc.	Record	Ref.
Toomore	Creggagh	Fair John	corn	-	-	-	Fair John - Cannon Eliz	1834	-	dd/	1834 2 126
Turlough	Crillaun	-	mill	-	-	-	-	-	-	6"os/	60
Turlough	Crillaun	- E. side Tobergal R.	mill	-	-	-	-	-	hz wheel	sv/	CLawless
Kilmore	Cross	-	corn kiln	-	-	-	-	-	-	6"os/	16
Kilmore	Cross	-	mill	-	-	-	-	2003	-	pWEH	R
Aghmore	Crossard :	-	corn & kiln	-	-	-	-	-	-	6"os/	93
Aghamore	Crossbeg	Cassidy Patrick	corn	-	-	-	-	-	13x2x4	vmb/	15
Kilbride	Crott	Flanagan Patrick	corn & tuck	-	-	-	-	-	-	hob/	5.4179
Kilbride	Crott	Flanagan Patrick	corn GIG	-	-	-		-	3x - x3	vmb/	15
Kilcolman	Cuilmore	McGrath Thomas	corn	-	-	-	-	-	15x3x5	vmb/	15
Kilcolman	Cuilmore :	-	corn & dam	-	-	-	-	-	-	6"os/	102
Addergoole	Cuilmullagh	-	corn kiln	-	-	-	-	-	-	6"os/	59
Bekan	Cullentragh	Flatley William	corn GIG	-	-	-	-	-	-	hob/	5.4132
Bekan	Cullentragh	Flatley William	corn GIG	-	-	-	-	-	- x - x4	vmb/	15
Bekan	Cultycreaghan	Kilroy John	corn	-	-	-	-	-	- x - x4	vmb/	15
Addergole	Cum	-	malt kiln	-	-	-	-	-	-	6"os/	47
Ballyhean	Cunnaker	-	mill	-	-	-	-	-	-	VOms/	5.4093 (+MS)
Ballyhean	Cunnaker :	-	corn	-	-	-	-	-	-	6"os/	89
Aglish	Curragh	- on Robe R.	mill	-	-	-	-	-	-	1"os/	85
Crossboyne	Curraghadooey	- on Robe R.	tuck & race	-	-	-	-	-	-	6"os/	111
Kilconduff	Curraun	-	mill & corn kiln	-	-	-	-	-	-	6"os/	72
Mayo	Currymacmanus	-	mill	-	-	-	-	-	-	6"os/	90
Mayo	Currymacmanus	Ward John	gig & kiln	19.6x14x5 & kilns :	-	11.4.0	-	-	3ft 10ins. GIG :	hob/	5.4087
Kilcommon	Darraragh	-	old corn kiln	-	-	-	-	-	-	6"os/	26
Crossmolina	Derry Upper	- at Derry Vge.	mill	-	-	-	-	-	-	6"os/	37
Addergoole	Derryfadda	-	corn kiln	-	-	-	-	-	-	6"os/	59
Aghagower	Derryherbert	-	corn kiln	-	-	-	-	-	-	6"os/	107
Kilgeever	Derrylahan	-	mill	-	-	-	-	2003	-	mmSv/	wh - Z
Kilgeever	Derrylahan :	-	corn	-	-	-	-	-	-	6"os/	86
Aglish	Derrylea	- nr Pheasant Hill	tuck	-	-	-	-	-	-	6"os/	78
Aglish	Derrylea :	-	tuck	-	-	-	-	-	-	6"os/	78
Bekan	Devlis	- SE. of Ballyhaunis	corn	-	-	-	-	1844	-	6"os/	103
Aghill	Doogart East	Nagle Rev Edward	corn	-	-	-	-	-	13x3x13	vmb/	15
Achill	Doogart East	Nagle Rev Edward	corrn & tuck	-	-	-	-	-	-	hob/	5.4077
Achill	Doogort	- nr Fisheen Vge.	corn	-	-	-	-	-	-	6"os/	40
Achill	Doogort	- nr Fisheen Vge.	tuck	-	-	-	-	-	-	6"os/	40
Kilvine	Doonamacreena	Maning Daniel	mill & kiln	-	-	-	-	-	-	hob/	5.4085
Crossmolina	Doonbreedia	-	corn kiln	-	-	-	-	-	-	6"os/	38
Kilvine	Doonmacreena	Manion Daniel	corn	-	-	-	-	-	14x1x4	vmb/	15
Kilvine	Doonmacreena	Manion Daniel	tuck	-	-	-	-	-	14x1x4	vmb/	15
Kilvine	Doonmacreena	Manning Daniel	corn & tuck	(1B) 53x22x9.6 :	-	6.6.0	-	-	corn 14x1.6x4.6 :	hob/	5.4085
Kilvine	Doonmacreena :	- on Dangan R.	mill	-	-	-	-	-	-	6"os/	112
Drum	Drum	Cannon Michael	corn GIG	(3B) 19X19X5.6 :	-	7/6d.	-	-	-	hob/	5.4106
Drum	Drum	Connor Michael	new corn	-	-	-	-	-	-	hob/	5.4107
Drum	Drum :	-	corn & kiln	-	-	-	-	-	-	6"os/	90
Oughval	Drummin East :	-	tuck	-	-	-	-	-	-	6"os/	107
Kilmore	Drumreagh	-	corn kiln	-	-	-	-	-	-	6"os/	16
Aglish	Drumshinagh	-	windmill stump	-	-	-	-	-	-	6"os/	78
Aglish	Drumshinagh	- N./ Castlebar L.	windmill stump	-	-	-	-	-	-	6"os/	78
Mayo	Drymills	Warren Mathias	mills	-	-	-	Warren M - Daly Bernard :	1785	-	dd/	470 34 299096
Mayo	Duckanelly	Caulfiend Thomas	mills	-	-	-	Caulfield - Clendenning :	1835	-	dd/	1835 13 255
Mayo	Duckanelly	Moore Sir Hugh Jas	mills	-	-	-	Moore - Towers Thos	1828	-	dd/	835 267 651202

PARISH	TOWNLAND	MILLER	TYPE	HOUSE	Land	£Val	PROPRIETORS	Date	WHEEL etc.	Record	Ref.
Mayo	Duckanelly	Moore Sir Hugh Jas	mills	-	-	-	Moore - Dunne Joseph	1828	-	dd/	835 279 561214
Mayo	Duckanelly	Sligo Margaret	mills	-	-	-	Sligo M - O`Donel Richd	1835	-	dd/	1835 18 263
Bekan	Eden	-	corn kiln	-	-	-	-	1844	-	6"os/	92
Bekan	Eden	Horgan Patrick	corn GIG	-	-	-	-	-	- x - x3	vmb/	15
Kilgarvan	Ellagh-More	-	corn	-	-	-	-	-	-	6"os/	40
Kilcolman	Eskerlavally	-	mill	-	-	-	-	2003	-	pWEH	D
Kilcolman	Eskerlevally	-	mill	-	-	-	-	-	-	1"os/	86
Kilcolman	Eskerlevally	Brown	mill	-	-	-	Brown - Feeny	c1751	-	dd/	557 28 368297
Kilcolman	Eskerlevally	Brown Hon. Denis :	mill	-	-	-	Brown D - Altamount John :	1790	-	dd/	431 530 281659
Kilcolman	Eskerlevally	Brown Hon. Denis :	mill	-	-	-	Brown D - Mahon Robert :	1791	-	dd/	437 10 281660
Kilcolman	Eskerlevally	Feeny John	corn	-	-	-	-	-	13x2x -	vmb/	15
Kilcolman	Eskerlevally	Young Owen :	mill	-	-	-	Young E - Brown John :	1752	-	dd/	154 101 102929
Aghamore	Falleighter	-	mill & mill dam	-	-	-	-	-	-	6"os/	81
Kilmore	Fallmore	-	corn kiln	-	-	-	-	-	-	6"os/	33
Kilturra	Flughany	-	mill & kiln	-	-	-	-	-	-	6"os/	52
Kilturra	Flughany	Doyle Andrew	corn GIG	-	-	-	-	-	-	hob/	5.4144
Moygawnagh	Forrew	-	corn	-	-	-	-	-	-	6"os/	29
Kilmanbeg	Fountain Hill	-	corn & hz	old house ruins :	-	-	-	2003	Mrs. McDonnell	pWEH	R
Kilmanbeg	Fountain Hill	-	corn & pond	-	-	-	-	-	-	6"os/	121
Kilmanbeg	Fountain Hill	Jennings Ulick	horizontal	-	-	-	-	-	-	hob/	5.4158
Toomore	Foxford	Bingham Henry	mills	-	-	-	Bingham - Banks Susan. :	1759	-	dd/	321 557 217727
Toomore	Foxford	Bingham Henry Hon.	iron works	-	-	-	Bingham - Ruttledge Andr.	1738	-	dd/	106 439 74604
Toomore	Foxford	Bingham Henry Hon.	iron works	-	-	-	Bingham - Ruttledge Andr.	1745	-	dd/	122 556 85395
Toomore	Foxford	Bingham Jno	mills	-	-	-	Bingham - Kildare Jas. Earl	1744	-	dd/	115 333 806654
Toomore	Foxford	Bingham John :	iron works	-	-	-	Bingham J - Bingham Henry	1780	-	dd/	336 118 224083
Toomore	Foxford	Bingham John :	mills	-	-	-	Brown John - Grogan :	1755	-	dd/	177 189 117987
Toomore	Foxford	Blake Walter & Wife :	mills	-	-	-	Blake & W - Irvine James :	1797	-	dd/	492 400/ 329034
Toomore	Foxford	Brown James :	mills	-	-	-	Brown Jas - Leigh Fras :	1749	-	dd/	132 546 91305
Toomore	Foxford	Harward William	mills	-	-	-	Harward - Lambert Chas :	1702	-	dd/	225 232 145881
Toomore	Foxford	Hutchinson	land	-	-	-	Hutchinson - Pemberton	c1751	?	dd/	111 75 75670
Toomore	Foxford	Lambert	mills	-	-	-	Lambert - Dillon & ano	c1780	?	dd/	335 260 223403
Toomore	Foxford	Ormsby Charles	iron works	-	-	-	Ormsby C - Moore George	1741	-	dd/	112 23 76587
Toomore	Foxford	Ormsby Charles	iron works	-	-	-	Ormsby - Sweeny Denis	1752	-	dd/	204 219 135107
Toomore	Foxford	Ruttledge	iron works	-	-	-	Ruttledge - Ruttledge	c1750	?	dd/	191 384 128272
Toomore	Foxford Town	- Foxford Mills	woollen	modernised now :	-	-	-	1999	-	mmSv/	wh - A
Toomore	Foxford Town	Corley John	mill	-	-	-	-	-	-	hob/	5.3136
Toomore	Foxford Town	Deane Edward H :	corn kiln	91x18.6x20 & store :	-	13.0	-	-	-	hob/	5.3137
Ballinrobe	Friars Quarter W	Flair Camble	flour	-	-	-	-	-	17x3x5	vmb/	15
Ballinrobe	Friars Quarter W	Kenny Courtney :	old brewery	78x21.6x8 & offs :	-	-	-	-	-	hob/	5.3122
Ballinrobe	Friars Quarter W	unoc., Bridge Street	old flour mill	69.6x25x32 :	-	-	-	-	-	hob/	5.3122
Burrishoole	Furnace	-	gig	-	-	-	-	-	-	6"os/	67
Burrishoole	Furnace	-	tuck	-	-	-	-	-	-	6"os/	67
Burrishoole	Furnace	Ryan Thomas	corn & tuck	-	-	-	-	-	-	hob/	5.4080
Moygawnagh	Garranard	Gallagher Peter	hz - corn	(2B) 18x14x6	-	3/1d	-	1853	old turbine hz wheel	hob/	5.4187
Moygawnagh	Garranard	Wills Robert	corn	(2C) 16x13x5	-	-	-	1853	old turbine dia. 5.6 :	hob/	5.4187
Tagheen	Garravlagh	-	mill	-	-	-	-	-	-	6"os/	90
Kilcolman	Glebe	- nr Ballahadareen	corn & pond	-	-	-	-	-	-	6"os/	74
Castlemore	Glebe	Flynn David	corn	-	-	-	-	-	11x1x -	vmb/	15
Castlemore	Glebe	Flynn David	tuck	-	-	-	-	-	11x1x- 1 stock	vmb/	15
Kilmovee	Glentavraun	-	corn	-	-	-	-	-	-	1"os/	75
Kildacommoge	Gneeve	- on Manulla R.	mill	-	-	-	-	-	-	1"os/	75
Kildacommoge	Gneeve	- sited in mid-river :	tuck	-	-	-	-	-	-	6"os/	79

PARISH	TOWNLAND	MILLER	TYPE	HOUSE	Land	£Val	PROPRIETORS	Date	WHEEL etc.	Record	Ref.
Kildacommoge	Gneeve :	-	tuck	-	-	-	-	-	-	6"os/	79
Myo ?	Gorlough	- nr Cloghermore	mill	- plaque date 1847	-	-	J. Donnellan	2003	-	pWEH	D?
Shrule	Gortbrack	- on Black R. :	mill	-	-	-	-	-	-	6"os/	123
Templemore	Gorteen	- SW. rd./ Foxford	corn & kiln	-	-	-	-	-	-	6"os/	71
Kildacommoge	Gortlahan	-	mill	-	-	-	-	-	-	6"os/	60
Kilcolman	Gortnarahan	Downey Anthony	corn	-	-	-	-	-	11x2x7	vmb/	15
Killasser	Grallagh	-	mill & kiln	-	-	-	-	-	-	6"os/	71
Ardagh	Greenaun	- E. Crannagh Vge.	corn	-	-	-	-	-	-	6"os/	30
Ardagh	Greenaun	- W. Crannagh Vge.	corn	-	-	-	-	-	-	6"os/	30
Kilcolman	Hawksford	-	corn & kiln	-	-	-	-	-	-	6"os/	64
Kilcolman	Hawksford	Dillon Dow Vc`tess	mill	-	-	-	Dillon V`ss - Squire Jn	1834	-	dd/	1834 11 56
Kilcolman	Hawksford	Dillon Dow Vc`tess	mill	-	-	-	Dillon V`ss - Squire Jn	1834	-	dd/	1834 11 56
Kilcolman	Hawksford	Dillon Henry	mill	-	-	-	Dillon H - Musgrave Lord	1807	-	dd/	588 33 398428
Kilcolman	Hawksford	Dillon Ld Chas Visc.	mill	-	-	-	Dillon Lord - Warren Peter :	1800	-	dd/	528 493 347509
Kilcolman	Hawksford	Dillon Lord	mill	-	-	-	Dillon Lord - Warren	c1790	-	dd/	528 493 347509
Kilcolman	Hawksford	Dillon Lord	mill	-	-	-	Dillon Lord - Trustees	c1800	?	dd/	561 459 37812
Kilcolman	Hawksford	Dillon Visc.	mill	-	-	-	Dillon V - Dunsany Ld	1834	-	dd/	1834 6 24
Kilturra	Hughany	Doyle Andrew	corn	-	-	-	-	-	-	vmb/	15
Doonfeeny	Inagh Village	-	corn kiln ruins	-	-	-	-	-	-	6"os/	13
Ballintober	Kilbree Lower	- site intact :	-	no evidence of mill	-	-	John Cooper	2003	old small dia stone	pWEH	Z
Ballintober	Kilbree Lower	Fahy William	gig & forge	-	-	-	-	-	-	hob/	5.4078
Kilconduff	Kilbride	Staunton Patrick	corn & kiln	-	-	-	-	-	-	hob/	5.4146
Kilmovee	Kilcashel	- near Glebe Ho.	mill & kiln	-	-	-	-	-	-	6"os/	73
Kilmovee	Kilcashel	Dillon Dow Vc`tess	mill	-	-	-	Dillon V`ss - Squire Jn	1834	-	dd/	1834 11 56
Attymass	Kildermot	- E. of Vge.	corn kiln	-	-	-	-	1844	-	6"os/	40
Kilmovee	Kilkelly	- at Kilkelly Town	corn & kiln	-	-	-	-	1844	-	6"os/	72
Kilmovee	Kilkelly	Dillon	mills	-	-	-	Dillon - Delafield	c1725	-	dd/	58 207 39197
Bekan	Kilknock	Barnacle Patrick	corn	-	-	-	-	-	-	hob/	5.4132
Bekan	Kilknock	Barnacle Patrick	corn	-	-	-	-	-	12x2x1	vmb/	15
Bekan	Kilknock	Barnacle Patrick	tuck	-	-	-	-	-	13x2x -	vmb/	15
Kilmovee	Killaclare	-	mill	-	-	-	-	-	-	1"os/	75
Knock	Killeen	-	corn kiln	-	-	-	-	-	-	6"os/	92
Oughaval	Killeencoff	beside Aghamore Br.	corn	-	-	-	-	2003	-	pWEH	Z
Oughaval	Killeencoff :	- near Owenwee R.	corn	-	-	-	-	-	-	6"os/	87
Oughaval	Killeencoff :	- near Owenwee R.	corn	-	-	-	-	-	-	6"os/	87
Oughaval	Killeencoff :	-	corn	-	-	-	-	-	-	pWEH	R
Moygawnagh	Killeennashask	- on R. Cloonamore	mill	-	-	-	-	-	-	6"os/	21
Moygawnagh	Killeennashask	Robinson George	corn	(2B) 18x14x6.6 :	-	2.3.0	-	-	12x2x4 floats 9ins.:	hob/	5
bo. Gallen	Killinasash	Brown Andrew :	mill	-	-	-	Brown A - Martin Edward :	1804	-	dd/	559 185 372?818
Islandeady	Kilmaglasser	Coffey Martin	corn & tuck	-	-	-	-	-	-	hob/	5.4082
Kilmovee	Kilmovee	Knox John	mill	-	-	-	Knox - Oxmantown Ld	1835	-	dd/	1835 21 204
Kilcommon	Kilrush	Lowrie Francis	threshing	-	-	-	-	-	-	hob/	5.4157
Kilvine	Kilvine	Kerrane David	gig	(4C) 20.6x13.6x4 :	-	1.4.0	-	-	4ft. 14 float bds :	hob/	5.4085
Kilvine	Kilvine :	-	mill	-	-	-	-	-	-	6"os/	112
Crossmolina	Kinard	-	corn kiln	-	-	-	-	-	-	6"os/	38
Aghagower	Knappa	-	gig	- :	-	-	-	2003	-	pWEH	Z
Aghagower	Knappa	- W. rd. to Linaunn	iron foundry	-	-	-	Michael o`Byrne	2003	-	pWEH	Z
Aghagower	Knappa More	-	old iron mill	-	-	-	-	-	-	6"os/	88
Aghagower	Knappa More	- near main road	old foundry	demolished	-	-	-	-	-	mmSv/	wh - Z
Aghagower	Knappa More :	- site among trees	gig mill	-	-	-	-	-	-	6"os/	88
Aglish	Knockacroghery	- in Castlebar :	brewery	-	-	-	-	-	-	6"os/	78
Aglish	Knockacroghery	- in Castlebar :	distillery	-	-	-	-	-	-	6"os/	78

PARISH	TOWNLAND	MILLER	TYPE	HOUSE	Land	£Val	PROPRIETORS	Date	WHEEL etc.	Record	Ref.
Aglish	Knockacroghery :	-	distillery	-	-	-	-	-	-	6"os/	78
Ballinrobe	Knockanotish	Maguire Isaac	bleach	-	-	-	-	-	-	vmb/	15
Ballinrobe	Knockanotish :	-	bleach	-	-	-	-	-	-	6"os/	118
Ballinrobe	Knockanotish :	-	bleach	solid old building :	-	-	-	2003	-	pWEH	B
Ballinrobe	Knockanotish :	- W. side of river :	mill	-	-	-	-	1844	-	6"os/	118
Kilfian	Knockaskeehaun	- near Millpark Ho.	old mill	-	-	-	-	-	-	6"os/	29
Kilmeena	Knockballagh	- on Morney R.	corn	-	-	-	-	-	-	6"os/	76
Knock	Knockbaun	-	corn	-	-	-	-	-	-	6"os/	92
Killasser	Knockfadda	-	corn kiln	-	-	-	-	-	-	6"os/	149
Kilbefad	Knockfree	-	-	- demolished	-	-	John J Kavanagh (land)	2003	-	pWEH	Z
Kilbefad	Knockfree	-	corn & kiln	-	-	-	-	-	-	6"os/	39
Kilbefad	Knockfree	-	tuck	-	-	-	-	-	-	6"os/	39
Addergoole	Knockmaria	- near L. Conn	corn & kiln	-	-	-	-	-	-	6"os/	47
Ballynahaglish	Knockmore	-	corn & kiln	-	-	-	-	-	-	6"os/	48
Myo	Knockmore	near to Mill Field :	corn	-	-	-	-	2003	-	pWEH	Z
Ballynahaglish	Knockmore	Ormsby	mills	-	-	-	Ormsby - Monk	c1775	?	dd/	316 315 214127
Ballynahaglish	Knockmore	Ormsby Henry	mills	-	-	-	Ormsby - Ruttledge Wm	1782	-	dd/	344 243 231251
Ballynahaglish	Knockmore	Ormsby Henry	mills	-	-	-	Ormsby Henry - Carter :	1794	-	dd/	350 155 234773
Ballynahaglish	Knockmore	Ormsby Henry	mills	-	-	-	Ormsby H - Peacock Bryce	1791	-	dd/	437 224 282599
Ballynahaglish	Knockmore	Ormsby Henry	mills	-	-	-	Ormsby - Peacock Bryce	1793	-	dd/	467 200 297831
Ballynahaglish	Knockmore	Perry Henry	mills	-	-	-	Perry Henry & Setlement	1780	-	dd/	350 155 234773
Oughval	Knockranny :	-	flour & pond	-	-	-	-	-	-	6"os/	88
Kildacomoge	Knocktemple	-	corn	-	-	-	-	-	-	6"os/	71
Myo	Laghtamacdurcan	- S. of R. Moy	corn kilns (2)	-	-	-	-	-	-	6"os/	61
Oughval	Leckanvy :	-	corn & pond	-	-	-	-	-	-	6"os/	86
Oughval	Leckanvy :	- not heard of local	corn	- assumed demol.	-	-	-	2003	-	pWEH	Z
Turlough	Leckneen	-	-	large bds. o`grown	-	-	Gerry Kearney	2003	-	pWEH	D
Turlough	Leckneen	-	bleach	-	-	-	-	-	-	6"os/	60
Turlough	Leckneen	-	bleach & corn	-	-	-	-	-	-	6"os/	70
Turlough	Leckneen	-	tuck & corn	-	-	-	-	-	-	6"os/	70
Turlough	Leckneen	-	watch tower	-	-	-	-	-	-	6"os/	60
Turlough	Leckneen	-	watch tower	-	-	-	-	-	-	6"os/	70
Turlough	Leckneen	Malley William	beetling	-	-	-	-	-	-	hob/	5.4125
Turlough	Leckneen	Malley William	corn	-	-	-	-	-	-	hob/	5.4125
Crossboyne	Leedaun	- Brookhill	Flour Mill	-	-	-	-	-	-	6"os/	101
Crossboyne	Leedaun	Lambert Joseph	flour	walls good & strong :	-	-	-	-	13x5x14	vmb/	15
Balla	Legaun	- nr L. Naminoo	tuck & corn	-	-	-	-	-	-	6"os/	79
Balla	Legaun	- site located ? :	corn	old house :	-	-	-	2003	-	pWEH	R
Balla	Legaun	Flanagan Michael	corn	-	-	-	-	-	11x2x3	vmb/	15
Balla	Legaun :	-	mill gulph	-	-	-	-	-	-	6"os/	79
Turlough	Levallinree	-	mill	-	-	-	-	-	hz wheel	sv/	CLawless
Turlough	Levallinree	stream to Derryhick Lo	mill & corn kiln	-	-	-	-	1844	-	6"os/	70
Kilmovee	Leveelick	-	corn & kiln	-	-	-	-	-	-	6"os/	74
Meelick	Lisbrogan	-	corn & kiln	-	-	-	-	-	-	6"os/	61
Aghagower	Liscarney :	-	corn & tuck	-	-	-	-	-	-	6"os/	97
Islandeady	Lisclonaun	-	gig mill & kiln	-	-	-	-	-	-	6"os/	77
Kilmeenagh	Lisclovaun	-	gig & kiln	-	-	-	-	-	-	6"os/	77
Kilmeenagh	Lisclovaun	- site near bridge :	gig	-	-	-	-	2003	-	pWEH	Z
Annagh	Lisduff	Dillon Edward :	mill	-	-	-	Dillon Ed - Taffe Edmond	1791	-	dd/	443 238 285930
Annagh	Lisduff	Higgins Andrew :	mill	-	-	-	Higgins A - O`Hara Chas :	1806	-	dd/	576 422 392842
Annagh	Lisduff	Kelly Hugh :	mill	-	-	-	Kelly H - Clonbrock Rt. Hon.	1802	-	dd/	549 357 364110
Killasser	Lismoran	-	mill & corn kiln	-	-	-	-	-	-	6"os/	71

PARISH	TOWNLAND	MILLER	TYPE	HOUSE	Land	£Val	PROPRIETORS	Date	WHEEL etc.	Record	Ref.
Aglish	Lisnageeha	Lucan Earl	kiln (circular)	(3B) 58ft circ. x 8ft :	-	-	-	-	-	hob/	5.4090
Bekan	Lissaniska	-	corn kiln	-	-	-	-	-	-	6"os/	48
Bekan	Lissaniska	Folliard Patrick	corn	-	-	-	-	-	-	hob/	5.4132
Bekan	Lissaniska	Tolard Patrick	corn	-	-	-	-	-	11x2x -	vmb/	15
Kilgeever	Louisburgh Glebe	-	corn	-	-	-	-	2003	-	pWEH	R
Kilgeever	Louisburgh Glebe	-	mill, kiln & race	-	-	-	-	-	-	6"os/	86
Kilgeever	Louisburgh Tn	McGin Patrick	gig	-	-	-	-	-	-	hob/	5.3141
Kilgeever	Louisburgh Tn	McGin Patrick Jun	gig	-	1a.	-	-	-	does no work :	hob/	5.3141
Castlemore	Lung	- near Lung Ho.	corn & tuck	-	-	-	-	-	-	6"os/	74
Annagh	Lurgan	-	corn, kiln & :	-	-	-	-	1844	-	6"os/	93
Annagh	Lurgan	Higgins John	corn	-	-	-	-	-	- x - x4	vmb/	15
Kilcolman	Magheraboy	-	corn & kiln	-	-	-	-	-	-	6"os/	74
Mayo	Mayo	-	corn	-	-	-	-	-	-	1"os/	85
Mayo	Millcross	Butler Stephen C :	mills	-	-	-	Butler S - McHugh Patrick	1761	-	dd/	211 438 140706
Doonfeeny	Milltown	-	no mill	-	-	-	-	-	-	1"os/	53
Turlough	Milltown	Courtney David	land	-	-	-	Courtney - Clendenning	1835	-	dd/	1835 9 58
Turlough	Milltown	Fitzgerald Edward	land	-	-	-	Fitzgerald E - Kirwan C	1833	-	dd/	1833 3 269
Turlough	Milltown	Fitzgerald George	land	-	-	-	Fitzgerald G - Lyster Thos	1754	-	dd/	174 170 115665
Doonfeeny	Milltown :	-	no mill	-	-	-	-	-	-	6"os/	7
Kildacommoge	Moyhenna	- at Glebe	corn	-	-	-	-	-	-	6"os/	79
Kildacommoge	Moyhenna	Becket Isaac	corn & kiln	-	-	-	-	-	-	hob/	5.4112
Kildacommoge	Moyhenna	Becket Isaac	corn & kiln	-	-	-	-	-	-	hob/	5.4114
Kildacommoge	Moyhenna	Fitzgerald	mills	-	-	-	Fitzgerald - Brown	c1751	-	dd/	180 291 120583
Kildacommoge	Moyhenna :	-	corn	-	-	-	-	-	-	6"os/	79
Kildacommoge	Moyheny	Blake Mark :	mills	-	-	-	-	-	-	6"os/	79
Attymass	Mullaghawny	-	corn kiln	-	-	-	-	-	-	6"os/	39
Kilmoremoy	Mullauns	Daly James	corn	-	-	-	-	-	10x2x8	vmb/	15
Crossmolina	Mullenmore N.	-	corn & kiln	-	-	-	-	-	-	6"os/	38
Crossmolina	Mullinmore	Blaney Andrew	corn	-	-	-	-	-	11x2x3	vmb/	15
Crossmolina	Mullinmore	Blaney Andrew	tuck	-	-	-	-	-	12x4x1 2 wheels	vmb/	15
Burrishoole	Murracoagh	Heffernan Luke	corn GIG	-	-	-	-	-	-	hob/	5.4080
Burrishoole	Murrevagh	- nr Bunnahowna Br.	tuck	-	-	-	-	-	-	6"os/	66
Burrishoole	Murrevagh	Heffernan Luke	corn GIG	-	-	-	-	-	-	hob/	5.4080
Burrishoole	Newport	Medlycott	tuck	-	-	-	Medlycott - O`Donnell	c1751	?	dd/	294 516 195589
Burrishoole	Newport	Medlycott John	tuck	-	-	-	Medlycott J - French	c1751	?	dd/	295 369 197006
Burrishoole	Newport	Medlycott Thos J :	tuck	-	-	-	Medlycott - Hennen Matt.	1772	-	dd/	290 520 194070
Burrishoole	Newport	Medlycott Thos John :	tuck	-	-	-	Medlycott - Hennen Matt.	1772	-	dd/	290 519 194069
Burrishoole	Newport	Medlycott Thos John :	tuck	-	-	-	Medlycott TJ - Smith Thos :	1768	-	dd/	280 112 179728
Burrishoole	Newport	Medlycott Thos John :	tuck	-	-	-	Medlycott - Donnell Neal :	1769	-	dd/	282 375 184146
Burrishoole	Newport	Wilkes Anthony :	tuck	-	-	-	Wilkes A - Lendrum Richd :	1757	-	dd/	270 272 171435
Burriscarra	Newtown	-	corn	-	-	-	-	-	-	1"os/	75
Meelick	Oldcastle	-	flax & corn	-	-	-	-	-	-	6"os/	61
Crossmolina	Owenboy	- near Deel R.	mill	-	-	-	-	-	-	6"os/	37
Killedan	Oxford	- on Pollagh R.	corn & pond :	-	-	-	-	-	-	6"os/	80
Killedan	Oxford	- on Pollagh R.	corn & race	-	-	-	-	-	-	6"os/	80
Killedan	Oxford	Flanagan Thomas	corn & kiln	-	-	-	-	-	-	hob/	5.4148
Kilcommon	Pollaweela	McDermot Martin	corn	-	-	-	-	-	-	hob/	5.4156
Tagheen	Polldrain	-	kiln	-	-	-	-	-	-	6"os/	101
Kilcommon	Portacloy	- nr Vge. Portacloy	old corn mill	-	-	-	-	-	-	6"os/	-
Kilmoremoy	Quignashee	- on R. Moy	mill	-	-	-	-	-	-	1"os/	- (?Sligo)
Ballinrobe	Rahard	Bunadober Mill :	hz	well preserved :	-	-	OPW (formerly ?)	2003	in good condition :	pWEH	A?
Ballinrobe	Rahard :	-	corn HZ mill	-	-	-	-	-	-	6"os/	117

PARISH	TOWNLAND	MILLER	TYPE	HOUSE	Land	£Val	PROPRIETORS	Date	WHEEL etc.	Record	Ref.
Aghamore	Rath	-	mill	-	-	-	-	-	-	6"os/	81
Aghamore	Rath /Falleighter :	-	mill & corn kiln	-	-	-	-	-	-	6"os/	81
Templemurry	Rathbaun	- nr Palmerstown R.	Tully Mills	-	-	-	-	-	-	6"os/	14
Templemurry	Rathbaun	Browne Michael	corn	-	-	-	-	-	11x1x8	vmb/	15
Templemurry	Rathbaun	Browne Michael	tuck	-	-	-	-	-	11x1x8	vmb/	15
Templenurry	Rathbaun	Lindsay Ellen	corn & tuck	(1B) 23.6x22.6x11 :	-	-	-	-	-	hob/	5.4190
Kilgarvan	Rathreedaun	-	corn kiln	-	-	-	-	1843	-	6"os/	29
Kilconduff	Rathscanlon	Maunteen Patrick	corn	-	-	-	-	-	12x1x7	vmb/	15
Kilbeagh	Roosky	-	corn	-	-	-	-	2003	-	pWEH	Z
Kilbeagh	Roosky	- (? hz mill -)	corn & tuck	-	-	-	-	-	-	6"os/	81
Knock	Roosky	Behany Thady	corn & tuck	-	-	-	-	-	-	hob/	5.4145
Knock	Roosky	Behany Thady	corn GIG	-	-	-	-	-	-	vmb/	15
Knock	Roosky	Horkan Patrick	corn GIG	-	-	-	-	-	-	hob/	5.4145
Knock	Rosserk	-	corn	in fine order	-	-	-	2003	-	pWEH	B
Knock	Rosserk	on Rosserk R. :	flax	old & dangerous	-	-	-	2003	-	pWEH	D
Kilcommon	Roy	-	corn kiln	-	-	-	-	-	-	6"os/	33
Achill	Salia	- at Cashel Vge.	corn kiln	-	-	-	-	-	-	6"os/	55
Tagheen	Sessiagh	-	mill	-	-	-	-	-	-	1"os/	85
Shrule	Shrule	Cradock Thomas	corn	-	-	-	-	-	14x2x3	vmb/	15
Shrule	Shrule Town	Craddock Thomas	corn & tuck	-	-	-	-	-	-	hob/	5.3144
Shrule	Shrule Town	Golding Richard	brewery	78x26x18 :	-	-	-	-	-	hob/	5.3147
Shrule	Shrule Town	Golding Richard	mill	-	-	-	-	-	-	hob/	5.3144
Shrule	Shrule Town :	- on Black R.	mill	-	-	-	-	-	-	6"os/	122
Shrule	Shrule Town :	- nr Milford House :	brewery	-	-	-	-	-	-	6"os/	122
Kilmovee	Sonvolaun	-	corn kiln	-	-	-	-	1844	-	6"os/	73
Aglish	Springfield	- nr (E./Castlebar)	mill	-	-	-	-	-	-	6"os/	78
Aglish	Springfield :	-	old bleach	-	-	-	-	-	-	6"os/	78
Kilvine	Springvale	Tierney Patrick	bleach	-	-	-	-	-	-	hob/	5.4085
Kilmaine	Springvale	Tierney Patrick	bleach & corn	-	-	-	-	1843	-	hob/	5.4151
Templemore	Strade	-	corn & kiln	-	-	-	-	1844	-	6"os/	70
Kilconduff	Swinford Glebe	-	corn & pond	-	-	-	-	-	-	6"os/	62
Kilcommon	Tarsaghaun Beg	-	kiln	-	-	-	-	-	-	6"os/	35
Kilcommon	Tarsaghaunbeg	-	kiln	-	-	-	-	-	-	6"os/	35
Kilmovee	Tauraun	- nr Tauraun Ho.	mill & pond	-	-	-	-	-	-	6"os/	73
Kilmovee	Tauraun	Brett Michael	corn GIG	-	-	-	-	-	- x - x4	vmb/	15
Aghamore	Tawnagh	- on Glore R.	old mill	-	-	-	-	-	-	6"os/	81
bo. Gallen	Tawndressoge	Browne John W	mill	-	-	-	Browne - Brabazon W	1834	-	dd/	1834 20 82
Oughval	Tawnycrower :	-	old smelting ho.	-	-	-	-	-	-	6"os/	107
Turlough	Tawnylaheen	-	corn	-	-	-	-	-	hz wheel	sv/	CLawless
Turlough	Tawnylaheen	- on Clydagh R.	corn	-	-	-	-	-	-	6"os/	69
Kilbeagh	Temple	- on Mullaghanoe R.	mill & kiln	-	-	-	-	-	-	6"os/	63
Kilbeagh	Temple	Cavan Patk & John	corn GIG	-	-	-	-	-	-	hob/	5.4139
Kilbeagh	Temple	Swan Dominick	corn GIG	-	-	-	-	-	- x - x6	vmb/	15
Aglish	The Triangle	- at Aile	mill	-	-	-	-	-	-	1"os/	75
Oughaval	Thornhill	- on Polla R.	corn	-	-	-	-	-	-	1"os/	75
Bekan	Togher Lough	-	mill	-	-	-	-	-	-	1"os/	75
Kilcolman	Toobracken	McDonnell Roger	corn	-	-	-	-	-	13x2x7	vmb/	15
Toomore	Toomore	-	corn GIG	- :	-	-	John Burke	2003	-	pWEH	Z
Toomore	Toomore	-	mill & kiln	-	-	-	-	-	-	1"os/	64
Toomore	Toomore	-	mill & kiln	-	-	-	-	-	-	6"os/	61
Toomore	Toomore	-	mill ruins	- :	-	-	John Burke	2003	-	pWEH	R
Toomore	Toomore :	-	mill ruin	-	-	-	John Burke	-	-	(nil ?)	R

PARISH	TOWNLAND	MILLER	TYPE	HOUSE	Land	£Val	PROPRIETORS	Date	WHEEL etc.	Record	Ref.
Toomore	Toomore :	-	mill site	-	-	-	-	-	-	pWEH	Z
Crossmolina	Tooreen	- on Tooreen R.	corn	-	-	-	-	-	-	6"os/	29
Bohola	Treanfohanavan	-	mill	-	-	-	-	-	-	6"os/	71
Crossboyne	Treangarve :	-	mill	-	-	-	-	-	-	6"os/	111
Killedan	Treankeel	- S. side Glore R.	corn	-	-	-	-	-	-	6"os/	80
Killeden	Treankeel	Brehany Michael	corn	-	-	-	-	-	13x2x6	vmb/	15
Killedan	Treankeel	Brehany Michael	corn & kiln	-	-	-	-	-	-	hob/	5.4148
Killeden	Treankeel	Brehany Michael	tuck	-	-	-	-	-	12x2x6	vmb/	15
Killeden	Treankeel	- Gore Mill	corn	restored as res. & :	-	-	-	2003	Sally Mckenna	mmSv/	wh - Cr
Killeden	Treankeel	- on Glore River	corn	-	-	-	-	-	-	6"os/	80
Kilbeagh	Trouthill	- on Sonnagh R.	mill	-	-	-	-	-	-	map/	-
Kilgeever	Tully	-	tuck & corn	-	-	-	-	-	-	6"os/	96
Kilgeever	Tully	- above Tully Br.	mill	old & overgrown	-	-	-	2003	-	pWEH	R
Kilgeever	Tully	Browne Dodwell :	mills	-	-	-	Browne D - O`Donnell Sir :	1797	-	dd/	511 414 332623
Kilgeever	Tully	Browne Michael :	mill	-	-	-	Browne Mcl - Nolan Jas	1805	-	dd/	617 90 421616
Kilgeever	Tully	Garvey Nicholas	mills	-	-	-	Garvey N - Gervey Maria :	1801	-	dd/	545 516 360711
Kilgeever	Tully	Gore St Geo Ralph :	mill	-	-	-	Gore St G - Palmer Roger :	1782	- Cons. £608	dd/	213 512 142482
Kilgeever	Tully	Kilmaine Lord James :	mills	-	-	-	Kilmaine Ld - Browne :	1794	-	dd/	489 385 309857
Kilgeever	Tully	Palmer Roger :	mill	-	-	-	Palmer R - O`Neil Chas :	1747	Agmt. 11 June	dd/	123 351 86019
Kilgeever	Tully	Palmer Roger :	mill	-	-	-	Palmer R - Gardiner Chas :	1764	L&R. 1 Nov.	dd/	239 18 152695
Kilgeever	Tully	Palmer Roger :	mill	-	-	-	Palmer R - Granaghan :	1764	Lse. 24 Mar.	dd/	240 7 152717
Kilgeever	Tully	Palmer Roger :	mill	-	-	-	Palmer R - Goodwin Fran :	1765	lse. 6 Apl.	dd/	241 545 160836
Kilgeever	Tully	Palmer Francis :	mill	-	-	-	Palmer Francis - Elizabeth	1769	Instrumt.:10 Oct. :	dd/	278 206 177799
Kilgeever	Tully	Palmer Francis :	mill	-	-	-	Palmer F - Cuthbert John :	1753	-	dd/	168 21 142483
Turlough	Turlough	-	mill	demolished	-	-	-	-	-	rep/LR	Z
Turlough	Turlough	Cuffe James :	mills	-	-	-	Cuffe J - Courtney David :	1775	-	dd/	179 117 119082
Turlough	Turlough	Fitzgerald	mill	-	-	-	Fitzgerald - Curnes	-	- (error)	dd/	592 467 375046
Turlough	Turlough	Fitzgerald George :	mills	-	-	-	Fitzgerald - McDonnell Jas :	1748	Lse. 28 July	dd/	131 412 89641
Turlough	Turlough	Fitzgerald George	mills	-	-	-	Fitzgerald G - Cormick Mcl :	1754	-	dd/	162 580 111591
Turlough	Turlough	Fitzgerald George :	mills	-	-	-	Fitzgerald G - Browne Jn :	1756	-	dd/	180 291 120587
Turlough	Turlough	Fitzgerald George R.	mill	-	-	-	Fitzgerald - Knox Fran	1786	-	dd/	397 185 263964
Turlough	Turlough	Kirwan Patrick :	mill	-	-	-	Kirwan Pat - Fitzgerald :	1805	M. Arts. 20 Sep. :	dd/	574 218 388124
Turlough	Turlough	Kirwan Christopher	mills	-	-	-	Kirwan C - Dillon James :	1750	-	dd/	141 208 95057
Turlough	Turlough	Lynch Eustace :	mill	-	-	-	Lynch E - Kilkelly Patrick :	1801	-	dd/	542 9 355696
Turlough	Turlough	Moore	mills	-	-	-	Moore - Kirwan	-	-	dd/	130 443 94927
Turlough	Turlough	Ruttledge Andrew :	mill	-	-	-	Ruttledge A - Tully William:	1800	23 July.	dd/	539 52 353815
Turlough	Turlough ?	-	flour	-	-	-	-	-	-	6"os/	78
Kilmeena	Westport :	-	mill	-	-	-	-	-	-	6"os/	87
Kilmeena	Westport Dems.	Sligo Marquess	brew house	(cont. -) offices :	-	-	-	-	-	hob/	5.4083
Kilmeena	Westport Dems.	Sligo Marquess	threshing	(1B) 72x22x22 :	-	68.7	-	-	-	hob/	5.4083
Oughaval	Westport Town :	-	flour	-	-	-	-	2003	-	pWEH	Z
Oughaval	Westport Town :	-	mill	-	-	-	-	2003	-	pWEH	Z?
Oughaval	Westport Town :	- Quay Flour Mills	flour	-	-	-	-	-	-	6"os/	88
Oughaval	Westport Town :	-	flour	- :	-	-	-	2003	-	pWEH	D
Oughaval	Westport Town :	- Riverside Res.	distillery	recently renovated :	-	-	-	2003	-	pWEH	Cr
Oughaval	Westport Town :	- Old Mill Hostel	distillery	recently renovated	-	-	-	2003	-	pWEH	Cr
Oughaval	Westport Town :	-	brewery	-	-	-	-	-	-	6"os/	88
Oughaval	Westport Town :	-	no mill	-	-	-	-	-	-	6"os/	88
Oughaval	Westport Town :	-	mill	- :	-	-	-	2003	-	pWEH	B
Oughaval	Westport Town :	-	distillery	-	-	-	-	-	-	6"os/	88
Kilbelfad	Wherrew	- near coast	corn kiln	-	-	-	-	1844	-	6"os/	38

PARISH	TOWNLAND	MILLER	TYPE	HOUSE	Land	£Val	PROPRIETORS	Date	WHEEL etc.	Record	Ref.
Navan Lower	Abbeyland	Forde James	wool	-	1a.	-	-	-	-	gr/	-
Navan Lower	Abbeyland	Skelly RH & J	corn	-	37a.	-	-	-	-	gr/	-
Navan Lower	Abbeyland :	Murphy Peter	mills	-	-	-	Murphy Peter - Skelly Wm	1846	-	dd/	1846 13 229
Navan Lower	Abbeylands	- N. side R. Boyne :	mill in ruins		-	-	-	-	-	6"os/	25
Navan Lower	Abbeylands	- S. side R. Boyne :	corn	-	-	-	-	-	-	6"os/	25
Navan Lower	Abbeylands	Bradley Patrick :	corn	(1B) 74x26x23 :	-	31	-	1852	12x5.9x3.6 & :	hob/	5.3160
Navan Lower	Abbeylands :	- Millbrook :	Paper Mill	-	-	-	-	-	-	6"os/	25
Navan Lower	Abbeylands :	- N. side R. Boyne :	mill & distillery	-	-	-	-	-	-	6"os/	25
Navan Lower	Abbeylands :	-	distillery & :	-	-	-	-	-	-	6"os/	25
Enniskeen	Aghaloaghan	- NW/ Newcastle Lo.	corn & kiln	-	-	-	-	-	-	6"os/	2
Enniskeen	Aghaloaghan	- NW/ Newcastle Lo.	tuck	-	-	-	-	-	-	6"os/	2
Enniskeen	Aghaloaghan	Shiels Eleanor	mill & kiln	-	58a.	-	-	-	-	gr/	-
Meath	Altboystown	-	mill	-	-	-	-	-	-	1"os/	90
Moynalty	Annsborough	Tyrell Thomas	flour	-	-	-	Tyrell Thos - Tyrell James	1845	-	dd/	1845 17 29
Moynalty	Annsborough	Tyrell Thomas	flour	-	-	-	Tyrell & Deed	1847	-	dd/	1847 16 48
Kilbeg	Ardlonan	Smith Henry	corn	29x22.9x8 & kiln :	-	5.14	-	1838	-	hob/	5.4196
Ardmulchan	Ardmulchan	-	corn mills & :	-	-	-	-	-	-	6"os/	25
Ardmulchan	Ardmulchan	Dunne Patrick	corn	-	-	-	-	-	-	gr/	-
Ardsallagh	Ardsallagh :	- nr Ballintee Br.	corn	-	-	-	-	-	-	6"os/	31
Athboy	Athboy T`parks	- N. side Bridge St.	corn & flour	-	-	-	-	-	-	6"os/	29
Athboy	Athboy Town	Bell Rev Andrew	bleach yard	-	-	-	Bell Andrew - Roper Jno	1845	-	dd/	1845 7 140
Athboy	Athboy Town	Crawford John	mill & fields	-	-	-	Crawford Jn - Stephens H	1875	-	dd/	1875 40 284
Athboy	Athboy Town	Darnley Earl of	Athboy Mills	-	-	-	Darnley E - Newman Thos	1898	-	dd/	1898 84 11
Athboy	Athboy Town	Darnley Earl of	Athboy Mills	-	-	-	Darnley E - Pryor Edward	1899	-	dd/	1899 92 212
Athboy	Athboy Town	Darnley Earl of	mills	-	-	-	Darnley - Stevens Hos Gvs	1896	-	dd/	1896 78 118
Athboy	Athboy Town	Darnley Earl of	mills & weirs	-	-	-	Darnley E - Walsh fras	1850	-	dd/	1850 7 299
Athboy	Athboy Town	Fegan Michael	mill	-	-	-	Fegan Mcl - Nat.Bank Ltd	1876	-	dd/	1876 35 263
Athboy	Athboy Town	Hopkins Francis	mill & holding	-	-	-	Hopkins fras - Webb Wm	1840	-	dd/	1840 23 39
Athboy	Athboy Town	Massey William N	mill	-	-	-	Massey Wm - Cassidy Jn	1880	-	dd/	1880 3 13
Athboy	Athboy Town	Pryor Edward	mills				Pryor E - Rashleigh Geo	1904		dd/	1904 92256
Athboy	Athboy Town	Stevens Hos Govrs	mills	-	-	-	Stevens - Darnley Earl of	1896	-	dd/	1896 78 119
Athboy	Athboy Town	Stevens Hospital	mill	-	-	-	Stevens - Darnley Earl of	1875	-	dd/	1875 33 13
Athboy	Athboy Town	Stevenson Blackwood	mills				Stevenson - Rashleigh Geo	1904		dd/	1904 92 257
Athboy	Athboy Town	Walsh John	flour & corn	(1B) 41x36x33 :	-	47	-	-	flour : 11x5.6 :	hob/	5.3152
Athboy	Athboy Town	Warren Edward	mill	-	-	-	Warren Ed - Crawford Robt	1878	-	dd/	1878 27 226
Athlumney	Athlumney	- c1 mile NE/ Tn	corn	-	-	-	-	-	-	6"os/	25
Athlumney	Athlumney	- imed. NE/ New Br.	corn & flour	-	-	-	-	-	-	6"os/	25
Athlumney	Athlumney	- mid-field E. of Tn	factory & mill dam		-	-	-	-	-	6"os/	25
Athlumney	Athlumney	- S. side R. Boyne	flax, corn & flour		-	-	-	-	-	6"os/	25
Athlumney	Athlumney	- S/ Somerville Br.	old corn mill	-	-	-	-	-	-	6"os/	25
Athlumney	Athlumney	Chadwick J & F	corn	-	-	-	-	-	-	gr/	-
Athlumney	Athlumney	Delaney Patrick	corn & kilns	83x36x75 & 29x18x75	-	-	-	1838	16x15x5 4 pr st.	hob/	5.4214
Athlumney	Athlumney	Delaney Patrick	flour	98x24x19 & 21x24x17	-	168		-	18x6x6 5 pr st.	hob/	5.4214
Athlumney	Athlumney	Delaney Patrick	flour	-	-	-	M/s Mullen & Malcomson	1860	-	loc./	history
Athlumney	Athlumney	Gradwell, Chadwick :	spinning	-	5a.	-	-	-	-	gr/	-
Balfeaghan	Balfeaghan	- Calgath Mill	corn & dam	-	-	-	-	-	-	6"os/	49
Ardcath	Balgeeth	-	corn	-	-	-	-	1841	-	6"os/	33
Ardcath	Balgeeth	- at Micknanstown	corn	small 3 sty. building :	-	-	-	2002	-	mmSv/	wh - B
Ardcath	Balgeeth	- near Ardcath	corn	-	-	-	-	-	-	1"os/	91
Ardcath	Balgeeth	Sherlock Patrick	mill	-	17a.	-	-	1856	-	gr/	-
Ardcath	Balgeeth	Sherlock Patrick	mill	house, office & land	4.2.6	26	-	1889	-	Val.cb/	1
Oldcastle	Ballinvally	-	corn	-	-	-	-	1841	-	6"os/	9

PARISH	TOWNLAND	MILLER	TYPE	HOUSE	Land	£Val	PROPRIETORS	Date	WHEEL etc.	Record	Ref.
Oldcastle	Ballinvally	Reilly Bryan	corn	-	19a.	-	-	-	-	gr/	-
Killyon	Ballyadams	- on R. Deel	mill	-	-	-	-	1841	-	6"os/	41
Killyon	Ballyadams	Treacy John	corn	-	2a.	-	-	-	-	gr/	-
Meath	Ballyann	Smith	mill	-	-	-	Smith - Whelan	-	?	dd/	385 318 224177
Meath	Ballyann	Smith John	mill	-	-	-	Smith John - Webb John	1748	-	dd/	168 505 114 233
Meath	Ballyann	Smith Joseph	mill	-	-	-	Smith Jos - Kane Nathaniel	1748	-	dd/	132 314 89443
Meath	Ballyann	Smith Joseph	mill	-	-	-	Smith Joseph - Thos Sam	1749	-	dd/	139 262 94068
Meath	Ballyann	Smith Joseph	mill	-	-	-	Jos Smith - Browne Henry	1752	-	dd/	160 170 106074
Meath	Ballyann	Smith Joseph	mill	-	-	-	Smith Jos - Mottley James	1753	-	dd/	166 366 111880
Meath	Ballyann	Smith Thomas	mill	-	-	-	Smith T - Hendley Earbery	1779	-	dd/	331 682 224250
Meath	Ballyann	Taylor Thomas	mill	-	-	-	Taylor T - Bridges William	1739	-	dd/	98 308 68527
Meath	Ballyann	Whelan Thomas	mill	-	-	-	Whelan T - Whelan Pilsw`th	1772	-	dd/	325 99 21886
Ballyboggan	Ballyboggan ? :	Saliner	mill	-	-	-	Saliner & ano - Boyne	-	?	dd/	529 40 340207?
Ballyboggin	Ballyboggin	Palmer Willaim	mill	-	-	-	Palmer W - Palmer Jno (Sor	1778	-	dd/	326 481 216705
Dunboyne	Ballymacoll	-	wind mill :	-	-	-	-	-	-	6"os/	50
Killeagh	Ballynacree	-	corn mill :	-	-	-	-	-	-	6"os/	8
Killeagh	Ballynacree	Forde Joseph	woollen fcty.	-	13a.	-	-	-	-	gr/	-
Kildalkey	Ballynadrimma	Potterton James	corn	-	97a	-	-	-	-	gr/	-
Rathcore	Ballynaskea	- nr Rathcors Church	corn	-	-	-	-	-	-	6"os/	48
Meath	Ballyroghan	-	mill	-	-	-	-	-	-	6"os/	46
Kells	Balnagon	- Kells	corn	-	-	-	-	-	-	1"os/	90
Kells	Balnagon	- nr Seymourstown	corn	-	-	-	-	-		1"os/	80
Kells	Balnagon	Henry	mills	-	-	-	Henry - Henry	-	?	dd/	528 497 344987
Kells	Balnagon	Henry John	mills	-	-	-	Henry Jo & L - Henry John	1755	-	dd/	192 336 127865?
Kells	Balnagon	Henry John :	mills	-	-	-	Henry J - Henry Rvv John	1755	-	dd/	192 236 127865
Kilskeer	Balnagon Upper	-	corn & mill dam	-	-	-	-	-	-	6"os/	16
Kilskeer	Balnagon Upper	Kelly Hugh	corn	45.6x22x23.6 & dw. :	-	9.19	-	1853	17x4.10x16.9 :	hob/	5.4203
Kilskeer	Balnagon Upper	Reilly Hugh	corn	-	35a	-	-	-	-	gr/	-
Kileskeer	Balnagon Upper	Reilly Mary	corn	27.6x18x7 kiln :	-	3.3.1	-	1838	11x2.3x13 1 pr st	hob/	5.4203
Painstown	Balrath	McKenna Margaret	mills & lands	-	-	-	McKenna Margt. her will	1789	-	dd/	414 313 270749
Painstown	Balrath	Seagrave Thomas :	mill	-	-	-	Seagrava T - Walsh Richd	1812	-	dd/	639 390 442389
Painstown	Balrath	Segrave	mills & lands	-	-	-	Segrave - Walsh	-	- [? error parties	dd/	431 178 279496
Painstown	Balrath	Strong Jno :	mill	-	-	-	Strang J - Osborne Thos :	1970	-	dd/	423 221 275023
Painstown	Balrath	Strong John Rev.	mills & lands	-	-	-	Strong Jn - Barnwall Nich	1785	-	dd/	369 507 249449
Painstown	Balrath	Tighe Sarah :	mill	-	-	-	Tighe s - Fenner Edmond	1782	-	dd/	349 183 233537
Painstown	Balrath	Walsh	windmill	80ft. x 46ft. dia. stump	-	-	-	-	-	sv/	C.Ellison
Painstown	Balrath	Walsh Jane	corn	-	26a.	-	-	-	-	gr/	-
Piercetown	Balrath	Walsh Jane	windmill	-	-	-	-	-	-	gr/	-
Painstown	Balrath	Walsh Michael :	mill	-	-	-	Walsh M - Walsh Catherine	1791	-	dd/	647 184 442775
Painstown	Balrath	Walsh Michael :	mill	-	-	-	Walsh Mcl - Walsh Cath :	1791	-	dd/	441 170 284083
Painstown	Balrath	Walsh Richard :	mill	-	-	-	Walsh R - Seagrave Thos. :	1812	-	dd/	647 184 442775
Painstown	Balrath	Walsh Richard :	mill	-	-	-	Walsh R- Fitzsimons Chris	1813	-	dd/	662 458 457088
Meath	Balrath or :	Ballyhack	windmill stump :	-	-	-	-	2002	-	mmSv/	jl - B
Burry	Balrath Dems.	Nicholson John	brewing	80x22x20 granary :	-	154	-	1853	-	hob/	5.4198
Trim or Kells?	Balreask	-	Old Windmill	-	-	-	-	-	-	1"os/	90
Balsoon	Balsoon	Crooke	mill	- Broadfords Mill	-	-	Crooke - Warren	-	?	dd/	62 130 42478
Ardcath	Bartramstown	Gordon Jas, Yeoman	mills	-	-	-	Gordon J - Georges Ham	1773	-	dd/	298 148 196854
Ardcath	Bartramstown	Langan James	mills	-	-	-	Langan James - Curtis Mk	1750	-	dd/	144 144 96820
Ardcath	Bartramstown	Langan John	corn	- mill being repaired	-	-	-	1871	-	VOcb/	1
Ardcath	Bartramstown	Langan Patrick	corn	-	18a.	-	-	1856	-	gr/	-
Ardcath	Bartramstown	Langan Patrick	windmill	- and land	7a.	7.10.	-	1864	-	VOcb/	1
Ardcath	Bartramstown	Langan Reps John	corn (at rest)	-	-	-	-	1882	-	VOcb/	1

PARISH	TOWNLAND	MILLER	TYPE	HOUSE	Land	£Val	PROPRIETORS	Date	WHEEL etc.	Record	Ref.
Ardcath	Bartramstown	Langan Richard	mills	-	-	-	Langan R - Dillon William	1785	Mort. 4 Jan.	dd/	363 422 244996
Ardcath	Bartramstown :	-	corn	-	-	-	-	1841	-	6"os/	33
Ardcath	Bartramstown :	-	mill	- neat 3 sty. bld	-	-	-	2001	-	mmSv/	wh - B
Duleek	Beaumont	- at Baumont Bridge	mill	-	-	-	-	-	-	1"os/	92
Duleek	Beaumont	- Bemond Mill	corn	- demolished 1936	-	-		2002		mmSv/	wh - Z
Duleek	Beaumont	- S. of B`mont Br.	flour	-	-	-	-	1841	-	6"os/	27
Duleek	Beaumont	Courtney	mill	-	-	-	Courtney - Cullen	-	?	dd/	46 361 29542
Duleek	Beaumont	Doran Edward	mill	-	-	-	Doran Edwd - Tonge Jas	1794	-	dd/	485 348 305721
Duleek	Beaumont	Langan	mill	-	-	-	Langan - Boylan	-	?	dd/	376 520 250317
Duleek	Beaumont	Tonge Edward :	mill	-	-	-	Tonge Ed - McCann John :	1799	-	dd/	494 641 339142
Duleek	Beaumont :	M`Cann John	corn	-	-	-	-	-	-	gr/	-
Bective	Bective	-	corn & :	-	-	-	-	-	-	6"os/	31
Bective	Bective	- on R. Boyne	mill	-	-	-	-	-	-	1"os/	101
Bective	Bective	Bolton Robert Chas :	mill	-	-	-	Bolton R - Garnett John :	-	-	dd/	546 36 358599
Bective	Bective	Byrne Thomas	corn	-	36a.	-	-	-	-	gr/	-
Bective	Bective	Garnett	mill	-	-	-	Garnett - Thompson	-	-	dd/	538 414 358598
Bective	Bective	Gosson Thomas	corn	-	-	-	-	-	-	fdb/	4.1415
Meath	Bedlow`s Mill	Maxton William	mill	-	-	-	Maxton Wm - McKay Wm	1849	-	dd/	1849 8 199
Bo. Ratoath	Bedlow`s Mill	Tara John Rt. Hon. :	mill	-	-	-	Tara Lord - Preston Jos :	1816	-	dd/	706 208 483743
Broadford	Behanagh	Broderick Michael	mill	37.6x19x18 15x17.6x8	-	-	-	-	11x2.8x - 24 bkts	hob/	5.4030
Broadford	Beheenagh	Bailey William	bolting & grist	-	267a.	-	-	1851	-	fdb/	4.2586
Broadford	Beheenagh	Bailey William	tuck	-	-	-	-	-	-	fdb/	4.2586
Trim	Bellewstown	-	corn	-	-	-	-	-	-	6"os/	27
Trim	Bellewstown	- on R. Boyne :	tuck	-	-	-	-	-	-	6"os/	36
Duleek	Bellewstown	- near Duleek	mill	-	-	-	-	2002	-	mmSv/	wh - Z
Trim	Bellewstown	Brown Simon	paper	61x12x8, rag room :	-	2.16	-	1853	- (as woollen)	hob/	5.1306
Trim	Bellewstown	Brown Simon	woollen	-	-	-	-	-	-	hob/	5.1306
Trim	Bellewstown	Brown Simon	woollen	61x19x12 & water :	-	5.11	-	1853	10.8x4.6x2 24 fl.	hob/	5.1306
Trim	Bellewstown	Browne Simon	woollen	-	5a.	-	-	-	-	gr/	-
Duleek	Bellewstown	Callaghan Andrew	mill	-	44a.	-	-	-	-	gr/	-
Navan	Blackcastle Dem.	Morgan James	corn :	-	-	-	-	-	-	loc./	history
Navan	Blackcastle Dem.	Morgan William	flour	64X21X48.6 & kiln :	-	84.9	-	1838	14x4x6 & 14x3x6 :	hob/	5.4214
Donaghmore	Blackcastle Dem.	Morgan William :	flour & corn	- detail and tab Val	-	60	-	1852	12x1.6x4 24 bkts	hob/	5.3160
Donaghmore	Blackcastle Dem.	Morgan William :	scutch	(1A) 63x24x30 & :	-	-	-	1852	12x2 & works	hob/	5.3160
Navan	Blackcastle Dem.	Morgan William :	corn :	-	-	-	-	-	-	loc./	history
Navan	Blackcastle Dem.	Ormonde Earl	mill	- mill rebuilt :	-	-	-	-	-	sv/	CEllison
Navan	Blackcastle Dem.	Tallon John	mill	-	-	-	- leased from E. Ormonde	1543	-	sv/	CEllison
Crickstown	Blackwater R.	Coddington John	mill	-	-	-	Coddington - Phepoe Sam	1733	-	dd/	72 267 50698
Crickstown	Blackwater R.	Georges Richard	mill	-	-	-	Georges R - Coghill Hon.	1730	-	dd/	62 305 42960
Crickstown	Blackwater R.	Kildare Eliz C`tess	mill	-	-	-	Kildare E - Coddington Jn	1730	-	dd/	64 230 43598
Crickstown	Blackwater R.	Newton Michael	mill	-	-	-	Newton M - French Jeoff	1719	-	dd/	62 417 43464
Meath	Boltray	Audley Lord George :	mill	-	-	-	Audley Ld Geo - Cummins :	1822	-	dd/	777 120 526255
Meath	Boyne	Irwin Eliz Judy Darcy :	mills	- of Drumow / Drumoe	-	-	Irwin Eliz - Blacker William :	1818	Rent ú316.8.4 :	dd/	729 520 497855
Meath	Boyne	Irwin George Darcy :	mills	-	-	-	Irwin Geo - Keaguick :	1815	-	dd/	726 78 495613
Meath	Boyne	Blake Anthony Richd :	mill	-	-	-	Blake A - Maguire Alex :	1823	Conv. 10 Dec.	dd/	801 482 451017
Meath	Boyne River	Beckett Sir George	mill	-	-	-	Beckett G - Black Thos :	1831	-	dd/	879 376 583376
Trim	Brannockstown	- Boards Mill	mill	-	-	-	-	-	-	1"os/	100
Trim	Brannockstown	Flood William & James	corn	-	213a.	-	-	-	-	gr/	-
Trim	Brannockstown	Flood William & James	corn	32.6x31x22 & kiln :	-	19.12	-	1853	12x4.8x8 40 bkts :	hob/	5.1306
Trim	Brannockstown	Flood William & James	corn & kiln	(1A)32.6x18.6x8 kiln :	-	19.12	-	1853	12x4x8 3 pr st. :	hob/	5.1306
Trim	Brannockstown	Fox John :	mills	-	-	-	Fox John - Fox Joseph :	1797	-	dd/	518 223 341343
Trim	Brannockstown	Fox William :	(mills	-	-	-	Fox W - Kingston Arthur :	1817	-	dd/	718 77 490812

PARISH	TOWNLAND	MILLER	TYPE	HOUSE	Land	£Val	PROPRIETORS	Date	WHEEL etc.	Record	Ref.
Trim	Brannockstown	Griffin	mills	-	-	-	Griffin - Grace	-	?	dd/	364 27 242693
Trim	Branockstown	- E side. R. Boyne :	Boards Mill	-	-	-	-	-	-	6"os/	36
Trim	Branockstown	- E. side R. Boyne :	corn	-	-	-	-	-	-	6"os/	36
Trim	Broad	- at Broadboyne Br.	Old Cotton Mill	- v. dilap & cottages	-	-		2001	-	mmSv/	wh - D
Trim	Broad	Caulfield	mill	-	-	-	Caulfield - Earl of Drigheda	1742	-	dd/	109 382 76795
Trim	Broad	Drogheda Edward E.	mill	-	-	-	Drogheda E - Stewart Ch	1732	-	dd/	69 343 48655
Trim	Broad	Drogheda Edward E.	mill	-	-	-	Drogheda E - Leland Ralph	1733	-	dd/	73 268 51018
Trim	Broad	Drogheda Edward E.	mill	-	-	-	Drogheda E - Caulfield Toby	1733	-	dd/	80 40 55237
Trim	Broad	Drogheda Edward Lord	mill	-	-	-	Drogheda Ld - Gardiner L	1729	-	dd/	63 160 43049
Trim	Broad	Lum	mill	-	-	-	Lum - Staunton	-	(? error)	dd/	60 278 42867
Staffordstown	Brownstown	Henderson Thomas :	mill	-	-	-	Henderson - Wilkinson - :	1794	Mort. 25 Oct.	dd/	483 117 310431
Staffordstown	Brownstown	Kelly	mill	-	-	-	Kelly - Heniston	-	?	dd/	622 502 148388
Staffordstown	Brownstown	Kelly Thomas	mill	-	-	-	Kelly T- Pellisser Rev John	1765	Mort. 11 Apl.	dd/	233 417 154808
Staffordstown	Brownstown	McKenna Patrick :	mill	-	-	-	McKenna P - McKenna	1788	-	dd/	397 205 264027
Staffordstown	Brownstown	Somerswell Quaile	mill	-	-	-	Somerswell Q - Kelly Andr	1740	-	dd/	102 236 70563
Staffordstown	Brownstown	Strong John Rev. :	mill	-	-	-	Strong John - Finlay Geo :	1791	-	dd/	454 189 291305
Staffordstown	Brownstown :	-	corn	-	-	-	-	-	-	6"os/	32
Siddan	Caddelstown	Reilly Thomas	corn & kilns	-	44a	-	-	-	-	gr/	-
Siddan	Caddlestown	- at Yellowford Br.	corn	-	-	-	-	-	-	6"os/	6
Siddan	Caddlestown	- on R. Dee	corn	-	-	-	-	-	-	1"os/	81
Siddan	Caddlestown	Reilly Thomas	corn	30x24x10 8.6x20x10 :	-	12	-	1853	14x4.3x8.6 u`shot	hob/	5.4211
Rodanstown	Calgarth	Woods Samuel	corn	-	3a.	-	-	-	-	gr/	-
Rodanstown	Calgath	- Calgath	Corn Mill	-	-	-	-	1841	-	6"os/	49
Rodanstown	Calgath	Moore Denis	corn	-	2a.	-	-	-	-	gr/	-
Kilbride	Castlecor	- S/ R. Blackwater	mill	-	-	-	-	1841	-	6"os/	8
Kilbride	Castlecor	Webb Samuel	corn	-	3a.	-	-	-	-	gr/	-
Castlejordan	Castlejordan	- W. side C'jordan R.	corn	-	-	-		1841	-	6"os/	52
Castlejordan	Castlejordan	Gifford Thomas	corn & tuck	-	-	-	Gifford T - Hackett John	1717	-	dd/	19 407 10452
Ardcath	Clatterstown	-	corn	-	-	-	-	-	-	1"os/	91
Ardcath	Clatterstown	-	mill	- solid building	-	-	-	2001	Mgr. Sean Byrne	mmSv/	wh - B
Ardcath	Clatterstown	-	mill race (only) :	-	-	-	-	1841	-	6"os/	33
Ardcath	Clatterstown	Bowes John	mill	-	-	-	Bowes John - Fox James	1738	-	dd/	90 234 54023
Ardcath	Clatterstown	Fox George	mill	-	-	-	Fox G - Fox James	1733	-	dd/	71 350 51195
Ardcath	Clatterstown	Fox George	mill	-	-	-	Fox G - Fox James	1732	-	dd/	72 203 50402
Ardcath	Clatterstown	Fox James	mill	-	-	-	Fox Jas - Bowes John	1734	-	dd/	79 117 54879
Bective	Cliftonlodge Dem.	-	kiln	-	-	-	-	-	-	6"os/	30
Meath	Cloghagh	Pitcher Augustus	mills	-	-	-	Pitcher Aug - Sturgeon JK	1833	-	dd/	1833 5 297
Meath	Cloghagh	Sturgeon James Kemp :	mill	-	-	-	Sturgeon Jas - Pitcher :	1829	-	dd/	847 384 567384
Dunboyne	Clonee	-	-	The Mill House	-	-	Brown`s (Clarke /20s)	1997	print house	pWEH	Cc
Dunboyne	Clonee	-	corn	-	-	-	-	-	-	6"os/	51
Dunboyne	Clonee	- E. of Town	corn & race	-	-	-	-	-	-	6"os/	51
Dunboyne	Clonee	Halligan Margaret	corn	-	3.0.8	-	-	-	-	gr/	-
Rathcore	Clonguiffin	- near Longwood :	corn	-	-	-	-	1841	-	6"os/	47
Rathcore	Clonguiffin	Edgeworth Edward	mill	-	-	-	Edgeworth E - Swift Meade	1717	-	dd/	19 372 10382
Rathcore	Clonguiffin	Edgeworth Robert	mill	-	-	-	Edgeworth R - Lackington	1729	-	dd/	67 116 45507
Rathcore	Clonguiffin	Newell	mill	-	-	-	Newell - Sullivan	-	-	dd/	41 209 25423
Rathcore	Clonguiffin	Newell John	mill	-	-	-	Newell J - Sullivan Philip	1721	-	dd/	36 316 22598
Rathcore	Clonguiffin	Swift John	mill	-	-	-	Swift J - Swift Rev Jno	1731	-	dd/	69 144 47653
Rathcore	Clonguiffin	Swift Mead	mill	-	-	-	Swift M - Edgeworth Robt	1717	-	dd/	20 252 10514
Rathcore	Clonguiffin	Swift Meade	mill	-	-	-	Swift M - Lyons Chas	1728	-	dd/	60 82 39996
Mitchelstown	Clontail	M`Cann John	corn	-	44a	-	-	-	-	gr/	-
Mitchelstown	Clontail	M`Cann John	corn	(1B) 34x20.6x14.6 :	-	17.10	-	1853	13.8x5x10 u`shot	hob/	5.4210

PARISH	TOWNLAND	MILLER	TYPE	HOUSE	Land	£Val	PROPRIETORS	Date	WHEEL etc.	Record	Ref.
Mitchelstown	Clontail	- N/ Mitchelstown Br.	mill	-	-	-	-	-	-	6"os/	12
Mitchelstown	Clontail	- on R. Dee	mill	-	-	-	-	-	-	1"os/	81
Killeen	Clowanstown	-	mill	-	-	-	-	-	-	1"os/	101
Killeen	Clowanstown	- W. C`stown Bridge	corn	-	-	-	-	1841	-	6"os/	38
Killeen	Clowanstown	- Teeling's Mill	corn	- large building :	-	-	-	2002	Kelly	gr/	-
Killeen	Clowanstown	M`Namara Patrick	mill	-	10a.	-	-	-	-	gr/	-
Duleek	Commons	- NE of Town	corn & pond	-	-	-	-	1841	-	6"os/	27
Duleek	Commons	Beahan Owen	corn	-	14a.	-	-	-	-	gr/	-
Navan Lower	Cookstown	Clarke John	corn	-	42a	-	-	-	-	gr/	-
Balrathboyne	Cookstown Great	-	corn & mill race	-	-	-	-	1841	-	6"os/	17
Balrathboyne	Cookstown Great	Clarke John	corn	small corn mill	-	6.16	-	-	13ft dia. works :	hob/	5.4196
Moynalty	Coolnahinch	-	corn	-	-	-	-	-	-	6"os/	4
Moynalty	Coolnahinch	Martin James	mill	-	34a.	-	-	-	-	gr/	-
Lune	Coolronan	Bligh John	mills	-	-	-	Bligh John - Gibson Jos	1711	-	dd/	19 84 9723
Lune	Coolronan	Gibson Joseph	mills	-	-	-	Gibson Jos - Brown Richd	1717	-	dd/	20 71 9798
Lune	Coolronan	Gibson Joseph	mills	-	-	-	Gibson Jos - Tandy John	1726	-	dd/	61 142 40901
Lune	Coolronan	Gibson Joseph :	mills	-	-	-	Gibson Jos - Gibson Richd	1728	-	dd/	57 281 38475
Kildalkey	Corballis	-	corn	-	-	-	-	-	-	6"os/	35
Kildalkey	Corballis	M`Garry Michael	corn	-	65a.	-	-	-	-	gr/	-
Moynalty	Corboggy	-	corn	-	-	-	-	-	-	6"os/	4
Moynalty	Corboggy	Cahill Thomas	mill & kiln	-	31a.	-	-	-	-	gr/	-
Moybolgue	Corcarra (?)	-	tuck	-	-	-	-	-	-	6"os/	4
Moynalty	Cormeen	- at W. edge County	tuck	-	-	-	-	-	-	6"os/	1
Moynalty	Cormeen	Clinton Patrick	mill & kiln	-	100a.	-	-	-	-	gr/	-
Enniskeen	Corratober	- nr Corratober Br.	corn & kiln	-	-	-	-	-	-	6"os/	2
Stackallan	Cruicetown	-	windmill :	-	-	-	-	-	-	6"os/	5
Stackallan	Cruicetown	Carney John	tuck	-	-	-	-	-	-	fdb/	4.1467
Stackallan	Cruicetown :	- N. side R. Boyne	tuck	-	-	-	-	-	-	6"os/	19
Stackallan	Cruicetown :	- on R. Boyne	corn	-	-	-	-	-	-	6"os/	19
Rathmoylon	Cullentry	Crook John	mill	-	-	-	Crook Jno - Warren Edw	1729	-	dd/	62 189 42478
Rathmoylon	Cullentry	Crook John :	mill	-	-	-	Crook J - Warren Edward :	1727	(Mort.)	dd/	55 237 36732
Laracor	Dangan Manor	Preston John	mill	- Bedlow`s Mill	-	-	Preston J - Noy William	1733	-	dd/	78 24 52850
Laracor	Dangan Manor	Preston John	mill	- Bedlow`s Mill	-	-	Preston J - Noy Edward	1734	-	dd/	80 188 55455
Monknewtown	Dardistown	- on R. Nanny :	corn	-	-	-	-	-	-	6"os/	27
Monknewtown	Dardistown	- S.side R. Nanny :	tuck	-	-	-	-	-	-	6"os/	28
Monknewtown	Dardistown	- Sandyhall Mill	corn	refurbished as res.	-	-	- Leo Monaghan	2002	- pho. taken	mmSv/	wh - Cr
Monknewtown	Dardistown	Coyle James	corn	-	9a.	-	-	-	-	gr/	-
Monknewtown	Dardistown	Coyle James	tuck	-	-	-	-	-	-	gr/	-
Monknewtown	Dardistown	Dowd James	corn & flour	-	55a.	-	-	-	-	gr/	-
Castletownd`n	Delvin`s Br.	- on Devlins R.	mill	-	-	-	-	-	-	1"os/	-
Diamor	Diamor	- W. Roachtown X	corn & dam	-	-	-	-	-	-	6"os/	15
Navan	Dillonsland	Spicer John :	corn store & :	-	-	17.1.1	-	1852	-	hob/	5.3160
Navan	Dillonsland :	-	distillery	-	-	-	-	-	-	6"os/	25
Rodanstown	Dolanstown	-	wind mill :	-	-	-	-	-	-	6"os/	49
Rodanstown	Dolanstown	- at Knockatulla X	corn & dam	-	-	-	-	-	-	6"os/	49
Donaghmore	Donaghmore	Eiffe Valentine	corn	-	120a.	-	-	-	-	gr/	-
Donaghpatrick	Donaghpatrick	- nr R. Blackwater	old mill	-	-	-	-	-	-	6"os/	17
Dowth	Dowth	- Dowth Corn Mill :	corn & dam	-	-	-	-	-	-	6"os/	20
Dowth	Dowth	Elcock Mary	corn	-	-	-	-	-	-	gr/	-
Oldcastle	Drumlerry	-	corn	-	-	-	-	-	-	6"os/	9
Loughcrew	Drumone	-	old mill	stone arch & mill race	-	-	- [not in 6" O.S. 15]	2006	-	mmSv/	wh - R
Duleek	Duleek Commons	- E. end Town	corn	-	-	-	-	-	-	6"os/	27

PARISH	TOWNLAND	MILLER	TYPE	HOUSE	Land	£Val	PROPRIETORS	Date	WHEEL etc.	Record	Ref.
Duleek	Duleek Town	Beahan Owen & :	corn	-	-	-	-	-	-	sv/	CEllison
Duleek	Duleek Town	Woodroofe Richard	mill	-	-	-	Woodroofe - Hamilton Josh	1849	-	dd/	1849 7 60
Dunboyne	Dunboyne	- Dunboyne Mill	corn	-	-	-	-	-	-	6"os/	51
Dunboyne	Dunboyne	Herbert John	corn, millpond	-	11a.	-	-	-	-	gr/	-
Donaghmore	Dunmoe	- N. side R. Boyne :	corn	-	-	-	-	1841	-	6"os/	18
Donaghmore	Dunmoe	- on R. Boyne	mill	-	-	-	-	-	-	1"os/	91
Dunmoe	Dunmoe	Commons Edmond	corn	-	9a.	-	-	-	-	gr/	-
Dunmoe	Dunmoe :	-	corn mill & weir	-	-	-	-	-	-	6"os/	25
Dunsany	Dunsany	-	corn	-	-	-	-	-	-	6"os/	37
Kilmainham	Eden	- in Kilmainham Tn	corn & tuck :	-	-	-	-	-	-	6"os/	5
Kilmainham	Eden	Corbally Richard	mill	-	19a.	-	-	-	-	gr/	-
Meath (?)	Esker *	- near R. Bridge	mill	3 sty. roofless	-	-	-	2001	-	mmSv/	wh - R
Bartramstown	Fennor	- near Johnstown Ho.	corn	-	-	-	-	-	-	6"os/	33
Bartramstown	Fennor	Andrews Christopher	corn	-	-	-	-	1856	-	gr/	-
Bartramstown	Fennor	Andrews John	corn	-	-	7.5.0	-	1883	-	VOcb/	1
Bartramstown	Fennor	Andrews Nicholas	corn	-	-	7.5.0	-	1880	-	VOcb/	1
Athlumney	Ferganstown	-	corn & flour	-	-	-	-	-	-	6"os/	25
Athlumney	Ferganstown :	-	factory	-	-	-	-	-	-	6"os/	25
Athlumney	Ferganstown :	-	flax	-	-	-	-	-	-	6"os/	25
Moynalty	Fertagh	-	corn	-	-	-	-	-	-	6"os/	1
Meath	Formays	Gurney Samuel :	mill	-	-	-	Gurney S - Ball Jn Wm :	1825	-	dd/	815 519 549454
Meath	Formays	Gurney Samuel :	mill & lands :	-	-	-	Gurney Sam - Ball William :	1826	-	dd/	815 520 549455
Meath	Formays	Taylor Hon. Thomas :	mill	- cabbins, gardens :	-	-	E of Bective - Gurney Sam	1826	-	dd/	815 513 549448
Meath	Formays	Taylor Hon. Thomas :	mill	-	-	-	E of Bective - Evans John	1826	-	dd/	815 514 549449
Meath	Formays	Taylor Hon. Thomas :	mill	-	-	-	E of Bective - Taylor Edw :	1820	-	dd/	815 515 549450
Trim	Friars Park	Smart John	corn	39x22.6x13	-	-	-	1853	-	hob/	5.1306
Trim	Friarspark	- Trim Town :	tuck & weir	-	-	-	-	-	-	6"os/	36
Trim	Friarspark	Smart John	corn	-	-	-	-	-	-	gr/	-
Trim	Friarspark	Smartt John	corn	39x22.6x13	-	19.3	-	1853	3 pair st. (1 Irish)	hob/	5.1306
Nobber	Garmanagh	-	old malt house :	-	-	-	-	-	-	6"os/	5
Trevet	Garristown :	-	windmill	o/ dia. 21m X 20ft ht.							
Stamullan	Gormanstn Vge.	Boylan Patrick	corn	-	52a.	-	-	-	-	gr/	-
Stamullan	Gormanstown	-	corn	-	-	-	-	-	-	1"os/	92
Stamullan	Gormanstown	Arnold William	corn & kiln	-	124a.	-	-	-	-	gr/	-
Stamullan	Gormanstown :	- near Delvin R.	corn	-	-	-	-	-	-	6"os/	28
Stamullan	Gormanstown :	- on Delvin R.	corn	-	-	-	-	-	-	6"os/	28
Killeagh	Halfcarton	-	mill	-	-	-	-	-	-	1"os/	90
Killeagh	Halfcartron	-	corn & kiln	-	-	-	-	1841	-	6"os/	8
Kells	Headford Dems.	-	old corn mill	-	-	-	-	-	-	6"os/	17
Kells	Headford Dems.	-	old windmill	-	-	-	-	-	-	6"os/	17
Slane	Higggginstown	Norman John :	mill	-	-	-	Norman Jn - Allen John :	1826	Mort. 2 Aug.	dd/	817 114 550249
Slane	Higginstown	- near Delvin`s Br.	corn	-	-	-	-	-	-	6"os/	
Slane	Higginstown	- near Slane	corn	fine restoration for :	-	-	-	1999	- pho. taken	mmSV/	wh - Ca
Stamullin	Hodgestown	- imed. E. Old Mill Br	Old Mill	-	-	-	-	-	-	JRoc	1760
Siddan	Howthstown	-	windmill ruins	-	-	-	-	-	-	6"os/	6
Laracor	Ifferknock	-	corn	-	-	-	-	-	-	6"os/	36
Laracor	Ifferknock	- Knock Mills	mills	-	-	-	-	-	-	6"os/	36
Laracor	Ifferknock	- near R. Boyne :	tuck	-	-	-	-	-	-	6"os/	36
Laracor	Ifferknock	Keefe Richard	flour	64x21.6x37 wht. kiln :	-	33.12	-	1853	19x8x15 48 bkts.	hob/	5.1303
Laracor	Iffernock	-	mill	-	-	-	-	-	-	1"os/	101
Laracor	Iffernock	Keeffe Richard	flour	-	2a.	-	-	-	-	gr/	-
Laracor	Iffernock	Keeffe Richard	flour	64.0x21.6x37 & kiln	-	-	-	-	19x8x15 48 bkts	hob/	5.1303

PARISH	TOWNLAND	MILLER	TYPE	HOUSE	Land	£Val	PROPRIETORS	Date	WHEEL etc.	Record	Ref.
Laracor	Iffernock	Shiel John	corn	-	9a.	-	-	-	-	gr/	-
Ardcath	Irishtown	- near Ardcath	Old Windmill	-	-	-	-	-	-	1"os/	91
Girley	Johnsbrook	- near J`sbrook Ho.	water engine :	-	-	-	-	-	-	6"os/	23
Rathcor	Jordanstown	Rynd Robert F	threshing	62x21x13.9, boliing ho.	767a.	-	-	-	-	hob/	5.1304
Julianstown	Julianstown	- on R. Gabher :	mill	-	-	-	-	2008	- (Local History)	holten	-
Julianstown	Julianstown	Barnes Thomas :	mill	-	-	-	Barnes T - Clare Joshua :	1828	-	dd/	831 391 558926
Julianstown	Julianstown	Moore William :	mill	-	-	-	Moore William - George	1827	-	dd/	832 54 559189
Julianstown	Julianstown W.	Moran John	mill & kiln	-	0.0.3	-	-	-	-	gr/	-
Kells	Kells	Floody Thomas :	Cusacks Mills	-	-	-	Floody Thos - Duffe Patrick	1719	-	dd/	70 524 49361
Kells	Kells T`nparks	-	flour & corn	-	-	-	-	1841	-	6"os/	17
Kells	Kells T`nparks	Farelly Thomas	corn & kiln	-	75a.	-	-	-	-	gr/	-
Kells	Kells T`nparks :	-	brewery	-	-	-	-	-	-	6"os/	17
Kells	Kells Town	Headford Marq. of	Formays Mill	-	-	-	Headford - Richardson Ths	1834	-	dd/	1834 20 37
Kells	Kells Town	Headford Marq. of	mills	-	-	-	Headford - Richardson Ths	1834	-	dd/	1834 20 37
Kilclone	Kemmins Mill	-	mill ?	-	-	-	-	-	-	1"os/	101
Kilclone	Kemmins Mill	-	no mill	-	-	-	-	-	-	6"os/	49
Kilclone	Kemmins Mill	-	old mill race	-	-	-	-	-	-	6"os/	49
Kentstown	Kentstown	- Daly's Mill	saw	-	-	-	-	-	- (Local History)	holten	-
Kentstown	Kentstown		mill	-	-	-	-	2001	- pho. taken	mmSv/	wh - Ca
Kells	Kestown Glebe :	-	old corn mill	-	-	-	-	-	-	6"os/	17
Rathmolyon	Kilballyporter	-	corn	-	-	-	-	-	-	1"os/	100
Rathmolyon	Kilballyporter	-	corn	-	-	-	-	-	-	6"os/	42
Rathmolyon	Kilballyporter	-	old windmill	-	-	-	-	-	-	6"os/	42
Nobber	Kilbride	-	Old Nobber	-	-	-	-	-	-	1"os/	81
Kilcarn	Kilcarn	Barry Charles :	mill	-	-	-	Barry Chas - Barry Neville :	1826	-	dd/	811 434 546969
Kilcarn	Kilcarn :	- E. side R. Boyne	corn	-	-	-	-	-	-	6"os/	31
Kilcarn	Kilcarn Lower	-	corn ('big')	-	-	-	-	2008	- (Civil Survey)	holten	41
Kilcarn	Kilcarn Upper	- Delvin's Mill :	corn ('small')	-	-	-	-	2008	- (Local History)	holten	41
Killallon	Killacroy	- Killallon Mill :	mill	-	-	-	-	-	-	6"os/	22
Killallon	Killacroy	Glennon Thomas	corn	-	49a.	-	-	-	-	gr/	-
Rathmoylon	Killballyporter	Keeffe Richard	threshing	32x20.6x18 & :	-	12.11	-	-	11x4x12.9 35 bkts	hob/	5.1305
Rathmoylon	Killballyporter :	-	corn	-	-	-	-	-	-	6"os/	42
Rathmoylon	Killballyporter :	-	old windmill	-	-	-	-	-	-	6"os/	42
Ratoath	Killrue :	- site of	old windmill	-	-	-	-	-	-	6"os/	45
Kilmessan	Kilmessan	- Arnold's Mill :	corn & kiln	-	-	-	-	2008	- (Local History)	holten	-
Kilmessan	Kilmessan	- in deserted locality	corn	-	-	-	-	2002	-	mmSv/	od - B
Kilmessan	Kilmessan	- on County border	corn	-	-	-	-	-	-	6"os/	37
Kilmessan	Kilmessan	Arnold Christopher	corn & kiln	-	28a.	-	-	-	-	gr/	-
Trim	Kilnagross	- close to R. Boyne	corn & weir	-	-	-	-	-	-	6"os/	36
Trim	Kilnagross	Barnwell Charles	mill	-	-	-	Barnwell Chas - :	1847	-	dd/	1847 5 280
Trim	Kilnagross	Michael Patrick	mill	-	-	-	Michael Patrick - :	1847	-	dd/	1847 5 42
Kilsharvan	Kilsharvan	- nr Kilsharvan Ho.	mill	-	-	-	-	-	-	6"os/	27
Kilsker	Kilsker	-	Milltown Ho. & :	-	-	-	-	1841	-	6"os/	16
Kilsker	Kilsker	Carney John	threshing	(2B) 32x18x8 & dw. :	-	-	-	-	-	hob/	5.4203
Knock	Knock	- stream to Killary Wt.	corn & kiln	-	-	-	-	-	-	6"os/	12
Knock	Knock	Flood James	corn & kiln	-	-	-	-	-	-	gr/	
Knockmark	Knockmark	- near Drumree Br.	corn & race	-	-	-	-	1841	-	6"os/	44
Knockmark	Knockmark	Boylan John	corn	-	21a.	-	-	-	-	gr/	-
Dunshaughlin	Leshemstown	-	mill	-	-	-	-	-	-	1"os/	101
Dunshaughlin	Leshemstown :	- .	corn	-	-	-	-	-	-	1"os/	101
Castlerickard	Lionsden	- on R. Boyne :	corn	-	-	-	-	-	-	6"os/	41
Liscartan	Liscartan	- nr R. Blackwater	corn	-	-	-	-	-	-	6"os/	25

PARISH	TOWNLAND	MILLER	TYPE	HOUSE	Land	£Val	PROPRIETORS	Date	WHEEL etc.	Record	Ref.
Liscartan	Liscartan	Carogan Lord	corn	-	-	-	- leased to Everards	-	-	sv/	CEllison
Liscartan	Liscartan	Cullen James	corn	-	4.1.0	-	-	-	-	gr/	-
Lismullin	Lismullin	Burns James	saw	-	-	-	-	-	-	fdb/	4.1445
Lismullin	Lismullin	Byrne Patrick	corn	-	27a.	-	-	-	-	gr/	-
Lismullin	Lismullin :	- 'The King's Mill'	mill	-	-	-	-	2008	- (Local History)	holten	-
Lismullin	Lismullin :	-	corn	-	-	-	-	-	-	6"os/	31
Enniskeen	Lisnagrow	-	tuck	-	-	-	-	-	-	6"os/	2
Enniskeen	Lisnagrow	- nr Lakeview Ho.	corn & kiln	-	-	-	-	-	-	6"os/	2
Killary	Lobinstown	Brinkley Matt	treshing	(2C) 28.6x15x7 & :	-	10	-	-	-	hob/	5.4209
Castlekeeran	Loughan	-	corn	-	-	-	-	-	-	6"os/	10
Castlekeeran	Loughan	Miles Anne Mary	corn & kiln	-	29a.	-	-	-	-	gr/	-
Diamor	Loughcrew	-	corn & wool	- roof replaced	-	-	-	2006	remains of wheel	mmSv/	wh - R
Diamor	Loughcrew	- Loughrew Demse.	corn	-	-	-	-	-	-	6"os/	15
Kilberry	Louth	-	mill	-	-	-	-	-		pWEH	C
Macetown	Macetown	-	corn	- restored as res.	-	-	Clive & Prudence Symmons	2001	-	mmSv/	wh - Cc
Macetown	Macetown	- on Hurley R.	mills	-	-	-	-	-	-	1"os/	101
Macetown	Macetown	Flanagan Mary	corn	-	17a.	-	-	-	-	gr/	-
Macetown	Macetown	Flanagan Peter	corn	-	-	-	-	-	-	fdb/	4.1446
Athboy	Martinstown	- near Athboy	mill	-	-	-	-	-	-	1"os/	90
Athboy	Martinstown	M`Cormick Michael	corn & kiln	-	7a.	-	-	-	-	gr/	-
Athboy	Martinstown :	-	corn	-	-	-	-	-	-	6"os/	29
Martry	Martry	-	corn	-	-	-	-	-	-	1"os/	91
Martry	Martry	-	corn	- well preserved	-	-	James Tallon	1999	- wheel inactive :	mmSv/	wh - A
Martry	Martry	Darcy Nicholas :	mill	-	-	-	-	1640	-	sv/	CEllison
Martry	Martry	Lee M (Nugentstown)	mill	- buildings renovated	-	-	-	1745	-	sv/	CEllison
Martry	Martry	Tallon James	mill	-	-	-	- proprietor of mill since	1859	-	sv/	CEllison
Martry	Martry	Tallon Thomas	mill	-	-	-	- beq. to son James	1977	-	mmSv/	jt
Martry	Martry	Tisdall Henrietta	mill	-	-	-	Tisdall H`etta - Erskine Wm	1835	-	dd/	1835 3 84
Martry	Martry	Tisdall Michael	mill	-	-	-	- pursd. from Plattins	1668	-	sv/	CEllison
Loughan	Meenlagh	- on R. Blackwater	corn	-	-	-	-	-	-	6"os/	16
Loughan	Meenlagh	- on R. Blackwater	tuck	-	-	-	-	-	-	6"os/	16
Inishmot	Mentrim	-	corn & kiln	-	-	-	acquired by s McCallion	2008	-		
Inishmot	Mentrim	-	mill	-	-	-	-	-		pWEH	C
Inishmot	Mentrim	- on Keeran R.	corn	-	-	-	-	-	-	1"os/	81
Inishmot	Mentrim	- W. side Keeran R.	corn & dam	-	-	-	-	-	-	6"os/	7
Inishmot	Mentrim	Callan Philip	corn	-	56a.	-	-	-	-	gr/	-
Inishmot	Mentrim	Callan Phillip	corn & kiln	32.0x20.0x19 & kiln	-	-	-	1853	15x5x11 32 bkts.	hob/	5.4208
Inishmot	Mentrim	Slevin Nicholas	corn & kiln	- for restoration	-	-	acquired by John Lynch	1980	wheel intact		
Rathbeggan	Millland	-	no mill	-	-	-	-	-	-	6"os/	44
- (7)	Milltown	Burke William :	mill	-	-	-	Burke Wm - Atkin Martha :	1825	Asgt. 24 Nov.	dd/	809 536 545871
- (7)	Milltown	Howth Earl of	mill	-	-	-	E of Howth - Dowse	-	-	dd/	810 1 545934
- (7)	Milltown	Moore	mills	-	-	-	Moore & ors - Nesbitt	-	-	dd/	835 475 561360
- (7)	Milltown	St George Arthur	mill	-	-	-	St George Arth - Styles Wm	1835	-	dd/	1835 4 206
Killegland	Milltown :	-	no mill	-	-	-	-	-	-	6"os/	45
Mitchelstown	Mitchelstown	-	corn	-	-	-	-	-	-	6"os/	12
Monknewtown	Monknewtown	-	corn & kiln	-	-	-	-	-	-	6"os/	19
Monknewt`n	Monknewtown	Hill Richard R	corn & flour	-	9a.	-	-	-	-	gr/	-
Monknewt`n	Monknewtown	Rogers Wiliam	corn	Incumb Est consisting	-	-	- sold to Earl of Sheffield	1860	30 HP, 6 pair st. :	mlyIE/	167
Monknewt`n	Monknewtown	Rogers Wiliam	corn & flour	-	-	-	-	-	-	fdb/	4.1464
Trim	Monktown	-	corn	-	-	-	-	-	-	6"os/	32
Trim	Monktown	McNamara Chris	corn	-	-	-	-	-	-	fdb/	4.1447
Moorechurch	Mosney :	Pepper Thomas	corn & flour	-	-	-	-	-	-	sv/	CEllison
Moynalty	Moynalty	Rathbourne :	flour	acquired for renovation by		-	Ronan & Odette Jacob	1999	wheel & m/cy :	mmSv/	rj - B

PARISH	TOWNLAND	MILLER	TYPE	HOUSE	Land	£Val	PROPRIETORS	Date	WHEEL etc.	Record	Ref.
Kilmore	Moynalvy :	- on Moynalvy R. :	old corn mill	-	-	-	-	-	-	6"os/	43
Rathkenny	Mullagha	- at Mullagha Ho.	corn	-	-	-	-	1841	-	6"os/	18
Rathkenny	Mullagha	Morris Joseph Wm	corn	-	-	-	-	-	-	fdb/	4.1465
Siddan	Mullaghwillin	- near Hogs Hill	corn	-	-	-	-	-	-	6"os/	7
Siddan	Mullaghwillin	M`Kenna John	old corn mill	-	-	-	-	-	-	gr/	-
Clonalvy	Naul	- N. side R. Delvin	flour & pond	-	-	-	-	-	-	6"os/	34
Clonalvy	Naul	- S. side R. Delvin	flour & pond	-	-	-	-	-	-	6"os/	33
Clonalvy	Naul	Ennis James	flour & corn	-	129a.	-	-	-	-	gr/	-
Clonalvy	Naul :	Mervyn Arthur	flour & corn	-	129a.	-	- built by Nich Freemantle	1761	-	sv/	CEllison
Athlumney	Navan	- at Nevinstown Ho.	mill	-	-	-	-	-	-	1"os/	91
Athlumney	Navan	- on R. Boyne	corn	-	-	-	-	-	-	1"os/	91
Athlumney	Navan Abby Lds	Skelly Robert	Bridge Mill	-	-	-	Skelly Robt - Dowd Eliza	1835	-	dd/	1835 8 253
Navan Lr	Navan T`nparks	- W. side R. Boyne	corn	-	-	-	-	-	-	6"os/	25
Navan Lr	Navan T`nparks	Byrne Patrick	corn	83x25x48 & kilns :	-	15.10.	-	1838	13.6x4.6x5 :	hob/	5.4214
Navan Lr	Navan T`nparks	Mullen James	corn	46x24x35 & 80x24x28	-	-	-	1838	17x6x4 3 pr st.	hob/	5.4214
Navan Lr	Navan T`nparks :	Byrne Patrick	corn	-	-	21	-	1852	large 16x1.3x4.6	hob/	5.3160
Navan Lr	Navan T`nparks :	Mullen James	corn	add office 27x14x8 :	-	18	-	1852	13x6x3.6 32 bkts	hob/	5.3160
Navan Lr	Navan Town	Byrne Patrick	corn	-	-	-	-	-	-	gr/	-
Navan Lr	Navan Town	Chadwick Francis	flax	-	-	-	Chadwick Francis - John	1890	-	dd/	1890 43 38
Navan Lr	Navan Town	Clayton's Mill	cotton	-	-	-	-	2001	-	mmSv/	wh - R
Navan Lr	Navan Town	Ireland Bank Govs.	Mullens Mills :	-	-	-	Ire. Bk - Geoghegan Wm	1888	-	dd/	1898 42 192
Navan Lr	Navan Town	Maconchy John A	Byrnes Mills	-	-	-	Maconchy J - Smyth Luke	1888	-	dd/	188 43 148
Navan Lr	Navan Town	McCann Thomas	Byrnes Mills	-	-	-	McCann Thomas - James	1885	-	dd/	1885 12 106
Navan Lr	Navan Town	Mullen James	corn	-	-	-	-	-	-	gr/	-
Navan Lr	Navan Town	Spicer's Mill	flour	massive refurbishment	-	-	-	2001	-	mmSv/	wh - Cr
Navan Lr	Navan Town :	O`Reilly Matthew	mills	-	-	-	O`Reilly M - Barker Richd	1841	-	dd/	1841 19 244
Athlumney	Navan Town :	Murphy Peter	mills	-	-	-	Murphy Peter - Skelly Wm	1846	-	dd/	1846 14 229
Navan Lr	Navan Town :	Chadwick John	flax	-	-	-	Chadwick John - Francis	1883	-	dd/	1883 41 3
Navan Lr	Navan Town :	Ford William	flour :	-	-	-	Ford Wm - McCann James	1838	-	dd/	1838 23 69
Navan Lr	Navan Town :	Spicer John	mills	-	-	-	Spicer Jn - McCann Thos	1884	-	dd/	1884 59 219
Navan Lr	Navan Town :	Gradwell John	flax	-	-	-	Gradwell Jn - Ire. Bank of	1850	-	dd/	1850 19 81
Navan Lr	Navan Town :	Millar George	flour, corn :	-	-	-	-	-	9 pr. cn & 6 fl. st.	hob/	5.3160
Navan Lr	Navan Town :	Spicer John	mills	-	-	-	Spicer Jn - Ire. Bank Govs.	1884	-	dd/	1884 6 197
Navan Lr	Navan Town :	Elliott's Mill	flour	dilapidated, pt. burned	-	-	-	2001	-	mmSv/	wh - R
Navan Lr	Newbridge	Mullan George	flour & corn	-	-	-	-	-	-	gr/	-
Oldcastle	Newcastle	- on E. edge County	corn	-	-	-	-	-	-	6"os/	9
Trim	Newhaggard	-	flour	6 sty. large building :	-	-	-	2002	-	mmSv/	wh - D
Trim	Newhaggard	- on R. Boyne :	flour	-	-	-	-	-	-	6"os/	36
Trim	Newhaggard	Odlum R & Michael	flour	-	1.3.0	-	-	-	-	gr/	-
Trim	Newhaggard	Odlum Richard & Mcl	flour	104x34x49, boiler ho	-	83.10	-	1853	15x21x4 40 float	hob/	5.1306
Drumcondra	Newstone	-	corn & kiln	-	-	-	-	-	-	6"os/	3
Meath	Newtown (11)	- on Owenro R.	corn	-	-	-	-	-	-	6"os/	11
Duleek	nr Bellewstn Ho.	- at Blackditch	corn	-	-	-	-	-	-	1"os/	91
Kilbeg	nr Carlanstown	-	mill	-	-	-	-	-	-	1"os/	90
Dunmoe	nr Dunmoe Castle	- on R. Boyne	mill	-	-	-	-	-	-	1"os/	91
Teltown	Nugentstown	-	old corn mill	-	-	-	-	-	-	6"os/	17
Oldcastle	Oldcastle	- Henry's Mill	flour	-	-	-	-	1777	-	AB'bg	-
Ardsallagh	Philpotstown	- at Dillon`s Bridge	corn	-	-	-	-	-	-	6"os/	31
Dunboyne	Piercetown	-	old race dry	-	-	-	-	-	-	6"os/	50
Dunboyne	Piercetown	- S. Black Bull Br.	old corn mill	-	-	-	-	-	-	6"os/	50
Kilskeer	Portlereagh	Daly John	corn	-	91a.	-	-	-	-	gr/	-
Kileskeer	Potteragh	- on R. Blackwater	corn	-	-	-	-	-	-	6"os/	10

PARISH	TOWNLAND	MILLER	TYPE	HOUSE	Land	£Val	PROPRIETORS	Date	WHEEL etc.	Record	Ref.
Kileskeer	Pottleragh	Daly John	corn	old mill 45x22.6x7 :	-	36.4	-	1853	15.3 undershot :	hob/	5.4203
Dowth	Proudsfoottown	- SW of New Bridge :	corn	-	-	-	-	1841	-	6"os/	20
Dowth	Proudsfoottown	Drew James	corn	-	43a.	-	-	-	-	gr/	-
Meath	Rahad	-	mill	-	-	-	-	-	-	1"os/	90
Donapatrick	Randalstown	- nr Whitest`n Br.	mill	-	-	-	-	-	-	1"os/	? (? Mea.)
Killary	Rathbranchuch	-	corn & kiln :	-	-	-	-	-	-	6"os/	12
Killary	Rathbranchurch	Carpenter Catherine	old mill	-	60a	-	-	-	-	gr/	-
Nobber	Rathe	- E. side Rathe Br.	corn	-	-	-	-	-	-	6"os/	5
Rathfeigh	Rathfeigh	-	corn	mill roof in bad order :	-	-	-	2001	-	mmSv/	wh - B
Rathfeigh	Rathfeigh	Leany Patrick	corn	-	21a.	-	-	-	-	gr/	-
Rathfeigh	Rathfeigh	Leary Patrick	corn & kiln	-	-	-	-	-	-	fdb/	4.1448
Rathfeigh	Rathfeigh :	-	corn	-	-	-	-	-	-	6"os/	32
Rathkenny	Rathkenny	-	corn :	-	-	-	-	-	-	6"os/	12
Rathkenny	Rathkenny	-	mill	-	-	-	-	-		pWEH	C
Rathkenny	Rathkenny	- Slevin.s Mill	corn	- small building :	-	-	-	1999		pWEH	B
Rathkenny	Rathkenny	Slevin Thomas	corn	-	-	-	-	-	-	fdb/	4.1465
Kilcooly	Rathnally	-	corn	- substantial blds :	-	-	-	2002	-	pWEH	R
Kilcooly	Rathnally	-	granary	-	-	-	-	2002	-	pWEH	D
Kilcooly	Rathnally	-	mill house	-	-	-	-	2002		pWEH	-
Kilcooly	Rathnally	- on R. Boyne :	flour	-	-	-	-	-	-	6"os/	37
Kilcooly	Rathnally	Hopkins Eleanor	mill	-	-	-	Hopkins Dame Eleanor - :	1845	-	dd/	1845 12 157
Kilcooly	Rathnally	Hopkins Eleanor	mill	-	-	-	Hopkins Dame Eleanor - :	1845	-	dd/	1845 12 158
Kilcooly	Rathnally	Hopkins Eleanor	mill	-	-	-	Hopkins Dame Eleanor - :	1845	-	dd/	1845 12 254
Kilcooly	Rathnally	McCann John :	mills	-	-	-	McCann J - Thompson Jn :	1828	-	dd/	835 367 561302
Kilcooly	Rathnally	Skeffington Th`son	mill	-	-	-	Skeffington Thomas - :	1845	-	dd/	1846 7 194
Ratoath	Ratoath	-	mill	-	-	-	-	-	-	1"os/	101
Ratoath	Ratoath	- SW of Town	corn & mill race	-	-	-	-	1841	-	6"os/	101
Ratoath	Ratoath	- SW of Town	Mill Tree	-	-	-	-	1841	-	6"os/	101
Ratoath	Ratoath	Ready James	corn	-	0.0.30		-	-	-	gr/	-
Ratoath	Ratoath Town	-	mill	-	-	-	-	-	-	1"os/	101
Ratoath	Ratoath Town :	Mockler Jno	mill	-	-	-	Mockler Jno - Graham Wm	1838	-	dd/	1838 10 7
Ratoath	Ratoath Town :	Dickens Craven H	mill	-	-	-	Dickens C - Dickens	1898	-	dd/	1898 2 145
Ratoath	Ratoath Town :	-	corn & race	-	-	-	-	-	-	6"os/	44
Ratoath	Raystown	-	horizontal	- wooden structure :	-	-	-	c900	-	pWEH	-
Ratoath	Raystown	-	horizontal	- wooden structure :	-	-	-	1200	-	pWEH	-
Mitchelstown	Ricetown	-	mill	-	-	-	-	-	-	1"os/	81
Mitchelstown	Ricetown	- N./ Killary Vge.	corn	-	-	-	-	-	-	6"os/	12
Mitchelstown	Ricetown	Slevin John	corn	31.6x21x15 29x19x14	-	3.6	-	1853	13.6x3x13 2 pr st.	hob/	5.4210
Mitchelstown	Ricetown	Slevin John	corn & kiln	-	-	-	-	-	-	gr/	-
Meath	Roachtown	-	mill	-	-	-	-	-	-	1"os/	90
Meath	Rockstown	Andrews John	corn	-	-	-	-	-	-	fdb/	4.1462
Rodanstown	Rodanstown	- W. side of road	old mill dam	-	-	-	-	-	-	6"os/	49
Dunshaughlin	Roestown	-	corn & kiln	-	-	-	-	-	-	6"os/	18
Julianstown	Rogerstown :	Norman John :	mill	-	-	-	Norman Jn - Allen John :	1826	Mort. 2 Aug.	dd/	817 114 550249
Kn`common	Rossnaree	-	corn & kiln	- building fair	-	-	-	2002	- wheel intact	mmSv/	jl - B
Knockcommon	Rossnaree	- on R. Boyne	mill	-	-	-	-	-	-	1"os/	91
Knockcommon	Rossnaree	- S. side R. Boyne	corn	-	-	-	-	1841	-	6"os/	26
Kn`common	Rossnaree	Johnston Walter	corn & kiln	-	41a.	-	-	-	-	gr/	-
Kn`common	Rossnaree	Osborne Thomas	mill	-	-	-	Osborne T - Ball Fras	1823	-	dd/	836 91 561626
Duleek	Roughrange	- betw. R. & canal	corn	-	-	-	-	-	-	6"os/	19
Duleek	Roughrange	- S. side R. Boyne	corn	-	-	-	-	-	-	6"os/	26
Duleek	Roughrange	Norris William	corn	-	8.1.5	-	-	-	-	gr/	-

PARISH	TOWNLAND	MILLER	TYPE	HOUSE	Land	£Val	PROPRIETORS	Date	WHEEL etc.	Record	Ref.
Duleek	Scatternagh	-	mill	- not located	-	-	-	2001	-	mmSv/	?Z
Scurlockstown	Scurlockstown	- near R. Boyne :	corn	-	-	-	-	-	-	6"os/	37
Scurlockstown	Scurlockstown	Cassidy Thomas	corn	-	16a.	-	-	-	-	gr/	-
Moynalty	Skearke	- nr Annesbrook :	corn	-	-	-	-	-	-	6"os/	4
Moynalty	Skearke	Rathburn John	mill	-	80a.	-	-	-	-	gr/	-
Staffordstown	Slanduff	-	copper mine	-	-	-	-	-	-	6"os/	32
Staffordstown	Slanduff	-	corn	-	-	-	-	-	-	6"os/	32
Monktown	Slanduff	- near Kentstown	saw	-	-	-	-	-	-	1"os/	91
Slane	Slane	-	mill	-	-	-	-	-	-	pWEH	B
Slane	Slane	- Slane Mills	flour	-	-	-	buildings in poor order :	1998	-	mmSv/	wh - B
Slane	Slane	French John :	Slane Mills	-	-	-	French J - Balfour Blaney :	1821	-	dd/	772 21 523156
Slane	Slane	Jebb David	mill	-	-	-	Visc. Conyngham	1764	-	sv/	LMCullen
Slane	Slane	Wetherill & Powell	flour	-	36a.	-	-	-	-	gr/	-
Slane	Slane Demense	Conyngham Marq.	saw	-	182a.	-	-	-	-	gr/	-
Slane	Slane Manor	Cunningham William	Stamps Mill	-	-	-	Cunningham - Browne Ulick	1726	-	dd/	51 160 32787
Slane	Slane Manor	Cunningham William	Stamps Mill	-	-	-	Cunningham - Hansard Nich	1727	-	dd/	54 457 36403
Slane	Slane Manor	Cunningham William :	Stamps Mill	-	-	-	Cunningham - Hansard Nch	1727	-	dd/	54 492 36533
Slane	Slane Manor	Norman Henry :	Stamps Mill	-	-	-	Norman H - Hansard Nich :	1729	Mort. 29Apl.	dd/	59 261 40397
Slane	Slane Town	- Slane Flour Mills :	flour	-	-	-	-	-	-	6"os/	19
Nobber	Spiddal	- Old Mill of Nobber :	mill	-	-	-	-	-	-	6"os/	6
Stackallan	Stackallan	- on R. Boyne	woollen	-	-	-	-	-	-	1"os/	91
Stackallan	Stackallan	Grimshaw :	cotton	-	-	-	-	-	-	sv/	C.Ellison
Stamullan	Stadalt	-	flour & pond	-	-	-	-	-	-	6"os/	34
Stamullan	Stadalt	- N. side Delvin R.	flour	-	-	-	-	-	-	6"os/	34
Stamullan	Stadalt	Walsh William	flour & kiln	-	382a.	-	-	-	-	gr/	-
Staholmog	Staholmog	-	Wind Mill Farm	-	-	-	-	-	-	1"os/	81
Donore	Staleen	- E. side R. Boyne	corn	-	-	-	-	-	-	6"os/	20
Donore	Staleen	Carroll Edward	mill	-	-	-	Caroll Ed - Graham William	1730	-	dd/	64 208 43493
Donore	Staleen	Hamilton Sophia Hon.	mill	-	-	-	Hamilton S - Boyne Gustav.	1733	-	dd/	73 520 52283
Donore	Staleen	M`Cullagh Peter	corn & kiln	-	43a.	-	-	-	-	gr/	-
Colp	Stameen	-	corn & dam	-	-	-	-	-	-	6"os/	20
Colp	Stameen	-	windmill	-	-	-	-	-	-	6"os/	21
Collon	Starinagh	- near Matock R.	flax	-	-	-	-	-	-	6"os/	13
Collon	Starinagh	Byrne Patrick	flax	-	4a.	-	-	-	-	gr/	-
Castletown	Stephenstown	Dowling Mary :	mill	-	-	-	Dowling M - Shaw James :	1825	Mort. 16 Dec.	dd/	809 214 545549
Castletown	Stephenstown	Fleming Michael :	mill	-	-	-	Fleming Mcl - Card Ralph :	1742	-	dd/	104 554 74112
Castletown	Stephenstown	Fleming Richard	mill	-	-	-	Fleming R - Woodward Ben	1794	-	dd/	476 149 311038
Castletown	Stephenstown	Tuke Francis	mill	-	-	-	Tuke Fran - Owens George	1786	-	dd/	381 404 252249
Oldcastle	Stonefield	Cadden Bernard	corn	-	16a.	-	-	-	-	gr/	-
Moymet	Stonestown	Harman Wesley :	mill	-	-	-	Harman W - Kane Redmonc	1752	-	dd/	162 316 109612
Moymet	Stonestown	Irvine Christy :	mill	-	-	-	Irvine C - Brooke Henry :	1749	-	dd/	135 423 92078
Moymet	Stonestown	Irvine James & Wife	mill	-	-	-	Mervyn J - Mervyn Arthur	1749	-	dd/	135 495 92389
Moymet	Stonestown	Mervyn James	mill	-	-	-	Mervyn James & his Will	1752	-	dd/	162 319 109436
Meath	Strahan	-	mill	-	-	-	-	-	-	1"os/	80
Teltown	Teltown	- R. Blackwater :	corn	-	-	-	-	-	-	6"os/	17
Teltown	Teltown	Garrett Louisa	corn	20x18x10, ho., offs(3) :	-	-	-	1853	11 ft. & 2 pr st.	hob/	5.4204
Teltown	Teltown	Kellett John	corn	-	4a.	-	-	-	-	gr/	-
Kilbeg	Thomastown	-	mill	-	-	-	-	-	-	hob/	5.4196
Clonard	Ticroghan	-	old mill & :	-	-	-	-	-	-	6"os/	46
Moybolgue	Tirawinnea	-.	corn	-	-	-	-	-	-	6"os/	2
Moybolgue	Tirawinnea	Williamson Edward	mill	-	13a.	-	-	-	-	gr/	-
Meath	Townland ?	Connolly	mill	-	-	-	Connolly - Connolly	-	-	dd/	439 340 285024

PARISH	TOWNLAND	MILLER	TYPE	HOUSE	Land	£Val	PROPRIETORS	Date	WHEEL etc.	Record	Ref.
Meath	Townland ?	Connolly, Clarke & Fay	mills	-	-	-	-	-		loc/	history
Broadford	Townland ?	Crook John	mill	-	-	-	Crook Jno - Warren Edw	1729	-	dd/	62 189 42478
Meath	Townland ?	Maxton William	Bedlow`s Mill	-	-	-	Maxton Wm - McKay Wm	1849	-	dd/	1849 8 199
Navan	Townland ?	Morgan James	mill & distillery	-	-	-	-	-	-	loc./	history
Meath	Townland ?	Murphy Patrick	distillery	-	-	-	-	-		loc/	history
Ratoath (bo.)	Townland ?	Tara Lord	Bedlows Mill	-	-	-	Lord Tara - Preston	-	-	dd/	706 298 483743
Meath	Townland ?	Trimbleston	mill	-	-	-	Trimbleston - Connolly	-	-	dd/	391 359 261601
Trim	Trim T`nparks	- Trim Town :	flour	-	-	-	-	-	-	6"os/	36
Trim	Trim T`nparks	Kennedy Patrick	corn & tuck	-	-	-	-	-	-	gr/	-
Trim	Trim T`nparks	Kennedy Patrick	flour	-	-	-	-	-	-	gr/	-
Trim	Trim T`nparks	Kennedy Patrick	flour & corn	-	-	-	-	-	-	gr/	-
Trim	Trim Town	Skeffington Thompson	Rathnally Mills	-	-	-	Skeffington T - Henry Dan	1834	-	dd/	1834 10 243
Navan Lower	Trim Town	Trim Town Commrs.	The Brewery	-	-	-	Trim Cmrs. - P. Works Cmrs	1891	-	dd/	1891 6 116
Trim	Trim Town :	Devins Patrick	brewery	(1B) 67.6x20x18 :	-	-	-	-	-	hob/	5.3167
Killeagh	Tubrid	- at Millbrook Vge.	flax	-	-	-	-	-	-	6"os/	9
Killeagh	Tubrid	- at Millbrook Vge.	flour	-	-	-	-	-	-	6"os/	9
Stamullan	Tullog	- on R. Delvin	flour	-	-	-	-	-	-	6"os/	34
Stamullan	Tullog	Ennis James	corn & kiln	-	30a.	-	-	-	-	gr/	-
Stamullan	Tullog	Killian	flour	-	-	-	Killian - Simon Lancaster	1992	conv. for. Res.	p/SL	C
Killeagh	Tully	- W. of Castlecor	corn	-	-	-	-	-	-	6"os/	8
Killeagh	Tully	Tormy John	corn	-	20a.	-	-	-	-	gr/	-
Killeagh	Tully	Tormy John	tuck	-	-	-	-	-	-	gr/	-
Dunboyne	Warrenstown	- at W`town Ho.	threshing	-	-	-	-	-	-	6"os/	37
Kilberry	Wilkinstown	-	mill	demolished some time	-	-	-	-		pWEH	D
Kilberry	Wilkinstown	- near Brookville	corn	-	-	-	-	-	-	6"os/	18
Kilberry	Wilkinstown	- on Yellow R.	mill	-	-	-	-	-	-	1"os/	91
Kilberry	Wilkinstown :	Fegan Patrick	mill	-	-	-	-	-	-	sv/	CEllison
Siddan	Woodtown	- near Fort :	corn	-	-	-	-	-	-	6"os/	35
Siddan	Woodtown	Carey Patrick	tuck	-	32a.	-	-	-	-	gr/	-
Drumcondra	Woodtown :	- Drumcondra Vge.	tuck & dam	-	-	-	-	-	-	6"os/	6
Meath	Yellowleas	- SW of Killary Br.	corn	-	-	-	-	-	-	6"os/	12

PARISH	TOWNLAND	MILLER	TYPE	HOUSE	Land	£Val	PROPRIETORS	Date	WHEEL etc.	Record	Ref.
Monaghan	Adelought	Ley Wiliam	mill	-	-	-	Ley W - Mitchell Blayow	1792	-	dd/	450 93 287562
Tedavnet	Aghaclogha	Fitzpatrick	mill	-	-	-	Fitzpatrick - Fitzpatrick	-	-	dd/	635 254 437219
Tedavnet	Aghaclogha	Fitzpatrick	mill	-	-	-	Fitzpatrick - Fitzpatrick	-	-	dd/	635 2544 437219
Donaghgmoyne	Aghadreenan	-	mill & mill dam	-	-	-	-	1836	-	6"os/	25
Donaghgmoyne	Aghadreenan	-	tuck	-	-	-	-	1836	-	6"os/	25
Donaghgmoyne	Aghadreenan	- close/ co. b'dry.	corn	-	-	-	-	1836	-	6"os/	26
Donaghgmoyne	Aghadreenan	M`Math Hamilton	corn	-	-	-	-	-	-	gr/	-
Donaghgmoyne	Aghadreenan	M`Math Hamilton	flax & land	-	80a.	139	-	-	-	gr/	-
Donaghgmoyne	Aghadreenan	McMath Mr	corn	-	-	-	-	-	28x - x - undershot	osm/	-
Donaghgmoyne	Aghadreenan	McMath Mr	mills (several)	-	-	-	-	-	-	osm/	-
Monaghan	Aghalaverty	-	mill	-	-	-	-	-	-	1"os/	58
Agabog	Aghalough	-	corn & mill race	-	-	-	-	1836	-	6"os/	18
Monaghan *	Aghalough	Roe	-	-	-	-	Roe - Roe	-	-	dd/	57 157 37781
Donagh	Aghaloughan	Wilson John	flax & land	-	5a.	18.5	-	1856	-	gr	-
Monaghan	Agher *	Erwin	-	-	-	-	Erwin - Erwin	-	-	dd/	177 425 118736
Monaghan	Agherybeggan *	Barlow	mill	-	-	-	Barlow - Dawson	-	-	dd/	178 472 119645
Monaghan	Agherybeggan *	Barlow John	mill	-	-	-	Barlow J - Mitchell John	1754	-	dd/	187 8 123042
Monaghan	Agherybeggan *	Pockrich Richard :	mill	-	-	-	Pockrich R - Green Wm	1757	-	dd/	184 516 124112
Monaghan	Agherybeggan *	Scott Barlow Rev.	mill	-	-	-	Scott B - Scott John :	1774	-	dd/	299 582 119418
Monaghan	Aghillagh *	Dawson Ralph :	mill	-	-	-	Dawson - Pratt Mervyn :	1786	-	dd/	375 433 251537
Monaghan	Aghillagh *	Ley Wiliam	mill	-	-	-	Ley W - Mitchell Blayow	1792	-	dd/	450 93 287562
Monaghan	Aghintamy	-	corn	-	-	-	-	-	-	6"os/	10
Monaghan	Aghintamy	-	mill	-	-	-	-	-	-	1"os/	58
Monaghan	Aghintamy	Hanna James	corn	-	-	-	-	-	14x1.10x3	osm/	-
Monaghan	Aghintamy	Malone Patrick	corn & kiln & land	-	1.2.0	7	-	1856	-	gr	-
Agabog	Aghnacue	-	corn & dam	-	-	-	-	1836	-	6"os/	18
Agabog	Aghnacue	-	flax	-	-	-	-	1836	-	6"os/	18
Donagh	Aghnagap	Macklin Samuel	corn & land	-	2a.	9.5.0	-	1856	-	gr	-
Donagh	Aghnagap	McCanagh Bern	corn	-	-	-	Leslie Mrs	1835	15x2x0.4	osm/	-
Donagh	Aghnagap	on Mountain Water	corn & mill dam	-	-	-	-	-	-	6"os/	7
Errigal trough	Aghnaha	Leslie	corn	& moulture & toll	-	-	Leslie - Fleming	-	-	dd/	86 437 61149
Tedavnit	Aghnameena	Duffy Hugh	corn & land	-	3a.	8	-	1865	-	gr	-
Aghnamullan	Aghnamullan	Ker	-	-	-	-	Ker - Ellis	-	-	dd/	348 459 234772
Aghnamullan	Aghnamullan	Wallace	-	-	-	-	Wallace - Holt	-	-	dd/	353 401 239660
Aghnamullen	Aghnamullen	-	corn	-	-	-	-	1836	-	6"os/	23
Aghnamullen	Aghnamullen	-	corn	-	-	-	-	-	12x2.6x -	osm/	-
Aghnamullen	Aghnamullen	- at Rockmount	corn	-	-	-	-	-	-	1"os/	69
Aghnamullen	Aghnamullen	- nr Cremorne Ho.	corn	-	-	-	-	-	-	1"os/	69
Aghnamullen	Aghnamullen	Corby	mill	-	-	-	Corby - Smith	-	?	dd/	526 443 345319
Aghnamullen	Aghnamullen	Johnston	mills	-	-	-	Johnston - Johnston	-	-	dd/	636 223 437242
Aghnamullen	Aghnamullen	Johnston James :	mills	-	-	-	Johnston - Johnston Dav.	1811	-	dd/	636 223 437242
Aghnamullen	Aghnamullen	Ker John, Cornet :	corn	-	-	-	Ker John - Ellis Henry :	1783	Mort. 24 Jan.	dd/	348 459 234772
Aghnamullen	Aghnamullen	Sherrif Co. Mon.	mill	-	-	-	Co. Sherrif - McClelland	-	-	dd/	743 542 506277
Aghnamullen	Aghnamullen	Wallace Robert :	mill	-	-	-	Wallace R - Thompson R	1796	-	dd/	501 559 326841
Aghnamullen	Aghnamullen	Wallace William	mill	-	-	-	Wallace W - Holt William	1783	-	dd/	353 401 239660
Monaghan	Agkellough	Ley	-	-	-	-	Ley - Lucas	-	-	dd/	236 528 155354
Monaghan	Analore	Kerr Robert :	mils	-	-	-	Kerr Robert - Alex	1790	-	dd/	418 296 273517
Monaghan	Analore	McCauley James :	mills	-	-	-	McCauley - Whiteside Jas	1791	-	dd/	441 10 203074
Monaghan	Anlore Bridge	- on Finn R.	mill	-	-	-	-	-	-	1"os/	58
Clones	Annaghkilly	-	mill pond	-	-	-	-	-	-	6"os/	12
Clones	Annaghkilly	Moore Marshall	corn & flour	(1B)40x20x23 :	-	-	-	-	Breast 14x3.4x12 :	hob/	5.1310
Currin	Annaveagh	Mears Abraham :	mills	-	-	-	Mears A - Mears William	1760	-	dd/	204 512 136688

PARISH	TOWNLAND	MILLER	TYPE	HOUSE	Land	£Val	PROPRIETORS	Date	WHEEL etc.	Record	Ref.
Currin	Annaveagh	Mears John	mills	-	-	-	Mears - Linn George	1768	-	dd/	257 531 169730
Currin	Annaveagh	Mears John	mills	-	-	-	Mears Jn - Mears Sam	1766	-	dd/	276 248 177197
Aghnamullen	Anveyerg	Mullen William	corn & land		26a.	32.10	-	1856	-	gr	-
Errigal Trough	Attiduff	-	mill & mill race	-	-	-	-	1836	-	6"os/	22
Augh	Aughalorigh	Gorrell William :	mill	-	-	-	Gorrell - Crawford Arch	1792	-	dd/	479 433 307982
Aghnamullen	Aughnahaveyarig	-	corn	-	-	-	-	-	-	osm/	-
Ballybay	Ballybay Town	Rosse D	corn	-	-	-	-	-	13.6x2.6x -	osm/	-
Ballybay	Ballybay Town	Rosse D	flax	-	-	-	-	-	12x2.6x -	osm/	-
Monaghan	Ballycranog	Baker John (ano)	mill	-	-	-	Baker J - Johnston Thos	1762	-	dd/	216 557 144346
Monaghan	Ballycranog	Clarke John, Newry	mill	-	-	-	Clarke Jn - Bredin Jerome	1751	-	dd/	145 486 99523
Monaghan	Ballycranog	Fleming Michael :	mill	-	-	-	Fleming M - Lucas Fran :	1740	-	dd/	97 510 69362
Monaghan	Ballycranog	Lucas Francis & Edw	mill	-	-	-	Lucas - Smith Thos Rev. :	1717	-	dd/	147 224 99522
Monaghan	Ballycranog	Witcraft William	mill	-	-	-	Whitcraft - Johnston Th	1762	-	dd/	216 557 144346
Monaghan	Ballynode	Shaw William	mill	-	-	-	Shaw Wm - Forster Jane :	1779	D.Poll 1 Jul.	dd/	340 460 230938
Killeevan	Ballynure	Gore Richard Hon. :	mills	-	-	-	Gore R - Forster Jane :	1782	D.Poll 1 Jul.	dd/	340 460 230938
Inishkeen	Ballyrush	Clement Dixie :	mill	-	-	-	Clement Dixie - Steele :	1807	29 Apl.	dd/	592 65 400491
Inishkeen	Ballyrush	Clement Dixie :	mill	-	-	-	Clement - Clement Sus'ah :	1806	Mort. 23 May	dd/	576 418 392827
Inishkeen	Ballyrush	Clement Dixie :	mill	-	-	-	Clement - Clement Sus'ah :	1806	Mort. 23 May	dd/	592 64 400490
Monaghan	Beagh	Marlin	mills	-	-	-	Marlin - Kennedy	-	-	dd/	650 414 445847
Aghnamullen	Bellatrain	Corry Isiah :	mill	-	-	-	Corry I - Drew Ambrose :	1781	Lse. 10 Aug.	dd/	342 192 229283
Aghnamullen	Bellatrain	Corry James :	mill with malt ho.	-	-	-	Corry J - Corry Isiah :	1781	Lse. 4 Apl.	dd/	338 249 277407
Aghnamullen	Bellatrain	Corry Jno Rev. :	mill	-	-	-	Corry J - Corry James :	1769	-	dd/	270 521 175135
Aghnamullen	Bellatrain	McMahon	-	-	-	-	McMahon - Barton	-	-	dd/	78 328 56191
Annagh	Bessbrook	-	mill	-	-	-	-	-	-	1"os/	58
Monaghan	Bodgaranroch *	Fleming Michael :	mill	-	-	-	Fleming M - Maxwell Jn :	1743	L&R. 11 Feb.	dd/	114 173 78495
Aghnamullen	Bowelk	-	beetling	-	-	-	-	1836	-	6"os/	23
Aghnamullen	Bowelk	Brien Andrew	land (& mill?)	-	-	-	Brien - Dawson	-	M. Arts.	dd/	672 536 465078
Aghnamullen	Bowelk	Dawson	mill (?)	-	-	-	Dawson - Hall - Taggart	-	Trust (1821/25)	dd/	782 337 532472
Aghnamullen	Bowelk	Jackson Eleanor	mill (?)	-	-	-	Jackson El - Johnston :	1825	Mort. 4 Jne.	dd/	803 459 542194
Aghnamullen	Bowelk	Jackson Hugh Yngr.	land (& mill?)	-	-	-	Jackson H - Jackson Hugh,	1809	Smt. 5 Mar.	dd/	602 379 416467
Aghnamullen	Bowelk	Jackson Hugh Yngr.	mill (?)	-	-	-	Jackson H - Bell James :	1814	Rel. 1 May	dd/	676 24 465564
Aghnamullen	Bowilk	Dawson William Rev.	mill (?)	-	-	-	Dawson W - Jebbs Thos :	1817	5 Jul.	dd/	726 367 495902
Aghnamullen	Bowilk	Jebbs Thomas :	mill (?)	-	-	-	Jebbs - McClelland Thos :	1814	Mort. L&R. 1 Jul.	dd/	718 563 491298
Aghnamullen	Bowilk	McClelland John :	mill	-	-	-	McClellend - Jebb Thos :	1826	Asgt. Mort. 23 Nov.	dd/	819 23 551358
Ematris	Boyher	-	millrace 1.25m	-	-	-	-	1836	-	6"os/	18
Ematris	Boyher	- 1/8m E/ Town	flax	-	-	-	-	1836	-	6"os/	18
Ematris	Boyher	Swann Robert	corn	-	26a.	-	-	-	-	gr/	-
Monaghan	Bradoge :	Fleming	miln	-	-	-	Fleming - Maxwell	-	-	dd/	114 173 78495
Monaghan	Bradoge :	Fleming Michael :	miln	-	-	-	Fleming M - White Mark :	1741	-	dd/	102 455 71767
Monaghan	Bryanlitter	-	mill	-	-	-	-	-	-	1"os/	58
Magheraclone	Camaghy	-	mill & kiln	-	-	-	-	1836	-	6"os/	30
Inishkeen	Candlefort	- S. side Fane R.	flax	-	-	-	-	1836	-	6"os/	29
Drumsnat	Carnbane	-	corn	-	-	-	-	-	-	6"os/	13
Drumsnat	Carnbane	Dawson	-	-	-	-	Dawson - Willoman	-	-	dd/	14 230 6122
Drumsnat	Carnbane	Dawson William :	mill	-	-	-	Dawson - Dawson Wm :	1758	-	dd/	200 96 132129
Drumsnat	Carnbane	McKeever James	corn & kiln & land	-	17a.	15.5	-	1865	-	gr	-
Clontibret	Carrickaddery	-	Millmount House	-	-	-	-	-	-	6"os/	14
Clontibret	Carrickaddery	- at Milltown Vge.	corn & mill pond	-	-	-	-	-	-	6"os/	14
Clontibret	Carrickaderry	Lucas Francis :	mill	-	-	-	Lucas F - McGinn Mary :	1796	-	dd/	502 205 324674
Clontibret	Carrickaderry	Lucas Frans :	mill	-	-	-	Lucas F - Hillis James :	1796	-	dd/	497 392 324672
Clontibret	Carrickaderry	Lucas Wm & Fras :	-	-	-	-	Lucas W - Leysan Wm	1796	-	dd/	505 337 326398?
Clontibret	Carrickaderry	Swanzy Andrew	mill	-	-	-	Swanzy A - Lewis Robt	1795	-	dd/	487 168 312305
Ematris	Carrickaslane	-	flax, corn, mill dan	-	-	-	-	1836	-	6"os/	20
Ematris	Carrickaslane	-	mill	-	-	-	-	-	-	1"os/	59

PARISH	TOWNLAND	MILLER	TYPE	HOUSE	Land	£Val	PROPRIETORS	Date	WHEEL etc.	Record	Ref.
Muckno	Carrickasliam	-	corn & flax	-	-	-	-	-	14x2.6x3	osm/	-
Magheross	Carrickmaclim	-	corn	-	-	-	-	-	-	1"os/	70
Carrickmacross	Carrickmacr`s Tn	-	distillery	-	-	-	-	-	15x7x8 14x1.8x10	osm/	-
Carrickmacross	Carrickmacr`s Tn	Mieg Thomas	flour	-	-	-	-	-	-	gr/	-
Carrickmacross	Carrickmacross	-	distillery disused	-	-	-	-	-	-	1"os/	58
Clones	Carrivettragh	-	windmill	-	-	-	-	-	-	1"os/	58
Clones	Carrivettragh	Windmill Hill :	windmill	- imed. S/ Vge.	-	-	-	-	-	6"os/	11
Monaghan	Caryaghlissanery	Moore Jno :	mil	-	-	-	Moore - Noble Brabazon :	1787	Mort. 4 Jne	dd/	380 525 257418
Monaghan	Castleshane	-	flax	-	-	-	-	-	-	1"os/	59
Errigal Trough	Cavan (Cope)	McCosker Edward	corn & kiln (unfin.)	-	16a.	13	-	1856	-	gr	-
Clones	Cavanacross	Herst John	mill pond	-	1.1.0		-	1865	-	gr	-
Errigall	Cavancope	Fleming John :	mill	-	-	-	Fleming Jn - Fleming Wm	1775	-	dd/	309 9 204822
Errigall	Cavancope	Fleming William	mill	-	-	-	Fleming W - Pringle Alex :	1780	Mort. 10 Jne.	dd/	331 372 222572
Errigall	Cavancope	Fleming William :	corn	-	-	-	Fleming W - Barton Gus	1795	-	dd/	490 243 313708
Errigall	Cavancope	McKenna James :	mill	-	-	-	Mckenna J - McKenna Pat	1805	Marr. Smt.	dd/	580 285 395279
Monaghan	Cherry Vale	-	flax	-	-	-	-	-	-	1"os/	70
Kilmore	Clonavarn	Johnston	mill & grist	-	-	-	Johnston - Johnston	-	-	dd/	668 71 460433
Kilmore	Clonavarn	Johnston	mills	-	-	-	Johnston - Hamilton	-	-	dd/	608? 175 61300
Kilmore	Clonavarn	Johnston William :	mill & grist	-	-	-	Johnston William - Wm	1813	-	dd/	668 71 460438
Tehallan	Clonlonan	-	corn	-	-	-	-	-	-	6"os/	10
Tehallan	Clonlonan	-	mill dam	-	-	-	-	-	-	6"os/	10
Tehallan	Clonlonan	McDonnell Patrick	corn & kiln	(1B) 37x22x26 :	-	-	-	-	18x4.4x19 2 pair st.	hob/	5.1312
Tehallan	Clonlonan	McDonnell Patrick Jur	corn	Ho. offs., & land	16a.	33.15	-	1856	-	gr	-
Clones	Clonmore	- SW/ Cumber Br.	corn	-	-	-	-	-	-	6"os/	16
Clontibret	Clontibret	- nr Castleshane	mill	-	-	-	-	-	-	1"os/	58
Tedavnet	Clontoe	-	mill	-	-	-	-	-	-	1"os/	58
Magheracloone	Clontrain	Wood Peter	corn	-	-	-	-	-	14x4x6	osm/	-
Aghnamullen	Cooas	-	corn	-	-	-	-	-	18x2.6x -	osm/	-
Killanny	Coolaha	- NW/ small river	old mill	-	-	-	-	1836	-	6"os/	31
Drumsnat	Coolcorragh	-	mill	-	-	-	-	-	-	1"os/	58
Drumsnat	Cooldarragh	-	corn	-	-	-	-	-	-	6"os/	13
Aghnamullen	Coose	-	corn	-	-	-	-	-	-	1"os/	70
Aghnamullen	Coose	-	corn & mill dam	-	-	-	-	1836	-	6"os/	25
Aghnamullen	Coose	McMahon Owen	corn & miller's ho.	-	17a.	22.5	-	1856	-	gr	-
Monaghan	Corad *	- W/ Corad Ho.	corn & flax	-	-	-	-	1836	-	6"os/	23
Errigal Trough	Corclare	-	mill	-	-	-	-	-	-	1"os/	46
Kilmore	Corcreeghy	- W/ White Br.	corn	-	-	-	-	-	-	6"os/	9
Killeevan	Corcummins	-	corn & mill pond	-	-	-	-	-	-	6"os/	16
Aughnamullen	Cordevlis	-	Peat Hole Mill	-	-	-	-	1836	-	6"os/	18
Aughnamullen	Cordevlis	- NE/ Town Cen.	corn	-	-	-	-	1836	-	6"os/	18
Aghnamullen	Cordevlish	-	flax & corn	-	-	-	-	-	14x4.6x -	osm/	-
Aghnamullen	Corfad	-	corn	-	-	-	-	-	-	6"os/	14
Aghnamullen	Corfad	McCullagh Mr	corn	-	-	-	-	-	12x4x -	osm/	-
Aghnamullen	Corfad	McCullagh Mr	flax	-	-	-	-	-	12x2.6x -	osm/	-
Tullycorbet	Corfinlough	Clarke James	corn & kiln & land	-	22a.	27.15	-	1865	-	gr	-
Tullycorbet	Corfinlough	Jones Humphrys	flax (as office)	-		1.0.0	-	1865	-	gr	-
Tullycorbet	Corfinlough	Shegog John	-	-	-	-	Shegog John - James	1794	-	dd/	477 537 303267
Tullycorbet	Corfinlough	Shegog John :	mill	-	-	-	Shegog John Revocation:	1800	-	dd/	534 307 350475
Magherooo	Corlea	-	corn & pond	-	-	-	-	1836	-	6"os/	30
Magherooo	Corlea	-	corn & pond	-	-	-	-	1836	-	6"os/	30
Clontibret	Corlealacka	-	corn & kiln	-	-	-	-	1836	-	6"os/	19
Clontibret	Corlealacka	-	dam & mill pond	-	-	-	-	1836	-	6"os/	19

PARISH	TOWNLAND	MILLER	TYPE	HOUSE	Land	£Val	PROPRIETORS	Date	WHEEL etc.	Record	Ref.
Clontibret	Corlealacka	Farrell Patrick	corn & kiln & land	-	6a.	13.10	-	1856	-	gr	-
Clontibret	Corleanamaddy	- W/ small bridge	site Beggar's Mill	-	-	-	-	1836	-	6"os/	19
Monaghan	Corliglacka * :	Shegog George :	mill	-	-	-	Shegog - Swanzy Anne :	1817	-	dd/	718 448 491183
Tullycorbet	Cornanure	-	corn	-	-	-	-	-	-	1"os/	70
Errigal Trough	Cornanure	Doogan John	corn & kilns & lanc	-	17a.	19.5	-	1856	-	gr	-
Tullycorbet	Cornanure	on Mountain Water	corn	-	-	-	-	-	-	6"os/	6
Aghnamullen	Corncarrow	Davidson Mr	beetling	-	-	-	-	-	24x - x -	osm/	-
Aghnamullen	Corncarrow	McKean Elizabeth	spinning	-	-	50	-	1856	-	gr	-
Currin	Corneparte	-	corn	-	-	-	-	-	-	osm/	-
Currin	Corragarry ? :	-	corn	-	-	-	-	1836	-	6"os/	25
Currin	Corrinshigo	-	mill	-	-	-	-	1836	-	6"os/	22
Drummully	Corvaghan	-	corn & mill race	-	-	-	-	-	-	6"os/	16
Aghnamullen	Corwillin	-	beetling	-	-	-	-	1836	-	6"os/	23
Aghnamullen	Corwillin	-	beetling	-	-	-	-	1836	-	6"os/	24
Aghnamullen	Corwillin	-	flax threshing	-	-	-	-	1836	-	6"os/	24
Clontibret ? :	Cossabey	Hall James	mills	-	-	-	Hall Jas - Steel Jno Eld :	1761	-	dd/	209 586 189616
Clontibret ? :	Cossabey	Hall James	mills	-	-	-	Hall Jas - Steel James	1784	-	dd/	369 278 274102
Clontibret ? :	Cossabey	Lucas Edward	mills	-	-	-	Lucas Ed - Steel Walter	1765	-	dd/	252 136 162059
Clontibret ? :	Cossabey	Steen John :	mills	-	-	-	Steen J - Moore Thomas :	1757	-	dd/	189 429 126053
Aghnamullen	Creeve	-	beetling	-	-	-	-	-	-	osm/	-
Aghnamullen	Creeve	-	beetling	-	-	-	-	-	-	osm/	-
Aghnamullen	Creeve	-	beetling	-	-	-	-	-	-	osm/	-
Aghnamullen	Creeve	-	beetling	-	-	-	-	-	-	osm/	-
Aghnamullen	Creeve	-	beetling	-	-	-	-	-	-	osm/	-
Aghnamullen	Creeve	-	beetling	-	-	-	-	-	-	osm/	-
Aghnamullen	Creeve	-	beetling	-	-	-	-	-	-	osm/	-
Aghnamullen	Creeve	-	beetling	-	-	-	-	-	-	osm/	-
Aghnamullen	Creeve	- 1/2m S/ Creeve Ho	beetling	-	-	-	-	1836	-	6"os/	24
Aghnamullen	Creeve	- 1/4m S/ Creeve Ho	beetling	-	-	-	-	1836	-	6"os/	24
Aghnamullen	Creeve	imed. E/ Creeve Ho.	beetling	-	-	-	-	1836	-	6"os/	24
Aghnamullen	Creeve	imed. NE/ Creeve Ho	beetling	-	-	-	-	1836	-	6"os/	24
Aghnamullen	Creeve	imed. S/ Creeve Ho.	beetling	-	-	-	-	1836	-	6"os/	24
Aghnamullen	Creeve	Brunker Robert :	mill	-	-	-	Brunker R - Nelson Jos :	1817	-	dd/	718 471 491006
Aghnamullen	Creeve	Cunningham M/s	bleach green	-	50a	-	-	-	-	osm/	-
Aghnamullen	Creeve	Fowler John	bleach gn & mill	-	-	-	Fowler J - Prentice Thos	1785	-	dd/	364 223 244500
Aghnamullen	Creeve	Matier Daniel	corn & flax & land	-	73a.	96.10	-	1856	-	gr	-
Aghnamullen	Creeve	Montgomery Arthur	flax & lands	-	58a.	83.15	-	1856	-	gr	-
Aghnamullen	Creeve	Murdock Robert	beetling	-	-	20	-	1856	-	gr	-
Aghnamullen	Creeve	Murdock Robert	bleach	-	-	20	-	1856	-	gr	-
Aghnamullen	Creeve	Phibbs Mary :	mill	-	-	-	Phibbs M - Jackson John	1815	-	dd/	697 427 478517
Aghnamullen	Creeve	Phibbs Mary :	mill	-	-	-	Phibbs M - Jackson John :	1815	-	dd/	697 426 478514
Aghnamullen	Creeve	Thompson David	corn & kiln (unfin.)	-	-	-	-	1856	-	gr	-
Aghnamullen	Creeve	Tyler Walter :	bleach gn & mills	-	-	-	Tyler W & W - Cole Eliz :	1816	-	dd/	740 464 504399
Donaghmore	Creevy	Oliver	mil	-	-	-	Oliver - Jackson		-	dd/	305 312 202140
Donaghmore	Creevy	Sherrif Co. Mon.	mill	-	-	-	Co. Sherrif - Oliver	-	-	dd/	316 107 210086
Donaghmoyne	Creevy (Oliver)	-	mill, kiln & mill rac	-	-	-	-	1836	-	6"os/	28
Clontibret	Cremartin	Caraher Arth & Mary	corn & flax & kiln	-	-	26	-	1856	-	gr	-
Tullycorbet	Crevagh	-	flax	-	-	-	-	-	-	1"os/	58
Tehallon	Crumlin	-	corn	-	-	-	-	-	-	1"os/	58
Tehallon	Crumlin	- on Blackwater R.	corn	-	-	-	-	-	-	6"os/	9
Tehallon	Crumlin	Brien Andrew	corn, flax & kiln	(1B) 30x23x12 :	-	-	-	-	12x3x4	hob/	5.1312
Tehallon	Crumlin	Bryans Andrew	corn & flax	steward's ho, offs :	-	-	-	1856	-	gr	-

PARISH	TOWNLAND	MILLER	TYPE	HOUSE	Land	£Val	PROPRIETORS	Date	WHEEL etc.	Record	Ref.
Tehallon	Crumlin	Quigly	mill	-	-	-	Quigley - Nicholson	-	-	dd/	688 142 472874
Tehallon	Crumlin	Quigly	mill	-	-	-	Quigly - Nicholson	-	-	dd/	688 142 472874
Currin	Crunchigo	-	corn	-	-	-	-	-	-	osm/	-
Monaghan	Cumber *	Kerr Robert :	-	-	-	-	Kerr Robert - Alex	1790	-	dd/	418 296 273517
Aghnamullen	Cumry	-	beetling	-	-	-	-	-	16x4x - overshot	osm/	-
Tedavnet	Curnanure	Ankell Rodger	corn	-	-	-	Singleton Mrs	-	16x2.8x3	osm/	-
Kilmore	Darraghlan	-	mill	-	-	-	-	-	-	1"os/	58
Kilmore	Darraghlan	Meakin Samuel	corn & kiln	-		7	-	1865	-	gr	-
Monaghan	Deanagola	-	flax	-	-	-	-	-	-	1"os/	46
Clontibret	Dernaglug	-	flax & mill pond	-	-	-	-	1836	-	6"os/	19
Clontibret	Dernaglug	Farlon George	corn & flax & kiln	-	68a.	63.10	-	1836	-	6"os/	19
Donagh	Derrilla	-	mill	-	-	-	-	-	-	1"os/	46
Aghnamullen	Derrygooney	-	corn	-	-	-	-	-	- formerly bleach	osm/	-
Aghnamullen	Derrygooney	- NW/ D'moyne Ho.	mill & mill dam	-	-	-	-	1836	-	6"os/	28
Aghnamullen	Derrygooney	- SE/ Vicar's Br.	corn	-	-	-	-	1836	-	6"os/	26
Aghnamullen	Derrygooney	Adams	mills	-	-	-	Adams - Gresson	-	-	dd/	650 207 453193
Aghnamullen	Derrygooney	Adams	water & mill	-	-	-	Adams - Jackson	-	-	dd/	625 293 438206
Aghnamullen	Derrygooney	Jackson John Elder :	water & mill	-	-	-	Jackson J - Bell Alicia :	1817	-	dd/	718 266 491001
Magheross	Derrylavan	-	Derrylavan Mills	-	-	-	-	-	-	1"os/	70
Magheross	Derrylavan	Lane William	corn & kiln	-	11a.	-	-	-	-	gr/	-
Donagh	Derrylea	- near Clones	mill	-	-	-	-	-	-	1"os/	58
Aghnamullen	Derryroosk	-	flax	-	-	-	-	1836	-	6"os/	23
Aghnamullen	Derryroosk	-	flax	-	-	-	-	-	12x2.6x -	osm/	-
Monaghan *	Dondroman	Leister	-	-	-	-	Leister - Wright	-	-	dd/	29 283 17266
Monaghan *	Dondroman	Lester	-	-	-	-	Lester - Wright	-	-	dd/	35 456 23230
Clontibret	Doohamlat	-	flax	-	-	-	-	-	-	1"os/	58
Clontibret	Doohamlat	-	mill x2	-	-	-	-	-	-	1"os/	58
Clontibret	Dooskey	-	mill, kiln & pond	-	-	-	-	-	-	6"os/	13
Clontibret	Dooskey	Smith Owen	corn & kiln & land	-	28a	20.10	-	1856	-	gr	-
Tehallan	Dromore	-	flax	-	-	-	-	-	-	1"os/	58
Tehallan	Dromore	Blaney	-	-	-	-	Blaney - McMath	-	-	dd/	89 79 62155
Tehallan	Dromore	Evans Francis	corn	-	-	-	Hurchell Mr	-	16x3x3	osm/	-
Currin	Drum	- N. side Fane R.	corn & tuck	-	-	-	-	1836	-	6"os/	29
Ematris	Drumacreeve	-	mill	-	-	-	-	-	-	1"os/	-
Muckno	Drumacribb	-	flax	-	-	-	-	-	12x2.8x2	osm/	-
Muckno	Drumagelvin	Blaney	-	-	-	-	Blaney - McMath	-	-	dd/	89 79 62155
Kilmore	Drumalt	McCullagh Thomas	corn & flax & land	-	3a.	35	-	1865	-	gr	-
Kilmore	Drumalt	McCullagh Thomas	flax	-	-	15	-	1865	-	gr	-
Nishkeen	Drumass	-	flax & tuck	-	-	-	-	1835	12x - x -	osm/	-
Nishkeen	Drumass	-	mill	-	-	-	-	-	12x - x -	osm/	-
Nishkeen	Drumass	-	mill	-	-	-	-	-	12x - x -	osm/	-
Nishkeen	Drumass	-	mill	-	-	-	-	-	-	osm/	-
Nishkeen	Drumass	-	mill	-	-	-	-	-	-	osm/	-
Nishkeen	Drumass	Hamill Bernard	corn	-	15a.	-	-	-	-	gr/	-
Donagh	Drumbanagher	Leslie Charles P.	flax	-	0.2.5	30	-	-	-	gr/	-
Monaghan	Drumbear	-	mill	-	-	-	-	-	-	1"os/	58
Clones	Drumcru Renwick	-	corn	-	-	-	-	-	-	6"os/	12
Clones	Drumcrue	McDonnell Steph	corn	-	-	-	-	-	16x4 2 pr st.	hob/	5.1310
Aghnamullen	Drumfaldra	-	beetling	-	-	-	-	-	16x4x - overshot	osm/	-
Aghnamullen	Drumfaldra	-	corn & flour	-	-	-	-	1836	-	6"os/	23
Aghnamullen	Drumfaldra	Cunningham John	corn & 2 kilns	- 4 storey	-	-	-	-	22x4x -	osm/	-
Aghnamullen	Drumfaldra	Cunningham John	flour	-	-	-	-	-	17x4.6x -	osm/	-

COUNTY MONAGHAN

PARISH	TOWNLAND	MILLER	TYPE	HOUSE	Land	£Val	PROPRIETORS	Date	WHEEL etc.	Record	Ref.
Aghnamullen	Drumfaldra	Jackson John :	mill	-	-	-	Jackson John - Jackson :	1816	-	dd/	697 432 478520
Clontibret	Drumgallan	Haire George :	mill	-	-	-	Haire G & Lynton Eliz :	1814	-	dd/	752 199 511334
Tedavnit	Drumgarran	Adams Francis	flour & corn	- herd's house :	70a.	283	-	1865	-	gr	-
Drumsnat	Drumgarve	-	corn	-	-	-	-	-	-	6"os/	13
Drumsnat	Drumgarve	Hughes mary	corn & kiln	house, offs. & ld.	2.3.20		-	1856	-	gr	-
Monaghan	Drumgoony *	Jackson	mill	-	-	-	Jackson & Bell marr.	-	-	dd/	718 266 490001
Monaghan	Drumgoony *	Jackson	mill	-	-	-	Jackson & Bell marr.	-	-	dd/	718 266 491001
Aghnamullen	Drumgor	Conlon Patrick	corn & land	-	21a.	16.5	-	1856	-	gr	-
Aghnamullen	Drumgor	Shegog William :	mill	-	-	-	Shegog - Courtney Ed :	1817	-	dd/	714 162 488497
Drumsnat	Drumguill	-	corn	-	-	-	-	-	-	6"os/	13
Drumsnat	Drumguill	Hare James	corn & flax & land	-	1.3.0	3.15	-	1865	-	gr	-
Monaghan	Drumhirk	-	mill	-	-	-	-	-	-	1"os/	58
Ballybay	Drumlane	-	corn & mill pond	-	-	-	-	1836	-	6"os/	24
Ballybay	Drumlane	Keenan D	corn	-	-	-	-	-	12x2.6x -	osm/	-
Muckno	Drumleck	McWatty James	corn	-	-	-	-	-	18x4x15	osm/	-
Muckno	Drumleek South	-	corn	-	-	-	-	1836	-	6"os/	20
Tehallan	Drumleig	Blaney	-	-	-	-	Blaney - McMath				89 79 62155
Monaghan	Drumlog *	-	mill	-	-	-	-	-	-	1"os/	58
Clones	Drummans	-	mill & kiln	-	-	-	-	-	-	6"os/	8
Clones	Drummans	- from Drumloo Lo.	mill race	-	-	-	-	-	-	6"os/	8
Clones	Drummans	Ballagh Anthony	corn & flax & land	-	12a.	22	-	1865	-	gr	-
Magheracloone	Drummond :	- due S/ Town	flax	-	-	-	-	1836	-	6"os/	31
Magheracloone	Drummond :	- due S/ Town	old mill	-	-	-	-	1836	-	6"os/	31
Magheracloone	Drummond :	- E. side River	brewery	-	-	-	-	1836	-	6"os/	31
Magheross	Drummond Otra :	M`Evoy Thomas	distillery	-	0.1.25		-	-	-	gr/	-
Magheross	Drummond Otra :	McEvoy Thomas	distillery	(B) 32x16x3 :	-	-	-	1860	-	hob/	5.3173
Killevan	Drummullan	-	corn	-	-	-	-	-	-	6"os/	12
Donaghmoyne	Drumnavaddy	Levingston	-	-	-	-	Levingston - Campbell	-	-	dd/	55 155 36321
Tedavnet	Drumscor	-	mill	-	-	-	-	-	-	1"os/	46
Tedavnet	Drumscor	Duffy John	corn	-	-	-	Hamilton James	-	14x3x4 breast	osm/	-
Monaghan	Drumucky *	Verner	mills	-	-	-	Verner & ors - Kerr	-	-	dd/	750 591 510526
Monaghan	Drumulla *	- 3/8m W/ Town	old windmill stump	-	-	-	-	1836	-	6"os/	18
Donagh	Drumully	Collins John	corn	-	-	-	Ankatell William	-	13x1.11x1.6 o`shot	osm/	-
Donagh	Drumully	Collins John	flax	- house	-	7.0.0	-	1865	-	gr	-
Donagh	Drumully	Collins John	flax	-	-	-	Ankatell William	-	13x2.8x - overshot	osm/	-
Currin	Drumurcher	-	corn	-	-	-	-	1836	-	6"os/	22
Currin	Drumurcher	-	tuck	-	-	-	-	-	- long since unempl.	osm/	-
Clontibret	Dunfelimy	-	mill	-	-	-	-	-	-	1"os/	58
Drumglass (Tyr)	Dungannnon	Cairns	mills	-	-	-	Cairns - Falls	-	-	dd/	708 467 485211
Monaghan	Dunsinare	- S/ Monaghan Tn	corn	-	-	-	-	-	-	6"os/	9
Tullycorbet	Edenaferkin	-	flax	-	-	-	-	1836	-	6"os/	18
Monaghan	Edenaferkin	-	mill	-	-	-	-	-	-	1"os/	58
Nishkeen	Edenamagh	-	flax & tuck	-	-	-	-	-	12x - x -	osm/	-
Aghnamullen	Edenbrone	-	tuck	-	-	-	-	-	13x2 not working	osm/	-
Aughnamullen	Edenbrone	- 3/8m S/ Moyle Ch.	old mill	-	-	-	-	1836	-	6"os/	23
Aghnamullen	Edenforran	Cremorne Green	bleach	-	57a	-	-	-	-	osm/	-
Donagh	Emy	Leslie	corn	& moulture & toll	-	-	Leslie - Fleming	-	-	dd/	86 437 61149
Donagh	Emyvale Town	-	flax	-	-	-	-	-	-	1"os/	46
Donagh	Emyvale Town	Wright Thomas	corn	-	-	-	-	1860	-	hob/	5.3177
Monaghan	Enveyarig *	Rogers	mill	-	-	-	Rogers - Cunningham	-	-	dd/	665 491 458186
Aghabog	Faltagh	- near Newbliss	corn	-	-	-	-	-	-	1"os/	58
Monaghan *	Fermilly	Blaney	-	-	-	-	Blaney - McMath	-	-	dd/	89 79 62155

PARISH	TOWNLAND	MILLER	TYPE	HOUSE	Land	£Val	PROPRIETORS	Date	WHEEL etc.	Record	Ref.
Donaghmoyle	Fincarn	-	scutching ruins	-	-	-	-	1836	-	6"os/	25
Clontibret	Fintully	-	corn	-	-	-	-	-	-	1"os/	-
Clontibret	Fintully	-	corn & mill pond	-	-	-	-	-	-	6"os/	14
Clontibret	Fintully	Johnston James	mill & kiln	(2C)61x21x9 :	-	8.0.0	-	-	[no dia.] 19ft fall & :	hob/	5.1308
Clontibret	Fintully	Johnston James	mill & land	house & offices	20a.	24	-	1856	-	gr	-
Monaghan	Gallanagh	- at Milltown Vge.	corn	-	-	-	-	-	-	6"os/	9
Donagh	Glannan	-	corn	-	-	-	-	-	-	6"os/	7
Donagh	Glannan	Aiken Robert	corn	-	-	-	-	-	12x2	osm/	-
Donagh	Glannan	Eakin William	flax & corn	-	-	3	-	1865	-	gr	-
Donagh	Glaslough	-	saw	-	-	-	-	-	-	1"os/	46
Newbliss	Glenbrook	- near Newbliss	corn	-	-	-	-	-	-	1"os/	58
Newbliss	Glenbrook	- near Newbliss	mill	-	-	-	-	-	-	1"os/	58
Clones	Gola	Gilles Thomas	corn & kiln	-	-	-	-	1865	-	gr	-
Aghnamullen	Gragarnagh	-	corn & mill race	-	-	-	-	1836	-	6"os/	24
Carrickmacross	Greenmount	-	corn & mill race	-	-	-	-	-	-	6"os/	10
Carrickmacross	Greenmount	Maxwell John	corn	-	-	-	Maxwell Edward	-	14x2.8x1.6 overshot	osm/	-
Monaghan	Greenmount	McCraren Owen	corn	ho., offs. & gdn	0.0.20	ú4.10	-	1856	-	gr	-
Aghnamullen	Grigorna	-	corn	-	-	-	-	-	12x2.6x -	osm/	-
Monaghan	Inishkeen	McCabe Owen	corn	-	11a.	-	-	-	-	gr/	-
Donagh	Kilcran	- at New Mills	flax & corn	-	-	-	-	-	-	6"os/	7
Donagh	Kilcran	- on Blackwater R.	New Mills Town	-	-	-	-	-	-	6"os/	7
Donagh	Kilcran	Cargil William	corn & threshing	(1B) 72x23x28 :	-	8.7	-	1859	15X5.6X7.6 2 pair st	hob/	5.1313
Donagh	Kilcran	Cargil William	flax	(1B) 44x24x8 :	-	1.7.1	-	1859	15x5.6 3 rs. 10stks.	hob/	5.1313
Donagh	Kilcran	Young William	corn	-	-	-	Leslie Mrs	-	15x4x -	osm/	-
Donagh	Kilcran	Young William	flax	-	-	-	Leslie Mrs	-	14x2.4x -	osm/	-
Clones	Kilcreen	-	mill	-	-	-	-	-	-	1"os/	58
Donagh	Kileran	Cargill Wilson	corn & flax & kilns	- caretaker's ho.	-	-	-	1856	-	gr	-
Donagh	Kileran	Cargill Wilson	thrashing & land	-	38a.	80	-	1856	-	gr	-
Killanny	Killanny	-	corn	-	-	-	-	-	15.6x - x -	osm/	-
Killeevan	Killeevan	-	corn	-	-	-	-	-	-	6"os/	12
Killeevan	Killeevan	McGinty	mill & millholding	-	-	-	McGinty - Irwin	-	-	dd/	732 583 499718
Monaghan	Killiercrom * :	McGinty James :	mill	-	-	-	McGinty J - Irwin Geo :	1818	Rent ú34.2.6	dd/	732 581 499718
Clones	Killycoghill	-	corn	-	-	-	-	-	-	6"os/	12
Donagh	Killycooly	-	flour	-	-	-	-	-	-	6"os/	3
Donagh	Killycooly	Ryan William	flour	(1B) 43x36x64 :	-	-	-	1859	25x11x - 3 pair st.	hob/	5.1313
Clontibret	Killycrom	Brennan	mill	-	-	-	Brennan - Irwin	-	-	dd/	734 327 500662
Clontibret	Killycrom	Lennan Bernard	corn & land	-	11a.	15.5	-	1856	-	gr	-
Monaghan	Killycrummy * :	Brennan Charles	mill	-	-	-	Brennan C - Irwin Geo :	1816	-	dd/	734 327 500662
Currin	Killyfargy	-	corn	-	-	-	-	-	-	osm/	-
Currin	Killyfargy	-	corn kiln	-	-	-	-	-	-	6"os/	16
Currin	Killyfargy	-	mill	-	-	-	-	-	-	6"os/	16
Killeevan	Killyfuddy	-	corn	-	-	-	-	-	-	6"os/	12
Killosolan	Killygrom	- nr Castleblaney	mill	-	-	-	-	-	-	1"os/	59
Errigal Trough	Killyloughavoy	-	corn	-	-	-	-	-	-	6"os/	3
Tedavnet	Killymaran	-	mills & mill dam	-	-	-	-	-	-	6"os/	9
Tedavnet	Killymaran	Read James	corn	-	-	-	Rose James	-	14x2.6x -	osm/	-
Tedavnet	Killymaran	Read James	flax	-	-	-	Rose James	-	-	osm/	-
Tedavnit	Killymarran	Reid Thomas	corn & flax & land	-	8a.	18	-	1865	-	gr	-
Errigal Trough	Killyslavan	- due S/ Drumbirn	old mill ruins	-	-	-	-	-	-	6"os/	3
Donagh	Killyveley	Fleming William	corn	-	-	-	Fleming W - Barton Gus	1795	-	dd/	490 243 313708
Drumsnat	Kilnaclay	-	mill	-	-	-	-	-	-	1"os/	-
Clontibret	Kilycrom	-	corn & mill pond	-	-	-	-	-	-	os/	19

PARISH	TOWNLAND	MILLER	TYPE	HOUSE	Land	£Val	PROPRIETORS	Date	WHEEL etc.	Record	Ref.
Monaghan	Kincorragh	-	corn	-	-	-	-	-	-	6"os/	8
Ballybay	Knappagh	Lillion Mary	corn	-	-	-	-	-	13x3.6x -	osm/	-
Ballybay	Knappagh	Lillion Mary	flax	-	-	-	-	-	8x3.6x -	osm/	-
Ballybay	Knappagh	McClleland Jane	corn & miller's ho.	-	-	-	-	1856	-	gr	-
Ballybay	Knappagh	McClleland Jane	flax & land	-	13a.	13.10	-	1856	-	gr	-
Monaghan	Knockowen *	-	flax	-	-	-	-	-	-	1"os/	59
Aghnamullen	Laraagh	-	beetling & green	-	-	-	-	1836	-	6"os/	27
Aghnamullen	Laraagh	-	corn	-	-	-	-	1836	-	6"os/	27
Aghnamullen	Laraagh	-	watch house	-	-	-	-	1836	-	6"os/	27
Aghnamullen	Laragh	-	mill	-	-	-	-	-	-	1"os/	70
Aghnamullen	Laragh	Davidson Mr	bleach	-	-	-	-	-	-	osm/	-
Aghnamullen	Laragh	McKean Eliza	beetling mills (3)	-	-	58	-	1856	-	gr	-
Aghnamullen	Laragh	McKean Eliza	corn & land	-	9a.	5.10	-	1856	-	gr	-
Aghnamullen	Laragh	Oliver Mr	corn	-	-	-	-	-	-	osm/	-
Aghnamullen	Laragh	Oliver Mr	flax	-	-	-	-	-	-	osm/	-
Clones	Latgallon	-	spade m'fty	-	-	-	-	-	-	6"os/	12
Clones	Latgallon	Benson Samuel	corn	-	-	-	-	-	breast 14x6x6 :	hob/	5.1310
Clones	Latgallon	Benson Samuel	hammer	-	-	-	-	-	breast 14x6x6 :	hob/	5.1310
Clones	Latgallon	Benson Samuel	scutch	-	-	-	-	-	breast 14x6x6 :	hob/	5.1310
Kilmore	Leck	-	mill	-	-	-	-	-	-	1"os/	58
Tullycorbet	Legacurry	-	corn & flax	-	-	-	-	1836	-	6"os/	19
Tullycorbet	Legacurry	Richardson	-	-	-	-	Richardson - Galbraith	-	-	dd/	83 506 60017
Clones	Legarhill	- SW/ Town	brewery	-	-	-	-	-	-	6"os/	11
Magheross	Lisacullion	-	mill	-	-	-	-	1836	-	6"os/	27
Magheross	Lisacullion	Martin Henry	corn & kiln	-	10a	-	-	-	-	gr/	-
Clontibret	Lisaginny	Carson Charles	flax & land	house & offices	49a.	48.5	-	-	-	gr/	-
Killeevan	Lisdaragh	-	corn	-	-	-	-	-	-	6"os/	17
Killeevan	Lisdaragh	-	mill race & pond	-	-	-	-	-	-	6"os/	17
Muckno	Liseenan	-	corn & mill dam	-	-	-	-	1836	-	6"os/	20
Muckno	Liseenan	Kenner John :	mill	-	-	-	Kenner J - Neill William :	1816	-	dd/	706 43 483570
Clones	Lisgall	-	corn, kiln & dam	-	-	-	-	1836	-	6"os/	28
Aghnamullen	Lisnagalliagh	-	bleach	-	-	-	-	-	-	osm/	-
Aghnamullen	Lisnalong	-	corn	-	-	-	-	-	11x2.6x -	osm/	-
Aghnamullen	Lisnalong	Delaney	-	-	-	-	Delaney - Akle	-	-	dd/	74 264 51067
Monaghan	Lissanery	Moore Jno :	mill	-	-	-	Moore - Noble Brabazon :	1787	Mort. 1 Jne.	dd/	380 525 257418
Muckno	Lurganearly	-	flax	-	-	-	-	-	-	1"os/	59
Muckno	Lurganearly	-	flax	-	-	-	-	-	12x2x3	osm/	-
Muckno	Lurganearly	-	mill	-	-	-	-	-	-	1"os/	59
Magheross	Lurganmore	-	corn	-	-	-	-	1836	-	6"os/	20
Magheross	Lurganmore	-	corn	-	-	-	-	-	14x1.3x -	osm/	-
Maghernacloone	Maghernacloone	-	mill	-	-	-	-	-	-	1"os/	70
Maghernacloone	Maghernacloy	- imed. NW/ Castle	threshing machine	-	-	-	-	1836	-	6"os/	34
Inishkeen	Magoney	Filgate William :	mill	-	-	-	Filgate W - Hughes John :	1811	-	dd/	661 373 455606
Inishkeen	Magoney	Hughes John :	mill	-	-	-	Hughes J - Atkinson Jas :	1814	Lse. 29 Aug.	dd/	679 99 467432
Inishkeen	Magoney River	Hughes John :	mill	-	-	-	Hughes J - Sandys Thos :	1816	Mort. 19 Dec.	dd/	712 92 487227
Castleblaney	Milltown	-	corn	-	-	-	-	-	-	1"os/	59
Castleblaney	Milltown	-	flax	-	-	-	-	-	-	1"os/	59
Ematris	Milltown	-	mil & corn kiln	-	-	-	-	1836	-	6"os/	18
Monaghan	Milltown	-	mill	-	-	-	-	-	-	1"os/	58
Ematris	Milltown	Nesbitt Robert	corn & kiln	-	50a.	-	-	-	-	gr/	-
Inishkeen	Miskish	Filgate	mills	-	-	-	Filgate - Hughes	-	?	dd/	661 373 455606
Inishkeen	Miskish	Hughes	mills	-	-	-	Hughes - Atkinson	-	?	dd/	679 99 467432

PARISH	TOWNLAND	MILLER	TYPE	HOUSE	Land	£Val	PROPRIETORS	Date	WHEEL etc.	Record	Ref.
Monaghan	Monaghan Town	Travers	malt kiln & fcty	-	-	-	Travers & W - Hamilton	-	-	dd/	743 534 506269
Monaghan	Monaghan Town :	Monaghan G. Jury	tread mill	(B+) 10.4x6x6	-	1-16	-	-	-	hob/	5.3180
Ematris	Monneill	-	old w mill	-	-	-	-	-	-	1"os/	58
Clontibret	Moy Otra	-	corn & kiln	-	-	-	-	-	-	6"os/	14
Moy Otra	Moy Otra	-	flax & mill pond	-	-	-	-	-	-	6"os/	14
Clontibret	Moy Otra	Davison John	flax & land	labourer's ho, off.	4a.	18	-	1856	-	gr	-
Donaghmoynw	Moyles	-	mill	-	-	-	-	-	-	1"os/	70
Donaghmoynw	Moyles	- W. side Fane R.	corn	-	-	-	-	1836	-	6"os/	29
Errigal Trough	Mullabryan	-	mill	-	-	-	-	-	-	1"os/	46
Ballybay	Mullaghanee	Fenning Rose	corn & land		17a.	19.10	-	1856	-	gr	-
Monaghan	Mullaghmonaghan :	Adams Francis	corn-store	- & offices	-	10	-	1856	-	gr	-
Monaghan	Mullaghmonaghan :	- NE/ Sparks Lake	brewery	-	-	-	-	-	-	6"os/	9
Tedavnet	Mullaghmore	Forster	milltate	-	-	-	Forster - Fortescues	-	-	dd/	716 485 498020
Tedavnet	Mullaghmore	Wright Robert	corn	-	-	-	Foster Sir Thomas	-	16x3x4 14.6x2.8x6.6	osm/	-
Tedavnet	Mullaghmore West	- on Blackwater R.	corn	-	-	-		-	-	6"os/	9
Tedavnit	Mullaghmore West	Tenants	mill houses (12) :	-			-	1865	-	gr	-
Tedavnit	Mullaghmore West	Wright Robert	corn & land	-	56a.	93	-	1865	-	gr	-
Donagh	Mullaliss	-	mill	-	-	-	-	-	-	1"os/	46
Errigal Trough	Mullan	-	flax	-	-	-	-	-	-	1"os/	46
Errigal Trough	Mullan	Smyth Robert	spinning	house, offs., land :	4.3.6	132	-	-	-	gr	-
Monaghan	Mullanacask *	-	mill dam	-	-	-	-	-	-	6"os/	3
Mon ?	Newtownhamilton	-	mill x2	-	-	-	-	-	-	1"os/	59
Monaghan	nr Harry Mount Ho	-	mill	-	-	-	-	-	-	1"os/	58
Monaghan	nr The Burrow	-	mill	-	-	-	-	-	-	1"os/	58
Muckno	Oram	- nr Castleblaney	mill	-	-	-	-	-	-	1"os/	59
Tedavnet	Quiglough	-	corn	-	-	-	-	-	-	6"os/	9
Tedavnit	Quiglough	Jamison Robert	corn & flax & kiln	- ho., offices, ld.	11a.	15	-	1865	-	gr	-
Tedavnet	Quiglough	Thomas Humphry	corn	-	-	-	Foster Andrew	-	13.6x2.8x2	osm/	-
Monaghan	Rackwallace	Clarke Margaret	corn & land	-	27a.	16.10	-	1856	-	gr	-
Tedavnet	Rafeenan	-	mill	-	-	-	-	-	-	1"os/	58
Tedavnet	Rafeenan	- on Blackwater R.	corn	-	-	-	-	-	-	6"os/	9
Tedavnit	Rafeenan	M'Cague John	corn & kiln & land	-	74a.	79.10	Forster William	1865	-	gr	-
Tedavnet	Rafeenan	McCague Andrew	corn	-	-	-	-	-	14.6x2.8x3	osm/	-
Magheross	Raferagh	-	corn	-	-	-	-	1836	-	6"os/	30
Magheross	Raferagh	-	corn kilns (2)	-	-	-	-	1836	-	6"os/	30
Magheross	Raferagh	-	mill	-	-	-	-	-	-	1"os/	69
Magheross	Raferagh	Martin Myles :	mills	-	-	-	Martin M - Kennedy Jno :	-	?	dd/	650 114 445847
Donaghmoyne	Rahans	-	corn	-	-	-	-	1836	-	6"os/	28
Donaghmoyne	Rahans	-	Cox's Mill	-	-	-	-	1836	-	6"os/	28
Donaghmoyne	Rahans	-	mill & mill dam	-	-	-	-	1836	-	6"os/	28
Magheross	Rakeragh	Johnston James	corn & kiln	-	-	-	-	-	-	gr/	-
Magheross	Rakeragh	Johnston James	scutch mill & ld	-	14a.	-	-	-	-	gr/	-
Monaghan	Readuffe *	Hyndman Margaret :	mill	-	-	-	Hyndman M - Kerr Robert	1811	Lse. 22 Oct.	dd/	643 107 440797
Aghnamullen	Reduff	- NW/ cross roads	corn	-	-	-	-	1836	-	6"os/	27
Aghnamullen	Reduff	Oliver Joseph	corn & flax	-	5a.	21	-	1856	-	gr	-
Aghnamullen	Reduff	- N. of cross roads	mill race& pond :	-	-	-	-	-	-	6"os/	27
Aghnamullen	Reduff	- S. Farm Hill Ho.	corn	-	-	-	-	-	-	6"os/	27
Aghnamullen	Reduff	Harrison	corn	-	-	-	-	2010	- Sheridan	mmSv/	pc
Aghnamullen	Reduff	Fleming John	scutch	-	-	-	-	-	-	mmSv/	pc
Aghnamullen	Reduff	Ward Peter	scutch	-	-	-	-	-	-	mmSv/	pc
Aghnamullen	Reduff	- NW/ cross roads		-	-	-	-	2008	- Patsy Connolly	mmSv/	pc
Ematris	Rockcorry	Brunker	mills	-	-	-	Brunker - Adams	-	-	dd/	695 424 477355

PARISH	TOWNLAND	MILLER	TYPE	HOUSE	Land	£Val	PROPRIETORS	Date	WHEEL etc.	Record	Ref.
Ematris	Rockcorry Town	-	mill	-	-	-	-	-	-	1"os/	58
Ematris	Rockcorry Town	Browne James	corn	-	1.1.0	-	-	-	-	gr/	-
Killeevan	Roosky	-	flour & mill pond	-	-	-	-	-	-	6"os/	12
Killeevan	Roosky	-	mill	-	-	-	-	-	-	1"os/	58
Drumsnat	Roosky	Hare James	miller's house	-	0.3.0	1.5.0	-	1865	-	gr	-
Killeevan	Roosky	McKenna Catherine :	mill	-	-	-	McKenna C - McQuaid Jn:	1817	Mort. 29 Mar.	dd/	713 297 488032
Clontibret	Rossollus	-	corn	-	-	-	-	1836	-	6"os/	24
Aghnamullen	Royduff	Robinson Mr	corn	-	-	-	-	-	18x5x -	osm/	-
Aghnamullen	Royduff	Robinson Mr	corn	-	-	-	-	-	12x4.6x -	osm/	-
Monaghan	Sallycrum	Kerr	mill	-	-	-	Kerr - Hudson	-	-	dd/	709 357 495692
Donagh	Scarnageeragh	Murdoch William	corn	-	-	-	Leslie Mrs	-	16x4x -	osm/	-
Donagh	Scarnageeragh	on Mountain Water	corn	-	-	-	-	-	-	6"os/	6
Mon	Scotshouse	-	mill	-	-	-	-	-	-	1"os/	57
Tehallan	Seaveagh	- on Blackwater R.	flax	-	-	-	-	-	-	6"os/	10
Tehallan	Seaveagh	McElhone Arthur	flax & land	-	19a.	20.10	-	1856	-	gr	-
Tehallan	Seaveagh	McGlone Thomas	flax	-	-	-	Richarson Edward	-	14x4.6x -	osm/	-
Inishkeen	Seeola	-	corn & sluice	-	-	-	-	1836	-	6"os/	29
Clones	Selloo	Smith James	corn & land	- house & offices	20a.	31.5	-	1865	-	gr	-
Ballybay	Shane	-	corn	-	-	-	-	-	-	1"os/	69
Clontibret	Shanmullagh	-	corn	-	-	-	-	-	-	6"os/	14
Ballybay	Shantonagh	-	flax & corn	-	-	-	-	1836	-	6"os/	18
Ballybay	Shantonagh	Thompson John	flax & corn	- miller's house	1.3.0	58	-	1856	-	gr	-
Donagh	Sillis at Newmills	-	mill	-	-	-	-	-	-	1"os/	46
Muckno	Skerrymore	-	flax & mill dam	-	-	-	-	1836	-	6"os/	20
Kilmore	Slieveroe	-	flax	-	-	-	-	-	-	6"os/	13
Errigal Trough	Tamlat	- SE/ Monaghan	corn	-	-	-	-	-	-	6"os/	9
Errigal Trough	Tamlat	Clarke Margaret	corn & kiln	-	-	-	-	-	14x3.6x13 42 bkts.	hob/	5.1311
Errigal Trough	Tamlat	MacKlim Robert	corn & kiln	-	-	19/-	-	-	15x3x14 48 bkts.	hob/	5.1311
Errigal Trough	Tamlat	Wilson William	corn	(1A)42x22x30 :	-	-	-	-	o`shot 20x3.6x19 :	hob/	5.1311
Errigal Trough	Tamlat	Wilson William	corn & kiln	-	-	26.5	-	1856	-	gr	-
Currin	Tatenacake	-	corn	-	-	-	-	-	-	osm/	-
Muckno	Tatinclave	-	flax	-	-	-	-	-	14x3.6x -	osm/	-
Currin	Tattincake	-	mill	-	-	-	-	1836	-	6"os/	22
Muckno	Tattintlieve	-	mill	-	-	-	-	-	-	1"os/	59
Muckno	Tattintlieve	- W. side Keady Rd.	flax	-	-	-	-	1836	-	6"os/	20
Donaghmore	Tattyboy	- nr Magoney Br.	corn	-	-	-	-	-	-	1"os/	70
Monaghan	Team *	Cunningham William :	mill	-	-	-	Cunnungham - Kineer Jas	1811	-	dd/	634 493 437500
Monaghan	Tenary	McMorran John :	mils	-	-	-	McMorran - Armstrong :	1817	-	dd/	717 170 490305
Tedavnet	Teraverty	- on Blackwater R.	flax	-	-	-	-	-	-	6"os/	9
Tedavnet	Teraverty	Read Thomas	corn	-	-	-	Westenra Richard	-	12.6x2.2x4	osm/	-
Tedavnet	Teraverty	Read Thomas	flax	-	-	-	Westenra Richard	-	13.6x3x4 :	osm/	-
Tedavnet	Teraverty	Read Thomas	flax & corn	- ho., office, land	17a.	-	-	-	-	gr	-
Kilmore	Tetoppa	-	corn & flax	-	-	-	-	-	-	6"os/	13
Monaghan	Thornford	-	mill	-	-	-	-	-	-	1"os/	70
Aghnamullen	Tieneleney	-	corn	-	-	-	-	-	10x2.4x -	osm/	-
Aghnamullen	Tievanely	McGuire Terence	corn & kiln & land	-	1.2.0	7.10	-	-	-	gr	-
Aghabog	Tinary	-	flax & mill dam	-	-	-	-	-	-	6"os/	12
Magheross	Tirnadrola	Johnston James	corn	-	3a.	-	-	-	-	gr/	-
Monaghan	Toam *	Shegog William :	grist	-	-	-	Shegog - Clourtney Ed :	1817	-	dd/	714 162 488491
Aghnamullen	Tooay	Forbes Mr	bleach	-	-	-	-	-	- discontinued	osm/	-
Clontibret	Toome	- NW/ B'larnan Br.	corn, kiln & pond	-	-	-	-	1836	-	6"os/	19
Clontibret	Toome	Fitzpatrick Patrick	corn & flax	-	-	8	-	1856	-	gr	-

PARISH	TOWNLAND		MILLER	TYPE	HOUSE	Land	£Val	PROPRIETORS	Date	WHEEL etc.	Record	Ref.
Donaghmore	Townland ?		-	-	-	-	-	-	-	-	osm/	-
Donaghmore	Townland ?		-	-	-	-	-	-	-	-	osm/	-
Donaghmore	Townland ?		-	-	-	-	-	-	-	-	osm/	-
Magheross	Townland ?		-	mill	-	-	-	-	-	-	osm/	-
Magheross	Townland ?		-	mill	-	-	-	-	-	-	osm/	-
Magheross	Townland ?		-	mill	-	-	-	-	-	-	osm/	-
Errigal Trough	Tullyard		-	corn & mill dam	-	-	-	-	-	-	6"os/	13
Errigal Trough	Tullyard		McCormack Thomas	corn & kiln & land	-	25a.	32.10	-	1865	-	gr	-
Errigal Trough	Tullyard		McCormack Thos	corn & kiln	(1A) 79x25x26.6	-	-	-	-	23.6x3x23 72 bkts.	hob/	5.1311
Monaghan	Tullycelase	*	- E/ Shantonagh L.	beetling	-	-	-	-	1836	-	6"os/	27
Monaghan	Tullyear	*	-	mill	-	-	-	-	-	-	1"os/	58
Aghnamullen	Tullyglass		-	beetling & mill rac	-	-	-	-	1836	-	6"os/	27
Aghnamullen	Tullyglass		-	corn & pond	-	-	-	-	1836	-	6"os/	27
Aghnamullen	Tullyglass		Forbes Mr	beetling, bleach	-	-	-	-	-	-	osm/	-
Aghnamullen	Tullyglass		Rothwell Thomas	flax	-	-	15	-	1856	-	gr	-
Aghnamullen	Tullyglass		Rothwell Thomas	spinning	-	-	-	-	1856	-	gr	-
Aghnamullen	Tullyglish		Forbes Jno :	mills	-	-	-	Forbes J - Stevenson Jn :	1811	Mort. 23 Feb.	dd/	636 254 437291
Tehallan	Tullynanure		-	corn & mill pond	-	-	-	-	-	-	6"os/	10
Tehallan	Tullynanure		Campbell George	corn	ho., offs. & land	35a.	34.5	-	1856	-	gr	-
Tehallan	Tullynanure		Campbell George	corn	-	-	-	Maxwell John	-	13x3x2	osm/	-
Tehallan	Tullynanure		Campbell George	corn & land	-	35a.	26.5	-	26.5	-	gr	-
Aghnamullen	Tullyrain		Roe Michael	corn & flax mills :	-	93a.	122	-	1856	-	gr	-

PARISH	TOWNLAND	MILLER	TYPE	HOUSE	Land	£Val	PROPRIETORS	Date	WHEEL etc.	Record	Ref.
bo/Ballyboy	Aanard	Doyle (as Master)	mils	-	-	-	Doyle - Connell	-	-	dd/	374 159 248525
bo/Ballyboy	Aanard	Lucas	mils	-	-	-	Lucas - Champaigne	-	-	dd/	192 486 128424
bo/Ballyboy	Aanard	Lucas Samuel :	mils	-	-	-	Lucas S - Coleman Chas :	1748	-	dd/	131 230 88809
bo/Ballyboy	Aanard	Saxten James :	mils	-	-	-	Saxten J - Lucas Sam :	1747	-	dd/	128 491 87705
Durrow	Acantha	-	corn & mill race	-	-	-	-	1841	-	6"os/	9
Durrow	Acantha	-	distillery	-	-	-	-	1841	-	6"os/	9
Durrow	Acantha	Scully Edward	corn	37.0x20.0x10 :	-	-	-	1853	- outside wheel :	hob/	5.1339
Durrow	Acantha	Woods Christopher	tuck	26.6x23x7 & dw :	-	-	-	1852	7x4 c.30 buckets :	hob/	5.1339
Durrow	Acantha	Woods Edward	corn	-	-	-	-	-	12x3x10	vmb/	14
bo/Ballyboy	Accurard	Connell	mill	-	-	-	Connell - Chenevix	-	-	dd/	367 414 248820
Offaly	Acklin Big *	-	corn & corn kiln	-	-	-	-	1841	-	6"os/	9
Offaly	Acklin Big *	-	mill stream	-	-	-	-	1841	-	6"os/	9
Offaly	Acklin Little *	-	corn in ruins, pond	-	-	-	-	1841	-	6"os/	9
Killagally	Aghaboy	- E. side R. Brosna	flour	-	-	-	-	1841	-	6"os/	14
Killagally	Aghaboy	Delaney Robert	flour	-	-	-	-	-	14x6x5	vmb/	14
Killagally	Aghaboy	Delaney Robert	oat	-	-	-	-	-	14x5x5	vmb/	14
Seirkieran	Aghagurty	- N side small R.	corn	-	-	-	-	1841	-	6"os/	39
Seirkieran	Aghagurty	Carey Edward	corn	-	90a.	-	-	-	-	gr/	-
Seirkieran	Aghagurty	Carrey Edward	corn	37x25x28	-	-	-	1850	14x5x10 48 bkts :	hob/	5.1336
Croghan	Aghamore	-	corn & corn kiln	-	-	-	-	1841	-	6"os/	10
Offaly	Aghanore *	Kearney Patrick	corn	-	11a.	-	-	-	-	gr/	-
Offaly	Aghanvilla	- at Bloomfield	corn	-	-	-	-	-	-	1"os/	118
Tisaran	Annaghmore	Armitt ?	mills	-	-	-	Armit - Shaw	-	-	dd/	574 525 394777
Tisaran	Annaghmore	Armstrong	mills	-	-	-	Armstrong - Craven	-	-	dd/	266 339 171224
Tisaran	Annaghmore	Armstrong	mills	-	-	-	Armstrong - Clarke	-	-	dd/	279 629 184674
Gallen	Annaghmore	Bagnal Abraham	oat	-	-	-	-	-	14x4x4	vmb/	14
Tisaran	Annaghmore	Lestrange	mills	-	-	-	Lestrange - Carlton	-	-	dd/	265 264 175058
Tisaran	Annaghmore	Lestrange	mills	-	-	-	Lestrange - Weir	-	-	dd/	494 459 322474
Tisaran	Annaghmore	Lestrange	mills	-	-	-	Lestrange - Lestrange	-	-	dd/	507 16 326871
Tisaran	Annaghmore	Lestrange	mills	-	-	-	Lestrange - Moloney	-	-	dd/	512 153 333078
Tisaran	Annaghmore	O`Connor	mills	-	-	-	O`Connor - Lambert	-	-	dd/	563 225 375655
Gallen	Annaghmore	Seale Thomas	oat	-	-	-	-	-	14x2x3	vmb/	14
Tisaran	Annaghmore	Upton	mills	-	-	-	Upton - Buxton	-	-	dd/	528 17? 339076
Tisaran	Annaghmore	Upton	mills	-	-	-	Upton - Redington	-	-	dd/	574 515 394727
Tisaran	Annaghmore	Wilson	mills	-	-	-	Wilson - Whitfield	-	-	dd/	206 386 136550
Reynagh	Ballaghanogher	-	corn	-	-	-	-	1841	-	6"os/	30
Reynagh	Ballaghanogher	-	large mill pond	-	-	-	-	1841	-	6"os/	30
Reynagh	Ballaghanogher	-	rape & corn kiln	-	-	-	-	1841	-	6"os/	30
Reynagh	Ballaghanogher	-	Rapemill Vge.	-	-	-	-	1841	-	6"os/	30
Reynagh	Ballaghanoher	Dillon Frederick	corn & oats	39x21.6x21 kiln :	-	-	-	1845	-	hob/	5.1377
Reynagh	Ballaghanoher	Dillon Frederick	mill	-	12a.	-	-	-	-	gr/	-
Reynagh	Ballaghanoher	Dillon Frederick	rape	19x21.6x21 mill & :	-	-	-	-	-	hob/	5.1377
Reynagh	Ballaghanoher	Dillon W F	oat	-	-	-	-	-	15x4x7	vmb/	14
Kilmanaghan	Ballinaminton	Henderson	mill	-	-	-	Henderson - Robinson	-	-	dd/	599 236 410963
Kilmanaghan	Ballinaminton	Robinson Samuel :	corn	-	-	-	Robinson - Simmons Thos	1810	-	dd/	604 117 413731
Kilmanaghan	Ballinaminton	Robinson Samuel :	mill	-	-	-	Robinson - Simmons Thos	1810	-	dd/	622 128 428648
Kinnitty	Ballincur	Foster Maria	flour	-	-	-	-	-	16x4x16	vmb/	14
Kinnitty	Ballincur	Glass Andrew	corn	-	28a.	-	-	-	-	gr/	-
Offaly	Ballingladdy *	-	Castle in ruins	-	-	-	-	1841	-	6"os/	35
Offaly	Ballingladdy *	-	malt house	-	-	-	-	1841	-	6"os/	39
Offaly	Ballingladdy *	-	old malt mill	-	-	-	-	1841	-	6"os/	35
Offaly	Ballingladdy *	-	old malt mill	-	-	-	-	1841	-	6"os/	35

PARISH	TOWNLAND	MILLER	TYPE	HOUSE	Land	£Val	PROPRIETORS	Date	WHEEL etc.	Record	Ref.
Birr / Drumcullen	Ballinree	-	corn & corn kiln	-	-	-	-	1841	-	6"os/	35
Birr / Drumcullen	Ballinree+B102	Clements Griffith	corn	-	14a.	-	-	-	-	gr/	-
Ballyboy	Ballyboy	-	flour	-	-	-	-	1841	-	6"os/	31
Ballyboy	Ballyboy	-	mill race (long)	-	-	-	-	1841	-	6"os/	31
Ballyboy	Ballyboy	- at Mount Erin	rape mills	-	-	-	-	-	-	1"os/	117
Ballyboy	Ballyboy	Delaney William	corn	-	-	-	-	-	14x4x7	vmb/	14
Ballyboy	Ballyboy	Delaney William	flour	-	-	-	-	-	14x3x7	vmb/	14
Ballyboy	Ballyboy Town	-	mill	-	-	-	-	-	-	hob/	5.3184
Ballyboy	Ballyboy Town	Delany William	corn	81x21.6x30 & kiln :	-	33		1842	14x3.9x7 2 pr st. :	hob/	5.3184
Offaly	Ballycomber *	- W/ B'cumber Br.	linen factory	-	-	-	-	1841	-	6"os/	7
Kiladerry	Ballycommon Beg	McIlray John	corn	-	-	-	-	-	10x2x4	vmb/	14
Lemanaghan	Ballycumber	Armstrong	mill	-	-	-	Armstrong - Wetherell	-	?	dd/	172 50 114977
Lemanaghan	Ballycumber	Armstrong	mill	-	-	-	Armstrong - McGuire	-	-	dd/	490 61 311041
Lemanaghan	Ballycumber	Armstrong	mills	-	-	-	Armstrong - Armstrong	-	-	dd/	197 482 131353
Lemanaghan	Ballycumber	Bever	mill	-	-	-	Bever - Armstrong	-	-	dd/	585 300 390810
Lemanaghan	Ballycumber	Chambre Calcot	mill	-	-	-	Chambre Calcot - Wolfe	-	?	dd/	146 501 98565
Lemanaghan	Ballycumber	Clarke	mill	-	-	-	Clarke - Smith	-	-	dd/	498 124 316228
Lemanaghan	Ballycumber	Clarke	mill	-	-	-	Clarke - Clark	-	-	dd/	558 418 370291
Lemanaghan	Ballycumber	Horne	mill	-	-	-	Horne - Horne	-	-	dd/	384 496 256248
Lemanaghan	Ballycumber	Maguire	mill	-	-	-	Maguire - Esamond	-	-	dd/	535 131 350131
Lemanaghan	Ballycumber	Marsh	mill	-	-	-	Marsh - Armstrong	-	?	dd/	147 264 99705
Lemanaghan	Ballycumber	Marsh	mill	-	-	-	Marsh - Wilson	-	?	dd/	173 52 115329
Lemanaghan	Ballycumber	Mulloy Dr Thos H	blue mill	-	-	-	-	-	14x4x3	vmb/	14
Lemanaghan	Ballycumber	Robins Patrick	corn	-	38a.	-	-	-	-	gr/	-
Lemanaghan	Ballycumber	Rolle	mill	-	-	-	Rolle - Armstrong	-	?	dd/	157 476 105524
Lemanaghan	Ballycumber	Wetherell	mill	-	-	-	Wetherell - Boland	-	?	dd/	170 242 113858
Lemanaghan	Ballycumber	Wetherell	mill	-	-	-	Wetherell - Brown	-	-	dd/	198 543 133524
Lemanaghan	Ballycumber Tn	Armstrong Capt.	mill (not working)	-	-	7	-	1844	- [no dims.] note :	hob/	5.3185
Lemanaghan	Ballycumber Tn	Mulloy Dr Thomas H	blue & drying ho.	-	-	-	-	-	-	gr/	-
Lemanaghan	Ballycumber Tn	Mullroy Dr Thomas	blue	29.6x24x16 & :	-	8.17	-	-	-	hob/	5.3185
Roscrea	Ballyduff	-	corn	-	-	-	-	1841	-	6"os/	16
Roscrea	Ballyduff	-	corn & mill race	-	-	-	-	1841	-	6"os/	43
Roscrea	Ballyduff	Hanlon John	corn	39x17.6x16.6 kiln :	-	-	-	1853	16x4x12 2 pr. st. :	hob/	5.1334
Roscrea	Ballyduff	Hanlon John	mills	-	-	-	Hanlon John - Rudd W	1862	-	dd/	1852 29 96
Roscrea	Ballyduff	Hanlon Marcus	mills	-	-	-	Hanlon M - Going John	1864	-	dd/	1864 14 183
Kilbride	Ballyduff	Molloy Denis	corn	27.6x26x12 :	-	-	-	1842	- breast 30 bkts :	hob/	5.1341
Kilbride	Ballyduff	Molloy Denis	corn	-	-	-	-	-	10x4x7	vmb/	14
Roscrea	Ballyduff	Whitten Edward	mills	-	-	-	Whitten Ed - Hanlon Mark	1863	-	dd/	1862 15 21
	Ballyglass	-	corn & mill dam	-	-	-	-	1841	-	6"os/	18
Monasteroris	Ballyhugh	- NW/ Newtown Br.	corn & mill pond	-	-	-	-	1841	-	6"os/	11
Monasteroris	Ballyhugh	Gillard Richard	corn & kiln	-	31a.	-	-	-	-	gr/	-
Monasteroris	Ballyhugh	Gilliard Richd (miller)	corn	48.6x22.6x20 & kiln	-	-	-	1842	10x3x4 all wood :	hob/	5.1365
Ballyboy	Ballynacarrig	-	cloth	-	-	-	-	1841	-	6"os/	32
Ballyboy	Ballynacarrig	-	flour	-	-	-	-	1841	-	6"os/	32
Ballyboy	Ballynacarrig	Delaney William	flour	66.0x20.0x24 & :	-	-	-	1853	13x3x8 3 pr. st. dia :	hob/	5.1316
Ballyboy	Ballynacarrig	Delaney William	flour	-	-	-	-	-	13x3x8 3 pr st. :	vmb/	14
Ballyboy	Ballynacarrig	Delaney William	cloth	-	-	-	-	-	12x2x7	vmb/	14
Ballyboy	Ballynacarrig	Delaney William	tuck	-	-	-	-	-	mill is in ruins :	vmb/	14
Ballyboy	Ballynacarrig	Delany William	mill	-	79a.	-	-	-	-	gr/	-
Ballyboy	Ballynacarrig	Jackson James	mill	-	180a.	-	-	-	-	gr/	-
Eglish	Ballynaghuilsha	-	corn & kiln	-	-	-	-	1841	-	6"os/	30
Eglish	Ballynaguisha	Smith M Berry	corn	-	-	-	-	-	14x5x6	vmb/	14

PARISH	TOWNLAND	MILLER	TYPE	HOUSE	Land	£Val	PROPRIETORS	Date	WHEEL etc.	Record	Ref.
Offaly	Ballynahinch *	-	corn & kiln	-	-	-	-	1841	-	6"os/	1
Kilbride	Ballynasrah or :	Kelly Thomas	corn	-	-	-	-	-	10x6x14	vmb/	14
Kilbride	Ballynasrah or :	Bryen Daniel	corn & kiln	21x19.6x14.6 kiln :	-	-	-	1842	- breast good fall :	hob/	5.1341
Ballyboy	Ballyoran	- at Ballyboy	corn	-	-	-	John Flynn	1999	-	ph/wh	B
Ballyboy	Ballyoran	- at Ballyboy	mill	-	-	-	-	-	-	1"os/	117
Ballyboy	Ballyoran	Delaney William	corn	-	-	-	-	-	12x4x5 not worked :	vmb/	14
Ballyboy	Ballyoran	Jackson James	corn & kiln	55.6x19x15 & mill :	-	-	-	1853	12x5x2 32 bkts. :	hob/	5.1314
Aghancon	Ballyrickard Beg	Evans John	thrashing & bone	173x21.6x18 :	-	-	-	-	bone grinding m/c. :	hob/	5.1355
Kinnitty	Ballyshane	-	corn & mill pond	-	-	-	-	1841	-	6"os/	36
Offaly	Ballyshear	-	mill	-	-	-	-	-	-	1"os/	118
Offaly	Ballystrig	-	old windmill	-	-	-	-	-	-	1"os/	110
Kilcolmin	Ballytoran	-	old distillery	-	-	-	-	1841	-	6"os/	41
Offaly	Ballywilliamreagh	- on Silver R	corn	-	-	-	-	-	-	1"os/	118
Reynagh	Banagher Town	Harton John L	flour, corn (steam)	81.6x23.6x33 :	-	53	-	-	wheel is ruined :	hob/	5.3186
Reynagh	Banagher Town	Haughton's mill	flour	- large, ruinous : :	-	-	-	2009	-	mmSv/	wh - R
Reynagh	Banagher Town	Mulloy Keran	distillery	46x23.6x20 incl. :	-	-	-	1844	no wheel, this is :	hob/	5.3186
Reynagh	Banagher Town	Scott Adam (1884 :	distillery	-	-	-	-	2009	-	mmSv/	wh - Z
Reynagh	Banagher Town	Trench Henry	flour, corn (steam)	-	0.1.34	-	-	-	-	gr/	-
Offaly	Barrynaguilsha	Berry Smith M	corn	-	49a.	-	-	-	-	gr/	-
Tisaran	Bellmount	-	tuck	-	-	-	-	1841	-	6"os/	14
Tisaran	Bellmount	- on Brosna R	mill	-	-	-	-	-	-	1"os/	117
Tisaran	Bellmount	- W/ Belmount Br.	flour	-	-	-	-	1841	-	6"os/	14
Tisaran	Bellmount	Atkinson Charles	flour & oat	-	-	-	-	-	15x5x5	vmb/	14
Tisaran	Bellmount	Atkinson Charles	old tuck mill	-	-	-	-	-	12x3x5	vmb/	14
Tisaran	Belmont	- imed. SW B'm Br.	corn	- nicely restored	-	-	John Dolan	2009	- turbine installed	mmSv/	wh - Ce
bo/Coolyst`n	Belmont Mill	Holmes	mill	-	-	-	Holmes - Holmes	-	-	dd/	296 405 1976?82
bo/Coolyst`n	Belmont Mill	Holmes	mill	-	-	-	Holmes - Holmes	-	-	dd/	319 150 211394
bo/Coolyst`n	Belmont Mill	Holmes	mill	-	-	-	Holmes - Deveril	-	-	dd/	320 461 219643
bo/Coolyst`n	Belmont Mill	Holmes	mill	-	-	-	Holmes - Lestrange	-	-	dd/	415 474 273399
bo/Coolyst`n	Belmont Mill	Marsh	mill	-	-	-	Marsh - Wetherell	-	-	dd/	203 566 136747
bo/Coolyst`n	Belmont Mill	Marsh	mill	-	-	-	Marsh - Armstrong	-	-	dd/	217 303 144014
bo/Coolyst`n	Belmont Mill	Marsh	mill	-	-	-	Marsh - Keeran	-	-	dd/	222 24 145211
Tisaran	Belmount	Perry R. & Son	Belmount Mills	-	-	-	-	-	Francis 67kw open :	turb/	c1947
Tisaran	Belmount /Lisderg	Collins John	steam	-	200a.	-	-	-	-	gr/	-
Tisaran	Belmount /Lisderg	L`Estrange Thomas	corn (dilapidated)	-	57a.	-	-	-	-	gr/	-
Tisaran	Belmount /Lisderg	L`Estrange Thomas	tuck	-	-	-	-	-	-	gr/	-
Tisaran	Belmount Dem.	Perry Henry	mills	-	-	-	Perry Henry - Perry W J	1864	-	dd/	1864 29 292
Tisaran	Belmount Dem.	Perry Henry	mills	-	-	-	Perry Henry - Perry Wm	1864	-	dd/	1864 30 13
Birr	Birr	Elliott	bleach yard	-	-	-	Elliott - Short	-	-	dd/	389 27 255539
Birr	Birr	Elliott	bleach yard	-	-	-	Elliott - Short	-	-	dd/	389 27 255539
Birr	Birr	Rosse Lord	Birr Castle	-	-	-	-	-	Francis Craig /8 :	turb/	c1947
Birr	Birr Town	-	The Maltings	-	-	-	-	-	-	ph/wh	Cp
Birr	Birr Town	Hackett Jemina	Birr Distillery & Id.	-	-	-	Hackett J - Wallace Richd	1876	-	dd/	1876 26 67
Birr	Birr Town	Robinson Thomas	Manor Mills	-	-	-	-	1849	-	dd/	1849 15 208
Birr	Birr Town	Robinson Thomas	Manor Mills	-	-	-	Robinson T - Butler Luke	1849	-	dd/	1849 15 295
Birr	Birr Town :	Froste Richard	Burkes Mill	-	-	-	Froste R - King Sir Richd	1876	-	dd/	1876 2 238
Birr	Birr Town :	Robinson Chris	Manor Mill	-	-	-	Robinson - Warburton Jn	1842	-	dd/	8142 2 164
Birr	Birr Town :	Booth Wiliam	Burkes Mill	-	-	-	Booth Wm - Gerard Thos	1886	-	dd/	1886 7 288
Birr	Birr Town :	Fair James W	Burkes Mill	-	-	-	Fair James - Booth Wm S	1887	-	dd/	1887 20268
Birr	Birr Town :	Maher Jeremiah & :	flour	66x37.6x34 :	-	54	-	1854	20x12x11.9 64 bkts :	hob/	5.3205 (*)
Birr	Birr Town :	Robinson Chris	flour	66x37.6x34 part :	-	-	-	1854	20x12x11.4 new :	hob/	5.3202 (*)
Birr	Birr Townsparks	-	mill	-	-	-	-	-	-	hob/	5.3203

PARISH	TOWNLAND	MILLER	TYPE	HOUSE	Land	£Val	PROPRIETORS	Date	WHEEL etc.	Record	Ref.
Birr	Birr Townsparks	-	mill	-	-	-	-	-	-	hob/	5.3203
Birr	Birr Townsparks	Hackett Michael	corn & malt stores	-	-	-	-	-	-	gr/	-
Birr	Birr Townsparks	Maher & Sutherland	flour	-	2.3.0	-	-	-	-	gr/	-
Birr	Birr Townsparks	Robinson Chris	corn	-	-	-	-	-	-	vmb/	14
Birr	Birr Townsparks	Robinson Chris	flour	-	-	-	-	-	18x15x10 4 pr st.	vmb/	14
Birr	Birr Townsparks	Robinson Robert	corn	-	-	-	-	-	15x3x6	vmb/	14
Birr	Birr Townsparks	Robinson Robt & S.	distillery (dilap.)	-	-	-	-	-	-	gr/	-
Birr	Birr Townsparks	Robinson Robt & S.	malt stores	-	-	-	-	-	-	gr/	-
Birr	Birr Townsparks	Robinson Robt & S.	old brewery	-	-	-	-	-	-	gr/	-
Ballykean	Bogtown	-	corn & mill pond	-	-	-	-	1841	-	6"os/	26
Ballykean	Bogtown	-	old mill	-	-	-	-	1841	-	6"os/	26
Ballykean	Bogtown	Adamson	mill	-	-	-	Adamson - Adamson	-	?	dd/	155 38 103434
Ballykean	Bogtown	Adamson	mill	-	-	-	Adamson - Hancock	-	?	dd/	173 244 116083
Ballykean	Bogtown	Conner Thos & M	corn	-	-	-	-	-	14x3x7	vmb/	14
Ballykean	Bogtown	Connor Thos & Mk	corn	26x20.6x9 new :	31a.	-	-	1846	14x3.6x7 breast :	hob/	5.1403
Ballykean	Bogtown	Gilliard	mill	-	-	-	Giliard - Smith	-	-	dd/	506 412 332347
Ballykean	Bogtown	Tuthill	mill	-	-	-	Tuthill & W - Adamson	-	?	dd/	160 114 106660
Ballykean	Bogtown	Tuthill	mill	-	-	-	Tuthill - Labal	-	-	dd/	207 525 138220
Rahan	Boheraugrisha	Molloy Thomas	corn	37x25x25 & kiln :	-	-	-	1853	14.6x8 undershot :	hob/	5.1346
Rahan	Bohernagrisna	-	corn & corn kiln	-	-	-	-	1841	-	6"os/	7
Rahan	Bohernagrisna	Molloy Thomas	corn	-	-	-	-	-	15x8x1	vmb/	14
Offaly	Bolart	-	mill	-	-	-	-	-	-	1"os/	109
Ballycommon	Bracklin Big	McIlroy Terence	corn	23x17.6x9 & kiln :	15a.	-	-	-	- 2 pair stones :	hob/	5.1396
Ballycommon	Bracklin Little	-	corn	-	-	-	-	-	-	1"os/	109
Clonsast	Bracknagh	- SW/ Johnville Br.	flour	-	-	-	-	1841	-	6"os/	27
Clonsast	Bracknagh	Abbot John	flour	-	-	-	-	-	-	gr/	-
Clonsast	Bracknagh	Abbot John	flour	62.6x19x23 & ret. :	-	-	-	1842	15.6 u`shot 30 bkts.	hob/	5.1363
Clonsast	Bracknagh	Montgomery	bolting	-	-	-	Montgomery - Despard	-	-	dd/	453 63 288615
Clonsast	Bracknagh	O`Reilly	bolting	-	-	-	O`Reilly - Bellew	-	-	dd/	592 390 403100
Clonsast	Bracknagh	Poole	bolting	-	-	-	Poole - Dempley	-	-	dd/	528 155 345631
Offaly	Bunakeeran	-	corn	-	-	-	-	-	-	1"os/	118
Reynagh	Bunrevan	-	Bunrevan Mill	-	-	-	-	-	-	ph/wh	B
Reynagh	Bunrevan	- Bunrevan Mill	corn	- old large blds. :	-	-	-	1998	-	mmSv/	wh - B
Reynagh	Bunrevan	Cruise John	oat	-	-	-	-	-	13x3x4	vmb/	14
Reynagh	Bunrevan	Leicester H. & J.	corn	-	-	-	-	-	-	gr/	-
Letterluna	Cadamstown	-	mill	-	-	-	-	1841	-	6"os/	37
Letterluna	Cadamstown	-	mill pond	-	-	-	-	1841	-	6"os/	37
Letterluna	Cadamstown	- near Tullamore	corn	walls only remain :	-	-	- Paddy Heany	1999	- phos. taken	mmSv/	wh - D
Letterluna	Cadamstown	nr Tullamore :	corn	-	-	-	-	-	-	ph/wh	D
Letterluna	Cadamstown	Manifold George	corn	68.6x19.6x32.6 :	-	-	-	1853	14.3x2.8x14.3 new :	hob/	5.1328
Letterluna	Cadamstown	Manifold George	mill	-	37a.	-	-	-	-	gr/	-
Letterluna	Cadamstown	Maryfold Daniel	corn	-	-	-	-	-	14x3x14	vmb/	14
Killoughy	Cappagowlan	-	corn	-	-	-	-	1841	-	6"os/	32
Killoughy	Cappagowlan	- on Silver R	mills	-	-	-	-	-	-	1"os/	118
Killoughy	Cappagowlan	Assatis Jonathan	corn & kiln	24x19.6x14.6 kiln :	-	-	-	1853	13.6x3.3x4.6 3 pr. :	hob/	5.1317
Geashill	Cappancur	Flanagan William	corn & kiln	53x21.6x17.6 kiln :	-	-	-	1842	12.8x4.8x10 2 pr. :	hob/	5.1386
Geashill	Cappancur	O`Flanagan James	corn	-	-	-	-	-	13x5x10	vmb/	14
Ardnurcher	Cappydonnell Little	-	corn	-	-	-	-	-	10x3x7	vmb/	14
Ardnurcher	Cappydonnell Little	Buckley Timothy	corn	-	-	-	-	-	10x3x7	vmb/	14
Ofly	Cartron East	- nr Gormagh Br.	corn	-	-	-	-	-	-	1"os/	109
Killaderry	Castlebarnagh	-	old windmill	-	-	-	-	1841	-	6"os/	18
Ofly	Castlegarry *	Armstrong Wm B	distillery, not in use		-	-	-	-	-	gr/	-

PARISH	TOWNLAND	MILLER	TYPE	HOUSE	Land	£Val	PROPRIETORS	Date	WHEEL etc.	Record	Ref.
Ofly	Castlegarry *	Armstrong Wm B	flour & corn	-	7a.	-	-	-	-	gr/	-
Ofly	Castletown	- nr Kilmaine Ho.	mill	-	-	-	-	-	-	1"os/	117
Kilbride	Clara	- Clara Mills	flour	old mill & chimney	-	-	-	1999	-	mmSv/	wh - D
Kilbride	Clara	- in Clara Village :	flour	-	-	-	-	-	-	ph/wh	D
Kilbride	Clara	Robinson Samuel	bone	-	-	-	-	-	16x4x5	vmb/	14
Kilbride	Clara	Robinson Samuel	corn	-	-	-	-	-	16x3x5	vmb/	14
Kilbride	Clara	Robinson Samuel	corn	-	-	-	-	-	14x5x5	vmb/	14
Kilbride	Clara	Robinson Samuel	flour	-	-	-	-	-	16x2x5	vmb/	14
Kilbride	Clara & Town	-	flour and corn	-	-	-	-	1841	-	6"os/	8
Kilbride	Clara Charlestn	Goodbody Jonathan	flour	41x25x49 also :	-	-	-	1844	no. 1: 36 float bds. :	hob/	5.3190
Kilbride	Clara Charlestn	Perry Robert & Co	flour	84x46x52 kilns :	82a.	-	-	1844	96 float boards :	hob/	5.3190
Kilbride	Clara Town	Robinson Samuel	flour (Bridge St.)	53x27x21 also :	71a.	-	-	1844	18x3, 16x2.9, 18x8 :	hob/	5.3190
Kilbride	Clara Town :	Robinson Samuel	lace factory	-	-	4	-	1856	-	gr/	a.a.Ire.ie
Offaly	Clonahenoge	- on R Shannon	mill	-	-	-	-	-	-	1"os/	117
Clonsast	Clonavoe	- S/ Figile R.	corn & mill pond	-	-	-	-	1841	-	6"os/	19
Clonsast	Clonavoe	Ryan Margaret	corn & kiln	-	-	-	-	-	-	gr/	-
Clonsast	Clonavoe	Ryan Margaret wid.	corn	29.6x20.6x9 & kiln :	-	-	-	-	9x2.6x6 30 bkts. :	hob/	5.1363
Drumcullen	Clonbrone	Mills Nathaniel	corn	mill & kiln 38x17.6x9	-	-	-	1843	10x2.6x2 very old :	hob/	5.1367
Drumcullen	Clonbrone	Mills Nathaniel	corn	-	-	-	-	-	13x2x3	vmb/	14
Clonsast	Clonbulloge	- NW/ Clonbull' Br.	corn	-	-	-	-	1841	-	6"os/	19
Clonsast	Clonbulloge	Downshire Marq.	corn (dilapidated)	-	-	-	-	-	-	gr/	-
Offaly	Clondallon	- on Brosna R	mill	-	-	-	-	-	-	1"os/	117
Kilcomin	Clonlisk	-	corn	-	-	-	-	1841	-	6"os/	45
Kilcomin	Clonlisk	Kelly Michael	flour	-	-	-	-	-	14x3x7	vmb/	14
Clonmacnoise	Clonmacnoise	-	corn	-	-	-	-	1845	-	1"os/	5
Clonmacnoise	Clonmacnoise	Connor John	oat & wheat	-	-	-	-	-	10x2x11 mill is	vmb/	14
Clonmacnoise	Clonmacnoise	Connor Thomas	corn & kiln	-	38a.	-	-	-	-	gr/	-
Birr	Clonoghil Upper	-	Millbrook Cottage	-	-	-	-	1841	-	6"os/	35
Birr	Clonoghill Upper	Hackett Michael	corn mill	-	-	-	-	-	16x11x6	vmb/	14
Birr	Clonoghill Upper	Hackett Michael	distillery	-	40a.	-	-	-	-	gr/	-
Birr	Clonoghill Upper	Hackett Michael	distillery	-	-	-	-	-	-	vmb/	14
Birr	Clonoghill Upper	Hackett Michael	malt & stores	-	-	-	-	-	-	gr/	-
Birr	Clonoghill Upper	Hackett Thomas	flour & corn	-	23a.	-	-	-	-	gr/	-
Birr	Clonoghill Upper	Palmer John	corn	-	17a.	-	-	-	-	gr/	-
Birr	Clonoghill Upper	Palmer John	flour	-	-	-	-	-	13x4x5	vmb/	14
Birr	Clonoghill Upper	Palmer John	rape	-	-	-	-	-	-	gr/	-
Birr	Clonoghill Upper	Palmer John	rape	-	-	-	-	-	13x3x5 = 1 corn st.	vmb/	14
Rahan	Clonshanny	-	tuck & corn	-	-	-	-	1841	-	6"os/	7
Clonsast	Clonvara	Ryan Margaret	corn	-	-	-	-	1853	9x7 wood & iron :	hob/	5.1364
Ballykean	Clonygowan	-	brewery	-	-	-	-	1841	-	6"os/	33
Ballykean	Clonygowan	Odlum Wiliam Jun	old malt mill	26x24x8 bake ho :	35a.	24	holds from Mrs Dunne	1846	no dimensions	hob/	5.1403
Offaly	Cloughjordan	-	corn	-	-	-	-	-	-	1"os/	126
Kilcolman	Clucka North	Kelly Michael	mill & malt house	18x18x13.6 & :	-	-	-	-	no dimensions	hob/	5.1357
Clonsast	Clunbulloge	Downshire Marquis	corn	35x23x15 & kiln :	-	-	-	1842	no outside wheel :	hob/	5.1363
Offaly	Colehill	Sadlier Thomas	charcoal	13.6x15.6x21 also	-	-	-	1852	- the machinery :	hob/	5.1385
Offaly	Comms. Clonlish	Joynt Henry	mills	-	-	-	Joynt Henry - Richard	1864	-	dd/	1864 7 208
Birr	Crinkill	-	corn kiln, flour mill	-	-	-	-	1841	-	6"os/	36
Birr	Crinkill	-	mill	-	-	-	-	-	-	1"os/	117
Birr	Crinkill	Hackett Thomas	flour	-	-	-	-	-	24x6x24	vmb/	14
Birr	Crinkill	Hackett Thomas	flour & corn	95x19.6x30	-	-	-	-	14x7x8 32 bkts :	hob/	5.1321
Birr	Crinkill Town	Hackett Thomas	flour	100x33x44 & kiln :	-	75.5	-	1843	24x6.6x24 4 pr st. :	hob/	5.3188
Croghan	Croghan Demesne	-	corn & corn kiln	-	-	-	-	1841	-	6"os/	10

PARISH	TOWNLAND	MILLER	TYPE	HOUSE	Land	£Val	PROPRIETORS	Date	WHEEL etc.	Record	Ref.
Reynagh	Curraghavarna	Molloy Kiran	distillery	-	-	-	-	-	-	gr/	-
Drumcullen	Curraghmore	Warren Edward	mill	-	44a.	-	-	-	-	gr/	-
Drumcullen	Curraghmore	Warren Edward	mill	38.6x18x7.6 & :	-	-	-	1853	16x5x11 48 bkts. :	hob/	5.1366
Drumcullen	Curraghmore	Whitfield Abraham	corn	24x18x20 & kilns :	-	-	-	-	[no dims.] supplied :	hob/	5.1367
Drumcullen	Curraghmore	Whitfield Abraham	corn	-	-	-	-	-	16x5x12	vmb/	14
Offally	Curraghvarna *	-	brewery	-	-	-	-	1841	-	6"os/	21
Offally	Curraghvarna *	-	corn	-	-	-	-	1841	-	6"os/	21
Offally	Curraghvarna *	-	distillery	-	-	-	-	1841	-	6"os/	21
Offally	Curraghvarna *	- W/ Banagher Br.	Haughton's Mills	-	-	-	-	1841	-	6"os/	21
Ballyburly	Derryiron	Mooney Jn & Thos	corn	-	-	-	-	-	8x3x3	vmb/	14
Ballyburly	Derryiron	Mooney Jn & Thos	corn & kiln	-	91a.	-	-	-	-	gr/	-
Ballyburly	Derryiron	Mooney Jn & Thos	corn & kiln	26.6x20x11 kiln :	-	-	-	1852	no dimensions 3 pr. :	hob/	5.1409
Killoughy	Derrymore	Finamore Thomas	corn	-	-	-	-	-	14x6x9	vmb/	14
Offaly	Doon (? Qns)	Lyons John	oat	-	-	-	-	-	12x2x6	vmb/	14
Offaly	Doon (? Qns)	Lyons John	old tuck mill	-	-	-	-	-	12x1x6	vmb/	14
Lemanaghan	Doon Demesne	-	corn & corn kiln	-	-	-	-	1841	-	6"os/	6
Lemanaghan	Doon Demesne	Lyons John	corn	-	10a.	-	-	-	-	gr/	-
Kiladerry	Down	-	corn & mill pond	-	-	-	-	1841	-	6"os/	10
Kiladerry	Down	Mullagan James	corn	-	-	-	-	-	13x2x10	vmb/	14
Kiladerry	Down	Mulligan James	corn	46x22x19 also :	-	-	-	-	[no dims.] 2 pr st. :	hob/	5.1401
Roscrea	Drumakeenan	-	flour, mill pond, mill	-	-	-	-	1841	-	6"os/	42
Roscrea	Drumakeenan	-	mill, flour mill	-	-	-	-	1841	-	6"os/	42
Roscrea	Drumakeenan	-	oat mill & cloth fact	-	-	-	-	1841	-	6"os/	42
Roscrea	Drumakeenan	- SW/ Brosna Ho.	Brosna Flour Mill	-	-	-	-	1841	-	6"os/	42
Roscrea	Drumakeenan	Acres Adam	flour	-	-	-	-	-	16x6x10 3 pr st. :	vmb/	14
Roscrea	Drumakeenan	Buckley Henry	cloth factory	45x24x34 &16x18.6:	-	-	-	1850	10x4.6x15 50 bkts :	hob/	5.1359
Roscrea	Drumakeenan	Buckley Henry	cloth factory	-	-	-	-	-	18x4x14 1 willy :	vmb/	14
Roscrea	Drumakeenan	Buckley Henry	flour	-	-	-	-	1850	18x4.6x16 56 bkts :	hob/	5.1359
Roscrea	Drumakeenan	Buckley Henry	flour	-	-	-	-	-	18x4x16	vmb/	14
Roscrea	Drumakeenan	Dowd Richard	flour	-	-	-	-	-	20x10x4 5 pr st. :	vmb/	14
Roscrea	Drumakeenan	Dowd Robert	flour	48x34.6x26 & shed	-	-	-	1850	16.6x8x8 40 floats :	hob/	5.1359
Ettagh	Drumakeenan	Dowd Robert	flour	Hos., offs. & land	65a.	131	-	1856	-	gr/	a.a.Ire.ie
Ettagh	Drumakeenan	Dowd Robert	flour & kilns	64x38x37 return :	-	-	-	-	20x10x- breast :	hob/	5.1355
Ettagh	Drumakeenan	Fitzpatrick Patrick	corn	-	-	-	-	-	13x2x14	vmb/	14
Ettagh	Drumakeenan	Fitzpatrick Patrick	corn & kiln	54x20x21 & miller`s	-	-	-	-	12x2.6x12 overshot :	hob/	5.1355
Roscrea	Drumakeenan	Loughman Dn & Wm	corn & kiln	39.4x22x23.6 kiln :	-	-	-	1850	16x2.4x11 breast :	hob/	5.1359
Roscrea	Drumakeenan	Richard Dowd	flour	-	-	-	-	-	18x7x 7 4 pr st. :	vmb/	14
Roscrea	Drumakeeran	Acres George	flour	38x19x34 & :	-	-	-	1850	16x6x15 50 bkts. :	hob/	5.1359
Offaly	E./ Phillipstown	-	corn & mill dam	-	-	-	-	1841	-	6"os/	18
Ballykean	Eanaghan	Conner Thos & M	corn	-	-	-	-	-	13x3x7	vmb/	14
Ballykean	Eanaghan	Conner Thos & M	tuck	-	-	-	-	-	12x3x6	vmb/	14
Monasteroris	Edenderry	-	silver mine	-	-	-	-	1841	-	6"os/	12
Monasteroris	Edenderry	-	tanyard	-	-	-	-	1841	-	6"os/	12
Monasteroris	Edenderry Town	Andrews Mr	damask factory	88x23x21 more :	-	-	-	-	-	hob/	5.3193
Eglish	Eglish	- E/ Eglish Castle	flour	-	-	-	-	1841	-	6"os/	30
Eglish	Eglish	Berry Smith M	bleach	-	6a.	-	-	-	-	gr/	-
Ballykean	Enaghan	-	corn kiln, mill	-	-	-	-	1841	-	6"os/	26
Ballykean	Enaghan	-	mill pond	-	-	-	-	1841	-	6"os/	26
Ballykean	Enaghan	GoodwinJohn	corn	46x19x11.6 kiln :	-	-	formerly: Hanah Milner	1846	13.6x2 revs.7 /min.:	hob/	5.1403
Ballykean	Enaghan	GoodwinJohn	tuck	-	-	-	-	1846	12ft dia. 1 pr. feet :	hob/	5.1403
Kilbride	Erry : Maryborough	Dugdale John & Co	flour	-	-	-	-	-	28x7x13 6 pr st.	vmb/	14
Kilbride	Erry : Maryborough	Robert Perry & Co.	corn	- offices & Land	8a.	192	-	1856	-	gr/	a.a.Ire.ie

PARISH	TOWNLAND	MILLER	TYPE	HOUSE	Land	£Val	PROPRIETORS	Date	WHEEL etc.	Record	Ref.
Kilbride	Erry Marlbororough	-	flour & kiln	-	-	-	-	1841	-	6"os/	8
Offaly	Esker	-	corn	-	-	-	-	-	-	1"os/	108
Skeirkieran	Fancroft	-	flour & pond	-	-	-	-	1841	-	6"os/	43
Seirkieran	Fancroft	Bergin John	corn	34.6x24x34.6 7 &	-	-	-	1853	18x4.6x8 2 pair st.	hob/	5.1325
Seirkieran	Fancroft	Bergin John	corn	-	-	-	-	-	18x4x8	vmb/	14
Skeirkieran	Fancroft	Dupe Angela	flour	- for restoration	-	-	acq. by Marcus Sweeney	2006	- wheel repair : ar	Pho/	ms - B
Offaly	Fanure *	Landed Est. Court	mill	-	-	-	L.E.Ct - Jackson Fred	1863	-	dd/	1863 19 254
Gallen	Ferbane Town	Bagnal A	oat	46x23x16.6 return :	-	3.18	-	-	-	hob/	5.3195
Dunkerrin	Franckfort	Kelly James	kiln (addition)	16x14x8	-	-	-	-	(revsd.) 14x3.6x8 :	hob/	5.1354
Dunkerrin	Franckfort	Kelly Thomas	corn & store	31.6x22.6x18 & :	-	-	-	-	13.6x2x7 36 bkts. :	hob/	5.1354
Ballyboy	Frankford	-	brewery	-	-	-	-	1841	-	6"os/	31
Ballyboy	Frankford	-	corn	-	-	-	-	1841	-	6"os/	31
Ballyboy	Frankford	-	distillery	-	-	-	-	1841	-	6"os/	31
Ballyboy	Frankford	-	flour	-	-	-	-	1841	-	6"os/	31
Ballyboy	Frankford	Burris Charles	flour	-	-	-	-	-	15x7x4	vmb/	14
Ballyboy	Frankford	Kelly Thomas	corn	-	-	-	-	-	15x2x13	vmb/	14
Ballyboy	Frankford Town	Burris Charles	flour	52x21.6x20 & do. :	-	-	-	1842	15.6x6.10x4 2 pr. :	hob/	5.3195
Ballyboy	Frankford Town	Delaney William	corn & kiln	81x21.6x30 & kiln :	-	-	-	1853	15x7x7 32 bkts. :	hob/	5.1513
Ballyboy	Frankford Town	Little Charlotte	flour	52x21.6x20.6 dw :	-	-	-	1853	- no wk done 3 yrs :	hob/	5.1315
Ballyboy	Frankford Town	Little Charlotte	mill & stores	-	2a.	-	-	-	-	gr/	-
Ballyboy	Frankford Town	Mitchell Robert	brewery	-	-	-	-	-	-	gr/	-
Ballyboy	Frankford town	Mitchell Robert	brewery	78.6x15x10.6 & :	-	16.17	-	1842	-	hob/	5.3195
Ballyboy	Frankford Town	Mitchell Robert	brewery & stores	70x18.0x10.6 & :	-	-	-	1853	-	hob/	5.1315
Ballyboy	Frankford Town	Mitchell Robert	distillery	-	2a.	-	-	-	-	gr/	-
Ballyboy	Frankford Town	Mitchell Robert	distillery & malt ho.	78.4x26x17.6 dw :	-	-	-	1853	-	hob/	5.1315
Ballyboy	Frankford Town	Mitchell Robert	malt	29.6x29.6x21 & :	-	-	-	1853	-	hob/	5.1315
Ballyboy	Frankford Town	Mitchell Robert	steam distillery	78x26x17.6 & :	-	-	-	1842	-	hob/	5.3195
Ballyboy	Freagh	Drought Robert	corn & kiln	14.6x28.0x43 & :	-	-	-	1853	16x8x8 3 pr. st. :	hob/	5.1316
Gallen	Gallen	- SE/ Ferbane Br.	flour	-	-	-	-	1841	-	6"os/	14
Gallen	Gallen	Bagnall Abraham	corn & kiln	-	11a.	-	-	-	-	gr/	-
Reynagh	Garrycastle	-	corn kilns, mill ponc	-	-	-	-	1841	-	6"os/	29
Reynagh	Garrycastle	-	distillery	-	-	-	-	-	-	1"os/	117
Reynagh	Garrycastle	-	flour, corn, mill race	-	-	-	-	1841	-	6"os/	29
Reynagh	Garrycastle	Armstrong Wm B	corn & flour	42.6x21x34 & :	-	-	-	1845	[no dims.] or blds. :	hob/	5.1377
Reynagh	Garrycastle	Armstrong Wm B	distillery	140x24.6x40 & :	-	-	-	-	- [no dims] has - :	hob/	5.1377
Reynagh	Garrycastle	Armstrong Wm B	flour	-	-	-	-	-	30x6x24	vmb/	14
Reynagh	Garrycastle	Armstrong Wm B	oat	-	-	-	-	-	18x4x18	vmb/	14
Clonyhurk	Garryhinch	-	New Mill Land	-	-	-	-	1841	-	6"os/	33
Clonyhurk	Garryhinch	-	old mill in ruins	-	-	-	-	1841	-	6"os/	33
Offaly	Garrymona	- on Cushina R	mill	-	-	-	-	-	-	1"os/	119
Ettagh	Glasderry More	-	Mill Park	-	-	-	-	1841	-	6"os/	42
Kilcolman	Glasshouse	Tracy John	flour & kiln	44.0x21.0x29 also :	-	-	-	-	22x718 breast :	hob/	5.1357
Templeharry	Gorraun	-	flour	-	-	-	-	1841	-	6"os/	44
Templeharry	Gorraun	Armitage Benjamin	corn	66.6x21.6x19.6 & :	-	-	-	-	14x4.9x15 40 bkts.:	hob/	5.1361
Templeharry	Gorraun	Armitage Benjamin	corn	-	-	-	-	-	14x4x15	vmb/	14
Geashill	Gorteenard	-	corn & mill race	-	-	-	-	1841	-	6"os/	26
Geashill	Gorteenard	Wire Daniel	corn	-	-	-	-	-	12x2x14	vmb/	14
Geashill	Gorteenard	Wyre Daniel	corn	16x20x10 kiln :	-	-	-	1844	12x2x14 overshot :	hob/	5.1407
Offaly	Grogan	-	mill	-	-	-	-	-	-	1"os/	108
Horseleap	Horseleap	- nr Spittalstown :	mill	-	-	-	-	-	-	ph/wh	R
Horseleap	Horseleap	- on Gageboro` R	corn	-	-	-	-	-	-	1"os/	109
Garrygastle	Incherky	- nr Marlboro` Br.	mill	-	-	-	-	-	-	1"os/	117

PARISH	TOWNLAND	MILLER	TYPE	HOUSE	Land	£Val	PROPRIETORS	Date	WHEEL etc.	Record	Ref.
Shinrone	Keeloge	Woods Thomas	flour	62x24.6x35 & :	-	-	-	1845	1st mill: 14x6 40 bkts	hob/	5.1360
Shinrone	Keeloge	Woods Thomas	flour	-	-	-	-	-	18x3x10 3 pair st. :	vmb/	14
Shinrone	Keeloge	Woods Thomas	flour	-	-	-	-	-	16x4x10 1 pair st. :	vmb/	14
Shinrone	Keeloge Glebe	-	flour & mill race	-	-	-	-	1841	-	6"os/	42
Kilbeggan	Kilbeggan	-	Distillery Lock`s :	-	-	-	-	-	-	ph/wh	A
Kilcomin	Kilcomin	- at Gaybrook	mill	-	-	-	-	-	-	1"os/	117
Kilcomin	Kilcomin	- N. of Abbey	corn mill (disused)	-	-	-	-	1888	-	25"os/	41
Kilcomin	Kilcomin	- N. of Abbey	flour & millrace	-	-	-	-	-	-	6"os/	41
Kilcomin	Kilcomin	- nr Milltown	old corn mill	-	-	-	-	-	-	1"os/	117
Kilcomin	Kilcomin	Tracy John	flour	-	-	-	-	-	15x3x8	vmb/	14
Kilcomin	Kilcomin & Village	-	flour & mill race	-	-	-	-	1841	-	6"os/	41
Kilbride	Kilcoursey	-	flour & kiln	-	-	-	-	1841	-	6"os/	8
Kilbride	Kilcoursey	Goodbody L, M, & J	cotton factory	offices & yard	1a.	45	-	1856	-	gr/	a.a.lre.ie
Kilbride	Kilcoursey	Goodbody L, M, & J	flour & kilns	offices & yard	1a.	135	-	1856	-	gr/	a.a.lre.ie
Kilbride	Kilcoursey	Goodbody Robert	flour	-	-	-	-	-	13x10x4 5 pr st.	vmb/	14
Kilbride	Kilcoursey	Goodbody Robert	flour	-	-	-	-	-	15x11x4 5 pr st.	vmb/	14
Offaly	Kildangan	- on Silver R	mill	-	-	-	-	-	-	1"os/	109
Geashill	Killeenmore	Casey Michael	corn	22.6x19x13 & dw :	-	-	-	1842	no dimensions 2 pr. :	hob/	5.1386
Geashill	Killenmore	Grogan Thomas	corn	-	-	-	-	-	11x2x11	vmb/	14
Rahan	Killina	- SW/ B'cowan	mill pond, corn milll	-	-	-	-	1841	-	6"os/	16
Rahan	Killina	Boake William	corn	28x20x17 & kiln :	-	-	-	1844	12x3.9x8 overshot :	hob/	5.1346
Rahan	Killina	Boake William	corn	-	-	-	-	-	9x4x10	vmb/	14
Rahan	Killina	Galvin Martin	corn & kiln	26x19x17 & kiln :	-	-	-	-	9x4x10 42 bkts. :	hob/	5.1347
Ballyboy	Killnagall	Mooney Andrew	corn & kiln	28x21x12 & kiln :	-	-	-	1853	13x2.4x30 2 pr. st.	hob/	5.1314
Killoughy	Killoughy	-	corn	-	-	-	-	1841	-	6"os/	32
Killoughy	Killoughy	Malone James	corn	27x20x17 & kiln :	-	-	-	1853	13x2.6x13.6 1 pr st.	hob/	5.1317
Killoughy	Killoughy	Malone Thomas	corn	-	-	-	formerly Malone James		13x2x13	vmb/	14
Geashill	Killurin	Carroll George	corn	-	-	-	-	-	13x4x8	vmb/	14
Kilbride	Kilmacormack	- Park Mill	flour	-	-	-	-	2009	-	mmSv/	wh - D
Kilbride	Kilmacormack	- at Tullamore Park	ruins :	-	-	-	-	-	-	ph/wh	R
Kilbride	Kilmacormack	- near the town	ruin (ivy-covered)	-	-	-	-	-	-	ph/wh	R
Ballyboy	Kilmaine	Foster Charles	corn	-	5a.	-	-	-	-	gr/	-
Ballyboy	Kilmaine	Foster Charles	corn	mill & offices	-	-	-	1850	-	hob/	5.1336
Ballyboy	Kilmaine	Foster Charles	mill	29.6x19.6x24.6 & :	-	-	-	1853	16x4x16 46 bkts. :	hob/	5.1335
Clonburk	Kilmalogue	Odlum Henry	flour	-	-	-	-	-	12x10x2	vmb/	14
Clonburk	Kilmalogue :	Odlum Henry	flour & corn	50x20x25 & new :	-	25	-	-	12x10x2 36 floats :	hob/	5.321
Ballyboy	Kilnagall	-	flour	-	-	-	-	1841	-	6"os/	31
Ballyboy	Kilnagall	-	kiln & mill	-	-	-	-	1841	-	6"os/	31
Ballyboy	Kilnagall	-	mill race	-	-	-	-	1841	-	6"os/	31
Ballyboy	Kilnagall	Mooney Andrew	corn	-	-	-	-	-	13x2x3	vmb/	14
Ballyboy	Kilnagall	Mooney Andrew	corn & kiln	-	10a.	-	-	-	-	gr/	-
Roscomroe	Knockarley	-	corn	-	-	-	-	1841	-	6"os/	39
Roscomroe	Knockarley	Mitchell Thomas	corn	59x21.6x17 kiln :	-	-	-	-	14x3x14.6 (2) :	hob/	5.1331
Roscomroe	Knockarley	Mitchell Thomas	corn	-	-	-	-	-	14x3x14-	vmb/	14
Roscomroe	Knockarley	Mitchell Thomas	flour	-	-	-	-	-	14x3x14	vmb/	14
Roscomroe	Knockarley	Mitchell William	mill	-	-	-	Mitchell William - Jane	1862	-	dd/	1862 28 192
Roscrea	Laurel Hill	- nr Roscrea	corn	-	-	-	-	-	-	1"os/	126
Lusmagh	Lavagh	-	flour	-	-	-	-	1841	-	6"os/	29
Lusmagh	Lavagh	Killeen Timothy	- (note)	-	-	-	-	-	12x4x4 not worked:	vmb/	14
Lusmagh	Lavagh	Scott Richard	mill	-	2.2.31	-	-	-	-	gr/	-
Killagally	Leamore	-	mill	-	-	-	-	-	-	1"os/	117
Killagally	Leamore	Scott William	tuck	-	-	-	-	-	6x3x7	vmb/	14

PARISH	TOWNLAND	MILLER	TYPE	HOUSE	Land	£Val	PROPRIETORS	Date	WHEEL etc.	Record	Ref.
Kilbride	Lehinch	-	corn	-	-	-	-	1841	-	6"os/	8
Kilbride	Lehinch	Hackett John	corn	-	-	-	-	-	10x4x6ins.	vmb/	14
Tisaran	Lissaniska	-	Bleach Hill	-	-	-	-	1841	-	6"os/	13
Roscomroe	Longford	- at Aghagurty Br.	mill	-	-	-	-	-	-	1"os/	126
Roscomroe	Longford	- SE/ Loftus Br.	Big Mill	-	-	-	-	1841	-	6"os/	39
Durrow	Loughan	Belton Philip	corn	56x21x20 & kiln :	-	-	-	1844	-	hob/	5.1338
Durrow	Loughan	Slater Robt B	corn	53.0x19.6x20 kiln :	-	-	-	1852	15.6x4 2 pr. sts. :	hob/	5.1339
Durrow	Loughaun	-	Coleraine Flour Mill		-	-	-	1841	-	6"os/	8
Durrow	Loughaun	Bolton Philip	corn	-	-	-	-	-	13x4x6	vmb/	14
Geashill	Lugmore	-	corn & corn kiln	-	-	-	-	1841	-	6"os/	18
Geashill	Lugmore	Bartle Yarr	corn	-	-	-	-	-	13x4x10	vmb/	14
Geashill	Lugmore	Yarr Bartle	corn	27x21.6x20.6 kilns	-	-	-	1841	- 1 pair stones	hob/	5.1387
Gallen	Lumcloon	- near Millbrook Br.	Millbrook Flour Mill	-	-	-	-	1838	-	6"os/	23
Gallen	Lumcloon	Callaghan Peter	corn	-	552a.	-	-	-	-	gr/	-
Geashill	Meelaghans	-	corn	-	-	-	-	1841	-	6"os/	17
Geashill	Meelaghans	Owens Owen	corn	-	-	-	-	-	12x3x4 2 pr st. :	vmb/	14
Geashill	Meelaghans	Owens Owen	corn & kiln	41x20x9 & dw. ho :	-	-	-	1841	12x3.6x4 2 pr st. :	hob/	5.1387
Aghancon	Mill Park Ballybritt	Kenny	mill	-	-	-	Kenny - Bank Court	1864	-	dd/	1864 15 51
Ballykean	Millbrook	Tarleton Robert	corn	-	-	-	now Abernethy John		15x4x13	vmb/	14
Clonsast	Millgrove	-	Millgrove Bridge	-	-	-	-	1841	-	6"os/	27
Clonsast	Millgrove	- S/ Millgrove Br.	flour mill	-	-		-	1841	-	6"os/	27
Clonsast	Millgrove	Byrne Maria (miller)	corn	17.6x19x13 & :	13a.	-	-	1842	wheel wood v. old :	hob/	5.1363
Shinrone	Milltown	-	flour & mill pond	-	-	-	-	1841	-	6"os/	42
Shinrone	Milltown	-	Milltown (House)	-	-	-	-	1841	-	6"os/	42
Reynagh	Milltown	-	Milltown House	-	-	-	-	1841	-	6"os/	30
Shinrone	Milltown	- on R Brosna	no mill	-	-	-	-	-	-	1"os/	117
Shinrone	Milltown	Bergin James	flour	65x22x31	-	-	-	1845	15x4.3x15 32 bkts :	hob/	5.1360
Shinrone	Milltown	Bergin James	flour	-	-	-	-	-	14x3x15	vmb/	14
Garrycastle	Milltown	Cowan Joseph	mill	-	-	-	Cowan J - Greene Richd.	1864	-	dd/	1864 4 171
Eglish	Milltown	L`Estrange	mill	-	-	-	L`Estrange - Manifold Thac	1864	-	dd/	1864 9 115
Eglish	Milltown	O`Conor Maria	mills	-	-	-	O`Connor M - Cassidy Jno	1862	-	dd/	1862 35 156
Monasteroris	Monasteroris	Jackson M & J	corn	66x21x15 & kiln :	36a.	-	-	-	14x4x10 breast :	hob/	5.1365
Monasteroris	Monasteroris	Jackson Robt Wm	corn	-	92a.	-	-	-	-	gr/	-
Kilmmanaghan	Moyally	-	Marchbrook Mill	-	-	-	-	1841	-	6"os/	1
Kilmanaghan	Moyally	-	woollen factory	-	-	-	-	1841	-	6"os/	2
Tisaran	Moyestown Dem.	-	flax	-	-	-	-	1841	-	6"os/	22
Tisaran	Moyestown Dem.	- SW/ Moyst'n Br.	flour	-	-	-	-	1841	-	6"os/	22
Tisaran	Moyestown Dem.	- N. side R. Brosna	flour	-	-	-	-	1841	-	6"os/	22
Gallen	Moyestown Dem.	Callaghan Peter	flour	-	-	-	-	-	16x6x10	vmb/	14
Gallen	Moyestown Dem.	L`Estrange G B	corn	-	-	-	-	-	15x5x4	vmb/	14
Gallen	Moyestown Dem.	L`Estrange G B	flour	-	-	-	-	-	15x4x4	vmb/	14
Lusmagh	Muckinish	-	Still Island (0.1.4)	-	-	-	-	1841	-	6"os/	21
Lynally	Mucklagh	- SW/ Mucklagh Br.	corn & tuck mill	-	-	-	-	1841	-	6"os/	16
Lynally	Mucklagh	Molloy John	corn	-	-	-	-	-	11x3x3	vmb/	14
Lynally	Mucklagh	Molloy John	corn & tuck	27.6x19.6x9 & kiln :	-	-	-	1845	10x3x5 breast :	hob/	5.1344
Lynally	Mucklagh	Molloy John	tuck	-	-	-	-	-	10x2x5 2 beetles	vmb/	14
Lemanaghan	Mullaghans	Owens Owen	mill	- [no dimensions]	-	-	-	1852	mill out of repair :	hob/	5.1385
Clonsast	Nahana	- on Figile R	mill	-	-	-	-	-	-	1"os/	119
Geashill	Newtown	-	brewery	-	-	-	-	1841	-	6"os/	25
Geashill	Newtown	-	corn & mill pond	-	-	-	-	1841	-	6"os/	25
Lusmagh	Newtown	- nr Gortarevagh	old windmill	-	-	-	-	-	-	1"os/	117
Kilcoursey	Newtown	Gibbons John	corn & land	-	8a.	10	-	1856	-	gr/	a.a.Ire.ie

PARISH	TOWNLAND	MILLER	TYPE	HOUSE	Land	£Val	PROPRIETORS	Date	WHEEL etc.	Record	Ref.
Geashill	Newtown	Sadler Fran	corn	-	-	-	-	-	14x4x13	vmb/	14
Geashill	Newtown	Yarr Bartholomew	corn	30x20x18 & kilns :	-	-	-	1841	14x4.6x13 2 pr st. :	hob/	5.1387
Ballyboy	Park	Crawley George	corn & kilns	74.6x28x43 & kiln :	-	-	-	1853	16x8x8 3 pair.st. :	hob/	5.1314
Ballyboy	Park	Drought Robert	corn	-	-	-	-	-	16x8x8	vmb/	14
Ballyboy	Park	Drought Robert S	mill	-	119a.	-	-	-	-	gr	-
Kilcoursey	Parkwood	Byrne Daniel	corn	-	-	-	-	-	16x4x4	vmb/	14
Kilcoursey	Parkwood	Collins samuel	mill	- offices & land	21a.	-	-	-	-	gr/	a.a.Ire.ie
Killaderry	Philipstown	-	corn	-	-	-	-	-	-	1"os/	109
Killaderry	Philipstown	-	tannery	-	-	-	-	1841	-	6"os/	18
Killaderry	Philipstown T'pks	-	distillery ruins	-	-	-	-	1841	-	6"os/	18
Offaly	Purefoy`s Place	Purefoy James R	mill	-	-	-	Purefoy J - Marq Dns	1864	-	dd/	1864 7 215
Offaly	Quarter Mill (not)	Landed Est Court	mill	-	-	-	L.E.Ct - Smallman James	1863	-	dd/	1863 40 293
Rahan	Rahan Demense	Cahill Patrick	corn	-	-	-	-	-	8x4x1	vmb/	14
Rahan	Rahan Demense	Cahill Patrick	corn & tuck	37.0x21.6x19.6 :	-	-	-	1844	11.6x4.6x2.6 floats :	hob/	5.1346
Rahan	Rahan Demense	Cahill Patrick	tuck	-	-	-	-	-	11x3x - 2 beetles	vmb/	14
Rahan	Rahan Demense	Grennan William	corn & kiln	-	-	-	-	1853	no.1: grist 10x5x2 :	hob/	5.1348
Rahan	Rahan Demense	Grennan William	wheat & bere	-	-	-	-	1853	no.2: wheat & bere :	hob/	5.1348
Rahan	Rahan Demesne	-	old corn mill	-	-	-	-	1841	-	6"os/	16
Kilcolman	Rathmore	Synge Edward	threshing	-	-	-	-	-	13x4x5	vmb/	14
Ballyburly	Rathmoyle	Rait Silvester	new kiln	66x20x23.6 :	-	-	-	1852	-	hob/	5.1409
Offaly	Riverstown *	- on R Brosna	mill	-	-	-	-	-	-	1"os/	117
Offaly	Roanville *	Murphy Michael	mill	-	-	-	Murphy M - Shaw Richd	1864	-	dd/	1864 28 18
Ballydyff	Roscrea	Hanlon John	corn	-	-	-	-	-	16x4x12	vmb/	14
Kilcomin	Rusheen	Tiguin Mary	corn	-	-	-	-	-	16x3x3	vmb/	14
Kilcomin	Rusheen	Tiguin Maryanne	corn	house, offs. & land	46a.	30	-	1856	-	gr/	a.a.Ire.ie
Offaly	Seven Churches *	-	site of Temple Killir	-	-	-	-	1841	-	6"os/	5
Clonyhurk	Shanderry	-	flour, mill race	-	-	-	-	1841	-	6"os/	34
Shinrone	Shinrone Glebe	-	brewery	-	-	-	-	1841	-	6"os/	42
Birr	Singfield	- near Birr :	corn	-	-	-	Martin Dobson	1998	- photos taken	mmSv/	wh - B
Birr	Singfield	- S of Birr Town	brewery	- large building :	-	-	-	2005	-	mmSv/	wh - R
Killagally	Skehanagh	-	corn & corn kiln	-	-	-	-	1841	-	6"os/	14
Killagally	Skehanagh	Bayley Geo & Co	tuck	-	-	-	-	-	13x3x4	vmb/	14
Killagally	Skehanagh	Gallagher Bernard	flour	-	-	-	-	-	4x3x6	vmb/	14
Offaly	Springmount *	Murphy Michael	mills	-	-	-	Murphy M - Shaw Jno	1864	-	dd/	1864 12 215
Drumcullen	Streamstown	Corcoran Patrick	mill	28x28x7	-	-	-	-	-	hob/	5.1366
Birr	Syngfield *	- on Camcor R.	mill	-	-	-	-	-	-	1"os/	117
Offaly	Tld. ? /Xx-cloon	-	Millbrook Bridge	-	-	-	-	1841	-	6"os/	23
Offaly	Tld. ? /Xx-cloon	-	Millbrook Flour Mills	-	-	-	-	1841	-	6"os/	23
Castlejordan	Toberdaly	-	threshing mill	-	-	-	-	1841	-	6"os/	11
Gallen	Tonlemone	-	Gaybrook Flour Milll		-	-	-	1841	-	6"os/	22
Gallen	Tonlemone	Doorley Denis	corn	- [no dimensions]	-	-	-	-	16x4.4x12 48 bkts.:	hob/	5.1371
Gallen	Toulemone	Doorley Dennis	oat	-	-	-	-	-	15x4x10	vmb/	14
-	Townland ?	at Palmer`s Br. :	ruin	-	-	-	-	-	-	ph/wh	R
Kiladerry	Townsparks	Barry Thomas	corn	27x17.6x19.6 :	-	-	-	-	12x4x1 2 pr st. :	hob/	5.1401
Kiladerry	Townsparks	Denis Mrs	corn	-	-	-	formerly Baynhasm Benj		12x4x6	vmb/	14
Birr	Townsparks	Hackett George	brewery	130x26x21 part :	-	19.15	-	1854	-	hob/	5.3203
Birr	Townsparks	Robinson Robert	brewery	51.6 x 22.6 x 16 :	-	-	-	1843	15.6x6.6x3, pr st :	hob/	5.3202
Kilbride	Tullamore	-	brewery	-	-	-	-	1841	-	6"os/	17
Kilbride	Tullamore	-	brewery	-	-	-	-	1841	-	6"os/	17
Kilbride	Tullamore	-	tannery	-	-	-	-	1841	-	6"os/	17
Kilbride	Tullamore	Flavan Joseph	domestic	-	-	-	-	-	Francis 12kw	turb/	c1947
Kilbride	Tullamore	Molloy Michael	flour	-	-	-	-	-	12x7x7 3 pr st.	vmb/	14

PARISH	TOWNLAND	MILLER	TYPE	HOUSE	Land	£Val	PROPRIETORS	Date	WHEEL etc.	Record	Ref.
Kilbride	Tullamore	Ryan Thomas	corn	-	-	-	-	-	14x3x2	vmb/	14
Kilbride	Tullamore	Ryan Thomas	corn	-	-	-	-	-	10x3x2	vmb/	14
Kilbride	Tullamore :	Joughin Charlotte	wheatmeal :	-	-	-	-	1963	-	lic./17	wheat
Kilbride	Tullamore T/pks	-	brewery	-	-	-	-	1841	-	6"os/	17
Kilbride	Tullamore T/pks	-	corn	-	-	-	-	1841	-	6"os/	17
Kilbride	Tullamore T/pks	-	distillery	-	-	-	-	1841	-	6"os/	17
Kilbride	Tullamore T/pks	-	flour	-	-	-	-	1841	-	6"os/	17
Kilbride	Tullamore T/pks	-	flour	-	-	-	-	1841	-	6"os/	17
Kilbride	Tullamore Town	Allison John	old brewery	53x17.6x13.6 & :	-	7.17	-	1853	no machinery detail :	hob/	5.3214
Kilbride	Tullamore Town	Doyle Bernard	distillery (Br. St.)	still ho. 43x25x17 :	-	-	-	1853	worked by steam :	hob/	5.3214
Kilbride	Tullamore Town	Molloy Michael	flour	65x232x23 kiln :	-	-	-	1853	open, all metal :	hob/	5.3214
Kilbride	Tullamore Town	Pentland Henry	distillery	23x32x11 kiln & :	-	52.1	-	1853	no machinery detail :	hob/	5.3215
Kilbride	Tullamore Town	Ryan Thomas	corn	53x20x25 & part :	-	19.13	-	1853	wheel undershot :	hob/	5.3214
Kilbride	Tullamore Town :	Manly Henry	brewery	35x29x16 :	-	1.1.0	-	1853	-	hob/	5.3214
Kilbride	Tullamore Town :	Ryan Thomas	corn	38x22x30	-	-	-	1853	outside wheel has :	hob/	5.3214
Kilmanaghen	Tully	- SW/ Old Bridge	woollen factory	-	-	-	-	1841	-	6"os/	2
Kilmanaghen	Tully	Gibbons John	woollen factory	-	-	-	-	-	30x6x20 6 stocks	vmb/	14
Gallen	Tumcloon	Caliaghan Peter	flour	62.6x27x28 & kiln :	-	-	-	-	-	hob/	5.1370
Ballycommon	Wood Of O	Cobb John	old mill	44x17.6x23 also :	-	-	-	-	- Irish st. 3 sets :	hob/	5.1396

PARISH	TOWNLAND	MILLER	TYPE	HOUSE	Land	£Val	PROPRIETORS	Date	WHEEL etc.	Record	Ref.
Tibohine	Aghaderry	-	corn & kiln	-	-	-	-	-	-	6"os/	14
Kilteevan	Annaghmore	-	corn kiln	-	-	-	-	-	-	6"os/	40
Drum	Ardkeenan	-	malt kiln	-	-	-	-	-	-	6"os/	51
Aughrim	Ardleckna	-	corn	-	-		-	-	-	1"os/	77
Elphin	Ardnagowna	-	brewery	-	-	-	-	-	-	6"os/	16
Elphin	Ardnagowna	-	corn & kiln	-	-	-	-	-	-	6"os/	16
Elphin	Ardnagowna	-	corn kilns (2)	-	-	-	-	-	-	6"os/	16
Boyle	Ardsallagh	Crofton Henry Rev :	mills	-	-	-	Crofton Henry - Lloyde Wm	1803	-	dd/	553 130 366263
Boyle	Ardsallagh	Crofton Henry Rev.	mills	-	-	-	Crofton H - Yeeden John	1786	-	dd/	383 116 253120
Boyle	Ardsallagh	Yeeden John Loyd :	mills	-	-	-	Veeden J - Crofton Henry :	1786	-	dd/	378 334 253129
Creagh	Articorra	Harney Patrick	corn	-	61a.	-	-	-	-	gr/	-
Creagh	Ashford	- on R. Suck nr :	corn	-	-	-	-	-	-	6"os/	53
Athleague	Athleague	- Athleague Town :	corn	-	-	-	-	-	-	6"os/	41
Athleague	Athleague	Healy Patrick	wheatmeal :	-	-	-	-	1963	-	lic./13	wheat
Athleague	Athleague	Hood John	corn & kiln	-	-	-	-	-	-	gr/	-
Athleague	Athleague	Lennon William	mill	-	-	-	Lennon W - Taffe Chris	1780	-	dd/	342 247 220842
Athleague	Athleague	Murray James :	mill		-	-	Murray J - Fetherston Margt	1808	-	dd/	600 510 412337
Athleague	Athleague	O`Gilvie George :	mill	-	-	-	O`Gilvie - Devine & Nolan	1810	-	dd/	621 426 423980
Athleague	Athleague	Smith	mill	-	-	-	Smith - Smith	-	?	dd/	533 389 354466
Athleague	Athleague	Taffe Anthony :	mill	-	-	-	Taffe A - Ryan Thomas :	1801	Mort. 5 Mar.	dd/	549 482 364740
Athleague	Athleague Manor	Gunning George :	mill	-	-	-	Gunning G - Lester John :	1753	-	dd/	159 408 107482
Athleague	Athleague Manor	Lyster	mill	-	-	-	Lyster - Bryan	1743	-	dd/	166 81 110425
Athleague	Athleague Manor	Lyster John	mill	-	-	-	Lyster J - Dillon James :	1752	-	dd/	158 102 105069
Athleague	Athleague Manor	Lyster John	mill	-	-	-	Lyster - Dempsey Robt	1753	-	dd/	159 409 107483
Athleague	Athleague Manor	Lyster Margaret	mill	-	-	-	Lyster M - Rumbold Eliz	1799	-	dd/	494 672 339422
St Mary`s	Athlone	-	tuck	-	-	-	Jones L - Thomas Edwin	1707	Lse. 16 Oct.	dd/	61 395 41756
St Mary`s	Athlone	Dalton John :	gins & mills	-	-	-	Dalton J - Potts Jno	1772	-	dd/	300 575 201319?
St Mary`s	Athlone	Sproule Sam., Wm. :	gins & mills	-	-	-	Sproule S - Burke Peter :	1752	-	dd/	164 383 111046
St Mary`s	Athlone	Sproule Samuel :	gins & mills	-	-	-	Sproule S - Sproule Wm :	1758	-	dd/	197 249 130287
St Mary`s	Athlone	St George Henry Rev :	mill (at Bridge)	-	-	-	St George H - Sproule Wm	1818	-	dd/	726 278 495813
St Mary`s	Athlone Town :	-	distillery	-	-	-	-	-	-	6"os/	52
St Mary`s	Athlone Town :	-	distillery	-	-	-	-	-	-	6"os/	52
Kiltoom	Atteagh	- O'Briens Mill	mill	-	-	-	John O'Brien	2001	-	mmSv/	wh - B
Kiltoom	Atteagh	- E./ Milltown Pass :	corn & kiln	-	-	-	-	-	-	6"os/	48
Kiltoom	Atteagh	O`Brien Bartholomew	corn	-	-	-	-	-	-	gr/	-
Creagh	Atticorra	-	corn & kiln	-	-	-	-	1841	-	6"os/	53
Roscommon	Balingaglass	French John :	mill	-	-	-	French J - Hawkes Chas :	1742	-	dd/	111 150 76020
Roscommon	Balingaglass	Hawkes Charles :	mill	-	-	-	Hawkes C - Hull Richard :	1746	-	dd/	126 37 85330
Roscommon	Balingaglass	Hawkes Margaret :	mill	-	-	-	Hawkes M - Kelly John :	1768	D.Poll 9 Mar.	dd/	260 444 173950
Aughrim	Ballagh	-	old corn kiln	-	-	-	-	-	-	6"os/	17
Creagh	Ballinasloe	Berne William :	mills	-	-	-	Berene W - Mannett Dom :	1812	-	dd/	641 456 447921
Creagh	Ballinasloe	Dunbo	mills	-	-	-	Dunbo Lord - Reeves	-	?	dd/	666 459 458762
Creagh	Ballinasloe	Dunne Thomas :	mills	-	-	-	Dunne T - Armstrong Robt :	1813	-	dd/	664 373 456524?
Creagh	Ballinasloe T`parks	- mid. Town	corn	-	-	-	-	-	-	6"os/	53
Creagh	Ballinasloe T`parks	- nr B`sloe Bridge	corn	-	-	-	-	-	-	6"os/	53
Creagh	Ballinasloe T`parks	- E./ Town nr Castle	corn	-	-	-	-	-	-	6"os/	53
Creagh	Ballinasloe Town	Hood John	corn & kiln	-	-	-	-	-	-	gr/	-
Creagh	Ballinasloe Town	Lancaster John	corn & kiln	-	3.0.30		-	-	-	gr/	-
Kilronan	Ballyfarnan Vge. :	Clarke Michael	corn	(1B) 26x18x8 & :	-	3.7.6	-	1846	- [no detail]	hob/	5.3222
Kilronan	Ballyfarnan Vge. :	Clarke Michael	mill	-	-	-	-	-	-	gr/	-
Taghboy	Ballyforan	Kenny Thomas H	corn	-	-	-	-	-	-	gr/	-
Taghboy	Ballyforan :	-	flour & corn	-	-	-	-	-	-	6"os/	46

PARISH	TOWNLAND	MILLER	TYPE	HOUSE	Land	£Val	PROPRIETORS	Date	WHEEL etc.	Record	Ref.
Roscommon	Ballyfornet * :	McCawley Clarenda :	mills & weir	-	-	-	McCawley Clar - Patrick :	1817	-	dd/	717199 490334
Dysart	Ballyglass	- nr Ballyglass Br.	mill in ruins :	-	-	-	-	-	-	6"os/	46
Dysart	Ballyglass	Elphin Lord Bishop	mills	-	-	-	Elphin Ld. B - Westenra :	1717	L&R. 20 Mar.	dd/	21 60 10762
Cloontuskert	Ballyleague	-	mill	- site not located	-	-	-	2003	-	mmSv/	wh - Z?
Roscommon	Ballymartin	Plunket Jane	corn	-	22a.	-	-	-	-	gr/	-
Roscommon	Ballymartin More :	-	mill & mill pond		-	-	-	-	-	6"os/	39
Kiltoom	Ballymullavill	- near Milltownpass	mill	- building good	-	-	-	2001	narro' wh. arch	mmSv/	hw - B
Roscommon	Ballypheasan :	-	brewery	-	-	-	-	-	-	6"os/	39
Shankill	Ballyroddy	-	corn & kiln	-	-	-	-	-	-	6"os/	16
Shankill	Ballyroddy	-	mill	-	-	-	-	-	-	1"os/	77
Shankill	Ballyroddy	Griffin Joseph :	mills	-	-	-	Griffin J - Dodwell Henry :	1760	-	dd/	205 434 135833
Shankill	Ballyroddy	Griffin Joseph :	mills	-	-	-	Griffin J - Simpson George :	1760	Mort. 21 Feb.	dd/	206 51 134856
Shankill	Ballyroddy	Griffin Margaret	mills	-	-	-	Griffin M - Daly Cath	1784	-	dd/	353 431 239863
Shankill	Ballyroddy	Robbins Richard :	mills	-	-	-	Robbins R - Griffin Joseph	1760	-	dd/	202 478 134855
Termonbarry	Ballytoohey	-	old corn kiln :	-	-	-	-	-	-	6"os/	30
Termonbarry	Ballytoohey :	- on the island :	old tuck mill	-	-	-	-	-	-	6"os/	30
Termonbarry	Ballytoohey :	- S. of Br. & Rd.	corn	-	-	-	-	-	-	6"os/	30
Tibohine	Barnacawley	-	corn kiln	-	-	-	-	-	-	6"os/	14
Kilteevan	Belderg	Finneran James	corn	-	-	-	-	-	-	gr/	-
Kilteevan	Belderg	Finneran James	tuck	-	-	-	-	-	-	gr/	-
Kilcorkey	Bellanagare :	French John :	mills		-	-	French J - Hawkes Chas :	1723	L&R. 3 Dec.	dd/	30 282 17887
Kilcorkey	Bellanagare :	O'Connor Denis :	mills		-	-	O'Connor D - French Robt :	1720	L&R. 11 Dec.	dd/	29 338 17888
Kilcorkey	Bellanagare	-	corn & tuck		-	-	-	-	-	6"os/	15
Kilcorkey	Bellanagare	Clarke Thomas	corn	-	2.3.6	-	-	-	-	gr/	-
Kilcorkey	Bellanagare	Clarke Thomas	tuck	-	-	-	-	-	-	gr/	-
St Peter`s	Bellanamullia	-	corn & kiln	-	-	-	-	1841	-	6"os/	52
St Peter`s	Bellanamullia	-	mill	-	-	-	-	-	-	1"os/	98
St Peter`s	Bellanamullia	- at Millbrook	flour & kiln	-	-	-	-	1841	-	6"os/	52
St Peter`s	Bellanamullia	Bannon Michael	corn	-	27a.	-	-	-	-	gr/	-
St Peter`s	Bellanamullia	Kelly Peter	corn	-	25a.	-	-	-	-	gr/	-
T`maconnell	Bellaneeny	-	corn & pond	-	-	-	-	-	-	6"os/	51
Kiltulagh	Benmore	Folliott Robert	corn & kilns	-	9a.	-	-	-	-	gr/	-
Boyle	Boyle	Day	mills	-	-	-	Day - Glover	-	-	dd/	733 543 500278
Boyle	Boyle Town	Mulhall Joseph	mills & kiln	-	3.2.10	-	-	-	-	gr/	-
Boyle	Boyle Town :	-	brewery	-	-	-	-	-	-	6"os/	6
Boyle	Boyle Town :	-	corn	-	-	-	-	-	-	6"os/	6
Boyle	Boyle Town :	Mulhall Joseph :	corn, flour	(1A) 79x29x39 :	-	101	-	1846	- flour mill new	hob/	5.3225
Boyle	Boyle Town :	Mulhall Joseph	tuck	(1A) 79x29x39 :	-	101	-	1846	16x6x1.6 fall 5ft.	hob/	5.3225
Cl`gormican	Brierfield	- above Shadlough	old kiln	-	-	-	-	-	-	6"os/	27
Athleague	Buckfield	- nr Castlestrange	corn kiln	-	-	-	-	-	-	6"os/	41
Roscommon	Burne Brooke *	Kelly John (Elder) :	mills	-	-	-	Kelly John - Kealy Julia :	1814	4 May	dd/	673 398 464407
Roscommon	Burne Brooke *	Kelly John (Elder) :	mills	-	-	-	Kelly John - Killy Denis :	1814	4 May	dd/	673 387 464406
Moore	Camcloon	-	corn & tuck	-	-	-	-	1841	-	6"os/	54
Moore	Camcloon	Murray Patrick	corn & kiln	-	30a.	-	-	-	-	gr/	-
Roscommon	Canagh *	Flood George :	mill	-	-	-	Flood G - Nurney John :	1778	-	dd/	317 287 217497
Roscommon	Canagh *	Reilly James :	mill	-	-	-	Reilly Jas - Kelly Richard :	1776	-	dd/	315 96 208825?
Roscommon	Canagh *	Reilly James :	mill	-	-	-	Reilly Jas - Flood George :	1776	-	dd/	308 526 207 163
St Peter`s	Canal & Banks	Swain & Holton	flour	-	-	-	-	-	-	gr/	-
St John`s	Carnagh East	- near Lecarrow	corn & tuck	-	-	-	-	-	-	6"os/	46
Roscommon	Carricknorrue	Gore Booth :	mills	-	-	-	Gore B - Corkran Francis :	1741	-	dd/	109 106 75153
Boyle	Carrigeenagowna	-	corn kiln	-	-	-	-	-	-	6"os/	5
Rahara	Carrowmoney	-	old windmill	-	-	-	-	-	-	1"os/	97
Kilteevan	Carrowmore	-	crockery kiln	-	-	-	-	-	-	6"os/	40

PARISH	TOWNLAND	MILLER	TYPE	HOUSE	Land	£Val	PROPRIETORS	Date	WHEEL etc.	Record	Ref.
Kilteevan	Carrowmore :	-	corn kiln	-	-	-	-	-	-	6"os/	40
Tibohine	Carrownakn`kaun	-	corn kiln	-	-	-	-	-	-	6"os/	13
Tibohine	Carrownakn`kaun	-	mill (? pond)	-	-	-	-	-	-	6"os/	13
Shankill	Carrownam`heny	-	corn kiln	-	-	-	-	-	-	6"os/	16
Aughrim	Carrowreagh	-	corn	-	-	-	-	-	-	1"os/	77
Aughrim	Carrowreagh	-	corn	-	-	-	-	-	-	6"os/	11
Aughrim	Carrowreagh	Caddell	mills	-	-	-	Caddell - Willens	-	?	dd/	682 469 469642
Aughrim	Carrowreagh	Caddell	mills	-	-	-	Caddell - Boylan	-	-	dd/	704 83 482418
Aughrim	Carrowreagh	Caddell Richard	mills	-	-	-	Caddell R - Arnold Rev. :	1820	Mort. 5 July	dd/	753 512 512247
Killumod	Cartron	Barrett Patrick	corn	-	8.0.10		-	-	-	gr/	-
Tibohine	Cartron More	-	corn kiln	-	-	-	-	-	-	6"os/	14
Fuerty	Castlecoote	- on R. Suck	mill	-	-	-	-	-	-	1"os/	87
Fuerty	Castlecoote	- W. side R. Suck :	flour	-	-	-	-	-	-	6"os/	39
Fuerty	Castlecoote	M`Loughlin William Jn	corn & kilns	-	-	-	-	-	-	gr/	-
Fuerty	Castlecoote	M`Loughlin William Jn	eel weir	-	-	-	-	-	-	gr/	-
Fuerty	Castlecoote	M`Loughlin William Jn	flour	-	-	-	-	-	-	gr/	-
Fuerty	Castlecoote	M`Loughlin William Jn	miller`s house	-	-	-	-	-	-	gr/	-
Fuerty	Castlecoote	Nolan	mills	-	-	-	Nolan - Nolan	-	-	dd/	662 546 457601
Kilkeevin	Castlereagh	-	mill :	-	-	-	McLoughnin	-	-	sv04	Z
Kilkeevin	Castlereagh	- formerly Farrelly`s	Mill	-	-	-	McLoughlin	2004	-	pWEH	B
Kilkeevin	Castlereagh	Silke Michael Sen. :	mills	-	-	-	Silke M - Silke Michael Jun :	1814	Sale 5 Nov.	dd/	681 139 468690
Kilkeevin	Castlereagh Town	-	brewery	-	-	-	-	-	-	6"os/	26
Kilkeevin	Castlereagh Town	-	corn & dam	-	-	-	-	-	-	6"os/	26
Kilkeevin	Castlereagh Town	-	distillery	-	-	-	-	-	-	6"os/	26
Kilkeevin	Castlereagh Town	- W. of Bridge	mill	recently demol. :	-	-	-	2004	-	mmSv/	wh - Z
Kilkeevin	Castlereagh Town :	Henry Laurence	corn & kiln	(1A) 22x21.6x19 :	-	20	-	1846	- [no detail]	hob/	5.3226
Kilkeevin	Castlereagh Town :	Dillon Peter	corn & kiln	(1A) 52x21.6x21 :	-	23	-	1846	- [no detail]	hob/	5.3226
Kilkeevin	Castlereagh Town :	Sweeny Patrick	corn & kiln	(1A) 88x23.6x15.6 :	-	14	-	1846	- [no detail]	hob/	5.3226
Kilmacumsy	Cleeraugh	-	corn	-	-	-	-	-	-	6"os	20
T`maconnell	Clonakille	- at Vge. Burnsbrook	flour & kiln	-	-	-	-	-	-	6"os/	51
Tibohine	Clonard	Dunne Thomas :	mill			-	Dunne T - Armstrong Robt :	1813	-	dd/	664 373 458321
Tibohine	Clonard	French Jeff :	mill	-	-	-	French J - Hogan William :	1813	-	dd/	670 21 459574
St Peter`s	Cloonakille	St George Edw Capt :	mills	-	-	-	St George E - Plummer Jn :	1744	-	dd/	122 499 85050
St Peter`s	Cloonakille	St George Richard :	mills	-	-	-	St George R - Molyneux :	1791	-	dd/	434 301 281416
Kilbride	Cloonaragh	Caulfield George :	mill	-	-	-	Caulfield G - Sandys Neherr	1769	-	dd/	272 250 17471
Kilbride	Cloonaragh	Hicks Elizabeth	corn & kiln	-	34a.	-	-	-	-	gr/	-
Kilbride	Cloonaragh	Hodson	mill	-	-	-	Hodson - Hodson	-	?	dd/	303 603 202390
Kilbride	Cloonaragh	Murray Bryan :	mill	-	-	-	Murray B - Hodson Daniel :	1769	-	dd/	270 577 175270
Kilbride	Cloonaragh	Reynolds Edwin S.	mill	-	-	-	Reynolds E - Dillon James	1755	-	dd/	178 374 119269
Kilbride	Cloonarragh	-	corn kilns	-	-	-	-	-	-	6"os/	36
Kilbride	Cloonarragh	-	corn, mill race	-	-	-	-	-	-	6"os/	36
Kilbride	Cloonarragh	-	mill	-	-	-	-	-	-	1"os/	87
Tibohine	Cloonbunny	-	corn kiln	-	-	-	-	-	-	6"os/	20
Kilkeevan	Clooncan	-	corn & kiln	-	-	-	-	-	-	6"os/	19
Kilkeevan	Clooncan	-	corn kilns (2)	-	-	-	-	-	-	6"os/	19
Kilkeevan	Clooncan	Fitzgerald James	mill & kiln	-	0.2.39		-	-	-	gr/	-
Kiltullagh	Clooncrim	-	mill dam & kiln	-	-	-	-	-	-	6"os/	25
Fuerty	Clooneenbaun	-	corn & kiln	-	-	-	-	1841	-	6"os/	35
Fuerty	Clooneenbaun	O`Brien Denis	corn	-	12a.	-	-	-	-	gr/	-
Fuerty	Clooneenbaun	O`Brien Denis	tuck	-	-	-	-	-	-	gr/	-
Kiltulagh	Cloonfad	-	corn	-	-	-	-	-	-	1"os/	86
Kiltulagh	Cloonfad East	Gannon Peter	corn & kilns	-	-	-	-	-	-	gr/	-

PARISH	TOWNLAND	MILLER	TYPE	HOUSE	Land	£Val	PROPRIETORS	Date	WHEEL etc.	Record	Ref.
Kiltulagh	Cloonfad West	-	corn & dam	-	-	-	-	-	-	6"os/	31
Kiltulagh	Cloonfad West	-	corn kiln	-	-	-	-	-	-	6"os/	31
Cloonfinlough	Cloonfinlough	- at Cloonfinloogh Br.	corn	-	-	-	-	-	-	6"os/	29
Kiltevan	Cloonlarge	-	corn kiln	-	-	-	-	1841	-	6"os/	40
Tisrara	Cloonlaughan :	-	corn & kiln	-	-	-	-	-	-	6"os/	44
Kilnamanagh	Cloonmagunnaun	Eccles John :	mill	-	-	-	Eccles J - Ecles Gilbert :	1750	-	dd/	190 512 127995
Kilnamanagh	Cloonmagunnaun	Espinalse Richard :	mills	-	-	-	Espinalse R - Rennell Cath	1817	-	dd/	717 274 790411
Kilnamanagh	Cloonmagunnaun	Espinalse Richard :	mill	-	-	-	Espinalse R - Reynell Cath	1817	-	dd/	717 276 490411
Kilnamanagh	Cloonmagunnaun	French Arthur :	mill	-	-	-	French A - French Richard	1820		dd/	758 183 514918
Kilnamanagh	Cloonmagunnaun	French Arthur :	mill	-	-	-	French Arthur - Kelly Dan	1816	-	dd/	700 569 480 409
Kilnamanagh	Cloonmagunnaun	French Arthur :	mill	-	-	-	French A - Eccles Jno :	1751	-	dd/	148 252 99375
Kilnamanagh	Cloonmagunnaun	French Arthur Jun :	mill	-	-	-	French Arthur - Arthur Jun.	1812	Annuity 20 Nov.	dd/	657 69 450070
Kilnamanagh	Cloonmagunnaun	French John :	mill	-	-	-	French J - Hughes George	1819	-	dd/	737 596 502731
Kilnamanagh	Cloonmagunnaun	French Robt. Henry :	mill	-	-	-	French R H - Goff Robert :	1820	-	dd/	749 252 509587
Kilnamanagh	Cloonmagunnaun	O`Hara Charles :	mill	-	-	-	O`Hara C - French Arthur :	1817	-	dd/	720 377 492312
Kilteevan	Cloonmore	-	corn kilns (2)	-	-	-	-	-	-	6"os/	40
Cloonfinlough	Cloonrane	-	corn (in ruins)	-	-	-	-	-	-	6"os/	29
Cloonfinlough	Cloonrane	-	corn kiln	-	-	-	-	-	-	6"os/	29
Kilteevan	Cloonsellan :	-	pottery	-	-	-	-	-	-	6"os/	40
Tibohine	Cloonshanville	N./ Carricknabraher R.:	gig mill	-	-	-	-	-	-	6"os/	15
Kilteevan	Cloontimullan :	-	corn & kiln	-	-	-	-	-	-	6"os/	40
Tibohine	Cloontowart	-	mill & kiln	-	-	-	-	-	-	6"os/	19
Tibohine	Cloontowart	Sandford Elizabeth	corn	-	41a.	-	-	-	-	gr/	-
Tibohine	Cloonylatttan	-	corn kilns (2)	-	-	-	-	-	-	6"os/	17
Elphin	Commeen	-	corn	-	-	-	-	-	-	1"os/	77
Tibohine	Coolagarry	-	corn kiln	-	-	-	-	-	-	6"os/	20
Kiltulagh	Coolaugher	Daly Nicholas	corn	-	23a.	-	-	-	-	gr/	-
Clooncraff	Coolmeen	-	corn kiln	-	-	-	-	-	-	6"os/	17
Boyle	Copse	Kennedy John	corn-mill & kiln	-	-	-	-	-	-	gr/	-
Kilglass	Corgowan	Blakeney	mills	-	-	-	Blakeney - Hughes	-	- [? error]	dd/	710 390 48632185
Ardcarn	Cornagrea	-	paper & pond	-	-	-	-	-	-	6"os/	3
	Cornagrea	East Wiliam	corn & kiln	-	-	-	-	-	-	gr/	-
Boyle	Cornameelta	-	corn kiln	-	-	-	-	-	-	6"os/	5
KIltoom	Corrantotan	-	corn & kiln	-	-	-	-	1841	-	6"os/	48
KIltoom	Corrantotan	- at Cross Roads	corn	-	-	-	-	-	-	1"os/	98
KIltoom	Corrantotan	Mongan Denis & Dom	corn	-	3a.	-	-	-	-	gr/	-
Tisrara	Correal	- SW of main rd. :	windmill	-	-	-	-	-	-	6"os/	44
Drum	Crannagh	- nr Crannagh Ho.	corn kiln	-	-	-	-	-	-	6"os/	52
Drum	Crannagh	- nr Crannagh Ho.	flour & kiln	-	-	-	-	-	-	6"os/	52
Drum	Crannagh	McMullen Irvine T	mill	-	-	-	McMullen I - Lloyd Thomas	1784	-	dd/	360 110 242001?
Creeve	Creevemully	-	corn kiln	-	-	-	-	1841	-	6"os/	40
Creeve	Creevemully	Caulfield Burne Rev. :	mills	-	-	-	Caulfield B - Radcliff Thos :	1802	-	dd/	549 538 365320
Creeve	Creevemully	Caulfield George Rev.	mills	-	-	-	Caulfield G - Moran Edmonc	1804	-	dd/	568 76 378730
Fuerty	Creevemully	Caulfield St George :	mills	-	-	-	Caulfield J - O`Gilvie Geo :	1806	-	dd/	699 15 419 346
Creeve	Creevemully	Coote Henry	mills	-	-	-	Coote H - Coote Sir Chas H	1814	-	dd/	683 192 469932
Creeve	Creevemully	Coote Sir Chas Henry	mills	-	-	-	Coote H - Crosbie Chidley C	1814	-	dd/	683 269 470018
Creeve	Creevemully	Coote Sir Chas Henry	mills	-	-	-	Coote C - Coote Robt Carr :	1814	-	dd/	683 270 470019
Creeve	Creevemully	Kennedy	mills	-	-	-	Kennedy - Connor	-	?	dd/	568 -?- 378731
Creeve	Creevemully	Mountrath Earl of	mills	-	-	-	Mountrath - Caulfield	-	?	dd/	300 415 230464
Fuerty	Creevemully	O`Gilvie John Geo :	mills	-	-	-	O`Gilvie - Nolan Thos & Jas	1815	-	dd/	698 408 479113?
Creeve	Creevemully	Sanders Lancellot :	mills	-	-	-	Sanders & Coote M. Arts.	1814	-	dd/	684 191 470535
Kilkevin	Creggameen	-	corn kilns	-	-	-	-	-	-	6"os/	26

PARISH	TOWNLAND	MILLER	TYPE	HOUSE	Land	£Val	PROPRIETORS	Date	WHEEL etc.	Record	Ref.
T`maconnell	Cregganycarna	- nr Vge C`carna :	corn	-	-	-	-	-	-	6"os/	50
T`maconnell	Cregganycarna	Murray Peter, Jn & Ed	eel-weir	-	-	-	-	-	-	gr/	-
T`maconnell	Cregganycarna	Murray Peter, Jn & Ed	tuck	-	-	-	-	-	-	gr/	-
Creagh	Culliaghbeg	-	corn & kiln	-	-	-	-	-	-	6"os/	56
Ros	Cunmeen	- near Elphin	corn	-	-	-	-	-	-	1"os/	77
Creagh	Curriaghbeg	Doland Martin	corn	-	28a.	-	-	-	-	gr/	-
Killumod	Danesfort	Thrilfall Richard	corn	-	14a.	-	-	-	-	gr/	-
Killumod	Danesfort	Thrilfall Richard	miller`s house	-	-	-	-	-	-	gr/	-
Killinvoy	Demesne :	-	corn & kiln	-	-	-	-	-	-	6"os/	42
Kilronan	Derreenavoggy	- Arigna Iron Works	iron	-	-	-	-	-	-	6"os/	2
Kilronan	Derreenavoggy	Lyons	mills	-	-	-	Lyons - Jones	-	?	dd/	286 20 184420
Kilronan	Derreenavoggy	Lyons Myles :	mills	-	-	-	Lyons M - McDermott Chas	1783	-	dd/	375 203 250740
Kilronan	Derreenavoggy	Tenison Thomas :	mills	-	-	-	Tenison T - Lyons Myles :	1761	Lse. 15 Mar.	dd/	238 258 154341
Tibohine	Derry	- site of	old iron works	-	-	-	-	1841	-	6"os/	19
Kilbryan	Derryvunny	Peyton John	corn & kiln	-	0.0.30		-	-	-	gr/	-
Kilcolagh	Dooneen	-	corn kiln	-	-	-	-	-	-	6"os/	16
Tumna	Drumboylan	O`Brien William	corn & kiln	-	-	-	-	-	-	gr/	-
Kilbride	Drumdaff	- Hick`s Mill	flour	- converting	-	-	D & B Pftherrick	2004	-	pWEH	Cr
Clooncraff	Drummullin	-	corn & kiln	-	-	-	-	-	-	6"os/	17
Clooncraff	Drummullin	-	corn kilns (2)	-	-	-	-	-	-	6"os/	17
Clooncraff	Drummullin	Fox Arthur	mill	-	38a.	-	-	-	-	gr/	-
Elphin	Emlagh	-	corn kiln	-	-	-	-	-	-	6"os/	16
Elphin	Emlagh	Howard Jno :	mill	-	-	-	Howard J - Sandford Robt :	1773	-	dd/	293 105 194226?
Elphin	Emlagh	Sandford Henry :	mill	-	-	-	Sandford - Mahon Maurice	1789	-	dd/	410 11 267568
Elphin	Emlagh	Sandford Robert :	mill	-	-	-	Sandford R - Kildare E.	1750	-	dd/	145 47 96708
Elphin	Emlagh	Sandford Robert :	mills	-	-	-	Sandford R - Owen Sam :	1741	-	dd/	105 124 73123
Elphin	Emlagh (5)	Hartland Maurice :	mill	-	-	-	Hartland Lord - Lloyd Thos	1803	-	dd/	558 294 371436
Oran	Emlaghnagree	-	corn kiln	-	-	-	-	-	-	6"os/	39
Ballintober	Enfield	French Thomas :	bleach	-	-	-	French T - Kelly William :	1813	-	dd/	660 198 455847
Creeve	Erriblagh	Acheson William	corn	-	1.0.30	-	-	-	-	gr/	-
	Farankelly	-	corn kiln	-	-	-	-	-	-	6"os/	41
Bumlin	Farnbeg	- N. side river :	brewery	-	-	-	-	-	-	6"os/	29
Ballintober	Frenchlawn :	-	old corn mill	-	-	-	-	-	-	6"os/	34
Ballintober	Frenchlawn :	-	old corn mill	-	-	-	-	2004	-	pWEH	R
Fuerty	Fuerty	Henry Joseph	bleach green	-	-	-	Henry Jos - Montgomery	1792	-	dd/	452 102 291704
Fuerty	Fuerty	Mitchell	bleach green	-	-	-	Mitchell & ano - Mallsen	-	?	dd/	540 482 354574
Fuerty	Fuerty	Mitchell Thomas :	bleach green	-	-	-	Mitchell T - Nisbitt :	1748	-	dd/	126 470 88403
Fuerty	Fuerty	Mitchell Thomas :	bleach green	-	-	-	Mitchell T - Henry Ann :	1774	Mort. 23 Apl.	dd/	300 381 200276
St John`s	Galey Beg :	-	corn & kiln	-	-	-	-	-	-	6"os/	45
Killinvoy	Gally	Downey	mills & kilns	-	-	-	Downey - Pim	-	?	dd/	686 395 471918
Killinvoy	Gally	Fairbrother George :	mills & kilns	-	80a.	-	Fairbrother Geo - Fox John :	1815	Mort. 29 Apl.	dd/	686 395 471918
Killinvoy	Gally	Fairbrother George :	mills & kilns	-	-	-	Fairbrother G - Fox John :	1815	Mort. 29 Apl.	dd/	869 17 4733348
Roscommon	Ganlys	Abbot	mill	-	-	-	Abbot - Kelly	-	-	dd/	709 96 485431
Kilglass	Gillstown	-	corn & kiln	-	-	-	-	1841	-	6"os/	23
Kilglass	Gillstown	Blakeney	mills	-	-	-	Blakeney - Greavy	-	-	dd/	663 271 456124
Kilglass	Gillstown	Cope	mill	-	-	-	Cope - Walsh	-	- [error]	dd/	386 559 259536
Kilglass	Gillstown	E. side Scranmoge R.	old corn mill	-	-	-	-	1841	-	6"os/	23
Kilglass	Gillstown	French Robert	mill	-	-	-	French R - Bruen Henry	1792	-	dd/	442 546 288629
Kilglass	Gillstown	Johnston Samuel :	mills	-	-	-	Johnston S - Stafford :	1747	-	dd/	128 193 86554
Kilglass	Gillstown	Ritchie Robert :	mills	-	-	-	Ritchie R - Cocking Henry :	1774	-	dd/	303 427 201749
Kilglass	Gillstown	Stafford Eliz & Bridgid	mill	-	-	-	Stafford Eliz & Br. - Margt.	1782	-	dd/	349 279 234168
Kilglass	Gillstown	Stafford John	mills	-	-	-	Stafford J - Bruen Moses :	1748	-	dd/	133 129 89878/9

PARISH	TOWNLAND	MILLER	TYPE	HOUSE	Land	£Val	PROPRIETORS	Date	WHEEL etc.	Record	Ref.
Kilglass	Gillstown	Stafford Margaret	mill	-	-	-	Stafford M - Cope Henry	1782	-	dd/	345 440 234182
Kilglass	Gillstown	Wynne Jno (of Dublin)	mills	-	-	-	Wynne J - Stafford John	1747	-	dd/	130 4 87140
Kilglass	Glen	-	corn kiln	-	-	-	-	-	-	6"os/	3
Kilmacumsy	Gortnacloy	-	corn kiln	-	-	-	-	-	-	6"os/	16
Kilbride	Grange	-	corn	-	-	-	-	-	-	6"os/	23
Kilbride	Grange	-	tuck	-	-	-	-	-	-	6"os/	23
Kilbride	Grange	- ab. Shadlough :	corn	-	-	-	-	-	-	6"os/	28
Kilbride	Grange	Blackall Jane Dame :	mills	-	-	-	Blackall J - Kelly Henry :	1801	-	dd/	534 260 350115
Kilbride	Grange	Cary William :	mills	-	-	-	Cary W - Cary Rev Oliver :	1786	-	dd/	408 469 271487
Kilbride	Grange	Dunn James Rev :	mills	-	-	-	Dunn J & ors - Swan John :	1800	-	dd/	529 309 347254
Kilrustan	Grange	Fox Arthur	corn	-	61a.	-	-	-	-	gr/	-
Kilbride	Grange	Knot William :	mills	-	-	-	Knot W - Hastings Percival	1800	-	dd/	534 22 350175
Kilbride	Grange	Knott William :	mills	-	-	-	Knott WM - Elwood	1800	-	dd/	528 400 347114
Kilbride	Grange	Spelman Stephen	corn	-	8.3.3	-	-	-	-	gr/	-
Roscommon	Greganaharney *	Plunkett Richard :	mill	-	-	-	Plunket R - Plunkett Ann :	1791	-	dd/	443 267 286034
Roscommon	Greganaharney *	Shanly Francis :	mill	-	-	-	Shanly - Plunkett Michael	1749	-	dd/	137 454 94025
Kileevan	Greglahan	Grady John	mill	-	24a.	-	-	-	-	gr/	-
Roscommon	Hatley *	Moore George :	mills	-	-	-	Moore Geo - Parvisol John	1803	-	dd/	557 242 370165
Roscommon	Hatley *	Moore George :	mills	-	-	-	Moore G - Moore Philip :	1806	-	dd/	594 208 402764
Roscommon	Hatley *	Moore Philip	mills	-	-	-	Moore P - Moore Geo	1806	-	dd/	594 207 402763
Roscommon	Hatley *	Hallam Edward :	mills	-	-	-	Hallam Ed - Moore Geo :	1800	Conv. 30 Sep.	dd/	588 564 401443
Roscommon	Hatley *	Parvisol John Esq.	mills	-	-	-	Parvisol J - Moore George :	1807	-	dd/	588 482 401016
Roscommon	Hatley Manor *	Moore George :	mill	-	-	-	Moore G - Chamley Jno :	1811	-	dd/	643 216 442621
Kilcorkey	Kilcorkey	-	corn & tuck	-	-	-	-	1841	-	6"os/	21
Kilcorkey	Kilcorkey	O`Conor Denis	corn	-	206a.	-	-	-	-	gr/	-
Kilcorkey	Kilcorkey	O`Conor Denis	tuck	-	-	-	-	-	-	gr/	-
Roscommon	Killakin *	Bucknall	mills	-	-	-	Bucknall - Vesey	-	-	dd/	592 ? 401623
Roscommon	Killakin *	Cary	mills	-	-	-	Cary - Cary	-	?	dd/	580? 482 401067
Roscommon	Killakin *	Cary William :	mills	-	-	-	Cary W - Cary Rev. Oliver :	1786	-	dd/	408 469 271487
Roscommon	Killakin *	Hallam Edward :	mills	-	-	-	Hallam Ed - Moore Geo :	1800	Conv. 30 Sep.	dd/	588 564 401443
Roscommon	Killakin *	French Arthur :	mills	-	-	-	French A - Cary William :	1776	-	dd/	416 125 275010
Roscommon	Killakin *	Scott John :	mills	-	-	-	Scott J - Lawder Edward :	1806	Leasae 31 June	dd/	586 17 394529
Killumod	Killappoge	Brown John :	mill	-	-	-	Brown J - Spencer Harry :	1749	-	dd/	114 194 78597
Killumod	Killappoge	French Henry	mill	-	-	-	French H - Dodwell H	1740	-	dd/	103 458 72046
Killumod	Killappoge	French Jeffery :	mill	-	-	-	French - Talbot Chs & Chr	1750	-	dd/	141 284 95437
Killumod	Killappoge	French Kathleen	mill	-	-	-	French K - Lloyd Thomas	1784	-	dd/	375 229 250827
Killumod	Killappoge	Lloyd Guy :	mill	-	-	-	Lloyd G - Talbot Henry :	1750	-	dd/	143 35 95438
Killumod	Killappoge	Lloyd Guy :	mills	-	-	-	Lloyd Guy - Lloyd Owen	1740	-	dd/	102 103 698891
Killumod	Killappoge	Lloyd Owen :	mill	-	-	-	Lloyd O - Lloyd William :	1751	-	dd/	147 55 98730
Killumod	Killappoge	Lloyd Owen :	mill	-	-	-	Lloyd Owen - Owen Ygr.	1740	-	dd/	103 205 71433
Killumod	Killappoge	Spencer Harry :	mill	-	-	-	Spencer - Brown Dorothy :	1753	-	dd/	160 204 106996
Kilglass	Killegan	-	corn	-	-	-	-	-	-	1"os/	107
T`maconnell	Killeglan	- nr Vge. Killeglan	corn & pond	-	-	-	-	-	-	6"os/	50
Roscommon	Killendniell *	Fry Henry :	mill	-	-	-	Fry H - Fraser George :	1754	-	dd/	174 332 116419
Killuken	Killukin	Bond James Rev. :	mills	-	-	-	Bond Jas - Little James :	1816	-	dd/	706 243 483799
Killuken	Killukin	Bond	mills	-	-	-	Bond	1819	-	dd/	741 46 584581
Killuken	Killukin	Moore George :	mill	-	-	-	Moore G - Chamley Jno :	1811	-	dd/	643 216 442621
Elphin	Killynagh Beg	-	corn & tuck	-	-	-	-	1841	-	6"os/	22
Elphin	Killynagh Beg	-	corn kilns (2)	-	-	-	-	1841	-	6"os/	22
Elphin	Killynagh Beg	Stroker John	tuck	-	-	-	-	-	-	gr/	-
Elphin	Kilmaclumsy	- near Elphin	old windmill	-	-	-	-	-	-	1"os/	77
Tibohine	Kilrooddan	-	corn kiln	-	-	-	-	-	-	6"os/	20

PARISH	TOWNLAND	MILLER	TYPE	HOUSE	Land	£Val	PROPRIETORS	Date	WHEEL etc.	Record	Ref.
Kilgeefin	Kilroosky	-	corn & kiln	-	-	-	-	-	-	6"os/	36
Kilgeefin	Kilroosky	-	mill	old buildings	17a.	-	-	2004	- & waterway	mmSv/	wh - R
Kilgeefin	Kilroosky	- 1/4 mile from PO	corn	-	-	-	-	-	-	pWEH	R
Kilgeefin	Kilroosky	Fineran Mary	corn	-	17a.	-	-	-	-	gr/	-
Roscommon	Kiltymaine	Dillon Charles H. Hon.	mill	-	-	-	Dillon C - Colebroke Sir Geo	1771	-	dd/	284 449 185349
Roscommon	Knockabeast *	-	corn	-	-	-	-	-	-	6"os/	10
Kilronan	Knockadryan	-	corn & kiln	-	-	-	-	-	-	6"os/	2
Kilronan	Knockadryan	Timon Charles	corn	-	6.0.0	-	-	-	-	gr/	-
Baslick	Knockalegan	Kelly	mills	-	-	-	Kelly - Kelly	-	?	dd/	112 218 77760
Baslick	Knockalegan	Kelly John :	mills	-	-	-	Kelly & Son - French Arth :	1753	-	dd/	160 504 108617
St John`s	Knockanyconor	- E. side of road	flour & pond	-	-	-	-	-	-	6"os/	45
St John`s	Knockanyconor	- W. side of road	corn & kiln	-	-	-	-	-	-	6"os/	45
St John`s	Knockanyconor	Barbor James :	mills	-	-	-	Barbor J - Bond William :	1811	-	dd/	636 338 437803
St John`s	Knockanyconor	Bond James Rev. :	mills	-	-	-	Bond J - Blackhall Robt. :	1816	Mort. 15 May.	dd/	741 46 584581
St John`s	Knockanyconor	Bond Richard	corn	-	7.0.10		-	-	-	gr/	-
Roscommon	Knocklagharry *	Kelly Wid. Hon Mary	mills	-	-	-	Kelly Mary - Kelly Jno :	-	?	dd/	112 218 77760
Killumod	Knockroe	-	corn	-	-	-	-	-	-	6"os/	10
Killumod	Knockroe	Cox Mark	corn	-	61a.	-	-	-	-	gr/	-
Cloontuskert	Lanesborough Tn	Costello John	ruins & store	-	-	-	-	-	-	gr/	-
Cloontuskert	Lanesborough Tn	Shannon Commrs.	corn	-	-	-	-	-	-	gr/	-
Cloontuskert	Lanesborough Tn :	- unoccupied :	corn - old :	s (1A) 51x34x16.6	-	5.1.	-	1846	works out of order :	hob/	5.3229
Cloontuskert	Lanesborough Tn :	Russell J A	corn store	(1B) 33.6x16.6x15 &	-	7	-	1846	-	hob/	5.3229
Kilglass	Lavagh	- at Dereen Vge.	corn kiln	-	-	-	-	1841	-	6"os/	18
Drumatemple	Leabeg	-	corn kiln	-	-	-	-	-	-	6"os/	34
Ballintober	Lecarrow	- on streem to L. Ree	orn	old, v. dilapidated	-	-	-	2004	- pho. taken	mmSv/	wh - D
Tibohine	Leggatinty	- near Frenchpark	mill	-	-	-	-	-	-	1"os/	77
Tibohine	Leggatinty	- Cloonshanville Mill :	mill	-	-	-	-	-	-	6"os/	15
Kilbride	Lisgobban	Finniran Laurence	corn & kiln	-	10a.	-	-	-	-	gr/	-
Kilbride	Lisgobban	Finniran Laurence	tuck	-	-	-	-	-	-	gr/	-
Tibohine	Lissacurkia	-	corn kiln	-	-	-	-	-	-	6"os/	14
Aughrim	Lissadorn	Colingsby Lady	mill	-	-	-	Colingsby - Gunning	1775	-	dd/	309 16 204064
Aughrim	Lissadorn	Colingsby Lady Fran	mill	-	-	-	Colingsby F - Gunning Jn	1775	-	dd/	309 16 204065
Aughrim	Lissadorn	Gunning John :	mill	-	-	-	Gunning J - Wade Phelim :	1754	-	dd/	194 458 130368
Aughrim	Lissadorn	Hamilton James Hon :	mill	-	-	-	Hamilton J - Kirkwood Sam	1758	-	dd/	196 19 18922
Tibohine	Lissydaly	- N. of Lissydaly Br.	corn, mill dam :	-	-	-	-	1841	-	6"os/	13
Tibohine	Lissydaly	Breheny Andrew	corn & kilns	-	11a.	-	-	-	-	gr/	-
Killinvoy	Longnamuck	- near L. Ree :	corn	-	-	-	-	-	-	6"os/	42
Kilcolagh	Loughbally	-	corn kiln	-	-	-	-	-	-	6"os/	15
Tisrara	Lyscallagh (?)	Gore Hon. Richard :	mill	-	-	-	Gore R - Lloyd Thomas :	1787	-	dd/	388 68 255371
Tisrara	Lyscallagh (?)	Gore Hon. Richard :	mill	-	-	-	Gore R - Phibbs William :	1786	-	dd/	384 210 254695
Tisrara	Lyscallagh (?)	Gore Hon. Richard :	mill	-	-	-	Gore R - Guffe Robt	1789	-	dd/	411 544 212600
Tisrara	Lyscallagh (?) :	French Austi :	mill	-	-	-	French A - French Robt	1809	-	dd/	622 103 428608
Tisrara	Lysgallagh	French Arthur & Son	mill	-	-	-	French A - Gore Richard	1786	-	dd/	380 142 254245
Tisrara	Lysgallagh	Gore Richard	mill	-	-	-	Gore R - Phibbs William	1786	-	dd/	384 210 254695
Termonbarry	Meelick	-	corn kiln	-	-	-	-	1841	-	6"os/	19
Termonbarry	Meelick	-	old mill & dam	-	-	-	-	-	-	6"os/	15
Kiltullagh	Meeltraun	-	corn & dam	-	-	-	-	-	-	6"os/	32
Boyle Town	Mill Park	King Sir Robert Bt. :	tuck	-	-	-	King R - Croghan Owen :	1746	-	dd/	125 449 85651
Boyle Town	Mill Park Boyle Tn	King Robert Sir :	tuck	-	-	-	King R - Croghen Owen :	1746	-	dd/	124 511 86549
Boyle Town	Mill Park Boyle Tn	King Robert Sir :	tuck	-	-	-	King R - Lynch Stephen	1746	-	dd/	124 512 85653
Boyle Town	Mill Park Boyle Tn	King Robert Sir :	tuck	-	-	-	King R - Croghen Owen :	1741	-	dd/	125 449 85650
Boyle Town	Mill Park Boyle Tn	King Robert Sir :	tuck	-	-	-	King R - Lynch Stephen :	1746	-	dd/	127 4 85652

PARISH	TOWNLAND	MILLER	TYPE	HOUSE	Land	£Val	PROPRIETORS	Date	WHEEL etc.	Record	Ref.
Boyle Town	Mill Park Boyle Tn	King Robert Sir :	tuck	-	-	-	King R - Lynch Mary Wid.	1740	-	dd/	127 5 85654
Kiltullagh	Milltown	-	mill & mill dam	-	-	-	-	-	-	6"os/	32
Roscommon	Milltown	Burke Reps. Mary	corn & kiln	-	-	-	-	-	-	gr/	-
Kiltulagh	Milltown	Burke Reps. Mary	mill & kiln	-	144a.	-	-	-	-	gr/	-
Roscommon	Milltown	Burne James :	land	-	-	-	Burne J - Nugent Richard :	1746	-	dd/	128 26 85804
Roscommon	Milltown	Irvin John :	mill	-	-	-	Irvin Jn - Connolly Daniel :	1812	?	dd/	641 349 447463?
Roscommon	Milltown	O`Reilly Dom. Wm :	mill	-	-	-	O`Reilly D - Connolly John :	1817	Mort. 4 Jan.	dd/	710 16 485951
Dysart	Milltown :	Dillon Richard :	land	-	-	-	Dillon R - French Jefferys :	1750	-	dd/	155 554 105805
Roscommon	Milltown B`robe	Wills Thomas :	land	-	-	-	Wills Thomas - Burke Ulick :	1786	-	dd/	394 155 258608
Roscommon	Milltown Pass	-	mill	-	-	-	-	-	-	1"os/	98
Boyle	Mocmoyne	- N. side of river	corn	-	-	-	-	1841	-	6"os/	5
Boyle	Mocmoyne	- S. side R. Boyle	brewery	-	-	-	-	1841	-	6"os/	5
Roscommon	Moher (3)	Nerheny Hugh	mill	-	-	-	Nerheny H - Nerheny Hugh	1808	-	dd/	632 373 433666
St Peter`s	Monksland	- at Milltown Pass :	pond	-	-	-	-	-	-	6"os/	48
St Peter`s	Monksland	Walsh William	mill & kiln	-	47a.	-	-	-	-	gr/	-
St Peter`s	Monksland :	-	brewery	-	-	-	-	-	-	6"os/	52
Roscommon	Mount Delvin	-	mill	-	-	-	-	-	-	1"os/	86
Tibohine	Mullen	-	mill & tuck mill	-	-	-	-	-	-	6"os/	15
Tibohine	Mullen	Darcy John	corn & kiln	-	-	-	-	-	-	gr/	-
Kilgeefin	N. of Kilroosky)	-	corn & kiln	-	-	-	-	-	-	6"os/	36
Kilmacumsy	Oldtown	- Rd. to Shannon Br.	corn	-	-	-	-	-	-	1"os/	107
Aughrim	Pollnamoghill	M`Donnell Michael	corn	-	19a.	-	-	-	-	gr/	-
Aughrim	Pollnamoghill	M`Donnell Michael	corn & kiln	-	-	-	-	1841	-	6"os/	17
Rahara	Rahara	-	old mill	-	-	-	-	-	-	6"os/	45
Kiltoom	Ratawragh	- at Milltown Pass	corn & kiln	-	-	-	-	-	-	6"os/	48
Creeve	Rathardeagher	Mulvey James :	mill	-	-	-	Mulvey J - Carey William	1757	-	dd/	188 565 126706
Creeve	Rathardeigher	Bartley Charles :	mill	-	-	-	Bartley C - McDonnell Edw :	1767	-	dd/	261 384 171889?
St Johns	Rinnagan	-	corn kiln	-	-	-	-	1841	-	6"os/	243
Roscommon	Rockfield *	-	mill	-	-	-	-	-	-	1"os/	87
T`maconnell	Rockwell	Finneran John	corn	-	2.2.30		-	-	-	gr/	-
T`maconnell	Rockwell	Finneran John	tuck	-	-	-	-	-	-	gr/	-
Kilmore	Roo	- on shore Tully Lo.	corn kiln	-	-	-	-	-	-	6"os/	17
Ballintober N.	Roosky Town	- S. of Market Ho :	corn	-	-	-	-	-	-	6"os/	24
Roscommon	Roscommon Tn	- Casey`s Mill	foundry	-	-	-	-	2004	-	pWEH	Z
Kilcolagh	Runnaboll	-	corn kiln	-	-	-	-	-	-	6"os/	16
Killinvoy	Scregg	-	corn & pond	-	-	-	-	-	-	6"os/	42
Tibohine	Sheepwalk	M`Gunn James	corn - bad rep.	-	-	-	-	-	-	gr/	-
Ballintober	Snipe Hill	Hanly Daniel :	mill	-	-	-	Hanly Dan - Feely John :	1801	-	dd/	536 65 351557
Ballintober	Snipe Hill	Wills Thomas :	mill	-	-	-	Wills Thos - Tracy John :	1790	-	dd/	501 590 327116
Killinvoy	Srah	Alexander Joseph	corn & kiln	-	5a.	-	-	-	-	gr/	-
Killinvoy	Srah :	-	flour	-	-	-	-	-	-	6"os/	42
Killinvoy	Srah :	-	corn	-	-	-	-	-	-	6"os/	42
Tibohine	Stonepark	on road Frenchpark :	corn	-	-	-	-	-	-	6"os/	20
Roscommon	Stonepark	on road Roscommon :	mill & pond	-	19a.	-	-	-	-	gr/	-
Roscommon	Stonepark	Wade Henry	corn	-	19a.	-	-	-	-	gr/	-
Kiltulagh	Swinefield	-	mill	-	-	-	-	-	-	1"os/	86
Kiltulagh	Swinefield	Corcoran Patrick	corn kilns	-	-	-	-	-	-	gr/	-
Roscommon	Tanidrissoge *	Athenry Fras Lord :	mill	-	-	-	Athenry Ld - Bermingham :	1743	-	dd/	114 234 78770
Roscommon	Tanidrissoge *	Baldwin Richard :	mill	-	-	-	Baldwin N - Swift Michael :	1761	-	dd/	212 281 139237
Roscommon	Tanidrissoge *	Louth Earl of	mill	-	-	-	Louth E. - Bermingham	-	?	dd/	271 451 179178
Roscommon	Tanidrissoge *	Radford Newton :	mill	-	-	-	Radford N - Bill against Daly	1760	-	dd/	209 530 139437
Tibohine	Tibohine	-	corn kiln	-	-	-	-	-	-	6"os/	14

PARISH	TOWNLAND	MILLER	TYPE	HOUSE	Land	£Val	PROPRIETORS	Date	WHEEL etc.	Record	Ref.
Boyle	Tivannagh	-	corn kiln	-	-	-	-	-	-	6"os/	5
Drumatemple	Tobermakee	-	corn kiln	-	-	-	-	-	-	6"os/	34
Drumatemple	Tobermakee :	-	crockery kiln	-	-	-	-	-	-	6"os/	34
Drumatemple	Tobermakee :	-	old mill	-	-	-	-	-	-	6"os/	34
Clooncraff	Toomore	-	corn kiln	-	-	-	-	-	-	6"os/	17
Roscommon	Townland ? :	-	corn & kiln		-	-	-	-	-	6"os/	40
Killinvoy	Townland ? :	-	tuck & race	-	-	-	-	-	-	6"os/	42
Tibohine	Tully	- nr Tully Bridge	corn kiln	-	-	-	-	-	-	6"os/	19
Tibohine	Tully	- nr Tully Bridge	gig mill	-	-	-	-	-	-	6"os/	19
Kilkeevin	Willsbrook	- on R. Suck	corn & kiln	-	-	-	-	-	-	6"os/	26
Roscommon	Windmill Field :	King Edwd & Elinor :	land	-	-	-	King Ed & W - Crofton Ed :	1787	Rel. 26 Jne.	dd/	392 117 257986
Roscommon	Windmill Field :	Plunkett Arthur :	land	-	-	-	Plunkett A - Shanly Thos :	1743	-	dd/	108 385 76713

PARISH	TOWNLAND	MILLER	TYPE	HOUSE	Land	£Val	PROPRIETORS	Date	WHEEL etc.	Record	Ref.
Kilmoremoy	Abbeyhalfquarter	Knoxgore Colfa	flax & water	-	4-1-8	-	-	-	-	gr/	-
Kilmoremoy	Abbeyhalfquarter N.	- E. end Linenhall St.	distillery	-	-	-	-	1841	-	6"os/	14
Achonry	Achonry	Creeveen Thomas	corn	-	11a.	-	-	-	-	gr/	
Kilmacteigue	Aclare Village	Burns John & Evans W	corn & kiln	-	0-1-25		-	-	-	gr/	
Kilmacteigue	Aclare Village :	Burns John & Evans W	corn & kiln	(2C) 31x18.6x8 :	-	8/7d	-	-	14x2x5 1 pair st.	hob/	5.3235
Kilmacallan	Aghoo	-	corn	-	-	-	-	-	-	1"os/	66
Kilfree	Annaghmore	-	corn kiln	-	-	-	-	-	-	6"os/	44
Ballysadare	Ardcurley	at Toberscanavan Vge.	mill	-	-	-	-	-	-	6"os/	26
Ballysadare	Ardcurley	Hort Patrick	corn & kilns	-	-	-	-	-	-	gr/	-
Kilmacallan	Ardkeeran	- at Riverstown	tuck	-	-	-	-	-	-	6"os/	27
Kilmacallan	Ardkeeran	- S. side Riverstown	corn & kiln	-	-	-	-	-	-	6"os/	27
Kilmacallan	Ardkeeran	Clarkin James	corn	-	2-0-35		-	-	-	gr/	
Kilmacallan	Ardkeeran	Clarkin James	tuck	-	-	-	-	-	-	gr/	
Kilmacallan	Ardkeeran	Clerkin James	corn	-	-	-	-	-	14x2x -	vmb/	17
Kilmacallan	Ardkeeran	Clerkin James	tuck	-	-	-	-	-	12x2x -	vmb/	17
Kilshalvy	Ardminnan	-	corn kiln	-	-	-	-	-	-	6"os/	39
Kilmoremoy	Ardnaree	- E. side R. Moy	brewery	-	-	-	-	-	-	6"os/	29
Kilmoremoy	Ardnaree Town	Hearne John	old brewery	-	-	-	-	-	-	gr/	-
Kilmoremoy	Ardnaree Town :	Bredin Richard	mill	(1B) 74x39x36 :	-	18	-	-	16x7x7 32 bkts.	hob/	5.3236
Kilmoremoy	Ardnaree Town :	Fair John (in chancery)	corn & kiln	(1B) 74x39x36 :	-	18	-	-	16ft. dia. u'shot :	hob/	5.3236
Kilmoremoy	Ardnaree Town :	- unoccupied : s	flour	(1B) 65x34x36	-	-	-	-	17x7x6 breast :	hob/	5.3237
Kilmoremoy	Ardnaree Town :	Verscoyle Robert	flour	(1B) 65x34x36	-	8	-	-	17x7x6 32 bkts. :	hob/	5.3236
Kilmoremoy	Ardnaree Town :	Bredin Mrs. Margaret	kiln & store	(1B) 47x18x23 :	-	21	-	-	-	hob/	5.3236
Drumcliff	Ardtermon :	Gore Nathaniel :	manor (? mill)	-	-	-	Gore Nath - Gore John :	1715	L&R. 4/5 July	dd/	14 450 6560
Drumcliff	Ardtermon :	Gore Nathaniel Bt. :	manor (? mill)	-	-	-	Gore Nath - Ormsby John :	1714	Lse. 6 Aug. (1yr.)	dd/	13 123 5371
Kilterra	Ballanalock	Biern Phillis	corn	-	-	-	-	-	11x1x6	vmb/	17
Cloonoghill	Ballanecarron S	Lennox Robert	corn	called a GIG mill	-	-	-	-	3ft 9ins x 6"x 8" :	vmb/	17
Aghanagh	Ballinafad	- 1/4m WxN B'afad Vg.	corn mill	-	-	-	-	-	-	6"os/	40
Aghanagh	Ballinafad	- 5/8 mile ex Surgal R.	mill race	-	-	-	-	-	-	6"os/	40
Drumcliff	Ballincar	- S./ Millbrook Ho.	flour, race 1m.	-	-	-	-	-	-	6"os/	8
Drumcliff	Ballincar	Simpson Edward	corn	-	17a.	-	-	-	-	gr/	-
Dromard	Ballinlig	- on stream to bay	corn & kiln	-	-	-	-	1841	-	6"os/	19
Dromard	Ballinlig	Beatty Charles	corn	-	33a.	-	-	-	-	gr/	-
Dromard	Ballinlig	Beatty Charles	corn	-	-	-	-	-	no information	vmb/	17
Killoran	Ballinvally	- N. side Owenboy R.	corn mill	-	-	-	-	-	-	6"os/	25
Killoran	Ballinvally	Bruin James	corn	-	-	-	-	-	-	gr/	
Killoran	Ballinvally	Bruin James	corn	-	-	-	-	-	4x1x4	vmb/	17
Killoran	Ballinvally	Bruin James	tuck	-	-	-	-	-	-	gr/	
Killoran	Ballinvally		mill dam	-	-	-	-	-	-	6"os/	25
Achonry	Ballyara	-	corn kiln	-	-	-	-	-	-	6"os/	37
Kilmoremoy	Ballyholan	Wingfield Edward	corn	-	-	-	-	-	-	gr/	-
Emlaghfad	Ballymote	-	mill	-	-	-	-	-	-	1"os/	66
Emlaghfad	Ballymote	Baker Andrew	mill	-	-	-	Baker Andr - Gorman Jno	1846	-	dd/	1846 20 188
Kilvarnet	Ballynacarrow	Gilbert Charles	bleach	-	-	-	-	-	-	gr/	
Kilvarnet	Ballynacarrow	Gilbert Charles	corn	-	159a.	-	-	-	-	gr/	
Kilvarnet	Ballynacarrow N.	-	mill race	-	-	-	-	-	-	6"os/	26
Kilvarnet	Ballynacarrow N.	- E./ Thornhill bridge	corn	-	-	-	-	-	-	6"os/	26
Kilvarnet	Ballynacarrow N.	- 1/8 m NW./ Thornhill	bleach	-	-	-	-	-	-	6"os/	26
Kilvarnet	Ballynacarrow N.	- 1/8m/sq. S side river	bleach gn	-	-	-	-	-	-	6"os/	26
Cloonoghill	Ballynaraw S.	nr. Bunnanaddan Vge.	corn, corn kiln : &	-	-	-	-	1841	-	6"os/	38
Cloonoghill	Ballynaraw S.	Scanlan James	corn	-	25a.	-	-	-	-	gr/	
Ballysadare	Ballysadare Town	- (vacant)	old corn mill	(1C) 34x22.6x14 :	-	2.8.9	-	1838	- [no dims.}	hob/	5.3239
Ballysadare	Ballysadare Town	- (vacant)	old corn mill	(1C) 36x16x12 :	-	1	-	1838	- [no dims.}	hob/	5.3239

PARISH	TOWNLAND	MILLER	TYPE	HOUSE	Land	£Val	PROPRIETORS	Date	WHEEL etc.	Record	Ref.
Ballysadare	Ballysadare Town	Benson Margaret	tuck	(2B) 11x20x8 :	-	5.5.6	-	1838	18x4x7 1 pr. feet :	hob/	5.3239
Ballysadare	Ballysadare Town	Broder Michael	tuck	unroofed 20x12x8 :	-	3.1.0	-	1838	- 1 pair feet	hob/	5.3239
Ballysadare	Ballysadare Town	Culbertson Robert	corn & kiln	-	-	-	-	-	-	gr/	-
Ballysadare	Ballysadare Town	Culbertson Robert	corn & kiln	(1A) 105x35x48.6 :	-	149	-	1838	18x5x7 6 pr. st. :	hob/	5.3239
Ballysadare	Ballysadare Town	Culbertson Robert	corn & kiln	(1A) 71x31x46 :	-	113	-	1838	- [no dims.}	hob/	5.3239
Ballysadare	Ballysadare Town	Litton Edward	mill	-	-	-	Litton Ed - Culbertson Robt	1845	-	dd/	1845 10 1
Ballysadare	Ballysadare Town	Mostyn Thomas	mil	-	-	-	Mostyn T - Culbertson Robt	1846	-	dd/	1846 13 204
Ballysadare	Ballysadare Town	Pollexfen W. & G.	flour	Avena Mills	-	-	-	1963	-	lic./20	flour
Ballysadare	Ballysadare Town	Wynne James	mil	-	-	-	Wynne J - Culbertson Robt	1846	-	dd/	1846 13 65
Ballysadare	Ballysadare Town :	Broder Michael	tuck	20x12x8 unroofed :	-	3.1.0	-	-	- 1 pair feet :	hob/	5.3239
Ballysadare	Ballysadare Town :	- vacant	old corn mill	(1C) 34x22.6x14 :	-	2.8.9	-	1838	- (no information)	hob/	5.3239
Ballysadare	Ballysadare Town :	- vacant	old corn mill	(1C) 36x16x12 :	-	1	-	1838	- (no information)	hob/	5.3239
Ballysadare	Ballysadare Town :	Culbertson Robert	barley & flour	(1A) 71x34x46 & :	-	62	-	1838	- (no information)	hob/	5.3239
Ballysadare	Ballysadare Town :	Culbertson Robert	tuck	- (no dimensions)	-	-	-	1838	- 1 pair feet :	hob/	5.3239
Ballysadare	Ballysadare Town :	Culbertson Robert	corn & kilns	(1A) 105x35x48.6 :	-	94	-	1838	- 6 pair stones :	hob/	5.3238
Ballysadare	Ballysadare Town :	Culbertson Robert	flour & corn	stores& yard	-	300	-	1856	-	gr/	a.a.lre.ie
Kilmacteigue	Banada	-	corn kiln	-	-	-	-	-	-	6"os/	37
Kilmacteigue	Banada	- 1/10m W. Banada Br.	mill	-	-	-	-	-	-	6"os/	37
Kilmacteigue	Banada	Doyle Peter	corn	-	-	-	-	-	12x2x5	vmb/	17
Kilmacteigue	Banada	Doyle Thomas	corn & kiln	-	-	-	-	-	-	gr/	
Bohola	Barley Mill	Culbertson Robert	mill	-	-	-	Culbertson - Rendall Henry	1846	-	dd/	1846 13 205
Bohola	Barley Mill	Harvey Agnes	mill	-	-	-	Harvey Agnes - Harvey Jno	1849	-	dd/	1849 13 229
Drumcliff	Barnaderg	- S. of Grange P.O.	corn	-	-	-	-	1841	-	6"os/	5
Drumcliff	Barnaderg	M`Clean Thomas	corn	-	14a.	-	-	-	-	gr/	-
Toomour	Battlefield	-	corn & tuck	-	-	-	-	-	-	6"os/	39
Toomour	Battlefield	-	kiln	-	-	-	-	-	-	6"os/	39
Toomour	Battlefield	-	mill race (1/2 mile	-	-	-	-	-	-	6"os/	39
Toomour	Battlefield	Doyle Patrick	corn	-	10a.	-	-	-	-	gr/	-
Toomour	Battlefield	Doyle Patrick	tuck	-	-	-	-	-	-	gr/	-
Kilmacteigue	Belclare	- S./ Bellanameen R.	corn & dam	-	-	-	-	-	-	6"os/	36
Kilmacteigue	Belclare	Commins Charles & P	corn	-	-	-	-	-	12x1x8	vmb/	17
Kilmacteigue	Belclare	Commons Patrick	corn	-	9a.	-	-	-	-	gr/	
Kilturra	Bellanalack	-	mill race, no mill	-	-	-	-	-	-	6"os/	39
Kilturra	Bellanalack	O`Byrne Philip	corn	-	79a.	-	-	-	-	gr/	
Kilmacallan	Bellanascarva	-	mill race	-	-	-	-	-	-	6"os/	34
Kilmacallan	Bellanascarva	- stream to Unshin R.	corn	-	-	-	-	-	-	6"os/	34
Kilmacallan	Bellanascarva	Harper Munns	mill	-	0-1-30	-	-	-	-	gr/	
Kilmacallan	Bellangarrigreeny	1/5m SE./Casltebaldwin	corn	-	-	-	-	-	-	6"os/	34
Kilmacallan	Bellangarrigreeny	Brehony Michael	old mill	-	9a.	-	-	-	-	gr/	
Kilmacshalgan	Belville	- 1.2m.S. of br.	old corn mill	-	-	-	-	-	-	6"os/	18
Ballysadare	Bleachgreen	- N. side R.	mill	-	-	-	-	-	-	6"os/	20
Ballysadare	Bleachgreen	- SW of Town Br.	mill	-	-	-	-	-	-	6"os/	20
Ballysadare	Bleachgreen	Kelly Andrew	beetling	-	-	-	-	-	4x4x24	vmb/	17
Ballysadare	Bleachgreen	Kelly Andrew	bleach	-	-	-	-	-	20x2x24	vmb/	17
Ballysadare	Bleachgreen	Madden Martin	bleach	-	55a.	64	-	-	-	gr/	-
Ballysadare	Bleachgreen	Madden Martin	corn	-	-	-	-	-	-	gr/	-
Ballysadare	Bleachgreen	Madden Martin J	corn	(1A) 61x25.6x43 & :	-	35	-	1838	8 pairs stones :	hob/	5.3239
Ballysadare	Bleachgreen	Madden Thomas	flour & kiln	-	-	120	-	-	-	gr/	-
Ballysadare	Bleachgreen	Mangan Richard	beetling	-	-	-	-	-	24x2x25	vmb/	17
Ballysadare	Bleachgreen		mill	-	-	-	-	-	-	6"os/	20
Kilmacowen	Breeoge	- NE / Bösadare Bay	corn (ruins)	-	-	-	-	-	-	6"os/	20
Dromard	Buninna	Griffith Henry	thrashing	-	124a.	-	-	-	-	gr/	-

PARISH	TOWNLAND	MILLER	TYPE	HOUSE	Land	£Val	PROPRIETORS	Date	WHEEL etc.	Record	Ref.
Achonry	Bunnacranagh	-	corn kiln	-	-	-	-	-	-	6"os/	42
Aghanagh	Bunnadober	-	corn kiln	-	-	-	-	-	-	6"os/	40
Kilmoremoy	Bunree	-	mil	-	-	-	-	-	-	1"os/	53
Kilmoremoy	Bunree	Gallagher Andrew	corn	-	-	-	-	-	15x5x5 3 pr st.	vmb/	17
Kilglass	Cabrakeel	Finton Michael	corn	-	89a.	-	-	-	-	gr/	-
Killoran	Carha	-	corn & kiln	-	-	-	-	1841	-	6"os/	25
Killoran	Carha	-	tuck	-	-	-	-	1841	-	6"os/	25
Killoran	Carha	Mullan Patrick	corn	-	-	-	-	-	11x1x7	vmb/	17
Killoran	Carha	Mullan Patrick	tuck	-	-	-	-	-	11x1x7	vmb/	17
Killoran	Carha	Reilly Patrick	corn	-	1-1-30	-	-	-	-	gr/	
Killoran	Carha	Reilly Patrick	tuck	-	-	-	-	-	-	gr/	
Toomour	Carowcrory	- from Tövanny Lo.	mill race	-	-	-	-	-	-	6"os/	40
Dromard	Carrowbleagh E.	- opp. Longford Ho.	corn & kiln	-	-	-	-	-	-	6"os/	19
Achonry	Carrowcarragh	-	corn kiln	-	-	-	-	-	-	6"os/	32
Achonry	Carrowcarragh	-	corn mill	-	-	-	-	-	-	6"os/	32
Achonry	Carrowcarragh	Crosby Peter	mill	-	0-1-20	-	-	-	-	gr/	
Achonry	Carrowcarragh	Sloan James	corn	-	-	-	-	-	11x1x4 no empl.	vmb/	17
Toomour	Carrowcrory	1/4m SW Templevanny Lo.	corn mill	-	-	-	-	-	-	6"os/	40
Toomour	Carrowcrory	Leonard Matthew	corn	-	35a.	-	-	-	-	gr/	-
Kilmoremoy	Carrowcushlaun W.	1/4 m S Ardnaree Vge.	foundry	-	-	-	-	-	-	6"os/	29
Kilmoremoy	Carrowcushlaun W.	1/5m S Ardnaree Tn. Br.	flour	-	-	-	-	-	-	6"os/	29
Kilmoremoy	Carrowcushlawn	Hearne Fair & Co.	corn	-	-	-	-	-	17x8x6 4 pair st.	vmb/	17
Kilmoremoy	Carrowcushlawn	Hearne Fair & Co.	flour	-	-	-	-	-	18x7x7 3 pair st.	vmb/	17
Aghanagh	Carrowkeel	-	corn kiln	-	-	-	-	-	-	6"os/	40
Dromard	Carrowmorris		corn & tuck	-	-	-	-	-	-	6"os/	19
Dromard	Carrowmorris		mill dam	-	-	-	-	-	-	6"os/	19
Kiloran	Carrownacleigha	- S of Coolaney Vge.	corn mill	-	-	-	-	-	-	6"os/	25
Kiloran	Carrownaskeagh	- S. of R. Owenboy	cloth & corn	-	-	-	-	-	-	6"os/	25
Kiloran	Carrownaskeagh	- S/ R. Owenboy	corn kiln	-	-	-	-	-	-	6"os/	2
Kilfree	Carrowntemple	- close NW of Abbey	corn kiln	-	-	-	-	-	-	6"os/	44
Kilmacteigue	Carrowreagh	-	corn	-	-	-	-	-	-	6"os/	36
Kilmacteigue	Carrowreagh	-	corn kiln	-	-	-	-	-	-	6"os/	40
Kilmacteigue	Carrowreagh	-	malt kiln	-	-	-	-	-	-	6"os/	36
Kilmacteigue	Carrowreagh	-	mill	-	-	-	-	-	-	1"os/	66
Kilmacteigue	Carrowreagh	Quin Edward	corn	-	-	-	-	-	4x1x4	vmb/	17
Castleconnor	Castleconnor	Rutledge George	corn	-	-	-	-	-	12x2x12	vmb/	17
Kilmacteigue	Castlerock	Doyle Thomas	corn	-	23a.	-	-	-	-	gr/	
Kilmacteigue	Castlerock	Doyle Thomas	corn	-	-	-	-	-	13x1x5	vmb/	17
Kilmacteigue	Castlerock	Doyle Thomas	tuck	-	-	-	-	-	-	gr/	
Kilmacteigue	Castlerock	Doyle Thomas	tuck	-	-	-	-	-	12x2x5	vmb/	17
Kilmacteigue	Castlerock	W./ Crow Isl. Vge. X	kiln & mill	-	-	-	-	-	-	6"os/	31
Easky	Castletown	Ormsby William :	Ye Mill Park :	- (no mill O.S. 11)	-	-	Ormsby W - Shannon Jn :	1734	Lse. 28 Aug.	dd/	84 220 59672
Sligo	Chasefield *	-	corn kiln	-	-	-	-	-	-	6"os/	45
Sligo	Churchland	Culbertson Robert	mill	-	-	-	Culbertson R - Mostyn Thos	1845	-	dd/	1845 17 179
Sligo	Churchland	Harvey Agnes	mil	-	-	-	Harvey Agnes - Harvey Jno	1849	-	dd/	1849 13 229
Kilmactranny	Cloghmine	-	malt kiln	-	-	-	-	-	-	6"os/	41
Achonry	Cloonacool	- S side R. Moy	corn	-	-	-	-	-	-	6"os/	31
Achonry	Cloonacool	- S./ Cloonacool Vge.	corn kiln	-	-	-	-	-	-	6"os/	31
Achonry	Cloonacool	Brennan Dominick	mill & kiln	-	30a.	-	-	-	-	gr/	
Achonry	Cloonacool	Brennan Domnick	corn	-	-	-	-	-	14x2xx4	vmb/	17
Achonry	Cloonacool	Brennan Luke	mill & kiln	-	12a.	-	-	-	-	gr/	
Achonry	Cloonacool	Doyle Martin	mill	-	11a.	-	-	-	-	gr/	

PARISH	TOWNLAND	MILLER	TYPE	HOUSE	Land	£Val	PROPRIETORS	Date	WHEEL etc.	Record	Ref.
Ballysadare	Cloonacurra	-	corn	-	-	-	-	-	-	6"os/	26
Ballysadare	Cloonacurra	-	mill race	-	-	-	-	-	-	6"os/	26
Ballysadare	Cloonacurra	- 1/8m SW Ardcree Br.	tuck	-	-	-	-	-	-	6"os/	26
Ballysadare	Cloonacurra	Doyle James	corn	-	0-0-30	-	-	-	-	gr/	
Kilfree	Cloonanure	-	corn kiln (2)	-	-	-	-	-	-	6"os/	44
Killaraghy	Clooncunny	-	corn kiln	-	-	-	-	-	-	6"os/	46
Kilross	Clooneenroe	-	engine house	-	-	-	-	1841	-	6"os/	26
Kilfree	Cloonlaheen	-	corn kiln	-	-	-	-	-	-	6"os/	44
Achonry	Cloonlaughil	-	corn kiln	-	-	-	-	-	-	6"os/	42
Achonry	Cloonlaughil	-	corn mill	-	-	-	-	-	-	6"os/	42
Achonry	Cloonlaughil	-	sluice	-	-	-	-	-	-	6"os/	42
Achonry	Cloonlaughil	E. side Mullaghanoe R.	mill	-	-	-	-	-	-	6"os/	42
Achonry	Cloonloughil	Henny Mrs.	corn	-	-	-	-	-	4x2x2	vmb/	17
Kilfree	Cloonsillagh	-	corn kiln (2)	-	-	-	-	-	-	6"os/	44
Kilfree	Cloonsillagh	-	mill	-	-	-	-	-	-	1"os/	66
Kilfree	Cloontycarn	-	corn kiln (3)	-	-	-	-	-	-	6"os/	44
Kilfree	Cloontycarn	-	kiln	-	-	-	-	-	-	6"os/	45
Kilfree	Cloontycarn	W. side rd. /Drunlushma	corn mill	-	-	-	-	-	-	6"os/	45
Drumcliff	Collinsford	- S./ Drumcliff R	corn	-	-	-	-	-	-	6"os/	8
Drumcliff	Collinsford	- S./ Drumcliff R	tuck	-	-	-	-	-	-	6"os/	8
Drumcliff	Collinsford	Goggins Thomas	tuck	-	-	-	-	-	-	gr/	-
Drumcliff	Collinsford	M`Hugh Michael	old mill	-	53a.	-	-	-	-	gr/	-
Colloney	Colloney	Sims Alex	flour	-	-	-	-	-	36x8x28	vmb/	17
Colloney	Colloney Town	Sims Alexander	flour, corn, kiln	ho., offs., store & ld.	1.3.0	902	-	1856	-	gr/	a.a.lre.ie
Killoran	Coolaney	- in Coolaney Vge.	mill	-	-	-	-	-	-	6"os/	25
Killoran	Coolaney	Burrows Henry	corn	-	-	-	-	-	16x5x9	vmb/	17
Killoran	Coolaney	Doyle Patrick	corn & kiln	-	-	-	-	-	-	gr/	
Killoran	Coolaney Town	- (name unclear)	corn (no. 2 :	(1A) 71x46.6x46 :	-	94.10	-	1838	10x1.9 91 r.p.m.	hob/	5.3239
Killoran	Coolaney Town	- (name unclear)	flour (no. 1 :	(1A) 105x41.6x46.6 :	-	76	-	1838	35.6x8x28 8 pr. st.	hob/	5.3239
Coolany	Coolany Town :	Doyle Patrick	corn & kilns	(1B) 54.6x24x25 :	-	9.15.1	-	-	-	hob/	5.3254
	Coolbeg	- on shore :	old salt pans	-	-	-	-	-	-	6"os/	8
Sligo	Coollaughil ?	Henry Myles	corn	-	22a.	-	-	-	-	gr/	
Sligo	Coollaughil ?	Scally Martin	corn & kiln	-	32a.	-	-	-	-	gr/	
Kilmacallan	Cooperhill	1/4m. W./ Riverstown X	tuck	-	-	-	-	-	-	6"os/	27
Kilmacallan	Cooperhill	1/5m W. / Riverstown X	corn & kiln	-	-	-	-	-	-	6"os/	27
Kilmacallan	Cooperhill	1/8m. W./ Riverstown X	corn & kiln	-	-	-	-	-	-	6"os/	27
Kilmacallan	Cooperhill	Cooper Charles Wm	corn & kiln	-	460a.	-	-	-	-	gr/	-
Kilmacallan	Cooperhill	Fahy Patrick	corn	-	-	-	-	-	14x2x3	vmb/	17
Kilmoremoy	Corimla South	Durkin Hugh	corn	-	56a.	-	-	-	-	gr/	-
Drumcliff	Cregg	- close to shore :	mill	-	-	-	-	-	-	6"os/	14
Drumcliff	Cregg	- near shore Ballincar	Mill	-	-	-	-	1890	-	25"os/	5
Kilfree	Cuilmore	-	corn kiln (5)	-	-	-	-	-	-	6"os/	4
Kilfree	Cuilprughlish	-	corn kiln (2)	-	-	-	-	-	-	6"os/	45
Drumcliff	Cullabeg	- 1m S./ Milltown	corn	-	-	-	-	-	-	6"os/	8
Drumcliff	Cullabeg	Allen Matthew	corn	-	23a.	-	-	-	-	gr/	-
Killglass	Culleens	Gordon Patrick	corn	-	36a.	-	-	-	-	gr/	-
Killglass	Culleens	Ryan Patrick & Thos	corn	-	-	-	-	-	11x1x5	vmb/	17
Killglass	Culleens	S./ Cloonycarney Vge.	mill	-	-	-	-	1841	-	6"os/	17
Achonry	Cully	-	corn kiln	-	-	-	-	-	-	6"os/	42
Easky	Curraghnagap	M`Nama John	tuck	-	-	-	-	-	-	gr/	-
Easky	Curraghnagap	W./ Easky R. above Vge.	corn & pond	-	-	-	-	1841	-	6"os/	11
Easky	Curraghnagap :	Gore Nathaniel Bt. :	mill	-	-	-	Gore Nath - Jones Wm :	1730	-	dd/	65 2 44054
Easky	Curraghnagap :	Gore Nathaniel Bt. :	mill	-	-	-	Gore Nath - Gore Boothe :	1733	L&R. 13/14 Jul.	dd/	71 371 51426

PARISH	TOWNLAND	MILLER	TYPE	HOUSE	Land	£Val	PROPRIETORS	Date	WHEEL etc.	Record	Ref.
Easky	Curraghnagap :	Humphry	mill	-	-	-	Humphry - Gilmore Wm :	1735	Lse. 4 Aug.	dd/	79 444 56803
Easky	Curraghnagap :	Gore Nathaniel Sir :	mill	-	-	-	Gore Nath - Gore Boothe :	1733	L&R. 31 July	dd/	72 436 51427
Easky	Curraghnagass	Cullen Domnick	corn	-	-	-	-	-	12x1x10	vmb/	17
Achonry	Curry	-	mill	-	-	-	-	1841	-	6"os/	42
Achonry	Curry	- on Coarse R.	corn	-	-	-	-	-	-	1"os/	65
Achonry	Curry	Brehany Patrick	corn	-	18a.	-	-	-	-	gr/	
Achonry	Curry	Filan James	corn	-	-	-	-	-	13x1x5	vmb/	17
Achonry	Curry	Filan James	tuck	-	-	-	-	-	13x1x6	vmb/	17
Achonry	Curry	Filon James	corn	-	5.2.4	-	-	-	-	gr/	
Drumral	Daghloanagh	Clarkin Michael	corn	-	-	-	-	-	13x2x6	vmb/	17
Drumral	Daghloonagh	-	corn & tuck	-	-	-	-	-	-	6"os/	39
Drumral	Daghloonagh	-	mill race	-	-	-	-	-	-	6"os/	39
Killaraght	Derrinoghran	- SE. of Gorteen Br.	corn kiln	-	-	-	-	-	-	6"os/	45
Templeboy	Donaghintraine	- 2m N./ Dunne. Br	corn & kiln	-	-	-	-	-	-	6"os/	12
Templeboy	Donaghintraine	John Ryan	corn	-	-	-	-	-	15x1x9	vmb/	17
Templeboy	Donaghintraine		mill dam	-	-	-	-	-	-	6"os/	12
Kilfree	Doon	-	corn kiln (4)	-	-	-	-	-	-	6"os/	44
Templeboy	Doonycoy	on small R. near coast	corn	-	-	-	-	-	-	6"os/	12
Castleconor	Dooyeaghny	Dempsey Michael	corn	-	19a.	-	-	-	-	gr/	-
Kilmacteigue	Drimina	-	corn kiln	-	-	-	-	-	-	6"os/	37
Kilmacteigue	Drimina	-	mill dam	-	-	-	-	-	-	6"os/	37
Kilmacteigue	Drimina	- NE./ R. Moy	corn mill	-	-	-	-	-	-	6"os/	37
Kilmacteigue	Drimina	Kennan Frank	corn	-	-	-	-	-	- a small GIG mill	vmb/	17
Kilmacteigue	Drimina	M`Vey James	corn	-	c20a.	-	-	-	-	gr/	
Kilmacshalgan	Dromore	Fenton John	corn	-	-	-	-	-	-	gr/	-
Kilmacshalgan	Dromore West	-	mill	-	-	-	-	-	-	1"os/	55
Drumcliff	Drumcliff South	- E Drumcliff Br.	tuck	-	-	-	-	-	-	6"os/	8
Drumcliff	Drumcliff South	- on Drumcliff R.	corn	-	-	-	-	-	-	6"os/	8
Drumcliff	Drumcliff South	Stewart Charles	tuck	-	1.3.10	-	-	-	-	gr/	-
Screen	Drumnagoal	Bruen Mark	corn	-	1.3.10	-	-	-	-	gr/	-
Screen	Drumnagoal		corn	-	-	-	-	-	-	6"os/	19
Kilmactiege	Eskragh	-	corn	-	-	-	-	-	-	6"os/	37
Screen	Farranyharpy	Golden Robert	corn	-	18a.	-	-	-	-	gr/	-
Screen	Farranyharpy	Golden Robert	tuck	-	-	-	-	-	-	gr/	-
Screen	Farranyharpy		corn kilns	-	-	-	-	-	-	6"os/	18
Screen	Farranyharpy		old corn mill	-	-	-	-	-	-	6"os/	18
Kilmacteigue	Glenawoo	- W. of Aclare Vge.	mill, mill dam & :	-	-	-	-	1841	-	6"os/	'36
Kilmacteigue	Glenawoo	Clarke Michael	corn	-	23a.	-	-	-	-	gr/	
Kilmacteigue	Glenawoo	Clarke Patrick	corn	-	-	-	-	-	4x1x4	vmb/	17
Kilmacteigue	Glenawoo	O`Brien Henry	corn	-	29a.	-	-	-	-	gr/	
Kilfree	Gorteen	- W. of Gorteen Br.	mill	-	-	-	-	-	-	6"os/	44
Kilfree	Gorteen	Leonard Mark	corn	-	15a.	-	-	-	-	gr/	-
Kilfree	Gorteen	Leynard Mark	corn	-	-	-	-	-	11x1x8	vmb/	17
Kilmacteigue	Gorterslin	Quin Martin	corn	-	20a.	-	-	-	-	gr/	
Kilmacteigue	Gorterslin	Quin Martin	corn	-	-	-	-	-	13x2x5	vmb/	17
Drumcliff	Gortnagrelly	Parke William :	mill	-	-	-	Parke - Ormsby Mathew :	1719	M. Arts. 27 Aug. :	dd/	47 439 31620
Drumcliff	Grange	- 1.2m from Grange	tuck	-	-	-	-	-	-	6"os/	5
Templeboy	Grangemore	-	corn	-	-	-	-	1841	-	6"os/	18
Drumcliff	Gregg	Kieghron Patrick	corn	-	8a.	-	-	-	-	gr/	-
Kilfree	Greyfield	-	corn kiln	-	-	-	-	-	-	6"os/	44
Calry	Hazelwood Dems.	Wynne John	saw	-	814a.	-	-	-	-	gr/	-
Calry	Hazlewood Dems.	-	saw	-	-	-	-	-	-	6"os/	15

PARISH	TOWNLAND	MILLER	TYPE	HOUSE	Land	£Val	PROPRIETORS	Date	WHEEL etc.	Record	Ref.
Rossinver	Keeloges	- S Ballanatrillick Br.	corn	-	-	-	-	-	-	6"os/	6
Rossinver	Keeloges	Booth Sir Robert G	corn	-	-	-	-	-	-	gr/	-
Emlaghfad	Keenaghan	3/8m S. of Town centre	corn	-	-	-	-	-	-	6"os/	33
Emlaghfad	Keenaghan	Gorman John & Henry	corn	-	18a.	-	-	-	-	gr/	
Kilfree	Kilfree	-	corn kiln (4)	-	-	-	-	-	-	6"os/	44
Kilfree	Kilfree	Brewin James	mill & kiln	-	4a.	-	-	-	-	gr/	-
Kilfree	Kilfree	Brien James	corn	-	-	-	-	-	11x1x7	vmb/	17
Kilshalvy	Killavil	-	kiln	-	-	-	-	-	-	6"os/	39
Kilshalvy	Killavil	- SE./ Black River	mill ruin	-	-	-	-	-	-	6"os/	39
Kilshalvy	Killavil	Morrison James	corn	-	22-0-1	-	-	-	-	gr/	-
Kilross	Killeenduff	Ormsby John	corn & kiln	offices & land	32a.	25	-	1856	-	gr/	a.a.ire.ie
Sligo	Killian	-	corn	-	-	-	-	-	-	1"os/	65
Sligo	Killmorgan *	- W. of Camus Bridge	mill	-	-	-	-	-	-	6"os/	34
Sligo	Killmure * :	French Jno :	mill	-	-	-	French Jno - Irwin Jno :	1725	Lse. 1 Apl.	dd/	90 377 64936
Kilmacteigue	Kilmacteigue	-	corn kiln	-	-	-	-	-	-	6"os/	36
Kilmacteigue	Kilmacteigue	- in Glebe	tuck	-	-	-	-	-	-	6"os/	36
Kilmacteigue	Kilmacteigue	Quin Michael	corn	-	-	-	-	-	4x2x5	vmb/	17
Kilmacteigue	Kilmacteigue	Quinn Michael	corn & kiln	-	-	-	-	-	-	gr/	
Kilmorgan	Kilmorgan	Fahy John	mill	-	1-1-35	-	-	-	-	gr/	
Ballysadare	Kiloglashery	Beatty George & Richd	barley	-	-	-	-	-	15x6x7	vmb/	17
Ballysadare	Kiloglashery	Beatty George & Richd	shelling	-	-	-	-	-	16x4x6	vmb/	17
Ballysadare	Kiloglashery	Bolan Thomas	corn	-	-	-	-	-	14x4x4	vmb/	17
Ballysadare	Kiloglashery	not occ. 15 years	grain store	-	-	-	-	-	-	vmb/	17
Ballysadare	Kiloglashery	Tucker John	beetling	-	-	-	-	-	15x2x8	vmb/	17
Ballysadare	Kiloglashery	Tucker John	bleach	-	-	-	-	-	131x8	vmb/	17
Sligo	Kiloye *	Ormsby	mill	-	-	-	Ormsby - Ward	-	-	dd/	36 143 21830
Templeboy	Kilrusheighter	Ryan Thomas	tuck	-	4a.	-	-	-	-	gr/	-
Kilfree	Kilstraghlan	1/2m SSW Gorteen Vge.	mill in ruins	-	-	-	-	-	-	6"os/	44
Emlaghfad	Kinaghan	Lester Charworth	corn	-	-	-	-	-	15x5x8 & 15x5x8	vmb/	17
Kilmacshalgan	Knockaculleen	Jones Louis G	corn (unfin.)	-	62a.	-	-	-	-	gr/	-
Castleconnor	Knockagower	- WNW/ Kn'gower Br.	corn	-	-	-	-	-	-	6"os/	16
Castleconnor	Knockagower	Howley Edward	mill & kiln	-	-	-	-	-	-	gr/	-
Castleconnor	Knockagower	Rafter John	corn	-	-	-	-	-	13x1x13	vmb/	17
Ballysadare	Knockbeg West	- S. side Owenbeg R.	mill	-	-	-	-	-	-	6"os/	26
Ballynakill	Knockbrook	Rorke Patrick	corn	-	-	-	-	-	13x1x -	vmb/	17
Ballysadare	Knockmuldoney	-	mll	-	-	-	-	-	-	6"os/	20
Ballysadare	Knockmuldoney	- 1/8 m above br.	mill	-	-	-	-	-	-	6"os/	20
Ballysadare	Knockmuldoney	- E of river in Town	mill	-	-	-	-	-	-	6"os/	20
Ballysadare	Knockmuldoney	- W. Bösadare R.	bleach mill	-	-	-	-	-	-	6"os/	20
Ballysadare	Knockmuldoney	- W. Bösadare R.	mill	-	-	-	-	-	-	6"os/	20
Ballysadare	Knockmuldoney	Beatty George & Rich	corn	-	-	-	-	-	12x1x6	vmb/	17
Ballysadare	Knockmuldoney	Beatty George & Rich	tuck	-	-	-	-	-	13x2x6	vmb/	17
Ballysadare	Knockmuldoney	Cooper Edward J	old corn mills (2)	- & kiln (both unoc.)	-	3 & 2	-	1856	-	gr/	a.a.Ire.ie
Ballysadare	Knockmuldoney	Culbertson Robert	corn & kiln	- & offices	-	300	-	1856	-	gr/	a.a.Ire.ie
Ballysadare	Knockmuldoney	Culbertson Robert	mil	-	-	-	Culbertson - Ashlin Darmida	1848	-	dd/	1848 11 159
Ballysadare	Knockmuldoney	Young J & Mitchell J	corn	-	-	-	-	-	13x2x5	vmb/	17
Ballysadare	Knockmuldoney	Young J & Mitchell J	tuck	-	-	-	-	-	13x2x5	vmb/	17
Ballysadare	Knockmuldoney :	Benson James	tuck	-	-	-	-	-	10x2x6	vmb/	
Ballysadare	Knockmuldoney :	Benson Margaret	tuck	-	-	-	-	-	-	gr/	-
Ballysadare	Knockmuldoney :	Broder Michael	tuck	-	-	-	-	-	-	gr/	-
Ballysadare	Knockmuldoney :	Broder Michael	tuck	house & garden	0.0.25	3.5.0	-	1856	-	gr/	a.a.Ire.ie
Kilmoremoy	Knocknalyre	- 1/8m E./ Bunree Br.	Bunree Corn Mills	-	-	-	-	-	-	6"os/	29

PARISH	TOWNLAND	MILLER	TYPE	HOUSE	Land	£Val	PROPRIETORS	Date	WHEEL etc.	Record	Ref.
Kilfree	Knocknaskeagh	-	corn kiln	-	-	-	-	-	-	6"os/	39
Kilmorgan	Lackagh	Scanlan James	mill	-	1-0-10	-	-	-	-	gr/	
Sligo	Lareen	- on Drowes R	mill	-	-	-	-	-	-	1"os/	43
Ballysadare	Lark Hill	- E. of Deescart Glebe	corn, kiln & dam	-	-	-	-	1841	-	6"os/	19
Ballysadare	Lark Hill	McGrath Terence	corn	-	-	-	-	-	3x1x4	vmb/	17
Kilglass	Leaffony	- W./ R. Leaffony	tuck	-	-	-	-	-	-	6"os/	11
Killglass	Leaffony	Carroll George	corn	-	-	-	-	-	12x1x11	vmb/	17
Kilglass	Leaffony	Carroll Thomas	corn	-	-	-	-	-	-	gr/	-
Kilglass	Leaffony	Carroll Thomas	tuck	-	-	-	-	-	-	gr/	-
Kilglass	Leaffony		corn	-	-	-	-	-	-	6"os/	11
Kilfree	Lisbaleely	-	corn kiln	-	-	-	-	-	-	6"os/	44
Drumcolumb	Lisconny	- E. side Unshin R.	old mill	-	-	-	-	1841	-	6"os/	26
Drumcolumb	Lisconny	Mortimer John :	mill	Plantation measure :	119a.	-	Mortimor John - Hanlan :	1709	L&R. 30 Apl.	dd/	4 458 1158
Ahamlish	Lislary	- stream to Pollmosha	old corn mill	-	-	-	-	-	-	6"os/	4
Kilmacteigue	Lislea	- E. side Lo. Talt R. :	corn & kiln	-	-	-	-	-	-	6"os/	36
Kilmacteigue	Lislea	Burns John	corn & kiln	-	0-0-12	-	-	-	-	gr/	
Kilmacteigue	Lislea	Mrs Elizabeth	corn	-	-	-	-	-	14x2x5	vmb/	17
Cloonoghil	Lisnagore	-	corn kiln	-	-	-	-	-	-	6"os/	32
Drumcliff	Lissadill	Booth Sir Robert G	saw	-	-	-	-	-	-	gr/	-
Killoran	Lissalough	- SSW/Coolaney Vge.	mill in ruins	-	-	-	-	-	-	6"os/	25
Killoran	Lissalough		corn kiln	-	-	-	-	-	-	6"os/	25
Achonry	Montiagh	-	corn kiln	-	-	-	-	-	-	6"os/	42
Achonry	Montiagh	-	mill race	-	-	-	-	-	-	6"os/	42
Achonry	Montiagh	1/2m NW Curry Vge. X	corn mill	-	-	-	-	-	-	6"os/	42
Achonry	Montiagh	Doyle Patrick	corn	-	14a.	-	-	-	-	gr/	
Achonry	Montiagh	Doyle Patrick	corn	-	-	-	-	-	4x1x3	vmb/	17
Achonry	Montiagh	E side R. nr Vge. Curry	mill	-	-	-	-	-	-	6"os/	42
Kilfree	Moygara	M`Keown James	corn	-	24a.	-	-	-	-	gr/	-
Sligo	Moygha	-	corn kiln (4)	-	-	-	-	-	-	6"os/	44
Kilfree	Mullaghroe	-	corn kiln	-	-	-	-	-	-	6"os/	45
Achonry	Mullanabreena	-	no mill	-	-	-	-	-	-	gr/	
Killadoon	Rannatruffaun W.	- at bottomof farm	corn	-	-	-	-	-	-	6"os/	35
Calry	Rathbraghan	Byrne John :	mills	-	-	-	Byrne J - Wynne Owen : I	1729	7 Jan.	dd/	64 117 42882
Calry	Rathbraghan	Greene William	corn & flour	-	6a.	-	-	-	-	gr/	-
Calry	Rathbraghan	Leicester	mills	-	-	-	Leicester - Wynne	-	-	dd/	36 275 22279
Calry	Rathbraghan	Ward John :	mills	-	-	-	Ward J - Wynne Owen : R	-	-	dd/	63 110 42881
Calry	Rathbraghan	Wynne	mills	-	-	-	Wynne - Warden	-	-	dd/	34 110 20784
Calry	Rathbraghan	Wynne Owen :	mills	-	-	-	Wynne Owen - Knox : I	1736	Lse. 27 mar.	dd/	94 193 65866
Calry	Rathbraghan		flour, mill race	-	-	-	-	-	-	6"os/	14
St John's	Rathedmond	- due W/ Sligo Tn Br.	old brewery	-	-	-	-	-	-	6"os/	14
Kilmoremoy	Rathkid	Brogan James	tuck	-	19a.	-	-	-	-	gr/	-
Kilfree	Rathmadder	-	corn kiln	-	-	-	-	-	-	6"os/	44
Kilfree	Rathmadder	- at Gorteen Vge.	corn mill	-	-	-	-	-	-	6"os/	44
Castlrconor	Rathmurphy	- at Castleconor Vge	corn	-	-	-	-	-	-	6"os/	22
Sligo	Ratkip *	- 1/4m above White Br.	tuck	-	-	-	-	-	-	6"os/	29
Kilshalvy	Riverstown	Clarkin James	corn & tuck	(2B) 35.6x19x9.6 :	-	3.7.10	-	-	1 pair stones :	hob/	5.3254
Kilshalvy	Riverstown	Cooper C W	mill	(1A) 31x19x22 & :	-	7	-	-	1 pair stones :	hob/	5.3254
allynakill	Rockbrook	- above Rockbrook Ho.	corn	-	-	-	-	-	-	6"os/	27
Killaspugbrone	Scardanmore	- due N. St. Patös Well	flour	-	-	-	-	-	-	6"os/	14
Killaspugbrone	Scardanmore	M`Intyre Alex	corn & flour	-	-	-	-	-	-	gr/	-
Achonry	Sessuacommon	-	corn kiln	-	-	-	-	-	-	6"os/	31
Achonry	Sessuacommon	-	old mill	-	-	-	-	-	-	6"os/	31
Achonry	Sessuegilroy	1/4m N. Crow Isl. Vge.	mill	-	-	-	-	-	-	6"os/	31

PARISH	TOWNLAND	MILLER	TYPE	HOUSE	Land	£Val	PROPRIETORS	Date	WHEEL etc.	Record	Ref.
Achonry	Sessuegilroy	Finan James	corn	-	9a.	-	-	-	-	gr/	
Achonry	Sessuegilroy	Finan James	tuck	-	-	-	-	-	-	gr/	
Achonry	Sessuigilroy	Finman James	corn	-	-	-	-	-	4x8x4	vmb/	17
Achonry	Sessuigilroy	Finman James	tuck	-	-	-	-	-	12x1x4	vmb/	17
Kilmacranny	Shaduff	Keough Mr	corn	-	-	-	-	-	20x1x-	vmb/	17
Easky	Shannon	Parke William :	mill	-	-	-	Parke - Ormsby Mathew :	1719	M. Arts. 27 Aug. :	dd/	47 493 31620
Calry	Shannon Oughter	M`Donnell Thomas	bleach	-	9a.	-	-	-	-	gr/	-
St John`s	Sligo Town	Martin James	distillery	-	-	-	-	-	-	gr/	-
St John`s	Sligo Town	Martin James	mill	-	-	-	-	-	-	gr/	-
St John`s	Sligo Town	Pollexfen Charles W	Sligo Mills	-	-	-	Pollexfen C - Ire. Bk. Govs.	1886	-	dd/	1886 45 100
St John`s	Sligo Town	Pollexfen Charles W	Sligo mills :	-	-	-	Pollexfen Charles - William	1887	-	dd/	1887 508
St John`s	Sligo Town :	Martin James Capt.	flour & kilns	stores,offs, yard	-	240	-	-	-	gr/	-
St John`s	Sligo Town :	Martin Abraham	distillery	-	-	-	Martin Abraham - Gregory	1834	-	gr/	1834 19 156
Calry	Sligo Town :	Carroll John	bewery	stores & offices	-	85	-	-	-	gr/	-
St John`s	Sligo Town :	Martin Capt. James	flour & kilns	(1B) 110x28x29 :	-	49	-	-	16x4.64, 27 float b(	hob/	5.3251
St John`s	Sligo Town :	-	tread mill	(1A) 24x33.6x37 :	-	104	-	-	-	hob/	5.3247
St John`s	Sligo Town :	Ramsay John	corn store	(1B) 78x22x30 :	-	95	-	-	-	hob/	5.3248
St John`s	Sligo Town :	Anderson John	brewery	(1B) 30.6x21.6x23 :	-	24	-	-	- (no information)	hob/	5.3244
St John`s	Sligo Town :	Martin Abraham :	distillery	mill lofts, cooperage	-	-	-	-	18x4.6 breast :	hob/	5.3244
St John`s	Sligo Town :	- unoccupied	distillery & mill	malt house & kilns :	-	-	-	-	-	hob/	5.3247
St John`s	Sligo Town :	Wynne John	corn market	sheds & yard	-	13	-	-	-	gr/	-
St John`s	Sligo Town :	Wynne John	corn market	gateho. & stores	-	30	-	-	-	gr/	-
St John`s	Sligo Town :	- Town of Sligo	tolls on oats	weighbridge & offs.	-	-	-	-	-	hob/	5.3251
St John`s	Sligo Town :	Burton	mill	-	-	-	Burton - Dirany	-	-	dd/	79 260 55717
St John`s	Sligo Town :	Burton Benjamin :	mill	-	-	-	Burton B - Burton Fras :	1734	L&R. 9/10 Jan.	dd/	76 392 55021
St John`s	Sligo Town :	Burton Benjamin :	mill	-	-	-	Burton B - Burton Fras :	1734	L&R. 9/10 Jan.	dd/	76 392 55021
St John`s	Sligo Town :	Burton Benjamin :	mill	-	-	-	Burton B - Macartney Jas :	1708	L&R. 10/11 Jne.	dd/	1 331 209
Drumard	Spring Garden	-	corn & tuck & :	-	-	-	-	-	-	6"os/	19
Drumard	Spring Garden	Scanlan Julia	corn	-	-	-	-	-	-	gr/	-
Drumcliff	St Helens	- nr Rosses Point	mill	-	-	-	-	-	-	1"os/	43
Kilmactranny	Straduff	- on Cammoge R.	mill race	-	-	-	-	-	-	6"os/	36
Kilmactranny	Straduff	3/8m NNW of Bömashee L(	corn	-	-	-	-	-	-	6"os/	36
Ballysadare	Streamstown	-	windmill	-	-	-	-	-	-	1"os/	55
Ballysadare	Streamstown	- S./ Bösadare Bay	old salt pans	-	-	-	-	-	-	6"os/	20
Shancough	Tap	-	malt kiln	-	-	-	-	-	-	6"os/	35
Achonry	Tobertelly	-	corn kiln	-	-	-	-	-	-	6"os/	32
Toomour	Toomour	-	corn kiln	-	-	-	-	-	-	6"os/	40
Drumral	Toomour-Carrow	Lorton Lord	corn	-	-	-	-	-	13x1x6	vmb/	17
Kilmacshalgan	Toorboy	- E. side Easky R.	mill	-	-	-	-	-	-	6"os/	11
Sligo	Townland ?	- due W./ Mullanyös X	corn	-	-	-	-	-	-	6"os/	37
Sligo	Townland ?	- N./ Mullany's Cross	corn kiln	-	-	-	-	-	-	6"os/	37
Sligo	Townland ?	- W./ jctn. Ballina rd.	mill pond	-	-	-	-	-	-	6"os/	14
Sligo	Townland ?		old corn mill	-	-	-	-	-	-	6"os/	14
Shancough	Ummeryroe	-	corn	-	-	-	-	-	-	6"os/	34
Calry	Willowbrook	Benson James	tuck	-	3a.	-	-	-	-	gr/	-

PARISH	TOWNLAND		MILLER	TYPE	HOUSE	Land	£Val	PROPRIETORS	Date	WHEEL etc.	Record	Ref.
Inishlounaght	Abbeyville	*	- S. of Lacken Castl	mill	-	-	-	-	-	-	iaa/	AI2287 os4.12.1
Aghnameadle	Aghnameadle		Cormack Thomas	corn	-	10a.	10.13	-	-	-	gr/	-
bo./ Ormond L&U	Allitrim	*	Sheddon Barbara	mill	-	-	-	Shedon B - Barbara	1884	-	dd/	1884 58 187
bo./ Ormond L&U	Annaghnerigge	*	Clebwine Margaret	mills	-	-	-	Clebwine M - LusterJn	1882	-	dd/	18842 20 113
Rahelty	Archerstown		-	mill	-	-	-	-	-	-	iaa/	AI2288 os41.15.6
Rahelty	Archerstown		- E. side manor R.	Archerstown Brewery		-	-	-	-	-	6"os/	41
Rahelty	Archerstown		- E/ Archerst'n Br.	flour	-	-	-	-	-	-	6"os/	41
Rahelty	Archerstown		Knaggs Matthew	flour	-	16a.	74	-	-	-	gr/	-
Rahelty	Archerstown		Langley Henry	mill	-	-	-	Langley Henry - Chas	1885	-	dd/	1885 42 116
Rahelty	Archerstown		Ruddy James	brewery	(1B) 20x10x5.6 & :	-	-	-	1847	18x6x2.6 40 floats :	hob/	5.1493
Rahelty	Archerstown		Ruddy James	flour	(1B) 39x26x27.6 :	-	21.11	-	1847	18x6x2.6 40 floats :	hob/	5.1493
Ardfinnan	Ardfinnan		- on bridge R. Suir	flour	-	-	-	-	-	-	6"os/	86
Ardfinnan	Ardfinnan		Prendergast James :	flour	(1B) 93.6x26.6x46 :	-	39	-	-	- [no dimensions]	hob/	5.1558
Ardmayle	Ardmayle		- E/ Ardmayle Br.	old woollen factor	-	-	-	-	-	-	6"os/	52
Tipperary	Arnora	*	-	flour	-	-	-	-	-	-	6"os/	75
Templebeg	Atshanbo Cahill		Ryan Anthony	corn	-	-	-	-	-	13x3x6	vmb/	20
Templebeg	Atshanboe		Ryan Anthony	corn	-	1a.	4.15	-	-	-	gr/	-
Knigh	Ballanny More		- N. side Nenagh R.	old flour mill	-	-	-	-	1841	-	6"os/	14
Knigh	Ballanny More		Maher James	old flour mill	(1B) 66x24.9x41.6 :	-	31.18	-	-	-	hob/	5.1763
Tipp (3 tlds)	Ballinderry		-	Ballinderry Mills	-	-	-	-	-	-	1"os/	125
Ballingarry	Ballingarry Lower		- SW/Ballingarry Br.	corn	-	-	-	-	-	-	6"os/	55
Ballingarry	Ballingarry Lower		McGrath Thomas	corn	-	-	-	-	-	15x4x11	vmb/	20
Ballingarry	Ballingarry Lower		McGrath Thomas	corn & kiln	-	4a.	12.15	-	-	-	gr/	-
Tullaghorton	Ballinhalla		- N./ R. Tar	corn & kiln	-	-	-	-	-	-	6"os/	86
Templeree	Ballinroe		- NW./ Washpin Br.	Castleiny Mill	-	-	-	-	-	-	6"os/	29
Templeree	Ballinroe		Laffan John	flour	-	19a.	34.15	-	-	-	gr/	-
Templeree	Ballinroe		Laffan John	flour	-	-	-	-	-	15x - x8	vmb/	20
Graystown	Ballinunty		- Ballinunty	Mill	-	-	-	-	1841	-	6"os/	54
Graystown	Ballinunty		Lawless Robert	flour, Indian corn	-	1a.	20.10	-	-	-	gr/	-
Graystown	Ballinunty		Lawless Robert	flour, Indian corn	-	-	-	-	-	20x6x19 4 pr st.	vmb/	20
Knigh	Ballyanny		-	mill	-	-	-	-	-	-	map	DownSurv.
Knigh	Ballyanny		- E. bank Nenagh R	mill	-	-	-	-	1655	-	iaa/	AI2289 os14.16.4
Knigh	Ballyanny		Stapleton James	corn	-	-	15	-	-	-	gr/	-
Knigh	Ballyanny More		- NE/ Nenagh R	old flour mill	-	-	-	-	-	-	6"os/	14
Knigh	Ballyanny More		Maher James	old flour mill	(1B) 66x24.9x41.6 :	-	31	-	1846	- (no information)	hob/	5.1763
Kilcomenty	Ballyard		Kingscote Fitzharding	bleach	-	-	-	Kingcote - Thomas Pet.	1882	-	dd/	1882 17 84
Dromineer	Ballyartella		- W / Nenagh R	flour	-	-	-	-	-	-	6"os/	14
Dromineer	Ballyartella		Minnitt	mill	-	-	-	innitt - Moilse	-	-	dd/	821 453 552988
Dromineer	Ballyartella		O`Keeffe Patrick	flour	-	41a.	101	-	-	-	gr/	-
Dromineer	Ballyartella		O`Keeffe Patrick	flour	(1B) 50x17x18.6 :	-	26.4	-	-	16x11.6 48 floats	hob/	5.1766
Dromineer	Ballyartella		O`Keeffe Patrick	flour	-	-	-	-	-	16x11x6 3 pr st.	vmb/	20
Dromineer	Ballyartella		O`Keeffe Patrick	old flour mill	(1B) 23x28.6x19 :	-	9.2	-	-	16x5.6 48 floats	hob/	5.1766
Templemore	Ballycahill		Morkin John	corn	-	13a.	18.5	-	-	-	gr/	-
Lismalin	Ballydonnell		McCarthy William	corn	-	-	-	-	-	19x8x-	vmb/	20
Lismalin	Ballydonnell		McCarty William	corn	-	22a.	27.10	-	-	-	gr/	-
Dorrha	Ballyduff		Gwydir Daniel	mill	-	-	-	Gwydir D - Barry McI	1889	-	dd/	1889 22 192
Moyne	Ballyerk		-	mill (site)	-	-	-	-	1654	-	iaa/	AI2290 os36.5.5
Moyne	Ballyerk		- SW/ Lislacy Br.	old mill	-	-	-	-	-	-	6"os/	36
Twomileborris	Ballyerk		Grimes William	corn	(2B) 23x18x7	-	4	-	1847	11.6x1.6 undershot	hob/	5.1492
Kilmore	Ballygown		Ryan Patrick	corn	-	1a.	6.2.0	-	-	-	gr/	-
Monsea	Ballyhimiken		- E/ Nenagh R.	flour	-	-	-	-	-	-	6"os/	14
Monsea	Ballyhimiken		McDonnell James	flour	-	-	-	-	-	16x6x- 4 pr st.	vmb/	20

PARISH	TOWNLAND	MILLER	TYPE	HOUSE	Land	£Val	PROPRIETORS	Date	WHEEL etc.	Record	Ref.
Loughkeen	Ballykinash		windmill	N. of Carrig Village :	-	-	-	-	-	6"os/	5
Ballymackey	Ballyknockane	-	flour	-	-	-	-	-	-	6"os/	22
Ballymackey	Ballyknockane	Kennedy Edward	corn	(1B) 33.6x22x29 &	-	44.12	-	1848	shelling - 15x4x13 :	hob/	5.1796
Loughkeen	Ballyloughnane	- 1/8m SW/ Bridge	flour	-	-	-	-	-	-	6"os/	5
Loughkeen	Ballyloughnane	Abernethy William	flour	(1B) 58x21.9x29 :	-	46	-	1846	-	hob/	5.1766
Loughkeen	Ballyloughnane	Abernethy William	flour	(1B) 58x21.9x29 :	-	-	-	1846	11.6x4 o`shot :	hob/	5.1766
Loughkeen	Ballyloughnane	Hackett John	flour	-	-	-	-	-	14x5x-	vmb/	20
Loughkeen	Ballyloughnane	Hackett John & :	flour & kiln	-	-	40	-	-	-	gr/	-
Loughkeen	Ballyloughnane	Hackett Simpson	flour	(1B) 126.6x23.3x26.9	-	35	-	1846	11x2 27 bkts. :	hob/	5.1767
Loughkeen	Ballyloughnane	Hackett Simpson	flour	(1B) 126.6x23.3x26.9	-	35	-	1846	(2) - large 11x4.9 :	hob/	5.1767
Carrick	Ballylynch	- W. side Lingaun R.	corn	-	-	-	-	1841	-	6'os/	85
Carrick	Ballylynch	O`Neill Thomas	corn	-	-	7.6.0	-	-	-	gr/	-
Iffa & Offa East	Ballylynch	Shaw	mill	-	-	-	Shaw - Shaw	-	?	dd/	641 551 448156
Tipperary	Ballymillard	Dalton Richard (Dick)	corn	-	-	-	-	-	20x5x14	vmb/	20
Ballynaclough	Ballynaclogh	- imed. W.of Vge.	mill & mill race	-	-	-	-	1841	-	6"os/	27
Ballynaclogh	Ballynaclogh	Going Caleb	carding	-	-	-	-	-	-	gr/	-
Ballynaclogh	Ballynaclogh	Going Caleb	corn	-	0.1.1	21	-	-	-	gr/	-
Ballynaclogh	Ballynaclogh	Gowing Caleb	corn	(1B) 33x16x23 :	-	25.2	-	1847	17x5 48 bkts. drives	hob/	5.1801
Kilmurry	Ballynacloona	-	mill		-	-	-	-	-	1"os/	156
Bruis	Ballynahow	- N. side of road	brick kiln	-	-	-	-	1841	-	6"os/	66
Kilruane	Ballynamurragh S.	-	Ralpa Mills	-	-	-	-	-	-	6"os/	15
Kilruane	Ballynamurragh S.	Dunn Edward	flour	(1B) 55x19x17 :	-	5.10	-	1847	17x3.6x13.6 1 pr. :	hob/	5.1819
Kilruane	Ballynamurragh S.	Dunne Edmond	corn	-	-	6.12	-	-	-	gr/	-
Tipperary	Ballynilard	Dalton Richard (Dick)	corn	-	29a.	43	-	-	-	gr/	-
Lorrha	Ballyquirk	- E/ Carrigahorig Vge.	corn	-	-	-	-	1841	-	6"os/	4
Newtowntennan	Ballyrichard	- N./ Carrick Br.	Wilmar Mill, mill pond		-	-	-	-	-	6"os/	85
Newtowntennan	Ballyrichard	Barry Jno, Callan, Kky.	mill		-	-	-	1812	-	dd/	643 263 442670
Newtowntennan	Ballyrichard	Bourke	mill		-	-	Bourke - O'Donnell	-	-	dd/	774 303 524638
Newtowntennan	Ballyrichard	Cassin	mill		-	-	Cassin - Morris	-	-	dd/	696 87 477613
Carrick	Ballyrichard [2nd]	- N./ Carrick Br.	bleaching racks	-	-	-	-	-	-	6"os/	85
Newtowntennan	Ballyrickard	Brown Thomas	flour	-	-	-	formerly John Neill	-	14x4x3 4 pr st.	vmb/	
Ballysheehan	Ballysheehan	- N/ B'sheehan Ho.	old corn mill	-	-	-	-	-	-	6"os/	53
	Ballyvartane										
Templeneiry	Bansagh * (?) :	Bannister	mills	-	-	-	Bannister - Sadlier	-	-	dd/	1 11 11
Templeneiry	Bansagh * (?) :	Butler Pierce O.B	mills	-	-	-	Butler P - Power Luke	1810	-	dd/	632 207 433024
Templeneiry	Bansagh * (?) :	Butler Pierce O.B	mills	-	-	-	Butler - Ryan	-	-	dd/	649 531 452393
Templeneiry	Bansagh * (?) :	Butler Pierce O.B	mills	-	-	-	Butler P - Power	-	-	dd/	655 446 452407
Templeneiry	Bansagh * (?) :	Butler Pierce O.B	mills	-	-	-	Butler - Sadlier	-	-	dd/	798 512 539247
Templeneiry	Bansagh * (?) :	Co. Tipp Barrister	mills	-	-	-	Co Tipp Bar - Decree	-	-	dd/	131 11 11
Templeneiry	Bansagh * (?) :	Power	mills	-	-	-	Power - Dalton	-	-	dd/	718 175 191210
Templeneiry	Bansagh * (?) :	Power	mills	-	-	-	Power - Falkiner	-	-	dd/	755 185 513120
Templeneiry	Bansha	- nr Bansha Castle	mill	-	-	-	-	-	-	1"os/	155
Templeneiry	Bansha	Turner Robert	flour	-	-	-	-	-	16x6x10	vmb/	20
Templeneiry	Bansha Village	Turner Robert	flour	-	1a.	59.10	-	-	-	gr/	-
Templeneiry	Bansha West	- SW/ Bansha Br.	flour & pond	-	-	-	-	-	-	6"os/	67
Templeneiry	Bansha West	- SW. of Bansha Br.	flour & mill pond	-	-	-	-	1841	-	6"os/	67
Templeneiry	Bansha West	Bansha Woollen Mill	mills	-	-	-	BWMC - Anderson Geo	1886	-	dd/	1886 13 74
Templeneiry	Bansha West	Bourke John	mills	-	-	-	Bourke Jn - Bansha :	1885	-	dd/	1885 23 43
Templeneiry	Bansha West	Royal Ld. Bd. Inv. Co.	mill	-	-	-	R.LBI. Co. - Bourke Jn	1882	-	dd/	1882 36 123
Ballygibbon	Bantis	- NW / rd. to Nenagh	distillery	-	-	-	-	-	-	6"os/	15
Ballygibbon	Bantis	Kennedy Edward	brewy	-	220a.	98.18	-	-	-	gr/	-
Roscrea	Barnagree	- at Springville Ho.:	corn	-	-	-	-	1841	-	6"os/	12

PARISH	TOWNLAND	MILLER	TYPE	HOUSE	Land	£Val	PROPRIETORS	Date	WHEEL etc.	Record	Ref.
Roscrea	Barnagree	Feehan Keeran	corn	-	-	-	-	-	12x4x4	vmb/	20
Rathnavoge	Barnagree	Feehan Kieran	corn	-	28a.	85.15	-	-	-	gr/	-
Barnaneely	Barnane	Bohan James	corn	-	-	-	-	-	no measurements	vmb/	20
Caher	Barnora	- on R. Suir	mill	-	-	-	-	-	-	1"os/	155
Caher	Barnora	- Suir Mill	flour	mill, kiln & bakehouse	-	-	-	-	-	rep./	nc - A
Caher	Barnora	Barton	land	-	-	-	Barton - Fitzgerald	-	-	dd/	874 258 580758
Caher	Barnora	Barton & Wife	land	-	-	-	Barton - Hempill	-	?	dd/	808 122 544857
Caher	Barnora	Caher Lord	land	-	-	-	Caher Ld - Furlong	-	-	dd/	690 418 474329
Caher	Barnora	Glengall Earl of	land	-	-	-	Glengall E. - Barton	1834	-	dd/	1834 19 29
Caher	Barnora	Glengall Earl of	land	-	-	-	Glengall E. - Barton	-	-	dd/	826 29 555614
Cahir	Barnora	Going William	flour	(1C) 73x28x36 :	-	23.13	-	1847	18x15, floats 2ft. :	hob/	5.1558
Caher	Barnora	Going William	Suir Mills	mill, bake ho etc.	-	-	- (bakery in 1994)	-	18x1.3x4	hob/	per J.W.
Caher	Barnora	Grubb Richard	mills	-	-	-	Grubb R - Going Charles	1847	-	dd/	829 278 557613
Caher	Barnora	Penefather Richard	Manor & Land	-	-	-	Penefather - Quin Thos	1837	-	dd/	1837 20 236
Caher	Barnora	Wall	land	-	-	-	Wall - Wall	-	-	dd/	770 364 516299
Caher	Barnora	Young William	flour	-	-	-	-	-	18x15x4	vmb/	20
Barrettsgrange	Barrettstown	Maher	mill	-	-	-	Maher - Carroll	-	-	dd/	759 187 515552
Relickmurry	Baurstooken	-	flour mills	-	-	-	-	-	-	6"os/	60
Relickmurry	Baurstooken	-	mill pond	-	-	-	-	-	-	6"os/	60
Relickmurry	Baurstooken	Matthews Margaret	flour & stores	-	-	45.15	-	-	-	gr/	-
Holycross	Beakstown	- W. bank R. Suir	mill (site)	-	-	-	-	1654	-	iaa/	AI2291 os47.1.6
Holycross	Beakstown	- W. side R. Suir	B'tn Woollen Mill	-	-	-	-	1841	-	6"os/	47
Holycross	Beakstown	- W. side R. Suir	B'town Flour Mill	-	-	-	-	1841	-	6"os/	47
Holycross	Beakstown	Mullvany Mcl Esq.	Flour Mills :	[no mill dims.] ho. :	-	-	-	-	18x6.6x3.6 2 pair :	hob/	5.1478
Holycross	Beakstown	Mullvany Mcl Esq.	flour mills & kiln :	ho. over machinery :	-	17.2	-	-	18x6.6x3.6 :	hob/	5.1478
Holycross	Beakstown	Mulvaney Michael	flour	-	4a.	83.5	-	-	-	gr/	-
Holycross	Beakstown	Mulvaney Michael	flour	(1B) 58.6x42x33 :	-	17	-	-	18x6.6 u`shot :	hob/	5.1478/1674
Holycross	Beakstown	Shortall Michael	corn	-	0.5a.	22.18	-	-	-	gr/	-
Holycross	Beakstown	Shortall Michael	spinning	-	-	-	-	-	-	gr/	-
Holycross	Beakstown	Shortall Michael	spinning :	(1B) 27.6x20.9x9 :	0.25a.	17	-	-	17.6x4.8x3.6 head :	hob/	5.1478
Holycross	Beakstown	Shorthall Michael	spinning	(1B) 42.6x18.3x21 :	3/4a.	7.9.9	-	-	17.6x4.8x3.6 revs.:	hob/	5.1478
Bourney	Behaghglas	- 4m. S. of Roscrea	mill in ruins	-	-	-	-	1841	-	6"os/	23
Bourney	Behaghglas	Maher James	corn	-	-	-	-	-	14x2x11	vmb/	20
Bourney	Behaghlass	Maher James	corn	-	19a.	16.5	-	-	-	gr/	-
Corbally	Birchgrove	- SE/ Roscrea Town	large distillery	-	-	-	-	-	-	6"os/	12
Corbally	Birchgrove	Birch George & Co.	distillery	-	-	66	-	-	-	gr/	-
Corbally	Birchgrove	Birch George & Co.	distillery	-	-	-	-	-	12x2x13 wheel :	vmb/	20
Tipperary	Blackmills *	Reynolds Nicholas :	mills	-	-	-	Reynolds - Watson Geo	1825	Mortgage	dd/	818 857 551322
Tipperary	Bohercrow	- E. end Henry St.	corn	-	-	-	-	-	-	6"os/	67
Tipperary	Bohercrow	Coleman Michael	corn	-	-	-	-	-	22x5x14	vmb/	20
Tubrid	Bohernamore	vacant	corn	-	-	-	-	-	13x3x13	vmb/	20
Tubrid	Bohernarnane	Glengall Earl of	corn	-	-	-	-	-	-	gr/	-
Glenkeen	Borrisland	Ryan Stephen	corn	-	-	-	-	-	16x3x17	vmb/	20
Glenkeen	Borrisland North	Ryan Stephen	corn & kiln	-	8a.	24.5	-	-	-	gr/	-
Glenkeen	Borrisland North :	- at Milmount Cottge	corn & kiln	-	8a.	24.5	-	-	-	gr/	-
Glenkeen	Borrisland South	-	old distillery	-	-	-	-	1841	-	6"os/	34
Glenkeen	Borrisland South	-	old malt kiln	-	-	-	-	1841	-	6"os/	34
Ardcrony	Borrisokane Town	Humphry Thomas	flour	-	-	-	-	-	18x5x11 3 pr st.	vmb/	20
Glenkeen	Borrisoleigh North	- N/ Town centre	corn	-	-	-	-	-	-	6"os/	34
Glenkeen	Borrisoleigh North	- at Millmount Cottag	corn mills	-	-	-	-	1841	-	6"os/	34
Glenkeen	Borrisoleigh Town	Fogarty Mary	old corn mill	-	-	3.10.0	-	-	-	gr/	-
Glenkeen	Borrisoleigh Town :	Walpole Geoorge	mill & kiln	(1B) 42.6x22.6x22 :	-	21	-	1853	18x5.6x14 3 pr. st.	hob/	5.3267

PARISH	TOWNLAND	MILLER	TYPE	HOUSE	Land	£Val	PROPRIETORS	Date	WHEEL etc.	Record	Ref.
Tipperary (2 tlds)	Brodeen	- nr Station	mill	-	-	-	-	-	-	1"os/	155
Kilbarron	Brookfield	Talbot Edward	corn	-	-	-	-	-	20x1x -	vmb/	20
Tipperary	Brookhill	O'Ryan	mill	-	-	-	O'Ryan - Wade	-	-	dd/	740 126 504061
St Mary`s	Burgagery Lands	Grubb Thomas Saml	flour	-	-	-	-	-	18x3x - 18x5x -	vmb/	20
Relickmurry	Burnstookeen :	Matthews Margaret	flour	-	-	-	-	-	22x7x4	vmb/	20
Fertiana	Cabragh	Sullivan John	mills	-	-	-	Sullivan J - Magrath Jn	1886	-	dd/	1886 30 160
Caher	Caher : T`parks	- S. Castle Street	flour	-	-	-	-	-	-	6"os/	75
Caher	Caher : T`parks	- imed. W. of Bridge	flour	-	-	-	-	-	-	6"os/	75
Caher	Caher : T`parks	Sargeant William :	flour	-	-	-	-	-	14x7x5	vmb/	20
Caher	Caher : T`parks	Sargeant William :	flour	-	-	-	-	-	19x9x5 5 revs./min	vmb/	20
Caher	Caher Abbey	Grubb Richard Sen	flour	-	-	-	- (demolished 1994)	-	2 large u`shot	hob/	per J.W.
Caher	Caher Abbey	Grubb Richard Sen	flour	-	-	-	-	-	27x7x26 drives	vmb/	20
Caher	Caher Abbey	Grubb Richard Sen	flour	-	-	-	-	-	19x12 & 19x12x5	vmb/	20
Caher	Caher Prems.	Sargent	mills	-	-	-	Sargent - Sadlier	-	?	dd/	701 419 484554
Caher	Caher Town	Sargeant Wm & Henry	flour	-	-	-	-	-	19x12x5	vmb/	20
Caher	Caher Town	Sargeant Wm & Henry	flour	-	-	-	-	-	20x16x -	vmb/	20
Caher	Caher Town :	Sargent Wm & Henry	flour	-	-	160	-	-	-	gr/	-
Caher	Caher Town :	Walpole John	flour	mill, dw. & kilns :	-	-	- (demolished 1994)	-	-	hob/	per J.W.
Caher	Caher Town :	Going & Smith Ltd.	Cahir Mills flour	-	-	-	-	1963	-	lic./	11
Caher	Caher Town :	Sargeant William :	flour	-	-	160	- (remodled 1994)	-	4 wheels	hob/	per J.W.
Caher	Caher Town :	-	& kilns	- demolished 1994	-	-	-	-	-	rep./	nc - Z
Caher	Caherabbey Lr	- W/ R. Suir	large flour mill	-	-	-	-	-	-	6"os/	75
Ardmayle	Camus	-	corn (in ruins)	-	-	-	-	-	-	6"os/	60
Ardmayle	Camus	- NW/ Camus Br.	flour	-	-	-	-	-	-	6"os/	60
Ardmayle	Camus	Connell Joseph	corn	-	19a.	41.14	-	-	-	gr/	-
Ardmayle	Camus	Connell Joseph	flour	(1A) 42.6x28x27.6 :	-	-	-	1846	16x5.8x - 2 pr. st.	hob/	5.1032
Patricksrock	Camus	Meehan Patrick	corn & carding	-	2a.	15.7	-	-	-	gr/	-
Tipperary	Carragharnen	- nr Happygrow Ho.	disused mill	-	-	-	-	-	-	1"os/	134
Carrick	Carrick-on-Suir :	Dalton William	corn	-	-	-	-	-	-	gr/	-
Carrick	Carrick-on-Suir :	Dalton William	flour & corn	-	4a.	52.7	-	-	-	gr/	-
Carrick	Carrick-on-Suir :	-	corn	-	-	-	-	-	-	6"os/	85
Carrick	Carrick-on-Suir :	- N. side R. Suir	bleach yard	-	-	-	-	-	-	6"os/	85
Carrick	Carrick-on-Suir :	- N. side R. Suir :	flour	-	-	-	-	-	-	6"os/	85
Carrick	Carrick-on-Suir :	- NNW/ Carrick Br.	mill	-	-	-	-	-	-	6"os/	85
Carrick	Carrick-on-Suir :	Dalton William	mill	-	-	-	Dalton Wim - Dooly Jno	1846	-	dd/	1846 14 38
Tipperary	Carrig	-	old windmill	-	-	-	-	-	-	1"os/	126
Tipperary	Carrigahorig	- nr Santa Cruise	mill	-	-	-	-	-	-	1"os/	125
Burgesbeg	Carrigatogher	- coach rd. to Limk.	toll gate	-	-	-	-	-	-	6"os/	20
Caher	Carrigeen	- W. (Island) Bridge	old mill	-	-	-	-	1841	-	6"os/	75
Kilmore	Carrow	-	mill (site)	-	-	-	-	1654	-	iaa/	AI2293 os26.7.1
Ballymackey	Carrowea	- N. side Ollatrim R.	Clash Mills	-	-	-	-	-	-	6"os/	22
Ballymackey	Carrowea	Toher Michael	new corn mill	[no measurements]	-	-	-	1849	mc/y taken down	hob/	5.1797
Ballymackey	Carrowea	Towers Michael	corn	-	9a.	11.8.0	-	-	-	gr/	-
St John`s	Cashel Town	Gordon Avary	old brewery	-	-	-	Gordon - P L Comms.	1850	-	dd/	1850 10 179
St John`s	Cashel Town	Walter	field & windmill	-	-	-	Walter - Bloomfield	-	-	dd/	871 115 589115
St John`s	Cashel Town :	Sadlier Thomas	premises	-	-	-	Sadlier T - Lewis Wm	1834	-	dd/	1834 10 172
Kilmastulla	Castlecranna	-	flour & mill pond	-	-	-	-	-	-	6"os/	26
Kilmastulla	Castlecranna	Bolands George	flour	(1B) 44.6x24x36 & :	-	-	-	-	17x4.6x12. 46 bkts.	hob/	5.1840
Athassel	Castleflake	Matthews Mary	corn	-	63a.	85.9	-	-	-	gr/	-
Tullaghorton	Castlegrace	-	Mill River	-	-	-	-	-	-	6"os/	86
Tullaghorton	Castlegrace	- 1/16m N./ R. Tar	flour	-	-	-	-	-	-	6"os/	86
Tullaghorton	Castlegrace	Grubb Samuel	flour	-	98a.	240	-	-	-	gr/	-

PARISH	TOWNLAND	MILLER	TYPE	HOUSE	Land	£Val	PROPRIETORS	Date	WHEEL etc.	Record	Ref.
Tullaghorton	Castlegrace	Grubb Samuel	flour	-	-	-	-	-	19x9x5 20x10x5:	vmb/	20
Tullaghorton	Castlegrace	Grubb Samuel Richard	mill	convert to grain store	-	-	-	1882	-	mlyIE	p137
Relickmurry	Castlelake	-	Castlelake Distille	-	-	-	-	-	-	6"os/	60
Relickmurry	Castlelake	-	corn & large pon	-	-	-	-	-	-	6"os/	60
Relickmurry	Castlelake	Mathews Mrs Mary	flour & corn	(1B) 46.6x42x35 :	-	32.16	-	-	16x8x1 42 bkts. :	hob/	5.1675
Glenkeen	Castlequarter	Fogarty Maria	corn kiln	-	-	-	-	1849	-	hob/	5.1624
Glenkeen	Castlequarter :	-	brewery	-	-	-	-	-	-	6"os/	34
Glenkeen	Castlequarter :	- NE /Town centre	malt & mill weir	-	-	-	-	-	-	6"os/	34
Castletownnarra	Castletown	-								iaa/	
Castletownnarra	Castletown	- 1.75m W/ Portroe	old mill	-	-	-	-	-	-	6"os/	19
Kiltinan	Clare More	- W/ Anner R.	corn	-	-	-	-	-	-	6"os/	70
Kiltinan	Clare More	Clancy John	corn	-	30a.	40.3	-	-	-	gr/	-
Tipperary	Clariana *	Pepper	mill & hill	-	-	-	Pepper - O'Leary	-	-	dd/	739 285 503620
Neddans	Clocully	- on isle in R. Suir	site of old mill	-	-	-	-	-	-	6"os/	86
Knockgraffon	Cloghabreedy	- E/ R. Suir	Cloghabreedy Mil	-	-	-	-	-	-	6"os/	75
Knockgraffon	Cloghabreedy	- stream to R. Suir	Cloghabre Mill	-	-	-	-	-	-	1"os/	155
Knockgraffon	Cloghabreedy	Keating William	corn	-	20a.	30.4	-	-	-	gr/	-
Knockgraffon	Cloghabreedy	Keating William	corn	mill, kiln, chaff ho.	-	36	- (ruins in 1994)	1846	12x5x8 2 pr st.	hob/	per JW
Shanrahan	Clogheen Market	-	brewery	-	-	-	-	-	-	6"os/	86
Shanrahan	Clogheen Market	- E./ Clogh Br. :	flour	-	-	-	-	-	-	6"os/	86
Shanrahan	Clogheen Market	- ENE/ Old Bridge	flour	-	-	-	-	-	-	6"os/	86
Shanrahan	Clogheen Market	- SW/ Clogheen Br.	flour & pond	-	-	-	-	-	-	6"os/	86
Shanrahan	Clogheen Market	Fennell William & Jas	flour	-	16a.	69.15	-	-	-	gr/	-
Shanrahan	Clogheen Market	Grubb Richard	flour	-	79a.	286	-	-	-	gr/	-
Shanrahan	Clogheen Market	Mahony William	corn	-	20a.	47.15	-	-	-	gr/	-
Templederry	Cloghinch	Gleeson John	corn	-	13a.	13	-	-	-	gr/	-
Bourney	Clonakenny	Maher John	corn	-	-	-	-	-	- new mill	vmb/	20
Bourney	Clonakenny	Mara John	corn & kiln	-	-	1.15.0	-	-	-	gr/	-
Corbally	Cloneen	- on Anner R.	mill	-	-	-	-	-	-	1"os/	156
Kilvemnon	Clonlaghy	Irvine Isabella	Mill Common	-	-	-	Irvine I - Going Arabella	1887	-	dd/	1887 46 64
Kilvemnon	Clonlaghy	Smith	mill	-	-	-	Smith - Disreal	-	?	dd/	635 72 435140
St Mary`s	Clonmel	Castle	mills	-	-	-	Castle - Castle	-	?	dd/	580 577 400403
St Mary`s	Clonmel	Collins Edward :	Corp Mills & :	-	-	-	Collins Edw - Maude Sir	-	-	dd/	362 434 245928
St Mary`s	Clonmel	Collins Edward :	Corp Mills & :	-	-	-	Collins Edw - Havell Edw	1785	-	dd/	371 320 249356
St Mary`s	Clonmel	English Philip :	mills	-	-	-	English P - Grubb Fran :	-	?	dd/	589 398 403443
St Mary`s	Clonmel	Grubb Francis :	mills	-	-	-	Grubb F - Grubb Thomas	1807	?	dd/	489 399 403444
St Mary`s	Clonmel	Howel	Corp Mills & :	-	-	-	Howel - Morton	-	-	dd/	557 20 371470
St Mary`s	Clonmel	Hughes Thomas	Burnt Mills & land	-	-	-	Hughes T - Malone Sarah	1810	-	dd/	644 41 440457
St Mary`s	Clonmel	Latouche Dav Rt. Hon.	Corp Mills & :	-	-	-	Latouche D - Morton Jas	1795	Mort. 21 Jne.	dd/	499 123 315345
St Mary`s	Clonmel	Lycester James :	mills	-	-	-	Lycester J - Baker Sam	1807	-	dd/	592 229 402111
St Mary`s	Clonmel	Maude	Corp Mills & :	-	-	-	Maude - Latouche	-	?	dd/	364 381 245991
St Mary`s	Clonmel	Mitchell	mills	-	-	-	Mitchell - Coman	-	?	dd/	583? 91 394729
St Mary`s	Clonmel	Moore William Hon. :	Corp Mills & :	-	-	-	Moore W - Hammil John	1795	-	dd/	485 561 315467
Whitechurch	Clonmel	Roe Andrew :	rape	-	-	-	Roe A - Cooke James :	1759	-	dd/	165 425 112604
Whitechurch	Clonmel	Roe Mary Widow	rape mills	-	-	-	Roe Mary - Bryen John	1723	-	dd/	36 414 23258
Whitechurch	Clonmel	Tothall Osborn	rape mills	-	-	-	Tothall O - McGrath Tce	-	-	dd/	73 241 50724
St Mary`s	Clonmel Corp.	Malcolmson David	mills	-	-	-	Malcolmson D - Pim Jno	1834	-	dd/	1834 18 145
St Marys	Clonmel Town	Byrne Marianne B	Manor Mills	-	-	-	Byrne M B - Grubb Thos	1890	-	dd/	1890 25080
St Mary`s	Clonmel Town	Grubb Josh	Manor Mill :	-	-	-	Grubb Josh - Thomas	1845	-	dd/	1845 17 78
St Marys	Clonmel Town	Grubb Thomas C	Suir Island Mills	-	-	-	Grubb Thos - SuirIsland	1891	-	dd/	1891 46 17
St Marys	Clonmel Town	Hughes George	The Burned Mills	-	-	-	Hughes Geo - Irish Nat.	1893	-	dd/	1893 663 191
St Mary`s	Clonmel Town	Hughes Thomas	flour	15.6x24.6x48 :	-	-	-	1850	17x12 27 floats :	hob/	5.3382

PARISH	TOWNLAND	MILLER	TYPE	HOUSE	Land	£Val	PROPRIETORS	Date	WHEEL etc.	Record	Ref.
St Marys	Clonmel Town	Malcolmson Marcalla	Corporation Mills	-	-	-	Malcolmson M - Myles Ja	1890	-	dd/	1890 9119
St Marys	Clonmel Town	Malcolmson Nannie	Corporation Mills	-	-	-	Malcolmson N - Myers Ja	1890	-	dd/	1890 27 62
St Marys	Clonmel Town	Malcolmson Nannie	The Barons Mills	-	-	-	Malcolmson N - Myers Ja	1890	-	dd/	1890 27 61
St Marys	Clonmel Town	Malcolmson Robert	Corporation Mills	-	-	-	Malcolmson R - Myers Ja	1887	-	dd/	1887 39 279
St Marys	Clonmel Town	Malcolmson William	flour	-	-	-	Malcolmson - Grubb Thos	1891	-	dd/	1891 46 84
St. Mary`s	Clonmel Town	Perry Samuel	Figgans Mill	-	-	-	Perry - Bannantyne Jas	1898	-	dd/	1898 70 283
St. Mary`s	Clonmel Town	Shannon Mary Anne	Abbey Mills	-	-	-	-	1846	-	dir/	Slator
St Marys	Clonmel Town	White William	Manor Mills	-	-	-	White Wm - Byrne M`ann	1887	-	dd/	1887 15 131
St Mary`s	Clonmel Town :	Greer Thomas & Wm	grinding	47.6x21x47 51x27x4	-	-	-	-	18x6.4 32 bkts. :	hob/	5.3382
St Mary`s	Clonmel Town :	Mallinson John	mills	-	-	-	Malinson John - Robert	1879	-	dd/	1879 54 52
St Mary`s	Clonmel Town :	Malcolmson George	mills	-	-	-	Malcolmson George P -	1882	-	dd/	1882 43 7
St Mary`s	Clonmel Town :	Landed Estate Court	mill	-	-	-	Ld. E. Ct. - Hackett Henr	1876	-	dd/	1876 33 148
St. Mary`s	Clonmel Town :	Hughes John	flour	-	-	194	-	-	-	gr/	-
St. Mary`s	Clonmel Town :	Banfirld Peter	flour	-	-	63	-	-	-	gr/	-
St. Mary`s	Clonmel Town :	Collett John M	mill	-	-	-	-	1846	-	dir/	Slater
St Mary`s	Clonmel Town :	Murray Abraham	mill	-	-	-	Murray A - Grubb Thos	1880	-	dd/	1880 51 154
St Mary`s	Clonmel Town :	Murray Anne B	mill	-	-	-	Murray A - Murray Abr.	1876	-	dd/	1876 5 84
St Mary`s	Clonmel Town :	Hughes	burnt mill	-	-	-	Hughes & ors - Hill	-	?	dd/	883 238 858238
St. Mary`s	Clonmel Town :	Murphy Thomas. & Co	brewery	-	-	202	-	-	-	gr/	-
St. Mary`s	Clonmel Town :	Grubb Samuel	flour	-	0.1.3	136	-	-	-	gr/	-
St. Mary`s	Clonmel Town :	Murray Abraham	mill	-	-	-	Murray A - Grubb Thos	1880	-	dd/	1880 17 154
St. Mary`s	Clonmel Town :	Byrne William	corn store, fcty	-	-	63	-	-	-	gr/	-
St Mary`s	Clonmel Town :	Greer Thomas	mill	-	-	-	Greer Thomas - Jno	1851	-	dd/	1851 6 102
St Mary`s	Clonmel Town :	Power Edward	mill	-	-	-	-	1846		dir/	Slator
St Mary`s	Clonmel Town :	Clonmel Mayor	mills	-	-	-	Clonmel Mayor - Nat Bk.	1850	-	dd/	1850 16 49
St Mary`s	Clonmel Town :	Hughes Thos & Jas	mill	-	-	-	-	1846	-	dir/	Slator
Inisglounaght	Clonmore	- S/ Dolla Br.	Happygrove Mill	-	-	-	-	-	-	6"os/	26
Dolla	Clonmore	Brindley Samuel	corn	(1A) 40.6 29x14 :	-	-	-	-	17x3.8x- 1 pr. st. :	hob/	5.1804
Inisglounaght	Clonmore	Charteris Margaret :	mill	-	-	-	Charteris - Wemyss & :	1888	-	dd/	1888 27 31
Toem	Clonmurragha	-	copper mines	-	-	-	-	-	-	6"os/	45
Templemore	Clontaaffe	-	old corn mill	-	-	-	-	-	-	6"os/	22
Ardmayle	Cloon	- SW/ Arglo Br.	flour	-	-	-	-	-	-	6"os/	52
Ardmayle	Cloon	- SW/ Arglo Br.	MILL	(1B) 71x19x30 :	-	8.11.4	-	-	16x6x12 44 bkts.	hob/	5.1675
Ardmayle	Cloon	- SW/ Arglo Br.	old starch m/fy	-	-	-	-	-	-	6"os/	52
Killardry	Cloonfinglass	Bourke John	mill race & strean	-	-	-	Bourke John - Bansha :	1885	-	dd/	1885 23 43
Ballymackey	Cloonmore	- SW/ Ollatrim R.	old mill	-	-	-	-	-	-	6"os/	21
Shaurahan	Clougheenmarket	Fennell James & Wm	flour	-	-	-	-	-	14x5x13 3 pr st.	vmb/	20
Shaurahan	Clougheenmarket	Fennell James & Wm	flour	-	-	-	-	-	16x4x13	vmb/	20
Shaurahan	Clougheenmarket	Grubb Richard	corn	-	-	-	-	-	20x15x5 5 elevs.	vmb/	20
Shaurahan	Clougheenmarket	Gruff Samuel	flour	-	-	-	-	-	16x4x14 4 pr st.	vmb/	20
Shaurahan	Clougheenmarket	Mahoney William	corn	-	-	-	-	-	16x6x4	vmb/	20
Rathnancoge	Clybanane	- 1/2m. W/ Roscrea	old mill, mill race	-	-	-	-	-	-	6"os/	12
Rathnancoge	Clybanane	Smallman William	corn	-	-	-	-	-	-	vmb/	20
Roscrea	Clybanane	Smallman William	flour	-	11a.	12	-	-	-	gr/	-
Rathnancoge	Clybanane	Smallman William	flour	-	-	-	-	-	new mill	vmb/	20
Rathnancoge	Clybanane Roscrea	- W/ Burgoo Bridge	flour mill ruins	-	-	-	-	-	-	6"os/	12
Thurles	Commons	- E/ Cabragh Bridge	corn	-	-	-	-	-	-	6"os/	47
Thurles	Commons	Sullivan Stephen	corn	-	13a.	23.3.0	-	-	-	gr/	-
Thurles	Commons	Sullivan Stephen	tuck	-	-	-	-	-	-	gr/	-
Thurles	Commons									iaa/	
bo./ Compsey	Compsey	* Brady James	Compsey Mills	-	-	-	Brady Jas - Jones Wm	1881	-	dd/	1881 26 140
Castletownarra	Corbally	-	R.I. Mining Co.	-	-	-	-	-	-	6"os/	19
Cordangan	Cordangan	-	Cordangan Hous	-	-	-	-	-	-	6"os/	67

PARISH	TOWNLAND	MILLER	TYPE	HOUSE	Land	£Val	PROPRIETORS	Date	WHEEL etc.	Record	Ref.
Cordangan	Cordangan	-	mill race	-	-	-	-	-	-	6"os/	67
Cordangan	Cordangan	- S/ Deer Park	corn	-	-	-	-	-	-	6"os/	67
Knigh	Cornamult	Turney William	mill	(1B) 30x20.6x17 :	-	-	-	1846	13.9x3 32 buckets	hob/	5.1764
Knigh	Cornamult	Turney William	mill (used as off.)	(1B) 30x20.6x17	-	-	-	1846	13.9x3 - 32 bkts.:	hob/	5.1765
Tubrid	Crannavone	Ryan Edward	corn	-	41a.	47.5	-	-	-	gr/	-
Tubrid	Crannavone	Ryan Edward	corn	-	-	-	-	-	13x4x3	vmb/	20
Newtowntennan	Cregg	-	long mill race :	-	-	-	-	-	-	6"os/	79
Newtowntennan	Cregg	- on Lingaun R.	flour	-	-	-	-	-	-	6"os/	79
Newtowntennan	Cregg	Felix O`Neill Felix	flour	-	-	-	-	-	18x4x12 3 pr st.	vmb/	20
Newtownlennon	Cregg	Kennedy James	flour & corn	-	2a.	15.11	-	-	-	gr/	-
Newtownlennon	Cregg	O`Neil Felix	flour	-	2a.	34.10	-	-	-	gr/	-
Dorrha	Derinsallow	- S. side R. Brosna	Mill Ville (no mill)	-	-	-	-	1841	-	6"os/	2
Dorrha	Derinsallow	Gordon John	mill	-	-	-	Gordon Jn - Lyster Wm	1884	-	dd/	1884 48 145
Dorrha	Derrinsallow	-	flour	-	-	-	- built 1830, rebuilt	1850	Ross & Parsons	mmSv/	D
Dorrha	Derrinsallow	Leicester Ham P & J	flour	house, offs. & land	32a.	146	- [+ tenant's house]	1856	-	gr/	a.a.ire.ie
Dorrha	Derrinsallow	Leister Hamilton	mill	(1A) 120x38x50 :	-	12.13	-	-	18.8x11.9 56 bkts.	hob	5.1743&5
Dorrha	Derrinsallow	Lyster H & I	flour	-	-	-	-	-	19x12x9 8 pr st.	vmb/	20
Loughkeen	Doughkill	- NW Carrig Ho.	flour	-	-	-	-	-	-	6"os/	8
Loughkeen	Doughkill	Abernethy William	corn	-	-	-	-	-	- 3 pr stones	vmb/	20
Loughkeen	Doughkill	Abernethy William	corn & store	-	-	15.5	-	-	-	gr/	-
Loughkeen	Doughkill	Abernethy William	flour	(1B) 58x21.9x29 :	-	46.4	-	1853	11.6x4 overshot :	hob/	5.1767
Kilfaakle	Dromline	- N/ R. Ara	cloth	-	-	-	-	-	-	6"os/	67
Moyaliff	Drumbane	- NW/ Mulgrave Br.	tuck	-	-	-	-	-	-	6"os/	40
Moyaliff	Drumbane	Hayes John	corn & tuck	(2B) 32.6x13x10 :	-	15	-	1849	13x2.6x14 36 bkts. :	hob/	5.1617/26
Moyaliff	Drumbane	Hayes John & Thos	corn	-	-	-	-	-	13x2x14	vmb/	20
Moyaliff	Drumbane	Hayes John & Thos	tuck	-	-	-	-	-	13x2x14	vmb/	20
Moyaliff	Drumbane	Hayes Thos & John	corn & tuck	-	20a.	18.15	-	-	-	gr/	-
Emly	Duncummin	Hennasy Maurice	corn	-	-	-	-	-	14x4x11	vmb/	20
Emly	Duncummin	Hennessy Maurice	corn	(1A) 28x18x10 :	-	1	-	1848	14x4.2x11.6 36 bkts.	hob/	5.1455
Emly	Duncummin	Hennessy Maurice	corn & kiln	-	0.2.2	7.5.0	-	-	-	gr/	-
Ballintemple	Dundrum	Hawarden Viscount	corn	-	1602a.	1731	-	-	-	gr/	-
Ballintemple	Dundrum	Howarden Wm Visc.	corn, wheat meal	-	-	-	-	-	14x3x13	vmb/	20
Ballintemple	Dundrum	- S/ Pound Cross	flour	-	-	-	-	-	-	6"os/	51
Ardcrony	Feemore	-	Ballyfinboy Mills	-	-	-	-	-	-	6"os/	10
Ardcrony	Feemore	-	tuck	-	-	-	-	-	-	6"os/	10
Ardcrony	Feemore	- N/ B'finboy Castle	grist & pond	-	-	-	-	-	-	6"os/	10
Ardcrony	Feemore	Dagg William	corn	-	-	-	-	-	16x3x6	vmb/	20
Fethard	Fethard	-	Mill View	-	-	-	-	-	-	6"os/	70
Fethard	Fethard	- W. end main St	flour	-	-	-	-	-	-	6"os/	70
Fethard	Fethard	- E/ Clashawaley R	corn	-	-	-	-	-	-	6"os/	70
Fethard	Fethard	Wilson Charles	corn	-	2a.	22.3	-	-	-	gr/	-
Fethard	Fethard Town	- W. end main St.	corn	-	-	-	-	-	-	6"os/	70
Fethard	Fethard Town	- W. end main St.	flour & mill weir	-	-	-	-	-	-	6"os/	70
Fethard	Fethard Town	Harvey Julia	flour & corn	-	1a.	54.4	-	-	-	gr/	-
Fethard	Fethard Town	Holmes John	corn & kiln	-	-	24	-	-	-	gr/	-
Fethard	Fethard Town	O`Connor Edmund	corn & kiln	-	-	14.9	-	-	-	gr/	-
Kilmurry	Figlash	-	corn & mill pond	-	-	-	-	1841	-	6"os/	79
Kilmurry	Figlash	Rockett Mary	corn	-	19a.	29.9	-	-	-	gr/	-
Terryglass	Firmount	- San ta Cruise	Flour Mill	-	-	-	-	1841	-	6"os/	4
Terryglass	Firmount	Palmer Samuel	flour	-	52a.	82	-	-	-	gr/	-
Terryglass	Firmount	Palmer Samuel	flour	-	-	-	-	-	18x5x2 3 pr st.	vmb/	20
Shanrahan	Flemingstown	-	flour	-	-	-	-	-	-	6"os/	86

PARISH	TOWNLAND	MILLER	TYPE	HOUSE	Land	£Val	PROPRIETORS	Date	WHEEL etc.	Record	Ref.
Shanrahan	Flemingstown	Grubb Samuel	flour	-	-	61	-	-	-	gr/	-
Shanrahan	Flemingstown	Grubb Samuel	flour	-	-	-	-	-	18x6x6 4 pair st.	vmb/	20
Shanrahan	Flemingstown	Grubb Samuel	flour	-	-	-	-	-	18x8x14	vmb/	20
Aglishcloghane	Fortmoy	Slattery John	corn	-	-	10	-	-	-	gr/	-
Aglishcloghane	Fortmoy	Slattery John	grist	-	-	-	-	-	14x3x -	vmb/	20
Latteragh	Garane	Slattery Matthew	mill	-	-	-	Slattery - Brereton Den	1880	-	dd/	1880 57 49
Latteragh	Garrane	-	Garrane Mill	-	-	-	-	-	-	6"os/	27
Latteragh	Garrane	-	Mill Farm	-	-	-	-	-	-	6"os/	27
Latteragh	Garrane	Coghlan James	corn, tuck, cardin	(1B) 70x18.9x14 :	-	-	-	-	14x2.6x14 2 pr. st.	hob/	5.1821
Latteragh	Garrane	Coghlan James & Wm	corn	-	991a.	97.6	-	-	-	gr/	-
Latteragh	Garrane	Coghlan James & Wm	tuck & carding	-	-	-	-	-	-	gr/	-
Knockgraffon	Garranlea	-	flour, mill pond	-	-	-	-	-	-	6"os/	67
Knockgraffon	Garranlea	Keating James	corn & flour	-	27a.	68.11	-	-	-	gr/	-
Terryglass	Garrycloghy	E./ Carrigahorig Vge.	corn	-	0.1.3	14.10	-	-	-	gr/	-
Terryglass	Garrycloghy	Palmer Samuel	corn	-	0.1.3	14.10	-	-	-	gr/	-
Terryglass	Garrycloghy	Palmer Samuel	corn	-	-	-	formerly Doolen John	-	16x7x10 3 pair st.	vmb/	20
Corbally	Glenbeha	-	mill in ruins	-	-	-	-	-	-	6"os/	17
Thurles	Glengarriff	-	Thurles Malt House		-	-	-	-	-	6"os/	41
Glenkeen	Glenkeen	-	-	-	-	-	-	-	-	iaa/	AI2296 os34.2.6
Conoulty	Glenough Upper	-	copper mines	-	-	-	-	-	-	6"os/	45
Boulick	Gorteenraine	McNamara James	corn	-	-	-	-	-	18x3x12	vmb/	20
Boulick	Gorteenrainee	-	corn & mill pond	-	-	-	-	-	-	6"os/	49
Loughmoe East	Graiguefrahane	- E. side og R. Suir :	tuck	-	-	-	-	1841	-	6"os/	35
Loughmoe East	Graiguefrahane	Reid Minchin	flour	(1A) 65.6x29x40 :	-	20	-	-	13x8.3x3.6 u`shot :	hob/	5.1481
Loughmoe East	Graiguefrahane	Rudd Minchin	flour	-	12a.	66	-	-	-	gr/	-
Loughmore E.	Graiguefrahane	Rudle Minchin	flour	mill about 3 yrs. built:	-	-	-	1847	13x8.3 u'shot : fl	hob/	5.1486
Holycross	Graiguenoe	-	distillery	-	-	-	-	-	-	6"os/	48
Holy Cross	Graiguenoe	Power Michael	distillery	(1A) 49.6x27x21 7 :	-	30.13	-	1845	17x10x -	hob/	5.1671
Thurles	Grange	-	lime kiln	-	-	-	-	-	-	6"os/	41
Grangemockler	Grangemockler	- Mulleenaglogh Vge	no mill	-	-	-	-	-	-	6"os/	71
Grangemockler	Grangemockler	- on Linganun R.	mill	-	-	-	-	-	-	1"os/	156
Grangemockler	Grangemockler	Barnes John	corn	-	55a.	41.5	-	-	-	gr/	-
Grangemockler	Grangemockler	Barns John	corn	-	-	-	-	-	14x4x -	vmb/	20
Ballingarry	Gurteen	- nr Pallas Glebe	mill	-	-	-	-	-	-	6"os/	4
Ballingarry	Gurteen		mill in ruin							6"os/	5
Ballingarry	Gurteen									iaa/	
Holycross	Holycross	- W. side R. Suir	old mill	-	-	-	-	-	-	6"os/	47
Holycross	Holycross	Blacker Robert S. C.	Manor	-	-	-	Blacker - Murdoch Rbt	1884	-	dd/	1884 14 214
Holycross	Holycross	Bourke Richard	Abbey fields	-	-	-	Bourke Richard - Patk	1885	-	dd/	1885 10 111
Holy Cross	Holycross	Dwan M.	mill	-	-	-	-	-	Francis av. 0.9 GW/h	turb	c1947
Holycross	Holycross	O`Brien Jeremiah	corn	-	1.0.2	15.14	-	-	-	gr/	-
Holy Cross	Holycross	O'Brien Jeremiah	grinding	(1B) 50x23x17.6 :	-	-	-	1847	-	hob/	5.1674
Holycross	Holycross	Phillips Richard	tythes	-	-	-	Phillips - Armstrong R	1884	-	dd/	1884 53 43
Holycross	Holycross	Ryan John	mill	-	-	-	Ryan J - Ryan Daniel	1881	-	dd/	1881 40 196
Holycross	Holycross	Ryan Michael	mill	-	-	-	Ryan M - Ryan Daniel	1881	-	dd/	1881 16 6
Holy Cross	Holycross	Shorthall Michael	spinning	(1A) 42.6x18.3x21 :	-	16.8.9	-	1847	-	hob/	5.1674
Holy Cross	Holycross									iaa/	
Relickmurry	Hymenstown	-	old mills	-	-	-	-	-	-	6"os/	67
Lisbunny	Islandbawn	- N/ Ollatrim R.	Islandbawn Mills	-	-	-	-	1843	-	6"os/	21
Lisbunny	Islandbawn	Ryan Malachi	flour	-	76a.	157	-	-	-	gr/	-
Lisbunny	Islandbawn	Ryan Malachi	flour	(1B) 64x25x41 &	-	71	-	1848	large 21x4x14 & :	hob/	5.1824
Tipperary	Johnstown *	- N/ St.J'town Castle	corn	-	-	-	-	-	-	6"os/	62

PARISH	TOWNLAND	MILLER	TYPE	HOUSE	Land	£Val	PROPRIETORS	Date	WHEEL etc.	Record	Ref.
Cahir	Kilconly	Going Thomas	mill	(1C) 37.6x24.6x33.6 :	-	13.3	-	1847	21x4x20.6 o'shot :	hob/	5.1558
Kilcooly	Kilcoolyabbey	- near Abbey	thrashing m/c	-	-	-	-	-	-	6"os/	43
Cahir	Kilemly	Going Thomas Esq.	flour	(1C) 37.6x24x33.6 :	-	15.3 :	-	-	21x4x20.6 48 bkts. :	hob/	5.1554
Cahir	Kilemly *	- E. of R. Suir	corn	-	-	-	-	-	-	6"os/	75
Kiltinan	Killavally	- E side Anner R.	old mill	-	-	-	-	-	-	6"os/	77
bo./ Ormond L&U	Killeen (4)	Kennedy Edward	mill	-	-	-	Kennedy - Markey Patk	1885	-	dd/	1885 44 75
Caher	Killemly	- E. of Suir R. :	corn	-	-	-	-	1841	-	6"os/	75
Caher	Killemly	Going Thomas	corn	-	198a.	160	-	-	-	gr/	-
Caher	Killemly	Going William	corn	mill, barn, stables	-	-	- (derelict in 1994)	1848	21ft. 1pr st. Irish	hob/	per J.W.
Dorrha	Killenaule Tn&Tld.	- on River St.	old distillery	-	-	-	-	-	-	6"os/	54
Glenkeen	Killeroe	Burke Patrick	corn	-	32a.	21.5	-	-	-	gr/	-
Killea	Killoskehan	Hennessy Patrick	corn	-	-	4.15	-	-	-	gr/	-
Killea	Killoskenan	Hennessy Patrick	corn & mill race	-	-	-	-	1841	-	6"os/	67
Lisronagh	Kilmore	- on R. Moyle	flour	-	-	-	-	-	-	6"os/	77
Lisronagh	Kilmore	Morrisey	corn	-	-	-	-	-	15x5x7	vmb/	20
Lisronagh	Kilmore	Morrisey Michael	corn	-	18a.	31	-	-	-	gr/	-
Loughmoe East	Kilnaseer	- on R. Suir	tuck	-	-	-	-	-	-	6"os/	35
Kilshane	Kilshane	- N. side of R. Ard	corn & mill race	-	-	-	-	1841	-	6"0s/	67
Kilshane	Kilshane	- N. side R. Ara	corn	-	-	-	-	-	14x4x4	vmb/	20
Kilshane	Kilshane	M`Curtin William	corn	-	13a.	17.5.0	-	-	-	gr/	-
Kilshane	Kilshane	McCurtin William	corn	-	-	-	-	-	14x4x4	vmb/	20
Kilsheelan	Kilsheelan	- N side R. Suir :	corn	-	-	-	-	-	-	6"os/	84
Kilsheelan	Kilsheelan	Power James	corn	-	9a.	20.18	-	-	-	gr/	-
Knigh	Knigh	Stapleton James	corn	-	-	-	-	-	16x10x10ins.	vmb/	20
Tipperary	Knocheenbaun	- in Kilmanagh Tn	mill	-	-	-	-	-	-	1"os/	-
Ballymackey	Knockane	Kennedy Edward	flour & corn	-	21a.	62.14	-	-	-	gr/	-
Youghalarra	Knockanfoilemore	- on Newtown R	grist	-	-	-	-	-	-	6"os/	20
Youghalarra	Knockanfoilemore	Omentage William	flour	(1B) 23.6x17.6x9.6 :	-	4.17	-	1846	overshot 11.6x1.6 :	hob/	5.1852
Ballymackey	Knockanglass	-	grist & tuck	-	-	-	-	-	-	6"os/	21
Tipperary	Knockaunmullan	- stream/ Multeeen R.	saw	-	-	-	-	-	-	1"os/	155
Tipperary	Knocknoe Estate	- COS	mill	-	-	-	-	-	-	1"os/	167
Ballynaclogh	Kylebeg	Boland Anne	corn	-	15.3.7	16.17	-	-	-	gr/	-
Ballynaclogh	Kylebeg	Boland Jennie Widow	corn	(1C) 21x29.6 18 &	-	8.8.5	-	1848	17x4x7 40 bkts. :	hob/	5.1801
Ballynaclogh	Kylebeg	on mill race S/ Nenagh	mill	-	-	-	-	1841	-	6'os/	27
Borrisokane	Kyletombrickane	- (per Down Survey)	mill (site)	-	-	-	-	-	-	iaa/	AI2299 os6.16.3
Kilvellane	Lackamore	-	copper mines	-	-	-	-	-	-	6"os/	38
Cordangan	Lacken	-	mill race (no mill)	-	-	-	-	1841	-	6"os/	67
Cordangan	Lacken	- Bansha Woods	mill	-	-	-	-	-	-	1"os/	155
Cordangan	Lacken	Bansha Woollen Co.	mill	-	-	-	BWMC - Anderson Geo	1886	-	dd/	1886 13 74
Cordangan	Lacken	Bourke Elizabeth	mill	-	-	-	Bourke Eliz -Eliz	1885	-	dd/	1885 23 43
Cordangan	Lacken	Ryan Timothy	corn	-	-	-	-	-	13x2x5	vmb/	20
Cordangan	Lacken	Ryan Timothy	corn & flour	(2B) 32x19.6x9 :	-	5.0.3	-	1848	13x2.6x8 wood :	hob/	5.1421
Cordangan	Lacken	Ryan Timothy	corn & kiln	-	3.1.7	9.10	-	-	-	gr/	-
Donohill	Lackenacreena	-	copper mines	-	-	-	-	-	-	6"os/	45
Killenaule	Lanespark	Hanrahan William	corn	-	-	-	-	-	14x4x10	vmb/	20
Killenaule	Lanespark	Hanrahan William	corn & kiln	-	4a.	9.5.0	-	-	-	gr/	-
Slieveardagh	Lickfinn	- NW/Colliery cross	mill (in ruins)	-	-	-	-	-	-	6"os/	54
Lisbunny	Lisbunny	-	mill (site)	-	-	-	-	-	-	iaa/	AI2300 os21.5.6
Inch	Liscreagh	Vice Chancellor	Liscreagh Mills	-	-	-	Chancellor - Major Geo	1885	-	dd/	1885 46 98
Kilruane	Lisgarode	- W. side Ollatrim R	grist & tuck	-	-	-	-	1841	-	6"os/	21
Kilruane	Lisgarode	Magrath Patrick	corn	-	9a.	12.11	-	-	-	gr/	-
Kilruane	Lisgarode	Magrath Patrick	corn	(1B) 21x34x19 :	-	-	-	-	-	hob/	5.1818

PARISH	TOWNLAND	MILLER	TYPE	HOUSE	Land	£Val	PROPRIETORS	Date	WHEEL etc.	Record	Ref.
Kilruane	Lisgarode	Magrath Patrick	tuck	-	-	-	-	-	-	gr/	-
Kilruane	Lisgarode	Magrath Patrick	tuck	(2A) 30x16x6	-	-	-	-	12x2.8x - 36 bkts.	hob/	5.1818
Dolla	Lisgarrif East	- NW Bennett's Br.	grist	-	-	-	-	-	-	6"os/	27
Clogheen	Lissava	- SW/ New Bridge	old mill	-	-	-	-	-	-	6"os/	75
Clonbeg	Longford	- stream/ R.Aherlow	old tuck mill	-	-	-	-	-	-	6"os/	71
Clonbeg	Longford	Dawson Rev. John M	corn & flax	-	14a.	27	-	-	-	gr/	-
Clonbeg	Longford	Massey Jno Rev.	corn & flax	(1A) 46x24x22 :	-	-	-	1846	21x5.6 2 pr. st. :	hob/	5.1420
Glenbane	Longford	Massey John Rev.	corn & flax	(1A) 46x24x22 :	-	-	-	-	22x5x22 2pr.st. :	hob/	5.1420
Clonbeg	Longford	McDawson John Rev.	corn	-	-	-	-	-	22x5x20 4 in mill	vmb/	20
Clonbeg	Longford	McDawson John Rev.	flax	-	-	-	-	-	same wheel	vmb/	20
Lorrha	Lorrha	- at Kildodan :	mill	-	-	-	-	-	-	1"os/	4
Lorrha	Lorrha	- on Abbeylands :	mill	-	-	-	-	1841	-	6"os/	4
Lorrha	Lorrha	- at Vge. Abbey Mill	corn	-	-	-	-	1841	-	6"os/	4
Lorrha	Lorrha	Reddan Timothy	corn	-	-	-	-	-	14x3x10	vmb/	20
Lorrha	Lorrha	Reddin Timothy	corn	-	115a.	64.5	-	-	-	gr/	-
Kilnaneave	Loughane Lower	- S. side Nenagh R.	corn & mill race	-	-	-	-	1841	-	6"os/	33
Kilnaneave	Loughane Lower	Ardell John	corn	-	39a.	41	-	-	-	gr/	-
Kilnaneave	Loughane Lower	Ardill John	corn	(1B) 23x18.6x9.6 &	-	-	-	-	14x2.2x14 36 bkts. :	hob/	5.1815
Kilnaneave	Loughane Lower :	- Riverfiel	Mill	-	-	-	-	1841	-	6"os/	33
Tipperary	Loughmoe	-	mill	-	-	-	-	-	-	1"os/	135
Graystown	Mardyke	-	coal pits (3)	-	-	-	-	-	-	6"os/	54
Graystown	Mardyke	-	steam engine	-	-	-	-	-	-	6"os/	54
Inishlounaght	Marlfield	- W/ Clonmel Town	distillery, lge ponc	-	-	-	-	-	-	6"os/	83
Inishlounaght	Marlfield	Stein John & Co.	distillery	-	-	-	-	1846	-	dir/	Slator
Inishlounaght	Marlfield	Murray John	distillery	-	-	-	-	-	20x5x1 20x3x1/2 :	vmb/	20
Inishlounaght	Marlfield	Murray John & Co.	distillery & -	-	-	-	-	1856	-	gr/	a.a.Ire.ie
Inishlounaght	Marlfield	Murray John & Co.	mills	house, offs. & land	10a.	339	-	1856	-	gr/	a.a.Ire.ie
Inishlounaght	Marlfield	Shannon Mary	flour	-	-	-	-	-	19x7x12 3 pr st.	vmb/	20
Inishlounaght	Marlfield	Shannon Mary Anne	flour	house, offs. & land	2a.	44.13	-	1856	-	gr/	a.a.Ire.ie
Killea	Mein	Sweeney John	corn	-	-	-	-	-	11x3x13	vmb/	20
Killea	Mien	-	Garret`s Mill	-	-	-	-	-	-	1"os/	135
Killea	Mien	- on R. Suir	Garrell's Mill	-	-	-	-	-	-	6"os/	22
Killea	Mien	Sweeny John	corn	-	6.1.8	9	-	-	-	gr/	-
Ballyhomuck	Milestown	- NE/ Melbourne Br.	corn	-	-	-	-	-	-	6"os/	71
Ballyhomuck	Milestown	Shea William	corn	-	59a.	75.14	-	-	-	gr/	-
Clooneen	Milestown	Shea William	corn	(1A) 34x24x25 & :	-	8.13	-	-	16x4x - 32 bkts. :	hob/	5.1675
bo./ Ormond L&U	Mill Grove *	Kennedy Edward	mill	-	-	-	Kennedy - Markey Patk	1885	-	dd/	1885 44 75
bo./ Ormond L&U	Mill Grove *	Stoney Margaret	mill holding	-	-	-	Stoney M - St Sadlier	1882	-	dd/	1882 6 161
bo./ Clanwilliam	Mill Place Old	Eccles William	mill & race	-	-	-	Eccles W - Grey Edwadr	1884	-	dd/	1884 59 300
Kilnaneave	Millbrook	-	Millbrook House	-	-	-	-	-	-	6"os/	27
Kilnaneave	Millbrook	Gleeson Michael	corn	-	33a.	23.16	-	-	-	gr/	-
Kilnaneave	Millbrook	Gleeson Michael	tuck	(1B) 18x19x14 & :	-	4.9	-	-	12.4x2x13 36 bkts.	hob/	5.1817
Tipperary	Millgrove	- Millgrove Mill	corn	- ruins since 1949	-	-	-	-	-	rep./	nc - R
Roscrea	Millpark	- at Millpark House	flour	-	-	-	-	1841	-	6"os/	12
Roscrea	Millpark	Grubb Jonathan	mills	-	-	-	Grubb Jno - Joshua	1880	-	dd/	1880 9 194
Roscrea	Millpark	Lyster Hamilton	flour	-	6a.	5.6.0	-	-	-	gr/	-
Roscrea	Millpark	Lyster Hamilton	flour	-	-	-	-	-	22x6x19 3 pr st.	vmb/	20
bo./ Clanwilliam	Milltown	Harding Patrick	land	-	-	-	Harding - Moriarty Jas	1880	-	dd/	1880 3 275
Mora	Milltown Beg	-	(no mill 2m)	-	-	-	-	-	-	6"os/	69
Tipperary	Monegall	- nr Ollatrim Bridge	mills	-	-	-	-	-	-	1"os/	135
Tipperary	Mount Falcon	-	mill	-	-	-	-	-	-	1"os/	125
Shanrahan	Mountanglesby	Wade James	flour	-	56a.	53	-	-	-	gr/	-

PARISH	TOWNLAND	MILLER	TYPE	HOUSE	Land	£Val	PROPRIETORS	Date	WHEEL etc.	Record	Ref.
Shanrahan	Mountanglesby	Wade James	flour	-	-	-	-	-	17x7x14 3 pr st.	vmb/	20
Shanrahan	Mountanglesby	Wade James	flour	-	-	-	-	-	17x7x14 mill :	vmb/	20
Ardcrony	Mountfalcon		Killoganny Mill	-	-	-	-	-	-	6"os/	10
Moyaliff	Moyaliff	- W. of Clodiagh R.	mill (site)	- on a farm site	-	-	-	-	-	iaa/	AI2302 os46.3.3
Moyaliff	Moyaliff	- SW/ Ballyoughter Br.	flour	-	-	-	-	1845	-	6"os	40
Moyaliff	Moyaliff	Dwyer Pierce	corn	-	33a.	41.5	-	-	-	gr/	-
Moyaliff	Moyaliff	Dwyer Pierce	corn	(2B) 27x20x13 kiln :	-	5.6.7	-	1849	13x3x13 38 bkts. :	hob/	5.1626
Moyaliff	Moyaliff	Dwyer Pierce	corn	-	-	-	-	-	13x3x13	vmb/	20
Moyne	Moynetemple	- E. of Moyne Vge.	wind mill (ruins)	-	-	-	-	1848	-	6"os	
Moyne	Moynetemple	Ryan William	wind mill	ho., offs., piggery & :	-	-	-	1847	-	hob/	5.1492
Durrow	Muckloon :	- N./ Village of :	flour	-	-	-	-	-	-	6"os/	4
Thurles	Mullauns	-	old corn mill	-	-	-	-	-	-	6"os/	41
Thurles	Mullauns	- NE/ Tortulla Br.	old tuck mill	-	-	-	-	-	-	6"os/	41
Thurles	Mullauns	- on Manor R.	Old Mills Bridge	-	-	-	-	-	-	6"os/	41
Thurles	Mullauns	- SW/ Drish Br.	flour	-	-	-	-	-	-	6"os/	41
Thurles	Mullauns	- SW/ Drish Br.	large mill pond	-	-	-	-	-	-	6"os/	41
Thurles	Mullauns	Burns William	corn & kiln	-	-	10.15	-	-	-	gr/	-
Thurles	Mullauns	Meihin John	mill	-	27a.	34.16	-	-	-	gr/	-
Thurles	Mullauns		woollen factory	-	-	-	-	-	-	6"os/	41
Modreeny	Mullenkeagh	- E. end Cloughjordan	distillery	-	-	-	-	1841	-	6"os/	15
Mooreeny	Mullenkeagh	Kennedy Edmond	distillery	-	-	-	-	-	16x4x9	vmb/	20
Mooreeny	Mullenkeagh	Kennedy Edmond	oats, malt, barley	-	-	-	-	-	16x4x9	vmb/	20
Modreeny	Mullenkeagh	Kennedy Edward	corn	-	-	-	-	-	-	gr/	-
Modreeny	Mullenkeagh	Kennedy Edward	distillery	-	3a.	47	-	-	-	gr/	-
Kilvemnon	Mullinahone	- on Anner R.	Beeverstown Mill	-	-	-	-	-	-	1"os/	156
Kilvemnon	Mullinolly	-	large mill pond	-	-	-	-	-	-	6"os/	63
Kilvemnon	Mullinolly	- S/ Mullinahone Vge.	flour & corn	-	-	-	-	-	-	6"os/	63
Kilvemnon	Mullinolly	Wright George	flour, Indian corn	-	24a.	55	-	-	-	gr/	-
Kilvemnon	Mullinolly	Wright George	flour, Indian corn	-	-	-	-	-	18x5x10 6 pr st. :	vmb/	20
Nenagh	Nenagh	- at Bennets Bridge	corn	-	-	-	-	-	-	1"os/	134
Nenagh	Nenagh	- N. of Bennets Br.	corn	-	-	-	-	-	-	6"os/	21
Nenagh	Nenagh	- S. side Dublin St.	brewery	-	-	-	-	-	-	6"os/	21
Nenagh	Nenagh	- W/ Kyleeragh Br.	brick fields (2)	-	-	-	-	-	-	6"os/	21
Nenagh	Nenagh	Bolton George	grist	-	-	-	Bolton G - Harty John	1880	-	dd/	1880 46 263
Nenagh	Nenagh	Bolton George	grist	-	-	-	Bolton G - Tennant Dav	1883	-	dd/	1883 42 232
Nenagh	Nenagh	Fayle Samuel	grist	-	-	-	Fayle Sam - Benjamin	1881	-	dd/	1881 6 62
Nenagh	Nenagh North	Bennett William	corn	-	-	-	-	-	15x6x5 3 pair st.	vmb/	20
Nenagh	Nenagh North	Deegan William	mill & store	-	-	54.10	-	-	-	gr/	-
Nenagh	Nenagh North :	-	brewery	-	-	-	-	-	-	6"os/	20
Nenagh	Nenagh Town :	Pine Thomas	spinning	-	-	25.10	-	-	-	gr/	-
Nenagh	Nenagh Town :	-	toll gate	-	-	-	-	-	-	6"os/	20
Knigh	Newbawn	Egan William	distillery	(1B) 74x24x11.9 :	-	90.14	-	1846	-	hob/	5.1765
Knigh	Newbawn	Egan William	distillery (part)	(1B) 68x53x36.9 :	-	-	-	1846	17.9x5 40 bkts. :	hob/	5.1765
Knigh	Newbawn	Egan William	flour	(1B) 57x23.6x30 :	-	-	-	1846	27x8 64 bkts. :	hob/	5.1765
Tipperary	Newbawn *	Egan William	distillery	(1B) 74x24x11.9 :	-	-	-	1846	-	hob/	5.1764
Tipperary	Newbawn *	Egan William	flour	(1B) 57x23.6x30 :	-	-	-	1846	-	hob/	5.1764
Tipperary	Newbawn *	Egan William	still house	(1B) 16.6x14x8 :	-	-	-	1846	-	hob/	5.1764
Galbooly	Newbrook	-	mill (site)	-	-	-	-	-	-	iaa/	AI2304 os47.4.1
Terryglass	Newlands	Egan William	distillery	-	-	-	-	-	-	gr/	-
Terryglass	Newlands	Egan William	flour	-	51a.	127	-	-	-	gr/	-
Terryglass	Newlawn	- on Ballyfinboy R. :	distillery	-	-	-	-	-	-	6"os/	6
Terryglass	Newlawn	Brereton Denis	mill & bog	-	-	-	Brereton - Hogan Patk	1888	-	dd/	1888 17 94

PARISH	TOWNLAND	MILLER	TYPE	HOUSE	Land	£Val	PROPRIETORS	Date	WHEEL etc.	Record	Ref.
Terryglass	Newlawn	Egan William	distillery	-	-	-	-	-	18 5 -	vmb/	20
Terryglass	Newlawn	Egan William	flour	-	-	-	-	-	27x8x -	vmb/	20
Terryglass	Newlawn	-	Ballinderry Mills	-	-	-	-	-	-	6"os/	6
Terryglass	Newlawn	-	still house	-	-	-	-	-	-	6"os/	6
Youghalarra	Newtown	- S/ Newtown Br.	grist	-	-	-	-	-	-	6"os/	20
Newtownlennan	Newtown Lower	-	weir & mill dam	-	-	-	-	-	-	6"os/	79
Tipperary	nr Knockonoe Ho	- COS	mill	-	-	-	-	-	-	1"os/	167
Aghnameadle	Ollatrim	- S/ Ollatrim Br.	Victoria Mills	-	-	-	-	-	-	6"os/	22
Aghnameadle	Ollatrim	Touhy Jeremiah	flour	-	6.3.5	39.5	-	-	-	gr/	-
St Johnstown	St Johnstown	-	mill pond	-	-	-	-	-	-	6"os/	62
Nenagh	Pallas Beg	-	mill	-	-	-	-	-	-	1"os/	134
Rathnancoge	Parkmore	Jackson Robert	corn	-	-	-	-	-	13x3x3	vmb/	20
Rathnancoge	Parkmore	Jackson Robert	tuck	-	-	-	-	-	-	vmb/	20
Rathnancoge	Parkmore	Rudd William	flour	-	-	-	-	-	14x8x -	vmb/	20
Rathnancoge	Parkmore, Roscrea	- S. side (main) St. :	flour & pond							6"os/	12
Rathnancoge	Parkmore, Roscrea	- S. side of Town :	tuck							6"os/	12
Rathnancoge	Parkmore, Roscrea	- S. of Burgoo Br.	brewery							6"os/	12
Donohill	Philipston	-	tuck	-	-	-	-	-	-	6"os/	51
b./Owney & Arra	Pollogbane *	Waller Edmond Sir	mill	-	-	-	Waller Ed - Maunsell Jn	1885	-	dd/	1885 8 284
b./Owney & Arra	Polloghbane *	Warburton Henry	mill	-	-	-	Warburton - Birch Hen.	1881	-	dd/	1881 36 137
Whitechurch	Poulaculleare	- ENE/ Kilcoran Br.	old factory	-	-	-	-	-	-	6"os/	81
Coolmundry	Quartercross	- W/ Anner R.	corn	-	-	-	-	-	-	6"os/	70
Corbally	Rackethall	- beside Racket :	brewery	-	-	-	-	1841	-	6"os/	12
Corbally	Rackethall	Birch George & Co.	brewery	-	33a.	52.15	-	-	-	gr/	-
Caher	Raheen	Chaytor	threshing	-	68a.	38.10	-	-	-	gr/	-
Caher	Raheen	Chaytor John	threshing	-	-	-	-	-	-	vmb/	20
Glenkeen	Rathcarden	- [no name - note :]	corn	-	2.2	-	-	1848	-	hob/	5.1624
Glenkeen	Rathcardon	Chadwick Michael	corn	-	29a.	21.10	-	-	-	gr/	-
Borrisokane	Rathmore	Humphries Thomas	flour	-	-	64	-	-	-	gr/	-
Rathronan	Rathmore :	- Mill Street	- (no mill)	-	-	-	-	1841	-	6"os/	7
Rathronan	Rathronan	- S/ Albert Bridge	flour & mill pond	-	-	-	-	-	-	6"os/	77
Rathronan	Rathronan	O`Connor John	flour & corn	-	3a.	38.9	-	-	-	gr/	-
Rathronan	Rathronan	O`Connor John	flour & corn	-	-	-	formerly O`Keeffe Richd	-	25x7x13 5 pr st.	vmb/	20
Toem	Reafadda	Minnis Hollyford Co. :	pumping wheel	house (1A) 40x28x7	-	-	34x4.6x38 100 bkts. :	1847	-	hob/	5.1629
Toem	Reafadda	Minnis Hollyford Co. :	pumping wheel	-	-	-	-	-	34x4x31	vmb/	20
Shanrahan	Rearoe	- on stream to R. Dua	cloth	-	-	-	-	1841	-	6"os/	90
Shanrahan	Rearoe	Lynch William	corn	-	7a.	15.5	-	-	-	gr/	-
Shanrahan	Rearoe	Lynch William	corn	-	-	-	-	-	9x2x9	vmb/	20
Shanrahan	Rearoe	Lynch William	tuck	-	-	-	-	-	-	gr/	-
Shanrahan	Rearoe	Lynch William	tuck	-	-	-	-	-	8x2x8	vmb/	20
Kilgrant	Redmondstown	- 1/2m N./ R. Suir	flour mills	-	-	-	-	-	-	6"os/	83
Shanrahan	Rehill	-	-	-	-	-	-	1850	-	mlyIE	p76
Shanrahan	Rehill	- W/ Glennyreea R. :	flour	-	-	-	-	-	-	6"os/	81
Shanrahan	Rehill	Mulcahy James	corn	-	29a.	21.15	-	-	-	gr/	-
Shanrahan	Rehill	Mulcahy James	corn	-	-	-	-	-	17x5x16	vmb/	20
Kilnarath	Rockvale	- S/ Mulkear R.	Rockvale Mill	-	-	-	-	-	-	6"os/	31
Kilnarath	Rockvale	O'Keeffe Patrick	flour	(1C) 44.6x25x33 :	-	-	-	-	13.6x2.11 o'shot :	hob/	5.1841
Roscrea	Roscrea	- nr Bunnow Bridge	mill	-	-	-	-	-	-	1"os/	-
Roscrea	Roscrea T`parks	Smallman William	flour	-	-	-	-	-	14x3x10 & 14x3x10	vmb/	20
Roscrea	Roscrea Town	-	Black Mills	-	-	-	-	-	-	6"os/	12
Roscrea	Roscrea Town	- S/ Burgoo Bridge	brewery	-	-	-	-	-	-	6"os/	12
Roscrea	Roscrea Town	- E/ Burgoo Bridge	flour & pond	-	-	-	-	-	-	6"os/	12

COUNTY TIPPERARY

PARISH	TOWNLAND	MILLER	TYPE	HOUSE	Land	£Val	PROPRIETORS	Date	WHEEL etc.	Record	Ref.
Roscrea	Roscrea Town :	Jackson Robert	corn	-	-	17.10	-	-	-	gr/	-
Roscrea	Roscrea Town :	Jackson Robert	tuck	-	-	-	-	-	-	gr/	-
Roscrea	Roscrea Town :	Rudd William	flour	-	-	67	-	-	-	gr/	-
Roscrea	Roscrea Town :	-	large pond	-	-	-	-	-	-	6"os/	12
Roscrea	Roscrea Town :	-	flour & corn	-	-	-	-	-	-	6"os/	12
Roscrea	Roscrea Town :	-	malt store	-	-	-	-	-	-	6"os/	12
Roscrea	Roscrea Town :	-	tuck	-	-	-	-	-	-	6"os/	12
Donohill	Rossacrow	- NW/ Turks Br.	Millbrook House	-	-	-	-	-	-	6"os/	51
Donohill	Rossacrow	- on R. Multen	corn	-	-	-	-	-	-	6"os/	51
Donohill	Rossacrow	Millet Dammer	corn & kiln	-	-	7.5.0	-	-	-	gr/	-
Donohill	Rossacrow	Millett Danner	corn	(1C) 64x28.8x36.6 :	-	9.6.6	-	-	18.6x2.10x11 u'shot:	hob/	5.1610
Donohill	Rossacrow	Millett Danner	corn	-	-	-	-	-	18x3x9	vmb/	20
Clonoulty	Rossmore	-	carding	-	-	-	-	-	-	6"os/	45
Clonoulty	Rossmore	- SW Rossmore Br.	tuck	-	-	-	-	-	-	6"os/	45
Clonoulty	Rossmore	Daly John	carding	-	-	-	-	-	12x3x12 also :	vmb/	20
Clonoulty	Rossmore	Daly John	carding & tuck	-	2a.	11	-	-	-	gr/	-
Clonoulty	Rossmore	Daly John	tuck	-	-	-	-	-	8x2x 8	vmb/	20
bo./ Ormond L&U	Santacruse *	Palmer Robert	Santacruse Mills	-	-	-	Palmer R - Prov. B O Ire	1885	-	dd/	1885 10 238
Killoscully	Shalee	-	mine works	-	-	-	-	-	-	6"os/	26
Aghacrew	Shanaknock	- Iron Mill Br.	(no mill)	-	-	-	-	-	-	6"os/	51
Cloghprior	Shanavally	Slattery Joseph	corn	-	19a.	19.5	-	-	-	gr/	-
Cloghprior	Shanavally	Slattery Joseph	corn	-	-	-	-	-	17x3x -	vmb/	20
Rahelty	Shanballyduff	Godfrey Thomas	flour	-	-	39.8	-	-	-	gr/	-
Rahelty	Shenballyduff	-	mill pond	-	-	-	-	-	-	6"os/	42
Rahelty	Shenballyduff	- W/ Drish R.	flour & corn	-	-	-	-	-	-	6"os/	42
Borrisokane	Shesheragh More	- E/ Main St, Borris'k	distilery	-	-	-	-	-	-	6"os/	10
Magorban	Silverfort	- NE/ Silverfort Ho.	old mill	-	-	-	-	-	-	6"os/	61
Kilshane	Springhouse	M`Curtin William	corn	-	-	5.15	-	-	-	gr/	-
Dorrha	Sraduff	-	mill (site)	-	-	-	-	-	-	iaa/	AI2305 os5.2.6
Dorrha	Sraduff	- in Ho. Demesne	mill in ruins	-	-	-	-	-	-	6"os/	4
St Johnstown	St Johnstown	-	corn & mill pond	-	-	-	-	1841	-	6"os/	62
St Johnstown	St Johnstown	Hanrahan Mary	corn	-	12a.	21	-	-	-	gr/	-
St Johnstown	St Johnstown	Hanrahan Mrs Mary	corn	(1A) 45x17x17 & :	-	5.4.9	-	-	14x3.3x - 40 bkts.	hob/	5.1675
Coolmundry	Strike Lower	- W/ Clash. R.	flour	-	-	-	-	-	-	6"os/	70
St Mary`s	Suir Island	- R.Suir N side Isle.	flour	-	-	-	-	-	-	6"os/	83
St Mary`s	Suir Island	- R.Suir S side Isle	flour	-	-	-	-	-	-	6"os/	83
St Mary`s	Suir Island	Hughes John	flour	-	-	-	-	-	16x6x - 6 pair st.	vmb/	20
Rathnavoge	Summerhill	Meara John	corn & kiln	-	-	16.10	-	-	-	gr/	-
Templemore	Templemore	Walsh Stephen	mill	-	-	-	Walsh - Connolly Thos	1880	-	dd/	1880 32 21
Templemore	Templemore Town	Rudd Minchin	old brewery	-	-	5.14	-	-	-	gr/	-
Terryglass	Terryglass Vge.	- at Loughnagow	malt kiln	-	-	-	-	-	-	6"os/	6
Thurles	Thurles : Mill Road	- Doran's Mill	mill	all timber now decayed		-	also k/a Byrne's	-	-	iaa/	IAA?6/00
Thurles	Thurles T'parks	- ENE/ Barry's Br.	brewery	-	-	-	-	-	-	6"os/	41
Thurles	Thurles T'parks	O`Keeffe Dixon	brewery	-	-	28.5	-	-	-	gr/	-
Whitechurch	Tincurry	E/ Kilcoran Br.	flour & mill pond	-	-	-	-	-	-	6"os/	81
Whitechurch	Tincurry	Walpole William	corn	-	87a.	118	-	-	-	gr/	-
Whitechurch	Tincurry	Walpole William	corn	-	-	-	-	-	20x4x19	vmb/	20
Carrick	Tinvane	Dooley John	Mill Quarter	-	-	-	Dooly - Grubb Llewellyn	1886	-	dd/	1886 14 253
Carrick	Tinvane	Dooley John & Denis	flour & corn	-	11a.	26.14	-	-	-	gr/	-
Tipperary	Tipperary Town	Dobbin R & Burke P	corn	-	-	-	-	-	16x -x -	vmb/	20
Tipperary	Tipperary Town :	Michael Coleman	corn & kiln	-	1a.	46.10	-	-	-	gr/	-
Tipperary	Tipperary Town :	Dobbyn & Burke	corn, kiln, stores	-	-	34.10	-	-	-	gr/	-

PARISH	TOWNLAND	MILLER	TYPE	HOUSE	Land	£Val	PROPRIETORS	Date	WHEEL etc.	Record	Ref.
Loughmoe W.	Whitefield	-	mill pond & mill race		-	-	-	-	-	6"os/	29
Loughmoe W.	Whitefield	Whitefield	Flour Mill		-	-	-	-	-	6"os/	29
Inishlounaght	Toberaheena	- N/ R. Suir :	flour	-	-	-	-	-	-	6"os/	83
Inishlounaght	Toberahena	- N. side R. Suir	flour & mill pond	-	-	-	-	1841	-	6"os/	83
Inishlounaght	Toberahena	Collett John Maera	corn	-	-	-	-	-	16x4x17	vmb/	20
Inishlounaght	Toberahena	Collett John Meara	corn & kiln	-	4a.	36	-	-	-	gr/	-
Gaile	Toberdora	on Toberadora Stream	old mill	-	-	-	-	1841	-	6"os/	53
Gaile	Toberdora	Commons Denis	corn	-	49a.	44.11	-	-	-	gr/	-
Tipperary	Town Lot	- W. end Main St.	tan yard	-	-	-	-	-	-	6"os/	67
Kilvemnon	Town Mullinahone	-	no mill	-	-	-	-	-	-	6"os/	62
bo./ Ikerrin	Townland ?	Jackson Phoebe	St. Cronan`s Mill	-	-	-	Jackson - Stanley Richd	1884	-	dd/	1884 41 231
Tipperary	Townland ?	- at Clarialia	Mill View (ho)	-	-	-	-	-	-	6"os/	14
Emly	Townland ?	Hennessy Maurice	corn	(1A) 28x18x10 :	-	1.18	-	1848	14x4.2x11.6 36 bkts	hob/	5.1435
bo./ Iffa & Offa	Townland ?	Malcolmson William	Factory Fields	-	-	-	Malcolmson - Cleeve Th	1889	-	dd/	1889 23 37
Burgesbeg	Townland ?	McGrath James	tuck	(3C) 29.6x18x13 &	-	5.16	-	1839	10x2.6x - 36 bkts. :	hob/	5.1834
Tipperary	Townland ?	- rd. to Cloughjordan	distillery	-	-	-	-	-	-	6"os/	15
Tipperary	Townsparks ?	-	flour	-	-	-	-	-	-	6"os/	75
Tipperary	Townsparks ?	-	Mill View	-	-	-	-	-	-	6"os/	75
Dolla	Tullamoylin	-	mill (site)	-	-	-	-	-	-	iaa/	Ai2306 os27.5.1
Kilvellane	Tullow	- E. bank Mulkear R	mill (site)	-	-	-	-	1654	-	iaa/	AI2307 os37.2.6
Kilvellane	Tullow	- E/ Mulkear R.	old mill & mill rac	-	-	-	-	-	-	6"os/	37
Kilvellane	Tullow	- E/ Mulkear R.	tuck	-	-	-	-	-	-	6"os/	37
Kilvellane	Tullow	- NE/ Mulkear Br.	corn	-	-	-	-	-	-	6"os/	37
Kilvellane	Tullow	Carey John	corn	(1C) 65.6x23x19 :	-	1.18	-	1846	14x2.6x15 2 pr. st.	hob/	5.1844
Thurles	Turtulla	- N/ Turtulla Br.	Turtulla Flour Mill	-	-	-	-	-	-	6"os/	41
Inishlounaght	Twomilebridge	- from Anner R.	mill race & dam	-	-	-	-	-	-	6"os/	83
Inishlounaght	Twomilebridge	- N side R. Suir	flour factory	-	-	-	-	-	-	6"os/	83
Inishlounaght	Twomilebridge	- on Anner R. :	Anner Mills	-	-	-	-	-	-	6"os/	83
Inishlounaght	Twomilebridge	Clibborn John B	flour	-	41a.	276	-	-	-	gr/	-
Inishlounaght	Twomilebridge	Clibborn John Barclay	flour	-	-	-	-	-	18x2x17, 18x5x4 :	vmb/	20
Nenagh	Tyone	- W/ Nenagh R.	Tyone Mill	-	-	-	-	-	-	6"os/	21
Nenagh	Tyone	Ryan Malachi	flour	(1B) 78x48x36 &	-	-	-	1848	17.6x8 & 17x3 :	hob/	5.1824/9
Nenagh	Tyone	Ryan Malachy	flour	-	6.2.6	84	-	-	-	gr/	-
Templebeg	Ushanbo Cahill	Ryan Anthony	corn	(1B) 21x18.6x16.6 :	-	5.1.7	-	1849	13x3x6 38 bkts. :	hob/	5.11627
bo./ Ikerrin	Wayside *	Birch William	brewery	-	-	-	Birch Wm- Smaith Mary	1880	-	dd/	1880 58 102
Loughmoe West	Whitefield	-	Whitefield Flour M	-	-	-	-	1835	-	6"os/	29
Loughmoe West	Whitefield	-	Whitefield mill	-	-	-	-	-	-	1"os/	135
Loughmoe West	Whitefield	Connolly John	mill	-	-	-	Connolly - McCraith Ml	1880	-	dd/	1880 23 31
Loughmoe West	Whitefield	Connolly John	mill	-	-	-	Connplly - McCraith Ml	1882	-	dd/	1882 23 31
Loughmoe West	Whitefield	Rudd Minchin	flour	-	135a.	107	-	-	-	gr/	-
Loughmoe West	Whitefield	Walsh Stephen	mill	-	-	-	Walsh - Connolly Thos	1880	-	dd/	1880 23 31
St Patricksrock	Windmill	-	(no mill)	-	-	-	-	-	-	1"os/	155
St Patricksrock	Windmill	- Rd. Cashel /Newinn	(no mill)	-	-	-	-	1841	-	6"os/	61
St Patricksrock	Windmill	Barry Richard H S	land	-	-	-	Barry R - Riddiford Geo	1882	-	dd/	1882 16 135
bo./ Ormond L&U	Windmill Field	Birmingham William	land	-	-	-	Birmingham W - Visc. :	1889	-	dd/	1889 44 300

PARISH	TOWNLAND	MILLER	TYPE	HOUSE	Land	£Val	PROPRIETORS	Date	WHEEL etc.	Record	Ref.
Drumragh	Aghadulla (Harper)	-	corn kilns (3)	-	-	-	-	1834	-	6"os/	42
Drumragh	Aghadulla (Harper)	- on stream to :	corn & pond	-	-	-	-	1834	-	6"os/	42
Donaghedy	Aghafad	-	corn	-	-	-	-	1834	-	6"os/	6
Tullyniskan	Aghakinsallagh Glebe	-	mill dam, mill race	-	-	-	-	1834	-	6"os/	46
Tullyniskan	Aghakinsallagh Glebe	E/ road to Armagh	spade m'factory	-	-	-	-	1834	-	6"os/	46
Cappagh	Aghalane	-	flax	-	-	-	-	1834	-	6"os/	26
Cappagh	Aghalane	-	old kiln, mill pond	-	-	-	-	1834	-	6"os/	27
Termonamongan	Aghascreragh	-	corn kiln (2)	-	-	-	-	1834	-	6"os/	19
Ardstraw	Aghasessy	-	corn kiln (2)	-	-	-	-	1834	-	6"os/	24
Dromore	Aghee	-	corn kiln	-	-	-	-	1834	-	6"os/	49
Clogher	Aghintain	M`Clean William	corn	-	8a.	-	-	-	-	gr/	-
Dromore	Aghlisk	-	corn	-	-	-	-	1834	-	6"os/	50
Termonamongan	Aghnahoo	- SE/ R. Derg	corn	-	-	-	-	1834	-	6"os/	23
Bodoney Lower	Aghnamirigan	- on Aghnacree R.	corn & kiln	-	-	-	-	1834	-	6"os/	19
Dromore	Aghnamoe	-	corn kiln	-	-	-	-	1834	-	6"os/	50
Desertcreat	Allen	- on Rocky R.	mill	-	-	-	-	-	-	1"os/	34
Clogher	Altanavera	-	corn kiln (2)	-	-	-	-	1834	-	6"os/	51
Errigal K`ogue	Altcloghfin	Campbell Patrick	corn	-	-	-	-	-	-	gr/	-
Errigal K`ogue	Altcloghfin	E. side small river	corn & corn kiln	-	-	-	-	1834	-	6"os/	52
Termonmaguirk	Altdrumman	-	corn kiln	-	-	-	-	1834	-	6"os/	36
Termonmaguirk	Altdrumman	- S/ Lo. Macrory	corn & corn kiln	-	-	-	-	1834	-	6"os/	36
Clonfeacle	Altnavannog	Barcroft William J	corn & kiln	-	66a.	-	-	1856	-	gr/	-
Clonfeacle	Altnavannog	Hogg Jonathan :	mills & water	-	-	-	Hogg Jno & Barcroft Sarah	1820	Mort. 27 Oct.	dd/	756 523 514058
Donaghedy	Altrest	-	flax	-	-	-	-	1834	-	6"os/	2
Donaghedy	Altrest	-	flax & millrace	-	-	-	-	1834	-	6"os/	2
Donaghedy	Altrest	Smith William	flax	-	-	-	-	-	-	gr/	-
Donaghedy	Altrest	Stewart William :	mill	-	-	-	Stewart Wm - Stewart Jas :	1817	-	dd/	734 386 500721
Donaghedy	Altrest	Stewart William :	flax	-	-	-	Stewart Wm - Stewart Jas :	1812	-	dd/	645 367 448760
Clogher	Annagarvey	Gervais Francis J	corn	-	85a.	-	-	-	-	gr/	-
Clogher	Annagarvey	Gervais Francis J	flour	-	-	-	-	-	-	gr/	-
Clonoe	Annagher	-	mill race	-	-	-	-	1834	-	6"os/	47
Clonoe	Annagher	- at Coalisland	mill	-	-	-	-	-	-	1"os/	35
Clonoe	Annagher	E/ Coal Island	mill	-	-	-	-	1834	-	6"os/	47
Clonoe	Annagher	Eccles John	corn	-	22a.	-	-	-	-	gr/	-
Clonoe	Annaghmore	N. side of Canal	pottery	-	-	-	-	1834	-	6"os/	47
Ardstraw	Ardbarren Upper	-	corn kiln	-	-	-	-	1834	-	6"os/	24
Clogher	Ardunshin	Gervais Francis J	thrashing	-	154a	-	-	-	-	gr/	-
Leckpatrick	Artigarvan	-	bleach	-	-	-	-	1834	-	6"os/	5
Leckpatrick	Artigarvan	-	bleach	-	-	-	-	1834	-	6"os/	5
Leckpatrick	Artigarvan	-	flax	-	-	-	-	1834	-	6"os/	5
Leckpatrick	Artigarvan	- near Sion Mills	flax	-	-	-	-	-	- [not located]	mmSv/	?
Leckpatrick	Artigarvan	Burgoyne Sir J. or :	bleach	66x24x11 & : (	-	13.7	-	1833	-	v1B/	640
Leckpatrick	Artigarvan	Cox James	flax	-	-	-	-	-	-	gr/	-
Leckpatrick	Artigarvan	Ovens Hugh :	mills	-	-	-	Ovens H - Burgyne Sir :	1820	-	dd/	754 498 512833
Tyrone	Arvagh *	-	corn	-	-	-	-	1834	-	6"os/	52
Tyrone	Aughalough * :	Fitzpatrick James :	mill	-	-	-	Fitzpatrick James - Jno	1811	-	dd/	635 223 437242
Clonoe	Aughamullin	Crawford Richard :	mill	-	-	-	Crawford R - Johnston :	1819	-	dd/	744 92 506428
Clonoe	Aughamullin	Hadley Eliz. Widow :	corn	-	-	-	Hadley E - Hadley Francis	1817	-	dd/	724 90 494425
Clonoe	Aughamullin	Mayne John :	mills	-	-	-	Mayne J - McClennan :	1819	-	dd/	743 542 506277
Clogher	Augher	Alexander William Sir :	mill	-	-	-	Alexander W - Cairnes Jas:	1814	-	dd/	682 42 469182
Clogher	Augher	Bunbury James Sir	Mill of Augher	-	-	-	Bunbury Jas - Bunbury Jn	1835	-	dd/	1835 15 71
Clogher	Augher	Falls James :	mill	-	-	-	Falls Jas - Cairns James :	1814	Mort. 25 Oct.	dd/	681 116 448663

PARISH	TOWNLAND	MILLER	TYPE	HOUSE	Land	£Val	PROPRIETORS	Date	WHEEL etc.	Record	Ref.
Clogher	Augher	Hamilton John :	mills	-	-	-	Hamilton - Richardson Wm	1807	Mort. 22 Aug.	dd/	671 300 461482
Clogher	Augher	Richardson	mill	-	-	-	Richardson - Richardson	-	?	dd/	755 211 513146
Clogher	Augher	Richardson	mill	-	-	-	Richardson - Richardson	-	?	dd/	755 212 513147
Clogher	Augher	Tener John K	corn & kiln	-	5a.	-	-	-	-	gr/	-
Termonmaguirk	Aughnacloy	Coote James & :	mill	-	-	-	Coote J - Moore Edward :	1816	-	dd/	701 476 480981
Termonmaguirk	Aughnacloy	Curry Wiliam :	mill	-	-	-	Curry Wm - Moore Edwd. :	1816	-	dd/	700 484 480338
Termonmaguirk	Aughnacloy	Falls James	mill	-	-	-	Falls J - Matthews John :	1816	-	dd/	700 468 480327
Termonmaguirk	Aughnacloy	Matthews John :	mill & miller's ho. :	-	-	-	Matthews J - Falls James :	1818	Mort. 6 Mar.	dd/	725 239 495174
Termonmaguirk	Aughnacloy	Ms. Cready's	corn	Restoration :	-	-	-	1999	-	mmSv/	wh - Ca
Termonmaguirk	Aughnacloy Town :	Fiddes James	corn	-	-	-	-	-	-	gr/	-
Clonoe	Aughrimderg	-	spade forge, dam	-	-	-	-	1834	-	6"os/	47
Ballyclog	Back Lower	Miller Thomas	flax	-	33a.	-	-	-	-	gr/	-
Tyrone	Balloughy *	-	flax	-	-	-	-	-	-	1"os/	-
Kilskeery	Ballyard	-	corn kiln	-	-	-	-	1834	-	6"os/	50
Errigal Keerogue	Ballygawly	Armstrong Andrew	distillery	-	-	-	-	1782	1 still - 228g.	hcJ	lic.
Errigal Keerogue	Ballygawly	Falls Alexander	distillery	-	-	-	-	1782	1 still - 203g.	hcJ	lic.
Errigal Keerogue	Ballygawly	Means Alexander	distillery	-	-	-	-	1782	1 still - 218g.	hcJ	lic.
Errigal Keerogue	Ballygawly	O'Neal Terence	distillery	-	-	-	-	1782	1 still - 210g.	hcJ	lic.
Errigal Keerogue	Ballygawly	Patterson John	corn	-	-	-	-	-	-	gr/	-
Donaghedy	Ballyheather	-	flax	-	-	-	-	1834	-	6"os/	2
Donaghedy	Ballyheather	M`Crea John	flax	-	43a.	-	-	-	-	gr/	-
Cappagh	Ballykeel	-	corn kiln	-	-	-	-	1834	-	6"os/	17
Urney	Ballylennan Mercer	-	mill pond	-	-	-	-	1834	-	6"os/	16
Leckpatrick	Ballymagorry	Devlin Thomas	corn & kiln	-	-	-	-	-	-	gr/	-
Clogher	Ballymagowan	Rigney David	distillery	-	-	-	-	1782	1 still - 209g.	hcJ	lic.
Tyrone	Ballymagrane *	Moore Hugh :	mill	-	-	-	Moore H - Muligan Stuart :	1814	-	dd/	668 435 465227
Termonamongan	Ballymongan	-	corn kiln	-	-	-	-	1834	-	6"os/	23
Donaghedy	Ballynabwee	-	flax	-	-	-	-	1834	-	6"os/	2
Donaghedy	Ballynabwee	Kilgore James & Jos	flax	-	-	-	-	-	-	gr/	-
Donaghedy	Ballynabwee	Kilgore William	flax	-	-	-	-	-	-	gr/	-
Cappagh	Ballynamullan	- S/ Cookstown rd.	corn & corn kiln	-	-	-	-	1834	-	6"os/	35
Cappagh	Ballynatubbrit	-	corn kiln	-	-	-	-	1834	-	6"os/	26
Cappagh	Ballynatubbrit	-	corn kiln	-	-	-	-	1834	-	6"os/	26
Dungannon Uppe	Ballyreagh	-	mill	-	-	-	-	-	-	1"os/	34
Camus	Ballyrenan	Watson David	flax	-	76a.	-	-	-	-	gr/	-
Ardstraw	Ballyrennan	-	corn & kiln	-	-	-	-	1834	-	6"os/	25
Ardstraw	Ballyrennan	-	flax & pond	-	-	-	-	1834	-	6"os/	25
Donaghmore	Ballysaggart	Belfast Banking Co.	spinning	-	-	-	-	-	-	gr/	-
Leckpatrick	Ballyskeagh	-	spade	-	-	-	-	1834	-	6"os/	5
Leckpatrick	Ballyskeagh	Gordon AAron	corn kiln	34x18x6 & :	-	14	-	1833	-	v1B/	640
Dungannon Uppe	Bardahessiagh	-	mill	-	-	-	-	-	-	1"os/	34
Clogherny	Beagh	-	corn mill	-	-	-	-	1834	-	6"os/	51
Clogherny	Beagh	N. side R.	mill	-	-	-	-	1834	-	6"os/	51
Camus	Bearney Glebe	-	old mill walls	-	-	-	-	1834	-	6"os/	10
Camus	Bearney Glebe	-	old mill walls	-	-	-	-	1834	-	6"os/	10
Donacavey	Belnagarnan	NE/ Fintona	mill	-	-	-	-	1834	-	6"os/	51
Bodeney lower	Beltrim	-	corn kiln	-	-	-	-	1834	-	6"os/	18
Clonfeacle	Benburb	- Benburb Valley	cotton	Restoration :	-	-	Erskine Holmes	1999	-	mmSv/	wh - Ce
Clonfeacle	Benburb	Eyre John	corn & kiln	-	11a.	-	-	-	-	gr/	-
Clonfeacle	Benburb	McKane Robert	corn	-	-	-	-	-	-	gr/	-
Clonfeacle	Benburb	McKane Robert	corn & kiln	-	11a.	-	-	-	-	gr/	-
Cappagh	Beragh	-	corn kiln	-	-	-	-	1834	-	6"os/	25

PARISH	TOWNLAND	MILLER	TYPE	HOUSE	Land	£Val	PROPRIETORS	Date	WHEEL etc.	Record	Ref.
Cappagh	Beragh	S/ Cloghfin R.	corn	-	-	-	-	1834	-	6"os/	44
Clogherny	Beragh Town	- on Cloghfin R.	flax	-	-	-	-	-	-	1"os/	34
Clogherny	Beragh Town	- on Cloghfin R.	mill	-	-	-	-	-	-	1"os/	34
Omagh	Berrysfort	-	old distillery	-	-	-	-	1834	-	6"os/	16
Ardstraw	Binnawooda	-	corn & mill pond	-	-	-	-	1834	-	6"os/	24
Ardstraw	Binnawooda	-	corn kiln	-	-	-	-	1834	-	6"os/	23
Ardstraw	Birnaghs	Baskin John	flax	-	60a.	-	-	-	-	gr/	-
Ardstraw	Birnaghs	Dogue John	flax	-	3.2.0	-	-	-	-	gr/	-
Donacavey	Blackfort	- on R. Quiggery	mill	-	-	-	-	1834	-	6"os/	43
Donacavey	Blackfort	Morton Joseph	corn & kiln	-	-	-	-	-	-	gr/	-
Donacavey	Blackfort	Morton Joseph	flax	-	-	-	-	-	-	gr/	-
Drumragh	Blacksessagh	Early Samuel :	corn :	-	-	-	Early S - Huston Ross :	1818	-	dd/	723 211 499346
Drumragh	Blacksessagh	Early Samuel :	corn & flax	-	-	-	Early Sam - Huston Ross :	1817	-	dd/	723 230 493965
Drumragh	Blacksessagh	White John :	mills	-	-	-	Whittie J&M - Stewart Jno :	1811	-	dd/	640 455 440821
Drumragh	Blacksessagh	Young James	corn	-	-	-	-	-	-	gr/	-
Drumragh	Blacksessagh	Young James	flax	-	-	-	-	-	-	gr/	-
Drumragh	Blacksessiagh	-	corn kiln	-	-	-	-	1834	-	6"os/	42
Drumragh	Blacksessiagh	- S/ B'sessiagh Br.	flax & corn	-	-	-	-	1834	-	6"os/	42
Cappagh	Boheragh	-	corn kiln	-	-	-	-	1834	-	6"os/	35
Clonfeacle	Boland	Jackson Robert	flax	-	10a.	-	-	-	-	gr/	-
Longfield West	Bomacktall Lower	-	flax kiln, corn kiln	-	-	-	-	1834	-	6"os/	24
Tyrone	Bonds Mill *	Hamilton	mill	-	-	-	Hamilton - Frank	-	-	dd/	673 42 462859
Drumragh	Botera Lower	-	flax & mill pond	-	-	-	-	1834	-	6"os/	34
Kilskeery	Brackagh	-	corn kiln	-	-	-	-	1834	-	6"os/	49
Donaghenry	Brackaville	-	ruins of bleach mill		-	-	-	1834	-	6"os/	47
Donaghenry	Brackaville	Sloan Andrew :	mills	-	-	-	Sloan T & Co-partnership	1814	30 Apl.	dd/	679 420 467777
Donaghenry	Brackaville	Sloane George	saw	-	-	-	-	-	-	gr/	-
Donaghenry	Brackaville	Sloane George	thrashing	-	-	-	-	-	-	gr/	-
Donaghenry	Brackaville	Wilson John	spinning	-	-	-	-	-	-	gr/	-
Termonmaguirk	Bracky	-	corn & corn kilns	-	-	-	-	1834	-	6"os/	36
Termonmaguirk	Bracky	-	corn kiln	-	-	-	-	1834	-	6"os/	36
Termonmaguirk	Bracky	- SE/ Archer's Br.	flax kiln (8)	-	-	-	-	1834	-	6"os/	36
Arboe	Brookend	-	corn & mill dam (large)		-	-	-	1834	-	6"os/	40
Arboe	Brookend	-	corn kiln	-	-	-	-	1834	-	6"os/	40
Clonfeacle	Brossloy	Donaghy Francis	corn & kiln	-	28a.	-	-	-	-	gr/	-
Clonfeacle	Brossloy	Donaghy Francis	flax	-	-	-	-	-	-	gr/	-
Lissan	Broughderg	- N/ Owenkillew R.	malt kiln	-	-	-	-	1834	-	6"os/	20
Donaghedy	Bunowen	- nr Altinagree Burn	corn	-	-	-	-	1834	-	6"os/	3
Donaghedy	Bunowen	- on Altinagree Burn	flax	-	-	-	-	1834	-	6"os/	3
Donaghedy	Bunowen	Roddy James	corn & kiln	-	27a.	-	-	-	-	gr/	-
Donaghedy	Bunowen	Roddy James	flax	-	-	-	-	-	-	gr/	-
Aghaloo	Caledon	Brown William	flour & corn	-	-	-	-	-	-	gr/	-
Aghaloo	Caledon	Cryer James	distillery	-	-	-	-	1782	1 still - 209g.	hcJ	lic.
Aghaloo	Caledon	Irwin Thomas	distillery	-	-	-	-	1782	1 still - 207g.	hcJ	lic.
Aghaloo	Caledon	Marshall Cornelus	distillery	-	-	-	-	1782	1 still - 220g.	hcJ	lic.
Aghaloo	Caledon	Norris Charles	distillery	-	-	-	-	1782	1 still - 223g.	hcJ	lic.
Dromore	Camderry	-	mill	-	-	-	-	1834	-	6"os/	42
Cappagh	Camowen	- E/ Camowen R.	mill	-	-	-	-	1834	-	6"os/	43
Cappagh	Camowen		old bleach green	-	-	-	-	1834	-	6"os/	43
Cappagh	Cappagh	-	mill	-	-	-	-	-	-	1"os/	34
Clogher	Carnagatt	Mountjoy Luke Hon.	mill	-	-	-	Mountjoy - Montgomery :	1789	-	dd/	416 361 272756
Clogher	Carnagatt	Mountjoy Luke Hon.	mill	-	-	-	Mountjoy - Stawell Wm :	1792	-	dd/	444 548 289599

PARISH	TOWNLAND	MILLER	TYPE	HOUSE	Land	£Val	PROPRIETORS	Date	WHEEL etc.	Record	Ref.
Arboe	Carnan	Hunter James	corn	-	15a.	-	-	-	-	gr/	-
Arboe	Carnan	Hunter James	flax	-	-	-	-	-	-	gr/	-
Ardstraw	Carncoran Glebe	-	corn	-	-	-	-	1834	-	6"os/	16
Ardstraw	Carncoran Glebe	-	corn	-	-	-	-	1834	-	6"os/	16
Ardstraw	Carncoran Glebe	-	flax	-	-	-	-	1834	-	6"os/	16
Tyrone	Carrickaness Br	- on Black Water	mill	-	-	-	-	-	-	1"os/	33
Tyrone	Carrickmore	-	mill	-	-	-	-	-	-	1"os/	34
Camus	Carrigullin	-	old mill walls	-	-	-	-	1834	-	6"os/	10
Camus	Carrigullin	- in Sion Town	Sion Mills	-	-	-	-	-	-	1"os/	25
Bodoney Upper	Carrowoaghtragh	- on Glenelly R.	corn kiln (/ mill)	-	-	-	-	1834	-	6"os/	13
Ardstraw	Cashty	-	corn kiln	-	-	-	-	1834	-	6"os/	25
Donaghmore	Castlecaulfield	Charlemont Lord	mill	-	-	-	Charlemont - Cuddy Alex :	1751	-	dd/	153 286 102810
Urney	Castlederg Town	- on Back Burn	mill	-	-	-	-	-	-	1"os/	25
Urney	Castlegore	- SE/ Derg R.	ruins of old mill	-	-	-	-	1834	-	6"os/	16
Kilskeery	Castleirvine Dems.	-	corn kiln	-	-	-	-	1834	-	6"os/	49
Kilskeery	Castleirvine Dems.	- NE. of Castle	mill	-	-	-	-	1834	-	6"os/	49
Cappagh	Castleroddy	-	corn kiln	-	-	-	-	1834	-	6"os/	26
Urney	Castlesessiagh	-	mill pond & race	-	-	-	-	1834	-	6"os/	16
Urney	Castlesessiagh	-	rorn & kiln	-	-	-	-	1834	-	6"os/	16
Donacavey	Cavan	Mullen Daniel	corn	-	13a.	-	-	-	-	gr/	-
Donacavey	Cavan	Stewart Jn Rt. Hon. :	mill	-	-	-	Stewart J & Hugh Son & :	1813	-	dd/	663 371 456575
Donacavey	Cavan	Stewart John Bart.	mill	-	-	-	Stewart J - Buchanan Dan :	1806	-	dd/	601 621 413115
Donacavey	Cavan	Stewart John Sir	mill	-	-	-	Stewart John - Osborne A	1806	-	dd/	601 622 413115
Drumragh	Cavanacaw	-	corn kiln	-	-	-	-	1834	-	6"os/	34
Pomeroy	Cavanakeeran	-	mill pond	-	-	-	-	1834	-	6"os/	37
Drumragh	Cavancaw Upper	-	corn kiln	-	-	-	-	1834	-	6"os/	34
Camus	Cavanlee	Young John	flax	-	20a.	-	-	-	-	gr/	-
Urney	Claddy Town	-	corn & mill pond	-	-	-	-	1834	-	6"os/	9
Urney	Clady	Killen James :	mill	-	-	-	Killen Jas - Craig James :	1764	-	dd/	282 215 182844
Urney	Clady	Kinkead Charles :	mill	-	-	-	Kinkead C - McElhenny :	1768	-	dd/	282 211 182837
Termonamongan	Clagernagh	- S/ Tillyred Vge.	ruins of corn kiln	-	-	-	-	1834	-	6"os/	23
Tyrone	Clanburns *	Stewart James	mill	-	-	-	Stewart Jas - Stewart W	1742	-	dd/	106 282 73770
Longfield East	Claraghmore	-	corn kiln	-	-	-	-	1834	-	6"os/	34
Tyrone	Clare Bridge	- on Fairy Water	mill	-	-	-	-	-	-	1"os/	25
Tyrone	Claudy *	Maxwell	mill	-	-	-	Maxwell - Black	-	?	dd/	721 447 493000
Errigal K`ogue	Cleanally	Martin Patrick	corn	-	-	-	-	-	-	gr/	-
Clonoe	Clintycracken	-	mill & mill race	-	-	-	-	1834	-	6"os/	47
Leckpartick	Cloghcor	-	old mill	-	-	-	-	1834	-	6"os/	2
Termonmaguirk	Cloghfin	NW/ Cloghfin R.	corn & corn kiln	-	-	-	-	1834	-	6"os/	44
Drumragh	Cloghog Lower	O`Kane Susanna	corn & kiln	-	-	-	-	-	-	gr/	-
Donaghmore	Clonavaddy	-	mill	-	-	-	-	-	-	1"os/	34
Tyrone	Clonavarn *	Falls	mills	-	-	-	-	-	-	dd/	708 238 484973
Kildress	Clontyferagh	- S/ Ballinderry R.	ruins of old mill	-	-	-	-	1834	-	6"os/	29
Tyrone	Clough Lower *	- str./ Fairy Water	corn	-	-	-	-	1834	-	6"os/	34
Longfield West	Clunahill Glebe	-	still house in ruins	-	-	-	-	1834	-	6"os/	33
Tamlaght	Coagh	Hamilton	mill	-	-	-	Hamilton - Newton Andrew	1812	-	dd/	656 121 460477
Tamlaght	Coagh	Hannyngton	mill	-	-	-	Hannyngton - Newton	-	-	dd/	656 121 450477
Tamlaght	Coagh	Hanyngston Thos :	mill	-	-	-	Hanyngston - Newton Andr	1812	-	dd/	656 21 460477
Tamlaght	Coagh	Hogg James :	mill	-	-	-	Hogg Jas - Clerk Alex :	1814	-	dd/	690 40 473983
Tamlaght	Coagh	Lawson	mill	-	-	-	Lawson - Newton	-	-	dd/	653 59 450121
Tamlaght	Coagh	McCarter	mills	-	-	-	McCarter - McCarter	-	-	dd/	751 409 510944
Tamlaght	Coagh	Vance James :	mill	-	20a.	-	Vance James - Duff Jas :	1805	-	dd/	571 349 386308

COUNTY TYRONE

PARISH	TOWNLAND	MILLER	TYPE	HOUSE	Land	£Val	PROPRIETORS	Date	WHEEL etc.	Record	Ref.
Donaghenry	Coalisland	-	corn	Restoration :	-	-	-	1999	-	mmSv/	wh - Cc
Derryloran	Cookstown Town	-	no mill	-	-	-	-	1834	-	6"os/	29
Ardstraw	Coolaghy	Ramsay Robert :	flax	-	-	-	Ramsay R - Ramsay Wm	1814	Conv. 3 Sep. :	dd/	727 38 496 174
Longfield West	Coolavannagh	-	mill	-	-	-	-	-	-	1"os/	33
Longfield West	Coolavannagh	- W/ R. Blackwater	mill & mill pond	-	-	-	-	1834	-	6"os/	33
Dungannon	Coolhill	- near Dungannon	Old Windmill	-	-	-	-	-	-	1"os/	35
Derryloran	Coolkeeghan	-	wv. factory	-	-	-	-	-	-	1"os/	35
Ardstraw	Coolnacrun	- NW/ Fairy Water	mill & mill pond	-	-	-	-	1834	-	6"os/	24
Dromore	Corbally	-	corn kiln	-	-	-	-	1834	-	6"os/	41
Donacavey	Corbally	-	kiln	-	-	-	-	1834	-	6"os/	50
Kildress	Corchoney	-	mill	-	-	-	-	-	-	1"os/	26
Kildress	Corchoney		corn & mill race	-	-	-	-	1834	-	6"os/	29
Clogher	Corcreevy	Davidson Robert	corn	-	1a.	-	-	-	-	gr/	-
Kilskerry	Cordromedy	Bleakney Robert	corn	-	-	-	-	-	-	gr/	-
Kildress	Corkhill	- SW/ Wellbrook	mill & mill race	-	-	-	-	1834	-	6"os/	29
Kildress	Corkill	- on Ballinderry R.	flax	-	-	-	-	-	-	1"os/	26
Kildress	Corkill	Black William	flax	-	-	-	-	-	-	gr/	-
Kildress	Corkill	Irwin Caroline	beetling	-	-	-	-	-	-	gr/	-
Kilskerry	Corkragh	Armstrong Charles	corn	-	-	-	-	-	-	gr/	-
Kilskerry	Corkragh	O`Brien Hugh	tuck	-	-	-	-	-	-	gr/	-
Dromore	Corlaghdergan	-	brick kiln	-	-	-	-	1834	-	6"os/	49
Dromore	Corlaghdergan	-	corn kiln	-	-	-	-	1834	-	6"os/	49
Dromore	Corlaghdergan	-	corn kiln & brick kiln	-	-	-	-	1834	-	6"os/	49
Kilskerry	Corlea	Armstrong John	corn	-	-	-	-	-	-	gr/	-
Tyrone	Cormamucklagh	Lendrum John	mulcture	-	-	-	Lendrun Jn - Hamilton Jas	1808	-	dd/	637 519 440306
Dromore	Cornamuck	-	corn kiln	-	-	-	-	1834	-	6"os/	49
Longfield East	Cornavarrow	-	corn kiln	-	-	-	-	1834	-	6"os/	42
Killyman	Corr	NE/ road to Armagh	Cranebrok Pottery	-	-	-	-	1834	-	6"os/	47
Dromore	Corrasheskin	-	corn kiln (2)	-	-	-	-	1834	-	6"os/	42
Tyrone	Corrogan Water	Scott John & Margt	corn	-	-	-	Scott John - McMinn Sam	1740	-	dd/	103 47 70554
Kildress	Corvanaghan	-	corn & mill dam	-	-	-	-	1834	-	6"os/	28
Kildress	Corvanaghan	Charles Thomas	corn	-	-	-	-	-	-	gr/	-
Kildress	Corvanaghan	Charles Thomas	flax	-	-	-	-	-	-	gr/	-
Cappagh	Cranny	- N/ Cranny Br.	mill & mill stream	-	-	-	-	1834	-	6"os/	35
Ballyclog	Cratley	Spear Robert :	lands	-	-	-	Spear R - Ledlie William	1750	-	dd/	156 210 105 139
Termonamongan	Creeduff	Kyle William	mills	-	-	-	Kyle Wm - Norris William :	1813	-	dd/	661 250 454756
Termonamongan	Creeduff	Kyle William	mills	-	-	-	Kyle & Marr Arts. - Norris :	1809	-	dd/	662 334 456335
Tullyniskan	Creenagh	NE/ road to Armagh	pottery (3)	-	-	-	-	1834	-	6"os/	47
Tullyniskan	Creenagh	Nicholson James :	mill	-	-	-	Nicholson J - Clibborn Ed :	1819	-	dd/	742 477 505612
Tullyniskan	Creenagh	Nicholson Joseph	mill	-	-	-	Nicholson J - Clibborn Ed	1810	-	dd/	629 185 432429
Donaghmore	Creevagh Lower	-	corn kiln	-	-	-	-	1834	-	6"os/	46
Lissan	Creeve	-	mill race	-	-	-	-	1834	-	6"os/	21
Lissan	Creeve	-	old bleach mill	-	-	-	-	1834	-	6"os/	29
Cappagh	Creevenagh	Ellis Thomas :	mill	-	-	-	Ellis Thos - Stewart Sir Jn :	1811	-	dd/	646 485 447026
Cappagh	Creevenagh	Stewart James Hon.	mill	-	-	-	Stewart Jas - Burrowes : T	1812	Mort. 1 Jul.		652 117 447207
Tyrone	Creevy	-	flax	-	-	-	-	-	-	1"os/	25
Tyrone	Creevy	-	mill	-	-	-	-	-	-	1"os/	25
Termonmaguirk	Creggan	-	corn kiln	-	-	-	-	1834	-	6"os/	27
Termonmaguirk	Creggan	-	old corn kiln	-	-	-	-	1834	-	6"os/	27
Termonamongan	Crighdenis	-	corn kiln	-	-	-	-	1834	-	6"os/	22
Kilskeery	Crossan	- nr Drumbinnion Br.	mill	-	-	-	-	-	-	1"os/	33
Pomeroy	Crossdernot	Browne John	corn	-	-	-	-	-	-	gr/	-

PARISH	TOWNLAND	MILLER	TYPE	HOUSE	Land	£Val	PROPRIETORS	Date	WHEEL etc.	Record	Ref.
Pomeroy	Crossdernot	Browne John	flax	-	-	-	-	-	-	gr/	-
Pomeroy	Crossdernot	Cowan	mills	-	-	-	Cowan - Shaw	-	-	dd/	665 261 458999
Pomeroy	Crossdernot	Cowan James	mills	-	-	-	Cowan Jas - Shaw Edw	1809	-	dd/	665 261 450999
Pomeroy	Crossdernot	SW/ Mill Cross Rds.	corn & mill dam	-	-	-	-	1834	-	6"os/	46
Clonfeacle	Crossteely	Loughran John	flax	-	11a.	-	-	-	-	gr/	-
Tyrone	Cullinean	Lendrum James :	mill	-	-	-	Lendrum J - Lendrum J :	1797	-	dd/	511 330 332070
Tyrone	Cullinean	Lendrum John	mill	-	-	-	Lendrum Jn - Lendrum Jn	1766	-	dd/	271 649 182233
Tyrone	Cullinean	Lendrum John	mill	-	-	-	Lendrum - Miller Jno	1795	-	dd/	552 209 365772
Aghalurcher	Cullynane	Montgomery Reps.	corn	-	1a.	-	-	-	-	gr/	-
Tyrone	Culnagrew	-	mill	-	-	-	-	-	-	1"os/	35
Bodeney Lower	Culvacullion	-	corn kiln (2)	-	-	-	-	1834	-	6"os/	18
Dromore	Derganny (Maguire)	-	corn kiln & mill pond		-	-	-	1834	-	6"os/	49
Termonmaguirk	Deroran	-	corn kiln	-	-	-	-	1834	-	6"os/	35
Tullyniskan	Derry	-	tile manufactory	-	-	-	-	1834	-	6"os/	47
Tullyniskan	Derry	Hall William :	mills & grist	-	-	-	Hall Wm - Pike Wm & Jno	1811	-	dd/	647 61 441363
Tullyniskan	Derry	Hogg Jno, Redford :	mills & grist	-	-	-	Hogg & ano - Hall William :	1811	-	dd/	647 64 441364
Tullyniskan	Derry	Sloan	mills & grist	-	-	-	Sloan - Pepper	-	?	dd/	650 138 446470
Tullyniskan	Derry	Sloane George	corn	-	-	-	-	-	-	gr/	-
Tullyniskan	Derry	Sloane George	spade	-	-	-	-	-	-	gr/	-
Tullyniskan	Derry	SW/ Coal Island	flour, mill dam & race		-	-	-	1834	-	6"os/	47
Tullyniskan	Derry Drumy	Hogg	mill	-	-	-	Hogg - Hall	-	-	dd/	647 64 441364
Ballinderry	Derrycrin Eglish	- nr Ballinderry Br.	corn & mill pond	-	-	-	-	1834	-	6"os/	31
Ballinderry	Derrycrin Eglish	McGuckin John	corn	-	25a.	-	-	-	-	gr/	-
Artrea	Derrygonian	Sloan John	bleach	-	-	-	-	-	-	gr/	-
Artrea	Derrygonian	Sloan John	flax	-	12a.	-	-	-	-	gr/	-
Dromore	Derrynaseer	-	corn kiln	-	-	-	-	1834	-	6"os/	41
Dromore	Derrynaseer	-	corn mill (ruins)	-	-	-	-	1834	-	6"os/	41
Dromore	Derryvaghorn	-	corn kiln	-	-	-	-	1834	-	6"os/	43
Desertcreat	Desertcreat	Kenny Robon & Mary :	mills	-	-	-	Kenny R - Kenny Samuel	1800	-	dd/	637 541 440332
Desertcreat	Desertcreat	Kenny William	bleach	-	-	14	-	1833	-	v1B/	623
Desertcreat	Desertcreat	Kenny William	corn & kiln	-	-	6.3	-	1833	-	v1B/	623
Desertcreat	Desertcreat	Walsh Robert	beetling	-	8a.	-	-	-	-	gr/	-
Desertcreat	Desertcreat	Walsh Robert	flax	-	-	-	-	-	-	gr/	-
Donaghenry	Donaghenry	Stewart's	corn	Restored	-	-	-	1999		mmSv/	wh - C
Donaghmore	Donaghmore	N/ Town	mill	-	-	-	-	1834	-	6"os/	46
Donaghmore	Donaghmore	Ball	mill	-	-	-	Ball - Mackenzie	-	-	dd/	667 368 460737
Donaghmore	Donaghmore	E. end Town	brewery	-	-	-	-	1834	-	6"os/	46
Donaghmore	Donaghmore	Mackenzie	mill	-	-	-	Mackenzie - Dickson	-	-	dd/	474 382 446137
Donaghmore	Donaghmore	Mackenzie Alex :	mill	-	-	-	Mackenzie A - Shaw John :	1816		dd/	701 536 481038
Donaghmore	Donaghmore	Sloan Thomas K :	mill (known as :	-	-	-	Sloan T - Sloan Thos :	1815	-	dd/	689 385 472722
Donaghmore	Donaghmore	Vincent Rev Richard	mill	-	-	-	Vincent - Mackenzie Alex	1815	-	dd/	690 507 441743
Desertcreat	Donaghrisk	-	mill race	-	-	-	-	1834	-	6"os/	38
Desertcreat	Donaghrisk	- S/ Des'creat Br.	bleach	-	-	-	-	1834	-	6"os/	38
Desertcreat	Donaghrisk	- SW/ Des'creat Br.	bleach	-	-	-	-	1834	-	6"os/	38
Desertcreat	Donaghrisk	Daniel Capt.	old flax mill	-	-	3.17	-	1833	-	v1B/	623
Desertcreat	Donaghrisk	Lindsay Frederick	corn & kiln	-	117a.	-	-	-	-	gr/	-
Desertcreat	Donaghrisk	Lindsay Frederick	flax	-	-	-	-	-	-	gr/	-
Tyrone	Donemanna	Silverbrook Mill	corn & flax	Restoration :	-	-	-	2001	-	mmSv/	wh - Ce
Urney	Donnygowen	-	corn	-	-	-	-	1834	-	6"os/	9
Urney	Donnygowen	-	old mill ruins	-	-	-	-	1834	-	6"os/	9
Urney	Donnygowen	Lafferty Owen	flax	-	-	-	-	-	-	gr/	-
Dromore	Doocrock	-	corn kiln	-	-	-	-	1834	-	6"os/	49

PARISH	TOWNLAND	MILLER	TYPE	HOUSE	Land	£Val	PROPRIETORS	Date	WHEEL etc.	Record	Ref.
Kildress	Doons	-	mill	-	-	-	-	-	-	1"os/	26
Dromore	Dressoge	-	corn kiln	-	-	-	-	1834	-	6"os/	34
Dromore	Dressoge	-	corn kiln	-	-	-	-	1834	-	6"os/	41
Tempanroe	Drumaspil	Strain Alex	flax	-	-	-	-	-	-	gr/	-
Tempanroe	Drumaspill	Edwards George :	mill	-	-	-	Edwards - Stewart Alex :	1817	-	dd/	754 280 512615
Tempanroe	Drumaspill	Stewart George :	mill	-	-	-	Stewart G - Todd Wm :	1816	-	dd/	708 225 484960
Longfield East	Drumbarley	-	corn kiln	-	-	-	-	1834	-	6"os/	34
Dromore	Drumconnis	-	corn kiln (2)	-	-	-	-	1834	-	6"os/	50
Drumglass	Drumcoo	Jackson James	corn	-	-	-	-	-	-	gr/	-
Drumglass	Drumcoo :	- S. of Town :	corn	-	-	-	-	1834	-	6"os/	54
Clonfeakle	Drumderg Glebe	-	corn kiln	-	-	-	-	1834	-	6"os/	50
Derryloran	Drumgarrell	-	bleach green	-	-	-	-	1834	-	6"os/	30
Donaghedy	Drumgauty	-	flax	-	-	-	-	1834	-	6"os/	2
Kilskeery	Drumharvey	-	corn kiln	-	-	-	-	1834	-	6"os/	49
Clonfeacle	Drumlee	-	flax	-	-	-	-	-	-	1"os/	35
Clonfeacle	Drumlee	Bartley John	flax	-	18a.	-	-	-	-	gr/	-
Camus	Drumlegagh	-	corn	-	-	-	-	1834	-	6"os/	24
Camus	Drumlegagh	-	flax & corn kiln	-	-	-	-	1834	-	6"os/	24
Camus	Drumlegagh	M`Coy Hugh	flax	-	50a.	-	-	-	-	gr/	-
Camus	Drumlegagh	Maxwell Joseph	flax	-	43a.	-	-	-	-	gr/	-
Camus	Drumlegagh	Maxwell Joseph	flax	-	-	-	-	-	-	gr/	-
Camus	Drumlegagh	Moody Samuel	flax	-	43a.	-	-	-	-	gr/	-
Dromore	Drumlish	-	corn kiln	-	-	-	-	1834	-	6"os/	42
Termonamongan	Drummahon	-	ruins of corn kiln	-	-	-	-	1834	-	6"os/	23
Longfield Wedt	Drummenagh	-	corn kiln	-	-	-	-	1834	-	6"os/	33
Tyrone	Drummuck	Atkinson Jackson	corn	-	-	-	-	-	-	gr/	-
Kildress	Drumnaglogh	-	mill dam	-	-	-	-	1834	-	6"os/	29
Cappagh	Drumnakilly	-	brick kiln	-	-	-	-	1834	-	6"os/	36
Cappagh	Drumnakilly	-	corn kiln	-	-	-	-	1834	-	6"os/	36
Cappagh	Drumnakilly	-	corn kiln (2)	-	-	-	-	1834	-	6"os/	36
Cappagh	Drumnakilly	-	mill	-	-	-	-	-	-	1"os/	34
Cappagh	Drumnakilly	-	tuck & mill race	-	-	-	-	1834	-	6"os/	36
Cappagh	Drumnakilly	- mid-townland	spade	-	-	-	-	1834	-	6"os/	36
Cappagh	Drumnakilly	- NE/ Archer's Br.	scutch	-	-	-	-	1834	-	6"os/	36
Cappagh	Drumnakilly	Kyle James	tuck	-	42a.	-	-	-	-	gr/	-
Longfield West	Drumowen	- NW/ Black Water	corn	-	-	-	-	1834	-	6"os/	33
Longfield West	Drumowen	- W/ Black Water	still house in ruins	-	-	-	-	1834	-	6"os/	33
Longfield West	Drumquin	-	mill	-	-	-	-	1834	-	6"os/	33
Longfield West	Drumquin	Bateman John :	mill	-	-	-	Bateman J - Balfe Edmond	1819	-	dd/	743 40 505775
Longfield West	Drumquin Town		mill	-	-	-	-	-	-	1"os/	-
Tullyniskan	Drumreagh Otra	-	New Mills	-	-	-	-	1834	-	6"os/	46
Tullyniskan	Drumreagh Otra	-	spade factory	-	-	-	-	1834	-	6"os/	46
Tullyniskan	Drumreaghotra	Stevenson Robert	corn	-	-	-	-	-	-	gr/	-
Kilskeery	Drumsonnus	Johnson	mills	-	-	-	Johnson & Butler M.Arts	-	-	dd/	717 528 482658
Tempanroe	Drumuck	Verner	mill	-	-	-	Verner - Kerr	-	-	dd/	750 591 510526
Tyrone	Drumullen	Hannyngton Thos :	mill	-	-	-	Hannyngton T - Harkness :	1814	Mort. 15 Aug.	dd/	678 148 466898?
Tyrone	Drumullen	Harryngton	mills (2) :	-	-	-	Harryngton - Sloan Thos	1815	Mort. 12 May	dd/	689 383 474722
Tyrone	Drumush		mill	-	-	-	-			1"os/	33
Dromore	Dullaghan	Cunningham Robert	corn & kiln	-	-	-	-	-	-	gr/	-
Clonfeacle	Dunamony	Holmes William	corn & kiln	-	17a.	-	-	-	-	gr/	-
Clonfeacle	Dunamony	Holmes William	flax	-	-	-	-	-	-	gr/	-
Tyrone	Dunamore	-	mill	-	-	-	-	-	-	1"os/	26

PARISH	TOWNLAND	MILLER	TYPE	HOUSE	Land	£Val	PROPRIETORS	Date	WHEEL etc.	Record	Ref.
Cappagh	Dunbreen	-	corn	-	-	-	-	1834	-	6"os/	26
Cappagh	Dunbreen	-	corn kiln (3)	-	-	-	-	1834	-	6"os/	26
Cappagh	Dunbreen	Crawford Oliver	corn	-	9a.	-	-	-	-	gr/	-
Cappagh	Dunbreen	Crawford Oliver	flax	-	-	-	-	-	-	gr/	-
Drumglass	Dungannon	Cairns James :	mill	-	-	-	Cairns James - Falls Jas :	1816	-	dd/	708 475 485211
Drumglass	Dungannon	Falls	mills	-	-	-	Falls - Hamilton	-	-	dd/	653 267 453236
Drumglass	Dungannon	Knox Thomas	mills	-	-	-	Knox Thos & Stewart :	1815	-	dd/	686 21 471558
Drumglass	Dungannon	Knox William :	mills	-	-	-	Knox Wm - Stewart Mary	1815	Annuity 24 Feb.	dd/	686 308 471849
Drumglass	Dungannon	Northland Hon Lord :	mill	-	-	-	Northland Ld - Falls Jas :	1811	-	dd/	640 390 440243
Drumglass	Dungannon L`ships	Knox Charles Hon :	mill	-	-	-	Knox C - Knox Hon Vesey :	1819	Asgt. 7 Apl.	dd/	739 311 503646
Drumglass	Dungannon L`ships	Knox Vesey Hon. :	mill	-	-	-	Knox V - Ball Benjamin :	1819	-	dd/	742 217 505352
Drumglass	Dungannon L`ships	Northland Thomas :	mills	-	-	-	Northland Ld - Knox Vesey	1819	-	dd/	739 189 503524
Drumglass	Dungannon Town	- SW road to Moy	distillery	-	-	-	-	1834	-	6"os/	54
Drumglass	Dungannon Town	O`Neill John	Milltown	-	-	-	O`Neill J - Loughreen Dav	1878	-	dd/	1878 48 247
Kildress	Dungate	-	dam & mill race	-	-	-	-	1834	-	6"os/	28
Kildress	Dungate	-	ruins of old corn mill		-	-	-	1834	-	6"os/	28
Lissan	Dunmore	-	old bleach mill	-	-	-	-	1834	-	6"os/	21
Donaghedy	Dunnamanagh	- on Burn Dennet	old mill	-	-	-	-	1834	-	6"os/	3
Donaghedy	Dunnamanagh	- on Burn Dennet	paper	-	-	-	-	1834	-	6"os/	3
Donaghedy	Dunnamanagh	Connison Walter	flax	-	-	-	-	-	-	gr/	-
Donaghedy	Dunnamanagh	Connison Walter	paper	-	-	-	-	-	-	gr/	-
Donaghedy	Dunnamanagh	Hamilton Charles :	mill - Bond's Mill	-	-	-	Hamilton C - Frank Thos T	1814	Annuity 17 Mar.	dd/	673 42 462859
Aghaloo	Dyan	Caledon Earl of	corn	-	5a.	-	-	-	-	gr/	-
Aghaloo	Dyan	Caledon Earl of	flax	-	-	-	-	-	-	gr/	-
Aghaloo	Dyan	Wilson	corn & kilns	Restoration :	-	-	Edward & Pr. Wilson	2000	-	pWEH	B
Tyrone	Eden	- on Eden R.	mill	-	-	-	-	-	-	1"os/	26
Baldonney Upper	Eden Mill	-	corn	-	-	-	-	1834	-	6"os/	11
Baldonney Upper	Eden Mill	-	corn kiln & pond	-	-	-	-	1834	-	6"os/	11
Cappagh	Edenderry	- NW/ Camowen R.	Leap Mill	-	-	-	-	1834	-	6"os/	43
Cappagh	Edenderry	Bellmore Earl	mill	-	-	-	Belmore E - Stack	-	-	dd/	705 452 483387
Cappagh	Edenderry	Bellmore Rt. Hon Earl	mill	-	-	-	Belmore E - Caldwell John	1815	Mort. 3 Dec.	dd/	696 501 472998
Cappagh	Edenderry	Bellmore Rt. Hon. :	mill	-	-	-	Belmore E - Ankettle Oliver	1815	-	dd/	695 209 477134
Cappagh	Edenderry	Bellmore Rt. Hon. :	mill	-	-	-	Belmore E - Johnson Robt	1815	-	dd/	698 466 479174
Desertcreat	Edendroit	Adair Thomas	beetling	-	2a.	-	-	-	-	gr/	-
Desertcreat	Edendroit	Carruthers James	bleach	-	-	17.2	-	-	-	v1B/	623
Desertcreat	Edendroit	Carruthers James	corn & kiln	-	-	3	-	-	-	v1B/	623
Desertcreat	Edendroit	Crowthers James	corn	-	25a.	-	-	-	-	gr/	-
Drumragh	Edergoole Lower	McDonnell James	corn	-	-	-	-	-	-	gr/	-
Artrea	Edernagh	-	King's Mill & mill dam		-	-	-	1834	-	6"os/	39
Artrea	Edernagh	M`Reynolds Thomas	corn	-	47a.	-	-	-	-	gr/	-
Artrea	Edernagh	M`Reynolds Thomas	flax	-	-	-	-	-	-	gr/	-
Camus	Edymore	-	corn kiln	-	-	-	-	1834	-	6"os/	10
Killeeshill	Ennish	Burgess John Y	corn	-	-	-	-	-	-	gr/	-
Ardstraw	Envagh	-	corn kiln (2)	-	-	-	-	1834	-	6"os/	25
Kildress	Ergannagh	-	flax holes (2)	-	-	-	-	1834	-	6"os/	16
Dromore	Esker	-	corn kiln (3)	-	-	-	-	1834	-	6"os/	49
Donaghmore	Eskragh	- nr Eskragh Water	mill	-	-	-	-			1"os/	34
Donaghmore	Eskragh	Corry Geo & Matt :	use of water	-	-	-	Corry Geo - Hogg John :	1817	Mort. 22 Dec.	dd/	724 432 494767
Cappagh	Faccary	-	flax kiln	-	-	-	-	1834	-	6"os/	26
Cappagh	Faccary	M`Farland Charles	corn	-	8a.	-	-	-	-	gr/	-
Donacavey	Fallaghearn	-	corn kiln	-	-	-	-	1834	-	6"os/	42
Donacavey	Fallaghearn	-	corn kiln	-	-	-	-	1834	-	6"os/	52

PARISH	TOWNLAND	MILLER	TYPE	HOUSE	Land	£Val	PROPRIETORS	Date	WHEEL etc.	Record	Ref.
Tullyniskan	Farlough	-	bleach & mill race	-	-	-	-	1834	-	6"os/	46
Tullyniskan	Farlough	Tuckey Davys :	bleach & lands :	-	-	-	Tuckey D - Tuckey Chas :	1813	Mort. 1 Jan.	dd/	654 871 541160
Tullyniskan	Farlough	W. side of R.	bleach & mill dam	-	-	-	-	1834	-	6"os/	46
Donaghedy	Fawney	-	old bleach	-	-	-	-	1834	-	6"os/	3
Kilskeery	Feglish	-	corn kiln (2)	-	-	-	-	1834	-	6"os/	49
Cappagh	Fernagh		mill	-	-	-	-	-	-	1"os/	34
Donacavey :	Fintona Town	Houston Henry	corn & kilns	-	-	-	-	-	-	gr/	-
Clogher	Fivemiletown	- 1/2 m. S. of Town	mill	-	-	-	-	1834	-	6"os/	64
Clogher	Fivemiletown	Birney William	distillery	-	-	-	-	1782	1 still - 200g.	hcJ	lic.
Clogher	Fivemiletown	Boyd Mathew	distillery	-	-	-	-	1782	1 still - 200g.	hcJ	lic.
Errigal K`ogue	Foremass		mill	-	-	-	-	-	-	1"os/	34
Errigal K`ogue	Foremass		mills	-	-	-	-	-	-	1"os/	34
Errigal K`ogue	Foremass Lower	Crossle Charles	corn	-	-	-	-	-	-	gr/	-
Bodoney Lower	Formil	-	corn kiln (2)	-	-	-	-	1834	-	6"os/	27
Urney	Freughlough	-	old lime kilns (2)	-	-	-	-	1834	-	6"os/	16
Tyrone	Freughmore (3)		mill	-	-	-	-	-	-	1"os/	-
Pomeroy	Galbally	- on Altmore R.	mill	-	-	-	-	-	-	1"os/	34
Pomeroy	Galbally	SW/ rd. to Dungannon	corn & mill pond	-	-	-	-	1834	-	6"os/	45
Drumragh	Gammy	- SW/ Drumragh R.	flax	-	-	-	-	1834	-	6"os/	43
Dromore	Gardrum	-	corn kiln	-	-	-	-	1834	-	6"os/	50
Kilskeery	Gargadis	-	corn kiln	-	-	-	-	1834	-	6"os/	49
Bodoney Lower	Garvagh	-	corn kiln (2)	-	-	-	-	1834	-	6"os/	18
Termonamongan	Garvagh	-	ruins of kiln	-	-	-	-	1834	-	6"os/	15
Bodoney Lower	Garvagh Blane	-	ruins of corn kiln	-	-	-	-	1834	-	6"os/	14
Errigal K`ogue	Garvaghy	-	corn kiln	-	-	-	-	1834	-	6"os/	49
Errigal K`ogue	Garvaghy	Cammock John	corn	-	-	-	-	-	-	gr/	-
Errigal K`ogue	Garvaghy		mill	-	-	-	-	-	-	1"os/	34
Donacavey	Garvallagh	S/ R. near S'ore	mill	-	-	-	-	1834	-	6"os/	51
Drumragh	Gillygooly	-	corn kiln	-	-	-	-	1834	-	6"os/	34
Drumragh	Gillygooly	- nr Meeting House	corn kiln & mill, pond		-	-	-	1834	-	6"os/	34
Drumragh	Gillygooly	Glass Galbraith	corn	-	-	-	-	-	-	gr/	-
Drumragh	Gillygooly	Glass Galbraith	flax	-	-	-	-	-	-	gr/	-
Drumragh	Gillygooly	Smith William Jun	flax	-	-	-	-	-	-	gr/	-
Tyrone	Glasmullagh		mill	-	-	-	-	-		1"os/	34
Kilskeery	Glasmullagh North	road SE ex Trillick	bark	-	-	-	-	1834	-	6"os/	50
Tyrone	Glenchiel	- Oughtdoorish R.	mill	-	-	-	-	-	-	1"os/	26
Cappagh	Glengawna	-	corn kiln	-	-	-	-	1834	-	6"os/	26
Bodoney Lower	Glenmacoffer	-	corn & corn kiln	-	-	-	-	1834	-	6"os/	18
Bodoney Lower	Glenroan	Hamilton James :	mill	-	-	-	Hamilton J - Sinclair Jas :	1817	-	dd/	711 371 486906
Urney	Glentown	-	flax	-	-	-	-	1834	-	6"os/	9
Urney	Glentown		flax	-	-	-	-			1"os/	25
Cappagh	Golan	-	corn	-	-	-	-	1834	-	6"os/	26
Cappagh	Golan	Sproule Andrew :	mill	-	-	-	Sproule A - Sproule Edw :	1811	-	dd/	646 54 441536
Tyrone	Gorta Lower	- on Ballinderry R.	bleach & mill race	-	-	-	-	1834	-	6"os/	29
Tyrone	Gortacashel	-	corn kiln (2)	-	-	-	-	1834	-	6"os/	19
Tyrone	Gortacashel	-	tan yard	-	-	-	-	1834	-	6"os/	19
Clogherny	Gortaclare	-	flax	-	-	-	-	1834	-	6"os/	43
Clogherny	Gortaclare		flax	-	-	-	-	-		1"os/	34
Derryloran	Gortalowry	- W/King's Br.	mill	-	-	-	-	1834	-	6"os/	38
Tyrone	Gorticashel	- on G`cashel B.	flax	-	-	-	-	-	-	1"os/	26
Leckpatrick	Gorticrum	- on Glenmoran R.	spade	-	-	-	-	1834	-	6"os/	5
Derryloran	Gortin	- NE/ Oritor	corn	-	-	-	-	1834	-	6"os/	29

PARISH	TOWNLAND	MILLER	TYPE	HOUSE	Land	£Val	PROPRIETORS	Date	WHEEL etc.	Record	Ref.
Bodoney Lower	Gortin	- S/ Main St. Gortin	distillery	-	-	-	-	1834	-	6"os/	18
Desertcreat	Gortindarragh	McKee William	flax	-	-	-	-	-	-	gr/	-
Termonamongan	Gortnagross	-	corn kiln	-	-	-	-	1834	-	6"os/	23
Tullyniskan	Gortnaskea	Frizell Patrick	corn	-	-	-	-	-	-	gr/	-
Tullyniskan	Gortnaskea	McCann Robert :	mills	-	-	-	McCann R - Coruth Jas :	1815	-	dd/	692 356 475494
Tullyniskan	Gortnaskea	Sloan Andrew	mills	-	-	-	Sloan A - Sloan Thomas :	1815	-	dd/	692 301 475436
Tullyniskan	Gortnaskea	Sloane George	flax	-	-	-	-	-	-	gr/	-
Tullyniskan	Gortnaskea	Sloane George	saw	-	-	-	-	-	-	gr/	-
Tullyniskan	Gortnaskea	W/ Coal Island	flour	-	-	-	-	1834	-	6"os/	47
Leckpatrick	Gortycrum Irish	Donaghy Bryan	spade	40x25x9 & :	-	4.15	-	1833	-	v1b/	640
Termonmaguirk	Granagh	-	corn kiln	-	-	-	-	1834	-	6"os/	36
Dromore	Greenan	-	old still house	-	-	-	-	1834	-	6"os/	41
Tyrone	Greyduff	Kyle James	mills	-	-	-	Kyle James - Gay Henry :	1810	-	dd/	619 590 425194
Leckpatrick	Holly Hill	Legerson William	spade	80x17x7 & :	-	7.0	-	1833	-	v1B/	640
Leckpatrick	Holly Hill	Sigerson William	spade	-	-	-	-	-	-	gr/	-
Urney	Inchenny	Inch William	flax	-	-	-	-	-	-	gr/	-
Carnteel	Innishmagh	Crossle James	corn	-	18a.	-	-	-	-	gr/	-
Kildress	Kildress Upper	- NW/ Kildress Br.	corn & mill race	-	-	-	-	1834	-	6"os/	29
Tyrone	Kilfaddy *	Maxwell John W.	mill	-	-	-	Maxwell J - Maxwell Robt.	1815	-	dd/	696 466 477965
Ardstraw	Killeen	-	flax	-	-	-	-	1834	-	6"os/	16
Ardstraw	Killeen	-	Mill pond & corn kiln		-	-	-	1834	-	6"os/	16
Termonamongan	Killen Far	-	flax kiln	-	-	-	-	1834	-	6"os/	23
Termonamongan	Killeter	- on Derry R.	mill	-	-	-	-	-	-	1"os/	25
Pomeroy	Killey	- SW. of Town	corn	-	-	-	-	1834	-	6"os/	37
Cappagh	Killins	-	corn	-	-	-	-	1834	-	6"os/	26
Longfield West	Killoan	-	corn kiln	-	-	-	-	1834	-	6"os/	33
Cappagh	Killybrack	-	corn kiln	-	-	-	-	1834	-	6"os/	35
Desertcreat	Killycolp		wv. factory	-	-	-	-	-	-	1"os/	35
Derryloran	Killymam	Falls John :	mills	-	-	-	Falls John - Ball Benjamin	1816	Mort. 4 Nov.	dd/	708 238 484973
Derryloran	Killymam	Mackenzie Alex :	mills	-	-	-	Mackenzie A - Falls John :	1816	-	dd/	707 314 484449
Derryloran	Killymam	Northland Lord	mills	-	-	-	Northland Lord - Falls	-	-	dd/	640 390 440243
Derryloran	Killymoon	Stewart Col William	flax & thrashing	Incumb Est :	-	-	-	1851	-	mlylE	p.8/9
Drumglass	Killyneill		mill	-	-	-	-	-	-	1"os/	35
Drumragh	Kilmoore	- S/ Glenelly R.	corn & pond	-	-	-	-	1834	-	6"os/	17
Drumragh	Kilmore	-	corn kiln	-	-	-	-	1834	-	6"os/	34
Drumragh	Kilmore	- str./ Fairy Water	corn & mill pond	-	-	-	-	1834	-	6"os/	34
Clogher	Kilnaheery	- on Routing Burn	mills	-	-	-	-	-	-	1"os/	34
Clogher	Kilnaheery	Gervais Francis J	corn	-	4a.	-	-	-	-	gr/	-
Clogher	Kilnaheery	Gervais Francis J	flax	-	-	-	-	-	-	gr/	-
Clogher	Kilnaheery	SE/ river	mills	-	-	-	-	1834	-	6"os/	51
Ardstraw	Kilstrule	-	flax holes	-	-	-	-	1834	-	6"os/	16
Dromore	Knockahorn	Osborne Thomas	corn & kiln	-	-	-	-	-	-	gr/	-
Kildress	Knockaleery	-	corn & mill race	-	-	-	-	1834	-	6"os/	42
Leckpatrick	Knockanbrack	-	corn	-	-	-	-	1834	-	6"os/	5
Leckpatrick	Knockanbrack	-	old still ho.	-	-	-	-	1834	-	6"os/	5
Leckpatrick	Knockanbrack	Christie Thomas	corn	-	-	-	-	-	-	gr/	-
Dromore	Knockaraven	-	corn kiln	-	-	-	-	1834	-	6"os/	42
Cappagh	Knockmore	- close E/ corn mill	large pond	-	-	-	-	1834	-	6"os/	25
Cappagh	Knockmoyle	Scott Robert	corn	-	19a.	-	-	-	-	gr/	-
Clogher	Knocknacarney	McClean William	flax	-	5a.	-	-	-	-	gr/	-
Dromore	Knocknahorn	-	corn & mill pond	-	-	-	-	1834	-	6"os/	41
Camus	Knockniller	-	corn	-	-	-	-	1834	-	6"os/	10

COUNTY TYRONE

PARISH	TOWNLAND	MILLER	TYPE	HOUSE	Land	£Val	PROPRIETORS	Date	WHEEL etc.	Record	Ref.
Camus	Knockniller	-	flax	-	-	-	-	1834	-	6"os/	10
Camus	Knockniller	-	flax & mill dam	-	-	-	-	1834	-	6"os/	10
Donacavey	Lackagh	Gorman Terence	corn	-	21a.	-	-	-	-	gr/	-
Donacavey	Lackagh	Gorman Terence	corn & store	-	-	-	-	-	-	gr/	-
Donacavey	Lackagh	Gorman Terence	spade	-	-	-	-	-	-	gr/	-
Donacavey	Lackagh	W/ fort	corn	-	-	-	-	1834	-	6"os/	51
Termonamongan	Laghtmorris	-	corn kiln	-	-	-	-	1834	-	6"os/	14
Termonamongan	Laghtmorris	-	old still house	-	-	-	-	1834	-	6"os/	14
Bodoney Upper	Leaghs	- on Glenelly R.	old still house	-	-	-	-	1834	-	6"os/	13
Bodoney Upper	Learden Lower	-	corn kiln	-	-	-	-	1834	-	6"os/	18
Ballyclog	Leck	-	corn	-	-	-	-	1834	-	6"os/	39
Ballyclog	Leck	Spear Robert :	mill	-	-	-	Spear R - Ledlie William	1750	-	dd/	156 210 105 139
Leckpatrick	Leckpatrick	-	corn & mill pond	-	-	-	-	1834	-	6"os/	5
Leckpatrick	Leckpatrick	- on Glenmoran R.	corn	-	-	-	-	1834	-	6"os/	5
Leckpatrick	Leckpatrick	Ferris John	corn	-	-	-	-	-	-	gr/	-
Leckpatrick	Leckpatrick	Ferris John	flax	-	-	-	-	-	-	gr/	-
Leckpatrick	Leckpatrick	Grainger & Co.	paper	60x24x25 & :	-	9.2	-	1833	-	v1B/	640
Leckpatrick	Leckpatrick	McCrea William	corn kiln	34x24x15 & :	-	5.7	-	1833	-	v1B/	640
Leckpatrick	Leckpatrick Town :	McKinley James	saw	-	-	-	-	-	-	gr/	-
Leckpatrick	Leckpatrick Town :	Scott Walter	corn (steam)	-	-	-	-	-	-	gr/	-
Longfield West	Legpup	-	corn kiln	-	-	-	-	1834	-	6"os/	33
Donaghedy	Leitrim	-	flax	-	-	-	-	1834	-	6"os/	3
Donaghedy	Leitrim	- on Altinaghree B.	corn	-	-	-	-	1834	-	6"os/	3
Bodoney Lower	Lenamore	-	corn kiln	-	-	-	-	1834	-	6"os/	18
Bodoney Lower	Lenamore	-	mill	-	-	-	-	-	-	1"os/	26
Dromore	Lettery	-	corn kiln	-	-	-	-	1834	-	6"os/	41
Urney	Liggarstown	-	corn	-	-	-	-	1834	-	6"os/	10
Urney	Liggarstown	- on Mourne R.	old mill	-	-	-	-	1834	-	6"os/	10
Urney	Liggarstown	Herdman James	flax spinning	-	-	-	-	-	-	gr/	-
Bodoney Lower	Liggins	-	corn kiln	-	-	-	-	1834	-	6"os/	19
Cappagh	Lisboy	-	corn kiln	-	-	-	-	1834	-	6"os/	35
Donaghedy	Liscloon	- on Altinaghree B.	corn	-	-	-	-	1834	-	6"os/	3
Donaghedy	Liscloon Lower	Deery William	corn & kiln	-	-	-	-	-	-	gr/	-
Donaghedy	Liscloon Lower :	-	flax	-	-	-	Brown Madge Mrs	1900	20x4x -	sv/	2006/NC
Clonfeacle	Lisdermot	Woods Charles	flax	-	1a.	12	-	-	-	gr/	-
Termonmaguirk	Lisdoart	Stewart George V	corn	-	-	-	-	-	-	gr/	-
Tyrone	Lisdoart	Stewart George V	flax	-	-	-	-	-	-	gr/	-
Kilskeery	Lisdoo	-	corn kiln	-	-	-	-	1834	-	6"os/	49
Cappagh	Lislea		mill	-	-	-	-	-	-	1"os/	34
Termonamongan	Lisnacloon	- 'pipe' ex R. Derg	flax	-	-	-	-	1834	-	6"os/	15
Ardstraw	Lisnacreaght	- N/ Fairy Water	corn	-	-	-	-	1834	-	6"os/	25
Ardstraw	Lisnacreaght	Rollestone Robert	corn	-	15a.	-	-	-	-	gr/	-
Ardstraw	Lisnacreaght	Rollestone Robert	flax	-	-	-	-	-	-	gr/	-
Donaghmore	Lisnagowan	-	mill	-	-	-	-	1834	-	6"os/	46
Donaghmore	Lisnagowan	Morrough Samuel	corn	-	-	-	-	-	-	gr/	-
Cappagh	Lisnamallard	-	Millbank (House)	-	-	-	-	1834	-	6"os/	35
Cappagh	Lisnamallard	race ex Camowen R.	brewery	-	-	-	-	1834	-	6"os/	35
Cappagh	Lisnamallard	Scott William	corn	-	7a.	-	-	-	-	gr/	-
Cappagh	Lisnamallard	Scott William	flour	-	-	-	-	-	-	gr/	-
Cappagh	Lisnamallard	Scott William	saw	-	-	-	-	-	-	gr/	-
Tyrone	Lisnasoragh	Colhoun Crawford :	mill	-	-	-	Colhour C - Cross Hamilton	1817	-	dd/	710 269 486205
Dromore	Lissaneden	-	corn kiln (2)	-	-	-	-	1834	-	6"os/	50

PARISH	TOWNLAND	MILLER	TYPE	HOUSE	Land	£Val	PROPRIETORS	Date	WHEEL etc.	Record	Ref.
Tyrone	Little Bridge	Harrington	mill	-	-	-	Harryngton - Sloan	-	-	dd/	869 383 473722
Tyrone	Littlebridge	Harryngton Dunganno	mill	-	-	-	Harryngton D - Sloan	1815	Mort. 12 May	dd/	689 383 473722
Tyrone	Loughash	Enery	mill	-	-	-	Enery - Enery & ano	-	-	dd/	746 537 508072
Tyrone	Loughash	Enery John Sen. :	mill	-	-	-	Enery John - Enery John :	1819	-	dd/	746 536 508072
Tyrone	Loughash	Hamilton	mill	-	-	-	Hamilton - Frank	-	-	dd/	673 42 462859
Tyrone	Loughash	Hamilton	mill	-	-	-	Hamilton - Frank & ano	-	-	dd/	763 42 462859
Termonmaguirk	Loughmacrory	- at Milltown	mill	-	-	-	-	-	-	1"os/	34
Termonmaguirk	Loughmacrory	Mann Ann Jane	corn & kiln	-	-	-	-	-	-	gr/	-
Termonmaguirk	Loughmacrory :	-	flax hole (3)	-	-	-	-	1834	-	6"os/	27
Tempanroe	Loughmuck	Edwards	mill	-	-	-	Edwards - Stuart M/Arts	-	-	dd/	754 280 512615
Tempanroe	Loughmuck	Stewart	mill	-	-	-	Stewart - Todd m. arts.	-	-	dd/	708 225 484960
Tempanroe	Loughmuck	Stewart George :	mill	-	-	-	Stewart G - Todd Wm :	1816	-	dd/	708 225 484960
Leckpatrick	Loughneas	-	corn kiln	-	-	-	-	1834	-	6"os/	2
Leckpatrick	Loughneas	-	flax	-	-	-	-	1834	-	6"os/	2
Derryloran	Loughry	- S/ New bridge	old mill in ruins	-	-	-	-	1834	-	6"os/	38
Leckpatrick	Mac Crackens	Gourley William	paper	79x28x21 & :	-	8.0	-	1833	-	v1B/	640
Leckpatrick	Maccrackens	-	paper	-	-	-	-	1834	-	6"os/	5
Leckpatrick	Maccrackens	Lyon George	corn	-	-	-	-	-	-	gr/	-
Leckpatrick	Maccrackens	Lyon George	corn & kiln	-	-	-	-	-	-	gr/	-
Leckpatrick	Maccrackens	Lyon George	thrashing	-	-	-	-	-	-	gr/	-
Ardstraw	Magheracreggan	-	mill pond	-	-	-	-	1834	-	6"os/	24
Ardstraw	Magheracreggan	- N. side of road	corn mills (2)	-	-	-	-	1834	-	6"os/	24
Ardstraw	Magheracreggan	- N. side of road	flax	-	-	-	-	1834	-	6"os/	24
Dromore	Magheragart (Donnell)	- S./ Sheephill Lo.	corn	-	-	-	-	1834	-	6"os/	50
Termonamongan	Magherakeel	-	flax kiln	-	-	-	-	1834	-	6"os/	23
Ardstraw	Magheralough	- E/ Village	flax & mill pond	-	-	-	-	1834	-	6"os/	24
Kilskeery ? :	Magheralough ?	Quin	mill	-	-	-	Quin - Alexanders	-	-	dd/	715 87 489022
Donaghedy	Magheramason	-	old mill	34.6x12.9x16	-	-	-	1834	-	6"os/	1
Cappagh	Maine	-	brick kiln	-	-	-	-	1834	-	6"os/	35
Ardstraw	Meaghy	-	corn kiln	-	-	-	-	1834	-	6"os/	16
Bodoney Lower	Meenadoo	-	corn kiln	-	-	-	-	1834	-	6"os/	18
Dromore	Meenagar	-	corn kiln (2)	-	-	-	-	1834	-	6"os/	50
Clonoe	Meenagh	-	mill	-	-	-	-	1834	-	6"os/	47
Clonoe	Meenagh	- near Coalislend	flax	-	-	-	-	-		1"os/	35
Clonoe	Meenagh	King Robert	flax	-	38a.	-	-	-	-	gr/	-
Clonoe	Meencargagh	-	corn kiln (2)	-	-	-	-	1834	-	6"os/	24
Tyrone	Megna *	Annesley Arthur :	mill	-	-	-	Annesley Arth & Arthur :	1811	-	dd/	639 80 439636
Tyrone	Megna *	Annesley Francis :	mill	-	-	-	Annesley Fran - Le Grice :	1811	-	dd/	637 565 440918
Tyrone	Millown House	- near Dungannon	-	-	-	-	-	-	-	1"os/	35
Donaghedy	Milltown	-	bleach	-	-	-	-	1834	-	6"os/	2
Donaghedy	Milltown	-	corn	-	-	-	-	1834	-	6"os/	2
Leckpatrick	Milltown	-	corn	-	-	-	-	1834	-	6"os/	6
Donaghedy	Milltown	-	flax	-	-	-	-	1834	-	6"os/	2
Drumquin	Milltown	-	mill - 1 mile	-	-	-	-	-		1"os/	25
Ardstraw	Milltown	-	Milltown Village	-	-	-	-	1834	-	6"os/	17
Ardstraw	Milltown	- on R. Derg	spade foundry	-	-	-	-	1834	-	6"os/	17
Ardstraw	Milltown	- S/ R. Derg	flax & mill pond	-	-	-	-	1834	-	6"os/	17
Strabane	Milltown	- on Glenmoran R.	old mill	-	-	-	-	1834	-	6"os/	5
Tyrone	Milltown	- stream to R. Derg	flax	-	-	-	-	-		1"os/	25
Leckpatrick	Milltown	Barhill Thomas & Co.	corn	50x22x8 & :	-	3.14	-	1833	-	v1B/	640
Ardstraw	Milltown	Bradly John	corn	48x21x7	-	2.1	-	1833	14x1/6 works :	v1B/	673A
Ardstraw	Milltown	Carson	mill	-	-	-	Carson - Eakings M. Arts.	-	-	dd/	722 273 493408

PARISH	TOWNLAND	MILLER	TYPE	HOUSE	Land	£Val	PROPRIETORS	Date	WHEEL etc.	Record	Ref.
Ardstraw	Milltown	Dudgeon	mill	-	-	-	Dudgeon - Dudgeon	-	-	dd/	704 108 482443
Donaghedy	Milltown	Edie Alex	corn & kiln	36x23x16 & :	-	6.2.0	-	1833	-	v1B/	639
Donaghedy	Milltown	Edie Alex	corn & kiln	36x23x16 & :	-	6.2	-	1833	-	v1B/	639A
Donaghedy	Milltown	Kelly Mrs or Edie A.	beetling	52x27x19 & :	-	9.8	-	1833	-	v1B/	147
Aghaloo	Milltown	Kewn John	flax	-	-	-	-	1833	-	v1B/	639a
Ardstraw	Milltown	King, Barton & Co.	spade	23x30x11	-	2.12	-	1833	13x2.6	v1B/	673A
Camus	Milltown	Lowther Galbraith	corn & kiln	-	-	-	-	-	-	gr/	-
Leckpatrick	Milltown	Lynch John & ors	corn & kiln	-	-	-	-	-	-	gr/	-
Donaghedy	Milltown	McNeill Godfrey	corn & kiln	-	-	-	-	-	-	gr/	-
Donaghedy	Milltown	McNeill Godfrey	flax	-	-	-	-	-	-	gr/	-
Upper Comber	Milltown	O'Neill Francis	bleach	60x27x9 :	-	9.9	-	1833	-	v1B/	639A
Ardstraw	Milltown	Sheriffe Co. Tyrone	mill	-	-	-	Sheriffe - Neilson	-	-	dd/	719 376 491711
Ardstraw	Milltown	Smith John	flax	33x18x13	-	2.1	-	1833	13x2.6	v1B/	673A
Donaghedy	Milltown	White George	flax	-	-	-	-	-	-	gr/	-
Tyrone	Monbeg	Bateman	mill	-	-	-	Bateman - Johnson	-	-	dd/	736 547 502082
Tyrone	Monbeg	Bateman	mill	-	-	-	Bateman - Balfe	-	-	dd/	743 40 505775
Cappagh	Mountjoy Forest :	- NE. of Struce R.	corn	-	-	-	-	1834	-	6"os/	25
Termonamongan	Mournbeg	-	mill & mill race	-	-	-	-	1834	-	6"os/	15
Termonamongan	Mournbeg	- on R. Derg	tuck	-	-	-	-	1834	-	6"os/	15
Clonfeacle	Moygashel	Boardman	mills	-	-	-	Boardman - Greer	-	-	dd/	668 117 460827
Clonfeacle	Moygashel	Duffin Charles :	mill	-	-	-	Duffin C - Ferguson Patk. :	1811	-	dd/	627 472 434447
Clonfeacle	Moygashel	Orr Jacob	beetling	-	23a.	-	-	-	-	gr/	-
Clonfeacle	Moygashel	Woods Charles	beetling	-	24a.	-	-	-	-	gr/	-
Clonfeacle	Moygashel	Woods Charles	flax	-	-	-	-	-	-	gr/	-
Clonfeacle	Moygashell	-	fabric	Restoration :	-	-	P. Costello & others	1999	-	mmSv/	wh - Cc
Clonfeacle	Moygashell	Boardman Thomas :	mills	-	-	-	Boardman T - Greer Thos :	1813	Mort. 22 Dec.	dd/	668 117 460827
Clogherny	Moylagh	- E/ rd. to Clogher	corn & mill pond	-	-	-	-	1834	-	6"os/	43
Clogherny	Moylagh	Mackey Samuel	corn & kiln	-	5a.	-	-	-	-	gr/	-
Dromore	Mullaghbane	-	corn kiln	-	-	-	-	1834	-	6"os/	42
Cappagh	Mullaghmore	-	brick kiln (2) & brick field		-	-	-	1834	-	6"os/	35
Cappagh	Mullaghmore	- on Torrent R.	mill	-	-	-	-	-	-	1"os/	34
Cappagh	Mullaghmore	Carson John	corn	-	30a.	-	-	-	-	gr/	-
Cappagh	Mullaghmore	Donnelly John	corn	-	29a.	-	-	-	-	gr/	-
Cappagh	Mullaghmore	Donnelly John	flax	-	-	-	-	-	-	gr/	-
Tempanroe	Mullaghteige	Mc Clean Frederick	flax	-	-	-	-	-	-	gr/	-
Tyrone	Mullaghtitoney	- NE/ Artrea Vge.	bleach & mill race	-	-	-	-	1834	-	6"os/	38
Tyrone	Mullan Beg	-	corn kiln	-	-	-	-	1834	-	6"os/	36
Tyrone	Mullanahoe	-	mill	-	-	-	-	-	-	1"os/	35
Dromore	Mullanboy	-	corn kiln	-	-	-	-	1834	-	6"os/	42
Tyrone	Mullanbreen	- on R. Derg	mill	-	-	-	-	-	-	1"os/	25
Donacavey	Mullawinny	-	corn kiln	-	-	-	-	1834	-	6"os/	42
Clonfeakle	Mullybrannon	Falls James :	mills & kilns	-	-	-	Falls Jas - Hamilton John :	1813	-	dd/	653 267 453324
Clonfeakle	Mullybrannon	Knox Thomas Hon. :	mills & kilns	-	-	-	Knox - Stewart M.Arts	1815	10 Feb.	dd/	686 21 471558
Clonfeakle	Mullybrannon	Knox William :	mills & kilns	-	-	-	Knox - Stewart marr arts.	1815	Smt. 24 Feb.	dd/	686 308 471849
Clonfeakle	Mullybrannon & :	Northland Hon Lord :	mills	-	-	-	Northland Ld - Falls Jas :	1811	-	dd/	640 390 440243
Aghaloo	Mullyneill	- c1 mile W./ Dyan	scutch	-	-	-	-	-	-	pWEH	R
Desertcreat	Mullynure	-	corn, dam & mill race		-	-	-	1834	-	6"os/	38
Killeeshill	Mullyroddan	- on Oona Water	flax	-	-	-	-	-	-	1"os/	34
Killeeshill	Mullyroddan	Reid Mary	corn	-	-	-	-	-	-	gr/	-
Killeeshill	Mullyroddan	Reid Mary	flax	-	-	-	-	-	-	gr/	-
Termonmaguirk	Mulnafye	-	mill dam & flax kiln		-	-	-	1834	-	6"os/	27
Dromore	Mulnagoagh	-	corn kiln (2)	-	-	-	-	1834	-	6"os/	50

PARISH	TOWNLAND	MILLER	TYPE	HOUSE	Land	£Val	PROPRIETORS	Date	WHEEL etc.	Record	Ref.
Tyrone	Mulnagore	- at Cross Roads	The Mill	-	-	-	-	-	-	1"os/	34
Aghaloo	Mulnahorn	Moore Cecil	flax	-	56a	-	-	-	-	gr/	-
Pomeroy	Munderry	NE Gortnavoy Br.	mill, mill stream :	-	-	-	-	1834	-	6"os/	46
Tyrone	Newmills	- on Torrent R.	-	-	-	-	-	-	-	1"os/	35
Dromore	Newpark	-	corn kiln (2)	-	-	-	-	1834	-	6"os/	49
Ardstraw	Newtownstewart	-	mill pond & corn kiln		-	-	-	1834	-	6"os/	17
Clogher	Nurchossy Scotch	Hornridge Robert	corn	-	-	-	-	-	-	gr/	-
Baldonney Upper	Oughtdoorish	- on Glenelly R.	corn	-	-	-	-	1834	-	6"os/	12
Baldonney Upper	Oughtdoorish	- str. to Glenelly R.	corn	-	-	-	-	1834	-	6"os/	12
Desertcreat	Oughterard	-	corn kiln	-	-	-	-	1834	-	6"os/	41
Desertcreat	Oughterard	- S/ The Rock cross.	corn	-	-	-	-	1834	-	6"os/	38
Desertcreat	Oughterard	Boyd Joseph	corn & kiln	-	-	4.7	-	-	-	v1B/	623
Desertcreat	Oughterard	Robinson Bariah	corn & kiln	-	21a.	-	-	-	-	gr/	-
Bodoney Upper	Oughtnamwella	-	old still house	-	-	-	-	1834	-	6"os/	8
Tyrone	Parkmount	- near Dungannon	linen factory	-	-	-	-	-	-	1"os/	35
Tyrone	Pluck *	Gorman William :	mills	-	-	-	Gorman - Fleetwood Chas	1819	4 May.	dd/	741 8 504543
Tyrone	Pluck *	Gorman William :	mills	-	-	-	Gorman W - Gorman Wm :	1820	Asgt. 15 Mar.	dd/	750 147 510082
Tyrone	Pluck *	Gorman William Elder	mills	-	-	-	Gorman &son - Knox Ann :	1817	Mort. 3 Dec.	dd/	722 54 493189
Tyrone	Pluck *	Gorman William Elder	mills	-	-	-	Gorman W - Knox Geo :	1817	Mort. 1 Dec.	dd/	721 600 493135
Tyrone	Pluck *	Gorman William Elder	mills	-	-	-	Gorman - Knox Sarah :	1817	Mort. 2 Dec.	dd/	722 37 493172
Longfield West	Prughlish	-	still house in ruins	-	-	-	-	1834	-	6"os/	33
Clogherny	Radergan	-	corn kiln	-	-	-	-	1834	-	6"os/	44
Tyrone	Raghony	-	corn kiln	-	-	-	-	1834	-	6"os/	50
Dromore	Rakeeran	-	corn kiln (2)	-	-	-	-	1834	-	6"os/	50
Dromore	Rakeeran	SW/ fort	corn & mill stream	-	-	-	-	1834	-	6"os/	50
Dromore	Rakeeranbeg	Landrum Richard	corn & kilns	-	-	-	-	-	-	gr/	-
Dromore	Rakeeranbeg	Lendrum John	mill	-	-	-	Lendrun Jn - Hamilton Jas	1808	-	dd/	637 519 449306
Termonmaguirk	Ramacan	-	flax kiln	-	-	-	-	1834	-	6"os/	44
Clogherny	Ranelly	- S/ Bloody Bridge	corn & mill pond	-	-	-	-	1834	-	6"os/	43
Clogherny	Ranelly	Donnell James	mill dam	-	9a.	-	-	-	-	gr/	-
Clogherny	Ranelly	Perry	mills	-	-	-	Perry - Simpson	-	-	dd/	709 206 485511
Clogherny	Ranelly	Wilson Thomas	corn	-	46a.	-	-	-	-	gr/	-
Donacavey	Raveagh	Barr George	corn & kiln	-	0.3.0	-	-	-	-	gr/	-
Donacavey	Raveagh	Brabazon	mill	-	-	-	Brabazon Martha her will	-	-	dd/	694 1 476336
Donacavey	Raveagh	SW/ br. Tld/ Beagh	mill	-	-	-	-	1834	-	6"os/	51
Donacavey	Raveagh	Wallace	mill	-	-	-	Wallace - Moyne	-	-	dd/	657 238 451107
Clogherny	Raw	-	corn kiln	-	-	-	-	1834	-	6"os/	43
Cappagh	Recarson	-	corn kiln	-	-	-	-	1834	-	6"os/	35
Tyrone	Redford	- C664 on Rhone R.	wv	-	-	-	-	-		1"os/	35
Errigal K`ogue	Rough Hill	Moutray Anketell	corn	-	-	-	-	-	-	gr/	-
Donaghenry	Roughan	S/ road to Coalisl.	bleach	-	-	-	-	1834	-	6"os/	46
Donaghenry	Roughan	S/ road to Coalisl.	bleach & pond	-	-	-	-	1834	-	6"os/	46
Donaghenry	Roughan	Wilson John	bleach	-	-	-	-	-	-	gr/	-
Donaghenry	Roughan	Wilson John	spinning	-	-	-	-	-	-	gr/	-
Leckpatrick	Rousky	-	corn	-	-	-	-	1834	-	6"os/	6
Leckpatrick	Rousky	- on Burn Dennet	corn	-	-	-	-	1834	-	6"os/	6
Kilskerry	Scallan	Douglas	mill	-	-	-	Douglas - Johnson	-	?	dd/	693 557 476266
Kilskerry	Scallen	- S. side of road :	corn	-	-	-	-	-	-	6"os/	49
Kilskerry	Scallen	Beacon Lowther	corn & kiln	-	-	-	-	-	-	gr/	-
Ardstraw	Scarvagherin	-	flax hole	-	-	-	-	1834	-	6"os/	16
Derryloran	Scotchtown	- on Owenaillew R.	flax	-	-	-	-	-	-	1"os/	26
Termanamongan	Scraghy	-	old corn kiln	-	-	-	-	1834	-	6"os/	32

PARISH	TOWNLAND	MILLER	TYPE	HOUSE	Land	£Val	PROPRIETORS	Date	WHEEL etc.	Record	Ref.
Termanamongan	Scraghy	-	riuins of corn kiln	-	-	-	-	1834	-	6"os/	32
Clogherny	Seskinore	W/ S'ore Vge.	corn & corn kiln	-	-	-	-	1834	-	6"os/	51
Clogherny	Seskinore	Walsh Louis	corn	-	7a.	-	-	-	-	gr/	-
Termanamongan	Shanaghy	-	old malt kiln	-	-	-	-	1834	-	6"os/	23
Donaghenry	Shankey	-	mill & mil race	-	-	-	-	1834	-	6"os/	39
Kilskerry	Shanmullagh	Fleming Andrew	corn	-	-	-	-	-	-	gr/	-
Kilskerry	Shanmullagh East	-	corn, corn kiln, stream		-	-	-	1834	-	6"os/	49
Dromore	Shannaragh	-	corn & corn kiln	-	-	-	-	1834	-	6"os/	42
Dromore	Shannaragh	-	flax	-	-	-	-	-		1"os/	33
Dromore	Shannaragh	Wilson James	corn	-	-	-	-	-	-	gr/	-
Dromore	Shannaragh	Wilson James	flax	-	-	-	-	-	-	gr/	-
Tyrone	Shilen	Falls	mill	-	-	-	Falls - Cairns	-	?	dd/	681 116 448663
Leckpatrick	Silverhill	-	old still ho.	-	-	-	-	1834	-	6"os/	5
Tyrone	Sion Mills	Herdman & Co.	spinning	Restoration :	-	-	-	2001	-	mmSv/	wh - B
Camus	Skinboy	- near Douglas Br.	large mill ponds	-	-	-	-	1834	-	6"os/	10
Camus	Skinboy	- on Douglas Burn	flax	-	-	-	-	1834	-	6"os/	10
Omagh West	Sloughan	-	corn kiln in ruins	-	-	-	-	1834	-	6"os/	33
Omagh West	Spamount	- on R. Derg	bleach	-	-	-	-	1834	-	6"os/	16
Omagh West	Speerholme	- on R. Derg	corn & mill race	-	-	-	-	1834	-	6"os/	23
Clonfeacle	Stiloga	Anderson Andrew	corn	-	-	-	-	-	-	gr/	-
Clonfeacle	Stiloga	Knock Robert	corn & kiln	-	56a.	-	-	-	-	gr/	-
Clonfeacle	Stiloga	Knock Robert	flax	-	-	-	-	-	-	gr/	-
Camus	Strabane Town	Majoriebanks Edwd	mill	-	-	-	M`banks - Broughton Robt	1887	-	dd/	1887 23 266
Camus	Strabane Town :	Boyd William	mill	-	-	-	Boyd Wm - Craig James	1853	-	dd/	1853 22 89
Camus	Strabane Town :	Craig Thomas	mill	-	-	-	Craig Thos - Boyd Wm	1850	-	dd/	1850 9 90
Camus	Strabane Townp`ks	-	brewery	-	-	-	-	1834	-	6"os/	5
Camus	Strabane Townp`ks	Smith David	corn (steam)	-	-	-	-	-	-	gr/	-
Kilskeery	Stralongford	-	corn	-	-	-	-	-		1"os/	33
Kilskeery	Stralongford	-	corn kiln	-	-	-	-	1834	-	6"os/	49
Cumber	Stranaghalwilly	-	tuck	-	-	-	-	1834	-	6"os/	7
Cumber	Stranaghalwilly	- on Glernrandsal R.	corn & kiln	-	-	-	-	1834	-	6"os/	7
Clonfeacle	Strangmore	Barcroft John P	beetling	-	-	-	-	-	-	gr/	-
Clonfeacle	Strangmore	Barcroft John P	bleach green	-	5a.	-	-	-	-	gr/	-
Clonfeacle	Strangmore	Boardman	mill	-	-	-	Boardman - Greer	-	-	dd/	668 117 460827
Clonfeacle	Strangmore	Burrowes	mill	-	-	-	Burrowes - Hannington	-	-	dd/	670 317 461420
Termonmaguirk	Sultan	-	corn kiln	-	-	-	-	1834	-	6"os/	36
Tyrone	Tabananmatt *	McClintock James :	mill	-	-	-	McClintock J - McClintock	1786	-	dd/	375 303 251391
Tyrone	Tabananmatt *	McClintock John :	mill	-	-	-	McClintock - McCullagh Jas	1762	-	dd/	243 7 155769
Tamlaght	Tamlaght	-	mill dam	-	-	-	-	1834	-	6"os/	29
Kildress	Tamnaskeeny	-	mill dam, mill race		-	-	-	1834	-	6"os/	38
Kildress	Tamnaskeeny	-	mill in ruins	-	-	-	-	1834	-	6"os/	38
Kildress	Tamnaskeeny	Black James	mill	-	-	-	Black Jas - Reynolds Wm	1791	-	dd/	442 425 287820
Kildress	Tamnaskeeny	Morris John :	mill	-	-	-	Morris John - Holmes Wm :	1742	-	dd/	111 134 75943
Termonmaguitk	Tanderagee	-	corn kiln	-	-	-	-	1834	-	6"os/	44
Tempanroe	Tartlaghan	-	paper	-	-	-	-	-	-	gr/	-
Tempanroe	Tartlaghan	-	spade m`fty	-	-	-	-	-		1"os/	35
Drumragh	Tattykeel	Rodgers Alex & :	mill	-	-	-	Rodgers A - Rodgers Robt	1736	-	dd/	111 461 77579
Drumragh	Tattykeel	Rodgers William :	mill	-	-	-	Rodgers W - Knight James	1759	-	dd/	201 363 133183
Drumragh	Tattykeel (Buchannon)	- E/ Tattykeel Vge.	corn kiln	-	-	-	-	1834	-	6"os/	42
Clogherny	Tattykeeran	-	corn kiln	-	-	-	-	1834	-	6"os/	43
Donacavey	Tattymoyle Upper	Monaghan Arthur	corn & kiln	-	14a.	-	-	-	-	gr/	-
Drumragh	Tattysallagh	-	corn & mill pond	-	-	-	-	1834	-	6"os/	42

PARISH	TOWNLAND	MILLER	TYPE	HOUSE	Land	£Val	PROPRIETORS	Date	WHEEL etc.	Record	Ref.
Drumragh	Tattysallagh	-	corn kiln	-	-	-	-	1834	-	6"os/	42
Drumragh	Tattysallagh	- W/ Wid Magee's Br.	corn	-	-	-	-	1834	-	6"os/	42
Drumragh	Tattysallagh	Allen Thomas	corn	-	-	-	-	-	-	gr/	-
Bodley Lower	Teebane	-	corn kiln	-	-	-	-	1834	-	6"os/	19
Bodley Lower	Teebane East	- on Owenaillew R.	mill	-	-	-	-	-	-	1"os/	26
Killyman	Tempanroe	Hamilton John :	mill	-	-	-	Hamilton J - Makenzie Sir :	1816	-	dd/	707 300 484435
Killyman	Tempanroe	Mackenzie	mills	-	-	-	Mackenzie - Falls	-	-	dd/	707 314 484449
Killyman	Tempanroe	McDonnell James	corn	-	-	-	-	-	-	gr/	-
Killyman	Tempanroe	McElroy William :	bleach green	-	-	-	Milroy Wm - McEroy Patk	1774	-	dd/	302 476 201010
Donaghenry	Templereagh	-	mill	-	-	-	-	-		1"os/	35
Donaghenry	Templereagh	- W/ Cratley Br.	mill & kiln	-	-	-	-	1834	-	6"os/	39
Clogher	Terrew	Brackenridge G. C.	corn	-	-	-	-	-	-	gr/	-
Clogher	Terrew	Dickey James :	corn	-	-	-	Dickey J - Hurst James	1767	-	dd/	355 240 239295
Clogher	Terrew	Dickey James :	corn	-	-	-	Dickey J - Rees John :	1763	M.Arts.	dd/	309 638 208781
Cappagh	Tirmurty	-	corn kiln	-	-	-	-	1834	-	6"os/	26
Cappagh	Tirmurty	Donnelly Charles	corn	-	23a.	-	-	-	-	gr/	-
Cappagh	Tirmurty	Donnelly Charles	flax	-	-	-	-	-	-	gr/	-
Desertcreat	Tirnaskea	-	beetling	-	-	-	-	-		1"os/	34
Desertcreat	Tirnaskea	-	mill	-	-	-	-	-		1"os/	34
Termonmaguirk	Tironoy	-	corn & corn kiln	-	-	-	-	1834	-	6"os/	36
Cappagh	Tirquin	-	brick kiln (2)	-	-	-	-	1834	-	6"os/	35
Donacavey	Tonnaghmore	-	mill & mill stream	-	-	-	-	1834	-	6"os/	50
Donacavey	Tonnaghmore	Eecles Daniel	tuck	-	-	-	Eecles Dan - Archdall Nick	1744	-	dd/	119 17 80530
Donacavey	Tonnaghmore	McClintock Alex :	tuck	-	-	-	McClintock A - Sampson R	1744	-	dd/	117 257 80686
Donacavey	Tonnaghmore	Ross Daniel	corn	-	1a.	-	-	-	-	gr/	-
Kilskery	Trillick	-	corn mills (2)	-	-	-	-	1834	-	6"os/	56
Ardstraw	Tuckmill Quarter	Dick David :	mill	-	-	-	Dick D - Smith Robert :	1798	-	dd/	530 292 384144?
Ardstraw	Tuckmill Quarter	Smith Robert	mill	-	-	-	Smith Robt - Smith John	1809	-	dd/	614 265 419081
Ardstraw	Tuckmill Quarter	Smyth John :	flax	-	40a	-	Smyth J - Stephenson Edw	1818	-	dd/	726 18 495553
Ardstraw	Tuckmill Quarter	Smyth John :	flax	-	5a.	-	Smyth J - Stephenson Edw	1818	-	dd/	726 78 495613
Donaghenry	Tullagh Beg	Hogg	tolls & grist	-	-	-	Hogg - Hall & ano	-	-	dd/	647 64 441364
Tyrone	Tullaghon *	-	bleach	-	-	-	-	1834	-	6"os/	38
Tyrone	Tullaghon *	-	Milltown Village	-	-	-	-	1834	-	6"os/	38
Tyrone	Tullinure *	Mackenzie	mills	-	-	-	Mackenzie A - Shaw John :	1816	Mort. 20 Apl.	dd/	701 536 481038
Donaghmore	Tullyallen	-	mill	-	-	-	-	-	-	1"os/	34
Donaghedy	Tullyard	-	bleach & mill race	-	-	-	-	1834	-	6"os/	38
Donaghedy	Tullyard	-	flax	-	-	-	-	1834	-	6"os/	2
Donaghedy	Tullyard	-	mill	-	-	-	-	1834	-	6"os/	2
Donaghedy	Tullyard	Glynn Robert	corn	-	-	-	-	-	-	gr/	-
Donaghedy	Tullyard	Glynn Robert	flax	-	-	-	-	-	-	gr/	-
Donaghedy	Tullyard	Greer Thomas	bleach	-	-	11.14	-	1833	-	v1B/	623
Tyrone	Tullycrin *	-	corn & con kiln	-	-	-	-	1834	-	6"os/	49
Tyrone	Tullycrin *	-	mill pond	-	-	-	-	1834	-	6"os/	49
Drumragh	Tullycunny	-	corn kiln	-	-	-	-	1834	-	6"os/	42
Clonfeacle	Tullydowey	Jackson James E	old bleach mill	-	145a.	-	-	-	-	gr/	-
Desertcreat	Tullylagan	Brown John	beetling	-	25a.	-	-	-	-	gr/	-
Desertcreat	Tullylagan	Greer	mills	-	-	-	Greer - Phenix	-	-	dd/	662 337 456340
Desertcreat	Tullylagan	Greer Thomas	beetling	-	67a.	-	-	-	-	gr/	-
Donaghedy	Tullylagan	Greer Thomas	bleach	-	-	24.17	-	1833	-	v1B/	623
Desertcreat	Tullylagan	Greer Thomas	mill	-	-	-	Greer Thos - Greer Thos	1798	-	dd/	530 317 348234
Desertcreat	Tullylagan	Reilly Jno :	mill	-	-	-	Reilly J - Greer Thomas :	1811	-	dd/	636 154 436548
Desertcreat	Tullylagan	Sanderson	mills	-	-	-	Sanderson - Greer	-	-	dd/	633 299 434270?

COUNTY TYRONE

PARISH	TOWNLAND		MILLER	TYPE	HOUSE	Land	£Val	PROPRIETORS	Date	WHEEL etc.	Record	Ref.
Desertcreat	Tullylagan		Saunderson	mills	-	-	-	Saunderson - Boyd	-	-	dd/	402 105 265085
Desertcreat	Tullylagan		Saunderson Alex :	mills	-	-	-	Saunderson - Huggins Max	1801	-	dd/	534 444 350891?
Desertcreat	Tullylagan		Saunderson Robert :	mills	-	-	-	Saunderson - Wakefield :	1775	-	dd/	318 443 218345
Desertcreat	Tullylagan		Saunderson Robert :	mills	-	-	-	Saunderson R - Greer Jas :	1777	-	dd/	319 348 214903
Kilskerry	Tullynincrin		McMullen Gilbert	corn & kiln	-	-	-	-	-	-	gr/	-
Donaghmore	Tullynure		McKinsey Anne	flax	-	-	-	-	-	-	gr/	-
Artrea	Tullyveagh		- SW Artrea Vge.	bleach & mill race	-	-	-	-	1834	-	6"os/	39
Artrea	Tullyveagh		Glasgow B & W	flax	-	20a.	-	-	-	-	gr/	-
Dromore	Tullywee		-	corn kiln	-	-	-	-	1834	-	6"os/	49
Urney	Tullywhisker		Lindsay John :	mill	-	-	-	Lindsay John - Lendrum :	1757	-	dd/	187 504 126255
Urney	Tullywhisker		Mount Castle James :	mill	-	-	-	Mount Castle J - Keon A	1739	-	dd/	94 496 67400
Derryloran	Tullywiggan		-	corn	-	-	-	-	-	-	1"os/	35
Derryloran	Tullywiggan		-	flax	-	-	-	-	-	-	1"os/	35
Derryloran	Tullywiggan		-	mill	-	-	-	-	-	-	1"os/	35
Derryloran	Tullywiggan		- N/ Wooden Bridge	flax & corn	-	-	-	-	1834	-	6"os/	38
Derryloran	Tullywiggan		King Andrew Rev :	mill	-	-	-	King A - Creighton Ab'ram :	1762	-	dd/	218 227 143168
Clogherny	Tulyrush		-	corn kiln	-	-	-	-	1834	-	6"os/	43
Dromore	Tummery		-	corn kiln (2)	-	-	-	-	1834	-	6"os/	49
Dromore	Tummery		E/ School Ho.	corn & mill pond	-	-	-	-	1834	-	6"os/	49
Tamlaght	Urbal		-	spade	-	-	-	-	1834	-	6"os/	30
Tyrone	Waterard	*	Boyle	mills	-	-	-	-	-	-	dd/	708 292 485027
Tyrone	Waterard	*	Huey	mill	-	-	-	-	-	-	dd/	708 531 485266
Tyrone	Waterard	*	Huey	mills	-	-	-	-	-	-	dd/	748 600 509385

PARISH	TOWNLAND	MILLER	TYPE	HOUSE	Land	£Val	PROPRIETORS	Date	WHEEL etc.	Record	Ref.
Kilculliheen	Abbeylands :	Grubb Thomas	flour (steam)	-	-	-	-	-	-	hob/	5.3399
Kilculliheen	Abbeylands :	- N. side R. Suir	flour	-	-	-	-	1842	-	6"os/	9
Kilmeadan	Adamstown	-	mill	- [NB site uncertain]	-	-	-	2003	-	mmSv/	wh - Z
Kilmeadan	Adamstown	-	toll gate	-	-	-	-	1841	-	6"os/	17
Kilmeadan	Adamstown	- S. of Whelan's Br.	flour (in ruins)	-	-	-	-	1841	-	6"os/	16
Kilmeadan	Adamstown	- on Whelansbridge R.	paper (ruins)	-	-	-	-	1841	-	6"os/	16
Kilmeadan	Adamstown	Harduin Henry :	mill (paper ?)	-	-	-	Harduin H - Harduin Robt :	1809	-	dd/	615 544 422869
Kilmeadan	Adamstown	Merrick	mill	-	-	-	Merrick - Merrick	-	?	dd/	595 467 398472
Aglish	Aglish	Cotton John Hynde	mill	-	-	-	Cotton J - Assleck Gilbert	1733	-	dd/	73 481 52081
Aglish	Aglish	Grandison George Hon.	mill	-	-	-	Grandison - Beauchamp :	1784	-	dd/	362 113 242767
Aglish	Aglish	Grandison John E.	mill	-	-	-	Grandison - Cotton J H :	1730	-	dd/	65 372 45941
Aglish	Aglish	Grandison John E.	mill	-	-	-	Grandison - Cotton Jn H	1730	Mort. 15 Jan.	dd/	77 196 53325
Aglish	Aglish	Grubbleton Richard	mill	-	-	-	Grubbleton - Sowton Steph	1732	Sale 10 Oct.	dd/	77 287 53716
Aglish	Aglish	Hill Andrew	mill	-	-	-	Hill Andr - Duggan Fras	1739	D.Poll	dd/	71 62 48780
Aglish	Aglish	Middleton Anne	mill	-	-	-	Midddleton A - Shelley H	1726	-	dd/	69 53 47205
Aglish	Aglish	Parsons	mill	-	-	-	Parsons - Barron	-	-	dd/	560? 64 37163?
Aglish	Aglish	Southwell Hon. Lord	mill	-	-	-	Southwell - Butler Jas :	1787	-	dd/	393 463 26096?
Aglish	Aglish	Steuart William	mill	-	-	-	Steuart W - Shelley Henry	1726	-	dd/	51 58 32781
Aglish	Aglish	Villiers Lady	mill	-	-	-	Villiers L - Seymour Geo	-	-	dd/	-
Ballynamuck	Ballinamuck Middle	-	corn & race	-	-	-	-	-	-	6"os/	31
Kilbarry	Ballindud	-	-	-	-	-	-	-	-	1"os/	168
Kilbarry	Ballindud	-	corn	-	-	-	-	-	-	6"os/	16
Kilbarry	Ballindud	-	corn	-	-	-	-	-	-	6"os/	17
Kilbarry	Ballindud	-	mill race :	-	-	-	-	-	-	6"os/	16
Kilbarry	Ballindud	Carew	land	-	-	-	Carew - Newton	-	-	dd/	103 495 72296
Kilbarry	Ballindud	Carew Thomas	corn	-	4a.	-	Carew T - Shanahan Wm	1816	-	dd/	?
Kilbarry	Ballindud	Carew Thomas	tuck	-	-	-	Carew T - Shanahan Wm	1816	-	dd/	-
Kilbarry	Ballindud	Maher Mary Annie	corn	22.6x18.0x23.0 :	-	-	-	-	16x2x13.6	hob/	5.2014
Kilmolera	Ballindysert	-	cloth	-	-	-	-	-	-	6"os/	6
Kilmolera	Ballindysert	-	cloth	-	-	-	-	-	-	6"os/	6
Dysert	Ballindysert	-	factory	-	-	-	-	-	-	1"os/	167
Dysert	Ballindysert	- near Carrickbeg	mill	-	-	-	-	-	-	1"os/	167
Dysert	Ballindysert	- stream to R Suir	cloth	-	-	-	-	-	-	1"os/	167
Dysert	Ballindysert	- on Aughnablane Str.	cloth	-	-	-	-	1842	-	6"os/	3
Kilmolera	Ballindysert	Slattery Pierce	napping	(1&3C) 33.6x18x8	-	-	-	-	O`shot 11.6x1.4x12	hob/	5.2121
Kilmolera	Ballindysert	Slattery Pierce	spinning	(1C) 23.6x54x25 :	-	-	-	-	gravity 16x4x13.6 :	hob/	5.2121
Kilmolera	Ballindysert	Slattery Pierce	tuck (part)	-	-	-	-	-	o`shot 11.6x2x12 :	hob/	5.2121
Kilmolera	Ballindysert	Slattery Pierce	tuck (part)	-	-	-	-	-	part sp. mill m/cy :	hob/	5.2121
K`macleague	Ballinvella	-	windmill ruins	-	-	-	-	-	-	iaa/	AI1171os27.1.6
Lismore & M	Ballinwillin	- on Owenbeg R.	mill	-	-	-	-	-	-	1"os/	-
Kill St Nicholas	Ballycanavan	-	mill	-	-	-	-	2000	-	mmSv/	wh - R
Kill St Nich	Ballycanavan	- In King`s Channel.	mill tidal	-	-	-	-	-	-	iaa/	AI1712os -
Kill St Nich	Ballycanavan Big :	-	flour & dam	-	-	-	-	-	-	6"os/	18
Kilwatermoy	Ballyclement	Evans William	flour	26x19.6x23.6	-	-	-	-	-	hob/	5.1937
Rathgormuck	Ballycullane	- Shanakill	Tuck Mill	-	-	-	-	1842	-	6"os/	6
Ballylaneen	Ballydownane W	-	mill hz	-	-	-	-	1841	-	iaa/	AI1281os24.16.4
Waterford	Ballyduff	-	factory	-	-	-	-	-	-	1"os/	168
Bo.Cosh & M.	Ballyeen	Cork & Burlington :	mill	-	-	-	Cork E - Musgrave Chris :	1738	-	dd/	93 439 66248
Bo.Cosh & M.	Ballyeen	Cork Richard E. of	mill	-	-	-	Cork E - Keane	-	-	dd/	113 223 78084
Bo.Cosh & M.	Ballyeen	Cork Richard E. of	mill	-	-	-	Cork E - Musgrave	-	-	dd/	169 536 114846
Bo.Cosh & M.	Ballyeen	Musgrave	mill	-	-	-	Musgrave - Poole	-	-	dd/	376 168 250175
Bo.Cosh & M.	Ballyeen	Musgrave Chris Fred :	mill	-	-	-	Musgrave C - Scott John :	1801	-	dd/	545 224 359137

PARISH	TOWNLAND	MILLER	TYPE	HOUSE	Land	£Val	PROPRIETORS	Date	WHEEL etc.	Record	Ref.
Lismore & M	Ballyin Lower	- near Tourtane Ho.	corn & kiln	- blds. well restored :	-	-	Chas. Twigg	2003	-	mmSv/	wh - B
Lismore & M	Ballyin Lower	Foley Nelson T	flour	55.6x30.9x46.6	-	-	-	-	15.6x5.10	hob/	5.1935
Lismore & M	Ballyin Lower	Foley Nelson T	flour	-	-	-	-	-	15x6x9 5 pair st.	vmb/	25
Lismore & M	Ballyin Lower	Foley Nelson T :	flour	-	-	110	-	1851		gr/	Ld.Est.db
Lismore & M	Ballyin Lower :	-	flour		-	-	-	-	-	6"os/	18
Kilronan	Ballymacarby	Coates Abraham	flour	63x28x29	-	-	-	-	20x8x13 42 bkts. :	hob/	5.2069
Kilronan	Ballymacarby	-	mill	-	-	-	-	2011	still extant in use	Sv/-	Ld.Est.db
Ballygunner	Ballymaclode	Manning Thos & Wm	corn	Newport Corn Mill :	-	31	-	1856	-	gr/	Ld.Est.db
Ballygunner	Ballymaclode	Barron Anne & Cath :	mill	-	-	-	Barron A & C - Barron Wm	1809	-	dd/	610 214 419776
Ballygunner	Ballymaclode	Esmond Mary Widow :	mill	-	-	-	Esmond M - Penrose Geo	1794	-	dd/	479 523 308953
Ballygunner	Ballymaclode	Keefe William :	mill	-	-	-	Keefe - Delahunty Richard	1801	-	dd/	539 342 35567
Ballygunner	Ballymaclode	Keefe William :	mill	-	-	-	Keefe Wm - Morgan John	1796	-	dd/	506 229 329284
Ballygunner	Ballymaclode	Ward Isobel :	mill	-	-	-	Ward - Cotton George	1799	-	dd/	519 461 341035
Ballygunner	Ballymaclode :	-	corn	-	-	-	-	-	-	6"os/	18
Waterford	Ballynacourty (4)	-	mill	-	-	-	-	-	-	1"os/	-
Kilmacleague	Ballynamoyntagh	- B`namoyntagh	Flour Mill	-	-	-	-	-	-	6"os/	27
K`macleague	Ballynamoyntragh	-	flour		-	-	-	-	-	6"os/	27
K`macleague	Ballynamoyntragh	Quinn James	corn	45x23.6x15 basem`t :	-	-	-	-	16x3.3x -	hob/	5.2042
Ballynamuck	Ballynamuck	-	corn	-	-	-	-	-	-	6"os/	31
Ballynamuck	Ballynamuck Mid.	Walsh John	corn	26x22.6x7	-	-	-	-	11.4x3x	hob/	5.1961
Ballynamuck	Ballynamuck Mid.	Walsh William	corn	38.6x22x12	-	-	-	-	11x3.7x	hob/	5.1961
Ballynamuck	Ballynamuck West	-	corn	-	-	-	-	-	-	6"os/	31
Ballynamuck	Ballynamuck West	-	corn	-	-	-	-	-	-	6"os/	31
Ballynamuck	Ballynamuck West	Walsh John	corn	26.0x22.6x7.0 & kiln :	-	-	-	1848	11.4x3x - 30 bkts.	hob/	5.1961
Ballynamuck	Ballynamuck West	Walsh John	corn	-	-	-	-	-	11x3x7	vmb/	25
Ballynamuck	Ballynamuck West	Walsh William	corn	38.6x22.0x12	-	-	-	1848	11x3.7x - 30 bkts.	hob/	5.1961
Ballynamuck	Ballynamuck West	Walsh William	corn	-	-	-	-	-	11x3x7	vmb/	25
Templemichael	Ballynatray	Smith Richard	flour	32.6x21x26.6	-	-	-	-	16x5.9x	hob/	5.1959
Templemichael	Ballynatrayde	-	flour		-	-	-	-	-	6"os/	37
Fews	Ballyristeen	-	corn	-	-	-	-	-	-	6"os/	25
Fews	Ballyristeen	Phelan Thomas	corn	23.6x17.0x7.0 :	-	-	-	-	9.10x2.6x2	hob/	5.1968
Fews	Ballyristeen	Whelan Thomas	corn	-	-	-	-	-	14x3x15	vmb/	25
Fews	Ballyristeen	Whitlaw Thomas	corn	39.0x19.6x6.6 & kiln	-	-	-	-	14x3.6x15.3	hob/	5.1970
Waterford	Ballyroe	Neville John	corn	24x17x11	-	-	-	-	14x3.6	hob/	5.1928
Islandikane	Ballyscanlan	-	corn		-	-	-	-	-	6"os/	26
Stradbally	Ballyvoyle	-	corn		-	-	-	-	-	6"os/	32
Stradbally	Ballyvoyle	- near coast	corn	-	-	-	-	-	[local information] :	mmSv/	Z
Stradbally	Ballyvoyle	Anthony Murphy	corn	-	-	-	-	-	12x3x11	vmb/	25
Stradbally	Ballyvoyle	James Houlahan	corn	-	-	-	-	-	14x3x8	vmb/	25
Stradbally	Ballyvoyle	Ryan Edward	corn	35.6x22x12	-	-	-	-	12x3x13.6	hob/	5.1982
Lismore & M	Ballywillin	-	flour		-	-	-	-	-	6"os/	29
Lismore & M	Ballywillin	-	mill	- mill (with iron roof) :	-	-	-	2003	John Scanlon	mmSv/	wh - B
Lismore & M	Ballywillin	- N. side Owenbeg R.	flour, mill race	-	-	-	-	-	-	6"os/	29
Lismore & M	Ballywillin	Purcell Thomas	grinding	34.0x19.9x24.6 & ret :	-	-	-	1850	14x4x10.6 30 bkts.	hob/	5.3374
Lismore & M	Ballywillin	Purcell Thomas	mill	-	14a.	2	-	-	-	gr/	-
Waterford	Bellicka *	Allin Samuel	mill	-	-	-	Allin S - Collender Richd	1838	-	dd/	1838 2 254
Waterford	Blantesure *	Barron Philip	mill, mill lands	-	-	-	Barron P - Chearnly Ant	1834	-	dd/	1834 5 251
Aglish	Bleach	-	mill	large ruin & thatched :	-	-	- res. Mary T Rowan	2003	-	mmSv/	wh - R
Aglish	Bleach	- stream to Goish R.	flour	-	-	-	-	-	-	6"os/	29
Aglish	Bleach	Charles Graves	flour	-	-	-	-	-	-	vmb/	25
Killrossanty	Boolattin	-	corn		-	-	-	-	-	6"os/	23
Killrossanty	Boolattin	Callaghan Mary	corn & kiln	(1B) 18.6x20x13.6 :	-	4	-	1848	16.9x3.6x2.6 :	hob/	5.4221
Killrossanty	Boolattin	Kennedy Edward	mill	-	-	-	Kennedy ED - Callaghan :	1835	-	dd/	1835 7 24

PARISH	TOWNLAND	MILLER	TYPE	HOUSE	Land	£Val	PROPRIETORS	Date	WHEEL etc.	Record	Ref.
Killrossanty	Boolattin	Mary Callaghan	corn	-	-	-	-	-	17x3x18	vmb/	25
Killrossanty	Boolattin	Mary Callaghan	flour & corn	24.6x20.0x13.6 :	-	-	-	-	16.6x3.6x16 gr st.:	hob/	5.1959
Templemichael	Bridgequarter	- on Tourig R.	old corn mill		-	-	-	-	-	6"os/	37
? S.Tip C`mel	Burgagerylands W	-	flour		-	-	-	-	-	6"os/	1
Lismore & Mo.	Capoquin	-	mill	-	-	-	-	-	-	dd/	?
Lismore & Mo.	Capoquin	Peter Daly	-	-	-	-	-	-	-	vmb/	25
Lismore & Mo.	Capoquin	Purcell Thomas	-	-	-	-	-	-	14x4x10	vmb/	25
Lismore & Mo.	Capoquin Town	Leopold Keane	corn & flour	-	-	-	-	-	28x6x28 3 pr st.	vmb/	25
Lismore & Mo.	Cappoquin	- at Demesne	mill	- site bulldozed :	-	-	-	2003	-	mmSv/	wh - Z
Lismore & Mo.	Cappoquin	Brown Robert	mills	-	-	-	Brown Robt - Allin Sam	1834	-	dd/	1834 2 251
Lismore & Mo.	Cappoquin	Cork Richard E.	mill	-	-	-	Cork Richd E of - Roche	1718	-	dd/	47 229 30333
Lismore & Mo.	Cappoquin	Fuller William	mills	-	-	-	Fuller William - Roche Jn	1835	-	dd/	1835 19 189
Lismore & Mo.	Cappoquin	Keane	mill	-	-	-	Keane - Jones	-	-	dd/	170 535 115037
Lismore & Mo.	Cappoquin	Keane	mill	-	-	-	Keane - Coughlan	-	-	dd/	178 370 119255
Lismore & Mo.	Cappoquin	Keane Jno	mill	-	-	-	Keane J - Jones Jno	1752	-	dd/	179 123 119111
Lismore & Mo.	Cappoquin	Keane Jno	mill	-	-	-	Keane J - Jones John :	1749	-	dd/	179 124 119112
Lismore & Mo.	Cappoquin	Keane John	mill	-	-	-	Keane - Greatrakes Val :	1746	-	dd/	146 10 96440
Lismore & Mo.	Cappoquin D`mse	Purcell Thomas	grinding	34x19.9x24.6	-	-	-	-	11.8x4x9.6	hob/	5.1937
Lismore & Mo.	Cappoquin Town	Keane Leopold	corn & flour	48.10x28.10x21.0 & :	-	-	-	-	27.7x6x28.6 :	hob/	5.3375
Kilmoleran	Carickbeg	-	mill	-	-	-	-	-	-	1"os/	167
Kilmoleran	Carickbeg	-	mill	-	-	-	-	-	-	1"os/	167
Kilmoleran	Carrickbeg Town	Boyle Mary	woollen	64x18.6x12.6 - wv.ho :	-	-	-	-	-	hob/	5.3376
Kilmoleran	Carrickbeg Town	Feehan Thomas	brewery	36x27x6x19 :	-	-	-	-	- m/cy etc. v old	hob/	5.3376
Kilmoleran	Carrickbeg Town	Slattery Pierce	woollen	24x24.6x16.6 :	-	-	-	-	no wh. - manual :	hob/	5.3376
Ballylanneen	Carrickcastle	Anthony Joseph	mills	-	-	-	Anthony J - Power Jos	1800	-	dd/	533 66 351191
Ballylanneen	Carrickcastle	Mandeville Edward :	mills	-	-	-	Mandeville - Smith Fran :	1800	-	dd/	532 140 348443
Ballylanneen	Carrickcastle	Mandeville Edward :	mills	-	-	-	Mandeville E - Smith Fras :	1801	-	dd/	540 124 354472
Ballylanneen	Carrickcastle	Power	mills	-	-	-	Power - Johnston	-	-	dd/	525?381 345083
Ballylanneen	Carrickcastle	Power Joseph	mills	-	-	-	Power J - Johnston Benj :	1800	-	dd/	526 465 345074
Ballylanneen	Carrickcastle	Power Pierce :	mills	-	-	-	Power P - Merrigan Mcl :	1799	-	dd/	536 98 351922
Ballylanneen	Carrigcastle	- W./ Aughshemus Br.	corn	-	-	-	-	1842	-	6"os/	24
Ballylanneen	Carrigcastle	Mining Co. of Ireland	corn & kiln	(1A) 44.6x28x39 :	-	15	-	-	-	hob/	5.4220
Ballylanneen	Carrigcastle	Richard Purdy	flour	-	-	-	-	-	12x10x5 3 pr st.	vmb/	25
Colligan	Carrowgarriff	-	corn		-	-	-	-	-	6"os/	22
Colligan	Carrowgarriff	Flyng Francis	corn	26x20x19	-	-	-	-	15.6x3	hob/	5.1950
Colligan	Carrowgarriff	Flyng Francis	tuck & kiln	26x20x19 mill in ruin	-	-	-	-	in ruins	hob/	5.1950
Colligan	Carrowgarriff	Power Edward	mill	52x20x19	-	-	-	-	16x3x14	hob/	5.1952
Whitechurch	Clashnagoneen	- on Magaha R.	mill	-	-	-	-	-	-	1"os/	167
Mothel	Clonea	- below village	mill	- on farm concealed	-	-	-	2003	Mr Moore	mmSv/	wh - R
Mothel	Clonea	- on Clodiagh R.	mill	-	-	-	-	-	-	1"os/	167
Mothel	Clonea	O`Flinn James	corn & flour	23.0x33.0x12.6 & kiln	-	-	-	-	14.6x3x12.9	hob/	5.2135
St Marys Clonmel	Clonmel	Anderson John	Corp. Mills	-	-	-	Anderson J - Hamil John	1795	-	dd/	485 561 315467
St Marys Clonmel	Clonmel	Anderson John	Corp. Mills	-	-	-	Anderson J - Hamil John	1795	-	dd/	485 561 315467
St Marys Clonmel	Clonmel	English Richard	mills	-	-	-	English R - Grubb Fran :	1807	-	dd/	589 389 403443
St Marys Clonmel	Clonmel	Grubb Francis	mills	-	-	-	Grubb F - Grubb Thos :	1807	-	dd/	589 399 403444
St Marys Clonmel	Clonmel	Latouche David Rt Hon.	Corp. Mills	-	-	-	Latouche D - Morton Jas	1795	-	dd/	499 123 315345
St Marys Clonmel	Clonmel	Lycester William :	mills	-	-	-	Lycester W - Baker Sam :	1807	-	dd/	592 229 402111
Bo. Midthird	Colbeck`s	Congreve Ambrose	mill	-	-	-	Congreve A - Smith Wm	1726	-	dd/	57 112 375341
Bo. Midthird	Colbeck`s	Smith William	mill	-	-	-	Smith Wm - West Robt	1727	-	dd/	55 411 37535
Clashmore	Coolbooa	- Clashmore Vge.	flour	-	-	-	-	-	-	6"os/	37
Dysert	Coolnamuck	- on Aughnablane Str.	corn & tuck	-	-	-	-	1842	-	6"os/	3
Kilmolera	Coolnamuck East	Boyle John	spinning	(1B) 50x24.6x25.3 :	-	-	-	-	o`shot 11.6x1.4x12	hob/	5.2121

PARISH	TOWNLAND	MILLER	TYPE	HOUSE	Land	£Val	PROPRIETORS	Date	WHEEL etc.	Record	Ref.
Waterford	Coolnanan	-	mill hz	-	-	-	-	-	-	iaa/	AI1282 os -
Clonagam	Coolroe	- on Clodiagh R.	cotton factory		-	-	-	-	-	6"os/	8
Clongan	Coolroe	Malcolmson Joseph	boiling ho.	Ho. (1A) 47x43x22.6 :	-	-	-	-	-	hob/	5.2117
Waterford	Coolroe	Malcolmson Joseph	cotton factory	142x46x63 & 122x46x6	-	-	-	1846	34x17x26 :	hob/	5.3391
Waterford	Coraginna * :	-	tuck		-	-	-	-	-	6"os/	3
Waterford	Coraginna * :	-	corn		-	-	-	-	-	6"os/	3
Kilmacleague	Coreballymore	- E. end Back Strand	corn mill site	-	-	-	-	-	-	6"os/	27
Dysert	Corragina	- on Aughnablane Str.	corn	-	-	-	-	1842	-	6"os/	3
Kilmolera	Corragina	Bohill Richard	corn	(1B) 44x25.6x19.6 :	-	-	-	-	O`shot 12x2x12.6 :	hob/	5.2121
Fews	Coumahon	Stack Patrick	churning	office 52.6x18x8 & :	-	-	-	-	dia. 6ft 6in. fall 5ft. :	hob/	5.4226
Kill St L`rence	Couse	-	corn	2 sty. buildg. neat, ruin	-	-	-	-	-	mmSv/	wh - R
Kill St L`rence	Couse	-	corn & pond		-	-	-	-	-	6"os/	17
Kill St L`rence	Couse	Power Richard	corn	47x21.6x21.6	-	-	-	-	15.6x3.6x - breast :	hob/	5.2026
Waterford	Coushmacale	Welsh Matthew	mill	-	-	-	Welsh M - Welsh Edm. :	1762	-	dd/	226 407 148207
St Marys Clonmel	Croan	Hughes James & Thos	corn	(1B) 88.6x24.6x35.6 :	-	-	-	-	breast 20x5x15 :	hob/	5.4225
St Marys Clonmel	Croan Lower	- E. end Clonmel	Millbrook Ho.	-	-	-	-	1842	-	6"os/	1
St Marys Clonmel	Croan Lower	- S./ River Suirville	Mills	-	-	-	-	1842	-	6"os/	1
Drumcannon	Crobally Lower	McGrath John	old mill	27.6x18.0x8.6	-	-	-	-	-	hob/	5.2077
Drumcannon	Crobally Lower :	-	corn in ruins		-	-	-	-	-	6"os/	26
Crooke	Crooke	-	windmill ruins	5.3m dia (ext.) :	-		-	-	-	iaa/	AI1713 os18.4.4
Crooke	Crooke	-	windmill ruins	5.3m dia (ext.) :	-		-	-	-	ph/	OPW (AI1713)
Crooke	Crooke	-	windmill ruins	5.3m dia (ext.) :	-		-	-	-	ph/	WEH
Crooke	Crooke	- near Suir estuary	windmill ruins	-	-	-	-	-	-	iaa/	AI1713os18.4.4
Bo.Middlethird	Cullinagh	Caulfield Joun & Wife	mill	-	-	-	Caulfiend - Roderick Dav	1774	-	dd/	120 12 80667
Bo.Middlethird	Cullinagh	Gamble	mill	-	-	-	Gamble - Gamble	-	?	dd/	196 291 136043
Bo.Middlethird	Cullinagh	Gamble Richard :	mill	-	-	-	Gamble R - Gamble Robt	1748	-	dd/	136 245 91237
Bo.Middlethird	Cullinagh	Gamble Robert :	mill	-	-	-	Gamble Robt - Gamble R	1746	-	dd/	134 342 91239
Bo.Middlethird	Cullinagh	Gamble Wm & Richard	mill	-	-	-	Gamble W&R - Denis Wm	1739	-	dd/	98 22 67490
Currabaha	Currabaha	Power "Benjamin	corn	-	-	-	-	-	18x5x9	vmb/	25
Waterford	Curraeigh North	-	mill	-	-	-	-	-	-	1"os/	167
Kinsalebeg	Drumgullane	Page Thomas	Glenlicky Mill	- & house	-	44	-	1856	-	gr/	Ld.Est.db
Kinsalebeg	Drumgullane	-	Glenlicky Mill	-	-	-	-	2011	now ruinous	Sv/	Ld.Est.db
Kinsalebeg	Drumgullane W.	Page Thomas	flour & corn	-	-	-	-	-	- 4 pair stones	vmb/	25
Tallon	Duck`s	Carroll	mill meadow	-	-	-	Carrol - Carney	-	-	dd/	224 497 180791
Dungarvan	Dungarvan Town	-	flour	buildings restored now	-	-	-	2000	-	mmSv/	wh - Cc
Dungarvan	Dungarvan Town	Anderson John	Milltown	-	-	-	Anderson - Dickson Thos	1890	-	dd/	1890 661 28
Dungarvan	Dungarvan Town	Dunphy Edmd. Rev	brewery	-	-	-	Dunphy Edmund - Michael	1885	-	dd/	1885 18 210
Dungarvan	Dungarvan Town	Dunphy Michael	Brewery Lodge		-	-	Dunphy Ml - Haines John	1890	-	dd/	1890 61 28
Dungarvan	Dungarvan Town	Kelly John	mills	-	-	-	KellyJn - Waterford Marq.	1834	-	dd/	1834 5283
Dungarvan	Dungarvan Town	Loughran David	Milltown	-	-	-	Loughran - Reynolds Wm	1890	-	dd/	1890 8 101
Dungarvan	Dungarvan Town :	McCreagh	mill	-	-	-	McCragh John - Fonlone	1755	-	dd/	179 284 120187
Dungarvan	Dungarvan Town :	Power	brewery, mill	-	-	-	Power - Terry	-	-	dd/	550 6 362891
Dungarvan	Dungarvan Town :	Ronayne Elinor Spin.	brewery, mill	-	-	-	Ronayne - Power Richd :	1798	-	dd/	513 245 336612
Dungarvan	Dungarvan Town :	Terry	brewery, mill	-	-	-	Terry - Power	-	-	dd/	594 448 465429
Dungarvan	Dungarvan Town :	Osbone	mill	-	-	-	Osborne - Cox	-	-	dd/	176 156 118337
Dungarvan	Dungarvan Town :	Cork Earl	mill	-	-	-	Cork Earl - Rylan	-	-	dd/	100 173 70038
Dungarvan	Dungarvan Town :	Browne	mill	-	-	-	Browne - Russell	-	-	dd/	376 276 243434
Dungarvan	Dungarvan Town :	Dower John	kilns (2)	(1A) 26.6x26.6x29 & :	-	-	-	-	-	hob/	5.3383
Dungarvan	Dungarvan Town :	Baker Roger	mill	-	-	-	-	1846	-	dir/	Slater
Stradbally	Durrow	Foley Michael	mill	-	-	-	FoleyM - Power Robert :	1790	-	dd/	416 496 277790
Stradbally	Durrow	Foley Michael	mill	-	-	-	FoleyM - Power Robert :	1790	-	dd/	416 496 277790
Stradbally	Durrow	Roberts	mill	-	-	-	Roberts - Travers	-	-	dd/	102 347 71805
Stradbally	Durrow	Sheehy Edmond	mill	-	-	-	Sheehy E - Kane Richard :	1760	-	dd/	204 362 135941

PARISH	TOWNLAND	MILLER	TYPE	HOUSE	Land	£Val	PROPRIETORS	Date	WHEEL etc.	Record	Ref.
Stradbally	Durrow	Travers	mill	-	-	-	Travers - Roberts	-	-	dd/	112 5 75962
Stradbally	Durrow	Travers	mill	-	-	-	Travers - Roberts	-	-	dd/	126 242 86814
Stradbally	Durrow (Millerstn.)	Whiteman Richard :	mill	-	-	-	Whiteman R - Travers Mcl :	1742	-	dd/	114 390 79332
Dungarvan	Fairlane :	-	brewery	-	-	-	-	-	-	6"os/	32
Dungarvan	Fairlane :	-	brewery	-	-	-	-	-	-	6"os/	32
Faithlegg	Faithlegg	-	corn (ruins)	-	-	-	-	1842	-	6"os/	10
Fews	Farragleigh	Palliser Col.	flour	-	-	-	-	-	31x7x25	vmb/	25
Waterford	Fox`s Castle	-	mill hz	-	-	-	-	-	-	iaa/	AI1283 os -
Fews	Furraleigh	- E. side R. Mahon	saw	Comeragh Saw Mills	-	-	-	1841	-	25"os/	15.09
Waterford	Garran	Power Thomas	mill lands	-	-	-	Power T - Keoarney Jas	1834	-	dd/	1834 14 25
Bo.Middlethird	Garrancrobally	Alcock	mill	-	-	-	Alcock - Rogers	-	?	dd/	188 421 126194
Bo.Middlethird	Garrancrobally	Hagherine Thomas :	mill	-	-	-	Hagherine - McGuire Wm	1759	-	dd/	199 188 131927
Bo.Middlethird	Garrancrobally	Lyon	mill	-	-	-	Lyon - Bachas	-	?	dd/	237 135 152840
Bo.Middlethird	Garrancrobally	McGuire William :	mill	-	-	-	McGuire Wm - Lyon Jno :	1759	-	dd/	199 189 131928
Bo.Middlethird	Garrancrobally	Rogers	mill	-	-	-	Rogers - Alcock	-	?	dd/	188 420 126193
Bo.Middlethird	Garrancrobally	Rogers John :	mill	-	-	-	Rogers J - Rogers Thos :	1763	-	dd/	223 278 148239
Bo.Middlethird	Garrancrobally	Rogers Susanna :	mill	-	-	-	Rogers S - Rogers John :	1761	-	dd/	212 274 139228
Trinity Without	Gibbethill	- S. side R. Suir	brewery	-	-	-	-	1842	-	6"os/	9
Waterford	Glanavaddra	-	corn kiln	-	-	-	-	-	-	iaa/	AI1284os22.15.5 -
Aglish	Glenassy	- at Cooneen Ferry	corn & flour	-	-	-	-	-	-	6"os/	34
Aglish	Glenassy	Musgrave Charles	mill	-	-	-	-	-	-	gr/	Ld.Est.db
Aglish	Glenassy	-	mill	-	-	-	-	-	ruins still remain	Sv/-	Ld.Est.db
Aglish	Glenassy	Musgrave Chris	corn	-	-	-	-	-	- 4 pair stones	vmb/	25
Waterford	Goose Island	Grubb Robert	mill	-	-	-	Grubb Robt - Jones Richd	1843	-	dd/	1843 18 82
kilmeadan	Gortaclare	-	old mill		-	-	-	-	-	6"os/	8
Waterford	Gortaclare	-	old mill		-	-	-	-	-	6"os/	8
Kilmeadan	Gortaclare	-	tuck		-	-	-	-	-	6"os/	-
Waterford	Gortaclare :	-	tuck		-	-	-	-	-	6"os/	6
Ballymacart	Gowlan	Gleeson Jeremiah	corn	-	-	-	-	-	-	vmb/	25
Ballymacart	Gowlaun	-	tuck		-	-	-	-	-	6"os/	39
Rathgormuck	Graigavalla	-	corn & tuck		-	-	-	-	-	6"os/	6
Rathgormuck	Graigavalla	Ryan John	corn	(1B) 21x18.6x9 & :	-	4	-	1846	o`shot 11x1.6x11.9	hob/	5.4224
Rathgormuck	Graigavalla	Ryan John	tuck	- (same as above)	-	-	-	-	o`shot 12x1.6x12.6	hob/	5.4214
Rathgormuck	Graigavalla	Ryan Widow	tuck	-	-	-	-	-	12.6x1.8x13 24 bkt.	hob/	5.2137
Rathgormuck	Graigavalla	Whelan Patrick	corn	(1B) 20x18.6x8.6	-	-	-	-	10.8x1.6x12 24 bkt.	hob/	5.2137
Rathgormuck	Graigavalla	Whelan Patrick	tuck	-	-	-	-	-	12.6x1.8x13 24 bkt.	hob/	5.2137
Waterford	Graigvearush	- on Mahon R.	saw	-	-	-	-	-	-	1"os/	167
Kilbarry	Kilbarry	-	Bleach Bridge	-	-	-	-	-	-	6"os/	16
Waterford	Kilclooney	-	mill hz	-	-	-	-	1849	-	iaa/	AI1285os -
Waterford	Kilcooney	-	old corn mill		-	-	-	-	-	6"os/	22
Seskinan	Kilkeany	John Mulcahy	corn	-	-	-	-	-	9x2x10	vmb/	25
Waterford	Kilkeenans	Barron Philip	mill & mill lds	-	-	-	Barron P - Chearnly Ant	1834	-	dd/	1834 5 251
Kill S Lawrence	Kill St Laurence	-	mill	-	-	-	-	-	-	1"os/	168
Kill S Lawrence	Kill St Lawrence	Hayden Henry	mill	-	-	-	Hayden - Walsh Edmond	1782	-	dd/	347 389 233483
Kill S Lawrence	Kill St Lawrence	Walsh	mill	-	-	-	Walsh - Foran	-	-	dd/	123 346 84840
Kilgobnet	Killadangan	-	woollen		-	-	-	-	-	6"os/	30
Kilgobnet	Killadangan	- on Colligan R.	woollen	-	-	-	-	-	-	1"os/	178
Kilgobnet	Killadangan	- on Colligan R.	woollen fcty	-	-	-	-	-	-	6"os/	30
Kilgobnet	Killadangan	Barron Pierce	mills	-	-	-	Barron P - McGrath Mary :	1806	-	dd/	616 314 422217
Kilgobnet	Killadangan	Burke	mills	-	-	-	Burke - Boyle	-	?	dd/	593 8 400665
Kilgobnet	Killadangan	Neville William :	mills	-	-	-	Neville W - Hackett Saml :	1807	-	dd/	593 8 400664
Kilgobnet	Killadangan	Stephen Baker	Indian corn	-	-	-	-	-	16x8x4	vmb/	25

PARISH	TOWNLAND	MILLER	TYPE	HOUSE	Land	£Val	PROPRIETORS	Date	WHEEL etc.	Record	Ref.
Whitechurch	Killeeshal	- NW. of R. Douglas	corn	-	-	-	-	-	-	6"os/	30
Whitechurch	Killeeshal	Congreve	mills	-	-	-	Congrece & W - Hearn	-	-	dd/	200 54 131930
Whitechurch	Killeeshal	Hurley Mary	corn	22.0x18.0x8.0 & kiln	-	-	-	-	12x2.9x12	hob/	5.1983
Whitechurch	Killeeshal	Hurley Mary	tuck	16.6x19x7	-	-	-	-	11.6x1.9x12	hob/	5.1983
Whitechurch	Killeeshal	Keane Richard :	mills	-	-	-	Keane - Green Rodolphus :	1756	-	dd/	178 521 119796
Whitechurch	Killeeshal	Laughnam Connell	mills	-	-	-	Laughnam - O`Keefe Mgt	1845	-	dd/	1845 7 161
Whitechurch	Killeeshal	Mary Hurly	corn	-	-	-	-	-	12x4x13	vmb/	25
Whitechurch	Killeeshal	O`Keefe Margaret	mill	-	-	-	O`Keefe ors Sargent Mgt :	1842	-	dd/	1842 21 152
Whitechurch	Killeeshal	Usher Arthur :	mills	-	-	-	Usher - Musgrave Chris :	1761	-	dd/	209 172 138000
Whitechurch	Killeeshal	Usher Beverley :	mills	-	-	-	Usher B - Usher Arthur :	1741	-	dd/	120 389 82963
Whitechurch	Killeeshal	Usher Beverley :	mills	-	-	-	Usher B - Usher Bev :	1755	-	dd/	172 224 115794
Whitechurch	Killeeshal	Usher Beverley :	mills	-	-	-	Usher B - Keane John :	1731	-	dd/	174 419 116834
Whitechurch	Killeeshal	Usher Beverley :	mills	-	-	-	Usher Beverley - Arthur	1757	-	dd/	191 9 127357
Inishlounaght	Kilmacomma	- on Glenary R.	flannel (ruins)	-	-	-	-	1842	-	6"os/	1
Rossmire	Kilmacthomas	-	corn		-	-	-	-	-	6"os/	15
Rossmire	Kilmacthomas	- near Bridge	flour	- replaced by modern	-	-	John Flavahan	-	-	mmSv/	wh - A
Rossmire	Kilmacthomas	Mathew Hughes	corn	-	-	-	-	-	- wheel enclosed	vmb/	25
Rossmire	Kilmacthomas	Moore Christopher	flour & corn	(1B) 72.6x25x35 :	-	-	-	-	15.6x4x- 3 pr. st.	hob/	5.3385
Rossmire	Kilmacthomas	Thomas Barton	flour	-	-	-	-	-	14x4x10 3 pr st.	vmb/	25
Rossmire	Kilmacthomas	Walsh John	corn	36x25x29	-	-	-	-	13.9x4x13.6	hob/	5.1977
Rossmire	Kilmacthomas	Walsh John	flour	41x25x30.9	-	-	-	-	13.9x4x13.6	hob/	5.1977
Waterford	Kilmalloo	-	corn		-	-	-	-	-	6"os/	37
Kilronan	Kilmanahan	- on Russelstown R.	corn	-	-	-	-	1842	-	6"os/	1
Kilronan	Kilmanahan	Greene William	saw	Incumb Est consisting of :		-	sold to Andrew Glasgow -	1855	-	mlyIE	p137
Kilmeadan	Kilmeadan	-	corn		-	-	-	-	-	6"os/	16
Kilmeadan	Kilmeadan	-	tuck		-	-	-	-	-	6"os/	8
Kilmeadan	Kilmeadan	Bachas	mill	-	-	-	Bachas - Bachas	-	-	dd/	573 476 392143
Kilmeadan	Kilmeadan	Bollon Robert Lt. Col. :	mill	-	-	-	Bollon R - Hamon George :	1801	-	dd/	542 104 356438
Kilmeadan	Kilmeadan	Downrayl Elizabeth :	tuck	-	-	-	Downrayl E - Douse Wm	1729	-	dd/	64 435 44566
Kilmeadan	Kilmeadan	Downrayl Elizabeth :	tuck	-	-	-	Downrayl E - Baccus Pet	1728	-	dd/	65 99 44565
Kilmeadan	Kilmeadan	Hearne Michael :	mill	-	-	-	Hearne M - Cashin Roger	1795	-	dd/	488 416 311551
Kilmeadan	Kilmeadan	Hearne Michael :	mill	-	-	-	Hearne M - Cashin Roger	1795	-	dd/	488 416 311551
Kilmeadan	Kilmeadan	Marchant	mill	-	-	-	Marchant - Fleming	-	?	dd/	460 224 29322?
Kilmeadan	Kilmeadan	Morris Abigail	tuck	-	-	-	Morris R & A - Douse Wm :	1724	-	dd/	63 493 44567
Kilmeadan	Kilmeadan	Morris Richard	tuck	-	-	-	Morris R - Douse William :	1724	-	dd/	63 493 44567
Kilmeadan	Kilmeadan	Morris William	mill	-	-	-	Morris Wm & his will :	1782	-	dd/	365 518 246175
Kilmeadan	Kilmeadan	O`Brien	mill	-	-	-	O`Brien - O`Brien	-	-	dd/	486 76 302516
Kilmeadan	Kilmeadan	O`Brien Denis :	mill	-	-	-	O`Brien D - O`Brien Cons.	1790	-	dd/	429 382 287579
Kilmeadan	Kilmeadan	O`Brien Denis :	mill	-	-	-	O`Brien D - O`Brien Cons.	1790	-	dd/	429 382 287579
Kilmeadan	Kilmeadan	St Leger Richard :	mill	-	-	-	St Leger - Phelan James	1802	-	dd/	547 377 361007
Kilmeadan	Kilmeadan	Wallis Henry	mill	-	-	-	Wallis Henry - John	1796	-	dd/	502 323 324891
Kilmeadan	Kilmeadan	Wallis Henry	mill	-	-	-	Wallis Henry - John	1796	-	dd/	507 323 324891
Kilmeadan	Kilmeadan	Wallis Henry :	mill	-	-	-	Wallis Henry - Henry	1788	-	dd/	405 194 265720
Kilmeadan	Kilmeadan	Wallis Henry :	mill	-	-	-	Wallis Henry - Henry	1788	-	dd/	405 194 265720
Fews	Kilnagrange	-	corn		-	-	-	-	-	6"os/	8
Fews	Kilnagrange	-	mill	-	-	-	-	-	-	1"os/	167
Fews	Kilnagrange	Catherine Dunne	corn	-	-	-	-	-	13x4x13	vmb/	25
Fews	Kilnagrange	Dunn Mrs.	corn & kiln	(1C) 34x21x17 :	-	-	-	-	13.6x4.6x13.6 :	hob/	5.4226
Fews	Kilnagrange	Dunne Catherine	corn	34x21x17.6 kiln :	-	-	-	-	13.6x4.6x14	hob/	5.1955
Fews	Kilnagrange	Catheine Dunn Mrs.	mill	-	-	14	-	-	-	gr/	Ld.Est.db
Kilrush	Kilrush	Walter Collinder	corn & flour	-	-	-	-	-	-	vmb/	25
Waterford	Knockanenoffriney	Mansfield Walter	mill	-	-	-	Mansfield Walt - Brady Jn	1839	-	dd/	?

PARISH	TOWNLAND	MILLER	TYPE	HOUSE	Land	£Val	PROPRIETORS	Date	WHEEL etc.	Record	Ref.
Colligan	Knockanpower Up	- on Clodiagh R	mill hz	-	-	-	-	-	-	iaa/	AI1285os22.8.1
Kilbarrymeadan	Knockmahon	-	engine ho. (2)	-	-	-	-	1842	-	6"os/	25
Kilronan	Knockmeal	Kiely Denis	corn	63.0x21.0x29 :	-	-	-	-	14x2.6x12	hob/	5.2067
Kilronan	Knockmeal :	-	flour		-	-	-	-	-	6"os/	13
Rathgormuck	Knocknacreha	-	mill hz	-	-	-	-	-	-	iaa/	AI1287 os7.1.1
Dungarvan	Knocknagranagh	Power Mary	tuck	- dw : 60x19x7	-	-	-	-	10x1.6x -	hob/	5.1953
Waterford	Lackandara	Barron Philip	mill, mill lands	-	-	-	Barron Phil - Chearnly Ant	1834	-	dd/	1834 5 251
Drumcannon	Lisselan	-	corn	-	-	-	-	-	-	6"os/	26
Lisnakill	Loughdeheen	Carn Patrick	corn	43.6x23.8x8 - mill & kil	-	-	-	-	10.3x1.11x7.6	hob/	5.2104
St Marys Clonmel	Lyranearla	-	corn & pond	-	-	-	-	1842	-	6"os/	2
Clonagam	Mayfield	Forbes James :	mills	-	-	-	Forbes & ors - Daniel Jas	1802	-	dd/	545 391 359775
Clonagam	Mayfield	May Edward :	mills	-	-	-	May - Bernal Isaac	1794	-	dd/	498 90 316010
Clonagam	Mayfield	May Edward, York	mills	-	-	-	May E - Medlicott John Th	1799	-	dd/	418 234 273292
Clonagam	Mayfield	Medlicott	mills	-	-	-	Medlicot - Daniel	-	-	dd/	439 450 285216
Clonagam	Mayfield	Medlicott Jno Thomas	mills	-	-	-	Medlicott - Edwards Jno	1788	-	dd/	395 339 261956
Clonagam	Mayfield	Medlicott Jno Thomas	mills	-	-	-	Medlicott - Edwards Jno	1788	-	dd/	395 339 261956
Clonagam	Mayfield	Pierce Rogers :	mills	-	-	-	Pierce R - Joy Nicholas :	1789	-	dd/	505 229 325479
Clonagam	Mayfield	Pierce Rogers :	mills	-	-	-	Pierce R - Joy Nicholas :	1789	-	dd/	505 229 325479
Stradbally	Millerstown	-	(none)	-	-	-	-	-	-	6"os/	24
Stradbally	Millerstown	Pierse	mill	-	-	-	Pierse - Kennedy	-	-	dd/	754 461 104488
Stradbally	Millerstown	Roberts	mill	-	-	-	Roberts - Travers	-	-	dd/	102 347 71085
Stradbally	Millerstown	Travers	mill	-	-	-	Travers - Roberts	-	-	dd/	112 5 75962?
Stradbally	Millerstown	Travers	mill	-	-	-	Travers - Roberts	-	-	dd/	126 242 80814
Stradbally	Millerstown	Walsh	mill	-	-	-	Walsh - Pierse	-	-	dd/	111 359 76978
Stradbally	Millerstown	Welsh Thomas :	mill	-	-	-	Welsh T - Matthew Geo	1724	-	dd/	55 160 36370
Stradbally	Millerstown	Whiteman Richard :	mill	-	-	-	Whiteman R - Travers Mcl :	1742	-	dd/	114 390 79332
bo. Mid.1/3	Millfort	Uniacke Norman :	-	-	-	-	Uniacke N - Johnson Benj	1810	-	dd/	617 422 424882
Tallow	Moanfune	Allen Prenderby	corn	17x19x5.0	-	-	-	-	8x4	hob/	5.1939
Lismore & Mo.	Mocollup	Drew Fras, Mocollop :	mill	-	-	-	Drew F - Heard (m. smt.)	1791	-	dd/	438 250 282607
Lismore & Mo.	Mocollup	Drew William Chas :	mill	-	-	-	Drew W - Drew Samuel :	1799	-	dd/	527 9 342953
Lismore & Mo.	Mocollup	Pigott & Phillpot	mill	-	-	-	Pigott - Drew John :	1754	-	dd/	167 337 112705
Kilculliheen	Mount Misery :	White George	corn (steam)	(1A) 30x29x19.6 & :	-	-	-	-	12 H.P. engine :	hob/	5.3399
Ardmore	Mountstuart	- N. side Goish R. :	corn (disused)	-	-	-	-	1888	-	25"os/	35.06
Ardmore	Mountstuart	William Brien	corn	-	-	-	-	-	-	vmb/	25
Kilburne	Munahoge	-	corn	-	-	-	-	-	-	6"os/	17
Kilburn	Munmahoge	Brien Michael	corn	(3B) 21.6x23.0x7.6 & :	-	3.14	-	-	12x2.7x13.6	hob/	5.2093 & 4223
Kilmeadan	Newtown	-	dam, reservoir	-	-	-	-	-	-	6"os/	16
Kilmeadan	Newtown	-	paper	-	-	-	-	-	-	6"os/	16
Kilmeadan	Newtown	- Fairview	Paper Mill	-	-	-	-	-	-	6"os/	16
Kilrush	Nicholastown	Cullinder Walter	corn	25.6x20	-	-	-	-	-	hob/	5.1983
Waterford	Park (2)	- near Rathgormuck	mill hz	-	-	-	-	-	-	iaa/	AI1288os2.12.4
Kinsalebeg	Pilltown	Arundel Hill	mill	-	-	-	Arundel H - Conner Richd	1839	-	dd/	1839 7 1
Kinsalebeg	Pilltown	Moore Peter	mill & lands	-	-	-	Moore Pet - Fisher Abr`m	1835	-	dd/	1835 12 42
Kinsalebeg	Pilltown	Peter M Fisher	flour & corn	-	-	-	-	-	- 3 pr st.	vmb/	25
Kinsalebeg	Pilltown	Fisher Peter Moor	mill	-	-	-	-	1846	-	dir/	Slater
Kinsalebeg	Piltown	-	flour & ponds	-	-	-	-	-	-	6"os/	37
Kinsalebeg	Piltown	Berney	mill	-	-	-	Berney - Ahern	-	-	dd/	349 171 362888
Kinsalebeg	Piltown	Connery	mill	-	-	-	Connery - Connery	-	-	dd/	491 410 319164
Kinsalebeg	Piltown	Deaggan Connery :	mill	-	-	-	Deaggan - Fisher Ruben :	1795	-	dd/	503 151 321964
Kinsalebeg	Piltown	Deaggan Connery :	mill	-	-	-	Deaggan - Fisher Ruben :	1795	-	dd/	503 151 321964
Kinsalebeg	Piltown	Renney Willam :	mill	-	-	-	Renney - Kennedy Chas	1761	-	dd/	210 379 13956
Kinsalebeg	Piltown	Welsh	mill	-	-	-	Welsh - Bernard	-	-	dd/	41 132 24994

PARISH	TOWNLAND	MILLER	TYPE	HOUSE	Land	£Val	PROPRIETORS	Date	WHEEL etc.	Record	Ref.
Kinsalebeg	Piltown	Welsh	mill	-	-	-	Welsh T - Grandison Jn	-	-	dd/	55 109 36370
Kinsalebeg	Piltown	Welsh Thomas :	mill	-	-	-	Welsh T - Coughlan Wm	1719	-	dd/	26 252 15373
Kinsalebeg	Piltown	Welsh Thomas :	mill	-	-	-	Welsh T - Bernard Fran	1720	-	dd/	26 457 16272
Clonagam	Portlaw	-	cotton	-	-	-	-	-	-	1"os/	167
Clonagam	Portlaw	-	cotton factory	-	-	-	-	1842	-	6"os/	8
Clonagam	Portlaw	-	gas house	-	-	-	-	1842	-	6"os/	8
Clonagam	Portlaw	Connolly William	land (only)	-	-	-	Connolly - Malcolmson Jos	1849	-	dd/	1849 14 50
Clonagam	Portlaw	Curtis Thomas	land (only)	-	-	-	Curtis T - Malcolmson Dav	1834	-	dd/	1834 20 27
Clonagam	Portlaw	Fowley Matthew	mills	-	-	-	Fowley M- Quinn John	1803	-	dd/	559 151 373080
Clonagam	Portlaw	Kennedy James :	mills	-	-	-	Kennedy James - Peter :	1795	-	dd/	498 169 316448
Clonagam	Portlaw	Kennedy James :	mills	-	-	-	Kennedy James - Peter :	1795	-	dd/	498 169 316448
Clonagam	Portlaw		cotton factory	- v. derelict & untidy	-	-	-	2000	-	mmSv/	pg - D
Clonagam	Portlaw Bridge	Malcolmson David	mill prems	-	-	-	Malcolmson - Connolly W	1836	-	dd/	1836 14 293
Fenoagh	Portnaboe	-	mill	-	-	-	-	-	-	1"os/	167
St Marys Clonmel	Poulboy	-	corn & pond	-	-	-	-	-	-	6"os/	2
St Marys Clonmel	Poulboy	-	mill & pond	-	-	-	-	-	-	6"os/	2
St Marys Clonmel	Poulboy	-	mill & pond	-	-	-	-	1842	-	6"os/	2
St Marys Clonmel	Poulboy	Daniel Edmond	tuck	-	-	-	Daniel E - Griffin Thomas :	1790	-	dd/	455 515 293941
St Marys Clonmel	Poulboy	Daniel Edmond	tuck	-	-	-	Daniel E - Griffin Thomas :	1790	-	dd/	455 515 293941
St Marys Clonmel	Poulboy	Daniel Jno	tuck	-	-	-	Daniel J - Gordon Thomas	-	-	dd/	469 287 299952
St Marys Clonmel	Poulboy	Daniel Jno :	tuck	-	-	-	Daniel J - Gordon Thomas	-	-	dd/	469 287 299952
St Marys Clonmel	Poulboy	Gordon Thomas :	tuck	-	-	-	Gordon T - Daniel Honora :	1802	-	dd/	544 44 363786
Waterford	Pouldrew *	Beresford Claudius :	mill	-	-	-	Beresford - O`Neill John :	1802	-	dd/	547 497 361565
Waterford	Pouldrew *	Wise Thomas :	mill	-	-	-	Wise Thos - O`Neill John	1800	-	dd/	530 306 348190
Lismore & M	Quarter	- quay, on Finisk R.	corn store	-	-	-	-	-	-	6"os/	29
St Marys Clonmel	Raheen	- JB Hearn's Mill	mill	- now Albatross Fcty.	-	-	-	2003	-	mmSv/	pg - Cc
St Marys Clonmel	Raheen	- at Butler's Bridge	mill	-	-	-	Rothwell's Mill	2003	-	mmSv/	pg - B
St Marys Clonmel	Raheen	Dudley	mills	-	-	-	Dudley - Jacob	-	-	dd/	572 525 3922217
St Marys Clonmel	Raheen	Mandeville	mills	-	-	-	Mandeville - Newport	-	-	dd/	455 116 367620
St Marys Clonmel	Raheen	Mandeville	mills	-	-	-	Mandeville - Newport	-	-	dd/	560 28 371970
St Marys Clonmel	Raheen	McCreighton James :	mills	-	-	-	McCreighton - Donovan :	1790	-	dd/	426 400 278228
St Marys Clonmel	Raheen	McCreighton James :	mills	-	-	-	McCreighton - Donovan :	1790	-	dd/	426 400 278228
St Marys Clonmel	Raheen	McCreighton William :	mills	-	-	-	McCreighton - Landiford :	1799	-	dd/	537 190 352490
St Marys Clonmel	Raheen	Middleton Anne	mill	-	-	-	Middleton A - Shelley Hen	1726	-	dd/	69 53 47205
St Marys Clonmel	Raheen	Stuart Henry	mills	-	-	-	Stuart Henry - Homan Wm	1833	-	dd/	1833 11 175
St Marys Clonmel	Raheen	Waterford Marq.	mills	-	-	-	Waterford Mq - Newpport	-	-	dd/	579 310 392001
Islandikane	Rehill Manor	Grandison George Hon.	mills	-	-	-	Grandison - Weston Ambr	1787	-	dd/	396 65 260381
Islandikane	Rehill Manor	McCreight Cecilia	mills	-	-	-	McCreight Cecilia - Wm	1786	-	dd/	378 405 253574
Islandikane	Rehill Manor	McCreight William	mills	-	-	-	McCreight Wm - Wm Ygr	1782	-	dd/	350 88 233867
Islandikane	Rehill Manor	Southwell Lord	mills	-	-	-	Southwell Ld - Butler	-	-	dd/	393 463 260961?
Newcastle	Ross	-	engine house	-	-	-	-	-	-	6"os/	16
St Mary`s Clonme	Scrothea West :	- Parknaglough	Mill	-	-	-	-	1842	-	6"os/	1
Rathgormuck	Shanakill	-	tuck	-	-	-	-	-	-	6"os/	7
Rathgormuck	Shanakill	Addy William :	mill	-	-	-	Addy W - Heathcote Geo :	1748	-	dd/	133 312 91258
Rathgormuck	Shanakill	Hearn John	mill	-	-	-	Hearn J - Walsh Thomas :	1762	-	dd/	248 229 159851
Rathgormuck	Shanakill	Heathcote George :	mill	-	-	-	Heathcote G - Morgan Jno	1760	-	dd/	206 427 136729
Rathgormuck	Shanakill	Ryan Michael	corn	(1C) 26.6x18x10.6 :	-	-	-	-	12X1.6X13 24 bkts	hob/	5.2137
Rathgormuck	Shanakill	Ryan Michael	tuck	-	-	-	-	-	13x1.8x13.6 24 bkt.	hob/	5.2137
Rathgormuck	Shanakill	Ryan Michael	tuck	-	-	-	-	-	13x1.8x14 23 bkts. :	hob/	5.2137
Rathgormuck	Shanakill	Ryan Michael :	tuck	mill, house, barn & :	-	-	-	1846	2 wheels o`shot	hob/	5.4224
Rathgormuck	Shanakill	Tomb	mill	-	-	-	Tomb - Morgan	-	-	dd/	620 430 136730
Seskinan	Shanballyanne	Barron Philip	mill, mill lands	-	-	-	Barron Phil - Chearnly Ant	1834	-	dd/	1834 5 251

PARISH	TOWNLAND	MILLER	TYPE	HOUSE	Land	£Val	PROPRIETORS	Date	WHEEL etc.	Record	Ref.
St Mary`s	Spa	- ESE. / Island Bridge	corn	-	-	-	-	1842	-	6"os/	1
St Mary`s	Spa	- ESE. / Island Bridge	corn & flour	-	-	-	-	1842	-	6"os/	1
St Mary`s	Spa	- ESE. / Island Bridge	corn & pond	-	-	-	-	1842	-	6"os/	1
St Mary`s	Spa	Smith William	mill	-	-	-	-	-	o`shot 40x4x - :	hob/	5.4225
Kilmeadan	Stonehouse	-	mill	-	-	-	-	-	-	1"os/	168
Clonagam	Stonehouse	- on Pouldree R.	flour & pond	-	-	-	-	-	-	6"os/	8
Kilmeadan	Stonehouse	Eakes Edward	mill	-	-	95	-	1856	(now demolished)	gr/	Ld.Est.db
Kilmeadan	Stonehouse	O`Neil	mill	-	-	-	O`Neil - O`Neil	-	-	dd/	564 331 378926
Kilmeadan	Stonehouse	O`Neil	mill	-	-	-	O`Neil - O`Neil	-	-	dd/	564 345 328950
Kilmeadan	Stonehouse	Roche	mill	-	-	-	Roche - Holmes Pomeroy	-	-	dd/	104 459 73907
St Marys Clonmel	Suir Island	- R. Suir N. side Isle	flour	-	-	-	-	1842	-	6"os/	1
St Marys Clonmel	Suir Island	- R. Suir S. side Isle	flour	-	-	-	-	1842	-	6"os/	1
St Marys Clonmel	Suir Island	Collins Edward	Corp. Mills	-	-	-	Collins Ed - Maude Sir C	1785	-	dd/	362 434 245928
St Marys Clonmel	Suir Island	Collins Edward	Corp. Mills	-	-	-	Collins Edw - Havell Edw	1785	-	dd/	371 320 249365
St Marys Clonmel	Suir Island	Grubb Robert	mill	-	-	-	Grubb R - Murray Anne B	1842	-	dd/	1842 14 194
St Marys Clonmel	Suir Island	Grubb Robert	rape	-	-	-	Grubb R - Grubb Sam	1838	-	dd/	1838 3 233
St Marys Clonmel	Suir Island	Grubb Robert	rape	-	-	-	Grubb R - Grubb Thomas	1844	-	dd/	1844 12 26
St Marys Clonmel	Suir Island	Grubb Samuel	mill	-	-	-	Grubb Sam - Grubb Robert	1841	-	dd/	1842 14 79
St Marys Clonmel	Suir Island	Grubb Samuel	rape	-	-	-	Grubb Sam - Grrubb Robt	1842	-	dd/	1842 14 79
St Marys Clonmel	Suir Island	Grubb Samuel	rape	-	-	-	Grubb Saml - Phelan Bern	1844	-	dd/	1844 1 18
St Marys Clonmel	Suir Island	Grubb Thomas	mill	-	-	-	Grubb Thos - Greer Thos	1840	-	dd/	1840 2 186
St Marys Clonmel	Suir Island	Phelan Bernard	rape	-	-	-	Phelan Bern - Greer Thos	1844	-	dd/	1844 3 16
Ballynakill	Summerville	-	corn mill site	-	-	-	-	-	-	6"os/	27
Tallow	Tallow	-	brewery	-	-	-	-	-	-	6"os/	28
Tallow	Tallow	- 1/8 m. SSW Town	flour & pond	-	-	-	-	-	-	6"os/	28
Tallow	Tallow	Gully Nicholas :	Dukes Mills	-	-	-	Gully N - Green Luke :	1753	-	dd/	160 549 109727
Tallow	Tallow	Hallahan Robert :	Dukes Mills	-	-	-	Hallahan R - Dean Peter :	1771	-	dd/	317 545 218874
Tallow	Tallow Tn`parks	-	flour	-	-	-	-	-	-	6"os/	28
Tallow	Tallow Town	Woodley Francis	mill	-	-	-	Woodley F - Hopper Fran	1879	-	dd/	1879 37 170
Tallow	Tallow Town	Woodley Francis	mill	-	-	-	Woodley F - Martin Jas R	1879	-	dd/	1879 37 171
Tallow	Tallow Town :	O`Hea Elizabeth	mill	-	-	-	O`Hea E` - Woodley Ellen	1846	-	dd/	1846 5 233
Waterford :	Tiercullen *	Henchy Donal	mill	-	-	-	Henchy D - Connor D	1807	-	dd/	579 340 392415
Waterford :	Tiercullen *	Henchy Donal	mill	-	-	-	Henchy D - Connor	1807	-	dd/	592 1 400406
Waterford :	Tiercullen *	Kelly	mill	-	-	-	Kelly - Parker	-	?	dd/	624 269 428807
Waterford :	Tiercullen *	Morrisey John :	mills	-	-	-	Morrisey - Walker Thos :	1805	Mort. 2 May	dd/	571 270 384982
Waterford :	Tiercullen *	Walker	mill	-	-	-	Walker - Henchy	-	-	dd/	584 16 393922
Fenoagh	Tinhalla	- unoc.	new	36.6x26.0x25.6 & :	-	-	-	-	-	hob/	5.2122
Drumcannon	Tramore	Doneraile Arthur :	tuck	-	-	-	Doneraile - Massereene :	1719	-	dd/	99 68 67952
Drumcannon	Tramore	Doneraile Lord	tuck	-	-	-	Doneraile Ld - Wyse	-	-	dd/	131 300 89144
Drumcannon	Tramore	Rogers	tuck	-	-	-	Rogers - Mason	-	-	dd/	130 316 87211
Drumcannon	Tramore	Rogers	tuck	-	-	-	Rogers - Alcock	-	-	dd/	188 420 126193
Fews	Turraleigh	Palliser Col.	flour	(1A) 48x28x40 :	-	7	-	-	31x7.6x - 4 pr. st. :	hob/	5.4226
Rossmire	Villierstown	-	mill	-	-	-	-	-	-	1"os/	-
Rossmire	Villierstown	- near Village	bleach	- demolished 1900:	-	-	(J.Stuart, Drumona Ho.)	2003	-	mmSv/	wh - Z
St John`s	Waterford City	Arthur Robert	mill (John`s)	-	-	-	Arthur R ano - Russell Jn	1834	-	dd/	1834 13 101
Trinity	Waterford City	Mayor Waterford	mill field :	-	5a.	-	Mayor - Christmas Thos	1725	-	dd/	46 467 30012
Waterford	Waterford City :	Evans Henry	kiln & yard	-	-	-	Evans H - Weekes Edw	1721	-	dd/	28 495 18499
Trinity Without	Waterford City :	Strangman Davis	brewery :	(1C) 27.6x30x23.6 & :	-	-	-	-	-	hob/	5.3409
Trinity Without	Waterford City :	Strangman Davis	brewery :	(1B) 39x96.6x38 & :	-	-	-	-	-	hob/	5.3409
St John`s	Waterford City :	Swean	malthouse	-	-	-	Swean - Hobbs	1736	-	dd/	90 49 62810
St John`s	Waterford City :	Thompson William	windmill	-	-	-	Thompson - Anderson Jn	1726	-	dd/	61 109 40788
Waterford	Waterford City :	Wyse Thomas	Boggs Mill	-	-	-	Wyse T - Teame Robt	1727	-	dd/	54 326 35923

COUNTY WATERFORD

PARISH	TOWNLAND	MILLER	TYPE	HOUSE	Land	£Val	PROPRIETORS	Date	WHEEL etc.	Record	Ref.
St John`s	Waterford City :	McMurren Henry	windmill	-	-	-	McMurren H - Alcock Alex	1725	-	dd/	39 256 25116
Trinity Without	Waterford City :	Power John	flour	1B) 77x25x28 & :	-	-	-	-	12 H.P. engine :	hob/	5.3409
Trinity	Waterford Town :	Rogers Geale	brewhouse	-	-	-	Rogers G - Grant Thos :	1767	-	dd/	261 60 166740
St John`s	Waterford Town :	May James :	Bricken`s Mill	-	-	-	May James - Whitby Jno :	1760	-	dd/	207 123 136275
St John`s	Waterford Town :	Roche William :	Bricken`s Mill	-	-	-	Roche W - Ryan Charles :	1765	-	dd/	241 508 160646
St John`s	Waterford Town :	Ryan Charles :	Bricken`s Mill	-	-	-	Ryan C - Kearney Patk :	1776	-	dd/	241 509 160674
St John`s	Waterford Town :	Warren John	Bricken`s Mill	-	-	-	Warren J - Roche Wm	1763	-	dd/	237 377 153246
St John`s	Waterford Town :	Bachas Charles	Bricken`s Mill	-	-	-	Bachas C - Murphy Thos :	1774	-	dd/	312 193 208044
St John`s	Waterford Town :	Waterford County	Bricken`s Mill	-	-	-	Waterford - Bachas Geo :	1759	-	dd/	205 593 113599
St John`s	Waterford Town :	Rogers	thread mills & :	-	-	-	Rogers & Wiley	-	-	dd/	296 228 194622
St John`s	Waterford Town :	Shanginan	thread mills & :	-	-	-	Shanginan - Lyons	-	-	dd/	327 485 219475
St John`s	Waterford Town :	Walls	thread mills & :	-	-	-	Walls - Shanginan	-	-	dd/	320 422 219472
St John`s	Waterford Town :	Bolton Bridget Widow :	malthouse	-	-	-	Bolton B - Coursey Dom.	1753	-	dd/	164 414 111168
St John`s	Waterford Town :	Rogers William :	thread mills :	-	-	-	Rogers W & McCord Jas :	1749	-	dd/	137 26 92221

PARISH	TOWNLAND	MILLER	TYPE	HOUSE	Land	£Val	PROPRIETORS	Date	WHEEL etc.	Record	Ref.
Kilcleagh	Aghnasullivan	-	-	- [no mill 6" O.S.]	-	-	-	1611	-	sv/moc	Inquis.Jac.I.
bo. Kilkenny W.	Aghnatemple *	Dawson	Anthonys Mill	-	-	-	Dawson - Robinson	-	-	dd/	159 247 1865?
bo. Kilkenny W.	Aghnatemple *	Dawson	Anthonys Mill	-	-	-	Dawson - Cooke	-	-	dd/	421 174 274230
bo. Kilkenny W.	Aghnatemple *	Devenish	Anthonys Mill	-	-	-	Devenish - Handcock	-	-	dd/	419 449 83194
bo. Kilkenny W.	Aghnatemple *	Handcock Gustavus	Anthonys Mill	-	-	-	Handcock G - Dawson Rich :	1746	Mort. 18 Apl.	dd/	120 449 83221
bo. Kilkenny W.	Aghnatemple *	Harman Frances :	Anthonys Mill	-	-	-	Harman F - Morgan Marcus :	1751	L&R. 19 Jul.	dd/	148 299 99665
bo. Kilkenny W.	Aghnatemple *	Harman	Anthonys Mill	-	-	-	Harman - La Touche	-	-	dd/	290 256 191665
bo. Kilkenny W.	Aghnatemple *	Oxmantown Lord	Mill	-	-	-	Oxmantown - Mountcharles	-	-	dd/	521 302 343726
bo. Kilkenny W.	Aghnatemple *	Robinson Anthony's	Mill	-	-	-	Robinson - Vigors	-	-	dd/	262 415 173071
Kilkenny West	Annagh :	-	corn	- [no mill 6" O.S.]	-	-	-	1624	-	sv/moc	Inquis.Jac.I.
Kilkenny West	Annagh :	Dillon Robert	corn	-	-	-	-	-	-	sv/moc	-
Kilkenny West	Annagh :	O'Neill Anthony	mill	-	-	-	O'Neil A - Kilmurray Henry	1889		dd/	1889 42 181
Kilkenny West	Annaghagny	Jones Edward	corn	- [no mill 6" O.S.]	-	-	-	-	-	sv/moc	Inquis.Jac.I.
Ballyloughloe	Annaghgortagh	NW/ Bealin Vge.	corn	-	-	-	-	1838	-	6"os/	29
Ballyloughloe	Annaghgortagh	NW/ Bealin Vge.	tuck	-	-	-	-	1838	-	6"os/	29
Ballyloughloe	Annaghgortagh	Swain Jonas	corn	-	-	-	-	-	-	sv/moc	V.O.Field Book
Moylisker	Anneville	-	threshing	-	-	-	-	-	-	sv/moc	-
Castletowndelvin	Archerstown	-	corn	-	-	-	-	1620	-	sv/moc	Inquis.Jac.I.
Castletowndelvin	Archerstown	Fitzgerald Patrick	corn	-	-	-	-	1840	-	sv/moc	V.O.Field Book
Castletowndelvin	Archerstown	Hogan Edward	corn	-	-	-	-	-	13x3x13	vmb/	21
Castletowndelvin	Archerstown	on co. bdry.	corn	-	-	-	-	1838	-	6"os/	9
Killare	Ardbrennan	-	corn	-	-	-	-	-	-	1"os/	99
Killare	Ardbrennan	-	corn	-	-	-	-	1611	-	sv/moc	Inquis.Jac.I.
Killare	Ardbrennan	Casey Thomas	corn	-	-	-	-	-	16x2x16	vmb/	21
Killare	Ardbrennan	Pettit Thomas	corn	-	-	-	-	1840	-	sv/moc	
Noughaval	Ardnacranny :	Harman Edward	mill	-	-	-	Harman Edw - Ruxton Willian	1886		dd/	1886 5 166
Drumraney	Ardnagragh Digby	Nugent Alice	corn & corn kiln	-	-	-	-	1838	-	6"os/	23
Drumraney	Ardnagrath Gray	Bertles Richard	corn	-	-	-	-	-	-	sv/moc	O.S.
Lickbla	Ardnagross	-	horizontal	-	-	-	- (discovered 1950's)	-	-	sv/moc	V.O.Field Book
Ardnurcher	Ardnurcher	Clavan James	tuck	-	-	-	-	-	-	sv/moc	V.O.Field Book
Drumraney	Ardracragh	Bartles Richard	corn	-	-	-	-	-	12x2x12	vmb/	21
St Marys	Athlone Town	- at Workhouse	push mill	-	-	-	-	-	-	sv/moc	-
St Marys	Athlone Town	beside North Gate :	brewery	-	-	-	-	1837	-	6"os/	29
St Marys	Athlone Town	Egan Mary	Mills of Athlone	-	-	-	Egan M - Ferguson Jno	1854	-	dd/	1854 14 172
St Peters	Athlone Town	Gleeson Gerard	Shannon Mills				Gleeson - Athlone Woollen C	1900		dd/	1900 32 40
St Peters	Athlone Town	Gleeson Gerard	Shannon Mills				Gleeson - Gleeson Patk	1900		dd/	1900 37 108
St Marys	Athlone Town	O`Beirne Charles	distillery	-	-	-	O`Beirne - Stephen Henry	1887	-	dd/	1887 20 114
St Marys	Athlone Town	Ryan Charles R	distillery	-	-	-	Ryan C R - O`Beirne Chas	1887	-	dd/	1887 20 113
St Marys	Athlone Town	S/ side Athlone Bridge	flour	-	-	-	-	1838	-	6"os/	29
St. Peters	Athlone Town	Swain & Halton	flour	-	-	-	-	-	-	sv/moc	-
St Marys	Athlone Town	Wilson Joshua	distillery	-	-	-	Wilson J - Wilson Bros Ltd.	1889	-	dd/	188947 43
St Marys	Athlone Town :	Woolseley Richd Sir	mills	-	-	-	Woolesley - Castlemore	1833	-	dd/	1833 10 240
St Marys	Athlone Town :	Wilson Bros Ltd.	distillery	-	-	-	Wilson Bros - Smith Wm	1895	-	dd/	1895 32 54
St Marys	Athlone Town :	Jones Lewis :	mills & land	-	-	-	Jones L - Sproule Joseph :	1717	-	dd/	20 404 11046
St Marys	Athlone Town :	Jones	mills & land	-	-	-	Jones - Sproule	-	-	dd/	21 152 11047
St Marys	Athlone Town :	Jones	mills & land	-	-	-	Jones - Thomas	-	-	dd/	61 395 41796
St Marys	Athlone Town :	Ganly's Mill	flour	-	-	-	-	-	-	sv/moc	-
St Marys	Athlone Town :	St George Edward :	mills	-	-	-	St George E - Dubois Anna :	1735	L&R. 8 Nov.	dd/	81 381 57992
St. Peters	Athlone Town :	Potts William T	distillery	-	-	-	-	-	-	sv/moc	-
St. Peters	Athlone Town :	Kelly Denis	distillery	-	-	-	-	-	-	sv/moc	-
St Marys	Athlone Town :	St George	mills	-	-	-	St George - Morris	-	-	dd/	47 422 31278
Kilkenny West	Ballaghkeeran	Murthagh James	flour	-	29a.	-	-	-	-	gr/	-
Kilkenny West	Ballaghkeeran	Murthagh John	flour	-	29a.	-	-	-	-	gr/	-
Killare	Ballinacor	Nugent Count	threshing	-	-	-	-	-	14x4x5	vmb/	21
Portnashangan	Ballinagall	-	-	-	-	-	-	-	-	sv/moc	-
Castletown	Ballinagore Vge.	Perry John	flour & stores	-	-	-	-	-	-	gr/	-
Castletown	Ballinagore Vge.	Perry William	flour & stores	-	-	-	-	-	-	gr/	-
Ardnurcher	Ballinamill	-	-	-	-	-	-	-	-	sv/moc	-

PARISH	TOWNLAND	MILLER	TYPE	HOUSE	Land	£Val	PROPRIETORS	Date	WHEEL etc.	Record	Ref.
Mullingar	Ballinderry	Hopp Thomas :	mill	-	-	-	-	1609	-	sv/moc	Inquis.Jac.I.
Multifarnham	Ballindurrow	Gaynor Walter	corn	-	19a.	-	-	-	-	gr/	-
Killare	Ballinkeeny	Pettit Thomas	corn	-	-	-	-	-	-	sv/moc	-
Kilbeggan	Ballinwire	Connolly John	flour	-	-	-	-	-	-	sv/moc	Inquis.Jac.I.
Faughalstown	Ballybeg	-	mill	-	-	-	-	1808	-	sv/moc	LarkinMap
Kilcumreragh	Ballybornia	-	mill	-	-	-	-	-	-	1"os/	98
Kilcumreragh	Ballybrickoge	-	corn	-	-	-	-	-	-	sv/moc	-
Kilcumreragh	Ballybrickoge	-	old corn mill & kil	-	-	-	-	1838	-	6"os/	31
Durrow	Ballycahan	- S/ R. Brosna	old bleach green	- (no mill)	-	-	-	1808	-	6"os/	37
Durrow	Ballycahan	Magan Arthur	mill & bl. green	-	-	-	-	-	-	sv/moc	-
Drumraney	Ballycloughduff	Buckley William	corn	-	8-3-4	-	-	-	-	gr/	-
Drumraney	Ballycloughduff	Buckley William	corn	-	-	-	-	-	14x4x14	vmb/	21
Drumraney	Ballycloughduff	Dillon Robert	corn & tuck	-	-	-	-	-	-	sv/moc	-
Drumraney	Ballycloughduff	NE/ B'cloughduff Br.	corn & tuck	-	-	-	-	1838	-	6"os/	30
Drumraney	Ballycloughduff	McAulay Patrick	corn	-	-	-	-	1840	-	sv/moc	V.O.Field Book
Ballyloughloe	Ballydoogan	- nr B`cloughduff Br.	corn	-	-	-	-	-	-	1"os/	98
Killucan	Ballyhaw	Rally Matthew	mill	-	26a.	-	-	-	-	gr/	-
Kilbixy	Ballyhoreen	Bennett John Sir	corn	-	-	-	-	1845	-	sv/moc	-
Kilbixy	Ballyhoreen	-	corn & kiln	-	-	-	-	1838	-	6"os/	11
Killare	Ballykeeny	Claver Laurence	corn	-	-	-	-	-	11x2x12	vmb/	21
Killare	Ballykeeny	Pettit Thomas	corn	-	-	-	-	1630	-	sv/moc	Inquis.Jac.I.
St Marys	Ballykeeran	Murtagh John	corn & bleach	-	-	-	-	1853	-	sv/moc	V.O.Field Book
St Marys	Ballykeeran	- on Breensford R.	mill	-	-	-	-	-	-	1"os/	98
St Marys	Ballykeeran	Darnley C'tess Hon.	mill	-	-	-	Darnley Countess - Mitchell:	1784	Rel. 30 Apl.	dd/	356 379 240738
St Marys	Ballykeeran	Darnley Countess	mill	-	-	-	Darnley Countess - Lennox	-	-	dd/	442 23 285774
St Marys	Ballykeeran	Dillon Christopher :	mill	-	-	-	Dillon C - Dillon Walter :	1808	-	dd/	596 285 406660
St Marys	Ballykeeran	Forster & Wife	mill	-	-	-	Forster - Glover	-	-	dd/	496 512 320308
St Marys	Ballykeeran	Forster Charles :	mill	-	-	-	Forster C - Kearney William :	1793	-	dd/	494 261 323504
St Marys	Ballykeeran	Murtagh John	corn & store	-	23a.	-	-	-	-	gr/	-
St Marys	Ballykeeran	W/ Breensford R.	bleach	-	-	-	-	1838	-	6"os/	29
St Marys	Ballykeeran	W/ Breensford R.	corn	-	-	-	-	1838	-	6"os/	29
St Marys	Ballykeeran Big	-	flour	-	-	-	-	-	-	sv/moc	-
Street	Ballykildevin	-	threshing	-	-	-	-	1838	-	6"os/	2
Street	Ballykildevin	-	threshing (?)	-	-	-	-	-	-	sv/moc	-
Castlet`nkindalen	Ballykilroe	-	corn	-	-	-	-	-	-	sv/moc	-
Noughaval	Ballymahon	- on R. Inny	flour	-	-	-	-	2004	-	pWEH	Cr
Kilmacnevan	Ballynacarrow	-	corn & corn kiln	-	-	-	-	1838	-	6"os/	17
Rathconrath	Ballynacarrow	Ballasty Owen	corn	-	-	-	-	-	13x3x13	vmb/	21
Rathconrath	Ballynacarrow	Ballasty Patrick	corn & kiln	-	129a.	-	-	-	-	gr/	-
Kilmacnevan	Ballynacarrow	Dooley John	mill & kiln	-	43a.	-	-	-	-	gr/	-
Kilmacnevan	Ballynacarrow	Dooly John	corn	-	-	-	-	-	13x2x2	vmb/	21
Killulagh	Ballynacor	-	wind pump	-	-	-	- on O.S. 1914 edition	-	-	sv/moc	-
Killulagh	Ballynacor	Fetherston Richard	threshing	-	-	-	-	-	-	sv/moc	V.O.Field Book
Castlet`nkindalen	Ballynagore	-	mill dam	-	-	-	-	-	-	sv/moc	-
Castlet`nkindalen	Ballynagore	- on R. Brosna	corn	-	-	-	-	-	-	1"os/	109
Castlet`nkindalen	Ballynagore	E/ R. Brosna	bleach	-	-	-	-	1838	-	6"os/	32
Castlet`nkindalen	Ballynagore	E/ R. Brosna	corn & kiln	-	-	-	-	1838	-	6"os/	32
Castlet`nkindalen	Ballynagore	Garden	mill	-	-	-	Garden - Evans	-	-	dd/	550 329 369973
Castlet`nkindalen	Ballynagore	Low	mill	-	-	-	Low - Garden	-	-	dd/	377 429 250727
Castlet`nkindalen	Ballynagore	Low	mill	-	-	-	Low - Brennan	-	-	dd/	435 399 284108
Castlet`nkindalen	Ballynagore	N/ B'nagorer Br.	mill dam & mill race		-	-	-	1838	-	6"os/	32
Castlet`nkindalen	Ballynagore	on R. Brosna	flour	-	-	-	-	1838	-	6"os/	32
Castlet`nkindalen	Ballynagore	Richardson	mill	-	-	-	Richardson - Low	-	-	dd/	368 486 250588

PARISH	TOWNLAND	MILLER	TYPE	HOUSE	Land	£Val	PROPRIETORS	Date	WHEEL etc.	Record	Ref.
Castlet`nkindalen	Ballynagore	Wade	mill	-	-	-	Wade - Mullock	-	-	dd/	591 515 404843
Castlet`nkindalen	Ballynagore	Hamilton George	mill	-	-	-	-	1891	-	sv/moc	-
Kilcleagh	Ballynahown	-	-	-	-	-	-	-	-	sv/moc	-
Ardnurcher	Ballynamullen	-	corn & tuck	-	-	-	-	1841	-	6"os/	31
Ardnurcher	Ballynamullen	Clavin James	tuck	-	39a.	-	-	-	-	gr/	-
bo. Fertulla	Ballywhite	Milward Edward :	mill	-	-	-	Millward E - Hughes Henry :	1734	L&R. 30 Sep.	dd/	80 353 56150
Wm	Balnacart	-	corn	-	-	-	-	-	-	1"os/	-
bo. Kilkenny W.	Balnamill	Haltam	mill	-	-	-	Haltam - Shanahan	-	?	dd/	x y 340550
Rathconnell	Balrath	N/ Clonlost Ho.	corn & mill dam	-	-	-	-	1838	-	6"os/	20
Rathconnell	Balrath East	Connolly James	corn	-	44a.	-	-	-	-	gr/	-
Street	Barradrum	-	saw	-	-	-	-	-	-	sv/moc	-
Drumraney	Baskin Low	Dillon Theobald	corn	-	-	-	-	-	-	sv/moc	-
Drumraney	Baskin Low	W/ Baskin Bridge	corn	-	-	-	-	1838	-	6"os/	23
Enniscoffey	Blackislands	-	-	-	-	-	-	-	-	sv/moc	-
Westmeath	Bleachlawn *	-	no mill	-	-	-	-	1838	-	6"os/	23
Kilcleagh	Boyanagh	Daly	mill	-	-	-	Daly - Daly	-	-	dd/	533 531 355338
Kilcleagh	Boyanagh	Handcock	mill	-	-	-	Handcock - Stoney	-	?	dd/	183 53 121494
Kilcleagh	Boyanagh	Handcock	mill	-	-	-	Handcock - Stoney	-	-	dd/	260 91 166596
Kilcleagh	Boyanagh	Handcock	mill	-	-	-	Handcock - Hewetson	-	-	dd/	451 468 29036
Kilcleagh	Boyanagh :	Larkin Elizabeth	corn	-	24a.	-	-	-	-	gr/	-
Kilcleagh	Boyanagh :	S/ Constabulary	corn	-	-	-	-	1838	-	6"os/	36
Kilcleagh	Boyanagh :	Malone Edmond	corn	-	-	-	-	1840	-	sv/moc	V.O.Field Book
Rathmoylan	Brownstown	-	corn	-	-	-	-	-	-	sv/moc	-
Noughaval	Cannorstown	Doonigan Thomas	corn	-	-	-	-	-	11x2x12	vmb/	21
Noughaval	Cannorstown :	NE/ Cannorstown Br.	corn	-	-	-	-	1838	-	6"os/	15
Noughaval	Cannorstown :	Dillon Robert	corn	-	-	-	-	1838	-	sv/moc	V.O.Field Book
Noughaval	Cannorstown :	E/ Castletown Br.	windmill	-	-	-	-	1838	-	6"os/	16
Carrick	Carrick	Fraine Walter	corn & tuck	-	-	-	-	1839	-	sv/moc	V.O.Field Book
Carrick	Carrick	-	tuck & corn	-	-	-	-	1838	-	sv/moc	Inquis.Jac.I.
Carrick	Carrick	- near Ballinalack	corn	-	-	-	-	-	-	1"os/	-
Carrick	Carrick	Battersby George	corn & kiln	-	-	-	-	-	-	gr/	-
Carrick	Carrick	Battersby George	miller`s ho, lo.	-	235a.	-	-	-	-	gr/	-
Carrick	Carrick	Dempsey Arthur	corn & kiln	-	19a.	-	-	-	-	gr/	-
Carrick	Carrick	Dempsey Patrick	corn	-	-	-	-	-	12x3x11	vmb/	21
Carrick	Carrick	Grattan	mill	-	-	-	Grattan - Nugent	-	-	dd/	118 144 80320
Carrick	Carrick	Grattan James :	mill	-	-	-	Grattan J - Marlay Anthony :	1740	L&R. 24 May	dd/	96 482 69064
Carrick	Carrick	SE/ Ballinalack Vge.	corn & kiln	-	-	-	-	1838	-	6"os/	6
Carrick	Carrick	Sherlock Wiliam :	mill	-	-	-	Sherlock W - Fetherston :	1743	11 Feb.	dd/	111 552 78353
Carrick	Carrick	Sherlock Wiliam :	mill	-	-	-	Sherlock W - Pierson Thos	1739	Lse. 20 Jne.	dd/	114 33 77865
Carrick	Carrick	Sherlock Wiliam :	mill	-	-	-	Sherlock W - Fetherston :	1746	-	dd/	122 416 84622
Kilkenny West	Carrick :	Dillon Robert	mill	-	-	-	-	1611	-	sv/moc	Inquis.Jac.I.
Carrick	Carrrick	Gallagher Peter	-	-	-	-	-	-	Gilkes 10"	turb/	c1947
Carrick	Carrrick	Lynch	mills	-	-	-	Lynch - Lynch	-	-	dd/	586 44 3946?57
Carrick	Carrrick	-	corn & kiln	-	-	-	-	1838	-	6"os/	4
Lacken	Carrrick	Gaynor Michael Sen.	corn	-	-	-	-	1829	-	sv/moc	FreeholdersList
Noughaval	Cartroncroy	-	Old Windmill	-	-	-	-	-	-	1"os/	98
Kilcleagh	Cartronkeel	-	old brewery	-	-	-	-	1838	-	6"os/	30
Kilkenny West	Cartronkeel :	- near Pass Kilbride	brewery	-	-	-	-	-	-	-	
Rahanne	Castlelost	Kelly Matthew	corn	-	-	-	-	-	12x3x6	vmb/	21
Rathgarve	Castlepollard	- at Millcastle	corn	-	-	-	-	-	-	1"os/	-
Castlet`nkindalen	Castletown	Jessop William	corn & kiln	-	31a.	-	-	-	-	gr/	-
Castlet`nkindalen	Castletown	Nugent Robert :	mill	-	-	-	Nugent R - Nugent Robert :	1737	Lse. 16 Jan.	dd/	89 197 62820
Castlet`nkindalen	Castletown		corn, kiln, mill rac	-	-	-	-	1838	-	6"os/	32

PARISH	TOWNLAND	MILLER	TYPE	HOUSE	Land	£Val	PROPRIETORS	Date	WHEEL etc.	Record	Ref.
Enniscoffey	Claremount	Rynd John	threshing	-	-	-	-	1840	-	sv/moc	V.O.Field Book
Noughaval	Clogher	Dawson Thomas	mill	-	-	-	Dawson T - Murtagh Chas	1784	Lse. 24 Apl.	dd/	403 508 270102
Noughaval	Clogher	Lennon	mill	-	-	-	Lennon - St George	-	-	dd/	346 158 231158
Killare	Clonaboy	-	flour	-	-	-	-	-	-	sv/moc	-
Killare	Clonaboy	-	threshing	-	-	-	-	-	-	sv/moc	-
Killucan	Clonfad	- near Pass Kilbride	mill	-	-	-	-	-	-	1"os/	
Rathconnell	Clonikilivant	-	horizontal	-	-	-	-	1985	-	sv/moc	Arch. Surv.No.20
Kilcleagh	Clonlonan	-	horizontal	-	-	-	-	-	-	sv/moc	-
Castlet`nkindalen	Clonmaskil	Cusack John	mill	-	-	-	-	1895	-	sv/moc	Arch. Surv.No.28
Castlet`nkindalen	Clonmaskil	-	-	-	-	-	-	1631	-	sv/moc	Inquis.Jac.I.
Street	Clonmore	-	corn & kiln	-	-	-	-	1838	-	6"os/	2
Street	Clonmore	-	corn & tuck	-	-	-	-	-	-	sv/moc	-
Street	Clonmore	Tuite Richard	tuck & corn	-	-	-	-	1840	-	sv/moc	V.O.Field Book
Street	Clonmore	Gilligan John	corn	-	-	-	-	-	12x3x10	vmb/	21
Street	Clonmore	M`Keown James	corn & kiln	-	26a.	-	-	-	-	gr/	-
Street	Clonmore	M`Keown James	tuck	-	-	-	-	-	-	gr/	-
Street	Clonmore	Maguire	mill	-	-	-	Maguire - Maguire	-	-	dd/	138 103 92362
Street	Clonmore	Maguire	mill	-	-	-	Maguire - Kelly	-	-	dd/	245 543 163004
Castletowndelvin	Clonnagapple	Greville Col. Fulke S.	saw	-	58a.	-	-	-	-	gr/	-
Killare	Clonnalynagh Up.	-	corn	-	-	-	-	-	-	1"os/	99
Conry	Clonown	-	corn	-	-	-	-	-	-	1"os/	99
Kilcumreragh	Clonrellick	- unoc.	old mill house	-	27a.	-	-	-	-	gr/	-
Kilcumreragh	Clonrellick	Kilduff Edward	bleach & corn	-	-	-	-	1840	-	sv/moc	V.O.Field Book
Castlet`nkindalen	Cloonagh	-	corn & flax	-	-	-	-	-	-	sv/moc	-
St Feighins	Collinstown	- near Mountain Vge.	mill	-	-	-	-	-	-	1"os/	90
Wm	Comermills	-	-	-	-	-	-	-	-	sv/moc	-
bo. Clanlonan	Connyborrons	Giffard Thomas :	mill	-	-	-	Giffard Thos - Pollard Dillon :	1735	-	dd/	78 381 56680
bo. Clanlonan	Connyborrons	Pollard Hampson	mill	-	-	-	Pollard H - Mervyn	-	- [error]	dd/	79 30 54404
bo. Clanlonan	Connyborrons	Pollard Hampson	mill	-	-	-	Pollard H - Dagnan Thos :	1735	-	dd/	82 42 56953
bo. Clanlonan	Connyborrons	Pollard Walter :	mill	-	-	-	Pollard W - Reynolds Richd :	1734	-	dd/	84 459 61969
Rathconnell	Cooksborough	Donnellan John	mill	-	-	-	Donnellan J - Donnellan Phili	1889		dd/	1889 11 174
Kilbeggan	Coola	Green William	flour	-	-	-	-	1840	-	sv/moc	V.O.Field Book
Kilbeggan	Coola	-	saw	-	-	-	-	1840	-	sv/moc	V.O.Field Book
Kilbeggan	Coola	Delaney William Bern	mill	-	-	-	-	-	-	gr/	-
Kilbeggan	Coola	S/ flour mill	Coola Cottage	-	-	-	-	1838	-	6"os/	38
Kilbeggan	Coola	SE/ Coola Bridge	corn	-	-	-	-	1838	-	6"os/	38
Kilbeggan	Coola	SW/ Coola Bridge	flour & kiln	-	-	-	-	1838	-	6"os/	38
Mayne	Coole	Scott John	windmill	-	17a.	-	-	-	-	gr/	-
Mayne	Coole	Smith Thomas Rev.	windmill	-	-	-	-	1810	-	sv/moc	Arch. Surv.No.53
Ballyloughloe	Cooleen	-	corn	-	-	-	-	-	-	sv/moc	-
Ballyloughloe	Cooleen	SE/ B'cloughduff Br.	corn & corn kiln	-	-	-	-	1838	-	6"os/	30
Street	Coolnagun	-	windmill	-	-	-	-	-	-	sv/moc	-
Templeoran	Coolnahay	Nugent John :	millrace	-	-	-	-	1808	-	sv/moc	-
Mayne	Coolure	Lilli	mill	-	-	-	Lili - Parker	-	-	dd/	475 36 305516
Mayne	Coolure	Longford Lord Henry	mill	-	-	-	Longford Ld. - E. of Bective	-	-	dd/	314 272 218077
Mayne	Coolure	McCally Andrew :	mill	-	-	-	McCally A - Newcomen Wm :	1784	Asgt. 10 Jne.	dd/	359 197 242318
Pass of Kilbride	Corcloon	-	corn & mill pond	-	-	-	-	1838	-	6"os/	33
Pass of Kilbride	Corcloon	Geraghty James	corn & tuck	-	-	-	-	-	-	sv/moc	-
Pass of Kilbride	Corcloon	-	tuck	-	-	-	-	1838	-	6"os/	33
bo. Fertulla	Corduff	Handcock Richard	mill	-	-	-	Handcock R - Smith Henry :	1742	Lse. 2 Sep.	dd/	114 349 79345
bo. Clanlonan	Corduff	Handcock	mill	-	-	-	Handcock - Dunstervill	-	?	dd/	44 240 28867
bo. Fertulla	Corduff	Smith Henry	mill	-	-	-	Smith H - Hewetson William :	1748	Asgt. 19 Sep.	dd/	124 111 83979
Rathconrath	Corkan	-	corn	-	-	-	-	-	-	1"os/	99

PARISH	TOWNLAND	MILLER	TYPE	HOUSE	Land	£Val	PROPRIETORS	Date	WHEEL etc.	Record	Ref.
Rathconrath	Corkan	-	corn	-	-	-	-	1838	-	6"os/	17
Rathconrath	Corkan	Donaho James	corn	-	-	-	-	-	12x3x12	vmb/	21
Rathconrath	Corkan	Donoghue James	corn & kiln	-	58a.	-	-	-	-	gr/	-
Street	Cornacausk	Monaghan Patrick	mill & kiln	-	0-1-25	-	-	-	-	gr/	-
Street	Cornacausk	Monaghan Patt	corn	-	-	-	-	-	16x1x17	vmb/	21
Street	Cornacausk	W. of Village	corn, kiln, pond	-	-	-	-	1838	-	6"os/	2
Street	Cornacausk	Wilson William	corn	-	-	-	-	1899	-	sv/moc	Wm.W. Diary
bo. Clonlonan	Corner	Nettelvill Nich. Hon. :	mills & land	-	-	-	Nettelvill N Ld. - Donagh Jn :	1743	Dem. 1 Jul.	dd/	110 243 76922
Drumraney	Corrlore	Geraghty James	tuck	-	-	-	-	-	11x2x8	vmb/	21
Rathaspick	Corry	-	corn	-	-	-	-	-	-	sv/moc	-
Rathaspick	Corry	-	corn & kiln	-	-	-	-	1838	-	6"os/	6
Rathaspick	Corry	Tormey Denis	corn	-	-	-	-	-	12x2x2	vmb/	21
Ballyloughloe	Creeve	-	corn & corn kiln	-	-	-	-	1838	-	6"os/	30
Ballyloughloe	Creeve	-	corn, kiln & pond	-	-	-	-	1838	-	6"os/	30
Ballyloughloe	Creeve	Donoghue Andrew	corn	-	42a.	-	-	-	-	gr/	-
Ballyloughloe	Creeve	Ward James	corn	-	-	-	-	1840	-	sv/moc	V.O.Field Book
St Marys	Creggan Upper	Allen George	corn	-	16a.	-	-	-	-	gr/	-
bo. Fertulla	Crievebeg/ -more	Handcock Thomas :	mill	-	-	-	Handcock Thos - Handcock :	1722	Lse. 18 Sep.	dd/	34 283 21606
bo. Fertulla	Crievebeg/ -more	Handcock Thomas :	mill	-	-	-	Handcock Thos - Dunstervill :	1725	-	dd/	44 240 28867
Tyfarnham	Crookedwood	- near Parsonstown	corn	-	-	-	-	-	-	1"os/	99
Castletowndelvin	Crowinstown		corn & corn kiln	-	-	-	-	1838	-	6"os/	14
Castletowndelvin	Crowinstown Gt.	Tormey Patrick	corn	-	-	-	-	-	10x3x12	vmb/	21
Castletowndelvin	Crowinstown Gt.	Tormy Patrick	corn	-	45a.	-	-	-	-	gr/	-
Rathaspick	Crumoin	Crawford Matthew	steam	-	-	-	-	-	6 h.p.	sv/moc	V.O.Field Book
bo. Moyeshall	Cullenmore	Dillon	mill (Lady Margaret's)		-	-	Dillon - Mitchell	-	-	dd/	182 208 xxxxx
bo. Moyeshall	Cullenmore	Leigh	mill	-	-	-	Leigh - Reynell	-	-	dd/	180 376 120985
bo. Moyeshall	Cullenmore	Maguire	mill (Lady Margaret's)		-	-	Maguire - Cashell	-	-	dd/	206 281 136001
bo. Moyeshall	Cullenmore	Swift James :	mill	-	-	-	Swift Jas - Barlow James :	1741	L&R. 20 Jul.	dd/	120 371 82849
bo. Moyeshall	Cullenmore	Blaquiere Jno Rt. :	mill	-	-	-	Blaquiere Jno - Black Jos :	1788	13 Aug.	dd/	399 420 264362
bo. Moyeshall	Cullenmore	Wilkinson	mill (Lady Margaret's)		-	-	Wilkinson - Lynch	-	-	dd/	569 205 380776
Street	Culvin Rathowen	- on R. Riffey	mill	-	-	-	-	-	-	1"os/	-
St Marys	Cummerstown	-	bleach & flax	-	-	-	-	-	-	sv/moc	-
St Marys	Cummerstown	-	corn	-	-	-	-	-	-	sv/moc	-
St Marys	Cummerstown	-	corn & mill pond	-	-	-	-	1838	-	6"os/	8
Kilcleagh	Curries	Adamson Richard	corn	-	-	-	-	-	-	gr/	-
Killucan	Cushingtown	on Riverstown R.	mill & corn kiln	-	-	-	-	1838	-	6"os/	27
Killucan	Cushinstown	-	corn	-	-	-	-	-	-	sv/moc	-
Killucan	Cushinstown	Daniel	mill	-	-	-	Daniel - Smith	-	?	dd/	164 578 111930
Killucan	Cushinstown	Garty William	mill & kiln	-	20a.	-	-	-	-	gr/	-
Killucan	Cushinstown	Geale Daniel :	mill	-	-	-	Geale D - Purdon Edward :	1785	Reconv. 28 Nov	dd/	360 516 244856
Killucan	Cushinstown	Nugent	mill	-	-	-	Nugent - Daniel	-	?	dd/	144 268 97440?
Killucan	Cushinstown	Purdon	mill	-	-	-	Purdon - Gaynor	-	-	dd/	566?46?384740
Killucan	Cushinstown	Purdon	mill	-	-	-	Purdon - Geale	-	-	dd/	358 429 241659
Killucan	Cushinstown	Purdon Edward	mill	-	-	-	Purdon Ed - Purcell Andrew :	1790	-	dd/	445 402 287075
Killucan	Cushinstown	Smith	mill	-	-	-	Smith - Browne	-	-	dd/	376 363 251390
Killagh	Dardistown		brick kiln	-	-	-	-	1838	-	6"os/	13
St Feighin`s	Deerpark	Dewar Alexander	scutch & corn	-	-	-	-	-	-	sv/moc	-
Castletowndelvin	Delvin	-	thread	-	-	-	-	-	-	sv/moc	-
Faughalstown	Derrynagarragh	-	corn & kiln	-	-	-	-	1841	-	6"os/	7
Faughalstown	Derrynagarragh	Tormey James	corn & kiln	-	39a.	-	-	-	-	gr/	-
Noughaval	Doonamona	-	corn	-	-	-	-	-	-	1"os/	98
Noughaval	Doonamona	-	mill dam & mill ra	-	-	-	-	1838	-	6"os/	23
Noughaval	Doonamona	Bracken Timothy	corn	-	20a.	-	-	-	-	gr/	-

PARISH	TOWNLAND	MILLER	TYPE	HOUSE	Land	£Val	PROPRIETORS	Date	WHEEL etc.	Record	Ref.
Noughaval	Doonamona	Bracken Timothy	corn	-	-	-	-	-	12x2x14	vmb/	21
Noughaval	Doonamona	NE/ Crocktoctha Br.	corn & corn kiln	-	-	-	-	1838	-	6"os/	23
Wm	Drumcroe	-	mill	-	-	-	-	-	-	1"os/	90
Dysart	Dysart	-	corn	-	-	-	-	-	-	sv/moc	-
Dysart	Dysart	Nugent Sir Roberte	mill	manor, lands etc..	-	-	-	1610	-	sv/moc	Inquis.Jac.I.
Dysart	Dysart	on R.from L. Ennell	corn, corn kiln :	-	-	-	-	1838	-	6"os/	25
Rathconell	Edmondstown	-	threshing	-	-	-	-	-	-	sv/moc	-
Rathconell	Edmondstown	at Edmondstown	threshing m/c	-	-	-	-	1838	-	6"os/	13
St Feighins	Fore	- Priory Mill	corn	-	-	-	-	-	-	sv/moc	-
St Feighins	Fore	Kiernan Patrick	corn & kiln	-	17a.	-	-	-	-	gr/	-
St Feighins	Fore	NW/ Fore Vge.	mill & dam	-	-	-	-	1838	-	6"os/	4
St Feighins	Fore	St Feighin`s	corn	-	-	-	-	-	-	sv/moc	-
Westmeath	Fowlerstown	Dillon Robert	mill & land	-	-	-	-	1611	-	sv/moc	Inquis.Jac.I.
Foyran	Foyran	Dermody William	corn	-	32a.	-	-	-	-	gr/	-
Foyran	Foyran	Nugent Robert :	mill	-	-	-	Nugent Robt - Reilly Myles	1837	-	dd/	89 200 62831
Foyran	Foyran	S/ Balnacart Vge.	corn, kiln, mill po	-	-	-	-	1838	-	6"os/	1
Lackan	Fulmort	-	corn kiln	-	-	-	-	1838	-	6"os/	6
Enniscoffey	Gaybrook Dems	Smyth Robert	threshing	-	-	-	-	1839	-	sv/moc	V.O.Field Book
Killviagh	Gigginstown	Busby Elizabeth	corn	-	-	-	-	1840	-	sv/moc	V.O.Field Book
Killviagh	Gigginstown	-	corn	-	-	-	-	1663	-	sv/moc	Sm.PapersChas.II
Lickbla	Gilbertstown	Mulvey Nicholas	corn	-	-	-	-	1811	-	sv/moc	LWT. Nich.M
Killviagh	Gigginstown	-	corn & corn kiln	-	-	-	-	1838	-	6"os/	13
Killviagh	Gigginstown	Dermody William	corn	-	-	-	-	-	11x2x13	vmb/	21
Killviagh	Gigginstown	Tormey Edward	corn	-	13a.	-	-	-	-	gr/	-
Lickbla	Gilbertstown	Callaghan	corn & tuck	-	-	-	-	-	-	sv/moc	-
Lickbla	Gilbertstown	Callaghan Matthew	corn	-	60a.	-	-	-	-	gr/	-
Lickbla	Gilbertstown	Hampson	mill	-	-	-	Hampson - Napper	-	-	dd/	99 481 70117
Lickbla	Gilbertstown	Mulvey	corn	-	-	-	-	-	-	sv/moc	-
Lickbla	Gilbertstown	Pollard Hampson	corn & tuck	-	-	-	Pollard - Stott	-	-	dd/	62 381 12326
Lickbla	Gilbertstown	Pollard Hampson :	mill	-	-	-	Pollard Hampson Dillon :	1734	Marr. 28 Aug.	dd/	93 508 66580
Lickbla	Gilbertstown	Pollard H'son Lettice :	corn & tuck	-	-	-	Pollard H L - Mervyn Arthur :	1734	L&R 21 May	dd/	79 38 54404
Kilkenny West	Glassan	-	corn & mill pond	-	-	-	-	1838	-	6"os/	22
Bunown	Glassan	Brackan Thomas	corn	-	-	-	-	-	14x3x1	vmb/	21
Bunown	Glassan	Carty William	corn	-	-	-	-	1840	-	sv/moc	V.O.Field Book
Bunown	Glassan	Manny Patrick	corn	-	0-1-0	-	-	-	-	gr/	-
Kilkenny West	Glassan	Wiley Alex	corn	-	-	-	-	-	13x3x8	vmb/	21
Kilkenny West	Glassan (south)	N/ Glassan PO	corn & corn kiln	-	-	-	-	1838	-	6"os/	22
St Marys	Glenidan	McDaniel Thomas	corn & kiln	-	42a.	-	-	-	-	gr/	-
Kilcurry	Gormanstown	Tormey Edward	corn & tuck	-	15a.	-	-	-	-	gr/	-
Kilcurry	Gormanstown	Tormey Mary	corn	-	-	-	-	-	15x3x11	vmb/	21
Kilcurry	Gormanstown	Tormey Mary	tuck	-	-	-	-	-	12x1x11	vmb/	21
Noughval	Gortmore	Langstaff	threshing	-	-	-	-	1840	-	sv/moc	V.O.Field Book
Noughval	Gortmore	Dillon Richard	mill	-	-	-	-	1619	-	sv/moc	Inquis.Jac.I.
Killucan	Grangemore	Weir John	threshing	-	-	-	-	1840	-	sv/moc	V.O.Field Book
Castletowndelvin	Grangestown	-	corn & tuck	-	-	-	-	-	-	sv/moc	-
Castletowndelvin	Grangestown	E/ R. Dee	corn & kiln	-	-	-	-	1838	-	6"os/	8
Castletowndelvin	Grangestown	E/ R. Dee	tuck	-	-	-	-	1838	-	6"os/	8
Castletowndelvin	Grangetown	Martin Thomas	corn	-	-	-	-	-	12x2x5	vmb/	21
Killucan	Grehanstown	Leavy Patrick	corn	-	63a.	-	-	-	-	gr/	-
Ballymore	Harrystown	Farrell John	cleaning wheel	-	-	-	-	-	12x2x12	vmb/	21
Ballymore	Harrystown	Farrell John	flour	-	-	-	-	-	14x4x14	vmb/	21
Killucan	Hightown	-	corn	-	-	-	-	-	-	sv/moc	-
Killucan	Hightown	Flynn Peter	corn & kiln	-	141a.	-	-	-	-	gr/	-

PARISH	TOWNLAND	MILLER	TYPE	HOUSE	Land	£Val	PROPRIETORS	Date	WHEEL etc.	Record	Ref.
Killucan	Hightown :	-	corn & corn kiln	-	-	-	-	1838	-	6"os/	27
Killucan	Hightown :	Landys Patrick :	mill	-	-	-	Landys P - Whyte Mark :	1744	-	dd/	116 49 79387
bo. Fertullagh	Hill	Pollard Hampson Letti	mill	-	-	-	Pollard H L - Mervyn Arthur :	1734	L&R 21 May	dd/	79 38 54404
bo. Fertullagh	Kibber	Rochfort Robert	mill	-	-	-	Rochfort R - Sandys Edwin	1731	-	dd/	65 46 46404
bo. Fertullagh	Kibber	Rochfort Robert	mill	-	-	-	Rochfort R - Moore Henry :	1731	-	dd/	70 58 47341
bo. Fertullagh	Kibber	Rochfort Robert :	mill	-	-	-	Rochfort - Molesworth Lord	1736	5 Aug.	dd/	84 208 59565
bo. Fertullagh	Kibber	Rochfort Robert :	mill	-	-	-	Rochfort R - Bonning Fran	1736	Lse. 16 Apl.	dd/	92 2 83658
Kilbeggan	Kilbeggan	-	corn & tuck	-	-	-	-	-	-	sv/moc	-
Kilbeggan	Kilbeggan	- on R. Brosna	mill	-	-	-	-	-	-	1"os/	109
Kilbeggan	Kilbeggan	Dowdall	mill	-	-	-	Dowdall - Nevill	-	-	dd/	157 163 104297
Kilbeggan	Kilbeggan	Horan William	mill & kiln	-	0-1-15	-	-	-	-	gr/	-
Kilbeggan	Kilbeggan	Lambert Charles	mill	-	-	-	Lambert C - Lambert Gus :	1749	-	dd/	109 208?75977
Kilbeggan	Kilbeggan	Lambert Charles :	mill	-	-	-	Lambert C - Rochfort Geo :	1743	L&R. 4 Feb.	dd/	110 44 78588
Kilbeggan	Kilbeggan	Rochfort George :	mill	-	-	-	Rochfort George - Lambert :	1746	L&R. 4 Jne.	dd/	115 44 79210
Kilbeggan	Kilbeggan	Lambert Oliver	tuck & corn	-	-	-	-	1618	-	sv/moc	Inquis.Jac.I.
Kilbeggan	Kilbeggan	Locke John	distillery	-	-	-	-	-	-	gr/	-
Kilbeggan	Kilbeggan	Fallon Charles	distillery	-	-	-	-	1841	-	sv/moc	"Wme. Guardian'
Kilbeggan	Kilbeggan	N/ Church	distillery (small)	-	-	-	-	1838	-	6"os/	38
Kilbeggan	Kilbeggan	on R. Brosna	distillery	-	-	-	-	1838	-	6"os/	38
Kilbeggan	Kilbeggan	Caddle William :	malt ?	-	-	-	-	1840	-	sv/moc	V.O.Field Book
Kilbeggan	Kilbeggan	Pole	mill	-	-	-	Pole - Berry	-		dd/	304 430 205682
Kilbeggan	Kilbeggan	Rochfort	mill	-	-	-	Rochfort - Lambert	-	-	dd/	115 44 79210
Kilbeggan	Kilbeggan	Usher	mill	-	-	-	Usher - Owen	-		dd/	118 270 80712
Kilbeggan	Kilbeggan	Mullen James G	brewery	-	-	-	-	1840	-	sv/moc	V.O.Field Book
Kilcleagh	Kilbillaghan	Dillon Robert	mill	-	-	-	-	1611	-	sv/moc	Inq.
Kilcleagh	Kilbillaghan	Golden James	corn	-	5-1-2	-	-	-	-	gr/	-
Kilbixy	Kilbixy	-	-	-	-	-	-	-	-	sv/moc	-
Kilcleagh	Kilcleagh	Daly Joseph M	tuck	-	-	-	-	-	-	sv/moc	Arch. Surv.No.20
Kilcumreragh	Kilcumreragh	Buckley Timothy	corn	-	95a.	-	-	-	-	gr/	-
Kilcumreragh	Kilcumreragh	SW/ B,naberna Vge.	corn & corn kiln	-	-	-	-	1838	-	6"os/	31
Templeoran	Kildallan North	-	corn & tuck	-	-	-	-	-	-	6"os/	18
Kilkenny Weat	Kilfaughny	-	corn	-	-	-	-	1650	-	sv/moc	Inq. Car. I
Ballyloghloe	Kill	Darcy William J	mill	-	-	-	-	1838	-	sv/moc	"Wme. Guardian'
Killagh	Killagh	- S/ Killagh Br.	corn & corn kiln	-	-	-	-	1838	-	6"os/	13
Killviagh	Killagh	Hagarty Maurice	corn & tuck	-	79a.	-	-	-	-	gr/	-
Killviagh	Killagh	Haggerty John	corn	-	-	-	-	-	10x2x10	vmb/	21
Killviagh	Killagh	Haggerty John	tuck	-	-	-	-	-	10x2x10	vmb/	21
Killviagh	Killagh	S/ Killagh Br.	tuck	-	-	-	-	1838	-	6"os/	13
Castlet`nkindalen	Killalea	-	-	-	-	-	-	-	-	sv/moc	-
Templeoran	Killdallan North	-	corn & tuck	-	-	-	-	-	-	6"os/	18
Kilcumreagh	Killeenboylegan	-	saw	-	-	-	-	-	-	sv/moc	-
Rathconell	Killynan	-	corn	-	-	-	-	-	-	sv/moc	-
Rathconell	Killynan	-	corn, dam & kiln	-	-	-	-	1838	-	6"os/	20
St Marys	Kilmacuagh	English Robert	corn	-	17a.	-	-	-	-	gr/	-
St Marys	Kilmacuagh	Martin Patrick	corn	-	18a.	-	-	-	-	gr/	-
St Marys	Kilmacuagh	SW Garrycastle Br.	corn & mill race	-	-	-	-	1838	-	6"os/	29
Tyfarnham	Kilmaglish	-	corn	-	-	-	-	-	-	sv/moc	-
Street	Kilmore	-	corn, kiln, mill po	-	-	-	-	1838	-	6"os/	2
Street	Kilmore	Carrigy John	corn kilns	-	1-1-0	-	-	-	-	gr/	-
Mullingar	Kilpatrick	-	corn	-	-	-	-	-	-	sv/moc	-
Mullingar	Kilpatrick	Daly Hugh	mill	-	22a.	-	-	-	-	gr/	-
Faughalstown	Kiltoom	-	corn	-	-	-	-	-	-	sv/moc	-
Rathgarve	Kinturk	Fitz-Symons Edwd	corn	-	-	-	-	1618	-	sv/moc	Inquis.Jac.I.

PARISH	TOWNLAND	MILLER	TYPE	HOUSE	Land	£Val	PROPRIETORS	Date	WHEEL etc.	Record	Ref.
Newtown	Knockycosker	-	bleach	-	-	-	-	-	-	sv/moc	-
Newtown	Knockycosker	-	corn	-	-	-	-	-	-	sv/moc	-
Newtown	Knockycosker	-	flour	-	-	-	-	-	-	sv/moc	-
Newtown	Knockycosker	-	scutch	-	-	-	-	-	-	sv/moc	-
Newtown	Knockycosker	Perry William	mill & kiln	-	57a.	-	-	-	-	gr/	-
Newtown	Knockycosker	Perry William	flour	-	-	-	-	1827	-	sv/moc	Wme. Journal'
Lickbla	Lickbla	-	bleach	-	-	-	-	1838	-	6"os/	3
Lickbla	Lickbla	-	flax	-	-	-	-	-	-	sv/moc	-
Lickbla	Lickbla	Booker George	corn	-	19a.	-	-	-	-	gr/	-
Lickbla	Lickbla	Booker George	flour	-	-	-	-	-	-	gr/	-
Lickbla	Lickbla	Fagan Thomas	bleach	-	295a.	-	-	-	-	gr/	-
Lickbla	Lickbla	Fagan Thomas	corn	-	-	-	-	-	-	gr/	-
Lickbla	Lickbla	NW/ Rockbrook Ho	corn	-	-	-	-	1838	-	6"os/	3
Lickbla	Lickbla	W/ church	flax	-	-	-	-	1838	-	6"os/	3
Street	Lismacaffry	Ranelagh Ld. Chas	mill	-	-	-	Ranelagh Ld - Webb Chas	1795	Lse. 10 Jul.	dd/	510 50 328591
Street	Lismacaffry	Ranelagh Lord	mill	-	-	-	Ranelagh - Gilligan	-	-	dd/	502 404 325641?
St Mary's	Lissywollen	Handcock Richd :	mill	-	-	-	Handcock R - Cooke Thos	1787	Lse. 14 Jne.	dd/	360 452 244404
St Mary's	Lissywollen	Holmes Gilbert :	mill	-	-	-	Holmes Gilbert - Tully Ross :	1774	-	dd/	400 123 263188
St Mary's	Lissywollen	Kelly Daniel :	mill	-	-	-	Kelly D - Cooke Thomas :	1700	Lse. 2 May	dd/	356 158 239083
St Mary's	Lissywollen	Palmer	mill	-	-	-	Palmer - Thomas	-	-	dd/	318 517 218701
Conry	Lockardstown	-	corn	-	-	-	-	-	-	sv/moc	-
Conry	Lockardstown	nr Clonown Vge.	corn, mill-stream	-	-	-	-	1838	-	6"os/	24
Wm	Loughanesker	- near Carrig Ho.	corn	-	-	-	-	-	-	1"os/	99
Killucan	Mill Land	-	flour	-	-	-	-	-	-	sv/moc	-
Killucan	Mill Land	N/ Riverstown R.	flour	-	-	-	-	1838	-	6"os/	27
Rathgarve	Millcastle	Cusack John	corn	-	-	-	-	-	horizontal	sv/moc	-
Killucan	Millerstown	-	no mill	-	-	-	-	1838	-	6"os/	20
Rathconrath	Milltown	-	corn	- preserved :	-	-	Karl Eppendorfer & Denise :	2004	-	pWEH	Cr
Churchtown	Milltown	-	corn	-	-	-	-	-	-	sv/moc	-
Faughalstown	Milltown	-	corn	-	-	-	-	-	-	sv/moc	-
Ballymore	Milltown	-	flour	-	-	-	-	-	-	sv/moc	-
Pass of Kilbride	Milltown	-	Milltown Village	-	-	-	-	1838	-	6"os/	33
Pass of Kilbride	Milltown	Levinge Mark A	corn	-	-	-	-	1808	-	sv/moc	Larkin Map
Pass of Kilbride	Milltown	Boyd George A	flour & corn	-	-	-	-	1837	-	sv/moc	Wme.Guardian'
Rathconrath	Milltown	-	no mill	-	-	-	-	1838	-	6"os/	17/18
Ballymore	Milltown	Blake John	corn	-	-	-	-	-	15x6x5	vmb/	21
Kilbride	Milltown	Dunne Thomas	corn	-	3-3-17	-	-	-	-	gr/	-
Kilbride	Milltown	Geraghty Andrew	corn & kiln	-	1-0-30	-	-	-	-	gr/	-
Drumraney	Milltown	Geraghty James	corn	-	-	-	-	-	11x2x8	vmb/	21
Kilbride	Milltown	Geraghty James	flour & corn	-	-	-	-	-	-	sv/moc	-
Pass of Kilbride	Milltown	SE/ Milltown Br.	flour (in ruins)	-	-	-	-	1838	-	6"os/	33
Ballymore	Milltown p/B'more	SE/ Baskin Br.	corn	-	-	-	-	1838	-	6"os/	23
Kilcleagh	Moate (nr Town)	-	corn	- blds. restored :	-	-	-	2001	-	mmSv	wh - Cc
Kilcleagh	Moate town	-	-	-	-	-	-	-	-	sv/moc	-
Kilcleagh	Moategranogue	Clibborn Thomas	corn	-	-	-	-	-	-	sv/moc	-
Kilcleagh	Moategranogue	Clibborn Thomas	frieze	-	-	-	-	-	-	sv/moc	-
Ardnurcher	Monaduff	-	corn	-	-	-	-	-	-	1"os/	99
Ardnurcher	Monaduff	-	mill	-	-	-	-	-	-	1"os/	-
Rahugh	Monasset	on Silver River	New Mill Bridge	-	-	-	-	1838	-	6"os/	40
Rahugh	Monasset :	no mill	mill pond	-	-	-	-	1838	-	6"os/	40
Rathconnell	Moneylea	Mitchell John	corn & kiln	-	1-1-20	-	-	-	-	gr/	-
Rathconnell	Moneylea	Mitchell John	corn	-	-	-	-	1828	-	sv/moc	Wme.Journal'
bo. Brawny	Monksland	Bridges Catherine : o	mill	-	-	-	Bridges C - Brown John :	1731	4 Jan.	dd/	68 141 47352

PARISH	TOWNLAND	MILLER	TYPE	HOUSE	Land	£Val	PROPRIETORS	Date	WHEEL etc.	Record	Ref.
bo. Corkery	Monksland	Brown	tuck	-	-	-	Brown - Mayo Lord	-	-	dd/	56 74 37822
bo. Brawny	Monksland	Brown John :	mill	-	-	-	Brown J - Cormick Richd :	1735	L&R. 1 Mar.	dd/	81 505 58507
bo. Corkery	Monksland	Cosby Pole :	tuck	-	-	-	Cosby W - Digby John :	1730	Conv. 16 Feb.	dd/	67 129 45546
bo. Corkery	Monksland	Digby John :	tuck	-	-	-	Digby Jn - French Robert	1730	L&R. 25 Nov.	dd/	65 24 45329
bo. Brawny	Monksland	Dodwell Mary Spin.	mill	-	-	-	Dodwell M - Warburton :	1727	L&R. 8 Feb.	dd/	68 142 47358
bo. Corkery	Monksland	Elphin Bo. of	tuck	-	-	-	Elphin Bo - Westenra	-	-	dd/	21 60 10767
bo. Brawny	Monksland	French	mill	-	-	-	French - Stone	-	-	dd/	70 109 47667
bo. Corkery	Monksland	Kenny	tuck	-	-	-	Kenny - Brown	-	-	dd/	64 70 42657
bo. Corkery	Monksland	Kenny Henry :	tuck	-	-	-	Kenny Henry - Brown Jn :	1726	Lse. 26 Nov.	dd/	52 42 33432
Castletowndelvin	Mooretown	-	watch tower	-	-	-	-	1838	-	6"os/	13
Killare	Mosstown	Clavin Laurence	corn & kiln	-	38a.	-	-	-	-	gr/	-
Killare	Mosstown	Judge & Wife	mill	-	-	-	Judge - Carroll	-		dd/	137 348 93738
Killare	Mosstown	Judge & Wife	mill	-	-	-	Judge - Cary als Conagan	-		dd/	139 539 96068
Killare	Mosstown	Judge & Wife	mill	-	-	-	Judge - Casey	-		dd/	151?83 100504
Street	Mount Land	- near Street Vge.	corn	-	-	-	-	-	-	1"os/	-
Kilmicheal	Mountmurray	- S. side Goulden R.	mill	-	-	-	- (record map Geo. Marshall	1655)	-	sv/moc	(1)
Kilmicheal	Mountmurray	- S. side Goulden R.	mill	-	-	-	- (record map Geo. Marshall	1655)	-	sv/moc	(2)
St Marys	Moydrum	-	-	-	-	-	-	-	-	sv/moc	-
Templepatrick	Moyvore	Bonham Francis :	mills	-	-	-	Bonham F - Carty John :	1731	L&R. 12 Aug.	dd/	67 349 46514
Templepatrick	Moyvore	Burton	mills	-	-	-		1728	Mort. Mar. 1728	dd/	60 83 40004
Templepatrick	Moyvore	Carty John Dublin	mills	-	-	-	Carty John - Bonham Fran :	1728	Lse. Mar. 1728	dd/	60 105 40088
Templepatrick	Moyvore	Rochfort	mills	-	-	-	Rochfort - Moore	-	-	dd/	70 58 47344
Templepatrick	Moyvore	Rochfort Robert :	mills	-	-	-	Rochfort R - Moore Henry :	1731	L&R.5 Dec.173	dd/	70 58 47344
Templepatrick	Moyvore	Rochfort Robert :	mills	-	-	-	Rochfort R - Sandys Irwin	1731	-	dd/	65 461 46454
Templepatrick	Moyvore	Smith	mills	-	-	-	Smith - Carty	-	-	dd/	72 88 49864
Templepatrick	Moyvore	Smith James	mills	-	-	-	Smith James - Carty John :	1732	Mort. 23 Dec.	dd/	72 88 49864
Templepatrick	Moyvore	Smith James	mills	-	-	-	Smith James - Carty John :	-	-	dd/	60 117 40140
Templepatrick	Moyvore	Smith James	mills	-	-	-	Smith James - Carty John :	-	-	dd/	60 117 40140
Ballymore	Moyvoughly	Ennis John	tile m/fcty	-	7-3-3	-	-	-	-	gr/	-
Lickbla	Mullagh	-	corn	-	-	-		-	-	sv/moc	-
Lickbla	Mullagh	-	corn kiln	-	-	-	-	1838	-	6"os/	3
bo. Brawney	Mullamoran :	Baldwin Richard :	mills	-	-	-	Baldwin R - Piers John :	1739	L&R 21 Jul.	dd/	96 142 66884
bo. Brawney	Mullamoran :	Palmer	mills	-	-	-	Palmer - Stock	-		dd/	510 124 330559
Ballymore	Mullenmeehan	-	corn	-	-	-	-	-	-	1"os/	99
Ballymore	Mullenmeehan	Buckley Catherine	corn	-	-	-	-	-	12x2x13	vmb/	21
Ballymore	Mullenmeehan	Buckley Catherine	corn & kiln	-	39a.	-	-	-	-	gr/	-
Mullingar	Mullingar	-	flax	-	-	-	-	-	-	sv/moc	Wme.Guardian'
Mullingar	Mullingar	-	windmill	-	-	-	-	-	-	1"os/	99
Mullingar	Mullingar	-	Manor mills	-	-	-	-	1611	-	sv/moc	Inquis.Jac.I.
Mullingar	Mullingar	Fagan Mrs.	Manor mills	-	-	-	-	-	-	sv/moc	-
Mullingar	Mullingar	- St Colman`s Mill	corn	-	-	-	-	-	-	sv/moc	-
Mullingar	Mullingar	- (at Jail)	corn	-	-	-	-	-	-	sv/moc	-
Mullingar	Mullingar	- (at Jail)	thread	-	-	-	-	1827	-	sv/moc	Rep. Gaols Inspr.
Mullingar	Mullingar	- at Loretto Convent	windmill	-	-	-	-	-	-	sv/moc	-
Mullingar	Mullingar	Daly James	corn & tuck	-	0-1-30	-	-	-	-	gr/	-
Mullingar	Mullingar	on R. Brosna	tuck	-	-	-	-	1838	-	6"os/	19
Mullingar	Mullingar & Town	N/ Barrack St.	corn	-	-	-	-	1838	-	6"os/	19
Mullingar	Mullingar Town :	-	flax	-	-	-		1865	-	dd/	
Mullingar	Mullingar Town	- The Freyer's	Mill	-	-	-	Forbes - Sagan	-	-	dd/	52 263 34512
Mullingar	Mullingar Town	Daly James	corn & tuck	Friars Mill	-	-	-	1650	-	sv/moc	Allen's Map
Mullingar	Mullingar Town	Fitzgerald	old brewery	-	-	-	-	-	-	gr/	-
Mullingar	Mullingar Town	Midland Railway Co.	Friars Mill	-	-	-	M R Co - Greville Baron	1895	-	dd/	1895 9 290
Mullingar	Mullingar Town :	Johnson & Co. Ltd.	old brewery	-	-	-	Johnson - Downes Chr	1897	-	dd/	1897 69 36
Mullingar	Mullingar Town :	Forbes	mill	-	-	-	Forbes - Sagan	-	-	dd/	52 263 34512
Noughaval	Mullinmeehan	-	corn	-	-	-	-	-	-	sv/moc	-
Multyfarnham	Multyfarnham	- (at Friary)	corn	-	-	-	-	-	-	sv/moc	-
Multyfarnham	Multyfarnham	Gaynor	mills	-	-	-	Gaynor - Gaynor	-	-	dd/	53 129 34739
Multyfarnham	Multyfarnham	Gaynor	mills	-	-	-	Gaynor - Reynell	-	-	dd/	63 297 43627

PARISH	TOWNLAND	MILLER	TYPE	HOUSE	Land	£Val	PROPRIETORS	Date	WHEEL etc.	Record	Ref.
Kilkenny West	near Annagh Ho.	- on Breenstord R.	mill	-	-	-	-	-	-	1"os/	98
Newtown	Newtownlow	Mageoghegan Hugh	mill	-	-	-	-	-	-	sv/moc	-
Noughaval	Noughaval	Dawson	mill	-	-	-	Dawson - Robinson	-		dd/	159 247 106830
Noughaval	Noughaval	Harman	mill	-	-	-	Harman - Morgan	-		dd/	148 299 99665
Noughaval	Noughaval	Hoar James L	corn	-	-	-	-	-	12x4x4	vmb/	21
Noughaval	Noughaval	Longworth Frances	mill	-	170a.	-	-	-	-	gr/	-
Noughaval	Noughaval	Longworth Frances	old mill	-	-	-	-	-	-	gr/	-
Dysart	Nure	-	-	-	-	-	-	-	-	sv/moc	-
Dysart	Nure or Lillyput	-	corn kiln	-	-	-	-	1838	-	6"os/	32
Castlelost	Oldtown	Kelly Matthew	-	-	-	-	-	1832	-	sv/moc	Voters List
Mayne	Pakenham Hall	Longford Earl	saw	-	-	-	-	-	-	sv/moc	V.O. Field Book
Templeoran	Parcellstown	Fitzsimons	mill	-	-	-	Fitzsimons - Stearne	-	-	dd/	31 215 18804
Templeoran	Parcellstown	Smith	mill	-	-	-	Smith - Fitzsimons	-	-	dd/	31 195 18746
Templeoran	Parcellstown	Stearne	mill	-	-	-	Stearne - Smith	-	-	dd/	43 23 27113
Templeoran	Parcellstown	Tighe	mill	-	-	-	Tighe - Tighe	-	-	dd/	41 507 27114
Templeoran	Parcelstown	-	mill	-	-	-	-	-	-	1"os/	99
Templeoran	Parcelstown	Gormley Edward	corn	-	-	-	-	-	12x1x14	vmb/	21
Tyfarnham	Parsonstown	-	corn	-	-	-	-	-	-	1"os/	99
Drumraney	Pass of Kilbride	Cole Catherine	corn	-	44a.	-	-	-	-	gr/	-
Drumraney	Pass of Kilbride	Cole Catherine	corn	-	-	-	-	-	10x3x10	vmb/	21
Mullingar	Pettitswood	-	mill	-	-	-	-	-	-	sv/moc	-
Portnashangan	Piercefield	- S. side Goulden R.	mill	-	-	-	- (record map Geo. Marshal	1655)	-	sv/moc	(1)
Portnashangan	Piercefield	- S. side Goulden R.	mill	-	-	-	- (record map Geo. Marshal	1655)	-	sv/moc	(2)
Castlelost	Piercetown	- near Hilltown Ho.	mill	-	-	-	-	-	-	1"os/	-
Killare	Rackvara	- near Mosstown Ho	mill	-	-	-	-	-	-	1"os/	99
Castlelost	Rahanine	Kelly Matthew	corn	-	122a.	-	-	-	-	gr/	-
Killucan	Raharney Little	-	corn	-	-	-	-	-	-	sv/moc	-
Killucan	Raharney Little	E. of R. Deel	corn & corn kiln	-	-	-	-	1838	-	6"os/	21
Killucan	Raharney Little	Keefe Christopher	mill	-	54a.	-	-	-	-	gr/	-
Newtown	Rahinmore	-	corn & tuck, kiln	-	-	-	-	1838	-	6"os/	38
Newtown	Rahinmore	Hackett Thomas	corn & tuck	-	5a.	-	-	-	-	gr/	-
Rahugh	Rahugh	-	-	-	-	-	-	-	-	sv/moc	-
Roscommon	Ranelagh :	- on Athlone Bridge	distillery	-	-	-	-	1838	-	6"os/	29
Roscommon	Ranelagh :	- W. side R. Shanno	distillery	-	-	-	-	1838	-	6"os/	29
Kilbixy	Rath	-	Caher Corn Mill	-	-	-	-	1838	-	6"os/	11
Kilbixy	Rath	West James	corn	-	-	-	-	-	13x3x3	vmb/	21
Kilbixy	Rath	West Thomas Wm	corn & kilns	-	63a.	-	-	-	-	gr/	-
Leny	Rathbennett	Hampson Pollard	mill	-	-	-	Pollard Hampson - Mervyn	-	-	dd/	79 38 54404
Leny	Rathbennett	Moran Michael :	mill	-	-	-	Moran M - Wilson Andrew :	1708	L&R 10 Mar.	dd/	7 71 1639
Lenny	Rathbennett	Pollard Hampson :	mill	-	-	-	Pollard Hampson Dillon :	1734	Inter Mg. 28 Au	dd/	93 508 66580
Lenny	Rathbennett	Pollard Hamson :	mill	-	-	-	Pollard Hampson - Latouche	-		dd/	208 237 138191
Lenny	Rathbennett	Pollard Urquhart :	mill	-	-	-	Pollard H - Alexander Robt :	1888		dd/	1888 33 273
Leny	Rathbennett	Roddy	mill	-	-	-	Roddy - Wilsin	-	-	dd/	7 71 1640
Castlet`nkindalen	Rathdrishogue	Keenan John	corn	-	-	-	-	1840	-	sv/moc	V.O.Field Book
Rathconrath	Rathduff	Dillon Robert	-	-	-	-	-	1611	-	sv/moc	Inquis.Jac.I.
Multifarnham	Rathganny	Nugent Peter Sir	corn	-	-	-	-	1832	-	sv/moc	Voters List
Rathaspick	Rathowen	- nr Loughanstown	mill	-	-	-	-	-	-	1"os/	-
Killucan	Rathwire Lower	Badge Thomas :	mill	-	-	-	Badge T - Hamilton Baker :	1799		dd/	524 270 348895
Killucan	Rathwire Lower	Larken	mill	-	-	-	Larken - Hylan	-		dd/	585 511 413921
Killucan	Rathwire U.& Lr.	Frayne	mill	-	-	-	Frayne - Purdon	-		dd/	259 132 165780
Killucan	Rathwire U.& Lr.	Longford Lady	mill	-	-	-	Longford Lady - Lord	-		dd/	243 481 68?651
Killucan	Rathwire U.& Lr.	Packenham	mill	-	-	-	Packenham - Kildare Earl	-		dd/	96 373 68353
Killucan	Rattin	Hagarty Denis	mill	-	56a.	-	-	-	-	gr/	-
Killucan	Rattin	S/ Vge. cross	corn & corn kiln	-	-	-	-	1838	-	6"os/	34
Killucan	Riverstown	Hannon Benj	mill	-	-	-	Hannon Benj - Hannon Mary	1886		dd/	1886 53 96
Killucan	Riverstown	Hibernian Bank Ltd.	mill	-	-	-	Hibernian - Hannan Benjamir	1885		dd/	1885 37 151
Killucan	Riverstown	Purdon	mill	-	-	-	Purdon - Geale	-		dd/	349 372 234708
Killucan	Riverstown	Purdon	mill	-	-	-	Purdon - Falkiner	-		dd/	349 373 234707

PARISH	TOWNLAND	MILLER	TYPE	HOUSE	Land	£Val	PROPRIETORS	Date	WHEEL etc.	Record	Ref.
Moylescan	Rochford Dems.	-	corn & tuck	-	-	-	-	-	-	sv/moc	-
Moylescan	Rochford Dems.	Daly Matthew	corn	-	-	-	-	-	10x2x13	vmb/	21
Moylescan	Rochford Dems.	Daly Matthew	corn & kiln	-	9a.	-	-	-	-	gr/	-
Moylescan	Rochford Dems.	on R. to L. Ennell	corn, corn kiln, pc	-	-	-	-	1838	-	6"os/	26
Rathgarve	Rockbrook	- nr Castlepollard	corn	-	-	-	-	-	-	1"os/	-
Rathconrath	Rowlandstown	-	corm	-	-	-	-	1838	-	6"os/	17
Rathconrath	Rowlandstown	Nairn William	corn	-	-	-	-	-	12x2x11	vmb/	21
Rathconrath	Rowlandstown	Nairn William	tuck	-	-	-	-	-	122x11 1 stocl	vmb/	21
Russagh	Russagh	-	corn & kiln	-	-	-	-	1838	-	6"os/	6
Russagh	Russagh	-	tuck	-	-	-	-	1838	-	6"os/	6
Russagh	Russagh	Daly John	corn	-	-	-	-	-	12x2x9	vmb/	21
Russagh	Russagh	Daly Nicholas	corn & kiln	-	13a.	-	-	-	-	gr/	-
Russagh	Russagh	Daly Nicholas	tuck	-	13a.	-	-	-	-	gr/	-
Taghmon	Sheefin	Coffey Ann	corn	-	76a.	-	-	-	-	gr/	-
Taghmon	Sheefin	SSW Crokedwood Br.	corn, kiln, mill rac	-	-	-	-	1838	-	6"os/	12
Taghmon	Sraduff	W/ Rockfield Ho.	mill	-	-	-	-	1838	-	6"os/	31
Castlet`nkindalen	Sraneg	-	tuck	-	-	-	-	1841	-	6"os/	31
Castlet`nkindalen	Sraneg	M`Laughlin Martin	tuck	-	-	-	-	-	-	gr/	-
Castlet`nkindalen	Sraneg	M`Laughlin Martin	corn	-	-	-	-	-	-	gr/	-
Castlet`nkindalen	Sraneg	M`Laughlin Patrick	corn	-	-	-	-	-	-	gr/	-
Castlet`nkindalen	Sraneg	M`Laughlin Patrick	tuck	-	-	-	-	-	-	gr/	-
Mulingar	Stokestown	Kerrigan Michael	corn	-	26a.	-	-	-	-	gr/	-
Mullingar	Stokestown	NE/ Dysart Ho.	corn & mill dam	-	-	-	-	1838	-	6"os/	25
Castlet`nkindalen	Stradduff	-	corn & tuck	-	-	-	-	-	-	sv/moc	-
Castlet`nkindalen	Stradduff	Clavin James	corn	(1B) 25x20x17 :	-	-	-	-	o`shot 11.6x1.8	hob/	5.2144
Castlet`nkindalen	Stradutt	Colgan Marcus	old mill	(1C) 41x20x16.6 :	-	-	-	-	- mc/y gone	hob/	5.2144
Castlet`nkindalen	Stradduff	Jessop William	corn	(2B) 31x21.6x10 :	-	-	-	-	o`shot 13x3x -	hob/	5.2144
Ardnurcher	Streamstown	-	windmill	-	-	-	-	-	-	sv/moc	-
Ardnurcher	Syonan	(no mill)	mill pond	-	-	-	-	1838	-	6"os/	4
Ardnurcher	Syonan	NE/ Syona Castle	corn & mill dam	-	-	-	-	1838	-	6"os/	31
Ardnurcher	Syonan	Walsh Bridget	corn & kiln	-	-	-	-	-	-	gr/	-
Ardnurcher	Syonan	Walsh Thomas	corn & kiln	-	-	-	-	-	-	gr/	-
Taghmon	Taghmon	-	corn & tuck	-	-	-	-	-	-	sv/moc	-
Wm	Tang	- on Tang R.	mill	-	-	-	-	-	-	1"os/	98
St Feighin`s	Templanstown	-	corn	-	-	-	-	-	-	sv/moc	-
St Feighin`s	Templanstown	Fagan John	mill & kiln	-	99a.	-	-	-	-	gr/	-
Templepartick	Templepartick	Sherrif of County	mill	-	-	-	Sherrif - Darcy	-		dd/	117 488 81550
Templepatrick	Templepatrick	Sherrif of County	mill	-	-	-	Darcy - Smith	-		dd/	117 489 81551
Templepatrick	Templepatrick	Kean James	corn & kiln	-	72a.	-	-	-	-	gr/	-
Templepatrick	Templepatrick	S/ Vge. Moyvore	corn, kiln, mill rac	-	-	-	-	1838	-	6"os/	17
Templepatrick	Templepatrick	Wynne Thomas	corn	-	-	-	-	-	15x4x8	vmb/	21
Killucan	Thomastown	-	corn	-	-	-	-	-	-	sv/moc	-
Killucan	Thomastown	Purdon Edward :	corn	-	-	-	Purdon Ed- Geale Daniel :	1784		dd/	358 429 241659
Killucan	Thomastown	Purdon	mill	-	-	-	Purdon - Gaynor	-		dd/	556?46 384740
Street	Tinode	-	corn	-	-	-	-	-	-	sv/moc	-
Westmeath	Tld? (in M17)	SW/ Washford Br.	flour	-	-	-	-	1838	-	6"os/	24
Taghmon	Toberaquill		horizontal	-	-	-	-	-	-	sv/moc	-
Ballymoran	Tobercormick	-	woollen	-	-	-	-	-	-	1"os/	99
Ballymoran	Tobercormick	Murtagh Michael	mill buildings	-	-	-	-	-	-	gr/	-
Ballymoran	Tobercormick	Watson James	flour	-	-	-	-	-	28x6x28 3 pr st	vmb/	21
Foyran	Togher	-	corn	-	-	-	-	-	-	sv/moc	-
Westmeath	Tolcan	Dillon Theobald	mill	-	-	-	-	1610	-	sv/moc	Jac.1.Reg (1)
Kilcleagh	Toorydonnellin	Fox Margaret	corn	-	42a.	-	-	-	-	gr/	-
bo. Fertulla	Townland ?	Fryer's	Mill	-	-	-	Fagan - Peppard	-	-	dd/	422 113 275628
bo. Rathgunrath	Tubber	Farrell James	mill	-	-	-	Farrell J - Reilly Margaret	1886		dd/	1886 7 40
Kilpatrick	Tuitestown	Tormey Edward	corn & kiln	-	86a.	-	-	-	-	gr/	-
Kilkenny West	Tullaghan	Dillon Theobald	mill	-	-	-	-	-	-	sv/moc	Inq. Car. I
Ballyloughloe	Tullaghgeeragh	W/ Moate Ch	distillery	-	-	-	-	1838	-	6"os/	30

PARISH	TOWNLAND	MILLER	TYPE	HOUSE	Land	£Val	PROPRIETORS	Date	WHEEL etc.	Record	Ref.
Ballyloughloe	Tullynageeragh	-	distillery	-	-	-	-	-	-	sv/moc	
Clonfad	Tyrellspass	Grant William Jun. :	mill	-	-	-	Grant W - Wetherell John :	1736	L&R. 19 Nov.	dd/	83 480 59876
Clonfad	Tyrellspass	Rochfort Robert :	mills	-	-	-	Rochfort R - Sandys Irwin :	1731	-	dd/	65 461 46404
Clonfad	Tyrellspass	Rochfort Robert :	mill	-	-	-	Rochfrot R - Moore Henry :	1731	L&R. 5 Dec.	dd/	70 58 46344
Clonfad	Tyrellspass	Rochfort Robert :	mill	-	-	-	Rochfort - Molesworth Lord :	1736	L&R. 19 Nov.	dd/	84 208 59565
Clonfad	Tyrrellspass	-	linen / cotton	-	-	-	-	-	-	sv/moc	-
Drumraney	Walderstown	Townsend Thomas	mill	-	-	-	-	1810	-	sv/moc	Bog. Map
Enniscoffey	Windmill or Blackislands		no mill	-	-	-	-	1838	-	6"os/	33

PARISH	TOWNLAND	MILLER	TYPE	HOUSE	Land	£Val	PROPRIETORS	Date	WHEEL etc.	Record	Ref.
Moyacomb	Abbeydown	- on Derry R.	mill (in ruins)	-	-	-	-	-	-	6"os/	4
Tellarought	Aclamon	- near Aghboy Br.	mill	-	-	-	-	-	-	1"os/	168
Tellarought	Aclamon	O`Brien Laurence	corn	-	-	-	-	-	11x2x11	vmb/	24
Tellarought	Aghclare	- nr Teliarought Br.	mill	-	-	-	-	-	-	1"os/	168
Ambrosetowm	Ambrosetown	-	mill	-	-	-	-	-	-	1"os/	169
Ambrosetowm	Ambrosetown	-	windmill	-	-	-	-	-	-	1"os/	169
Ambrosetowm	Ambrosetown	NW/ Bridge	corn & mill race	-	-	-	-	1841	-	6"os/	46
Ambrosetowm	Ambrosetown	NW/ Bridge	windmill	-	-	-	-	1841	-	6"os/	46
Ambrosetowm	Ambrosetown	Parle John	corn	-	-	-	-	-	17x2x18	vmb/	24
Ambrosetowm	Ambrosetown	Parle John	wind & water	circum. 53 ft x 22 :	-	-	-	1853	12x2x18 each mill :	hob/	5.2191
Ambrosetowm	Ambrosetown	White Matthew	corn	29x21x14 & :	-	-	-	-	11x2x11 2 pr st.	hob/	5.2191
Ambrosetowm	Ambrosetown :	Parle John	flour	-	-	-	-	-	- <1,000 barrels	lic/23	wh.meal
Taghmon	Ardenagh	- stream / Corock R.	mill x 2	-	-	-	-	-	-	1"os/	169
St Mary`s	Arnestown	- NW/ B'macar Br.	A'stown Corn Mill	-	-	-	-	-	-	6"os/	30
St Mary`s	Arnestown	Howlett Martin	corn	-	-	-	-	-	13x3x16	vmb/	24
St Mary`s	Arnestown	NW/ Arnestown Ho.	thrashing	-	-	-	-	1841	-	6"os/	34
St Mary`s	Arnestown	Roche Patrick	corn	-	-	-	-	-	10x3x12	vmb/	24
Carnew	Aska More	- Askamore	Corn Mill	-	-	-	-	-	-	6"os/	5
Carnew	Aska More	- on trib. to Mine R.	corn	-	-	-	-	-	-	1"os/	148
Carnew	Aska More	Byrnes James	oat	-	-	-	-	-	10x2x10	vmb/	24
Killann	Askinvillar	-	Devil's Mill	-	-	-	-	-	-	6"os/	18
Killann	Askinvillar Lr	Morris Martin	reaping hook	24x12x5.6 & :	-	-	-	1851	dia. 9ft. bkts 34 :	hob/	5.2178
Killann	Askinvillar Lr	Morrissey Martin	reaping hook	-	-	-	-	-	8x6x3	vmb/	24
Monart	Aughathlappa	- near mine shaft :	pulverising :	-	-	-	-	-	-	6"os/	19
Ballybrazil	Aughclare	-	corn	-	-	-	-	1841	-	6"os/	34
Ballybrazil	Aughclare	Cormick James	corn	-	-	-	-	-	14x1x14	vmb/	24
Kilmakeloge	Balekale	Young Edward	corn	-	-	-	-	-	14x3x12	vmb/	24
Kilturk	Ballask	NxW/ Kilmore Vge.	windmill	-	-	-	-	1841	-	6"os/	52
Kilnahue	Ballinacoola	- E/ Craanford Br.	carding	-	-	-	-	-	-	6"os/	6
Kilnahue	Ballinacoola	Murphy John	corn	-	-	-	-	-	11x3x5	vmb/	24
Kilnahue	Ballinacoola	Redmond Daniel	carding	(1B) 25x14x9 :	-	6-18	-	-	11x3.6x6 36 bkts. :	hob/	5.2240
Ballyvalden	Ballinaglogh	Tobin Patrick & Wm	carding, sp. & tuck	-	-	-	-	-	11x2x12 wheel & :	hob/	5.2151
Ballyvalden	Ballinamona	Connoy Denis	corn	-	-	-	-	-	11x2x12	vmb/	24
Clonmore	Ballinavary	- on Boro R.	saw	-	-	-	-	-	-	1"os/	158
Kilcormick	Ballincash Lower	-	corn	-	-	-	-	-	-	6"os/	21
Kilcormick	Ballincosh	Dempsey Miles	corn	-	-	-	-	-	16x5x13	vmb/	24
Carrick	Ballindinas	Leared Richard	flour	(1B) 48x24x42 :	-	-	-	-	13x5x6.6 float bds.:	hob/	5.2286
Carrick	Ballindinas	Leared Richard	flour	-	-	-	-	-	13x4x6	vmb/	24
Ballycarney	Ballingale	-	corn	-	-	-	-	-	-	6"os/	15
Ballycarney	Ballingale	Myles Joseph	corn	-	-	-	-	-	11x3x11	vmb/	24
Ballycarney	Ballingale	Myles Joseph	tuck	-	-	-	-	-	11x1x12	vmb/	24
Ballingly	Ballingly	Crosbie Thomas	corn	(1A)40x17x20	-	-	-	1852	20x3x20 o`shot :	hob/	5.2283
Toome	Ballintim	-	old corn mill	-	-	-	-	-	-	6"os/	11
Toome	Ballintim	Carton Patrick	corn & hook	- [no dims.]	-	2-10	-	-	mc/y removed :	hob/	5.2246
Toome	Ballintine	McCarthy Charles	corn & carding	-	-	-	-	-	12x2x11	vmb/	24
Ardamine	Ballintray	Dennies James	flour	-	-	-	-	-	13x4x6	vmb/	24
Ardamine	Ballintray	Dunne James	corn	30x19.6x16 & :	-	-	-	1846	13x3x5.6 breast :	hob/	5.2148
Ballyvaldon	Ballintubrid	-	corn & mill race	-	-	-	-	-	-	6"os/	28
Ballyvaldon	Ballintubrid	-	salt house	-	-	-	-	-	-	6"os/	28
Wexford	Ballinvella	-	windmill (ruins)	- conical tower :	-	-	-	-	-	iaa/	AI1711 os27.1.6
Kilmecridge	Ballyadam	- W/ B'adam Br.	Ballyadam Mill	-	-	-	-	-	-	6"os/	22
Kilmecridge	Ballyadam	Bolton William	corn	33.6x20.6x7.6 :	-	-	-	-	15x2.6x15 o`shot :	hob/	5.2161

PARISH	TOWNLAND	MILLER	TYPE	HOUSE	Land	£Val	PROPRIETORS	Date	WHEEL etc.	Record	Ref.
Kilmecridge	Ballyadam	Botten William	corn	-	-	-	-	-	15x3x15	vmb/	24
Ballyanne	Ballyanne	- E/ Anne's Br	corn & mill race	-	-	-	-	-	-	6"os/	29
Ballyanne	Ballyanne	- on R. Barrow	mill	-	-	-	-	-	-	1"os/	157
Ballyanne	Ballyanne	Roche John	corn & flour	34.6x22.0x23.6 :	14a	-	-	-	14x2.4x14 2 pr. st.	hob/	5.2170
Ballyanne	Ballyanne	Roche John	corn & flour	-	-	-	-	-	12x3x15	vmb/	24
Wexford	Ballybane *	Ram Abel	mill	-	-	-	Ram Abel - Trotter Thomas	1723	-	dd/	36 500 23809
Wexford	Ballybane *	Ram Abel	mill	-	-	-	Ram Abel - Ram Humphrey	1736	-	dd/	84 912 60510
Wexford	Ballybane *	Ram Humphry	mill	- (leased to) :	30a.	-	Ram Humphry - Ram Abel	1738	-	dd/	92 42 63851
Wexford	Ballybane *	Trotter Thomas	mill	-	-	-	Trotter Thos - Ram Stephen	1724	-	dd/	41 513 27165
Templeudigan	Ballybaun	- on Boro R.	corn	-	-	-	-	-	-	6"os/	18
Templeudigan	Ballybawn	Cuigley Patrick	corn	-	-	-	-	-	13x4x16	vmb/	24
Killisk	Ballybeg Small	N/ Garryhubbock Br.	Ballylucas Corn Mill	-	-	-	-	1841	-	6"os/	33
Kilscoran	Ballybing	Nun John	mill	-	-	-	Nun John - Hughes Pierce	1734	-	dd/	91 140 63679
Tikillen	Ballybogg Lower	- SE/ Castle Bridge	mill in ruins	-	-	-	-	-	-	6"os/	32
Tikillen	Ballyboggan Lr	Murphy Patrick	corn & flour	-	-	-	-	-	16x3x17	vmb/	24
Tikillin	Ballyboggan Lr	Murphy Patrick	flour	(1A) 11.6x20x19	-	-	-	1852	16x3x19	hob/	5.2281
Castle-ellis	Ballybought	Adams William	corn	-	-	-	-	-	13x2x14	vmb/	24
Castle-ellis	Ballybought	Addams William	corn	-	-	-	-	-	-	hob/	5.2152
Castle-ellis	Ballybregagh	- W/ B'bregagh Br.	corn & mill race	-	-	-	-	-	-	6"os/	27
Castle-ellis	Ballybregagh	Prendergast James	corn mill & kiln	30.0x16.6x8.6 :	-	-	-	-	11x2x11 wood :	hob/	5.2152
Castle-ellis	Ballybregagh	Prendergast Laurence	house & corn mill	55x18x7.6 & :	-	-	-	-	-	hob/	5.2152
Ballybrennan	Ballybrennan	SE/ Ballybrennan Ho.	windmill	-	-	-	-	1841	-	6"os/	48
Ballybrennan	Ballybrennan Big	-	windmill	8.8m dia (ext.) :	-	-	-	-	-	iaa/	AI1638 os48.1.2
Castle-ellis	Ballybugagh	Dempsey Honor	corn	-	-	-	-	-	12x3x12	vmb/	24
Ballycanew	Ballycanew	-	corn & flour	-	-	-	-	-	-	6"os/	16
Ballycanew	Ballycanew	Furney Henry	corn	-	-	-	-	1846	14x6x15	vmb/	24
Wex	Ballycanvan	-	grist - tidal mill	13m x 6.9m 3 bay :	-	-	-	-	- millpond filled :	iaa/	AI1712 os18.2.2
Newbawn	Ballyclemock	Martin Thomas	corn	(1B) 18z22.6x9.6 :	-	6-7	-	1851	12X3.6X12.6 :	hob/	5.2294
Newbawn	Ballyclemock	Martin Thomas	corn	-	-	-	-	-	11x3x11	vmb/	24
Newbawn	Ballyclemock	Martin Thomas	tuck	- (no house)	-	6-7		1851	- (m/cy only)	hob/	5.2294
Newbawn	Ballyclemock	Martin Thomas	tuck	-	-	-	-	-	8x1x11	vmb/	24
Newbawn	Ballyclemock	SW/ Cullenstown Br.	corn	-	-	-	-	1841	-	6"os/	35
Inch	Ballyconlore	-	corn	-	-	-	-	-	-	6"os/	3
Inch	Ballyconlore	Kinsella Andrew	corn & flax	-	-	-	-	-	12x4x -	vmb/	24
c	Ballyconlore	Kinshela Andrew	corn & flour	(1B) 35x21x20 :	16a.	rt/21	- Kinshela built all	-	13x4x13.6 1pr. st. :	hob/	5.2234
Templeshanboe	Ballycristal	- not working	corn	-	-	-	-	-	12x4x13	vmb/	24
Templeshanboe	Ballycrystal	- on Urrin R.	corn	-	-	-	-	-	-	6"os/	14
Templeshanboe	Ballycrystal	- on Urrin R.	mill race & weir	-	-	-	-	-	-	6"os/	14
Tintern	Ballycullane	- at Taylorstown Br.	corn	-	-	-	-	-	-	1"os/	169
Toome	Ballydaniel	- near Medop Hall	mill	-	-	-	-	-	-	1"os/	149
Wexford	Ballydrum	Lear James	mill	33.6x20.6x7.6 :	-	-	-	-	15x2.6x15 42 bkts.:	hob/	5.2161
Kilnamanagh	Ballyedmond	- on B'edmond R.	corn	-	-	-	-	-	-	6"os/	21
Kilnamanagh	Ballyedmond	- on B'edmond R.	mill	-	-	-	-	-	-	1"os/	149
Kilnamanagh	Ballyedmond	Ormond Duke James	mill	-	-	-	Ormond Jas - Burdett Thos	1697	-	dd/	88 488 63405
Kilnamanagh	Ballyedmond	Swiny Shapland	mill	-	-	-	Swiny S - Bolton Henry	1738	-	dd/	88 335 72788
Kilnamanagh	Ballyedmond	Virgors Sir William	mill	-	-	-	Vigors Wm - Alexander Jn	1738	-	dd/	88 488 63405
Kilnamanagh	Ballyedmond	Walsh Cath	corn	19x22x17 & :	-	-	-	-	12.6x3.6x13.2 :	hob/	5.2162
Clonleigh	Ballygalvert	- E/ Ballinvegga Br.	corn, pond & race	-	-	-	-	-	-	6"os/	24
Clonleigh	Ballygalvert	Devereux Widow	corn	-	-	-	-	-	9x2x12	vmb/	24
Owenduff	Ballygarvan	E/ Nash Bridge	Shannon's Mill & mill race		-	-	-	1841	-	6"os/	39
Kilscoran	Ballygarvey	-	mill	-	-	-	-	-	-	1"os/	170
Kilscoran	Ballygarvey	-	windmill	-	-	-	-	-	-	1"os/	170

PARISH	TOWNLAND	MILLER	TYPE	HOUSE	Land	£Val	PROPRIETORS	Date	WHEEL etc.	Record	Ref.
Owenduff	Ballygavan	Shannon Thomas	corn	-	-	-	-	-	13x3x10	vmb/	24
Kilrane	Ballygerry	NW Grenore Point	windmill stump	-	-	-	-	1841	-	6"os/	48
Rossdroir	Ballygillistown	- stream to Boro R.	corn (x2)	-	-	-	-	-	-	1"os/	158
St James & Dun.	Ballygow	-	mill	-	-	-	-	-	-	1"os/	168
St James & Dun.	Ballygow	- near Chapel	mill	-	-	-	-	-	-	1"os/	168
Gorey	Ballygullen	Warren John	thrashing m/c	(5A) 14x20x7.6 :	-	14-15	-	-	9.8x3x10 30 bkts. :	hob/	5.2243
St James & Dun.	Ballyhack	-	mill-stone quarry	-	-	-	-	-	- record states :	iaa/	AI1639 os44.6.5
Kilmore	Ballyharty	-	windmill (ruins)	4.85m dia (ext.) :	-	-	-	-	-	iaa/	AI1640 os47.13.5
Rossdroit	Ballyhighland	- at Demesne	threshing	-	-	-	-	1888	-	25"os/	19.09
Rossdroit	Ballyhighland	Howlett John	bone	-	-	-	-	-	15x2x16	vmb/	24
Lady`s Island	Ballyhit	-	mill	-	-	-	-	-	-	1"os/	170
Lady`s Island	Ballyhit	-	mill	-	-	-	-	1841	-	6"os/	48
Lady`s Island	Ballyhit	-	Old Windmill	-	-	-	-	-	-	1"os/	170
Lady`s Island	Ballyhit	Barry Thomas	corn	-	-	-	-	-	12x2x13	vmb/	24
Lady`s Island	Ballyhit	S?/ Kisha Bridge	windmill	-	-	-	-	1841	-	6"os/	48
Ballyhoge	Ballyhoge	Cliffe Anthony	threshing & corn	- [no mill meas.] :	-	-	-	-	30x7x- wheel :	hob/	5..2283
Castle-ellis	Ballyhought	-	corn & mill race	-	-	-	-	-	-	6"os/	27
Kilmakilloge	Ballykale	- N/ B'walter Bridge	corn	-	-	-	-	-	-	6"os/	12
Togmon	Ballykennigan	- Brownscastle Br.	mill	-	-	-	-	-	-	1"os/	169
Killiane	Ballykilliane	-	windmill stump	-	-	-	-	1841	-	6"os/	42
Inch	Ballylarkin	- SW/ B'lrkin Bridge	corn & kiln	-	-	-	-	-	-	6"os/	3
Inch	Ballylarkin	Doyle Peter	corn	(1B) 30.6x20.6x17 :	-	9-16	-	-	12x3.10x11 36 bkts.	hob/	5.2234/5
Inch	Ballylarkin	Doyle Peter	corn	-	-	-	-	-	13x4x12	vmb/	24
St Mulins	Ballyleigh	- on R. Slaney	Pollymont Bridge	-	-	-	-	-	-	6"os/	23
Kilrisk	Ballylucas	Lacy Nicholas	corn	-	-	-	-	-	12x2x12	vmb/	24
Ballymetty	Ballymetty	-	corn, pond & mill race		-	-	-	1841	-	6"os/	41
Ballymetty	Ballymetty	Coddy Alex	corn	-	-	-	-	-	11x2x12	vmb/	24
St Peters	Ballymorris	-	windmill (ruins)	6.6m dia. (ext.) :	-				-	25"os/	37 - 15
Ballyhuskard	Ballymoty More	- SW/ Ballymoty Br.	woollen factory	-	-	-	-	-	-	6"os/	20
Ballyvalden	Ballynaglogh	- N/ Blackwater Br.	corn	-	-	-	-	-	-	6"os/	27
Killilla	Ballynaglogh	Curtis Patrick	corn	-	-	-	-	-	12x3x13	vmb/	24
Ballyvalden	Ballynaglogh	Dobbin Patrick & Wm	machine	-	-	-	-	-	10x2x11	vmb/	24
Ballyvalden	Ballynaglogh	Dobbin Patrick & Wm	woollen	-	-	-	-	-	9x2x10	vmb/	24
Wexford	Ballynahask (3)	Connors Denis	corn	22x16x8	-	-	-	1852	overshot very old	hob/	5.2151
Templeshanboe	Ballynaminnan	- on Urrin R.	corn, pond & race	-	-	-	-	-	-	6"os/	19
Templeshanboe	Ballynaminnan	Farrell Robert	corn	-	-	-	-	-	11x2x12	vmb/	24
Ballyvalden	Ballynamona	-	mill	-	-	-	-	-	-	1"os/	159
Ballynaslaney	Ballynaslaney	- S/ Oilgate Cross Rd	corn	-	-	-	-	-	-	6"os/	32
Ballynaslaney	Ballynaslaney	Whitty Edward	corn	-	-	-	-	-	17x2x18	vmb/	24
Ballynaslaney	Ballynaslaney	Whitty James :	corn	(1C) 28x20x17	-	-	-	1845	19X3.6X19	hob/	5.2276
Kilcavan	Ballynestragh	Redmond John	corn & flour	-	-	-	-	-	14x4x15	vmb/	24
Kilcavan	Ballynestragh Dem.	-	corn & mill race	-	-	-	-	-	-	6"os/	7
Kilcavan	Ballynestragh Dem.	Redmond William	corn	(1A) 31.6x14x18 :	-	15.6	-	-	18x5x13.6 40 bkts.	hob/	5.2235
Kilmore	Ballyseskin	-	windmill	-	-	-	-	1841	-	6"os/	4
Kilmore	Ballyseskin	-	windmill (ruins)	4.7m dia height :	-	-	-	1749	-	iaa/	AI1642 os47.14.5
Kilmore	Ballyseskin	-	windmill (ruins)	4.7m dia height :	-	-	-	-	-	pOPW/	(AI1642)
Wexford	Ballyshancarry	Masterson John	mill	-	-	-	Masterson J - Murphy Patk.	1725	-	dd/	44 429 29973
Newbawn	Ballyshannon	Kavanagh Richard	carding	-	-	-	-	-	12x2x12	vmb/	24
Newbawn	Ballyshannon	Kavanagh Richard	corn	-	-	-	-	-	15x2x15	vmb/	24
Newbawn	Ballyshannon	W/ Ballyshannon Br.	corn	-	-	-	-	1841	-	6"os/	35
Carn	Ballysheen	-	windmill (ht. 52)	-	-	-	-	1841	-	6"os/	53
Carn	Ballysheen	- nr Carnsore Pt. :	windmill (corn)	- 3 sty (ruins) :	-	-	-	-	-	iaa/	AI1643 os53.3.4

PARISH	TOWNLAND	MILLER	TYPE	HOUSE	Land	£Val	PROPRIETORS	Date	WHEEL etc.	Record	Ref.
Carn	Ballysheen or :	- nr Carnsore Pt. :	windmill	- location :	-	-	-	-	-	1"os/	170
Tacumshin	Ballytory Upper	-	windmill	2.87m dia (int.)	-	-	-	-	-	iaa/	AI1644 os48.13.6
Kilcormick	Ballytracey	-	corn	-	-	-	-	1841	-	6"os/	16
Templeudigan	Ballywilliam	-	corn	-	-	-	-	-	-	6"os/	23
Templeudigan	Ballywilliam	- at Ballinyegga Br.	mill	-	-	-	-	-	-	1"os/	158
Templeudigan	Ballywilliam	Lawlor Michael	corn	-	-	-	-	-	12x3x13	vmb/	24
Templeudigan	Ballywilliam	Lawlor Michael	tuck	-	-	-	-	-	11x2x13	vmb/	24
Wexford	Banoge	- at Ballinatray Br.	mill	-	-	-	-	-	-	1"os/	149
Wexford	Banoge	- on Banoge R.	saw	-	-	-	-	-	-	1"os/	149
Wexford	Barglany *	Swiny Shapland	mill & mill lands	-	-	-	Swiny S - Denross John	1730	-	dd/	64 468 44731
Wexford	Barglany *	Swiny Shapland	mill & mill lands	-	-	-	Swiny S - Sandwith Wm	1731	-	dd/	65 441 46301
Wexford	Barglany *	Swiny Shapland	mill & mill lands	-	-	-	Swiny S - Sandwith Wm	1730	-	dd/	67 316 46300
Wexford	Barglany *	Swiny Shapland	mill & mill lands	-	-	-	Swiny S - Sandwith Henry	1734	-	dd/	77 264 53626
Wexford	Barglany *	Swiny William	mill & mill lands	-	-	-	Swiny Wm ano - Reilly Jas	1724	-	dd/	42 337 26564
Wexford	Barglany *	Swiny William	mill & mill lands	-	-	-	Swiny Wm - Bolton Henry	1717	-	dd/	64 66 42636
Tomhaggard	Bargy	-	windmill (ruins)	4.65m dia (ext.) :	-	-	-	-	-	iaa/	AI1645 os47.15.3
St Mary`s	Bawnmore	- SE/ Bishopsmill Br.	Bishop's Mill (ruins)	-	-	-	-	-	-	6"os/	29
St Mary`s	Bawnmore	- SE/ Bishopsmill Br.	corn	-	-	-	-	-	-	6"os/	29
St Mary`s	Bawnmore	- SE/ Bishopsmill Br.	tuck (in ruins)	-	-	-	-	-	-	6"os/	29
St Mary`s	Bawnmore	Dunphy John	corn	-	-	-	-	-	14x3x12	vmb/	24
Monart	Bessmount	Brown Catherine	corn	-	-	-	-	-	15x3x5	vmb/	24
St Helens	Bing	-	windmill (ruins)	4.05m dia (ext.) :	-	-	-	-	-	iaa/	AI1647 os48.8.5
St Helens	Bing	- near Greenor Pt.	Old Windmill	-	-	-	-	-	-	1"os/	170
St Helens	Bing	W/ Grenore Point	windmill	-	-	-	-	1841	-	6"os/	48
Ballyvaldon	Blackwater Town	-	mill	-	-	-	-	-	-	1"os/	159
Ballynaslaney	Bleachlands	-	no mill	-	-	-	-	-	-	hob/	5.2150
Ballynaslaney	Bleachlands	Kehoe Edward	old flax mill	16.6x16.0x12 :	-	-	-	-	9x2x- drives :	hob/	5.1250
Enniscorthy	Bloomfield	- on Urrin R.	tuck	-	-	-	-	-	-	1"os/	158
Wex	Bolabradda	- on Clonough R.	mill	-	-	-	-	-	-	1"os/	139
Rossdroit	Boolabaun	- nr Aughsallagh Br.	mill	-	-	-	-	-	-	6"os/	25
Rossdroit	Boolabawn	Kennedy Richard	corn & wheat	-	-	-	-	-	9x2x11	vmb/	24
Clonmore	Borrmount	- E/ Borromount Br.	Borrmount Bridge	-	-	-	-	-	-	6"os/	26
Clonmore	Borrmount	Caughy Martin	corn & flour	-	-	-	-	-	11x3x13	vmb/	24
Clonmore	Borrmount	Quigley michael	corn	39x22x10 :	-	-	-	-	11x2.6x - o`shot	hob/	5.2175
Wex	Bortins *	- at Kilmannan X	mill	-	-	-	-	-	-	1"os/	169
Clonmore	Bridgetown	-	mill	-	-	-	-	-	-	1"os/	169
Clonmore	Bridgetown North	NE/ bridge	corn	-	-	-	-	1841	-	6"os/	47
Dunganstown	Brittas	Kinsella J	Ballyconlore Mill	-	-	-	-	-	Cross flow 8kw	turb/	c1947
Eardowney	Broadway	- near Carnsore Pt.	Old Windmill	- location :	-	-	-	-	-	1"os/	170
Togmon	Browncastle	Fortune Edward	corn	-	-	-	-	-	11x3x11	vmb/	24
Togmon	Browncastle	Fortune Edward	tuck	-	-	-	-	-	10x2x11	vmb/	24
Togmon	Brownscastle	NW/ Brownscastle Br.	corn & mill race	-	-	-	-	1841	-	6"os/	36
Togmon	Brownscastle	NW/ Brownscastle Br.	tuck	-	-	-	-	1841	-	6"os/	36
St Iberin`s	Butlerstown	-	corn	-	-	-	-	1841	-	6"os/	48
St Iberin`s	Butlerstown	-	windmill	-	-	-	-	1841	-	6"os/	48
St Iberin`s	Butlerstown	Wall Alicia	corn	-	-	-	-	-	13x2x14	vmb/	24
Toame	Camolin	-	corn & flour	-	-	-	-	-	-	6"os/	11
Toame	Camolin	-	mill pond & sluice	-	-	-	-	-	-	6"os/	11
Toame	Camolin	Rock Samuel	corn	-	-	-	-	-	12x3x13	vmb/	24
Toame	Camolin	Rock Samuel	flour	-	-	-	-	-	12x3x13	vmb/	24
Bannow	Carrick	-	Old Windmill	-	-	-	-	-	-	1"os/	169
Bannow	Carrick	- N. / Bannow Bay	mill	-	-	-	-	-	-	1"os/	169

PARISH	TOWNLAND	MILLER	TYPE	HOUSE	Land	£Val	PROPRIETORS	Date	WHEEL etc.	Record	Ref.
Killurgan	Carrigmannan	Waddy William	corn	-	-	-	-	-	12x1x12	vmb/	24
Ardcavan	Castlebridge	- W. side River	flour	-	-	-	-	-	-	6"os/	32
Ardcavan	Castlebridge	- The Miller's Rest	corn	- part restored :	-	-	-	1998	-	mmSv/	wh - Cc
Ardcavan	Castlebridge	Breen Patrick	corn	(1B) 36.6x57x17.6	-	-	-	1845	24ft.	hob/	5.2274
Ardcavan	Castlebridge	Breen Patrick	corn	-	-	-	-	-	24x6x14	vmb/	24
Ardcavan	Castlebridge	Breen Patrick	flour	-	-	-	-	-	- 4 pair stones	vmb/	24
Whitechurch G.	Castlehayestown	McDaniel John	corn	-	-	-	-	-	10x1x14	vmb/	24
Whitechurch G.	Castlehayestown	N./ Camaross Vge.	corn, mill pond & race		-	-	-	1841	-	6"os/	36
Tikillin	Castlesow	Eveligh William	corn & tuck	-	-	-	Eveligh Wm - Williams Jos	1718	-	dd/	62 109 42113
Kilgorman	Castletown	- on Kilgorman R.	mill	-	-	-	-	-	-	1"os/	139
Kilgorman	Castletown	- SE/ Castletown Br.	corn & kiln	-	-	-	-	-	-	6"os/	7
Kilgorman	Castletown	Hanlon Lewis	corn	(1B) 33.6x21x20 :	-	10-3	-	-	13.6x4x4.6 36 bkts.	hob/	5.2737
Tintern	Castleworkhouse	SW/ Abbey Bridge	corn	-	-	-	-	1841	-	6"os/	45
Chapel	Chapel	-	windmill disused	7.6m dia (ext.) :	-	-	-	-	-	iaa/	AI1648 os52.5.5
Liskinfere	Clogh	-	corn & mill pond	-	-	-	-	-	-	6"os/	11
Liskinfere	Clogh	- near railway	mill	-	-	-	-	-	-	1"os/	149
Liskinfere	Clogh	Moles Thomas	corn	-	-	-	-	-	13x3x14	vmb/	24
Liskinfere	Clogh	Moles Thomas	corn & kiln	(1B) 47x20x12.6 :	18a.	8	-	1846	12x2.9x36 1 pr. st. :	hob/	5.2243
Wexford	Cloghnagleraghy *	Alcock William	mills	-	-	-	Alcock W - Alcock Wm Jun	1734	-	dd/	78 104 53663
Kilrush	Clohamon	- on R. Slaney	cotton	-	-	-	-	-	-	1"os/	148
Kilrush	Clohamon	- on R. Slaney	flour	-	-	-	-	-	-	1"os/	148
Kilrush	Clohamon	- E. side R. Slaney	cotton factory	-	-	-	-	-	-	6"os/	9
Kilrush	Clohamon	- E. side R. Slaney	flour	-	-	-	-	-	-	6"os/	9
Kilrush	Clohamon	Lewis William	cotton factory	-	-	-	-	-	15x15x6	vmb/	24
Rossminogue	Clonamona Lower	- SW/ Craanford Br.	corn	-	-	-	-	-	-	6"os/	6
Rossminogue	Clonamona Lower	Doyle John	corn	-	-	-	-	-	13x3x14	vmb/	24
Rossminogue	Clonamona Lower	Doyle John :	corn	(3B) 32x20x11 :	-	2-9	-	1845	13x3x13.6 48 bkts.	hob	5.2245
Kilturk	Clongaddy	-	windmill disused	5.15m dia (ext.) :	-	-	-	-	-	iaa/	AI1649 os52.5.3
Kilturk	Clongaddy	NE/ Brandy Cr. Rds.	windmill (ht 35)	-	-	-	-	1841	-	6"os/	52
Donaghmore	Clonganny	-	corn & mill race	-	-	-	-	-	-	6"os/	22
Donaghmore	Clonganny	-	mill pond	-	-	-	-	-	-	6"os/	22
Wexford	Clonganny	Connor Myles	mill	-	-	-	-	-	-	hob/	5.2153
Clonmines	Clonmines	-	windmill (ruins)	4.83m dia (ext.) :	-	-	-	-	-	iaa/	AI1650 os45.7.3
Kilcavan	Cloonagloose	- near Inch	old mill	mill & ho. good order		-	-	1998	-	mmSv/	wh - B
Kilcavan	Cloonagloose	McDermot Denis	reaping hook	(1A) 24x10.4x6 :	-	19/11	-	-	12x3x8 36 bkts. :	hob/	5.2235
Clonmore	Clough	- on Boro R.	corn & mill race	-	-	-	-	-	-	6"os/	25
Clonmore	Clough	Doyle James	corn	38.0x19.0x15.6 :	-	-	-	1846	12x3x13 36 bts :	hob/	5.2175
Clonmore	Clough	Doyle James	corn & flour	-	-	-	-	-	10x3x14	vmb/	24
Carn	Clough East	-	windmill corn	4.6m. dia. 5m :	-	-	-	-	-	iaa/	AI1651 os53.7.2
Carn	Clough East	NW Churchtown	windmill	-	-	-	-	1841	-	6"os/	53
St James	Coleman	Fitzgerald James	corn	-	-	-	-	-	16x2x17	vmb/	24
Carrick	Colestown	- near Wexford	Glenville Mills	-	-	-	-	-	-	1"os/	169
Ballyvalden	Cooladine	Doyle Matthew	corn	-	-	-	-	-	9x3x10	vmb/	24
Rossdroit	Coolamurry	-	mill	-	-	-	-	-	-	1"os/	158
St Mary`s	Coolatin	- on R. Glasha	corn	-	-	-	-	-	-	1"os/	148
St Mary`s	Coolatin	- on R. Glasha	spinning	-	-	-	-	-	-	1"os/	148
St Mary`s	Coolatin	Chalke Isaac	mill	-	-	-	Chalke Isaac - Vesey Theo	1726	-	dd/	48 396 31995
St Mary`s	Coolatin	Doyle James & Richd	corn	50.0x20.0x15.6 :	-	-	-	1852	9.9x2.9 wood :	hob/	5.2149
St Mary`s	Coolatin	Hogan Michael	carding	-	-	-	-	-	15x2x -	vmb/	24
St Mary`s	Coolatin	Hogan Michael	oat	-	-	-	-	-	14x4x12	vmb/	24
St Mary`s	Coolatin	Hogan Michael	tuck	-	-	-	-	-	10x2x11	vmb/	24
Kiltrick	Coolatrindle	-	mill	-	-	-	-	-	-	1"os/	149

PARISH	TOWNLAND	MILLER	TYPE	HOUSE	Land	£Val	PROPRIETORS	Date	WHEEL etc.	Record	Ref.
Carrick	Coolcots	Leared Richard	flour	(1B) 34x23x34.6 :	-	10-13	-	-	16x4.6x16 drives :	hob/	5.2286
Carrick	Coolcots	Leared Richard	flour	-	-	-	-	-	15x4x7	vmb/	24
Carrick	Coolcots	S/ Newtown Bridge	Glenville Mills	-	-	-	-	1841	-	6"os/	37
Inch	Coolgreany	-	corn & mill pond	-	-	-	-	-	-	6"os/	3
Inch	Coolgreeny	Kinch John	corn	-	-	-	-	-	13x4x14	vmb/	24
Kilcavan	Coolnagloose	McDermot James	reaping hook	- [no mill meas.]	-	-	-	-	- [no details]	hob/	5.2235
Rossdroit	Courtnacuddy	- W/ Monehore Br.W	Courtnecuddy Mill	-	-	-	-	-	-	6"os/	25
Rossdroit	Courtnacuddy	Fitzhenry William	corn	-	-	-	-	-	8x2x12	vmb/	24
Gorey	Craanford	-	corn	-	-	-	-	1998	John Lyons	mmSv/	wh - A
St Mary`s	Craywell	- E. side R. Barrow	Craywell Brewery	-	-	-	-	-	-	6"os/	29
Templeshannon	Crefoge	- near Enniscorthy	flour	-	-	-	-	-	-	1"os/	158
Astramon	Crory Lower	- SE/ Randallsmill Br.	corn	-	-	-	-	-	-	6"os/	32
Astramon	Crory Lower	Shortall Michael	corn	-	-	-	-	-	17x4x13	vmb/	24
Astramon	Crory Lower	Shortall Michael	flour	(1A) 54x21.6x25	-	-	-	1845	16x5.9x13.6 bkts :	hob/	5.2275
Astramon	Crory, Ferns Town	- N side R. Bann	corn & mill race	-	-	-	-	-	-	6"os/	15
Bannow	Cullenstown	-	windmill (ruins)	5.3m dia (ext.) :	-	-	-	-	-	iaa/	AI1652 os46.15.2
Drinagh	Drinagh	-	Cortnacuddy Mill	-	-	-	-	-	-	1"os/	158
Drinagh	Drinagh	- on coast	Old Windmill	-	-	-	-	-	-	1"os/	169
Drinagh	Drinagh South	-	windmill (ruins)	5.57m dia (ext.) :	-	-	-	-	-	iaa/	AI1653
St James & D	Dunbrody	-	salt & tidal	- nr Abbey ruins	-	-	-	1654	-	iaa/	Monastic
St James & D	Dunbrody	-	tidal	- large mill house	-	-	-	-	-	iaa/	AI1654 os39.14.2
St James & D	Dunbrody Manor	Chichester John	mills	-	-	-	Chichester J - Newdigate R	1726	-	dd/	52 237 34374
St James & D	Dunbrody Manor	Chichester John :	mills	-	-	-	Chichester J - Jordan Jn :	1734	-	dd/	78 261 55300
Duncormack	Duncormack	N/ Bridge	grist & mill race	-	-	-	-	1841	-	6"os/	46
Duncormack	Duncormack	Shudall John	corn	21.0x22.0x17.6 :	-	-	-	-	14x3x14.6 drives :	hob/	5.2194
Duncormack	Duncormack	Shudall John	corn & flour	-	-	-	-	-	14x3x16	vmb/	24
Whitechurch	Dunganstown	-	mill	-	-	-	-	-	-	1"os/	168
Fethard	Dungulf	- near Dungulf Castle	mill	-	-	-	-	-	-	1"os/	168
Fethard	Dungulph	-	flour	-	-	-	-	1841	-	6"os/	45
Fethard	Dungulph	-	windmill	-	-	-	-	1841	-	6"os/	45
Fethard	Dungulph	Clooney Thomas	corn	-	-	-	-	-	16x3x16	vmb/	24
Monart	East Monart	Pounder Thomas	tuck	-	-	-	-	-	-	vmb/	24
Edermine	Edermine	Kelly James	corn	-	-	-	-	-	14x3x15	vmb/	24
(Enniscorthy) -	Enniscorthy	- W side R. Slaney	flour & mill pond	-	-	-	-	-	-	6"os/	20
Kilrush	Enniscorthy	Freeman I E	corn	-	-	-	-	-	10x6x10	vmb/	24
Kilrush	Enniscorthy	Freeman I E	flour	-	-	-	-	-	13x3x14	vmb/	24
Kilrush	Enniscorthy	Pounder Thomas	corn	-	-	-	-	-	13x4x13	vmb/	24
(Enniscorthy) -	Enniscorthy :	-	distillery	-	-	-	-	-	-	6"os/	20
(Enniscorthy) -	Enniscorthy :	-	brewery	-	-	-	-	-	-	6"os/	20
(Enniscorthy) -	Enniscorthy :	-	flour	-	-	-	-	-	-	6"os/	20
St John`s ?	Enniscorthy Town	Breen Michael	mills	-	-	-	Breen Mcl - Kavanagh Edw	1899	-	dd/	1899 3 129
St Mary`s	Enniscorthy Town	Clegg Isabella	Windmill Hill	-	-	-	Clegg I - Hunter Hamilton	1889	-	dd/	1889 12 279
St Mary`s	Enniscorthy Town	Freeman George	Manor & Mill	-	-	-	Freeman Geo - Davis Sam	1880	-	dd/	1880 7 143
Kilrush	Enniscorthy Town	Freeman Thos Edw :	mill & land	-	-	-	Freeman T - Ryan Mary :	-	?	dd/	888 480 587980
St Mary`s	Enniscorthy Town	Lett Josephine	brewery & mill	-	-	-	Lett Josephine - George	1893	-	dd/	1893 25 130
St Mary`s	Enniscorthy Town	Pounder John :	V mills	-	-	-	Pounder - McMahon Peter :	1829	-	dd/	853 351 570351
St John`s	Enniscorthy Town :	Hill Charles :	mill & land	-	-	-	Hill Chas - Dallas Anne :	1831	Mort. 25 Jan.	dd/	876 28 581528
Kilrush	Enniscorthy Town :	Wheelock James	wheatmeal :	-	-	-	-	1963	-	lic/7	wheat
Kilrush	Enniscorthy Town :	-	flour	-	-	-	-	1963	-	lic/5	wheat
Tacumshin	Fence	-	windmill corn	- 3 sty. tapering :	-	-	-	-	-	iaa/	AI1655
Tacumshin	Fencering Park	Barrington John	mill	-	-	-	Barrington J - Wainwright R	1728	-	dd/	57 508 39477
Tacumshin	Fencering Park	Barrington Richard	mill	-	-	-	Barrington R - Harvey Jas	1735	-	dd/	82 114 57204

PARISH	TOWNLAND	MILLER	TYPE	HOUSE	Land	£Val	PROPRIETORS	Date	WHEEL etc.	Record	Ref.
Killegney	Forestalstown	Leary Mary	reaping hook	29x17x8	-	-	-	-	10.6 dia . 34 bkts :	hob/	5.2179
Killegney	Forestalstown	Leary Patrick	-	-	-	-	-	-	11x4x9	vmb/	24
Monart	Forge Lands	- not working	flour	-	-	-	-	-	15x9x12	vmb/	24
Monart	Forge Lands	Hogan Michael	oat	-	-	-	-	-	14x8x7	vmb/	24
Monart	Forgelands :	- N/ Verona Br.	corn & kiln	-	-	-	-	-	-	6"os/	19
Ballylannan	Foulkesmill	Scott John	mill	-	-	-	Scott Jn - Read Geo & ors	1719	-	dd/	25 137 14386
Ballylannan	Foulksmill Vge.	W/ Foulksmill Bridge	mill	-	-	-	-	1841	-	6"os/	40
Ballylannan	Foulksmills	- on Corock R.	mill	-	-	-	-	-	-	1"os/	169
Tacumshin	Furziestown	NW/ Bunargatestrand	windmill (ht 59)	-	-	-	-	1841	-	6"os/	53
Moyglass	Gardamus Great	Conor Patrick	corn	-	-	-	-	-	14x2x -	vmb/	24
Moyglass	Gardamus Great	NE/ Wolfesfort Br.	corn	-	-	-	-	1841	-	6"os/	47
Clonmore	Garr	- E/ Garr Bridge	corn	-	-	-	-	-	-	6"os/	25
Clonmore	Garr	Larkin James	corn	-	-	-	-	1851	14x3x8 breast :	hob/	5.2175
Clonmore	Garr	Larkin James	corn & flour	-	-	-	-	-	12x1x6	vmb/	24
Ballyhoge	Garranstackle	- near R. Barrow	mill	-	-	-	-	-	-	1"os/	158
Kilcormick	Garrybrit Upper	-	Garrybritt Corn Mill	-	-	-	-	-	-	6"os/	21
Kilcormick	Garrybrit Upper	Webster Robert	corn	(1B) 25x19x14 :	-	10-1	-	1845	15x2.2x18 56 bkts.:	hob/	5.2236
Kilcormick	Garrybrit Upper	Webster Robert	corn	-	-	-	-	-	14x2x15	vmb/	24
St Nichol`s	Garrylough	SE/ Garryhubbock Br.	corn & mill race	-	-	-	-	1841	-	6"os/	33
St Nichol`s	Garrylough Lr	Roche Maurice	corn	34x17x30 & :	-	-	-	-	18.4x6x12 49 bkts.:	hob/	5.2155
St Nichol`s	Garrylough Lr	Roche Patrick	corn	-	-	-	-	-	11x4x10	vmb/	24
St Nichol`s	Garrylough Lr	Shortall Peter	corn	-	-	-	-	1937	-	hist/	Journal.WHS
Wexford	Garrymadder	Morris Philip	tuck	-	-	-	-	-	10x1x12	vmb/	24
Wexford	Garrymadder	Morris Philip	corn	-	-	-	-	-	12x2x13	vmb/	24
Castle-ellis	Garrynisk	-	mill	-	-	-	-	-	-	1"os/	159
Clongeen	Garryrichard	-		-	-	-	-	1841	-	6"os/	40
Castle-ellis	Garryvadden	- E/ B'bregagh Br.	corn & mill race	-	-	-	-	-	-	6"os/	27
Castle-ellis	Garryvadden	Morris Phillip	corn	27.6x16.0x8.0 :	-	-	-	-	12x2x12 o`shot :	hob/	5.2152
Duncormick	Gibbeapatrick	Murphy Michael	windmill	circum. 53 x 21ft :	34a.	-	-	-	- 2 pr stones	hob/	5.2194
Duncormick	Gibberpatrick	E/ Village	windmill	-	-	-	-	1841	-	6"os/	46
Wexford	Glynn	- at Killurin Vge.	mill	-	-	-	-	-	-	1"os/	158
Kilmakilloge	Gorey	Ram Abel & Abel Jnr	grist	-	-	-	Ram Abel - Donovan Robt	1736	-	dd/	94 23 65288
Duncormick	Gortins	- at Kilmannan X	mill	-	-	-	-	-	-	1"os/	169
St. James	Grange	W/ Ingard Point	Ingard Windmill	-	-	-	-	1841	-	6"os/	50
Wexford	Grange (8)	- nr Dunbrody Castle	salt mills	-	-	-	-	-	-	1"os/	168
Kilnahue	Grovemill	- E. side Bann R.	- no mill	-	-	-	-	-	-	6"os/	6
Mayglass	Hardygregan	-	windmill	-	-	-	-	1841	-	6"os/	47
Mayglass	Hardygregan	-	windmill corn	- 3 storey :	-	-	-	-	-	iaa/	AI1655 os47.3.5
Hook	Harrylock	- on Hook Head	Old Windmill	- location :	-	-	-	-	-	1"os/	179
Rathaspick	Hayenstown	-	windmill	-	-	-	-	1841	-	6"os/	42
Rathaspick	Hayestown Gt	-	windmill	4.9m dia (ext.) :	-	-	-	-	-	iaa/	AI1657 os42.2.5
Wexford	Hedges *	- W./ Carnsore Pt.	Old Windmill	- location :	-	-	-	-	-	1"os/	181
Wexford	Hedges *	Geering Richard	mill & mill land	-	-	-	Geering R - Radford Benj	1720	-	dd/	32 12 18699
Wexford	Hedges *	Granville Rebecca	mill	-	-	-	Granville R - Knox Andrew	1717	-	dd/	21 9 10640
Wexford	Hedges *	Jacob William	mill & mill land	-	-	-	Jacob William - Knox Thos	1726	-	dd/	58 259 39405
Wexford	Hedges *	Jefferys James Hon.	mill	-	24a.	-	Jefferys J - Geering Richd	1714	-	dd/	13 274 5744
Wexford	Hedges *	Knox Andrew	mill & mill land	-	-	-	Knox Andrew - his will	1737	-	dd/	87 459 62580
Wexford	Hedges *	Knox Sidney	mill & mill land	-	-	-	Knox Sidney - Knox Andr	1737	-	dd/	84 431 61791
Wexford	Hedges *	Radford Benjamin	mill & mill land	-	-	-	Radford Benj - Jacob Wm	1726	-	dd/	59 63 39404
Rathmacnee	Hoagesmill	Deegan Laurence	corn	-	-	-	-	-	11x3x11	vmb/	24
Rathmacnee	Hodgesmill	- SE/ Kildavin Br.	corn	-	-	-	-	1841	-	6"os/	42
Kilbrideglynn	Holmestown	- at Muchwood X	mill	-	-	-	-	-	-	1"os/	169

PARISH	TOWNLAND	MILLER	TYPE	HOUSE	Land	£Val	PROPRIETORS	Date	WHEEL etc.	Record	Ref.
Kilmokea	Horeswood	-	mill	-	-	-	-	-	-	1"os/	168
Kilmokea	Horeswood	Reville John	corn	-	-	-	-	-	12x2x12	vmb/	24
Horetown	Horetown	Purcell Richard	flour	(1B) 39x19x30.6 :	-	18-14	-	1852	10x5.6x14 40 bkts.:	hob/	5.2287
Horetown	Horetown South	Parcel Richard	corn	(1B) 22x20x16 :	-	21-13	-	1851	14x4x14.6 42 bkts. :	hob/	5.2290
Horetown	Horetown South	Parcel Richard	corn	-	-	-	-	-	13x3x13	vmb/	24
Horetown	Horetown South	Parcel Richard	flour	-	-	-	-	-	16x5x16	vmb/	24
Horetown	Horetown South	W/ Goff's Bridge	corn, dam, mill race		-	-	-	1841	-	6"os/	41
Horetown	Horewood	NW Campile Bridge	corn, pond, mill race		-	-	-	1841	-	6"os/	39
Templetown	Houseland	-	windmill (ruins)	8.7m dia (ext.) :	-	-	-	-	-	iaa/	AI1658 os49.16.2
Templetown	Houseland	- E./ Harrylock Vge.	windmill	-	-	-	-	-	-	6"os/	49
Templetown	Houseland	- W/ rd. Hook Head	windmill	-	-	-	-	-	-	6'os/	49
Iberins	Iberins (parish)	Wexford Corp.C437	Old Windmill	-	-	-	Wexford Corp - Bryan Andr	1723	-	dd/	36 431 23389
Killilla	Inch	- on Inch R.	corn	-	-	-	-	-	-	1"os/	139
Killilla	Inch	- on R.	corn	-	-	-	-	-	-	6"os/	27
Killilla	Inch	Tobin James	carding	-	-	-	-	-	12x2x8	vmb/	24
Killilla	Inch	Tobin James	tuck	-	-	-	-	-	10x2x7	vmb/	24
Ballycarney	Ioneganon	Doyle Peter	corn	-	-	-	-	-	11x2x12	vmb/	24
St Mary's	Irishtown	- NE/ Wooden Br.	Sutton's Brewery	-	-	-	-	-	-	6"os/	29
Moyacomb	Johnstown	-	Watchhouse Vge. :	-	-	-	-	-	-	6"os/	4
Moyacomb	Johnstown	Thompson John	oat & flour	-	-	-	-	-	16x5x7	vmb/	24
Inch	Kayle	- near Carrick Town	mill	-	-	-	-	-	-	1"os/	169
Rathaspick	Kellystown	-	corn & dam	-	-	-	-	1841	-	6"os/	42
Rathaspick	Kellystown	Fortune Laurence	corn	-	-	-	-	-	14x2x14	vmb/	24
Ballyhoge	Kereight	-	corn	-	-	-	-	-	-	6"os/	31
Ballyhoge	Kereight	Doyle James	corn	-	-	-	-	-	9x2x12	vmb/	24
Ballyhoge	Kereight	Farday Thomas	corn	24.7x17.6x10.6 :	-	-	-	1846	10x2x11 overshot :	hob/	5.2171
Kerloge	Kerloge	-	corn	-	-	-	-	1841	-	6"os/	42
Kerloge	Kerloge	Codd David	corn & flour	-	-	-	-	-	17x2x17	vmb/	24
Clongeen	Kilbraney	-	thrashing mill	-	-	-	-	1841	-	6"os/	40
Clongeen	Kilbraney	- on Owenduff R.	mill	-	-	-	-	-	-	1"os/	169
Clongeeny	Kilbraney	Cormick Simon	carding	(1A) 18x29.6x13.6	-	2-3	-	1852	10.10x3.10x11.6 :	hob/	5.2287
Clongeeny	Kilbraney	Cormick Simon	mill & kilns	(1C) 22x21x10 :	-	9-9	-	1852	11x3x12 2 pr.st. :	hob/	5.2287
Clongeeny	Kilbraney	Cormick Simon	tuck	(3C) 18x29x8	-	19/6d	-	1852	10.6x1.5x11.6 :	hob/	5.2287
Clongeen	Kilbraney	Gemick Simon	corn	-	-	-	-	-	11x3x11	vmb/	24
Clongeen	Kilbraney	Gemick Simon	woollen	-	-	-	-	-	11x3x11	vmb/	24
Clongeen	Kilbraney	on Owenduff R.	mill & mill race	-	-	-	-	1841	-	6"os/	40
Wexford *	Kilcooly Beg	- SW/ K'cooly Ch.	flour & mill race	-	-	-	-	-	-	6"os/	28
Kilcowan	Kilcowan Upper	-	mill race [illegible] mile	-	-	-	-	1841	-	6"os/	46
Kilcowan	Kilcowan Upper	Codd Nicholas	corn & flour	-	-	-	-	-	16x4x12	vmb/	24
Kilcowan	Kilcowan Upper	SW/ Mulchtown Bridge	grist	-	-	-	-	1841	-	6"os/	46
Kildavin	Kildavin Upper	Crampton John	tuck	-	-	-	-	-	18x2x18	vmb/	24
Kildavin	Kildavin Upper	Crampton John	woollen	-	-	-	-	-	13x2x14	vmb/	24
Killincooly	Killincooly	Kavanagh James	corn	-	-	-	-	-	12x2x12	vmb/	24
Killmecridge	Killmecridge	Hatton John	corn	-	-	-	-	-	11x2x12	vmb/	24
Inch	Killybegs	- S/ Clonlough Br.	corn & mill race	-	-	-	-	-	-	6"os/	3
Kilgormack	Killybegs	Conneron Sarah	corn & kiln	(1B) 30.6x21x17.6	-	8	-	-	- [no detail]	hob/	5.2237
Kilgormack	Killybegs	Cowan David	corn	-	-	-	-	-	13x5x7	vmb/	24
Kilgormack	Killybegs	Cowan David	corn & kiln	(1A) 30.6x21x17 & :	-	19-7	-	-	13x5x7 42 bkts. :	hob/	5.2237
Kilmakilloge	Killynann	Foley William	bark & tan yard	(1B) 20x20x11.6 :	-	10-1	-	1845	all idle [no wh. detail]	hob/	5.2238
Kilmannan	Kilmannan	-	mill	-	-	-	-	1841	-	6"os/	42
Kilmannan	Kilmannan	Rockfort Moses	corn	-	-	-	-	-	12x2x13	vmb/	24
Kilnahue	Kilmichael	- W. side Bann R.	corn	-	-	-	-	-	-	6"os/	6

PARISH	TOWNLAND	MILLER	TYPE	HOUSE	Land	£Val	PROPRIETORS	Date	WHEEL etc.	Record	Ref.
Kilnahue	Kilmichael	Parsons	mill	-	-	-	Parsons - Man	-	?	dd/	92 239 64431
Kilmakilloge	Kilmichael	Ram Abel & Abel Jnr	mill	-	-	-	Ram Abel - Donovan Robt	1736	-	dd/	94 23 65288
Kilnahue	Kilmichael Lower	Fitzsimons William	corn	-	-	-	-	-	12x2x12	vmb/	24
Kilnahue	Kilmichael Lower	Fitzsimons William	corn & kiln	(1A) 39x20.6x25 :	-	-	-	-	12x2x13 36bkts. :	vmb/	24
Kilscanlan	Kilscanlan	-	corn	-	-	-	-	1841	-	6"os/	35
Kilscanlan	Kilscanlan	-	mill	-	-	-	-	-	-	1"os/	169
Kilscanlan	Kilscanlan	Foley David	corn	21.6x17.0x9.6 :	-	-	-	-	9x2x - 30 buckets	hob/	5.2180
Kilscanlan	Kilscanlan	Koley David	corn	-	-	-	-	-	8x2x11	vmb/	24
Bannow	Kiltra	-	corn & mill race	-	-	-	-	1841	-	6"os/	45
Bannow	Kiltra	-	windmill (ruins)	6.5m dia (ext.) :	-	-	-	-	-	iaa/	AI1659 os45.8.6
Bannow	Kiltra	Colfer Elizabeth	corn	23.0x18.0x12.6 :	-	-	-	-	12.3xx4.2x12 :	hob/	5.2193
Bannow	Kiltra	Colfer Elizabeth	windmill	circum.: 56 x 27 ft.	-	-	-	1852	not yet finished :	hob/	5.2193
Bannow	Kiltra	Culfer Elizabeth	corn	-	-	-	-	-	12x4x13	vmb/	24
Bannow	Kiltra	E/ Waterloo Bridge	corn & mill pond	-	-	-	-	1841	-	6"os/	45
Bannow	Kiltra	Flix Johanna	corn	-	-	-	-	-	17x2x11	vmb/	24
Bannow	Kiltra	Hore Mary	mill	48x22x22 kiln :	-	-	-	-	17x2.6x12.6 :	hob/	5.1250
Tintern	Kinnagh	- nr Bayeystown Ho.	mill	-	-	-	-	-	-	1"os/	168
Kilmakilloge	Knockmiullen	- due S. Town	Millmount House	-	-	-	-	-	-	6"os/	7
Kilmakilloge	Knockmullen	Walsh George	starch	-	-	-	-	-	13x2x16 :	vmb/	24
Kilrush	Knocknalour	-	thrashing machine	-	-	-	-	-	-	6"os/	5
Wex (? Wick)	Knocknamunion	Evans William	woollen factory	26.6x22.0x20 :	-	-	-	1844	14x3.4x6.6 breast :	hob/	5.2154
Kimore	Libgate	- W/ Nat. School	windmill	-	-	-	-	1841	-	6"os/	52
Kimore	Libgate	- W/ Nat. School	windmill	-	-	-	-	1841	-	6"os/	52
Ishartmon	Lingstown	Cliffe Loftus	mill	-	110a.	-	Cliffe L - Jeffrreys Jas	1715	-	dd/	16 75 6945
Ishartmon	Lingstown	Sealy Richard	mill	-	87a.	-	Sealy Richd - Boxwell John	1720	-	dd/	29 404 18119
Ishartmon	Lingstown	Thresher William	mill	-	-	-	Thresher W - Sealy Richd	1717	-	dd/	22 74 11437
Kilscoran	Lough (3)	- near Hill Castle	Old Windmill	-	-	-	-	-	-	1"os/	170
Clongeeny	Loughanur	Delaney James	corn & kiln	(3C) 32x19x18 :	-	-	-	1852	o`shot 10x4x10 :	hob/	5.2287
Clongeen	Loughnageer	E/ Taylorstown Br.	Cullen's Mill	-	-	-	-	1841	-	6"os/	40
St John`s	Lucas Park	- near Enniscorthy	flour	-	-	-	-	-	-	1"os/	158
Ballyhoge	Lucas Park	- S/ St. John Br.	Urrin Flour Mill	-	-	-	-	-	-	6"os/	26
Wexford	Lyngstown	Thresher William	mill	-	-	-	Thresher W - Cliffe Loftus	1713	-	dd/	11 120 4144
Clonmore	Mackmine	Muray John	corn	-	-	-	-	-	15x2x15	vmb/	24
Wexford	Marny	Monk Charles :	mills	-	-	-	Monk C - Adair Robert :	1733	-	dd/	78 28 52892
Ballynaslaney ?	Martingalls	Allen John	mill	-	-	-	Allen John - Davis John	1730	-	dd/	74 127 50532
Ballynaslaney ?	Martingalls	Hill Edward	mill	-	-	-	Hill Ed - Smyth Katherine	1735	-	dd/	76 504 55615
Ballynaslaney ?	Martingalls	Ludlow William	mill	-	-	-	Ludlow Wm - Hill Edward	1723	-	dd/	41 245 25641
Ballynaslaney ?	Martingalls	Winckworth John	mill	-	-	-	Winckworth J - Ludlow Wm	1721	-	dd/	31 191 18736
Ballynaslaney ?	Martingalls	Winkworth John	mill	-	-	-	Winkworth J - Warburton G	1726	-	dd/	50 473 33865
Templeshannon	Matabeg	Allen Mr	flour	-	-	-	-	-	24x4x24	vmb/	24
St Mary`s	Maudlins	- W/ Maudlins Br.	Maudlins Corn Mill	-	-	-	-	-	-	6"os/	29
St Mary`s	Maudlins	Cheevers Patrick	corn	-	-	-	-	-	10x3x12	vmb/	24
St Mary`s	Maudlins	Roche Patrick	corn	-	-	-	-	-	10x2x13	vmb/	24
St Mary`s	Maudlins :	- SE/ Maudlins Br.	corn	-	-	-	-	-	-	6"os/	29
Templeudigan	Meelgarrow	-	corn & mill pond	-	-	-	-	1888	-	25"os/	24.11
Templeudigan	Meelgarrow	Condon Patrick	corn	-	-	-	-	-	11x3x14	vmb/	24
Kilmakilloge	Mill Lands	-	brewery	-	-	-	-	-	-	6"os/	7
Ballynaslaney	Mill Lands	-	flax & mill race	-	-	-	-	-	-	6"os/	32
Ballynaslaney	Mill Lands	- N/ Coolmain Br.	bleach green	-	-	-	-	-	-	6"os/	32
Ballynaslaney	Mill Lands	- N/ Coolmain Br.	corn	-	-	-	-	-	-	6"os/	32
Kilmakilloge	Mill Lands	Brownrigg Henry	mill	-	80a.	-	Brownrigg - Harrison Fran	1716	-	dd/	17 209 8560
Kilmakilloge	Mill Lands	Coulthurst Nicholas	mill	-	20a.	-	Coulthirst N - Harrison Fran	1711	-	dd/	8 386 2977

PARISH	TOWNLAND	MILLER	TYPE	HOUSE	Land	£Val	PROPRIETORS	Date	WHEEL etc.	Record	Ref.
Kilmakilloge	Mill Lands	Harrison Marth	mill	-	-	-	Harrison M - Arthur Bendct	1726	-	dd/	53 136 34767
Ballynaslaney	Mill Lands	Keogh Edward	corn	-	-	-	-	-	14x3x5	vmb/	24
Ballynaslaney	Mill Lands	Keogh Edward	flax	-	-	-	-	-	12x2x5 5 stocks :	vmb/	24
Kilmakilloge	Mill Lands	Redmond John	corn	-	-	-	-	-	13x4x13	vmb/	24
Kilmakilloge	Mill Lands	Redmond John	flour	-	-	-	-	-	16x10x12	vmb/	24
Kilmakilloge	Mill Lands	Stopford James	mill	-	80a.	-	Stopford J - Harrison Fran	1711	-	dd/	15 239 7369
Kilmakilloge	Mill Lands	Stopford James	mill	-	-	-	Stopford J - Chichester Jn	1711	-	dd/	74 308 51315?
Kilmakilloge	Mill Lands	William	mill	-	-	-	Swiny Wm - Reilly James	1724	-	dd/	42 337 26564
Old Ross	Mill Quarter	- near Old Ross	mill	-	-	-	-	-	-	1"os/	158
Kilnahue	Mill Quarter	Brown Edward	corn	-	-	-	-	-	11x3x14	vmb/	24
Old Ross	Mill Quarter	Cloney Garret	woollen	-	-	-	-	-	9x3x11	vmb/	24
Old Ross	Mill Quarter	Clooney Garrett	carding	32.0x18.0x12	-	-	-	1846	10x5x10 30 bkts. :	hob/	5.2182
Old Ross	Mill Quarter	Clooney Garrett	new corn mill	33.0x22.0x18.0 :	-	-	-	-	14x3x - 40 bkts :	hob/	5.2182
Ballynaslaney	Milllands	Atkins Jn & Kehoe Ed	corn	25x22x19 & :	-	-	-	-	14x3.6x5 40 bkts. :	hob/	5.2150
Kilnahue	Millquarter	- E. side R. Lask	corn & mill race	-	-	-	-	-	-	6"os/	6
Oldross	Millquarter	- W/ Miller's Bridge	corn	-	-	-	-	1841	-	6"os/	35
Kilnahue	Millquarter	Browne Michael	corn & kiln	(1B) 20x22.6x18.8 :	28a.	10-3	-	-	11x3x12 36 bkts. :	hob/	5.2239
Wexford	Millroad	-	windmill	-	-	-	-	-	-	1"os/	180
Kilbride	Milltown	- E. side R. Bann	corn	-	-	-	-	-	-	6"os/	15
Killann	Milltown	- on Milltown Stream	corn & mill race	-	-	-	-	-	-	6"os/	18
Kilbride	Milltown	- on R. Bann	Milltown Vge.	-	-	-	-	-	-	6"os/	15
Fiescoran	Milltown	Boggin John	corn	-	-	-	-	-	13x2x14	vmb/	24
Kilbride	Milltown	Furney Henry	corn & flour	-	-	-	-	-	14x5x5	vmb/	24
Tintern	Milltown	NW/ Milltown Br.	flour	-	-	-	-	1841	-	6"os/	44
Tintern	Milltown	Ryan William	corn	-	-	-	-	-	18x3x10	vmb/	24
Rathmacnee	Milltown :	-	no mill	-	-	-	-	1841	-	6"os/	42
Templeshanboe	Mocurry	Doyle Edward	-	-	-	-	-	-	12x4x12	vmb/	24
Templeshanboe	Mocurry	Doyle Edward	tuck	-	-	-	-	-	12x2x12	vmb/	24
Templeshanboe	Mocurry West	-	carding & tuck	-	-	-	-	-	-	6"os/	14
Monamolin	Monagreany Lr.	-	corn	-	-	-	-	-	-	6"os	16
Monamolin	Monagreany Lr.	Gahon Arthur (deld. :	corn	(1B) 20.6x23x11 :	-	1-18	-	-	14x2.6x16 48 bkts.	hob/	5.2244
Monamolin	Monagreany Lr.	Roche Henry	corn	-	-	-	-	-	16x2x17	vmb/	24
Ballycanew	Monroe	- near Ballycanew	Milltown	-	-	-	-	-	-	1"os/	149
Carn/ Mayglass	Moortown	-	windmill	-	-	-	-	1841	-	6"os/	47
Carn/Mayglass	Moortown	-	windmill (ruins)	4.9m dia (ext.) :	-	-	-	-	-	iaa/	AI1660 os47.7.6
Templeshannon	Motabeg or Salville	- E/ side R. Slaney	flour	-	-	-	-	-	-	6"os/	26
Carnew	Motabower	-	millstone quarry :	-	-	-	-	-	-	iaa/	AI1661 os5.4.6
Templeshannon	Motebegg	Hatton	mill	-	-	-	Hatton - Phaire	-	?	dd/	92 426 65228
Templeshannon	Motebegg	Parsons William	mill	-	-	-	Parsons W - Gamble Ones	1737	-	dd/	89 135 62500
Templeshannon	Motebegg	Parsons Judith :	mill	-	-	-	Parsons J - Hatton Jack :	1738	-	dd/	93 151 65227
Templeshannon	Motebegg	Parsons Lowther	mills	-	-	-	Parsons L - Parsons Wm	1722	-	dd/	34 163 21033
Templeshannon	Motebegg	Parsons William	mill	-	-	-	Parsons W - Gamble Ones	1737	-	dd/	86 227 60126
Templeshannon	Motebegg	Parsons William	mill	-	-	-	Parsons W - Gamble Ones	1737	-	dd/	87 437 62499
Templeshannon	Motebegg	Phair Thomas :	mill	-	-	-	Phaire Thomas - Gamble :	1738	-	dd/	92 427 65229
Moyglass	Moyglass	- near Mount Pl. Ho.	windmill	-	-	-	-	-	-	1"os/	169
Maudlinstown	Mulgannon	-	windmill	-	-	-	-	1841	-	6"os/	42
Inch	Mullinderry	Byrne Thomas	corn	-	-	-	-	-	13x2x13	vmb/	24
inch	Mullinderry	Leslie Edward Rev. :	corn & kiln	(1B) 18x22.6x9.6 :	-	-	-	1851	16x2.2x10 o`shot :	hob/	5.2290
Inch	Mullinderry	Ryan Martin	corn	-	-	-	-	-	16x6x7	vmb/	24
inch	Mullinderry	Ryan Martin	mill, kiln, carding	(1B) 44x22x26.6 :	-	24-4	-	1851	16x5..8x7 2 pr st. :	hob/	5.2290
inch	Mullinderry	S/ Mullindery Bridge	carding machine	-	-	-	-	1841	-	6"os/	40
inch	Mullinderry	SE/ Mullindery Br.	corn	-	-	-	-	1841	-	6"os/	40

PARISH	TOWNLAND	MILLER	TYPE	HOUSE	Land	£Val	PROPRIETORS	Date	WHEEL etc.	Record	Ref.
Togmon	Mulmontry	N/ Brownscastle Br.	woollen factory	-	-	-	-	1841	-	6"os/	36
Togmon	Mulmonty	Fortune Edward	woollen spinning	-	-	-	-	-	13x2x7 drives :	vmb/	24
Mulrankin	Mulrankin	Parle Mary	corn	-	-	-	-	-	18x3x10	vmb/	24
St Mary`s	New Ross	-	Shallows Park Mill	-	-	-	-	-	-	1"os/	157
Templeludigan	New Ross :	Bailey Mills Ltd.	flour	-	-	-	-	1963	- <1,000 barrels	lic/ 1	wh.meal
St Peter's	Newbawn	SE/ Newbawn Cr.Rd.	corn mill (in ruins)	-	-	-	-	1841	-	6"os/	35
St Peter's	Newbay	Cleary Mary Ann	corn	-	-	-	-	-	18x2x20	vmb/	24
Wex	Newborough	Ram Abel	mill	-	-	-	Ram Abel - Donovan Robt	1736	-	dd/	94 28 65288
St Peter's	Newtown	NW/ Newtown Br.	corn & mill dam	-	-	-	-	1841	-	6"os/	37
St Mary`s	Newtownbarry	- not working	flour	-	-	-	-	-	17x6x5	vmb/	24
St Mary`s	Newtownbarry	- not working	oat	-	-	-	-	-	15x4x4	vmb/	24
St Mary`s	Newtownbarry	- on R. Slaney	corn & mill pond	-	-	-	-	-	-	6"os/	9
St Mary`s	Newtownbarry	- on R. Slaney	corn & mill pond	-	-	-	-	-	-	6"os/	9
St Mary`s	Newtownbarry	- on R. Slaney	flour & mill dam	-	-	-	-	-	-	6"os/	9
St Mary`s	Newtownbarry	- on R. Slaney	Mill View Cottage	-	-	-	-	-	-	6"os/	9
St Mary`s	Newtownbarry	- on R. Slaney	New Mills	-	-	-	-	-	-	6"os/	9
Enniscorthy	nr Kiltealy	- on Urrin R.	mill	-	-	-	-	-	-	1"os/	148
St Mary`s	nr New Ross	-	mill	-	-	-	-	-	-	1"os/	157
Kilmacree	Orristown	-	corn	-	-	-	-	1841	-	6"os/	47
Kilmacree	Orristown	Scallion Johanna	corn & flour	-	-	-	-	-	12x3x -	vmb/	24
Oldross	Palace	Burdett Thomas	mill	-	-	-	Burdett T Naylor John	1721	-	dd/	47 444 31388
Oldross	Palace	Burdett Thomas	mill	-	-	-	Burdett T - Dillon John	1726	-	dd/	49 324 32164
Oldross	Palace	Burdett William :	mill	-	-	-	Burdett W - Chamney Jn :	1730	-	dd/	64 413 44434
Oldross	Palace	Esmond	mill	-	-	-	Esmond - Putland	-	?	dd/	74 426 51891
Oldross	Palace	Esmond Laurence	mill	-	-	-	Esmond L - Hatton Henry	1717	-	dd/	19 267 10130
Oldross	Palace	Esmond Laurence	mill	-	-	-	Esmond L - Doyle John	1717	-	dd/	21 336 11686
Kilnenor	Pallis Lower	-	corn	-	-	-	-	-	-	1"os/	139
Kilnenor	Pallis Upper	- SW/ Pallis Bridge	corn & mill race	-	-	-	-	-	-	6"os/	2
Kilnenor	Pallis Upper	Sullivan Patrick	corn	-	-	-	-	-	11x3x12	vmb/	24
Kilnenor	Pallis Upper	Sullivan Patrick	corn & kiln	(1B) 21x20x14.4 :	-	13-12	-	1846	10x3x12 2 pr. st. :	hob/	5.2239
Kilnenor	Pallis Upper	Sullivan Patrick	corn & kiln	(1B) 49x20x15 :	-	13-12	-	-	10.6x3x11.6 36 bkts	vmb/	24
St Mary`s	Pigats & Tanyard	- SE/ Maudlins Br.	corn	-	-	-	-	-	-	6"os/	29
St Mary`s	Pigats & Tanyard	Faunia & Haurick :	corn	-	-	-	-	-	11x3x15	vmb/	24
St Mary`s	Pigats & Tanyard	Faunia & Haurick :	starch	-	-	-	-	-	5x18x6	vmb/	24
Ardcandrisk	Polehore	Cullen William	corn	(1A) 18x21x16	-	-	-	1852	13x2x13.6 2 pr.st. :	hob/	5.2282
Ardcandrisk	Polehore	Cullen William	corn	-	-	-	-	-	12x2x13	vmb/	24
Ardcandrisk	Polehore	W. side R. Slaney	corn & mill race	-	-	-	-	1841	-	6"os/	37
Ardcolm	Pollregan	- on R. Slaney	corn & mill dam	-	-	-	-	-	-	6"os/	32
Ardcolm	Pollregan	Dickson George & Ed	corn & flour	-	-	-	-	-	13x4x9	vmb/	24
Hook	Portersgate	-	Haye's Quay	-	-	-	-	-	-	6'os/	49
Killenagh	Raheen Beg	-	Kileena Corn Mill :	- E./ Kileena Br.	-	-	-	-	-	6"os/	17
Killenagh	Raheen Beg	Redmond James	corn	-	-	-	-	-	14x3x7	vmb/	24
Adamstown	Raheenduff	-	Foulkes mills	-	-	-	-	-	Breast 74.6kw	turb/	c1947
Kilmakilloge	Raheengurren	Stopford James	mill	-	-	-	Stopford J - Chichester Jn	1711	-	dd/	72 334 50955
St Jas & Dunb'	Ramsgrange	NW/ Kilbride Br. (new)	corn	-	-	-	-	1841	-	6"os/	44
Tikillin	Randallsmill	- imed. NW/ R'mill Br.	corn	-	-	-	-	-	-	6"os/	32
Tikillen	Randals Mills	Williams Jack	corn	-	-	-	-	-	12x4x14	vmb/	24
Tikillen	Randals Mills	Williams Jack	flour	-	-	-	-	-	12x2x14	vmb/	24
Tikillin	Randalsmill	Williams Joseph	corn	(2B) 25x16.6x7 :	-	-	-	1852	12x4x12 2 pr.st. :	hob/	5.2281
Duncormick	Rath	-	windmill	-	-	-	-	1841	-	6"os/	46
Duncormick	Rath	-	windmill corn	9.65m dia (ext.) :	-	-	-	-	-	iaa/	AI1662 os46.10.6
Duncormick	Rath	- near Duncormick	windmill	-	-	-	-	-	-	1"os/	169

PARISH	TOWNLAND	MILLER	TYPE	HOUSE	Land	£Val	PROPRIETORS	Date	WHEEL etc.	Record	Ref.
Duncormick	Rath	Jeffers Richard	windmill	26.6 dia. x 22 ft :	13a.	-	-	1853	2 pr. pretty good st.	hob/	5.2194
Killann	Rathduff	Chapman Graham	corn	-	-	-	-	-	14x3x17	vmb/	24
Kinawley	Rathfylane	- at Boro Bridge	flour	-	-	-	-	-	-	1"os/	158
Kinawley	Rathfylane	- E/ Boro Bridge	flour & mill race	-	-	-	-	-	-	6"os/	25
Rathmacnee	Rathmacnee Gt	Kelly James	corn	-	-	-	-	-	12x3x13	vmb/	24
Ballybrennan	Ratholm	-	mill	-	-	-	-	1841	-	6"os/	48
Ballybrennan	Ratholm	E. side river	Foulkes Mill Little	- (ruins)	-	-	-	1841	-	6"os/	40
Ballybrennan	Ratholm	Percivall Jno	mill race	-	-	-	Percivall J - Neale Denis	1734	-	dd/	89 37 61967
Ballybrennan	Ratholm	W/ Dalton Cottage	mill race & small po	-	-	-	-	1841	-	6"os/	40
Tacumshin	Rathshillane	due W/ Inish (isle.)	windmill (ruins)	-	-	-	-	1841	-	6"os/	53
Rossdroit	Rathylane	Graham John	corn & wheat	- The Boro Mill	-	-	-	-	12x2x6	vmb/	24
Duncormick	Robinstown	-	windmill	-	-	-	-	-	-	1"os/	169
St Mary`s	Ross Town	Altham Arthur Hon.	old horse mill	-	-	-	Altham Arth - Lower John	1721	-	dd/	34 38 20376
St Mary`s	Ross Town	Altham Arthur Hon.	old horse mill	-	-	-	Altham A - Barrett Fras	1721	-	dd/	36 114 21759
St Mary`s	Ross Town	Carew Lord	Earls Mills	-	-	-	Carew Ld - Huntingdon E.	1844	-	dd/	1844 15 43
St Mary`s	Ross Town	Cherry Elizabeth	Grey Well Brewery	-	-	-	Cherry Elizabeth - Hannah	1888	-	dd/	1888 43 249
St Mary`s	Ross Town	Harman Thomas	tuck	-	-	-	Harman T -Ticehurst Rowl	1887	-	dd/	1887 46 38
St Mary`s	Ross Town	Harman Wilhelmina	tuck	-	-	-	Harman Wilhelmina - Rel.	1887	-	dd/	1887 46 41
St Mary`s	Ross Town	Ld Judges Cp & Co	tuck & tan ho.	-	-	-	Ld Judges - Harman Sam	1881	-	dd/	1881 17 283
St Mary`s	Ross Town	Stevelly Robert Rev.	Martingales Mill	-	-	-	Stevelly R - Sankey Robt	1836	-	dd/	1836 7 97
St Mary`s	Ross Town	Stevelly Robert Rev.	Safes Mill	-	-	-	Stevelly R - Sankey Robt	1836	-	dd/	1836 7 97
St Mary`s	Ross Town	Ticehurst Rowland	tuck mill & tan ho.	-	-	-	Ticehurst - Clayton Emma	1890	-	dd/	1890 6 38
St Mary`s	Ross Town	Winkworth John :	tuck	-	-	-	Winkworth J - Piggott M :	1728	-	dd/	61 204 41112
St Mary`s	Ross Town :	Pigott William	mills	-	-	-	Pigott W - Sutton Cousar	1834	-	dd/	1834 15 138
St Mary`s	Ross Town :	Polwheele Robt Rev.	tuck	-	-	-	Polwheele Robt - Little Geo	1839	-	dd/	1839 21 72
Rossminogue	Rossminogue S.	-	corn & mill race	-	-	-	-	-	-	6"os/	11
Rossminogue	Rossminogue S.	Doyle Thomas	corn	(3C) 22x18x8 :	-	1-3	-	1845	11x2.2x14 36 bkts.	hob/	5.2245
Rossminogue	Rossminogue S.	Doyle Thomas	corn	-	-	-	-	-	12x2x14	vmb/	24
St John`s	Saintjohn`s	Davis Francis	flour	-	-	-	- 3 pr stones	-	12x12x10	vmb/	24
St John`s	Saintjohn`s	Parsons	mill & mill lands	-	-	-	Parsons - Man	-	-	dd/	2 23 64431
St John`s	Saintjohn`s	Parsons	mill & toll	-	-	-	Parsons - Wall	-	?	dd/	57 101 60754?
St John`s	Saintjohn`s	Parsons Lowther	mill & toll	-	-	-	Parsons L - Parsons Wm	1722	-	dd/	34 163 21033
St John`s	Saintjohn`s	Parsons William	mill & toll	-	-	-	Parsons W - Gamble Ones	1736	-	dd/	83 525 60125
St John`s	Saintjohn`s	Parsons William	mill & toll	-	-	-	Parsons W - Gamble Ones	1737	-	dd/	88 262 62498
St John`s	Saintjohn`s	Parsons William	mill & toll	-	-	-	Parsons W - Gamble Ones	1737	-	dd/	89 135 62500
Tintern	Saltmills Village	SW/ Tintern Br.	salt	-	-	-	-	1841	-	6"os/	45
Templeshannon	Salville or Motabeg	Preston Alex	mills	not recently used	-	-	Mr A Preston from 1847	-	22x4x - wood :	hob/	5.1268
Duncormick	Scar	- near Knocktown X	windmill	-	-	-	-	-	-	1"os/	169
Duncormick	Scar	NW/ Sour Bridge	corn & mill race	-	-	-	-	1841	-	6"os/	46
Duncormick	Scar	Stafford John	corn	20.0x19.0x11.6 :	-	-	-	-	14x2.8x14.3 :	hob/	5.2194
Duncormick	Seal	Keeffe Edward	corn	-	-	-	-	-	13x2x14	vmb/	24
Wexford	Shanb`agherine *	Barnewall Nicholas	salt	-	-	-	Barnewall - Beauchamp Jn	1722	-	dd/	36 320 22617
Wexford	Shanb`agherine *	Barnewall Nicholas	salt	-	-	-	Barnewall - Barnes Caleb	1722	-	dd/	37 252 22616
Wexford	Shanb`agherine *	Coleclough Cesar	salt	-	-	-	Coleclough C - Vesey Thos	1719	-	dd/	31 206 18787
Tacumshin	Sigginstown	Pierce Andrew	corn	-	-	-	-	-	12x2x13	vmb/	24
Tacumshin	Sigginstown	WxN/ Glebe	corn	-	-	-	-	1841	-	6"os/	53
Tacumshin	Sigginstown Upr	Marshall Peter	corn	-	-	-	-	-	15x3x9	vmb/	24
Ardcavan	Sinnottsmill	-	corn	-	-	-	-	1841	-	6"os/	33
Ardcavan	Sinnottsmill	Breen Patrick	corn	-	-	-	-	-	13x4x15 drives :	vmb/	24
Shelmaliere	Sinnottsmill	Breen Patrick	corn & kiln	39x22x26	-	-	-	1845	13x3x17 30 bkts. :	hob/	5.2274
Fiescoran	Slad	Codd William	corn	-	-	-	-	-	11x2x13	vmb/	24
Fiescoran	Slad	Nun Joshua :	mill	-	-	-	Nun Josh - Sinnott Mary :	1722	-	dd/	36 445 23518

COUNTY WEXFORD

PARISH	TOWNLAND	MILLER	TYPE	HOUSE	Land	£Val	PROPRIETORS	Date	WHEEL etc.	Record	Ref.
Fiescoran	Slad	Sinnott Mary	mill	-	-	-	Sinnott M - Hughes Pierce	1723	-	dd/	38 111 23520
Fiescoran	Slad	Sinnott Mary & Margt	mill	-	-	-	Sinnott M & M - Nun Richd	1723	-	dd/	35 509 23510
Hook	Slade	-	salt mfty (in ruins)	-	-	-	-	1845	-	6"os/	47
Hook	Slade	-	salt mfty (ruins)	- 18th c. complex :	-	-	-	-	-	iaa/	AI1663 os54.8.1
Hook	Slade	- near Hook Head	salt mfty (ruins)	-	-	-	-	-	-	6'os/	49
Kilmannan	Sledagh	-	tuck	-	-	-	-	1841	-	6"os/	49
Kilmannan	Sledagh	Compton Nathaniel	corn	-	-	-	-	-	15x2x16	vmb/	24
Ballyhuskard	Slievenagorea	- at Ballaghkeen Vge.	mill	-	-	-	-	-	-	6"os/	27
Ballyhuskard	Slievenagorea	Murphy Nicholas	old mill	30x18x11	-	-	-	1852	-	hob/	5.2149
Kilturk	Soughane	-	windmill corn	- 3 storey :	-	-	-	-	-	iaa/	AI1664 os52.2.3
St John`s	St John`s (Taigh)	Ivory John	mills & mill lands	-	-	-	Ivory Jn - Jones Edward	1713	-	dd/	12 103 4551
St John`s	St John`s (Taigh)	Jones Edward	mills & mill lands	-	-	-	Jones Ed - Neal Rev Benj	1717	-	dd/	21 92 10858
St John`s	St John`s (Taigh)	Jones Edward	mills & mill lands	-	-	-	Jones Ed - Baisley Diana	1720	-	dd/	30 41 16279
St John`s	St John`s (Taigh)	Napper William	mills & mill lands	-	-	-	Napper Wm - Ivory John	1712	-	dd/	11 374 4766
Kilrush	St Mary`s	Lewis William	flour	-	-	-	-	-	34x5x27 drives :	vmb/	24
Whitechurch	Stokestown	-	corn	-	-	-	-	1841	-	6"os/	34
Whitechurch	Stokestown	Shallow James	corn	-	-	-	-	-	11x2x14	vmb/	24
St John`s	Sweetfarm	- N/ Kilcarbry Br.	flour	-	-	-	-	-	-	6"os/	26
St John`s	Sweetfarm	Davis Fran	flour	-	-	-	- 3 pr stones	-	11x9x8	vmb/	24
Tacumshin	Tacumshin	-	windmill	-	-	-	-	-	-	1"os/	170
Taghmon	Taghmon	-	Old Windmill	-	-	-	-	-	-	1"os/	169
Wexford	Tagoat *	-	mill	-	-	-	-	-	-	1"os/	170
Wexford	Tagoat *	-	windmill	-	-	-	-	-	-	1"os/	170
Tintern	Taylorstown	Anderson James	corn	-	-	-	-	-	11x3x12	vmb/	24
Tintern	Taylorstown	W side Owenduff R.	corn	-	-	-	-	1841	-	6"os/	40
Templeshannon	Templeshannon	-	windmill (ruins)	4.6m dia (ext.) :	-	-	-	-	-	iaa/	AI1665 os52.2.3
Templeshannon	Templeshannon	- on Vinegar Hill 389	windmill in ruins	-	-	-	-	-	-	6"os/	20
Templetown	Templetown	-	millstone quarry	- rock platform :	-	-	-	-	-	iaa/	AI1666 os49.12.4
Templetown	Templetown	- at Harrylock Bay	I.G. Survey site	-	-	-	-	-	-	6'os/	49
Wexford	The Moor	-	windmill	-	-	-	-	-	-	1"os/	169
Wexford	Tinnock	- at Glensmill Br.	mill	-	-	-	-	-	-	1"os/	168
Wexford	Tinnock	SE/ Campile Bridge	corn & mill race	-	-	-	-	1841	-	6"os/	39
Gorey	Toberanierin	Hill John	bark & tan yard	(2B) 26.5x20x8 :	-	6-6	-	-	no wheel detail :	hob/	5.2243
St John`s	Tomduff	Robinson John	woollen spinning	-	-	-	-	-	12x6x6	vmb/	24
Adamstown	Tomgarrow	- on R. Slaney	mill	-	-	-	-	-	-	1"os/	148
Adamstown	Tomgarrow	- on R. Slaney	corn & kiln	-	-	-	-	-	-	6"os/	15
Adamstown	Tomgarrow	- S/ Adamstown Br.	corn & mill dam	-	-	-	-	-	-	6"os/	30
Adamstown	Tomgarrow	Downes George	corn	-	-	-	-	-	10x3x13	vmb/	24
Adamstown	Tomgarrow	Downes Gregory	corn	24.6x20.0x17.6 :	-	-	-	-	12x2.6x11 o`shot :	hob/	5.2169
Ballycarney	Toneybrackwood	Keogh Moses	corn	-	-	-	-	-	- drives 4 pair st.	vmb/	24
Ballycarney	Toneybrackwood	Keogh Moses	flour	-	-	-	-	-	13x5x13	vmb/	24
Horetown	Tottenhamgreen	-	flour	-	-	-	-	1841	-	6"os/	36
Horetown	Tottenhamgreen	Parle Pat & Roach Jn	corn	-	-	-	-	-	10x2x10	vmb/	24
Horetown	Tottenhamgreen	Parle Pat & Roach Jn	flour	-	-	-	-	-	13x3x14	vmb/	24
Taghmon	Traceystown E.	-	mill	-	-	-	-	-	-	1"os/	169
Toome	Tullabeg	-	corn & mill pond	-	-	-	-	-	-	6"os/	11
Toome	Tullabeg	Bryan Thomas	corn	-	-	-	-	-	12x2x13	vmb/	24
Ambrosetowm	Tullucanna	- nr Tullycanna Br.	mill	-	-	-	-	-	-	1"os/	169
Ambrosetowm	Tullycanna	E/ Tullycanna BrIDGE	corn & mill race	-	-	-	-	1841	-	6"os/	41
Ambrosetowm	Tullycanna	White Matthew	corn	-	-	-	-	-	11x2x12	vmb/	24
Ballycormick	Waddingsland	Edwards	mill	-	-	-	Edwards - Maddock	-	-	dd/	38 59 19655
Ballycormick	Waddingsland	Edwards Cadwallad :	mill	-	-	-	Edwards C - Roberts Wm :	1726	-	dd/	76 319 54618

PARISH	TOWNLAND	MILLER	TYPE	HOUSE	Land	£Val	PROPRIETORS	Date	WHEEL etc.	Record	Ref.
Ballycormick	Waddington	-	corn	-	-	-	-	1841	-	6"os/	41
Ballycormick	Waddington	-	mill	-	-	-	-	-	-	1"os/	169
Ballycormick	Waddington	Cram Patrick	corn	-	-	-	-	-	13x2x14	vmb/	24
Ballycormick	Waddington	Stafford Patrick	mill & kiln	13x17.6x11 & :	-	-	-	-	12.6x2.6 oveshot	hob/	5.2192
Ballycormick	Waddington	Stafford Patrick	old mill	Is in bad repair :	-	-	-	-	-	hob/	5.2192
Wexford	Walshestown (2)	- near Assaly Br.	corn	-	-	-	-	-	-	1"os/	169
Wexford	Wexford	-	flour	-	-	-	-	1841	-	6"os/	37
Wexford	Wexford	-	windmill	-	-	-	-	1841	-	6"os/	37
Wexford	Wexford	- 2 m. S of Town	windmill	-	-	-	-	-	-	1"os/	169
St Marys	Wexford T'nparks	- on Spawell Road	Spawell Brewery	-	-	-	-	1841	-	6"os/	37
St Marys	Wexford T'nparks :	- N/ St Mary's Church	brewery	-	-	-	-	1841	-	6"os/	37
Wexford	Wexford Town	-	Glenville Mills	-	-	-	-	-	-	1"os/	169
Wexford	Wexford Town	Baillis Mayor :	wind mill lands	-	-	-	Wexford Tn - Hatton Loftus	1734	-	dd/	79 242 55612
Wexford	Wexford Town	Carroll Frederick	mill	-	-	-	Carroll Fred - Warren Mary	1899	-	dd/	1899 74 221
Wexford	Wexford Town	Chambers Benjamin	mill	-	-	-	Chambers B - White Robt	1833	-	dd/	1833 12 280
Wexford	Wexford Town	Davis Francis Sen	mill	-	-	-	Davis Fran - Seaver John P	1885	-	dd/	1885 16 53
Wexford	Wexford Town	Ld. Estate Court	Folly Mills Fdry	-	-	-	Ld Est Court - Pierce Philip	1876	-	dd/	1876 13 158
Wexford	Wexford Town	Maddock John	Windmill Hills	-	-	-	Maddock Jn - Warren Mcl	1876	-	dd/	1876 43 166
Wexford	Wexford Town	Pierce John	Folly Mills	-	-	-	Pierce John - Pierce Martin	1896	-	dd/	1896 5 116
Wexford	Wexford Town	Taylor Christopher	Wind Mills Hill	-	-	-	Taylor Chris - William	1836	-	dd/	1836 7 108
Wexford	Wexford Town	Wakefield George	Spa Well Mill	-	-	-	Wakefield G - Rowe Thos	1876	-	dd/	1876 29 174
Wexford	Wexford Town :	Harris Walter	mill	-	-	-	Harris Walter - Juliette	1897	-	dd/	1897 77 217
Wexford	Wexford Town :	Brown James Rev.	distillery	-	-	-	Brown jas - Barry John E	1899	-	dd/	1899 39 254
Wexford	Wexford Town :	Warburton George	mill	-	-	-	Warburton G - Booker Jn J	1877	-	dd/	1877 53 128
Wexford	Wexford Town :	Furlong Thomas	mills	-	-	-	FurlongThos - Perceval Jn	1875	-	dd/	1875 24 299
Wexford	Wexford Town :	O`Flaherty William	mill garden	-	-	-	O`Flaherty - McDonald Dan	1898	-	dd/	1898 62 33
Wexford	Wexford Town :	Harvey Jaffrey	mill	-	-	-	Harvey J - Hamilton Maxwel	1845	-	dd/	1845 9 95
Wexford	Wexford Town :	Pearce Angela	mills	-	-	-	Pearce A - Walker Charles	1845	-	dd/	1845 14 31
Wexford	Wexford Town :	O`Keeffe Laurence	old malt house	-	-	-	O`Keeffe - B of I Govs.	1893	-	dd/	1893 25 210
Wexford	Wexford Town :	Rowe Howard & S	flour	-	-	-	-	1963	-	lic/10	flour
Kilcavan ?	Wingstown	E/ Tomhagan Vge	corn & mill dam	-	-	-	-	1841	-	6"os/	47
Fethard	Winningtown	-	corn	-	-	-	-	1841	-	6"os/	45
Owenduff	Yoletown	- on Owenduff R.	corn	-	-	-	-	-	-	1"os/	169
Owenduff	Yoletown	- on Owenduff R.	mill	-	-	-	-	-	-	1"os/	169
Owenduff	Yoletown	Caddigan Walter	carding	-	-	-	-	-	11x3x11	vmb/	24
Owenduff	Yoletown	Caddigan Walter	flour	-	-	-	-	-	13x7x13	vmb/	24
Owenduff	Yoletown	due W/ Mullinderrl Br.	mill (in ruins)	-	-	-	-	1841	-	6"os/	40
Owenduff	Yoletown	NW/ Mullinderry Br.	corn & carding mills	-	-	-	-	1841	-	6"os/	40
Owenduff	Yoletown	Powel James	bleach	-	-	-	-	-	11x2x4	vmb/	24
Owenduff	Yoletown	Ryan Patrick	bleach	-	-	-	-	-	15x3x13	vmb/	24
Owenduff	Yoletown	W. side Owenduff R.	bleach greens	-	-	-	-	1841	-	6"os/	40
Owenduff	Yoletown :	Murphy Reps James	flour	-	-	-	-	1963	- <1,000 barels	lic/20	wh.meal
Coolstuff	Youngstown	Brady Edward	corn	-	-	-	-	1844	14x3x14	vmb/	24
Coolstuff	Youngstown	Bready Edward	corn	(1B) 17.6x19.6x17:	-	3-9-10		1852	10x2.8x15 o`shot :	hob/	5.2288

PARISH	TOWNLAND	MILLER	TYPE	HOUSE	Land	£Val	PROPRIETORS	Date	WHEEL etc.	Record	Ref.
Derrylossary	Aragh East	Lamb John	corn & flour	-	-	25	-	1853	-	gr	-
Arklow	Arklow	- nr Killinskyduff Ho.	corn	-	-	-	-	-	-	1"os/	139
Rathnew	Ashford	-	saw & pond	-	-	-	-	-	-	6"os/	24
Ballykine	Aughrim Town	- on railway siding	flour	Large Old Blds. :	-	-	-	1999	- has old turbine :	mmS/	wh - B
Ballykine	Aughrim Town		mills	-	-	-	-	-	-	1"os/	139
Rathdrum	Avondale	- near Kingston Ho.	saw	-	-	-	-	-	-	1"os/	130
Ballykine	Bahana	-	corn mill in ruins	-	-	-	-	-	-	6"os/	35
Rathdrum	Ballinacarrig	- on Avondale R.	corn	-	-	-	-	-	-	1"os/	130
Rathdrum	Ballinacarrig Lr	- N. side Avonbeg R.	corn	-	-	-	-	-	-	6"os/	35
Ballykine	Ballinaclash	-	site iron works	-	-	-	-	-	-	6"os/	35
Ballykine	Ballinaclash	Darby Joseph Leonard :	mill	-	-	-	Darby J - Disney Thomas	1807	-	dd/	594 547 406149
Ballykine	Ballinaclash	Darby Thomas of :	mill	-	31a.	-	Darby T - Parsons Matt :	1805	-	dd/	578 416 389410
Ballinacor	Ballinacor	- at Annamore	mill	-	-	-	-	-	-	mssH/	11,343
Calary	Ballinacor North	McDonnell Charles	old mill	(2B) 30x19.6x8.6 :	-	3-16	-	1843	11x2.6 :	hob/	5.2310
Calary	Ballinacor North	McDonnell Charles	tuck	-	-	1-10	-	1843	2 wash ft. m/cy B :	hob/	5.2310
Ballinacor	Ballinacorbeg	- E. side Annamoe R.	mill	-	-	-	-	-	-	6"os/	18
Derrylossary	Ballinacorbeg	Murphy James	corn & kiln	(1B) 44x20x29 :	-	5-12	-	1848	12x2.3x6 1 pr.st.	hob/	5.2311
Derrylossary	Ballinacorbeg	Murphy James	corn & kiln	(1B) 23x16x12.6 :	-	5-12	-	1843	12x3x6 1pr st. :	hob/	5.2311
Derrylossary	Ballinacorbeg	Murphy James	corn & kiln, land	-	77a.	20.15	-	1853	-	gr	-
Dunganstown	Ballinameesda	- at Ballinameesda Br.	corn	-	-	-	-	-	-	6"os/	31
Dunganstown	Ballinameesda	Galvin William	corn, offs., land	-	49a.	62.10	-	1853	-	gr	-
Dunganstown	Ballinameesda Lr	Galvin William	corn & kiln	(1A) 40x20x22 :	-	-	-	-	gravity 14x4.6 :	hob/	5.3200
Dunganstown	Ballinameesda Lr	Timmons Sarah :	corn	(3C) 19.6x18x6.6	-	1-3	-	1848	12x3x11 1 pr. st. :	hob/	5.2300
Castlemacadam	Ballinamona	-	site of smelting ho.		-	-	-	-	-	6"os/	40
Castlemacadam	Ballinamona	- on Aughrim R.	corn	-	-	-	-	-	-	6"os/	40
Calary	Ballinastoe	- W. side Vartry R.	cloth	-	-	-	-	-	-	6"os/	12
Calary	Ballinastoe	M'Donnell Christopher	corn & tuck mills :	-	65a.	34.10	-	1853	-	gr	-
Redcross	Ballinaston	McDonnell Chris	old mill	(2B) 30x19.6x8.6 :	-	-	-	1852	11x2.6 2 wash ft. :	hob/	5.2310
Rathdrum	Ballincurrig Lower	Lamb Michael :	corn	(1B) 25x16.6x12.6	-	6-10	-	1853	12.6x1.6 1 pr.st. :	hob/	5.2313
Preban	Ballinglen	-	corn	-	-	-	-	-	-	6"os/	39
Preban	Ballinglen	-	corn &pond	-	-	-	-	-	-	6"os/	39
Preban	Ballinglen	Blake William	corn & kiln	-	-	-	-	1853	-	gr	-
Preban	Ballinglen	Gilbert Robert	corn & flour & ld.	-	26a.	75	-	1853	-	gr	-
Killahurler	Ballinvally	Erly Fran & Hester :	mill	-	-	-	Erly F & H - Bomford Wm	1788	-	dd/	406? 57 265778
Killahurler	Ballinvally	Rose John	mill	-	-	-	Rose John - Jones [NB] :	1784	-	dd/	353 385 239606
Killahurler	Ballinvally	Shiel James of :	mill	-	-	-	Shiel Jas - Coonan John	1780	-	dd/	330 593 225276
Killahurler	Ballinvally	Shiel Thomas	mill	-	-	-	Shiel Th - Meath James	1780	-	dd/	334 567225375
Wicklow	Ballybrittan *	Byrne John, Dublin	mills	-	-	-	Byrne J - Alexander Hu :	1741	-	dd/	104 64 71959
Wicklow	Ballybrittan *	Byrne Matthew :	mills	-	-	-	Byrne R - Kain Terrence :	1790	-	dd/	441 409 284725
Wicklow	Ballybrittan *	Byrne Michael :	mills	-	-	-	Byrne - Leycester Ralph :	1772	-	dd/	286 573 190615
Wicklow	Ballybrittan *	Byrne Robert :	mills	-	-	-	Byrne - Dunsany Jas :	1790	-	dd/	429 248 278055
Wicklow	Ballybrittan *	Clancurry Nicholas :	mill	-	-	-	Clancurry N - Byrne Robt :	1791	-	dd/	431 279 280046
Wicklow	Ballybrittan *	Keogh John :	mill	-	-	-	Keogh John - Hayes John	1743	-	dd/	111 260 76485?
Wicklow	Ballybrittan *	Keoghoe	mill	-	-	-	Keoghoe - Keoghoe	-	-	dd/	307 70 203017
Wicklow	Ballybrittan *	Lycester	mill	-	-	-	Lycester - Lawless	-	?	dd/	530 52 233556
Ballinacon	Ballycarnew Lr.	Foley Matthew	corn	-	-	-	-	-	-	vmb/	23
Rathnew	Ballycullen	-	corn & pond	-	-	-	-	-	-	6"os/	24
Rathnew	Ballycullen	Quinians Anthony	corn	-	-	-	-	-	14x2x15	vmb/	23
Arklow	Ballyduff	- on Avoca R.	mill	-	-	-	-	-	-	1"os/	139
Arklow	Ballyduff	Allen Joshua Hon Lord	mills & mill race	-	-	-	Allen J Lord - Revill Fras	1734	-	dd/	78 302 55870
Arklow	Ballyduff North	-	bed of mill race	-	-	-	-	-	-	6"os/	40
Arklow	Ballyduff North	-	corn & mill dam	-	-	-	-	-	-	6"os/	40

PARISH	TOWNLAND	MILLER	TYPE	HOUSE	Land	£Val	PROPRIETORS	Date	WHEEL etc.	Record	Ref.
Arklow	Ballyduff North	Newsom George	corn & kiln	(1B) 45x21x16.6 :	-	-	-	-	14.8x3.11x11.8 :	hob/	5.2295
Arklow	Ballyduff North	Nuzam John & Robert	corn & land	-	19a.	24.10	-	1853	-	gr	-
Castlemacadam	Ballygahan	- NxW of New Br.	stamp mill in ruins	-	-	-	-	-	-	6"os/	35
Castlemacadam	Ballygahan Lr.	Hodgson Henry	copper mine	-	21a.	32	-	1853	-	gr	-
Killiskey	Ballymaghroe :	Synge John Esq.	printing	(1B) 19.6x17.6x17	-	140	-	1842	-	hob/	5.2324
Kilpipe	Ballymanus	Byrne	mill	-	-	-	Byrne - Coates	1810	-	dd/	276 346 432521
Kilpipe	Ballymanus	Byrne Garrett	mill	-	-	-	Byrne G - Harvey Jas :	1810	-	dd/	627 347 432522
Kilpipe	Ballymanus	Holmes Hugh :	mill	-	-	-	Holmes H - Byrne Edw :	1810	-	dd/	625 184 432677
B'more Eustace	B'more Eustace	Burton Charles :	mill & kiln	-	-	-	Burton C - Meredith Jos :	1807	-	dd/	596 133 405179
B'more Eustace	B'more Eustace	Miley James :	mill & kiln	. - with brew ho. :	-	-	Miley Jas - Lynch James	1809	Lse. 1 Sep.	dd/	623 264 428227
B'more Eustace	B'more Eustace	Wolfe Elizabeth :	mill & kiln	-	-	-	Wolfe E - Wolfe John	1811	Mort. 5 Nov.	dd/	644 304 442870
B'more Eustace	B'more Eustace	White	mill & kiln	-	-	-	White - Day	-	-	dd/	673 467 464595
Mullinacuff	Ballymultagh	Hopkins Joseph	flour, corn & land	-	10a.	53	-	1853	-	gr	-
Castlemacadam	Ballymurtagh	Wicklow C. Mining Co.	copper mine, land	-	67a.	54	-	1853	-	gr	-
Kilcommon	Ballynamanoge	-	corn & mill race	-	-	-	-	-	-	6"os/	38
Arklow	Ballynernon	Eaton Thomas	windmill field	-	-	-	Eaton Thos - Elliott Geo	1731	-	dd/	69 491 49351
Mullinacuff	Ballynultagh	-	mill dam	-	-	-	-	-	-	6"os/	43
Mullinacuff	Ballynultagh	-	mill race (>1mile) :	-	-	-	-	-	-	6"os/	43
Mullinacuff	Ballynultagh	- Shillelagh	Flour Mills	-	-	-	-	-	-	6"os/	43
Mullinacuff	Ballynultagh	- Newtown	Flour Mill	-	-	-	-	-	-	6"os/	43
Mullinacuff	Ballynultagh	Bradell Thos & Nich :	mill	-	-	-	Braddel T - Moore John :	1979	Mort. 25Jne.	dd/	506 317 330840
Mullinacuff	Ballynultagh	Carleton George :	mill	-	-	-	Carleton G - Ford Roger :	1766	-	dd/	309 657 209057
Mullinacuff	Ballynultagh	Forde Roger	mill	-	-	-	Forde R - Rothwell Wm	1778	-	dd/	328 72 216861
Mullinacuff	Ballynultagh	Furlong Cloney	mill	-	-	-	Furlong C - Kelly James :	1724	-	dd/	486? 310 308418
Mullinacuff	Ballynultagh	Hopkins Joseph	2nd bleach	-	-	-	-	-	16x11x13	vmb/	23
Mullinacuff	Ballynultagh	Hopkins Joseph	beetling	-	-	-	-	-	16x11x13	vmb/	23
Mullinacuff	Ballynultagh	Hopkins Joseph	bleach	-	-	-	-	-	14x5x15 15x5x15	vmb/	23
Mullinacuff	Ballynultagh	Hopkins Joseph	bleach green :	-	-	-	-	1853	-	gr	-
Mullinacuff	Ballynultagh	Hopkins Joseph	corn	-	-	-	-	-	18x4x19 4 pr sts.	vmb/	23
Mullinacuff	Ballynultagh	Hopkins Joseph	flour	-	-	-	-	-	18.7x4x7	vmb/	23
Mullinacuff	Ballynultagh	Hopkins Joseph	flour, corn mills, land		15a.	56	-	1853	-	gr	-
Mullinacuff	Ballynultagh	Hopkins Joseph	starching mayle	-	-	-	-	-	-	vmb/	23
Mullinacuff	Ballynultagh	Hopkins Joseph	wool carding	-	-	-	-	-	-	vmb/	23
Mullinacuff	Ballynultagh	Ireland George	mill	-	-	-	Ireland G - Ireland Henry	1780	-	dd/	332 125 223 630
Mullinacuff	Ballynultagh	Robinson	mill	-	-	-	Robinson - Tighe	-	?	dd/	592 4 409411?
Mullinacuff	Ballynultagh	Rockingham Charles :	mill	-	-	-	Rockingham C - Jones :	1763	-	dd/	226 474 148575
Preban	Baltinglass	Blake William	corn	-	-	-	-	-	14x2x14	vmb/	23
Preban	Baltinglass	Gibney Robert	corn	-	-	-	-	-	14x5x14	vmb/	23
Preban	Baltinglass	Gibney Robert	flour	-	-	-	-	-	14x4x14	vmb/	23
Preban	Baltinglass Town	- W. side R. Slaney	flour	-	-	-	-	-	-	6"os/	27
Baltinglass	Baltinglass W.	Anderson Robert H	flour & corn	-	-	65	-	1853	-	gr	-
Preban	BaltinglassTown	- N. side Main St.	brewery	-	-	-	-	-	-	6"os/	27
Wcklow	Bannoqueroe *	Garner Francis	mill	-	-	-	Garner F - Savage Fran	1717	-	dd/	55 496 37991
Ballinacor	Baravore	Baravore Mining Co.	crushing mill	-	-	4	-	1853	-	gr	-
Delgany	Bellevue	-	corn	-	-	-	-	-	-	1"os/	121
Blessington	Blessington	- on R. Liffey	corn	-	-	-	-	1845	-	6"os/	5
Blessington	Blessington	Blesinton	mills	-	-	-	Blesinton - Sargeant		?	dd/	43 79 27927
Blessington	Blessington	Ebbs Thomas	corn	-	-	-	-	-	14x6x5	vmb/	23
Blessington	Blessington	Ebbs William	corn & land	-	6a.	17.10	-	1853	-	gr	-
Blessington	Blessington	Farquharson	mills	-	-	-	Farquhason - Stewart	-	?	dd/	72 149 50160
Blessington	Blessington	Merrey William :	needle m/facture	-	-	-	-	1824	-	surv/	B`tonFHS
Blessington	Blessington	Sargeant William :	Sourgade Mill	-	-	-	Sargeant - Wilkinson Jn :	1773	DD Poll	dd/	76 48 52682

PARISH	TOWNLAND	MILLER	TYPE	HOUSE	Land	£Val	PROPRIETORS	Date	WHEEL etc.	Record	Ref.
Blessington	Blessington :	- submerged	corn	-	-	-	-	2010	-	mmSv/	wh - Z
Blessington	Blessington Tn :	Trustees Turnpike Rd.	toll-house	-	-	-	-	1853	-	gr	-
Dunganstown	Bonagrew	-	bed of mill race	-	-	-	-	-	-	6"os/	36
Dunganstown	Bonagrew	- Castletimon	Corn Mill	-	-	-	-	-	-	6"os/	36
Dunganstown	Bonagrew	Nolan & Perrin :	corn	(1B) 27x21x17 :	-	9-0-4	-	1845	13.6x4.4x3.6 :	hob/	5.2300
Kiltegan	Borkill Beg	- S. side Douglas R.	corn & race	-	-	-	-	-	-	6"os/	32
Kiltegan	Borkill Beg	Chandler Thomas	corn & flour	-	-	-	-	-	- 3 pr stones	vmb/	23
Kiltegan	Borkill Beg	Giltrap William	corn	-	-	-	-	-	11x211	vmb/	23
Kilbride	Borkill Beg Weel	Molloy Partick	corn	-	-	-	-	-	11x2x12	vmb/	23
Bray	Bray	-	corn	-	-	-	-	-	-	6"os/	4
Bray	Bray	Barnier Joshua :	mill	-	-	-	Bernier J - Prendergast :	1805	-	dd/	596 146 405602
Bray	Bray	Bernier	mill	-	-	-	Bernier - Quin	-	?	dd/	596 107 405603
Bray	Bray	Donnellan John	mill	-	-	-	Donnellan J - Barnier Jos	1807	-	dd/	586 381 397787
Bray	Bray	Donnellan John	mill	-	-	-	Donnellan J - Farrell Danl	1801	-	dd/	619 92 423691
Bray	Bray	Doyle Thomas	mill	-	-	-	Doyle T - Clooney Denis :	1807	-	dd/	590 350 401588
Bray	Bray	Farrell Daniel :	mill	-	-	-	Farrell D - Roberts Thos :	1809	-	dd/	619 289 423584
Bray	Bray	Keating	mill	-	-	-	Keating - Farrell	-	?	dd/	619 228 423583
Bray	Bray	Norris S & Co.	flour	-	-	-	-	-	15x6x 3	vmb/	23
Bray	Bray	Salheren	mill	-	-	-	Salheren - Sothern	-	?	dd/	618 41 423045
Bray	Bray	Salheren George	mill	-	-	-	Salheren - Culloden Jem'a	1809	-	dd/	619 422 424344
Bray	Bray	Sharkey Thomas :	mill	-	-	-	Sharkey T - Roberts Jno :	1807	-	dd/	590 466 403244
Bray	Bray	Southern Thomas :	corn	- kn/a Bray Mill :	-	-	Southern Thomas - Geo	1809	-	dd/	615 151 420613
Bray	Bray	Toole Margret Widow	mill	-	-	-	Toole - Cunningham Geo	1808	-	dd/	603 109 410884
Bray	Bray Great	Hill Abraham :	mills	-	-	-	Hill A- Donnellan John :	1777	-	dd/	317 147 211719
Bray	Bray Great	Hill Elizabeth	mills	-	-	-	Hill E - Toole Tobias	1782	-	dd/	340 494 231276
Bray	Bray Great	Hill William :	mills	-	-	-	Hill William to Robert :	1775	-	dd/	309 193 205310
Bray	Bray Great	Toole Tobias :	maltho. & distillery	-	-	-	Toole T - Exshaw Thos :	1777	-	dd/	319 312 214487
Dunganstown	Brittas	-	bed of mill race	-	-	-	-	-	-	6"os/	36
Dunganstown	Brittas	- Brittas	Flour Mill	-	-	-	-	-	-	6"os/	36
Dunganstown	Brittas	McCormack Mr.	-	-	-	-	-	-	Pelton	turb/	c1947
Dunganstown	Brittas	Nevins Archibald :	mills	-	-	-	Nevins A - Nevins Thos :	1806	-	dd/	580 179 393844
Dunganstown	Brittas	Nolan & Perrin :	corn & kiln :	(1A) 72x22.6x26 :	-	42-15	-	1850	25x9x19 bkts. 75 :	hob/	5.2299
Dunganstown	Brittas	Nolan & Perrin Mssrs	flour & land	-	5a.	43.10	-	1853	-	gr	-
Donaghmore	Brittas	O'Toole Eoin	The Fish Farm	-	-	-	-	-	o/shot 2kw	turb/	c1947
Derrylossary	Brockagh	Mining Co. of Ireland	crushing mill & forge		-	10/-	-	1853	-	gr	-
Derrylossary	Brocklagh	Mining Co. of Ireland	Legannon Mines	turf ho. shed, etc.	-	-	-	1853	3 wheels - o`shot :	hob/	5.2311
Kilranelagh	Brockna	-	mill in ruins	-	-	-	-	-	-	6"os/	3
Donard	Broomfield	-	mill & pond	-	-	-	-	-	-	6"os/	21
Donard	Broomfield	Meath Robt & Robt	corn	-	-	-	-	-	11x3x10	vmb/	23
Donard	Broomfield	Proprietor Samuel	tuck	-	-	-	-	-	11x2x10	vmb/	23
Carnew	Carnew	-	brewery	-	-	-	-	-	-	1"os/	148
Carnew	Carnew	-	corn & pond	-	-	-	-	-	-	6"os/	4
Carnew	Carnew	-	mill race to coast :	-	-	-	-	-	-	6"os/	4
Carnew	Carnew	- E. of Tombreen Br.	corn	-	-	-	-	-	-	6"os/	4
Carnew	Carnew	Graham John	corn	-	-	-	-	-	13x3x13	vmb/	23
Carnew	Carnew	Stone Ralph	corn & land		25a.	26.10	-	1853	-	gr	-
Newcastle	Cloro	Synge Mr	saw	-	-	-	-	-	13x4x12 4 saws	vmb/	23
Castlemacadam	Connary Upper	Connary Mining Co.	copper mine, land	-	14a.	10.10	-	1853	-	gr	-
Castlemacadam	Connary Upper	Salkeld Joseph	Royalty of copper mine		-	1000	-	1853	-	gr	-
Rathnew	Coolawinnia	-	mill	-	-	-	-	-	-	6"os/	25
Rathnew	Coolawinnia	-	old mill stream	-	-	-	-	-	-	6"os/	25
Rathnew	Coolawinnia	Flynn Michael	old mill	(1C0 51x20.6x24 :	-	-	-	-	not used some yrs.	hob/	5.2329

PARISH	TOWNLAND	MILLER	TYPE	HOUSE	Land	£Val	PROPRIETORS	Date	WHEEL etc.	Record	Ref.
Glenealy	Coolbeg	-	churning & pond	-	-	-	-	-	-	6"os/	31
Arklow	Coolgarrow	Stedman Richard	corn & land	-	68a.	50	-	1853	-	gr	-
Castlemacadam	Cronebane	Brooke Richard	Royalty of copper mine		-	2000	-	1853	-	gr	-
Castlemacadam	Cronebane	Williams & Sons	engine house, ld. :	-	65a.	7.5.0	-	1853	-	gr	-
Mullinacuff	Cronelea	-	corn	-	-	-	-	-	-	6"os/	43
Mullinacuff	Cronelea	Twamley Thomas	corn	-	-	-	-	-	14x3x14	vmb/	23
Mullinacuff	Cronelea	Twamley Thomas	corn & land	-	71a.	44	-	1853	-	gr	-
Donard	Donard	-	mill	-	-	-	-	-	-	1"os/	129
Powerscourt	Enniskerry	- S. side Cookst`n R.	mill ruin	-	-	-	-	-	-	6"os/	7
Powerscourt	Enniskerry	Williams William	corn	-	-	-	-	-	12x2x14	vmb/	23
Kilcommon	Glasnaigirt N.	Comerford Mr	flour	-	-	-	-	-	11x5x 4	vmb/	23
Rathdrum	Glasnarget	- E. of Rathdrum Br.	flour	-	-	-	-	-	-	6"os/	30
Kilcommon	Glasnarget North	Comerford James :	flour	(1B) 46x24x31 :	-	-	-	1842	16x8 wh. & m/cy :	hob/	5.2320
Knockrath	Grenan Beg	-	mill	-	-	-	-	1606	-	iaa/	AI1184os29.12.5
Boystown	Homphrystown	Shannon Robt & Bridge	corn	-	-	3	-	1853	-	gr	-
Boystown	Humphreystown	- W. side Kings R.	mill	-	-	-	-	-	-	6"os/	10
Boystown	Humphreystown	Shannon Robt & Jno	corn	-	-	-	-	-	12x2x5	vmb/	23
Mullinacuff	Kellynure	Moore Thomas	corn	-	-	-	-	-	12x3x8	vmb/	23
Kilbride	Kilbride	-	corn	-	-	-	-	-	-	6"os/	5
Kilbride	Kilbride	Molley Patrick	corn & land	-	32a.	32	-	1853	-	gr	-
Newcastle	Kilcoole	- 1/8 mile E. of Vge.	corn	-	-	-	-	-	-	6"os/	13
Newcastle	Kilcoole	Anderson Francis	mills	-	-	-	Anderson F - Byrne Jn	1716	-	dd/	16 358 7710
Newcastle	Kilcoole	Darlington Mr	corn	-	-	-	-	-	12x2x13	vmb/	23
Newcastle	Kilcoole	Ross Hon Richard	mills	-	-	-	Ross R - Anderson Fran	1716	-	dd/	16 333 7641/2
Newcastle	Kilcoole	Ross Richard Hon.	mills	-	-	-	Ross R - Hayes John	1723	-	dd/	38 143 23719
Newcastle	Kilcoole	Ross Richard Ld Visc.	mills	-	-	-	Ross Richd - Ryder John	1716	-	dd/	15 340 7689
Newcastle	Kilcoole	Ryder John :	mills & fairs	-	-	-	Ryder J - Woodcock Sm	1716	-	dd/	15 341 7693
Aghowle	Killabeg	-	corn	- seems quite old	-	-	-	1999	- has recent turbine	mmSv/	wh - D
Aghowle	Killabeg	-	old mill dam	-	-	-	-	-	-	6"os/	42
Aghowle	Killabeg	- Killabeg	Old Corn Mill	-	-	-	-	-	-	6"os/	42
Carnew	Killabeg	Maguire	corn	-	-	-	-	-	14x4x14	vmb/	23
Aghowle	Killabeg	M'Guire Patrick	corn & land	-	7a.	11	-	1853	-	gr	-
Kilpipe	Killacloran	-	site iron works	-	-	-	-	-	-	6"os/	34
Kilpipe	Killacloran	- W. of Kilpipe Br.	corn	-	-	-	-	-	-	6"os/	39
Kilpipe	Killacloran	Kirwan Ann	corn	-	-	-	-	-	10x2x10	vmb/	23
Kilpipe	Killacoran	Doyle John	corn & kiln & land	-	66a.	43.5	-	1853	-	gr	-
Kilpipe	Killancanny	Rothwell George	corn	-	-	-	-	-	10x2x10	vmb/	23
Kilpipe	Killaveny	Rothwell George	corn & kiln & land	-	27a.	20.15	-	1853	-	gr	-
Delgany	Killincarrig	- 1/4 mile S. of Vge.	mill & race	-	-	-	-	-	-	6"os/	13
Delgany	Killincarrig	Dunne Peter	flour	(1B) 58.3x25.9x40	-	-	-	1843	18x6x16 4pr. st. :	hob/	5.2334
Delgany	Killincarrig	Dunne Peter	flour	-	-	-	-	-	18x6x16	vmb/	23
Kilbride	Killinskyduff	- Ticknock	Corn Mill	-	-	-	-	-	-	6"os/	40
Aghowle	Killinure	-	corn & mill dam	-	-	-	-	-	-	6"os/	42
Aghowle	Killinure	-	mill race (1/2 mile)	-	-	-	-	-	-	6"os/	42
Aghowle	Killinure	Laurenson Michael	corn & kiln	-	-	-	-	1853	-	gr	-
Newcastle	Kilmaccullagh	Bower & Galway	corn	-	-	-	-	-	13x2x15	vmb/	23
Newcastle	Kilmaccullagh	Bower & Galway	corn	-	-	-	-	-	14x3x15	vmb/	23
C`macadam	Kilmacon Upper	Boswell Robert	mill & kiln	-	-	-	Boswell R - Boswell Alex	1735	-	dd/	80 216 55527
C`macadam	Kilmacon Upper	Heyden	mill & kiln	-	-	-	Hayden - Waters	1737	-	dd/	88 519 63542
C`macadam	Kilmacon Upper	Heyden Samuel	mill & kiln	-	-	-	Hayden S - Salkeld John	1731	-	dd/	68 228 47820
C`macadam	Kilmacon Upper	Heyden Samuel	mill & kiln	-	-	-	Hayden - Sandes Richd	1731	-	dd/	83 27 57400
Newcastle Up	Kilmacullagh	-	flour	-	-	-	-	-	-	6"os/	13

PARISH	TOWNLAND	MILLER	TYPE	HOUSE	Land	£Val	PROPRIETORS	Date	WHEEL etc.	Record	Ref.
Newcastle Up	Kilmacullagh	-	mill race & pond	-	-	-	-	-	-	6"os/	13
Castlemacadam	Kilmagig Lower	-	old corn mill	-	-	-	-	-	-	6"os/	35
Castlemacadam	Kilmagig Lower	- at Millmount	flour	-	-	-	-	-	-	6"os/	35
Castlemacadam	Kilmagig Lower	Johnson Richard	corn & land	-	14a.	38	-	1853	-	gr	-
Ennerielly.	Kilpatrick	-	mill race (no mill)	-	-	-	-	-	-	6"os/	36
Killiskey	Kiltimon	-	brewery	-	-	-	-	-	-	6"os/	19
Rathdrum	Knockadosan	-	brewery	-	-	-	-	-	-	6"os/	30
Rathdrum	Knockadosan	Darley & Co. :	old brewery & :	(1B) 88x17.6x19 :	-	26-2	-	1853	- in bad order :	hob/	5.2313
Arklow	Knockanree	-	corn mill in ruins	-	-	-	-	-	-	6"os/	35
Liscolman	Knockeen	- on Derreen R.	mill	-	-	-	-	-	-	1"os/	-
Killahurler	Knockmiller	-	corn	-	-	-	-	-	-	6"os/	40
Kilcommon	Knocknaboy	Darcy Thomas	corn	-	-	-	-	-	12x2x10	vmb/	23
Rathnew	Knocknacrumpa	- near Ashford	butter	old walls still stand	-	-	-	2007	- machinery parts	mmSv/	p&mc
Bolin Valley *	Lady Park *	Blesinton Charles :	mill	-	-	-	Blessington - Malone Rich	1727	-	dd/	52 390 34997
Derrylossary	Laragh	-	lead mines	-	-	-	-	-	-	6"os/	23
Derrylossary	Laragh	-	ore grinding mill	-	-	-	-	-	-	6"os/	23
Derrylossary	Laragh	Lamb John	corn & flour	(1A) 44x20x29	-	3	-	1843	14x6x- all metal :	hob/	5.2311
Baltinglass	Lathaleere	-	bleach	-	-	-	-	-	-	6"os/	1
Newcastle Lr.	Leabeg Lower	-	lime kiln	-	-	-	-	-	-	6"os/	13
Wicklow	Limekiln Park *	Blessington Chas Hon.	mill	-	-	-	Blessington - Sargint W	1724	-	dd/	45 79 27927
Kilbride	Lisheens	- W. bank of Brittas R.	hz mill	- oak timbers :	-	-	-	-	-	iaa/	AI1188 os1.11.6
Shillelagh	Lumcloon	-	mill	-	-	-	-	-	-	1"os/	-
Dunlavin	Milltown	- stream to R.Grease	corn	-	-	-	-	-	-	6"os/	14
Dunlavin	Milltown	Byrne Elizabeth	corn	-	-	-	-	-	12x2x12	vmb/	23
Dunlavin	Milltown	Byrne Elizabeth	corn & land	-	31a.	40	-	1853	-	gr	-
Talbotstown	Milltown	Carter Thomas Hon.	land	-	-	-	Carter T - Kingsbury Th	1738	-	dd/	89 501 64316
Talbotstown	Milltown	Carter Thomas Hon.	land	-	-	-	Carter - Dowling Ann :	1738	-	dd/	91 301 64317
Dunlavin	Milltown	Deering Barry	corn	buildings fine	-	-	-	2000	wheel removed	pWEH	B
Dunlavin	Milltown	Deering Barry	domestic	-	-	-	-	-	Ossberger 9.3kw :	turb/	c1947
Coneroe	Milltown	Eccles John Sir	land	-	-	-	Eccles Jn - Forth James	1720	-	dd/	29 261 17142
Coneroe	Milltown	Eccles John Sir	land	-	-	-	Eccles J - Robnett Robt :	1722	-	dd/	35 361 22802
Talbotstown	Milltown	Leyland	land	-	-	-	Leyland - Kingsbury	-	?	dd/	92 105 64315
Dunlavin	Milltown	Tynte Hon. James :	mill	-	-	-	Tynte J - Woods John :	1723	-	dd/	37 508 23671
Coneroe	Milltown	Walsh Philip Rev.	land	-	-	-	Walsh P - Howard Wm	1720	-	dd/	51 442 34292
Rathnew	Milltown North	Moran Mr	corn	-	-	-	-	-	12x3x13	vmb/	23
Rathnew	Milltown North	Moran Simon	corn	-	-	23-19	-	1852	-	hob/	5.2328
Rathnew	Milltown North	Moran Simon	corn	(3B) 23.6x20.6x6 :	-	18-19	-	1842	12x3.4x13 2 pr. st.	hob/	5.2329
Newcastle Up.	Mountkennedy Dm.	Bowes Andrew	corn	(1B) 37x24.6x17 :	-	25-10	-	1842	13x3 & 13x4 ea. :	hob/	5.2327
Newcastle Up.	Mountkennedy Dm.	Cunningham Robt G.	old threshing mill	(1B) 32.6x12x6 :	-	164	-	1842	- [no wheel]	hob/	5.2327
Rathnew	Mountusher	- E. side R. Vartry	corn	-	-	-	-	-	-	6"os/	25
Rathnew	Mountusher	Sutton Samuel	corn	-	-	15-0	-	1853	-	hob/	5.2328
Rathnew	Mountusher	Sutton Samuel	corn	-	-	14-13	(1C) 20x18x13 & :	1842	14x3x9.6 38 bkts. :	hob/	5.2329
Rathnew	Mountusher	Sutton Samuel	corn	-	-	-	-	-	14 x3x9	vmb/	23
Rathnew	Mountusher	Walpole Edward :	corn	-	-	-	-	1868	-	l.hist	sc
Derrylossary	Moyntiagh	-	corn & dam	-	-	-	-	-	-	6"os/	24
Derrylossary	Moyntiagh	Byrne Andrew & Wm	bark	(2B) 27x22x8 :	-	13-2	-	1853	14x4x14.6 B :	hob/	5.2317
Derrylossary	Moyntiagh	Byrne Andrew & Wm	bark (old) :	(1B) 62x30x8.6 :	-	41-9	-	1842	-	hob/	5.2318
Rathnew	Mullinacuff *	-	mill	- no trace found	-	-	-	1998	-	mmSv/	wh - Z
Newcastle	Newcastle	-	corn	-	-	-	-	-	-	6"os/	19
Newcastle	Newcastle Mid	-	mill (site)	-	-	-	-	-	-	iaa/	AI1189 os19.2.6
Newcastle	Newcastle Mid	Doyle Mr	flour	-	-	-	-	-	13x415	vmb/	23
Newcastle	Newcastle Upr	-	hz	-	-	-	Glen Golf Club	2001	horizontal, dia. ?	gr/	-

PARISH	TOWNLAND	MILLER	TYPE	HOUSE	Land	£Val	PROPRIETORS	Date	WHEEL etc.	Record	Ref.
Newcastle	Newcastle Upr	-	hz mill	-	-	-	-	-	-	iaa/	AI1190 os19.2.5
Wcklow	Newmills	Bourice	mill	-	-	-	Bourice - Nutley	-	?	dd/	48 477 30104
Wcklow	Newmills	Fairfax Thos RtH. Gen.	mill	-	-	-	Fairfax Th - Alcock Wm	1709	-	dd/	3 233 870
Wcklow	Newmills	Robinson Ann	mill	-	-	-	Robinson A - Prior Thos	1738	-	dd/	91 382 64509
Mullinacuff	Newtown	-	The Old Mill	-	-	-	-	-	-	6"os/	43
Mullinacuff	Newtown	- near Forttown Ho.	mill	-	-	-	-	-	-	1"os/	-
Mullinacuff	Newtown	Tomkin Charles	corn	-	-	-	-	-	14x4x12	vmb/	23
Mullinacuff	Newtown	Tomkins Charles	corn & land	-	102a.	50	-	1853	-	gr	-
Powerscourt	Powerscourt Dem.	Powerscourt Lord	saw & thrashing	-	-	-	-	-	16x3x13	vmb/	23
Donaghmore	Randalstown	- near Whitestown Br.	mill	-	-	-	-	-	-	1"os/	129
Delgany	Rathdown	Monk Chas & Agneta	Redmond`s Mills	-	-	-	Monk C - Stephens Jn	1712	-	dd/	17 180 8489?
Delgany	Rathdown	Stephens John	Redmond`s Mills :	-	-	-	Stephens J - Adair Robt	1713	-	dd/	12 229 4865
Delgany	Rathdown	Wingfield Edward :	mills	-	-	-	Wingfield E - Kavanagh:	1728	-	dd/	61 32 40528
Delgany	Rathdrum	-	brewery	-	-	-	-	-	-	6"os/	30
Rathdrum	Rathdrum	- on Avondale R.	mill	-	-	-	-	-	-	1"os/	130
Redcross	Redcross	- N/ Redcrosss Tn	corn	-	-	-	-	-	-	6"os/	35
Redcross	Redcross	Ruskell Thomas	corn, offs. & land	-	16a.	22.10	-	1853	-	gr	-
Redcross	Redcross	Russell Thomas	corn & kiln	(3B) 24x18.6x8 :	-	2-17	-	1843	13x2.10x12 :	hob/	5.2309
Derrylossary	Roundwood	Clotworthy Robert	-	Clohoge, Luggala	-	-	-	-	Gilkes 22kw Turgo :	turb/	c1947
Roundwood	Roundwood	Collins Edward	old corn mill	(1B) 25x16.6x12 :	-	4-10	-	1843	10x1.6x- mill idle	hob/	5.2311
Roundwood	Roundwood	Collins Edward	old tuck mill	(3C) 19x16.6x6.6	-	-	-	1853	1 pair wash feet :	hob/	5.2311
Rathbran	Saundergrove	- to Saundersville	mill race & stream	-	-	-	-	-	-	1"os/	129
Rathbran	Saundersville	-	tuck	-	-	-	-	-	-	1"os/	129
Rathbran	Saundersville	- close to Bridge	tuck	-	-	-	-	-	-	6"os/	21
Derrylossary	Sevenchurches :	Mining Co. of Ireland	lead mines	-	-	500	-	1853	-	gr	-
Derrylossary	Sevenchurches :	Mining Co. of Ireland	mill for crushing ore		-	11.10	-	1853	-	gr	-
Kilbride	Shelton	Wicklow Earl of	mill & land, offs. :	-	86a.	113	-	1853	-	gr	-
Castlemacadam	Sroughmore	Connary Mining Co.	engine house & ld.	-	17a.	4.5.0	-	1853	-	gr	-
Rathbran	Stratford	-	bleach	-	-	-	-	-	-	6"os/	21
Rathbran	Stratford	-	cotton print fcty	-	-	-	-	-	-	6"os/	21
Rathbran	Stratford	- near Factory Bridge	mill	-	-	-	-	-	-	1"os/	129
Baltinglass	Stratfordlodge	-	bleach & mill dam	-	-	-	-	-	-	6"os/	27
Baltinglass	Stratfordlodge	-	bleach green	-	-	-	-	-	-	6"os/	27
Killiskey	The Grange Vge.	-	old corn mill	-	-	-	-	-	-	6"os/	20
Kilbride	Ticknock	-	site of smelting ho	-	-	-	-	-	-	6"os/	40
Kilbride	Ticknock	- Ovoca	Brewery	-	-	-	-	-	-	6"os/	40
Kilbride	Ticknock	Galvin William	flour & corn	(1B) 30.6x20.6x20	-	90-4	-	1845	12.10x5x12 36 bkts:	hob/	5.2304
Kilbride	Ticknock	Gavin William	flour mills & land	-	28a.	42	-	1853	-	gr	-
Castlemacadam	Tigroney	-	mill	-	-	-	-	-	-	6"os/	35
Kilcommon	Tinahely	-	mill race (1 mile)	-	-	-	-	-	-	6"os/	38
Kilcommon	Tinahely	- near Killaveny Br.	mill	-	-	-	-	-	-	1"os/	-
Kilcommon	Tinahely	- Town / W. side R.	corn	-	-	-	-	-	-	6"os/	38
Kilcommon	Tinahely	- Town / W. side R.	flour	-	-	-	-	-	-	6"os/	38
Kilcommon	Tinahely	Dowse Henry & Thos	corn	-	-	-	-	-	14x3x14 14x5x14	vmb/	23
Ballykine	Tinakelly Upper	Fogarty Owen	flour, kiln & land	-	5a.	27.10	-	1856	-	gr	-
Ballykine	Aughrim Upper	Fogarty Owen	hos., offs., land	- (18 sections)	250a.	140	-	1856	-	gr	a.a.ire.ie
Ballykine	Tinakelly Upper	Fogerty Matthew	flour	-	-	-	-	1843	14x4x14	vmb/	23
Castlemacadam	Tinnahinch	Cooper John	corn & land	-	30a.	32.5	-	1853	-	gr	-
Ballykine	Tinnakelly	-	flour	-	-	-	-	-	-	6"os/	34
Wcklow	Tobber *	Morecroft James Rev.	mill	-	-	-	Morecroft - Stotthard Jn	1722	-	dd/	37 361 23053
Wcklow	Tobber *	Percy Henry	mill	-	-	-	Percy H - Powell Chas	1722	-	dd/	37 286 22745
Blessington	Tober	Wall James	corn	-	-	-	-	-	14x2x14	vmb/	23

PARISH	TOWNLAND	MILLER	TYPE	HOUSE	Land	£Val	PROPRIETORS	Date	WHEEL etc.	Record	Ref.
Kilpipe	Toherpatrick	Hobson Abraham	corn	-	-	-	-	-	10x2x10	vmb/	23
Carnew	Tombreen	- WxN Cronyhorn Br.	corn	-	-	-	-	-	-	6"os/	47
Carnew	Tombreen	Nolan Jno	corn	-	-	-	-	-	9x3x9	vmb/	23
Carnew	Tombreen	Nolan Jno	reaping hook mill	-	-	-	-	-	8x2x8 seldom empl.	vmb/	23
Carnew	Tombreen	Nolan John	corn & land	-	19a.	13.10	-	1853	-	gr	-
Preban	Tomcoyle	- at Tankersley House	saw	-	-	-	-	-	-	25"os/	39.06
Wick	Townland ?	- near Belleview Ho.	corn	-	-	-	-	-	-	6"os/	8
Kilcommon	Townland ?	McDonald Francis	corn	-	-	-	-	1852	-	hob/	5.2322
Wcklow	Tubber *	Essington Richard	mill	-	-	-	Essington R - Lingen Wm	1731	-	dd/	67 147 45619
Rathbran	Tuckmill Upper	-	corn	-	-	-		-	-	6"os/	27
Rathbran	Tuckmill Upper	-	tuck	-	-	-	-	-	-	6"os/	27
Carnew	Umrygar	-	corn	-	-	-	-	-	-	6"os/	47
Carnew	Umrygar	-	mill race (>1 mile)	-	-	-	-	-	-	6"os/	47
Carnew	Umrygar	Graham Elizabeth	corn	-	-	-	-	-	10x1x10	vmb/	23
Carnew	Umrygar	Tyndall James	corn & land	-	48a.	27	-	1853	-	gr	-
Donaghmore	Whitestown	-	corn & race	-	-	-	-	-	-	6"os/	21
Donaghmore	Whitestown Lr.	Doyle James	corn	-	-	-	-	-	10x2x10	vmb/	23
Rathnew	Wicklow Town	Blessinton Charles :	Limekiln Park mills	-	-	-	Blessinton - Sargeant Wm	1725	-	dd/	45 79 27927
Rathnew	Wicklow Town	Carroll Frederick	mill	-	-	-	Carroll F - Warren Mary	1899	-	dd/	1899 28 21
Rathnew	Wicklow Town	Sargeant	Limekiln Park Mills	-	-	-	Sargeant - Wilkinson Jn :	1773	DD Poll	dd/	76 48 52682
Kilpoole	Wicklow Town :	Perrin & Nolan	corn store & kiln	-	-	16	-	1853	-	gr	-
Kilpoole	Wicklow Town :	Edwards John	corn stores :	-	38	-	-	1853	-	gr	-
Kilpoole	Wicklow Town :	Edwards John	flour & corn :	-	45	-	-	1853	-	gr	-
Kilpoole	Wicklow Town :	Porter Richard	corn store & kiln	-	-	32	-	1853	-	gr	-
Kilpoole	Wicklow Town :	Perrin & Nolan	corn stores :	-	-	28	-	1853	-	gr	-

PARISH	TOWNLAND	MILLER	TYPE	HOUSE	Land £Val	PROPRIETORS	Date	WHEEL etc.	Record	Ref.

More than 15,00 names of the mill proprietors, in many cases that of the miller, are provided. With time-span being approximately 1700 to year 1900. The index lists these names in A - Z order, giving notes of the County and Townland for each mill.

INDEX FOLLOWS -

CO.	TOWNLAND	MILLER
		A
ROS	Ganlys	**Abbot**
DUB	Finglas	**Abbot Chrisopher**
OFF	Bracknagh	**Abbot John**
DUB	Milltown	**Abercorn Earl**
DON	Glensmill	**Abercorn Marq.**
DON	Sion Mill	**Abercorn Marq.**
TIP	Ballyloughnane	**Abernethy William**
TIP	Doughkill	**Abernethy William**
FER	Rosscolban	**Acheson Guy**
LDY	Timaconway	**Acheson James**
FER	Rosscolban	**Acheson John**
ROS	Erriblagh	**Acheson William**
ARM	Lisbane	**Achison James**
OFF	Drumakeenan	**Acres Adam**
OFF	Drumakeeran	**Acres George**
GAL	Kilcreevanty	**Acton Patrick**
DWN	Belvor *	**Adair**
DUB	Dublin City	**Adair Archibald**
LDY	Ballygurk	**Adair Bell**
LDY	Ballyness	**Adair Bell**
LDY	Bellaghy	**Adair Bell**
DWN	Balloo	**Adair James**
WW	Rathdown	**Adair Robert**
WEX	Marny	**Adair Robert**
DWN	Ballygowan	**Adair Thomas B**
ANT	Carnearney	**Adair Thomas Benj**
DWN	Ballygowan	**Adair William**
CAV	Townland ?	**Adame Francis**
LOU	Banktown Up & Lr	**Adams**
LOU	Comm. Corp. Lds	**Adams**
MON	Derrygooney	**Adams**
MON	Derrygooney	**Adams**
LOU	Kercock	**Adams**
LAO	Rathdowney	**Adams**
MON	Rockcorry	**Adams**
ANT	Magherahoney	**Adams Alex**
CAV	Drumhillagh	**Adams Charles Jas**
ANT	Stranocum	**Adams Dav**
CAV	Drumaraw	**Adams Francis**
MON	Drumgarran	**Adams Francis**
MON	Mullaghmonaghan	**Adams Francis**
LDY	Ballydevitt	**Adams John**
LDY	Boghilboy	**Adams John**
LDY	Loughan Water	**Adams John**
MON	Aghillagh *	**Adams Richard**
CAV	Killan	**Adams Robert**
DUB	Stubbins Mill	**Adams Thomas**
CAV	Drumaraw	**Adams William**
LAO	Ballybuggy	**Adamson**
DWN	Ballydown	**Adamson**
OFF	Bogtown	**Adamson**
WME	Curries	**Adamson Richard**
WEX	Ballybought	**Addams William**
LOU	Ardee Town	**Addy**

CO.	TOWNLAND	MILLER
LOU	Ardee	**Addy Edward**
LOU	Ardee Town	**Addy Edward**
LOU	Ardee Town	**Addy John**
LOU	Ardee Town	**Addy John**
WAT	Shanakill	**Addy William**
CAR	Carlow Town	**Ager John**
ANT	Ballygalley	**Agnew Jones**
ANT	Rory`s Glen	**Agnew William**
CRK	Kinsale Town	**Ahearne John**
CRK	Kinsale Town	**Ahearne Thomas**
WAT	Piltown	**Ahern**
ARM	Annsborough	**Aicken Graves**
ANT	Ballygally	**Aiken Robert**
LDY	Clagan	**Aiken Robert**
MON	Glannan	**Aiken Robert**
KILD	Osberstown	**Aikens**
DWN	Ballynavally	**Aikin John**
DWN	Carlingford	**Aithin William**
ANT	Ballygolan	**Aitken James**
ANT	Drumnadrough	**Aitken James**
KILD	Blackchurch	**Aitken Samuel**
MON	Lisnalong	**Akle**
WAT	Garrancrobally	**Alcock**
WAT	Tramore	**Alcock**
WAT	Waterford City	**Alcock Alex**
WAT	Ballymaclode	**Alcock William**
WEX	Cloghnagleraghy	**Alcock William**
WW	Newmills	**Alcock William**
WEX	Cloghnagleraghy *	**Alcock William Jun.**
KILD	Belan	**Aldborough Earl**
DUB	Islandbridge	**Alderman Mandera**
CRK	Gortroche	**Aldworth John**
ARM	Ardressel	**Alexander**
CAR	Ballyellen	**Alexander**
CAR	Ballygowan	**Alexander**
DWN	Ballylisbredan	**Alexander**
DWN	Listooder	**Alexander**
ANT	Mullinsallagh	**Alexander**
CAR	Strongstream	**Alexander**
DWN	Comber T`parks	**Alexander Alex**
DON	Cloghfin	**Alexander David**
DWN	Dundonnell	**Alexander Eliz Lady**
DWN	Owenocork	**Alexander Eliz Lady**
DUB	Balbriggan	**Alexander George**
CAR	Milford	**Alexander George**
LAO	Barraghcore	**Alexander Harriet**
CAR	Cloghristick	**Alexander Harrietta**
CAR	Strongstream	**Alexander Henry**
WW	Ballybrittan *	**Alexander Hugh**
ANT	Ed`derry Falls Rd	**Alexander James**
CAR	Milford	**Alexander James**
CAR	Strongstream	**Alexander Jas**
CAR	Ballygowan	**Alexander Jn Yngr**
LDY	Articlave Village	**Alexander John**
LDY	Articlave Village	**Alexander John**
WEX	Ballyedmond	**Alexander John**

CO.	TOWNLAND	MILLER
CAR	Ballygowan	**Alexander John**
ANT	Belfast Town	**Alexander John**
CAR	Carlow Town	**Alexander John**
CAR	Cloghristick	**Alexander John**
ANT	Edenderry	**Alexander John**
KILD	Ladycastle	**Alexander John**
CAR	Milford	**Alexander John**
CAR	Strongstream	**Alexander John**
ROS	Srah	**Alexander Joseph**
ANT	Ed`derry Falls Rd	**Alexander Lor**
ANT	Milllands	**Alexander Marquis**
DON	Drummanon	**Alexander Mr**
DON	Balleeghan	**Alexander Nath**
TYR	Augher	**Alexander Robert**
ANT	Carrickfergus Tn	**Alexander Robert**
WME	Rathbennett	**Alexander Robert**
TYR	Tempanroe	**Alexander Robert**
DUB	Milltown	**Alexander Robert Sir**
LDY	Bolean	**Alexander Robt**
GAL	Ahascragh Town	**Alexander Samuel**
LDY	Bolea	**Alexander William**
TYR	Augher	**Alexander William Sir Bt.**
TYR	Magheralough ?	**Alexanders**
KILD	Ardree Town	**Alfred Haughton**
LEI	Glenboy	**Algeo Lewis**
DON	Cratlagh	**Algeo William**
DON	Cratlagh	**Algeo William**
ANT	Ballymather Lr	**Algie Thomas**
GAL	Olter	**Alice Stephny Widow**
DUB	Donnybrook	**Alkin William**
DUB	Red Mills	**Alkin William**
DUB	Feltrim	**Allan Thomas**
WME	Creggan Upper	**Allen George**
DWN	Unicarval	**Allen George**
DWN	Belvor *	**Allen Hugh**
CRK	Grillagh	**Allen James**
CRK	Scartagh	**Allen James**
DON	St Johnstown	**Allen James**
CRK	Tawnies Lower	**Allen James**
LDY	Termonbacca	**Allen Jane**
LDY	Londonderry	**Allen Jane Widow**
DWN	Ballygowan	**Allen John**
ARM	Drumachee	**Allen John**
MEA	Higgginstown	**Allen John**
WEX	Martingalls	**Allen John**
MEA	Rogerstown	**Allen John**
ANT	Tildarg	**Allen John**
LONG	Ballycloghan	**Allen Joseph**
ARM	Carrickduff	**Allen Joseph**
ARM	Drumachee	**Allen Joseph**
WW	Ballyduff	**Allen Joshua Hon Lord**
CRK	Clashanure	**Allen Kyree**
KILD	Newtown O`More	**Allen Lord Visc.**
SLI	Cullabeg	**Allen Matthew**
WEX	Matabeg	**Allen Mr.**
CRK	Middleton Town	**Allen Mr.**

CO.	TOWNLAND	MILLER
WAT	Moanfune	**Allen Prenderby**
DON	Convoy	**Allen Robert**
KKY	Coolnamuck	**Allen Robert**
LDY	Edenballymore	**Allen Robert**
DON	Milltown	**Allen Robert**
LDY	Whitehouse	**Allen Robert**
DON	Milltown	**Allen Robert**
DON	Kiltole	**Allen Robt**
ANT	Lisconnan	**Allen Saml**
CRK	Grillagh	**Allen Thomas**
CRK	Grillagh	**Allen Thomas**
CRK	Scartagh	**Allen Thomas**
TYR	Tattysallagh	**Allen Thomas**
CRK	Tawnies Lower	**Allen Thomas**
CRK	Tawnies Lower	**Allen Thomas**
ANT	Antrim Town	**Allen William**
ARM	Mullanture	**Allen William**
LAO	Donaghmore	**Alley Patrick**
LAO	Donaghmore	**Alley Peter**
WAT	Cappoquin	**Allin Sam**
WAT	Bellicka *	**Allin Samuel**
LOU	Drogheda Town	**Allison Evan**
OFF	Tullamore Town	**Allison John**
DON	Monfad	**Allison Richard**
CRK	Knocknagarrane	**Allman George**
CRK	Moanarone	**Allman George**
CRK	Coolfadda	**Allman R Lord**
CRK	Bandon Town	**Allman Richard**
CRK	Moanarone	**Allman Richard**
CRK	Moanarone	**Allman Richard L**
CRK	Bandon	**Allman Richd**
CRK	Bandon	**Allman Richd Lord**
CRK	Clogheenavodig	**Allman Robert**
CRK	Moanarone	**Alman Richard**
MYO	Eskerlevally	**Altamount John Hon. Earl**
CAR	St Mullins	**Altham**
WEX	Ross Town	**Altham Arthur Hon.**
LONG	Clooneen	**Amuty Samuel**
DUB	Loaders Park	**Andersen John**
ANT	Ballaghmore	**Anderson**
ARM	Lisadian	**Anderson**
CAV	Lurgan	**Anderson**
TYR	Stiloga	**Anderson Andrew**
WW	Kilcoole	**Anderson Fran**
WW	Kilcoole	**Anderson Francis**
TIP	Bansha West	**Anderson Geo**
TIP	Lacken	**Anderson Geo**
CAR	Carlow Town	**Anderson Geo W**
DUB	Inchicore	**Anderson George**
LDY	Coleraine Town	**Anderson Hen**
DWN	Ballyinran	**Anderson James**
DWN	Carlingford Town	**Anderson James**
LOU	Carlingford Town	**Anderson James**
CAV	Knocknalosset	**Anderson James**
DON	Moleng	**Anderson James**
LDY	Primity	**Anderson James**
WEX	Taylorstown	**Anderson James**
TIP	Clonmel	**Anderson John**
WAT	Clonmel	**Anderson John**
WAT	Dungarvan Town	**Anderson John**
CAR	Kilcarry	**Anderson John**
CRK	Rouryglen	**Anderson John**
SLI	Sligo Town	**Anderson John**
WAT	Waterford City	**Anderson John**
DON	Gulladoo	**Anderson Richard**
LDY	Killygullib Glebe	**Anderson Robert**
CAV	Knocknalosset	**Anderson Robert**
WW	Baltinglass W.	**Anderson Robert H**
ANT	Bushmills	**Anderson Stewart**
ANT	Eagry	**Anderson Stewart**
ANT	Rosnashane	**Anderson W**
DWN	Ballyvicnacally	**Anderson William**
ARM	Lisadian	**Anderson William**
DWN	Balloo	**Andrew**
GAL	Tormaun	**Andrew Griffin**
MEA	Fennor	**Andrews Christopher**
ANT	(bo. BELFAST)	**Andrews James**
ANT	Bracknamuckley	**Andrews James**
MEA	Fennor	**Andrews John**
MEA	Rockstown	**Andrews John**
ARM	Ballyloughan	**Andrews Joseph**
ANT	Kilroot	**Andrews Mlichael**
ANT	Kilroot	**Andrews Mr**
ANT	Edenderry	**Andrews Mr.**
OFF	Edenderry Town	**Andrews Mr.**
MEA	Fennor	**Andrews Nicholas**
DWN	Comber T`parks	**Andrews Reps Jas**
DWN	Mountalexander	**Andrews Reps Jas**
ARM	Ballyloughan	**Andrews Robert**
LDY	Coleraine Town	**Andrews William**
DWN	Comber T`parks	**Andrews William**
CRK	Cork City	**Anglesea Road**
MON	Drumully	**Ankatell William**
MON	Curnanure	**Ankell Rodger**
ARM	Augher Town	**Ankettell F`mne**
TYR	Edenderry	**Ankettle Oliver**
MYO	Cloonkee	**Annally Hon. Lady Mary**
MYO	Cloonkee	**Annally Hon. Lord John**
MYO	Cloongee	**Annally Lord John**
DUB	Diswellstown	**Annaly Baron**
DUB	Woodlands	**Annaly Baron**
DWN	Drumnagally	**Anne Dunbar**
DWN	Rumnagally	**Anne Dunbar**
CAR	Kilcarrig	**Anne McKinney**
CAR	St Mullins	**Annesley**
TYR	Megna *	**Annesley Arththur Jun.**
TYR	Megna *	**Annesley Arthur**
DWN	Aughnacloy	**Annesley Francis**
TYR	Megna *	**Annesley Francis Rev.**
TYR	Megna *	**Annesley Fras.**
DWN	Ballydugan	**Annesley Lord**
LDY	Ballykellaghan	**Annesley William**
WAT	Carrickcastle	**Anthony Joseph**
WAT	Ballyvoyle	**Anthony Murphy**
DUB	Diswellstown	**Antrobus Hugh**
DUB	Templogue	**Antrobus John Rev.**
DWN	Conlig	**Appleton Arthur**
DUB	Corkagh	**Arabin John Ladaveze**
DWN	Ballygowan	**Arbuckle Sherriff**
DWN	Balleny	**Archbishop of Dublin**
DUB	Balheary	**Archbold**
DUB	Balheary	**Archbold Eliz Widow**
DUB	Balheary	**Archbold Elizabeth**
LAO	Clonagh	**Archdall**
FER	Derrihalla	**Archdall**
FER	Island *	**Archdall**
LAO	Mountmellick	**Archdall**
FER	Dooederny	**Archdall Angel**
FER	Island *	**Archdall Angel**
FER	Dooederny	**Archdall Edward**
DWN	Ballydargan	**Archdall Henry**
FER	Dooederny	**Archdall Mervyn**
LAO	Sampsons Court	**Archdall Mervyn**
LAO	Clonagh	**Archdall Mervyn Rev.**
FER	Crevinish	**Archdall Nicholas**
FER	Dooederny	**Archdall Nicholas**
FER	Island *	**Archdall Nicholas**
TYR	Tonnaghmore	**Archdall Nicholas**
DUB	Lucan	**Archer George**
DUB	Dublin City	**Archer Richard**
DUB	Haroldscross	**Archer Richard**
DUB	St Sepulchre	**Archer Richard**
DUB	Templeogue	**Archibald Widow**
FER	Drumawillin	**Archrall**
CAR	Carlow Town	**Ardagh**
TIP	Loughane Lower	**Ardell John**
DWN	Coolsallagh	**Ardery Robert**
GAL	Galway Town	**Ardilaun Baron**
TIP	Loughane Lower	**Ardill John**
LOU	Ardee Town	**Armitage**
OFF	Gorraun	**Armitage Benjamin**
OFF	Annaghmore	**Armitt ?**
OFF	Annaghmore	**Armstrong**
OFF	Ballycumber	**Armstrong**
ARM	Balteagh	**Armstrong**
OFF	Belmont Mill	**Armstrong**
LAO	Cardtown	**Armstrong**
LAO	Rathdowney	**Armstrong**
FER	Rathmore	**Armstrong**
FER	Enniskillen	**Armstrong A**
FER	Cappy	**Armstrong Adam**
TYR	Ballygawly	**Armstrong Andrew**
ARM	Drumgane	**Armstrong Archibald**
OFF	Ballycumber Tn	**Armstrong Capt.**
TYR	Corkragh	**Armstrong Charles**
LONG	Cullynore	**Armstrong Charles**
FER	Cloy	**Armstrong David**
ARM	Ballaghy	**Armstrong George**

INDEX

CO.	TOWNLAND	MILLER
GAL	Ballynahivnia	Armstrong Grey
FER	Bellanmallard	Armstrong J
FER	Craghan	Armstrong J
ANT	Ballyquillan	Armstrong James
LEI	Blackmill Farm	Armstrong James
CAV	Gartylough	Armstrong James
FER	Ballylucas	Armstrong John
TYR	Corlea	Armstrong John
ANT	Mill Quarter	Armstrong John
CAR	Clashganny	Armstrong M
DUB	Haroldscross	Armstrong Mr
ARM	Drumgane	Armstrong Mr.
TIP	Holycross	Armstrong R
LONG	Cullynore	Armstrong Richard
LONG	Cullynore	Armstrong Richard Eldr
ROS	Ballinasloe	Armstrong Robert
ANT	Belfast Town	Armstrong Robert
LAO	Cardtown	Armstrong Robert
ROS	Clonard	Armstrong Robert
LAO	Clonaslee	Armstrong Robert
MON	Tenary	Armstrong Thomas
ARM	Balteagh	Armstrong Thos Knox
CLE	Deerpark	Armstrong William
DON	Drumaneel	Armstrong William
DON	Urbalshinny	Armstrong William
OFF	Garrycastle	Armstrong Wm B
MEA	Kilmessan	Arnold Christopher
ROS	Carrowreagh	Arnold Rev.
MEA	Gormanstown	Arnold William
CRK	bo./ Ballymore	Arnott Sir John
ANT	Kilbride	Arthur Alex
WEX	Mill Lands	Arthur Bendct
ROS	Cloonmagunnaun	Arthur Jun.
WAT	Waterford City	Arthur Robert
ANT	Ballymurphy	Arthur William
DUB	Irishtown	Arthur William
CRK	Garrane	Artkinson Susanna
WAT	Pilltown	Arundel Hill
CRK	Curraghgrane Beg	Arundel Mills
CRK	Dromihill *	Ash
LDY	Ballykellaghan	Ash Benjamin
DWN	Claragh	Ash Hugh
LDY	Tullylinkisee	Ash Wiliamm
LDY	Pennyburn	Ash William
LDY	Windmill Perches	Ash William
LAO	Old Mill	Ashe
LDY	Ballyness	Ashe Benjamin
KILD	Moone	Ashe Martha
KILD	Moone	Ashe Mary
GAL	Knockglass	Ashe Norman
SLI	Knockmuldoney	Ashlin Darmida
KRY	Dillons	Ashton
DUB	Palmerston Lr	Ashton John
GAL	Woodlawn	Ashton Lord
DUB	Donnybrook	Ashwood S
GAL	Galway Town	Ashworth Edmond
DUB	Donnybrook Lr	Ashworth Margaret
DUB	Edmondstown	Ashworth Thomas
GAL	Galway Town	Ashworth Thomas
OFF	Cappagowlan	Assatis Jonathan
WAT	Aglish	Assleck Gilbert
ROS	Tanidrissoge *	Athenry Fras Lord
WME	Athlone Town	Athlone Woollen Co.
MEA	Milltown	Atkin Martha Widow
WEX	Millands	Atkins John
ARM	Tullyallen	Atkinsin William
ARM	Aghory	Atkinson
KILD	Ardnaree	Atkinson
MYO	Ardnaree	Atkinson
KILD	Ardree	Atkinson
DWN	Ballygowan	Atkinson
MYO	Belleek	Atkinson
MON	Miskish	Atkinson
DWN	Mountpanther	Atkinson
ARM	Mullaghycasey	Atkinson
LAO	Rathdowney	Atkinson Richard
LAO	Rathdowney	Atkinson Robert
DWN	Mullartown	Atkinson Arthur
ARM	Ballynewry	Atkinson Benjamin
ARM	Clonmain	Atkinson C
MYO	Belesker	Atkinson Charles
MYO	Belleek	Atkinson Charles
OFF	Bellmount	Atkinson Charles
ARM	Clonmain	Atkinson Charles
ARM	Ballynahone	Atkinson Edward
MYO	Belleek	Atkinson George
DWN	Mullartown	Atkinson Henry
TYR	Drummuck	Atkinson Jackson
DWN	Ballygowan	Atkinson James
ANT	Bruslee	Atkinson James
MON	Magoney	Atkinson James
ARM	Aghory	Atkinson John
ARM	Aughariel	Atkinson John
DWN	Ballydugan	Atkinson John
DWN	Drumguillan	Atkinson John
DWN	Saul	Atkinson John
ARM	Tullyallen	Atkinson Mr
DUB	Red Mills	Atkinson Mr.
LAO	Ballybuggy	Atkinson Robert
KILD	Ladycastle	Atkinson Thomas
LAO	Maryborough	Atkinson Thomas
KILD	Turnings	Atkinson Thomas
ARM	Aghory	Atkinson William
ARM	Clare	Atkinson William
ARM	Glassdrummond	Atkinson William
ARM	Lisdrumchor Lr	Atkinson William
ARM	Lisdrumchor Upr.	Atkinson William
ARM	Mullaglass	Atkinson William
ARM	Tullyallan	Atkinson William
MYO	Ardnaree	Attwod Mathias
GAL	Galway Town	Atwood Mathias
DWN	Ballydugan	Auchenleck
DUB	Loaders Park	Auchmuty C
MEA	Boltray	Audley Lord George Rt. Hon.
WW	Bray	Audouin Gorge
CRK	Blarney	Austen Samuel
GAL	Streamstown	Austim William Esq.
LDY	Pennyburn	Averell Isabella Widow.
KILD	Pluckerstown	Aylmer
KILD	Pluckerstown	Aylmer Fitzgerald Sir
CLE	Craggbryen	Aylmer James
KILD	Pluckerstown	Aylmer Lucy
KILD	Celbridge	Aylward
KKY	Ballinlough	Aylward William
		B
LAO	Mounteagle	B. of Waterford
LIM	Hingesmill *	Babington
DON	Ballylast	Babington Richard
KILD	Hinges	Babington William
KILD	Townland ?	Babington Wm Chas
WAT	Kilmeadan	Baccus Peter
WAT	Garrancrobally	Bachas
WAT	Kilmeadan	Bachas
WAT	Waterford Town	Bachas Charles
WAT	Waterford Town	Bachas George
ANT	Islandbane	Back James
LDY	Gregardvardan *	Bacon
ARM	Shancrackan Beg	Bacon
LDY	Coleraine Libs	Bacon Robert
LDY	Loghran	Bacon Robert
WME	Rathwire Lower	Badge Thomas
CRK	Finagh	Baeey
CAR	Bagnelstown	Bagenal
CAR	Oldtown	Bagenal
CAR	Rosdellig	Bagenal Beauchamp
CAR	Staples Mill	Bagenal Beauchamp
CAR	Staplestown	Bagenal Beauchamp
CAR	Staples Mill	Bagenal Maria
DUB	Mill Hill	Bagenal Walter
CAR	Rosdellig	Bagenal Walter
CAR	Rosdellig	BagenalBeauchamp
DUB	Kilmainham	Baggs Isham
DWN	Ballygowan	Baggs Islam
OFF	Ferbane Town	Bagnal A
OFF	Annaghmore	Bagnal Abraham
OFF	Gallen	Bagnall Abraham
LONG	Crane Grove	Bagnall Timothy
LAO	Heath	Bagnell John
KILD	Mountrice	Bagot
CAR	Tobinstown	Bagot
CAR	Tobinstown	Bagot Eleanor Wid
CAR	Tobinstown	Bagot James John
KILD	Turnings Lower	Bagwell Charles
KILD	Turnings Lower	Bagwell Mrs.
WEX	New Ross	Bailey
LAO	Garrymaddock	Bailey John
KKY	Graignamanagh	Bailey John

CO.	TOWNLAND	MILLER
LAO	Tonfarna	**Bailey John**
KRY	Beheenagh	**Bailey William**
MEA	Beheenagh	**Bailey William**
DWN	Ballywalter	**Bailie John**
DWN	Ballycreevy	**Baillie**
CAR	Cloghristick	**Baillie**
DWN	Ballycreevy	**Baillie Ann**
DWN	Ballycreevy	**Baillie James**
DWN	Bishops Court	**Baillie Jno**
DWN	Ballylisbredan	**Baillie John**
WEX	Wexford Town	**Baillis Mayor**
KKY	Graiguenamanagh	**Baily John**
ANT	Glynn	**Baines George**
LDY	Ballynacally	**Baird Alexander**
ANT	Ballywee	**Baird Jackson**
DUB	Hibernian Mills	**Baird Jasper**
ANT	Ballywee	**Baird John**
ANT	Ballywee	**Baird John (Miller)**
LDY	Ballynacally Beg	**Baird William**
DON	Mullinbuoy Farm	**Baird William**
LDY	Ballynacally Beg	**Baird William Alex**
WEX	St John`s (Taigh)	**Baisley Diana**
ANT	Creggan	**Baker**
SLI	Ballymote	**Baker Andrew**
KKY	Callan Town	**Baker George**
DUB	Gallagh	**Baker Henry**
MON	Ballycronog	**Baker John (ano)**
WAT	Dungarvan Town	**Baker Roger**
TIP	Clonmel	**Baker Samuel**
WAT	Clonmel	**Baker Samuel**
CAR	Staples Mill	**Baker Sir Walter**
KKY	Callan Town	**Baker William**
KKY	Minnauns	**Baker William**
ANT	Belfast Town	**BakerJames**
KILD	Bonglass *	**Baldwin**
LAO	Coolkerry	**Baldwin**
LAO	Doon	**Baldwin**
LAO	Aughnahorna	**Baldwin James**
LAO	Coolkerry	**Baldwin John**
ROS	Tanidrissoge *	**Baldwin Richard**
ROS	Tanidrissoge *	**Baldwin Richard Jun.**
WME	Mullamoran	**Baldwin Richard Rev.**
LAO	Aughnahorna	**Baldwin Robert**
LAO	Coolkerry	**Baldwin Robert**
TYR	Monbeg	**Balfe**
TYR	Drumquin	**Balfe Edmond**
LOU	Stephenstown	**Balfour**
LOU	Stephenstown	**Balfour**
MEA	Slane	**Balfour Blaney**
FER	Cushwash	**Balfour William**
KILD	Boycetown	**Balhurst**
KILD	Boycetown	**Balhurst**
TYR	Donaghmore	**Ball**
LOU	Little Mill	**Ball (as Master)**
TYR	Dungannon L`ships	**Ball Benjamin**
TYR	Killymam	**Ball Benjamin**
MEA	Rossnaree	**Ball Francis**
MEA	Formays	**Ball Jn William**
CAR	Carlow Town	**Ball Jno**
CAR	Carlow Town	**Ball Jno**
LOU	Ardee Town	**Ball Thomas (as Master)**
CRK	Clashganniv	**Ball Valentine**
MEA	Formays	**Ball William**
MON	Drummans	**Ballagh Anthony**
ARM	Ballyloughan	**Ballantine Adam**
LDY	Ardlough	**Ballantine Thomas**
CRK	Ballygarvan	**Ballard John**
WME	Ballynacarrow	**Ballasty Owen**
WME	Ballynacarrow	**Ballasty Patrick**
MYO	Ballina Town	**Ballina Flour Mills Ltd.**
LDY	Waterside	**Ballintine Thomas**
ARM	Ballyards	**Ballyards Bleach Wks**
KILD	Johnstown South	**Bamberry Thomas**
LAO	Castletown	**Bambrick Henry**
KKY	Naglesland	**Bambrick James**
LAO	Castletown	**Bambrick John**
LAO	Grange	**Bambrick John**
CLE	Lifford	**Banantine Cloghlea**
CLE	Lifford	**Banantine Cloghlea**
CRK	Ahgamilla	**Bandon Earl**
CRK	Ardkitt	**Bandon Earl**
CRK	Bealick	**Bandon Earl**
TIP	Clonmel Town	**Banfirld Peter**
ANT	Harphall	**Banford**
DWN	Bangor	**Bangor Lord**
DWN	Castleward	**Bangor Viscount**
ANT	Old Forge	**Bank Liverpool B`ro**
DWN	Newry Town	**Bank of Ire. Govs.**
DWN	Ballyholme	**Banking Co. North.**
MYO	Foxford	**Banks Clive**
MYO	Foxford	**Banks Robert**
MYO	Foxford	**Banks Susan ors Blake**
MYO	Foxford	**Banks Thomas**
DWN	Ardaghy	**Bann Reservoir Co.**
CLE	Knockalehia	**Bannantine James**
CLE	Ennis Town	**Bannantyne Alex**
CLE	EnnisTown	**Bannantyne Alex**
LIM	Ballyclough	**Bannantyne James**
TIP	Clonmel Town	**Bannantyne James**
CLE	Cloughleagh	**Bannantyne James**
CLE	Ennis Town	**Bannantyne James**
CLE	Lifford	**Bannantyne James**
LIM	Limerick City	**Bannantyne James**
CLE	Cloughleagh	**Bannantyne James Jun.**
CLE	Ennis Town	**Bannatyne Alex**
TIP	Bansagh	**Bannister**
ROS	Bellanamullia	**Bannon Michael**
TIP	Lacken	**Bansha Woollen Co.**
TIP	Bansha West	**Bansha Woollen Mill**
LAO	Doon	**Banting John**
WW	Baravore	**Baravore Mining Co.**
KILD	Boycetown	**Barber**
ANT	Lambeg South	**Barber William**
ROS	Knockanyconor	**Barbor James**
ANT	Antrim Town	**Barbour James**
ANT	Lisburn Town	**Barbour James**
DWN	Ballymacarret	**Barbour John**
ANT	Dunmurry	**Barbour William**
ANT	Lisburn Town	**Barbour William**
ANT	Antiville	**Barclay Archibald**
ANT	Inver	**Barclay Archibald**
TYR	Strangmore	**Barcroft John P**
TYR	Altnavannog	**Barcroft Sarah**
TYR	Altnavannog	**Barcroft William J**
LDY	Drumard	**Barfoot Henry**
TYR	Milltown	**Barhill Thomas**
LIM	Ballingarry	**Barker**
MEA	Navan Town	**Barker Richard**
ANT	Kildrum	**Barker Robert**
CRK	Killavarrig	**Barkley John**
ANT	Antiville	**Barklie**
DWN	Monlehegolly	**Barklie**
LDY	Mullaghmore	**Barklie Alex**
ANT	Inver	**Barklie Archibald**
LDY	Mullaghmore	**Barklie George**
ARM	Darkley	**Barklie James**
WME	Cullenmore	**Barlow James**
MON	Agherybeggan *	**Barlow John**
MYO	Kilknock	**Barnacle Patrick**
ARM	Ballyards	**Barnes**
ARM	Crossdened	**Barnes**
CAR	Rosdellig	**Barnes Bart**
CAR	Staples Mill	**Barnes Bartholomew**
WEX	Shanb`agherine *	**Barnes Caleb**
ARM	Ballyards	**Barnes George**
LAO	Doon	**Barnes George**
TIP	Grangemockler	**Barnes John**
MEA	Julianstown	**Barnes Thomas**
ANT	Carrickfergus Irish	**Barnet James**
DWN	Ballynahinch	**Barnett**
ANT	Carrickfergus	**Barnett James**
DWN	Ballynahinch	**Barnett James Robt**
DWN	Ballynahinch	**Barnett Jno**
WEX	Shanb`agherine *	**Barnewall Nicholas**
DON	Tirharon	**Barnhill John**
WW	Bray	**Barnier Joseph**
WW	Bray	**Barnier Joshua**
DWN	Ballymoney	**Barns John**
DWN	Ballybawne	**Barnsley Richard**
MEA	Balrath	**Barnwall Nicholas**
GAL	Cregg (6)	**Barnwall Thomas**
MEA	Kilnagross	**Barnwell Charles**
ANT	(bo. BELFAST)	**Barr David-**
TYR	Raveagh	**Barr George**
LDY	Drumsteeple	**Barr Higginbotham**
DWN	Ballymaconnell	**Barr Samuel**
LAO	Aghmacart	**Barrett**
WEX	Ross Town	**Barrett Francis**

CO.	TOWNLAND	MILLER
ANT	Cloghanduff	Bell David
CAR	Clonegall	Bell Edward
ARM	Donnybeg	Bell Edward
LAO	Abbeyleix	Bell Elizabeth
FER	Drumadraghy	Bell Francis
ANT	Ballyclare	Bell George
ANT	Drumnadrough	Bell J
MON	Bowelk	Bell James
FER	Drummadraghy	Bell James
ANT	Ballyclare	Bell John
ANT	Belfast Town	Bell John
ARM	Cloghreagh	Bell John
MON	Derrygooney	Bell John
ARM	Donnybeg	Bell John Sen
DON	Eskymeen	Bell Joseph
KILD	Mount Blarney *	Bell Marmaduke
LAO	Abbeyleix	Bell Mary
ARM	Lurgy Valley	Bell Matthew
ANT	Ballynure Village	Bell Mrs
ANT	Drumnadrough	Bell R
MEA	Athboy Town	Bell Rev Andrew
ANT	Ballykeel	Bell Robert
ANT	Kirkinriola T`parks	Bell Robert
GAL	Ahascragh	Bell Samuel
CAR	Clonegall	Bell Susanna
DWN	Ballyminstragh	Bell Thomas
LAO	Mounteagle	Bell Wellington
GAL	Abbey	Bell William
LAO	Abbeyleix	Bell William
MON	Aghillagh	Bellamont Hon. Chas. E.
MYO	Cloonagh	Bellamount Earl of
LDY	Coleraine Town	Bellas Hugh
LDY	Coleraine Town	Bellas Thomas
OFF	Bracknagh	Bellew
LOU	Aghaboys	Bellew James
ARM	Shean	Bellew John
ARM	Thean	Bellew John
KILD	Gorteen	Bellew Lord
DUB	Milltown	Bellew Thomas
TYR	Edenderry	Bellmore Rt. Hon Earl
ANT	Drumnadrough	Bells
ANT	Whitehouse Upr	Bells
DUB	Rathmines	Bellwood Mr.
OFF	Loughan	Belton Philip
CAV	Doon	Benison Capt.
DON	Ballyshannon Tn	Benison John
DON	Ballyshannon Tn	Benison Joseph
LOU	Doolargy	Benison Mrs Nichola
LOU	Doolargy	Benison Richard
DON	Ballyshannon Tn	Benison Thomas
DUB	Kilmainham	Benkein
DUB	Kilmainham	Benkein John
DUB	Inchicore	Benkier Andrew
CRK	Newberry	Benn Walter
KRY	Tralee Town	Benner Henry
ANT	Gortnacor	Bennet John
CAV	Bellananagh	Bennett
CRK	Clonakilty Town	Bennett
LAO	Cullenaghbegg	Bennett
CRK	Grillagh	Bennett family
DWN	Glassdrumman	Bennett James
DWN	Ballyknockan	Bennett John
ARM	Brannock	Bennett John
DWN	Edenslate	Bennett John
ANT	Gortnacor Upr	Bennett John
DWN	Monlough	Bennett John
DWN	Tullyhubbert	Bennett John
LDY	Ardvarness	Bennett Mary
ANT	Carrickfergus Tn	Bennett Robert
LDY	Macleary	Bennett Stephen
LDY	Ballydevit	Bennett Thomas
LDY	Ballywillin	Bennett Thomas
CRK	Townland ?`	Bennett Thomas
TIP	Nenagh North	Bennett William
CAV	Bellananagh	Bennett`s
ARM	Lisdrumgullion	Bennie John
CAV	Doon	Bennison Capt.
SLI	Knockmuldoney	Benson James
FER	Lacky	Benson James
SLI	Willowbrook	Benson James
LIM	Limerick City	Benson John
SLI	Ballysadare Town	Benson Margaret
SLI	Knockmuldoney	Benson Margaret
ANT	Islandreagh	Benson Robert S
MON	Latgallon	Benson Samuel
ANT	Belfast Town	Bentley George
DUB	Woodlock`s Gr	Benyon Samuel
KILD	Mount Blarney *	Bere
DUB	Feltrim	Beresford
WAT	Pouldrew *	Beresford Claudius
CAR	Clonmisk *	Beresford J
DUB	Feltrim	Beresford Jn Rt. Hon.
DUB	Feltrim	Beresford John
CAR	Clonmisk *	Beresford John G
DWN	Balleny	Beresford Lord.
OFF	Milltown	Bergin James
OFF	Fauncroft	Bergin John
DUB	Kilmainham	Berkby Nicholas
DUB	Kilmainham	Berkby Nicholas
DUB	Haroldscross	Bermingham
ROS	Tanidrissoge *	Bermingham
KRY	Ardagh	Bermingham Edward
GAL	Galway Liberties	Bermingham John
GAL	Lack	Bermingham John
GAL	Galway Town	Bermingham Mary
ROS	Tanidrissoge *	Bermingham Thomas Hon.
WAT	Mayfield	Bernal Isaac
LOU	Ardee Town	Bernard
DWN	Cregagh	Bernard
WAT	Piltown	Bernard
LDY	Arlogh	Bernard Anthony
WAT	Piltown	Bernard Francis
CRK	Ardkitt	Bernard Kath F Hon.
CRK	Ahgamilla	Bernard Percy B
CRK	Ardkitt	Bernard Percy B
CAR	Carlow Town	Bernard Philip
ROS	Ballinasloe	Berne William
WAT	Piltown	Berney
WW	Bray	Bernier
LAO	Cardtown	Berry
WME	Kilbeggan	Berry
WW	Bray Great	Berry Edward
ANT	Carrickfergus Tn	Berry James
CAV	Killywilly	Berry James
LOU	Doolargy	Berry John
OFF	Barrynaguilsha	Berry Smith M
OFF	Eglish	Berry Smith M
LDY	Altagasky *	Besnard Peter
KKY	Milltown	Bessborough Earl
CRK	Castletrasna	Besuard Mr
KRY	Ardagh	Betham Sir William
KRY	Deewnagh *	Betham Sir Wm
DUB	Gracedieu	Betson John
LIM	Reboge	Bevan Mrs G
LIM	Singland	Beven Mrs G
OFF	Ballycumber	Bever
DUB	Feltrim	Bever Edward
DUB	Feltrim	Bever Samuel Capt.
DUB	Feltrim	Bever Samuel J Capt.
ANT	Carrickfergus	Beverley Alex
ANT	Carrickfergus Tn	Beverly Alex
DUB	Conagh	Bewley Samuel
DUB	Haroldscross	Bewley Samuel
DUB	Whitechurch	Bewley Thomas
CAR	Carlow Town	Bewly James
KILD	Athy Town	Bibby Thomas
SLI	Ballanalock	Biern Phillis
KILD	Harristown	Bierne Patrick
DON	Corkey	Biers John
CRK	Bantry Town	Biggs
CRK	Bandon	Biggs Christopher
CRK	Bandon	Biggs Jacob
CRK	Bandon Town	Biggs Jacob
CRK	Bandon	Biggs John
CRK	Bandon	Biggs William
LDY	Bolea	Bigham John of Bolea
DUB	Dublin City	Bignell Thomas
DUB	Dublin City	Bignoll Thos
CLE	Kiltenanlea	Bindon Samuel
CLE	Kiltenanlea	Bindon Samuel
CLE	Waterpark	Bindon Samuel
MYO	Carrownoultore	Bingham
FER	Crevinish	Bingham
MYO	Foxford	Bingham Henry
MYO	Foxford	Bingham Henry Hon.
MYO	Foxford	Bingham Jno
MYO	Foxford	Bingham John
DWN	Ballyroney	Birch

CO.	TOWNLAND	MILLER
CAR	St Mullins	**Birch**
DWN	Ballyroney	**Birch - McCardle**
TIP	Rackethall	**Birch George**
TIP	Birchgrove	**Birch George.**
TIP	Polloghbane *	**Birch Henry**
DWN	Ballydown	**Birch John**
DUB	Portmarnock	**Birch Robert**
TIP	Wayside *	**Birch William**
CRK	Bandon Town	**Bird Kate R**
CRK	Desert	**Bird Robert G**
ANT	Antrim Town	**Birkhead Matthew**
TIP	Windmill Field	**Birmingham William**
TYR	Fivemiletown	**Birney William**
LIM	Galbally	**Bishop John**
LIM	Park	**Bishop John**
ANT	Belfast Town	**Black**
TYR	Claudy *	**Black**
DWN	Newtown	**Black**
DWN	Newtown	**Black**
DWN	Dromara Town	**Black Christopher**
DWN	Magheraconluce	**Black Henry**
ANT	Ballygrooby	**Black James**
ANT	Donegore	**Black James**
TYR	Tamnaskeeny	**Black James**
DON	Drumgumberland	**Black James Rev**
DON	Aughagault	**Black John**
DWN	Ballynahinch	**Black John**
ANT	Dunaird	**Black John**
FER	Shannock	**Black John**
ANT	Artogues	**Black Joseph**
ANT	Broughshane Tn	**Black Joseph**
WME	Cullenmore	**Black Joseph**
ANT	Derryhollagh	**Black Joseph**
ANT	Donegore	**Black Mr**
ARM	Ballylane	**Black Samuel**
MYO	Belleek	**Black Thomas**
MEA	Boyne River	**Black Thomas**
TYR	Corkill	**Black William**
ANT	Dervock	**Black William**
LDY	Dundoonan	**Black William**
ROS	Grange	**Blackall Jane Widow.**
CRK	Ardarostig	**Blackall Robert**
DWN	Ballyhackmore	**Blackburn Henry**
TIP	Holycross	**Blacker Robert S. C.**
ARM	Ballymacranagan	**Blacker Samuel**
LDY	Ballykellaghan	**Blacker Stewart Rev.**
ARM	Drominikelly	**Blacker Stuart**
ARM	Ballynaghy	**Blacker William**
MEA	Boyne	**Blacker William**
ROS	Knockanyconor	**Blackhall Robtert**
LONG	Killincastra	**Blackman Patrick**
KILD	Athgarvan	**Blackrath**
DWN	Ballydugan	**Blackwood**
DWN	Tullychin	**Blackwood**
DWN	Tullycreely	**Blackwood**
CAV	Lisboduff	**Blackwood Anne Spin.**
CAV	Lisboduff	**Blackwood Dorcas**
CAV	Shankill	**Blackwood Dorcas**
DWN	Ballygowan	**Blackwood James**
DWN	Ballyholme	**Blackwood James**
CAV	Lisboduff & Latt	**Blackwood James**
DWN	Ballyhemlin	**Blackwood John**
CAV	Lisboduff	**Blackwood Letitia Spin.**
DWN	Ballyward	**Blackwood Robert**
LOU	Ardee Town	**Blair Edw S**
FER	Carran West	**Blair Edward**
LDY	Ballywildrick	**Blair James**
ANT	Glenstall	**Blair James**
LDY	Keely & Rusky	**Blair John**
ANT	Knockanully	**Blair John**
LDY	Ballywildrick	**Blair John Jun**
LDY	Ballywildrick	**Blair Matthew**
DUB	Lucan	**Blair Mr**
DUB	Palmerstown	**Blair Mr**
DON	Ballyholy Near	**Blair Thomas**
KRY	Ballylongford Town	**Blair William**
FER	Carran West	**Blair William**
MYO	Cordroon	**Blake**
GAL	Tuam Town	**Blake Alicia**
GAL	Tuam T`parks	**Blake Alicia Mary**
MEA	Boyne	**Blake Anthony Richd**
MYO	Clooneencarra	**Blake Edward**
GAL	Carragh	**Blake Ethelslane H**
GAL	Drumgriffin	**Blake Frances**
LONG	Cullynore	**Blake Francis**
GAL	Galway T`nsparks	**Blake James**
GAL	Tuam Town	**Blake James**
WME	Milltown	**Blake John**
GAL	Ruford	**Blake John Henry**
MYO	Foxford	**Blake Letitia**
MYO	Moyheny	**Blake Mark**
WME	Lissivollen	**Blake Mary ors Molloy**
MYO	Foxford	**Blake Walte**
WME	Lissivollen	**Blake Walter**
WW	Ballinglen	**Blake William**
WW	Baltinglass	**Blake William**
ROS	Corgowan	**Blakeney**
ROS	Gillstown	**Blakeney**
GAL	Galway Town	**Blakeney Arabella**
CAR	Ballygowan	**Blakeney Walter**
GAL	Galway Town	**BlakeThomas**
LDY	Ballywoodock	**Blanchcard**
DON	Killybegs Town	**Blane Thomas**
MON	Dromore	**Blaney**
MON	Drumagelvin	**Blaney**
MON	Drumleig	**Blaney**
MON	Fermilly	**Blaney**
MYO	Mullinmore	**Blaney Andrew**
FER	Knocks	**Blaney Leslie**
WME	Cullenmore	**Blaquiere Jno Sir**
LDY	Ardkill	**Blaquire John Rt. Hon.**
TYR	Cordromedy	**Bleakney Robert**
CRK	Killavarrig	**Bleazby John**
CRK	Dromcorragh	**Blecher**
KRY	Ballycarty	**Blenerhasset**
ANT	Islandreagh	**Blenerhasset**
KRY	Clashcommon	**Blenerhasset Arthur**
KRY	Ballycarty	**Blenerhasset William**
KRY	Clashcommon	**Blenerhasset William**
KRY	Ballycarty	**Blenerhassett John**
KRY	Mill Lands	**Blennerhasset**
KRY	Cloghercade	**Blennerhasset Dorcas**
KRY	Cloghercade	**Blennerhasset Georgina Spin.**
KRY	Tralee Town	**Blennerhassett Arthur**
WW	Blessington	**Blesinton**
WW	Lady Park	**Blesinton Chas Hon.**
CRK	Douglas	**Blesinton Lord**
WW	Limekiln Park *	**Blessington Chas Hon.**
WW	Wicklow Town	**Blessinton Charles Visc.**
MEA	Coolronan	**Bligh John**
DUB	Feltrim	**Bligh Robert**
LIM	Caherass	**Blood Neptune**
KILD	Greatconnell	**Bloomer William**
TIP	Cashel Town	**Bloomfield**
FER	Ballymagaghran	**Bloomfield John C**
FER	Ballymaghran	**Bloomfield John C**
DUB	Dundrum	**Bloomfield William**
DWN	Cabragh	**Blosinton**
ANT	Dunadry	**Blow**
ANT	Malone Lower	**Blow Edward**
ANT	Dunadry	**Blow Edwin**
ANT	Cromack	**Blow James**
ANT	Belfast Town	**Blow Ward**
ANT	Malone Lower	**Blow William**
LAO	Aughnahorna	**Blunden**
OFF	Killina	**Boake William**
ANT	Antrim Town	**Boal Hugh**
ANT	Antrim Town	**Boal John**
KILD	Parsonstown	**Boardman**
TYR	Strangmore	**Boardman**
KILD	Parsonstown	**Boardman Joseph**
TYR	Moygashell	**Boardman Thomas**
LDY	Boveagh	**Bodkin James**
LDY	Longfield	**Bodkin James**
WEX	Milltown	**Boggin John**
FER	Boyhill	**Bogues James**
TIP	Barnane	**Bohan James**
GAL	Gortawullaun	**Bohan Michael**
WAT	Corragina	**Bohill Richard**
CAR	Bendinstown	**Boileau**
CRK	Moore Park	**Boileau Francis**
CAR	Bendinstown	**Boileau Wilson**
SLI	Kiloglashery	**Bolan Thomas**
OFF	Ballycumber	**Boland**
TIP	Kylebeg	**Boland Anne**
TIP	Kylebeg	**Boland Jennie Widow**
CLE	Clooncool	**Boland John**
CLE	Clooncool	**Boland Matthew**

CO.	TOWNLAND	MILLER
CLE	Clooncool	**Boland Matthew**
DUB	Dublin City	**Boland's**
DUB	Dublin City	**Boland's Flour Mill**
TIP	Castlecranna	**Bolands George**
DUB	Ringsend	**Bolands Ltd.**
DUB	Ringsend	**Bolands Patrick**
WAT	Kilmeadan	**Bollon Robert Lt. Col.**
LDY	Templemoyle	**Bolson**
CRK	Curraghbower	**Bolster George**
CRK	Lombardstown	**Bolster Thomas**
WAT	Waterford Town	**Bolton Ann Spin.**
WAT	Waterford Town	**Bolton Bridget Widow**
KILD	Bonglash *	**Bolton Edward**
TIP	Nenagh	**Bolton George**
WEX	Ballyedmond	**Bolton Henry**
WEX	Barglany *	**Bolton Henry**
OFF	Loughaun	**Bolton Philip**
MEA	Bective	**Bolton Robert Charles**
WEX	Ballyadam	**Bolton William**
KILD	Kilmore	**Bomford Mary**
KKY	Milltown	**Bomford Samuel**
KILD	Gorteen	**Bomford Stephen**
KILD	Gurty (?)	**Bomford Stephen**
KILD	Kilmore	**Bomford Stephen**
WW	Ballinvally	**Bomford William**
CRK	Cork City	**Bonbounous John**
CRK	Ballyrusheen	**Bond**
ROS	Killukin	**Bond**
ARM	Middletown Manor	**Bond**
LONG	Clonaghill	**Bond James**
LONG	Cloraghill	**Bond James**
ROS	Killukin	**Bond James Rev.**
ROS	Knockanyconor	**Bond James Rev.**
DUB	Dolphins Barn	**Bond John**
LDY	Pennyburn	**Bond Oliver**
LONG	Woodlawn	**Bond R W**
ROS	Knockanyconor	**Bond Richard**
LONG	Moygh	**Bond Richard**
ROS	Knockanyconor	**Bond William**
DUB	Milltown	**Bond William**
LONG	Clonaghill	**Bond Winsley**
ANT	Connor	**Bones James**
KILD	Ballintaggart	**Bonham Francis**
KILD	Ballykelly	**Bonham Francis**
KILD	Ballyntagart *	**Bonham Francis**
WME	Moyvore	**Bonham Francis**
WME	Kibber	**Bonning Francis**
DUB	Hibernian Mills	**Bonsall Jno**
WME	Lickbla	**Booker George**
WEX	Wexford Town	**Booker John J**
ANT	Belfast Town	**Boomer James**
ANT	Edenderry	**Boomer James**
SLI	Keeloges	**Booth Sir Robert G**
SLI	Lissadill	**Booth Sir Robert G**
OFF	Birr Town	**Booth Wiliam**
OFF	Birr Town	**Booth William S**
DUB	Edmondstown	**Borr Christian**
CAR	Carlow Town	**Borroughs George**
CAR	Carlow Town	**Borroughs George**
MEA	Balrath	**Borroughs Thomas**
KILD	Brannockstown	**Borrowes Robert**
DUB	Ballyboden	**Boswell**
WW	Kilmacon Upper	**Boswell Alex**
DUB	Dublin City	**Boswell Catherine**
WW	Kilmacon Upper	**Boswell Robert**
WEX	Ballyadam	**Botten William**
KILD	Mountrice	**Boughal**
CAR	Bagnelstown	**Boulger William**
LDY	Ballygurk	**Boune Andrew**
WW	Newmills	**Bourice**
TIP	Ballyrichard	**Bourke**
KILD	Moone	**Bourke**
GAL	Raford	**Bourke Edward**
TIP	Lacken	**Bourke Elizabeth**
DUB	Bluebell	**Bourke Henry**
TIP	Bansha West	**Bourke John**
TIP	Cloonfinglass	**Bourke John**
MYO	Ballina Town	**Bourke John JP**
TIP	Holycross	**Bourke Patrick**
TIP	Holycross	**Bourke Richard**
MYO	Aghaleague	**Bourke Walter**
KILD	Maynooth	**Bourne**
CLE	O'Callaghansmills	**Bourne Lucinda**
KKY	Tifeaghna	**Bowden John**
LOU	ArdeeTown	**Bowden William**
LAO	Eglish	**Bowe Patrick**
CRK	Cullen	**Bowen Jno**
CRK	Cullen	**Bowen William**
WW	Kilmaccullagh	**Bower**
KILD	Parsonstown	**Bowers**
KKY	Clogga	**Bowers Edward**
WW	Mountkennedy Dm.	**Bowes Andrew**
MEA	Clatterstown	**Bowes John**
KRY	The Wood	**Bowler Widow Mary**
ANT	Ballysillan	**Bowles C**
CAR	Rosdellig	**Bowycar Fran**
LDY	Ardkill	**Bowyer Francis**
CAR	Carlow Town	**Box Edward**
WEX	Lingstown	**Boxwell John**
DON	Ballaghderg	**Boyce Anthony**
DON	Bohirril Park	**Boyce Daniel**
LDY	Drumagoosker	**Boyce John**
DWN	Ballyroney	**Boyd**
DWN	Ballyroney	**Boyd**
ANT	Belfast T`parks	**Boyd**
DWN	Dalmolly	**Boyd**
ARM	Derry	**Boyd**
ANT	Dunadry	**Boyd**
ARM	Lisdrumgullion	**Boyd**
CAV	Lisnageer	**Boyd**
ARM	Tannagh	**Boyd**
ARM	Tannagh More S.	**Boyd**
TYR	Tullylagan	**Boyd**
CAV	Cabragh	**Boyd**
DWN	Ballyroney	**Boyd - Carr**
DWN	Ballyroney	**Boyd - Gilmer**
ANT	Cloghanmurry	**Boyd Andrew**
CRK	Ballycroneen	**Boyd Charles**
CRK	Ballyrobin	**Boyd Charles**
CRK	Maytown	**Boyd Charles**
DWN	Downpatrick Town	**Boyd Edm - Keith Andrew**
DWN	Downpatrick Town	**Boyd Edmond**
ARM	Tassagh	**Boyd Elizabeth**
ANT	Bonamargy	**Boyd Hugh**
ARM	Lisdrumgullion	**Boyd Hugh**
ARM	Demoan	**Boyd Isaac**
ARM	Balleer	**Boyd James**
LIM	Ballysimon	**Boyd James**
ARM	Tassagh	**Boyd James**
ARM	Tassagh	**Boyd James B**
ANT	Lisnagarvey	**Boyd Jane**
FER	Enniskillen Town	**Boyd Jno**
LDY	Coleraine Town	**Boyd John**
ANT	Shankill T`parks	**Boyd John**
LDY	Terrydremont N.	**Boyd John**
ANT	Shankill T`parks	**Boyd John C**
DON	Letterkenny Town	**Boyd John R**
DON	Letterkenny Town	**Boyd John R**
TYR	Oughterard	**Boyd Joseph**
DWN	Downpatrick Town	**Boyd K - Phillmore Walter**
DWN	Downpatrick Town	**Boyd Keown**
TYR	Fivemiletown	**Boyd Mathew**
DUB	Newtown	**Boyd Patk**
DWN	Downpatrick Town	**Boyd R - McClurg Margt.**
DWN	Downpatrick Town	**Boyd Richard**
MON	Corliglacka	**Boyd Robert**
ARM	Marlacoo Beg	**Boyd Robert**
ARM	Marlacoomore	**Boyd Robert**
MON	Toam *	**Boyd Robert**
ARM	Ballinlare	**Boyd Samuel**
DWN	Ballywilliam	**Boyd William**
TYR	Strabane Town	**Boyd William**
DON	Kiltoy	**Boyd William Rev.**
ARM	Knockbane	**Boyde**
ARM	Unshog	**Boyde**
DWN	Crossgar	**Boyde John B**
MEA	Beaumont	**Boylan**
ROS	Carrowreagh	**Boylan**
KILD	Parsonstown	**Boylan**
MEA	Knockmark	**Boylan John**
DUB	Gormanstown	**Boylan Mr**
MEA	Gormanstn Vge.	**Boylan Patrick**
WAT	Killadangan	**Boyle**
TYR	Waterard *	**Boyle**
WAT	Mocollup	**Boyle Amy**
KRY	Ardfert	**Boyle Charles Lord**
KILD	Newtown	**Boyle Christopher**
ARM	Drumnarriff	**Boyle Denis**

INDEX

CO.	TOWNLAND	MILLER
ANT	Belfast Town	**Broadley Benj**
LEI	Carrickevy	**Brock Patrick**
CRK	Cork City	**Brockelsby St.**
KRY	Maulykeevane	**Brocklebank Thomas**
ARM	Augher Town	**Brockman Edward**
SLI	Ballysadare Town	**Broder Michael**
GAL	Carrowroe	**Broder Michael**
SLI	Knockmuldoney	**Broder Michael**
LIM	Behanagh	**Broderick Michael**
MEA	Behanagh	**Broderick Michael**
CRK	Killavarrig	**Brodhead Collins**
KILD	Celbridge	**Broe James**
MYO	Bellass	**Brogan Denis**
MYO	Corroy	**Brogan Dennis**
SLI	Rathkid	**Brogan James**
FER	Gubbacrock	**Brogue Bernard**
DWN	Ballydugan	**Bromley C**
DWN	Ballydugan	**Bromley Chester**
MYO	Brookhill :	**Broockhill Flour Mill**
FER	Derrihalla *	**Brook Henry**
ANT	Antrim Town	**Brooke Basil**
MEA	Stonestown	**Brooke Henry**
WW	Cronebane	**Brooke Richard**
DON	Lougheask Dem.	**Brooke Thomas**
SLI	Sligo Town :	**Brooks Henry**
DUB	Dublin City	**Brooks Joseph**
DON	Eighterross	**Brooks Mrs.**
LOU	Ardee Town	**Brooks William James**
CAR	Carlow Town	**Brophy**
DUB	Kilmainham	**Brophy Wiliam**
CAR	Wells	**Brosnan Pierce**
CAR	Carlow Town	**Brough**
CAR	Carlow Town	**Brough**
KILD	Tuckmilltown	**Broughall Nicholas**
TYR	Strabane Town	**Broughton Robert**
CLE	Ballykilty	**Brown**
ANT	Carrickfergus W	**Brown**
DUB	Dublin City	**Brown**
MYO	Eskerlevally	**Brown**
WME	Monksland	**Brown**
MYO	Moyhenna	**Brown**
ANT	Shankill T`parks	**Brown A**
ANT	Glengormly	**Brown Allen G**
MYO	Killinasash	**Brown Andrew**
DWN	Rossconor	**Brown Arthur**
WEX	Bessmount	**Brown Catherine**
DUB	Dublin City	**Brown Daniel**
GAL	Carriglass	**Brown Dom**
GAL	Athernell	**Brown Domnick**
GAL	Carriglass	**Brown Domnick**
MYO	Ardnaree	**Brown Dorcas Hon.**
KILD	Ardnaree	**Brown Dorcas Hon. (Moore)**
LOU	Ardnaree	**Brown Dorcas Hon .Widow**
ROS	Killappoge	**Brown Dorothy**
WEX	Mill Quarter	**Brown Edward**
KRY	Milltown	**Brown Edward**
GAL	Carriglass	**Brown Henry**
KRY	Ardagh	**Brown Hon. Chas.**
MYO	Eskerlevally	**Brown Hon. Denis**
DWN	Ballymacarn S	**Brown James**
DWN	Donaghcloney	**Brown James**
MYO	Foxford	**Brown James**
WEX	Wexford Town	**Brown James Rev.**
CAR	Carlow	**Brown Jane**
LONG	Bellanchowen	**Brown John**
LONG	Bellemack	**Brown John**
MYO	Eskerlevally	**Brown John**
LAO	Graigue Town	**Brown John**
ROS	Killappoge	**Brown John**
ARM	Mohan	**Brown John**
FER	Monaghan	**Brown John**
LONG	Sheeroe	**Brown John**
TYR	Tullylagan	**Brown John**
MYO	Turlough	**Brown John**
WME	Monksland	**Brown John**
LIM	Castlematrix	**Brown John S**
KRY	Ardagh	**Brown Lord**
TYR	Liscloon Lower	**Brown Madge Mrs.**
WME	Monksland	**Brown Margaret**
DUB	Dublin City	**Brown Matthew**
GAL	Bullenfoule	**Brown Michael Jos**
DUB	Dolphins Barn	**Brown Mr**
MYO	Killinasash	**Brown Nicholas**
DUB	Gracedieu	**Brown Patrick**
LOU	Dundalk Town	**Brown Paul**
DUB	Newtown	**Brown Paul**
MEA	Coolronan	**Brown Richard**
WAT	Cappoquin	**Brown Robert**
ANT	Carrickfergus Tn	**Brown Robert**
LOU	Dundalk Town	**Brown Robert**
CAR	Borris	**Brown Robin**
DWN	Legacurry	**Brown Samuel**
MEA	Bellewstown	**Brown Simon**
DON	Carrowkeel	**Brown Susan**
TIP	Ballyrickard	**Brown Thomas**
LOU	Dundalk Town	**Brown Thomas**
ANT	Brookfield	**Brown William**
TYR	Caledon	**Brown William**
LDY	Coleraine Libs	**Brown William**
KILD	Ardree	**Browne**
CRK	Ballyrusheen	**Browne**
CAR	Carlow Town	**Browne**
KILD	Clonard	**Browne**
WME	Cushinstown	**Browne**
LOU	Dundalk Town	**Browne**
WAT	Dungarvan Town	**Browne**
KILD	Kilcock	**Browne**
LIM	Kilfergus	**Browne**
CAR	Newacre	**Browne**
CLE	O`Callaghans	**Browne**
ANT	Glengormley	**Browne Allen**
GAL	Galway Town	**Browne Charles**
GAL	Galway Town	**Browne Charles**
GAL	Galway Town	**Browne Denis Rt. Hon.**
MYO	Tully	**Browne Dodwell**
GAL	Athenry Town	**Browne Dominick**
GAL	Galway Town	**Browne Dominick**
CLE	Cartron	**Browne Emill**
CRK	Ballyrusheen	**Browne Fran Widow**
GAL	Athenry Town	**Browne Georgina Dorcas**
MEA	Ballyann	**Browne Henry**
ANT	Ballyvorally	**Browne Hugh**
MON	Rockcorry Town	**Browne James**
DWN	Rossconnor	**Browne James**
ANT	Ballyvorally	**Browne John**
CAR	Carlow Town	**Browne John**
LDY	Cregg	**Browne John**
TYR	Crossdernot	**Browne John**
LONG	Sheeroe	**Browne John**
MYO	Tawndressoge	**Browne John W**
MYO	Turlough	**Browne John W**
MYO	Ardnaree	**Browne Katherine**
LOU	Dundalk	**Browne Malcolm**
GAL	Athenry Town	**Browne Margaret Widow.**
FER	Monaghan	**Browne Mary**
DUB	Kiltiernan	**Browne Michael**
WEX	Millquarter	**Browne Michael**
MYO	Rathbaun	**Browne Michael**
MYO	Tully	**Browne Michael**
DUB	Gracedieu	**Browne Patrick**
MYO	Ardnaree	**Browne Robert**
CAR	Carlow Town	**Browne Robert**
ANT	Kells	**Browne Robert**
GAL	Teeranea	**Browne Sam & Thad.**
LOU	Dundalk Town	**Browne Stephen**
LOU	Dundalk	**Browne Thomas**
CLE	Cartron	**Browne Thos**
MEA	Slane Manor	**Browne Ulick**
LIM	Hospital	**Browne Valentine**
CAR	Carlow Town	**Browne William**
LDY	Loghran	**Browne William**
LIM	Milltown	**Browne William**
CRK	Castle-land	**Browning David R**
ARM	Keady	**Brownlee Richard**
LIM	Rylanes	**Brownrick**
KILD	Moorhill	**Brownrigg Cath**
WEX	Mill Lands	**Brownrigg Henry**
LIM	Ballyclough	**Brownrigg Joseph**
LDY	Ballywoodock	**Bruce**
ANT	Carrickfergus Mid.	**Bruce**
LIM	Castlematrix	**Bruce Jno Rev.**
LDY	Ballymadigan	**Bruce Sir Henry Bt.**
LDY	Ballywoodock	**Bruce Sir Henry Bt.**
DWN	Ballycreely	**Bruce William**
CAR	Orchard	**Bruen**
CAR	Old Park *	**Bruen H**
ROS	Gillstown	**Bruen Henry**
CAR	Old Park *	**Bruen Henry**

CO.	TOWNLAND	MILLER
CAR	Staplestown	**Bruen Henry**
SLI	Drumnagoal	**Bruen Mark**
ROS	Gillstown	**Bruen Moses**
SLI	Ballinvally	**Bruin James**
LAO	Cartown	**Brundram**
MON	Rockcorry	**Brunker**
MON	Creeve	**Brunker John**
MON	Creeve	**Brunker Rober**
DWN	Downpatrick Town	**Brunker Thomas**
GAL	Woodford	**Brunskill Henry**
LOU	Ballymascanlan	**Brush**
LOU	Ballynamenan	**Brush**
LOU	Dromod	**Brush**
ROS	Athleague Manor	**Bryan**
KILD	Johnstown	**Bryan**
DUB	Palmerstown	**Bryan**
WEX	Iberins (parish)	**Bryan Andrew**
KKY	Mill Island	**Bryan Eilliam**
KKY	Woollengrange	**Bryan George**
KKY	Woollengrange	**Bryan George**
CLE	Inchiquin Manor	**Bryan John**
WEX	Tullabeg	**Bryan Thomas**
KKY	Mill Island	**Bryan William B**
LOU	Balregan	**Bryans**
LOU	Castletown	**Bryans**
MON	Crumlin	**Bryans Andrew**
FER	Gortgor	**Bryans Capt.**
LOU	Dundalk Town	**Bryans Richard**
OFF	Tinnycross	**Bryen Daniel**
TIP	Clonmel	**Bryen John**
DUB	Blanchardstown	**Bryson John**
TYR	Cavan	**Buchanan Dan**
DON	Keeloges	**Buchanan Fran**
TYR	Cavan	**Buchanan John**
LEI	Tormahoony	**Buchanan PatRICK**
TYR	Cavan	**Buchanan Robert**
DON	Keeloges	**Buchanan Robert**
TYR	Cavan	**Buchanan William**
WME	Mullenmeehan	**Buckley Catherine**
CRK	Blarney	**Buckley Daniel**
OFF	Drumakeenan	**Buckley Henry**
LONG	Sheeroe	**Buckley Henry**
DUB	Kingsmillstown	**Buckley Jno**
OFF	Cappydonnell Little	**Buckley Timothy**
WME	Kilcumreragh	**Buckley Timothy**
WME	Ballycloughduff	**Buckley William**
ROS	Killakin *	**Bucknall**
LAO	Maryborough Town	**Budda**
KKY	Thomastown	**Budds Charles**
LAO	Timogue	**Budds Thomas**
LOU	Dundalk Town	**Builder G. Kelso**
CRK	Kinsale Town	**Builen William**
GAL	Middleline North	**Bulger James**
CLE	Blackwater	**Bull**
CAR	Clashganny	**Bull**
CAR	Clashganny	**Bull**

CO.	TOWNLAND	MILLER
KKY	Grennan	**Bull William**
KKY	Thomastown :	**Bull William**
LDY	Balteagh Lower	**Bullion John**
DON	Drimennan	**Bullockshed James**
ARM	Augher Town	**Bunbery Emily R**
CAR	Lisnevagh	**Bunbury**
ARM	Augher Town	**Bunbury Diana R**
KILD	Pluckerstown	**Bunbury George**
ARM	Augher Town	**Bunbury James**
TYR	Augher	**Bunbury James Sir**
TYR	Augher	**Bunbury John**
ARM	Augher Town	**Bunbury John**
ARM	Augher Town	**Bunbury John A**
ARM	Augher Town	**Bunbury Mervyn**
KILD	Pluckerstown	**Bunbury Thomas**
CAR	Lisnevagh	**Bunbury William C**
LDY	Annagh	**Bunton John**
KILD	Greatconnell	**Burchell Peter**
KILD	Clane	**Burdett George Capt.**
WEX	Ballyedmond	**Burdett Thomas**
WEX	Palace	**Burdett Thomas**
WEX	Palace	**Burdett William**
ARM	Tullyelmer	**Burges**
CAR	Rosdellig	**Burgess Elizabeth**
TYR	Ennish	**Burgess John Y**
CAR	Carlow Town	**Burgess William**
CAR	Tullow	**Burgess William**
KILD	Corbans *	**Burgh**
KILD	Corbans *	**Burgh**
KILD	Oldtown	**Burgh**
TYR	Artigarvan	**Burgoyne Sir J.**
TYR	Artigarvan	**Burgyne John J Sir**
MYO	Ardnaree	**Burke**
WAT	Killadangan	**Burke**
DUB	Milltown	**Burke**
KILD	Newtown	**Burke A**
GAL	Athenry Town	**Burke Bartholomew**
ROS	Tanidrissoge *	**Burke Dominick**
GAL	Galway Town	**Burke Ed. Cussen**
DUB	Edmondstown	**Burke Edmund**
GAL	Galway Town	**Burke Edward**
GAL	Galway Town	**Burke Edward C**
GAL	Galway Town	**Burke Edward C**
GAL	Galway Town	**Burke Edwd**
DUB	Templeogue	**Burke Francis**
GAL	Galway Town	**Burke James**
GAL	Ballinderry	**Burke James U**
ROS	Burne Brooke *	**Burke John**
GAL	Galway Town	**Burke John**
GAL	Galway Town	**Burke Josephine**
GAL	Galway Town	**Burke Marcella**
GAL	Annaghbeg	**Burke Martin**
ROS	Milltown	**Burke Mary**
CLE	Killaloe town	**Burke Michael**
MYO	Killinasash	**Burke Michael**
CAV	Bawnboy	**Burke Mrs.**

CO.	TOWNLAND	MILLER
TIP	Tipperary Town	**Burke P**
TIP	Killeroe	**Burke Patrick**
ROS	Athlone	**Burke Peter**
MYO	Bunnadober	**Burke Peter**
GAL	Galway Town	**Burke Richard**
ROS	Milltown B`robe	**Burke Ulick**
MYO	Ballyduffy	**Burke Walter**
DUB	Milltown	**Burke Walter**
KILD	Grange Beg	**Burke William**
MEA	Milltown	**Burke William**
DUB	Templeogue	**Burke William J**
DON	Carrowkeel	**Burn James**
ROS	Milltown	**Burne James**
DUB	Dublin City	**Burne John**
CAV	Mullagh Cuilcagh	**Burns Denis**
SLI	Aclare Village	**Burns John**
SLI	Lislea	**Burns John**
TIP	Mullauns	**Burns William**
ARM	Anagh	**Burnside James**
GAL	Cloonlaghan Geo	**Burrell Charles W G**
OFF	Frankford	**Burris Charles**
OFF	Frankford Town	**Burris Charles**
KKY	Goresbridge :	**Burris W.K. Rev.**
KILD	Ardree	**Burroughs Thomas**
KILD	Ardree	**Burroughs Thos Master**
ARM	Granemore	**Burrowes**
TYR	Strangmore	**Burrowes**
KILD	Ballyaghmoone *	**Burrowes Eliz Lady**
DUB	Templeogue	**Burrowes Mr**
TYR	Creevenagh	**Burrowes Thomas**
KILD	Corbans *	**Burrows Dixon**
SLI	Coolaney	**Burrows Henry**
ANT	Craigs	**Burrows James**
CAV	Raheelagh	**Burrows Robert**
LAO	Ballyger	**Burry Willam**
KILD	B`more Eustace	**Burton**
WME	Moyvore	**Burton**
DUB	Islandbridge	**Burton Benjamin**
SLI	Sligo Town :	**Burton Benjamin**
WW	B'more Eustace	**Burton Charles Bart.**
WW	B'more Eustace	**Burton Charles Jun.**
SLI	Sligo Town :	**Burton Fras Rt. Hon.**
DUB	Feltrim	**Burton John**
DUB	Inchicore North	**Burton Mr**
SLI	Sligo Town :	**Burton Samuel**
KILD	Pluckerstown	**Burton Sir Charles**
WAT	Shanakill	**Burwood Jno**
DUB	Dublin City	**Busby John**
KRY	Milltown	**Bushe Gervais**
DWN	Ballyharley	**Bustard**
DWN	Ballyharley	**Bustard**
DWN	Ballyharley	**Bustard Andrew**
DWN	Ballyharley	**Bustard John**
DWN	Ballyharley	**Bustard Robert**
CRK	Douglas	**Bustead**
CRK	Killingly	**Busteed**

CO.	TOWNLAND	MILLER
MEA	Mentrim	Callan Phillip
LOU	Balriggan	Callon John
LOU	Castletown	Callon Patrick
DWN	Drumbo	Callwell Robert
ANT	Belfast Town	Calvert
ANT	Drumnadrough	Calvert
ANT	Whitehouse Upr	Calvert
CAR	Carlow Town	Calwell Nathaniel
DUB	Red Mills	Camac - Malone
DUB	Red Mills	Camack John
LIM	Milltown	Cameron Alexander
ANT	Ballymoney	Cameron James
ANT	Millquarter	Cameron James
ANT	Molusk	Cameron James
ANT	Ballybentragh	Cameron Robert
TYR	Garvaghy	Cammock John
LAO	Coolkerry	Campbell
MON	Drumnavaddy	Campbell
GAL	Galway Town	Campbell & Miller
SLI	Sligo Town :	Campbell Ann
DWN	Ballylisbredan	Campbell Charles
DWN	Ballylisbredan	Campbell Charles
DWN	Cabragh	Campbell Charles
KKY	Dunkit	Campbell Charles
SLI	Sligo Town :	Campbell Charles
KKY	Strangsmill	Campbell Charles
MON	Tullynanure	Campbell George
MON	Tullynanure	Campbell George
ARM	Armagh Town	Campbell Henry
ANT	Ballyhenry	Campbell Henry
ANT	Carntall	Campbell Henry
ANT	Carrickfergus Tn	Campbell Henry
ANT	Shankill T`parks	Campbell Henry
FER	Derrihalla	Campbell Hugh
ANT	Ed`derry Falls Rd	Campbell James
DWN	Saul	Campbell James
ANT	Carntall	Campbell John
ANT	Corkey Little S.	Campbell John
ANT	Shankill T`parks	Campbell John
TYR	Altcloghfin	Campbell Patrick
LOU	Ballinfull	Campbell Peter
FER	Windmill Hill *	Campbell Robert W
CLE	O'Callaghansmills	Campbell W
FER	Drumbane	Campbell William
LDY	Galvally	Campbell William
LDY	Lisnagroat	Campbell William
LAO	Ballycarnan	Campion Samuel
GAL	Killaan	Cannon Dudley
GAL	Killaan	Cannon Dudley
MYO	Creggagh	Cannon Elizabeth
MYO	Drum	Cannon Michael
ANT	Shaneoguestown	Cantwell
CRK	Ballindresrough	Canty
CRK	Ballindresrough	Canty Johanna
CRK	Cappaghglass	Capppagh
MON	Cremartin	Caraher Arth & Mary
MEA	Stephenstown	Card Ralph
KILD	Coolsickin	Card Samuel
CRK	Broomfield	Carden John
MYO	Ballysakeery	Cardin John
ARM	Tullyelmer	Cardwell
ARM	Tullyelmer	Cardwell John
ARM	Tullyelmer	Cardwell William
WAT	Ballindud	Carew
KKY	Tinakelly	Carew E
KKY	Tinakelly	Carew I
WEX	Ross Town	Carew Lord
WAT	Ballindud	Carew Thomas
CRK	Careysville	Carey Edward
CRK	Coreysville	Carey Edward K
LAO	Curragh	Carey John
TIP	Tullow	Carey John
MEA	Woodtown	Carey Patrick
ROS	Rathardeagher	Carey William
MON	Kilcran	Cargil William
MON	Kileran	Cargill Wilson
ANT	Lisburn Town	Carleton
ANT	Lisburn Town	Carleton
WW	Ballynultagh	Carleton Alex
LDY	Bovagh	Carleton Cornelius
CAV	Drumsheil	Carleton Edward
WW	Ballynultagh	Carleton George
FER	Maghernegeragh *	Carleton George
LDY	Mawillian	Carleton William Jun
LEI	Balscarra	Carlisle Henry
OFF	Annaghmore	Carlton
DUB	Crumlin	Carmach Jno
DWN	Ballymacruise	Carmichael D
DWN	Ballycopeland	Carmichael D & W
DWN	Donaghadee T`pk	Carmichael David
ANT	Grange Park	Carmichael Hugh
CRK	Mallow Town	Carmichael J
DWN	Ballymacruise	Carmichael W
WAT	Loughdeheen	Carn Patrick
CRK	Ballymee	Carney John
MEA	Cruicetown	Carney John
MEA	Kilsker	Carney John
CRK	Rearour	Carney John
KRY	Shannow *	Carney John
CRK	Rearour	Carney John Jun.
LOU	Cappocks	Carnhampton Earl
MEA	Liscartan	Carogan Lord
KILD	Kilacolla	Caroll Patrick
CAR	Carlow Town	Carpenter
MEA	Rathbranchurch	Carpenter Catherine
LOU	Drogheda Town	CarpenterThomas
ANT	Craigs	Carr Henry
DWN	Killyleagh Town	Carr John
DWN	Tullygarvan	Carr John
DWN	Killyleagh Town	Carr Joseph
LAO	Maryborough Town	Carr Richard
MYO	Ballynew	Carr Thomas
LONG	Freaghmeen	Carragig John
OFF	Aghagurty	Carrey Edward
DUB	Island R. Liffey	Carrick Thomas
LEI	Urbal	Carrigan Farell
CAV	Clarebane	Carrigan Peter
KRY	Ballintourtone	Carrigue James
KRY	Ballintourtone	Carrigue Lansby
WME	Kilmore	Carrigy John
TIP	Barrettstown	Carroll
WAT	Duck`s	Carroll
ARM	Moneyquin	Carroll
WME	Mosstown	Carroll
DUB	Kilmainham	Carroll Alex
CRK	Farahy	Carroll Anthony
ARM	Ballyards	Carroll Edward
MEA	Staleen	Carroll Edward
KILD	Clane	Carroll Ephram
WEX	Wexford Town	Carroll Frederick
WW	Wicklow Town	Carroll Frederick
OFF	Killurin	Carroll George
LIM	Bruree	Carroll Honora
LIM	Knockfenora	Carroll Honoria Mrs
CRK	Ballygarvan	Carroll John
LIM	Bruff	Carroll John
KILD	Milltown	Carroll John
CRK	Rathmorgan	Carroll John
SLI	Sligo Town	Carroll John
LIM	Drumacummer E.	Carroll Martin
DUB	Dolphins Barn	Carroll Mchl
CRK	Park South	Carroll Michael
LIM	Killacolla	Carroll Patrick
CRK	Rusheen	Carroll Patrick
CRK	Loriga *	Carroll Theodore
CRK	Ballygarvan	Carroll Thomas
SLI	Leaffony	Carroll Thomas
LAO	Templequain	Carroll Thomas
CRK	Fermoy	Carroll William
CRK	Fermoy Town	Carroll William
ARM	Brannock	Carrothers Alex
ARM	Tullynacross	Carrothers Alex
ARM	Tullynacross	carrothers William
TYR	Edendroit	Carruthers James
MYO	Ardnaree	Carshore Thomas
DWN	Ballydugan	Carson
TYR	Milltown	Carson
DWN	Ballywalter	Carson Agnes
MON	Lisaginny	Carson Charles
LDY	Edenballymore	Carson James
TYR	Mullaghmore	Carson John
DWN	Ballyviggis	Carson Joseph
DWN	Grangewalls	Carson Joseph
ARM	Ballaghy	Carson Thomas
DWN	Greenan	Carswell John
LOU	Ballynamenan	Carter
CAR	Carlow Town	Carter
CAR	Carlow Town	Carter

CO.	TOWNLAND	MILLER
DUB	Mounttown	**Coleman Charles**
ANT	Antrim Town	**Coleman James**
ANT	Antrim Town	**Coleman Jas**
LOU	Balregan	**Coleman John**
TIP	Bohercrow	**Coleman Michael**
LOU	Dundalk Town	**Coleman Neil**
LDY	Tullans	**Coleraine Corporation**
LDY	Tullans	**Coleraine Mayor**
KILD	Pluckerstowm	**Coles Barry**
DUB	Lucan	**Coley Edward**
KILD	Kilcock	**Colgan**
LAO	Rathendock	**Colgan**
KILD	Kilcock Town	**Colgan Edward**
KILD	Kilcock Town	**Colgan Henry**
LAO	Rathdowney	**Colgan James**
WME	Straduff	**Colgan Marcus**
KILD	Kilcock Town	**Colgan Samuel**
TYR	Blacksessagh	**Colham Margt. ors Davies**
TYR	Lisnasoragh	**Colhoun Alex Wm**
TYR	Lisnasoragh	**Colhoun Crawford**
ROS	Lissadorn	**Colingsby Lady Fran**
DON	Carn Lower	**Colins Edward**
WAT	Bellicka *	**Collender Richd**
KILD	Townland ?	**Colles**
KRY	Dromthacker E.	**Colles Edward**
KKY	Gallowshill	**Colles Richard**
KKY	Maddoxtown	**Colles Richard**
KKY	Maddoxtown	**Colles Richd Colles**
TIP	Clonmel	**Collett John**
TIP	Toberahena	**Collett John Meara**
KILD	Kilmore	**Colley Elizabeth Spin.**
KILD	Kilmore	**Colley Mary**
KILD	Kilmore	**Colley Mary,**
LOU	Cruisetown	**Collier John**
CAR	Carlow Town	**Collier Peter**
LOU	Cruisetown	**Collier Peter**
LAO	Clonaslee	**Collins**
TIP	Clonmel	**Collins Edward**
WW	Roundwood	**Collins Edward**
WAT	Suir Island	**Collins Edward**
CRK	Blarney	**Collins Jeremiah**
OFF	Belmount /Lisderg	**Collins John**
MON	Drumully	**Collins John**
KILD	Naas Town	**Collins John**
OFF	Parkwood	**Collins samuel**
TIP	Clonmel	**Collins Stephen**
KRY	Knockanenore	**Collis Maurice**
KRY	Milltown	**Collis Maurice**
KKY	Highrath	**Collis Richard**
KRY	Clashcommon	**Collis Thomas**
FER	Doon	**Collum A**
FER	Tullybellina	**Collum Archibald**
LOU	Castletown	**Colman John**
LOU	Balregan	**Colman Michael**
DON	Carrickballydooey	**Colquhoun Robt**
DON	Rooskey	**Colquohoon John**
DON	Carrickballydooey	**Colquohoon Robt**
LOU	Ballymascanlan	**Colter Launcelot**
CRK	Slievreagh	**Colthurst George**
KRY	Shinnagh	**Coltsman Daniel C.**
DWN	Ballyhalbert	**Colvill**
DWN	Ballyhalbert	**Colvill**
DUB	Willbrook Lr	**Colvill**
CAR	Bagenalstown	**Colvill Hester**
CAR	Bagenalstown	**Colvill Hugh**
DUB	Templeogue	**Colvill James**
DUB	Templeogue	**Colvill James**
CAR	Bagenalstown	**Colvill Martha**
CAR	Knockmill *	**Colvill Martha**
DWN	Ballystockart	**Colvill Robert**
DWN	Ballystockart	**Colvill Robert**
FER	Cushwash	**Colvill Robert**
KILD	Athgarvan	**Colvill William**
DWN	Ballylisbredan	**Colvill William**
DUB	Willbrook Lr	**Colvill William C**
KILD	Athgarvan	**Colville**
KILD	Blackrath	**Colville**
ANT	Cullybackey	**Colville**
KILD	Moone	**Colville**
KILD	Osberstown	**Colville**
DWN	Ten Towns	**Colville**
CAR	Bagnelstown	**Colville William**
DWN	Ballydargan	**Colville William**
FER	Cushwash	**Colville William**
DWN	Ballydargan	**Colville William.**
LOU	Ardree	**Colville Wm Charg**
TIP	Clonmel	**Coman**
LONG	Bellanchowen	**Combermere Hon. Stapleton.**
LONG	Bellemack	**Combermere Hon. Stapleton.**
LAO	Borris	**Combie Sol.**
LAO	Borris	**Combie Solomon**
WW	Glasnarget North	**Comerford James**
LAO	Old Mill	**Comerford John**
CAR	Carlow Town	**Comerford Michael**
WW	Glasnaigirt N.	**Comerford Mr**
SLI	Belclare	**Commins Charles**
SLI	Belclare	**Commins P**
TIP	Toberdora	**Commons Denis**
MEA	Dunmoe	**Commons Edmond**
SLI	Belclare	**Commons Patrick**
WEX	Sledagh	**Compton Nathaniel**
LEI	Sheena	**Comyn William**
GAL	Tuam Townsparks	**Concannon Edmond**
GAL	Attyflynn	**Concannon Fran**
GAL	Attiflynn	**Concannon Francis**
GAL	Attiflynn	**Concannon John**
GAL	Glenamaddy	**Concannon William**
GAL	Galway Town	**Concanon Matthew**
CAR	Newacre	**Condell**
CRK	Glananoudig *	**Condon**
KKY	Greenville	**Condon James**
KKY	Greenville	**Condon John**
WEX	Meelgarrow	**Condon Patrick**
LAO	Rathdowney	**Condran Thomas**
CAV	Rassudan	**Conell Patrick**
WAT	Killeeshal	**Congreve**
WAT	Colbeck`s	**Congreve Ambrose**
LDY	Tirkeeran	**Coningham**
ANT	Glynn	**Conliffe John**
ANT	Glynn	**Conliffe Mr**
LDY	Clagan	**Conlon Mathew**
MON	Drumgor	**Conlon Patrick**
KILD	Walterstown	**Conlon Patrick**
LDY	Gortin	**Conn Samuel**
WW	Connary Upper	**Connary Mining Co.**
WW	Sroughmore	**Connary Mining Co.**
OFF	Aanard	**Connell**
OFF	Accurard	**Connell**
KILD	Milltown	**Connell**
CRK	Dromgarrif	**Connell Charles**
CRK	Madame	**Connell Charles**
KRY	Dromthacker	**Connell James**
KILD	Kilcullen	**Connell John**
TIP	Camus	**Connell Joseph**
GAL	Gortaganny	**Connell Michael**
CRK	Lahanaght	**Connelly Cornelius**
OFF	Eanaghan	**Conner M**
WAT	Pilltown	**Conner Richard**
OFF	Bogtown	**Conner Thomas**
OFF	Eanaghan	**Conner Thomas**
WEX	Killybegs	**Conneron Sarah**
WAT	Piltown	**Connery**
LOU	Dundalk	**Connick John**
LOU	Dundalk Town	**Connick Thomas**
TYR	Dunnamanagh	**Connison Walter**
KILD	Ardree	**Connolly**
CAR	Cloghristick	**Connolly**
DUB	Haroldscross	**Connolly**
CAR	Millford	**Connolly**
DUB	Saggart	**Connolly**
CAR	St Mullins	**Connolly**
CAR	Strongstream	**Connolly**
MEA	Townland ?	**Connolly**
CAR	Ballygowan	**Connolly Andrew**
CAR	Milford	**Connolly Andrew**
KILD	Ardree	**Connolly Arthur Rev**
GAL	Galway Town	**Connolly Bartholomew**
GAL	Galway Town	**Connolly Bartholomew**
ROS	Milltown	**Connolly Daniel**
DUB	Rathfarnham	**Connolly Elinor**
CAR	Bagenalstown	**Connolly Elizabeth**
DUB	Haroldscross	**Connolly H**
DON	Abbeylands	**Connolly Hamilton**
CAR	Ballygowan	**Connolly James**
WME	Balrath East	**Connolly James**
CAR	Strongstream	**Connolly James**
CAR	Ballygowan	**Connolly John**
ROS	Milltown	**Connolly John**

CO.	TOWNLAND	MILLER
TIP	Whitefield	**Connolly John**
KILD	Alliganstown	**Connolly Patrick**
MON	Reduff	**Connolly Patsy**
CAR	Ballygowan	**Connolly Richard**
DON	Abbey Mill	**Connolly Thomas**
DON	Abbey Mill	**Connolly Thomas**
DON	Casellard *	**Connolly Thomas**
DON	Knader	**Connolly Thomas**
DON	Rathbalskinney *	**Connolly Thomas**
DON	Scotch *	**Connolly Thomas**
TIP	Templemore	**Connolly Thomas**
DON	Tuckmill & Island	**Connolly Thomas**
DON	Tuckmill & Island	**Connolly Thomas**
TIP	Whitefield	**Connolly Thomas**
LDY	Ballyness	**Connolly Thomas Hon.**
LDY	Ballyness	**Connolly Thos Rt. Hon.**
WAT	Portlaw Bridge	**Connolly W**
WAT	Portlaw	**Connolly William**
CAR	Ballygowan	**Connolly William**
LDY	Bellaghy	**Connolly William Hon.**
LDY	Bellaghy	**Connolly William Hon.**
LDY	Curran	**Connolly William Hon.**
LDY	Vintners Propn.	**Connolly William Rt. Hon.**
KRY	Caunguillet	**Connor**
ROS	Creevemully	**Connor**
WAT	Tiercullen *	**Connor**
ARM	Middletown	**Connor Anne**
CRK	Ballyduff	**Connor Cornelius**
WAT	Tiercullen *	**Connor D**
LIM	Ballydonohoe	**Connor Elen**
KRY	Tralee Town	**Connor Ellen**
ANT	Ballygrooby	**Connor Foster**
KILD	Johnstown	**Connor George**
LOU	Dunleer	**Connor Gerard**
LOU	Dunleer	**Connor Gerard**
CRK	Derrygalun	**Connor James**
LDY	Tullyverry	**Connor James**
LDY	Ballydarrog	**Connor John**
OFF	Clonmacnoise	**Connor John**
DUB	Swords Town	**Connor Johnds.**
OFF	Bogtown	**Connor Mark**
CLE	Kilvoyran	**Connor Martin**
DWN	Ballydugan	**Connor Mary**
WEX	Clonganny	**Connor Myles**
GAL	Cloonatleva	**Connor Patrick**
GAL	Cloonatleva Lower	**Connor Patrick**
LONG	Shrule	**Connor Roderick**
CAR	Carlow Town	**Connor Roderick**
LDY	Learmount	**Connor Samuel**
LDY	Straid	**Connor Samuel**
OFF	Clonmacnoise	**Connor Thomas**
DUB	Collegeland	**Connor Thomas**
KRY	Counguilly *	**Connor Timothy**
DUB	Dolphins Barn	**Connor William**
LIM	Ballinlyna Lower	**Connors Brian**
LIM	Ballinlyna Lower	**Connors Bryan**
WEX	Ballynahask	**Connors Denis**
LIM	Drewscourt East	**Connors William**
WEX	Ballinamona	**Connoy Denis**
WEX	Gardamus Great	**Conor Patrick**
LONG	Shrule	**Conran**
LONG	Garrynagh	**Conran Patrick**
CAR	Carlow Town	**Constantine Thomas**
DON	Milltown	**Convoy Woollen Co**
LAO	Donaghmore	**Conway**
CLE	Coolmeen	**Conway Edmond**
LAO	Mountmellick T'pks	**Conway Edward**
CLE	Glenconaun More	**Conway John**
DUB	Chapelizod	**Conway Mr**
MEA	Slane Demense	**Conyngham Marq.**
DUB	Whitetown	**Coogan**
WME	Aghnatemple *	**Cooke**
KILD	Moone	**Cooke**
CAR	Rathvilly	**Cooke**
CAR	St Mullins	**Cooke**
KILD	Moone	**Cooke Deborah ors Ashe**
FER	Creevehill	**Cooke Edward**
TIP	Clonmel	**Cooke James**
KILD	Mount Blarney *	**Cooke James**
LDY	Derrychrier	**Cooke Margaret**
WME	Lissiwollen	**Cooke Thomas**
KILD	Moone	**Cooke Thomas,**
LAO	Aghmacart	**Cooksey**
WW	Ballinvally	**Coonan John**
LAO	Pass	**Cooney Alex**
LAO	Heath	**Cooney John**
DUB	Goldenbridge	**Cooney Michael**
LOU	Cappocks	**Cooper**
DUB	Feltrim	**Cooper**
DUB	Feltrim	**Cooper Austin**
SLI	Riverstown	**Cooper C W**
SLI	Cooperhill	**Cooper Charles Wm**
SLI	Knockmuldoney	**Cooper Edward J**
LEI	Creaveleagh	**Cooper Eward**
CAR	Carlow Town	**Cooper George**
MON	Bowelk	**Cooper Grace**
DWN	Cunningburn	**Cooper Hugh**
KILD	Kilcullen	**Cooper James**
DUB	Haroldscross	**Cooper Jane**
ANT	Ballygrooby	**Cooper John**
DUB	Dublin City	**Cooper John**
DUB	Haroldscross	**Cooper John**
ANT	Monkstown	**Cooper John**
WW	Tinnahinch	**Cooper John**
DUB	Glasnevin	**Cooper Richd.**
DWN	Balloo	**Cooper William**
DWN	Ballygowan	**Cooper William**
DWN	Owencork	**Cooper William**
ANT	Monkstown	**Cooper William**
CAR	Poorestown *	**Cooper William**
CRK	Corrydorregan *	**Coosheen district**
LAO	Borris	**Coote**
ROS	Creevemully	**Coote**
DUB	Windmill Land	**Coote**
TYR	Aughnacloy	**Coote Margery (Barclay)**
LAO	Olar Esker	**Coote Charles Rev**
ROS	Creevemully	**Coote Henry**
TYR	Aughnacloy	**Coote James**
ROS	Creevemully	**Coote Mary Spinster**
LAO	Borris	**Coote Rev. Chas**
ROS	Creevemully	**Coote Robt Carr**
LAO	Bally	**Coote Sir Charles**
ROS	Creevemully	**Coote Sir Chas H**
ROS	Creevemully	**Coote Sir Chas Henry**
GAL	Castletown	**Coouchan Michael**
WAT	Waterford Town	**Coursey Domnick**
ROS	Gillstown	**Cope**
KILD	Kilcock	**Cope**
KILD	Coolsickin	**Cope Henry**
ROS	Gillstown	**Cope Henry**
DON	Ballyshannon Tn	**Cope James**
FER	Mullybritt	**Copeland James**
DWN	Shannaghan	**Copes Thomas**
KILD	B'more Eustace	**Copleton John**
LDY	Edenballymore	**Coppin William**
DUB	Portmarnock	**Coppinger Charles**
MEA	Eden	**Corbally Richard**
CRK	Maryville	**Corban Laurence**
CRK	Maryville	**Corban Lucas Arthur**
DWN	Ballyward	**Corbett John**
LIM	Askeaton Town	**Corbett Nicholas**
DWN	Glaskermore	**Corbett Robt**
DWN	Ballywalter	**Corbitt Michael**
MON	Aghnamullen	**Corby**
GAL	Addergoolemore	**Corcoran Augustine**
GAL	Drumbane	**Corcoran John**
GAL	Drumbane	**Corcoran Michael**
GAL	Drumleane	**Corcoran Michael**
CAR	Clonmacshane	**Corcoran Patrick**
OFF	Streamstown	**Corcoran Patrick**
ROS	Swinefield	**Corcoran Patrick**
GAL	Townsparks	**Corcoran William**
WAT	Dungarvan Town	**Cork Earl**
WAT	Ballyeen	**Cork Richard E.**
WAT	Cappoquin	**Cork Richard E.**
DUB	Corkagh Dems.	**Corkagh House**
KRY	Charleville	**Corke**
KRY	Ballinirу	**Corkerry Michael**
ROS	Carricknorrue	**Corkran Francis**
MYO	Foxford Town	**Corley John**
TIP	Aghnameadle	**Cormack Thomas**
WME	Ballykeeran	**Cormick ElizABETH**
WME	Ballykeeran	**Cormick Hester Wid.**
WEX	Aughclare	**Cormick James**
MYO	Turlough	**Cormick Micheal**
WME	Monksland	**Cormick Richard**
LIM	Ballingarry	**Cormody**
CRK	Knockbrogan	**Cornwall Henry**

CO.	TOWNLAND	MILLER
KILD	Blackchurch	**Crawford Andrew**
MON	Aughalorigh	**Crawford Arch**
TYR	Blacksessagh	**Crawford Colham**
DWN	Colenecran	**Crawford Geo**
DWN	Balleevy	**Crawford George**
DWN	Coose	**Crawford George**
DWN	Tullylish	**Crawford George**
DWN	Balleevy	**Crawford Gilbert**
ANT	Carneal	**Crawford James**
MEA	Athboy Town	**Crawford John**
LEI	Drumherriff	**Crawford John**
DWN	Ballymullan	**Crawford John S**
LDY	Straw	**Crawford Joseph**
DON	Gobnacastle	**Crawford Margt**
TYR	Dunbreen	**Crawford Oliver**
TYR	Aughamullin	**Crawford Richard**
MEA	Athboy Town	**Crawford Robt**
DON	Ballyshannon	**Crawford Samuel**
DWN	Colenecran	**Crawford Thomas**
ANT	Antrim Town	**Crawford William**
DUB	Dublin City	**Crawford William**
OFF	Park	**Crawley George**
LOU	Drumgoolstown	**Crawley Robert**
TYR	Aughnacloy	**Cready**
LIM	Deebert	**Creed Edmond**
LIM	Deebert	**Creed James**
LIM	Deebert	**Creed James (1807)**
LIM	Deebert	**Creed Jane**
CRK	Carrigagulla	**Creed John**
SLI	Achonry	**Creeveen Thomas**
ARM	Tullycross	**Creevy John**
ARM	Tullyhugh	**Creevy John**
LIM	Milltown South	**Cregan Thomas**
CRK	Kilbrittan	**Crehan Michael**
KILD	Boycetown	**Creighton**
GAL	Ardbear	**Creighton Abraham**
GAL	Clifden Town	**Creighton Abraham**
TYR	Tullywiggan	**Creighton Abraham**
DWN	Lappoges	**Creighton Alex**
LOU	Cappocks	**Cremorne**
LDY	Ballynian	**Crilly John**
ARM	Ballynaclosha	**Crilly Thomas**
KRY	Drumyrourk	**Crimmen Denis**
KRY	Pallis	**Crimmin Patrick**
KRY	Headfort	**Crimmin Timothy**
KRY	Curraghnanav	**Crimmins Andrew**
KRY	Dunloe Upper	**Crimmins Catherine**
KRY	Dunloe Upper	**Crimmins Denis**
LAO	Mountmellick	**Crips**
LAO	Mountmellick	**Crips George**
LAO	Mountmellick	**Crips John**
KKY	Kilree	**Croak James**
DWN	Ballyvally	**Croathers**
ROS	Grange	**Crofton Ann Spin.**
ROS	Windmill Field	**Crofton Edward**
ROS	Ardsallagh	**Crofton Henry Rev.**
DUB	Ballyboden	**Crofton M**
CAV	Corbeagh	**Crofton Morgan**
CAV	Drumbarry	**Crofton Morgan**
ROS	Grange	**Crofton Morgan Yngr.**
LAO	Heath	**Crofts**
DUB	Glasnevin	**Crofts Alice**
CRK	Knockabehy	**Crofts James**
CAR	Carlow Town	**Croghan Edward**
CAR	Carlow Town	**Croghan Edward**
CAR	Carlow Town	**Croghan Richard**
ROS	Mill Park Boyle Tn	**Croghen**
LIM	Ballingarry	**Croker**
LIM	Bruff	**Croker**
DUB	Dolphins Barn	**Croker Edward**
CAR	Grangewat	**Croker Jno**
WME	Aghnatemple *	**Croker Thomas**
DWN	Donaghadee	**Cromellin**
DWN	Donaghadee	**Cromellin Nicholas**
DON	Haugh	**Cromer John**
ARM	Ballinliss	**Cromey Thomas**
MYO	Cordroon	**Cromie**
KILD	Irishtown	**Cromie**
ARM	Ballinliss	**Cromie James**
LDY	Ballygalagh	**Cromie John**
LDY	Galvally	**Cromie John**
DWN	Grallaghgreenan	**Cromie John**
DWN	Seafin	**Cromie John**
DWN	Ballynamagna	**Cromie Mary Anne**
MYO	Cardroon	**Cromie William**
MYO	Cordroon	**Cromie William**
ANT	Shankill T`parks	**Crommelin Michael**
ANT	Newt`ncrommelin	**Crommelin Mr**
DON	Haugh	**Crommer John**
LDY	Tamniarin	**Crommie James**
DWN	Ballyhemlin	**Cromwel Price**
ANT	Magheralave	**Crone John**
DUB	St Sepulchre	**Cronheim Theo**
CAV	Clareboy	**Cronin John**
KKY	Dangan	**Cronin Owen**
MEA	Cullentry	**Crook John**
MEA	Townland ?	**Crook John**
MEA	Balsoon	**Crooke**
ANT	Inishloughlin	**Crooks George**
LDY	Coleraine Town	**Crookshank R**
LDY	Coleraine Town	**Crookshank William**
KRY	Ballycarty	**Crosbie Arthur**
ROS	Creevemully	**Crosbie Chidley C**
KRY	Odorny *	**Crosbie David**
DUB	Finglas	**Crosbie Henry**
KRY	Ardfert	**Crosbie Jno**
KRY	Currens *	**Crosbie Maurice**
KRY	Liscahane	**Crosbie Maurice**
KRY	Ardfert	**Crosbie Sir Maurice**
WEX	Ballingly	**Crosbie Thomas**
CAR	Carlow Town	**Crosbie Thomas**
DUB	Milltown	**Crosbie W**
KRY	Ardfert	**Crosbie William**
KRY	Ardfert	**Crosbie William**
KRY	Shannow *	**Crosbie William**
KRY	Knockanenore	**Crosbie William T**
KRY	Milltown	**Crosbie William T**
LAO	Old Mill	**Crosby Emily**
SLI	Carrowcarragh	**Crosby Peter**
LAO	Old Mill bo:Ossory	**Crosby Poly**
LAO	Old Mill	**Crosby Robert**
CAR	Carlow Town	**Cross**
TYR	Lisnasoragh	**Cross Hamilton**
ARM	Carrickaness	**Cross Richard**
DWN	Ballylisbredan	**Cross Silvester**
ANT	Belfast Town	**Crossen James**
ANT	Belfast Town	**Crossen William**
ANT	Magheragall	**Crossin James**
TYR	Foremass Lower	**Crossle Charles**
TYR	Innishmagh	**Crossle James**
DUB	Chapelizod	**Crosthwaite**
LONG	Kilnplot	**Crosthwaite John Rev.**
LONG	Cloonkeen	**Crosthwaite Rev. J**
CAR	Bagenalstown Tn	**Crosthwaite Samuel**
CAR	Moneybeg	**Crosthwaite Samuel**
LONG	Cloonkeen	**Crosthwaite Sarah (Davenport)**
LONG	Kilnplot	**Crosthwaite Sarah (Davenport)**
ARM	Brannock	**Crothers Thomas**
CLE	Clooncool	**Crowe**
CLE	O'Callaghansmills	**Crowe**
KILD	Ardree	**Crowe Anne Widow**
LAO	Cardtown	**Crowe William**
CRK	Gurteen	**Crowley John**
KKY	Kilmacoliver	**Crowley Michael**
CRK	Roundhill	**Crowley Timothy**
CRK	Bandon Town	**Crowley Timothy J.**
CRK	Roundhill	**Crowley William**
DON	Newtowncunningha	**Crowther James**
FER	Bellanmallard	**Crozier A**
FER	Craghan	**Crozier A**
FER	Maghernegeragh *	**Crozier John**
FER	Bellanmallard	**Crozier Robert**
ANT	Antrim Town	**Crozier Wm**
DON	Culdaff	**Crudden Owen**
KILD	Boycetown	**Cruise**
LOU	Newtown Bog	**Cruise**
OFF	Bunrevan	**Cruise John**
ANT	Ballyportery S	**Cruit Robert**
TYR	Caledon	**Cryer James**
TYR	Castlecaulfield	**Cuddy Alex**
CAR	Grangewat	**Cudmore Henry**
LIM	Ballyclough	**Cudmore Paul**
MYO	Ballinrobe	**Cuffe**
MYO	Ballina	**Cuffe James**
MYO	Turlough	**Cuffe James**
LAO	Grange	**Cuffe Maurice**
LAO	Monksgrange	**Cuffe Maurice**
WEX	Ballybawn	**Cuigley Patrick**

CO.	TOWNLAND	MILLER
DON	Kildrum	Culbert Mr
SLI	Ballysadare Town	Culbertson Robert
SLI	Barley Mill	Culbertson Robert
SLI	Churchland	Culbertson Robert
SLI	Knockmuldoney	Culbertson Robert
WEX	Kiltra	Culfer Elizabeth
MEA	Beaumont	Cullen
CLE	Inverstown	Cullen
LDY	Bellaghy Town	Cullen Andrew
SLI	Curraghnagass	Cullen Domnick
CAR	Ballyellin	Cullen Edmond
LAO	Doon	Cullen Edward
LEI	Rossclogher	Cullen Henry
CAR	Ballyellin	Cullen James
MEA	Liscartan	Cullen James
LAO	Eglish	Cullen John
DUB	Shanganagh	Cullen Patrick
WEX	Polehore	Cullen William
WAT	Nicholastown	Cullinder Walter
WW	Bray	Culloden Jemima, Spin.
GAL	Kilconnell	Cummins George
ARM	Drumnakelly	Cummins John
MEA	Boltray	Cummins Robert
MEA	Boltray	Cummins Robert King
GAL	Millplot	Cummins Thomas
ANT	Glynn Village	Cunliffe William
ANT	Carnlea	Cunning Robert
DWN	Ballyhemlin	Cunningham
ANT	Cromack	Cunningham
DUB	Dublin City	Cunningham
MON	Enveyarig *	Cunningham
KRY	Milltown	Cunningham
DUB	Willbrook	Cunningham
DUB	Willbrook	Cunningham Dan
DON	Castletown	Cunningham Eliza
ANT	Aughnamullan	Cunningham George
WW	Bray	Cunningham George
DON	Castletown	Cunningham Jane
ANT	Belfast Town	Cunningham John
MON	Drumfaldra	Cunningham John
ANT	Fenaghy	Cunningham John
MON	Creeve	Cunningham Joseph
DON	Meenachallow	Cunningham Lord
MON	Creeve	Cunningham M/s
DWN	Newry Town	Cunningham Michael
LEI	Carrickanurroo	Cunningham Patrick
LEI	Newtown	Cunningham Peter
DON	Castletown	Cunningham Rev
TYR	Dullaghan	Cunningham Robert
LDY	Grillagh	Cunningham Robert
LDY	Londonderry Tn	Cunningham Robert
WW	Mountkennedy Dm	Cunningham Robt G.
ANT	Belfast Town	Cunningham Thomas
DON	Castletown	Cunningham William
ANT	Craigs	Cunningham William
ANT	Moylarg	Cunningham William

CO.	TOWNLAND	MILLER
MEA	Slane Manor	Cunningham William
MON	Team *	Cunningham William
DWN	Ballymacarret	Cunninghan C
LDY	Drumlamph	Cunnungham David
ANT	Tavnaghdrissagh	Cuppage Edmond F
KILD	Clane	Cuppaidge George
DUB	Haroldscross	Cuppaidge Mr
ANT	Doonbought	Cupples Henry
LAO	Ballybuggy	Curleton
MYO	Turlough	Curnes
DWN	Ravara	Curragh Saml
DWN	Ravara	Curragh William J
DUB	Rathfarnham	Curraghan
CAR	Carlow Town	Curran Jno
DWN	Tullyboard	Curran William
KRY	Ballybrack	Currane Patrick
ANT	Ballygarvey	Currell Andrew
ANT	Craigs	Currell Andrew
ANT	Ballygarvey	Currie Daniel
ANT	Broughshane Upr	Currie Daniel
ANT	Ballygarvey	Currill Daniel
CAR	Carlow Town	Currin Jno
DWN	Sheepland Beg	Currin William
ANT	Killygore	Curry John
TYR	Aughnacloy	Curry Wiliam
LAO	Aghmacart	Curtis
DUB	Welshestown	Curtis George
MEA	Bartramstown	Curtis Mark
ANT	Dunmurry	Curtis Mr
ANT	Old Forge	Curtis Mr
WEX	Ballynaglogh	Curtis Patrick
WAT	Portlaw	Curtis Thomas
DUB	Willbrook	Curtis Thomas
WAT	Garrancrobally	Curtis Wiliam
CAV	Corrawillin	Cussack Patrick
DUB	Boddin *	Cuthbert John
FER	Maghernegeragh *	Cuthbert John
MYO	Tully	Cuthbert John
FER	Maghernegeragh *	Cuthbert Sid Widow
FER	Maghernegeragh *	Cuthbert Sidney
		D
TIP	Feemore	Dagg William
WME	Connyborrons	Dagnan Thomas
DUB	Dolphins Barn	Daker George
MYO	Ballina	Daky James
ANT	Ballyruther	Dale Jane
ARM	Doogarry	Daley Thomas
WEX	Enniscorthy Town	Dallas Anne
TIP	Bansha	Dalton
ROS	Athlone	Dalton John
TIP	Ballymillard	Dalton Richard (Dick)
TIP	Ballynilard	Dalton Richard (Dick)
DUB	Feltrim	Dalton Thomas
KKY	Birchwood	Dalton William
TIP	Carrick-on-Suir	Dalton William

CO.	TOWNLAND	MILLER
ANT	Bellahill	Dalway Marriot
WME	Boyanagh	Daly
KILD	Castletown	Daly
KILD	Greatconnell	Daly
GAL	Killian	Daly
KILD	Castletown	Daly - McNally
GAL	Carrowroe	Daly Arthur
MYO	Drymills	Daly Bernard
ROS	Ballyroddy	Daly Cath
KILD	Greatconnell	Daly Denis
ROS	Tanidrissoge *	Daly Denis
GAL	Cregg	Daly George Rt. Hon.
KILD	B`more Eustace	Daly Hon. Justice
WME	Kilpatrick	Daly Hugh
ROS	Tanidrissoge *	Daly Hyacinth
MYO	Ballina Town	Daly James
CRK	Ballincroney	Daly James
KILD	Bonglash *	Daly James
GAL	Kilconnell	Daly James
MYO	Mullauns	Daly James
WME	Mullingar	Daly James
GAL	Kilconnell	Daly James.
CRK	Cork City	Daly John
MEA	Portlereagh	Daly John
TIP	Rossmore	Daly John
WME	Russagh	Daly John
CRK	Townland ?`	Daly John
WME	Rochford Dems.	Daly Matthew
KRY	Tralee Town	Daly Myles
ROS	Coolaugher	Daly Nicholas
WME	Russagh	Daly Nicholas
GAL	Ballinlass	Daly Patrick
KILD	Milltown	Daly William
KKY	Greenville	Dan Laffan
CRK	Garranenagappul	Danaghy
CRK	Garranenagappul	Danaghy John
LAO	Heath	Dancer
DUB	Haroldscross	Danford Willaim
LOU	Corcreaghagh	Daniel
WME	Cushinstown	Daniel
KKY	Ennisnag	Daniel
WAT	Mayfield	Daniel
TYR	Donaghrisk	Daniel Capt.
WAT	Poulboy	Daniel Edmond
WAT	Poulboy	Daniel Honora
WAT	Mayfield	Daniel James
WAT	Poulboy	Daniel Jno
CAV	Mully Maher	Daniel John Lt. Gen.
KKY	Kilmacow	Daniel Loughry
LDY	Raspberry Hill	Danton Henry
LONG	Ballyrohan	Darby Jane Widow
WW	Ballinaclash	Darby Joseph Leonard
WW	Ballinaclash	Darby Thomas
LAO	Rathendock	Darcey
CAR	Carlow Town	Darcy
KILD	Clonard	Darcy

CO.	TOWNLAND	MILLER
WME	Templepartick	**Darcy**
GAL	Eden Hill	**Darcy James**
ROS	Mullen	**Darcy John**
MEA	Martry	**Darcy Nicholas**
CAR	Borough	**Darcy Thomas**
WW	Knocknaboy	**Darcy Thomas**
FER	Castle Irvine Dem.	**Darcy William**
CAR	Carlow Town	**Dargan Andrew**
WW	Knockadosan	**Darley**
DUB	Walterstown	**Darley Henry**
WW	Kilcoole	**Darlington Mr**
WME	Ballykeeran	**Darnley Countess**
MEA	Athboy Town	**Darnley Earl**
WME	Ballywhite	**Darnley Earl Hon. Robert.**
LIM	Castlematrix	**Dartnell William**
DUB	Rathgar	**Dartry Dye Works**
ANT	Ballycregagh	**David**
KILD	Prumpelstown	**David Cope**
DWN	Welshtown	**David Good**
DWN	Ballynamagna	**David Hanna**
CAR	Patrickswell	**David Whitty**
DWN	Dromaness	**Davidson**
LDY	Vintners Propn.	**Davidson**
ANT	Aghaboy	**Davidson Adam**
ANT	Broughshane Upr	**Davidson Alex**
DWN	Drumaness	**Davidson Jno**
ANT	Broughshane Upr	**Davidson John**
DWN	Drumaness	**Davidson John**
MON	Corncarrow	**Davidson Mr**
MON	Laragh	**Davidson Mr**
ANT	Randalstown	**Davidson Mr**
TYR	Corcreevy	**Davidson Robert**
DWN	Downpatrick Town	**Davidson William**
CRK	Blarney	**Davies**
CRK	Cork City	**Davies Rev.Boyle**
CRK	Coolfadda	**Davis**
DUB	Crumlin	**Davis**
FER	Island *	**Davis**
CLE	O'Briensbridge	**Davis**
DUB	Doddsborough	**Davis Anne**
FER	Dooederny	**Davis Ferdinand**
WEX	Sweetfarm	**Davis Fran**
LOU	Ardee	**Davis Frances L**
WEX	Saintjohn`s	**Davis Francis**
WEX	Wexford Town	**Davis Francis Sen.**
DON	Aghlehard	**Davis John**
KKY	Dangan	**Davis John**
WEX	Martingalls	**Davis John**
KKY	Purcellsinch	**Davis Martin**
CAR	Cloghristick	**Davis Richard**
WEX	Enniscorthy Town	**Davis Samuel**
KKY	Mount Argula	**Davis Syd**
KKY	Mount Argula	**Davis Syd**
KKY	Dangan	**Davis Sydenham**
KKY	Ballyduff	**Davis Sydnam**
ARM	Ballinlare	**Davis Thomas**

CO.	TOWNLAND	MILLER
ANT	Knockboy	**Davison Alex**
MON	Moy Otra	**Davison John**
CRK	Cork City	**Dawly John**
LAO	Acreavock	**Dawson**
MON	Aghery beggan *	**Dawson**
LAO	Ballyegle	**Dawson**
LAO	Ballyroan	**Dawson**
LAO	Cappanard	**Dawson**
MON	Carnbane	**Dawson**
LAO	Clarahill	**Dawson**
LAO	Clonagh	**Dawson**
LAO	Mountmellick	**Dawson**
WME	Noughaval	**Dawson**
MON	Bowelk	**Dawson Charlotte**
MON	Bowelk	**Dawson Elizabeth**
ANT	Kilraghts	**Dawson James**
MON	Aghillagh	**Dawson Jane (Coote)**
LAO	Sampsons Court	**Dawson Jos Hon.**
LAO	Clonagh	**Dawson Joseph Hon.**
MON	Carnbane	**Dawson Letice**
MON	Aghillagh	**Dawson Ralph**
TIP	Longford	**Dawson Rev. John M**
WME	Aghnatemple *	**Dawson Richard**
DUB	Donnybrook	**Dawson Richd**
KILD	Glassely	**Dawson Robert**
WME	Clogher	**Dawson Thomas**
CRK	Kilnap	**Dawson Thomas**
LAO	Cardtown	**Dawson Wiliam Hon. Lord**
MON	Carnbane	**Dawson William**
LAO	Cullenagh (bo.)	**Dawson William H**
LAO	Ballyroan	**Dawson William Henry**
MON	Carnbane	**Dawson William Rev.**
KRY	Ballintourtone	**Day**
WW	B'more Eustace	**Day**
ROS	Boyle	**Day**
KRY	Liscahane	**Day Edward**
KRY	Liscahane	**Day Edward**
KRY	Keelerisky Manor	**Day Sir Robt**
GAL	Galway Town	**De Caen George**
LEI	Limerick Manor	**De Clifford Sophia Rt. Hon.**
KRY	Ballintourtane	**De Moleyns D**
DUB	Luttrelstown	**De Notingham Robert**
DUB	Astagob	**De Sallie Charles**
LAO	Clonenagh Dems.	**de Vesci Lord**
WAT	Piltown	**Deaggan Connery**
KILD	Milltown	**Dealy William**
WAT	Tallow	**Dean Peter**
MYO	Foxford Town	**Deane Edward H**
LIM	Windmill Hill	**Deane Matthew**
LONG	Gaigue	**Deane Sarah (Drake)**
LAO	Ballynakill	**Dease**
KILD	Boycetown	**Dease**
KILD	Kilcock	**Dease**
LAO	Old Mills	**Dease**
CRK	Youghals	**Deasy Jane**
CRK	Cork City	**Deeble Benjamin**

CO.	TOWNLAND	MILLER
WEX	Hoagesmill	**Deegan Laurence**
TIP	Nenagh North	**Deegan William**
WW	Milltown	**Deering Barry**
TYR	Liscloon Lower	**Deery William**
KILD	Ballykelly	**Deey Christopher**
KILD	Blackhall	**Deey Christopher**
LAO	Corbally	**Degan John**
LAO	Clonaslee	**Deigan William**
CRK	Townland ?`	**Delacour James**
CRK	Townland ?`	**Delacour Robert**
MYO	Kilkelly	**Delafield**
KKY	Kilcross	**Delahunt Bridget**
WAT	Ballymaclode	**Delahunty Richard**
DUB	Lockswood *	**Delandre Bart**
DUB	Lockswood *	**Delandre William Elder.**
DUB	Lockswood *	**Delandre William Yngr.**
MON	Lisnalong	**Delaney**
DUB	Shipping`s Mill	**Delaney Cornelius**
DUB	Willbrook	**Delaney Cornelius**
DUB	Blanchardstown	**Delaney Emma**
KKY	Goodwinsgarden	**Delaney James**
WEX	Loughanur	**Delaney James**
MEA	Athlumney	**Delaney Patrick**
OFF	Aghaboy	**Delaney Robert**
KKY	Ballylowra	**Delaney Thomas**
OFF	Ballyboy	**Delaney William**
OFF	Ballynacarrig	**Delaney William**
OFF	Ballyoran	**Delaney William**
OFF	Frankford Town	**Delaney William**
DUB	Woodlands	**Delaney William**
WME	Coola	**Delaney William Bern**
DUB	Diswellstown	**Delany - Moran**
KKY	Goodwinsgarden	**Delany James**
DUB	Diswellstown	**Delany Jno**
LAO	Aghmacart	**Delany John**
KKY	Kilnagranny Town	**Delany John**
KKY	Newtown (Baker)	**Delany John**
KKY	Jerpoint Abbey	**Delany Patrick**
CAR	Carlow Town	**Delany Thomas**
OFF	Ballyboy Town	**Delany William**
ARM	Ballykeel	**Delany William**
LAO	Course	**Delany William**
KKY	Newtown (Baker)	**Delany William**
DUB	Stopping`s Mill	**Dellany Cornelius**
DUB	Lucan	**Delvin W**
DWN	Ballydown	**Delzel**
DWN	Ballykeel	**Delzel**
OFF	Bracknagh	**Dempsey**
LAO	Portnahinch	**Dempsey**
WME	Carrick	**Dempsey Arthur**
KILD	Woodlands East	**Dempsey Edward**
WEX	Ballybugagh	**Dempsey Honor**
KILD	Woodlands E	**Dempsey John**
LAO	Ballinolart	**Dempsey John**
LAO	Ballinolart	**Dempsey Margt (Dunn)**
LAO	Clarahill	**Dempsey Martin**

CO.	TOWNLAND	MILLER
CAR	Cloghristick	**Disney**
KILD	Kilkea	**Disney Moore**
WW	Ballinaclash	**Disney Thomas**
CAR	Bendinstown	**Disrael Bergin**
TIP	Clonlaghy	**Disreal**
DUB	Diswellstown	**Diswells**
ARM	Annsborough	**Dixon**
LIM	Hingesmill *	**Dixon**
KILD	Hinges	**Dixon Amy (Green)**
KILD	Townland ?	**Dixon Amy (ors Green)**
DWN	Gilford Town	**Dixon Bebjamin**
DWN	Loughans	**Dixon Benjamin**
ANT	Calisnagh *	**Dixon Daniel**
KILD	Hinges	**Dixon Henry**
KILD	Townland ?	**Dixon Henry**
LAO	Rathdowney	**Dixon James**
LDY	Moneyguiggy	**Dixon John**
ANT	Carndonaghy	**Dixon Joseph**
DUB	Comberry	**Dixon Mr**
LDY	Ballymagrorty	**Doak James**
DWN	Kinallen Common	**Doake Samuel**
DON	Ballymaghy	**Doaks Samuel**
ARM	Maydown	**Dobbin**
ARM	Drumarg	**Dobbin John**
LDY	Lemnaboy	**Dobbin John**
ARM	Ballymahon More	**Dobbin Leo**
ARM	Ballynahone More	**Dobbin Leonard**
DUB	Oldbawn	**Dobbin Matthew**
WEX	Ballynaglogh	**Dobbin Patrick**
TIP	Tipperary Town	**Dobbin R**
ANT	Ballymatuskerty	**Dobbin William**
WEX	Ballynaglogh	**Dobbin William**
CAR	Carlow Town	**Dobbyn**
CAR	Rathvilly	**Dobie**
DUB	Dublin City	**Dobson Mr.**
LDY	Ardkill	**Dobson Anna Maria (Tomkins)**
LDY	Ardkill	**Dobson Anne Maria**
DUB	Dundrum Manor	**Dobson Isaac**
LDY	Ardkill	**Dobson Robert**
LDY	Ardkill	**Dobson Robert Capt.**
DUB	Dublin City	**Dodd W**
LAO	Timahoe	**Dodsworth**
ROS	Killappoge	**Dodwell H**
ROS	Ballyroddy	**Dodwell Henry**
WME	Monksland	**Dodwell Mary Spin.**
DON	Magheranappan	**Dogherty Charles**
DON	Ballycallan	**Dogherty Hugh**
DWN	Magheradrool	**Dogherty Patrick**
TYR	Birnaghs	**Dogue John**
KILD	Ardree	**Doherty**
KILD	Ardree	**Doherty**
DON	Ballycallan	**Doherty**
DON	Kildrum	**Doherty**
LIM	Ballylanders	**Doherty Patrick**
CRK	Ahgamilla	**Doherty Richardd**
CRK	Bealick	**Doherty Richardd**
CAV	Derrynatruan	**Dolan Charles**
CAR	Milford	**Dolan Fran**
CAR	Ballygowan	**Dolan Francis**
DUB	Kilmashogue	**Dolan Mr**
ROS	Curriaghbeg	**Doland Martin**
ROS	Kiltymaine	**Dolebroke Sir Geo Bt.**
DUB	Edmondstown	**Dollard Margaret**
DUB	Edmondstown	**Dollard Richard**
GAL	Loughrea Town	**Dolphin Henry**
LONG	Ballyrohan	**Domty**
CAV	Drumcalpin	**Donachs Mrs**
WME	Corner	**Donagh John**
DUB	Drimnagh	**Donagh John**
LONG	Ballyduffy	**Donaghoe James**
TYR	Gortycrum Irish	**Donaghy Bryan**
TYR	Brossloy	**Donaghy Francis**
ARM	Clarbane	**Donaghy Terence**
WME	Corkan	**Donaho James**
ARM	Allistragh	**Donaldson**
ARM	Glassdrumman	**Donaldson**
CLE	Inverstown	**Donaldson**
ARM	Killrockan	**Donaldson**
CLE	Ieverstown	**Donaldson Alexander**
CLE	Sixmilebridge Town	**Donaldson Alexander**
DON	Cloghore	**Donaldson Geo**
DUB	Willbrook	**Donaldson Jno**
KRY	Derrymore West	**Donavan Richard Esq.**
LAO	Maryborough Town	**Dond Robert**
LDY	Ballyness	**Donegal Hon. Marq.**
DON	Garvary	**Donegal Marq of**
ANT	Carrickfergus Tn	**Donegall George Marq.**
ANT	Carrickfergus Tn	**Donegall Marq. of**
FER	Killymackacrean	**Donegan James**
LONG	Cloonker	**Donelan Barnabas**
CRK	Dromaskill *	**Doneraile**
WAT	Tramore	**Doneraile Arthur Hon.**
WAT	Tramore	**Doneraile Lord**
CRK	Ballinhassig	**Donigan James**
CRK	Brownsmills	**Donnan**
GAL	Cloonreleagh E.	**Donnelan John**
KILD	Kilrush	**Donnell**
TYR	Ranelly	**Donnell James**
MYO	Newport	**Donnell Neal**
KILD	Newtown	**Donnellan**
LIM	Ryevale *	**Donnellan**
KILD	Ryevale *	**Donnellan Charles T**
WW	Bray	**Donnellan John**
WW	Bray Great	**Donnellan John**
WME	Cooksborough	**Donnellan John**
WME	Cooksborough	**Donnellan Philip**
KILD	Ryevale *	**Donnellan William**
CAV	Cornagee	**Donnelly**
DON	Laherdan	**Donnelly**
LDY	Straw	**Donnelly Bernard**
TYR	Tirmurty	**Donnelly Charles**
TYR	Mullaghmore	**Donnelly John**
ARM	Cashel	**Donnelly Michael**
LDY	Culnagrew	**Donnelly Patrick**
LDY	Straw	**Donnelly Philip**
ARM	Aghory	**Donnelly Robert**
MYO	Cloghermore (?)	**Donnelly Thomas**
DON	Drumherrive	**Donnelly Thomas**
LDY	Vintners Propn.	**Donnington Wiliam**
CRK	Newmill	**Donoghoe Michael**
GAL	Aggard More	**Donoghue**
WME	Creeve	**Donoghue Andrew**
CAR	Tullowbeg	**Donoghue Daniel**
KRY	Aughacasla South	**Donoghue Henry**
GAL	Aggard More	**Donoghue James**
WME	Corkan	**Donoghue James**
CRK	Ahgamilla	**Donoghue Jn**
CAV	Drumcalpin	**Donoghue Mary**
CAR	Tullowbeg	**Donohoe Daniel**
GAL	Kilroe West	**Donohoe Thomas**
WAT	Kilmanahan	**Donoughmore Earl**
KRY	Derrymore	**Donovan**
CRK	Driminidy South	**Donovan Con**
WAT	Raheen	**Donovan Eliz Widow**
LIM	Mullagh	**Donovan Ellen**
LAO	Abbeyleix	**Donovan James**
WAT	Raheen	**Donovan Jeremiah**
KRY	Tralee Town	**Donovan John**
LONG	Cloonkern	**Donovan Ned**
KKY	Ballynavoragh	**Donovan Patrick**
KRY	Tralee Town	**Donovan Richard**
WEX	Gorey	**Donovan Robert**
WEX	Kilmichael	**Donovan Robert**
WEX	Newborough	**Donovan Robert**
MON	Cornanure	**Doogan John**
CAR	Ballyknockan	**Doolan Edward**
LAO	Moat	**Doolan John**
LAO	Gortnaclea	**Doolan Thomas**
TIP	Garrycloghy	**Doolen John**
TIP	Tinvane	**Dooley Denis**
WME	Ballynacarrow	**Dooley John**
TIP	Tinvane	**Dooley John**
TIP	Carrick-on-Suir	**Dooly Jno**
WME	Ballynacarrow	**Dooly John**
WME	Cannorstown	**Doonigan Thomas**
OFF	Tonlemone	**Doorley Denis**
DUB	Windmillhill	**Doran Carlton**
KILD	Kilkea	**Doran Denis**
LAO	Timahoe Manor	**Doran Edmund**
MEA	Beaumont	**Doran Edward**
ARM	Corkley	**Doran George**
ARM	Brannock	**Doran Peter**
ARM	Lislea	**Doran Terence**
LIM	Kilfergus	**Dore**
LDY	Curragh	**Dorrety William**
KRY	Cagriga *	**Dorset Henry Chas**
KRY	Cagriga *	**Dorset Henry Duke**
DUB	Dublin City	**Dorty**

INDEX

CO.	TOWNLAND	MILLER
DUB	Ballsbridge	**Duffy John**
MON	Drumscor	**Duffy John**
LONG	Monadarragh	**Duffy John**
DUB	Donnybrook Lr	**Duffy Patrick**
LAO	Donaghmore	**Dugdale John**
OFF	Erry	**Dugdale John**
WAT	Aglish	**Duggan Francis**
LDY	Ballywoolen	**Duggan isaac**
LDY	Dunboe	**Duggan Isaac Jun**
KKY	Dangan	**Duggan Patrick**
DWN	Carrickmannan	**Duggan Willaim**
CAR	Carlow Town	**Duggan William**
CAR	Newacre	**Duigan John**
CAV	Shankill	**Duigan John**
LONG	Sheeroe	**Duigan John**
LONG	Sheeroe	**Duigan Sidney Wid.**
KRY	Ardfert	**Duke Dorset**
KRY	Charleville	**Duke Manchester**
KILD	Milltown	**Duke of Leinster**
LOU	Stranacarry	**Dullaghan James**
LOU	Killincoole	**Dullahane Patrick**
LDY	Arlogh	**Dumeny John**
ANT	White Head	**Dunan John**
DWN	Ballymacarret	**Dunbar**
LDY	Drummullan	**Dunbar John**
ROS	Ballinasloe	**Dunbo**
GAL	Galway Town	**Duncan Alexander**
ANT	Carrickfergus NE	**Duncan Dr**
ANT	Legoneil	**Duncan William**
CAR	Milltown	**Duncannon**
LOU	Dundalk Town	**Dundalk Woollen M Co.**
DUB	Castleknock bo.	**Dundas L**
LIM	Askeaton	**Dundon Philip**
DWN	Dundonnell	**Dungannon Arth Hon.**
DWN	Belvor *	**Dungannon Lord**
ANT	Derriaghy	**Dunlap Samuel**
DWN	Downpatrick Town	**Dunleath Baron**
DWN	Ballyhemlin	**Dunlop**
ANT	Ballykeel	**Dunlop**
ANT	Buckna	**Dunlop Charles**
ANT	Ballycastle Town	**Dunlop John**
ANT	Magheraboy	**Dunlop John**
LDY	Tullyheran	**Dunlop John**
ANT	Townsparks R`mn	**Dunlop Mrs**
ANT	Derryaghy	**Dunlop Samuel**
LAO	Ballynakill	**Dunn**
LAO	Clonaslee	**Dunn**
KILD	Newland	**Dunn**
DUB	Windmillhill	**Dunn James**
ROS	Grange	**Dunn James Rev**
LAO	Ballyroan	**Dunn John**
CRK	Kinsale Town	**Dunn Josias**
WAT	Kilnagrange	**Dunn Mrs**
LAO	Orchard	**Dunn Patrick**
CAR	Carlow Town	**Dunn Richard**
LAO	Orchard	**Dunn Richard**

CO.	TOWNLAND	MILLER
LAO	Clonaslee	**Dunn Samuel**
LAO	Ballinolart	**Dunn Timothy**
LAO	Clonaslee	**Dunn Watkins**
LAO	Milltown M`boro	**Dunn William**
KILD	Belan	**Dunne**
LAO	Clonaslee	**Dunne**
ROS	Ballinasloe	**Dunne Cath (Armstrong)**
WAT	Kilnagrange	**Dunne Catherine**
TIP	Ballynamurragh S.	**Dunne Edmond**
CAR	Carlow Town	**Dunne Isbella**
WEX	Ballintray	**Dunne James**
CAR	Carlow Town	**Dunne James**
GAL	Duckanelly	**Dunne Joseph**
MYO	Duckanelly	**Dunne Joseph**
LEI	Limerick Manor	**Dunne Josias**
CAR	Carlow Town	**Dunne Kate**
CAR	Carlow Town	**Dunne Michael**
MEA	Ardmulchan	**Dunne Patrick**
WW	Killincarrig	**Dunne Peter**
CAR	Carlow Town	**Dunne Richard**
CAR	Carlow Town	**Dunne Richard**
LAO	Orchard	**Dunne Richard**
ANT	Carrickfergus Tn	**Dunne Stewart**
ANT	Carrickfergus Tn	**Dunne Stewart**
ROS	Ballinasloe	**Dunne Thomas**
ROS	Clonard	**Dunne Thomas**
WME	Milltown	**Dunne Thomas**
WW	Bray	**Dunnflann Jno**
LAO	Rathdowney	**Dunphy**
WAT	Dungarvan Town	**Dunphy Edmond Rev.**
WEX	Bawnmore	**Dunphy John**
WAT	Dungarvan Town	**Dunphy Michael**
GAL	Ballynahivnia	**Dunsandla Lord**
WW	Ballybrittan *	**Dunsany James Baron**
MYO	Baghtiduffe	**Dunsany Lord**
MYO	Hawksford	**Dunsany Lord**
WME	Corduff	**Dunstervill**
WME	Crievebeg/ -more	**Dunstervill Charles**
CRK	Youghal Town	**Durdin Alexander**
SLI	Corimla South	**Durkin Hugh**
LAO	Portarlington	**Duron Isaac**
TIP	Holycross	**Dwan M.**
CAR	Tullow	**Dwyer Garrett**
GAL	Lavally	**Dwyer Michael**
CRK	Middleton Town	**Dwyer Mrs**
TIP	Moyaliff	**Dwyer Pierce**
LIM	Toomalene Upr	**Dwyer Thomas**
CAR	Newacre	**Dyer**
KILD	Inchemcquethyr	**Dyer John**
KILD	Inchemcquethyr	**Dyer John**
CRK	Mansion Ho Ward	**Dyke Parade**

E

CO.	TOWNLAND	MILLER
KILD	Colbinstown	**Eager William**
DUB	Feltrim	**Eagle**
WAT	Stonehouse	**Eakers Edward**
LDY	Tirglassan	**Eakin Andrew Jun**
MON	Glannan	**Eakin William**
TYR	Milltown	**Eakings**
CRK	Burrane	**Earl Barrymore**
DWN	Ballystockart	**Earl Londnderry**
WME	Coolure	**Earl of Bective**
MEA	Broad	**Earl of Drigheda**
CAV	Coldrum	**Earl of Farnham**
DWN	Ballykine	**Earls James**
TYR	Blacksessagh	**Early John**
TYR	Blacksessagh	**Early Samuel**
LEI	Aughrim	**Early Thady**
LIM	Askeaton	**Eason**
ROS	Cornagrea	**East Wiliam**
ARM	Ballinaclosh	**Eastwood Francis**
ARM	Ballinaclosha	**Eastwood James**
ARM	Ballinaclosha	**Eastwood John**
ARM	Ballinaclosha	**Eastwood Samuel**
WW	Ballynernon	**Eaton Thomas**
KILD	Rathmore E.	**Ebb Thomas**
WW	Blessington	**Ebbs Thomas**
LAO	Ironmills / Kilrush	**Ebury Baron**
FER	Dooederny	**Eccles Dan**
FER	Island *	**Eccles Daniel**
LDY	Ballykellaghan	**Eccles James (1834)**
LEI	Rossclogher	**Eccles Jemmina**
ROS	Cloonmagunnaun	**Eccles Jno**
TYR	Annagher	**Eccles John**
ROS	Cloonmagunnaun	**Eccles John**
WW	Milltown	**Eccles John Sir**
ANT	Broughshane	**Eccles Thos**
TIP	Mill Place Old	**Eccles William**
DWN	Ballydugan	**Echlin**
DWN	Ballyhalbert	**Echlin**
DWN	Ballyhemlin	**Echlin**
CAR	Aghade	**Echlin Alice**
MYO	Turlough	**Echlin Elizabeth**
DWN	Ballyhemlin	**Echlin Godfrey**
DWN	Cloughy	**Echlin John**
DUB	Feltrim	**Echlin Richard**
MYO	Turlough	**Echlin Robert Sir**
ROS	Cloonmagunnaun	**Ecles Gilbert**
ROS	Cloonmagunnaun	**Ecles Gilbert Jno**
ROS	Cloonmagunnaun	**Ecles Gilbert Robert**
ROS	Cloonmagunnaun	**Ecles James**
ARM	Ballaghy	**Edgar James**
LAO	Clonbrock	**Edge John Esq.**
LAO	Clonbrock	**Edge John Sen**
LAO	Timahoe	**Edge Joseph**
LONG	Cranally	**Edgewoorth**
LONG	Cullynore	**Edgewoorth Henry**
LONG	Cullynore	**Edgewoorth Henry Rev.**
LONG	Sheeroe	**Edgeworth Connell**
LONG	Forgney	**Edgeworth Frances Wid.**
LONG	Ballyrohan	**Edgeworth Jno**
LONG	Forgney	**Edgeworth Lovell**

CO.	TOWNLAND	MILLER
DUB	Willbrook	**Evans William**
WEX	Castlesow	**Eveligh William**
MEA	Liscartan	**Everard**
LONG	Forgney	**Evers Denis**
DWN	Ganaway	**Ewart Francis**
DWN	Ballyhaskin	**Ewart Jane Sen.**
DWN	Tullygarvan	**Ewart Thomas**
ANT	Ballygomartin	**Ewart William**
ANT	Ballysillan Vge.	**Ewart William**
ANT	Shankill T`parks	**Ewart William**
ANT	Tildarg	**Ewart William**
ANT	Shankill T`parks	**Ewart Wm**
DON	Labbadish	**Ewing Alex**
CLE	Ballykilty	**Exre**
CAR	Bendinstown	**Exshaw John**
WW	Bray Great	**Exshaw Thomas**
DUB	Milltown	**Eyre**
GAL	Galway Town	**Eyre Catherine Lady**
GAL	Lisfinny	**Eyre Giles**
GAL	Lismafada	**Eyre Gyles**
TYR	Benburb	**Eyre John**
GAL	Listinny	**Eyre John**
GAL	Galway Town	**Eyre Lady C**
GAL	Galway Liberties	**Eyre Robert Hedges**
GAL	Clifden Town	**Eyre Thomas**
KILD	Hortland	**Eyre Thomas**
ARM	Maydown	**Eyres**
ARM	Drumduff	**Eyres Thomas**
ARM	Maydown	**Eyres Thomas**
		F
WME	Ballycarty	**Fagan**
WME	Goldenbridge	**Fagan**
DUB	Templanstown	**Fagan John**
GAL	Lickbla	**Fagan Thomas**
SLI	Goldenbridge	**Fagan William**
GAL	Killaguile	**Fahy**
GAL	Kilmorgan	**Fahy John**
SLI	Cosmona	**Fahy Laurence**
GAL	Mountross	**Fahy Margaret**
GAL	Cooperhill	**Fahy Patrick**
MYO	Woodford	**Fahy Patrick**
GAL	Loughrea Town	**Fahy Rep. Laurence**
MYO	Kilbree Lower	**Fahy William**
SLI	Cong	**Fair James Jun**
MYO	Ardnaree	**Fair John**
GAL	Ardnaree Town	**Fair John**
DUB	Creggagh	**Fair John**
ROS	Cong	**Fair William**
DUB	Dolphins Barn	**Fairbrother Abraham**
DUB	Gally	**Fairbrother George**
CAR	Dolphins Barn	**Fairbrother Mr**
CAR	Dublin City	**Fairbrother Samuel**
WW	Ratheeran	**Fairbrother Sarah**
DWN	Carlow Town	**Faircloth George**
DWN	Newmills	**Fairfax Thos Hon.**
KRY	Carnany	**Fairlie**
DUB	Ballybawne	**Fairlie William**
DWN	Ballyroney	**Fairlie William**
DWN	Bo. Castlereagh	**Fairly**
DUB	Butlers Meadow	**Falconberg Hen**
DUB	Dolphins Barn	**Falkener Margaret**
TIP	Bansha	**Falkiner**
WME	Riverstown	**Falkiner**
DUB	Shipping`s Mill	**Falkiner Daniel**
LONG	Ballywillin	**Falkiner Thomas**
ROS	Killakin *	**Fallon**
KILD	Mullantine	**Fallon Cherry**
KKY	Fahy	**Fallon James**
GAL	Galway Town	**Fallon James**
CLE	Ardnacullia N.	**Fallon John**
CLE	Ardnacullia N.	**Fallon John**
TYR	Clonavarn *	**Falls**
TYR	Dungannon	**Falls**
TYR	Killymam	**Falls**
TYR	Shilen	**Falls**
TYR	Tempanroe	**Falls**
TYR	Ballygawly	**Falls Alexander**
TYR	Augher	**Falls James**
TYR	Aughnacloy	**Falls James**
TYR	Aughnacloy	**Falls James**
TYR	Dungannon	**Falls James**
TYR	Mullybrannon	**Falls James**
TYR	Mullybrannon	**Falls James**
TYR	Killymam	**Falls John**
CRK	Cloghane	**Falvey Thomas**
LAO	Stradbally	**Falye**
LAO	Ironmills / Kilrush	**Fannan James**
LAO	Ironmills / Kilrush	**Fannin David**
LOU	Ardree	**Farance Sophia Wid.**
KILD	Ardree	**Farange**
KILD	Ardree	**Farange**
WEX	Kereight	**Farday Thomas**
MEA	Kells T`nparks	**Farelly Thomas**
DWN	Ballymacarret	**Faren Joseph**
DWN	Portavoe	**Fargie James**
MON	Dernaglug	**Farlon George**
KILD	Inchaquire	**Farmer**
ARM	Allistragh	**Farnham**
LAO	Olar Esker	**Farnham Lady E.**
CAV	Cavan Town	**Farnham Ld Baron**
CAV	Cavan Town	**Farnham Ld Baron**
WW	Blessington	**Farquharson**
DUB	Feltrim	**Farran**
LAO	Pass	**Farrar John**
DUB	Rush	**Farrel Patrick**
GAL	Ahascragh	**Farrell**
WW	Bray	**Farrell**
GAL	Kilshanvy	**Farrell**
KILD	Moone	**Farrell**
KILD	Mountrice	**Farrell Christopher**
WW	Bray	**Farrell Daniel**
CAR	Carlow Town	**Farrell Edward**
ROS	Milltown	**Farrell Henry**
DWN	Ballymaconaghy	**Farrell James**
CAV	Coldrum	**Farrell James**
GAL	Coolrevagh	**Farrell James**
KILD	Mullantine	**Farrell James**
WME	Tubber	**Farrell James**
GAL	Conagher	**Farrell John**
WME	Harrystown	**Farrell John**
GAL	Lack	**Farrell John**
GAL	Mount Bellew	**Farrell John**
GAL	Grange	**Farrell Michael**
KKY	Jerpointchurch	**Farrell Mrs**
CAR	Carlow Town	**Farrell Myles**
GAL	Ahgloragh	**Farrell P**
MON	Corlealacka	**Farrell Patrick**
GAL	Tuam Town	**Farrell Patrick**
GAL	Tuam Townsparks	**Farrell Patrick**
WEX	Ballynaminnan	**Farrell Robert**
KILD	Connell	**Farrell Thomas**
KILD	Greatconnell	**Farrell Thomas**
TYR	Tullinure *	**Farrell William**
LEI	Ballinamore Town	**Farrelly Jno**
KILD	Clane	**Farrin Richard**
LONG	Cooleroy	**Farris Thos**
DUB	Inchicore North	**Farris Walter**
CAV	Cloggy	**Farris William**
CAR	Bathbrumill *	**Faulkner**
CAR	Patrickswell	**Faulkner Thomas**
CAR	Patrickswell	**Faulkner Thomas S**
WEX	Pigats & Tanyard	**Faunia**
LOU	Cappocks	**Faviere**
MEA	Townland ?	**Fay**
CAV	Drumakeenan	**Fay Bernard**
CAV	Drumakeenan	**Fay Luke**
KILD	Moone	**Fayle**
KILD	Moone Manor	**Fayle**
LAO	Rathendock	**Fayle**
CAR	Scortreen	**Fayle**
TIP	Nenagh	**Fayle Benjamin**
TIP	Nenagh	**Fayle Samuel**
LONG	Longford Town	**Fee Thomas**
LONG	Longford Town	**Fee Thomas**
LOU	Castletowncooley	**Feehan John**
TIP	Barnagree	**Feehan Keeran**
WAT	Carrickbeg Town	**Feehan Thomas**
ROS	Snipe Hill	**Feely John**
GAL	Leitrim More	**Feenarty Michael**
MYO	Eskerlevally	**Feeny**
MYO	Eskerlevally	**Feeny John**
GAL	Bleachgreen	**Feeny Ptk**
ARM	Allistragh	**Fegan Daniel**
MEA	Athboy Town	**Fegan Michael**
MEA	Wilkinstown	**Fegan Patrick**
ARM	Tullyglush	**Feir**
TIP	Cregg	**Felix O`Neill Felix**

CO.	TOWNLAND	MILLER
DUB	Lucan	**Fellows Charles**
KKY	Woollengrange	**Fenlon Patrick**
TIP	Clogheen Market	**Fennell James**
TIP	Clonmel Town	**Fennell LLewellyn**
DWN	Ballyvally	**Fennell Robert**
DWN	Tullyyear	**Fennell Robert**
TIP	Clogheen Market	**Fennell William**
MEA	Balrath	**Fenner Edmond**
DUB	Donnybrook	**Fenner Richardd**
MON	Mullaghanee	**Fenning Rose**
ANT	Ballygrooby	**Fenton**
ANT	Brookfield	**Fenton**
ARM	Tullyhugh	**Fenton**
SLI	Dromore	**Fenton John**
ANT	Carrickfergus Tn	**Fenton Samuel**
ARM	Tassagh	**Ferdon, Kidd**
ANT	Antrim T`parks	**Ferguson**
ANT	Ballycor	**Ferguson**
DWN	Belvor *	**Ferguson**
ARM	Knockbeg	**Ferguson**
ANT	Clontyfinnan	**Ferguson Hugh**
ANT	Ballycor	**Ferguson J C**
ANT	Culbane	**Ferguson James**
ANT	Drumdallagh	**Ferguson James**
ANT	Ferguson`s Land	**Ferguson James**
ANT	Malone Upper	**Ferguson James**
ANT	Antrim Town	**Ferguson Jno**
WME	Athlone Town	**Ferguson Jno**
LDY	Articrunaght	**Ferguson John**
FER	Derrygonnelly	**Ferguson John**
ANT	Islandreagh	**Ferguson John**
ANT	Shankill T`parks	**Ferguson John**
ARM	Tynan	**Ferguson John**
ANT	Antrim Town	**Ferguson John**
ANT	Antrim T`parks	**Ferguson John F**
ANT	Ferguson`s Land	**Ferguson Margaret**
LIM	Croagh	**Ferguson Maria**
LIM	Croagh	**Ferguson Maria Mrs**
ANT	Islandreagh	**Ferguson Mr**
TYR	Moygashel	**Ferguson Patrick**
ARM	Balleer	**Ferguson Thomas**
DWN	Edenderry	**Ferguson Thomas**
ANT	Ballymurphy	**Ferguson William**
LEI	Manor Hamilton	**Ferguson William**
LONG	Ballykenny	**Ferrall Edw**
LONG	Cloonker	**Ferrall James**
CAR	Carlow Town	**Ferrall John**
CAR	Carlow Town	**Ferrall Robert**
DWN	Ballymacarn	**Ferren Terence**
TYR	Leckpatrick	**Ferris John**
FER	Milltownblaney	**Ferris Matthew**
ARM	Latt	**Ferris Robert**
FER	Milltown	**Ferris Thomas**
ANT	Aghalee	**Ferris William**
LONG	Forgney	**Fetherston**
LONG	Forgney	**Fetherston George**
ROS	Athleague	**Fetherston Margt**
LONG	Arboula	**Fetherston Ralph Bt.**
LONG	Arboula	**Fetherston Sir Geo Ralph**
WME	Carrick	**Fetherston William**
TYR	Aughnacloy Town	**Fiddes James**
FER	Tullycreevy	**Fiddis Alexander**
MYO	Cloonagh	**Fielden John**
DUB	Feltrim	**Fierran**
DUB	Haroldscross	**Figgis Samuel**
LIM	Ballingarry	**Filaan**
SLI	Curry	**Filan James**
MYO	Cogaula	**Filbin Patrick**
DWN	Drumacanagher	**Filcock Jno**
LOU	Ardee	**Filgate**
LOU	Little Mill	**Filgate**
MON	Miskish	**Filgate**
LOU	Thomastown	**Filgate**
LOU	Ardee Town	**Filgate Alex**
LOU	Ardee Town	**Filgate Townly**
MON	Magoney	**Filgate William**
ANT	Shankill T`parks	**Filson Robert**
OFF	Derrymore	**Finamore Thomas**
SLI	Sessuegilroy	**Finan James**
ROS	Kilroosky	**Fineran Mary**
LAO	Orchard	**Fingleton Michael**
LAO	Orchard	**Fingleton Thomas**
ANT	Belfast Town	**Finlay Alexander**
DUB	Corkagh	**Finlay Colley**
MEA	Brownstown	**Finlay George**
ANT	Belfast T`parks	**Finlay Robert**
DUB	Diswellstown	**Finlay Thomas**
ANT	Ballymartin	**Finlay William**
SLI	Sessuigilroy	**Finman James**
CAR	Carlow Town	**Finn**
CRK	Sallybrook	**Finn James**
GAL	Ballygowan	**Finn John**
LAO	Derrycappy	**Finn John**
LAO	Irishtown	**Finn John**
CAR	Carlow Town	**Finn Michael**
CAR	Carlow Town	**Finn Susanna**
CAV	Garrymore	**Finnegan John**
ROS	Belderg	**Finneran James**
ROS	Rockwell	**Finneran John**
KRY	Tralee Town	**Finnerty Henry**
GAL	Leitrim	**Finnerty Vincent**
KILD	Irishtown	**Finnigan Thomas**
ROS	Lisgobban	**Finniran Laurence**
SLI	Cabrakeel	**Finton Michael**
ARM	Tullyglush	**Finton S**
ANT	Freemanstown	**Finton Samuel G**
CAR	Carlow Town	**Fishborne Wm Elder**
CAR	Carlow Town	**Fishbourne Gordon**
CAR	Rathvilly	**Fishbourne Joseph**
CAR	Carlow Town	**Fishbourne W**
CAR	Carlow Town	**Fishbourne William**
LAO	Coolhenry	**Fishbourne William**
LIM	Inch *	**Fisher**
DUB	Mounttown	**Fisher - Colaman**
WAT	Pilltown	**Fisher Abraham**
KILD	Pluckerstown	**Fisher Lucy (Aylmer)**
WAT	Pilltown	**Fisher Peter**
KILD	Pluckerstown	**Fisher Robert**
LAO	Rathdowney	**Fisher Robert**
WAT	Piltown	**Fisher Ruben**
LDY	Ballykelly	**Fishmongers W`full Co.**
LDY	Walworth	**Fishmongers W`full Co.**
LDY	Killycor	**Fishmongers` Co.**
CAR	Carlow Town	**Fitsimmons Thomas**
CAR	Carlow Town	**Fitsimmons Thos**
DWN	Ballycashan	**Fitsimons James**
LIM	Limerick City	**Fitt Mathew**
CRK	Cornmarket Ward	**Fitton St.**
TIP	Barnora	**Fitzgerald**
CAR	Carlow	**Fitzgerald**
CRK	Castledodde *	**Fitzgerald**
MYO	Clogher	**Fitzgerald**
MYO	Cloonagh	**Fitzgerald**
KILD	Kilrush	**Fitzgerald**
KILD	Milltown	**Fitzgerald**
KRY	Milltown	**Fitzgerald**
KILD	Mountrice	**Fitzgerald**
MYO	Moyhenna	**Fitzgerald**
WME	Mullingar Town	**Fitzgerald**
CAR	Paupish	**Fitzgerald**
DWN	Strangford	**Fitzgerald**
MYO	Turlough	**Fitzgerald**
LAO	Stradbally	**Fitzgerald (High.Sher.)**
CAR	Ballymurphy	**Fitzgerald Anne**
KILD	Rathangan Manor	**Fitzgerald C'tess Margaretta.**
MYO	Turlough	**Fitzgerald Dorothea**
MYO	Turlough	**Fitzgerald Dot. B162Maria**
KILD	Kilrush	**Fitzgerald Ed Lord**
MYO	Milltown	**Fitzgerald Edward**
GAL	Galway Town	**Fitzgerald Francis**
MYO	Clogher	**Fitzgerald George**
MYO	Turlough	**Fitzgerald George**
MYO	Turlough	**Fitzgerald George R.**
GAL	Galway Town	**Fitzgerald Gerald**
GAL	Galway Town	**Fitzgerald Gerald**
DWN	Blakans	**Fitzgerald Henry Rt.**
KILD	Greenhills	**Fitzgerald Hon. Charles**
ROS	Clooncan	**Fitzgerald James**
WEX	Coleman	**Fitzgerald James**
LIM	Kilmallock Town	**Fitzgerald James**
CRK	Kilnatoora	**Fitzgerald James**
KKY	Mill Island	**Fitzgerald James**
KILD	Nurney	**Fitzgerald Jas W**
DWN	Black Causway *	**Fitzgerald Ld Henry**
LIM	Greenmills *	**Fitzgerald Lord**
CAR	Paupish	**Fitzgerald Martin**
CRK	Cloughmacsimon	**Fitzgerald Maurice**
KRY	Odorny *	**Fitzgerald Maurice**

CO.	TOWNLAND	MILLER
KRY	Garraun	**Fitzgerald Patrick**
CAR	Straboe	**Fitzgerald Patrick**
ANT	Antrim Town	**Fitzgerald Percy**
KRY	Tralee Town	**Fitzgerald Rev Jas**
LIM	Castlematrix	**Fitzgerald Thomas**
CAR	Milltown	**Fitzgerald Thomas**
LAO	Cullenaghbegg	**Fitzgerald William**
CAR	Paupish	**Fitzgerald William**
CAR	Rosdellig	**Fitzhenry**
KILD	Inchemcquethyr	**Fitzhenry David**
WEX	Courtnacuddy	**Fitzhenry William**
LAO	Monksgrange	**Fitzmaurice**
LAO	Monksgrange	**Fitzmaurice James**
MON	Aghaclogha	**Fitzpatrick**
LIM	Milletstown *	**Fitzpatrick**
KILD	Newhall	**Fitzpatrick**
CAV	Aghadreenagh	**Fitzpatrick Daniel**
CAV	Shankill Lower	**Fitzpatrick Daniel**
TYR	Aghalougher	**Fitzpatrick James**
TYR	Aghalougher	**Fitzpatrick Jno**
KILD	Johnstown	**Fitzpatrick John**
CRK	Scartagh	**Fitzpatrick John**
OFF	Drumakeenan	**Fitzpatrick Patrick**
CAV	Leaghin	**Fitzpatrick Patrick**
MON	Toome	**Fitzpatrick Patrick**
KILD	Maudlins	**Fitzpatrick Thos**
DWN	Carrickmaddyroe	**Fitzsimmons Richd**
WME	Parcellstown	**Fitzsimons**
MEA	Balrath	**Fitzsimons Christopher**
CAR	Carlow Town	**Fitzsimons Thos**
WEX	Kilmichael Lower	**Fitzsimons William**
DUB	Donnybrook	**Fitzwiliam Richd**
DWN	Newry Town	**Fivey William**
LONG	Clondra	**Fladgate William**
MYO	Friars Quarter W	**Flair Camble**
DUB	Rathfarnham	**Flanagan**
CLE	Ballycorney	**Flanagan John**
KILD	Gilltown	**Flanagan John**
MEA	Macetown	**Flanagan Mary**
KILD	Garrisker	**Flanagan Matthew**
MYO	Legaun	**Flanagan Michael**
MYO	Crott	**Flanagan Patrick**
FER	Drumnagalliagh	**Flanagan Patrick**
MEA	Macetown	**Flanagan Peter**
KILD	Hartwell Upper	**Flanagan Thomas**
MYO	Oxford	**Flanagan Thomas**
OFF	Cappancur	**Flanagan William**
DUB	Ringsend	**Flanigan**
GAL	Galway Town	**Flatley Catherine**
GAL	Galway Town	**Flatley Catherine**
MYO	Cullentragh	**Flatley William**
OFF	Tullamore	**Flavan Joseph**
TYR	Pluck *	**Fleetwood Charles**
MON	Aghnaha	**Fleming**
LOU	Ardee	**Fleming**
LONG	Clondra	**Fleming**

CO.	TOWNLAND	MILLER
MON	Emy	**Fleming**
WAT	Kilmeadan	**Fleming**
TYR	Shanmullagh	**Fleming Andrew**
LONG	Clondra	**Fleming David**
LONG	Clondra	**Fleming Eliz Spin.**
ANT	Ballinlea Lr	**Fleming George**
KKY	Duninga	**Fleming H**
KKY	Barraghcore	**Fleming Handy**
CLE	Inchiquion	**Fleming Helen**
ANT	Aughnamullan	**Fleming James**
DWN	Ballymacarret	**Fleming John**
MON	Cavancope	**Fleming John**
MON	Reduff	**Fleming John**
GAL	Athenry	**Fleming Margaret M**
MON	Cavancope	**Fleming Mary**
DWN	Ballymacarret	**Fleming Mary Widow**
MON	Ballycronog	**Fleming Michael**
MON	Bradoge	**Fleming Michael**
MON	Bradoge	**Fleming Michael**
MEA	Stephenstown	**Fleming Michael**
MEA	Stephenstown	**Fleming Richard**
DON	St Johnstown	**Fleming Robert**
KILD	Naas East	**Fleming Thomas**
DON	Carrowreagh	**Fleming William**
MON	Cavancope	**Fleming William**
LONG	Clondra	**Fleming William**
LONG	Clonloman	**Fleming William**
MON	Killyveley	**Fleming William**
CAR	Barragh	**Fletcher John**
DUB	Leybstowm	**Fletcher John.**
GAL	Galway Town	**Fletcher Thomas**
DUB	Kimmage	**Flinn John**
DUB	Doolagh	**Flinn Mr**
LAO	Rathdowney	**Flintoff Albert**
LAO	Rathdowney	**Flintoff Anne**
WEX	Kiltra	**Flix Johanna**
LAO	Ballynakill	**Flood**
DUB	Black Mills	**Flood**
LIM	Milletstown *	**Flood**
KILD	Parsonstown	**Flood**
KILD	Johnstown	**Flood Anne Spin.**
CAV	Derryhum	**Flood Bridget**
CAV	Derryhum	**Flood Edward**
KKY	Thomastown	**Flood Edward**
KKY	Thomastown	**Flood Edward**
KKY	Thomastown	**Flood Edward**
KKY	Thomastown	**Flood Edwd**
LAO	Ballybuggy	**Flood Francis**
ROS	Canagh *	**Flood George**
ROS	Canagh *	**Flood George**
MEA	Knock	**Flood James**
DUB	Inchicore	**Flood Sir Frederick**
KILD	Newhall	**Flood Thomas**
MEA	Brannockstown	**Flood Willlam**
MEA	Kells	**Floody Thomas**
DUB	St Margarets	**Flower William**

CO.	TOWNLAND	MILLER
DWN	Magheramurphy	**Floyd William**
WAT	Carrowgarriff	**Flyng Francis**
GAL	Our	**Flynn Bernard**
DUB	Skerries T`pks	**Flynn Bridget**
MYO	Glebe	**Flynn David**
CLE	Shantrand	**Flynn Edmond**
CLE	Feakle	**Flynn Hugh**
GAL	Galway Town	**Flynn James**
GAL	Galway Town	**Flynn James & Co.**
LIM	Ashroe	**Flynn John**
LONG	Creelaghta	**Flynn John**
LIM	Cullenagh	**Flynn John**
CAR	Grangewat	**Flynn John**
KRY	Tralee Town	**Flynn John**
WW	Coolawinnia	**Flynn Michael**
LONG	Ballymacroly	**Flynn Patrick**
CLE	Raheen	**Flynn Patrick**
CLE	Raheen Town	**Flynn Patrick**
CLE	Raheen Town	**Flynn Patrick**
LIM	Scart	**Flynn Paul**
WME	Hightown	**Flynn Peter**
CLE	Shantrand	**Flynn Philip Jnr.**
CLE	Shantrand	**Flynn Philip Jnr.**
CLE	Shantraud	**Flynn Philip Jun.**
TIP	Castlequarter	**Fogarty Maria**
TIP	Borrisoleigh Town	**Fogarty Mary**
WW	Tinakelly Upper	**Fogarty Owen**
WW	Tinakelly Upper	**Fogerty Matthew**
DUB	Castleknock	**Foley**
WEX	Kilscanlan	**Foley David**
WW	Ballycarnew Lr.	**Foley Matthew**
WAT	Durrow	**Foley Michael**
WAT	Ballyin Lower	**Foley Nelson T**
WEX	Killynann	**Foley William**
MYO	Lissaniska	**Folliard Patrick**
ROS	Benmore	**Folliott Robert**
WAT	Dungarvan Town	**Fonlone Jno**
WAT	Dungarvan Town	**Fonlone Maurice**
LIM	Ballingarry	**Foot Jeffrey**
CRK	Ballymacmoy	**Foote B.**
WAT	Kill St Lawrence	**Foran**
WME	Mullingar Town	**Forbes**
CAR	Monebeg	**Forbes Edward**
WAT	Mayfield	**Forbes James**
MON	Tullyglish	**Forbes Jno**
CAR	Bagenalstown	**Forbes Matthew**
MON	Tooay	**Forbes Mr**
MON	Tullyglass	**Forbes Mr**
DUB	Dublin City	**Forbes William**
LDY	Ballywoodock	**Ford**
DUB	Dublin City	**Ford**
LDY	Ballywoodock	**Ford James**
ARM	Derryadd	**Ford James**
DUB	Windmillhill	**Ford James**
DUB	Windmillhill	**Ford James**
LONG	Bellamock	**Ford Mathew**

CO.	TOWNLAND	MILLER
LONG	Bellanchower	**Ford Mathew**
LAO	Abbeyleix	**Ford Matthew**
DUB	Dublin City	**Ford Mr.**
DUB	Dublin City	**Ford Robert**
WW	Ballynultagh	**Ford Roger**
LDY	Ballywoodock	**Ford William**
DUB	Dublin City	**Ford William**
DUB	Milltown	**Ford William**
MEA	Navan Town	**Ford William**
DWN	Dromaness	**Forde**
DWN	Balleny	**Forde Chathew**
DWN	Annadorn	**Forde Col.**
ARM	Derryadd	**Forde Francis**
LONG	Ballykenny Upr	**Forde Henry**
LONG	Creagh	**Forde Henry**
MEA	Abbeyland	**Forde James**
MEA	Ballynacree	**Forde Joseph**
WW	Ballynultagh	**Forde Roger**
LDY	Dromore	**Forrest D**
MON	Mullaghmore	**Forster**
LOU	Newtown Bog	**Forster**
WME	Ballykeeran	**Forster Anne ors Colville**
WME	Ballykeeran	**Forster Charles**
MON	Ballynode	**Forster Jane**
MON	Ballynure	**Forster Jane**
MON	Ballynure	**Forster John**
MON	Rafeenan	**Forster William**
ANT	Millfield	**Forsyth**
DWN	Ballyroney	**Forsyth Ann**
DWN	Ballyroney	**Forsyth Ann Widow**
DWN	Ballymakilbrick	**Forsyth John**
DWN	Ballyroney	**Forsyth John**
DWN	Ballyward	**Forsyth John**
LDY	Maine North	**Forsythe Andrew**
LDY	Newt`nlimavady	**Forsythe Mary Anne**
LAO	Acreavock	**Fortescue**
LOU	Ballymascanlan	**Fortescue**
LOU	Ballynamenan	**Fortescue**
LOU	Chanonrock	**Fortescue Faithful**
LOU	Killincoole	**Fortescue Faithful**
LOU	Stephenstown	**Fortescue Matthew**
DWN	Carlingford	**Fortescue William**
LOU	Carlingford Town	**Fortescue William**
MON	Mullaghmore	**Fortescues**
WW	Milltown	**Forth James**
DUB	Palmerstown	**Fortick Tristrum**
WEX	Browncastle	**Fortune Edward**
WEX	Mulmonty	**Fortune Edward**
WEX	Kellystown	**Fortune Laurence**
LIM	Brudy *	**Foster**
KILD	Corbans *	**Foster**
CLE	Inchiquin Manor	**Foster**
DWN	Tullychin	**Foster**
DWN	Tullycreely	**Foster**
CRK	Dromore(2)	**Foster Alfred**
MON	Quiglough	**Foster Andrew**
LOU	Ardee	**Foster Baron**
LOU	Ardee Town	**Foster Breen**
OFF	Kilmaine	**Foster Charles**
LOU	Ardee Town	**Foster Jno**
OFF	Ballincur	**Foster Maria**
MON	Mullaghmore	**Foster Sir Thomas**
DUB	Shallows Mill	**Foster Sir Wm**
LONG	Aghnashannagh	**Foster William**
DUB	Dolphins Barn	**Fottrell John**
ANT	Antrim T`parks	**Fowke**
CAR	Clonegall	**Fowkke Sydn.**
CAR	St Mullins	**Fowler**
FER	Littlemount	**Fowler George**
DUB	St Margarets	**Fowler James**
MON	Creeve	**Fowler John**
DUB	St Margarets	**Fowler William**
DUB	Rathfarnham	**Fowles**
WAT	Portlaw	**Fowley Matthew**
LDY	Ballyness	**Fox**
ROS	Drummullin	**Fox Arthur**
ROS	Grange	**Fox Arthur**
MEA	Clatterstown	**Fox George**
LONG	Clondra	**Fox George**
LONG	Barnacor	**Fox George Lane**
LDY	Ballyness	**Fox Henry Hon.**
LONG	Barnacor	**Fox James**
MEA	Clatterstown	**Fox James**
LONG	Cooleroy	**Fox James**
MEA	Brannockstown	**Fox John**
ROS	Gally	**Fox John**
MEA	Brannockstown	**Fox Joseph**
WME	Toorydonnellin	**Fox Margaret**
LONG	Cloonkeen	**Fox Richard**
DUB	Finglas	**Fox Richard**
LONG	Sheeroe	**Fox Richard**
LONG	Tinnynarr	**Fox Richard**
LONG	Treely	**Fox Richard**
KRY	Tarbert	**Fox Samuel**
CAR	Butlersgrange	**Fox Thomas**
CAR	Knockloe	**Fox Thomas**
CAR	Tullow Town	**Fox Thomas**
CAR	Tullowphelim	**Fox Thomas**
MEA	Brannockstown	**Fox William**
LAO	Abbeyleix	**Foxhall Esther**
LAO	Abbeyleix	**Foxhall Zachariah**
CAV	Bunnoe	**Foy**
CAV	Drumnakenan	**Foy Bernard**
CAV	Drumsheil	**Foy Charles**
CAV	Killycreeny	**Foy Charles**
CAV	Killycreeny	**Foy Charles**
CAV	Lisboduff	**Foy Owen**
CAR	Scartreene	**Foyle Joseph**
CLE	Rossmadda	**Fran Gore**
CLE	Gortafeane	**Fran McNamara**
ROS	Ballyglass	**Francis Harrison**
DUB	Goldenbridge	**Francis Journaux**
TYR	Bonds Mill *	**Frank**
TYR	Loughash	**Frank**
LOU	Ardee	**Frank Aiken**
TYR	Dunnamanagh	**Frank George**
TYR	Dunnamanagh	**Frank Thos T**
GAL	Galway Town	**Franklin Walter**
GAL	Galway Town	**Franklin Walter**
KRY	Cagrigh *	**Franks**
KRY	Clashcommon	**Franks**
KRY	Milltown	**Franks**
KRY	Cagriga *	**Franks Matt**
KRY	Cagriga *	**Franks Robert**
KRY	Clashcommon	**Franks Thomas**
CRK	Townland ?`	**Franks Thomas**
CAR	Clashganny	**Fraser**
ROS	Killendniell *	**Fraser George**
FER	Mulakeran	**Fraser William**
CAR	Clashganny	**Fraser William B**
LIM	Cloghanarold	**Frauly Ellen**
DUB	Dublin City	**Fraut R**
LIM	Cloghanarold	**Frawley Ellen**
LIM	Cloghanarold	**Frawley Maurice**
WME	Rathwire U.& Lr.	**Frayne**
DUB	Windmillhill	**Frayne**
DWN	Cabbragh	**Frazer John**
FER	Mullanmeen Under	**Frazer Thomas**
CLE	Inchiquin Manor	**Freake Jno**
KRY	Knockreagh	**Freeman**
LAO	Timahoe	**Freeman**
WEX	Enniscorthy Town	**Freeman George**
WEX	Enniscorthy Town	**Freeman I E**
DUB	Rathfarnham	**Freeman Mr**
DUB	Willbrook	**Freeman Richard**
WEX	Enniscorthy Town	**Freeman Thos Edward**
KRY	Knockreer	**Freeman William**
MEA	Naul	**Freemantle Nich (builder)**
ANT	Dunadry	**Fremantle Arth**
LAO	Aghmacart	**French**
WME	Monksland	**French**
MYO	Newport	**French**
LOU	Stephenstown	**French**
ROS	Knockalegan	**French Arth**
KILD	Bonglash *	**French Arthur**
ROS	Cloonmagunnaun	**French Arthur**
ROS	Killakin *	**French Arthur**
ROS	Lysgallagh	**French Arthur**
ROS	Cloonmagunnaun	**French Arthur Eldr.**
ROS	Cloonmagunnaun	**French Arthur Jun**
ROS	Cloonmagunnaun	**French Arthur Yngr.**
ROS	Lyscallagh (?) :	**French Austin Eldr.**
ROS	Killappoge	**French Catherine**
DUB	Killossery	**French Edmdmond**
ROS	Cloonmagunnaun	**French George**
ROS	Killappoge	**French Henry**
DUB	Milltown	**French Humphry**
ROS	Clonard	**French Jeff**

INDEX

CO.	TOWNLAND	MILLER
ROS	Killappoge	French Jeffery
ROS	Milltown	French Jefferys
MEA	Blackwater R.	French Jeoff
SLI	Killmure *	French Jno
ROS	Balingaglass	French John
ROS	Bellnagare	French John
MEA	Slane	French John
ROS	Cloonmagunnaun	French John Eldr.
ROS	Cloonmagunnaun	French John Rev.
ROS	Killappoge	French Kathleen
GAL	Newtownsmith	French Nicholas
GAL	Newtownsmith	French Peter
ROS	Cloonmagunnaun	French Richard
ROS	Bellnagare	French Robert
KILD	Blackchurch	French Robert
ROS	Gillstown	French Robert
CLE	Inchiquin Manor	French Robert
ROS	Lyscallagh	French Robert
ROS	Cloonmagunnaun	French Robt. Henr
ROS	Enfield	French Thos Lord Baron.
LAO	Baunbeagh	French William S
WW	Ballincurrig Lower	Freney Thomas
DWN	Ballyminstragh	Frew John
ANT	Tullycreenaght	Frew John
ANT	Tullycreenaght	Frew William
WME	Mullingar Town	Freyer
FER	Tonystick	Frith Richard
TYR	Gortnaskea	Frizell Patrick
DUB	Edmondstown	Frizell Richard
CAR	Clashganny	Frizell Richd
KILD	Kilrush	Frizzell
KILD	Coolsickin	Frost
KILD	Coolsickin	Frost
KILD	Ballyaghmoone *	Frost Leonard
OFF	Birr Town	Froste Richard
ROS	Killendniell *	Fry Henry
DUB	Rockbrook *	Fry Mr
LIM	The Mill Holding	Fry William
WME	Townland ?	Fryer
WAT	Drumgulliane W.	Fuge Thomas
ANT	Drumwillin	Fulerton Marcella
WAT	Cappoquin	Fuller William
ANT	Drumwillin	Fullerton
ANT	Drumawillin	Fullerton Dug
DON	Carn Low	Fullerton John
ANT	Tullymore	Fulton Adam
ANT	Mill Five Acre	Fulton Hugh
DWN	Donaghadee	Fulton James
DWN	Millisle	Fulton James
GAL	Kilroe	Furey
TIP	Barnora	Furlong
WW	Ballynultagh	Furlong Cloney
CRK	Cork City	Furlong John
DUB	Dolphins Barn	Furlong Nicholas
WW	Bray Great	Furlong Richard
WEX	Wexford Town	Furlong Thomas

CO.	TOWNLAND	MILLER
CAR	Carlow Town	Furney
CAR	Carlow Town	Furney Benjamin
LAO	Castletown	Furney Benjamin
LAO	Castletown	Furney Benjamin
WEX	Ballycanew	Furney Henry
WEX	Milltown	Furney Henry
LAO	Ballickmoyler	Furney James
LAO	Ballickmoyler	Furney Robert
KILD	Parsonstown	Fury
GAL	Bunatober	Fury Simon
CAR	Tullow Castleqtr.	Fury William
GAL	Galway Town	Fynn James
GAL	Loughrea Town	Fynn John

G

CO.	TOWNLAND	MILLER
CLE	Rossmadda	Gabbett William
CAV	Crumlin	Gaffney Bernard
DUB	Feltrim	Gaffney James
KKY	Clonassy	Gaffney William
KKY	Robinstown	Gafney Nicholas
KKY	Coolroe	Gafney Thomas
LDY	Belareena	Gage Connolly
LDY	Duncrun	Gage Connolly
ANT	Kinkeel	Gage Robert
CRK	Cork City N. Libs	Gaggin Francis
CRK	Cork City N. Libs	Gaggin Francis
WEX	Monagreany	Gahon Arthur
ARM	Ballycrummy	Gainford George
MON	Legacurry	Galbraith
DWN	Lissara	Galbraith Hugh
DON	Labbadish	Galbraith Mr
CAR	Staples Mill	Galbraith Samuel
LAO	Grange	Gale
LAO	Monksgrange	Gale
LAO	Sampsons Court	Gale
LAO	Grange	Gale Anthony
LAO	Grange	Gale Peter
LAO	Monksgrange	Gale Peter
LAO	Grange	Gale William
KKY	Listerlin	Gall James
DON	Port Lough	Gallagher
SLI	Bunree	Gallagher Andrew
OFF	Skehanagh	Gallagher Bernard
DON	Ardfarn	Gallagher Conlly
DON	Knock	Gallagher Corns
DON	Knock	Gallagher Corns
DON	Liscooly	Gallagher Hugh
DON	Carricknashane	Gallagher James
LEI	Millacre	Gallagher James
CAV	Moneen	Gallagher John
DON	Rooskey	Gallagher John
LDY	Templemoyle	Gallagher Martha
DON	Aughagault	Gallagher Mary
DON	Carrigans	Gallagher Mr
DON	Milltown	Gallagher Patrick
KILD	Strafan	Gallagher Patrick

CO.	TOWNLAND	MILLER
WME	Carrrick	Gallagher Peter
MYO	Garranard	Gallagher Peter
CAR	Carlow Town	Gallagher Thos Elder
MYO	Castlebar	Galloghly Thomas
KRY	Coolclogher	Gallwey John
KRY	Ballincarrig West	Gallwey Thomas
OFF	Killina	Galvin Martin
WW	Ballinameesda	Galvin William
WW	Ballinameesda Lr	Galvin William
KRY	Coolclogher	Galway
WW	Kilmaccullagh	Galway
KRY	Coolclogherl	Galway - Betham
KRY	Ballymallis	Galway Chris
KRY	Derreen	Galway Christopher
KRY	Ardagh	Galway Lucinda
KRY	Deewnagh *	Galway Lucinda Spin.
KRY	Deewnagh *	Galway Stephen
KRY	Ballincarrig West	Galway Thomas
DWN	Ballylisbredan	Galway William
DWN	Balleny	Gamble
ANT	Carrickfergus Mid.	Gamble
WAT	Cullinagh	Gamble
ANT	Edenderry	Gamble
LDY	Enniskillen Town	Gamble Baptist
ANT	Carrickferfus Tn	Gamble James
ANT	Carrickfergus Tn	Gamble James
WEX	Motebegg	Gamble Ones
WEX	Saintjohn`s	Gamble Ones
WEX	Motebegg	Gamble Onesipheris
WAT	Cullinagh	Gamble Richard
WAT	Cullinagh	Gamble Robt
ANT	Carrickfergus Tn	Gamble William
WAT	Cullinagh	Gamble William
LONG	Cordivin	Ganley James
LOU	Drumin	Gannon Michael
ROS	Cloontad East	Gannon Peter
CRK	Sallybrook	Garde Mary
WME	Ballynagore	Garden
DON	Milltown	Gardiner Catherine
MYO	Tully	Gardiner Charles
MEA	Broad	Gardiner L
ARM	Annavale	Gardiner William
ARM	Ballyards	Gardiner William
ARM	Green	Gardiner William
ARM	Racarby	Gardiner William
ARM	Tassagh	Gardiner William
MYO	Ardnaree	Gardner Charles
DON	Monclick	Gardner James
LOU	Ardee Town	Gare Francis
ARM	Ballynarea	Garmoney Hugh
ARM	Cortamlat	Garmoney Hugh
WW	Bannoqueroe *	Garner Francis
MEA	Bective	Garnett
KILD	Quinsborough	Garnett
KILD	Johnstown	Garnett Ann
MEA	Bective	Garnett John

CO.	TOWNLAND	MILLER
DWN	Ardkeen	**Garratt Joseph**
MEA	Teltown	**Garrett Louisa**
DUB	Dublin City	**Garrod Joseph**
DUB	Feltrim	**Garstin John**
LEI	Cavan Park	**Garstin Wm**
CRK	Kinsale Town	**Garton Patrick**
WME	Cushinstown	**Garty William**
KKY	Knocktopher Mano	**Garvey John**
KKY	Knocktopher Mano	**Garvey Mr**
MYO	Tully	**Garvey Nicholas**
LIM	Ballingoola	**Garvey Timothy**
LDY	Craigavole	**Garvin James**
LIM	Kilfinnane	**Gascoigne**
LIM	Kilfinnane	**Gascoigne E O Miss**
LIM	Kilfinnane	**Gascoigne Miss**
ARM	Cladymore	**Gass William**
ARM	Claddymore	**Gass William Jnr.**
LAO	Coolkerry	**Gasson Stephen**
ANT	Killycreen	**Gaston David**
MYO	Ballyscanlan	**Gate Hugh**
KILD	Greatconnell	**Gates Rober**
KILD	Greatconnell	**Gates Thomas**
LONG	Bleach Green	**Gauldsbury Catherine**
LDY	Ardmore	**Gault Thomas**
KKY	Newtown	**Gault`s Mill**
CRK	Ardkitt	**Gaussen Willia**
LDY	Ballyronan Beg	**Gaussen William**
KILD	Coolsickin	**Gaven Luke**
KILD	Greatconnell	**Gaven Robert**
WW	Ticknock	**Gavin William**
TYR	Greyduff	**Gay Frederick**
TYR	Greyduff	**Gay Henry**
DUB	Dublin City	**Gay Letitia**
GAL	Ardane East	**Gaynard Peter**
WME	Cushinstown	**Gaynor**
WME	Multyfarnham	**Gaynor**
WME	Thomastown	**Gaynor**
WME	Ballindurrow	**Gaynor Walter**
LAO	Grange	**Geale Anthony**
CAR	Carlow Town	**Geale Daniel**
WME	Cushinstown	**Geale Daniel**
WME	Riverstown	**Geale Daniel**
LAO	Rathdowney	**Geale Hannah Wid.**
DUB	Woodmills	**Geals Benjamine**
WEX	Hedges *	**Geering Richard**
ANT	Lisnafillon	**Gehan John**
ANT	Kirkinriola T`parks	**Gehon Andrew**
WEX	Kilbraney	**Gemick Simon**
ANT	Belfast Town	**Gemmill Robert**
CAR	Bagnelstown	**Geoghan John**
MEA	Navan Town	**Geoghegan Wiliam**
DUB	Donnybrook	**George**
ANT	Ballyginniff	**George Alex**
CAR	Bendinstown	**George John**
LDY	Terrydremount	**George William**
MEA	Bartramstown	**Georges Ham**
MEA	Blackwater R.	**Georges Richard**
WME	Milltown	**Geraghty Andrew**
WME	Corrlore	**Geraghty James**
WME	Milltown	**Geraghty James**
LEI	Rhadermott	**Geraghty Laurence**
DUB	Dublin City	**Gerard Jno**
OFF	Birr Town	**Gerard Thos**
KILD	Gorteen	**Gernon**
LOU	Philipstown	**Gernon**
CLE	O'Callaghansmills	**Gerran**
LEI	Boeeshil	**Gerrard Charles**
LEI	Boeeshil	**Gerrard Charles**
DUB	Finglas	**Gerrard Elloner**
DUB	Dublin City	**Gerrard Jno**
DUB	Dublin City	**Gerrard Samuel**
CAR	Carlow Town	**Gerrard Thomas**
MYO	Leckneen	**Gerry Kearney**
TYR	Annagarvey	**Gervais Francis J**
TYR	Ardunshin	**Gervais Francis J**
TYR	Kilnaheery	**Gervais Francis J**
DUB	Feltrim	**Gervais Peter**
MYO	Tully	**Gervey Maria (Burke) Wid.**
ARM	Tullyglush	**Gervin**
DUB	Dublin City	**Gibbon William**
GAL	Kilbeg Upper	**Gibbons James**
CRK	Glanworth	**Gibbons John**
OFF	Newtown	**Gibbons John**
OFF	Tully	**Gibbons John**
DUB	Mill Hill Farm	**Gibbons Mary Widow**
MYO	Ballycarra	**Gibbons Patrick**
GAL	Kilbeg Upper	**Gibbons Thomas**
WW	Baltinglass	**Gibney Robert**
DUB	Willbrook	**Gibney Robert**
LAO	Cappanapp	**Gibson**
LDY	Coshquin	**Gibson Charles**
MEA	Coolronan	**Gibson Joseph**
ARM	Tullyallan	**Gibson Messrs**
MEA	Coolronan	**Gibson Richard**
ARM	Tullyallen	**Gibson Robert Wm**
ANT	Belfast Town	**Gibson Samuel**
LDY	Dungorkin	**Gibson Thomas**
WME	Connyborrons	**Giffard Thomas**
ANT	Crevilly-valley	**Giffin William**
MEA	Castlejordan	**Gifford Thomas**
ANT	Ballymena	**Gihon Andrew**
ANT	Ballymena T`pks	**Gihon William Jun**
ANT	Lisnafillon	**Gihon William Jun**
SLI	Ballynacarrow	**Gilbert Charles**
DUB	Dolphins Barn	**Gilbert Claudins**
DUB	Feltrim	**Gilbert J**
WW	Ballinglen	**Gilbert Robert**
CAV	Killyconnan	**Gilcreest John (Andy)**
MYO	Carrownoultore	**Gildea**
DWN	Downpatrick Town	**Giles John**
LDY	Dromore	**Gilfillen J**
LDY	Dromore	**Gilfillen John**
GAL	Killoscobe	**Gilhooly Michael**
DUB	Barons Mills	**Gill**
OFF	Ballyhugh	**Gillard Richard**
ANT	Galgorm Parks	**Gillen George**
MON	Gola	**Gilles Thomas**
DWN	Ballycreevy	**Gillespie William**
OFF	Bogtown	**Gilliard**
OFF	Ballyhugh	**Gilliard Richd (miller)**
WME	Lismacaffry	**Gilligan**
WME	Clonmore	**Gilligan John**
LOU	Dundalk	**Gillighan Mr.**
DON	Terioddy ?	**Gillilan John**
ANT	Doagh	**Gilliland**
ANT	Doonans	**Gillin Alex**
CRK	Ballynacarrigga	**Gillman Edward**
CRK	Ahgamilla	**Gillman Henry**
CRK	Cloontiquirk	**Gillman Herbert**
CRK	Ballygarvan	**Gillman James**
CRK	Ballynacarrigga	**Gillman James**
CRK	Cork City	**Gillman John Jun**
LEI	Blackmill Farm	**Gillmor Gowan**
ARM	Lisadian	**Gillon George**
LEI	Annagheurly	**Gilmartin Owen**
DWN	Ballycreevy	**Gilmer**
MYO	Brickeens	**Gilmor James**
LDY	Lismoyle	**Gilmore John**
GAL	Lettera	**Gilmore Joseph**
GAL	Lettera	**Gilmore Michael**
DON	Cratlagh	**Gilmore Patrick**
SLI	Curraghnagap	**Gilmore William**
DWN	Downpatrick Town	**Gilmour William**
CAV	Bawnboy	**Gilroy Owen**
CAV	Moneen	**Gilroy Owen**
WW	Borkill Beg	**Giltrap William**
ARM	Roughan	**Girvan Mary**
ANT	Carrickfergus Tn	**Girwood John**
ANT	Ballymurphy	**Girwood Thomas**
ANT	Old Park	**Girwood William**
LDY	Ballygurk	**Given**
LDY	Ballyness	**Given**
LDY	Bellaghy	**Given**
LDY	Coleraine Town	**Given Andrew**
LDY	Terrydremont S.	**Given Andrew**
LDY	Ballygurk	**Given James**
LDY	Ballyness	**Given James**
LDY	Bellaghy	**Given James**
DUB	Wey Mills	**Given Lewis**
DON	Knockdoagh	**Glackin James**
GAL	Kilconnell	**Glascock Talbo**
KKY	Cilcomb	**Glascor William B**
KKY	Cilcomb	**Glascot William**
LDY	Cloghog	**Glascow Robert**
WAT	Kilmanahan	**Glasgow Andrew**
TYR	Tullyveagh	**Glasgow B**
TYR	Tullyveagh	**Glasgow W**
OFF	Ballincur	**Glass Andrew**

CO.	TOWNLAND	MILLER
FER	Litlemount	**Glass Andrew**
TYR	Gillygooly	**Glass Galbraith**
CRK	Burrane	**Gleadon**
MYO	Cloonkee	**Gledstones Thomas**
CLE	Clooncool	**Gleeson Batt**
CLE	Ballymulcashel	**Gleeson D**
WME	Athlone Town	**Gleeson Gerard**
CLE	Ballymulcashel	**Gleeson J**
WAT	Gowlan	**Gleeson Jeremiah**
TIP	Cloghinch	**Gleeson John**
LIM	Meanns	**Gleeson Michael**
TIP	Millbrook	**Gleeson Michael**
WME	Athlone Town	**Gleeson PatRICk**
CLE	Newmarket Town	**Gleeson William**
GAL	Garden Blake	**Glenane Patrick**
MYO	Milltown	**Glendenning**
MYO	Duckanelly	**Glendenning George**
ARM	Aghory	**Glendenning Henry**
LDY	Brackagh	**Glendenning Robert**
GAL	Athenry Town	**Glendinning George**
CAV	Corradarren	**Glendinning Misses**
TIP	Barnora	**Glengall Earl**
TIP	Bohernarnane	**Glengall Earl**
LDY	Annagh	**Glenholme Mr**
LDY	Glenmanus	**Glenn Hugh**
DON	Moneymore	**Glenn James**
DON	Dooish	**Glenn John**
LDY	Dundoonan	**Glenn Wiliam**
LDY	Coleraine	**Glenn William**
LONG	Forthill	**Glennon Peter**
MEA	Killacroy	**Glennon Thomas**
ARM	Ballynahone	**Glenny**
DWN	Dalmolly	**Glenny**
ARM	Lisdrumgullion	**Glenny**
DWN	Ardarragh	**Glenny Isaac**
DWN	Desert	**Glenny Isaac**
DWN	Saval More	**Glenny Isaac**
CAR	Borris	**Gliborn Ed**
DUB	Castleknock	**Glorney Benjamin**
WME	Ballykeeran	**Glover**
ROS	Boyle	**Glover**
GAL	Lisduff	**Glynn James**
KILD	Moone	**Glynn Joseph**
CLE	Kilrush Town	**Glynn M**
TYR	Tullyard	**Glynn Robert**
GAL	Ballingarry	**Glynn Thomas**
KILD	Oldtown	**Goddard**
KILD	Oldtown (5)	**Goddard**
ANT	Carrickfergus Tn	**Goddard James**
ARM	Lisdrumgullion	**Godfrey**
KRY	Milltown	**Godfrey**
ANT	Mullinsallagh	**Godfrey**
DWN	Downpatrick Town	**Godfrey Lyle**
TIP	Shanballyduff	**Godfrey Thomas**
LOU	Philipstown	**Godley**
ROS	Cloonmagunnaun	**Goff Robert**

CO.	TOWNLAND	MILLER
CAR	Scartreene	**Goff Tadd**
CAR	Scortreen	**Goffe**
KKY	Grannagh	**Gogane Mabel**
CAR	Carlow Town	**Goggin Richard**
CAR	Carlow Town	**Goggin Stephen**
CAR	Carlow Town	**Goggin William**
DUB	Woodlands	**Goggins James**
SLI	Collinsford	**Goggins Thomas**
TIP	Caher Town	**Going**
TIP	Clonlaghy	**Going Arabella**
TIP	Ballynaclogh	**Going Caleb**
TIP	Barnora	**Going Charles**
OFF	Ballyduff	**Going John**
TIP	Kilconly	**Going Thomas**
TIP	Killemly	**Going Thomas**
TIP	Barnora	**Going William**
TIP	Killemly	**Going William**
WME	Kilbillaghan	**Golden James**
SLI	Farranyharpy	**Golden Robert**
MYO	Shrule Town	**Golding Richard**
CRK	Townland ?`	**Good James**
CRK	Skibbereen	**Good Robert**
CAR	Carlow Town	**Good William**
LAO	Mountmellick	**Goodbody**
OFF	Kilcoursey	**Goodbody J**
OFF	Clara Charlestn	**Goodbody Jonathan**
OFF	Kilcoursey	**Goodbody L**
OFF	Kilcoursey	**Goodbody M**
OFF	Kilcoursey	**Goodbody Robert**
LIM	Limerick City	**Goodbodys (1893)**
CAV	Clodrum	**Goodfellow Isbla, Spin.**
CAV	Clodrum	**Goodfellow James**
CAV	Clodrum	**Goodfellow Margt Sen. Wid.**
CAR	Paupish	**Goodison O'Neill**
KILD	Athgarvan	**Goodman**
KILD	Blackrath and :	**Goodman**
KILD	Johnstown	**Goodshaw**
KILD	Millestown ?	**Goodshaw**
DUB	Leixlip	**Goodshaw Mr**
DUB	Loaders Park	**Goodwin F**
MYO	Tully	**Goodwin Francis**
DON	Tuckmill & Island	**Goodwin Lizie**
ANT	Grange Park	**Goodwin Wilkin**
OFF	Enaghan	**GoodwinJohn**
OFF	Enaghan	**GoodwinJohn**
CRK	Gully East	**Gookin**
KRY	Knockreer	**Goold Francis**
CAR	Orchard	**Goold Mary**
KRY	Knockreer	**Goold Nicholas**
LDY	Ballygurk	**Goold Pierce Rev.**
LDY	Ballyness	**Goold Pierce Rev.**
LDY	Bellaghy	**Goold Pierce Rev.**
KKY	Greenville	**Goough Benjamin**
DWN	Ballywalter	**Gordon**
TYR	Ballyskeagh	**Gordon AAron**
TIP	Cashel Town	**Gordon Avary**

CO.	TOWNLAND	MILLER
DWN	Ballycashan	**Gordon David**
DWN	Carmeen	**Gordon George**
ANT	Belfast Town	**Gordon James**
LDY	Fallahogy	**Gordon James**
MEA	Bartramstown	**Gordon Jas, Yeoman**
TIP	Derinsallow	**Gordon John**
CAR	Old Leighlin	**Gordon John**
DUB	Feltrim	**Gordon Nicholas**
SLI	Culleens	**Gordon Patrick**
ANT	Ed`derry Falls Rd	**Gordon Robert**
DWN	Ballyrobert	**Gordon Robert F**
WAT	Poulboy	**Gordon Thomas**
DWN	Lisduff	**Gordon William**
DUB	Edmondstown	**Gore**
LAO	Heath	**Gore**
KILD	Ardnaree	**Gore Arthur**
MYO	Ardnaree	**Gore Arthur**
MYO	Ballina	**Gore Arthur**
KILD	Ardnaree	**Gore Arthur Isaac**
ROS	Carricknorrue	**Gore Booth**
SLI	Curraghnagap	**Gore Boothe**
CLE	Ennis Town	**Gore Edward**
CLE	Ennis Town	**Gore Edward A**
KILD	Ardnaree	**Gore Elizabeth**
CLE	Ennis	**Gore Fran Hon. Brig.**
CLE	Ennis Town	**Gore Francis**
CLE	Ennis Town	**Gore Francis**
MYO	Ballina	**Gore Hon Richard**
SLI	Ardtermon	**Gore John**
SLI	Ardtermon	**Gore Nathaniel**
SLI	Ardtermon	**Gore Nathaniel Bt.**
SLI	Curraghnagap	**Gore Nathaniel Bt.**
SLI	Curraghnagap	**Gore Nathaniel Sir**
SLI	Curraghnagap	**Gore Nathaniel.**
FER	Crevinish	**Gore Ralph Rt Hon.**
KILD	Ardnaree	**Gore Richard**
ROS	Lysgallagh	**Gore Richard**
ROS	Lyscallagh	**Gore Richard Hon.**
DUB	Willbrook	**Gore Robert**
KILD	Ardnaree	**Gore Sophia**
MYO	Tully	**Gore St Geo Ralph**
CAR	Staples Mill	**Gorman Ferdinand**
SLI	Keenaghan	**Gorman Henry**
SLI	Ballymote	**Gorman Jno**
SLI	Keenaghan	**Gorman John**
CAR	Staplestown	**Gorman Patrick**
CAR	Staplestown	**Gorman Patrick**
TYR	Lackagh	**Gorman Terence**
KILD	Johnstown	**Gorman Timothy**
TYR	Pluck *	**Gorman William Eld.**
TYR	Pluck *	**Gorman William Yng.**
WME	Parcelstown	**Gormley Edward**
MON	Aughalorigh	**Gorrell William**
LAO	Old Mill bo:Ossory	**Gosby**
ARM	Markethill	**Gosford Earl**
ARM	Mohan	**Gosford Earl**

CO.	TOWNLAND	MILLER
WME	Clonnagapple	**Greville Col. Fulke S.**
LONG	Bellanchowen	**Greville William**
LONG	Bellemack	**Greville William**
TIP	Mill Place Old	**Grey Edward Sir**
ARM	Bryandrum	**Grey John**
LDY	Coleraine Town	**Gribben Edward**
LDY	Coleraine Town	**Gribben John**
ARM	Lisaveague	**Grier Moses**
DUB	Corkagh	**Grierson Philip**
MEA	Brannockstown	**Griffin**
LIM	Bruree	**Griffin Benedict**
CAR	Grangewat	**Griffin Edward**
LIM	Bruree	**Griffin Jessie**
KRY	Kilcumminbeg	**Griffin John**
ROS	Ballyroddy	**Griffin Joseph**
ROS	Ballyroddy	**Griffin Margaret**
GAL	Galway Town	**Griffin Michael**
GAL	Galway Town	**Griffin Michael**
GAL	Gortmore	**Griffin Michael**
KRY	Ballynabooley	**Griffin Patrick**
LIM	Cullenagh	**Griffin Patrick**
CAR	Grangewat	**Griffin Patrick**
LIM	Altavilla	**Griffin Peter G**
LEI	Greaghnaguillaun	**Griffin Philip**
WAT	Poulboy	**Griffin Thomas**
GAL	Gortmore	**Griffin Widow**
SLI	Buninna	**Griffith Henry**
DUB	Inchicore	**Griffitts Walter**
DUB	Islandbridge	**Griffitts Walter**
TIP	Ballyerk	**Grimes William**
ANT	Ballyhowne	**Grimshaw**
MEA	Stackallan	**Grimshaw**
ANT	Ballyhenry	**Grimshaw Edmund**
ANT	Ballygolan	**Grimshaw James**
ANT	Ballygoland W`ho	**Grimshaw James**
ANT	Ballygowan	**Grimshaw James**
ANT	Drumnadrough	**Grimshaw James**
ANT	Drumnadrough	**Grimshaw John T**
ANT	Drumnadrough	**Grimshaw M/s**
ANT	Ballyhenry	**Grimshaw Mr**
ANT	Linfield	**Grimshaw Nich**
ANT	Whitehouse Upr	**Grimshaw Nicholas**
ANT	Ballyhowne	**Grimshaw Robert**
ANT	Ballygolan	**Grimshaw Thomas**
ANT	Drumnadrough	**Grimshaw Thomas**
ANT	Linfield	**Grimshaw William H**
ANT	Ballygolan	**Grimshaw William P**
LOU	Cappocks	**Grimwood**
LDY	Ballyness	**Grocers Company**
KILD	Celbridge	**Grogan**
MYO	Foxford	**Grogan**
KILD	Newland	**Grogan**
LAO	Monksgrange	**Grogan Edward**
MYO	Clonbullig	**Grogan Muchael**
OFF	Killenmore	**Grogan Thomas**
TYR	Megna *	**Groom William**

CO.	TOWNLAND	MILLER
CAR	Staples Mill	**Grose Edward**
DON	Corcreggan	**Grove Jas G**
DON	Mass More	**Grove Jas G**
ANT	Muckamore	**Groves**
WAT	Clonmel	**Grubb Fran**
TIP	Clonmel	**Grubb Francis**
WAT	Clonmel	**Grubb Francis**
TIP	Millpark	**Grubb Jonathan**
TIP	Clonmel Town	**Grubb Josh**
TIP	Millpark	**Grubb Joshua**
TIP	Tinvane	**Grubb Llewellyn**
TIP	Barnora	**Grubb Richard**
TIP	Clogheen Market	**Grubb Richard**
TIP	Caher Abbey	**Grubb Richard Sen**
TIP	Clonmel	**Grubb Robert**
WAT	Goose Island	**Grubb Robert**
WAT	Suir Island	**Grubb Robert**
WAT	Suir Island	**Grubb Sameul**
TIP	Castlegrace	**Grubb Samuel**
TIP	Clonmel Town	**Grubb Samuel**
TIP	Flemingstown	**Grubb Samuel**
TIP	Castlegrace	**Grubb Samuel Richard**
WAT	Abbeylands	**Grubb Thomas**
TIP	Clonmel	**Grubb Thomas**
WAT	Clonmel	**Grubb Thomas**
TIP	Clonmel Town	**Grubb Thomas C**
TIP	Burgagery Lands	**Grubb Thomas Saml**
TIP	Clonmel Town	**Grubb Thos**
WAT	Aglish	**Grubbleton Richard**
LIM	Rivers	**Grubbs Robert**
TIP	Clogheen Market	**Gruff Samuel**
CAR	Carlow Town	**Grumly John**
LIM	Askeaton	**Gubbins George**
CRK	Aghakeiny *	**Gubbins Joseph**
ROS	Lyscallagh (?)	**Guffe Robt**
DUB	Woodpark	**Guidon Christopher**
GAL	Galway Town	**Guiness Benjamin**
CRK	Ahgamilla	**Guiness Henry**
LOU	ArdeeTown	**Guiness Henry**
CRK	Ardkitt	**Guiness Henry**
DUB	Red Mills	**Guiness Hon Arth**
WAT	Tallow	**Gully Nicholas**
KRY	Milltown	**Gun**
GAL	Galway Town	**Guning John**
DON	Ballymagowan	**Gunn Ezekiel**
DON	Ballymagowan	**Gunn Ezekiel**
ROS	Lissadorn	**Gunning**
DWN	Ballywallon	**Gunning Arthur**
ROS	Athleague Manor	**Gunning George**
LONG	Clondra	**Gunning George**
GAL	Galway T`nsparks	**Gunning J.**
DWN	Ballycopeland	**Gunning James**
GAL	Galway Town	**Gunning James**
GAL	Galway Town	**Gunning Jno**
GAL	Galway Town	**Gunning John**
GAL	Inish	**Gunning John**

CO.	TOWNLAND	MILLER
ROS	Lissadorn	**Gunning John**
ROS	Lissadorn	**Gunning John Capt. i**
LONG	Clondra	**Gunning Robert**
LONG	Clonloman	**Gunning Robert**
LONG	Clondra	**Gunning Robert King**
LONG	Clondra	**Gunning Sir Robert**
CRK	Ballincollig	**Gunpowder Mills**
CAR	Carlow Town	**Gurley**
MEA	Formays	**Gurney Samuel**
ARM	Ballinlare	**Guy George**
DON	Monellan	**Guy James**
DUB	Dolphins Barn	**Guy Robert**
DUB	Wey Mills	**Gwin**
TIP	Ballyduff	**Gwydir Daniel**
ANT	Clogher North	**Gwymae John**
DUB	Dunsoghly Mnr	**Gwyn Lewis Capt.**
DUB	Wey Mills	**Gwyn Lewis Capt.**
LIM	Glenduff	**Gwynn John Rev.**
		H
LIM	Ryevale *	**Hackett**
CRK	Middleton T'parks	**Hackett Bart Jas.**
CRK	Broomfield	**Hackett Bart. James**
KILD	Newtown	**Hackett Esther Wid.**
OFF	Townsparks	**Hackett George**
TIP	Clonmel Town	**Hackett Henry**
OFF	Birr Town	**Hackett Jemina**
MEA	Castlejordan	**Hackett John**
OFF	Lehinch	**Hackett John**
TIP	Ballyloughnane	**Hackett John**
CRK	Middleton T'parks	**Hackett Maria**
OFF	Birr Townsparks	**Hackett Michael**
KILD	Ryevale *	**Hackett Michael**
KILD	Newabbey	**Hackett Patrick**
WAT	Killadangan	**Hackett Samuel**
TIP	Ballyloughnane	**Hackett Simpson**
OFF	Clonoghill Upper	**Hackett Thomas**
OFF	Crinkill Town	**Hackett Thomas**
WME	Rahinmore	**Hackett Thomas**
CRK	Middleton T'parks	**Hackett William**
TYR	Aughamullin	**Hadley Eliz. Widow**
TYR	Aughamullin	**Hadley Eliz., Spin.**
TYR	Aughamullin	**Hadley Francis**
DWN	Ballywalter	**Haemill**
DWN	Ballydugan	**Haemill Hans Mark**
WME	Milltown	**Hagan Denise**
ARM	Drumacanver	**Hagan Frances**
ARM	Drumnacanner	**Hagan Frances**
ARM	Ballaghy	**Hagan Patrick**
LDY	Killea	**Hagan Patrick**
WME	Rattin	**Hagarty Denis**
WME	Killagh	**Hagarty Maurice**
CAV	Corravohy	**Hagerty Patrick**
WME	Killagh	**Haggerty John**
WAT	Garrancrobally	**Hagherine Thomas**
CAV	Cavan Town :	**Hague William**

CO.	TOWNLAND	MILLER
CRK	Glanmire	**Hail**
CRK	Rathgoggan Mid	**Haines Edward**
WAT	Dungarvan Town	**Haines John**
CRK	Ballygarvan	**Hains Charles**
MON	Drumgallan	**Haire George**
LOU	Dawson`s Dems.	**Hale Henry**
LOU	Dawson`s Dems.	**Hale Nathaniel**
DWN	DownpatrickTown	**Hale Robert H B**
DWN	DownpatrickTown	**Hale Robt**
FER	Enniskillen Town	**Hales John**
DUB	Miltown Kings	**Haliday George**
FER	Craghan	**Haliday William A**
FER	Salloon	**Haliday William A**
DWN	Ballydugan	**Hall**
DWN	Ballyharley	**Hall**
ARM	Ballynahone	**Hall**
MON	Bowelk	**Hall**
DUB	Channon Hill	**Hall**
ARM	Copes Mill	**Hall**
TYR	Derry Drumy	**Hall**
TYR	Tullagh Beg	**Hall**
DWN	Black Causway *	**Hall Anne Widow**
CAV	Coppanagh	**Hall David**
CAV	Corravilla	**Hall Isaac**
MON	Cossabey	**Hall James**
MON	Cossabey	**Hall James**
ARM	Drominikelly	**Hall Letitia**
ARM	Townland ?	**Hall Letitia**
ARM	Copes Mill	**Hall Letitia Widow**
DUB	Dundrum	**Hall Mrs**
CRK	East Gully	**Hall Robert**
DWN	Ballyhemlin	**Hall Roger**
CAV	Corraceeran	**Hall Thomas**
CAV	Corravilla	**Hall Thomas**
ARM	Carryhugh	**Hall William**
LONG	Creagh	**Hall William**
TYR	Derry	**Hall William**
DUB	Dolphins Barn	**Hall William**
LONG	Creelaghta	**Hall William, Miller**
WAT	Tallow	**Hallahan Robert**
FER	Laragh	**Halliday John**
FER	Laragh	**Halliday William A**
MEA	Clonee	**Halligan Margaret**
LIM	Kilmallock Town	**Hallinan John Jun**
CRK	Ardarostig	**Hallinan Timothy**
LOU	Ardee	**Halpenny M**
LOU	Ardee Town	**Halpenny Peter**
DUB	Drumcondra	**Halpin Mr**
WME	Balnamill	**Haltam**
DWN	Ballyroney	**Haltridge John**
DWN	Ballywalter	**Hamel Hans**
DWN	Milltown	**Hamieon**
DWN	Aghiohill	**Hamieon Hans**
DWN	Aghiohill	**Hamieon James**
CAR	Barrow River	**Hamil**
ANT	Moycraig Upr	**Hamil Dan**
DUB	Donnybrook Lr	**Hamil Hugh**
WAT	Clonmel	**Hamil John**
DUB	Ballsbridge	**Hamill**
MON	Drumass	**Hamill Bernard**
DWN	Ballywalter	**Hamill Frances**
DWN	Ballywalter	**Hamill Fras**
ANT	Ballymurphy	**Hamill Thomas**
ANT	Moycraig Upr	**Hamill William**
DWN	Annalong	**Hamilton**
DWN	Ballydargan	**Hamilton**
DWN	Ballydugan	**Hamilton**
DWN	Ballymacarret	**Hamilton**
DWN	Ballymullan	**Hamilton**
TYR	Bonds Mill *	**Hamilton**
CAR	Carlow Town	**Hamilton**
DUB	Channon Hill	**Hamilton**
MON	Clonavarn	**Hamilton**
TYR	Cough	**Hamilton**
ANT	Cross	**Hamilton**
DWN	Cullontrogh	**Hamilton**
TYR	Dungannon	**Hamilton**
TYR	Loughash	**Hamilton**
MON	Monaghan Town	**Hamilton**
LIM	Mountblainey *	**Hamilton**
CAR	Orchard	**Hamilton**
DWN	Quilly & Moss	**Hamilton**
CAR	Staplestown	**Hamilton**
CAV	Lisboduff	**Hamilton : Stewart, Dublin City**
LAO	Abbeyleix	**Hamilton Alev Rev.**
DWN	Ballydargan	**Hamilton Alex**
DWN	Ballywalter	**Hamilton Alex**
LDY	Bolea	**Hamilton Alex**
DON	Ballyshannon Tn	**Hamilton Andrew**
DWN	Ballyknockan	**Hamilton Ann Hon.**
DWN	Ballydollaghan	**Hamilton Ann Hon. Wid.**
DWN	Annalong	**Hamilton Archibald**
WME	Rathwire Lower	**Hamilton Baker**
CAR	Carlow Town	**Hamilton Benedict**
ARM	Townland ?	**Hamilton Benedict**
CAR	Carlow Town	**Hamilton Bernard**
DON	Fahan *	**Hamilton Catherine**
DON	Fahan *	**Hamilton Catherine**
TYR	Dunnamanagh	**Hamilton Charles**
DUB	Manor N`castle	**Hamilton Charles**
DON	Fahan *	**Hamilton David**
MON	Bowelk	**Hamilton Fran**
DWN	Clonknaverty	**Hamilton Francis**
MYO	Turlough	**Hamilton Francis Rev.**
DUB	Mount Pl Manor	**Hamilton Fredk**
ANT	Carrickfergus Tn	**Hamilton G**
DUB	Balbriggan	**Hamilton Geo Alex**
LDY	Ballykellaghan	**Hamilton George**
ARM	Ballyshiel More	**Hamilton George**
DUB	Knock	**Hamilton George**
DWN	Ballydargan	**Hamilton George**
DWN	Ballydargan	**Hamilton George Rev.**
TYR	Creevenagh	**Hamilton Georges**
LDY	Ballyness	**Hamilton H. T. Sir**
DWN	Ballyhalbert	**Hamilton Hans**
DWN	Ballylisbredan	**Hamilton Hans**
DWN	Drennans	**Hamilton Hans**
DWN	Kircubbin	**Hamilton Hans**
DWN	Listooder	**Hamilton Hans**
ARM	Townland ?	**Hamilton Henrietta**
LDY	Ballyness	**Hamilton Henry**
KILD	Johnstown	**Hamilton Henry**
DON	Kinnacally	**Hamilton Henry**
KILD	Mountblairnet	**Hamilton Henry**
KILD	Kilmore	**Hamilton Hon.**
DWN	Ballynahinch	**Hamilton Hugh**
DWN	Black Causway *	**Hamilton Hugh Rev.**
CRK	Bandon Town	**Hamilton James**
CAR	Carlow Town	**Hamilton James**
LDY	Coleraine Town	**Hamilton James**
TYR	Cormamucklagh	**Hamilton James**
MON	Drumscor	**Hamilton James**
DUB	Dublin City	**Hamilton James**
TYR	Glenroan	**Hamilton James**
FER	Mullycovet	**Hamilton James**
TYR	Rakeeranbeg	**Hamilton James**
ANT	Carrickfergus Tn	**Hamilton James**
ROS	Lissadorn	**Hamilton James Hon**
DWN	Ballyhemlin	**Hamilton James Rev**
CAR	Carlow Town	**Hamilton Jno**
CAR	Carlow Town	**Hamilton Jno**
LIM	Askeaton Town	**Hamilton John**
LIM	Askeaton Town :	**Hamilton John**
CAR	Carlow Town	**Hamilton John**
ANT	Catrucktergus Tn	**Hamilton John**
ANT	Larne Town	**Hamilton John**
DON	Muckross	**Hamilton John**
LDY	Muladonagh	**Hamilton John**
TYR	Mullybrannon	**Hamilton John**
FER	Mullynavannoge	**Hamilton John**
TYR	Tempanroe	**Hamilton John**
TYR	Augher	**Hamilton John Brig.**
MEA	Duleek Town	**Hamilton Joshua**
WEX	Wexford Town	**Hamilton Maxwll**
DON	Townland	**Hamilton Mrs**
DWN	Ballyharley	**Hamilton Robert**
DWN	Ballyharley	**Hamilton Robert**
CAR	Staplestown	**Hamilton Robert**
MEA	Staleen	**Hamilton Sophia Hon.**
CAV	Drumlon	**Hamilton Stewart**
CAV	Latt	**Hamilton Stewart**
ANT	Antrim Town	**Hamilton Thos**
ANT	Carrickfergus Tn	**Hamilton William**
KILD	Irishtown	**Hamilton William**
LDY	Curryfree	**Hamilton William J**
TIP	Clonmel	**Hammil John**
MYO	Ardnaree	**Hammon William**
WAT	Kilmeadan	**Hamon Georgetain.**

CO.	TOWNLAND	MILLER
KRY	Caunguillet	**Hamott William**
WME	Gilbertstown	**Hampson**
KILD	Ballyaghmoone *	**Hampton James**
KKY	Kilkenny City	**Hampton Thomas**
LAO	Ballyroan	**Hanay**
OFF	Bogtown	**Hancock**
ARM	Lisdrumgullion	**Hancock William**
WME	Aghnatemple *	**Handcock**
WME	Boyanagh	**Handcock**
LAO	Drinagh	**Handcock**
WME	Lissywolan	**Handcock**
WME	Aghnatemple *	**Handcock Gustavus**
WME	Crievebeg/ -more	**Handcock Gustavus**
LAO	Borris	**Handcock James**
LAO	Borris	**Handcock Joseph**
WME	Corduff	**Handcock Richard**
WME	Crievebeg/ -more	**Handcock Thomas**
KKY	Glencloghlea	**Handrick Laurence**
KKY	Duninga	**Handy John**
GAL	Killuney	**Haneran Michael**
DUB	Rathfarnham	**Hankison John**
SLI	Lisconny	**Hanlan**
SLI	Lisconny	**Hanlan Redmond**
CAR	Carlow Town	**Hanlen**
GAL	Inish	**Hanley James**
OFF	Ballyduff	**Hanlon John**
OFF	Roscrea	**Hanlon John**
WEX	Castletown	**Hanlon Lewis**
OFF	Ballyduff	**Hanlon Marcus**
CAR	Carlow Town	**Hanlon Patrick**
KILD	Cherrymills	**Hanlon Patrick**
CAR	Carlow Town	**Hanlon Thomas**
CRK	Ardarostig	**Hanlon Timothy**
CAR	St Mullins	**Hanly**
ROS	Snipe Hill	**Hanly Daniel**
LDY	Ardlogh	**Hanly Peter**
ANT	Ballycregagh	**Hanna Andrew**
ANT	Ballycregagh	**Hanna David**
DWN	Drumballyroney	**Hanna David**
ANT	Carrickfergus Tn	**Hanna Dr (Belfast)**
ARM	Ballydogherty	**Hanna Hugh**
MON	Aghintamy	**Hanna James**
DWN	Clarkill	**Hanna James**
ANT	Ballycregagh	**Hanna John**
ARM	Ballydogherty	**Hanna John**
ANT	Kildrum	**Hanna John**
DWN	Kilcliet	**Hanna Patrick**
LDY	Moyheeland	**Hanna Samuel**
DWN	Legananny	**Hanna William**
KRY	Tralee Town	**Hannafin James**
KILD	Johnstown	**Hannan James**
KILD	Johnstown South	**Hannan James**
TYR	Strangmore	**Hannington**
WME	Riverstown	**Hannon Benjamin**
KILD	Athy Town	**Hannon Ellen**
KILD	Athy Town	**Hannon Georgina**
KILD	Athy Town	**Hannon Henry**
KILD	Athy Town	**Hannon John**
KILD	Athy Town	**Hannon John**
WME	Riverstown	**Hannon Mary**
TYR	Cough	**Hannyngton**
TYR	Drumullen	**Hannyngton Thos Knox**
TIP	St Johnstown	**Hanrahan Mary**
TIP	St Johnstown	**Hanrahan Mrs Mary**
TIP	Lanespark	**Hanrahan William**
MEA	Slane Manor	**Hansard Nicholas**
LDY	Ballylintagh	**Hanson George**
DON	Meenatoal ?	**Hanson George**
TYR	Coagh	**Hanyngston Thomas**
LDY	Londonderry	**Harbour Commrs.**
ARM	Ballylane	**Harcourt**
ARM	Ballysheil Beg	**Harden Robert**
ARM	Druminure	**Harden Robert**
KILD	Ardrigh	**Harding**
LAO	Ballyroan	**Harding**
CAR	Milltown	**Harding**
KILD	Ardree	**Harding Ambrose**
TIP	Milltown	**Harding Patrick**
CRK	Bealick	**Hardings of Firville**
CRK	Ballydulogher *	**Hardman**
WAT	Adamstown	**Harduin Henry**
WAT	Adamstown	**Harduin Robert**
ARM	Moodoge	**Hardy George**
DWN	Ballydugan	**Hardy Isaac**
ANT	Ballybeg	**Hardy Joseph**
ANT	Carnearney	**Hardy Joseph**
GAL	Magheramore	**Hardy Joseph**
DON	Garvary	**Hardyman**
MON	Drumguill	**Hare James**
MON	Roosky	**Hare James**
LIM	Abington	**Hargrave Ab'ram**
KRY	Maghancoosaun	**Hargrave Joshua**
DUB	Shanganagh	**Hargrave Thomas**
KILD	Greatconnell	**Harinan Robert**
KRY	Castleisland	**Harington John**
DWN	Hazel Park	**Haris**
ARM	Ballycargan	**Harison Cartwell**
DON	Stramackilmartin	**Harkin Charles**
DON	Ards Beg	**Harkin Jas. (John)**
DON	Ards Beg	**Harkin John**
ARM	Middletown	**Harkness**
TYR	Drumullen	**Harkness William**
WME	Noughaval	**Harman**
WME	Ardnacranny	**Harman Edward**
LAO	Coolkerry	**Harman Frances**
WME	Aghnatemple *	**Harman Frances, Widow**
LAO	Coolkerry	**Harman Robert**
LAO	Coolkerry	**Harman Robert**
WEX	Ross Town	**Harman Samuel**
WEX	Ross Town	**Harman Thomas**
MEA	Stonestown	**Harman Wesley**
WEX	Ross Town	**Harman Wilhelmina**
KILD	Athy Town	**Harmon Henry**
KRY	Meanus	**Harnett Thomas**
ROS	Articorra	**Harney Patrick**
KRY	Charleville	**Harper Jn**
SLI	Bellanascarva	**Harper Munns**
LAO	Grange	**Harpole**
KILD	Newtown	**Harpur**
KKY	Barraghcore	**Harriet Alexander**
LAO	Mountrath Manor	**Harrin John Mr.**
TYR	Little Bridge	**Harrington**
KILD	Millquarter Timolin	**Harrington**
ARM	Tullyglush	**Harrington John**
KILD	Naas Town	**Harrington Mary**
KRY	Tralee Town	**Harrington Maurice**
ARM	Blackwatertown	**Harrington Prudence**
CRK	Cork City :	**Harrington Robert**
LAO	Monksgrange	**Harrington W**
DWN	Ballytogher *	**Harris**
ARM	Middletown Manor	**Harris**
DWN	Carncally	**Harris Arthur**
DWN	Cornakelly	**Harris Arthur**
ANT	Mill Quarter	**Harris Charlotte**
LAO	Mountrath Manor	**Harris John**
ANT	Millquarter	**Harris Joseph**
WEX	Wexford Town	**Harris Juliette**
DON	Abbey Mill	**Harris Lewis**
KILD	Kilcullen	**Harris Mary Wid.**
KILD	Kilcullen	**Harris Mary Widow**
DWN	Cornakelly	**Harris Robert**
KILD	Kilcullen	**Harris Robert**
WEX	Wexford Town	**Harris Walter**
CRK	Ballygarvan	**Harris William**
CRK	Kilcully	**Harris William**
DWN	Ballydugan	**Harrison**
DWN	Ballydugan	**Harrison**
CLE	Clooncool	**Harrison**
CLE	O'Callaghansmills	**Harrison**
MON	Reduff	**Harrison**
CAR	St Mullins	**Harrison**
ARM	Mohan	**Harrison Cartwell**
CRK	Clashganniv	**Harrison Christina**
WEX	Mill Lands	**Harrison Fran**
WEX	Mill Lands	**Harrison Francis**
CRK	Clashganniv	**Harrison Geo**
CRK	Clashganniv	**Harrison George**
DWN	Newtownards Tn	**Harrison George**
DUB	Manor	**Harrison Henry J**
DWN	Ballyhemlin	**Harrison Henry Yngr**
LIM	Prospect	**Harrison Joseph**
WEX	Mill Lands	**Harrison Marth**
LONG	Garvagh	**Harrison Mrs Alex**
DWN	Ballyhemlin	**Harrison Nichholas**
DWN	Ballydugan	**Harrison Nicholas**
DWN	Ballyhemlin	**Harrison Nicholas**
CRK	Clashganniv	**Harrison Standish**
TYR	Drumullen	**Harryngton**

CO.	TOWNLAND	MILLER
TYR	Littlebridge	**Harryngton Dunganon**
DON	Craig	**Hart George**
DON	Townland ?	**Hart George**
DWN	Lisnoe	**Hart Henry**
DWN	Ravernet	**Hart Henry**
MYO	Ballycastle	**Hart Phelim**
DON	Townland ?	**Hart William**
ANT	Vow	**Harte Solomon**
DON	Glenalla	**Harte Thos B**
ANT	Lisnagarvey	**Hartford Marq.**
ANT	Lisburn Town	**Hartford Marquess of**
DUB	Woodpark	**Hartford Patrick**
ROS	Emlagh	**Hartland Maurice Rt.Hon.**
GAL	Clanbruckley	**Hartland Rt. Hon. Thos**
CAR	Ballynebranagh	**Hartley Humphry**
DUB	Milltown Village	**Hartnett Maurice**
CLE	Clooncool	**Hartney**
CLE	O'Callaghansmills	**Hartney**
OFF	Banagher Town	**Harton John L**
LAO	Monksgrange	**Hartpole**
LAO	Ironmills / Kilrush	**Hartpole George**
LAO	Monksgrange	**Hartpole Robert**
LAO	Doon	**Hartt Charles**
TIP	Nenagh	**Harty John**
KILD	Kilcock	**Harvey Francis**
SLI	Barley Mill	**Harvey Agnes**
SLI	Churchland	**Harvey Agnes**
DON	Carrowmore	**Harvey Edward**
DON	Carrowmore	**Harvey G**
DON	Carrowmore	**Harvey George M**
WEX	Wexford Town	**Harvey Jaffrey**
WW	Ballymanus	**Harvey James**
WEX	Fencering Park	**Harvey James**
DUB	Swords Town	**Harvey Jn**
SLI	Barley Mill	**Harvey Jno**
SLI	Churchland	**Harvey Jno**
DUB	Mountdown	**Harvey John**
TIP	Fethard Town	**Harvey Julia**
LIM	Freelane	**Harvey Reuban**
LIM	Sreelane	**Harvey Reuben**
ANT	Antrim Town	**Harvey Sir Robt J**
KKY	Bennetsbridge	**Harvey Thomas & Jn**
ANT	Lisburn Tn`parks	**Harvey William**
ANT	Lisburn Tn`parks :	**Harvey William**
MYO	Foxford	**Harward William**
DUB	Mardyke	**Haskins Mr**
LDY	Ballyness	**Haslett Wiliam**
LDY	Bellaghy	**Haslett William**
LAO	Ballymowland	**Haslins Haniball**
MEA	Boyne	**Hassard Geo Ch Remr.**
CAV	Drumcor	**Hassard Minor**
ROS	Grange	**Hastings Percival**
MON	Bowelk	**Hatchell**
DUB	Diswellstown	**Hatchell Henry**
CAR	Ballypierce	**Hatchell John Rt. Hon.**
WEX	Motebegg	**Hatton**
WEX	Palace	**Hatton Henry**
WEX	Motebegg	**Hatton Jack**
WEX	Killmecridge	**Hatton John**
WEX	Wexford Town	**Hatton Loftus**
CAR	Clashganny	**Haughton**
LOU	Ardree	**Haughton Alfred**
LOU	Ardree Town	**Haughton Alfred**
DWN	Tullylish	**Haughton B**
LAO	Graigue Town	**Haughton Benjamin**
DWN	Loughans	**Haughton Benjamin**
DWN	Moyallan	**Haughton Benjamin**
DWN	Tullylish	**Haughton Benjamin**
LAO	Graigue Town	**Haughton John**
CAR	Carlow Town	**Haughton Samuel**
DWN	Tullylish	**Haughton Thomas**
CAR	Carlow Town	**Haughton William**
OFF	Banagher Town	**Haughton's mill**
WEX	Pigats & Tanyard	**Haurick J**
TIP	Clonmel	**Havell Edward**
WAT	Suir Island	**Havell Edward**
TIP	Clonmel	**Havell John**
DWN	Annadorn	**Haven Armatilda Spin.**
DWN	Annadorn	**Haven Grace Spin.**
OFF	Roanville *	**haw Richd**
ROS	Balingaglass	**Hawkes Charles**
ROS	Bellnagare	**Hawkes Charles**
CRK	Kinsale Town	**Hawkes Isaac**
DUB	Willbrook	**Hawkins John**
DUB	Luttrellstown	**Hawkins William**
DON	Carrowmore	**Hawkshaw Cath E**
DON	Cratlagh	**Hay Charles**
LOU	Skibbolmore	**Hay Eugene**
DON	Moyle	**Hay Robert**
DON	Tully (4)	**Hay Robert**
WAT	Kill St Lawrence	**Hayden Henry**
DON	Craig	**Hayden James**
CRK	Cork City	**Hayes Atwell**
DON	Pluck	**Hayes Edmund**
DON	Pluck	**Hayes Edmund**
DON	Millers Holding	**Hayes Henry**
CRK	Ballinrougher	**Hayes Jayes**
WW	Ballybrittan *	**Hayes John**
GAL	Creggaree	**Hayes John**
TIP	Drumbane	**Hayes John**
WW	Kilcoole	**Hayes John**
LEI	Rhadermott	**Hayes Lyndon**
CRK	Kilcully	**Hayes Mr**
KKY	Ballyhimmin	**Hayes Nathaniel**
KKY	Deerpark	**Hayes Patirck**
KRY	Tralee Town	**Hayes Patrick**
DWN	Edenderry	**Hayes Richard**
LEI	Rhadermott	**Hayes Richard**
LDY	Coleraine Town	**Hayes Robert**
TIP	Drumbane	**Hayes Thomas**
LOU	Ardee Town	**Hayes Wiliam**
CRK	Kilcully	**Hayes William**
DWN	Kilpike	**Hayes William**
DWN	Milltown	**Hayes William**
CRK	Lyhe	**Hayes William H**
KILD	Rathangan	**Haynes George**
CRK	Kilcully	**Haynes William**
CRK	Kilcully	**Hays William**
LOU	Lagan Water	**Hazelwood**
FER	Tullycreevy	**Hazlett**
FER	Tullycreevy	**Hazlett Jane**
FER	Brookhill	**Hazlett William**
DON	Omlick	**Hazlett William**
ARM	Corkley	**Hazlip Thomas**
CLE	O'Callaghansmills	**Head Eliz**
CLE	O'Callaghansmills	**Head Samuel**
MEA	Kells Town	**Headford Marq.**
KRY	Dillons	**Headley**
KRY	Beheenagh	**Headley Lady A**
DUB	Coolock	**Healy Edward**
KRY	Knockaboul	**Healy John**
ROS	Athleague	**Healy Patrick**
DUB	Donore Liberty	**Healy William**
FER	Keeran Beg	**Hean Counseller**
ANT	Anticur	**Heany James**
ANT	Clady Lower	**Heany William**
WAT	Mocollup	**Heard**
CRK	Kinsale Town	**Heard Edward**
CRK	Kinsale Town	**Heard Isaac**
CRK	Kinsale Town	**Heard John**
WAT	Killeeshal	**Hearn**
WAT	Shanakill	**Hearn John**
SLI	Carrowcushlawn	**Hearne Fair**
SLI	Ardnaree Town	**Hearne John**
WAT	Kilmeadan	**Hearne Michael**
GAL	Cahertinny	**Heary John**
LDY	Terrydremount	**Heaslit Henry**
CAV	Clarebane	**Heaslop Samuel**
WAT	Shanakill	**Heathcote George**
DUB	Dublin City	**Heavin R**
DUB	Dublin City	**Heavy B**
CRK	Inchafune	**Heazel John**
CRK	Inchafune	**Heazel John**
CRK	Bandon Town	**Heazle Henry**
CRK	Ballynacarriga	**Heazle John**
CRK	Cork City	**Hedges Richard**
LOU	Drogheda Town	**Heeny Patrick**
MYO	Belfarsad	**Heffernan Benjamin**
GAL	Garrafrauns	**Heffernan David**
MYO	Murrevagh	**Heffernan Luke**
GAL	Bleachgreen	**Heffernan Mary**
GAL	Cloon	**Heffernan Michael**
MYO	Ballybeg	**Heffernan Thomas**
ANT	Artogues	**Heffron John**
CAV	Corravohy	**Hegarty Patrick**
KRY	Knockreagh	**Hehir**
DWN	Aghiohill	**Heir Rober**
KKY	Foulks Court	**Hely George**

INDEX

CO.	TOWNLAND	MILLER
KKY	Foulks Court	Hely Georges
LDY	Aghadowey	Hempill
LDY	Ballybritain	Hempill
TIP	Barnora	Hempill
LDY	Mullan	Hempill
ARM	Armagh	Henchey Pat
WAT	Tiercullen *	Henchy
WAT	Tiercullen *	Henchy Donal
OFF	Ballinaminton	Henderson
LDY	Clady Village	Henderson
FER	Faughard	Henderson
LDY	Londonderry	Henderson J
LDY	Ardkill	Henderson James
ANT	Ballyhowne	Henderson James
LDY	Clondermot	Henderson James
DUB	Faranboley	Henderson James
DWN	Hillsborough	Henderson James
DWN	Ravernet	Henderson Jno
ANT	Bracknamuckley	Henderson John
MEA	Brownstown	Henderson Thomas
ANT	Topp Lower	Henderson William
MEA	Ballyann	Hendley Earbery
MYO	Ballina	Hendry John
KKY	Inchalarran	Henebry John
CLE	O'Callaghansmills	Henessy Patrick
LAO	Cullenaghbegg	Heney
LAO	Clarahill	Heney Stephen
MEA	Brownstown	Heniston
LONG	Cloonkeen	Henn Jno
LONG	Treely	Henn Jno
LDY	Coleraine Town	Henn William
GAL	Cregg	Henn William
GAL	Ower	Hennelly James
MYO	Newport	Hennen Matthew
CLE	Clooncool	Hennessy
CRK	bo./ Carberry EW	Hennessy Daniel
TIP	Duncummin	Hennessy Maurice
TIP	Townland ?	Hennessy Maurice
TIP	Killoskenan	Hennessy Patrick
DWN	Magherana	Henning John
DWN	Tullyheron	Henning John
DUB	Knightsfield	Henning William
SLI	Cloonloughil	Henny Mrs.
MEA	Balnagon	Henry
LONG	Bellanchower	Henry
WAT	Kilmeadan	Henry
ARM	Lisbanoe	Henry
LOU	Little Mill	Henry
GAL	Clunbrucky	Henry Ann (Richardson)
ROS	Fuerty	Henry Ann Widow.
ARM	Kennedies	Henry Anne Widow
MEA	Trim Town	Henry Daniel
LIM	Abbeyfarm	Henry Dennis
ARM	Ballybrolly	Henry George
LEI	Limerick Manor	Henry George
LONG	Bellanchower	Henry Hugh
ARM	Ballybrolly	Henry John
MEA	Balnagon	Henry John
LDY	Culnady	Henry John
CAV	Drumhillagh N.	Henry John
CAV	Drumhillagh N.	Henry John
LDY	Culnady	Henry John Jun
ROS	Fuerty	Henry Joseph
DUB	Fairview	Henry Joseph Esq
MEA	Balnagon	Henry Laurence
ROS	Castlereagh Town	Henry Laurence
ANT	Ballycregagh Lr	Henry Mathew
GAL	Cappantruhaun	Henry Matthew
GAL	Cappantruhaun	Henry Michael
SLI	Coollaughil	Henry Myles
MEA	Balnagon	Henry Rev. John
LOU	Little Mill	Henry Robert
DWN	Balleevy	Henry Thos E
ANT	Ballycregagh	Henry Wiliam
ARM	Ballinlare	Henry William
ANT	Anticur	Henry Wmilliam
DUB	St Sepulchre	Henshaw Thomas
LOU	Philipstown	Henzell
DUB	Palmerstown	Henzell Josh
DUB	Palmerstown	Henzey Joshua
KRY	Cagrigh *	Herbert
KRY	Currens *	Herbert Arthur
CAR	Grangewat	Herbert Edw, Elder
KRY	Ardagh	Herbert Edward
KRY	Cagriga *	Herbert Edward
KRY	Cagrigh *	Herbert Henry
MEA	Dunboyne	Herbert John
ANT	Belfast Town	Herdman
TYR	Sion Mills	Herdman
TYR	Liggarstown	Herdman James
DWN	Ballydargan	Hereford Ralph Hon. Bish.
CAR	Carlow Town	Heron Edward
DWN	Cabragh	Heron Samuel
DUB	Haroldscross	Herron
DON	Breaghy	Herron David
DUB	Stubbins Mill	Herron Sir Robert
MON	Cavanacross	Herst John
ANT	Derryaghy	Hertford Marq.
DON	Malin Town	Hervey John
LONG	Forgney	Herview
LONG	Sheeroe	Herview Victor
LONG	Aghaboy	Heslin James
CAV	Killyteane	Heslop Henry
CAV	Killyteane	Heslop John
CLE	Lenercappagh *	Hester Clifford Widow
KKY	Castletown	Hetherington Mary
ANT	Ballyhill	Hevey Timothy
WME	Boyanagh	Hewetson
WME	Corduff	Hewetson
CLE	Ballykilty	Hewett Henry
LONG	Ballywillin	Hewison James
CRK	Fermoy (barony)	Hewson George
LIM	Askeaton Town	Hewson John
LIM	Askeaton Town	Hewson William
CAV	Aghadreenagh	Hewston Chas+B135
WW	Kilmacon Upper	Heyden
WW	Kilmacon Upper	Heyden Samuel
WW	Kilmacon Upper	Heyden Samuel
LIM	Colbans	Heydon
LDY	Ballyness	Heyland Rowley
CAR	Clashganny	Hickey
CLE	Roo East	Hickey James
CAR	Ouragh	Hickey Michael
CLE	Tarmon	Hickman
ROS	Cloonaragh	Hicks Elizabeth
DUB	Haroldscross W.	Hicks Richard
DUB	Haroldscross	Hicks Richard John
GAL	Canrawer West	Hicks William
KRY	Ardagh	Hickson James
KRY	Dingle Town	Hickson Robert
KRY	Milltown	Hickson Robert
LIM	Brudy *	Higgins
LAO	Timahoe	Higgins
ARM	Tullyglush	Higgins
CRK	Ballyderown	Higgins Elizabeth
KILD	Tully West	Higgins James
LAO	Stradbally Abbey	Higgins James Vicar
ARM	Tullyglush	Higgins Jno
MYO	Lurgan	Higgins John
KILD	Ballyaghmoone *	Higgins Patk
GAL	Galway Town	Higgins Terence
FER	Cappy	Higgins Thomas
ANT	Springmount	Higginson Jno O`N
KILD	Ardree	Hill
ARM	Ballynahone	Hill
DWN	Black Causway *	Hill
DWN	Cabragh	Hill
ARM	Lisdrumgullion	Hill
DUB	Lucan Town	Hill
ARM	Ballynahone	Hill - Mee
WW	Bray Great	Hill Abraham
WAT	Aglish	Hill Andrew
WEX	Enniscorthy Town	Hill Charles
GAL	Cregg	Hill Edward
WEX	Martingalls	Hill Edward
WW	Bray Great	Hill Elizabeth
DON	Bunbeg	Hill Geo Agustus
DWN	Ballybawne	Hill Geo Lord
DON	Ballyarr	Hill George A Lord
DON	Cavan Lower	Hill Henry
DWN	Black Causway *	Hill Hon. Arthur
ANT	Carneatly	Hill John
ANT	Clogh Mills	Hill John
WEX	Toberanierin	Hill John
DWN	Ballybawn	Hill Lord A
LOU	Drogheda Town	Hill R A
LOU	Drogheda Town	Hill R
LOU	Drogheda Town	Hill Richard R

CO.	TOWNLAND	MILLER
MEA	Monknewtown	**Hill Richard R**
WW	Bray Great	**Hill Robert**
DWN	Ballygallum	**Hill Samuel**
LDY	Tirkeeran	**Hill Sir George**
CRK	Clonakilty Town	**Hill Thomas**
CRK	Townland ?`	**Hill Thomas**
DWN	Ballymoney	**Hill Trevor**
DWN	Cabragh	**Hill Trevor**
DUB	Bluebell	**Hill William**
WW	Bray Great	**Hill William**
KRY	Tralee Town	**Hilliard Henry**
DUB	Dolphins Barn	**Hilliard Jno**
MON	Carrickaderry	**Hillis James**
DWN	Ballygowan	**Hillsborough Trevor Lord**
KKY	Kilkenny City	**Hilsham Geo Capt.**
ANT	Shankill T`parks	**Hind James**
ANT	Shankill T`parks	**Hind John**
ANT	Shankill T`parks	**Hind Joseph**
CAV	Boagh	**Hinds Robert**
DUB	Drishoge	**Hines Joseph**
LIM	Greenmills *	**Hippesley**
KILD	Greenhills	**Hippsley John Cox**
LAO	Rinn	**Hipwell James**
WME	Noughaval	**Hoar James L**
KRY	Cagrigh *	**Hoar Robert**
LDY	Ballyness	**Hoare**
CRK	Glanmire	**Hoare**
CRK	Ballinglanna	**Hoare Edward**
KILD	Pluckerstown	**Hoare Joseph**
KKY	Smithstown	**Hoban John**
KKY	Glendonnell	**Hoban Patrick**
KILD	Parsonstown	**Hobart Henry**
KILD	Parsonstown	**Hobart William**
WAT	Waterford City	**Hobbs**
WW	Toherpatrick	**Hobson Abraham**
LIM	Ballindra *	**Hodder William**
DON	Abbey Mill	**Hodges Harry**
LAO	Mountrath	**Hodgins**
DUB	Dublin City	**Hodgins Joseph**
ANT	Englishtown	**Hodgkinson Alfred**
ANT	Shankill T`parks	**Hodgkinson Alfred**
WW	Ballygahan Lr.	**Hodgson Henry**
ROS	Cloonaragh	**Hodson**
DUB	Dublin City	**Hoey George**
ARM	Ballyloughan	**Hoey James**
DUB	Chapelizod	**Hoey Robert**
DWN	Newry Town	**Hoey Thomas**
DON	Rathmullan	**Hoffman Francis**
WME	Archerstown	**Hogan Edward**
CLE	Caherhurley	**Hogan John**
WEX	Coolatin	**Hogan Michael**
WEX	Forge Lands	**Hogan Michael**
TIP	Newlawn	**Hogan Patrick**
ROS	Clonard	**Hogan William**
TYR	Derry Drumy	**Hogg**
LDY	Londonderry	**Hogg**
TYR	Tullagh Beg	**Hogg**
ANT	Kilcurry	**Hogg Edward**
ANT	Lisburn	**Hogg Edward**
TYR	Coagh	**Hogg James**
ANT	Lisburn	**Hogg James**
ANT	Portglenone	**Hogg James**
TYR	Derry	**Hogg Jno**
TYR	Eskragh	**Hogg John**
TYR	Altnavannog	**Hogg Jonathan**
ANT	Ballylig	**Hogg Quintin**
ANT	Lisburn	**Hogg Wiliam**
ARM	Corkley	**Hogg William**
ANT	Portglenone	**Hogg William**
LDY	Windmill Perches	**Hogg William**
ANT	Antrim Town	**Holford Thomas**
ANT	Antrim Town	**Holford Thos**
GAL	Tormaun	**Holland Michael**
GAL	Tormaun	**Holland Mick**
MEA	Duleek Town	**Holland Pat**
CRK	Ballyhandle	**Holland William**
ANT	Doagh	**Hollybank Sp. Co.**
OFF	Belmont Mill	**Holmes**
CAV	Swanlinbar Town	**Holmes**
ANT	Dunanney	**Holmes David**
CRK	Ballynacarrigga	**Holmes Francis**
WME	Lissywollen	**Holmes Gilbert**
LIM	Deebert	**Holmes Henry Rev. Bt.**
WW	Ballymanus	**Holmes Hugh**
TYR	Artigarvan	**Holmes J**
LONG	Abbeyshrule	**Holmes James**
LONG	Abbeyshrule	**Holmes Jane**
DWN	Balloo	**Holmes Jno**
DWN	Belvor *	**Holmes John**
TIP	Fethard Town	**Holmes John**
LEI	Tawnylea	**Holmes Mathew**
LEI	Tullinwillin	**Holmes Mathew**
WAT	Stonehouse	**Holmes Pomeroy**
LEI	Lisacoghil	**Holmes Robert**
LEI	Tullinwillin	**Holmes Robert**
ANT	Baloo	**Holmes Wiliam**
ANT	Carnspindle	**Holmes Wiliam**
ANT	Ballyhill	**Holmes William**
LIM	Deebert	**Holmes William**
TYR	Dunamony	**Holmes William**
TYR	Tamnaskeeny	**Holmes William**
KKY	Urlingford	**Holohan John**
LIM	Kilmore	**Holohan Michael**
KKY	Urlingford	**Holohan Thomas**
DUB	Wood Mills	**Holroyd Isaac**
MON	Aghnamullen	**Holt William**
ROS	Canal & Banks	**Holton**
DWN	Strangford Lr	**Holton William**
KILD	Ardinode	**Homan Henry**
WAT	Raheen	**Homan William**
LOU	Ardee Town	**Home Gustavus**
LEI	Lismackniff	**Hone Brindley**
DWN	Carlingford	**Hone Ele**
LOU	Carlingford Tn	**HoneEif**
CRK	Fermoy (barony)	**Honywood William**
LAO	Ballyroan	**Hood**
ANT	Tullaghbane	**Hood Adam**
DWN	Baven	**Hood Alex**
ROS	Athleague	**Hood John**
ROS	Ballinasloe Town	**Hood John**
ANT	Tullaghbane	**Hood John**
DWN	Cargygray	**Hook Campbell**
DWN	Downpatrick Town	**Hope James**
ANT	Lisburn Tn`parks :	**Hope Joseph**
DUB	Dublin City	**Hopkins**
MEA	Rathnally	**Hopkins Eleanor**
MEA	Athboy Town	**Hopkins Francis**
WW	Ballymultagh	**Hopkins Joseph**
WME	Ballinderry	**Hopp Thomas**
WAT	Tallow Town	**Hopper Fran**
LAO	Ballinolart	**Hopper Margt. (Dunn) Wid.**
GAL	Cloonlaghan Geo	**Horan Michael**
DUB	Dublin City	**Horan Mr**
WME	Kilbeggan	**Horan William**
WEX	Kiltra	**Hore Mary**
CAR	Ballykillane	**Hore Patrick**
MYO	Eden	**Horgan Patrick**
CRK	Carrigagulla	**Horgan Timothy O`C**
MYO	Roosky	**Horkan Patrick**
OFF	Ballycumber	**Horne**
CRK	Rockfort	**Hornebrell John I**
ANT	Belfast Town	**Horner Anthony**
TYR	Nurchossy Scotch	**Hornridge Robert**
GAL	Lisfinny	**Horsman Edward**
GAL	Listinny	**Horsman Edward**
GAL	Lismafada	**Horsman Edward**
GAL	Deerpark	**Horsman James E**
KILD	Hortland	**Hort Josiah Geo**
KILD	Hortland	**Hort Josiah George**
SLI	Ardcurley	**Hort Patrick**
KILD	Hortland	**Hortland Joseph+B168**
LEI	Dromahaire	**Hosey John**
CRK	Skibbereen Town :	**Hosford R J**
GAL	Galway Town	**Hosking Valentine**
GAL	Monacow	**Hosty Edward**
GAL	Drumaskin	**Hosty John**
DWN	Nutgrove	**Houghton**
KILD	Levitstown	**Houghton C**
KILD	Levitstown	**Houghton Fredk**
KILD	Celbridge	**Houghton Jeremiah**
DWN	Annadorn	**Houghton Joseph**
DUB	Dublin City	**Hoult Robert**
LDY	Ballymacilcur	**Houston David**
TYR	Fintona Town	**Houston Henry**
DWN	Cloughy	**Houston John**
LDY	Curragh	**Houston John**
DWN	Donaghadee	**Houston John**
LDY	Ballymacilcur	**Houston William**

CO.	TOWNLAND	MILLER
ANT	Belfast Town	**How John**
ANT	Carrickfergus Tn	**How Robert**
ANT	Toberdowney	**How Robert**
ANT	Belfast Town	**How Thomas**
ANT	Carrickfergus Tn	**How Thomas**
LAO	Cardtown	**Howard**
LAO	Clarahill	**Howard**
CRK	Crookstown	**Howard Bros Ltd.**
LAO	Cardtown	**Howard Hugh**
ROS	Emlagh	**Howard Jno**
LAO	Cardtown	**Howard Robert**
WW	Milltown	**Howard William**
TIP	Dundrum	**Howarden Wm Visc.**
CAV	Drumcannon	**Howden James**
CAV	Cornagee	**Howe**
ANT	Glenavy	**Howe John**
ANT	Ballynure Village	**Howe Robert**
ANT	Dunturkey	**Howe Robert**
ANT	Edenderry	**Howe Robert**
ANT	Glenavy Town	**Howe Thos**
TIP	Clonmel	**Howel**
CAV	Cornagee	**Howel John**
ANT	Buvolcan	**Howie Robert**
WEX	Ballyhighland	**Howlett John**
WEX	Arnestown	**Howlett Martin**
SLI	Knockagower	**Howley Edward**
CAV	Smithstown	**Howlin John**
MEA	Milltown	**Howth Ear**
ANT	Mullaghduff	**Hoy Michael**
DUB	Castleknock	**Hoyle**
DWN	Magheralagan	**Hozier James H**
DWN	Downpatrick Town	**Hozier James H C**
DWN	Downpatrick Town	**Hozier Jas H C**
ANT	Belfast Town	**Huddleson Fran**
DWN	Ballydown	**Hudson**
DWN	Belvor *	**Hudson**
MON	Sallycrum	**Hudson**
CRK	bo./ Barrymore	**Hudson Henry**
DWN	Balloo	**Hudson James**
DWN	Belvor *	**Hudson James**
DWN	Ballydown	**Hudson John**
DWN	Colenecran	**Hudson William**
DUB	Dublin City	**Huffey**
CRK	Desert	**Huggard Martin**
DWN	Ballydugan	**Huggins**
DWN	Ballywalter	**Huggins**
DWN	Ballydugan	**Huggins John**
TYR	Tullylagan	**Huggins Max**
KKY	Buston Mills	**Hugh Madden**
CAR	Bagenalstown	**Hughes**
TIP	Clonmel Town	**Hughes**
ROS	Corgowan	**Hughes**
CAR	Courmellan	**Hughes**
ARM	Edenappa	**Hughes**
KILD	Maynooth	**Hughes**
MON	Miskish	**Hughes**

CO.	TOWNLAND	MILLER
KILD	Parsonstown	**Hughes**
DWN	Raholp	**Hughes Bernard**
LAO	Cooleroan	**Hughes Frances**
ARM	Edenappa	**Hughes Francis**
TIP	Clonmel Town	**Hughes George**
ROS	Cloonmagunnaun	**Hughes George**
WME	Ballywhite	**Hughes Henry**
ARM	Aghayalloge	**Hughes James**
ARM	Baltarran	**Hughes James**
ARM	Baltarran	**Hughes James**
TIP	Clonmel Town	**Hughes James**
WAT	Croan	**Hughes James**
LONG	Longford Town	**Hughes James**
ARM	Middletown	**Hughes James**
ARM	Unshog	**Hughes James**
ANT	Antrim Town B76	**Hughes Jane**
CAR	Carlow Town	**Hughes John**
CAR	Carlow Town	**Hughes John**
TIP	Clonmel Town	**Hughes John**
MON	Magoney	**Hughes John**
MON	Magoney	**Hughes John**
TIP	Suir Island	**Hughes John**
GAL	Galway Town	**Hughes Maria**
CRK	Fenagh *	**Hughes Martin**
MON	Drumgarve	**Hughes Mary**
MYO	Ballynew	**Hughes Patrick**
ARM	Baltarran	**Hughes Patrick**
LOU	Castlering	**Hughes Patrick**
MYO	Cloghermore	**Hughes Patrick**
MYO	Carraghdooey	**Hughes Peter**
WEX	Ballybing	**Hughes Pierce**
WEX	Slad	**Hughes Pierce**
WW	Ballinaclash	**Hughes Robert**
TIP	Clonmel	**Hughes Thomas**
TIP	Clonmel Town	**Hughes Thomas**
WAT	Croan	**Hughes Thomas**
ARM	Baltarran	**Hughes William**
CAR	Carlow :	**Hughes William**
CRK	Ballycroneen	**Hugo Cherry Spin.**
ROS	Balingaglass	**Hull Richard**
LAO	Ballygor	**Hume**
FER	Clohonan *	**Hume**
FER	Drumawillin	**Hume**
FER	Derrihalla	**Hume Alice Rt. Hon.**
MYO	Ballina	**Hume Gustavus**
CAR	Carlow Town	**Humphrey**
CAR	Carlow Town	**Humphrey Alex**
CAR	Carlow Town	**Humphrey Michael**
ARM	Drumacanver	**Humphreys D**
LAO	Cardtown	**Humphries**
LAO	Clarahill	**Humphries**
FER	Drumhoney	**Humphries Chris**
ARM	Drumnacanner	**Humphries David**
DUB	Glasnevin	**Humphries John**
TIP	Rathmore	**Humphries Thomas**
SLI	Curraghnagap	**Humphry**

CO.	TOWNLAND	MILLER
DWN	Comber	**Humphry John**
TIP	Borrisokane Town	**Humphry Thomas**
FER	Crevinish	**Humphry William.**
DWN	Ballydugan	**Hungerford W**
DWN	Drumquillan	**Hungerford W**
DWN	Saul	**Hungerford W**
DWN	Kilmore	**Hungerford Winspeare**
GAL	Ahascragh Town	**Hunt**
LIM	Askeaton	**Hunt**
DUB	Johnstown	**Hunt John**
DUB	Milltown	**Hunt Mr**
LDY	Aghadowey	**Hunter**
LDY	Ballybritain	**Hunter**
DWN	Ballycreevy	**Hunter**
DWN	Ballyhalbert	**Hunter**
DWN	Ballymacarret	**Hunter**
ANT	Dunmurry	**Hunter**
ANT	Islandreagh	**Hunter**
DWN	Knock	**Hunter**
LDY	Mullan	**Hunter**
ANT	Ballymather	**Hunter & Elgee**
DWN	Drumbeg	**Hunter Alex**
ANT	Dunmurry	**Hunter Alex**
DWN	Ballycowan	**Hunter Andrew**
ARM	Ballynaghy	**Hunter David**
WEX	Enniscorthy Town	**Hunter Hamilton**
ANT	Ballygarvey	**Hunter Harris**
ANT	Ballynure Village	**Hunter Harris**
ANT	Ballyvorally	**Hunter James**
TYR	Carnan	**Hunter James**
CAV	Claddagh	**Hunter James**
CAV	Claddagh	**Hunter James**
ANT	Crosshill	**Hunter James**
DWN	Hillhall	**Hunter James S**
CAV	Cleffin	**Hunter John**
CAV	Cleffin	**Hunter John**
DWN	Mealough	**Hunter John**
LAO	Timahoe Manor	**Hunter John**
ANT	Ballymather Lr	**Hunter M**
LDY	Enniskillen Town	**Hunter Richard**
LAO	Timahoe Manor	**Hunter Thomas**
ANT	Dunmurry	**Hunter William**
ANT	Glenburn	**Hunter William Jun.**
WEX	Ross Town	**Huntingdon E.**
MON	Dromore	**Hurchell Mr**
ROS	Gillstown	**Hurd, William**
CRK	Fenagh *	**Hurges John**
CRK	Sraleigh	**Hurley Daniel**
CRK	Bandon Town	**Hurley Johanna**
CRK	Bandon Town	**Hurley John**
CRK	Shanaway E.	**Hurley John**
CRK	Clonakilty Town	**Hurley John J**
WAT	Killeeshal	**Hurley Mary**
CRK	Coolnagay	**Hurley Patrick**
CRK	Inchinattin	**Hurley Patrick**
CRK	Poulacurry South	**Hurley William**

INDEX

CO.	TOWNLAND	MILLER
LAO	Ironmills / Kilrush	**Jackson John**
CAV	Lisboduff	**Jackson John**
LONG	Sheeroe	**Jackson John**
DUB	Windmill House	**Jackson John**
MON	Derrygooney	**Jackson John Eldr.**
MON	Creeve	**Jackson John Jun.**
MON	Drumfaldra	**Jackson John Rev.**
OFF	Monasteroris	**Jackson M**
DUB	Dublin City	**Jackson Mr**
TIP	Townland /	**Jackson Phoebe**
ARM	Ballynahone Beg	**Jackson Robert**
TYR	Boland	**Jackson Robert**
TIP	Parkmore	**Jackson Robert**
TIP	Roscrea Town	**Jackson Robert**
ARM	Aughnacloy	**Jackson Robert Jun.**
OFF	Monasteroris	**Jackson Robt Wm**
KILD	Inchaquire	**Jackson S**
KILD	Inchaquire	**Jackson Samuel Jun**
ARM	Aughnacloy	**Jackson Thomas**
DWN	Barnamaghery	**Jackson Thomas**
ARM	Ballygasey	**Jackson Wiliam**
LDY	Altagasky *	**Jackson William**
LDY	Coleraine	**Jackson William**
LDY	Altagasky *	**Jackson William Jun**
LAO	Donaghmore	**Jacob**
WAT	Raheen	**Jacob**
KKY	Castlecomer Tn	**Jacob James**
LAO	Donaghmore	**Jacob John**
DUB	Dublin City	**Jacob John**
MEA	Moynalty	**Jacob Odette**
MEA	Moynalty	**Jacob Ronan**
KKY	Cappagh	**Jacob William**
WEX	Hedges *	**Jacob William**
KILD	Celbridge	**Jagger Joseph**
CRK	Kilbarry	**Jago John**
CRK	Kilmore	**Jago Richard**
CRK	Mullendunny	**Jago Robert J**
ANT	Lisburn Town	**James**
MYO	Creggagh	**James & Jack McGraoil**
CAV	Lisboduff	**James Blackwood**
KKY	Drumdowney	**James Butler**
ANT	Shankill T`parks	**James Carlisle**
DON	Drumpologe	**James Elizabeth**
GAL	Coolrevagh	**James Farrell**
KKY	Clogaralt	**James Fennelly**
WAT	Ballyvoyle	**James Houlahan**
CAR	Rosdellig	**James John**
KILD	Crookstown	**James Maher**
GAL	Olter	**James Manseragh**
GAL	Duckanelly	**James Moore**
CRK	Mount Keeffe	**James O`Keeffe**
CAR	Carlow Town	**James William**
DWN	Ballymacarret	**Jameson**
LOU	Drogheda Town	**Jameson**
DUB	Dublin City	**Jameson John**
LDY	Boughilboy *	**Jameson Robert**
ANT	Callisnagh	**Jameson Samuel**
ANT	(bo.GLENARM)	**Jamieson Daniel**
ANT	(bo.GLENARM)	**Jamieson John**
MON	Quiglough	**Jamison Robert**
MYO	Killinasash	**Jane Brown (O'Connor)**
KKY	Burrelspark	**Janis Henry**
KKY	Grennan	**Janis Henry**
DUB	Rathfarnham	**Jas Horan Alderman**
MEA	Slane	**Jebb David**
MON	Bowelk	**Jebbs Thomas**
LEI	Kilmallock	**Jeevers James**
LIM	Kilmallock	**Jeevers James**
KRY	Tralee Town	**Jeffcott Joseph**
WEX	Rath	**Jeffers Richard**
KILD	Newland	**Jefferys**
CLE	Ballycorney	**Jefferys Augustus**
WEX	Hedges *	**Jefferys James Hon.**
KILD	Levitstown	**Jeffries Edward**
WEX	Lingstown	**Jeffrreys James**
DUB	Way Mills	**Jellicoe James**
DUB	Irishtown	**Jemmat Samuel**
DWN	Bleary & B'doogan	**Jenney Henry**
DWN	Bleary	**Jenney Henry Rev. Dr.**
ARM	Clogharevan	**Jennings Andrew**
LDY	Vintners Propn.	**Jennings John**
CAV	Curraghmore	**Jennings John+B92**
CRK	Bishop's-mill-lands	**Jennings Thomas**
MYO	Fountain Hill	**Jennings Ulick**
DUB	Portmarnock	**Jenny Brabazon**
CRK	Roundhill	**Jeremiah Crowley**
LONG	Forgney	**Jerrard Joseph**
ARM	Dorsy	**Jerrfes Richard**
KILD	Greatconnell	**Jervis Augustin**
GAL	Galway Town	**Jesson Thomas**
LONG	Cloonkeen	**Jessop Fran**
LONG	Cloonkeen	**Jessop Robert**
WME	Castletown	**Jessop William**
WME	Straduff	**Jessop William**
KILD	Greatconnell	**Jevers Susannagh**
KILD	Greatconnell	**Jevers Susannagh Wid.**
ARM	Derryhaw	**Jiohnston James**
LONG	Smear	**Job David**
CAR	Milford	**John Alexander**
CAR	Bagenalstown Tn	**John Casey**
KKY	Greenville Lower	**John Laffan**
DON	Milltown	**John laird**
WAT	Kilkeany	**John Mulcahy**
TIP	Ballyrickard	**John Neill**
SLI	Donaghintraine	**John Ryan**
ANT	Carrickfergus NE	**Johns Alex**
ANT	Carrickfergus Tn	**Johns Alex**
ANT	Carrickfergus Tn	**Johns Alexander**
ANT	Carrickfergus Tn	**Johns Thomas**
ANT	Carrickfergus Tn	**Johns Thomas D**
DWN	Ballyharley	**Johnson**
LEI	Creaveleagh	**Johnson**
DWN	Cullintraw	**Johnson**
TYR	Drumsonnus	**Johnson**
KILD	Millestown ?	**Johnson**
TYR	Monbeg	**Johnson**
WME	Mullingar Town	**Johnson**
TYR	Scallan	**Johnson**
LEI	Tawnylea	**Johnson**
DWN	Downpatrick Town	**Johnson Beauchamp**
WAT	Millfort	**Johnson Benjamin**
MON	Bowelk	**Johnson Henry**
WW	Kilmagig Lower	**Johnson Richard**
DWN	Ballymonestown	**Johnson Robert**
FER	Cushwash	**Johnson Robert**
TYR	Edenderry	**Johnson Robert**
MON	Aghnamullen	**Johnston**
DWN	Ballymaconaghy	**Johnston**
LOU	Banktown Up & Lr	**Johnston**
WAT	Carrickcastle	**Johnston**
MON	Clonavarn	**Johnston**
LOU	Comm. Corp. Lds	**Johnston**
LOU	Kercock	**Johnston**
DON	Kildrum	**Johnston**
FER	Tullycreevy	**Johnston**
DWN	Ballymacarret	**Johnston Acheson**
LEI	Creaveleagh	**Johnston Andrew**
DWN	Downpatrick Town	**Johnston Arthur**
WAT	Carrickcastle	**Johnston Benjamin**
DON	Tullyleague	**Johnston Charles**
MON	Aghnamullen	**Johnston David**
DON	Ballyshannon Tn	**Johnston David**
LAO	Borris	**Johnston Edward**
FER	Drumbadmeen	**Johnston Edward**
TYR	Aughamullin	**Johnston Francis**
FER	Shallany	**Johnston Francis**
CRK	Duntahane	**Johnston Francis G**
DWN	Ballymegenaghie *	**Johnston George**
TYR	Coagh	**Johnston George**
FER	Drumcahy	**Johnston George**
LEI	Creaveleagh	**Johnston Hannah Wid.**
LOU	Dundalk Town	**Johnston Henry**
MON	Aghnamullen	**Johnston James**
DWN	Ballyhaft	**Johnston James**
FER	Boyhill	**Johnston James**
DWN	Carrickruskey	**Johnston James**
DWN	Clonknaverty	**Johnston James**
FER	Cooneen	**Johnston James**
FER	Corralongford	**Johnston James**
DON	Dreenan	**Johnston James**
MON	Fintully	**Johnston James**
LONG	Gaigue	**Johnston James**
ARM	Marlacoo More	**Johnston James**
DON	Naveeny	**Johnston James**
MON	Rakeragh	**Johnston James**
LEI	Rossclogher	**Johnston James**
FER	Shallany	**Johnston James**
MON	Tirnadrola	**Johnston James**

CO.	TOWNLAND	MILLER
ARM	Ballinaclosha	**Johnston John**
ANT	Ballyrobin	**Johnston John**
DON	Dreenan	**Johnston John**
DON	Dreenan	**Johnston John**
ARM	Lurgan	**Johnston John**
DON	Navenny	**Johnston John**
FER	Shallany	**Johnston John**
LONG	Sheeroe	**Johnston John**
FER	Stranadarriff	**Johnston John**
ARM	Tannagh	**Johnston John**
FER	Killyfoyle	**Johnston Joseph**
DON	Navenny	**Johnston Joseph**
ANT	Ballycreggy	**Johnston Margt**
ARM	Middleton Town	**Johnston Matthew**
ARM	Rathtrillick	**Johnston Matthew**
ARM	Tullybrick Hamilton	**Johnston Matthew**
ARM	Doogarry	**Johnston Messrs**
ANT	Derriaghy	**Johnston Mr.**
ANT	Glynn Village	**Johnston Mrs.**
ANT	Shankill T`parks	**Johnston Philip**
ANT	Glynn	**Johnston R W**
DWN	Carrickruskey	**Johnston Robert**
ARM	Derryhaw	**Johnston Robert**
ARM	Tullyvallon	**Johnston Robert**
LEI	Creaveleagh	**Johnston Robt**
ANT	Ballycreggy	**Johnston Robtert**
DWN	Drumaness	**Johnston Samuel**
ROS	Gillstown	**Johnston Samuel Eldr.**
FER	Braade	**Johnston Simon**
MON	Ballycronog	**Johnston Thomas**
MON	Ballycronog	**Johnston Thos**
ANT	Kells	**Johnston W C**
MEA	Rossnaree	**Johnston Walter**
MON	Clonavarn	**Johnston William**
LEI	Lismackniff	**Johnston William**
ANT	Lisnawhiggel	**Johnston William**
KRY	Tralee Town	**Johnston William**
ANT	Shankill T`parks	**Johnston William**
MON	Clonavarn	**Johnston William Eldr.**
MON	Cumber *	**Johnston William Jun.**
LOU	Dundalk Town	**Johnston, Murray**
DWN	Ballymonestown	**Johntson Robert**
CRK	Ballycurreen	**Joiners & Carps.**
ANT	Drumnakeel	**Jolly Charles**
ARM	Allistragh	**Jones**
ARM	Anaghgary	**Jones**
LOU	Ardmulchan	**Jones**
KILD	Ardree	**Jones**
ROS	Athlone	**Jones**
MYO	Ballina	**Jones**
WW	Ballinvally	**Jones**
LAO	Ballyegle	**Jones**
LAO	Ballyegle	**Jones**
KILD	Bonglash *	**Jones**
WAT	Cappoquin	**Jones**
CRK	Coolfadda	**Jones**

CO.	TOWNLAND	MILLER
ROS	Derreenavoggy	**Jones**
DUB	Dublin City	**Jones**
FER	Enniskillen	**Jones**
WW	Ballynultagh	**Jones Abraham**
LONG	Dring	**Jones David**
WEX	St John`s (Taigh)	**Jones Edward**
ARM	Anaghgary	**Jones Elizabeth Wid**
CAR	Grangewat	**Jones George**
KILD	Greatconnell	**Jones Henry**
MON	Corfinlough	**Jones Humphrys**
WAT	Cappoquin	**Jones Jno**
WAT	Cappoquin	**Jones John Yngr.**
ROS	Athlone	**Jones Levin**
WME	Athlone Town	**Jones Lewis**
SLI	Knockaculleen	**Jones Louis G**
ANT	Lealies	**Jones Miss**
ARM	Anaghgary	**Jones Richard**
DUB	Rathmines S	**Jones Richard**
WAT	Goose Island	**Jones Richd**
KILD	Bonglash *	**Jones Theophilus**
KILD	Ardnaree	**Jones Thomas**
MYO	Ardnaree	**Jones Thomas**
KILD	Ardree	**Jones Thomas**
MYO	Ballina	**Jones Thomas**
DUB	Glasnevin	**Jones Thomas**
KILD	Greatconnell	**Jones Thomas**
CRK	Mallow Town	**Jones Thomas**
KILD	Ardnaree	**Jones Vaughan**
MYO	Ballina	**Jones Vaughan**
KILD	Bonglash *	**Jones Walter**
TIP	Compsey *	**Jones William**
SLI	Curraghnagap	**Jones William**
CAV	Drummany	**Jones William**
CAR	Scortreen	**Jordan**
WEX	Dunbrody Manor	**Jordan John**
OFF	Tullamore	**Joughin Charlotte**
DUB	Goldenbridge S	**Journeaux Francis**
ANT	Belfast Town	**Joy James**
WAT	Mayfield	**Joy John**
WAT	Mayfield	**Joy Nicholas**
WAT	Mayfield	**Joy Richard**
ANT	Moorfields	**Joy Robert**
CAR	Ballymurphy	**Joyce Edward**
GAL	Galway Town	**Joyce James**
MYO	Ballycarra	**Joyce Martin**
GAL	Galway Town	**Joyce Patrick**
ARM	Ballydonaghy	**Joyce Thomas**
ARM	Ballynaghy	**Joyce Thomas**
KKY	Grange Lower	**Joyce Thomas**
GAL	Cregg	**Joyce Walter**
CRK	Ballynacarrigga	**Joye Windpear**
GAL	Galway Town	**Joyes James**
GAL	Galway Town	**Joyes John Richard**
GAL	Galway Town	**Joyes Patrick**
OFF	Comms. Clonlish	**Joynt Henry**
WME	Mosstown	**Judge**

CO.	TOWNLAND	MILLER
MYO	Carrowreagh	**Judge Edward**
MYO	Agloragh	**Judge Owen**
ANT	Antrim Town	**Judges Lord**
CAR	Carlow Town	**Juliana Michael**
		K
WW	Ballybrittan *	**Kain Terrence**
DUB	Dublin City	**Kane**
DUB	Stopping`s Mill	**Kane**
ARM	Tullyglush	**Kane John**
MEA	Ballyann	**Kane Nathaniel**
MEA	Stonestown	**Kane Redmond**
WAT	Durrow	**Kane Richard**
LDY	Derrylane	**Kane Thomas**
LDY	Ballymoney	**Kane William**
DUB	Donore Mills of	**Kappock Mcl**
DUB	Glasnevin	**Kathrens Samuel**
CAR	St Mullins	**Kavanagh**
LAO	Graigue Town	**Kavanagh Bridget Mrs.**
KKY	Kilrush	**Kavanagh Den**
CAR	Ballyknock	**Kavanagh Dudley**
WEX	Enniscorthy Town	**Kavanagh Edward**
KILD	Maynooth	**Kavanagh Edward**
WEX	Killincooly	**Kavanagh James**
CAR	Leighlinbridge	**Kavanagh John**
KILD	Athy Town	**Kavanagh Martin**
WW	Rathdown	**Kavanagh Murtagh**
WEX	Ballyshannon	**Kavanagh Richard**
CAR	Ballyedmond	**Kavanagh Thomas**
KKY	Greenville	**Kay Laffan**
DWN	Ballyculter	**Keagh Robert**
MEA	Boyne	**Keaguick**
CAR	Kilcloney	**Kealy James**
ROS	Burne Brooke *	**Kealy Julia**
ROS	Burne Brooke *	**Kealy Thomas**
DUB	Wildings Mill	**Kean**
ANT	Moyarget Lr	**Kean Bernard**
WME	Templepatrick	**Kean James**
WAT	Ballyeen	**Keane**
LIM	Bruff	**Keane**
WAT	Cappoquin	**Keane**
CRK	Ballybrack	**Keane Daniel**
CLE	Monreagh	**Keane Denis**
WAT	Cappoquin	**Keane Jno**
WAT	Cappoquin	**Keane John**
WAT	Killeeshal	**Keane John**
WAT	Cappoquin Town	**Keane Leopold**
WAT	Killeeshal	**Keane Richard**
DUB	Balheary	**Keany**
KILD	Millestown ?	**Kearney**
KILD	Parsonstown	**Kearney**
KILD	Moone	**Kearney James**
GAL	Galway Town	**Kearney Matthew**
OFF	Aghanore *	**Kearney Patrick**
KKY	Graguenakill	**Kearney Patrick**
WAT	Waterford Town	**Kearney Patrick**

CO.	TOWNLAND	MILLER
DUB	Diswellstown	Kennan Robert
DUB	Astagob	Kennan Thomas
DUB	Diswellstown	Kennan Thomas
DUB	Diswellstown	Kennan Thomas
MON	Beagh	Kennedy
ROS	Creevemully	Kennedy
DUB	Drishoge	Kennedy
KILD	Millestown ?	Kennedy
DWN	Saul	Kennedy Anne C
GAL	Bracklagh	Kennedy Bryan
WAT	Piltown	Kennedy Charles
ANT	Belfast Town	Kennedy Daniel
TIP	Mullenkeagh	Kennedy Edmond
TIP	Ballyknockane	Kennedy Edward
TIP	Bantis	Kennedy Edward
WAT	Boolattin	Kennedy Edward
TIP	Killeen	Kennedy Edward
TIP	Knockane	Kennedy Edward
TIP	Mill Grove *	Kennedy Edward
ANT	Shankill T`parks	Kennedy Ellen
LDY	Coleraine Town	Kennedy Hugh
LOU	Dundalk Town	Kennedy J J
ANT	Shankill T`parks	Kennedy Jame
TIP	Cregg	Kennedy James
DUB	Dolphins Barn	Kennedy James
WAT	Portlaw	Kennedy James
KRY	Tralee Town	Kennedy Jas & Co
MON	Raferagh	Kennedy Jno
ROS	Copse	Kennedy John
LOU	Dundalk Town	Kennedy John J
LOU	Dundalk Town	Kennedy John J
KRY	Ballinleague	Kennedy Maurice
ANT	Lisburn	Kennedy Mr
MEA	Trim T`nparks	Kennedy Patrick
WAT	Portlaw	Kennedy Peter
WEX	Boolabawn	Kennedy Richard
LAO	Rathdowney	Kennedy Richard
DWN	Downpatrick Town	Kennedy Robert
ANT	Lisnagarvey	Kennedy Samuel
LONG	Longford Town	Kennedy Thomas
ANT	Carnmoney	Kennedy Thos M.
ANT	Shankill T`parks	Kennedy Victor
ANT	Moorfields	Kennedy Wm
MON	Liseenan	Kenner John
DWN	Tullylish	Kenney Anne+B46
CLE	Sooreeny	Kennier Dennis
MYO	Ballinrobe	Kenny
DUB	Dublin City	Kenny
KILD	Kilbernon *	Kenny
OFF	Mill Park Ballybritt	Kenny
MYO	Friars Quarter W	Kenny Courtney
WME	Monksland	Kenny Eliz. als Dodwell
GAL	Derreen	Kenny Francis
WME	Monksland	Kenny Henry
TYR	Desertcreat	Kenny Mary, Spin.
TYR	Desertcreat	Kenny Robon, Spin.
TYR	Desertcreat	Kenny Samuel
ROS	Ballyforan	Kenny Thomas H
TYR	Desertcreat	Kenny William
DON	Abbeylands	Keo John
WAT	Garran	Keoarney James
CAR	Carlow Town	Keogh
CAR	Carlow Town	Keogh
KILD	Maynooth	Keogh
LEI	Umeryroe	Keogh Anthony
DUB	Edmondstown	Keogh Edward
WEX	Mill Lands	Keogh Edward
CAR	Carlow Town	Keogh Elizabeth
WW	Ballybrittan *	Keogh John
CAR	Carlow Town	Keogh John
KILD	B`more Eustace	Keogh Martin
WEX	Toneybrackwood	Keogh Moses
ANT	Brookfield	Keoghler
WW	Ballybrittan *	Keoghoe
TYR	Tullywhisker	Keon A
LONG	Clondora	Keon Ambrose
LONG	Clondra	Keon Ambrose
SLI	Shaduff	Keough Mr
DWN	Ballyherly	Keown James
CAR	Tullow Town	Keppel John
CAR	Aghade	Keppel Rober
MON	Aghnamullan	Ker
MON	Aghnamullan	Ker
DWN	Ballyhemlin	Ker
LDY	Bolea	Ker David
ANT	Redhall	Ker David
DWN	DownpatrickTown	Ker David
MON	Aghnamullen	Ker John
DWN	DownpatrickTown	Ker Margaret
DUB	Turvey	Kerby Thomas
LEI	Dromahaire	Kernaghan Thomas
LEI	Aghalough	Kernan James
LEI	Corryarga	Kernan William
LAO	Clonagh	Kerniss
DUB	Dublin City	Kerny J
TYR	Drumuck	Kerr
MON	Drumucky *	Kerr
MON	Sallycrum	Kerr
MON	Cumber *	Kerr Alex
MON	Analore	Kerr Alex
LDY	Glenkeen	Kerr Bernard
DWN	Ballynahinch	Kerr David
DWN	Magheraknock	Kerr David
ANT	Redhall	Kerr David
ANT	Kilbegs	Kerr James
DUB	Rahillion	Kerr John
ANT	Port Rush	Kerr Lord Mark
MON	Analore	Kerr Robert
LDY	Articlave Town	Kerr Robert
DON	Rafoarty	Kerr Robert
MYO	Kilvine	Kerrane David
WME	Stokestown	Kerrigan Michael
KRY	Mucknagh *	Kerry Thomas Lord
DUB	Dolphins Barn	Kevill Eamon
DUB	Dolphins Barn	Kevill Eamon John
TYR	Milltown	Kewn John
LIM	Dromeliagh	Keyes John
FER	Killynoogan	Keys J
DON	Dreenan	Keys Letitia
FER	Killynoogan	Keys Messrs.
ARM	Ballynahone Beg	Kid Thomas Osborne
ARM	Ballynahone	Kidd
ARM	Crossdened	Kidd
ARM	Drumarg	Kidd
ARM	Keady	Kidd
ARM	Racarby	Kidd
ARM	Tassagh	Kidd
ARM	Toagh	Kidd
LOU	Ardee Town	Kidd Wm
FER	Attyclannabryan	Kidd Anthony
ARM	Crossdened	Kidd Councillor
ARM	Crossdened	Kidd Count
LOU	Dundalk Town	Kidd Eliz.
LOU	Dundalk Town	Kidd F.W.
LOU	Dundalk Town	Kidd Frederick
DUB	Glasnevin	Kidd George
ARM	Tullyglush	Kidd George
LOU	Ardee Town	Kidd Hugh
DWN	Ballincraig	Kidd Hugh
LOU	Dundalk Town	Kidd Hugh
ARM	Tullyglush	Kidd J A
ARM	Crossdened	Kidd James
ARM	Tullyglush	Kidd James
ARM	Tullyglush	Kidd James A
ARM	Crossdened	Kidd Jo.
LOU	Dundalk Town	Kidd Louisa
LOU	Dundalk Town	Kidd Louisa S
ARM	Ballycrummy	Kidd Messrs
ARM	Racarby	Kidd Osborne
ARM	Darkley	Kidd S A
ARM	Dundrum	Kidd S A
ARM	Aughnagurgan	Kidd Samuel
ARM	Darkley	Kidd Samuel
ARM	Tassagh	Kidd Samuel
ARM	Aughnagurgan	Kidd Samuel A
ARM	Darkley	Kidd Samuel A
ARM	Ballynahone Beg	Kidd T O
ARM	Umgola	Kidd Thomas
LOU	Ardree Town	Kidd William
SLI	Gregg	Kieghron Patrick
WAT	Knockmeal	Kiely Denis
LOU	Balriggan	Kieran John
DUB	Skerries Town	Kieran Joseph
DUB	Balrothery	Kieran Louisa M
LOU	Dundalk	Kieran Owen
KKY	Ballyrowragh	Kieran Williams
CRK	Ballycurreen	Kiereen
LONG	Killeen	Kiernan

CO.	TOWNLAND	MILLER
LOU	Philipstown	**Kiernan**
LEI	Corryarga	**Kiernan William**
LONG	Aghnacliff	**Kiernan Edward**
DUB	Balbriggan	**Kiernan James**
DUB	Balbriggan	**Kiernan James**
LONG	Ballyduffy	**Kiernan James**
LOU	Chanonrock	**Kiernan John**
LONG	Killeen	**Kiernan Owen**
WME	Fore	**Kiernan Patrick**
DUB	Balbriggan	**Kiernan Robert**
ROS	Emlagh	**Kildare E.**
WME	Rathwire U.& Lr.	**Kildare Earl**
KILD	Mount Blarney *	**Kildare Earl James**
KILD	Rathangan Manor	**Kildare Earl Jas Rt. Hon.**
MEA	Blackwater R.	**Kildare Eliz C`tess**
MYO	Foxford	**Kildare James Earl**
KILD	Mount Blarney	**Kildare James Earl**
CLE	Inchiquin Manor	**Kildare James Hon.**
KILD	Rathangan Manor	**Kildare Jas Rt. Hon.**
DWN	Black Causway *	**Kildare Mary Rt. Hon.**
DWN	Black Causway *	**Kildare Robt Hoh. Ld**
DWN	Ardglass	**Kildare Robt Rt Hon.**
TYR	Ballynabwee	**Kilgore Joseph**
TYR	Ballynabwee	**Kilgore William**
MYO	Turlough	**Kilkelly Patrick**
KILD	Blackchurch	**Killarden John Lord**
KKY	Castle	**Kille Edward**
GAL	Ballingarry	**Killeen Edward**
GAL	Galway Town	**Killeen Edward**
GAL	Galway Town	**Killeen Edward**
DWN	Ballydugan	**Killeen Noel**
OFF	Lavagh	**Killeen Timothy**
CRK	Cork City :	**Killeher Cornelius**
TYR	Clady	**Killen James**
DWN	Ballydavey	**Killips Hugh**
ROS	Burne Brooke *	**Killy Denis**
MYO	Tully	**Kilmaine Lord James**
DON	Ardfarn	**Kilmartin James**
DWN	Newry Town	**Kilmorery C`tess**
DWN	Newry Town	**Kilmorery Earl of**
WME	Annagh	**Kilmurray Henry**
ANT	Craigs	**Kilpatrick George S**
DON	Adrmore	**Kilpatrick Isaac**
DON	Rath	**Kilpatrick J**
ANT	Culbane	**Kilpatrick James**
DON	Kildrum Lower	**Kilpatrick James**
DON	Rath	**Kilpatrick James**
DON	Rath	**Kilpatrick Jos Sen**
MYO	Cultycreaghan	**Kilroy John**
LONG	Longford Town	**Kincaird Joseph**
WEX	Coolgreeny	**Kinch John**
KKY	Warrington	**Kinchela Lewis**
CRK	bo./ Barrymore	**Kindham Edwd**
MON	Team *	**Kineer James**
MYO	Ardnaree	**King**
MYO	Ballina	**King**

CO.	TOWNLAND	MILLER
LIM	Ballindra *	**King**
CAV	Bawnboy	**King**
CAR	Carlow Town	**King**
LOU	Cushellstown	**King**
TYR	Milltown	**King**
LOU	Philipstown	**King**
TYR	Tullywiggan	**King Andrew Rev.**
CRK	Cork City N. Libs	**King Benjamin**
KRY	Charleville	**King Edward**
ROS	Windmill Field :	**King Edward**
ROS	Mill Park	**King Elinor (Shanley)**
KRY	Dromthacker	**King Elizabeth**
KILD	Athy Town	**King George**
ARM	Lurgyvallon	**King Irvin John+B388**
LIM	Ballindra *	**King James Wm Hon.**
KILD	Athy Town	**King Jno**
DUB	Knightsgreen	**King Jno**
LEI	Watercourse	**King Jno**
DUB	Balbriggan	**King Joseph**
ARM	Calan River	**King Michael**
LDY	Lakagh	**King Michael**
KRY	Cloghercade	**King Nicholas**
CAV	Drumhillagh N.	**King Peter (Miller)**
KKY	Foulks Court	**King Richard**
TYR	Meenagh	**King Robert**
ARM	Middletown	**King Robert**
ROS	Mill Park Boyle Tn	**King Robert Sir**
CAR	Carlow Town	**King Simon**
KRY	Mangerton	**King Sir R**
OFF	Birr Town	**King Sir Richd**
KILD	Ardnaree	**King Vesey**
CAR	Derren River	**Kinglsey Daniel**
WW	Milltown	**Kingsbury**
DUB	Kilmainham	**Kingsbury Thomas**
WW	Milltown	**Kingsbury Thomas**
TIP	Ballyard	**Kingscote Fitzharding**
LAO	Ballynakill	**Kingsmill**
LAO	Donaghmore	**Kingsmill**
LAO	Ironmills / Kilrush	**Kingsmill Luke**
MEA	Brannockstown	**Kingston Arthur**
LIM	Ballindra *	**Kingston Geo Rt. Hon. E.**
CRK	Clodagh	**Kingston Jane**
CRK	Glananoudig *	**Kingston Lord**
DUB	Riversdale	**Kinkaid John**
DWN	Drumaglis	**Kinkaird Jno**
TYR	Clady	**Kinkead Charles.**
KILD	Townland?	**Kinkead Thomas**
ANT	Magheraboy	**Kinley Mary**
WEX	Ballyconlore	**Kinsella Andrew**
WEX	Brittas	**Kinsella J**
WEX	Ballyconlore	**Kinshela Andrew**
KKY	Bleach Green	**Kinshela Lewis**
CAR	Ratheeran	**Kinsley Daniel**
LOU	Ardee Town	**Kinstry Lee**
ANT	Tawnybrack	**Kirk Daniel**
DWN	Ardkeen	**Kirk Ethel**

CO.	TOWNLAND	MILLER
DWN	Ardkeen	**Kirk Ethel E**
ARM	Corkley	**Kirk Henry**
ARM	Racarby	**Kirk Henry**
ARM	Tassagh	**Kirk Henry**
ARM	Corkley	**Kirk John**
ARM	Racarby	**Kirk John**
ARM	Tassagh	**Kirk John**
ARM	Corkley	**Kirk Wiliam**
ARM	Annavale	**Kirk William**
DWN	Ardbrin	**Kirk William**
ARM	Ballyards	**Kirk William**
ARM	Ballyards	**Kirk William**
ARM	Darkley	**Kirk William**
ARM	Green	**Kirk William**
ARM	Racarby	**Kirk William**
ARM	Tassagh	**Kirk William**
ARM	Tullynamollogue	**Kirk William**
ARM	Darkley	**Kirk William M**
DWN	Ballywillwill	**Kirkpatrick Andrew**
DWN	Cloughran	**Kirkpatrick Matthew**
ANT	Cross	**Kirks David**
ARM	Lisdrumgullion	**Kirkwood**
ROS	Lissadorn	**Kirkwood Samuel**
LAO	Ballydavin	**Kirwan**
MYO	Clogher	**Kirwan**
GAL	Conagher	**Kirwan**
GAL	Cregg	**Kirwan**
WW	Killacloran	**Kirwan Ann**
MYO	Milltown	**Kirwan C**
MYO	Clogher	**Kirwan Christopher**
MYO	Turlough	**Kirwan Christopher**
LOU	Townland ?	**Kirwan James**
GAL	Milltown	**Kirwan Louisa (Brown)**
GAL	Cregg	**Kirwan Patrick**
GAL	Lisduff	**Kirwan Patrick**
MYO	Turlough	**Kirwan Patrick**
MYO	Aghaleague	**Kirwan Thomas**
LDY	Crew	**Kissock William**
FER	Derrygonnelly	**Kitson James**
LAO	Donaghmore	**Knaggs**
LAO	Milltown M`boro	**Knaggs**
LAO	Doon	**Knaggs George**
LAO	Milltown M`boro	**Knaggs James**
LAO	Doon	**Knaggs Jno**
LAO	Mountrath Manor	**Knaggs Mary**
TIP	Archerstown	**Knaggs Matthew**
LAO	Milltown M`boro	**Knaggs Robert**
CAR	St Mullins	**Knapton Lord**
DUB	Templogue	**Knatchbull**
TYR	Tattykeel	**Knight James Rev.**
ARM	Ballaghy	**Knipe Thomas**
TYR	Stiloga	**Knock Robert**
ROS	Grange	**Knot William**
CAR	Badger	**Knott Abigail**
CAR	Badger	**Knott Sarah**
DWN	Ballydollaghan	**Knox**

CO.	TOWNLAND	MILLER
DWN	Ballydugan	**Knox**
DWN	Ballyknockan	**Knox**
DWN	Ballyvally	**Knox**
ARM	Balteagh	**Knox**
CLE	Callaghans	**Knox**
ARM	Clogharevan	**Knox**
LEI	Killynashinnagh	**Knox Alex**
LEI	Killynashinnagh	**Knox Alexander**
WEX	Hedges *	**Knox Andrew**
TYR	Pluck *	**Knox Ann**
MYO	Ardnaree	**Knox Annesley**
MYO	Castlereagh	**Knox Arthur E.**
TYR	Dungannon L`ships	**Knox Charles Hon.**
MYO	Castlereagh	**Knox Ernest**
MYO	Turlough	**Knox Fran**
MYO	Cloongee	**Knox Francis**
MYO	Cloonkee	**Knox Francis**
TYR	Pluck *	**Knox George**
LDY	Ballyquin	**Knox John**
MYO	Belleek	**Knox John**
MYO	Castlereagh	**Knox John**
MYO	Kilmovee	**Knox John**
TYR	Pluck *	**Knox John**
MYO	Castlereagh	**Knox Lawrence**
DON	Killygordon	**Knox Robert**
LOU	Ardee Town	**Knox Robert J**
TYR	Pluck *	**Knox Sarah**
WEX	Hedges *	**Knox Sidney**
DWN	Balleny	**Knox Thomas**
TYR	Dungannon	**Knox Thomas**
WEX	Hedges *	**Knox Thomas**
DUB	Walshestown	**Knox Thomas**
TYR	Mullybrannon	**Knox Thomas Bart.**
DWN	Ballydugan	**Knox Thomas Mr**
TYR	Mullybrannon	**Knox Thomas Visc.**
ANT	Park	**Knox Thos**
TYR	Dungannon L`ships	**Knox Vesey Hon.:**
KILD	Ardree	**Knox William**
CRK	Ballyrussell	**Knox William**
WME	Monksland	**Knox William**
DON	Leitter *	**Knox William**
DON	Maghery *	**Knox William**
DON	Oiley *	**Knox William**
TYR	Dungannon	**Knox William Rev.**
SLI	Abbeyhalfquarter	**Knoxgore Colfa**
DWN	Cregagh	**Koch**
WEX	Kilscanlan	**Koley David**
CAR	St Mullins	**Kough**
KILD	Abbyowthry *	**Kyd**
TYR	Drumnakilly	**Kyle James**
TYR	Greyduff	**Kyle James**
ANT	Magherahoney	**Kyle James**
DWN	Belvor *	**Kyle Robert**
TYR	Creeduff	**Kyle William**

CO.	TOWNLAND	MILLER
		L
OFF	Milltown	**L`Estrange**
OFF	Moyestown Dem.	**L`Estrange G B**
DUB	Blanchardstown	**L`Estrange John**
OFF	Belmount /Lisderg	**L`Estrange Thomas**
WME	Aghnatemple *	**La Touche**
OFF	Bogtown	**Labal**
LAO	Acreavock	**Laban**
DWN	Drumnescamp	**Lackard David**
MEA	Clonguiffin	**Lackington**
CAR	Ballynebranagh	**Lacy Mary Widow**
WEX	Ballylucas	**Lacy Nicholas**
TIP	Ballinroe	**Laffan John**
TYR	Donnygowen	**Lafferty Owen**
ANT	Dervock	**Laghlin Andr**
DON	Cross	**Laid Mr**
DON	Corraine	**Laird James**
DON	Carrygally	**Laird John**
DON	Tullyvinny	**Laird Robert**
CAR	Derren River	**Lalor Edward**
LAO	Ironmills / Kilrush	**Lalor James**
LAO	Doon	**Lalor Peter**
WW	Bray	**Lamb Hall**
WW	Aragh East	**Lamb John**
WW	Laragh	**Lamb John**
WW	Ballincurrig Lower	**Lamb Michael**
OFF	Annaghmore	**Lambert**
DWN	Cullintraw	**Lambert**
MYO	Foxford	**Lambert**
MYO	Foxford	**Lambert Charles**
WME	Kilbeggan	**Lambert Charles**
WME	Kilbeggan	**Lambert Gustavus**
MYO	Leedaun	**Lambert Joseph**
LAO	Coolkerry	**Lambert Robert**
ARM	Tassagh	**Lambert Thomas**
CRK	Ballyvolane	**Lambert William**
ANT	Ballywatt East	**Lamont Hugh**
DWN	Gransha	**Lamont John**
ROS	Ballinasloe Town	**Lancaster John**
MEA	Tullog	**Lancaster Simon**
ANT	Cloghanmurry	**Land Judges Co.**
OFF	Fanure *	**Landed Estate Court**
KKY	Thomastown	**Landed Estate Court**
CAR	Ballygowan	**Landed Estate Court**
TIP	Clonmel Town	**Landed Estate Court**
DWN	Downpatrick Town	**Landed Estate Court**
LAO	Old Mills	**Landers**
WAT	Raheen	**Landiford Thos Rev.**
TYR	Rakeeranbeg	**Landrum Richard**
ANT	Carrickfergus Tn	**Landys Lord**
WME	Hightown	**Landys Patrick**
CRK	Ballygarvan	**Lane**
CRK	Ballyrusheen	**Lane**
LEI	Creaveleagh	**Lane**
LEI	Tawnylea	**Lane**

CO.	TOWNLAND	MILLER
LDY	Ballycarton	**Lane Benjamin**
LDY	Coolessan	**Lane Hugh**
CRK	Ballybrack	**Lane James Rev.**
CRK	Ballygarvan	**Lane Maurice**
CRK	Douglas	**Lane Mr**
LAO	Ballymowland	**Lane Ralph**
CRK	Ballyrusheen	**Lane Richard**
CRK	Riverstown	**Lane Thomas B.**
CRK	Riverstown	**Lane Thomas Biggs**
CRK	Cork City :	**Lane William**
MON	Derrylavan	**Lane William**
MEA	Beaumont	**Langan**
KILD	Maynooth	**Langan**
MEA	Bartramstown	**Langan James**
MEA	Bartramstown	**Langan John**
MEA	Bartramstown	**Langan Patrick**
MEA	Bartramstown	**Langan Reps John**
MEA	Bartramstown	**Langan Richard**
TIP	Archerstown	**Langley Charles**
TIP	Archerstown	**Langley Henry**
KILD	Turnings Lower	**Langley Stephen**
LONG	Ballyrohan	**Langley Thomas**
WAT	Waterford Town	**Langrish Robert**
KILD	Parsonstown	**Langrishe**
LIM	Inch *	**Langton**
LAO	Mounteagle	**Langton John**
ARM	Ballyshiel Beg	**Langtree James**
ARM	Ballyshiel Beg	**Langtree John**
ARM	Richhill	**Langtree Mrs**
DWN	Ballymaconaghy	**Langtry**
CAV	Cabragh	**Langtry**
CAV	Lisnageer	**Langtry**
ANT	Dunamoy	**Langtry Charles**
DWN	Kilmore	**Langtry George**
ARM	Ballylane	**Langtry Jno**
LAO	Clarahill	**Large Samuel**
LAO	Cullenaghbegg	**Large Samuel**
WME	Rathwire Lower	**Larken**
WME	Boyanagh	**Larkin Elizabeth**
WEX	Garr	**Larkin James**
GAL	Derry	**Larkin Patrick**
ANT	Magheragall	**Larmor John**
ANT	Edenturcher	**Larmour Andrew**
ANT	Glenavy	**Larmour Andrew**
ANT	Magheragall	**Larmour John**
ANT	Mullaghcartin	**Larmour John**
DUB	Shanganagh	**Larney Bernard**
DON	New Mill	**Lasalles Henry**
DON	Salt Pans	**Lasalles Henry**
KRY	Milltown	**Latchfield Richard**
KILD	Carnalway	**Latouch Robert**
DWN	Annadorn	**Latouche**
TIP	Clonmel	**Latouche**
KILD	Moone	**Latouche**
WME	Rathbennett	**Latouche**
TIP	Clonmel	**Latouche Dav Rt. Hon.**

CO.	TOWNLAND	MILLER
CAR	Staples Mill	**Latouche David**
DUB	Haroldsgrange	**Latouche David Hon.**
WAT	Clonmel	**Latouche David Rt Hon.**
CAR	Ballygowan	**Latouche John**
CAR	Newtown	**Latouche Robt Lt. Col.**
DUB	Wood Mills	**Latouche William D**
KILD	Johnstown	**Lattin**
KILD	Mylerstown	**Lattin George**
KILD	Mylerstown	**Lattin Jane**
WAT	Killeeshal	**Laughnam Connell**
ARM	Rich Hill	**Laughy Charlotte**
DUB	Dublin City	**Laundy M**
LAO	Ballyroan	**Laurenson**
WW	Killinure	**Laurenson Michael**
CRK	Ballyrusheen	**Lavitt**
DWN	Ballyvally	**Law**
DWN	Gilford	**Law**
DWN	Ballyvally	**Law George**
DWN	Ballyvally	**Law James**
ANT	Gortaherran	**Law John**
DWN	Coose	**Law Samuel**
DWN	Lisnatifty	**Law Samuel**
KKY	Milltown	**Law Samuel**
KKY	Milltown	**Law Samuel**
CLE	Cragleagh	**Law Thomas P**
ANT	Gortaherran	**Law William**
ROS	Killakin *	**Lawder Edward**
CRK	bo./ Ballymore	**Lawe Alexander W**
KILD	Moone	**Lawler**
KILD	Moone	**Lawler John Henry**
WW	Ballybrittan *	**Lawless**
DUB	Palmerstown	**Lawless John**
DUB	Palmerstown	**Lawless Mr.**
CAR	Carlow Town	**Lawless Richard**
TIP	Ballinunty	**Lawless Robert**
DUB	Diswellstown	**Lawley Robert Bart**
LAO	Ballynakill	**Lawlor**
KILD	Kilrush	**Lawlor**
KILD	Mullaghboy	**Lawlor James**
WEX	Ballywilliam	**Lawlor Michael**
KILD	Maganey Upper	**Lawlor Patrick**
KILD	Castleroe West	**Lawlor Richard**
LDY	Coleraine Town	**Lawrence Samuel**
TYR	Cough	**Lawson**
ANT	Donegore	**Lawther C**
ANT	Donegore	**Lawther Charles**
ANT	Donegore	**Lawther Henry**
CRK	Youghal Town	**Ld Estate Court**
CRK	Youghal Town	**Ld Estate Court**
KKY	Thomastown	**Ld. Est Court**
WEX	Wexford Town	**Ld. Estate Court**
KKY	Grannagh	**Le Botiller James**
TYR	Megna *	**Le Grice**
CAV	Cornacarrow	**Leadbeater Garret**
LAO	Old Mill	**Leadbeater Richard**
LAO	Stradbally	**Leadbeater Richard**

CO.	TOWNLAND	MILLER
KRY	Coolclogher	**Leahy Charles**
KRY	Coolclogher	**Leahy Henry**
KRY	Flesk	**Leahy Henry**
KRY	Coolclogher	**Leahy John**
KRY	Tralee Town	**Leahy Richard**
KRY	Coolclogher	**Leahy Susanna**
KRY	Flesk	**Leahy Susanna**
DUB	Killossery	**Leany Joseph**
WEX	Ballydrum	**Lear James**
WEX	Ballindinas	**Leared Richard**
WEX	Coolcots	**Leared Richard**
CRK	Gurteen	**Leared William**
CRK	Kilmaloda	**Leary Daniel**
CRK	Carrig	**Leary John**
WEX	Forestalstown	**Leary Mary**
CRK	Barrane	**Leary Patrick**
WEX	Forestalstown	**Leary Patrick**
CRK	Kilmaloda	**Leary Patrick**
MEA	Rathfeigh	**Leary Patrick**
CRK	Reengarrigeen	**Leary Patrick**
LDY	Londonderry	**Leatham John**
LDY	Londonderry	**Leatham William**
DON	Bohullian Lower	**Leathan Samuel**
WME	Grehanstown	**Leavy Patrick**
LDY	Tirkeeran	**Lecky Henry**
ANT	Ballyboggy	**Lecky Hugh**
LAO	Monksgrange	**Lecky John**
DON	Carrickballydooey	**Lecky Robert**
DON	Pluck	**Lecky Samuel Alex**
ANT	Ballyclare	**Ledie George**
TYR	Cratley	**Ledlie William**
TYR	Leck	**Ledlie William**
KILD	Ardree	**Ledwick**
DUB	Whitetown	**Ledwidge William**
KILD	Kilrush	**Ledwith**
LONG	Curcunny	**Ledwith Edward**
LOU	Ardee Town	**Lee**
CAR	Clashganny	**Lee**
KILD	Tully West	**Lee Francis**
KILD	Tullywest	**Lee Francis**
DUB	Faranboley	**Lee John**
LAO	Poormansbridge	**Lee John**
MEA	Martry	**Lee M**
CAV	Lattagloghan	**Lee Peter**
CAV	Lattaloghan	**Lee Peter**
CRK	Bandon Town	**Lee Samuel G**
DWN	Ballyhemlin	**Leech**
CAR	Carlow Town	**Leech**
LAO	Boley	**Leech Alan**
ANT	Antrim Town	**Leech Arthur**
CAR	Rosdellig	**Leech George**
LDY	Coleraine Town	**Leech Hunt W**
LAO	Boley	**Leech Thomas**
LDY	Stranagard	**Leeper James**
ARM	Ballylane	**Leeper William**
LDY	Durnascallon	**Leeper William**

CO.	TOWNLAND	MILLER
DON	Ballylevin	**Lees John**
DUB	Milltown	**Leeson Ed**
DUB	Donnybrook	**Leeson Joseph**
GAL	Kilshanvy	**Leevin James**
MEA	Rathnally	**Lefroy Thomas**
KILD	Pluckerstown	**Lefroy Thos Hon.**
TYR	Holly Hill	**Legerson William**
CAR	Ardristan	**Leggett William**
LDY	Arlogh	**Legrand**
LDY	Arlough	**Legrand C J**
DUB	Feltrim	**Lehunte**
OFF	Bunrevan	**Leicester H.**
TIP	Derrinsallow	**Leicester Hamilton J**
TIP	Derrinsallow	**Leicester Hamilton P**
OFF	Bunrevan	**Leicester J.**
WME	Cullenmore	**Leigh**
ARM	Shancrackan Beg	**Leigh**
CAR	Tobinstown	**Leigh**
LAO	Poormansbridge	**Leigh John**
LDY	Moyletrakill	**Leighlin John**
LIM	Mountblainey *	**Leinster Duke**
KILD	Mountblairnet	**Leinster Duke**
KILD	Maynooth	**Leinster Duke**
KILD	Milltown	**Leinster Duke**
KILD	Mount Blarney *	**Leinster Duke**
KILD	Mount Blarney *	**Leinster Hon . Lady Hope.**
KILD	Mountblairnet	**Leinster Hon. Aug Fred**
LIM	Mountblainey	**Leinster Lady**
MON	Dondroman	**Leister**
CRK	St Patrick's Ward	**Leitrim St.**
LIM	Askeaton	**Leland**
MEA	Broad	**Leland Ralph**
TYR	Tullywhisker	**Lendrum George**
TYR	Cullinean	**Lendrum James Jun.**
TYR	Cullinean	**Lendrum James Sen.**
TYR	Cormamucklagh	**Lendrum John**
TYR	Cullinean	**Lendrum John**
TYR	Rakeeranbeg	**Lendrum John**
MYO	Newport	**Lendrum Richard**
MON	Killycrom	**Lennan Bernard**
WME	Clogher	**Lennon**
CAR	Aghade	**Lennon Maria**
CAR	Aghade	**Lennon Bernard**
KILD	Athy Town	**Lennon Landon**
CAR	Aghade	**Lennon Michael**
CAR	Carrickslaney	**Lennon Michael**
KRY	Toberananig	**Lennon R M**
ROS	Athleague	**Lennon William**
WME	Ballykeeran	**Lennox**
SLI	Ballanecarron S	**Lennox Robert**
DUB	Astagob	**Lennox Wiliam**
SLI	Carrowcrory	**Leonard Matthew**
WAT	Capoquin Town	**Leopold Keane**
ANT	Shankill T`parks	**Lepper Charles W**
ANT	Shankill T`parks	**Lepper John C.**
ANT	Shankill T`parks	**Lepper Robt C.**

CO.	TOWNLAND	MILLER
ANT	Shankill T`parks	Lepper William H
MON	Aghnaha	Leslie
MON	Emy	Leslie
FER	Knocks	Leslie Blaney
CRK	Ballincollig	Leslie Charles
DWN	Killough	Leslie Charles
DUB	Windmill Land	Leslie Charles
MON	Drumbanagher	Leslie Charles P.
WEX	Mullinderry	Leslie Edward Rev.
LDY	Drumslade	Leslie Henry
DUB	Feltrim	Leslie Jas Dr
DON	Ardnaglass	Leslie John
DON	Ardnaglass	Leslie John
KRY	Tarbert	Leslie John
MON	Aghnagap	Leslie Mrs
MON	Kilcran	Leslie Mrs
MON	Scarnageeragh	Leslie Mrs
DWN	Ballystockart	Leslie Rev Peter
ANT	Cullybackey	Leslie Rev Peter
DWN	Ten Towns	Leslie Rev Peter
DON	Corkey	Leslie Revd John
DON	Carrowan *	Leslie William
DUB	Feltrim	Lester Agnes Wid.
SLI	Kinaghan	Lester Charworth
ROS	Athleague Manor	Lester John
OFF	Annaghmore	Lestrange
OFF	Belmont Mill	Lestrange
KILD	Mount Blarney	Letablere Danl Rev.
WEX	Enniscorthy Town	Lett George
WEX	Enniscorthy Town	Lett Josephine
DON	Newmills	Letterkeny
WME	Gilbertstown	Lettice P Hamson Wid.
WME	Rathbennett	Lettice P Hamson Wid.
LAO	Cooleroan	Levin Charles
LONG	Cartrons	Levinge Sir Richard
ARM	Ballynahone More	Levingston
MON	Drumnavaddy	Levingston
MYO	Cahemamart	Levingston William
DON	Brickfield	Levins Mr
GAL	Kilshanvy	Lewin Carrigue
GAL	Kilshanvy	Lewin Frederick T
GAL	Kilshanvy	Lewin Thomas
LAO	Acreavock	Lewis
KILD	Kilkea	Lewis
LAO	Ballinfrase	Lewis Daniel
LAO	Ballinfrase	Lewis Henry
LAO	Little Mill	Lewis Henry
LONG	Kilnplot	Lewis John Rev.
MON	Carrickaderry	Lewis Robert
CAR	Ballygowan	Lewis Sam
ARM	Mohan	Lewis Samuel
TIP	Cashel Town	Lewis Wiliam
WEX	Clohamon	Lewis William
WEX	St Mary`s	Lewis William
ANT	Derriaghy	Lewson Mr
ANT	Poleglass	Lewson Mr
ANT	Poleglass	Lewson William
MON	Agkellough	Ley
MON	Agkellough	Ley
ARM	Augher	Ley George
KILD	Blackchurch	Ley James Smith
MON	Adelought	Ley Wiliam
MON	Aghillagh *	Ley Wiliam
WW	Ballybrittan *	Leycester Ralph
WW	Milltown	Leyland
LDY	Bovagh	Leyland Langford
SLI	Gorteen	Leynard Mark
MON	Carrickaderry	Leysan Wiliam
DWN	Donaghcloney	Liddal Morris
DWN	Donaghcloney	Liddal Williams
DWN	Banoge	Liddell
DUB	Astagob	Liddy Thomas
CAV	Cavan Town	Lifeforce Mill
CAR	Ardristan	Ligate Wiliam
CAR	Ardristan	Ligate William
DON	Millers Holding	Lighton Andrew
DON	St Johnstown	Lighton Andrew
DON	Townland ?	Lighton Andrew
DON	Townland ?	Lighton Andrew
WME	Coolure	Lilli
MON	Knappagh	Lillion Mary
LIM	Bruff	Limerick Chas Ld. Bish.
LDY	Glasvey	Limerick George
LIM	Bruff	Limerick Henry Hon. E.
DWN	Ballydollaghan	Limerick Hon. Jas Visc.
DWN	Ballydargan	Limerick James Hon. Lord
DWN	Ballydargan	Limerick Ld. Jas Rt. Hon.
DWN	Balloo	Limerick Lord
DWN	Ballydollaghan	Limerick Lord
DWN	Ballyknockan	Limerick Lord
DWN	Balloo	Limerick Lord Visc.
DWN	Ballyknockan	Limerick Thos Rt. Hon.
LIM	Singland	Limk. Manure Co
DWN	Colenecran	Lindasy John
ANT	Carrickfergus Tn	Lindon & Co.
DWN	Ballyaughian	Lindsay David
TYR	Tullywhisker	Lindsay Elizabeth
MYO	Rathbaun	Lindsay Ellen
LOU	Ravensdale Park	Lindsay Francis
TYR	Donaghrisk	Lindsay Frederick
DWN	Ballydown	Lindsay Geo & John
DWN	Ballyaughian	Lindsay James
DWN	Ballymagart	Lindsay James
DWN	Balleevy	Lindsay Jno
DWN	Balleevy	Lindsay John
LAO	Monksgrange	Lindsay John
TYR	Tullywhisker	Lindsay John
CRK	Hollybrook *	Lindsay Samuel
CRK	Mountmusic	Lindsay Samuel
WW	Tubber *	Lingen William
MON	Annaveagh	Linn George
ANT	Carrickfergus Tn	Linnet John
LDY	Carthabalintober	Linton William
ARM	Lisbanoe	Lisbane Mills
LAO	Tullyroe	Lister John
DWN	Downpatrick Town	Lithgow Robert T
CAR	Borris	Little
ARM	Glassdrumman	Little
ARM	Lisdrumgullion	Little
OFF	Frankford Town	Little Charlotte
DWN	Gransha	Little David
FER	Keeran Beg	Little Ellen
DWN	Drumbo	Little Frances (Young)
WEX	Ross Town	Little Geo
ROS	Killukin	Little James
LONG	Moor	Little John
ANT	Shankill T`parks	Little John
CLE	Cloonaleary	Little Michael
FER	Cushwash	Little Robert
DWN	Drumbo	Little Thomas
LAO	Aghmacart	Litton
SLI	Ballysadare Town	Litton Edward
DWN	Ballywalter	Litton Edward
DUB	Leabstown	Litton Thomas
GAL	Athenry Town	Livesay Richard
LDY	Carnalridge	Livingstone Hugh
CLE	O'Briensbridge	LLoyd
CRK	Castleland	LLoyd George
ROS	Killappoge	Lloyd Guy
ROS	Killappoge	Lloyd Owen
ROS	Killappoge	Lloyd Owen Eldr.
ROS	Crannagh	Lloyd Thomas
ROS	Killappoge	Lloyd Thomas
ROS	Lyscallagh (?)	Lloyd Thomas
ROS	Emlagh	Lloyd Thomas Rev.
ROS	Ardsallagh	Lloyd William
ROS	Killappoge	Lloyd William
KRY	Cagrigh *	Lloyde George
ROS	Ardsallagh	Lloyde Thomas
ROS	Ardsallagh	Lloyde William
ARM	Goragh	Lochart
DWN	Drumnascamph	Lockart David
WME	Kilbeggan	Locke John
DWN	Knocknagore	Lockhart David
DWN	Kernan Upr	Lockhart Thomas
CAR	Cloghristick	Lockington Christopher
KILD	Johnstown	Lodge
LAO	Cullenaghbegg	Lodge Christopher
LAO	Drinagh	Loftus
CAR	St Mullins	Loftus
MON	Ballycronog	Loftus Thomas
CRK	Riverstown	Logan Ellen
ANT	Knockboy	Logan James
LDY	Ballyagan	Logan John
ANT	Ballynashee	Logan John
CRK	Kinsale Town	Logan William
CRK	Ardarostig	Logan William & John
CRK	Liscahane	Logan William C

CO.	TOWNLAND	MILLER
LDY	Ballinamore	**Long William**
CRK	Ballycroneen	**Longfield Mountford**
KILD	Coolsickin	**Longfield Robert**
CRK	Ballycroneen	**Longfield Robert Rev.**
KILD	Coolsickin	**Longfield Robt Sen.**
CRK	Douglas	**Longford Earl**
LONG	Longford Town	**Longford Earl**
LIM	Milltown	**Longford Lord**
WME	Rathwire	**Longford Lord**
WME	Coolure	**Longford Lord Henry**
WME	Noughaval	**Longworth Frances**
DWN	Tullychin	**Lord Dufferin**
DWN	Tullycreely	**Lord Dufferin**
DWN	Ballylisbredan	**Lord Dungannon**
DWN	Listooder	**Lord Dungannon**
DWN	Owenocork	**Lord Dungannon**
DUB	Castleknock bo.	**Lorenzo D**
CLE	Lack West	**Lorihgan Jane**
CLE	Lack West	**Lorihgan Thomas**
ANT	Glenavy	**Lorimer John**
LIM	Ballindra *	**Lorton King Rt. Hon.**
SLI	Toomour-Carrow	**Lorton Lord**
ANT	Leymore	**Lougheridge J**
ANT	Leymore	**Lougheridge W**
KKY	Newtown	**Loughlin John**
KKY	Thomastown	**Loughlin Michael**
LDY	Moyletra	**Loughlin Thomas**
OFF	Drumakeenan	**Loughman Dan**
OFF	Drumakeenan	**Loughman William**
WAT	Dungarvan Town	**Loughran David**
TYR	Crossteely	**Loughran John**
TYR	Dungannon Town	**Loughreen David**
LDY	Drumgavenny Lr	**Loughry William**
ROS	Tanidrissoge *	**Louth Earl+C2955**
LOU	Lowrath	**Louth Lord**
LOU	Lowrath North	**Louth Lord**
ARM	Diving	**Love David**
ARM	Middletown	**Love Henry**
CAV	Clonkeiffy	**Love John**
CAV	Clonkeiffy	**Love Wiliam Mr.**
CAV	Clonkeiffy	**Love William**
CAV	Clonkeiffy	**Love Wm & Jno**
WME	Ballynagore	**Low**
CRK	Aghakeiny *	**Low Francis**
DWN	Carlingford Town	**Lowe William**
WEX	Ross Town	**Lower John**
LAO	Ballintrase	**Lowrenson**
MYO	Kilrush	**Lowrie Francis**
DWN	Ballykeel	**Lowry**
DWN	Shannaghan	**Lowry Alexander**
DWN	Ballymaconnell	**Lowry Elizabeth**
DON	Drumchrow	**Lowry Henry**
DWN	Ballydourne	**Lowry James**
DWN	Conlig	**Lowry John**
DON	Drumchrow	**Lowry John**
DON	Killyverry	**Lowry Moses**
FER	Crevinish	**Lowry Robert**
TYR	Milltown	**Lowther Galbraith**
KILD	Newhall	**Lowther Jno**
DWN	Milltown	**Lowthian**
KKY	Bleach Green	**Luby Cornelius**
MYO	Lisnageeha	**Lucan Earl of**
MYO	Ballynew	**Lucan Hon. Ld. Chas**
OFF	Aanard	**Lucas**
KILD	Osberstown	**Lucas**
MON	Ballycronog	**Lucas Edward**
MON	Cossabey	**Lucas Edward**
DWN	Ardkin	**Lucas Francis**
MON	Ballycronog	**Lucas Francis**
MON	Ballycronog	**Lucas Francis**
DWN	Ballylisbane	**Lucas Francis**
MON	Carrickaderry	**Lucas Frans**
OFF	Aanard	**Lucas Samuel**
MON	Carrickaderry	**Lucas William**
ANT	Lambeg North	**Lucen Samuel**
WEX	Martingalls	**Ludlow William**
MEA	Broad	**Lum**
KKY	Rathcubbin	**Lunnire John (?)**
CRK	bo./ Carberry EW	**Lupton Mary**
DWN	Ballywalter	**Lusk Arthur**
TIP	Annaghnerigge *	**Luster John**
KILD	Tomard	**Lutrell Alex**
LAO	Tonfarna	**Lutteral David**
KILD	Tomard	**Luttrell Andrew**
DUB	Diswellstown	**Luttrell Hon Simon**
DUB	Luttrellstown	**Luttrell Robert**
DUB	Diswellstown	**Luttrell Simon**
WW	Ballybrittan *	**Lycester**
TIP	Clonmel	**Lycester James**
WAT	Clonmel	**Lycester James**
WAT	Clonmel	**Lycester William**
ARM	Armagh	**Lyle Alex**
ARM	Armagh	**Lyle Andrew**
LDY	Moneysharvan	**Lyle Archibald**
LDY	Mormeal	**Lyle Martha**
DON	Corcreggan	**Lyle Robert**
DON	Mullenigar Millacre	**Lyle Robert**
LDY	Brackfield	**Lyle Samuel**
LDY	Legaghory	**Lyle Samuel**
ANT	Knockanboy	**Lyle Thomas**
CLE	Tarmon	**Lyllis**
ARM	Tullyvallon	**Lymes James**
KILD	B'more Eustace	**Lynch**
CRK	Blarney	**Lynch**
WME	Carrrick	**Lynch**
KILD	Clonard	**Lynch**
WME	Cullenmore	**Lynch**
MON	Reduff	**Lynch**
CAV	Drummallaght	**Lynch Bryan**
LEI	Ballinamore Town	**Lynch Edw**
MYO	Turlough	**Lynch Eustace**
DON	Drumskellan	**Lynch Henry**
DUB	Dublin City	**Lynch J**
CRK	Youghal Town	**Lynch James**
WW	B'more Eustace	**Lynch James**
CAR	Carlow Town	**Lynch John**
LDY	Derrycrummy	**Lynch John**
MEA	Mentrim	**Lynch John**
TYR	Milltown	**Lynch John**
CAR	Carlow Town	**Lynch Joseph**
GAL	Galway Town	**Lynch Mark**
KKY	Callan Town	**Lynch Michael**
KKY	Town of Callan	**Lynch Michael**
GAL	Galway Town	**Lynch Michael M**
GAL	Kilkieran	**Lynch Nicholas**
GAL	Galway Town	**Lynch Patrick**
FER	Mullans	**Lynch Peter**
ROS	Mill Park Boyle Tn	**Lynch Stephen**
TIP	Rearoe	**Lynch William**
LAO	Cardtown	**Lynes**
DUB	Dublin City	**Lynham M**
LDY	Killure	**Lynn John**
CAR	Aghade	**Lynnan John**
MON	Drumgallan	**Lynton Elizabeth Spin.**
WAT	Garrancrobally	**Lyon**
TYR	Maccrackens	**Lyon George**
WAT	Garrancrobally	**Lyon Jno**
WAT	Waterford Town	**Lyons**
LOU	Tullyallan	**Lyons Anne**
LIM	Bruree	**Lyons Barry**
MEA	Clonguiffin	**Lyons Charles**
WME	Kilbeggan	**Lyons Henry**
ANT	Old Park	**Lyons Henry**
DWN	Ballymacarn	**Lyons James**
LIM	Croom	**Lyons James D**
OFF	Doon (? Qns)	**Lyons John**
OFF	Doon Demesne	**Lyons John**
DWN	Drumbo	**Lyons John**
WAT	Garrancrobally	**Lyons John**
WAT	Garrancrobally	**Lyons Mary (Rogers)**
ROS	Derreenavoggy	**Lyons Myles**
LAO	Ironmills / Kilrush	**Lyons Myles**
LOU	Drogheda Town	**Lyons Peter**
LOU	Tullyallan	**Lyons Peter**
CRK	Knocknahoigane	**Lyons Thomas**
DWN	Drumbo	**Lyons William**
CLE	Caheraderry	**Lysaght Henry**
KKY	Fassadineen	**Lyster Charles**
KKY	Kilrush	**Lyster Charles**
CAR	Bendinstown	**Lyster Edmund**
TIP	Derrinsallow	**Lyster H**
TIP	Millpark	**Lyster Hamilton**
ROS	Athleague Manor	**Lyster John**
ROS	Athleague Manor	**Lyster Margaret**
CRK	Ballynahallisk	**Lyster Philip**
LAO	Cardtown	**Lyster Richard**
MYO	Milltown	**Lyster Thomas**
KKY	Clonmantagh Lowe	**Lyster William**

CO.	TOWNLAND	MILLER
TIP	Derinsallow	**Lyster William**
LDY	Culnady	**Lytle James**
LDY	Tullyheran	**Lytle James**
		M
DUB	Palmerston Lr	**M M`Garry Esq**
LDY	Tirekeran	**M`Alister Alexander**
ANT	Ballypatrick	**M`Aulay James**
DON	Ballyconnelly	**M`Aulay John**
FER	Belleek Town	**M`Birney David**
DON	Corraine	**M`Brerety Patrick**
DUB	Stephenstown	**M`Cabe Patrick**
ANT	Shankill T`parks	**M`Cammon Thomas**
LDY	Cregg	**M`Candless Thomas**
MEA	Clontail	**M`Cann John**
DUB	Kimmage	**M`Cann Mr**
ANT	Bracknamuckley	**M`Caw Thos**
DON	Tullywee	**M`Clay James**
TYR	Mullaghteige	**M`Clean Frederick**
SLI	Barnaderg	**M`Clean Thomas**
LDY	Ardmore	**M`Clelland Cary**
LDY	Ballymore	**M`Clelland James**
DON	Lurgy	**M`Clintock Sam**
DON	Lurgy	**M`Clintock Sam**
ANT	Legoneil WolfHill	**M`Clure Thomas**
LDY	Fincarn	**M`Cluskey Denis**
ANT	Belfast Town	**M`Connell William**
ANT	Tawnybrack	**M`Cord & Smith**
ANT	Connor	**M`Cormack Fran**
DON	Dreenan	**M`Cormack Saml**
LDY	Walworth	**M`Cormack William**
MEA	Martinstown	**M`Cormick Michael**
DUB	Knock	**M`Cormick Mr**
LDY	Craig	**M`Corstin George**
FER	Cavancarragh	**M`Court Patrick**
LDY	Ballyknock	**M`Coy Michael**
LONG	Smear	**M`Coy Thomas**
ANT	Belfast Town	**M`Cracken John**
DUB	Oldbawn	**M`Cracken John**
ANT	Belfast Town	**M`Cracken Margaret**
KILD	Carrigeen	**M`Cracken Peter**
ANT	Belfast Town	**M`Cracken William**
DUB	Dublin City	**M`Cready Edward**
FER	Drumadraghy	**M`Cready James**
GAL	Streamstown	**M`Creight James**
ANT	Belfast Town	**M`Crum John**
MEA	Staleen	**M`Cullagh Peter**
ANT	Shankill T`parks	**M`Cullough William**
TIP	Springhouse	**M`Curtin William**
GAL	Reynclamber	**M`Dermot John**
GAL	Ballycahill	**M`Dermot Martin**
DUB	Ballyboden	**M`Donagh John**
DUB	Killeen	**M`Donnell Chris**
TYR	Edergoole Lower	**M`Donnell James**
CAR	Rathcrogue	**M`Donnell John**
DUB	Saggart	**M`Donnell John**

CO.	TOWNLAND	MILLER
DUB	Templeogue	**M`Donnell Joseph**
DUB	Rathcreedan	**M`Donnell Mary A**
DUB	Oldbawn	**M`Donnell Michael**
DUB	Lucan	**M`Donnell Mr**
DUB	Templeogue	**M`Donnell Mr**
SLI	Shannon Oughter	**M`Donnell Thomas**
DUB	Backwestonpark	**M`Donnell William**
GAL	Baunyknav	**M`Donogh Conr.**
ANT	Ballymagarry	**M`Ewan John**
LDY	Muladonagh	**M`Fadden Archibald**
MEA	Corballis	**M`Garry Michael**
DON	Rath	**M`Gee William**
DON	Ardhane	**M`Gettigan**
DON	Ballyheerin	**M`Glinchy**
DON	Carrick	**M`Grenra Patrick**
GAL	Eskerroe	**M`Guire Luke**
LDY	Tamniaran	**M`Hugh Edward**
SLI	Collinsford	**M`Hugh Michael**
ANT	Belfast Town	**M`Ilroy Archibald**
DUB	Glasnevin	**M`Ilwrath Mr**
SLI	Scardanmore	**M`Intyre Alex**
LDY	Culrow	**M`Intyre William**
ANT	Edenderry	**M`Kavanagh John**
LDY	Clagan	**M`Keever John**
MEA	Mullaghwillin	**M`Kenna John**
DON	Knockbrack	**M`Kenny Henry**
DON	Knockbrack	**M`Kenny Henry**
SLI	Moygara	**M`Keown James**
LDY	Gobnascale	**M`Kinlay John**
ANT	Dunturkey	**M`Kinstry Thomas**
GAL	Galway T`nsparks	**M`Laughlin Lo`lan**
LDY	Ballynaheery	**M`Leod James**
LDY	Ballynaheery	**M`Leod William**
DON	Drumlonagher	**M`Logue Anthony**
DON	Donegal	**M`Loone Anthony**
ANT	Carnlough Town	**M`Loughlin Honoria**
FER	Tonity Bog	**M`Mahon John**
ANT	Belfast Town	**M`Millan Neil**
DUB	Corkagh	**M`Nally Mr**
DUB	Dublin Cityk Ward	**M`Nally Thomas**
MEA	Clowanstown	**M`Namara Patrick**
ANT	Ballybogy	**M`Naughten Catherine**
TYR	Milltown	**M`Neill Godfrey**
FER	Tonystick	**M`Neill Joseph**
LDY	Lismacarol	**M`Pherson Joseph**
LDY	Bellarena	**M`Quaid William**
TYR	Edernagh	**M`Reynolds Thomas**
LDY	Ardmore	**M`Rory Robert**
ANT	Creevamoy	**Mabin Patrick**
LDY	Granacohan	**MacAnellagh James**
DUB	Leabstown	**Macarell John**
ANT	Carrickfergus Tn	**MacArtney**
ANT	Dervog	**Macartney Catharnack**
ANT	Antrim Town	**Macartney Geo**
SLI	Sligo Town	**Macartney James Hon.**
MON	Ballynode	**Macash Daniel**

CO.	TOWNLAND	MILLER
FER	Rossole	**Macaulay John**
ANT	Larne Town	**Macaulay Robert**
DWN	Drumcaw	**Macauley William**
DWN	Knockstickeen	**Macauley William**
DON	Millsesalagh	**MacBith Andrew**
DON	Millsesalagh	**MacBith Andrew**
CAV	Clifferna	**MacChop John**
DUB	Templeogue	**MacDonnel Joseph**
DON	Cloon	**MacFarland Mr**
ARM	Carnally	**MacGeough Robert**
CLE	Ballycline River	**Macghee John**
KRY	Cagrigh *	**Machien Arthur**
DWN	Ballygowan	**Mackay**
ANT	Mosside	**Mackay Hugh**
ANT	Dervock town	**Mackay Hugh B**
DUB	Palmerstown	**Macken James**
TYR	Donaghmore	**Mackenzie**
TYR	Tullinure *	**Mackenzie**
TYR	Tempanroe	**Mackenzie**
TYR	Donaghmore	**Mackenzie Alex**
TYR	Killymam	**Mackenzie Alex**
KKY	Graguenakill	**Mackesy George**
KKY	Graguenakill	**Mackesy George**
KKY	Kilmacow	**Mackey Andrew**
KKY	Kilmacow	**Mackey Andrew**
KKY	Kilmacow	**Mackey John**
KKY	Kilmacow	**Mackey John**
KKY	Kilmacow	**Mackey John**
ANT	Ballysillan	**Mackey Mr**
TYR	Moylagh	**Mackey Samuel**
LDY	Tirkeeran	**Mackey William**
DON	Lishill	**Mackin Mr**
DON	Leitter *	**Mackinnon Wm**
DON	Maghery *	**Mackinnon Wm**
DON	Oiley *	**Mackinnon Wm**
CAV	Curraghmore	**MacKlern Robert**
MON	Tamlat	**MacKlim Robert**
MON	Aghnagap	**Macklin Samuel**
LDY	Tirkeeran	**Macky Patrick**
LDY	Tirkeeran	**Macky Patrick**
LDY	Ballyness	**Macky Robert**
DWN	Ballyroney	**Maclinchy John**
DWN	Tullylish	**Macolmson Thomas**
DUB	Templeogue	**Maconchy Charles**
LIM	Ballyclough	**Maconchy John**
LONG	Gaigue	**Maconchy John**
MEA	Navan Town	**Maconchy John A**
KRY	Shanakeale	**Maconochie**
FER	Cavancarragh	**Macort Patrick**
DWN	Quoile	**Macoubry**
ARM	Ballyards	**Macquay James**
DUB	Donnybrook Lr	**Madden**
MYO	Milltown	**Madden Daniel**
KKY	Buston Mills	**Madden Hugh**
DUB	Templogue	**Madden James**
DUB	Woodmills	**Madden James**

INDEX

CO.	TOWNLAND	MILLER
ARM	Ballynahone More	**Mathews Joseph**
TIP	Castlelake	**Mathews Mary Mrs.**
MON	Creeve	**Matier Daniel**
GAL	Clonmore	**Matt Donoghoe**
KILD	Pluckerstown	**Matther Simon**
WAT	Millerstown	**Matthew George**
KILD	Pluckerstown	**Matthew Isaac**
LAO	Aughnahorna	**Matthews**
ARM	Crossdened	**Matthews**
ARM	Knockbane	**Matthews**
ARM	Unshog	**Matthews**
DWN	Ballywalter	**Matthews George**
TYR	Aughnacloy	**Matthews John**
ARM	Ballymahon More	**Matthews Joseph**
TIP	Baurstooken	**Matthews Margaret**
TIP	Burnstookeen	**Matthews Margaret**
TIP	Castleflake	**Matthews Mary**
LDY	Lettermuck	**Matthews Robert**
ARM	Copes Mill	**Maturin**
LAO	Timahoe	**Maturin**
ARM	Townland ?	**Maturin William**
TIP	Clonmel	**Maude**
WAT	Suir Island	**Maude Sir C**
TIP	Clonmel	**Maude Sir Cornwallis**
KILD	Clane	**Maughan**
LDY	Altagasky *	**Mauleverer Bellingham**
LDY	Ballygurk	**Mauleverer Bellingham**
LDY	Bellaghy	**Mauleverer Bellingham**
LIM	Askeaton	**Maunsell**
CLE	Rossmadda	**Maunsell Dorothea**
LAO	Ballyger	**Maunsell Jno**
LAO	Ballyger	**Maunsell John**
TIP	Polloghbane *	**Maunsell John**
LIM	Caherass	**Maunsell William Reeves**
MYO	Rathscanlon	**Maunteen Patrick**
DUB	Whitechurch	**Maura Mullarney**
MEA	Bedlow`s Mill	**Maxton William**
MEA	Townland ?	**Maxton William**
DWN	Ballyhalbert	**Maxwell**
DWN	Ballyharley	**Maxwell**
TYR	Claudy *	**Maxwell**
LOU	Thomastown	**Maxwell**
DON	Altaghaderry	**Maxwell Alex**
DON	Garvary	**Maxwell Annabella**
DWN	Ballyherly	**Maxwell Benjamin**
MON	Greenmount	**Maxwell Edward**
CAV	Drumbarry	**Maxwell Henry**
CAV	Corbeagh	**Maxwell Henry Rev**
LONG	Cullynore	**Maxwell Henry Rev.**
CAV	Drumbarry	**Maxwell Henry Rev.**
MON	Bradoge/ Braddock	**Maxwell John**
MON	Greenmount	**Maxwell John**
MON	Tullynanure	**Maxwell John**
DWN	Finnabrogue	**Maxwell John W**
TYR	Kilfaddy *	**Maxwell John W.**
TYR	Drumlegagh	**Maxwell Joseph**

CO.	TOWNLAND	MILLER
ARM	Ballyards	**Maxwell Margaret**
DWN	Ballyholme	**Maxwell Robert**
LIM	Croom	**Maxwell Robert**
DON	Garvary	**Maxwell Robert**
TYR	Kilfaddy *	**Maxwell Robt.**
DWN	Ballyherly	**Maxwell William**
ANT	Carrickferfus Tn	**Maxwell William**
KRY	Knockreer	**May Charles**
WAT	Mayfield	**May Edward**
DWN	Ballygowan	**May Edward Rev.**
LDY	Ballyness	**May Edward Yngr.**
WAT	Waterford Town	**May James**
KRY	Dromaturk	**Mayberry George**
TYR	Aughamullin	**Mayne John**
CRK	bo./ Barrymore	**Mayne Sara**
WME	Monksland	**Mayo Lord**
WAT	Waterford City	**Mayor Waterford**
DWN	Welshtown	**Mayra Castle**
DWN	Welshtown	**Mayra Castle**
ARM	Ballynahone Beg	**Mazur Barth**
ANT	Cushendall	**Mc Donald R**
MYO	Ballyguin	**McAdam James**
CLE	Rossmadda	**McAdam Thomas**
LOU	Thomastown	**McAlister**
LDY	Killyvally	**McAlister Alexander**
LOU	Cambrickville	**McAlister James**
ANT	Currysheskin	**McAlister John**
DWN	Ballydugan	**McAlister Peter**
ANT	Lubitavish	**McAllister Alex**
ARM	Mullaglass	**McAllister Alex**
ANT	Lubitavish	**McAllister James**
ANT	Ballaghmore	**McAnally Robert Dr.**
LOU	Castletown	**M'Cann Richard**
LOU	Jenkinstown	**McArdle Edward**
CRK	Maulnarouga	**M'Carty Daniel**
ANT	Vow	**McAuley Alex**
FER	Rossole	**McAuley John**
ANT	Carrickfergus Tn	**McAuliffe George**
LIM	Knockbrack	**McAuliffe John**
CLE	Townland ?	**McAuliffe Synan**
DWN	Derryneill	**McAvoy Bernard**
DWN	Magherana	**M'Caw Joseph**
CLE	Ennis Town	**McBeath John**
FER	Drumbadmeen	**McBiren William**
FER	Rathmore	**McBirney**
DON	Rathbalskinney *	**McBirney David**
ANT	Dunminning	**McBirnie Thomas**
DWN	Moneyslane	**McBride James**
ARM	Allistragh	**McBride Robert**
ARM	Allistragh	**McBride Robert**
ARM	Crankey	**McBride Robert**
ANT	Ballycarry	**McBride Wm Alex**
DWN	Glassdrumman	**McBurnet Alex**
DWN	Carsonstown	**McBurney Alex**
DWN	Ballyhenry	**McBurney Thomas**
CAV	Knockataggart	**McCabe Edward**

CO.	TOWNLAND	MILLER
CAV	Carrickatobber	**McCabe James**
CAV	Carrickatober	**McCabe James**
CAV	Cleggan	**McCabe James**
CAV	Carrickatobber	**McCabe John**
CAV	Knockataggart	**McCabe John**
CAV	Knockataggart	**McCabe John]**
MON	Inishkeen	**McCabe Owen**
DUB	Stephenstown	**McCabe Patrick**
ARM	Lisavague	**McCaffrey**
DWN	Shanaghan	**McCaffrey Daniel**
MON	Rafeenan	**McCague Andrew**
MON	Rafeenan	**McCague John**
WME	Coolure	**McCaily**
ARM	Aughnagurgan	**McCaldin William**
ARM	Darkley	**McCaldin William**
ARM	Dundrum	**McCaldin William**
DWN	Ballydugan	**McCall Helena**
DUB	Glasnevin	**McCally Thomas**
ANT	Callisnagh	**McCambridge Arch**
DWN	Annadorn	**McCammon Andrew**
DWN	Edendarrif	**McCammon David**
DWN	Drumgooland	**McCammon John**
DWN	Ballygowan	**McCamon William**
ARM	Lurgyvallon	**McCan**
MON	Aghnagap	**McCanagh Bern**
ANT	Englishtown	**McCance**
DWN	Balleevy	**McCance John**
DWN	Ballyvally	**McCance John**
DWN	Ballyvally	**McCance John**
ANT	Dunmurry	**McCance John W S**
DWN	Ballyvally	**McCance Sarah (Law)**
LDY	Cregg	**McCandless Thomas**
DON	Corcreggan	**McCandlish John**
DON	Kilmackilloo	**McCandlish John**
LOU	Ardee	**McCann**
LOU	Drogheda Town	**McCann**
LOU	Drogheda Town	**McCann Ann**
LOU	Ardee	**McCann Anne**
MEA	Navan Town	**McCann James**
LOU	Beamond Mills	**McCann John**
MEA	Beaumont	**McCann John**
LOU	Drogheda Town	**McCann John**
MEA	Rathnally	**McCann John**
LONG	Tennalick	**McCann John**
TYR	Gortnaskea	**McCann Margt. ors Gillespie**
LONG	Tennalick	**McCann Mrs. Widow**
LOU	Grange	**McCann Neill**
TYR	Gortnaskea	**McCann Robert**
MEA	Navan Town	**McCann Thomas**
MEA	Navan Town	**McCann Thos**
ARM	Tamlaght	**McCarragher John**
DWN	Ballydugan	**McCartan**
DWN	Backaderry	**McCartan James**
LOU	Skibbolmore	**McCartan John**
TYR	Coagh	**McCarter**
LONG	Longford Town	**McCarthy Amarill**

INDEX

CO.	TOWNLAND	MILLER
ANT	Ballydonnelly	**McCulloch John**
ARM	Carnally	**McCullough John**
ARM	Mountnorris	**McCullough John**
ARM	Broughan	**McCullough Joseph**
CAV	Glasleck	**McCullough Joseph**
ARM	Armagh	**McCully Robert**
LDY	Coleraine Town	**McCurdy Jno**
TIP	Kilshane	**McCurtin William**
KILD	Clonard	**McCutchen**
DUB	Donnybrook	**McDaniel Christopher**
WEX	Castlehayestown	**McDaniel John**
WME	Glenidan	**McDaniel Thomas**
CAR	Carlow Town	**McDaniel Wm**
TIP	Longford	**McDawson John Rev.**
LONG	Shrule	**McDermot Christopher**
WEX	Cloonagloose	**McDermot Denis**
WEX	Coolnagloose	**McDermot James**
LONG	Shrule	**McDermot Lucy**
MYO	Pollaweela	**McDermot Martin**
LONG	Garrynagh	**McDermott**
LONG	Shrule	**McDermott**
GAL	Ballycahill	**McDermott Brenoll**
ROS	Derreenavoggy	**McDermott Charles**
LONG	Garrynagh	**McDermott Lucy Spin.**
LONG	Shrule	**McDermott Michael**
CAV	Mulloghoran	**McDermott Thomas**
GAL	Ballinastack	**McDonagh**
GAL	Galway Town	**McDonagh**
GAL	Galway Town	**McDonagh Mathew**
GAL	Galway Town	**McDonagh Matt**
GAL	Pollboy	**McDonagh Walter**
ANT	Revallagh N	**McDonald Andrew**
WEX	Wexford Town	**McDonald Daniel**
WW	Townland ?	**McDonald Francis**
CLE	Derry	**McDonald George**
ANT	Donegore	**McDonell**
ANT	Donegore	**McDonell Thomas**
DUB	Willbrook	**McDonnall Thomas**
DWN	Banoge	**McDonnell**
CAR	Carlow Town	**McDonnell**
MYO	Clogher	**McDonnell**
MYO	Cloonagh	**McDonnell**
GAL	Milltown	**McDonnell**
DWN	Ballygowan	**McDonnell Alex**
ANT	Culbane	**McDonnell Bernard**
WW	Ballinacor North	**McDonnell Charles**
WW	Ballinaston	**McDonnell Chris**
DUB	Gallanstown	**McDonnell Chris**
ANT	Glenarm Dem.	**McDonnell Edward**
ROS	Rathardeigher	**McDonnell Edward**
GAL	Bullenfoule	**McDonnell Fr**
CLE	Derry	**McDonnell George**
DUB	Glasnevin	**McDonnell Henry**
DWN	Cloughy	**McDonnell Hugh**
TIP	Ballyhimiken	**McDonnell James**
TYR	Tempanroe	**McDonnell James**

CO.	TOWNLAND	MILLER
DUB	Woodlands	**McDonnell James**
ANT	Broughanlea	**McDonnell John**
ARM	Crossmaglen	**McDonnell John**
DUB	Saggart	**McDonnell John**
GAL	Galway Town	**McDonnell Mary J**
DUB	Willbrook	**McDonnell Matt**
ARM	Cashel	**McDonnell Michael**
DUB	Oldbawn	**McDonnell Michael**
ROS	Pollnamoghill	**McDonnell Michael**
CRK	Ballinluig W.	**McDonnell Owen**
MON	Clonlonan	**McDonnell Patrick**
MON	Clonlonan	**McDonnell Patrick Jun.**
ARM	Lurgyvallon	**McDonnell Randall**
ARM	Edenkennedy	**McDonnell Robert**
MYO	Toobracken	**McDonnell Roger**
MON	Drumcrue	**McDonnell Steph**
DWN	Cloughy	**McDonnell Thomas**
CRK	Bandon Town	**McDonnell William**
CAR	Carlow Town	**McDonnell William**
LONG	Loughsheedan	**McDonnnell Laurence**
LDY	Ballyness	**McDougal Joseph**
DWN	Balloo	**McDowell**
CAV	Drummany	**McDowell Charles**
ANT	Ballywillin	**McDowell George**
DWN	Ballymegenaghie *	**McDowell Henry Rev.**
ANT	Ballyhunsley	**McElfatrick**
ANT	Kingariff	**McElhatten Armour**
TYR	Clady	**McElhenny James**
ANT	Clorey	**McElherin**
DON	Ballyness	**Mcelroy Edward**
DWN	Ballygowan	**McElroy Elizabeth**
DWN	Ballygowan	**McElroy Hugh**
FER	Knocks	**McElroy J**
TYR	Tempanroe	**McElroy William**
CAV	Tonyin	**McEnteer Terence**
TYR	Tempanroe	**McEroy Patrick**
LOU	Liberties	**McEvitty**
MON	Carrickmacross	**McEvoy Thomas**
MON	Carrickmacross	**McEvoy Thomas**
LDY	Coleraine Town	**McFadden J**
LDY	Coleraine Town	**McFadden John**
ARM	Aghory	**McFaden James**
LDY	Aghadowey	**McFarland**
LDY	Ballybritain	**McFarland**
LDY	Mullan	**McFarland**
TYR	Faccary	**McFarland Charles**
DON	Cloon	**McFarland William**
ANT	Tullynamullan	**McFarlane Andrew**
DUB	Palmerstown	**McGarry Bernard**
ANT	Ballyvenagh	**McGarry Neal**
DUB	Ashtown	**McGary Michael**
LEI	Tullinwillin	**McGaughren**
ARM	Annaghmore	**McGeogh William**
DWN	Newry Town	**McGeorge James**
ARM	Annaghmare	**McGeough**
ANT	Ballypatrick	**McGildowney C**

CO.	TOWNLAND	MILLER
ANT	Ballypatrick	**McGildowney E**
ANT	Carey Mill	**McGildowney Edmond**
DON	Craig	**McGilivay Wid. Sid.**
LOU	Carstown	**McGill William**
KRY	Milltown	**McGillicuddy Daniel**
DON	Glenmanagh	**McGilligan Patrick**
DWN	Ballycopeland	**McGilteen James**
DWN	Killinchy	**McGilton Hugh**
MYO	Louisburgh Town	**McGin Patrick**
MYO	Louisburgh Town	**McGin Patrick Jun**
DON	Ture	**McGinagle Widow**
LOU	Dundalk Town	**McGinity & Co.**
MON	Carrickaderry	**McGinn Mary**
LOU	Belpatrick	**McGinnis Patrick**
MON	Killeevan	**McGinty**
MON	Killeevan	**McGinty - Irwin**
MON	Killiercrom *	**McGinty James**
DWN	Lisnaliggan	**McGivern John**
LOU	Collon	**McGivey Luke**
DON	Scotch *	**McGivin James**
LOU	Collon	**McGivney L**
LOU	Collon Town	**McGivney Luke**
DWN	Carrowvanny	**McGlennon Patkick**
DON	Ballyheerin	**McGlinchy John**
MON	Seaveagh	**McGlone Thomas**
CAV	Leiter	**McGlure Robert**
LONG	Shrule	**McGlynn Philip**
CRK	Milleenannig	**McGovern Henry**
ARM	Derrycughan	**McGowan**
ARM	Keadybegg	**McGowan**
ARM	Knockbeg	**McGowan**
DON	Starritstown	**McGowan Wm**
MYO	Creggagh	**McGraoil Jack**
MYO	Creggagh	**McGraoil James**
CAR	St Mullins	**McGrath**
WAT	Killadangan	**McGrath Catherine**
TIP	Townland ?	**McGrath James**
WAT	Crobally Lower	**McGrath John**
WAT	Killadangan	**McGrath Mary Widow**
TIP	Clonmel	**McGrath Terence**
SLI	Lark Hill	**McGrath Terence**
TIP	Ballingarry Lower	**McGrath Thomas**
MYO	Cuilmore	**McGrath Thomas**
CAR	Nurney	**McGrath William**
TYR	Coagh	**McGuckan Laurence**
TYR	Derrycrin Eglish	**McGuckin John**
ANT	Dreen	**McGuigan Arthur**
ANT	Dunmurry	**McGuigan Jn**
DWN	Ballymoney	**McGuiness Arthur**
CAV	Drumrae	**McGuire Con**
ARM	Lisdrumgullion	**McGuire Dennis**
ARM	Brook	**McGuire Thomas**
WAT	Garrancrobally	**McGuire William**
ROS	Sheepwalk	**McGunn James**
DWN	Downpatrick Town	**McGusty William**
MYO	Carrowkeel	**McHugh James**

CO.	TOWNLAND	MILLER
MYO	Millcross	**McHugh Patrick**
GAL	Kilcreevanty	**McHugh Redmond**
DON	Eighterross	**McIlhenny Alex**
ANT	Dungonnell	**McIlrath William**
OFF	Ballycommon Beg	**McIlray John**
OFF	Bracklin Big	**McIlroy Terence**
DWN	Killarn	**McIlwain William**
DON	Mullinbuoy Farm	**McIlwaine James**
DWN	Ballyharley	**McIlwaine Thomas**
DWN	Carrowreagh	**McIlwaine William**
ANT	Dungonnell	**McIlwrath Deb**
CLE	Ballymulcashel	**McInerney Patrick**
CAV	Tonyin	**McIntee Terence**
LDY	Londonderry	**McIntyre**
ANT	Kilnadore	**McIntyre James**
ARM	Darkley	**McKane Henry**
ARM	Crossdened	**McKane James**
ANT	Stranocum	**McKane Neill**
TYR	Benburb	**McKane Robert**
MON	Laragh	**McKean Eliza**
MON	Corncarrow	**McKean Elizabeth**
ARM	Keady	**McKean James**
ANT	Carrickfergus Tn	**McKean William**
ARM	Tassagh	**McKee J**
ARM	Coolmillish	**McKee Joseph**
ARM	Tassagh	**McKee Joseph**
DWN	Ballynaskeagh	**McKee Rev David**
ARM	Corkley	**McKee William**
TYR	Gortindarragh	**McKee William**
DWN	Tullykevin	**McKee William**
MON	Carnbane	**McKeever James**
ANT	Gloonan	**McKelvey James**
LDY	Cavanreagh	**McKelvey Neill**
TYR	Creeduff	**McKelvey William**
ANT	Currysheskin	**McKenkie N**
MEA	Brownstown	**McKenna**
MON	Roosky	**McKenna Cath Widow**
LDY	Ballyknock	**McKenna Cornelius**
ARM	Brook	**McKenna James**
MEA	Brownstown	**McKenna James**
KRY	Dingle Town	**McKenna James**
MON	Cavancope	**McKenna Jas Baron**
DUB	St Margarets	**McKenna Jno**
MEA	Balrath	**McKenna Margaret**
MEA	Brownstown	**McKenna Patrick**
MON	Cavancope	**McKenna Patrick**
ANT	Carnmoney	**McKenny**
LDY	Beech Hill *	**McKenny Patrick**
LDY	Beech Hill *	**McKenny Thomas**
TYR	Mullybrannon	**McKenzie Alex**
CAV	Clarebane	**McKeon Frans**
LOU	Kilcurly	**McKeon Messrs**
ANT	Seneirl	**McKeon William**
WME	Clonmore	**McKeown James**
FER	Curraghfad	**McKeown Johnston**
LOU	Kilcurly	**McKeown Miss**

CO.	TOWNLAND	MILLER
DWN	Annadorn	**McKibben**
DWN	Ballyaltikilligan	**McKibben Agnes**
DWN	Lough	**McKibbon**
DWN	Loughanisland	**McKibbon**
ANT	Eagry	**McKibbon James**
LONG	Aghnacliff	**McKiernan**
LDY	Monegram	**McKiney John**
TYR	Leckpatrick Town	**McKinley James**
DWN	Drumbane	**McKinley Jno**
DON	Castlefinn	**McKinley Robert**
KRY	Tullaree	**McKinna Thomas**
ANT	Carnmoney	**McKinney Thomas**
TYR	Tullynure	**McKinsey Anne**
ARM	Knockbeg	**McKinstry**
ARM	Lisavague	**McKinstry**
ARM	Lisinacartie	**McKinstry**
ARM	Ballymoran	**McKinstry James**
LOU	Carlingford	**McKivitt Mr**
DUB	Finglas	**McKowen Alex**
DUB	Finglas	**McKowen Thomas**
ANT	Carnlough South	**McLaughlin Charles**
WME	Sraneg	**McLaughlin Patrick**
LAO	Coolanowle	**McLaughlin Peter**
LONG	Creelaghta	**McLaughlin Peter**
ANT	Stranocum	**McLean James**
ARM	Aughnagurgan	**McLennan John**
ARM	Darkley	**McLennan John**
ARM	Dundrum	**McLennan John**
CAV	Shankill Lower	**McLennon Bernard**
CRK	Kinsale Town	**McLeod R**
GAL	Galway Town	**McLoone Anthony**
ROS	Castlecoote	**McLoughlin William Jn**
ROS	Castlereagh	**McLoughnin**
MON	Bellatrain	**McMahon**
CAV	Rassudan	**McMahon**
LAO	Ballyroan	**McMahon Arthur**
KILD	Kilcullen	**McMahon James**
ARM	Balleer	**McMahon John**
ARM	Balleer	**McMahon Johnston**
CLE	Dough	**McMahon Martin**
CRK	Kilcronan	**McMahon Michael**
KILD	Kilcullen	**McMahon Patrick**
CAV	Rassudan	**McMahon Patrick**
WEX	Enniscorthy Town	**McMahon Peter**
ANT	Millq`r Manybrook	**McManus**
LEI	Corraleehan	**McManus Cornelius**
LEI	Ballinamore Town	**Mcmanus Jno**
LONG	Kilshruly	**McManus Jno**
LOU	Dundalk Town	**McMaster Anna**
LOU	Dundalk Town	**McMaster Anna C**
DWN	Loughans	**McMaster J**
DWN	Gilford Town	**McMaster James**
DWN	Loughans	**McMaster James**
DWN	Gilford Town	**McMaster Jno**
LOU	DundalkTown	**McMaster John**
LOU	DundalkTown	**McMaster William**

CO.	TOWNLAND	MILLER
DWN	Balloo	**McMath**
MON	Dromore	**McMath**
MON	Drumagelvin	**McMath**
MON	Drumleig	**McMath**
MON	Fermilly	**McMath**
MON	Aghadreenan	**McMath Hamilton**
MON	Aghadreenan	**McMath Mr**
DWN	Downpatrick Town	**McMechan Elizabeth**
DWN	Downpatrick Town	**McMechan James**
ANT	(bo. BELFAST)	**McMeekin William**
ANT	Culbane	**McMichael Anne**
TYR	Corrogan Water	**McMinn Samuel**
ARM	Tullymoreetra	**McMorran Edward**
ARM	Tullymoreetra	**McMorran James**
MON	Tenary	**McMorran John**
ARM	Tullymoreetra	**McMorran Widow I**
ANT	Cleggan	**McMullan John**
DWN	Ballooly More	**McMullen Daniel**
DWN	Shanrod	**McMullen Daniel**
TYR	Tullynincrin	**McMullen Gilbert**
ROS	Crannagh	**McMullen Irvine T**
DWN	Drumskee	**McMullen Joseph**
CRK	Mallow Town	**McMullen Josh**
CRK	Mallow Town	**McMullen Joshua**
DWN	Kearney	**McMullen William**
CRK	Quartertown	**McMullins Joseph**
ARM	Claddymore	**McMurdry Thomas**
ARM	Derrycughan	**McMurray**
DWN	Carrownacaw	**McMurray John**
KILD	Parsonstown	**McMurray Mary (Hobart)**
ANT	Carrickfergus Tn	**McMurray Robert**
DWN	Ballyinran	**McMurray Samuel**
DWN	Bangor Town	**McMurray Samuel**
DWN	Dromore Town	**McMurray Thomas**
DWN	Quilly	**McMurray William**
ARM	Tullymore	**McMurren**
WAT	Waterford City	**McMurren Henry**
DWN	Drumaghlis	**McMurry David**
ANT	Marshalstown	**McMurtry Jo`na**
ANT	Dunturkey	**McMurtry William**
LONG	Roseduff	**McNaboe Francis**
ARM	Lisdrumgullion	**McNaghten Rowan**
ARM	Copes Mill	**McNaghton Francis**
DUB	Fairview	**McNally Michael**
ANT	Lisburn Tn`parks	**McNally Willaim**
FER	Cloy	**McNalty M**
SLI	Curraghnagap	**McNama John**
CLE	Ballykilty	**McNamara**
MEA	Monktown	**McNamara Chris**
CLE	Ballycorney	**McNamara Danl**
TIP	Gorteenraine	**McNamara James**
KILD	Old Abbey	**McNamara Laur**
CRK	Carrigtishane	**McNamarra**
LDY	Coleraine Town	**McNaughten Barth.**
LDY	Kirkistown	**McNaughton Barth.**
ANT	Culbane	**McNaughton Jane**

CO.	TOWNLAND	MILLER
ANT	Ballyness	**McNaul Robert**
DWN	Ballystockart	**McNeale Daniel**
ANT	Kilwaughter	**McNeale Henry**
LDY	Coleraine Town	**McNeale Jno**
LOU	Ballymascanlan	**McNeale Wolfe**
LDY	Altagasky *	**McNeil Archibald**
LOU	Aghaboys	**McNeill John**
ANT	Ballynacaird	**McNeill Andrew**
LDY	Altagasky *	**McNeill Archibald**
LDY	Coleraine Town	**McNeill Jno**
ANT	Ballindam	**McNeill John**
DON	Craig	**McNickle Robert**
ARM	Tullymore Etrce	**McNorden**
ARM	Tullymore Etrce	**McNorden Widow**
ANT	Ballykeel	**McPeake William**
ANT	Old Park	**McPherson Dug**
DON	Kildrum	**McPherson Mr**
CAR	Carlow Town	**McPherson William**
ANT	Springmount	**McQuade William**
CAV	Leighan	**McQuaid James**
MON	Roosky	**McQuaid John**
ARM	Moneyquin	**McQuaide**
ARM	Ballyards	**McQuay James**
ARM	Ballyloughan	**McQuillan Ephraim**
DON	Carrigans	**McRea James**
LDY	Culnagrew	**McReynolds Thomas**
DWN	Baven	**McRobert James**
DWN	Magheralagan	**McRoberts James**
DWN	Rademan	**McRoberts James**
DWN	Downpatrick Town	**McRoberts John**
DWN	Listooder	**McRoberts John**
DWN	Magheralagan	**McRoberts John**
DWN	Rademan	**McRoberts John**
LDY	Ardmore	**McRory Robert**
ARM	Tullyvallon	**McShane**
KRY	Ballincarrig West	**McSherry Bryan**
KRY	Ballincarrig West	**McSherry Michael**
LDY	Derrylane	**McSparran John Arch**
CRK	Carrigrohan	**McSweeny Augustus**
CAR	Carlow Town	**McSweeny Marion**
KRY	Ardagh	**McSweeny Roger**
DWN	Longlands	**McTeer Alex**
CAR	Ballykeenan	**McTeir James**
LEI	Killavoggy	**McTiernan Edward**
LEI	Acre Park Five	**McTiernan J**
LEI	Creaneleagh	**McTiernan J**
LEI	Creaneleagh Abbe'	**McTiernan J**
GAL	Eden Hill	**McTighe John**
SLI	Drimina	**McVey James**
ANT	Calisnagh *	**McVicker Donald**
ANT	Moylarg	**McVicker John**
ANT	Aghislone	**McWaters John**
MON	Drumleck	**McWatty James**
LAO	Grange	**McWay Murtagh**
ARM	Ballynahone Beg	**McWilliams George**
ARM	Armagh	**McWilliams James**

CO.	TOWNLAND	MILLER
WW	Ballinastoe	**M'Donnell Christopher**
LAO	Mounteagle	**M'Donnell Mary**
DUB	Dublin City	**Mead Patrick**
LDY	Ballykellaghan	**Meade Jane**
LEI	Limerick Manor	**Meade Richard**
CRK	Ballindresrough	**Meade Richard Rev**
LAO	Coolkerry	**Meagher Thomas**
MON	Darraghlan	**Meakin Samuel**
TYR	Ballygawly	**Means Alexander**
CLE	Tarmon	**Meany James**
TIP	Summerhill	**Meara John**
MON	Annaveagh	**Mears Abraham**
DUB	Island R. Liffey	**Mears Charles**
MON	Annaveagh	**Mears John**
MON	Annaveagh	**Mears Samuel**
MON	Annaveagh	**Mears William**
LDY	Ballyartan	**Meath Bishop**
LDY	Killyvally	**Meath Bishop**
DWN	Bleary & B'doogan	**Meath Bishop Ralph Rev.**
WW	Ballinvally	**Meath James**
ANT	Lismacloskey	**Meath Ld. Bishop**
WW	Broomfield	**Meath Robert**
DUB	Dub Port & Cem.	**Mecredy Isabella**
WAT	Mayfield	**Medlicott**
WAT	Mayfield	**Medlicott Jno Thomas**
WAT	Mayfield	**Medlicott John T**
MYO	Newport	**Medlycott - O`Donnell**
MYO	Newport	**Medlycott John**
MYO	Newport	**Medlycott Thos John**
ARM	Ballynahone	**Mee**
DON	Mountcharles	**Meehan Hugh**
LDY	Clooney	**Meehan John**
LDY	Waterside	**Meehan John**
TIP	Camus	**Meehan Patrick**
CRK	Kilcully	**Meenan Cornelius**
DWN	Ballykinler Upr	**Megaw Bernard**
DWN	Grangewalls	**Megrann William**
GAL	Trean Park	**Mehan James**
CAR	Ballyknockan	**Meighan Patrick**
TIP	Mullauns	**Meihin John**
DUB	Palmerstown	**Meldon James**
GAL	Galway Town	**Meldon James D**
CAR	Ballygowan	**Meldon John**
GAL	Athenry Town	**Meldon Joseph**
MON	Seaveagh	**M'Elhone Arthur**
KILD	Athy Town	**Melia William+B56**
KKY	Warrington	**Mellea Still**
ANT	Marshalstown	**Melville William**
CRK	Reanascreena	**Mennis Hanora**
CRK	Reanascreena	**Mennis Michael**
CRK	Reen (2)	**Mennis Michael**
DUB	Swords	**Meras Mr**
CAR	Carlow Town	**Mercer**
CAR	Leighlandbridge	**Mercer**
DUB	Dunsoghly Mnr	**Mercer William**
ARM	Annsborough	**Mercer Ann**

CO.	TOWNLAND	MILLER
DWN	Drumbo	**Mercer Henry**
CAR	Bagnelstown	**Mercer Mounclierr**
CAR	Bagnelstown	**Mercer Richard**
CAR	Ballynebranagh	**Mercer Richard**
DWN	Cabragh	**Mercer Richard**
DUB	Wey Mills	**Mercer William**
LDY	Granacohan	**Mercers` Co.**
DWN	Loughans	**Mercier David**
DWN	Moyallan	**Mercier David**
KILD	Athy Town	**Meredith**
KILD	B`more Eustace	**Meredith**
CAR	Poorestown *	**Meredith**
DWN	Downpatrick Town	**Meredith Henry**
WW	B'more Eustace	**Meredith Joseph**
LAO	Cloondarrig	**Meredith S**
WW	B'more Eustace	**Meredith Susanna**
LAO	Cloondarrig	**Meredith T**
LOU	Ardee Town	**Meredith William**
DWN	Downpatrick Town	**Meredyth Harrietta A**
DWN	Downpatrick Town	**Meredyth Henrietta**
DWN	Magheralagan	**Meredyth Henry**
DWN	Downpatrick Town	**Meredyth Henry B**
KILD	Pluckerstown	**Meredyth Josh**
DWN	Downpatrick Town	**Meredyth Sir Henry**
KILD	Pluckerstown	**Meredyth Susanna**
WW	Blessington	**Merrey William**
WAT	Adamstown	**Merrick**
LDY	Altagasky *	**Merrifield Thos Rev.**
WAT	Carrickcastle	**Merrigan Michael**
WME	Rathbennett	**Mervyn**
WME	Gilbertstown	**Mervyn Arthur**
WME	Hill	**Mervyn Arthur**
MEA	Naul	**Mervyn Arthur**
MEA	Stonestown	**Mervyn Arthur**
MEA	Stonestown	**Mervyn Charles**
FER	Dooederny	**Mervyn Henry**
MEA	Stonestown	**Mervyn James**
DUB	Dundrum	**Meyler George**
LOU	Ardree	**Meyler Jno**
CAR	Carlow Town	**Meyler John**
DON	Maghery *	**MGarvey John**
WW	Killabeg	**M'Guire Patrick**
MON	Tievanely	**M'Guire Terence**
TIP	Tipperary Town	**Michael Coleman**
CAR	Craans	**Michael H. Watt**
DON	Kinaderry	**Michael Martin**
KKY	Gorteens	**Michael Murphy**
MEA	Kilnagross	**Michael Patrick**
GAL	Galway Town	**Michell Anne (Crawford)**
CAR	Carlow Town	**Michell George**
CAR	Carlow Town	**Michell Juliana Hon.**
LAO	Rathendock	**Middleton**
DWN	Cabragh	**Middleton Alan Hon.Visc.**
DUB	Shanganagh	**Middleton Alfred**
DWN	Cabragh	**Middleton Ann Hon. Lady**
WAT	Aglish	**Middleton Anne**

CO.	TOWNLAND	MILLER
DWN	Drumbane	Monroe Daniel
KKY	Maddoxtown	Monsarrat N
CLE	Ballykilty	Monsello William
WAT	Shanakill	Montague Jno
CAR	Shagten *	Montague Lord Henry
ANT	Lisnamurrikin	Montford John
LOU	Ardee	Montgomery
DWN	Ballydugan	Montgomery
OFF	Bracknagh	Montgomery
FER	Clohonan *	Montgomery
LDY	Coleraine Town	Montgomery
FER	Derrihalla	Montgomery
FER	Dooederny	Montgomery
FER	Drumawillin	Montgomery
CAV	Drumsillagh	Montgomery
ROS	Fuerty	Montgomery
FER	Island *	Montgomery
LDY	Kirkistown	Montgomery
DWN	Loughanisland	Montgomery
DWN	Nutgrove	Montgomery
KILD	Oldtown	Montgomery
KILD	Osberstown	Montgomery
LOU	Ardee Town	Montgomery Alex
ANT	Straidhaven	Montgomery Alex
KILD	Blackchurch	Montgomery Andrew
DWN	Magheradrool	Montgomery Arth H
MON	Creeve	Montgomery Arthur
ANT	Broughshane Upr	Montgomery Charles
ANT	Buckna	Montgomery Charles
DWN	Ballywalter	Montgomery Eliza
DWN	Greyabbey	Montgomery Elizabeth
CAR	Carlow Town	Montgomery Francis
TYR	Carnagatt	Montgomery Geo Sir
FER	Derrihalla	Montgomery Hercules
ANT	Ballyneely Upr	Montgomery Hugh
ANT	Dunaird	Montgomery Hugh
LDY	Coleraine Town	Montgomery Huugh
DWN	Greyabbey	Montgomery James
KILD	Annsborough *	Montgomery Jno
ANT	Ballyboggy	Montgomery John
CRK	Ballygarvan	Montgomery John
ANT	Breckagh	Montgomery John
DUB	Drumcondra	Montgomery Mr
DWN	Ballyhemlin	Montgomery Nathaniel
TYR	Cullynane	Montgomery Reps.
LOU	Ardee Town	Montgomery Richard
LDY	Coleraine Town	Montgomery Robert
DON	Convoy	Montgomery Robert
DON	Convoy Town	Montgomery Robt
DON	Wilson`s Mill	Montgomery Robt
LDY	Ardkill	Montgomery Sir Wiliam
LOU	Ardee Town	Montgomery Sophia
ARM	Aughnacloy	Montgomery Thomas
LIM	Ballindra *	Montgomery Thomas
ANT	Ballynacaird	Montgomery Thomas
FER	Derrihalla	Montgomery Thomas
KILD	Annsborough *	Montgomery William
DWN	Ardglass	Montgomery William
DWN	Ballylisbredan	Montgomery William
DWN	Ballywalter	Montgomery William
DON	Raymoghy	Montgomery Wm
DUB	Rathfarnham	Moody Jno
ARM	Lisraw	Moody John
DON	Kinnacally	Moody John
TYR	Drumlegagh	Moody Samuel
LONG	Ledwithstown	Moody William
ANT	Rashee	Moon William
ANT	Coggrey	Moone Wiliam
CLE	Inchiquin Manor	Mooney
OFF	Kilnagall	Mooney Andrew
OFF	Derryiron	Mooney John
LDY	Macosquin	Mooney John
KILD	Johnstown	Mooney Morgan
KILD	Haynestown	Mooney Mrs.
KILD	Mount Blarney *	Mooney Richard,
DUB	Edmondstown	Mooney Robert
CLE	Cloonomera	Mooney Thomas
CLE	Cloonomra	Mooney Thomas
OFF	Derryiron	Mooney Thomas
DON	Tullyhall	Moor Henry
ANT	Killyfad	Moor James
CRK	Ballinglanna	Moore
DWN	Balloo	Moore
LAO	Clonaslee	Moore
DUB	Dublin City	Moore
MEA	Milltown	Moore
DWN	Mountpanther	Moore
WME	Moyvore	Moore
LOU	Stephenstown	Moore
MYO	Turlough	Moore
LDY	Macknagh	Moore Alexander
ARM	Armagh Town	Moore Andrew
ANT	Broughshane Upr	Moore Archibald
TYR	Mulnahorn	Moore Cecil
WAT	Kilmacthomas	Moore Christopher
DON	Lurgy	Moore David
MEA	Calgath	Moore Denis
TYR	Aughnacloy	Moore Edward
CAR	Tullow	Moore Edward
CRK	Burranness	Moore Emanuel
ANT	Drumaheglis	Moore Fran
CAR	Carlow Town	Moore Garrett
ANT	Crookedstone	Moore George
MYO	Foxford	Moore George
ROS	Hatley *	Moore George
ROS	Hatley Manor *	Moore George
MEA	Julianstown	Moore George
ROS	Killakin *	Moore George
LIM	Ballindra *	Moore Henry
WME	Kibber	Moore Henry Hon. Dr.
WME	Tyrellspass	Moore Henry Rev.
TYR	Ballymagrane *	Moore Hugh
LOU	Carlingford Town	Moore Hugh
LOU	Yellowbatter	Moore Isaiah
LDY	Upperlands	Moore Jacob
ANT	Ballygomartin	Moore James
ANT	Ballymoney	Moore James
MYO	Belleek	Moore James
FER	Brookhill	Moore James
ANT	Carntall	Moore James
ANT	Chathamhall	Moore James
MYO	Clogher	Moore James
LDY	Coleraine Town	Moore James
DWN	Craigogantlet	Moore James
ANT	Crookedstone	Moore James
LDY	Loghran	Moore James
ANT	Shankill T`parks	Moore James
LDY	Tullans	Moore James Jun
ANT	Ballintoy Upr	Moore James S
MON	Caryaghlissanery	Moore Jno
DWN	Drumcaw	Moore Jno
MON	Lissanery	Moore Jno
DWN	Balloo	Moore John
DON	Ballycushion	Moore John
DWN	Ballymorran	Moore John
WW	Ballynultagh	Moore John
ANT	Ballysillan	Moore John
CRK	Cork City	Moore John
DWN	Dromore	Moore John
DWN	Greencastle	Moore John
LAO	Maryborough	Moore John
ANT	Mullaghduff	Moore John
CAR	Tullow	Moore John
LAO	Clonaslee	Moore John
ANT	Ballyboylands	Moore Lawrence
LAO	Ballyguille	Moore Lewis
DON	Milltown	Moore Margaret
MON	Annaghkilly	Moore Marshall
CRK	Bandon Town	Moore Mary
DUB	Knockengen	Moore Mr
CAV	Balloughly	Moore Patrick
CAV	Ballyloughly	Moore Patrick
LAO	Ironmills / Kilrush	Moore Patrick
WAT	Pilltown	Moore Peter
ROS	Hatley *	Moore Philip
WME	Moyvore	Moore Rev Henry
MYO	Brockagh	Moore Richard
ANT	Ballygowan	Moore Robert
ANT	Clogh Mills	Moore Sampson
LOU	Annaloughan	Moore Samuel
DUB	Milltown	Moore Samuel
MYO	Duckanelly	Moore Sir Hugh Jas
MON	Cossabey	Moore Thomas
LOU	Drogheda Town	Moore Thomas
WW	Kellynure	Moore Thomas
LOU	Yellowbatter	Moore Thomas
CRK	Baurleigh	Moore Walter B
DWN	Ballywalter	Moore William

CO.	TOWNLAND	MILLER
CLE	Cloonlaheen	**Muggevin Patrick**
CLE	Finor Bog	**Muggevin Patrick**
FER	Clohonan *	**Mulala John**
KKY	Russelstown	**Mulally Mrs**
DON	Mountcharles	**Mulbreary Hugh**
TIP	Rehill	**Mulcahy James**
KRY	Shanakeale	**Mulchinock Edward**
ROS	Boyle Town	**Mulhall John**
ROS	Boyle Town	**Mulhall Joseph**
DUB	HaroldsCross	**Mulhall Lewis**
KKY	Clintstown	**Mulhall Patrick**
DON	Drumskellan	**Mulhern Thomas**
ANT	Shankill T`parks	**Mulholland John**
DWN	Downpatrick Town	**Mulholland William**
KKY	Graiguenamanagh	**Muligan Rebecca**
TYR	Ballymagrane *	**Muligan Stuart**
KKY	Garrynamann Lr	**Mulins Bridget**
OFF	Down	**Mullagan James**
KILD	Gorteen	**Mullally John**
KILD	Gorteen	**Mullally Thomas**
KKY	Russellstown	**Mullally Widow Mary**
MEA	Newbridge	**Mullan George**
ANT	Cloghanmurry	**Mullan Hugh**
SLI	Carha	**Mullan Patrick**
LDY	Coolnasillagh	**Mullan Patrick**
LONG	Moor	**Mullaniff James**
MEA	Athlumney	**Mullen**
DUB	Milltown	**Mullen Barnaby**
TYR	Cavan	**Mullen Daniel**
ANT	Carnamenagh	**Mullen Felix**
DWN	Tullylish	**Mullen George**
MEA	Navan T`nparks	**Mullen James**
KRY	Ballintourtone	**Mullen Sir Thos**
MON	Anveyerg	**Mullen William**
GAL	Galway Town	**Mullens Denis V**
LDY	Vintners Propn.	**Mullhollan Bernard**
LDY	Vintners Propn.	**Mullholland Dan**
LDY	Vintners Propn.	**Mullholland Elinor Wid.**
LDY	Lemnaboy	**Mullholland Henry**
LDY	Vintners Propn.	**Mullholland Henry**
DWN	Downpatrick Town	**Mullholland John**
DWN	Balleevy	**Mulligan**
ARM	Tullycondraught	**Mulligan**
DWN	Carbet	**Mulligan Fran M J**
DWN	Tullyconnaught	**Mulligan Fran M J**
DWN	Tullyconnaught	**Mulligan Fras**
DWN	Carbet	**Mulligan G**
DWN	Tullyconnaught	**Mulligan G**
DWN	Tullyconnaught	**Mulligan George**
LDY	Vintners Propn.	**Mulligan George**
DWN	Tullyconnaught	**Mulligan Gilbert**
CAV	Drumnabeg	**Mulligan James**
DWN	Tullyconnaught	**Mulligan John**
ANT	Shankill T`parks	**Mulligan Montague**
ARM	Camlyball	**Mulligan Qwen**
KKY	Graignamanagh	**Mulligan Rebecca**
LONG	Smear	**Mulligan William**
LAO	Maryborough Town	**Mullin Geroge**
DUB	Haroldscross	**Mullin Jno**
KKY	Garrynamann Lr	**Mullins Bridget**
CRK	Coole	**Mullins Hannah**
CRK	Coole	**Mullins Hannah**
CRK	Coole	**Mullins Henry**
CRK	Coole	**Mullins Henry**
CRK	Sallybrook	**Mullins Henry**
CRK	Sallybrook	**Mullins Henry**
CRK	Coole	**Mullins James**
CAV	Graddum	**Mullins Owen**
WME	Ballynagore	**Mullock**
MYO	Ballybaun	**Mulloy James**
OFF	Banagher Town	**Mulloy Keran**
LAO	Bohernagrisna	**Mulloy Thomas**
OFF	Ballycumber	**Mulloy Thomas H**
OFF	Ballycumber Tn	**Mullroy Thomas Dr.**
DON	Mountcharles	**Mulrany Hugh**
DON	Mountcharles	**Mulrany Hugh**
DON	Mountcharles	**Mulreany Hugh**
DON	Mountcharles	**Mulreany Hugh**
CAR	Ballyknockan	**Mulroony John**
TIP	Beakstown	**Mulvaney Michael**
WME	Gilbertstown	**Mulvey**
ROS	Rathardeagher	**Mulvey James**
LEI	Drumcroman	**Mulvey Jas & Son**
LOU	Ardee Town	**Munkillrick William**
LOU	Ardee Town	**Munkittriick Alex**
LDY	Londonderry	**Munn John Jun**
ANT	Ballyrobin	**Munniss John**
GAL	Coolrevagh	**Munroe John**
GAL	Gerraun	**Munroe Simon**
KILD	Gilltown	**Muray Andrew**
WEX	Mackmine	**Muray John**
DWN	Balloo	**Murdagh**
DWN	Ballymacarret	**Murdoch**
TIP	Holycross	**Murdoch Robert**
MON	Scarnageeragh	**Murdoch William**
MON	Creeve	**Murdock Robert**
LOU	Dungooly	**Murdock William**
DUB	Dublin City	**Murgitroide Jno**
DWN	Ballylough	**Murland Charles**
DWN	Clarkill	**Murland Charles**
DWN	Ballylough	**Murland James**
DWN	Downpatrick Town	**Murland James**
DWN	Ballylough	**Murland Samuel**
DWN	Clarkill	**Murland Samuel**
LAO	Abbeyleix	**Murphy**
CAR	Barrow River	**Murphy**
KRY	Derrymore	**Murphy**
KILD	Greatconnell	**Murphy**
DUB	Haroldscross	**Murphy**
DUB	Haroldscross	**Murphy**
LOU	Newtown Bog	**Murphy**
DWN	Tullybranigan	**Murphy**
DUB	Goldenbridge	**Murphy Anthony**
CAV	Cabragh	**Murphy Charles**
DWN	Shanaghan	**Murphy David**
CRK	Ballyvolane	**Murphy Denis**
CRK	Kilbarry	**Murphy Denis**
DUB	Balheary	**Murphy Edward**
CRK	Kinsale Town	**Murphy Edward**
KRY	Knockreer	**Murphy Elenor Spin.**
GAL	Galway Town	**Murphy Hen**
WW	Ballinacorbeg	**Murphy James**
KILD	Greatconnell	**Murphy James**
CAR	Knockagundarragh	**Murphy James**
CAR	Knockagundarragh	**Murphy James**
CRK	Middleton Town	**Murphy James**
DWN	Shannaghan	**Murphy James**
DUB	Willbrook	**Murphy Jane**
DWN	Ballintogher	**Murphy Jno**
DWN	Ardmillan	**Murphy John**
WEX	Ballinacoola	**Murphy John**
MYO	Ballyglass	**Murphy John**
MYO	Ballyglass E.	**Murphy John**
LOU	Castletowncooley	**Murphy John**
KILD	Greatconnell	**Murphy John**
CAR	Portrushen Lr	**Murphy John**
CAR	Carlow Town	**Murphy John**
DWN	Ballynewport	**Murphy John Sen.**
ARM	Corporation	**Murphy Joseph**
ARM	Drumcarn	**Murphy Joseph**
DWN	Ballintogher	**Murphy Mary**
CAR	Ballyellin	**Murphy Matt**
KKY	Gorteens	**Murphy Michael**
KILD	Kilcullen Town	**Murphy Michael**
OFF	Roanville *	**Murphy Michael**
OFF	Springmount *	**Murphy Michael**
CAV	Lisnageer	**Murphy Mr**
DUB	Red Mills	**Murphy Mr**
WEX	Slievenagorea	**Murphy Nicholas**
CAV	Graddum	**Murphy Owen**
KILD	Irishtown	**Murphy Partick**
KKY	Warrington	**Murphy Partick**
WEX	Ballyboggan Lr	**Murphy Patrick**
CAR	Ballyellin	**Murphy Patrick**
WEX	Ballyshancarry	**Murphy Patrick**
MEA	Townland ?	**Murphy Patrick**
MEA	Abbeyland	**Murphy Peter**
DUB	Haroldscross	**Murphy Peter**
CAV	Keadew	**Murphy Peter**
MEA	Navan Town	**Murphy Peter**
MYO	Ballyglass E.	**Murphy Phil**
WEX	Yoletown	**Murphy Reps James**
LOU	Ballybinaby	**Murphy Thomas**
DWN	Ballynewport	**Murphy Thomas**
TIP	Clonmel Town	**Murphy Thomas**
LOU	Tarnadarra	**Murphy Thomas**
WAT	Waterford Town	**Murphy Thomas**
DUB	Willbrook	**Murphy Thomas**

CO.	TOWNLAND	MILLER
CAR	Knockagundarragh	**Murphy Timothy**
KKY	Brownstown	**Murphy Widow**
KILD	Carburry	**Murphy William**
ANT	Malone Lower	**Murphy William**
ANT	Shankill T`parks	**Murphy Wm**
LAO	Ballygor	**Murray**
ARM	Augher Town	**Murray Abraham**
TIP	Clonmel Town	**Murray Abraham**
TIP	Clonmel Town	**Murray Anne B**
WAT	Suir Island	**Murray Anne B**
ROS	Cloonaragh	**Murray Bryan**
ROS	Athleague	**Murray James**
DWN	Annalong	**Murray John**
LAO	Ballygor	**Murray John**
ROS	Creggganycarna	**Murray John**
LOU	Dundalk Town	**Murray John**
TIP	Marlfield	**Murray John**
LAO	Orchard	**Murray John**
ANT	Clogh Mills	**Murray Mary**
GAL	Mountross	**Murray Matthew**
CRK	Ballincrossig	**Murray Maurice**
CRK	Cork City	**Murray Maurice**
GAL	Galway Town	**Murray Nicholas**
ROS	Camcloon	**Murray Patrick**
ROS	Cregganycarna	**Murray Peter**
ROS	Cregganycarna	**Murray Peter Edward**
DWN	DownpatrickTown	**Murray Robt**
DUB	Rathfarnham	**Murray Thomas**
WME	Clogher	**Murtagh Charles**
LONG	Longford Town	**Murtagh Elizabeth**
LOU	Dundalk Town	**Murtagh James**
LONG	Longford Town	**Murtagh James**
DUB	St Sepulchre	**Murtagh Jno**
WME	Ballykeeran	**Murtagh John**
LONG	Garrynagh	**Murtagh Michael**
LONG	Longford Town	**Murtagh Michael**
WME	Tobercormick	**Murtagh Michael**
WME	Ballaghkeeran	**Murthagh James**
WME	Ballaghkeeran	**Murthagh John**
WAT	Ballyeen	**Musgrave**
WAT	Ballyeen	**Musgrave Chris**
WAT	Ballyeen	**Musgrave Chris Fred**
KRY	Cagrigh *	**Musgrave Christopher**
KRY	Cagrigh *	**Musgrave Christopher**
KRY	Cogreig	**Musgrave Christopher**
WAT	Killeeshal	**Musgrave Christopher**
WAT	Killeeshal	**Musgrave Jane, Spin.**
MYO	Hawksford	**Musgrave Lord**
KRY	Cogreig	**Musgrave Richard**
KRY	Cuyrigns *	**Musgrave Richard**
TIP	Clonmel Town	**Myles James**
DON	Ballyshannon Tn	**Myles John**
WEX	Ballingale	**Myles Joseph**
		N
ANT	Carrickferfus Tn	**N. Bank**
ANT	Carrickfergus Tn	**N. Banking Co.**
ANT	Ballyclare	**N.I. Paper Mill Co.**
DUB	Newtown	**N`tn Gt Paper Mill**
ROS	Knockalegan	**Nachton L.**
MYO	Doogart East	**Nagle Rev Edward**
WME	Rowlandstown	**Nairn William**
DUB	Dub Port & Cem.	**Naish Redmond**
DWN	Ballyharley	**Napier**
KILD	Celbridge	**Napier Emily Louisa Spin.**
ANT	Belfast T`parks	**Napier William**
WME	Gilbertstown	**Napper**
WEX	St John`s (Taigh)	**Napper William**
LIM	Ballyclough	**Nash Cornelius**
LOU	Dundalk Town	**Nat. Bank Ltd.**
CLE	Milltown	**National Bank Ltd.**
WEX	Palace	**Naylor John**
LAO	Coolrain	**Neal George**
WEX	St John`s (Taigh)	**Neal Rev Benjamin**
LAO	Aughnahorna	**Neale**
LAO	Ballybuggy	**Neale**
LAO	Rathdowney	**Neale**
WEX	Ratholm	**Neale Denis**
LAO	Mountrath	**Neale Richard**
DWN	Ballydonety	**near Ballydugan**
DWN	Legacurry	**near Hillsborough**
KKY	Ballyduff	**near Inistioge**
DWN	Annalong	**near Kilkeel**
CAV	Carrick	**near L. Sheelin**
KRY	Maulykeevane	**Neave S**
DWN	Ballygowan	**Nedham**
DWN	Ballygowan	**Nedham Robert**
LDY	Ballyness	**Nedham Robert**
DWN	Newry Town	**Needham Fran Visc.**
DON	Ballyshannon Tn	**Neely William**
DUB	Oldbawn	**Neil Kate**
DUB	Oldbawn	**Neil Samuel**
DWN	Ballymacarret	**Neill**
LAO	Coolrain	**Neill George**
DUB	Dub Port & Cem.	**Neill John**
DUB	Haerlem *	**Neill John**
ARM	Ballybreagh	**Neill Mrs**
ARM	Ballybreagh	**Neill Widow**
MON	Liseenan	**Neill William**
TYR	Milltown	**Neilson**
ANT	Cappobeg	**Neilson James**
LAO	Heath	**Nelands**
CLE	Kilmaley	**Nellan Patrick**
MON	Creeve	**Nelson Joseph**
MON	Creeve	**Nelson Mary**
KILD	Mount Blarney *	**Nelson Oliver**
KILD	Mount Blarney *	**Nelson Richard**
MON	Creeve	**Nelson Samuel**
ROS	Moher	**Nerheny Hugh**
FER	Drumawillin	**Nesbitt**
MEA	Milltown	**Nesbitt**
FER	Shannock	**Nesbitt**
FER	Clohonan *	**Nesbitt Alex**
FER	Crevinish	**Nesbitt Alex**
FER	Windmill Hill	**Nesbitt Alex**
LDY	Ballygonny Beg	**Nesbitt Hugh**
MON	Milltown	**Nesbitt Robert**
MYO	Ballinaster	**Nestor Patricia**
WME	Corner	**Nettelvill Nich. Lord**
DWN	Ballymaconaghy	**Netterville Patk**
WME	Kilbeggan	**Nevill**
DWN	Strangford	**Neville**
DUB	Kilgobbin	**Neville Benjamin**
DWN	Blakans	**Neville Brent Yngr.**
CRK	Cloghina *	**Neville Henry Rev.**
WAT	Ballyroe	**Neville John**
FER	Ballymagaghran	**Neville Robert**
WAT	Killadangan	**Neville William**
ANT	Greenshields Up	**Nevin John**
GAL	Ballygasty	**Nevin Michael**
GAL	Ballygasty	**Nevin Patrick**
ANT	Lisnisk	**Nevin Robert A**
ANT	Ballybogy	**Nevin Thomas**
DWN	Ballydugan	**Nevin William**
DWN	Ballydugan	**Nevin William Rev.**
KKY	Strangsmill	**Nevine Thomas F**
WW	Brittas	**Nevins Archibald**
WW	Brittas	**Nevins Thomas**
WME	Coolure	**Newcomen**
WAT	Waterford Town	**Newcomen William**
WEX	Dunbrody Manor	**Newdigate R**
MEA	Clonguiffin	**Newell**
MEA	Clonguiffin	**Newell John**
ANT	Derryaghy	**Newell Wiliam**
CRK	Ballinglanna	**Newenham**
CRK	Killingly	**Newenham**
CRK	bo./ Barrymore	**Newenham Edward**
DWN	Ardarragh	**Newham Robert Jun.**
DUB	Tallaght	**Newman Mr**
DUB	Templeogue	**Newman Mr**
DUB	Rathfarnham	**Newman Mr & Co.**
MEA	Athboy Town	**Newman Thomas**
WAT	Raheen	**Newpport**
DWN	Annalong	**Newry County Council**
DWN	Tullybranigan	**Newsom**
WW	Ballyduff North	**Newsom George**
WAT	Ballindud	**Newton**
CAR	Carlow Town	**Newton**
TYR	Coagh	**Newton Andrew**
DON	Cullion	**Newton Andrew**
CLE	Ballycorney	**Newton Edward**
CAR	Ballinure	**Newton Henry**
CAR	Carlow Town	**Newton Jno**
CAR	Carlow Town	**Newton John**
ANT	Carrickfergus Tn	**Newton Josh**
MEA	Blackwater R.	**Newton Michael**
LDY	Gobnascale	**Newton Robert William**
DUB	Dublin City	**Neynoe**

INDEX

CO.	TOWNLAND	MILLER
ANT	Cullybackey	**Nichol Joseph**
DWN	Eden Ballycoggill	**Nicholl**
LEI	Doogree	**Nicholls George**
LEI	Doogree	**Nicholls John**
CAR	Carlow Town	**Nicholson**
MON	Crumlin	**Nicholson**
LDY	Magherafelt	**Nicholson**
LAO	Rathdowney	**Nicholson**
MYO	Foxford	**Nicholson Edward**
CAR	Carlow Town	**Nicholson James**
TYR	Creenagh	**Nicholson James**
MEA	Balrath Dems.	**Nicholson John**
DWN	Downpatrick Town	**Nicholson John**
CRK	Ballycroneen	**Nicholson Joseph**
ARM	Clogharavan	**Nicholson Joseph**
TYR	Creenagh	**Nicholson Joseph**
DWN	Banoge	**Nicholson Mr**
DWN	Downpatrick Town	**Nicholson William**
CRK	Garransduff	**Niern Richard**
CRK	Curraghalicky	**Nihan John**
CRK	Curraghalicky	**Nihan John**
ROS	Fuerty	**Nisbitt**
ANT	Lisnisk	**Nivan Thomas**
ANT	Carrickfergus Tn	**Niven Richard**
FER	Killywillin	**Nixon Alex**
DON	Ray	**Nixon Alex Rev.**
DON	Townland ?	**Nixon Alex Rev.**
DON	Tullaghobegly Irish	**Nixon Alex Revd.**
DUB	Castleknock	**Nixon Frederick**
FER	Derrihalla	**Nixon George**
CAR	Old Leighlin	**Nixon James**
FER	Derrygonnelly	**Nixon John**
DUB	Donnybrook	**Nixon John**
DUB	Donnybrook	**Nixon John**
FER	Derrygonnelly Tn	**Nixon John Jun.**
DUB	Red Mills	**Nixon Mr**
CAV	Darna	**Nixon Mrs**
CAV	Kiltomulty	**Nixon Mrs**
CAV	Kiltumulty	**Nixon Mrs**
DUB	Glasnevin	**Nixon Robert**
LAO	Ironmills / Kilrush	**Noble Benjamin**
MON	Caryaghlissanery	**Noble Brabazon**
MON	Lissanery	**Noble Brabazon**
DON	Milltown	**Noble John**
DWN	Banbridge Town	**Noble M/s**
TYR	Lisnasoragh	**Noble Wiliam**
GAL	Kilmeen	**Nokely Patrick**
ROS	Athleague	**Nolan**
WW	Bonagrew	**Nolan**
WW	Brittas	**Nolan**
ROS	Castlecoote	**Nolan**
LDY	Killykergan	**Nolan**
WW	Wicklow Town	**Nolan**
DUB	Goldenbridge	**Nolan Andrew**
LDY	Enniskillen Town	**Nolan Elizabeth**
ROS	Creevemully	**Nolan James**
GAL	Galway Town	**Nolan James**
DUB	Killeek	**Nolan James**
CAR	Rathnapish	**Nolan James**
KILD	Timolin	**Nolan James**
MYO	Tully	**Nolan James**
WW	Tombreen	**Nolan Jno**
WW	Tombreen	**Nolan John**
KILD	Moatstown	**Nolan Michael**
KILD	Osberstown	**Nolan Simon**
ROS	Creevemully	**Nolan Thomas**
GAL	Killoscobe	**Noon Martin**
CAR	Gilbertstown	**Noonan Anne**
CRK	Ballinglen North	**Noonan John**
MYO	Ballinaster	**Noone John**
GAL	Derrynabrin	**Noone Martin**
GAL	Derrynabrin	**Noone Martin**
GAL	Killian	**Noone Patrick & Tom**
GAL	Killian	**Noone Timothy & Patk**
LIM	Askeaton	**Nordblad**
MEA	Slane Manor	**Norman Henry**
MEA	Higgginstown	**Norman John**
MEA	Rogerstown	**Norman John**
DON	Convoy Town	**Norman Mr**
DUB	Droultuin *	**Norman Robert**
CLE	O'Briensbridge	**Norris**
KILD	Pluckerstown	**Norris**
LEI	Carnacannon	**Norris Alex**
LEI	Balscarra	**Norris Berry**
LEI	Carnacannon	**Norris Berry**
LEI	Keeldra	**Norris Berry**
TYR	Creeduff	**Norris Jane**
TYR	Creeduff	**Norris John**
KILD	Pluckerstown	**Norris John**
CAR	Tobinstown	**Norris Margaret**
LOU	Carntown	**Norris Nicholas**
WW	Bray	**Norris S**
DWN	Aghiohill	**Norris Toby**
MEA	Roughrange	**Norris William**
CAR	Clashganny	**North**
LOU	Ardee Town	**North Letitia**
ANT	Carrickfergus Tn	**Northern Bank Co.**
LDY	Coleraine Town	**Northern Bank Co.**
TYR	Mullybrannon	**Northland Hon. Ld. Visc.**
TYR	Dungannon	**Northland Hon. Lord**
TYR	Killymam	**Northland Lord**
TYR	Dungannon L`ships	**Northland Thos Rt. Hon.**
CAR	Dunleckny	**Norton John**
CAR	Ballygowan	**Norton Patrick**
CAR	Milford	**Norton Patrick**
CRK	Fananashesherry	**Norwood William**
CRK	Murragh	**Norwood William**
CRK	Townland ?`	**Norwood William**
LEI	Drumcree	**Notley R**
LEI	Drumcree	**Notley Robert**
OFF	Millbrook	**now Abernethy John**
KILD	Maynooth	**Nowlan**
KILD	Moone Manor	**Nowlan**
CAR	Grangewat	**Nowlan Gerard**
CAR	Tullow	**Nowlan John**
KILD	Moone	**Nowlan Michael**
DUB	Chapelizod	**Nowlan Mr**
DUB	Gormanstown	**Nowlan Mr**
CAR	Rathvilly	**Nowlan Thomas**
MEA	Dangan Manor	**Noy Edward**
MEA	Dangan Manor	**Noy William**
CAR	Ballygowan	**Nugenr John**
LOU	Carlingford	**Nugent**
WME	Carrick	**Nugent**
CAR	Cloghristick	**Nugent**
WME	Cushinstown	**Nugent**
CAR	St Mullins	**Nugent**
DWN	Portaferrey Town	**Nugent Andrew**
WME	Ballinacor	**Nugent Count**
DUB	Windmillhill	**Nugent Edmond H S**
CAR	Ballygowan	**Nugent James**
CAR	Ballygowan	**Nugent John**
CAR	Milford	**Nugent John**
KILD	Quinsborough	**Nugent John**
CAR	Ballygowan	**Nugent Kathleen**
CAR	Milford	**Nugent Kathleen**
ARM	Tandragee	**Nugent Peter**
ROS	Milltown	**Nugent Richard**
WME	Castletown	**Nugent Robert**
WME	Foyran	**Nugent Robert**
WME	Dysart	**Nugent Sir Roberte**
DWN	Carlingford Town	**Nugent Thomas**
DWN	Carlingford	**Nugent Thomas John**
LOU	Carlingford Town	**Nugent Thos**
DUB	Freestone	**Nun James**
WEX	Ballybing	**Nun John**
WEX	Slad	**Nun Joshua**
DUB	Rockbrook *	**Nun Mr**
DUB	Freestone	**Nun Richard**
WEX	Slad	**Nun Richd**
DUB	Edmondstown	**Nunn James**
DUB	Edmondstown	**Nunn Theresa**
CRK	Ballinglanna N.	**Nunnan John**
ROS	Canagh *	**Nurney John**
WW	Newmills	**Nutley**
DUB	Edmondstown	**Nutley Richard**
WW	Ballyduff North	**Nuzam John**
WW	Ballyduff North	**Nuzam Robert**
		O
WME	Athlone Town	**O`Beirne Charles**
CLE	Tarmon	**O`Brian John**
KILD	Boycetown	**O`Brien**
CAR	Carlow Town	**O`Brien**
LAO	Clonmore	**O`Brien**
GAL	Clough House	**O`Brien**
KILD	Gorteen	**O`Brien**
KILD	Gorteen	**O`Brien**

CO.	TOWNLAND	MILLER
KILD	Gorteen	O`Brien
WAT	Kilmeadan	O`Brien
KILD	Newtown	O`Brien
KILD	Parsonstown	O`Brien
LAO	Stradbally	O`Brien
LEI	Aghavas	O`Brien Achison
LEI	Watercourse	O`Brien Achison
ROS	Atteagh	O`Brien Bartholomew
WAT	Kilmeadan	O`Brien Conelius
ROS	Clooneenbaun	O`Brien Denis
WAT	Kilmeadan	O`Brien Denis
CAR	Derren River	O`Brien Edwd
SLI	Glenawoo	O`Brien Henry
TYR	Corkragh	O`Brien Hugh
TIP	Holycross	O`Brien Jeremiah
CRK	Ballinadee	O`Brien John
WEX	Aclamon	O`Brien Laurence
CLE	Ennis Town	O`Brien Michael
GAL	Knockanarra	O`Brien Morgan
DUB	Palmerstown	O`Brien Mr
MYO	Bekan	O`Brien Patrick
LIM	Clonkeen	O`Brien Patrick
LIM	Glenduff	O`Brien Robert
DUB	Kings Miltown	O`Brien Robert
CLE	Ardrahine *	O`Brien Robt.
GAL	Loughrea Town	O`Brien Samuel
KILD	Moone	O`Brien Simon
CLE	Milltown	O`Brien Thomas
ROS	Drumboylan	O`Brien William
GAL	Knockanarra	O`Brien William
ANT	Ballynacree More	O`Bryan James T
SLI	Bellanalack	O`Byrne Philip
LOU	Philipstown	O`Callaghan
KKY	Thomastown	O`Callaghan Corns
CAR	Tobinstown	O`Callaghan Ellen
KKY	Sheastown	O`Callaghan Owen
CRK	Cloghina *	O`Callaghan Thos
KRY	Dromthacker	O`Connell James
KRY	Dromthacker E.	O`Connell James
LONG	Longford Town	O`Connell Maurice
CAR	Orchard	O`Connell Maurice
KRY	Morakiffe	O`Connell Richard
DUB	Drishoge	O`Connell Thos
OFF	Annaghmore	O`Connor
CLE	Kilbane	O`Connor
DUB	Diswellstown	O`Connor Arthur
DUB	Diswellstown	O`Connor Charles
TIP	Fethard Town	O`Connor Edmund
ANT	Lisburn Town	O`Connor Jn
TIP	Rathronan	O`Connor John
CAR	Carlow Town	O`Connor Mary
LONG	Clondra	O`Connor Michael
LIM	Drewscourt East	O`Connor William
ROS	Bellnagare	O`Conor Denis
ROS	Kilcorkey	O`Conor Denis
OFF	Milltown	O`Conor Maria
GAL	Rinneen	O`Dea Daniel
MYO	Duckanelly	O`Donel Richard
LIM	Ryevale *	O`Donnell
CLE	Tullycrine	O`Donnell Dick
CRK	Liscahane	O`Donnell Herbert
MYO	Tully	O`Donnell Mary Spinster
GAL	Duckanelly	O`Donnell Sir Hugh
MYO	Tully	O`Donnell Sir Neal
MYO	Barrack Hill	O`Donnell Sir Richard
KRY	Gortonora	O`Donoghue Thomas
CRK	Broomfield West	O`Donohoe Mrs
LONG	Cullynore	O`Farrell Roger
CAR	Tobinstown	O`Ferral Richard
CAR	Tobinstown	O`Ferrall Ambrose
WEX	Wexford Town	O`Flaherty William
OFF	Cappancur	O`Flanagan James
WAT	Clonea	O`Flinn James
DUB	Holmpatrick	O`Flynn Patrick
LDY	Ballykellaghan	O`Gilby Robert
ROS	Creevemully	O`Gilvie Geo
ROS	Athleague	O`Gilvie George
ROS	Creevemully	O`Gilvie John Geo
CLE	Killadysert Town	O`Grady Daniel
LOU	Dundalk Town	O`Hagan Patk
DUB	Balbriggan	O`Hara Ann
ROS	Cloonmagunnaun	O`Hara Charles
LOU	Ram Park	O`Hara Eugene
GAL	Galway Town	O`Hara Jno
GAL	Galway Town	O`Hara John
GAL	Galway Town	O`Hara John
GAL	Galway Town	O`Hara John
LOU	Doolargy O`Hara	O`Hara Owen
LOU	Doolargy O`Hara	O`Hara Patrick
WAT	Tallow Town	O`Hea Elizabeth
TYR	Cloghog Lower	O`Kane Susanna
WAT	Killeeshal	O`Keefe Margaret
WAT	Killeeshal	O`Keefe Margt. ors Sargent
CRK	Youghal Town	O`Keeffe David
TIP	Thurles T'parks	O`Keeffe Dixon
WEX	Wexford Town	O`Keeffe Laurence
TIP	Ballyartella	O`Keeffe Patrick
TIP	Rathronan	O`Keeffe Richardd
CLE	Ennis Town	O`Kelly
CLE	Ennis Town	O`Kelly Jno
KRY	Tralee Town	O`Kelly Thomas
KRY	Ardagh	O`Leary Cornelius
LIM	Milltown South	O`Leary Henry
GAL	Ballymantan	O`Loughlin John
GAL	Ballymantan	O`Loughton Murty
CRK	Upton	O`Mahony Barth.
GAL	Galway Town	O`Malley Martin
GAL	Cong	O`Malley Michael
MYO	Castlebar	O`Malley Owen
MYO	Bellavarry	O`Mally William
LAO	Rathendock	O`Meara
CLE	Ennis Town	O`Meara Eyre
CLE	Ennis Town	O`Meara Phillipa
ANT	Carnamenagh	O`Mullan Felix
WAT	Stonehouse	O`Neil
MYO	Tully	O`Neil Charles
TIP	Cregg	O`Neil Felix
DUB	Swords Town	O`Neil Laurence
DWN	Ballyaughian	O`Neill
DWN	Ballyaughian	O`Neill
ANT	Ballybollen	O`Neill Ambrose
DWN	Grangewalls	O`Neill Ambrose
DON	Ballyshannon Tn	O`Neill Charles
ANT	Ballynacaird	O`Neill Chas
ANT	Ballymatoskerty	O`Neill Earl
ANT	Derryhollagh	O`Neill Earl
LOU	Dundalk Town	O`Neill Elizabeth
DWN	Ballymoney	O`Neill Francis
ANT	Antrim Town	O`Neill Hon. Edward
TYR	Dungannon Town	O`Neill John
WAT	Pouldrew *	O`Neill John
TIP	Ballylynch	O`Neill Thomas
KKY	Castletown	O`Neill Thomas
WAT	Pouldrew *	O`Neill William
CRK	Millstreet	O`Regan Andrew
OFF	Bracknagh	O`Reilly
KILD	Millestown ?	O`Reilly
ROS	Milltown	O`Reilly Dom. Wm
CAV	Lackan Lower	O`Reilly John
MEA	Navan Town	O`Reilly Matthew
CAR	Carlow Town	O`Reilly Michael M
DUB	Astagob	O`Reilly Mr.
LONG	Aghara	O`Reilly Richard
LOU	Little Mill	O`Rourke Michael
WW	Bonagrew	O`Rourke Owen
LIM	Kilmallock Town :	O`Shaughnessy
CRK	Clashganniv	O`Shaughnessy William
LIM	Drewscourt East	O`Shaughnessy William
CRK	Clashganniv	O`Shaughnessy Wm
CRK	Boulapatrick *	O`Sullivan Bart
KRY	Killarney Town	O`Sullivan Jeremiah
CRK	Youghal Town	O`Sullivan Michael
KRY	Milltown	O`Sullivans
CLE	Inchiquion	O'Brien Catherine
CLE	Ardrahine *	O'Brien Edward
CAR	Hacketstown	O'Brien Edward
CLE	Ardrahine *	O'Brien Michael
LIM	Limerick City	O'Brien Patrick
CRK	Ballinadee	O'Brine John
CLE	Clonassy	O'Callaghan
CLE	Coogy West	O'Callaghan
CLE	Coshery island	O'Callaghan
CLE	Dromin	O'Callaghan
CLE	O'Callaghansmills	O'Callaghan
CLE	O'Callaghansmills	O'Callaghan
CLE	O'Callaghansmills	O'Callaghan Cornelius
CLE	O'Callaghansmills	O'Callaghan Donal
CLE	O'Callaghansmills	O'Callaghan Donalus

INDEX

CO.	TOWNLAND	MILLER
CAV	Magheraboy Upr	**Plunkett Henry**
CAV	Cormeen	**Plunkett John**
DUB	Dub Port & Cem.	**Plunkett John**
CAV	Cormeen	**Plunkett Joseph**
ROS	Greganaharney *	**Plunkett Michael**
DUB	Leybstown	**Plunkett Patrick**
ROS	Greganaharney *	**Plunkett Richard**
GAL	Cosmona	**Plunkett Walter**
MON	Agherybeggan *	**Pockrich Richard**
WME	Kilbeggan	**Pole**
WME	Connyborrons	**Pollard Dillon**
WME	Connyborrons	**Pollard H**
WME	Connyborrons	**Pollard Hampson**
WME	Gilbertstown	**Pollard Hampson**
WME	Gilbertstown	**Pollard Hampson Dillon**
WME	Hill	**Pollard Hampson Dillon**
WME	Gilbertstown	**Pollard Hampson Lettice Wid.**
WME	Hill	**Pollard Hampson Lettice Wid.**
WME	Rathbennett	**Pollard Hamson Dillon**
WME	Rathbennett	**Pollard Urquhart**
WME	Connyborrons	**Pollard Walter**
SLI	Sligo Town	**Pollexfen Charles W**
SLI	Ballysadare Town	**Pollexfen G.**
SLI	Ballysadare Town	**Pollexfen W.**
DWN	Ballyvally	**Pollock**
ARM	Goragh	**Pollock**
GAL	Oghillmore	**Pollock Allan**
ARM	Goragh	**Pollock B**
CAR	Old Park *	**Pollock Henry**
LDY	Muladonagh	**Pollock Samuel**
LDY	Englishtown	**Pollock William**
WEX	Ross Town	**Polwheele Robt Rev.**
CRK	Ballinglanna	**Pomeroy**
KILD	Carbury	**Pomeroy**
KILD	Windmill Land	**Pomeroy**
KILD	Kilmore	**Pomeroy Arthur**
KILD	Kilmore	**Pomeroy Arthur**
KILD	Kilmore	**Pomeroy Henry**
KILD	Carberry & Castle :	**Pomeroy John**
KILD	Kilmore	**Pomeroy Mary**
KILD	Kilmore	**Pomeroy Mary (ors Colley)**
DON	Ballylast	**Ponsonby Frances**
KRY	Ballintourtone	**Ponsonby Richard**
KRY	Ballintourtone	**Ponsonby Thomas**
WAT	Ballyeen	**Poole**
OFF	Bracknagh	**Poole**
DUB	Dublin City	**Poole**
DUB	Dublin City	**Poole Jacob**
DUB	Dundrum Manor	**Poole Jacob**
LAO	Ballyroan	**Porter**
LOU	Newtown Bog	**Porter**
DWN	Shannaghan	**Porter Alex**
DWN	Shanaghan	**Porter Andrew**
KILD	Gurty *	**Porter Cooke Wm**
ANT	Belfast Town	**Porter Edward**
KRY	Castleisland	**Porter Edward**

CO.	TOWNLAND	MILLER
DON	Townland ?	**Porter James**
CAV	Ryefield	**Porter John**
FER	Attyclannabryan	**Porter John G**
FER	Mullybritt	**Porter John G**
CAV	Townland ?	**Porter John Sen.**
FER	Attyclannabryan	**Porter Rev John G**
FER	Lisbellaw Town	**Porter Rev John G**
WW	Wicklow Town	**Porter Richard**
DWN	Shannaghan	**Porter Robert**
CRK	Cork City	**Porter Samuel**
DON	Tuckmill & Island	**Porter Thomas**
CRK	Killeen	**Porter William**
LOU	White Mill	**Porteus Matthew**
DWN	Balloo	**Potter**
DWN	Balloo	**Potter Jno Yngr.**
DWN	Balloo	**Potter John**
DWN	Balloo	**Potter John (Elder)**
CRK	Farsha	**Potter Leonard**
MEA	Ballynadrimma	**Potterton James**
DWN	Ballymacarret	**Pottinger**
DWN	Ballymacarret	**Pottinger Joseph**
DWN	Annaclone *	**Potts**
DWN	Derrylough	**Potts**
DWN	Cappagh	**Potts Andrew**
ROS	Athlone	**Potts Jno**
WEX	Enniscorthy Town	**Pounder John**
WEX	East Monart	**Pounder Thomas**
WEX	Enniscorthy Town	**Pounder Thomas**
WEX	Yoletown	**Powel James**
KILD	Greatconnell	**Powell**
MEA	Slane	**Powell**
WW	Tobber *	**Powell Charles**
DUB	Tubber	**Powell Charles**
LAO	Portarlington	**Powell George**
LAO	Portarlington	**Powell Jno Rev.**
DUB	Islandbridge	**Powell Michael**
LAO	Mountrath	**Powell William**
TIP	Bansagh	**Power**
TIP	Bansha	**Power**
WAT	Carrickcastle	**Power**
WAT	Dungarvan Town	**Power**
WAT	Currabaha	**Power Benjamin**
WAT	Carrowgarriff	**Power Edward**
TIP	Clonmel	**Power Edward**
DUB	Tallaght	**Power George**
TIP	Kilsheelan	**Power James**
CRK	Ballyvolane	**Power John**
CRK	Grenagh North	**Power John**
CRK	Kilnap	**Power John**
WAT	Waterford City	**Power John**
WAT	Carrickcastle	**Power Joseph**
TIP	Bansha	**Power Luke**
CAV	Corbeagh	**Power Margaret**
CAV	Drumbarry	**Power Margaret**
WAT	Knocknagranagh	**Power Mary**
TIP	Graiguenoe	**Power Michael**

CO.	TOWNLAND	MILLER
CRK	Morefieldstown	**Power Mr**
WAT	Shanakill	**Power Patt**
KRY	Ballycarty	**Power Pierce**
WAT	Carrickcastle	**Power Pierce**
WAT	Couse	**Power Richard**
WAT	Dungarvan Town	**Power Richard**
WAT	Durrow	**Power Robert**
KILD	Inchaquire	**Power Robert**
TIP	Clonmel	**Power Thomas**
KRY	Clooncarrig	**Power Thomas**
WAT	Garran	**Power Thomas**
DUB	Gallagh	**Powerscourt**
LAO	Old Mill bo:Ossory	**Powerscourt**
KILD	Milltown	**Powerscourt Lady**
WW	Powerscourt Dem.	**Powerscourt Lord**
LAO	Abbeyleix	**Powerscourt Richard Rt. Hon.**
LOU	Knock	**Powis**
KILD	Grange Beg	**Pratt Fitzmaurics**
CRK	Youghal Town	**Pratt James**
CRK	Ahgamilla	**Pratt Robert**
CRK	Ardkitt	**Pratt Robert**
CRK	Youghal Town	**Pratt Robert**
DUB	Pelletstown	**Pratt William**
WW	Bray	**Prendergast**
TIP	Ardfinnan	**Prendergast James**
WEX	Ballybregagh	**Prendergast James**
GAL	Ballooly	**Prendergast John**
GAL	Ballooly Kelly	**Prendergast John**
WEX	Ballybregagh	**Prendergast Laurence**
ANT	Burnside	**Prenter Nath A**
ANT	Walk Mill	**Prenter Nathaniel A**
ANT	Walkmill	**Prenter Nathaniel A**
ARM	Ballynahone More	**Prentice**
ARM	Ballynahone Beg	**Prentice**
ARM	Ennislare	**Prentice Henry L**
MON	Creeve	**Prentice Thomas**
ANT	Brookfield	**Prentor Nath**
LOU	Ardee Town	**Prescott Robert**
LIM	Askeaton	**Prescottt Robt**
MEA	Townland ?	**Preston**
WEX	Salville or Motabeg	**Preston A (1847)**
WEX	Salville or Motabeg	**Preston Alex**
ANT	Carrickfergus Tn	**Preston George**
ANT	Carrickfergus NE	**Preston John**
MEA	Dangan Manor	**Preston John**
MEA	Bedlow`s Mill	**Preston Joseph Rev.**
ARM	Ballynahone Beg	**Price**
CAR	Ballypierce	**Price**
DWN	Ballytogher *	**Price**
CAR	Carlow Town	**Price**
KILD	Newhall	**Price**
LONG	Bleach Green	**Price Richard**
CAV	Drumsillagh	**Prichard Alicia Boyle**
CAV	Drumsillagh	**Prichit Mary**
MON	Cavancope	**Pringle Alex**
LAO	Stradbally	**Pringle George**

INDEX

CO.	TOWNLAND	MILLER
ARM	Aughnacloy	**Pringle Michael**
LAO	Ballybuggy	**Prior**
LAO	Grelagh	**Prior**
LAO	Monlisheal	**Prior**
LAO	Rathdowney	**Prior**
LAO	Rathdowney	**Prior Eliz. ors Palmer**
LAO	Rathdowney	**Prior John Murray**
LAO	Rathdowney	**Prior Murray**
LAO	Cullenaghbegg	**Prior Robert**
LAO	Raheenah	**Prior Robert**
LAO	Rathdowney	**Prior Thomas**
WW	Newmills	**Prior Thommas**
LAO	Ballybuggy	**PriorThomas**
CAR	Carlow Town	**Proctor**
CAR	Carlow Town	**Proctor Bridget**
CAR	Carlow Town	**Proctor Nathaniel**
CAR	Carlow Town	**Proctor Thomas**
CAR	Carlow Town	**Proctor Thomas Lieut.**
WW	Broomfield	**Proprietor Samuel**
LAO	Aghmacart	**Prossan**
LAO	Aghmacart	**Prossan John**
CAR	Carlow Town	**Prossor James**
CRK	Milltown b/ Imokilly	**Prov Bank of Ireland**
DWN	Ballydugan	**Prow Patrick**
DWN	Ballyhemlin	**Prow Stephen**
LIM	Rylanes	**Pruderman Barry**
CAV	Aghadreenagh	**Prunty John**
MEA	Athboy Town	**Pryor Edward**
ANT	Craigarogan	**Pullen Matt**
LAO	Ballybuggy	**Purcell**
LAO	Clonaslee	**Purcell**
WME	Cushinstown	**Purcell Andrew**
KRY	Ardagh	**Purcell Hannan**
LAO	Clonaslee	**Purcell Philip**
WEX	Horetown	**Purcell Richard**
WAT	Ballywillin	**Purcell Thomas**
WAT	Capoquin	**Purcell Thomas**
LAO	Ballybuggy	**Purcell Tobias**
LDY	Rathbrady	**Purcell William K**
WME	Rathwire U.& Lr.	**Purdon**
WME	Riverstown	**Purdon**
DUB	Manor	**Purdon Arabella**
WME	Cushinstown	**Purdon Edward**
WME	Thomastown	**Purdon Edward**
DWN	Balloo	**Purdy**
OFF	Purefoy`s Place	**Purefoy James R**
WEX	Palace	**Putland**
CAR	Clonegall	**Putland John**

Q

CO.	TOWNLAND	MILLER
LOU	Collon	**Qiun Henry**
DWN	Tobermoney	**Quaile Thomas**
KILD	Parsonstown	**Queade**
CLE	Ballymacooda	**Quealy John**
WEX	Borrmount	**Quigley michael**
MON	Crumlin	**Quigly**
WW	Bray	**Quin**
ARM	Lisavague	**Quin**
TYR	Magheralough ?	**Quin**
ANT	Millquarter	**Quin**
KILD	Quinsborough	**Quin**
ARM	Ballynewry	**Quin Arthur**
LAO	Lea	**Quin Bridget**
SLI	Carrowreagh	**Quin Edward**
ARM	Lurgyvallon	**Quin John**
KKY	Milltown	**Quin John**
SLI	Gorterslin	**Quin Martin**
DUB	Glasnevin	**Quin Mary**
LIM	Askeaton Town	**Quin Michael**
GAL	Conagher	**Quin Michael**
SLI	Kilmacteigue	**Quin Michael**
GAL	Lackfinna South	**Quin Patrick**
KILD	B`more Eustace	**Quin Terence**
TIP	Barnora	**Quin Thomas**
LAO	Lea	**Quin widow**
WW	Ballycullen	**Quinians Anthony**
CRK	Cork City	**Quinlan Edmond**
CRK	Glanduff	**Quinlan Timothy**
CRK	Kilbrittan	**Quinlan Timothy**
ANT	Creggan	**Quinn**
GAL	Dalgin	**Quinn**
WAT	Ballynamoyntragh	**Quinn James**
LDY	Granaghan	**Quinn James**
DWN	Leitrim	**Quinn James**
WAT	Portlaw	**Quinn John**
CLE	Summerhill	**Quinn John**
ARM	Tullyglush	**Quinn John**
LONG	Gorteenora	**Quinn Patrick**
KILD	Ballinure	**Quinn Thomas**

R

CO.	TOWNLAND	MILLER
ROS	Creevemully	**Radcliff Thomas Rev.**
ANT	Belfast Town	**Radcliffe**
CLE	Ennis Town	**Radcliffe Jos**
WEX	Hedges *	**Radford Benjamin**
ROS	Tanidrissoge *	**Radford Newton**
KRY	Ross	**Rae Edward**
GAL	Castlemoyle	**Raferty**
SLI	Knockagower	**Rafter John**
KKY	Owning & Town	**Rafter William**
GAL	Attiregan	**Raftery Thomas**
KKY	Kiltorcan	**Raftis Patrick**
DWN	Cullintraw	**Rainey**
DWN	Mountpanther	**Rainey**
DWN	Drumbo	**Rainey John**
DWN	Greencastle	**Rainey Robert**
DWN	Drumbo	**Rainey William**
DWN	Ballygallum	**Rainey William Ash**
LOU	Carlingford	**Rainsford Joseph**
DWN	Carlingford Town	**Rainsford Joseph**
DUB	Woodlands	**Rainsford Richard**
KILD	Ballyaghmoone *	**Rainsford Thomas**
KILD	Coolsickin	**Rainsford Thomas**
OFF	Rathmoyle	**Rait Silvester**
WME	Ballyhaw	**Rally Matthew**
WEX	Ballybane *	**Ram Abel**
WEX	Gorey	**Ram Abel**
WEX	Kilmichael	**Ram Abel**
WEX	Newborough	**Ram Abel**
WEX	Gorey	**Ram Abel Jnr.**
WEX	Kilmichael	**Ram Abel Jnr.**
WEX	Ballybane	**Ram Humphry**
WEX	Ballybane *	**Ram Stephen**
DUB	Kilmashogue	**Ramor Samuel**
LDY	Clagan	**Ramsay John**
SLI	Sligo Town	**Ramsay John**
TYR	Coolaghy	**Ramsay Robert**
DON	Kiln Hills *	**Ramsay Robert**
LDY	Clagan	**Ramsay William**
TYR	Coolaghy	**Ramsay William**
DON	Ballyederowen	**Ramsy Henry**
DWN	Drumbo	**Ramsy James**
KILD	Parsonstown	**Randell**
KILD	Parsonstown	**Randell**
CLE	O'Callaghansmills	**Ranelagh Hon. Arthur**
WME	Lismacaffry	**Ranelagh Ld. Charles**
CRK	Grillagh	**Rank Company**
DWN	Ballymacarret	**Ranken**
LDY	Vintners Propn.	**Rankin**
LDY	Ballyagan	**Rankin David**
LDY	Inshaleen	**Rankin David**
DON	Lustical Lower	**Rankin Samuel**
DON	Haw	**Rankin William**
LDY	Clagan	**Ransay John**
CAR	Clonegall	**Ransford Michael**
LDY	Vintners Propn.	**Ransterne William**
ANT	Ballyhamage	**Raphael**
ANT	Ballynamage	**Raphael**
ANT	Craiginorne	**Raphael Mrs.**
MEA	Athboy Town	**Rashleigh George**
KKY	Cappagh	**Rasstus William**
GAL	Ahascragh Town	**Rathbourne**
MEA	Skearke	**Rathburn John**
DUB	Rathgar	**Rathgar Calico Print**
DWN	Ballynahinch	**Rawdon Hon. John**
KILD	Milltown	**Rawley**
LAO	Cloghrennan	**Rawson**
KILD	Inchaquire	**Rawson Richard**
KILD	Inchaquire	**Rawson William**
KRY	Counguilly *	**Raymond**
KRY	Galey *	**Raymond Samuel**
ANT	Crookedstone	**Rea John**
KILD	Quinsborough	**Read**
WEX	Foulke`s Mill	**Read George**
KKY	Kilkenny City	**Read Inditt**
ARM	Blackwatertown	**Read James**
MON	Killymaran	**Read James**
DUB	Red Mills	**Read James**

CO.	TOWNLAND	MILLER
ANT	Tullycreenaght	**Read James**
DUB	Ballyboden	**Read John**
DUB	Edmondstown	**Read John**
DWN	Drumnascamph	**Read Mary**
MON	Teraverty	**Read Thomas**
MON	Teraverty	**Read Thomas**
ANT	Carrickfergus Tn	**Reade Robert**
MEA	Ratoath	**Ready James**
GAL	Galway Town	**Reagan Michael**
KKY	Graignamanagh	**Rebecca Mulligan**
TIP	Lorrha	**Reddin Timothy**
DUB	Lucan	**Redford**
OFF	Annaghmore	**Redington**
CAR	Carlow Town	**Redmond**
WEX	Ballinacoola	**Redmond Daniel**
ARM	Legacurry	**Redmond David**
WEX	Raheen Beg	**Redmond James**
WEX	Ballynestragh	**Redmond John**
WEX	Mill Lands	**Redmond John**
DUB	Diswellstown	**Redmond L**
CAR	Carlow Town	**Redmond Matt**
LAO	Grange	**Redmond Morris**
WEX	Ballynestragh	**Redmond William**
KILD	Osberstown	**Reed Robert**
LONG	Cullynore	**Reel John**
LONG	Cullynore	**Reel Mary Widow**
LOU	Reaghstown	**Reenan Peter**
TYR	Terrew	**Rees John**
ROS	Ballinasloe	**Reeves**
KILD	Connell	**Reeves Jos Robt**
KILD	Athgarvan	**Reeves Joseph R**
LONG	Longford Town	**Reeves Thomas**
DUB	Shanganagh	**Reeves Thomas**
LIM	Caherass	**Reeves Wiliam M**
DUB	Windmillhill	**Refues Richard C**
CRK	Brownsmills	**Regan**
GAL	Galway Town	**Regan Ann**
GAL	Galway Town	**Regan Anne**
CRK	Ballycroneen	**Regan Edward**
CRK	Carrigbaun	**Regan John**
GAL	Galway Town	**Regan Mary**
GAL	Galway Town	**Regan Michael**
DUB	Stubbins Mill	**Regan Patk**
DUB	Kimmage	**Regan Patrick**
DUB	Stubbins Mill	**Regan Patrick**
DUB	Tinkers Mill	**Regan Patrick**
ANT	Belfast Town	**Reid**
ANT	Whiteabbey	**Reid**
DWN	Ballygowan	**Reid Alex Orr**
ARM	Lurgana	**Reid Capt.**
DWN	Ballystockart	**Reid James**
ANT	Carrickfergus Tn	**Reid James**
ANT	Carrickfergus Tn	**Reid James J**
DWN	Ballygowan	**Reid Jane**
DON	Ballygay	**Reid Jas & Alex**
DWN	Drumnascamph	**Reid Joseph**
ANT	Carrickfergus Tn	**Reid Mary**
TYR	Mullyroddan	**Reid Mary**
TIP	Graiguefrahane	**Reid Minchin**
LOU	Dundalk Town	**Reid or Brown Margt**
DON	Rathmullan	**Reid Robert**
MON	Killymarran	**Reid Thomas**
ARM	lurgana	**Reid William**
CLE	Newmarket	**Reidy John**
DWN	Ballybawne	**Reilly**
DWN	Lisnamulligan	**Reilly**
CAV	Lurgan	**Reilly**
CAV	Lurganboy	**Reilly**
KILD	Newtown O`More	**Reilly**
CLE	Ballycorney	**Reilly**
ANT	Belfast Town	**Reilly & Co.**
CAV	Darkley	**Reilly Anne**
LEI	Kilmakeeny	**Reilly Bernard**
MEA	Ballinvally	**Reilly Bryan**
CAV	Greaghnadarragh	**Reilly Felix**
DUB	Edmondstown	**Reilly Hugh**
ARM	Aughnacloy	**Reilly James**
WEX	Barglany *	**Reilly James**
DUB	Blanchardstown	**Reilly James**
ROS	Canagh *	**Reilly James**
CRK	Edencurra	**Reilly James**
WEX	Mill Lands	**Reilly James**
TYR	Tullylagan	**Reilly Jno**
DWN	Ballygowan	**Reilly John**
DWN	Carnany	**Reilly John**
DWN	Clonknaverty	**Reilly John**
CAV	Drummany	**Reilly John**
CAV	Lackan	**Reilly John**
ARM	Lisdrumullion	**Reilly John**
TYR	Pluck	**Reilly John**
LEI	Kilmakeeny	**Reilly John**
WME	Tubber	**Reilly Margaret**
MEA	Balnagon Upper	**Reilly Mary**
CAV	Drumhillagh	**Reilly Michael**
DWN	Clonknaverty	**Reilly Miles**
CAV	Darkley	**Reilly Mrs.**
WME	Foyran	**Reilly Myles**
SLI	Carha	**Reilly Patrick**
CAV	Lurganboy	**Reilly Patrick**
CAV	Drumcassidy	**Reilly Peter**
CAV	Drumrush	**Reilly Terence**
MEA	Caddlestown	**Reilly Thomas**
CAV	Drumrush	**Reilly Thomas (Miler)**
CAV	Darkley	**Reilly Widow**
CAV	Darkley	**Reilly Widow**
DWN	Ballybawne	**Reilly Willaim**
DWN	Ballybawne	**Reilly William E**
ANT	Carrickfergus Tn	**Reilly William E**
DUB	Dublin City	**Reily James**
DWN	Baven	**Reily W**
SLI	Barley Mill	**Rendall Henry**
ROS	Cloonmagunnaun	**Rennell Catherine**
WAT	Piltown	**Renney Willam**
ANT	Ballygalley	**Rennie Hugh**
LDY	Coleraine Town	**Rennie John**
LDY	Coleraine	**Rennie John Hill**
DON	Abbey Mill	**Reoper George**
KILD	Castletown	**Revell**
CRK	Ballycroneen	**Reves Robert**
WW	Ballyduff	**Revill Francis**
WEX	Horeswood	**Reville John**
WME	Cullenmore	**Reynell**
WME	Multyfarnham	**Reynell**
KILD	Johnstown	**Reynolds**
CRK	Ballygarvan	**Reynolds Benjamin**
DUB	Dublin City	**Reynolds Benjamin**
ROS	Cloonaragh	**Reynolds Edwin S.**
CLE	Ardrahine *	**Reynolds Francis**
ARM	Markethill, Mohan	**Reynolds Geo**
CRK	KinsaleTown	**Reynolds Jno**
TIP	Blackmills *	**Reynolds Nicholas**
WME	Connyborrons	**Reynolds Richard**
LEI	Rossclogher	**Reynolds Richard**
DUB	Dundrum Manor	**Reynolds Thomas**
WAT	Dungarvan Town	**Reynolds William**
TYR	Tamnaskeeny	**Reynolds William**
DUB	Welshestown	**Ribton**
ROS	Clonard	**Ribtonward William**
KILD	Clonard	**Ricards**
KRY	Ballycarty	**Rice**
CRK	Gully East	**Rice**
LOU	Ballintiskin	**Rice Bernard**
KRY	Clashcommon	**Rice Stephen Edw**
KILD	B`more Eustace	**Rice Stephen Henry**
CAR	Wells	**Rice William**
DWN	Milltown	**Rich**
OFF	Comms. Clonlish	**Richard**
OFF	Drumakeenan	**Richard Dowd**
GAL	Shrulegrove	**Richard Golding**
KRY	Coolclogher	**Richard Leahy**
WAT	Carrigcastle	**Richard Purdy**
KILD	Ardree	**Richards**
LEI	Acre Park Five	**Richards Georgina**
LEI	Creaneleagh	**Richards Georgina**
LEI	Creaneleagh Abbey	**Richards Georgina**
ARM	Aghory	**Richardson**
TYR	Augher	**Richardson**
WME	Ballynagore	**Richardson**
ANT	Ballysillan	**Richardson**
ANT	Carrickfergus W	**Richardson**
MON	Legacurry	**Richardson**
ANT	Lisnagarvey	**Richardson**
LOU	Little Mill	**Richardson**
KILD	Moone	**Richardson**
GAL	Woodlands	**Richardson**
GAL	Woodlands	**Richardson**
DON	Tullarville *	**Richardson A. M.**
DON	Tullarville *	**Richardson Alex**

CO.	TOWNLAND	MILLER
DWN	Ballymacarret	**Richardson J**
DWN	Lisburn Island	**Richardson J Joseph**
ANT	Lisburn Town	**Richardson J N**
ANT	Tullynacross	**Richardson J N**
ANT	Magheralave	**Richardson J N R**
DWN	Tullynacross	**Richardson J.N.R.**
GAL	Clunbrucky	**Richardson James**
ANT	Lambeg	**Richardson James**
ANT	Lambeg South	**Richardson James**
ANT	Lisburn Millbrook	**Richardson James**
ANT	Lisburn Town	**Richardson James**
ANT	Magheralin	**Richardson James**
GAL	Woodlands	**Richardson James**
ANT	Lisburn Town	**Richardson James N**
ANT	Lisnagarvey	**Richardson Jas N**
ANT	Aghislone	**Richardson Jas N.**
DWN	Balyskeagh	**Richardson Jno**
DWN	DownpatrickTown	**Richardson Jno**
ANT	Lisburn Town	**Richardson Jno**
DWN	Saul	**Richardson Jno**
DWN	Taghnabrick	**Richardson Jno**
DWN	Tullynacross	**Richardson Jno**
ANT	Aghislone	**Richardson John**
KKY	Banagher	**Richardson John**
DUB	Dublin	**Richardson John**
ANT	Tullynacross	**Richardson Jonathan**
ANT	Aghislone	**Richardson Joseph,**
ANT	Lisburn Town	**Richardson Josh**
LOU	Thomastown	**Richardson M/As**
MEA	Kells Town	**Richardson Thomas**
TYR	Augher	**Richardson Wiliam**
ARM	Augher	**Richardson William**
ARM	Ballylane	**Richardson William**
GAL	Clunbrucky	**Richardson William H**
GAL	Clunbrucky	**Richardson Wm Henry**
MON	Seaveagh	**Richarson Edward**
ARM	Crossdened	**Richey John**
KILD	Greatconnell	**Rickard**
DUB	Whitestown	**Rickard Walter**
DUB	Whitestown	**Rickards Mr**
DUB	Whitestown	**Rickards Walter**
TIP	Windmill	**Riddiford Geo**
LOU	Drogheda Town	**Ridgeway Thomas**
LOU	Newtownstalaban	**Ridley Stephen**
LEI	Drumcree	**Riggs Ann Spinster**
LEI	Drumcree	**Riggs Robert**
LEI	Drumcree	**Riggs Thomas**
TYR	Ballymagowan	**Rigney David**
DWN	Ballynahinch	**Ringland John**
CRK	Macroney Lower	**Riordan James**
LOU	White Mill	**Rispin**
LDY	Derrylane	**Ritchie John**
ROS	Gillstown	**Ritchie Robert**
FER	Emmerroo *	**Ritchie William**
DUB	Dublin City	**Rivers J**
LONG	Barnacor	**Rivers Lord Geo Bt.**

CO.	TOWNLAND	MILLER
WEX	Tottenhamgreen	**Roach John**
KKY	Garrynarea	**Roade John**
LAO	Stradbally	**Roan James**
ARM	Derrybrughas	**Robb Mrs**
DUB	Diswellstown	**Robbins Joseph**
ROS	Ballyroddy	**Robbins Mary ors Griffin**
ROS	Ballyroddy	**Robbins Richard**
DWN	Tullylish	**Robbins Robert**
CRK	Baurnahulla	**Robbinson George**
LAO	Old Mill	**Robert**
LAO	Cullenagh (bo.)	**Roberts**
LAO	Donaghmore	**Roberts**
CRK	Dromcorragh	**Roberts**
WAT	Durrow	**Roberts**
DWN	Gransha	**Roberts**
WAT	Millerstown	**Roberts**
LAO	Rathdowney	**Roberts**
CLE	Cragleagh	**Roberts Arthur**
CLE	Cragleagh	**Roberts Arthur**
LAO	Rathdowney	**Roberts Arthur**
LAO	Stradbally	**Roberts Arthur**
DUB	Dublin City	**Roberts J F**
WW	Bray	**Roberts Jno**
ANT	Ballycollin	**Roberts John**
ANT	Collin Mountain	**Roberts John**
ANT	Mullaglass	**Roberts John**
ARM	Sheernageragh	**Roberts John**
KILD	Johnstown	**Roberts John Cramer Rev.**
KILD	Johnstown	**Roberts John Rev**
KILD	Johnstown	**Roberts Marmaduke**
CRK	Carrigaline West	**Roberts Michael**
WAT	Millerstown	**Roberts Peter**
DUB	Donnybrook	**Roberts Robert**
WAT	Mayfield	**Roberts Robert**
LAO	Ballycullenbeg	**Roberts Thomas**
WW	Bray	**Roberts Thomas**
LAO	Clonagheen	**Roberts Thomas**
LAO	Nore Mills	**Roberts Thomas**
WAT	Durrow (Millerstn.)	**Roberts Walter**
WEX	Waddingsland	**Roberts Wiliam**
ARM	Balteagh	**Robertson John**
CRK	Youghal Town	**Robertson Thomas**
OFF	Ballycumber	**Robins Patrick**
WME	Aghnatemple *	**Robinson**
OFF	Ballinamintown	**Robinson**
WW	Ballynultagh	**Robinson**
KILD	Belan	**Robinson**
LAO	Borris	**Robinson**
WME	Noughaval	**Robinson**
WW	Newmills	**Robinson Ann**
TYR	Oughterard	**Robinson Bariah**
KILD	Carberry & Castle :	**Robinson Caroline Spin.**
OFF	Birr Town	**Robinson Chris**
OFF	Birr Townsparks	**Robinson Chris**
FER	Dooederny	**Robinson David**
MYO	Banagher	**Robinson Edward**

CO.	TOWNLAND	MILLER
DUB	Dolphins Barn	**Robinson Elizabeth**
MYO	Killeennashask	**Robinson George**
DWN	Lisnamaul	**Robinson George**
ANT	Killydonnelly	**Robinson Hugh**
ARM	Artabrackagh	**Robinson James**
DWN	Ballynagarrick	**Robinson Jno**
LOU	Dundalk Town	**Robinson Jno**
DWN	Cunningburn	**Robinson John**
LOU	Dundalk Town	**Robinson John**
DUB	Hollybrook	**Robinson John**
WEX	Tomduff	**Robinson John**
DON	Legnachiny Lr *	**Robinson John Rev**
KILD	Carberry & Castle :	**Robinson John Rev.**
DUB	Beggarsbush	**Robinson Mr**
MON	Royduff	**Robinson Mr**
DWN	Dundrum	**Robinson Richard**
DUB	Mounttown	**Robinson Richard**
OFF	Birr Townsparks	**Robinson Robert**
OFF	Birr Townsparks	**Robinson S.**
ANT	Beltoy	**Robinson Sam**
OFF	Ballinamintown	**Robinson Samuel**
OFF	Clara Town	**Robinson Samuel**
OFF	Birr Town	**Robinson Thomas**
DON	Killult	**Robinson Thomas**
KILD	Greatconnell	**Robinson William**
ANT	Turreagh	**Robinson William**
WW	Milltown	**Robnett Robert**
DWN	Ballymacarret	**Roche**
WAT	Cappoquin	**Roche**
CLE	Clonassy	**Roche**
KILD	Milltown	**Roche**
WAT	Stonehouse	**Roche**
LIM	Caherass	**Roche David**
LIM	Caherass	**Roche David Yngr.**
WEX	Monagreany	**Roche Henry**
WEX	Monagreany	**Roche Henry (1846)**
CRK	Milltown b/ Imokilly	**Roche James**
CLE	Ballycline River	**Roche Jno**
WEX	Ballyanne	**Roche John**
WAT	Cappoquin	**Roche John**
CRK	Doonawanly	**Roche John**
CAR	Milford	**Roche John**
WEX	Garrylough Lr	**Roche Maurice**
CRK	Straw Hall	**Roche Nicholas Wm**
WEX	Arnestown	**Roche Patrick**
WEX	Garrylough Lr	**Roche Patrick**
WEX	Maudlins	**Roche Patrick**
KKY	Newtown	**Roche Patrick**
LIM	Mahoonagh	**Roche R**
LIM	Mahoonagh More	**Roche Richard**
LIM	Mahoonagh More	**Roche Robert**
LIM	Caherass	**Roche Sir David Bart.**
LIM	Skeagh	**Roche Sir David Bart.**
LIM	Milltown	**Roche William**
WAT	Waterford Town	**Roche William**
DUB	Roebuck	**Rochford John**

CO.	TOWNLAND	MILLER
LAO	Cloghrennan	Rochfort
WME	Moyvore	Rochfort
WME	Kibber	Rochfort Arthur
WME	Tyrellspass	Rochfort Arthur
CRK	Ballycroneen	Rochfort Boyd Chas
DUB	Dublin City	Rochfort D
WME	Kilbeggan	Rochfort George
CAR	Cloghristick	Rochfort Horace
WME	Tyrellspass	Rochfort Richard
WME	Kibber	Rochfort Robert
WME	Moyvore	Rochfort Robert
WME	Tyrellspass	Rochfort Robert
WEX	Camolin	Rock Samuel
TIP	Figlash	Rockett Mary
WEX	Kilmannan	Rockfort Moses
WW	Ballynultagh	Rockingham Charles Hon.
TYR	Bunowen	Roddy James
LOU	Killanny	Roddy John
DWN	Millisle	Roddy John
WME	Rathbennett	Roddy John
DWN	Millisle	Roddy Robert
WAT	Cullinagh	Roderick David
TYR	Tattykeel	Rodgers Alex
TYR	Tattykeel	Rodgers Frances
LDY	Curran	Rodgers George
LOU	Listulk	Rodgers John
LDY	Carrick East	Rodgers Marcus
LDY	Terrydremount	Rodgers Marcus
TYR	Tattykeel	Rodgers Margaret
LEI	Kilmakeeny	Rodgers Patrick
TYR	Tattykeel	Rodgers Robert
LONG	Drumlish Vge.	Rodgers Thomas
TYR	Tattykeel	Rodgers William
MON	Agnaglogh	Roe
CAR	Clashganny	Roe
CAR	Cloghristick	Roe
TIP	Clonmel	Roe Andrew
CAR	Cloghristick	Roe James
TIP	Clonmel	Roe Mary Widow
MON	Tullyrain	Roe Micharl
DUB	Dublin	Roe Mr, Coome
LAO	Mountrath	Roe Peter
DUB	Dublin City	Roe R
LONG	Gaigue	Roe William
DUB	Dundrum	Rogan Nichholas
GAL	Galway Town	Rogan William
GAL	Galway Town	Rogan William
DON	Ginsurry	Roger Mr
MYO	Ardnaree	Roger Palmer+B91
MON	Enveyarig *	Rogers
WAT	Garrancrobally	Rogers
WAT	Tramore	Rogers
WAT	Waterford Town	Rogers
WAT	Waterford Town	Rogers Geale
DON	Killyverry	Rogers George
DON	Killyverry	Rogers James
WAT	Garrancrobally	Rogers John
WAT	Waterford Town	Rogers Mary ors Bachus
ANT	Derryaghy	Rogers Robert
WAT	Garrancrobally	Rogers Susanna Wid.
WAT	Garrancrobally	Rogers Thomas
LONG	Garvagh	Rogers Thomas
CAV	Legwee	Rogers Thomas
WAT	Waterford Town	Rogers W
MEA	Monknewtown	Rogers Wiliam
CAV	Drumrish	Rogers William
MEA	Rogerstown	Rogers William
WAT	Waterford Town	Rogers William
GAL	Ballylee	Roland John
MYO	Brackley	Roland William
GAL	Strongfort	Roland William
DON	Ardagh	Rolestone Andrew
OFF	Ballycumber	Rolle
TYR	Lisnacreaght	Rollestone Robert
CRK	Newmarket Town	Ronaldson Eben'zer
ANT	Shankill T`parks	Ronan John,
ANT	Shankill T`parks	Ronan William
WAT	Dungarvan Town	Ronayne Elinor, Spin.
CRK	Youghal Town	Ronayne Thomas
KILD	Clonard	Rooke John Jun
LOU	ArdeeTown	Rooke W. Bart.
GAL	Ballylee	Roonan Patrick
GAL	Brownville	Rooney Alexander
GAL	Corcullen	Rooney Alexander
LDY	Vintners Propn.	Rooney Elizabeth
DUB	Dublin City	Rooney M
MYO	Ballinamona	Rooney Patrick
LDY	Vintners Propn.	Rooney Thomas
DUB	Dublin City	Rooney W
MEA	Athboy Town	Roper Jno
LAO	Ballyroan	Rorke
SLI	Knockbrook	Rorke Patrick
KILD	Johnstown	Rose
MON	Killymaran	Rose James
WW	Ballinvally	Rose John
LIM	Castlematrix	Rose Richard
DWN	Ballyhalbert	Ross
DWN	Ballyharley	Ross
DWN	Ballyhemlin	Ross
LOU	Carlingford Town	Ross
LAO	Clonmore	Ross
DWN	Newtown	Ross
DUB	Clondalkin	Ross Alex
DUB	Dub Port & Cem.	Ross Alex
TYR	Tonnaghmore	Ross Daniel
WW	Kilcoole	Ross Hon Richard
LEI	Ballinamore Town	Ross James
DWN	Ballyhemlin	Ross James
ANT	Inver	Ross James
ANT	Larne Town	Ross James
ANT	Belfast Town	Ross John
ANT	Millquarter	Ross John
WW	Kilcoole	Ross Richard Hon.
WW	Kilcoole	Ross Richard Ld Visc.
DWN	Ardkeen	Ross Thos C
ANT	Shankill T`parks	Ross William
MON	Ballybay Town	Rosse D
OFF	Birr	Rosse Lord
CRK	Cork City	Roth John
CRK	Cork City	Roth Philip
WW	Killancanny	Rothwell George
WW	Killaveny	Rothwell George
MON	Tullyglass	Rothwell Thomas
WW	Ballynultagh	Rothwell William
KRY	Ballyheabought	Rourk Michael
DUB	Edmondstown	Rourke
KILD	Clonkeen	Rourke Francis
CAR	Knockbarragh	Rourke Hugh
GAL	Kilnaborris	Rourke John
LOU	Little Mill	Rourke Michael
DUB	Milltown	Rourke P
KILD	Ballynabought *	Rourke Peter
LOU	Kercock	Rourke Peter
KILD	Ballynabought *	Rourke Thomas
KILD	Bonglass *	Rourke Thomas
KRY	Ballintourtone	Rowan
ANT	Belfast Town	Rowan Henry
ANT	Doagh	Rowan James
ANT	Ballyhamage	Rowan John
ANT	Toberdowney	Rowan John
WAT	Bleach	Rowan Mary T
DWN	Tobermoney	Rowan Thomas
DWN	Cloghskelt	Rowan William
LDY	Loughan Water	Rowan William
DWN	Moneyslane	Rowan William
WEX	Wexford Town	Rowe Howard
WEX	Wexford Town	Rowe S
WEX	Wexford Town	Rowe Thomas
GAL	Ballygarraun	Rowland John
GAL	Ballygarraun	Rowland Thomas
GAL	Caheradangan	Rowland William
DUB	Channon Hill	Rowley
LEI	Limerick Manor	Rowley Josias Sir
LEI	Cavan Park	Rowley Rev Jno
LEI	Cavan Park	Rowley William
ARM	Marlacoo	Rowntree James
TIP	Bansha West	Royal Ld. Bd. Inv. Co.
KILD	Millquarter Timolin	Roycroft
DON	Kiln Hills *	RReid Robert
CRK	Ballinacarriga	Rucklet John
TIP	Graiguefrahane	Rudd Minchin
TIP	Templemore Town	Rudd Minchin
TIP	Whitefield	Rudd Minchin
OFF	Ballyduff	Rudd W
TIP	Parkmore	Rudd William
TIP	Roscrea Town	Rudd William
TIP	Archerstown	Ruddy James
TIP	Graiguefrahane	Rudle Minchin

CO.	TOWNLAND	MILLER
ROS	Athleague Manor	**Rumbold Eliz**
GAL	Galway Town	**Rush A**
GAL	Galway Town	**Rush Ambrose**
ARM	Balleer	**Rusk William**
ANT	Skerry East	**Russel Thomas H**
ANT	Belfast Town	**Russell**
DWN	Belvor *	**Russell**
LAO	Clonaslee	**Russell**
LAO	Drinagh	**Russell**
WAT	Dungarvan Town	**Russell**
LOU	Dundalk Town	**Russell A (Millwright)**
DON	Burnside	**Russell Alex**
ARM	Ballinlare	**Russell Arthur**
DWN	Ballykinler Upr	**Russell Charles**
LIM	Askeaton Town	**Russell Edmond**
LIM	Limerick City	**Russell Francis P**
KILD	Bushfield	**Russell Henry**
DWN	Edenderry	**Russell Houston**
ROS	Ballyleague	**Russell J A**
DON	Burnside	**Russell James**
LIM	Aghalacka	**Russell Jn Norris**
LIM	Askeaton	**Russell Jno**
LIM	Askeaton Town	**Russell Jno**
LIM	Aghalacka	**Russell John**
LIM	Askeaton Town	**Russell John**
DWN	Belvor *	**Russell John**
DON	Drumcavan	**Russell John**
WAT	Waterford City	**Russell John**
LIM	Aghalacka	**Russell John Norris**
LIM	Limerick City	**Russell John R**
KKY	The Mill Field	**Russell John W**
KKY	The Mill Field	**Russell John W**
LIM	Askeaton Town	**Russell Richard**
ARM	Derrycushan	**Russell Robert**
DWN	Ballooly More	**Russell Samuel**
KILD	Bushfield	**Russell Samuel**
KILD	Bushfield	**Russell Solomon**
ARM	Lislanly	**Russell Thomas**
WW	Redcross	**Russell Thomas**
ANT	Limavallaghan	**Russell Thomas H**
LOU	Dundalk Town	**Russell W (Millwright)**
DON	Moleng	**Russell William**
DON	Ballyarr	**Russell`s Mill**
KKY	Freshford Lots	**Ruth Martin**
KKY	Kilrush	**Ruth Patrick**
ANT	Belfast Town	**Rutherford John**
DUB	Donnybrook	**Rutland A**
KILD	Mount Blarney *	**Rutledge Edward**
SLI	Castleconnor	**Rutledge George**
KILD	Mount Blarney *	**Rutledge Thomas**
MYO	Foxford	**Ruttledge**
MYO	Foxford	**Ruttledge Andrew**
MYO	Turlough	**Ruttledge Mr.**
KILD	Kilkea	**Ruttledge Thomas**
MYO	Knockmore	**Ruttledge William**
MYO	Turlough	**Ruttledge William**

CO.	TOWNLAND	MILLER
LOU	Ardee	**Ruxton**
LOU	Ballynamenan	**Ruxton**
LOU	Ardee Town	**Ruxton William**
LOU	Ardee Town	**Ruxton Arthur**
LOU	Ardee Town	**Ruxton Clarges**
CAR	Tobinstown	**Ruxton Clarges**
ARM	Newt`nhamilton	**Ruxton Henry**
LOU	ArdeeTown	**Ruxton Jno**
LOU	Ardee Town	**Ruxton John**
LOU	Ardee Town	**Ruxton Mary**
LOU	ArdeeTown	**Ruxton Wiliam**
LOU	Ardee Town	**Ruxton William**
WME	Ardnacranny	**Ruxton William**
TIP	Bansha	**Ryan**
LIM	Brudy *	**Ryan**
CAR	Carlow Town	**Ryan**
KILD	Millestown ?	**Ryan**
CLE	O'Briensbridge	**Ryan**
LAO	Timahoe	**Ryan**
CAR	Carlow Town	**Ryan - Hamilton**
CAR	Carlow Town	**Ryan - Redmond**
ROS	Athleague	**Ryan Thomas**
LAO	Rathdowney	**Ryan Andrew**
TIP	Atshanbo Cahill	**Ryan Anthony**
TIP	Atshanboe	**Ryan Anthony**
TIP	Ushanbo Cahill	**Ryan Anthony**
WAT	Waterford Town	**Ryan Charles**
WME	Athlone Town	**Ryan Charles R**
TIP	Holycross	**Ryan Daniel**
CAR	Ballyknockan	**Ryan David**
WAT	Ballyvoyle	**Ryan Edward**
TIP	Crannavone	**Ryan Edward**
CAR	Carlow Town	**Ryan Henry**
CAR	Carlow Town	**Ryan James**
GAL	Galway Liberties	**Ryan James**
KRY	Kilfountan	**Ryan James**
CAR	Carlow Town	**Ryan John**
CRK	Clashganniv	**Ryan John**
WAT	Graigavalla	**Ryan John**
TIP	Holycross	**Ryan John**
LIM	Kilmallock Town :	**Ryan John**
CRK	Rathgoggan Middle	**Ryan Kennedy**
TIP	Islandbawn	**Ryan Malachi**
TIP	Islandbawn	**Ryan Malachi**
TIP	Tyone	**Ryan Malachi**
OFF	Clonavoe	**Ryan Margaret**
OFF	Clonvara	**Ryan Margaret**
OFF	Clonbrone	**Ryan Margaret Wid.**
WEX	Mullinderry	**Ryan Martin**
KILD	Athy Town	**Ryan Mary**
WEX	Enniscorthy Town	**Ryan Mary**
LIM	Bruree	**Ryan Michael**
LIM	Bruree Town	**Ryan Michael**
TIP	Holycross	**Ryan Michael**
WAT	Shanakill	**Ryan Michael**
DUB	Ballyboden	**Ryan Nicholas**

CO.	TOWNLAND	MILLER
TIP	Ballygown	**Ryan Patrick**
SLI	Culleens	**Ryan Patrick**
WEX	Yoletown	**Ryan Patrick**
DUB	Edmondstown	**Ryan Richard**
TIP	Borrisland	**Ryan Stephen**
TIP	Borrisland North	**Ryan Stephen**
SLI	Culleens	**Ryan Thomas**
MYO	Furnace	**Ryan Thomas**
SLI	Kilrusheighter	**Ryan Thomas**
OFF	Tullamore Town	**Ryan Thomas**
TIP	Lacken	**Ryan Timothy**
WAT	Graigavalla	**Ryan Widow**
KILD	Johnstown	**Ryan William**
MON	Killycooly	**Ryan William**
WEX	Milltown	**Ryan William**
TIP	Moynetemple	**Ryan William**
WW	Kilcoole	**Ryder John**
DUB	St Cath`s Park	**Ryder Thomas**
WAT	Dungarvan Town	**Rylan**
MEA	Jordanstown	**Rynd Robert F**
		S
KILD	Newhall	**Sabine**
KILD	Newhall	**Sabine Joshua**
ANT	Ballysillan	**Saddler B G**
ARM	Tassagh	**Sadler**
OFF	Newtown	**Sadler Fran**
TIP	Bansagh	**Sadlier**
TIP	Bansha	**Sadlier**
TIP	Caher Prems.	**Sadlier**
CRK	Hollybrook *	**Sadlier John G**
TIP	Cashel Town	**Sadlier Thomas**
OFF	Colehill	**Sadlier Thomas**
WME	Mullingar Town	**Sagan**
WW	Bray	**Salheren**
WW	Bray	**Salheren George**
MEA	Ballyboggan	**Saliner**
WW	Kilmacon Upper	**Salkeld John**
DWN	Ballymegenaghie *	**Salkeld Joseph**
WW	Connary Upper	**Salkeld Joseph**
DWN	Ballymegenaghie *	**Salkeld Thomas**
CLE	O'Callaghansmills	**Sampson**
TYR	Tonnaghmore	**Sampson R**
LIM	Deebert	**Sanders John**
ROS	Creevemully	**Sanders Lancellot**
DUB	Inchicore	**Sanders Richard**
TYR	Tullylagan	**Sanderson -**
WW	Kilmacon Upper	**Sandes Richardd**
ROS	Cloontowart	**Sandford Elizabeth**
ROS	Emlagh	**Sandford Henry**
ROS	Emlagh	**Sandford Robert**
DWN	Newry Town	**Sands Robert**
DUB	Dolphins Barn	**Sands William**
KRY	Ashtown	**Sandview Ltd**
WEX	Barglany *	**Sandwith Henry**
WEX	Barglany *	**Sandwith William**

INDEX

CO.	TOWNLAND	MILLER
WW	Humphreystown	Shannon Jno
SLI	Castletown	Shannon John
LAO	Mountmellick	Shannon Joseph
TIP	Marlfield	Shannon Mary
TIP	Marlfield	Shannon Mary Anne
WW	Homphrystown	Shannon Robert
DWN	Aghiohill *	Shannon Samuel
WEX	Ballygavan	Shannon Thomas
DWN	Aghiohill *	Shannon William
WW	Bray	Sharkey Robert
WW	Bray	Sharkey Thomas
KKY	Skeard	Sharman John
KKY	Skeard	Sharman Joseph
DUB	Swords Town	Sharp Edward
DUB	Templeogue	Sharp James
DUB	Templeogue	Sharpe James
DUB	Templeogue	Sharpe James
LEI	Ballinamore Town	Sharpley Charles
LEI	Rhadermott	Sharpley Charles
LIM	Kilmallock	Shaughnessy
CRK	Coolhane	Shaughnessy Andr
GAL	Fiddaun	Shaughnessy John
GAL	Fiddaun	Shaughnessy William
OFF	Annaghmore	Shaw
TIP	Ballylynch	Shaw
LAO	Ballyroan	Shaw
ANT	Cappobeg	Shaw
KILD	Celbridge Town	Shaw
LIM	Limerick City	Shaw
MEA	Stephenstown	Shaw Charles
TYR	Crossdernot	Shaw Edward
DWN	Kilmood	Shaw Frew
LDY	Tamniaran	Shaw George
DWN	Drumaroad	Shaw Hugh
ANT	Ballynacaird	Shaw James
LONG	Cloonturk	Shaw James
DON	Convoy	Shaw James A
MEA	Stephenstown	Shaw James Eldr.
MEA	Stephenstown	Shaw James Yngr.
ANT	Belfast	Shaw Jno
OFF	Springmount *	Shaw Jno
TYR	Donaghmore	Shaw John
TYR	Tullinure *	Shaw John
DUB	Feltrim	Shaw John P
CRK	Ballyvolane	Shaw Joseph
CRK	Cahergal	Shaw Joseph
KILD	Newtown	Shaw Joseph
DON	Kinnacally	Shaw Mr
ANT	Ballywillin	Shaw Richard
LEI	Umeryroe	Shaw Richard
DWN	Cullintraw	Shaw Robert
ANT	Limavallaghan	Shaw Robert
DUB	Willbrook	Shaw Robert
LAO	Clarahill	Shaw Silvester
DON	Kinnacally	Shaw Widow
DWN	Ballycloghan	Shaw William
MON	Ballynode	Shaw William
MON	Ballynure	Shaw William
CRK	Bandon	Shaw William
CRK	Bandon Town	Shaw William
DON	Milltown	Shaw William
LEI	Umeryroe	Shaw William
DUB	Milltown	Shaw William Alex
CRK	Kilnap	Shaw William J
LONG	Cloonturk	Shaw`s Mill
MON	Ballynode	Shaw+B136
KRY	Derreennamucklagl	Shea Cornelius
KRY	Gortaneden	Shea James
KKY	Parksgrove	Shea James
KKY	Mullen Beg	Shea Jeoffry
KKY	Columbkille	Shea John
KKY	Dangan	Shea John
CRK	Cahergal	Shea Joseph
CRK	Kilnap	Shea Joseph
CRK	Ringroe	Shea L I
KRY	Ballard Upper	Shea Timothy
TIP	Milestown	Shea William
ARM	Brannock	Sheals Michael
ARM	Brannock	Sheals Neal
LAO	Mountmellick T`pks	Sheane James
KRY	Ballycasheen	Shebee Michael
LOU	Collon	Sheckleton James
LOU	Collon	Sheckleton Margaret
TIP	Allitrim *	Shedon Barbara
CLE	Moys	Sheehan Joseph
KRY	Ballincarrig West	Sheehy Bart
WAT	Durrow	Sheehy Edmond
MEA	Monknewtown	Sheffield Earl
MON	Corliglacka	Shegog George
MON	Corfinlough	Shegog James
MON	Corealacka	Shegog John
MON	Corfinlough	Shegog John
MON	Drumgor	Shegog William
MON	Toam *	Shegog William
WW	Ballinvally	Sheil Mary Widow
WW	Ballinvally	Sheil Osborne Rev.
LOU	Ardnaree	Sheil Phillipa (Moore) Wid.
DUB	Dublin City	Sheill
LOU	Drogheda Town	Sheils John Joseph
LOU	Collon Town	Shekleton James
LOU	Collon Town	Shekleton Margaret
LOU	Collon	Shekleton Mrs
LONG	Clondra	Shelburn Lord Henry
LONG	Clondora	Shelburne Earl
LAO	Maryborough Town	Shelburne Earl
WAT	Aglish	Shelley H
WAT	Aglish	Shelley Henry
WAT	Raheen	Shelley Henry
DUB	Dublin City	Shepheard
KILD	Newhall	Sherdley
MON	Reduff	Sheridan
DWN	Tullychin	Sheridan
DWN	Ardkeen	Sheridan Augustine
LOU	Balregan	Sherif Co Louth
LOU	White Mill	Sherif Co. Louth
LOU	Balregan	Sheriff Co. Louth
DUB	Dublin City	Sherigley
KILD	Ardee	Sherlock
DUB	Drumcondra	Sherlock Mr
MEA	Balgeeth	Sherlock Patrick
DUB	Drishoge	Sherlock Patrick
DUB	Killerough	Sherlock Richard
DUB	Edmondstown	Sherlock Robert
KILD	Ardee	Sherlock Thomas
LOU	Ardree	Sherlock Thomas
LOU	Ardree	Sherlock Thomasl
WME	Carrick	Sherlock William
MON	Aghnamullen	Sherrif Co. Monaghan
LOU	Balregan	Sherry
DUB	Feltrim	Sherry Patrick
DUB	Donnybrook	Sherwin
WW	Ballinvally	Shiel James
MEA	Iffernock	Shiel John
KILD	Ardnaree	Shiel Phillipa (Moore) Wid.
WW	Ballinvally	Shiel Thomas
MEA	Aghaloaghan	Shiels Eleanor
LAO	Killinure	Shiels Patrick
DON	Disslin	Shildon Alex
DON	Disslin	Shildon Alexander
ARM	Garvaghy	Shillington Thomas
CRK	Ballygarvan	Shimmick John
CRK	Ballygarvan	Shimmick Yahine
LIM	Ballynoe	Shine Michael
LEI	Kilmallock	Shinkwin Capt.
LIM	Kilmallock	Shinkwin Capt.
ARM	Tullycondraught	Shirges
DUB	Dublin City	Shirigley
KKY	Killinny	Shirley Thomas
CRK	Coolkellure	Sholdam General
OFF	Birr	Short
KILD	Irishtown	Short John
TIP	Beakstown	Shortall Michael
WEX	Crory Lower	Shortall Michael
WEX	Garrylough Lr.	Shortall Peter
CRK	Townland ?	Shorten Joseph
CRK	Townland ?	Shorten Thomas
TIP	Holycross	Shorthall Michael
LEI	Stradermot	Shortley Charles
WEX	Duncormack	Shudall John
MYO	Ballynew	Shuffle Robert
LONG	Garrynagh	Shuldam
ANT	Millq`r Manybrook	Shuldam
LONG	Kilnplot	Shuldam Jn Brady
LONG	Ballymulvey	Shuldam John
LONG	Kilnplot	Shuldam John
LONG	Shrule	Shuldam John Brady
KILD	Parsonstown	Shuldan
LONG	Cloonkeen	Shuldham John

CO.	TOWNLAND	MILLER
ROS	Gillstown	**Stafford Andrew**
ROS	Gillstown	**Stafford Bridgid**
ROS	Gillstown	**Stafford Elizabeth**
FER	Gubbacrock	**Stafford Gerrard**
KILD	Clane	**Stafford Hugh**
ROS	Gillstown	**Stafford John**
WEX	Scar	**Stafford John**
ROS	Gillstown	**Stafford Margaret**
ROS	Gillstown	**Stafford Matthew**
WEX	Waddington	**Stafford Patrick**
CLE	Craggbryen	**Stakpoole John**
WW	B'more Eustace	**Standish William**
GAL	Coololla	**Stanford Robert**
ARM	Tavanagh	**Stanley Henry**
ARM	Kennedies	**Stanley James**
CRK	Bandon Town	**Stanley Joseph**
CRK	Bandon Town	**Stanley Joseph**
TIP	Townland /	**Stanley Richard**
CRK	Desert	**Stannard James E**
TIP	Ballyanny	**Stapleton James**
TIP	Knigh	**Stapleton James**
DON	Rathmullan	**Starratt**
MEA	Broad	**Staunton**
LDY	Lismoney	**Staunton John**
MYO	Kilbride	**Staunton Patrick**
GAL	Esker Roe	**Staunton Peter**
KILD	Kilmore	**Staunton Thomas**
CRK	Horseclose	**Stawel George**
TYR	Carnagatt	**Stawell William**
WME	Parcellstown	**Stearne**
WW	Coolgarrow	**Stedman Richard**
MON	Cossabey	**Steel James**
MON	Cossabey	**Steel Jno Eld**
MON	Cossabey	**Steel Walter**
MON	Ballyrush	**Steele**
CLE	Clonassy	**Steele**
MON	Cossabey	**Steen John**
ANT	Stradballymorris	**Steen A**
ANT	Stradballymorris	**Steen Alex**
LDY	Ballinacanon	**Steen James**
DWN	Ballyhackmore	**Steen James**
ANT	Stradbally	**Steen James**
DON	Little Dromore	**Steen Joseph**
DON	Little Dromore	**Steen Matthew**
ANT	Stradballymorris	**Steen Mr**
DUB	Inchicore	**Steering James**
WAT	Killadangan	**Stephen Baker**
WME	Athlone Town	**Stephen Henry**
KRY	Killerisk	**Stephen Samuel**
CRK	Castledodde *	**Stephens**
DUB	Chapelizod	**Stephens**
KRY	Killerisk	**Stephens**
CAR	Scortreen	**Stephens**
FER	Belleek Town	**Stephens Felix**
FER	Rathmore	**Stephens Felix**
MEA	Athboy Town	**Stephens H**

CO.	TOWNLAND	MILLER
GAL	Galway Town	**Stephens James**
WW	Rathdown	**Stephens John**
DUB	Dublin City	**Stephens Mr**
DON	Aighan	**Stephens Mrs**
LAO	Abbeyleix	**Stephens William**
DUB	Glasnevin	**Stephens William**
ARM	Ballyards	**Stephenson**
TYR	Tuckmill Quarter	**Stephenson Edward**
DWN	Ballynagarrick	**Stephenson John**
LDY	Tullyally Lower	**Stephenson Margaret**
DON	Lignathraw	**Stephenson Mr**
DUB	Glasnevin	**Sterling Dorothea Spin.**
WAT	Aglish	**Steuart William**
ANT	Carnbrock	**Stevelly Edward**
ANT	Ballyportery S	**Stevelly John**
WEX	Ross Town	**Stevelly Robert Rev.**
ANT	Ballyportery S	**Stevelly William**
ANT	Ballymagarry	**Stevenson**
ANT	Loaning	**Stevenson**
MEA	Athboy Town	**Stevenson Blackwood**
LDY	Carnanbane	**Stevenson James**
LDY	Gallany	**Stevenson John**
MON	Tullyglish	**Stevenson John Ygr.**
ANT	Shankill T`parks	**Stevenson Peter**
DON	Carrowkeel	**Stevenson Robert**
TYR	Drumreaghotra	**Stevenson Robert**
DON	Ballylevin	**Stevenson Robt**
DWN	Ballymacarret	**Stevenson S**
ANT	Kilroot	**Stevenson Samuel**
ARM	Acton Manor	**Stewart**
DWN	Balloo	**Stewart**
DWN	Ballydugan	**Stewart**
CAR	Ballyellen	**Stewart**
WW	Blessington	**Stewart**
TYR	Dungannon	**Stewart**
LDY	Gregardvardan *	**Stewart**
DWN	Portaferrey Town	**Stewart**
DON	Cavan	**Stewart A**
DON	Corcreggan	**Stewart A**
DON	Kilmackilloo	**Stewart A**
LDY	Edenballymore	**Stewart Abraham H**
DWN	Ballystockart	**Stewart Alex**
ARM	Brannock	**Stewart Alex**
DON	Cashelshanaghan	**Stewart Alex**
DON	Cashelshanaghan	**Stewart Alex**
DON	Cavan	**Stewart Alex**
DON	Corcreggan	**Stewart Alex**
DON	Corcreggan	**Stewart Alex**
TYR	Drumaspill	**Stewart Alex**
DON	Kilmacrenan	**Stewart Alex**
ANT	Legoneil	**Stewart Alex**
DON	Mass More	**Stewart Alex**
DON	Mullenigar Millacre	**Stewart Alex**
ANT	Tullaghbane	**Stewart Alex**
CAR	Bendinstown	**Stewart Andrew**
CAR	Bendinstown	**Stewart Andrew**

CO.	TOWNLAND	MILLER
DUB	Feltrim	**Stewart Annesley**
MEA	Broad	**Stewart Charles**
CAR	Carlow Town	**Stewart Charles**
SLI	Drumcliff South	**Stewart Charles**
TYR	Killymoon	**Stewart Col William**
TYR	Drumaspill	**Stewart Geo Rector**
TYR	Loughmuck	**Stewart George**
TYR	Lisdoart	**Stewart George V**
TYR	Drumaspill	**Stewart Hamilton Rev.**
LDY	Carndaisy	**Stewart Hannah**
CAR	Bagnelstown	**Stewart Henry**
ANT	Chathamhall	**Stewart Henry**
DUB	Gallagh	**Stewart Henry**
TYR	Cavan	**Stewart Hugh**
DWN	Shannaghan	**Stewart Hugh**
ANT	Tullaghbane	**Stewart Hugh**
DWN	Ballymurphy	**Stewart J**
TYR	Altrest	**Stewart James**
TYR	Clanburns *	**Stewart James**
DON	Meenatoal ?	**Stewart James**
LDY	Moykeeran	**Stewart James**
CRK	Douglas	**Stewart James**
TYR	Creevenagh	**Stewart James Hon.**
DON	Fortstewart	**Stewart James Sir**
ANT	Tullaghbane	**Stewart Jane**
TYR	Blacksessagh	**Stewart Jno Rt. Hon.**
TYR	Cavan	**Stewart John Bart.**
TYR	Cavan	**Stewart John Rt. Hon.**
TYR	Cavan	**Stewart John Sir**
TYR	Creevenagh	**Stewart John Sir**
TYR	Dungannon	**Stewart Mary**
TYR	Mullybrannon	**Stewart Mary J**
TYR	Altrest	**Stewart Robert**
ARM	Glaslough	**Stewart Robert**
DON	Rathmillor	**Stewart Samuel**
LIM	Kilmallock Town	**Stewart Spencer**
DWN	Ballymorran	**Stewart Thomas**
TYR	Clanburns *	**Stewart W**
CAR	Ballygowan	**Stewart Wiliam**
TYR	Altrest	**Stewart William**
CAR	Ballyknockan	**Stewart William**
DWN	Ballyward	**Stewart William**
TYR	Mullybrannon	**Stewart William**
DON	Newmills	**Stewart William**
CAR	Poorestown *	**Stewart William**
DON	Rathmelton	**Stewart William**
TYR	Donaghenry	**Stewart's**
ARM	Balleer	**Stitt Alex**
WME	Mullamoran	**Stock**
LAO	Ballyroan	**Stoker**
DUB	Dundrum	**Stoker**
LAO	Ballyroan	**Stokes**
CLE	Cragleagh	**Stokes George B**
GAL	Galway Town	**Stokes Michael**
DUB	Dundrum	**Stokes Mr.**
DUB	Clonskeagh	**Stokes Mr. & Co.**

CO.	TOWNLAND	MILLER
DUB	Kiltiernan	**Stokes P**
DUB	Droultuin *	**Stokes William**
WME	Monksland	**Stone**
WW	Carnew	**Stone Ralph**
WME	Boyanagh	**Stoney**
DWN	Tullylish	**Stoney Issac**
TIP	Mill Grove *	**Stoney Margaret**
WEX	Mill Lands	**Stopford James**
WEX	Raheengurren	**Stopford James**
CAR	Shagten *	**Stoppford Lord**
FER	Dinnydoon	**Storey Joseph**
DUB	Dublin City	**Story Thomas**
WME	Gilbertstown	**Stott**
DWN	Quilly & Moss	**Stott**
KRY	Cuyrigns *	**Stotten**
WW	Tobber *	**Stotthard John**
ANT	Ballyreagh	**Strachan John**
ANT	Ballyloughan	**Strahan George**
TYR	Drumaspil	**Strain Alex**
KKY	Graguenakill	**Strangham Samuel**
WAT	Waterford City	**Strangman Davis**
LAO	Irishtown	**Strangman Joshua**
LAO	Maryborough Bo.	**Strangman Sam**
LAO	Monksgrange	**Stratford**
LAO	Monksgrange	**Stratford Benjamin**
LOU	Dundalk Town	**Straton John**
LOU	Dundalk Town	**Stratton Isabella**
LDY	Ballygurk	**Strean Samuel**
LDY	Ballyness	**Strean Samuel**
LDY	Bellaghy	**Strean Samuel**
CLE	Ballykilty	**Strettle Ambrose**
GAL	Galway Town	**Strickland Jar**
LAO	Timahoe	**Stringer**
ARM	Allistragh	**Stringer Francis**
ARM	Tassagh	**Stringer Francis**
ARM	Armagh	**Stringer Thomas**
ROS	Killynagh Beg	**Stroker John**
CAR	Poorestown *	**Stronde**
ARM	Tynan	**Strong James Sir**
MEA	Balrath	**Strong Jno**
MEA	Brownstown	**Strong John Rev.**
DWN	Ballyhemlin	**Stronge Thomas Rev.**
CAR	Milford	**Strongstream Ltd.**
ANT	Ballylig	**Stuart**
TYR	Loughmuck	**Stuart**
WAT	Raheen	**Stuart Henry**
DWN	Ballyhemlin	**Stuart William**
GAL	Galway Town	**Stubber Eleanor**
DUB	Edmondstown	**Stubbs**
DUB	Ballyboden	**Stubbs Jno**
DUB	Newbrook Mill	**Stubbs Jno**
DUB	Ballyboden	**Stubbs Robert**
LAO	Ballynakill	**Stubdel**
CLE	Ennis Town	**Studdert Richard**
MYO	Boherhallagh	**Sturgeon Hubert**
MEA	Cloghagh	**Sturgeon James Kemp**
MEA	Cloghagh	**Sturgeon JK**
FER	Moneen	**Stutt James**
DUB	Islandbridge	**Stuttart Elis, Miller**
MEA	Milltown	**Styles William**
DUB	Drimnagh	**Sulivan Daniel P**
ANT	Carrickfergus E	**Sullatober B&D Wks**
CRK	Ardclare *	**Sullivan**
CRK	Ballinhassig	**Sullivan**
MEA	Clonguiffin	**Sullivan**
DUB	Goldenbridge N	**Sullivan Bart**
KRY	Castledrum	**Sullivan Daniel**
DUB	Drimnagh	**Sullivan Daniel**
DUB	Goldenbridge N	**Sullivan Daniel P**
DUB	Kilmainham	**Sullivan Edward**
CRK	Blarney	**Sullivan Jas Bart**
DUB	Ballyboden	**Sullivan Jeremiah.**
CRK	Kinsale Town	**Sullivan Jno**
TIP	Cabragh	**Sullivan John**
CRK	Carrigboy	**Sullivan John**
KILD	Mount Blarney *	**Sullivan John**
CRK	Tubridtown	**Sullivan John**
CRK	Carrigagulla	**Sullivan Mary**
CRK	Garanes South	**Sullivan Michael**
DUB	Rockbrook *	**Sullivan Mr**
WEX	Pallis Upper	**Sullivan Patrick**
KRY	Tralee Town	**Sullivan Patrick**
MEA	Clonguiffin	**Sullivan Philip**
KKY	Archersgrove	**Sullivan Richard**
TIP	Commons	**Sullivan Stephen**
CRK	Ballea	**Sullivan Thomas**
KRY	Inchiboy	**Sullivan Timothy**
CRK	Knockbrogan	**Sullivan William**
CRK	Kinsale Town	**Sullivan William C**
DUB	Kilmainham	**Summers Jno**
DUB	Kilmainham	**Summers John**
FER	Milltown	**Surphlis Richard**
OFF	Birr Town	**Sutherland John**
WEX	Ross Town	**Sutton Cousar**
WW	Mountusher	**Sutton Samuel**
CRK	Cork City :	**Suttons Ltd.**
ROS	Canal & Banks	**Swain**
MYO	Barrack Hill	**Swaine Jonas**
ANT	Doagh	**Swan**
ANT	Shaneoguestown	**Swan**
MYO	Temple	**Swan Dominick**
DUB	Dublin City	**Swan J**
ROS	Grange	**Swan John**
ANT	Stradballymorris	**Swan Mr**
DWN	Grallaghgreenan	**Swan Robert**
ANT	Stradballymorris	**Swann Hugh**
MON	Boyher	**Swann Robert**
CRK	Carrigtishane	**Swanton**
CRK	Lurriga	**Swanton James**
CRK	Townland ?`	**Swanton James**
ARM	Lisdrumgullion	**Swanzy**
MON	Carrickaderry	**Swanzy Andrew**
TIP	Mein	**Sweeney John**
MON	Corliglacka * :	**Swanzy Anne Widow.**
LOU	Ardee Town	**Swanzy Thomas**
WAT	Waterford City	**Swean**
OFF	Fancroft	**Sweeney Marcus**
DON	Moyle	**Sweeney Samuel**
DUB	Dublin City	**Sweeny B**
MYO	Foxford	**Sweeny Denis**
CRK	Bandon Town	**Sweeny Fran Bern**
TIP	Mien	**Sweeny John**
CAR	Carlow Town	**Sweeny Marion**
ROS	Castlereagh Town	**Sweeny Patrick**
CRK	Youghal Town	**Sweeny Patrick**
CRK	Youghal Town	**Sweeny Thomas**
DUB	Drishoge	**Sweetman**
KILD	Kilrush	**Sweetman**
DWN	Milltown	**Sweetman**
DUB	Dublin City	**Sweetman A**
DUB	Dublin	**Sweetman Mr**
CRK	Townland ?`	**Sweetman Wm**
CAR	Ballyknockan	**Swift**
CAR	Leighlandbridge	**Swift**
DUB	Swords	**Swift**
WME	Cullenmore	**Swift James**
MEA	Clonguiffin	**Swift Jno Rev.**
MEA	Clonguiffin	**Swift John**
MEA	Clonguiffin	**Swift Meade**
ROS	Tanidrissoge *	**Swift Michael**
CAR	Ballyknockan	**Swift Robert**
FER	Cushwash	**Swindell Francis**
MYO	Ballymagauna	**Swiney Edward**
DON	Moyle	**Swiney John**
DON	Moyle	**Swiney John**
DON	Tully	**Swiney John**
WEX	Ballyedmond	**Swiny Shapland**
WEX	Barglany *	**Swiny Shapland**
WEX	Barglany *	**Swiny William**
KILD	Maynooth	**Swords**
LAO	Olar Esker	**Sydney Lord Crosbie**
CAR	Carlow Town	**Sykes George**
DUB	Dundrum	**Sykes George**
CAR	Paupish	**Sykes George Sen.**
CAR	Paupish	**Sykes John**
LAO	Cardtown	**Symes Jeremiah**
MEA	Macetown	**Symmons Clive**
MEA	Macetown	**Symmons Prudence**
CRK	Knocknahorgan	**Symons Mr**
OFF	Rathmore	**Synge Edward**
CLE	Carhoo	**Synge Francis H**
WW	Ballymaghroe	**Synge John**
WW	Cloro	**Synge Mr**
CAR	Tullow	**Synott Patk Rev.**

T

CO.	TOWNLAND	MILLER
ARM	Ballynaghy	**Tade**
LDY	Killykergan	**Taffe**

CO.	TOWNLAND	MILLER
ROS	Athleague	**Taffe Anthony**
ROS	Athleague	**Taffe Chris**
MYO	Lisduff	**Taffe Edmond**
ROS	Enfield	**Taffe Henry E**
DON	Killygordon	**Tagert Robert**
DWN	Saul	**Taggarh Bernard**
CAV	Ballyness	**Taggart**
ANT	Antrim Town	**Taggart J**
ANT	Ballybogy	**Taggart John**
ANT	Lisconnan	**Taggart John**
ROS	Killappoge	**Talbot Charles**
ROS	Killappoge	**Talbot Chris**
TIP	Brookfield	**Talbot Edward**
ROS	Killappoge	**Talbot Henry**
LAO	Kyle	**Talbot John**
DUB	Swords Town	**Talbot Richard**
KKY	Castlemarket	**Talien John**
LOU	Ballynamenan	**Tallan**
LOU	Dromad	**Tallan**
CRK	Youghal Town	**Tallon**
DWN	Ballynahinch	**Tallon Frances**
MEA	Martry	**Tallon James**
MEA	Martry	**Tallon James Jun.**
MEA	Martry	**Tallon Thomas**
MEA	Blackcastle Dem.	**Tallon John**
CRK	Cloghane	**Talvey Thomas**
MEA	Coolronan	**Tandy John**
MEA	Bedlow`s Mill	**Tara Harriett Rt. Hon. Lady**
MEA	Bedlow`s Mill	**Tara John Rt. Hon.**
MEA	Townland ?	**Tara Lord**
LAO	Mountmellick	**Tarleton**
OFF	Millbrook	**Tarleton Robert**
KILD	Belan	**Tate John**
KILD	Moone	**Taylor**
WEX	Wexford Town	**Taylor Christopher**
LDY	Coleraine Town	**Taylor Daniel**
MEA	Formays	**Taylor Edward Rev.**
MEA	Formays	**Taylor Hon.Thos E. Bective**
ANT	Ardihannon	**Taylor James**
DWN	Ballydugan	**Taylor James**
ANT	Ballyhone	**Taylor James**
DWN	Ballywalter	**Taylor James**
ANT	Carrickfergus NE	**Taylor James**
ANT	Carrickfergus Tn	**Taylor Jas**
DWN	Balloo	**Taylor Jno**
DON	Castlefinn	**Taylor John**
LDY	Coleraine Town	**Taylor John**
DUB	Dublin City	**Taylor John**
DON	Knockrawer	**Taylor John**
DUB	Shipping`s Mill	**Taylor John**
DUB	Stopping`s Mill	**Taylor John**
DWN	Cabragh	**Taylor John Sen.**
DUB	Rockbrook *	**Taylor Mr.**
KKY	Rathpatrick	**Taylor Nathaniel**
LDY	Coleraine Town	**Taylor Paul**
ROS	Milltown	**Taylor Rebecca**
LDY	Coleraine Town	**Taylor Robert**
DON	Castlefinn	**Taylor Samuel**
GAL	Galway Town	**Taylor Samuel**
DON	Knockrawer	**Taylor Samuel**
DON	Knockrawer	**Taylor Samuel**
MEA	Ballyann	**Taylor Thomas**
DUB	Dundrum Manor	**Taylor Thomas**
GAL	Galway Town	**Taylor Walter**
GAL	Mulpit	**Taylor Walter**
KRY	Charleville	**Taylor William**
DON	Knockrawer	**Taylor William**
WEX	Wexford Town	**Taylor William**
WAT	Waterford City	**Teame Robert**
DON	Carnatreantragh	**Teas John**
DUB	Milltown	**Teeling Jno**
DUB	Naul	**Teeling Mr.**
DUB	Rathfarnham	**Teeling Mr.**
DUB	Finglas	**Teeling Walter**
FER	Glasdrumman	**Tegart John**
CAV	Boffealan	**Tegart William**
CAV	Crover	**Telford Henry**
GAL	Woodford	**Tempany John**
GAL	Woodford Village	**Tempany John**
DWN	Ballyvally	**Templeton**
MON	Mullaghmore West	**Tenants**
TYR	Augher	**Tener John K**
ROS	Derreenavoggy	**Tenison Thomas**
LAO	Ironmills / Kilrush	**Tenison Thomas**
TIP	Nenagh	**Tennant David**
DWN	Ardkeen	**Tennent Robert**
ARM	Augher Town	**Tenner John K Jun**
LOU	Drogheda Town	**Ternan Patrick**
DUB	Balbriggan	**Ternan Richard**
WAT	Dungarvan Town	**Terry**
LAO	Mountmellick	**Thacker Thomas**
KKY	Bennetsbridge	**The Big Mill**
ANT	Dunadry	**The Old Mill**
KKY	Bennetsbridge	**The Small Mill**
WME	Athlone Town	**Thomas**
WME	Lissywolan	**Thomas**
KILD	Moone	**Thomas Amyas**
WAT	Kilmacthomas	**Thomas Barton**
CRK	Ballygarvan	**Thomas Casey**
KILD	Ryevale *	**Thomas Donnellan**
ROS	Athlone	**Thomas Edwin**
KILD	Greatconnell	**Thomas H G Ld Primate**
KILD	Moone	**Thomas Henry**
MON	Quiglough	**Thomas Humphry**
LDY	Ballywillin	**Thomas James**
GAL	Abbert Demesne	**Thomas Kavanagh**
ROS	Athlone	**Thomas Levin**
LAO	Killeen	**Thomas Matthew D**
GAL	Durrow	**Thomas N Baggot**
TIP	Ballyard	**Thomas Peter**
DUB	Dundrum Manor	**Thomas William**
CAR	Carlow Town	**Thomond Lord**
LOU	Annagassan	**Thompson**
LOU	Ardee	**Thompson**
DWN	Ballymaconaghy	**Thompson**
LOU	Ballynamenan	**Thompson**
MEA	Bective	**Thompson**
LAO	Cardtown	**Thompson**
CAR	Carlow Town	**Thompson**
KILD	Celbridge	**Thompson**
LAO	Clarahill	**Thompson**
LOU	Dromod	**Thompson**
DWN	Gransha	**Thompson**
KILD	Maynooth	**Thompson**
KILD	Quinsborough	**Thompson**
CAR	Staplestown	**Thompson**
LOU	Sundayswell	**Thompson**
LOU	Annaverna	**Thompson B**
LOU	Doolargy	**Thompson Benjamin**
ANT	Drumdallagh	**Thompson Daniel**
MON	Creeve	**Thompson David**
CAV	Manor Mill	**Thompson David**
DUB	Milltown	**Thompson David**
DON	Tullydonnell Lower	**Thompson Galbr.**
CRK	Cork City :	**Thompson George**
ANT	Greenshields	**Thompson George**
ANT	Moycraig Ham	**Thompson George**
ANT	Carrickfergus Tn	**Thompson Henry**
DWN	Annadorn	**Thompson James**
KILD	Ballyaghmoone *	**Thompson James**
ANT	Ballynacreeskein	**Thompson James**
LDY	Londonderry	**Thompson James**
DON	Newtowncunninghа	**Thompson James**
CAV	Sraheglin	**Thompson Jn Dixon**
ARM	Ballyloughan	**Thompson John**
DWN	Gilford Town	**Thompson John**
DWN	Glassdrumman	**Thompson John**
WEX	Johnstown	**Thompson John**
MEA	Rathnally	**Thompson John**
ANT	Shankill T`parks	**Thompson John**
MON	Shantonagh	**Thompson John**
KILD	Quinsborough	**Thompson Mary (Garnett)**
ANT	Ballyhenry W`ho	**Thompson Mr**
ANT	Legoneil	**Thompson Mr**
MON	Aghnamullen	**Thompson R**
KILD	Castletown	**Thompson Robert**
LOU	Dillonstown	**Thompson Robert**
LDY	Dunderg	**Thompson Robert**
ANT	Derriaghy	**Thompson Ross**
DON	Ardnagannagh	**Thompson Thomas**
DON	Ballyshannon	**Thompson Thomas**
DWN	Annadorn	**Thompson William**
ARM	Ballyloughan	**Thompson William**
DWN	Ballymaconaghy	**Thompson William**
ANT	Ballynacaird	**Thompson William**
KRY	Dirreen *	**Thompson William**
KILD	Johnstown	**Thompson William**
DWN	Largymore	**Thompson William**

CO.	TOWNLAND	MILLER
DON	Milltown	**Thompson William**
KILD	Quinsborough	**Thompson William**
ARM	Richhill	**Thompson William**
WAT	Waterford City	**Thompson William**
DON	Milltown	**Thompson Wm Jn**
CAR	Staplestown	**Thompson Wm Rev**
LOU	Sundayswell	**Thompsonn**
ANT	Carrickfergus Tn	**Thomson Charles**
KILD	Celbridge	**Thomson Robert**
LIM	Windmill Hill	**Thomson Robt**
DON	Cavan	**Thomson William**
CRK	Riverstown	**Thorley Samuel**
CRK	Poulacurrys	**Thorley William**
CRK	Riverstown	**Thorley William**
ANT	Ballyclare	**Thornley Thos**
DON	Ballyboe	**Thorp Margaret**
CAR	Borris	**Thorpe**
LOU	Ardee	**Thorpe Francis**
LOU	Ardee	**Thorpe Frank**
LOU	Ardee	**Thorpe Richard Hon.**
CAR	Corries	**Thorpe Samuel**
CAR	Corries	**Thorpe Samuel**
DUB	Dublin City	**Thresher**
WEX	Lingstown	**Thresher William**
ROS	Danesfort	**Thrilfall Richard**
DUB	Donnybrook	**Thwaite Margaret**
DUB	Donnybrook	**Thwaite George**
LAO	Drinagh	**Thwaites**
WEX	Ross Town	**Ticehurst Rowl**
WEX	Ross Town	**Ticehurst Rowland**
LONG	Cartrons	**Tickell Edward**
DUB	Balbriggan	**Tiernan Mr**
LOU	Mellifont Park	**Tiernan Thomas**
LEI	Lavaur	**Tiernan William**
GAL	Ahgloragh	**Tierney J**
MYO	Springvale	**Tierney Patrick**
MYO	Springvale	**Tierney Patrick**
WW	Ballynultagh	**Tighe**
WME	Parcellstown	**Tighe**
DUB	Balbriggan	**Tighe Laurence**
MYO	Ballinrobe Town	**Tighe Robert**
MYO	Castle Bourke	**Tighe Robert**
KILD	Kilcullen	**Tighe Robert**
MEA	Balrath	**Tighe Sarah**
CRK	Ruineen	**Tighe St Laurence**
OFF	Rusheen	**Tiguin Mary**
OFF	Rusheen	**Tiguin Maryanne**
LDY	Londonderry	**Tillie W**
LDY	Clady Village	**Tillis**
WW	Ballinameesda Lr	**Timmons Michael**
KILD	Athy Town	**Timmons Patrick**
WW	Ballinameesda Lr	**Timmons Sarah**
ROS	Knockadryan	**Timon Charles**
DON	Slievebuck	**Tinny James**
ARM	Rockmacreeny	**Tinton William**
ARM	Anaghgary	**Tipping**

CO.	TOWNLAND	MILLER
DWN	Ballydargan	**Tipping**
ARM	Anaghgary	**Tipping Francis**
LOU	Bellurgan	**Tipping Richard**
KILD	Mount Blarney *	**Tisdall Charles**
MEA	Martry	**Tisdall Henrietta**
KILD	Irishtown	**Tisdall Hester**
MEA	Martry	**Tisdall Michael**
DWN	Drennans	**Tisdall Richard**
DWN	Kircubbin	**Tisdall Richard**
DWN	Listooder	**Tisdall Richard**
DWN	Ballyhalbert	**Tisdall Richd**
DWN	Ballylisbredan	**Tisdall Richd**
WEX	Inch	**Tobin James**
CRK	Kilbelogue	**Tobin John**
CRK	Townland ?`	**Tobin Mark**
WEX	Ballinaglogh	**Tobin Patrick**
KKY	Lismateige	**Tobin Peter**
CRK	Ballincollig	**Tobin Thomas**
CRK	Coolyduff	**Tobin Thomas**
WEX	Ballinaglogh	**Tobin William**
DWN	Derrylough	**Todd**
KILD	Kilcullen	**Todd**
TYR	Loughmuck	**Todd**
TYR	Drumaspill	**Todd E Rt. Hon.**
LDY	Coleraine Town	**Todd Isaac**
TYR	Drumaspill	**Todd William**
TYR	Loughmuck	**Todd William**
KILD	Parsonstown	**Todhunter John**
TIP	Carrowea	**Toher Michael**
MYO	Lissaniska	**Tolard Patrick**
DWN	Ballywalter	**Tomb**
WAT	Shanakill	**Tomb**
DWN	Ballywalter	**Tomb Margaret Spin.**
DWN	Ballywalter	**Tomb Olivia Spim.**
CLE	O'Briensbridge	**Tomkin**
CLE	O'Briensbridge	**Tomkin**
LDY	Ardkill	**Tomkins Anna Maria**
WW	Newtown	**Tomkins Charles**
ARM	Carrinane	**Toner Loughlin**
ARM	Corrinure	**Toner Loughlin**
LDY	Magheraboy	**Toner Thomas**
MEA	Beaumont	**Tonge Edward**
MEA	Beaumont	**Tonge James**
CAR	Rarhvilly	**Tononi Enrico**
CRK	Dromaskill *	**Toogood**
GAL	Athenry Town	**Toole Charles**
DUB	Templeogue	**Toole Charles**
WW	Bray	**Toole Denis**
LAO	Stradbally	**Toole Joseph**
WW	Bray	**Toole Margret Widow**
WW	Bray Great	**Toole Tobias**
WME	Corry	**Tormey Denis**
WME	Gigginstown	**Tormey Edward**
WME	Gormanstown	**Tormey Edward**
WME	Tuitestown	**Tormey Edward**
WME	Derrynagarragh	**Tormey James**

CO.	TOWNLAND	MILLER
WME	Gormanstown	**Tormey Mary**
WME	Crowinstown Gt	**Tormey Patrick**
CAV	Ballaghanna	**Tormey Walter**
CAV	Ballaghanna	**Tormey Walter**
CAV	Kilnaleck	**Tormey Widow**
CAV	Ballaghanea	**Tormry Walter**
MEA	Tully	**Tormy John**
KILD	Parsonstown	**Toss Eliz (Tuton) Widow**
TIP	Clonmel	**Tothall Osborn**
LEI	Lismackniff	**Tottenham Nicholas**
LEI	Millacre	**Tottenham Nicholas**
LIM	Ballygeagoge	**Touchstone**
KILD	Ballygegorge	**Touchstone**
CLE	Rathmeehan	**Toughey Andrew**
CLE	Rathmeehan	**Toughey Daniel**
TIP	Ollatrim	**Touhy Jeremiah**
TIP	Carrowea	**Towers Michael**
GAL	Duckanelly	**Towers Thomas**
MYO	Duckanelly	**Towers Thomas**
CRK	Blarney	**Towgood Mat**
CRK	Boulapatrick *	**Towgood Mattew**
CRK	Boulapatrick *	**Towgood Matthew**
CAV	Drumnagran	**Townley John**
LOU	Dundalk Town	**Townley John**
CAV	Drumnagran	**Townly John**
LIM	Kilmallock Town	**Townsend Henry**
LDY	Bovagh	**Tracy Athur**
LONG	Lislea	**Tracy Cornelius**
OFF	Glasshouse	**Tracy John**
OFF	Kilcomin	**Tracy John**
ROS	Snipe Hill	**Tracy John**
DWN	Ballymacarret	**Trail Hamilton Rev**
WAT	Durrow	**Travers**
WAT	Millerstown	**Travers**
MON	Monaghan Town	**Travers**
WAT	Durrow (Millerstn.)	**Travers Michael**
CRK	Newmill	**Travers Robert**
DUB	Feltrim	**Traviere Max**
LOU	Collon	**Traynor Mary Ann**
LOU	Collon Town	**Traynor Mary Anne**
LOU	Collon Town	**Traynor Mrs Mary A**
LONG	Lislea	**Treacy Cornelius**
MEA	Ballyadams	**Treacy John**
GAL	Durrow	**Treans Patrick**
LONG	Grillagh	**Trelford Edward**
LAO	Ballyroan	**Trench**
LIM	Kilfinnane	**Trench**
LIM	Ballynoe Lower	**Trench Chas F**
LIM	Clovers	**Trench Chas Fred Esq.**
LIM	Kilfinnane	**Trench Fred Charles**
OFF	Banagher Town	**Trench Henry**
DWN	Ballyvally	**Trevor Edward**
DWN	Balloo	**Trevor Jno**
ARM	Derrycughan	**Trew Andrew**
KRY	Cottoners	**Trewell**
MEA	Trim Town	**Trim Town Commrs.**

CO.	TOWNLAND	MILLER
KILD	Celbridge	**Watts John**
DWN	Edenordinary	**Watts William**
ARM	Ballynahone Beg	**Waugh John**
DWN	Tullycarn	**Waugh Mrs**
WME	Lismacaffry	**Webb Charles**
LOU	Ardee	**Webb Hugh**
MEA	Ballyann	**Webb John**
CRK	Ballyadeen	**Webb Robert**
MEA	Castlecor	**Webb Samuel**
CAR	Ballynebranagh	**Webb Stawell**
MEA	Athboy Town	**Webb Wiliam**
WEX	Garrybrit Upper	**Webster Robert**
KKY	Strangsmill	**Webster Robert**
WAT	Waterford City	**Weekes Edward**
DUB	Diswellstown	**Wegg Samuel**
OFF	Annaghmore	**Weir**
DWN	Ballydugan	**Weir**
ARM	Lisdrumgullion	**Weir**
GAL	Woodlands	**Weir**
ANT	Dunmurry	**Weir A**
ANT	Straid	**Weir Alex**
GAL	Clunbrucky	**Weir Christopher**
CAR	Ballykeenan	**Weir James**
ANT	Gloonan	**Weir John**
DON	Mullaboy	**Weir John**
DUB	Glasnevin	**Weir Robert**
ANT	Straid	**Weir Robert**
ANT	Ahoghill	**Weir Robt**
DWN	Desert	**Weir William**
ANT	Springfield	**Weir William**
CAR	Bagenalstown	**Weld Edmond**
CAR	Carlow Town	**Weld Edmond**
CAR	Monebeg	**Weld Edmond**
CAR	Carlow Town	**Weld Georgina**
KILD	Ardnaree	**Weld Isaac**
CAR	Bagenalstown	**Weld Matt**
CAR	Knockmill *	**Weld Matt**
CAR	Bagnelstown	**Weld Matthew**
DUB	Stopping`s Mill	**Weld Nathaniel**
CAR	Bagnelstown	**Weld Richard**
CAR	Ballynebranagh	**Weld Richard**
DUB	Kilmainham	**Weldon Arthur**
LIM	Kilmallock	**Weldon Thomas**
LEI	Aghavas	**Weldon Wm S**
DWN	Balleny	**Wells Lord Baron**
CAR	Cloghristick	**Wellwood**
WAT	Piltown	**Welsh**
WAT	Coushmacale	**Welsh Edmond**
WAT	Coushmacale	**Welsh Matthew**
WAT	Millerstown	**Welsh Thomas**
WAT	Piltown	**Welsh Thomas**
TIP	Clonmore	**Wemyss**
DWN	Ballydugan	**West**
DUB	Dublin City	**West**
DWN	Ballydugan	**West Batt**
DWN	Ballydugan	**West Henry**
DWN	Ballyhemlin	**West Henry**
DWN	Ye King's Fields	**West Henry**
DWN	Ballyhemlin	**West Henry Jun.**
WME	Rath	**West James**
LEI	Balscarra	**West John**
LEI	Keeldra	**West John**
LEI	Balscarra	**West Joihn B**
DWN	Ballyhemlin	**West Patrick**
DWN	Ballydugan	**West Richard Henry**
WAT	Colbeck`s	**West Robert**
DUB	Feltrim	**West Robert**
DWN	Ballydugan	**West Roger**
WME	Rath	**West Thomas Wm**
LAO	Iron Mills	**Westbury**
LONG	Clonaghlis	**Westby Willia**
LAO	Dysart	**Westenra**
WME	Monksland	**Westenra**
ROS	Ballyglass	**Westenra Henry**
MON	Teraverty	**Westenra Richard**
MYO	Cloonkee	**Westly Edward Master**
WAT	Rehill Manor	**Weston Ambr**
MYO	Clogher	**Westport Water Wks.**
KILD	Johnstown	**Wetherall Hannah**
KRY	Ballycarty	**Wetherall Joseph**
DUB	Wey Mills	**Wetherall Thomas**
OFF	Ballycumber	**Wetherell**
OFF	Ballycumber	**Wetherell**
OFF	Belmont Mill	**Wetherell**
WME	Tyrellspass	**Wetherell John**
MEA	Slane	**Wetherill**
LOU	Drogheda Town	**Wetherill Thomas B**
WEX	Iberins (parish)	**Wexford Corp.**
CLE	Inchiquin Manor	**Wheeler**
CLE	Inchiquin Manor	**Wheeler**
LIM	Ballynacurra Hart	**Wheeler Robert**
LAO	Maryborough	**Wheelock Henry**
WEX	Enniscorthy Town	**Wheelock James**
MEA	Ballyann	**Whelan**
KILD	Moone	**Whelan**
DUB	Dublin City	**Whelan E Rev.**
KKY	Jerpoint Abbey	**Whelan Margaret**
WAT	Graigavalla	**Whelan Patrick**
MEA	Ballyann	**Whelan Pilsworth**
MEA	Ballyann	**Whelan Thomas**
WAT	Ballyristeen	**Whelan Thomas**
CAR	Carlow Town	**Whelan Thomas**
KILD	Moone	**Whelan William**
DON	Legnachiny Lr *	**Wheler Margaret**
DWN	Downpatrick Town	**Whisker James**
WAT	Waterford Town	**Whitby Jno**
DWN	Ballykeel	**White**
LAO	Ballyroan	**White**
WW	B'more Eustace	**White**
LAO	Cardtown	**White**
DUB	Clonskeagh	**White**
LAO	Cullenagh (bo.)	**White**
ARM	Lisdrumgullion	**White**
ANT	Shaneoguestown	**White**
CRK	Ballycureen	**White Edmond**
LAO	Grange	**White Francis**
LAO	Little Mill	**White Francis**
DUB	Woodlands	**White Francis**
TYR	Milltown	**White George**
WAT	Waterford Citl	**White George**
KILD	Clane	**White Henry**
DON	Moyle	**White Henry**
ANT	Drumrankin	**White James**
ANT	Muckamore	**White James**
ANT	Belfast Town	**White John**
TYR	Blacksessagh	**White John**
DWN	Downpatrick Town	**White John**
KRY	Milltown	**White John**
DWN	Ballybawne	**White John Nevin**
KILD	B`more Eustace	**White John Sir**
LONG	Cooleroy	**White Luke**
TYR	Blacksessagh	**White Margt. ors Bohamon**
DUB	Boddin *	**White Mark**
KILD	Kilkea	**White Mark**
DUB	Woodlock`s Gr	**White Mark**
MON	Bradoge	**White Mark.**
WEX	Ambrosetown	**White Matthew**
WEX	Tullycanna	**White Matthew**
DUB	Luttrelstown	**White Mr**
KKY	The Mill Field	**White Patrick**
DUB	Diswellstown	**White R**
LAO	Rathdowney	**White Robert**
CAV	Virginia Town :	**White Robert**
WEX	Wexford Town	**White Robert**
LEI	Rossclogher	**White Saml**
LEI	Balscarra	**White Samuel**
LAO	Ironmills / Kilrush	**White Simon**
LAO	Doon	**White Thomas**
TIP	Clonmel Town	**White William**
ANT	(bo. BELFAST)	**Whitehouse Sp. Co**
WAT	Durrow (Millerstn.)	**Whiteman R**
WAT	Durrow (Millerstn.)	**Whiteman Richard**
WAT	Millerstown	**Whiteman Richard**
ARM	Tullymore	**Whiteside**
MON	Analore	**Whiteside Jas**
DUB	Woodlock`s Gr	**Whiteside Mary**
OFF	Annaghmore	**Whitfield**
OFF	Curraghmore	**Whitfield Abraham**
CRK	Ballinglanna	**Whiting John**
ANT	Ballyloran	**Whitla George**
ANT	Inver	**Whitla H**
WAT	Ballyristeen	**Whitlaw Thomas**
CAV	Corbeagh	**Whitley Charles**
CAV	Killycreeny	**Whitley Joseph**
FER	Cooneen	**Whitley Robert**
MEA	Bedlow`s Mill	**Whitley Stokes**
CAR	Borris Town	**Whitney George**
CAR	Borris Town	**Whitney Thomas**

INDEX

Y

Z

[Zero]